The Grants Register 2024

The Grants Register 2024

The Complete Guide to Postgraduate Funding Worldwide

Forty-Second Edition

Volume 2

N–Z

palgrave
macmillan

Palgrave Macmillan
Macmillan Publishers Ltd.

ISBN 978-1-349-96072-9 ISBN 978-1-349-96073-6 (eBook)
https://doi.org/10.1057/978-1-349-96073-6

Paper in this product is recyclable.The Palgrave imprint is published by Springer Nature.
The registered company is Macmillan Publishers Ltd. London.

Paper in this product is recyclable.

Preface

The forty-second edition of *The Grants Register* provides a detailed, accurate and comprehensive survey of awards intended for students at or above the postgraduate level, or those who require further professional or advanced vocational training.

Student numbers around the world continue to grow rapidly, and overseas study is now the first choice for many of these students. *The Grants Register* provides comprehensive, up-to-date information about the availability of, and eligibility for, non-refundable postgraduate and professional awards worldwide.

We remain grateful to the institutions which have supplied information for inclusion in this edition, and would also like to thank the International Association of Universities for continued permission to use their subject index within our Subject and Eligibility Guide to Awards.

The Grants Register database is updated continually in order to ensure that the information provided is the most current available. **Therefore, if your details have changed or you would like to be included for the first time, please contact the Senior Editor, at the address below.** If you wish to obtain further information relating to specific application procedures, please contact the relevant grant-awarding institution, rather than the publisher.

The Grants Register
Palgrave Macmillan
Springer Nature Campus
4 Crinan St
London
N1 9XW
United Kingdom
Tel: 144 (0)207 843 4634
Fax: 144 (0)207 843 4650
Email: Grants.Register@spi-global.com

Ruth Lefèvre
Senior Editor

How to Use *The Grants Register*

For ease of use, *The Grants Register 2024* is divided into four sections:

- The Grants Register
- Subject and Eligibility Guide to Awards
- Index of Awards
- Index of Awarding Organisations

The Grants Register

Information in this section is supplied directly by the awarding organisations. Entries are arranged alphabetically by name of organisation, and awards are listed alphabetically within the awarding organisation. This section includes details on subject area, eligibility, purpose, type, numbers offered, frequency, value, length of study, study establishment, country of study, and application procedure. Full contact details appcar with cach awarding organisation and also appended to individual awards where additional addresses are givcn.

A

AACR - American Association for Cancer Research

615 Chestnut St., 17th Floor, Philadelphia, PA 19106-4404, United States of America.

Tel: (1) 215 440 9300
Email: ayacr@aacr.org
Website: www.aacr.org/

From the simple beginning of a few scientists gathering to share information to the multifaceted organization that exists today, the growth of the AACR reflects the increasing complexity of our our understanding of the collection of devastating diseases we now know as cancer.

AACR Cancer Disparities Research Fellowships

Purpose: The AACR Cancer Disparities Research Fellowships represent an effort to encourage and support postdoctoral or clinical research fellows to conduct cancer disparities research and to establish a successful career path in this field. The research proposed for funding may be basic, translational, clinical, or epidemiological in nature and must have direct applicability and relevance to cancer disparities.
Eligibility: Applicants must have a doctoral degree (PhD, MD, MD/PhD, or equivalent) in a related field and not currently be a candidate for a further doctoral degree. At the start of the grant term applicants must hold a mentored research position with the title of postdoctoral fellow, clinical research fellow, or the equivalent; have completed their most recent doctoral degree within the past five years (i.e., degree cannot have been conferred before July 1, 2018); and work under the auspices of a mentor at an academic, medical, or research institution anywhere in the world. Applicants with a medical degree must have completed their most recent doctoral degree or medical residency - whichever date is later - within the past five years. If eligibility is based on a future position, the position must be confirmed at the time of application and cannot be contingent upon receiving this grant. Investigators may submit only one application for the AACR Cancer Disparities Research Fellowships but may concurrently apply for other AACR grants. However, applicants are expected to accept the first grant they are awarded. Individuals may accept and hold only one AACR grant at a time. Employees or subcontractors of a U.S. government entity or for-profit private industry are not eligible. Postdoctoral or clinical research fellows conducting research in a U.S. government laboratory (e.g., NIH, CDC, FDA, etc.), are not eligible. Any individual who currently holds an active AACR grant may not apply. Past grantees may apply if they complied with all progress and financial report requirements. Investigators currently or previously holding the rank of instructor, adjunct professor, assistant professor, research assistant professor, the equivalent or higher are not eligible. Qualified researchers are invited to apply for an AACR Career Development Award.
Level of Study: Doctorate
Type: Grant
Value: US$120,000
Length of Study: 2 Years
Frequency: Annual
Country of Study: Any country
Application Procedure: The AACR requires applicants to submit an online application, using the ProposalCentral website at proposalcentral.com/.
Closing Date: 7 January

For further information contact:

Email: grants@aacr.org

 1
Palgrave Macmillan (ed.), *The Grants Register 2024*,
https://doi.org/10.1057/978-1-349-96073-6

Subject and Eligibility Guide to Awards

Awards can be located through the Subject and Eligibility Guide to Awards. This section allows the user to find an award within a specific subject area. *The Grants Register* uses a list of subjects endorsed by the International Association of Universities (IAU), the information centre on higher education, located at UNESCO, Paris. It is further subdivided into eligibility by nationality. Thereafter, awards are listed alphabetically within their designated category, along with a page reference where full details of the award can be found.

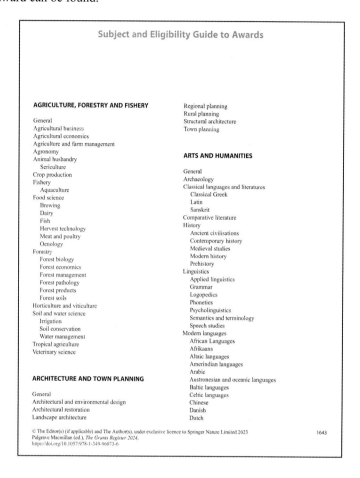

Subject and Eligibility Guide to Awards

AGRICULTURE, FORESTRY AND FISHERY

General
Agricultural business
Agricultural economics
Agriculture and farm management
Agronomy
Animal husbandry
  Sericulture
Crop production
Fishery
  Aquaculture
Food science
  Brewing
  Dairy
  Fish
  Harvest technology
  Meat and poultry
  Oenology
Forestry
  Forest biology
  Forest economics
  Forest management
  Forest pathology
  Forest products
  Forest soils
Horticulture and viticulture
Soil and water science
  Irrigation
  Soil conservation
  Water management
Tropical agriculture
Veterinary science

ARCHITECTURE AND TOWN PLANNING

General
Architectural and environmental design
Architectural restoration
Landscape architecture
Regional planning
Rural planning
Structural architecture
Town planning

ARTS AND HUMANITIES

General
Archaeology
Classical languages and literatures
  Classical Greek
  Latin
  Sanskrit
Comparative literature
History
  Ancient civilisations
  Contemporary history
  Medieval studies
  Modern history
  Prehistory
Linguistics
  Applied linguistics
  Grammar
  Logopedics
  Phonetics
  Psycholinguistics
  Semantics and terminology
  Speech studies
Modern languages
  African Languages
  Afrikaans
  Altaic languages
  Amerindian languages
  Arabic
  Austronesian and oceanic languages
  Baltic languages
  Celtic languages
  Chinese
  Danish
  Dutch

 1643
Palgrave Macmillan (ed.), *The Grants Register 2024*,
https://doi.org/10.1057/978-1-349-96073-6

Index of Awards

All awards are indexed alphabetically with a page reference.

Index of Awarding Organisations

A complete list of all awarding organisations, with country name and page reference.

List of Contents

Preface v

How to Use *The Grants Register* vii

The Grants Register 1

Subject and Eligibility Guide to Awards 1643

Index of Awards 1763

Index of Awarding Organisations 1805

N

Nan Tien Institute

Nan Tien Institute - Wollongong Campus, 231 Nolan Street, Unanderra, NSW 2526, Australia.

Tel: (61) 02 4258 0700
Email: info@nantien.edu.au
Website: www.nantien.edu.au

Nan Tien Institute (NTI) is a private, not for profit, government accredited higher education provider offering studies in the areas of Buddhist studies, health and wellbeing, within an environment that incorporates contemplative education. NTI offers postgraduate programs in Applied Buddhist Studies, Health and Social Wellbeing, Humanistic Buddhism, and Mental Health as well as customised Continuing Professional Development (CPD) programs and special interest subjects across the areas of meditation, mindfulness and health.

Hsing Yun Education Foundation (HYEF) Scholarship for Domestic Students

Purpose: To honour Venerable Master Hsing Yun, HYEF is offering this scholarship to assist high achieving domestic students to undertake the Graduate Certificate in Humanistic Buddhism course at Nan Tien Institute (NTI)
Eligibility: 1. The applicant must have been admitted or been offered admission to the Graduate Certificate in Humanistic Buddhism at NTI. 2. The applicant must be an Australian or New Zealand citizen, or a permanent resident of Australia
Type: Scholarship
Value: Tuition fees, Vegetarian meals provided by Nan Tien Temple during the period of stay
Frequency: Annual
Country of Study: Any country
Application Procedure: Download the 'Domestic Scholarship' Application Form: www.nantien.edu.au/wp-content/uploads/2020/07/Hsing-Yun-Education-Foundation-Domestic-Scholarship-Application-Form-1.pdf
No. of awards offered: 10
Closing Date: 14 April
Additional Information: www.nantien.edu.au/admissions/scholarships/

For further information contact:

Tel: (61) 2 4258 0700
Email: cholarships@nantien.edu.au

Hsing Yun Education Foundation (HYEF) Scholarship for International Students

Purpose: To honour Venerable Master Hsing Yun, HYEF is offering this scholarship to assist high achieving international students to undertake Applied Buddhist Studies and Humanistic Buddhism programs at Nan Tien Institute (NTI). We hope that people with similar visions can contribute to this great initiative
Eligibility: 1. Master of Arts (Applied Buddhist Studies) 2. Graduate Diploma of Applied Buddhist Studies 3. Graduate Certificate in Applied Buddhist Studies 4. Graduate Certificate in Humanistic Buddhism
Eligible Country: Any Country
Type: Scholarship
Value: Tuition fees, accommodation, Vegetarian meals
Country of Study: Any country
Application Procedure: Download the 'International Scholarship' Application Form: www.nantien.edu.au/wp-content/uploads/2020/09/Hsing-Yun-Education-Foundation-International-Scholarship-Application-Form.pdf
No. of awards offered: 10
Closing Date: 15 April

Palgrave Macmillan (ed.), *The Grants Register 2024*,
https://doi.org/10.1057/978-1-349-96073-6

Additional Information: www.nantien.edu.au/admissions/scholarships/

For further information contact:

Tel: (61) 2 4258 0700
Email: scholarships@nantien.edu.au

Nan Tien Institute Postgraduate Scholarship

Eligibility: Open to Australian domestic students only.
Level of Study: Graduate, Postgraduate
Type: Scholarship
Value: AU$13,800.00 covers tuition costs only (not text books, learning materials or accommodation) plus research supervision
Length of Study: Up to 3 years from commencement, unless otherwise agreed
Frequency: Annual
Study Establishment: Nan Tien Institute
Country of Study: Australia
Application Procedure: Complete and submit the application form, along with your application for admission form by the closing date
Closing Date: December
Contributor: Nan Tien Institute
Additional Information: Please check for more information at www.scholarshipdb.net/jobs-in-Australia/Nan-Tien-Institute-Postgraduate-Scholarship-Applied-Buddhist-Studies-Research-Pathway-Pgabssrp-Nan-Tien-Institute=Ox4iZhJ75RGUPAAlkGUTnw.html

For further information contact:

Tel: (61) 4258 0700

Nansen Fund

77 Saddlebrook Lane, Houston, TX 77024, United States of America.

Tel: (1) 713 686 3963
Contact: Fellowships Office

John Dana Archbold Fellowship

Purpose: To support educational exchange between the United States and Norway
Eligibility: Eligibility is limited to those aged between 20 and 35, in good health, of good character, and citizens of the United States of America, who are not recent immigrants from Norway
Level of Study: Postdoctorate, Postgraduate, Professional development
Type: Fellowship
Value: Grants vary, depending on costs and rates of exchange. The University of Oslo will charge no tuition and the Nansen Fund will pay up to US$10,000 for supplies, maintenance and travel. The maintenance stipend is sufficient to meet expenses in Norway for a single person. Air fare from the United States of America to Norway is covered
Length of Study: 1 year
Frequency: Every 2 years
Study Establishment: The University of Oslo
Country of Study: Norway
Application Procedure: Applicants must complete and submit an application form with references and transcripts.
Closing Date: 31 January
Additional Information: Every other year the Norway-America Association, the sister organisation of the Nansen Fund, offers fellowships for Norwegian citizens wishing to study at a university in the United States of America. For further information please contact The Norway-America Association. www.scholarshipdb.net/jobs-in-Australia/Nan-Tien-Institute-Postgraduate-Scholarship-Applied-Buddhist-Studies-Research-Pathway-Pgabssrp-Nan-Tien-Institute=Ox4iZhJ75RGUPAAlkGUTnw.html

For further information contact:

The Norway-American Association, Drammensveien 20c, N-0271 Oslo, Norway.

Tel: (47) 2 244 7716
Fax: (47) 2 244 7716
Email: cg.newyork@mfa.no

Nanyang Technological University (NTU)

50 Nanyang Avenue, 639798, Singapore.

Tel: (65) 67911744
Email: qsmanager@ntu.edu.sg
Website: www.ntu.edu.sg
Contact: Director

A research-intensive public university, Nanyang Technological University, Singapore (NTU Singapore) has 33,000 undergraduate and postgraduate students in the colleges of

Engineering, Business, Science, and Humanities, Arts and Social Sciences, and its Graduate College. NTU's Lee Kong Chian School of Medicine was established jointly with Imperial College London.

Asia Journalism Fellowship

Eligibility: At least five years of professional journalism experience, not including student journalism, who are currently working as a journalist. Freelancers are eligible, if journalism is their main activity. Applicants should be residing in Asia and should be able to operate in English which is the working language of the programme. Journalists working in non-English media are welcomed, but they will have to show their proficiency in English through a telephone interview. Permission is required from their employers to be away for the full three months of the Fellowship
Type: Fellowship
Value: Stipend of Singaporean S$1,500 per month for the duration of the three month programme. Travel to and from Singapore will also be covered. There is no extra funding for spouses and children to visit. Free accommodation is provided in service apartments. Two or three Fellows share one apartment with kitchen to cook meals. Fellows will have access to the library, computer, internet and athletic facilities of the NTU campus. NTU will apply for Training Employment Passes for the Fellows to come to Singapore. Any visiting family members must handle their own entry permit applications
Country of Study: Singapore
Application Procedure: The mode of applying is electronically send to applications@ajf.sg
Closing Date: 25 October
Contributor: Temasek Foundation and Nanyang Technological University
Additional Information: The Fellowship brings around 15 journalists from across Asia to Singapore for three months www.ajf.sg/applying/

For further information contact:

Email: applications@ajf.sg

Asian Communication Resource Centre (ACRC) Fellowship Award

Purpose: To encourage in-depth research, promote cooperation and support scholars who wish to pursue research in communication, information and ICT-related disciplines in Asia
Eligibility: All applicants should possess or be working towards a postgraduate degree from a reputable academic institution and Applicants should be working on a research project in communication, media, information or related areas that would be able to exploit the materials in the ACRC
Level of Study: Postgraduate, Research
Type: Fellowships
Value: Up to US$1,500 (economy class return air ticket), on-campus accommodation will be provided and weekly allowance of US$210 will be provided
Length of Study: 1 to 3 months
Frequency: Annual
Application Procedure: Applicants can download the application form from the website and send in their completed application form along with a copy of their latest curriculum vitae
Closing Date: 1 October

For further information contact:

Tel: (65) 6790 4577
Fax: (65) 6791 5214
Email: acrc_fellowship@ntu.edu.sg

Nanyang Technological University HASS International PhD Scholarship (HIPS) for Singaporean Students

Purpose: HIPS aims to encourage outstanding Singapore citizens and Singapore permanent residents to pursue an academic career in HASS by supporting their doctoral studies abroad
Eligibility: Under HIPS, the successful candidates will be employed as University staff. They will be granted paid leave to pursue a sponsored PhD programme in an approved overseas university or in NTU with an extended period of research in an approved overseas partner university. Upon successful completion of the PhD programme, they will be appointed as tenure-track Assistant Professors of the University
Type: Scholarship
Frequency: Annual
Application Procedure: Interested applicants should first get in touch with the relevant School and Division. Send all applications, through the respective Heads of Divisions/Groups and School Chairs, to Dean's Office (or to the Dean's office). Applicants who wish to submit their documents electronically should email their application form and complete dossier to Ms Chan Bee Kwang email BKCHAN@ntu.edu.sg
Closing Date: 31 December

Additional Information: All late and/or incomplete applications will not be considered. A check list is included in the application package www.cohass.ntu.edu.sg/Programmes/Pages/HIPS2020.aspx

For further information contact:

Email: wpseeto@ntu.edu.sg

Singapore Education – Sampoerna Foundation MBA in Singapore

Purpose: To help Indonesian citizens below 35 years pursue their MBA studies
Eligibility: Applicant must be an Indonesian citizen under 35 years, hold a local Bachelor's degree from any discipline with a minimum GPA of 3.00 (on a 4.00 scale), have a minimum of 2 year full-time professional work experience after the completion of the undergraduate degree, currently not enrolled in graduate or post-graduate program, or obtained a Master's degree or equivalent; not be a graduate from overseas tertiary institutions, unless was on a full scholarship, not receive other equivalent award or scholarship offering similar or other benefits at the time of the award
Level of Study: MBA
Type: Award
Value: US$70,000 to 150,000
Country of Study: Singapore
Closing Date: 1 February
Additional Information: www.postgraduatefunding.com/award-3961

Singapore International Graduate Award

Purpose: The Singapore International Graduate Award (SINGA) is a collaboration between the Agency for Science, Technology & Research (A*STAR), the Nanyang Technological University (NTU), the National University of Singapore (NUS) and the Singapore University of Technology and Design (SUTD)
Eligibility: Open for application to all international graduates with a passion for research and excellent academic results. Good skills in written and spoken English. Good reports from academic referees
Level of Study: Doctorate
Type: Award
Value: Tuition fees Monthly stipend of S$2,200 which will be increased to S$2,700 after the passing of the Qualifying Examination One-time airfare grant of up to S$1,500 One-time settling-in allowance of S$1,000
Length of Study: 4 years
Frequency: Annual
Country of Study: Singapore
Application Procedure: Online application form should be submitted. Go to Research Areas to browse the projects you are interested in. Valid Passport. A recent passport-sized photo (in.jpeg or.png format). ALL transcripts need to be in English translation. Bachelor's and/or Master's academic transcripts. Bachelor's Degree certificate(s) / scroll(s) or a letter of certification from the university on your candidature if your degree certificate / scroll has not yet been conferred. 2 recommendation reports (to be completed and submitted online by the referees). Apply now via this link here: sms-applicant-app.a-star.edu.sg/
Closing Date: 1 June
Additional Information: www.a-star.edu.sg/Scholarships/for-graduate-studies/singapore-international-graduate-award-singa

Spring Management Development Scholarship (MDS)

Purpose: To nurture the next generation of leaders for the trailblazing companies of tomorrow
Eligibility: Those who are currently working in an SME or are interested to join one, are citizens or permanent residents of Singapore, have less than 5 years of working experience and successfully apply for one of the approved MBA programmes.
Level of Study: MBA
Type: Scholarship
Value: Full-time/Part-time MBA SPRING will provide grant value of up to 70 % of tuition fees, and other related expenses for full-time MBA scholars up to a maximum qualifying cost of S$52,000
Study Establishment: Nanyang Business School
Country of Study: Singapore
Application Procedure: Applicants will have to go through a joint selection process by SPRING and the participating SME, serve a 3 month internship in the SME prior to embarking on the approved MBA course (performance must be deemed satisfactory by the SME), and serve a bond of up to 2 years in the SME upon completion of studies. For more information on government assistance programmes, please contact the Enterprise One hotline at Tel (65) 6898 1800 or email enterpriseone@spring.gov.sg or visit their website at www.spring.gov.sg/mds
Funding: Private
Contributor: SPRING Singapore and small medium enterprises.
Additional Information: For more information on government assistance programmes, please contact the Enterprise One hotline at Tel: (65) 6898 1800 or email enterpriseone@spring.gov.sg or visit their website at www.spring.gov.sg/mds

For further information contact:

Tel: (65) 6898 1800
Email: enquiry@enterprisesg.gov.sg

The Lien Foundation Scholarship for Social Service Leaders

Purpose: To provide scholarships to support education and professional development
Eligibility: The scholarship is open to candidates with academic excellence, notable performance record and the potential to take up leadership positions in voluntary welfare organizations
Level of Study: Professional development
Type: Scholarship
Value: The award includes tuition fees, maintenance allowance (for full-time studies), book allowance and any other compulsory fees
Country of Study: Any country
Application Procedure: For more information on the scholarship do visit the websites www.ncss.org.sg/lien
Closing Date: 22 June

For further information contact:

Email: Pamela_biswas@ncss.gov.sg

Narotam Sekhsaria Foundation

1st Floor, Nirmal Building, Nariman Point, Mumbai, Maharashtra 400021, India.

Tel: (91) 22 6132 6200
Email: admin@nsfoundation.co.in
Website: nsfoundation.co.in/
Contact: Narotam Sekhsaria Foundation

Narotam Sekhsaria Foundation is a non-profit initiative created to support enterprising individuals and innovative organizations.

Narotam Sekhsaria Postgraduate Scholarship

Purpose: The aim of the scholarship is to help high achieving students to pursue postgraduate studies at prestigious Indian and international universities
Eligibility: 1. Applicant must be an Indian national, residing in India 2. Applicant must be below 30 years of age as of January 31, 2024 3. Applicant must have graduated from an accredited Indian University Students in their final year of the degree course or those awaiting results are also eligible 4. Applicants planning to pursue Postgraduate studies at top ranking institutions from Fall 2024 5. Applicants who have applied and are awaiting an acceptance from the university are also eligible to apply 6. The award of scholarship is subject to securing admission
Level of Study: Postgraduate
Type: Postgraduate scholarships
Value: The award of scholarship is subject to securing admission
Study Establishment: The scholarship is awarded in the fields offered by the university
Country of Study: India
Application Procedure: All applications for the Narotam Sekhsaria's scholarships for post-graduation are invited by the Foundation in the month of January for every academic year. webportalapp.com/sp/login/narotam_application_portal
Closing Date: 16 March
Additional Information: For more details please see the website pg.nsfoundation.co.in/ pg.nsfoundation.co.in/application-process/

For further information contact:

Tel: (91) 22 61326200
Email: pgscholarship@nsfoundation.co.in

National Academies

500 5th Street NW, Washington, DC 20001, United States of America.

Tel: (1) 202 334 2000
Email: infofell@nas.edu
Website: www.nationalacademies.org

The National Academies of Sciences, Engineering, and Medicine provide independent, objective advice to inform policy with evidence, spark progress and innovation, and confront challenging issues for the benefit of society.

American Board of Emergency Medicine Fellowship

Purpose: The overall purpose of the ABEM Emergency Medicine Fellowship is to provide talented, early-career

health science scholars in emergency medicine with the opportunity to experience and participate in evidence-based healthcare or public health studies that improve the care and access to care of patients in domestic and global health care systems. The ABEM Emergency Medicine Fellowship is part of the NAM Fellowships for Health Science Scholars program
Eligibility: Nominees for the ABEM Emergency Medicine Fellowship must: 1. Be nominated by a member of the NAM or a board member of the ABEM 2. Be an ABEM Diplomate or meet the emergency medicine credential requirements for board certification 3. Hold an M.D. or D.O. 4. Be two-to-ten years out from completion of post-graduate work 5. Be able to dedicate 10 to 20 percent of time to the fellowship for two years Hold U.S. citizen or permanent resident status at the time of the nomination
Level of Study: Doctorate
Type: Fellowship
Value: US$25,000
Length of Study: 2 years
Country of Study: United States of America
Closing Date: June
Additional Information: nam.edu/programs/health-policy-educational-programs-and-fellowships/nam-fellowship-program/american-board-of-emergency-medicine-fellowship/

For further information contact:

Email: yphillips@nas.edu

Christine Mirzayan Science & Technology Policy Graduate Fellowship Program

Purpose: To engage students in science and technology policy
Eligibility: Graduate students and postdoctoral scholars and those who have completed graduate studies or postdoctoral research within the last 5 years are eligible to apply
Level of Study: Postgraduate
Type: Fellowship
Value: The stipend for a 10-week program is US$11,000
Length of Study: 12 weeks
Frequency: Annual
Country of Study: United States of America
Application Procedure: A completed application form must be submitted. Application forms are available on the website
Closing Date: 29 October
Additional Information: mirzayanfellow.nas.edu/

Ford Foundation Fellowship Programs

Purpose: Through its program of fellowships, the Ford Foundation seeks to increase the diversity of the nation's college and university faculties by increasing their ethnic and racial diversity, maximize the educational benefits of diversity, and increase the number of professors who can and will use diversity as a resource for enriching the education of all students
Eligibility: 1. All U.S. citizens, U.S. nationals, and U.S. permanent residents (holders of a Permanent Resident Card); individuals granted deferred action status under the Deferred Action for Childhood Arrivals Program;1 Indigenous individuals exercising rights associated with the Jay Treaty of 1794; individuals granted Temporary Protected Status; asylees; and refugees, regardless of race, national origin, religion, gender, age, disability, or sexual orientation; 2. Individuals with evidence of superior academic achievement (such as grade point average, class rank, honors or other designations); and 3. Individuals committed to a career in teaching and research at the college or university level in the U.S.
Eligible Country: United States of America
Level of Study: Doctorate
Type: Fellowship
Value: Annual stipend: Pre-doctoral US$27,000, Dissertation US$28,000, Postdoctoral US$50,000
Country of Study: United States of America
Closing Date: 5 January
Additional Information: sites.nationalacademies.org/PGA/FordFellowships/index.htm

For further information contact:

Email: FordApplications@nas.edu

Ford Foundation Senior Fellowship

Eligibility: The Ford Foundation Senior Fellowship award is open only to individuals who have previously held a Ford Foundation Predoctoral, Dissertation, or Postdoctoral Fellowship administered by the National Academies and currently hold a faculty appointment at an accredited U.S. academic institution. Applicants must have held the PhD/Sc.D. for at least seven years by the application deadline
Eligible Country: United States of America
Level of Study: Doctorate, Postdoctorate
Type: Fellowship
Value: annual stipend of US$80,000 and US$5,000 for travel and other research expenses.
Length of Study: 6 to 12 months

Country of Study: United States of America
Closing Date: 31 January
Additional Information: sites.nationalacademies.org/PGA/FordFellowships/PGA_171447

For further information contact:

Email: FordApplications@nas.edu

Gilbert S. Omenn Fellowship

Purpose: The Omenn Fellowship aims to foster a cadre of physician-scientists who will integrate biomedical research, population health, and health policy and will expand the nation's capacity for research, leadership, and policy development that advances health. The program especially welcomes nominations of historically underrepresented candidates
Eligibility: Nominees for the Omenn Fellowship must: 1. Be nominated by a member of the NAM 2. Hold an M.D. or D.O. with additional study in the medical sciences, public health, and/or public policy 3. Be one-to-five years out from completion of residency and fellowship training or receiving the terminal doctoral degree, in an appropriate faculty position or its equivalent 4. Be able to dedicate 10 to 20 percent of time to the fellowship for two years, including all the specified experiences 5. Be endorsed by the department chair, institute director, or equivalent 6. Hold U.S. citizen or permanent resident status at the time of the nomination
Level of Study: Doctorate
Type: Fellowship
Value: US$25,000
Length of Study: 2 years
Country of Study: United States of America
Closing Date: June
Additional Information: nam.edu/programs/health-policy-educational-programs-and-fellowships/nam-fellowship-program/gilbert-s-omenn-fellowship/

For further information contact:

Email: yphillips@nas.edu

Greenwall Fellowship in Bioethics

Purpose: The Greenwall Fellowship in Bioethics enables young investigators to participate actively in the work of the National Academies of Sciences, Engineering, and Medicine (the National Academies) and to further their careers as future leaders addressing bioethics issues in clinical care, biomedical research, and public policy
Eligibility: Nominees for the Greenwall Fellowship in Bioethics must: 1. Be nominated by a member of the NAM 2. Hold an M.D., D.O., J.D., PhD, or an equivalent degree, with completion of post-graduate work two to ten years prior to the award 3. Have demonstrated interest in, focus on, and scholarship on addressing bioethics issues in clinical care, biomedical research, public health, or public policy 4. Be able to dedicate 10 to 20 percent of time to the fellowship for two years 5. Be endorsed by the department chair, institute director, or equivalent
Level of Study: Doctorate
Type: Fellowship
Value: US$25,000
Length of Study: 2 year
Country of Study: United States of America
Closing Date: June
Additional Information: nam.edu/programs/health-policy-educational-programs-and-fellowships/nam-fellowship-program/greenwall-fellowship-in-bioethics/

For further information contact:

Email: yphillips@nas.edu

Jefferson Science Fellowship

Purpose: To offset the costs of temporary living quarters in the Washington, DC area
Eligibility: Applicants must be United States citizens and holding a tenured faculty position at a United States degree granting academic institution of higher learning. For terms and conditions as well as further details log on to the website.
Level of Study: Postgraduate
Value: The Jefferson Science Fellow will be paid a per diem of up to US$50,000 by the United States Department of State and US$10,000 will be made available to the Fellow for travel associated with their assignment(s)
Length of Study: 1 year
Frequency: Annual
Application Procedure: A complete nomination/application package consists of nomination/application form in PDF format and in word format; curriculum vitae (limit 10 pages); statements of qualifications (limit 2 pages each); and at least 3, and no more than 5, letters of recommendation from peers of the nominee/applicant
Closing Date: 18 October
Contributor: National Academies supported through a partnership between American philanthropic foundations, the United States STE academic community, professional scientific societies, and the United States Department of State
Additional Information: Applicants should notify their institution while applying and encourage them to initiate

a JSF/MOU as described on the website. Incomplete nomination/application packages, or those received after the deadline, will not be reviewed sites.nationalacademies.org/PGA/Jefferson/index.htm

For further information contact:

Tel: (1) 202 334 2643
Email: jsf@nas.edu

National Energy Technology Laboratory Methane Hydrates Fellowship Program (MHFP)

Purpose: The National Academies of Sciences, Engineering, and Medicine, in association with the U.S. Department of Energy's National Energy Technology Laboratory (NETL), administers a Research Fellowship Program designed to support the development of Methane Hydrate science and enable highly qualified graduate and postgraduate students to pursue advanced degrees and training in an area of increasing national interest
Eligibility: M.S., PhD, and Postdoctoral applicants. Open to U.S. citizens only
Level of Study: Doctorate, Postdoctorate, Postgraduate
Type: Fellowship
Value: Stipend Rates Master's Level (Fellow) begins at US$30,000 with a maximum 2-year tenure, PhD Level (Fellow) begins at US$35,000 with a maximum 3-year tenure and Postdoctoral Level (Research Associate) begins at US$60,000 with a maximum 2-year tenure, Travel Allowance of US$6,000
Country of Study: United States of America
Application Procedure: The online application system will close on the deadline date at 500 PM Eastern Time. All application components, including letters of recommendation, must be submitted by this deadline. Access to the online application system will not be available to applicants and letter writers after this time
Closing Date: 1 February
Additional Information: sites.nationalacademies.org/pga/rap/pga_050408

For further information contact:

Tel: (1) 304 285 4714
Email: richard.baker@netl.doe.gov

NRC Research Associate Programs (RAP)

Purpose: The National Academies of Sciences, Engineering, and Medicine administers competitive postdoctoral and senior research awards on behalf of U.S. federal research agencies and affiliated institutions with facilities at over 100 locations throughout the U.S. and abroad
Eligibility: Awards are available for scientists and engineers at all stages of their career. Applicants should hold, or anticipate receiving, an earned doctorate in science or engineering. Degrees from universities abroad should be equivalent in training and research experience to a degree from a U.S. institution. Many awards are open to foreign nationals as well as to U.S. citizens
Level of Study: Postdoctorate, Research
Type: Award
Value: NRC Research Associates receive annual stipends ranging from US$45,000 to US$80,000 for recent doctoral recipients and are proportionally higher for Senior Associates
Length of Study: More than 5 years
Frequency: Annual
Country of Study: Any country
Application Procedure: Apply online
Closing Date: 1 May
Funding: Government
Additional Information: sites.nationalacademies.org/PGA/RAP/index.htm

For further information contact:

The National Academies of Sciences, Engineering, and Medicine, 500 Fifth Street, NW, Washington, DC 20001, United States of America.

Tel: (1) 202 334 2000

NRC Research Associateship Programs (RAP)

Purpose: The NRC Research Associateship Programs (RAP) promote excellence in scientific and technological research conducted by the U.S. government through the administration of programs offering graduate, postdoctoral, and senior level research opportunities at sponsoring federal laboratories and affiliated institutions
Eligibility: Awards are available for scientists and engineers at all stages of their career. Applicants should hold, or anticipate receiving, an earned doctorate in science or engineering. Degrees from universities abroad should be equivalent in training and research experience to a degree from a U.S. institution. Many awards are open to foreign nationals as well as to U.S. citizens
Eligible Country: Any Country
Level of Study: Postdoctoral
Type: Award

Value: US$45,000 to US$80,000
Length of Study: 5 years
Frequency: Annual
Country of Study: United States of America
Application Procedure: An application is submitted through the NRC Research Associateship Programs online application system
Closing Date: 1 May
Additional Information: sites.nationalacademies.org/PGA/RAP/index.htm

For further information contact:

NRC Research Associateship Programs, 500 Fifth Street, NW, Washington, DC 20001, United States of America.

Tel: (1) 202 334 2760
Email: rap@nas.edu

The Optical Society, Amplify Scholarship

Purpose: The Amplify Scholarship is awarded annually to 10 Black undergraduate or graduate level students. This grant is both merit and need-based. In addition to the funding, recipients gain access to our global network of mentors and the supporting companies
Eligibility: Self-identify as Black Be currently enrolled as an undergraduate or graduate student at a university Undergraduates have a major in physics, math or engineering and a demonstrated interest in optics and photonics. Graduates have a major and/or concentration in optics or photonics demonstrated with your research and coursework. Demonstrate academic potential (GPA, publications, references, other awards/merits) Program requirements recognize and exclude career breaks from timelines (eg, eldercare; maternity or paternity leave)
Level of Study: Graduate
Type: Scholarship
Value: US$7,500 One-year Optica Student Membership Access to mentorship platform and connection with a mentor
Frequency: Annual
Country of Study: Any country
Application Procedure: Application is now open. Apply here today: apply.osa.org/
No. of awards offered: 10
Closing Date: 9 December
Contributor: 3DEO Gary Bjorklund Jason Eichenholz Fibertek Inc Optica Executive Team 2016-2020 Optica Ambassadors
Additional Information: www.optica.org/en-us/foundation/opportunities/scholarships/amplify_scholarship/

The Optical Society, Chang Pivoting Fellowship

Purpose: The Milton and Rosalind Chang Pivoting Fellowship provides unrestricted funding to talented, early-career optical scientists and engineers who believe their expertise can improve society outside of the lab. We encourage those with vision and exceptional talent to apply and pursue a newfound passion
Eligibility: Be a current early career member who has received a terminal degree within the last five - seven years or will receive a terminal degree by the application deadline
Type: Fellowship
Value: US$50,000
Length of Study: five - seven years
Frequency: Annual
Country of Study: Any country
Application Procedure: Visit apply.optica.org.
Closing Date: 23 September
Additional Information: www.optica.org/en-us/foundation/opportunities/fellowships/milton_and_rosalind_chang_pivoting_fellowship/#SELECT

For further information contact:

Global Headquarters, 2010 Massachusetts Ave. NW, Washington, DC 20036, United States of America.

Tel: (1) 202 223 8130
Fax: (1) 202 223 1096
Email: info@optica.org

N

The Optical Society, Corning Women in Optical Communications Scholarship

Subjects: Be recognized for excellence in optical communications
Purpose: The Corning Women in Optical Fiber Communications Scholarship supports gender diversity in the optical communications industry, this scholarship is a merit-based prize recognizing outstanding women studying optical communications and networking
Eligibility: 1. Be a current member 2. Self Identify as a woman 3. Be currently enrolled as a graduate student at a university 4. Have a field of study/research focused on one of the following areas: optical components, devices and fiber, networks, applications and access or photonic systems and subsystems 5. Demonstrate academic excellence (GPA, publications, references, other awards/merits) 6. Program requirements recognize and exclude career breaks from career timelines (eg, eldercare; maternity or paternity leave)
Type: Scholarship

Value: US$3,000 scholarship, and up to US$2,000 toward travel expenses
Frequency: Annual
Country of Study: Any country
Application Procedure: Application Requirements: 1. Essay response: How would attending OFC support your career advancement and goals? 2. CV/resume 3. Personal statement 4. GPA certification (unofficial transcript) Apply when open at apply.optica.org
No. of awards offered: 3
Closing Date: 15 November
Contributor: Corning Incorporated.
Additional Information: Website: www.optica.org/en-us/foundation/opportunities/scholarships/corning_women_in_optical_communications_scholarshi/

For further information contact:

Global Headquarters, 2010 Massachusetts Ave. NW, Washington, DC 20036, United States of America.

Tel: (1) 202 223 8130
Fax: (1) 202 223 1096
Email: info@optica.org

The Optical Society, Deutsch Fellowship

Purpose: This one-year multidisciplinary fellowship specifically fosters interactions between researchers from diverse fields of science and medicine and supports post-doctoral investigators pursuing training in either basic or clinical research. It is offered in partnership with the Massachusetts General Hospital (MGH) Wellman Center for Photomedicine
Eligibility: Select one or more positions available for the fellowship 2024 Position Descriptions Hold a PhD, M.D. or M.D./PhD degree Be at the postdoctoral training level at the time of the award and within 5 years of completion of your degree, excluding breaks in a career timeline (e.g., eldercare, maternity or paternity leave)
Level of Study: Postdoctorate
Type: Fellowship
Value: One year fellowship
Length of Study: 5 Years
Country of Study: Any country
Application Procedure: Applications will be available at apply.optica.org
Closing Date: 5 August
Contributor: Massachusetts General Hospital (MGH) Wellman Center for Photomedicine
Additional Information: www.optica.org/en-us/foundation/opportunities/fellowships/thomas_f_deutsch_fellowship/

For further information contact:

Global Headquarters, 2010 Massachusetts Ave. NW, Washington, DC 20036, United States of America.

Tel: (1) 202 223 8130
Fax: (1) 202 223 1096
Email: info@optica.org

The Optical Society, Foundation Fellowships

Purpose: The Optical Society of America Foundation inspires future optics innovators, supports career development for optics students, recent graduates, and young professionals and recognizes distinguished achievement in the field through the presentation of awards and honors. OSAF Fellowships are intended to provide career enhancing experiences to recent PhDs through postdoctoral research at an OSAF sponsoring company
Eligibility: Open to all nationalities; subject to visa requirements. Foreign nationals will be sponsored under a J-1 visa by the National Academy of Sciences
Level of Study: Postgraduate
Type: Fellowship
Value: Stipend, health insurance allowance, relocation reimbursement, and funding for attendance and participation in OSA meetings and committees
Length of Study: One year with the possibility of renewal for additional year(s) based on adequate research progress and availability of funds
Additional Information: www.sites.nationalacademies.org/PGA/osaff/index.htm

For further information contact:

The Optical Society, Foundation Fellowships, 500 Fifth Street NW, Keck 516, Washington, DC 2000, United States of America.

Tel: (1) 202 334 3478
Email: OSAFFellowships@nas.edu

The Optical Society, Optica Women Scholars

Purpose: Empowering the next generation of women leaders in optics and photonics
Eligibility: Self-identify as a woman. Be currently enrolled as an undergraduate or graduate student at a university. Undergraduates have a major in optics, physics, math or engineering and a demonstrated interest in optics and photonics. Graduates have a major and/or concentration in optics or photonics demonstrated with your research and coursework.

Demonstrate academic potential (GPA, publications, references, other awards/merits). Program requirements recognize and exclude career breaks from timelines (eg, eldercare; maternity or paternity leave)
Level of Study: Graduate
Type: Scholarship
Value: US$10,000. One-year Optica Student Membership Access to mentorship platform and connection with a mentor
Frequency: Annual
Country of Study: Any country
No. of awards offered: 20
Closing Date: 31 January
Contributor: Marvell Semiconductors Inc Edmund Optics Joseph Goodman James Wyant
Additional Information: www.optica.org/en-us/foundation/opportunities/scholarships/optica_women_scholars/

National Aeronautics and Space Administration (NASA)

NASA Headquarters, Suite 5R30, Washington, DC 20546, United States of America.

Tel: (1) 202 358 0001
Email: hfinquiry@stsci.edu
Website: www.nasa.gov
Contact: Public Communications Office

The National Aeronautics and Space Administration is America's civil space program and the global leader in space exploration. The agency has a diverse workforce of just under 18,000 civil servants, and works with many more U.S. contractors, academia, and international and commercial partners to explore, discover, and expand knowledge for the benefit of humanity. With an annual budget of US$23.2 billion in Fiscal Year 2021, which is.5% of the overall U.S. federal budget, NASA supports more than 312,000 jobs across the United States, generating more than US$64.3 billion in total economic output (Fiscal Year 2019).

Hubble Fellowships for Postdoctoral Scientists

Purpose: The Hubble Fellowship Program provides an opportunity for highly qualified recent postdoctoral scientists to conduct independent research that is broadly related to the NASA Cosmic Origins scientific goals as addressed by any of the missions in that program the Hubble Space Telescope, Spitzer Space Telescope, Stratospheric Observatory for Infrared Astronomy (SOFIA), the Herschel Space Observatory, and the James Webb Space Telescope. The research will be carried out at United States Host Institutions chosen by each Fellow
Eligibility: Applicants must have received a PhD or equivalent doctoral-level research degree in astronomy, physics, or a related discipline on or after 1 January (previous year). Graduate-student awardees who have not yet received their doctoral degree at the time of application must present evidence of having completed all requirements for the degree before commencing their Fellowships. Hubble Fellowships are open to citizens of the United States and to English-speaking citizens of other countries. Qualified applicants will receive consideration without regard to race, creed, color, age, gender, or national origin. Women and members of minority groups are strongly encouraged to apply. Incomplete applications and/or applications received after the deadline will not be considered
Type: Fellowship
Value: An annual stipend of approx. US$75,000, health insurance (up to a maximum of US$20,000 for a family plan), up to US$8,500 for relocation costs, and up to US$19,000 in the first year and US$15,000 in the second and third years for research-related travel, hardware, computing services, publications, and other direct costs
Length of Study: Up to 3 years
Frequency: Annual
Country of Study: United States of America
Application Procedure: Application website: catcopy.ipac.caltech.edu/nhfp/application.php
Closing Date: 3 November
Additional Information: The Hubble Fellowship Program is administered for NASA by the Space Telescope Science Institute (STScI), operated by the Association of Universities for Research in Astronomy, Inc., working in cooperation with astronomical institutions throughout the United States. Awards will be made to support each Hubble Fellow through a designated Host Institution www.stsci.edu/stsci-research/fellowships/nasa-hubble-fellowship-program

National Air and Space Museum (NASM), Smithsonian Institution

655 Jefferson Drive, SW, Washington, DC 20560, United States of America.

Tel: (1) 202 633 2214
Email: colette.williams@nasm.si.edu
Website: www.nasm.si.edu

The Smithsonian's National Air and Space Museum maintains the world's largest and most significant collection of aviation and space artifacts, encompassing all aspects of human flight, as well as related works of art and archival materials. It operates two landmark facilities that, together, welcome more than eight million visitors a year, making it the most visited museum in the country. It also is home to the Center for Earth and Planetary Studies.

Charles A Lindbergh Chair in Aerospace History

Purpose: The Charles A. Lindbergh Chair in Aerospace History is a competitive 12-month fellowship open Oct 15, to senior scholars with distinguished records of publication who are at work on, or anticipate being at work on, books in aerospace history
Level of Study: Research
Type: Fellowship
Value: US$100,000
Length of Study: 1 year
Frequency: Annual
Study Establishment: Smithsonian Institution
Country of Study: United States of America
Application Procedure: Before beginning your application, you must create an account. As you work on your application, you can save your progress and resume your application as needed. As part of the application, you will be required to include the following supplemental files 1. Three letters of reference. 2. A summary description, not longer than 250 words, of your proposed research. 3. A research proposal not more than 1,500 words. This statement should set forth your research plan, indicating the importance of the work both in relation to the larger discipline and to your own intellectual goals. The proposal must contain your evaluation of the contributions that Museum staff members are expected to make to your studies, and indicate what Museum collections, special facilities, and other resources are needed. In addition, the proposal must also provide justification for the research-related expenses included in the research budget. We encourage the inclusion of an annotated historiographical introduction to the subject field of your proposal. 4. An estimated schedule for each phase of the proposed research. 5. A curriculum vitae or resume, not longer than three pages, including pertinent publications, fellowships or accomplishments relevant to your proposal
Closing Date: 1 November
Funding: Private
Contributor: Smithsonian restricted funds
Additional Information: www.airandspace.si.edu/support/get-involved/fellowships/charles-lindbergh-chair-aerospace-history

For further information contact:

Email: kinneyj@si.edu

Engen Conservation

Purpose: The Engen fellowship will introduce the candidate to conservation techniques for a wide range of composite objects, metals, organic materials, and painted surfaces. This fellowship is intended to contribute to the education of recent graduates by allowing them to delve into the complexities of working with modern composite materials, refine treatment process, learn management, and conduct a small-scale research project. The Fellow's independent research will be derived from our diverse collection materials. Fellows will be encouraged to publish or present their research at the end of their tenure. Access to other Smithsonian conservators, conservation scientists, and analytical capabilities at the Museum Conservation Institute (MCI) may also be available
Eligibility: The ideal candidate will have a Master's degree in Objects Conservation from a recognized program and is able to multi-task, work collaboratively as well as conduct treatments and research independently. The candidate should have knowledge of ethical and professional principles and concepts related to the preservation of objects in a wide variety of media and knowledge of the theories, principles, techniques, practices, and methodologies used to examine, study, treat, and preserve historic objects. Applicants should have a proven record of research, writing ability, and proficiency in English language skills (written and spoken)
Level of Study: Research
Type: Fellowship
Value: Stipend amount: US$45,000 Research allowance: US$5,000
Length of Study: 1 year
Country of Study: United States of America
Application Procedure: Applications are submitted through the Smithsonian Online Academic Appointment System (SOLAA)
Closing Date: 15 February
Additional Information: We are excited about the opportunity to provide this fellowship experience and look forward to receiving your application. airandspace.si.edu/collections/conservation/fellowships

For further information contact:

Email: HorelickL@si.edu

Guggenheim Fellowship

Subjects: Space history
Purpose: The Guggenheim Fellowships are competitive three- to twelve-month in-residence fellowships for pre- or postdoctoral research in aviation and space history
Eligibility: Applicants who have received a PhD degree or equivalent within seven years of the beginning of the Fellowship period are eligible to apply for a Postdoctoral

Guggenheim Fellowship. The limitation may be waived upon demonstration that a Fellowship appointment would further the applicant's research training. Recipients must have completed that degree at the time the Fellowship commences. Students who have completed preliminary course work and examinations and are engaged in dissertation research are eligible to apply for a Pre-doctoral Guggenheim Fellowship. All applicants must be able to speak and write fluently in English
Level of Study: Research
Type: Fellowship
Value: An annual stipend of US$30,000 for predoctoral candidates and US$45,000 for postdoctoral candidates
Study Establishment: NASM
Country of Study: United States of America
Application Procedure: Before beginning your application, you must create an account. As you work on your application, you can save your progress and resume your application as needed. As part of the application, you will be required to include the following supplemental files 1. Three letters of reference. 2. A summary description, not longer than 250 words, of your proposed research. 3. A research proposal not more than 1,500 words. This statement should set forth your research plan, indicating the importance of the work both in relation to the larger discipline and to your own intellectual goals. The proposal must contain your evaluation of the contributions that Museum staff members are expected to make to your studies, and indicate what Museum collections, special facilities, and other resources are needed. In addition, the proposal must also provide justification for the research-related expenses included in the research budget. We encourage the inclusion of an annotated historiographical introduction to the subject field of your proposal. 4. An estimated schedule for each phase of the proposed research. 5. A curriculum vitae or resume, not longer than three pages, including pertinent publications, fellowships or accomplishments relevant to your proposal
Closing Date: 1 December
Additional Information: airandspace.si.edu/support/get-involved/fellowships/guggenheim

For further information contact:

Email: NASM-Fellowships@si.edu

National Air and Space Museum Aviation/Space Writers Award

Purpose: To support research on aerospace topics. The product created as a result of the grant must be in any form suitable for potential public dissemination in print, electronic, broadcast, or other visual medium, including, but not limited to, a book manuscript, video, film script, or monograph
Type: Award
Value: US$5,000
Frequency: Annual
Application Procedure: 1. Maximum two-page, single-spaced proposal stating the subject of their research and their research goals 2. One- to two-page curriculum vitae 3. One-page detailed budget explaining how the grant will be spent
Closing Date: March
Additional Information: www.airandspace.si.edu/support/get-involved/fellowships/aviation-space-writers-foundation-award

For further information contact:

National Air and Space Museum, Independence Ave at Sixth Street, SW, Rm 3313, MRC 312, P.O. Box 37012, Washington, DC 20013-7012, United States of America.

Email: NASM-Fellowships@si.edu

Postdoctoral Earth and Planetary Sciences Fellowship

Purpose: To support scientific research.
Level of Study: Postdoctorate
Type: Fellowship
Value: Stipend, compatible with National Research Council Awards
Length of Study: 1 or more years
Frequency: Dependent on funds available
Study Establishment: NASM
Country of Study: United States of America
Application Procedure: Applicants must complete an application form
Closing Date: 15 January
Funding: Private
Contributor: Smithsonian restricted funds
Additional Information: www.airandspace.si.edu/support/get-involved/fellowships/postdoctoral-earth-and-planetary-sciences

National Association for Core Curriculum, Inc.

1640 Franklin Avenue, Suite 104, Kent, OH 44240-4324, United States of America.

Tel: (1) 330 677 5008
Email: gvarsnacc@aol.com
Contact: Dr Gordon F Vars, Executive Secretary & Treasurer

The National Association for Core Curriculum, Inc. has promoted integrative person centred education at all levels since 1953.

Bossing-Edwards Research Scholarship Award

Purpose: To encourage research on core curriculum and other interdisciplinary or integrative approaches to education
Eligibility: Must be a postgraduate student attend a university; by race for Black students; not be attending high school currently; study full-time; to students studying Nursing; be affiliated with National Black Nurses' Association
Level of Study: Doctorate, Postgraduate
Type: Scholarship
Value: US$2,500
Frequency: Dependent on funds available
Study Establishment: An appropriate institution
Country of Study: United States of America
Application Procedure: Applicants should write explaining intended research and how they meet the criteria of eligibility
No. of awards offered: 5
Closing Date: 1 May
No. of awards given last year: 1
No. of applicants last year: 5
Additional Information: www.petersons.com/scholarship/lynne-edwards-research-scholarship-111_228423.

For further information contact:

Email: canada@berkeley.edu

National Association for Gifed Children

1300 I Street, NW, Suite 400E, Washington, DC 20005, United States of America.

Tel: (1) 202 785 4268
Website: www.nagc.org/
Contact: National Association for Gifted Children

NAGC's mission is to support those who enhance the growth and development of gifted and talented children through education, advocacy, community building, and research. We aim to help parents and families, K-12 education professionals including support service personnel, and members of the research and higher education community who work to help gifted and talented children as they strive to achieve their personal best and contribute to their communities.

Davis Scholarship

Purpose: Lewis & Clark is pleased to announce its continuing commitment to the Davis United World College (UWC) Scholars program for the academic year
Level of Study: Postgraduate
Type: Scholarship
Value: US$25,000
Length of Study: 4 year
Frequency: Annual
Country of Study: Any country
Closing Date: 15 February
Funding: Foundation
Additional Information: www.lclark.edu/offices/international/financial_aid/davis_scholarship/

For further information contact:

Associate Dean of Students, Lewis & Clark College, 0615 SW Palatine Hill Road, Portland, OR 97219, United States of America.

Tel: (1) 503 768 7305
Fax: (1) 503 768 7301
Email: iso@lclark.edu

Distinguished Scholarship

Purpose: The National Association for Gifted Children (NAGC) annually presents the Distinguished Scholar Award to an individual who has made significant contributions to the field of knowledge regarding the education of gifted and talented individuals. This individual should have a continued record of distinguished scholarship and contributions to the field of gifted education for more than 10 years, and must show a record of ongoing scholarly productivity as recognized by experts in the field
Eligibility: 1. Evidence of research in the field of gifted and talented. 2. Evidence that the contributions reflect a continuous and noted record of involvement in the field of gifted and talented education. 3. Evidence of recognition by peers of the importance of the above-mentioned contributions
Level of Study: Postgraduate
Type: Scholarship
Value: US$30,000
Length of Study: 4 year
Frequency: Annual
Country of Study: Any country
Closing Date: 1 February
Funding: Foundation
Additional Information: www.nagc.org/about/awards-recognition/distinguished-scholar-award

Goodrich Scholarship Program

Purpose: Goodrich students establish a dynamic presence on campus. They come hungry, ready to learn and eager to join the UNO community. Many recipients are the first in their families to attend college. They come from underrepresented populations and have earned an opportunity to continue their education
Type: Scholarship
Value: Financial aid in the form of tuition and general fees.
Frequency: Annual
Country of Study: United States of America
Application Procedure: The Goodrich scholarship is both merit-and-need-based. Merit and financial aid are evaluated based on a composite of selection criteria, including 1. Application data 2. Financial analysis 3. Academic record 4. In-person interview 5. English Placement and Proficiency Exam (EPPE) 6. Personal life-experience essay 7. References
Closing Date: 1 March

For further information contact:

UNO Campus, 6001 Dodge Street, CPACS 123, Omaha Nebraska, NE 68182, United States of America.

Tel: (1) 402 554 2274
Email: unogoodrich@unomaha.edu

Javits-Frasier Scholars Program

Subjects: Teachers, school counselors, or school psychologists
Purpose: The Javits-Frasier Teacher Scholars program is a unique professional development opportunity for teachers, school counselors/psychologists, and others who work in Title I schools and are passionate about helping all gifted children
Eligibility: 1. Teachers, school counselors, or school psychologists should apply. Educators from culturally and ethnically diverse backgrounds are especially encouraged to apply. 2. Applicant must work in a Title I School. 3. Applicant has not previously attended an NAGC Convention. 4. Applicant must be new (1-2 years of experience) to teaching and/or new to gifted/talented education
Type: Scholarship
Frequency: Annual
Country of Study: United States of America
Application Procedure: 1. Personal Contact & School Information (school demographic information will be available in the school report card or through your state's department of education). 2. Personal Statement (no more than two [2] single-spaced pages). 3. Professional Resume 4. One (1) Administrative Recommendation (Have your administrator recommender go to www.nagc.org/javits-frasier-scholar-recommendation. 5. One (1) Recommendation form from another source (Have the recommender go to www.nagc.org/javits-frasier-scholar-recommendation
Closing Date: 14 May

National Association of Teachers of Singing (NATS)

9957 Moorings Drive, Suite 401, Jacksonville, FL 32257, United States of America.

Tel: (1) 904 992 9101
Email: info@nats.org
Website: www.nats.org

The National Association of Teachers of Singing (NATS) is now the largest association of teachers of singing in the world. NATS offers a variety of lifelong learning experiences to its members, such as workshops, intern programmes, master classes, and conferences, all beginning at the chapter level and progressing to national events.

Clifton Ware Group-Voice Pedagogy Award

Purpose: The Group-Voice Pedagogy Award has been established by Clifton Ware, professor emeritus (voice, voice pedagogy), University of Minnesota Twin Cities and a long-time NATS member. It is designed to highlight the concept of "Class Voice" and its potential impact for singers through offerings in community, independent, and academic settings
Eligibility: Applicants for this award must be currently active NATS members who want to advance the idea of learning to sing together in group instructional settings such as group-voice classes, studio classes, choral and musical-theater ensembles; small group lessons of 2-3 similar voice types for students taking private lessons; student and teacher practicums, workshops; or other innovative group teaching
Level of Study: Professional development
Type: Award
Value: up to US$1,000
Country of Study: Any country
Application Procedure: www.nats.org/Clifton_Ware_Group-Voice_Pedagogy_Award_Application.html
Closing Date: 8 May
Additional Information: www.nats.org/Clifton_Ware_Group-Voice_Pedagogy_Award.html

Emerging Leaders Awards

Purpose: Designed to recognize and support NATS teachers with no more than 10 years of teaching experience, this grant will help selected recipients attend sessions, network with colleagues, and enjoy all the benefits available at the NATS Conference
Eligibility: 1. Applicants must be FULL members in good standing, with no more than 10 years of full-time teaching, or the part-time equivalent. 2. Applicants should be active in NATS Chapter and Regional activities. 3. For 2024, applicants must be from the Cal-Western, Mid-Atlantic, Mid-South, New England, Southeastern, Southern, or Texoma regions. Applicants from other regions will be eligible for the 2026 awards. 4. Prior participants in the NATS Intern Program and winners of the YOUNG LEADERS AWARD will not be eligible to apply.
Type: Award
Value: Up to US$750
Country of Study: Any country
Application Procedure: https://www.nats.org/emerging-leaders-awards.html
Closing Date: 21 January
Additional Information: www.nats.org/emerging-leaders-awards.html

For further information contact:

National Association of Teachers of Singing, 9957 Moorings Drive, Suite 401, Jacksonville, FL 32257, United States of America.

Tel: (1) 904 992 9101
Fax: (1) 904 262 2587

Joan Frey Boytim Awards for Independent Teachers

Purpose: In summer 2015, the NATS Foundation announced a new opportunity for independent teachers
Eligibility: In order to be eligible, ALL of the following requirements must apply: 1. The applicant must be a NATS member in good standing at the time of application and time of conference; 2. The applicant must never have attended a NATS National Conference previously; 3. Applicant must teach at least 5 private students per week; 4. Applicant must not work for a college or university as a voice instructor. Recipients will not receive the funds until after the conference and will be required to write a short essay detailing their experience in order to receive disbursement of the funds
Type: Award
Value: US$1,000
Country of Study: Any country
Application Procedure: PROCEDURE: 1. Complete the online application. 2. Provide name and contact information for 1 letter of reference (to be requested and submitted through www.nats.org/cgi/page.cgi/independent-teacher-submit.html
No. of awards offered: 14
Closing Date: 1 February
Additional Information: www.nats.org/independent-teacher-fellowship.html

For further information contact:

National Association of Teachers of Singing, 9957 Moorings Drive, Suite 401 Jacksonville, FL 32257, United States of America.

Tel: (1) 904 992 9101
Fax: (1) 904 262 2587

National Association of Teachers of Singing Art Song Competition Award

Purpose: To stimulate the creation of quality vocal literature through the cooperation of singer and composer
Eligibility: 1. A song cycle, group of songs, or extended song approximately 20' in length-13' to 25' acceptable. (Genres other than the classical "art song" are discouraged.) 2. For single voice and single instrument (neither synthesized) Solo instruments, other than piano, may be used as the collaborative/accompanying instrument with the voice. The genre and style remains that of the art song. Compositions must be scored for voice and ONE accompanying instrument, i.e., voice & piano, voice & flute, voice & violin, etc. ("Compositions may not be scored for three or more instruments, i.e. voice, piano, & violin; voice, guitar, & flute; etc.") 3. To a text written in English, for which the composer has secured copyright clearance-only text setting permission necessary. (If the poem is not in the public domain, the composer must be able to show proof that the proper rights from the appropriate person in control of the copyright-either the poet, the poet's estate or the publisher-have been secured.) 4. Composed within the past two years
Type: Cash prize
Value: 1st place - US$2,000 plus the composer expenses (US$500 airfare reimbursement plus hotel) and for 2nd place - US$1,000
Country of Study: United States of America
Application Procedure: All applications for the Art Song Composition Award are submitted electronically via www.NATS.org.

Closing Date: 1 December
Additional Information: www.nats.org/art-song-composition.html

For further information contact:

Email: cmikkels@valdosta.edu

NATS Artist Awards

Purpose: The NATS Artist Awards (NATSAA) competition is designed to assist singers prepared to launch a professional career and, to that end, substantial monetary and performance prizes are offered
Eligibility: 1. Applicant must be at least 21 but not more than 35 years of age on the deadline entry date September 13, 2024. 2. The applicant's most recent teacher must be a full or associate member of NATS (in good standing) with whom the applicant must have studied continuously for at least one academic year. The applicant must be a full or associate member of NATS in good standing for at least one year prior to September 13, 2024. 3. Applicants must enter in the region audition (dates and locations TBA) of their legal residence or where they are currently studying singing. EXCEPTIONS: applicants who reside outside the continental United States enter an At-Large (Virtual) NATSAA 4. First-place winners in prior NATSAA national auditions are ineligible. 5. A contestant entering the auditions for a second or third time will be expected to present a reasonable amount of new repertoire. 6. Applicants must be available to perform at live, national semifinal auditions in early January 2025 in New York City, should they be named a national semifinalist. 7. Semifinalists must agree to be available for appearance and not be booked during the dates of the NATS 59th National Conference (dates and location TBA). The national NATSAA winner typically presents a live performance as a feature in each biennial NATS National Conference. 8. The final decision on all matters of eligibility rests with the Vice President of Auditions contacted via email at vpaudition@nats.org.
Type: Award
Value: A total of over US$50,000 in cash and other prizes is awarded!
Frequency: Annual
Country of Study: United States of America
Application Procedure: All applications must be submitted electronically
No. of awards offered: 6
Closing Date: 9 November
Additional Information: www.nats.org/nats-artist-awards.html

Van L. Lawrence Fellowship

Purpose: The Van L. Lawrence Fellowship was created to honor Van L. Lawrence, M.D. for his outstanding contribution to voice, and particularly to recognize the importance of the interdisciplinary education he fostered among laryngologists and singing teachers
Eligibility: Candidates for the Van L. Lawrence Fellowship must be members of National Association of Teachers of Singing and actively engaged in teaching. The Fellowship will be awarded to candidates who have demonstrated excellence in their professions as singing teachers, and who have shown interest in, and knowledge of, voice science
Type: Fellowship
Value: US$2,000
Country of Study: Any country
Application Procedure: Members of NATS wishing to apply for the fellowship should write an electronic letter of intent to The Voice Foundation along with your CV — combined into one PDF document. Include the area and methods of your proposed study. E-mail: office@voicefoundation.org
Closing Date: 15 November
Additional Information: www.nats.org/van-lawrence-fellowship.html

For further information contact:

National Association of Teachers of Singing, 9957 Moorings Drive, Suite 401, Jacksonville, FL 32257, United States of America.

Tel: (1) 904 992 9101
Fax: (1) 904 262 2587
Email: office@voicefoundation.org

Voice Pedagogy Award

Eligibility: Candidates must submit a request for funds to the NATS executive director no later than February 15 of the year in which the seminar will take place. A committee from NATS will select the winning candidates
Level of Study: Professional development
Type: Award
Value: US$500
Country of Study: Any country
Application Procedure: To make a submission login or register.: www.nats.org/cgi/page.cgi/Voice_Pedagogy_Award_App_-_CFP.html
Closing Date: 15 February
Additional Information: www.nats.org/voice-pedagogy-award.html

National Breast Cancer Foundation (NBCF)

GPO Box 4126, Sydney, NSW 2001, Australia.

Tel: (61) 1300 737 086
Email: info@nbcf.org.au
Website: www.nbcf.org.au
Contact: National Breast Cancer Foundation

The National Breast Cancer Foundation (NBCF) is Australia's leading national body funding game-changing breast cancer research with money raised entirely by the Australian public. Since NBCF's inception in 1994, the five-year survival rates for breast cancer has increased from 76% to 91%. It's proof our strategy is working. Identifying new and effective models of funding and ensuring that we don't stand alone but work collaboratively and creatively to achieve our mission of Zero Deaths by breast cancer by 2030.

National Breast Cancer Foundation Doctoral Scholarship

Purpose: To provide outstanding graduates with a strong interest in breast cancer research with an opportunity to pursue full-time PhD studies at an Australian University
Eligibility: Open to applicants who are permanent residents of Australia
Level of Study: Doctorate, Postgraduate, Research
Type: Scholarship
Value: Scholars will receive a stipend of approx. AU$33,240
Length of Study: 3 years
Frequency: Annual
Country of Study: Australia
Application Procedure: The applications are judged under peer review by experts in the field for their scientific merit and contribution to either new knowledge or building on existing knowledge of breast cancer
No. of awards offered: 15
Funding: Foundation
Contributor: Australian community and corporate funding
No. of awards given last year: 4
No. of applicants last year: 15

For further information contact:

Email: lhan.gannon@nbcf.org.au

Novel Concept Awards

Purpose: To provide investigators with the opportunity to pursue serendipitous observations and explore new, innovative, and untested ideas
Eligibility: Open to applicants undertaking research in the entire continuum of breast cancer research. Residing in Australia throughout the funding period. Must meet all eligibility criteria outlined in guidelines and application form. Please check at www.nbcf.org.au
Level of Study: Unrestricted
Type: Research grant
Value: Maximum value of AU$100,000 per grant per year
Length of Study: 1 to 2 years
Country of Study: Australia
Application Procedure: Please contact the Research Administrator or check the website for further details
Closing Date: 20 June
Funding: Foundation, Trusts
Contributor: NBCF, Australian Community and Corporate
Additional Information: Each year NBCF board will decide when to call for application and closing dates in late February

Pilot Study Grants

Purpose: To financially assist investigators to obtain preliminary data regarding methodology, effect sizes and possible findings relating to new research ideas relevant to breast cancer
Eligibility: Applicants must be Australian citizens, or be graduates from overseas with permanent Australian resident status, must reside in Australia throughout the funding period and not under bond to any foreign government
Level of Study: Research, Unrestricted
Type: Grant
Value: A maximum of AU$100,000 for up to 2 years
Length of Study: Up to 2 years
Frequency: Every 2 years
Country of Study: Australia
Application Procedure: Check website for further details
No. of awards offered: 76
Closing Date: 10 May
Funding: Foundation
Contributor: Australian Community and Corporate
No. of awards given last year: 3
No. of applicants last year: 76
Additional Information: NBCF Board will decide whether to offer this grant scheme again when they meet annual in late February researchfunding.duke.edu/pilot-study-grants

National Bureau of Asian Research (NBR)

600 University Street, Suite 1012, Seattle, WA 98101, United States of America.

Tel: (1) 206 632 7370
Email: nbr@nbr.org
Website: www.nbr.org
Contact: George F Russell

NBR is an independent research institution based in Seattle and Washington, D.C. We bring world-class scholarship to bear on the evolving strategic environment in Asia through original, policy-relevant research, and we invest in our future by training the next generation of Asia specialists.

Chinese Language Fellowship Program

Purpose: The Chinese Language Fellowship Program seeks to train a new generation of scholars who possess deep understanding of China's contemporary politics, society, and modern history, as well as fluency in Chinese language
Eligibility: Qualified applicants for the Chinese Language Fellowship will: 1. Be a U.S. citizen or permanent resident. 2. Be a PhD student, with a focus on China and policy. 3. Demonstrate an intermediate Chinese language ability (e.g., through course transcripts and/or the results of language assessment tests) and a clear commitment to expand these language skills. The fellowship is NOT intended to help beginner students of Chinese. 4. Desire to advance public policy toward China through improved expertise and understanding, or to contribute to scholarly research and teaching on China in order to develop future generations of China specialists
Eligible Country: United States of America
Level of Study: Doctorate, Postdoctorate
Type: Fellowship
Value: PhD Track (up to US$50,000, Prospective PhD Track (up to US$40,000)
Length of Study: 1 year
Country of Study: United States of America
Closing Date: 21 February
Additional Information: www.nbr.org/chinese-language-fellowship-program/

For further information contact:

Email: clfp@nbr.org

The Next Generation: Leadership in Asian Affairs Fellowship

Purpose: The Next Generation Leadership in Asian Affairs Fellowship (Next Generation) is a post-master's degree one-year program that is cultivating a new generation of Asian affairs specialists committed to and capable of bridging the gap between the best scholarly research and the pressing needs of U.S. foreign policy toward a rapidly changing Asia
Eligibility: Eligible applicants must be U.S. citizens or permanent residents
Level of Study: Research
Type: Fellowships
Value: Each fellow will receive a US$32,500 fellowship award (with benefits), as well as a reimbursement for some relocation expenses
Length of Study: 1 year
Frequency: Annual
Country of Study: United States of America
Closing Date: 15 January
Funding: Corporation, Foundation, Government
Additional Information: www.honorsociety.org/scholarships/next-generation-leadership-asian-affairs-fellowship

For further information contact:

Tel: (1) 866 313 6311
Email: nextgen@nbr.org

N

National Cattleman Foundation

9110 E Nichols Ave Ste 300, Centennial, CO 80112, United States of America.

Tel: (1) 303 850 3457
Email: ncf@beef.org
Website: www.nationalcattlemensfoundation.org/
Contact: General Foundation Information & Scholarships

The American Cattlemen's Foundation was first organized in 1972 with the stated purpose of providing "Charitable, scientific and educational activities to benefit the cattle industry." The foundation was later renamed the National Cattlemn's Foundation (NCF).

Continuing Medical Education Beef Industry Scholarship

Subjects: Beef industry, which may include education, communications, production, and research

Purpose: The CME Beef Industry Scholarships are awarded to students pursuing careers in the beef industry, which may include education, communications, production, and research. The purpose of this program is to identify and encourage talented and thoughtful students who will emerge as industry leaders
Eligibility: 1. Be a graduating high school senior or full-time undergraduate student who will be enrolled in a two- or four-year institution for the 2024–2025 school year. 2. Have demonstrated a commitment to a career in the beef industry through classes, internships or life experiences. 3. Include a Letter of Intent-write a one-page letter expressing/indicating your future career goals related to the beef industry. 4. Write an original essay-750 words or less describing an issue confronting the beef industry and offering a solution(s). 5. Provide two Letters of Recommendation-two letters of reference from current or former instructors or industry professionals. 6. Previous scholarship winners are eligible to apply
Level of Study: Graduate
Type: Scholarship
Value: US$1,500
Length of Study: 2–4 years
Frequency: Annual
Country of Study: United States of America
Closing Date: 13 November
Funding: Foundation, Private
Additional Information: www.nationalcattlemensfoundation.org/scholarships/cme-beef-industry-scholarship

For further information contact:

9110 East Nichols Ave., Suite #300, Centennial, CO 80112, United States of America.

National Education Association (NEA) Foundation

1201 16th Street, North West, Washington, DC 20036, United States of America.

Tel: (1) 202 822 7840
Email: NEAFoundation@nea.org
Website: www.neafoundation.org

The NEA Foundation offers programs and grants that support public school educators' efforts to close the achievement gaps, increase student achievement, salute excellence in education and provide professional development.

Envision Equity Grants

Purpose: Envision Equity Grants enable educators to test creative new ideas and innovations, demonstrating exemplary teaching and learning
Type: Grant
Value: US$1,500 and US$5,000
Length of Study: 12 Months
Country of Study: United States of America
Application Procedure: Scholarship website: www.cybergrants.com/pls/cybergrants/ao_login.login?x_gm_id=2862&x_proposal_type_id=73220
Closing Date: 27 April
Additional Information: www.neafoundation.org/for-educators/envision-equity-grants/

Learning & Leadership Grants

Purpose: Educators frequently need outside resources to engage in meaningful professional development due to limited district funding. Through our Learning & Leadership grants, we support the professional development of NEA members by providing grants
Eligibility: Applicants must be teachers, education support professionals, or specialized instructional support personnel and must be current NEA members. Current NEA Foundation grantees are ineligible for this funding opportunity. A successful proposal will also make an individual ineligible for other NEA Foundation funding opportunities, until the grant is successfully completed and closed out
Type: Grant
Value: US$2,000 and US$5,000
Length of Study: 12 Months
Country of Study: Any country
Closing Date: 1 June
Additional Information: www.neafoundation.org/for-educators/learning-and-leadership-grants/

For further information contact:

1201 16th Street, NW Washington, DC 20036, United States of America.

Tel: (1) 202 822 7840
Fax: (1) 202 822 7779

Student Achievement Grants

Purpose: The NEA Foundation believes public education should stimulate students' curiosity and excitement about

learning and help them become successful 21st-century global citizens
Eligibility: Applicants must be teachers, education support professionals, or specialized instructional support personnel and must be current NEA members
Type: Grant
Value: US$2,000 and US$5,000
Length of Study: 12 months
Frequency: Annual
Country of Study: United States of America
Closing Date: 1 June
Additional Information: www.neafoundation.org/for-educators/student-success-grants/

National Education Union (NEU)

Hamilton House, Mabledon Place, London WC1H 9BD, United Kingdom.

Tel: (44) 20 7388 6191
Email: enquiries@neu.org.uk
Website: neu.org.uk/

The NEU was formed in 2017 following the amalgamation of the National Union of Teachers (NUT) and the Association of Teachers and Lecturers (ATL). As the largest education union, we have a powerful voice and have been effective in winning improvements to our members' working conditions and shaping an education system that works for all.

National Union of Teachers Page Scholarship

Purpose: To promote the exchange of educational ideas between Britain and America
Eligibility: Open to teaching members of the NUT aged 25–60 years, although 25–55 is preferred
Level of Study: Graduate
Type: Scholarship
Value: Each up to £1,700 pro rata daily rate with complete hospitality in the United States of America provided by the English- Speaking Union of the United States of America
Length of Study: 2 weeks. The scholarship must be taken during the American academic year, which is September–May
Frequency: Annual
Country of Study: United Kingdom
Application Procedure: Applicants must complete an application form. An outline and synopsis of the project must accompany the form along with a curriculum vitae and scholastic and personal testimonials
No. of awards offered: 2
Funding: Private
No. of awards given last year: 2
No. of applicants last year: 100
Additional Information: It is a discontinued award type. The scholarship is limited to the individual teacher and neither the spouse nor partner can be included in the travel, accommodation or study arrangements. Recipients are required to report on their visit to teacher groups and educational meetings in the United States and on their return home. www.chegg.com/scholarships/national-tour-associationluray-caverns-graduate-research-scholarship-2345

For further information contact:

Tel: (44) 1 812 277 9670
Fax: (44) 20 7388 6191

National Endowment for the Humanities (NEH)

400 7th Street, SW, Washington, DC 20506, United States of America.

Tel: (1) 202 606 8400
Email: questions@neh.gov
Website: www.neh.gov

The National Endowment for the Humanities (NEH) is an independent federal agency created in 1965. It is one of the largest funders of humanities programs in the United States. NEH grants typically go to cultural institutions, such as museums, archives, libraries, colleges, universities, public television, and radio stations, and to individual scholars.

Awards for Faculty at Hispanic-Serving Institutions

Purpose: The Awards for Faculty program strengthens the humanities at Hispanic-Serving Institutions by encouraging and expanding humanities research opportunities for individual faculty and staff members. Awards support individuals pursuing scholarly research that is of value to humanities scholars, students, and/or general audiences
Eligibility: Eligible projects include: 1. research in primary and secondary materials leading to the development of books,

monographs, peer-reviewed articles, e-books, digital materials, translations with annotations or a critical apparatus, critical editions, or other scholarly resources 2. research related to institutional or community goals or interests, such as projects that draw on archival collections, collection and interpretation of oral histories, or the development of materials in support of culture or language preservation and revitalization 3. research leading to the improvement of a single existing undergraduate course, including the development of humanities resources (for example, oral histories, identification and preparation of previously unavailable archival sources, or newly compiled historical or literary collections) research leading to digital or web-based products intended to supplement a course revision or publication project
Type: Award
Value: US$5,000 per month
Length of Study: 2 to 12 months
Country of Study: Any country
Application Procedure: Apply Now on Grants.gov: grants.gov/
Closing Date: 12 April
Additional Information: www.neh.gov/grants/research/awards-faculty-hispanic-serving-institutions

For further information contact:

Email: FacultyAwards@neh.gov

Awards for Faculty at Historically Black Colleges and Universities

Subjects: Archaeological Report; Article; Basic research leading to improvement of existing course; Basic research related to goals and interests of the institution or community; Book; Digital Material and Publication; Edition; Other Scholarly Resource; Translation
Purpose: The NEH Awards for Faculty program seeks to strengthen the humanities at Historically Black Colleges and Universities (HBCUs) by encouraging and expanding humanities research opportunities for individual faculty and staff members. Awards support individuals pursuing scholarly research that is of value to humanities scholars, students, and/or general audiences
Eligibility: humanities research in primary and secondary materials leading to the development of books, monographs, peer-reviewed articles, e-books, digital materials, translations with annotations or a critical apparatus, critical editions, or other scholarly resources humanities research related to institutional or community goals or interests, such as projects that draw on institutional or community archival collections, or the development of materials in support of culture or language preservation and revitalization humanities research leading to the improvement of an existing undergraduate course, including the development of humanities resources (for example, oral histories, identification of previously unavailable primary sources, historical or literary collections)
Type: Award
Value: US$5,000 per month
Length of Study: Two to twelve months
Country of Study: Any country
Closing Date: 12 April
Additional Information: www.neh.gov/grants/research/awards-faculty-historically-black-colleges-and-universities

For further information contact:

400 7th Street, SW Washington, DC 20506, United States of America.

Tel: (1) 202 606 8200
Email: FacultyAwards@neh.gov

Awards for Faculty at Tribal Colleges and Universities

Subjects: Archaeological Report; Article; Basic research leading to improvement of existing course; Basic research related to goals and interests of the institution or community; Book; Digital Material and Publication; Edition; Other Scholarly Resource; Translation
Purpose: The Awards for Faculty program seeks to strengthen the humanities at Tribal Colleges and Universities by encouraging and expanding humanities research opportunities for individual faculty and staff members
Eligibility: earch related to tribal or institutional priorities, goals or interests, such as projects that draw on cultural or institutional archival collections the development of materials in support of sustaining, preserving and revitalizing culture or language research leading to the improvement of an existing undergraduate or graduate course travel to and research in archival or cultural collections with significant holdings in the researcher's area of expertise or in an area of tribal or institutional priority or interest
Type: Award
Value: US$5,000 per month
Length of Study: Two to twelve months
Country of Study: Any country
Closing Date: 12 April
Additional Information: www.neh.gov/grants/research/awards-faculty-tribal-colleges-and-universities

For further information contact:

400 7th Street, SW Washington, DC 20506, United States of America.

Tel: (1) 202 606 8200
Email: FacultyAwards@neh.gov

Fellowships for Advanced Social Science Research on Japan

Purpose: The Fellowships for Advanced Social Science Research on Japan program is a joint activity of the Japan-United States Friendship Commission (JUSFC) and the National Endowment for the Humanities (NEH). The goals of the program are to promote Japan studies in the United States, to encourage U.S.-Japanese scholarly exchange, and to support the next generation of Japan scholars in the United States
Type: Fellowship
Value: US$60,000 (US$5,000 per month)
Length of Study: Six to twelve months
Country of Study: Any country
Closing Date: 26 April
Additional Information: www.neh.gov/grants/research/fellowships-advanced-social-science-research-japan

For further information contact:

400 7th Street, SW Washington, DC 20506, United States of America.

Tel: (1) 202 606 8200
Email: fellowships@neh.gov

Fellowships Open Book Program

Subjects: Digital Material and Publication
Purpose: The Fellowships Open Book Program is a limited competition designed to make outstanding humanities books available to a wide audience. By taking advantage of low-cost e-book technology, the program will allow teachers, students, scholars, and the public to read humanities books that can be downloaded or redistributed for no charge
Eligibility: Organizations
Type: Fellowship
Value: US$5,500
Length of Study: Up to 12 months
Country of Study: Any country
Closing Date: 15 March
Additional Information: www.neh.gov/grants/odh/FOBP

For further information contact:

Email: odh@neh.gov

National Endowment for the Humanities Fellowships

Purpose: NEH Fellowships are competitive awards granted to individual scholars pursuing projects that embody exceptional research, rigorous analysis, and clear writing. Applications must clearly articulate a projects value to humanities scholars, general audiences, or both
Eligibility: The Fellowships program accepts applications from individuals who meet the following requirements. 1. Citizenship 2. Currently enrolled students
Level of Study: Postdoctorate
Type: Fellowship
Value: US$60,000 (US$5,000 per month)
Length of Study: Six to twelve months
Frequency: Annual
Country of Study: United States of America
Application Procedure: Applicants are required to apply online through www.Grants.gov Workspace
Closing Date: 12 April
Funding: Government
Additional Information: www.neh.gov/grants/research/fellowships

For further information contact:

Tel: (1) 202 606 8200
Email: fellowships@neh.gov

N

NEH-Mellon Fellowships for Digital Publication

Purpose: Through NEH-Mellon Fellowships for Digital Publication, the National Endowment for the Humanities and The Andrew W. Mellon Foundation jointly support individual scholars pursuing interpretive research projects that require digital expression and digital publication
Type: Fellowship
Value: US$5,000 per month
Length of Study: Six to twelve months
Country of Study: Any country
Closing Date: 19 April
Additional Information: www.neh.gov/grants/research/neh-mellon-fellowships-digital-publication

For further information contact:

400 7th Street, SW Washington, DC 20506, United States of America.

Tel: (1) 202 606 8200
Email: fellowships@neh.gov

Public Scholars

Type: Award
Value: US$5,000 per month
Length of Study: 6 to 12 months
Country of Study: Any country
Closing Date: 29 November
Additional Information: www.neh.gov/grants/research/public-scholar-program

For further information contact:

Email: publicscholar@neh.gov

Scholarly Editions and Scholarly Translations

Purpose: The Scholarly Editions and Scholarly Translations program provides grants to organizations to support collaborative teams who are editing, annotating, and translating foundational humanities texts that are vital to learning and research but are currently inaccessible or are available only in inadequate editions or translations
Eligibility: Projects must be undertaken by at least two scholars working collaboratively. While international collaboration is permitted, projects must maintain an equitable balance between scholars at U.S. institutions and scholars at non-U.S. institutions
Type: Scholarship
Value: US$300,000; up to US$450,000
Length of Study: One to three years
Country of Study: Any country
Closing Date: 29 November
Additional Information: www.neh.gov/grants/research/scholarly-editions-and-translations-grants

For further information contact:

Tel: (1) 202 606 8200
Email: editions@neh.gov

Summer Stipends

Type: Stipendiary
Value: US$6,000
Length of Study: 2 months
Country of Study: Any country
Application Procedure: Apply Now on Grants.gov: grants.gov/
Closing Date: 20 September
Additional Information: www.neh.gov/grants/research/summer-stipends

For further information contact:

Email: stipends@neh.gov

National Foundation for Infectious Diseases (NFID)

7201 Wisconsin Avenue, Suite 750, Bethesda, MD 20814, United States of America.

Tel: (1) 301 656 0003
Email: info@nfid.org
Website: www.nfid.org

The National Foundation for Infectious Diseases (NFID) is a non-profit, non-governmental organization whose mission is public and professional education and promotion of research on the causes, treatment and prevention of infectious diseases.

National Foundation for Infectious Diseases Postdoctoral Fellowship in Nosocomial Infection Research and Training

Purpose: To encourage a qualified physician researcher to become a specialist and investigator in the field of nosocomial infections
Eligibility: Open to citizens of the United States
Level of Study: Postgraduate
Type: Fellowship
Value: US$40,000
Frequency: Annual
Country of Study: United States of America
Application Procedure: Applicants must submit their application form and curriculum vitae
Closing Date: 6 January
Additional Information: Contact Grants Manager. Priority will be given to Fellows in or entering into infectious diseases training www.neh.gov/grants/research/fellowships

For further information contact:

Email: nfid@aol.com

National Health and Medical Research Council (NHMRC)

NHMRC, GPO Box 1421, Canberra, ACT 2601, Australia.

Tel: (61) 2 6217 9000
Email: grantnet.help@nhmrc.gov.au
Website: www.nhmrc.gov.au
Contact: Executive Director

At NHMRC we are excited by the huge potential benefits of the research we fund and by the opportunities we have to ensure Australians have access to evidence-based, authoritative health advice.

National Health and Medical Research Council Equipment Grants

Purpose: To provide funding support for the purchase of items of equipment required for biomedical research
Eligibility: Open to individuals, groups or institutions which are normally eligible for NHMRC support. Grants will be made on the basis of scientific merit, taking into consideration factors including whether the applicants hold NHMRC grants, the institutional ranking of the application, and institutional or regional availability of major equipment
Level of Study: Unrestricted
Type: Grant
Value: AU$10,000 to cover the cost of equipment in excess
Frequency: Annual
Country of Study: Australia
Application Procedure: Applicants must complete an application form
Funding: Government

For further information contact:

MDP 33, Project Grants Office, GPO Box 9848, Canberra, ACT 2601, Australia.

Tel: (61) 2 6289 8278
Fax: (61) 2 6289 8617
Email: jean.sewell@hhlgcs.ausgovhhcs.telememo.au

National Health and Medical Research Council Public Health Travelling Fellowships

Purpose: To enable Fellows to make postgraduate study tours abroad or within Australia, which relate to their work and speciality and which will be of benefit to public health in Australia
Eligibility: Open to all personnel working in the field of public health, who are suitably qualified at a level appropriate for fulfilment of the objectives of the study and for implementation of its benefits. The applicant may be employed in government or industry, or may be self-employed. Preference will be given to those applicants who would not normally, in the course of their employment, have the opportunity, as part of their normal duties, for overseas travel and experience
Level of Study: Unrestricted
Type: Other
Value: Not exceeding AU$19,700 plus an agreed annual allowance to cover cost increases
Length of Study: 2–12 months
Frequency: Annual
Country of Study: Any country
Application Procedure: Please write for details
No. of awards offered: 18
Closing Date: 31 July
Funding: Government
No. of awards given last year: 8
No. of applicants last year: 18
Additional Information: Preference will be given to public health practitioners www.neh.gov/grants/research/fellowships

For further information contact:

Secretariat & Training Awards, GPO Box 9848, Canberra, ACT 2601, Australia.

Tel: (61) 2 6289 7945
Fax: (61) 2 6289 6957
Email: trevorlord@hhlgcs.ausgovhhcs.telememo.au

R Douglas Wright Awards

Purpose: To provide outstanding researchers at an early stage in their career with an opportunity for independent research together with improved security
Eligibility: Open to applicants who have completed postdoctoral research training or have equivalent experience, and are seeking to establish themselves in a career in medical research in Australia
Level of Study: Doctorate, Postdoctorate, Professional development
Type: Award
Value: Salary in the range of Senior Research Officer Level 1 to Senior Research Officer Level 4, with annual increments, plus an allowance of AU$10,000 per year

Length of Study: 4 years
Frequency: Annual
Study Establishment: Australian research institutions
Country of Study: Australia
Application Procedure: Applicants must complete an application form, available from Ms H Murray
No. of awards offered: 43
Closing Date: 30 April
Funding: Government
No. of awards given last year: 6
No. of applicants last year: 43
Additional Information: staff.unimelb.edu.au/mdhs/research-development/research-collaboration-and-funding/faculty-trust-fellowships/r-douglas-wright-research-fellowship

For further information contact:

Fellowships Unit - Mail Drop Point, 33GPO Box 9848, Canberra, ACT 2601, Australia.

Tel: (61) 2 6289 5034
Fax: (61) 2 6289 1329
Email: helen.murray@hhlgcs.ausgovhhcs.telememo.au

National Heart, Lung, and Blood Institute

Building 31, 31 Center Drive, Bethesda, MD 20892, United States of America.

Tel: (1) 877 645 2448
Website: www.nhlbi.nih.gov/

The NHLBI's Strategic Vision rests on four mission-driven goals that will benefit from sustained Institute focus. Eight objectives organize the 132 Research Priorities. The goals are Understand Human Biology, Reduce Human Disease, Develop Workforce and Resources and Advance Translational Research.

Immersive Training in the Glycosciences - Fellowship

Subjects: Glycosciences
Purpose: The ultimate goal of the program is to transform the study of glycoscience from a specialized domain into mainstream biology. This fellowship is expected to provide scholars with an unparalleled opportunity to participate in cross-disciplinary research, obtain advanced knowledge, skills, and professional exposure within the glycosciences, as well as to develop a research portfolio from which to launch independent careers
Eligibility: Scholars must be citizens or non-citizen nationals of the United States or have been lawfully admitted for permanent residence at the time of appointment. At the time of appointment scholars should hold an M.D. and/or PhD degree
Type: Fellowship
Value: up to US$100,000 per year (inclusive of benefits), research supplies (US$25,000)
Length of Study: 2 years
Study Establishment: John Hopkins University
Country of Study: United States of America
Closing Date: 15 June
Additional Information: glycocareers.cclinic.jhu.edu/styled/index.html

For further information contact:

Email: GlycoED@jhmi.edu

National Institute for Health and Care Excellence (NICE)

2nd Floor, 2 Redman Place, London E20 1JQ, United Kingdom.

Tel: (44) 300 323 0140
Email: nice@nice.org.uk
Website: www.nice.org.uk
Contact: National Institute for Health and Care Excellence

We provide national guidance and advice to improve health and social care. The history, structure and key responsibilities of NICE. Contains governance information, up-to-date policies, procedures and publications. Our guidance, advice, quality standards and information services for health, public health and social care. Contains resources to help maximise use of evidence and guidance.

National Institute for Health and Care Excellence Scholarships

Purpose: NICE Scholarships are one-year opportunities for qualified health and social care professionals to find out about the inner workings of NICE and undertake a supported

improvement project, related to NICE guidance, within their local organization
Eligibility: NICE Scholarships are typically awarded to specialist registrars, senior nurses, pharmacists and allied health professionals, service improvement leads, public health and social care specialists and health service managers. In addition to their project-based activities, NICE Scholars are expected to act as local ambassadors for clinical and public health and social care excellence; promote the principles and the recommendations of NICE guidance-through teaching activities, for example
Type: Scholarship
Value: NICE Scholars are supported in their project via a series of workshops, access to a very experienced senior mentor and contact with the expert teams at NICE. NICE Scholars are not paid. NICE will, however, meet all reasonable expenses (e.g. travel, accommodation) incurred in the course of carrying out Scholarship activities
Length of Study: 1 year
Frequency: Annual
Country of Study: United Kingdom
Application Procedure: The mode of applying is by post
Closing Date: 1 November
Additional Information: Scholars are expected to devote approximately 7.5 hours per week to their Scholarship project. For detailed information, visit www.nice.org.uk/getinvolved/nice_fellows_and_scholars/scholars/NICEScholarships.jsp scientistsolutions.com/forum/jobs-clinicaldiagnostic/national-institute-health-and-care-excellence-scholarships

National Institute of General Medical Sciences (NIGMS)

45 Center Drive, MSC 6200, Bethesda, MD 20892-6200, United States of America.

Tel: (1) 301 496 7301
Email: info@nigms.nih.gov
Website: www.nigms.nih.gov
Contact: Ms Jilliene Drayton, Information Development Specialist

The National Institute of General Medical Sciences (NIGMS) supports basic research that increases our understanding of biological processes and lays the foundation for advances in disease diagnosis, treatment, and prevention. NIGMS-funded scientists investigate how living systems work at a range of levels from molecules and cells to tissues and organs, in research organisms, humans, and populations.

High-End Instrumentation (HEI) Grant Program

Purpose: The High-End Instrumentation (HEI) Grant Program encourages applications from groups of NIH-supported investigators to purchase or upgrade a single item of high-end, specialized, commercially available instruments or integrated systems
Eligibility: Higher Education Institutions Public/State Controlled Institutions of Higher Education Private Institutions of Higher Education The following types of Higher Education Institutions are always encouraged to apply for NIH support as Public or Private Institutions of Higher Education Hispanic-serving Institutions Historically Black Colleges and Universities (HBCUs) Tribally Controlled Colleges and Universities (TCCUs) Alaska Native and Native Hawaiian Serving Institutions Asian American Native American Pacific Islander Serving Institutions (AANAPISIs) Nonprofits Other Than Institutions of Higher Education Nonprofits with 501(c)(3) IRS Status (Other than Institutions of Higher Education) Nonprofits without 501(c)(3) IRS Status (Other than Institutions of Higher Education)
Type: Grant
Value: The minimum award is US$600,001. the maximum award is US$2,000,000
Frequency: Annual
Country of Study: Any country
Closing Date: 1 June
Additional Information: grants.nih.gov/grants/guide/pa-files/PAR-22-079.html

For further information contact:

Karen Brummett Office of Research Infrastructure Programs (ORIP).

Tel: (1) 301 945 7573
Email: GrantsInfo@nih.gov

IDeA Networks of Biomedical Research Excellence (INBRE) (P20 Clinical Trial Optional)

Eligibility: Any individual(s) with the skills, knowledge, and resources necessary to carry out the proposed research as the Program Director(s)/Principal Investigator(s) (PD(s)/PI(s)) is invited to work with his/her organization to develop an application for support. Individuals from diverse backgrounds, including underrepresented racial and ethnic groups, individuals with disabilities, and women are always encouraged to apply for NIH support
Type: Grant
Value: one-time funding of up to US$250,000
Length of Study: 5 years

Country of Study: Any country
Closing Date: 26 June
Additional Information: grants.nih.gov/grants/guide/pa-files/PAR-23-100.html

National Institute of General Medical Sciences Research Project Grants (R01)

Purpose: To support a discrete project related to the investigator's area of interest and competence
Eligibility: Research project grants may be awarded to non-profit organizations and institutions; governments and their agencies; occasionally, though rarely, to individuals who have access to adequate facilities and resources for conducting the research; and to profit-making organizations. Foreign institutions and international organizations are also eligible to apply for these grants
Level of Study: Postgraduate
Type: Grant
Value: These grants may provide funds for reasonable costs of the research activity, as well as for salaries, equipment, supplies, travel and other related expenses
Length of Study: 12 months
Frequency: Annual
Country of Study: United States of America
Application Procedure: Applicants must contact the Office of Extramural Outreach for details
Closing Date: 5 February
Funding: Government
Additional Information: grants.nih.gov/grants/funding/r01.htm

For further information contact:

Office of Extramural Outreach, NIH 6701 Rockledge Drive Msc 7760, Bethesda, MD 20892-7760, United States of America.

Tel: (1) 301 435 0714
Email: grantsinfo@nih.gov

National Road Safety Authority Individual Postdoctoral Fellowships (F32)

Purpose: NIGMS welcomes NRSA applications from eligible individuals who seek postdoctoral biomedical research training in areas related to the scientific programmes of the Institute
Eligibility: Applicants must have received the doctoral degree (PhD, M.D., D.O., D.C., D.D.S., D.V.M., O.D., D.P.M., Sc.D., Eng.D., Dr.P.H., D.N.S., N.D., Pharm.D., D.S.W., Psy.D. or equivalent doctoral degree from an accredited domestic or foreign institution) by the beginning date of the proposed award. For applicants holding the PhD degree, this award is designed to provide support for advanced and specialized training in basic research, in basic research associated with clinical problems or in clinical research. For applicants holding the M.D. or other clinical-professional degree, this program is intended to provide at least 2 years of rigorous basic or clinical research training.
Level of Study: Doctorate, Postdoctorate
Type: Award
Value: NIGMS provides an annual stipend to postdoctoral fellows, and an institutional allowance to cover training-related expenses
Length of Study: Up to 3 years
Frequency: Annual
Study Establishment: The institutional setting may be domestic or foreign, public or private
Country of Study: Any country
Application Procedure: Applicants must write to the main address for details or telephone Dr Michael Sesma, at (1) 301 594 2772. Further details are also available from the website www.nigms.nih.gov
Closing Date: 8 April
Funding: Government
Additional Information: www.nigms.nih.gov/training/indivpostdoc/Pages/PostdocFellowshipDescription.aspx

---

National Institutes of Health

9000 Rockville Pike, Bethesda, MA 20892, United States of America.

Tel: (1) 301 496 4000
Website: www.nih.gov
Contact: Dr Belinda Seto, Acting Deputy Director for Extramural Research

The National Institutes of Health (NIH), a part of the U.S. Department of Health and Human Services, is the nation's medical research agency - making important discoveries that improve health and save lives. Life expectancy in the United States has jumped from 47 years in 1900 to 78 years as reported in 2009, and disability in people over age 65 has dropped dramatically in the past 3 decades. In recent years, nationwide rates of new diagnoses and deaths from all cancers combined have fallen significantly.

Hitchings-Elion Postdoctoral Fellowships for United States Scientist

Purpose: The purpose of these fellowships is to promote scientific collaboration between British and American scientists for the conduct of biomedical and behavioral research. The Hitchings-Elion Fellowships will support two years of collaborative research by a U.S. scientist at a sponsor's laboratory in the United Kingdom and a third year at a sponsor's laboratory in the United States
Eligibility: The applicant must be a United States citizen or permanent United States resident, hold a doctorate level degree in one of the medical or veterinary clinical, behavioral, or biomedical sciences, and be within ten years of the last doctoral degree
Level of Study: Doctorate, Research
Type: Fellowship
Value: US$7,500 per annum for research expenses in the United States
Frequency: Annual
Application Procedure: Applications must be sent to the Division of Research Grants, NIH, to meet receipt dates of January 10, May 10 and September 10 each year. Special application forms must be used and are available, along with detailed instructions
Closing Date: 10 September
Funding: Private
Additional Information: Website: www.grants.nih.gov/grants/guide/pa-files/PA-92-030.html

For further information contact:

Chief, International Research and Awards Branch Fogarty International Center, Building 31, Room B2C21, Bethesda, MD 20892, United States of America.

Tel: (1) 301 496 1653

Ruth L. Kirschstein National Research Service Award (NRSA) Individual Postdoctoral Fellowship

Subjects: 1. Engineering and Physical Sciences 2. Environmental & Life Sciences 3. Medical 4. Medical - Basic Science 5. Medical - Clinical Science 6. Medical - Translational 7. Social Sciences
Purpose: The purpose of the Ruth L. Kirschstein National Research Service Award (NRSA) Individual Postdoctoral Fellowship (Parent F32) is to support research training of highly promising postdoctoral candidates who have the potential to become productive, independent investigators in scientific health-related research fields relevant to the missions of the participating NIH Institutes and Centers. Applications are expected to incorporate exceptional mentorship
Level of Study: Postdoctoral
Type: Fellowships
Value: Stipend, allowance & tuition
Frequency: Annual
Country of Study: Any country
Closing Date: 8 January
Additional Information: www.grants.nih.gov/grants/guide/pa-files/PA-19-188.html

National Library of Medicine (NLM)

8600 Rockville Pike, Bethesda, MD 20894, United States of America.

Tel: (1) 301 594 5983
Email: NLMCommunications@nih.gov
Website: www.nlm.nih.gov
Contact: Mr Dwight Mawrery, Grants Management Officer

The National Library of Medicine (NLM), on the campus of the National Institutes of Health in Bethesda, Maryland, has been a center of information innovation since its founding in 1836. The world's largest biomedical library, NLM maintains and makes available a vast print collection and produces electronic information resources on a wide range of topics that are searched billions of times each year by millions of people around the globe. It also supports and conducts research, development, and training in biomedical informatics and health information technology. In addition, the Library coordinates a 6,500-member Network of the National Library of Medicine that promotes and provides access to health information in communities across the United States.

National Library of Medicine Fellowship in Applied Informatics

Purpose: The National Library of Medicine (NLM) wishes to increase the national pool of health professionals capable of managing the knowledge and techniques of medical informatics in health science organizations. Medical informatics provides the theoretical and scientific basis for the application of computer and automated information systems to biomedicine

Eligibility: Open to individuals with a BA, BSc, MA, MSc or PhD in a field related to health, who are United States nationals or permanent residents of the United States of America
Level of Study: Doctorate, Graduate, Postdoctorate, Postgraduate
Type: Fellowship
Value: Up to US$58,000 per year, based on the salary or remuneration the individual would have been paid from their home institution
Length of Study: Varies
Frequency: Annual
Study Establishment: Universities, colleges, hospitals, laboratories, units of State and certain agencies of the Federal Government in the United States
Country of Study: United States of America
Application Procedure: Applications must be submitted by an organisation on behalf of the individual seeking the grant, on the standard grant application form PHS 416-1 (rev 8/95)
Closing Date: 10 May
Additional Information: The NLM encourages potential applicants to clarify any issues or questions. For enquiries regarding programmatic issues, please contact Mr Peter Clepper, Program Officer. For enquiries regarding Division of Nursing programmatic issues, please contact the Division of Nursing. For enquiries regarding fiscal matters, please contact Ms Shelley Carow, Grants Management Officer. www.grants.nih.gov/grants/guide/pa-files/PA-92-090.html

For further information contact:

Division of Nursing, Parklawn Building, Room 9-36, 5600 Fishes Lane, Rockville, MD 20852, United States of America.

Tel: (1) 301 443 5786
Fax: (1) 301 443 8586

National Library of Medicine Investigator Initiated Project Grant

Purpose: To support individual investigators and their colleagues to pursue a discreet, circumscribed line of investigation to its logical conclusion
Type: Project grant
Length of Study: Up to 3 years
Frequency: 3 times each year
Study Establishment: United States universities or research institutions
Country of Study: United States of America
Application Procedure: Applications must be submitted on the PHS form 398 (ref 5/95)
Closing Date: 15 February
Additional Information: www.grants.nih.gov/grants/guide/pa-files/PA-96-001.html

For further information contact:

Division of Extramural Programmes, National Library of Medicine, Rockledge One Building, 6705 Rockledge Drive Suite 301, Bethesda, MD 20817, United States of America.

Tel: (1) 301 594 4882
Fax: (1) 301 402 2952
Email: bean@nlm.nih.gov

National Library of Medicine Postdoctoral Informatics Research Fellowships

Purpose: To promote researchers interested in informatics research training wishing to identify their own mentor and host institution
Eligibility: Open to applicants who have a PhD relevant to biomedicine or computer science or an equivalent degree from an accredited domestic or foreign institution
Level of Study: Postdoctorate
Type: Fellowship
Value: Based on established NIH schedules.
Frequency: Annual
Study Establishment: United States universities or research institutions.
Country of Study: United States of America
Application Procedure: Applicants must contact the organisation.
Additional Information: For a complete list of NLM factsheets, please contact Factsheets, Office of Public Information. www.grants.nih.gov/grants/guide/pa-files/PA-96-001.html

For further information contact:

Factsheets Office of Public Information National Library of Medicine, 8600 Rockville Pike, Bethesda, MD 20894, United States of America.

Fax: (1) 301 496 4450
Email: publicinfo@nlm.nih.gov

National Library of Medicine Publication Grant Program

Purpose: To provide assistance for the preparation of book length manuscripts and, in some cases, the publication of important scientific information needed by United States health professionals

Eligibility: Open to public or private, non-profit institutions and individuals, who are involved in research
Type: Project grant
Value: US$35,000 direct costs per year over a period of three years maximum
Length of Study: 1–3 years
Frequency: 3 times each year
Country of Study: United States of America
Application Procedure: Applications must be submitted on the PHS FORM 398 (Rev 5/95) grant application kit
Closing Date: 1 October
Additional Information: Potential applicants are strongly encouraged to discuss projects early with the Program staff, who will discuss programme status and experience with them, provide additional information in response to specific application plans and review draft proposals for completeness if desired. For a complete list of NLM Factsheets, please contact Factsheets, Office of Public Information. www.grants.nih.gov/grants/guide/pa-files/PA-96-001.html

For further information contact:

Fax: (1) 301 402 2952
Email: sparks@nlm.nih.gov

NLM Research Grants in Biomedical Informatics and Data Science

Purpose: The National Library of Medicine (NLM) supports innovative research and development in biomedical informatics and data science. The scope of NLM's interest in these research domains is broad, with emphasis on new methods and approaches to foster data driven discovery in the biomedical and clinical health sciences as well as domain-independent, reusable approaches to discovery, curation, analysis, organization and management of health-related digital objects. Biomedical informatics and data science draw upon many fields, including mathematics, statistics, information science, computer science and engineering, and social/behavioral sciences
Eligibility: Any individual(s) with the skills, knowledge, and resources necessary to carry out the proposed research as the Program Director(s)/Principal Investigator(s) (PD(s)/PI(s)) is invited to work with his/her organization to develop an application for support. Individuals from diverse backgrounds, including underrepresented racial and ethnic groups, individuals with disabilities, and women are always encouraged to apply for NIH support
Type: Grant
Value: US$250,000 per year
Length of Study: 4 years
Frequency: Annual
Country of Study: Any country
Closing Date: 5 February
Additional Information: www.nlm.nih.gov/ep/GrantResearch.html

National Multiple Sclerosis Society (MS)

National MS Society, P.O. Box 4527, New York, NY 10163, United States of America.

Tel: (1) 310 479 4456
Website: www.nationalmssociety.org/

The National Multiple Sclerosis Society (NMSS) is a non-profit organization based in New York City with chapters located throughout the United States. The organization funds research, advocates for social and political change, provides education, and sponsors services that help people with multiple sclerosis and their families.

Biostatistics/Informatics Junior Faculty Award

Purpose: As part of our commitment to building a workforce of research leaders to drive pathways to MS cures, the National MS Society established a junior faculty award in biostatistics/ informatics/computational biology, with funding from the Marilyn Hilton MS Research Fund
Eligibility: Eligible candidates hold a doctoral degree (PhD or equivalent) in biostatistics, data science, or informatics, and are within five years of completion of their terminal degree. They must have been offered or hold an academic appointment at the assistant professor (or equivalent) level at the initiation of the award
Type: Award
Value: three years of partial (25-50%) salary support, up to US$20,000 per year for access to datasets
Length of Study: 3 years
Frequency: Annual
Country of Study: Any country
Application Procedure: To submit a proposal, investigators must first register with our online portal (nmss.fluxx.io) and complete a pre-application. Staff will review the pre-application to determine whether the research plan is appropriate and relevant to our goals
Closing Date: 17 August
Additional Information: www.nationalmssociety.org/For-Professionals/Researchers/Society-Funding/Training-Grants-and-Fellowships/Biostatistics-Informatics-Junior-Faculty-Award

N

For further information contact:

Email: Bruce.Bebo@nmss.org

Career Transition Fellowships

Purpose: The Society's Career Transition Fellowship addresses this need by fostering the development and productivity of young scientists who have potential to make significant contributions to MS research and help ensure the future and stability of MS research. The Career Transition Fellowship targets current postdoctoral trainees who demonstrate both commitment and exceptional potential to conduct MS-related research
Eligibility: 1. Applicants must hold a doctoral degree (M.D., PhD or equivalent) and must be in a research-oriented postdoctoral training program at an academic, government, or non-profit research institution. 2. Applicants must have more than two years of postdoctoral research experience and no more than five years of postdoctoral research experience at the time of application. (Clinically related training periods such as medical residencies or sub-specialty fellowships will not be counted towards postdoctoral research experience.)
Level of Study: Doctorate, Postdoctorate
Type: Fellowships
Value: US$550,000
Length of Study: 5 years
Frequency: Annual
Country of Study: Any country
Application Procedure: The application process for this award involves two levels of review, preliminary and full applications. To submit a proposal for research support, investigators must first register with our Apply Online site (nmss.fluxx.io) and complete a pre-application. Staff will review the pre-applications and selected applicants will be invited to submit a full proposal
Closing Date: August
Additional Information: www.nationalmssociety.org/For-Professionals/Researchers/Society-Funding/Training-Grants-and-Fellowships/Career-Transition-Fellowships

For further information contact:

Email: douglas.landsman@nmss.org

MS Clinical Mentorship for Medical Students

Purpose: to raise awareness of the challenges experienced by people with MS to generate interest in a career in MS care
Eligibility: The student must make their own living arrangements. They must also have their own daily transportation and the ability to travel to the assigned mentorship sites. The mentorship is open to all graduate students attending school who are U.S. citizens or candidates lawfully admitted to the U.S. for permanent residence
Type: Studentship
Value: US$3,000
Length of Study: 4 weeks
Country of Study: Any country
Application Procedure: nms2cdn.azureedge.net/cmssite/nationalmssociety/media/msnationalfiles/professionals/clinical-mentorship-programs-application-instructions_12-21-22.pdf
Closing Date: 25 January
Additional Information: www.nationalmssociety.org/For-Professionals/Researchers/Society-Funding/Training-Grants-and-Fellowships/MS-Clinical-Mentorship-for-Students

For further information contact:

Tel: (1) 800 344 4867

National Research Council (NRC)

500 Fifth Street NW, Washington, DC 20001, United States of America.

Tel: (1) 202 334 2644

The National Research Council was organized by the National Academy of Sciences in 1916 to associate the broad community of science and technology with the Academy's purposes of further knowledge and advising the federal government. The Council has become the principal operating agency of both the National Academy of Sciences and the National Academy of Engineering in providing services to the government, the public, and the scientific and engineering communities.

Christine Mirzayan Science & Technology Policy Graduate Fellowship Program

Subjects: Social/behavioral sciences, health and medicine, physical or biological sciences, engineering, law/business/public administration, or relevant interdisciplinary fields
Purpose: The fellowship program, which operates under the auspices of the Policy and Global Affairs Division, a program unit within the Academies, is designed to engage early career

professionals in the analytical processes that inform U.S. science and technology policy. Fellows obtain the essential skills and knowledge needed to work in science policy at the federal, state, or local levels
Eligibility: Graduate and professional school students and those who have completed graduate studies within the last five years may apply. Areas of study may include social/behavioral sciences, health and medicine, physical or biological sciences, engineering, law/business/public administration, or relevant interdisciplinary fields
Type: Fellowship
Value: A stipend is provided to offset expenses during the fellowship period
Length of Study: 12 weeks
Country of Study: Any country
Application Procedure: 1. Apply using the register/login buttons at the top right of this page under "How to Apply". If you are a first time visitor, click the 'register' button. If you have applied in the past or already started your application, click Log In. 2. Review your eligibility. This is an early career fellowship program. Graduate and professional school students and those who have completed graduate studies (degree awarded) within the last five years may apply. Areas of study may include social/behavioral sciences, health and medicine, physical or biological sciences, engineering, law/business/public administration, or relevant interdisciplinary fields. 3. Review Prospective Units and select up to 7 that interest you. 4. Review all sections of the application prior to submission. 5. Notify Referees. TWO references are required. These must be relevant to your academic, professional, volunteer, or other related experience. Towards the beginning of the application form, you will be asked to provide an email address for each referee. Complete this section right away to ensure that your referees have adequate time to submit their reference before the application deadline. Mailed reference letters will NOT be accepted. 6. In order to submit your application successfully, you must upload ALL required materials, ensure that your recommendation letters are attached, and hit the SUBMIT button by the deadline
Closing Date: 31 October
Additional Information: www.nationalacademies.org/our-work/the-christine-mirzayan-science–technology-policy-graduate-fellowship-program

For further information contact:

500 5th Street, NW, Keck 574, Washington, DC 20001, United States of America.

Tel: (1) 202 334 2455
Email: policyfellows@nas.edu

National Research Foundation (NRF)

PO Box 2600, Pretoria 0001, South Africa.

Tel: (27) (0)12 481 4000
Email: info@nrf.ac.za
Website: www.nrf.ac.za
Contact: Ms HA Michau, Manager, Student Support

The NRF is an independent statutory body established through the National Research Foundation Act (Act No 23 of 1998), following a system-wide review conducted for the Department of Arts, Culture, Science and Technology (DACST). The new entity incorporated the functions of the research funding agencies that were previously servicing various sections of the research community, namely the former Centre for Science Development (CSD) of the Human Sciences Research Council (HSRC) and the former Foundation for Research Development (FRD) that included several National Research Facilities.

Innovation Masters and Doctoral Scholarships

Eligibility: Scholarships are open to South African citizens, South African permanent residents as well as a limited percentage of non-South African citizens registered at a South African public university
Level of Study: Postgraduate
Type: Scholarship
Value: Masters scholarships worth R80,000 per annum and doctoral scholarships worth R110,000 per annum
Country of Study: South Africa
Application Procedure: Please check website for more details
Closing Date: 7 August
Contributor: Funded by Department of Science and Technology (DST) and managed by the National Research Foundation (NRF)

For further information contact:

Email: futurestudents@bournemouth.ac.uk

National Research Foundation Fellowships for Postdoctoral Research

Purpose: To foster postdoctoral research in the natural and applied sciences, engineering, social sciences and the humanities

Eligibility: Open to any nationals who have received their PhD within the last 5 years
Level of Study: Postdoctorate
Type: Fellowship
Value: Up to R60,000 plus a contribution of R10,000 towards the running cost of the project
Length of Study: Up to 2 years
Frequency: Twice a year
Study Establishment: Any university, technikon or research institute for full-time research
Country of Study: South Africa
Application Procedure: Applicants must complete and submit an application form, full academic record and the names of referees. Forms are available from the bursary offices of universities and technikons or can be downloaded from the website
No. of awards offered: 150
Closing Date: 31 July
Funding: Government
No. of awards given last year: 50
No. of applicants last year: 150

For further information contact:

Email: fellowships@twas.org

National Research Foundation Free-standing Masters and Doctoral Scholarships

Eligibility: Scholarships are open to South African citizens, South African permanent residents as well as a limited percentage of non-South African citizens registered at a South African public university. All applicants for full-time Masters or Doctoral studies in South Africa must be registered or intending to register at a South African public university. Applicants that already hold a degree at the level for which they are applying for funding are not eligible
Level of Study: Doctorate
Type: Scholarship
Value: Masters scholarships worth R50,000 per year and doctoral scholarships worth R70,000 per year
Frequency: Annual
Country of Study: South Africa
Application Procedure: Applications must be submitted through an online application process to the NRF
Closing Date: 7 August
Funding: International office

For further information contact:

Email: CGSMSFSS-SEEMSBESC@cihr-irsc.gc.ca

National Research Foundation Targeted Research Awards Competitive Industry Programme

Purpose: To support research in priority areas where expertise is lacking
Eligibility: Open to South African citizens only, who qualify for postgraduate support. Postdoctoral support is available for any nationality
Level of Study: Doctorate, Postdoctorate, Postgraduate
Type: Research grant
Value: From a total of approximately R20 million per year.
Frequency: Annual
Study Establishment: Any tertiary educational institution in South Africa
Country of Study: Other
Application Procedure: Applicants must complete an electronic application form. For further information please contact Ms Jill Sawers
No. of awards offered: 200
Closing Date: 31 July
Funding: Government
No. of awards given last year: 181
No. of applicants last year: 200
Additional Information: Joint ventures and collaboration with industry are strongly encouraged. www.mirzayanfellow.nas.edu/

For further information contact:

Tel: (27) 12 481 4104
Email: jill@frd.ac.za

National Research Foundation Visiting Fellowships

Purpose: To strengthen areas of expertise needed in South Africa
Eligibility: Open to senior scientists of any nationality
Level of Study: Postdoctorate
Type: Fellowship
Value: To cover air fares and accommodation.
Length of Study: Up to 3 months
Frequency: Annual, if funds are available
Study Establishment: Any South African university, technikon, museum or scientific society
Country of Study: South Africa
Application Procedure: Applications should be submitted by a South African counterpart attached to a South African university, technikon, museum or scientific society

For further information contact:

Meiring Naude Rd, Gauteng, Pretoria 0184, South Africa.

Tel: (27) 12 481 4122
Email: ferdi@frd.ac.za

Vrije University Amsterdam-NRF Desmond Tutu Doctoral Scholarships

Eligibility: Be in possession of a research Master's degree, or be in the process of completing requirements for such a degree. Should be South African citizens or permanent residents
Level of Study: Doctorate, Postgraduate
Type: Scholarship
Value: R240,000
Length of Study: The VUA-NRF Desmond Tutu Training Programme provides funding for up to four (4) years of study, depending on satisfactory progress each year
Country of Study: South Africa
Application Procedure: Check website for more details
Closing Date: 17 July
Contributor: Vrije Universiteit Amsterdam (VUA)

For further information contact:

Email: danielle.nel@nrf.ac.za

National Science Foundation (NSF)

2415 Eisenhower Avenue, Alexandria, VA 22314, United States of America.

Tel: (1) 703 292 5111
Email: info@nsf.gov
Website: www.nsf.gov
Contact: Division Director

The National Science Foundation (NSF) is an independent federal agency created by Congress in 1950 to promote the progress of science; to advance the national health, prosperity, and welfare; to secure the national defense. NSF is vital because we support basic research and people to create knowledge that transforms the future.

Cultural Anthropology Program Senior Research Awards

Purpose: The primary objective of the Cultural Anthropology Program is to support fundamental, systematic anthropological research and training to increase understanding of the causes, consequences, and complexities of human social and cultural variability
Eligibility: The categories of proposers eligible to submit proposals to the National Science Foundation are identified in the NSF Proposal & Award Policies & Procedures Guide
Level of Study: Graduate
Type: Award
Value: US$4,000,000
Frequency: Annual
Country of Study: Any country
No. of awards offered: 30 to 40
Closing Date: 15 August
Funding: Foundation
Additional Information: The Cultural Anthropology Program cannot support research that takes as its primary objective improved clinical practice, applied policy, or other immediate application www.nsf.gov/funding/pgm_summ.jsp?pims_id=505513

For further information contact:

Tel: (1) 703 292 7783
Email: jmantz@nsf.gov

Directorate for Education and Human Resources Core Research

Purpose: The ECR program places emphasis on the rigorous development of theory and accumulation of knowledge to inform efforts to address challenges in STEM interest, learning, and participation, for all groups and all ages in formal and informal settings. This emphasis includes research on advancing evaluative methodologies to support research efforts funded through ECR
Level of Study: Graduate
Type: Research
Value: Level I proposals may request up to US$500,000; Level II proposals may request up to US$1,500,000; Level III proposals may request up to US$2,500,000
Length of Study: 3 to 5 years
Frequency: Annual
Country of Study: Any country
No. of awards offered: 40 Estimated number of awards description- approximately 15 awards at level I; 12 awards at level II; 5 awards at level III, and 9 other awards
Closing Date: 5 October
Funding: Foundation
Additional Information: 1. Level 1 and Level 2 proposals have a maximum grant duration of three years. 2. Level 3 proposals have a maximum grant duration of five years. ECR Proposals may fall within three levels of funding. Level 1 Proposals: have a maximum award size of US$5,00,000.

Synthesis proposals may only be budgeted at Level 1 or 2. Level 2 Proposals: have a maximum award size of US$1,500,000. Synthesis proposals may only be budgeted at Level 1 or 2. Level 3 Proposals: have a maximum award size of US$2,500,000 www.nsf.gov/funding/pgm_summ.jsp?pims_id=504924

For further information contact:

Email: ECR@nsf.gov

Enabling Discovery through GEnomic Tools (EDGE)

Purpose: Enabling Discovery through GEnomics (EDGE) program, the National Science Foundation (NSF) and the National Institutes for Health (NIH) support research to advance understanding of comparative and functional genomics. The EDGE program supports the development of innovative tools, technologies, resources, and infrastructure that advance biological research focused on the identification of the causal mechanisms connecting genes and phenotypes. The EDGE program also supports functional genomic research that addresses the mechanistic basis of complex traits in diverse organisms within the context (environmental, developmental, social, and/or genomic) in which they function
Eligibility: The categories of proposers eligible to submit proposals to the National Science Foundation are identified in the NSF Proposal & Award Policies & Procedures Guide (PAPPG), Chapter I.E.
Level of Study: Graduate
Type: Award
Value: US$10,000,000
Frequency: Annual
Country of Study: Any country
Application Procedure: Step 1 Download a Grant Application Package and Application Instructions link and enter the funding opportunity number, (the program solicitation number without the NSF prefix) and press the Download Package button
No. of awards offered: 10 to 15
Closing Date: 17 February
Funding: Private
Additional Information: www.nsf.gov/pubs/2021/nsf21546/nsf21546.htm

For further information contact:

2415, Eisenhower Avenue, Alexandria, VA 22314, United States of America.

Tel: (1) 301 312 3276
Email: jennifer.troyer@nih.gov

Faculty Early Career Development Program (CAREER)

Purpose: The Faculty Early Career Development (CAREER) Program is a Foundation-wide activity that offers the National Science Foundation's most prestigious awards in support of early-career faculty who have the potential to serve as academic role models in research and education and to lead advances in the mission of their department or organization. Activities pursued by early-career faculty should build a firm foundation for a lifetime of leadership in integrating education and research. NSF encourages submission of CAREER proposals from early-career faculty at all CAREER-eligible organizations and especially encourages women, members of underrepresented minority groups, and persons with disabilities to apply
Level of Study: Foundation programme
Type: Award
Value: subject to availability of funds
Frequency: Annual
Country of Study: Any country
No. of awards offered: 500
Closing Date: 26 July
Funding: Foundation
Additional Information: www.nsf.gov/funding/pgm_summ.jsp?pims_id=503214

For further information contact:

Tel: (1) 703 292 5111
Email: nsf-ccc@nsf.gov

Macrosystems Biology and NEON-Enabled Science (MSB-NES)

Purpose: The Macrosystems Biology and NEON-Enabled Science (MSB-NES) Research on Biological Systems at Regional to Continental Scales program will support quantitative, interdisciplinary, systems-oriented research on biosphere processes and their complex interactions with climate, land use, and changes in species distribution at regional to continental scales as well as training activities to broaden participation of researchers in Macrosystems Biology and NEON-Enabled Science
Type: Award
Value: US$300,000
Length of Study: (MRA)-5 years; (MSA)-3 years
Frequency: Annual
Country of Study: Any country
No. of awards offered: 15 to 25
Closing Date: 13 November

Additional Information: www.nsf.gov/funding/pgm_summ.jsp?pims_id=503425

For further information contact:

Tel: (1) 703 292 7186
Email: mkane@nsf.gov

National Science Foundation Research Traineeship (NRT) Program

Purpose: The NSF Research Traineeship (NRT) program seeks proposals that explore ways for graduate students in research-based master's and doctoral degree programs to develop the skills, knowledge, and competencies needed to pursue a range of STEM careers. The program is dedicated to effective training of STEM graduate students in high priority interdisciplinary or convergent research areas, through a comprehensive traineeship model that is innovative, evidence-based, and aligned with changing workforce and research needs
Level of Study: Doctorate, Masters Degree
Type: Grant
Value: 14 to 16 awards US$3,000,000 4 to 6 awards US$2,000,000
Length of Study: 5 years
Frequency: Annual
Country of Study: Any country
No. of awards offered: 18 to 20
Closing Date: 6 September
Funding: Foundation
Additional Information: www.nsf.gov/funding/pgm_summ.jsp?pims_id=505015

For further information contact:

Tel: (1) 703 292 8072
Email: ddenecke@nsf.gov

Robert Noyce Teacher Scholarship Program

Purpose: The National Science Foundation Robert Noyce Teacher Scholarship Program seeks to encourage talented science, technology, engineering, and mathematics (STEM) majors and professionals to become K-12 mathematics and science (including engineering and computer science) teachers. The program invites creative and innovative proposals that address the critical need for recruiting and preparing highly effective elementary and secondary science and mathematics teachers in high-need local educational agencies
Level of Study: Graduate
Type: Scholarship
Value: Up to US$3,000,000
Length of Study: 6 years
Frequency: Annual
Study Establishment: This program provides educational opportunities for Undergraduate Students, Graduate Students, K-12 Educators
Country of Study: Any country
No. of awards offered: 55 to 70
Closing Date: 29 August
Funding: Private
Additional Information: www.nsf.gov/funding/pgm_summ.jsp?pims_id=5733

For further information contact:

Tel: (1) 703 292 4657
Email: srichard@nsf.gov

Scalable Parallelism in the Extreme (SPX)

Purpose: The Scalable Parallelism in the Extreme (SPX) program aims to support research addressing the challenges of increasing performance in this modern era of parallel computing. This will require a collaborative effort among researchers in multiple areas, from services and applications down to micro-architecture
Eligibility: Proposals may only be submitted by the following 1. Institutions of Higher Education (IHEs) - Two- and four-year IHEs (including community colleges) accredited in, and having a campus located in the United States, acting on behalf of their faculty members. 2. Non-profit, non--academic organizations Independent museums, observatories, research labs, professional societies and similar organizations in the United States associated with educational or research activities
Level of Study: Graduate
Type: Grants, work-study (not just grants)
Value: US$10,000,000
Length of Study: 3 to 4 years
Frequency: Annual
Country of Study: Any country
No. of awards offered: 4 to 10
Closing Date: 17 January
Funding: Private
Additional Information: www.nsf.gov/funding/pgm_summ.jsp?pims_id=505348&org=NSF

For further information contact:

Tel: (1) 703 292 7885
Email: abanerje@nsf.gov

National Sea Grant College

1315 East-West Highway, Silver Spring, MD 20910, United States of America.

Tel: (1) 301 734 1066
Email: sgfellow@ucsd.edu
Website: www.seagrant.noaa.gov
Contact: Jim Eckman, Director

The National Sea Grant College program was established by the U.S. Congress in 1966 and works to create and maintain a healthy coastal environment and economy. The Sea Grant network consists of a federal/university partnership between the National Oceanic and Atmospheric Administration (NOAA) and 34 university-based programs in every coastal and Great Lakes state, Puerto Rico, and Guam. The network draws on the expertise of more than 3,000 scientists, engineers, public outreach experts, educators and students to help citizens better understand, conserve and utilize America's coastal resources.

Sea Grant/NOAA Fisheries Graduate Fellowship

Purpose: To encourage qualified applicants to pursue careers in either population and ecosystem dynamics and stock assessment or in marine resource economics. To increase available expertise related to these fields. To foster closer relationships between academic scientists and NOAA Fisheries. To provide real-world experience to graduate students and accelerate their career development
Eligibility: The NMFS-Sea Grant Fellowships are available to U.S. citizens who are graduate students enrolled in PhD degree programs in academic institutions in the United States and its territories. Only U.S. citizens are eligible to apply
Eligible Country: United States of America
Level of Study: Postdoctorate
Type: Fellowship
Value: Up to US$54,166
Length of Study: 3 years
Frequency: Annual
Country of Study: United States of America
Application Procedure: Applicants are strongly encouraged to reach out to the Sea Grant program in their state/territory at least one month prior to the state application deadline to receive application support and provide notification of intent to apply
No. of awards offered: stipend, tuition, fees, equipment, supplies, and travel necessary
Closing Date: 25 January
Funding: Government
Additional Information: www.seagrant.noaa.gov/NMFS-SG-Fellowship

For further information contact:

Tel: (1) 240 507 3712
Email: OAR.SG.Fellows@noaa.gov

National Sun Yat-Sen University (NSYSU)

70 Lien-hai Road, Kaohsiung 804, Taiwan.

Tel: (886) 7 525 2633
Website: www.oia.nsysu.edu.tw

National Sun Yat-sen University (NSYSU) is one of the few universities in the world to feature its very own on-campus beach. Built in the coastal city of Kaohsiung which boasts almost year-round sunshine, the campus is bordered to the east by the slopes of the beautifully-named Longevity mountain and to the west by the sandy beach, clear blue water and coral reefs of Sizi Bay and beyond that the Strait of Taiwan.

National Sun Yat-sen University International Fellowship

Purpose: To pursue academic excellence combining theory and practice
Eligibility: Open to candidates who are pursuing their Master's or Doctoral degrees
Level of Study: Doctorate, Postgraduate
Type: Fellowships
Value: Varies
Length of Study: 2–3 months
Frequency: Annual
Country of Study: Any country
Application Procedure: Applications along with a curriculum vitae, research proposal, name of the corresponding member in the Kuroshio Research Group and 2 letters of recommendation must be mailed
Additional Information: "Recommendation to Kuroshio Application" must appear as the subject line. www.seagrant.noaa.gov/NMFS-SG-Fellowship

For further information contact:

Email: keryea@mail.nsysu.edu.tw

National Tax Association

1100 Vermont Avenue, NW, Suite 650, Washington, DC 20005, United States of America.

Tel: (1) 202 737 3325
Email: nta@ntanet.org
Website: ntanet.org/

The National Tax Association serves as the leading association of scholars and professionals dedicated to advancing the theory and practice of public finance, including public taxing, spending and borrowing. The National Tax Association is a nonpartisan, nonpolitical educational association. As a 501(c)(3) organization, the NTA does not promote any particular tax program or policy. The enormous public benefit that can come from sound tax policy and wise administration of public finances is a prime reason for the work of NTA.

Tax Institute of America Doctoral Dissertations in Government and Taxation

Subjects: Finance
Purpose: To award original, innovative, clear and analytical dissertations written by scholars and practitioners of government finance
Eligibility: The award will be granted to exceptional dissertations written by scholars and practitioners of government finance
Type: Award
Value: The winning entry will receive US$2,000 and the opportunity to publish a paper based on the dissertation in the National Tax Journal. There will also be two honorable mentions of US$1,000 each for outstanding entries
Country of Study: Any country
Closing Date: 30 June
Additional Information: ntanet.org/awards/phd-dissertation-award/

National Tour Association

101 Prosperous Place, Suite 190, Lexington, KY 40509, United States of America.

Tel: (1) 859 264 6540
Website: ntaonline.com/

NTA is the leading business association for companies and organizations that serve customers traveling to, from and within North America. Our 700 buyer members are tour operators and travel planners who package travel product domestically and around the world. Our seller members - 500 destinations and 1,100 tour suppliers - represent product in all 50 U.S. states, each Canadian province and more than 40 other countries.

National Tour Association (NTA) Luray Caverns Graduate Research Scholarship

Purpose: To aid graduate students who are conducting tourism-related research
Eligibility: 1. Applicants can be permanent residents of any country but must be enrolled at an accredited U.S. or Canadian four-year postsecondary institution. 2. They must be entering or returning graduate students who are conducting research that focuses on tourism. They must have a proven commitment to the tourism industry, and must have a GPA of 3.0 or higher on a four-point scale. Selection is based on the strength of the research project
Level of Study: Graduate
Type: Scholarship
Value: US$3,000
Frequency: Annual
Country of Study: Any country
Application Procedure: Applications are available online. An application form, proof of residency, a personal essay, a resume, a research proposal, an official transcript and one letter of recommendation are required
No. of awards offered: 1
Closing Date: 3 April
Funding: Private
Additional Information: www.chegg.com/scholarships/national-tour-associationluray-caverns-graduate-research-scholarship-2345

National University of Ireland Galway

Postgraduate Admission Office, University Road, Galway, H91 TK33, Ireland.

Tel: (353) 91 524 411
Email: info@it.nuigalway.ie
Website: www.nuigalway.ie
Contact: Mairead Faherty

NUI Galway has grown massively in size and reputation over the past 175 years, with a student population today of over

N

18,000. According to QS World University Rankings, we are ranked 259 in the world and have been increasing our global reach and reputation over the past decade.

Charles Parsons Energy Research Award

Purpose: To focus on investigation and optimization of electron transfer reactions in biological fuel cells that can generate energy from diverse substrates. To focus the research on applications of pure- and mixed-culture microbial fuel cells, and biocatalytic enzyme-based fuel cells
Eligibility: Open to engineering graduates
Level of Study: Doctorate
Type: Research award
Value: Salary scale €55,000–80,486 per year for researchers, stipend of €18,000 per year plus tuition fees for PhD studentship and undergraduate engineering students €1,500 per month
Application Procedure: Applicants should include a curriculum vitae and the names of two academic referees
Closing Date: October
Additional Information: The research will involve liaison with international collaborators, bench research and reporting. To this end, good inter-personal, written communication and networking skills are advantageous. www.chegg.com/scholarships/national-tour-associationluray-caverns-graduate-research-scholarship-2345

For further information contact:

Email: donal.leech@nuigalway.ie

Hardiman PhD Scholarships

Purpose: The Scholarships offer opportunities for suitably qualified individuals to pursue a Structured PhD focused on the five key areas of research in which the University offers leading expertise; Engaging with our partners locally, nationally and worldwide, we invite ambition in research that underpins the following areas 1. Enhancing policy and society 2. Enriching creativity and culture 3. Improving health and wellbeing 4. Realising potential through data and enabling technologies 5. Sustaining our planet and people
Eligibility: 1. Successful applicants will be expected to have a first or upper second class honours primary degree or equivalent. 2. Applications will not be accepted from persons currently registered as PhD students. 3. English Language Requirements - please go to this webpage www.nuigalway.ie/international-students/entry-requirements/
Level of Study: Postgraduate
Type: Scholarship
Value: stipend of €18,500
Length of Study: 4 years
Country of Study: Any country
Application Procedure: Applicants must read the Applicant's Guide prior to completing the application form
Closing Date: 11 February
Additional Information: www.nuigalway.ie/hardiman-scholarships/

For further information contact:

Email: hrscholar@nuigalway.ie

Irish Research Council Scholarships-Ulysses

Purpose: The aim of the Ulysses scheme is to foster new collaborations between Ireland and France-based researchers by providing seed funding for reciprocal travel visits. The scheme thus facilitates the exchange of innovative ideas and approaches across all disciplines. The Irish Research Council and the Embassy of France in Ireland are committed to supporting continued knowledge exchange between Irish and French researchers through appropriate forms of collaboration
Eligibility: Eligible Irish-based partner(s) include postdoctoral researchers and Principal Investigators in eligible third level institutions or publicly-funded research institutions with contracts that will cover their employment during the two year period of the award. Postgraduate researchers are not eligible to be applicants or Project Leaders, but their participation is encouraged as part of the wider research team
Level of Study: Postdoctorate
Type: Scholarship
Value: Irish based researcher may receive up to €5,000, and the French based researcher may also receive up to €5,000
Length of Study: 2 years
Country of Study: Any country
Application Procedure: One electronic copy of the application form and all related attachments must be submitted via email to ulysses@research.ie by a person authorised by their institution to hold responsibility for research grants
Closing Date: 13 April
Additional Information: research.ie/funding/ulysses/?f=postdoctoral

For further information contact:

Email: ulysses@research.ie

PhD Student Scholarship in Atmospheric Science

Purpose: To study the effect of ambient relative humidity on aerosol radiative parameters aerosol light scattering coefficient and aerosol absorption coefficient
Eligibility: Open to candidates who have obtained a good Honours Degree (grade 2.1 at least) in physics or in a cognate subject
Level of Study: Doctorate
Type: Scholarship
Value: Stipend and tuition fees
Length of Study: 3 years
Country of Study: Ireland
Application Procedure: Applicants must submit a covering letter, curriculum vitae and the names of at least two referees

For further information contact:

Tel: (353) 91 492 704
Fax: (353) 91 495 515
Email: gerard.jennings@nuigalway.ie

Postgraduate Research Funding-China

Eligibility: This funding is available to students undertaking full-time PhD study. This funding is available to students with a Chinese passport
Level of Study: Doctorate
Type: Scholarship
Value: CSC will cover the living costs and flight tickets
Country of Study: China
No. of awards offered: 12 PhD tuition-fee waivers from University of Galway with no subject restrictions
Closing Date: 24 February
Additional Information: www.universityofgalway.ie/international-students/studyinireland/yourcountry/china/#tab5

For further information contact:

Email: cheryl.xu@universityofgalway.ie

Student Research Scholarship in Occupational Hygiene

Purpose: To enhance GSK's exposure assessment strategy, to look at current occupational hygiene data collected from across all GSK sites and to apply Bayesian statistics to optimize the exposure assessment strategy
Eligibility: Candidates for the degree of PhD or MSc by research must have reached a high honours standard (minimum H2.2 [or equivalent international qualification] for an MSc) at the examination for the primary degree or presented such other evidence as will satisfy the Head of School and the College of his/her fitness
Level of Study: Doctorate, Postgraduate
Type: Scholarship
Value: Monthly stipend
Country of Study: Ireland
Application Procedure: Applicants must submit a covering letter, a curriculum vitae and the names of at least two referees
Closing Date: 31 August
Contributor: GlaxoSmithKline (GSK)
Additional Information: www.universityofgalway.ie/courses/research-postgraduate-programmes/phd-and-masters/occupational-health-hygiene.html

For further information contact:

Department of Experimental Physics, National University of Ireland, University Road, Galway, H91 TK33, Ireland.

Email: marie.coggins@nuigalway.ie

Taught Postgraduate Scholarships

Purpose: NUI Galway has established a Postgraduate Scholarship Scheme to support and facilitate students wishing to register for a Fulltime Taught Postgraduate Masters programme in the academic
Eligibility: In order to be eligible for the award of a scholarship, students must: 1. Have submitted a valid online scholarship application form by the deadline; 2. Be registered in Year 1 of a Fulltime Taught Masters programme for the academic year subsequent to the scholarship application (repeat students are not eligible to apply); 3. Have attained a first class honours (or equivalent) in a Level 8 primary degree.
Eligible Country: East European Countries
Level of Study: Postgraduate
Type: Scholarship
Value: €1,500 for EU students
Country of Study: Any country
Application Procedure: Applications must be made using the online application form
Closing Date: 31 August
Additional Information: The Admissions Office will review applications and will verify submitted documentary evidence provided, during the summer months. Once the applicant is notified of her/his eligibility, they will then be required to complete the registration requirements of the University by the due date. www.nuigalway.ie/media/registry/admissions/files/Scholarship_criteria.pdf

National University of Ireland, Maynooth

Co. Kildare, Maynooth, W23 X021, Ireland.

Tel: (353) 1 708 3868
Email: international.office@mu.ie
Website: www.maynoothuniversity.ie/

The Maynooth University International Office supports over 1000 students of different nationalities and cultures, and facilitates the applications of international undergraduate and postgraduate students from outside of the European Union to study at the University. In addition the Office coordinates and provides support to approximately 600 visiting students from North America and the European Union each year, while also encouraging all current Maynooth students to incorporate a period of study or work placement abroad into their degree.

John and Pat Hume Doctoral Scholarships

Purpose: John & Pat Hume doctoral awards will be offered to successful doctoral applicants with demonstrated excellence in academic course work and research. Consideration will be given to the relevance of the proposed doctoral research to departmental and university research priorities. Applicants will also be expected to have some prior non-academic engagement such as volunteering, outreach activities or similar, in line with the university's strategic plan
Eligibility: The minimum standards for eligibility for MU John & Pat Hume doctoral awards of any type are 1. All applicants must have a first class or upper second-class honours bachelor's degree, or the equivalent, in the discipline of the department of application, or in a cognate discipline approved by the proposed supervisor. 2. If undergraduate examination results are not known at the time of application, Maynooth University may make a provisional offer of a scholarship on condition that the scholar's bachelor's (equivalent) degree result is a first class or upper second-class honours. 3. If a scholar does not have a first class or upper second-class honours bachelor's degree (or equivalent), they must possess a master's degree in the discipline of the department of application or cognate discipline as approved by proposed supervisor. 4. Applicants of any nationality are eligible to apply
Level of Study: Doctorate
Type: Scholarship
Value: offering €18,500 stipend, €2,000 for research expenses plus fees for four years
Length of Study: 4 years
Country of Study: Any country
Application Procedure: Completed and signed applications should be submitted via the online application system
Closing Date: 30 January
Additional Information: www.maynoothuniversity.ie/graduate-studies/john-pat-hume-doctoral-awards

For further information contact:

John Hume Building, 3rd Floor, Maynooth University, Co. Kildare, Ireland.

Email: humephdscholarship@mu.ie

John and Pat Hume Research Scholarships

Purpose: To build on excellence in areas across the arts, humanities, social sciences, sciences and engineering
Eligibility: Applicants must have a First or Upper Second-Class Honours Primary Degree (or equivalent) from Ireland, the European Union or from any overseas university and intend to pursue a PhD degree at the University. Those who have commenced a research degree at NUI Maynooth prior to application will not be eligible
Level of Study: Postgraduate, Research
Type: Scholarship
Value: €5,000 per year plus payment of fees at European Union level. In some cases an additional fund of €3,000 is also provided to the student researcher for activities undertaken in support of the Department including tutorials and laboratory demonstration
Length of Study: Up to 4 years
Frequency: Annual
Study Establishment: NUI Maynooth
Country of Study: Ireland
Application Procedure: Applicants must first make contact with a NUI Maynooth department or centre to discuss their suitability for a PhD programme. A list of departmental contacts is available on the website. Application for the scholarship can then be filed
Closing Date: May
No. of awards given last year: 30
Additional Information: Supplement the scholarship with an additional €3,000 for tutorial or demonstrating duties www.maynoothuniversity.ie/study-maynooth/postgraduate-studies/fees-funding-scholarships/john-and-pat-hume-doctoral-awards.

For further information contact:

Tel: (353) 1 708 6018
Fax: (353) 1 708 3359
Email: pgdean@nuim.ie

Maynooth University Teaching Studentships

Purpose: Funded student teaching assistant opportunities are offered across a range of disciplines at Maynooth University. Successful applicants will commence PhD Doctoral studies at Maynooth University in the Autumn semester and will have 5 years to complete their PhD
Level of Study: Postdoctorate
Type: Scholarship
Value: 1. Full annual tuition fees support (approximately €6,500 per annum); 2. A fixed stipend of €9,007 per annum
Length of Study: 5 years
Country of Study: Ireland
Additional Information: In addition to their PhD research, the recipient of the Teaching Studentship will support the teaching and assessment duties of their Department up to a maximum of 455 hours per annum. www.maynoothuniversity.ie/study-maynooth/postgraduate-studies/fees-funding-scholarships/maynooth-university-teaching-studentship#main-content

Taught Master's Scholarships

Eligibility: Applicants must intend to pursue a full-time taught master's degree at the university commencing in the academic year 2024–25 and meet the following eligibility criteria: 1. Satisfy the entry requirements of the Maynooth University taught master's programme they intend to undertake in 2024–25 and have applied on v2.pac.ie/institute/2 before 30 June 2024. 2. All applicants must have achieved a minimum 2.1 honours undergraduate degree (NFQ Level 8) in order to be considered for a Taught Master's Scholarship. Results from Level 8 Higher Diplomas are not eligible. 3. Applicants who are not graduates/alumni of Maynooth University will be requiredto upload their final undergraduate degree transcripts for their Level 8 degree to PAC.ie as part of the standard PAC.ie application process for a Taught Master's programme at Maynooth University by the 1 July 2024. 4. Only students who have applied for a full-time taught master's programme at Maynooth University by the scholarship closing date are considered eligible for the scholarship. 5. Applicants must have received a firm or conditional offer of a place on their chosen programme by 26 July 2024 in order for their scholarship application to be assessed
Level of Study: Postgraduate
Type: Scholarship
Value: €2000 to students across all disciplines in recognition of academic excellence.. A further €2000 scholarship will be awarded to applicants ordinarily resident in Ireland and registered with their Higher Education Institution Access Office and meet the eligibilty requirement
Country of Study: Ireland
Application Procedure: Apply online in conjunction with your application for your chosen postgraduate programme: v2.pac.ie/institute/2
Closing Date: 30 June
Additional Information: www.maynoothuniversity.ie/study-maynooth/postgraduate-studies/fees-funding-scholarships/taught-masters-scholarships

For further information contact:

Email: pgstudies@mu.ie

National University of Singapore (NUS)

21 Lower Kent Ridge Road, 119077, Singapore.

Tel: (65) 6516 6666
Email: research@nus.edu.sg
Website: www.nus.edu.sg

The National University of Singapore aspires to be a vital community of academics, researchers, staff, students and alumni working together in a spirit of innovation and enterprise for a better world. Our singular focus on talent will be the cornerstone of a truly great university that is dedicated to quality education, influential research and visionary enterprise, in service of country and society.

Asian Development Bank-Japan Scholarship Program

Purpose: To find further study in public policy implementation
Eligibility: 1. A national of an ADB borrowing member country (applicants from countries that are no longer borrowing from ADB are not eligible for the ADB-JSP Scholarship) 2. A Bachelor's degree or its equivalent with superior academic record. 3. At least two (2) years of full-time professional working experience (acquired after a university degree) at a time of application. 4. Proficiency in oral and written English communication skills to be able to pursue studies. 5. Not more than 35 years old at the time of application. In exceptional cases, for programs which are appropriate for senior officials and managers, the age limit is 45 years old. 6. In good health. 7. Should agree to return to his/her home county after completion of studies under the Program. 8. Executive Directors, Alternate Directors, management and staff of ADB, consultants, and relatives of the aforementioned are not eligible for the Scholarship. 9. Staff of AIT are

not eligible for the Scholarship. 10. Applicants living or working in a country other than his/her home country are not eligible for the scholarships. 11. ADB-JSP does not support applicants who are already enrolled in graduate degree programs. 12. ADB-JSP does not sponsor undergraduate studies, distance learning programs, short-term training, conferences, seminars, thesis writing, and research projects
Type: Scholarship
Value: Tuition fees (actual costs) See website
Frequency: Annual
Study Establishment: Lee Kuan Yew School of Public Policy, National University of Singapore
Country of Study: Singapore
Application Procedure: See Website: ait.ac.th/financial/joint-japan-world-bank-graduate-scholarship-program/
No. of awards offered: 350
Closing Date: 31 March
Funding: Government
Contributor: Government
No. of awards given last year: 3
No. of applicants last year: 350
Additional Information: Website: www.ait.ac.th/admissions/scholarships/asian-development-bank-japan-scholarship-program/

Law/Faculty Graduate Scholarship (FGS)

Purpose: To reward an outstanding student of the faculty of Law
Eligibility: Outstanding applicants of any nationality (including Singapore citizens and permanent residents) may be awarded the FGS to pursue the LLM coursework degrees LLM, LLM (Asian Legal Studies), LLM (Corporate & Financial Services Law), LLM (Intellectual Property & Technology Law), LLM (International & Comparative Law), LLM (Maritime Law)
Level of Study: Postgraduate
Type: Scholarship
Value: The scholarship will cover tuition fees
Frequency: Annual
Study Establishment: National University of Singapore
Country of Study: Singapore

Lee Kuan Yew School of Public Policy Graduate Scholarships (LKYSPPS)

Purpose: To find further study in public policy and administration implementation
Eligibility: Open to all nationalities (except Singapore)
Level of Study: Postgraduate
Type: Scholarship
Value: A monthly stipend, a one-time book allowance, a one-time settling-in allowance, shared housing, tuition, health insurance, examination and other approved fees, cost of travel from home country to Singapore on award of the scholarship and from Singapore to home country on graduation
Length of Study: 1 year (for public administration) and 2 years (for public policy)
Frequency: Annual
Study Establishment: Lee Kuan Yew School of Public Policy, National University of Singapore
Country of Study: Singapore
Application Procedure: Apply online
Funding: Government
Contributor: Government

For further information contact:

Email: LKYSPPmpp@nus.edu.sg

Master of Business Administration Programme

Application Procedure: Applicants must complete an application form supplying US$15 fee.
Closing Date: 1 April

For further information contact:

Graduate School of Business, MBA Programme, FBA2, Level 5, Room 6, 17 Law Link, 117592, Singapore.

Tel: (65) 6874 6149
Fax: (65) 6778 2681
Email: fbagrad@nus.edu.sg

National University of Singapore Design Technology Institute Scholarship

Eligibility: Open to all nationalities with good Bachelor's degree with Honours in Engineering or Science
Level of Study: Postgraduate
Type: Scholarship
Value: A monthly stipend S$1,500 with a possible monthly top-up of S$500 and all approved NUS fees
Length of Study: 2 years
Frequency: Annual
Study Establishment: National University of Singapore
Country of Study: Singapore
Closing Date: November
Additional Information: DTI Scholars who are international students will be required to serve a 2 years bond in Singapore upon graduation. www.ait.ac.th/admissions/scholarships/asian-development-bank-japan-scholarship-program/

For further information contact:

Tel: (65) 6874 1227
Fax: (65) 6873 2175
Email: dtibox@nus.edu.sg

NUS Research Scholarship

Purpose: The NUS Research Scholarship ("Scholarship") is awarded to outstanding graduate students for research leading to a higher degree at the University. The Scholarship consists of a monthly stipend plus a tuition fee subsidy
Eligibility: The Scholarship is open to candidates who meet the following criteria: 1. have graduated with an undergraduate degree with at least Second Class Honours (Upper division)/Honours (Distinction) or equivalent; 2. have been offered admission to/or already admitted to a full-time graduate research programme at NUS; and 3. must be eligible for MOE Subsidy
Level of Study: Doctorate, Postdoctorate
Type: Scholarship
Value: 1. Singapore Citizen: PhD/postgraduate-S$2,800, 2. Singapore Permanent Resident: PhD-S$2,400, Postgraduate-S$2,000. 3. International Student: PhD-S$2,200, Postgraduate-S$1,900
Length of Study: 2 to 4 years
Country of Study: Singapore
Closing Date: October
Additional Information: nusgs.nus.edu.sg/scholarships-list/?lkys

President's Graduate Fellowship

Purpose: The President's Graduate Fellowship ("Fellowship") is awarded to PhD candidates who show exceptional promise or accomplishment in research. A number of PhD candidates are selected each semester by the University for the award
Eligibility: The Fellowship is open to new, incoming PhD candidates who meet the following criteria: 1. Exemplary academic record. Top performance in undergraduate/postgraduate studies, graduation from top programs, and other academic/research achievements. 2. Strong research potential. Potential to be a future leader in their respective fields based on the strength and originality of research proposal, credible signs of research ability, and expertise/interests that might lead to a path-breaking piece of work. Research interests that are aligned and/or complementary with the strengths of NUS faculty is a plus. 3. Strong ethical character and high potential to succeed in our PhD program
Level of Study: Doctorate
Type: Scholarship
Value: 1. Singapore Citizen S$3,600, 2. Singapore Permanent Resident S$3,400, 3. International Student S$3,100
Length of Study: 1 to 4 years
Country of Study: Singapore
Closing Date: October
Additional Information: nusgs.nus.edu.sg/scholarships-list/?lkys

Singapore-MIT Alliance Graduate Fellowship

Purpose: The SMA Graduate Fellowship is established by the Singapore Ministry of Education in January 2009 to attract the best and most talented PhD students from Singapore, the region and beyond, and educate them to be future leaders in the areas of science and technology. The selection of candidates will take place twice a year, in time for the start of the semesters in August and January
Eligibility: The Scholarships are open to students of all nationalities who gain admission to any PhD programme at the University whose research interest fits within one or more of the projects currently being carried out in one of the SMART Interdisciplinary Research Groups (IRGs)
Level of Study: Graduate, Postgraduate
Type: Fellowship
Value: A monthly stipend of Singaporean S$3,200; Tuition fees at NUS; and Scholarship allowance of up to S$12,000 to help cover the expenses associated with a 6-month research residency at MIT
Length of Study: The award is tenable for 1 year in the first instance; but subject to the scholar's satisfactory progress, it may be renewed each semester. The maximum period of award is 4 years
Frequency: Annual
Study Establishment: National University of Singapore and Nanyang Technological University
Country of Study: Singapore
Application Procedure: Applicants must apply separately to both MIT and NUS/NTU for the dual degrees and only to NUS or NTU for direct PhD degree; applicants must also apply directly to SMA for an SMA Graduate Fellowship
No. of awards offered: 120
Closing Date: March
Funding: Government
Contributor: A*Star, Economic and Development Board (EDB), Ministry of Education (MOE), National University of Singapore (NUS) and Nanyang Technological University (NTU)
No. of applicants last year: 120
Additional Information: smart.mit.edu/fellowships/for-graduates-smart-graduates

For further information contact:

Tel: (65) 6516 4787
Fax: (65) 6775 2920
Email: smart@nus.edu.sg

Natural Environment Research Council (NERC)

Polaris House, North Star Avenue, Swindon SN2 1EU, United Kingdom.

Tel: (44) 1793 411500
Website: www.nerc.ac.uk/funding
Contact: Studentships & Training Awards Group (STAG)

NERC - the Natural Environment Research Council - is the driving force of investment in environmental science in the UK. NERC advances the frontier of environmental science by commissioning new research, infrastructure and training that delivers valuable scientific breakthroughs. We do this because understanding our changing planet is vital for our wellbeing and economic prosperity.

Knowledge Asset Grant Fund: Expand 2023

Eligibility: This competition is open to single applicants. To lead a project your organisation must be a UK government public sector organisation headed by an accounting officer responsible for upholding managing public money. This includes: 1. UK government departments 2. arms-length bodies 3. public sector research establishments
Type: Grant
Value: £5,000,000
Country of Study: United Kingdom
Closing Date: 16 March
Additional Information: www.ukri.org/opportunity/knowledge-asset-grant-fund-expand-2023/

Natural Environment Research Council Independent Research Fellowships (IRF)

Purpose: To develop scientific leadership among the most promising early-career environmental scientists, by giving all Fellows 5 year's support, which will allow them sufficient time to develop their research programmes, and to establish international recognition
Eligibility: You must: 1. be an early career researcher 2. hold a PhD qualification or expect to submit your thesis before the fellowship interview
Level of Study: Research
Type: Fellowship
Value: £7,400,000
Length of Study: 5 years
Frequency: Annual
Country of Study: United Kingdom
Application Procedure: Please refer to the Research Grants and Fellowships Handbook at www.nerc.ac.uk/funding/available/fellowships/apply/
Closing Date: 11 October
Funding: Government
Contributor: Natural Environment Research Council (NERC)
Additional Information: www.ukri.org/opportunity/nerc-independent-research-fellowship-2022/

For further information contact:

Email: fellowships@nerc.ac.uk

Natural Environment Research Council Research Grants

Purpose: To support a specific investigation in which the applicant will be engaged personally, to enter promising new or modified fields of research, or to take advantage of developments in apparatus offering improved techniques in promising lines of research already established
Eligibility: Open to research workers ordinarily resident in the United Kingdom who are also members of the academic staff of universities, colleges and similar institutions within the United Kingdom recognised by the NERC. Research assistants and technicians are not eligible to apply. Holders of Research Council Fellowships at an Institute of Higher Education are eligible to apply for research grants
Level of Study: Postdoctorate, Professional development
Type: Grant
Value: The Standard Research Grant offers amounts over £30,000, for periods not usually in excess of three years. The Small Research Grant offers a more rapid response for applications costing £2,000–30,000. Applications for less than £2,000 will not be accepted. The new investigator scheme offers up to the £50,000
Frequency: Throughout the year
Study Establishment: Any approved Institute of Higher Education in the United Kingdom
Country of Study: United Kingdom
Application Procedure: Applicants must complete an application form, available on request. Application forms and further information can be found on the NERC website

Closing Date: 1 October
Funding: Government
No. of awards given last year: 307

For further information contact:

Email: researchcareers@nerc.ac.uk

UKRI Policy Fellowships 2024

Eligibility: This funding opportunity is open to academics who hold a PhD or equivalent research experience. As well as relevant subject matter or methodological expertise, experience of working in a policy and knowledge exchange context is beneficial. Policy fellowship funding opportunities with a UK or devolved government host are aimed at early to mid-career academics. Fellowships with a What Works Network centre host are open to all career stages. Please refer to fellowship funding opportunity specifications for detailed eligibility requirements. Please see the full list of specific fellowship funding opportunities in 'additional information' section. These include: 1. an overview of the proposed research areas and policy challenges that the fellowship will focus on 2. the person specification for each fellowship 3. any relevant eligibility criteria, including any security clearance requirements
Type: Fellowship
Value: £170,000 to £210,000
Length of Study: 18 months
Country of Study: United Kingdom
Closing Date: 20 April
Additional Information: www.ukri.org/opportunity/ukri-policy-fellowships-2023/

For further information contact:

Email: ukripolicyfellowships@ukri.org

Natural Hazards Center-University of Colorado

483 UCB, Boulder, CO 80309-0483, United States of America.

Tel: (1) 303 735 5844
Email: hazctr@colorado.edu
Website: hazards.colorado.edu/

The mission of the Natural Hazards Center at the University of Colorado at Boulder is to advance and communicate knowledge on hazards mitigation and disaster preparedness, response and recovery. Using an all hazards and interdisciplinary framework, the Center fosters information- sharing and integration of activities among researchers, practitioners and policy makers from around the world, supports and conducts research and provides educational opportunities for the next generation of hazards scholars and professionals.

Annual Hazards and Disasters Student Paper Competition

Purpose: The Natural Hazards Center created the Annual Hazards and Disasters Student Paper Competition for undergraduate and graduate students in 2004 as a way to recognize and promote the next generation of hazards and disaster researchers
Eligibility: Author(s) must be enrolled as an undergraduate or graduate student for at least one term in the 2023–24 academic year. Papers must be authored by one or more students and cannot be co-authored by faculty or colleagues who are not students. Papers cannot be under consideration or accepted for publication at the time of submission. Papers presented or submitted for presentation at professional meetings are allowable. Papers must be edited, double-spaced (including references), and less than 25 pages, including notes, references, and tables. Single-spaced papers or papers over 25 pages will be disqualified. Papers must include a brief abstract that provides an overview of the paper. Submissions should be submitted in a Word document format using 12-point Arial font. Winning submissions will be edited for Natural Hazards Center style and length before publication
Type: Competition
Value: winner each will receive US$100
Frequency: Annual
Country of Study: Any country
Closing Date: 15 May
Additional Information: hazards.colorado.edu/awards/paper-competition

For further information contact:

Natural Hazards Center, 483 UCB, Boulder, CO 80309-0483, United States of America.

Tel: (1) 303 735 5844
Email: hazctr@colorado.edu

Dissertation Fellowship in Hazards, Risks, and Disaster

Purpose: To provide financial support for research that is crucial to advancing the knowledge in the hazards field, as well as ensure that the next generation of interdisciplinary hazards professional has a source of financial and academic support to foster sound development

Eligibility: Open to candidates who already have a dissertation at an institution in the United States. Non-United States citizens may apply as long as the Doctorate degree will be granted by a United States institution

Level of Study: Postgraduate

Type: Fellowships

Value: US$10,000

Frequency: Annual

Country of Study: United States of America

Application Procedure: The applicant must submit a curriculum vitae along with a dissertation summary

Closing Date: September

Additional Information: freestudiesabroad.blogspot.com/2006/06/dissertation-fellowship-in-hazards.html

For further information contact:

Email: periship@riskinstitute.org

Natural Sciences and Engineering Research Council of Canada (NSERC)

Ontario Regional Office, 125 Zaida Eddy Private, 2nd floor, Ottawa, ON K1A 0E3, Canada.

Tel: (1) 877 767 1767
Email: nserc-ontario@nserc-crsng.gc.ca
Website: www.nserc.ca
Contact: Corporate Account Executive

The Natural Sciences and Engineering Research Council of Canada funds visionaries, explorers and innovators who are searching for the scientific and technical breakthroughs that will benefit our country. We are Canada's largest supporter of discovery and innovation. We work with universities, colleges, businesses and not-for-profits to remove barriers, develop opportunities and attract new expertise to make Canada's research community thrive. We give Canadian scientists and engineers the means to go further because we believe in research without borders and beyond frontiers.

Canada Graduate Scholarships – Michael Smith Foreign Study Supplements Program

Purpose: The Canada Graduate Scholarships - Michael Smith Foreign Study Supplements (CGS-MSFSS) support high-calibre Canadian graduate students in building global linkages and international networks through the pursuit of exceptional research experiences at research institutions abroad. By accessing international scientific research and training, CGS-MSFSS recipients will contribute to strengthening the potential for collaboration between Canadian and foreign institutions

Eligibility: 1. Have accepted or currently hold one of the following CGS a. Joseph-Armand Bombardier (SSHRC). b. Alexander Graham Bell (NSERC). c. Frederick Banting and Charles Best (CIHR). d. Vanier (if eligible). 2. Undertake your proposed trip abroad no earlier than the competition deadline date; 3. Not hold, or have held, any other CGS-MSFSS during the course of your graduate studies

Level of Study: Postgraduate

Type: Award

Value: Up to CA$6,000 for a period of research study abroad

Frequency: Annual

Country of Study: Canada

Application Procedure: You will be required to provide the following information 1. The name and contact information of your CGS or Vanier CGS research supervisor and of the proposed host supervisor. 2. The name and location of the proposed host institution. 3. A maximum two-page description of your intended research activities during your research study period abroad (including objectives, methodology, timelines and expected outcomes) and how they relate to your main graduate research topic, and a description of the potential benefits you will derive from the host institution in relation to your current research objectives. 4. A budget that provides estimates for costs of travel, living and other expenses during your research study period abroad. 5. A letter from your CGS or Vanier CGS research supervisor detailing their support for your research study period abroad and confirming that your proposed research aligns with the research from your CGS award (maximum one page). 6. A letter from your host supervisor detailing their support for your research study period abroad and the resources they have available-financial (if any), supervision time, equipment, library access, etc.-to support your planned research activities (maximum one page)

No. of awards offered: A total of 250 awards, in which 45 for CIHR, 80 for NSERC and 125 for SSHRC.

Closing Date: 10 October

Additional Information: www.nserc-crsng.gc.ca/Students-Etudiants/PG-CS/CGSForeignStudy-BESCEtudeEtranger_eng.asp#applicationinstructions

For further information contact:

Email: schol@nserc-crsng.gc.ca

Canada Graduate Scholarships-Master's (CGS M) Program

Purpose: The objective of the Canada Graduate Scholarships – Master's (CGS M) program is to help develop research skills and assist in the training of highly qualified personnel by supporting students who demonstrate a high standard of achievement in undergraduate and early graduate studies
Eligibility: 1. Open to be a Canadian citizen or a permanent resident of Canada, as of the application deadline date. 2. Be enrolled in, have applied for or will apply for full-time admission to an eligible graduate program at the master's or doctoral level at a Canadian institution with a CGS M allocation. 3. Respect the internal deadline to apply for admission for your intended program of study contact the faculty of graduate studies (or its equivalent) at the selected Canadian institution(s) for more detailed information. 4. Not have previously held a CGS M. 5. Have achieved a first-class average**, as determined by the host institution, in each of the last two completed years of study (full-time equivalent) 6. Submit a maximum of one scholarship application per academic year to either CIHR, NSERC or SSHRC
Level of Study: Postgraduate
Type: Scholarship
Value: CA$17,500
Length of Study: 1 year
Frequency: Annual
Country of Study: Canada
Application Procedure: To apply to the CGS M program, applicants must complete and submit an application to up to three institutions using the research portal. Applicants should consult the Canada Graduate Scholarships - Master's program Instructions for completing an application
No. of awards offered: 3,000
Closing Date: 1 December
Funding: Government
Contributor: CIHR, NSERC and SSHRC
Additional Information: www.nserc-crsng.gc.ca/Students-Etudiants/PG-CS/CGSM-BESCM_eng.asp

For further information contact:

Email: schol@nserc-crsng.gc.ca

Canada Postgraduate Scholarships (PGS)

Eligibility: Open to a Canadian citizen or a permanent citizen of Canada, with a university degree in science or engineering, intending to pursue year full-time graduate study and research at the Master's or Doctorate level in one of the areas supported by NSERC with a first-class average in each of the last two completed years of study
Level of Study: Postgraduate
Type: Fellowship
Value: CA$17,300 (Masters) per year for 1 year and CA$21,000 (Doctoral) per year for a period of 2–3 years
Length of Study: 1 year
Frequency: Annual
Country of Study: Canada
Application Procedure: Check website for further details
Closing Date: 15 October
Contributor: Natural Sciences and Engineering Research Council of Canada (NSERC)

For further information contact:

Scholarships and Fellowships Division National Sciences and Engineering Research Council of Canada, 350 Albert Street (for courier mailings, add 10th Floor), Ottawa, ON K1A 1H5, Canada.

Fax: (1) 613 996 2589
Email: schol@nserc.ca

Defence Research and Development Canada Postgraduate Scholarship Supplements

Purpose: To encourage and support graduates to carry out research of interest to DRDC; to increase contact between DRDC researchers and those at Canadian universities; and to foster graduate training potential candidates for possible employment at DRDC
Eligibility: Open to candidates possessing a CGS, PGS or IPS award
Level of Study: Postgraduate
Type: Scholarship
Value: CA$5,000 per year
Length of Study: 2 years
Frequency: Annual
Country of Study: Canada
Application Procedure: Applicants must submit a copy Notification of Award document from NSERC, a copy of successful scholarship application (Form 200), and a statement of interest in R&D for defence/national security. Check website for further details
Closing Date: 1 June
Contributor: Defence Research and Development Canada.

For further information contact:

DRDC Postgraduate Scholarship Supplements Program, Department of National Defence, 305 Rideau Street, Ottawa, ON K1N 5Y6, Canada.

Tel: (1) 613 992 0563
Fax: (1) 613 996 7063
Email: hr-rh@drdc-rddc.gc.ca

Japan Society for the Promotion of Science Postdoctoral Fellowships

Purpose: The Japan Society for the Promotion of Science (JSPS) has established the JSPS Postdoctoral Fellowships for Foreign Researchers. A limited number of promising early career researchers are given the opportunity, through this fellowship, to conduct research in Japanese universities and in designated research institutions and laboratories. NSERC is responsible for recommending Canadian nominees for JSPS Postdoctoral Fellowships
Eligibility: To be considered eligible for support, as of the application deadline date, you must: 1. be a Canadian citizen or a permanent resident of Canada 2. not have Japanese nationality or be a permanent resident of Japan 3. hold or expect to hold a doctorate degree in one of the fields of research that NSERC supports prior to the proposed start date of the postdoctoral fellowship 4. not hold, or have held, any other JSPS postdoctoral fellowship
Type: Fellowship
Value: ¥362,000 per month. A settling-in allowance of ¥200,000, Overseas travel insurance, etc.
Frequency: Annual
Country of Study: Any country
Closing Date: 1 February
Additional Information: www.nserc-crsng.gc.ca/Students-Etudiants/PD-NP/JSPS-SJPS_eng.asp#value

For further information contact:

Email: schol@nserc-crsng.gc.ca

NSERC Indigenous Student Ambassadors

Purpose: The NSERC Indigenous Student Ambassadors (NISA) grant aims to engage Indigenous students and fellows in promoting interest and participation in the natural sciences and engineering (NSE) by visiting Indigenous communities and schools in Canada and sharing their research and education experiences or participating in science promotion events and activities
Eligibility: To be eligible, you must be: 1. an Indigenous person in Canada 2. registered at a Canadian postsecondary institution, polytechnic, college or CEGEP in the NSE or have been registered last term and plan to return next term to one of those institutions for studies in the NSE or be a postdoctoral fellow in the NSE at a Canadian postsecondary institution
Level of Study: Postgraduate
Type: Award
Value: Up to CA$5,000
Country of Study: Canada
Application Procedure: Applications must be submitted electronically using NSERC's ICSP Secure Submission Site. The application must be submitted in Portable Document Format (PDF) as a single document
Funding: Government
Additional Information: If your activity is planned for March or April, please submit your application earlier than two months in advance due to a potential delay of your payment as a result of NSERC's fiscal year-end processes. www.nserc-crsng.gc.ca/students-etudiants/aboriginal-autochtones_eng.asp

For further information contact:

Email: ambassadors@nserc-crsng.gc.ca

NSERC Postgraduate Scholarships-Doctoral Program

Purpose: The NSERC Postgraduate Scholarships - Doctoral (PGS D) program provides financial support to high-calibre scholars who are engaged in an eligible doctoral program (see Eligibility criteria for students and fellows) in the natural sciences or engineering. This support allows these scholars to fully concentrate on their studies and seek out the best research mentors in their chosen fields
Eligibility: 1. Be a Canadian citizen or a permanent resident of Canada, as of the application deadline date. 2. Have completed no more than 24 months of full-time study in their doctoral program by December 31 of the calendar year of application if previously enrolled in a master's program. 3. Have completed no more than 36 months of full-time study in their doctoral program by December 31 of the calendar year of application if enrolled in a joint program; for example, MD/PhD, MA/PhD. 4. Have completed no more than 36 months of full-time study in their doctoral program by December 31 of the calendar year of application if enrolled directly from a bachelor's to a PhD program (with no time spent in a master's program)
Level of Study: Postgraduate
Type: Scholarship
Value: CA$21,000 per year
Length of Study: 3 years
Country of Study: Canada
Application Procedure: Refer to the CGS D program description for information on applying to the PGS D program www.nserc-crsng.gc.ca/Students-Etudiants/PG-CS/CGSD-BESCD_eng.asp
Closing Date: 17 October
Additional Information: www.nserc-crsng.gc.ca/Students-Etudiants/PG-CS/BellandPostgrad-BelletSuperieures_eng.asp

Netherlands Organization for Scientific Research (NWO)

Lann van Nieuw Oost Indie 300, PO Box 93138, NL-2509 The Hague AC, Netherlands.

Tel: (31) 70 344 0640
Email: nwo@nwo.nl
Website: www.nwo.nl
Contact: F.A.O. Grants Department

The Dutch Research Council (NWO) is one of the most important science funding bodies in the Netherlands and realises quality and innovation in science. Each year, NWO invests almost 1 billion euros in curiosity-driven research, research related to societal challenges and research infrastructure. The Dutch Research Council advances world-class scientific research. NWO facilitates excellent, curiosity-driven disciplinary, interdisciplinary and multidisciplinary research.

Rubicon Programme

Purpose: Rubicon aims to encourage talented researchers who recently received their PhD to spend some time at top research institutes outside the Netherlands to further their scientific career. Rubicon bridges the phase between obtaining a PhD and being eligible for funding from the Talent Scheme
Eligibility: Postgraduates who are currently engaged in doctoral research or who have been awarded a doctorate in the twelve months. Women especially are urged to apply
Level of Study: Postdoctorate
Type: Award
Value: €1,067,500
Length of Study: Up to 2 years
No. of awards offered: Varies
Closing Date: 28 March
Additional Information: www.nwo.nl/en/calls/rubicon-2023-1

For further information contact:

Tel: (31) 70 3440989

WOTRO DC Fellowships

Purpose: To support high-quality PhD and postdoctorate research projects
Eligibility: Open to project researchers with the appropriate degrees
Level of Study: Doctorate
Type: Fellowship
Value: A contribution to personal living costs and research costs
Length of Study: 4 years for PhD research and 2 years for postdoctorate research
Frequency: Annual
Application Procedure: Applications must be formally submitted by a senior researcher employed at a Dutch research institution, together with a senior researcher from the home country as a co-applicant and as part of the supervising them.
Contributor: WOTRO

For further information contact:

Tel: (31) 70 344 0945
Email: dijk@nwo.nl

Neurosurgery Research & Education Foundation (NREF)

5550 Meadowbrook Industrial Ct., Rolling Meadows, IL 60008, United States of America.

Email: info@nref.org
Website: www.nref.org/

Cerebrovascular Traveling Fellowship

Purpose: The objective of the grant is to fund travel of mid-career (see eligibility below) fellowship-trained cerebrovascular/endovascular specialist (applicant/fellow) to another institution (host) for five (5) days
Eligibility: Applicant/Fellow Fellowship-trained cerebrovascular/endovascular specialist, board certified in his/her specialty and holds a CAST certificate in neuroendovascular surgery or is able to demonstrate significant open cerebrovascular experience and practice, who has practiced independently for at least five (5) years and is a dues-paying member in good standing of the AANS/CNS Joint Cerebrovascular Section or the Society of NeuroInterventional Surgery (SNIS). Host Any practice that demonstrates significant volumes and outcomes in the area that the applicant is seeking experience. The presence of a CAST-approved fellowship training program may be used as an indicator of such practice focus but may not be sufficient. The selection committee will reserve the right to make a final decision regarding the eligibility of a specific applicant or host

N

Type: Fellowship
Value: stipend of US$5,000, travel and lodging expenses up to US$2,500, award of US$1,000
Length of Study: 5 Days
Frequency: Annual
Country of Study: Any country
Closing Date: 1 November
Additional Information: www.nref.org/-/media/Files/NREF/CV_Traveling_Fellowship-Application_Instructions_and_FAQs.ashx

For further information contact:

Lauren Coleman NREF Development Coordinator.

Tel: (1) 847 378 0535
Email: lcoleman@nref.org

CV Section/CNS Foundation Young Investigator Research Grant

Purpose: The objective of the grant is to provide sustained research startup funding for early-stage academic neurosurgeon-scientists in the field of cerebrovascular disease
Eligibility: Board-eligible cerebrovascular and/or endovascular fellowship-trained neurosurgeon, in the first three (3) years of full-time faculty position at the start of the funding period. Applicant must be an active member in good standing of the AANS/CNS Cerebrovascular Section ("CV Section"). Fellows may apply in the final year of fellowship, as long as a faculty position is confirmed prior to the start of the funding period. Faculty position must be at a teaching institution in North America
Type: Grant
Value: US$50,000 per year for three (3) years; total US$150,000 of direct costs
Length of Study: Three years
Country of Study: Any country
Closing Date: 31 March
Additional Information: www.nref.org/-/media/Files/NREF/2022_CV_Section_Research_Grant-Application_Instructions_and_FAQs.ashx

For further information contact:

Tel: (1) 847 378 0500
Email: info@nref.org

Directed Residency Scholarships

Purpose: The objective of the scholarship grant is to fund clinical scholarships in a subspecialty of neurosurgery
Eligibility: Neurosurgical residents in ACGME-accredited neurosurgery residency training programs interested in expanded subspecialty exposure with a rotation away from their home program prior to their Chief Resident year. Rotation must be spent in a neurosurgery residency program with Accreditation Council for Graduate Medical Education (ACGME) certification or the international equivalent. The applicant institution must provide proof of qualification as a non-profit, charitable entity (IRS determination letter)
Type: Scholarship
Value: US$30,000
Length of Study: Three (3) months to one (1) year
Country of Study: Any country
Closing Date: 1 December
Additional Information: www.nref.org/-/media/files/nref/NREFDirectedResidencyScholarshipApplicationInstructionsandFAQs82721

For further information contact:

Lauren Coleman Kathryn A. Dattomo, MNA, CAE, CFRE NREF Development Coordinator.

Tel: (1) 847 378 0535
Email: kam@nref.org

NREF Clinical Fellowship Grant

Purpose: The objective of the fellowship grant is to fund post-residency clinical fellowships in the specialty of neurosurgery. Any academic institution or group practice with an established neurosurgery residency program in North America that qualifies as a non-profit, charitable entity may apply. A for-profit entity is not eligible unless affiliated with a non-profit entity. The NREF strongly encourages institutions to be accredited by CAST, but exceptions may be considered by the selection committee
Eligibility: Applicants must be neurosurgeons, no more than two years from having completed their neurosurgical residency training, and/or clinical fellowship, who are full-time faculty in North American teaching institutions
Level of Study: Postdoctorate
Type: Award
Value: Up to US$75,000
Length of Study: 1 year
Frequency: Annual
Country of Study: Any country
Application Procedure: Complete an application for each subspecialty for which funding is requested. However, based on an evaluation of proposals from recent awardees, here are factors to consider when applying 1. Is the training environment supportive? Does the institution offer strong mentorship? 2. Does the institution have Accreditation Council for

Graduate Medical Education (ACGME) certification for neurosurgery residency program or the Canadian equivalent? 3. Has the institution applied for CAST accreditation, but not yet received CAST accreditation? Have they submitted a copy of the CAST accreditation request with the application? The NREF strongly encourages institutions to be accredited by CAST, but exceptions may be considered by the selection committee. 3. NOTE Including these elements should not be interpreted as a guarantee of an award
Closing Date: 1 November
Funding: Private
Contributor: Corporations and membership
Additional Information: www.nref.org/-/media/Files/NREF/2022-23_CFG_Application_Instructions-FAQs.ashx

For further information contact:

5550 Meadowbrook Industrial Ct., Rolling Meadows, IL 60008, United States of America.

Tel: (1) 847 378 0535
Email: lcoleman@nref.org

NREF Research Fellowship Grant

Purpose: Open to residents only, the NREF Research Fellowship Grant provides funding for neurosurgeons preparing for academic careers as clinician investigators. Applicants must be physicians who are currently accepted into an approved residency training program in neurological surgery within North America. One hundred percent of the resident's research effort during the funding period of this grant should be devoted to the project
Eligibility: Applicants must be neurosurgeons, no more than two years from having completed their neurosurgical residency training, and/or clinical fellowship, who are full-time faculty in North American teaching institutions
Level of Study: Postdoctorate
Type: Award
Value: Up to US$50,000
Length of Study: 1 year
Frequency: Annual
Country of Study: Any country
Application Procedure: Complete an application for each category for which funding is requested. The format of the application is flexible. However, based on an evaluation of proposals from recent awardees, here are factors to consider when applying 1. Does the research have potential for extramural funding? Is there strong preliminary data? 2. Does the project represent a new direction from existing research efforts? Is the study innovative? 3. What is the societal impact and potential applications of the research? Would a positive outcome contribute to the field? 4. Are the goals, objective and anticipated results clearly defined, logical and well-described in the proposal? Is the scope of the project realistic for timeframe? 5. Is the research environment supportive? Does the institution offer strong mentorship? 6. NOTE Including these elements should not be interpreted as a guarantee of an award
Closing Date: 1 November
Funding: Private
Contributor: Corporations and membership
Additional Information: www.nref.org/research/medical-student-fellowships

For further information contact:

5550 Meadowbrook Industrial Ct., Rolling Meadows, IL 60008, United States of America.

Tel: (1) 847 378 0535
Email: lcoleman@nref.org

NREF Young Clinician Investigator Award

Purpose: The NREF Young Clinician Investigator Award supports junior faculty pursuing careers as clinical investigators. Applicants must be neurosurgeons, no more than two years from completing neurosurgical residency training or clinical fellowship, who are full-time faculty in North American teaching institutions. Fifty percent of the young clinician investigator's efforts during the funding period of this grant should be devoted to research, but exceptions can be considered
Eligibility: Applicants must be neurosurgeons, no more than two years from having completed their neurosurgical residency training, and/or clinical fellowship, who are full-time faculty in North American teaching institutions
Level of Study: Postdoctorate
Type: Award
Value: Up to US$50,000
Length of Study: 1 year
Frequency: Annual
Country of Study: Any country
Application Procedure: Complete an application for each category for which funding is requested. The format of the application is flexible. However, based on an evaluation of proposals from recent awardees, here are factors to consider when applying 1. Does the research have potential for extramural funding? Is there strong preliminary data? 2. Does the project represent a new direction from existing research efforts? Is the study innovative? 3. What is the societal impact and potential applications of the research? Would a positive outcome contribute to the field? 4. Are the goals, objective and anticipated results clearly defined, logical and well-described in the proposal? Is the scope of the project realistic

for timeframe? 5. Is the research environment supportive? Does the institution offer strong mentorship? 6. NOTE Including these elements should not be interpreted as a guarantee of an award
Closing Date: 1 November
Funding: Private
Contributor: Corporations and membership
Additional Information: www.nref.org/-/media/Files/NREF/2022-23_RG-YCI_Application_Instructions-FAQs.ashx

For further information contact:

5550 Meadowbrook Industrial Ct., Rolling Meadows, IL 60008, United States of America.

Tel: (1) 847 378 0535
Email: lcoleman@nref.org

The William P. Van Wagenen Fellowship

Purpose: The William P. Van Wagenen Fellowship was established by the estate of Dr. Van Wagenen, one of the founders and the first President of the Harvey Cushing Society, now the AANS
Eligibility: Application should be submitted with letters of reference, including one from the applicant's Program Director. A letter from the proposed sponsor and documentation of intent to pursue an academic career, while not required, will strengthen the application
Type: Fellowship
Value: Up to US$120,000 stipend, travel and living allowance of US$6,000, US$15,000 of research support, US$5,000 for medical insurance
Frequency: Annual
Country of Study: Any country
Closing Date: 1 October
Additional Information: www.aans.org/en/Trainees/Grants-and-Fellowships/Van-Wagenen-Fellowship

New England Culninary Institute (NECI)

Admissions Office, 56 College Street, Montpelier, VT 05602, United States of America.

Tel: (1) 877 223 324
Website: www.neci.edu

New England Culinary Institute (NECI) opened in 1980, the school offered an experience that was different from any other culinary school. NECI is small and intimate by design. NECI is student centered and students participate in shared governance. A NECI education propels you out into the real world, building your professional network and finding your place in the fascinating food and beverage industry. A NECI education opens a world of possibilities!

Cabot Scholarships

Purpose: To encourage and support students who are committed to furthering their education and enhancing their careers in the restaurant and food service industry
Eligibility: Open to candidates who are current resident of Vermont, New York, Maine, New Hampshire, Connecticut, Rhode Island or Massachusetts
Level of Study: Professional development
Type: Scholarship
Value: US$100,000
Length of Study: 1 year
Frequency: Annual
Study Establishment: New England Culinary Institute
Country of Study: United States of America
Application Procedure: Applicant must submit a complete application form to New England Culinary Institute
Closing Date: 3 December
Additional Information: www.cabotschools.org/news/10159/cabot+scholarship+foundation+application++deadline+20212022

For further information contact:

Tel: (1) 501 843 3562
Email: lindac@neci.edu

New South Wales Architects Registration Board

NSW Architects Registration Board, Level 2, 156 Gloucester Street, Sydney, NSW 2000, Australia.

Tel: (61) 2 9241 4033
Email: mail@architects.nsw.gov.au
Website: www.architects.nsw.gov.au
Contact: Ms Mae Cruz, Deputy Registrar

The NSW Architects Registration Board (ARB) administers the Architects Act - the legislation regulating architects in NSW. When the Act was introduced in to NSW parliament, the aim was a community actively discussing architecture that is contributing to its wellbeing, a community that is serviced by architects who have a robust professional framework and a flexible system of professional discipline.

For further information contact:

Email: awards@rcsa.com.au

Byera Hadley Travelling Scholarships

Purpose: The purpose of the Byera Hadley Travelling Scholarships (BHTS) is to provide financial support for the promotion and encouragement of students and/or graduates in architecture to undertake a course of study, research, or other activity approved by the Board
Eligibility: Applicants for the Scholarship must be a student or a graduate of an accredited architecture program offered by a NSW university
Level of Study: Masters Degree, Research
Type: Scholarship
Value: US$30,000
Frequency: Annual
Country of Study: Any country
Closing Date: 31 August
Additional Information: www.architects.nsw.gov.au/download/Byera%20Hadley%20Application%20Form.pdf?v=20210521

For further information contact:

Tel: (61) 2 9241 4033
Email: mail@architects.nsw.gov.au

Client Service Excellence Award

Purpose: To encourage excellence in the professional services offered by architects
Eligibility: Open to all architects registered in New South Wales (NSW) who have completed projects in the last 2 years in NSW not exceeding AU$4 million
Level of Study: Unrestricted
Type: Award
Value: AU$5,000
Frequency: Annual
Country of Study: Any country
Application Procedure: For further information about the Client Service Excellence Award contact the Registrar of the NSW Architects Registration Board on (61) 2 9241 4033. Check website for further details
Closing Date: 28 September
Contributor: Victorian Architects Registration Board
Additional Information: Architect, architect corporations, and firms should have two nominations from clients www.nserc-crsng.gc.ca/Students-Etudiants/PG-CS/BellandPostgrad-BelletSuperieures_eng.asp

New South Wales Ministry of the Arts

Level 9 St James Centre, 111 Elizabeth Street, PO Box A226, Sydney, NSW 1235, Australia.

Tel: (61) 1800 358 594, (61) 2 8218 2222
Email: mail@arts.nsw.gov.au
Website: www.arts.nsw.gov.au

New South Wales Ministry of the Arts works closely with the State's 8 major cultural institutions, providing policy advice to Government on their operations.

Western Sydney Artists Fellowship

Purpose: To encourage artists and students in the field of creative arts
Eligibility: Open to applicants who are residents of Western Sydney or whose practice is located primarily in Western Sydney
Level of Study: Postgraduate
Type: Fellowship
Value: AU$5,000 to AU$25,000
Length of Study: 1 year
Frequency: Annual
Study Establishment: New South Wales, Sydney Western Suburbs
Country of Study: Australia
Closing Date: September

For further information contact:

Email: mail@create.nsw.gov.au

New York Foundation for the Arts (NYFA)

38th Street, Suite 740, 9th Floor, NY 10018, United States of America.

Tel: (1) 212 366 6900
Email: hr@nyfa.org
Website: www.nyfa.org

New York Foundation for the Arts (NYFA) is a 501(c)(3) service organization that provides artists, emerging arts organizations, arts administrators, and students with critical support, professional development tools, and resources for defining and achieving career success.

Canadian Women Artists' Award

Purpose: The Canadian Women Artists' Award is open to emerging or early career artists in New York State. The CA$5,000 award is designed to provide financial support to an emerging or early career artist working in any discipline, and can be used in any manner the recipient deems necessary to further their artistic goals
Eligibility: The Canadian Women Artist's Award is open to women artists who meet the following requirements Must be a Canadian citizen, and able to provide proof of citizenship with legal documentation upon receipt of the award; Must be between the ages of 21 and 35 before the application deadline; Must be a current resident of New York, New Jersey, or Connecticut; Must apply in only one of the eligible discipline categories; Must be the originators of the work, i.e. choreographers or playwrights; not awarded to interpretative artists such as dancers or actors; Must not be a previous recipient of the Canadian Women Artist's Award; Must not be a NYFA employee, member of the NYFA Board of Trustees or Artists' Advisory Committee, and/or an immediate family member of any of the previous
Level of Study: Unrestricted
Type: Award
Value: CA$5,000
Frequency: Annual
Country of Study: Any country
Application Procedure: All applicants must apply online at www.apply.nyfa.org/submit. The application cycle runs through the Spring, opening in March and closing in May.
Closing Date: May
Funding: Foundation, Private
Contributor: The Canadian Women's Club (CWC) of New York
No. of awards given last year: 1
No. of applicants last year: 82
Additional Information: www.nyfa.org/awards-grants/canadian-women-artists-award/

"Made in NY" Women's Film, TV and Theatre Fund

Purpose: "Made in NY" Women's Film, TV and Theatre Fund provides grants to encourage and support the creation of film, television, digital, and live theatre content that reflects the voices and perspectives of all who identify as women
Eligibility: In addition to being made by, for, or about all who identify as women, projects are eligible if they feature a strong female perspective; and/or include a female director; and/or include a meaningful female producer credit; and/or include a meaningful female writing credit; and/or include a female protagonist(s). Projects must also meet the "Made in NY" criteria as described in the program guideline
Level of Study: Unrestricted
Type: A variable number of grants
Value: CA$50,000
Frequency: Annual
Country of Study: Any country
Application Procedure: All applications must be submitted online at apply.nyfa.org/submit. Applications open in the summer, and close in the fall
No. of awards offered: 568
Closing Date: October
Funding: Government
Contributor: The City of New York Mayor's Office of Media and Entertainment (MOME)
No. of awards given last year: 60
No. of applicants last year: 568

New York State Council on the Arts/New York Foundation for the Arts Artist Fellowship

Purpose: This grant is awarded in fifteen different disciplines over a three-year period (five categories a year) and the application is free to complete. The NYSCA/NYFA Artist Fellowship is not a project grant, but is intended to fund an artist's vision or voice, at all levels of their artistic development
Eligibility: 1. 25 years or older 2. Current residents of New York State and/or one of the Indian Nations located in New York State 3. Must have maintained New York State residency, and/or residency in one of the Indian Nations located therein, for at least the last two consecutive years 4. Cannot be enrolled in a degree-seeking program of any kind 5. Are the originators of the work, i.e., choreographers or playwrights, not interpretive artists such as dancers or actors 6. Did not receive a NYSCA/NYFA Artist Fellowship in any discipline in the past five consecutive years 7. Cannot submit any work samples that have been previously awarded a NYSCA/NYFA Artist Fellowship 8. While collaborating artists are eligible to apply, the total number of collaborators cannot exceed three 9. Are not a current NYFA employee or have been in the last 12 months, a member of the NYFA Board of Trustees or Artists' Advisory Committee, immediate family member of any of the aforementioned, or an immediate family member of a 2024–2025 panelist 10. Artists that have

been awarded five NYSCA/NYFA Artist Fellowships receive Emeritus status and are no longer eligible for the award
Type: Fellowship
Value: US$8,000
Length of Study: Unrestricted
Frequency: Annual
Country of Study: Any country
Application Procedure: NYFA only accepts applications online via apply.nyfa.org/submit www.apply.nyfa.org/submit
Closing Date: 25 January
Additional Information: www.nyfa.org/awards-grants/artist-fellowships/

For further information contact:

New York Foundation for the Arts, 20 Jay Street, Suite 740, Brooklyn, NY 11201, United States of America.

Rauschenberg Emergency Grants

Purpose: New York Foundation for the Arts (NYFA) is proud to partner with the Robert Rauschenberg Foundation to administer a new emergency grant program called Rauschenberg Emergency Grants. This marks the first phase of a program that will be in the tradition of Change, Inc., a non-profit foundation established in 1970 by Robert Rauschenberg to assist professional artists of all disciplines in need of emergency medical aid
Eligibility: Open to visual and media artists and choreographers. If you aren't sure if your artistic discipline fits within these guidelines, please contact emergencyfunds@nyfa.org. 1. Open to artists who are U.S. citizens or permanent residents in the United States, District of Columbia, or U.S. Territories. 2. Applicants must demonstrate current and ongoing activity in artistic discipline/s. 3. Applicants cannot be enrolled in any degree-seeking program
Type: Grant
Value: US$5,000 ($100,000)
Frequency: Annual
Country of Study: Any country
No. of awards offered: 20
Closing Date: 31 July
Additional Information: www.nyfa.org/awards-grants/rauschenberg-dancer-emergency-grants/

For further information contact:

New York Foundation for the Arts, 20 Jay Street, Suite 740, Brooklyn, NY 11201, United States of America.

Email: emergencyfunds@nyfa.org

Recharge Foundation Fellowship for New Surrealist Art

Purpose: The New York Foundation for the Arts (NYFA) created the Recharge Foundation Fellowship for New Surrealist Art, a US$5,000 award for painters living in the United States and U.S. Territories who are working in the New Surrealist style. The award program is administered by NYFA with funding provided by the Gu Family of the Recharge Foundation
Type: Award
Value: US$5,000
Frequency: Annual
Application Procedure: The JGS Fellowship for Photography is open to New York State photography artists, living and working anywhere in the following regions of New York State Western New York, Finger Lakes, Southern Tier, Central New York, North Country, Mohawk Valley, Capital District, Hudson Valley, and Long Island. 1. Applicants must work in photography. 2. Applicants can work in traditional and experimental photography or any form in which photography or photographic techniques are pivotal, if not exclusive. 3. Applicants must be a current full-time resident of New York State and have lived full-time in one of the regions listed above for a minimum of 12 months at the time applications close. 4. Applicant must be at least 25 years of age at the time the application closes. 5. Students in bachelor's or master's degree programs of any kind are not eligible to apply. 6. All past recipients of any NYFA grant or Fellowship are eligible to apply. 7. NYFA employees, members of the NYFA Board of Trustees or Artists' Advisory Committee, and/or an immediate family member of any of the above cannot apply
Closing Date: 15 May
Additional Information: www.nyfa.org/Content/Show/The-Recharge-Foundation-Fellowship-for-New-Surrealist-Art

N

New York University

27 West Fourth Street, New York, NY 10003, United States of America.

Tel: (1) 212 998 4550
Email: admissions.ops@nyu.edu
Website: www.nyu.edu/

NYU has been an innovator in higher education, reaching out to an emerging middle class, embracing an urban identity and professional focus, and promoting a global vision that informs its 19 schools and colleges. Today, that trailblazing spirit makes NYU one of the most prominent and respected research universities in the world, featuring top-ranked academic programs and accepting fewer than one-in-five undergraduates.

Provost's Postdoctoral Fellowship Program

Purpose: New York University's Provost's Postdoctoral Fellowship Program was created to attract and support a wide range of brilliant young scholars and educators from diverse backgrounds whose research experience, life experience, and employment background can significantly contribute to academic excellence. The program provides fellows with faculty mentoring, professional development, and academic networking opportunities. The ultimate goal of the program is for participants to join the ranks of faculty at competitive institutions
Eligibility: 1. Individuals who have completed their dissertation within the last three years or who will have completed their dissertation by next year; or 2. Professionals transitioning to academic careers (for those in a field for which the doctorate is not the terminal degree) 3. Priority is given to candidates who do not currently hold postdoctoral fellowships or traineeships. As part of its selection process, our selection committee looks for evidence of superior scholarly achievement (honors, awards, publications), commitment to teaching and research, mention of a clear mentorship plan, and promise of continuing achievement as scholars and teachers 4. NYU does not sponsor visa application for this Fellowship. Fellowship recipients must provide proof of authorization to work in the United States
Level of Study: Postgraduate
Type: Fellowship
Value: US$62,000 nine-month salary, research allowance ($2,000), one-time relocation fees (up to US$3,000)
Frequency: Annual
Country of Study: Any country
Application Procedure: Application Requirements: 1. curriculum vitae; 2. candidate information form; 3. a statement of research and goals; 4. a personal statement detailing reasons for applying for the fellowship; 5. three letters of recommendation; and 6. one of the following: A dissertation abstract (postdoctoral applicants); or a statement of how your professional experience prepares you for a faculty position (professionals)
Funding: Private
Additional Information: Website: www.nyu.edu/faculty/faculty-diversity-and-inclusion/mentoring-and-professional-development/provosts-postdoctoral-fellowship-program/about.html

For further information contact:

383 Lafayette Street, New York, NY 10003, United States of America.

Email: admissions.ops@nyu.edu

University Distinguished Teaching Awards

Purpose: Established in 1987, the Distinguished Teaching Award (DTA) highlights New York University's commitment to teaching excellence and is given annually to selected outstanding members of the faculty. Recipients are presented with a research stipend
Eligibility: Only full-time faculty members with at least ten years of service at NYU. Please note that while current adjuncts are not eligible for consideration, current full-time faculty may count past adjunct service towards the ten-year eligibility requirement. Past winners of the award may not be renominated. Please review the list of previous winners before nominating. Faculty members must hold one of the following job titles Professor, Associate Professor, Assistant Professor Clinical Professor, Clinical Associate Professor, Clinical Assistant Professor Research Professor, Research Associate Professor, Research Assistant Professor Industry Assistant Professor, Industry Associate Professor, Industry Full Professor, Lecturer and Senior Lecturer Master Teacher, Teacher Arts Professor, Arts Associate Professor, Arts Assistant Professor
Type: Award
Value: Recipients are presented with a research stipend.
Frequency: Annual
Country of Study: Any country
Closing Date: 16 February
Additional Information: docs.google.com/document/d/1ZhfsctdkTnFmr9GLKUP9kp1vSlBWNXlJl_KSmGfMfx8/edit#

For further information contact:

Email: facultyadvance@nyu.edu.

New York University Academic and Science

Tel: (1) 212 998 6880
Email: cas.alumni@nyu.edu

NYU has been an innovator in higher education, reaching out to an emerging middle class, embracing an urban identity and professional focus, and promoting a global vision that informs its 19 schools and colleges. The core of New York University is the academic enterprise. The best students and faculty are drawn to the University by the allure of being part of a compelling intellectual and creative enterprise - a community of scholars characterized by collaboration, innovation, and incandescent teaching.

Rangel Graduate Fellowship Program

Subjects: Foreign Service
Purpose: The Rangel Graduate Fellowship is a program that aims to attract and prepare outstanding young people for careers in the Foreign Service of the U.S. Department of State in which they can help formulate, represent and implement U.S. foreign policy
Eligibility: 1. Applicants must be seeking admission to enter graduate school in the fall for a two-year program at a United States university in an area of relevance to the Foreign Service. They can be in their senior year of their undergraduate studies, graduating by June, or they can be college graduates. 2. Applicants must have a cumulative grade point average of 3.2 or higher on a 4.0 scale at the time of application. 3. Applicants must be United States citizen
Eligible Country: United States of America
Level of Study: Masters Degree
Type: Fellowship
Value: Up to US$42,000 annually for a two year period for tuition, room, board, books and mandatory fees
Length of Study: 2 year
Frequency: Annual
Country of Study: United States of America
Application Procedure: Applicants apply to two-year graduate programs at U.S. universities simultaneously with their application to the Rangel Program
No. of awards offered: 45
Closing Date: 14 October
Funding: Private
Additional Information: www.rangelprogram.org/graduate-fellowship-program/

For further information contact:

2218 6th Street NW, Washington, DC 20059, United States of America.

Tel: (1) 202 806 4367
Email: rangelprogram@howard.edu

New Zealand Aid Programme

195 Lambton Quay, Private Bag 18 901, Wellington 6160, New Zealand.

Tel: (64) 4 439 8000
Website: www.govt.nz/organisations/new-zealand-aid-programme/
Contact: Ministry of Foreign Affairs and Trade

The purpose of New Zealand's aid is to develop shared prosperity and stability in the Pacific and beyond, drawing on the best of New Zealand's knowledge and skills. We support sustainable development in developing countries to reduce poverty and contribute to a more secure, equitable and prosperous world.

New Zealand Pacific Scholarships

Purpose: A particular focus of NZPS is to increase the number of young pacific people studying in New Zealand and to build a new generation of Pacific leadership with strong links to New Zealand
Type: Scholarship
Country of Study: Any country
Application Procedure: For application procedure, please refer website www.mfat.govt.nz/en/aid-and-development/scholarships/how-to-apply/
Closing Date: 28 March
Additional Information: scholarship-positions.com/new-zealand-pacific-scholarships-for-pacific-countries/2011/06/11/

For further information contact:

Email: studentinfo@auckland.ac.nz

Newberry Library

60 West Walton Street, Chicago, IL 60610-3380, United States of America.

Tel: (1) 312 943 9090
Email: research@newberry.org
Website: www.newberry.org
Contact: Research and Education

The Newberry Library supports and inspires research, teaching, and learning in the humanities. The Newberry collection some 1.6 million books, 600,000 maps, and 5 million manuscript pages is a portal to more than six centuries of human history, from the Middle Ages to the present. We connect researchers and visitors with our collection in the Newberry's reading rooms, exhibition galleries, program spaces, classrooms, and online digital resources.

Associated Colleges of the Midwest/the Great Lakes Colleges Association Faculty Fellowships

Purpose: This fellowship supports faculty from the colleges of the Associated Colleges of the Midwest and the Great Lakes Colleges Association, Inc.
Eligibility: Applicants can come from any of the colleges in ACM or GLCA, from any discipline
Type: Fellowship
Value: Fellows teach a small group of select undergraduate students in an advanced research seminar.
Application Procedure: Potential applicants should contact Joan Gillespie at the ACM
Closing Date: 15 March
Additional Information: For more information, visit the Associated Colleges of the Midwest's call for proposals at www.acm.edu/programs/14/newberry/index.html

For further information contact:

535 West William, Suite 301, Ann Arbor, Michigan 48103, United States of America.

Tel: (1) 734 661 2350

Long-Term Fellowships

Purpose: Long-Term Fellowships are intended to support individual scholarly research and promote serious intellectual exchange through active participation in the Newberry's scholarly activities, including Fellows' Seminars and Weekly Colloquium
Eligibility: Long-Term Fellowships are open only to postdoctoral scholars who have been awarded the PhD degree or other equivalent terminal degree by the Newberry's application deadline. United States citizens are eligible for all Newberry Fellowships. Permanent United States residents who have had at least three years of continuous residence in the U.S. are eligible for all fellowships. Recent United States residents who have had less than three years of continuous residence in the U.S. are eligible for all fellowships except the National Endowment for the Humanities (NEH) Fellowships. Citizens of foreign nations are eligible for all fellowships except the National Endowment for the Humanities (NEH) Fellowships. Only applicants of North American Indian heritage are eligible for the Susan Kelly Power and Helen Hornbeck Tanner and Frances C. Allen Fellowships
Level of Study: Postgraduate
Type: Fellowships
Value: US$5,000 per month
Length of Study: 4 to 9 months
Frequency: Annual
Study Establishment: The Newberry Library
Country of Study: United States of America
Application Procedure: For more information on eligibility, guidelines, and the application process, please visit www.newberry.org/how-apply. Fellowship applicants are required to submit the following material 1. A project abstract of no more than 300 words (approximately 2000 characters) that communicates the significance of the project to the Newberry's review panel, which consists of humanities scholars with wide areas of expertise. 2. A project description of no more than 1500 words. 3. A current Curriculum Vitae (CV) of no more than 5 pages. 4. Letter(s) of recommendation
Closing Date: 1 November
Funding: Private
Additional Information: www.newberry.org/long-term-fellowships

Rudolph Ganz Fellowship

Purpose: The Rudolph Ganz Fellowship supports researchers using the Rudolph Ganz Papers and other late nineteenth- and early twentieth-century materials related to Chicago music in that period. Ganz's papers include musical compositions of the world-renowned concert pianist, composer, conductor, and educator, as well as articles, speeches, lectures and essays by him, and two recordings
Eligibility: Having a PhD (or equivalent terminal degree) by the application deadline is required
Type: Scholarship
Value: US$5,000/month
Length of Study: 4 to 9 months
Country of Study: United States of America
Closing Date: 1 November
Additional Information: www.networks.h-net.org/node/73374/announcements/85457/rudolph-ganz-fellowship

Weiss/Brown Publication Subvention Award

Subjects: Music, theater, cultural studies, or French or Italian literature

Purpose: The purpose of this award is to enable the publication of works of the highest quality either by making it possible to publish a work in a particularly appropriate way (with special typography plates, or appendices, for example) that would otherwise be prohibitively expensive; or by significantly reducing the cover price, allowing the publication to reach a wider audience
Eligibility: 1. United States citizens are eligible for all Newberry Fellowships. 2. Permanent United States residents who have had at least three years of continuous residence in the U.S. are eligible for all fellowships. 3. Recent United States residents who have had less than three years of continuous residence in the U.S. are eligible for all fellowships except the National Endowment for the Humanities (NEH) Fellowships. 4. Citizens of foreign nations are eligible for all fellowships except the National Endowment for the Humanities (NEH) Fellowships. 5. Only applicants of North American Indian heritage are eligible for the Susan Kelly Power and Helen Hornbeck Tanner and Frances C. Allen Fellowships
Type: Award
Value: Up to US$8,000
Frequency: Annual
Country of Study: United States of America
Application Procedure: For more information, please see www.newberry.org/how-apply. Fellowship applicants are required to submit the following material 1. A project abstract of no more than 300 words (approximately 2000 characters) that communicates the significance of the project to the Newberry's review panel, which consists of humanities scholars with wide areas of expertise. 2. A project description of no more than 1500 words. 3. A current Curriculum Vitae (CV) of no more than 5 pages. 4. Letter(s) of recommendation.
Closing Date: 15 December
Additional Information: www.newberry.org/publication-subvention

Newcastle University

Manager, Student Financial Support, Newcastle University, King's Gate, Newcastle upon Tyne NE1 7RU, United Kingdom.

Tel: (44) 191 208 6000
Website: www.ncl.ac.uk/
Contact: Mrs Rencesova Irena, Student Financial Support Officer

Newcastle University experts are protecting cultural property and preserving unique archives around the world We are a world-leading university, advancing knowledge, providing creative solutions, and addressing global problems.

Advancing Women in Leadership Scholarship (MBA)

Purpose: The scholarship will support innovative business women who aspire to higher levels of influence and professional development
Eligibility: To be eligible for this full-fee scholarship you must meet the following criteria (MBA Full-Fee Regulations 23 (PDF:206.6KB)): 1. identify as female 2. hold an offer (conditional or unconditional) for admission in September 2023 to the Full-time MBA programme 3. have substantive managerial experience of 3 years or more 4. hold the equivalent of a UK 2:1 honours degree (applicants who do not meet this requirement but can demonstrate relevant work experience above the minimum plus significant career progression may also be considered) 5. perform well at interview across all competency areas 6. hold an English language qualification of IELTS 6.5 or its equivalent with no subskill below 6.0 (if your first language is not English) 7. completed the scholarship application form including submitting an essay of no more than 1,500 words in response to the question listed. Submissions need to be in English
Level of Study: MBA
Type: Scholarship
Value: A full fee award of £27,600
Frequency: Annual
Study Establishment: Newcastle University Business School
Country of Study: United Kingdom
Application Procedure: Applications and essays will be reviewed by a panel of judges. Candidates need to complete the online application form. www.forms.ncl.ac.uk/view.php?id=2981403
Closing Date: 10 April
Funding: Private
Contributor: Newcastle University Business School
Additional Information: www.ncl.ac.uk/business/study/scholarships/

For further information contact:

Tel: (44) 191 208 1589
Email: mba@ncl.ac.uk

British Marshall Scholarships

Purpose: The British Marshall Scholarships will finance two years of postgraduate and occasionally, undergraduate study

N

in the UK. The scholarships cover fares to and from the United States, university tuition fees, cost of living expenses, book, thesis, research and daily travel allowances, and where applicable, a contribution towards the support of a dependent spouse
Eligibility: You may be eligible to apply for one of 40 competitive awards if you meet the following criteria 1. You are a United States citizen (at the time you take up your Scholarship). 2. Hold a first degree from an accredited four-year college or university in the United States with a minimum GPA of 3.7. 3. Aged under 26
Level of Study: Postgraduate
Type: Scholarship
Value: Varies
Length of Study: Two years duration.
Frequency: Annual
Country of Study: United Kingdom
Application Procedure: For further information about the scholarship and details on eligibility and applications, contact the Marshall Aid Commemoration Commission.
No. of awards offered: 40
Funding: Private
Contributor: The Marshall Aid Commemoration Commission
Additional Information: www.ncl.ac.uk/postgraduate/funding/sources/internationalnoneustudents/bmarshall.html

For further information contact:

Woburn House 20-24 Tavistock Square, London WC1H 9HF, United Kingdom.

Email: apps@marshallscholarship.org

European Excellence Scholarship (MBA)

Purpose: Our MBA provides an inclusive, diverse and collaborative learning community that educates and develops our students to be creative, innovative, enterprising and global in their outlook
Eligibility: To be eligible for this full-fee scholarship you must meet the following criteria 1. Completed the scholarship application form including submitting an essay of no more than 1,500 words in response to the question listed. Submissions need to be in English. 2. Hold a conditional or unconditional offer of admission to the Full-time MBA programme entry. 3. Have substantive managerial experience (minimum 3 years prior to starting the MBA) preferably hold the equivalent of a United Kingdom 21 honours degree (however, applicants who do not meet this requirement but can demonstrate relevant work experience above the minimum plus significant career progression may also be considered). 4. Perform well at interview across all competency areas. 5. Hold an English language qualification of IELTS 6.5 or its equivalent with no subskill below 6.0 (if your first language is not English). 6. Be assessed as an European Union student for fee paying purposes
Level of Study: Postgraduate
Type: Scholarship
Frequency: Annual
Country of Study: Any country
Application Procedure: Applications and essays will be reviewed by a panel of judges. Candidates need to complete the online application form
Closing Date: 5 April
Funding: Private
Additional Information: www.ncl.ac.uk/business-school/courses/scholarships/mba/

For further information contact:

Tel: (44) 191 208 1589
Email: mba@ncl.ac.uk

Humanities and Social Sciences Postgraduate Scholarships

Purpose: The Faculty of Humanities and Social Sciences at Newcastle University is pleased to offer Humanities and Social Sciences Postgraduate scholarships to assist non-UK European Union nationals to study a postgraduate Master's degree
Eligibility: To be considered for awards applicants must 1. Hold the equivalent of a first class UK honours degree. 2. Have an offer for an eligible, full time, taught postgraduate degree programme within the Faculty of Humanities and Social Sciences. Applicants applying to Newcastle University Business School are not eligible for these awards. 3. Must be non UK European Union nationals and must be classed as EU for fee paying purposes. 4. Eligible candidates will be assessed as part of their academic application
Level of Study: Postgraduate
Type: Scholarship
Value: £2,000 tuition fee awards
Frequency: Annual
Country of Study: United Kingdom
Application Procedure: Eligible candidates will automatically be considered for a Humanities and Social Sciences Postgraduate Scholarship as part of their academic course application
Closing Date: September
Funding: Private
Additional Information: www.ncl.ac.uk//postgraduate/funding/sources/ukeustudents/hsspgs20.html

Indonesia Endowment Fund for Education (LPDP)

Purpose: The Indonesia Endowment Fund (LPDP) provides funding for high achieving Indonesian students undertaking Master's or PhD study. It forms part of the Indonesian government's aim to nurture young talented individuals, enabling them to become future leaders
Eligibility: For detailed information about the eligiblity, check the website
Level of Study: Postgraduate
Type: Funding support
Value: The scholarship covers tuition fees and living expenses
Frequency: Annual
Study Establishment: Ministry of Finance and Minister of Research, Technology and Higher Education
Country of Study: Any country
Application Procedure: For detailed information grants, check the following link, www.lpdp.kemenkeu.go.id
Closing Date: October
Funding: Private
Contributor: Lembaga Pengelolaan Dana Pendidikan (LPDP)
Additional Information: www.ncl.ac.uk/postgraduate/funding/sources/internationalnoneustudents/lpdp19.html

For further information contact:

Email: cso.lpdp@kemenkeu.go.id

International Family Discounts (IFD)

Purpose: We offer discounts to encourage relatives of our current international students, and past international graduates, to pursue their studies at Newcastle University
Eligibility: 1. This discount is only available to students studying at the Newcastle city campus. 2. The University offers partial discounts to close relatives (husband, wife, brother, sister, mother, father, son or daughter) of students and graduates, who have been assessed as International for fees purposes, and who wish to pursue their studies at Newcastle University in currently studying here. 3. Students may only apply for a discount if they are registered as a student at the University or after they have been offered a place to study on their chosen degree programme, and have been assessed as International for fees purposes
Level of Study: Postgraduate
Type: Award
Value: 10% of the tuition fee per year
Length of Study: Duration of the degree programme
Frequency: Annual
Country of Study: Any country
Application Procedure: Please complete the online International Family Discount application form in accordance with the IFD regulations
Funding: Private
Additional Information: www.ncl.ac.uk/postgraduate/funding/sources/internationalnoneustudents/ifd.html

For further information contact:

Newcastle upon Tyne NE1 7RU, United Kingdom.

Tel: (44) 191 208 5537
Email: scholarship.applications@ncl.ac.uk

Master of Arts (Taught Masters) Scholarships in the School of Modern Languages

Purpose: The School of Modern Languages is offering competitive scholarships to outstanding applicants for the following programmes MA programmes in Translating and Interpreting (Chinese) MA in Professional Translating for European Languages (French, German, Italian, Spanish) MA Film Theory and Practice
Eligibility: Home, European Union and International Students are eligible to apply
Level of Study: Postgraduate
Type: Scholarship
Value: £5,000
Frequency: Annual
Country of Study: Any country
Application Procedure: In order to apply for the scholarship, check the website. www.ncl.ac.uk/sml/study/funding/#currentopportunities
Closing Date: 7 June
Funding: Private
Contributor: SML Postgraduate Officer

For further information contact:

Tel: (44) 191 208 5867
Email: modlang.pgadmin@ncl.ac.uk

Master of Arts in Art Museum and Gallery Studies Scholarship

Purpose: The Art Museum and Gallery Studies MA provides students with the opportunity to develop skills as a curator or gallery educator in the fields of both historical and contemporary art
Eligibility: The studentships are open to United Kingdom, European Union and international applicants who hold, or expect to achieve a minimum of a 2.1 Honours degree

N

(or international equivalent) in fine art or an art related subject. We welcome applications from all sections of the community regardless of race, ethnicity, gender or sexuality, and wish to encourage applications from traditionally underrepresented groups in United Kingdom higher education. International students If your first language is not English you must also meet our English language requirements
Level of Study: Professional development
Type: Scholarship
Value: £3,000
Frequency: Annual
Country of Study: Any country
Application Procedure: You must apply through the University's online postgraduate application system. To do this please 'Create a new account'. All relevant fields should be completed, but fields marked with a red asterisk must be completed. The following information will help us to process your application. You will need to 1. Insert the programme code 4138F in the programme of study section. 2. Select 'Art Museum and Gallery Studies (full time)' as the programme of study. 3. Insert the studentship code SAC025 in the studentship/partnership reference field. 4. Attach a personal statement of no more than 500 words outlining. i. Your preparedness to undertake the Art Museum and Gallery Studies MA. ii. Your aspirations for a career in the art museum and gallery sector
Closing Date: 30 April
Funding: Private
Additional Information: www.ncl.ac.uk/postgraduate/courses/degrees/art-museum-gallery-studies-ma-pgdip/#profile

For further information contact:

Email: gerard.corsane@ncl.ac.uk

Master of Business Administration Business Excellence Scholarships

Purpose: The main aim of this programme is to provide financial help and support candidates in achieving their career goals by providing awards of £8,000, payable towards the cost of tuition fees. So, all the interested candidates can apply for the programme
Eligibility: 1. Eligible Countries Applications are accepted from around the world. 2. Eligible Course or Subjects MBA degree programme in Business Excellence at the Newcastle University. 3. Must hold a conditional or unconditional offer of admission to the MBA programme. 4. Must have substantive managerial experience (normally four years or more, minimum of three years). 5. Must preferably hold the equivalent of a UK 21 honours degree. 6. Must have to perform well at interview across all competency areas
Level of Study: MBA
Type: Scholarship
Value: £8,000
Frequency: Annual
Study Establishment: Newcastle University Business School
Country of Study: Any country
Application Procedure: To be considered for the programme applicants must have to take admission at the university. After that No other application required. All candidates will be assessed at the time of interview for this Scholarship. Applicants must submit the following documents previous year degree, a CV, Certificates to confirm your degree or highest qualification - if your degree is complete, a copy of passport, and a personal statement. Interested students must be met out of the university admission requirement page. University's programs are in the English Language; if the student hasn't met the English Level requirements, he/she will be required to take the English Proficiency Exam
No. of awards offered: Various
Funding: Private
Additional Information: www.scholarship-positions.com/mba-business-excellence-scholarships-at-newcastle-university-in-the-uk/2020/11/18/

For further information contact:

Northways Parade, 28 College Cres, London NW3 5DN, United Kingdom.

Tel: (44) 756 390 4978
Email: mba@ncl.ac.uk

Newcastle University - English Language Excellence Scholarships (Business School Masters)

Purpose: Newcastle University Business School offers a number of partial scholarship awards to outstanding and high-quality Masters students each year to assist them to study for a Masters degree
Eligibility: You will be considered for an English Language Excellence Scholarship if you hold an unconditional offer for one of the following Masters courses 1. Arts, Business and Creativity MA. 2. Innovation, Creativity and Entrepreneurship MSc. 3. Global Human Resource Management MSc. 4. International Economics and Finance MSc. 5. Banking and Finance MSc. 6. Finance MSc. 7. Quantitative Finance and Risk Management MSc. 8. International Business Management MSc. 9. International Marketing MSc. 10. Operations, Logistics

and Supply Chain Management MSc. 11. Accounting, Finance and Strategic Investment MSc. 12. International Financial Analysis MSc. 13. E-Business MSc. 14. E-Business (Information Systems) MSc. 15. E-Business (E-Marketing) MSc
Level of Study: Postgraduate
Type: Scholarship
Value: Partial awards of £5,000 towards the cost of tuition fees.
Frequency: Annual
Country of Study: Any country
Application Procedure: Regulations and application details are available on the below link, www.ncl.ac.uk/media/wwwnclacuk/postgraduate/funding/files/English%20Language%20Excellence%20Scholarships%20Regulations%202019%20Entry.pdf
Funding: Private

For further information contact:

Tel: (44) 191 208 1503
Email: nubs@ncl.ac.uk

Newcastle University - United States of America Athlete Scholarship

Purpose: Newcastle University offers partial scholarship awards to encourage USA and Canadian athletes to undertake Master's level study. Awards have a value of £4000–£8000 payable to the student's tuition fee account (40% or 20% fee reduction) and include a comprehensive support package including Free gym membership, Unlimited strength and conditioning support, Professional coaching, Physiotherapy and sports massage, Lifestyle support and mentoring
Eligibility: Applicants should ideally have NCAA D1- D3 playing experience in one of the following sports Basketball, Lacrosse, Volleyball, Tennis, Golf, Women's Soccer, Waterpolo. They must also be 1. Registered at Newcastle University for the academic year. 2. Registered for one of the following eligible Master's courses MA; MBA; MClinRes; MEd; MMedEd; LLM; LLM (by research); MLitt; MMus; MPH; MRes; MSc. 3. Defined as international for fee purposes. 4. Resident in the USA or Canada. 5. Registered to study at Newcastle University city centre campus. 6. Students new to the University and not those transferring or repeating courses
Level of Study: Graduate
Type: Scholarship
Value: 40% or 20% fee reduction. £4,000 - £8,000 payable towards the first year of tuition fees and a comprehensive support package on eligible Master's courses
Length of Study: September for one year of study
Frequency: Annual
Country of Study: Any country
Application Procedure: Complete the application form using the following www.ncl.ac.uk/sport/performance/scholarships/application/
No. of awards offered: 20 at 40% 10 at 20%
Closing Date: 31 July
Funding: Private
Contributor: Newcastle University

For further information contact:

Tel: (44) 191 208 5230
Email: performance.sport@ncl.ac.uk

Newcastle University - Vice-Chancellor's Excellence Scholarships - Postgraduate

Purpose: Newcastle University is pleased to offer 39 Vice-Chancellor's Excellence Scholarships (VCES) for outstanding international applicants who apply to commence full-time Master's studies. There are 37 50% tuition fee scholarships and 2 100% tuition fee scholarships
Eligibility: To be considered for the Vice-Chancellor's Global Scholarships applicants must: 1. be assessed as international for fee purposes 2. hold an offer for an eligible Master's degree programme at the University's Newcastle city centre campus for the 2024/25 academic year 3. already have or expect to receive the equivalent of an upper second class UK honours degree or above
Level of Study: Postgraduate
Type: Scholarship
Value: £4,000 tuition fee awards
Length of Study: September for the full duration of the degree programme.
Frequency: Annual
Study Establishment: Newcastle University
Country of Study: United Kingdom
Application Procedure: Applications must be submitted on the Apply to Newcastle Portal: applyto.newcastle.ac.uk/
No. of awards offered: 10
Closing Date: 27 April
Funding: Private
Contributor: Newcastle University
Additional Information: www.ncl.ac.uk/postgraduate/fees-funding/search-funding/?code=vcgs23

For further information contact:

Tel: (44) 191 208 5537/8107
Email: scholarship.applications@ncl.ac.uk

Newcastle University International Postgraduate Scholarship (NUIPS)

Purpose: To provide a partial scholarship for international students
Eligibility: Candidates for scholarships must already have been offered a place to study at Newcastle University. See webpages www.ncl.ac.uk/postgraduate/funding/search/list/nuips
Level of Study: Postgraduate
Type: Partial scholarship
Value: £2,000 per year
Length of Study: 1st year of study only
Frequency: Annual
Study Establishment: Newcastle University
Country of Study: United Kingdom
Application Procedure: All eligible applicants who are offered a place to study at Newcastle University are invited to apply for one of these scholarships. Applicants must check the website for details or contact the Student Financial Support Team
No. of awards offered: 800
Closing Date: 27 May
Contributor: Newcastle University
No. of awards given last year: 100
No. of applicants last year: 800
Additional Information: www.scholarshipsads.com/newcastle-university-international-postgraduate-scholarship-nuips-uk/

For further information contact:

Email: international-scholarships@ncl.ac.uk

Newcastle University Overseas Research Scholarship (NUORS)

Purpose: Newcastle University is committed to offering support to the very best international students hoping to pursue a programme of research. We are pleased to offer a small number of University funded NUORS awards for outstanding international students who apply to commence PhD studies in any subject
Eligibility: You could be eligible to apply for a NUORS award if 1. You have been offered a place on a PhD research programme. 2. You have been assessed as international/overseas for fees purposes, and are wholly or partially self-financing. 3. Applicants must already have been offered a place on a PhD research programme before applying
Level of Study: Postgraduate
Type: Scholarship
Value: value approximately £14,004 to £22,104 per annum
Length of Study: The award is valid for the normal duration of the PhD (not longer than 3 years)
Frequency: Annual
Country of Study: Any country
Application Procedure: You must have already applied for and been offered a place to study at Newcastle University before you apply for a NUORS award. Please complete the online NUORS application form and in accordance with the NUORS regulations. You will also be required to provide details of an academic referee; the University will then contact your referee directly
No. of awards offered: 15
Closing Date: 23 April
Funding: Private
Contributor: Newcastle University
Additional Information: www.ncl.ac.uk/postgraduate/funding/sources/internationalnoneustudents/nuors21.html

For further information contact:

Newcastle upon Tyne NE1 7RU, United Kingdom.

Tel: (44) 191 208 5537/8107
Email: scholarship.applications@ncl.ac.uk

Newcastle University Scholarship – Thailand - GREAT

Purpose: This year, in partnership with the British Council and the GREAT Britain Campaign, Newcastle University is offering scholarships to students in Thailand applying for postgraduate taught courses listed below. This scholarship scheme is part of the "GREAT Scholarships - East Asia" campaign, which has been launched by the British Council together with 28 United Kingdom universities to support more students in East Asia to get access to the excellent United Kingdom higher education opportunities
Eligibility: To be considered for awards applicants must 1. Must be passport holders of Thailand. 2. Be assessed as international for fee purposes. 3. Hold an offer for an eligible Master's degree programme listed below. 4. MSc Sustainable Chemical Engineering. 5. MSc REFLEX (Renewable Energy Flexible Training Programme)
Level of Study: Postgraduate
Type: Scholarship
Value: £10,000
Frequency: Annual
Study Establishment: Newcastle University
Country of Study: Any country

Application Procedure: Applications must be submitted using the application form. Other applications will not be accepted. Application link is available below www.app.geckoform.com/public/#/modern/FOEU01c3zJ6qAVgh
Closing Date: 25 May
Funding: Private
Contributor: British Council and Newcastle University
Additional Information: www.app.geckoform.com/public/#/modern/FOEU01c3zJ6qAVgh, www.wemakescholars.com/scholarship/newcastle-university-great-scholarships-thailand

For further information contact:

Email: scholarship.applications@newcastle.ac.uk

Newcastle Vice-Chancellor's Global Scholarships - Postgraduate

Purpose: Newcastle University is pleased to offer 5 Vice-Chancellor's Global Scholarships (VCGS) for outstanding international applicants who apply to commence full-time Master's studies
Eligibility: To be considered for the Vice-Chancellor's Global Scholarships applicants must 1. Be assessed as international for fee purposes. 2. Hold an offer for an eligible Master's degree programme at the University's Newcastle city centre campus for the academic year. 3. Already have or expect to receive the equivalent of an upper second class United Kingdom honours degree or above
Level of Study: Postgraduate
Type: Scholarship
Value: £4,000 tuition fee awards
Length of Study: September for the full duration of degree programme
Frequency: Annual
Country of Study: Any country
Application Procedure: Applications must be submitted using the online application form. Other applications will not be accepted
No. of awards offered: 10
Closing Date: 27 April
Funding: Private
Contributor: Newcastle University
Additional Information: www.ncl.ac.uk/undergraduate/fees-funding/scholarships-bursaries/vc-global/

For further information contact:

Tel: (44) 191 208 5537/8107
Email: scholarship.applications@ncl.ac.uk

Postgraduate Master's Loan Scheme (Students from United Kingdom and non-United Kingdom European Union Countries)

Purpose: The Loan is non means-tested and is considered as a contribution towards your tuition fees and living expenses. It is available to students under the age of 60. If you already have a Master's level qualification (including an integrated Master's), an equivalent qualification or a higher level qualification, you will not be eligible to receive the Master's Student Loan. This applies even if your previous qualification was entirely self-funded and/or achieved outside the UK. If you already have a lower postgraduate qualification, such as a Postgraduate Diploma or Postgraduate Certificate, you will be eligible to receive the loan if you choose to undertake a standalone Master's course
Eligibility: 1. You must have most recently been resident in England and must not have moved from elsewhere in the UK and Islands solely for the purposes of attending the course. 2. You may be eligible for the Loan if you've had temporary absences from your home address, such as for education and travelling. 3. You may be eligible if you are an EU national or family member of an EU national, or hold other specific statuses (eg have refugee residency status, an EEA migrant worker or are a 'British Overseas Territories' resident)
Level of Study: Postgraduate
Type: Award
Value: £11,570
Length of Study: 1 to 2
Frequency: Annual
Country of Study: Any country
Application Procedure: The quickest way to apply is online. www.gov.uk/masters-loan/apply
Closing Date: June
Funding: Private
Additional Information: www.ncl.ac.uk/postgraduate/funding/sources/ukeustudents/mastersloan.html

For further information contact:

Email: ltds@ncl.ac.uk

Postgraduate Masters Scholarships in the School of Geography, Politics and Sociology

Purpose: The scholarships are open to United Kingdom, European Union and international applicants who Hold an offer of admission on one of the eligible programmes Hold, or expect to achieve, at least a 2.1 honours degree (or international equivalent), in a related discipline

N

Eligibility: The scholarships are open to United Kingdom, European Union and international applicants who 1. Hold an offer of admission on one of the eligible programmes. 2. Hold, or expect to achieve, at least a 2.1 honours degree (or international equivalent), in a related discipline
Level of Study: Postgraduate
Type: Scholarship
Value: £7,410
Frequency: Annual
Country of Study: Any country
Closing Date: 7 June
Funding: Private
Additional Information: www.ncl.ac.uk/gps/about/funding/schoolfunding/#phdscholarships

For further information contact:

Email: gps.pgr@ncl.ac.uk

Postgraduate Opportunity Scholarships

Purpose: The scholarships are available as part of Newcastle University's Postgraduate Support Scheme for Master's students. They have been designed to enable students from under-represented groups to progress to higher level study
Eligibility: 1. have been offered a place to study full time for one year or a maximum of two years part time on one of the University's eligible taught or research Master's courses commencing in September 2024. 2. are UK students progressing from undergraduate courses for which they were charged the higher tuition fee applying since 2012/13 and falling into the following categories: 3. a student living in England when they entered undergraduate study at any UK institution 4. a student living in Scotland when they entered undergraduate study at any English, Northern Irish or Welsh institution 5. a student living in Northern Ireland when they entered undergraduate study at any English, Scottish or Welsh institution 6. UK domiciled students (Newcastle and non-Newcastle graduates) who have paid fees at the 'home' rate since commencing undergraduate study from 2012 onwards. 7. meet at least one of the following criteria 8. a woman studying an eligible engineering or computing science course 9. have been in Local Authority care, or supported by the Foyer Federation, for at least three months in the last 10 years before September 2024 10. have been in receipt of Disabled Students' Allowances (DSA) while an undergraduate 11. have been in receipt of the maximum Maintenance Loan from the Student Loans Company in their final academic year 12. were from a neighbourhood which has a low progression rate to higher education (as determined by individual postcode on entry to undergraduate study)
Level of Study: Postgraduate
Type: Scholarship
Value: £5,000 award per student
Frequency: Annual
Country of Study: United Kingdom
Application Procedure: To apply for the Postgraduate Opportunity Scholarship, please complete the online application form: app.geckoform.com/public/#/modern/21FO00cjrmmby800l72ryrjrhq
No. of awards offered: 40
Closing Date: 23 June
Funding: Private
Additional Information: www.ncl.ac.uk/postgraduate/fees-funding/search-funding/?code=C0000031

For further information contact:

Email: uk.postgraduate-scholarships@ncl.ac.uk

Regional Impact Scholarship (MBA)

Purpose: To support aspiring and established leaders from the region to continue their professional development. The Regional Impact Scholarship is aimed at MBA candidates who can demonstrate their potential to the economy and society of the North East of United Kingdom
Eligibility: To be eligible for this full-fee scholarship you must meet the following criteria 1. Completed the scholarship application form including submitting an essay of no more than 1,500 words in response to the question listed. Submissions need to be in English. 2. Hold a conditional or unconditional offer of admission to the Full-time MBA programme of current year entry. 3. Have substantive managerial experience (minimum 3 years prior to starting the MBA). 4. Preferably hold the equivalent of a United Kingdom 21 honours degree (however, applicants who do not meet this requirement but can demonstrate relevant work experience above the minimum plus significant career progression may also be considered). 5. Perform well at interview across all competency areas hold an English language qualification of IELTS 6.5 or its equivalent with no subskill below 6.0 (if your first language is not English)
Level of Study: Postgraduate
Type: Scholarship
Value: A full fee award of £22,800, payable towards the cost of tuition fees
Frequency: Annual
Country of Study: United Kingdom
Application Procedure: Applications and essays will be reviewed by a panel of judges. Candidates need to complete the online application form. www.forms.ncl.ac.uk/view.php?id=2981068

Closing Date: 5 April
Funding: Private
Additional Information: www.ncl.ac.uk/business-school/courses/scholarships/mba/

For further information contact:

Tel: (44) 191 208 1589
Email: mba@ncl.ac.uk

Newcastle University in the United Kingdom

Newcastle upon Tyne, Tyne and Wear NE1 7RU, United Kingdom.

Tel: (44) 191 208 6000
Website: www.ncl.ac.uk/
Contact: Newcastle University

Newcastle University experts are protecting cultural property and preserving unique archives around the world

13 PhD International Studentships at Northumbria University in UK

Purpose: This is a 3.5 years funded studentship available to Home/EU/ Worldwide students who will commence the PhD study at the university in the UK
Eligibility: Eligible Countries Applications are accepted from around the world. Acceptable Course or Subjects PhD degree will be awarded in any subject offered by the university Admissible Criteria To be eligible, the applicants must meet all the following criteria You must have or expect to gain a First Class or high 21 Honours degree or international equivalent in a relevant subject or subject relevant to the proposed PhD project. Enthusiasm for research, the ability to think and work independently, excellent analytical skills, and strong verbal and written communication skills are also essential requirements
Level of Study: Postdoctorate
Type: Studentship
Value: Full tuition fees, living allowance of £15,609
Length of Study: 3.5 Years
Frequency: Annual
Country of Study: Any country
No. of awards offered: 13
Closing Date: 24 January
Additional Information: scholarship-positions.com/13-phd-international-studentships-at-northumbria-university-in-uk/2022/01/19/

For further information contact:

Northways Parade, 28 College Cres, London NW3 5DN, United Kingdom.

Tel: (44) 756 390 4978
Email: help@scholarship-positions.com

40 Fully-Funded Postgraduate Scholarships at Newcastle University in the United Kingdom

Purpose: Students need a good level of English language to study at Newcastle University. English will be the main language you use socially and for study. If English is not their first language they will need to provide a recognised English language test or qualification
Eligibility: Citizens of China, United States of America, Canada, India, Indonesia, Malaysia, Thailand, Singapore, Jordan, Lebanon, Egypt, Turkey, Algeria, Morocco, India, Nigeria, Ghana, Kenya and Uganda are eligible to apply
Type: Postgraduate scholarships
Value: 50% or 100% of tuition fees
Study Establishment: Scholarships are awarded to study the subjects offered by the university
Country of Study: United Kingdom
Application Procedure: International preparation courses and graduate diplomas have a different application method. Students apply online through partner INTO. Applications must be submitted using the online application app-eu.geckoform.com/public/#/modern/FOEU01c3yyTyxhy4
No. of awards offered: 40
Closing Date: 29 June
Additional Information: For more details please browse the website scholarship-positions.com/fully-funded-postgraduate-scholarships-newcastle-university-uk/2017/11/14/

For further information contact:

Email: scholarship.applications@ncl.ac.uk

International PhD Fellowships in Environmental Chemistry, Denmark

Subjects: PhD degree study in the Department of Plant and Environmental Sciences
Purpose: The University of Copenhagen has collaborated with the Department of Ecoscience at Aarhus University to

N

offer the International PhD fellowships in Environmental Chemistry
Eligibility: 1. Eligible Countries: Students from Denmark and all other foreign countries are eligible to apply. 2. Eligible Course or Subjects: PhD degree study in the Department of Plant and Environmental Sciences 3. Eligibility Criteria: To be eligible, the applicants must meet all the following/given criteria: 4. Professional qualifications relevant to the PhD project 5. Relevant publications 6. Relevant work experience Other relevant professional activities 7. The curious mindset with a strong interest in biogeochemistry as the basis for developing solutions for sustainable and climate-smart land use 8. Good language skills
Level of Study: Doctorate, Postdoctorate
Type: Fellowship
Value: Salary
Country of Study: Any country
Application Procedure: employment.ku.dk/phd/?show=155599
Closing Date: 30 January
Contributor: Department of Ecoscience at Aarhus University
Additional Information: scholarship-positions.com/international-phd-fellowships-in-environmental-chemistry-denmark/2022/01/27/

For further information contact:

Tel: (44) 191 208 6000
Email: scholarship.applications@ncl.ac.uk

International PhD Student Positions in Mathematics, Sweden

Purpose: Awards are another resource to help students afford the degree. To cover educational expenses, the University of Gothenburg is offering International PhD Student Positions in Mathematics
Eligibility: Eligible Countries All countries candidates can join this program. Acceptable Course or Subjects The PhD scholarship will be awarded in Mathematics Admissible Criteria The eligibility for academic positions is given in the Swedish Higher Education Ordinance. To qualify for the position, you must have obtained a master's degree or a 4-year bachelor's degree, or expect to complete that degree by the time the employment starts
Level of Study: Postdoctorate
Type: Studentship
Value: Salary
Length of Study: 4 Years
Frequency: Annual
Country of Study: Any country
Application Procedure: web103.reachmee.com/ext/I005/1035/job?site=7&lang=UK&validator=9b89bead79bb7258ad55c8d75228e5b7&job_id=23732
No. of awards offered: 3
Closing Date: 25 February
Additional Information: scholarship-positions.com/international-phd-student-positions-in-mathematics-sweden/2022/01/21/

For further information contact:

Tel: (44) 191 208 6000
Email: scholarship.applications@ncl.ac.uk

PhD (via MPhil) International Studentships in Cyber Security in UK

Subjects: School of Psychology and Computer Science
Purpose: The University of Central Lancashire is offering financial support to high-potential students through its PhD (via MPhil) Studentships in Cyber Security in the UK
Eligibility: Eligible Countries All nationalities Acceptable Course or Subjects PhD degree in Towards Securing Connected and Autonomous Vehicles (CAV) infrastructure to mitigate Virtual Vehicle Hijacking Admissible Criteria To be eligible, the applicants must meet all the given criteria Applicants must have to enroll in the PhD degree programme
Level of Study: Doctorate, Postdoctorate
Type: Studentship
Value: £15,609 per year
Length of Study: 3 years
Country of Study: Any country
Application Procedure: www.uclan.ac.uk/research/research-degrees/studentships
Closing Date: 23 February
Additional Information: scholarship-positions.com/phd-via-mphil-international-studentships-in-cyber-security-in-uk/2022/01/25/

For further information contact:

Tel: (44) 191 208 6000
Email: scholarship.applications@ncl.ac.uk

PhD Excellence Scholarships for International Students at Walailak University, Thailand

Purpose: Walailak University is pleased to announce the PhD Excellence Scholarships to help foreign students conduct studies in order to develop new knowledge in Thailand

Eligibility: Eligible Countries Foreign and home country national students are eligible to apply. Eligible Course or Subjects International PhD programmes offered at Walailak are eligible to be applied for. Eligibility Criteria To be eligible, the applicants must meet all the following/given criteria The applicants must have at least 2 research articles written by scholarship recipients MUST be published or have been formally accepted for publication in peer-review academic journals indexed in the Scopus database ranked in the 1stquartile (Q1) or 2nd quartile (Q2)
Level of Study: Postdoctorate
Type: Scholarship
Value: Tuition fee
Frequency: Annual
Country of Study: Any country
Application Procedure: grad.wu.ac.th/ph-d-excellence-scholarships/
Closing Date: 19 January
Additional Information: scholarship-positions.com/phd-excellence-scholarships-for-international-students-at-walailak-university-thailand/2022/01/19/

For further information contact:

Northways Parade, 28 College Cres, London NW3 5DN, United Kingdom.

Tel: (44) 756 390 4978
Email: help@scholarship-positions.com

PhD International Scholarships in Quantitative Genetics of Senescence in Seychelles Warblers, Netherlands

Purpose: The University of Groningen is looking for a student who wishes to design their PhD research project researching the Genomics of Senescence. It has established the PhD Scholarships in Quantitative Genetics of Senescence in Seychelles Warblers in the Netherlands
Eligibility: 1. Home country national and international students can both apply. 2. PhD degree studies in Quantitative genetics of senescence in Seychelles warblers at Groningen can be undertaken. 3. Eligibility Criteria: To be eligible, the applicants must meet all the following/given criteria: 4. The applicants must have experience extracting and analyzing data from databases (e.g., Access) or large datasets (training provided)
Level of Study: Postdoctorate
Type: Scholarship
Value: €2,249 per month
Length of Study: 4 Years
Frequency: Annual
Country of Study: Any country
Application Procedure: www.rug.nl/phd-scholarships?details=00347-02S0008U8P
Closing Date: 24 January
Contributor: University of Groningen
Additional Information: scholarship-positions.com/phd-international-scholarships-in-quantitative-genetics-of-senescence-in-seychelles-warblers-netherlands/2022/01/24/

For further information contact:

Tel: (44) 191 208 6000
Email: scholarship.applications@ncl.ac.uk

PhD International Studentships in Control of Mitosis in Calcium in Mammalian Cells, UK

Purpose: This funding scheme aims to cover the costs of studying for a PhD degree in the Biological and Medical Sciences at the Faculty of Health and Life Sciences at the University of Liverpool
Eligibility: Eligible Countries All students from all countries can apply. Eligible Course or Subjects PhD study programmes in Biological and Medical Sciences at the University of Liverpool. Eligibility Criteria To be eligible, the applicants must meet all the following/given criteria The applicants must be self-funded students
Level of Study: Doctorate, Postdoctorate
Type: Studentship
Value: £24,250 and £4,500
Frequency: Annual
Country of Study: Any country
Application Procedure: www.liverpool.ac.uk/study/postgraduate-research/studentships/mitosis-calcium-mammalian-cells/
Closing Date: 21 January
Additional Information: scholarship-positions.com/phd-international-studentships-in-control-of-mitosis-in-calcium-in-mammalian-cells-uk/2022/01/21/

For further information contact:

Tel: (44) 191 208 60008
Email: scholarship.applications@ncl.ac.uk

PhD International Studentships in Physical Layer Algorithm Design in 6G Non-Terrestrial Communications, UK

Purpose: The role will include both theoretical and applied research in the well-equipped 6GIC/ICS at the University of

N

Surrey. Future wireless communication networks are expected to provide a much more satisfying service to people by building uninterrupted and ubiquitous connectivity to everyone, everything, and everywhere with ultra-high data rate, extremely high reliability, and low latency
Eligibility: Eligible Countries All nationalities. Eligible Course or Subjects PhD degree in Physical layer algorithm design in 6G non-terrestrial communications Eligibility Criteria To be eligible, the applicants must meet all the following/given criteria The applicants must be the UK or international students holding a relevant master's degree qualification
Level of Study: Postdoctorate
Type: Studentship
Value: Tuition fee
Frequency: Annual
Country of Study: Any country
Application Procedure: www.surrey.ac.uk/fees-and-funding/studentships/physical-layer-algorithm-design-6g-non-terrestrial-communications-sure-fund-studentships
Closing Date: 27 January
Contributor: University of Surrey
Additional Information: scholarship-positions.com/phd-international-studentships-in-physical-layer-algorithm-design-in-6g-non-terrestrial-communications-uk/2022/01/27/

For further information contact:

Tel: (44) 191 208 6000
Email: scholarship.applications@ncl.ac.uk

PhD Studentship in Liquid Metal Catalysts for Green Fuels, Australia

Purpose: This studentship is open to all applicants that wish to work on a project that will investigate novel catalytic systems with applications in CO2 reduction
Eligibility: Eligible Countries Australian national and other international students can apply. Eligible Course or Subjects PhD study in Liquid Metal Catalysts for Green Fuels and CO2 Mitigation at RMIT is eligible to apply for. Eligibility Criteria To be eligible, the applicants must meet all the following/given criteria The applicants must meet the university's research degree requirements
Level of Study: Doctorate
Type: Studentship
Value: AU$31,000 per annum
Length of Study: 3 Years
Frequency: Annual
Country of Study: Any country
Application Procedure: www.rmit.edu.au/students/careers-opportunities/scholarships/research/phd-liquid-metal-catalysts
No. of awards offered: 1
Closing Date: 20 January
Additional Information: scholarship-positions.com/phd-studentship-in-liquid-metal-catalysts-for-green-fuels-australia/2022/01/20/

For further information contact:

Northways Parade, 28 College Cres, London NW3 5DN, United Kingdom.

Tel: (44) 756 390 4978
Email: help@scholarship-positions.com

Sam and Nina Narodowski PhD International Scholarships in Australia

Purpose: Aiming to support new commencing PhD candidates financially throughout their PhD study, RMIT University has decided to award deserving students the Sam and Nina Narodowski PhD Scholarships in Australia
Eligibility: 1. Domestic and International students are both eligible to apply. 2. PhD study programme in Food Production and Agribusiness, Sustainability and Environment or Clothing Textiles and Health Disability and Aged Care, Urban Transport and Social Planning or Migration and Settlement Services at RMIT can be applied for. 3. To be eligible, the applicants must meet all the following/given criteria: 4. The applicants must meet the eligibility criteria for admission into the PhD program
Level of Study: Postdoctorate
Type: Scholarship
Value: AU$33,000 per annum
Frequency: Annual
Country of Study: Any country
Application Procedure: www.rmit.edu.au/students/careers-opportunities/scholarships/research/sam-nina-narodowski-phd-scholarships
No. of awards offered: 2
Closing Date: 24 January
Additional Information: scholarship-positions.com/sam-and-nina-narodowski-phd-international-scholarships-in-australia/2022/01/24/

For further information contact:

Tel: (44) 191 208 6000
Email: scholarship.applications@ncl.ac.uk

School of Social Sciences and Humanities International PhD Studentships in UK

Purpose: Applications are welcomed from high calibre students wishing to apply for the International PhD Studentships based in the School of Social Sciences and Humanities at Loughborough University
Eligibility: 1. Applications are accepted from around the world. 2. PhD degree programme in creative arts by the university. 3. To be eligible, the applicants must have first-class honours, upper second-class honours, and lower second-class honours
Level of Study: Postdoctorate
Type: Studentship
Value: £15609 per annum
Frequency: Annual
Country of Study: Any country
Closing Date: 16 March
Contributor: Loughborough University
Additional Information: scholarship-positions.com/school-of-social-sciences-and-humanities-international-phd-studentships-in-uk/2022/01/22/

For further information contact:

Tel: (44) 191 208 6000
Email: scholarship.applications@ncl.ac.uk

Test Scholarships for International Students at Free University of Berlin, Germany

Purpose: International students alone can make applications for this scholarship scheme. PhD degree programme applicants are eligible
Eligibility: Eligible Countries All international students are eligible to apply. Eligible Course or Subjects Students can undertake PhD degree study programmes at FU Berlin. Eligibility Criteria To be eligible, the applicants must meet all the following/given criteria The applicants must submit a project report to the Center for International Cooperation within six weeks of project completion
Level of Study: Doctorate
Type: Scholarship
Value: €1,300
Length of Study: 3 Months
Frequency: Annual
Country of Study: Any country
Closing Date: 1 April
Additional Information: scholarship-positions.com/test-scholarships-for-international-students-at-free-university-of-berlin-germany/2022/01/21/

For further information contact:

Tel: (44) 191 208 6000
Email: scholarship.applications@ncl.ac.uk

University of Copenhagen International PhD Fellowships in Food Biotechnology, Denmark

Subjects: Department of Food Science
Purpose: The PhD position aims to explore the potential to release and extract seed storage proteins in a mild, controlled, and sustainable way by using enzymatic methods inspired by the pea plant's mechanism to mobilize the storage proteins during germination
Eligibility: Eligible Countries All nationalities Acceptable Course or Subjects PhD program in Microbial Interactions Admissible Criteria To be eligible for the regular PhD programme, you must have completed a degree programme, equivalent to a Danish master's degree (180 ECTS/3 FTE BSc + 120 ECTS/2 FTE MSc) related to the subject area of the project, e.g. biochemistry, molecular biology, biotechnology or bioengineering
Level of Study: Doctorate, Postdoctorate
Type: Fellowship
Value: DKK 27,871.40 per month
Country of Study: Any country
Closing Date: 25 January
Additional Information: scholarship-positions.com/university-of-copenhagen-international-phd-fellowships-in-food-biotechnology-denmark/2022/01/25/

For further information contact:

Tel: (44) 191 208 6000
Email: scholarship.applications@ncl.ac.uk

University of Newcastle International PhD Scholarships in Geomicrobial Biosensors, Australia

Purpose: The educational programme is available for highly motivated domestic and international students to apply for this PhD degree programme
Eligibility: An applicant for admission to candidature for a Doctoral Degree (Research) shall Have satisfied all of the requirements for admission to the degree of Bachelor with Honours Class 1 or Honours Class II, Division 1 or any other degree approved for this purpose by the Assistant Dean (Research Training); or Have satisfied all of the requirements for admission to the degree of Bachelor in the University or any other degree approved for this purpose by the Assistant

N

Dean (Research Training), and have achieved by subsequent work and study a standard recognized by the Assistant Dean (Research Training) as equivalent to at least Honours Class II, Division 1; or In exceptional cases, submit evidence of possessing such other academic or professional qualifications and experience as may be approved by the Assistant Dean (Research Training) on the recommendation of the relevant School; or In the disciplines of education, medical physics, nursing, social work, social sciences and surgery have completed a minimum standard of professional experience as required by the Assistant Dean (Research Training) on the recommendation of the School; An Australian honours degree with Class 1 or Class 2 division
Level of Study: Doctorate
Type: Scholarship
Value: US$28,092
Frequency: Annual
Country of Study: Any country
Application Procedure: www.newcastle.edu.au/study/research/phd-scholarships/phd-scholarships/geomicrobial-biosensors-microbial-diversity-and-the-genetics-of-heavy-metal-resistance-in-regolith
Closing Date: 28 February
Additional Information: scholarship-positions.com/university-of-newcastle-international-phd-scholarships-in-geomicrobial-biosensors-australia/2022/01/20/

For further information contact:

Tel: (44) 191 208 6000
Email: scholarship.applications@ncl.ac.uk

Newcomen Society of the United States

211 Welsh Pool Road, Suite 240, Exton, PA 19341, United States of America.

Tel: (1) 610 363 6600
Email: mstoner@newcomen.org
Website: www.newcomen.org
Contact: Ms Marcy J. Stoner, Executive Assistant

The Newcomen Society of the United States is a non-profit business educational foundation that studies and supports outstanding achievement in American business.

Harvard/Newcomen Postdoctoral Award

Purpose: To improve the scholar's professional acquaintance with business and economic history, to increase his or her skills as they relate to this field, and to enable him or her to engage in research that will benefit from the resources of the Harvard Business School and the Boston scholarly community
Eligibility: Open to Scholars who have received a PhD in history, economics or a related discipline within the past 10 years, and who would not otherwise be able to attend Harvard Business School
Level of Study: Postdoctorate
Type: Award
Value: US$46,000
Length of Study: 1 year
Frequency: Annual
Study Establishment: Harvard Business School in Cambridge, Massachusetts
Country of Study: United States of America
Application Procedure: Applicants must contact Harvard University for further details
Closing Date: 1 November

For further information contact:

Graduate School of Business Administration, Straus Professor of Business History Harvard University, Soldiers Field Road, Boston, MA 02163, United States of America.

Tel: (1) 617 495 6354
Email: tmccraw@hbs.edu

RMIT- CSIRO PhD International Scholarship in Mineral Resources and Environmental Science, Australia

Purpose: RMIT University is looking for excellent, highly motivated early-career researchers that are keen on studying in Australia to apply for the CSIRO PhD International Scholarship in Mineral Resources and Environmental Science
Eligibility: Eligible Countries Australian or international students are eligible. Acceptable Course or Subjects PhD degree in Chemical and Rheological Assessment of Rejuvenated Asphalt Material. Admissible Criteria To be eligible, the candidates must meet all the following criteria Applicants with an honours degree or graduates with a research master in experimental and analytical work with a civil engineering or chemical engineering background are invited to apply. Previous experience in the rheology and chemistry of bituminous products is highly regarded
Level of Study: Doctorate, Postdoctorate
Type: Scholarship
Value: US$31,260 per annum
Length of Study: 3 years
Frequency: Annual
Country of Study: Any country

Application Procedure: www.rmit.edu.au/students/careers-opportunities/scholarships/research/phd-rmit-csiro-mineral-resources-environmental-sciences
No. of awards offered: 1
Additional Information: scholarship-positions.com/rmit-csiro-phd-international-scholarship-in-mineral-resources-and-environmental-science-australia/2022/01/21/

For further information contact:

Northways Parade, 28 College Cres, London NW3 5DN, United Kingdom.

Tel: (44) 756 390 4978

North Atlantic Treaty Organization (NATO)

Public Diplomacy Division, Office Nb 106, Boulevard Leopold III, B-1110 Brussels, Belgium.

Tel: (32) 2 811 4000
Website: www.nato.int
Contact: Academic Affairs Officer

NATO's purpose is to guarantee the freedom and security of its members through political and military means. NATO promotes democratic values and enables members to consult and cooperate on defence and security-related issues to solve problems, build trust and, in the long run, prevent conflict.

Manfred Wörner Fellowship

Purpose: To honour the memory of the late Secretary General by focusing attention on his leadership in the transformation of the alliance, including efforts at extending NATO's relations with CEE countries and promoting the principles and image of the Transatlantic partnership
Eligibility: Open to applicants who are citizens of the EAPC countries with proven experience to carry out an important scholarly endeavour within the time limit of the Fellowship
Level of Study: Professional development
Type: Fellowship
Value: €5,000 (including all travel costs)
Frequency: Annual
Country of Study: Any country
Application Procedure: Application forms can be downloaded from the NATO website
Closing Date: 25 January
Funding: Government

For further information contact:

Fax: (32) 2 707 5457
Email: leadershipprograms@gmfus.org

North Central College

Graduate Programs MBA Program, 30 North Brainard Street, Naperville, IL 60540, United States of America.

Tel: (1) 630 637 5100
Email: grad@noctrl.edu
Website: www.noctrl.edu
Contact: MBA Admissions Officer

Since 1861, North Central has been a place where new ideas lead to unlimited possibilities. We're an independent college dedicated to the power of the liberal arts and sciences to transform students into leaders both in their careers and communities. Our nearly 3,000 students study across more than 65 undergraduate and graduate programs, with their education made richer by supportive faculty and staff, world-class facilities and countless opportunities to learn beyond the classroom.

N

North Central Association for Counselor Education and Supervision Research Grant Awards

Purpose: The call for proposals is to fund studies that increase understanding of the counselor education profession (including research, teaching, supervision, leadership and advocacy). Research grant awards will be presented at the business meeting at the NCACES
Eligibility: Proposed topic is within the scope of this Research Award program. Need for the proposed topic is clearly outlined through review of the research. Objectives are clear and attainable in the proposed study. Methodology proposed is appropriate for the research questions. Outcomes are consistent with objectives and method. Research proposed adheres to ACA/ACES ethical standards for research with human subjects
Level of Study: Graduate
Type: Study grant
Value: US$1,000
Frequency: Annual
Country of Study: Any country
Application Procedure: The competition is open to both professional and student members of NCACES. The primary investigator must be an ACES/NCACES member at the time

the application is submitted. Individuals may submit (or be part of a submission team) for only one proposal. www.ncaces.org/awards/general/gsubmit
No. of awards offered: 3
Closing Date: 29 June
Funding: Private

North Dallas Bank & Trust Company

12900 Preston Rd, ST 300 Dallas, TX 75230, United States of America.

Tel: (1) 972 716 7100
Email: customer.service@ndbt.com
Website: www.ndbt.com/

North Dallas Bank & Trust aims to provide banking for smarter choices in business and life. This means engaging with our customers and communities through personalized and excellent service, returning a fair and reasonable profit to our shareholders, acting at all times with dignity, honor and respect and providing an environment in which each of our employees can excel in the spirit of mutual respect, accountability, creativity and teamwork.

James W. Tyra Memorial Scholarship

Purpose: High school seniors who have a grade point avearage of 3.0 or higher and are in the top 25 percent of their graduating class are eligible for this award. Students must be attending high schools located inside the North Dallas Bank & Trust Company service area and have a annual family income no higher than US$58,720
Level of Study: Graduate
Type: Scholarship
Value: US$4,000
Frequency: Annual
Country of Study: United States of America
Application Procedure: Application requirements for the James W. Tyra Memorial Scholarship are Application form. Official Transcript. Recommendation letters (2). Personal statement
No. of awards offered: 2
Closing Date: 1 April
Funding: Private
Additional Information: Applicants must demonstrate financial need. Selection will be judged by an internal North Dallas Bank committee, representing a cross-section of the bank's communities. The decision of the committee will be final. The bank will notify all recipients. Family members and employees of North Dallas Bank and its affiliates are not eligible. www.gmfus.org/transatlantic-leadership-initiatives/manfred-w%C3%B6rner-seminar

North West Cancer Research Fund

200 London Road, Liverpool L3 9TA, United Kingdom.

Tel: (44) 151 709 2919
Email: info@nwcr.org
Website: www.nwcr.org/
Contact: Mr A W Renison, General Secretary

As the only independent charity dedicated to tackling cancer across the North West and North Wales, our goal is simple: to put our region's cancer needs first.

North West Cancer Research Fund Research Project Grants

Purpose: To support fundamental research into the cause of cancers and the mechanisms by which cancers arise and exert their effects
Eligibility: Open to candidates undertaking cancer research studies at one of the universities named below in the Northwest. Grants are only available for travel costs associated with currently funded 3-year cancer research projects. No grants are awarded for buildings or for the development of drugs
Level of Study: Research
Type: Project
Value: Approx. £35,000 per year
Length of Study: Usually 3 years
Frequency: Dependent on funds available
Study Establishment: The University of Liverpool, Lancaster University and the University of Wales, Bangor
Country of Study: Any country
Application Procedure: The NWCRF Scientific Committee meets twice a year. All applications are subject to peer review
No. of awards offered: 50
Closing Date: 1 October
Funding: Individuals, Private
Contributor: Voluntary donations
No. of awards given last year: 10
No. of applicants last year: 50

For further information contact:

NWCRF Scientific Committee, Department of Medicine, Duncan Building, Daulby Street, Liverpool L7 8XW, United Kingdom.

Email: ricketts@liverpool.ac.uk

NWCR & Tenovus PhD Studentship Award

Purpose: We invite applications from principal investigators, with a track record of successful PhD supervision, to submit proposals for this jointly funded research award. NWCR and Tenovus Cancer Care (Tenovus) seek to fund a health services PhD research award which will aim to impact cancer policy or practice through the targeted area of psycho-social oncology
Level of Study: Research
Type: Studentship
Value: £75,000
Length of Study: 3 years
Closing Date: 22 June
Funding: Individuals, Private

Northeast Florida Phi Beta Kappa Alumni Association

1606 New Hampshire Ave NW, Washington, DC 20009, United States.

Website: pbkaa.blogspot.com/

Northeast Florida Phi Beta Kappa Alumni Association Scholarship

Purpose: The Fall Program provides a social and intellectual opportunity for members and their guests
Eligibility: Winners will be honored at the association's Spring Banquet. For further details, see the website
Level of Study: Postgraduate
Type: Scholarship and Research award
Value: US$2,000
Frequency: Annual
Country of Study: Any country
Application Procedure: Application information is available online at the Phi Beta Kappa Alumni Association of Northeast Florida website
No. of awards offered: 2
Closing Date: 1 March
Funding: Private
Additional Information: www.unigo.com/scholarships/merit-based/merit-scholarships/northeast-florida-phi-beta-kappa-alumni-association-scholarship

For further information contact:

1606 New Hampshire Ave NW, Washington, DC 20009, United States of America.

Tel: (1) 2022653808
Email: mroberts@unf.edu

Northeastern University

Graduate School of Business Administration, 350 Dodge Hall, 360 Huntington Ave, Boston, MA 02115, United States of America.

Tel: (1) 617 373 2000
Email: gsba@neu.edu
Contact: MBA Admissions Officer

Located in Boston and founded in 1898, Northeastern is a private, nonprofit university that offers degree programs at the undergraduate and graduate levels. Home to more than 35 specialized research and education centers, we are a leader in worldwide experiential learning, urban engagement and interdisciplinary research that responds to global and societal needs

Expanding Capacity in Quantum Information Science and Engineering (ExpandQISE)

Purpose: The NSF Expanding Capacity in Quantum Information Science and Engineering (ExpandQISE) program aims to increase research capacity and broaden participation in Quantum Information Science and Engineering (QISE) and related disciplines through the creation of a diversified investment portfolio in research and education that will lead to scientific and engineering breakthroughs, while securing a talent pipeline in a field where workforce needs of industry, government and academia continue to outgrow the available talent
Type: Award
Value: Track1-US$800,000; Track 2-US$5,000,000.
Length of Study: 3-5 years
Country of Study: Any country

No. of awards offered: 4 to 25
Closing Date: 24 April
Additional Information: beta.nsf.gov/funding/opportunities/expanding-capacity-quantum-information-science-and-engineering-expandqise

For further information contact:

360 Huntington Ave, Boston, MA 02115, United States of America.

Tel: (1) 617 373 2000
Email: beta-nsf-feedback@nsf.gov

National Robotics Initiative 2.0: Ubiquitous Collaborative Robots (NRI-2.0)

Purpose: The goal of the National Robotics Initiative (NRI) is to support fundamental research that will accelerate the development and use of robots in the United States that work beside or cooperatively with people
Eligibility: 1. An investigator may participate as PI, co-PI, or Senior Personnel in no more than two proposals submitted in response to this solicitation each year. 2. In the event that an individual exceeds this limit, proposals received within the limit will be accepted based on earliest date and time of proposal submission (i.e., the first two proposals received will be accepted and the remainder will be returned without review). No exceptions will be made. 3. The above limit applies only to proposals to the NRI-2.0 solicitation, not to the totality of proposals submitted to NSF
Level of Study: Graduate
Type: Grant
Value: US$250,000 to US$1,500,000
Length of Study: 4 Years
Frequency: Annual
Country of Study: Any country
No. of awards offered: 15–30
Closing Date: 22 February
Funding: Private
Additional Information: www.nsf.gov/funding/pgm_summ.jsp?pims_id=503641

For further information contact:

360 Huntington Ave, Boston, MA 02115, United States of America.

Tel: (1) 617 373 2000
Email: beta-nsf-feedback@nsf.gov

Norway – the Official Site in the United States

2720 34th Street NW, Washington, DC 20008, United States of America.

Tel: (1) 202 333 6000
Email: cg.newyork@mfa.no
Website: www.norway.org
Contact: Grants and Scholarships Department

Al Fog Bergljot Kolflats Stipendfond

Purpose: To provide a stipend for those who want to take a trip to the United States to get practical experience within their fields of interest
Eligibility: Open to Norwegian citizens only, especially for a Norwegian engineer or architect. The applicant must have worked for at least 3 years after graduation, and he/she must present a detailed plan for the trip when they apply. Also, a budget for the trip must be included as well as references
Level of Study: Postgraduate
Value: Up to 40,000 NOK
Length of Study: 3 years
Country of Study: Any country
Closing Date: 1 April
Additional Information: noram.no/noram_stipend/andre-stipend/

For further information contact:

The Norway–America Association, Rådhusgaten 23B, N-0158 Oslo, Norway.

Tel: (47) 233 571 60
Fax: (47) 233 571 75
Email: info@noram.no

American-Scandinavian Foundation Scholarships (ASF)

Purpose: To encourage Scandinavians to undertake advanced study and research programmes in the United States
Eligibility: Applicants must be United States citizens or permanent residents. Team projects are eligible, but each member must apply as an individual, submitting a separate, fully-documented application. Applicants must have completed their undergraduate education by the start of their project in the Nordic region

Level of Study: Postgraduate
Type: Fellowship
Value: US$23,000
Length of Study: 1 year
Frequency: Annual
Country of Study: United States of America
Application Procedure: Applicants must complete an application on ASF application forms. More information available on our website - www.amscan.org/fellowships-and-grants/fellowships-and-grants-for-advanced-study-or-research-in-the-usa/
Closing Date: 1 November
Funding: Foundation
Additional Information: www.amscan.org/fellowships-and-grants/fellowshipsgrants-to-study-in-scandinavia/

For further information contact:

58 Park Ave, New York, NY 10016, United States of America.

Tel: (1) 212 879 9779
Fax: (1) 212 249 3444
Email: grants@amscan.org

John Dana Archbold Fellowship Program

Purpose: To support educational exchange between the United States of America and Norway
Eligibility: Open to citizens of the United States of America citizens aged 20–35, in good health and of good character. Qualified applicants must show evidence of a high level of competence in their chosen field, indicate a seriousness of purpose, and have a record of social adaptability. There is ordinarily no language requirement
Eligible Country: United States of America
Level of Study: Postgraduate, Professional development, Research
Type: Fellowship
Value: US$5,000
Length of Study: 1 year
Frequency: Annual
Study Establishment: University of Oslo International Summer School
Country of Study: United States of America
Application Procedure: Applicants must write to the Nansen Fund, Inc. for an application form
Closing Date: 1 November
Funding: Private
Additional Information: The University of Oslo International Summer School offers orientation and Norwegian languages courses 6 weeks before the start of the regular academic year. For Americans, tuition is paid. Attendance is required. Americans visit Norway in even-numbered years and Norwegians visit the United States of America in odd-numbered years. For further information please contact the Nansen Fund, Inc. www.amscan.org/fellowships-and-grants/fellowshipsgrants-to-study-in-scandinavia/

For further information contact:

Rådhusgata 23B, N-0158 Oslo, Norway.

Tel: (47) 23 35 71 60

Memorial Fund of 8 May

Purpose: To promote cultural exchange between foreign countries and Norwegian residential experiential colleges by providing scholarships for residence, and to help prepare young people for everyday life in the community
Eligibility: Open to candidates aged 18–22 years who do not have a permanent residence in Norway, and do not hold a Norwegian passport. Candidates must be planning to return to their home country after a year in Norway. Candidates must be aware of the kind of education the Memorial Fund bursaries cover, that being a year in a Norwegian residential colleges, not admission to education on a higher level, such as a university, or specialized training
Type: Scholarship
Value: The scholarship will cover board and lodging. In addition it is possible to apply for extra funds. Applicants from some countries may apply for required books and excursions arranged by the school. Also, extra support may be provided for short study trips and short courses before or after the school year. A fixed amount towards spending money may also be given. Normally the students must pay their own travelling expenses. The colleges do not charge tuition fees
Length of Study: 1 year
Frequency: Annual
Study Establishment: Norwegian residential experiential colleges.
Country of Study: Norway
Application Procedure: Applicants must request more information and application forms from the Memorial Fund of 8 May or to the nearest Norwegian Embassy. Applicants who require a scholarship to attend a Norwegian college should not apply to a them directly. In this case, the Board will place successful applicants at a college school based on their hobbies and interest. Residence permits must

be applied for by each individual student when a scholarship has been granted
No. of awards offered: 700
Closing Date: 1 November
No. of awards given last year: 25
No. of applicants last year: 700
Additional Information: A residential experiential college is a 1-year independent residential school, primarily for young adults, offering many non-traditional subjects of study. Each college has its own profile, but as a group, the Norwegian colleges teach classes covering almost all areas, including history, arts, crafts, music, sports, philosophy, theatre, photography etc. www.grad.uchicago.edu/fellowship/john-dana-archbold-fellowship-in-norway/

For further information contact:

IKF, Grensen 9a, N-0159 Oslo, Norway.

Email: ikf@ikf.no

Norwegian Emigration Fund

Purpose: To support for advanced or specialized study in Norway
Eligibility: Open to citizens and residents of the United States of America. The fund may also give grants to institutions in the United States of America whose activities are primarily centred on the subjects mentioned
Level of Study: Doctorate, Graduate, Professional development
Type: Grant
Value: NOK 5,000–20,000
Frequency: Annual
Country of Study: Norway
Application Procedure: Applicants must complete an application form and return it clearly marked Emigration Fund to Nordmanns-Forbundet. Applications as well as enclosures will not be returned
Closing Date: 1 February
Funding: Government

For further information contact:

Email: norseman@online.no

Norwegian Marshall Fund

Purpose: To provide financial support for Americans to come to Norway to conduct postgraduate study or research in areas of mutual importance to Norway and the United States of America, thereby increasing knowledge, understanding and strengthening the ties of friendship between the two countries
Eligibility: Open to citizens of the United States of America, who have arranged with a Norwegian sponsor or research institution to pursue a research project or programme in Norway. Under special circumstances, the awards can be extended to Norwegians for study or research in the United States of America
Level of Study: Postgraduate
Type: Award
Value: US$1,500 to 4,500
Length of Study: Varies
Frequency: Annual
Country of Study: Norway
Application Procedure: Applicants must contact the Norway-America Association to receive an application. Application forms must be typewritten either in English or Norwegian and submitted in duplicate, including all supplementary materials. Each application must also be accompanied by a letter of support from the project sponsor or affiliated research institution in Norway. There is an application fee of Norwegian Krone 350
No. of awards offered: 5 to 15
Closing Date: 15 March
Funding: Private
Additional Information: www.postgraduatefunding.com/award-2647

For further information contact:

Rådhusgata 23B, N-0158 Oslo, Norway.

Tel: (47) 23 35 71 60

Norwegian Thanksgiving Fund Scholarship

Purpose: To provide eligible students to pursue their studies.
Eligibility: The applicant must be a US citizen doing graduate level work in Norway. The student must be working on social medicine, Norwegian culture, fisheries, geology, glaciology or astronomy at a Norwegian university
Eligible Country: United States of America
Level of Study: Graduate
Type: Scholarship
Value: US$3,000
Frequency: Annual
Country of Study: United States of America
Application Procedure: Candidates must contact the American Scandinavian Foundation.
No. of awards offered: 1
Closing Date: 15 March
Contributor: Former Norwegian students and friends

Scholarships for Americans to Study in Norway

Purpose: The purpose of the scholarships is to provide financial support for Americans to study in Norway. By supporting post-graduate study or research in areas of mutual importance to Norway and the United States, we hope to bring the two countries closer
Eligibility: The applicant must be American citizen, planning to study/currently studying in Norway
Type: Scholarship
Value: NOK 10 000– 40 000
Frequency: Annual
Country of Study: Any country
No. of awards offered: 10
Closing Date: 1 April
Additional Information: noram.no/en/scholarship-americans/

For further information contact:

The Norway-America Association Rådhusgaten 23 B, N-0158 Oslo, Norway.

Tel: (47) 23 35 71 60
Email: info@noram.no

The Norway-America Association Awards

Purpose: Norwegians who wish to study in the United States on the graduate level
Eligibility: Open to Norwegian who wish to study in the United States on the graduate level, must have completed their Bachelor's Degree before applying for these scholarships. The applicants must also be members of the Norway-America Association, and the membership fee is NOK 200 per year
Level of Study: Graduate, Research
Type: Award
Value: US$2,000 to US$20,000
Frequency: Annual
Country of Study: United States of America
Application Procedure: Check website for further details
Closing Date: 22 September

The Norway-America Association Graduate & Research Stipend

Purpose: To give the student substantial financial support for 1 year of studies in the United States
Eligibility: Open to Norwegians and members of the Norway-America Association, and he/she must pay NOK 250 in administrative fees and are currently living in Norway, and intend to return to Norway after their graduation
Level of Study: Graduate, Research
Type: Award
Value: NOK$2,000 to NOK$25,000
Country of Study: Norway
Application Procedure: Check website for further details.
Closing Date: 22 September

The Professional Development Award

Purpose: To help established professionals with a higher education who want to study within their own field of interest
Eligibility: Open to Norwegian professionals who worked for at least 3 years after finishing his or her education as well as planning on doing special research or further study in their fields
Level of Study: Postgraduate
Type: Award
Value: US$250 and maximum of US$1,000
Frequency: Annual
Country of Study: Any country
Application Procedure: Check website for further details.
No. of awards offered: 2
Additional Information: Candidates must be invited to apply for this award. There is also an administrative fee of NOK 250, which must be deposited in bank account with number 7878.05.23025. Please contact the American-Scandinavian Foundation or the Norway-America Association directly in order to find the appropriate scholarship. www.grad.uchicago.edu/fellowship/john-dana-archbold-fellowship-in-norway/

The Torskeklubben Stipend

Purpose: To promote Norwegian-American relations through helping Norwegians come to the United States to study
Eligibility: Open to Norwegians and must already be accepted at the Graduate School at the University of Minnesota before applying for the award
Level of Study: Graduate
Type: Award
Value: NOK$15,000
Frequency: Annual
Country of Study: Norway
Application Procedure: Application forms are available upon request from the Norway-America Association and the Graduate School at the University of Minnesota or it can be downloaded from the website
Closing Date: 1 March
Funding: Private

For further information contact:

2720 34th Street NW, Washington, DC 20008, United States of America.

Tel: (1) 202 333 6000

Novo Nordisk A/S

Novo Alle 1, DK-2880 Bagsvaerd, Denmark.

Tel: (45) 44 44 88 88
Website: www.novonordisk.com
Contact: Director

Novo Nordisk A/S develops, produces, and markets pharmaceutical products. The Company focuses on diabetes care and offers insulin delivery systems and other diabetes products. Novo Nordisk also works in areas such as haemostatis management, growth disorders, and hormone replacement therapy. The Company offers educational and training materials. Novo Nordisk markets worldwide.

National Fellowship and Scholarship for Higher Education of ST Students

Purpose: National Fellowship and Scholarship for Higher Education of ST Students is offered by Ministry of Tribal Affairs. This is a central sector scheme for the ST students who are selected for pursuing MPhil and PhD. The application form is available online and students can apply via the link given on this page. The scholarship has emerged as two different schemes i.e. Rajiv Gandhi National Fellowship for ST students and top class education for ST students. The fellowship covers under Rajiv Gandhi National Fellowship programme and scholarship is covered by top-class education
Eligibility: 1. Candidates must belong to ST category. 2. Candidates should get registered for the full-time Mphil and PhD course. 3. Scholarship, the students must have taken admission in their notified institution. 4. Family income should not exceed more than 6 Lac per annum
Level of Study: Postdoctorate
Type: Scholarship
Value: Tuition Fees, Books & Stationery-Rs.3000/-; Living expenses-2200/- per month; Computer & Accessories-Rs.45000/
Frequency: Annual
Country of Study: Any country
No. of awards offered: 1000
Closing Date: 31 December
Funding: Foundation
Additional Information: www.vikaspedia.in/education/policies-and-schemes/scholarships/p-g-and-above-scholarships/national-fellowship-and-scholarship-for-higher-education-of-st-students

For further information contact:

Tel: (45) 44 44 88 88
Email: info@vidhyaa.in

Novo Nordisk Foundation

Tuborg Havnevej 19, DK-2900 Hellerup, Denmark.

Tel: (45) 3527 6600
Email: info@novonordiskfonden.dk
Website: novonordiskfonden.dk/en/

The Novo Nordisk Foundation dates back to 1922, when Nobel laureate August Krogh returned home from the United States and Canada with permission to produce insulin in the Nordic countries. This marked the beginning of the development of world-class diabetes medicine and a subsequent Danish business and export venture. It also led to the establishment of several foundations that, many years later, merged into today's Novo Nordisk Foundation.

Postdoc Fellowship for Research Abroad - Bioscience and Basic Biomedicine

Purpose: The Novo Nordisk Foundation invites young, ambitious researchers in Denmark to apply for a post-doctoral fellowship to conduct research outside of Denmark, with the purpose of obtaining knowledge, training and research experience in an international research environment. Associating the fellow to a Danish research institution throughout the fellowship, and thereby facilitating the return to, and integration in, the Danish academic research environment
Eligibility: The successful candidate: 1. will carry out research at least 3 years abroad, followed by up to 1 year in Denmark 2. has obtained a PhD degree within 5 years of the fellowship start date 3. can apply as a PhD-student if the supervisor signs a declaration stating that the applicant is expected to graduate before the start date of the fellowship 4. can apply if he/she has already started a postdoctoral stay abroad. However, the time spent as postdoc abroad must not exceed 1 year at the time of application 5. has established

contact with the laboratory abroad and has support from the principal investigator/lab head at the foreign research institution 6. has considerable prior association to the Danish education or research community
Level of Study: Postdoctorate
Type: Fellowship
Value: The Novo Nordisk Foundation awards DKK 1 million per year, that is, for a total of up to DKK 4 million/fellowship
Length of Study: 4 years
Frequency: Annual
Country of Study: Denmark
Application Procedure: The applicant has to submit application via the foundation's application system (the green 'Apply' button at the top of the screen) from the indicated 'Application opens' date
No. of awards offered: 3
Closing Date: 11 January
Contributor: Novo Nordisk Foundation
Additional Information: novonordiskfonden.dk/en/grant/postdoc-fellowship-for-research-abroad-bioscience-and-basic-biomedicine/

For further information contact:

Tel: (45) 35 27 66 00

Nuffic

Kortenaerkade 11, 2518 AX Den Haag, PO Box 29777, NL-2502 LT The Hague, Netherlands.

Tel: (31) 70 4260 260
Email: nuffic@nuffic.nl
Website: www.nuffic.net

We are Nuffic, the Dutch organization for internationalization in education. From primary and secondary education to MBO, higher education and research, and adult education.

Netherlands Organization for International Cooperation in Higher Education-Natural Family Planning Fellowships for PhD Studies

Purpose: To allow candidates to pursue a PhD at one of 18 Dutch universities and institutes for international education
Eligibility: Candidate must be a national of one of 61 developing countries and have been admitted to a Dutch institution as a PhD fellow. Priority will be given to female candidates and candidates from sub-Saharan Africa
Level of Study: Doctorate
Type: Fellowship
Value: €595 to €1190
Length of Study: 4 years
Frequency: Annual
Country of Study: Any country
Application Procedure: After being accepted for admission to a Dutch institution, the candidate may submit a request for a PhD fellowship. Applicant must present a completed NFP PhD study application form to the Netherlands embassy or consulate in his/her own country. The application must be accompanied by the necessary documentation and by a research proposal that is supported by the supervisor(s). Form can be downloaded from website
No. of awards offered: Varies
Closing Date: 1 February
No. of applicants last year: Varies
Additional Information: www.european-funding-guide.eu/other-financial-assistance/14452-nfp-fellowships-phd-studies

O

Office of International Affairs at Ohio State University (OIA)

140 Enarson Classroom Building, 2009 Millikin Rd, Columbus, OH 43210, United States of America.

Tel: (1) 614 292 6101
Email: bock.126@osu.edu
Website: oia.osu.edu/
Contact: Jennifer Bock, Student Immigration Coordinator

OIA provides leadership and international expertise to ensure a coordinated and dynamic strategy for university-wide global engagement. To further Ohio State's international goals and to advance the university's reputation world-wide, OIA facilitates international experiences for students and faculty, supports academic programs and research, coordinates international partnerships, administers grants and scholarships for global engagement and contributes to enriching the Ohio State experience for the university's international student and scholar population.

Dr. Suguru Furuichi Memorial Scholarship General Information

Purpose: OIA is pleased to make available a partial tuition scholarship on behalf of and in memory of Dr. Suguru Furuichi. There is a limit of one scholarship per academic year.
Eligibility: An eligible student must meet all of the following criteria: 1. Be a non-immigrant international student (F-1 or J-1 status) 2. Be a citizen of Japan 3. Be currently enrolled full time in a degree granting program – undergraduate or graduate 4. Making satisfactory academic progress. Preference will be given to: 1. Students who majored or are majoring in Physical Education 2. Students who attended Waseda University
Level of Study: Graduate
Type: Scholarship
Value: Between US$500 - US$3,000 based on need
Frequency: Annual
Application Procedure: Application Details: oia.osu.edu/media/ikal2r0f/sugurufuruichi.pdf
Closing Date: January
Additional Information: Website: oia.osu.edu/grants-and-scholarships/graduate/

Everett And Florence Drumright Scholarship

Purpose: The awarding of scholarships is based on a combination of academic merit and financial need. Students in all fields are eligible
Eligibility: Check the official website.
Level of Study: Graduate
Type: Scholarship
Value: US$1,000
Frequency: Annual
Country of Study: Any country
Funding: Private

For further information contact:

509 University Hall (M/C 590), 601 South Morgan Street, Chicago, IL 60607-7128, United States of America.

Tel: (1) 312 996 5455
Email: oia@uic.edu

Palgrave Macmillan (ed.), *The Grants Register 2024*,
https://doi.org/10.1057/978-1-349-96073-6

International Student Grant

Purpose: OIA awards partial tuition grants each semester to international students at The Ohio State University. These grants are intended to help international students who are within two semesters of graduation and who have demonstrated financial need to complete their degrees.
Eligibility: Be a non-immigrant international student (F-1 or J-1 status) 1. Be currently enrolled in a degree granting program 2. Have never received an OIA grant before in current degree level 3. Be within one semester of graduation or have a compelling, unforeseen emergency 4. Have demonstrated financial need to complete current degree 5. Have a minimum cumulative grade point average (GPA) of 2.5 (for undergraduates) or 3.0 (for graduates)
Level of Study: Graduate
Type: Grant
Value: See website
Application Procedure: Application: oia.osu.edu/media/1akactja/international-student-grant.pdf. Please submit the following documentation when applying for an International Student Grant: 1. International Student Grant Application 2. Letter explaining in specific terms why this grant is needed and how you intend to use it, as well as what you have done and are doing to meet your financial needs. 3. Any additional documentation you wish to submit to support your case, if necessary. Email the completed application and supporting documentation to Devan Gibson at gibson.734@osu.edu.
Additional Information: Note: You will not be interviewed for an OIA grant. Therefore, take full advantage of this opportunity to explain your financial situation in writing. However, limit your statement to a maximum of one page. Website: oia.osu.edu/grants-and-scholarships/graduate/international-student-grant/

For further information contact:

Email: gibson.734@osu.edu

Mershon Center Graduate Student Grants

Purpose: The Mershon Center for International Security Studies seeks applications from Ohio State graduate students for grants to support travel and research on topics related to international security.
Eligibility: Funds may be used for a variety of purposes related to the conduct of research including travel costs, food and lodging expenses, interview or library fees, survey costs, and other expenses.
Level of Study: Graduate, Research
Type: Grant
Application Procedure: All application materials should be sent via email attachments (coversheet saved as a Word document) to mershon.student@osu.edu. All other items can be sent separately or as one combined PDF. Please identify each electronic document with your last name, the grant, and document type (i.e. smithGRvita.doc or smithGRproposal.doc).
Closing Date: 1 March
Additional Information: For questions regarding the application process or budget, allowable expenses, travel, or disbursement of funds, please contact Kyle McCray, Business & Operations Manager at the Mershon Center, at mccray.44@osu.edu or at 614-292-3810. Website: oia.osu.edu/grants-and-scholarships/graduate/mershon-center-graduate-student-grants/

For further information contact:

Email: mershon.student@osu.edu

Ohio Arts Council

Rhodes State Office Tower, 30 E. Broad Street, 33rd Floor, Columbus, OH 43215-3414, United States of America.

Tel: (1) 614 466 2613
Email: communications@oac.ohio.gov
Website: oac.ohio.gov/

The Ohio Arts Council is a state agency that funds and supports quality arts experiences to strengthen Ohio communities culturally, educationally and economically. It was created in 1965 to foster and encourage the development of the arts and assist the preservation of Ohio's cultural heritage.

Ohio Arts Council Individual Excellence Awards

Purpose: The Individual Excellence Awards program recognizes outstanding accomplishments by artists in a variety of disciplines. Individual artists will be supported through programs that recognize excellence, preserve cultural traditions, and offer developmental support.
Eligibility: Creative artists who are residents of Ohio may apply to this program. Applicants must have lived in Ohio for one year prior to the deadline, and must remain in the state throughout the grant period. Applicants must be at least eighteen years of age.
Level of Study: Postgraduate

Type: Award/Grant
Value: US$4,000
Frequency: Annual
Country of Study: United States of America
Application Procedure: Individual Excellence Awards program applications must be submitted via the ARTIE system (ohioartscouncil.smartsimple.com/s_Login.jsp) refer to ARTIE Individual Artist Grant Applications oac.ohio.gov/Portals/0/grants/Guidelines/Guidelines_ARTIE_Inds.pdf) for a description of the process.
Closing Date: 1 September
Funding: Government
Additional Information: NOTE: Up to two artists who worked together to create a body of work, and who plan to continue working together, may apply collaboratively, with each artist retaining creative ownership of the completed artwork. If awarded an Individual Excellence Award, the collaborative applicants split the award equally. Collaborative artists must each submit an application with the same narrative on each application, and each must submit the same required support materials. For more details please refer oac.ohio.gov/grants#4436-individual-artists, oac.ohio.gov/Portals/0/grants/Guidelines/Individual_Excellence.pdf

For further information contact:

30 E. Broad Street, 33rd Floor, Columbus, OH 43215-3414, United States of America.

Tel: (1) 614 728 4421
Email: katie.davis@oac.ohio.gov

Omohundro Institute of Early American History and Culture

Omohundro Institute, P.O. Box 8781, Williamsburg, VA 23187-8781, United States of America.

Tel: (1) 757 221 1114
Email: OIdirector@wm.edu; oieahc@wm.edu
Website: oieahc.wm.edu/
Contact: Karin Wulf, Executive Director

Our scope encompasses the history and cultures of North America from circa 1450 to 1820 and includes related developments in Africa, the British Isles, the Caribbean, Europe, and Latin America. In a rapidly changing academic and economic environment, we promote scholars and their scholarship via our publications, conferences, and fellowships. Through a variety of media and formats we curate conversations among junior and senior scholars and a broad range of interested intellectuals.

Omohundro Institute-NEH Postdoctoral Fellowship

Purpose: The Omohundro Institute of Early American History & Culture (OI) offers an expanded residential postdoctoral fellowship program in any area of early American studies and funded by a grant from the National Endowment of the Humanities' Fellowship Programs at Independent Research Institutions (FPIRI) program
Eligibility: Applicants must have met all requirements for the doctorate, including a successful defense, by the application deadline. Foreign nationals must have been in continuous residence in the United States for the three years immediately preceding the date of application for the fellowship in order to be eligible for NEH funding.
Level of Study: Postdoctorate
Type: Fellowship
Value: US$5,000 per month
Length of Study: 1 Year
Frequency: Annual
Study Establishment: Omohundro Institute
Country of Study: United States of America
Application Procedure: The following documents in PDF format in order to complete your application 1. Curriculum Vitae. 2. Abstract (a one-paragraph summary of your project). 3. Statement of proposed work (4 to 7 pages). 4. Manuscript (up to 100 pages). 5. Three references. You will need to provide contact information for the three scholars who have agreed to serve as references for you. All letters of recommendation should be addressed to Chair, OI-NEH Postdoctoral Fellowship Committee and sent by email to oieahc@wm.edu. Apply online oieahc.wm.edu/postdoctoral-fellowship-application/
No. of awards offered: 2
Closing Date: 15 November
Funding: Foundation
Contributor: Omohundro Institute and National Endowment of the Humanities
Additional Information: For more information: oieahc.wm.edu/fellowships/neh/

For further information contact:

P.O. Box 8781, Williamsburg, VA 23187-8781, United States of America.

Email: oieahc@wm.edu

Oncology Nursing Society Foundation (ONS)

125 Enterprise Drive, Pittsburgh, PA 15275-1214, United States of America.

Tel: (1) 866 257 4667
Email: info@onfgivesback.org
Website: www.onsfoundation.org/
Contact: Director of Research

The mission of the ONS is to support cancer nursing excellence. The ONS is a national public, non-profit, tax-exempt, charitable organization dedicated to oncology nurses from around the world. This funding has translated to career development awards, academic scholarships, research grants, a myriad of specialized educational initiatives, as well as nurse wellness support.

Doctoral Scholarships

Purpose: To provide scholarships to registered nurses who are interested in and committed to oncology nursing to continue their education by pursuing a research doctoral degree (PhD or DNSc) or clinical doctoral degree (DNP).
Eligibility: 1. The candidate must be currently enrolled in (or applying to) a Ph.D. or DNP nursing degree program for the forthcoming academic year. 2. The candidate must have a current license to practice as a registered nurse and must have a commitment to oncology nursing. 3. The candidate must provide a letter of reference from the current work supervisor or academic advisor on organizational letterhead, signed by the individual providing recommendation. The letter must address the applicant's ability to perform doctoral-level work.
Level of Study: Doctorate
Type: Scholarship
Value: US$5,000 and US$7,500
Frequency: Dependent on funds available
Country of Study: Any country
Application Procedure: Two professional letters of support are required. One of these letters must address the applicant's ability to perform doctoral level work. Apply Online. Required Submit US$5 application fee (www.ons.org/store/oncology-nursing-foundation-academic-scholarship-application-fee) payable to Oncology Nursing Foundation through ONS. www.onsfoundation.org/funding-for-nurses/education/doctoral-scholarships
Closing Date: 30 January

For further information contact:

Tel: (1) 866 257 4667
Email: info@onfgivesback.org

Master's Scholarships

Purpose: To provide scholarships to registered nurses who are interested in and committed to oncology nursing to continue their education by pursuing a master's degree in nursing.
Eligibility: 1. The candidate must be enrolled in (or applying to) a master's degree program at an accredited institution in the forthcoming academic year. and in good academic standing 2. The candidate must be a registered nurse. 3. The candidate must have a commitment to oncology nursing 4. The candidate must provide a letter of reference.
Level of Study: Masters Degree
Type: Scholarship
Value: US$5,000 each
Frequency: Dependent on funds available
Country of Study: Any country
Application Procedure: Required Submit a US$5 application fee made payable to Oncology Nursing Foundation through ONS. www.ons.org/store/oncology-nursing-foundation-academic-scholarship-application-fee?pk_vid=df085644dbc1665116430923107b580c
Closing Date: 30 January
No. of awards given last year: 39

For further information contact:

Tel: (1) 866 257 4667
Email: info@onfgivesback.org

Oncology Doctoral Scholarships

Purpose: To provide scholarships to registered nurses who are committed to oncology nursing to continue their education by pursuing a research doctoral degree (Ph.D.) or clinical doctoral degree (DNP).
Eligibility: 1. The applicant must be currently enrolled in, accepted to, or have applied to a Ph.D. or DNP nursing degree program at an accredited institution in the forthcoming academic year. 2. The candidate must be in good academic standing. 3. The candidate must be a registered nurse. 4. The candidate must have a commitment to oncology. 5. The candidate must provide a letter of reference from the current work supervisor or academic advisor on organizational letterhead, signed by the individual providing the recommendation. 6. Agree to participate in a post-graduation survey.

Level of Study: Doctorate
Type: Scholarship
Value: US$7,500
Frequency: Annual
Country of Study: United States of America
Application Procedure: 1. Email grants@onfgivesback.org with any questions. 2. All questions must be submitted to the Foundation prior to 4:30 pm Eastern Time on the day of the application due date in order to receive a response prior to the deadline. 3. No late applications will be accepted, and all applications must be submitted through the application platform.
Closing Date: 1 February
Funding: Foundation, Private
Additional Information: www.onsfoundation.org/funding-for-nurses/education/doctoral-scholarships

Oncology Nursing Society Breast Cancer Research Grant

Purpose: To increase breast cancer awareness in communities by supporting nurse-directed and community-focused educational programs.
Eligibility: 1. Program must be an ONS Chapter activity and focus on community education. 2. Grant is not intended to support work-based community education programs. Program cannot limit attendance to an institution, hospital, or hospital network, or nurse work setting. 3. Individual programs and/or Chapters can only receive one grant.
Level of Study: Research
Type: Grant
Value: Up to US$1,000
Frequency: Annual
Country of Study: United States of America
Application Procedure: Apply Online. First-time users must create an account using the link below. Returning users may access the application directly. 1. Register by creating a username and password on the Closerware Grantmaker site. 2. Access the online application. www.closerware.com/intake/bo/grant/ApplicationEdit.do?ownerKey=onsf&intakeFormId=36&opportunityId=8295
Funding: Foundation
Contributor: ONS Foundation
Additional Information: Open applications accepted but must be received by the Oncology Nursing Foundation no later than two weeks prior to the program start date. Applications will remain open until funds are expended. For more details please refer: www.onfgivesback.org/funding-nurses/chapter-funding/breast-cancer-community-education-grants-ons-chapters

For further information contact:

125 Enterprise Drive, Pittsburgh, PA 15275, United States of America.

Email: info@onfgivesback.org

Oncology Nursing Society Foundation Research Grant Awards

Purpose: To support oncology nursing research addressing cancer health disparities, including in the topic areas of breast, colorectal, lung or prostate cancer. To support oncology nursing research in symptom science addressing the adverse effects of immunotherapy and emerging therapies used in the treatment of cancer patients. Symptom science in immunotherapy and emerging therapies has been identified as one of the top cancer nursing research priorities in need of new knowledge.
Eligibility: The principal investigator must be a registered nurse actively involved in some aspect of cancer patient care, education or research and be PhD or DNSc prepared that has received and completed at least one research study of at least US$50,000 as PI.
Level of Study: Postgraduate
Type: Grant
Value: Grant up to US$100,000 will be awarded with funding period of up to two years for Addressing Cancer Health Disparities Through Evidence-Based Cancer Nursing Research. Grant up to US$150,000 will be awarded with funding period of up to two years for Addressing the Adverse Effects of Immunotherapy and Emerging Therapies on Cancer Patients
Frequency: Annual
Country of Study: United States of America
Application Procedure: Apply online www.onsfoundation.org/funding-for-nurses/research/research-grant
Closing Date: 17 May
Funding: Foundation
Additional Information: For more information, contact the ONS Foundation Research Department www.onsfoundation.org/funding-for-nurses/research/research-grant

For further information contact:

Email: info@onfgivesback.org

Oncology Research Grant

Purpose: To support rigorous scientific oncology nursing research. Research projects may include investigator-initiated research, pilot or feasibility studies, supplements to current

funded projects, or developing a new aspect of a program of research. Funding preference is given to projects that involve nurses in the design and conduct of the research activity and that promote theoretically based oncology practice.
Eligibility: The principal investigator (individual primarily responsible for implementing the proposal and reporting to Oncology Nursing Foundation) must be a registered nurse actively involved in some aspect of cancer patient care, education, or research and be PhD or DNSc prepared (only one PI can appear on the grant).
Level of Study: Graduate
Type: Research grant
Value: US$50,000 over 2 years. At least one member of the research team must have received and completed research study funding of at least US$100,000 as PI
Frequency: Annual
Country of Study: Any country
Application Procedure: Apply online www.onsfoundation.org/funding-for-nurses/research/research-grant
Closing Date: 15 April
Funding: Private

For further information contact:

Tel: (1) 866 257 4667
Email: info@onfgivesback.org

Sandy Purl Mentorship Scholarship

Purpose: To support an additional ONS Chapter member to attend the ONS Chapter Leadership Workshop.
Eligibility: 1. Must be a current ONS Chapter Board or committee member supported by a Chapter Leader Sponsor. (A Chapter Leader Sponsor is a current Chapter Board member who has agreed that the applicant has the approval of the Chapter to attend). 2. Chapter Leaders Sponsors may support more than one individual, however the grant is restricted to support only one individual. 3. Applicants must share their goal for attending the Chapter Leadership Workshop and how they plan to use the information they gained by attending. Applicants must identify the other Chapter member who is attending the Chapter Leadership Workshop
Level of Study: Graduate
Type: Scholarship
Value: Up to US$1,000
Frequency: Annual
Country of Study: Any country
Application Procedure: Apply online www.onfgivesback.org/apply-now. Kindly view the following link for further details www.onfgivesback.org/funding-nurses/chapter-funding/sandy-purl-mentorship-scholarship
Closing Date: 15 May
Funding: Private
Additional Information: Note: An individual cannot receive this award more than one time. www.onfgivesback.org/funding-nurses/chapter-funding/sandy-purl-mentorship-scholarship

For further information contact:

Email: info@onfgivesback.org

Ontario Council on Graduate Studies (OCGS)

Council of Ontario Universities, 180 Dundas St West, Suite 1800, Toronto, ON M5G 1Z8, Canada.

Tel: (1) 416 979 2165
Email: contact@ontariosuniversities.ca
Website: cou.ca/members-groups/affiliates/ocav/ocgs/
Contact: Katarina Todic, Senior Policy Analyst, Policy and Sector Collaboration

The Council of Ontario Universities (COU) provides a forum for Ontario's universities to collaborate and advocate in support of their shared mission to the benefit and prosperity of students, communities and the province of Ontario.

Ontario Graduate Scholarship (OGS)

Purpose: The Scholarships are designed to encourage excellence in graduate studies at the master's and doctoral levels.
Eligibility: 1. Plan to be enrolled full-time in a graduate program at an Ontario university 2. Canadian citizen, permanent resident or an international student studying on a study permit 3. A- (80%) average over the last two years of study if less than two years of graduate work OR the cumulative graduate average, if more than two years 4. Have not exceeded the lifetime maximum of 6 years of government-funded awards including OGS, and awards from CIHR, NSERC and SSHRC
Level of Study: Doctorate, Masters Degree, Postdoctorate
Type: Scholarship
Value: CA$15,000
Application Procedure: Application Form: www.nipissingu.ca/sites/default/files/2022-10/OGS%20application%202023-2024%20Full%20-%20All%20Pages-v1_1.pdf. Students applying to or currently enrolled in a graduate program at Nipissing will apply using the application form above and submit all documents to sgs@nipissingu.ca

Closing Date: 13 January
Contributor: Ontario Ministry of Training, Colleges and Universities and Nipissing University
Additional Information: website: www.nipissingu.ca/academics/school-graduate-studies/awards-and-funding/types-funding/ogs

For further information contact:

Email: sgs@nipissingu.ca
Website: www.nipissingu.ca/sites/default/files/2022-10/OGS%20application%202023-2024%20Full%20-%20All%20Pages-v1_1.pdf

Ontario Graduate Scholarship (OGS) Program

Purpose: The Ontario Graduate Scholarship (OGS) Program recognizes academic excellence in graduate studies at the master's and doctoral levels in all disciplines of academic study. The program is jointly supported by funds provided by the Ministry of Training, College and Universities ('ministry') and funds provided by the University of Guelph. The ministry contributes two-thirds of the value of the award and the university provides one-third.
Eligibility: 1. Be registered or intend to register in an eligible program on a full-time basis. 2. Be registered or intend to register full-time in the Summer, Fall, or Winter semester following the OGS application deadline. 3. Have not exceeded the lifetime maximum of government-funded support or maximum OGS support available for their current level of study (see Maximum Support) 4. Master's students must have completed, as of December 31 prior to the application deadline, between zero and 12 months of full-time studies at the master's level. Visit website for more information: graduatestudies.uoguelph.ca/current/funding/scholarships/gov-fundedawards/ogs
Level of Study: Doctorate, Graduate, Masters Degree
Type: Scholarship
Value: The OGS is valued at CA$15,000 for one year. A recipient will be awarded CA$5,000 per semester for up to three semesters.
Length of Study: 1 Year
Application Procedure: A complete OGS application consists of the following: 1. A complete OGS Application Form, submitted to your Graduate Program Assistant via email. As we all continue to work remotely, mailed or other hard copies will NOT be accepted. 2. Two (2) Academic Assessments, submitted directly by your referees to your Graduate Program Assistant via email, from the referees' official institutional or corporate email addresses (i.e., assessments may not be submitted from gmail, hotmail or similar email accounts). As previously noted, assessments must be e-mailed directly to the Graduate Program Assistant, and mailed or other hard copies will not be accepted. 3. Students not currently registered in a graduate program at Guelph must submit a complete application for admission to a graduate program at Guelph prior to the OGS application deadline; it takes quite some time to fully complete an application for admission, so please start your admission application well in advance of the OGS deadline. 4. Current University of Guelph master's students applying for doctoral funding who are not eligible as master's applicants must also submit a online OUAC application for admission to a doctoral program.
Closing Date: 31 January
Contributor: Ministry of Training, College and Universities, University of Guelph
Additional Information: Website: graduatestudies.uoguelph.ca/current/funding/scholarships/gov-fundedawards/ogs

Ontario Women's Health Scholars Award

Purpose: The community of women's health scholars fostered by this Awards program will excel, according to internationally accepted standards of scientific excellence, in the creation of new knowledge about women's health and its translation into improved health for women, more effective health services and products for women, and a strengthened heath care system.
Eligibility: See website: cou.ca/wp-content/uploads/2022/09/OWHS-Awards-Announcement-2023-24-English.pdf
Level of Study: Doctorate, Masters Degree, Postdoctorate
Type: Award
Value: 1. Master's Awards - CA$25,000 plus CA$1,000 research allowance. 2. Doctoral Awards - CA$35,000 plus CA$2,000 research allowance. 3. Postdoctoral Awards - CA$50,000 plus CA$5,000 research allowance.
Frequency: Annual
Country of Study: Canada
Application Procedure: Application Form: cou.ca/wp-content/uploads/2022/09/OWHS-Awards-Application-2023-24-English-Electronic-form.pdf
No. of awards offered: 8
Closing Date: 1 December
Funding: Government
Contributor: Ontario Ministry of Health and Long-Term Care
No. of awards given last year: 9
Additional Information: If you wish to enquire about any aspect of the Ontario Women's Health Scholars Awards, send an email to ExecDirectorQA@cou.ca or call 416-979-2165, extension 235. Note: In our experience, most applicant questions can be answered by reading the announcement; we do

not provide advice on improving an application, or provide feedback on an application. Please see the website for further details cou.ca/resources/awards/

For further information contact:

Tel: (1) 416 979 2165 ext 235
Email: SeniorDirectorQA@cou.ca

Ontario Federation of Anglers & Hunters (OFAH)

4601 Guthrie Drive, PO Box 2800, Peterborough, ON K9J 8L5, Canada.

Email: ofah@ofah.org
Website: www.ofah.org/

OFAH is, Canada's largest nonprofit, charitable fish and wildlife conservation organization. It strives ensure the protection of our hunting and fishing heritage and the enhancement of hunting and fishing opportunities; encourage safe and responsible participation; and champion the conservation of Ontario's fish and wildlife resources.

OFAH/Fleming College Fish & Wildlife Scholarship

Eligibility: The OFAH/Fleming College Fish & Wildlife Scholarship is open to Fleming College students who: 1. are in their final year of the Fish and Wildlife Program (Technician or Technology Graduate). 2. are continuing further studies in a related University Degree or College Diploma program (e.g. third-year Fish and Wildlife Technology, or Ontario College Graduates Certificates – Aquaculture, and Conservation and Environmental Law Enforcement Programs, etc.). 3. have a minimum GPA of 3.0.
Level of Study: Graduate
Type: Scholarship
Value: CA$2,000
Frequency: Annual
Country of Study: Canada
Application Procedure: Scholarship website: www.ofah.org/wp-content/uploads/2023/01/OFAH-FC-scholarship-outline-and-application.pdf
Closing Date: 26 February
Additional Information: www.ofah.org/programs/ofah-student-research-grants/reader-sportsmens-fleming-scholarship/

For further information contact:

Tel: (1) 705 748 6324 Ext 240
Email: chris_robinson@ofah.org

Ontario Federation of Anglers & Hunters/Oakville and District Rod & Gun Club Conservation Research Grant

Purpose: The OFAH is committed to supporting students and their research, which provides the science needed to inform and support sound fish and wildlife conservation management in Ontario. Preference will be given to projects utilizing the funds for equipment and field support.
Eligibility: Any graduate or post-graduate university student currently researching a fish and wildlife topic, and whose findings would benefit Ontario's fish and/or wildlife management.
Level of Study: Research
Type: Research grant
Value: CA$4,000
Frequency: Annual
Country of Study: Canada
Application Procedure: Apply online www.ofah.org/programs/ofah-student-research-grants/
Closing Date: 12 February
Additional Information: For more details: www.ofah.org/programs/ofah-student-research-grants/

For further information contact:

Ontario Federation of Anglers & Hunters, PO Box 2800 / 4601 Guthrie Dr, Peterborough, ON K9J 8L5, Canada.

Tel: (1) 705 748 6324

Ontario Ministry of Education and Training

Ministry of Education, 315 Front Street, 14th Floor, Toronto, Ontario M7A 0B8, Canada.

Tel: (1) 416 325 2929
Email: Ingrid.E.Anderson@ontario.ca
Website: www.ontario.ca/page/education-and-training
Contact: Ingrid Anderson, Communications Branch

Ontario Ministry of Education and Training works to make Ontario's publicly funded education and child care systems the world's best, where all children and students have the opportunity to achieve success.

Ontario Ministry of Education and Training Graduate Scholarship Programme

Purpose: OGS is a merit-based scholarship. Students in graduate studies at the master's and doctoral levels can apply for a merit-based scholarship through the Ontario Graduate Scholarship (OGS) Program. Awards are available to graduate students for all disciplines of academic study at participating schools in Ontario.
Eligibility: 1. You'll be in graduate studies in the master's or doctoral level. 2. You'll be enrolled in a full-time program for 2 or more terms (21 to 52 weeks in total) for the academic year you're submitting your application. 3. You'll be attending one of the participating Ontario school in following link osap.gov.on.ca/OSAPPortal/en/A-ZListofAid/PRDR019245.html
Level of Study: Doctorate, Masters Degree
Type: Scholarship
Value: CA$10,000 for 2 consecutive study terms and CA$15,000 for 3 consecutive study terms.
Frequency: Annual
Study Establishment: A university in Ontario
Country of Study: Canada
Application Procedure: Use your school's OGS application. They are normally available in October. If you're applying to more than one graduate program at different schools, submit an OGS application for each school. Contact the Graduate Studies Office: cou.ca/resources/graduate-studies/ at the school you're planning to attend for details on their application process.
Funding: Government
Contributor: Province of Ontario (two thirds) and the school offering the award (one third)
Additional Information: website: osap.gov.on.ca/OSAPPortal/en/A-ZListofAid/PRDR019245.html

Ontario Student Assistance Program (OSAP)

Student Financial Assistance Branch, Ministry of Colleges and Universities, PO Box 4500, 189 Red River Road, 4th Floor, Thunder Bay, ON P7B 6G9, Canada.

Tel: (1) 807 343 7260
Email: webmaster.tcu@ontario.ca
Website: www.ontario.ca/page/osap-ontario-student-assistance-program

Minister of Education and the Minister of Training, Colleges and Universities are responsible for the administration of laws relating to education and skills training in Ontario.

Ontario Graduate Scholarship Program

Purpose: Students in graduate studies at the master's and doctoral levels can apply for a merit-based scholarship through the Ontario Graduate Scholarship (OGS) Program. Each award is jointly funded by the Province of Ontario (two thirds) and the school offering the award (one third).
Eligibility: Candidates must be citizens or permanent residents of Canada. To be considered, you must also meet the following criteria 1. You'll be in graduate studies in the master's or doctoral level. 2. You'll be enrolled in a full-time program for 2 or more terms (21 to 52 weeks in total) for the academic year you're submitting your application. 3. You'll be attending one of the participating Ontario school in website
Level of Study: Doctorate, Masters Degree, Postgraduate
Type: Scholarships
Value: CA$10,000 for 2 consecutive study terms and CA$15,000 for 3 consecutive study terms.
Length of Study: Master's students 2 academic years; Doctoral students 4 academic years; Lifetime limit (all students) 6 academic years
Frequency: Annual
Country of Study: Canada
Application Procedure: Use your school's OGS application. They are normally available in October. If you're applying to more than one graduate program at different schools, submit an OGS application for each school. Contact the Graduate Studies Office (cou.ca/resources/graduate-studies/) at the school you're planning to attend for details on their application process
Funding: Government, Private
Additional Information: For more details: osap.gov.on.ca/OSAPPortal/en/A-ZListofAid/PRDR020870.html

Open Society Foundation - Sofia

56 Solunska Str., BG-1000 Sofia, Bulgaria.

Tel: (359) 2 930 6619
Email: info@osi.bg
Website: osis.bg/?page_id=849&lang=en
Contact: Ms Iliana Bobova, Education Consultant

Open Society Institute – Sofia is a non-governmental organization, acting for the public benefit, defending the values of

O

the open society in Bulgaria and supporting the integration of the country to the European Union. The Institute was founded to promote, develop and support the values, dispositions and practices of the open society in Bulgaria.

Open Society Institute's Global Supplementary Grant Program (Grant SGP)

Purpose: To enable qualified students to pursue doctoral studies in the humanities and social sciences
Eligibility: Open to candidates from selected countries from Eastern and Central Europe and the former Soviet Union. Bulgarian nationals under the age of 40 who have been accepted into a full-time doctoral programme at an accredited university in Western Europe, Asia, Australia or North America and have already been awarded partial or full tuition, room and board stipends or other types of financial aid are also eligible
Level of Study: Doctorate
Type: Grant
Value: 50% of tuition and fees or living expenses or additional expenses
Length of Study: Up to 1 year of study with the option to apply for a second year
Frequency: Annual
Study Establishment: Accredited universities
Country of Study: Other
Application Procedure: Applicants must complete an application form and provide the required supporting documents
Closing Date: 1 April
Funding: Private
Contributor: The Open Society Institute in New York
No. of awards given last year: 22
Additional Information: Programme availability and format are reviewed on an annual basis. Changes may occur from year to year. For the most up to date information please contact the Open Society Institute in New York www.european-funding-guide.eu/scholarship/12229-open-society-foundations%C2%A0-%E2%80%93-global-supplementary-grant-program

For further information contact:

Open Society Institute, Network Scholarship Programs, 400 West 59th Street, New York, NY 10019, United States of America.

Tel: (1) 212 548 0175
Fax: (1) 212 548 4652
Email: vjohnson@sorosny.org

Oxford Colleges Hospitality Scheme for East European Scholars

Purpose: To enable overseas scholars to work in Oxford or Cambridge libraries or to consult Oxbridge specialists in their subjects
Eligibility: Open to Scholars from Eastern and Central Europe, who have a good knowledge of English and who are in the process of completing work for an advanced degree, or who are working on a book, or a new course of lectures
Level of Study: Professional development
Type: Scholarship
Value: Full scholarship
Length of Study: 1–3 months
Frequency: Annual
Study Establishment: The University of Oxford and the University of Cambridge
Country of Study: United Kingdom
Application Procedure: Applicants must submit a completed application form, a curriculum vitae, a list of publications and two recommendation letters
No. of awards offered: 45
Closing Date: November
Funding: Government, Private
Contributor: FCO, OSI-Budapest, University of Oxford
No. of awards given last year: 7
No. of applicants last year: 45
Additional Information: Programme availability and format are reviewed on an annual basis. Changes may occur from year to year. For the most up to date information, please contact the Open Society Institute in Budapest www.eac.md/scholarships/soros/oxford_hospitality/index.html

For further information contact:

Open Society Institute, Network Scholarship Programmes, Nador Utca 11, H-1051 Budapest, Hungary.

Email: mariefergusonsmith@hotmail.com

Soros Equality Fellowship

Purpose: Open Society-U.S.'s Soros Equality Fellowship seeks to support emerging midcareer professionals whom we believe will become long-term innovative leaders impacting racial justice.
Eligibility: Applicants must be able to devote at least 35 hours per week to the project if awarded a Fellowship; and the project must be the applicant's only full-time work during the course of the Fellowship.
Type: Fellowship

Value: US$130,000 stipend
Length of Study: 18 months
Country of Study: Any country
Application Procedure: See www.opensocietyfoundations.org/uploads/423f3678-1988-4ed7-8e19-702da82e2ee9/2022-soros-equality-fellowship-guidelines-20211129.pdf
Closing Date: 14 February
Funding: Individuals

For further information contact:

Email: equality.fellowships@opensocietyfoundations.org

Soros Justice Fellowships

Purpose: Open Society-U.S.'s Soros Justice Fellowships fund outstanding individuals to undertake projects that advance reform, spur debate, and catalyze change on a range of issues facing the U.S. criminal justice system.
Eligibility: All projects must, at a minimum, relate to one or more of the following U.S. criminal justice reform goals reducing the number of people who are incarcerated or under correctional control, challenging extreme punishment, and promoting fairness and accountability in our systems of justice. Please carefully review the complete guidelines for more details on the specific requirements for each category of fellowships.
Type: Fellowship
Frequency: Annual
Country of Study: United States of America
Application Procedure: Applications must be submitted online via the application
Closing Date: 8 February
Funding: Individuals

For further information contact:

Email: sorosjusticefellowships@opensocietyfoundations.org

Organization for Autism Research (OAR)

2111 Wilson Boulevard, Suite 401, Arlington, VA 22201, United States of America.

Tel: (1) 866 366 9710
Email: info@researchautism.org
Website: researchautism.org/
Contact: 2111 Wilson Boulevard, Suite 401 Arlington, VA 22201

OAR was founded in December 2001 by seven individuals whose lives and families had been directly impacted by autism. The studies we fund and the information resources we provide have meaning in the day-to-day lives of autistic people and those who support them personally and professionally. Rather than fund research on what causes autism, we fund studies on topics of more everyday relevance such as education, parent and teacher training, communication, self-care, social skills, employment, behavior, and adult and community issues.

Applied Research Competition

Purpose: OAR seeks to fund studies that expand the body of knowledge related to autism intervention and treatment, produce practical and clearly objective results, have the potential to positively affect public policy, and provide outcomes that offer to enhance quality of life for persons with autism and their families.
Eligibility: At least one member of the research team must hold a Ph.D., M.D., or equivalent degree and maintain a faculty position or equivalent at a college, university, medical school, or other research facility. International researchers are eligible to apply.
Level of Study: Doctorate, Postgraduate
Type: Grant
Value: Grant awards for US$40,000 each
Length of Study: 1-2 year
Frequency: Annual
Application Procedure: This application is available online at: researchautism.smapply.org/prog/2023_applied_research_competition/
No. of awards offered: 8
Closing Date: 20 March
Additional Information: Website: researchautism.org/research-grants/apply-for-a-grant/applied-research/

For further information contact:

Tel: (1) 703 243 9762
Email: research@researchautism.org

Organization of American Historians (OAH)

Data Protection Officer, Organization of American Historians, 112 North Bryan Avenue, Bloomington, Indiana 47408-4141, United States of America.

Tel: (1) 812 855 7311
Email: oah@oah.org
Website: www.oah.org/

O

OAH is the largest professional society dedicated to the teaching and study of American history. The mission of the organization is to promote excellence in the scholarship, teaching, and presentation of American history, and to encourage wide discussion of historical questions and the equitable treatment of all practitioners of history.

ALA Library History Round Table Davis Article Award

Subjects: The round table is particularly interested in articles that place the subject within its broader historical, social, cultural, and political context and make interdisciplinary connections with print culture and information studies.
Purpose: The Library History Round Table (LHRT) of the American Library Association (ALA) invites submissions for the Donald G. Davis Article Award. The Davis Award is given every even-numbered year to the best article written in English in the field of United States and Canadian library history.
Type: Award
Frequency: Annual
Country of Study: Any country
No. of awards offered: 1
Closing Date: 15 February
Additional Information: Website: www.oah.org/insights/opportunities-for-historians/ala-library-history-round-table-davis-article-award/

For further information contact:

Email: julie8park@gmail.com

Avery O. Craven Award

Purpose: Since 1985, the Avery O. Craven Award has been presented annually by the OAH for the most original book on the coming of the Civil War, the Civil War years, or the Era of Reconstruction, with the exception of works of purely military history.
Eligibility: Each entry must be published during the period mentioned in the website.
Type: Award
Frequency: Annual
Country of Study: Any country
Application Procedure: One copy of each entry, clearly labeled must be mailed directly to the committee members listed below. Each committee member must receive all submissions. Applicants must visit the website www.oah.org/awards/book-awards/civil-war-and-reconstruction-award/
Closing Date: 1 October
No. of awards given last year: 1
Additional Information: For more information www.oah.org/awards/book-awards/avery-o-craven-award/. www.oah.org/awards/book-awards/civil-war-and-reconstruction-award/

For further information contact:

Diane Miller Sommerville, Committee Chair, 18 East Country Gate Place, Vestal, NY 13850, United States of America.

China Residency Program

Purpose: Thanks to a generous grant from the Ford Foundation, the Organization of American Historians and the American History Research Association of China (AHRAC) are pleased to announce the third year of the teaching seminars in the People's Republic of China
Eligibility: The OAH International Committee seeks applications from OAH members with strong records of research and teaching excellence who are interested in leading an advanced seminar in the People's Republic of China, focused on one of the following three topics constitutional history, cultural/gender history or history of the American West
Level of Study: Research
Type: Residency
Length of Study: 3 week-long intensive seminars
Frequency: Annual
Country of Study: United States of America
Application Procedure: The application consists of a short (3–5 pages) curriculum vitae, the name and contact information of 3 references who can speak to the applicant's teaching and scholarship, and an outline of the proposed intensive week-long seminar. Applications should be submitted electronically, in Microsoft Word format, to prizes@oah.org. Please indicate, China Residency Program in the subject line. If you do not receive an email confirmation that your application has been received within 3 days, please contact the OAH Committee Coordinator at khamm@oah.org
Additional Information: www.oah.org/programs/residencies/china/

Civil War and Reconstruction Book Award

Purpose: The Civil War and Reconstruction Book Award is given annually by the Organization of American Historians to the author of the most original book on the coming of the Civil War, the Civil War years, or the Era of Reconstruction.
Level of Study: Graduate
Type: Award
Value: US$500

Frequency: Annual
Country of Study: Any country
Application Procedure: One copy of each entry, clearly labeled "2024 Civil War and Reconstruction Book Award Entry," must be mailed directly to the committee members listed below. Each committee member must receive all submissions postmarked by October 1, 2023.
No. of awards offered: 1
Closing Date: 1 October
No. of awards given last year: 1
No. of applicants last year: 42
Additional Information: Website: www.oah.org/awards/book-awards/civil-war-and-reconstruction-award/

Darlene Clark Hine Award

Purpose: The Award is given annually by the Organization of American Historians to the author of the best book in African American women's and gender history.
Level of Study: Postgraduate
Type: Award
Value: US$2,000
Frequency: Annual
Country of Study: Any country
No. of awards offered: 1
Closing Date: 1 October
Funding: Private
No. of awards given last year: 1
No. of applicants last year: 20
Additional Information: www.oah.org/awards/book-awards/darlene-clark-hine-award/

David Montgomery Award

Purpose: The Award is given annually by the OAH with co-sponsorship by the Labor and Working-Class History Association (LAWCHA) for the best book on a topic in American labor and working-class history.
Eligibility: Eligible works shall be written in English and deal with United States history in significant ways but may include comparative or transnational studies that fall within these guidelines.
Type: Award
Value: US$500
Frequency: Annual
Country of Study: Any country
Application Procedure: One copy of each entry, clearly labeled "2024 David Montgomery Award Entry," must be mailed directly to the committee members listed below. Each committee member must receive all submissions postmarked by October 1, 2023.
No. of awards offered: 1
Closing Date: 1 October
No. of awards given last year: 1
No. of applicants last year: 35
Additional Information: www.oah.org/awards/book-awards/david-montgomery-award/

For further information contact:

David Roediger, Committee Chair, 1501 Rhode Island, Lawrence, KS 66044, United States of America.

Ellis W. Hawley Prize

Purpose: The Prize is given annually by the Organization of American Historians to the author of the best book-length historical study of the political economy, politics, or institutions of the United States, in its domestic or international affairs, from the Civil War to the present. The prize honors Ellis W. Hawley, Emeritus Professor of History, University of Iowa, an outstanding historian of these subjects.
Type: Prize
Value: US$500
Frequency: Annual
Country of Study: Any country
Application Procedure: One copy of each entry, clearly labeled "2024 Ellis W. Hawley Prize Entry," must be mailed directly to the committee members listed below. Each committee member must receive all submissions postmarked by October 1, 2023.
No. of awards offered: 1
Closing Date: 1 October
Contributor: OAH
No. of awards given last year: 1
No. of applicants last year: 78
Additional Information: For more details please check at www.oah.org/awards/book-awards/ellis-w-hawley-prize/

For further information contact:

Email: eyellin@richmond.edu

Erik Barnouw Award

Purpose: Awards are given annually by the Organization of American Historians in recognition of outstanding programming on television, or in documentary film, concerned with American history, the study of American history, and/or the promotion of American history.
Eligibility: Only films and video programs released January 1 through December 31 are eligible for entry.
Type: Award

O

Value: US$500
Frequency: Annual
Country of Study: Any country
Application Procedure: Applicants should visit the website for complete application requirements. One copy of each entry, clearly labeled must be sent directly to the committee members listed in website. Each committee member must receive all submissions. www.oah.org/awards/uncategorized-awards/erik-barnouw-award/
No. of awards offered: 2
Closing Date: 7 January
No. of awards given last year: 1
No. of applicants last year: 42
Additional Information: Please check at www.oah.org/awards/uncategorized-awards/erik-barnouw-award/

For further information contact:

Daniel Blake Smith (Committee Chair), DBS Films, 5234 Nottingham Avenue, Saint Louis MO 63109-2963, United States of America.

Email: dblakesmitty13@gmail.com; Eduardo.Pagan@asu.edu

Frederick Jackson Turner Award

Purpose: The Frederick Jackson Turner Award is given annually by the Organization of American Historians to the author of a first scholarly book dealing with some aspect of American history.
Eligibility: The rules and terms of the competition are as follows 1. Eligible books must be published during the calendar year preceding that in which the award is given; 2. The author may not have previously published a book-length work of history; 3. Submissions will be made by publishers, who may submit such books as they deem eligible; 4. Co-authored works are eligible, as long as neither author has previously published a book of history; 5. Authors who have previously co-authored a book of history are not eligible.
Type: Award
Value: US$1,000
Frequency: Annual
Country of Study: Any country
Application Procedure: One copy of each entry, clearly labeled "2024 Frederick Jackson Turner Award Entry" must be mailed directly to the committee members listed below and must include a complete list of the author's publications OR a statement from the publisher verifying this is the author's first book. No submission will be considered without this proof of eligibility. Each committee member must receive all submissions postmarked by October 1, 2023.
No. of awards offered: 1
Closing Date: 1 October
No. of awards given last year: 1
No. of applicants last year: 81
Additional Information: Website: www.oah.org/awards/book-awards/frederick-jackson-turner-award/

Germany Residency Program

Purpose: Thanks to a generous grant from the Fritz Thyssen Foundation, the OAH International Committee is pleased to announce the continuation of the Residency Program in American History–Germany (Germany Residency Program) at the University of Tübingen
Eligibility: The committee seeks applications from OAH members who are established scholars affiliated with an American or Canadian University interested in leading an advanced undergraduate/graduate student seminar in Tübingen. The seminar will cover a topic of U.S. History or the History of Transatlantic Relations of an applicant's design. All fields and methodologies are welcome. The language of instruction is English.
Type: Residency
Value: The Residency Program will provide round-trip airfare, housing for thirty days, a modest honorarium (around US$1,000), support by a graduate assistant, and office space.
Length of Study: 4 to 5 Weeks
Frequency: Annual
Country of Study: Any country
Application Procedure: The application process for the Germany residency program requires a short CV and an outline of the planned seminar. The application materials must be sent electronically (PDF) to germanyresidency@oah.org. Please indicate "Germany Residency Program" in the subject line.
Closing Date: 1 October
Contributor: OAH
No. of awards given last year: 1
Additional Information: For more details, please visit: www.oah.org/awards/residencies/germany/

For further information contact:

Email: georg.schild@uni-tuebingen.de

Huggins-Quarles Award

Purpose: For graduate students of color to assist them with expenses related to travel to research collections for the completion of the PhD dissertation. These awards were established to promote greater diversity in the historical profession.

Eligibility: 1. applicant must be advanced ABD, minimum 5th year in program. 2. Applicant must be ALANA (African American, Latino/a, Asian American, Native American) scholar. 3. Applicant's dissertation must focus on U.S. history. 4. U.S. residency is not required
Level of Study: Doctorate
Type: Award
Value: US$1,500 for one award/US$750 each for two awards
Frequency: Annual
Country of Study: Any country
Application Procedure: To apply, the student should submit the following items in one PDF document and in the following order 1. cover letter, which should also indicate the candidate's progress on the dissertation, including ABD status. 2. CV. 3. abstract: a five-page dissertation proposal (double spaced), which should include a definition of the project, an explanation of the project's significance and contribution to the field, and a description of the most important primary sources. 4. a one-page itemized budget explaining travel and research plans. Each application must include a letter from the dissertation adviser attesting to the student's status and the ways in which the Huggins-Quarles Award will facilitate the completion of the dissertation project. Advisers should e-mail their letters separately to the committee chair. Please refer www.oah.org/awards/dissertation-awards/huggins-quarles-award/
No. of awards offered: 2
Closing Date: 1 November
No. of awards given last year: 1
No. of applicants last year: 7
Additional Information: Please check at www.oah.org/awards/dissertation-awards/huggins-quarles-award/

For further information contact:

Email: francoise_hamlin@brown.edu

James A. Rawley Prize

Purpose: The Prize is given annually by the Organization of American Historians to the author of the best book dealing with the history of race relations in the United States. The prize is given in memory of Professor James A. Rawley, Carl Adolph Happold Professor of History Emeritus at the University of Nebraska, Lincoln.
Type: Prize
Value: US$1,000
Frequency: Annual
Country of Study: Any country
Application Procedure: One copy of each entry, clearly labeled "2024 James A. Rawley Prize Entry," must be mailed directly to the committee members listed below. Each committee member must receive all submissions postmarked by October 1, 2023.
No. of awards offered: 1
Closing Date: 1 October
Contributor: OAH
No. of awards given last year: 1
No. of applicants last year: 80
Additional Information: Please check at www.oah.org/awards/book-awards/organization-of-american-historians-oah-james-a-rawley-prize/

For further information contact:

Deborah Cohen, Committtee Chair, 3943 Fairview Avenue, St. Louis, MO 63116, United States of America.

Japanese Residencies for United States of America Historians

Purpose: To facilitate scholarly dialogue and contribute to the expansion of scholarly networks among students and professors of American history in both countries.
Eligibility: Applicants must be members of the OAH, have a PhD, and be scholars of American history. Applicants from previous competitions are welcome to apply again.
Level of Study: Postgraduate
Type: Residency
Value: Round-trip airfare to Japan, housing, and modest daily expenses are covered by the award (note: if the host university is unable to provide housing, award recipients are expected to use the daily stipend to pay hotel expenses). Award winners are also encouraged to explore Japan before or after their two-week residency at their own expense.
Length of Study: 2 weeks
Frequency: Annual
Country of Study: Japan
Application Procedure: Please send all materials (in one PDF labeled with your name) and indicate "Japan Residencies Program-[UNIVERSITY NAME]" in the subject line. If you would like to apply for both residencies, please send a separate application for each. 1. A two-page curriculum vitae emphasizing teaching experience and publications. 2. The institution for which you would like to be considered. 3. A personal statement, no longer than two pages, describing your interest in this program and the issues that your own scholarship and teaching have addressed. Please devote one or two paragraphs to why you understand this residency to be central to your development as a scholar in the world community. You may include comments on any previous collaboration or work with non-U.S. academics or students. If you wish, you may comment on your particular interest in Japan. 4. A letter of recommendation, to be solicited by the applicant

and sent directly by the recommender to OAH (japanresidency@oah.org), which should also address the applicant's teaching skill. The subject line of the e-mail should say "Recommendation for [NAME OF APPLICANT]."
No. of awards offered: 2
Closing Date: 1 October
Additional Information: For more detials, please visit: www.oah.org/awards/residencies/japan/

For further information contact:

Email: japanresidency@oah.org

John D'Emilio LGBTQ History Dissertation Award

Purpose: This Award is given annually by the Organization of American Historians to the best PhD dissertation in U.-S. LGBTQ history. The award is named for John D'Emilio, pioneer in LGBTQ history.
Type: Award
Value: US$500
Length of Study: 1 Year
Frequency: Annual
Country of Study: Any country
Application Procedure: Please send an electronic attachment (PDF) of your complete dissertation, abstract, and table of contents in one e-mail to the committee members listed below. The subject line should be "2024 John D'Emilio LGBTQ History Dissertation Award.
No. of awards offered: 1
Closing Date: 1 October
No. of awards given last year: 1
No. of applicants last year: 9
Additional Information: Website: www.oah.org/awards/dissertation-awards/john-demilio-lgbtq-history-dissertation-award/#:~:text=The%20John%20D'Emilio%20LGBTQ,Emilio%2C%20pioneer%20in%20LGBTQ%20history.

John Higham Research Fellowship

Purpose: This fellowship is open to all graduate students writing doctoral dissertations for a PhD in American history. Applicants pursuing research in those fields most congenial to the research and writing interests of John Higham will receive special consideration
Level of Study: Graduate
Type: Fellowship
Value: US$3,000
Frequency: Annual
Country of Study: Any country
Application Procedure: Applications should include the following components 1. Project proposal of no more than 1,000 words describing the applicant's research project and detailing how the funds will be used. 2. An updated curriculum vitae with a list of the names and addresses of references. 3. Two signed letters of recommendation on official letterhead submitted independently by referees. Letters in the form of a signed PDF should be e-mailed to the chair of the John Higham Research Fellowship Committee at the address listed below. We ask that recommenders use the subject line "Recommendation for [APPLICANT'S NAME].". Complete all application components (including project proposal, names and addresses of recommenders, and curriculum vitae), in a recent version of Microsoft Word or PDF (preferable), and e-mail the entire electronic file to the chair of the John Higham Research Fellowship Committee at the address listed in website. For more details please refer www.oah.org/awards/uncategorized-awards/john-higham-fellowship/
No. of awards offered: 2
Closing Date: 1 November
Funding: Private
No. of awards given last year: 2
No. of applicants last year: 25
Additional Information: Applicants pursuing research in those fields most congenial to the research and writing interests of John Higham will receive special consideration. These topics include U.S. social and intellectual history broadly considered, with preference given to research projects on American immigration and ethnic history as well as American historiography, and the cultural history of the nineteenth-century U.S. www.oah.org/awards/uncategorized-awards/john-higham-fellowship/

For further information contact:

Patrick Chung, University of Maryland, College Park, MD 20742, United States of America.; Julian Lim, Arizona State University, Phoenix, AZ 85004, United States of America.

Tel: (1) 812 855 7311
Email: pchung10@umd.edu

Lawrence W. Levine Award

Purpose: This Award is given annually by the Organization of American Historians to the author of the best book in American cultural history.
Type: Award
Frequency: Annual
Country of Study: Any country

Application Procedure: One copy of each entry, clearly labeled "2024 Lawrence W. Levine Award Entry," must be mailed directly to the committee members listed below. Each committee member must receive all submissions postmarked by October 1, 2023.
Closing Date: 1 October
Additional Information: Please check at www.oah.org/awards/book-awards/lawrence-w-levine-award/

For further information contact:

112 N. Bryan Avenue, Bloomington, IN 47408-4141, United States of America.

Email: kah@umich.edu

Lerner-Scott Prize

Purpose: This Prize is given annually by the Organization of American Historians for the best doctoral dissertation in U.-S. women's history. The prize is named for Gerda Lerner and Anne Firor Scott, both pioneers in women's history and past presidents of the OAH.
Eligibility: See website
Level of Study: Postdoctorate
Type: Award
Value: US$1,000
Frequency: Annual
Country of Study: Any country
Application Procedure: Please send an electronic attachment (PDF) of your complete dissertation (including abstract and table of contents) to the committee chair listed below by midnight (PST) on October 1, 2023 with "2024 OAH Lerner-Scott Prize Entry" in the subject line.
No. of awards offered: 1
Closing Date: 1 October
No. of awards given last year: 1
No. of applicants last year: 12
Additional Information: Website: www.oah.org/awards/dissertation-awards/lerner-scott-prize/

Liberty Legacy Foundation Award

Purpose: Inspired by OAH President Darlene Clark Hine's call in her 2002 OAH presidential address for more research on the origins of the civil rights movement in the period before 1954, this Award is given annually by the Organization of American Historians to the author of the best book by a historian on the civil rights struggle from the beginnings of the nation to the present.
Type: Award
Value: US$2,000
Frequency: Annual
Country of Study: Any country
Application Procedure: One copy of each entry, clearly labeled "2024 Liberty Legacy Foundation Award Entry," must be mailed directly to the committee members listed below. Each committee member must receive all submissions postmarked by October 1, 2023.
No. of awards offered: 1
Closing Date: 1 October
Contributor: OAH
No. of awards given last year: 1
No. of applicants last year: 41
Additional Information: website: www.oah.org/awards/book-awards/liberty-legacy-foundation-award/

Louis Pelzer Memorial Award

Purpose: The Louis Pelzer Memorial Award Committee of the Organization of American Historians invites candidates for graduate degrees to submit essays for the Louis Pelzer Memorial Award competition. Essays may deal with any period or topic in the history of the United States.
Level of Study: Graduate
Type: Award
Value: US$500
Frequency: Annual
Country of Study: Any country
Application Procedure: Essays, including footnotes, should not exceed 10,000 words. An abstract and the electronic version of the essay should be sent to jahms@oah.org with "2024 Louis Pelzer Memorial Award Entry" noted in the subject line, and one hard copy should be submitted to the address below. Because manuscripts are judged anonymously, the author's name and graduate program should appear only on a separate cover page.
No. of awards offered: 1
Closing Date: 1 November
No. of awards given last year: 1
No. of applicants last year: 21
Additional Information: Website: www.oah.org/awards/article-essay-awards/louis-pelzer-memorial-award/

For further information contact:

Benjamin H. Irvin, Executive Editor, OAH/Editor, Journal of American History, Journal of American History, 1215 East Atwater Avenue, Bloomington, IN 47401, United States of America.

Email: jahms@oah.org

Mary Nickliss Prize in United States Women's and/or Gender History

Purpose: This Prize is given for "the most original" book in United States Women's and/or Gender History (including North America and the Caribbean prior to 1776). The best book recognizes the ideas and originality of the significant historical scholarship being done by historians of United States Women's and/or Gender History and makes a significant contribution to the understanding of United States Women's and/or Gender History
Eligibility: Each entry must be published during the calendar year preceding that in which the award is given.
Type: Award
Value: US$1,000
Frequency: Annual
Country of Study: Any country
Application Procedure: One copy of each entry, clearly labeled "Mary Nickliss Prize Entry" must be mailed directly to the committee members listed in website. Each committee member must receive all submissions postmarked by 1 October. If a book carries a copyright date that is different from the publication date, but the actual publication date falls during the correct timeframe making it eligible, please include a letter of explanation from the publisher with each copy of the book sent to the committee members. Applicants should contact by e-mail for mailing address
No. of awards offered: 1
Closing Date: 1 October
No. of awards given last year: 2
No. of applicants last year: 48
Additional Information: www.oah.org/awards/book-awards/mary-nickliss-prize/

For further information contact:

112 N. Bryan Avenue, Bloomington, IN 47408-4141, United States of America.

Email: mchavezgarcia@history.ucsb.edu

Merle Curti Award in American Intellectual History

Purpose: To recognise books in the fields of american social, intellectual, and/or cultural history
Type: Award
Value: US$500
Frequency: Annual
Country of Study: Any country
Application Procedure: Applicants must send a copy of each entry to the committee members. Publishers are urged to enter one or more books in the competition. For further application details, candidates should visit the website
No. of awards offered: 73
Closing Date: 1 October
Contributor: OAH
No. of awards given last year: 1
Additional Information: www.oah.org/awards/book-awards/merle-curti-award-intellectual-history/

Merle Curti Intellectual History Award

Purpose: One award is given annually to the author of the best book in American intellectual history.
Type: Award
Value: US$500
Frequency: Annual
Country of Study: Any country
Application Procedure: One copy of each entry, clearly labeled "2024 Merle Curti Intellectual History Award Entry," must be mailed directly to the committee members listed below. Each committee member must receive all submissions postmarked by October 1, 2023.
No. of awards offered: 1
Closing Date: 1 October
Contributor: OAH
No. of awards given last year: 1
No. of applicants last year: 45
Additional Information: Please check at www.oah.org/awards/book-awards/merle-curti-award-intellectual-history/

Merle Curti Social History Award

Purpose: One award is given annually to the author of the best book in American social history.
Level of Study: Graduate
Type: Award
Value: US$500
Frequency: Annual
Country of Study: Any country
Application Procedure: 1. One copy of each entry, clearly labeled "Merle Curti Social History Award Entry," must be mailed directly to the committee members listed below. Each committee member must receive all submissions postmarked by 1 October. 2. Bound page proofs may be used for books to be published after 1 October and before 1 January. If a bound page proof is submitted, a bound copy of the book must be received by each committee member postmarked no later than 7 January. (Please see "Submission Policy") 3. If a book carries a copyright date that is different from the publication date, but the actual publication date falls during the correct timeframe making it eligible, please include a letter of explanation from the publisher with each copy of the book sent to the committee members.
No. of awards offered: 1

Closing Date: 1 October
Funding: Private
No. of awards given last year: 1
No. of applicants last year: 81
Additional Information: The final decision will be made by the Merle Curti Social History Award Committee by February. The winner will be provided with details regarding the OAH Annual Meeting and awards presentation. www.oah.org/awards/book-awards/merle-curti-award-social-history/

Presidents' Travel Fund

Purpose: The fund provides travel stipends to five graduate students and recent PhDs in history (no more than four years from date of degree) whose papers or panels/sessions have been accepted by the OAH Program Committee for inclusion on the annual meeting program
Eligibility: PhDs in history (no more than four years from date of degree) whose papers or panels/sessions have been accepted by the OAH Program Committeefor inclusion on the OAH Conference on American History program. Preference will be given to those who are presenting at the conference for the first time.
Level of Study: Doctorate, Postgraduate
Type: Travel grant
Value: The fund provides travel stipends of up to US$750
Frequency: Annual
Country of Study: Any country
Application Procedure: Please e-mail your paper title or panel title, with an abstract and a CV (indicating your anticipated year of completion of the PhD or the year your PhD was granted), and a paragraph describing why it is important for you to attend the conference (besides presenting your paper if you are doing so) as a PDF by midnight PST on November 1, 2022 to the OAH Presidents' Travel Fund for Emerging Historians Committee at presidentstravelfund@oah.org.
No. of awards offered: 5
Closing Date: 1 November
Additional Information: For more information: www.oah.org/awards/travel-grants/presidents-travel-fund/

For further information contact:

Email: presidentstravelfund@oah.org

Ray Allen Billington Prize

Purpose: This Prize is awarded biennially by the Organization of American Historians to the author of the best book on the history of native and/or settler peoples in frontier, border, and borderland zones of intercultural contact in any century to the present and to include works that address the legacies of those zones.
Eligibility: Author of the best book on the history of native and/or settler peoples in frontier, border, and borderland zones of intercultural contact in any century to the present and to include works that address the legacies of those zones.
Type: Award
Value: US$1,000
Frequency: Every 2 years
Country of Study: Any country
Application Procedure: Applicants must visit the website www.oah.org/awards/book-awards/ray-allen-billington-prize/
No. of awards offered: 1
Closing Date: 1 October
Contributor: OAH
No. of awards given last year: 1
No. of applicants last year: 62
Additional Information: Please check at www.oah.org/awards/book-awards/ray-allen-billington-prize/

For further information contact:

Andrés Reséndez (Committee Chair), University of California, Davis, Department of History, One Shields Avenue, Davis CA 95616-5270, United States of America.

Email: adubcovs@ucr.edu

Richard W. Leopold Prize

Purpose: This Prize is given biennially by the Organization of American Historians to the author or editor of the best book on foreign policy, military affairs, historical activities of the federal government, documentary histories, or biography written by a U.S. government historian or federal contract historian.
Eligibility: U.S Government or Federal Contract Historians (current or former)
Type: Prize
Value: US$1,500
Frequency: Every 2 years (even-numbered years)
Country of Study: Any country
Application Procedure: Verification of current or past employment with the U.S. government (in the form of a letter or e-mail sent to the publisher from the office that employs or has employed the author) must be included with each entry for the Leopold Prize. One copy of each entry, clearly labeled "2024 Richard W. Leopold Prize Entry," must be mailed directly to the committee members listed. Applicants should contact by e-mail for mailing address. Applicants must visit the website www.oah.org/awards/book-awards/richard-w-leopold-prize/

Closing Date: 1 October
Funding: Government
No. of awards given last year: 1
No. of applicants last year: 7
Additional Information: Please check at www.oah.org/awards/book-awards/richard-w-leopold-prize/

For further information contact:

Rebecca Tinio McKenna, Department of History, University of Notre Dame, 434 Decio Hall, Notre Dame, IN 46556, United States of America.

Email: mbradley@uchicago.edu

Society of American Archivists' Mosaic Scholarship Opportunity

Purpose: The Mosaic Scholarship provides financial and mentoring support to students of color pursuing graduate education in archival science, encourages students to pursue a career as an archivist, and promotes the diversification of the American archives profession
Eligibility: 1. Must be a citizen or permanent resident of the United States or Canada. 2. Must be of American Indian/Alaska Native, Asian, Black/African American, Hispanic/Latinx, Middle Eastern/North African, or Native Hawaiian/Other Pacific Islander descent. 3. Must be currently enrolled in a graduate program or a multi-course program in archival administration, or have applied to such a program for the next academic year. (The graduate program must offer at least three courses in archival science or be listed in the current SAA Directory of Archival Education. If the program is not listed in the SAA Directory of Archival Education, the applicant must provide proof of the three-course standard by submitting copies of course descriptions from the institution's current course catalog.) 4. Shall have completed no more than half of the credit requirements toward her/his graduate degree at the time of award (i.e., June 1). 5. Must be enrolled in a graduate program and begin school no later than September 1 or the fall semester/quarter immediately following the award. Otherwise the award will be rescinded. 6. May have full-time or part-time status. 7. Must submit a 500-word report to the SAA Council upon completion of the second semester.
Type: Scholarship
Value: US$5,000 each
Length of Study: one-year
Frequency: Annual
Country of Study: Any country
Application Procedure: Apply app.smarterselect.com/programs/45830-Society-Of-American-Archivists
No. of awards offered: 2
Closing Date: 28 February
Additional Information: Website: www.oah.org/insights/opportunities-for-historians/society-of-american-archivists-mosaic-scholarship-opportunity/

Stanton-Horton Award for Excellence in National Park Service History

Purpose: The award recognizes excellence in National Park Service historical efforts that make the NPS a leader in promoting public understanding of and engagement with American history. Please share exemplary projects that encourage civic dialogue in all areas of public history
Type: Award
Value: Varies
Frequency: Annual
Application Procedure: Application Form: www.oah.org/
Closing Date: 1 December
Additional Information: Website: www.petersons.com/scholarship/stanton-horton-award-for-excellence-in-national-park-service-history-111_222444.aspx#eligibility

Tachau Teacher of the Year Award

Purpose: The Mary K. Bonsteel Tachau Teacher of the Year Award is given annually by the Organization of American Historians in recognition of the contributions made by precollegiate teachers to improve history education within the field of American history
Eligibility: Precollegiate teachers engaged at least half time in U.S. history teaching, whether in history or social studies, are eligible. Successful candidates shall demonstrate exceptional ability in one or more of the following kinds of activities 1. Initiating or participating in projects which involve students in historical research, writing, or other means of representing their knowledge of history. 2. Initiating or participating in school, district, regional, state, or national projects which enhance the professional development of history teachers. 3. Initiating or participating in projects to build bridges between precollegiate and collegiate history or social studies teachers. 4. Working with museums, historical preservation societies, or other public history associations to enhance the place of public history in precollegiate schools. 5. Developing innovative history curricula which foster a spirit of inquiry and emphasize critical skills. 6. Publishing or otherwise publicly presenting scholarship that advances history education or historical knowledge.
Type: Award
Value: US$500
Frequency: Annual
Country of Study: Any country

Application Procedure: Applicants must visit the website www.oah.org/awards/uncategorized-awards/tachau-teacher-of-the-year-award/. Please fill out the nomination form here. www.oah.org/awards/uncategorized-awards/tachau-teacher-of-the-year-award/submission-form/
Closing Date: 1 November
No. of awards given last year: 1
No. of applicants last year: 9
Additional Information: Please check at www.oah.org/awards/uncategorized-awards/tachau-teacher-of-the-year-award/

The Japan Residencies Program

Purpose: The purpose of this program is to facilitate scholarly dialogue and contribute to the expansion of scholarly networks among students and professors of American history in both countries.
Eligibility: Applicants must be members of the OAH, have a PhD, and be scholars of American history. Applicants from previous competitions are welcome to apply again.
Type: Residency
Value: Round-trip airfare to Japan, housing, and modest daily expenses are covered by the award (note: if the host university is unable to provide housing, award recipients are expected to use the daily stipend to pay hotel expenses).
Length of Study: 2 weeks
Frequency: Annual
Country of Study: Any country
Application Procedure: Please send all materials (in one PDF labeled with your name) by midnight PST on October 1, 2023 to japanresidency@oah.org and indicate "Japan Residencies Program-[UNIVERSITY NAME]" in the subject line. If you would like to apply for both residencies, please send a separate application for each. See website for details
No. of awards offered: 2
Closing Date: 1 October
Additional Information: For more detials, please visit: www.oah.org/awards/residencies/japan/

For further information contact:

Email: japanresidency@oah.org

Willi Paul Adams Award

Purpose: The Willi Paul Adams Award is given biennially by the Organization of American Historians to the author of the best book on American history published in a language other than English.
Eligibility: Please write a one- to two-page essay (in English, along with the title in English) explaining why the book is a significant and original contribution to our understanding of American history, and include a summary of the book's main argument.
Type: Award
Value: See website
Frequency: Every 2 years
Country of Study: Any country
Application Procedure: Please write a one- to two-page essay (in English, along with the title in English) explaining why the book is a significant and original contribution to our understanding of American history, and include a summary of the book's main argument. The application should also include the following information 1. Name. 2. Mailing address. 3. Institutional affiliation. 4. Fax number. 5. E-mail address. 6. Language of submitted book. 7. Table of contents in English. Copies of the book and essay will be reviewed by contributing editors of the Journal of American History who are proficient in the language of the submission as well as by referees (proficient in the language of the submitted book) who are experts on its subject matter. Four copies of the essay and book, clearly labeled "2025 OAH Willi Paul Adams Award Entry," must be mailed to the following address and postmarked by May 1, 2024
No. of awards offered: 1
Closing Date: 1 May
Contributor: OAH
No. of awards given last year: 1
No. of applicants last year: 4
Additional Information: Please check at www.oah.org/awards/book-awards/willi-paul-adams-award/

For further information contact:

Willi Paul Adams Award Committee, c/o Organization of American Historians, 112 North Bryan Avenue, Bloomington IN 47408-4141, United States of America.

Email: khamm@oah.org

Organization of American States (OAS)

17th Street and Constitution Ave., NW, Washington, D.C. 20006-4499, United States of America.

Tel: (1) 202 370 5000
Email: Scholarships@oas.org
Website: www.oas.org/en/

The OAS is the world's oldest regional organization came into being in 1948 with the signing in Bogotá, Colombia, of the Charter of the OAS, which entered into force in December

1951. The Organization uses a four-pronged approach to effectively implement its essential purposes, based on its main pillars: democracy, human rights, security, and development.

Stanton-Horton Award for Excellence in National Park Service History

Purpose: The award recognizes excellence in National Park Service historical efforts that make the NPS a leader in promoting public understanding of and engagement with American history. Please share exemplary projects that encourage civic dialogue in all areas of public history
Level of Study: Graduate
Type: Award
Value: Varies
Frequency: Annual
Country of Study: Any country
Application Procedure: Application Form: www.oah.org/
Closing Date: 1 December
Funding: Private
Additional Information: Website: www.petersons.com/scholarship/stanton-horton-award-for-excellence-in-national-park-service-history-111_222444.aspx#eligibility

For further information contact:

Email: khamm@oah.org
Website: www.oah.org/

Oriel College

Oriel College, Oriel Square, Oxford OX1 4EW, United Kingdom.

Tel: (44) 1865 276555
Email: lodge@oriel.ox.ac.uk
Website: www.oriel.ox.ac.uk/

Oriel College is the fifth oldest of the University of Oxford's constituent colleges, founded in 1326. The College prides itself on being a welcoming academic community, home to world-class teaching, learning and research.

Basil Reeve DPhil Scholarship in Physical or Biomedical Sciences

Subjects: DPhil in Physical or Biomedical Sciences
Eligibility: open to Clarendon Scholarship holders only. To find out more about the Clarendon Scholarships: www.ox.ac.uk/clarendon.
Value: up to £40,000, paired with Clarendon Scholarship funds
Length of Study: usually 3 years
Application Procedure: See website: www.oriel.ox.ac.uk/study-with-us/postgraduates/postgraduate-scholarships/
Additional Information: Note: Students who receive the Basil Reeve DPhil Scholarship will be expected to relocate to Oriel College if originally accepted at another College. Website: www.oriel.ox.ac.uk/study-with-us/postgraduates/postgraduate-scholarships/

Black Academic Futures DPhil Scholarship in History

Subjects: DPhil in History
Purpose: As part of Oxford University's Black Academic Futures scholarship programme, Oriel offers a Black Academic Futures DPhil Scholarship in History for a talented postgraduate student of Black or Mixed Back ethnicity who is ordinarily resident in the UK.
Eligibility: postgraduate students of Black or Mixed Black ethnicity ordinarily resident in the UK. For more details: www.ox.ac.uk/admissions/graduate/access/academic-futures
Level of Study: Postgraduate
Type: Scholarship
Value: Minimum £15,609/yr
Length of Study: TBC
Application Procedure: To apply for the Black Academic Futures Scholarship, submit your completed graduate course application, including ethnicity information, by either the December or January deadline (whichever is relevant for your course) and you will automatically be considered. You do not need to submit any additional documents and there is no separate scholarship application form for these awards.
Closing Date: January
No. of applicants last year: Up to 30 scholarships are available
Additional Information: Website: www.oriel.ox.ac.uk/study-with-us/postgraduates/postgraduate-scholarships/

David N. Lyon Scholarship in Politics – The Politics of Sex and Gender Equality in Diverse Societies

Purpose: This scholarship will support one student to undertake research at Oriel into the politics of sex and gender equality in diverse societies in the field of Politics, broadly construed. These questions reward investigation from a number of different approaches: historical and contemporary, theoretical and empirical.
Eligibility: The Scholarship is open to candidates of any nationality for the MPhil, MSc or DPhil in Politics at the University of Oxford. Current University of Oxford MPhil

and DPhil students are also welcome to apply, and would be expected to migrate to Oriel College if successful in their application.
Level of Study: Masters Degree, Postgraduate, Postgraduate (MSc)
Type: Scholarship
Value: £8,500 per year
Country of Study: Any country
Closing Date: 31 December
Funding: Private
Additional Information: website: www.oriel.ox.ac.uk/study-with-us/postgraduates/postgraduate-scholarships/david-n-lyon-scholarship/

For further information contact:

Joseph Cole, Academic Registrar, Oriel College, Oxford OX1 4EW, United Kingdom.

Email: teresa.bejan@oriel.ox.ac.uk

James Mellon DPhil Scholarship in Longevity Research

Purpose: Based within Professor Lynne Cox's lab, this scholarship is intended to support a DPhil candidate in the area of longevity science and healthy ageing.
Eligibility: Must have a research focus on Longevity, Ageing or Cell senescence
Level of Study: Postgraduate, Research
Type: Scholarship
Value: Covers full fees and stipend in line with RCUK rate.
Length of Study: up to 3 years
Application Procedure: See website
Additional Information: Website: www.oriel.ox.ac.uk/study-with-us/postgraduates/postgraduate-scholarships/

Keith Hawkins Graduate Research Scholarship in English or American Legal History

Subjects: Graduate Research Degree in Legal History (MPhil or DPhil)
Purpose: This scholarship in English or American Legal History, named following a benefaction in honour of Emeritus Professor Keith Hawkins, provides financial support for a student undertaking a graduate research degree in the field of English or American Legal History at the University of Oxford.
Eligibility: open to new applicants or existing students of any nationality. For more information: www.oriel.ox.ac.uk/study-with-us/postgraduates/postgraduate-scholarships/keith-hawkins-scholarship-legal-history/
Level of Study: Masters Degree, Postgraduate
Value: £5,000/yr and guaranteed accommodation in first year
Length of Study: 1 year with potential to renew
Application Procedure: See website
Additional Information: Note: Current University of Oxford MPhil and DPhil students are also welcome to apply, and would be expected to migrate to Oriel College if successful in their application. Website: www.oriel.ox.ac.uk/study-with-us/postgraduates/postgraduate-scholarships/

Oriel and Institute for New Economic Thinking (INET) Graduate Scholarship

Subjects: DPhil candidate affiliated with INET
Eligibility: Must be studying on a graduate course affiliated with INET. To find more about INET: www.inet.ox.ac.uk/
Level of Study: Graduate
Type: Scholarship
Value: £5,000/yr for fees or living costs
Length of Study: up to 3 years
Application Procedure: see website
Additional Information: Website: www.oriel.ox.ac.uk/study-with-us/postgraduates/postgraduate-scholarships/

Oriel DPhil Scholarship in Engineering Science

Subjects: DPhil in Engineering Science
Purpose: Following a generous benefaction by an Orielensis and their family, we are able to offer the Oriel DPhil Scholarship in Engineering Science, which is open to candidates applying to study any discipline of Engineering, with a preference for Environmental Engineering.
Eligibility: Preference for Environmental Engineering. Applicants must list Oriel as their College preference. To learn more: www.oriel.ox.ac.uk/study-with-us/postgraduates/postgraduate-scholarships/graduate-scholarship-engineering-science/
Level of Study: Graduate, Postgraduate
Type: Scholarship
Value: £3,400/yr
Length of Study: up to 3 years
Application Procedure: See website
Additional Information: Website: www.oriel.ox.ac.uk/study-with-us/postgraduates/postgraduate-scholarships/

Oriel Graduate Scholarship in Science and Religion

Subjects: Any discipline with a research focus on the intersection between Christian theology and scientific thought.

Purpose: To a postgraduate student whose research focuses on the intersection of Christian theology and scientific thought.
Eligibility: Open to new applicants of any nationality. Candidates from other colleges will be considered provided that they migrate to Oriel upon acceptance of the scholarship. New postgraduate students who have applied to Oriel are also eligible. for more information: www.oriel.ox.ac.uk/study-with-us/postgraduates/postgraduate-scholarships/oriel-graduate-scholarship-in-science-religion/
Level of Study: Graduate, Postgraduate, Research
Type: Scholarship
Value: £3,400/yr
Length of Study: up to 3 years
Application Procedure: See website
Additional Information: Website: www.oriel.ox.ac.uk/study-with-us/postgraduates/postgraduate-scholarships/

Oriel Graduate Student Scholarships for Academic Merit

Subjects: Any current Oriel graduate student
Eligibility: Current graduate students on research degrees of at least 1 year in duration who have shown academic merit.
Level of Study: Graduate
Type: Scholarship
Value: £3,205 plus High Table dining rights once per week during term time. Accommodation (subject to availability).
Length of Study: 1 year
Application Procedure: see website
Closing Date: 16 March
Additional Information: Website: www.oriel.ox.ac.uk/study-with-us/postgraduates/postgraduate-scholarships/

Sir Walter Raleigh MSc Scholarship in Environmental Change and Management

Subjects: MSc in Environmental Change and Management
Eligibility: Open to applicants of any nationality. The selection criteria for the Scholarship are: 1. Academic achievement and potential 2. Breadth of vision 3. Career aspirations and commitment 4. Global orientation 5. Potential as Leader/Agent/Manager of Change 6. Multi-disciplinary training in relevant fields prior to graduation (vacation jobs etc) 7. Range and depth of experience relevant to the MSc course. To find more: www.oriel.ox.ac.uk/study-with-us/postgraduates/postgraduate-scholarships/sir-walter-raleigh-scholarship/
Level of Study: Postgraduate (MSc)
Type: Scholarship
Value: £4,000
Length of Study: 1 year
Application Procedure: Students who have successfully applied for the MSc in Environmental Change and Management will be contacted with information about how to apply for the scholarship.
Additional Information: Website: www.oriel.ox.ac.uk/study-with-us/postgraduates/postgraduate-scholarships/

The Oriel Graduate Scholarship for Sub-Saharan African Scholars

Subjects: Any graduate course (taught or research)
Purpose: The prize exists to support students from sub-Saharan Africa who are interested in solving the biggest problems currently facing the African continent, be that public health, ensuring stable economic growth, mitigating the worst effects of the climate crisis, or something else.
Eligibility: Open to applicants normally resident in a Sub-Saharan African country (as defined by NATO). For more information: www.oriel.ox.ac.uk/study-with-us/postgraduates/postgraduate-scholarships/graduate-sub-saharan-african-scholarship/
Level of Study: Graduate
Type: Scholarship
Value: £1,500/yr
Length of Study: TBC
Application Procedure: See website
Additional Information: Website: www.oriel.ox.ac.uk/study-with-us/postgraduates/postgraduate-scholarships/

Yalda Hakim Graduate Scholarship for Female Afghan Scholars

Subjects: Any 1-year Masters course
Purpose: It is intended that the scholarship, for the 2022-23 academic year, will benefit a student from an economically and socially disadvantaged background.
Eligibility: Open to Female applicants from Afghanistan only. for more information: www.oriel.ox.ac.uk/study-with-us/postgraduates/postgraduate-scholarships/yalda-hakim-scholarship-female-afghan-scholars/
Level of Study: Masters Degree
Type: Scholarship
Value: Full finding for 1 year
Length of Study: 1 year only
Additional Information: Website: www.oriel.ox.ac.uk/study-with-us/postgraduates/postgraduate-scholarships/

Orthopaedic Research and Education Foundation (OREF)

9400 W. Higgins Road, Suite 215, Rosemont, IL 60018-4975, United States of America.

Tel: (1) 847 698 9980
Email: communications@oref.org
Website: www.oref.org/

Our Mission: To fund and facilitate outstanding research and mentor researchers to improve the lives of patients with musculoskeletal conditions. Our Vision: OREF will be the leader in developing and disseminating the evidence needed to improve clinical practices, including treatment and recovery, and ultimately, patient outcomes. OREF is a charitable 501(c)(3) organization committed to improving lives by supporting excellence in orthopaedic research. OREF is dedicated to being the leader in supporting research that improves function, eliminates pain and restores mobility, and is the premier orthopaedic organization funding research across all specialties.

Friedenberg Mentored Clinician Scientist Grant

Purpose: Promotes the development of new clinician scientists who have demonstrated success as both a clinician and a researcher.
Eligibility: 1. Orthopaedic surgeons licensed to practice and working at an institution in the United States. 2. Applicants who have demonstrated success in research by receiving extramural research funding under one or more K08 or K23 awards from the National Institutes of Health or an equivalent funding source. 3. Recipients with multiyear NIHK08 or K23 awards may reapply to continue support
Level of Study: Research
Type: Grant
Value: US$20,000
Frequency: Annual
Country of Study: Any country
Application Procedure: To Access the Request for Application, you will need a proposalCENTRAL account. If you don't already have one, go to proposalCENTRAL by clicking the button below, then click the "Create an Account" link, which is located in the top right corner of the page.
Closing Date: 11 May
Additional Information: www.oref.org/grants-and-awards/grant-programs/general-grants/friedenberg-mentored-clinician-scientist-grant

For further information contact:

Email: grants@oref.org

Grants Programs

Subjects: Orthopaedic research
Purpose: Orthopaedic Research and Education Foundation offers both Investigator-Initiated and Research Specific Grants. Read each program for details.
Eligibility: OREF invites applications for funding for qualified, clinically relevant orthopaedic research projects. Please visit website.
Type: Grant
Value: 1. US$300,000 over 2 years for OREF Total Joint Replacement Research Grant in Memory of Jorge O. Galante, MD. 2. US$50,000 for OREF New Investigator Grant. 3. US$50,000 for OREF Multimodal Musculoskeletal Perioperative Pain Management Grant. 4. US$20,000 for Friedenberg Mentored Clinician Scientist Grant. 5. US$100,000 over 2 years for OREF and The Aircast Foundation Orthopaedic Research Grant. 6. US$300,000 over 3 years for OREF Career Development Grant. 7. US$5,000 for Resident Research Project Grant Round 2.
Frequency: Annual
Country of Study: Any country
Application Procedure: Please visit www.oref.org/grants-and-awards/grant-programs
Closing Date: 11 May
Additional Information: Grant programs for funding will be offered in two cycles with RFAs going live in November or May. There are research-specific grants as well as investigator-initiated grants. See website for details. www.oref.org/grants-and-awards/grant-programs

For further information contact:

Tel: (1) 847 430 5109
Email: grants@oref.org

Otaru University of Commerce

Business Administration, 3-5-21, Midori, Otaru-shi, Hokkaido 047-0034, Japan.

Tel: (81) 134 27 5206
Website: www.otaru-uc.ac.jp/news/167411/
Contact: MBA Admissions Officer

Otaru University of Commerce is located in Hokkaido one of the main ports in Japan. The university was established in this city to support the development of international trade. It has kept its fame during its history of ninety years because of its academic achievement, and distinguished graduates.

Bamforth Postgraduate Scholarship

Purpose: Doctoral scholarships are awarded by the University Council, on the recommendation of the Senate, to candidates proceeding to a course of supervised doctoral study at this University. These scholarships are normally available only to students seeking to obtain their first doctoral qualification. Candidates may be awarded one University of Otago doctoral scholarship only
Eligibility: In the case of an applicant for a doctoral scholarship who has completed a Master's degree by papers and thesis (at least 0.75 EFTS), the grades of all relevant advanced level papers counting towards the award of the degree and the thesis will be taken into account. An explanation of the time taken for completion of the thesis may be requested and considered by the Scholarships and Prizes Committee if the thesis has taken more than 2 EFTS (2 fulltime years) to complete
Level of Study: Postgraduate
Type: Scholarship
Value: NZ$28,600 stipend per annum
Length of Study: 3 year
Frequency: Annual
Country of Study: New Zealand
Funding: Foundation

For further information contact:

Email: scholarships@otago.ac.nz

Ovarian Cancer Research Fund

14 Pennsylvania Plaza, Suite 2110, New York, NY 10122, United States of America.

Tel: (1) 212 268 1002
Email: info@ocrahope.org
Website: ocrahope.org/

Ovarian Cancer Research Alliance (OCRA) is the leading organization in the world fighting ovarian cancer from all fronts, including in the lab and on Capitol Hill, while supporting women and their families. OCRA's ongoing investment in the most promising scientific research is funding discoveries, creating new treatments, and hastening desperately needed breakthroughs.

Ann and Sol Schreiber Mentored Investigator Award

Subjects: Ovarian cancer research
Purpose: This award provides funding for trainees (postdoctoral fellows or clinical fellows) who are working under the supervision of a mentor who is a recognized leader in the field of ovarian cancer research.
Eligibility: Applicants must have an MD or a PhD degree.
Level of Study: Doctorate, Postdoctorate
Type: Award
Value: The award provides a total of US$75,000 to be used over one or two years
Length of Study: One or two years
Country of Study: Any country
Application Procedure: Requests for Proposals (RFPs) are issued every spring. We use a two step application and peer review process. Letters of Intent (LOIs) are due in May and undergo a rigorous peer review by our Scientific Advisory Committee. After LOI review, a subset of those applicants are invited to submit full applications. Full applications are due in July. Final grant notifications are made in October. RFPs are available for future grant cycles, please send an email to grants@ocrahope.org.
Closing Date: May
No. of awards given last year: 10
Additional Information: ocrahope.org/grant/ann-schreiber-mentored-award/

For further information contact:

Email: grants@ocrahope.org

Oxford Brookes University, School of Business

Headington Campus, Oxford OX3 0BP, United Kingdom.

Tel: (44) 1865 485858
Email: business@brookes.ac.uk
Website: www.brookes.ac.uk/business/

Oxford Brookes Business School is a place of inspiration and transformation. Our students embark on a supported journey of learning and self-development to become highly effective practitioners and responsible leaders operating in global markets.

Alumni Discount Scheme

Eligibility: You must: 1. Hold an offer and register on a degree-awarding postgraduate course at Oxford Brookes University. The majority of courses qualify for the award, but please check the exception list below. 2. Be a graduate of Oxford Brookes University. That is, you must have qualified on a full undergraduate or postgraduate degree.
Level of Study: Postgraduate, Research
Value: 10% Discount from tuition fees
Application Procedure: Please complete the application form: docs.google.com/forms/d/e/1FAIpQLSdI9m4mN1HN1KqoCprbU8I5SpYpnuuhNOLItnm4YkwlDqRSFg/viewform
No. of applicants last year: Unlimited
Additional Information: website: www.brookes.ac.uk/Study/Funding/Alumni-Discount-Scheme

Oxford Brookes University MBA Programme

Purpose: These scholarships aim to support those who are based in lower-income countries, to provide enhanced opportunities and to celebrate the truly global reach of our MBA programme.
Eligibility: They are offered to all students who live and work in specific countries based on the UN Development Index. Please visit website
Type: Scholarship
Value: £2,000
Country of Study: Any country
Application Procedure: Please apply using our application form. www.brookes.ac.uk/courses/postgraduate/oxford-brookes-mba
Additional Information: These scholarships do not apply to ACCA members, who already receive a substantial discount on the Oxford Brookes Global MBA fees. www.brookes.ac.uk/courses/postgraduate/oxford-brookes-mba

For further information contact:

Tel: (44) 1865 48 58 00
Email: mbaoxford@brookes.ac.uk

P

Paloma O Shea Santander International Piano Competition

C / Luis Martinez 21, E-39005 Santander, Spain.

Tel: (34) 942 31 14 51
Email: concurso@albeniz.com
Website: www.santanderpianocompetition.com
Contact: Foundation Albeniz

Non-profit institution founded in 1987. It directs and governs the set of programs sponsored by the Albeniz Foundation in Cantabria. Organization 19th International Piano Competition of Santander.

Gold, Silver and Bronze Medals

Subjects: Musical instrument (piano)
Purpose: To give support to young pianists of exceptional talents.
Eligibility: Competition is open to all pianists born on 1st January, 1994 and after
Level of Study: Unrestricted
Type: Prize
Value: Cash prizes totalling more than €90,000
Frequency: Annual
Study Establishment: ANY
Country of Study: Any country
Application Procedure: Apply online
No. of awards offered: 7
Closing Date: November
Funding: Commercial, Foundation, Government, Private
No. of applicants last year: 241
Additional Information: www.santanderpianocompetition.com/C_Premios.aspx

For further information contact:

Calle Luis Martínez, 21, Santander, E-39005 Cantabria, Spain.

Paralyzed Veterans of America (PVA)

801 Eighteenth Street NW, Washington, DC 20006-3517, United States of America.

Tel: (1) 800 424 8200
Email: info@pva.org
Website: www.pva.org
Contact: Paralyzed Veterans of America

PVA was originally founded by a band of service members who came home from World War II with spinal cord injuries. They returned to a grateful nation, but also to a world with few solutions to the major challenges they faced. Paralyzed Veterans of America, a congressionally chartered veterans service organization founded in 1946, has developed a unique expertise on a wide variety of issues involving the special needs of our members - veterans of the armed forces who have experienced spinal cord injury or dysfunction.

Paralyzed Veterans of America Fellowships in Spinal Cord Injury Research

Purpose: The Research Foundation is focused on funding projects grounded in basic laboratory science and the education of scientists working on breakthroughs directed toward a cure for paralysis, secondary health effects and technologies associated with spinal cord injury or disease (SCI/D).

Palgrave Macmillan (ed.), *The Grants Register 2024*,
https://doi.org/10.1057/978-1-349-96073-6

Eligibility: 1. Eligible grantee institutions must be located in the United States or Canada. 2. However, investigators and fellows are not required to be U.S. or Canadian citizens. 3. All grant applicants must have a professional degree Ph.D. or M.D. preferred. 4. Senior fellows are encouraged to apply as principal investigators. 5. Post-doctoral scientists are eligible to apply for fellowship support within four years of receiving a Ph.D. or completing M.D. residency. 6. Graduate students can participate in Foundation-related research and be paid from a Foundation award. 7. However, graduate students cannot apply for a Foundation grant as a fellow or as a principal investigator.
Level of Study: Postdoctorate, Postgraduate, Research
Type: Fellowship
Value: US$746,293
Length of Study: Two-year period
Frequency: Annual
Country of Study: United States of America
No. of awards offered: 5
Closing Date: 1 July
Funding: Foundation
No. of applicants last year: 83
Additional Information: pva.org/news-and-media-center/recent-news/paralyzed-veterans-spinal-cord-injury-research-grant/

For further information contact:

Tel: (1) 202 416 7611
Email: LindsayP@pva.org

Research Grants & Fellowships

Eligibility: Eligible grantee institutions must be located in the United States or Canada. However, investigators and fellows are not required to be U.S. or Canadian citizens. All grant applicants must have a professional degree Ph.D. or M.D. preferred. Senior fellows are encouraged to apply as principal investigators. Post-doctoral scientists are eligible to apply for fellowship support within four years of receiving a Ph.D. or completing M.D. residency. Graduate students can participate in Foundation-related research and be paid from a Foundation award. However, graduate students cannot apply for a Foundation grant as a fellow or as a principal investigator.
Level of Study: Postgraduate
Type: Fellowship or Grant
Value: US$796,402
Country of Study: Any country
Application Procedure: Lindsay Perlman, Associate Director, Research and Education
Closing Date: 1 January

For further information contact:

Tel: (1) 202 416 7611
Email: LindsayP@pva.org

Parapsychology Foundation, Inc.

PO Box 1562, New York, NY 10021, United States of America.

Tel: (1) 212 628 1550
Email: office@parapsychology.org
Website: www.parapsychology.org
Contact: Parapsychology Foundation

The Parapsychology Foundation is a not-for-profit foundation which provides a worldwide forum supporting the scientific investigation of psychic phenomena. The Foundation gives grants, publishes pamphlets, monographs, conference proceedings and the International Journal of Parapsychology, hosts the Perspectives Lecture Series, conducts the Outreach Program, maintains the Eileen J. Garrett Library with its collection of more than 12,000 volumes and 100 periodicals on parapsychology and related topics, and is proud of its quality paperback imprint, Helix Press.

Eileen J Garrett Scholarship

Purpose: To assist students attending an accredited college or university in pursuing the academic study of the science of parapsychology
Eligibility: 1. Must be an undergraduate student, a graduate student or a postgraduate student. 2. Must attend a university, a four-year college or two-year college. 3. Citizenship requirements US. 4. Must not be attending high school currently. 5. Must study full-time. 6. Restricted to students studying Social Sciences.
Level of Study: Unrestricted
Type: Scholarship
Value: US$3,000
Length of Study: 1 year
Frequency: Annual
Study Establishment: An accredited college or university
Country of Study: United States of America
Application Procedure: Applicants must submit samples of writings on the subject with an application form from the Foundation. Letters of reference are required from three individuals, familiar with the applicant's work and/or studies in parapsychology.

No. of awards offered: 1
Closing Date: 15 July
Additional Information: parapsychology.org/garrett/

For further information contact:

Tel: (1) 212 628 1550
Fax: (1) 212 628 1559

Paris School of International Affairs (PSIA)

28 Rue des Saints-Peres, F-75007 Paris, France.

Website: www.sciencespo.fr/psia/

At Sciences Po's Paris School of International Affairs (PSIA), our goal is to train and shape global actors to understand and respond to the complexities of our world. Attracting the best and brightest students worldwide, PSIA has a population of 1500 students representing over 110 countries. With 70% of courses taught in English, students may take a full course of study in English.

Kuwait Program at Sciences Po Excellence Scholarship for Arab Students and Kuwait Nationals

Purpose: The Kuwait Excellence Scholarship program supports outstanding students coming from the Arab world and Kuwait to pursue Master's level graduate studies at Sciences Po. Multiple scholarships will be awarded to the best candidates on a competitive basis.
Eligibility: 1. Nationals from Arab countries, Kuwaiti National including the Gulf Region, may apply. 2. Applicants must a. be first-time degree-seeking students in France. b. submit a full application to Sciences Po for the 2024/2025 intake (including all supporting documents and references) via the Sciences Po Admissions Portal. c. apply to any of the 7 graduate schools of Sciences Po, in any of the two-year Master programs. 3. Students applying to a dual degree program are not eligible. Students applying to a one-year Master program are not eligible.
Level of Study: MBA, Masters Degree, Postgraduate, Postgraduate (MSc)
Type: Scholarship
Value: For Arab students Each recipient is awarded up to 20,000 Euros for two years of study. For Kuwait Nationals 25,000 Euros for the two years of study.
Length of Study: 2 years
Frequency: Annual
Country of Study: United States of America
Application Procedure: To apply, please send the following materials by email to program.kuwait@sciencespo.fr with "Kuwait Excellence Scholarship Application 2024/2025" in the subject line CV in English, cover letter in English of 1000 words addressed to the members of the joint selection committee (this letter must be different from your letter of motivation to Sciences Po, describing your motivations for applying to the Kuwait Excellence Scholarship). copy of passport.
No. of awards offered: Multiple
Closing Date: 14 February
No. of applicants last year: Multiple
Additional Information: www.sciencespo.fr/kuwait-program/student-activities/scholarship/

For further information contact:

27, rue Saint Guillaume, F-75337 Paris Cedex 07, France.

Tel: (33) 1 45 49 50 50
Email: program.kuwait@sciencespo.fr

Parkinson's United Kingdom

215 Vauxhall Bridge Road, London SW1V 1EJ, United Kingdom.

Tel: (44) 20 7931 8080
Email: hello@parkinsons.org.uk
Website: www.parkinsons.org.uk

We have come a long way since 1969, when Mali Jenkins founded the Parkinson's Disease Society - now Parkinson's UK. Together we will find a cure, and improve life for everybody affected by Parkinson's. Our core values show the way we all work together to bring forward the day when no one fears Parkinson's.

Clinician Scientist Fellowship

Purpose: To support MDs and other health professionals studying for a PhD.
Level of Study: Doctorate
Type: Fellowship
Value: Up to £250,000
Length of Study: 3 years

Frequency: Annual
Country of Study: United Kingdom
Application Procedure: Please see website
Additional Information: mrc.ukri.org/skills-careers/fellowships/clinical-fellowships/clinician-scientist-fellowship-csf/

For further information contact:

Email: cindy@cmscfoundation.org

Parkinson's UK drug accelerator grant

Purpose: These awards will help pioneer and accelerate novel drug development for the treatment of Parkinson's, providing researchers the opportunity to plug essential gaps in existing datasets to get their projects/compounds ready to enter full scale drug discovery with an industry partner or the Parkinson's Virtual Biotech. We are looking for projects that will have a clear focus on translational drug development to make a difference to those affected by Parkinson's.
Eligibility: 1. Grants are tenable only at a UK university, NHS Trust or small start-up biotech companies. 2. Principal applicants should hold employment contracts that extend beyond the period of the grant. 3. Co-applicants and collaborators may be based at institutions outside the UK or biotech companies.
Type: Grant
Value: There is no minimum value and the maximum award amount is £100,000.
Length of Study: Maximum of 12 months
Country of Study: United Kingdom
Closing Date: 17 March
Additional Information: www.parkinsons.org.uk/research/drug-accelerator-awards

For further information contact:

Email: researchapplications@parkinsons.org.uk

Parkinson's UK non-drug approaches grant

Eligibility: 1. Grants are tenable only at a UK university, NHS Trust, statutory social care organisation or other research institution. 2. Principal applicants should hold employment contracts that extend beyond the period of the grant. 3. Co-applicants and collaborators may be based at institutions outside the UK or biotech companies.
Type: Grant
Value: There is no minimum value and the maximum award amount is £200,000.
Length of Study: Maximum of 2 years
Country of Study: United Kingdom
No. of awards offered: 2
Closing Date: 14 September
No. of awards given last year: 8
No. of applicants last year: 19
Additional Information: www.parkinsons.org.uk/research/grants-non-drug-approaches

For further information contact:

Email: researchapplications@parkinsons.org.uk

Parkinson's UK project grant

Purpose: Our project grants tackle major Parkinson's research challenges with groundbreaking studies that get right to the heart of complex problems.
Eligibility: 1. Grants are tenable only at a UK university, NHS Trust, statutory social care organisation or other UK research institution. 2. Principal applicants should hold employment contracts that extend beyond the period of the grant. 3. Co-applicants and collaborators may be based at institutions outside the UK or at pharmaceutical or biotech companies.
Level of Study: Research
Type: Grant
Value: the cost of applications is usually up to £400,000 and the average amount awarded is £240,000.
Length of Study: Maximum of 3 years
Country of Study: United Kingdom
No. of awards offered: 4
Closing Date: 31 March
No. of awards given last year: 19
No. of applicants last year: 30
Additional Information: www.parkinsons.org.uk/research/project-grants

Paul & Daisy Soros Fellowships for New Americans

11 West 42nd Street, 3rd floor, New York, NY 10036, United States of America.

Tel: (1) 212 405 8234
Email: pdsoros_fellows@sorosny.org
Website: www.pdsoros.org

In its near 20 year history, The Paul & Daisy Soros Fellowships for New Americans has built a community of

655 immigrants and children of immigrants. The Fellowship has supported New Americans with heritage in 89 countries. India, China, and Mexico are the most well represented.

The Paul & Daisy Soros Fellowship for New Americans

Purpose: To provide opportunities for continuing generations of able and accomplished New Americans to achieve leadership in their chosen fields
Eligibility: Open to New Americans resident aliens (Green Card Holders) naturalized United States citizens and/or children of 2 naturalized parents
Level of Study: Postdoctorate
Type: Fellowship
Value: US$25,000 up to US$20,000 in tuition support for each year
Length of Study: 2 years
Study Establishment: Any accredited graduate University in the United States
Country of Study: United States of America
Application Procedure: Apply online
No. of awards offered: 77
Closing Date: 12 November
Funding: Private
Contributor: Paul and Daisy Soros
No. of awards given last year: 30
No. of applicants last year: 77
Additional Information: www.pdsoros.org/apply

For further information contact:

Email: pdsoros@pdsoros.org

Paul Lowin Prizes

Perpetual Trustees Australia Limited, 39 Hunter Street, Sydney, NSW 2000, Australia.

Email: lowinprizes@perpetual.com.au
Website: www.paullowin.perpetual.com.au

The Paul Lowin Prizes are administered by the Perpetual Trustees Australia Limited, which is a public trustee company operating in all mainland states of Australia. Income generated from investment of this capital is distributed annually to charitable organisations to fulfil the intent of the trusts under management.

Paul Lowin Prizes - Song Cycle Prize

Purpose: To recognise original composition. For the purposes of the competition, a song cycle is music suitable for chamber performance
Eligibility: The composer must be at least 18 years of age and an Australian citizen or a resident of Australia for not less than three years prior to the closing date
Level of Study: Unrestricted
Type: Prize
Value: AU$15,000
Frequency: Every 2 years
Country of Study: Any country
Application Procedure: Applicants must refer to the website for details
No. of awards offered: 10
Closing Date: 30 June
Funding: Private
No. of awards given last year: 1
No. of applicants last year: 10
Additional Information: Works should use no more than one-eight independent vocal lines, which may be accompanied by up to 10 instrumental players. The text of the work may have a unifying theme, and the composer and the author of the text may or may not be different people, but the author of the text is not eligible for the prize. The work may be no less than 15 minutes and no more than 60 in duration taitmemorialtrust.org/tag/paul-lowin-song-cycle-prize/

For further information contact:

Australian Music Centre, Level 4, The Arts Exchange, 18 Hickson Road, Dawes Point, NSW 2000, Australia.

Email: info@australianmusiccentre.com.au

P

Peninsula School of Medicine and Dentistry

Plymouth Science Park, Research Way, Plymouth PL6 8BT, United Kingdom.

Tel: (44) 345 155 8109
Email: info@psmd.ac.uk
Website: www.pcmd.ac.uk

Peninsula College of Medicine and Dentistry (PCMD) is a Medical and Dental school in England, run in partnership with the University of Exeter, the University of Plymouth and the NHS in Devon and Cornwall.

Peninsula College of Medicine and Dentistry PhD Studentships

Purpose: To attract PhD candidates of outstanding ability to join their exciting and rapidly expanding programme of internationally rated research
Eligibility: Open to the suitably qualified graduates
Level of Study: Doctorate
Type: Studentship
Value: £13,290 (Research Council Rate)
Frequency: Dependent on funds available
Study Establishment: Peninsula College of Medicine & Dentistry
Country of Study: United Kingdom
Application Procedure: Check website for the details
Closing Date: 8 November
Contributor: Various sources

Penn State, College of Communications

201 Carnegie Building, State College, PA 16803, United States of America.

Tel: (1) 814 863 1484
Email: bellisarioinfo@psu.edu
Website: www.bellisario.psu.edu/

The Donald P. Bellisario College of Communications at Penn State provides the opportunities and resources of a large university with the personalized feel and support of a small school. As one of the largest accredited programs of its kind in the nation, students can find a place where they can fit and succeed.

Call for Proposals: Narratives in Public Communications

Purpose: Donald P. Bellisario College of Communications at Penn State has announced its annual Page/Johnson Legacy Scholar Grant competition for the study of integrity in public communication. This year, the Center is issuing three research calls 1. Proposals for research projects on Corporate Social Advocacy. 2. Proposals for research projects on Ethics of Care. 3. Proposals for curriculum development on Activism.
Eligibility: This call therefore seeks grant proposals that will examine the uses and implications of stories and storytelling in public communications.
Level of Study: Graduate
Type: Grant
Value: US$2,000
Frequency: Annual
Country of Study: United States of America
Application Procedure: Check the application procedure at the link below. The proposal requires the below information to process further 1. Narrative (up to 5 pages). 2. Abstract (1 page). 3. Coversheet (1 page). 4. Budget (1 page). 5. Curriculum Vitae or Professional Resume. bellisario.psu.edu/page-center/grants/legacy-scholar-grants/guidelines-for-grant-applications.
No. of awards offered: 3
Closing Date: 15 January
Funding: Private

Perkins School of Theology

Southern Methodist University, PO Box 750133, Dallas, TX 75275-0133, United States of America.

Tel: (1) 214 768 8436
Email: theology@smu.edu
Website: www.smu.edu/perkins

Perkins School of Theology is one of the 13 seminaries of The United Methodist Church and one of only five university-related United Methodist theological schools, located in the heart of Dallas, Texas, with an extension program in Houston/Galveston. The primary mission of Perkins School of Theology, as a community devoted to theological study and teaching in the service of the church of Jesus Christ, is to prepare women and men for faithful leadership in Christian ministry.

Diaconia Graduate Fellowships

Purpose: This fellowship was established to support deacons in full or provisional membership and diaconal ministers planning to teach or serve as an administrator in a school of theology, college, or university or in another institution or agency of the church. Applicants must be graduate students at an accredited academic institution. Demonstration of academic ability and financial need is a must.
Eligibility: 1. Applicant must be a full-time doctoral student in an accredited academic institution and have been accepted for work in a doctoral program (preferably Ph.D.) prior to the year for which the award is granted in an institution. 2. Applicant must be a full-time doctoral student in an accredited academic institution. 3. Applicant must be an ACTIVE, full member of The United Methodist Church for at least ONE

year. Membership is determined by the date the applicant was confirmed and took membership vows with a United Methodist church.
Level of Study: Doctorate, Graduate
Type: Fellowships
Value: US$1,000 - US$10,000
Frequency: Annual
Country of Study: United States of America
Application Procedure: 1. Award selection is based on intellectual competence, academic achievements, promise of usefulness, personal qualities, and clarity of spiritual purpose and commitment. 2. A completed online application.
No. of awards offered: 1
Closing Date: March

For further information contact:

Tel: (1) 615 340 7344
Email: umscholar@gbhem.org

Petro Jacyk Central & East European Resource Centre (PJRC)

130 St George St, Room 3008 (3rd floor), Toronto, Ontario M5S 1A5, Canada.

Tel: (1) 416 978 0588
Email: jacyk.centre@utoronto.ca
Website: pjrc.library.utoronto.ca/content/

Petro Jacyk's contributions to the University of Toronto Library include funding the microfilming of the Peter Jacyk Collection of Ukrainian Serials in 1983, establishing an endowment to support annual subscriptions to Ukrainian periodicals in 1994, and support for the creation of the Petro Jacyk Central and East European Resource Centre in 1995.

Petro Jacyk Program

Purpose: The objective of the Post-Doctoral Fellowship is to support annually one of the most promising junior scholars studying contemporary Ukraine and thereby to advance academic understanding of Ukrainian politics, culture, and society
Eligibility: The Petro Jacyk Post-Doctoral Fellowship is available to junior scholars in the social sciences and humanities with a research and teaching focus on contemporary Ukraine. The fellowship is open to recently awarded PhDs (persons holding doctorates for no more than three years at the time of application)
Level of Study: Postdoctorate
Type: Fellowship
Value: CA$40,000, which includes payment for teaching a semester-long course, and separately an allowance of up to CA$2,500 for research and travel expenses
Length of Study: 1 year
Study Establishment: University of Toronto
Country of Study: Canada
Application Procedure: Please send applications by email to the Foundation at pjef@bellnet.ca and the Petro Jacyk Program for the Study of Ukraine at the University of Toronto at jacyk.program@utoronto.ca simultaneously
Closing Date: 1 February
Contributor: Petro Jacyk Education Foundation

Pfizer

235 East 42nd Street, New York, NY 10017, United States of America.

Tel: (1) 212 733 2323
Email: MAPinfo@clinicalconnexion.com
Website: www.pfizermap.com

Pfizer supports the global healthcare community's independent initiatives to improve patient outcomes in areas of unmet medical need that are aligned with Pfizer's medical and/or scientific strategies.

Acromegaly/Growth Hormone Excess Research

Purpose: Pfizer Global Medical Grants (GMG) supports the global healthcare community's independent initiatives (e.g., research, quality improvement or education) to improve patient outcomes in areas of unmet medical need that are aligned with Pfizer's medical and/or scientific strategies. Pfizer's GMG competitive grant program involves a publicly posted Request for Proposal (RFP) that provides detail regarding a specific area of interest, sets timelines for review and approval, and uses an external review panel (ERP) to make final grant decisions. Organizations are invited to submit an application addressing the specific gaps in research, practice or care as outlined in the specific RFP. For all Investigator Sponsored Research (ISRs) and general research grants, the grant requester (and ultimately the grantee) is responsible for the design, implementation, sponsorship, and conduct of the independent initiative supported by the

grant, including compliance with any regulatory requirements. Pfizer must not be involved in any aspect of study protocol or project development, nor the conduct or monitoring of the research program.
Eligibility: The institution and principal investigator (PI) must be based in one of the eligible countries noted above. 1. Only organizations are eligible to receive grants, not individuals or medical practice groups. 2. The applicant (PI) must have a medical or postdoctoral degree (MD, PhD, or equivalent), an advanced nursing degree (BSN with a MS/PhD), or a degree in Pharmacy, Physiotherapy, or Social Work. 3. Applicant must be affiliated with a host institution 4. Both early career and experienced investigators are encouraged to apply and consideration will be given to all proposals meeting the selection criteria
Level of Study: Postgraduate
Type: Grant
Value: Individual projects requesting up to US$100,000 will be considered. Pfizer anticipates awarding up to 1 grant. The amount of the grant Pfizer will be prepared to fund for any project will depend upon the external review panel's evaluation of the proposal and costs involved, and will be stated clearly in the approval notification
Frequency: Annual
Country of Study: United States of America
Application Procedure: 1. Please go to www.cybergrants.com/pfizer/Research and sign in. First-time users should click "Create your password". Requirements for submission 2. Select the following Competitive Grant Program Name RD LAcromegaly/Growth Hormone Excess Research US 3. Complete all required sections of the online application. See Appendix A for additional details 4. If you encounter any technical difficulties with the website, please click the "Technical Questions" link at the bottom of the page
No. of awards offered: 1
Closing Date: 28 May
Additional Information: www.pfizer.com/purpose/independent-grants/competitive-grants

For further information contact:

Email: amanda.j.stein@pfizer.com

Breast Cancer Competitive Research Grant Program

Purpose: Pfizer Global Medical Grants (GMG) supports the global healthcare community's independent initiatives (e.g., research, quality improvement or education) to improve patient outcomes in areas of unmet medical need that are aligned with Pfizer's medical and/or scientific strategies. Pfizer's GMG competitive grant program involves a publicly posted Request for Proposal (RFP) that provides detail regarding a specific area of interest, sets timelines for review and approval, and uses an external review panel (ERP) to make final grant decisions. Organizations are invited to submit an application addressing the specific gaps in research, practice or care as outlined in the specific RFP. For all Investigator Sponsored Research (ISRs), general research and medical education grants, the grant requester (and ultimately the grantee) is responsible for the design, implementation, sponsorship, and conduct of the independent initiative supported by the grant, including compliance with any regulatory requirements. Pfizer must not be involved in any aspect of study protocol or project development, nor the conduct or monitoring of the project.
Eligibility: The principal investigator (PI) and institution must be based in one of the eligible regions noted above. 1. The applicant (PI) must have a medical or postdoctoral degree (MD, PhD, or equivalent). 2. Applicant must be affiliated with a host institution. 3. Both early career and experienced investigators are encouraged to apply and consideration will be given to all proposals meeting the selection criteria. 4. If the project involves multiple departments within an institution and/or between different institutions/organizations/associations, all institutions must have a relevant role and the requesting organization must have a key role in the project.
Level of Study: Postgraduate
Type: Grant
Value: A total of US$3 million is allocated to this grants program. 1. Applications will be reviewed by an independent review panel. Up to 15 projects will be selected for funding. 2. The amount of the grant Pfizer will be prepared to fund for any project will depend upon the external review panel's evaluation of the proposal and costs involved, and will be stated clearly in the approval notification.
Frequency: Annual
Country of Study: United States of America
Application Procedure: Please go to www.cybergrants.com/pfizer/Research and sign in. Firsttime users should click "REGISTER NOW". Requirements for submission 1. Select the following Competitive Grant Program Name Breast Cancer Competitive Research for AfME, Asia, LatAm 2. Complete all required sections of the online application. See Appendix A for additional details. All applications must be in English. 3. If you encounter any technical difficulties with the website, please click the "Technical Questions" link at the bottom of the page
Closing Date: 7 April
Additional Information: www.pfizer.com/about/programs-policies/grants/competitive-grants

For further information contact:

Email: Jessica.Romano@pfizer.com

Global Hemophilia ASPIRE

Purpose: Projects that will be considered for Pfizer support will focus on the following areas in Gene Therapy for Hemophilia A or B Basic Science of Gene Therapy for Hemophilia; Basic Science of TFPI & Anti-TFPI Monoclonal Antibodies; ross talk among regulators (e.g., Protein S being a co-factor for both Protein C and TFPI); AND Patients with MILD Hemophilia A or B.
Eligibility: The applicant (PI) must have a medical or postdoctoral degree (MD, PhD, or equivalent), an advanced nursing degree (BSN with a MS/PhD), or a degree in Pharmacy, Physiotherapy, or Social Work.
Level of Study: Masters Degree, Postdoctorate, Postgraduate, Postgraduate (MSc)
Type: Grant
Value: US$90,000
Length of Study: 1 to 2 year
Frequency: Annual
Country of Study: Any country
Closing Date: 1 March
Additional Information: cdn.pfizer.com/pfizercom/2021-11/2022-RD-G_GlobalHemophiliaASPIRE.pdf?i9KTO8LQkwd0.6WPjji0GapVHAvXbc9h

For further information contact:

Email: amanda.j.stein@pfizer.com

Growth Hormone Research

Purpose: Pfizer Global Medical Grants (GMG) supports the global healthcare community's independent initiatives (e.g., research, quality improvement or education) to improve patient outcomes in areas of unmet medical need that are aligned with Pfizer's medical and/or scientific strategies. Pfizer's GMG competitive grant program involves a publicly posted Request for Proposal (RFP) that provides detail regarding a specific area of interest, sets timelines for review and approval, and uses an external review panel (ERP) to make final grant decisions. Organizations are invited to submit an application addressing the specific gaps in research, practice or care as outlined in the specific RFP. For all Investigator Sponsored Research (ISRs) and general research grants, the grant requester (and ultimately the grantee) is responsible for the design, implementation, sponsorship, and conduct of the independent initiative supported by the grant, including compliance with any regulatory requirements. Pfizer must not be involved in any aspect of study protocol or project development, nor the conduct or monitoring of the research program.
Eligibility: The institution and principal investigator (PI) must be based in one of the eligible countries noted above. 1. Only organizations are eligible to receive grants, not individuals or medical practice groups. 2. The applicant (PI) must have a medical or postdoctoral degree (MD, PhD, or equivalent), an advanced nursing degree (BSN with a MS/PhD), or a degree in Pharmacy, Physiotherapy, or Social Work. 3. Applicant must be affiliated with a host institution 4. Both early career and experienced investigators are encouraged to apply and consideration will be given to all proposals meeting the selection criteria
Level of Study: Postgraduate
Type: Grant
Value: Individual projects requesting up to US$100,000 will be considered. Pfizer anticipates awarding up to one grant. The amount of the grant Pfizer will be prepared to fund for any project will depend upon the external review panel's evaluation of the proposal and costs involved, and will be stated clearly in the approval notification
Frequency: Annual
Country of Study: United States of America
Application Procedure: Please go to www.cybergrants.com/pfizer/Research and sign in. First-time users should click "Create your password". Requirements for submission 1. Select the following Competitive Grant Program Name RD LPediatric Growth Hormone Deficiency Research US 2. Complete all required sections of the online application. See Appendix A for additional details 3. If you encounter any technical difficulties with the website, please click the "Technical Questions" link at the bottom of the page
No. of awards offered: 1
Closing Date: 28 May
Additional Information: www.pfizer.com/purpose/independent-grants/competitive-grants

For further information contact:

Email: amanda.j.stein@pfizer.com

Pfizer Scholar

Purpose: To support cancer development in epidemiology
Eligibility: Open to individuals who are pursuing research in epidemiology relevant to human health
Level of Study: Postgraduate
Type: Grant
Value: US$130,000

P

Length of Study: 2 years
Frequency: Annual
Country of Study: Any country
Application Procedure: A completed application form must be submitted
Closing Date: 6 January
Funding: Commercial
Additional Information: www.collegescholarships.org/scholarships/companies/pfizer.htm

For further information contact:

Email: mzebrowski@metrohealth.org

Pfizer Scholars Grants in Clinical Epidemiology

Purpose: To support the career development of junior faculty
Eligibility: Citizens or permanent residents of the United States of America who have a doctoral degree, relevant research experience and postdoctoral clinical training appropriate for the proposed research are encouraged to apply. The applicant should hold a junior faculty position (with 2 years of appointment as an instructor, an assistant professor or an equivalent junior faculty rank) at an accredited academic medical institution
Level of Study: Professional development
Type: Grant
Value: US$195,000
Length of Study: 3 years
Frequency: Annual
Country of Study: United States of America
Application Procedure: Applicants must visit the website for full details on the application process
Closing Date: 5 January
Funding: Corporation
Contributor: Pfizer Inc

For further information contact:

Email: mzebrowski@metrohealth.org

Pfizer Scholars Grants in Clinical Psychiatry

Purpose: To support the development of junior faculty
Eligibility: Citizens or permanent residents of the United States of America who are junior faculty with a doctoral degree (with 2 years of appointment as an instructor, an assistant professor or an equivalent junior faculty rank) at an accredited academic medical institution are encouraged to apply
Level of Study: Professional development
Type: Grant
Value: US$130,000
Length of Study: 2 years
Frequency: Annual
Country of Study: United States of America
Application Procedure: Applicants must visit the website for full details
Closing Date: 5 January
Funding: Corporation
Contributor: Pfizer Inc

For further information contact:

Email: mzebrowski@metrohealth.org

Pfizer Scholars Grants in Clinical Rheumatology

Purpose: To support the career development of junior faculty
Eligibility: Citizens or permanent residents of the United States of America who have a doctoral degree, relevant research experience and postdoctoral clinical training appropriate for the proposed research are encouraged to apply. The applicant should hold a junior faculty position (with 2 years of appointment as an instructor, an assistant professor or an equivalent junior faculty rank) at an accredited academic medical institution
Level of Study: Professional development
Type: Grant
Value: Up to US$130,000
Length of Study: 2 years
Frequency: Annual
Country of Study: United States of America
Application Procedure: Applicants must visit the website for details on the application process
Closing Date: 24 February
Funding: Corporation
Contributor: Pfizer Inc

For further information contact:

Email: Amanda.solis@pfizer.com

Pfizer Scholars Grants in Pain Medicine

Purpose: To support the career development of junior faculty
Eligibility: Citizens or permanent residents of the United States of America who have a doctoral degree, relevant research experience are encouraged to apply. The applicant should hold a junior faculty position (with 2 years of appointment as an instructor, an assistant professor or an equivalent junior faculty rank) at an accredited academic medical institution
Level of Study: Professional development
Type: Grant
Value: US$130,000

Length of Study: 2 years
Frequency: Annual
Country of Study: United States of America
Application Procedure: Applicants must visit the website for details on the application process
Closing Date: 5 January
Funding: Corporation
Contributor: Pfizer Inc

For further information contact:

Email: mzebrowski@metrohealth.org

Pfizer Visiting Professorships Program

Purpose: To create opportunities for selected institutions to invite a distinguished expert for three days of teaching
Eligibility: Open to accredited medical schools and/or affiliated teaching hospitals
Level of Study: Postgraduate
Type: Grant
Value: US$7,500 each
Frequency: Annual
Country of Study: Any country
Application Procedure: Applications available online
Closing Date: 12 February
Additional Information: researchfunding.duke.edu/pfizer-visiting-professorship-program

For further information contact:

Email: mzebrowski@metrohealth.org

Transthyretin Amyloidosis (ATTR) Competitive Grant Program/ ASPIRE

Subjects: Transthyretin Amyloidosis (ATTR) including cardiomyopathy, peripheral neuropathy, and mixed phenotypes
Purpose: The intent of this Request for Proposal (RFP) is to improve the care of patients with ATTR by improving our understanding of disease epidemiology, pathophysiology, early diagnosis, prognosis, and emerging treatment paradigms.
Eligibility: Only organizations are eligible to receive grants, not individuals or medical practice groups. The principal investigator (PI) and institution must be based in one of the eligible countries noted above. The applicant (PI) must have a medical or postdoctoral degree (MD, PhD, or equivalent), an advanced nursing degree (BSN with a MS/PhD), or a degree in Pharmacy, Physiotherapy, or Social Work. Applicant must be affiliated with a host institution. Both early career and experienced investigators are encouraged to apply and consideration will be given to all proposals meeting the selection criteria
Type: Grant
Value: Up to US$75,000
Country of Study: United States of America
Application Procedure: Go to www.cybergrants.com/pfizer/Research and sign in. First-time users should click "REGISTER NOW"
No. of awards offered: Up to four
Closing Date: 17 May
Additional Information: arci.org/pfizer-aspire-ttr-amyloidosis-grants-program/

Phi Beta Kappa Society

1606 New Hampshire Avenue, NW, Washington, DC 20009, United States of America.

Tel: (1) 202 265 3808
Email: info@pbk.org
Website: www.pbk.org

Since 1776, Phi Beta Kappa has championed education in the arts and sciences, fostered freedom of thought, and recognized academic excellence. Phi Beta Kappa grew along with American higher education into an organization grounded in liberal arts and sciences learning and freedom of inquiry.

The Mary Isabel Sibley Fellowship

Purpose: This fellowship was designed to reward women pursuing graduate work in one of two fields of study, French or Greek, with the experience of researching and living abroad.
Eligibility: The fellowship is intended, according to the donor's wishes, for women in the early stages of their research careers who 1. Demonstrate ability to carry on original research. 2. Hold a doctorate/have fulfilled all requirements for doctorate except the dissertation (ABD). 3. Plan to devote full-time work to research during the fellowship year. Under appropriate circumstances, if approved by Phi Beta Kappa, candidates may hold other positions concurrently with the Sibley Fellowship.
Level of Study: Research
Type: Fellowship
Value: US$20,000
Length of Study: 1 year, non-renewable
Frequency: Annual
Country of Study: Any country
Application Procedure: Applications must include 1. A work proposal. 2. Transcripts from all institutions

(Transcripts do not need to come directly from the institution). 3. Three letters of recommendation should be uploaded directly by each recommender at this link.
Closing Date: 1 January
Funding: Private
Additional Information: www.pbk.org/Sibley

For further information contact:

Email: asherman@pbk.org

PhRMA Foundation

950 F Street, N.W. Suite 300, Washington, DC 20004, United States of America.

Tel: (1) 202 572 7756
Email: foundation@phrma.org.
Website: www.phrmafoundation.org/
Contact: PhRMA Foundation

The PhRMA Foundation works to improve public health by proactively investing in innovative research, education and value-driven health care. Supporting and encouraging young scientists to pursue novel projects to advance innovative and transformative research efforts. Using data, sound methodologies and advanced technology to inform decisions.

Patient-Centered Outcomes Challenge Award

Subjects: Health economics, outcomes research, clinical sciences, health care evaluation, public health
Purpose: The PhRMA Foundation is committed to driving real change in health care delivery and recognizes the benefit of shared knowledge.
Level of Study: Postdoctorate, Postgraduate (MSc)
Type: Award
Value: The winner will receive US$50,000; The runner up will receive US$25,000; Third place will receive US$5,000
Frequency: Annual
Country of Study: Any country
Closing Date: 1 March

Postdoctoral Fellowship in Health Outcomes Research

Purpose: To seek further development and refine their research skills through formal postdoctoral training. These fellowships are designed for individuals engaged in a multidisciplinary research training program that will create or extend their credentials.
Eligibility: 1. Applicants (U.S. and non-U.S. citizens) attending schools of medicine, pharmacy, public health, nursing, and dentistry are eligible for this award. 2. Applicants (U.S. and non-U.S. citizens) must have a firm commitment from a sponsor (a.k.a. mentor) at an accredited U.S. university. 3. Applicants must hold a PhD, PharmD, or MD degree. 4. If you do not hold one at the time of application submission, please state in your extended letter when you expect to receive it, as it must be received before funding could begin. 5. Applicants are encouraged to apply at the earliest point possible in their postdoctoral research. 6. Applicants requesting funds to continue an existing postdoctoral program for a third to fifth year will not be considered, nor will preference be given to those applying for funds to support postdoctoral work in the laboratory where their graduate work was performed. 7. Applicants must write and submit a research plan and provide the mentor's research record, as well as a description of how the mentoring experience will enhance their career development in Health Outcomes Research.
Level of Study: Doctorate, Masters Degree, Postdoctorate, Postgraduate (MSc)
Type: Fellowship
Value: US$60,000 per year
Length of Study: two-year
Frequency: Annual
Country of Study: United States of America
Application Procedure: We look forward to receiving your application. Items needed 1. General Registration Information 2. Applicant Biosketch (should be NIH or NSF format) 3. Extended Letter 4. Project/Research Title 5. Project/Research Abstract 6. Project/Research Description 7. Transcripts
Closing Date: 10 February
Additional Information: www.phrmafoundation.org/awards/post-doctoral-fellowships/value-assessment-health-outcomes/

For further information contact:

Email: info@phrmafoundation.org

Postdoctoral Fellowship in Translational Medicine

Purpose: This award supports individuals engaged in multidisciplinary/collaborative research training programs that will extend their credentials in Translational Medicine. To support research that can readily translate into positively impacting patients and physicians.

Eligibility: 1. Applicants (U.S. and non-U.S. citizens) must have a firm commitment from a sponsor (a.k.a. mentor) at an accredited U.S. university or research institution. 2. Applicants must hold a PhD, DSc, DEng, or MD degree, and seek to further develop and refine their skills and understanding of Translational Medicine through postdoctoral training. If you do not hold one at the time of application submission, please state in your extended letter when you expect to receive it, as it must be received before funding could begin. 3. Applicants are encouraged to apply at the earliest point possible in their postdoctoral research. 4. Applicants must write and submit a research plan and provide the mentor's research record, as well as a description of how the mentoring experience will enhance the applicant's career development in Translational Medicine. 5. A key component of Translational Medicine involves collaborative programs that span non-clinical and clinical domains, potentially involving multiple laboratories, advisers, and institutions.
Level of Study: Doctorate, Masters Degree, Postdoctorate
Type: Fellowship
Value: US$60,000
Length of Study: Two years
Frequency: Annual
Country of Study: United States of America
Application Procedure: Items needed 1. General Registration Information 2. Applicant Biosketch (should be NIH or NSF format) 3. Extended Letter 4. Project/Research Title 5. Project/Research Abstract 6. Research Plan
Closing Date: 10 February
Additional Information: www.phrmafoundation.org/awards/post-doctoral-fellowships/translational-medicine/

Pierre Elliott Trudeau Foundation

600 - 1980 Sherbrooke Street West, Montreal, Quebec H3H 1E8, Canada.

Tel: (1) 514 938 0001
Email: competition@trudeaufoundation.ca
Website: www.trudeaufoundation.ca/

The Pierre Elliott Trudeau Foundation is an independent and non-partisan charity established in 2001 as a living memorial to the former prime minister. The Pierre Elliott Trudeau Foundation represents much more than a Scholarship. We are a gateway for bold, cutting-edge doctoral researchers to become Engaged Leaders who have meaningful impact in their communities and institutions.

Pierre Elliott Trudeau Foundation Doctoral Scholarships

Purpose: This three-year leadership program is designed to train engaged leaders, equipping outstanding doctoral candidates with the skills to translate their ideas into action, for the betterment of their communities, Canada, and the world. Up to 16 doctoral Scholars are selected each year and receive generous funding for their studies in addition to leadership training in the context of Brave Spaces.
Eligibility: 1. You must be already accepted into or in year one, two, or three of a full-time doctoral program in the humanities or social sciences. 2. Your doctoral work must relate to at least one of the Foundation's Four Themes Human Rights and Dignity, Responsible Citizenship, Canada and the World, People and their Natural Environment. 3. Be a Canadian citizen studying at a Canadian or foreign institution, or a non-Canadian (permanent resident or foreign national) enrolled in a doctoral program at a Canadian institution.
Level of Study: Doctorate, Postdoctorate
Type: Scholarship
Value: Up to CA$40,000 per year
Length of Study: 3 years
Frequency: Annual
Country of Study: Canada
Application Procedure: In order to complete your application, you will need to provide 1. Demographic information on yourself The Foundation gathers demographic information for statistical purposes, in order to fulfill its commitment to diversity and inclusion. This information will only be used by the Pierre Elliott Trudeau Foundation. 2. Essay Questions Provide answers (200 to 400 words) to four essay questions. 3. Doctoral Projects and Themes Provide information on your doctoral project, with answers ranging from 200 to 400 words in length. 4. Upload Transcripts Upload transcripts for all your post-secondary education, except information related to CEGEP in Quebec, should you have attended CEGEP in Quebec.
No. of awards offered: three years
Closing Date: 5 January

Pine Tree State 4-H Foundation

York Complex #1, Orono, ME 04469, United States of America.

Tel: (1) 207 581 3739
Email: extension@maine.edu
Website: extension.umaine.edu/4hfoundation/

P

Since 1961 the Maine 4-H Foundation has played an active role in supporting the University of Maine Cooperative Extension 4-H program. With your help it will continue to do so for many years into the future.

Azure Dillon 4-H Memorial Scholarship

Purpose: The purpose of scholarship is for the graduating high school seniors and for the female members.
Eligibility: 1. This scholarship is available for female 4-H members in Maine who are active in 4-H activities. 2. Students must be graduating high school seniors or have previously graduated from high school but delayed going to college for no more than one year.
Level of Study: Graduate
Type: Scholarship
Value: US$1,000
Frequency: Annual
Country of Study: United States of America
Application Procedure: Application requirements for the Azure Dillon 4-H Memorial Scholarship are 1. Recommendation letter 2. Application form 3. Official Transcript 4. Story 5. Resume
No. of awards offered: 1
Closing Date: 1 March
Funding: Private
Additional Information: extension.umaine.edu/4hfoundation/wp-content/uploads/sites/18/2020/11/scholarship-application-form-2021.pdf

Plymouth University

Drake Circus, Plymouth, Devon PL4 8AA, United Kingdom.

Tel: (44) 1752 600 600
Email: india@plymouth.ac.uk
Website: www.plymouth.ac.uk

The University of Plymouth is a public university that was established in 1862 as a polytechnic institute. The institute gained the status of a university in 1992 and is also the first contemporary university to start a private medical and dental school. It is affiliated to ACU, EUA, CHUC, and Universities UK. The university has academic collaborations with several renowned institutes including GSM London, Highlands College, Weymouth College, Strode College, City of Bristol College, and Exeter College.

International Postgraduate Gaza Scholarships

Purpose: These scholarships will be awarded on a competitive basis to prospective masters students.
Eligibility: To be considered for the scholarship you must 1. be a citizen of Gaza. 2. be self-funding and classified as overseas for tuition fee purposes. 3. hold a conditional or unconditional offer from the University of Sheffield before the specified deadline to study a full-time postgraduate taught Master's course starting in September 2024.
Level of Study: Postgraduate, Postgraduate (MSc)
Type: Scholarship
Value: Each scholarship will be for a fee discount of £5,000 on a masters programme at Plymouth University.
Frequency: Annual
Country of Study: United Kingdom
Application Procedure: Please send completed application form as an attachment to internationalscholarships@plymouth.ac.uk along with a copy of your offer letter; a copy of final transcript/marks sheet from undergraduate degree (if final transcript is not available at the time of application please send the most recent or provisional results); a reference letter, from a suitable source, supporting this scholarship application (please do not supply the same reference as that submitted with the postgraduate application). www.plymouth.ac.uk/uploads/production/document/path/5/5758/GazaScholarship2016.docx
Closing Date: 31 May

For further information contact:

Tel: (44) 114 222 1319
Email: financialhelp@sheffield.ac.uk

International Student Merit Scholarship

Purpose: This scholarship is available to international students who have met the conditions of their University of Plymouth offer of study for the following programmes MSc Advanced Psychology, MSc/PgDip Psychology.
Eligibility: Applicants must have received a conditional offer of a place for a postgraduate taught programme commencing in September and be holding the equivalent of a United Kingdom university 1 class Bachelors degree in a relevant subject.
Level of Study: Masters Degree, Postgraduate, Postgraduate (MSc)
Type: Scholarship
Value: £2,500
Frequency: Annual
Country of Study: United Kingdom

Application Procedure: Applicants can apply via email. For detailed information, please visit website.
Closing Date: 31 May

International Student PGT Scholarship

Purpose: Scholarships are available for international students who wish to study postgraduate taught degree courses.
Eligibility: 1. Applicants should hold a conditional offer of a place on a postgraduate taught degree programme at Plymouth University. 2. The University will automatically consider applicants with relevant Bachelor degree grades as stipulated in the list. Please note this eligibility criteria list is not exhaustive and graduates from all non-EU countries will be considered for these scholarships. 3. The Bachelor's degree must be the equivalent of a United Kingdom Honours degree, as specified by United Kingdom NARIC.
Level of Study: Postgraduate, Postgraduate (MSc)
Type: Scholarship
Value: £1,500
Frequency: Annual
Country of Study: United Kingdom
Application Procedure: If the student has applied for a postgraduate taught degree programme, they will automatically be considered for this scholarship if their final transcript or marks sheet was submitted with their application.
Closing Date: 31 May
Additional Information: www.plymouth.ac.uk/study/fees/scholarships-bursaries-and-funding/international-students/postgraduate-scholarships-for-international-students

For further information contact:

Tel: (44) 1274 236637
Email: scholarships@bradford.ac.uk

Poets Essayists Novelists American Center

588 Broadway, Suite 303, New York, NY 10012, United States of America.

Tel: (1) 212 334 1660
Email: pen@pen.org
Website: www.pen.org

PEN America stands at the intersection of literature and human rights to protect free expression in the United States and worldwide. We champion the freedom to write, recognizing the power of the word to transform the world. Our mission is to unite writers and their allies to celebrate creative expression and defend the liberties that make it possible.

The PEN Translation Fund Grants

Purpose: Its purpose is to promote the publication and reception of translated international literature in English.
Eligibility: 1. The PEN/Heim Translation Fund provides grants to support the translation of book-length works of fiction, creative nonfiction, poetry, or drama that have not previously appeared in English in print or have appeared only in an outdated or otherwise flawed translation. 2. Works should be translations-in-progress, as the grant aims to provide support for completion. 3. There are no restrictions on the nationality or citizenship of the translator, but the works must be translated into English. 4. The Fund seeks to encourage translators to undertake projects they might not otherwise have had the means to attempt. 5. Works with multiple translators, literary criticism, and scholarly or technical texts do not qualify. 6. Translators who have previously been awarded grants by the Fund are ineligible to reapply for three years after the year in which they receive a grant. 7. Please note that projects that have been previously submitted and have not received a grant are unlikely to be reconsidered in a subsequent year. 8. Projects may have up to two translators. 9. Translators may only submit one project per year.
Level of Study: Unrestricted
Type: Grant
Value: US$2,000 to US$4,000
Frequency: Annual
Country of Study: United States of America
Application Procedure: 1. The application form, with all items completed: a. A 1-2 page, single-spaced statement outlining the work and describing its importance. b. A biography and bibliography of the author, including information on translations of his or her work into other languages. c. A CV of the translator, no longer than 3 pages. d. If the book is not in the public domain and the project is not yet under contract, please include a photocopy of the copyright notice on the original (the copyright notice is a line including the character, a date, and the name of the copyright holder, which appears as part of the front matter in every book), and a letter from the copyright holder stating that English-language rights to the book are available. A letter or copy of an email from the copyright holder is sufficient. e. If the translation is currently under contract with a publisher, please submit a copy of the contract. 2. An 8–10 page, single-spaced sample of the translation. For prose, this should be within the range of 3,000-

5,000 words. For poetry, please include 1–2 poems per page, within the 8–10 page range. 3. The same passage in the original language (and, if the work has been previously translated, the same passage in the earlier version).
Closing Date: 1 June
Additional Information: pen.org/pen-heim-grants/

For further information contact:

Email: awards@pen.org.

Polycystic Kidney Disease Foundation

1001 E 101st Terrace Suite 220, Kansas City, MO 64131, United States of America.

Tel: (1) 816 931 2600
Email: pkdcure@pkdcure.org
Website: www.pkdcure.org
Contact: PKD Foundation

We are the only organization in the U.S. solely dedicated to finding treatments and a cure for polycystic kidney disease (PKD). We fund research, education, advocacy, support, and awareness on a national and local level. We fund basic and clinical research, nephrology fellowships, and scientific meetings. We fund research, advocate for patients, and build a community for all impacted by PKD.

Polycystic Kidney Disease Foundation Grant-In-Aid

Purpose: The principal goal of our research grant program is the development of clinical interventions for the treatment of PKD. This program funds basic laboratory research aimed at increasing understanding of the genetic and pathological processes involved in PKD as well as research with an obvious or direct potential to accelerate the development of potential therapies.
Eligibility: 1. Applicants must have an M.D., Ph.D. or equivalent degree and hold a faculty appointment at the institution where the research will be conducted at the time of award. 2. Applicants need not be United States citizens. 3. No fellowships will be awarded under this RFA, although salary support for personnel working on the project may be requested. 4. Applicants may only submit one grant proposal per funding cycle.
Level of Study: Doctorate, Masters Degree, Postdoctorate
Type: Research grant
Value: Award amounts will equal US$80,000 direct costs per year for two years, for a total grant award of US$160,000 (or US$240,000 for a three-year Young Investigator Award).
Length of Study: 2 or 3 years
Frequency: Annual
Country of Study: Any country
Application Procedure: 1. Applicants will be asked to submit a project proposal, letters of support, and budget details through the Proposal Central platform. 2. If the application is a resubmission, a response to reviewers will be requested. 3. If eligible, applicants may also submit justification to be considered for the Young Investigator Award.
Closing Date: 19 January
Funding: Foundation, Individuals, Private

Population Council

One Dag Hammarskjold Plaza, New York, NY 10017, United States of America.

Tel: (1) 877 339 0500
Email: pubinfo@popcouncil.org
Website: www.popcouncil.org

The Population Council conducts research to address critical health and development issues. Our work allows couples to plan their families and chart their futures. We conduct research and programs in more than 50 countries. Our New York headquarters supports a global network of offices in Africa, Asia, Latin America, and the Middle East.

Health and Population Innovation Fellowship Program

Purpose: To support mid-career individuals who have innovative ideas and the capacity to help shape public debate in the field of population, rights and reproductive health
Level of Study: Postdoctorate, Professional development
Type: Fellowship
Length of Study: 1 year
Frequency: Annual
Study Establishment: The Population Council, New Delhi
Country of Study: India
Application Procedure: Request application form
Closing Date: 15 September
Funding: Foundation
Contributor: John D. and Catherine T. MacArthur Foundation
No. of awards given last year: 12

Additional Information: nursing.duke.edu/centers-institutes/center-nursing-research/postdoctoral-fellowship-health-innovation

For further information contact:

Zone 5A, Ground Floor India Habitat Centre, Lodi Road, New Delhi, Delhi 110003, India.

Tel: (91) 11 2464 2901
Fax: (91) 11 2464 2903
Email: fellowships@pcindia.org

Transmission of Immunodeficiency Viruses: Postdoctoral Research Position

For further information contact:

Tel: (1) 212 327 7794
Fax: (1) 212 327 7764
Email: mpope@popcouncil.org

Prehistoric Society

Institute of Archaeology, University College London, 31-34 Gordon Square, London WC1H 0PY, United Kingdom.

Email: prehistoric@ucl.ac.uk
Website: www.prehistoricsociety.org

The Prehistoric Society's interests are world-wide and extend from the earliest human origins to the emergence of written records. Founded in 1935, we currently have around 1500 members in over 40 countries. The Society is registered in England and Wales as a company limited by guarantee and is a registered charity.

Collections Study Award

Eligibility: The award will be available to partnerships between a museum and a named early-stage researcher (post-graduate, post-doctorate or equivalent experience) and both parties will be eligible for a contribution to the costs incurred. Third-party ('external') costs will also be eligible where essential to the successful outcome of the project. Applications may be submitted by the named researcher or by the museum. The named researcher is required to be a member of the Prehistoric Society.
Level of Study: Postdoctorate, Postgraduate
Type: Award
Value: Up to £3000
Frequency: Annual
Country of Study: Any country
Closing Date: 31 January
Funding: Private
Additional Information: www.prehistoricsociety.org/grants/collections-study-award

For further information contact:

Email: admin@prehistoricsociety.org

Prehistoric Society Conference Fund

Purpose: It's aim is to further the development of prehistory as an international discipline. To offer funding to those who might not otherwise be able to travel to an international conference.
Eligibility: There are no eligibility restrictions.
Level of Study: Unrestricted
Type: Scholarship
Value: £200–300
Frequency: Annual
Country of Study: Any country
Application Procedure: Applications from both members and non-members will be considered. Applications may also be made by conference organisers, on behalf of attending scholars. Please check website for application www.prehistoricsociety.org/grants/conference_fund/
Closing Date: 31 January
Funding: Private
Additional Information: www.prehistoricsociety.org/grants/conference-fund

For further information contact:

Email: admin@prehistoricsociety.org

Research Fund

Purpose: The Research Grant aims to offer small "pump-primer" grants to projects in their early stages. A further aim is to give preference to projects showing innovation in the field of prehistory research and to those scholars in the earliest stages of their research careers.
Eligibility: The Research Fund is open only to members of the Prehistoric Society. The Prehistoric Society cannot accept applications for salaries or student funding. Post-excavation work relating to excavations not originally sponsored by the Society will only be considered in situations of exceptional research potential that exceed reasonable, initial planning

P

expectations. Where applications are being made to help fund an excavation, the Society will only consider funding the project to assessment stage. The society may, however, consider an application to fund post-excavation work in the following year.
Level of Study: Unrestricted
Type: Award
Value: £100-£1,500 per award
Frequency: Annual
Country of Study: Any country
Application Procedure: Applications will only be considered from members of the society.
Closing Date: 31 January
Funding: Private
Additional Information: www.prehistoricsociety.org/grants/research-fund

For further information contact:

Email: admin@prehistoricsociety.org

The John and Bryony Coles Bursary (Student Travel Award)

Purpose: The purpose of the bursary is to permit the recipients to travel abroad (i.e. outside their countries of residence and registered study) to gain a better understanding of prehistoric archaeology, through the active study of archaeology, whether by taking part in excavations, surveys or other fieldwork, by working in museums, or by travelling to visit sites.
Eligibility: Applicants must be registered students of archaeology (either part or full time) in the later stages of undergraduate study or in the early years of postgraduate study, or other equivalent status, without restriction on age. All applicants must provide proof of their student status (i.e. a letter from their institution). Student cards will not be accepted.
Level of Study: Unrestricted
Type: Award
Value: £200 and £300 each are usually given each year.
Frequency: Annual
Country of Study: Any country
Application Procedure: Applications will only be considered from members of the society.
Closing Date: 31 January
Funding: Private
Additional Information: www.prehistoricsociety.org/grants/the_john_and_bryony_coles_bursary_student_travel_award/

For further information contact:

Email: admin@prehistoricsociety.org

President's Commission on White House Fellowships

1600 Pennsylvania Ave NW, Washington, DC 20500, United States of America.

Tel: (1) 202 395 4522
Email: comments@whitehouse.gov
Website: www.whitehouse.gov/
Contact: The White House

The White House is where the President and First Family of the United States live and work - but it's also the People's House, where we hope all Americans feel a sense of inclusion and belonging. Thousands of people work in the West Wing, the East Wing, the Cabinet, and the Executive Office of the President.

White House Fellowships

Purpose: The purpose of the White House Fellows program is to provide gifted and highly motivated emerging leaders with some first-hand experience in the process of governing the Nation and a sense of personal involvement in the leadership of society.
Eligibility: 1. Applicants must be U.S. citizens. 2. Employees of the Federal government are not eligible unless they are career military personnel. 3. Applicants must have completed their undergraduate education by the time they begin the application process. 4. There are no formal age restrictions. However, the Fellowship program was created to give selected Americans the experience of government service early in their careers.
Level of Study: Postgraduate
Type: Fellowships
Length of Study: 1 year
Frequency: Annual
Country of Study: United States of America
Application Procedure: 1. If you have additional questions about the program, please contact our program office at whitehousefellows@who.eop.gov 2. If you encounter technical difficulties with your application, please contact WHFApplication@opm.gov.
Closing Date: 6 January
Funding: Government
Additional Information: www.whitehouse.gov/briefing-room/statements-releases/2022/11/03/2023-2024-white-house-fellowship/

For further information contact:

Email: whitehousefellows@who.eop.gov

Prime Minister's Research Fellowship

Hauz Khas, New Delhi, Delhi 110 016, India.

Email: pmrfsupport@iitd.ac.in
Website: www.pmrf.in/

Prime Minister's Research Fellowship scheme aims to attract the talent pool of the country to doctoral programmes of Indian Institute of Science (IISc), Indian Institutes of Science Education & Research (IISERs), Indian Institutes of Technology (IITs), National Institute of Technology (NITs) and Central Universities for carrying out research in cutting edge science and technology domains, with focus on national priorities.

Prime Minister's Research Fellowship Scheme

Purpose: The aim of this fellowship is to promote technical research studies and attract meritorious students to pursue doctoral programmes at leading institutions in India. Selected students will get admission in Ph.D. programmes at IISc/IISERs/IITs and Central Universities.
Eligibility: To be eligible, an applicant must 1. Apply for a PhD programme at one of the PMRF granting institutes either through direct entry channel or lateral entry channel. For Direct Entry Channel the following criteria 1. Have completed or been pursuing the final year of 4- (or 5) year undergraduate or 5-year integrated M.Tech or 5-year integrated M.Sc. or 2-year M.Sc. or 5-year undergraduate-postgraduate dual degree programs in Science and Technology streams from IISc/IITs/NITs/IISERs/IIEST and centrally funded universities with a CGPA/CPI of at least 8.0 (on a 10 point scale). 2. Have completed or been pursuing the final year of 4- (or 5) year undergraduate or 5-year integrated M. Tech or 5-year integrated M.Sc. or 2-year M.Sc. or 5-year undergraduate-postgraduate dual degree programs in Science and Technology streams from any other (not covered in the first point) Institute/University recognized in India with a CGPA/CPI of at least 8.0 (on a 10-point scale). 3. Have qualified GATE and be pursuing or have completed M.Tech./MS by Research at one of PMRF granting institutions having a minimum CGPA or CPI of 8.0 (on a 10-point scale) at the end of the first semester with a minimum of four courses. For Lateral Entry Channel the following criteria are 1. Be pursuing PhD in one of the PMRF granting institutions and have completed at most 12 months in the PhD programme (if they have joined the programme with a Master's degree), OR have completed at most 24 months in the PhD programme (if they have joined the programme with a Bachelor's degree). 2. Have completed at least four courses in the PhD programme, each of which should be a full-semester course. 3. Have obtained an aggregate CGPA of 8.5 (out of 10) or higher.
Level of Study: MBA, Masters Degree, Postgraduate, Postgraduate (MSc), Undergraduate
Type: Fellowship
Value: Up to ₹80,000
Frequency: Annual
Country of Study: India
Application Procedure: 1. Click the 'Apply Online' button below. 2. Then click the 'Apply Now' button. 3. Register on the site, if not registered. 4. Log in to begin the application process. 5. Fill the required details in the online application form. 6. Upload the necessary documents as part of the application process. 7. Click on the 'Submit' button to complete the application process.
Closing Date: December
Funding: Government
Additional Information: www.pmrf.in/fellowship

Prince Charles Hospital Foundation's

GPO Box 3175, Brisbane, QLD 4001, Australia.

Tel: (61) 1800 501 269
Email: info@thecommongood.org.au
Website: www.thecommongood.org.au

The Common Good is all of us working together to give precious time to researchers, so they can give more time to us and those we love to live happier, healthier, longer lives.

Prince Charles Hospital Foundation's PhD Scholarship

Purpose: The aim of the scholarship is to support educational academic research and high-quality research training at TPCH or in the significant partnership with TPCH and its associated community programs. The scholarship provides the applicant with a living stipend to undertake research at or in significant association with, The Prince Charles Hospital

Eligibility: Applicants from Australia are eligible to apply for the scholarship. Applicants must be enrolled, or soon to be enrolled, full-time in a PhD program at an Australian University
Type: Scholarship
Value: The scholarship will be valued at AU$27,082 per annum. The scholarship provides the applicant with a living stipend to undertake research at or insignificant association with, The Prince Charles Hospital
Country of Study: Australia
Application Procedure: See the website
Closing Date: 24 February
Additional Information: tpchfoundation.smartygrants.com.au/PhD2023

For further information contact:

Email: Megan.Grace@tpchfoundation.org.au

Q

Qalaa Holdings Scholarship Foundation (QHSF)

Qalaa Holdings Scholarship Foundation, P.O Box: 29, Cairo EG-11516, Egypt.

Tel: (20) 2 2794 5553
Email: info@qalaascholarships.org
Website: qalaascholarships.org/

The Qalaa Holdings Scholarship Foundation was created in 2007, out of a strong will to contribute to national development through creating high caliber professionals to help enhance Egypt's growth in all sectors. The Foundation is funded by an endowment from Qalaa Holdings to grant academic scholarships for talented and promising young Egyptian men and women to pursue master degrees abroad in all fields of study.

Citadel Capital Scholarship

Eligibility: Students from Egypt can apply
Level of Study: Postgraduate
Type: Scholarship
Value: US$50,000
Frequency: Annual
Country of Study: Egypt
Application Procedure: Application form is only accepted by postal mail or through the FedEx account.
Closing Date: 15 April

For further information contact:

Qalaa Holdings Scholarship Foundation, P.O Box: 29, Cairo EG-11516, Egypt.

Email: info@citadelscholarships.org

Queen Elisabeth International Music Competition of Belgium

20 rue aux Laines, B-1000 Brussels, Belgium.

Tel: (32) 2 213 4050
Email: info@queenelisabethcompetition.be
Website: queenelisabethcompetition.be/
Contact: Secretariat

One of the most demanding and also one of the most widely publicised international competitions, the Queen Elisabeth Competition, ever since its creation in 1937, has established itself as a springboard for young violinists, pianists, singers, and cellists on the threshold of an international career. The competition aims, above all, to serve as an intermediary between those young virtuosos and the world's great musical venues.

Queen Elisabeth International Music Competition of Belgium

Purpose: To provide career support for young pianists, singers, violinists and cellists
Eligibility: Open to musicians of any nationality who are at least 17 years of age and not older than 30 years for violin, piano, singing and cellists. The competition is made up of a first round, a semi-final and a final round
Level of Study: Unrestricted
Type: Competition
Value: Prizes, awards and certificates along with cash prizes will be awarded
Frequency: Annual
Country of Study: Any country
Application Procedure: Applicants must obtain an application form from the Secretariat of the Competition or via the website

Palgrave Macmillan (ed.), *The Grants Register 2024*,
https://doi.org/10.1057/978-1-349-96073-6

No. of awards offered: Unrestricted
Closing Date: November
Funding: Private
No. of applicants last year: Unrestricted
Additional Information: queenelisabethcompetition.be/en/competitions/cello-2022/

Queen Margaret University

Queen Margaret University Drive, Musselburgh, Edinburgh EH21 6UU, United Kingdom.

Tel: (44) 131 474 0000
Email: rilo@qmu.ac.uk
Website: www.qmuc.ac.uk
Contact: Professor Anthony Cohen, Principal

We aim to shape a better world through education, research and innovation. Our person-centred approach to learning makes us stand out from other universities, along with our focus on making society better. We dedicate ourselves to subjects where we can offer a distinctive offering - in healthcare; social sciences; creative arts; business, management and enterprise; and primary and secondary teaching.

Students Awards Agency for Scotland Postgraduate Students' Allowances Scheme (PSAS)

Purpose: Under the scheme, students may receive support for certain full-time vocational courses, mostly at diploma level.
Eligibility: To be eligible for postgraduate support students must meet the residence and previous study conditions; and take an eligible course.
Level of Study: Postgraduate
Type: Award
Value: £10,000
Frequency: Annual
Study Establishment: Queen Margaret University College
Country of Study: United Kingdom
No. of awards offered: 7
Closing Date: 8 April
Contributor: Students Awards Agency for Scotland (SAAS)
Additional Information: www.postgraduatestudentships.co.uk/opportunity/postgraduate-student-allowance-scheme/22237

Queen Mary, University of London

Admissions and Research Student Office, Mile End Road, London E1 4NS, United Kingdom.

Tel: (44) 20 7882 5555
Email: admissions@qmul.ac.uk
Website: www.qmul.ac.uk

Queen Mary has a long, proud and distinctive history built on four historic institutions stretching back to 1785 and beyond.

ANID (Becas Chile)

Subjects: PhD or Masters study in any subject.
Purpose: Queen Mary has an agreement with ANID Becas Chile (formerly known as CONICYT), which allows us to offer funding for postgraduate students (Master's and PhDs). This co-funded scholarship is available across all of our full-time Masters and PhD programmes.
Level of Study: Doctorate, Masters Degree
Type: Award
Value: Tuition fee, stipend and airfare.
Frequency: Annual
Country of Study: Other
Country of Study: Chile
Application Procedure: Please visit the ANID website for information about the scholarships and how to apply.
No. of awards offered: Variable
Additional Information: www.qmul.ac.uk/scholarships/items/anid-becas-chile-1.html

For further information contact:

Email: f.mckay@qmul.ac.uk

ANII Becas

Purpose: ANII and Queen Mary have formally partnered to fund Uruguayan Master's and Doctoral students to study at Queen Mary.
Level of Study: Doctorate, Masters Degree
Type: Scholarships
Value: US$20,000 per year
Frequency: Annual
Country of Study: United Kingdom
Application Procedure: Applicants should first apply to Queen Mary for admission and then to ANII for the scholarship.

No. of awards offered: Up to 5
Closing Date: 22 March
Additional Information: www.qmul.ac.uk/scholarships/items/anii-becas.html

For further information contact:

Email: f.mckay@qmul.ac.uk

Associate Alumni Bursary

Subjects: All Taught Masters courses in Humanities and Social Sciences
Purpose: Queen Mary offers students who have studied as an Associate Student a bursary of 20% reduction on tuition fees when returning for a postgraduate taught programme from September 2023. This award is automatically awarded and students are not required to submit a formal application.
Eligibility: 1. Must have studied on an Associate Student Programme in the last three academic years - the scheme is currently open to students who have studied with us between September 2014 - present. 2. Must have successfully completed their semester or year abroad at Queen Mary. 3. Must enrol on a postgraduate taught programme in the Faculty of Humanities and Social Sciences.
Level of Study: Postgraduate
Type: Award
Value: 20% tuition fee discount
Frequency: Annual
Country of Study: Any country
Application Procedure: Students should submit an application for their programme of study using the following application link www.qmul.ac.uk/postgraduate/taught/applyfortaughtprogrammes/ and inform us via email following submitting the application to scholarships@qmul.ac.uk
No. of awards offered: Unlimited
Additional Information: www.qmul.ac.uk/scholarships/items/associate-alumni-bursary.html

For further information contact:

Email: scholarships@qmul.ac.uk

B.A. Krukoff Fellowship in Systematics

Subjects: MSc Plant and Fungal Taxonomy, Diversity and Conservation
Purpose: The bursary is provided by the Bentham-Moxon Trust B.A. Krukoff Fund to support a student wishing to focus their MSc research project on Tropical African botany. The bursary itself will be administered by RBG Kew.
Eligibility: Applicants must 1. Have received an offer of a place on the Kew/QMUL Plant and Fungal Taxonomy Diversity and Conservation MSc programme for the 2023–24 academic year. Applicants who have received a conditional offer are also eligible to apply but, if awarded the bursary, they must fulfil all conditions of the offer no later than 31 August 2023. 2. Demonstrate their experience in Tropical African botany*. 3. Demonstrate how they will continue to work and have an impact in Tropical African Botany* after they complete the course. *Note - In this context, we consider tropical Africa to comprise those countries that are members of the African Union. The bursary recipient must 1. Be eligible to study in the UK. All applicants are advised to check the UK visa requirements and application processes as early as possible, to ensure that they fulfil any requirements before the start of the course in September. 2. Not be in receipt of any other bursaries or grants for completion of an MSc in the 2023–24 academic year.
Type: Fellowship
Value: Full tuition fees, and up to £21,000 maintenance and travel costs
Country of Study: Any country
No. of awards offered: 1
Closing Date: 31 March

For further information contact:

Email: kewmsc@kew.org

BASF (Ludwigshafen/Germany)

Purpose: BASF (Ludwigshafen/Germany) are offering three fee waivers
Level of Study: Masters Degree
Type: Scholarships
Value: £9,950 each
Frequency: Annual
Country of Study: United Kingdom
No. of awards offered: 2
Closing Date: 1 May
Additional Information: For further information about the programme, and to apply, please visit: www.qmul.ac.uk/postgraduate/taught/coursefinder/courses/121436.html www.qmul.ac.uk/scholarships/items/basf-ludwigshafengermany-.html

For further information contact:

Tel: (44) 20 7882 5555
Email: r.goerner@qmul.ac.uk

Q

Blockchain in Business and Society Scholarships

Subjects: MSc Blockchain in Business and Society Scholarships.
Eligibility: Eligible students will contacted by Queen Mary after receiving an offer and invited to apply for a scholarship. We will consider applicants that have achieved a UK 2:1 degree (Upper Second) (or equivalent), and those who are on course to achieve a 2:1.
Level of Study: Masters Degree
Type: Scholarship
Value: £10,000
Frequency: Annual
Country of Study: Any country
No. of awards offered: 3
Additional Information: www.qmul.ac.uk/scholarships/items/blockchain-.html

Business and Management Postgraduate Scholarships

Subjects: MSc and MA programmes in the School of Business and Management.
Purpose: Business and Management Postgraduate Scholarships are £3000 awards for outstanding students enrolling on a full time Master's programme in the School of Business and Management in September.
Eligibility: Eligible students will be contacted by Queen Mary after receiving an offer and invited to apply for a scholarship. We will consider applicants that have achieved a UK first class honours degree (or equivalent), and those who are on course to achieve a First. Applicants must be domiciled in one of the eligible countries.
Level of Study: Masters Degree
Type: Scholarships
Value: £5000
Frequency: Annual
Country of Study: United Kingdom
Application Procedure: There is no separate application for this scholarship. We will consider all applicants that have achieved a UK first class honours degree (or equivalent), and those who are on course to achieve a First. Applicants must be domiciled in one of the eligible countries.
No. of awards offered: 10
Additional Information: www.qmul.ac.uk/scholarships/items/business-and-management-postgraduate-scholarships.html

Children of Alumni Award

Subjects: The Children of Alumni Loyalty Award is those enrolling on a full Bachelors, Master's or Doctoral degree programme.
Purpose: The Children of Alumni Loyalty Award gives £1000 of year-1 overseas fees for children of international alumni.
Eligibility: To be eligible you must: 1. be enrolling on a full Bachelors, Master's or Doctoral degree. 2. be the child of a Queen Mary alumnus. 3. be paying at least £1000 of your fees (i.e. not full sponsored). 4. be an overseas fee payer (i.e. not paying the cheaper "Home Fee" rate).
Level of Study: Doctorate, Masters Degree, Undergraduate
Type: Award
Value: £1000 one-off fee discount
Country of Study: United Kingdom
No. of awards offered: Unlimited
Additional Information: www.qmul.ac.uk/scholarships/items/children-of-alumni-award.html

China Scholarship Council Scholarships

Subjects: All PhDs in the Faculties of Science and Engineering and Humanities and Social Sciences
Purpose: Queen Mary will provide scholarships to cover all tuition fees, whilst the CSC will provide living expenses and one return flight ticket to successful applicants. This scholarship is available to both new and continuing (current 1st year) students.
Level of Study: Postdoctorate
Type: Scholarship
Value: Full tuition fee waiver and living stipend (£1350/month)
Length of Study: 4 years
Frequency: Annual
Country of Study: Any country
No. of awards offered: 60
Closing Date: 30 January

For further information contact:

Email: international-partnerships@qmul.ac.uk

Colfuturo Scholarships

Subjects: Any Masters course and any PhD programme except those in Medicine and Dentistry
Purpose: COLFUTURO is a Colombian non-profit foundation that was established in 1991 with the support of the National Government and some of the most important companies of the private sector in the country at that time. Its main objective is to provide financial support and increase the possibilities of Colombian citizens to access high-quality postgraduate study programs abroad.
Eligibility: See website www.colfuturo.org
Level of Study: Doctorate, Masters Degree

Type: Award
Value: Up to US$50,000
Length of Study: 2 years
Country of Study: Colombia
Application Procedure: The COLFUTURO application form and terms and conditions can be found at www.colfuturo.org
No. of awards offered: Unlimited
Closing Date: 28 February
Additional Information: www.qmul.ac.uk/scholarships/items/colfuturo.html

For further information contact:

Email: f.mckay@qmul.ac.uk

DeepMind Scholarship

Subjects: MSc in Artificial Intelligence (FT) MSc in Computer Science (FT) MSc in Machine Learning for Visual Data Analytics (FT) MSc Computer Games (FT)
Purpose: The DeepMind Scholarship at Queen Mary University of London is a programme to support and encourage underrepresented groups to pursue postgraduate education in the field of Artificial Intelligence, Machine Learning and Computer Science. The scholarships are for female and/or black students as these students are currently underrepresented in these areas of study.
Eligibility: To be eligible to apply for a DeepMind Scholarship you must 1. Be a UK or International student. 2. Identify as female or have one of the following categories of ethnicity Black African; Black Caribbean; Black Other; Mixed – White and Black Caribbean; Mixed – White and Black African; or Other mixed background (to include Black African, Black Caribbean or Black Other). 3. Have a confirmed offer to study on one of the following programmes MSc in Artificial Intelligence (Full Time), MSc Computer Science (Full Time), MSc Computer Games (Full Time), and MSc in Machine Learning for Visual Data Analytics (Full Time) at Queen Mary University of London.
Level of Study: Masters Degree
Type: Scholarship
Value: Each DeepMind Scholarship will cover the cost of tuition fees, £11,850 (International fees - £27,250), a living allowance of £15,480, an annual £2,000 travel scholarship and a one-off equipment grant of £1,500.
Frequency: Annual
Country of Study: Any country
Application Procedure: 1. First, please check your eligibility to apply. The panel will not consider any applications that do not meet eligibility criteria, and awards may be withdrawn if applicants are later found not to have met eligibility criteria or to have provided false information. 2. Please download, complete and submit the application form to ioc@qmul.ac.uk. Download the DeepMind Scholarship Application Form 2023 [www.qmul.ac.uk/media/eecs/ioc/scholarship-application-forms/2022_AF_The-DeepMind-Scholarship-in-the-School-of-Electronic-Engineering-and-Computer-Science-2022.docx] here. 3. To complete your application, you will need to provide A copy of your offer letter to study on one of the following programmes at Queen Mary MSc in Artificial Intelligence (Full Time), MSc Computer Science (FT), MSc Computer Games, or MSc in Machine Learning for Visual Data Analytics (FT) programme. A completed application form, including a short statement of no more than 500 words detailing why you should be considered for the award and what motivated your interest in this area of study at Queen Mary University of London.
No. of awards offered: 4
Closing Date: 13 July

For further information contact:

Email: ioc@qmul.ac.uk

Dhaka PhD Scholarships

Subjects: Any PhD in the Faculty of Science and Engineering
Purpose: This award covers full tuition fees and if the scholar is a current Faculty member at University of Dhaka they will receive their basic salary to cover living expenses. Any shortfall between the salary and living expenses set by UKVI will need to be covered by the student.
Level of Study: Masters Degree, Postdoctorate
Type: Scholarship
Value: Full tuition fees and partial living stipend.
Frequency: Annual
Country of Study: Any country
No. of awards offered: 3
Closing Date: 31 January

Herchel Smith Scholarship in Intellectual Property

Purpose: The award will cover all tuition fees whether at the Home/EU rate or the overseas rate. It is therefore open to both UK and non-EU applicants.
Eligibility: The award is for new applicants who will enrol at the start of the coming academic year.
Level of Study: Doctorate, Postdoctorate
Type: Scholarship
Value: £19,000
Length of Study: 3 years
Frequency: Annual
Country of Study: United Kingdom
Application Procedure: Submit online application.

Closing Date: 2 June
Additional Information: www.qmul.ac.uk/law/postgraduate/funding/phd-ip/

For further information contact:

Email: g.skehan@qmul.ac.uk

Historic Royal Palaces Heritage Scholarships

Purpose: Historic Royal Palaces (HRP) wishes to make careers in the heritage sector more accessible to people from UK-resident Black, Asian, and Minority Ethnic (BAME) communities to help ensure everyone feels the palaces are for them and make them accessible and relevant for all.
Eligibility: The scholarships will cover your part-time course fees
Level of Study: Masters Degree, Postgraduate
Type: Scholarships
Value: Part-time course fees and a living allowance of £12,273 per annum
Frequency: Annual
Country of Study: United Kingdom
No. of awards offered: 2
Closing Date: 3 July
Additional Information: www.qmul.ac.uk/scholarships/items/historic-royal-palaces-heritage-scholarships.html

For further information contact:

Email: john.davis@hrp.org.uk

Marshall Scholarships

Purpose: The QMUL Marshall Scholarship offers support for candidates wishing to pursue up to two years of postgraduate study, on any Masters or PhD programme across the University. A third year of funding may be available for students engaged in doctoral degrees.
Eligibility: The award is open to US citizens
Level of Study: Masters Degree, Postgraduate
Type: Scholarships
Value: Full tuition and living costs.
Frequency: Annual
Country of Study: United Kingdom
Application Procedure: Applications are made online directly to the www.marshallscholarship.org/applications/apply
No. of awards offered: Up to 2 each year
Closing Date: September
Additional Information: www.qmul.ac.uk/scholarships/items/marshall-scholarships.html

For further information contact:

Tel: (1) 202 538 3885
Email: americas@qmul.ac.uk

Snowdon Masters Scholarship

Purpose: The Snowdon Masters Scholarship has been designed to identify and accelerate talented disabled students through higher education, creating the influencers of the future.
Eligibility: 1. Exceptional leaders, with the ability to create change within and beyond their academic field 2. Individuals that have shown excellence within their chosen subjects 3. Those that have demonstrated leadership potential with a proven drive for success 4. Ability to create change and drive disability issues 5. Proven achievements in academia, employment or voluntary activities.
Level of Study: Masters Degree
Type: Scholarships
Value: Up to £30,000
Length of Study: 1 year
Frequency: Annual
Country of Study: Any country
Application Procedure: Apply online
Closing Date: 1 April
Contributor: Snowdon Trust
Additional Information: www.qmul.ac.uk/scholarships/items/snowdon-masters-scholarship.html

Queen's Nursing Institute

1A Henrietta Place, London W1G 0LZ, United Kingdom.

Tel: (44) 20 7549 1400
Email: rosemary.cook@qni.org.uk
Website: www.qni.org.uk

The Queen's Nursing Institute is a registered charity dedicated to improving the nursing care of people in the home and community. We promote excellent nursing care for everyone, where and when they need it, provided by nurses and their teams with specific skills and knowledge.

Queen's Nursing Institute Fund for Innovation and Leadership

Purpose: Implementation of good practice, or a project or an idea, within the community

Level of Study: Graduate, Postgraduate
Type: A variable number of grants
Value: Up to £5,000
Length of Study: 1 year
Frequency: Annual
Country of Study: United Kingdom
Closing Date: 17 October
No. of awards given last year: 12
Additional Information: This content is password protected. To view it please enter your password. www.qni.org.uk/explore-qni/nurse-led-projects/fund-for-innovation-ld-leaders-2/

Queen's University of Belfast

University Road, Belfast, Northern Ireland BT7 1NN, United Kingdom.

Tel: (44) 28 9024 5133
Email: pg.office@qub.ac.uk
Website: www.qub.ac.uk/

The Queen's University of Belfast has provided a stimulating environment for postgraduate students since the 1850s. It has a reputation as a centre of academic excellence, embracing the most effective technologies and techniques of the 21 century. Queen's has 14 subjects in the top 200 in the world.

International Office Postgraduate Scholarship

Purpose: This award is exclusively for new International students beginning their first year of full-time postgraduate taught study at Queen's University Belfast in the academic year who meet the conditions of their academic offer.
Eligibility: If you are holding an offer for an eligible programme and meet the criteria as set out in these terms & conditions, you will automatically be awarded an International Office Postgraduate Taught Scholarship upon enrolment.
Level of Study: Postgraduate
Type: Award
Value: Year one award of £2,000 (fee rate 1) or £3,000 (fee rate 2)
Length of Study: 1 year
Frequency: Annual
Country of Study: United Kingdom
Application Procedure: No application necessary.
Funding: International office
Additional Information: www.qub.ac.uk/International/International-students/International-scholarships/taught-masters-scholarships/

For further information contact:

Email: internationalscholarships@qub.ac.uk

International PhD Awards

Subjects: Arts, Humanities and Social Sciences
Purpose: To support more International and EU students the Faculty of Arts, Humanities and Social Sciences (AHSS) is offering 2 PhD scholarships for September entry.
Eligibility: To qualify for an international/EU scholarship, students must be in receipt of an offer to study for a PhD degree at Queen's University Belfast within the Faculty of Arts, Humanities and Social Sciences and meet the eligibility criteria below 1. Students must not be in receipt of funding from any other organisation. 2. Students must be in a position to commence their studies in September. 3. Students must be classified as international fee paying students paying the international tuition fee rate OR be classified as EU fee paying students paying the EU tuition fee rate in order to be considered for these awards. 4. Students must hold an offer of a place on a full-time programme at the Queen's University Belfast campus, and meet any academic and language conditions attached to their offer as stated in their offer letter.
Level of Study: Postgraduate
Type: Award
Length of Study: 3 years
Frequency: Annual
Country of Study: Any country
Application Procedure: Please complete an application for admission to PhD study via the Direct Application Portal.
No. of awards offered: 2
Closing Date: 22 January

For further information contact:

Email: G.ODonnell@qub.ac.uk

Kyle Scholarship

Purpose: This postgraduate scholarship has been established by Terence Kyle, former chief executive of Linklaters. Terence went to school in Belfast and is a keen supporter of Queen's University Belfast in its efforts to provide increased opportunity for postgraduate study.
Eligibility: To be eligible for the scholarship an applicant must 1. Be classified in residency terms for fees at UK or EU status only; 2. Have received an offer of study for the

postgraduate LLM International Business Law programme in the School of Law.
Level of Study: Postgraduate
Type: Scholarship
Value: £5,000
Frequency: Annual
Country of Study: United Kingdom
Application Procedure: Applicants for the Kyle Scholarship should also submit a written statement outlining, in not more than 750 words 1. Why they want to undertake the LLM International Business Law at Queen's; 2. What they hope to achieve through this opportunity and the impact they think this will have on their career and/or future ambitions. This statement should be submitted to law.office@qub.ac.uk by the stipulated deadline.
No. of awards offered: 1
Closing Date: 9 July
Additional Information: www.qub.ac.uk/Study/funding-scholarships/ahss/SchoolofLaw/TheKyleScholarship.html

For further information contact:

Tel: (44) 28 9097 3597
Email: a.brady@qub.ac.uk

Leverhulme (LINCS) PhD Scholarship

Purpose: To support pioneering research at the interface between the social sciences and electronic engineering and computer science
Eligibility: 1. Applicants must hold a minimum 2 Class Upper Degree (21) or equivalent qualification in a relevant Technology, Social Science or Humanities Based subject. 2. Applicants must be a United Kingdom or European Union citizen. 3. Applications from non-United Kingdom or non-European Union citizens may be accepted on an exceptional basis but additional funding to cover International student fees is not available and must be secured by the applicant prior to starting. 4. Applicants must be proficient in both writing and speaking in English
Type: Scholarship
Value: Full tuition fees at standard United Kingdom rates (currently £4,195 per annum) for 3 years; a maintenance award at the Research Councils United Kingdom national rate. £1,000 per annum research training and expenses to fund the costs of study abroad, conference attendance and fieldwork
Frequency: Annual
Country of Study: United Kingdom
Closing Date: 15 January
Additional Information: worldscholarshipforum.com/fully-funded-leverhulme-scholarship-queens-university-belfast-uk-20182019/

Mary McNeill Scholarship in Irish Studies

Purpose: Two scholarships to the value of £3,000 each are available for well–qualified students enrolling in the one-year MA in Irish Studies at the Queen's University of Belfast in September. This scholarship is open only to residents of the USA or Canada, enrolling as overseas students on this MA course, and will take the form of a fee bursary covering part of their student fees.
Eligibility: Open to well-qualified United States of America or Canadian students enrolled in the MA (Irish Studies) programme
Level of Study: Postgraduate
Type: Scholarship
Value: £5000
Frequency: Annual
Study Establishment: Queen's University of Belfast
Country of Study: United Kingdom
Application Procedure: Applications will be judged by a panel chaired by the Director of Irish Studies on the basis of academic merit and reasons for taking the course. Download an Application Form McNeill Bursary Form
No. of awards offered: 2
Closing Date: 22 April
Additional Information: www.qub.ac.uk/schools/IrishStudiesGateway/Study/MAIrishStudies/FeesFundingAccommodation/

PhD Studentships in Astrophysics Research Centre

Subjects: Astrophysics
Purpose: These scholarships are available for students wishing to undertake a PhD in the Astrophysics Research Centre
Level of Study: Postgraduate
Type: Scholarship
Value: fully funded PhD studentships
Length of Study: 3 years
Frequency: Annual
Country of Study: United Kingdom
Application Procedure: Applications for post-graduate studies must be made via the QUB portal
Closing Date: 26 January
Contributor: Queen's University Belfast
Additional Information: www.qub.ac.uk/research-centres/astrophysics-research-centre/EducationandOpportunities/PHDStudentships/PhDstudentshipsintheARC/

For further information contact:

Email: e.demooij@qub.ac.uk

Queen's Loyalty Scholarship

Purpose: The Queen's Loyalty Scholarship is a 20% reduction on first year gross tuition fees available exclusively to students who have been assessed as paying International tuition fee rates and are Queen's University Belfast alumni or Exchange, Study Abroad or International Summer School students progressing to a full duration postgraduate programme at the Queen's University Belfast campus in the academic year.
Eligibility: 1. Students must hold an offer of a place on a full-time and complete duration programme at the Queen's University Belfast campus, starting in the academic year and prior to commencement of study have met any academic and language conditions attached to their offer as stated in their offer letter. 2. Students must register on their degree programme by the start date outlined in their offer.
Level of Study: Postgraduate
Type: Scholarship
Value: 20% reduction on first year gross tuition fees
Frequency: Annual
Country of Study: United Kingdom
Application Procedure: Complete the online application form to verify your previous studies at Queen's University Belfast.
Additional Information: www.qub.ac.uk/Study/funding-scholarships/Non-facultydepartments/international-office/international-office-postgraduate-loyalty-scholarship-undergraduate.html

Vice-Chancellor's International Attainment Scholarship

Purpose: Four scholarships offering a 50% reduction on full international tuition fee rates available to exceptionally talented international students starting full-time undergraduate studies in the academic year.
Eligibility: Students must hold an offer for a place on a full-time eligible undergraduate programme at the Queen's University Belfast campus which has been confirmed as their FIRM choice by their UCAS deadline, and prior to commencement of study have met any academic and language conditions attached to their offer as stated in their offer letter.
Level of Study: Undergraduate
Type: Scholarship
Value: 50% reduction on full tuition fees paid for all years of a programme, up to a maximum of four years (including advanced entry into Year 2 or Year 3)
Length of Study: 4 years
Frequency: Annual
Country of Study: United Kingdom
Application Procedure: Applicants must complete the online application form and submit a video as detailed on the application form within the deadline. response.questback.com/isa/qbv.dll/bylink?p=NbqJlAKfOA7uB8uLPyAWIBPaJT9X8Rt2ZU6dCPk3ktx2A6BtrtoMyVhwNC2W6u3zrTUU5-dZvI2RDT4JZsIEqQ2
No. of awards offered: 4
Closing Date: 8 June
Additional Information: www.qub.ac.uk/International/International-students/International-scholarships/undergraduate-scholarships/vice-chancellors-international-attainment-scholarship/

For further information contact:

Email: internationalscholarships@qub.ac.uk

Queensland University of Technology (QUT)

Research Students Centre, GPO Box 2434, Brisbane, QLD 4001, Australia.

Tel: (61) 3138 2000
Email: askqut@qut.edu.au
Website: www.qut.edu.au/

Queensland University of Technology (QUT) is a major Australian university with a truly global outlook. Home to nearly 50,000 students, we're providing real-world infrastructure, learning and teaching, and graduate skills to the next generation of change-makers.

Australian Postgraduate Award Industry Scholarships within Integrative Biology

Eligibility: Open to citizens of Australia or permanent residents having Honours 1 Degree or equivalent
Level of Study: Postgraduate
Type: Scholarship
Value: AU$25,627
Length of Study: 3 years
Frequency: Annual
Application Procedure: Check website for further details
Closing Date: 2 March

For further information contact:

Email: susanne.schmidt@uq.edu.au

Australian Research Council Australian Postgraduate Award Industry – Alternative Engine Technologies

Purpose: The multidisciplinary nature of the project will provide the student with a significant intellectual challenge, to assimilate the required background research and to integrate this knowledge to achieve the aims of the current project
Eligibility: Open to citizens of Australia or New Zealand or permanent residents who have achieved Honours 1 or equivalent, or Honours 2a or equivalent
Level of Study: Postdoctorate, Postgraduate
Type: Scholarship
Value: AU$26,140 per year
Length of Study: 3 years
Frequency: Annual
Country of Study: Australia
Application Procedure: Check website for further details
Closing Date: 28 September
Additional Information: Please check website for more details scholarship-positions.com/australian-postgraduate-award-industry-apai-phd-scholarship/2009/03/31/

For further information contact:

Tel: (61) 7 3138 5174
Email: rong.situ@qut.edu.au

Institute of Health and Biomedical Innovation Awards

Purpose: To support living expenses
Eligibility: Open for citizens of Australia or permanent residents who have achieved Honours 1 or equivalent, or Honours 2a or equivalent
Level of Study: Doctorate, Postgraduate
Type: Award
Value: AU$36,140
Length of Study: 2 years (Masters) or 3 years (PhD)
Frequency: Annual
Country of Study: Australia
Application Procedure: Check website for further details
Closing Date: 12 October

For further information contact:

Tel: (61) 7 3138 6056
Fax: (61) 7 3138 6039
Email: s.winn@qut.edu.au

International Postgraduate Research Scholarship at Queensland University of Technology

Purpose: We are building research excellence by supporting students of exceptional research potential with QUTPRAs. The number of QUTPRAs offered varies from year to year.
Eligibility: Applicant must apply for and be accepted into a PhD or professional doctorate.
Level of Study: Postgraduate
Type: Postgraduate scholarships
Value: AU$28,597
Frequency: Annual
Country of Study: Australia
No. of awards offered: Varies
Additional Information: www.qut.edu.au/study/fees-and-scholarships/scholarships/qut-postgraduate-research-award-qutpra-international

R

Radboud University Nijmegen

Houtlaan 4, NL-6525 XZ Nijmegen, The Netherlands.

Tel: (31) 24 361 61 61
Email: info@ru.nl
Website: www.ru.nl/english/

Radboud University Nijmegen was established on 17 October 1923 under the name Catholic University Nijmegen. With their own university, Dutch Catholics sought to promote the emancipation of Roman Catholics in the Netherlands, who at that time were strongly underrepresented in public administration, the legal profession, medicine and other sectors. The Radboud Foundation was the body behind this initiative. Today, Radboud University continues its commitment to the emancipation of certain groups. For example, the University has an above average percentage of female professors, compared to other Dutch universities. And of all the general universities, it has the highest relative number of students for whom neither parent had a university education (source: WO-instroommonitor, 1999-2000 t/m 2014-2015).

Orange Tulip Scholarship

Eligibility: You are eligible if you: 1. are admitted to an English-taught Master's degree programme at Radboud University, starting 1 September 2024 (and at the time of your scholarship application you need to have at least applied for this Master's programme at Radboud University) 2. have applied for an Orange Tulip Scholarship at your Nuffic NESO office before the deadline 3. have (will obtain) a Bachelor's degree achieved outside the Netherlands, have no degrees achieved in the Netherlands and did not receive any previous education in the Netherlands (exchange programmes excluded, provided that they are part of the bachelor degree achieved outside the Netherlands) 4. are a citizen of India or Indonesia and are not currently studying or working in the Netherlands 5. meet the English language proficiency requirement for the Master's programme you applied for at Radboud University 6. are not eligible for the lower EU/EEA tuition fee. 7. Eligible countries or regions: India, Indonesia.
Level of Study: Postgraduate
Type: Scholarship
Value: A reduction of the institutional tuition fee for non-EEA students (to €2.314)
Length of Study: 2 years
Country of Study: Any country
No. of awards offered: 4
Closing Date: 28 February
Additional Information: www.ru.nl/en/education/scholarships/orange-tulip-scholarship

For further information contact:

Email: scholarships@ru.nl

Radboud Encouragement Scholarship

Eligibility: You will only be eligible to apply for a Radboud Encouragement Scholarship if you: 1. hold a non-EU/non-EEA passport 2. are not eligible for the lower EEA tuition fee for other reasons 3. do not have sufficient funds or access to grants or loans to finance your studies at Radboud University 4. have (will obtain) a Bachelor's degree achieved outside the Netherlands, have no degrees achieved in the Netherlands and did not receive any previous education in the Netherlands (exchange programmes excluded, provided that they are part of the bachelor degree achieved outside the Netherlands) 5. meet the English language proficiency requirement for the Master's programme of your choice 6. are fully admitted to the English-taught Master's degree programme starting 1 September 2024 as stated in the formal letter of admission 7. are able to comply with the conditions for obtaining a visa

Palgrave Macmillan (ed.), *The Grants Register 2024*,
https://doi.org/10.1057/978-1-349-96073-6

for the Netherlands 8. are enrolled at Radboud University as a full-time student for the academic year and Master's degree programme for which the scholarship will be awarded.
Type: Scholarship
Value: Covers the full tuition fee and living costs of €11,220
Country of Study: Any country
No. of awards offered: 16
Closing Date: 28 February
Additional Information: www.ru.nl/en/education/scholarships/radboud-encouragement-scholarship

For further information contact:

Email: scholarships@ru.nl

Radboud Scholarship Programme

Purpose: The Radboud Scholarship Programme is a very selective scholarship programme. It offers talented, highly motivated, non-EEA students with outstanding study results the opportunity to be awarded a scholarship for a complete English-taught Radboud University Master's degree programme.
Eligibility: You can apply for a Radboud Scholarship if you 1. Hold a non-EU/EEA passport. 2. Are not eligible for the lower EEA tuition fee for other reasons. 3. Have (will obtain) a Bachelor's degree achieved outside the Netherlands, have no degrees achieved in the Netherlands and did not receive any previous education in the Netherlands (exchange programmes excluded, provided that they are part of the bachelor degree achieved outside the Netherlands). 4. Meet the English language proficiency requirement for the Master's programme of your choice. 5. Have been fully admitted to the English-taught Master's degree programme starting 1 September as stated in the formal letter of admission. 6. Are able to comply with the conditions for obtaining a visa for the Netherlands. 7. Are enrolled at Radboud University as a full-time student for the academic year and Master's degree programme for which the scholarship will be awarded.
Level of Study: Masters Degree
Type: Scholarship
Value: The Scholarship will reduce your tuition fee to € 2.314
Frequency: Annual
Country of Study: Any country
Application Procedure: You can apply by indicating during your application for admission (www.ru.nl/english/education/masters-programmes/application-procedure-master-pre-master/) for a Master's programme in the OSIRIS Application system that you wish to apply for a Radboud Scholarship. You will then be requested to upload three additional documents two reference letters and a curriculum vitae. For more details please visit website.
No. of awards offered: 37
Closing Date: 28 February
Funding: Private
Additional Information: For more information: www.ru.nl/english/education/masters-programmes/international-masters-students/financial-matters/scholarships-grants/read_more/rsprogramme/

For further information contact:

Houtlaan 4, NL-6525 XZ Nijmegen, Netherlands.

Tel: (31) 24 361 60 55
Email: scholarships@ru.nl; internationaloffice@io.ru.nl

Radboud Scholarship Programme for International Students

Purpose: The Radboud Scholarship Programme is a very selective scholarship programme. It offers talented, highly motivated, non-EEA students with outstanding study results the opportunity to be awarded a scholarship for a complete English-taught Radboud University Master's degree programme.
Eligibility: You are eligible to apply for a Radboud Scholarship if you 1. Hold a non-EU/EEA passport. 2. Are not eligible for the lower EEA tuition fee for other reasons. 3. Have (will obtain) a Bachelor's degree achieved outside the Netherlands, have no degrees achieved in the Netherlands and did not receive any previous education in the Netherlands (exchange programmes excluded, provided that they are part of the bachelor degree achieved outside the Netherlands). 4. Meet the English language proficiency requirement for the Master's programme of your choice. 5. Have been fully admitted to the English-taught Master's degree programme starting 1 September as stated in the formal letter of admission. 6. Are able to comply with the conditions for obtaining a visa for the Netherlands. 7. Are enrolled at Radboud University as a full-time student for the academic year and Master's degree programme for which the scholarship will be awarded.
Level of Study: Masters Degree
Type: Scholarships
Value: A partial scholarship will reduce your tuition fee to € 2.314.
Frequency: Annual
Country of Study: Netherlands
Application Procedure: You can apply by indicating during your application for admission for a Master's programme in the OSIRIS Application system that you wish to apply for

a Radboud Scholarship. You will then be requested to upload three additional documents two reference letters and a curriculum vitae. For details please vist website.
No. of awards offered: 37
Closing Date: 28 February
Additional Information: www.ru.nl/english/education/masters-programmes/financial-matters/scholarships-grants/read_more/rsprogramme/. www.scholars4dev.com/6127/radboud-university-scholarships-for-international-students/

For further information contact:

Houtlaan 4, NL-6525 XZ Nijmegen, Netherlands.

Tel: (31) 24 361 6161
Email: scholarships@ru.nl

Radboud Scholarships Programme for Masters Students

Purpose: The Radboud Scholarship Programme is a very selective scholarship programme. It offers talented, highly motivated, non-EEA students with outstanding study results the opportunity to be awarded a scholarship for a complete English-taught Radboud University Master's degree programme.
Eligibility: You are eligible to apply for a Radboud Scholarship if you 1. Hold a non-EU/EEA passport. 2. Are not eligible for the lower EEA tuition fee for other reasons. 3. Have (will obtain) a Bachelor's degree achieved outside the Netherlands, have no degrees achieved in the Netherlands and did not receive any previous education in the Netherlands (exchange programmes excluded, provided that they are part of the bachelor degree achieved outside the Netherlands). 4. Meet the English language proficiency requirement for the Master's programme of your choice. 5. Have been fully admitted to the English-taught Master's degree programme starting 1 September as stated in the formal letter of admission. 6. Are able to comply with the conditions for obtaining a visa for the Netherlands. 7. Are enrolled at Radboud University as a full-time student for the academic year and Master's degree programme for which the scholarship will be awarded.
Level of Study: Masters Degree
Type: Scholarship
Value: A partial scholarship will reduce your tuition fee to € 2.314
Frequency: Annual
Country of Study: The Netherlands
Application Procedure: You can apply by indicating during your application for admission for a Master's programme in the OSIRIS Application system that you wish to apply for a Radboud Scholarship. You will then be requested to upload three additional documents two reference letters and a curriculum vitae. For details please vist website.
No. of awards offered: 37
Closing Date: 28 February
Additional Information: For more information about the scholarship programme, you may contact the International Office via scholarships@ru.nl. www.ru.nl/english/education/masters-programmes/international-masters-students/financial-matters/scholarships-grants/read_more/rsprogramme/

For further information contact:

Houtlaan 4, NL-6525 XZ Nijmegen, Netherlands.

Tel: (31) 24 361 6161
Email: scholarships@ru.nl

Radcliffe Institute for Advanced Study

10 Garden Street, Fay House, Suite 330, Cambridge, MA 02138, United States of America.

Tel: (1) 617 496 3078
Email: info@radcliffe.harvard.edu; jane_huber@radcliffe.harvard.edu
Website: www.radcliffe.harvard.edu/
Contact: Jane F. Huber, Director of Communications

The Radcliffe Institute for Advanced Study at Harvard University, known as Harvard Radcliffe Institute, is one of the world's leading centers for interdisciplinary exploration. Harvard Radcliffe Institute is an interdisciplinary community of students, scholars, researchers, practitioners, artists, and others committed to pursuing curiosity-driven research, expanding human understanding, and grappling with questions that demand insight from across disciplines.

Radcliffe Institute Fellowship

Purpose: The Fellowship Program annually selects and supports artists, scholars, and practitioners who bring both a record of achievement and exceptional promise to the Institute.
Eligibility: Applicants may apply as individuals or in a group of two to three people working on the same project. For eligibility guidelines, please refer website www.radcliffe.harvard.edu/radcliffe-fellowship

Level of Study: Doctorate
Type: Fellowship
Value: A stipend with the possibility of an additional US$750 for travel related to conferences and job interviews. The stipend will be equal to or greater than the standard GSAS stipend amount
Frequency: Annual
Country of Study: United States of America
Application Procedure: A complete application with all necessary documents must be uploaded to CARAT. Applicants for Radcliffe Institute Dissertation Completion Fellowships must include a brief statement describing how an affiliation with the Radcliffe Institute Fellowship Program would benefit them; a two-page resume; a dissertation abstract and a table of contents; two letters of recommendation, one of which must be written by the dissertation advisor; and two faculty evaluation forms. Apply via CARAT www.pin1.harvard.edu/cas/login?service=https%3A%2F%2Fcarat.fas.harvard.edu%2Flogin%2Fcas.
No. of awards offered: 50
Closing Date: 10 February
Additional Information: www.radcliffe.harvard.edu/radcliffe-fellowship

For further information contact:

Radcliffe Institute Fellowship Program, 8 Garden Street, Byerly Hall, Cambridge, MA 02138, United States of America.

Tel: (1) 617 495 8212 or (1) 617 495 8213
Email: fellowships@radcliffe.harvard.edu; claudia_rizzini@radcliffe.harvard.edu

Radiological Society of North America, Inc. (RSNA)

820 Jorie Blvd., Suite 200, Oak Brook, IL 60523-2251, United States of America.

Tel: (1) 630 571 2670
Email: customerservice@rsna.org
Website: www.rsna.org/
Contact: Mr Scott Walter, Assistant Director, Grant Administration

The Radiological Society of North America (RSNA) is a non-profit organization with over 52,000 members from 153 countries around the world. We provide high-quality educational resources, including continuing education credits toward physicians' certification maintenance, host the world's largest radiology conference and publish five top peer-reviewed journals. Our Research and Education Foundation, which has funded US$66 million in grants since its inception, our solutions to support standards development or educational outreach to low-resource nations.

Derek Harwood-Nash International Education Scholar Grant

Eligibility: 1. Applicant must be an RSNA Member (at any level) at the time of application, and throughout duration of award. If the applicant's membership category is Member-in-Training or any other non-dues paying category, the scientific advisor or one of the coinvestigators must be a dues paying member. 2. Applicant/co-principal investigator(s) must not be agents of any for-profit, commercial company in the radiologic sciences. 3. Applicants may not submit more than one research or education grant application to the RSNA R&E Foundation per year. 4. Recipients may not have concurrent RSNA grants. 5. Supplementation of funding from other grant sources must be approved by Foundation staff if not described in the original research plan. Awards from other sources may be approved by Foundation staff if the investigator submits a satisfactory plan to address any budgetary overlap.
Level of Study: Research
Type: Grant
Value: US$75,000
Length of Study: 1 year
Country of Study: Any country
Application Procedure: All grant applications are completed online: www.rsna.org/research/funding-opportunities
Closing Date: 12 January
Additional Information: www.rsna.org/research/funding-opportunities/education-grants/derek-harwood-nash-international-scholar-grant

For further information contact:

Email: rortiz@rsna.org

Education Project Award

Eligibility: Applicant Eligibility: 1. Applicant must be an RSNA member at the time of application and the duration of the award. Faculty, residents, and fellows are encouraged to apply. 2. Applicant/co-applicant(s) must not be agents of any for-profit, commercial company in the radiologic sciences 3. Recipients may not have concurrent RSNA grants or awards.
Type: Award

Value: US$10,000 to US$20,000
Length of Study: 1 year
Country of Study: Any country
Closing Date: 12 January
Additional Information: www.rsna.org/research/funding-opportunities/education-grants/education-project-award

Medical Student Research Grant

Subjects: Projects may include any of the following 1. Hypothesis-driven basic science. 2. Clinical investigation. 3. Drug, device or therapy development. 4. Comparative effectiveness. 5. Evidence-based radiology. 6. Ethics and professionalism. 7. Quality improvement. 8. Clinical practice efficiency. 9. Imaging informatics
Purpose: This R&E Foundation grant gives medical students the opportunity to gain research experience in medical imaging while they're still in school. Recipients will define objectives, develop research skills and test hypotheses, all before even choosing a residency program. Ultimately, this experience gives students a chance to consider academic radiology as a future career option.
Eligibility: Any area of research in the radiologic sciences is eligible for funding. 1. You must be an RSNA member to apply for the Medical Student Research Grant. If you're a non dues-paying member, your scientific advisor or your co-investigator must be a dues-paying member. 2. You must be a full-time medical student at an accredited North American medical school. 3. You must commit to work full-time for at least 10 weeks on your research project. 4. Your research project must take place in a department of radiology, radiation oncology or nuclear medicine in a North American medical institution, but this doesn't have to be the same institution where you're enrolled as a student. 5. You cannot have been a principal investigator on a grant or contract totaling more than US$60,000 in a single year. This includes single and combined grants and contracts from government, private and commercial sources. 6. You and your principal investigators cannot be employed by any for-profit, commercial company in the radiologic sciences. 7. You cannot submit more than one grant application to the RSNA R&E Foundation a year, and cannot have a concurrent RSNA grant. 8. Funding from other grant sources must be approved by foundation staff if it wasn't described in the original research plan.
Level of Study: Research
Type: Research grant
Value: Grant recipients receive US$3,000, which is matched by the sponsoring department, equaling US$6,000 total.
Frequency: Annual
Country of Study: Any country
Application Procedure: All grant applications are completed online: www.rsna.org/research/funding-opportunities
No. of awards offered: 10
Closing Date: 2 February
Funding: Private
Additional Information: For more information: www.rsna.org/research/funding-opportunities/research-grants/medical-student-research-grant

For further information contact:

820 Jorie Blvd # 200, Oak Brook, IL 60523, United States of America.

Tel: (1) 630 571 7816
Email: grants@rsna.org

Radiological Society of North America Education Seed Grant

Purpose: To provide funding opportunities for individuals with an active interest in radiologic education
Eligibility: Any investigator from anywhere in the world with an academic appointment may apply for this grant, as long as you are an RSNA member. If you're a non dues-paying member, your scientific advisor or your co-investigator must be a dues-paying member. You must also meet the following criteria: 1. You must hold a full-time faculty position in a radiology, radiation oncology or nuclear medicine department at an educational institution. 1a. If you aren't currently a full-time faculty member, but will be by the time funding starts, a letter from the department chair must be included in your application. 2. You cannot have been a principal investigator on a grant or contract totaling more than US$60,000 in a single year. This includes single and combined grants and contracts from government, private and commercial sources. 3. You and your principal investigators cannot be employed by any for-profit, commercial company in the radiologic sciences. 4. You cannot submit more than one grant application to the RSNA R&E Foundation a year and cannot have a concurrent RSNA grant. 5. Funding from other grant sources must be approved by foundation staff if it wasn't described in the original research plan.
Level of Study: Research
Type: Grant
Value: Up to US$60,000
Length of Study: 1 year
Frequency: Annual
Country of Study: Any country
Application Procedure: All grant applications are completed online: www.rsna.org/research/funding-opportunities
Closing Date: 19 January
Funding: Foundation

For further information contact:

Email: rmurray@rsna.org

Radiological Society of North America Institutional Clinical Fellowship in Cardiovascular Imaging

Purpose: To provide opportunities for radiologists early in their careers to gain experience and expertise in cardiovascular imaging
Eligibility: Open to citizens or permanent residents of a North American country who have completed their residency training in the radiological sciences. Fellows must also hold an MD or the equivalent as recognized by the American Medical Association and must be ACGME-certified in radiology or be eligible to sit for such certification
Type: Fellowship
Value: US$50,000 per year paid to a department. The Foundation does not pay overhead or indirect costs
Length of Study: 3 years
Frequency: Annual
Country of Study: Any country
Application Procedure: Applications must be submitted by a department in preparation for the recruitment of a Fellow into an existing cardiovascular imaging training programme. Application forms are available from the website
Closing Date: 1 June

For further information contact:

Department of Radiology Northwestern University Feinberg School of Medicine, Cardiovascular Imaging Fellowship Program, 676 N. Saint Clair St., Suite 800, Chicago, IL 60611, United States of America.

Email: bcartalino@rsna.org

Radiological Society of North America Medical Student Grant Program

Purpose: This R&E Foundation grant gives medical students the opportunity to gain research experience in medical imaging while they're still in school. Recipients will define objectives, develop research skills and test hypotheses, all before even choosing a residency program. Ultimately, this experience gives students a chance to consider academic radiology as a future career option.
Eligibility: You must be an RSNA member to apply for the Medical Student Research Grant. If you're a non dues-paying member, your scientific advisor or your co-investigator must be a dues-paying member. You must also meet the following criteria 1. You must be a full-time medical student at an accredited North American medical school. 2. You must commit to work full-time for at least 10 weeks on your research project. 3. Your research project must take place in a department of radiology, radiation oncology or nuclear medicine in a North American medical institution, but this doesn't have to be the same institution where you're enrolled as a student. 4. You cannot have been a principal investigator on a grant or contract totaling more than US$60,000 in a single year. This includes single and combined grants and contracts from government, private and commercial sources. 5. You and your principal investigators cannot be employed by any for-profit, commercial company in the radiologic sciences. 6. You cannot submit more than one grant application to the RSNA R&E Foundation a year, and cannot have a concurrent RSNA grant. 7. Funding from other grant sources must be approved by foundation staff if it wasn't described in the original research plan. For UIM applicants please refer website.
Level of Study: Research
Type: Grant
Value: Grant recipients receive US$3,000, which is matched by the sponsoring department, equaling US$6,000 total.
Length of Study: 1 year
Frequency: Annual
Country of Study: Any country
Application Procedure: All grant applications are completed online: www.rsna.org/research/funding-opportunities
No. of awards offered: 10
Closing Date: 2 February
Funding: Foundation
Additional Information: www.rsna.org/research/funding-opportunities/research-grants/medical-student-research-grant

For further information contact:

820 Jorie Blvd # 200, Oak Brook, IL 60523, United States of America.

Tel: (1) 630 571 7816
Email: grants@rsna.org

Radiological Society of North America Research Resident Program

Purpose: To provide opportunities for individuals to gain further insight into scientific investigation, and to develop competence in research and educational techniques and methods
Eligibility: Open to citizens or permanent residents of a North American country. Applicants should be in residency training so that the award can occur during any year after the 1st year

of training and should have an academic degree acceptable for a radiology residency
Level of Study: Postgraduate
Type: Grant
Value: US$30,000 designed to replace a portion of the resident
Length of Study: 1 year, non-renewable
Frequency: Annual
Country of Study: Any country
Application Procedure: Applicants must complete an application form, available from the website
Closing Date: 1 April
Additional Information:. www.rsna.org/research/research-awards/roentgen-resident-fellow-research-award#:~:text=Eligibility,with%20an%20ACGME%2Dapproved%20program.&text=Nominations%20are%20limited%20to%20one,nuclear%20medicine%20program%20per%20year

For further information contact:

820 Jorie Blvd., Suite 200, Oak Brook, IL 60523-2251, United States of America.

Tel: (1) 6305712670
Email: REfoundation@rsna.org

Radiological Society of North America Research Resident/Fellow Program

Purpose: To provide young investigators an opportunity to gain further insight into scientific investigation and to gain competence in research techniques and methods in anticipation of establishing a career in academic radiologic science.
Eligibility: Any resident or fellow may apply for this grant, as long as you are an RSNA member. If you're a non dues-paying member, your scientific advisor or your co-investigator must be a dues-paying member.
Level of Study: Research
Type: Fellowship
Value: Resident grant recipients receive up to US$50,000 fellow grant recipients receive up to US$75,000 for research projects.
Length of Study: 1 year
Frequency: Annual
Country of Study: Any country
Application Procedure: To apply for this grant, please log in and use our online: www.rsna.org/research/funding-opportunities
Closing Date: 19 January
Funding: Foundation
Additional Information: For more detailed information, including application instructions, please review the policies and procedures (PDF) for this grant. www.rsna.org/research/funding-opportunities/research-grants/resident-fellow-research-grant

For further information contact:

Tel: (1) 630 571 7816
Email: grants@rsna.org

Radiological Society of North America Research Scholar Grant Program

Purpose: This R&E Foundation grant supports junior faculty members who have completed resident and fellowship programs, but haven't been recognized as independent investigators
Eligibility: As a junior radiology faculty member, you may apply for the Research Scholar Grant, as long as you are an RSNA member and meet the following criteria 1. You must hold a full-time faculty position in a department of radiology, radiation oncology or nuclear medicine within a North American educational institution. 2. You must have been hired within the last 5 years with an academic rank of instructor, assistant professor or an equivalent title. 3. You must have completed advanced training and be certified by either the American Board of Radiology (ABR), The Royal College of Physicians and Surgeons of Canada or are on track for certification. 4. You cannot have been a principal investigator on a grant or contract totaling more than US$60,000 in a single year. This includes single and combined grants and contracts from government, private and commercial sources. 5. You and your principal investigators cannot be employed by any for-profit, commercial company in the radiologic sciences. 6. You cannot submit more than one grant application to the RSNA R&E Foundation a year and cannot have a concurrent RSNA grant. 7. Funding from other grant sources must be approved by Foundation staff if it wasn't described in the original research plan. 8. You cannot have previously accepted any of the following grants ARRS Scholar Award, AUR GE-Radiology Research Academic Fellowship (GERRAF), RSNA Research Scholar Grant.
Level of Study: Doctorate, Postdoctorate
Type: Research grant
Value: US$100,000 per year
Length of Study: 2 years
Frequency: Annual
Country of Study: Any country
Application Procedure: All grant applications are completed online: www.rsna.org/research/funding-opportunities
Closing Date: 19 January
Funding: Private

Additional Information: www.rsna.org/research/funding-opportunities/research-grants/research-scholar-grant

For further information contact:

Keshia Osley, Assistant Director, Grant Administration Radiological Society of North America, 820 Jorie Boulevard, Oak Brook, IL 60523, United States of America.

Email: grants@rsna.org

Research Scholar Grant

Purpose: This R&E Foundation grant supports junior faculty members who have completed resident and fellowship programs, but haven't been recognized as independent investigators.
Eligibility: Any junior radiology faculty member may apply for the Research Scholar Grant, as long as you are an RSNA member and meet the following criteria 1. You must hold a full-time faculty position in a department of radiology, radiation oncology or nuclear medicine within a North American educational institution. 2. You must have been hired within the last 5 years with an academic rank of instructor, assistant professor or an equivalent title. 3. You must have completed advanced training and be certified by either the American Board of Radiology (ABR), The Royal College of Physicians and Surgeons of Canada or are on track for certification. 4. You cannot have been a principal investigator on a grant or contract totaling more than US$60,000 in a single year. This includes single and combined grants and contracts from government, private and commercial sources. 5. You and your principal investigators cannot be employed by any for-profit, commercial company in the radiologic sciences. 6. You cannot submit more than one grant application to the RSNA R&E Foundation a year and cannot have a concurrent RSNA grant. 7. Funding from other grant sources must be approved by Foundation staff if it wasn't described in the original research plan. 8. You cannot have previously accepted any of the following grants ARRS Scholar Award, AUR GE-Radiology Research Academic Fellowship (GERRAF), RSNA Research Scholar Grant.
Level of Study: Research
Type: Research grant
Value: US$100,000 per year
Length of Study: 2 Year
Frequency: Annual
Country of Study: Any country
Application Procedure: All grant applications are completed online: www.rsna.org/research/funding-opportunities
Closing Date: 19 January
Funding: Private
Additional Information: www.rsna.org/research/funding-opportunities/research-grants/research-scholar-grant

For further information contact:

Tel: (1) 630 571 7816
Email: grants@rsna.org

Research Seed Grant

Purpose: This R&E Foundation Research Seed Grant gives investigators around the world the chance to define objectives and test hypotheses in preparation for larger grant applications at corporations, foundations and government agencies.
Eligibility: Any investigator from anywhere in the world with an academic appointment may apply for this grant, as long as you are an RSNA member. If you're a non dues-paying member, your scientific advisor or your co-investigator must be a dues-paying member.
Level of Study: Research
Type: Research grant
Value: Up to US$60,000
Length of Study: 1 year
Frequency: Annual
Country of Study: Any country
Application Procedure: All grant applications are completed online: www.rsna.org/research/funding-opportunities
Closing Date: 19 January
Funding: Private
Additional Information: www.rsna.org/research/funding-opportunities/research-grants/research-seed-grant

For further information contact:

Tel: (1) 630 571 7816
Email: grants@rsna.org

Ragdale

1260 North Green Bay Road, Lake Forest, IL 60045, United States of America.

Tel: (1) 847 234 1063
Email: info@ragdale.org
Website: www.ragdale.org/

Ragdale is a nonprofit artists' community located on the former country estate of architect Howard Van Doren Shaw.

Our residents represent a cross-section of ages, cultures, experience, and mediums for a diverse and vibrant community.

Sybil Shearer Fellowship: Dancemakers

Purpose: This fellowship opportunity to dancemakers will support an individual choreographer and/or dance artist by offering residency at Ragdale along with a cash stipend, the creation of a brief video documentary/interview, and the presentation of a public program. The residency may be awarded to a collaborative duo if they share a live/work studio. Open to emerging and established practitioners. This fellowship is made possible by the Morrison-Shearer Foundation.
Eligibility: Ragdale encourages applications from artists representing the widest possible range of perspectives and demographics, and to that end, emerging as well as established artists are invited to apply. While there are no publication, exhibition or performance requirements for application, applicants should be working at the professional level in their fields. Ragdale encourages artists of all backgrounds to apply.
Type: Fellowship
Value: 18-day residency at Ragdale along with a cash stipend of US$1000
Length of Study: 18-day
Frequency: Annual
Country of Study: Any country
Application Procedure: All applicants submit electronic materials through the Submittable application portal. Please note the following requirements to complete your application 1. A completed online application form. 2. Two current letters of reference OR surveys completed by people who know you personally and can address your professional capacity and suitability for a residency in a working community with other artists. Reference letters and survey responses are confidential and are submitted electronically through Submittable when you submit your application. Letters of reference/ Reference Surveys are due 1159 PM CST June 1. A 10-15 minute survey option has been added to residency applications. Instructions for completing the survey or letter of recommendation will be automatically sent to your references when you submit your application. 3. A one-page artist's statement and work plan explaining your work and what you plan to do while in residence. 4. A one-page CV or resume that summarizes your professional background. 5. Work samples that show previous work from the past 2-3 years. All media is acceptable. Most electronic file types and sizes are accepted. 6. Some fellowships require an eligibility statement of 500 words or less. Please refer www.ragdale.org/residencies
Closing Date: 15 May
Additional Information: www.ragdale.org/fellowships

For further information contact:

Email: info@ragdale.org

Rebecca Skelton Fund

Dance Department Administrator, University of Chichester, Bishop Otter Campus, College Lane, Chichester, Sussex PO19 6PE, United Kingdom.

Tel: (44) 1243 812137
Email: rebeccaskeltonfund@chi.ac.uk
Website: www.rebeccaskeltonfund.org
Contact: The Rebecca Skelton Fund Administrator

The fund provides financial assistance towards the cost of postgraduate dance study in experiential/creative work to include dance improvization and those training methods such as Skinner Releasing Technique, Alignment Therapy, Feldenkrais Technique, Alexander Technique and other body-mind practices that focus on an inner awareness and use the proprioceptive communication system or an inner sensory mode.

The Rebecca Skelton Scholarship

Purpose: To assist students to pursue a course of specific or advanced performance studies or an appropriate dance research and performance
Eligibility: Open to anyone pursuing dance studies at post-graduate level
Level of Study: Doctorate, Postdoctorate, Postgraduate, Professional development, Research
Type: Scholarships and fellowships
Value: £500
Frequency: Annual
Country of Study: United Kingdom
Application Procedure: Application form on request
No. of awards offered: 1–4
Closing Date: 12 January
Funding: Foundation
Contributor: The Rebecca Skelton Fund

For further information contact:

Email: artsresearch@chi.ac.uk

Regent's Park College

Pusey Street, Oxford OX1 2LB, United Kingdom.

Tel: (44) 1865 288120
Email: enquiries@regents.ox.ac.uk
Website: www.rpc.ox.ac.uk/

Regent's Park College is a small, dynamic community at the heart of the City and University of Oxford, specialising in the Arts and Humanities. The College offers places in a range of Arts and Humanities disciplines, with an outstanding record in Theology, Philosophy, History and English, as well as preparing men and women for ordained ministry in the Baptist Union of Great Britain. Everyone admitted to read for a degree is matriculated into the University and has full access to its rich resources. The College also has award-winning tutors, who are teaching members of multiple faculties and departments, encouraging students to aim high and providing excellent academic support.

Greyfriars Postgraduate Scholarship

Purpose: Regent's Park College is offering a postgraduate scholarship worth up to £2000 for a UK student who is currently engaged in, or has been accepted for, masters-level studies in a humanities subject at the University of Oxford.
Eligibility: 1. UK student who is currently engaged in, or has been accepted for, masters-level studies in a humanities subject at the University of Oxford. 2. The holder of the scholarship is required to be, or to become, a member of Regent's Park College, Oxford.
Level of Study: Postgraduate
Type: Scholarship
Value: Up to £2000
Country of Study: Any country
Application Procedure: Application materials: (i) covering letter, including an explanation of any special circumstances in relation to financial need that may otherwise prohibit or make it difficult to undertake postgraduate studies at Oxford University. Also state any other postgraduate grants or scholarships applied for and awarded; (ii) current CV, including the names and contact details of two referees; (iii) research proposal written for a non-specialist audience (no longer than two pages). Send to: Academic Administrator (academic.administrator@regents.ox.ac.uk)
Closing Date: 5 May
Additional Information: Website: www.rpc.ox.ac.uk/study-here/postgraduate-study/scholarships/

For further information contact:

Pusey St, Oxford OX1 2LB, United Kingdom.

Tel: (44) 1865 288120
Email: academic.administrator@regents.ox.ac.uk

The Pamela Sue Anderson Studentship for the Encouragement of the Place of Women in Philosophy

Purpose: Regent's Park College is offering a postgraduate studentship who is currently engaged in or has been accepted for post graduate study in the University of Oxford
Eligibility: The holder of the scholarship is required to be, or to become, a member of Regent's Park College, Oxford.
Level of Study: Postgraduate
Type: Studentship
Value: Up to £4,000
Frequency: Annual
Study Establishment: University of Oxford
Country of Study: Any country
Application Procedure: 1. Covering letter, explaining how the candidate's proposed research relates to the vision of the studentship; 2. Current CV, including the names and contact details of two referees; 3. Research proposal; 4. Writing sample of no more than 5,000 words. Send application materials to Jennifer Taylor, Academic Administrator by email.
No. of awards offered: 1
Closing Date: 29 April
Funding: Private
Additional Information: www.rpc.ox.ac.uk/study-here/postgraduate-study/scholarships/

For further information contact:

Pusey Street, Oxford, OX1 2LB, United Kingdom.

Tel: (44) 1865 288120
Email: academic.administrator@regents.ox.ac.uk

The Tim Collins Scholarship for the Study of Love in Religion

Purpose: The Project for the Study of Love in Religion is offering a scholarship worth £5,000 per annum for a student at Oxford who is writing, or intending to write a thesis that relates in some way to the place or meaning of love in religion.
Eligibility: DPhil in Theology (Full-time or Part-time); Philosophy; Oriental Studies; Anthropology; Archaeology; Archaeology (Part-time) (Continuing Education); Archaeological Science; Ancient History (Full-time or Part-time);

Classical Languages and Literature (Full-time or Part-time); General Linguistics and Comparative Philology; Classical Archaeology; International Development; Education (Full-time or Part-time); English (all subjects); English Local History (Part-time); Geography and the Environment; Fine Art (Full-time or Part-time); Continuing Education (Part-time); History of Art (Full-time or Part-time); History (History of Science and Medicine and Economic and Social History); History (HSM and ESH) (Part-time); History (Full-time and part-time); Literature and Arts; Law; Socio-Legal Studies; Music (Part-time); Politics; Medieval and Modern Languages (Full-time and Part-time); Sustainable Urban Development; Social Policy; Social Intervention; Sociology; Economics; International Relations.
Level of Study: Research
Type: Scholarship
Value: £5,000 per annum
Frequency: Annual
Country of Study: Any country
Application Procedure: Applicants should supply: 1. A current CV, with the names of two referees; 2. An abstract of the intended thesis; 3. A letter explaining how the thesis relates to the Study of Love in Religion, and giving an account of the applicant's interest in the subject. Applications should be sent to: academic.administrator@regents.ox.ac.uk
Closing Date: 30 June
Additional Information: www.rpc.ox.ac.uk/study-here/postgraduate-study/scholarships/

For further information contact:

Pusey St, Oxford OX1 2LB, United Kingdom.

Tel: (44) 1865 288120
Email: academic.administrator@regents.ox.ac.uk

Regent's University London

Inner Circle, Regent's Park, London NW1 4NS, United Kingdom.

Tel: (44) 20 7487 7700
Email: enquiries@regents.ac.uk
Website: www.regents.ac.uk/
Contact: Regent's University London

Regent's University London is a private non-profit university located in London, United Kingdom. Regent's University is only the second institution in the United Kingdom to be granted the status of a private university.

Greyfriars Postgraduate Scholarship

Purpose: In recognition of the historic commitment of the Greyfriars and of Regent's Park College to philanthropy and the inclusion of those whose life chances have been limited through no fault of their own, preference will be given to applicants whose financial needs are greatest and may otherwise prohibit their studies. The intention is that the Scholarship be applied to student fees.
Level of Study: Postgraduate
Type: Scholarship
Value: Up to £2,000
Frequency: Annual
Country of Study: Any country
Application Procedure: 1. Covering letter, including an explanation of any special circumstances in relation to financial need that may otherwise prohibit or make it difficult to undertake postgraduate studies at Oxford University. Also state any other postgraduate grants or scholarships applied for and awarded; 2. Current CV, including the names and contact details of two referees; 3. Research proposal
Closing Date: 6 May
Funding: Private

For further information contact:

Inner Cir, London NW1 4NS, United Kingdom.

Tel: (44) 20 7487 7700
Email: academic.administrator@regents.ox.ac.uk

Robert McKee International Screenwriting Scholarships

Subjects: BA (Hons) Screenwriting and Producing and BA (Hons) Screenwriting and Producing with Foundation
Purpose: In partnership with Robert McKee, Regent's is honoured to offer this scholarship to one student studying BA (Hons) Screenwriting and Producing or BA (Hons) Screenwriting and Producing with Foundation
Eligibility: All nationalities
Level of Study: Undergraduate
Type: Scholarship
Value: £7,000 towards fees
Length of Study: One standard programme duration
Country of Study: Any country
Application Procedure: Please complete the following task and send your statement and script as attachments to study@regents.ac.uk. Please include your full name, nationality and student number within the email. Please submit a short drama script, of up to 5 minutes in length and a 1,000 word statement answering the following question:

'Why would being a Robert McKee International Screenwriting scholar be important to you?'
Closing Date: 30 June
Additional Information: Website: www.regents.ac.uk/study/scholarships-funding-and-bursaries/robert-mckee#overview

For further information contact:

Email: scholarships@regents.ac.uk

The Dean of Humanities, Arts & Social Sciences Excellence Scholarship

Purpose: The Dean of the Faculty of Humanities, Arts & Social Sciences has established three scholarships that celebrate the University's independent, cosmopolitan and enterprising spirit
Level of Study: Graduate
Type: Scholarship and award
Value: The Scholarship award will cover a quarter of the tuition fees for the selected course
Frequency: Annual
Country of Study: Any country
Application Procedure: Applications must be emailed to scholarships@regents.ac.uk
No. of awards offered: 3
Closing Date: 31 May
Funding: Private
Additional Information: For any queries, please contact: Regent's University London, Tel: (44) 20 7487 7505, Email: enquiries@regents.ac.uk www.regents.ac.uk/study/scholarships-funding-and-bursaries/the-dean-of-humanities-arts-social-sciences-excellence-scholarship

For further information contact:

Email: scholarships@regents.ac.uk

Regional Institute for Population Studies

University of Ghana, PO Box 96, Legon, Accra, Ghana.

Tel: (233) 302 906800
Email: rips@ug.edu.gh
Website: www.rips-ug.edu.gh/
Contact: Director

The Regional Institute for Population Studies (RIPS) was established in 1972 jointly by the United Nations in partnership with the Government of Ghana, and is located at the University of Ghana. Since its establishment, the Institute has served as a regional centre for teaching and research training at the post-graduate level of population scientists in English-speaking countries in Africa. The Institute enjoyed enormous funding from the United Nations Population Fund (UNFPA), was the leading demographic research and teaching centre has trained more than 600 population scientists since its inception in 1972. RIPS is committed to training and development of the intellect, independence and character of the most competitive graduate students and faculty from across the continent and the globe and playing a leading role in research in population health by ardently pursuing excellence in education.

Respective Government Fellowships

Purpose: To enable fellows to obtain advanced training through study or research leading to a Master of Arts, Master of Philosophy or PhD degree
Eligibility: Open to English speaking Sub-Saharan Africans, nominated by their governments, who are capable of pursuing a course of study or research using English as a medium of expression. Candidates should have a good first degree in population studies for the Master of Arts degree course or the Master of Population Studies degree, a Master of Arts in population studies or its equivalent for the Master of Philosophy degree, a Master of Philosophy in population studies or its equivalent for a PhD course
Level of Study: Doctorate, Postgraduate
Type: Fellowship
Value: Approx. US$13,840 per year including stipend, fees, costs for books, minor equipment and production of dissertations and theses
Length of Study: At least 1 year for Master of Arts, at least 18 months for MPhil and 36 months for PhD
Frequency: Annual
Study Establishment: Regional Institute for Population Studies at the University of Ghana
Country of Study: Ghana
Application Procedure: United Nations Fellows must complete an application form, available at any United Nations Development Programme Office in the capital city of each English speaking Sub Saharan African country, through which all applications should be routed. Applications must be filled out in triplicate and submitted together with the relevant admission requirement through the government ministry responsible for recruiting candidates for the Institute. Non United Nation Fellows should send an application letter directly to the Director of the Institute. All seven students were sponsored through country programme budgets of governments of three of the member states of the Institute

No. of awards offered: 22
Closing Date: 30 June
Funding: Government
No. of awards given last year: 13
No. of applicants last year: 22
Additional Information: 20 of last year's candidates were sponsored directly by the Institute and 10 through country programme budgets of governments of four of the member states of the Institute

For further information contact:

Tel: (233) 21 773 8906
Fax: (233) 21 772 829
Email: fo.gha@undp.org

Religious Scholarships

513 Central Avenue, Suite 300, Highland Park, IL 60035, United States of America.

Website: www.scholarships.com/financial-aid/college-scholarships/scholarships-by-type/religious-scholarships/

Religious scholarships reward students who are actively involved with faith-related activities, pursuing religious-affiliated careers or ministry work, or even those who simply belong to the church. If you are active in your church community or strong in your religious faith, there are religious scholarships for you. Providing scholarship opportunities and financial aid are ideal ways for churches and religious organizations to show their commitment to helping its members go to college. Religious organizations sponsor a variety of national, regional, and local scholarships.

American Atheists Chinn Scholarships

Purpose: American Atheists celebrates activism by awarding scholarships to students who engage in atheist activism in their communities and schools. American Atheists is proud to award Chinn Scholarships for LGBTQ Atheist Activism that recognize atheist activism in the area of LGBTQ equality
Eligibility: 1. You do not have to be a U.S. citizen to be awarded a scholarship, but you do have to attend a U.S.-based institution. 2. Scholarships are open to current college or vocational students and to high school students entering college in the upcoming year. 3. Full-time graduate and law school students are also eligible. 4. Applicants for all awards must be atheists and must have a cumulative GPA of 2.5 or higher in academic subjects. 5. Applicants of all races, ethnicities, genders, and sexual orientations are encouraged to apply.
Level of Study: Graduate
Type: Scholarship
Value: US$1,000
Length of Study: 1 year
Frequency: Annual
Country of Study: Any country
Application Procedure: Apply online. For more information or to apply, please visit the scholarship provider's website. www.atheists.org/activism/scholarships/
Closing Date: 15 March
Funding: Foundation
Contributor: American Atheists
Additional Information: www.scholarships.com/financial-aid/college-scholarships/scholarship-directory/religion/atheist/american-atheists-scholarships

For further information contact:

P.O. Box 158, Cranford, NJ 07016, United States of America.

Tel: (1) 908 276 7300
Email: scholarships@atheists.org

American Atheists O'Hair Award

Purpose: American Atheists celebrates activism by awarding scholarships to students who engage in atheist activism in their communities and schools. American Atheists awards O'Hair Scholarships to atheist students in the United States.
Eligibility: 1. You do not have to be a U.S. citizen to be awarded a scholarship, but you do have to attend a U.S.-based institution. 2. Scholarships are open to current college or vocational students and to high school students entering college in the upcoming year. 3. Full-time graduate and law school students are also eligible. 4. Applicants for all awards must be atheists and must have a cumulative GPA of 2.5 or higher in academic subjects. 5. Applicants of all races, ethnicities, genders, and sexual orientations are encouraged to apply.
Level of Study: Graduate
Type: Award
Value: NZ$1,000
Length of Study: 1 year
Frequency: Annual
Country of Study: New Zealand
Application Procedure: Apply online. For more information or to apply, please visit the scholarship provider's website. www.atheists.org/activism/scholarships/

No. of awards offered: 8
Closing Date: 31 May
Funding: Foundation
Contributor: American Atheists
Additional Information: www.scholarships.com/financial-aid/college-scholarships/scholarship-directory/religion/atheist/american-atheists-scholarships

For further information contact:

Scholarship Committee, P.O. Box 158, Cranford, NJ 07016, United States of America.

Tel: (1) 908 276 7300
Email: scholarships@atheists.org

Anna Schiller Scholarship

Purpose: Anna Schiller Memorial Scholarship provides educational resources to a graduating Rockford Christian High School senior to further their education. Rockford Christian High School graduating senior who demonstrates a strong commitment to improving the quality of life for people in their school, community and/or world at large through their community service and demonstrates the same strong love for others that Anna exemplified through her life
Eligibility: To be eligible, you must be a Rockford Christian High School graduating senior who demonstrates a strong commitment to improving the quality of life for people in their school, community and/or world at large through their community service and demonstrates the same strong love for others. Minimum GPA of 2.0 GPA is required.
Level of Study: Graduate
Type: Scholarship
Frequency: Annual
Application Procedure: For more information or to apply, please visit the scholarship provider's website.
Closing Date: 1 February
Funding: Foundation
Additional Information: Website: www.scholarships.com/financial-aid/college-scholarships/scholarship-directory/religion/christian/anna-schiller-scholarship

For further information contact:

Scholarship Committee, 946 N. Second Street, Rockford, IL 61107, United States of America.

Tel: (1) 779 210 8209
Email: cstahly@cfnil.org

Associated Women for Pepperdine (AWP) Scholarship

Purpose: AWP was established in 1958 and is the largest, most active women's group supporting colleges and universities in Southern California. For over 50 years, members have been primary contributors to scholarships for Christian students and have forged a strong link between the University and the Churches of Christ across the country
Eligibility: Applicants must meet the following criteria 1. Be a current, active member of a Church of Christ congregation. 2. Submit the general Pepperdine admission application by the January 5 deadline. 3. Submit the Free Application for Federal Student Aid (FAFSA) (studentaid.gov/h/apply-for-aid/fafsa) by February 15. 4. Submit an additional recommendation from a Church of Christ leader (minister, youth minister, elder, or deacon) by February 15.
Type: Scholarship
Value: US$5,000
Frequency: Annual
Country of Study: United States of America
Application Procedure: Apply online
Closing Date: 15 February
Funding: Foundation
Contributor: The Associated Women for Pepperdine (AWP)
Additional Information: www.seaver.pepperdine.edu/admission/financial-aid/undergraduate/assistance/awp-scholarship-exception.htm www.scholarships.com/financial-aid/college-scholarships/scholarships-by-type/federal-scholarships/associated-women-for-pepperdine-awp-scholarship/

For further information contact:

Scholarship Committee, 24255 Pacific Coast Hwy, Malibu, CA 90263, United States of America.

Tel: (1) 310 506 4000

Republic of South Africa

Tel: (27) 12 312 5372
Email: internationalscholarships@dhet.gov.za
Website: www.internationalscholarships.dhet.gov.za/

There are a number of scholarship opportunities currently available for South African students to undertake studies, research and exchanges in other countries. The Department of Higher Education and Training (DHET) coordinates several such scholarships, while others are managed by other international, national and provincial departments or government agencies. Scholarships are for South African citizens and require a commitment to return to South African upon completion of studies.

Azerbaijan: Azerbaijan Diplomatic Academy University Scholarship

Purpose: The Government of the Republic of Azerbaijan and ADA University are offering scholarships to foreign students. The ADA University is committed to grooming world class leaders
Eligibility: Be South African citizens in good health, with a strong academic record. 1. Meet the entry criteria for their selected programme at the ADA University. 2. Meet the minimum academic requirement for entry into a similar programme at a South African university. 3. Applicants must be proficient in English
Level of Study: Postgraduate
Type: Scholarship
Value: Offers tuition fees, travel expenses, medical benefits and monthly stipend
Frequency: Annual
Country of Study: Any country
Application Procedure: Information on the application process is available on the website. www.ada.edu.az/en-us/pages/admission_fellowships.aspx
Closing Date: 1 July
Funding: Private

For further information contact:

Email: admissions@ada.edu.az

Research Corporation for Science Advancement

4703 East Camp Lowell Drive, Suite 201, Tucson, AZ 85712, United States of America.

Tel: (1) 520 571 1111
Email: awards@rescorp.org
Website: rescorp.org/
Contact: Editor, Science Advancement Programme

Research Corporation for Science Advancement (RCSA) is a foundation providing catalytic funding for innovative scientific research and the development of academic scientists since 1912. RCSA is a private foundation that aids basic research in the physical sciences (astronomy, chemistry, physics, and related fields) at colleges and universities through its Cottrell Scholar and Scialog programs. It supports research independently proposed by faculty members and convenes conferences. RCSA is a strong supporter of improvements in science education.

Research Corporation (United States of America) Research Innovation Awards

Purpose: To assist innovative research programmes for faculty of PhD granting departments
Eligibility: Open to faculty members whose first tenure track position began in either the preceding or the current calendar year are eligible to apply
Level of Study: Doctorate
Type: Research grant
Value: US$35,000 for equipment and supplies, graduate stipends and some other expenses. The award does not cover overheads
Frequency: Annual
Study Establishment: Research universities with PhD granting departments of physics, chemistry and astronomy
Country of Study: United States of America or Canada
Application Procedure: Applicants must complete an application form. Guidelines and an application request forms are available from the website
No. of awards offered: 200
Closing Date: 1 May
Funding: Private
Contributor: Foundation endowment
No. of awards given last year: 45
No. of applicants last year: 200

For further information contact:

Email: awards@ria.ie

Research Council of Norway

Drammensveien 288, N-0283 Oslo, Norway.

Tel: (47) 22 03 70 00
Email: post@forskningsradet.no
Website: www.forskningsradet.no/en/

The Research Council works to promote research and innovation of high quality and relevance and to generate knowledge in priority areas to enable Norway to deal with key challenges to society and the business sector.

Collaborative Project in Global Health

Subjects: Global development and international relations
Purpose: The purpose of this call for proposals is to support research on health improvements for disadvantaged populations in low- and lower-middle income countries (LLMICs). The research must be relevant to Sustainable Development Goal 3 'Good health for all' and its targets. Projects where it is expedient and beneficial to establish collaboration outside academia should apply under this call.
Eligibility: The call is open to approved Norwegian research organisations in effective collaboration with relevant actors from public sector bodies, non-governmental organisations and/or other private organisations.
Value: NOK 48,000,000
Length of Study: 32–72 months
Country of Study: Any country
No. of awards offered: 5
Closing Date: 9 February
Additional Information: www.forskningsradet.no/en/call-for-proposals/2022/collaborative-project-global-health/

For further information contact:

Drammensveien 288, N-0283 Oslo, Norway.

Tel: (47) 22 03 70 00

Collaborative Project relating to Antimicrobial Resistance from a One Health Perspective

Subjects: Cross-cutting topics
Purpose: The purpose of this call is to generate new knowledge about measures that can help us to understand, handle and prevent the development of antimicrobial resistance (AMR) from a One Health perspective, both nationally and internationally. The call is open to approved Norwegian research organisations in collaboration with non-research organisations from Norway and/or developing countries (LLMIC countries), India and China.
Eligibility: The call is open to approved Norwegian research organisations in effective collaboration with relevant actors from public sector entities, non-governmental organisations, the business sector and/or other private organisations.
Value: NOK 60,000,000
Length of Study: 24–48 months
Country of Study: Any country
No. of awards offered: 5
Closing Date: 9 February
Additional Information: www.forskningsradet.no/en/call-for-proposals/2022/collaborative-project-antimicrobial-resistance/

For further information contact:

Drammensveien 288, N-0283 Oslo, Norway.

Tel: (47) 22 03 70 00

Collaborative Project to Meet Societal and Industry-related Challenges

Subjects: Cross-cutting topics, Democracy, Administration and renewal, Energy, Transport and low emissions, Oceans, Health, Land-based food, The environment and bioresources, Enabling technologies, Petroleum, Education and competence, Welfare, Culture and society
Purpose: The purpose of this call is to develop new knowledge and generate research competence needed by society or the business sector to address important societal challenges. The projects are to encourage and support collaboration between research organisations and stakeholders from outside the research sector that represent societal and/or industry-related needs for knowledge and research competence.
Eligibility: The call is open to approved Norwegian research organisations in effective cooperation with relevant actors from public sector entities, non-governmental organisations, the business sector and/or other private organisations.
Value: NOK 1,028,000,000
Length of Study: 24–48 months
Frequency: Annual
Country of Study: Any country
No. of awards offered: 5
Closing Date: 9 February
Additional Information: www.forskningsradet.no/en/call-for-proposals/2022/collaborative-project-industry/

For further information contact:

Drammensveien 288, N-0283 Oslo, Norway.

Tel: (47) 22 03 70 00

Knowledge-building Project for Industry

Subjects: Energy, transport and low emissions; Petroleum
Purpose: The purpose of this call is to develop new knowledge and generate competence in the research organisations needed by society or the business sector to address important societal challenges. The projects are to encourage and support collaboration between research organisations and stakeholders from outside the research sector that represent societal and/or industry-related needs for knowledge and research competence.

Eligibility: The call is open to approved Norwegian research organisations in effective cooperation with relevant actors from public sector entities, non-governmental organisations, the business sector and/or other private organisations.
Value: NOK 305,000,000
Length of Study: 24–60 months
Country of Study: Any country
No. of awards offered: 5
Closing Date: 9 February
Additional Information: www.forskningsradet.no/en/call-for-proposals/2022/knowledge-building-project-industry/

For further information contact:

Drammensveien 288, N-0283 Oslo, Norway.

Tel: (47) 22 03 70 00

Research Council of Norway Senior Scientist Visiting Fellowship

Purpose: To enable Norwegian research institutions to receive foreign scientists to participate in research groups, discuss research arrangements and give lectures within their special fields
Eligibility: Open to well established and internationally recognised scientists who are at a professional or equivalent level
Level of Study: Professional development
Type: Fellowship
Value: NOK 25,000 per month for the first two months, NOK 10,000 for each succeeding month. Travelling expenses may also be defrayed
Length of Study: 1–12 months
Frequency: Annual
Study Establishment: A Norwegian research institution
Country of Study: Norway
Application Procedure: Applications must be filed by Norwegian institutions, so individual scientists should contact the Norwegian research institution or university department of their choice
Funding: Government
Additional Information: The Research Council of Norway also administers the following: Research Programmes of the European Union (EU), Bilateral Scholarship Agreements, and the Nordic Scheme for the Baltic Countries and North West Russia www.dhet.gov.za/internationalScholarships/AZERBAIJAN2.html

For further information contact:

Email: post@forskningsradet.no

Researcher Project for Scientific Renewal

Subjects: Ground-breaking research, Cross-cutting topics, Global development and international relations, Oceans, Health, Climate and polar research, Petroleum, Sámi society and culture, Education and competence, Welfare, culture and society
Purpose: Funding is intended to support scientific renewal and development in research that can help to advance the international research front. This call is therefore targeted towards researchers who have demonstrated the ability to conduct research of high scientific quality. Grant proposals will be accepted for projects within all disciplines and research areas.
Eligibility: Only approved Norwegian research organizations may apply
Type: Research grant
Value: NOK 1 467 000 000
Length of Study: 36–72 months
Country of Study: Any country
Closing Date: 2 February
Additional Information: www.forskningsradet.no/en/call-for-proposals/2022/researcher-project-scientific-renewal/

For further information contact:

Drammensveien 288, N-0283 Oslo, Norway.

Tel: (47) 22 03 70 00
Email: ResearcherProject@rcn.no

Researcher Project for Young Talents

Subjects: Ground-breaking research, Oceans, Climate and polar research
Purpose: Funding is intended to give talented young researchers, under the age of 40 in all disciplines and thematic areas, the opportunity to pursue their ideas and lead a research project. This call is targeted towards researchers in the early stages of their careers, 2–7 years after defence of an approved doctorate, who have demonstrated the potential to conduct research of high scientific quality.
Eligibility: Only approved Norwegian research organizations may apply
Level of Study: Research
Type: Grant
Value: NOK 3,06,000,000
Length of Study: 36–48 months
Country of Study: Any country
Closing Date: 2 February
Additional Information: www.forskningsradet.no/en/call-for-proposals/2022/researcher-project-young-talents/

For further information contact:

Drammensveien 288, N-0283 Oslo, Norway.

Tel: (47) 22 03 70 00
Email: ResearcherProject@rcn.no

Three-year Researcher Project with International Mobility

Purpose: Funding is intended to increase international mobility and promote career development among researchers at an early stage in their careers, as well as to facilitate knowledge transfer to research groups in Norway. The call is targeted towards researchers at the post-doctoral level who are to spend two years at a research organisation abroad and the third year at a research organisation in Norway. Grant proposals will be accepted for projects within all disciplines and research areas.
Eligibility: Only approved Norwegian research organizations may apply
Level of Study: Research
Type: Research grant
Value: NOK 40,000,000
Length of Study: 36–36 months
Frequency: Annual
Country of Study: Any country
Closing Date: 2 February
Additional Information: www.forskningsradet.no/en/call-for-proposals/2022/researcher-project-international-mobility/

For further information contact:

Drammensveien 288, N-0283 Oslo, Norway.

Tel: (47) 22 03 70 00

Reserve Bank of New Zealand

2 The Terrace, PO Box 2498, Wellington 6140, New Zealand.

Tel: (64) 4 472 2029
Email: rbnz-info@rbnz.govt.nz
Website: www.rbnz.govt.nz/

The Reserve Bank of New Zealand is New Zealand's central bank. They promote a sound and dynamic monetary and financial system. They work towards our vision by operating monetary policy to achieve and maintain price stability, assisting the functioning of a sound and efficient financial system, meeting the currency needs of the public, overseeing and operating effective payments systems and providing effective support services to the Bank.

Māori and Pacific Islands Scholarship

Purpose: Enabling and supporting diversity in our talent, pipeline is important to the Bank. One of the ways we do this is by offering Māori and Pacific Island scholarships, to those studying towards the afore mentioned qualifications.
Eligibility: The scholarships are available each year to students majoring in Economics, Finance, Mathematics, Law and Accounting studies, who attained at least a B+ grade point average and who intend to continue studying to Honours or Master's level. Please note that students who are entering their first year of university are not eligible. We're looking for future leaders who're interested in becoming well-rounded central bankers and who demonstrate our values of integrity, innovation and inclusion. A key focus for us is attracting diversity of thought and experience, to enable our vision of 'Great Team, Best Central Bank'
Type: Scholarship
Value: NZ$3,000 for each of the first year and second years of study and NZ$5,000 in the final year of study.
Frequency: Annual
Country of Study: Any country
Application Procedure: Applying is easy. Email these documents to Early.Careers@rbnz.govt.nz: 1. Your CV 2. Your completed application form 3. Your official academic transcript. www.rbnz.govt.nz/-/media/project/sites/rbnz/careers/scholarship-application-2023.docx
Closing Date: 24 March
Additional Information: www.rbnz.govt.nz/grads/scholarships#māori-pacific-scholarship

For further information contact:

2 The Terrace, Wellington Central, Wellington 6140, New Zealand.

Tel: (64) 4 472 2029
Email: Early.Careers@rbnz.govt.nz

Reserve Bank of New Zealand Scholarships

Purpose: The RBNZ scholarships is open to all students.
Eligibility: The scholarships are available each year to students majoring in Economics, Finance, Mathematics, Law and Accounting studies, who attained at least a B+ grade

point average and who intend to continue studying to Honours or Master's level.
Type: Scholarship
Value: NZ$3,000 for each of the first year and second years of study and NZ$5,000 in the final year of study
Country of Study: New Zealand
Application Procedure: Applying is easy. Email these documents to Early.Careers@rbnz.govt.nz: 1. Your CV 2. Your completed application form 3. Your official academic transcript. www.rbnz.govt.nz/-/media/project/sites/rbnz/careers/scholarship-application-2023.docx
Closing Date: 24 March
Additional Information: www.rbnz.govt.nz/grads/scholarships#māori-pacific-scholarship

For further information contact:

2 The Terrace, Wellington Central, Wellington 6140, New Zealand.

Tel: (64) 4 472 2029
Email: recruitment@rbnz.govt.nz

Reserve Bank of New Zealand Scholarships for International Students

Purpose: The Reserve Bank of New Zealand offers scholarships for students studying at a New Zealand University. The scholarships are available each year to students majoring in Economics, Finance, Mathematics, Law and Accounting studies, who intend to continue studying to Honours or Master's level.
Eligibility: 1. To be eligible, applicants must be studying full-time at a New Zealand University and are a NZ Citizen or have NZ Permanent Residency status. 2. The RBNZ scholarships is open to all students. 3. The scholarships are available each year to students majoring in Economics, Finance, Mathematics, Law and Accounting studies, who attained at least a B+ grade point average and who intend to continue studying to Honours or Master's level.
Type: Scholarship
Value: The scholarship is valued at NZ$3,000 for each of the first year and second years of study and NZ$5,000 in the final year of study. These funds will be paid fortnightly during the academic year.
Frequency: Annual
Country of Study: New Zealand
Application Procedure: Applying is easy. Email these documents to Early.Careers@rbnz.govt.nz: 1. Your CV. 2. A copy of your official academic transcript. 3. A recent essay or assessment (to demonstrate your written work) you have submitted as part of your degree. 4. Details of 2 - 3 referees who are able to give verbal references. www.rbnz.govt.nz/-/media/project/sites/rbnz/careers/scholarship-application-2023.docx
Closing Date: 24 March
Contributor: Any New Zealand University
Additional Information: Please note that students who are entering their first year of university are not eligible. www.rbnz.govt.nz/grads/scholarships#rbnz-scholarship

For further information contact:

2 The Terrace, Wellington Central, Wellington 6140, New Zealand.

Tel: (64) 4 472 2029
Email: working@rbnz.govt.nz

The Roger Perry Memorial Scholarship

Purpose: The Roger Perry Memorial scholarship is for those students entering their final year of study and working towards Honours or Masters. This scholarship has been established as an enduring recognition of the immense contribution Roger made to the Reserve Bank.
Eligibility: The scholarships are available each year to students majoring in Economics, Finance, Mathematics, Law and Accounting studies, who attained at least a B+ grade point average and who intend to continue studying to Honours or Master's level.
Type: Scholarship
Value: NZ$10,000
Country of Study: New Zealand
Application Procedure: Applying is easy. Email these documents to Early.Careers@rbnz.govt.nz. Application address: www.rbnz.govt.nz/-/media/project/sites/rbnz/careers/scholarship-application-2023.docx
Closing Date: 24 March
Additional Information: www.rbnz.govt.nz/grads/scholarships#māori-pacific-scholarship

For further information contact:

2 The Terrace, Wellington Central, Wellington 6140, New Zealand.

Tel: (64) 4 472 2029
Email: recruitment@rbnz.govt.nz

Women in Central Banking Scholarship

Purpose: This scholarship is aimed at increasing opportunities for women in central banking and forms part of our wider commitment to diversity and inclusion.

R

Eligibility: The scholarships are available each year to students majoring in Economics, Finance, Mathematics, Law and Accounting studies, who attained at least a B+ grade point average and who intend to continue studying to Honours or Master's level.
Type: Scholarship
Value: NZ$3,000 for each of the first year and second years of study and NZ$5,000 in the final year of study
Frequency: Annual
Country of Study: New Zealand
Closing Date: 24 March
Additional Information: www.rbnz.govt.nz/grads/scholarships#maori-pacific-scholarship

For further information contact:

2 The Terrace, Wellington Central, Wellington 6140, New Zealand.

Tel: (64) 4 472 2029
Email: recruitment@rbnz.govt.nz

Resuscitation Council (United Kingdom)

5th Floor, Tavistock House North, Tavistock Square, London WC1H 9HR, United Kingdom.

Tel: (44) 20 7388 4678
Website: www.resus.org.uk/
Contact: Dr Sara Harris, Assistant Director

Resuscitation Council UK is the national expert in resuscitation. Formed in 1983, Resuscitation Council UK is committed to ensuring that survival rates for in and out of hospital cardiac arrest improve. We're doing this by driving CPR education, and encouraging everyone, from healthcare workers to the general public, to learn life-saving resuscitation skills.

Resuscitation Council (United Kingdom) Research & Development Grant

Purpose: The purpose of this grant funding is to support high-quality medical education research and/or clinical research involving people (patients, staff, relatives), and the generation of new knowledge in resuscitation science and education. The purpose is also to support future resuscitation specialists developing their interest and expertise through high quality research.
Eligibility: 1. Applications must be methodologically robust. Advice on research design may be available from the regional NIHR Research Design Services. 2. RCUK does not fund animal research or purely basic science research. 3. Project proposers and project leads must be based in the UK. 4. Applications where the applicant is registered for a higher degree (e.g. MSc by Research, MPhil, PhD will be considered if associated with high quality research. 5. Applicants should have a credible track record of conducting such research projects or have appropriate supervision. 6. The lead investigator must hold a tenured position within an official health or social care setting, NHS setting or UK university organisation. 7. The research project should normally be completed within 1-3 years.
Level of Study: Doctorate, Masters Degree, Postgraduate, Research
Type: Grant
Value: £20,000
Frequency: Annual
Country of Study: United Kingdom
Application Procedure: Applications should be submitted by a department or institution for a defined project to be undertaken by a specified individual. The researcher must be working within an official health or social care setting, NHS setting or UK university organisation within the UK and hold qualifications appropriate to their grade. Such individuals will usually be doctors, nurses, resuscitation officers or other professions allied to medicine. If the application is submitted by the supervisor of the research project the CV and reference will be required in respect of the appointed individual. Applications must be submitted using the RCUK Research and Development Grant applications online system.
Closing Date: 6 January
Additional Information: For more details www.resus.org.uk/about-us/resuscitation-research

For further information contact:

Email: research@resus.org.uk

Rheumatology Research Foundation

2200 Lake Boulevard NE, Atlanta, GA 30319, United States of America.

Tel: (1) 404 365 1373
Email: foundation@rheumatology.org
Website: www.rheumresearch.org/
Contact: Sarah Barksdale, Senior Specialist, Awards and Grants

The Rheumatology Research Foundation is the largest private funding source for rheumatology research & training in the U.S. The mission of the Rheumatology Research Foundation is to advance research and training to improve the health of patients living with rheumatic disease. We award grants to scientists conducting innovative research that will lead to a future with more options for patients with rheumatic disease to live longer, healthier lives.

American College of Rheumatology REF Rheumatology Scientist Development Award

Purpose: To encourage qualified physicians without significant prior research experience to embark on careers in biomedical and/or clinical research in arthritis and rheumatic diseases
Eligibility: Candidates must be an ACR or ARHP member, have a doctoral level degree, must be clinician scientists
Level of Study: Doctorate, Postdoctorate, Professional development, Research
Type: Award
Value: US$50,000 for first year, US$75,000 for second year and US$100,000 for third year
Length of Study: 3 years
Frequency: Annual
Country of Study: United States of America
Application Procedure: Application forms are available on the website
No. of awards offered: 12
Closing Date: 1 June
Funding: Foundation
Contributor: Centocor Inc
Additional Information: For any questions regarding eligibility, contact the REF www.rheumresearch.org/career-development-research-awards

For further information contact:

Email: Foundation@rheumatology.org

American College of Rheumatology/REF Arthritis Investigator Award

Purpose: To provide support to physicians and scientists in research fields related to arthritis for the period between the completion of postdoctoral fellowship training and establishment as an independent investigators
Level of Study: Research
Type: Award
Value: US$75,000 for the first 2 years and US$90,000 per year after renewal
Length of Study: 2–4 years
Frequency: Annual
Country of Study: United States of America
Application Procedure: Application forms are available on the website
Closing Date: 1 September
Funding: Foundation
Contributor: The Arthritis Foundation

For further information contact:

Email: acrnominations@rheumatology.org

Amgen Fellowship Training Award

Purpose: To help ensure an adequate supply of (a) rheumatology providers meeting the needs of children and adults with rheumatic diseases in all areas of the country and (b) rheumatology educators and investigators to train future clinicians and advance research in rheumatic and musculoskeletal diseases. The Amgen Fellowship Training Award may be used to support the salary of any fellow in an ACGME-accredited rheumatology fellowship training program.
Eligibility: Applicant (Program Director) must be an ACR or ARP member at the time of submission and for the duration of the award. 1. Only Program Directors at ACGME-accredited institutionsin good standing may apply. 2. The rheumatology fellowship training Program Director at the institution will be responsible for the overall direction, management and administration of the program. 3. By submitting an application, the Program Director and sponsoring institution agree funds will be used ONLY for salary support of one fellow in their first or second year (or third year fellow in pediatric rheumatology). 4. Multiple applications from a single institution will not be permitted unless they are for separate training programs (e.g., adult and pediatric rheumatology). 5. Programs may not apply for the Amgen Fellowship Training Award and Fellowship Training Award- Workforce Expansion within the same application cycle. 6. Current recipients of the Fellowship Training Award for Workforce Expansion are not eligible to apply for this award. 7. Supported fellows do not need to be U.S. citizens or non-citizen nationals. If you have questions about your eligibility, please inquire by email.
Type: Award
Value: US$50,000
Length of Study: 1 year
Frequency: Annual
Country of Study: United States of America
Application Procedure: All applications must be submitted online by 5 PM ET on the deadline day through ProposalCentral at proposalcentral.com/. Before starting the

R

online application, you will be required to create a Professional Profile in ProposalCentral, if you have not already. To do so, visit this link (proposalcentral.com/register.asp) to begin creating your account. Please refer website.
Closing Date: 2 May
Contributor: Amgen, Inc
Additional Information: www.rheumresearch.org/education-and-training-awards

Career Development Bridge Funding Award: K Bridge

Purpose: To provide bridge funding for promising investigators as they are revising outstanding individual career development award applications (i.e., applications for NIH K series awards or VA CDA-2 awards or any equivalent career development awards). Through this bridge funding award, the Foundation will support young faculty members so that they have the highest likelihood of achieving success in obtaining longerterm career development awards.
Eligibility: 1. All applicants must meet citizenship/permanent resident status and other eligibility requirements as outlined in the Awards and Grants policies. 2. Applicants must be ACR or ARP members with an MD, DO, PhD or equivalent doctoral level degree from an accredited institution. 3. The Foundation does not currently support non-MD/DO scientists working on basic science research. 4. Bridge funds are not intended to bridge the period between review and funding. 5. Previous recipients of this award are not eligible to apply. 6. In addition to an excellent application, applicantsmust be capable of becoming independent researchers with a clear and firm institutional commitment to their career development, including a faculty position and other supporting resources.
Level of Study: Professional development
Type: Award
Value: US$75,000
Length of Study: 1 year
Frequency: Annual
Country of Study: United States of America
Application Procedure: All applications must be submitted by 5 PM ET on the deadline day through ProposalCentral proposalcentral.com/. Before starting the online application, you will be required to create a Professional Profile in ProposalCentral, if you have not already. To do so, visit this link to begin creating your account. proposalcentral.com/register.asp. Please refer website.
Closing Date: 3 October
Funding: Foundation
Additional Information: For more details: www.rheumresearch.org/career-development-research-awards. www.rheumresearch.org/file/FY22_Career-Development-Bridge-Funding-Award_K-Bridge_3.3.2021.pdf

For further information contact:

Email: Foundation@rheumatology.org

Career Development Bridge Funding Award: K Supplement

Purpose: The NIH K Series and VA CDA awards provide limited resources to cover research costs, such as essential laboratory supplies or supportstaff (e.g. salary support for research technician, database assistant or statistician), which are crucial to the successful transition of junior investigators to independent investigators. This award is designed to address the needs of these investigators and serve as a supplement to the NIH individual K series, VA CDA, or equivalent 4- or 5-year award mechanism.
Eligibility: 1. All applicants must meet citizenship/permanent resident status and other eligibility requirements as outlined in the Awards and Grants policies. 2. Applicants must be ACR or ARPmembers with an MD, DO, PhD or equivalent doctoral level degree from an accredited institution. ACR members must meet the following criteria a. Applicant must be an NIH K08, K23, K25, VA CD, or equivalent 4- or 5-year award recipient. The applicant must be in years 2, 3 or 4 of their award at the time of application. b. Have earned a DO, MD, MD/PhD, or DO/PhD degree or be currently enrolled in an ACGME accredited clinical training program. c. MDs and DOs who are not licensed to perform clinical care may not apply. ARP members must meet the following criteria a. Applicant must be an NIH K01, K08, K23, K25, VA CD, or equivalent 4- or 5-year award recipient. The applicant must be in years 2, 3 or 4 of their award at the time of application. b. Have earned a PhD, DSc, or equivalent doctoral degree. 3. The Foundation does not currently support non- MD/DO scientists working on basic science research. 4. In addition to an excellent application, applicants must be capable of becoming independent researchers with a clear and firm institutional commitment to their career development, including a faculty position and other supporting resources.
Level of Study: Doctorate, Professional development, Research
Type: Award
Value: US$100,000
Length of Study: 2 years
Frequency: Annual
Country of Study: United States of America
Application Procedure: All applications must be submitted by 5 PM ET on the deadline day through ProposalCentral. proposalcentral.com/. Please visit website.

Closing Date: 1 August
Funding: Foundation
Additional Information: For more details: www.rheumresearch.org/career-development-research-awards. www.rheumresearch.org/file/FY22_Career-Development-Bridge-Funding-Award_K-Supplement_2.16.21.pdf

For further information contact:

Email: Foundation@rheumatology.org

Career Development Bridge Funding Award: R Bridge

Purpose: To provide funding to NIH R01, VA Research Career Scientist (RCS) or Merit Award applicants whose application received a priority score but was not funded, and who are at risk of running out of research support.
Eligibility: 1. All applicants must meet citizenship/permanent resident status and other eligibility requirements as outlined in the Awards and Grants policies. 2. Applicants must be ACR or ARP members with an MD, DO, PhD or equivalent doctoral level degree from an accredited institution. ACR members must meet the following criteria a. Applicants must have less than one year (or a lapse) remaining on one of the following awards NIH K08, K23, K25, K99/R00, VA CDA, institutional K, or Rheumatology Research Foundation Investigator Award. b. Have earned a DO, MD, MD/PhD, or DO/PhD degree and have completed a Rheumatology fellowship. c. MDs and Dos who are not licensed to perform clinical care in the U.S. may not apply. ARP members must meet the following criteria a. Applicants must have less than one year (or a lapse) remaining on one of the following awards NIH K01, K08, K23, K25, K99/R00, VA CDA, institutional K, or Rheumatology Research Foundation Investigator Award. b. Have earned a PhD, DSc, or equivalent degree. 3. The Foundation does not currently support non- MD/DO scientists working on basic science research. 4. Previous recipients of an NIH R01 or VA RCS/ORD are not eligible to apply. 5. Applicants must have received a priority score, summary statement, and funding decision on their NIH R01 or VA RCS/ORD award. Applicants whose career development applications were triaged, and therefore, not discussed during peer review, are not eligible. Bridge funds are not intended to bridge the period between review and funding. 6. Applications from individuals from groups underrepresented (diversity.nih.gov/about-us/population-underrepresented) in medicine are particularly encouraged. 7. Previous recipients of this award are not eligible to apply. 8. In addition to an excellent application, applicants must be capable of becoming independent, researchers with a clear and firm institutional commitment to their continued career development, including a faculty position and other supporting resources.
Level of Study: Doctorate, Masters Degree, Postdoctorate
Type: Award
Value: US$200,000
Length of Study: 2 years
Frequency: Annual
Country of Study: United States of America
Application Procedure: All applications must be submitted by 5 PM ET on the deadline day through ProposalCentral. proposalcentral.com/. Please visit website.
Closing Date: 3 October
Additional Information: For more information: www.rheumresearch.org/career-development-research-awards. www.rheumresearch.org/file/FY22_Career-Development-Bridge-Funding-Award_R-Bridge_3.3.2021.pdf

For further information contact:

Email: Foundation@rheumatology.org

Career Development in Geriatric Medicine Award

Purpose: To support career development for junior faculty in the early stages of their research career
Eligibility: The candidate must be a member of the ACR; have completed a rheumatology fellowship leading to certification by the ABIM and be within the first 3 years of his/her faculty appointment; and possess a faculty appointment at the time of the award. Award applicant must be a citizen or non-citizen national of the United States of America, or be in lawful possessions of a permanent resident card. Individuals on temporary (J1, H1) or student visas are not eligible
Level of Study: Doctorate, Professional development, Research
Type: Research award
Value: US$75,000 per year plus US$3,000 in travel grants
Length of Study: 2 years
Frequency: Annual
Country of Study: United States of America
Application Procedure: Application forms are available on website www.rheumatology.org/foundation/index.asp
No. of awards offered: 1
Closing Date: 1 December
Funding: Foundation
Contributor: Association of Subspecialty Professors
No. of awards given last year: 1
No. of applicants last year: 1
Additional Information: www.rheumresearch.org/career-development-research-awards

For further information contact:

Email: ysong@hrsa.gov

Clinician Scholar Educator Award

Purpose: The purpose of the Clinician Scholar Educator (CSE) Award is to enhance education in musculoskeletal diseases for future doctors and rheumatology health professionals. Recipients of the award have demonstrated that they want to develop a career in education and are devoted to providing effective and efficient training. Recipients of the CSE Award devote themselves to developing products and processes using new technologies and methods to better train future rheumatologists.
Eligibility: 1. Applicant must meet citizenship and other eligibility requirements as outlined in the Awards and Grants policies. 2. Must propose educational projects related to rheumatic disease. 3. Applicant must be affiliated with an accredited graduate or medical school. 4. Applicant must be able to devote at least 25 percent full-time effort (including this project and other educational endeavors) to educational and scholarly activity for the duration of the award. Note this time is independent of any program administrative time for teaching faculty, Assistant Program Directors or Program Directors. 5. Applicant must be an ACR or ARP member at the time of submission and for the duration of the award. For ACR members must meet the following criteria 1. Have earned a DO, MD, or MD/PhD degree and completed a Rheumatology fellowship by the time of award start, 2. Have experience in the education or training of medical students, and/or residents and fellows, 3. Be licensed to perform clinical care, 4. Have experience seeing patients AND currently see patients; For ARP members must meet the following criteria 1. Have earned an advanced degree (Masters or above), 2. Have experience in the education or training of health professionals, 3. Have experience seeing patients AND currently see patients.
Type: Award
Value: US$180,000
Length of Study: 3 years
Frequency: Annual
Country of Study: United States of America
Application Procedure: All applications must be submitted online by 5 PM ET on the deadline day through ProposalCentral at proposalcentral.com/. If you have any questions about your eligibility or submitting your application, please contact Award & Grants staff. Before starting the online application, you will be required to create a Professional Profile in ProposalCentral. Please refer website www.rheumresearch.org/education-and-training-awards
Closing Date: 2 May
Additional Information: www.rheumresearch.org/education-and-training-awards

For further information contact:

Email: Foundation@rheumatology.org

Fellowship Training Award for Workforce Expansion

Purpose: To help ensure an adequate supply of rheumatology providers meeting the needs of children and adults with rheumatic diseases in all areas of the country, particularly those currently underserved
Eligibility: 1. The Fellowship Training Award for Workforce Expansion may be used to support the salary of any fellow in an ACGME-accredited rheumatology fellowship training program meeting any of the criteria below a. Program has been unable to fill all of its ACGME-approved slots due to funding constraints, b. An existing program that is creating a new slot, c. A new ACGME-accredited program (prepared to participate in the NRMP match for the first year of funding). 2. Applicant (Program Director) must be an ACR or ARP member at the time of submission and for the duration of the award. 3. Only Program Directors at ACGME-accredited institutions in good standing may apply. 4. The rheumatology fellowship training Program Director at the institution will be responsible for the overall direction, management and administration of the program. 5. By submitting an application, the Program Director and sponsoring institution agree funds will be used ONLY for salary support of one fellow in their first or second year (or third year fellow in pediatric rheumatology). 6. Multiple applications from a single institution will not be permitted unless they are for separate training programs (e.g. adult and pediatric rheumatology). 7. Programs may not apply for the Amgen Fellowship Training Award and Fellowship Training Award for Workforce Expansion within the same application cycle. Preference will be given to programs not supported by fellowship training awards granted by other organizations. 8. If there is no fellow available to appoint to this award between July 1 and June 30, recipient may request a one-year deferral. 9. Supported fellows do not need to be U.S. citizens or non-citizen nationals.
Type: Award
Value: US$100,000 for adult programs; US$150,000 for pediatric programs
Length of Study: 2 to 3 Years
Frequency: Annual
Country of Study: United States of America
Application Procedure: All applications must be submitted online by 5 PM ET on the deadline day through

ProposalCentral at proposalcentral.com/. Please refer www.rheumresearch.org/file/FY23-Fellowship-Training-Award-for-Workforce-Expansion_2.16.21.pdf
Closing Date: 2 May
Additional Information: For more information www.rheumresearch.org/file/FY23-Fellowship-Training-Award-for-Workforce-Expansion_2.16.21.pdf

For further information contact:

Email: foundation@rheumatology.org

Health Professional Online Education Grant

Purpose: To increase the knowledge and skills of non-physician rheumatology health professionals to meet the needs of a growing rheumatology patient population by reimbursing the cost of registration for the Advanced Rheumatology Courses or the Fundamentals of Rheumatology Courses
Eligibility: 1. Applicants must meet citizenship and other eligibility requirements as outlined in the Awards and Grants Policies. 2. Applicants must be ARP members at the time of submission and for the duration of the award. 3. Nurse practitioners, physician assistants, nurses, pharmacists, physical therapists, occupational therapists, social workers, psychologists, practice management staff, other licensed non-physician health professionals with an interest in rheumatology.
Type: Grant
Value: Up to US$799 for the Fundamentals of Rheumatology Course
Frequency: Annual
Country of Study: United States of America
Application Procedure: All applications must be submitted by 5 PM ET on the deadline day through ProposalCentral at proposalcentral.com/. Please refer www.rheumresearch.org/file/HPOEG-21.pdf
Additional Information: For more information www.rheumresearch.org/file/awards/2019/FY20-HPOEG-RFA_FINAL.pdf

Innovative Research Award

Purpose: Supporting innovative research ideas is essential to better understanding rheumatic diseases, their cause, and the best way to treat them. The Innovative Research Award provides independent academic investigators with the funding they need to pursue ideas that could lead to important breakthroughs in discovering new treatments and, one day, a cure. This award provides essential support for innovative studies focused on generating new insights into the cause, progression, treatment, and outcomes of rheumatic and musculoskeletal diseases.
Eligibility: To be eligible, the applicant must 1. Be a member of the ACR or ARP at the time of submission and for the duration of the award, 2. Hold a doctoral-level degree (MD, PhD, DO, MBBS or equivalent), 3. Have a faculty appointment (instructor, assistant professor, etc.) at an academic center or research institution at the time of application and for the duration of the award, 4. Must exhibit evidence of research independence, scientific productivity and career accomplishments, 5. Be able to devote a minimum of 20% full-time professional research effort to the project (see details in Award Eligibility and Guidelines in website), 6. Meet citizenship and other eligibility requirements as outlined in the Awards and Grants policies.
Level of Study: Doctorate, Postdoctorate, Professional development
Type: Award
Value: Up to US$200,000 per year
Length of Study: 2 years
Frequency: Annual
Country of Study: United States of America
Application Procedure: All applications must be submitted by 5 PM ET on the deadline day through ProposalCentral at www.proposalcentral.com/ Please refer website. www.rheumresearch.org/innovative-research-award
Closing Date: December
Funding: Foundation
Additional Information: www.rheumresearch.org/innovative-research-award

Innovative Research Award for Community Practitioners

Purpose: Through our innovative research program, the Foundation is committed to funding research ideas that are essential to improve understanding of rheumatic diseases, including their causes and optimal treatments. The Innovative Research Award for Community Practitioners will enable research that has the potential to improve treatment of rheumatic diseases, patient outcomes, and/or quality of care. This award is targeted to community practitioners who, in addition to being engaged in patient care, conduct or are interested in conducting research.
Eligibility: To be eligible, the applicant must 1. Be a member of the ACR or ARP at the time of submission and for the duration of the award; 2. Hold a doctoral-level degree (MD, DO, PhD, DNP, PsyD, EdD); 3. Have a current license to practice medicine or other interprofessional specialty and be in good medical standing; 4. Be employed in a community practice setting including a. Solo practice. b. Single specialty

group practice. c. Multi-specialty group practice. d. Hospital system-based practice. 5. Have the ability to manage a grant award administratively and fiscally, 6. Demonstrate certification of training in human subjects research and the ability to obtain human subjects research approval and oversight for the proposed research for the duration of the award; 8. Meet citizenship and other eligibility requirements as outlined in the Awards and Grants policies.
Level of Study: Doctorate, Postdoctorate, Professional development, Research
Type: Award
Value: US$$80,000
Length of Study: 1 year
Frequency: Annual
Country of Study: United States of America
Application Procedure: All applications must be submitted by 5 PM ET on the deadline day through ProposalCentral at www.proposalcentral.com/ Please refer website www.rheumresearch.org/innovative-research-award
Closing Date: 1 June
Funding: Foundation
Additional Information: For more information: www.rheumresearch.org/document.doc?id=491

For further information contact:

Email: Foundation@rheumatology.org

Lawren H. Daltroy Health Professional Preceptorship

Purpose: The Lawren H. Daltroy Preceptorship in Health Communication was established with the aim of improving patient-clinician interactions and communications. Dr. Daltroy was an internationally recognized authority on health education and enhancing communication between physicians and patients. He performed groundbreaking studies on patient selfmedication in hospitals, spousal support for cardiac patients and worksite health education. This award provides resources to support the training, career development, and/or enhancement of research skills of researchers and clinicians.
Eligibility: 1. Preceptee must meet citizenship and other eligibility requirements as outlined in the Awards and Grants policies. 2. Preceptor must be an ACR or ARP member. 3. This mentored award is intended for trainees and junior researchers or health professionals with no current or prior R01 or R01-equivalent funding. Both ACR and ARP members are eligible to apply.
Level of Study: Professional development, Research
Type: Award
Value: Up to US$15,000 for one year
Length of Study: 1 year
Frequency: Annual
Country of Study: United States of America
Application Procedure: All applications must be submitted by 5 PM ET on the deadline day through Proposal Central at www.proposalcentral.com/. Please refer www.rheumresearch.org/file/FY22-Lawren-H.-Daltroy-Health-Professional-Preceptorship.pdf.
Funding: Corporation
Contributor: Funding for this award is made possible through an endowment established by Rheuminations, Inc.
Additional Information: Please check website www.rheumresearch.org/preceptorships#LHDP

For further information contact:

Email: Foundation@rheumatology.org

Medical and Graduate Student Preceptonship

Purpose: The purpose of the preceptorship program is to introduce medical and graduate students to rheumatology-related health care by supporting a 4-Week or 8-Week, full-time clinical or research experience in the broad area of rheumatic disease.
Eligibility: 1. Preceptor must be an ACR or ARP member at the time of submission and for the duration of the award (students are not required to be members). 2. A preceptor may be eligible to receive the award multiple times; however, they must work with a different student each time. 3. Students enrolled in LCME or AOA COCA accredited medical schools, undergraduate students who have been accepted into medical school, students enrolled in an accredited graduate school, or undergraduate students who have been accepted into graduate school, are eligible to apply. 4. Students may apply during any year of their medical or graduate studies and must have identified a preceptor by the time of the application. 5. Individuals who are personally related to the proposed student are not eligible to serve as the student's preceptor.
Level of Study: Research
Type: Award
Value: US$2,000-$4,000 plus US$1,000 for travel expenses and complimentary registration to ACR Convergence
Length of Study: 4 to 8 Weeks
Frequency: Annual
Country of Study: United States of America
Application Procedure: Applicants have the option to select Clinical or Research when applying. All applications must be

submitted by 5 PM ET on the deadline day through ProposalCentral at www.proposalcentral.com/. For details please refer www.rheumresearch.org/file/FY22-Medical–Graduate-Student-Preceptorship.pdf
No. of awards offered: 3
Funding: Private
Contributor: Marc R. Chevrier, MD, PhD, FACR, Lupus Research Memorial Fund
Additional Information: www.rheumresearch.org/file/FY21-Medical–Graduate-Student-Preceptorship_FINAL.pdf

For further information contact:

Email: Foundation@rheumatology.org

Mentored Nurse Practitioner/Physician Assistant Award for Workforce Expansion

Purpose: The purpose of the Mentored Nurse Practitioner/Physician Assistant (NP/PA) Award for Workforce Expansion is to increase the supply of rheumatology healthcare providers to better meet the needs of people with rheumatic diseases across the United States, particularly in geographically underserved areas. This award provides resources and the framework of knowledge, skills, and attitudes needed by NP/PAs, new to rheumatology, to facilitate their integration into a rheumatology practice under the supervision of a rheumatologist.
Eligibility: 1. Eligible applicant ("Mentor") must be a board-certified rheumatologist employed in clinical rheumatology practice. The NP or PA does not have to be identified at the time of application but must be identified at the time of award contract. Eligible NP/PA must be new to the field of rheumatology (employed in a rheumatology practice setting for fewer than 18 months). 2. Mentor must meet citizenship and other eligibility requirements as outlined in the Awards and Grants policies. 3. Mentor must be an ACR member at the time of submission and for the duration of the award. 4. Mentor is eligible to receive the award multiple times; however, the mentor must work with a new NP or PA each time. The mentor may have only one active NP/PA award at a time. 5. NP or PA must be a graduate from a program accredited by either the Commission on Collegiate Nursing Education (CCNE) or the Accreditation Review Commission on Education for the Physician Assistant. 6. NP or PA must have current state licensure. 7. NP or PA must have national Board certification by one or more of the following a. American Nurses Credentialing Center b. American Academy of Nurse Practitioners c. Pediatric Nursing Certification Board d. National Certification Corporation e. National Commission on Certification of Physician Assistants 8. NP or PA must be a member of the Association for Rheumatology Professionals for the duration of the award.
Type: Award
Value: US$25,000
Length of Study: 1 year
Frequency: Annual
Country of Study: United States of America
Application Procedure: Apply Now: proposalcentral.com/ProposalGI.asp?SectionID=9646&ProposalID=-1
Closing Date: 1 March
Contributor: Rheumatology Research Foundation
Additional Information: For more information: www.rheumresearch.org/education-and-training-awards

Paula de Merieux Fellowship Training Award

Purpose: Paula de Merieux grant is awarded to support a trainee who belongs to an underrepresented minority within rheumatology, or is a woman. For the purposes of this program, "underrepresented minority within rheumatology" shall mean Black, Hispanic, or Native American.
Eligibility: 1. To qualify, the trainee must be a member of an underrepresented minority within rheumatology, or a woman. 2. Applicant (Program Director) must be an ACR or ARP member at the time of submission and for the duration of the award. 3. Only Program Directors at ACGME-accredited institutionsin good standing may apply. 4. The rheumatology fellowship training Program Director at the institution will be responsible for the overall direction, management and administration of the program. 5. By submitting an application, the Program Director and sponsoring institution agree funds will be used ONLY for salary support of one fellow in their first orsecond year (or third year fellow in pediatric rheumatology). 6. Multiple applicationsfrom a single institution will not be permitted unless they are for separate training programs (e.g., adult and pediatric rheumatology). 7. Programs may not apply for the Amgen Fellowship Training Award and Fellowship Training Award- Workforce Expansion within the same application cycle. 8. Current recipients of the Fellowship Training Award for Workforce Expansion are not eligible to apply for this award. 9. Supported fellows do not need to be U.S. citizens or non-citizen nationals.
Type: Award
Value: US$50,000
Length of Study: 1 year
Frequency: Annual
Country of Study: United States of America
Application Procedure: All applications must be submitted online by 5 PM ET on the deadline day through ProposalCentral at www.proposalcentral.com/. Please refer

www.rheumresearch.org/file/FY23_Fellowship-Training-Award-PDM_2.16.21.pdf
No. of awards offered: 1
Closing Date: 2 May
Contributor: Paula de Merieux estate
Additional Information: For more details: www.rheumresearch.org/file/FY23_Fellowship-Training-Award-PDM_2.16.21.pdf

For further information contact:

Email: foundation@rheumatology.org

Rheumatology Future Physician Scientist Award

Purpose: The purpose of this pre-doctoral scholar award is to enhance the research training of promising students who are enrolled in a combined MD/PhD or DO/PhD dual-doctoral degree training program and who intend careers as physician-scientists. This grant mechanism aims to support the nation's top emerging physician scientists and promote their interest in investigative careers in rheumatology. This award will support dissertation research projects in scientific health-related fields relevant to the mission of the Rheumatology Research Foundation. The research training experience is expected to tangibly enhance the individuals' potential to develop into a productive, independent physician-scientist in the field of rheumatology.
Eligibility: The Foundation encourages applications from students early in the research training phase of their dual degree training so that they can substantively benefit from the mentored research training opportunities. 1. Applicant must meet citizenship and other eligibility requirements as outlined in the Awards and Grants policies. 2. The applicant must have a baccalaureate degree, show evidence of high academic performance in the sciences, and commitment to a career as an independent physician-scientist. Applicants should demonstrate a strong interest in pursuing a career in rheumatology research. 3. This program is specifically designed to support combined, dual-degree training leading to award of both a health professional doctoral degree (MD, DO) that would make the awardee eligible for future training as a rheumatologist; and a research doctoral degree (PhD) from an accredited program. Thus, the applicant must be enrolled in an MD/PhD or DO/PhD program. The entirety of the award period must be devoted to full-time graduate research training leading to the doctoral research degree. This award will not support full-time clinical training during the years of the MD/PhD or DO/PhD program. Program-required preceptorships during graduate training are allowed. 4. To encourage timely completion of dual degree training, this award is generally not intended to support students after year 5 of their training program. Ideally, support will be for 2 years during years 3-6 of the dual degree program (after the initial 2 years of classwork but prior to the clinical rotations/medical training). 5. The applicant must have identified a dissertation research project and a primary mentor. The primary mentor must be a faculty member actively engaged in basic, translational, clinical or health services research with a strong record of peer-reviewed research relevant to rheumatology. 6. The primary mentor must be a member of the American College of Rheumatology (ACR) at the time of the application and for the duration of the award.
Level of Study: Doctorate, Postdoctorate, Professional development
Type: Award
Value: Up to US$60,000
Length of Study: 2 years
Frequency: Annual
Country of Study: United States of America
Application Procedure: All applications must be submitted by 5 PM ET on the deadline day through ProposalCentral at www.proposalcentral.com/. Please refer www.rheumresearch.org/file/FY23-Rheumatology-Future-Physician-Scientist-Award.pdf
Closing Date: 1 December
Additional Information: For more details: www.rheumresearch.org/file/FY23-Rheumatology-Future-Physician-Scientist-Award.pdf

For further information contact:

Email: foundation@rheumatology.org

Scientist Development Award

Purpose: This award is designed for individuals in the early stages of their career (typically Fellows) or those without significant prior research experience who plan to embark on careers in rheumatic diseases. The purpose of this award is to provide support for a structured research training program for rheumatologists or health professionals in the field of rheumatology.
Eligibility: 1. Applicant must meet citizenship and other eligibility requirements as outlined in the Awards and Grants policies. 2. Applicant must be an ACR or ARP member at the time of submission and for the duration of the award. For ACR members must meet the following criteria a. Have earned a DO, MD, or degree and by the start of the award term have completed at least one year of training in an ACGME accredited rheumatology training program. b. Individuals more than 4 years from the beginning of fellowship (or 5 years for pediatric rheumatologists) at the

time of award start date may not apply. c. MDs and DOs who are not licensed to perform clinical care may not apply. For ARP members must meet the following criteria a. Have earned a PhD, DSc, or equivalent doctoral degree. b. Must be within 3 years of terminal degree at the time of award start date. 3. The Foundation does NOT currently support non-MD/DO scientists working on basic science projects. 4. Applicant must be affiliated with an accredited graduate or medical school. 5. Applicant must be able to commit a minimum of 75 percent full-time professional effort to research, academic career development, and other research related activities. Candidates may not spend more than 25 percent in clinical and/or teaching activities. It is expected that about 50 percent full-time professional effort will be spent on the Foundation funded project. 6. Receive acceptance by a mentor who will oversee the training and research experience. 7. Former or current recipients of research grants (at the K level or higher, including institutional K) and past awardees of this or equivalent Foundation grants are NOT eligible to apply. 8. Applicants may not apply for the Investigator Award in the same funding cycle. 9. Individuals may not apply for more than one Scientist Development Award per funding cycle. 10. Investigators interested in using data from the ACR's RISE registry as part of their proposed research project need to get their data use request approved before applying for funding. Please visit RISE for Research (www.rheumatology.org/I-Am-A/Rheumatologist/RISE-Registry/RISE-for-Research) for more information on RISE data. RISE data requests should be submitted at least 2 months prior to the Foundation's application deadline.

Level of Study: Professional development
Type: Award
Value: Up to US$225,000
Length of Study: 2 to 3 Years
Frequency: Annual
Country of Study: United States of America
Application Procedure: All applications must be submitted by 5 PM ET on the deadline day through ProposalCentral at www.proposalcentral.com/. Please refer www.rheumresearch.org/file/FY23-Scientist-Development-Award_2.16.21.pdf
Closing Date: 1 July
Funding: Foundation
Contributor: Rheumatology Research Foundation
Additional Information: For more information: www.rheumresearch.org/career-development-research-awards. www.rheumresearch.org/file/FY23-Scientist-Development-Award_2.16.21.pdf

For further information contact:

Email: foundation@rheumatology.org

Rhode Island Foundation

One Union Station, Providence, RI 02903, United States of America.

Tel: (1) 401 274 4564
Email: info@rifoundation.org
Website: rifoundation.org/

The Foundation was organized at the Rhode Island Hospital Trust Co. in June 1916 by a small group of prominent Rhode Islanders. For more than 100 years, the Rhode Island Foundation has been dedicated to improving the lives of Rhode Islanders. We partner with generous individuals, families, organizations, and corporations that share our commitment to the state, as well as with nonprofit organizations that provide the "boots-on-the-ground" services that make Rhode Island a better place to live, work, and play.

AAA Northeast Scholarship

Purpose: The scholarship program provides financial assistance to children and legal dependents of current employees of AAA Northeast who have been employed full-time for at least one year at the time of application (initial or renewal).
Eligibility: You are eligible if you: Are the child and legal dependent of a current AAA Northeast employee who has been employed full-time for at least one year at the time of application. Are a high school senior or first, second, or third-year student at an accredited post-secondary institution enrolling full-time in an associate or bachelor's degree program. If a high-school senior, you must enroll in and attend such institution in the first academic term following graduation from high school. Demonstrate academic achievement as evidenced by a GPA of at least 2.5 on a 4.0 scale (or its equivalent). Demonstrate unmet financial need. Demonstrate good character and potential as evidenced by the application responses and a required essay of up to 300 words.
Type: Scholarship
Value: US$2,500
Frequency: Annual
Country of Study: United States of America
Application Procedure: To apply for a AAA Northeast Scholarship, click the link: www.grantinterface.com/Home/Logon?urlkey=rifs
No. of awards offered: 12
Closing Date: 17 April
Additional Information: rifoundation.org/grants-scholarships/browse-scholarships/aaa-northeast-scholarship

For further information contact:

1 Union Station, Providence, RI 02903, United States of America.

Tel: (1) 401 274 4564
Email: mbenson@rifoundation.org

Carter Roger Williams Scholarship

Purpose: This annual scholarship program is intended to inspire students and their parents to think big about what's possible for their future. Students who appreciate and embody Roger Williams's values and legacy are encouraged to apply.
Eligibility: Currently reside in Rhode Island; Be current seniors at any high school (public, independent, or private) in Rhode Island; and Have been accepted by an accredited post-secondary institution (by the date of the award).
Type: Scholarship
Value: US$20,000
Frequency: Annual
Country of Study: United States of America
Closing Date: 28 February
Additional Information: rifoundation.org/grants-scholarships/browse-scholarships/carterscholarship

For further information contact:

1 Union Station, Providence, RI 02903, United States of America.

Tel: (1) 401 274 4564
Email: mbenson@rifoundation.org

Cataract Fire Company #2 Scholarship

Purpose: This scholarship is open to residents of Warwick, Rhode Island, who are entering their first year of a two-year, four-year, or vocational/technical postsecondary institution.
Eligibility: 1. Must be a High school seniors. 2. Must be a Warwick, Rhode Island residents. 3. Academic excellence not necessary, preference given to students not in the top 10% of their graduating class. 4. Students must demonstrate financial need.
Level of Study: Graduate
Type: Scholarship
Value: US$1,500 - US$2,000; non-renewable
Frequency: Annual
Country of Study: United States of America
Application Procedure: Applications must be submitted through Rhode Island Foundation Online Application System.
Closing Date: 10 April
Funding: Foundation
Additional Information: rifoundation.org/grants-scholarships/browse-scholarships#cataract-fire-company-2-scholarship

For further information contact:

1 Union Station, Providence, RI 02903, United States of America.

Tel: (1) 401 427 4028
Email: kriley@rifoundation.org

Major Jeremiah P. Murphy Scholarship

Purpose: This scholarship is open to children of active, retired, or deceased Providence (RI) police officers who are or will be attending postsecondary institutions offering two-year associate's or four-year college degree
Eligibility: 1. Children of active, retired, or deceased Providence police officers. 2. Attending post-secondary institutions offering two-year associate or four-year college degree.
Type: Scholarship
Value: US$1,000 - US$2,500; renewable
Frequency: Annual
Country of Study: United States of America
Application Procedure: Applications must be submitted through Rhode Island Foundation Online Application System.
Closing Date: 10 April
Additional Information: www.rifoundation.org/grants-scholarships/browse-scholarships?l=54&s=1&q=Jeremiah+

For further information contact:

1 Union Station, Providence, RI 02903, United States of America.

Tel: (1) 401 427 4028
Email: kriley@rifoundation.org

Michael P. Metcalf Memorial Fund and Christine T. Grinavic Adventurer

Purpose: These funds provide grants to college students to subsidize experiences intended to broaden their perspective and enhance personal growth.
Eligibility: Applications will be accepted from college freshmen, sophomores, juniors, and seniors who are legal residents of Rhode Island.

Type: Scholarship
Value: US$2,000 to US$5,000
Country of Study: United States of America
Closing Date: 21 February
Additional Information: rifoundation.org/grants-scholarships/browse-scholarships/metcalf-memorial-fund-and-grinavic-adventurers-fund

For further information contact:

1 Union Station, Providence, RI 02903, United States of America.

Tel: (1) 401 274 4564
Email: mbenson@rifoundation.org

Nursing Scholarships

Purpose: The Foundation awards scholarships from five nursing funds each year. One application may be used to apply for all five programs, as long as an applicant qualifies for at least one of the programs described below.
Eligibility: To be eligible you must be either a Rhode Island resident or attending a nursing program in Rhode Island.
Type: Scholarship
Value: US$500 to US$5000
Country of Study: United States of America
Application Procedure: Click here to apply: www.grantinterface.com/Home/Logon?urlkey=rifs
Closing Date: 8 May
Additional Information: rifoundation.org/grants-scholarships/browse-scholarships/nursing-scholarships

For further information contact:

1 Union Station, Providence, RI 02903, United States of America.

Tel: (1) 401 274 4564
Email: mbenson@rifoundation.org

Rhodes College

2000 North Parkway, Memphis, TN 38112, United States of America.

Tel: (1) 901 843 3000
Email: adminfo@rhodes.edu
Website: www.rhodes.edu/

Rhodes College was founded in 1848 in Clarksville, Tennessee. Rhodes College aspires to graduate students with a lifelong passion for learning, a compassion for others, and the ability to translate academic study and personal concern into effective leadership and action in their communities and the world.

Carnegie Endowment Junior Fellows Program

Eligibility: Graduating seniors or seniors who have graduated in the past year and are interested in international affairs
Eligible Country: Any Country
Level of Study: Postgraduate, Research
Type: Fellowship
Value: US$1,875.00 per semi-monthly pay period
Length of Study: 1 year
Country of Study: United States of America
Closing Date: 15 January
Additional Information: www.rhodes.edu/academics/experiential-applied-learning/postgraduate-scholarships/scholarship-opportunities#Carnegie carnegieendowment.org/about/jr-fellows/faq#citizen

Emerson National Hunger Fellows Program

Purpose: The Emerson Hunger Fellow Program is a social justice program that trains, inspires, and sustains leaders.
Eligibility: Eligibility: US citizen or permanent resident; BA or equivalent by beginning of grant period, language proficiency.
Eligible Country: United States of America
Type: Scholarship
Value: US$16,000 annual living allowance; Health insurance; Travel expenses; Housing during field placement; US$3,500 end of service award; US$4,000 housing subsidy in DC
Frequency: Annual
Country of Study: United States of America
Closing Date: 30 December
Additional Information: www.rhodes.edu/academics/postgraduate-scholarships/scholarship-opportunities#Carnegie

For further information contact:

Rhodes College, 2000 North Parkway, Memphis, TN 38112, United States of America.

Tel: (1) 800 844 5969

Lilly Fellows Program in the Humanities and the Arts

Subjects: Eligible disciplines are art; art history; creative writing; history; interdisciplinary studies; languages and literature; music; music history; philosophy; religion; rhetoric; theater history; theater arts, and theology.
Purpose: Nominees must have earned or be in the process of earning a baccalaureate degree from a LFP network institution.
Eligibility: 1. Nominees must have earned or be in the process of earning a baccalaureate degree from a LFP network institution. 2. Eligibility is open to seniors graduating during the current academic year, or to anyone having received a baccalaureate from a network institution within the last five years. 3. Nominees must be U.S. Citizens. 4. Eligible disciplines are: art; art history; creative writing; history; interdisciplinary studies; languages and literature; music; music history; philosophy; religion; rhetoric; theater history; theater arts, and theology. 5. Notes: To be eligible for the Lilly Graduate Fellowship, nominees must intend to enter a Ph.D., M.F.A., D.M.A., Th.D., or equivalent program the school of their choice in fall, 2013, that will lead to a teaching career in humanities or the arts within the academy. Nominees should also want to explore the connections between Christianity and higher education and have an interest in teaching at a church-related school.
Eligible Country: United States of America
Level of Study: Doctorate, Postgraduate
Type: Fellowship
Value: Provides US$3,000 stipend, mentorship, and intellectual network for students
Length of Study: 5 Years
Frequency: Annual
Country of Study: United States of America
Closing Date: 1 March
Additional Information: www.rhodes.edu/academics/postgraduate-scholarships/scholarship-opportunities#Fulbright

For further information contact:

Rhodes College, 2000 North Parkway, Memphis, TN 38112, United States of America.

Tel: (1) 800 844 5969

Watson Fellowship

Purpose: To offer college graduates a year of independent study and travel outside the United States
Eligibility: Must be graduating senior to apply; U.S. citizenship NOT required
Type: Fellowship
Value: US$40,000
Length of Study: 1 year
Frequency: Annual
Country of Study: Any country
Application Procedure: 1. Ensure eligibility. 2. Meet with your campus advisor. 3. Complete the application including a. Your Personal Statement - What has convinced you to apply for the Watson? What do you hope to benefit from the year? b. Your Project Proposal - Your project must sustain your interest amidst the highs and lows of a year in unfamiliar places. What is your plan for the 12-month period? What opportunities and challenges are unique to your project? 4. 2 Recommendations. 5. Transcript. 6. Complete the campus selection process.
Closing Date: 7 October
Contributor: Thomas J. Watson Foundation
Additional Information: www.rhodes.edu/academics/experiential-and-applied-learning/postgraduate-scholarships/internal-and-national-deadlines

For further information contact:

2000 North Pkwy, Memphis, TN 38112, United States of America.

Tel: (1) 901 843 3249
Email: saxer@rhodes.edu

Rhodes Trust

Rhodes House, South Parks Road, Oxford OX1 3RG, United Kingdom.

Tel: (44) 1865 270901
Email: admin@rhodeshouse.ox.ac.uk
Website: www.rhodeshouse.ox.ac.uk/
Contact: Porters' Lodge

The Rhodes Trust, based at the University of Oxford, brings together and develops exceptional people from all over the world, and in all fields of study, who are impatient with the way things are and have the courage to act. The Rhodes Trust is an educational charity which supports exceptional students from around the world to study at the University of Oxford.

Rhodes Scholarship

Purpose: Rhodes Scholarships are the oldest and perhaps most prestigious international scholarship programme in the

world, enabling outstanding young people from around the world to undertake full-time postgraduate study at the University of Oxford.
Eligibility: 1. Literary and scholastic attainments (academic excellence) 2. energy to use one's talents to the full (as demonstrated by mastery in areas such as sports, music, debate, dance, theatre, and artistic pursuits, particularly where teamwork is involved) 3. truth, courage, devotion to duty, sympathy for and protection of the weak, kindliness, unselfishness and fellowship 4. moral force of character and instincts to lead, and to take an interest in one's fellow beings. 5. The detailed eligibility criteria varies slightly depending on which constituency you are applying for. You can use our eligibility checker tool to find out if you meet the criteria and are eligible to apply for the Scholarship. www.rhodeshouse.ox.ac.uk/scholarships/applications/
Level of Study: Doctorate
Type: Scholarship
Value: the stipend is £18,180 per annum (£1,515 per month)
Length of Study: 2 year
Frequency: Annual
Country of Study: United Kingdom
Application Procedure: Apply online. Please visit website www.rhodeshouse.ox.ac.uk/scholarships/application-overview/.
No. of awards offered: 100
Funding: Trusts
Additional Information: For more information: www.rhodeshouse.ox.ac.uk/scholarships/the-rhodes-scholarship/

For further information contact:

Email: scholarship.queries@rhodeshouse.ox.ac.uk

Rhodes University

PO Box 94, Makhanda, Eastern Cape 6140, South Africa.

Tel: (27) 46 603 8111
Email: communications@ru.ac.za
Website: www.ru.ac.za/
Contact: John Gillam, Manager

Founded in 1904, the University has a well-established reputation for academic excellence. With just over 8200 students, Rhodes is a small University, which enjoys the distinction of having among the best undergraduate pass and graduation rates in South Africa, outstanding postgraduate success rates, and the best research output per academic staff member.

Andrew W. Mellon Foundation Masters & Doctoral Scholarships

Purpose: The focus of Dr Thando Njovane's project is History, Memory and Trauma in African Fiction. Working within this interdisciplinary lense, the project investigates how works of fiction may help us theorise trauma, history and memory from an African perspective. This may include comparative studies with other postcolonial, post-conflict and/or African-American fictions in which questions of race and/or embodiment feature prominently.
Eligibility: Preference will be given to designated groups. Honours degree in English literature/Literary Studies for MA applicants, and MA in English literature/Literary Studies for PhD applicants (candidates must have studied or show a keen interest in African literature or comparative postcolonial literature). Candidates may select to work on either the short story, novels or poetry.
Level of Study: Masters Degree, Postdoctorate
Type: Scholarship
Value: MA scholarship (two years) R105,000 per annum PhD scholarship (three years) R135,000 per annum
Country of Study: Any country
Closing Date: 5 November
Contributor: Dr Thando Njovane, Department of Literary Studies in English, Rhodes University, Makhanda
Additional Information: www.ru.ac.za/researchgateway/postgraduates/funding/internal/

For further information contact:

PO Box 94 Makhanda (Grahamstown) 6140 Eastern Cape, South Africa.

Tel: (27) 46 603 8111

R

Global Partnership Network Masters Scholarships

Subjects: The politics of NGO work; Post-development thinking and Africa; and/or Alternative knowledge production about Africa.
Purpose: The Global Partnership Network (GPN) funds research on development cooperation, the global economy, and knowledge production.
Eligibility: In line with the GPN scholarship requirements, preference will be given to candidates from countries in the Global South (including but not limited to South Africa)
Type: Scholarship
Value: R100 000.00 per annum
Length of Study: Two years
Frequency: Annual
Country of Study: Any country

Closing Date: 30 September
Additional Information: www.ru.ac.za/researchgateway/postgraduates/funding/internal/

For further information contact:

Drosty Rd, Grahamstown, Makhanda, 6139, South Africa.

Tel: (27) 46 603 8111
Email: s.matthews@ru.ac.za or pgfunding@ru.ac.za

GUS LIPSCHITZ BURSARY

Purpose: This Bursary was established in 2021 by the family of the late Gustav Lipschitz. He was a graduate of Rhodes University (BCom 1941 (majoring in Accounting an Economics) and MCom Economics 1946). He had a strong belief in education and this bursary is established in his memory.
Eligibility: Acceptance for postgraduate course (full-time in attendance) in Economics at Rhodes University, proven financial need and academic merit.
Type: Bursary
Value: R130,000
Length of Study: Maximum of two years.
Frequency: Annual
Country of Study: Any country
Closing Date: 30 September
Additional Information: www.ru.ac.za/researchgateway/postgraduates/funding/internal/

For further information contact:

PO Box 94 Makhanda (Grahamstown) 6140 Eastern Cape, South Africa.

Tel: (27) 46 603 8111

Guy Butler Research Award

Subjects: English Language, English Literature, English-in-Education, South African English Drama, South African Journalism in English, Cultural studies focusing on English-related topics in Southern Africa and research in the area of English bilingualism, as an additional language.
Purpose: Rhodes University invites all students with a strong academic record (grades 70% and above) who intend pursuing full-time Postgraduate studies in 2024, to apply for the Guy Butler Research Award.
Eligibility: Applicants must pursue research in one of the following fields English Language, English Literature, English-in-Education, South African English Drama, South African Journalism in English, Cultural studies focusing on English-related topics in Southern Africa and research in the area of English bilingualism, as an additional language. Period Initially for one year, but renewable depending on satisfactory progress for a further year at Masters level and two years at Doctoral level. Tenable Full-time attendance and registration at Rhodes University (Departments of English, English Languages and Linguistics and ISEA).
Level of Study: Doctorate, Masters Degree, Postgraduate
Type: Award
Value: Honours - R90 000, Masters - R100 000, Doctoral - R120 000
Length of Study: 1 to 3 years
Frequency: Annual
Country of Study: Any country
Application Procedure: Guy Butler Application Form: www.ru.ac.za/media/rhodesuniversity/content/research/documents/funding/Butler_app_form.docx
Closing Date: 11 October
Additional Information: www.ru.ac.za/researchgateway/postgraduates/funding/internal/

For further information contact:

Drosty Rd, Grahamstown, Makhanda, 6139, South Africa.

Tel: (27) 46 603 8111
Email: pgfunding@ru.ac.za

Hobart Houghton Research Fellowship

Purpose: The Fellowship is intended to promote work relevant to the economic problems of the Eastern Cape, and which could contribute to the development of the region. Funding for the establishment of the Fellowship has been provided by Hobart Houghton's former students and associates and by the Liberty Life Educational Foundation.
Eligibility: Prospective Fellows should have had research experience, and hold at least a Masters degree in Economics or Agricultural Economics. They should have a sound knowledge of economic analysis and be capable of independent, innovative work. Candidates may either be established scholars (possibly on sabbatical leave) or young, promising economists.
Level of Study: Research
Type: Fellowship
Value: A typical package includes return airfare to Grahamstown, accommodation in university visitor's flats, plus a monthly cost of living stipend, all determined by the availability of funds and the background and status of the fellow. Limited funds will be available for travel and other research expenses

Length of Study: 6–8 weeks
Frequency: Annual
Study Establishment: Rhodes University, Grahamstown
Country of Study: South Africa
Application Procedure: The Hobart Houghton Fellowship Application Form should include a full statement of research interest.
Closing Date: 30 September
Funding: Foundation, Private
Contributor: Hobart Houghton's former students and associates and by the Liberty Life Educational Foundation
Additional Information: www.ru.ac.za/economics/hobarthoughtonresearchfellowship/

For further information contact:

Email: h.nel@ru.ac.za

Makabongwe Ndzwayiba Bursary

Purpose: This Bursary was established in 2012 by the Vice-Chancellor in memory of the late Makabongwe Ndzwayiba. An outstanding student, a sub-warden and Community Engagement representative, Makabongwe was an inspiration to all who came to know him.
Eligibility: Acceptance for Honours in Economics, proven financial need, demonstrable hardships overcome and leadership in assisting in the "upliftment" of local communities.
Type: Bursary
Value: R44 000 per annum
Frequency: Annual
Country of Study: Any country
Closing Date: 21 October
Additional Information: www.ru.ac.za/researchgateway/postgraduates/funding/internal/

For further information contact:

Drosty Rd, Grahamstown, Makhanda, 6139, South Africa.

Tel: (27) 46 603 8111
Email: pgfunding@ru.ac.za

Nicholas Iain Paumgarten Scholarship for Postgraduate Studies in Accounting

Purpose: This scholarship for Postgraduate studies in Accounting has been established through the generous support from the family of the late Nicholas Iain Paumgarten. His special interests were music, fishing, nature, spending time with family and friends.
Eligibility: South African citizenship, Full-time (in attendance) Honours, HDAC or Masters in Accounting Academic merit In addition, the Committee will consider the applicant's active participation in sporting, cultural and altruistic activities during their undergrad while still managing to maintain an academic record that makes them eligible for Honours/HDAC or Masters. Academic CV Certified copies of academic transcripts Motivation/Essay not exceeding 300 words explaining why you have chosen your field of study & what you propose to do in South Africa once qualified.
Level of Study: Postgraduate
Type: Scholarship
Value: R100 000 each
Length of Study: 1 year
Country of Study: South Africa
No. of awards offered: 2
Closing Date: 21 October
Additional Information: www.ru.ac.za/research/postgraduates/funding

For further information contact:

Drosty Rd, Grahamstown, Makhanda, 6139, South Africa.

Tel: (27) 46 603 8111
Email: pgfunding@ru.ac.za

Rhodes University African Studies Centre (RASC)

Subjects: All research projects must align to at least one of the following themes (1) Moralities; (2) Knowledge; (3) Arts and Aesthetics; (4) Mobilities; (5) Affiliations; and (6) Learning.
Purpose: We are pleased to announce the launch of the RHODES UNIVERSITY AFRICAN STUDIES CENTRE (RASC) DOCTORAL SCHOLARSHIPS IN AFRICAN STUDIES.
Level of Study: Doctorate
Type: Scholarship
Value: R130000
Study Establishment: African Studies
Country of Study: Any country
Closing Date: 5 November
Additional Information: For additional information about the Rhodes University African Studies Centre, visit our website: www.ru.ac.za/africanstudiescentre/

For further information contact:

Drosty Rd, Grahamstown, Makhanda, 6139, South Africa.

Tel: (27) 46 603 8111

Ruth First Scholarship

Purpose: The Ruth First Scholarship is intended to support candidates whose research is in the spirit of the life and work of Ruth First, whose research poses difficult social questions, and who are interested in linking knowledge and politics and scholarship and action.
Eligibility: All Doctoral and Masters candidates accepted at Rhodes University in the focus areas of this scholarship will be eligible to apply. South African and Mozambican black and women candidates will be particularly encouraged to apply, and will be shown preference in situations where short listed candidates are deemed to be equally suitable for the award of the scholarship. Preference will also be given to candidates who are able to demonstrate financial need and disadvantaged social origins.
Level of Study: Doctorate, Masters Degree
Type: Scholarship
Value: PhD R130 000 per annum or R120 000 per annum for Masters
Frequency: Annual
Study Establishment: Rhodes University, Grahamsdown
Country of Study: South Africa
Application Procedure: Ruth First Scholarship Application Process downloadable from www.ru.ac.za/researchgateway/postgraduates/funding/internal/. Submit a SINGLE PDF document clearly marked as your "surname_RFirst_Schol.pdf" no later than the closing date to pgfunding@ru.ac.za
Closing Date: 19 August
Funding: Private
Contributor: Donor and Investments
Additional Information: www.ru.ac.za/researchgateway/postgraduates/funding/internal/

For further information contact:

Tel: (27) 46 603 8755
Email: pgfunding@ru.ac.za

Robert Wood Johnson Foundation

50 College Road East, Princeton, NJ 08540-6614, United States of America.

Tel: (1) 609 627 6000
Website: www.rwjf.org/

The Robert Wood Johnson Foundation (RWJF) is working alongside others to build a national Culture of Health. Our goal is to help raise the health of everyone in the United States to the level that a great nation deserves, by placing well-being at the center of every aspect of life. Since 1972, RWJF supported research and programs targeting some of America's most pressing health issues—from substance abuse to improving access to quality health care.

Culture of Health Prize

Eligibility: 1. City, town, village, borough, or other municipality with a publicly elected governing body; 2. County or parish; 3. Federally recognized tribe or a state-designated American Indian reservation; 4. Native Hawaiian organization serving and representing the interests of Native Hawaiians or other Pacific Islanders in Hawaii; 5. Region, defined as geographically contiguous municipalities, counties, and/or reservations.
Level of Study: Postgraduate
Type: Award
Closing Date: 29 March
Additional Information: www.rwjf.org/en/grants/active-funding-opportunities/2023/2023-culture-of-health-prize.html

For further information contact:

Email: cultureofhealthprize@hria.org

Harold Amos Medical Faculty Development Program

Purpose: The Harold Amos Medical Faculty Development Program (AMFDP) offers four-year postdoctoral research awards to physicians, dentists, and nurses from historically marginalized backgrounds. Scholars should be committed to working toward eliminating health disparities by achieving senior rank in academic medicine, dentistry, or nursing.
Eligibility: Applicants must be physicians, dentists, or nurses who 1. are from historically marginalized backgrounds; 2. are U.S. citizens, permanent residents at the time of application, or individuals granted Deferred Action for Childhood Arrivals (DACA) status by the U.S. Citizenship and Immigration Services at the time of application (changes in federal policy or law may necessitate that we consider adjustments in eligibility and grant terms); 3. are completing or have completed their formal clinical training (we will give preference to those who have recently completed their formal clinical training or–in the case of nurses–their research doctorate); 4. are not related by blood or marriage to any Officer or Trustee of the Robert Wood Johnson Foundation, or a descendant of its founder, Robert Wood Johnson. 5. Federal, state, tribal, and local government employees who are not considered

government officials under Section 4946 of the Internal Revenue Code are eligible to apply. 6. Physicians must be Board-eligible to apply for this program. A dental applicant must be a general dentist with a master's or a doctoral degree or have completed advanced dental education. Nurse applicants must be registered nurses with a research doctorate in nursing or a related discipline completed by the application deadline. 7. Detailed research plans and budgets for selected finalists must be submitted by the university, school of medicine, dentistry, nursing, or research institution with which the prospective scholar will be affiliated during the term of the fellowship. 8. The university, school, or research institution must meet the following criteria a. Be either a public entity or nonprofit organization that is tax-exempt under Section 501(c)(3) of the Internal Revenue Code and is not a private foundation or nonfunctionally integrated Type III supporting organization; b. Be based in the United States or its territories.
Eligible Country: United States of America
Level of Study: Doctorate, Postdoctorate
Type: Scholarships
Value: RWJF will fund up to 10 four-year awards of up to US$420,000 each. Scholars will receive an annual stipend of up to US$75,000 each, complemented by a US$30,000 annual grant to support research activities.
Length of Study: 4 Year
Country of Study: United States of America
Application Procedure: Apply online.
No. of awards offered: 10
Closing Date: 15 March
No. of awards given last year: 88
Additional Information: www.rwjf.org/en/library/funding-opportunities/2022/harold-amos-medical-faculty-development-program.html

For further information contact:

Harold Amos Medical Faculty Development Program, 340 W. 10th St., Suite FS5110, Indianapolis, IN 46202, United States of America.

Tel: (1) 317 278 0500
Email: amfdp@indiana.edu

Healthy Eating Research

Eligibility: 1. Applicant organizations must be based in the United States or its territories. 2. Awards will be made to organizations, not to individuals. 3. Preference will be given to applicants that are either public entities or nonprofit organizations that are tax-exempt under Section 501(c)(3) of the Internal Revenue Code and are not private foundations or Type III supporting organizations. Additional documentation may be required by Duke University.
Level of Study: Postgraduate
Type: Award
Value: Up to US$2.5 million will be awarded through this CFP, with each award up to a maximum of US$275,000 and 24 months in duration
Length of Study: 24 months
Country of Study: United States of America
Closing Date: 5 April
Additional Information: www.rwjf.org/en/grants/active-funding-opportunities/2023/healthy-eating-research.html

Roberta Sykes Indigenous Education Foundation

100 Botany Road, Alexandria, NSW 2015, Australia.

Tel: (61) 2 9310 8402
Email: scholarships@aurorafoundation.com.au
Website: www.robertasykesfoundation.com/
Contact: The Roberta Sykes Indigenous Education Foundation

The Roberta Sykes Indigenous Education Foundation partners with the Aurora Education Foundation to support Aboriginal and Torres Strait Islander students to undertake postgraduate study abroad. This support falls under two broad categories: Scholarships to study full time postgraduate programs at recognised overseas universities and Bursaries to study Short Executive Programs at leading overseas academic institutions.

R

Roberta Sykes Bursary

Purpose: The Roberta Sykes Indigenous Education Foundation provides partial funding for Indigenous Australians to undertake short, executive education courses at leading overseas academic institutions.
Eligibility: Applicants must 1. Be of Aboriginal or Torres Strait Islander descent, identify as Aboriginal and/or Torres Strait Islander and be accepted as such by the community in which they live or have lived. 2. Provide confirmation of Aboriginal or Torres Strait Islander descent through a signed statement (including common seal) from the Aboriginal or Torres Strait Islander Heritage Association, Aboriginal or Torres Strait Islander Corporation or Land Council of your ancestors. If applicable, candidates are encouraged to provide a written statement from the Aboriginal or Torres Strait

Islander Heritage Association, Aboriginal or Torres Strait Islander Corporation or Land Council of the community in which they live or have lived and/or are connected to. 3. Be accepted into an executive program at a recognised overseas academic institution. 4. Be able to demonstrate that their studies will be of benefit to their community upon their return to Australia.
Type: Bursary
Value: The value of the Bursary is up to AU$20,000
Country of Study: Australia
Application Procedure: To apply you will need to submit 1. A completed application form. Please contact scholarships@aurorafoundation.com.au for an application form. 2. A personal statement outlining mentioned in website. 3. Your curriculum vitae. 4. Academic transcript/s if you completed your studies in the last 6 years. 5. Three written references, which highlight your capabilities, your past contribution to the Indigenous community, and the perceived future benefit of doing your chosen course. These should be a. One academic/professional; b. One from an Elder in your community, (which should highlight your connection to the community); c. One personal. 6. A written statement confirming Aboriginal or Torres Strait Islander heritage. In addition, applicants are required to provide a signed statement in writing from the Aboriginal Heritage Association, Aboriginal Corporation or Land Council of the community in which they live or have lived, also confirming the above. 7. A passport sized photo. 8. A financial budget. Please check your application thoroughly as any errors may delay the process. You can send your application to the Scholarships Team at Aurora.
Closing Date: 8 November
Additional Information: www.robertasykesfoundation.com/roberta-sykes-bursary.html

For further information contact:

Email: scholarships@aurorafoundation.com.au

Roberta Sykes Scholarship

Purpose: The Roberta Sykes Scholarship provides partial funding to Aboriginal and/or Torres Strait Islander postgraduate students who wish to undertake studies at recognised overseas universities.
Eligibility: Applicants must 1. Usually have an undergraduate degree with a strong academic record. 2. Be accepted into a postgraduate coursework or research degree at a recognised overseas university. 3. Be of Aboriginal and/or Torres Strait Islander descent, identify as Aboriginal and/or Torres Strait Islander and be accepted as such by the community in which they live or have lived. 4. Be able to demonstrate that alongside a Roberta Sykes Scholarship, they will have sufficient funds to support themselves during the course of their postgraduate degree (such as through another scholarship, private sponsorship or personal funds). 5. Be able to demonstrate that their studies will be of benefit to their community upon their return to Australia. 6. Applications for part-time study will be considered in special circumstances.
Type: Scholarship
Value: The value of the Scholarship is up to AU$30,000 per year
Country of Study: Australia
Application Procedure: Applicants need to apply directly to the overseas academic institution first, and then to the Trust for a Scholarship. To apply, you will need to submit 1. A completed application form downloadable from website. 2. A personal statement outlining a. Why you want to do the course. b. How you identify with the Aboriginal and/or Torres Strait Islander community in which you live or have lived and past contributions you have made within the community. c. Ways in which undertaking your chosen course will benefit the Aboriginal and/or Torres Strait Islander community, and future contributions you plan to make to the Aboriginal and/or Torres Strait Islander community (and wider community) following completion of the course. 3. Your curriculum vitae. 4. Academic transcript(s). 5. Four written references, which highlight you capabilities, your past contribution to the Indigenous community, and the perceived future benefit of doing your chosen course. These should be a. Two academic; b. One from and Elder in your community (which should highlight your connection to the community); c. One personal. 6. Confirmation of Aboriginal or Torres Strait Islander descent through a signed statement (including common seal) from and Aboriginal or Torres Strait Islander Heritage Association, Aboriginal or Torres Strait Islander Corporation or Land Council.
Closing Date: 8 November
Additional Information: https://aurorafoundation.com.au/our-work/indigenous-pathways-portal/scholarships/roberta-sykes-scholarship/

For further information contact:

Email: scholarships@aurorafoundation.com.au

Rotterdam School of Management Erasmus University

Burgemeester Oudlaan 50, Rotterdam, NL-3062 PA, The Netherlands.

Tel: (31) 10 408 2222
Email: info@rsm.nl

Website: www.rsm.nl/
Contact: Denise Chasney van Dijk, Financial Aid Manager

Rotterdam School of Management, Erasmus University (RSM) has firmly established its reputation over almost 50 years as one of Europe's most international and innovative business schools. RSM's primary focus is on developing business leaders with international careers who can become a force for positive change by carrying their innovative mindset into a sustainable future. Our first-class portfolio of bachelor, master, MBA, PhD and executive programmes encourage people to become critical, creative, caring and collaborative thinkers and doers.

Erasmus Trustfonds Scholarship

Eligibility: 1. Your nationality is EEA. 2. You are a prospective student, starting your studies in the academic year 2024/2025; 3. You are applying for a full-time master's programme at RSM; 4. You meet the specific requirements of the programme you are applying for; 5. You do not already have a degree from an educational institution in the Netherlands (excluding exchange programmes in the Netherlands).
Level of Study: Postgraduate
Type: Scholarship
Value: up to € 15,000
Length of Study: 12 months
Country of Study: Netherlands
Closing Date: 1 March
Additional Information: https://www.rsm.nl/education/scholarships/msc-scholarships/erasmus-trustfonds-scholarship/

For further information contact:

Email: scholarships@rsm.nl

Erasmus University Holland Scholarship

Eligibility: 1. Your nationality is non-EEA; 2. You are a prospective student, starting your studies in the academic year 2024/2025; 3. You are applying for a full-time master's programme at RSM; 4. You meet the specific requirements of the programme you are applying for; 5. You do not have a degree from an educational institution in the Netherlands (excluding exchange programmes in the Netherlands).
Level of Study: Postgraduate
Type: Scholarship
Value: €10,000
Length of Study: 12 months
Closing Date: 1 February
Additional Information: www.rsm.nl/education/master/scholarships/detail/?tx_rsmfinancialaid%5Bidentifier%5D=607&cHash=9af15746051cc32c8734c4805d4c1402

For further information contact:

Email: scholarships@rsm.nl

Rotterdam School of Management Master of Business Administration Asia & Australia Regional Scholarship

Purpose: To assist candidates from the Asia & Australasia Region in financing their MBA study in the Netherlands
Eligibility: The scholarship is open to high potential candidates who are a citizen or hold permanent residence status in one of the following listed countries Australia, Bangladesh, Bhutan, Brunei, Burma, Cambodia, China, Fiji, Hong Kong, India, Indonesia, Japan, Kiribati, Laos, Macau, Malaysia, Micronesia, Mongolia, Nepal, New Zealand, Palau, Papua New Guinea, Philippines, Samoa, Singapore, Solomon Islands, Sri Lanka, Thailand, Timor-Leste, Tonga, Tuvalu, Vietnam, Yemen
Level of Study: MBA
Type: Scholarship
Value: 20% tuition fee waiver
Length of Study: 12 months
Frequency: Annual
Study Establishment: Erasmus University
Country of Study: Netherlands
Application Procedure: Complete application form to be considered
No. of awards offered: 36
Closing Date: 30 September
Funding: Private
Contributor: RSM Erasmus University
No. of awards given last year: 1
No. of applicants last year: 36
Additional Information: Eligible to nationals of Asia and Australasia

RSM non-EEA Scholarship of Excellence (MSc)

Purpose: Rotterdam School of Management, Erasmus University offers scholarships to prospective MSc students from non-EEA countries who are not entitled to pay the EEA tuition fee, provided their grades are considered 'excellent'.
Eligibility: Application is open for prospective MSc students from all non-EEA countries who do not have a degree yet

from an educational institution in the Netherlands, starting their studies in 2024/2025. In principle, a fair distribution of scholarships over the various MSc programmes will take place. This principle may be deviated from and priority may be given to applicants for certain MSc programmes. The school may strive for a certain distribution over the continents.
Type: Scholarship
Value: up to 50% of the non-EEA tuition fee (€ 21,500 in 2023–2024)
Length of Study: 12 months
Country of Study: Netherlands
Closing Date: 1 March
Additional Information: https://www.rsm.nl/education/scholarships/iba-scholarships/rsm-non-eea-scholarship-of-excellence-iba/

For further information contact:

Email: scholarships@rsm.nl

Rotterdam School of Management, Erasmus Graduate School of Business

Burgemeester Oudlaan 50, Rotterdam, NL-3062 PA, The Netherlands.

Tel: (31) 10 408 2222
Email: info@rsm.nl
Website: www.rsm.nl/

Rotterdam School of Management, Erasmus University (RSM) has firmly established its reputation over almost 50 years as one of Europe's most international and innovative business schools. RSM's primary focus is on developing business leaders with international careers who can become a force for positive change by carrying their innovative mindset into a sustainable future. Our first-class portfolio of bachelor, master, MBA, PhD and executive programmes encourage people to become critical, creative, caring and collaborative thinkers and doers.

Holland Government Scholarship/Upcoming Year for School of Management

Purpose: The Erasmus University Holland Scholarship is financed by the Dutch Ministry of Education, Culture and Science as well as Rotterdam School of Management, Erasmus University. This scholarship is meant for international students from outside the European Economic Area (EEA) who want to do their master's at RSM.
Eligibility: To be eligible, fulfill the following 1. Your nationality is non-EEA; 2. You are a prospective student, starting your studies in the current academic year; 3. You are applying for a full-time master's programme at RSM; 4. You meet the specific requirements of the programme you are applying for; 5. You do not have a degree from an educational institution in the Netherlands (excluding exchange programmes in the Netherlands).
Level of Study: Masters Degree
Type: Scholarship
Value: €10,000
Length of Study: 12 months
Frequency: Annual
Country of Study: Any country
Application Procedure: First step is to register for the Master programme in Studielink. Once you have registered yourself, you will receive a link to our Online Application Form (OLAF). Required documents 1. A scholarship application letter in OLAF of maximum 1 A4 size page, including the following information a. an explanation why you would need a scholarship, comprising a description of your current financial situation; b. an explanation why you would deserve a scholarship, comprising a description of academic excellence and if applicable other merits. 2. A budget plan using this template www.rsm.nl/fileadmin/Images_NEW/Master/Admissions/Budget_Plan_RSM_MSc.pdf. 3. If applicable certified copies of other scholarships granted. Please note that we can only take a scholarship application into consideration if it is complete and meets all of the requirements. This includes a GMAT score, English language test results, a scholarship application letter and a budget plan.
Closing Date: 1 February
Funding: Government, Private
Contributor: The Dutch Ministry of Education, Culture and Science
Additional Information: The scholarship amount will be paid in 10 installments after you have paid the full tuition fee amount. www.rsm.nl/master/msc-programmes/scholarships/scholarships/?tx_rsmfinancialaid%5Bidentifier%5D=607&
cHash=4f21fd9a7db8ae5e813341cceef75da9

For further information contact:

Burgemeester Oudlaan 50, NL-3062 PA Rotterdam, Netherlands.

Tel: (31) 10 408 2222
Email: scholarships@rsm.nl

Royal Academy of Engineering

Prince Philip House, 3 Carlton House Terrace, London SW1Y 5DG, United Kingdom.

Tel: (44) 20 7766 0600
Email: research@raeng.org.uk
Website: www.raeng.org.uk/
Contact: Dr Mark Bambury, Scheme Manager

The Royal Academy of Engineering is a charity that harnesses the power of engineering to build a sustainable society and an inclusive economy that works for everyone. In collaboration with our Fellows and partners, we're growing talent and developing skills for the future, driving innovation and building global partnerships, and influencing policy and engaging the public.

ExxonMobil Excellence in Teaching Awards

Purpose: To encourage able young engineering and Earth science lecturers to remain in the education sector in their early years
Eligibility: Open to well-qualified graduates, preferably with industrial experience and full-time lecturing posts at Institutes of Higher Education in the United Kingdom. Applicants should have been in their current posts for at least 1 year. The post must include the teaching of chemical, petroleum or mechanical engineering to undergraduates through courses that are accredited for registration with professional bodies for qualifications such as chartered engineer. For applicants whose career path has been graduation at the age of 22 years, followed by academic or industrial posts, the age limit is generally 32 years (at the closing date). Older candidates who have taken time out, e.g. for industrial experience, parenthood or voluntary service, will also be considered. Applicants should preferably be chartered engineers, or of equivalent professional status, or should be making progress towards this qualification
Level of Study: Postdoctorate
Type: Fellowship
Value: A range of benefits in addition to the £10,000 prize
Length of Study: 12 months
Frequency: Annual
Study Establishment: The applicant's current university in the United Kingdom
Country of Study: United Kingdom
Application Procedure: Applicants must complete an application form
Closing Date: 31 October
Funding: Commercial
Contributor: Exxon Mobile
Additional Information: A brochure is available on request. Enquiries about Exxon mobile university contacts should be sent via email and please see the website for further details.

For further information contact:

Email: bowbricki@raeng.co.uk

Royal Academy Engineering Professional Development

Purpose: To ensure that the skills and knowledge of employees reflect the very latest in technological advances
Eligibility: Open to United Kingdom citizens with a degree or HND/HNC in engineering or a closely allied subject. OND/ONC or City and Guilds Full Technological Certificate or NVQ level III qualifications are acceptable provided the individual has substantial industrial experience
Level of Study: Professional development
Type: Grant
Value: £10,000 and £5,000 and prospective applicants should indicate for which level of award they are applying
Length of Study: 1 year
Frequency: Annual
Country of Study: United Kingdom
Application Procedure: For further information please contact the scheme manager lan Bowbrick at the Academy
Closing Date: 24 October

For further information contact:

Email: lan.bowbrick@raeng.org.uk

Royal Academy Sir Angus Paton Bursary

Purpose: To study water and environmental management
Eligibility: The bursary supports a suitably qualified engineer study a full-time Masters' degree course specifically related to water resources engineering or some other environmental technology
Level of Study: Postgraduate
Type: Bursary
Value: £8,000
Length of Study: 1 year
Frequency: Annual
Country of Study: United Kingdom
Application Procedure: For further information please contact the scheme manager Ian Bowbrick at the Academy
Funding: Private
Contributor: Sir Angus Paton

Additional Information: www.raeng.org.uk/publications/other/panasonic-trust-fellowships-guidance-notes

For further information contact:

Email: ian.bowbrick@raeng.org.uk

Royal Academy Sir Henry Royce Bursary

Eligibility: Open to qualified engineers enrolled on part-time modular Master's courses
Level of Study: Postgraduate
Type: Bursary
Value: £1,000
Length of Study: 1 year
Frequency: Annual
Country of Study: United Kingdom
Application Procedure: For further information please contact the scheme manager Ian Bowbrick at the Academy
Funding: Foundation
Contributor: Sir Henry Royce Memorial Foundation
Additional Information: Each awardee will receive a commemorative certificate and, on successful completion of their studies and award of the degree, a medal from the Sir Henry Royce Memorial Foundation www.raeng.org.uk/publications/other/issue-10

For further information contact:

Email: ian.bowbrick@raeng.org.uk

Sainsbury Management Fellowships

Purpose: The Sainsbury Management Fellowship scheme, funded by the Gatsby Charitable Foundation, enables engineers of high career potential to undertake full time MBA courses at major international business schools. The overall objective of the scheme is to improve the economic performance of UK engineering, manufacturing and construction businesses by providing a resource of highly-motivated engineers who have complemented their technical qualifications and skills with a first-class business education in an international environment.
Eligibility: 1. Applicants must have a confirmed place on a full-time MBA programme at one of the 14 eligible business schools 2. You may apply before a place is confirmed but will not be invited to interview until a Business school place is confirmed 3. Applicants must have a first degree in an engineering, allied technology or science discipline, preferably a first or upper second class 4. Applicants must demonstrate a strong commitment to both UK engineering/business/industry and their respective engineering communities 5. Applicants must be a UK / EU / EEA citizen, normally domiciled in the United Kingdom 6. Applicants do not need to have Chartered Engineer status (or equivalent), however this qualification or progress towards it will be viewed favourably 7. Applicants would usually have 4–10 years professional experience post-degree
Level of Study: Postgraduate
Type: Fellowships
Value: £50,000 to be used towards an eligible, full-time MBA
Frequency: Annual
Country of Study: United Kingdom
Application Procedure: Applying for a Sainsbury Management Fellowship, please contact Veronica Frincu
Closing Date: 11 April
Funding: Foundation
Contributor: Gatsby Charitable Foundation
Additional Information: For more details: www.raeng.org.uk/grants-prizes/grants/schemes-for-students/sainsbury-management-fellowship

For further information contact:

3 Carlton House Terrace, St. James's, London SW1Y 5DG, United Kingdom.

Tel: (44) 20 7766 0625
Email: lauren.pattle@raeng.org.uk

Royal Agricultural University

Royal Agricultural University, Gloucestershire, Cirencester GL7 6JS, United Kingdom.

Tel: (44) 1285 652531
Email: international@rau.ac.uk
Website: www.rau.ac.uk/

The Royal Agricultural University has always been at the forefront of agricultural education since 1845. Today, the RAU has more than 1,100 students studying agriculture, business, environment, equine science, farm management, food, real estate and rural land management. The University, which is based in Cirencester, Gloucestershire, prides itself on its links with industry and all courses are designed to meet the demands of the employment market for land-based expertise, both in the UK and worldwide.

Africa Land and Food Masters Fellowship

Eligibility: Fellowships are open to Africans from Sub-Saharan Africa who have experience in agriculture,

agri-business, food or natural resource management; an interest in land reform; and a desire to make a strategic and sustainable contribution to Africa's development
Level of Study: Postgraduate
Type: Fellowship
Value: Since the Fellowship was launched in 2005, over £1,800,000 has been generously provided by the private sector, foundations and charities in support of the programme
Country of Study: United Kingdom
Application Procedure: Nationals from sub-Saharan Africa are invited to apply for a Fellowship
Closing Date: 31 October
Funding: International office

Royal College of Midwives

10-18 Union Street, London SE1 1SZ, United Kingdom.

Tel: (44) 207 3123 535
Email: info@rcm.org.uk
Website: www.rcm.org.uk/

The RCM was established in 1881 as the Matron's Aid or Trained Midwives Registration Society, but has existed under its present name since 1947. A charity for maintaining and improving standards of professional midwifery. The Trust conducts and commissions research, publishes information, provides education and training and organises conferences, campaigns and other events.

Royal College of Midwives Annual Midwifery Awards

Purpose: To recognize and celebrate innovation in midwifery practice, education and research
Eligibility: Applicants may be individuals or small groups but should meet the criteria of 1 of the 10 categories. Check the website for complete details
Level of Study: Postgraduate, Professional development, Research
Type: Award
Value: Varies (up to £20,000 in total)
Frequency: Annual
Country of Study: United Kingdom
Application Procedure: Applicants must apply in writing or email to the address given below. The application must be accompanied by a 500-word description of the project. Shortlisted candidates will be asked to attend an interview
No. of awards offered: 13
Closing Date: 1 November
Funding: Commercial
Contributor: Several

For further information contact:

Gothic House, 3 The Green, Richmond, Surrey TW9 1PL, United Kingdom.

Email: mail@chamberdunn.co.uk

Ruth Davies Research Bursary

Purpose: To promote and develop midwifery research and practice
Eligibility: Open to practicing midwives who are RCM members, who have basic knowledge, skills and understanding of the research process, have access to research support in their trust or Institutes of Higher Education and who have been in practice for 2 years or more
Level of Study: Doctorate, Graduate, Postdoctorate, Postgraduate, Predoctorate, Professional development, Research
Type: Bursary
Value: £5,000 per bursary
Length of Study: 1 year
Frequency: Annual
Country of Study: United Kingdom
Application Procedure: Applicants must submit a succinct curriculum vitae covering the previous 5 years, a research proposal of no more than 2,500 words and letters of support from both employers and academics who are familiar with the applicant's work
No. of awards offered: 3
Closing Date: 30 July
Funding: Commercial
Contributor: Bounty
Additional Information: https://www.postgraduatefunding.com/award-714

For further information contact:

Tel: (44) 20 7312 3463
Email: marlyn.gennace@rcm.org.uk

Royal College of Nursing Foundation

20 Cavendish Square, London W1G 0RN, United Kingdom.

Tel: (44) 20 7647 3645
Email: rcnfoundation@rcn.org.uk
Website: rcnfoundation.rcn.org.uk/
Contact: Ms Grants Officer Awards Officer

R

In 2010, the Royal College of Nursing (RCN) set up an independent charity – the RCN Foundation. The RCN Foundation is here to support every member of the nursing team as they care for patients and improve the UK's health and wellbeing.

Education Grants

Subjects: Nursing
Purpose: We offer two types of education grants professional development grants and student grants
Eligibility: Open to nurses, midwives and HCAs in United Kingdom
Level of Study: Doctorate, Postgraduate
Type: Award
Value: Up to £1,600 for professional development grants, £2,500 for student grants
Length of Study: Unrestricted
Frequency: Twice a year
Study Establishment: Unrestricted
Country of Study: United Kingdom
Application Procedure: Online rcnfoundation.rcn.org.uk/apply-for-funding/educational-grants
No. of awards offered: Up to 100
Closing Date: October
Funding: Private
No. of awards given last year: 69
No. of applicants last year: 771
Additional Information: https://rcnfoundation.rcn.org.uk/Grants-and-funding/Educational-grants

For further information contact:

Email: grants@rcnfoundation.org.uk

Mary Seacole Leadership and Development Awards

Purpose: To provide funding for a project, or other educational/development activity that benefits the health needs of people from black and minority ethnic communities
Eligibility: Open to nurses, midwives and health visitors in United Kingdom
Level of Study: Doctorate, Graduate, Postdoctorate, Postgraduate, Predoctorate, Professional development, Research
Type: Award
Value: Up to £12,500 for Mary Seacole Leadership Award and up to £6,250 for Mary Seacole Development Award
Length of Study: Unrestricted
Frequency: Annual
Study Establishment: Unrestricted
Country of Study: United Kingdom
Application Procedure: Applicants must send a stamped addressed envelope to the Royal College of Nursing (RCN) to obtain details and an application form
No. of awards offered: 16
Closing Date: 23 March
Funding: Government
Contributor: Department of Health
No. of awards given last year: 6
No. of applicants last year: 16
Additional Information: www.rcn.org.uk/professional-development/scholarships-and-bursaries/mary-seacole-awards

For further information contact:

Email: governance.support@rcn.org.uk

Royal College of Obstetricians and Gynaecologists (RCOG)

10-18 Union Street, London SE1 1SZ, United Kingdom.

Tel: (44) 20 7772 6200
Email: info@rcog.org.uk
Website: www.rcog.org.uk/

RCOG founded in 1929, works to improve health care for women everywhere, by setting standards for clinical practice, providing doctors with training and lifelong learning, and advocating for women's health care worldwide.

Annual Academic Award

Purpose: The award recognises distinguished service to academic obstetrics and gynaecology.
Eligibility: 1. Outstanding contribution to the academic aspects of our speciality (scientific discovery, pre-clinical and clinical research, academic education and training). 2. UK RCOG Fellows or Members, RCOG Fellows ad eundem or others of equivalent academic distinction (professorial level), at the discretion of the Academic Board. 3. Award exclusions Current members of the Academic Board. 4. Nominators to be UK Fellows. 5. Nominees can self-nominate with the support of 2 UK Fellows.
Type: Award
Frequency: Annual
Country of Study: United Kingdom
Application Procedure: Please complete the nomination form word document downloadable from website. www.

rcog.org.uk/en/careers-training/awards-grants-prizes/annual-academic-award/. Please ensure that the nominee is aware of this nomination. Please email the nomination form, written statement and abbreviated CV to awards@rcog.org.uk
Closing Date: 13 March
Additional Information: For more information: www.rcog.org.uk/en/careers-training/awards-grants-prizes/annual-academic-award/

For further information contact:

Email: academic@rcog.org.uk

Bernhard Baron Travelling Fellowship

Purpose: The Bernhard Baron Charitable Trust has generously endowed to the RCOG two travel scholarships in obstetrics and gynaecology for Fellows and Members of the College worth up to £6000 each
Eligibility: 1. Travel must take place within 12 months of the award being made. 2. The award may only be used for the purpose outlined in your original application. 3. A detailed report (maximum 1,000 words), including pictures if necessary, must be submitted to the RCOG Awards Administrator within eight weeks after the elective
Level of Study: Postdoctorate
Type: Fellowships
Value: Up to £6,000
Length of Study: 1 year
Frequency: Annual
Country of Study: Any country
Closing Date: 31 May
Funding: Foundation

For further information contact:

27 Sussex Place Regent's Park, London NW1 4RG, United Kingdom.

Fax: (44) 20 7723 0575
Email: awards@rcog.org.uk

Bruggeman Postgraduate Scholarship in Classics

Purpose: Doctoral scholarships are awarded by the University Council, on the recommendation of the Senate, to candidates proceeding to a course of supervised doctoral study at this University. These scholarships are normally available only to students seeking to obtain their first doctoral qualification
Level of Study: Postgraduate
Type: Scholarship
Value: NZ$25,000
Frequency: Annual
Country of Study: New Zealand
Funding: Foundation

For further information contact:

Email: scholarships@otago.ac.nz

Eden Travelling Fellowship in Obstetrics and Gynaecology

Purpose: The RCOG through the generous endowment of the late Dr Thomas Watts is able to offer a travel fellowship. The winner can use the funds to visit another O&G department or a related discipline to gain additional O&G knowledge and experience.
Eligibility: This Fellowship is open to medical graduates (who graduated within the last 2 years) who are currently undertaking a research project. This award may only be used for the purposes outlined in your original application.
Type: Travelling fellowship
Value: Up to £5,000
Frequency: Annual
Country of Study: Any country
Application Procedure: Please complete the online application via Oxford Abstracts app.oxfordabstracts.com/login?redirect=/stages/2102/submitter This application is hosted by Oxford Abstracts platform. Please register for an account using your email address. For further guidance on how to submit your application, please see Oxford Abstracts' guidance on making a submission oxfordabstracts.freshdesk.com/support/solutions/articles/8000072762-making-a-submission.
Closing Date: 11 May
Additional Information: For more details: https://www.rcog.org.uk/careers-and-training/awards-grants-and-prizes/awards-grants-and-prizes-open-to-all/eden-travelling-fellowship-in-obstetrics-and-gynaecology/

For further information contact:

Email: awards@rcog.org.uk

Edgar Gentilli Prize

Purpose: Through the kind and generous bequest of the late Mr and Mrs Gilbert Edgar, the RCOG is delighted to offer this award to the candidate who submits the best piece of original work on the cause, nature, recognition and treatment of any form of cancer of the female genital tract.

Eligibility: 1. The Edgar Gentilli Prize is open to both members and non-members of the RCOG. 2. Applicants should submit results of their research by way of an original manuscript, adequately referenced and written in a format comparable to that used for submission to a learned journal, or by means of a reprint of the published article.
Type: Prize
Value: First prize £750 and Second prize £250
Frequency: Annual
Country of Study: Any country
Application Procedure: Please complete the online application via Oxford Abstracts app.oxfordabstracts.com/login?redirect=/stages/2102/submitter. This application is hosted by Oxford Abstracts platform. Please register for an account using your email address. For further guidance on how to submit your application, please see Oxford Abstracts' guidance on making a submission oxfordabstracts.freshdesk.com/support/solutions/articles/8000072762-making-a-submission. Applicants must submit a maximum of 2,000 words, with a maximum of 10 references. Applications that are over the word limit will be marked down.
No. of awards offered: 2
Closing Date: 11 May
Additional Information: For more details: https://www.rcog.org.uk/careers-and-training/awards-grants-and-prizes/awards-grants-and-prizes-open-to-all/edgar-gentilli-prize/

For further information contact:

Email: awards@rcog.org.uk

Elizabeth Garrett Anderson Hospital Charity Travelling Fellowship in Memory of Anne Boutwood

Purpose: Through the generosity of the EGA Hospital Charity, we award a prize of £5,000 to one United Kingdom trainee in the field of obstetrics and gynaecology in memory of Miss Anne Boutwood FRCOG
Eligibility: 1. Travel must take place within 12 months of the award being made. 2. The award may only be used for the purpose outlined in your original application. 3. A detailed report (maximum 1,000 words), including pictures if necessary, must be submitted to the RCOG Awards Administrator within eight weeks after the elective
Level of Study: Postgraduate
Type: Fellowship
Value: £5,000
Frequency: Annual
Country of Study: Any country
Closing Date: 31 May
Funding: Foundation

For further information contact:

Email: awards@rcog.org.uk

Endometriosis Millenium Fund

Purpose: The RCOG is proud to support the Organising Committee of the World Congress of Endometriosis who, through a generous donation, have established the Endometriosis Millennium Fund. Available to RCOG Members and Trainees working in the UK and Republic of Ireland, the RCOG is able to offer in order to stimulate and encourage research (clinical or laboratory based) in the field of endometriosis.
Eligibility: The Fund is available to RCOG members and trainees working in the British Isles. Applications are invited for the following 1. To provide monies to fund a pilot project, clinical or laboratory based in the field of endometriosis, or to provide monies to fund an extension of an existing project researching endometriosis, or 2. To provide a contribution towards a travelling fellowship to attend a recognised training centre, preferably overseas, to obtain surgical training in the management of cases of endometriosis, beyond the skills expected of core training. 3. If the application is for travel funding, travel must take place within 12 months of the award being made. 4. The award may only be used for the purpose outlines in your original application. 5. Clinicians are encouraged, with the use of the funds to acquire extra clinical skills in order to more efficiently manage patients with the disease.
Level of Study: Postgraduate
Type: Funding support
Value: Up to £5,000
Frequency: Annual
Country of Study: United Kingdom
Application Procedure: Please complete the online application via Oxford Abstracts app.oxfordabstracts.com/login?redirect=/stages/2102/submitter. This application is hosted by Oxford Abstracts platform. Please register for an account using your email address. For further guidance on how to submit your application, please see Oxford Abstracts' guidance on making a submission oxfordabstracts.freshdesk.com/support/solutions/articles/8000072762-making-a-submission.
Closing Date: 24 March

For further information contact:

Email: awards@rcog.org.uk

Ethicon Foundation Fund Travelling Fellowship

Purpose: The objective of the Ethicon Foundation Fund Travelling Fellowship, established through the generosity of Ethicon Limited, is to promote international goodwill in medicine and surgery by means of grants to assist the overseas travel of surgeons
Eligibility: 1. Applicants must be MRCS(Glasg) or FRCS (Glasg) and in a higher training post in the United Kingdom, or equivalent elsewhere in the world. 2. The proposed work experience, research or other study should be of clear benefit to the individual's training and to the NHS- or equivalent- on return. 3. Periods abroad should generally be between 1-12 months. 4. Awards will not be given for the sole purpose of attending meetings, or conferences to present papers or for undertaking a series of brief visits to multiple centres
Level of Study: Postgraduate
Type: Travel grant
Value: Up to £900
Frequency: Annual
Country of Study: United Kingdom
Application Procedure: Download and complete the application form and return the completed form to the address given. Make sure to include in your application Your CV A signed letter of support from your current supervisor A signed letter from the centre you will be visiting confirming that you are welcome
No. of awards offered: 2
Closing Date: 24 November
Additional Information: Travel must take place within 6 months of the award being made. www.rcpsg.ac.uk/awards-and-scholarships/ethicon-foundation-fund-travelling-fellowship

For further information contact:

Royal College of Physicians and Surgeons of Glasgow, 232 - 242 St Vincent Street, Glasgow G2 5RJ, United Kingdom.

Tel: (44) 141 221 6072
Fax: (44) 141 221 1804
Email: scholarships@rcpsg.ac.uk

Ethicon Student Elective Award

Purpose: The RCOG, with the kind and generous support of Ethicon, is pleased to offer funding towards approved student medical electives in obstetrics and gynaecology taking place between autumn current and upcoming year.
Eligibility: This award is open to students wishing to pursue a career in obstetrics and gynaecology. Applicants undertaking/planning to undertake their elective in a subject associated with this specialty in a low-resource country are particularly encouraged to apply. The successful applicants will have submitted a well-planned and well-presented application demonstrating clear objectives and detailed information about the project they wish to undertake. 1. The award may only be used for the purpose outlined in your original application. 2. Travel must take place within 12 months of the award being granted. 3. Retrospective applications will not be accepted.
Type: Award
Value: Up to £500
Frequency: Annual
Country of Study: United Kingdom
Application Procedure: Please complete the online application via Oxford Abstracts app.oxfordabstracts.com/login?redirect=/stages/2098/submitter. This application is hosted by Oxford Abstracts platform. Please register for an account using your email address. For further guidance on how to submit your application, please see Oxford Abstracts' guidance on making a submission oxfordabstracts.freshdesk.com/support/solutions/articles/8000072762-making-a-submission
Closing Date: 11 May
Additional Information: www.rcog.org.uk/en/careers-training/awards-grants-prizes/ethicon-student-elective-award/

For further information contact:

Email: awards@rcog.org.uk

Florence and William Blair Bell Research Fellowship

Purpose: The funding has been donated in order to stimulate and encourage research (clinical or laboratory based) in the field of O&G. Clinicians are encouraged, with the use of funds, to acquire extra clinical or research skills to improve patient management or develop their postdoctoral research.
Eligibility: The research fellowship will be awarded to a Member or Trainee on the RCOG Trainees' Register pre-CCT in obstetrics and gynaecology within a year of MD or PhD award at the time of application. 1. If the application is for travel funding, travel must take place within 12 months of the award being made. 2. The award may only be used for the purpose outlined in your original application. 3. A detailed report (maximum 1,000 words), including pictures if appropriate, must be submitted to the RCOG Awards at the end of the grant period. 4. An undertaking must be given that the source of the grant will be acknowledged in any related publications

Level of Study: Doctorate, Postdoctorate, Postgraduate
Type: Fellowship
Value: Up to £5,000
Frequency: Annual
Country of Study: United Kingdom
Application Procedure: Please complete the online application via Oxford Abstracts app.oxfordabstracts.com/login?redirect=/stages/2102/submitter. This application is hosted by Oxford Abstracts platform. Please register for an account using your email address. For further guidance on how to submit your application, please see Oxford Abstracts' guidance on making a submission oxfordabstracts.freshdesk.com/support/solutions/articles/8000072762-making-a-submission.
No. of awards offered: 1
Closing Date: 11 May
Additional Information: https://www.rcog.org.uk/careers-and-training/awards-grants-and-prizes/awards-grants-and-prizes-for-rcog-fellows-members-and-trainees/florence-and-william-blair-bell-research-fellowship/

For further information contact:

Email: awards@rcog.org.uk

Green-Armytage and Spackman Travelling Scholarship

Purpose: Through the generosity of the late Mr V B Green-Armytage and of the late Colonel W C Spackman, Council is able to award a biennial travelling scholarship up to £4,000 to a Fellow or Member of the College
Eligibility: Applicants should have shown a special interest in some particular aspect of obstetrical or gynaecological practice. The donors' wishes are that the awards should be used for the purpose of visiting centres where similar work is being carried out. Your application will be judged on the following criteria 1. Presentation well planned and presented. 2. Relevance of project to career development in O&G. 3. Level of involvement. 4. References. 5. Value to the NHS/local community. 6. Value to personal development
Level of Study: Postgraduate
Type: Scholarship
Value: £5,000 to 10,000
Frequency: Annual
Country of Study: United Kingdom
Application Procedure: Applicants must include information on qualifications, areas of interest and/or publications in a specified area, centres to be visited with confirmation from the head of that centre, estimated costs and the names of two referees
Closing Date: 24 May
Funding: Private

Herbert Erik Reiss Memorial Case History Prize

Purpose: The Herbert Erik Reiss is comprised of prizes which are available for FY1 and FY2 doctor or specialist training Years 1 and 2 in the UK and the republic of Ireland.
Eligibility: Open to FY1 and FY2 doctors or Specialist Training Years 1 and 2 in the UK and the Republic of Ireland. The prizes are awarded to candidates who submit the most outstanding presentation of clinical case, including critical assessment and literature research on a topic in obstetrics and gynaecology.
Type: Prize
Value: First prize £400 and Second prize £200
Frequency: Annual
Country of Study: United Kingdom
Application Procedure: Please complete the online application via Oxford Abstracts app.oxfordabstracts.com/login?redirect=/stages/2100/submitter. This application is hosted by Oxford Abstracts platform. Please register for an account using your email address. For further guidance on how to submit your application, please see Oxford Abstracts' guidance on making a submission oxfordabstracts.freshdesk.com/support/solutions/articles/8000072762-making-a-submission
No. of awards offered: 2
Closing Date: 11 May
Additional Information: For more details: https://rcog.org.uk/careers-and-training/awards-grants-and-prizes/awards-grants-and-prizes-for-medical-students-and-foundation-year-doctors/herbert-erik-reiss-memorial-case-history-prize/

For further information contact:

Email: awards@rcog.org.uk

John Lawson Prize

Purpose: The prize will be awarded through the kind generosity of the late Mr John Lawson FRCOG, for the best article on obstetric and/or gynaecological work carried out in Africa between the tropics of Capricorn and Cancer.
Eligibility: This award is open to Members and non-members of the RCOG. The record of work can be submitted by way of an original manuscript, adequately referenced and written in a format comparable to that used for submission to a learned journal, or by means of a reprint of the published article.
Type: Prize
Value: £150
Frequency: Annual
Country of Study: United Kingdom
Application Procedure: Please complete the online application via Oxford Abstracts app.oxfordabstracts.com/login?redirect=/stages/2102/submitter. This application is hosted

by Oxford Abstracts platform. Please register for an account using your email address. For further guidance on how to submit your application, please see Oxford Abstracts' guidance on making a submission oxfordabstracts.freshdesk.com/support/solutions/articles/8000072762-making-a-submission. A maximum of 2,000 words with a maximum of 10 references should be submitted. Applications that are over the word limit will be marked down.
Closing Date: 11 May
Additional Information: https://www.rcog.org.uk/careers-and-training/awards-grants-and-prizes/awards-grants-and-prizes-open-to-all/john-lawson-prize/

For further information contact:

Email: awards@rcog.org.uk

Kolkata Eden Hospital Annual Prize

Purpose: The Calcutta (Kolkata) Eden Hospital is notable because it is where the highly reputed Professor Green Armytage spent his professional career for 25 years. During his tenure, he designed 'uterine haemostatic forceps' which are still widely used around the world in caesarean sections. The Kolkata Eden Hospital, a major maternity and gynaecological hospital and part of the Kolkata Medical College Hospital was the medical school of Mr Prabhat Chattopadhyay FRCOG. His generosity has enabled the RCOG to offer an annual prize to final year medical students or junior doctors (FY1) in the UK and Republic of Ireland.
Eligibility: This prize is open to final year medical students or FY1 junior doctors in the UK and Republic of Ireland. The prize is awarded for the best submission of an article that outlines your insight into any aspect of obstetrics and gynaecology undertaken during your training.
Type: Prize
Value: £350
Frequency: Annual
Country of Study: United Kingdom
Application Procedure: Please complete the online application via Oxford Abstracts app.oxfordabstracts.com/login?redirect=/stages/2100/submitter. This application is hosted by Oxford Abstracts platform. Please register for an account using your email address. For further guidance on how to submit your application, please see Oxford Abstracts' guidance on making a submission oxfordabstracts.freshdesk.com/support/solutions/articles/8000072762-making-a-submission.
Closing Date: 11 May
Additional Information: For more information: https://www.rcog.org.uk/careers-and-training/awards-grants-and-prizes/awards-grants-and-prizes-for-medical-students-and-foundation-year-doctors/kolkata-eden-hospital-annual-prize/

For further information contact:

Email: awards@rcog.org.uk

Malcolm Black Travel Fellowship

Purpose: The purpose of the fellowship is to enable a College Member of up to 5 years' standing or a Fellow at the time of application, to travel either to the British Isles or from the British Isles abroad, for a period of time to attend postgraduate training courses or to visit centres of research or of particular expertise within the specialty of obstetrics and gynaecology.
Eligibility: This Fellowship is open to college Members and Fellows
Level of Study: Postgraduate
Type: Fellowship
Value: This biennial travel fellowship awards up to £1,000 to RCOG Members and Fellows
Length of Study: 12 months
Frequency: Annual

Overseas Fund

Purpose: The purpose of this fund is to make grants available to International Fellows and Members of the College working in obstetrics and gynaecology overseas who wish to travel to the UK for further training.
Eligibility: The award may only be used for the purpose outlined in the original application. Travel must take place within 12 months of the award being made.
Type: Travel grant
Value: Up to £2,500 of grants towards travel, accommodation and subsistence
Frequency: Annual
Country of Study: United Kingdom
Application Procedure: Please complete the online application via Oxford Abstracts app.oxfordabstracts.com/login?redirect=/stages/2102/submitter. This application is hosted by Oxford Abstracts platform. Please register for an account using your email address. For further guidance on how to submit your application, please see Oxford Abstracts' guidance on making a submission oxfordabstracts.freshdesk.com/support/solutions/articles/8000072762-making-a-submission.
No. of awards offered: 8
Closing Date: 24 May

Peter Huntingford Memorial Prize

Purpose: The British Pregnancy Advisory Service (BPAS) has generously endowed the Peter Huntingford Memorial Prize to mark the late Professor Peter Huntingford's contribution to O&G.
Eligibility: This award is for FY1 or FY2 doctors across the UK and Republic of Ireland. The prize will be awarded to the best presentations of either 1. A case history focused on women with complications of pregnancy and giving birth. 2. A clinical audit of report of a research project with any aspect of sexual health and fertility control in which they have been directly involved.
Type: Prize
Value: First prize £150 and Second prize £75
Frequency: Annual
Country of Study: Any country
Application Procedure: Please complete the online application via Oxford Abstracts app.oxfordabstracts.com/login?redirect=/stages/2100/submitter. This application is hosted by Oxford Abstracts platform. Please register for an account using your email address. For further guidance on how to submit your application, please see Oxford Abstracts' guidance on making a submission oxfordabstracts.freshdesk.com/support/solutions/articles/8000072762-making-a-submission
No. of awards offered: 2
Closing Date: 30 April
Contributor: British Pregnancy Advisory Service (BPAS)

For further information contact:

Email: awards@rcog.org.uk

Professor Geoffrey Chamberlain Award

Purpose: This award was established in memory of Professor Geoffrey Chamberlain who was a President of the College, Editor-in-Chief of BJOG and Head of the O&G Department at St George's Hospital London. The award consists of two separate awards.
Eligibility: 1. The first award is open to Trainees in the sub-continent Nepal, Bhutan, Pakistan, India, Bangladesh or Sri Lanka. (Not open for current year.). 2. The second award is open to all Trainees worldwide. The essay for the second award should be no more than 800 words and must be adequately referenced and written in a format comparable to that used for submission to a learned journal. Applications that are over the word limit will be marked down.
Type: Award
Value: First award £1,000 will be awarded every 3 years, Second award £150 will be awarded an annual basis
Frequency: Annual
Country of Study: Any country
Application Procedure: Please complete the online application via Oxford Abstracts app.oxfordabstracts.com/login?redirect=/stages/2102/submitter. This application is hosted by Oxford Abstracts platform. Please register for an account using your email address. For further guidance on how to submit your application, please see Oxford Abstracts' guidance on making a submission oxfordabstracts.freshdesk.com/support/solutions/articles/8000072762-making-a-submission.
Closing Date: 30 April

For further information contact:

Email: awards@rcog.org.uk

Royal College of Obstetricians and Gynaecologists Edgar Research Fellowship

Purpose: To encourage research, especially into chorion carcinoma or other forms of malignant disease
Eligibility: Open to candidates of high academic standing either in obstetrics and gynaecology, or related fields
Level of Study: Postgraduate
Type: Fellowship
Value: Up to a maximum of £35,000
Length of Study: Initially for 1 year's research but a further year's funding may be offered
Frequency: Annual
Country of Study: Any country
Application Procedure: Please contact the Research Administrator at the WellBeing address
Closing Date: December
Additional Information: In making the award the Council of the College will bear in mind the original intention of the fellowship, which was to encourage research into chorion carcinoma or other forms of malignant disease. Where applications of equal merit are received, priority will be given to the project most closely related to this condition. Fellows are required to submit a report on the work carried out as soon as the tenure of the fellowship is completed.

For further information contact:

WellBeing 27 Sussex Place Regent's Park, London NW1 4SP, United Kingdom.

Tel: (44) 20 7772 6338
Fax: (44) 20 7724 7725
Email: mary.stanton@wellbeing.org.uk

Royal College of Obstetricians and Gynaecologists Research Training Fellowships

Purpose: To further the training of a young medical graduate in research techniques and methodology in a subject in a subject of direct or indirect relevance to obstetrics and gynaecology
Eligibility: Candidates will have had their basic training in obstetrics and gynaecology, preferably having passed their MRCOG. Candidates will be expected to enrol for a higher degree
Type: Fellowship
Value: Up to a maximum of three years salary
Length of Study: Up to 3 years
Frequency: Annual
Application Procedure: Enquiries about this award should be directed to The Research Administrator, WellBeing
Closing Date: October
Additional Information: www.rcog.org.uk/en/careers-training/academic-og/research-funding-opportunities/mrcrcog-clinical-research-training-fellowship/

For further information contact:

WellBeing 27 Sussex Place Regent's Park, London NW1 4SP, United Kingdom.

Tel: (44) 20 7772 6338
Fax: (44) 20 7724 7725
Email: mary.stanton@wellbeing.org.uk

Royal College of Obstetricians and Gynaecologists WellBeing Grants

Purpose: To fund research into all aspects of Obstetrics and Gynaecology with emphasis on increasing safety of childbirth for mother and baby and prevention of handicap
Eligibility: Open to specialists in any obstetrics and gynaecology inter-related field
Level of Study: Professional development, Research
Type: Grant
Value: Maximum of £80,000 over three years, with not more than £45,000 in the first year
Frequency: Annual
Application Procedure: Applicants must write for details
Funding: Private
Additional Information: www.rcog.org.uk/en/careers-training/academic-og/research-funding-opportunities/

For further information contact:

WellBeing 27 Sussex Place Regent's Park, London NW1 4SP, United Kingdom.

Tel: (44) 20 7772 6338
Fax: (44) 20 7724 7725
Email: mary.stanton@wellbeing.org.uk

Sims Black Travelling Proffesorship

Purpose: The purpose of the Sims Black Travelling Professorship is to Contribute to postgraduate education by presenting lectures, participating in seminars, group discussions and clinical demonstrations (if appropriate)
Eligibility: he College welcomes applications from O&G Colleges, International Representative Committees, professional bodies and groups, and similar organisations in the specialty. Applications must come from centres outside of the UK and Republic of Ireland. The application must include details of the programme and schedule of activities for the proposed visit. Nominators may name an RCOG Fellow or Member in their application, but the College will ultimately decide on a suitable candidate and the length of their stay.
Level of Study: Postgraduate
Type: Professorship
Frequency: Annual
Country of Study: United Kingdom
Closing Date: 11 May
Funding: Private
Additional Information: www.rcog.org.uk/careers-and-training/awards-grants-and-prizes/other-awards/sims-black-travelling-professorship/

For further information contact:

10-18 Union Street, London, SE1 1SZ, United Kingdom.

Tel: (44) 20 7772 6200
Fax: (44) 20 7723 0575
Email: awards@rcog.org.uk

R

Target Ovarian Cancer Essay Prize

Purpose: The Target Ovarian Cancer essay prize is supported by The Royal College of Obstetricians and Gynaecologists. The prize is open to all undergraduate medical students across the United Kingdom. Its aim is to encourage students to read more widely on ovarian cancer, to think about some of the current issues and learn about recent research.
Eligibility: The prize is open to all undergraduate medical students studying at a UK medical school. It aims to encourage students to read more widely on ovarian cancer, to think about some of the current issues and learn about recent research. Funding of the Target Ovarian Cancer essay prize

is made possible due to the kind generosity of the Annette Mills Charitable Trust.
Level of Study: Undergraduate
Type: Prize
Value: First prize £750, Second prize £500 and Third prize £250
Frequency: Annual
Country of Study: United Kingdom
Application Procedure: Please complete the online application via Oxford Abstracts app.oxfordabstracts.com/stages/2103/submitter. This application is hosted by Oxford Abstracts platform. Please register for an account using your email address. For further guidance on how to submit your application, please see Oxford Abstracts' guidance on making a submission oxfordabstracts.freshdesk.com/support/solutions/articles/8000072762-making-a-submission.
No. of awards offered: 3
Closing Date: 25 June
Contributor: Annette Mills Charitable Trust
Additional Information: For more information: www.rcog.org.uk/en/careers-training/awards-grants-prizes/target-ovarian-cancer-essay-prize/

For further information contact:

Email: essay@targetovariancancer.org.uk

Tim Chard Case History Prize

Purpose: The Tim Chard Case History Prize has been generously endowed by the Bart's and The London school of Medicine to further the contribution of the late professor Tim Chard in obstetrics and gynaecology. To award students showing the greatest understanding of a clinical problem in obstetrics and gynaecology.
Eligibility: The prize is open to all medical students from the UK and the Republic of Ireland. 1. The successful applicants will show the greatest understanding of a clinical problem in O&G by submitting a case history with an intelligent discussion. 2. The successful applicants are invited to present their submission in a short lecture or a poster presentation at an RCOG event.
Type: Prize
Value: First prize: £500 Second prize: £250 Third prize: £150
Frequency: Annual
Country of Study: United Kingdom
Application Procedure: Please complete the online application via Oxford Abstracts app.oxfordabstracts.com/login?redirect=/stages/2100/submitter. This application is hosted by Oxford Abstracts platform. Please register for an account using your email address. For further guidance on how to submit your application, please see Oxford Abstracts' guidance on making a submission oxfordabstracts.freshdesk.com/support/solutions/articles/8000072762-making-a-submission
No. of awards offered: 3
Closing Date: 17 June
Contributor: Bart's and The London school of Medicine
Additional Information: For more information: www.rcog.org.uk/careers-and-training/awards-grants-and-prizes/awards-grants-and-prizes-for-medical-students-and-foundation-year-doctors/tim-chard-case-history-prize/

For further information contact:

Royal College of Obstetricians and Gynaecologists, United Kingdom.

William Blair Bell Memorial Lecture

Purpose: William Blair Bell, the first president of the RCOG, called for the award of an annual lectureship in a gynaecological or obstetric subject to a developing clinician scientist. The purpose of the lectureship is to allow a clinician or scientist who is at any stage of their career between award of an MD / PhD and the completion of their second year as a Senior Lecturer or its equivalent (e.g. Clinician Scientist), at the time of application, to give a lecture describing research in any area pertaining to Women's Health at the RCOG Annual Academic Meeting.
Eligibility: 1. Clinician or scientist between the award of their MD/PhD thesis and completion of their second year as a Senior Lecturer or its equivalent. 2. Proposed lecture describes their personal research in any area pertaining to Women's Health. 3. Applicants must declare that the lecture is entirely their own work and whether they have applied for other prizes for the same work.
Level of Study: Doctorate, Postgraduate
Type: Lectureship/Prize
Value: The winner of the lecture will be awarded a free place at the RCOG's Annual Academic Meeting and will have the opportunity to present a lecture.
Frequency: Annual
Country of Study: United Kingdom
Application Procedure: Please complete the online application via Oxford Abstracts app.oxfordabstracts.com/login?redirect=/stages/2102/submitter. This application is hosted by Oxford Abstracts platform. Please register for an account using your email address. For further guidance on how to submit your application, please see Oxford Abstracts' guidance on making a submission oxfordabstracts.freshdesk.com/support/solutions/articles/8000072762-making-a-submission.
Closing Date: 5 January
Funding: Foundation

Additional Information: https://www.rcog.org.uk/careers-and-training/awards-grants-and-prizes/lectureship/william-blair-bell-memorial-lecture/

For further information contact:

Email: awards@rcog.org.uk

Women's Visiting Gynaecological Club Prize

Purpose: Through the generosity of the Women's Visiting Gynaecological Club, the RCOG is able to offer prize to a medical student in the UK or Republic of Ireland towards an overseas elective in obstetrics and gynaecology.
Eligibility: This prize is awarded to a medical student who presents an application that best articulates the rationale and objectives for wanting to complete an overseas elective. The award may only be used for the purposes outlines in the original application. Travel must take place within 12 months of the award being made.
Type: Prize
Value: £500
Frequency: Annual
Country of Study: Any country
Application Procedure: Please complete the online application via Oxford Abstracts. app.oxfordabstracts.com/login?redirect=/stages/2098/submitter. This application is hosted by Oxford Abstracts platform. Please register for an account using your email address. For further guidance on how to submit your application, please see Oxford Abstracts' guidance on making a submission oxfordabstracts.freshdesk.com/support/solutions/articles/8000072762-making-a-submission
No. of awards offered: 1
Closing Date: 17 June
Additional Information: For more information https://www.rcog.org.uk/careers-and-training/awards-grants-and-prizes/awards-grants-and-prizes-for-medical-students-and-foundation-year-doctors/womens-visiting-gynaecological-club-prize/

For further information contact:

Email: awards@rcog.org.uk

Royal College of Ophthalmologists

18 Stephenson Way, Euston, London NW1 2HD, United Kingdom.

Tel: (44) 20 3770 5327
Email: communications@rcophth.ac.uk; liz.price@rcophth.ac.uk
Website: www.rcophth.ac.uk/
Contact: Vanda Fadda, Deputy Head of Education and Training

The College was originally formed from the Ophthalmological Society of the United Kingdom and the Faculty of Ophthalmologists. The Royal Charter creating the College of Ophthalmologists was granted on the 14 April 1988 and the Royal Licence was granted five years later. The Royal College of Ophthalmologists believes that everyone should have access to high quality eye care. The College acts as the voice of the profession, set the curriculum and examinations for trainee ophthalmologists, provide training in eye surgery, maintain standards in the practice of ophthalmology, and promote research and advance science in the specialty. Ophthalmologists are at the forefront of eye health services because of their extensive training and experience.

Bayer Educational Grant Awards

Purpose: Supporting ophthalmologists to present work at educational meetings in the United Kingdom and overseas
Eligibility: Application from any grade of ophthalmologist working in the United Kingdom. Members and fellows of the Royal College of Ophthalmologists
Level of Study: Postgraduate
Type: Travel award
Value: Varies
Country of Study: United Kingdom
No. of awards offered: 37
Closing Date: 28 February
Funding: Commercial
Contributor: Bayer HealthCare, Bayer plc
No. of awards given last year: 11
No. of applicants last year: 37
Additional Information: www.fund.bayer.us/grant/2016/7/1/education

For further information contact:

Email: helen.sonderegger@rcophth.ac.uk

Essay Prize for Foundation Doctors

Purpose: Entries are now invited to the Essay Prize for Foundation Doctors on the essay "Discuss the impact of multi professional working on eye care"
Eligibility: 1. The competition is open to all those currently in a United Kingdom Foundation Programme. (F1, F2) at the time of submission, as well as those who have completed the United

R

Kingdom Foundation Programme but have not yet achieved an OST1 post. 2. Entries are invited on the essay "Discuss the impact of multi professional working on eye care"
Level of Study: Postgraduate
Type: Grant
Frequency: Annual
Country of Study: United Kingdom
Application Procedure: Essays of up to 1,500 words should be submitted to education@rcophth.ac.uk
Closing Date: 5 September
Funding: Private
Additional Information: curriculum.rcophth.ac.uk/wp-content/uploads/2016/08/Essay-prize-for-foundation-doctors-2016-FINAL-VERSION-5.pdf, www.rcophth.ac.uk/professional-resources/awards-and-prizes/

For further information contact:

18 Stephenson Way, Kings Cross, London NW1 2HD, United Kingdom.

Email: education@rcophth.ac.uk

Glaucoma UK and The Royal College of Ophthalmologists Research Award

Eligibility: Applicants may be trainees seeking support for a fellowship or senior researchers seeking a grant for a project. Applications are invited from departments and individuals based in the UK and Ireland, but the research studies may be carried out elsewhere.
Level of Study: Postgraduate
Type: Award
Value: Up to £100,000
Country of Study: Any country
Application Procedure: The application form can be found here: www.rcophth.ac.uk/wp-content/uploads/2023/01/Glaucoma-UK-and-The-Royal-College-of-Ophthalmologists-Research-Award-2023-Form.docx
Closing Date: 11 April
Additional Information: www.rcophth.ac.uk/events-courses/scholarships-awards-prizes/

For further information contact:

Email: education@rcophth.ac.uk

Keeler Scholarship

Purpose: To enable the scholar to study, research or acquire special skills, knowledge or experience at a suitable location in the United Kingdom or elsewhere for a minimum period of 6 months
Eligibility: Applicants must be Fellows, Members or Affiliates of the Royal College of Ophthalmologists, those Fellows, Members and Affiliates being in good standing. Potential applicants who have received substantial (usually meaning amounts greater than the value of the scholarship) funding for their project are not eligible for the Keeler Scholarship. The trustees will give special consideration to candidates intending to make a career in ophthalmology in the United Kingdom. Applicants may apply retrospectively but should not be more than 3 months into the fellowship for which they are applying for support by 10 February (application closing date)
Level of Study: Postgraduate
Type: Scholarship
Value: Up to £30,000
Length of Study: 2 years
Frequency: Every 2 years (even-numbered years)
Country of Study: United Kingdom
Application Procedure: 5 copies each of the application form duly completed and the candidate's curriculum vitae should be submitted
Closing Date: 10 February
Funding: Private
Contributor: Keeler Ltd
Additional Information: Funds will be paid to the Scholar two months before the start date of the project or fellowship. www.eyedocs.co.uk/ophthalmology-clinical-awards/1078-keeler-scholarship, www.rcophth.ac.uk/professional-resources/awards-and-prizes/

For further information contact:

The Royal College of Ophthalmologists Education and Training Department – Awards and Prizes, 18 Stephenson Way, Kings Cross, London NW1 2HD, United Kingdom.

Email: training@rcophth.ac.uk

Nettleship Medal

Eligibility: The applicant should be British, a member of The Royal College of Ophthalmologists, and the work must be undertaken under the auspices of a British institution.
Type: Monetary award and medal
Value: £500.00
Country of Study: Any country
Closing Date: 7 January
Additional Information: www.rcophth.ac.uk/news-views/2022-nettleship-medal/

For further information contact:

18 Stephenson Way, London NW1 2HD, United Kingdom.

Email: laurelle.bygraves@rcophth.ac.uk.

Patrick Trevor-Roper Undergraduate Award

Purpose: Applications are invited for the Patrick Trevor-Roper Award, which is open to all undergraduate medical students from the United Kingdom and Ireland who have an interest in the specialty. The money may be used to fund electives in Ophthalmology, and may be spent on traveling or subsistence
Eligibility: Medical Undergraduates
Level of Study: Postgraduate
Type: Award
Value: £550
Frequency: Annual
Country of Study: United Kingdom
Application Procedure: Please post 4 hard copies of your application form and CV to The Royal College of Ophthalmologists, Education and Training Department – Awards and Prizes, 18 Stephenson Way, NW1 2HD, London, United Kingdom
No. of awards offered: 2
Funding: Private
Additional Information: www.eyedocs.co.uk/undergraduate-ophthalmology-awards/1076-patrick-trevor-roper-award www.rcophth.ac.uk/professional-resources/awards-and-prizes/

For further information contact:

The Royal College of Ophthalmologists, Education and Training Department – Awards and Prizes, 18 Stephenson Way, Kings Cross, London NW1 2HD, United Kingdom.

Email: education@rcophth.ac.uk

The Ulverscroft David Owen Award

Purpose: The Ulverscroft Foundation gives financial help to Universities that research the causes of eye diseases; funds eye clinics, hospitals, schools, libraries and other organisations which help visually impaired people.
Eligibility: The first author and senior author should apply together. Either the first or lead author must be an ophthalmologist. At least one of the authors must be a member of the RCOphth. The applicants should be based and have undertaken the research reported at a British institution. The paper must have been published in a peer reviewed scientific journal after 1 January 2020.
Type: Award
Value: £500
Country of Study: Turkey
Application Procedure: Ulverscroft David Owen Prize Application Form – 2023: www.rcophth.ac.uk/wp-content/uploads/2022/10/Ulverscroft-David-Owen-Prize-Application-Form-2023-1.doc
Closing Date: 6 January
Additional Information: www.rcophth.ac.uk/news-views/ulverscroft-david-owen-award-2022/

For further information contact:

18 Stephenson Way, London NW1 2HD, United Kingdom.

Email: aurelle.bygraves@rcophth.ac.uk.

Royal College of Ophthalmologists-Bayer Research

18 Stephenson Way, London NW1 2HD, United Kingdom.

Tel: (44) 20 3770 5341
Email: gareth.brennan@rcophth.ac.uk
Website: www.rcophth.ac.uk/
Contact: Gareth Brennan, Education and Training Administrator

The Royal College of Ophthalmologists believes that everyone should have access to high quality eye care. We champion excellence in the practice of ophthalmology through standards in training, education and assessment of ophthalmologists; supporting the promotion of research and innovation throughout the ophthalmic community.

Royal College of Ophthalmologists-Bayer Research Award

Purpose: The Royal College of Ophthalmologists and Bayer have come together in a partnership to launch a grant to promote research in ophthalmology
Eligibility: Any Ophthalmic Specialist Trainee, Member or Fellow of The RCOphth with an interest in research
Level of Study: Postgraduate
Type: Award
Value: £8,000
Frequency: Annual

Country of Study: Any country
Closing Date: 30 March
Funding: Foundation

For further information contact:

Email: education@rcophth.ac.uk

Royal College of Organists (RCO)

PO Box 7328, New Milton, Hampshire BH25 9DU, United Kingdom.

Tel: (44) 20 3865 6998
Email: admin@rco.org.uk
Website: www.rco.org.uk/

The College was established in 1864, the result of an idea by Richard Limpus, organist of St Michael's, Cornhill in the City of London. The Royal College of Organists has supported and represented organists and choral directors for more than 150 years. With members in nearly 40 countries around the world, we work together to promote the best in organ playing and choral directing, to encourage anyone who is interested to learn more about this fascinating and versatile musical instrument, and to explore its history and repertoire.

Royal College of Organists Scholarships and Awards

Purpose: To assist organists with professional playing
Eligibility: Open to members of the College. Only in exceptional circumstances will awards be made to non members. Membership is open to all upon payment of an annual subscription
Level of Study: Unrestricted
Type: Grant
Length of Study: 2 year, renewable
Frequency: Annual
Study Establishment: Varies
Country of Study: Any country
Application Procedure: Applicants must write for an application form
Closing Date: 17 February
Funding: Private
Contributor: College trusts
Additional Information: www.rca.ac.uk/studying-at-the-rca/fees-funding/financial-help-/preentry-scholarships-and-awards/

For further information contact:

Tel: (44) 207 590 4108
Email: scholarships@rca.ac.uk

Royal College of Organists Various Open Award Bequests

Purpose: To assist students who are training to become organists and/or choral directors.
Eligibility: Students in serious organ study, and in particular study devoted to the attainment of the College's diplomas
Level of Study: Postgraduate, Professional development
Type: Award
Value: Various; each award usually between £100 and £400
Frequency: Annual
Country of Study: Any country
Application Procedure: Applications for an RCO award should be made through this form RCO Awards & Bursaries Application Form downloadable from website. This application form should be accompanied by a letter of recommendation from your current organ teacher or suitable person. Please print and complete this Bursary Application form either post to Andrew McCrea or send by e-mail as a scanned file to andrew.mccrea@rco.org.uk.
Closing Date: 18 April
Additional Information: Open Awards Group A: 1. Mrs Alice Bonwick Bequest; 2. Miss Agnes Ethel Freeth Bequest; 3. Mrs Nellie Parnaby Bequest; 4. Noel Bonavia-Hunt Bequest. For more information www.rco.org.uk/education_scholarships.php#awards

For further information contact:

Andrew McCrea, Director of Academic Development, Royal College of Organists, RCO Bookings and Accounts, PO Box 7328, New Milton BH25 9DU, United Kingdom.

Email: andrew.mccrea@rco.org.uk

Royal College of Organists Various Open Awards

Purpose: These awards, each of which is available to more than one applicant, will normally be made to full-time music students (i.e. students pursuing to some extent organ and/or choral directing studies) at postgraduate level. They may also be used towards the cost of additional courses or lessons for which the holder receives little or no other funding, and may be used in this country or abroad.
Eligibility: Full-time music students (i.e. students pursuing to some extent organ and/or choral directing studies) at postgraduate level.
Level of Study: Postgraduate

Type: Award
Value: Various; each award from at least £400
Country of Study: Any country
Application Procedure: Applications for an RCO award should be made through this form RCO Awards & Bursaries Application Form downloadable from website. This application form should be accompanied by a letter of recommendation from your current organ teacher or suitable person. Please print and complete this Bursary Application form, either post or send by e-mail as a scanned file to Andrew McCrea.
Closing Date: 1 February
Additional Information: Open Awards Group B: 1. Lady Aline Cholmondeley Award. 2. Barbara Maude Osborne Award. 3. Samuel Paterson Baird Award. www.rco.org.uk/education_scholarships.php

For further information contact:

Andrew McCrea, Director of Academic Development, Royal College of Organists, RCO Bookings and Accounts, PO Box 7328, New Milton BH25 9DU, United Kingdom.

Email: andrew.mccrea@rco.org.uk

The Harry Moreton Memorial Scholarship

Purpose: The Scholarship grants towards graduate and postgraduate studies in the UK or abroad and also for grants towards local courses of organ lessons with teachers approved by the College.
Eligibility: Tenable only by students whose home is in either Devon or Cornwall.
Level of Study: Graduate, Postgraduate
Type: Scholarship
Value: At least £800 per annum
Country of Study: Any country
Application Procedure: Applications for an RCO award should be made through this form RCO Awards & Bursaries Application Form downloadable from website. This application form should be accompanied by a letter of recommendation from your current organ teacher or suitable person. Please print and complete this Bursary Application form, either post or send by e-mail as a scanned file to Andrew McCrea.
Closing Date: 1 May
Additional Information: www.rco.org.uk/education_scholarships.php

For further information contact:

Andrew McCrea, Director of Academic Development, Royal College of Organists, RCO Bookings and Accounts, PO Box 7328, New Milton BH25 9DU, United Kingdom.

Email: andrew.mccrea@rco.org.uk

The Leonard Freestone Scholarship

Purpose: This scholarship is available to a student pursuing postgraduate (taught or research based) course related to organ playing and/or choral direction.
Level of Study: Postgraduate
Type: Scholarship
Value: £4,750 per annum
Length of Study: 3 Years
Frequency: Annual
Country of Study: United Kingdom
Application Procedure: Applications for an RCO award should be made through this form RCO Awards & Bursaries Application Form downloadable from website. This application form should be accompanied by a letter of recommendation from your current organ teacher or suitable person. Please print and complete this Bursary Application form, either post or send by e-mail as a scanned file to Andrew McCrea.
Closing Date: 1 May
Additional Information: www.rco.org.uk/education_scholarships.php

For further information contact:

Andrew McCrea, Director of Academic Development, Royal College of Organists, RCO Bookings and Accounts, PO Box 7328, New Milton BH25 9DU, United Kingdom.

Email: andrew.mccrea@rco.org.uk

The Peter Wiles Scholarship

Purpose: This scholarship is available annually to a student in higher education pursuing postgraduate course related to organ playing and/or choral direction, or pursuing vocational training as an organist and/or choral director.
Level of Study: Postgraduate
Type: Scholarship
Value: £1,500 per annum
Frequency: Annual
Country of Study: United Kingdom
Application Procedure: Applications for an RCO award should be made through this form RCO Awards & Bursaries Application Form downloadable from website. This application form should be accompanied by a letter of recommendation from your current organ teacher or suitable person. Please print and complete this Bursary Application form, either post or send by e-mail as a scanned file to Andrew McCrea.
Closing Date: 1 May
Additional Information: www.rco.org.uk/education_scholarships.php

For further information contact:

Andrew McCrea, Director of Academic Development, Royal College of Organists, RCO Bookings and Accounts, PO Box 7328, New Milton BH25 9DU, United Kingdom.

Email: andrew.mccrea@rco.org.uk

Royal College of Physicians and Surgeons of Canada (RCPSC)

Office of Fellowship Affairs, 774 Echo Drive, Ottawa, ON K1S 5N8, Canada.

Tel: (1) 613 730 8177
Email: feedback@royalcollege.ca
Website: www.royalcollege.ca/
Contact: Dr James Hickey, FRCPC, Director

In June 1929, a special act of Parliament established the Royal College of Physicians and Surgeons of Canada to oversee postgraduate medical education. We serve patients, diverse populations and our Fellows by setting the standards in specialty medical education and lifelong learning, and by advancing professional practice and health care. The Royal College sets the highest standards for specialty medical education in Canada. The Royal College distributes more than CA$1 million a year in awards, grants, fellowships and visiting professorship programs. Funds are provided by member donations, through a portion of membership dues, through the Royal College's Education Fund and from private endowments.

Canadian Research Awards for Specialty Residents (Medicine, Surgery)

Purpose: We serve patients, diverse populations and our Fellows by setting the standards in specialty medical education and lifelong learning, and by advancing professional practice and health care.
Type: Award
Country of Study: Canada
Closing Date: 18 January
Additional Information: www.vascular.org/career-tools-training/awards-and-scholarships/resident-research-award

For further information contact:

774 Echo Drive, Ottawa, ON K1S 0R4, Canada.

Fax: (1) 613 730 8830
Email: llocas@rcpsc.edu

Duncan Graham Award for Outstanding Contribution to Medical Education

Purpose: One of the notable and outstanding awards that The Royal College of Physicians and Surgeons of Canada may bestow upon an individual is the Duncan Graham Award in Medical Education.
Eligibility: 1. The Award is conferred upon any individual, whether physician or not, in recognition of outstanding contribution to medical education. 2. Self-applications are ineligible.
Type: Award
Value: CA$1,000
Country of Study: Canada
Closing Date: 2 October
Additional Information: https://www.royalcollege.ca/ca/en/awards-grants/awards/duncan-graham-award-lifelong-contribution-medical-education.html

For further information contact:

Email: awards@royalcollege.ca

International Medical Educator of the Year Award

Purpose: This award is given annually to an international medical educator who has demonstrated a commitment to enhancing residency education as evidenced by innovation and impact beyond their program.
Eligibility: A nominee must be a current medical educator of a postgraduate program residing outside of Canada.
Type: Award
Country of Study: Canada
Closing Date: 8 April
Additional Information: https://www.royalcollege.ca/ca/en/awards-grants/awards/international-medical-educator-year-award.html

For further information contact:

Tel: (1) 613 730 8177
Email: icreawards@royalcollege.ca

International Resident Leadership Award

Purpose: This award is given to an international resident who has demonstrated leadership in specialty education and encourages the development of future leaders in medicine. Up to two awards will be presented annually. Award winners receive a plaque recognizing their contribution as well as travel and registration to the International Conference on Residency Education.

Eligibility: The resident must be enrolled in a postgraduate medical or surgical training program outside of Canada
Type: Award
Country of Study: Any country
Closing Date: 8 April
Additional Information: https://www.royalcollege.ca/ca/en/awards-grants/awards/international-resident-leadership-award.html

For further information contact:

Tel: (1) 613 730 8177
Email: icreawards@royalcollege.ca

James H. Graham Award of Merit

Purpose: This honorary award of merit was named for Dr. James H. Graham, secretary-general of the Royal College from 1953 to 1979. In 1987, the Council of The Royal College of Physicians and Surgeons of Canada recommended that an award of merit be given to a person whose outstanding career achievements reflect the aims and objectives of the Royal College.
Eligibility: This person need not be a physician. Self-applications are ineligible. The recipient's career achievements must be outstanding, enduring, and must be reflective of the Royal College strategic priorities. Potential candidates, who need not be physicians, could be long-serving contributors in a wide variety of areas
Type: Award
Value: The recipient will be presented with an engraved memento at Royal College event.
Country of Study: Canada
Application Procedure: Please submit your application via our online platform: royalcollege.ungerboeck.com/prod/app85.cshtml?AppCode=SPA&OrgCode=10&CC=82&AppMode=0
Closing Date: 2 October
Additional Information: https://www.royalcollege.ca/ca/en/awards-grants/awards/james-h-graham-award-merit-commitment-royal-college.html

For further information contact:

Email: awards@royalcollege.ca

Kristin Sivertz Resident Leadership Award

Purpose: This award is given to a resident who has demonstrated leadership in Canadian specialty education and encourages the development of future leaders in medicine. Up to two awards will be presented annually. Award winners will receive a plaque recognizing their contribution as well as complimentary travel and registration to the International Conference on Residency Education.
Eligibility: The resident must be enrolled in a Royal College-accredited residency program.
Type: Award
Country of Study: Canada
Closing Date: 8 April
Additional Information: https://www.royalcollege.ca/ca/en/awards-grants/awards/kristin-sivertz-resident-leadership-award.html

For further information contact:

Tel: (1) 613 730 8177
Email: icreawards@royalcollege.ca

Program Administrator Award for Excellence

Purpose: This award is given to a residency Program Administrator who has demonstrated a commitment to excellence in supporting all aspects of residency education, and works with all aspects of the program and with peers to exemplify the professional role of the Program Administrator and may be evidenced by innovation and/or improved or newly implemented processes within their program(s).
Eligibility: 1. Nominee must be a current postgraduate residency Program Administrator 2. Current members of the Royal College Program Administrator Conference Steering Committee are not eligible 3. Self-nominations are not accepted 4. Individuals may be re-nominated in subsequent years; however, previous winners of the award will not be eligible to win again.
Type: Award
Country of Study: Canada
Closing Date: 8 April
Additional Information: https://www.royalcollege.ca/ca/en/awards-grants/awards/program-administrator-award-for-excellence.html

For further information contact:

Tel: (1) 613 730 8177
Email: paconference@royalcollege.ca

Royal College AMS Donald Richards Wilson Award for CanMEDS Integration

Purpose: The Royal College of Physicians and Surgeons of Canada, in collaboration with Associated Medical Services, Inc. has established an award to honour and acknowledge the contribution of Dr. Donald R. Wilson (President, RCPSC, 1988-1990) to medical education.

Eligibility: Any medical educator (not necessarily a Fellow) or an identified leader of a team, program, or department who has demonstrated excellence in integrating the CanMEDS roles into a Royal College or other health related training programs. Nominations should be accompanied by a statement describing the relevant educational program; how the particular innovations have been implemented; the impact of the innovations for integrating CanMEDS roles into the program. A curriculum vitae along with two letters of support are required one from the Dean of Medicine, or the Dean responsible for postgraduate education; and a second from an individual acquainted with the particulars of the innovation leading to the program changes. Self-applications are ineligible.
Type: Award
Value: US$2,000
Country of Study: Canada
Application Procedure: Please submit your application via our online platform: royalcollege.ungerboeck.com/prod/app85.cshtml?ppCode=SPA&OrgCode=10&CC=83&AppMode=0
Closing Date: 2 October
Additional Information: https://www.royalcollege.ca/ca/en/awards-grants/awards/royal-college-associated-medical-services-donald-r-wilson-award.html

For further information contact:

Email: awards@royalcollege.ca

Royal College Award for Early-Career Leadership

Purpose: The Award for Early-Career Leadership honours new Royal College Fellows (with 7 or fewer years of post-training full-time practice) who have shown outstanding leadership, initiative, service and/or innovation in areas aligned with one of three key areas of the Royal College mandateMedical Education and/or Continuing Professional Development (CPD);Health Policy / Health Systems Professional Practice / Patient Care
Eligibility: The nominee must currently be a Fellow of the Royal College, and has been so for at least one year; Has been in full-time practice (clinical or academic) for not more than seven years post-training (not including any leaves of absence such as maternity leave); Self-applications are ineligible; Unsuccessful nominees may be re-submitted, however recipients are not eligible for future nomination.
Type: Award
Value: CA$1,000.
Country of Study: Canada
Closing Date: 2 October
Additional Information: https://www.royalcollege.ca/ca/en/awards-grants/awards/early-career-leadership-in-medical-education.html

For further information contact:

Email: awards@royalcollege.ca

Royal College Dr. Thomas Dignan Indigenous Health Award

Purpose: The Royal College Dr. Thomas Dignan Indigenous Health Award was founded in 2014 in honour of the late Thomas Dignan, CM, OOnt, MD, co-chair of the Indigenous Health Committee of the Royal College.
Eligibility: The award may be bestowed upon physicians, residents or medical students who self-identify as Indigenous, Aboriginal, First Nations, Inuit or Métis and are Canadian residents (International applicants are not eligible). The award may be bestowed upon Elders and Knowledge Keepers who self-identify as Indigenous, Aboriginal, First Nations, Inuit or Métis and are Canadian residents (International applicants are not eligible). Nominators will be asked to describe the nominee's exceptional contribution, as well as to provide a curriculum vitae for the nominee and at least two letters of support. It is strongly preferred but not essential that at least one of the letters be from a Fellow of the Royal College. Self-applications are ineligible.
Type: Award
Value: CA$1,000, Travel and related expenses
Country of Study: Canada
Closing Date: 2 October
Additional Information: https://www.royalcollege.ca/ca/en/awards-grants/awards/royal-college-dr-thomas-dignan-indigenous-health-award.html

For further information contact:

Email: awards@royalcollege.ca

Royal College of Surgeons

35-43 Lincoln's Inn Fields, London WC2A 3PE, United Kingdom.

Tel: (44) 20 7405 3474
Email: reception@rcseng.ac.uk
Website: www.rcseng.ac.uk/

The Royal College of Surgeons of England is a professional membership organisation and registered charity, which exists to advance patient care. We support over 25,000 members in the UK and internationally by improving their skills and knowledge, facilitating research and developing policy and guidance. The College was set up by Royal Charter in 1800 and has a unique heritage and collections, including the Hunterian Museum, surgeons' library and Wellcome Museum of Anatomy and Pathology. The RCS relies heavily on charitable support to fund surgical research, training and conserving our heritage collections. Legacies and support from grant-giving trusts, companies and individuals play a crucial role in maintaining and improving surgical care for patients.

Ethicon Travel Award

Purpose: Ethicon Foundation Fund travel awards for overseas visits are awarded to fellows and members of the College who are in good standing
Eligibility: Applicants must demonstrate that the period overseas relates directly to their home country's surgical training scheme's objectives and/or an opportunity to obtain relevant surgical experience that is not normally available in their home country. They must have obtained prior approval for the visit from the appropriate training authority in the country of application where appropriate. UK trainees must produce confirmation/evidence of prospective approval from the GMC if the post is to count towards the award of a Certificate of Completion of Training (CCT).
Type: Award
Value: The awards are for travel costs only, economy class travel, up to a value of £1,000
Length of Study: 3–12 Months
Frequency: Annual
Country of Study: United Kingdom
Application Procedure: Please email the following documents to Linda at lslater@rcseng.ac.uk. 1. Completed application form (download from website). 2. A letter of support from the head of department, or consultant, under whom the applicant is currently working. 3. A letter of support from another, independent referee. 4. Confirmation from the Institute you are visiting.
Closing Date: 16 March
Contributor: Ethicon Foundation Fund
Additional Information: As a condition of the award, successful applicants are required to submit a report of their visit within two months of return. Applicants who do not submit a report may have the award withdrawn. For more information www.rcseng.ac.uk/standards-and-research/research/fellowships-awards-grants/awards-and-grants/travel-awards/ethicon-grants/

For further information contact:

38–43 Lincoln's Inn Fields, London WC2A 3PE, United Kingdom.

Tel: (44) 20 7405 3474
Email: lslater@rcseng.ac.uk

Sir Ratanji Dalal Research Scholarship

Eligibility: 1. The scholarship is open to all consultants, senior lecturers, SAS doctors and trainee fellows/members of the Royal College of Surgeons of England. 2. Successful applicants must remain in a good standing order with their membership fees throughout the tenure of the award. 3. If the research will not be carried out in a tropical country, the relevance of the project to tropical surgery should be made clear. 4. Candidates must be sponsored by the head of the department where the research will be conducted, who can offer facilities and technical assistance for research in the appropriate field. 5. Must not have received a travelling scholarship from RCS England before.
Level of Study: Postgraduate
Type: Scholarship
Value: £20,00
Length of Study: 1 year
Country of Study: United Kingdom
Application Procedure: Application form: www.rcseng.ac.uk/-/media/files/rcs/standards-and-research/research/fellowships-awards-grants/sir-r-dalal/sir-ratanji-dalal-research-scholarship-app-form-2023.docx
Closing Date: 30 April
Additional Information: www.rcseng.ac.uk/standards-and-research/research/fellowships-awards-grants/awards-and-grants/travel-awards/ratanji-scholarship/

For further information contact:

Email: fellowshipapplication@rcseng.ac.uk

R

Royal College of Surgeons of United Kingdom

35–43 Lincoln's Inn Fields, London WC2A 3PE, United Kingdom.

Tel: (44) 20 7405 3474
Email: reception@rcseng.ac.uk
Website: www.rcseng.ac.uk
Contact: Miss Bumbi Singh, Research Department

The Royal College of Surgeons of England is a professional membership organisation and registered charity, which exists to advance patient care. The College was set up by Royal Charter in 1800 and has a unique heritage and collections, including the Hunterian Museum, surgeons' library and Wellcome Museum of Anatomy and Pathology. We support over 25,000 members in the UK and internationally by improving their skills and knowledge, facilitating research and developing policy and guidance.

Cutlers' Surgical Fellowship

Purpose: The Worshipful Company of Cutlers' Surgical Fellowship is to allow fellows and members of the Royal College of Surgeons working in hospitals throughout the UK to undertake a period of time overseas to learn a surgical technique, procedure or treatment which they can then practice on their return to the UK to benefit NHS patients.
Eligibility: Particular emphasis in determining the recipient of this fellowship is placed on the career progress of the applicant to date, their CV, the opportunities provided at the centre of excellence where the fellowship will be undertaken, the innovative qualities of the skills to be learnt and how gaining such skills will be applied in the UK for the benefit for patient care.
Level of Study: Doctorate
Type: Fellowship
Value: £10,000
Country of Study: Any country
Closing Date: September
Additional Information: www.rcseng.ac.uk/standards-and-research/research/fellowships-awards-grants/awards-and-grants/cutlers-surgical-fellowship/

For further information contact:

Email: lslater@rcseng.ac.uk

Cutlers' Surgical Prize

Purpose: The Cutlers' Surgical Prize was instituted in 1981 and has become established as one of the most prestigious annual prizes for original innovation in the design or application of surgical instruments, equipment or practice to improve the health and recovery of surgical patients.
Level of Study: Postgraduate
Type: Prize
Value: Elegant mounted Victorian silver-gilt medal and £5,000
Country of Study: United Kingdom
Application Procedure: The applications must include the following: 1. Evidence of originality, innovation, date of development, clinical usage and an explanation of benefits in patient care and benefit. 2. Written evidence from one or more independent referees as to the surgical application is essential and must be attached. Please email your completed application form to Linda Slater: www.rcseng.ac.uk/-/media/files/rcs/standards-and-research/research/fellowships-awards-grants/cutlers/cutlers-prize-entry-form-2023.doc
Closing Date: September
Additional Information: www.rcseng.ac.uk/standards-and-research/research/fellowships-awards-grants/awards-and-grants/cutlers-surgical-prize/

For further information contact:

Email: lslater@rcseng.ac.uk

Ethicon Foundation Fund

Purpose: Ethicon Foundation Fund travel awards for overseas visits are awarded to fellows and members of the College who are in good standing.
Eligibility: Applicants must demonstrate that the period overseas relates directly to their home country's surgical training scheme's objectives and/or an opportunity to obtain relevant surgical experience that is not normally available in their home country. They must have obtained prior approval for the visit from the appropriate training authority in the country of application where appropriate. UK trainees must produce confirmation/evidence of prospective approval from the GMC if the post is to count towards the award of a Certificate of Completion of Training (CCT).
Type: Travel grant
Value: The awards are for travel costs only, economy class travel, up to a value of £1,000.
Frequency: Annual
Country of Study: United Kingdom
Application Procedure: Please email the following documents to Linda at lslater@rcseng.ac.uk 1. Completed application form (download from website). 2. A letter of support from the head of department, or consultant, under whom the applicant is currently working. 3. A letter of support from another, independent referee. 4. Confirmation from the Institute you are visiting.
Closing Date: 16 March
Additional Information: As a condition of the award, successful applicants are required to submit a report of their visit within two months of return. Applicants who do not submit a report may have the award withdrawn. For more information www.rcseng.ac.uk/standards-and-research/research/fellowships-awards-grants/awards-and-grants/travel-awards/ethicon-grants/

For further information contact:

38-43 Lincoln's Inn Fields, London WC2A 3PE, United Kingdom.

Tel: (44) 20 7405 3474
Email: lslater@rcseng.ac.uk

Ronald Raven Barbers

Eligibility: 1. You should be affiliated to this College and a resident in the UK. 2. You should not already have received a Ronald Raven Award.
Type: Award
Value: £2,500 each
Length of Study: 1 to 2 years
Frequency: Annual
Country of Study: United Kingdom
Application Procedure: a completed application form; www.rcseng.ac.uk/-/media/files/rcs/standards-and-research/research/fellowships-awards-grants/ronald-raven/ronaldravenbarberswordapplicationform.doc
No. of awards offered: 2
Additional Information: www.rcseng.ac.uk/standards-and-research/research/fellowships-awards-grants/awards-and-grants/travel-awards/ronald-raven-barbers-award/

Royal Geographical Society (with the Institute of British Geographers)

1 Kensington Gore, London SW7 2AR, United Kingdom.

Tel: (44) 20 7591 3000
Email: enquiries@rgs.org
Website: www.rgs.org/
Contact: Juliette Scull, Grants Officer

The Royal Geographical Society (with the Institute of British Geographers) is the UK's learned society and professional body for geography. We advance geography and support geographers in the UK and across the world. As a charity, learned society and professional body, we reach millions of people each year through our work in advancing geography and supporting geographers. With over two million items, our Collections provide an unparalleled resource tracing 500 years of geographical discovery and research. Equality, diversity and inclusion are core values for the Society and for the practice, study and teaching of geography.

30th International Geographical Congress Award

Purpose: To assist with the cost of attending a conference organised by a geographical scientific Union or Association formally affiliated with the International Science Council (ISC)
Eligibility: Applicants must be UK/EU nationals. Applicants are early career researchers (post PhD) currently affiliated with a UK Higher Education Institution. Preference will be given to applicants within 6 years of completion of a PhD, presenting papers and seeking to cover travel expenses, although help with conference fees, accommodation, and maintenance costs will also be considered. Applicants must demonstrate the geographical nature of both the conference and the work they will present.
Level of Study: Research
Type: Award
Value: Up to £750
Frequency: Annual
Country of Study: Any country
Application Procedure: All prospective grant applicants should read our Advice and Resources: www.rgs.org/in-the-field/in-the-field-grants/advice-and-resources/ pages, which include more information about the grants programme, its conditions, and what is expected if your application is successful. Please read this information carefully and send your completed application form, or any enquiries, by email to grants@rgs.org. Application form: www.rgs.org/in-the-field/in-the-field-grants/research-grants/thirtieth-international-geographical-congress/downloads/30th-igc-award-application-form.doc/
No. of awards offered: 5
Closing Date: 31 October
Additional Information: For more details www.rgs.org/in-the-field/in-the-field-grants/research-grants/thirtieth-international-geographical-congress/

R

For further information contact:

Tel: (44) 20 7591 3073
Email: grants@rgs.org

Environment and Sustainability Research Grants

Purpose: To support researchers investigating some of the bigger issues in environmental sustainability.
Eligibility: Applicants may be researches of any nationality but must be affiliated with a UK Higher Education Institution. Individuals or groups may apply.
Type: Grant
Value: £15,000
Frequency: Annual

Country of Study: Any country
Application Procedure: All prospective grant applicants are encouraged to read our Advice and Resources pages, which include more information about the grants programme, its conditions, how to apply for a grant and what is expected if your application is successful. Please read this information carefully and send your application, or any enquiries, by email to grants@rgs.org.
No. of awards offered: 3
Closing Date: 8 March
Contributor: Deutsche Post-Stiftung and SUN Institute Environment and Sustainability
No. of awards given last year: 4
Additional Information: For more information www.rgs.org/in-the-field/in-the-field-grants/research-grants/environment-and-sustainability-research-grants/

For further information contact:

Tel: (44) 207 591 3073
Email: grants@rgs.org

Geographical Club Award

Purpose: The Geographical Club Award is given through the RGS-IBG Postgraduate Research Awards scheme to support PhD students undertaking geographical fieldwork or other forms of data collection in the UK or overseas.
Eligibility: Applicants must be registered at a UK Higher Education Institution. Preference is given to students who do not receive full funding from a research council, university or comparable levels of support from other sources for fieldwork and data collection.
Level of Study: Doctorate, Postgraduate
Type: Award
Value: £1,000
Frequency: Annual
Country of Study: Any country
Application Procedure: The Geographical Club Award is given through the RGS-IBG Postgraduate Research Awards scheme. All prospective grant applicants are encouraged to read our Advice and Resources pages, which include more information about the grants programme, its conditions, how to apply for a grant and what is expected if your application is successful. Please read this information carefully and send your application, or any enquiries, by email to grants@rgs.org.
No. of awards offered: 2
Closing Date: 23 November
No. of awards given last year: 2
Additional Information: www.rgs.org/in-the-field/in-the-field-grants/students/phd/geographical-club-award-(1)/

For further information contact:

Tel: (44) 207 591 3073
Email: grants@rgs.org

Innovative Geography Teaching Grants

Purpose: The aim is to serve both geography pupils and the wider teaching community through the creation of teaching materials. The materials produced will be published on the Society's website.
Eligibility: Two supporting statements are required. One referee statement must be signed by the Head of Department, Head Teacher or Employer of the lead applicant.
Type: Grant
Value: £1,000
Country of Study: Any country
Application Procedure: All prospective grant applicants should read our Advice and Resources pages: www.rgs.org/in-the-field/in-the-field-grants/advice-and-resources/, which include more information about the grants programme, its conditions, and what is expected if your application is successful. Please read this information carefully and send your application, or any enquiries, by email to grants@rgs.org.
No. of awards offered: 2
Closing Date: 15 February
Additional Information: www.rgs.org/in-the-field/in-the-field-grants/teacher-grants/innovative-teaching-geography-grants/

For further information contact:

1 Kensington Gore, South Kensington, London SW7 2AR, United Kingdom.

Tel: (44) 20 7591 3000
Email: grants@rgs.org.

Ray Y. Gildea Jr Award

Purpose: The Ray Y Gildea Jr Award supports innovation in teaching and learning in higher and secondary education.
Eligibility: Applicants must be currently employed in the higher education (college) sector and/or secondary school level, either in the UK or the USA, actively teaching students.
Type: Grant
Value: Up to £1,000

Frequency: Annual
Country of Study: Any country
Application Procedure: All prospective grant applicants are encouraged to read our Advice and Resources pages, which include more information about the grants programme, its conditions, how to apply for a grant and what is expected if your application is successful. Please read this information carefully and send your application, or any enquiries, by email to grants@rgs.org
Closing Date: 30 November
Additional Information: For more information www.rgs.org/in-the-field/in-the-field-grants/teacher-grants/ray-y-gildea-jr-award/

For further information contact:

Tel: (44) 207 591 3073
Email: grants@rgs.org

Walters Kundert Fellowship

Purpose: The Walters Kundert Fellowship offers awards to support field research in physical geography within Arctic and/or high mountain environments, with preference for field studies that advance the understanding of environmental change past or present.
Eligibility: Applications are open to post-PhD researchers affiliated with a UK university or research institute, or Fellows and members of the Society who are employed outside the UK.
Level of Study: Research
Type: Grant
Value: £10,000
Frequency: Annual
Country of Study: Any country
Application Procedure: All prospective grant applicants are encouraged to read our Advice and Resources pages, which include more information about the grants programme, its conditions, how to apply for a grant and what is expected if your application is successful. Please read this information carefully and send your application, or any enquiries, by email to grants@rgs.org. Apply Now: www.rgs.org/in-the-field/in-the-field-grants/research-grants/kundert-fellowship/#
No. of awards offered: 1
Closing Date: 23 November
No. of awards given last year: 1
Additional Information: For more information www.rgs.org/in-the-field/in-the-field-grants/research-grants/kundert-fellowship/

For further information contact:

Email: grants@rgs.org

Royal Holloway, University of London

Egham Hill, Egham, Surrey TW20 0EX, United Kingdom.

Tel: (44) 1784 434 455
Email: international@royalholloway.ac.uk
Website: www.royalholloway.ac.uk/
Contact: Ms Claire Collingwood, Schools & International Liaison Officer

Royal Holloway is formed from two colleges, Bedford College in London and Royal Holloway College was founded by two social pioneers, Elizabeth Jesser Reid and Thomas Holloway. In 1900, the colleges became part of the University of London and in 1985 they merged to form what is now known as Royal Holloway. As one of the UK's leading research-intensive universities, we are home to some of the world's foremost authorities in the sciences, arts, business, economics and law. As teachers and researchers they change lives, expand minds and help current and future leaders understand power and responsibility.

American Foundation of RHBNC International Excellence Scholarship

Purpose: This scholarship is available to students from the United States with outstanding academic ability studying any taught Masters course.
Eligibility: 1. US citizen 2. Offer to study for a taught Masters course at Royal Holloway 3. Achieved, or on target to achieve, a First Class degree, or equivalent.
Eligible Country: United States of America
Level of Study: Masters Degree
Type: Scholarships
Value: £3,000
Frequency: Annual
Country of Study: United Kingdom
Application Procedure: Apply via our online system Royal Holloway Direct (admissions.royalholloway.ac.uk/#/login), where you will be able to complete your statement and upload any required documents including your grades transcript.
Closing Date: 3 July

Additional Information: For further details www.royalholloway.ac.uk/studying-here/fees-and-funding/postgraduate/scholarships/american-foundation-of-rhbnc-international-excellence-scholarship/

For further information contact:

Egham Hill, Egham TW20 0EX, United Kingdom.

Tel: (44) 1784 414944
Email: rhps@rhul.ac.uk

Bedford Society Scholarship

Purpose: The scholarships are awarded to new full-time or part-time students with Home or International fee status who are studying for a taught Masters degree within one of the academic departments listed. The scholarships are funded by the alumni and friends of Bedford College, one of the founding colleges of Royal Holloway and Bedford New College. Formed in 2013, the Bedford Society aims to ensure the spirit of Bedford College lives on by providing new scholars with access to financial support and opportunities for networking.
Eligibility: You must have achieved, or be on target to achieve, a First Class Honours degree or equivalent (PDF link available in website). You must have a conditional or unconditional offer to study a Masters course within 1. Department of Classics. 2. Department of English. 3. Department of History. 4. Department of Languages, Literatures and Cultures. 5. Department of Economics. 6. Department of Law and Criminology. 7. Department of Politics, International Relations and Philosophy. 8. Department of Social Work. 9. Department of Biological Sciences. 10. Department of Earth Sciences. 11. Department of Geography. 12. Department of Psychology.
Level of Study: Masters Degree, Postgraduate
Type: Scholarships
Value: Scholarships are offered as a tuition fee reduction of £8,100
Country of Study: United Kingdom
Application Procedure: You must apply via our online system Royal Holloway Direct admissions.royalholloway.ac.uk/#/login, where you will be able to complete your statement and upload any required documents including your grades transcript. You must provide a supporting statement of no more than 400 words, which should include 1. Academic achievements you are particularly proud of and why these really matter to you. 2. Why you have chosen to do the degree you have applied for. 3. What your future aspirations are and how the scholarship will help you to achieve your future goals. 4. It should also demonstrate an enthusiastic and authentic spirit of enquiry and indicate clearly how this scholarship would help you share and advance knowledge of future generations. As well as your statement, you will need to upload your most recent grades transcript from your undergraduate degree.
No. of awards offered: 3
Closing Date: 3 July
Funding: Private
Contributor: Bedford College
Additional Information: For more information vist www.royalholloway.ac.uk/studying-here/fees-and-funding/postgraduate/scholarships/bedford-society-scholarships/

For further information contact:

Egham Hill, Egham TW20 0EX, United Kingdom.

Tel: (44) 1784 414944
Email: study@royalholloway.ac.uk

Brian Harris Scholarship

Purpose: The scholarship was established by entrepreneur Brian Harris to provide an opportunity for a student from a low-income background to study a Masters degree in History.
Eligibility: 1. You must be a full or part-time student from the UK applying for one of the following Masters degrees a. MA History. b. MA Public History. 2. To be eligible for the scholarship your focus of study, including the MA dissertation, must be on British and/or European History. 3. You are expected to have achieved, or be on target to achieve, at least a 21 degree or equivalent, with preference given to those with, or expected to achieve, a First Class Honours Degree. 4. You must be able to demonstrate financial need. 5. You must also hold a conditional or unconditional offer to study at Royal Holloway.
Level of Study: Postgraduate
Type: Scholarship
Value: Tuition fee reduction and contribution to living costs worth £10,000
Frequency: Annual
Country of Study: United Kingdom
Application Procedure: You will need to apply using our online system Royal Holloway Direct admissions.royalholloway.ac.uk/#/login. You must provide a supporting statement of up to 1,000 words which should include 1. How and why you feel you qualify for the scholarship. 2. What you want to achieve by completing a Masters in History. 3. Details of your career plans and how your degree will help you fulfil your goals. 4. Details of what you think you gained from your undergraduate degree. 5. Details of your educational

background prior to your undergraduate degree. 6. Details of both your academic and personal background, including financial need. 7. Evidence of resilience e.g. an example of a difficult period in your life, how you overcame it and what you learnt from your experience. 8. How you will give back to the university community. You must also provide 1. Evidence of the financial support you received at undergraduate level and the basis on which this was received and why. The sources this could be from are Student Finance England, Student Awards Agency Scotland, Student Finance Wales, Student Finance Northern Ireland, or a university-funded bursary (where this has been awarded on the basis of financial need). 2. Evidence of having achieved or expected to achieve a 21 or First Class undergraduate degree or equivalent. 3. An up-to-date CV. 4. You must provide two written academic references (up to 200 words each). These must be from academics who have previously supported, taught or worked with you. Please ask your reference to email their statement to RHPS@rhul.ac.uk directly. 5. The piece of work from your undergraduate degree that you are most proud of.
No. of awards offered: 2
Closing Date: 3 July
Additional Information: For more information www.royalholloway.ac.uk/studying-here/fees-and-funding/postgraduate/scholarships/brian-harris-scholarship/

For further information contact:

Egham Hill, Egham TW20 0EX, United Kingdom.

Tel: (44) 1784 434455
Email: study@rhul.ac.uk

Computer Science Scholarships

Eligibility: 1. International fee status. 2. Achieved a First Class Honours degree in a technical subject or 3. Achieved a First Class Masters Degree in a technical subject accompanied by a 2:1 Bachelors degree in any subject Studying one of the following degrees with the Department of Computer Science: 2a. MSc Artificial Intelligence b. MSc Computational Finance c. MSc Data Science and Analytics d. MSc Machine Learning.
Level of Study: Postdoctorate
Type: Scholarship
Value: Eligible Indian nationals who are domiciled in India (living in India at the point of application) will receive a £4,000 tuition fee reduction. All other eligible international students will receive a £2,000 tuition fee reduction.
Country of Study: United Kingdom
Application Procedure: All eligible applicants are automatically considered.

Dr Pirkko Koppinen Scholarship

Eligibility: 1. Home or international fee status 2. Achieved, or be expected to achieve, a 2:1 degree or higher 3. Offer to study MA Medieval Studies at Royal Holloway.
Eligible Country: United Kingdom
Level of Study: Postgraduate
Type: Scholarship
Value: £12,000
Country of Study: United Kingdom
Application Procedure: You must submit your application via RH Direct: admissions.royalholloway.ac.uk/#/login
Closing Date: 3 July
Additional Information: www.royalholloway.ac.uk/studying-here/fees-and-funding/postgraduate/scholarships/dr-pirkko-koppinen-scholarship/

For further information contact:

Email: rhps@rhul.ac.uk

Headley Trust Scholarship

Eligibility: 1. Living and educated in the UK 2. Offer to study MMus Music 3. Achieved, or expected to achieve, a First Class Honours degree.
Type: Scholarship
Value: £10,000 plus contribution to living costs.
Country of Study: United Kingdom
Application Procedure: You must submit your application via RH Direct: admissions.royalholloway.ac.uk/#/login
Closing Date: 3 July
Additional Information: www.royalholloway.ac.uk/studying-here/fees-and-funding/postgraduate/scholarships/headley-trust-scholarship/

For further information contact:

Email: rhps@rhul.ac.uk

Manju Mehrotra Scholarship

Eligibility: 1. Offer to study one of the following degrees: a. MSc Artificial Intelligence (including the Autonomous Intelligent Systems module) b. MSc Artificial Intelligence with a Year in Industry (including the Autonomous Intelligent Systems module) c. MSc Logistics and Supply Chain Management MSc Engineering Management d. MSc Project Management 2. Indian national, resident in India, with preference given to students with a connection to Uttar Pradesh. 3. Achieved, or be expected to achieve, a First Class Honours degree or equivalent.
Level of Study: Postgraduate

R

Type: Scholarship
Value: Tuition fee reduction of £10,000
Country of Study: United Kingdom
No. of awards offered: 2
Closing Date: March
Additional Information: royalholloway.ac.uk/studying-here/fees-and-funding/postgraduate/scholarships/manju-mehrotra-scholarship/

For further information contact:

Email: rhps@rhul.ac.uk.

Music Scholarships-Choral Scholarship

Level of Study: Postgraduate
Type: Scholarship
Value: up to £700 a year and performance opportunities for strong choral singers
Country of Study: United Kingdom
Application Procedure: You will need to follow the links below to complete an application form and submit a recording. Application www.chapelchoir.co.uk/apply. Submit as recording: www.royalholloway.ac.uk/studying-here/fees-and-funding/undergraduate/scholarships-and-bursaries/scholarships/music-scholarships/choral-scholarship/choral-scholarships-submit-recording/
Closing Date: 3 March
Additional Information: www.royalholloway.ac.uk/studying-here/fees-and-funding/undergraduate/scholarships-and-bursaries/scholarships/music-scholarships/choral-scholarship/

For further information contact:

Email: choraladmin@royalholloway.ac.uk

RHBNC Trust Scholarship

Purpose: These scholarships provide a tuition fee reduction and are for new full-time or part-time taught Masters students with Home or International status, studying for a postgraduate degree within one of the academic departments listed.
Eligibility: You must have achieved, or be expected to achieve, a First Class Honours degree or equivalent. This scholarship is open to Home and International fee paying students with a conditional or unconditional offer to study a course within 1. School of Business and Management. 2. Department of Drama, Theatre and Dance. 3. Department of Media Arts. 4. Department of Music. 5. Department of Computer Science. 6. Department of Electronic Engineering. 7. Department of Information Security. 8. Department of Mathematics. 9. Department of Physics. Only students applying to study for their first Masters degree will be considered for this scholarship.
Level of Study: Masters Degree, Postgraduate
Type: Scholarships
Value: Tuition fee reduction of £7,000 for taught postgraduate degrees in selected subjects
Frequency: Annual
Country of Study: United Kingdom
Application Procedure: You must apply via our online system Royal Holloway Direct admissions.royalholloway.ac.uk/#/login, where you will be able to complete your statement and upload any required documents including your grades transcript. You must provide a supporting statement of no more than 400 words, which should include 1. Academic achievements you are particularly proud of and why these really matter to you. 2. Why you have chosen to do the degree you have applied for. 3. What your future aspirations are and how the scholarship will help you to achieve your future goals. As well as your statement, you will need to upload your most recent grades transcript from your undergraduate degree.
No. of awards offered: 3
Closing Date: 3 July
Additional Information: www.royalholloway.ac.uk/studying-here/fees-and-funding/postgraduate/scholarships/rhbnc-trust-scholarship/

For further information contact:

Egham Hill, Egham TW20 0EX, United Kingdom.

Tel: (44) 1784 434455
Email: study@royalholloway.ac.uk

Royal Holloway Principal's Masters Scholarship

Eligibility: 1. Offer to study a taught postgraduate degree 2. (Home fee status) Achieved, or expected to achieve, a First Class Honours Degree. 3.(International fee status) Achieved, or expected to achieve the equivalent to a UK First Class degree, or a 2:1 degree in countries where an equivalent of a First is not possible.
Eligible Country: Any Country
Level of Study: Postgraduate
Type: Scholarship
Value: Tuition fee reduction of £4,000 for Home and International students.
Country of Study: United Kingdom
Closing Date: 3 July

Additional Information: www.royalholloway.ac.uk/studying-here/fees-and-funding/postgraduate/scholarships/royal-holloway-principals-masters-scholarship/

For further information contact:

Email: rhps@rhul.ac.uk

Royal Holloway, University of London MBA Programme

Application Procedure: Applicants must complete an application form
Closing Date: 30 June
Additional Information: studyabroad.shiksha.com/uk/universities/royal-holloway-university-of-london/mba-international-management

For further information contact:

School of Management Royal Holloway University of London, Egham TW20 0EX, United Kingdom.

Tel: (44) 1784 443 780
Fax: (44) 1784 439 854
Email: school-management@rhul.ac.uk

Sports Scholarships

Eligibility: 1. Offer to study any undergraduate or postgraduate degree at Royal Holloway 2. Competing in a BUCS recognised sport 3. Competing at minimum national level, with potential to represent internationally.
Value: Package of benefits to help talented student athletes balance sport and academic life at university.
Country of Study: United Kingdom
Closing Date: 12 May
Additional Information: royalholloway.ac.uk/studying-here/fees-and-funding/undergraduate/scholarships-and-bursaries/sports-scholarships/

For further information contact:

Email: sports@royalholloway.ac.uk

Royal Horticultural Society (RHS)

80 Vincent Square, London SW1P 2PE, United Kingdom.

Tel: (44) 20 3176 5800
Email: customercare@rhs.org.uk
Website: www.rhs.org.uk/
Contact: Secretary of RHS Bursaries Committee

The Royal Horticultural Society is the world's leading gardening charity. We aim to enrich everyone's life through plants, and make the UK a greener and more beautiful place - we are committed to inspiring everyone to grow. As a charity, we want to inspire a passion for gardening and growing plants, promote the value of gardens, demonstrate how gardening is good for us and explain the vital role that plants play.

Blaxall Valentine Bursary Fund

Purpose: To help finance horticultural study tours and projects that will provide real benefits to horticulture.
Eligibility: Open to applicants worldwide, but preference is given to UK citizens. Financial sponsorship will be available to both professional and amateur horticulturists and consideration for an award is not restricted to RHS members. Proposals may be made by individuals or group of individuals.
Level of Study: Unrestricted
Type: Bursary
Value: Funds are limited. High-cost projects are expected to receive supplementary finance from other sources, including personal contributions
Frequency: Annual
Country of Study: Any country
Application Procedure: Applicants must complete an application form downloaded from the RHS website www.rhs.org.uk/bursaries.
Closing Date: 30 September
Funding: Private
Additional Information: Please contact at for applying and deadline. bursaries@rhs.org.uk

Royal Horticultural Society Financial Awards

Purpose: To help finance horticulture-related projects and to further the interests of horticultural education along with horticultural work experience
Eligibility: Submissions are welcomed from applicants worldwide, but preference is given to United Kingdom and Commonwealth citizens. Applicants should preferably be within the age bracket of 20 and 35 years and satisfy the Society that their health enables them to undertake the project proposed. Financial sponsorship will be available to both

professional and amateur horticulturists, and consideration for an award is not restricted to RHS members. Proposals may be made by individuals or groups
Level of Study: Unrestricted
Type: Bursary
Value: Funds are limited. High-cost projects are expected to receive supplementary finance from other sources, including personal contributions
Frequency: Annual
Country of Study: Any country
Application Procedure: Applicants must complete an application form, available on request. Candidates may be called for interview
Closing Date: 30 September
Funding: Private
No. of awards given last year: 6
Additional Information: Recipients must submit a brief factual report within 3 months of completion, along with an outline of achievements or difficulties, including any unusual problems, e.g. medical or political, and an account of expenses bursaries@rhs.org.uk

Royal Horticulture Society Bursary Scheme

Purpose: To broaden skills, increase knowledge and enhance career opportunities related to Horticulture
Eligibility: United Kingdom citizens may apply for projects worldwide. Others may only apply for projects based in the United Kingdom
Level of Study: Unrestricted
Type: Bursary
Value: Funds are limited. High-cost projects are expected to receive supplementary finance from other sources
Frequency: Annual
Country of Study: United Kingdom
Application Procedure: Applicants must complete an application form downloadable from the RHS website www.rhs.org.uk/bursarie
Closing Date: 15 December
Funding: Private
Additional Information: www.rhs.org.uk/education-learning/bursaries-grants

For further information contact:

RHS Garden, Wisley, Woking, Surrey GU23 6QB, United Kingdom.

Email: bursanes@rhs.org.uk

Royal Irish Academy

19 Dawson Street, Dublin 2, D02 HH58, Ireland.

Tel: (353) 1 609 0600
Email: info@ria.ie
Website: www.ria.ie/
Contact: Ms Laura Mahoney, Assistant Executive Secretary

The Royal Irish Academy is Ireland's leading body of experts in the sciences and humanities. We identify and recognise Ireland's world class researchers. It was founded in 1785, with the Earl of Charlemont as first president. Its royal charter, granted the following year, declared its aims to be the promotion and investigation of the sciences, polite literature, and antiquities, as well as the encouragement of discussion and debate between scholars of diverse backgrounds and interests. We support scholarship and promote awareness of how science and the humanities enrich our lives and benefit society. The Academy is run by a Council of its members. Membership is by election and considered the highest academic honour in Ireland.

R.J. Hunter Research Bursary Scheme

Purpose: The R.J. Hunter Grants Scheme was established in 2014 using funding generously made available by his daughter, Ms Laura Hunter Houghton, through the Community Foundation for Northern Ireland.
Eligibility: 1. Researchers who are resident in Ireland (North or South) or Britain may apply 1a. Irish based researchers (including those based in Northern Ireland) may apply for funding for research in libraries, archives or museums within Ireland or abroad. 1b. British based researchers may only apply for funding for research in libraries, archives or museums in Ireland (including Northern Ireland). 2. We are seeking applications from researchers across all career stages 3. There is no requirement for an applicant to be a university graduate however applicants must demonstrate that their research is likely to constitute a significant and scholarly contribution to historical knowledge on aspects of Ulster History during the period 1500-1800. 4. Applications from researchers active in local learned and historical societies are welcome.
Level of Study: Postgraduate
Type: Bursary
Value: Maximum of €2,500
Country of Study: United Kingdom
Closing Date: 30 March

Additional Information: www.ria.ie/grants-and-awards/rj-hunter-research-bursary-scheme

For further information contact:

Email: grants@ria.ie

Royal Irish Academy Senior Visiting Fellowships

Purpose: To enable a new scientific research technique or development to be introduced into the Republic of Ireland
Eligibility: Open to senior researchers from member countries of the Organisation for Economic Co-operation and Development (OECD) only
Level of Study: Postdoctorate, Professional development
Type: Fellowship
Value: Varies
Frequency: Annual
Country of Study: Other
Application Procedure: Applicants must complete an application form
Closing Date: 15 October
Funding: Government
No. of awards given last year: 10
Additional Information: Senior Visiting Fellowships are made on behalf of the Irish government www.rics.org/en-in/news-insight/research/research-trust/

For further information contact:

Email: grants@ria.ie

Royal Literary Fund RLF

3 Johnson's Court, off Fleet Street, London EC4A 3EA, United Kingdom.

Tel: (44) 20 7353 7150
Email: rlitfund@btconnect.com
Website: www.rlf.org.uk/
Contact: Steve Cook, Fellowship Officer

The Royal Literary Fund is a British charity that has been supporting authors since 1790. The Royal Literary Fund is a benevolent fund for professional published authors; it is funded exclusively by bequests and donations from writers and others who wish to help writers. We provide grants and pensions to writers in financial difficulty: novelists, poets, playwrights, screenwriters and translators. As writers struggle in the current situation, we are here to help. We also run education programmes where writers deploy their talents for the wider benefit. Our Fellowship scheme funds writers to work one-to-one with university students. We also provide writing development workshops to schools and our community projects nurture resilience, engagement and empowerment.

Royal Literary Fund Grant

Purpose: To support prolific writers suffering financial hardship
Eligibility: You are eligible to apply for financial assistance if you have published several works.
Type: Grant
Value: £15,000
Length of Study: 36 weeks
Frequency: Annual
Country of Study: United Kingdom
Application Procedure: The application form requests details of income and expenditure and applicants are requested to send copies of published work with the completed form. For application form please contact Eileen Gunn and provide a list of your publications including names of publishers, dates, and whether sole author.
Closing Date: 8 April
Additional Information: www.rlf.org.uk/helping-writers/fellowships/

For further information contact:

The Royal Literary Fund, 3 Johnson's Court, London EC4A 3EA, United Kingdom.

Tel: (44) 20 7353 7159

R

Royal Melbourne Institute of Technology University

Info Corner - Office for Prospective Students, GPO Box 2476, Melbourne, VIC 3001, Australia.

Tel: (61) 3 9925 2000
Email: study@rmit.edu.au
Website: www.rmit.edu.au/

RMIT was established in 1887 as the Working Men's College with the aim of bringing education to the working people of Melbourne. RMIT University has excellent opportunities for talented employees across academic, professional, teaching and research areas. RMIT is a world leader in Art and Design; Architecture; Education; Engineering; Development; Computer Science and Information Systems; Business and Management; and Communication and Media Studies.

Aboriginal Social and Emotional Wellbeing Scholarship

Purpose: For Aboriginal and/or Torres Strait Islander students working, or intending to work in the social and emotional well-being workforce, enrolled in related programs; worth up to US$135,000 for tuition fees, SSAF and financial support.
Eligibility: Identify as Aboriginal and/or Torres Strait Islander have applied for admission or be continuing study in one of the following programs at RMIT with enrolments in semester 1, 2024 1. Bachelor of Applied Science (Psychology) 2. Bachelor of Social Science (Psychology) 3. Bachelor of Applied Science (Psychology) (Honours) 4. Bachelor of Social Work (Honours) 5. Bachelor of Youth Work and Youth Studies 6. Graduate Certificate in Domestic and Family Violence 7. Online Graduate Diploma in Psychology 8. Graduate Diploma in Mental Health Nursing 9. Master of Mental Health Nursing 10. Master of Clinical Psychology 11. Master of Social Work 12. be an Australian citizen or permanent resident13. be currently employed by an ACCO or a mainstream health organisation in a Victorian Aboriginal SEWB (social and emotional wellbeing) team or role OR 14. if not currently employed, intend to work in a Victorian Aboriginal SEWB team or role in the future.
Eligible Country: Australia
Type: Scholarship
Value: AU$12,000 to AU$31,000 per year. Student Services and Amenities fees (SSAF) paid, up to AU$326 per annum. Financial assistance of up to AU$10,000 per annum for full-time enrolment or AU$5,000 per annum for part-time enrolment, paid fortnightly.
Length of Study: 8 years
Country of Study: Australia
Closing Date: 30 January
Additional Information: www.rmit.edu.au/students/careers-opportunities/scholarships/coursework/sewb

For further information contact:

Tel: (61) 3 9925 2811
Email: scholarships@rmit.edu.au

Arcadia Landscape Architecture Scholarship in Landscape Architecture Design

Purpose: For Aboriginal and/or Torres Strait Islander student commencing a Bachelor of Landscape Architecture Design. If you are an Australian Aboriginal and/or Torres Strait Islander student commencing a Bachelor of Landscape Architecture Design, this scholarship could provide assistance for three years.
Eligibility: 1. Be an Aboriginal and/or Torres Strait Islander student 2. Be an Australian citizen 3. Be commencing full-time study in semester 1, 2024 in your first year of the Bachelor of Landscape Architecture Design (BP256) at RMIT University.
Type: Scholarship
Value: The scholarship provides AU$5,000 per year
Length of Study: 3 Years
Frequency: Annual
Country of Study: Australia
Closing Date: 14 January
Additional Information: www.rmit.edu.au/students/careers-opportunities/scholarships/coursework/arcadia

For further information contact:

124 La Trobe St, Melbourne, VIC 3000, Australia.

Tel: (61) 3 9925 2000
Email: scholarships@rmit.edu.au

Destination Australia Scholarship

Eligibility: To be eligible for this scholarship you must: 1. be an Australian citizen, an Australian permanent resident or a permanent humanitarian visa holder 2. be commencing full-time study in semester 1, 2024 in: a. Bachelor of Aviation (Pilot Training) (BP345) (scholarship application extended), or b. Associate Degree in Aviation (Professional Pilots) (AD023) (scholarship application closed) 3. be studying/taking the flying component at RMIT's Bendigo campus (not at RMIT's Point Cook campus) 4. be residing in a regional area 5. be committed to becoming a commercial pilot 6. interested after graduating in a flying career that includes regional Australia 7. Preference will be given to applicants who can demonstrate financial disadvantage.
Eligible Country: Australia
Type: Scholarship
Value: AU$15,000 per annum
Length of Study: 2 to 3 years
Country of Study: Australia

Application Procedure: Complete the online application by the close date: courseworkscholarshipsoffice.formstack.com/forms/destinationaustralia_2023
Closing Date: 13 March
Additional Information: www.rmit.edu.au/students/careers-opportunities/scholarships/coursework/destinationaustralia

Interior Design-Masters of Arts by Research

Purpose: To offer a space within which candidates develop and contribute to the knowledge and possibilities of interior design
Eligibility: Open to the candidates of any country who have a First Degree of RMIT with at least a credit average in the final undergraduate year or a deemed equivalent by RMIT to a First Degree of RMIT with at least a credit average in the final undergraduate year or evidence of experience
Level of Study: Postgraduate
Length of Study: 2 years full-time (Masters) and 4 years part-time (PhD)
Application Procedure: Check website for further details
Closing Date: 31 October
Funding: Government
Contributor: Commonwealth Government
Additional Information: Please check the website for more details www.rlf.org.uk/

For further information contact:

Tel: (61) 3 9925 2819
Email: suzie.attiwill@rmit.edu.au

Royal Melbourne Institute of Technology PhD Scholarship in the School of Electrical and Computer Engineering

Eligibility: To be eligible, you must be enroled in a higher degree by research (HDR) at the RMIT School of Electrical and Computer Engineering; be a top ranking student using the RMIT University Scholarships Ranking Model; awarded an APA or RMIT PhD Scholarship and/or an RTS place; be aligned to one of the school's areas of strategic focus; not previously have held any Electrical and Computer Engineering (ECE) scholarship over the past 3 years (or more); demonstrate excellent academic results and research capability
Type: Scholarship
Value: AU$12,000
Frequency: Annual
Country of Study: Australia
Application Procedure: International applicants are expected to apply for the RMIT International PhD Scholarship. If successful, the school may supplement the scholarship stipend
Additional Information: Preference will be given to PhD students but high ranking Masters by Research students may also be eligible for the top-up scholarship www.rmit.edu.au/study-with-us/levels-of-study/research-programs/phd/phd-electrical–electronic-engineering-dr220

For further information contact:

Tel: (61) 3 9925 3174
Email: elecengresearch@rmit.edu.au

Royal Over-Seas League ARTS

Over-Seas House, Park Place, St James's Street, London SW1A 1LR, United Kingdom.

Tel: (44) 20 7408 0214
Email: roslarts@rosl.org.uk
Website: www.rosl.org.uk/rosl-arts
Contact: Mandy Murphy, Administrative Assistant

The Royal Over-Seas League is dedicated to championing international friendship and understanding throughout the Commonwealth and beyond. A not-for-profit private members' club, we've been bringing like-minded people together since our launch in 1910. ROSL is a self-funded organisation which operates under a Royal Charter. ROSL ARTS A cultural organisation providing performance opportunities, and support for young musicians and artists throughout the commonwealth. ROSL's renowned ARTS programme has worked for nearly 70 years to support the careers of emerging talent in the fields of music, visual arts and literature, and the programme continues to grow. We run competitions, scholarships, residencies and concerts and events at our headquarters in London and around the world.

Royal Over-Seas League Annual Music Competition

Purpose: To support and promote young Commonwealth musicians
Eligibility: The age limit for all competitors is 30 years. The solo awards are open to UK and Commonwealth citizens, and

at least one member of an ensemble must also be a UK or Commonwealth citizen.
Level of Study: Professional development
Type: Competition
Value: The competition offers more than £75,000 in awards with a £15,000 first prize for solo performers and chamber ensemble awards of £10,000. The winners of the Wind and Brass, Singers, Strings, and Keyboard solo sections and the collaborative piano prize receive £5,000 each.
Frequency: Annual
Country of Study: Any country
Application Procedure: Applicants must see the website www.rosl.org.uk/amc/for-applicants
Closing Date: 6 January
Funding: Commercial, Individuals, Private, Trusts
No. of awards given last year: 19
No. of applicants last year: 500
Additional Information: www.rosl.org.uk/amc/for-applicants

For further information contact:

Royal Over-Seas League St James's St, Over-Seas House, Park Pl, London SW1A 1LR, United Kingdom.

Email: roslarts@rosl.org.uk

Royal Over-Seas League Travel Scholarship

Purpose: To support and promote young United Kingdom and Commonwealth artists
Eligibility: Open to citizens of Commonwealth, including the United Kingdom, and former Commonwealth countries, who are up to 35 years of age, on year of application
Level of Study: Graduate, Postgraduate, Professional development, Unrestricted
Value: £3,000
Frequency: Annual
Country of Study: United Kingdom or Commonwealth
Application Procedure: Applicants must see the website www.roslarts.co.uk
No. of awards offered: 450
Closing Date: 31 March
Funding: Commercial, Private, Trusts
No. of awards given last year: 5
No. of applicants last year: 450
Additional Information: Each artist may be represented by one recent work only, any medium. Works must not exceed 152 cm in their largest dimension, inclusive of frame

For further information contact:

Email: Membership@rosl.org.uk

Royal Scottish Academy (RSA)

The Mound, Edinburgh EH2 2EL, United Kingdom.

Tel: (44) 131 624 6110
Email: info@royalscottishacademy.org
Website: www.royalscottishacademy.org/
Contact: Secretary

The Royal Scottish Academy (RSA) was founded in 1826 by a group of eleven eminent artists. The RSA runs a year-round programme of exhibitions, artist opportunities and related educational talks and events which support artists at all stages of their careers. Over the last decade, every aspect of the RSA has been interrogated to ensure that the Academy remains relevant to the needs of today's artists and architects. Importantly, the Academy continues to evolve, electing new Members, exhibiting new work, developing its collections and supporting and promoting excellence in contemporary Scottish art and architecture.

The Barns-Graham Travel Award

Subjects: Painting, sculpture or printmaking
Purpose: The RSA Barns-Graham Travel Award provides a travel and research opportunity for graduating and postgraduate students.
Eligibility: 1. Entrants must be painters, printmakers or sculptors. 2. Entrants must either be undergraduates graduating in summer 2024 or currently studying at postgraduate level at one of the following Scottish art schools: Gray's School of Art, Aberdeen, Duncan of Jordanstone Collage of Art, Dundee, Edinburgh College of Art, Glasgow School of Art, and University of the Highlands & Islands.
Level of Study: Postgraduate
Type: Travel award
Value: £2,000
Frequency: Annual
Country of Study: Scotland
Application Procedure: Apply online. royalscottishacademy.submittable.com/submit. A collaborative application must only include one CV and be in keeping with the exact same guidelines and limits as a single artist application.
No. of awards offered: 1
Closing Date: 26 March
Funding: Trusts
Contributor: Barns-Graham Charitable Trust
Additional Information: Please see the website for further details www.royalscottishacademy.org/artist/rsa-barns-graham-travel-award/

For further information contact:

The Mound, Edinburgh EH2 2EL, United Kingdom.

Tel: (44) 131 624 6110
Email: opportunities@royalscottishacademy.org

The Royal Scottish Academy John Kinross Scholarships to Florence

Purpose: The RSA John Kinross Scholarships are for final year and postgraduate artists and architects to spend a period of 6 to 12 weeks in Florence to research and develop their practice.
Eligibility: 1. Applicants must be students in their Honours or Postgraduate years of study at one of the following art schools in Scotland Gray's School of Art, Aberdeen, Duncan of Jordanstone Collage of Art, Dundee, Edinburgh Collage of Art, Glasgow School of Art, and University of the Highlands and Islands. 2. Applicants must be RIBA Part 2 students in their final year, or currently attending a Masters programme, at one of the five Scottish Schools of Architecture. Group work is not admissible.
Level of Study: Masters Degree, Postgraduate
Type: Scholarship
Value: £3000 (Ten artists receive an initial payment of £2,800 for travel, accommodation and subsistence, with the remaining £200 awarded on the satisfactory completion of the scholarship.)
Length of Study: 6 to 12 weeks
Frequency: Annual
Country of Study: Scotland
Application Procedure: Apply online royalscottishacademy.submittable.com/submit
No. of awards offered: 12
Closing Date: 3 April
No. of awards given last year: 10
Additional Information: For more details www.royalscottishacademy.org/artist/the-rsa-john-kinross-scholarships/

For further information contact:

The Mound, Edinburgh EH2 2EL, United Kingdom.

Tel: (44) 131 624 6110
Email: opportunities@royalscottishacademy.org

The Royal Scottish Academy William Littlejohn Award for Excellence and Innovation in Water-Based Media

Purpose: To provide young professional artists who are Scottish or have studied in Scotland, with a period for personal development and the exploration of new directions
Eligibility: 1. Entrants must be working in water-based media (any pigment mixed with water). 2. Entrants must either be born in Scotland or have been resident in Scotland for at least 3 years. 3. In the case of students applying, entrants must either be graduating in 2023 or currently studying at post-graduate level at one of the following art schools in Scotland - Gray's School of Art, Aberdeen, Duncan of Jordanstone Collage of Art, Dundee, Edinburgh Collage of Art, Glasgow School of Art, and University of the Highlands and Islands.
Level of Study: Postgraduate
Type: Residency
Value: £2,000
Frequency: Annual
Study Establishment: Hospitalfield House, Arbroath
Country of Study: Scotland
Application Procedure: Applicants must contact the RSA
Funding: Private
Contributor: The Bequest Fund administered by the RSA
Additional Information: www.royalscottishacademy.org/opportunities/rsa-william-littlejohn-award/

For further information contact:

Email: opportunities@royalscottishacademy.org

The RSA David Michie Travel Award

Purpose: The RSA David Michie Travel Award (£2,500) provides a travel and research opportunity for graduating and postgraduate drawing and painting students
Eligibility: 1. Entrants must be painters. 2. Entrants must either be undergraduates graduating in summer 2024 or currently studying at postgraduate level at one of the following Scottish art schools: Gray's School of Art, Aberdeen, Duncan of Jordanstone Collage of Art, Dundee, Edinburgh College of Art, Glasgow School of Art, and University of the Highlands & Islands.
Type: Award
Value: £2,500
Country of Study: Any country
Application Procedure: Please read the guidelines on Submittable in full before applying: royalscottishacademy.submittable.com/submit Click here to apply: royalscottishacademy.submittable.com/submit
Closing Date: 26 March
Contributor: Michie Family and administered by the Royal Scottish Academy
Additional Information: www.royalscottishacademy.org/opportunities/rsa-david-michie-award/

For further information contact:

The Mound, Edinburgh EH2 2EL, United Kingdom.

Tel: (44) 131 624 6110
Email: opportunities@royalscottishacademy.org

Royal Society

6–9 Carlton House Terrace, London SW1Y 5AG, United Kingdom.

Tel: (44) 207 451 2500
Email: webmanager@royalsociety.org
Website: royalsociety.org/

The Royal Society is a Fellowship of many of the world's most eminent scientists and is the oldest scientific academy in continuous existence. The Society's fundamental purpose, reflected in its founding Charters of the 1660s, is to recognise, promote, and support excellence in science and to encourage the development and use of science for the benefit of humanity. The Society has played a part in some of the most fundamental, significant, and life-changing discoveries in scientific history and Royal Society scientists continue to make outstanding contributions to science in many research areas.

Charles Fleming Publishing Award

Purpose: To support the preparation of scientific books and relevant publications.
Eligibility: The fund will give preference to those who do not normally have access to funds through their place of employment for assisting with the writing and publication of their research or a review of a particular area of scientific endeavour.
Level of Study: Post graduate
Type: Award
Value: Up to NZ$8,000
Frequency: Annual
Country of Study: New Zealand
Application Procedure: A Charles Fleming Publishing Fund Application form (downloaded from website) must be completed. Applicants should 1. Describe the project for which the funding is being applied, and explain how funding will assist in meeting its objectives (1000 words maximum). Please include start and estimated end dates for the project. 2. Include a budget with details of other funding received or applied for. 3. Include a brief Curriculum Vitae (1 page) plus a list of any refereed publications for the previous 5 years. 4. Include contact details. Please email the application to awards@royalsociety.org.nz.
No. of awards offered: 1
Closing Date: 31 March
No. of awards given last year: 2
Additional Information: www.royalsociety.org.nz/what-we-do/funds-and-opportunities/charles-fleming-fund/charles-fleming-publishing-award/#:~:text=Annual%20award%20worth%20up%20to,of%20the%20Academy%20Executive%20Committee

For further information contact:

11 Turnbull St Thorndon, Wellington, 6011 Aotearoa, New Zealand.

Email: awards@royalsociety.org.nz

Charles Fleming Senior Scientist Award

Purpose: To support the research of a senior scientist at a university, Crown Research Institute, polytechnic or other research organisation in New Zealand, and that of their research group.
Eligibility: The fund will give preference to requests for research expenses over and above those that a university or Crown Research Institute in New Zealand would normally be expected to cover. Examples include expenses to 1. Cover a visit to an institution in New Zealand or overseas; 2. Expenses related to specialist assays or methodologies; 3. Research assistance to carry out a specific task; or 4. Expenses relating to a visit to the research group of a visitor.
Level of Study: Post Doctoral
Type: Grant
Value: Up to NZ$10,000
Frequency: Annual
Country of Study: New Zealand
Application Procedure: A Senior Scientist Application Form (downloaded from website) must be completed. Applicants should provide the following information 1. Project description (suitable for a non-specialist scientist; one page maximum); 2. Method, resources, collaboration (one page maximum, excluding references); 3. Expected outcomes from this project (This section should NOT be used to discuss scientific outcomes which should be covered in the previous two sections; one page maximum.); 4. Researcher experience; 5. Curriculum Vitae (one page maximum for each named research person); 6. Budget details and justification; 7. Approvals. Please email the application.
No. of awards offered: 1
Closing Date: 31 March
No. of awards given last year: 1
Additional Information: www.royalsociety.org.nz/what-we-do/funds-and-opportunities/charles-fleming-fund/charles-fleming-senior-scientist-award/

For further information contact:

11 Turnbull St Thorndon, Wellington, 6011 Aotearoa, New Zealand.

Email: awards@royalsociety.org.nz

Global Challenges Research Fund Challenge-led Grants (GCRF)

Purpose: The scheme provided funding to support research consortia involving groups in the UK and developing countries to address global challenges.
Eligibility: 1. Your proposed research must address two or more GCRF thematic areas. The proposal must ultimately benefit the economic development and welfare of developing countries (i.e. be compliant with the ODA guidelines). 2. Your proposal must fall within the remit of the United Kingdom academies and must be interdisciplinary. 3. The consortia must consist of one United Kingdom research group and two research groups from developing countries
Level of Study: Graduate
Type: Grant
Value: £500,000
Length of Study: 2.5 years
Country of Study: Any country
Application Procedure: Application should be submitted through the Royal Society's grants and awards management system (Flexi-Grant®). The weblink is www.grants.royalsociety.org/
Closing Date: 11 September
Funding: Private
Additional Information: royalsociety.org/grants-schemes-awards/grants/challenge-led-grants/

For further information contact:

Email: ChallengeGrants@royalsociety.org

Hutton Fund

Subjects: Zoology, Botany, Geology
Purpose: To encourage research in New Zealand zoology, botany and geology.
Eligibility: Please note that funding is not available for fees, thesis production or conference attendance.
Type: Grant
Value: NZ$1,000
Frequency: Annual
Country of Study: New Zealand
Closing Date: 31 March
Additional Information: www.royalsociety.org.nz/what-we-do/funds-and-opportunities/hutton-fund/

For further information contact:

Email: awards@royalsociety.org.nz

Industry Fellowships

Eligibility: You can apply for this scheme if you: 1. have a PhD or are of equivalent standing in your profession 2. hold a permanent post or have an 'open-ended contract' in either a university, not-for-profit research organisation or industry in the UK 3. are at a stage in your career when you would particularly benefit from establishing or strengthening personal or corporate links between academia and industry as a foundation for long-term collaboration and development
Level of Study: Doctorate
Type: Fellowship
Value: £4,000 per year
Country of Study: Scotland
Closing Date: 29 March
Additional Information: royalsociety.org/grants-schemes-awards/grants/industry-fellowship/

For further information contact:

Email: innovationgrants@royalsociety.org

International Exchanges

Eligibility: You can apply for this scheme if both you and the overseas co-applicant: 1. hold a PhD or have equivalent research experience 2. hold a fixed or permanent contract at an eligible organisation for the duration of the project (ineligible organisations include industrial, private and commercial organisations, university spin-out companies and government bodies) 3. are based in the respective countries at the time of the application.
Level of Study: Doctorate
Type: Fellowship
Value: up to £3,000 for one-off travel lasting up to three months, up to £6,000 for multiple visits to be completed within one year. up to £12,000 for multiple visits to be completed within two years
Length of Study: 2 years
Country of Study: Scotland
Closing Date: 8 March
Additional Information: royalsociety.org/grants-schemes-awards/grants/international-exchanges/

For further information contact:

Email: international.exchanges@royalsociety.org

Newton International Fellowships

Eligibility: To be eligible to apply you must: 1. have a PhD, or will have a PhD by the time the funding starts 2. have no

more than seven years of active full time postdoctoral experience at the time of application (discounting career breaks, but including teaching experience and/or time spent in industry on research) 3. be working outside the UK 4. not hold UK citizenship 5. be competent in oral and written English
Eligible Country: Any Country
Level of Study: Doctorate
Type: Scholarship
Value: £420,000
Length of Study: 3 years
Country of Study: United Kingdom
Closing Date: 28 March
Additional Information: royalsociety.org/grants-schemes-awards/grants/newton-international/

For further information contact:

Email: info@newtonfellowships.org

Olga Kennard Research Fellowship Scheme

Purpose: The Royal Society Olga Kennard Research Fellowship is a privately funded award through the University Research Fellowship for early career researchers working in the field of crystallography. This award is supported by a donation in the name of Professor Olga Kennard OBE FRS by the Cambridge Crystallographic Data Centre.
Eligibility: Applicants must be citizens of the EU, Norway, Israel or Switzerland. There are no UK residency requirements for this appointment. Applicants must have at least three years' postdoctoral experience and should be at least 26 years but should not have passed their 40th birthday on 1 October in the year of application
Level of Study: Postdoctorate
Type: Fellowship
Value: Salary with London allowance where appropriate, together with annual research expenses, travel expenses and a contribution to baggage costs for overseas applicants
Length of Study: 5 years
Study Establishment: Appropriate university departments
Country of Study: United Kingdom
Application Procedure: Applications can only be submitted online on the Royal Society's E-gap system. For further information on this scheme or the E-gap process, submit an enquiry to ukgrants@royalsoc.ac.uk
No. of awards offered: 1
Additional Information: Further information is available on the website www.royalsociety.org/people/olga-kennard-11735/, www.royalsociety.org/grants-schemes-awards/grants/university-research/jon-agirre/

For further information contact:

Tel: (44) 207 451 2547
Email: ukresearch.appointments@royalsoc.ac.uk

Raewyn Good Study Award for Māori and Pasifika Social Science Research

Subjects: Social Science
Purpose: For Māori and Pasifika postgraduate student undertaking a Master's which involves social sciences research.
Eligibility: Māori and Pasifika postgraduate students at any New Zealand university/wānanga
Level of Study: Postgraduate
Type: Grant
Value: NZ$6,000
Length of Study: 1 year
Frequency: Annual
Country of Study: New Zealand
No. of awards offered: 1
Closing Date: 31 August
Funding: Foundation
Additional Information: www.royalsociety.org.nz/what-we-do/funds-and-opportunities/raewyn-good-study-award/

For further information contact:

Email: awards@royalsociety.org.nz

RHT Bates Postgraduate Scholarship

Subjects: Physical Sciences and Engineering
Purpose: For a PhD in the Physical Sciences and Engineering in a New Zealand university.
Eligibility: Applicants must have physical sciences or engineering as a significant part of their undergraduate degree. For the purposes of this scholarship, physical sciences shall be deemed to mean physics, chemistry and mathematical and information sciences. At the time of application students must be engaged in postgraduate studies (honours, masters or doctorate). Students in their final year of undergraduate study are ineligible to apply.
Level of Study: Postgraduate
Type: Grant
Value: NZ$6,000
Frequency: Annual
Country of Study: New Zealand
No. of awards offered: 1
Closing Date: 31 August
Additional Information: www.royalsociety.org.nz/what-we-do/funds-and-opportunities/r-h-t-bates-postgraduate-scholarship/

For further information contact:

Email: awards@royalsociety.org.nz

Royal Society South East Asia Rainforest Research Project - Travel Grants

Eligibility: Open to scientists and nationals of European Union countries and South East Asia countries who are PhD or MSc students
Level of Study: Postgraduate
Type: Travel grant
Value: Economy air fare plus two weeks subsistence for European scientists travelling to South East Asia or three months subsistence for South East Asian scientists travelling to Europe
Length of Study: Varies
Country of Study: Other
Application Procedure: Applicants must apply for information, available on request from Programme Research Coordinator, Dr Stephen Sutton email sutton@hh.edi.co.uk

For further information contact:

Department of Zoology, University of Cambridge, Downing Street, Cambridge CB2 3EJ, United Kingdom.

Fax: (44) 8 988 4046
Email: ajdavis@pc.jaring.my

Sir Henry Dale Fellowships

Purpose: This scheme is for outstanding post-doctoral scientists wishing to build their own UK-based, independent research career addressing an important biomedical question. It supports research ranging from molecules and the cells vital to life, to the spread of diseases and vectors of disease around the world, to public health research.
Eligibility: You can apply for this scheme if you: 1. have a PhD and significant postdoctoral research experience have made important contributions to your area of research, eg publications, patents, software development or an impact on policy 2. have sponsorship from a head of department or equivalent at an eligible host organisation in the UK (applicants who want to be based in the Republic of Ireland should apply for a Research Career Development Fellowship instead) 3. are conducting research within the biomedical sciences and are aligned to the remit of one of the review panels.
Level of Study: Postdoctorate, Research
Type: Research grant
Value: The scheme covers 1. A basic salary for the Fellow, as determined by the host organisation. 2. Wellcome Trust fellowship supplement of £7,500 per annum for your personal support. 3. Research expenses, normally including research post (postdoctoral research assistant or technician)
Length of Study: 5 Years
Frequency: Every 5 years
Country of Study: Any country
Application Procedure: Applications should be submitted through the Wellcome Trust Grant Tracker (WTGT) wtgrants.wellcome.org/Login.aspx?ReturnUrl=%2f
Closing Date: 24 June
Additional Information: This scheme is not open to individuals who wish to combine research with a continuing clinical career in medicine, psychology, dentistry or veterinary practice. For more information royalsociety.org/grants-schemes-awards/grants/henry-dale/

For further information contact:

Tel: (44) 207 451 2500
Email: grants@royalsociety.org

Skinner Fund

Subjects: History, art, culture, physical and social anthropology of the Māori and other Polynesian people
Purpose: To encourage research in the study of the history, art, culture, physical and social anthropology of the Māori and other Polynesian people
Eligibility: The results of research aided by grants from the fund, shall, where possible, be published in New Zealand, with due acknowledgement of the source of financial assistance, and one copy of any report stemming from such research shall be sent to the Society.
Type: Grant
Value: NZ$1,000
Frequency: Annual
Country of Study: New Zealand
Closing Date: 31 March
Additional Information: www.royalsociety.org.nz/what-we-do/funds-and-opportunities/skinner-fund/

For further information contact:

Email: awards@royalsociety.org.nz

The Sir Hugh Kawharu Masters Scholarship for Innovation in Science

Subjects: Sciences
Purpose: Supporting and encouraging masters level study by Māori in the sciences

Eligibility: To be eligible applicants must be enrolled full-time in a one or two year masters degree in a science discipline; and be persons of Māori descent able to explain their tribal connections.
Level of Study: Masters
Type: Scholarship
Value: NZ$10,000
Length of Study: 1–2 Years
Frequency: Annual
Country of Study: New Zealand
No. of awards offered: 1
Funding: Foundation
Contributor: Sir Hugh Kawharu Foundation
Additional Information: www.royalsociety.org.nz/what-we-do/funds-and-opportunities/the-sir-hugh-kawharu-masters-scholarship-for-innovation-in-science/

For further information contact:

Email: awards@royalsociety.org.nz

Royal Society of Chemistry

Thomas Graham House (290), Science Park, Milton Road, Cambridge CB4 0WF, United Kingdom.

Tel: (44) 1223 420066
Website: www.rsc.org/

Our origins can be traced through the history of our predecessor societies: the Chemical Society, the Society for Analytical Chemistry, the Royal Institute of Chemistry and the Faraday Society. These four bodies merged in 1980 to form The Royal Society of Chemistry, which was granted a new Royal Charter in 1980. The Royal Society of Chemistry's purpose is to advance excellence in the chemical sciences – to improve the lives of people around the world now and in the future. As a not-for-profit organisation, we invest our surplus income to achieve our charitable objectives in support of the chemical science community and advancing excellence in the chemical sciences.

Royal Society of Chemistry Journals Grants for International Authors

Purpose: To allow international authors to visit other countries in order to collaborate in research, exchange research ideas and results, and to give or receive special expertise and training
Eligibility: Open to anyone with a recent publication in any of the Society's journals. Those from the United Kingdom or Republic of Ireland are excluded
Level of Study: Professional development
Type: Grant
Value: Up to £2,500 cover travel and subsistence (but not research related costs) and are available
Length of Study: Normally 1–3 months
Country of Study: Any country
Application Procedure: Candidates must apply for application forms, together with full details, from the International Affairs Officer
No. of awards offered: 107
Closing Date: 1 October
No. of awards given last year: 83
No. of applicants last year: 107
Additional Information: Please see the website for further details pubs.rsc.org/en/content/articlehtml/2003/dt/b211852c

Royal Society of Edinburgh

22-26 George Street, Edinburgh EH2 2PQ, United Kingdom.

Tel: (44) 131 240 5000
Email: scarcassonne@therse.org.uk
Website: www.rse.org.uk/
Contact: Sasha Carcassonne, Research Awards Officer

The RSE is an educational charity, registered in Scotland, operating on a wholly independent and non-party-political basis and providing public benefit throughout Scotland. The RSE was created in 1783 by Royal Charter for "the advancement of learning and useful knowledge" and since then have drawn upon the considerable strengths and varied expertise of our Fellows, of which there are currently around 1600, who are based in Scotland, the rest of the UK and beyond.

Royal Society of Edinburgh Personal Research Fellowships

Purpose: To provide outstanding researchers, who have the potential to become leaders in their chosen field, with the opportunity to build an independent research career
Eligibility: Open to persons of all nationalities who have 2 to 6 years postdoctoral experience. They must also show that they have the capacity for innovative research and the potential to become leaders in their field
Level of Study: Doctorate
Type: Fellowship
Value: Salary up to £55k plus research costs of £10k per year
Length of Study: 12 months
Frequency: Annual

Study Establishment: Any Higher Education Institution in Scotland
Country of Study: Scotland
Application Procedure: Applicants must complete an application form, available on the RSE website. Applicants should negotiate directly with their host institution
Closing Date: 28 March
Contributor: Scottish Government, BP and Caledonian Research Fund
Additional Information: Please note: this scheme is no longer running. www.rse.org.uk/awards/rse-personal-research-fellowships/

For further information contact:

22-26 George Street, Edinburgh EH2 2PQ, United Kingdom.

Email: Awards@theRSE.org.uk

RSE Fulbright Scholar Award

Purpose: We are delighted to accept applications for the RSE Fulbright Scholar Award, in partnership with the US-UK Fulbright Commission.
Eligibility: You are a resident in the UK and have a clear and continuing connection with Scotland and that you hold a PhD (or equivalent professional training or experience) in a relevant area before departure to the US.
Type: Award
Value: US$5,000 per month
Length of Study: Maximum 3 months
Country of Study: Any country
Closing Date: 8 November
Additional Information: https://rse.org.uk/funding-collaboration/fulbright-rse-scholar-award/

For further information contact:

Tel: (44) 131 240 5000
Email: fulbrightprogrammes@fulbright.org.uk.

RSE Research Network Grants

Purpose: RSE Research Network Grants are designed to create and/or to consolidate collaborative partnerships over a two-year period.
Eligibility: The awards are open to applications from Principal Investigators from all academic disciplines and all career stages who are eligible as one of the following a full or part-time academic in any academic discipline and are tenured and/or salaried staff of a Higher Education Institution (HEI), Research Institute (RI) or Cultural Institution (CI) in Scotland. Applicants must be on open-ended, continuing, or fixed-term contracts which extend three months beyond the end date of the envisaged grant period. The RSE grant cannot be used to extend an applicant's contract. a retired academic in any academic field who retains demonstrable links with a Scottish HEI, RI or CI with a demonstrable commitment to teaching and research within that institution. a full or part-time practitioner or research-active member of staff in any academic field employed by a Scottish Cultural Institution with a demonstrable commitment to teaching and research within that institution. Applicants on short or fixed-term contracts should ensure their contracts extend for at least three months after the end of the proposed project. Early career researchers on staged contracts to permanent lectureship positions are eligible but must be in contract for the duration of the award. Joint applications are accepted for the RSE Research Network Grants where there is evidence of the partners having worked together successfully previously to bring together complementary skills and expertise. Collaborations may be between Scottish or overseas HEIs and/or practitioners, policy makers, Research Institutions and Cultural Institutions provided that the lead applicant is based in Scotland; the key principles of the awards scheme are recognised; and the application is interdisciplinary. A new application will not be considered when a report on a previous RSE grant is overdue.
Type: Grant
Value: £20,000
Length of Study: 24 months
Country of Study: Any country
Closing Date: 28 March
Additional Information: rse.org.uk/funding-collaboration/award/rse-research-network-grants/

For further information contact:

Email: Awards@theRSE.org.uk

R

RSE Research Workshop Grants

Purpose: RSE Research Workshop Grants are designed to encourage collaborative investigation into a research proposition at an early stage of development.
Eligibility: The awards are open to applications from Principal Investigators from all academic disciplines and all career stages who are eligible as one of the following a full or part-time academic in any academic discipline and are tenured and/or salaried staff of a Higher Education Institution (HEI), Research Institute (RI) or Cultural Institution (CI) in Scotland. Applicants must be on open-ended, continuing, or fixed-term contracts which extend three months beyond the end date of the envisaged grant period. The RSE grant cannot be used to extend an applicant's contract. a retired academic in

any academic field who retains demonstrable links with a Scottish HEI, RI or CI with a demonstrable commitment to teaching and research within that institution. a full or part-time practitioner or research-active member of staff in any academic field employed by a Scottish Cultural Institution with a demonstrable commitment to teaching and research within that institution. Applicants on short or fixed-term contracts should ensure their contracts extend for at least three months after the end of the proposed project. Early career researchers on staged contracts to permanent lectureship positions are eligible but must be in contract for the duration of the award. Joint applications are accepted for the RSE Research Workshop Grants where there is evidence of the partners having worked together successfully previously to bring together complementary skills and expertise. Collaborations may be between Scottish or overseas HEIs and/or practitioners, policy makers, Research Institutions and Cultural Institutions provided that the lead applicant is based in Scotland; the key principles of the awards scheme are recognised; and the application is interdisciplinary. A new application will not be considered when a report on a previous RSE grant is overdue.
Type: Grant
Value: £10,000
Length of Study: 12 months
Country of Study: Any country
Closing Date: 28 March
Additional Information: rse.org.uk/funding-collaboration/award/rse-research-workshop-grants/

For further information contact:

Email: Awards@theRSE.org.uk

RSE Small Research Grants

Purpose: RSE Small Research Grants are designed to support personally conducted high-quality research. The awards are available to cover eligible costs arising from a defined research project.
Eligibility: The awards are open to applications from Principal Investigators from all academic disciplines and all career stages who are eligible as one of the following a full or part-time academic in any academic discipline and are tenured and/or salaried staff of a Higher Education Institution (HEI), Research Institute (RI) or Cultural Institution (CI) in Scotland. Applicants must be on open-ended, continuing, or fixed-term contracts which extend three months beyond the end date of the envisaged grant period. The RSE grant cannot be used to extend an applicant's contract. a retired academic in any academic field who retains demonstrable links with a Scottish HEI, RI or CI with a demonstrable commitment to teaching and research within that institution. a full or part-time practitioner or research-active member of staff in any academic field employed by a Scottish Cultural Institution with a demonstrable commitment to teaching and research within that institution. Applicants on short or fixed-term contracts should ensure their contracts extend for at least three months after the end of the proposed project. Early career researchers on staged contracts to permanent lectureship positions are eligible but must be in contract for the duration of the award. Collaborations may be between Scottish or overseas HEIs and/or practitioners, policymakers, Research Institutions and Cultural Institutions provided that the lead applicant is based in Scotland; the key principles of the awards scheme are recognised; and the application is interdisciplinary. A new application will not be considered when a report on a previous RSE grant is overdue.
Type: Grant
Value: £500 to £5,000
Length of Study: 12 months
Country of Study: Any country
Closing Date: 28 March
Additional Information: rse.org.uk/funding-collaboration/award/rse-small-grants/

For further information contact:

Tel: (44) 131 240 5000
Email: Awards@theRSE.org.uk

Royal Society of Medicine (RSM)

1 Wimpole Street, London W1G 0AE, United Kingdom.

Tel: (44) 20 7290 2900
Email: info@rsm.ac.uk
Website: www.rsm.ac.uk/
Contact: Awards Manager, Aldemic Department

The Royal Society of Medicine is a leading provider of high-quality continuing postgraduate education and learning to the medical profession. Its mission is to advance health, through education and innovation. Independent and apolitical, the RSM also aims to actively encourage and support those who are entering medicine and healthcare.

Adrian Tanner Prize

Purpose: To encourage surgical trainees to submit the best clinical case reports

Eligibility: Open to all surgical trainees.
Type: Prize
Value: £250
Frequency: Annual
Study Establishment: Royal Society of Medicine–Surgery section
Country of Study: United Kingdom
Application Procedure: Apply online www.rsm.ac.uk/prizes-and-awards/prizes-for-trainees/. Clinical case reports should be submitted for this prize focusing upon the multidisciplinary nature of the care of a surgical patient. The report should be no longer than 500 words and have a maximum of 5 references. Abstracts previously presented at another meeting should be declared.
Closing Date: 1 June
Additional Information: www.rsm.ac.uk/prizes-and-awards/prizes-for-trainees/

Alan Emery Prize

Purpose: To reward the best published research article in Medical Genetics in the past 2 years
Eligibility: Open to candidates in an accredited training or research post in the United Kingdom
Type: Prize
Value: £500 or £300 or 1 year membership of Royal Society of Medicine
Frequency: Annual
Application Procedure: Candidates must submit full copy of the article, curriculum vitae or covering letter explaining the significance of the publication
No. of awards offered: 7
Closing Date: 5 March
No. of awards given last year: 1
No. of applicants last year: 7

For further information contact:

Email: genetics@rsm.ac.uk

BMDST-RSM Student Elective Awards

Purpose: Medical and dental students of UK and other EU medical and dental schools intending to go on an elective including a research element in the next academic year
Eligibility: Medical and dental students of UK and other EU medical and dental schools intending to go on an elective including a research element in the next academic year
Type: Award
Value: Successful applicants will receive funding
Country of Study: Any country
Closing Date: 31 July
Additional Information: www.rsm.ac.uk/prizes-and-awards/prizes-for-students/

For further information contact:

1 Wimpole St, London W1G 0AE, United Kingdom.

Tel: (44) 20 7290 2900

Cardiology Section Presidents Prize

Purpose: The President's prize will be given for original research from specialist registrars in cardiology.
Eligibility: Open to Cardiology trainees who have received all or part of their training at recognised centres in the UK are eligible.
Level of Study: Research
Type: Prize
Value: 1st prize Medal and £1,000 and 2nd prize £500
Frequency: Annual
Country of Study: United Kingdom
Application Procedure: Please submit an abstract of no more than 200 words, based on a subject which represents original work. Apply online www.shocklogic.com/scripts/jmevent/Abstract.asp?Client_Id=%27RSM%27&Project_Id=%2706CDP234%27&System_Id=1
Closing Date: 9 April
Additional Information: www.rsm.ac.uk/prizes-and-awards/prizes-for-trainees/

Catastrophes & Conflict Forum Medical Student Essay Prize

Eligibility: Open to candidates who are enroled full-time at a United Kingdom medical school
Level of Study: Postgraduate
Type: Prize
Value: £250 plus encouragement and advice on submitting the essay for publication in the JRSM
Frequency: Annual
Study Establishment: Royal Society of Medicine
Country of Study: United Kingdom
Application Procedure: Candidates should submit an essay no longer than 1,500 words, emailed in Word format
No. of awards offered: 9
Closing Date: 1 March
No. of awards given last year: 2
No. of applicants last year: 9

For further information contact:

Email: catastrophes@rsm.ac.uk

Clinical Forensic and Legal Medicine Section Poster Competition

Purpose: Postgraduate students who have been working for qualifications in forensic and legal medicine or medical law to present a case or a poster in clinical studies
Eligibility: Open to anyone who is undertaking or has completed a post graduate qualification in a clinical forensic or legal field related to forensic medicine.
Level of Study: Postgraduate
Type: Prize
Value: £250
Frequency: Annual
Country of Study: United Kingdom
Application Procedure: Apply online www.shocklogic.com/scripts/jmevent/Abstract.asp?Client_Id=%27RSM%27&Project_Id=%2706CLP387%27&System_Id=1
Closing Date: 7 September
Additional Information: Students studying other specialities may submit their work to be considered for presentation purposes but are NOT eligible for the prize. All presenters will receive a certificate after the event. www.rsm.ac.uk/prizes-and-awards/prizes-for-trainees/

Clinical Forensics and Legal Medicine: Postgraduate Poster Prize

Eligibility: Postgraduate students who have been working for qualifications in forensic and legal medicine or medical law.
Type: Prize
Value: £250
Country of Study: Any country
Closing Date: 7 September
Additional Information: www.rsm.ac.uk/prizes-and-awards/prizes-for-students/

For further information contact:

1 Wimpole St, London W1G 0AE, United Kingdom.

Tel: (44) 20 7290 2900

Clinical Immunology & Allergy President's Prize

Purpose: To support training grade doctors, young scientists and medical students with an immunological or allergy component of their clinical research.
Eligibility: Open to training grade doctors and young scientists (not above Specialist Registrar, Grade B Clinical Scientist or equivalent grade) with an immunological or allergy component of their clinical research
Level of Study: Research
Type: Prize
Value: £300 (First prize); two prizes of £100 (Second prize)
Frequency: Annual
Country of Study: United Kingdom
Application Procedure: Check website for further details
No. of awards offered: 3
Closing Date: 19 January
No. of awards given last year: 3
Additional Information: www.rsm.ac.uk/prizes-and-awards/prizes-for-trainees/

Clinical Neurosciences Gordon Holmes Prize

Purpose: To award a research prize in clinical neurosciences
Eligibility: Trainees in neurosciences, including neurology, neurosurgery, neurophysiology, neuropathology or neuroradiology
Type: Prize
Value: £300
Frequency: Every 2 years
Country of Study: Any country
Application Procedure: Please check the website www.rsm.ac.uk/prizes-awards/trainees.aspx
Closing Date: 7 March
Additional Information: www.rsm.ac.uk/prizes-and-awards/prizes-for-trainees/

For further information contact:

Email: cns@rsm.ac.uk

Clinical Neurosciences President's Prize

Purpose: To encourage clinical neurosciences case presentation
Eligibility: Open to Trainees in all areas of clinical neurosciences, including neurology, neurosurgery, neurophysiology, neuropsychiatry, neuropathology or neuroradiology.
Type: Prize
Value: 1. Official President's prize Best oral presentation of case report(s) £300. 2. Live popular vote prize Certificate
Frequency: Every 2 years
Country of Study: United Kingdom
Application Procedure: The Clinical Neurosciences Section would like to welcome summary abstracts of up to

250 words of a clinical paper on an unusual case report or a short case series which should not be derived from a supervised research project. Please ensure your abstract is anonymous - i.e. your name and the name of the institution are not mentioned or included in the text.
Closing Date: 25 January
Additional Information: Please note: An individual can submit more than one case report but no more than one abstract will be eligible - abstract receiving the highest mark will be selected. www.rsm.ac.uk/prizes-and-awards/prizes-for-trainees/

Coloproctology John of Arderne Medal

Purpose: To award the presenter of the best paper presented at the short papers meeting of the section of coloproctology.
Eligibility: Open to all coloproctology and surgery trainees and medical students.
Type: Award
Value: The John of Arderne medal and a travelling fellowship
Frequency: Annual
Study Establishment: Varies
Country of Study: Any country
Application Procedure: Apply online. Abstracts should state briefly and clearly the purpose, methods, results and conclusions of the work and must not exceed 200 words.
Closing Date: 18 November
Additional Information: www.rsm.ac.uk/prizes-and-awards/prizes-for-trainees/

Critical Care Medicine Section: Audit and Quality Improvement Project Prize

Eligibility: All UK & Eire junior doctors in Intensive Care Medicine
Type: Prize
Value: annual subscription to CRIT-IQ (an excellent resource for the FFICM) and 1 year free RSM membership.
Country of Study: Any country
No. of awards offered: 3
Closing Date: 20 January
Additional Information: www.rsm.ac.uk/prizes-and-awards/prizes-for-trainees/

For further information contact:

1 Wimpole St, London W1G 0AE, United Kingdom.

Tel: (44) 20 7290 2900

Dermatology Clinicopathological Meetings

Eligibility: Open to all dermatology trainees.
Type: Prize
Value: First prize £50 and RSM certificate
Frequency: Annual
Country of Study: United Kingdom
No. of awards given last year: 1
Additional Information: For more details, please refer the website: www.rsm.ac.uk/prizes-and-awards/prizes-for-trainees/

Dermatology Section: Hugh Wallace Essay Prize

Eligibility: Dermatology registrars.
Type: Prize
Value: First prize £250
Country of Study: Any country
Closing Date: 10 March
Additional Information: www.rsm.ac.uk/prizes-and-awards/prizes-for-trainees/

For further information contact:

1 Wimpole St, London W1G 0AE, United Kingdom.

Tel: (44) 20 7290 2900

Dermatology Section: Trainee Research Prize

Eligibility: All dermatology trainees in the United Kingdom and Ireland. Newly qualified consultants whose research was completed as a trainee in the previous year are also eligible.
Type: Prize
Value: £250
Country of Study: United Kingdom
Closing Date: 31 March
Additional Information: www5.shocklogic.com/scripts/jmevent/Abstract.asp?Client_Id=%27RSM%27&Project_Id=%2706DER379%27&System_Id=1

Dermatology Section: Trainee Research Prize

Eligibility: All dermatology trainees in the United Kingdom and Ireland. Newly qualified consultants whose research was completed as a trainee in the year before the submission date.
Type: Prize
Value: First prize £250
Country of Study: Any country

R

Closing Date: 10 March
Additional Information: www.rsm.ac.uk/prizes-and-awards/prizes-for-trainees/

For further information contact:

1 Wimpole St, London W1G 0AE, United Kingdom.

Tel: (44) 20 7290 2900

Ellison-Cliffe Travelling Fellowship

Purpose: The award is intended to cover expenses for travel abroad, to one or two centres, for a period of not less than six months, in pursuit of further study, research or clinical training relevant to the applicant's current interests.
Eligibility: Fellows of the Royal Society of Medicine who are of specialist registrar or lecturer grade or equivalent, or who are consultants within three years of their first consultant appointment.
Type: Prize
Value: First prize £15,000
Country of Study: Any country
Closing Date: 4 October
Additional Information: www.rsm.ac.uk/prizes-and-awards/travel-grants-and-bursaries/

For further information contact:

1 Wimpole St, London W1G 0AE, United Kingdom.

Tel: (44) 20 7290 2900

Emergency Medicine Section: Innovation in ED Education for Students

Subjects: Students, nurses and doctors all grades working in Emergency Departments
Purpose: The aim of this prize is to recognise and promote educational initiatives in Emergency Departments.
Eligibility: The top 3 entrants will be invited to deliver a presentation on their initiative at a designated Emergency Medicine Section meeting at the Royal Society of Medicine.
Type: Prize
Value: £100
Country of Study: Any country
No. of awards offered: 3
Closing Date: 3 April
Additional Information: www.rsm.ac.uk/prizes-and-awards/travel-grants-and-bursaries/

Emergency Medicine section: Innovation in ED Education for Trainers

Purpose: The aim of this prize is to recognise and promote educational initiatives in Emergency Departments.
Eligibility: Students, nurses and doctors all grades working in Emergency Departments
Type: Prize
Value: £100
Country of Study: Any country
No. of awards offered: 3
Closing Date: 3 April
Additional Information: www.rsm.ac.uk/prizes-and-awards/prizes-for-trainees/

For further information contact:

1 Wimpole St, London W1G 0AE, United Kingdom.

Tel: (44) 20 7290 2900

Emergency Medicine Section: Innovation in ED Education Prize

Purpose: The aim of this prize is to recognize and promote educational initiatives in Emergency Departments.
Eligibility: Students, nurses and doctors all grades working in Emergency Departments
Type: Prize
Value: £100 will be awarded
Country of Study: Any country
No. of awards offered: 3
Closing Date: 3 April
Additional Information: www.rsm.ac.uk/prizes-and-awards/prizes-for-students/

For further information contact:

1 Wimpole St, London W1G 0AE, United Kingdom.

Tel: (44) 20 7290 2900

Emergency Medicine Section: Students' Prize for Students

Purpose: This prize is to contribute towards the cost of an elective abroad, with the intention of gaining experience in the practice of emergency medicine.
Eligibility: Medical students
Type: Prize
Value: £1 x £250 and one year
Country of Study: Any country

Closing Date: 3 April
Additional Information: www.rsm.ac.uk/prizes-and-awards/prizes-for-students/

For further information contact:

1 Wimpole St, London W1G 0AE, United Kingdom.

Tel: (44) 20 7290 2900

Emergency Medicine Section: Students' Prize for Trainers

Purpose: This prize is to contribute towards the cost of an elective abroad, with the intention of gaining experience in the practice of emergency medicine.
Eligibility: Medical students
Type: Prize
Value: £1 x £250 and one year
Country of Study: Any country
Closing Date: 3 April
Additional Information: www.rsm.ac.uk/prizes-and-awards/prizes-for-trainees/

For further information contact:

1 Wimpole St, London W1G 0AE, United Kingdom.

Tel: (44) 20 7290 2900

Epidemiology & Public Health Young Epidemiologists Prize

Purpose: To reward outstanding papers in epidemiology and public health section
Eligibility: Open to any medical and non-medical epidemiologist or public health practitioner under the age of 40 years.
Type: Award
Value: First prize £250
Frequency: Annual
Country of Study: United Kingdom
Application Procedure: Download the application form from website. Submit a 1,000-word paper addressing a public health issue which relates to a project conducted. Your paper should include an introduction, methodology used and results, discussion headings and a conclusion.
Additional Information: www.rsm.ac.uk/prizes-and-awards/prizes-for-trainees/

Gastroenterology & Hepatology Section: Gut Club Prize

Eligibility: Medical students and pre-registrar junior doctors
Type: Prize
Value: 1st prize - £100 and 50% discount on RSM membership for 1 year; Other Runners-up will receive 50% discount on RSM membership for 1 year
Country of Study: Any country
Closing Date: 10 February
Additional Information: www.rsm.ac.uk/prizes-and-awards/prizes-for-students/

For further information contact:

1 Wimpole St, London W1G 0AE, United Kingdom.

Tel: (44) 20 7290 2900

General Practice with Primary Healthcare John Fry Prize

Purpose: To award best examples of practice-based research involving members of the primary health and social community, demonstrating and promoting effective team work
Eligibility: Open to GP registrars, postgraduate students based in primary care, medical students and other undergraduates from professional groups involved in primary care and patients with experiences from primary care.
Type: Prize
Value: £300
Frequency: Annual
Country of Study: United Kingdom
Application Procedure: Title of the essay When Dr John Fry started his pioneering research he was a single handed GP. Today general practice is delivered by the primary care team comprising a broad group of healthcare professionals. Giving referenced examples, show how this has influenced current research in primary care. The essay submission should be between 2500-3000 words and well referenced. Apply online www5.shocklogic.com/scripts/jmevent/Abstract.asp?Client_Id=%27RSM%27&Project_Id=%2706GPQ231%27&System_Id=1
Closing Date: 1 July
Additional Information: www.rsm.ac.uk/prizes-and-awards/prizes-for-students/

For further information contact:

RSM, 1 Wimpole Street, Marylebone, London W1G 0AE, United Kingdom.

Geriatrics & Gerontology Section: Clinical Audit and Governance Prize

Eligibility: The prize is open to all trainees involved in the field of geriatrics and care of older people - including trainee nurses, allied health professionals and social workers.
Type: Prize
Value: First prize - for best oral presentation £100 and certification recognition and a 1-year membership to the British Geriatrics Society; First prize - for best poster presentation £50 and certification recognition and a 1-year membership to the British Geriatrics Society.
Country of Study: Any country
Closing Date: 14 February
Additional Information: www.rsm.ac.uk/prizes-and-awards/prizes-for-trainees/

For further information contact:

1 Wimpole St, London W1G 0AE, United Kingdom.

Tel: (44) 20 7290 2900

Geriatrics & Gerontology Section: President's Essay Prize for Students

Eligibility: Students or postgraduates of 5 years standing from disciplines involved in the care of older people
Type: Prize
Value: One year
Country of Study: Any country
Closing Date: 30 April
Additional Information: www.rsm.ac.uk/prizes-and-awards/prizes-for-students/

For further information contact:

1 Wimpole St, London W1G 0AE, United Kingdom.

Tel: (44) 20 7290 2900

Geriatrics & Gerontology Section: President's Essay Prize for Trainers

Eligibility: Students or postgraduates of 5 years standing from disciplines involved in the care of older people
Type: Prize
Value: One year
Country of Study: Any country
Closing Date: 30 April
Additional Information: www.rsm.ac.uk/prizes-and-awards/prizes-for-trainees/

For further information contact:

1 Wimpole St, London W1G 0AE, United Kingdom.

Tel: (44) 20 7290 2900

Geriatrics & Gerontology Section: Trainees' Prize, Clinical Presentations

Eligibility: Trainees in elderly medicine and old age psychiatry
Type: Prize
Value: First prize - for best oral presentation £100; First prize - for best poster presentation £50
Country of Study: Any country
Closing Date: 13 October
Additional Information: www.rsm.ac.uk/prizes-and-awards/prizes-for-students/

For further information contact:

1 Wimpole St, London W1G 0AE, United Kingdom.

Tel: (44) 20 7290 2900

Geriatrics & Gerontology Section: Trainees' Prize, Clinical Presentations for Trainers

Eligibility: Trainees in elderly medicine and old age psychiatry
Type: Prize
Value: First prize - for best oral presentation £100; First prize - for best poster presentation £50
Country of Study: Any country
Closing Date: 13 October
Additional Information: www.rsm.ac.uk/prizes-and-awards/prizes-for-trainees/

For further information contact:

1 Wimpole St, London W1G 0AE, United Kingdom.

Tel: (44) 20 7290 2900

History of Medicine Society: Norah Schuster Essay Prize

Purpose: This prize will be awarded for the best essay or essays submitted on any subject related to the history of medicine, including medical science.

Eligibility: Pre-clinical, clinical medical and dental students. Please note that you must be a medical student to be eligible to submit for this prize.
Type: Prize
Value: £100 Amazon voucher and a year's membership of the RSM
Country of Study: Any country
Closing Date: 17 January
Additional Information: www.rsm.ac.uk/prizes-and-awards/prizes-for-students/

For further information contact:

1 Wimpole St, London W1G 0AE, United Kingdom.

Tel: (44) 20 7290 2900

Laryngology & Rhinology Section: Rhinology Essay Prize

Purpose: This prize is to be awarded for an original essay on 'The nasal septum should never be touched before the age of sixteen. Discuss.'
Eligibility: All trainees and consultants within 1-2 years of appointment in the UK or Republic of Eire
Type: Prize
Value: £1,000
Country of Study: Any country
Closing Date: 25 March
Additional Information: www.rsm.ac.uk/prizes-and-awards/prizes-for-trainees/

For further information contact:

1 Wimpole St, London W1G 0AE, United Kingdom.

Tel: (44) 20 7290 2900

Laryngology & Rhinology Section: Short Paper and Poster Prize

Eligibility: All trainees and consultants within 2 years of appointment in the UK and Ireland.
Type: Prize
Value: 1st £250 and a year's free RSM membership 2nd £100 and a year's free RSM membership 3rd £50 and a year's free RSM membership
Country of Study: Any country
Closing Date: 25 March
Additional Information: www.rsm.ac.uk/prizes-and-awards/prizes-for-trainees/

For further information contact:

1 Wimpole St, London W1G 0AE, United Kingdom.

Tel: (44) 20 7290 2900

Laryngology & Rhinology Travel and Equipment Grants

Purpose: To assist with the cost of travel to overseas centres
Eligibility: Open to trainee RSM members with an interest in laryngology and rhinology who live–more than 50 miles from the RSM.
Level of Study: Postdoctorate
Type: Travel grant
Value: A grant of up to £100 towards attending a Laryngology and Rhinology meeting at the RSM
Frequency: Annual
Country of Study: United Kingdom
Application Procedure: Applicants should submit a letter of no more than two A4 pages in length detailing their expenses and which Laryngology & Rhinology meeting they would like to attend and why. Email your application letter to laryngology@rsm.ac.uk
Additional Information: Applications will be accepted up to two weeks before each meeting. www.rsm.ac.uk/prizes-and-awards/travel-grants-and-bursaries/

For further information contact:

Email: laryngology@rsm.ac.uk

Maternity & the Newborn Forum: Basil Lee Bursary for Innovation in Communication

Purpose: This bursary is to honour Basil Lee a GP who was a founding member of the Forum and an innovator in maternity care.
Eligibility: Students, trainees and other professionals who specialise in maternity and/or surrounding disciplines who are registered in the UK. Please note those who work for commercial operations will not be eligible for the bursary. This bursary is to enable the successful applicant to develop their new media skills which relate to the subject of maternity care or care of the newborn.
Type: Bursary
Value: £500 and a year's free RSM membership for students
Country of Study: Any country
Closing Date: 28 March
Additional Information: www.rsm.ac.uk/prizes-and-awards/travel-grants-and-bursaries/

For further information contact:

Email: maternity@rsm.ac.uk

Maternity & the Newborn Forum: Wendy Savage Bursary

Purpose: This bursary is to honour Wendy Savage, a long-standing member of the Forum and an innovator in maternity care.
Eligibility: Students, trainees and other professionals who specialise in maternity and/ or surrounding disciplines who are registered in the UK. Please note those who work for commercial operations will not be eligible for the bursary. The bursary is to enable the successful applicant to attend a conference to present a paper based on their research in the field of maternity care or care of the newborn.
Value: One prize of £750 to cover overseas travel or £500 to cover travel within the UK and a year's free RSM membership for students
Country of Study: Any country
Closing Date: 4 February
Additional Information: www.rsm.ac.uk/prizes-and-awards/travel-grants-and-bursaries/

For further information contact:

Email: maternity@rsm.ac.uk

Military Medicine Colt Foundation Research Prize

Purpose: To recognize the best abstract by a serving military medical officer
Eligibility: Open to medical officers in any training grade in general practice, occupational medicine, public health or hospital-based specialties.
Level of Study: Postgraduate
Type: Prize
Value: First prize £200 and Second prize Five £100 prizes
Frequency: Annual
Study Establishment: Royal Society of Medicine
Country of Study: United Kingdom
Application Procedure: Candidates should email the abstracts.
No. of awards offered: 6
Closing Date: 6 November
Funding: Foundation
Contributor: Colt Foundation
Additional Information: www.rsm.ac.uk/prizes-and-awards/prizes-for-trainees/

For further information contact:

Email: united.services@rsm.ac.uk

Nephrology Section Rosemarie Baillod Clinical Award

Purpose: To support trainees and research fellows in the area of clinical research, case series or individual case history in nephrology
Eligibility: Open to any trainees or fellows training in nephrology and wider specialties.
Level of Study: Research
Type: Research award
Value: £200
Frequency: Annual
Country of Study: United Kingdom
Application Procedure: Trainees and research fellows are invited to submit clinical abstracts in the area of clinical research, case series or individual case histories. Clinical cases or pedigrees should demonstrate novel clinical findings, illustrate classic conditions in new or unusual ways, and illuminate or expand knowledge concerning physiology, cell biology, genetics, radiology, or molecular mechanisms. Abstracts should be no more than 300 words. Submissions will be shortlisted for oral presentation at a Section meeting. The prize will be awarded to the best 15 minute presentation.
Additional Information: www.rsm.ac.uk/prizes-and-awards/prizes-for-trainees/

Obstetrics & Gynaecology Section: Dame Josephine Barnes Award

Eligibility: All medical students
Type: Prize
Value: £100
Country of Study: Any country
Closing Date: 21 January
Additional Information: www.rsm.ac.uk/prizes-and-awards/prizes-for-students/

For further information contact:

1 Wimpole St, London W1G 0AE, United Kingdom.

Tel: (44) 20 7290 2900

Obstetrics & Gynaecology Section: Herbert Reiss Trainees' Prize

Eligibility: SpRs in obstetrics and gynaecology
Type: Prize

Value: Oral first prize £150 Oral second prize £100 Poster first prize £100 Poster second prize £75
Country of Study: Any country
Closing Date: 14 January
Additional Information: www.rsm.ac.uk/prizes-and-awards/prizes-for-trainees/

For further information contact:

1 Wimpole St, London W1G 0AE, United Kingdom.

Tel: (44) 20 7290 2900

Occupational Medicine Section Malcolm Harrington Prize

Purpose: To award the work that is most likely to advance the study of occupational medicine in its broadest sense
Eligibility: Open to occupational physician in training or within an year of achieving specialist accreditation
Type: Prize
Value: £250
Frequency: Annual
Application Procedure: Candidates should submit an abstract of their own work (no longer than 200 words)
No. of awards offered: 9
Closing Date: 9 March
Funding: Private
Contributor: Professor Harrington
No. of awards given last year: 1
No. of applicants last year: 9

For further information contact:

Email: occupational@rsm.ac.uk

Oncology Section Sylvia Lawler Prize

Purpose: To encourage scientists and clinicians in training to present the best scientific paper and best clinical paper on oncology
Eligibility: Open to all clinicians in training
Type: Prize
Value: £250 to oral presenters
Frequency: Annual
Country of Study: United Kingdom
Application Procedure: Abstracts of no more than 200 words are invited from clinicians in training, themed on a clinical research project. Apply online www.rsm.ac.uk/prizes-and-awards/prizes-for-trainees/.
No. of awards offered: 6
Closing Date: 25 April
Additional Information: The top 6 abstracts (3x clinical, 3x scientific) will be selected for oral presentations; a panel of judges will determine the best oral presentation and 1 applicant will be awarded the Sylvia Lawler Prize for the best scientific paper and 1 applicant will be awarded the Sylvia Lawler Prize for the best clinical paper. www.rsm.ac.uk/prizes-and-awards/prizes-for-trainees/

Ophthalmology Section Travelling Fellowships

Purpose: To enable British ophthalmologists to travel abroad with the intention of furthering the study or advancement of ophthalmology, or to enable foreign ophthalmologists to visit the United Kingdom for the same purpose
Eligibility: Open to British based ophthalmologists travelling abroad and foreign ophthalmologists travelling to the UK.
Level of Study: Professional development
Type: Travelling fellowship
Value: Up to the value of £1,000 towards travelling abroad to further the study or advancement of ophthalmology.
Frequency: Every 2 years
Country of Study: Any country
Application Procedure: Submit a CV and an application letter detailing the intended purpose of travelling abroad, along with a budget outline of your travelling costs and any supporting statements and letters. Apply online www.shocklogic.com/scripts/jmevent/Abstract.asp?Client_Id=%27RSM%27&Project_Id=%2706OPP25A%27&System_Id=1
Closing Date: 1 May
Additional Information: Travelling Fellows may be required by the Ophthalmology Section Council to lecture at an Ophthalmology meeting on their experiences during the period of the award. www.rsm.ac.uk/prizes-and-awards/travel-grants-and-bursaries/

Oral & Maxillofacial Surgery Section: Short Paper Prize

Eligibility: All trainees in relevant specialties - to be eligible for the prize the candidate must be registered with the General Medical Council and/or the General Dental Council in the United Kingdom or be studying medicine or dentistry at a United Kingdom university. The candidate need not be a member of the Royal Society of Medicine. Candidates must register for and attend the meeting if short-listed.
Type: Prize
Value: £100
Country of Study: Any country
Closing Date: 11 September
Additional Information: www.rsm.ac.uk/prizes-and-awards/prizes-for-trainees/

R

For further information contact:

1 Wimpole St, London W1G 0AE, United Kingdom.

Tel: (44) 20 7290 2900

Oral & Maxillofacial Surgery Section: UMAX Poster Prize for students

Eligibility: All trainees without dual qualification including students as well as singly-qualified and second degree medical and dental students
Type: Prize
Value: 1 year
Country of Study: Any country
Closing Date: 26 February
Additional Information: www.rsm.ac.uk/prizes-and-awards/prizes-for-students/

For further information contact:

1 Wimpole St, London W1G 0AE, United Kingdom.

Tel: (44) 20 7290 2900

Oral & Maxillofacial Surgery Section: UMAX Poster Prize for trainers

Eligibility: All trainees without dual qualification including undergraduate students as well as singly-qualified and second degree medical and dental students
Type: Prize
Value: 1 year's RSM membership
Country of Study: Any country
Closing Date: 26 February
Additional Information: www.rsm.ac.uk/prizes-and-awards/prizes-for-trainees/

For further information contact:

1 Wimpole St, London W1G 0AE, United Kingdom.

Tel: (44) 20 7290 2900

Orthopaedics Section FOSC (Future Orthopaedic Surgeons Conference) Prize for Research for Students

Eligibility: 1. Medical Students 2. Foundation 1 and 2 doctors 3. Core surgical trainees
Type: Prize
Value: £100 cash prize for 1st place + and a 1-year subscription to the RSM £50 for the Runner up and a 1-year subscription to the RSM, which will be awarded at the FOSC
Country of Study: Any country
Closing Date: 28 January
Additional Information: www.rsm.ac.uk/prizes-and-awards/prizes-for-students/

For further information contact:

1 Wimpole St, London W1G 0AE, United Kingdom.

Tel: (44) 20 7290 2900

Orthopaedics Section FOSC (Future Orthopaedic Surgeons Conference) Prize for Research for Trainers

Eligibility: 1. Medical Students 2. Foundation 1 and 2 doctors 3. Core surgical trainees
Type: Prize
Value: £100 cash prize for 1st place + and a 1-year subscription to the RSM £50 for the Runner up and a 1-year subscription to the RSM, which will be awarded at the FOSC
Country of Study: Any country
Closing Date: 28 January
Additional Information: www.rsm.ac.uk/prizes-and-awards/prizes-for-trainees/

For further information contact:

1 Wimpole St, London W1G 0AE, United Kingdom.

Tel: (44) 20 7290 2900

Orthopaedics Section President's Prize Papers

Purpose: To encourage research in the area of Orthopaedics
Eligibility: Open to medical students and trainees.
Type: Prize
Value: First prize £600, Second prize £400 and Third prize £200
Frequency: Annual
Study Establishment: Royal Society of Medicine
Country of Study: United Kingdom
Application Procedure: Submit a 300-word abstract describing original (not previously published) work exploring clinical case studies and case reports. Apply online
No. of awards offered: 3
Closing Date: 20 October
Additional Information: www.rsm.ac.uk/prizes-and-awards/prizes-for-trainees/

Orthopaedics Section: President's Prize

Eligibility: Students and trainees
Type: Prize
Value: First prize £600 Second prize £400 Third prize £200
Country of Study: Any country
Closing Date: 14 January
Additional Information: www.rsm.ac.uk/prizes-and-awards/prizes-for-trainees/

For further information contact:

1 Wimpole St, London W1G 0AE, United Kingdom.

Tel: (44) 20 7290 2900

Otology Section Norman Gamble Grant

Purpose: This prize is awarded to the best original work in otology in the preceding four years, as evidenced by published papers.
Eligibility: Open to British citizens, both lay and medics.
Level of Study: Unrestricted
Type: Prize grant
Value: £100
Frequency: Annual
Country of Study: United Kingdom
Application Procedure: Submissions should include copies of these papers, along with a supporting letter from a proposer or a cover letter from the researcher themselves. Apply online
Closing Date: 1 May
Additional Information: www.rsm.ac.uk/prizes-and-awards/prizes-for-trainees/

Otology Section: Matthew Yung Short Paper and Poster Prize

Eligibility: All trainees and consultants within 2 years of appointment
Type: Prize
Value: 1st place £1,000 to be used in support of travel to centres of otology overseas 2nd place CWJ Short Fellowship to the International Otology Course at the Causse clinic in Beziers, France sponsored by the TWJ Foundation Poster prize ENT book to be confirmed
Country of Study: Any country
Closing Date: 21 January
Additional Information: www.rsm.ac.uk/prizes-and-awards/prizes-for-trainees/

For further information contact:

1 Wimpole St, London W1G 0AE, United Kingdom.

Tel: (44) 20 7290 2900

Otology Section: Training Scholarships

Eligibility: RSM Trainee Members interested in Otology
Type: Prize
Value: Up to £1,000
Country of Study: Any country
Closing Date: 26 January
Additional Information: www.rsm.ac.uk/prizes-and-awards/prizes-for-trainees/

For further information contact:

1 Wimpole St, London W1G 0AE, United Kingdom.

Tel: (44) 20 7290 2900

Paediatrics & Child Health Section: Overseas Bursary

Eligibility: Priority will be given to Paediatric Consultants in clinical practices who have not attended an overseas meeting in the past 5 years.
Type: Prize
Value: covering the registration fee plus a contribution of £500 towards travel and hotel costs
Length of Study: Six years
Country of Study: Any country
Application Procedure: Applicants should complete the submission form - detailing: 1. a brief description of the overseas conference they wish to attend- including title, dates and venue 2. a brief summary of no more than 500 words outlining why they wish to attend the conference and how will it benefit the work of their clinical teams 3. the conferences attended (both national and international) in the past 5 years.
No. of awards offered: 5
Closing Date: 23 April
Additional Information: www.rsm.ac.uk/prizes-and-awards/prizes-for-trainees/

Paediatrics & Child Health Section Trainees Tim David Prize

Purpose: To encourage research in the area of Paediatrics and Child Health

Eligibility: Open to medical trainees.
Level of Study: Research
Type: Prize
Value: First prize £250 and a year's free RSM membership Second prize £200 Third prize £150
Frequency: Annual
Country of Study: United Kingdom
Application Procedure: Submit a 750-word case report on a general paediatric case. A maximum of four general paediatric case reports will be shortlisted to presented at a Paediatrics & Child Health meeting. Apply online
Closing Date: 14 December
Additional Information: www.rsm.ac.uk/prizes-and-awards/prizes-for-trainees/

Paediatrics & Child Health Section: President's Prize for Students

Eligibility: Students and paediatrics trainees.
Type: Prize
Value: First prize £250 Second prize £150 The two runner ups will receive a £20 Amazon voucher
Country of Study: Any country
Closing Date: 18 January
Additional Information: www.rsm.ac.uk/prizes-and-awards/prizes-for-students/

For further information contact:

1 Wimpole St, London W1G 0AE, United Kingdom.

Tel: (44) 20 7290 2900

Paediatrics & Child Health Section: President's Prize for Trainers

Eligibility: Students and paediatrics trainees.
Type: Prize
Value: First prize £250 Second prize £150 The two runner ups will receive a £20 Amazon voucher
Country of Study: Any country
Closing Date: 18 January
Additional Information: www.rsm.ac.uk/prizes-and-awards/prizes-for-trainees/

For further information contact:

1 Wimpole St, London W1G 0AE, United Kingdom.

Tel: (44) 20 7290 2900

Pain Medicine Section: Andrew Lawson Prize

Eligibility: All medical students and trainees in pain medicine up to APT level, submissions from trainees of other specialities will also be accepted.
Type: Prize
Value: First prize £200 and one year free RSM membership and free attendance to the meeting Second prize £100 Third prize £50
Country of Study: Any country
Closing Date: 16 November
Additional Information: www.rsm.ac.uk/prizes-and-awards/prizes-for-students/

For further information contact:

1 Wimpole St, London W1G 0AE, United Kingdom.

Tel: (44) 20 7290 2900

Pain Medicine Section: Andrew Lawson Prize for Trainers

Eligibility: All medical students and trainees in pain medicine up to APT level, submissions from trainees of other specialities will also be accepted.
Type: Prize
Value: First prize £200 and one year free RSM membership and free attendance to the meeting Second prize £100 Third prize £50
Country of Study: Any country
Closing Date: 16 November
Additional Information: www.rsm.ac.uk/prizes-and-awards/prizes-for-trainees/

For further information contact:

1 Wimpole St, London W1G 0AE, United Kingdom.

Tel: (44) 20 7290 2900

Palliative Care Section MSc/MA Research Prize

Purpose: To support healthcare students and healthcare professionals with master's level research projects, quality improvement or audit in the field of palliative medicine.
Eligibility: Open to Healthcare students and healthcare professionals with master's level research projects, quality improvement or audit in the field of palliative medicine
Level of Study: Masters Degree

Type: Prize
Value: 1st prize - £250 plus a year's free membership, 2nd prize - £100, 3rd prize - £50 and Poster prize - £50
Frequency: Annual
Application Procedure: Submissions of abstracts for poster and/or oral presentations to showcase current research in palliative care from master's research or quality improvement/audit projects (no more than 300 words). Apply online.
No. of awards offered: 4
Closing Date: 15 October
Additional Information: www.rsm.ac.uk/prizes-and-awards/prizes-for-students/

Patient Safety Section: Student and Trainees' Prize

Eligibility: All students and trainees.
Type: Prize
Value: 1 year RSM membership and a cash award for outstanding contributions
Country of Study: Any country
Closing Date: 1 September
Additional Information: www.rsm.ac.uk/prizes-and-awards/prizes-for-trainees/

For further information contact:

1 Wimpole St, London W1G 0AE, United Kingdom.

Tel: (44) 20 7290 2900

Psychiatry Section Mental Health Foundation Research Prize

Purpose: This prize is to be awarded for the most outstanding published paper reporting original research work by the principal author in the last year.
Eligibility: Open to Juniors (excluding consultants or senior academic staff)
Type: Prize
Value: £750 and £100
Frequency: Annual
Country of Study: United Kingdom
Application Procedure: Entries should consist of a covering letter explaining, the significance of the publication and attachments of 1. The published article or the article and a letter of acceptance from the publisher. 2. A short CV of the applicant. Apply online.
Closing Date: 4 March
Additional Information: www.rsm.ac.uk/prizes-and-awards/prizes-for-trainees/

Radiology Section: Finzi Prize

Eligibility: All SpRs radiologists and radiotherapists training in the UK and Northern Ireland with a limit of one paper from each hospital
Type: Prize
Value: First prize £500
Country of Study: Any country
Closing Date: 27 February
Additional Information: www.rsm.ac.uk/prizes-and-awards/prizes-for-trainees/

For further information contact:

1 Wimpole St, London W1G 0AE, United Kingdom.

Tel: (44) 20 7290 2900

Radiology: BSHNI Annual Oral Presentation

Eligibility: All delegates (the presenting author should register for the meeting)
Type: Prize
Value: First prize £500, Second prize 2 x £125
Country of Study: Any country
Closing Date: 30 April
Additional Information: www.rsm.ac.uk/prizes-and-awards/prizes-for-trainees/

For further information contact:

1 Wimpole St, London W1G 0AE, United Kingdom.

Tel: (44) 20 7290 2900

Respiratory Medicine Section: Foundation Year and Internal Medicine Trainee Award

Eligibility: Junior doctors currently in foundation training or SHO level (IMT trainees, JCF, trust-grade SHO)
Type: Prize
Value: £100 and one free admission to an RSM Respiratory Section event
Country of Study: Any country
Closing Date: 1 December
Additional Information: www.rsm.ac.uk/prizes-and-awards/prizes-for-trainees/

For further information contact:

1 Wimpole St, London W1G 0AE, United Kingdom.

Tel: (44) 20 7290 2900

Respiratory Medicine Section: Respiratory Specialist Registrar Award

Eligibility: ST3 and above who have received all or part of their training in the UK. Registrars from any speciality may apply.
Type: Prize
Value: £100 and one free admission to an RSM Respiratory Section event
Country of Study: Any country
Closing Date: 1 December
Additional Information: www.rsm.ac.uk/prizes-and-awards/prizes-for-trainees/

For further information contact:

1 Wimpole St, London W1G 0AE, United Kingdom.

Tel: (44) 20 7290 2900

Respiratory Medicine Section: Student Award

Eligibility: All current UK medical students and FY1 doctors who completed the research whilst at medical school.
Type: Prize
Value: £100 and one year's free RSM membership
Country of Study: Any country
Closing Date: 1 December
Additional Information: www.rsm.ac.uk/prizes-and-awards/prizes-for-students/

For further information contact:

1 Wimpole St, London W1G 0AE, United Kingdom.

Tel: (44) 20 7290 2900

Rheumatology & Rehabilitation Section: Barbara Ansell Prize

Eligibility: Specialist registrars and research fellows in all specialities
Type: Prize
Value: First prize £200; Second prize £100; Third prize £50
Country of Study: Any country
Closing Date: 9 May
Additional Information: www.rsm.ac.uk/prizes-and-awards/prizes-for-trainees/

For further information contact:

1 Wimpole St, London W1G 0AE, United Kingdom.

Tel: (44) 20 7290 2900

Rheumatology & Rehabilitation Section: Eric Bywaters Prize

Eligibility: Specialist registrars, research fellows, scientists and allied health professionals in all specialities
Type: Prize
Value: First prize £200 Second prize £100 Third prize £50
Country of Study: Any country
Closing Date: 9 May
Additional Information: www.rsm.ac.uk/prizes-and-awards/prizes-for-trainees/

For further information contact:

1 Wimpole St, London W1G 0AE, United Kingdom.

Tel: (44) 20 7290 2900

Sexuality & Sexual Health Section: Medical Student Essay Prize

Eligibility: Medical students, all medical specialities, all training levels and allied health professionals.
Type: Prize
Value: First prize £250 and a year
Country of Study: Any country
Closing Date: 16 February
Additional Information: www.rsm.ac.uk/prizes-and-awards/prizes-for-students/

For further information contact:

1 Wimpole St, London W1G 0AE, United Kingdom.

Tel: (44) 20 7290 2900
Email: sexmed@rsm.ac.uk.

Sexuality & Sexual Health Section: Trainee Essay Prize

Eligibility: Medical students, all medical specialities, all training levels and allied health professionals.

Type: Prize
Value: First prize £250 and a year's free RSM membership Second prize A year's free RSM membership
Country of Study: Any country
Closing Date: 16 February
Additional Information: www.rsm.ac.uk/prizes-and-awards/prizes-for-trainees/

For further information contact:

1 Wimpole St, London W1G 0AE, United Kingdom.

Tel: (44) 20 7290 2900

Sleep Medicine Section: Student Essay Prize

Type: Prize
Value: First prize £300; Second prize £200 Third prize £100
Country of Study: Any country
Application Procedure: Pre-clinical, clinical medical and dental students
Closing Date: 7 December
Additional Information: www.rsm.ac.uk/prizes-and-awards/prizes-for-students/

For further information contact:

1 Wimpole St, London W1G 0AE, United Kingdom.

Tel: (44) 20 7290 2900

Surgery Section Norman Tanner Prize and Glaxo Travelling Fellowship

Purpose: To encourage clinical registrars submit the best clinical paper
Eligibility: Open to all surgical trainees.
Type: Prize
Value: £250 and the Norman Tanner Medal
Frequency: Annual
Country of Study: United Kingdom
Application Procedure: Candidates must submit clinically oriented papers detailing original clinical research, multi-disciplinary care and audit leading to improved patients' care. Submissions should be no longer than 500 words +/− 10%. Apply online.
Closing Date: 1 November
Additional Information: www.rsm.ac.uk/prizes-and-awards/prizes-for-trainees/

Trainees' Committee John Glyn Trainees' Prize

Purpose: The John Glyn trainees audit prize is awarded for an audit project undertaken during training.
Eligibility: Open to trainees working in any hospital or primary care specialty.
Type: Prize
Value: Oral presentation 1st - £250, 2nd - £100 Poster presentation 1st - £100, 2nd - £50
Frequency: Annual
Country of Study: Any country
Application Procedure: Submit a 200-word abstract describing an audit project that was undertaken during your training. The abstract should include the objective, methods used and results, discussion topics and conclusion. Applicants must be the primary authors of the original project. Apply online www.shocklogic.com/scripts/jmevent/Abstract.asp?Client_Id=%27RSM%27&Project_Id=%2706TRN224%27&System_Id=1
Closing Date: 30 June
Additional Information: www.rsm.ac.uk/prizes-and-awards/prizes-for-trainees/

Urology

Eligibility: Medical students and doctors not yet in core or specialist training
Type: Prize
Value: 1st: Up to £500, 2nd: £250, 3rd: £100
Country of Study: Any country
Closing Date: 31 March
Additional Information: www.rsm.ac.uk/prizes-and-awards/prizes-for-trainees/

For further information contact:

1 Wimpole St, London W1G 0AE, United Kingdom.

Tel: (44) 20 7290 2900

Urology Professor Geoffrey D Chisholm CBE Communication Prize

Purpose: To reward the best abstract at the Short Papers Prize Meeting
Eligibility: Open to urological trainees.
Type: Prize
Frequency: Annual
Country of Study: Any country
Application Procedure: Please send a brief abstract of no more than 200 words summarising your planned presentation. Apply online.

Closing Date: 24 March
Additional Information: www.rsm.ac.uk/sections/urology-section/, www.rsm.ac.uk/prizes-and-awards/prizes-for-trainees/

Urology Section Professor John Blandy Essay Prize for Medical Students

Purpose: To enable the holder to enhance his or her knowledge and experience by visiting an overseas unit
Eligibility: Medical students
Type: Fellowship
Value: A bursary of £1,000 and an RSM award certificate
Frequency: Annual
Closing Date: 8 March
Additional Information: Candidates must be available on the May 16th for presentation of their short paper to be eligible for this prize www.baus.org.uk/professionals/sections/essay_competition.aspx

For further information contact:

Email: urology@rsm.ac.uk

Urology Section Winter Short Papers Prize (Clinical Uro-Radiological Meeting)

Purpose: To reward the best clinicopathological short paper
Eligibility: Open to UK-based Urology Specialty or urologically inspired core surgical trainees.
Type: Prize
Value: 1. First prize £2,000 towards attending the Urology Section overseas winter meeting. 2. Second prize Campbell's Urology and RSM certificate. 3. Third prize Smith's Urology and RSM certificate.
Frequency: Annual
Country of Study: United Kingdom
Application Procedure: Submit a 250-word abstract on a topic such as latest academic or clinical research topics, interesting case collections in the context of diagnosis and management or audit projects and their application to urological practice. Apply online.
Closing Date: 18 September
Additional Information: Submissions must not have been presented previously at any national or international meeting. www.rsm.ac.uk/sections/urology-section/, www.rsm.ac.uk/prizes-and-awards/prizes-for-trainees/

Urology Section: Malcolm Coptcoat Spring Short Papers Prize

Purpose: The Malcolm Coptcoat Prize was established in the early 2000s to celebrate the enormous contribution of Malcolm Coptcoat to British Urology during his relatively short professional career. He was a great innovator and a pioneer of laparoscopic urology in the UK.
Eligibility: Urological trainees
Type: Prize
Value: First prize Up to £2,000; Second prize £750; Third prize £500
Country of Study: Any country
Closing Date: 15 February
Additional Information: www.rsm.ac.uk/prizes-and-awards/prizes-for-trainees/

For further information contact:

1 Wimpole St, London W1G 0AE, United Kingdom.

Tel: (44) 20 7290 2900

Urology Section: Secretary's Prize

Eligibility: All pre-SpRs training grades
Type: Prize
Value: First prize £200 plus an RSM certificate
Country of Study: Any country
Closing Date: 24 March
Additional Information: www.rsm.ac.uk/prizes-and-awards/prizes-for-trainees/

For further information contact:

1 Wimpole St, London W1G 0AE, United Kingdom.

Tel: (44) 20 7290 2900

Venous Forum: Annual Meeting Prize

Purpose: To recognize the best original paper in the field of venous disease
Eligibility: Open to medical students and trainees.
Type: Prize
Value: First prize £250, Second prize £200, Third prize £150 and Poster prize £200
Frequency: Annual
Country of Study: United Kingdom

Application Procedure: Submit a 250-word abstract on a topic relating to the Venous Forum annual meeting. The abstract should be structured to include aims, methods, results and conclusions. Apply online.
No. of awards offered: 4
Closing Date: 13 April
Additional Information: www.rsm.ac.uk/sections/venous-forum/, www.rsm.ac.uk/prizes-and-awards/prizes-for-trainees/

Royal Town Planning Institute (RTPI)

41 Botolph Lane, London EC3R 8DL, United Kingdom.

Tel: (44) 370 774 9494
Email: contact@rtpi.org.uk
Website: www.rtpi.org.uk/

The Royal Town Planning Institute (RTPI) was founded in 1914 and is a registered charity, leading membership organisation and a Chartered Institute responsible for maintaining professional standards and accrediting world class planning courses nationally and internationally.

George Pepler International Award

Purpose: The George Pepler International Award is a bursary granted biennially to a person in their first ten years of post-qualification experience wishing to undertake a short period of study (3-4 weeks) on a particular aspect of spatial planning. The study consists of live blog posts, images and video during the visit and a written report at completion.
Eligibility: Open to those that are wishing to travel to either the UK or anywhere in the world that supports their study.
Level of Study: Professional development, Research
Type: Bursary
Value: Up to £1,500
Length of Study: 3–4 weeks
Frequency: Every 2 years
Country of Study: Any country
Application Procedure: Applicants must submit a statement showing the nature of the study visit proposed, together with an itinerary. Application forms are available on request from the RTPI
Closing Date: 31 March
Funding: Private
Contributor: Trust fund
No. of awards given last year: 1
No. of applicants last year: 20
Additional Information: At the conclusion of the visit the recipient must submit a report. Please see the website for further details www.rtpi.org.uk/events-training-and-awards/awards/george-pepler-award/

For further information contact:

Email: marketing@rtpi.org.uk

Rural Health Information Hub

School of Medicine and Health Sciences, Suite E231, 1301 N. Columbia Road, Stop 9037, Grand Forks, ND 58202-9037, United States of America.

Tel: (1) 800 270 1898
Email: info@ruralhealthinfo.org
Website: www.ruralhealthinfo.org/

The Rural Health Information Hub, formerly the Rural Assistance Center, is funded by the Federal Office of Rural Health Policy to be a national clearinghouse on rural health issues. We are committed to supporting healthcare and population health in rural communities.

National Board for Certified Counselors Minority Fellowship Program for Mental Health Counselors

Purpose: The NBCC Foundation provides fellowships for master's and doctoral degree-level counseling students from minority backgrounds. The purpose of the program is to ensure that the behavioral health needs of all Americans are met, regardless of language or culture, thereby reducing health disparities and improving overall community health and well-being. For the purpose of this program, minorities include racial, ethnic, cultural, religious, gender, sexual orientation, rural, and military groups.
Eligibility: Eligible applicants are U.S. citizens or permanent residents that are currently enrolled and in good standing in an accredited graduate level counseling program. Other specific eligibility and service requirements are listed in the application instructions for master's level fellowships and doctoral level fellowships. Please check the website link for further details
Level of Study: Doctorate, Masters Degree

Type: Fellowship
Value: For masters degree-level students: 30 fellowships for US$10,000, plus travel expenses to participate in other program-related training. For doctoral degree-level students: 20 fellowships for US$20,000, plus travel expenses to participate in other program-related training.
Frequency: Annual
Country of Study: Any country
Application Procedure: Links to application instructions are available on the program website: nbccf.org/programs/scholarships.
No. of awards offered: 50
Closing Date: 31 December
Funding: Foundation
Contributor: National Board for Certified Counselors (NBCC) Foundation
Additional Information: Website: www.ruralhealthinfo.org/funding/4510

For further information contact:

NBCCF, 3 Terrace Way, Greensboro, NC 27403, United States of America.

Tel: (1) 336 232 0376
Email: foundation@nbcc.org

Rural Maternity Care Research

Suite 530-1501 West Broadway, Vancouver, BC V6J 4Z6, Canada.

Tel: (1) 604 742 1796
Email: leslie@ruralmatresearch.net
Website: www.ruralmatresearch.net

Rural Maternity Care Research is a team of academic and community based researchers interested in rural maternity care. They believe their diversity of expertise, backgrounds and interests enhance their ability to comprehensively investigate the complexity of challenges and opportunities for rural maternity care in British Columbia.

Rural Maternity Care Doctoral Student Fellowship

Purpose: To enable a motivated Doctoral student researcher to join the interdisciplinary team investigating rural maternity care in British Columbia
Eligibility: Open to citizens or permanent residents of Canada who are registered in a Doctoral programme in Canada
Level of Study: Doctorate
Type: Fellowship
Value: Up to CA$45,000 (benefits included)
Length of Study: 18 months
Frequency: Annual
Country of Study: Canada
Application Procedure: Applicants must include the following documents in the application cover letter, transcripts, curriculum vitae, contact information of 3 research referees and sample of the candidates writing preferably from an article published in a referred journal
Closing Date: 1 October
Additional Information: The fellow will be provided with office space in Vancouver, as well as access to and use of internet, printers and telephone and fax lines. Candidates from all academic disciplines are invited to apply. Candidates who may be completing coursework for their PhD programme, will be expected to contribute sufficient time to the RM-NET to develop a research focus area www.multicare.org/rural-fellowship/

For further information contact:

Email: clin2@cw.bc.ca

Ryerson University

350 Victoria Street, Toronto, ON M5B 2K3, Canada.

Tel: (1) 416 979 5000
Website: www.ryerson.ca/

Ryerson University is currently recognized as a leading institution for research and innovation, being ranked the top institution for undergraduate research in Canada. At Ryerson University we're dedicated to creating a culture of action. We believe that education and experience go hand-in-hand. What our students learn in the classroom is enhanced by real-world knowledge through internships and co-ops, or amplified through zone learning, specialized minors and graduate programs.

Autism Scholars Award

Purpose: With the support of the Ministry of Training, Colleges and Universities, a scholar awards program in autism has been established to ensure that Ontario attracts and retains

pre-eminent scholars. The community of autism scholars fostered by this awards program will excel, according to internationally accepted standards of scientific excellence, in the creation of new knowledge concerning child autism, and its translation into improved health for children, more effective services and products for children with autism, and increase the province's capacity in diagnosis and assessment of autism and a strengthened treatment system.
Eligibility: 1. An applicant must be a. A Canadian citizen or a permanent resident of Canada at the time of the application deadline. b. Registered as a full-time student in a master's or doctoral program at an Ontario university at the beginning of the award period, and remain registered as a full-time student throughout the term of the award. 2. A master's student remains eligible until the end of the sixth term of full-time study. 3. A doctoral student remains eligible until the end of the 15th term of full-time study. 4. During the year an Autism Scholars Award is held, the recipient is precluded from holding any other award that offers financial support of more than CA$20,000 for that same year (subject to the university's own policies).
Level of Study: Doctorate, Masters Degree
Type: Award
Value: Master awards - CA$18,000 Doctoral awards - CA$20,000
Frequency: Annual
Country of Study: Any country
Application Procedure: Each applicant must submit an electronic copy of the following documents in a single PDF package by December 1st to Natasha Mills. 1. The completed application form. 2. A curriculum vitae (including information concerning eligibility criteria). 3. A statement of research to be undertaken during the period of graduate study (maximum 1,000 words). There must also be an additional non-technical summary (maximum 500 words). These statements must be written by the candidate.
Closing Date: 1 December
Funding: International office
Additional Information: For further information visit www.ryerson.ca/graduate/future-students/financing-your-studies/scholarships-awards/autism-scholars-award/

For further information contact:

Email: ExecDirectorQA@cou.on.ca

C. Ravi Ravindran Outstanding Doctoral Thesis Award

Purpose: The C. Ravi Ravindran Outstanding Doctoral Thesis Award was established in 2008 (the 60th year of the creation of Ryerson as an educational institution) by his family in recognition of his long and distinguished industrial and academic career. This Award recognizes the excellence of the winning doctoral dissertation from the points of originality, contribution to better understanding of the theory, philosophy, science, practice or their interrelationship, application of theory and impact on society, industry or some aspect of national value.
Eligibility: 1. registration as a graduate studies student in a program of study leading to a PhD; 2. a nominated student must have applied to graduate at the upcoming Fall Convocation ceremonies or have already graduated at the previous Spring Convocation ceremonies; 3. one student may be nominated by a Program Director from each PhD program.
Level of Study: Doctorate
Type: Award
Value: CA$2,500
Frequency: Annual
Application Procedure: Please email your nomination to Natasha Mills.
No. of awards offered: 1
Closing Date: 31 March
Funding: Foundation
Additional Information: For more information: www.ryerson.ca/graduate/future-students/financing-your-studies/scholarships-awards/ravindran-outstanding-doctoral-thesis/

For further information contact:

Email: natasha.mills@ryerson.ca

Canada's Distinguished Dissertation Awards

Purpose: The CAGS/ProQuest Distinguished Dissertation Awards recognize Canadian doctoral dissertations that make unusually significant and original contributions to their academic field. They were established in 1994 and are presented annually
Eligibility: Eligible Dissertations include 1. A dissertation in any discipline in engineering, medical sciences, and natural sciences completed and accepted by the Graduate School between 1 January and 31 December. 2. A dissertation in any discipline in the fine arts, humanities, and social sciences completed and accepted by the Graduate School between 1 January and 31 December.
Level of Study: Graduate
Type: Award
Value: CA$1,500 prize, a Citation Certificate, and an awards ceremony at the CAGS Annual Conference in Quebec City.
Frequency: Annual
Country of Study: Any country
Application Procedure: Complete nomination packages must be received by YSGS as a single PDF document from

the nominating program, 1. A letter from the student's supervisor or program director describing the reasons for the nomination, and why the dissertation constitutes a significant piece of original work. 2. A copy of the external examiner's pre-defence report. The examiner's report must be dated and signed or otherwise authenticated by the Dean of Graduate Studies. 3. An abstract of the dissertation, not exceeding 350 words, written by the candidate in non-technical language. 4. An up-to-date c.v. of the nominee. Please submit required documents to Natasha Mills.
Funding: International office
Additional Information: For further details: www.ryerson.ca/graduate/future-students/financing-your-studies/scholarships-awards/distinguished-dissertation-awards/

For further information contact:

Email: info@cags.ca; natasha.mills@ryerson.ca

Doctoral Completion Award

Purpose: Funding amount is determined on a year-to-year basis and is a one-time-only award
Eligibility: In addition to graduate unit criteria, applicants for the DCA must be: 1. beyond the funded cohort as established by graduate unit practice 2. within time limit for the degree 3. in good academic standing as defined by the graduate unit 4. a full-time PhD or SJD student (DMA, EdD, and flexible-time PhD students are ineligible).
Level of Study: Doctorate
Type: Award
Value: Up to CA$10,000
Frequency: Annual
Country of Study: Any country
Closing Date: 19 November
Funding: International office
Additional Information: www.sgs.utoronto.ca/awards/doctoral-completion-award-dca/

Edward S. Rogers Sr. Graduate Student Fellowships

Purpose: The Edward S. Rogers Sr. Graduate School Fellowship, first awarded in 2001, was established by Ted and Loretta Rogers to honour the contributions of Edward S. Rogers Sr. to the Canadian communications industry. The fellowships are available annually to recognize the accomplishments of master's and doctoral level students in the Communication and Culture program who have demonstrated outstanding academic accomplishments in the communications field.
Eligibility: All Canadian PhD students in the Communication & Culture program.
Eligible Country: Canada
Level of Study: Doctorate
Type: Fellowship
Value: CA$20,000
Frequency: Annual
Country of Study: Canada
Additional Information: www.ryerson.ca/graduate/future-students/financing-your-studies/scholarships-awards/rogers-graduate-student-fellowships/

For further information contact:

Email: grdadmit@ryerson.ca

Fulbright Canada Scholarship

Purpose: The mandate of Fulbright Canada is to enhance mutual understanding between the people of Canada and the United States of America by providing support to outstanding graduate students, faculty, professionals, and independent researchers. These individuals conduct research, lecture, or enroll in formal academic programs in the other country. In doing so, Fulbright Canada aims to grow intellectual capacity, increase productivity, and assist in the shaping of future leaders in both countries.
Eligibility: 1. Be a Canadian citizen (Permanent residence is not sufficient). 2. Hold a Bachelor's degree prior to the proposed start date of the grant. 3. Be proficient in English. 4. Be in compliance with all J. William Fulbright Foreign Scholarship Board (FFSB) guidelines. 5. Be in compliance with all governmental regulations regarding visas, immigration, travel and residence.
Eligible Country: Canada
Level of Study: Graduate
Type: Scholarship
Value: Annual value CA$15,000
Frequency: Annual
Country of Study: Canada
Application Procedure: Applicants interested in applying for a Traditional Fulbright Student award are asked to complete an online application through the Embark system www.fulbright.ca/programs/canadian-students/traditional-awards/how-to-apply-traditional-fulbright-student-awards.html
Closing Date: 15 November
Funding: International office
Additional Information: www.ryerson.ca/graduate/future-students/financing-your-studies/scholarships-awards/fulbright-canada-scholarship/

Governor General Gold Medal

Purpose: The Governor General Gold Medal (GGGM), Ryerson University's most prestigious academic award, is awarded annually to the graduate student who achieves the highest academic standing in a graduate degree program
Eligibility: All master's and doctoral program students, who are in their first Master's or Doctoral program respectively, are eligible for this award. The student must have completed his/her program within the normal time frame (as deemed by the Yeates School of Graduate Studies)
Level of Study: Graduate
Type: Award
Value: No nominal value
Frequency: Annual
Country of Study: Any country
Application Procedure: Candidates must be nominated by their program. Please direct inquiries to Natasha Mills
Closing Date: 6 September
Funding: International office
Additional Information: www.ryerson.ca/graduate/future-students/financing-your-studies/scholarships-awards/governor-general-gold-medal/

For further information contact:

Email: natasha.mills@ryerson.ca

Graduate Student Stipend

Purpose: A graduate student stipend provides financial support to a graduate student while completing their graduate studies. Normally the stipend is paid from the research funding of a faculty supervisor. Stipends are not payment for employment
Level of Study: Graduate
Type: Stipendiary
Value: Dollar amounts vary by program and/or discipline
Frequency: Annual
Country of Study: Any country
Funding: International office
Additional Information: www.ryerson.ca/graduate/future-students/financing-your-studies/scholarships-awards/graduate-stipend/

For further information contact:

Email: grdadmit@ryerson.ca

John Charles Polanyi Prizes

Purpose: In honour of the achievement of John Charles Polanyi, recipient of the 1986 Nobel Prize in Chemistry, the Government of the Province of Ontario has established a fund to provide annually up to five (5) prizes to outstanding researchers in the early stages of their careers who are continuing to postdoctoral studies or have recently started a faculty appointment at an Ontario university. The John Charles Polanyi Prizes are available in the areas broadly defined as Physics, Chemistry, Physiology or Medicine, Literature and Economic Science
Eligibility: An applicant must 1. Be normally resident in Ontario; 2. Have received their doctoral degree from any recognized university in the world on or after September 1, 2017, or, if the doctoral degree has not yet been awarded, be confident that they will have completed all degree requirements by May 31, current year (an applicant who was on parental leave between the time of completion of the doctorate and the time of application may have their period of eligibility extended by six months); 3. Either be planning to continue to post-doctoral studies, or hold a faculty appointment, in a recognized publicly assisted university in Ontario.
Level of Study: Postdoctorate
Type: Grant
Value: Prizes have a value of CA$20,000 each.
Frequency: Annual
Country of Study: Any country
Application Procedure: All applicants must submit an electronic copy of the following documents in a single PDF package by December 1st to Natasha Mills. 1. The completed application form. 2. Curriculum vitae, including information concerning the application. Updates to curriculum vitae will not be accepted after submission. 3. A brief summary of the doctoral thesis (1 page, to be written by the applicant). 4. A statement of research (or writing) to be undertaken during the period of the award (maximum of 2 pages, plus an additional 1 page for diagrams, bibliography, etc., to be prepared by the applicant). 5. A non-technical summary (maximum 500 words, to be written by the applicant). 6. Confidential letters from four assessors. These should focus on an evaluation of the applicant's research (or writing) to date, and the research (or writing) being undertaken. The applicant must ask for the appraisals to be transmitted electronically directly to the Dean of Graduate Studies. Two of the assessors must not have been associated with the candidate as either a supervisor, or a member of the applicant's supervisory committee, or a co-author and should preferably be from another university.
No. of awards offered: 5
Closing Date: 1 December
Funding: Government
Contributor: The Government of the Province of Ontario
Additional Information: www.torontomu.ca/graduate/future-students/financing-your-studies/scholarships-awards/john-charles-polanyi-prizes/

For further information contact:

Email: natasha.mills@ryerson.ca

Sandbox Student Grant Program

Purpose: The DMZ Sandbox Student Grant Program (also known as the "Grant Program") will financially support and provide eligible Ryerson led startups with the crucial grant funding and mentorship they need
Eligibility: 1. The Grant Program is open for applications from Toronto Metropolitan undergraduate and graduate students registered in a full-time degree-granting academic program, or a recent (up to eight months after the date of graduation). Toronto Metropolitan graduate from a full-time undergraduate or graduate program. 2. The Toronto Metropolitan student or recent alumni applying must have at least a 25% stake in the company/solution/idea either as an inventor or founder. 3. Co-inventors, or co-founders must have the permission of their co-inventors/co-founders to apply and must demonstrate this permission through the inclusion of a letter of support for the application signed by the co-inventor/co-founders.
Level of Study: Postgraduate
Type: Grant
Value: Stage 1: up to CA$5,000 for 12 months Stage 2: up to CA$10,000 for 18 months Stage 3: up to CA$15,000 for 24 months.
Frequency: Annual
Country of Study: Canada
Closing Date: 29 January
Funding: International office
Additional Information: www.torontomu.ca/zone-learning/member-resources/awards-funding/zone-learning-awards/sandbox-student-grant-program/

For further information contact:

Email: sandbox@ryerson.ca

Senior Women Academic Administrators of Canada Awards

Purpose: The Senior Women Academic Administrators of Canada (SWAAC), organization was founded in 1987 to provide a forum and a collective voice for women in senior administrative ranks in Canadian universities, colleges and technical institutes. The primary purpose of SWAAC is the promotion of female leadership in Canadian universities, colleges and technical institutes.
Eligibility: Women registered in master's or PhD programs at any Member Institution of Universities Canada within a designated region are eligible to be nominated. Regions and number of awards are defined as follows, and eligibility shall rotate among them: 1. Ontario (2023) - five (5) awards 2. Western Provinces (2024) - four (4) awards 3. Quebec (2025) - four (4) awards 4. Atlantic Provinces (2026) - four (4) awards
Level of Study: Doctorate, Graduate, Masters Degree
Type: Award
Value: CA$4,000
Frequency: Annual
Country of Study: Canada
Application Procedure: Applicants must provide the following 1. Biographical data - includes information about former and current studies, areas of interest, research, publications, other awards, interests outside the university, and community or volunteer work. It's usually in a narrative form, about 1–2 pages in length, and is an opportunity for the nominee to tell the adjudication committee some things about herself, and to explain at greater length her background/interests/passions/ambitions/volunteer work. 2. Curriculum vitae. 3. All post-secondary transcripts. 4. Three letters of reference.
No. of awards offered: 4
Closing Date: 20 January
Funding: Foundation
Contributor: The Senior Women Academic Administrators of Canada (SWAAC)
Additional Information: www.ryerson.ca/graduate/future-students/financing-your-studies/scholarships-awards/swaac-awards/

For further information contact:

Email: natasha.mills@ryerson.ca

Social Sciences and Humanities Research Council Impact Awards

Purpose: SSHRC Impact Awards are designed to build on and sustain Canada's research-based knowledge culture in all research areas of the social sciences and humanities. The awards recognize outstanding researchers and celebrate their research achievements, research training, knowledge mobilization, and outreach activities funded partially or entirely by SSHRC.
Eligibility: A nominee must 1. Be a citizen or permanent resident of Canada at the time of nomination; 2. Be an active social sciences and humanities researcher or student; 3. Hold or have held SSHRC funding pertinent to the award category; 4. Be in good standing with SSHRC; 5. Be affiliated with an eligible institution; and 6. If the recipient of an award, maintain affiliation with an eligible institution for the duration of the award. Nominees 1. Cannot nominate themselves; 2. Can

be nominated in two sequential years for the same award, following which two years must pass before they can next be nominated in the same category; 3. Can be nominated in only one category in any year; and 4. Can be nominated in a subsequent year for a different SSHRC Impact Award. To be eligible to hold an award, winning institutions must provide SSHRC with a promotion strategy (two pages maximum) outlining a proposed approach for promoting and celebrating the impact and outcomes of the award winners' and project's achievements.
Eligible Country: Canada
Type: Award
Value: CA$50,000 or CA$100,000
Frequency: Annual
Country of Study: Canada
Application Procedure: Every nomination package must include all of the components listed below 1. Institutional nomination letter and rationale (three pages maximum). 2. Information supporting the nomination. 3. SSHRC CVs and consent forms. 4. Letters of support, two pages maximum each, from three referees. Please visit website for more information.
Closing Date: 1 April
Contributor: Social Sciences and Humanities Research Council
Additional Information: www.ryerson.ca/graduate/future-students/financing-your-studies/scholarships-awards/sshrc-impact-awards/

For further information contact:

Social Sciences and Humanities Research Council, 350 Albert Street, P.O. Box 1610, Ottawa, ON K1P 6G4, Canada.

Tel: (1) 613 943 7777
Email: impactawards-priximpacts@sshrc-crsh.gc.ca

The Dennis Mock Graduate Scholarship

Purpose: The Dennis Mock Graduate Scholarship is available annually to recognize the accomplishments of a first-year Master's student. This award was established in the name of Dennis Mock to honour his commitment to higher education, to recognize his leadership and dedication demonstrated during his 28 years at Ryerson, and to acknowledge his role in developing graduate studies at the university, as vice-president, academic. The funds have been provided by the Peter Bronfman Scholarship Program and the Ontario Student Opportunities Trust Fund.
Eligibility: Students must meet the following criteria: 1. Completion of an undergraduate degree program at TMU; 2. Full-time enrollment in the first year of a master's program at TMU, with a course load of at least two graded, one-term courses in the fall term; 3. First-time enrollment in a graduate program; 4. Canadian Citizen or Permanent Resident; 5. Must meet the Ontario Residency Requirement (see application form for details) and 6. Demonstrated financial need.
Eligible Country: Canada
Level of Study: Graduate
Type: Scholarship
Value: CA$5,000
Frequency: Annual
Country of Study: Canada
Application Procedure: Download and complete the application PDF file Dennis Mock Graduate Scholarship Application from website. Please email applications to g2guerci@ryerson.ca. The following must be included along with your application form 1. Graduate student budget form. 2. A grade report; RAMSS web version will suffice. 3. A progress report for fall 2023, signed by your Supervisor. Some programs/streams do not utilize progress reports. Please provide a note from your Program Director (www.ryerson.ca/graduate/contact/#tab-1466025665344-program-contacts) indicating this. 4. Please contact your Program Administrator (www.ryerson.ca/graduate/contact/#tab-1466025665344-program-contacts) if you require assistance regarding your grade report and progress report.
Closing Date: 17 March
Funding: Private, Trusts
Contributor: Peter Bronfman Scholarship Program and the Ontario Student Opportunities Trust Fund
Additional Information: NOTE: Incomplete applications will not be considered. Paper applications will NOT be accepted. www.ryerson.ca/graduate/future-students/financing-your-studies/scholarships-awards/dennis-mock-graduate-scholarship/

For further information contact:

Email: g2guerci@ryerson.ca

The Dennis Mock Student Leadership Award

Purpose: The Dennis Mock Student Leadership Awards recognize graduating students who have made outstanding voluntary extracurricular contributions to their school or academic program department, their faculty, or to Toronto Metropolitan University as a whole.
Eligibility: Graduating students who have made outstanding voluntary extracurricular contributions to their school or academic program department, their faculty, or to Toronto Metropolitan University as a whole
Level of Study: Graduate
Type: Award

Frequency: Annual
Country of Study: Any country
Application Procedure: The Dennis Mock Student Leadership Awards program recognizes graduating students who have made outstanding volunteer extracurricular contributions to their school, faculty or to the Toronto Met community as a whole. 1. Program/faculty-level: one recipient per program is recommended A. Faculty/staff do not need to submit formal nomination applications to our office - names of meritorious graduands is sufficient
Additional Information: Website: www.ryerson.ca/graduate/future-students/financing-your-studies/scholarships-awards/dennis-mock-student-leadership-award/

For further information contact:

Yeates School of Graduate Studies, 1 Dundas St. West (11th floor), Toronto, ON M5B 2K3, Canada.

Tel: (1) 416 979 5365
Email: awards@ryerson.ca

The Geoffrey F. Bruce Fellowship in Canadian Freshwater Policy

Purpose: Geoffrey F. Bruce was a distinguished Canadian, dedicated public servant and diplomat who devoted his career to advancing multilateral cooperation in pursuit of environmental protection and sustainable development practices. Geoffrey was passionate about the stewardship of Canadian water resources. The Geoffrey F. Bruce Fellowship is designed to generate research recommendations that shape public policy related to freshwater resources in Canada. Research projects should be rooted in the social sciences and contribute to interdisciplinary analysis and discussion of freshwater governance and policy in Canada.
Eligibility: 1. Projects must align with the spirit of the fellowship and relevant research areas. 2. Students at Ryerson University. 3. Graduate students involved in collaborative research co-supervised by Ryerson faculty.
Level of Study: Graduate
Type: Fellowship
Value: CA$25,000
Length of Study: 2 year
Frequency: Annual
Country of Study: Any country
Application Procedure: Interested applicants should submit an application package by September 30 including 1. Resume 2. Transcripts; 3. Statement of interest; 4. Two (2) letters of reference. All application documents can be submitted to Dr. Carolyn Johns.
Closing Date: 30 September
Additional Information: For more information www.ryerson.ca/graduate/future-students/financing-your-studies/scholarships-awards/geoffrey-bruce-fellowship/

For further information contact:

Dr. Carolyn Johns, Chair, Geoffrey F. Bruce Fellowship, Selection Committee, Ryerson University, 350 Victoria Street, Toronto, ON M5B 2K3, Canada.

Email: cjohns@ryerson.ca

The Hydro One Aboriginal Award for Graduate Studies in Public Policy and Administration

Purpose: The Hydro One Aboriginal Award for Graduate Studies in Public Policy and Administration provides financial assistance and recognizes the academic achievement of an Aboriginal student entering the Master of Arts in Public Policy and Administration program at Ryerson University.
Eligibility: To be eligible for this award, students must be of Aboriginal descent. In keeping with the admission requirements of the Master of Arts in Public Policy and Administration program and the requirements of the Ontario Trust for Student Support initiative (OTSS), the applicant must also have 1. A four year degree with a least a B+ average in the last two years of study; 2. Demonstrated competence in the English Language; 3. Canadian citizenship or be a protected person; 4. Ontario residency (in accordance with OTSS requirements); and 5. Demonstrated financial need as determined by Ryerson University.
Level of Study: Graduate
Type: Award
Value: Up to US$10,000
Frequency: Annual
Country of Study: Any country
Application Procedure: Applicants will need to supply A - one-page cover letter describing why they are an ideal candidate. The letter should address the applicant's reasons for pursuing graduate studies in this program, research interests which the applicant may wish to pursue, how the applicant's previous studies and experience have prepared him/her for the MA program, and the applicant's career objectives and how this program relates to them. 2. Three Letters of support from both academic and community-based references. A student may substitute one letter from an employer for one of the academic references. A letter of recommendation from an Aboriginal community or organization supporting the applicant's future contributions may enhance the award application. 3. Resume. 4. OTSS budget form.
No. of awards offered: 2
Funding: Private, Trusts

Contributor: Hydro One Networks Inc. and the Ontario Trust for Student Support (OTSS)
Additional Information: Applicants may be self-nominated, nominated by their peers or nominated by faculty or staff from the Department of Politics and Public Administration. Contact the program for deadline. The Committee will prepare a ranked list of qualified award recipients and will make the final selection of the recipient based on the weighted criteria. If, in the opinion of the selection committee, no applicants meet the outlined criteria, the award shall not be given to any applicant that year. www.torontomu.ca/graduate/future-students/financing-your-studies/scholarships-awards/hydro-one-indigenous-award/

For further information contact:

Tuna Baskoy, PhD, Department Chair, Ryerson University, Department of Politics & Public Administration, 350 Victoria Street JOR-700, Toronto, ON M5B 2K3, Canada.

Tel: (1) 416 979 5000 Ext 552702
Email: tbaskoy@ryerson.ca

The Pierre Elliott Trudeau Foundation Scholarship

Purpose: The award supports interdisciplinary research and original fieldwork by providing a substantial yearly allowance for research and travel, enabling the Scholars to gain first-hand contact with the diverse communities that can enrich their studies. Moreover, each Scholar is paired with a distinguished Trudeau Mentor selected by the Foundation among the most eminent Canadian practitioners in all sectors of public life. The Scholarship also offers the opportunity to interact with an exceptional community of leaders and committed individuals in every field of the social sciences and humanities, to participate in events organized by the Foundation and to hold their own workshops, through available financial support.
Eligibility: 1. Be a Canadian citizen or landed immigrant applying to a doctoral program in the social sciences and humanities or registered full-time in the first or second year of such a program at a Canadian university. OR; 2. Be a Canadian citizen applying to a doctoral program in the social sciences and humanities or registered full-time in the first or second year of such a program at a foreign university. OR; 3. Be a foreign national [with a preference for candidates from the developing world] applying to a doctoral program in the social sciences and humanities or registered full-time in the first or second year of such a program at a Canadian university. 4. Present a research project linked to one of the Foundation's four themes (Human rights and dignity; Responsible citizenship; Canada in the world; People and their natural environment). 5. Be nominated by a university.
Level of Study: Doctorate, Graduate
Type: Scholarship
Value: Annual value up to US$60,000 (including an annual travel allowance of US$20,000) per Scholar for a maximum of three years
Length of Study: 3 year
Frequency: Annual
Country of Study: Any country
Application Procedure: Interested students must complete and submit their electronic application package through the Trudeau Foundation website online application system by the internal deadline stated above. Create an account and follow instructions fdnpetf.smartsimple.ca/s_Login.jsp.
Closing Date: 21 December
Funding: International office
Additional Information: Ryerson can offer editorial support if applications are submitted to natasha.mills@ryerson.ca for review by December 14. www.ryerson.ca/graduate/future-students/financing-your-studies/scholarships-awards/trudeau-foundation/

For further information contact:

Natasha Mills, Coordinator, Graduate Scholarships and Awards, Yeates School of Graduate Studies, Ryerson University, 1 Dundas St. West (11th floor), Toronto, ON M5B 2K3, Canada.

Tel: (1) 416 979 5000 ext. 3648
Email: natasha.mills@ryerson.ca

The W. L. Mackenzie King Scholarships

Purpose: The Mackenzie King Scholarships were established as an independent trust under the will of the late Rt. Hon. William Mackenzie King (1874-1950). Two classes of Mackenzie King Scholarship are available to graduates of Canadian universities the Open Scholarship and the Travelling Scholarship. Both are to support graduate study.
Eligibility: 1. The Mackenzie King Open Scholarship is open to graduates of any Canadian university who engage in (commence or continue) graduate study (master's or doctoral) in any field, in Canada or elsewhere. 2. The Mackenzie King Travelling Scholarship is open to graduates of any Canadian university who engage in (commence or continue) postgraduate study (master's or doctoral) in the United States or the United Kingdom, of international relations or industrial relations (including the international or industrial relations aspects of law, history, politics and economics).
Level of Study: Doctorate, Masters Degree

Type: Scholarship
Value: 1. The Mackenzie King Open Scholarship - US$8,500 (value subject to change). 2. The Mackenzie King Travelling Scholarship - US$10,500 (value subject to change).
Frequency: Annual
Country of Study: Any country
Application Procedure: 1. The completed and signed application form (including attached sheets A and B as described on that form). 2. Three letters of reference from persons who have an intimate knowledge of your record and ability and are able to give a critical evaluation of your plans for graduate study. Note At least two of these testimonials must be from persons under whom you have taken your major work at university, or from senior colleagues with whom you have been associated in academic teaching or research. 3. Information for Referees Reference letters must be signed, dated, on letterhead and sent directly by the referee(s) to Natasha Mills - natasha.mills@ryerson.ca in a PDF format. 4. Certified copies or official transcripts of marks and other academic records from each university you have attended. If a transcript is not available, you may substitute a certified statement by the Registrar or the Faculty concerned. Each applicant must submit an electronic copy of their application (completed application form and certified or official transcripts) in a single PDF package by February 1 to Natasha Mills
No. of awards offered: 5
Closing Date: 1 February
Additional Information: Note: This is the internal YSGS Ryerson deadline for all candidates to submit their application packages. www.ryerson.ca/graduate/future-students/financing-your-studies/scholarships-awards/mackenzie-king/

For further information contact:

Email: natasha.mills@ryerson.ca

S

Sacramento State

6000 J Street, Sacramento, CA 95819, United States of America.

Tel: (1) 916 278 6011
Email: infodesk@csus.edu
Website: www.csus.edu
Contact: Timothy Hodson, Executive Director

Center for California Studies, CSU-Sacramento, California Legislature (CSUS) was founded in 1984. It is located on the capital campus of the California State University. Center for California Studies is a public service, educational support and applied research institute of CSUS. It is dedicated to promoting a better understanding of California's government, politics, people, cultures and history.

California Senate Fellows

Purpose: The California Senate Fellows program was established in 1973 to provide participants with insight into the legislative process. The fellowship program's primary goals include exposing people with diverse life experiences and backgrounds to the legislative process and providing research and other professional staff assistance to the Senate.
Eligibility: Anyone who will be at least 20 years of age and a graduate of a four-year college or university is eligible to apply. There is no preferred major. Individuals with advanced degrees and those in mid-career are encouraged to apply. Although no previous political or legislative experience is necessary, applicants should have a strong interest in public policy and politics. A five-week orientation provides background on state government, the legislative process, and major policy issues.
Level of Study: Professional development
Type: Fellowships
Value: Fellows receive a monthly stipend of US$2964 plus full health, vision and dental benefits.
Length of Study: 11 months
Frequency: Annual
Country of Study: United States of America
Application Procedure: Applicants can download the application form from the website
No. of awards offered: 18
Closing Date: 7 February
Funding: Government
Additional Information: sfela.senate.ca.gov/home

For further information contact:

1020 N Street, Room 525, Sacramento, CA 95814, United States of America.

Tel: (1) 916 651 4950
Email: Jamie.Taylor@sen.ca.gov

Jesse M. Unruh Assembly Fellowship Program

Purpose: The Assembly Fellowship seeks highly motivated individuals who are passionate about the state of California, public policy and politics. Fellowship alumni have gone on to positions of leadership in both the public and private sectors, including federal, state, and local elected office. The program successfully provides fellows with the professional development, support and mentorship needed to continue legislative work post-fellowship while also developing transferrable skills that can be applied to other career or academic pursuits.
Eligibility: 1. Be at least 20 years of age by September 1st of the fellowship year. 2. Have a bachelor's degree by September 1st of the fellowship year and either a cumulative undergraduate GPA of 2.5 or higher or a GPA of 2.5 or higher in the last 60 (semester) or 90 (quarter) units. 3. Demonstrated interest in state government and public policy. 4. Be authorized to work

Palgrave Macmillan (ed.), *The Grants Register 2024*,
https://doi.org/10.1057/978-1-349-96073-6

in the United States for the duration of the fellowship program.
Type: Fellowship
Value: Monthly stipend of US$3,253 and health, dental and vision benefits.
Length of Study: 11 months
Frequency: Annual
Study Establishment: Center for California Studies
Country of Study: United States of America
Application Procedure: Applicants must submit the following by the February deadline: 1. Completed online application at www.csus.edu/calst/assembly. 2. College transcript(s). 3. Personal statement and policy statement. 4. Three current, original letters of recommendation.
Closing Date: February
Additional Information: www.assembly.ca.gov/fellowship

For further information contact:

Email: Ambar.Carlisle@asm.ca.gov

Saint Louis University

1 N. Grand Blvd., St Louis, MO 63103, United States of America.

Tel: (1) 314 977 2500
Email: admission@slu.edu
Website: www.slu.edu/
Contact: MBA Admissions Officer

Saint Louis University is one of the nation's oldest and most prestigious Catholic universities. SLU, which also has a campus in Madrid, Spain, is recognized for world-class academics, life-changing research, compassionate health care, and a strong commitment to faith and service.

Saint Louis University International MBA Programme

Length of Study: More than 2 years
Country of Study: Any country
Application Procedure: Applicants must return a completed application, with personal essays, a non-refundable US$55 application fee, two letters of recommendation, official transcripts from all previously attended colleges and universities, Graduate Management Admission Test score, and a curriculum vitae. Overseas students must also provide evidence of financial support and a TOEFL score
Closing Date: 15 April

For further information contact:

Tel: (1) 314 977 3630
Fax: (1) 314 977 7188
Email: biib@slu.edu

Samuel H. Kress Foundation

174 East 80th Street, New York, NY 10075, United States of America.

Tel: (1) 212 861 4993
Email: info@kressfoundation.org
Website: www.kressfoundation.org/
Contact: Wyman Meers, Program Administrator

The Samuel H. Kress Foundation devotes its resources to advancing the study, conservation, and enjoyment of the vast heritage of European art, architecture, and archaeology from antiquity to the early 19th century.

History of Art Institutional Fellowships

Subjects: History
Purpose: The Kress History of Art Institutional Fellowships are intended to provide promising emerging art historians with the opportunity to experience just this kind of immersion.
Eligibility: Restricted to pre-doctoral candidates in the history of art and related disciplines (such as archaeology, architecture, or classics). Nominees must be U.S. citizens or individuals matriculated at an American university. Dissertation research must focus on European art from antiquity to the early 19th century and applicants must be ABD by the time their fellowship begins. Candidates must be nominated by their academic department. Each nomination should be formally confirmed in a letter of recommendation from the department chair.
Level of Study: Postdoctorate
Type: Fellowship
Value: US$30,000
Length of Study: 2 year
Frequency: Annual
Country of Study: United States of America
Application Procedure: Scholarship website: kressfoundation.fluxx.io/user_sessions/new
No. of awards offered: 6

Closing Date: 30 November
Funding: Foundation
Additional Information: www.kressfoundation.org/Programs/Fellowships/History-of-Art-Institutional-Fellowships

For further information contact:

174 East 80th Street, New York, NY 10075, United States of America.

Interpretive Fellowships at Art Museums

Subjects: Mentored professional development opportunity within American art museums
Purpose: The purpose of the Kress Interpretive Fellowships at Art Museums program is to provide a new kind of mentored professional development opportunity within American art museums.
Eligibility: Application must be made by the art museum proposing to host a Kress Interpretive Fellow. These Interpretive Fellowships are intended as an opportunity for individuals who have completed a degree (B.A., M.A., or Ph.D.) in art history, art education, studio art or museum studies and who are pursuing or contemplating graduate study or professional placement in these or related fields. The appropriate level of educational achievement will be determined by the host museum and be dependent upon the needs of the proposed fellowship project. The Fellowship candidate may be identified in advance of application by the host institution or recruited subsequently.
Type: Fellowship
Value: US$30,000
Length of Study: 9-12 month
Frequency: Annual
Country of Study: United States of America
Application Procedure: Scholarship website: kressfoundation.fluxx.io/user_sessions/new.
Closing Date: 1 April
Additional Information: www.kressfoundation.org/Programs/Fellowships/Interpretive-Fellowships-at-Art-Museums

Kress Conservation Fellowships

Purpose: The purpose of the Kress Conservation Fellowship program is to provide a wide range of post-graduate fellowship opportunities that will help develop the skills of emerging conservators.
Eligibility: Applications must be made by the museum or conservation facility at which the fellowship will be based. Prior to beginning the fellowship, fellows should have completed a masters-level degree in conservation. The fellowship candidate may be identified in advance of application by the host institution or recruited subsequently.
Level of Study: Postgraduate
Type: Fellowship
Value: US$37,000
Length of Study: 9 to 12 months
Frequency: Annual
Country of Study: United States of America
Application Procedure: The Kress Conservation Fellowships are administered by the Foundation for Advancement in Conservation (FAIC). Please visit the FAIC website for detailed application instructions. For answers to additional questions, you may also wish to review the Fellowship FAQs.
No. of awards offered: 6
Closing Date: 22 January
Funding: Foundation
Contributor: Foundation for Advancement in Conservation (FAIC)
Additional Information: www.kressfoundation.org/Programs/Fellowships/Conservation-Fellowships

San Antonio Nathan Shock Center

7703 Floyd Curl Drive, San Antonio, TX 78229, United States of America.

Tel: (1) 210 562 6140
Website: nathanshock.barshop.uthscsa.edu/

The San Antonio Nathan Shock Center provides critical support to investigators locally, nationally and abroad. With its existing and growing intellectual capital, the Center is poised to provide (1) an enhanced platform to conduct horizontally-integrated (lifespan, healthspan, pathology) transformative research in the biology of aging, and (2) a springboard for advanced educational and training activities.

S

Awards Supported by the San Antonio Nathan Shock Center

Subjects: Biomedical and Clinical; physiology; pharmacology; pathology
Purpose: To support the research of any investigator who is developing a new project in the basic biology of aging.
Eligibility: Any investigator who is eligible to receive NIH grants according to the rules of their home institution.
Type: Research grant
Value: Contingent on the availability of funds

Frequency: Annual, if funds are available
Study Establishment: Any US Academic Institution
Country of Study: United States of America
Application Procedure: The projects should utilize one or more Cores of the Center. Projects that propose creative uses of more than one Core are encouraged. Center Cores and their capabilities are listed at nathanshock.barshop.uthscsa.edu Applications must include a one-page hypothesis and specific aims of your project. Include a title for your project. This can be very brief, sufficient for the reader to understand the importance of what is being proposed. Specifics such as numbers of animals, etc., are not initially needed because this will be determined in conjunction with the Core Leaders if the proposal is selected for further consideration. Please indicate which Cores of the Center will be needed for your studies. It is strongly suggested that you contact the Core Leaders (see above) in advance of submitting your proposal. If you have consulted with one or more Core Leaders during the development of your proposal, please state it in your application. Please include your NIH biosketch and the biosketches of any proposed collaborators. A budget is not initially required. If your proposal is selected for further consideration, a budget will be developed based on a power analysis of the number of samples, animals, etc., that will be needed for the successful development of your project. The budget will be used for internal planning purposes only. Costs of the entire project, including purchase of animals and their housing, will be borne by the Center. Some parts of the project may be more appropriately performed in the applicant's lab, in which case it will be expected that the PI will bear the cost of those studies.
Closing Date: 15 April

San Francisco Foundation (SFF)

One Embarcadero Center, Suite 1400, San Francisco, CA 94111, United States of America.

Tel: (1) 415 733 8500
Email: info@sff.org
Website: www.sff.org

The San Francisco Foundation is one of the nation's largest community foundations - a grantmaking public charity dedicated to improving life within a specific local region. Our mission is to mobilize resources and act as a catalyst for change to build strong communities, foster civic leadership, and promote philanthropy in the San Francisco Bay Area.

Koshland Young Leader Awards

Purpose: It recognizes young leaders who balance extraordinary challenges, including family separation and homelessness, yet continue to show academic promise and community leadership.
Eligibility: 1. be a junior in a San Francisco Unified School District High School. 2. have demonstrated academic excellence (at least a 3.0 cumulative GPA) and be college-bound. 3. have demonstrated significant leadership in their community, school, work, and/or home including active participation in school clubs, sports, volunteer work, religious community, college prep programming, family responsibilities, etc. 4. have overcome significant hardship (e.g., unstable housing, non-native English speaker, economic insecurity, health issues, immigrant story, family situation, etc.). 5. have a recommendation from a teacher, counselor, school administrator, or college prep program staff who can speak to their qualifications.
Level of Study: Postgraduate
Type: Award
Value: US$10,000
Frequency: Annual
Country of Study: United States of America
Application Procedure: Scholarship website: sff.submittable.com/submit
No. of awards offered: 11
Closing Date: 7 April
Funding: Foundation
Contributor: San Francisco Foundation
No. of awards given last year: 11
Additional Information: sff.org/what-we-do/leadership-programs-awards/kyla/

San Francisco State University (SFSU)

1600 Holloway Avenue, San Francisco, CA 94132, United States of America.

Tel: (1) 415 338 1111
Email: outreach@sfsu.edu
Website: sfsu.edu/

SF State is a major The University offers comprehensive, rigorous, and integrated academic programs that require students to engage in open-minded inquiry and reflection. SF State encourages its students, faculty, and staff to engage fully with the community and develop and share knowledge.

Robert Westwood Scholarship

Purpose: To assist SFSU students who are living with HIV and plan to make a contribution in any field to communities affected by HIV
Level of Study: Postgraduate
Type: Scholarship
Value: US$1,000
Frequency: Annual
Study Establishment: San Francisco State University
Country of Study: United States of America
Application Procedure: Applicants must submit a copy of the most recent SFSU academic transcript, along with a brief, typed essay discussing plans to incorporate academic work and degree at SFSU with service in the HIV community or in the area of HIV prevention
Closing Date: 7 May
Additional Information: Applicants must submit a verification from the physician sfsu.academicworks.com/opportunities/2089

For further information contact:

Tel: (1) 415 338 7339
Email: mritter@sfsu.edu

Sanskriti Pratishthan

Head Office C-11 Qutab Institutional Area, New Delhi, Delhi 110016, India.

Tel: (91) 8130968700
Email: kendra@sanskritifoundation.org
Website: www.sanskritifoundation.org

Sanskriti Pratishthan is a non-profit organization established in 1978. Sanskriti Pratishthan perceives its role as that of a catalyst, in revitalizing cultural sensitivity in contemporary times.

Geddes Scholarship

Purpose: The objective of the scholarship is to promote and advance interest in and understanding of Patrick Geddes' principles of town planning. This scholarship will provide an opportunity to create awareness among young planners and architects of Geddes' principle of 'place, work, and folk'.
Eligibility: The scholarship is only open to Indian Nationals in the age group of 20 to 30. The applicant must be a student of planning and architecture at a graduate/postgraduate/research level from a recognized university or institution and /or young practicing professionals. The applicants can be an individual or can be a collaborative work of a group of individuals.
Level of Study: Professional development
Type: Scholarships
Value: ₹45,000 will be given in two phases
Length of Study: 6 months
Frequency: Annual
Country of Study: India
Application Procedure: Interested Candidates should send a two page with full postal, telephone and email details. The proposal should not merely be a compilation of reports but should contain a well researched proposal which would advance the application of the Geddes ideas, a plan of action including field visits and the availability of archival material relevant to that study. A bibliography of the reports, websites browsed should accompany the proposal. The proposal can also focus on a section of the city/mohalla. The applicant has to expose the methodology of diagnostic survey and conservative surgery as a visible strategic option for the renewal of cities in India. Priority will be given to such proposals which traces and advances the relevance of Geddes' ideas and work The project proposal should be written in 1500 words with reference to the specific city /section/mohalla. The names and contact addresses/telephone of two referees should also be sent. The application should bear the title 'Sanskriti – Geddes Scholarship' on the envelope if sent by post on head office address and in the subject line if e-mailed on fellowships@sanskritifoundation.org
Funding: Foundation
Additional Information: www.sanskritifoundation.org/Geddes-Fellowship.htm

For further information contact:

Sanskriti Kendra / Sanskriti Museums, Anandagram, Mehrauli Gurgaon Road, Opposite Metro Pillar No. 165, Nearest Metro Station Arjangarh, New Delhi, Delhi 110047, India.

Tel: (91) 11 2696 3226, 2652 7077 / 8130968700
Email: info@sanskritifoundation.org

Kalakriti Fellowship in Indian Classical Dance

Purpose: The purpose is to encourage young artists to develop their potential and enhance their skills through intensive practice and or incorporating different facets of their art.

S

Eligibility: 1. The fellowship is only open to Indian Nationals in the age group of 25 to 40. 2. While this fellowship specially encourages women applicants, all proposals that further the objectives of the program are welcome. The candidate should have at least ten years of initial training in Indian classical dance. The fellow would be required to have given at least 2-3 solo performances to his/her credit in recognized forums. 3. The candidate will be required to take guidance from another senior guru and enhance the existing style. It would be a residency programme for a period of three months, which can be spread over the period of ten months. This will require the candidate to take consent from her current guru and the guru he/she would want to go to.
Level of Study: Professional development
Type: Fellowships
Value: ₹50,000 in two instalments
Length of Study: 10 months
Frequency: Annual
Country of Study: India
Application Procedure: Candidates should send their two page CV and a write up of approximately 500 words explaining their project. Full postal and telephonic contact details together with any e-mail address should be submitted to facilitate contact. Few samples of previous work, project or performances should be submitted. The names and contact addresses/telephones of two referees should also be sent. The application should bear the title 'Sanskriti - Kalakriti Fellowship' on the envelope when sent by post and in subject line if sent through email on fellowships@sanskritifoundation.org
Funding: Foundation
Additional Information: www.sanskritifoundation.org/Kalakriti-Fellowship.htm

For further information contact:

Mehrauli Gurgaon Road, Opposite Metro Pillar No. 165, Nearest Metro Station Arjangarh, New Delhi, Delhi 110047, India.

Email: fellowships@sanskritifoundation.org

Madhobi Chatterji Memorial Fellowship

Purpose: The objective is to encourage promising young artists to develop their potential and perfect their skills by providing them the resources and time to dedicate to the art.
Eligibility: The Fellowship is open to Indian Nationals from any genre of Indian Classical Music (Vocal or Instrumental) or Dance (any form or choreography). Proposals that further the objectives of the program are welcome. The candidate should have at least some years of formal training in Indian classical Music or Dance. The fellow would be required to have given at least 2-3 solo performances to his/her credit. The candidate will be facilitated to take guidance from a source unavailable to him/her to enhance his existing style. It can be a residency programme for a period of minimum three months, which can be spread over the period of ten months.
Level of Study: Professional development
Type: Fellowships
Value: The grant of ₹1,00,000 will be given in two instalments
Length of Study: 10 Months
Frequency: Annual
Country of Study: India
Application Procedure: Candidates should send a two – page CV, a CD of their recitals and a write up of approximately 500 words explaining their project. The project proposal should explain how the fellowship will provide an opportunity to express their creativity and technical competence and expand the repertoire of their style. Full postal and telephonic contact details together with any E-mail id should be submitted to facilitate contact. Few samples of previous work, project or performances should be submitted. The names and contact addresses/telephones of two referees should also be sent. The application should bear the title 'Sanskriti – Madhobi Chatterji Memorial Fellowship' on the envelope when sent by post.
Funding: Foundation
Additional Information: www.sanskritifoundation.org/Madhobi-Chatterji-Memorial.htm

For further information contact:

Sanskriti Kendra / Sanskriti Museums, Anandagram, Mehrauli Gurgaon Road, Opposite Metro Pillar No. 165, Nearest Metro Station Arjangarh, New Delhi, Delhi 110047, India.

Email: fellowships@sanskritifoundation.org

Mani Mann Fellowship

Purpose: This Fellowship has been instituted to encourage promising young artists to advance in their field. This fellowship will enable the recipient to have the resources and time to dedicate to the art.
Eligibility: 1. The Fellowship is only open to Indian Nationals in the age group of 25 to 40. 2. While this fellowship specially encourages women applicants, all proposals that further the objectives of the program are welcome. The applicant must hold a degree/diploma from a recognized university or institution in the field and/or the candidate should

have at least ten years of initial training in Indian classical music. The fellow would be required to have given at least 2-3 solo performances to his/her credit in recognized forums. 3. The candidate will be required to take guidance from another senior guru and enhance the existing style. It would be a residency programme for a period of three months, which can be spread over the period of one year. This will require the candidate to take consent from his/her current guru and the guru he/she would want to go to.
Level of Study: Professional development
Type: Fellowships
Value: ₹100,000 will be given in two phases
Length of Study: 1 year
Frequency: Annual
Country of Study: India
Application Procedure: Candidates should send their two page CV and a write up of approximately 500 words explaining their project. Full postal and telephonic contact details together with any E-mail id should be submitted to facilitate contact. Few samples of previous work, project or performances should be submitted. The names and contact addresses/telephones of two referees should also be sent. The application should bear the title 'Mani Mann Fellowship' on the envelope when sent by post and in subject line if sent through email on fellowships@sanskritifoundation.org
Funding: Foundation
Additional Information: www.sanskritifoundation.org/Mani-Mann-Fellowship.htm

For further information contact:

Sanskriti Kendra / Sanskriti Museums, Anandagram, Mehrauli Gurgaon Road, Opposite Metro Pillar No. 165, Nearest Metro Station Arjangarh, New Delhi, Delhi 110047, India.

Email: fellowships@sanskritifoundation.org

Prabha Dutt Fellowship

Purpose: The purpose of the fellowship is to encourage young mid career women journalists to develop their potential by pursuing meaningful projects without having to work under the pressures of short deadlines.
Eligibility: The Fellowship is only open to women who are Indian Nationals in the age group of 25 to 40. It is exclusively for print journalists. The Fellows will be required to publish a stipulated number of articles in established publications. The Fellow may work on a book or monograph for subsequent publication within the given time frame.
Level of Study: Professional development
Type: Fellowships
Value: ₹1,00,000 including travel expenses
Length of Study: 10 months
Frequency: Annual
Country of Study: India
Application Procedure: Candidates should send a two - page CV and a write up of about 250 - 300 words explaining their project. Full postal and telephonic contact details together with any e-mail id should be submitted to facilitate contact. Five samples of work published. The names and contact addresses/telephones of two referees should also be sent. The application should bear the title 'Sanskriti - Prabha Dutt Fellowship' on the envelope when sent by post or can be emailed on fellowships@sanskritifoundation.org with 'Sanskriti - Prabha Dutt Fellowship' in subject line.
Funding: Foundation
Additional Information: www.sanskritifoundation.org/prabha-dutt-fellowship.htm

For further information contact:

Sanskriti Kendra / Sanskriti Museums, Anandagram, Mehrauli Gurgaon Road, Opposite Metro Pillar No. 165, Nearest Metro Station Arjangarh, New Delhi, Delhi 110047, India.

Email: fellowships@sanskritifoundation.org

Pt. Vasant Thakar Memorial Fellowship

Purpose: The objective of the Fellowship is to recognize and provide a platform to excellent but lesser known artists and to bring them to larger audiences.
Eligibility: 1. The Fellowship is open to Indian Nationals from any genre of Indian Classical Music (Vocal or Instrumental). Proposals that further the objectives of the program are welcome. 2. The duration of the fellowship will be 10 months followed by a performance in Delhi.
Level of Study: Professional development
Type: Fellowships
Value: ₹1,00,000 will be given in two instalments
Length of Study: 10 months
Frequency: Annual
Country of Study: India
Application Procedure: All candidates should mail their CV and a short synopsis of their project proposal to Sanskriti Head Office. The application should bear the title 'Sanskriti-Pt Vasant Thakar Memorial Fellowship' on the envelope when sent by post and in subject line if sent through email on Pt vasant Thakar Memorial Fellowship at fellowships@sanskritifoundation.org

Funding: Foundation
Additional Information: www.sanskritifoundation.org/Pt-Vasant-Thakar-Memorial-Fellowship.htm

For further information contact:

Sanskriti Kendra / Sanskriti Museums, Anandagram, Mehrauli Gurgaon Road, Opposite Metro Pillar No. 165, Nearest Metro Station Arjangarh, New Delhi, Delhi 110047, India.

Email: fellowships@sanskritifoundation.org

Sasakawa Fund

School of Economics, University of São Paulo 908, FEA 1, room D105, São Paulo, Buntantã, SP 055 (080) 10, Brazil.

Tel: (55) 11 3091 6075
Email: sylff@usp.br

Generally known as SYLFF, The Ryoichi Sasakawa Young Leaders Fellowship Fund, aims to nurture future leaders who will transcend the geopolitical, religious, ethnic, and cultural boundaries and actively participate in the world community for peace and the well-being of humankind.

Sasakawa Young Leader Fellowship (SYLFF) Program

Subjects: Humanities and Social Sciences
Purpose: The Ryoichi Sasakawa Young Leaders Fellowship Fund, or SYLFF, is a fellowship program initiated in 1987 to support students pursuing graduate studies in the humanities and social sciences.
Eligibility: Open to postgraduate students from the university of Sao Paulo with research projects proposals that relate to approved subject areas and aim to assist Brazil in its global insertion.
Level of Study: Postgraduate
Type: Fellowship
Length of Study: 2 years
Frequency: Annual
Study Establishment: São Paulo University
Country of Study: Japan
Funding: Foundation
Contributor: The Tokyo Foundation
No. of awards given last year: 9
Additional Information: www.sylff.org/about/

For further information contact:

Sylff Association Secretariat c/o The Tokyo Foundation for Policy Research, Roppongi Grand Tower, 34th Fl., 3-2-1 Roppongi, Minato-ku, Tokyo 106-6234, Japan.

Tel: (81) 3 5797 8402
Fax: (81) 3 5570 6032
Email: sylff@tkfd.or.jp

Savoy Foundation

230 Foch Street, Saint-Jean-sur-Richelieu, QC J3B 2B2, Canada.

Tel: (1) 450 358 9779
Email: info@savoy-foundation.ca
Website: savoy-foundation.ca/
Contact: Vivian Downing, Assistant to Vice President/ Secretary

The Savoy Foundation is a non-profit organization established by the Savoy family with the stated mission to raise funds to be used for the sole purpose of financing research into epilepsy. The Foundation works principally with Canadian researchers or with foreign nationals who conduct projects in Canada.

Savoy Foundation International Grant

Purpose: To improve the situation of people with epilepsy where medical care is not readily available.
Eligibility: Only available to clinicians and established scientists
Level of Study: Postdoctorate, Postgraduate, Research
Type: Research grant
Value: Up to CA$30,000
Length of Study: 1 year
Frequency: Annual
Study Establishment: An affiliated University
Country of Study: Any country
Application Procedure: Applicants must contact the Foundation or visit the website for application forms and further information
No. of awards offered: 1
Closing Date: 15 January
Funding: Private
Contributor: The Savoy Foundation endowments
No. of awards given last year: 1
No. of applicants last year: 1

Additional Information: One grant is available per year. All applications are evaluated by the medical board of the Savoy Foundation for epilepsy www.savoy-foundation.ca/

Savoy Foundation Postdoctoral and Clinical Research Fellowships

Purpose: Awarded to scientists or medical specialists (Ph.D. or M.D.) wishing to carry out a full-time research project, which must be focused on epilepsy.
Eligibility: Candidates must be scientists or medical specialists with a PhD or MD.
Level of Study: Postgraduate, Research
Type: Fellowship
Value: The fellow with the highest marks will be awarded CA$1,500.
Length of Study: 1 year (non-renewable)
Frequency: Annual
Country of Study: Canada
Application Procedure: Applicants must contact the Foundation or visit the website for application forms and further information.
No. of awards offered: 2-3
Closing Date: 31 January
Funding: Foundation
Contributor: The Savoy Foundation endowments
Additional Information: savoy-foundation.ca/doctoral.asp

Savoy Foundation Research Grants

Purpose: These grants will be awarded for the following purposes 1. Launching of a project operating costs in the expectation of funds already requested from government agencies. In this category, the description of the project should bear mainly on the initial stages (and/or reorientation) rather than the whole research program. 2. Pre-research. 3. Pursuit or completion of a project. 4. Contribution to the funding of a research project of particular interest in the field of epilepsy. 5. Contribution to the funding of a scientific activity (e.g. workshop, symposium) related to the field of epilepsy.
Level of Study: Research
Type: Research grant
Value: Up to CA$5,000
Frequency: Annual
Country of Study: Canada
Application Procedure: Applicants must contact the Foundation or visit the website for application forms and further information.
No. of awards offered: 2-3
Closing Date: 31 January
Funding: Foundation, Private
Contributor: The Savoy Foundation endowments
Additional Information: savoy-foundation.ca/researchgrants.asp

Savoy Foundation Studentships

Purpose: To meritorious applicants wishing to acquire training and pursue research in a biomedical discipline, the health sciences or social sciences related to epilepsy in an MSc or PhD program.
Eligibility: Candidates must have a good university record, e.g. a BSc, MD or equivalent diploma and have ensured that a qualified researcher affiliated to a university or hospital will supervise his or her work. Concomitant registration in a graduate programme is encouraged. The awards are available to Canadian citizens or for projects conducted in Canada.
Level of Study: Doctorate, Postgraduate, Predoctorate
Type: Studentship
Value: The stipend will be CA$15,000 per year for masters studies and CA$17,000 for PhD studies. The student with the highest mark will receive in addition the prestigious Van Gelder-Savoy award worth CA$1,500.
Length of Study: 1
Frequency: Annual
Country of Study: Canada
Application Procedure: Applicants must contact the Foundation or visit the website for application forms and further information.
No. of awards offered: 2-3
Closing Date: 31 January
Funding: Foundation
Contributor: The Savoy Foundation endowments
Additional Information: savoy-foundation.ca/studentship.asp

Scholarship Foundation of the League of Finnish-American Societies

Mechelininkatu 10, Helsinki, FI-00100 Helsinki, Finland.

Tel: (358) 9 4133 3700
Email: sayl@sayl.fi
Website: www.sayl.fi
Contact: Ms Tuula Nuckols, Project Manager

American Society of Naval Engineers (ASNE) Scholarship

Purpose: The American Society of Naval Engineers began its scholarship program in 1979 in order to promote the

S

profession of naval engineering and to encourage college students to enter the field. Since the inception of the Scholarship Program, ASNE has since awarded more than 500 scholarships to undergraduate and graduate students interested in pursuing an education and career in naval engineering.
Eligibility: You must be a United States citizen to be eligible for an ASNE Scholarship. Graduate candidates must be a member of ASNE to apply for a scholarship. Student membership applications can be submitted with the scholarship application. Undergraduate candidates do not have to be a member of ASNE to apply.
Level of Study: Professional development
Type: Scholarship
Value: US$4,000
Frequency: Annual
Country of Study: United States of America
Application Procedure: www.navalengineers.org/Portals/16/Students/Scholarship/ASNE_Scholarship_Application_2022-2023.pdf
Closing Date: 7 February
Funding: Private
Additional Information: www.navalengineers.org/Education/Scholarships

For further information contact:

1452 Duke Street, Alexandria, VA 22314, United States of America.

Email: scholarships@navalengineers.org

School of Oriental and African Studies (SOAS)

University of London, 10 Thornhaugh Street, Russell Square, London WC1H 0XG, United Kingdom.

Tel: (44) 20 7637 2388
Website: www.soas.ac.uk/
Contact: Miss Alicia Sales, Scholarships Officer, Registry

SOAS University of London is the leading higher education institution in Europe specialising in the study of Asia, Africa and the Near and Middle East. Programmes are taught by respected academics engaged in fieldwork and research which influences government policy and the lives of individuals across the globe. SOAS scholars grapple with the pressing issues confronting two-thirds of humankind today: democracy, development, economy, finance, public and corporate policy, human rights, migration, identity, legal systems, poverty, religion, and social change.

Academy of Korean Studies Postgraduate Bursaries

Eligibility: Open to United Kingdom/European Union and overseas applicants. See the website for details
Level of Study: Postgraduate
Type: Bursary
Value: Up to £6,000 towards tuition fees
Length of Study: 1 year
Frequency: Annual
Study Establishment: SOAS
Country of Study: United Kingdom
Application Procedure: See website www.soas.ac.uk/scholarships
Closing Date: 24 May
Funding: Private
Contributor: Academy of Korean Studies
No. of awards given last year: 1
Additional Information: If you have any questions about the bursary application, please contact the Scholarships Officer www.petersons.com/scholarship/babe-ruth-scholarship-program-111_179153.aspx

For further information contact:

Email: ak49@soas.ac.uk

Allan and Nesta Ferguson Scholarships

Eligibility: 1. Be nationals of and resident in an African country, 2. Hold an undergraduate degree at the first class level, 3. New scholarship applicants must have applied to SOAS but are not required to have received an offer of admissions by the scholarship deadline. An offer will need to have been received by the time the relevant panel meets to discuss scholarship applications, 4. Applicants must meet the English language condition of their offer of admission to study at SOAS as soon as possible but no later than 1 June. If your offer is conditional on English, please arrange your English test and ensure you meet the English requirement as soon as possible. 5. Please note that most scholarships do not cover funding or even allow for Pre-sessionals. Please check the wording of your scholarship offer carefully to see if you are eligible for a Pre-sessional course or whether you need to achieve SOAS direct entry scores by the deadline specified in your scholarship terms and conditions.
Level of Study: Postgraduate
Type: Scholarship
Value: £30,555
Frequency: Annual
Country of Study: United Kingdom
Closing Date: 1 May

Additional Information: www.soas.ac.uk/study/student-life/finance/scholarships/allan-and-nesta-ferguson-scholarships

For further information contact:

Tel: (44) 20 7074 5106
Email: scholarships@soas.ac.uk

Arts and Humanities Research Council Studentships

Purpose: Up to 56 Arts and Humanities studentships available from CHASE Doctoral Training Partnership. CHASE Studentships are for PhD-level study only and successful applicants will have their fees paid, as well as receiving a stipend to cover living expenses (where eligible, see below) and access to further funds for skills training and research.
Eligibility: CHASE AHRC funding is only available to Home or EU students. Both Home and EU students must satisfy the standard research council eligibility criteria. Please see page 12 of the Research Councils Terms and Conditions for Training Grants to check eligibility.
Level of Study: Postgraduate
Type: Studentship
Value: Maintenance plus approved tuition fees
Frequency: Annual
Study Establishment: SOAS
Country of Study: United Kingdom
Application Procedure: You must apply for the CHASE studentships via the studentship application. (www.chase.ac.uk/apply)
No. of awards offered: 56
Closing Date: 28 January
Funding: Government
Additional Information: www.soas.ac.uk/study/student-life/finance/scholarships/chase-ahrc-studentship

For further information contact:

Tel: (44) 20 7074 5106
Email: scholarships@soas.ac.uk

Bernard Buckman Scholarship

Purpose: The Bernard Buckman Scholarship was established in 1992 with generous support by Mrs Buckman in memory of her late husband who was a Governor of the School. There is one Scholarship available.
Eligibility: 1. Open to applicants paying fees at the UK/EU rate only. 2. Applicants must possess a good honours degree from a UK university or an equivalent institution recognised by SOAS. 3. Applicants must have an offer of admission to pursue the full-time MA Chinese Studies or MA Advanced Chinese Studies programme at SOAS by the scholarship application deadline. 4. Applicants must meet the English language condition of their offer of admission to study at SOAS. If your offer is conditional on English, please arrange your English test and ensure you meet the English requirements as soon as possible.
Level of Study: Postgraduate
Type: Scholarship
Value: £6,000
Frequency: Annual
Study Establishment: SOAS
Country of Study: United Kingdom
Application Procedure: Candidates can apply for this scholarship via the online scholarship application form.
No. of awards offered: 2
Closing Date: 30 April
Funding: Private
Additional Information: www.soas.ac.uk/study/student-life/finance/scholarships/bernard-buckman-scholarship

For further information contact:

Tel: (44) 20 7074 5106
Email: scholarships@soas.ac.uk

Brough Sanskrit Awards

Purpose: There are 3 awards of up to £1,200 for SOAS postgraduate research and master's students who use Sanskrit in their work and will use the funds for research activity such as fieldwork trips.
Eligibility: 1. The funding is for students who use Sanskrit in their work. Evidence of this should be provided in your application. 2. We cannot normally hold an award over into the next academic year if a candidate does not make the trip or attend the conference or workshop when intended a re-application has to be made. 3. For research degree applicants only 4. Any student accepting a Brough Sanskrit award for fieldwork, workshops and conference must be enrolled 5. The student must submit a brief report, signed by the supervisor, to the Scholarships Officer within one month of the end of the fieldwork visit, conference or workshop. 6. Retrospective applications for a Brough Sanskrit Award will be considered but will not be given priority. 7. If you have already had a Brough Sanskrit Award, you can be considered for another award in a different academic year. 8. For conference funding, priority may be given to students who have been invited to present a paper at the conference
Level of Study: Postgraduate
Type: Award
Value: £1,200

Length of Study: 1 year
Frequency: Annual
Study Establishment: SOAS
Country of Study: United Kingdom
Application Procedure: Please apply online via the on-line application form. (docs.google.com/forms/d/e/1FAIpQLSciNs4iyr1IJ293OUamoABPLWifocGTDFPpANCHyvgCIxVgVw/viewform)
No. of awards offered: 3
Closing Date: 9 April
Additional Information: www.soas.ac.uk/study/student-life/finance/scholarships/brough-sanskrit-awards

For further information contact:

Email: scholarships@soas.ac.uk

CSJR Postgraduate Student Bursary

Purpose: The Centre for the Study of Japanese Religions offers a CSJR Postgraduate Student Bursary in Japanese Religions to be held at SOAS, University of London.
Eligibility: 1. Applicants must possess an outstanding academic record. 2. Taught Masters (MA) applicants must focus on Japanese Religions / Japanese Buddhism. Evidence of this should be included in the statement of their application and reflected in their choice of modules. 3. Taught Masters (MA) and Research Degree (MPhil/PhD) applicants should give evidence in the statement of their application of their ability to use sources in Japanese. 4. Open to UK/EU and Overseas candidates. 5. Applicants must have an offer of admission for one of the eligible programmes at SOAS by the scholarship application deadline. 6. Applicants must meet the English language condition of their offer of admission to study at SOAS as soon as possible.
Level of Study: Doctorate, Postgraduate
Type: Bursary
Value: £5,000
Length of Study: 1 year
Frequency: Annual
Study Establishment: SOAS
Country of Study: United Kingdom
Application Procedure: Applicants must apply for this scholarship via the online application form.
Closing Date: 28 April
Funding: Foundation
Additional Information: www.soas.ac.uk/study/student-life/finance/scholarships/csjr-postgraduate-student-bursary

For further information contact:

Tel: (44) 20 7074 5090
Email: scholarships@soas.ac.uk

Felix Scholarship

Subjects: Any full time PhD programme or Taught Masters programmes
Purpose: A number of Felix Scholarships will be available to Indian nationals with first class degrees to pursue graduate studies at SOAS, University of London.
Eligibility: 1. Must be Indian nationals and not currently be living or studying outside of India. 2. Must not have previously studied for one year or more outside India. 3. Felix Master's Alumni who have obtained a distinction at Masters may apply for a PhD Felix scholarship. 4. Candidates must have at least a first class Bachelor's degree from an Indian University or comparable institution. We may give priority applicants with a higher first class Bachelor's degree. 5. Exceptionally those with an upper second-class degree at the Bachelor's level may be considered for PhD if they hold a first class degree at the Master's level.
Level of Study: Doctorate, Postgraduate
Type: Scholarship
Value: Covers the full cost of tuition fees; living costs and a return air fare
Frequency: Annual
Study Establishment: SOAS
Country of Study: United Kingdom
Closing Date: 28 January
Funding: Private
Contributor: Felix Scholarship Trust
Additional Information: www.soas.ac.uk/study/student-life/finance/scholarships/felix-scholarships

For further information contact:

Tel: (44) 20 7074 5090
Email: scholarships@soas.ac.uk

Hong Kong and Shanghai Banking Corporation School of Oriental and African Studies Scholarships

Purpose: To support United Kingdom or European Union fee payers commencing a full-time master's course in Sinology or Chinese literature.
Eligibility: Applicants must possess or be about to complete a good honours degree, preferably first class, from a United Kingdom institution or overseas equivalent
Level of Study: Postgraduate
Type: Scholarship
Value: £16,650 plus tuition fees at the home European Union rate
Length of Study: 1 year
Frequency: Annual

Study Establishment: SOAS
Country of Study: United Kingdom
Application Procedure: Candidates can apply for this scholarship via the online scholarship application form. For enquiries, please contact Scholarships Officer
Closing Date: 22 March
Funding: Trusts
Contributor: HSBC educational trust
No. of awards given last year: 2
Additional Information: www.soas.ac.uk/registry/scholarships/hsbc-soas-scholarships.html

For further information contact:

Tel: (44) 20 7074 5094/5091

International Postgraduate Scholarships

Purpose: The International Postgraduate Scholarship is designed to award new entry Postgraduate students with outstanding academic performance.
Eligibility: 1. Accepted an offer to study a Postgraduate taught (on-campus) degree. 2. Overseas fee-paying student who is a national of China, Hong Kong, or Taiwan. 3. Minimum UK upper second-class (21) or international equivalent.
Level of Study: Postgraduate
Type: Scholarship
Value: £3,000
Frequency: Annual
Study Establishment: SOAS
Country of Study: United Kingdom
Application Procedure: Apply for the International Scholarship via the online form. (docs.google.com/forms/d/e/1FAIpQLSd3dRxz_SdPARVCzG8AeNOBPXelEw2ItS2hodRD1qO7wBL3kQ/viewform)
No. of awards offered: 15
Closing Date: 31 May
Funding: Foundation
Additional Information: www.soas.ac.uk/study/student-life/finance/scholarships/international-postgraduate-scholarships-2023

For further information contact:

Tel: (44) 20 3510 6974
Email: scholarships@soas.ac.uk

Shapoorji Pallonji Scholarships

Purpose: The Shapoorji Pallonji Scholarships will provide a contribution to fees and living costs calibrated according to merit and availability of funds.
Eligibility: 1. Applicants for the MA Scholarships must possess or expect to be awarded a First Class Honours Degree or equivalent. Applicants with a non UK masters degree must be in the top rank as evidenced by references and transcripts. Applicants with a 2.1 may also apply but will not be given preference. 2. Applicants for the MPhil/PhD scholarships must possess or expect to be awarded a Masters degree with a mark of Distinction from a UK university. Applicants with a non UK masters degree must be in the top rank as evidenced by references and transcripts. Applicants with a mark of merit may also apply but will not be given preference. 3. Applicants for the MPhil/PhD scholarships must have demonstrated in the research proposal of their application for admission that their research is in one of the following subject areas i) Zoroastrianism, both ancient and modern ii) Zoroastrianism with Avestan, Pahlavi, Persian or Gujarati languages. 4. Applicants for the MA scholarship must complete the compulsory 60 credit dissertation in Zoroastrianism and the 30-credit module Zoroastrianism, Historical and Contemporary Perspectives. In addition to this, applicants may wish to take one further 30-credit language module (e.g. Avestan language module). 5. The scholarship is open to UK/EU and overseas fee-paying full time students.
Level of Study: Doctorate, Postgraduate
Type: Scholarship
Value: contribution to fees and living costs calibrated according to merit and availability of funds.
Length of Study: The MPhil/PhD scholarship is paid for 3 years. The MA is paid for one year (or over two years if part-time).
Frequency: Annual
Study Establishment: SOAS
Country of Study: United Kingdom
Application Procedure: Applicants must apply for this scholarship via the online scholarship application form.
Closing Date: 28 April
Funding: Foundation
Additional Information: www.soas.ac.uk/study/student-life/finance/scholarships/shapoorji-pallonji-scholarships

For further information contact:

Tel: (44) 20 7074 5090
Email: scholarships@soas.ac.uk

SOAS Master's Scholarship

Purpose: The SOAS Masters Scholarships are designed to recognise applicants with outstanding academic achievements.
Eligibility: 1. UK 'Home fees' applicants only. 2. Holding offer (conditional or unconditional) for full-time Postgraduate Taught (on campus) programmes. Part-time programmes are

not eligible. 3. Assessed on academic merit and work experience.
Level of Study: Postgraduate
Type: Scholarship
Value: £4,000
Length of Study: 1 year, non-renewable
Frequency: Annual
Study Establishment: SOAS
Country of Study: United Kingdom
Application Procedure: Applicants must submit a complete online application for admission. (www.soas.ac.uk/admissions/pg/howtoapply/)
No. of awards offered: 44
Closing Date: 30 April
Funding: Government
Additional Information: www.soas.ac.uk/study/student-life/finance/scholarships/soas-masters-scholarships

For further information contact:

Tel: (44) 20 7074 5106
Email: scholarships@soas.ac.uk

SOAS Research Scholarship

Purpose: To support full-time research study at SOAS
Eligibility: 1. Any full-time MPhil/PhD programme (new admissions only). 2. Be UK-permanent residents (UK fee-paying students) from the following ethnic group 3. Black (Black or Black British African, Black or Black British Caribbean, Black or Black British other or Mixed Black or Black British).
Level of Study: Doctorate
Type: Scholarship
Value: £17,285
Length of Study: 3 years
Frequency: Annual
Study Establishment: SOAS
Country of Study: United Kingdom
Application Procedure: Applicants must complete and submit an application form that can be downloaded from the website
Closing Date: 30 April
Funding: Government
No. of awards given last year: 4
Additional Information: For enquiries, please contact Scholarships Officer www.afterschoolafrica.com/35577/soas-research-studentships/

For further information contact:

Email: scholarships@soas.ac.uk

SOAS Sanctuary Scholarship

Purpose: The SOAS Sanctuary scheme to support displaced people.
Eligibility: 1. Any full-time undergraduate degree of 3 years duration. 2. Any full-time one year or part-time two year postgraduate taught Master's degree on campus (not distance learning). 3. In addition, a package of support will be provided to contribute towards the living costs (which includes accommodation, travel and study materials) for the student to take up their place.
Level of Study: Postgraduate
Type: Scholarship
Value: Tuition fee and £12,000 maintenance
Frequency: Annual
Study Establishment: SOAS
Country of Study: United Kingdom
Application Procedure: Apply for this Sanctuary Scholarship via the online form.
Closing Date: 30 April
Funding: Foundation
Additional Information: www.soas.ac.uk/study/student-life/finance/scholarships/soas-sanctuary-scholarships-2022/23

For further information contact:

Tel: (44) 20 7074 5090
Email: scholarships@soas.ac.uk

Sochon Foundation Scholarship

Purpose: The Sochon Foundation has generously provided SOAS with scholarships for students undertaking a full-time post-graduate programmes in Korean Studies.
Eligibility: 1. Open to UK/EU and overseas applicants. Priority will be given to Overseas applicants. 2. Applicants must have an offer of admission to the degree programme by the scholarship application deadline. 3. Applicants must meet the English language condition of their offer of admission to study at SOAS as soon as possible. If your offer is conditional on English, please arrange your English test and ensure you meet the English requirements as soon as possible.
Level of Study: Doctorate, Postgraduate
Type: Scholarship
Value: Up to £3,000 (Home or EU student) for fees, Up to £6,000 (Overseas student) for fees
Length of Study: 1 year
Frequency: Annual
Study Establishment: SOAS
Country of Study: United Kingdom

Application Procedure: Applicants must apply for this scholarship via the online application form.
Closing Date: 28 April
Funding: Foundation
Additional Information: www.soas.ac.uk/study/student-life/finance/scholarships/sochon-foundation-scholarship

For further information contact:

Tel: (44) 20 7074 5090
Email: scholarships@soas.ac.uk

Tibawi Trust Awards

Purpose: Dr Abdul-Latif Tibawi left a gift in his will to establish a Trust for a postgraduate award. The award is to assist Palestinians undertaking a postgraduate course at SOAS and may be used towards conference visits or field-work in the UK or Overseas.
Eligibility: 1. Any postgraduate degree programme at SOAS. 2. Candidates must be of Palestinian origin. 3. Candidates must be enrolled in a programme at SOAS.
Level of Study: Postgraduate
Type: Award
Value: Up to £1,300 each
Frequency: Annual
Study Establishment: SOAS
Country of Study: United Kingdom
Application Procedure: In order to be considered for the scholarship, you must have submitted an online application to The Tibawi Trust Awards.
No. of awards offered: 2
Closing Date: 28 February
Funding: Foundation
Additional Information: www.soas.ac.uk/study/student-life/finance/scholarships/tibawi-trust-award

For further information contact:

Tel: (44) 20 7074 5090
Email: scholarships@soas.ac.uk

VP Kanitkar Memorial Scholarship

Purpose: The V P Kanitkar Memorial Scholarships are available for postgraduates to support a taught masters in Religious Studies with reference to Hinduism and a taught masters in Anthropology with reference to Hindu culture in South Asia. Each scholarship covers the cost of tuition fees and provides a maintenance.
Eligibility: 1. The scholarship is open to UK/EU and overseas applicants. 2. Applicants must possess or expect to be awarded a First Class Honours Degree or equivalent. Students with a non-UK degree to be adjudged in the top rank by their referees and transcript.
Level of Study: Postgraduate
Type: Scholarship
Value: Tuition fees, plus a maintenance
Frequency: Annual
Study Establishment: SOAS
Country of Study: United Kingdom
Application Procedure: You must apply for this scholarship via the online scholarship application form.
Closing Date: 28 April
Funding: Foundation
Additional Information: www.soas.ac.uk/study/student-life/finance/scholarships/vp-kanitkar-memorial-scholarships

For further information contact:

Tel: (44) 20 7074 5090
Email: scholarships@soas.ac.uk

William Ross Murray Scholarship

Purpose: To support a student of high academic achievement from a developing country unable to pay overseas tuition fees and attend the full-time LLM degree at SOAS
Eligibility: 1. Must be domiciled in a developing country. 2. Possess a good honours degree, preferably first class, from a UK institution or overseas equivalent. 3. Have an unconditional offer of admission to pursue the full-time LLM at SOAS by the scholarship application deadline. If your offer is conditional, please ensure you meet the conditions and receive an unconditional offer by the deadline.
Level of Study: Postgraduate
Type: Scholarship
Value: Overseas tuition fees. Free accommodation at International Student House and food vouchers
Length of Study: 1 year
Frequency: Annual
Study Establishment: SOAS
Country of Study: United Kingdom
No. of awards offered: 1
Closing Date: 20 February
Funding: Foundation
No. of awards given last year: 1
Additional Information: www.afterschoolafrica.com/159/william-ross-murray-scholarship/

Science and Engineering Research Board

3rd & 4th Floor, Block II, Technology Bhawan, New Mehrauli Road, New Delhi, Delhi 110 016, India.

Tel: (91) 11 2655 2199
Website: serb.gov.in/
Contact: Science and Engineering Research Board

Promoting basic research in Science and Engineering and to provide financial assistance to persons engaged in such research, academic institutions, research and development laboratories, industrial concerns and other agencies for such research and for matters connected therewith or incidental thereto are the primary and distinctive mandate of the Board. SERB aims to build up best management systems which would match the best global practices in the area of promotion and funding of basic research.

J C Bose National Fellowship

Subjects: All areas of Science
Purpose: The JC Bose fellowship is awarded to active scientists in recognition for their outstanding performance. The fellowship is scientist-specific and very selective.
Eligibility: 1. Should be an active scientist with a record of outstanding performance apparent from the award of SS Bhatnagar prize and or fellowship of science academies (including engineering, agriculture and medicine). 2. The scientist should be in service at the time of nomination to this fellowship. 3. The nominee should be an Indian national working in institutions in India. The nominee should not be receiving any other fellowship from any other Government sources.
Level of Study: Postgraduate
Type: Fellowship
Value: The fellowship amount is ₹25,000 per month in addition to regular income. Research grant of ₹15,00,000 per annum. Overhead of ₹1,00,000 per annum to the host institute.
Length of Study: 5 years
Frequency: Twice a year
Country of Study: India
Funding: Government
Additional Information: serb.gov.in/page/awards_fellowship#J%20C%20Bose%20National%20Fellowship

National Post Doctoral Fellowship (N-PDF)

Purpose: The SERB-National Post Doctoral Fellowship (N-PDF) is aimed to identify motivated young researchers and provide them support for doing research in frontier areas of science and engineering. The fellows will work under a mentor, and it is hoped that this training will provide them a platform to develop as an independent researcher
Eligibility: 1. The applicant should be an Indian citizen. 2. The applicant must have obtained Ph.D./M.D./M.S. degree from a recognized University. Those who have submitted their PhD/M.D/M.S thesis and are awaiting award of the degree are also eligible to apply. However, such candidates, if selected, will be offered lower fellowship amount till they qualify the eligible degree. 3. The upper age limit for the fellowship is 35 years at the time of the submission of application, age will be calculated by taking the date of closure of the respective call. Age relaxation of 5 (five) years will be given to candidates belonging to SC/ST/OBC/Physically Challenged & Women candidates. 4. NPDF can be availed only once by a candidate in his/her career. 5. Mentor must hold a regular academic / research position in a recognized institution in India. Should hold Ph.D. degree in Science or Engineering. 6. A mentor shall not have more than two SERB NPDF fellows at any given time. 7. Aspirants of NPDF, ECRA and CRG (EMR) can submit their proposal only once in a calendar year in any one of these schemes.
Level of Study: Postdoctorate
Type: Fellowship
Value: Fellowship ₹55,000 per month + HRA. Research Grant ₹2,00,000 per annum. Overheads ₹1,00,000 per annum
Length of Study: 2 years
Frequency: Annual
Country of Study: India
Application Procedure: Applicants should first register into the online website www.serbonline.in click here to register. After log-in, applicants are required to fill all the mandatory fields in Profile Detail section under User Profile, which includes Bio data, photo, Institute Address, etc. Details including Project Title (max 500 characters), Project summary (max 3000 characters), Keywords (max 6), Objectives of the proposal (max 1500 characters), Expected output and outcome of the proposal (max 1500 characters) should be provided online at the time of submission of the application. Work Methodology and Research plan has to be uploaded in single PDF file not more than 3 pages (max 10 MB). For details one may visit serbonline.in/SERB/npdf?HomePage=New
Funding: Government
Additional Information: serb.gov.in/page/awards_fellowship#National%20Post%20Doctoral%20Fellowship

Prime Minister's Fellowship Scheme for Doctoral Research

Purpose: This scheme is aimed at encouraging young, talented, enthusiastic and result-oriented scholars to take up industry-relevant research. Under this scheme, full-time PhD scholars get double the money that they would otherwise get for doing research.
Eligibility: The applicants for the Prime Minister's Fellowship for Doctoral Research Scheme should: 1. Indian National. 2. Full time PhD registered with any academic or research institution offering PhD degree. 3. Apply within 14 months of PhD admission/registration whichever date is earlier. 4. Complete all required academic qualification in past. 5. Have an industry partner to sponsor 50% of the fellowship (Rs. 4lakhs per annum).
Level of Study: Research
Type: Fellowship
Length of Study: 4 years
Frequency: Annual
Country of Study: India
Application Procedure: Candidates may apply for the SERB's Prime Minister's Fellowship for Doctoral Research Scheme at any time of the year at www.serbficci-iirrada.in
No. of awards offered: 100
Funding: Government
Contributor: Department of Science & Technology (DST) and Science & Engineering Research Board (SERB) with The Confederation of Indian Industry (CII)
Additional Information: www.serbficci-iirrada.in/PrimeMinisterFellowshipResearch.html

For further information contact:

Federation of Indian Chambers of Commerce and Industry (FICCI), Tansen Marg, New Delhi, Delhi 110001, India.

Email: info@serbficci-iirrada.in

Ramanujan Fellowship

Subjects: Researchers scientists/engineers
Purpose: The scheme provides support to active researchers/scientists/engineers who want to return to India from abroad and contribute their work for the country.
Eligibility: 1. The Fellowship is open to brilliant Indian scientists and engineers working abroad and are below the age of 40 years. 2. The nominee should possess a higher degree or equivalent, such as Ph.D. in Science/ Engineering, Masters in Engineering or Technology/ MD in Medicine, etc. and have adequate professional experience. 3. These Fellowships are very selective and only those who have a proven/ outstanding track-record as evident from their research publications and recognition's would be eligible. 4. In case of selection of the candidate for regular position in the University/ Institute, the candidate will not be eligible for receiving grant under the Ramanujan Fellowship. 5. The Fellowship is only for those scientists who are not holding any permanent/ tenure track/ contractual position in any Indian Institute/ University. 6. The nominee should be working abroad at the time of nomination.
Level of Study: Postgraduate
Type: Fellowship
Value: Fellowship will be ₹1,35,000 per month. Research grant of ₹7,00,000 per annum and ₹60,000 per annum as overhead charges
Length of Study: 5 years
Frequency: Annual
Country of Study: India
Application Procedure: The project proposal should be prepared according to the guidelines and submitted online through the website www.serbonline.in
Funding: Government
Additional Information: serb.gov.in/page/awards_fellowship#Ramanujan%20Fellowship

S.N Bose Scholar Program

Purpose: S.N Bose Scholar Program is organized by the Science and Engineering Board (SERB), Department of science and technology (DST), Govt. of India, Indo–US Technology Forum and Win Step Forward. The scholarship envisages providing a world-class research platform in top US universities. It also aims at making Indo-US long-term collaboration in the field of research
Eligibility: 1. Students pursuing a Bachelor's or Master's degree program from a recognized institution of India can apply for this scheme. 2. The disciplines of pursuing UG and PG degree are Atmospheric and Earth Sciences, Chemical Sciences, Engineering Sciences, Mathematical and Computational Sciences, and Physical Sciences. 3. Candidates who are studying PhD cannot apply
Level of Study: Postdoctorate
Type: Scholarship
Length of Study: 1 year
Frequency: Annual
Closing Date: May
Funding: Foundation
Additional Information: The program will not be accepting applications for this year. www.iusstf.org/program/for-indian-students

For further information contact:

Indo-US Science and Technology Forum, Fulbright House, 12, Hailey Road, New Delhi, 110001, India.

Tel: (91) 11 42691712
Email: bose@indousstf.org

Science and Engineering Research Board Distinguished Fellowship

Purpose: This fellowship is especially to encourage and provide financial support to those senior scientists who find it difficult to continue their research because of financial limitations, and those who are forced to stop their research against their will.
Eligibility: Superannuated scientist who is active in research. Must have received recognition for his/her work from National and/or International scientific bodies
Level of Study: Research
Type: Fellowship
Value: A research grant of ₹5,00,000 per annum and a fellowship amount of ₹60,000 per month will be given to each fellow
Length of Study: 3 years
Country of Study: India
Application Procedure: Call for nomination is made from time to time. Nominations are accepted only when the call is made
No. of awards offered: 20
Closing Date: 30 November
Funding: Government
Additional Information: www.scholarshipsinindia.com/fellowship/serb-distinguished-fellowship.html

For further information contact:

Email: keerti.serb@gmail.com

Science and Engineering Research Board Overseas Postdoctoral Fellowship (OPDF)

Purpose: SERB Overseas Postdoctoral fellowship (SERB-OPDF) aims to build national capacity in frontier areas of Science and Engineering, which are of interest to India by providing postdoctoral fellowship
Eligibility: The applicant should have completed PhD in science and engineering not earlier than the preceding 2 years from recognized institutions in India. For researchers who are in regular employment, the 2 years period may be relaxed
Level of Study: Postdoctorate
Type: Fellowship
Length of Study: 1 year, extendable to 1 more year subject to good performance
Application Procedure: The format, guidelines and other details of the SERB-OPDF Program details are also available at www.dst.gov.in
Additional Information: The programme admits candidates in identified areas and sends them to top institutions around the globe, other than United States of America and also to institutions where internationally acclaimed scientists are working www.serb.gov.in/opf.php

Science and Engineering Research Board Women Excellence Award

Purpose: SERB Women Excellence Award is a one-time award given to women scientists below 40 years of age and who have received recognition from any one or more of the following national academies such as Young Scientist Medal, Young Associate etc.
Eligibility: 1. Only for Women Scientists. 2. The age of the applicant should not exceed 40 years as on submission date. 3. Applicant must be having recognition from any one or more of the following national academies such as Young Scientist Medal, Young Associate etc. a. Indian National Science Academy, New Delhi. b. Indian Academy of Science, Bangalore. c. National Academy of Science, Allahabad. d. Indian National Academy of Engineering, New Delhi. e. National Academy of Medical Sciences, New Delhi. f. National Academy of Agricultural Sciences, New Delhi.
Level of Study: Research
Type: Award
Value: ₹5,00,000 per annum
Length of Study: 3 years
Frequency: Annual
Country of Study: India
Application Procedure: A copy of the proposal (in one file in PDF) may also be sent by email to: shilpipaul@serb.gov.in
Funding: Government
Additional Information: serb.gov.in/page/awards_fellowship#SERB%20-%20Women%20Excellence%20Research%20Grant

For further information contact:

Email: shilpipaul@serb.gov.in

Science and Technology Facilities Council (STFC)

Polaris House, North Star Avenue, Swindon SN2 1SZ, United Kingdom.

Tel: (44) 1793 442 000
Email: enquiries@stfc.ac.uk
Website: stfc.ukri.org/

STFC's Strategic Context and Future Opportunities takes into account the Government's renewed focus on the importance of UK Industrial Strategy and the impact of the UK's decision to leave the European Union. We have also taken the opportunity to consider STFC's contribution to UK Research and Innovation's (UKRI's) ambitions. This replaces our existing Corporate Strategy but provides a current document on which to base our engagement with stakeholders.

Daphne Jackson Fellowships

Purpose: Daphne Jackson fellowships are retraining fellowships open to all researchers across science, technology, engineering, mathematics, social sciences, arts and humanities, and other related disciplines. Daphne Jackson Fellowships are retraining fellowships for anyone who has taken a break of two years or more from research for family, caring or health reasons.
Eligibility: 1. A career break of at least two years' duration, taken for family, health or caring reasons. 2. A good first degree in a research subject. 3. A PhD, or at least three years research experience (academic or industrial) prior to the career break (with evidence of research impacts and outcomes). 4. UK residency status / right to remain in the UK indefinitely and based in the UK on application. 5. Good command of English (spoken and written). 6. Good computer skills. 7. Your application will be stronger if you also have post-doctoral experience and research impacts and outcomes.
Level of Study: Research
Type: Fellowship
Frequency: Annual
Country of Study: United Kingdom
Application Procedure: There are two main application routes for Daphne Jackson Fellowships. Whichever route you choose, please read 'Are you eligible to apply for a Fellowship' and 'Application process' before submitting your application. (daphnejackson.org/about-fellowships/apply-here/)
Funding: Government
Contributor: Daphne Jackson Trust
Additional Information: www.ukri.org/opportunity/daphne-jackson-fellowship/

For further information contact:

The Daphne Jackson Trust, Department of Physics, University of Surrey, Guildford, Surrey GU2 7XH, United Kingdom.

Tel: (44) 1483 689166
Email: djmft@surrey.ac.uk

Ernest Rutherford Fellowship

Purpose: The Ernest Rutherford Fellowships will enable early career researchers with clear leadership potential to establish a strong, independent research programme
Eligibility: Ernest Rutherford Fellowships are intended for early career researchers who do not have a permanent academic position. You are not eligible if you currently hold a permanent academic position or the equivalent in institutions other than universities. Fellowships are open to applicants of any nationality
Level of Study: Research
Type: A variable number of fellowships
Value: Fund the proposal at 80% of the full economic cost
Length of Study: 5 years
Frequency: Annual
Country of Study: United Kingdom
Application Procedure: Please refer to the application details on the STFC website stfc.ukri.org/funding/fellowships/ernest-rutherford-fellowship/
No. of awards offered: 160
Closing Date: 16 September
Funding: Government
No. of awards given last year: 11
No. of applicants last year: 160
Additional Information: stfc.ukri.org/funding/fellowships/ernest-rutherford-fellowship/

For further information contact:

Email: fellowships@stfc.ukri.org

Industrial CASE Studentships

Purpose: Provides support for PhD students to work in collaboration with a non-academic partner on projects that aim to apply technologies or techniques developed within the programme into other areas
Eligibility: Organisations eligible to receive STFC grant funding
Level of Study: Postgraduate
Type: Studentship
Value: Stipend, fees, research training and fieldwork travel
Length of Study: 3.5 years
Frequency: Annual
Country of Study: United Kingdom
Application Procedure: Call opens in August. Applications must be submitted by the academic partner through the Je-S system. Proposals may be led by either the academic supervisor at an eligible United Kingdom University or research institute or supervisor/supervisors at the non-academic partner organisation, but the application process must be

S

completed by the academic partner, who will then be the recipient of the award
Closing Date: October
Funding: Commercial
Additional Information: www.ukri.org/opportunity/science-and-technology-projects-industrial-case-and-case-plus-studentship/

For further information contact:

Tel: (44) 1793 444164
Email: studentships@stfc.ukri.org

Industrial CASE-Plus Studentship

Purpose: Industrial CASE-Plus extends the Industrial CASE competition to help students become more effective in promoting technology transfer, should their chosen career path take them into either academic research or industry.
Eligibility: Proposals should be submitted by a supervisor from a research organisation eligible to be the academic partner through Je-S. Proposals may be led by either the academic supervisor at an eligible UK university or research institute or supervisor/supervisors at the non-academic partner organisation. The application process must be completed by the academic partner, who will then be the recipient of the award. Before preparing and submitting a proposal it is essential you ensure the non-academic partner and academic institution are both eligible.
Level of Study: Postgraduate
Type: Grant
Value: £500,000
Length of Study: 3.5 years
Frequency: Annual
Study Establishment: Science and Technology Facilities Council
Country of Study: United Kingdom
Closing Date: 29 September
Funding: Government
Additional Information: www.ukri.org/opportunity/science-and-technology-projects-industrial-case-and-case-plus-studentship/

For further information contact:

Tel: (44) 1793 444164
Email: studentships@stfc.ukri.org

PPARC Communications/Media Programme

Purpose: To support students undertake communications training
Eligibility: Either (a) Upper second class honours (21) degree or equivalent in social science, or (b) Upper second class (21) degree or equivalent in another field with professional experience in the media and communications field.
Level of Study: Postgraduate
Type: Bursary
Value: £25,920
Length of Study: 12 months full-time, 24 months part-time
Frequency: Annual
Study Establishment: Any approved university
Country of Study: United Kingdom
Application Procedure: Scholarship website: www.lse.ac.uk/study-at-lse/Graduate/Prospective-students/Supporting-documents
Additional Information: www.lse.ac.uk/study-at-lse/Graduate/Degree-programmes-2020/MSc-Media-and-Communications

For further information contact:

Tel: (44) 20 7405 7686
Email: pr.pus@pparc.ac.uk

PPARC Royal Society Industry Fellowships

Purpose: To enhance interaction between those in industry and the research base, to the benefit of United Kingdom industry
Eligibility: 1. have a PhD or are of equivalent standing in your profession. 2. hold a permanent post or have an 'open-ended contract' in either a university, not-for-profit research organisation or industry in the UK. 3. are at a stage in your career when you would particularly benefit from establishing or strengthening personal or corporate links between academia and industry as a foundation for long-term collaboration and development.
Level of Study: Postdoctorate
Type: Fellowship
Value: Varies
Length of Study: 6 months–2 years full-time, or part-time over a period of up to 4 years
Frequency: Annual
Study Establishment: An appropriate academic institution or position in the industry
Country of Study: United Kingdom
Application Procedure: Applications should be submitted through the Society's grant management system Flexi-Grant®. Your application will go through the process detailed on the Making a grant application page overseen by the Industry Fellowship panel.
Closing Date: 29 March
Funding: Commercial, Private

Contributor: The Royal Society, EPSRC, BBSRC, Rolls-Royce and PPARC
Additional Information: Apart from the Royal Society Fellowships Programme the following fellowship programmes are administered by the PPARC in collaboration with other partners: The European Organisation for Nuclear Research (CERN) Fellowships, The European Space Agency (ESA) Fellowships, The Anglo-Australian Postdoctoral Research Fellowships, and the Daphne Jackson Fellowships. Further information on these programmes is available on the PPARC website royalsociety.org/grants-schemes-awards/grants/industry-fellowship/

For further information contact:

Tel: (44) 20 7451 2666
Email: innovationgrants@royalsociety.org

PPARC Standard Research Studentship

Purpose: To enable promising scientists and engineers to continue training
Eligibility: Advice on eligibility should be sought from the Registrar's Office
Level of Study: Postgraduate
Type: Studentship
Value: Tuition fees only
Length of Study: 3 years
Frequency: Annual
Country of Study: United Kingdom
Application Procedure: Contact the PPARC
Closing Date: 31 March

For further information contact:

Tel: (44) 1793 442026
Email: steve.cann@pparc.ac.uk

Science and Technology Facilities Council Postgraduate Studentships

Subjects: Particle physics, accelerator science, nuclear physics, particle astrophysics, solar system science and astronomy.
Purpose: STFC postgraduate studentships are awarded to enable promising scientists and engineers to continue training beyond a first degree.
Eligibility: Open to postgraduates from the UK and EU countries. All studentship projects supported through STFC funding must fall within STFC remit.
Level of Study: Postgraduate
Type: Studentship
Value: Stipend (excluding fees only students), approved fees, research training support grant, conference and U.K. fieldwork element, fieldwork expenses, long term attachments, other allowances (where applicable).
Length of Study: 3.5 years
Frequency: Annual
Country of Study: United Kingdom
Application Procedure: If you are interested in applying for an STFC-funded PhD, please contact the institution at which you wish to undertake a research degree directly.
No. of awards offered: Approx. 220
Closing Date: 31 March
Funding: Government
Additional Information: Please check at www.stfc.ac.uk/funding/studentships/types-of-postgraduate-studentship/

For further information contact:

Email: studentships@stfc.ukri.org

University of Canterbury Pasifika Doctoral Scholarship

Purpose: This scholarship supports Pasifika students for study towards a research doctoral degree at the University of Canterbury
Eligibility: 1. Candidates must be Pasifika. 2. Intending students who already hold a research doctoral degree are not eligible for the scholarship. 3. Students may not take up the scholarship until any non-academic requirements for the qualifying degree have been completed and credited. Offers of scholarships to candidates whose qualifying degree is the BE (Hons) are conditional on the completion and crediting of ENGR 200 no later than 12 months after the formal offer of a place in a doctoral programme has been accepted.
Level of Study: Doctorate
Type: Scholarship
Value: Up to NZ$21,000 per annum plus tuition fees at domestic rate
Length of Study: Up to 3 years
Frequency: Annual
Country of Study: New Zealand
Application Procedure: Apply through webpage approximately 8 weeks before applications close. If the link is not provided, please download and complete the application form located below. However, if the scholarship is managed by Universities NZ or another department of the University an External Website link will appear below and application instructions will be available through that link. Apply through online link. www.canterbury.ac.nz/scholarshipsearch/ScholarshipDetails.aspx
No. of awards offered: 2

Closing Date: 15 May
Funding: Private
Additional Information: www.canterbury.ac.nz/scholarshipsearch/ScholarshipDetails.aspx?ScholarshipID=6935.1640

For further information contact:

Email: scholarships@canterbury.ac.nz

Science Foundation Ireland

Three Park Place, Hatch Street Upper, Dublin 2 D02 FX65, Ireland.

Tel: (353) 1 607 3200
Email: info@sfi.ie
Website: www.sfi.ie/
Contact: Professor Mark W. J. Ferguson, Director

SFI funds oriented basic and applied research in the areas of science, technology, engineering and mathematics. SFI provides awards to support scientists and engineers working in the fields of science and engineering that underpin biotechnology, information and communications technology and sustainable energy and energy-efficient technologies.

President of Ireland Young Research Award (PIYRA)

Purpose: The purpose of the PIYRA programme is to recruit and retain outstanding early career investigators with leadership potential. Its aim is to enable those at an earlier career stage who already hold permanent academic positions to advance their careers and build up their research teams and activities; to allow researchers in temporary positions to advance their careers and provide them with enhanced opportunities to move into a permanent academic position; to enable the award holder, together with his/her team, to carry out their work in Ireland's public research bodies; to offer funding opportunities that help third-level institutions attract and develop researchers and their careers; to allow earlier-career investigators of all nationalities to enhance their experience in Irish HEIs and to allow those employed outside of Ireland to return to work in an Irish HEI
Eligibility: The lead applicant must have completed a minimum of 36 months of active postdoctoral research. The lead applicant must have been awarded a PhD or MD within the last 8 years, in the normal case, or up to a maximum of 12 and a half years for applicants who have taken documented eligible leave, as described below. The lead applicant has an exceptional record of internationally recognized independent research accomplishments for their career stage. The lead applicant must be an individual who will be recognized by the research body upon receipt of the SFI grant as an independent investigator who will have an independent office and research space at the host research body for which he/she will be fully responsible for at least the duration of the SFI grant.
Level of Study: Postdoctorate, Research
Type: Grant
Value: Up to €1,000,000 of total value (inclusive of the host institution contribution) in direct costs
Length of Study: 5 years
Frequency: Annual
Study Establishment: Host Research Bodies must be situated in the Republic of Ireland. Research Bodies will include Universities, Institutes of Technology and independent not-for-profit public research organizations that receive a significant share of their total funding from public sources
Country of Study: Ireland
Application Procedure: Applicants are invited to submit the following documentation expression of Interest and if invited to do so after the Expression of Interest evaluation stage; full proposal. Application must be submitted via an eligible research body. Application must be submitted online via SESAME
Closing Date: December
Funding: Government
Contributor: Science Foundation Ireland
Additional Information: www.sfi.ie/funding/funding-calls/sfi-president-of-ireland/

For further information contact:

Email: frl@sfi.ie

Science Foundation Ireland Career Development Award (CDA)

Purpose: The SFI Career Development Award (CDA) aims to support early- and mid-career researchers who already hold a salaried, independent research post and who are looking to expand their research activities. Its aims is to support excellent scientific research that has potential economic and societal impact; to enable those at an earlier career stage who already hold permanent academic positions to advance their careers and build up their research teams and activities; to allow researchers in temporary positions to advance their careers and provide them with enhanced opportunities to move into a permanent academic position; to provide the

support and infrastructure to carry out novel research in areas that underpin SFI's legal remit; to enable the award holder, together with his/her team, to carry out their work in Ireland's public research bodies, including Universities and Institutes of Technology; to offer funding opportunities that help third-level institutions attract and develop researchers and their careers; to allow earlier-career investigators of all nationalities to enhance their experience in Irish HEIs
Eligibility: The applicant will be a researcher with 3–15 years of relevant experience beyond the award of their doctoral degree, who at the time of application will be either in a permanent, full-time academic position (either within the institution at which they wish to base their CDA-funded research or another elsewhere in Ireland or overseas), or employed on a temporary (fixed-term) contract where it is evident that the role being carried out is an independent research position (i.e., Postdoctoral Research Associates (or equivalent) or Research Fellows working under the guidance of a supervisor and who have never held an independent position are not eligible to apply to the CDA Programme)
Level of Study: Research
Type: Award
Value: Between €300,000 and €500,000 direct costs
Length of Study: 4 years
Frequency: Every 2 years
Study Establishment: Host Research Bodies must be situated in the Republic of Ireland. Research Bodies will include Universities, Institutes of Technology and independent not-for-profit public research organizations that receive a significant share of their total funding from public sources
Country of Study: Ireland
Application Procedure: Application must be submitted via an eligible research body. Application must be submitted online via SESAME (www.sfi.ie/funding/award-management-system)
Closing Date: 10 December
Funding: Government
Contributor: Science Foundation Ireland
No. of awards given last year: 20
Additional Information: Please write to cda@sfi.ie www.sfi.ie/funding/funding-calls/sfi-career-development-award/

For further information contact:

Email: cda@sfi.ie

Science Foundation Ireland Investigator Programme

Purpose: To fund scientific research projects of excellence in focused areas. To build capacity, expertise and relationships so as to enable researchers to compete in future SFI Research Centre Programmes or in other funding programmes such as ERC and Horizon 2020. To encourage researchers to build capacity, expertise, collaborations and relationships in areas of strategic economic importance through themed calls. To facilitate partnerships with other agencies. To support collaborations and partnerships between academia and industry
Eligibility: The lead applicant and any co-applicant(s) must hold a PhD/MD or equivalent for at least 5 years by the proposal deadline. The lead applicant and any co-applicant (s) are required to have demonstrated that they are each senior author on at least 10 international peer reviewed articles. The lead applicant and any co-applicant(s) are required to have demonstrated research independence through securing at least one independent research grant as a lead investigator or as co-investigator
Level of Study: Research
Type: Grant
Value: €400,000–2,500,000 per year
Length of Study: 3–5 years
Frequency: Annual
Study Establishment: Host Research Bodies must be situated in the Republic of Ireland. Research Bodies will include Universities, Institutes of Technology and independent not-for-profit public research organizations that receive a significant share of their total funding from public sources
Country of Study: Ireland
Application Procedure: Application must be submitted via an eligible research body. Application must be submitted online via SESAME (www.sfi.ie/funding/award-management-system)
Closing Date: 26 June
Funding: Government
Contributor: Science Foundation Ireland
No. of awards given last year: 40
Additional Information: www.sfi.ie/funding/funding-calls/sfi-investigators-programme/

For further information contact:

Email: investigators@sfi.ie

S

Starting Investigator Research Grant (SIRG)

Purpose: The SIRG programme supports excellent postdoctoral researchers who wish to take steps towards a fully independent research career. Aims to support excellent scientific research that has potential economic and societal impact. To enable those at an early career stage to establish themselves as independent researchers; to provide the support and infrastructure to carry out novel research in areas that underpin SFI's legal remit; to gain important experience towards a full-time academic position, including the supervision of the

postgraduate student supported by the award; to enable the award holder, together with his/her postgraduate student, to carry out their work in Ireland's public research bodies, including Universities and Institutes of technology; to offer funding opportunities that help third-level institutions attract and develop researchers and their careers; to allow early-career investigators of all nationalities to enhance their experience in Irish HEIs; to allow early-career investigators who have been employed outside of Ireland to return to work in an Irish HEI
Eligibility: The applicant will be a researcher with 3 to 8 years of relevant experience beyond the award of their doctoral, who is currently employed as a Postdoctoral Research Associate (or equivalent) or a Research Fellow under the guidance of a named supervisor, and who has never previously held an independent research position of any kind where they were primarily responsible for a research team and its financial support. Allowances will be made for documented leave, including maternity leave, paternity leave, parental leave, military service, sick/disability leave and carer's leave
Level of Study: Research
Type: Grant
Value: €425,000 direct costs over a period of four years
Length of Study: 4 years
Study Establishment: Host Research Bodies must be situated in the Republic of Ireland. Research Bodies will include Universities, Institutes of Technology and independent not-for-profit public research organizations that receive a significant share of their total funding from public sources
Country of Study: Ireland
Application Procedure: Application must be submitted via an eligible research body. Application must be submitted online via SESAME
Closing Date: 26 November
Funding: Government
Contributor: Science Foundation Ireland
No. of awards given last year: 20
Additional Information: www.sfi.ie/funding/funding-calls/sirg/

For further information contact:

Email: sirg@sfi.ie

Sciences Po

27, rue Saint Guillaume, Cedex 07, F-75337 Paris, France.

Tel: (33) 1 45 49 50 50
Website: www.sciencespo.fr/en/
Contact: Sciences Po

Sciences Po stands is a world-class university with over 478 partner universities within its network.

David Gritz Scholarship

Purpose: The Scholarship is meant to attract undergraduate and graduate Israeli citizens who wish to study at Sciences Po
Eligibility: The scholarship is awarded every year to 1 Israeli citizen. The candidates must be admitted to an undergraduate or a masters programme or have submitted an application for admission to Sciences Po
Level of Study: Postgraduate
Type: Scholarship
Value: €15,000 per year
Length of Study: 1 year
Country of Study: France
Application Procedure: Applicants must send the forms to caterina.sabbatini@sciencespo.fr
Closing Date: 1 June
Contributor: Sciences Po Foundation
Additional Information: For more details contact Caterina Sabbatini-Clec'h, caterina.sabbatini@sciencespo.fr www.sciencespo.fr/students/en/finance/financial-aid/bourse-david-gritz.html

For further information contact:

Tel: (33) 1 45 49 55 46
Email: lea.albrieux@sciencespo.fr

Emile Boutmy Scholarships

Purpose: The Emile Boutmy Scholarships was created after the founder of Sciences Po in order to attract the very best international students from outside of the European Union who are first time applicants and who have been admitted to an undergraduate or master's programme offered at the University
Eligibility: To be eligible for the scholarship, students must be first time applicants from a non-European Union state, whose household does not file taxes within the European Union, and who have been admitted to the Undergraduate or Master's programme.
Level of Study: Postgraduate
Type: Scholarship
Value: €12,200 per year
Length of Study: 2 years
Frequency: Annual
Country of Study: France
Application Procedure: Visit the official website to access the application form and for detailed information on how to apply for this scholarship. Students must indicate that they are

applying for the Emile Boutmy scholarship in their Sciences Po application
Closing Date: 30 November
Contributor: Science Po Foundation
Additional Information: www.sciencespo.fr/students/en/fees-funding/financial-aid/emile-boutmy-scholarship.html

KSP Fund for Innovative Projects

Purpose: The KSP Fund for Innovative Projects supports extra-curricular student-led initiatives taking place in countries of the Arab World and the Gulf Region. It is aimed at fostering innovation and providing funding for the realization of creative ideas benefiting the region in all sectors
Level of Study: Postgraduate
Value: €5,000–€10,000
Application Procedure: To apply, please send an email with 'KSP Fund for Innovative Projects' in the subject line, to the Kuwait Program Assistant fatima.iddahamou@sciencespo.fr
Closing Date: 28 February
Additional Information: Proposed projects must take place in a country of the Arab World or the Gulf Region. For further details, please contact Kuwait Program Assistant, Fatima Iddahamou: fatima.iddahamou@sciencespo.fr

For further information contact:

Email: kancelaria@ksplegal.pl

KSP Joint Research Projects

Purpose: KSP Joint Research Projects are funded by the Kuwait Program at Sciences Po to foster research links between faculty members at Sciences Po and in Kuwait, in the interest of building a unique scholarly network
Level of Study: Research
Value: Up to €50,000
Length of Study: 1 year
Application Procedure: Application files should be sent to the Kuwait Program Manager at mariezenaide.jolys@sciencespo.fr
Closing Date: 31 October
Funding: Foundation
Contributor: Sciences Po and the Kuwait Foundation for the Advancement of Sciences (KFAS)
Additional Information: For details, please check the website: www.sciencespo.fr/psia/kuwait-program www.cnr.it/en/joint-research-projects

For further information contact:

Email: info@itsr.ir

Kuwait Excellence Scholarship for Arab Students and Kuwait Nationals

Purpose: The Kuwait Excellence Scholarship program supports outstanding students coming from the Arab world and Kuwait to pursue Master's level graduate studies at Sciences Po. Multiple scholarships will be awarded to the best candidates on a competitive basis.
Eligibility: 1. Applicants must be first-time degree-seeking students in France. 2. Nationals from Arab countries, including the Gulf Region, may apply. 3. Kuwaiti National
Level of Study: Masters Degree
Type: Scholarship
Value: Arab students £10, 000 per year (ie. £20, 000 for two years of study). and for Kuwait students £12,500 per year (i.e. £25,000 for the two years of study).
Country of Study: France
Application Procedure: To apply, please send the following materials contact by email program.kuwait@sciencespo.fr with Kuwait Excellence Scholarship Application for Kuwaiti Nationals in the subject line.
Closing Date: 14 February
Additional Information: www.sciencespo.fr/kuwait-program/student-activities/scholarship/

For further information contact:

Email: program.kuwait@sciencespo.fr

Seoul National University

1 Gwanak-ro, Gwanak-gu, Seoul 08826, Korea.

Tel: (82) 2 880 5114
Email: snuadmit@snu.ac.kr
Website: en.snu.ac.kr/
Contact: MBA Admissions Officer

S

Seoul National University became the first comprehensive university of independent Korea, founded with the primary aim of producing intellectual elites who would lead the newly liberated country.

Korea Foundation Fellowship

Eligibility: Preference is given to Korean nationals residing abroad
Level of Study: Postdoctorate, Postgraduate, Research
Type: Fellowship

Value: To be determined by the review committee
Length of Study: 1 academic year
Frequency: Annual
Study Establishment: Seoul National University
Country of Study: Korea
Application Procedure: Contact the Office of international Affairs
Closing Date: January
Funding: Foundation
Contributor: The Korean Foundation
Additional Information: en.snu.ac.kr/admission/undergraduate/scholarships/before_admission

For further information contact:

Tel: (82) 2 880 8635
Fax: (82) 2 880 8632
Email: yss@snu.ac.kr

Korea-Japan Cultural Association Scholarship

Eligibility: Japanese students enroled in undergraduate programs who are not in 1st-year
Level of Study: Postdoctorate, Postgraduate, Research
Type: Scholarship
Value: KRW 3,500,000
Length of Study: 1 academic year
Frequency: Annual
Study Establishment: Seoul National University
Country of Study: Korea
Application Procedure: Contact the Office of International Affairs
Closing Date: March
Funding: Foundation
Contributor: Korea-Japan Cultural Association
Additional Information: en.snu.ac.kr/about/overview/vision

For further information contact:

Tel: (82) 2 880 8638
Fax: (82) 2 880 8632
Email: sjlim@snu.ac.kr

Overseas Koreans Scholarship

Purpose: To support students with an outstanding academic record
Eligibility: Overseas Korean students who wish to earn graduate degrees at SNU.
Level of Study: Postdoctorate, Postgraduate, Research
Type: Scholarship
Value: Full tuition exemption for a maximum of 4 semesters (when conditions are met). Living expenses: KRW 900,000 per month 4 semesters (maximum). Airfare for one economy round trip. Korean language training fee: fee exemption at the Language Education Institute for 6 months. Medical insurance subscription (private company).
Frequency: Annual
Country of Study: Korea
Application Procedure: Contact the Overseas Korean Foundation.
Closing Date: March
Additional Information: en.snu.ac.kr/admission/graduate/scholarships/before_application

For further information contact:

Tel: (82) 64 786 0274
Email: scholarship@okf.or.kr

Sher-Gil-Sundaram Arts Foundation

3/9, Sector 3, Shanti Niketan, New Delhi, Delhi 110021, India.

Tel: (91) 11 46170894
Email: contact@ssaf.in
Website: ssaf.in/

The Sher-Gil Sundaram Arts Foundation (SSAF) seeks to enable conjunctions of artistic and cultural practice that deal with historical memory, and to build expectations for the future. It commits itself to advancing creative independence for art that is founded on freedom of expression, and which is secular. It will work in solidarity with initiatives addressing concerns of the marginalized; it will support alternative and heterodox practices.

Sher-Gil Sundaram Arts Foundation: Installation Art Grant

Purpose: The Grant is premised on the fact that Indian art has been energized since the 1990s by what is broadly termed installation art, but that there is, until today, limited infrastructural and institutional support for such projects
Eligibility: 1. Individuals of Indian origin residing in India, or collectives whose members are Indian nationals residing in India. Preference will be given to applicants who lack access to networks of national and international sponsorships. 2. Artists who currently do not hold a grant or a residency where the proposed project has been developed.
Level of Study: Postgraduate

Type: Grant
Value: ₹8 lakhs
Length of Study: 18 months
Frequency: Annual
Country of Study: India
Application Procedure: The Grant invites applications from artists or artists' collectives of Indian origin residing in India. Preference will be given to applicants who lack access to networks of national and international sponsorships. The Grant will support an individual artist or an artists' collective to conceptualize and produce a new work within the parameters of installation art.
Closing Date: 20 February
Funding: Foundation
Additional Information: ssaf.in/grant-details-ssaf-open-call/

For further information contact:

Email: ssaf.installationart@gmail.com

Shorenstein Asia-Pacific Research Center (APARC)

616 Jane Stanford Way, Stanford University, Stanford, CA 94305-6055, United States of America.

Tel: (1) 650 723 4581
Website: aparc.fsi.stanford.edu/

The Walter H. Shorenstein Asia-Pacific Research Center is Stanford University's hub for contemporary Asia studies. The Walter H. Shorenstein Asia-Pacific Research Center (Shorenstein APARC) addresses critical issues affecting the countries of Asia, their regional and global affairs, and U.S.-Asia relations. As Stanford University's hub for the interdisciplinary study of contemporary Asia, we produce policy-relevant research, provide education and training to students, scholars, and practitioners, and strengthen dialogue and cooperation between counterparts in the Asia-Pacific and the United States.

Shorenstein Fellowships in Contemporary Asia

Purpose: Each year the Walter H. Shorenstein Asia-Pacific Research Center (Shorenstein APARC) offers two postdoctoral fellowship positions to junior scholars for research and writing on contemporary Asia. The primary research areas focus on political, economic, or social change in the Asia-Pacific region (including Northeast, Southeast, and South Asia), or on international relations and international political economy in the region. The fellowships are made possible through the generosity of APARC's benefactor, Walter H. Shorenstein.
Eligibility: 1. Applicants must be recent Ph.D.s and cannot be more than 3 years past the awarding of their doctoral degree when the fellowship begins. 2. Must have dissertation submission and approval for conferral by June 30. 3. Certification of degree completion and conferral must be submitted no later than August 31.
Level of Study: Doctorate, Postdoctorate
Type: Fellowships
Value: Approximately US$60,000 (annual rate of US$72,000) + US$2,000 for research expenses.
Length of Study: 10 months
Frequency: Annual
Country of Study: Asia
Application Procedure: Apply through Online.
No. of awards offered: 2
Closing Date: 3 January
Funding: Private
Additional Information: aparc.fsi.stanford.edu/education/fellowship-and-training-opportunities/shorenstein-postdoctoral-fellowship

For further information contact:

Email: shorensteinfellowships@stanford.edu

Sidney Sussex College

Cambridge University, Sidney Street, Cambridge CB2 3HU, United Kingdom.

Tel: (44) 1223 338800
Email: gradtutor@sid.cam.ac.uk
Website: www.sid.cam.ac.uk
Contact: Sidney Sussex College Tutor for Graduate Students

Evan Lewis-Thomas Law Studentships

Purpose: For research or advanced courses in law or cognate subjects. There are three current award-holders (PhD, Law).
Eligibility: There are no eligibility restrictions. Candidates must have shown proficiency in Law and Jurisprudence, normally by obtaining a university degree in Law by August, and they must be or become candidates for the PhD Degree, the Diploma in Legal Studies, the Diploma in International Law, the MPhil Degree (1 year course) in Criminology, or the

S

LLM Degree. Students from other Cambridge Colleges may apply, but if successful they would be expected to transfer their membership to Sidney Sussex College. In the competition for the studentship, no preference will be given to candidates who nominate Sidney Sussex College as their college of first or second choice on their application form
Level of Study: Postgraduate
Type: Studentship
Value: The value depends on the candidate's needs in the light of support from other sources and on the availability of income from the Evan Lewis Thomas Fund.
Length of Study: 1–3 years
Frequency: Annual
Study Establishment: The University of Cambridge
Country of Study: United Kingdom
Application Procedure: Further details of these competitions, including deadlines, can be found at www.admin.cam.ac.uk/students/studentregistry/fees/funding/index.htm
Funding: Private
Contributor: Sidney Sussex College
Additional Information: www.sid.cam.ac.uk/apply/postgraduate-study/studentships-and-funding

For further information contact:

Sidney Street, Cambridge CB2 3HU, United Kingdom.

Email: graduate.funding@admin.cam.ac.uk

Sievert Larsson Foundation

Box 23415, CY-1683 Nicosia, Cyprus.

Email: info@sievertlarssonscholarships.org
Website: www.sievertlarssonscholarships.org/
Contact: The Sievert Larsson Scholarship Foundation

The Sievert Larsson Scholarship Foundation's primary purpose is to facilitate the education of promising students from disadvantaged backgrounds. The Foundation will also facilitate the education of a few high calibre students that have exhibited excellence through their academic achievements.

The Sievert Larsson Scholarship

Purpose: To support students who come from financially vulnerable homes and who would not otherwise have the opportunity to study in Sweden
Eligibility: 1. Citizens of Thailand only. 2. Students with a completed or soon to be completed Bachelor's Degree, with a minimum grade of 3.0 (CGPA) from a prestigious Thai University, with a high position on international ranking lists.
Level of Study: Postgraduate
Type: Scholarship
Value: Version 1 Full tuition fee waiver (covers 100% of the tuition fees) during the 2-year programme (4 semesters). Version 2 Full tuition fee waiver (covers 100% of the tuition fees) and SEK 230,000 for costs of living during the 2-year programme (4 semesters)
Length of Study: 2 years
Frequency: Annual
Study Establishment: Chalmers University of Technology
Country of Study: Thailand
Application Procedure: Applications for the Sievert Larsson Scholarship are made online via the Chalmers scholarship application form
Contributor: The Sievert Larsson Foundation
Additional Information: www.chalmers.se/en/education/application-and-admission/scholarships-for-fee-paying-students/

Sigma Theta Tau International

550 W. North Street., Indianapolis, IN 46202, United States of America.

Tel: (1) 888 634 7575
Email: memserv@sigmanursing.org
Website: www.sigmanursing.org/

Sigma Theta Tau International exists to promote the development, dissemination and utilization of nursing knowledge. It is committed to improving the health of people worldwide through increasing the scientific base of nursing practice. In support of this mission, the society advances nursing leadership and scholarship, and furthers the utilization of nursing research in healthcare delivery as well as in public policy.

Sigma Theta Tau International/Association of Operating Room Nurses Foundation Grant

Purpose: The AORN Foundation awards scholarships to students who are pursuing a career in perioperative nursing, and to registered nurses who are continuing their education in perioperative nursing by pursuing a bachelor's, master's or doctoral degree.
Level of Study: Doctorate
Type: Grant
Frequency: Annual
Country of Study: United States of America

Application Procedure: Applicants should submit a completed application package for the relevant institution for that year
Closing Date: 15 June
Funding: Private
Additional Information: www.aorn.org/aorn-foundation/foundation-scholarships

For further information contact:

Association of Operating Room Nurses, 2170 South Parker Road, Suite 300, CO 80231, United States of America.

Tel: (1) 800 755 2676
Email: foundation@aorn.org

Sigma Theta Tau International/Association of Perioperative Registered Nurses Foundation Grant

Purpose: To encourage qualified nurses to conduct research related to perioperative nursing practice and contribute to the development of perioperative nursing science.
Eligibility: 1. Principal investigator is required to be a registered nurse (with a current license) in the perioperative setting or a registered nurse who demonstrates interest in or significant contributions to perioperative nursing practice. 2. Principal investigator must have, at a minimum, a master's degree in nursing. 3. Membership in either organization is acceptable but not required.
Type: Grant
Value: US$5,000 (max)
Frequency: Annual
Country of Study: United States of America
Application Procedure: All applications are accepted by AORN. View additional details. (www.aorn.org/guidelines/clinical-resources/nursing-research)
No. of awards offered: 1
Closing Date: 31 August
Contributor: The Association of Perioperative Registered Nurses and Sigma Theta Tau International
Additional Information: www.sigmanursing.org/advance-elevate/research/research-grants/association-of-perioperative-registered-nurses-(aorn)-grant

For further information contact:

2170 S. Parker Road, Suite 400, Denver, CO 80231-571, United States of America.

Tel: (1) 303 755 6304 ext. 207
Fax: (1) 800 755 2676 ext. 207
Email: lspruce@aorn.org

Sigma Theta Tau International/Rehabilitation Nursing Foundation Grant

Purpose: The Sigma Theta Tau International/Rehabilitation Nursing Foundation (RNF) Grant encourages research related to rehabilitation nursing.
Eligibility: The applicant must be a registered nurse in rehabilitation or a registered nurse who demonstrates interest in and significantly contributes to rehabilitation nursing. Proposals that address the clinical practice, educational or administrative dimensions of rehabilitation nursing are requested. Quantitative and qualitative research projects will be accepted for review. The principal investigator must have a Master's degree in nursing and an ability to complete the project within 2 years of initial funding
Level of Study: Doctorate, Postdoctorate, Postgraduate, Predoctorate
Type: Research grant
Value: Up to US$4,500
Length of Study: 1 year
Frequency: Annual
Application Procedure: Applicants must write to the Rehabilitation Nursing Foundation for details
Closing Date: 1 March
Funding: Foundation, Private
Contributor: The Rehabilitation Nursing Foundation and Sigma Theta Tau International
Additional Information: The funding month is the following January www.sigmanursing.org/advance-elevate/research/research-grants/rehabilitation-nursing-foundation-grant-(rna)

For further information contact:

Rehabilitation Nursing Foundation, 4700 West Lake Avenue, Glenview, IL 60025, United States of America.

Tel: (1) 800 229 7530
Fax: (1) 847 375 4710
Email: info@rehabnurse.org

S

Silicon Valley Community Foundation

2440 West El Camino Real, Suite 300, Mountain View, CA 94040-1498, United States of America.

Tel: (1) 650 450 5400
Email: donate@siliconvalleycf.org
Website: www.siliconvalleycf.org/

Silicon Valley Community Foundation is a regional catalyst, connector and collaborator. We bring the resources and skills of donors, business, government and community to solve some of our region's toughest challenges. We promote philanthropy in our region and support philanthropists to invest with impact. Through advocacy, research, policy and grantmaking, we seek systemic solutions to drive enduring community change.

Western Digital Scholarship Program

Subjects: Science
Purpose: For students pursuing a Bachelor of Science degree in a STEM major, particularly those from underrepresented populations and/or those demonstrating financial need or hardship. A portion of the scholarships awarded through this fund are reserved for the dependents of Western Digital employees.
Eligibility: 1. Legal dependent of a Western Digital Employee with an Employee Level of 109 or below. 2. Undergraduate student enrolled on a full-time basis at an accredited four year college / university. 3. Minimum grade point average of 3.0 on a 4.0 scale or equivalent. 4. Financial need or hardship.
Level of Study: Graduate
Type: Scholarship
Value: US$5,000
Frequency: Annual
Country of Study: United States of America
No. of awards offered: Up to 500 one-time scholarships
Closing Date: 24 March
Funding: Foundation
Additional Information: www.siliconvalleycf.org/scholarships/westerndigital

Simon Fraser University

8888 University Drive, Burnaby, BC V5A 1S6, Canada.

Tel: (1) 778 782 5567
Email: sfubeedie_undergrad@sfu.ca
Website: beedie.sfu.ca/
Contact: Ms Preet Virk, Manager, Donor Relations

Since the creation of Canada's first Executive MBA in 1968, Simon Fraser University's Beedie School of Business has emerged as a dynamic teaching and learning setting with a reputation for producing global-class research for the knowledge economy. Our undergraduate, graduate and PhD programs demonstrate a spirit of innovation, flexibility and relevance. Supported by extensive partnerships with public, private and not-for-profit organizations, our goal is to produce broadly educated, enterprising and socially responsible managers capable of making lasting contributions to their communities.

Natural Sciences and Engineering Research Council of Canada - Postdoctoral Fellowship Program

Purpose: The Postdoctoral Fellowships (PDF) program provides support to a core of the most promising researchers at a pivotal time in their careers. The fellowships are also intended to secure a supply of highly qualified Canadians with leading-edge scientific and research skills for Canadian industry, government and academic institutions.
Eligibility: 1. Be a Canadian citizen or a permanent resident of Canada. 2. Hold or expect to hold a doctorate in one of the fields of research that NSERC supports.
Level of Study: Postdoctorate
Type: Fellowship
Value: CA$45,000 per year
Length of Study: 2 years
Frequency: Annual
Study Establishment: Simon Fraser University (SFU)
Country of Study: Canada
Application Procedure: You can apply for a PDF by completing and submitting form 201, and attaching supporting documents if necessary. For further information, check with the below link., www.nserc-crsng.gc.ca/OnlineServices-ServicesEnLigne/Index_eng.asp
Closing Date: 17 October
Additional Information: www.nserc-crsng.gc.ca/Students-Etudiants/PD-NP/PDF-BP_eng.asp

For further information contact:

350 Albert Street, 16th Floor, Ottawa, ON K1A 1H5, Canada.

Email: schol@nserc-crsng.gc.ca

Natural Sciences and Engineering Research Council of Canada Industrial Post-Graduate Scholarships (IPS)

Purpose: The NSERC Postgraduate Scholarships – Doctoral (PGS D) program provides financial support to high-calibre scholars who are engaged in an eligible doctoral program in the natural sciences or engineering. This support allows these scholars to fully concentrate on their studies and seek out the best research mentors in their chosen fields.

Eligibility: Open to highly qualified science and engineering graduates.
Level of Study: Postgraduate
Type: Scholarship
Value: CA$21,000 per year for three years
Length of Study: 3 years
Frequency: Annual
Country of Study: Canada
Application Procedure: Form 201 - Application for a Postgraduate Scholarship or Postdoctoral Fellowship. To create or access an application, select online system login. (www.nserc-crsng.gc.ca/OnlineServices-ServicesEnLigne/Index_eng.asp).
Closing Date: 17 October
Additional Information: www.nserc-crsng.gc.ca/Students-Etudiants/PG-CS/BellandPostgrad-BelletSuperieures_eng.asp

Winter Pilot Award

Purpose: The goal of the Pilot Award is to provide early support for exploratory ideas, particularly those with novel hypotheses.
Eligibility: All applicants and key collaborators must hold a Ph.D., M.D. or equivalent degree and have a faculty position or the equivalent at a college, university, medical school or other research facility. Applications may be submitted by domestic and foreign nonprofit organizations; public and private institutions, such as colleges, universities, hospitals, laboratories, and units of state and local government; and eligible agencies of the federal government. There are no citizenship or country requirements.
Level of Study: Postgraduate
Type: Award
Value: The total budget of a Pilot Award is US$300,000 or less
Length of Study: 2 years
Frequency: Annual
Country of Study: United States of America
Application Procedure: Applications must be completed electronically and submitted using forms provided at proposalCENTRAL. Please log in as an applicant, go to the "Grant Opportunities" tab, scroll to Simons Foundation and click "Apply Now" for the Simons Foundation Autism Research Initiative – Pilot Award program.
Closing Date: 17 March
Additional Information: www.sfari.org/grant/pilot-awards-request-for-applications/

For further information contact:

Tel: (1) 646 654 0066
Email: sfarigrants@simonsfoundation.org

Simons Foundation

160 Fifth Avenue, 7th Floor, New York, New York 10010, United States of America.

Tel: (1) 646 654 0066
Email: info@simonsfoundation.org
Website: www.simonsfoundation.org/

The Simons Foundation's mission is to advance the frontiers of research in mathematics and the basic sciences. The Foundation's support of science takes two forms: We support research by making grants to individual investigators and their projects through academic institutions, and, with the launch of the Flatiron Institute in 2016, we now conduct scientific research in-house, supporting teams of top computational scientists.

Bridge to Independence Award Program

Purpose: SCGB's Bridge to Independence (BTI) Award aims to facilitate the transition of the next generation of systems and computational neuroscientists to research independence.
Eligibility: 1. Applicants must hold a Ph.D., M.D., or equivalent degree. 2. Applicants must be currently in non-independent, mentored training positions, as recognized by their institution. 3. Applicants must be actively seeking a tenure-track position at an institution of higher education during the next job cycle. 4. Applicants are not eligible if they are recipients of other career development awards with similar budgetary scopes as the SCGB BTI Award. 5. Applicants must not have accepted a formal offer for a tenure-track faculty position. 6. There are no citizenship requirements.
Level of Study: Postdoctorate
Type: Award
Value: US$495,000 over three years, as well as a designated US$10,000 gift
Length of Study: 3 years
Frequency: Annual
Country of Study: United States of America or Canada
Application Procedure: The Simons Foundation uses an electronic grants submission process. All interested grant applicants must submit their applications online through proposalCENTRAL. (proposalcentral.com/)
Closing Date: 28 February
Additional Information: www.simonsfoundation.org/grant/bridge-to-independence-award/?tab=rfa

S

For further information contact:

Tel: (1) 800 875 2562
Email: pcsupport@altum.com

Sir Richard Stapley Educational Trust

The Sir Richard Stapley Educational Trust, Clerk SRSET, PO Box 76132, London E8 9HE, United Kingdom.

Email: admin@stapleytrust.org
Website: www.stapleytrust.org/
Contact: The Administrator

The Sir Richard Stapley Educational Trust supports the work of students of proven academic merit, and in financial need, who are pursuing further degrees or certain postgraduate qualifications at an institution in the UK. Open to students from all countries, applicants must be living in the UK at the time of applying, as well as during their course of study. The Trust supports courses in medicine, dentistry or veterinary studies taken as a second degree, as well as certain postgraduate courses in any subject.

Sir Richard Stapley Educational Trust Grants

Purpose: To support postgraduate study
Eligibility: Open to graduates holding a First Class (Honours) degree or a good Second Class (Honours) degree (65% or above, or its overseas equivalent, or a Masters or PhD) and who are more than 24 years of age on October 1st of the proposed academic year. Students in receipt of a substantial award from local authorities, the NHS Executive, Industry, Research Councils, the British Academy or other similar public bodies will not normally receive a grant from the Trust. Courses not eligible include electives, diplomas, placements, professional training and intercalated degrees. The Trust does not support students for full-time PhD studies beyond year 3, or part-time PhD studies beyond year 6. Applicants must already be resident in the United Kingdom at the time of application
Level of Study: Postgraduate
Type: Grant
Value: £500 and £1,300
Length of Study: Grants are awarded for 1 full academic year in the first instance
Frequency: Annual
Study Establishment: Any appropriate University
Country of Study: United Kingdom
Application Procedure: Electronic applications are available in early January. The trust will consider either the first 300 complete applications or all applications received on or before deadline
No. of awards offered: 300
Closing Date: March
Funding: Trusts
No. of awards given last year: 133
No. of applicants last year: 300
Additional Information: www.stapleytrust.org/applications

Sir William Lister/Dorey Bequest

18 Stephenson Way, London NW1 2HD, United Kingdom.

Sir William Lister/Dorey Bequest

Purpose: The award is for ophthalmologists in training who are citizens of the United Kingdom as well as Members and Fellows of the Royal College of Ophthalmologists, in good standing. The number and value of the awards will be determined by the state of the funds and the candidate's requirements;
Eligibility: 1. UK citizen. 2. Members/Fellows of RCO in good standing.
Level of Study: Postgraduate
Type: Grant
Value: £300 to £600
Frequency: Annual
Country of Study: United Kingdom
Application Procedure: Retrospective applications will not be considered. All award recipients are required to submit a written report within three months of the completion of their Fellowship/research, to be circulated to the RCOphth Education Committee and the awarding body.
No. of awards offered: Varies
Closing Date: September
Funding: Private
Additional Information: www.eyedocs.co.uk/ophthalmology-travel-awards/1110-dorey-bequest-and-sir-william-lister-travel-awards

For further information contact:

Email: training@rcophth.ac.uk

Smeal College of Business

351 Business Building, University Park, Pennsylvania 16802, United States of America.

Tel: (1) 814 865 7669
Website: www.smeal.psu.edu/

The Penn State Smeal College of Business is a vibrant intellectual community offering highly ranked undergraduate, graduate, doctoral, and executive education opportunities to more than 6,000 students from across the country and around the world. We are a destination of choice for top global organizations seeking talent that will make a positive difference.

Edward & Susan Wilson Graduate Scholarship in Business

Subjects: Business
Purpose: The purpose of this program is to identify and honor full-time graduate students enrolled or planning to enroll in Smeal College of Business.
Eligibility: Consideration for this scholarship shall be given to all full-time graduate students who are currently enrolled or are planning to enroll in Smeal College of Business and have achieved superior academic standing.
Type: Scholarship
Value: The amount of the awards will depend on the performance of the endowment.
Study Establishment: Smeal College of Business, The Pennsylvania State University
Country of Study: United States of America
Application Procedure: Nominations should be made by the Department Chair (attach copy of transcript and resume) and send to Hans Baumgartner, 483-A Business Building.
Closing Date: 1 May
Additional Information: phdstudents.smeal.psu.edu/scholarship-fellowship-opportunities/internal-awards/wilson.html

For further information contact:

The Pennsylvania State University, 483-A Business Building, University Park, PA 16802, United States of America.

Tel: (1) 814 865 7669

Jeanne and Charles Rider Graduate Fellowship

Subjects: Business
Purpose: The purpose of this fellowship shall be to recognize and support outstanding graduate students enrolled or planning to enroll in The Smeal College of Business Administration.
Eligibility: Selection is based on academic merit.
Type: Fellowship
Value: To be determined
Length of Study: One academic year and may be renewed for subsequent years providing the recipient continues to meet the conditions of eligibility and funds are available.
Study Establishment: Smeal College of Business, The Pennsylvania State University
Country of Study: United States of America
Application Procedure: Nominations should be made by Department Chair to Hans Baumgartner, PhD Director. Recipient shall be selected by the Graduate Fellowship Committee.
No. of awards offered: To be determined
Closing Date: 1 May
Additional Information: phdstudents.smeal.psu.edu/scholarship-fellowship-opportunities/internal-awards/rider.html

For further information contact:

483-A Business Building, University Park, PA 16802, United States of America.

Tel: (1) 814 865 7669

Ossian R. MacKenzie Teaching Award

Subjects: Business Administration
Purpose: To identify and honor an exceptional doctoral candidate who demonstrates a high degree of promise toward making significant teaching contributions in business administration.
Eligibility: Be an exceptional doctoral candidate with demonstrable experience working towards a career teaching business administration.
Level of Study: Doctorate
Type: Award
Value: The amount of each award shall be determined by a selection committee and shall depend upon the amount of income earned by the Ossian R. MacKenzie Doctoral Award Fund.
Length of Study: One academic year

Frequency: Annual
Study Establishment: Smeal College of Business, The Pennsylvania State University
Country of Study: United States of America
Application Procedure: To nominate a graduate student, faculty are encouraged to send their letters of recommendation to 351 Business Building.
Closing Date: 1 May
Additional Information: phdstudents.smeal.psu.edu/scholarship-fellowship-opportunities/internal-awards/ossian.html

For further information contact:

The Pennsylvania State University, 351 Business Building, University Park, PA 16802, United States of America.

Tel: (1) 814 865 7669

Peter E. Liberti and Judy D. Olian Scholarship

Subjects: Business
Purpose: To provide recognition and financial assistance to outstanding PhD students enrolled or planning to enroll in The Smeal College of Business.
Eligibility: Selection is based on superior academic records or who manifest promise of outstanding academic success.
Level of Study: Postdoctorate
Type: Scholarship
Value: To be determined.
Length of Study: One academic year and may be renewed for subsequent years providing the recipient continues to meet the conditions of eligibility and funds are available.
Frequency: Annual
Study Establishment: Smeal College of Business, The Pennsylvania State University
Country of Study: United States of America
Application Procedure: Nominations should be made by Department Chair to Hans Baumgartner, PhD Director. Recipient shall be selected by the Graduate Fellowship Committee.
No. of awards offered: 2
Closing Date: 1 May
Additional Information: phdstudents.smeal.psu.edu/scholarship-fellowship-opportunities/internal-awards/liberti.html

For further information contact:

483-A Business Building, University Park, PA 16802, United States of America.

Tel: (1) 814 865 7669

Smithsonian Environmental Research Center (SERC)

Smithsonian Institution, PO Box 28, 647 Contees Wharf Road, Edgewater, MD 21037-0028, United States of America.

Tel: (1) 443 482 2217
Email: gustafsond@si.edu
Website: serc.si.edu/
Contact: Daniel E Gustafson, Jr, Professional Training & Volunteer Coordinator

The Smithsonian Environmental Research Center (SERC) provides science-based knowledge to meet critical environmental challenges. SERC leads objective research on coastal ecosystems where land meets the sea to inform real-world decisions for wise policies, best business practices, and a sustainable planet.

Postdoctoral Fellowships

Purpose: The Smithsonian Institution offers several Postdoctoral Fellowships annually to outstanding early career scientists.
Eligibility: Applicants currently working at SERC should dedicate one page of the proposal to describing their research progress. This progress report should include publications and presentations at conferences and meetings.
Level of Study: Postdoctorate
Type: Fellowship
Value: US$55,000 plus health, relocation and research expenses
Length of Study: 1 year
Frequency: Annual
Country of Study: United States of America
Closing Date: 1 November
Additional Information: serc.si.edu/fellowships

Predoctoral Fellowships

Purpose: Predoctoral fellowships are offered for students enrolled in a university as candidates for a Ph.D. or equivalent doctoral candidates who have completed preliminary course work and examinations.
Eligibility: Applicants currently working at SERC should dedicate one page of the proposal to describing their research progress. This progress report should include publications and presentations at conferences and meetings.

Level of Study: Predoctorate
Type: Fellowship
Value: US$40,000 plus allowances
Length of Study: 1 year
Frequency: Annual
Country of Study: United States of America
Closing Date: 1 November
Additional Information: serc.si.edu/fellowships

Smithsonian Environmental Research Center Graduate Student Fellowship

Subjects: Research Topics Include Biodiversity & Conservation, Biological Invasions, Ecosystems Ecology, Environmental Pollution, Food Webs, Global Change, Parasite & Disease Ecology and Watersheds & Land Use
Purpose: Graduate student fellowships are offered for students formally enrolled in a graduate program who have completed at least one semester and not yet been advanced to candidacy if in a Ph.D. program.
Eligibility: Students must be formally enroled in a graduate program of study at a degree granting institution must have completed at least one full-time semester. Intended for students who have not yet been advanced to candidacy if in a doctoral program.
Level of Study: Graduate
Type: Fellowship
Value: US$8,000
Length of Study: 10 weeks
Frequency: Annual
Country of Study: United States of America
Application Procedure: Complete online fellowship application form with the Smithsonian Office of Fellowships and Internships (click "Smithsonian Institution Fellowship Program" for application instructions)
Closing Date: 1 November
Additional Information: serc.si.edu/fellowships

Smithsonian Institution-National Air and Space Museum

6th St. and Independence Ave, SW, Washington, DC 20560, United States of America.

Tel: (1) 202 633 2214
Email: NASM-Fellowships@si.edu
Website: airandspace.si.edu/
Contact: Ms Collette Williams, Fellowships Programme Coordinator

The Smithsonian's National Air and Space Museum maintains the world's largest and most significant collection of aviation and space artifacts, encompassing all aspects of human flight, as well as related works of art and archival materials. It operates two landmark facilities that, together, welcome more than eight million visitors a year, making it the most visited museum in the country. It also is home to the Center for Earth and Planetary Studies.

Charles A Lindbergh Chair in Aerospace History

Subjects: Aerospace History
Purpose: The Charles A. Lindbergh Chair in Aerospace History is a competitive 12-month fellowship open Oct 15, to senior scholars with distinguished records of publication who are at work on, or anticipate being at work on, books in aerospace history.
Eligibility: Open to senior scholars with distinguished records of publication who are at work on, or anticipate being at work on, books in aerospace history
Type: Fellowship
Value: US$100,000
Length of Study: 12 months
Frequency: Annual
Country of Study: United States of America
Closing Date: 1 December
Additional Information: airandspace.si.edu/support/get-involved/fellowships/charles-lindbergh-chair-aerospace-history

For further information contact:

Email: NASM-Fellowships@si.edu.

The Aviation Space Writers Foundation Award

Purpose: The product created as a result of the grant must be in any form suitable for potential public dissemination in print, electronic, broadcast, or other visual medium, including, but not limited to, a book manuscript, video, film script, or monograph. Potential topics might be contemporary aviation or space events that are of interest to the general public; significant persons, historical events, or trends that illuminate the history of human flight in air and space; records; or compendia of aerospace source material.
Type: Grant
Value: US$5,000
Frequency: Every 2 years
Country of Study: United States of America
Application Procedure: Maximum two-page, single-spaced proposal stating the subject of their research and their research

goals. One- to two-page curriculum vitae. One-page detailed budget explaining how the grant will be spent.
Additional Information: Award winners are required to provide a summary report in the form of a memorandum to Ms Collette Williams that outlines how the grant was used to accomplish the goals of the project airandspace.si.edu/support/get-involved/fellowships/aviation-space-writers-foundation-award

For further information contact:

Email: NASM-Fellowships@si.edu

Smithsonian National Air and Space Museum

6th St. and Independence Ave, SW, Washington, DC 20560, United States of America.

Tel: (1) 202 633 2214
Website: airandspace.si.edu/
Contact: Miss Collette Williams

The Smithsonian's National Air and Space Museum maintains the world's largest and most significant collection of aviation and space artifacts, encompassing all aspects of human flight, as well as related works of art and archival materials. It operates two landmark facilities that, together, welcome more than eight million visitors a year, making it the most visited museum in the country. It also is home to the Center for Earth and Planetary Studies.

A. Verville Fellowship

Purpose: To pursue programs of research and writing professional in tone and substance, but addressed to an audience with broad interests
Eligibility: The A. Verville Fellowship is open to all interested candidates who can provide a critical analytical approach to major trends, developments, and accomplishments in some aspect of aviation and/or space history. Good writing skills are required. An advanced degree is not a requirement.
Type: Fellowship
Value: US$55,000 per year
Length of Study: 9 months to 1 year
Country of Study: United States of America
Application Procedure: All applications for the Verville Fellowships must be submitted electronically through the Smithsonian Online Academic Appointment System (SOLAA) (solaa.si.edu/solaa/#/public)
Closing Date: 1 December
Additional Information: airandspace.si.edu/support/get-involved/fellowships/verville

For further information contact:

Email: NASM-Fellowships@si.edu

Charles A. Lindbergh Chair in Aerospace History

Purpose: The Charles A. Lindbergh Chair in Aerospace History is a competitive 12-month fellowship open 15 October, to senior scholars with distinguished records of publication who are at work on, or anticipate being at work on, books in aerospace history
Eligibility: The Lindbergh Chair is open to established and recognized senior scholars with distinguished records of publication who are at work on, or anticipate being at work on, books in aerospace history
Type: Award
Value: US$100,000 per year
Length of Study: 1 year
Frequency: Annual
Country of Study: United States of America
Application Procedure: All applications for the Lindbergh Fellowships must be submitted electronically through the Smithsonian Online Academic Appointment System (SOLAA)
Closing Date: 1 December
Additional Information: airandspace.si.edu/support/get-involved/fellowships/charles-lindbergh-chair-aerospace-history

For further information contact:

Email: NASM-Fellowships@si.edu

Engen Conservation

Purpose: The Engen fellowship will introduce the candidate to conservation techniques for a wide range of composite objects, metals, organic materials, and painted surfaces. This fellowship is intended to contribute to the education of recent graduates by allowing them to delve into the complexities of working with modern composite materials, refine treatment process, learn management, and conduct a small-scale research project. The Fellow's independent research will be derived from our diverse collection materials. Fellows will be encouraged to publish or present their research at the end of their tenure. Access to other Smithsonian conservators,

conservation scientists, and analytical capabilities at the Museum Conservation Institute (MCI) may also be available.
Eligibility: The ideal candidate will have a Master's degree in Objects Conservation from a recognized program, is able to multi-task, work collaboratively, and conduct treatments and research independently. The candidate should have knowledge of ethical and professional principles and concepts related to the preservation of objects in a wide variety of media. They must have the ability to apply theories, principles, techniques, practices, and methodologies used to examine, study, treat, and preserve historic objects. Applicants should have a proven record of research, writing ability, and proficiency in English language skills (written and spoken).
Type: Award
Value: US$45,000 per year in addition to US$5,000 for Research allowance
Length of Study: 1 year
Frequency: Annual
Country of Study: United States of America
Application Procedure: Applications are submitted through the Smithsonian Online Academic Appointment System (SOLAA) Scholarship website: solaa.si.edu/solaa/#/public
Closing Date: 15 February
Additional Information: airandspace.si.edu/collections/conservation/fellowships

For further information contact:

Email: HorelickL@si.edu

Guggenheim Fellowships

Purpose: To pursue programs of research and writing that support publication of works that are scholarly in tone and substance and intended for publication as articles in peer-reviewed journals or in book form from a reputable publisher (in the case of post postdoctoral applicants) or in a doctoral dissertation (in the case of pre-docs)
Eligibility: Predoctoral applicants should have completed preliminary course work and examinations and be engaged in dissertation research. Postdoctoral applicants should have received their PhD within the past seven years.
Level of Study: Postdoctorate, Predoctorate
Type: Fellowship
Value: US$30,000 for predoctoral candidates and US$45,000 for postdoctoral candidates
Length of Study: 1 year
Frequency: Annual
Country of Study: United States of America
Application Procedure: All applications for the Guggenheim, Verville and Lindbergh Fellowships must be submitted electronically through the Smithsonian Online Academic Appointment System (SOLAA)
Closing Date: 1 December
Additional Information: airandspace.si.edu/support/get-involved/fellowships/guggenheim

For further information contact:

John Simon Guggenheim Memorial Foundation, 90 Park Avenue, New York, NY 10016, United States of America.

Email: NASM-Fellowships@si.edu

National Air and Space Museum

Purpose: To support research on aerospace topics
Value: US$5,000
Frequency: Every 2 years
Country of Study: United States of America
Closing Date: 15 January
Additional Information: airandspace.si.edu/visit

For further information contact:

6th Street and Independence Ave, SW, Washington, DC 20560, United States of America.

Tel: (1) 202 633 2214
Email: karafantisl@si.edu

Smithsonian Tropical Research Institution (STRI)

Smithsonian Tropical Research Institute, P.O. Box 37012, MRC 705, Washington, DC 20013-7012, United States of America.

Tel: (1) 507 212 8000
Email: fellows@si.edu
Website: www.stri.org

The Institute was founded with the purpose of increasing and sharing knowledge about the past, present and future of tropical ecosystems and their relevance to human welfare. This work began in Panama in 1910, when the Smithsonian led one of the world's first major environmental impact studies, which surveyed and catalogued the flora and fauna of the lowland tropical forests that would be flooded with the creation of the Panama Canal. A century later, the Smithsonian in Panama is a standard-setting global platform for groundbreaking research on tropical forests and marine ecosystems and their astounding biodiversity.

RaMP-UP -Research and Mentoring Program – Understanding and Preserving Tropical BioDiversity Fellowship

Purpose: The Smithsonian Tropical Research Institute has partnered with Global Sustainability Scholars to launch an NSF funded program for RaMP-UP Fellows to spend a year engaged in BioDiversity studies. The fellows will be embedded in the tropical landscapes of Panamá, practicing cutting-edge and rigorous methodologies to make lasting impact on Tropical BioDiversity.
Eligibility: 1. STRI-GSS RaMP-Up Fellows must have completed a bachelor's degree focused on Biology or similar fields, for example, environmental sciences, within the past four years. 2. Applicants must be U.S. citizens and have the proper legal documentation to travel abroad (passport) or apply for a passport by April 2023.
Level of Study: Research
Type: Fellowship
Value: The program offers a stipend of US$32,000 for a full year of participation. Round trip ticket to Panamá and lodging while at Smithsonian Tropical Research Institute facilities.
Length of Study: Twelve months
Country of Study: United States of America
Closing Date: 25 March
Additional Information: stri.si.edu/academic-programs/fellowships

STRI Postdoctoral Research in Hydrology

Eligibility: Open to applicants with a PhD in spatial analysis applied to soils or hydrology, hands-on programming skills, fluency in English and Spanish
Level of Study: Postdoctorate
Type: Research grant
Value: Minimum salary of US$40,000
Length of Study: 2 years
Frequency: Annual
Country of Study: United States of America
Application Procedure: Applicants should send an electronic copy of the current curriculum vitae, statement of research accomplishments and goals, names and contact information of three references, and reprints to Helmut Elsenbeer. Review of applications begins by July 15th
Additional Information: stri.si.edu/academic-programs/fellowships

For further information contact:

Email: ElsenbeerH@si.edu

Social Science Research Council (SSRC)

One Pierrepont Plaza, 15th Floor, 300 Cadman Plaza West, Brooklyn, NY 11201, United States of America.

Tel: (1) 212 377 2700
Email: info@ssrc.org
Website: www.ssrc.org/
Contact: Director

SSRC is an independent, international, nonprofit organization founded in 1923. It fosters innovative research, nurtures new generations of social scientists, deepens how inquiry is practiced within and across disciplines, and mobilizes necessary knowledge on important public issues.

African Peacebuilding Network (APN) Residential Postdoctoral Fellowship Program

Purpose: To support independent African research and its integration into regional and global policy communities
Eligibility: Applicants must be African citizens currently residing in an African country. Researchers based in conflict-affected African countries or those recently emerging from conflict are especially encouraged to apply. Applicants must hold a faculty or research position at an African university and have completed their PhD within 7 years of the application deadline
Level of Study: Research
Type: Fellowships
Value: A maximum of US$20,000
Frequency: Annual
Application Procedure: All applications must be uploaded through our online portal. For enquiries or technical questions pertaining to the portal, please contact APN staff (apn@ssrc.org)
Closing Date: December
Additional Information: If you have questions, please contact APN program staff by telephone at (1) 212 377 2700 or by email at apn@ssrc.org www.ssrc.org/programs/component/apn/residential-postdoctoral-fellowships/

For further information contact:

Email: apn@ssrc.org

African Peacebuilding Network Fellowships

Eligibility: All applicants must be African citizens currently residing in an African country. This competition is open to African academics, as well as policy analysts and practitioners. Applicants who are academics must hold a faculty or research position at an African university or research organization, and have a PhD obtained no earlier than January 2012.
Level of Study: Postdoctorate
Type: Fellowship
Value: US$15,000 each
Frequency: Annual
Country of Study: United States of America
Application Procedure: All applications must be uploaded through our Online Open Water portal ssrc.secure-platform.com/.
No. of awards offered: 18
Closing Date: 1 February
Additional Information: www.ssrc.org/programs/african-peacebuilding-network/apn-individual-research-fellowships/

For further information contact:

Email: apn@ssrc.org

Berlin Program Fellowship

Purpose: To support doctoral dissertation research as well as postdoctoral research leading to the completion of a monograph
Eligibility: Applicants for a dissertation fellowship must be full-time graduate students who have completed all coursework required for the PhD and must have achieved ABD status by the time the proposed research stay in Berlin begins. Also eligible are United States of America and Canadian PhD's who have received their doctorates within the past two calendar years
Level of Study: Postdoctorate
Type: Fellowship
Value: €1,100 per month for dissertation fellows, €1,400 per month for postdoctoral fellows
Length of Study: 10 months–1 year
Frequency: Annual
Study Establishment: Freie Universität Berlin
Country of Study: Germany
Closing Date: 25 March
Additional Information: grad.uchicago.edu/fellowship/berlin-program-for-advanced-german-and-european-studies-fellowship/

For further information contact:

Berlin Program for Advanced German and European Studies, Freie Universität Berlin, Kaiserswerther Str. 16-18, D-14195 Berlin, Germany.

Tel: (49) 30 838 56671
Fax: (49) 30 838 56672
Email: bprogram@zedat.fu-berlin.de

ESRC/SSRC Collaborative Visiting Fellowships

Purpose: To encourage communication and cooperation between social scientists in Great Britain and the Americas
Eligibility: Open to PhD scholars in the Americas, ESRC-supported centres, and holders of large grants awards or professorial fellowships in Britain
Level of Study: Doctorate, Research
Type: Fellowship
Value: Up to US$9,500
Length of Study: 1–3 months
Frequency: Annual
Application Procedure: Check website for further details
Closing Date: 16 April
Additional Information: www.scholarshipsinindia.com/esrc-ssrc.html

For further information contact:

Email: international@esrc.ac.uk

Japan Society for the Promotion of Science (JSPS) Fellowship

Purpose: To provide qualified researchers with the opportunity to conduct research at leading universities and other research institutions in Japan
Eligibility: 1. Scholars who have previously been awarded a fellowship under the JSPS Postdoctoral Fellowship Program for Foreign Researchers are not eligible. However, previous short-term fellowship recipients may apply for the long-term fellowship. 2. JSPS does not extend fellowships to scholars employed in institutions under the jurisdiction of the U.S. Department of Defense. 3. Japanese nationals are not eligible. 4. Japanese permanent residents are not eligible. 5. Those who have resident cards with mailing addresses in Japan at the application deadline are not eligible for the short-term fellowship.
Level of Study: Doctorate, Postdoctorate, Research
Type: Fellowship

Value: Round-trip international airfare for fellows originating in the U.S.; Insurance coverage for accidents and illness; A monthly stipend of ¥362,000 for fellows with a PhD at the start of their tenure and ¥200,000 for fellows without it. A settling-in allowance of ¥200,000 for fellowships over three months in duration; Additional research expenses may be made available for long-term fellows only.
Length of Study: 1 month to 2 years
Frequency: Annual
Study Establishment: An approved institution
Country of Study: Japan
Application Procedure: Applicants must submit the application, including all supporting documents, through the portal (www.ssrc.org/fellowships/jsps-fellowships)
No. of awards offered: 11
Closing Date: 5 January
Funding: Government
Contributor: The Japan Society for the Promotion of Science
Additional Information: www.ssrc.org/fellowships/view/jsps-fellowship/

For further information contact:

Email: japan@ssrc.org

Mellon Mays Predoctoral Research Grants

Purpose: The Graduate Initiatives Program offers three predoctoral grant opportunities the Graduate Studies Enhancement Grant (GSE), the Predoctoral Research Development Grant (PRD), and the Dissertation Completion Grant (DCG). These grants are only open to Ph.D. students who were selected as Mellon Mays Undergraduate Fellows.
Eligibility: Applicants must be a Mellon fellow enroled in a doctoral program. Applicants must have been selected as Mellon Mays Fellows as undergraduates. Fellows may apply for one grant per year and must be enroled in a doctoral program in one of the fields listed in the website or have filed a petition for inclusion of another field
Level of Study: Predoctorate
Type: Grant
Value: Maximum of US$6,500 and in GSE up to US$2,000; PRD up to US$3,000; DCG up to US$2,500.
Country of Study: United States of America
Application Procedure: Applicants should use the online application portal to apply. For detailed information, please visit www.ssrc.org/fellowships/mellon-mays-predoctoral-research-grants/
Closing Date: 1 November
Additional Information: www.ssrc.org/fellowships/view/mellon-mays-predoctoral-research-grants/

Religion, Spirituality, and Democratic Renewal Fellowship

Purpose: The Religion, Spirituality, and Democratic Renewal (RSDR) Fellowship of the Social Science Research Council (SSRC) aims to bring knowledge of the place of religion and spirituality into scholarly and public conversations about renewing democracy in the United States. These fellowships are offered by the SSRC Program on Religion and the Public Sphere with the support and partnership of the Fetzer Institute.
Eligibility: The grant competition is open to doctoral students who have advanced to candidacy and to postdoctoral researchers within five years of their PhD at the time of application. Applicants working as professional researchers or university faculty without the PhD outside of the United States may be eligible, if they are not concurrently enrolled in an MA program, and are within five years of the commencement of their professional position, as demonstrated by their curriculum vitae. Applications are welcome from scholars at these career stages from any country in the world, but all application materials must be submitted in English.
Level of Study: Doctorate, Postdoctorate
Type: Fellowship
Value: Doctoral candidates can receive between US$8,000 and US$15,000; Postdoctoral researchers can receive between US$10,000 and US$18,000 toward research-related expenses.
Length of Study: 12 Months
Country of Study: United States of America
Application Procedure: Scholarship website: ssrc.secure-platform.com/a/solicitations/login/1096?returnUrl=https%3A%2F%2Fssrc.secure-platform.com%2Fa%2Fsolicitations%2F1096%2Fhome
Closing Date: 20 March
Additional Information: www.ssrc.org/programs/religion-and-the-public-sphere/religion-spirituality-and-democratic-renewal-fellowship/

For further information contact:

Email: religion@ssrc.org

Social Science Research Council Abe Fellowship Program

Purpose: To encourage international multidisciplinary research on topics of pressing global concern and to foster the development of a new generation of researchers who are interested in policy-relevant topics of long-range importance and who are willing to become key members of a bilateral and global research network built around such topics

Eligibility: Open to citizens of Japan and the United States of and to other nationals who can demonstrate serious and long-term affiliations with research communities in Japan or the United States. Applicants must hold a PhD or have attained an equivalent level of professional experience. Applications from researchers in non-academic professions are welcome
Level of Study: Postdoctorate
Type: Fellowship
Value: Research and travel expenses as necessary for the completion of the research project in addition to limited salary replacement
Length of Study: Up to 1 year
Frequency: Annual
Study Establishment: An appropriate institution
Country of Study: United States of America
Application Procedure: Applicants must submit an online application along with a writing sample, letter of reference and an optional language evaluation form
No. of awards offered: 60–100
Closing Date: 1 September
Funding: Foundation
Contributor: The Japan Foundation Center for Global Partnership
No. of awards given last year: 14
No. of applicants last year: 60 to 100
Additional Information: www.ssrc.org/programs/abe-fellowship-program/abe-fellowship/

For further information contact:

Email: abe@ssrc.org

Social Science Research Council Eurasia Program Postdoctoral Fellowships

Purpose: To support research and/or publication records and to further the recipients academic career
Eligibility: Applicants for Postdoctoral Fellowships must have the PhD in hand at the time of application (ABDs will not be considered), and must have received the degree no more than 5 years prior to the application deadline. They must be citizens or permanent residents of the United States of America. Detailed information on eligibility criteria and conditions of awards will be in the application materials
Level of Study: Doctorate
Type: Fellowship
Value: Up to US$20,000
Length of Study: 18–24 months
Frequency: Annual
Application Procedure: Awards are made on the basis of evaluations and recommendations by the Title III Program Committee, an interdisciplinary committee and composed of scholars of the region. The committee rewards proposals with clarity of argument, purpose, theory, and method, written in a style accessible to readers outside the applicant's discipline. Applicants must submit a completed application, a narrative statement, a curriculum vitae and references. Full information is available online
No. of awards offered: Approx. 30
Closing Date: 13 November
Funding: Government
Contributor: United States Department of State under the Program for Research and Training on Eastern Europe and the Independent States of the Former Soviet Union (Title VIII)
No. of awards given last year: Approx. 3
No. of applicants last year: Approx. 30
Additional Information: No funding is available for research on the Baltic States www.ssrc.org/programs/view/eurasia-program/

For further information contact:

Email: eurasia@ssrc.org

Social Science Research Council Eurasia Program Predissertation Training Fellowships

Purpose: To provide graduate students with the opportunity to enhance their research skills in the field of Eurasian Studies
Eligibility: Applicants for Predissertation Training Fellowships must be enrolled in a doctoral programme in the social sciences or humanities or equivalent degree, but not yet advanced to the PhD candidacy. ABD's are not eligible for these fellowships. They must be citizens or permanent residents of the United States of America. Detailed information on eligibility criteria and conditions of awards will be available in the application materials
Level of Study: Doctorate, Graduate
Type: Fellowship
Value: Up to US$7,000
Length of Study: Up to 9 months
Frequency: Annual
Country of Study: United States of America
Application Procedure: Awards are made on the basis of evaluations and recommendations by the Title VIII Program Committee, an interdisciplinary committee composed of scholars of the region. The committee rewards proposals with clarity of argument, purpose, theory, and method, written a style accessible to readers outside the applicant's discipline. Applicants must submit a completed application, a narrative statement, transcripts, a course list and language evaluation form and references. Full information is available online
No. of awards offered: Approx. 20
Closing Date: 13 November

S

Funding: Government
Contributor: United States Department of State under the Program for Research and Training on Eastern Europe and the Independent States of the Former Soviet Union (Title VIII)
No. of awards given last year: 2
No. of applicants last year: Approx. 20
Additional Information: No funding is available for research on the Baltic States www.ssrc.org/programs/view/eurasia-program/

For further information contact:

Email: eurasia@ssrc.org

Social Science Research Council Eurasia Program Teaching Fellowships

Purpose: To encourage and support faculty members at all career levels in their efforts to impart their own knowledge and expertise to their students
Eligibility: Applicants for the Teaching Fellowships must have the PhD in hand and currently be teaching full-time in an accredited United States of America university, and the must be citizens or permanent residents of the United States of America. The home institution of the teaching fellowship recipient is expected to provide a letter of intent stating that the institution or relevant department intends to support the implementation of the Fellow's new course into the offered curriculum at least once within a period of no more than 2 years. Detailed information on eligibility criteria and conditions of awards will be available in the application materials
Level of Study: Postdoctorate
Type: Fellowship
Value: US$10,000
Length of Study: Maximum 2 years
Frequency: Annual
Country of Study: United States of America
Application Procedure: Awards are made on the basis of evaluations and recommendations by the Title III Programme Committee, an interdisciplinary committee and composed of scholars of the region. The committee rewards proposals with clarity of argument, purpose, theory, and method, written in a style accessible to readers outside the applicant's discipline. Applicants must submit a completed application, a narrative statement, a curriculum vitae and references. Full information is available online
No. of awards offered: 15
Closing Date: 1 November
Funding: Government
Contributor: United States Department of State (Title VIII)
No. of awards given last year: 3
No. of applicants last year: 15
Additional Information: www.ssrc.org/programs/view/eurasia-program/

For further information contact:

Email: eurasia@ssrc.org

Social Science Research Council International Dissertation Research Fellowship

Purpose: To support distinguished graduate students in the humanities and social sciences conducting dissertation research outside the United States
Eligibility: The program is open to graduate students in the humanities and humanistic social sciences regardless of citizenship enrolled in PhD programs in the United States. Applicants to the 2023 IDRF competition must complete all PhD requirements except on-site research by the time the fellowship begins or by December 2023, whichever comes first.
Level of Study: Doctorate
Type: Fellowship
Value: US$23,000
Length of Study: 6 to 12 months
Frequency: Annual
Country of Study: United States of America
No. of awards offered: 60
Closing Date: December
Funding: Private
Additional Information: www.ssrc.org/programs/idrf/international-dissertation-research-fellowship/

For further information contact:

Email: idrf@ssrc.org

Social Science Research Council Summer Institute on International Migration

Purpose: To enable attendance at a workshop/conference training young scholars in the field of migration studies
Eligibility: Open to advanced doctoral candidates currently involved in research or writing for their dissertations and recent PhDs revising their dissertations for publication or initiating new research
Level of Study: Postdoctorate, Postgraduate, Predoctorate
Type: Award
Value: Flights, meals and lodging necessary for participation in the institute are fully subsidized
Length of Study: 1 Week

Frequency: Dependent on funds available
Study Establishment: The University of California at Irvine
Country of Study: United States of America
Application Procedure: Applicants must download the application form from the website www.cri.uci.edu
No. of awards offered: 250
Closing Date: 18 February
Funding: Private
Contributor: UCT and SSRC
No. of awards given last year: 20
No. of applicants last year: 250
Additional Information: The Institute is a collaboration between the SSRC and the Center for Research on Immigration, Population and Public Policy (CRI) at the University of California, Irvine www.ssrc.org/programs/view/migration-program/

For further information contact:

Center for Research on International Migration, United States of America.

Tel: (1) 949 824 1361
Email: cbramle@uci.edu

SSRC/ACLS Eastern European Program Dissertation Fellowships

Purpose: To fund dissertation research
Eligibility: Open to United States citizens or permanent legal residents
Level of Study: Postgraduate
Type: Varies
Value: Up to US$15,000 plus expenses
Length of Study: 1 academic year
Frequency: Annual, if funds are available
Study Establishment: Any university or institution
Country of Study: Other
Application Procedure: Applicants must contact the American Council of Learned Societies (ACLS) for further information
Closing Date: November
Additional Information: The product of the proposed work must be disseminated in English www.ssrc.org/programs/view/eurasia-program/

For further information contact:

228 East 45th Street, New York, NY 10017, United States of America.

Email: grants@acls.org

Social Sciences and Humanities Research Council of Canada (SSHRC)

125 Zaida Eddy Private, 2nd Floor, Ottawa, Ontario K1R 0E3, Canada.

Tel: (1) 855 275 2861
Website: www.sshrc-crsh.gc.ca/

SSHRC is the federal research funding agency that promotes and supports postsecondary-based research and research training in the humanities and social sciences. Through its Talent, Insight and Connection programs, and through partnerships and collaborations, SSHRC strategically supports world-leading initiatives that reflect a commitment to ensuring a better future for Canada and the world. SSHRC also oversees the delivery of a number of tri-agency programs, including the Canada Research Chairs and other research chairs programs, and the New Frontiers in Research Fund, which supports international, interdisciplinary, fast-breaking and high-risk research

Aid to Scholarly Journals

Purpose: To promote the sharing of research results by assisting the publication of individual works that make an important contribution to the advancement of knowledge
Eligibility: Applicants must consult the Canadian Federation for the Humanities and Social Sciences website for eligibility requirements
Level of Study: Postdoctorate, Research
Type: Grant
Value: Up to CA$30,000 per year
Length of Study: 3 years
Frequency: Annual
Country of Study: Canada
Application Procedure: Applicants must refer to the website or email the Humanities and Social Sciences Federation of Canada
Closing Date: 2 June
Funding: Government
Additional Information: The program is administered on behalf of SSHRC by the Humanities and Social Sciences Federation of Canada www.sshrc-crsh.gc.ca/news_room-salle_de_presse/latest_news-nouvelles_recentes/2018/aid_to_scholarly_journals-aide_aux_revues_savantes-eng.aspx

For further information contact:

The Humanities and Social Sciences Federation of Canada, 151 Slater Street, Ottawa, ON K1P 5H2, Canada.

Tel: (1) 613 238 6112 ext 350
Email: scholarlyjournals@sshrc-crsh.gc.ca

Canada Graduate Scholarships – Doctoral Program

Eligibility: To be eligible to apply, you must 1. be a Canadian citizen, a permanent resident of Canada or a Protected Person under subsection 95(2) of the Immigration and Refugee Protection Act (Canada), as of the application deadline 2. have completed no more than 24 months of full-time study in your doctoral program by December 31 of the calendar year of application if previously enrolled in a graduate program 3. have completed no more than 36 months of full-time study in your doctoral program by December 31 of the calendar year of application if enrolled in a joint program; for example, MD/PhD, MA/PhD. 3a. if you fall into this category, you have access to the 36-month window whether or not you were previously enrolled in a Master's program 4. have completed no more than 36 months of full-time study in your doctoral program by December 31 of the calendar year of application if enrolled directly from a bachelor's to a PhD program (not previously enrolled in a graduate program) 4a. direct-entry applicants must be enrolled in their doctoral program at the time of application.
Level of Study: Doctorate
Type: Scholarship
Value: CA$35,000
Length of Study: 3 years
Frequency: Annual
Country of Study: Canada
Closing Date: 17 October
Additional Information: www.nserc-crsng.gc.ca/Students-Etudiants/PG-CS/CGSD-BESCD_eng.asp

For further information contact:

Email: fellowships@sshrc-crsh.gc.ca

Canada Graduate Scholarships – Master's Program

Purpose: The objective of the Canada Graduate Scholarships – Master's (CGS M) program is to help develop research skills and assist in the training of highly qualified personnel by supporting students who demonstrate a high standard of achievement in undergraduate and early graduate studies.
Eligibility: To be eligible to apply, you must 1. be a Canadian citizen, a permanent resident of Canada or a Protected Person under subsection 95(2) of the Immigration and Refugee Protection Act (Canada) as of the application deadline date 2. be enrolled in, have applied for or will apply for full-time admission to an eligible graduate program at the Master's or Doctoral level at a Canadian institution with a CGS M allocation. 3. respect the internal deadline to apply for admission for your intended program of study—contact the faculty of graduate studies (or its equivalent) at the selected Canadian institution (s) for more detailed information 4. have completed the following, as of December 31 of the year of application 4a. either between 0 and 12 months of full-time studies (or full-time equivalent) in the program for which you are requesting funding or 4b. between 4 and 12 months of full-time study (or full-time equivalent) in an eligible master's program for which the degree requirements will be completed before activation of the award, allowing it to be activated during the first 12 months of the subsequent doctoral program for which you are requesting funding.
Level of Study: Postgraduate
Type: Scholarship
Value: CA$17,500
Length of Study: 1 year
Frequency: Annual
Country of Study: Canada
Closing Date: 1 December
Additional Information: www.nserc-crsng.gc.ca/Students-Etudiants/PG-CS/CGSM-BESCM_eng.asp

For further information contact:

Email: fellowships@sshrc-crsh.gc.ca

Canadian Forest Service Graduate Supplements

Purpose: To promote Canadian doctoral research into forestry, to encourage the use of Canadian Forest Service (CFS) centres and to increase contacts between CFS researchers and Canadian universities
Eligibility: Open to SSHRC Doctoral Fellows who are conducting research in an area related to forestry in Canada and who are in the 3rd or 4th year of their programme. Candidates must have at least one CFS scientist on their supervisory committee and must carry out all or part of their research at a CFS forestry centre
Level of Study: Doctorate, Predoctorate, Research
Type: Supplement or Fellowship
Value: CA$5,000 supplement to the CA$20,000 doctoral fellowship
Length of Study: Up to 2 years
Frequency: Annual

Country of Study: Canada
Application Procedure: Applicants must visit the website
Funding: Foundation, Government
Contributor: The Canadian Forest Service

For further information contact:

Canadian Forest Service Graduate Supplements Science Branch, Natural Resources Canada, 580 Booth Street, Ottawa, ON K1A 0E4, Canada.

Tel: (1) 613 947 8992
Fax: (1) 613 947 9090
Email: mlamarch@nrcan.gc.ca

Canadian Tobacco Control Research Initiative Planning Grants

Purpose: To support investigators in developing strong proposals for grants in tobacco control research
Eligibility: Open to experts in programme and policy development as well as researchers
Level of Study: Research
Type: Grant
Value: Up to CA$30,000
Length of Study: Up to 1 year
Frequency: Dependent on funds available
Country of Study: Canada
Application Procedure: Applicants must complete an application form available with instructions on the National Cancer Institute of Canada website www.ncic.cancer.ca
Closing Date: 1 March
Funding: Government, Private
No. of awards given last year: 6
Additional Information: www.idrc.ca/en/funding

For further information contact:

Research Programs Department National Cancer Institute of Canada (NCIC), 10 Alcorn Avenue Suite 200, Toronto, ON M5V 1L9, Canada.

Tel: (1) 416 961 7223
Email: mwosnick@cancer.ca

SSHRC Doctoral Fellowships

Purpose: This support allows scholars to fully focus on their doctoral studies, to seek out the best research mentors in their chosen fields, and to contribute to the Canadian research ecosystem during and beyond the tenure of their awards.
Eligibility: To be eligible to apply, an applicant must 1. be a Canadian citizen or a permanent resident of Canada or a "protected person" under subsection 95(2) of Canada's Immigration and Refugee Protection Act by the application deadline; 2. not have already received a doctoral-level scholarship or fellowship from the Canadian Institutes of Health Research (CIHR), the Natural Sciences and Engineering Research Council (NSERC) or SSHRC; 3. not have submitted more than one scholarship or fellowship (Masters or Doctoral) application per academic year to either CIHR, NSERC or SSHRC—nominations to the Vanier CGS program do not count toward this limit (see SSHRC's regulations on multiple applications and on holding multiple awards for more information); and 4. have completed no more than 48 months of full-time study in their doctoral program by December 31 of the calendar year of application.
Level of Study: Doctorate
Type: Fellowship
Value: CA$20,000 per year up to a total of CA$80,000
Length of Study: 1 to 4 years
Frequency: Annual
Country of Study: Canada
Closing Date: 17 October
Additional Information: Both the SSHRC Doctoral Fellowships and the Canada Graduate Scholarships—Doctoral Program (CGS D) are offered through one annual national competition. Applicants need to submit only one application to be considered for one or both awards. As each award has notable differences, applicants must read the descriptions for each award carefully to determine if they are eligible to apply and hold each award. Applicants eligible for both the SSHRC Doctoral Fellowships and CGS D Scholarships will automatically be considered for both awards. www.sshrc-crsh.gc.ca/funding-financement/programs-programmes/fellowships/doctoral-doctorat-eng.aspx

S

For further information contact:

Tel: (1) 855 275 2861
Email: fellowships@sshrc-crsh.gc.ca

SSHRC Impact Awards

Purpose: SSHRC Impact Awards are designed to build on and sustain Canada's research-based knowledge culture in all research areas of the social sciences and humanities.
Eligibility: A nominee must: 1. be a citizen or permanent resident of Canada, or a "protected person" under subsection 95(2) of Canada's Immigration and Refugee Protection Act,

by the nomination deadline. 2. be an active social sciences and humanities researcher or student. 3. hold or have held SSHRC funding relevant to the award category. 4. be in good standing with SSHRC. 5. be affiliated with an institution that meets the institutional eligibility requirements. 6. maintain affiliation with an eligible institution for the duration of the Impact Award.
Type: Award
Value: CA$50,000 or CA$100,000
Frequency: Annual
Country of Study: Canada
Closing Date: 1 April
Additional Information: www.sshrc-crsh.gc.ca/funding-financement/programs-programmes/impact_awards-prix_impacts-eng.aspx

For further information contact:

Tel: (1) 855 275 2861
Email: impactawards-priximpacts@sshrc-crsh.gc.ca

SSHRC Postdoctoral Fellowships

Purpose: These fellowships support the most promising Canadian new scholars in the social sciences and humanities, and assist them in establishing a research base at an important time in their research careers.
Eligibility: To apply to this funding opportunity, applicants must 1. be a citizen or permanent resident of Canada or a "protected person" under subsection 95(2) of Canada's Immigration and Refugee Protection Act by the application deadline; 2. not hold a permanent faculty position or a faculty position leading to permanency; 3. have finalized arrangements for affiliation with a recognized university or research institution; 4. not have applied more than twice before to the SSHRC Postdoctoral Fellowships funding opportunity;
Level of Study: Postdoctorate
Type: Fellowship
Value: CA$45,000 per year
Length of Study: 1 to 2 years
Frequency: Annual
Country of Study: Canada
Closing Date: 15 September
Additional Information: www.sshrc-crsh.gc.ca/funding-financement/programs-programmes/fellowships/postdoctoral-postdoctorale-eng.aspx

For further information contact:

Tel: (1) 855 275 2861
Email: fellowships@sshrc-crsh.gc.ca

Society for Academic Emergency Medicine Foundation

1111 East Touhy Ave, Suite 540, Des Plaines, IL 60018, United States of America.

Tel: (1) 847 813 9823
Website: www.saem.org/saem-foundation/lowerfootermenu/

The Society for Academic Emergency Medicine (SAEM) is the founding member and parent organization of the SAEM Foundation. SAEM serves over 6,500 members and has a mission to create and promote scientific discovery, advancement of education, and the highest professional and ethical standards for clinicians, educators, and researchers.

Education Research Grant

Subjects: Emergency medicine
Purpose: The SAEMF Education Research Grant strives to foster innovation in teaching, education, and educational research in emergency medicine for faculty-, fellow-, resident- and medical student-level learners. The mission of the grant is to develop the academic potential of the selected fellow by providing support for a dedicated two-year training period, including pursuit and preferably completion of an advanced degree in education.
Eligibility: 1. Be a member of SAEM in good standing at application deadline and during the entire award period. 2. Be board eligible or certified by the American Board of Emergency Medicine, American Board of Osteopathic Emergency Medicine, or the American Board of Pediatrics and practicing in an emergency care setting. Senior/final year residents (3rd or 4th year, as applicable to the applicant's residency program) in good standing to graduate from an ACGME accredited emergency medicine residency program may also apply but must complete their residency program before the start of the award period. 3. Not have received an Education Research Training Grant (formerly Education Fellowship grant) previously. 4. Express and, if possible, provide evidence of a commitment to leadership in emergency medicine education in his/her current or prior work, or show potential for serving as a future leader in emergency medicine education. 5. Demonstrate a sustained interest in and commitment to emergency medicine education and an education career. This demonstrated commitment may include previous participation in educational activities related to emergency medicine or another field, peer-reviewed publications, current or previous educational research, presentations of educational

scholarly activity at scientific meetings, and engagement in local, regional, national and international activities focused on research and emergency medicine-focused education. Applicants will be judged and scored according to their expressed and demonstrated commitment to these areas. Greater consideration and potentially higher scores will be given to applicants who can demonstrate this commitment. 6. Demonstrate evidence of involvement in SAEM activities and functions. Demonstrated involvement includes number of years as a member of SAEM and participation in SAEM activities and functions (e.g., SAEM presentations and committee membership). Applicants will be judged and scored according to their expressed and demonstrated commitment to SAEM. Greater consideration and potentially higher scores will be given to applicants who can demonstrate this commitment.
Type: Grant
Value: US$50,000
Length of Study: 2 years
Frequency: Annual
Country of Study: United States of America
Closing Date: 1 August
Additional Information: www.saem.org/saem-foundation/grants/funding-opportunities/what-we-fund/education-fellowship-grant

For further information contact:

Email: grants@saem.org

Research Training Grant

Subjects: Emergency medicine
Purpose: The SAEMF Research Training Grant is intended to provide funding to support the development of a scientist in emergency medicine.
Eligibility: 1. Be a member of SAEM in good standing at application deadline and during the entire award period. 2. Be board eligible or certified by the American Board of Emergency Medicine, American Board of Osteopathic Emergency Medicine, or the American Board of Pediatrics and practicing in an emergency care setting. Senior/final year residents (3rd or 4th year, as applicable to the applicant's residency program) in good standing to graduate from an ACGME accredited emergency medicine residency program may also apply but must complete their residency program before the start of the award period. 3. Hold a university appointment (e.g., faculty, fellow, or similar) in or be actively involved (e.g., have an adjunct appointment) with a department or division of emergency medicine or pediatric emergency medicine at the start of the Research Training Grant award period. Emergency medicine residents in their final year of residency may apply for the Research Training Grant, subject to the same stipulation of holding a university appointment at the start of the Research Training Grant award period. The applicant may work as a clinician at an institution other than the host institution or the institution at which the project will be conducted. 4. Not have previously received a SAEMF Research Training Grant, an Emergency Medicine Foundation (EMF) grant with similar purpose as the SAEMF Research Training Grant, a federally funded individual career development award (K-series or VA CDA), a federally funded R01 or equivalent, or a similar research training grant from another entity, prior to the start of the Research Training Grant period. If an applicant has received funding for an institutional training grant (K12, KL2 or similar), he/she should provide a detailed description of the currently funded project and any similarities or overlap with the SAEMF application. Eligibility will be assessed at the time of the award decision, so applicants funded by a disqualifying source after submission of their application may become ineligible as a result of subsequent funding decisions.
Level of Study: Research
Type: Grant
Value: US$150,000
Length of Study: 2 years
Frequency: Annual
Country of Study: United States of America
Application Procedure: All application components, including letters of support, must be submitted through the SAEM Foundation Grant Portal. (auth.saem.org/openid/authenticate?state=7e5c1964-30bd-11ea-bf93-002590ebe516&redirect_uri=https%3A%2F%2Fsaem.smapply.io%2Fsso%2Foauth%2F&response_type=code&client_id=39b29911-9e25-4416-b0cb-bd33a0d2dd45)
Closing Date: 1 August
Additional Information: www.saem.org/saem-foundation/grants/funding-opportunities/what-we-fund/research-training-grant

For further information contact:

Email: grants@saem.org

Society for Promotion of Roman Studies

Room 252, South Block, Senate House, Malet Street, London WC1E 7HU, United Kingdom.

Tel: (44) 20 7862 8727
Email: office@romansociety.org
Website: www.romansociety.org/
Contact: Dr Fiona Haarer, Secretary of Society

S

The Society is the sister society to the Society for the Promotion of Hellenic Studies. The Roman Society is the leading organisation in the United Kingdom for those interested in the study of Rome and the Roman Empire. Its scope is wide, covering Roman history, archaeology, literature and art down to about A.D. 700. It has a broadly based membership, drawn from over forty countries and from all ages and walks of life.

Hugh Last Fund and General Fund

Purpose: To assist in the undertaking, completion, or publication of works relating to the general scholarly purposes of the Roman Society, excluding expenses in connection with archaeological projects. The Hugh Last Fund also excludes travelling, hotel, conference, or other living expenses of scholars
Level of Study: Postdoctorate
Type: Funding support
Value: Varies £500 or £1,000
Frequency: Annual
Country of Study: United Kingdom
Application Procedure: Applications should be made using the application form – the completed application should not exceed two sides of A4. Applicants should give a concise and clear outline of the project, including publication plans if relevant, and itemise the costs requested. They must declare any other applications being made for the same project. Completed applications should be sent to the Secretary by email office@romansociety.org
Closing Date: 31 January
Additional Information: Individuals may not make more than one application in any year www.romansociety.org/Grants-Prizes/Hugh-Last-Fund-General-Fund

For further information contact:

Email: office@romansociety.org

Society for the Arts in Religious and Theological Studies (SARTS)

United Theological Seminary of the Twin Cities, 3000 5th Street NW, New Brighton, MN 55112, United States of America.

Tel: (1) 651 255 6117, (1) 651 255 6190
Email: wyates@unitedseminary-mn.org
Website: www.societyarts.org/
Contact: Wilson Yates

The Society was organized to provide a forum for scholars and artists interested in the intersections among theology, religion, spirituality, and the arts, to share thoughts, challenge ideas, strategize approaches in the classroom, and to advance the discipline in theological and religious studies curricula.

Luce Fellowships

Purpose: To enhance and expand the conversation on theology and art
Eligibility: Open to candidates teaching theology as a faculty member at an accredited postsecondary educational institution or graduate students
Level of Study: Graduate, Research
Type: Fellowships
Value: Awards are up to US$3,000 each
Length of Study: 1 year
Frequency: Annual
Country of Study: United States of America
Application Procedure: Applicants must submit an information sheet, curriculum vitae, a project abstract, a formal proposal, a budget and 2 letters of recommendation
Closing Date: 20 February
Additional Information: www.societyarts.org/fellowships.html

For further information contact:

University of St Thomas, Mail JRC 153 2115 Summit Avenue, MN 55105, United States of America.

Email: office@societyarts.org

Society for the Psychological Study of Social Issues (SPSSI)

700 7th St SE, Washington, DC 20003, United States of America.

Tel: (1) 877 310 7778
Email: spssi@spssi.org
Website: www.spssi.org/
Contact: Anila Balkissoon, Executive Director

SPSSI is an organization of social scientists that has historically brought research to bear on a wide array of societal problems. SPSSI was organized during the Depression of the 1930s, in an attempt to bring together a "national group of socially minded psychologists" to address social and economic issues (Finison, 1979). While maintaining its status as an independently incorporated society, SPSSI also became an affiliated organization of the American Psychological Association from 1937 to 1945, and Division 9 of the APA from 1945 to the present (Kimmel, 1997).

Society for the Psychological Study of Social Issues Grants-in-Aid Program

Purpose: To support scientific research in social problem areas related to the basic interests and goals of SPSSI
Eligibility: The applicant must be a member of SPSS-I. Applicants may submit only one application per deadline. If an applicant has applied to the Clara Mayo Grant in the same award year (July 1 – June 30), she or he is not eligible to apply for GIA. Individuals may submit a joint application.
Level of Study: Doctorate, Graduate, Postdoctorate, Postgraduate
Type: Grant
Value: The usual grant is for up to US$2000 for post-doctoral work and up to US$1000 for pre-doctoral work.
Frequency: Twice a year
Country of Study: United States of America
Application Procedure: 1. A cover sheet with your name, address, phone number, e-mail address and title of the proposal. 2. An abstract of 100 words or less summarizing the proposed research. 3. Project purposes, theoretical rationale, and research methodology and analytical procedures to be employed. 4. Relevance of research to SPSSI goals and Grants-in-Aid criteria. Applicants are encouraged to describe why SPSSI funding is useful for their research. 5. Status of human subjects review process (which must be satisfactorily completed before grant funds can be forwarded). 6. Resume of investigator (a faculty sponsor's recommendation must be provided if the investigator is a graduate student; support is seldom awarded to students who have not yet reached the dissertation stage). 7. Specific amount requested, including a budget. For co-authored submissions, please indicate only one name and institution to whom a check should be jointly issued if selected for funding. Scholarship website: www.spssi.org/index.cfm?fuseaction=Workflow.skipSave&WorkflowID=12&opportunityType_id=1&ApplyFlag=1
Closing Date: 15 October
Funding: Private
Additional Information: www.spssi.org/index.cfm?fuseaction=page.viewpage&pageid=730

For further information contact:

Email: awards@spssi.org

The Clara Mayo Grants

Purpose: The Clara Mayo Grant program was set up to support Masters' theses or pre-dissertation research on aspects of sexism, racism, or prejudice, with preference given to students enrolled in a terminal Master's program.
Eligibility: Individuals who are SPSSI members and who have matriculated in graduate programs in psychology, applied social science, and related disciplines. A student who is applying for a Grants-In-Aids may not apply for the Clara Mayo award in the same award year. Applicants may submit only one Clara Mayo grant application per calendar year.
Level of Study: Research
Type: Grant
Value: US$1,000
Frequency: Twice a year
Country of Study: United States of America
Application Procedure: Scholarship website: www.spssi.org/index.cfm?fuseaction=Workflow.skipSave&WorkflowID=12&opportunityType_id=1&ApplyFlag=1
No. of awards offered: 6
Closing Date: 15 October
Additional Information: www.spssi.org/index.cfm?fuseaction=page.viewpage&pageid=727

For further information contact:

Email: awards@spssi.org

Society for the Scientific Study of Sexuality (SSSS)

1874 Catasauqua Road, #208, Allentown, PA 18109, United States of America.

Tel: (1) 610 443 3100
Email: Thesociety@SexScience.org
Website: www.sexscience.org/
Contact: Dawn Laubach, Director of Operations

The Society for the Scientific Study of Sexuality is dedicated to advancing knowledge of sexuality and communicating scientifically based sexuality research and scholarship to professionals, policy makers, and the general public. SSSS fosters a worldwide community of diverse professionals committed to a scholarly and scientific approach to acquiring and disseminating accurate knowledge of sexuality.

Society for the Scientific Study of Sexuality Student Research Grants

Purpose: SSSS has a strong commitment to "the next generation" through the support of a vigorous student membership program, and as a member benefit to its students, SSSS offers two grants to be awarded each year - one to a graduate student and one to an undergraduate student.
Eligibility: Applicants must be a member of the SSSS
Level of Study: Graduate, Undergraduate
Type: Grant
Value: Graduate Student Research Grant up to US$1,500 and for Undergraduate Student Research Grant up to US$1,000. Both US$500 for travel
Length of Study: 1 year
Frequency: Annual
Country of Study: Any country
Application Procedure: Contact the society or check website for details
Contributor: The Foundation for the Scientific study of sexuality
Additional Information: www.sexscience.org/content.aspx?page_id=22&club_id=173936&module_id=455311

For further information contact:

Email: TheSociety@SexScience.org

Society of Apothecaries of London

Apothecaries Hall, Black Friars Lane, London EC4V 6EJ, United Kingdom.

Tel: (44) 20 7236 1189
Email: clerksec@apothecaries.org
Website: www.apothecaries.org/
Contact: Wallington Smith, Clerk

The Worshipful Society of Apothecaries lies at the heart of the early foundations of modern-day medicine and remains an important, active and innovative medical institution today. The Society plays a key role in the advancement of specialist areas of medicine, and in the ongoing post-graduate education and qualification of practitioners. Steeped in history and tradition, the Society was founded by Royal Charter in 1617 and is one of the few livery companies in the City of London to remain professionally based with over 85 per cent of its membership belonging to professions allied to medicine.

Gillson Scholarship in Pathology

Purpose: To encourage original research in any branch of pathology
Eligibility: Open to candidates under 35 years of age who are either licenciates or freemen of the Society, or who will obtain the licence or the freedom within 6 months of election to the scholarship
Level of Study: Postgraduate
Type: Scholarship
Value: £1,800 in total. Payments are made twice annually for the duration of the scholarship
Length of Study: 3 years, renewable for a second term of 3 years
Frequency: Every 3 years
Country of Study: Any country
Application Procedure: Applicants must submit two testimonials and present evidence of their attainments and capabilities as shown by any papers already published, and a detailed record of any pathological work already done. Candidates should also state where the research will be undertaken
Closing Date: 1 December
Funding: Private
Additional Information: Preference is given to the candidate who is engaged in the teaching of medical science or in its research. Scholars are required to submit an interim report at the end of the first 6 months of tenure, and a complete report 1 month prior to the end of the 3rd year. Any published results should also be submitted to the Society phd.northeastern.edu/opportunity/society-for-the-scientific-study-of-sexuality-ssss-graduate-research-grant/

For further information contact:

Email: admin@scholarship-positions.com

Society of Architectural Historians (SAH)

1365 North Astor Street, Chicago, IL 60610, United States of America.

Tel: (1) 312 573 1365
Email: info@sah.org
Website: www.sah.org/

SAH is an international not-for-profit membership organization that promotes the study and preservation of the built environment worldwide. The society serves scholars, professionals in allied fields and the interested general public.

American Council of Learned Societies Digital Extension Grants

Purpose: ACLS invites applications for ACLS Digital Extension Grants, made possible by the generous assistance of The Andrew W. Mellon Foundation. This program supports digitally based research projects in all disciplines of the humanities and related social sciences. It is hoped that these grants will advance humanistic scholarship by enhancing established digital projects and extending their reach to new communities of users
Eligibility: The project must be hosted by an institution of higher education in the United States. The project's principal investigator must be a scholar in a field of the humanities and the; humanistic social sciences. The principal investigator must have a PhD degree conferred prior to the application; deadline. (An established scholar who can demonstrate the equivalent of the PhD in publications and professional experience may also qualify.)
Level of Study: Graduate
Type: Grant
Length of Study: 12 to 18 months
Frequency: Annual
Country of Study: Any country
Application Procedure: 1. Applicants must list current and past funding sources for their projects; in the case of joint funding sources for the project. 2. Applicants should indicate clearly in their budget plans how each source of project funding will be used during the ACLS grant period. 3. Awards provide funding of up to US$150,000 for project costs. A portion of grant funds must go towards collaborations with new project partners who could benefit from access to the infrastructure at the project's host site or from substantive participation in the development of the project. 4. Grants may be used to cover salary replacement, staffing, equipment, and other costs. 5. Tenure 12–18 months, to be initiated between 1 July and 31 December
Closing Date: 31 December
Funding: Private
Additional Information: www.acls.org/programs/digitalextension/

For further information contact:

Email: fellowships@acls.org

Edilia and François-Auguste de Montequin Fellowship in Iberian and Latin American Architecture

Purpose: To fund travel for research into Spanish, Portuguese and Ibero American architecture
Eligibility: Open to SAH members who are junior scholars, including graduate students
Level of Study: Doctorate, Postdoctorate, Postgraduate
Type: Fellowship
Value: US$2,000 for junior scholars awarded each year and US$6,000 for senior scholars offered every 2 years
Application Procedure: Applicants must complete an application form, available on request by writing to SAH for guidelines or visiting the SAH website
No. of awards offered: 5
Closing Date: 16 October
Funding: Private
No. of awards given last year: 1
No. of applicants last year: 5
Additional Information: eahn.org/2017/08/fellowship-edilia-and-francois-auguste-de-montequin-fellowship/

For further information contact:

Email: vnelson@unm.edu

Society of Naval Architects and Marine Engineers

99 Canal Center Plaza, Suite 310, Alexandria, VA 22314, United States of America.

Tel: (1) 703 997 6701
Email: sname@sname.org
Website: www.sname.org/

SNAME is an internationally recognized non-profit, professional society of individual members serving the maritime and offshore industries and their suppliers. For many, SNAME has been absolutely essential to career development and success in the industry.

John W. Davies Scholarship

Subjects: Marine transportation, development of offshore resources, eco-systems interaction with development of Arctic/cold ocean resources, climate change impact in marine cold regions, or special areas of research for Arctic/cold ocean environments.
Purpose: The competition is open to any full time graduate student at a recognized University in Canada or the US State of Alaska whose research will assist in providing solutions to problems encountered in the Arctic or in cold ocean environments.

Eligibility: The competition is open to any full time graduate student at a recognized University in Canada or the US State of Alaska
Type: Scholarship
Value: CA$3,000
Study Establishment: Any recognized University in Canada or the US State of Alaska
Country of Study: United States of America or Canada
Application Procedure: An abstract of approximately 500 words is to be submitted explaining the objectives of the research being undertaken, progress to date, and how this research is to be applied in the Arctic or to cold ocean environments. Applicants are also encouraged to describe how their research is placed within the context of broader Arctic issues. In addition, the selection pancl will require a resume, a transcript of marks, sent by the university directly to the Awards Committee (for the most recent degree completed and degree in progress), and three letters of reference, two of which being former or current professors, to be sent by the referees directly to the Awards Committee.
Closing Date: 26 June
Additional Information: www.sname.org/arcticsection/home

Society of Women Engineers (SWE)

130 East Randolph Street, Suite 3500, Chicago, IL 60601, United States of America.

Tel: (1) 312 596 5223
Email: hq@swe.org
Website: swe.org/
Contact: Ms Karen Horting, Executive Director

SWE was founded in 1950, and is a non-profit educational service organization. SWE is the driving force that establishes engineering as a highly desirable career aspiration for women. SWE empowers women to succeed and advance in those aspirations and be recognized for their life-changing contributions and achievements as engineers and leaders.

Society of Women Engineers Past Presidents Scholarships

Purpose: Past Presidents Scholarship is open to sophomore, junior, senior undergraduate and graduate students taking up engineering or engineering technology related majors. Two scholarships worth US$2000 will be given to the chosen recipients
Eligibility: 1. Gender: Female. 2. Age/Grade Level: Sophomore, Junior, Senior, Graduate. 3. Minimum GPA: 3.0. 4. Financial Need: Not Mentioned. 5. Citizenship: US citizenship required. 6. Major/Career: Engineering, Engineering Technology.
Level of Study: Doctorate, Graduate, Postgraduate
Type: Scholarship
Value: US$2,000
Frequency: Annual
Country of Study: United States of America
Application Procedure: Scholarship website: scholarships.swe.org/applications/login.asp
Closing Date: February
Funding: Private
No. of awards given last year: 2
Additional Information: www.smartscholar.com/scholarship/past-presidents-scholarship-swe/

For further information contact:

Tel: (1) 312 596 5223
Email: scholarships@swe.org

Södertörn University

Alfred Nobels allé 7, 141 89 Huddinge, Sweden.

Tel: (46) 8 608 40 00
Website: www.sh.se/english/sodertorn-university
Contact: Södertörn University Registrator

Sodertorn University is a public university located in Flemingsberg, which is located in Huddinge Municipality, and the larger area called Södertörn, in Stockholm County, Sweden.

Södertörn University Tuition Fee Waive

Purpose: Södertörn University is offering tuition fee waiver for pursuing master's programme studies
Eligibility: Applicants from countries outside the EU/EEA/Switzerland are eligible to apply, Applicant should hold degree from a Swedish higher education institution, Applicants is currently enrolled in a study programme at a Swedish higher education institution, more priority will be given to Sweden students. Applicant should have English Language requirements, Applicant should have ability to qualify in TOEFL, IELTS or equivalent tests.
Level of Study: Postgraduate
Type: Scholarship

Length of Study: 1 to 2 years
Country of Study: Sweden
Application Procedure: All the eligible applicants must send application form along with supporting documents via e-mail registrator@sh.se on or before deadline, Incomplete application forms will not be accepted.
Closing Date: 10 March
Additional Information: scholarship-fellowship.com/sodertorn-university-tuition-fee-waiver/

For further information contact:

Email: studentservice@sh.se

Soil and Water Conservation Society (SWCS)

945 SW Ankeny Road, Ankeny, IA 50023, United States of America.

Tel: (1) 515 289 2331
Email: swcs@swcs.org
Website: www.swcs.org/

SWCS fosters the science and the art of soil, water and related natural resource management to achieve sustainability. The SWCS promotes and practices an ethic recognizing the interdependence of people and the environment.

Melville H. Cohee Student Leader Conservation Scholarship

Purpose: The Scholarship provides financial assistance to members of SWCS who are in their junior or senior year of full-time undergraduate study or are pursuing graduate level studies with a natural resources conservation orientation at a properly accredited college or university.
Eligibility: 1. Applicants must be a member of SWCS at the time of application. 2. In junior or senior year of full-time undergraduate study by the fall of 2022 or pursuing graduate level studies in a natural resource field. 3. Have demonstrated integrity, ability, and leadership in the natural resources field. 4. Members of the SWCS Awards Committee and their immediate families are not eligible.
Level of Study: Graduate, Postgraduate
Type: Scholarship
Value: US$2000
Country of Study: United States of America
Application Procedure: Scholarship website: swcs.formstack.com/forms/2023_cohee_scholarship
No. of awards offered: 1
Closing Date: 31 March
Additional Information: swcs.formstack.com/forms/2023_cohee_scholarship

For further information contact:

Email: awards@swcs.org

The Kenneth E. Grant Scholarship

Purpose: The Scholarship provides financial aid to members of SWCS for interdisciplinary graduate-level research on a conservation topic that will extend the SWCS mission of fostering the science and the art of soil, water, and related natural resource management research.
Eligibility: 1. Applicants must be a member of SWCS at the time of application. 2. Applicants should be pursuing interdisciplinary graduate-level research on a conservation topic that will extend the SWCS mission. 3. Have demonstrated integrity, ability, and competence to complete the specified study topic. 4. Members of the SWCS Awards Committee and their immediate families are not eligible.
Level of Study: Postgraduate
Type: Grant
Value: US$500
Frequency: Annual
Country of Study: United States of America
Application Procedure: Scholarship website: swcs.formstack.com/forms/2023_grant_scholarship
No. of awards offered: 1
Closing Date: 31 March
Additional Information: swcs.formstack.com/forms/2023_grant_scholarship

For further information contact:

Email: awards@swcs.org

S

South African Association of Women Graduates (SAAWG)

SAAWG NATIONAL OFFICE, Suite 329, Rondebosch 7701, South Africa.

Tel: (27) 21 4478989
Email: fellowships@saawg.org
Website: www.saawg.org/
Contact: Miss Margaret Edwards, National President

SAAWG promotes the tertiary education of women and their self-development over their life span. It seeks and facilitates equity for women graduates, cross-cultural insights and co-operation and societal advancement. Its great underlying purpose is world peace, brought about through education and international friendship. SAAWG is affiliated to the International Federation of University Women (IFUW) and is a member of the Federation of University Women of Africa (FUWA).

Hansi Pollak Scholarship

Purpose: To assist postgraduate study or research devoted to the practical purpose of ameliorating social conditions in South Africa
Eligibility: Open to South African women graduates of all races who are, or have become, members of the Association
Level of Study: Doctorate, Postgraduate
Type: Scholarship
Value: R6,000 paid in 6-month installments
Length of Study: 2 years, non-renewable
Frequency: Every 2 years
Study Establishment: Any recognized university
Country of Study: Any country
Application Procedure: Applicants must write for application forms
No. of awards offered: 50
Closing Date: 25 March
Funding: Private
No. of awards given last year: 1
No. of applicants last year: 50
Additional Information: www.saawg.org/Bursaries.html

For further information contact:

Email: fellowships@saawg.org

Isie Smuts Research Award

Purpose: To assist postgraduate women in research
Eligibility: 1. For a female applicant undertaking postgraduate studies/research in any field. 2. Applicants must be studying in South African Universities or Universities of Technology. 3. There is option for renewal of scholarship.
Level of Study: Postgraduate
Type: Award
Value: R1,300
Frequency: Annual
Study Establishment: Any university
Country of Study: South Africa
Application Procedure: Applicants must write to Miss V Henley
Closing Date: 25 March
Funding: Private
No. of awards given last year: 1
Additional Information: www.saawg.org/Bursaries.html

For further information contact:

Email: fellowships@saawg.org

South African Council for English Education (SACEE)

1261 Storey Street, Queenswood 0186, South Africa.

Tel: (27) 82 4488 372
Email: sacee.national@gmail.com
Website: sacee.org.za/
Contact: Treasurer/Secretary

SACEE is a registered non-profit association mainly consisting of voluntary members. SACEE was established in 1955 by a small group of people who were dedicated to the protection of English usage. Our mission statement - to support the teaching, learning and appreciation of English. Today, through a network of branches and membership, the Council succeeds in initiating and sustaining a wide variety of worthwhile activities and projects, undertaken voluntarily by members and aimed at benefiting teachers, learners and college and university students. SACEE provides a practical means for individuals and organisations to participate in the development of skills and in the enjoyment of the English language. SACEE draws together people with an appreciation of the richness of the language, a concern for clarity of thought and a respect for the multilingual diversity of South Africa.

South African Council for English Education's EX-PCE Bursary

Purpose: The bursary is available for course fees, the purchase of books, printing costs and, at the Bursary Committee's discretion, any other incidental expenses which may be incurred. The applicant will need to show that he/she is a 'deserving' case.
Eligibility: Applicants must be South African citizens or residents. The applicant's normal place of residence must be in the PRETORIA area.
Level of Study: Postgraduate
Type: Bursary
Value: Course fees, the purchase of books, printing costs

Frequency: Annual
Study Establishment: Any academic institution
Country of Study: South Africa
Application Procedure: Scholarship website: sacee.org.za/wp-content/uploads/ExPCE-App-form.pdf
Closing Date: 31 July
Funding: Private
Additional Information: sacee.org.za/bursary-news/

Southern Cross University

Graduate Research College, PO Box 157, Lismore, NSW 2480, Australia.

Tel: (61) 2 6620 3876
Email: jrussell@scu.edu.au
Website: www.scu.edu.au
Contact: Mr John Russell, Administrative Officer

Southern Cross University is one of Australia's most modern, creative and innovative universities founded on traditions of academic excellence, with national and international industry links. The University's courses emphasize real-world skills and vocational training, and are designed to give graduates a competitive edge in today's demanding employment market.

Master of Business Administration Programme

Length of Study: Please contact the Organisation
Application Procedure: Applicants must complete the application form, supply evidence of any previous academic qualifications, as well as a curriculum vitae and a letter of support from your employer
Closing Date: 30 November

For further information contact:

Fax: (61) 2 6620 3227
Email: intoff@scu.edu.au

Space Environment Research Centre (SERC)

AITC2 Mount Stromlo Observatory, Cotter Road, Weston Creek, ACT 2611, Australia.

Tel: (61) 7 3365 1111
Website: www.serc.org.au/

SERC brings together expertise and resources from leading universities, international space agencies and commercial research providers to mitigate and ultimately remove the risk of space debris collisions.

Space Environment Research Centre Scholarships

Purpose: The CRC for Space Environment Management (SEMCRC), managed by the Space Environment Research Centre (SERC) has been established to build on Australian and international expertise. Students can receive additional support and opportunities provided by the Space Environment Research Centre. Successful scholarship candidates will also have the opportunity to apply for exciting short-term placements in space research centres internationally and within Australia
Eligibility: Consideration of all candidates will be given based on academic merit, relevance of studies to SERC objectives and potential for long-term contribution to research outcomes. Priority is given to students with first class honours (or equivalent) from participating countries, currently Australia, Japan and the United States of America
Level of Study: Graduate, Postgraduate
Type: Scholarship
Value: Will cover an additional support and opportunities provided by the Space Environment Research Centre and an opportunity to apply for exciting short-term placements in space research centres internationally and within Australia.
Country of Study: Australia
Application Procedure: Applicants can apply through online system at the link scholarships.uq.edu.au/scholarship/space-environment-research-centre-scholarships
Closing Date: 31 December
Additional Information: The applicant is or will be enrolled in academic studies at a reputable Australian University. In the case of an international applicant, the applicant is required to have a valid passport, appropriate visa and may not be from a country subject to Trade Controls www.scholarshipsads.com/space-environment-research-centre-scholarships-international-students-australia-2017/

For further information contact:

Email: admissions@gradschool.uq.edu.au

Spencer Foundation

The Spencer Foundation, 625 N Michigan Ave, Suite 1600, Chicago, IL 60611, United States of America.

Tel: (1) 312 337 7000
Website: www.spencer.org/
Contact: Fellowships Office

The Spencer Foundation has been a leading funder of education research since 1971 and is the only national foundation focused exclusively on supporting education research.

Research Grants on Education: Small

Purpose: The Small Research Grants Program supports education research projects that will contribute to the improvement of education, broadly conceived, with budgets up to US$50,000 for projects ranging from one to five years.
Eligibility: Proposals to the Research Grants on Education program must be for academic research projects that aim to study education. Proposals for activities other than research are not eligible (e.g., program evaluations, professional development, curriculum development, scholarships, capital projects). Additionally, proposals for research studies focused on areas other than education, are not eligible.
Level of Study: Postgraduate
Type: Grant
Value: US$50,000
Frequency: Annual
Country of Study: United States of America
Application Procedure: Scholarship website: spencer.smartsimple.us/s_Login.jsp
Closing Date: 5 April
Funding: Private
Additional Information: www.spencer.org/grant_types/small-research-grant

For further information contact:

Email: smallgrants@spencer.org

Spencer Foundation Dissertation Fellowship Program

Purpose: The fellowship is designed to provide fellows with support for the writing phase of the dissertation and to alleviate the need for significant other employment.
Type: Fellowship
Value: US$27,500
Frequency: Annual
Country of Study: United States of America
No. of awards offered: 35
Closing Date: 7 October
Additional Information: www.spencer.org/grant_types/dissertation-fellowship

For further information contact:

Email: fellows@spencer.org

Spinal Research

80 Coleman Street, London EC2R 5BJ, United Kingdom.

Tel: (44) 2038 247400
Email: info@spinal-research.org
Website: spinal-research.org/

Spinal Research is the UK's leading charity funding medical research around the world to develop effective treatments for paralysis caused by spinal cord injury. Spinal Research raises money to fund research into clinical treatments including vital scientific research such as clinical tools to better understand the injury caused, and for the devastating effects on daily living such as breathing, hand movement, and bladder and bowel control.

International Spinal Research Trust

Purpose: Healthcare Innovations that could have a significant impact on bladder, bowel and sexual function. The aim of the call is to support high-quality clinical research that develops and tests innovative ways to recover bladder, bowel or sexual function after spinal cord injury.
Eligibility: Any application is expected to have direct relevance to the fields of research discussed in the following published articles on the ISRT Research Strategy, copies are available Adams et al. International Spinal Research Trust Research Strategy a discussion document. Spinal Cord (2007) 45 2-14.
Level of Study: Graduate
Type: Grant
Value: Up to £250,000
Length of Study: 3 years
Frequency: Annual
Closing Date: 8 May
Funding: Private

For further information contact:

International Spinal Research Trust, 80 Coleman Street, London EC2R 5BJ, United Kingdom.

Email: research@spinal-research.org

Solomon Awards

Purpose: The Solomons' award is to help endorse quality experimental medicine, translational and reverse translational

research in the UK within the field of spinal cord injury. The purpose of the award is to support the development of an early career clinical researcher with either a science or medical training background.
Eligibility: The call is initially open to applicants from clinical units and allied research institutions that have an evident traumatic spinal cord injury case mix or demonstrable interest in SCI clinical research.
Level of Study: Research
Type: Award
Value: £10,000
Frequency: Annual
Country of Study: United Kingdom
Application Procedure: Our Solomons' awards are ongoing and open for applications. You can apply by completing our online application.
Additional Information: spinal-research.org/type-grant

St Cross College

61 St. Giles', Oxford OX1 3LZ, United Kingdom.

Tel: (44) 1865 278490
Email: master@stx.ox.ac.uk
Website: www.stx.ox.ac.uk/

St Cross College is a graduate college of the University of Oxford. It offers an outstanding academic environment dedicated to the pursuit of excellence within the Collegiate University. The St Cross College community is diverse with over 60% of students hailing from overseas; the common room is a wonderful mixture of language and cultures.

Clarendon Scholarship

Level of Study: Postgraduate
Type: Scholarship
Value: course fees in full-
Frequency: Annual
Country of Study: United Kingdom
Closing Date: January
Additional Information: www.ox.ac.uk/clarendon

Godfrey Tyler Scholarship in Economics

Eligibility: No separate application is required and all eligible offer-holders will be considered for this award.
Level of Study: Doctorate, Research
Type: Scholarship
Value: covers the full cost of the course fee for both Home/ROI and overseas students for three years, together with an annual stipend for living costs.
Length of Study: 3 years
Frequency: Annual
Country of Study: United Kingdom
Closing Date: January
Additional Information: www.stx.ox.ac.uk/godfrey-tyler-scholarship-in-economics

Hélène La Rue Scholarship in Music

Eligibility: All applicants who have submitted their DPhil course application by the relevant 2024 admissions deadline and who subsequently hold a College place offer from St Cross College will be considered automatically.
Level of Study: Doctorate, Research
Type: Scholarship
Value: a value of £6,000, which includes a grant of up to £500 per annum for travel and research expenses
Frequency: Annual
Country of Study: United Kingdom
Additional Information: www.stx.ox.ac.uk/helene-la-rue-scholarship-in-music

HAPP MSc Scholarship in the History of Science

Subjects: History of Science, Medicine and Technology
Purpose: The successful scholar and will be expected to engage with the termly activities of the St Cross Centre for the History and Philosophy of Physics (HAPP).
Eligibility: Applicants must have applied to study for an MSc in History of Science, Medicine and Technology
Level of Study: Masters Degree
Type: Scholarship
Value: £10,000 per annum.
Length of Study: 1 year
Frequency: Annual
Country of Study: Any country
Application Procedure: No separate application is required and all eligible offer-holders will be considered for these awards.
Closing Date: October
Funding: Private
Additional Information: www.stx.ox.ac.uk/happ-msc-scholarship-in-the-history-of-science

For further information contact:

Email: joanna.ashbourn@stx.ox.ac.uk

HAPP Scholarship in the History & Philosophy of Physics

Eligibility: Applicants must have applied to study for a DPhil in the History of Physics in the Faculty of History or a DPhil in the Philosophy of Physics in the Faculty of Philosophy by the relevant 2024 admissions deadline.
Level of Study: Postgraduate
Type: Scholarship
Value: full fee liability and has a value of £10,000 per annum
Length of Study: 3 year
Frequency: Annual
Country of Study: United Kingdom
Application Procedure: No separate application is required and all eligible offer-holders will be considered automatically.
Additional Information: www.stx.ox.ac.uk/the-happ-centre#/

Humanities St Cross College UK BAME PGT Studentship

Eligibility: Applicants must apply to the University of Oxford for admission to a Master's degree in the Humanities by the January 2024 application deadline.
Level of Study: Postgraduate
Type: Studentship
Value: All tuition fees and provide a grant for living expenses at UK Research Council rates
Frequency: Annual
Country of Study: United Kingdom
Application Procedure: No separate application is required to be considered for this award. All eligible applicants will be considered automatically.
Closing Date: January
Additional Information: www.stx.ox.ac.uk/humanities-st-cross-college-uk-bame-pgt-studentship

Jan-Georg Deutsch Scholarship in African Studies

Eligibility: No separate application is required and all eligible offer-holders will be considered for this award.
Level of Study: Postgraduate
Type: Scholarship
Value: value of £10,000
Frequency: Annual
Country of Study: United Kingdom
Additional Information: www.stx.ox.ac.uk/jan-georg-deutsch-scholarship-in-african-studies

Law Faculty Scholarships

Eligibility: To be considered for these scholarships, applicants must have applied to study for a Master's-level course by the January 2024 deadline.
Level of Study: Postgraduate
Value: £10,000
Length of Study: 1 year
Frequency: Annual
Country of Study: United Kingdom
Application Procedure: No separate application is required and all eligible offer-holders will be considered for these awards.
Closing Date: January
Additional Information: www.stx.ox.ac.uk/law-faculty-scholarships

Lorna Casselton Memorial Scholarships in Plant Sciences

Eligibility: Awarded purely on the basis of academic merit. Applicants must have applied for a DPhil in Interdisciplinary Bioscience by the January application deadline. No separate application is required and all eligible offer-holders will be considered for these awards.
Level of Study: Doctorate, Research
Type: Scholarship
Value: cover the annual cost of the course fee and the standard UKRI stipend for annual living costs
Frequency: Annual
Country of Study: United Kingdom
Closing Date: January
Additional Information: www.stx.ox.ac.uk/lorna-casselton-memorial-scholarships-in-plant-sciences

MPhil Scholarships in the Humanities and Social Sciences

Purpose: St Cross College offers two MPhil Scholarships for students studying at the University of Oxford for an MPhil degree in any of the humanities and social science disciplines or for the BPhil degree in Philosophy
Eligibility: To be considered for these scholarships, applicants must have applied to study for a Master's-level course
Level of Study: Postgraduate
Type: Scholarship
Value: £5,000 per annum
Length of Study: 2 years
Frequency: Annual

Country of Study: United Kingdom
Application Procedure: No separate application is required and all eligible offer-holders will be considered for these awards.
Closing Date: January
Funding: Private
Additional Information: www.stx.ox.ac.uk/mphil-scholarships-in-the-humanities-and-social-sciences

For further information contact:

Email: joanna.ashbourn@stx.ox.ac.uk

MSc Scholarships in Sustainability, Enterprise and the Environment

Eligibility: Applicants must have applied to study for the MSc in Sustainability, Enterprise and the Environment at the University of Oxford by the January 2024 deadline.
Level of Study: Postgraduate
Type: Scholarship
Value: £10,000
Frequency: Annual
Country of Study: United Kingdom
Application Procedure: No separate application is required and all eligible offer-holders will be considered for this award.
Closing Date: January
Additional Information: www.ox.ac.uk/admissions/graduate/courses/msc-sustainability-enterprise-environment

For further information contact:

Tel: (44) 1865 614963
Email: mscenquiries@smithschool.ox.ac.uk

St Cross MSc Scholarship in Biodiversity, Conservation and Management

Eligibility: Applicants must have applied to study for the MSc in Biodiversity, Conservation and Management by the January 2024 application deadline.
Level of Study: Postgraduate
Type: Scholarship
Value: £20,000
Frequency: Annual
Country of Study: United Kingdom
Closing Date: January
Additional Information: www.stx.ox.ac.uk/st-cross-msc-scholarship-in-biodiversity-conservation-and-management

St Cross MSc Scholarship in Global Health Science and Epidemiology

Eligibility: Applicants must have applied to study for the MSc in Global Health Science and Epidemiology by the December 2023 application deadline.
Level of Study: Postgraduate
Type: Scholarship
Value: the MSc course fee as well as providing a one-year maintenance grant to the value of the annual UKRI living allowance.
Frequency: Annual
Country of Study: United Kingdom
Closing Date: December
Additional Information: www.stx.ox.ac.uk/st-cross-msc-scholarship-in-global-health-science-and-epidemiology

The Robin & Nadine Wells Scholarship

Type: Scholarship
Value: £7,500
Length of Study: 1 year
Frequency: Annual
Country of Study: United Kingdom
Closing Date: March
Additional Information: www.stx.ox.ac.uk/the-robin

St John's College

St Johns Street, Cambridge CB2 1TP, United Kingdom.

Tel: (44) 1223 338600
Email: graduate-office@joh.cam.ac.uk
Website: www.joh.cam.ac.uk/

St John's is one of 31 Colleges at the University of Cambridge.

The Louis Cha Scholarship

Subjects: Literature and History
Purpose: Enables a student to undertake research in the University of Cambridge in literature, history, and culture of early and dynastic China (pre-1912).

Eligibility: 1. St John's College proposes to award a Louis Cha Scholarship commencing in October. 2. The successful applicant will be selected from those who have obtained a place at St John's College Cambridge to read for the MPhil or PhD degree in a relevant subject
Level of Study: Masters Degree, Postgraduate
Type: Scholarship
Value: A maintenance grant of £15,200 per annum and the approved University Composition fee
Length of Study: 3 years
Frequency: Annual
Country of Study: United Kingdom
Application Procedure: Candidates should apply to the University of Cambridge through the University's Graduate Admissions Office at the Board of Graduate Studies for admission as a graduate student, specifying St John's as their first choice of College For further information
Closing Date: 30 November
Funding: Private
Additional Information: www.joh.cam.ac.uk/louis-cha-scholarship

St. Baldricks Foundations

1333 South Mayflower Avenue, Suite 400, Monrovia, CA 91016, United States of America.

Tel: (1) 888 899 2253
Email: sbinfo@stbaldricks.org
Website: www.stbaldricks.org/

The St. Baldrick's Foundation is a volunteer and donor powered charity committed to supporting the most promising research to find cures for childhood cancers and give survivors long and healthy lives.

Research Grants

Eligibility: Applicants need not be American citizens; however, they must work at an academic, medical, or research institution within the United States. 1. Institutions that are actively involved in (sponsor, promote, or participate in) non-St. Baldrick's head-shaving fundraising events are not eligible to apply for St. Baldrick's funding. 2. St. Baldrick's funds may not be used for human embryonic stem cell research. 3. All awards will be payable to the Scholar's academic institution, non-profit research institution, or laboratory. 4. Applicants should hold a PhD, M.D., or D.O. degree in a field of research specialty by the date the award becomes effective. 5. Applicants must currently hold (for no longer than 7 years at the time the award begins), or will hold by start of the award, a title that is considered by the institution to be a fulltime, faculty position. Situations may occur where the institutions definition of "faculty" may differ from the Foundation's definition, this should be fully explained in the Scholar Applicant Checklist (required at LOI stage). 6. This is an early-career award. The Scholar award is intended to develop the independent pediatric cancer research careers of highly qualified investigators, not to support well established or senior investigators. 7. Scholars may receive funding from other sources to support their research. However, no other comparable or higher (monetary value) career development award may be held prior to or at the time the award begins. Scientific or budgetary overlap with other funded projects is not allowed. In the event of comparable or higher (monetary value) career development funding after the LOI has been approved, the Scholar must give up the remainder of their St. Baldrick's award, unless otherwise approved by the St. Baldrick's Foundation. 8. Applicants holding or awarded R01s at the time of the LOI are not eligible to apply. Applicants cannot hold a NIH K-award at the time that they apply (institutional K12 funding is allowable). 9. Applicants must have an appropriate sponsor who provides supervision, facilities, and research support. If appropriate for the project, applicants may have more than one (1) sponsor. 10. Research projects must have direct applicability and relevance to pediatric cancer. They may be in any discipline of basic, clinical, translational, or epidemiological research.
Level of Study: Postgraduate
Type: Grant
Value: This award is granted for three years with an opportunity to apply for an additional two years of funding based upon the demonstration of significant accomplishment. (Years 3-5, if funded, will be up to US$115,000/year).
Frequency: Annual
Country of Study: United States of America
Application Procedure: 1. Category/Cycle specific LOI Instructions/Requirements are available in ProposalCENTRAL upon starting the LOI and on the St. Baldrick's website (stbaldricks.org/for-researchers). 2. LOI, application, and required documents must be submitted by the Principal Investigator, in English, online through ProposalCENTRAL (proposalcentral.altum.com) before 5 p.m. EST on the deadline. 3. All application instructions and templates/requirements will be available in ProposalCENTRAL upon approval of an LOI. 4. Applicants can enable other users to access their proposal (e.g., department or grants administrators) in the full proposal section of ProposalCENTRAL. 5. It is the responsibility of the applicant to ensure and to verify that the application is received by the

deadline date and that the application is complete and correct prior to submission. 6. Eligible current St. Baldrick's Scholars applying for extended funding will be contacted by the St. Baldrick's Foundation Grants Administration staff with instructions for applying. Applications will be submitted via ProposalCENTRAL and reviewed for progress. Grantees can email Grants@StBaldricks.org with further questions about the optional funding. 7. St. Baldrick's Foundation funds biomedical research to better understand the causes of pediatric cancers and to advance its prevention, treatment, and cure. The main output of this research is new knowledge. To ensure this knowledge can be accessed, read, applied, and built upon in fulfillment of our goals, St. Baldrick's Foundation encourages researchers to share data with the research community in accordance with the NIH policy on data sharing and expects its grantees to publish their findings, including but not limited to publication in peer reviewed journals. Applicants will be asked about data sharing plans as part of the application. 8. All application evaluations are considered confidential and are available to scientific reviewers, the Foundation's Board of Directors, and the administrative personnel of the St. Baldrick's Foundation only. 9. Resubmissions Applicants with resubmissions have the option to check a box in ProposalCENTRAL on the title page of the application stating that it is a resubmission. Resbumissions are not marked in the Letter of Intent stage. You may mention it is a resubmission in your LOI. Applicants with a resubmission are asked to address the reviewer comments in the appendix. Be sure that the document addressing previous reviewer comments is listed in the table of contents for your appendix. Resubmission applicants will not have all three of the same reviewers. St. Baldrick's does ask at least one of the previous reviewers to re-review the resubmission. Once marked as a resubmission in ProposalCENTRAL, new reviewers will have access to the past reviewer comments. Resubmissions are still required to go through limited submission decisions per the institution.

Closing Date: 17 February

Additional Information: www.stbaldricks.org/file/sbf-research-grant-guidelines.pdf

For further information contact:

Tel: (1) 626 792 8247
Email: Laura@StBaldricks.org

St. Baldrick's International Scholars

Purpose: This three (3) year award, with an option for two (2) additional years based on progress, is to train researchers from low- and middle- income countries (as classified by the World Bank) to prepare them to fill specific stated needs in an area of childhood cancer research upon returning to their country of origin. Recipients are called St. Baldrick's International Scholars.

Eligibility: Applicants need not be American citizens; however, they must work at an academic, medical, or research institution within the United States. 1. A program/institution is defined as an entity essentially operating under one management. o Any questions or questionable situations will be reviewed by a subset of the Scientific Advisory Board of St. Baldrick's. Questions can be emailed to Grants@Stbaldricks.org, please include a copy of the potential Scholar's biosketch. 2. Institutions that are actively involved in (sponsor, promote, or participate in) non-St. Baldrick's head-shaving fundraising events are not eligible to apply for St. Baldrick's funding. 3. St. Baldrick's funds may not be used for human embryonic stem cell research. 4. All awards will be payable to the Scholar's academic institution, non-profit research institution, or laboratory. 5. Applicants should hold a PhD, M.D., or D.O. degree in a field of research specialty by the date the award becomes effective. 6. Applicants must currently hold (for no longer than 7 years at the time the award begins), or will hold by start of the award, a title that is considered by the institution to be a fulltime, faculty position. o Situations may occur where the institutions definition of "faculty" may differ from the Foundation's definition, this should be fully explained in the Scholar Applicant Checklist (required at LOI stage). 7. This is an early-career award. The Scholar award is intended to develop the independent pediatric cancer research careers of highly qualified investigators, not to support well established or senior investigators. 8. Scholars may receive funding from other sources to support their research. However, no other comparable or higher (monetary value) career development award may be held prior to or at the time the award begins. Scientific or budgetary overlap with other funded projects is not allowed. o In the event of comparable or higher (monetary value) career development funding after the LOI has been approved, the Scholar must give up the remainder of their St. Baldrick's award, unless otherwise approved by the St. Baldrick's Foundation. 10. Applicants holding or awarded R01s at the time of the LOI are not eligible to apply. Applicants cannot hold a NIH K-award at the time that they apply (institutional K12 funding is allowable). See "Conditions of Award" below regarding other awards received after the LOI is approved. 11. Applicants must have an appropriate Sponsor who provides supervision, facilities, and research support. If appropriate for the project, applicants may have more than one (1) Sponsor. 12. Research projects must have direct applicability and relevance to pediatric cancer. They may be in any discipline of basic, clinical, translational, or epidemiological research.

Level of Study: Postgraduate

Type: Grant

Value: This award is granted for three years with an opportunity to apply for an additional two years of funding based upon the demonstration of significant accomplishment. (Years 3-5, if funded, will be up to US$115,000/year).
Length of Study: 3 year
Frequency: Annual
Country of Study: United States of America
Application Procedure: Category/Cycle specific LOI Instructions/Requirements are available in ProposalCENTRAL upon starting the LOI and on the St. Baldrick's website (stbaldricks.org/for-researchers). 1. LOI, application, and required documents must be submitted by the Principal Investigator, in English, online through ProposalCENTRAL (proposalcentral.altum.com) before 5 p.m. EST on the deadline. 2. All application instructions and templates/requirements will be available in ProposalCENTRAL upon approval of an LOI. 3. Applicants can enable other users to access their proposal (e.g., department or grants administrators) in the full proposal section of ProposalCENTRAL. 4. It is the responsibility of the applicant to ensure and to verify that the application is received by the deadline date and that the application is complete and correct prior to submission. 5. Eligible current St. Baldrick's Scholars applying for extended funding will be contacted by the St. Baldrick's Foundation Grants Administration staff with instructions for applying. Applications will be submitted via ProposalCENTRAL and reviewed for progress. Grantees can email Grants@StBaldricks.org with further questions about the optional funding. 1. St. Baldrick's Foundation funds biomedical research to better understand the causes of pediatric cancers and to advance its prevention, treatment, and cure. The main output of this research is new knowledge. To ensure this knowledge can be accessed, read, applied, and built upon in fulfillment of our goals, St. Baldrick's Foundation encourages researchers to share data with the research community in accordance with the NIH policy on data sharing and expects its grantees to publish their findings, including but not limited to publication in peer reviewed journals. Applicants will be asked about data sharing plans as part of the application. 2. All application evaluations are considered confidential and are available to scientific reviewers, the Foundation's Board of Directors, and the administrative personnel of the St. Baldrick's Foundation only. 3. Resubmissions Applicants with resubmissions have the option to check a box in ProposalCENTRAL on the title page of the application stating that it is a resubmission. Resbumissions are not marked in the Letter of Intent stage. You may mention it is a resubmission in your LOI. Applicants with a resubmission are asked to address the reviewer comments in the appendix. Be sure that the document addressing previous reviewer comments is listed in the table of contents for your appendix. Resubmission applicants will not have all three of the same reviewers. St. Baldrick's does ask at least one of the previous reviewers to re-review the resubmission. Once marked as a resubmission in ProposalCENTRAL, new reviewers will have access to the past reviewer comments. Resubmissions are still required to go through limited submission decisions per the institution.
Closing Date: 18 February
Additional Information: www.stbaldricks.org/file/Research/2022-SBF-International-Scholar-Guidelines.pdf

For further information contact:

Tel: (1) 626 792 8247 (ext. 236)
Email: Laura@StBaldricks.org

St. Baldrick's Scholars

Purpose: The Scholar (Career Development) Award is meant to help develop the independent research of highly qualified individuals still early in their careers. Recipients are called St. Baldrick's Scholars.
Eligibility: Applicants need not be American citizens; however, they must work at an academic, medical, or research institution within the United States. 1. A program/institution is defined as an entity essentially operating under one management. o Any questions or questionable situations will be reviewed by a subset of the Scientific Advisory Board of St. Baldrick's. Questions can be emailed to Grants@Stbaldricks.org, please include a copy of the potential Scholar's biosketch. 2. Institutions that are actively involved in (sponsor, promote, or participate in) non-St. Baldrick's head-shaving fundraising events are not eligible to apply for St. Baldrick's funding. 3. St. Baldrick's funds may not be used for human embryonic stem cell research. 4. All awards will be payable to the Scholar's academic institution, non-profit research institution, or laboratory. 5. Applicants should hold a PhD, M.D., or D.O. degree in a field of research specialty by the date the award becomes effective. 6. Applicants must currently hold (for no longer than 7 years at the time the award begins), or will hold by start of the award, a title that is considered by the institution to be a fulltime, faculty position. o Situations may occur where the institutions definition of "faculty" may differ from the Foundation's definition, this should be fully explained in the Scholar Applicant Checklist (required at LOI stage). 7. This is an early-career award. The Scholar award is intended to develop the independent pediatric cancer research careers of highly qualified investigators, not to support well established or senior investigators. 8. Scholars may receive funding from other sources to support their research. However, no other comparable or higher (monetary value) career development award may be held prior to or at the time the award begins. Scientific or budgetary overlap with other funded projects is

not allowed. o In the event of comparable or higher (monetary value) career development funding after the LOI has been approved, the Scholar must give up the remainder of their St. Baldrick's award, unless otherwise approved by the St. Baldrick's Foundation. 9. Applicants holding or awarded R01s at the time of the LOI are not eligible to apply. Applicants cannot hold a NIH K-award at the time that they apply (institutional K12 funding is allowable). See "Conditions of Award" below regarding other awards received after the LOI is approved. 10. Applicants must have an appropriate Sponsor who provides supervision, facilities, and research support. If appropriate for the project, applicants may have more than one (1) Sponsor. 11. Research projects must have direct applicability and relevance to pediatric cancer. They may be in any discipline of basic, clinical, translational, or epidemiological research.

Level of Study: Postgraduate

Type: Fellowship

Value: This award is granted for three years with an opportunity to apply for an additional two years of funding based upon the demonstration of significant accomplishment. (Years 3-5, if funded, will be up to US$115,000/year).

Frequency: Annual

Country of Study: United Kingdom

Application Procedure: Category/Cycle specific LOI Instructions/Requirements are available in ProposalCENTRAL upon starting the LOI and on the St. Baldrick's website (stbaldricks.org/for-researchers). 1. LOI, application, and required documents must be submitted by the Principal Investigator, in English, online through ProposalCENTRAL (proposalcentral.altum.com) before 5 p.m. EST on the deadline. 2. All application instructions and templates/requirements will be available in ProposalCENTRAL upon approval of an LOI. 3. Applicants can enable other users to access their proposal (e.g., department or grants administrators) in the full proposal section of ProposalCENTRAL. 4. It is the responsibility of the applicant to ensure and to verify that the application is received by the deadline date and that the application is complete and correct prior to submission. 5. Eligible current St. Baldrick's Scholars applying for extended funding will be contacted by the St. Baldrick's Foundation Grants Administration staff with instructions for applying. Applications will be submitted via ProposalCENTRAL and reviewed for progress. Grantees can email Grants@StBaldricks.org with further questions about the optional funding. 1. St. Baldrick's Foundation funds biomedical research to better understand the causes of pediatric cancers and to advance its prevention, treatment, and cure. The main output of this research is new knowledge. To ensure this knowledge can be accessed, read, applied, and built upon in fulfillment of our goals, St. Baldrick's Foundation encourages researchers to share data with the research community in accordance with the NIH policy on data sharing and expects its grantees to publish their findings, including but not limited to publication in peer reviewed journals. Applicants will be asked about data sharing plans as part of the application. 2. All application evaluations are considered confidential and are available to scientific reviewers, the Foundation's Board of Directors, and the administrative personnel of the St. Baldrick's Foundation only. 3. Resubmissions Applicants with resubmissions have the option to check a box in ProposalCENTRAL on the title page of the application stating that it is a resubmission. Resbumissions are not marked in the Letter of Intent stage. You may mention it is a resubmission in your LOI. Applicants with a resubmission are asked to address the reviewer comments in the appendix. Be sure that the document addressing previous reviewer comments is listed in the table of contents for your appendix. Resubmission applicants will not have all three of the same reviewers. St. Baldrick's does ask at least one of the previous reviewers to re-review the resubmission. Once marked as a resubmission in ProposalCENTRAL, new reviewers will have access to the past reviewer comments. Resubmissions are still required to go through limited submission decisions per the institution.

Closing Date: 19 February

Additional Information: www.stbaldricks.org/file/Research/2021-SBF-Scholar-Guidelines.pdf

For further information contact:

Tel: (1) 626 792 8247
Email: Laura@StBaldricks.org

St. Catherine's College - University of Oxford

Manor Road, Oxford OX1 3UJ, United Kingdom.

Tel: (44) 1865 271 700
Email: admissions@stcatz.ox.ac.uk
Website: www.stcatz.ox.ac.uk/
Contact: Mrs Ben Nicholas, Graduate Funding Administrator

St Catherine's College is the largest college within Oxford University and teaches both undergraduate and graduate students.

Alan Tayler Scholarship (Mathematics)

Eligibility: For Overseas and EU fee status students who in October 2024 will be reading for an Oxford University DPhil degree in the Mathematical Institute.

S

Level of Study: Postgraduate
Type: Scholarship
Value: £5,000 per annum
Length of Study: 3 years
Frequency: Annual
Country of Study: United Kingdom
No. of awards offered: 1
Closing Date: 24 February
Additional Information: www.stcatz.ox.ac.uk/prospective-students/postgraduate-admissions/student-finance-and-scholarships/

Allen Senior Scholarship (Music)

Eligibility: For students who in October 2024 will be reading for an Oxford University graduate degree (MSt, MPhil or DPhil) in Music.
Type: Scholarship
Value: £3,300 per annum
Length of Study: 1 year
Frequency: Annual
Country of Study: United Kingdom
No. of awards offered: 1
Closing Date: 11 March
Additional Information: www.stcatz.ox.ac.uk/prospective-students/postgraduate-admissions/student-finance-and-scholarships/

Berlinski-Jacobson Graduate Scholarship (Humanities & Social Sciences)

Eligibility: For students who in October will be reading for any Oxford University graduate degree in the Arts (Humanities Division and Social Science Division) for which St Catherine's admits graduate students
Level of Study: Graduate
Type: Scholarship
Value: £4,000 per annum
Length of Study: 3 years
Frequency: Every 3 years
Country of Study: United Kingdom
Closing Date: 11 March
Funding: Private
Additional Information: studyqa.com/scholarships/view/257

For further information contact:

Email: development.office@stcatz.ox.ac.uk

College Scholarship (Arts)

Eligibility: For students who in October will be reading for any Oxford University research degree (DPhil, MLitt, or MSc by Research) in the Arts (Humanities Division and Social Science Division) for which St Catherine's admits graduate students.
Level of Study: Postgraduate
Type: Scholarship
Value: £3,300 per annum
Length of Study: 3 years
Frequency: Annual
Country of Study: United Kingdom
No. of awards offered: 2
Closing Date: 24 February
Additional Information: www.stcatz.ox.ac.uk/prospective-students/postgraduate-admissions/student-finance-and-scholarships/

College Scholarship (Sciences)

Eligibility: For students who in October will be reading for any Oxford University research degree (DPhil, or MSc by Research) in the Sciences (Mathematical, Physical and Life Sciences Division and Medical Sciences Division) for which St Catherine's admits graduate students.
Level of Study: Postgraduate
Type: Scholarship
Value: £3,300 per annum
Length of Study: 3 years
Frequency: Annual
Country of Study: United Kingdom
No. of awards offered: 2
Closing Date: 24 February
Additional Information: www.stcatz.ox.ac.uk/prospective-students/postgraduate-admissions/student-finance-and-scholarships/

Fletcher Graduate Scholarship (International Development & Social Enterprise)

Eligibility: For students who in October will be reading for any Oxford University taught degree (BCL, MBA, MJuris, MPhil, MPP or MSc by Coursework) in the Social Sciences Division for which St Catherine's admits graduate students, related to International Development or Social Enterprise. Applicants for this scholarship must explain in their application how their course is related to International Development or Social Enterprise.

Level of Study: Postgraduate
Type: Scholarship
Value: £5,000 per annum
Length of Study: 2 years
Frequency: Annual
Country of Study: United Kingdom
No. of awards offered: 1
Closing Date: 24 February
Additional Information: www.stcatz.ox.ac.uk/prospective-students/postgraduate-admissions/student-finance-and-scholarships/

Ghosh Graduate Scholarship (Humanities)

Eligibility: For students who in October will be reading for any Oxford University taught degree (BPhil, MFA, MSt, MSc by Coursework or MPhil) in the Humanities Division for which St Catherine's admits graduate students.
Level of Study: Postgraduate
Type: Scholarship
Value: £5,000 per annum
Length of Study: 2 years
Frequency: Annual
Country of Study: United Kingdom
No. of awards offered: 1
Closing Date: 24 February
Additional Information: www.stcatz.ox.ac.uk/prospective-students/postgraduate-admissions/student-finance-and-scholarships/

Great Eastern Scholarship (All Subjects)

Eligibility: For Indian nationals who in October will be reading for any Oxford University research degree (DPhil, MLitt, or MSc by Research) for which St Catherine's admits graduate students.
Level of Study: Postgraduate
Type: Scholarship
Value: £3,300 per annum
Length of Study: 3 years
Frequency: Annual
Country of Study: United Kingdom
No. of awards offered: 1
Closing Date: 24 February
Additional Information: www.stcatz.ox.ac.uk/prospective-students/postgraduate-admissions/student-finance-and-scholarships/

Leathersellers' Company Scholarship (Sciences)

Eligibility: For graduates of European (including UK) universities who in October will be reading for an Oxford University research degree (DPhil or MSc by Research) in Biochemistry, Chemistry, Computing, Earth Sciences, Engineering Science, Materials Science, Mathematics, Physics, Plant Sciences, Statistics or Zoology.
Level of Study: Postgraduate
Type: Scholarship
Value: £3,500 per annum
Length of Study: 3 years
Frequency: Annual
Country of Study: United Kingdom
No. of awards offered: 1
Closing Date: 24 February
Additional Information: www.stcatz.ox.ac.uk/prospective-students/postgraduate-admissions/student-finance-and-scholarships/

Mr and Mrs Kenny Lam's Graduate Scholarship (Law)

Eligibility: For students who in October will be reading for an Oxford University BCL, MJuris, MSt, MPhil or DPhil in Law for which St Catherine's admits graduate students.
Level of Study: Postgraduate
Type: Scholarship
Value: £5,000 per annum
Length of Study: 3 years
Frequency: Annual
Country of Study: United Kingdom
No. of awards offered: 1
Closing Date: 24 February
Additional Information: www.stcatz.ox.ac.uk/prospective-students/postgraduate-admissions/student-finance-and-scholarships/

Overseas Scholarship

Eligibility: For Overseas fee status students who in October will be reading for any Oxford University research degree (DPhil, MLitt, or MSc by Research) for which St Catherine's admits graduate students.
Level of Study: Postgraduate
Type: Scholarship
Value: £3,300 per annum
Length of Study: 3 years
Frequency: Annual
Country of Study: United Kingdom

No. of awards offered: 2
Closing Date: 24 February
Additional Information: www.stcatz.ox.ac.uk/prospective-students/postgraduate-admissions/student-finance-and-scholarships/

Wilfrid Knapp Scholarship (Arts)

Eligibility: For students who in October will be reading for any Oxford University research degree (DPhil, MLitt, or MSc by Research) in the Arts (Humanities Division and Social Science Division) for which St Catherine's admits graduate students.
Level of Study: Postgraduate
Type: Scholarship
Value: £5,000 per annum
Length of Study: 3 years
Frequency: Annual
Country of Study: United Kingdom
No. of awards offered: 1 or 2
Closing Date: 24 February
Additional Information: www.stcatz.ox.ac.uk/prospective-students/postgraduate-admissions/student-finance-and-scholarships/

Wilfrid Knapp Scholarship (Sciences)

Eligibility: For students who in October will be reading for any Oxford University research degree (DPhil, or MSc by Research) in the Sciences (Mathematical, Physical and Life Sciences Division and Medical Sciences Division) for which St Catherine's admits graduate students.
Level of Study: Postgraduate
Type: Scholarship
Value: £5,000 per annum
Length of Study: 3 years
Frequency: Annual
Country of Study: United Kingdom
No. of awards offered: 1 or 2
Closing Date: 24 February
Additional Information: www.stcatz.ox.ac.uk/prospective-students/postgraduate-admissions/student-finance-and-scholarships/

St. Mary's University

Waldegrave Rd, Strawberry Hill, Twickenham TW1 4SX, United Kingdom.

Tel: (44) 20 8240 4000
Email: scholarships@stmarys.ac.uk
Website: www.stmarys.ac.uk/

St Mary's has a long and distinguished history and a very modern outlook. With an original intake of just six students, St Mary's has now grown to around 6,000 undergraduate and postgraduate students across the four academic Schools.

Centre for Bioethics and Emerging Technologies PhD Funding

Purpose: The Centre for Bioethics and Emerging Technologies (CBET) at St Mary's University, Twickenham, offers a fully funded, full-time three year PhD programme commencing in October to support the successful applicant's research in bioethics
Eligibility: 1. The successful applicant would also expected to be involved with CBET activities, including conference organization and undergraduate teaching after a mandatory induction course. 2. The successful candidate may if they wish, carry out work with the Catholic Bishops' Conference of England and Wales. 3. It is also highly desirable that the successful applicant be located within the Greater London area during their studies
Level of Study: Graduate
Type: Funding support
Value: Provide full-time PhD fees at the current home/European Union rate of £4,375 p.a. and a bursary of £13,000 p.a
Length of Study: Up to 3 years
Frequency: Annual
Country of Study: United Kingdom
Application Procedure: To apply, download and complete a full registration PhD application and send it together with your 3,000-4,000 word research proposal, two academic references from your chosen referees, copies of your Master's qualification(s), a current CV and a covering letter stating the reasons you wish to be considered for the bursary to the physical address mentioned below
Closing Date: 26 April
Funding: Private

For further information contact:

Email: maggie.mayer@stmarys.ac.uk

Stanford University

450 Jane Stanford Way, Stanford, CA 94305–2004, United States of America.

Tel: (1) 650 723 2300
Website: www.stanford.edu

Stanford University, located between San Francisco and San Jose in the heart of California's Silicon Valley, is one of the world's leading teaching and research universities. Since its opening in 1891, Stanford has been dedicated to finding solutions to big challenges and to preparing students for leadership in a complex world.

School of Medicine Dean's Postdoctoral Fellowship

Purpose: The Fellowships encourage and support young investigators in the first two years of their postdoctoral research training at the School of Medicine and who are under the mentorship of faculty in the School of Medicine. With the goal to support current postdocs and to facilitate the recruitment of new scholars, the Dean's Fellowship is often used as seed money while outside funds are sought.
Eligibility: 1. Applicants must be postdoctoral scholars at the School of Medicine at the time the award begins. If applicant is not a postdoc at the application deadline, additional documents must be submitted with application. 2. Faculty sponsors must be appointed in the School of Medicine. Acting, consulting, and courtesy appointees are ineligible. 3. Awardees cannot be enrolled in a degree-granting program while funded. 4. Applicants in the first one or two years of postdoctoral research training are preferred. 5. Foreign fellows must have visas that allow stipend support (typically a J-1 & F-1 OPT). H1-B and TN visa holders are ineligible. Citizenship is not a selection factor. 6. This is a one-year fellowship and applications for a second year of funding will not be reviewed.
Level of Study: Postdoctorate
Type: Fellowship
Value: Stipend is US$34,119 for the entire award period.
Length of Study: 2 years
Frequency: Annual
Country of Study: United States of America
Application Procedure: Complete applications must be submitted online by the deadline. Start applications early to allow enough time for the system to solicit the required form from your faculty mentor which is due at the same time as your application. Applications due by 1159 PM PST on deadline date. A complete application consists of: 1. Complete online application form. 2. NIH Biosketch. 3. Research proposal Two page limit, including graphics/tables. Proposals are written by the fellow and reviewed by the faculty sponsor. Proposals must include a brief statement of proposed investigation including background, goals, hypothesis, and experimental methods. Use 1-inch margins and 12-point font. Include title of project on both numbered pages. Include references only if they are part of your two-page proposal. 4. Faculty Sponsor's Recommendation Form & Agreement. 5. Offer Letter only if not currently appointed as a postdoctoral scholar in the School of Medicine. This application does not go through RMG or OSR at Stanford.
Closing Date: 24 April
Additional Information: postdocs.stanford.edu/current/fellowship/deans

For further information contact:

Email: kanza@stanford.edu

Stanford Postdoctoral Recruitment Initiative in Sciences and Medicine (PRISM)

Purpose: PRISM invites students to explore our training environment and to consider whether advanced training at Stanford would support their career goals. Postdoctoral training is a critical period for establishing research independence. At Stanford, postdocs work alongside top scientists and at the same time develop their professional skills, explore career options, and prepare for independent careers. Stanford has one of the largest postdoc populations in the country and a strong commitment to making the postdoc experience the best it can possibly be.
Eligibility: 1. Eligible for NIH T-32 training grants, which are limited to US Citizens or Permanent Residents, by the time they will begin their postdoctoral appointment. 2. Currently at any institution in the US. Applications from students in Canada, Mexico, Puerto Rico, etc., may also be considered, pending funding availability. Travel funds are not available for those currently located overseas. 3. Intend to complete their PhD within 15 months of PRISM, though later graduation dates may be considered, at the discretion of the faculty or program.
Level of Study: Postgraduate
Type: Grant
Value: Travel funding through PRISM varies by School
Frequency: Annual
Country of Study: United States of America
Application Procedure: The PRISM Application consists of 2 parts, the Stanford Postdoc Diversity Common Application and the PRISM Application. (postdocs.stanford.edu/prism-application-guide)
Closing Date: 7 February
Additional Information: postdocs.stanford.edu/PRISM

For further information contact:

Email: stanfordprism@stanford.edu

The Helena Anna Henzl-Gabor Young Women in Science Fund for Postdoctoral Scholars Travel Grant

Purpose: The Helena Fund for Postdoctoral Scholars Travel Grant is open to currently appointed Stanford postdoctoral

S

scholars in the School of Medicine and School of Humanities & Sciences who have demonstrated a positive attitude through professional teamwork and collaborations of men and women. The Henzl-Gabor Travel Grant supports travel (airline tickets, accommodations, and registration expenses) for participation at scientific conferences. These travel grants are meant to help defray the costs of attending a national or international meeting for travel taking place during the period of December 1 - November 30
Eligibility: Applicants must have completed an MD or PhD degree within the past six years of fund application submission. Awards may be given in amounts up to US$2,000 based on the detailed expenses submitted. Total awards given and funding levels may vary depending on the size and strength of the applicant pool
Level of Study: Postgraduate
Type: Grant
Frequency: Annual
Closing Date: 22 October
Funding: Foundation
Additional Information: postdocs.stanford.edu/current/fellowship/henzlgabor

For further information contact:

Email: kanza@stanford.edu

The Katharine McCormick Advanced Postdoctoral Scholar Fellowship to Support Women in Academic Medicine

Purpose: The Fellowships are for advanced postdoctoral scholars who are pursuing faculty careers in academic medicine. The program aims to provide a bridge of the gap of support for advanced postdoctoral trainees who are competitive, yet have not yet been selected, for faculty positions
Eligibility: Eligibility requirements; Only individuals who are currently appointed as Postdoctoral Scholars at Stanford University are eligible to apply. Instructors and Research Associates may not apply. The applicant may be a United States citizen, permanent resident, or foreign national. Foreign scholar applicants must be a holder of a J1 visa or an F1 visa in OPT status. Applicants who hold H1B, TN, J2, O-1 or other visas are ineligible. The scholar's faculty mentor must have a primary appointment in the School of Medicine. Acting, consulting and courtesy faculty are not eligible. Commitment on the part of the applicant and his/her faculty mentor to hold monthly mentorship meetings with a focus on topics related to the job search process and starting out as an assistant professor. Candidate's willingness to make a presentation of their work to a large scientific audience. A progress report is required at the end of the fellowship
Level of Study: Graduate
Type: Fellowship
Value: US$65,000
Frequency: Annual
Country of Study: United Kingdom
Application Procedure: Application Process Complete online application Applicant's NIH Biosketch (uploaded by applicant online) Applicant's complete curriculum vitae (uploaded by applicant online) Research proposal (uploaded by applicant online) Two page limit, including any graphics or charts. The research proposal must be written by the fellow and reviewed by the faculty sponsor. These two pages should include a brief statement of proposed investigation in the following sections Background, Goals, Hypothesis, and Experimental methods. If the applicant chooses to include references in the two pages, the reference should include enough information to allow the reviewer to look up the paper. Three letters of reference. One letter is required from the faculty sponsor (mentor) at Stanford. Two letters are required from other faculty, at Stanford or elsewhere, who are familiar with the candidate's work and will likely serve as references for the candidate's anticipated job search. Letters will be submitted online by the reference writer directly to the application.
Closing Date: 16 January
Funding: Private
Additional Information: postdocs.stanford.edu/current/fellowship/katharine-mccormick-advanced-postdoctoral-scholar-fellowship-support-women#:~:text=Fellowships%20are%20awarded%20to%20women,are%20appointed%20in%20the%20SoM

For further information contact:

Email: jrebello@stanford.edu

The Walter V. and Idun Berry Postdoctoral Fellowship Program

Purpose: The fellowships aims to enhance research which utilizes the most advanced technologies and methodologies available to improve the health and wellness of children, including the latest opportunities in molecular and genetic medicine
Eligibility: 1. The applicant must be appointed as a postdoctoral scholar at the Stanford University School of Medicine at the time the award begins. If the applicant is not an appointed postdoctoral scholar at the time of the application deadline, additional documents must be submitted with the application (see application checklist below). Instructors and Research Associates may not apply. 2. Applicants must also hold an MD, PhD and/or a DVM/VMD degree(s); selection

preference will be given to physician scientists. 3. The faculty mentor/sponsor must be appointed in the School of Medicine. Acting, consulting and courtesy appointees are not eligible. 4. Foreign scholars may have J-1 or F-1 OPT (receiving stipends), or H1B visas (receiving the award as salary). Citizenship is not a selection factor. 5. Applicants must be available for an interview on the interview date listed on this website
Level of Study: Postgraduate
Type: Fellowship
Value: US$76,000/year
Frequency: Annual
Country of Study: United States of America
Application Procedure: 1. Complete online application form (application visible only when application period is open). 2. Applicant's NIH Biosketch (uploaded by applicant online). 3. Research Proposal (two page limit, including any graphics, charts or references). The research proposal must be written by the postdoc and reviewed by the faculty sponsor. These two pages should include a brief statement of proposed investigation in the following sections Background, Goals, Hypothesis, and Experimental methods. Formatting guidelines require at least 1-inch margins at the top, bottom, left and right; and 12 point or larger font Times New Roman, Times Roman, Arial, Helvetica, or Verdana. Include title of project and your name on both pages and number pages. If the applicant choses to include references, the reference should include enough information to allow the reviewer to look up the paper. 4. Three letters of recommendation one from the sponsoring Faculty Mentor at Stanford, and two additional letters from other recommenders. Letters are due the same day as the application, so please request these letters at the beginning of the application process via the online application
Closing Date: 6 June
Funding: Private
Additional Information: postdocs.stanford.edu/current/fellowship/walter-v-and-idun-berry-postdoctoral-fellowship-program

For further information contact:

Email: kanza@stanford.edu

Stanley Smith (United Kingdom) Horticultural Trust

770 Tamalpais Drive, Suite 309, Corte Madera, CA 94925, United States of America.

Tel: (1) 415 332 0166
Website: smithht.org/
Contact: Dr James Cullen, Director

The Stanley Smith Horticultural Trust was created in 1970 by May Smith, in honor of her late husband and in fulfillment of his vision. The Trust stewards Stanley Smith's philanthropic legacy, and seeks to nurture in others his enthusiasm for ornamental horticulture.

Stanley Smith (UK) Horticultural Trust Awards

Eligibility: Offered to charities, community and voluntary organisations and institutions for projects that meet the objectives of the Trust 1. to promote horticulture; 2. to promote the conservation of the physical and natural environment by promoting biological diversity 3. to promote the creation, development, preservation and maintenance of gardens (preference will normally, but not exclusively, be given 4. to gardens accessible to the public); and 5. the advancement of horticultural education.
Level of Study: Unrestricted
Type: Grant
Value: £3,000 to £4,000
Length of Study: Dependent on the nature of the project
Frequency: Annual
Country of Study: United Kingdom
Application Procedure: Applicants must apply to the Trust. Trustees allocate awards in Spring and Autumn
No. of awards offered: 200
Closing Date: 15 August
Funding: Private
Contributor: Donations
No. of awards given last year: 30
No. of applicants last year: 200
Additional Information: www.fundingforall.org.uk/funds/stanley-smith-uk-horticultural-trust/

For further information contact:

Email: tdaniel@calacademy.org

State Secretariat for Education, Research and Innovation SERI

Einsteinstrasse 2, CH-3005 Bern, Switzerland.

Tel: (41) 58 462 21 29
Email: info@sbfi.admin.ch
Website: www.sbfi.admin.ch

SERI is the national contact point for the recognition of professional qualifications in Switzerland.

Swiss Government Excellence Scholarships for Foreign Scholars and Artists

Purpose: The Swiss government, through the Federal Commission for Scholarships for Foreign Students (FCS), awards various postgraduate scholarships to foreign scholars and researchers
Eligibility: These scholarships provide graduates from all fields with the opportunity to pursue doctoral or postdoctoral research in Switzerland at one of the public funded universities or recognised institutions
Level of Study: Doctorate, Postdoctorate
Type: Scholarship
Frequency: Annual
Country of Study: Any country
Additional Information: Please check www.sbfi.admin.ch/scholarships_eng www.sbfi.admin.ch/sbfi/en/home/education/scholarships-and-grants/swiss-government-excellence-scholarships.html

For further information contact:

Tel: (41) 446326161
Email: exchange@ethz.ch

Statistical Society of Canada

219 - 1725 St. Laurent Blvd., Ottawa, ON K1G 3V4, Canada.

Tel: (1) 613 627 3530
Email: info@ssc.ca
Website: ssc.ca/
Contact: Sudhir Paul, Chair, Pierre Robillard Award

The Statistical Society of Canada provides a forum for discussion and interaction among individuals involved in all aspects of the statistical sciences. It publishes a newsletter, Liaison as well as a scientific journal, The Canadian Journal of Statistics. The Society also organizes annual scientific meetings and short courses on professional development.

Pierre Robillard Award

Purpose: The aim of the Pierre Robillard Award is to recognize the best PhD thesis defended at a Canadian university in a given year and written in the fields covered by The Canadian Journal of Statistics.
Eligibility: Open to all postgraduates who have made a potential impact on the statistical sciences
Level of Study: Doctorate, Postgraduate
Type: Award
Value: The award consists of a certificate, a monetary prize, and a one-year membership in the SSC.
Frequency: Annual
Country of Study: Canada
Application Procedure: Applicants must submit four copies of the thesis together with a covering letter from the thesis supervisor
Closing Date: 31 January
Additional Information: ssc.ca/en/award/pierre-robillard-award

For further information contact:

Department of Mathematical and Statistical Sciences University of Alberta, 632 Cab, AB T6G 2G1, Canada.

Tel: (1) 780 492 4230
Fax: (1) 780 492 6826
Email: kc.carriere@ualberta.ca

Stellenbosch University

Private Bay XI, Matieland 7602, South Africa.

Tel: (27) 21 808 9111
Email: info@sun.ac.za
Website: www.sun.ac.za

Stellenbosch University (SU) is home to an academic community of 29 000 students (including 4 000 foreign students from 100 countries) as well as 3 000 permanent staff members (including 1 000 academics) on five campuses.

Harry Crossley Doctoral Fellowship

Purpose: To reward academically above-average students
Eligibility: Individuals are not eligible who will be employed for more than 20 hours per week; who will register for part-time courses, the 4th year of an undergraduate degree, the LLB, postgraduate certificates and postgraduate diplomas and who will register for degrees in disciplines in Religious Studies and Political Studies
Level of Study: Doctorate
Type: Fellowship
Value: R80,000

Length of Study: 2 years
Frequency: Annual
Study Establishment: Stellenbosch University
Country of Study: South Africa
Application Procedure: Request application
No. of awards offered: 350
Closing Date: 29 September
Funding: Foundation
Contributor: Harry Crossley Foundation
No. of awards given last year: 50
No. of applicants last year: 350
Additional Information: www.validate-network.org/event/the-harry-crossley-foundation-research-fellowships-2020

For further information contact:

Level 3, Otto Beit Building, Upper Campus Rondebosch, 7700, South Africa.

Tel: (27) 21 650 3622
Fax: (27) 21 808 2739
Email: pgfunding@uct.ac.za

Harry Crossley Master

Purpose: To reward academically above-average students
Eligibility: To full-time students registered at Stellenbosch University in any postgraduate degree programme except theology and political science
Level of Study: Doctorate, Postgraduate
Type: Bursary
Value: R 75,000 (Honours), R 80,000 (Master)
Length of Study: 1 year
Frequency: Annual
Study Establishment: Stellenbosch University
Country of Study: South Africa
No. of awards offered: 500
Closing Date: 15 October
Funding: Foundation
Contributor: Harry Crossley Foundation
No. of awards given last year: 30
No. of applicants last year: 500
Additional Information: Please see the website further details www.scholarshubafrica.com/41257/harry-crossley-foundation-research-fellowship-uct-south-africa/

For further information contact:

Tel: (27) 21 808 4208
Fax: (27) 21 808 3799
Email: usbritz@sun.ac.za

Stellenbosch Fellowship in Polymer Science

Purpose: To fund further study in Polymer Science and synthetic Polymer chemistry
Eligibility: Open to students with a PhD in Polymer Science or Environmental Engineering and experience in membranes, membrane operations, polymer brushes, grafts and other nano particles
Level of Study: Postdoctorate
Type: Fellowship
Length of Study: 1 year
Frequency: Annual
Study Establishment: University of Stellenbosch
Country of Study: South Africa
Application Procedure: Request application.

For further information contact:

Department of Chemistry Division of Polymer Science University of Stellenbosch, Private Bag X1, Matieland, 7602, South Africa.

Email: rds@sun.ac.za

Stellenbosch Merit Bursary Award

Purpose: To reward academically above-average students
Eligibility: Available to full-time students registered at Stellenbosch University in any postgraduate degree programme
Level of Study: Postgraduate
Type: Bursary
Value: R 4,100 to 34,700
Length of Study: Up to 2 years
Frequency: Annual
Study Establishment: Stellenbosch University
Country of Study: South Africa
Application Procedure: Students must submit an application and a certified copy of a complete, official academic record
No. of awards offered: Approx. 700
Closing Date: 6 December
Contributor: Stellenbosch University
No. of awards given last year: 340
No. of applicants last year: Approx. 700
Additional Information: www.sun.ac.za/english/learning-teaching/undergraduate-bursaries-loans/su-funding/merit-bursaries

For further information contact:

Office for postgraduate student funding, Postgraduate and International Office Stellenbosch Central, Wilcocks Building, Room 3015, Stellenbosch, 7600, South Africa.

Tel: (27) 21 808 4208
Fax: (27) 21 808 3799
Email: postgradfunding@sun.ac.za

Stellenbosch Rector's Grants for Successing Against the Odds

Purpose: To award students who have achieved exceptional success despite difficult circumstances
Eligibility: Open to candidates who satisfy the admission requirements of the University and who can provide proof of exceptional achievement despite handicaps and/or specific physical, educational or social challenges
Level of Study: Postgraduate
Type: Grant
Value: R70, 000 per year
Length of Study: 1 to 3 years
Frequency: Annual
Study Establishment: Stellenbosch University
Country of Study: South Africa
Application Procedure: Students must submit a complete application form accompanied by a curriculum vitae and 2 references
No. of awards offered: 3
Closing Date: 10 September
Funding: Foundation
Contributor: Andrew Mellon Foundation
No. of awards given last year: 3
No. of applicants last year: 100

For further information contact:

Tel: (27) 21 8084208
Fax: (27) 21 808 2739
Email: beursnavrae_nagraads@sun.ac.za

Stockholm School of Economics

PO Box 6501, SE-11383 Stockholm, Sweden.

Tel: (46) 8 736 9000
Email: info@hhs.se
Website: www.hhs.se/

The Stockholm School of Economics is an academic hub for ambitious students and researchers from all over the world. By working closely with corporate partners and society at large, SSE has been creating opportunities for its graduates for over 100 years.

Consejo Nacional de Ciencia y Tecnologia (CONACYT) Scholarships

Eligibility: Open to Mexican students only
Level of Study: MBA
Type: Scholarship
Value: All agreed fees
Length of Study: 1 year
Frequency: Annual
Country of Study: Sweden
Application Procedure: Contact the Foundation
Funding: Foundation
Contributor: CONACYT
Additional Information: www.sussex.ac.uk/study/phd/doctoral/funding-support-international/conacyt

For further information contact:

Email: ochoa@buzon.main.conacyt.mx

Petra Och Kail Erik Hedborgs Stiftelse Scholarship

Level of Study: MBA
Type: Scholarship
Value: All tuition fees and travel costs
Length of Study: 1 year
Frequency: Annual
Country of Study: Sweden
Application Procedure: Contact the institute
Funding: Private
Additional Information: www.pkhedborg.com/english.html

For further information contact:

Grönstavägen 18, SE-18143 Lidingö, Sweden.

Tel: (46) 70 182 92 90
Email: info@pkhedborg.com

The Swedish Foundation for International Cooperation in Research and Higher Education (STINT) Scholarship

Eligibility: Open to Brazilian nationals only
Level of Study: MBA
Type: Scholarship
Length of Study: 1 year
Frequency: Dependent on funds available
Country of Study: Sweden
Application Procedure: Contact the institute
Closing Date: 31 May
Funding: Government

Contributor: STINT
Additional Information: www.european-funding-guide.eu/scholarship/5175-initiation

For further information contact:

STINT, Wallingatan 2, Stockholm, SE-111 60, Sweden.

Tel: (46) 46 8662 7690
Fax: (46) 46 8661 9210
Email: info@stint.se

Strathclyde University

16 Richmond Street, Glasgow G1 1XQ, United Kingdom.

Tel: (44) 141 552 4400
Website: www.strath.ac.uk/

Strathclyde University is a leading technological university with around 23,000 students from more than 100 nations. With an international reputation for teaching excellence, the university has a five-star Overall Rating in the QS Stars University Ratings, and seven Times Higher Education awards in as many years.

Carnegie Trust: St Andrew's Society Scholarships

Eligibility: Candidates must be Scottish by birth or descent, and will be expected to have current knowledge of Scotland and Scottish current affairs, and of the Scottish tradition generally. The Society expects its scholars to be good ambassadors for Scotland. Candidates must also be: 1. either graduates of a Scottish university, Glasgow School of Art, Royal Conservatoire of Scotland, or of Oxford or Cambridge, who have completed their first degree course (so as to be qualified to graduate) not earlier than 2022. 2. students of a Scottish university, Glasgow School of Art, Royal Conservatoire of Scotland, or of Oxford or Cambridge, who expect to complete their first degree course (so as to be qualified to graduate) in 2023. Preference will be given to candidates who have no previous experience of the United States and for whom a period of study there can be expected to be a life-changing experience. Selection will be on the basis of an all-round assessment, including character, experience and academic achievement.
Level of Study: Postgraduate
Type: Scholarship
Value: US$35,000
Frequency: Annual
Country of Study: United States of America
Application Procedure: Applications should be submitted through the student's UK university. Applications should NOT be submitted directly to the Saint Andrew's Society or to the Carnegie Trust. Applications should be submitted by email to rkes-pgrfunding@strath.ac.uk no later than Tuesday 28 February 2023.
No. of awards offered: 2
Closing Date: 28 February
Additional Information: www.strath.ac.uk/studywithus/scholarships/carnegietrust-standrewssocietyscholarships/

For further information contact:

Email: rkes-pgrfunding@strath.ac.uk

Faculty of Science Masters Scholarship for International Students

Eligibility: In order to be considered for a Faculty of Science International Masters Scholarship, candidates must: 1. Be a new, international fee-paying student holding an offer of admission for a full-time, taught masters degree in the Faculty of Science for the 2024/2025 academic year. 2. Be self-funded. Students who receive full scholarships, for example from a government office or embassy, will not be eligible.
Level of Study: Postgraduate
Type: Scholarship
Value: £4,000 to £6,000
Frequency: Annual
Country of Study: United Kingdom
Application Procedure: A link to the scholarship application form will be included in an applicant's offer of admission.
Closing Date: 3 July
Additional Information: www.strath.ac.uk/studywithus/scholarships/facultyofsciencemastersscholarshipsforinternationalstudents202324/

For further information contact:

Email: science-scholarships@strath.ac.uk

Mature Students Hardship Fund

Eligibility: Registered students of the University shall be eligible to apply to the Fund if they meet the following criteria: 1. are aged 21 or over at the start of their current course of study. 2. started their course with an appropriate funding arrangement in place but have fallen into hardship. 3. if eligible, have applied to the Discretionary Fund for support. 4. If eligible, have applied for all statutory funding

(Student loan, bursary, cost of living grant). 5. they have been recommended for support from the Fund by the Student Support Team on the basis of urgent or exceptional circumstances. 6. a payment from the fund will make a significant contribution to the student's ability to continue their studies successfully.
Level of Study: Postgraduate
Type: Award
Value: £500 to £1000
Frequency: Annual
Country of Study: United Kingdom
Application Procedure: Scholarship website: studentsupport.strath.ac.uk/finsup
Closing Date: 1 January
Additional Information: www.strath.ac.uk/studywithus/scholarships/maturestudentshardshipfund/

For further information contact:

Tel: (44) 141 548 2753
Email: financial-support@strath.ac.uk

MSc Psychology with a Specialisation in Business Scholarship

Eligibility: To be eligible for this award applicants must 1. Be available to commence their academic studies by the start of the academic year in September 2024. 2. Hold an unconditional academic offer to the MSc Psychology with a specialisation in Business at the University of Strathclyde (full-time, part-time and flexible route included).
Level of Study: Postgraduate
Type: Scholarship
Value: £6,700
Frequency: Annual
Country of Study: United Kingdom
Closing Date: 31 August
Additional Information: www.strath.ac.uk/courses/postgraduatetaught/psychologywithaspecialisation/

For further information contact:

Email: hass-pg-enquiries@strath.ac.uk

Strathclyde Research Studentship Scheme (SRSS)

Eligibility: Funding is provided for students with a good honours degree at a first- or upper second-class level, awarded within a relevant cognate discipline. Faculties may stipulate a first class honours degree
Level of Study: Postgraduate
Type: Scholarship
Value: Home fees and stipend at UKRI rate
Length of Study: 3 to 3.5 years
Frequency: Annual
Country of Study: Scotland
No. of awards offered: 150
Additional Information: www.strath.ac.uk/studywithus/scholarships/strathclyderesearchstudentshipschemesrss/

University of Strathclyde Performance Sport Scholarship

Eligibility: All applicants must be competing in a Sport Scotland-recognised sport, and priority will be given to students competing in a BUCS-sport who can demonstrate the potential to contribute toward the University's objective of being ranked in the top 20 in the UK. In addition, all applicants should be competing at least at Junior, if not senior, International level.
Level of Study: Postgraduate
Type: Bursary
Value: up to £1,000 (+ up to £3,750* in-kind support)
Length of Study: 1 year
Frequency: Annual
Country of Study: Scotland
Application Procedure: Scholarship website: strath.eu.qualtrics.com/jfe/form/SV_bIW66SQoeF9kyWO
Closing Date: 3 April
Additional Information: www.strath.ac.uk/studywithus/scholarships/performancesportscholarship/

For further information contact:

Email: dave.sykes@strath.ac.uk

Stroke Association

Stroke House, 240 City Road, London EC1V 2PR, United Kingdom.

Tel: (44) 20 7566 1543
Email: research@stroke.org.uk
Website: www.stroke.org.uk
Contact: Rachael Sherrington, Research Awards Officer

The Stroke Association funds research into stroke prevention, treatment, rehabilitation, and long term care. It also helps stroke patients and their families directly through community services. It campaigns, educates and informs to increase knowledge of stroke at all levels of society and it acts as a voice for everyone affected by stroke.

Priority Programme Awards

Purpose: This new funding stream is aimed at addressing the gaps in research in the following areas
Type: Award
Value: Up to the amount of £450,000
Length of Study: 3 to 5 years
Frequency: Annual
Country of Study: Any country
Closing Date: January
Additional Information: These awards will be made in July. Please contact research@stroke.org.uk www.stroke.org.uk/research/our-funding-schemes/priority-programme-awards

The Stroke Association Research Project Grants

Purpose: To advance research into stroke
Eligibility: 1. Stroke Association Awards must be carried out at Universities, NHS Trusts, Statutory Social Care Organisations or other Research Institutions within Great Britain and Northern Ireland. 2. The lead applicant must be a senior researcher holding a PhD (or equivalent) with a track record of managing grants, delivering research studies and a strong publication record. 3. The salary of the lead applicant has to be guaranteed for the duration of the proposed programme; the Lead applicant's salary cannot be requested in the budget. 4. For this funding call Masters, PhD studentships, and clinical fellowships are not eligible to be included in the budget.
Level of Study: Research
Type: Project grant
Value: Up to £250,000
Length of Study: 3 to 5 years
Frequency: Annual
Study Establishment: A suitable university or hospital in the United Kingdom
Country of Study: United Kingdom
Application Procedure: Application forms are available from the website
No. of awards offered: 20
Closing Date: 4 February
Funding: Private, Trusts
Contributor: Donations
No. of awards given last year: 3
No. of applicants last year: 20
Additional Information: Please visit www.stroke.org.uk/research/looking-funding/project-grants www.stroke.org.uk/research/our-funding-schemes/project-grants

Sugar Research Australia - SRA

50 Meiers Road, Indooroopilly QLD 4068, Australia.

Tel: (61) 7 3331 3333
Email: sra@sugarresearch.com.au
Website: sugarresearch.com.au/

Sugar Research Australia invests in and manages a portfolio of research, development and adoption projects that drive productivity, profitability and sustainability for the Australian sugarcane industry.

Sugar Industry Postgraduate Research Scholarships (SPRS)

Purpose: Sugar Research Australia (SRA) invests in and manages a portfolio of research, development and adoption (RD&A) projects that drive productivity, profitability and sustainability for the Australian sugarcane industry. SRA also invests significantly in industry capability with the ongoing future success of the sugar industry dependent upon improving the capability of existing industry employees. With respect to research funding and encouraging young scientists into our industry, SRA makes available a number of SPRS awards every year, tenable at Australian universities and institutions, for postgraduate research study. The purpose of these awards is to enable qualified graduates to undertake Research Doctorate or Research Masters study and to facilitate research and training in areas of value to the Australian sugarcane industry.
Eligibility: The purpose of the SPRS is to enable high calibre students to undertake a Masters or PhD research degree in disciplines relevant to the future of the Australian sugar industry. Scholarships are available for three years for PhD studies and two years for Research Masters studies and are awarded on the basis of academic excellence. Applicants should consult the SRA Strategic Plan document available on the SRA website and focus on inventive projects that address at least one of the following eight key focus areas of investment 1. Optimally-adapted varieties, plant breeding and release 2. Soil health, nutrient management and environmental sustainability 3. Pest, disease and weed management 4. Farming systems and harvesting 5. Milling efficiency and technology 6. Product diversification and value addition 7. Knowledge and technology transfer and adoption 8. Collaboration and capability development To be eligible for a full SPRS or a top-up scholarship, the candidate must be a citizen or permanent resident of Australia and must have acceptance at a recognised research institution. The principal supervisor

for the postgraduate study program must provide evidence that the host organisation supports the project and the applicant's candidature for the relevant study program. Awards are tenable at Australian universities/institutions; however for applicants of proven ability who are undertaking a PhD, training at overseas institutions may be approved where benefits will return to the Australian sugar industry and where overseas supervision will confer additional benefit. Awards are conferred on the student based on merit, with the evaluation criteria set out within this document. Generic applications from prospective supervisors requesting support for postgraduate research projects without identifying a specific candidate will not be considered. The SPRS award offers supplementary or full scholarships, the number and value of which are at the discretion of SRA. For a higher probability of success, the applicant is encouraged to also apply for a Research Training Program (RTP) scholarship or equivalent through their host university. Preference will be given to applicants who receive an RTP or equivalent scholarship. Successful applicants not holding an RTP scholarship or any other base scholarship will be provided a tax-free stipend of AU$32,000 per annum (exclusive of GST). Successful applicants with an RTP scholarship will be provided a tax free top-up set at a maximum of 75% of the RTP stipend rate which is determined by the Australian Government Department of Education and Training each year. All successful applicants will also be provided with an additional budget of AU$10,000 (excluding GST) per year to support research project operating expenses.
Level of Study: Postgraduate
Type: Scholarship
Value: AU$32,000
Length of Study: 2 to 3 years
Frequency: Annual
Country of Study: Australia
Application Procedure: The SRA SugarNet online submission system must be used for all SPRS applications. This can be accessed at sugarnet.sugarresearch.com.au. Applications will not be considered to be complete until the curriculum vitae (CV), certified copies of the academic record and academic transcript, letters of reference from at least two referees and proof of nationality or permanent residence visa are uploaded through SugarNet to accompany the application. The project title needs to be a concise statement of the aim of the proposed research project. The title, objectives and outcomes expected from the project may be published in the SRA Annual Report. Candidates are encouraged to consult their Principal Supervisor when completing this section of the online submission form. No additional information or attachments (such as images, diagrams, flow-charts, tables etc.) should be included unless a prior arrangement has been made with SRA
Closing Date: 31 October
Additional Information: sugarresearch.com.au/research/postgraduate/

Swansea University

Singleton Park, Swansea Wales SA2 8PP, United Kingdom.

Tel: (44) 1792 205 678
Email: sro@swansea.ac.uk
Website: www.swan.ac.uk
Contact: Dr Mark Skippen, Senior Postgraduate Recruitment Officer

Swansea University is a United Kingdom top 30 institution for research excellence that has been providing the highest quality postgraduate teaching since 1920. Our campuses are situated on the sandy beach of Swansea Bay. We have taught and research postgraduate funding for United Kingdom, European Union and international students: www.swansea.ac.uk/postgraduate/scholarships

International Excellence Scholarships

Eligibility: 1. Applicants must be non UK nationals and classed as overseas fee payers. If the fee status of the applicant changes after the scholarship application is made, then the University will need to remove the scholarship. 2. Applicants must have applied for and received an offer to study at Swansea University at Undergraduate or Master's level. 3. Students studying for a PhD, MPhil, Masters by Research, Graduate Diploma in Law, Postgraduate Diploma, Postgraduate Certificate or Erasmus Mundus programme are not eligible to apply for this scholarship. 4. Students on BSc, BA, BEng, LLB, MEng, MSci, MSc, MPharm, MBBCh, MA, LLM, MRes (not the same as Masters by Research) are eligible. 5. Students progressing from 'The College Swansea University' and students currently studying at the University are not eligible to apply for this scholarship. 6. Alumni are eligible to apply.
Level of Study: Postgraduate
Type: Scholarship
Value: Approx. £4,000
Length of Study: 1 year (Masters)
Frequency: Annual
Study Establishment: Swansea University
Country of Study: United Kingdom
Application Procedure: Complete application form, available online at website

MRes Scholarships

Purpose: An MRes Scholarship includes a fee waiver for one year. Associated costs – such as fieldwork and conference

attendance – may also be awarded if approved by the faculty during your research.
Eligibility: Candidates must demonstrate outstanding academic potential with preferably a 1st class honours degree and/or a Master's degree with distinction or equivalent Grade Point Average. An IELTS (Academic) score of 6.5 minimum (with a minimum 6.0 in each component) is essential for candidates for whom English is not their first language.
Type: Scholarship
Value: Each scholarship is worth £2,500, to be used towards the cost of tuition fees
Length of Study: 1 year
Country of Study: United Kingdom
Application Procedure: To apply, click the green Apply Now button on the Scholarship page and complete our online application form. science-scholarships@swansea.ac.uk

For further information contact:

Email: science-scholarships@swansea.ac.uk

PhD Fees-only Bursaries

Eligibility: Open to good Master's graduates from the United Kingdom/European Union who will be commencing PhD studies at Swansea University
Level of Study: Doctorate
Type: Scholarship
Value: Covers United Kingdom/European Union tuition fees
Length of Study: 3 years
Frequency: Annual
Study Establishment: Swansea University
Country of Study: United Kingdom
Application Procedure: Please contact us for an application form
No. of awards given last year: 10

For further information contact:

Email: admissions-enquiries@swansea.ac.uk

Swansea University Masters Scholarships

Eligibility: Open to students from the United Kingdom/European Union who will be starting an eligible master's course at Swansea University for the first time in September
Level of Study: Postgraduate
Type: Scholarship
Value: £2,900 towards tuition fees
Length of Study: 1 year full time or 2 to 3 years part-time
Frequency: Annual
Study Establishment: Swansea University
Country of Study: United Kingdom
Application Procedure: Eligible students are sent an application form when offered a place on a course
Closing Date: 17 July
No. of awards given last year: 100
Additional Information: www.swansea.ac.uk/science/postgraduatescholarships/swansea-science-masters-scholarships/

For further information contact:

Postgraduate Admissions Office Swansea University, Singleton Park, Sketty, Swansea SA2 8PP, United Kingdom.

Email: science-scholarships@swansea.ac.uk

Swansea University PhD Scholarships

Eligibility: Open to good Master's graduates from the United Kingdom/European Union who will be commencing PhD studies at Swansea University
Level of Study: Doctorate, Postgraduate
Type: Scholarship
Value: Annual stipend at Rcuk level (approx.£14,000)
Length of Study: 3 years
Frequency: Annual
Study Establishment: Swansea University
Country of Study: United Kingdom
Application Procedure: Please see individual scholarship listings on our website www.swansea.ac.uk/postgraduate/scholarships/research
No. of awards given last year: 15

For further information contact:

Postgraduate Admissions Office Swansea University, Singleton Park, Sketty, Swansea SA2 8PP, United Kingdom.

Email: postgraduate.admissions@swansea.ac.uk

Swansea University Research Excellence Scholarship

Purpose: The project aims to create novel approaches to contemporary challenges in theoretical and applied ecological and evolutionary biosciences
Level of Study: Doctorate
Type: Scholarship
Value: The scholarship covers the full cost of United Kingdom/European Union tuition fees, plus an annual stipend of £14,553 (in line with the RCUK stipend amount) for 3 years. There will also be £1,000 per annum available for research expenses such as travel, accommodation, field trips and conference attendance

Frequency: Annual
Country of Study: United Kingdom
No. of awards offered: 14
Closing Date: 8 January
Contributor: Swansea University
Additional Information: To apply please complete and return the following documents to Dr Vivienne Jenkins (pgrsures-at-swansea.ac.uk) using the quote reference COS2 www.postgrad.com/news/Applications-open-for-Swansea-University-Research-Excellence-Scholarships-SURES/2563/

For further information contact:

Email: pgrsures@swansea.ac.uk

The James Callaghan Scholarships

Eligibility: Research students from Commonwealth member countries are eligible to apply. Awards are available for full-time or part-time MPhil or PhD studies
Level of Study: Doctorate, Predoctorate
Type: Scholarship
Value: £1,700 (full-time) and £850 (half-time)
Length of Study: 1 year (MPhil) and 3 years (PhD)
Frequency: Annual
Study Establishment: Swansea University
Country of Study: United Kingdom
Application Procedure: Please contact us for an application form
Closing Date: 1 June
Additional Information: www.advance-africa.com/The-James-Callaghan-Scholarships.html

For further information contact:

Postgraduates Admissions Office Swansea University, Singleton Park, Sketty, Swansea SA2 8PP, United Kingdom.

Email: postgraduate.admissions@swansea.ac.uk

Swedish Institute

Swedish Institute, Virkesvägen 2, SE-120 30 Stockholm, Sweden.

Tel: (46) 8 453 7800
Email: si@si.se
Website: si.se/en/
Contact: The Swedish Institute

SISS is the Swedish government's international awards scheme aimed at developing global leaders. It is funded by the Ministry for Foreign Affairs of Sweden and administered by the Swedish Institute (SI). The programme offers a unique opportunity for future leaders to develop professionally and academically, to experience Swedish society and culture, and to build a long-lasting relationship with Sweden and with each other.

Swedish Institute Scholarships for Global Professionals (SISGP)

Purpose: The Swedish Institute (SI) Scholarships for Global Professionals aims to develop future global leaders that will contribute to the United Nations 2030 Agenda for Sustainable Development and contribute to a positive and sustainable development in their home countries and regions.
Eligibility: 1. You must be a citizen of a country that is eligible for SI scholarships. However, you do not need to reside in the country at the time of the application. 2. You must have a minimum of 3,000 hours of demonstrated work experience. In addition, you must have demonstrated leadership experience from your current or previous employer, or from civil society engagement. 3. You must be liable to pay tuition fees to Swedish universities, have followed the steps of University Admissions and be admitted to one of the eligible master's programmes by 30 of March 2024. 4. The master's programmes you apply for must be eligible for SI scholarships. We give priority to programmes within certain subject areas, depending on your country of citizenship.
Level of Study: Postgraduate
Type: Scholarship
Value: Full tuition fee coverage. A monthly payment of SEK 11,000 to cover your living expenses throughout the study period.
Length of Study: One academic year (2 semesters)
Frequency: Varies
Country of Study: Sweden
Application Procedure: Scholarship website: apply-scholarships.si.se/
No. of awards offered: 250
Closing Date: 28 February
Additional Information: si.se/en/apply/scholarships/swedish-institute-scholarships-for-global-professionals/

Swedish Institute Scholarships for the Western Balkans Programme

Purpose: The SI Scholarships for the Western Balkans Programme aims at supporting advanced level studies and research within the field of social sciences in order to forge closer links between the Western Balkans and the European

Union, and to contribute to strengthened democracy in the region

Eligibility: The scholarships are intended for PhD students and postdoctoral researchers from Albania, Bosnia-Herzegovina, Kosovo, Macedonia (FYROM), Montenegro and Serbia conducting part of their studies/research in Sweden within the field of social sciences with a special focus on any of the following thematic areas 1. Democratic accountability; 2. Gender equality, anti-discrimination; 3. Human rights, tolerance, minority groups; 4 Independent media; 5. Pluralistic civil society; 6. Rule of law; 7. Transparency, anti-corruption.

Level of Study: Doctorate, Postdoctorate

Type: Scholarship

Value: SEK 15,000 per month for PhD students, and SEK 18,000 per month for postdoctoral researchers and senior scientists

Length of Study: 1 year

Frequency: Annual

Country of Study: Sweden

Application Procedure: Online application portal

Contributor: Ministry for Foreign Affairs of Sweden and administered by the Swedish Institute (SI)

Swedish-Turkish Scholarship Programme for PhD Studies and Postdoctoral Research

Purpose: The Swedish-Turkish Scholarship Programme aims at supporting advanced level studies and research in order to forge closer links between Turkey and the European Union, and to contribute to strengthened democracy and a greater respect for human rights

Eligibility: The scholarships are intended for PhD students and postdoctoral researchers from Turkey conducting part of their studies/research in Sweden within the field of social sciences. You should not be a resident for more than 2 year in Sweden

Level of Study: Doctorate, Postdoctorate

Type: Scholarship

Value: SEK 15,000 per month for PhD students, and SEK 18,000 per month for postdoctoral researchers and senior scientists

Length of Study: 1 year

Frequency: Annual

Country of Study: Sweden

Contributor: Ministry for Foreign Affairs of Sweden and administered by the Swedish Institute (SI)

The Swedish Institute Study Scholarships (SISS)

Purpose: SISS is the Swedish government's international awards scheme aimed at developing global leaders

Eligibility: Applicants must be from an eligible country and have at least 3,000 hours of experience from full-time/part-time employment, voluntary work, paid/unpaid internship, and/or position of trust. Applicants must display academic qualifications and leadership experience. In addition, applicants should show an ambition to make a difference by working with issues which contribute to a just and sustainable development in their country, in a long term perspective. The travel grant is a one-time payment of SEK 15,000

Level of Study: Foundation programme

Type: Scholarship

Value: The scholarship covers both tuition fees (paid directly to the Swedish university/university college by the Swedish Institute) and living expenses to the amount of SEK 10,000 per month. There are no additional grants for family members

Length of Study: The scholarship is intended for full-time master's level studies of one or two years, and is only awarded for programmes starting in the autumn semester. The scholarship covers the whole duration of the master's programme

Country of Study: Any country

Closing Date: 19 February

Funding: Government

Contributor: Ministry for Foreign Affairs of Sweden

The Swedish Institute Study Scholarships for South Africa

Purpose: The programme offers a unique opportunity for future leaders to develop professionally and academically, to experience Swedish society and culture, and to build a long-lasting relationship with Sweden and with each other

Eligibility: Only citizens of South Africa are eligible for SISSA.

Level of Study: Masters Degree

Type: Scholarship

Value: The scholarship covers both tuition fees, Living expenses of SEK 10,000/month and Travel grant of SEK 15,000

Length of Study: Whole duration of the master's programme

Country of Study: Sweden

Application Procedure: Online application

No. of awards offered: 10

Closing Date: 19 February

Contributor: Ministry for Foreign Affairs of Sweden and administered by the Swedish Institute (SI)

Additional Information: si.se/en/apply/scholarships/swedish-institute-scholarships-for-south-africa/

For further information contact:

Email: sischolarships@si.se

S

Visby Programme Scholarships

Purpose: To support individual mobility, thereby contributing to increased contacts and collaborations between actors in Sweden and countries in the EU Eastern Partnership and Russia. The goal is to build an integrated, knowledge-based and research-intense region, centred on the Baltic Sea while also including EU Eastern Partnership countries and Russia
Eligibility: The candidates who are interested in applying for Masters degree program at university must possess a full time bachelor's degree from an accredited university in their nation with good academic score as the allotment of scholarships are completely merit based and the candidate should demonstrate good leadership skills and good oral and written skills in the languages that are mentioned compulsory to obtain education from Sweden.
Level of Study: Doctorate, Postdoctorate
Type: Scholarship
Value: monthly grant of SEK 9,000 covers tuition fees, insurance, travel expenses of SEK 5,000
Country of Study: Any country
No. of awards offered: 50
Additional Information: si.se/app/uploads/2019/09/4.visbyprog_invite_en.pdf

Swedish Natural Science Research Council (NFR)

Box 7142, SE-10387 Stockholm, Sweden.

Tel: (46) 85 464 400
Email: gfar-secretariat@fao.org
Website: www.gfar.net/
Contact: Grants Management Officer

GFAR makes agri-food research and innovation systems more effective, responsive and equitable, towards achieving Sustainable Development Goals. Partners in GFAR, at national, regional and international levels, advocate for, and catalyse Collective Actions that strengthen and transform agri-food research and innovation systems

NFR FRN Grants for Scientific Equipment

Purpose: To assist researchers
Eligibility: Open to individuals holding a research grant from any Swedish research council
Level of Study: Research
Type: A variable number of grants
Value: Up to SEK 10,000,000
Length of Study: Dependent on the requirements of the projects
Frequency: Annual
Study Establishment: Universities
Country of Study: Sweden
Application Procedure: Applicants must contact the organisation for details
Funding: Government

For further information contact:

Tel: (46) 84 544 254
Email: lars@nfr.se

NFR Travel Grants

Purpose: To give financial support to researchers attending conferences or wishing to undertake short-term research abroad
Eligibility: Open to Swedish researchers and foreign national researchers who have completed their PhD at a Swedish university and have embarked on postdoctoral studies
Level of Study: Postdoctorate, Research
Type: Travel grant
Value: Travelling expenses and subsistence
Length of Study: Up to 2 months
Frequency: Throughout the year
Study Establishment: Universities or academic institutions abroad
Country of Study: Sweden
Application Procedure: Applicants must complete an application form
Closing Date: 15 August
Funding: Government

For further information contact:

Tel: (46) 84 544 229
Email: elisa@nfr.se

Swinburne University of Technology

PO Box 218, Hawthorn, VIC 3122, Australia.

Tel: (61) 3 9214 8000
Email: webmaster@swin.edu.au
Website: www.swinburne.edu
Contact: MBA Admissions Officer

The University maintains a strong technology base and important links with industry, complemented by a number of innovative specialist research centres which attract a great deal of international interest. Swinburne was a pioneer of the Industry Based Learning (IBL) program which places students directly in industry for vocational employment as an integral part of the course structure. Swinburne is committed to the transfer of lifelong learning skills. It is heavily involved in international initiatives and plays a significant part in the internationalization of Australia's tertiary education system.

Chancellor's Research Scholarship

Purpose: To award students of exceptional research potential to undertake a higher degree by research (HDR)
Eligibility: Open to a local or an international student undertaking a higher degree by research (HDR) with Bachelor Degree with First Class Honours. For further details, please check the website
Level of Study: Doctorate, Postgraduate
Type: Research scholarship
Value: An annual stipend of US$30,000, an Establishment Grant of up to US$3,000, up to US$5,000 for a 6-month overseas placement, up to US$840 thesis allowance, Tuition fees and Relocation allowance
Length of Study: 3 years
Frequency: Annual
Application Procedure: Check website for further details
Additional Information: Please refer website for details: www.swinburne.edu.au/study/options/scholarships/215/chancellors-research-scholarship-/

For further information contact:

Email: HDRscholarships@swin.edu.au

PhD in Mechatronics

Purpose: To provide full time scholarships to undertake the degree of Doctor of Philosophy (PhD) at the Faculty of Engineering and Industrial Sciences of Swinburne University of Technology
Eligibility: Applicants should have completed an undergraduate course in engineering preferably in mechatronics or electrical engineering. Candidates with a Masters Degree in a related area or with previous research experience will be given priority
Level of Study: Doctorate
Type: Scholarship
Value: AU$19,616 per year
Length of Study: 3 years
Country of Study: Australia
Application Procedure: Check website for further details
Closing Date: 20 July

For further information contact:

Swinburne University of Technology, PO Box 218, VIC 3122, Australia.

Tel: (61) 61 3 9214 5659
Email: arad@swin.edu.au

Swinburne University Postgraduate Research Award (SUPRA)

Purpose: To assist with general living costs
Eligibility: Students must meet candidature requirements as set out in their proposed program. Please refer to the website for details.
Level of Study: Doctorate, Research
Type: Research award
Value: Annual stipend AU$30,000 (indexed) (2023 rate) for three years (with possible 6 month extension). Tuition fees for up to four years. Thesis allowance.
Length of Study: 3 years
Frequency: Annual
Country of Study: Australia
Application Procedure: Scholarship website: s1.swin.edu.au/eStudent/SM/eApplications/eAppLogin.aspx?f=%24S1.EAP.CI2LOGIN.WEB
Additional Information: www.swinburne.edu.au/study/options/scholarships/221/swinburne-university-postgraduate-research-award/

For further information contact:

Email: HDRscholarships@swin.edu.au

S

Vice Chancellor's Centenary Research Scholarship (VCRS)

Purpose: To assist with general living costs
Eligibility: Open to domestic or an international student who have completed a Bachelor degree with First Class Honours and are of exceptional research potential undertaking a higher degree by research (HDR). For further details, please check the website
Level of Study: Research
Type: Research scholarship
Value: The value of the VCRS will be up to AU$35,000 (tax-exempt) over a maximum period of up to 3.5 full-time

years, payable at the rate of AU$5,000 per year for the 1st year and AU$12,000 per year for the remaining 2.5 years
Length of Study: 3 years
Country of Study: Australia
Application Procedure: Check website for further details

For further information contact:

Building 60Wm, Level 7, 60 William Street, Hawthorn Campus, VIC 3122, Australia.

Tel: (61) 9214 5547 or 9214 8744
Email: ehill@swin.edu.au

Swiss National Science Foundation (SNSF)

Wildhainweg 3, P.O. Box 8232, CH-3001 Bern, Switzerland.

Tel: (41) 31 308 2222
Email: desk@snf.ch
Website: www.snf.ch/
Contact: Dr Benno G Frey, Office for Fellowship Programmes

SNSF supports scientific research at Swiss universities and other scientific institutions and awards fellowships to Swiss scientists or scientists living in Switzerland. The SNSF was established in 1952 as a private foundation entrusted with the promotion of basic non commercial research. While the SNSF supports research through grants given to established or promising researchers, it does not maintain its own research institutions. The main objectives are to support basic research in all areas of academic research and to support young scientists and researchers, with the intent of ensuring the continuing high quality of teaching and research in Swiss higher education. In addition to the general research funding, the SNSF is responsible for the National Research Programmes (NRP).

Swiss National Science Foundation Fellowships for Prospective Researchers

Purpose: To promote holders of MA or PhD degrees, who have had at least one year's experience in active research after the completion of their degree
Eligibility: Open to promising young scholars under the age of 33 who are Swiss nationals or permanent residents of Switzerland, hold an MA or PhD and can demonstrate at least one year's experience in active research. An exception to the age restriction (to a maximum of two years) can be made for candidates from clinical disciplines, or candidates who have interrupted their scientific careers due to family obligations. The main condition for such an exception is that the candidate has reached a high scientific level and will in the future pursue an active career in science and research. A high priority will be given to candidates who plan to return to Switzerland
Level of Study: Postdoctorate, Predoctorate
Type: A variable number of fellowships
Value: AU$35,000 (tax-exempt)
Length of Study: 3.5 years
Frequency: Annual
Study Establishment: Universities worldwide
Country of Study: Australia
Application Procedure: Applicants must complete an application form, available from the Local Research Commission. Candidates with a degree from a Swiss university should contact the Research Commission of their institution. Candidates with Italian as their native language, who have completed their studies in a foreign country should contact the Research Commission for the Italian speaking part of Switzerland. Swiss candidates who are residents of foreign countries, hold a degree from a foreign university, but who intend to return to Switzerland should contact the Swiss scientific academy responsible for their area of research
Additional Information: For further information please contact Benno Frey or Laurence at the Office for Fellowship Programmes, or refer to the website www.snf.ch/SiteCollectionDocuments/stip_ang_weisungen_mySNF_e.pdf

For further information contact:

Email: ehill@swin.edu.au

Syracuse University

900 South Crouse Ave, Syracuse, NY 13244, United States of America.

Tel: (1) 315 443 1870
Website: www.syracuse.edu/

Syracuse students work alongside leading scholars and have access to hands-on research and learning opportunities-all of which prepare them to shape their communities and become the change-makers of tomorrow.

Syracuse University Executive MBA Programme

Length of Study: 2 years
Application Procedure: Applicants must return a completed 'Independent Study MBA' application form
Closing Date: 7 May
Additional Information: onlinebusiness.syr.edu/mba/

For further information contact:

School of Management, Suite 100, Crouse-Hinds School of Management, Syracuse, NY 13244, United States of America.

Tel: (1) 315 443 3006
Fax: (1) 315 443 5389
Email: grad@gwmail.syr.edu

Syracuse University MBA

Purpose: All Syracuse MBA scholarships are awarded based on merit and the qualifications shown on a student's admission application. Applicants are not required to apply separately for merit-based scholarships
Eligibility: To be eligible for the MBA admission, listed below are the requirements. 1. A United States bachelor's degree or its equivalent from an accredited college or university Completed application. 2. Recommended minimum GPA is 3.0 on a 4.0 scale. 4. GMAT or GRE exam. 5. Recommended minimum GMAT score is 600. The 2016 entering class average was 623. 6. For those with GRE scores you can convert them to GMAT through the website www.ets.org/gre/institutions/about/mba/comparison_tool. 7. Program code for GMAT is NG0-SB-40. 8. Institution code for GRE is 2823. 9. English exam (for international students). 10. Minimum total score for TOEFL is 100, IELTS 7.0, PTE 68. 11. Preferred speaking score for TOEFL is 24, IELTS 7.5, PTE 65. 12. Institution code for TOEFL is 2823, department code is 02 if required. 13. PTE Academic program code is 5LD-BQ-15. 14. IELTS Whitman downloads IELTS scores that have been transmitted to our e-download account
Length of Study: 1 to 2 years
Country of Study: Any country
Application Procedure: Applicants must complete the application form (including the specified number of photocopies) with official academic transcripts, two letters of recommendation, personal essays, requested financial documents, Graduate Management Admission Test and TOEFL (if applicable) scores, and a fee of US$50. Applications may be fully completed online
Additional Information: whitman.syr.edu/programs-and-academics/programs/whitman-mba-experience/fulltime-mba-experience/index.aspx

For further information contact:

School of Management Syracuse University, Suite 100, Crouse-Hinds School of Management, Syracuse, NY 13244, United States of America.

Tel: (1) 315 443 4492
Fax: (1) 315 443 3423
Email: lescis@syr.edu

T

Tata Trusts

Bombay House, 24, Homi Mody Street, Mumbai 400 001, India.

Tel: (91) 22 6665 8282
Email: talktous@tatatrusts.org
Website: www.tatatrusts.org/

Tata Trusts endeavour to achieve societal and economic development for attaining self-sustained growth relevant to the nation. They support an assortment of causes such as health, nutrition, education, water and sanitation, livelihoods, social justice and inclusion, skilling, migration and urbanisation, environment, digital literacy, sports, arts, craft and culture, and disaster management to name a few.

Lady Meherbai D. TATA Education Trust

Purpose: The Lady Meherbai D Tata Education Trust awards scholarships to Indian women graduates of reputed universities who wish to pursue higher education abroad, as support towards their tuition fee component.
Eligibility: 1. Indian women graduates from a reputed university 2. A consistent and remarkable academic record 3. Must have applied for admission or preferably secured admission to reputed universities or institutions in the United States, UK or Europe for the year 2023 4. Relevant work experience of a minimum 2 years preferred
Level of Study: Graduate
Type: Grant
Value: Between Rupees three and six lakhs per selected student, is awarded, depending on the performance of the candidate
Frequency: Annual
Country of Study: Any country
Application Procedure: See website
Closing Date: 2 May
Funding: Private
Additional Information: Website: https://www.tatatrusts.org/Upload/pdf/scholarship-announcement-2023-2024.pdf

For further information contact:

Bombay House, 24, Homi Mody Street, Mumbai, Maharashtra 400 001, India.

Email: igpedulmdtet@tatatrusts.org

Te Pôkai Tara Universities New Zealand

PO Box 860, Manners Street, Wellington 6140, New Zealand.

Tel: (64) 4 381 8500
Email: contact@universitiesnz.ac.nz
Website: www.nzvcc.ac.nz
Contact: Kiri Manuera, Scholarships Manager

Universities New Zealand - Te Pôkai Tara is the sector voice for all eight universities, representing their collective views nationally and internationally, championing the quality education they deliver, and the important contribution they make to New Zealand, economically, socially and culturally.

William Georgetti Scholarships

Purpose: To encourage postgraduate study and research, normally in New Zealand, in a field that in the opinion of

Palgrave Macmillan (ed.), *The Grants Register 2024*,
https://doi.org/10.1057/978-1-349-96073-6

the Scholarship Board is important to the social, cultural or economic development of New Zealand.
Eligibility: Applicants must 1. Have resided in New Zealand for a period of at least five years immediately preceding the year of selection (refer to the Regulations for further information). 2. Be of good moral character and repute. 3. Be of good health. 4. Hold a degree from a university in New Zealand or elsewhere or any other academic qualification of a university or other institution of learning (in New Zealand or elsewhere) reasonably equivalent in the opinion of the Scholarship Board to a degree of a university in New Zealand.
Level of Study: Postgraduate
Type: Scholarship
Value: up to NZ$45,000 per year
Frequency: Annual
Study Establishment: Suitable universities
Country of Study: Any country
Application Procedure: Read the Regulations to confirm your eligibility to apply: www.universitiesnz.ac.nz/sites/default/files/uni-nz/documents/scholarships/William%20Georgetti%20Regulations_0.pdf. Apply on-line - the link to the application website is here: universitiesnz.communityforce.com/.
Closing Date: 1 February
Funding: Private
Contributor: The Georgetti Trust
Additional Information: Website: www.universitiesnz.ac.nz/scholarships/william-georgetti-scholarship

For further information contact:

Email: scholarshipscf@universitiesnz.ac.nz

Technische Universiteit Delft (TUD)

Post bus 5, NL-2600 AA Delft, Netherlands.

Tel: (31) 15 278 9111
Email: info@tudelft.nl
Website: www.tudelft.nl/msc

Founded in 1842, The Delft University of Technology is an establishment of both national importance and significant international standing. TU Delft collaborates with other educational establishments and research institutes, both within and outside of the Netherlands. TU Delft aims at being an, interactive partner to social issues, committed to answering its multifaceted demands and initiating changes to benefit people in the future.

The Shell Centenary Scholarship Fund, Netherlands

Purpose: To give students the opportunity to study at the TUD and gain skills that will make a long-term contribution to the further development of their countries
Eligibility: Open to candidates who are nationals of and resident in any country other than the ones listed in 'Additional Information' and aged 35 or under, intending to study a subject that will be of significant value in aiding the sustainable development of their home country, fluent in spoken and written English, and neither a current nor former employee of the Royal Dutch/Shell Group of companies.
Level of Study: Postgraduate
Type: Scholarship
Value: Full-cost scholarship including tuition fees, international travel, living allowances and health insurance
Length of Study: 2 years
Frequency: Annual
Country of Study: Netherlands
Application Procedure: Applicants must have been admitted to a MSc programme of TU Delft, the International Office will subsequently send you the application form by email, the International Office will check your application on the basis of the Royal Dutch/Shell criteria.
Closing Date: 15 December
Contributor: TUD with support from The Shell Centenary Scholarship Fund (TSCSF)
Additional Information: Website: www.postgraduatefunding.com/award-4026

For further information contact:

Tel: (31) 15 2789111
Email: info@tudelft.nl

Tel Aviv University (TAU)

PO Box 39040, Tel Aviv 6997801, Israel.

Tel: (972) 3 640 8111
Email: tauinfo@post.tau.ac.il
Website: www.tau.ac.il

TAU was founded in 1956 and is located in Israel's cultural, financial and industrial heartland. TAU offers an extensive range of programmes in the arts and sciences.

Tel Aviv University Scholarships

Purpose: To encourage innovative and interdisciplinary research that cuts across traditional boundaries and paradigms.
Eligibility: Open to candidates who have registered for their Doctoral or Postdoctoral degree.
Level of Study: Doctorate, Postdoctorate
Type: Scholarships
Value: Minimum award amount is US$500
Frequency: Annual
Application Procedure: Applicants can download the application form from the website. The completed application form along with a curriculum vitae and a description of research project with a list of publications is to be sent.
Closing Date: 30 April
Additional Information: Applications if sent by email, must be directed to ddprize@post.tau.ac. Website: il www.international.tau.ac.il/scholarship_programs

For further information contact:

The Lowy School for Overseas Students, Tel-Aviv University, Center Building, Israel.

Email: scholarship@tauex.tau.ac.il

Texas LBJ School

2300 Red River St., Stop E2700, Sid Richardson Hall, Unit 3, Austin, TX 78712-1536, United States of America.

Tel: (1) 512 471 3200
Email: lbjdeansoffice@austin.utexas.edu
Website: www.lbj.utexas.edu/

The LBJ School boasts of a dynamic community of students, faculty and staff all working toward the same goal of making an impact on the world. Sitting in on an actual LBJ class can be a great way to get a feel for the community and the program. Use the course schedule to find a course that interests you, and email the concerned professor directly for more details.

Barbara Jordan Baines Report Fellowship Fund

Purpose: The Barbara Jordan Baines Report Fellowship Fund is available to students interested in gaining skills in policy writing and storytelling, as well as exercising leadership through managing the student-run publication.
Eligibility: The Baines Report Fellowship supports a master's student pursuing skills in writing about public policy and experience in news media and content creation. Preference will be given to applicants with prior writing or journalism experience. All currently enrolled full-time LBJ School Master's students who are in good academic standing are eligible to apply.
Level of Study: Graduate
Type: Funding support
Value: Students are eligible up to US$750 fund and US$500 toward travel funds.
Frequency: Annual
Country of Study: Any country
Application Procedure: Apply using the common Current Student Endowed Fellowship Application form Students must also submit a current resume, a letter of interest, two writing samples and one well- planned story idea. Final candidates may be interviewed. For further details, check the following link www.lbj.utexas.edu/sites/default/files/BJBREligCriteria.pdf
Funding: Private
Additional Information: In addition, both the fall and spring fellowship awards provide US$500 towards travel to attend the Journal of Public and International Affairs (JPIA) reading weekend in February, contingent on JPIA's invitation. JPIA provides main meals and lodging www.lbj.utexas.edu/lbj-school-fellowships#Baines%20Report

For further information contact:

Lyndon B. Johnson School of Public Affairs, The University of Texas at Austin, P.O. Box Y, Austin, TX 78713-8925, United States of America.

Email: lbjdeansoffice@austin.utexas.edu

Elspeth D. Rostow Memorial Graduate Fellowship

Purpose: The LBJ Foundation is supporting the LBJ School of Public Affairs through the Elspeth Rostow Memorial Fellowship Fund.
Eligibility: To be considered for this fellowship, applicants must be degree-seeking master's students who have completed one year of full-time study at the LBJ School with a cumulative GPA of 3.0 or above. There are no exceptions to these requirements.
Level of Study: Graduate
Type: Fellowship
Value: US$3,000.
Frequency: Annual

Country of Study: Any country
Application Procedure: 1. Complete the Elspeth D. Rostow Memorial Graduate Fellowship application. 2. Submit a one-page statement describing your public service related commitments since enrolling in the LBJ School. Your statement should describe the needs of the community served, how the project pursued addressed those needs, the role you personally played in the public service activities, and the time commitment of the activity, and; 3. A current resume.
Closing Date: November
Funding: Private
Additional Information: www.lbj.utexas.edu/sites/default/files/RostowCriteria.pdf

For further information contact:

Email: lbjdeansoffice@austin.utexas.edu

Michael and Alice Kuhn Summer Fellowships

Purpose: The Kuhn Fellowship grant, made possible by the Michael and Alice Kuhn Foundation, awards each grantee US$6,000 to cover living expenses during their summer internship.
Eligibility: 1. A selection committee will review applications on a rolling basis and recommend applicants with demonstrated commitment to the goals of the Kuhn Summer Fellowship Program to promote social justice and fight poverty. 2. Students with diverse backgrounds receive priority consideration. 3. The selection committee may make requests in addition to the online application, such as official UT transcripts and/or interviews. 4. The selection committee will make its recommendations to the LBJ School leadership. Final selection is at the discretion of school leadership.
Level of Study: Graduate
Type: Fellowship
Frequency: Annual
Country of Study: Any country
Application Procedure: The student's summer work must be done for a nonprofit organization in Central Texas or the United States whose mission is related to social justice and alleviating poverty. There is an interest in supporting students whose placements involve leadership opportunities in the areas of public and legislative advocacy, program-related management, as well as opportunities to work with executive team members on strategic priorities and projects. Students will be asked to link to a Google Drive PDF copy of their 1. Resume. 2. Relevant three- to five-page writing sample from school or professional setting. 3. Offer letter from the nonprofit confirming the internship and description of work.
Closing Date: 30 April
Funding: Commercial, Private
Additional Information: www.lbj.utexas.edu/michael-and-alice-kuhn-summer-fellowships

For further information contact:

Email: LBJFellowships@austin.utexas.edu

Terrell Blodgett Fellowship for Government Services in Urban Management and Finance

Purpose: To encourage students to pursue careers in city management.
Eligibility: Applicants must be degree-seeking master's students in good academic standing who have not yet completed their internship requirement.
Level of Study: Graduate, Masters Degree
Type: Fellowship
Value: See website
Frequency: Annual
Country of Study: Any country
Application Procedure: Applications for the Blodgett Fellowship will be accepted during the internship fellowship application period. To apply, students must complete the LBJ Internship Fellowship application and turn it in along with their approved internship request form, a letter from the agency supervising the internship, a one-page essay on career goals, and a current resume.
Closing Date: April
Funding: Private
Additional Information: www.lbj.utexas.edu/sites/default/files/Blodgett%20Criteria%20PDF.pdf

For further information contact:

Email: lbjwriting@austin.utexas.edu

The Churchill Fellowship

Website: www.churchillfellowship.org
Contact: Communications Director

The Churchill Fellowship is a national network of 3,800 dynamic individuals who are inspiring change in every part of UK life. They may be a nurse promoting mental health in the NHS, a scientist monitoring pollution in the oceans, or a community leader training young entrepreneurs, but they are all united by a common mission: to develop new solutions for today's key challenges, based on learning from the world.

Churchill Fellowship

Subjects: Churchill Fellowships explore the whole spectrum of challenges facing the UK. They are focussed around eight universal themes in society Arts and culture, Community and citizenship, Economy and enterprise, Education and skills, Environment and resources, Health and wellbeing, Governance and public provision, and Science and technology. There is also an Open category for anything else.
Purpose: Churchill Fellowships fund UK citizens from all areas of society to travel overseas for 4-8 weeks in search of practical solutions for today's most pressing problems. On their return, Fellows are helped to make change happen in their community or sector in the UK.
Eligibility: Open to all UK citizens resident in the UK aged 18 years and above, regardless of their qualifications or background. We do not fund gap year activities, courses, volunteering, academic studies, degree placements, internships, medical electives or post-graduate studies.
Level of Study: Unrestricted
Type: Fellowship
Value: Average award is £7,000
Length of Study: 4 - 8 weeks
Frequency: Annual
Country of Study: Any country
Application Procedure: Applications must be made using the online form churchilltrust.force.com/app/s/
No. of awards offered: Up to 150 each year
Funding: Private, Trusts
No. of awards given last year: 141
No. of applicants last year: 1405
Additional Information: To hear when applications open, you can sign up for application alerts on our website at www.churchillfellowship.org

For further information contact:

The Winston Churchill Memorial Trust, GPO Box 1536, Canberra ACT 2601, Australia.

Email: office@churchillfellowship.org

The Community Foundation of South Alabama

P.O. Box 990, Alabama 36601-0990, United States of America.

Tel: (1) 251 438 5591
Email: lbolton@communityfoundationsa.org
Website: www.communityfoundationsa.org/

The Community Foundation of South Alabama is an Alabama not-for-profit corporation approved by the Internal Revenue Service as a publicly supported organization. We recognize the stewardship of the assets entrusted to us as one of our most important responsibilities.

Harry & Lula McCarn Nurses Scholarship

Subjects: Nursing Administration or other fields of nursing
Purpose: To offer financial assistance to a student pursuing a Master's degree in Nursing Administration or a related field.
Eligibility: For a student living in Mobile or Baldwin Counties and pursuing a master's degree in Nursing Administration or other field of nursing at USA. Applicants must have a minimum 3.0 GPA.
Type: Scholarship
Study Establishment: University of South Alabama
Country of Study: United States of America
Application Procedure: Applicants apply by utilizing the Foundation's online scholarship application portal. www.communityfoundationsa.org/apply-for-a-scholarship
Additional Information: www.communityfoundationsa.org/apply-for-a-scholarship

For further information contact:

Email: ndunn@communityfoundationsa.org

The Foundation for Advancement of Diversity in IP Law

1400 Crystal Drive, Suite 600, Arlington, VA 22202, United States of America.

Tel: (1) 703 412 4342
Email: admin@diversityinIPLaw.org
Website: www.diversityiniplaw.org/

For nearly two decades the Foundation—formerly the American Intellectual Property Law Education Foundation—has worked for the advancement of diversity in the IP profession. In 2020, the Foundation adopted its new name—Foundation for Advancement of Diversity in IP Law— to accompany an expansion of the Foundation's longstanding programming aimed at attracting more members of underrepresented racial and ethnic groups into the IP law profession—and advancing their opportunities for achievement in the profession once completing law school.

AIPLEF Sidney B. Williams Scholarship

Subjects: Law
Purpose: To increase the diversity of the IP bar by providing scholarships and mentoring to underrepresented minority law school students pursuing careers in IP law.
Eligibility: Be enrolled as an entering law school (1L) student. Have proven academic performance at the undergraduate, graduate, and law school levels (if applicable). Have a financial need. Have record of leadership, community activities, and/or special accomplishments. Demonstrate intent to engage in the full-time practice of patent law. Are currently enrolled in or have been accepted to an ABA-accredited law school.
Type: Scholarship
Value: Students will be selected to receive a three-year scholarship of up to US$30,000 (US$10,000 per academic year, US$5,000 per semester, which can only be applied to verifiable costs associated with average tuition and usual fees).
Length of Study: Three years
Country of Study: United States of America
Additional Information: The curriculum of law school, as it relates to intellectual property law, is not considered in awarding scholarships. Applicants related to a trustee of AIPLEF, a council member of the ABA-IPL Section, Officer or member of the Board of Directors of the AIPLA, or a member of the AIPLEF Scholarship Committee are ineligible to apply. Scholarship recipients are required to attend law school, day or evening, on either a full-time or part-time enrollment basis, and to maintain a grade point average of "B" (3.0) or better. Scholarship recipients are required to join and maintain membership in AIPLA. https://diversityiniplaw.org/sidney-b-williams-jr-scholar-program/

The Gerda Henkel Foundation

Malkastenstrasse 15, D-40211 Dusseldorf, Germany.

Tel: (49) 211 93 65 24 0
Email: info@gerda-henkel-stiftung.de
Website: www.gerda-henkel-stiftung.de/en/

The Gerda Henkel Foundation was established in June 1976 by Lisa Maskell. The Gerda Henkel Foundation concentrates its support on the historical humanities. In connection with funded projects, the Foundation also provides assistance for social support measures as part of complementary projects.

General Research Grants: Scholarships

Purpose: To support up-and-coming scholars. Special attention is made when approving grants to enable qualified young researchers of both sexes to conduct scientific work for a limited period of time and in order to improve their academic training. As part of its Ph.D. programme, the Foundation seeks to promote highly-qualified new academic talent. Only those candidates are considered whose study achievements and exam performances show them to be especially gifted and whose Ph.D. theses can be expected to yield well above-average results. At present, each year about 50 scholarships are awarded.
Eligibility: Criteria for applicants 1. Applications for a "research scholarship for post-doctoral researchers" may only be made if applicants received their PhD within the last ten years. The relevant date is that on the PhD certificate. (This restriction does not apply to research scholarships after Post Doctoral Lecture Qualification.) 2. The dissertation must have already been published at the time the application is made. The presentation of a publishing contract is not sufficient in this regard. 3. The topic of the proposed research project must clearly differ from the topic of the PhD thesis.
Level of Study: Postgraduate
Type: Scholarship
Value: Monthly scholarship award: €3,100
Length of Study: between one and 24 months
Application Procedure: Applications for research scholarships can be made directly by Postdocs or scholars with Post Doctoral Lecture Qualification. A research scholarship is usually applied for by one scholar who will work on a specific project on his own. An institutional affiliation is not necessary. The simultaneous receipt of salary or retirement pension and a research scholarship is not possible. see website for more information.
Closing Date: 17 May
Additional Information: Website: www.gerda-henkel-stiftung.de/en/researchscholarships

Lost Cities Funding Programme

Subjects: Abandoned cities
Purpose: The aim of the programme is to describe the tangible cultures of interpretation, knowledge and perception within these different contexts. Lost Cities are part of a distinct culture of memory, for example, which serves for the negotiation of identities, the preservation of knowledge cultures, the formulation of criticism of progress, or the construction of mythical or sacral topographies as part of

a veritable "ruin cult". On this basis, the focus here should not be on the question of which factors led to the city's abandonment. Rather, it is the abandoned cities themselves that are of particular interest, as well as the different forms of their interpretation, instrumentalization and coding in various cultures and time frames.
Eligibility: Post-doctoral researchers based in a university and working in the area of the humanities and the social sciences are eligible to apply. Funding can be provided for projects with a thematic focus being addressed by a group of researchers. The Foundation uses the term "group of researchers" to mean associations of at least two researchers actively involved in the project work which is to be funded by means of scholarships from the Foundation and who are carrying out research into the same issues. Applications can only be made for PhD or research scholarships. Applications for a research scholarship by the applicant (project leader) are also possible. A maximum total of three scholarships per group of researchers can be applied for, as well as funds for travel and materials. A fundamental prerequisite for a grant is that project staff conduct their own research, which is published under their name. Other contributors who are not financed by scholarships can also be involved in the project. Scholarship applications made by individual researchers outside of the group are not accepted. The funding programme also provides for the project partners to participate in a public "workshop discussion on Lost Cities" organised by the Foundation.
Level of Study: Postgraduate, Research
Type: Grant
Value: see website
Length of Study: 36 months
Country of Study: Any country
Application Procedure: The necessary application documents can be uploaded in the electronic application form. See website
Closing Date: 24 May
Additional Information: Website: www.gerda-henkel-stiftung.de/en/lost_cities

PhD Scholarships

Purpose: To support up-and-coming scholars. Special attention is made when approving grants to enable qualified young researchers of both sexes to conduct scientific work for a limited period of time and in order to improve their academic training.
Eligibility: Only those candidates are considered whose study achievements and exam performances show them to be especially gifted and whose Ph.D. theses can be expected to yield well above-average results.
Level of Study: Postgraduate, Research
Type: Scholarship
Value: Monthly scholarship award: € 1,600
Length of Study: up to 2 years
Application Procedure: It is only possible to apply electronically for the general research grants. The necessary application documents can be uploaded in the electronic application form. for more information see website
Additional Information: Website: www.gerda-henkel-stiftung.de/en/phd-scholarships

The Lynde and Harry Bradley Foundation

1400 N. Water Street, Suite 300, Milwaukee, WI 53202, United States of America.

Tel: (1) 414 291 9915
Website: www.bradleyfdn.org/

The Bradley Foundation envisions a nation invigorated by the principles and institutions that uphold our unalienable rights to life, liberty, and the pursuit of happiness. The Bradley Foundation seeks to further those beliefs by supporting the study, defense, and practice of the individual initiative and ordered liberty that lead to prosperity, strong families, and vibrant communities.

Grants

Subjects: Projects may address any arena of public life economics, politics, culture or civil society. As such, support is provided to schools of business, economics, public policy and more for activities including research, general operating expenses, graduate and post-graduate fellowships, seminars and speakers programs.
Purpose: Supports projects that "nurture a solid foundation of competent, self-governing citizens, who are capable of and responsible for making the major political, economic and moral decisions that shape their lives."
Eligibility: See website.
Type: Grant
Value: Varies
Country of Study: Any country
Application Procedure: The application process proceeds in two stages. First, brief letters of inquiry are required. If the foundation determines the project to be within its policy guidelines, the applicant will receive a brochure with further application instructions.
Closing Date: 1 December
Additional Information: www.bradleyfdn.org

The Marfan Foundation

22 Manhasset Avenue, Port Washington, NY 11050, United States of America.

Tel: (1) 516 883 8712
Email: research@marfan.org; media@marfan.org
Website: www.marfan.org/
Contact: Josephine Grima, PhD Chief Science Officer The Marfan Foundation

The Marfan Foundation's mission is to save lives and improve the quality of life of individuals with Marfan syndrome, Loeys-Dietz syndrome, Vascular Ehlers-Danlos syndrome (VEDS), and other genetic aortic and vascular conditions.

Faculty Grant Program

Purpose: We provide financial support for investigators studying any or all disciplines involving Marfan syndrome and related conditions.
Eligibility: The principal investigator must hold an MD, DO, PhD, ScD, DDS, DVM or equivalent degree. The investigator must have proven ability to pursue independent research as evidenced by original research publications in peer-reviewed journals and should hold a position of Associate Professor or above. Faculty members with less experience who have obtained an NIH R-01 grant are also eligible for the faculty grant award. Work can be performed in the U.S. or internationally and non U.S. appointments are acceptable.
Level of Study: Postgraduate
Type: Grant
Value: The Marfan Foundation will award up to three 2-year US$100,000 grant.
Frequency: Annual
Country of Study: Any country
Application Procedure: The application must be submitted electronically, including the application forms, additional pages, and appendices, as a single PDF file, via The Marfan Foundation website, www.marfan.org. Please name your application using the following format FacultyGrant_Lastname_FirstName.pdf Example FacultyGrant_Smith_Jane.pdf The application forms may be completed by using the free Adobe Reader program. If you do not already have it, you can download it at www.adobe.com/products/reader.html. The Title Page form requires dated signatures; you may either insert a digital signature and date or print the form and then scan it to include in your application PDF. Additional pages should be typed single-spaced using a font size of at least a 10 points and with one inch margins. Pages should be numbered at the bottom. Appendices should not be used to subvert the page limitation on the grant, however, figures, tables, diagrams and photographs can be placed in the appendices. Please present the proposal in the order that follows THE MARFAN FOUNDATION FACULTY GRANT GUIDELINES 5 1. Title Page 1 page Application form provided 2. Table of Contents 1 page Application form provided 3. Project Abstract and Lay Person Summary 1 page each On a single page, describe precisely and clearly the nature, objective, methods of procedure and significance of the proposed research project, and how it relates to the goal of providing a better understanding of Marfan syndrome, EDS, LDS, and other related disorders and/or improving the treatment or diagnosis of Marfan syndrome, EDS, LDS, and other related disorders (limit 300 words). Rewrite the abstract in abbreviated form in terms suitable for presentation to lay persons (limit 500 words). 4. Research Plan 3 pages a. Include Goals and Objectives; Rationale; Methodology; Evaluation. (Figures may be placed in appendix if needed). b. Please comment upon the importance of funding i. Will this funding allow you to pursue studies that would otherwise not be performed? Is funding meant to supplement other sources of support? ii. Do you anticipate that this funding will increase your competitiveness for other funding sources? c. Please comment upon the significance of the work that you propose i. Is it similar to or a direct extension of work that has been or is being performed elsewhere? ii. Does the work complement or extend other studies that are being performed at your institution? iii. How novel are the studies that you describe? iv. Would such a proposal be competitive for NIH funding in its current form, or would you require additional preliminary data? v. Do you anticipate that the support would lead to the generation of physical resources that might be useful to other investigators in the field? vi. If so, would you be willing to make them widely available? 5. Budget and Justification List full budget with amount requested. Include a. Names, titles, time/percentage effort of all participants, requested salaries and fringe benefits and total amount required. b. Statement that the institution or other funding sources will absorb indirect costs. c. A written budget justification. 6 The budget justification should be suited to the proposal. It is important that the investigators match the dollar award with the actual project. If funding from other sources is being used to cover certain parts of the study, please elaborate on what parts of the budget will not be completed with Foundation funding and what the approximate costs of the full project would be. No overhead or indirect costs will be considered. List the additional sources of funding if budget exceeds proposal amount. 6. Other Support 2 pages List other support received by principal and co-investigators for any projects (include yearly and total budget and duration of any grants) a. Current b. Pending c. Description (in a paragraph, describe each current or pending grant and whether it has scientific or

budgetary overlap with the present proposal). 7. Biographical Sketches 5 pages each. Using the supplied form, please provide biographical sketches for key personnel. Indicate the total number of publications in each of the (2) categories referenced articles and invited works. If you prefer, you may use the NIH biosketch form instead. 8. Facilities Description 1 page Describe the research facilities (laboratory space, clinical population, etc) available for the project. 9. Appendix a. Figures, tables etc. b. Literature cited c. Human subjects experimental approval d. Vertebrate animal experimental approval Letters of support.
Closing Date: January

For further information contact:

Email: jgrima@marfan.org

The National Academies of Sciences, Engineering and Medicine

500 Fifth St., N.W., Washington, DC 20001, United States of America.

Tel: (1) 202 334 2000
Email: worldwidewebfeedback@nas.edu; contact@nas.edu
Website: www.nationalacademies.org/

The National Academies of Sciences, Engineering, and Medicine provide independent, objective advice to inform policy with evidence, spark progress and innovation, and confront challenging issues for the benefit of society.

Gulf Research Program Science Policy Fellowships

Subjects: Science policy
Purpose: The Fellowship program helps scientists hone their skills by putting them to practice for the benefit of Gulf Coast communities and ecosystems. Fellows gain first-hand experience as they spend one year on the staff of federal, state, local, or non-governmental environmental, natural resource, oil and gas, and public health agencies in the Gulf of Mexico region.
Eligibility: See website
Type: Fellowship
Value: Fellows who have completed an MA, MS, or MPH/MSPH degree or who are currently enrolled in a doctoral program will receive an annual stipend of US$58,000. Fellows who have completed a PhD, ScD, EngD, MD, DrPH, or DVM will receive an annual stipend of US$63,000.
Frequency: Annual
Country of Study: Any country
Application Procedure: Applications submitted through the online application system: www.nationalacademies.org/gulf/fellowships/science-policy/index.htm?utm_source=direct&utm_medium=email&utm_campaign=2019_SPF_pathwaystoscience.
Closing Date: 1 March
Additional Information: website: pathwaystoscience.org/programhub.aspx?sort=GRD-NationalAcademies-GulfScPolicyFell

For further information contact:

Email: GulfFellowships@nas.edu

The Gulf Research Program's Early-Career Research Fellowship

Purpose: The Fellowship supports emerging scientific leaders as they take risks on research ideas not yet tested, pursue unique collaborations, and build a network of colleagues who share their interest in improving offshore energy system safety and the well-being of coastal communities and ecosystems.
Eligibility: 1. Hold a permanent, fully independent position as an investigator, faculty member, clinician scientist, or scientific team lead in industry, academia, or a research organization. A postdoc is not considered a fully independent position. 2. Be an early-career scientist who has received their eligible degree within the past 10 years (on or after January 1, 2013). 3. Hold a doctoral degree (e.g., PhD, ScD, EngD, MD, DrPH, or DVM) in the social and behavioral sciences, health sciences and medicine, engineering and physical sciences, earth and life sciences, or interdisciplinary scientific fields relevant to the charge of the Gulf Research Program. 4. Be affiliated with a non-federal U.S. institution that has a valid tax ID number. 5. Not be currently employed by the U.S. federal government. see website for more details
Level of Study: Doctorate, Masters Degree
Type: Fellowship
Value: US$76,000
Country of Study: Any country
Application Procedure: Applications can be submitted through our online application system: grpfellowships.smapply.io/.
Closing Date: 23 August
Additional Information: Website: www.nationalacademies.org/our-work/early-career-research-fellowship/for-

applicants#sl-three-columns-b0089821-e53f-4bfc-9062-1a3c752241b3

For further information contact:

Email: GulfFellowships@nas.edu

The National GEM Consortium

1430 Duke Street, Alexandria, VA 22314, United States of America.

Tel: (1) 703 562 3646
Email: info@gemfellowship.org
Website: www.gemfellowship.org/

The mission of The National GEM Consortium is to enhance the value of the nation's human capital by increasing the participation of underrepresented groups at the master's and doctoral levels in engineering and science.

MS Engineering and Science Fellowship Program

Subjects: Engineering
Purpose: The objective of this program is to promote the benefits of a Masters degree within industry.
Type: Fellowship
Value: 1. US$4,000 living stipend per full-time semester up to 4 semesters (US$8K per academic year – 3 quarters) 2. Minimum US$16,000 total stipend over the entire Master's program 3. Up to two paid summer internships with a GEM Employer Member 4. Full tuition and fees provided by a GEM University Member
Country of Study: United States of America
Application Procedure: See website.
Additional Information: www.gemfellowship.org/students/gem-fellowship-program/

PhD Engineering and Science Fellowship

Subjects: Engineering
Purpose: The objective of this program is to offer doctoral fellowships to underrepresented minority students who have either completed, are currently enrolled in a Master's in an Engineering program, or received admittance into a PhD program directly from a Bachelor's degree program.
Type: Fellowship
Value: During the first academic year of being awarded the GEM Fellowship, the GEM Consortium remits a stipend and a cost of instruction grant to the institution where the fellow is enrolled. Thereafter, up to the fifth year of the doctoral program, continued financial support of the GEM Fellow is borne by the GEM University through alternative sources of funding such as institutional awards, assistantships or other external fellowships. Fellows recieve US$16,000 stipend in the first academic year of the GEM Fellowship; GEM Member University provides a living stipend up to the 5th year of the PhD program, equivalent to other funded doctorate students in the department; a minimum of one paid summer internship with a GEM Employer Member; full tuition and fees at a GEM University Member
Country of Study: Any country
Application Procedure: See website.

PhD Science Fellowship

Subjects: Chemistry, physics, earth sciences, mathematics, biological sciences, and computer science.
Purpose: The goal of this program is to increase the number of minority students who pursue doctoral degrees in the natural science disciplines
Eligibility: Applicants to this program are accepted as early as their senior undergraduate year, as well as candidates currently enrolled in a Master's of Engineering program and working professionals.
Type: Fellowship
Value: During the first academic year of being awarded the GEM Fellowship, the GEM Consortium remits a stipend and a cost of instruction grant to the institution where the fellow is enrolled. Thereafter, up to the fifth year of the doctoral program, continued financial support of the GEM Fellow is borne by the GEM University through alternative sources of funding such as institutional awards, assistantships or other external fellowships. Fellows recieve US$16,000 stipend in the first academic year of the GEM Fellowship; GEM Member University provides a living stipend up to the 5th year of PhD program, equivalent to other funded doctorate students in the department; a minimum of one paid summer internship with a GEM Employer Member; full tuition and fees at a GEM University Member
Country of Study: Any country
Application Procedure: See website.
Closing Date: 15 November
Additional Information: Fellowships offered through this program are portable and may be used at any participating GEM Member University where the GEM Fellow is admitted. www.gemfellowship.org/students/gem-fellowship-program/

The National Hispanic Scholarship Fund

P.O. Box 160113, Orlando, FL 32816-0113, United States of America.

Tel: (1) 407 823 2827
Website: www.hsf.net/

Founded in 1975, the Hispanic Scholarship Fund empowers students and parents with the knowledge and resources to successfully complete a higher education, while providing support services and scholarships. HSF empowers students and parents with the knowledge and resources to successfully complete a higher education, while providing support services and scholarships to as many exceptional students, HSF Scholars, and Alumni as possible. Hispanics are a highly educated and influential community of courageous leaders, thriving and positively shaping all areas of a strong American society, from science and technology to entertainment, from finance to government.

BHW Women in STEM Scholarship

Purpose: The BHW Group is excited to announce our Women in STEM academic scholarship.
Eligibility: Women who are pursuing an undergraduate or master's degree and are majoring in science, technology, engineering, or mathematics during the 2023 school year.
Level of Study: Masters Degree
Type: Scholarship
Value: US$3,000
Application Procedure: Application: thebhwgroup.com/scholarship
Closing Date: 15 April
Additional Information: Website: thebhwgroup.com/scholarship

Critical Language Scholarship Program

Purpose: The program provides overseas foreign language instruction and cultural immersion experiences for American undergraduate and graduate students in fifteen critical need languages.
Eligibility: For eligibility criteria: exchanges.state.gov/cls
Level of Study: Graduate
Type: Scholarship
Value: Upto US$20,000
Application Procedure: See website
Additional Information: website: www.hsf.net/scholarship-finder/58

HSF Scholarship

Subjects: All
Purpose: To assist students of Hispanic heritage to obtain a university degree
Eligibility: 1. Must be of Hispanic heritage 2. U.S. citizen, permanent legal resident, or DACA 3. Minimum of 3.0 GPA on a 4.0 scale (or equivalent) for high school students; minimum of 2.5 GPA on a 4.0 scale (or equivalent) for college and graduate students 4. Plan to enroll full-time in an accredited, public or not-for-profit, four-year university, or graduate school, in the US, for the 2023–2024 academic year 5. Submit the FAFSA or state-based financial aid forms (if applicable)
Type: Scholarship
Value: Award amounts range from US$500 - US$5,000, based on relative need.
Country of Study: United States of America
Application Procedure: Sign in to apply: www.hsf.net/login
No. of awards offered: 10,000
Closing Date: 15 February
Additional Information: website: www.hsf.net/scholarship

The Thomas R. Pickering Foreign Affairs Fellowship Program

2216 6th Street NW, Washington, DC 20059, United States of America.

Tel: (1) 202 806 6495
Email: pickeringfellowship@howard.edu
Website: pickeringfellowship.org/

The Thomas R. Pickering Foreign Affairs Fellowship Program is a program funded by the U.S. Department of State, administered by Howard University, that attracts and prepares outstanding young people for Foreign Service careers in the U.S. Department of State. It welcomes the application of members of minority groups historically underrepresented in the State Department, women, and those with financial need. Based on the fundamental principle that diversity is a strength in our diplomatic efforts, the program values varied backgrounds, including ethnic, racial, social, and geographic diversity.

The Thomas R. Pickering Foreign Affairs Fellowship

Subjects: Public policy, international affairs, public administration, business, economics, political science, sociology, or foreign languages.

Purpose: Thomas R. Pickering Graduate Fellowship offers a unique opportunity to promote positive change in the world. Upon successful completion of a two-year master's degree program and fulfillment of fellowship and Foreign Service entry requirements, fellows have the opportunity to work as Foreign Service Officers with the U.S. Department of State, in accordance with applicable law and State Department policy, serving in Washington, DC or at a U.S. embassy, consulate, or diplomatic mission around the globe.
Eligibility: This is a highly selective program. To be eligible to participate, you must meet the following criteria: 1. Be a U.S. citizen. 2. Have a cumulative grade point average of at least 3.2 on a 4.0 scale at the time of application. 3. Seek admission to a two-year, full-time, on-campus, master's degree program at a U.S.-based graduate institution to begin in the fall of 2024 in an academic field relevant to the work of the Foreign Service (public policy, international affairs, public administration, business, economics, political science, management science, organizational development/leadership, sociology, or regional studies).
Type: Fellowship
Value: 45 fellowships of up to US$42,000 annually for a two-year period for tuition, room, board, books, and mandatory fees for completion of two-year master's degrees. This includes up to US$24,000 per year for tuition and mandatory fees and an academic year stipend of US$18,000.
Length of Study: Two years
Frequency: Annual
Study Establishment: Howard University
Country of Study: United States of America
Application Procedure: See website
No. of awards offered: 30
Closing Date: 29 September
No. of applicants last year: 45
Additional Information: website: pickeringfellowship.org/graduate-fellowship/overview-and-eligibility/

The White House

1600 Pennsylvania Ave NW, Washington, DC 20500, United States of America.

Website: www.whitehouse.gov/

The White House is where the President and First Family of the United States live and work, but it's also the People's House, where we hope all Americans feel a sense of inclusion and belonging.

The White House Fellowship

Subjects: All
Purpose: The White House Fellowship is a highly competitive opportunity to participate in and learn about the Federal Government from a unique perspective.
Eligibility: All applicants must be United States citizens, and must have completed their undergraduate education. With the exception of active duty military personnel, Federal Government employees are not eligible to apply.
Type: Fellowship
Value: see website
Country of Study: Any country
Application Procedure: Interested individuals may apply at: fellows.whitehouse.gov
Closing Date: 6 January
Additional Information: For more information, including details about the Fellowships, its history, and the selection process, please visit: www.whitehouse.gov/get–involved/fellows/. Any questions regarding the White House Fellowship program can be directed to whitehousefellows@who.eop.gov. Website: www.whitehouse.gov/briefing-room/statements-releases/2022/11/03/2023-2024-white-house-fellowship/

Third World Academy of Sciences (TWAS)

ICTP Enrico Fermi Building, ground and 1st floor, Via Beirut 6, I-34151 Trieste, Italy.

Email: info@twas.org
Website: www.twas.org

The Third Word Academy of Sciences (TWAS) is an autonomous international organization that promotes and supports excellence in scientific research and helps build research capacity in the South.

Council of Scientific and Industrial Research/ TWAS Fellowship for Postgraduate Research

Purpose: To enable scholars from developing countries (other than India) who wish to pursue postgraduate research to undertake research in laboratories or institutes of the CSIR
Eligibility: Candidates must have a Master's or equivalent degree in science or engineering and should be a regular employee in a developing country (other than India) and be holding a research assignment.

Level of Study: Postgraduate
Type: Fellowship
Value: Monthly stipend to cover for living costs, food and health insurance.
Length of Study: Up to 4 years
Frequency: Annual
Study Establishment: CSIR research laboratories or institutes.
Country of Study: India
Application Procedure: One copy of the application should be sent to TWAS and three copies to CSIR. Application forms are available on request or from the website.
Closing Date: 31 July
Funding: Government
Contributor: CSIR (India), the Italian Ministry of Foreign Affairs and the Directorate General for Development Co-operation
No. of awards given last year: 8

For further information contact:

International S&T Affairs Directorate, Council for Scientific and Industrial Research (CSIR), Anusandhan Bhavan, 2 Rafi Marg, New Delhi, Delhi 110001, India.

Tel: (39) 040 2240 314, (91) 11 2331 6751
Fax: (91) 11 2371 0618, (39) 040 2240 689
Email: fellowships@twas.org; anuradha@csir.res.in

OWSD PhD Fellowships for Women Scientists

Purpose: The PhD fellowship for women scientists from Science and Technology Lagging Countries (STLCs) supports them to undertake PhD research in the Natural, Engineering and Information Technology sciences at a host institute in the South.
Eligibility: The OWSD PhD Fellowship is offered only to women candidates. 1. Candidates must confirm that they intend to return to their home country as soon as possible after completion of the fellowship. 2. Eligible countries: The list of eligible countries is also available here: owsd.net/sites/default/files/OWSD%20Eligible%20Countries%202017.pdf.
Level of Study: Postgraduate
Type: Fellowship
Length of Study: Up to 4 years
Frequency: Annual
Country of Study: Any country
Closing Date: 15 April
Additional Information: website: owsd.net/career-development/phd-fellowship

Seed Grant for New African Principal Investigators (SG-NAPI)

Subjects: Agriculture, Biology, Chemistry, Earth Sciences, Engineering, Information Computer Technology, Mathematics, Medical Sciences and Physics
Purpose: With the support of the German Federal Ministry of Education and Research (BMBF), TWAS launches a new programme to strengthen the capacity of African countries lagging in science and technology. The new programme is aimed at young scientists who are getting established in their country or about to return home to an academic position. Under this scheme, grants are awarded to promising high-level research projects in Agriculture, Biology, Chemistry, Earth Sciences, Engineering, Information Computer Technology, Mathematics, Medical Sciences and Physics carried out in African countries lagging in science and technology identified by TWAS.
Eligibility: 1. Applying Principal Investigator must be a national of an eligible country, who holds a PhD and has good research experience. The grant should operate within a university or a research institution in one of the African countries lagging in science and technology. The PI must be 40 years or under. Any applicant turning 41 years in the year of application is not eligible. 2. The PI must have obtained their Ph.D. within the last 5 years in a country other than their home country. 3. The PI must have returned to their home country (refer to list in the guidelines) within the last 36 months or before the end of 2022. 4. The PI must hold, be offered or be in the process of accepting a position at an academic and/or research institution (including international research centers) in their home country. 5. The PI must be national of an eligible African country that is lagging in science and technology (refer to list in the giudelines). 6. Applicant must at the time of application NOT have an active research grant with TWAS or OWSD Early Career Women Scientists (ECWS) Fellowship. 7. Applications from women scientists and those working in Least Developed Countries are especially encouraged. 8. The applicant must submit a strong Research Proposal (you may find further information on how to write a strong proposal by visiting AuthorAID). Please be advised that applicants may apply for only one programme per calendar year in the TWAS and OWSD portfolio. Applicants will not be eligible to visit another institution in that year under the TWAS Visiting Scientists or the Visiting Professor programmes. One exception The head of an institution who invites an external scholar to share his/her expertise under the TWAS Visiting Professor programme or the TWAS Visiting Expert programme may still apply for another programme.
Level of Study: Postdoctorate
Type: Grant
Value: Maximum of US$67,700

Frequency: Annual
Country of Study: Any country
Application Procedure: SG-NAPI grant applications, once the call opens, will need to be submitted online by clicking on the "Apply Now" link at the bottom of this page. Please note the link will only be active once the call opens and not before (or after it is closed).

For further information contact:

Email: sgnapi@twas.org

The Council of Scientific and Industrial Research/ TWAS Fellowship for Postdoctoral Research

Subjects: 01-Agricultural Sciences, 02-Structural, Cell and Molecular Biology, 03-Biological Systems and Organisms, 04-Medical and Health Sciences incl. Neurosciences, 05-Chemical Sciences, 06-Engineering Sciences incl. Computing and IT, 07-Astronomy, Space and Earth Sciences, 08-Mathematical Sciences, 09-Physics
Purpose: To enable scholars from developing countries (other than India) who wish to pursue postdoctoral research to undertake research in laboratories or institutes of the CSIR.
Eligibility: The minimum qualification requirement is a PhD degree in science or technology. Applicants must be regular employees in a developing country (but not India) and should hold a research assignment. Be a maximum age of 45 years on December 31st of the application year.
Level of Study: Postdoctorate
Type: Fellowship
Value: Monthly stipend to cover for living costs, food and health insurance.
Length of Study: Up to 12 months
Frequency: Annual
Study Establishment: CSIR research laboratories or institutes
Country of Study: India
Application Procedure: Applicants must complete an application form, available on request or from the website.
Closing Date: 31 July
Funding: Government
Contributor: CSIR (India), the Italian Ministry of Foreign Affairs and the Directorate General for Development Co-operation.
No. of awards given last year: 4
Additional Information: CSIR is the premier civil scientific organization of India, which has a network of research laboratories covering wide areas of industrial research www.twas.org/opportunity/twas-csir-postdoctoral-fellowship-programme

For further information contact:

Tel: (39) 040 2240 314, (91) 11 2331 6751
Fax: (91) 11 2371 0618, (39) 040 2240 689
Email: fellowships@twas.org; anuradha@csir.res.in

TWAS-COMSTECH Science in Exile PhD Fellowship Programme for Displaced and Refugee Scientists

Subjects: 01-Agricultural Sciences 02-Structural, Cell and Molecular Biology 03-Biological Systems and Organisms 04-Medical and Health Sciences incl. Neurosciences 05-Chemical Sciences 06-Engineering Sciences incl. Computing and IT 07-Astronomy, Space and Earth Sciences 08-Mathematical Sciences 09-Physics
Purpose: UNESCO-TWAS has partnered with the Ministerial Standing Committee on Scientific and Technological Cooperation of the Organization of Islamic Cooperation (COMSTECH) for the UNESCO-TWAS-COMSTECH Science in Exile Fellowship Programme for displaced and refugee scholars and scientists. The PhD Fellowship Programme aims to provide displaced and refugee scholars and scientists who have not yet found a safe and long-term host country to pursue doctoral studies in Pakistan, at institutions members of the COMSTECH Consortium of Excellence (CCoE).
Eligibility: Applicants for these fellowships must meet the following criteria 1. They must be displaced or refugee scholars and scientists. 2. They must be currently living in Pakistan and holding the right to live and study in the country, OR able to travel to Pakistan. 3. Please note that the Programme is not suitable for scholars at risk who need specific assistance to leave their home country. Awardees are responsible for arranging the logistics and safety of their own relocation. Please note there is only a very small number of competitive travel bursaries available. 3. They must hold a Master's Degree as well as a Bachelors in the field of natural sciences, applied sciences, engineering and technology, health sciences, software engineering and computer.
Level of Study: Postdoctorate, Postgraduate (MSc)
Type: Fellowship
Length of Study: Up to 12 months
Frequency: Annual
Country of Study: Any country
Application Procedure: Applicants may apply for only one of the two types of the UNESCO-TWAS – COMSTECH Science in Exile Fellowships Programme. To learn about the Postdoctoral fellowships, please visit twas.org/opportunity/twas-comstech-postdoctoral-fellowship-programme-displaced-and-refugee-scientists
Closing Date: 4 February

For further information contact:

Email: displacedscientists@twas.org; events@comstech.org

TWAS-SN Bose Postgraduate Fellowship Programme

Subjects: Chemical Sciences, Mathematical Sciences, Physics
Purpose: TWAS-SN Bose Postgraduate Fellowships are tenable at the S.N. Bose National Centre for Basic Sciences in Kolkata, India for studies leading towards a PhD degree in the physical sciences for four years with the possibility of a one-year extension.
Eligibility: Candidates for these fellowships must meet the following criteria: 1. be a maximum age of 35 years on 31 December of the application year. 2. be nationals of a developing country (other than India). 3. must not hold any visa for temporary or permanent residency in India or any developed country. 4. hold a Masters Degree in physics, mathematics or chemistry. S/he must have completed at least a total 5 years of undergraduate and postgraduate studies in a recognized university or institute. 5. be accepted by a department of the S.N. Bose National Centre. Prospective applicants are advised to visit the S.N. Bose National Centre's website www.bose.res.in and seek to find a potential supervisor under whom they would like to pursue their research and contact them. However, requests for acceptance must be directed to the Dean (Academic Programme), S.N. Bose National Centre for Sciences by e-mail (deanap@bose.res.in) or fax (+91) 33 2335 3477. In contacting the Dean (Academic Programme), applicants must accompany their request for an Acceptance Letter with copy of their CV, a research proposal outline and two reference letters. See sample preliminary acceptance letter that can be downloaded below or included in the online application form. 6. provide evidence of proficiency in English, if medium of education was not English. 7. provide evidence that s/he will return to her/his home country on completion of the fellowship. 8. not take up other assignments during the period of her/his fellowship. 9. be financially responsible for any accompanying family members.
Level of Study: Postgraduate
Type: Fellowship
Length of Study: 5 years
Frequency: Annual
Study Establishment: S.N. Bose National Centre for Basic Sciences
Country of Study: Italy
Application Procedure: Scholarship website: onlineforms.twas.org/apply/219
Closing Date: 31 May
Additional Information: twas.org/opportunity/twas-sn-bose-postgraduate-fellowship-programme#:~:text=TWAS%2DSN%20Bose%20Postgraduate%20Fellowships,of%20a%20one%2Dyear%20extension.

For further information contact:

Tel: (39) 40 2240687
Email: fellowships@twas.org

Thomson Foundation

Thomson Foundation, 6 Greenland Place, London NW1 0AP, United Kingdom.

Email: enquiries@thomsonfoundation.org
Website: www.thomsonfoundation.org/

The Thomson Foundation provides practical, intensive training both in the United Kingdom and abroad, along with a wide range of consultancies to journalists, managers, technicians and production staff in television, radio and the press.

Thomson Foundation Scholarship

Purpose: To enable recipients to attend Thomson Foundation training courses in Britain.
Eligibility: Open to professional journalists and broadcasters with at least 3 years of full-time experience.
Level of Study: Professional development
Type: Scholarship
Value: Varies
Length of Study: Varies, usually a 12-week Summer course or a shorter 4-week course.
Study Establishment: The Thomson Foundation
Country of Study: United Kingdom
Application Procedure: Applicants must complete an application form, available from the Foundation, for the courses they wish to apply for
No. of awards offered: 20
Closing Date: 15 April
Funding: Government, Private
Contributor: The British Foreign Office Chevening Scholarship Scheme.
No. of awards given last year: 6
No. of applicants last year: 20
Additional Information: Annual 3-month courses in television, radio and press journalism run from June to September

Webpage not open www.twas.org/opportunity/twas-csir-postdoctoral-fellowship-programme

For further information contact:

Email: enquiries@thomsonfoundation.org

Thurgood Marshall College Fund (TMCF)

901 F Street NW, Suite 700, Washington, DC 20004, United States of America.

Tel: (1) 202 507 4851
Email: info@tmcfund.org
Website: www.tmcf.org/

The Thurgood Marshall College Fund (TMCF) was established in 1987 to carry on Justice Marshall's legacy of equal access to higher education by supporting exceptional merit scholars attending America's public historically Black colleges and universities. More than 5,000 Thurgood Marshall Scholars have graduated and are making valuable contributions to science, technology, government, human service, business, education and various communities

TMCF All Around Scholarship

Purpose: The Thurgood Marshall College Fund (TMCF) is proud to offer financial assistance to outstanding students attending one of TMCF's member-schools that include 47 publicly-supported Historically Black Colleges and Universities (HBCUs) and Predominantly Black Institutions (PBIs).
Eligibility: 1. Be enrolled full-time as a freshmen, sophomore, junior or senior at a TMCF member-school during the 2022-2023 academic school year. a. Preference will be given to students who attend the below institutions: 1. Albany State 2. Fort Valley 3. Savannah State 2. Current cumulative grade point average of 3.0 or higher. 3. Able to demonstrate a financial need. 4. Submitted the FAFSA to your selected university/college. 5. Be a U.S. Citizen or legal permanent resident with a valid permanent resident card or passport stamped I-551.
Type: Scholarship
Value: The award is US$10,000 for two (2) students.
Application Procedure: All applicants must: Create and provide the link to a two-minute video responding to this prompt: How will your education benefit you, your family, and the community?
Closing Date: 31 August
No. of applicants last year: 2
Additional Information: Website: www.tmcf.org/students-alumni/scholarship/tmcf-all-around-scholarship/

Center for Advancing Opportunity Doctorial Fellowship

Subjects: Education, criminal justice, and entrepreneurship
Purpose: CAO supports faculty and students at Historically Black Colleges and Universities (HBCUs) and other post-secondary institutions to develop research-based solutions to the most challenging issues in education, criminal justice, and entrepreneurship. Our constituency is people living in fragile communities and they are members of all races, ethnicities, and religions.
Eligibility: 1. Be a current doctoral student at an accredited college or university 2. Must have received a four-year undergraduate degree from an HBCU 3. Current cumulative grade point average of 3.0 or higher 4. Able to demonstrate leadership abilities 5. Able to demonstrate a financial need 6. Be a U.S. Citizen or legal permanent resident with a valid permanent resident card or passport stamped I-551
Type: Fellowship
Value: Scholars will be selected to receive a scholarship up to US$15,000 for the academic school year (US$7,500 per semester which can only be applied to verifiable costs associated with average tuition and usual fees).
Study Establishment: A Historically Black College and University (HBCU).
Country of Study: United States of America
Application Procedure: All applicants must: 1. Provide a copy of the FAFSA Student Aid Report. 2. Provide the transcript (official or unofficial) for your most recently completed academic term-this should include your end of Fall 2023 grades and cumulative GPA. 3. Upload two letters of recommendation from: a. Current doctoral advisor b. A former professor, college administrator, community leader, or another person supporting the academic ability, character, reputation or professional aptitude of the applicant. 4. Answer each of the following (Maximum of 1500 words): a. Tell us about yourself and why you are interested in becoming a CAO Scholar. b. Why does education reform, criminal justice reform, and entrepreneurship matter to your community? Describe something you have done in the past year that made a difference in your community under the purview of

criminal justice reform, education reform, or entrepreneurship. c. What solution would you propose to improve or resolve a current issue that relates to education, the economy, or criminal justice? How will your solution help remove barriers to opportunities for people living in fragile communities? (Use evidence and data from CAO's State of Opportunity in America report to support your solutions).
No. of awards offered: Up to five
Additional Information: Website: www.tmcf.org/students-alumni/scholarship/center-for-advancing-opportunity-doctoral-fellowship/

CVS Health Pharmacy Scholarship

Purpose: To offer financial assistance to outstanding students attending one of the three pre-selected publicly-supported Historically Black College and University (HBCU) and Predominantly Black Institution (PBI) Pharmacy Schools within the TMCF 47 member-school network.
Eligibility: 1. Enrolled as a full-time graduate or doctoral student in Spring and Fall at the following of TMCF's 47 member-schools: a. Florida A & M University – Pharmacy School b. University of Maryland Eastern Shore – Pharmacy School c. Texas Southern University – Pharmacy School 2. Open to Master of Science in Pharmaceutical Science, Doctor of Philosophy (PhD) in Pharmaceutical Sciences, or Doctor of Pharmacy majors 3. Current grade point average of 3.0 or higher 4. Demonstrate outstanding financial need 5. Demonstrate leadership ability through a variety of measures 6. Be a U.S. Citizen or legal permanent resident with a valid permanent resident card
Type: Scholarship
Value: One-year scholarship up to US$5,000 which will be used to cover the costs of tuition and fees, on-campus room and board, and required textbooks purchased from member schools.
Study Establishment: Florida A & M University, Pharmacy School; University of Maryland Eastern Shore, Pharmacy School; and Texas Southern University, Pharmacy School.
Country of Study: United States of America
Application Procedure: Applicants must submit the following documents for consideration: 1. Most recent transcript (unofficial or official copy) 2. Recommendation letter from current school professor or faculty member (must be completed online by the recommender) 3. Essay: a. Please answer the following (maximum 1,000 words): CVS Health is focused on being the leading healthcare innovation company whose purpose is to help people on a path to better health. How would your academic, community, and professional achievements help you achieve CVS Health's purpose? b. Video Interview Questions (Applicants: Be prepared to upload a YouTube video interview responding to these questions): CVS Health's values are innovation, collaboration, caring, integrity and accountability. Tell us about how you incorporate those values into your work with patients? Tell us about a time when you delivered an outstanding customer service experience, whether at work, school or in another setting.
Additional Information: website: www.tmcf.org/students-alumni/scholarship/tmcf-cvs-health-pharmacy-scholarship/

Thurgood Marshall College Fund Scholarships

Purpose: The Thurgood Marshall College Fund (TMCF) is proud to offer financial assistance to outstanding students attending one of the publicly-supported Historically Black Colleges and Universities (HBCUs) and Predominantly Black Institutions (PBIs) within the TMCF 47 member-school network.
Eligibility: 1. Be enrolled full-time as a freshman, sophomore, junior or senior at a TMCF member-school during the current academic school year. 2. Current cumulative grade point average of 3.0 or higher. 3. Able to demonstrate leadership abilities. 4. Able to demonstrate a financial need. 5. Be a U.S. Citizen or legal permanent resident with a valid permanent resident card or passport stamped I-551.
Type: Scholarship
Value: Varies
Frequency: Annual
Country of Study: Any country
Application Procedure: All Applicants Must Answer the following statement. (Video Question) How will your education benefit you, your family, and the community? to start the scholarship application: www.grantinterface.com/Home/Logon?urlkey=tmcf
Closing Date: 28 February
Additional Information: Refer to the website for details: https://www.tmcf.org/students-alumni/scholarship/tmcf-jcdrp-family-foundation-scholarship/

For further information contact:

AIPLEF Scholarship, 80 Maiden Lane, Suite 2204, New York, NY 1138, United States of America.

Email: jessica.barnes@tmcfund.org

WGRG Foundation Terri Grier Memorial Scholarship

Subjects: Public policy, public administration, political science, community engagement or other advocacy disciplines.
Purpose: To offer financial aid towards books, tuition and/or other college expenses.

T

Eligibility: 1. be a United States resident; 2. be a member of an ethnic minority group: 1. African-American (Black) 2. Asian and Pacific Islanders 3. Hispanic/Latin (Black, White or Asian) 4. Indians (Western and Eastern) 3. Be a high school senior and/or enrolled in an accredited college or university in the year of the award; 4. demonstrate a 3.0 or higher GPA 5. demonstrate leadership skills through participation in community/public service, issue advocacy, research, extracurricular, and/or other activities; 6. demonstrate the courage of conviction, persistence, and determination in the pursuit of his or her goals; and 7. demonstrate a commitment to a career in government or the nonprofit and advocacy sectors
Type: Scholarship
Value: At least US$5,000.00 towards your books, tuition and/or other college expenses.
Country of Study: United States of America
Application Procedure: 1. Complete the online application form. 2. Select one individual to complete a reference survey to be submitted by either an educator/college professor, administrator, counselor, employer, or individual with significant knowledge of the applicant's experience and public service engagement 3. An official and recent academic transcript with cumulative grade point average and a class standing/rank.* 4. Personal Essay In your essay, please answer the question directly in the application. 5. If you have any questions regarding the application, please contact Sean Burns at sean.burns@tmcf.org 6. The deadline to submit the application and receipt of supporting materials is Friday, May 10, 2019. Applications submitted and supporting materials postmarked after this date will not be considered.
Closing Date: 10 May
Additional Information: Website: www.tmcf.org/students-alumni/scholarship/wgrg-foundation-terri-grier-memorial-scholarship/

Toxicology Education Foundation (TEF)

4303 Kirby Ave, Cincinnati, OH 45223, United States of America.

Email: info@toxedfoundation.org
Website: www.toxedfoundation.org

The mission of TFE is to encourage, support and promote charitable and educational activities that increase the public understanding of toxicology.

Alleghery-ENCRC Student Research Award

Purpose: To support a student's thesis, dissertation and summer research project in toxicology and to encourage them to formulate and conduct meaningful research
Eligibility: Open to students who are members in good standing of AE-SOT. The student's advisor must also be a member in good standing and submit a letter concerning availability
Level of Study: Graduate
Type: Award
Value: Up to US$1,000
Frequency: Annual
Country of Study: United States of America
Application Procedure: Applicants must send four copies of completed application form along with a project description and budget.
Closing Date: 30 May
Additional Information: Website: www.postgraduatefunding.com/award-2368

For further information contact:

626 Admiral Drive, Ste. C, PMB 221, Annapolis, MD 21401, United States of America.

Tel: (1) 443 321 4654
Fax: (1) 443 321 8702
Email: tefhq@toxedfoundation.org
Website: www.toxedfoundation.org/

Colgate-Palmolive Grants for Alternative Research

Purpose: The Colgate-Palmolive Grant for Alternative Research will identify and support efforts that promote, develop, refine, or validate scientifically acceptable animal alternative methods to facilitate the safety assessment of new chemicals and formulations. Scientists at any stage of career progression may submit a proposal. High priority will be given to projects that use in vitro or non-animal models in one of the following research areas: (1) reproductive and developmental toxicology; (2) neurotoxicology; (3) systemic toxicology; (4) sensitization; or (5) acute toxicity.
Eligibility: To determine if you are eligible to submit an application for a Colgate-Palmolive Supported Award, you should be able to answer yes to the following statements. In my proposed research: 1. I will not use any animals in my research. 2. I will not use animal sacrifice to source cells for my research. 3. I will not use any cells derived from a human embryo. If you agree with all three of the statements above and meet the outlined criteria, you are eligible to submit an application. Please download the application materials and return the completed forms by the October 9 SOT Awards deadline.

Level of Study: Research
Type: Research grant
Value: Maximum cash award of US$40,000
Frequency: Annual
Country of Study: United States of America
Application Procedure: Apply by downloading application files, completing, and uploading to the SOT Awards System: www.toxicology.org/application/af/awardDocuments/CP%20Grant%20for%20Alternative%20Research%20Application.doc
Closing Date: 9 October
Funding: Private
Contributor: Colgate-Palmolive
No. of awards given last year: 5
Additional Information: www.toxicology.org/awards/sot/awards.aspx?AwardID=79

For further information contact:

Colgate-Palmolive Grants for Alternative Research, Society of Toxicology, 11190 Sunrise Valley Dr, Suite 300, Reston, VA 20191, United States of America.

Email: giuliana@toxicology.org

Food Safety SS Burdock Group Travel Award

Purpose: To cover travel expenses for a student to attend the Annual Meeting
Eligibility: Open to full-time graduate students with research interests in toxicology. Students in their early graduate training, who have not attended any SOT Annual Meeting are encouraged to apply
Level of Study: Graduate
Value: Up to US$1000 per student
Frequency: Annual
Country of Study: United States of America
Application Procedure: Applicants must send a letter of request indicating that he/she is enroled in good standing in a doctoral training programme. The applicant must also state how the research and training relate to food safety
Closing Date: 15 January

For further information contact:

Email: tberdum@burdockgroup.com

Regulation and Safety SS Travel Award

Purpose: To help defray the costs of travel to the SOT meeting
Eligibility: Open to students submitting a poster or making a presentation at the SOT meeting
Type: Travel award
Value: US$1,500 each
Frequency: Annual
Country of Study: United States of America
Application Procedure: Applicants must fill an application form and an abstract of work preserved
Closing Date: 15 December

For further information contact:

Email: jtmacgror@earthlink.net

Robert L. Dixon International Travel Award

Purpose: To financially assist students studying in the area of reproductive toxicology.
Eligibility: Open to applicants enroled full-time in a PhD programme studying reproductive toxicology and are student members of SOT.
Level of Study: Doctorate, Graduate
Type: Award
Value: Includes a stipend of US$2,000 for travel costs to enable students to attend the International Congress of Toxicology meeting.
Frequency: Every 3 years
Country of Study: United States of America and abroad
Application Procedure: Applicants must submit a completed application form, reference letter, graduate transcripts and lists of complete citations of the original work.
Closing Date: 9 October
Contributor: Toxicology Education Foundation
Additional Information: www.toxedfoundation.org/travel-awards/

For further information contact:

Email: crzymama17@gmail.com

Transport Research Laboratory

Crowthorne House, Nine Mile Ride, Wokingham, Berkshire RG40 3GA, United Kingdom.

Website: trl.co.uk/

TRL is a global centre for innovation in surface transport and mobility. TRL is a wholly owned subsidiary of the Transport Research Foundation (TRF), a non-profit distributing company limited by guarantee, and established for the impartial furtherance of transport and related research, consultancy, and expert advice. We are a world leader in creating the future of transport and mobility, using evidence-based solutions and innovative thinking.

A Master of Science Degree Scholarship

Purpose: To financially support postgraduate study
Eligibility: Open to part-time self-financing students only. Applicants must have applied for a place for graduate study at UCL
Level of Study: Postgraduate
Type: Scholarship
Value: United Kingdom/European Union tuition fees
Length of Study: Full time 1 year, Part time 2-3 years
Frequency: Annual
Study Establishment: University College London
Country of Study: United Kingdom
Application Procedure: Applicants should contact the department. If the applicants have not applied to UCL they complete a graduate application form and enclose it with the scholarship application

For further information contact:

Tel: (44) 20 7288 3548
Fax: (44) 20 7288 3322
Email: p.taylor@chime.ucl.ac.uk

Tropical Agricultural Research and Higher Education Center (CATIE)

Cartago, Turrialba 30501, Costa Rica.

Tel: (506) 2558 2000
Email: comunica@catie.ac.cr
Website: www.catie.ac.cr
Contact: Dean of the Graduate School

The Tropical Agricultural Research and Higher Education Center (CATIE) is an international, non-profit, regional, scientific and educational institution. Its main purpose is research and education in agricultural sciences, natural resources and related subjects in the American tropics, with emphasis on Central America and the Caribbean.

Scholarship Opportunities Linked to CATIE

Purpose: To develop specialized intellectual capital in clean technology, tropical agriculture, natural resources management and human resources in the American tropics
Eligibility: Priority is given to citizens of Belize, Guatemala, El Salvador, Honduras, Nicaragua, Panama, Costa Rica, Mexico, Venezuela, Colombia, the Dominican Republic, Bolivia and Paraguay
Level of Study: Doctorate, Postgraduate
Type: Scholarship
Value: Tuition and fees
Length of Study: 2 years for a Master
Frequency: Annual
Application Procedure: Applicants must undertake an admission process that constitutes 75% for curricular evaluation and 25% for a domiciliary examination. Please refer to the CATIE website for full instructions
No. of awards offered: 350
Funding: Foundation, Government, International office, Private
Contributor: ASDI, OAS, CATIE, DAAD, CONACYT (Mexico), Ford Foundation, Kellogg Foundation, Joint/ Japan World Bank. USAID provided the original donation for the endowment financing the Scholarship-Loan Program, SENACYT and Belgium Cooperation
No. of awards given last year: 32 in the Scholarship-Loan Program. Over 25 students received funding from alternative sources
No. of applicants last year: 350
Additional Information: Website: www.postgraduatefunding.com/award-1688

For further information contact:

Email: posgrado@catie.ac.cr
Website: www.catie.ac.cr/

Trust Company

Level 15, 20 Bond Street, GPO Box 4270, New South Wales, Sydney, NSW 2001, Australia.
A trust company is a legal entity that acts as a fiduciary, agent, or trustee on behalf of a person or business for a trust. A trust company is typically tasked with the administration, management, and the eventual transfer of assets to beneficiaries.

Miles Franklin Literary Award

Purpose: To reward the novel of the year that is of the highest literary merit and presents Australian life in any of its phases
Eligibility: Refer to the application form. The novel must have been first published in any country in the year preceding the award. Biographies, collections of short stories, children's books and poetry are not eligible. All works must be in English
Level of Study: Unrestricted
Type: Award
Value: AU$60,000
Frequency: Annual

Country of Study: Any country
Application Procedure: Applicants must complete an application form and send six copies of their novel
Funding: Trusts
Contributor: The estate of the late Miss SMS Miles Franklin
No. of awards given last year: 1
Additional Information: If there is no novel worthy of the prize, the award may be given to the author of a play. Please refer to the website for further details: www.milesfranklin.com.au/

For further information contact:

Email: trustawards@thetrustcompany.com.au

TU Delft

Postbus 5, NL-2600 AA Delft, Netherlands.

Tel: (31) 15 27 89111
Email: info@tudelft.nl
Website: www.tudelft.nl/en/

Delft University of Technology is a public legal entity in accordance with the Higher Education and Research Act. The main tasks include providing scientific education, conducting scientific research, transferring knowledge to society and promoting social responsibility.

Bert Enserink Scholarship EPA

Purpose: The Bert Enserink scholarship has been established with the aim of stimulating excellent international MSc students to study the Master EPA, and financially supporting them.
Eligibility: Excellent international applicants admitted to the two-year MSc programme Engineering and Policy Analysis (EPA). With a cumulative grade point average (GPA) of 80 percent or higher of the scale maximum in the bachelor's degree from an internationally renowned university outside The Netherlands.
Level of Study: Postgraduate (MSc)
Type: Scholarship
Value: covering the tuition fee and living expenses
Length of Study: 2 years
Application Procedure: See website: www.tudelft.nl/en/education/practical-matters/scholarships#c1015453
Closing Date: 1 February
Additional Information: PLEASE NOTE All documents required for the scholarship must be submitted together with the MSc Application. After submission no additional documents can be uploaded. Website: www.tudelft.nl/en/education/practical-matters/scholarships#c1015453

Holland Scholarship

Purpose: The Holland Scholarship is financed by the Dutch Ministry of Education, Culture and Science and Dutch research universities and universities of applied sciences. Part of the scholarships are meant for international students from outside the European Economic Area (EEA) who wish to study in Holland. The EEA consists of the EU countries and Iceland, Liechtenstein and Norway.
Eligibility: Excellent applicants from outside the European Economic Area (EEA) who have been (conditionally) admitted to one of the 2-year Regular TU Delft's MSc programmes with a bachelor's degree from an internationally renowned university outside The Netherlands
Level of Study: Postgraduate (MSc)
Type: Scholarship
Value: € 5.000 in the first academic year for Non EEA students, as contribution to living expenses for a TU Delft MSc programme based on the statutory fee or institutional rate, according to the registered nationality.
Application Procedure: Application Form: www.tudelft.nl/en/education/admission-and-application/msc-international-diploma/2-application-procedure/. See website for more details
Closing Date: 1 February
Additional Information: Note: A candidate can be awarded multiple Holland Scholarships, based on merit, to a maximum of 3 (€15.000). Website: www.tudelft.nl/en/education/practical-matters/scholarships/holland-scholarship

Justus & Louise van Effen Excellence Scholarships

Purpose: The Foundation Justus & Louise van Effen was established with the aim of stimulating excellent international MSc students and financially supporting them in their wish to study at TU Delft
Eligibility: Excellent international applicants (conditionally) admitted to one of the 2-year Regular TU Delft's MSc programmes. With a cumulative grade point average (GPA) of 80% or higher of the scale maximum in the bachelor's degree from an internationally renowned university outside The Netherlands
Level of Study: Graduate
Type: Scholarship

Value: €30.000 per year for Non-EU students and €11.500 per year for EU/EFTA students
Frequency: Annual
Country of Study: Any country
Application Procedure: Apply it online. Check with the below link for further information. www.tudelft.nl/en/education/admission-and-application/msc-international-diploma/1-admission-requirements/
No. of awards offered: 2
Closing Date: 1 December
Funding: Private
Additional Information: Membership to the Scholarship club giving access to personal development, workshops, seminars, etc www.tudelft.nl/en/education/practical-matters/scholarships/justus-louise-van-effen-excellence-scholarships/

For further information contact:

NL-2600 AA Delft, Netherlands.

Email: info@tudelft.nl

Turkiye Scholarships Burslari

Oguzlar Mah. Mevlana Boulevard No: 145, Balgat, TR-06520 ANKARA, Turkey.

Tel: (90) 850 455 0 982
Email: info@turkiyeburslari.gov.tr
Website: www.turkiyeburslari.gov.tr/

Through international students studying in Turkey, Turkey's aim is to raise generations that will produce solutions to problems of their countries as well as our world, have equality of opportunity and a supra-national perspective. Turkiye Scholarships is a scholarship program which not only provides financial support but also ensures university placement for students in their intended program of application. With this feature, it differs from other scholarship programs in the world. Apart from university education, it is aimed to provide students with the benefits of social, cultural and academic extra- curricular programs and activities while they are in Turkey.

Turkey Government Scholarships

Purpose: Türkiye Scholarships has designed different and specific scholarship programs for each education level. It offers many qualified scholarship opportunities ranging from long-term bachelor's, master's as well as PhD scholarships to research and merit-based scholarships, art scholarships to joint scholarship programs created with international reputable institutions.
Eligibility: Eligible Groups: 1. Citizens of all countries 2. Graduates or those who will graduate at the end of the current academic year 3. Researchers and academics
Level of Study: Masters Degree, Postgraduate, Undergraduate
Type: Scholarship
Value: See website
Frequency: Annual
Country of Study: Any country
Application Procedure: 5 Steps to Applying: www.turkiyeburslari.gov.tr/applysteps
Funding: Private
Additional Information: Website: www.turkiyeburslari.gov.tr/whyturkiyescholarships

For further information contact:

Email: intoffice@agu.edu.tr

U

UHasselt University

Hasselt University, Martelarenlaan 42, B-3500 Hasselt, Belgium.

Tel: (32) 11 268 111
Email: Info@uhasselt.be
Website: www.uhasselt.be/

Civic university, UHasselt, is more than its seven faculties, four research institutes, three research centres, 6,500 students and 1,400 researchers and staff. As civic university, we are strongly committed to the Region and the world. Better through education, research and technology transfer.

Master Mind Scholarships

Purpose: The Flemish Ministry of Education awards scholarships to outstanding students for Master programmes in Flanders and Brussels. The programme aims to promote Flanders and Brussels as a top study destination.
Eligibility: The applicant should have a high standard of academic performance: 1. a Grade Point Average of 3.5 out of 4.0: www.scholaro.com/gpa-calculator/. 2. a sufficient knowledge of the English language: a. an overall band score of min. 7.0 on the IELTS test. b. a min. total score of 94 on a TOEFL test. c. a C1 level on the Certificate in Advanced English (CAE). d. or similar results in another official English language test. e. online language tests of IELTS and TOEFL will also be accepted. 3. Only students who are currently not enrolled at a Flemish higher education institution are eligible (exception: international students who are enrolled in a preparatory programme in order to start a master's programme in September). 4. Students who enrol for only a preparatory programme, a bridging programme or a distance learning programme are not eligible. 5. All nationalities can apply, but the previous degree obtained should be from a higher education institution located outside Flanders. 6. Students can not combine this scholarship with another scholarship from the Flemish government or an Erasmus Mundus scholarship.
Level of Study: Masters Degree
Type: Scholarship
Value: €9,600 and a tuition fee waiver per academic year
Frequency: Annual
Country of Study: Belgium
Application Procedure: Step 1: Submit a completed application file (including all the mandatory documents) for the relevant Master programme at UHasselt (see application procedure) before the deadline of the specific master programme. Step 2: Complete this Master Mind application form by 15/03/2024 Please note that you need to upload the following documents in the application form: 2 recommendation letters from professors of your (previous) Home university, University or recent employer written in English. Please merge the 2 letters in 1 PDF document and upload the document here. Students applying for Master of Management or Master of Transportation Sciences also have to upload their admission letter from Hasselt University.
Closing Date: 15 March
Funding: Government
Additional Information: https://www.studyinflanders.be/scholarships/master-mind-scholarships

For further information contact:

Tel: (32) 11269082

Palgrave Macmillan (ed.), *The Grants Register 2024*,
https://doi.org/10.1057/978-1-349-96073-6

Union College

807 Union Street, Schenectady, NY 12308, United States of America.

Tel: (1) 518 388 6000
Website: www.union.edu/

Union College Board of Trustees Scholarship

Purpose: This scholarship is worth full tuition
Eligibility: 1. Must attend a college or university in the state of Nebraska. 2. Must be an incoming freshman. 3. Must enroll full-time. 4. Must have a grade point average of 3.9 or higher (or a GED score of 750 or higher). 5. Must have an ACT score of 32 or higher OR an SAT score of 1,500 or higher
Level of Study: Graduate
Type: Scholarship
Value: US$21,250
Length of Study: Varies. Addition of years is possible
Frequency: Annual
Country of Study: Any country
Application Procedure: 1. Admissions information is available on the Union College website by clicking on the 'Admissions Policy' link. Admissions applications are available in online and PDF formats. 2. In addition to a completed application, each student must submit an official high school transcript and ACT/SAT scores. 3. Students whose first language is not English must also submit TOEFL (Test of English as a Foreign Language) scores. 4. Admissions applications are available in online and PDF formats. In addition to a completed application, each student must submit an official high school transcript and ACT/SAT scores
Closing Date: 1 April
Funding: Private
Additional Information: www.unigo.com/scholarships/all/union-college-board-of-trustees-scholarship/1005990

For further information contact:

3800 S. 48th St., Lincoln, NE 68506-4386, United States of America.

Tel: (1) 402 486 2600
Email: enroll@ucollege.edu

United Nations Educational, Scientific and Cultural Organization (UNESCO)

7 place de Fontenoy, F-75352 Paris, France.

Tel: (33) 1 45 68 10 00 ext. 81507
Website: www.unesco.org/en
Contact: Ms F Abu-Shady, Director, Equipment & Fellowships Division

As early as 1951, a programme to promote and develop youth exchange for educational purposes has existed in UNESC-O. The Organization continued its action under the Fellowships Programme to respond to the needs of Member States in the field of human resources development and capacity building. This programme has up to date enabled more than 52,000 fellows from around the world to study in different countries contributing to intellectual solidarity, international cooperation and mutual understanding.

United Nations Educational, Scientific and Cultural Organization(UNESCO)/International Sustainable Energy DeISEDC Co-Sponsored Fellowships Programme

Purpose: To enhance the capacity-building and human resources development in the area of sustainable and renewable energy sources in developing countries and countries in transition
Eligibility: Holder of at least a BSc degree or BA in Economics; proficient in English language; not more than 35 years of age
Level of Study: Postgraduate
Value: Exempt of paying tuition fees for the entire duration, US$450 is intended to cover living expenses, one-time travel allowance amounting to US$100, cover the cost of the round-trip international travel
Length of Study: This is a four weeks fellowship programme
Country of Study: Any country
Application Procedure: All applications should be endorsed by the National Commission for UNESCO and must be duly completed in English or French
No. of awards offered: 20
Closing Date: 3 April
Contributor: UNESCO/ISEDC

For further information contact:

Email: info@oppurtunitydesk.org

United Nations University - Institute for the Advanced Study of Sustainability (UNU - IAS)

5-53-70 Jingumae, Shibuya-ku, Tokyo 150-8925, Japan.

Tel: (81) 3 5467 1212
Website: ias.unu.edu/

PhD in Sustainability Science

Purpose: The Japan Foundation for UNU (JFUNU) Scholarship is available for outstanding applicants from developing countries who can demonstrate a need for financial assistance and who are granted admissions to the PhD Programme in Sustainability Science at United Nations University Institute for the Advanced Study of Sustainability (UNU-IAS).
Eligibility: Applicants for the PhD in Sustainability Science are required to have met ALL of the following requirements by the application deadline in order to be considered 1. Strong interest in sustainability studies; 2. Demonstrated commitment to study and understand global issues; 3. A completed Master's degree in disciplines related to sustainability studies and a minimum of 2 years of practical field experience related to UNU-IAS research themes OR Two completed Master's degrees, at least one of which must be in disciplines related to sustainability studies; 4. A GPA of 3.5 or above on a 4.0 scale on at least one of the Master's degrees earned; and 5. English language proficiency; 6. Applicants must be from developing countries who can demonstrate a need for financial assistance; 7. Applicants who are currently living in Japan under a working visa are NOT eligible for the scholarship; 8. Applicants who want to pursue a second PhD degree at UNU-IAS are not eligible for the scholarship.
Level of Study: Postgraduate
Value: The scholarship provides a monthly allowance of ¥120,000 for living expenses for a maximum of 36 months. Travel costs to and from Japan, visa handling fees, and health/accident insurance costs must be covered by the student. The tuition fees are fully waived for the scholarship recipients
Country of Study: Japan
Application Procedure: It is important to visit the official website (link found below) to access the application form and for detailed information on how to apply for this scholarship. ias.unu.edu/en/admissions/degrees/phd-in-sustainability-science-2020.html#overview
Closing Date: 9 April
Additional Information: ias.unu.edu/en/admissions/degrees/phd-in-sustainability-science-2022.html#requirements

For further information contact:

53-70, Jingumae 5-chome, Shibuya-ku, Tokyo 150-8925, Japan.

Tel: (81) 3 5467 1212

United States Institute of Peace (USIP)

2301 Constitution Avenue, NW, Washington, DC 20037, United States of America.

Tel: (1) 202 457 1700
Email: grant_program@usip.org
Website: www.usip.org
Contact: Ms Cornelia Hoggart, Senior Programme Assistant

The United States Institute of Peace (USIP) is mandated by the Congress to promote education and training, research and public information programmes on means to promote international peace and resolve international conflicts without violence. The Institute meets this mandate through an array of programmes, including grants, fellowships, conferences and workshops, library services, publications and other educational activities.

Jennings Randolph Program for International Peace Dissertation Fellowship

Purpose: To support dissertations that explore the sources and nature of international conflict, and strategies to prevent or end conflict and to sustain peace
Eligibility: Open to applicants of all nationalities who are enroled in an accredited college or university in the United States of America. Applicants must have completed all requirements for the degree except the dissertation by the commencement of the award
Level of Study: Doctorate
Type: Fellowships
Value: Stipends of up to US$20,000 per academic year
Length of Study: 1 year
Frequency: Annual
Study Establishment: The student's home university or site of fieldwork
Country of Study: United States of America
Application Procedure: Application Applications must be submitted through the FLUXX online application system. On

the application form, please indicate the scholarship for which you would like to be considered the USIP Peace Scholar fellowship only; Minerva Research Initiative Peace and Security Fellowship only; or no preference. 1. Both fellowships have the same application form, deadline, award amount, and selection process; the only difference between the USIP and Minerva Fellowships is the source of funding. 2. Three letters of recommendation must be attached to your application in the FLUXX system. One letter must be from your dissertation advisor and two from current professors.
Closing Date: 15 October
Funding: Government
No. of awards given last year: 10
Additional Information: The programme does not support work involving partisan political and policy advocacy or policy making for any government or private organization www.usip.org/grants-fellowships/fellowships/jennings-randolph-peace-scholar-dissertation-fellowship-program

For further information contact:

Tel: (1) 202 429 3853
Email: jrprogram@usip.org

Jennings Randolph Program for International Peace Senior Fellowships

Purpose: To use the recipient's existing knowledge and skills towards a fruitful endeavour in the international peace and conflict management field, and to help bring the perspectives of this field into the Fellow's own career
Eligibility: Open to outstanding practitioners and scholars from a broad range of backgrounds. The competition is open to citizens of any country who have specific interest and experience in international peace and conflict management. Candidates would typically be senior academics, but applicants who hold at least a Bachelor's degree from a recognized university will also be considered
Type: Fellowship
Value: A stipend, an office with computer and voicemail and a part-time research assistant
Length of Study: Up to 10 months
Frequency: Annual
Study Establishment: USIP
Country of Study: United States of America
Application Procedure: Applicants must complete a web-based application form, available on request from the Institute or from the website
No. of awards offered: 136
Closing Date: January
No. of awards given last year: 10
No. of applicants last year: 136
Additional Information: www.usip.org/grants-fellowships/fellowships/jennings-randolph-senior-fellowship-program#:~:text=The%20U.S.%20Institute%20of%20Peace,foster%20rich%20communities%20of%20practice.

For further information contact:

Tel: (1) 202 429 3886
Email: jrprogram@usip.org

United States-India Educational Foundation (USIEF)

12 Hailey Road, New Delhi, Delhi 110001, India.

Tel: (91) 11 4209 0909/2332 8944
Email: info@usief.org.in
Website: www.usief.org.in/
Contact: Programme Officer

The activities of the United States Educational Foundation in India (USEFI) may be broadly categorized as the administration of the Fulbright Exchange Fellowships for Indian and United States of America scholars and professionals, and the provision of educational advising services to help Indian students wishing to pursue higher education in the United States. USEFI also works for the promotion of dialogue among fulbrighters and their communities as an outgrowth of educational exchange.

Fulbright Distinguished Awards in Teaching Program for International Teachers

Purpose: It is part of the overall Fulbright Program, named in honor of Senator J. William Fulbright, which promotes mutual understanding among people of the United States and other countries
Eligibility: The applicant should: 1. be a citizen of India and reside in India at the time of application. 2. live and teach in India. 3. hold at least a bachelor's degree. A teacher training degree is preferred. 4. be a full-time teacher teaching any subject at any level (primary, middle, secondary, or senior secondary). 5. primary and secondary level library media specialists, guidance counselors, curriculum specialists, special education coordinators, and administrators who spend at least fifty percent of their time teaching or working directly with students may also apply to the program. 6. Teacher trainers working with elementary, or secondary pre-service or in-service teachers are eligible to apply. 7. have completed

at least five years of full-time teaching experience at the program start. 8. demonstrate English language skills adequate to manage coursework, complete an inquiry project, and team-teach in U.S. schools. 9. demonstrate a commitment to continue teaching or working in their field after completion of the program. Candidates should be planning to continue working in elementary or secondary education for at least five years after the conclusion of the program. 10. plan to continue working in elementary or secondary education for at least five years after the conclusion of the program.
Type: Award
Value: J-1 visa support; A pre-departure orientation held in India; Round-trip airfare to and within the U.S.; A welcome and end of program workshop: Academic program fees; Housing and meals; Accident and sickness medical insurance coverage (does not cover pre-existing conditions); Transportation to local school (if necessary); A daily allowance for incidentals during the university academic program; A professional development allowance; A baggage allowance; A technology allowance; and The opportunity to apply for alumni small grants for alumni in good standing.
Frequency: Annual
Country of Study: United States of America
Application Procedure: Scholarship website: fulbright.irex.org/Account/Login?ReturnUrl=%2F
Closing Date: 30 March
Additional Information: www.usief.org.in/Distinguished-Fulbright-Awards-Teaching-Program.aspx

For further information contact:

Tel: (91) 9841122433
Email: usiefchennai@usief.org.in

Fulbright Indo-American Environmental Leadership Program

Purpose: To provide funding for Indian environment professionals to explore future links between American and Indian organisations with common agendas
Eligibility: Open to all Indian mid-level environment professionals with at least five years of professional experience in the respective field and a Master's or professional degree of at least four years duration. Applicants will preferably be under 50 years of age. Special attention will be given to applicants who can demonstrate involvement in co-operative efforts between academia, research institutions, government, industry and non governmental organisations to make practical contributions to environmental policies and programmes
Level of Study: Postdoctorate, Professional development
Type: Internship
Value: Round-trip travel from India to the United States of America, a monthly stipend, professional allowance, settling-in allowance plus health insurance. No allowance or travel is provided for dependants
Length of Study: 4 and 8 weeks
Frequency: Annual
Study Establishment: Selected Fellows will be placed at environmental public, private, non governmental organisations, academic institutions, research centres or environment related government agencies
Country of Study: United States of America
Application Procedure: Applicants must obtain an application form either in person from USEFI offices or by sending a stamped addressed envelope to the nearest local USEFI office. The envelope should be superscribed USEFI-IAELP. Application forms can also be downloaded from the website or requested via email specifying the relevant fellowship category. Although USEFI does not require applicants to have a letter of affiliation from a United States institution at the time of applying, it encourages all applicants to correspond, in advance, with potential host institutions
Closing Date: 15 July
Additional Information: usief.org.in/fellowships/2013-2014-Fulbright-Nehru-Environmental-Leadership-Program.aspx

For further information contact:

Email: lakshmi@fulbright-india.org

Fulbright-Kalam Climate Fellowships for Doctoral Research

Eligibility: In addition to the General Prerequisites: 1. Applicants registered for their Ph.D. should have conducted adequate research in the relevant field, especially in the identification of resources in India and the U.S. Applicant must be registered for a Ph.D. at an Indian institution on or before November 1, 2023. On the online application form, one of the recommendations should be from the Ph.D. supervisor that comments on the applicant's research, the need for the fellowship, and must indicate the Ph.D. registration date and topic. 2. This grant is intended for Ph.D. students to conduct research essential to their dissertations/thesis. Therefore, the expected Ph.D. thesis submission date should at least be three months after the Fulbright-Kalam grant end date. For example, if May 2025 is the grant end date, the applicant cannot submit his/her thesis before August 2025. Please indicate the Ph.D. registration date and the expected Ph.D. thesis submission date in the Applicant Annexure. The applicant can download the Applicant Annexure from the supplemental forms section of the online application. 3. If the applicant is

employed, s/he must follow the instructions carefully regarding employer's endorsement. If applicable, the applicant must obtain the endorsement from the appropriate administrative authority on the Employer's Endorsement Form. The employer must indicate that leave will be granted for the fellowship period. 4. The applicant must upload a copy of original published/presented paper or extracts from the Masters'/M.Phil. thesis in the online application form (not exceeding 20 pages).
Level of Study: Predoctorate
Type: Fellowship
Value: The fellowships provide J-1 visa support, a monthly stipend, Accident and Sickness Program for Exchanges per U.S. Government guidelines, round-trip economy class air travel, applicable allowances and modest affiliation fees.
Length of Study: 6 to 9 months
Country of Study: United States of America
Application Procedure: Scholarship website: apply.iie.org/apply/?sr=b29b205d-36bc-44e5-8e02-1d3e90c567a4
Closing Date: 17 July
Additional Information: www.usief.org.in/Fellowships/Fulbright-Kalam-Climate-Fellowship.aspx

For further information contact:

Email: dr-climate@usief.org.in

Fulbright-Kalam Climate Fellowships for Postdoctoral Research

Eligibility: In addition to the General Prerequisites: 1. Applicants must have a Ph.D. or D.M. degree within the past four years. S/he must have obtained a Ph.D. or D.M. degree between July 17, 2020 and July 16, 2024. The applicants are required to upload his/her Ph.D. or D.M. degree certificate/provisional Ph.D. or D.M. certificate on the online application. 2. Applicants must have a publication in reputed journals and demonstrate evidence of superior academic and professional achievement. S/he must upload a recent significant publication (copy of paper/article) on the online application (not exceeding 30 pages). 3. If applicant is employed, please follow the instructions carefully regarding employer's endorsement. If applicable, obtain the endorsement from the appropriate administrative authority on the Letter of Support from Home Institution. The employer must indicate that leave will be granted for the fellowship period. Candidates working under government-funded projects are also required to get endorsement from their affiliating institutions in India.
Level of Study: Postdoctorate
Type: Fellowship
Value: These fellowships provide J-1 visa support, a monthly stipend, Accident and Sickness Program for Exchanges per U.S. Government guidelines, round-trip economy class air travel between India and the U.S., a modest settling-in allowance, and a professional allowance.
Length of Study: 8 to 24 months
Country of Study: United States of America
Application Procedure: Scholarship website: apply.iie.org/apply/?sr=a1994ce9-7f75-44a0-8cb8-9dbbd79a40b0
Closing Date: 17 July
Additional Information: www.usief.org.in/Fellowships/Fulbright-Kalam-Postdoctoral-Research.aspx

For further information contact:

Email: postdoc@usief.org.in

Fulbright-Nehru Academic and Professional Excellence Fellowships

Purpose: The Fulbright-Nehru Academic and Professional Excellence Fellowships aim to provide Indian faculty, researchers, and professionals the opportunity to teach, conduct research, or carry out a combination of teaching and research at a U.S. institution.
Eligibility: In addition to the General Prerequisites: 1. faculty/researchers must have a Ph.D. degree with at least five years of relevant teaching/research/professional experience. 2. professionals outside academe must have a master's degree and at least five years of relevant experience. 3. the applicant should upload a recent significant publication (copy of paper/article) in the online application (not exceeding 30 pages). 4. if the applicant is employed, s/he must follow the instructions carefully regarding employer's endorsement. The employer must indicate that leave will be granted for the fellowship period. The applicant must obtain the endorsement from the appropriate administrative authority on the Letter of Support from Home Institution.
Level of Study: Research
Type: Fellowship
Value: The fellowships provide a J-1 visa support, a monthly stipend, Accident and Sickness Program for Exchanges per U.S. Government guidelines, round-trip economy class air travel, a modest settling-in allowance, and a professional allowance.
Length of Study: 4 to 9 months
Country of Study: United States of America
Application Procedure: Scholarship website: apply.iie.org/apply/?sr=a1994ce9-7f75-44a0-8cb8-9dbbd79a40b0
Closing Date: 17 July
Additional Information: www.usief.org.in/Fellowships/Fulbright-Nehru-Academic-Professional-Excellence-Fellowships.aspx

For further information contact:

Email: ape@usief.org.in

Fulbright-Nehru Doctoral Research Fellowships

Purpose: The Fulbright-Nehru Academic and Professional Excellence Fellowships aim to provide Indian faculty, researchers, and professionals the opportunity to teach, conduct research, or carry out a combination of teaching and research at a U.S. institution
Eligibility: In addition to the General Prerequisites: 1. the applicant should have done adequate research in the relevant field, especially in the identification of resources in India and the U.S. Applicant must be registered for Ph.D. at an Indian institution on or before November 1, 2023. On the online application form, one of the recommendation letters must be from the Ph.D. supervisor that comments on applicants' research, need for the fellowship, and must indicate the Ph.D. registration date and topic. 2. this grant is intended for Ph.D. students to conduct research essential to their dissertations/thesis. Therefore, the expected Ph.D. thesis submission date should at least be three months after the Fulbright-Nehru grant end date. For example, if May 2025 is the grant end date, the applicant cannot submit his/her thesis before August 2025. Please indicate the Ph.-D. registration date and the expected Ph.D. thesis submission date in the Applicant Annexure. 3. if the applicant is employed, s/he must follow the instructions carefully regarding employer's endorsement. If applicable, please obtain the endorsement from the appropriate administrative authority on the FNDR Employer's Endorsement Form. The employer must indicate that leave will be granted for the fellowship period. 4. the applicant must upload a copy of original published/presented paper or extracts from the Masters'/M.Phil. thesis on the online application form (not exceeding 20 pages).
Level of Study: Predoctorate
Type: Fellowship
Value: The fellowships provide J-1 visa support, a monthly stipend, Accident and Sickness Program for Exchanges per U.S. Government guidelines, round-trip economy class air travel, applicable allowances and modest affiliation fees.
Length of Study: 6 to 9 months
Frequency: Annual
Country of Study: United States of America
Application Procedure: Scholarship website: apply.iie.org/apply/?sr=b29b205d-36bc-44e5-8e02-1d3e90c567a4
Closing Date: 17 July
Additional Information: www.usief.org.in/Fellowships/Fulbright-Nehru-Doctoral-Research-Fellowships.aspx

For further information contact:

Email: dr@usief.org.in

Fulbright-Nehru Master's Fellowships

Purpose: The Fulbright-Nehru Master's Fellowships are designed for outstanding Indians to pursue a master's degree program at select United States of America colleges and universities in the areas of Arts and Culture Management including Heritage Conservation and Museum Studies; Environmental Science/Studies; Higher Education Administration; International Legal Studies.
Eligibility: In addition to the General Prerequisites, the applicant: 1. must have completed an equivalent of a U.S. bachelor's degree from a recognized Indian university with at least 55% marks. Applicants must either possess a four-year bachelor's degree or a completed master's degree; or a full-time postgraduate diploma from a recognized Indian institution, if the bachelor's degree is of less than four years' duration. 2. must have at least three years' full-time (paid) professional work experience relevant to the proposed field of study by the application deadline. 3. should demonstrate experience in leadership and community service. 4. must not have another degree from a U.S. university or be enrolled in a U.S. degree program. 5. if employed, should follow the instructions carefully regarding employer's endorsement. If applicable, obtain the endorsement from the appropriate administrative authority on the FNMasters Employer's Endorsement Form. The employer must indicate that leave will be granted for the fellowship period.
Level of Study: Postgraduate
Type: Fellowship
Value: The fellowship will provide J-1 visa support, round-trip economy class air travel from fellow's home city to the host institution in the U.S., funding for tuition and fees, living and related costs, and accident and sickness coverage per U.S. Government guidelines.
Length of Study: 1 to 2 years
Frequency: Annual
Country of Study: United States of America
Application Procedure: Scholarship website: apply.iie.org/apply/?sr=b29b205d-36bc-44e5-8e02-1d3e90c567a4
Closing Date: 17 May
Additional Information: www.usief.org.in/Fellowships/Fulbright-Nehru-Master-Fellowships.aspx

For further information contact:

Email: masters@usief.org.in

Fulbright-Nehru Postdoctoral Research Fellowships

Purpose: These fellowships are designed for Indian faculty and researchers who are in the early stages of their research careers in India.

Eligibility: In addition to the General Prerequisites: 1. the applicant must have a Ph.D. or a D.M. degree within the past four years. S/he must have obtained Ph.D. degree between July 17, 2020 and July 16, 2024. The applicant is required to upload his/her Ph.D. or D.M. degree certificate/provisional Ph.D. certificate on the online application. 2. the applicant must have a publication in a reputed journal and demonstrate evidence of superior academic and professional achievement. S/he must upload a recent significant publication (copy of paper/article) on the online application (not exceeding 30 pages). 3. if applicant is employed, please follow the instructions carefully regarding employer's endorsement. If applicable, obtain the endorsement from the appropriate administrative authority on the FNPostdoc Letter of Support from Home Institution. The employer must indicate that leave will be granted for the fellowship period. Candidates working under government-funded projects are also required to get endorsement from their affiliating institutions in India.
Level of Study: Doctorate, Postdoctorate, Postgraduate
Type: Fellowship
Value: These fellowships provide J-1 visa support, a monthly stipend, Accident and Sickness Program for Exchanges per U.S. Government guidelines, round-trip economy class air travel, a modest settling-in allowance, and a professional allowance.
Length of Study: 8 to 24 months
Frequency: Annual
Country of Study: United States of America
Application Procedure: Scholarship website: apply.iie.org/apply/?sr=a1994ce9-7f75-44a0-8cb8-9dbbd79a40b0
Closing Date: 17 July
Funding: Private
Additional Information: www.usief.org.in/Fellowships/Fulbright-Nehru-Postdoctoral-Research-Fellowship.aspx

For further information contact:

Email: postdoc@usief.org.in

United States-United Kingdom Fulbright Commission

3rd Floor Camelford House, 89 Albert Embankment, London SE1 7TP, United Kingdom.

Tel: (44) 20 7498 4010
Email: programmes@fulbright.co.uk
Website: www.fulbright.org.uk/
Contact: Mr Michael Scott-Kline, Director

The United States-United Kingdom Fulbright Commission has a programme of awards offered annually to citizens of the United Kingdom and United States of America.

The Fulbright-Edinburgh University Award

Purpose: To enable a United States citizen to pursue postgraduate study in the United Kingdom at the University of Bristol
Eligibility: Applicant must be a United States citizen (resident anywhere but the United Kingdom), and a graduating senior, holding a BS/BA degree, master's or doctoral degree candidate, young professional or artist
Level of Study: Doctorate, Graduate, Postgraduate
Type: Award/Grant
Value: £2,625 per month
Frequency: Annual
Country of Study: United Kingdom
Application Procedure: Please visit the website us.fulbrightonline.org/applynow.html
Closing Date: 18 October

For further information contact:

Tel: (44) 131 651 4221
Email: Robert.Lawrie@ed.ac.uk

Universities Canada

350 Albert St., suite 1710, Ottawa, ON K1R 1B1, Canada.

Website: www.univcan.ca/
Contact: Gabrielle Leblanc, Program Officer

Universities Canada manages government-funded international partnership programs and more than 130 scholarship programs on behalf of private sector companies.

ConocoPhillips Canada Centennial Scholarship Program

Purpose: To support young Canadian visionaries who have a drive to make a difference in the future. The scholarship programme encourages individuals with academic excellence and demonstrated leadership
Eligibility: Canadian citizens or permanent residents of Canada
Level of Study: Postgraduate
Type: Scholarship

Value: CA$2,500 to CA$10,000
Length of Study: 2 years
Frequency: Annual
Country of Study: Canada
Closing Date: 31 May

For further information contact:

Email: ucawards@ucalgary.ca

Fessenden-Trott Scholarship

Eligibility: 1. Candidates should be entering the second year of their first bachelor degree on a full-time basis in September. 2. Have Canadian citizenship or permanent residency by June 14th in the year of application. 3. Have completed the first year of their first bachelor degree program in a Canadian educational institution. 4. Have attained a high academic standing as defined by the nominating institution. 5. Be nominated by a Canadian educational institution where the first year of the first bachelor degree studies has been completed.
Type: Scholarship
Value: CA$9,000
Length of Study: 3 years
Country of Study: Canada
Closing Date: 1 April
Additional Information: www.univcan.ca/wp-content/uploads/2018/03/2018-fessenden-trott-guidelines.pdf

For further information contact:

Fessenden-Trott Scholarship, 1710-350 Albert Street, Ottawa, ON K1R 1B1, Canada.

Tel: (1) 613 563 1236
Email: awards@univcan.ca

L'Oréal Canada For Women in Science Research Excellence Fellowships

Purpose: The purpose of this fellowship program is to highlight the role of women in devising scientific solutions to problems confronting humankind in the 21st century. The program supports major research projects undertaken by Canadian women scientists at the postdoctoral level in Canada.
Eligibility: Applicants to the fellowship program must be: 1. female Canadian citizens or permanent residents by the application deadline. 2. planning to complete their doctoral degree by September 1, 2024, or have completed their degree within the last 5 years (i.e., applicants must have obtained their doctoral degree between September 1, 2019, and August 31, 2024. This window will be extended to the last six years if the applicant has taken a year off for parental or medical leave). 3. planning to start or currently involved in research at the postdoctoral level at a recognized Canadian institution/organization. 4. willing to participate in at least 2 events in support of women and girls in science (e.g., mentoring, classroom visits, media events, etc.) during their award tenure (September 1, 2024, to August 31, 2025). 5. available the week of November 20, 2024, to attend the "For Women in Science Award Ceremony" in Ottawa, Canada (travel expenses will be paid for by L'Oréal Canada). 6. willing to submit a brief report summarizing their research findings at the end of their award tenure.
Level of Study: Postdoctorate
Type: Fellowship
Value: CA$20,000
Length of Study: 1 year
Frequency: Annual
Country of Study: Canada
Application Procedure: Scholarship website: portal.scholarshippartners.ca/s_Login.jsp?&lang=1
No. of awards offered: 2
Closing Date: 18 April
Additional Information: www.univcan.ca/wp-content/uploads/2023/01/LOreal-Canada-2023-Application-guidelines.pdf

For further information contact:

1710-350 Albert Street, Ottawa, ON K1R 1B1, Canada.

Tel: (1) 844 567 1237
Email: loreal@univcan.ca

Multiple Sclerosis Society of Canada Scholarship Programs: John Helou Scholarship

Purpose: To encourage academic excellence and the pursuit of higher education among students who are directly affected by multiple sclerosis
Eligibility: Candidates must be female Canadian citizens or permanent residents
Level of Study: Postgraduate
Type: Fellowship
Value: CA$25,000 over four years
Length of Study: 4 years
Frequency: Annual
Country of Study: Canada
Application Procedure: Applicants must submit their own application electronically through the online platform www.fwis.fr
Closing Date: 31 March

For further information contact:

Email: lindsay.gulin@mssociety.ca

Universities Federation for Animal Welfare (UFAW)

The Old School, Brewhouse Hill, St Albans AL4 8AN, United Kingdom.

Tel: (44) 15 8283 1818
Email: ufaw@ufaw.org.uk
Website: www.ufaw.org.uk

The Universities Federation for Animal Welfare (UFAW), the international animal welfare science society, is a United Kingdom registered scientific and educational charity that brings together the animal welfare science community, educators, veterinarians and all concerned about animal welfare worldwide in order to achieve advances in the well-being of farm, companion, laboratory and captive wild animals, and for those animals with which we interact in the wild.

Universities Federation for Animal Welfare Student Scholarships

Purpose: To encourage students to develop their interests in animal welfare and their abilities for animal welfare research.
Eligibility: Applications are welcome from undergraduate or MSc students who are interested in carrying out a project in animal welfare and who are studying at universities or colleges at which there is a UFAW Link. Please note PhD students are not eligible to apply.
Level of Study: Postgraduate
Type: Scholarship
Value: Student Scholarships consist of £250 per week subsistence allowance for the Scholar and £100 per week project expenses.
Length of Study: 4 to 8 weeks
Frequency: Annual
Country of Study: United Kingdom
Country of Study: Any student in the UK or overseas where we have a UFAW University Link
Application Procedure: Scholarship website: ufaw.onlinesurveys.ac.uk/ufaw_awss2023
Closing Date: 28 February
Funding: Private
Additional Information: www.ufaw.org.uk/animal-welfare-student-scholarships/animal-welfare-student-scholarships

For further information contact:

Wendy Goodwin, UFAW, The Old School, Brewhouse Hill, Wheathampstead, Hertfordshire AL4 8AN, United Kingdom.

Tel: (44) 1582 831818
Email: grants@ufaw.org.uk

Universities New Zealand

Level 9, Pacific Radiology Building, 142 Lambton Quay, Wellington, PO Box 860, Wellington 6140, New Zealand.

Tel: (64) 4 381 8500
Email: contact@universitiesnz.ac.nz
Website: www.universitiesnz.ac.nz/

Universities New Zealand was established under the Education Act 1961 as the New Zealand Vice-Chancellors' Committee. Since 2010 we have operated as Universities New Zealand.

Auckland Council Research Scholarship in Urban Economics

Purpose: The purpose of this scholarship is to encourage and support postgraduate research into urban economics that has particular relevance to local government in New Zealand
Eligibility: 1. At the time of application, candidates must be enrolled or planning to enrol in a postgraduate programme at a New Zealand university (applicants may be enrolled as full-time students). 2. The postgraduate programme must be in the area of urban economics. Universities NZ and Auckland Council reserve the right to determine the eligibility of a particular area of study. 3. A thesis, dissertation, or research report must be a requirement of the postgraduate programme
Level of Study: Postgraduate
Type: Scholarship
Value: NZ$3,000
Length of Study: 1 year
Frequency: Annual
Country of Study: Any country
Application Procedure: Candidates must complete an application using the Universities NZ scholarships application website universitiesnz.communityforce.com/ Each year Auckland Council may grant one scholarship with an award of NZ$3,000. For candidates who are enrolled on a part-time basis, the value of the award will be NZ$1,500
No. of awards offered: 1

Closing Date: 1 February
Funding: Private
Additional Information: www.universitiesnz.ac.nz/sites/default/files/uni-nz/documents/scholarships/Auckland%20Council%20Economics%20Regulations.pdf

BayTrust Bruce Cronin Scholarship

Purpose: The scholarship is to support postgraduate study at masters or doctoral level at a New Zealand university.
Eligibility: Applicants must have links to the BayTrust geographical area. This area is shown on the BayTrust website www.baytrust.org.nz Applicants will be eligible if they were born in, or attended school in, or have whakapapa back to the area.
Level of Study: Postgraduate
Type: Scholarship
Value: NZ$5,000. each
Length of Study: 1 year
Frequency: Annual
Country of Study: New Zealand
No. of awards offered: 2
Closing Date: 1 February
Additional Information: www.universitiesnz.ac.nz/scholarships/baytrust-bruce-cronin-scholarship

Freyberg Scholarship

Purpose: Freyberg Scholarships are awarded to encourage graduate study into areas relevant to national security. Study should be undertaken at a recognised institution in New Zealand or an Asia-Pacific country, including Canada and the United States.
Eligibility: Applicants must be New Zealand citizens or permanent residents who meet the following academic requirements: they should normally have obtained at least second class honours, division A, or equivalent in their qualifying degree and have completed academic studies in political science, history, economics or some other discipline that may be considered an appropriate foundation for such study.
Level of Study: Postgraduate
Type: Scholarship
Value: NZ$50,000 per annum
Frequency: Annual
Country of Study: New Zealand
Country of Study: Any approved course
Application Procedure: Scholarship website: universitiesnz.communityforce.com/Login.aspx
No. of awards offered: Up to 3
Closing Date: 1 October
Additional Information: www.universitiesnz.ac.nz/scholarships/freyberg-scholarship

Gordon Watson Scholarship

Purpose: This scholarship is to enable New Zealanders to study international relationships or social and economic conditions at a university overseas. Candidates will be planning to study at Masters or PhD level.
Eligibility: Applicants must have graduated or be graduating with an Honours or Masters degree in arts, science, commerce, law or divinity from a New Zealand university, and be New Zealand citizens or permanent residents.
Level of Study: Doctorate, Masters Degree, Postgraduate
Type: Scholarship
Value: NZ$12,000 per year
Length of Study: 2 to 3 years
Frequency: Annual
Country of Study: New Zealand
Application Procedure: Scholarship website: universitiesnz.communityforce.com/Login.aspx
No. of awards offered: 1
Closing Date: 1 April
Funding: Private
Additional Information: www.universitiesnz.ac.nz/scholarships/gordon-watson-scholarship

Henry Kelsey Scholarship

Eligibility: Applicants will: 1. be New Zealand citizens or permanent residents. 2. have a Bachelors degree or equivalent, in a field appropriate to their nominated research degree at a New Zealand university.
Level of Study: Doctorate, Masters Degree
Type: Scholarship
Value: NZ$10,000 per annum
Length of Study: 2 to 3 years
Frequency: Annual
Country of Study: New Zealand
Application Procedure: Scholarship website: universitiesnz.communityforce.com/Login.aspx
No. of awards offered: 1
Closing Date: 1 October
Additional Information: www.universitiesnz.ac.nz/scholarships/henry-kelsey-scholarship

Kia Ora Foundation Patricia Pratt Scholarship

Purpose: The purpose of the Kia Ora Foundation Patricia Pratt Scholarship is to assist outstanding New Zealand musical performers who have completed the equivalent of an honours

degree in any field of musical performance in New Zealand to continue their musical development at a renowned international music school or conservatorium. The scholarship will be awarded for classical music performance including vocal or instrumental performance or conducting.
Eligibility: Applicants will be New Zealand citizens. Applicants may apply from outside New Zealand but must have resided in New Zealand for at least three of the last five years immediately preceding the year of selection. Applicants will have recently completed the requirements for an honours degree in musical performance at a New Zealand university (or an equivalent musical qualification).
Level of Study: Postgraduate
Type: Scholarship
Value: NZ$70,000 per annum
Length of Study: 2 years
Frequency: Annual
Country of Study: New Zealand
Application Procedure: Scholarship website: universitiesnz.communityforce.com/Login.aspx
Closing Date: 1 March
Additional Information: www.universitiesnz.ac.nz/scholarships/kia-ora-foundation-patricia-pratt-scholarship

Kiwi Music Scholarship

Purpose: This scholarship is to assist outstanding New Zealand musical performers or conductors to continue their musical development either in New Zealand or overseas.
Eligibility: Applicants will be New Zealand citizens who are normally resident in New Zealand. Applicants will have completed or are completing an honours or masters degree in musical performance (including vocal performance) or conducting at a New Zealand university, or an equivalent musical qualification.
Level of Study: Postgraduate
Type: Scholarship
Value: NZ$50,000 to NZ$60,000
Frequency: Annual
Country of Study: New Zealand
Application Procedure: Scholarship website: universitiesnz.communityforce.com/Login.aspx
Closing Date: 1 March
Additional Information: www.universitiesnz.ac.nz/scholarships/kiwi-music-scholarship

New Zealand Law Foundation Ethel Benjamin Scholarship (For Women)

Purpose: To support postgraduate research in law that will protect and promote the interests of the public in relation to legal matters in New Zealand.
Eligibility: A scholarship may be awarded to any woman scholar who is: 1. a New Zealand citizen or permanent resident. 2. the holder of a New Zealand university law degree (unless there are exceptional circumstances the award would normally be made to candidates who have gained the qualifying degree within the past five years). 3. accepted into a postgraduate course in law at either a New Zealand or an overseas university acceptable to the Selection Committee.
Level of Study: Postgraduate
Type: Scholarship
Value: Up to NZ$20,000 for study in New Zealand and up to NZ$30,000 for study overseas
Frequency: Annual
Country of Study: New Zealand
Application Procedure: Scholarship website: universitiesnz.communityforce.com/Login.aspx
No. of awards offered: 3
Closing Date: 1 March
Additional Information: www.universitiesnz.ac.nz/scholarships/new-zealand-law-foundation-ethel-benjamin-scholarship-women

Shirtcliffe Fellowship

Eligibility: Applicants must be: 1. New Zealand citizens. 2. ordinarily resident in New Zealand. 3. New Zealand university graduates. 4. planning to register or be currently registered as a doctoral candidate at a university in New Zealand or other Commonwealth country.
Level of Study: Doctorate, Predoctorate
Type: Scholarship
Value: NZ$5,000 per year
Length of Study: 3 years
Frequency: Annual
Country of Study: New Zealand
Application Procedure: Scholarship website: universitiesnz.communityforce.com/Login.aspx
No. of awards offered: 1
Closing Date: 1 April
Additional Information: www.universitiesnz.ac.nz/scholarships/shirtcliffe-fellowship

William Georgetti Scholarship

Eligibility: Applicants must 1. Have resided in New Zealand for a period of at least five years immediately preceding the year of selection (refer to the Regulations for further information). 2. Be of good moral character and repute. 3. Be of good health. 4. Hold a degree from a university in New Zealand or elsewhere or any other academic qualification of a university or other institution of learning (in New Zealand or elsewhere)

reasonably equivalent in the opinion of the Scholarship Board to a degree of a university in New Zealand.
Level of Study: Doctorate, Postdoctorate
Type: Scholarship
Value: Up to NZ$20,000 per year for Masters study and NZ$30,000 per year for doctoral study. NZ$45,000 per year for those students studying overseas.
Length of Study: 3 years
Frequency: Annual
Country of Study: New Zealand
Closing Date: 1 February
Additional Information: www.universitiesnz.ac.nz/scholarships/william-georgetti-scholarship

For further information contact:

Email: scholarshipscf@universitiesnz.ac.nz

University College London

Gower Street, London WC1E 6BT, United Kingdom.

Tel: (44) 20 7679 2000
Website: www.ucl.ac.uk

UCL was the first university to be established in United Kingdom after Oxford and Cambridge, providing a progressive alternative to those institutions social exclusivity, religious restrictions and academic constraints. UCL is the largest of over 50 colleges and institutes that make up the federal University of London.

Bartlett School of Planning Centenary Scholarship

Eligibility: The scholarships are available to students from the UK who have applied to study one of the nine eligible degree programmes concerned: 1. MSc Housing and City Planning. 2. MSc Infrastructure Planning, Appraisal and Delivery. 3. MSc International City Planning. 4. MSc Spatial Planning. 5. MSc Sustainable Urbanism. 6. MSc Transport and City Planning. 7. MSc Urban Regeneration. 8. MRes Inter-disciplinary Urban Design. 9. MPlan City Planning.
Level of Study: Postgraduate
Type: Scholarship
Value: £9,000
Length of Study: 1 year
Frequency: Annual
Study Establishment: University College London
Country of Study: United Kingdom
Application Procedure: Scholarship website: www.ucl.ac.uk/bartlett/planning/sites/bartlett_planning/files/scholarshipapplicationform24.doc
No. of awards offered: 5
Closing Date: 14 July
Funding: Individuals
Additional Information: www.ucl.ac.uk/bartlett/planning/funding-and-scholarships

For further information contact:

Email: a.n.patel@ucl.ac.uk

Brown Family Bursary

Eligibility: Candidates must fulfil all of the following criteria: 1. be ordinarily resident in the UK. 2. be in financial need (as determined by the UCL Student Funding Office). 3. AND have submitted an admission application for a full-time Master's degree at UCL in 2024/25 for one of the following programmes: a. MSc Environment and Sustainable Development. b. MSc Sustainable Resources: Economics, Policy and Transitions. c. MSc Climate Change. d. MPA Sustainable Infrastructures and Public Policy. e. MPA Energy, Technology and Public Policy. f. MSc Environmental Systems Engineering. g. MSc Global Management of Natural Resources. h. MSc Materials for Energy and Environment. i. MSc Biodiversity and Global Change. j. MSc Ecology and Data Science.
Level of Study: Postgraduate
Type: Bursary
Value: £15,000
Length of Study: 1 year
Frequency: Annual
Country of Study: United Kingdom
No. of awards offered: 1
Closing Date: 8 June
Additional Information: www.ucl.ac.uk/scholarships/brown-family-bursary

Child Health Research Appeal Trust Studentship

Purpose: To fund graduate students for MPhil/PhD research
Eligibility: Open to committed individuals wishing to do research in a clinical context, who expect to graduate with a United Kingdom first class or upper second class honours degree or equivalent from abroad
Level of Study: Doctorate, Postgraduate
Type: Studentship

Value: Tuition fees at the United Kingdom/European Union student rate, a stipend equivalent to MRC levels and £3,000 towards research costs
Length of Study: 3 years
Frequency: Annual
Study Establishment: UCL Institute of Child Health
Country of Study: United Kingdom
Application Procedure: Studentships are advertised on the department's vacancy website between November–January each year. Applicants should refer to www.ich.ucl.ac.uk/ich/humanresources/
Closing Date: January
Funding: Trusts
No. of awards given last year: Up to 4

For further information contact:

Email: chratapps@ich.ucl.ac.uk

Clara Collet Departmental Scholarships

Eligibility: 1. All PhD students who are registered on the Department's PhD programme and who have successfully completed the first year in the programme are eligible to apply for a Departmental Teaching Assistantship. 2. All eligible PhD students are considered for these positions.
Level of Study: Doctorate, Masters Degree
Type: Scholarship
Value: £18,062
Length of Study: 4 years
Frequency: Annual
Country of Study: United Kingdom
Application Procedure: After having read the application guidelines on the doctoral page, candidates should contact the PhD Manager polsci.admissions@ucl.ac.uk, to register their interest and for further information.
Closing Date: 30 April
Additional Information: www.ucl.ac.uk/political-science/study/post-graduate-research/funding-opportunities/clara-collet-departmental-scholarships

For further information contact:

Email: polsci.admissions@ucl.ac.uk

Common Wealth Shared Scholarship Scheme (CSSS)

Purpose: The aim of the Commonwealth Shared Scholarship Scheme (CSSS) is to assist students from developing Commonwealth countries who are of excellent academic calibre but for financial reasons would not otherwise be able to afford to study in the United Kingdom.
Eligibility: 1. Be a Commonwealth citizen, refugee, or British Protected Person; 2. Be permanently resident in an eligible Commonwealth country; 3. Be available to start your academic studies in the UK by the start of the UK academic year in September/October 2024; 4. By September 2024, hold a first degree of either first or upper second class (21) classification, or lower second class (22) classification plus a relevant postgraduate qualification (usually a Master's degree). If you are applying for a second UK Master's degree, you will need to provide justification as to why you wish to undertake this study; 5. Not have studied or worked for one (academic) year or more in a high-income country; 6. Be unable to afford to study in the UK without this scholarship;
Level of Study: Postgraduate
Type: Scholarship
Value: Tuition fees, living costs, flights to UK
Length of Study: 1 year
Frequency: Annual
Study Establishment: University College London
Country of Study: United Kingdom
Application Procedure: 1. You must separately apply for admission to UCL for one of the eligible programmes through the standard admissions procedure. 2. You must apply for the scholarship on the Commonwealth Scholarship Commission Electronic Application System (EAS) online following the procedures described on their website.
Closing Date: 13 December
Contributor: Department for International Development (DFID) and UCL
No. of awards given last year: 3
Additional Information: www.ucl.ac.uk/scholarships/commonwealth-shared-scholarship-scheme

Department of Communities and Local Government (formally Office of the Deputy Prime Minister)

Purpose: To financially support full-time study
Eligibility: Open to candidates who take up full time study only with residence restrictions, already holding or offer for the MSC spatial planning or MSC international planning, 21 or equivalent (except in exceptional circumstances)
Level of Study: Postgraduate
Type: Bursary
Value: Tuition fees at United Kingdom/European Union rate plus (For United Kingdom/European Union nationals only) along with a monthly stipend of £500
Length of Study: 1 year
Frequency: Annual
Study Establishment: University College London

Country of Study: United Kingdom
Application Procedure: Applications are available from www.esrc.ac.uk (ESRC) and should be sent to the department. Potentially eligible candidates will be contacted by the department
No. of awards offered: 16
Funding: Government
Contributor: Department of Communities and Local Government
No. of awards given last year: 7
No. of applicants last year: 16

For further information contact:

Tel: (44) 20 7679 7501
Email: j.hillmore@ucl.ac.uk

Digital Media Programme Bursary

Eligibility: Candidates must fulfil all of the following criteria 1. Be ordinarily resident in the UK and eligible to pay Home fee rate; 2. Hold an offer to study an MA Digital Media Critical Studies, MA Digital Media Education, or MA Digital Media Production in at UCL in 2023/24.
Level of Study: Postgraduate
Type: Bursary
Value: £5,000 (for one year)
Length of Study: 1 year
Frequency: Annual
Country of Study: United Kingdom
Closing Date: 9 June
Additional Information: www.ucl.ac.uk/scholarships/digital-media-programme-bursary

For further information contact:

Email: ma.dm.info@ucl.ac.uk

Graduate Research Scholarships

Eligibility: In order to APPLY, you must 1. have submitted an application to, or currently be registered on, a full- or part-time research degree programme at UCL by the scholarship deadline; 2. holding or expected to achieve at least an upper second-class Honours UK undergraduate degree or equivalent qualification.
Level of Study: Postgraduate
Type: Scholarship
Value: UK rate fees and maintenance stipend
Frequency: Annual
Country of Study: Any country
No. of awards offered: 1 year
Closing Date: 14 January
Additional Information: www.ucl.ac.uk/scholarships/graduate-research-scholarships

Graduate Research Scholarships for Cross-disciplinary Training (One-Year)

Eligibility: Eligible candidates must 1. be in receipt of an offer of admission to or currently registered at UCL on a full-time MPhil/PhD or EngD research programme*, and; 2. provide proof of three years of guaranteed funding for their normal MPhil/PhD or EngD programme. *Please note, students must be in the research phase of their degree and still paying fees. Students who have entered CRS are not eligible to apply.
Value: Full fees and maintenance stipend
Country of Study: United Kingdom
Closing Date: 28 January
Additional Information: www.ucl.ac.uk/scholarships/graduate-research-scholarships-cross-disciplinary-training-one-year

For further information contact:

Email: studentfundingadvice@ucl.ac.uk

GREAT Scholarship

Eligibility: 1. Candidates must be citizens of India, Mexico, Thailand, Ghana, Kenya, Indonesia, Nigeria or Vietnam. 2. Candidates must have made an application to study a full-time Master's degree at UCL in 2024/25, and hold an offer of a place at UCL by the scholarship closing date of 23rd May 2024. Please note distance learning and mod flex courses are not eligible.
Level of Study: Postgraduate
Type: Scholarship
Value: £10,000
Length of Study: 1 year
Frequency: Annual
Country of Study: United Kingdom
Application Procedure: Instructions for accessing the online scholarship application form: Login to Portico with your normal details. Click on the 'View' button for the 'Active Application' that you wish to apply for funding for. In the application screen, click on the 'Funding' in the menu at the top of the page. You are now on the funding page. To find out which funds you are eligible to apply for click 'Check and

apply' under 'Funds Available'. Click on the scholarship name of the scheme that you wish to apply for.
No. of awards offered: 4
Closing Date: 23 May
Additional Information: www.ucl.ac.uk/scholarships/great-scholarship

For further information contact:

Email: studentfunding@ucl.ac.uk

GREAT Scholarship for Justice and Law

Eligibility: 1. Candidates must be citizens of Indonesia. 2. Candidates must have submitted an application to study a full-time Master's degree in any LLM Law Programme, including LLM Specialist Law Degrees such as: Competition Law at UCL in 2024/25 and hold an offer by the scholarship closing date of 23rd May 2024. Please note distance learning and mod flex courses are not eligible.
Level of Study: Postgraduate
Type: Scholarship
Value: £10,000
Length of Study: 1 year
Frequency: Annual
Country of Study: United Kingdom
Application Procedure: Instructions for accessing the online scholarship application form: Login to Portico with your normal details. Click on the 'View' button for the 'Active Application' that you wish to apply for funding for. In the application screen, click on the 'Funding' in the menu at the top of the page. You are now on the funding page. To find out which funds you are eligible to apply for click 'Check and apply' under 'Funds Available'. Click on the scholarship name of the scheme that you wish to apply for.
No. of awards offered: 1
Closing Date: 23 May
Additional Information: www.ucl.ac.uk/scholarships/great-scholarship-justice-and-law

For further information contact:

Email: studentfunding@ucl.ac.uk

Institute of Education, University of London Centenary Masters Scholarships

Purpose: IOE is offering Centenary Masters Scholarships for students who plan to work either in their home country, or another, to improve the circumstances of disadvantaged, excluded or underachieving citizens.
Eligibility: In order to apply for the Centenary Master's Scholarships, candidates should: 1. Be domiciled in an eligible low or lower-middle income country according to the World Bank classification. 2. Have an official unconditional offer letter to study a full time Master's degree at IOE (letter issued by UCL Admissions). 3. Not have studied or lived in the UK before.
Level of Study: Postdoctorate
Type: Scholarship
Value: tuition fees and accommodation in a single room (shared bathroom) at International Students House
Frequency: Annual
Country of Study: Any country
Application Procedure: Scholarship website: https://www.ucl.ac.uk/ioe/about-ioe/global-reach/scholarships-and-funding
Closing Date: 2 May
Funding: Foundation
Additional Information: https://www.ucl.ac.uk/ioe/about-ioe/global-reach/scholarships-and-funding#IOE%20Centenary%20MA

For further information contact:

Email: IOEinternational@ucl.ac.uk

IOE Centenary Doctoral Scholarships

Eligibility: In order to apply for the Centenary Doctoral Scholarships, candidates should: 1. Be domiciled in an eligible low or lower-middle income country according to the World Bank classification. 2. Have received an official unconditional offer letter to study a full time PhD degree at IOE (letter issued by UCL Admissions).
Level of Study: Doctorate
Type: Scholarship
Value: tuition fees, accommodation in a single room (shared bathroom) at International Students House and an annual stipend of £7740 paid by monthly instalments.
Frequency: Annual
Country of Study: Any country
Application Procedure: Scholarship website: forms.office.com/pages/responsepage.aspx?id=_oivH5ipW0yTySEKEdmlwtT7sLiCUAJHj5KM_n5KyJ5UMVVUQVJWTVhWNEc0WEo3RUUwQU84U1Q0VC4u
Closing Date: 2 May
Additional Information: www.ucl.ac.uk/ioe/about-ioe/global-reach/scholarships-and-funding/scholarships-and-funding-faqs#IOE%20Centenary%20Doctoral%20Scholarships

Joseph Hume Scholarship

Purpose: To financially support LLM students or MPhil/PhD research
Eligibility: For all LLM or MPhil/PhD research students in the Department of Laws
Level of Study: Doctorate, Postgraduate, Research
Type: Scholarship
Value: £1,600
Frequency: Annual
Study Establishment: University College London
Country of Study: United Kingdom
Application Procedure: There is no application procedure. All eligible students will automatically be considered
Closing Date: 17 November
Additional Information: www.ucl.ac.uk/laws/study/mphilphd/mphilphd-fees-and-scholarships

For further information contact:

Email: phd-law@ucl.ac.uk

Keeling Scholarship

Purpose: To financially support MPhil/PhD research
Eligibility: United Kingdom, European Union and overseas students are eligible to apply
Level of Study: Doctorate, Postgraduate, Research
Type: Scholarship
Value: Up to £1,000
Length of Study: 3 years
Frequency: Annual
Study Establishment: University College London
Country of Study: United Kingdom
Application Procedure: No separate application is required. Applicants who are admitted to research programmes in philosophy will automatically be considered for the scholarship. Any queries should be directed to the department
Closing Date: 31 January
Additional Information: www.ucl.ac.uk/philosophy/keeling/scholarship

For further information contact:

Tel: (44) 20 7679 7115
Email: r.madden@ucl.ac.uk

Liver Group PhD Studentship

Purpose: To financially support students to pursue MPhil/PhD research
Eligibility: Open to United Kingdom and European Union applicants holding a relevant First or Upper Second Class
Level of Study: Doctorate, Postgraduate, Research
Type: Scholarship
Value: Home student fees plus a maintenance allowance (1st year approx. £14,500)
Length of Study: 3 years
Frequency: Dependent on funds available
Study Establishment: Royal Free and University College Medical School, UCL-Hampstead campus
Country of Study: United Kingdom
Application Procedure: Applicants should contact the department
Funding: Foundation
Contributor: The Liver Group Charity
No. of awards given last year: 1

For further information contact:

Centre for Hepatology, Department of Medicine (Royal Free Campus), Royal Free and University College Medicine School, Rowland Hill Street, London NW3 2PF, United Kingdom.

Tel: (44) 20 7433 2854
Fax: (44) 20 7433 2852
Email: c.selden@rfc.ucl.ac.uk

Master of the Rolls Scholarship for Commonwealth Students

Purpose: To financially support prospective LLM students
Eligibility: Applicants must be overseas students from the Commonwealth countries. An applicant must have accepted an offer (either conditional or unconditional) to read for the LLM at UCL
Level of Study: Postgraduate
Type: Scholarship
Value: £2,000
Frequency: Annual
Study Establishment: University College London
Country of Study: United Kingdom
Application Procedure: There is no application procedure. All eligible students who firmly accept the offer of admission by May 31st will be automatically considered
No. of awards given last year: 1

For further information contact:

Tel: (44) 20 7679 1441
Fax: (44) 20 7209 3470
Email: graduatelaw@ucl.ac.uk

Master's Degree Awards in Archaeology

Subjects: Archaeology.
Purpose: To financially support MA and MSc programmes in the Institute of Archaeology.
Eligibility: The Scholarship will be awarded on the basis of demonstrated academic excellence (taking into account the applicant's scholarship statement and CV along with references and transcripts submitted in the UCL admissions application form), only students who have, or are expected to have, a high upper second or first class degree will be considered.
Level of Study: Postgraduate
Type: Scholarship
Value: The value of the scholarship will be the equivalent to UK fees for the degree the successful applicant has been accepted onto.
Frequency: Annual
Study Establishment: University College London
Country of Study: United Kingdom
Application Procedure: Scholarship website: www.ucl.ac.uk/archaeology/sites/archaeology/files/ioa_funding_2022_23.docx
Closing Date: 1 March
Additional Information: www.ucl.ac.uk/archaeology/study/graduate-taught/applying/ucl-institute-archaeology-masters-award

For further information contact:

Tel: (44) 20 7679 7499
Email: l.daniel@ucl.ac.uk

Master's Degree Awards in Biochemical Engineering

Purpose: To financially support postgraduate study
Eligibility: 1. Normal entry requirements are at least a second-class Bachelor's degree from a UK university or the equivalent from an approved overseas institution. 2. Candidates offering recent industrial experience are also encouraged to apply.
Level of Study: Postgraduate
Type: Scholarship
Value: £18,000
Length of Study: 1 calendar year
Frequency: Annual
Study Establishment: University College London
Country of Study: United Kingdom
Application Procedure: Scholarship website: www.ucl.ac.uk/prospective-students/graduate/apply
Closing Date: 30 June
Additional Information: www.ucl.ac.uk/prospective-students/graduate/taught-degrees/biochemical-engineering-msc

For further information contact:

Email: biochemeng@ucl.ac.uk

Member Scholarship in Statistics

Purpose: To financially support full-time graduate study and research
Eligibility: Applicants should have graduated from UCL or be a candidate for graduation in the term in which the award is made. United Kingdom, European Union and overseas students are eligible to apply
Level of Study: Postgraduate, Research
Type: Scholarship
Value: £55
Frequency: Annual
Study Establishment: University College London
Country of Study: United Kingdom
Application Procedure: Applicants should write to the department indicating their intention to compete for the scholarship

For further information contact:

Tel: (44) 20 7679 1872
Fax: (44) 20 7383 4703
Email: marion@stats.ucl.ac.uk

Monica Hulse Scholarship

Purpose: This Scholarship, founded in 2004, is funded from a regular lifetime gift from Dr Paul Hulse, alumnus of UCL, in memory of his mother, Monica Hulse (1934-1999). One scholarship is awarded annually to a prospective graduate student from any country admitted to the Department of Mathematics for full-time Master's study or MPhil/PhD research
Eligibility: 1. University College London - Monica Hulse Scholarships in UK, is available to candidates from all nationalities. 2. Candidates intending to pursue their masters or PhD studies can apply. 3. The applicants of University College London - Monica Hulse Scholarships in UK, must be enrolled in a full-time program in the Department of Mathematics at UCL. 4. Candidates are not permitted to receive any other special funding
Level of Study: Doctorate, Masters Degree, Postgraduate, Research

Type: Scholarship
Value: £1,000
Length of Study: 1 year
Frequency: Annual
Country of Study: United Kingdom
Application Procedure: Candidates wishing to apply for the Scholarship must send written notice of their intention to apply for the Scholarship, along with an academic CV, to the Graduate Tutor in the Department of Mathematics. Applicants should not normally be in receipt of any other special funding (other than in exceptional circumstances).
Closing Date: 31 May
Funding: Private
No. of awards given last year: 1

For further information contact:

Email: h.higgins@ucl.ac.uk

National Health Service Bursaries

Purpose: To financially support postgraduate study
Eligibility: Open to United Kingdom and European Union applicants only who have applied for a place for graduate study at UCL
Level of Study: Postgraduate
Type: Bursary
Value: United Kingdom/European Union tuition fees. United Kingdom residents will also normally be eligible for a means tested bursary
Frequency: Annual
Study Establishment: University College London
Country of Study: United Kingdom
Application Procedure: There is no separate bursary application form. Application procedure is an automatic process once an offer of a place has been made

For further information contact:

Tel: (44) 20 7679 4202
Email: n.wilkins@ucl.ac.uk

Nederlandse Taalunie Scholarship

Purpose: To financially support postgraduate study
Eligibility: Applicants must have applied for a place for graduate study at UCL
Level of Study: Postgraduate
Type: Scholarship
Value: £2,500
Frequency: Annual
Study Establishment: University College London
Country of Study: United Kingdom
Application Procedure: Applicants should contact the department. If the applicant has not applied to UCL, they must complete a graduate application form and enclose it with the scholarship application
Closing Date: 15 July

For further information contact:

Tel: (44) 20 7679 3117
Fax: (44) 20 7616 6985
Email: t.hermans@ucl.ac.uk

Perren Studentship

Purpose: To financially support graduate study and research
Eligibility: Open to U.K. and EU applicants only who have applied for a place for graduate study at UCL.
Level of Study: Postgraduate, Research
Type: Studentship
Value: United Kingdom/European Union tuition fees. United Kingdom residents will also normally be eligible for a means tested bursary.
Frequency: Annual
Study Establishment: University College London
Country of Study: United Kingdom
Application Procedure: Applicants should provide particulars of their academic record and of the work that they intend to pursue to the department
Closing Date: 15 May
Funding: Trusts
Contributor: Perren Fund

For further information contact:

Tel: (44) 20 7679 473
Email: lahauestar@ucl.ac.uk

Professor Sir Malcolm Grant Postgraduate Scholarship

Eligibility: Candidates must fulfil all of the following criteria: 1. be ordinarily resident in the UK and eligible to pay Home fee rate. 2. have successfully completed or be currently completing undergraduate studies at UCL. 3. And have submitted an admission application for a full-time Master's degree at UCL in 2024/25.
Level of Study: Postgraduate
Type: Scholarship
Value: £25,000
Length of Study: 1 year
Frequency: Annual

Country of Study: United Kingdom
Application Procedure: Instructions for accessing the online scholarship application form: Login to Portico with your normal details. Click on the 'View' button for the 'Active Application' that you wish to apply for funding for. In the application screen, click on the 'Funding' in the menu at the top of the page. You are now on the funding page. To find out which funds you are eligible to apply for click 'Check and apply' under 'Funds Available'. Click on the scholarship name of the scheme that you wish to apply for.
No. of awards offered: 1
Closing Date: 8 June
Additional Information: www.ucl.ac.uk/scholarships/professor-sir-malcolm-grant-postgraduate-scholarship

For further information contact:

Tel: (44) 20 7679 8622
Fax: (44) 20 7679 8632
Email: ucsapga@ucl.ac.uk

Richard Chattaway Scholarship

Purpose: To financially support MPhil/PhD study
Eligibility: This scholarship is open to candidates from any country however candidates need to apply to a graduate programme in History by the relevant deadline to be eligible
Level of Study: Doctorate, Postgraduate
Type: Scholarship
Value: £2,000
Length of Study: 1 year
Frequency: Annual
Study Establishment: University College London
Country of Study: United Kingdom
Application Procedure: Applicants must contact the department. If the applicants have not already applied to UCL they must complete a graduate application form and enclose it with the scholarship application. Applicants must include particulars of the research work they intend to pursue in the event of the scholarship being awarded to them
Closing Date: 15 May
Funding: Individuals
Contributor: Private donation in honour of Richard Chattaway
No. of awards given last year: 1

For further information contact:

Email: n.miller@ucl.ac.uk

Research Degree Scholarship in Chemical Engineering

Purpose: To financially support MPhil/PhD research
Level of Study: Doctorate, Postgraduate, Research
Type: Scholarship
Value: £2,000
Frequency: Annual
Study Establishment: University College London
Country of Study: United Kingdom
Application Procedure: Applicants must contact the department

For further information contact:

Tel: (44) 20 7679 3835
Fax: (44) 20 7383 2348
Email: h.mahgerefteh@ucl.ac.uk

Research Degree Scholarships in Anthropology

Purpose: To financially support research in the field of anthropology
Eligibility: Please contact the Department of Anthropology for details
Level of Study: Doctorate, Postgraduate, Research
Type: Scholarship
Value: United Kingdom/European Union tuition fees
Frequency: Annual
Study Establishment: University College London
Country of Study: United Kingdom
Application Procedure: Applicants must contact the department
No. of awards offered: 12
Closing Date: 30 April
No. of awards given last year: 4
No. of applicants last year: 12

Royal National Orthopaedic Hospital Special Trustees Research Training Scholarship

Purpose: To give orthopaedic specialists of the future an early exposure to the first-class research culture at Stanmore
Eligibility: Open to students enrolled in the MSc in Surgical Sciences programme undertaking a research project at the Royal National Orthopaedic Hospital/Institute of Orthopaedic and Musculoskeletal Science.
Level of Study: Postgraduate
Type: Scholarship
Value: A stipend, tuition and bench fees
Frequency: Annual
Study Establishment: Royal National Orthopaedic Hospital, Stanmore
Country of Study: United Kingdom
Application Procedure: Once students have been accepted by a supervisor, they should contact the R&D office, Royal

National Orthopaedic Hospital. Applicants will be asked to send an outline of the research project and their curriculum vitae. Applicant should contact the department at the address given below
Funding: Private
Contributor: The RNOH Special Trustees and the R&D Subcommittee

For further information contact:

Royal National Orthopaedic Hospital, Brockley Hill, Stanmore, Middlesex HA7 4LP, United Kingdom.

Tel: (44) 20 8909 5752
Email: lphilpots@rnoh.nhs.uk

Score Africa/Allan & Nesta Ferguson Charitable Trust Scholarship

Purpose: To financially assist African nationals to undertake MSc/PhD studies at the Centre for International Health and Development (CIHD) at UCL
Eligibility: Applicants should refer to the website for full details on eligibility
Level of Study: Postgraduate
Type: Scholarship
Value: £30,555
Frequency: Annual
Country of Study: Any country
Application Procedure: Applicants should refer to the website for further information on application procedures, forms and deadlines
No. of awards offered: 10
Closing Date: 30 April

For further information contact:

Tel: (44) 20 7074 5094/5091
Email: scholarships@soas.ac.uk

Shell Petroleum Development Company Niger Delta Postgraduate Scholarship

Purpose: To provide opportunities for postgraduate study in the United Kingdom for young students and professionals, who demonstrate both academic excellence and the potential to become leading professionals in the oil and associated industries
Eligibility: The applicant must 1. have obtained a degree of at least an equivalent standard to a United Kingdom Upper Second Class (Honours Degree); 2. be neither a current nor former employee (who have left employment less than 5 years before) of SPDC, the Royal Dutch Shell Group of Companies or Wider Perspectives Limited, or current employee's relatives; 3. not already have had the chance of studying in the United Kingdom or another developed country; 4. be aged between 21 and 28 years; 5. originate from one of the Niger Delta States in Nigeria, namely Rivers, Delta or Bayelsa and currently reside in Nigeria
Level of Study: Postgraduate
Type: Scholarship
Value: Full tuition fee funding, maintenance allowance, return airfares and arrival allowance
Frequency: Annual
Study Establishment: University College London
Country of Study: United Kingdom
Closing Date: 15 March
No. of awards given last year: 10

For further information contact:

Student Funding Office, UCL, Gower Street, London WC1E 6BT, United Kingdom.

Email: studentfunding@ucl.ac.uk

Sir Frederick Pollock Scholarship for Students from North America

Purpose: To financially support prospective LLM students
Eligibility: Applicants must be overseas students from North America. An applicant must have accepted an offer (either conditional or unconditional) to read for the LLM at UCL to be eligible
Level of Study: Postgraduate
Type: Scholarship
Value: £2,000
Frequency: Annual
Country of Study: United Kingdom
Application Procedure: There is no application procedure. All eligible students will be automatically considered
Closing Date: 2 March

For further information contact:

Tel: (44) 20 7679 1441
Fax: (44) 20 7209 3470
Email: jane.ha@ucl.ac.uk

Sir George Jessel Studentship in Mathematics

Purpose: To financially support MPhil/PhD research
Eligibility: A candidate must have been an undergraduate student of UCL, and must have graduated, or be a candidate for graduation in the term in which the award is made. The

studentship may also be awarded to someone who has held it in the previous year.
Level of Study: Doctorate, Postgraduate, Research
Type: Studentship
Value: £1,800
Frequency: Annual
Study Establishment: University College London
Country of Study: United Kingdom
Application Procedure: Applicants must contact the department
Closing Date: 15 May
Additional Information: Please refer the website for further details www.ucl.ac.uk/prospective-students/scholarships/graduate/deptscholarships/mathematics www.scholarshipdesk.com/sir-george-jessel-studentship/

For further information contact:

Tel: (44) 20 7679 2839
Fax: (44) 20 7383 5519
Email: h.higgins@ucl.ac.uk

Sir James Lighthill Scholarship

Purpose: To financially support MPhil/PhD research
Eligibility: United Kingdom, European Union and overseas students are eligible to apply. All applicants who firmly accept a place for MPhil/PhD research in the Mathematics Department will be considered
Level of Study: Doctorate, Postgraduate, Research
Type: Scholarship
Value: £500 per year
Frequency: Annual
Study Establishment: University College London
Country of Study: United Kingdom
Application Procedure: Applicants must contact the department
Additional Information: www.ucl.ac.uk/lims/jameslighthill.htm

For further information contact:

Tel: (44) 20 7679 2839
Email: h.higgins@ucl.ac.uk

Sir John Salmond Scholarship for Students from Australia and New Zealand

Purpose: To financially support prospective LLM students
Eligibility: Applicants must be overseas students from Australia and New Zealand. An applicant must have accepted an offer (either conditional or unconditional) to read for the LLM at UCL to be eligible
Level of Study: Doctorate, Postgraduate
Type: Scholarship
Value: £2,000
Frequency: Annual
Study Establishment: University College London
Country of Study: United Kingdom
Application Procedure: There is no application

For further information contact:

Tel: (44) 20 7679 1441
Fax: (44) 20 7209 3470
Email: janc.ha@ucl.ac.uk

Sully Scholarship

Purpose: To financially support MPhil/PhD research
Eligibility: Open to the most outstanding candidate in the second year of their PhD research programme
Level of Study: Doctorate, Postgraduate, Research
Type: Scholarship
Value: £2,200
Frequency: Annual
Study Establishment: University College London
Country of Study: United Kingdom
Application Procedure: There is no separate application and the award is given to an outstanding student who is registered in the department's PhD programme and is in the second year of study
No. of awards given last year: 1

For further information contact:

Tel: (44) 20 7679 5332
Fax: (44) 20 7430 4276
Email: psychology-pg-enquiries@ucl.ac.uk

Teaching Assistantships (Economics)

Purpose: To financially support MPhil/PhD students
Eligibility: MPhil/PhD students who have successfully completed their 1st year in the department
Level of Study: Doctorate
Type: Assistantship
Value: £11,000
Frequency: Annual
Study Establishment: University College London
Country of Study: United Kingdom

Application Procedure: Contact the Department of Economics for details

For further information contact:

Email: d.fauvrelle@ucl.ac.uk

Thames and Hudson Scholarship

Purpose: To financially support postgraduate study
Level of Study: Postgraduate
Type: Scholarship
Value: A scholarship up to a maximum value of £15,000 or up to 4 scholarships totalling that value
Frequency: Annual
Study Establishment: University College London
Country of Study: United Kingdom
Application Procedure: Applicants must contact the department for details
Closing Date: July

For further information contact:

Tel: (44) 20 7679 7495
Fax: (44) 20 7383 2572
Email: k.thomas@ucl.ac.uk

The Bartlett Promise PhD Scholarship

Eligibility: Candidates must: 1. be UK domiciled with home fee status or a forced migrant (as defined by UCL) in the UK. 2. have an offer of admission to a Bartlett PhD programme to start in September 2024/25. 3. must not have completed a PhD at UCL or anywhere else previously.
Level of Study: Doctorate, Postgraduate
Type: Scholarship
Value: £19,668
Frequency: Annual
Country of Study: United Kingdom
Application Procedure: Scholarship website: forms.office.com/pages/responsepage.aspx?id=_oivH5ipW0yTySEKEdmlwpEeLY1xyWZAn7SHTUB4XchUOU0wTlZFS1Q4TFlQQlRURDdOWkxLTEFJMS4u
No. of awards offered: 4
Closing Date: 12 May
Additional Information: www.ucl.ac.uk/bartlett/study/funding-and-scholarships/bartlett-promise-scholarship/bartlett-promise-phd-scholarship

For further information contact:

Email: bartlett.promise@ucl.ac.uk

The George Melhuish Postgraduate Scholarship

Purpose: To financially support postgraduate research
Eligibility: Open to United Kingdom, European Union and overseas applicants
Level of Study: Postgraduate, Research
Type: Scholarship
Value: Up to £3,700
Frequency: Annual
Study Establishment: University College London
Country of Study: United Kingdom
Application Procedure: No separate application is required. Applicants who are admitted to research programmes in philosophy will automatically be considered for the scholarship. Any queries should be directed to the department
No. of awards given last year: 2

For further information contact:

Tel: (44) 20 7679 4451
Email: r.madden@ucl.ac.uk

Thomas Witherden Batt Scholarship

Eligibility: Candidates must fulfil all of the following criteria: 1. be ordinarily resident in the UK and eligible to pay Home fee rate. 2. And have submitted an admission application for a full-time Master of Science (MSc) degree at UCL in 2024/25.
Level of Study: Postgraduate
Type: Scholarship
Value: £10,000
Length of Study: 1 year
Frequency: Annual
Country of Study: United Kingdom
Application Procedure: Instructions for accessing the online scholarship application form: Login to Portico with your normal details. Click on the 'View' button for the 'Active Application' that you wish to apply for funding for. In the application screen, click on the 'Funding' in the menu at the top of the page. You are now on the funding page. To find out which funds you are eligible to apply for click 'Check and apply' under 'Funds Available'. Click on the scholarship name of the scheme that you wish to apply for.
No. of awards offered: 1
Closing Date: 8 June

Additional Information: www.ucl.ac.uk/scholarships/thomas-witherden-batt-scholarship

UCL Masters Bursary

Eligibility: Candidates must fulfill all of the following criteria: 1. be ordinarily resident in the UK or Ireland and eligible to pay Home fee rate. 2. have commenced undergraduate study no earlier than the 2013/14 academic session. 3. have an annual household income of £42,875 or less. 4. And have submitted an admission application for a full-time or part-time Master's degree at UCL in 2024/25. The flexible study mode is not eligible.
Level of Study: Postgraduate
Type: Bursary
Value: £10,000
Length of Study: 1 year
Frequency: Annual
Country of Study: United Kingdom
Application Procedure: Instructions for accessing the online scholarship application form: Login to Portico with your normal details. Click on the 'View' button for the 'Active Application' that you wish to apply for funding for. In the application screen, click on the 'Funding' in the menu at the top of the page. You are now on the funding page. To find out which funds you are eligible to apply for click 'Check and apply' under 'Funds Available'. Click on the scholarship name of the scheme that you wish to apply for.
No. of awards offered: 200
Closing Date: 8 June
Additional Information: www.ucl.ac.uk/scholarships/ucl-masters-bursary

University College London Department Awards for Graduate Students

Purpose: To financially support Master's and MPhil/PhD programmes
Eligibility: United Kingdom, European Union and overseas students are eligible to apply
Level of Study: Doctorate, Postgraduate
Type: Scholarship
Value: £500
Frequency: Annual
Study Establishment: University College London
Country of Study: United Kingdom
Application Procedure: Applicants must contact the department
Closing Date: 15 May

For further information contact:

Tel: (44) 20 7679 3262
Fax: (44) 20 7383 4108
Email: s.anyadi@ling.ucl.ac.uk

University College London-AET Undergraduate International Outreach Bursaries

Eligibility: Applicants must be a national of any African country (including Madagascar), currently living in an African country, and have one or both parents living in an African country, or are orphaned
Type: Bursary
Frequency: Annual
Country of Study: Any country

For further information contact:

Email: m.omona@africaeducationaltrust.org

William Blake Trust Bursary

Purpose: To financially support postgraduate or MPhil/PhD study
Eligibility: Applicants must have applied for a place for graduate study at UCL
Level of Study: Doctorate, Postgraduate
Type: Bursary
Value: £2,000
Frequency: Annual
Study Establishment: University College London
Country of Study: United Kingdom
Application Procedure: Applicants must contact the department. If the applicants have not already applied to UCL they must complete a graduate application form and enclose it with the scholarship application
Closing Date: 15 May

For further information contact:

Tel: (44) 20 7679 7546
Fax: (44) 20 7916 5939
Email: d.dethloff@ucl.ac.uk

William Moore Gorman Graduate Research Scholarship

Purpose: To financially support students entering the first year of the MPhil/PhD degree in department of Economics.

Eligibility: Open to candidates who have applied for a place for graduate study at University College London.
Level of Study: Doctorate, Postgraduate
Type: Scholarship
Value: £16,200
Length of Study: 1 year
Frequency: Annual
Study Establishment: University College London
Country of Study: United Kingdom
Application Procedure: All applicants for admission to our MRes programme are automatically considered for departmental funding at the time of application. There is no separate application process.
No. of awards offered: 4
No. of awards given last year: 9
Additional Information: www.ucl.ac.uk/economics/study/postgraduate/funding/funding/w-m-gorman-graduate-research-scholarships

University Commission for Development Academy of Research and Higher Education Scholarships

Rue Royale 180, B-1000 Brussels, Belgium.

Website: www.ares-ac.be/en/cooperation-au-developpement/bourses/masters-et-stages-en-belgique
Contact: ARES

Academy of Research and Higher Education Scholarships

Level of Study: Postgraduate
Value: The scholarship covers international travel expenses, living allowance, tuition fees, insurance, housing allowance
Country of Study: Any country
Application Procedure: To apply for the scholarship, complete the single form scholarship application and admission to one of the French-speaking universities of Belgium
Closing Date: 9 February
Additional Information: The scholarships are for nationals of: Benin, Bolivia, Burkina Faso, Burundi, Cambodia, Cameroon, Cuba, Ecuador, Ethiopia (only for courses in English), Haiti, Madagascar, Morocco, Niger, Peru, Philippines, DR Congo, Rwanda, Senegal, Vietnam. For more details, please visit official scholarship website: https://www.ares-ac.be/en/cooperation-au-developpement/scholarships/advanced-bachelor-s-and-master-s-degrees-or-continuing-education-courses-in-belgium#02-advanced-master-s-programs-for-2023-2024

For further information contact:

Email: scholarships-cooperation@ares-ac.be

University Institute of European Studies

Lungo Dora Siena 100, I-10153 Turin, Italy.

Tel: (39) 11 839 4660
Email: iuse@legalmail.it
Website: www.iuse.it
Contact: Ms Maria Grazia Goiettina, Course Secretariat

The University Institute of European Studies promotes international relations and European integration by organizing academic activities. The Institute has a comprehensive library in international law and economics. Since 1952 the Institute has been a European Documentation Centre (EDC), thus receiving all official publications of European institutions.

LLM in International Trade Law – Contracts and Dispute Resolution – Scholarships

Eligibility: Applicants must have successfully completed a first level university degree of at least 3 years' duration, either in law, economics, political sciences, business administration or equivalent
Level of Study: Postgraduate
Type: Scholarship
Country of Study: Any country
Funding: Foundation, Government, Individuals, Private

For further information contact:

Tel: (39) 11 69 36 945
Fax: (39) 11 69 36 369
Email: tradelaw@itcilo.org

University of Aarhus

Nordre Ringgade 1, Bygning 327 3, DK-8000 Aarhus, Denmark.

Tel: (45) 8715 0000
Email: au@au.dk
Website: www.au.dk
Contact: Faculty of Social Sciences

The University of Aarhus was founded in 1928 as Universitetsundervisningen i Jylland – University Teaching in Jutland in classrooms rented from the Technical College and a teaching corps consisting of 1 Professor of philosophy and 4 Readers of Danish, English, German and French. However, today the University has 20,000 students with 5,000 staff.

Doctor of Philosophy Scholarship in Globalisation and International Economics

Purpose: To enable students to take up research in the related fields
Eligibility: Open to applicants who have a Master's degree or to students who expect to obtain their Master's degree in the near future
Level of Study: Postgraduate, Research
Type: Scholarship
Value: Approx. salary of DKK2,700
Length of Study: 3 years
Frequency: Annual
Study Establishment: Aarhus School of Business
Country of Study: Denmark
Application Procedure: Application forms can be downloaded from the Aarhus website. The form should be sent with a curriculum vitae and an outline of a research project including a description of the proposed theory and methods
Closing Date: 19 February
Contributor: Danish Social Science Research Council

For further information contact:

Tel: (45) 89 486 482/392
Email: pje@asb.dk

University of Aberdeen

University Office, King's College, Aberdeen AB24 3FX, United Kingdom.

Tel: (44) 1224 272000
Email: ptgoff@abdn.ac.uk
Website: www.abdn.ac.uk
Contact: The Postgraduate Registry

The University of Aberdeen is the fifth oldest in the United Kingdom. Aberdeen is an international university serving one of the most dynamic regions of Europe with over 13,000 students and over 3,000 staff, and is at the forefront of teaching and research in medicine and the humanities and sciences.

Aberdeen International Masters Scholarship

Eligibility: Open to eligible self-funded taught Masters students who are classed as international fee status and domiciled in one of the countries listed below. The scholarship is not available to students studying PGDE degrees.
Level of Study: Masters Degree
Type: Scholarship
Value: £3,000 tuition fee discount
Frequency: Annual
Country of Study: United Kingdom
Application Procedure: You will be awarded your scholarships as a tuition fee discount and the value of the scholarship will be included in your CAS letter. Please check that you have firmly accepted an unconditional offer and that you have sent us confirmation of funding. Please note, you do not need to apply for this scholarship, all eligible students will receive the scholarship as a fee discount.
Additional Information: www.abdn.ac.uk/study/funding/341

For further information contact:

Email: study@abdn.ac.uk

AFZ Giles Scholarship

Eligibility: Students who are registered for an undergraduate or postgraduate degree in the School of Medicine, Medical Sciences and Nutrition at the University of Aberdeen are eligible to apply. Students must be researching issues directly affecting women's health. Preference will be given to projects supervised or co-supervised in the Aberdeen Centre for Women's Health Research. The scholarship is available to home or overseas students to assist with research project costs including research outputs (conference presentation, open access publication, etc). Fees for Master degree research projects supervised by ACWHR will also be considered.
Level of Study: Postgraduate
Type: Scholarship
Value: £2,000
Frequency: Annual
Country of Study: United Kingdom
Application Procedure: There is no set application form. Applications should include information about the course of study being undertaken, why financial support is needed, and

what the scholarship funds will be used for. The applications should be accompanied by: A copy of the applicant's curriculum vitae (max 2 page and can include link for google scholarly or PURE or similar for full list of publications), a max 500 word summary of the student's project in a scientific abstract format, a summary of how the funds will be used, and a letter of support from the student's supervisor.
Closing Date: 1 April
Additional Information: www.abdn.ac.uk/study/funding/165, https://www.abdn.ac.uk/acwhr/study-with-us-139.php

For further information contact:

Email: kelly.gray@abdn.ac.uk

Arnold Klopper Scholarship

Eligibility: 1. Students who are registered for an undergraduate or postgraduate degree in the School of Medicine, Medical Sciences and Nutrition at the University of Aberdeen are eligible to apply. Students must be researching issues directly affecting women's health. Preference will be given to projects supervised or co-supervised in the Aberdeen Centre for Women's Health Research. 2. The scholarship is available to home or overseas students to assist with research project costs including research outputs (conference presentation, open access publication, etc). Fees for Master degree research projects supervised by ACWHR will also be considered.
Level of Study: Postgraduate
Type: Scholarship
Value: £1,000
Frequency: Annual
Country of Study: United Kingdom
Application Procedure: There is no set application form. Applications should include information about the course of study being undertaken, why financial support is needed, and what the Scholarship funds will be used for. The applications should be accompanied by: A copy of the applicant's curriculum vitae (max 2 pages & can include link to google scholarly or PURE or similar for full list of publications), a max of 500-word summary of the student's project in a scientific abstract format, a summary of how the funds will be used, a letter of support from the student's supervisor.
Closing Date: 1 April
Additional Information: www.abdn.ac.uk/study/funding/620, https://www.abdn.ac.uk/acwhr/study-with-us-139.php

For further information contact:

Email: kelly.gray@abdn.ac.uk

Arts Humanities Research Council Collaborative Doctoral Partnership PhD Studentship

Purpose: The Collaborative Doctoral Partnership scheme gives non-higher education institutions with a proven track record in postgraduate research the opportunity to manage PhD students, with a minimum of three studentships per year
Eligibility: 1. Residency Students from the EU are normally eligible for a fees-only scholarship, unless they have been ordinarily resident in the UK for three or more years directly prior to the start of the studentship (with some further constraint regarding residence for education). 2. Projects These awards are attached to specific projects. Only students chosen by the project supervisors can apply.
Level of Study: Doctorate
Type: Studentship
Value: £15,009+ per annum, plus £550 enhancement, plus tuition fees
Length of Study: 3 years
Frequency: Annual
Country of Study: Any country
Application Procedure: You could use the website link www.ahrc-cdp.org
No. of awards offered: 3
Closing Date: 28 January

For further information contact:

Email: Lucie.Connors@ahrc.ukri.org

China Scholarship Council (CSC) Scholarship

Purpose: The CSC Scholarship is a scholarship programme for Chinese PhD students, who will take a full PhD at the University of Aberdeen
Eligibility: 1. To be eligible to apply for this scholarship in China, candidates must submit with their application, a conditional scholarship offer letter from Curtin University. 2. To ensure interested candidates meet the China Scholarship Council application deadline in March each year, Curtin University strongly encourage students submit their online e-application for admissions latest by 31 January of the applying year to avoid missing the deadline. 3. Scholarship Recipients must hold a conditional offer of enrolment subject to the CSC award and also fulfil the entry requirements of Curtin University, including a high level of English language proficiency
Level of Study: Doctorate
Type: Scholarship
Country of Study: Any country
Application Procedure: Applications for the CSC Scholarship should be submitted online at apply.csc.edu.cn/csc/main/person/login/index.jsf

For further information contact:

Email: study@abdn.ac.uk

Common Data Access MSc Petroleum Data Management Scholarships

Purpose: To pursue MSc programme
Eligibility: Open only to the citizens of Australia or permanent residents who have achieved Honours 1 or equivalent
Level of Study: Postgraduate
Value: Each scholarship is valued at £5,000 for the duration of the MSc Petroleum Data Management degree and will contribute towards the programme tuition fees
Frequency: Annual
Country of Study: Any country
Closing Date: 31 May

For further information contact:

Email: info@cdal.com

Elphinstone PhD Scholarships

Type: Scholarship
Value: Cover tuition fees for the duration of their supervised study
Country of Study: Any country

For further information contact:

Email: infohub@abdn.ac.uk

University of Adelaide

Graduate School of Management, 3rd Floor Security House, 233 North Terrace, Adelaide, SA 5005, Australia.

Tel: (61) 8 8313 4455
Email: cmchugh@gsm.adelaide.edu.au
Website: www.gsm.adelaide.edu.au
Contact: MBA Admissions Officer

Adelaide Postgraduate Coursework Scholarships

Eligibility: Open only to the citizens of Australia or permanent residents who have achieved Honours 1 or equivalent
Level of Study: Postgraduate
Type: Scholarship
Value: Covers 50% of the tuition fee costs
Length of Study: 2 years
Frequency: Annual
Study Establishment: University of Adelaide
Country of Study: Australia
Application Procedure: Applicants must apply directly to the scholarship provider. Check website for further details

For further information contact:

Adelaide Graduate Centre, Adelaide University, Adelaide, SA 5005, Australia.

Tel: (61) 8 8313 4455
Fax: (61) 8 8223 3394
Email: adrienne.gorringe@adelaide.edu.au

Asia Pacific Institute of Information Technology_IT PhDs in Grid Computing

Purpose: To enable high performance numerical computing on service-oriented architectures
Eligibility: Open only to the citizens of Australia and New Zealand or permanent residents who have achieved Honours 2a or equivalent
Level of Study: Postgraduate
Type: Scholarship
Value: AU$24,650 per year
Length of Study: 3 years and 6 months
Frequency: Annual
Study Establishment: The Australian National University, The University of Adelaide
Country of Study: Australia
Application Procedure: Check website for further details
Closing Date: 21 September
Contributor: Adelaide University and The Australian National University

For further information contact:

Email: Peter.Strazdins@cs.anu.edu.au

Australian Building Codes Board Research Scholarship

Purpose: The ABCB runs the Student Research Scholarship Program to encourage undergraduate and postgraduate research in the field of building regulatory reform in Australia, which can contribute to the ABCB fulfilling its charter
Eligibility: To be eligible for the scholarship, applicants must be students currently undertaking undergraduate or

postgraduate studies in building, building surveying, fire engineering, architecture, construction, plumbing, hydraulic design or similar at an Australian educational institution; and research that forms a component of a program or course at an educational institution (e.g. tertiary), such as a research project, thesis or dissertation
Level of Study: Graduate
Type: Scholarship
Value: Up to AU$5,000 one off payment
Length of Study: 1 year
Country of Study: Australia
Application Procedure: To apply for the scholarship, applicants are asked to submit an ABCB Research Scholarship Application Form together with a resume and academic transcript to date to the Research Scholarship Project Officer at abcb.scholarship@abcb.gov.au

For further information contact:

Email: abcb.scholarship@abcb.gov.au

Australian Federation of University Women SA Inc. (AFUW-SA) Diamond Jubilee Scholarship

Eligibility: This scholarship is available to: 1. Women students who are Australian citizens or permanent residents. 2. Must be enrolled at a South Australian University, undertaking a postgraduate Masters degree by research or including a thesis component. 3. Must have completed at least six (6) months full time equivalent of their masters program. 4. Must not be in full time paid employment or on fully paid leave. 5. Must not have received a scholarship or award in the same category in 2023.
Level of Study: Postgraduate, Research
Type: Scholarship
Value: AU$3,000
Length of Study: 1 year
Frequency: Annual
Country of Study: Australia
Application Procedure: Scholarship website: www.afuwsa-trust.com.au/wp-content/uploads/2023/01/AFUW-SA-DJ-Application-Form-2023.pdf
Closing Date: 31 March
Additional Information: scholarships.adelaide.edu.au/Scholarships/postgraduate-coursework/all-faculties/australian-federation-of-university-women-sa-inc

For further information contact:

Tel: (61) 8 8313 5208

Australian Rotary Health PhD Scholarships – Post Traumatic Stress Disorder (PTSD)

Eligibility: Applicants must be 1. an Australian citizen or have Australian Permanent Resident status, and not be under bond to any foreign government. Evidence of citizenship (citizenship certificate, birth certificate, passport) or residential status must accompany the application. 2. about to commence, or in their first year of a PhD only – studying full-time.
Level of Study: Postgraduate, Research
Type: Scholarship
Value: AU$30,000 per annum
Length of Study: 3.5 years
Frequency: Annual
Country of Study: Australia
Closing Date: 11 February

For further information contact:

Email: scholarships@adelaide.edu.au

Ferry Scholarship – UniSA

Purpose: To promote study and research into the scientific fields of physics and chemistry
Eligibility: Open only to the citizens of Australia below the age of 25 years who have achieved Honours or equivalent
Level of Study: Postgraduate
Type: Scholarship
Value: AU$7,500 per year
Length of Study: 1 year
Frequency: Annual
Study Establishment: Flinders University, The University of Adelaide, University of South Australia
Country of Study: Australia
Application Procedure: Applicants must apply directly to the university. Check the website for further details
Closing Date: 31 March
Funding: Individuals
Contributor: Late Cedric Arnold Seth Ferry

For further information contact:

Tel: (61) 8302 3967
Email: jenni.critcher@unisa.edu.au

U

Higher Education Scholarships (International)

Eligibility: To be eligible for this scholarship you must: 1. Either be an alumni (graduate) of an AQF-recognised Australian Higher Education institution or have completed an onshore Australian Year 12 qualification with a ATAR of

80 or an onshore IB Diploma with a total of 28. 2. Have a University of Adelaide offer of admission (full offer or conditional offer) as a full-fee-paying international student. 3. Complete the acceptance process as outlined in your offer of admission. 4. Enrol in a full time study load for each study period of your degree.
Level of Study: Postgraduate, Undergraduate
Type: Scholarship
Value: 25% tuition fee reduction
Frequency: Annual
Country of Study: Australia
Application Procedure: It is not necessary to apply for The University of Adelaide Higher Education Scholarship because this scholarship will be automatically awarded to students who meet the eligibility requirements. No separate Scholarship application form is required. Scholarship recipients will be confirmed at the point of acceptance.
Additional Information: international.adelaide.edu.au/admissions/scholarships/higher-education-scholarships

For further information contact:

Tel: (61) 8 8313 7335

Joint Postgraduate Scholarship Program

Eligibility: Open to applicants who are citizens and permanent residents of the People's Republic of China at the time of application; are less than 35 years old at the time of application (this is a CSC eligibility requirement); are a university student completing a master's degree, or enrolled as a first year PhD student, or new graduates from their university at the time of application; agree to return to China upon completion of their studies and/or research; hold an unconditional offer of enrolment at the University of Adelaide, which is subject to the applicant also being successful in applying for a CSC award. They must therefore fulfil the relevant academic entry requirements set by the University of Adelaide for all international scholarship holders, including a high level of English language proficiency; English is the language of instruction at the University of Adelaide and proficiency in speaking, listening to, reading and writing English is essential. The IELTS (International English Language Testing System) is the preferred English language proficiency although TOEFL scores are also accepted. Applicants who have not provided evidence that they have met the university's minimum English Language Proficiency requirements by the closing date are not eligible for a CSC scholarship. CSC applicants are not permitted to undertake Pre-Enrolment English programs as the CSC will not award scholarships to applicants who have not met the university's minimum ELP requirements for direct entry. The Scholarships will give priority to graduates of the Chinese universities listed as "985 Project" Universities. Eligible candidates will be assessed by the University of Melbourne and Karlsruhe Institute of Technology on the basis of their academic transcripts and their research work
Type: Scholarship
Value: Australia
Country of Study: Any country
Application Procedure: The mode of applying is electronically. For detailed information, please visit website
Closing Date: 31 March
Contributor: The China Scholarship Council (CSC) and The University of Adelaide (UA)

Rae and George Hammer Memorial Visiting Research Fellowship

Purpose: The fellowship is available to assist an Honours, Masters or PhD student who is interested in studying any of the collections held in the Fryer Library, University of Queensland, to support their studies.
Eligibility: 1. The fellowship is available to assist an Honours, Masters or PhD student who is interested in studying any of the collections held in the Fryer Library, University of Queensland, to support their studies. 2. The Library holds architecture, Australian art, Australian theatre, Australian literature, music and Aboriginal and Torres Strait Islander collections.
Level of Study: Doctorate, Masters Degree, Postgraduate
Type: Fellowship
Value: AU$2,500
Frequency: Annual
Country of Study: Australia
Application Procedure: Scholarship website: web.library.uq.edu.au/about-us/awards-and-fellowships/rae-and-george-hammer-memorial-visiting-research-fellowship
Additional Information: scholarships.adelaide.edu.au/Scholarships/honours/all-faculties/rae-and-george-hammer-memorial-visiting-research-fellowship

For further information contact:

Email: s.farley@library.uq.edu.au

The Eynesbury College High Achiever Progression Scholarship

Eligibility: To be eligible for this scholarship you must: 1. Be a graduate of Eynesbury College. 2. Minimum Grade average 85% or a GPA of 6.0/7.0. 3. Have a University of Adelaide

offer of admission (full offer or conditional offer) as a full-fee-paying international student. 4. Enrol in a full time study load for each study period of the degree. 5. Complete the acceptance process as outlined in your offer of admission.
Level of Study: Postgraduate, Undergraduate
Type: Scholarship
Value: 25% tuition fee reduction
Frequency: Annual
Country of Study: Australia
Application Procedure: It is not necessary to apply for The Eynesbury College High Achiever Progression Scholarship because this scholarship will be automatically awarded to students who meet the eligibility requirements. Scholarships will be confirmed at the point of acceptance.
No. of awards offered: 100
Additional Information: international.adelaide.edu.au/admissions/scholarships/the-eynesbury-college-high-achiever-progression-scholarship

For further information contact:

Tel: (61) 8 8313 7335

The Eynesbury College International Scholarship

Eligibility: To be eligible for this scholarship you must: 1. Be a graduate of Eynesbury College. 2. Minimum grade to be eligible is 319 or above for Foundation, or a GPA of 3.0 for Diploma. 3. Have a University of Adelaide offer of admission (full offer or conditional offer) as a full-fee-paying international student. 4. Enrol in a full time study load for each study period of the degree. 5. Complete the acceptance process as outlined in your offer of admission.
Level of Study: Postgraduate, Undergraduate
Type: Scholarship
Value: 10% or 5% tuition fee reduction
Frequency: Annual
Country of Study: Australia
Application Procedure: It is not necessary to apply for The Eynesbury College International Scholarship because this scholarship will be automatically awarded to students who meet the eligibility requirements. Scholarships will be confirmed at the point of acceptance.
Additional Information: international.adelaide.edu.au/admissions/scholarships/the-eynesbury-college-international-scholarship

For further information contact:

Tel: (61) 8 8313 7335

The Hugh Martin Weir Prize

Eligibility: The Prize is open to University of Adelaide students who are enrolled in an Honours thesis program or a postgraduate program by coursework or by research, either commencing or already in progress. Postdoctoral researchers are eligible to apply within three years of a doctoral award.
Level of Study: Doctorate, Postgraduate, Research
Type: Scholarship
Value: AU$2,000
Frequency: Annual
Country of Study: Australia
Closing Date: 28 February
Additional Information: scholarships.adelaide.edu.au/Scholarships/honours/all-faculties/hugh-martin-weir-prize

For further information contact:

Tel: (61) 8 8313 5208

The University of Adelaide Global Citizens Scholarship

Purpose: This scholarship rewards international students commencing an undergraduate or postgraduate qualification who have received academic merit in their studies.
Eligibility: To be eligible for this scholarship you must have a University of Adelaide offer or admission (full or conditional) as a full-fee paying international student.
Level of Study: Postgraduate, Undergraduate
Type: Scholarship
Value: The scholarship offers a reduction of between 15% and 30% of the tuition fee for the minimum standard duration of the scholars chosen undergraduate or postgraduate degree.
Frequency: Annual
Country of Study: Australia
Application Procedure: It is not necessary to apply for The University of Adelaide Global Citizen Scholarship because this scholarship will be automatically awarded to students who meet the eligibility requirements. No separate Scholarship application form is required. Scholarship recipients will be confirmed at the point of acceptance.
Additional Information: international.adelaide.edu.au/admissions/scholarships/the-university-of-adelaide-global-citizens-scholarship

For further information contact:

Tel: (61) 8 8313 7335

University of Adelaide Research Scholarship - The Elder Conservatorium of Music

Eligibility: Applicants will have a minimum of Honours 2A result or equivalent in Music Technology or a Digital Media discipline, and must be citizens or permanent residents of Australia, citizens of New Zealand, or permanent humanitarian visa holders at the time of application.
Level of Study: Doctorate
Type: Scholarship
Value: AU$28,854
Length of Study: 3 years
Frequency: Annual
Country of Study: Australia
Application Procedure: Applying Application for Admission must be submitted using the Online Application Form available at hdrapp.adelaide.edu.au/auth/login
Closing Date: 24 February
Additional Information: able.adelaide.edu.au/music/

For further information contact:

Tel: (61) 8 8313 5995
Fax: (61) 8 8313 4423
Email: music@adelaide.edu.au

University of Alabama

The University of Alabama, Tuscaloosa, AL 35487, United States of America.

Tel: (1) 205 348 6010
Website: www.ua.edu/

Alumni Heritage Graduate Scholarship (AHGS)

Subjects: All
Purpose: To recruit children and grandchildren of graduates of The University of Alabama. To send a clear signal to our graduates that want your children. To provide a tangible Alumni Association membership benefit for UA graduates.
Eligibility: 1. One time only (non-renewable) scholarship for first-year graduate students who are Alabama residents and who are children or grandchildren of a University of Alabama graduate. The scholarship is for the student's first term of graduate enrollment. 2. Parent or grandparent must be a degree holder (undergraduate, graduate, or law degree) from The University of Alabama. 3. The qualifying parent or grandparent must be an active member of the National Alumni Association for three of the past five years. (Parent or grandparent cannot write check for all three years in one year). 4. The student must be admitted to a graduate degree program at UA and may be enrolled part-time or full-time.
Level of Study: Graduate
Type: Scholarship
Value: US$500
Frequency: Annual
Study Establishment: University of Alabama
Country of Study: United States of America
Application Procedure: Scholarship website: slate.ua.edu/register/ahgs
Closing Date: 1 May
Additional Information: graduate.ua.edu/prospective-students/graduate-school-scholarships-fellowships/

For further information contact:

Email: amg@ua.edu

Graduate Council Fellowships

Purpose: To award University of Alabama Graduate School students.
Eligibility: Prospective and current University of Alabama students are nominated by their departments for our fellowships, so it is important that you are talking to the Graduate Program Director for your program. Prior to nomination, nominees who are prospective students must have been offered admission.
Type: Fellowship
Value: US$25,000/year for a maximum of 5 years
Length of Study: 5 years
Frequency: Annual
Study Establishment: University of Alabama
Country of Study: United States of America
No. of awards offered: 100
Closing Date: 13 January
No. of awards given last year: 15
Additional Information: graduate.ua.edu/prospective-students/graduate-school-scholarships-fellowships/#:~:text=Graduate%20Council%20Fellowships,-The%20University%20of&text=New%20and%20current%20UA%20students,a%20maximum%20of%205%20years

McNair Graduate Fellowships

Purpose: McNair Graduate Fellowships are specifically for entering graduate students who have either completed a McNair Undergraduate Scholars program or who are McNair eligible.

Eligibility: Low income (as defined by the US Department of Education) AND a first-generation college student or a member of a group traditionally underrepresented in graduate education (i.e. Hispanic, African American, Native American, Native Hawaiian, Pacific Islander). Although any prospective or current graduate student may be nominated for this fellowship, preference is given to students who have completed a McNair program and have been accepted into a Doctoral program at The University of Alabama. Exceptional current University of Alabama students may also be considered for this fellowship.
Level of Study: Doctorate, Masters Degree
Type: Fellowship
Value: The stipend for the McNair Graduate Fellowship is US$20,000 for the academic year (fall and spring semesters).
Length of Study: 1 year
Frequency: Annual
Study Establishment: University of Alabama
Country of Study: United States of America
Contributor: 2 years for doctoral and 1 year for masters
Additional Information: graduate.ua.edu/prospective-students/graduate-school-scholarships-fellowships/#:~:text=Graduate%20Council%20Fellowships,-The%20University%20of&text=New%20and%20current%20UA%20students,a%20maximum%20of%205%20years

University of Alaska Fairbanks (UAF)

University of Alaska Fairbanks, P.O. Box 757500, Fairbanks, AK 99775, United States of America.

Tel: (1) 907 474 7034
Email: uaf-admissions@alaska.edu
Website: www.uaf.edu/som/mba
Contact: MBA Admissions Officer

RFRC Graduate Student Fellowship Awards

Purpose: This fellowship is especially interested in seeing proposals on applied topics aligned with the research priorities and needs of the North Pacific Fishery Management Council.
Eligibility: 1. Awards will be made to support excellence in graduate student research. The award is not a research assistantship, but a fellowship in recognition of scholastic excellence. Awards are open to any full-time or prospective CFOS graduate student. 2. Research should produce findings with a potential for continued development as a scientific or applied initiative. 3. Projects should be distinctive and make an original contribution to existing knowledge. 4. Projects should have potential economic value to the fishing industry and contribute to long-term benefits for Alaska. 5. Awards may be contingent on receipt of research funding from other sources.
Level of Study: Doctorate, Postgraduate
Type: Fellowship
Value: US$47,000 for M.S. students and US$52,000 for Ph.D. students
Length of Study: 2 years for M.S. and 3 years for Ph.D. students
Frequency: Annual
Country of Study: United States of America
Closing Date: 19 March
Funding: Private
Additional Information: www.uaf.edu/cfos/research/rasmuson-fisheries-resear/rfrc-fellowships/#:~:text=Rasmuson%20Fellowships%20are%20annual%20awards,students%20and%20%2452%2C000%20for%20Ph.

For further information contact:

Email: clsutton3@alaska.edu

University of Alberta

Faculty of Graduate Studies & Research, Killam Centre for Advanced Studies, 2-29 Triffo Hall, Edmonton, AB T6G 2E1, Canada.

Tel: (1) 780 492 3111
Email: grad.services@ualberta.ca
Website: www.ualberta.ca/gradstudies

Opened in 1908, the University of Alberta has a long tradition of scholarly achievements and commitment to excellence in teaching, research and service to the community. It is one of Canada's five largest research-intensive universities, with an annual research income from external sources of more than CA$3,000,000,000. It participates in 18 of 21 of the Federal Networks of Centres of Excellence, which link industries, universities and governments in applied research and development.

U

Canadian Initiatives For Nordic Studies (CINS) Graduate Scholarship

Purpose: To provide financial assistance to students who wish to pursue higher studies.

Eligibility: The candidate must: 1. Be a Canadian citizen or landed immigrant. 2. Have completed a bachelor's degree with high scholastic achievement from a Canadian university or college. 3. Provide evidence in writing of acceptance of the proposed study/research from the proposed Nordic post-secondary institution. (Sometimes unavoidably late. Explain). 4. Be in residency at the Nordic destination for a minimum of six months. 5. Provide a summary of your experience to CINS no later than six months after completing the proposed programme of study.
Level of Study: Doctorate
Type: Scholarship
Value: CA$4,500
Frequency: Annual
Country of Study: Canada
Application Procedure: There is no official application form.
No. of awards offered: 1
Closing Date: 15 October
Additional Information: cins.artsrn.ualberta.ca/en/PhDscholarship.html

For further information contact:

Email: CINS@ualberta.ca

Izaak Walton Killam Memorial Scholarship

Purpose: It will be offered to outstanding students registered in, or admissible to, a doctoral program. No restrictions on citizenship
Eligibility: Offered to outstanding students registered in, or admissible to, a doctoral program. No restrictions on citizenship. All fields are eligible for funding. Applicants must have completed at least one year of graduate work (master's or doctoral level) before start of tenure; tenure may begin on 1 May or 1 September. Additional information regarding eligibility criteria can be found in the Applicant Instructions document below. Please note that the GPA is calculated over the current graduate program graded course work
Level of Study: Graduate
Type: Scholarship
Value: US$45,000
Length of Study: 2 years
Frequency: Annual
Country of Study: Any country
Application Procedure: Students complete the Izaak Walton Killam Memorial Scholarship application form and submit supporting documents to their department to be considered for both the Izaak Walton Killam Memorial Scholarship and the Dorothy J Killam Memorial Graduate Prizes. A complete Izaak Walton Killam Memorial Scholarship Application includes For Applicants Izaak Walton Killam Memorial Scholarship Applicant Instructions 1. Izaak Walton Killam Memorial Scholarship Application Form. 2. Two Letter of Reference to Support Application for Graduate Awards. 3. Transcripts (copies of official transcripts for all post-secondary study are required to support an application. Your home department may have copies in your department file. If your department does not have these transcripts, you are required to submit new transcripts. Unofficial copies of University of Alberta transcripts are acceptable)
Funding: Private
Contributor: Killam Trust Scholarships
Additional Information: www.ualberta.ca/graduate-studies/awards-and-funding/celebrating-our-killam-laureates/izaak-walton-killam-doctoral.html, https://killamlaureates.ca/

For further information contact:

School of Library and Information Studies, 7-104 Education North, University of Alberta, Edmonton, AB T6G 2R3, Canada.

Tel: (1) 780 492 7625
Email: slis@ualberta.ca

University of Alberta Graduate Entrance Scholarship

Purpose: The purpose of this scholarship is to provide funding and support to newly admitted graduate students that were highly ranked in their department at admission.
Eligibility: 1. The following admission terms are eligible: January 2024, May 2024, July 2024, and September 2024. 2. Must be a newly admitted student in one of the above terms in a master's or doctoral program. 3. Open to domestic and international students. 4. Open to course-based or thesis students. 5. Must have an Admission GPA of 3.7 or higher. 6. Must be full-time registered during the tenure of the award (Note: This award is payable in September 2024 regardless of the admit term of the student).
Level of Study: Doctorate, Masters Degree
Type: Scholarship
Value: CA$17,500 Master's and CA$21,000 Doctoral
Frequency: Annual
Country of Study: Canada
Application Procedure: There is no application form; students cannot apply for this scholarship. Eligible students are considered on the recommendation of the admitting department; students are to contact their admitting department for information.
Closing Date: 17 April

Additional Information: www.ualberta.ca/graduate-studies/awards-and-funding/scholarships/graduate-entrance.html

University of Alberta Graduate Recruitment Scholarship

Purpose: The purpose of the Recruitment Scholarship is to recruit superior graduate students who have the potential to contribute to the University of Alberta's community and research.
Eligibility: The scholarship will be awarded to students who: 1. Are Canadian citizens, permanent residents, or students on a study permit. 2. Are admitted to a doctoral or thesis-based master's graduate degree program by the department or transferred from a master's to a doctoral degree program. 3. Will be registered full-time in a doctoral degree or thesis-based master's degree program. 4. Have an admission GPA of at least 3.5.
Level of Study: Doctorate, Masters Degree
Type: Scholarship
Value: CA$5,000
Frequency: Annual
Country of Study: Canada
Application Procedure: There is no application form; students cannot apply for this scholarship. Eligible students are considered on the recommendation of the admitting department; students are to contact their admitting department for information.
Closing Date: 31 March
Additional Information: www.ualberta.ca/graduate-studies/awards-and-funding/scholarships/recruitment-scholarship.html

University of Alberta MBA Programme

Length of Study: 20 months; 72 months
Country of Study: Canada
Application Procedure: Applicants must complete and return the form, with two official academic transcripts, Graduate Management Admission Test scores, three letters of recommendation, a two page statement of intent, a detailed curriculum vitae, an application deposit of CA$60 (US$45), and a TOEFL score (if applicable) of 550+
Closing Date: 1 March
Additional Information: www.ualberta.ca/business/programs/mba/full-time/index.html

For further information contact:

Tel: (1) 780 492 3946
Fax: (1) 780 492 7825
Email: mba.programs@ualberta.ca

University of Amsterdam

Office of the Beadle, Handboogstraat 6, NL-1012 WX Amsterdam, Netherlands.

Tel: (31) 20 525 9111
Website: www.uva.nl/en

Amsterdam Excellence Scholarships (AES)

Purpose: The Amsterdam Excellence Scholarships (AES) awards scholarships to exceptionally talented students from outside Europe to pursue eligible Master's Programmes offered at the University of Amsterdam
Eligibility: Non-European Union students from any discipline who graduated in the top 10% of their class may apply. Selection is on the basis of academic excellence, ambition and the relevance of the selected Master's programme to a student's future career
Level of Study: Postgraduate
Type: Scholarship
Value: €25,000 per annum
Length of Study: 1 year
Frequency: Annual
Study Establishment: University of Amsterdam
Country of Study: Netherlands
Application Procedure: Applications are made through the Admissions Offices of the Graduate Schools
Closing Date: 15 January
Additional Information: For more details, please visit official scholarship website: https://www.uva.nl/en/education/fees-and-funding/masters-scholarships-and-loans/amsterdam-merit-scholarship/amsterdam-merit-scholarship.html

For further information contact:

P.O. Box 19268, NL-1000 GG Amsterdam, The Netherlands.

Email: servicedesk-ac@uva.nl

U

Amsterdam Science Talent Scholarship (ASTS)

Purpose: Scholarship is available for pursuing the masters degree programme at the University of Amsterdam.
Eligibility: To be eligible, an applicant must: 1. Be an international student. 2. Be registered or admissible to a full-time doctoral program. 3. Have completed at least one year of graduate work (master or doctoral level). 4. Have an intellect complemented by a sound character.
Level of Study: Masters Degree, Postgraduate

Type: Scholarship
Value: €15,000
Length of Study: 2 years
Frequency: Annual
Country of Study: Netherlands
Closing Date: 1 March
Additional Information: gss.uva.nl/scholarships/amsterdam-talent-scholarship/amsterdam-science-talent-scholarship.html#:~:text=The%20Amsterdam%20Science%20Talent%20Scholarship,previous%20year%20other%20amounts%20apply.

For further information contact:

Email: master-science@uva.nl

MacGillavry Fellowships

Purpose: These fellowships are available in the field of Biological Science and Biomedical Science, Earth Sciences (Physical Geography), Informatics and Logic, Physics, Chemistry, Astronomy, Mathematics, and Statistics
Eligibility: 1. A PhD degree in one of the scientific disciplines of their Faculty. 2. A scientific profile that links to one of the research fields eligible for application. 3. A publication record in international, high quality, peer-reviewed journals. 4. A few years of postdoctoral experience, preferably at the international level. 5. Well-developed organizational and communication skills. 6. Affinity for teaching at the undergraduate and graduate level
Level of Study: Postgraduate
Type: Fellowship
Value: The annual salary range for an assistant professor, including annual holiday allowance and the bonus is between €50,755 and €78,935 (before tax), depending on experience and past performance
Frequency: Annual
Country of Study: Any country
Application Procedure: To apply for the MacGillavry Fellowship you are invited to use the application form on the MacGillavry website of the Faculty of Science. www.uva.nl/en/faculty/faculty-of-science/macgillavry-fellowship/macgillavry-fellowship.html
Closing Date: 4 February
Funding: Private
Additional Information: www.uva.nl/en/about-the-uva/organisation/faculties/faculty-of-science/working-at-the-faculty/macgillavry-fellowship/macgillavry-fellowship.html

For further information contact:

Email: servicedesk-icts@uva.nl

University of Antwerp

Prinsstraat 13, B-2000 Antwerp, Belgium.

Tel: (32) 3 265 41 11
Email: internationalstudents@uantwerpen.be
Website: www.uantwerpen.be/en/

The Flemish Ministry of Education awards scholarships to outstanding students for Master programmes in Flanders and Brussels. The Master Mind programme aims to promote Flanders and Brussels as a top study destination. Students cannot apply directly. Applications need to be submitted by the Flemish host institution. The deadline for applications to the University of Antwerp is 1 March. Applications have to be done online through Mobility Online.

Master Mind Scholarships

Purpose: The Flemish Ministry of Education awards scholarships to outstanding students for Master programmes in Flanders and Brussels. The programme aims to promote Flanders and Brussels as a top study destination.
Eligibility: The applicant applies to study a Master degree programme at the University of Antwerp. The applicant should have a high standard of academic performance and/or potential. This means: 1. The student has a Grade Point Average (GPA) of 3.5 out of 4.0. You can use the GPA calculator here. 2. The student has a good knowledge of the English language, proven by one of the following situations: a. an overall band score of minimum 7.0 on the IELTS test. b. a minimum total score of 94 on a TOEFL test; a C1 level of the Common European Framework of Reference. c. a similar result in another official language test. d. or an exemption provided by the Master programme's Selection Committee.
Level of Study: Masters Degree
Type: Scholarships
Value: €8,400 + a tuition fee waiver per academic year
Frequency: Annual
Country of Study: Belgium
Application Procedure: The University of Antwerp screens all applicants and submits a shortlist of 20 candidates for the scholarship. The Flemish Government makes the final selection on the basis of this shortlist. To apply for the Master Mind scholarship, students need to complete the following steps: 1. Complete your application and upload all documents for the relevant Master programme at the University of Antwerp.

2. Click the link below to read more about the Admission and enrolment procedure. Please do not forget to upload your English test scores! 3. During your application indicate that you would also like to apply for the Master Mind Scholarship. In your motivation text, clearly specify why you are applying for the Master Mind scholarship and why you should be selected. Please address every selection criterium. In addition, specify your GPA score. 4. Applications without a motivation text will not be considered. Application process for candidates who do not need to submit a Master application in Mobility Online (previous degree from Wallonia, Netherlands or Luxembourg) or those currently enrolled in a preparatory or bridge programme at the University of Antwerp Please submit your application directly to the Master programme you are applying for. Your application should include a motivation letter addressing the selection criteria and clearly specifying your language test and GPA scores.
No. of awards offered: 30
Closing Date: 1 March
Additional Information: www.uantwerpen.be/en/study/scholarships/scholarships-with-uantwerp-participation/master-mind/

University of Auckland

Private Bag 92019, Auckland 1142, New Zealand.

Tel: (64) 9 373 7599
Email: alumni@auckland.ac.nz
Website: www.auckland.ac.nz
Contact: Ms S Codhersides, HR Manager

Anne Bellam Scholarship

Purpose: To assist students to further their musical education overseas.
Eligibility: The candidate must be under 30 years of age and a citizen of New Zealand, must have completed or will complete in the year of application any degree or diploma in performance or any postgraduate music degree at the University of Auckland.
Level of Study: Postgraduate
Type: Scholarship
Value: Up to NZ$30,000 for study overseas and up to NZ$20,000 for study at the University of Auckland
Length of Study: 1 year
Frequency: Annual
Study Establishment: University of Auckland
Country of Study: New Zealand
Application Procedure: Scholarship applications will usually open around six weeks before the closing date. Please read the regulations carefully to be sure you are eligible before you apply.
No. of awards offered: Varies
Closing Date: 1 November
Funding: Government
Additional Information: www.auckland.ac.nz/en/study/scholarships-and-awards/find-a-scholarship/anne-bellam-scholarship-68-cai.html

For further information contact:

Faculty of Creative Arts and Industries, School of Music, University of Auckland, Private Bag 92019, Auckland 1000, New Zealand.

Email: scholarships@auckland.ac.nz

Arthington Davy Scholarship

Purpose: To study and research in areas which will significantly contribute to the development of Tonga
Eligibility: The candidate must be a Tongan citizen, born to Tongan parents and possess a first University degree
Level of Study: Research
Type: Scholarship
Value: The Arthington Davy Scholarship may cover the cost of part of the cost of a postgraduate study or research programme
Study Establishment: Trinity College
Country of Study: United Kingdom
Application Procedure: The candidate must submit a complete curriculum vitae and academic record, proof of Tongan origin, details of the intended postgraduate study preferably with a letter of conditional acceptance from the University concerned, full details of tuition fees and living expenses and of finances available from the student's own resources or elsewhere and the names of two academic referees
Closing Date: 31 May
Funding: Commercial, Foundation, Individuals, Private
Additional Information: www.auckland.ac.nz/en/study/international-students/scholarships-loans-and-funding/country-specific-scholarships-and-funding0/tonga/arthington-davy-scholarship.html

For further information contact:

Tutor for Advanced Students, Trinity College, Cambridge CB2 1TQ, United Kingdom.

Email: gradtutor@trin.cam.ac.uk

Asian Development Bank Japan Scholarship

Purpose: The aim is to provide an opportunity for well-qualified citizens of ADB's developing member countries to undertake postgraduate studies in economics, management, science and technology, and other development-related fields at participating academic institutions in the Asia-Pacific region.
Eligibility: 1. Be a national of an ADB borrowing member. 2. Have gained admission to an approved masters at an approved academic institution. 3. Have a bachelors degree or its equivalent with a superior academic record. 4. Have at least two years of full-time professional work experience (acquired after a university degree) at the time of application. 5. Be proficient in oral and written English communication skills to be able to pursue studies. 6. Be under 35 years old at the time of application. In exceptional cases, for programmes which are appropriate for senior officials and managers, the age limit is 45 years. 7. Be in good health. 8. Agree to return to your home country after completing the programme.
Level of Study: Postgraduate
Type: Scholarship
Value: Tuition fee at the University of Auckland, Airfare from his or her home country to Auckland, New Zealand, Basic cost of living in Auckland, Health and medical insurance in New Zealand, and Airfare from Auckland, New Zealand, to the scholar's home country at the conclusion of his or her course of study
Study Establishment: University of Auckland
Country of Study: New Zealand
Application Procedure: 1. Completed ADB-JSP Information Sheet 2. Completed ADB-JSP Application Form 3. Copy of your offer letter to the University of Auckland 4. Academic documentation - both academic transcripts and degree certificates 5. Certificate of Employment for the duration of employment issued by the company 6. Certificate of Income issued by the company 7. Certificate of Family Income issued by the company. Must be either your parents or spouses annual/monthly income. 8. Copy of your Passport 9. Valid IELTS test
Closing Date: 21 July
Funding: Government, Private
Contributor: Asian Development Bank and Government of Japan
Additional Information: https://www.scholars4dev.com/12017/adb-scholarships-at-univeristy-of-auckland/

For further information contact:

Private Bag 92019, Auckland 1142, New Zealand.

Email: information@adbj.org

Beatrice Ratcliffe Postgraduate Scholarship in Music

Purpose: The main purpose of the Scholarship is to encourage and support students undertaking postgraduate study in the School of Music.
Level of Study: Postgraduate
Type: Scholarship
Value: Up to NZ$10,000
Length of Study: 1 year
Frequency: Annual
Country of Study: New Zealand
No. of awards offered: 1
Closing Date: 15 February
Additional Information: www.auckland.ac.nz/en/study/scholarships-and-awards/find-a-scholarship/beatrice-ratcliffe-postgraduate-scholarship-music-875-cai.html

For further information contact:

Email: scholarships@auckland.ac.nz

Commonwealth Scholarship

Purpose: The scholarships are available to students to be enroled at the University of Auckland for the Degree of Doctor of Philosophy; another approved Doctorate or a Master's degree
Eligibility: The candidate must be a citizen of Commonwealth of Nations, including Australian, British and Canadian citizens. The candidate must be tenable for a maximum of 36 months for a PhD candidate or 21 months for a Master's candidate
Level of Study: Doctorate, Postgraduate
Type: Scholarship
Value: Up to NZ$25,000 per year plus health insurance and fees at the domestic rate
Study Establishment: University of Auckland
Country of Study: New Zealand
Application Procedure: The candidate must send the application for UA Commonwealth Scholarships must be made through the appropriate organization in the scholar's home country on the Commonwealth Scholarship application form
Closing Date: 31 July
Funding: Government
Additional Information: www.auckland.ac.nz/en/study/scholarships-and-awards/find-a-scholarship/university-of-auckland-commonwealth-scholarship-266-all.html

For further information contact:

Email: scholarships@auckland.ac.nz

Doctoral Scholarships

Purpose: To assist and encourage students to pursue doctoral studies at The University of Auckland.
Eligibility: Any student who is to be offered a place in a doctoral programme will be eligible for scholarship consideration prior to receiving their offer of place.
Level of Study: Doctorate
Type: Scholarship
Value: NZ$33,000
Length of Study: 3 years
Frequency: Annual
Study Establishment: University of Auckland
Country of Study: New Zealand
Application Procedure: When you apply for a place at the University, you will have the opportunity to confirm whether or not you also wish to be considered for a University of Auckland Doctoral Scholarship — you don't need to apply separately.
Closing Date: 1 June
Funding: Government
Additional Information: www.auckland.ac.nz/en/study/scholarships-and-awards/scholarship-types/postgraduate-scholarships/doctoral-scholarships.html#schol-regs

For further information contact:

Email: scholarships@auckland.ac.nz

Dulcie Bowman Memorial Scholarship

Purpose: The main purpose of the Scholarship is to encourage hearing-impaired women students at either undergraduate or postgraduate levels.
Eligibility: Second or subsequent year of any year of postgraduate study
Level of Study: Postgraduate
Type: Scholarship
Value: Up to NZ$4,500 pa each
Length of Study: 1 year
Frequency: Annual
Country of Study: New Zealand
No. of awards offered: 2
Closing Date: 1 February
Additional Information: www.auckland.ac.nz/en/study/scholarships-and-awards/find-a-scholarship/dulcie-bowman-memorial-scholarship-96-all.html

For further information contact:

Email: scholarships@auckland.ac.nz

Fulbright Scholarship

Purpose: To encourage and facilitate study for approved postgraduate degrees at the University of Auckland by candidates already selected to hold Fulbright Awards.
Level of Study: Doctorate, Masters Degree
Type: Scholarship
Value: Up to NZ$33,000 pa for 2024 for a PhD and up to NZ$15,000 for Masters, plus compulsory fees and international health insurance.
Length of Study: For Masters up to 12 months and for PhD up to 2 years
Frequency: Annual
Study Establishment: University of Auckland
Country of Study: New Zealand
Application Procedure: Scholarship applications will usually open around six weeks before the closing date. Please read the regulations carefully to be sure you are eligible before you apply.
No. of awards offered: 3
Closing Date: 30 November
Funding: Government
Additional Information: www.auckland.ac.nz/en/study/scholarships-and-awards/find-a-scholarship/university-of-auckland-fulbright-scholarship-293-all.html

HC Russell Memorial Postgraduate Scholarship

Level of Study: Postgraduate, Predoctorate
Type: Scholarship
Value: Up to NZ$4,500 in total (MSc) or up to NZ$10,000 in total (PhD)
Length of Study: 3 years
Frequency: Annual
Country of Study: New Zealand
Application Procedure: Scholarship applications will usually open around six weeks before the closing date. Please read the regulations carefully to be sure you are eligible before you apply.
No. of awards offered: 1
Closing Date: 1 November
Additional Information: www.auckland.ac.nz/en/study/scholarships-and-awards/find-a-scholarship/hc-russell-memorial-postgraduate-scholarship-94-fmhs.html

Heather Leaity Memorial Award

Purpose: The main purpose of the Award is to recognise and encourage excellence in Marine Science research relating to sustainability and conservation.
Level of Study: Doctorate

Type: Scholarship
Value: NZ$1,000
Length of Study: 1 year
Frequency: Annual
Country of Study: New Zealand
Application Procedure: You do not need to apply for this scholarship, award or prize or complete an online application form. It is awarded on the recommendation of the relevant faculty or University of Auckland committee.
Additional Information: www.auckland.ac.nz/en/study/scholarships-and-awards/find-a-scholarship/heather-leaity-memorial-award-1051-sci.html

For further information contact:

Email: scholarships@auckland.ac.nz

Hope Selwyn Foundation Scholarship

Purpose: The HOPE Selwyn Foundation is a registered charitable trust established in 1996 to assist the funding of research and education essential to the health and welfare of older people in New Zealand.
Eligibility: 1. The purpose of the scholarships is to support or partially support the salaries of young scientists (the definition of "young" being reasonably flexible) who are in the early stages of their careers. 2. Candidates undertaking a Masters or doctoral thesis will be considered for support. Candidates will normally be working under supervision in a recognised research environment with a senior research leader. 3. HOPE Sewlyn Foundation scholarships may be held with any other bursary or award unless the candidate's other awards preclude this
Level of Study: Doctorate, Masters Degree
Type: Scholarship
Value: NZ$6,000 each
Length of Study: 1 year
Frequency: Annual
Country of Study: New Zealand
Application Procedure: Scholarship applications will usually open around six weeks before the closing date. Please read the regulations carefully to be sure you are eligible before you apply.
No. of awards offered: varies
Closing Date: 31 October
Funding: Foundation
Additional Information: www.auckland.ac.nz/en/study/scholarships-and-awards/find-a-scholarship/hope-foundation-research-on-ageing-scholarship-423-all.html

International College of Auckland PhD Scholarship in Plant Sciences

Purpose: To assist eminent Chinese scholars from nominated areas of China to study plant sciences at the University of Auckland and to promote links between China and New Zealand in the field of plant sciences
Eligibility: The candidate must possess a PhD in the field of plant science and who has paid the fees, or arranged to pay the fees, for full–time enrolment in the School of Biological Sciences
Level of Study: Postdoctorate
Type: Scholarship
Value: NZ$20,000 per year. The scholarship's emolument will be paid as a tuition/compulsory fees credit and the balance as a fortnightly stipend
Length of Study: 3 years
Frequency: Annual
Study Establishment: University of Auckland
Country of Study: New Zealand
Application Procedure: The candidate must submit the completed application form along with the curriculum vitae and at least two academic reference letters
Closing Date: 1 October
Funding: Government
Contributor: The International College of Auckland

For further information contact:

Email: scholarships@auckland.ac.nz

Māori and Pacific Graduate Scholarships (Masters/Honours/PGDIP)

Purpose: The Scholarship is offered each semester to Māori students enrolled in any Masters or postgraduate level Bachelors (Honours) degree, or any Postgraduate Diploma.
Eligibility: The University assesses your eligibility when you submit an Application for Admission. You will be advised of your eligibility once we have received your final grades and you have a firm offer of place for your chosen programme.
Level of Study: Postgraduate
Type: Scholarship
Value: NZ$13,655
Length of Study: 1 year
Frequency: Annual
Country of Study: New Zealand
Application Procedure: When you apply for a place at the University, you will automatically be considered for a University of Auckland Māori Postgraduate Scholarship—you don't need to apply separately.

No. of awards offered: Varies
Additional Information: www.auckland.ac.nz/en/study/scholarships-and-awards/scholarship-types/postgraduate-scholarships/maori-postgraduate-scholarships.html

Marie Clay Literacy Trust Literacy Learning Research Award

Purpose: The main purpose of the Award is to support an international or domestic doctoral student in the Faculty of Education and Social Work undertaking research which promotes literacy learning of the lowest achievers in primary schools in Aotearoa New Zealand.
Eligibility: Scholarship applications will usually open around six weeks before the closing date. Please read the regulations carefully to be sure you are eligible before you apply.
Level of Study: Doctorate, Predoctorate
Type: Scholarship
Value: Up to NZ$10,000 each
Length of Study: 1 year
Frequency: Annual
Country of Study: New Zealand
Closing Date: 11 July
Additional Information: www.auckland.ac.nz/en/study/scholarships-and-awards/find-a-scholarship/marie-clay-literacy-trust-literacy-learning-research-award-823-esw.html

For further information contact:

Email: scholarships@auckland.ac.nz

Masters/Honours/PGDIP Scholarships

Purpose: The Scholarship was established by the Dean of Arts in December 1994, and is offered annually to meritorious students enrolled for an approved masters degree, an approved Bachelors Honours degree, or an approved Postgraduate Diploma in the Faculty of Arts.
Eligibility: The candidate must be a citizen or a permanent resident of New Zealand. In case of a Master's degree, the candidate must be tenable until the date for completion of the requirements for the degree as specified in the General Regulations – Masters degrees
Level of Study: Graduate, Postgraduate
Type: Scholarship
Value: Up to NZ$10,000 per year including compulsory fees
Length of Study: 1 year
Frequency: Annual
Study Establishment: University of Auckland
Country of Study: New Zealand
Application Procedure: You do not need to apply for this scholarship, award or prize or complete an online application form. It is awarded on the recommendation of the relevant faculty or University of Auckland committee.
Funding: Government
Additional Information: www.auckland.ac.nz/en/study/scholarships-and-awards/find-a-scholarship/faculty-of-arts-masters-honours-pgdip-scholarship-50-art.html

For further information contact:

Email: scholarships@auckland.ac.nz

Mercer Memorial Scholarship in Aeronautics

Level of Study: Postgraduate
Type: Scholarship
Value: Up to NZ$6,000
Length of Study: 1 year
Frequency: Annual
Country of Study: New Zealand
Application Procedure: Scholarship website: aucklandscholars.communityforce.com/Funds/FundDetails.aspx?2B336C5030514338437752356A4D544E34392F54735773633033753434653446724D6E4D5638646D48733931765375766B2B54525942386741516E2F79766674
No. of awards offered: 1
Closing Date: 21 March
Additional Information: www.auckland.ac.nz/en/study/scholarships-and-awards/find-a-scholarship/mercer-memorial-scholarship-in-aeronautics-143-eng.html

New Zealand Agency for International Development Scholarship (NZDS) – Open Category

Eligibility: The candidate must possess minimum English language requirements for entry into the University of Auckland postgraduate study. IELTS (International English Language Testing System Certificate) with an overall score of 6.5 and no band less than 6.0 or a TOEFL (Test of English as a Foreign Language) paper based 575 with a TWE of 4.5 or computer based 233
Level of Study: Postgraduate
Type: Scholarship
Value: Tuition, enrollment/orientation fees, return economy fare travel, medical insurance and provision for students to meet course and basic living costs
Frequency: Annual
Study Establishment: University of Auckland
Country of Study: New Zealand

Application Procedure: Application form can be downloaded from the website
Closing Date: 1 June
Funding: Government
Contributor: New Zealand Agency for International Development and the Ministry of Foreign Affairs

For further information contact:

Tel: (64) 9 373 7599 ext 87556
Fax: (64) 9 373 7405
Email: rfatialofa.patolo@auckland.ac.nz

New Zealand International Doctoral Research (NZIDRS) Scholarship

Purpose: To provide financial support for postgraduate students from designated countries seeking doctoral degrees by research in New Zealand universities
Eligibility: The candidate must hold an A' average or equivalent in their studies, meet the requirements for entry into a research-based doctoral degree programme at a New Zealand university
Level of Study: Doctorate, Research
Type: Research scholarship
Value: Living allowance (NZ$25,000 per year), a travel allowance (NZ$2,000), a health insurance allowance (NZ$500), and a book and thesis allowance (NZ$800)
Length of Study: 3 years
Study Establishment: University of Auckland
Country of Study: New Zealand
Application Procedure: The candidate must complete the application form in English and attach supporting documents as stipulated in the application form
Closing Date: 16 July
Funding: Government
Contributor: Government of New Zealand

For further information contact:

Tel: (64) 4 472 0788
Fax: (64) 4 471 2828
Email: scholarships@educationnz.org.nz

Property Institute of New Zealand Postgraduate Scholarship

Purpose: The main purpose of the Award is to promote postgraduate study in the field of real property.
Eligibility: The candidate must possess a Master's degree or full-time PhD candidate and has the paid the fees, or arranged to pay the fees, for study in the Department of Property at Lincoln University, Massey University or The University of Auckland
Level of Study: Doctorate, Masters Degree
Type: Scholarship
Value: Up to NZ$2,000
Length of Study: 1 year
Frequency: Annual
Study Establishment: University of Auckland
Country of Study: New Zealand
No. of awards offered: 1
Funding: Government
Contributor: Property Institute of New Zealand
Additional Information: www.auckland.ac.nz/en/study/scholarships-and-awards/find-a-scholarship/property-institute-of-new-zealand-postgraduate-award-369-bus.html

For further information contact:

Tel: (64) 9 373 7599 ext 87494
Fax: (64) 9 308 2309
Email: scholarships@auckland.ac.nz

Reardon Postgraduate Scholarship in Music

Purpose: The main purpose of the Scholarship is to encourage and support postgraduate study in Music performance.
Eligibility: The candidate must possess a degree or diploma with a specialization in Performance in the year of the award
Level of Study: Postgraduate
Type: Scholarship
Value: NZ$8,000
Length of Study: 1 year
Frequency: Annual
Study Establishment: University of Auckland
Country of Study: New Zealand
No. of awards offered: 1
Closing Date: 1 November
Funding: Government
Contributor: Reardon Memorial Music Trust
Additional Information: www.auckland.ac.nz/en/study/scholarships-and-awards/find-a-scholarship/reardon-postgraduate-scholarship-in-music-74-cai.html

Senior Health Research Scholarships

Purpose: The main purpose of the Scholarship is to provide financial support so that health professionals can return to the University to study for a doctorate in health related areas.
Eligibility: The candidate must be a citizen or a permanent resident of New Zealand and who have worked for 3 years as a health professional
Level of Study: Doctorate

Type: Scholarship
Value: NZ$40,000 plus compulsory fees
Length of Study: 3 years
Frequency: Annual
Study Establishment: University of Auckland
Country of Study: New Zealand
Application Procedure: The candidate must submit an application form and send it to the Scholarships office. Selection shall be made on the basis of merit
No. of awards offered: 3
Funding: Government
Additional Information: www.auckland.ac.nz/en/study/scholarships-and-awards/find-a-scholarship/university-of-auckland-senior-health-research-scholarship-382-fmhs.html

The AUT Queen Elizabeth II Diamond Jubilee Doctoral Scholarship

Purpose: AUT Doctoral Scholarship AUT aims to Develop an internationally-aware, skilled future leader Establish enduring education and professional linkages
Eligibility: 1. The scholarship will be awarded annually to a doctoral student who is a citizen, and resident in, one of the following Pacific countries; Cook Islands, Fiji, Kiribati, Nauru, Niue, Papua New Guinea, Samoa, Solomon Islands, Tokelau, Tonga and Vanuatu to carry out doctoral study at AUT University. 2. Applicants must be a citizen and resident of one of the eligible countries. Applicants may not have citizenship or permanent residence status of New Zealand or any other developed country. Applicants who are New Zealand citizens from the Cook Islands, Niue, Tokelau and dual citizens of Samoa are exempt from this requirement; however, they must reside in the Cook Islands, Nuie, Tokelau or Samoa or another eligible country. Preference may be given to those applicants who have also been schooled in an eligible country. 3. The recipients of this scholarship will have strong academic references plus a strong academic record and/or have demonstrated the potential for quality research. Previous study should include research methodologies papers and an independent research project, including the writing of a report on that research
Level of Study: Postgraduate
Type: Scholarship
Value: NZ$25,000 annual stipend tuition fees and student services levies
Length of Study: 1 year
Frequency: Annual
Country of Study: New Zealand
Application Procedure: Application will be via the online scholarship application portal available from the link. It is not possible to submit incomplete scholarship applications through the online application process. In order for the application to be submitted all requested documentation must be included. The following documents or statements must be completed and uploaded in the application portal by the closing date. Incomplete applications will not be forwarded to the selection panel. 1. AUT Queen Elizabeth II Diamond Jubilee Doctoral Scholarship on-line application form. 2. Academic transcript(s) if any previous tertiary study has been completed at a university other than AUT. 3. A certified copy of the applicant's birth certificate or passport. 4. Two referee's reports are required. Applicants must not submit referee's reports directly. Nominated referees will be sent a request directly by the on-line application system. Please advise your referees that they will be receiving an email requesting a reference statement and that this must be submitted by the closing date or your application will be ineligible. If the referee declines to provide a reference before the closing date you will be able to nominate another referee. 5. A two page statement (maximum 1,000 words) outlining the applicant's research proposal using the template provided with the online application form. Please note this must be two pages only (plus one page for references). If a longer document is provided you will be asked to rewrite it. 6. Written support from the proposed primary supervisor if they have not acted as one of the referees above. 7. A brief C.V. (maximum three pages)
Closing Date: 1 November
Funding: Private
Additional Information: The scholarship is available every three years only. www.aut.ac.nz/study/fees-and-scholarships/scholarships-and-awards-at-aut/scholarships-database/detailpage?detailCode=500675&sessionID=32593825&sourceIP=&X_FORWARDED_FOR=scholarshipdb.net/scholarships-in-New-Zealand/The-Aut-Queen-Elizabeth-Ii-Diamond-Jubilee-Doctoral-Scholarship-Auckland-University-Of-Technology=Tc65tBC06BGUVQAlkGUTnw.html

For further information contact:

55 Wellesley St E, Auckland 1010, New Zealand.

Tel: (64) 9 921 9837
Email: scholars@aut.ac.nz

U

The Jackson Family Foundation Scholarship

Purpose: The main purpose of the Scholarship is to assist women students of Cook Island descent, who are experiencing challenging personal, family or financial circumstances that may prevent them from undertaking full-time study.
Eligibility: Women students of Cook Island descent enrolled in full-time study in any year of a postgraduate degree
Level of Study: Postgraduate
Type: Scholarship
Value: Up to NZ$11,000 pa

Length of Study: 1 year
Frequency: Annual
Country of Study: New Zealand
No. of awards offered: 4
Closing Date: 1 February
Additional Information: www.auckland.ac.nz/en/study/scholarships-and-awards/find-a-scholarship/the-jackson-family-foundation-scholarship-750-all.html

The Kate Edger Educational Charitable Trust Masters Degree Award

Purpose: The main purpose of the Award is to assist women graduates to carry out study for a masters degree at the University of Auckland.
Level of Study: Postgraduate
Type: Award
Value: Up to NZ$8,000
Length of Study: 1 year
Frequency: Annual
Country of Study: New Zealand
No. of awards offered: 8
Closing Date: 24 January
Additional Information: www.auckland.ac.nz/en/study/scholarships-and-awards/find-a-scholarship/the-kate-edger-educational-charitable-trust-masters-degree-award-787-all.html

The Kate Edger Educational Charitable Trust Vinka Marinovich Award in Music

Purpose: The main purpose of the Award is to support women enrolled in undergraduate or postgraduate study in the School of Music at the University of Auckland.
Level of Study: Doctorate, Postgraduate
Type: Award
Value: Up to NZ$8,000
Length of Study: 1 year
Frequency: Annual
Country of Study: New Zealand
Application Procedure: Scholarship website: aucklandscholars.communityforce.com/Funds/FundDetails.aspx?306D773059326330666D636F426873526F4876504B686A6A7A465A657267612B415671506C7770667A6C77474C302B6F4E5A447551685139487749626C2B734B
No. of awards offered: 2
Closing Date: 24 March
Additional Information: www.auckland.ac.nz/en/study/scholarships-and-awards/find-a-scholarship/the-kate-edger-trust-vinka-marinovich-award-music-912-cai.html

The University of Auckland International Doctoral Fees Bursary

Purpose: To assist international students from all countries who wish to pursue doctoral studies
Eligibility: Permanent citizens and residents of Australia and New Zealand are not eligible for the scholarship
Level of Study: Doctorate
Type: Bursary
Value: NZ$25,000
Frequency: Annual
Study Establishment: University of Auckland
Country of Study: New Zealand
Application Procedure: The application form can be obtained from the Scholarships Office, University of Auckland
Closing Date: 1 August
Funding: Government

University of Auckland International Doctoral Scholarship

Purpose: To assist international students from all countries who wish to pursue doctoral studies.
Eligibility: Any student who is to be offered a place in a doctoral programme will be eligible for scholarship consideration prior to receiving their offer of place.
Level of Study: Doctorate
Type: Scholarship
Value: NZ$$33,000
Frequency: Annual
Study Establishment: University of Auckland
Country of Study: New Zealand
Application Procedure: When you apply for a place at the University, you will have the opportunity to confirm whether or not you also wish to be considered for a University of Auckland Doctoral Scholarship — you don't need to apply separately.
Closing Date: 1 June
Funding: Government
Additional Information: www.auckland.ac.nz/en/study/scholarships-and-awards/scholarship-types/postgraduate-scholarships/doctoral-scholarships.html

University of Auckland International Student Excellence Scholarship

Purpose: The main purpose of the Scholarship is to attract new international students of high calibre to enrol in undergraduate or postgraduate taught study of one year or more at the University of Auckland.
Level of Study: Postgraduate

Type: Scholarship
Value: Up to NZ$10,000 for postgraduate study
Length of Study: 1 year
Frequency: Twice a year
Country of Study: New Zealand
Closing Date: 21 November
Additional Information: www.auckland.ac.nz/en/study/scholarships-and-awards/find-a-scholarship/university-of-auckland-international-student-excellence-scholarship-844-all.html

For further information contact:

Email: scholarships@auckland.ac.nz

University of Auckland Research Masters Scholarships

Eligibility: 1. The University assesses your eligibility when you submit an Application for Admission. You will be advised of your eligibility once we have received your final grades and you have a firm offer of place for your chosen programme. 2. Students previously awarded a University of Auckland Honours/PGDip Scholarship cannot subsequently be awarded a University of Auckland Research Masters Scholarship.
Level of Study: Masters Degree
Type: Scholarship
Value: NZ$13,655
Frequency: Annual
Country of Study: New Zealand
Application Procedure: Don't need to apply separately. Scholarship offers will be made soon after the confirmation of a place.
Additional Information: www.auckland.ac.nz/en/study/scholarships-and-awards/scholarship-types/postgraduate-scholarships/research-masters-scholarships.html

University of Auckland Business School

School of Business & Economics, Private Bag 92019, Auckland 1142, New Zealand.

Tel: (64) 9 373 7599
Email: alumni@auckland.ac.nz
Website: www.business.auckland.ac.nz
Contact: Dr Gary Cayton, Director MBA

Kupe Leadership Scholarships

Purpose: The Kupe Leadership Programme will involve a three-day Orientation in early March; two two-day workshops held during each mid-semester break; a one-day workshop in the inter-semester break and a concluding day-long workshop in November
Eligibility: The Kupe Leadership alumni will develop a reputation for embodying these values and for contributions they make, nationally and possibly internationally
Level of Study: Postgraduate
Type: Scholarship
Value: Scholars will receive either a NZ$22,000 stipend OR a NZ$10,000 stipend plus on-campus self-catered studio accommodation at 55 Symonds Street up to a total value of around NZ$25,000.
Length of Study: 1 year
Frequency: Annual
Country of Study: New Zealand
Closing Date: 30 August
Funding: Private
Additional Information: www.auckland.ac.nz/en/study/scholarships-and-awards/scholarship-types/postgraduate-scholarships/kupe-leadership-scholarships.html

For further information contact:

Tel: (64) 800 61 62 63
Email: pc.dasilva@auckland.ac.nz

University of Auckland Executive MBA Programme

Eligibility: To be eligible to apply for admission to the University of Auckland MBA you must have: 1. A relevant bachelors degree from a recognised university with a GPA/GPE of 5.0 or higher in at least 90 points in the most advanced courses. 2. Or have completed the Postgraduate Diploma in Business in Administration, or equivalent, with a GPA/GPE of 5.0 or higher. 3. Or a relevant bachelors degree and a Postgraduate Certificate in Business from this University with a GPA of 5.0 or higher.
Level of Study: Postgraduate
Type: Scholarship
Value: Indicative fees for the 180-point MBA for domestic students are NZ$43,727.45 (plus approximately NZ$2,500 for parking and textbooks etc and a Student Services Fee estimated at NZ$1,271 for 180 points).
Length of Study: Varies
Frequency: Other
Country of Study: New Zealand

Application Procedure: Scholarship website: iam.auckland.ac.nz/profile/SAML2/Redirect/SSO?execution=e1s1
Closing Date: 1 August
Additional Information: www.auckland.ac.nz/en/study/study-options/find-a-study-option/master-of-business-administration-mba.html

For further information contact:

Email: international@auckland.ac.nz

University of Bath

Claverton Down, Bath BA2 7AY, United Kingdom.

Tel: (44) 1225 388388
Website: www.bath.ac.uk
Contact: University of Bath

The University of Bath received its Royal Charter in 1966 and is now firmly established as a top ten United Kingdom university with a reputation for research and teaching excellence.

United Kingdom-India Year of Culture Great Postgraduate Scholarships

Purpose: The University of Bath is currently accepting applications for United Kingdom-India Year of Culture GREAT Scholarships. This scholarship is available to the international fee-paying student from India studying a full-time taught postgraduate masters programme
Eligibility: Indian students are eligible to apply for this scholarship. For most programmes, the requirement for non-native English speakers is 6.5 in the IELTS Academic English test, with no less than 6.0 in any element
Type: Postgraduate scholarships
Value: If you are an international fee-paying student you could be eligible for one of ten United Kingdom-India Year of Culture GREAT Scholarships each worth £5,000
Study Establishment: Scholarships are awarded in the Faculty of Humanities and Social Sciences, Faculty of Engineering and Design and in the Faculty of Science
Country of Study: United Kingdom
Application Procedure: If you are eligible for the scholarship scheme, we will let you know and invite you to apply. Queries for MSc students should be addressed to msc-mn-at-bath.ac.uk and for MBA students to mbaapps-at-management.bath.ac.uk
Closing Date: 1 June

University of Bern

Hochschulstrasse 6, CH-3012 Bern, Switzerland.

Tel: (41) 31 684 81 11
Email: info@imd.unibe.ch
Website: www.unibe.ch/

The University of Bern offers top quality teaching, special recognition in leading–edge disciplines, and a campus environment intimately linked to the social, economic, and political life of the city. The university's comprehensive offering includes 8 faculties and some 160 institutes with 12,500 students. Its academic and research organization prides itself on its interdisciplinarity. The university is actively involved in a wide range of European and worldwide research projects.

Excellence Scholarships for Postgraduate Study

Purpose: Scholarship for international students
Eligibility: Applicants must, by end of July, have graduated with at least a Bachelor's degree in the same field of study as the selected Master's programme and must be residing in their home country. The criteria for selection are previous academic excellence and the potential of the candidate
Level of Study: Graduate
Type: Scholarship
Value: CHF 1,600 per month for the entire duration of the course
Frequency: Annual
Country of Study: Any country
Application Procedure: Check website for specific details
Closing Date: 21 December
Funding: Commercial

For further information contact:

Tel: (41) 31 631 80 49
Email: claudine.rossi@int.unibe.ch

UniBE International

Purpose: To support for young researchers and to the university's internationalization
Level of Study: Doctorate, Postgraduate
Length of Study: 3 years
Study Establishment: University of Bern
Country of Study: Switzerland

Application Procedure: Please email your application including any related documents as one pdf to lenka.fehrenbach@entwicklung.unibe.ch
Closing Date: 17 May
Contributor: Swiss National Fund (SNF)
Additional Information: www.unibe.ch/university/organization/executive_board_and_central_administration/vice_rectorate_development/unibe_international/index_eng.html

For further information contact:

Hochschulstrasse 4, CH-3012 Bern, Switzerland.

Tel: (41) 31 684 41 75
Email: info.int@unibe.ch

University of Bologna

Via Zamboni, 33, I-40126 Bologna, Italy.

Tel: (39) 51 2088101
Website: www.unibo.it/

The origins of the University of Bologna go way back, and it is considered to be the oldest university in the Western world. Its history is intertwined with that of the great names of science and literature, it is a keystone and a point of reference for European culture.

University of Bologna Study Grants for International Students

Purpose: The University of Bologna awards study grants and full tuition fee waivers to deserving international students who wish to register for First, Single, and Second Cycle Degree Programmes at the University of Bologna for A.Y. 2024/2025.
Eligibility: You can apply for Unibo Action 1 & 2 if 1. you are in possession of (or about to obtain) a valid qualification for access to your chosen degree programme, issued by an Institution outside of the Italian education system. Students holding a diploma issued by an Italian school established outside Italy can apply as well. 2. you will take one of the following tests by the application deadline 2a. if you are interested in registering in a First or Single Cycle Degree Programme, the SAT and/or TOLC test; 2b. if you are interested in registering in a Second Cycle Degree Programme, the GRE test. 3. You are less than 30 years old upon the deadline of the call for application.
Level of Study: Bachelors/Masters Degree
Type: Scholarships
Value: Each Unibo Action 2 study grants are awarded for one academic year only and amounts to a total of €11.000, gross of all charges for the beneficiary account. Each Unibo Action 1 full tuition waivers are awarded for one academic year only.
Country of Study: Italy
Application Procedure: Applications must be submitted by 31 March (Second Cycle Programmes) or 29 April (First or Single Cycle Programmes), exclusively through Studenti Online, as explained in the call for applications. It is important to read the Call for Applications (GRE) or Call for Applications (SAT) and visit the official website (link found below) to access the online application system and for detailed information on how to apply for this scholarship.
Closing Date: 30 April
Additional Information: www.unibo.it/en/services-and-opportunities/study-grants-and-subsidies/exemptions-and-incentives/unibo-actions-1-2-study-grants-and-tuition-fee-waivers-for-international-students

For further information contact:

Via Filippo Re, 4, I-40126 Bologna, Italy.

Tel: (39) 51 2082550
Email: internationaldesk@unibo.it

University of Bristol

University of Bristol, Beacon House, Queens Road, Bristol BS8 1QU, United Kingdom.

Tel: (44) 117 928 9000
Email: student-funding@bris.ac.uk
Website: www.bristol.ac.uk
Contact: Ms Penny Rowe, Student Funding Advisor

The University of Bristol is committed to providing high-quality teaching and research in all its designated fields.

Future Leaders Postgraduate Scholarship

Eligibility: You can apply if you: 1. have applied to start one of the qualifying management MSc programmes in September 2024: a. MSc Management. b. MSc Management (CSR and Sustainability). c. MSc Management (Digitalisation and Big Data). d. MSc Management (Entrepreneurship and Innovation). e. MSc Management (International Business).

f. MSc Management (International HRM). g. MSc Management (Marketing). h. MSc Management (Project Management). i. MSc Business Analytics. j. MSc Global Operations and Supply Chain Management. k. MSc Human Resource Management and the Future of Work. l. MSc International Business and Strategy: Global Challenges. m. MSc Marketing. n. MSc Social Science Research Methods (Management). 2. are classed as an overseas student for fee purposes.
Level of Study: Postgraduate
Type: Scholarships
Value: Four scholarships of £13,000 and eight scholarships of £6,500 per year are available.
Length of Study: 1 year
Frequency: Annual
Country of Study: United Kingdom
Application Procedure: Scholarship website: www.bristol.ac.uk/international/fees-finance/scholarships/application-guidance/
No. of awards offered: 12
Closing Date: 24 April
Additional Information: www.bristol.ac.uk/students/support/finances/scholarships/future-leaders-postgraduate-scholarship/

Global Accounting and Finance Scholarship

Purpose: The Department of Accounting and Finance is offering eight scholarships worth £5,000 each to eligible international students studying for a postgraduate qualification in Accounting and Finance.
Eligibility: You can apply if you: 1. have applied to start one of the qualifying accounting and finance MSc programmes in September 2024: a. MSc Accounting and Finance. b. MSc Accounting, Finance and Management. c. MSc Banking, Regulation and Financial Stability. d. MSc Finance and Investment. 2. are classed as an overseas student for fee purposes.
Level of Study: Postgraduate
Type: Scholarship
Value: Four scholarships of £13,000 and eight scholarships of £6,500 per year are available.
Length of Study: 1 year
Frequency: Annual
Country of Study: United Kingdom
Application Procedure: Scholarship website: www.bristol.ac.uk/international/fees-finance/scholarships/application-guidance/
No. of awards offered: 12
Closing Date: 24 April
Funding: Private
Additional Information: www.bristol.ac.uk/students/support/finances/scholarships/global-accounting-finance/

Global Economics Postgraduate Scholarship

Purpose: The Department of Economics is offering five scholarships worth £5,000 each to eligible international students studying for a postgraduate qualification in Economics.
Eligibility: You can apply if you: 1. have applied to start one of the qualifying economics master's programmes in September 2024: a. MSc Economics. b. MSc Economics, Finance and Management. c. MSc Economics and Finance. d. MRes Economics. 2. are classed as an overseas student for fee purposes.
Level of Study: Postgraduate
Type: Scholarship
Value: Two scholarships of £13,000 per year and fifteen scholarships of £6,500 per year are available.
Length of Study: 1 year
Frequency: Annual
Country of Study: United Kingdom
Application Procedure: Scholarship website: www.bristol.ac.uk/international/fees-finance/scholarships/application-guidance/
No. of awards offered: 17
Closing Date: 24 April
Funding: Private
Additional Information: www.bristol.ac.uk/students/support/finances/scholarships/global-economics-pg/

International Postgraduate Scholarships – Taught Master's Programmes

Purpose: This programme provides plenty of offers for future research postgraduate researchers with access to studentships, supervision from world-class experts and excellent facilities on our PhD and doctoral programmes
Eligibility: Open to candidates holding an offer for a 1 year taught postgraduate programme at the University of Bristol
Level of Study: Postgraduate
Type: Scholarship (MSc)
Value: £2,000
Length of Study: 1 year
Frequency: Annual
Study Establishment: University of Bristol
Country of Study: United Kingdom
Application Procedure: Check website for further details
Closing Date: 30 June
Funding: Private

For further information contact:

International Recruitment Office, University of Bristol Union, Queens Road, Bristol BS8 1ND, United Kingdom.

Email: iro@bristol.ac.uk

Michael Wong Pakshong Bursary

Eligibility: You can apply if you are: 1. classed as an overseas student for fee purposes. 2. have applied to start a full-time one-year master's programme in the Faculty of Social Sciences and Law in September 2024.
Level of Study: Postgraduate
Type: Bursary
Value: £3,000
Length of Study: 1 year
Frequency: Annual
Country of Study: United Kingdom
Application Procedure: Scholarship website: www.bristol.ac.uk/international/fees-finance/scholarships/application-guidance/
No. of awards offered: 1
Closing Date: 24 April
Additional Information: www.bristol.ac.uk/students/support/finances/scholarships/wong-pakshong-bursary/

Phyllis Mary Morris Bursaries

Purpose: Phyllis Mary Morris née Doidge graduated with a degree in Geography in 1930.
Eligibility: You can apply if you are: 1. classed as an overseas student for fee purposes. 2. have applied to start a full-time postgraduate taught programme in the School of Geographical Sciences for 2024.
Level of Study: Postgraduate
Type: Bursary
Value: £2,000 each. The bursary can only be used towards living costs.
Frequency: Annual
Country of Study: United Kingdom
Application Procedure: Scholarship website: www.bristol.ac.uk/international/fees-finance/scholarships/application-guidance/
No. of awards offered: 6
Closing Date: 24 April
Funding: Private
Additional Information: www.bristol.ac.uk/students/support/finances/scholarships/phyllis-mary-morris-bursaries/

For further information contact:

Tel: (44) 117 928 9000
Email: graduation-office@bristol.ac.uk

School for Policy Studies International Postgraduate Scholarships

Eligibility: You can apply if you: 1. have applied to start one of the qualifying courses in September 2024: a. MSc Nutrition, Physical Activity and Public Health. b. MSc Public Policy. c. MSc Public Policy Analysis. d. MSc Social Work. 2. are classed as an overseas student for fee purposes.
Level of Study: Postgraduate
Type: Scholarship
Value: £13,000 per year
Frequency: Annual
Country of Study: United Kingdom
Application Procedure: Scholarship website: www.bristol.ac.uk/international/fees-finance/scholarships/application-guidance/
No. of awards offered: 4
Closing Date: 24 April
Additional Information: www.bristol.ac.uk/students/support/finances/scholarships/sps-pg-international-scholarships/

Think Big About Innovation Scholarships

Eligibility: You can apply if you: 1. have applied to start one of the qualifying MSc programmes in September 2024: a. MSc Innovation and Entrepreneurship. b. MSc Business Innovation and Entrepreneurship. c. MSc Social Innovation and Entrepreneurship. d. MSc Technology Innovation and Entrepreneurship. e. MA Creative Innovation and Entrepreneurship. 2. are classed as an overseas student for fee purposes.
Level of Study: Masters Degree, Postgraduate
Type: Scholarship
Value: £6,500
Length of Study: 1 year
Frequency: Annual
Country of Study: United Kingdom
Application Procedure: Apply using the international scholarships online application form. You can find more details about this form in our guidance on how to apply for international scholarships.
No. of awards offered: 4
Closing Date: 24 April
Additional Information: www.bristol.ac.uk/students/support/finances/scholarships/think-big-innovation/

U

Think Big Postgraduate Scholarships

Subjects: Any full-time Undergraduate programme (except Medicine, Dentistry and Veterinary Science) or any one-year, full-time taught postgraduate programme offered at the University.
Purpose: Helping and nurturing global talent to produce the future leaders of tomorrow.
Eligibility: You can apply if you: 1. are an overseas student for fee purposes. 2. have applied to start any one-year, full-time master's programme, or one of our eligible two-year

programmes - Social Work (MSc) and Law (MA), starting in September 2024.
Level of Study: Postgraduate
Type: Scholarships
Value: Scholarship awards for postgraduate international students are valued at £6,500, £13,000 and £26,000 per year and can only be used towards the cost of tuition fees.
Frequency: Annual
Country of Study: United Kingdom
Application Procedure: Scholarship website: www.bristol.ac.uk/international/fees-finance/scholarships/application-guidance/
Closing Date: 24 April
Additional Information: www.bristol.ac.uk/students/support/finances/scholarships/think-big-postgraduate/

University of British Columbia (UBC)

2329 West Mall, Vancouver, BC V6T 1Z4, Canada.

Tel: (1) 604 822 2211
Email: graduate.awards@ubc.ca
Website: www.ubc.ca
Contact: Ms Jiffin Arboleda, Awards Administrator

The University of British Columbia (UBC) is one of North America's major research universities. The Faculty of Graduate Studies has 6,500 students and is a national leader in interdisciplinary study and research, with 98 departments, 18 interdisciplinary research units, 9 interdisciplinary graduate programmes, 2 graduate residential colleges and 1 scholarly journal.

Izaak Walton Killam Predoctoral Fellowships

Purpose: To assist doctoral students with full-time studies and research
Eligibility: Open to students of any nationality, discipline, age or sex. This award is given at the PhD level only and is strictly based on academic merit. Students must have a First Class standing in their last 2 years of study
Level of Study: Doctorate
Type: Fellowship
Value: CA$22,000 per year and CA$1,500 travel allowance for the duration of the award
Frequency: Annual
Study Establishment: UBC
Country of Study: Canada
Application Procedure: Top ranked students are selected from the University Graduate Fellowship competition. Application forms can be obtained from individual departments, the Faculty of Graduate Studies or the website. Students must submit their applications to the departments, not to the Faculty of Graduate Studies
No. of awards offered: 200
Funding: Private
No. of awards given last year: 12
No. of applicants last year: 200

For further information contact:

Email: gsaward@ucalgary.ca

Killam Doctoral Scholarships

Eligibility: To be eligible to apply for Killam Doctoral Scholarship funding, applicants must have completed no more than 24 months of doctoral study as of the start date of the scholarship. Therefore, applicants to the 2024-2025 competition must have completed no more than 24 months of doctoral study as of 1 September 2024.
Level of Study: Doctorate
Type: Scholarship
Value: CA$30,000 per annum for two years, CA$2,000 allowance for research-related travel during the 24 months of the scholarship, and tuition.
Length of Study: 24 months
Frequency: Annual
Country of Study: Canada
Application Procedure: The Killam Doctoral Scholarships are part of the Affiliated Fellowships-Doctoral award competition. To be considered for the Killam Doctoral Scholarships, you must apply for the Affiliated Fellowships-Doctoral award competition.
No. of awards offered: 25
Closing Date: September
Additional Information: www.grad.ubc.ca/awards/killam-doctoral-scholarships

University of British Columbia Graduate Fellowship (UGF)

Purpose: To assist graduate students with their studies and research
Eligibility: Academic Standing 1. A progress report evaluated as satisfactory by the College of Graduate Studies based on established, articulated criteria; Number of Months of Study 1. Master's students must have completed, as of April 30 of the adjudication year, no more than 24 months of study in the program for which they are requesting funding 2. PhD

students must have completed, as of April 30 of the adjudication year, no more than 48 months of study in the program for which they are requesting funding
Level of Study: Masters and Doctoral
Type: Fellowship
Value: Awarded in a minimum base unit of CA$3,000 to a maximum of CA$24,000
Frequency: Annual
Study Establishment: UBC
Country of Study: Canada
Application Procedure: Annual progress reports must be completed and signed by both the student and supervisor/advisor, reviewed by the program coordinator, and submitted to the College of Graduate Studies by June 1 of each year to qualify for the fellowship
No. of awards offered: Approx. 2,500
Closing Date: 1 June
No. of awards given last year: 460
No. of applicants last year: Approx. 2,500
Additional Information: Please check for internal departmental deadlines https://www.grad.ubc.ca/scholarships-awards-funding/award-opportunities

For further information contact:

Okanagan Campus, EME2121 - 1137 Alumni Ave, Kelowna, BC V1V 1V7, Canada.

Tel: (1) 250 807 8772
Fax: (1) 250 807 8799
Email: graduateawards.ok@ubc.ca

University of California at Los Angeles (UCLA) Center for India and South Asia

Department of History, 11248 Bunche Hall, Los Angeles, CA 90095-1487, United States of America.

Tel: (1) 310 825 4811
Email: info-intl@international.ucla.edu
Website: www.international.ucla.edu
Contact: Professor Sanjay Subrahmanyam, Chair of Indian History

The main thrust behind the creation of the UCLA Center for India and South Asia is to raise the profile of South Asia on campus and more generally in southern California. The organization aims at transforming UCLA into one of the leading poles of integrated research activity on India and South Asia in the country.

University of California, Los Angeles (UCLA) Sardar Patel Award

Purpose: To award the best dissertation submitted at any American university on the subject of modern India
Eligibility: Open to candidates who have written their dissertations while being enrolled at any accredited university in the United States
Level of Study: Research
Type: Award
Value: US$10,000
Frequency: Annual
Country of Study: Any country
Application Procedure: Applicants must submit 2 hard copies of their dissertation, 7 copies of abstract, a copy of their curriculum vitae and a letter from the dissertation supervisor
Closing Date: 15 October

For further information contact:

Email: cisa@international.ucla.edu

University of California Berkeley - Haas School

S440 Student Services Building, Suite 1902, Berkeley, CA 94720-1900, United States of America.

Tel: (1) 510 642 1405
Website: www.haas.berkeley.edu
Contact: MBA Admissions Officer

Hellman Fellows Fund

Purpose: The purpose of the Hellman Fellows Fund is to support substantially the research of promising assistant professors who show capacity for great distinction in their research
Eligibility: In determining the allocation of awards, the Chancellor will seek the counsel of a panel of faculty comprised of tenured Hellman Fellows and a member of the Academic Senate Committee on Research, chaired by the Vice Provost for the Faculty. Applications should therefore include an introductory description which is accessible to someone who is not an expert in the given field
Level of Study: Postgraduate
Type: Funding support
Value: Maximum value of up to US$60,000
Frequency: Annual
Country of Study: United States of America

U

Application Procedure: 1. Applications should be brief, no more than 3 pages, and written with the understanding that they will be reviewed by a panel of faculty from the sciences and humanities that may not include specialists in the field of study. 2. Applications should therefore include an introductory description which is accessible to someone who is not an expert in the given field
Closing Date: May
Funding: Private

For further information contact:

Vice Provost for the Faculty, 200 California Hall, MC 1500, Berkeley, CA 94720-1500, United States of America.

Tel: (1) 510 642 6474
Email: yasyavg@berkeley.edu

Western Center for Agricultural Health and Safety

Purpose: The overarching goal of the WCAHS Small Grant Program is to encourage the development of creative research projects while nurturing researchers – particularly early-career researchers – interested in improving agricultural health and safety for the Western United States
Eligibility: 1. Faculty with PI eligibility in the Western region (AZ, CA, HI, NV). 2. PhD students or postdoctoral scholars in the Western region. 3. Applicants from AZ, HI, and NV are encouraged to apply
Level of Study: postdoctoral
Type: Grant
Value: Graduate students and postdoctoral scholars may request up to US$10,000. Faculty may request up to US$30,000
Frequency: Annual
Country of Study: United States of America
Application Procedure: For further information, check the website aghealth.ucdavis.edu/
Closing Date: 3 September

University of California, Berkeley

Graduate Services, Graduate Fellowships Office, 318 Sproul Hall #5900, Berkeley, CA 94720-5900, United States of America.

Tel: (1) 510 642 6000
Email: gradappt@berkeley.edu
Website: www.berkeley.edu

The University of California's flagship campus at Berkeley has become one of the preeminent universities in the world. Its early guiding lights, charged with providing education (both 'practical' and 'classical') for the state's people, gradually established a distinguished faculty (with 20 Nobel laureates to date), a stellar research library, and more than 350 academic programs.

Conference Travel Grants

Purpose: To allow students to attend professional conferences
Eligibility: Applicants must be registered graduate students in good academic standing. They must be in the final stages of their graduate work and planning to present a paper on their dissertation research at the conference they are attending
Level of Study: Doctorate, Graduate
Type: Grant
Value: Amount of the grant depends upon the location of conference (up to US$600 within California, US$900 elsewhere in North America, including Canada and Mexico, and US$1,500 outside of North America)
Frequency: Dependent on funds available
Study Establishment: University of California, Berkeley
Country of Study: United States of America
Application Procedure: Applicants must submit an application form and one letter of support from their graduate advisor attesting to the academic merit of the trip. Applications can be obtained from the website

For further information contact:

Email: aips@pakistanstudies-aips.org

University of California, Los Angeles (UCLA) Center for 17th and 18th Century Studies and the William Andrews Clark Memorial Library

10745 Dickson Plaza, 302 Royce Hall, Los Angeles, CA 90095-1404, United States of America.

Tel: (1) 310 206 8552
Email: c1718cs@humnet.ucla.edu
Website: www.c1718cs.ucla.edu/
Contact: Fellowship Co-ordinator

University of California, Los Angeles (UCLA) Center for 17th and 18th century Studies provides a forum for the discussion of central issues in the field of early modern studies, facilitates research and publication, supports scholarship and encourages the creation of interdisciplinary, cross-cultural programmes that advance the understanding of this important period. The William Andrews Clark Memorial Library, administered by the Center, is known for its collections of rare books and manuscripts concerning 17th and 18th-century Britain and Europe, Oscar Wilde and the 1890s, the history of printing, and certain aspects of the American West.

Clark-Huntington Joint Bibliographical Fellowship

Purpose: To support bibliographical research
Level of Study: Postdoctorate, Professional development
Type: Fellowship
Value: US$6,500
Length of Study: 2 months
Frequency: Annual
Study Establishment: The Clark Library and the Huntington Library
Country of Study: United States of America
Application Procedure: Applicants must submit an application form, a curriculum vitae, a proposal statement, a bibliography and three letters of reference
No. of awards offered: 15
Closing Date: 1 February
Funding: Private
No. of awards given last year: 1
No. of applicants last year: 15
Additional Information: www.1718.ucla.edu/research/postdoctoral/clark-huntington/

For further information contact:

Email: ortiz@humnet.ucla.edu

University of California, Los Angeles (UCLA) Institute of American Cultures (IAC)

2329 Murphy Hall, Los Angeles, CA 90095-7244, United States of America.

Tel: (1) 310 825 6815
Email: IACcoordinator@conet.ucla.edu
Website: iac.ucla.edu/
Contact: Dr N Cherie Francis, Co-ordinator

The UCLA Institute of American Cultures (IAC) is committed to advancing knowledge, strengthening and integrating interdisciplinary research and enriching instruction on African Americans, American Indians, Asian Americans and Chicanos. Since 1969, the IAC has been responsible for developing and expanding graduate studies, research and training in ethnic studies and is a major contributor to the academic and intellectual life of the University.

University of California at Los Angeles Institute of American Culture (IAC) Postdoctoral/Visiting Scholar Fellowships

Purpose: To enable PhD scholars wishing to work in association with the American Indian Studies Center, the BUNCHE Center for African American Studies, the Asian American Studies Center and the Chicano Studies Research Center, to conduct research and publish books or manuscripts relating to ethnic studies and interdisciplinary instruction
Eligibility: Open to citizens of the United States of America and permanent residents
Level of Study: Postdoctorate
Type: Fellowship
Value: US$29,000; US$34,000 stipend plus health benefits and up to US$4,000 in research support
Length of Study: Up to 1 year
Frequency: Annual
Country of Study: United States of America
Application Procedure: Applicants must complete an application form, available from one of the ethnic studies centres, the IAC, or from the website
Closing Date: 31 December
No. of awards given last year: 4
Additional Information: iac.ucla.edu/funding/visiting-scholars

For further information contact:

Tel: (1) 310 825 6815
Email: IACcoordinator@conet.ucla.edu

U

University of Cambridge

The Old Schools, Trinity Lane, Cambridge CB2 1TN, United Kingdom.

Tel: (44) 12 2333 7733
Email: dmh14@cam.ac.uk
Website: www.admin.cam.ac.uk
Contact: Hugo Hocknell, Student Registry

The University of Cambridge is a loose confederation of faculties, colleges and other bodies. The colleges are mainly concerned with the teaching of their undergraduate students through tutorials and supervisions and the academic support of both graduate and undergraduate students, while the University employs professors, readers, lecturers and other teaching and administrative staff who provide the formal teaching in lectures, seminars and practical classes. The University also administers the University Library.

Arthington-Davy Grants for Tongan Students for Postgraduate Study

Eligibility: 1. Hold a first University degree, 2. Have applied for admission, or already received an offer of admission, for a post-graduate study course at any University in the world, and 3. Be of Tongan origin
Level of Study: Postgraduate
Type: Grant
Value: Graduate Course Fees, and maintenance allowance, less any financial support received from elsewhere
Length of Study: For minimum further period required to complete PhD
Frequency: Annual
Country of Study: Any country
Application Procedure: A completed application form should be sent together with the following Proof of Tongan origin academic transcripts details of the intended postgraduate study, preferably with a letter of conditional acceptance from the University concerned 1. Clear and precise details of tuition fees, living expenses and finances available from the student's own resources and/or from other institutions. 2. Names and email addresses of two academic referees. 3. CV
Closing Date: 31 May
Funding: Private
Additional Information: https://www.trin.cam.ac.uk/postgraduate/funding-awards/

For further information contact:

Email: grad.tutor@trin.cam.ac.uk

Dorothy Hodgkin Postgraduate Award

Eligibility: Applicants must have already applied for and been accepted for a PhD place at the University of Cambridge, must be a national of one of the eligible countries (Russia plus all countries on the DAC List of ODA Recipients), must be intending to start their PhD that coming October and must hold a high-grade qualification, at least the equivalent of a United Kingdom First Class (Honours) Degree, from a prestigious academic institution
Type: Award
Value: Approx. £12,300 per year (university composition plus college fees and maintenance stipend)
Length of Study: 3 years
Frequency: Annual
Country of Study: Any country
Application Procedure: There is no separate application form for this competition
Closing Date: 15 December
Contributor: The United Kingdom Research Councils and Industrial Partners

For further information contact:

Email: kfw20@admin.cam.ac.uk

Evans Fund

Purpose: To support research.
Eligibility: 1. A Fellow shall be eligible for re-election for a year at a time subject to a maximum tenure, save in exceptional circumstances, of three years in all. 2. re-election shall be dependent on the receipt by the Advisory Committee by a specified date of a satisfactory report on the Fellow's diligence and progress in research during his or her tenure.
Level of Study: Doctorate, Postdoctorate, Postgraduate
Type: Funding support
Value: £6,000
Length of Study: 1 or 2 years
Frequency: Annual
Study Establishment: The University of Cambridge
Country of Study: United Kingdom
Application Procedure: Applicants should request the application form by e-mailing research@socanth.cam.ac.uk allowing plenty of time to receive the application form, complete it and return it by the deadline. Applicants should email their completed application form together with an outline of the proposed scheme of travel and research and their curriculum vitae, to the Secretary, Evans Fund Advisory Committee, at research@socanth.cam.ac.uk, so as to arrive no later than the annually announced deadline, usually the last week of April, confirmed each Michaelmas term. It is the applicants' responsibility to ensure that referees' confidential letters of support be emailed directly to the Fund Administrator before the deadline, at research@socanth.cam.ac.uk.
Closing Date: 26 April
Funding: Private
Contributor: Legacy
Additional Information: www.socanth.cam.ac.uk/about-us/funding/research-funding/evans-fund

For further information contact:

Email: research@socanth.cam.ac.uk

Fitzwilliam College Charlton Studentships

Purpose: Part-cost award for masters students.
Eligibility: 1. All full-time and part time Masters courses starting Michaelmas Term are eligible, with the exception of MRes, MBA, MFin and PGCE. 2. All nationalities and fee status. 3. Awards are made on academic merit.
Level of Study: Masters Degree, Postgraduate
Type: Scholarship
Value: £10,000 each
Length of Study: 1 year
Frequency: Annual
Study Establishment: Fitzwilliam College
Country of Study: United Kingdom
Application Procedure: All those eligible by the closing date will be automatically considered - no application form required.
No. of awards offered: 5
Closing Date: 15 March
Funding: Individuals
Contributor: Fitzwilliam College
Additional Information: www.fitz.cam.ac.uk/college-life/fees-funding-and-awards/postgraduate-scholarships-and-prizes

For further information contact:

Email: graduate.officer@fitz.cam.ac.uk

Fitzwilliam College Graduate Scholarship

Eligibility: 1. All full-time PhD courses are eligible. Arts students may be preferred. 2. All nationalities and fee status.
Level of Study: Postgraduate
Type: Fellowship
Value: £1,460
Length of Study: 1 year
Frequency: Annual
Study Establishment: Fitzwilliam College, University of Cambridge
Country of Study: United Kingdom
Application Procedure: Scholarship website: cambridge.eu.qualtrics.com/jfe/form/SV_djwm7zZcRg0SGIS
No. of awards offered: 1
Closing Date: 30 September
Funding: Private
Additional Information: www.fitz.cam.ac.uk/college-life/fees-funding-and-awards/postgraduate-scholarships-and-prizes

For further information contact:

Tel: (44) 12 2333 2035
Fax: (44) 12 2333 2082
Email: grad.scholarships@fitz.cam.ac.uk

Fitzwilliam College Leathersellers

Purpose: To support students who wish to undertake research
Eligibility: 1. Applicants must be Home fee status with a previous degree from a British university 2. PhD (including PhD probationary) students who will be in years 2 or 3 of their course at the start of the award period (Michaelmas Term) 3. Awards may be held for 2 or 3 years dependent on continued good progress. 4. Physical or Biological Sciences, Engineering and Mathematics subjects.
Level of Study: Doctorate
Type: Scholarship
Value: £3,500/year
Length of Study: 2 to 3 years dependent on continued good progress.
Frequency: Annual
Study Establishment: Fitzwilliam College, University of Cambridge
Country of Study: United Kingdom
Application Procedure: Scholarship website: cambridge.eu.qualtrics.com/jfe/form/SV_71hmBBO4bRk6tD0
Closing Date: 31 May
Funding: Commercial
Additional Information: cambridge.eu.qualtrics.com/jfe/form/SV_71hmBBO4bRk6tD0

For further information contact:

Email: graduate.office@fitz.cam.ac.uk

Fitzwilliam College Research Fellowship

Purpose: To enable scholars to carry out a programme of new research
Eligibility: Applicants should 1. have completed a PhD or have a clear expectation of doing so prior to 1 October 2024 2. have completed no more than two years (f.t.e.) of postdoctoral research at the time of application 3. have secured full research funding (including salary) for three years from 1 October 2024, or have a clear expectation of such funding 4. have secured an endorsement from a Department, Faculty, Institution, Laboratory or equivalent in the University of

Cambridge 5. have demonstrated to their funder their right to work in the UK.
Level of Study: Doctorate, Postdoctorate
Type: Fellowship
Value: The Fellowship is non-stipendiary. If available, rent-free single accommodation will be offered in College, with a charge to cover services; alternatively, if the Fellow is not resident in College, study facilities will be made available and an allowance (currently £3,469) paid. A Research Fellow is a member of the Governing Body, bringing responsibilities as a Trustee of the College, and is entitled to all meals at College expense when the kitchens are open. An annual allowance of £1000 may be claimed for academic purposes including the purchase of books and computing equipment, or attendance at conferences. Additional grants may be made to assist with certain approved research expenses which are not covered by departmental, faculty or other sources.
Length of Study: 3 years
Frequency: Annual
Study Establishment: Fitzwilliam College, University of Cambridge
Country of Study: United Kingdom
Application Procedure: www.fitz.cam.ac.uk/sites/default/files/2022-03/Non%20Stipendiary%20Research%20Fellowship%20Further%20Particulars%20March%202022%5B43%5D.pdf
Closing Date: 12 April
Additional Information: www.fitz.cam.ac.uk/non-stipendiary-research-fellowships

For further information contact:

Email: masters.assistant@fitz.cam.ac.uk

Fitzwilliam College: Cleaver-Wang Studentship

Eligibility: 1. All full-time and part time Masters courses starting Michaelmas Term are eligible, with the exception of MRes, MBA, MFin and PGCE. 2. All nationalities and fee status. 3. Awards are made on academic merit. 4. Preference given to those working across disciplines or with innovative methodologies.
Level of Study: Masters Degree, Postgraduate
Type: Studentship
Value: Between £5,000 and £10,000
Length of Study: 1 year
Frequency: Annual
Country of Study: United Kingdom
Application Procedure: All those eligible by the closing date will be automatically considered - no application form required.
No. of awards offered: 1
Closing Date: 15 March
Additional Information: www.fitz.cam.ac.uk/college-life/fees-funding-and-awards/postgraduate-scholarships-and-prizes#panel-2107856630

Fitzwilliam College: E D Davies Scholarship

Eligibility: 1. All full-time PhD courses are eligible. 2. All nationalities and fee status.
Level of Study: Doctorate
Type: Scholarship
Value: £1,460
Length of Study: 1 year
Frequency: Annual
Country of Study: United Kingdom
Application Procedure: Scholarship website: cambridge.eu.qualtrics.com/jfe/form/SV_djwm7zZcRg0SGIS
No. of awards offered: 3
Closing Date: 30 September
No. of awards given last year: 2
No. of applicants last year: 25
Additional Information: www.fitz.cam.ac.uk/college-life/fees-funding-and-awards/postgraduate-scholarships-and-prizes

Fitzwilliam College: Fitzwilliam Society JRW Alexander Law Book Grants

Eligibility: 1. All students starting the LLM or MCL course at Fitzwilliam receive a Law Book grant in the form of book tokens. 2. All eligible will receive the award.
Type: Grant
Value: £100 each
Frequency: Annual
Country of Study: United Kingdom
Application Procedure: No application is necessary.
Additional Information: www.fitz.cam.ac.uk/college-life/fees-funding-and-awards/postgraduate-scholarships-and-prizes#panel-775310585

Fitzwilliam College: Gibson Scholarship

Eligibility: 1. Applicant should be intending to work towards a doctorate in New Testament Studies. 2. Students naming Fitzwilliam as first choice are preferred but not exclusively.
Level of Study: Graduate, Postgraduate
Type: Scholarship
Value: £1,165
Length of Study: 1 year
Frequency: Annual
Country of Study: United Kingdom
No. of awards offered: 1

Closing Date: 30 September
Additional Information: www.fitz.cam.ac.uk/college-life/fees-funding-and-awards/postgraduate-scholarships-and-prizes

For further information contact:

Email: graduate.office@fitz.cam.ac.uk

Fitzwilliam College: Hirst-Player Scholarship

Eligibility: 1. Reading for a Degree or a Diploma in Theology. 2. Intention to take Holy Orders in a Christian Church preferred. 3. Students needing assistance with fees, who would otherwise be unable to study at Cambridge.
Level of Study: Postgraduate
Type: Scholarship
Value: £2,330 (maximum)
Length of Study: 1 year
Frequency: Annual
Country of Study: United Kingdom
No. of awards offered: 1 or 2
Closing Date: 30 September
Additional Information: www.fitz.cam.ac.uk/college-life/fees-funding-and-awards/postgraduate-scholarships-and-prizes

For further information contact:

Email: graduate.office@fitz.cam.ac.uk

Fitzwilliam College: Lee Kuan Yew PhD Studentships

Eligibility: 1. All full-time PhD courses are eligible 2. All nationalities and fee status 3. There are specific subject area criteria for this Studentship. More information. 4. Deadline for studentship application - 16 January 2024 (2400 hours) 5. Applicants must also apply for a place on their chosen course by the funding deadline and tick the box for inclusion in the funding competitions on their application. 6. Applicants may apply to any of the University's colleges as their first choice college. The awardee will be required to transfer college membership to Fitzwilliam College before the start of their course.
Level of Study: Doctorate
Type: Studentship
Value: Fully-funded (fees and maintenance).
Length of Study: 3.5 years
Frequency: Annual
Country of Study: United Kingdom
No. of awards offered: 2 to 3
Closing Date: 16 January

Fitzwilliam College: Peter Wilson Estates Gazette Studentships

Eligibility: 1. All full-time, one year Masters courses that are offered by the Department of Land Economy are eligible. 2. One of the Studentships will be prioritised for a Fitzwilliam undergraduate student who is applying for MPhil in Cambridge. 3. All nationalities and fee status.
Level of Study: Masters Degree, Postgraduate
Type: Studentship
Value: Three awards at £4,000 each or two awards at £6,000
Length of Study: 1 year
Frequency: Annual
Country of Study: United Kingdom
Application Procedure: All those eligible by the closing date will be automatically considered - no application form required.
No. of awards offered: 2 or 3
Closing Date: 31 May
Additional Information: www.fitz.cam.ac.uk/college-life/fees-funding-and-awards/postgraduate-scholarships-and-prizes#panel-1384001179

Fitzwilliam College: Quantedge – Lee Kuan Yew Masters Scholarship

Eligibility: 1. All full-time one year Masters courses are eligible, with the exception, MBA, MFin and PGCE. 2. Financially disadvantaged student of Singaporean nationality. 3. Deadline for studentship application - 16 January 2023 (12 noon). 4. Applicants must also apply for a place on their chosen course by the University funding deadline (either 3 December or 7 January depending on course). 5. Applicants may apply to any of the University's colleges as their first choice college. The awardee will be required to transfer college membership to Fitzwilliam College before the start of their course.
Type: Scholarship
Value: Fully-funded (fees and maintenance)
Length of Study: 1 year
Country of Study: United Kingdom
Application Procedure: Scholarship website: www.fitz.cam.ac.uk/onlineforms/view.php?id=287128
No. of awards offered: 1
Additional Information: www.fitz.cam.ac.uk/college-life/fees-funding-and-awards/postgraduate-scholarships-and-prizes

For further information contact:

Email: grad.scholarships@fitz.cam.ac.uk

U

Fitzwilliam College: Robert Lethbridge Scholarship in Modern Languages

Eligibility: 1. All full-time, one year Masters courses that are offered by the Faculty of Modern and Medieval Languages and Linguistics are eligible. 2. All nationalities and fee status.
Level of Study: Masters Degree, Postgraduate
Type: Scholarship
Value: £1,250
Length of Study: 1 year
Frequency: Annual
Country of Study: United Kingdom
Application Procedure: All those eligible by the closing date will be automatically considered - no application form required.
No. of awards offered: 1
Closing Date: 31 May
Additional Information: www.fitz.cam.ac.uk/college-life/fees-funding-and-awards/postgraduate-scholarships-and-prizes#panel-892737392

Fitzwilliam College: Shipley Studentship

Purpose: To enable graduates to undertake research
Eligibility: 1. Applicant should be undertaking / intending to undertake research at the Faculty of Divinity. 2. Exceptionally, research on a theological topic in another faculty also accepted.
Level of Study: Postgraduate
Type: Studentship
Value: £1,460
Length of Study: 1 year
Frequency: Annual
Study Establishment: Fitzwilliam College, University of Cambridge
Country of Study: United Kingdom
Application Procedure: Scholarship website: www.fitz.cam.ac.uk/onlineforms/view.php?id=278169
No. of awards offered: 1
Closing Date: 30 September
Funding: Private
Additional Information: www.fitz.cam.ac.uk/college-life/fees-funding-and-awards/postgraduate-scholarships-and-prizes

For further information contact:

Email: graduate.office@fitz.cam.ac.uk

Fitzwilliam College: The Hong Leong – Lee Kuan Yew Masters Scholarship

Eligibility: 1. All full-time one year Masters courses are eligible, with the exception of MBA, MFin, MRes and PGCE. 2. All nationalities and fee status. 3. There are specific subject area criteria for this Studentship. More information. 4. Applicants may apply to any of the University's colleges as their first choice college. The awardee will be required to transfer college membership to Fitzwilliam College before the start of their course.
Level of Study: Masters Degree, Postgraduate
Type: Scholarship
Value: Fully-funded (fees and maintenance)
Length of Study: 1 year
Frequency: Annual
Country of Study: United Kingdom
No. of awards offered: 1
Additional Information: www.fitz.cam.ac.uk/college-life/fees-funding-and-awards/postgraduate-scholarships-and-prizes#panel-661464388

Fitzwilliam Masters Studentship

Eligibility: 1. All full-time and part time Masters courses starting Michaelmas Term are eligible, with the exception of MRes, MBA, MFin and PGCE. 2. All nationalities and fee status. 3. Awards are made on academic merit.
Level of Study: Masters Degree, Postgraduate
Type: Studentship
Value: Fully-funded (fees and maintenance)
Frequency: Annual
Country of Study: United Kingdom
Application Procedure: All those eligible by the closing date will be automatically considered - no application form required.
No. of awards offered: 1
Closing Date: 15 March
Additional Information: www.fitz.cam.ac.uk/college-life/fees-funding-and-awards/postgraduate-scholarships-and-prizes#panel-1159453696

Girton College Graduate Research Scholarship

Eligibility: A first-class degree is almost always required and election will be conditional on the candidate being granted Graduate Student status by the University of Cambridge. The holder must become a member of the college and either be a candidate for a masters or a PhD degree
Level of Study: Doctorate, MBA, Postgraduate
Type: Scholarship

Value: The value of the award for this year is likely to be approximately £27,000
Frequency: Annual
Study Establishment: University of Cambridge
Country of Study: United Kingdom
Application Procedure: Application should be made online via www.girton.cam.ac.uk/graduates/research-awards
No. of awards offered: 200
Closing Date: 27 March
No. of awards given last year: 3
No. of applicants last year: 200
Additional Information: www.girton.cam.ac.uk/prospective-students/graduate/graduate-research-awards/

For further information contact:

Tel: (44) 1223 766673
Email: postgraduate.office@girton.cam.ac.uk

Girton College Overseas Bursaries

Eligibility: A first-class degree is almost always required and election will be conditional on the candidate being granted Graduate Student status by the University of Cambridge. The holder must become a member of the college
Level of Study: Doctorate, Graduate, MBA, Postgraduate
Type: Bursary
Value: £200 to £1,000 per year
Frequency: Dependent on funds available
Study Establishment: University of Cambridge
Country of Study: United Kingdom
Application Procedure: Application forms can be downloaded from www.girton.cam.ac.uk/graduates/research-awards or may be obtained from the Graduate Secretary, Girton College, Cambridge, CB3 0JG, United Kingdom (email graduate.office@girton.cam.ac.uk)
Closing Date: 28 March

For further information contact:

Email: graduate.office@girton.cam.ac.uk

Girton College: Doris Woodall Studentship

Eligibility: A first-class degree is almost always required and election will be conditional on the candidate being granted Graduate Student status by the University of Cambridge. The holder must become a member of the college
Level of Study: Doctorate, MBA, Postgraduate
Type: Studentship
Value: £6,400
Length of Study: 1 year
Frequency: Annual
Study Establishment: University of Cambridge
Country of Study: United Kingdom
Application Procedure: Application should be made online via www.girton.cam.ac.uk/graduates/research-awards
No. of awards offered: 1
Closing Date: 26 March
Additional Information: www.girton.cam.ac.uk/postgraduates/fees-finance-funding

For further information contact:

Tel: (44) 1223 766673
Email: postgraduate.office@girton.cam.ac.uk

Girton College: Ida and Isidore Cohen Research Scholarship

Eligibility: Open to students working in modern Hebrew studies. A first-class degree is almost always required and election will be conditional on the candidate being granted Graduate Student status by the University of Cambridge. The holder must become a member of the college
Level of Study: Doctorate, Graduate, Postgraduate
Type: Scholarship
Value: Between £3,000 and £5,000
Frequency: Annual
Study Establishment: University of Cambridge
Country of Study: United Kingdom
Application Procedure: Application forms can be downloaded from external link or may be obtained from the Graduate Secretary, Girton College, Cambridge, CB3 0JG, United Kingdom
Closing Date: 28 March
Additional Information: www.admin.cam.ac.uk/reporter/2005-06/special/06/175.html

For further information contact:

Email: jj216@cam.ac.uk

U

Girton College: Irene Hallinan Scholarship

Eligibility: A first-class degree is almost always required and election will be conditional on the candidate being granted Graduate Student status by the University of Cambridge. The holder must become a member of the college and either be a candidate for a masters or a PhD degree
Level of Study: Doctorate, MBA, Postgraduate

Type: Scholarship
Value: £6,500
Length of Study: 1 year
Frequency: Annual
Study Establishment: University of Cambridge
Country of Study: United Kingdom
Application Procedure: Application should be made online via www.girton.cam.ac.uk/graduates/research-awards
No. of awards offered: 200
Closing Date: 27 March
No. of awards given last year: 3
No. of applicants last year: 200
Additional Information: www.girton.cam.ac.uk/postgraduates/fees-finance-funding

For further information contact:

Tel: (44) 1223 766673
Email: postgraduate.office@girton.cam.ac.uk

Girton College: Maria Luisa de Sanchez Scholarship

Purpose: Available to students of Venezuelan nationality. The value is based upon University fees and the University recommended maintenance figure. It is awarded, in the first instance, for one year but may be renewed for further periods up to three years. In exceptional cases it can be extended to four years.
Eligibility: Applicants must be of Venezuelan nationality. A first-class degree is almost always required and election will be conditional on the candidate being granted Graduate Student status by the University of Cambridge. The holder must become a member of the college
Level of Study: Doctorate, Graduate, MBA, Postgraduate
Type: Scholarship
Value: £27,000
Length of Study: 1 Year
Frequency: Annual
Study Establishment: University of Cambridge
Country of Study: United Kingdom
Application Procedure: Application forms can be downloaded from app.casc.cam.ac.uk/fas_live/g_post.aspx or may be obtained from the Graduate Secretary, Girton College, Cambridge, CB3 0JG, United Kingdom (email graduate.office@girton.cam.ac.uk)
No. of awards offered: 2
Closing Date: 25 March
No. of awards given last year: 1
Additional Information: www.girton.cam.ac.uk/postgraduates/fees-finance-funding

For further information contact:

Tel: (44) 1223 766673
Email: postgraduate.office@girton.cam.ac.uk

Girton College: Ruth Whaley Scholarship

Eligibility: Open to outstanding students of non-European Union citizenship seeking admission to Girton. It is open to students following arts subjects. A first-class degree is almost always required and election will be conditional on the candidate being granted Graduate Student status by the University of Cambridge. The holder must become a member of the college
Level of Study: Doctorate, Postgraduate
Type: Scholarship
Value: £3,300
Length of Study: 1 year
Frequency: Annual
Study Establishment: University of Cambridge
Country of Study: United Kingdom
Application Procedure: Application forms can be downloaded from www.girton.cam.ac.uk/graduates/research-awards or may be obtained from the Graduate Secretary
No. of awards offered: 1
Closing Date: 26 March
No. of awards given last year: 1
Additional Information: www.girton.cam.ac.uk/students/graduate-scholarships/

For further information contact:

Tel: (44) 1223 766673
Email: postgraduate.office@girton.cam.ac.uk

Girton College: Sidney and Marguerite Cody Studentship

Purpose: Period of travel and study in continental Europe of up to 12 months and normally of not less than 6 months
Eligibility: Open to graduate members of any faculty except English who have completed less than nine terms in residence. A first-class degree is almost always required and election will be conditional on the candidate being granted Graduate Student status by the University of Cambridge. The holder must become a member of the college
Level of Study: Doctorate, Graduate, Postgraduate
Type: Studentship
Value: Up to £3,000
Frequency: Annual
Study Establishment: University of Cambridge
Country of Study: United Kingdom

Application Procedure: Application should be made online via www.girton.cam.ac.uk/graduates/research-awards
Closing Date: 28 March
No. of awards given last year: 1
Additional Information: https://www.girton.cam.ac.uk/postgraduates/financial-support/sports-travel-and-music-awards

Girton College: Stribling Award

Eligibility: Open to Girton students who are already members of the College, namely undergraduates coming into graduate status or current MPhil students who are going on to a PhD A first-class degree is almost always required and election will be conditional on the candidate being granted Graduate Student status by the University of Cambridge
Level of Study: Doctorate, Postgraduate
Type: Award
Value: £1,000, normally in addition to a studentship or any other funding for fees and maintenance
Length of Study: 1 year
Frequency: Annual
Study Establishment: University of Cambridge
Country of Study: United Kingdom
Application Procedure: Application should be made online via www.girton.cam.ac.uk/graduates/research-awards
No. of awards offered: 2
Closing Date: 28 March
No. of awards given last year: 2
Additional Information: www.girton.cam.ac.uk/postgraduates/fees-finance-funding

For further information contact:

Tel: (44) 1223 766673
Email: postgraduate.office@girton.cam.ac.uk

Girton College: The Chan and Mok Graduate Scholarship

Eligibility: 1. They are open to students who have graduated or will have graduated before 1st October of the year they apply, and who nominate Girton as their first or second choice College. 2. A first-class degree is almost always required and election will be conditional on the candidate being granted Postgraduate Student status by the University of Cambridge. 3. The holder must become a member of the College and be a candidate for either a Masters or a PhD degree. 4. Current Cambridge students who are members of another College are eligible to apply if they are moving from one course of study to another, however if they are part-way through a course they cannot apply for the awards. 5. available to students who are permanent residents of Hong Kong and with preference to those who have studied at schools affiliated to Po Leung Kuk.
Level of Study: Postgraduate
Type: Scholarship
Value: £10,000
Length of Study: 1 year
Frequency: Annual
Country of Study: Any country
Closing Date: 25 March
Additional Information: www.girton.cam.ac.uk/postgraduates/fees-finance-funding

For further information contact:

Tel: (44) 1223 766673
Email: postgraduate.office@girton.cam.ac.uk

Girton College: The Diane Worzala Memorial Fund

Eligibility: 1. They are open to students who have graduated or will have graduated before 1st October of the year they apply, and who nominate Girton as their first or second choice College. 2. A first-class degree is almost always required and election will be conditional on the candidate being granted Postgraduate Student status by the University of Cambridge. 3. The holder must become a member of the College and be a candidate for either a Masters or a PhD degree. 4. Current Cambridge students who are members of another College are eligible to apply if they are moving from one course of study to another, however if they are part-way through a course they cannot apply for the awards.
Type: Scholarship
Value: £600
Country of Study: United Kingdom
Closing Date: 25 March
Additional Information: www.girton.cam.ac.uk/postgraduates/fees-finance-funding

For further information contact:

Tel: (44) 1223 766673
Email: postgraduate.office@girton.cam.ac.uk

Girton College: The Dinah James Scholarship

Eligibility: 1. They are open to students who have graduated or will have graduated before 1st October of the year they apply, and who nominate Girton as their first or second choice College. 2. A first-class degree is almost always required and election will be conditional on the candidate being granted Postgraduate Student status by the University of Cambridge. 3. The holder must become a member of the College and be a candidate for either a Masters or a PhD degree. 4. Current

Cambridge students who are members of another College are eligible to apply if they are moving from one course of study to another, however if they are part-way through a course they cannot apply for the awards.
Level of Study: Postgraduate
Type: Scholarship
Value: £9,000
Frequency: Annual
Country of Study: United Kingdom
Closing Date: 25 March
Additional Information: www.girton.cam.ac.uk/postgraduates/fees-finance-funding

For further information contact:

Tel: (44) 1223 766673
Email: postgraduate.office@girton.cam.ac.uk

Girton College: The Girton Hong Kong Founder's Scholarship

Eligibility: 1. They are open to students who have graduated or will have graduated before 1st October of the year they apply, and who nominate Girton as their first or second choice College. 2. A first-class degree is almost always required and election will be conditional on the candidate being granted Postgraduate Student status by the University of Cambridge. 3. The holder must become a member of the College and be a candidate for either a Masters or a PhD degree. 4. Current Cambridge students who are members of another College are eligible to apply if they are moving from one course of study to another, however if they are part-way through a course they cannot apply for the awards.
Level of Study: Postgraduate
Type: Scholarship
Value: £10,000
Length of Study: 3 years
Frequency: Annual
Country of Study: United Kingdom
Closing Date: 25 March
Additional Information: www.girton.cam.ac.uk/postgraduates/fees-finance-funding

For further information contact:

Tel: (44) 1223 766673
Email: postgraduate.office@girton.cam.ac.uk

Girton College: The Joyce Biddle Scholarship

Eligibility: 1. They are open to students who have graduated or will have graduated before 1st October of the year they apply, and who nominate Girton as their first or second choice College. 2. A first-class degree is almost always required and election will be conditional on the candidate being granted Postgraduate Student status by the University of Cambridge. 3. The holder must become a member of the College and be a candidate for either a Masters or a PhD degree. 4. Current Cambridge students who are members of another College are eligible to apply if they are moving from one course of study to another, however if they are part-way through a course they cannot apply for the awards.
Level of Study: Postgraduate
Type: Scholarship
Value: £13,000, but may be renewed.
Length of Study: 1 year
Frequency: Annual
Country of Study: United Kingdom
Closing Date: 25 March
Additional Information: www.girton.cam.ac.uk/postgraduates/fees-finance-funding

For further information contact:

Tel: (44) 1223 766673
Email: postgraduate.office@girton.cam.ac.uk

Girton College: The Postgraduate Research Scholarship

Eligibility: 1. They are open to students who have graduated or will have graduated before 1st October of the year they apply, and who nominate Girton as their first or second choice College. 2. A first-class degree is almost always required and election will be conditional on the candidate being granted Postgraduate Student status by the University of Cambridge. 3. The holder must become a member of the College and be a candidate for either a Masters or a PhD degree. 4. Current Cambridge students who are members of another College are eligible to apply if they are moving from one course of study to another, however if they are part-way through a course they cannot apply for the awards.
Level of Study: Postgraduate
Type: Scholarship
Value: Approximately £10,500
Length of Study: 1 year, but may be renewed for further periods up to three years. In exceptional cases it can be extended to four years.
Frequency: Annual
Country of Study: United Kingdom
Closing Date: 25 March
Additional Information: www.girton.cam.ac.uk/postgraduates/fees-finance-funding

For further information contact:

Tel: (44) 1223 766673
Email: postgraduate.office@girton.cam.ac.uk

Girton College: Travel Grant

Level of Study: Postgraduate
Type: Grant
Value: Contribution to academic travel and
Frequency: Every 2 years
Country of Study: Any country
Application Procedure: Application should be made online via www.girton.cam.ac.uk/graduates/research-awards
Closing Date: 24 April
Additional Information: www.girton.cam.ac.uk/girton-community/travel-awards/

For further information contact:

Email: ns714@cam.ac.uk

Gonville and Caius College Gonville Bursary

Purpose: To help outstanding students from outside the European Union to meet the costs of degree courses at the University of Cambridge
Eligibility: Open to candidates who have been accepted by the College through its normal admissions procedures, and who are classified as overseas students for fees purposes. A statement of financial circumstances is required
Level of Study: Doctorate, Postgraduate
Type: Bursary
Value: Reimbursement of college fees
Length of Study: Up to 3 years, with a possibility of renewal, dependent on satisfactory progress
Frequency: Annual
Study Establishment: Gonville and Caius College, the University of Cambridge
Country of Study: United Kingdom
Application Procedure: Applicants must contact the Admissions Tutor for further information. There are no application forms

For further information contact:

Gonville and Caius College, Trinity Street, Cambridge CB2 1TA, United Kingdom.

Tel: (44) 12 2333 2447
Fax: (44) 12 2333 2456
Email: admissions@cai.cam.ac.uk

Gonville and Caius College Michael Miliffe Scholarship

Subjects: All Subjects
Eligibility: Applicants must apply to the University of Cambridge in the regular way and must have a first class/high second class (Honours) degree or equivalent. Must be under 26 years.
Level of Study: Post Graduate
Type: Scholarship
Value: £5,000 is awarded
Length of Study: 2 years
Frequency: Annual
Country of Study: United Kingdom
Additional Information: www.cai.cam.ac.uk/undergraduate/overseas

For further information contact:

Email: admissions@cai.cam.ac.uk

Gonville and Caius College W M Tapp Studentship in Law

Purpose: To encourage the study of law
Eligibility: Open to candidates who are not already members of the College, but who propose to register as graduate students at the University of Cambridge. Candidates must be under 30 years of age as of October 1st of the studentship year and be graduates or expect to be graduates no later than August of the same year. Preference is given to applicants nominating Gonville and Caius College as their first choice when applying under the Cambridge Intercollegiate Graduate Application Scheme
Level of Study: Doctorate, Postgraduate
Type: Studentship
Value: A stipend similar to that of a state studentship for research, plus fees and certain allowances, a dependent allowance, an allowance for a period of approved postgraduate experience, a travelling contribution for foreign students and a research allowance for research students
Length of Study: 1 year, renewable for up to a maximum of 3 years
Frequency: Annual
Study Establishment: Gonville and Caius College, University of Cambridge
Country of Study: United Kingdom
Application Procedure: Applicants must complete an application form, available from the Admissions Tutor
Closing Date: 31 December
Additional Information: www.cai.cam.ac.uk/postgraduate/finance/tapp-studentships

For further information contact:

Email: postgraduate.admin@cai.cam.ac.uk

Kings College: Stipendiary Junior Research Fellowships

Purpose: To support gifted young researchers
Level of Study: Postdoctorate, Research
Type: Fellowship
Value: Permit complete freedom to carry out research within the academic environment of the college
Length of Study: 4 years
Frequency: Annual
Study Establishment: University of Cambridge, Kings College
Country of Study: United Kingdom
Closing Date: October

For further information contact:

King's College, King's Parade, Cambridge CB2 1ST, United Kingdom.

Tel: (44) 1223 331 100
Email: info@kings.cam.ac.uk

Lucy Cavendish College: Becker Law Scholarships

Eligibility: Open to women accepted to read for the LLM and MCL by the law Faculty at the University of Cambridge
Level of Study: Postgraduate
Type: Scholarship
Value: At least £1,000 per year
Length of Study: Up to 3 years, conditional on satisfactory academic progress
Frequency: Annual
Study Establishment: Lucy Cavendish College, University of Cambridge
Country of Study: United Kingdom
Application Procedure: Please contact to the Secretary of the Studentship and Bursary Committee
Closing Date: 1 June
Additional Information: www.lucy.cam.ac.uk/study-us/postgraduates/studentships-and-awards

Lucy Cavendish College: Dorothy and Joseph Needham Studentship

Purpose: For studies in Natural Sciences
Eligibility: Check website or contact organisation for updates
Level of Study: Postgraduate
Type: Studentship
Value: £1,000 per year
Length of Study: Up to 3 years, conditional on satisfactory academic progress
Frequency: Annual
Study Establishment: Lucy Cavendish College, University of Cambridge
Country of Study: United Kingdom
Application Procedure: Please contact to the Secretary of the Studentship and Bursary Committee
Closing Date: 30 June
Additional Information: www.lucy.cam.ac.uk/study-us/postgraduates/studentships-and-awards

Lucy Cavendish College: Enterprise Studentship

Eligibility: 1. Candidates must select Lucy Cavendish as their first College choice. Candidates must have received an offer to join the programme starting in October and membership at Lucy Cavendish College before they can be considered for the studentship. 2. Applications are welcome from any candidate, irrespective of gender, nationality or geographical location. There are no restrictions on citizenship, country of residence, or fee status.
Level of Study: MBA, Postgraduate
Type: Studentship
Value: Either a single award of £12,000, or two half-awards of £6,000 each
Frequency: Annual
Study Establishment: Lucy Cavendish College, University of Cambridge
Country of Study: United Kingdom
Application Procedure: Please contact to the Secretary of the Studentship and Bursary Committee
Additional Information: www.lucy.cam.ac.uk/study-us/postgraduates/studentships-and-awards

For further information contact:

Email: mbe-admin@ceb.cam.ac.uk

Lucy Cavendish College: Evelyn Povey Studentship

Subjects: French Studies
Purpose: The Evelyn Povey Studentship for French Citizens and the Evelyn Povey Studentship in French Studies
Eligibility: The Evelyn Povey Studentship for French Citizens
Type: Studentship

Eligibility: Eligibility is confined to nationals of the fifty 'Least Developed Countries' as defined by the United Nations. The other is for nationals of the fifty 'Least Developed Countries' as defined by the United Nations.
Level of Study: Postgraduate
Type: Studentship
Value: University fees at least at the standard rate for Home/European Union students, plus college fees and a maintenance of £10,465
Frequency: Annual
Study Establishment: Pembroke College, University of Cambridge
Country of Study: Any country
Application Procedure: All applicants for any of these awards must apply in the first instance to the Board of Graduate Studies for their University place. Candidates should indicate that they are applying for a Pembroke College award. In making awards preference will be given to those who nominate Pembroke as their College of first choice. All candidates are expected to apply for Research Council funding where appropriate, and for University CHESS funding, if they are eligible. The College will take into account candidates' income from other sources when making awards
Closing Date: 31 January
Additional Information: www.admin.cam.ac.uk/reporter/2009-10/special/06/190.html

Pembroke College: The Bethune-Baker Graduate Studentship in Theology

Eligibility: Open to candidates who intend to register for the PhD degree at the University of Cambridge
Level of Study: Postgraduate
Type: Studentship
Value: College and university fees for three years
Length of Study: 3 years
Frequency: Annual
Study Establishment: University of Cambridge
Country of Study: United Kingdom
Application Procedure: All applicants for any of these awards must apply in the first instance to the Board of Graduate Studies for their University place. Candidates should indicate that they are applying for a Pembroke College award. In making awards preference will be given to those who nominate Pembroke as their college of first choice. All candidates are expected to apply for Research Council funding where appropriate, and for University CHESS funding, if they are eligible. The College will take into account candidates' income from other sources when making awards
Closing Date: 31 January
Contributor: HM the Sultan of Oman and Professor E.G. Browne
Additional Information: www.admin.cam.ac.uk/reporter/2009-10/special/06/190.html

Pembroke College: The Bristol-Myers Squibb Graduate Studentship in the Biomedical Sciences

Eligibility: Open to candidates who intend to register for a PhD degree at the University of Cambridge
Level of Study: Postgraduate
Type: Studentship
Value: The studentship will have a value sufficient to pay college fees for three years
Frequency: Annual
Country of Study: United Kingdom
Application Procedure: All applicants for any of these awards must apply in the first instance to the Board of Graduate Studies for their University place. Candidates should indicate that they are applying for a Pembroke College award. In making awards preference will be given to those who nominate Pembroke as their college of first choice. All candidates are expected to apply for Research Council funding where appropriate, and for University CHESS funding, if they are eligible. The College will take into account candidates' income from other sources when making awards

Pembroke College: The Grosvenor-Shilling Bursary in Land Economy

Eligibility: Applicants must normally reside in Australia and hold a qualification from an Australian tertiary institution. There is no restriction as to the academic field
Level of Study: Postgraduate
Type: Scholarship
Value: £500
Frequency: Annual
Country of Study: Any country
Application Procedure: All applicants for any of these awards must apply in the first instance to the Board of Graduate Studies for their University place. Candidates should indicate that they are applying for a Pembroke College award. In making awards preference will be given to those who nominate Pembroke as their college of first choice. All candidates are expected to apply for Research Council funding where appropriate, and for University CHESS funding, if they are eligible. The College will take into account candidates' income from other sources when making awards
Closing Date: 31 January
Additional Information: www.admin.cam.ac.uk/reporter/2009-10/special/06/190.html

Pembroke College: The Lander Studentship in the History of Art

Purpose: The College is very pleased to be able to offer one studentship for an outstanding art historian, supported by the estate of Professor J.R. Lander
Eligibility: Candidates must be applying to study for a PhD degree in the History of Art at the University of Cambridge, with Pembroke as first-choice college
Level of Study: Postgraduate
Type: Studentship
Value: The studentship will, if necessary, pay university and college fees, at the home rate, plus a maintenance allowance (approx. £10,140 a year), for a maximum of 3 years
Length of Study: 3 years
Frequency: Annual
Study Establishment: Pembroke College, University of Cambridge
Country of Study: United Kingdom
Application Procedure: All applicants for any of these awards must apply in the first instance to the Board of Graduate Studies for their University place. Candidates should indicate that they are applying for a Pembroke College award. In making awards preference will be given to those who nominate Pembroke as their College of first choice. All candidates are expected to apply for Research Council funding where appropriate, and for University CHESS funding, if they are eligible. The College will take into account candidates' income from other sources when making awards
Closing Date: 31 January
Additional Information: www.admin.cam.ac.uk/reporter/2009-10/special/06/190.html

Pembroke College: The Monica Partridge Studentship

Purpose: To offer a graduate studentship for a student from South-East Europe to study at Pembroke
Eligibility: Open to the students of the nationals of Albania, Bosnia and Herzegovina, Bulgaria, Croatia, Greece, Kosovo, Macedonia, Montenegro and Serbia. Applications from students from Romania, Slovenia and Turkey will be considered if there is no suitable candidate from the countries listed above. Preference will be given to fund students studying for a PhD, but MPhil applicants intending to continue to a PhD will also be considered
Level of Study: Postgraduate
Type: Studentship
Value: The studentship will have a value sufficient to cover college fees (£2,229) and maintenance (£10,140) for three years for a PhD student or, in the case of an MPhil student, one year
Frequency: Annual
Study Establishment: Pembroke College, University of Cambridge
Country of Study: United Kingdom
Application Procedure: All applicants for any of these awards must apply in the first instance to the Board of Graduate Studies for their University place. Candidates should indicate that they are applying for a Pembroke College award. In making awards preference will be given to those who nominate Pembroke as their college of first choice. All candidates are expected to apply for Research Council funding where appropriate, and for University CHESS funding, if they are eligible. The College will take into account candidates' income from other sources when making awards
Closing Date: 31 January
Additional Information: www.admin.cam.ac.uk/reporter/2009-10/special/06/190.html

Pembroke College: The Pembroke Australian Scholarship

Eligibility: Applicants must normally reside in Australia and hold a qualification from an Australian tertiary institution. There is no restriction as to the academic field
Level of Study: Postgraduate
Type: Scholarship
Value: £500
Frequency: Annual
Country of Study: Any country
Application Procedure: All applicants for any of these awards must apply in the first instance to the Board of Graduate Studies for their University place. Candidates should indicate that they are applying for a Pembroke College award. In making awards preference will be given to those who nominate Pembroke as their College of first choice. All candidates are expected to apply for Research Council funding where appropriate, and for University CHESS funding, if they are eligible. The College will take into account candidates' income from other sources when making awards
Closing Date: 31 January
Additional Information: www.admin.cam.ac.uk/reporter/2009-10/special/06/190.html

Pembroke College: The Thornton Graduate Studentship in History

Eligibility: Preference in awarding these studentships will be given to candidates who intend to register for a PhD degree at Pembroke. However, candidates registering to study for an

MPhil will also be considered for an award if they are intending to carry on to a PhD after they have finished their MPhil
Level of Study: Postgraduate
Type: Studentship
Value: The studentship will have a value sufficient to pay College fees for three years. Moreover, additional awards, of up to the equivalent of University fees for a Home student (£3,465), may be made to individual applicants, depending on need and the availability of funds
Frequency: Annual
Study Establishment: Pembroke College
Country of Study: United Kingdom
Application Procedure: All applicants for any of these awards must apply in the first instance to the Board of Graduate Studies for their University place. Candidates should indicate that they are applying for a Pembroke College award. In making awards preference will be given to those who nominate Pembroke as their college of first choice. All candidates are expected to apply for Research Council funding where appropriate, and for University CHESS funding, if they are eligible. The College will take into account candidates' income from other sources when making awards
Closing Date: 31 January
Additional Information: www.admin.cam.ac.uk/reporter/2009-10/special/06/190.html

Pembroke College: The Ziegler Graduate Studentship in Law

Eligibility: Preference in awarding studentships is given to candidates who intend to register for a PhD degree at Pembroke
Level of Study: Postgraduate
Type: Studentship
Value: Covers university and college fees (at the Home/European Union rate)
Frequency: Annual
Study Establishment: Pembroke College
Country of Study: United Kingdom
Application Procedure: All applicants for any of these awards must apply in the first instance to the Board of Graduate Studies for their University place. Candidates should indicate that they are applying for a Pembroke College award. In making awards preference will be given to those who nominate Pembroke as their college of first choice. All candidates are expected to apply for Research Council funding where appropriate, and for University CHESS funding, if they are eligible. The College will take into account candidates' income from other sources when making awards
Closing Date: 31 January
Additional Information: www.admin.cam.ac.uk/reporter/2009-10/special/06/190.html

Peterhouse: Research Studentships

Eligibility: Open to prospective PhD candidates
Level of Study: Postgraduate
Type: Studentship
Value: varies
Frequency: Annual
Study Establishment: Peterhouse College
Country of Study: United Kingdom
Application Procedure: Please contact at graduates@pet.cam.ac.uk
No. of awards offered: 57
Closing Date: January
No. of awards given last year: 5
No. of applicants last year: 57
Additional Information: www.pet.cam.ac.uk/graduate-studentships-0

For further information contact:

Peterhouse, Trumpington Street, Cambridge CB2 1RD, United Kingdom.

Email: graduates@pet.cam.ac.uk

Principal's Studentship

Purpose: To support an MPhil or PhD student
Level of Study: Graduate
Type: Studentship
Value: Approx. Between £3,000 and £12,000 per year
Length of Study: 1 to 3 years
Frequency: Dependent on funds available
Study Establishment: Newnham College, University of Cambridge
Country of Study: United Kingdom
Closing Date: 3 April
Funding: Private

For further information contact:

Email: studentfunding@ed.ac.uk

Ramanujan Research Studentship in Mathematics

Purpose: The Ramanujan Studentship is normally awarded for nine months in the first instance, while the student takes the course leading to the MASt in Mathematics

Eligibility: For students from India hoping to do research for a PhD degree in Cambridge. Students of any University or comparable institution in India who have not already begun residence in Cambridge and who hold a First Class Honours degree or its equivalent, or are likely to do so by the time of entry, are eligible to apply
Level of Study: Research
Type: Studentship
Value: £45,650
Length of Study: 1 year
Frequency: Annual
Country of Study: United Kingdom
Closing Date: 8 January
Additional Information: www.student-funding.cam.ac.uk/fund/ramanujan-research-studentship-in-mathematics-2022

For further information contact:

Tel: (44) 1223 761893

Ramanujan Research Studentship in Mathematics at Trinity College, Cambridge

Purpose: Trinity College, University of Cambridge is offering Ramanujan Research Studentship for students who wish to undertake research in Mathematics. Student should hold a first class honours degree or its equivalent from any university or comparable institution in India
Eligibility: Indian students can apply for this studentship. Applicants from outside the home country will often need to meet specific English language/other language requirements in order to be able to study there
Type: Research
Length of Study: 1 year
Study Establishment: Studentship is awarded in the field of Pure or Applied Mathematics of Cambridge
Country of Study: Any country
Application Procedure: Completed Preliminary Application Forms must be returned by post or email
No. of awards offered: 1
Closing Date: 8 January
Additional Information: www.student-funding.cam.ac.uk/ramanujan-research-studentship-mathematics-202021

Robinson College: Lewis Graduate Scholarship

Purpose: The College expects to award one Lewis Scholarship to a graduate student applying to read for a PhD degree in the humanities
Eligibility: Open to all applicants who name Robinson College as their college of first choice on the Board of Graduate Studies Application Form for Admissions as a Graduate student, or are prepared to change college if offered the scholarship. The scholarship is conditional on the candidate being offered a place at the University
Level of Study: Postgraduate
Type: Scholarship
Value: varies
Length of Study: The scholarship is tenable for up to 3 years, subject to satisfactory academic progress
Frequency: Annual
Study Establishment: University of Cambridge
Country of Study: United Kingdom
Application Procedure: Applicants should send a curriculum vitae and details of their intended programme of research including no more than one A4 page describing their proposed research project, together with details of other grant applications. Applications must be submitted by post to the Graduate Admissions Tutor
Additional Information: www.robinson.cam.ac.uk/alumni/fundraising-priorities/bursaries-scholarships/lewis-research-scholarship-fund

For further information contact:

Robinson College, Grange Road, Cambridge CB3 9AN, United Kingdom.

Tel: (44) 1223 339 100
Fax: (44) 1223 351 794
Email: graduate-admissions@robinson.cam.ac.uk

St John's College Benefactors' Scholarships for Research

Purpose: To fund candidates for PhD and MPhil degrees
Eligibility: Open to candidates of any nationality with a First Class (Honours) Degree or equivalent
Level of Study: Postgraduate
Type: Scholarship
Value: £9,000, plus approved college and university fees, a Scholar Book Grant of up to £100 and other expenses
Length of Study: Up to 3 years
Frequency: Annual
Study Establishment: St John College, University of Cambridge
Country of Study: United Kingdom
Application Procedure: Applicants must see the Cambridge University Graduate Studies prospectus for particulars
Closing Date: 1 March
No. of awards given last year: 3

Additional Information: www.student-funding.cam.ac.uk/fund/st-johns-college-benefactors-scholarships-for-postgraduate-students-2022

For further information contact:

St John's College, St John's Street, Cambridge CB2 1TP, United Kingdom.

Tel: (44) 12 2333 8612
Fax: (44) 12 2376 6419
Email: graduate_admissions@joh.cam.ac.uk

The Girton Singapore Scholarship

Eligibility: 1. They are open to students who have graduated or will have graduated before 1st October of the year they apply, and who nominate Girton as their first or second choice College. 2. A first-class degree is almost always required and election will be conditional on the candidate being granted Postgraduate Student status by the University of Cambridge. 3. The holder must become a member of the College and be a candidate for either a Masters or a PhD degree. 4. Current Cambridge students who are members of another College are eligible to apply if they are moving from one course of study to another, however if they are part-way through a course they cannot apply for the awards.
Level of Study: Postgraduate
Type: Scholarship
Value: £10,000
Length of Study: 3 years
Frequency: Annual
Country of Study: United Kingdom
Additional Information: www.girton.cam.ac.uk/postgraduates/fees-finance-funding

For further information contact:

Tel: (44) 1223 766673
Email: postgraduate.office@girton.cam.ac.uk

The Rhona Beare Award

Eligibility: 1. They are open to students who have graduated or will have graduated before 1st October of the year they apply, and who nominate Girton as their first or second choice College. 2. A first-class degree is almost always required and election will be conditional on the candidate being granted Postgraduate Student status by the University of Cambridge. 3. The holder must become a member of the College and be a candidate for either a Masters or a PhD degree. 4. Current Cambridge students who are members of another College are eligible to apply if they are moving from one course of study to another, however if they are part-way through a course they cannot apply for the awards.
Level of Study: Postgraduate
Type: Scholarship
Value: Approximately £1,500
Length of Study: 3 years
Frequency: Annual
Country of Study: United Kingdom
Closing Date: 25 March

For further information contact:

Email: graduate.office@girton.cam.ac.uk

Trinity College: Studentships in Mathematics

Purpose: The Trinity Studentship in Mathematics is a one-year studentship intended for students who wish to undertake research in Mathematics at the University of Cambridge but who are required by the Faculty of Mathematics to take, in the first instance, the course leading to the Master of Advanced Study (MASt)
Eligibility: Eligible candidates must; 1. Have applied for admission, or already received an offer of admission, to the University of Cambridge for the MASt degree. 2. Not yet have been members of the University of Cambridge as an undergraduate or graduate student
Level of Study: Postgraduate
Type: Studentship
Value: £25,000 to £45,000
Length of Study: 1 year of study
Frequency: Annual
Country of Study: Any country
No. of awards offered: 4
Closing Date: 8 January
Funding: Private
Additional Information: www.student-funding.cam.ac.uk/fund/trinity-studentship-in-mathematics-2022

For further information contact:

Tel: (1) 1223 761893
Email: gradfunding@trin.cam.ac.uk

Westminster College Lewis and Gibson Scholarship

Purpose: To enable Scholars to study for a theology degree at the University of Cambridge as an integral part of his or her

U

training for the ministry of a church in the reformed tradition which has a Presbyterian order
Eligibility: Open to graduates of a recognised university who are members of the United Reformed Church in the United Kingdom or of any church not established by the state which is a member of the World Alliance of Reformed Churches and has a Presbyterian form of government. Applicants must have been recognised by their churches as candidates for the Ministry of Word and Sacrament, but should not yet have been ordained
Level of Study: Postgraduate
Type: Scholarship
Value: One scholarship of £6,000 or two scholarships of £3,000 approx
Length of Study: 1 year, renewable for up to 2 further years
Frequency: Annual
Study Establishment: The University of Cambridge
Country of Study: United Kingdom
Application Procedure: If it is the intention to study at the postgraduate level, an application should be made at the same time to the Board of Graduate Studies of the university. The Scholar will normally study for one of the following degrees BA or MPhil in theology, or PhD. He or she will be a member of both Westminster College and one of the University's constituent colleges
Closing Date: 24 December
Funding: Private
Contributor: A legacy controlled by the United Reformed Church
No. of awards given last year: 2
Additional Information: www.divinity.cam.ac.uk/study-here/lewisgibson

For further information contact:

Westminster College, Madingley Road, Cambridge CB3 0AA, United Kingdom.

Tel: (44) 1223 741 084
Fax: (44) 1223 300 765
Email: arh26@cam.ac.uk

William Wyse Studentship in Social Anthropology

Purpose: To support study
Eligibility: Open to all students who wish to study for the degree of PhD, the Studentships are open to any person who is admitted to the University of Cambridge by the Board of Graduate Studies and intends to do research in Social Anthropology leading to the PhD Degree, regardless of whether they are liable for fees at the Home or Overseas rate. It is a condition of the Studentships that United Kingdom and European Union students are eligible for ESRC or Vice-Chancellor's Awards and that overseas students fulfil the eligibility criteria for Cambridge International Scholarships
Level of Study: Doctorate
Type: Studentship
Value: Varies
Length of Study: 3 years
Frequency: Annual
Study Establishment: The University of Cambridge
Country of Study: United Kingdom
Application Procedure: Applicants should contact the admissions secretary for details
No. of awards offered: 8
Closing Date: 11 January
Funding: Private
No. of awards given last year: 5 grants
No. of applicants last year: 8
Additional Information: www.student-funding.cam.ac.uk/fund/william-wyse-studentship-2022

For further information contact:

Email: tutorial.office@newn.cam.ac.uk

Wood Whistler Prize and Medal

Purpose: To reward an outstanding student
Level of Study: Graduate
Type: Prize
Value: Approx. £2,500
Length of Study: 3 years
Frequency: Annual
Study Establishment: Newnham College, University of Cambridge
Country of Study: United Kingdom
Application Procedure: There is no application form. Names are put forward by the English faculty of the University of Cambridge
Funding: Private

For further information contact:

Email: tutorial.office@newn.cam.ac.uk

University of Cambridge (Cambridge Commonwealth Trust, Cambridge Overseas Trust, Gates Cambridge Trust, Cambridge European Trust and Associated Trusts)

Benet Street, Cambridge CB2 3PT, United Kingdom.

Email: info@overseastrusts.cam.ac.uk
Website: www.cambridgetrust.org/

The Cambridge Commonwealth Trust and the Cambridge Overseas Trust (formerly the Chancellor's Fund) were established in 1982 by the University of Cambridge under the Chairmanship of his Royal Highness the Prime of Wales to provide financial assistance for students from overseas who, without help, would be unable to take up their places at Cambridge. Since 1982, the Cambridge Commonwealth Trust has brought 6,600 students from 51 countries to Cambridge, the Cambridge Overseas trust 4,252 students from 76 countries.

British Chevening Cambridge Scholarships for Postgraduate Study (Indonesia)

Purpose: To financially support those undertaking postgraduate study
Eligibility: Applicants must be citizens of Indonesia
Level of Study: Postgraduate
Type: Scholarship
Value: The University Composition Fee at the overseas rate, approved college fees, a maintenance allowance sufficient for a single student and a contribution towards return economy airfare
Length of Study: 1 year
Frequency: Annual
Study Establishment: The University of Cambridge
Country of Study: United Kingdom
Application Procedure: Applicants must apply directly to the British Embassy in Indonesia
Contributor: Offered in collaboration with the Malaysian Commonwealth Studies Centre and the Foreign and Commonwealth Office (FCO)

For further information contact:

Email: cambridge.trust@admin.cam.ac.uk

British Chevening Malaysia Cambridge Scholarship for PhD Study

Purpose: To financially support study towards a PhD
Eligibility: Open to students from Malaysia. Applicants must apply to the University of Cambridge and be offered a place at Cambridge in the normal way. All applicants must have a First Class or High Second Class (Honours) Degree or equivalent and normally be under 26. They must be successfully nominated for an Overseas Research Student (ORS) award
Level of Study: Doctorate
Type: Scholarship
Value: The University Composition Fee at the appropriate rate, approved college fees, a maintenance allowance sufficient for a single student and a contribution towards return economy airfare
Length of Study: Up to 3 years
Frequency: Annual
Study Establishment: The University of Cambridge
Country of Study: United Kingdom
Application Procedure: Applicants must complete a preliminary application form, which can be obtained from local universities, offices of the British Council or the Trust. Completed forms must be returned to the main address. Shortlisted candidates will be sent forms for admission to the University of Cambridge. The preliminary application form can also be downloaded from www.admin.cam.ac.uk/offices/gradstud/admissions/forms/
Contributor: Offered in collaboration with the Foreign and Commonwealth Office (FCO)

For further information contact:

Email: cambridge.trust@admin.cam.ac.uk

British Petroleum Research Bursaries for PhD Study

Purpose: To celebrate the Centenary for BP and New Hall College
Eligibility: For citizens of Russia, Ukraine, Countries of the former Soviet Union, China, The Middle East (particularly Egypt), Southern Africa, or South Asia
Level of Study: Doctorate
Type: Bursary
Value: £2,000 annually
Frequency: Annual

Study Establishment: BP and New Hall College, The University of Cambridge
Country of Study: United Kingdom
Application Procedure: Applicants for a place to do a PhD should apply for an ORS award and should normally be successfully nominated for an ORS award or an ORS equivalent award, which meets the difference between the higher overseas rate and the lower domestic rate of the University Composition Fee

For further information contact:

Email: enquiry@bpgraduates.co.uk

British Petroleum Research Bursaries for Postgraduate Study

Purpose: To celebrate the Centenary for BP and New Hall College
Eligibility: For citizens of Russia, Ukraine, Countries of the former Soviet Union, China, The Middle East (particularly Egypt), Southern Africa, or South Asia
Level of Study: Doctorate
Type: Bursary
Value: £2,000 annually
Length of Study: 1 year
Frequency: Annual
Study Establishment: BP and New Hall College, The University of Cambridge
Country of Study: United Kingdom

For further information contact:

Email: enquiry@bpgraduates.co.uk

Charles Wallace India Trust

Purpose: To financially assist postgraduate study for applicants who are not successful in winning a scholarship
Eligibility: This scholarship is only available for citizens of India. Applicants for a place to do a PhD should apply for an ORS award and should be successfully nominated for an ORS award or an ORS equivalent award, which meets the difference between the higher overseas rate and the lower domestic rate of the University Composition Fee
Type: Bursary
Value: Varies
Frequency: Annual
Study Establishment: The University of Cambridge
Country of Study: Any country
Contributor: Charles Wallace India Trust

For further information contact:

Email: cwit@in.britishcouncil.org

China Scholarship Council Cambridge Scholarships

Purpose: To financially assist study towards a PhD.
Eligibility: 1. Applicants should normally have a degree from a recognised university in the People's Republic of China. 2. Each year the China Scholarship Council sets a range of priority subjects.
Level of Study: Doctorate
Type: Scholarship
Value: University tuition fee, Annual stipend (sufficient for a single person), Contribution towards travel costs
Frequency: Annual
Study Establishment: The University of Cambridge
Country of Study: United Kingdom
Application Procedure: By statement in University of Cambridge application.
Contributor: In collaboration with the China Scholarship Council
Additional Information: www.cambridgetrust.org/scholarships/scholarship/?award=34

For further information contact:

Email: cambridge.trust@admin.cam.ac.uk

Corpus Christi Research Scholarship

Purpose: To financially assist study towards a PhD
Eligibility: Applicants must be from India, and already hold a degree equivalent to a first-class or a high upper second from a United Kingdom university
Level of Study: Doctorate
Type: Scholarship
Value: £13,000
Length of Study: 3 Years
Study Establishment: Corpus Christi College, The University of Cambridge
Country of Study: United Kingdom
Application Procedure: Applicants for a place to do a PhD should apply for an ORS award and should normally be successfully nominated for an ORS award or an ORS equivalent award, which meets the difference between the higher overseas rate and the lower domestic rate of the university composition fee
No. of awards offered: 6

Closing Date: 7 January
Contributor: In collaboration with the Corpus Christi College

For further information contact:

Email: graduate-tutorial@corpus.cam.ac.uk

David M. Livingstone (Australia) Scholarship

Purpose: To support students to undertake 1-year postgraduate degree course at the University of Cambridge
Eligibility: The scholarship is only available for citizens of Australia. Scholars must specify Jesus College as their first choice college
Level of Study: Postgraduate
Type: Scholarship
Value: University composition fee and college fee
Length of Study: 1 year
Frequency: Annual
Country of Study: Any country
Closing Date: 31 March
Contributor: Jesus College

For further information contact:

Tel: (44) 1223 760 606
Fax: (44) 1223 338 723
Email: admissions@gradstudies.cam.ac.uk

Developing World Education Fund Scholarships for PhD Study

Purpose: To financially support study towards a PhD
Eligibility: For citizens from Bangladesh, China, India, Pakistan, Sri Lanka or Zambia. Applicants must apply to the University of Cambridge and be offered a place at Cambridge in the normal way. All applicants must have a degree equivalent to a First Class from a United Kingdom university, and normally be under 26
Level of Study: Doctorate
Type: Scholarships and fellowships
Value: The University Composition Fee at the appropriate rate, approve College fees, a maintenance allowance sufficient for a single student, contribution towards an economy return airfare
Frequency: Annual
Study Establishment: The University of Cambridge
Country of Study: United Kingdom
Application Procedure: Applicants for a place to do a PhD should apply for an ORS award and should normally be successfully nominated for an ORS award or an ORS equivalent award, which meets the difference between the higher overseas rate and the lower domestic rate of the University Composition Fee

For further information contact:

Email: joe@advance-africa.com

International Club of Boston College Cambridge Scholarship

Purpose: To financially support those undertaking postgraduate study
Eligibility: Open to students from Chile
Level of Study: Postgraduate
Type: Scholarships and fellowships
Value: The University composition fee at the overseas rate, approved college fees, a maintenance allowance sufficient for a single student, contribution towards an economy return airfare
Length of Study: 1 year
Frequency: Annual
Study Establishment: The University of Cambridge
Country of Study: United Kingdom
Application Procedure: Apply directly to the British Council in Chile. Applicants are reminded that they will also need to apply to the Cambridge Trusts on the Scholarship Application Form (SAF) in the usual way
Contributor: Offered in collaboration with the Instituto Chileno Britanico de Cultura, the British Council, Chile and Cambridge Assessment (formerly the Local Examinations Syndicate), University of Cambridge

For further information contact:

Email: internationalstudents@admin.cam.ac.uk

Jawaharlal Nehru Memorial Trust Commonwealth Shared Scholarships

Purpose: To offer financial support
Eligibility: Open to citizens from India. All applicants must be under the age of 35 years on October 1st with priority given to those candidates under the age of 30 years. They must not be employed by a national or local government department or by a parastatal organization, nor at present be living or studying in a developed country and not have undertaken studies lasting a year or more in a developed country. Priority will be given to candidates wishing to pursue a study related to the economic and social development of their country

Level of Study: Postgraduate
Type: Scholarship
Value: The University Composition Fee, approved college fees, annual stipend sufficient for a single student and contribution towards travel costs
Length of Study: 1 year
Frequency: Annual
Study Establishment: The University of Cambridge, Trinity College
Country of Study: United Kingdom
Application Procedure: Applicants may obtain further details and a preliminary application form by writing before August 16th of the year before entry to the Joint Secretary of the Nehru Trust for Cambridge University, giving details of their academic qualifications
Closing Date: 28 February
Contributor: Offered in collaboration with the Jawaharlal Nehru Memorial Trust and the Commonwealth Scholarship Commission

For further information contact:

The Nehru Trust for Cambridge University, Teen Murti House, Teen Murti Marg 53 - 54 Sidney Street, Cambridge CB2 3HX, United Kingdom.

Email: cambridge.trust@admin.cam.ac.uk

Ministry of Education (Malaysia) Scholarships for Postgraduate Study

Purpose: To financially support those undertaking postgraduate study
Eligibility: Applicants must be from Malaysia, and must be nominated by the Ministry of Education. Applicants must apply to the University of Cambridge and be offered a place at Cambridge in the normal way. They must have a First Class or High Second Class (Honours) Degree or equivalent and normally be under 26
Level of Study: Postgraduate
Type: Scholarship
Value: The University Composition Fee at the overseas rate, approved college fees, a maintenance allowance sufficient for a single student and a contribution to return economy airfare
Length of Study: 1 year
Frequency: Annual
Study Establishment: The University of Cambridge
Country of Study: United Kingdom
Application Procedure: Applicants must complete a preliminary application form, which can be obtained from local universities, offices of the British Council or the Trust. Completed forms must be returned to the main address. Shortlisted candidates will be sent forms for admission to the University of Cambridge. The preliminary application form can also be downloaded from www.admin.cam.ac.uk/offices/gradstud/admissions/forms/
Closing Date: 28 February
Contributor: Offered in collaboration with the Malaysian Commonwealth Studies Centre and the Ministry of Education, Government of Malaysia

For further information contact:

Email: education.intoday@gmail.com

Ministry of Science, Technology and the Environment Scholarships for Postgraduate Study (Malaysia)

Purpose: To financially support those undertaking postgraduate study
Eligibility: Applicants must be from Malaysia, and must be nominated by the Ministry of Science, Technology and the Environment. Applicants must apply to the University of Cambridge and be offered a place at Cambridge in the normal way. They must have a First Class or High Second Class (Honours) Degree or equivalent and normally be under 26
Level of Study: Postgraduate
Type: Scholarship
Value: The University Composition Fee at the overseas rate, approved college fees, a maintenance allowance sufficient for a single student and a contribution to return economy airfare
Length of Study: 1 year
Frequency: Annual
Study Establishment: The University of Cambridge
Country of Study: United Kingdom
Application Procedure: Applicants must complete a preliminary application form, which can be obtained from local universities, offices of the British Council or the Trust. Completed forms must be returned to the main address. Shortlisted candidates will be sent forms for admission to the University of Cambridge. The preliminary application form can also be downloaded from www.admin.cam.ac.uk/offices/gradstud/admissions/forms/
Closing Date: 28 February
Contributor: Offered in collaboration with the Malaysian Commonwealth Studies Centre and the Ministry of Science, Technology and the Environment, Government of Malaysia

For further information contact:

Email: international_scholar@mohe.gov.my

Nehru Trust for the Indian Collections V&A Cambridge DFID Scholarship

Purpose: To financially support those undertaking postgraduate study
Eligibility: Applicants must be from India, and must be under the age of 35 years on October 1st with priority given to those candidates under the age of 30 years. Applicants must not be employed by a national or local government department or by a parastatal organization, nor at present be living or studying in a developed country. Priority will be given to candidates wishing to pursue a course of study related to the economic and social development of their country
Level of Study: Postgraduate
Type: Scholarship
Value: The University Composition Fee at the overseas rate, approved college fees, a maintenance allowance sufficient for a single student and a contribution to return economy airfare. In addition a supplementary allowance to cover a short period of practical training at the Victoria and Albert Museum, or other approved institution, will be given
Length of Study: 1 year
Frequency: Annual
Study Establishment: The University of Cambridge
Country of Study: United Kingdom
Application Procedure: Applicants may obtain further details and a preliminary application form by writing before August 16th of the year before entry to the Joint Secretary at the address given below with details of academic qualifications
Closing Date: 28 February
Contributor: Offered in collaboration with the Nehru Trust for the Indian Collections at the Victoria and Albert (V&A) Museum and the Department for International Development (DFID)

Oxford and Cambridge Society of Bombay Cambridge DFID Scholarship

Purpose: To financially support those undertaking postgraduate study
Eligibility: Open to a resident of Bombay City or the State of Maharashtra whose application is supported by the Oxford and Cambridge Society of Bombay. All applicants must be under the age of 35 on October 1st with priority given to those candidates under the age of 30. They must not be employed by a national or local government department or by a parastatal organization, nor at present be living or studying in a developed country. Priority will be given to candidates wishing to pursue a study related to the economic and social development of their country
Level of Study: Postgraduate
Type: Scholarship
Value: The University Composition Fee at the overseas rate, approved college fees, a maintenance allowance sufficient for a single student and a contribution to return economy airfare
Length of Study: 1 year
Frequency: Annual
Study Establishment: The University of Cambridge
Country of Study: United Kingdom
Application Procedure: Applicants may obtain further details and a preliminary application form by writing before August 16th of the year before entry to the Joint Secretary at address given below with details of academic qualifications
Closing Date: 28 February
Contributor: Offered in collaboration with the Department for International Development (DFID)

Pok Rafeah Cambridge Scholarship

Purpose: To financially support study towards a PhD
Eligibility: Applicants must be from Malaysia. The Trusts cannot admit students to the University or any of its colleges. Applicants for awards from the Trusts must therefore also apply to the University of Cambridge and be offered a place at Cambridge in the normal way. All applicants must have a First Class or High Second Class (Honours) Degree or equivalent and normally be under 26 years. Applicants for scholarships for study towards the degree of PhD must be successfully nominated for an Overseas Research Student (ORS) award, which covers the difference between the home and overseas rate of the University Composition Fee
Level of Study: Doctorate, Postgraduate, Predoctorate
Type: Scholarship
Value: The University Composition Fee at the approved rate, approved college fees, a maintenance allowance sufficient for a single student and a contribution to a return economy airfare
Length of Study: Up to 3 years for PhD study, and 1 year for postgraduate study
Frequency: Annual
Study Establishment: The University of Cambridge
Country of Study: United Kingdom
Application Procedure: Applicants must complete a preliminary application form, which can be obtained from local universities, offices of the British Council or the Trust. The preliminary application form can be downloaded from www.admin.cam.ac.uk/univ/gsprospectus/c7/overseas/schemes.html
Contributor: Offered in collaboration with the Pok Rafeah Foundation

For further information contact:

Email: cambridge.trust@admin.cam.ac.uk

University of Cambridge, Judge Business School

Trumpington Street, Cambridge CB2 1AG, United Kingdom.

Tel: (44) 1223 339 700
Email: enquiries@jbs.cam.ac.uk
Website: www.jbs.cam.ac.uk/
Contact: Mrs Natacha Wilson

The Judge Business School is the University of Cambridge's business school. Founded in 1990, it offers a portfolio of management programmes, including the Cambridge MB-A. Accredited by AMBA and EQUIS, the business school now hosts one of the largest concentrations of interdisciplinary business and management research activity in Europe.

Browns Restaurant Scholarships

Purpose: To provide funds for United Kingdom citizens with a strong interest in the hospitality and tourism industries to study for an MBA
Eligibility: Open to candidates with at least three years of experience in the hospitality or tourism industries. Candidates must show evidence of a career plan showing how they would use the skills and knowledge gained on the MBA course to develop their career within the hospitality or tourism industries. Where an applicant opts for the two year integrated version of the MBA course, arrangements should be in place for the placement year to be in an organisation in the hospitality or tourism industries. Applicants must be United Kingdom citizens
Level of Study: MBA
Type: Scholarship
Value: One scholarship of £20,000 to cover fees and two scholarships of £10,000 to cover roughly half the fees
Length of Study: 1 year
Frequency: Annual
Study Establishment: Judge Institute of Management, University of Cambridge
Country of Study: United Kingdom
Application Procedure: Applicants must complete and submit an application form, together with a covering letter indicating that they would like to apply for a Browns Restaurant Scholarship, to the Judge Institute of Management
Closing Date: March
Funding: Commercial
Contributor: Browns Restaurants Limited

For further information contact:

Email: financial_aid@brown.edu

University of Canberra

University of Canberra, Bruce, ACT 2617, Australia.

Tel: (61) 2 6201 5111
Website: www.canberra.edu.au/

Australia Awards

Purpose: Prestigious international scholarships and fellowships funded by the Australian Government offering the next generation of global leaders an opportunity to undertake study, research and professional development and provides funding and contacts for International students and organisational representatives to study in Australia.
Level of Study: Postgraduate
Type: Award
Value: Various
Country of Study: Australia
Application Procedure: Read through the available details and deadlines for this scholarship on the UC Scholarships website. Click on the Apply Now button and complete the external scholarships application form before the published deadline. www.dfat.gov.au/people-to-people/australia-awards/Pages/how-to-apply-for-an-australia-awards-scholarship
Additional Information: www.canberra.edu.au/scholarship/australia-awards.html

Australian Government Research Training Program (AGRTP) Stipend Scholarship

Purpose: Scholarships are offered in diverse fields to help students in upgrading their education
Eligibility: The Commonwealth Scholarship Guidelines (Research) 2017 set the basis for the conditions of award and outline the basic eligibility requirements for this scholarship. The ANU has established an RTP Policy & Procedure which outlines the standards, processes and conditions for this scholarship. These documents are available from the reference document section of this page.
Level of Study: Postgraduate
Type: Scholarship
Value: A$28,854 per annum
Length of Study: 3 years
Frequency: Annual
Country of Study: Australia
Application Procedure: Commencing students No application is required specifically for this scholarship as all eligible candidates will be considered. Note to ensure you are

considered please ensure you select the appropriate boxes in the admissions application form to note that you are interested in being considered for any available scholarships.
Closing Date: 31 August

For further information contact:

The Australian National University, Canberra, ACT 0200, Australia.

Tel: (61) 2 6125 5111
Email: gro@anu.edu.au

Bickerton-Widdowson Trust Memorial Scholarship

Level of Study: Postgraduate
Type: Scholarship
Value: NZ$2,000
Frequency: Annual
Country of Study: Any country
No. of awards offered: 1
Closing Date: 1 November

For further information contact:

Email: scholarships@canterbury.ac.nz

UC International Alumni Scholarship

Eligibility: 1. For international students who have completed a UC Bachelor degree and are commencing Master degree courses at the Bruce campus only. 2. Articulation, Sponsored and Diplomatic students not eligible.
Level of Study: Postgraduate
Type: Scholarship
Value: 10% off total tuition fee for duration of the course
Country of Study: Australia
Application Procedure: No scholarship application is required for this Scholarship. To be considered, submit an International student application to study at UC. www.canberra.edu.au/future-students/apply-to-uc/international-student-applications
Additional Information: www.canberra.edu.au/scholarship/uc-international-alumni.html

UC International Course Merit Scholarship

Eligibility: 1. Postgraduate students must have achieved 65% or higher from their Bachelor degree to be eligible for this scholarship. 2. Articulation, Sponsored and Diplomatic students not eligible.
Level of Study: Postgraduate
Type: Scholarship
Value: 25% off total tuition fee for duration of the course
Frequency: Other
Country of Study: Australia
Application Procedure: No scholarship application is required for this Scholarship. To be considered, submit an International student application to study at UC. www.canberra.edu.au/future-students/apply-to-uc/international-student-applications
Additional Information: www.canberra.edu.au/scholarship/uc-international-course-merit.html

UC International High Achiever Scholarship

Eligibility: 1. GPA 6 out of 7. 2. 80% (or equivalent grade) or higher for Masters degree.
Level of Study: Postgraduate
Type: Scholarship
Value: 20% off total tuition fee for duration of the course
Country of Study: Australia
Application Procedure: No scholarship application is required for this Scholarship. To be considered, submit an International student application to study at UC. www.canberra.edu.au/future-students/apply-to-uc/international-student-applications
Additional Information: www.canberra.edu.au/scholarship/uc-international-high-achiever.html

UC International Merit Scholarship

Eligibility: 1. GPA 5 out of 7. 2. 65% (or equivalent grade) or higher for Masters degree.
Level of Study: Postgraduate
Type: Scholarship
Value: 10% off total tuition fee for duration of the course
Frequency: Other
Country of Study: Australia
Application Procedure: No scholarship application is required for this Scholarship. To be considered, submit an International student application to study at UC. www.canberra.edu.au/future-students/apply-to-uc/international-student-applications
Additional Information: www.canberra.edu.au/scholarship/uc-international-merit.html

University of Canterbury

Level 9, 142 Lambton Quay, Wellington, PO Box 11915, Wellington 6142, New Zealand.

Tel: (64) 3 369 3999
Email: info@canterbury.ac.nz
Website: www.canterbury.ac.nz

The University of Canterbury offers a variety of subjects in a few flexible degree structures, namely, first and postgraduate degrees in arts, commerce, education, engineering, fine arts, forestry, law, music and science. At Canterbury, research and teaching are closely related, and while this feature shapes all courses, it is very marked at the postgraduate level.

Betty Wignall Scholarship in Chemistry

Purpose: The purpose of this scholarship is to support students for study towards a PhD in the Department of Chemistry at the University of Canterbury.
Level of Study: Postgraduate
Type: Scholarship
Value: NZ$5,000 per 120 points of enrolment
Length of Study: 3 years
Frequency: Annual
Country of Study: New Zealand
No. of awards offered: 1
Closing Date: 15 May
Additional Information: www.canterbury.ac.nz/scholarshipsforms/regulations/Betty_Wignall_Scholarship.pdf

For further information contact:

Email: scholarships@canterbury.ac.nz

Dennis William Moore Scholarship

Level of Study: Postgraduate
Type: Scholarship
Value: NZ$5,000
Length of Study: 1 to 3 years
Frequency: Annual
Country of Study: New Zealand
Closing Date: 1 November
Additional Information: www.canterbury.ac.nz/scholarshipsforms/regulations/Dennis_William_Moore_Scholarship.pdf

For further information contact:

Email: scholarships@canterbury.ac.nz

Dow Agrosciences Bursary in Chemical Engineering

Purpose: In 1990, DowElanco (NZ) Limited took over the bursary, formerly offered by Ivon Watkins-Dow Limited, for tenure in the Department of Chemical Engineering. In January 1998, DowElanco (NZ) Limited changed its name to Dow AgroSciences (NZ) Limited
Eligibility: Must be a full-time student who is enrolled for a BE(Hons) in Chemical & Process Engineering. The applicant must have completed, or been exempted from, the First Professional examination
Type: Bursary
Value: NZ$2,500
Length of Study: 1 year
Frequency: Annual
Country of Study: Any country
Application Procedure: You may apply through the webpage approximately 8 weeks before applications close. If it's possible to apply on-line for this scholarship there will be a link to the on-line system. If the link is not provided, please download and complete the application form. However, if the scholarship is managed by Universities NZ or another department of the University, an External Website link will appear and application instructions will be available through that link
No. of awards offered: 1
Closing Date: 31 March

For further information contact:

Tel: (64) 800 827 748
Email: enrol@canterbury.ac.nz

Ethel Rose Overton Scholarship

Level of Study: Postgraduate
Type: Scholarship
Value: PhD students Up to NZ$30,000 ($10,000 per annum) MFA students NZ$7,500
Length of Study: 1 to 3 years
Frequency: Annual
Country of Study: New Zealand
Closing Date: 1 November
Additional Information: www.canterbury.ac.nz/scholarshipsforms/regulations/Ethel_Rose_Overton_Scholarship.pdf

For further information contact:

Email: scholarships@canterbury.ac.nz

Farina Thompson Charitable Trust Music Scholarship

Level of Study: Postgraduate
Type: Studentship
Value: NZ$10,000
Length of Study: 1 year
Frequency: Annual
Country of Study: New Zealand
No. of awards offered: 1
Closing Date: 1 November
Additional Information: www.canterbury.ac.nz/scholarshipsforms/regulations/Farina_Thompson_Charitable_Trust_Music_Scholarship.pdf

For further information contact:

Email: scholarships@canterbury.ac.nz

Frank and Doris Bateson Memorial Graduate Scholarship

Level of Study: Postgraduate
Type: Scholarship
Value: NZ$2,500
Frequency: Annual
Country of Study: New Zealand
No. of awards offered: 1
Closing Date: 15 October
Additional Information: www.canterbury.ac.nz/scholarshipsforms/regulations/Frank_and_Doris_Bateson_Memorial_Graduate_Scholarship.pdf

For further information contact:

Email: scholarships@canterbury.ac.nz

Kitchener Memorial Scholarship

Purpose: The Kitchener Memorial Scholarship Fund offers scholarships to past or present members of the Armed Forces or their children, who are undertaking an agricultural course of study at a New Zealand university
Eligibility: Applicants must be either; 1. Past or present members of the Armed Forces or children of past or present members of the Armed Forces who have seen active service and who, at the time of enlistment, were domiciled in New Zealand, whether actually resident there or not, or. 2. Past or present members of the Armed Forces or their children to whom the above does not apply, or. 3. People resident in New Zealand for a period of not less than three years immediately before the award of the scholarship
Level of Study: Graduate
Type: Scholarship
Value: NZ$500
Frequency: Annual
Country of Study: New Zealand
Closing Date: 1 December
Funding: Private

Lighthouse Vision Trust Scholarship

Purpose: The scholarships support students with a vision impairment in undertaking study at the University of Canterbury. It was established in 2016 by the Lighthouse Vision Trust
Eligibility: Applicants must have a vision impairment that qualifies them to register with the Blind Foundation. By the closing date for applications, an applicant must have registered with the University's Disability Resource Service as a student with a vision impairment. Applicants must be citizens of New Zealand or holders of New Zealand residence class visas. Applicants must be enrolled, full-time or part-time, at the University at either undergraduate or postgraduate level.
Level of Study: Postgraduate
Type: Scholarship
Value: Up to NZ$10,000 can be received as total value
Length of Study: 1 year
Frequency: Annual
Country of Study: New Zealand
Application Procedure: 1 Applications must be made online at the Scholarships website by 31 March. 2 Applicants will be considered for both scholarships, and the decision on which of the top candidates will be offered which of the two scholarships will be made randomly. 3 A previous recipient of Lighthouse Vision Trust Scholarship or a Susan Barnes Memorial Scholarship may re-apply for the scholarship that they held, and a previous recipient of one of the scholarships may apply for the other scholarship in another year. However, no student may hold one of the scholarships or a combination of the two scholarships over a total period of more than three years
No. of awards offered: 1
Closing Date: March
Funding: Private
Additional Information: www.canterbury.ac.nz/scholarshipsforms/regulations/Lighthouse_Vision_Trust_Scholarship_&_Susan_Barnes_Memorial_Scholarship.pdf

For further information contact:

Email: scholarships@canterbury.ac.nz

Marian D Eve Memorial Scholarship

Purpose: This scholarship supports students studying, researching, or developing, resources for early-childhood special-needs education at the University of Canterbury
Eligibility: Recipients must be undergraduate or postgraduate students who are enrolled full-time at the University and studying, researching, or developing, in any discipline, resources for early-childhood special-needs education
Level of Study: Doctorate, Graduate, Postgraduate
Type: Scholarship
Value: NZ$2,000
Length of Study: 1 year
Frequency: Annual
Country of Study: Any country
Application Procedure: You may apply through the webpage approximately 8 weeks before applications close. If it's possible to apply on-line for this scholarship there will be a link above to the on-line system. Apply through online link. www.studyinnewzealand.govt.nz/how-to-apply/scholarship/details?scholarshipid=25668&institutionid=142318
Closing Date: March
Funding: Private
Additional Information: www.canterbury.ac.nz/scholarshipsforms/regulations/Marian_D'Eve_Memorial_Scholarship.pdf

For further information contact:

Email: scholarships@canterbury.ac.nz

McKelvey Award

Purpose: This award supports and PhD students in the New Zealand School of Forestry at the University of Canterbury. Normally, the award is available to assist students to present a paper at a relevant conference. However, in the absence of suitable applications, the applications may be opened to eligible students seeking support to meet other costs associated with their study
Eligibility: This award supports master's and PhD students in the New Zealand School of Forestry at the University of Canterbury. Normally, the award is available to assist students to present a paper at a relevant conference. However, in the absence of suitable applications, the applications may be opened to eligible students seeking support to meet other costs associated with their study. Students enrolled in a programme for a master's or PhD degree in the New Zealand School of Forestry
Level of Study: Postgraduate
Type: Scholarship
Value: NZ$1,000
Frequency: Annual
Country of Study: Any country
Application Procedure: Apply online www.fore.canterbury.ac.nz/people/index.shtml
No. of awards offered: 1
Closing Date: 1 April
Funding: Foundation

For further information contact:

Email: scholarships-cf@universitiesnz.ac.nz

Park and Paulay Scholarship

Purpose: This scholarship acknowledges and rewards a top performer in the first two Professional years of the programme for a Bachelor of Engineering (Honours) degree in Civil Engineering at the University of Canterbury
Eligibility: Full-time students in the Third Professional Year of the programme for the Bachelor of Engineering (Honours) degree in Civil Engineering (BE(Hons)(Civil)) at the University of Canterbury, who are enrolled in at least four courses related to Structural or Geotechnical or Earthquake Engineering
Level of Study: Graduate
Type: Scholarship
Value: NZ$2,500
Length of Study: 1 year
Frequency: Annual
Country of Study: New Zealand
Application Procedure: You may apply through the webpage approximately 8 weeks before applications close. If it's possible to apply on-line for this scholarship there will be a link above to the on-line system. If the link is not provided, please download and complete the application form located below. Closing dates are yet to be released for the same
No. of awards offered: 1
Closing Date: 31 March
Funding: Private
Additional Information: www.canterbury.ac.nz/scholarshipsforms/regulations/Park_and_Paulay_Undergraduate_Scholarship.pdf

For further information contact:

Tel: (64) 3 369 4900
Email: scholarships@canterbury.ac.nz

UC Te Kaupeka Ture Faculty of Law PhD Fees Scholarship

Level of Study: Doctorate
Type: Scholarship
Value: The prize is tuition fees for thesis enrolment
Length of Study: period necessary to complete up to 360 points of enrolment
Frequency: Annual
Country of Study: New Zealand
Closing Date: 1 December
Additional Information: www.canterbury.ac.nz/scholarshipsforms/regulations/UC_Te_Kaupeka_Ture_Faculty_of_Law_PhD_Fees_Scholarship.pdf

For further information contact:

Email: scholarships@canterbury.ac.nz

Wood Technology Research Centre – Postgraduate Scholarships

Purpose: To develop a computer model to simulate energy flow and energy efficiency in wood and wood product processing industry
Level of Study: Postgraduate
Type: Scholarship
Value: NZ$24,000 per year for PhD and NZ$18,000 per year for ME
Length of Study: 3 years for PhD and one and half year for ME
Country of Study: New Zealand
Application Procedure: To apply or for further information on the above scholarships, please contact Dr Shusheng Pang
Contributor: University of Canterbury
Additional Information: www.canterbury.ac.nz/engineering/schools/forestry/research/woodtech/

For further information contact:

Wood Technology Centre, Department of Chemical and Process Engineering, University of Canterbury, Christchurch 8041, New Zealand.

Tel: (64) 3 364 2538
Fax: (64) 3 364 2063
Email: shusheng.pang@canterbury.ac.nz

University of Canterbury, Department of Management

Private Bag 4800, Christchurch 8140, New Zealand.

Tel: (64) 3 369 3888
Email: studybusiness@canterbury.ac.nz
Website: www.canterbury.ac.nz/study/subjects/management/management.html
Contact: Mrs Suzanne Worrall, MBA Programme Director

Management involves organising teams of people and boosting business performance.

Auckland Council Chief Economist's Research Scholarship in Economics

Purpose: The purpose of this scholarship is to encourage and support postgraduate research into urban economics that has particular relevance to local government in New Zealand
Eligibility: 1. At the time of application candidates must be enrolled or planning to enrol in a postgraduate programme at a New Zealand university. 2. The postgraduate programme must be in the area of urban economics. Universities NZ and Auckland Council reserve the right to determine the eligibility of a particular area of study. 3. A thesis, dissertation, or research report must be a requirement of the postgraduate programme
Level of Study: Postgraduate
Type: Scholarship
Value: Each year Auckland Council may grant one scholarship with an award of NZ$4,000 or two scholarships with an award of NZ$2,000 each
Length of Study: 1 year
Frequency: Varies
Country of Study: New Zealand
Application Procedure: Apply online universitiesnz.communityforce.com/
No. of awards offered: 3
Closing Date: 1 February
Funding: Foundation

For further information contact:

Email: scholarships-cf@universitiesnz.ac.nz

U

Barbara Mito Reed Award

Purpose: The award was established in memory of Dr Barbara Mito Reed (1955-1990), a graduate in Japanese of the University of Canterbury, by her husband, Mr T. Mito, her family and her friends. It was established to help outstanding graduate students of Japanese, whose native language is not Japanese, to further their studies towards a higher degree in a field of Japanese language and/or culture
Eligibility: The scholarship is open to graduates of the University of Canterbury enrolled, or intending to enrol, in a postgraduate programme in a field of Japanese studies at the University of Canterbury or at a university in Japan. Normally, the programme will be for a BA(Hons), master's or doctoral degree. The scholarship is open to citizens or Permanent Residents of New Zealand, excluding native speakers of Japanese
Level of Study: Postgraduate
Type: Scholarship
Value: NZ$1,000
Length of Study: 1 year
Frequency: Annual
Country of Study: New Zealand
Application Procedure: Apply online universitiesnz.communityforce.com/
No. of awards offered: 1
Closing Date: 31 March
Funding: Foundation
Additional Information: https://scholarshipscanterbury.communityforce.com/Funds/Search.aspx

For further information contact:

Email: scholarships@canterbury.ac.nz

BayTrust Bruce Cronin Scholarship

Purpose: This scholarship has been established to recognise his service to the people of the Bay of Plenty
Eligibility: Applicants must have links to the BayTrust geographical area. This area is shown on the BayTrust website www.baytrust.org.nz Applicants will be eligible if they were born in, or attended school in, or have whakapapa back to the area.
Level of Study: Postgraduate
Type: Scholarship
Value: NZ$5,000
Length of Study: 1 year
Frequency: Annual
Country of Study: New Zealand
Application Procedure: Apply online
No. of awards offered: 2
Closing Date: 1 February
Funding: Foundation

For further information contact:

Level 9, 142 Lambton Quay, Wellington, PO Box 11915, Wellington 6142, New Zealand.

Tel: (64) 4 381 8500
Email: info@baytrust.org.nz

Christchurch City Council Antarctic Scholarship

Purpose: The Christchurch City Council offers a NZ$10,000 one-year scholarship for a University of Canterbury student to carry out Antarctic or Southern Ocean research at master's or PhD level. The scholarship includes one season of logistical support provided by Antarctica New Zealand
Eligibility: A candidate who, during the tenure of the scholarship, is studying for a PhD or is in the thesis year of a master's degree at the University of Canterbury in an Antarctic-related topic
Level of Study: Postgraduate
Type: Scholarship
Value: NZ$10,000
Length of Study: 1 year
Frequency: Varies
Country of Study: Any country
Application Procedure: Apply online through link www.antarcticanz.govt.nz/scholarships-and-fellowships
Closing Date: 31 March
Funding: Foundation

For further information contact:

International Antarctic Centre, 38 Orchard Road, Christchurch 8053, New Zealand.

Email: adrian.mcdonald@canterbury.ac.nz

Deutscher Akademischer Austauschdienst (German Academic Exchange Service) Scholarships

Purpose: The DAAD supports over 100,000 German and international students and researchers around the globe each year – making it the world's largest funding organisation of its kind
Eligibility: Graduates of all disciplines can apply for a scholarship to complete a postgraduate or Master's degree course at a German higher education institution and to gain a degree in Germany (Master's/Diploma)

Level of Study: Postgraduate
Type: Scholarship
Value: €750
Length of Study: 10-24 Months
Frequency: Annual
Country of Study: Any country
Application Procedure: See Website www.universitiesnz.ac.nz/scholarships/daad
Closing Date: 15 October
Funding: Trusts
Additional Information: https://scholarshipscanterbury.communityforce.com/Funds/Search.aspx

For further information contact:

Embassy of the Federal Republic of Germany, PO Box 1687, Wellington 6011, New Zealand.

Email: daad@auckland.ac.nz

Ernest William File Scholarship

Purpose: The purpose of the scholarship is to support the sons and daughters of members of the Rail and Maritime Transport Union (RMTU) in their first year of degree study at a New Zealand university
Eligibility: 1. Sons or daughters of financial members of the RMTU. 2. Enrolled or planning on enrolling in their first year of full time study for an undergraduate degree at a New Zealand university. Applications will not be accepted from anyone who already has a qualification from a tertiary institution in New Zealand or overseas
Level of Study: Graduate
Type: Scholarship
Value: The value of the scholarship is NZ$2,000 per year
Frequency: Annual
Country of Study: New Zealand
Application Procedure: Applications must be done online. universitiesnz.communityforce.com/Login.aspx
No. of awards offered: 2
Closing Date: 1 April
Funding: Private
Additional Information: https://scholarshipscanterbury.communityforce.com/Funds/Search.aspx

Francis Martin Baillie Reynolds Scholarship in Law to Oxford

Purpose: The purpose of the scholarship is to assist New Zealand Law graduates to commence postgraduate study in Law at the University of Oxford. It has been established to recognise the support that Emeritus Professor Francis Reynolds, Worcester College, Oxford, has provided to New Zealand Law students at the University of Oxford for over 40 years
Eligibility: 1. A New Zealand citizen or permanent resident. 2. Has completed the requirements for a LLB degree from a New Zealand University. 3. The date of application has applied for a place in a postgraduate programme in Law at the University of Oxford
Level of Study: Postgraduate
Type: Scholarship
Value: NZ$10,000
Length of Study: 1 year
Frequency: Annual
Country of Study: New Zealand
Application Procedure: Apply online through link universitiesnz.communityforce.com
Closing Date: 28 February
Funding: Trusts

Frank Knox Memorial Fellowships at Harvard University

Purpose: Annie Reid Knox set up these scholarships to honour her late husband and asked that future scholars be selected on the basis of future promise of leadership, strength of character, keen mind, a balanced judgement and a devotion to the democratic ideal
Eligibility: 1. New Zealand citizens at the time of application, normally resident in New Zealand. 2. Have completed or will complete a first or higher degree at a New Zealand university. 3. Studying for a first or higher degree; or have completed a first or higher degree and graduated no earlier than 2018
Level of Study: Postgraduate
Type: Fellowship
Value: US$32,000 plus tuition and health insurance fee per annum
Length of Study: 2 year
Frequency: Annual
Country of Study: Any country
Application Procedure: Apply online through the link universitiesnz.communityforce.com
Closing Date: 1 October
Funding: Trusts

For further information contact:

Email: emily@kennedytrust.org.uk

G B Battersby-Trimble Scholarship in Computer Science

Purpose: The scholarship supports postgraduate students in Computer Science at the University of Canterbury.
Eligibility: Eligibility criteria 2.1 Applicants must be enrolled full-time or part-time at the University in one of the following a. The final year of a programme for an honours degree in Computer Science. b. A programme for a master's degree in Computer Science. c. A programme for a PhD in Computer Science. 2.2 Current and former recipients may apply for new tenure of the scholarship.
Level of Study: Postgraduate
Type: Scholarship
Value: 1. US$2,000 for honours students and master students doing courses. 2. US$7,000 for masters thesis students. 3. US$8,000 for PhD thesis students
Length of Study: 1 year
Frequency: Annual
Country of Study: Any country
Application Procedure: Apply online universitiesnz.communityforce.com
Closing Date: 31 March
Funding: Trusts
Additional Information: scholarshipscanterbury.communityforce.com/Funds/FundDetails.aspx?3672424D4A4E5062613356565A6B4439525848446C4D4234444E636C62682F7559327070593730365070615 66C79686779366E7268312F306975724942415773

For further information contact:

Email: scholarships@canterbury.ac.nz

Gateway Antarctica's Ministry of Foreign Affairs and Trade Scholarship in Antarctic and Southern Ocean Studies

Purpose: The Ministry of Foreign Affairs and Trade (MFAT) Scholarship was founded in 2001 in support of research and teaching in Antarctic Studies in recognition of Antarctica as a continent devoted to peace and research.
Eligibility: The scholarship is awarded by the Board of Gateway Antarctica after considering the recommendation of a special committee, hereafter referred to as the Scholarship Committee, which shall consist of: a. The Director of Gateway Antarctica or nominee. b. One Representative from the Gateway Antarctica Teaching and Learning Working Group. c. One person nominated by the Antarctic Policy Division of the MFAT.
Level of Study: Doctorate, Postgraduate
Type: Scholarship
Value: NZ$5,000
Length of Study: 1 year
Frequency: Varies
Country of Study: New Zealand
Application Procedure: There is no application form. Applicants must provide the following: A Research Proposal, Curriculum Vitae (including contact details), Academic transcript, Two letters of support, Name of supervisor or supervisors, Details of any other scholarships held.
Closing Date: 28 February
Funding: Foundation
Additional Information: www.canterbury.ac.nz/scholarshipsforms/regulations/Gateway_Antarcticas_MFAT_Scholarship_in_Antarctic_and_Southern_Ocean_Studies.pdf

Geography Students Conference Fund

Purpose: The purpose of this fund is to financially assist Master's and PhD research thesis students in the Department of Geography with expenses involved in attending conferences.
Eligibility: Grants-in-aid may be made from the fund to master's and PhD research thesis students in the Department of Geography to assist with expenses involved in attending conferences.
Level of Study: Doctorate, Masters Degree, Postgraduate
Type: Scholarship
Value: NZ$500
Frequency: Varies
Country of Study: New Zealand
Application Procedure: Priority will be given to applications for assistance with attending conferences of the New Zealand Geographical Society.
No. of awards offered: Varies
Closing Date: 31 March
Funding: Trusts
Additional Information: scholarshipscanterbury.communityforce.com/Funds/FundDetails.aspx?3974434C474C374F385A7858596C4F766E4D712B725157446655416253444762707051546D7858494B5247744150696837 5A387858466E726F32657544523868

For further information contact:

Email: scholarships@canterbury.ac.nz

Gertrude Ardagh Holmes Bursary Fund

Purpose: The purpose of this fund is to assist students of ability and good character to commence or to continue their studies at the University of Canterbury, who would otherwise, by reason of their financial circumstances, be unable to do so or be seriously handicapped in doing so.
Eligibility: Applicants must be enrolled, or intending to enrol in the year following the year of application, full-time or part-time at the University in a health-related programme.
Level of Study: Doctorate, Masters Degree, Postgraduate
Type: Scholarship
Value: NZ$2,500
Frequency: Varies
Country of Study: New Zealand
Application Procedure: Applications must be made online at the Scholarships website1 by 31 March. Applications are accepted from previous recipients of the grant. All applications are given equal consideration.
No. of awards offered: Varies
Closing Date: 31 March
Funding: Foundation
Additional Information: scholarshipscanterbury.communityforce.com/Funds/FundDetails.aspx?68356E58436D4D544154345833507330546548414D78463863433773505353774930544657 4D4C476B656656793851564E30714C322B3962354837514F676231

For further information contact:

Email: scholarships@canterbury.ac.nz

Graduate Women Canterbury (Inc.) Trust Board Scholarship

Purpose: The purpose of this scholarship is to support female students at the University of Canterbury to complete bachelor's degrees, bachelor's with honours degrees, and non-thesis postgraduate study.
Eligibility: 1. Applicants must be female and citizens of New Zealand. 2. Applicants must be enrolled full-time at the University, mainly at 300, 400, 500, or 600 level, in: a. a programme for a bachelor's degree. b. a programme for a bachelor's with honours degree. c. postgraduate non-thesis study. 3. Scholarships are available in the following categories: a. For students who are enrolled mainly at 300 level (one scholarship). b. For students who are enrolled mainly at 400, 500, or 600 level (one scholarship).
Level of Study: Postgraduate
Type: Scholarship
Value: NZ$4,500
Length of Study: 1 year
Frequency: Annual
Country of Study: New Zealand
Application Procedure: Applications will not be accepted from previous holders of the scholarship.
No. of awards offered: 2
Closing Date: 31 March
Additional Information: scholarshipscanterbury.communityforce.com/Funds/FundDetails.aspx?496F49596D593768464E3537506B6F754D5442315A38496169665962654D776E4343703139 42656B666349533852704545707578397735 2B30676E456C4F6D67646342436B7631753355513D

For further information contact:

Email: scholarships@canterbury.ac.nz

Grant Lingard Scholarship

Purpose: These scholarships were established by the estate of Peter Lanini in memory of Grant Lingard (1961-1995), a graduate of the School of Fine Arts
Level of Study: Graduate
Type: Scholarship
Value: Full-time tuition fees at the New Zealand domestic rate
Length of Study: 1 year
Frequency: Annual
Country of Study: New Zealand
Application Procedure: You may apply through this webpage approximately 8 weeks before applications close. If it's possible to apply on-line for this scholarship there will be a link above to the on-line system. If the link is not provided, please download and complete the application form located below. Please check the website with the following link. scholarshipscanterbury.communityforce.com
Closing Date: 31 October
Funding: Private
Additional Information: www.canterbury.ac.nz/scholarshipsearch/ScholarshipDetails.aspx?ScholarshipID=6935.223

For further information contact:

Tel: (64) 800 827 748, (64) 3 369 4900
Email: scholarships@canterbury.ac.nz

Henry Kelsey Scholarship

Purpose: The purpose of the scholarship is to provide funds for individuals to undertake research towards a PhD at a New Zealand university or research institution, studying

U

muscular function, including the causes and treatment of muscular dysfunction
Eligibility: Applicants will be New Zealand citizens or permanent residents, and will have a Bachelor degree or equivalent, with honours where they are awarded, in a field appropriate to their intended doctoral study at a New Zealand university
Level of Study: Postgraduate
Type: Scholarship
Value: NZ$10,000
Length of Study: 3 year
Frequency: Varies
Country of Study: New Zealand
Application Procedure: Apply online universitiesnz.communityforce.com/Login.aspx
Closing Date: 1 October
Funding: Trusts

For further information contact:

Level 9, 142 Lambton Quay, Wellington, PO Box 11915, Wellington 6142, New Zealand.

Tel: (64) 4 381 8500

Joan Burns Memorial Scholarship in History

Purpose: The purpose of this scholarship is to recognise and support academic excellence by Honours and Master's students in History at the University of Canterbury.
Eligibility: 1. Applicants must be enrolled full-time or part-time in a Bachelor of Arts with Honours degree programme or in Part 1 of a Master of Arts degree programme. 2. Selection will be based on: a. Academic achievement. b. Academic potential.
Level of Study: Masters Degree, Postgraduate
Type: Scholarship
Value: Stipend equal to domestic tuition fees for 1.00 EFTS
Length of Study: 1 to 2 years
Frequency: Annual
Country of Study: New Zealand
Application Procedure: Applications for the scholarship must be made on the appropriate form, obtainable from the Scholarships website, and must be forwarded to the Scholarships Office, not later than 5pm on 31 March, or, if this is not a business day, not later than 5pm on the next business day.
No. of awards offered: One or more
Closing Date: 31 March
Funding: Private
Additional Information: scholarshipscanterbury.communityforce.com/Funds/FundDetails.aspx?306D773059326330666D667132454E7A65723552792F4C5045776F4C5A71766A46657A5330585664707550515934 6C355476464A7957644B536878622F774E43

For further information contact:

Email: scholarships@canterbury.ac.nz

Kia Ora Foundation Patricia Pratt Scholarship

Purpose: The purpose of the Kia Ora Foundation Patricia Pratt Music Scholarship is to assist outstanding New Zealand musical performers, who have completed the equivalent of an honours degree in musical performance in New Zealand, to continue their musical development at a renowned international music school or conservatorium
Eligibility: Applicants will be New Zealand citizens. Applicants may apply from outside New Zealand but must have resided in New Zealand for at least three of the last five years immediately preceding the year of selection. Applicants will have recently completed the requirements for an honours degree in musical performance at a New Zealand university (or an equivalent musical qualification).
Level of Study: Postgraduate
Type: Scholarship
Value: Funds available for the scholarship are up to NZ$70,000 per annum
Length of Study: 1 year
Frequency: Annual
Country of Study: New Zealand
Application Procedure: Apply online universitiesnz.communityforce.com
Closing Date: 1 March
Funding: Foundation
Additional Information: www.canterbury.ac.nz/scholarshipsearch/ScholarshipDetails.aspx?ScholarshipID=6935.1778

Kiwi Music Scholarship

Purpose: The purpose of the scholarship is to assist outstanding New Zealand musical performers or conductors who have completed or are completing an honours or master's degree in musical performance in New Zealand to continue their musical development either overseas or in New Zealand
Eligibility: Applicants will be New Zealand citizens who are normally resident in New Zealand. Applicants will have completed or are completing an honours or masters degree in musical performance (including vocal performance) or conducting at a New Zealand university, or an equivalent musical qualification.
Level of Study: Postgraduate
Type: Scholarship
Value: NZ$50,000 to NZ$60,000
Length of Study: 3 year
Frequency: Varies

Country of Study: New Zealand
Application Procedure: Apply online universitiesnz.communityforce.com/
Closing Date: 1 March
Funding: Trusts

L B Wood Travelling Scholarship

Purpose: The LB Wood Traveling Scholarship is awarded to supplement some other postgraduate scholarship held by the scholar supporting their studies in Britain. The scholarship can only be awarded for postgraduate study at a university or institution of university rank in Britain
Eligibility: Applicants must 1. be graduates of or graduating from a New Zealand university 2. apply for the scholarship within three years from the date of their graduation 3. have applied for or been awarded another postgraduate scholarship.
Level of Study: Postgraduate
Type: Scholarship
Value: NZ$3,000
Length of Study: 3 years
Frequency: Annual
Country of Study: New Zealand
Application Procedure: Apply online universitiesnz.communityforce.com/
No. of awards offered: 1
Closing Date: 1 April
Funding: Foundation

For further information contact:

Tel: (64) 3 369 3999
Email: info@canterbury.ac.nz

Master of Business Administration Programme

Length of Study: 1 to 5 years
Application Procedure: Applicants must complete an application form, a self-evaluation essay, supply an original transcript or a certified copy of grades and provide two references

For further information contact:

Tel: (64) 3 364 2657
Fax: (64) 3 364 2925
Email: international@regy.canterbury.ac.nz

New Zealand Law Foundation Ethel Benjamin Scholarship (for Women)

Purpose: To support postgraduate research in Law that encompasses the wider objectives of the NZ Law Foundation, in particular research that will protect and promote the interests of the public in relation to legal matters in New Zealand
Eligibility: A Scholarship may be awarded to any woman scholar who is 1. a New Zealand citizen or permanent resident 2. the holder of a New Zealand university law degree (unless there are exceptional circumstances the award would normally be made to candidates who have gained the qualifying degree within the past five years) 3. accepted into a postgraduate course in law at either a New Zealand or an overseas university acceptable to the Selection Committee.
Level of Study: Postgraduate
Type: Scholarship
Value: NZ$20,000 to NZ$30,000
Length of Study: 3 years
Frequency: Annual
Country of Study: Any country
Application Procedure: Apply online universitiesnz.communityforce.com/
No. of awards offered: 3
Closing Date: 1 March
Funding: Trusts
Additional Information: scholarshipscanterbury.communityforce.com/Funds/FundDetails.aspx?496F49596D593768464E3537506B6F754D5442315A34584949614244764D71365A4D68417235516D5A7A4570654E415337484E7A694C4A334E55645A796247595A646D666949744D5A706F3D

For further information contact:

Email: scholarships@canterbury.ac.nz

Prince of Wales' Cambridge International Scholarship

Purpose: To enable graduates of high academic ability to study at Cambridge University
Eligibility: These scholarships are open to graduates who are New Zealand citizens and who wish to pursue a course of research leading to the degree of PhD at Cambridge University
Level of Study: Doctorate, Postgraduate
Type: Scholarship
Value: Value determined by financial need of applicant.
Length of Study: 3 years
Frequency: Annual
Country of Study: New Zealand
Application Procedure: Apply online universitiesnz.communityforce.com
Closing Date: 1 October

Funding: Trusts
Contributor: Universities New Zealand – Te Pōkai Tara
Additional Information: www.canterbury.ac.nz/scholarshipsearch/ScholarshipDetails.aspx?ScholarshipID=6935.1593

For further information contact:

Email: cambridge.trust@admin.cam.ac.uk

Pukehou Poutu Scholarship

Purpose: The money for this scholarship has been made available by a bequest from the estate of Edith Fraser who wished that it be used for an award in agricultural or silvicultural sciences
Eligibility: Applicants must be graduates of a New Zealand university and be New Zealand citizens
Level of Study: Postgraduate
Type: Scholarship
Value: NZ$10,000
Length of Study: 1 year
Frequency: Annual
Country of Study: New Zealand
Application Procedure: Apply online universitiesnz.communityforce.com/Login.aspx
No. of awards offered: 1
Closing Date: 1 October
Funding: Foundation
Additional Information: www.canterbury.ac.nz/scholarshipsearch/ScholarshipDetails.aspx?ScholarshipID=6935.194

For further information contact:

Tel: (64) 3 369 3999
Email: info@canterbury.ac.nz

Roland Stead Postgraduate Scholarship in Biology

Purpose: This scholarship supports Masters research students of biology with an interest in ecology, freshwater fisheries and the Canterbury region.
Eligibility: Open to students who, in the year of application, are enrolled full-time in the School of Biological Sciences who are engaged in research in Part II of the Master of Science degree programme.
Level of Study: Postgraduate
Type: Scholarship
Value: NZ$5,000
Length of Study: 1 year
Frequency: Annual
Country of Study: New Zealand
Application Procedure: Applications for the scholarship must be made to the University of Canterbury Scholarships Office, on the approved form available from the Scholarships website, no later than 5.00 pm on 10 March, or, if this is not a business day, by 5.00 pm on the next business day.
No. of awards offered: 1
Closing Date: 10 March
Funding: Foundation
Additional Information: scholarshipscanterbury.communityforce.com/Funds/FundDetails.aspx?496F49596D593768464E3537506B6F754D5442315A334C3845524435652F4B4676506B56424874517669486676 2B706C672F614942706630392B6B436F51494977555974577532535066303D

For further information contact:

Email: scholarships@canterbury.ac.nz

Sir Douglas Myers Scholarship

Purpose: The Scholarship provides an opportunity for students who have already distinguished themselves academically to attend one of the most prestigious universities in the world
Eligibility: Candidates for the Scholarship must 1. Be entered for the Year 13 senior school examination (for example, NCEA Level 3, Cambridge exams, etc.) or equivalent senior school exam in the year of application. 2. Have a record of achievement sufficient to satisfy the academic criteria for entry to Cambridge University and Gonville and Caius College. 3. Be New Zealand citizens or permanent residents. 4. Normally have completed their five years of secondary schooling in New Zealand
Level of Study: Graduate
Type: Scholarship
Value: Provides tuition fees and a living allowance
Frequency: Annual
Country of Study: New Zealand
Application Procedure: See website universitiesnz.communityforce.com/Login.aspx
No. of awards offered: 1
Closing Date: 1 December
Funding: Private
Additional Information: www.canterbury.ac.nz/scholarshipsearch/ScholarshipDetails.aspx?ScholarshipID=6935.234

For further information contact:

Tel: (64) 3 369 3999
Email: info@canterbury.ac.nz

The Claude McCarthy Fellowships

Purpose: Claude McCarthy Fellowships (Category A) are available to candidates who are graduates of a New Zealand university and who are enrolled in a PhD programme at a New Zealand university.
Eligibility: 1. To enable graduates of a New Zealand university, who are registered and enrolled for a doctoral degree at a New Zealand university, and have been registered for their doctoral degree for at least one year at the closing date for applications. The original work or research must be in literature, science or medicine. Applicants should note that the committee will determine if an applicant's area of study falls within one of those disciplines. 2. If an applicant has previously held a Claude McCarthy Fellowship this does not preclude them from submitting another application however the selection committee will take the earlier fellowship into consideration when making their funding decisions. 3. Applications for overseas conference attendance are enhanced if combined with plans for overseas research activities.
Level of Study: Postgraduate
Type: Scholarship
Value: Varies
Length of Study: 1 year
Frequency: Annual
Country of Study: New Zealand
Application Procedure: Scholarship website: universitiesnz.communityforce.com/Login.aspx
Closing Date: 1 October
Funding: Trusts
Additional Information: www.universitiesnz.ac.nz/scholarships/claude-mccarthy-fellowship

For further information contact:

Tel: (64) 3 369 3999
Email: info@canterbury.ac.nz

The Dick and Mary Earle Scholarship in Technology

Purpose: The purpose of the scholarship is to provide funds for individuals to undertake research towards a masterate or doctorate degree at a New Zealand university or research institution in one or both of these fields: 1. Innovation and product development. 2. Bioprocess technology.
Eligibility: 1. Applicants will be New Zealand citizens or permanent residents who have resided in New Zealand for at least three years immediately preceding the year of selection. 2. Applicants will have a BTech, BEng, BE degree or equivalent from a NZ university, with honours where they are awarded, in a field appropriate to their intended postgraduate study.
Level of Study: Doctorate, Masters Degree
Type: Scholarship
Value: Up to NZ$17,000 per annum at Masters level and NZ$25,000 per annum at PhD level
Length of Study: 3 years
Frequency: Annual
Country of Study: New Zealand
Application Procedure: Scholarship website: universitiesnz.communityforce.com/Login.aspx
No. of awards offered: 2
Closing Date: 1 July
Funding: Trusts
Additional Information: www.universitiesnz.ac.nz/scholarships/dick-and-mary-earle-scholarship-technology

For further information contact:

Tel: (64) 3 369 3999
Email: info@canterbury.ac.nz

The Edward & Isabel Kidson Scholarship

Purpose: The purpose of the scholarships is to enable a graduate of a New Zealand university, who is of good character and who has shown an ability in physics or a combination of physics and mathematics, to undertake further advanced study or research in meteorology, either in New Zealand or elsewhere.
Eligibility: 1. Applicants should be graduates of a New Zealand university, be of good character and have shown ability in physics or a combination of physics and mathematics. 2. Preference will be given to (in order): a. past pupils of Nelson Boys' College. b. graduates of the University of Canterbury.
Level of Study: Postgraduate
Type: Scholarship
Value: NZ$6,000 per annum
Length of Study: 3 years
Frequency: Annual
Country of Study: New Zealand
Application Procedure: Scholarship website: universitiesnz.communityforce.com/Login.aspx
No. of awards offered: 3
Closing Date: 1 October
Funding: Trusts

Additional Information: www.universitiesnz.ac.nz/scholarships/edward-isabel-kidson-scholarship

For further information contact:

Tel: (64) 3 369 3999
Email: info@canterbury.ac.nz

The Judith Clark Memorial Fellowships

Purpose: The Judith Clark Memorial Fellowships have been established to assist music graduates undertake a special short-term project that will have long term benefits for their future professional careers as musicians
Eligibility: Applicants must hold New Zealand citizenship or permanent residency and must have recently graduated, or expect to graduate in the year of application, with an Honours degree, or equivalent, in music from a New Zealand university
Level of Study: Postgraduate
Type: Fellowship/Scholarship
Value: NZ$15,000
Length of Study: 1 year
Frequency: Varies
Country of Study: New Zealand
Application Procedure: See website universitiesnz.communityforce.com/Login.aspx
Closing Date: 15 February
Funding: Foundation
Additional Information: www.universitiesnz.ac.nz/scholarships/judith-clark-memorial-fellowship

For further information contact:

Tel: (64) 3 369 3999
Email: info@canterbury.ac.nz

The Kia Ora Foundation Patricia Pratt Music Scholarship

Purpose: The purpose of the Kia Ora Foundation Patricia Pratt Music Scholarship is to assist outstanding New Zealand musical performers, who have completed the equivalent of an honours degree in musical performance in New Zealand, to continue their musical development at a renowned international music school or conservatorium
Eligibility: Applicants will be New Zealand citizens. Applicants may apply from outside New Zealand but must have resided in New Zealand for at least three of the last five years immediately preceding the year of selection. Applicants will have recently completed the requirements for an honours degree in musical performance at a New Zealand university (or an equivalent musical qualification)
Level of Study: Postgraduate
Type: Scholarship
Value: NZ$70,000
Length of Study: 2 years
Frequency: Varies
Country of Study: Any country
Application Procedure: See Website www.universitiesnz.ac.nz/scholarships/kia-ora-foundation-patricia-pratt-scholarship
Closing Date: 1 March
Funding: Trusts
Additional Information: www.canterbury.ac.nz/scholarshipsearch/ScholarshipDetails.aspx?ScholarshipID=6935.1778

For further information contact:

Tel: (64) 3 369 3999
Email: info@canterbury.ac.nz

University of Canterbury Doctoral Scholarship

Purpose: These scholarships support students for study towards a research doctoral degree at the University of Canterbury. Approximately 60 scholarships are available each year, over two annual application rounds.
Eligibility: The scholarships are tenable by full-time and part-time students engaged in study for a research doctoral degree at UC. An applicant must have completed an appropriate qualification at a level judged to be equivalent to a bachelor's or master's degree with first-class honours at UC (equivalent to a UC GPA of at least 7.0)
Level of Study: Doctorate
Type: Scholarship
Value: NZ$21,000 per annum, domestic tuition fees
Frequency: Every 3 years
Country of Study: New Zealand
Application Procedure: Apply online thro below link. www.canterbury.ac.nz/scholarships/
Closing Date: 16 January
Funding: Private
Additional Information: scholarshipscanterbury.communityforce.com/Funds/FundDetails.aspx?58474831703852465071773470547 66A2B6C4A336441745544383251 4D7552506D52464B654345385570625635474F4D75634F497A724678376E6D4879556B4D

For further information contact:

Email: scholarships@canterbury.ac.nz

Woolf Fischer Scholarship

Purpose: The main objective of the Trust is that Woolf Fisher Scholars will make a significant commitment to New Zealand and become leaders in their fields.
Eligibility: Applicants must 1. be a New Zealand citizen. 2. be under the age of thirty in the year of application (i.e. will not have reached their thirtieth birthday by 31 December in the year the application is submitted) 3. have attended a secondary school in New Zealand for at least two years, and 4. have graduated or are expected to graduate with a first-class honours degree from a university in New Zealand.
Level of Study: Graduate
Type: Scholarship
Value: Approximately NZ$100,000 per annum
Length of Study: 3 years
Frequency: Every 3 years
Country of Study: New Zealand
Application Procedure: You may apply through this webpage approximately 8 weeks before applications close. If it's possible to apply on-line for this scholarship there will be a link above to the on-line system. For further details, visit the website. www.universitiesnz.ac.nz/scholarships/woolf-fisher-scholarship
Closing Date: 1 August
Funding: Private
Additional Information: www.canterbury.ac.nz/scholarshipsearch/ScholarshipDetails.aspx?ScholarshipID=6935.215

For further information contact:

Tel: (64) 3 369 3999
Email: info@canterbury.ac.nz

University of Cape Town

University of Cape Town, Private Bag X3, Rondebosch 7701, South Africa.

Tel: (27) 21 650 9111
Website: www.uct.ac.za/

University of Cape Town (UCT) is very similar to the city of Cape Town: it has a vibrant, cosmopolitan community. It is a cultural melting pot where each person contributes their unique blend of knowledge and thinking. Our staff and students come from over 100 countries in Africa and the rest of the world. The university has also built links, partnerships and exchange agreements with leading African and international institutions that further enrich the academic, social and cultural diversity of our campus.

University of Cape Town Masters Scholarships in Public Health

Purpose: To support the training of eye health professionals with strong public health skills, the Consortium offers scholarships for candidates from low- and middle-income African Commonwealth countries who have been accepted to study for a Masters Public Health, Community Eye Health at the University of Cape Town, South Africa
Eligibility: Applicants must come from a low- or middle-income African Commonwealth country to apply. Funding is available for postgraduate studies only. The bursaries are awarded on a yearly basis
Level of Study: Postgraduate
Type: Scholarship
Frequency: Annual
Country of Study: South Africa
Application Procedure: Check website for more details
Closing Date: 31 July
Funding: Trusts

University of Delaware

University of Delaware, Newark, DE 19716, United States of America.

Tel: (1) 302 831 2792
Email: dianec@udel.edu
Website: www.udel.edu
Contact: Ms Diane Clark, Administrative Assistant

The Department of History offers MA and PhD programmes in American and European history and more limited graduate study Ancient, African, Asian, Latin American, and Middle Eastern history. In conjunction with these, it offers special programmes in the history of industrialization, material culture studies, American Civilization, and museum studies.

U

Executive MBA Programme

Length of Study: 1 to 3 years
Country of Study: Any country
Application Procedure: Applicants must complete an application form supplying US$45 fee, transcripts, Graduate

Management Admission Test score, TOEFL score and two letters of recommendation

For further information contact:

Tel: (1) 302 831 2221
Fax: (1) 302 831 3329
Email: E-MBA@strauss.udel.edu

University of Derby

Kedleston Road, Derby DE22 1GB, United Kingdom.

Tel: (44) 1332 590 500
Website: www.derby.ac.uk
Contact: University of Derby

The University of Derby is a public university in the city of Derby, United Kingdom. It traces its history back to the establishment of the Derby Diocesan Institution for the Training of Schoolmistresses in 1851 and gained university status in 1992 as one of the new universities.

Great Scholarship

Purpose: The GREAT Scholarships programme, launched by the British Council together with 41 UK universities, supports postgraduate students to access world-class UK higher education opportunities.
Eligibility: The scholarship programme offers financial support of £11,000 to eligible students pursuing one year postgraduate study at the University of Derby and must be from one of the following countries: China, Ghana, Pakistan (2 scholarships available), India, Nigeria, Malaysia, Thailand.
Level of Study: Postgraduate
Type: Scholarship
Value: £11,000
Length of Study: 1 year
Frequency: Annual
Country of Study: United Kingdom
Application Procedure: Applications for the British Council GREAT scholarship should be made after you have received an offer, using the form below. As part of your application you will need to include an essay of no more than 500 words about a topic you have studied previously and why you found it interesting. This topic should be related to or have inspired you to apply for your chosen degree programme. This essay will be part of the shortlisting criteria, alongside previous academic achievement, and the potential you show. Scholarship website: www.derby.ac.uk/study/fees-finance/scholarships/great-scholarships/#d.en.121116
No. of awards offered: 8
Closing Date: 1 June
Additional Information: www.derby.ac.uk/study/fees-finance/scholarships/great-scholarships/

HLC MA in Chinese-English Translating and Interpreting Scholarships

Purpose: The Department of Modern Languages and Cultures is pleased to announce five scholarships for international students wishing to pursue the MA in Chinese-English Translating and Interpreting in 2024.
Eligibility: 1. International students studying the MA in Chinese-English Translating and Interpreting. 2. Applicants should have a good undergraduate degree (a 2:1 honours degree or equivalent). 3. Applicants with English as a second language should have a good IELTS score of at least 7.0 overall (with no less than 6.5 in any sub-score) for admission to the MA programme. Applicants with Chinese as a second language should have proficiency in Chinese (equivalent to the skills of HSK level 5).
Level of Study: Masters Degree
Type: Scholarship
Value: Two £10,000 scholarships, Three £5,000 scholarships
Application Procedure: Applications that will be considered for the scholarships should include the following: 1. Application form 2. CV 3. Relevant transcript and qualifications 4. A personal statement (500 words) that outlines the applicant's strengths and suitability for the MA, including (where appropriate) relevant translation and/or interpreting experience 5. A 300 word supporting statement on outlining why you should be awarded this scholarship sent to Dr Ting Guo at ting.guo@liverpool.ac.uk. Any other relevant supporting documents.
Closing Date: 31 January
No. of applicants last year: 5
Additional Information: Please note, however, that the deadline of 31st January 2024 applies. Those who apply for the MA after this date will not be considered for a scholarship. Website: www.liverpool.ac.uk/study/postgraduate-taught/finance/scholarships/

For further information contact:

Email: ting.guo@liverpool.ac.uk

International Scholarships at University of Derby

Purpose: The University of Derby is offering international scholarships for the academic year. These scholarships are available to apply for once you have received an offer on a course from the University
Eligibility: These scholarships are available to apply for once you have received an offer on a course from the University. International students are eligible to apply
Type: Postgraduate scholarships
Value: £5,00
Study Establishment: Scholarships are awarded to study the subjects offered by the university
Country of Study: United Kingdom
Application Procedure: Apply online www.derby.ac.uk/study/fees-finance/scholarships/#d.en.120869
Closing Date: 1 July
Additional Information: www.derby.ac.uk/study/fees-finance/scholarships/

For further information contact:

Email: iadmissions@derby.ac.uk

University of Dundee

Nethergate, Dundee DD1 4HN, United Kingdom.

Tel: (44) 1382 383838
Email: j.e.nicholson@dundee.ac.uk
Website: www.dundee.ac.uk
Contact: Postgraduate Office

The University of Dundee is one of United Kingdom's leading universities, named Scottish University of the Year 2004/2005 (Sunday Times) and ranked top for teaching quality in 2005 (THES). It is internationally recognised for its expertise across a range of disciplines including science, medicine, engineering and art and graduates more people into the professions than any other university in Scotland.

Al-Maktoum College Hamdan Bin Rashid Award

Eligibility: To be eligible for the scholarship, you must: 1. Have either a conditional or unconditional offer to study: a. International Business and Islamic Finance MSc. b. Islamic Banking and Finance MSc. c. Islamic Banking, Finance and International Business MSc. d. Islamic Finance MSc. 2. Be starting your course in September 2024. 3. Have been awarded the University of Dundee Global Excellence Scholarship.
Level of Study: Postgraduate
Type: Scholarship
Value: £6,000
Frequency: Annual
Country of Study: United Kingdom
Application Procedure: There is no separate application form for this scholarship as the University will review all offer holders who have received the Global Excellence scholarship.
No. of awards offered: 8
Closing Date: 31 July
Additional Information: https://www.dundee.ac.uk/scholarships/al-maktoum-college-hamdan-bin-rashid-scholarship-january-2024

For further information contact:

Email: scholarships@dundee.ac.uk.

Al-Maktoum College Living Support Bursary

Eligibility: To be eligible for the bursary, you must: 1. Have either a conditional or unconditional offer to study: a. Islamic Banking and Finance MSc. b. Islamic Banking, Finance and International Business MSc. c. Islamic Finance MSc. 2. Be starting your course in September 2024. 3. Have already been awarded one of the following University of Dundee scholarships: a. Global Citizenship Scholarship. b. Global Excellence Scholarship. c. Vice Chancellor's Regional Scholarship (Africa / South Asia / Indonesia / China). d. If you are an International College Dundee student, you must have received the International College Dundee Progressing with Excellence Scholarship. 4. Hold 'International' Fee Status.
Level of Study: Postgraduate
Type: Bursary
Value: £3,000
Frequency: Annual
Country of Study: United Kingdom
Application Procedure: There is no separate application form for this bursary.
Closing Date: 31 July
Additional Information: www.dundee.ac.uk/scholarships/al-maktoum-college-living-support-scholarship-september-2023

For further information contact:

Email: scholarships@dundee.ac.uk

U

Alumni Scholarship

Eligibility: 1. The University of Dundee provides up to £3,000 for Alumni Students. If you meet the following criteria, then you will be eligible to receive the scholarship: a. Have applied to study a full (180 credit) postgraduate taught course. b. Your course starts in September 2024. c. Have graduated from the University of Dundee, having previously completed a full undergraduate or postgraduate taught degree. 2. If you are not a direct graduate of the University of Dundee, but someone in your immediate family is, then you are also eligible for this Scholarship. If you meet the following criteria, then you will be eligible to apply for this scholarship: a. Have applied to study a full (180 credit) postgraduate taught course. b. Your course starts in September 2024. c. Have an immediate family member who has studied at the University of Dundee, having completed a full undergraduate or postgraduate taught degree. Immediate family members include Siblings, Children, Parents and Spouses. 3. Where eligible, this scholarship can be combined with one of the following scholarships: a. Global Excellence. b. Global Citizenship. c. Vice-Chancellor's Scholarships (one region only).
Level of Study: Postgraduate
Type: Scholarship
Value: £1,500 to £3,000
Length of Study: 1 year
Country of Study: United Kingdom
Application Procedure: There is no separate application form for this scholarship.
Closing Date: 31 July
Additional Information: www.dundee.ac.uk/scholarships/alumni-scholarship-september-2023

For further information contact:

Email: scholarships@dundee.ac.uk

Commonwealth Infection Prevention and Control Scholarship

Subjects: Nursing and Health Sciences
Eligibility: In order for candidate applications to be eligible for consideration, candidates will need the following 1. Copy of valid passport or national ID card showing photograph, date of birth, and country of citizenship - uploaded to the online application system 2. At least one reference - submitted directly by the referee to the online application system. Referees will be sent an email request however applicants are responsible for seeking permission from their referees in advance of submitting their application; for ensuring that their referees are available to complete the reference by the deadline; and that the referees have received the reference request email. 3. An offer letter to start chosen course of study - uploaded to the online application system 4. Full transcripts detailing all higher education qualifications (with certified translations if not in English) - uploaded to the online application system 5. The CSC will not accept supporting documentation submitted outside the online application system.
Level of Study: Postgraduate
Type: Scholarship
Value: £10,000
Length of Study: 1 year
Frequency: Throughout the year
Country of Study: Any country
Application Procedure: You can apply directly to the CSC cscuk.dfid.gov.uk/apply/distance-learning/
Closing Date: 7 May
Additional Information: www.dundee.ac.uk/scholarships/2020-21/commonwealth-ipc-scholarship/

For further information contact:

Email: contactus@dundee.ac.uk

Discover Business at Dundee

Eligibility: To be eligible for the Discover Business at Dundee scholarship, you must meet all the following criteria 1. You must have International fee status as determined by the University of Dundee 2. Have received an offer to study an eligible Undergraduate or Postgraduate Taught course in the School of Business 3. Begin studies in the 2024–2025 academic year. 4. September 2024 for Undergraduate 5. September 2024 or January 2025 for Postgraduate Taught
Type: Scholarship
Value: £2,000 per year
Length of Study: 4 years
Country of Study: Any country
Application Procedure: There is not a separate application form for this scholarship. You must apply to study a course at the University of Dundee first and your eligibility will be assessed as part of your course application.
Additional Information: www.dundee.ac.uk/scholarships/2022-23/discover-business-dundee/

For further information contact:

Email: scholarships@dundee.ac.uk

Global Citizenship Scholarship

Eligibility: To be considered for a scholarship, you must: 1. Have submitted an application to study at the University

of Dundee for September 2024, and received an Offer for a full-time, on campus Course. Please see our Terms and Conditions for exclusions. 2. Hold International Fee Status as determined by the University of Dundee, which is communicated in your Offer letter. 3. Not hold any other University of Dundee Scholarships.
Level of Study: Postgraduate
Type: Scholarship
Value: £5,000
Frequency: Annual
Country of Study: United Kingdom
Application Procedure: Scholarship website: forms.office.com/Pages/ResponsePage.aspx?id=OTEyrjoJKk2Bpl0zS82QGaHNPMcjD1RGk2YhA_mYzItUMU5VRzhDNzVKSjVESkQxQlZITlJTSDk2ViQlQCN0PWcu
Closing Date: 31 July
Additional Information: www.dundee.ac.uk/scholarships/global-citizenship-scholarship-september-2023

For further information contact:

Email: scholarships@dundee.ac.uk

Global Excellence Scholarship

Eligibility: To be considered for a scholarship, you must: 1. Have submitted an application to study at the University of Dundee for September 2024, and received an Offer for a full-time, on campus Course. Please see our Terms and Conditions for exclusions. 2. Have achieved either a 1st Class Honours Degree (if you are a Postgraduate Taught applicant), or BBB at A-Level (if you are an Undergraduate applicant). Grade equivalencies for International qualifications are determined by the University of Dundee. 3. Hold International Fee Status as determined by the University of Dundee, which is communicated in your Offer letter. 4. Not hold any other University of Dundee Scholarships.
Level of Study: Postgraduate
Type: Scholarship
Value: £6,000 per year
Frequency: Annual
Country of Study: United Kingdom
Application Procedure: You do not have to submit an application for this scholarship.
Closing Date: 31 August
Additional Information: www.dundee.ac.uk/scholarships/global-excellence-scholarship-september-2023

For further information contact:

Email: scholarships@dundee.ac.uk

GREAT Scholarship - Bangladesh

Eligibility: You are eligible if 1. You are a passport holder from Bangladesh 2. You have an offer to study a full time, on campus, postgraduate taught course 3. Your course starts in September 2024 4. You have International Fee status, as verified by the University of Dundee.
Level of Study: Postgraduate
Type: Scholarship
Value: £10,000
Length of Study: 1 year
Frequency: Annual
Country of Study: United Kingdom
Application Procedure: Please fill the online application form to complete your application
No. of awards offered: 1
Closing Date: 31 May

For further information contact:

Email: scholarships@dundee.ac.uk

GREAT Scholarship – Sri Lanka

Eligibility: You are eligible to apply for the GREAT Scholarship – Sri Lanka if you 1. Are a passport holder from Sri Lanka 2. Have an offer to study a full time, on campus, postgraduate taught course 3. Your course starts in September 2023 4. Have International Fee status, as verified by the University of Dundee.
Level of Study: Postgraduate
Type: Scholarship
Value: £10,000
Frequency: Annual
Country of Study: Any country
Closing Date: 31 May

For further information contact:

Email: scholarships@dundee.ac.uk

U

GREAT Scholarship for Justice & Law - Thailand

Eligibility: You are eligible to apply if you 1. Are a passport holder from Thailand 2. Have an offer to study one of the following full time, on campus, postgraduate taught courses International Commercial Law LLM, or Environmental Law LLM, 3. Your course starts in September 2024 4. Have International Fee status, as verified by the University of Dundee.

Level of Study: Postgraduate
Type: Scholarship
Value: £10,000
Length of Study: 1 year
Frequency: Annual
Country of Study: United Kingdom
Closing Date: 31 May

For further information contact:

Email: scholarships@dundee.ac.uk

GREAT Scholarships-China

Subjects: Anatomy / Forensic Anthropology / Forensic and Medical Art, Architecture and Urban Planning, Art and Design, Biological/Biomedical Sciences, Biomedical Engineering / Medical Imaging, Business (Accountancy / Economics / Finance / International Business), Civil Engineering / Structural Engineering, Computing / Applied Computing / Data Science / Data Engineering, Education, Electronic Engineering, Energy Petroleum and Mineral Law and Policy, English, Geography / Environmental Science, History, Law, Mathematics, Mechanical Engineering / Industrial Engineering, Nursing and Health Sciences, Philosophy, Physics, Politics and International Relations, Psychology, Social Work
Eligibility: You are eligible to apply for the GREAT Scholarship – China if you 1. Are a passport holder from mainland China; 2. Have an offer to study a full time, on campus, postgraduate taught programme at the University of Dundee, starting in September 2024; 3. Have International Fee Status, as verified by the University of Dundee.
Level of Study: Postgraduate
Type: Scholarship
Value: £10,000
Length of Study: 1 year
Frequency: Throughout the year
Country of Study: Any country
Closing Date: 7 May

For further information contact:

Email: contactus@dundee.ac.uk

GREAT Scholarships - Egypt

Subjects: Anatomy / Forensic Anthropology / Forensic and Medical Art, Architecture and Urban Planning, Art and Design, Biological/Biomedical Sciences, Biomedical Engineering / Medical Imaging, Business (Accountancy / Economics / Finance / International Business), Civil Engineering / Structural Engineering, Computing / Applied Computing / Data Science / Data Engineering, Education, Electronic Engineering, Energy Petroleum and Mineral Law and Policy, English, Geography / Environmental Science, History, Law, Mathematics, Mechanical Engineering / Industrial Engineering, Nursing and Health Sciences, Philosophy, Physics, Politics and International Relations, Psychology, Social Work
Eligibility: You are eligible to apply for the GREAT Scholarship – Egypt if you 1. Are a passport holder from Egypt; 2. Have an offer to study a full time, on campus, postgraduate taught programme at the University of Dundee, starting in September 2024; 3. Have International Fee Status, as verified by the University of Dundee.
Level of Study: Postgraduate
Type: Scholarship
Value: £10,000
Length of Study: 1 year
Frequency: Throughout the year
Country of Study: Any country
Closing Date: 7 May

For further information contact:

Email: contactus@dundee.ac.uk

GREAT Scholarships - Ghana

Subjects: Anatomy / Forensic Anthropology / Forensic and Medical Art, Architecture and Urban Planning, Art and Design, Biological/Biomedical Sciences, Biomedical Engineering / Medical Imaging, Business (Accountancy / Economics / Finance / International Business), Civil Engineering / Structural Engineering, Computing / Applied Computing / Data Science / Data Engineering, Education, Electronic Engineering, Energy Petroleum and Mineral Law and Policy, English, Geography / Environmental Science, History, Law, Mathematics, Mechanical Engineering / Industrial Engineering, Nursing and Health Sciences, Philosophy, Physics, Politics and International Relations, Psychology, Social Work
Eligibility: You are eligible to apply for the GREAT Scholarship – Ghana if you 1. Are a passport holder from Ghana; 2. Have an offer to study a full time, on campus, postgraduate taught programme at the University of Dundee, starting in September 2024; 3. Have International Fee Status, as verified by the University of Dundee.
Level of Study: Postdoctorate
Type: Scholarship
Value: £10,000

Length of Study: 1 year
Frequency: Throughout the year
Country of Study: Any country
Closing Date: 7 May

For further information contact:

Email: contactus@dundee.ac.uk

GREAT Scholarships - India

Subjects: Anatomy / Forensic Anthropology / Forensic and Medical Art, Architecture and Urban Planning, Art and Design, Biological/Biomedical Sciences, Biomedical Engineering / Medical Imaging, Business (Accountancy / Economics / Finance / International Business), Civil Engineering / Structural Engineering, Computing / Applied Computing / Data Science / Data Engineering, Education, Electronic Engineering, Energy Petroleum and Mineral Law and Policy, English, Geography / Environmental Science, History, Law, Mathematics, Mechanical Engineering / Industrial Engineering, Nursing and Health Sciences, Philosophy, Physics, Politics and International Relations, Psychology, Social Work
Eligibility: You are eligible to apply for the GREAT Scholarship – India if you 1. Are a passport holder from India; 2. Have an offer to study a full time, on campus, postgraduate taught programme at the University of Dundee, starting in September 2024; 3. Have International Fee Status, as verified by the University of Dundee
Level of Study: Postdoctorate
Type: Scholarship
Value: £10,000
Length of Study: 1 year
Frequency: Throughout the year
Country of Study: Any country
Closing Date: 7 May

For further information contact:

Email: contactus@dundee.ac.uk

GREAT Scholarships – Indonesia

Subjects: Anatomy / Forensic Anthropology / Forensic and Medical Art, Architecture and Urban Planning, Art and Design, Biological/Biomedical Sciences, Biomedical Engineering / Medical Imaging, Business (Accountancy / Economics / Finance / International Business), Civil Engineering / Structural Engineering, Computing / Applied Computing / Data Science / Data Engineering, Dentistry, Education, Electronic Engineering, Energy Petroleum and Mineral Law and Policy, English, Geography / Environmental Science, History, Law, Mathematics, Mechanical Engineering / Industrial Engineering, Medicine, Nursing and Health Sciences, Philosophy, Physics, Politics and International Relations, Psychology, Social Work
Eligibility: You are eligible to apply for the GREAT Scholarship – Indonesia if you 1. Are a passport holder from Indonesia; 2. Have an offer to study a full time, on campus, postgraduate taught programme at the University of Dundee, starting in September 2024; 3. Have International Fee Status, as verified by the University of Dundee.
Level of Study: Postdoctorate
Type: Scholarship
Value: £10,000
Length of Study: 1 year
Frequency: Throughout the year
Country of Study: Any country
Closing Date: 31 May

For further information contact:

Email: contactus@dundee.ac.uk

GREAT Scholarships - Kenya

Subjects: Anatomy / Forensic Anthropology / Forensic and Medical Art, Architecture and Urban Planning, Art and Design, Biological/Biomedical Sciences, Biomedical Engineering / Medical Imaging, Business (Accountancy / Economics / Finance / International Business), Civil Engineering / Structural Engineering, Computing / Applied Computing / Data Science / Data Engineering, Education, Electronic Engineering, Energy Petroleum and Mineral Law and Policy, English, Geography / Environmental Science, History, Law, Mathematics, Mechanical Engineering / Industrial Engineering, Nursing and Health Sciences, Philosophy, Physics, Politics and International Relations, Psychology, Social Work
Eligibility: You are eligible to apply for the GREAT Scholarship – Kenya if you 1. Are a passport holder from Kenya; 2. Have an offer to study a full time, on campus, postgraduate taught programme at the University of Dundee, starting in September 2024; 3. Have International Fee Status, as verified by the University of Dundee.
Level of Study: Postdoctorate
Type: Scholarship
Value: £10,000

Length of Study: 1 year
Frequency: Throughout the year
Country of Study: Any country
Closing Date: 7 May

For further information contact:

Email: contactus@dundee.ac.uk

GREAT Scholarships – Malaysia

Subjects: Anatomy / Forensic Anthropology / Forensic and Medical Art, Architecture and Urban Planning, Art and Design, Biological/Biomedical Sciences, Biomedical Engineering / Medical Imaging, Business (Accountancy / Economics / Finance / International Business), Civil Engineering / Structural Engineering, Computing / Applied Computing / Data Science / Data Engineering, Dentistry, Education, Electronic Engineering, Energy Petroleum and Mineral Law and Policy, English, Geography / Environmental Science, History, Law, Mathematics, Mechanical Engineering / Industrial Engineering, Medicine, Nursing and Health Sciences, Philosophy, Physics, Politics and International Relations, Psychology, Social Work
Eligibility: The University of Dundee is pleased to announce 1 scholarship opportunity, in conjunction with the British Council. You are eligible to apply for the GREAT Scholarship – Malaysia if you 1. Are a passport holder from Malaysia 2. Have an offer to study a full time, on campus, postgraduate taught course 3. Your course starts in September 2024. 4. Have International Fee status, as verified by the University of Dundee
Level of Study: Postdoctorate
Type: Scholarship
Value: £10,000
Length of Study: 1 year
Frequency: Throughout the year
Country of Study: Any country
Closing Date: 31 May

For further information contact:

Email: contactus@dundee.ac.uk

GREAT Scholarships – Pakistan

Subjects: Anatomy / Forensic Anthropology / Forensic and Medical Art, Architecture and Urban Planning, Art and Design, Biological/Biomedical Sciences, Biomedical Engineering / Medical Imaging, Business (Accountancy / Economics / Finance / International Business), Civil Engineering / Structural Engineering, Computing / Applied Computing / Data Science / Data Engineering, Dentistry, Education, Electronic Engineering, Energy Petroleum and Mineral Law and Policy, English, Geography / Environmental Science, History, Law, Mathematics, Mechanical Engineering / Industrial Engineering, Medicine, Nursing and Health Sciences, Philosophy, Physics, Politics and International Relations, Psychology, Social Work
Eligibility: You are eligible to apply for the GREAT Scholarship – Pakistan if you 1. Are a passport holder from Pakistan; 2. Have an offer to study a full time, on campus, postgraduate taught programme at the University of Dundee, starting in September 2024; 3. Have International Fee Status, as verified by the University of Dundee.
Level of Study: Postdoctorate
Type: Scholarship
Value: £10,000
Length of Study: 1 year
Frequency: Throughout the year
Country of Study: Any country
Closing Date: 7 May

For further information contact:

Email: contactus@dundee.ac.uk

GREAT Scholarships – Thailand

Subjects: Anatomy / Forensic Anthropology / Forensic and Medical Art, Architecture and Urban Planning, Art and Design, Biological/Biomedical Sciences, Biomedical Engineering / Medical Imaging, Business (Accountancy / Economics / Finance / International Business), Civil Engineering / Structural Engineering, Computing / Applied Computing / Data Science / Data Engineering, Dentistry, Education, Electronic Engineering, Energy Petroleum and Mineral Law and Policy, English, Geography / Environmental Science, History, Law, Mathematics, Mechanical Engineering / Industrial Engineering, Medicine, Nursing and Health Sciences, Philosophy, Physics, Politics and International Relations, Psychology, Social Work
Eligibility: You are eligible to apply for the GREAT Scholarship – Thailand if you 1. Are a passport holder from Thailand; 2. Have an offer to study a full time, on campus, postgraduate taught programme at the University of Dundee, starting in September 2024; 3. Have International Fee Status, as verified by the University of Dundee.
Level of Study: Postdoctorate
Type: Scholarship
Value: £10,000
Length of Study: 1 year
Frequency: Throughout the year
Country of Study: Any country
Closing Date: 7 May

For further information contact:

Email: contactus@dundee.ac.uk

Humanitarian Scholarship – The University of Dundee

Eligibility: 1. Hold an academic offer of entry for a postgraduate taught programme in any of our academic schools, beginning in September 2024. The programme must be a full 180 credit postgraduate taught course, on campus. 2. Have Refugee or Asylum Status, or Humanitarian Protection as recognised by the 1951 UN Convention on the Status of Refugees. 3. All fee status applicants are eligible: Scottish, RUK, EU, International.
Level of Study: Postgraduate
Type: Scholarship
Value: Full tuition fee waiver
Frequency: Annual
Country of Study: United Kingdom
Application Procedure: Scholarship website: forms.office.com/Pages/ResponsePage.aspx?id=OTEyrjoJKk2Bpl0zS82QGaHNPMcjD1RGk2YhA_mYzItUN0c3MUNMSk8wWlc4OFNWN0daRDA2N0MzNCQlQCN0PWcu
Closing Date: 26 March
Additional Information: www.dundee.ac.uk/scholarships/humanitarian-scholarship-september-2023

For further information contact:

Email: scholarships@dundee.ac.uk

International College Dundee Progressing with Excellence Scholarship (Taught Postgraduate)

Eligibility: To be considered for this scholarship, applicants must meet ALL the following eligibility criteria 1. Classified by the University of Dundee and Oxford International Education Group (OIEG) as an international student for tuition fees. 2. Students must have completed an ICD full time programme (online or on campus) AND be progressing to a full time (180 credits per year), on campus UoD programme. 3. Students must achieve one of the following during the study of their full programme at ICD overall, achieve an ‘A’ grade average in their academic performance show a significant uplift in academic performance during their time at ICD and achieve excellent (‘A’ grade average) academic performance in the final term.
Level of Study: Postgraduate
Type: Scholarship
Value: Up to £6000 per year
Frequency: Annual
Country of Study: United Kingdom
Additional Information: www.dundee.ac.uk/scholarships/2022-23/icd-progressing-with-excellence-tpg/

For further information contact:

Email: icd@dundee.ac.uk

JEP MSc Progression Scholarship

Eligibility: In order to be eligible for a JEP MSc Progression Scholarship, all applicants must be classified as an International Fee-paying student by the University of Dundee and not currently studying a PhD Course.
Level of Study: Postgraduate
Type: Scholarship
Value: £5,000 or £9,000 (grade based)
Country of Study: United Kingdom
Application Procedure: You do not need to apply for this scholarship.
Closing Date: 31 August
Additional Information: www.dundee.ac.uk/scholarships/jep-msc-progression-scholarship-september-2023

For further information contact:

Email: scholarships@dundee.ac.uk

Master of Business Administration Programme

Length of Study: 2 years; 5 years
Application Procedure: Applicants must complete an application form supplying £25 fee, two academic references, official transcripts and evidence of English Language proficiency if applicable

For further information contact:

Tel: (44) 1382 344300
Fax: (44) 1382 228578
Email: cepmlp@dundee.ac.uk

U

Steve Weston and Trust Scholarships

Eligibility: To be eligible for this scholarship, applicants must: 1. Already hold an Honours degree in Law, Economics, Geology, Petroleum, or mining Engineering, Finance at 2nd class upper level or above. Consideration will also be given to applicants with other academic backgrounds who clearly explain their motivation for undertaking the relevant LLM, outlining any relevant legal work experience. 2. Hold an offer

for September 2024 for LLM in International Mineral Law and Policy or LLM in International Oil and Gas Law and Policy. 3. Be able to demonstrate compliance with the University of Dundee English entry requirements. 4. Display intellectual ability and leadership potential. 5. Have a proven track record and potential to rise to positions of influence. 6. Preferably be qualified lawyers having had some post-degree work experience in energy or natural resource development in the government, private sector, or academia. 7. Go on to complete the degree within 12 months. Students from overseas are expected to return to their home country at the end of the period of study.
Level of Study: Postgraduate
Type: Scholarship
Value: Variable
Frequency: Annual
Country of Study: United Kingdom
Application Procedure: There is no separate application form for the Steve Weston Scholarship.
No. of awards offered: 3
Closing Date: 31 May
Additional Information: https://www.dundee.ac.uk/scholarships/steve-weston-and-trust-scholarships-september-2023

For further information contact:

Email: a.e.anderson@dundee.ac.uk

Vice Chancellor's Africa Scholarship

Eligibility: 1. Hold International Fee Status as determined by the University of Dundee, which is communicated in your Offer letter. 2. Be currently residing in an African Country as highlighted in the country list above.
Level of Study: Postgraduate
Type: Scholarship
Value: £5,000
Frequency: Annual
Country of Study: United Kingdom
Application Procedure: You do not have to submit an application for this scholarship.
Closing Date: 31 August
Additional Information: https://www.dundee.ac.uk/scholarships/vice-chancellors-africa-scholarship-january-2024

For further information contact:

Email: scholarships@dundee.ac.uk

Vice Chancellor's EU Scholarship

Eligibility: To be eligible for an award, you must meet all the following criteria 1. Have an offer to study 2. A full time, Undergraduate course excluding any courses in the School of Medicine or the School of Dentistry OR 3. A full time, 180 credit postgraduate taught course over the course of 1 year. If you are studying a 2-year full time postgraduate taught course, you may be eligible for the award in both years. 4. Be domiciled in an EU country (please see Key Facts document for full list of eligible countries). 5. Have International fee status as determined by the University of Dundee.
Level of Study: Postgraduate
Type: Scholarship
Value: £5,000 per year
Length of Study: 5 years
Frequency: Annual
Country of Study: Any country
Application Procedure: There is not a separate application form for this scholarship.
Additional Information: www.dundee.ac.uk/scholarships/2022-23/vc-eu-scholarship/

For further information contact:

Email: scholarships@dundee.ac.uk

Vice Chancellor's Indonesia Scholarship

Eligibility: To be considered for an award, you must: 1. Have submitted an application to study at the University of Dundee for September 2024, and received an Offer for a full-time, on campus Course. Please see our Terms and Conditions for exclusions. 2. Hold International Fee Status as determined by the University of Dundee, which is communicated in your Offer letter. 3. Be currently residing in Indonesia.
Level of Study: Postgraduate
Type: Scholarship
Value: £4,000
Country of Study: United Kingdom
Application Procedure: You do not have to submit an application for this scholarship.
Closing Date: 31 August
Additional Information: https://www.dundee.ac.uk/scholarships/vice-chancellors-indonesia-scholarship-january-2024

For further information contact:

Email: scholarships@dundee.ac.uk

Vice Chancellor's Mainland China Scholarship

Eligibility: To be considered for an award, you must: 1. Have submitted an application to study at the University of Dundee for September 2024, and received an Offer for a full-time, on campus Course. Please see our Terms and Conditions for

exclusions. 2. Hold International Fee Status as determined by the University of Dundee, which is communicated in your Offer letter. 3. Be currently residing in China as highlighted in the country list above.
Level of Study: Postgraduate
Type: Scholarship
Value: £4,000
Country of Study: United Kingdom
Application Procedure: You do not have to submit an application for this scholarship.
Closing Date: 31 August
Additional Information: www.dundee.ac.uk/scholarships/vice-chancellors-mainland-china-scholarship-september-2023

For further information contact:

Email: scholarships@dundee.ac.uk

Vice Chancellor's South Asia Scholarship

Eligibility: 1. Hold International Fee Status as determined by the University of Dundee, which is communicated in your Offer letter. 2. Be currently residing in a South Asia Country as highlighted in the country list above.
Level of Study: Postgraduate
Type: Scholarship
Value: £4,000
Frequency: Annual
Country of Study: United Kingdom
Application Procedure: You do not have to submit an application for this scholarship.
Closing Date: 31 August
Additional Information: www.dundee.ac.uk/scholarships/vice-chancellors-south-asia-scholarship-september-2023

For further information contact:

Email: scholarships@dundee.ac.uk

University of East Anglia (UEA)

University of East Anglia, Norwich Research Park, Norwich NR4 7TJ, United Kingdom.

Tel: (44) 1603 456161
Website: www.uea.ac.uk/
Contact: Fellowship Administrator

The University of East Anglia (UEA) is organized into 23 schools of study encompassing arts and humanities, health, sciences and social sciences. These are supported by central service and administration departments.

Chulalongkorn University (Thailand) LAW Scholarships

Eligibility: Chulalongkorn University (Thailand) LLM offer-holders.
Level of Study: Postgraduate
Type: Scholarship
Value: Up to £9,250
Frequency: Annual
Country of Study: United Kingdom
Application Procedure: Method of application: To be considered for the 50% Scholarship, LLM applicants should contact the Dean of Chula Law School explaining why they would like to apply, and include their current or anticipated LLB marks. All expressions of interest should be received by the Dean as early as possible, and in any event by 1st June 2024.
No. of awards offered: 1
Closing Date: 1 June
Additional Information: www.uea.ac.uk/study/fees-and-funding/scholarships-finder/scholarships-a-z/chulalongkorn-university-thailand-scholarships

Economics 50% Scholarships: Thammasat University (Thailand)

Eligibility: Any eligible applicant who has received an offer on one of the programmes by 30 April 2024, will be considered for this scholarship.
Level of Study: Postgraduate
Type: Scholarship
Value: £9,500
Frequency: Annual
Country of Study: United Kingdom
Application Procedure: Any eligible applicant who has received an offer on one of the MSc programmes by 30 April 2024 will be considered for this scholarship. No separate application is necessary. Applications will be judged on their academic merit. Scholarship website: www.uea.ac.uk/apply/postgraduate#masters
No. of awards offered: 1
Closing Date: 30 April
Additional Information: www.uea.ac.uk/study/fees-and-funding/scholarships-finder/scholarships-a-z/eco-50pc-scholarships-thailand

Economics: MSc Academic and Professional Scholarships (International)

Purpose: These programmes are ideally suited to those who seek advanced training in economics and those who wish to pursue an academic career.
Eligibility: Any eligible applicant who has received an offer on one of the MSc programmes by 30 April 2024 will be considered for this scholarship.
Level of Study: Postgraduate
Type: Scholarship
Value: £19,800 and £9,900
Frequency: Annual
Country of Study: United Kingdom
Application Procedure: Any eligible applicant who has received an offer on one of the MSc programmes by 30 April 2024 will be considered for this scholarship. No separate application is necessary. Applications will be judged on their academic merit.
Closing Date: 30 April
Additional Information: www.uea.ac.uk/study/fees-and-funding/scholarships-finder/scholarships-a-z/eco-msc-academic-and-professional-scholarships-international

Economics: MSc Applied Training Scholarships (International)

Eligibility: Any eligible applicant who has received an offer on one of the MSc programmes by 30 April 2024 will be considered for this scholarship.
Level of Study: Postgraduate
Type: Scholarship
Value: £5,000
Frequency: Annual
Country of Study: United Kingdom
Application Procedure: Any eligible applicant who has received an offer on one of the MSc programmes by 30 April 2024 will be considered for this scholarship. No separate application is necessary. Applications will be judged on their academic merit.
Closing Date: 30 April
Additional Information: www.uea.ac.uk/study/fees-and-funding/scholarships-finder/scholarships-a-z/eco-msc-applied-training-scholarships

Excellence in Education Scholarship

Eligibility: To be eligible for these scholarships, applicants will need to meet the following criteria: 1. Hold a conditional or unconditional offer for one of the full-time or part-time Master's courses listed above starting at UEA in September 2024. 2. Be independently funding your studies – i.e. students sponsored by organisations funding their fees are not eligible to apply. (Students applying for, or expecting to receive government loans, are eligible to apply).
Level of Study: Postgraduate
Type: Scholarship
Value: £4,000
Frequency: Annual
Country of Study: United Kingdom
Application Procedure: Scholarship website: app.geckoform.com/public/?&_ga=2.178501988.1939328296.1678159876-1645095867.1678159876#/modern/21FO0097rc0rm600ics8fi3j7x
No. of awards offered: 4
Closing Date: 15 June
Additional Information: www.uea.ac.uk/study/fees-and-funding/scholarships-finder/scholarships-a-z/excellence-in-education-scholarship

For further information contact:

Email: edu.pgt.admiss@uea.ac.uk

Global Talent Fellowships

Purpose: The UEA GCRF Global Talent Fellowships provide the opportunity for international researchers
Eligibility: Applicants must currently be based in an institution outside of the UK, with established or prospective research links to UEA researchers (a letter of recommendation from the host supervisor from UEA, as well as approval from the Head of School or Departmentare both required). To meet the funding conditions of the GCRF, the proposed impact of this research must also comply with requirements for Official Development Assistance (ODA)
Level of Study: Research
Type: Fellowship
Value: £637,000
Length of Study: 3 year
Frequency: Annual
Country of Study: Any country
Additional Information: www.uea.ac.uk/research/fellowships/uea-gcrf-qr-allocation

For further information contact:

Email: rin.international@uea.ac.uk

International Development*: Full Fees Scholarship

Eligibility: To apply for the School of International Development* Scholarship, candidates will need to meet the following eligibility criteria: 1. Be a graduate of any international

institution. 2. Hold a degree with a classification of 2:1 (or international equivalent). 3. To have secured an offer of a place to study your chosen MA or MSc course.
Level of Study: Postgraduate
Type: Scholarship
Value: £19,800
Frequency: Annual
Country of Study: United Kingdom
Application Procedure: Scholarship website: app.geckoform.com/public/?&_ga=2.83107286.1939328296.1678159876-1645095867.1678159876#/modern/21FO0097rlcj3900es7fjmqqqf
No. of awards offered: 5
Closing Date: 30 April
Additional Information: www.uea.ac.uk/study/fees-and-funding/scholarships-finder/scholarships-a-z/international-development-full-fees-scholarship

International Development*: Scholarships for Students from Bangladesh

Eligibility: To apply for the School of International Development* Scholarship, candidates will need to meet the following eligibility criteria: 1. Be a graduate of any International institution. 2. Hold a degree with a classification of 2:1 (or international equivalent). 3. To have secured an offer of a place to study your chosen MA or MSc course.
Level of Study: Postgraduate
Type: Scholarship
Value: £8,000
Frequency: Annual
Country of Study: United Kingdom
Application Procedure: Scholarship website: app.geckoform.com/public/?&_ga=2.124531018.1939328296.1678159876-1645095867.1678159876#/modern/21FO0097rlcj3900es7fjmqqqf
No. of awards offered: 1
Closing Date: 30 April
Additional Information: www.uea.ac.uk/study/fees-and-funding/scholarships-finder/scholarships-a-z/international-development-scholarships-for-students-from-bangladesh

International Development*: Scholarships for Students from Colombia

Eligibility: To apply for the School of International Development* Scholarship, candidates will need to meet the following eligibility criteria: 1. Be a graduate of any International institution. 2. Hold a degree with a classification of 2:1 (or international equivalent). 3. To have secured an offer of a place to study your chosen MA or MSc course.
Level of Study: Postgraduate
Type: Scholarship
Value: £8,000
Frequency: Annual
Country of Study: United Kingdom
Application Procedure: Scholarship website: app.geckoform.com/public/?&_ga=2.79437268.1939328296.1678159876-1645095867.1678159876#/modern/21FO0097rlcj3900es7fjmqqqf
No. of awards offered: 3
Closing Date: 30 April
Additional Information: www.uea.ac.uk/study/fees-and-funding/scholarships-finder/scholarships-a-z/international-development-scholarships-for-students-from-colombia

International Development*: Scholarships for Students from India

Eligibility: To apply for the School of International Development* Scholarship, candidates will need to meet the following eligibility criteria: 1. Be a graduate of any International institution. 2. Hold a degree with a classification of 2:1 (or international equivalent). 3. To have secured an offer of a place to study your chosen MA or MSc course.
Level of Study: Postgraduate
Type: Scholarship
Value: £8,000
Frequency: Annual
Country of Study: United Kingdom
Application Procedure: Scholarship website: app.geckoform.com/public/?&_ga=2.15301238.1939328296.1678159876-1645095867.1678159876#/modern/21FO0097rlcj3900es7fjmqqqf
No. of awards offered: 3
Closing Date: 30 April
Additional Information: www.uea.ac.uk/study/fees-and-funding/scholarships-finder/international-development-scholarships-for-students-from-india

International Development*: Scholarships for Students from Japan

Eligibility: To apply for the School of International Development* Scholarship, candidates will need to meet the following eligibility criteria: 1. Be a graduate of any International institution. 2. Hold a degree with a classification of 2:1 (or international equivalent). 3. To have secured an offer of a place to study your chosen MA or MSc course.
Level of Study: Postgraduate
Type: Scholarship
Value: £6,000

Frequency: Annual
Country of Study: United Kingdom
Application Procedure: Scholarship website: app.geckoform.com/public/?&_ga=2.125851853.1939328296.1678159876-1645095867.1678159876#/modern/21FO0097rlcj3900es7fjmqqqf
No. of awards offered: 3
Closing Date: 30 April
Additional Information: www.uea.ac.uk/study/fees-and-funding/scholarships-finder/scholarships-a-z/international-development-scholarships-for-students-from-japan

International Development*: Scholarships for Students from South Korea

Eligibility: To apply for the School of International Development* Scholarship, candidates will need to meet the following eligibility criteria: 1. Be a graduate of any International institution. 2. Hold a degree with a classification of 2:1 (or international equivalent). 3. To have secured an offer of a place to study your chosen MA or MSc course.
Level of Study: Postgraduate
Type: Scholarship
Value: £6,000
Frequency: Annual
Country of Study: United Kingdom
Application Procedure: Scholarship website: app.geckoform.com/public/?&_ga=2.83522134.1939328296.1678159876-1645095867.1678159876#/modern/21FO0097rlcj3900es7fjmqqqf
No. of awards offered: 2
Closing Date: 30 April
Additional Information: www.uea.ac.uk/study/fees-and-funding/scholarships-finder/scholarships-a-z/international-development-scholarships-for-students-from-south-korea

International Development*: Scholarships for Students from Sub Saharan Africa

Eligibility: To apply for the School of International Development* Scholarship, candidates will need to meet the following eligibility criteria: 1. Be a graduate of any International institution. 2. Hold a degree with a classification of 2:1 (or international equivalent). 3. To have secured an offer of a place to study your chosen MA or MSc course.
Level of Study: Postgraduate
Type: Scholarship
Value: £10,000
Frequency: Annual
Country of Study: United Kingdom
Application Procedure: Scholarship website: app.geckoform.com/public/?&_ga=2.24198522.1939328296.1678159876-1645095867.1678159876#/modern/21FO0097rlcj3900es7fjmqqqf
No. of awards offered: 3
Closing Date: 30 April
Additional Information: www.uea.ac.uk/study/fees-and-funding/scholarships-finder/scholarships-a-z/international-development-scholarships-for-students-from-sub-saharan-africa

LLM: E-Fellows Scholarship Programme

Eligibility: E-fellows scholarships are awarded on a first come, first served basis.
Level of Study: Postgraduate
Type: Scholarship
Value: Up to £5,500
Frequency: Annual
Country of Study: United Kingdom
Application Procedure: Method of Application: To be considered for one of the scholarships, LLM applicants should contact Nick Scharf at n.scharf@uea.ac.uk. Scholarship website: www.uea.ac.uk/apply/postgraduate#masters
Closing Date: 31 July
Additional Information: www.uea.ac.uk/study/fees-and-funding/scholarships-finder/scholarships-a-z/e-fellows-scholarship-programme

For further information contact:

Email: n.scharf@uea.ac.uk

University of East Anglia International Development Scholarships

Purpose: The University of East Anglia is offering one full fee scholarship for international students towards Masters Degree courses offered by the School of International Development.
Eligibility: To apply for the School of International Development* Scholarship, candidates will need to meet the following eligibility criteria: 1. Be a graduate of any international institution. 2. Hold a degree with a classification of 2:1 (or international equivalent). 3. To have secured an offer of a place to study your chosen MA or MSc course.
Level of Study: Postgraduate
Type: Scholarship
Value: £19,800
Frequency: Annual
Study Establishment: University of East Anglia
Country of Study: United Kingdom

Application Procedure: Scholarship website: app.geckoform.com/public/?_ga=2.117062214.1939328296.1678159876-1645095867.1678159876#/modern/21FO0097rlcj3900es7fjmqqqf
No. of awards offered: 5
Closing Date: 30 April
Funding: Corporation
Additional Information: www.uea.ac.uk/study/fees-and-funding/scholarships-finder/scholarships-a-z/international-development-full-fees-scholarship

Vietnam Scholarships – Ho Chi Minh City University and National Economics University, Hanoi

Eligibility: Any eligible applicant who has received an offer on one of the MSc programmes by 30 April 2024 will be considered for this scholarship.
Level of Study: Postgraduate
Type: Scholarship
Value: £9,900
Frequency: Annual
Country of Study: United Kingdom
Application Procedure: Any eligible applicant who has received an offer on one of the MSc programmes by 30 April 2024 will be considered for this scholarship. No separate application is necessary. Applications will be judged on their academic merit.
No. of awards offered: 1
Closing Date: 30 April
Additional Information: www.uea.ac.uk/study/fees-and-funding/scholarships-finder/scholarships-a-z/eco-vietnam-scholarship

University of Edinburgh

Old College, South Bridge, Edinburgh EH8 9YL, United Kingdom.

Tel: (44) 131 650 2159
Email: postgrad@ed.ac.uk
Website: www.ed.ac.uk/
Contact: Grants Management Officer

Alice Brown PhD Scholarships

Purpose: The Alice Brown Scholarship is a new 6-year PhD scholarship offering a programme of advanced study, ongoing research, professional training and development
Eligibility: Citizens of United Kingdom, European Economic Area and Switzerland are eligible to apply. A first class honours degree (or equivalent) in a subject relevant to the studentship OR a taught MSc degree at distinction level in a subject relevant to the studentship. Conditional offers can be made to applicants currently enrolled in a degree programme on the basis of anticipated results. 1. As comprehensive research training is integrated into the programme of this PhD, there will be no automatic preference given to those holding MSc qualifications covering research training. 2. Applications are encouraged from those nearing the end of an undergraduate degree in a subject relevant to the scholarship. 3. Due to constraints on part-time study for international students on visas, this award is only open to nationals of the United Kingdom, countries of the European Economic Area, or Switzerland
Level of Study: Postgraduate
Type: Scholarship
Value: The scholarship covers full payment of PhD tuition fees and provides an annual stipend of £10,000 each year
Length of Study: 6-year PhD programme
Country of Study: United Kingdom
Application Procedure: Applicants are invited to submit a current CV, a short research proposal/idea (max. 1,000 words) and a personal statement of up to 500 words explaining their suitability for the scholarship in the field to which they are applying
Closing Date: 3 February
Contributor: University of Edinburgh
Additional Information: www.ed.ac.uk/student-funding/postgraduate/uk-eu/humanities/social-political-science/alice-brown

For further information contact:

Email: pgresearch.sps@ed.ac.uk

Carnegie PhD Scholarships

Eligibility: Applicants must hold a First Class Honours undergraduate degree from an eligible Scottish University. This First-Class Honours degree must be in a subject related to the field of the proposed doctoral studies. Students in their final year of an undergraduate degree who are expected to obtain a First-Class Honours degree may also apply, but they will be required to withdraw from the competition if they fail to graduate with a First. Please note that no exemptions are made to this requirement except in faculties which do not award Honours e.g. Medicine, where the equivalent standard will be expected.
Level of Study: Doctorate
Type: Scholarship

U

Value: cover tuition fees, a maintenance allowance and a research expenses allowance
Length of Study: 3 years
Frequency: Annual
Country of Study: United Kingdom
Closing Date: 28 February
Additional Information: www.ed.ac.uk/student-funding/postgraduate/uk-eu/other-funding/carnegie-trust

For further information contact:

Tel: (44) 1383 724990
Email: admin@carnegie-trust.org

Clinical Management of Pain Scholarship

Eligibility: 1. The scholarships will be awarded to new applicants who have applied for admission to a postgraduate taught Masters or Masters by Research degree programme of study at the University commencing in September 2024. 2. Applicants must have, or expect to obtain, the equivalent of a UK first class or 2:1 Honours degree at undergraduate level. 3. Both taught Masters and Masters by Research programmes are eligible for this award. Applications will be considered from UK/Overseas applicants wishing to study full-time/part-time/online distance learning programmes.
Level of Study: Postgraduate
Type: Scholarship
Value: £1,000 each
Frequency: Annual
Country of Study: United Kingdom
Application Procedure: The online scholarship application form is located in EUCLID and can be accessed via MyEd our web based information portal at www.myed.ed.ac.uk. When logging in to MyEd, you will need your University User Name and password. If you require assistance, please go to www.ed.ac.uk/student-systems/support-guidance
No. of awards offered: 2
Closing Date: 5 July
Additional Information: www.ed.ac.uk/student-funding/postgraduate/e-learning/painnew

Commonwealth Distance Learning Scholarships

Eligibility: To apply for a Commonwealth Distance Learning Scholarship, candidates must: 1. Be a citizen of or be granted refugee status from an eligible Commonwealth country, or be a British Protected Person. 2. Be permanently and continually resident in an eligible Commonwealth country. 3. Hold a first degree of at least upper second class (2:1) standard. A lower qualification and sufficient relevant experience may be considered in certain cases. 4. All candidates must provide at least one reference. 5. All candidates must hold an offer to start their chosen course of study in the 2024.
Level of Study: Postgraduate
Type: Scholarship
Value: Each scholarship will cover full tuition fees
Length of Study: 3 years
Frequency: Annual
Country of Study: United Kingdom
Application Procedure: Apply to the programme at the university, search for your eligible On-line Masters of choice on our Degree Finder. Once you have received an offer from the University of Edinburgh, apply to the Commonwealth Scholarships, information on how to apply can be found here cscuk.fcdo.gov.uk/scholarships/commonwealth-distance-learning-scholarships-candidates/
Closing Date: 28 March
Additional Information: www.ed.ac.uk/student-funding/postgraduate/e-learning/common-distance-learning

DeepMind PhD Scholarships

Eligibility: The scholarships will be awarded to applicants who 1. are residents of a country and/or region underrepresented in AI; 2. identify as women including cis and trans people and non-binary or gender fluid people who identify in a significant way as women or female; 3. and/or identify as Black or other minority ethnicity
Type: Scholarship
Study Establishment: Annual stipend of £15,609 per annum
Country of Study: United Kingdom
Contributor: 4 years
Additional Information: www.ed.ac.uk/informatics/postgraduate/fees/research-scholarships/deepmind-phd-scholarships

For further information contact:

Email: neil.heatley@ed.ac.uk

Dr Lloyd John Ogilvie Scholarships

Eligibility: Two scholarships will be awarded to applicants who have applied for admission on a full-time basis to an on campus postgraduate Masters programme of study within the School of Divinity commencing in the 2024-2025 academic year. Awards are made on the basis of academic merit.
Level of Study: Postgraduate
Type: Scholarship

Value: 50% of the overseas tuition fee
Frequency: Annual
Country of Study: United Kingdom
Application Procedure: The online scholarship application form is located in EUCLID and can be accessed via MyEd our web based information portal at www.myed.ed.ac.uk. When logging in to MyEd, you will need your University User Name and password. If you require assistance, please go to www.ed.ac.uk/student-systems/support-guidance
No. of awards offered: 2
Closing Date: 5 April
Additional Information: www.ed.ac.uk/student-funding/postgraduate/international/humanities/divinity/dr-lloyd-john-ogilvie-scholarships

For further information contact:

Email: K.McLean@ed.ac.uk

Drever Trust MSc Scholarships

Eligibility: The scholarships will be awarded to students who are accepted for admission on one of the following programmes of study, within the School of Philosophy, Psychology & Language Sciences at the University of Edinburgh.
Level of Study: Postgraduate
Type: Scholarship
Value: cover the UK tuition fee level for MSc study
Length of Study: 1 year
Frequency: Annual
Country of Study: United Kingdom
Application Procedure: The online scholarship application form is located in EUCLID and can be accessed via MyEd our web based information portal at www.myed.ed.ac.uk. When logging in to MyEd, you will need your University User Name and password. If you require assistance, please go to www.ed.ac.uk/student-systems/support-guidance
No. of awards offered: 1
Closing Date: 31 May
Additional Information: www.ed.ac.uk/student-funding/postgraduate/uk-eu/humanities/philosophy-psychology-language/drever

For further information contact:

Email: pplspgoffice@ed.ac.uk

Edinburgh Dental Institute MSc Scholarship

Eligibility: Applications will be considered from both UK and overseas eligible candidates wishing to apply for a 3-year part time taught Masters in Restorative Dentistry by online learning. PG Development courses (PPD) and CPD (Continuing Professional Development) courses are excluded from the scholarship.
Value: The award will cover 10% of the total tuition fee
Length of Study: 1 year
Country of Study: United Kingdom
Closing Date: 31 July
Additional Information: www.ed.ac.uk/student-funding/postgraduate/international/medicine-vet-medicine/edinburgh-dental

Edinburgh Doctoral College Scholarships

Eligibility: The awards are open to UK and overseas students applying to start their first year of study for an on-campus research degree. Applicants must have already applied for admission to a full-time or part-time on campus PhD research programme of study at the University. We encourage applicants who wish to apply for this scholarship to make contact with their academic school regarding any admission deadlines.
Level of Study: Doctorate
Type: Scholarship
Value: £15,609p.a.
Length of Study: 4 years
Frequency: Annual
Country of Study: United Kingdom
Additional Information: www.ed.ac.uk/student-funding/postgraduate/international/other-funding/doctoral-college

Edinburgh Global Online Distance Learning Masters Scholarship

Eligibility: 1. Scholarships will be available for students commencing any online part-time learning Masters programme offered by the University in session 2024-2025. 2. Applicants should already have been offered a place at the University of Edinburgh and should have firmly accepted that offer or be intending to do so.
Level of Study: Postgraduate
Type: Scholarship
Value: Each scholarship will cover full tuition fees
Frequency: Annual
Country of Study: United Kingdom
No. of awards offered: 20
Closing Date: 5 June
Additional Information: www.ed.ac.uk/student-funding/postgraduate/e-learning/online-masters

Edinburgh Global Online Distance Learning Scholarships

Purpose: The University of Edinburgh will offer a number of scholarships for distance learning Master's programmes offered by the University
Eligibility: 1. Scholarships will be available for students commencing in session 2024–25 in any distance learning Masters programme offered by the University. Applicants must be nationals of the eligible countries. 2. Applicants should already have been offered a place at the University of Edinburgh and should have firmly accepted that offer or be intending to do so.
Level of Study: Postdoctorate
Type: Scholarship
Length of Study: 3 years
Frequency: Annual
Country of Study: Any country
Application Procedure: Eligible applicants should complete an online scholarship application. The scholarship deadline is 1 June.
No. of awards offered: 12
Closing Date: 1 June
Funding: Private
Contributor: University of Edinburgh

For further information contact:

Email: family.medicine@ed.ac.uk

Edinburgh Global Online Learning Masters Scholarships

Eligibility: 1. Scholarships will be available for students commencing any online part-time learning Masters programme offered by the University in session 2024-2025. 2. Applicants should already have been offered a place at the University of Edinburgh and should have firmly accepted that offer or be intending to do so.
Level of Study: Postgraduate
Type: Scholarship
Value: Each scholarship will cover full tuition fees
Frequency: Annual
Country of Study: United Kingdom
No. of awards offered: 20
Closing Date: 5 June
Additional Information: www.ed.ac.uk/student-funding/postgraduate/e-learning/online-masters

Edinburgh Global Research Scholarship

Purpose: These awards are designed to attract high quality overseas research students to the University of Edinburgh
Eligibility: 1. Must be a full-time Ph.D. student pursuing research work on any course of their choice from the university. 2. Must be an international student liable to pay the tuition fee. 3. Must be of outstanding academic merit. 3. students who receive upper second class in Bachelor's and Master's degrees are also considered for this scholarship, due to competition the chance of receiving the scholarship is broadened if they have better academic results. 4. Must provide proof of nationality, residence, the proposed field of study, and personal information. 5. Must not hold any other scholarship at the time of applying for this scholarship.
Level of Study: Postgraduate
Type: Scholarship
Value: Each scholarship will cover the difference between the tuition fee for a United Kingdom/European Union postgraduate student and that chargeable to an overseas postgraduate student. The awards do not cover maintenance expenses
Length of Study: Three years
Frequency: Annual
Country of Study: United Kingdom
No. of awards offered: 30
Closing Date: 17 February
Additional Information: www.ed.ac.uk/student-funding/postgraduate/international/global/research

For further information contact:

Tel: (44) 131 651 4070
Email: studentfunding@ed.ac.uk

Glenmore Medical Postgraduate Scholarship

Eligibility: The scholarships will be awarded to applicants who are accepted for admission in the 2024-2025 academic year on one of the listed eligible Human Medical programmes. The Glenmore Medical Postgraduate Scholarship would particularly welcome applications from students from Africa.
Level of Study: Postgraduate
Type: Scholarship
Value: The scholarship will cover full tuition fees for the duration of the programme of study.
Frequency: Annual
Country of Study: United Kingdom
No. of awards offered: 3
Closing Date: 1 June

Additional Information: www.ed.ac.uk/student-funding/postgraduate/international/medicine-vet-medicine/glenmore

For further information contact:

Email: isabel.lavers@ed.ac.uk

Haywood Doctoral Scholarship

Purpose: To offer Haywood Doctoral Scholarship to an outstanding doctoral research candidate in History of Art
Type: Scholarship
Value: As an international student, you will receive a reduction in tuition fees equivalent to the Home/European Union rate if successful
Country of Study: United Kingdom
Closing Date: 2 March

For further information contact:

Tel: (44) 1214 143 344
Email: calpg-research@contacts.bham.ac.uk

Informatics Global PhD Scholarships

Eligibility: Applications will be accepted from all candidates; there are no restrictions based on nationality or domicile. Candidates should be in receipt of, or expected to obtain, a high academic award from their most recent degree. In practice, this means a 1st class UK degree or a distinction at UK Masters level in a relevant discipline. Students with non-UK qualifications should check the equivalence of their degrees. Candidates must also meet certain minimum requirements for English language competency.
Level of Study: Doctorate
Type: Scholarship
Value: A stipend of £15,609 per year; all tuition fees, including overseas fees if applicable; an additional research support fund of £2,000 per year for the first three years
Length of Study: 3 years
Frequency: Annual
Country of Study: United Kingdom
Closing Date: 28 January
Additional Information: www.ed.ac.uk/informatics/postgraduate/fees/research-scholarships/informatics-global-phd-scholarships

For further information contact:

Email: studentsystems@ed.ac.uk

Institute for Advanced Studies in the Humanities Postdoctoral Fellowships

Subjects: We welcome applications on all topics and in all areas of the arts, humanities and social sciences to continue IASH's traditional interdisciplinary work.
Purpose: Applications are invited for postdoctoral bursaries from candidates in any area of the Arts, Humanities and Social Sciences.
Eligibility: Applicants must have been awarded a doctorate at the time of application, and normally within the last three years (i.e. you should have graduated between 2021 and 2024, although earlier graduates may be eligible if they have taken significant career breaks since completing their doctorate; if you have not yet graduated, you must be able to produce a transcript, testamur, or a letter of completion/eligibility to graduate as part of your application; you do not need to have actually graduated at the time you apply). You should not have held a permanent position at a university, or a previous Fellowship at the Institute for Advanced Studies in the Humanities. Those who have held temporary and/or short-term appointments are eligible to apply.
Level of Study: Postdoctorate
Type: Fellowship
Value: £15,000
Length of Study: 10 months
Frequency: Annual
Study Establishment: Institute for Advanced Studies in the Humanities
Country of Study: United Kingdom
Application Procedure: Scholarship website: www.iash.ed.ac.uk/application-form
No. of awards offered: 12 to 15
Closing Date: 28 April
Funding: Commercial, Private
Contributor: University of Edinburgh
No. of applicants last year: 200 Above
Additional Information: www.iash.ed.ac.uk/postdoctoral-fellowships-2023-24

For further information contact:

Tel: (44) 131 650 4671
Email: iash@ed.ac.uk

U

John L Paterson Postgraduate Design Scholarship

Eligibility: 1. The scholarship award is available to applicants with UK/Overseas status who apply for admission to the postgraduate taught MA Design for Change programme

commencing in the 2024-2025 academic year. 2. Applications for full-time study only will be considered.
Level of Study: Postgraduate
Type: Scholarship
Value: £8,000
Frequency: Annual
Country of Study: United Kingdom
Application Procedure: The online scholarship application form is located in EUCLID and can be accessed via MyEd our web based information portal at www.myed.ed.ac.uk. When logging in to MyEd, you will need your University User Name and password. If you require assistance, please go to www.ed.ac.uk/student-systems/support-guidance
No. of awards offered: 1
Closing Date: 13 March
Additional Information: www.ed.ac.uk/student-funding/postgraduate/uk-eu/humanities/edinburgh-college-of-art/john-l-paterson

LLM in European Law Scholarship

Eligibility: Any applicant to the LLM in European Law.
Level of Study: Postgraduate
Type: Scholarship
Value: Covers the full Home (UK) or International/EU tuition fee rate for 2024–25
Frequency: Annual
Country of Study: United Kingdom
No. of awards offered: 1
Closing Date: 1 May
Additional Information: www.ed.ac.uk/student-funding/postgraduate/uk-eu/humanities/law/llm-in-european

National Health Service Education for Scotland Primary Care Ophthalmology Scholarship

Eligibility: The scholarships will be awarded to students who are accepted for admission on to the online distance learning MSc in Primary Care Ophthalmology at the University of Edinburgh. Applicants should already have been offered a place at the University of Edinburgh and should have firmly accepted that offer or be intending to do so
Type: Scholarship
Value: The scholarship will have a total value of 50% of the course fees
Country of Study: United Kingdom
Closing Date: 27 July

For further information contact:

Email: studentfunding@ed.ac.uk

Perfect Storms: Leverhulme Doctoral Scholarships

Level of Study: Doctorate
Type: Scholarship
Value: Full fees, living and research costs
Length of Study: 3 years
Frequency: Annual
Study Establishment: University of Edinburgh
Country of Study: Scotland
Contributor: The Leverhulme Trusts
No. of awards given last year: 5
Additional Information: www.ed.ac.uk/student-funding/postgraduate/international/other-funding/leverdocintl

For further information contact:

Email: studentfunding@ed.ac.uk

PhD Social Work Scholarship at University of Edinburgh in United Kingdom

Purpose: This award is available to students intending to commence PhD Social Work study in September on either a full-time or part-time basis
Eligibility: Citizens of all nationalities are eligible to apply. If English is not your first language then you will need to show that your English language skills are at a high enough level to succeed in your studies
Level of Study: Postgraduate
Type: Scholarship
Value: One award covering tuition fees at the Home/European Union fee rate, a maintenance stipend of £14,000 and a research grant of £500 is on offer to applicants for PhD Social Work in the School of Social and Political Science
Frequency: Annual
Study Establishment: Social Work study
Country of Study: Any country
Application Procedure: The online scholarship application form is located in EUCLID and can be accessed via MyEd our web-based information portal. www.myed.ed.ac.uk/
Closing Date: 1 March

For further information contact:

Email: GradSchool.HCA@ed.ac.uk

PhD Studentship in Predicting Higher-Order Biomarker Interactions Using Machine Learning

Eligibility: 1. Minimum of 21 in first degree and/or Master's degree in physics/ mathematics/ statistics/ computer science

or similar. 2. Proficiency in English (both oral and written). 3. Advanced programming skills (Python, Pytorch or equivalent).4. Excellent verbal and written communication skills, both in terms of informal discussion and formal presentations. 5. Biomedical motivation. 6. Ability to work effectively and efficiently in a team.
Level of Study: Doctorate
Type: Studentship
Value: Full time PhD tuition fees for a overseas student £24,700 per annum. A tax free stipend of GBP £15,609 per year. Additional programme costs of £1000 per year.
Length of Study: 4 years
Frequency: Annual
Country of Study: United Kingdom
Closing Date: 23 February

Polish School of Medicine Memorial Fund Scholarships

Purpose: The scholarship enables medical scientists at the outset of their careers to undertake a period of further study or research at the University's Medical School and return to Poland.
Eligibility: The programme is open to Polish medical scientists: 1. in their early career (usually within 10 years of their medical graduation - MB ChB equivalent). 2. working in Polish Medical Academies/Universities and Research Institutes. 3. with excellent mastery of English. 4. committed to the further development of medical research expertise in Poland.
Level of Study: Postgraduate
Type: Scholarship
Value: Varies
Length of Study: 1 year
Frequency: Annual
Country of Study: United Kingdom
Application Procedure: The online scholarship application form is located in EUCLID and can be accessed via MyEd our web based information portal at www.myed.ed.ac.uk. When logging in to MyEd, you will need your University User Name and password. If you require assistance, please go to www.ed.ac.uk/student-systems/support-guidance
Closing Date: 26 June
Additional Information: www.ed.ac.uk/student-funding/postgraduate/uk-eu/medicine-vet-medicine/polish

For further information contact:

Email: PSMscourse@ed.ac.uk

President's Fund, Edinburgh Association of University Women

Eligibility: 1. Students must be in their final year of study and experiencing financial hardship. 2. Awards are not given for courses of one year's duration (undergraduate or postgraduate) 3. Awards are not given for access courses, diploma courses nor for certificate courses 4. Awards are not given for study or work overseas nor for tuition fees.
Level of Study: Postgraduate
Type: Scholarship
Value: £300 to £800
Length of Study: 1 year
Frequency: Annual
Country of Study: United Kingdom
Application Procedure: Applicants must request, complete and sign the application form. The printed form must be received by the Hon Secretary duly completed, dated, signed by the applicant and accompanied by two signed academic references. The application form and the references are to be posted to the Hon Secretary to the address specified in the application form. Email applications are not accepted.
No. of awards offered: 1
Closing Date: 8 October
Additional Information: www.ed.ac.uk/student-funding/hardship-funding/presidents-fund

For further information contact:

Email: eileencbrownlie2706@gmail.com

Principal Career Development PhD Scholarship

Purpose: To attract the best and brightest PhD students, the University seeks to offer not only unparalleled research facilities and superb supervision, but also to provide development opportunities which will support our research students as they progress beyond their PhD, through an innovative programme of integrated research, training, and career development
Type: Scholarship
Value: Each scholarship covers the United Kingdom/European Union rate of tuition fee as well as a stipend of £15,000
Country of Study: United Kingdom
Closing Date: 1 February

For further information contact:

Tel: (44) 131 651 4070
Email: studentfunding@ed.ac.uk

U

School of Divinity Postgraduate Masters Scholarships

Eligibility: 1. The scholarships will be awarded to new applicants who have applied for admission to a postgraduate taught Masters, Masters by Research or MPhil degree programme of study in the School of Divinity commencing in September 2024. 2. Applicants must have, or expect to obtain, the equivalent of a UK first class or 2:1 Honours degree at undergraduate level.
Level of Study: Postgraduate
Type: Scholarship
Value: cover full tuition fees (at both the UK, EU and Overseas rates)
Frequency: Annual
Country of Study: United Kingdom
Application Procedure: The online scholarship application form is located in EUCLID and can be accessed via MyEd our web based information portal at www.myed.ed.ac.uk. When logging in to MyEd, you will need your University User Name and password. If you require assistance, please go to www.ed.ac.uk/student-systems/support-guidance
Closing Date: 5 April
Additional Information: www.ed.ac.uk/student-funding/postgraduate/international/humanities/divinity/divinity-masters

For further information contact:

Email: K.McLean@ed.ac.uk

Shell Centenary Scholarships and Shell Centenary Chevening Scholarships at Edinburgh

Eligibility: Students from countries that are not present or applicant members of the Organization for Economic Co-operation and Development (OECD). Candidates should normally be aged 20–35, be resident in one of the non-OECD countries and be intending to return to the country concerned at the end of the period of study. They should normally already hold a degree equivalent to a United Kingdom First Class (Honours) Degree or be expecting to obtain such a degree before the start of their proposed course
Level of Study: Postgraduate
Type: Scholarship
Value: The scholarships covers tuition fees, accommodation, maintenance costs and a return airfare for the scholarship holder
Length of Study: 1 year
Frequency: Annual
Study Establishment: University of Edinburgh
Country of Study: Scotland
Application Procedure: Applicants must apply separately for admission to the University of Edinburgh making a clear statement that they wish to be considered for a Shell Scholarship
Closing Date: 1 March
No. of awards given last year: 6

For further information contact:

Email: scholarships@ed.ac.uk

The Anne Rowling Clinic Regenerative Neurology Scholarships

Purpose: The Anne Rowling Clinic will offer three online learning Masters scholarships for applicants commencing Stem Cells and Translational Neurology programmes in the academic year 2024-2025.
Eligibility: 1. The scholarships will be awarded to applicants who are accepted for admission on to the online learning postgraduate Certificate, Diploma, or Masters Stem Cell and Translational Neurology programme at the University of Edinburgh for the 2024-2025 academic session. Applicants should already have been offered a place at the University of Edinburgh and should have firmly accepted that offer or be intending to do so. 2. In addition, only applicants who are nationals of the following list of eligible countries will be considered for the International Anne Rowling Clinic Regenerative Neurology Scholarship (of which one scholarship is offered): Anne Rowling Clinic Regenerative Neurology International Scholarship - eligible countries (14.23 KB Word). Please note: the two Anne Rowling Clinic Regenerative Neurology Scholarships are available to all applicants regardless of nationality. 3. Students who are already enrolled on an eligible programme of study may also apply but if they are currently in receipt of a scholarship and still utilising it they will not be offered another.
Level of Study: Postgraduate
Type: Scholarship
Value: One International Anne Rowling Clinic Regenerative Neurology Scholarship will cover 60 credits towards your module fees. Two Anne Rowling Clinic Regenerative Neurology Scholarships will cover 30 credits worth of course fees.
Frequency: Annual
Country of Study: United Kingdom
Application Procedure: The scholarship deadline is Monday 21st August 2024. For information on how to apply please contact the Stem Cells and Translational Neurology programme directly at stemcell-msc@ed.ac.uk
No. of awards offered: 3
Closing Date: 21 August

Additional Information: www.ed.ac.uk/student-funding/postgraduate/e-learning/regenerative-neurology

For further information contact:

Email: stemcell-msc@ed.ac.uk

The Kirby Laing International Scholarships

Eligibility: 1. The scholarship will be awarded to a new applicant who has applied for admission to a postgraduate taught Masters or Masters by Research degree programme of study in the School of Divinity commencing in September 2024. 2. Applicants must have, or expect to obtain, the equivalent of a UK 2:1 honours degree in a relevant discipline or the international equivalent. 3. Both taught Masters and Masters by Research programmes are eligible for this award. Applications will be considered from 'Majority World' domiciled applicants wishing to study full-time.
Level of Study: Postgraduate
Type: Scholarship
Value: £17,500
Frequency: Annual
Country of Study: United Kingdom
Application Procedure: The online scholarship application form is located in EUCLID and can be accessed via MyEd our web based information portal at www.myed.ed.ac.uk. When logging in to MyEd, you will need your University User Name and password. If you require assistance, please go to www.ed.ac.uk/student-systems/support-guidance
Closing Date: 5 April
Additional Information: www.ed.ac.uk/student-funding/postgraduate/international/humanities/divinity/kirby-laing

For further information contact:

New College, Mound Place, Edinburgh EH1 2LX, United Kingdom.

Tel: (44) 131 650 8900
Email: Divinity.PG@ed.ac.uk

The Lt. Col Jack Wishart Scholarship

Eligibility: Eligible programmes of study 1. Any programme of study in the School of Chemistry 2. Final year undergraduate students studying MBChB 3. Postgraduate students in the Edinburgh Medical School.
Level of Study: Postgraduate
Type: Scholarship
Value: Up to £500 per academic year.
Length of Study: Two academic years
Frequency: Annual
Country of Study: United Kingdom
Application Procedure: The online scholarship application form is located in EUCLID and can be accessed via MyEd our web based information portal at www.myed.ed.ac.uk
No. of awards offered: 10
Closing Date: 1 June
Additional Information: www.ed.ac.uk/student-funding/hardship-funding/wishart#:~:text=The%20Lt%20Col%20Jack%20Wishart%20Scholarship%20has%20been%20amended%20with,of%20the%20Covid%2D19%20pandemic

For further information contact:

Email: studentfunding@ed.ac.uk

The Rev Dr Norma P Robertson Scholarship

Eligibility: The Scholarship will be awarded to student(s) accepted onto full-time or part-time postgraduate programmes in Christian History, Bible and Theology related subjects, taught in The School of Divinity, who have an excellent academic record. The scholarship will be awarded on the basis of academic merit. Candidates must have, or expect to obtain, a UK 21 honours degree in a relevant discipline or the international equivalent.
Level of Study: Postgraduate
Type: Scholarship
Value: The scholarship will have a maximum value of £7,500
Frequency: Annual
Country of Study: United Kingdom
Closing Date: 2 April

For further information contact:

Email: studentfunding@ed.ac.uk

University of Edinburgh - KU Leuven PhD Studentship

Eligibility: The studentship will be awarded competitively and is open to UK, EU and overseas students applying to start their PhD programme of study
Level of Study: Doctorate
Type: Studentship
Value: Full tuition fees, a stipend and provision of research costs
Length of Study: 4 years
Frequency: Annual
Study Establishment: The University of Edinburgh
Country of Study: Any country

Application Procedure: Applicants are required to provide the following information saved WITHIN ONE PDF FILE. 1. Personal statement about their research interests and their reasons for applying for the specified project Academic CV 2. Two signed referee letters of reference. Candidates are required to submit at least 1 academic reference. The second reference may be academic or professional. 3. Degree transcripts (translations should be provided if the originals are not in English).; Applicants wishing to apply for more than one project must submit an application for each project. Where information is missing, the application may not be considered.
No. of awards offered: 1
Closing Date: 26 February

For further information contact:

Email: pgawards@ed.ac.uk

Wellcome Trust 4-Year PhD Programme Studentships

Purpose: This scheme offers graduates outstanding training in scientific research
Eligibility: Studentship on one of Wellcome's four-year programmes if you're a graduate or student who has, or expects to obtain, a degree (or equivalent for EU and overseas candidates) in a relevant subject.
Level of Study: Postgraduate
Type: Studentship
Value: Studentship stipend, fees and other costs
Length of Study: 4 years
Frequency: Annual
Study Establishment: The University of Edinburgh
Country of Study: Scotland

University of Essex

Graduate Admissions Office, University of Essex, Wivenhoe Park, Colchester C04 3SQ, United Kingdom.

Tel: (44) 1206 873333
Email: pgadmit@essex.ac.uk
Website: www.essex.ac.uk
Contact: V Bartholomew, CRM Operations Manager

The University of Essex is one of the United Kingdom's leading academic institutions, ranked 10th nationally for research and 7th for teaching. It offers degrees and research opportunities across 19 academic departments (including government and sociology, which both have 6-star research ratings) and numerous research centres of world renown.

Academic Excellence International Masters Scholarship

Purpose: University of Essex is inviting applications for academic excellence international masters scholarship.
Eligibility: 1. These scholarships are restricted to students who are overseas fee payers and are entirely selffunded. 2. These scholarships may be awarded to students who have completed relevant university studies in one of the specified countries. Where a degree has been awarded by an institution based in the UK, students must have been domiciled in one of the other specified countries. 3. Graduates of the University of Essex are not eligible for this award, and for eligible students with a UK degree, the amount of the award will be set at £2,000. 4. Awards made by an institution based in one of the specified countries above, but delivered in another country, will also be eligible. 5. Students must have been awarded an undergraduate degree (this includes integrated Masters degrees) with the grade specified or above. A higher Masters grade cannot be taken to compensate for a lower Bachelors grade.
Level of Study: Masters Degree, Postgraduate
Type: Scholarship
Value: £5,000
Length of Study: first year of Masters study
Frequency: Annual
Study Establishment: Scholarships are awarded in the fields offered by the university
Country of Study: United Kingdom
Application Procedure: If you meet all the eligibility criteria, you will automatically be considered for this award. You don't need to complete an application form. The University will assess your eligibility based on the academic transcripts and certificates you submit with your application for your place at Essex.
Additional Information: www.essex.ac.uk/scholarships/academic-excellence-international-masters-scholarship

For further information contact:

Email: enquiries@essex.ac.uk

Academic Excellence Senior Status Law Scholarship

Purpose: These scholarships are restricted to students who are overseas fee payers and are entirely self-funded.

Eligibility: 1. These scholarships are restricted to students who are overseas fee payers and are entirely self-funded. 2. These scholarships are restricted to students studying on the LLB M103 Law (Senior Status) programme only. 3. Students must be starting their first year of study on the LLB M103 Law (Senior Status) programme at the University of Essex in 2024-25. 4. Students must have been awarded an equivalent of a UK 2.1 at undergraduate level.
Level of Study: Postgraduate
Type: Scholarship
Value: £3,000
Frequency: Annual
Country of Study: United Kingdom
Application Procedure: If you meet all the eligibility criteria, you will automatically be considered for this award. You don't need to complete an application form. The University will assess your eligibility based on the academic transcripts and certificates you submit with your application for your place at Essex.
No. of awards offered: 1
Additional Information: www.essex.ac.uk/scholarships/academic-excellence-senior-status-law-scholarship

For further information contact:

Email: enquiries@essex.ac.uk

Africa Postgraduate Regional Scholarship

Purpose: These scholarships are restricted to students who are overseas fee payers and are entirely self-funded.
Eligibility: 1. These scholarships are restricted to students who are overseas fee payers and are entirely self-funded. 2. Students must be ordinarily resident (see below for the definition of ordinary residence) in a member state of the African Union. 3. These scholarships may be awarded to applicants who have completed relevant school or university studies in one of the specified countries above. 4. Applicants must have been awarded an undergraduate degree (this includes integrated Masters degrees) with the grade specified or above. A higher Masters grade cannot be taken to compensate for a lower Bachelors grade. 5. Eligible courses are those which are full-time taught Masters courses leading to MA, MSc, MRES and LLM degree and start in October 2024 and January 2025.
Level of Study: Postgraduate
Type: Scholarship
Value: £4,500
Frequency: Annual
Country of Study: United Kingdom
Application Procedure: If you meet all the eligibility criteria, you will automatically be considered for this award. You don't need to complete an application form. The University will assess your eligibility based on your country of domicile and fee status that you submit on your application for your place at Essex.
No. of awards offered: 1
Additional Information: www.essex.ac.uk/scholarships/africa-scholarship-programme

For further information contact:

Email: enquiries@essex.ac.uk

Chinese-English Translation Scholarships

Subjects: Language and Linguistics
Purpose: If you're an international student studying one of our Chinese-English Translation and Interpreting programmes, you could be eligible for £3,000 through our Chinese-English Scholarship
Eligibility: 1. Be fully self-funding your studies 2. Hold a conditional offer of admission to one of the Chinese-English Translation and Interpreting courses 3. These scholarships are available to international students only.
Level of Study: Postgraduate
Type: Scholarship
Value: £3,000
Country of Study: Any country
No. of awards offered: 5
Closing Date: 31 May
Additional Information: www.essex.ac.uk/scholarships/chinese-english-translation-scholarships

For further information contact:

Email: enquiries@essex.ac.uk

Dowden Scholarship

Purpose: To help highly able students who otherwise would not be able to study at postgraduate level
Eligibility: Applicant must have settled status in the United Kingdom; been 'ordinarily resident' in the United Kingdom for the 3 years before the start of their studentship; not been residing in the United Kingdom wholly or mainly for the purpose of full-time education (United Kingdom and European Union nationals are exempt from this requirement). The Vera Dowden Baldwin Scholarship awards financial assistance to a resident of Dowden Hall who demonstrates financial need. The fund is named in honor of the late Vera Dowden Baldwin '34, whose connection with the University spanned more than seventy years
Level of Study: Postgraduate
Type: Scholarship

U

Value: Up to £5,000
Frequency: Annual
Study Establishment: University of Essex
Country of Study: United Kingdom
Application Procedure: Indicate on application for doctoral course

Drake Lewis Graduate Scholarship for Art History

Purpose: To support new MA students in art history
Eligibility: Open to postgraduate applicants
Level of Study: Postgraduate
Type: Scholarship
Value: £5,000
Frequency: Annual
Study Establishment: University of Essex
Country of Study: United Kingdom
Funding: Private
Contributor: Drake Lewis

For further information contact:

Email: scholarships@essex.ac.uk

Drake Lewis Graduate Scholarship for Health and Human Sciences

Purpose: To support students on full-time masters in public health or health studies
Eligibility: Open to postgraduate applicants
Level of Study: Postgraduate
Type: Scholarship
Value: £5,000
Frequency: Annual
Study Establishment: University of Essex
Country of Study: United Kingdom
Application Procedure: Applicants must contact the department concerned
Funding: Private
Contributor: Drake-Lewis

For further information contact:

Email: scholarships@essex.ac.uk

Essex Global Partner Scholarship

Purpose: These scholarships are restricted to students who are overseas fee payers and are entirely self-funded.
Eligibility: 1. These scholarships are restricted to students who are overseas fee payers and are entirely self-funded. 2. Applicants joining Essex from one of our Global Channel Partners listed above will be considered for this award.
Level of Study: Postgraduate
Type: Scholarship
Value: 20% tuition fee discount or a scholarship worth up to £3,000
Length of Study: First year of Masters study
Frequency: Annual
Country of Study: United Kingdom
Application Procedure: If you meet all the eligibility criteria, you will automatically be considered for this award. You don't need to complete an application form. The University will assess your eligibility based on the academic transcripts and certificates you submit with your application for your place at Essex. No alternative supporting evidence will be accepted.
No. of awards offered: 1
Additional Information: www.essex.ac.uk/scholarships/essex-global-partner-scholarship-masters

For further information contact:

Email: enquiries@essex.ac.uk

GREAT Scholarship

Purpose: The GREAT Scholarships programme is a joint initiative by the British Council and the UK Government, designed to attract some of the brightest postgraduates from around the world to study at UK universities.
Eligibility: 1. You must hold a passport from an eligible country (Bangladesh, Egypt, Ghana, India, and Pakistan). 2. Be classed as an overseas fee payer and entirely self-funded*. *Students receiving a repayable loan to fund their studies will be considered as self-funded. 3. Hold an offer (conditional or unconditional) to start a one-year full time masters degree on the provided subject list starting in October 2024. 4. Have a background of extracurricular activities relating to your subject area. 5. Only one scholarship award can be made per student and the award cannot normally be held in conjunction with other University of Essex awards.
Level of Study: Postgraduate
Type: Scholarship
Value: £10,000
Frequency: Annual
Country of Study: United Kingdom
Application Procedure: Scholarship website: www.essex.ac.uk/-/media/documents/directories/fees-and-funding/application-forms/great-scholarship-application-form.docx
No. of awards offered: 5
Closing Date: 31 May

Contributor: British Council and the GREAT Britain Campaign
Additional Information: www.essex.ac.uk/scholarships/great-scholarship

For further information contact:

Email: greatscholarships@essex.ac.uk

GREAT Scholarship for Justice and Law

Purpose: The GREAT Scholarships for Justice and Law programme is a new joint initiative by the British Council and the Ministry of Justice, designed to attract some of the brightest postgraduates from around the world to study at UK universities in Justice and Law related subjects.
Eligibility: You can apply if you 1. hold a passport from an eligible country (China) 2. are classed as an overseas student for fee purposes 3. already hold an offer (conditional or unconditional) to start a one-year full-time master's degree in October 2024 on the provided subject list 4. have a background of extracurricular activities relating to your chosen subject area.
Level of Study: Postgraduate
Type: Scholarship
Value: £10,000
Frequency: Annual
Country of Study: Any country
No. of awards offered: one
Closing Date: 31 May
Contributor: British Council and the GREAT Britain Campaign
Additional Information: www.essex.ac.uk/scholarships/great-scholarship-for-justice-and-law

For further information contact:

Wivenhoe Park, Colchester CO4 3SQ, United Kingdom.

Tel: (44) 1206 873333
Email: GREATScholarships2021@essex.ac.uk

Latin America Scholarship

Purpose: If you're from Latin America or the Caribbean and studying for our MA Translation, Interpreting and Subtitling or our MA Translation and Professional Practice, you could be eligible for £5,000 through our Latin American Scholarship.
Eligibility: 1. These scholarships are restricted to students who are from Latin America and are ordinarily resident in one of the following countries www.essex.ac.uk/-/media/documents/directories/fees-and-funding/pg-terms/latin-america-scholarship-2023-24.pdf?la=en. 2. Applicants from other English-speaking islands in the Caribbean will also be considered. 3. Applicants must have received a conditional firm or unconditional firm offer to study full time MA Translation, Interpreting & Subtitling or MA Translation & Professional Practice (Spanish or Portuguese strands only) at the University of Essex starting in the academic year 2024-25.
Level of Study: Postgraduate
Type: Scholarship
Value: £5,000
Frequency: Annual
Country of Study: United Kingdom
Application Procedure: Scholarship website: www.essex.ac.uk/-/media/documents/directories/fees-and-funding/application-forms/latin-america-scholarship-application-form-2023-24.pdf?la=en
No. of awards offered: 5
Closing Date: 30 June
Additional Information: www.essex.ac.uk/scholarships/latin-america-scholarship

For further information contact:

Email: enquiries@essex.ac.uk

Masters (PGT) EU Scholarship

Purpose: This scholarship scheme is for postgraduate taught (Masters) EU students studying as a new student in academic year 2024–2025 who are classified as international students for fees purposes.
Eligibility: 1. These scholarships are restricted to students who are overseas fee payers and are entirely self-funded*. 2. Students must be ordinarily resident (see below for the definition of ordinary residence) in an EU country.
Level of Study: Masters Degree, Postgraduate
Type: Scholarship
Value: £5,500
Length of Study: first year of study only
Frequency: Annual
Country of Study: United Kingdom
Application Procedure: If you meet all the eligibility criteria, you will automatically be considered for this award. You don't need to complete an application form. The University will assess your eligibility based on your country of domicile and fee status that you submit on your application for your place at Essex.
No. of awards offered: 1
Additional Information: www.essex.ac.uk/scholarships/masters-pgt-eu-scholarship

For further information contact:

Email: enquiries@essex.ac.uk

Masters Excellence Scholarship

Purpose: These scholarships are restricted to full-time students who are Home fee payers and are entirely self-funded.
Eligibility: 1. These scholarships are restricted to full-time students who are Home fee payers and are entirely self-funded*. 2. Students must have been awarded a first-class honours bachelor's degree from a UK university. 3. Eligible courses are those which are full-time Taught Masters programmes leading to the degree of MA, MSc, or LLM and start in October 2024 and January 2025. 4. Applicants who have firmly accepted an offer of a place by 14 July 2024 (for October 2024 start) or 13 October 2024 (for January 2025 start) and met the academic conditions of entry, will be considered for these scholarships. 5. The scholarship is offered in the form of a reduction on the annual tuition fee for the first year of full-time study only. 6. Only one scholarship award can be made per student and the award cannot be held in conjunction with any other University of Essex scholarships. 7. Successful applicants should be available for promotional activities.
Level of Study: Postgraduate
Type: Scholarship
Value: 25% discount on your Essex Masters tuition fee
Frequency: Annual
Country of Study: United Kingdom
Application Procedure: If you meet all the eligibility criteria, you will automatically be considered for this award. You don't need to complete an application form. The University will assess your eligibility based on the academic transcripts and certificates you submit with your application for your place at Essex. No alternative supporting evidence will be accepted.
No. of awards offered: 1
Additional Information: www.essex.ac.uk/scholarships/masters-excellence-scholarship

For further information contact:

Email: enquiries@essex.ac.uk

Postgraduate Conversion Courses in AI and Data Science Scholarships

Subjects: Data Sciences and Artificial Intelligence
Purpose: The Data Science and AI Scholarship is available to new Home, EU and International Postgraduate Taught (PGT) Masters students taking up a place to study in academic year 2024–25 on the following programmes
Eligibility: visit website.
Level of Study: Postgraduate
Type: Scholarship
Value: £10,000
Country of Study: Any country
Closing Date: 1 November
Additional Information: www.essex.ac.uk/scholarships/postgraduate-conversion-courses

For further information contact:

Email: enquiries@essex.ac.uk

Postgraduate Research EU Scholarship

Purpose: These scholarships are restricted to students who are overseas fee payers and are entirely self-funded.
Eligibility: visit website.
Level of Study: Postgraduate
Type: Scholarship
Value: £8,000 automatically deducted from your tuition fees.
Frequency: Annual
Country of Study: Any country
No. of awards offered: 1
Additional Information: www.essex.ac.uk/scholarships/postgraduate-research-eu-scholarship

For further information contact:

Email: enquiries@essex.ac.uk

Refugee Bursary

Purpose: The University is offering a Refugee Bursary to assist students who have UK refugee status or are a dependent of UK refugees.
Eligibility: 1. You are a current, full time or part-time registered student at the University of Essex. 2. You are eligible for UK home fees and funding, and ordinarily resident in the UK (overseas and EU students are not eligible). 3. You are undertaking Undergraduate or Postgraduate study. 4. You are able to provide evidence that you have UK refugee status or are a dependent of a UK refugee, including students who have been granted leave, or are the dependent of someone granted leave, under one of the following schemes: a. Afghan Citizens Resettlement Scheme. b. Afghan Relocations and Assistance Policy Scheme. c. Ukrainian Family Scheme. d. Homes for Ukraine Scheme. e. Ukraine Extension Scheme.
Level of Study: Postgraduate
Type: Bursary
Value: Up to £1,500 if you are studying full time or up to £750 if you are studying part time.
Frequency: Annual

Country of Study: United Kingdom
Application Procedure: To apply for the Refugee Bursary, you will need to do the following: Ensure that you meet the eligibility criteria above. Carefully read these Terms and Conditions. Register for the Blackbullion online money management website if you do not already have an account. Click the 'Funds' tab and select 'Refugee Bursary. Follow the instructions to complete the declaration form, upload the required evidence and submit your application.
Closing Date: 31 July
Additional Information: www.essex.ac.uk/scholarships/refugee-bursary

For further information contact:

Email: funding@essex.ac.uk

Sanctuary Scholarship

Purpose: The Sanctuary Scholarship scheme enables individuals seeking asylum and refugees who are not able access student finance to study at the University of Exeter.
Eligibility: 1. You have submitted a claim for asylum within the UK and are awaiting a response (this includes submission of a fresh claim) or 2. You have Limited Leave to Remain (formerly Discretionary Leave to Remain) in the UK and are not eligible for funding via Student Finance England or 3. You have been awarded 'Humanitarian Protection' or Refugee status in the UK but are not eligible for funding via Student Finance England or 4. You have left care in the UK and are assessed as international for tuition fee purposes and are not eligible for funding via Student Finance England or 5. (For applicants to postgraduate research programmes only) You have been granted refugee status* by the UK Home Office or 6. You are the family member of someone with one of the immigration statuses listed above with 'in line' or 'dependent' status
Level of Study: Postgraduate
Type: Scholarship
Value: Full tuition fee waiver plus annual living cost grant
Frequency: Annual
Country of Study: Any country
No. of awards offered: 3
Closing Date: 20 May

For further information contact:

Stocker Rd, Exeter EX4 4PY, United Kingdom.

Tel: (44) 1392 661000
Email: admissions-scholarships@exeter.ac.uk

Santander Masters Scholarship

Purpose: To support students from Santander network countries to undertake further study
Eligibility: Open to graduates residing in one of the Santander network countries who have an offer to study at Masters level
Level of Study: Postgraduate
Type: Scholarships
Value: £5,000
Frequency: Annual
Study Establishment: University of Essex
Country of Study: United Kingdom
Application Procedure: Please check website
Funding: Corporation
Contributor: Santander
Additional Information: www1.essex.ac.uk/fees-and-funding/masters/scholarships/santander-apply.aspx

For further information contact:

Email: pgtaught@lboro.ac.uk

The Eleonore Koch Fund

Subjects: School of Philosophy and Art History
Purpose: The School of Philosophy and Art History is offering a bursary of £5,000 to assist one student from Latin America to study the MA in Art History and Theory.
Eligibility: 1. These scholarships are restricted to students who are from Latin America. 2. Applicants must have received a conditional firm or unconditional firm offer to study full time MA Art History and Theory at the University of Essex starting in academic year 2024-25. 3. Applicants must have accepted their offer by 14 July 2024.
Level of Study: Postgraduate
Type: Funding support
Value: £5,000
Frequency: Annual
Country of Study: United Kingdom
Application Procedure: Scholarship website: www.essex.ac.uk/-/media/documents/directories/fees-and-funding/application-forms/eleanore-koch-fund-application-form-2023-24.pdf?la=en
No. of awards offered: 1
Closing Date: 14 July
Additional Information: www.essex.ac.uk/scholarships/the-eleonore-koch-fund

For further information contact:

Email: spahsm@essex.ac.uk

The Essex MBA Early Bird Discount

Subjects: Essex Business School
Purpose: Essex Business School is offering £3,000 to students starting their course in January 2024 who attend an interview with the MBA Team and accept their offer of a place on the full-time Essex MBA by 14 November 2022
Eligibility: visit website
Level of Study: MBA
Type: Scholarship
Value: tuition fee discount of £3,000.
Country of Study: Any country
Closing Date: 14 November
Additional Information: www.essex.ac.uk/scholarships/mba-early-bird-discount

For further information contact:

Wivenhoe Park, Colchester CO4 3SQ, United Kingdom.

Tel: (44) 1206 873333
Email: enquiries@essex.ac.uk

Tinson Fund Scholarship for Law

Purpose: To support students from the former Soviet Bloc interested in studying postgraduate law
Eligibility: Open to students from former Soviet Bloc countries, who have an offer on an LLM programme
Level of Study: Postgraduate
Type: Scholarship
Value: Tuition fees
Frequency: Annual
Study Establishment: University of Essex
Country of Study: United Kingdom
Application Procedure: See website for details
Closing Date: 31 May
No. of awards given last year: 1

For further information contact:

Email: lawpgtadmin@essex.ac.uk

University of Exeter

Postgraduate Administration Office, Northcote House, The Queen's Drive, Exeter EX4 4QJ, United Kingdom.

Tel: (44) 1392 723 044
Email: pg-ad@exeter.ac.uk
Website: www.exeter.ac.uk/postgraduate/money/funding/
Contact: Mrs Julie Gay, Scholarships Secretary

Anning Morgan Bursary

Purpose: An endowed scholarship is a major gift to a college or university used to fund scholarships.
Eligibility: To any student resident in Cornwall during their post-graduate studies and undertaking a post-graduate degree programme at the Penryn or Truro Campus. Students must be in receipt of an offer for the coming academic year to be considered for this bursary.
Level of Study: Postgraduate
Type: Bursary
Value: £2,000
Application Procedure: You can apply by completing and returning the Anning Morgan Bursary Application form: www.exeter.ac.uk/media/universityofexeter/funding/documents/Anning_Morgan_Bursary_Application_Form_2023.docx application form by email to advancement-scholarships@exeter.ac.uk
Closing Date: 11 August
Additional Information: Website: www.exeter.ac.uk/study/funding/endowed/

For further information contact:

Email: advancement-scholarships@exeter.ac.uk
Website: www.exeter.ac.uk/media/universityofexeter/funding/documents/Anning_Morgan_Bursary_Application_Form_2023.docx

Aziz Foundation Masters Scholarships

Subjects: Media & Journalism, Technology, Sustainability/Environment, Law, policy, Creative Content.
Purpose: The Scholarships Programme offers 100% tuition fee Masters scholarships to support British Muslims to study at UK universities. The scholarships are aimed at those who wish to advance in their careers and bring positive change to their communities and beyond.
Eligibility: 1. Be eligible for Home fees status 2. Be active within a Muslim community and demonstrate intimate knowledge of issues affecting British Muslim communities 3. Demonstrate long-term commitment to community/societal development within Britain 4. Show how the course will increase their effectiveness in one of the following areas relating to British Muslims.
Type: Scholarship
Value: 100% tuition fee

Frequency: Annual
Country of Study: Any country
Closing Date: 31 March
Additional Information: www.azizfoundation.org.uk/scholarships-application/

For further information contact:

Stocker Rd, Exeter EX4 4PY, United Kingdom.

Tel: (44) 1392 661000

Cornwall Heritage Trust Scholarship

Purpose: An endowed scholarship is a major gift to a college or university used to fund scholarships.
Eligibility: To post-graduate students at The Institute of Cornish Studies, University of Exeter to assist in study costs for one or more students producing a dissertation/thesis centred on any aspect of Cornwall's Heritage. This can include all aspects of human experience in Cornwall over the centuries.
Level of Study: Postgraduate
Type: Scholarship
Value: Study costs
Frequency: Annual
Application Procedure: For further details please contact: advancement-scholarships@exeter.ac.uk
Additional Information: Website: www.exeter.ac.uk/study/funding/endowed/

For further information contact:

Email: advancement-scholarships@exeter.ac.uk

Global Excellence Scholarships - Postgraduate Taught (Masters)

Purpose: Postgraduate Taught Global Excellence Scholarships have been created to support students wishing to develop their academic potential and contribute to our thriving University community of students and staff from over 140 countries.
Eligibility: You can apply for one of these scholarships if you: 1. are classified as an International student for fees purposes (including any EU students required to pay International fees in 2024/25); and 2. already hold an offer for an eligible Postgraduate taught degree at the University of Exeter, commencing in September 2024. If you are yet to make your Masters programme application then please visit our Postgraduate taught study pages for September 2024 entry.
Level of Study: Postgraduate
Type: Scholarship
Value: A range of £5,000, £10,000 and full scholarships are on offer.
Application Procedure: To be considered for one of these scholarships, once you have your offer, please apply using the webform here: www.exeter.ac.uk/study/funding/globalexcellence/form-2023/
Closing Date: 21 April
Additional Information: Website: www.exeter.ac.uk/study/funding/award/?id=4528

For further information contact:

Email: admissions-scholarships@exeter.ac.uk

'Green Futures' Postgraduate Taught Scholarships

Purpose: As part of our commitment to a Green Future, we want to make sure that the most capable and committed candidates from Low and Middle Income Countries have the opportunity to study at the University of Exeter
Eligibility: visit website
Level of Study: Postgraduate
Type: Scholarship
Value: The full tuition fees and a stipend for living costs.
Frequency: Annual
Country of Study: Any country
No. of awards offered: 9
Closing Date: 1 April
Additional Information: website: www.exeter.ac.uk/media/universityofexeter/funding/documents/Green_Futures_Postgraduate_Taught_Scholarship_2022_T&Css.pdf

For further information contact:

Stocker Rd, Exeter EX4 4PY, United Kingdom.

Tel: (44) 1392 661000
Email: isrscholarships@exeter.ac.uk

The Exeter MBA Better World Scholarship

Purpose: Our awards aim to recognise and support a range of factors to enable and support a fully diverse, able and enthusiastic cohort.
Eligibility: Offer of a place on The Exeter MBA programme. Students who can demonstrate outstanding academic merit or financial need and a commitment to the ethos of the programme.
Level of Study: MBA
Type: Scholarship
Value: £4,000-£12,000
Length of Study: For 1 year

Application Procedure: To apply for an MBA Better World scholarship, you will need to prepare and submit a video of yourself talking to camera, in which you address some key factors that support your application:- why you believe that you deserve a scholarship; what you will bring to the programme that will benefit others in the cohort; why responsible leadership is of particular interest to you; and how you'd plan to be an ambassador for the Exeter MBA programme after graduation.
Closing Date: 30 June
Additional Information: For more details Contact: Murray Scott: mba@exeter.ac.uk Website: www.exeter.ac.uk/study/funding/award/?id=4628

For further information contact:

Email: mba@exeter.ac.uk

The Exeter MBA SDG Scholarships

Purpose: The UN Sustainable Development Goals (SDGs) underpin the University of Exeter's Sustainability policy and targets for 2030. Aligning with this policy, The Exeter MBA is offering two new scholarships: 1. The Exeter MBA Women's Global Impact Scholarship (SDG5 - Gender Equality) 2. The Exeter MBA Inclusive and Sustainable Employment Scholarship (SDG8 - Decent Work and Economic Growth)
Eligibility: The 50% scholarships will be awarded to those offered a place on The Exeter MBA and awarded following successful application.
Level of Study: MBA
Type: Scholarship
Value: 50% scholarships
Application Procedure: To apply for these scholarships please click the links below: 1. Apply for The Exeter MBA Women's Global Impact Scholarship: www.exeter.ac.uk/studying/funding/apply/step1/?award=4426 2. Apply for The Exeter MBA Inclusive and Sustainable Employment Scholarship: www.exeter.ac.uk/study/funding/apply/step1/?award=4427
Closing Date: 30 April
Additional Information: Website: business-school.exeter.ac.uk/study/masters/mba/funding/#a1

University of Exeter Alumni Scholarship

Purpose: We are pleased to offer University of Exeter alumni beginning a taught Masters degree (eg MA, MSc, MRes, MFA, LLM) or research degree (eg MPhil, PhD) with us a scholarship towards the cost of their tuition fees.
Eligibility: Awards are available to all home and international University of Exeter alumni who have: 1. graduated from an undergraduate or postgraduate degree awarded by the University of Exeter; 2. completed an inbound Study Abroad semester/year at the University of Exeter; 3. completed a credit-bearing University of Exeter International Summer School. In order to be eligible for the scholarship, you must meet the entry requirements for your chosen postgraduate programme and enrol on this programme in 2024/25.
Level of Study: Masters Degree, Postgraduate
Type: Scholarship
Value: 10% reduction in first year tuition fee
Length of Study: 1 year
Frequency: Annual
Country of Study: Any country
Application Procedure: The scholarship will be applied automatically to eligible postgraduate applicants enrolling for study in 2024/25. A separate application is not required. When submitting your postgraduate programme application via our application portal: srs.exeter.ac.uk/urd/sits.urd/run/siw_ipp_lgn.login?process=siw_ipp_app_crs, please remember to complete the relevant section to indicate your previous Exeter study.
Closing Date: 31 August
Contributor: University of Exeter
Additional Information: Please use our enquiry form: www.exeter.ac.uk/enquiry/ Website: www.exeter.ac.uk/study/funding/award/?id=4033

For further information contact:

Stocker Rd, Exeter EX4 4PY, United Kingdom.

Tel: (44) 1392 661000

University of Exeter Chapel Choir Choral and Organ Scholarship

Purpose: Annual scholarships offered to choral and organ practitioners to aid in recitals on behalf of the chapel choir
Eligibility: If you are a University of Exeter student who will be studying at one of the Exeter campuses (Streatham and/or St Luke's) for a full academic year or longer, then you are very welcome to audition for the Chapel Choir. This opportunity is open to students in all years (not just first years),

undergraduates and postgraduates, and there is no age limit – mature students are very welcome to audition.
Level of Study: Postgraduate
Type: Scholarship
Value: The value of each full Choral Scholarship £650
Frequency: Annual
Study Establishment: The University of Exeter
Country of Study: United Kingdom
Application Procedure: See website
No. of awards offered: 60
Closing Date: 13 February
Funding: Corporation, Individuals, Trusts
No. of awards given last year: 10
No. of applicants last year: 60
Additional Information: website: www.exeter.ac.uk/study/funding/choral/

For further information contact:

Email: a.j.musson@exeter.ac.uk

University of Exeter Class of 2024 Progression Scholarship

Purpose: We are pleased to offer graduating University of Exeter students completing their degree in Summer 2024 and progressing direct to a standalone taught Masters degree (eg MA; MSc; MRes; MFA, LLM) or research degree (eg MPhil/PhD) with us a scholarship towards the cost of their tuition fees.
Eligibility: Awards are available to all home and international University finalists graduating from an undergraduate or postgraduate degree awarded by the University of Exeter. In order to be eligible for the scholarship, you must meet the entry requirements for your chosen postgraduate programme and enrol on this programme with us in 2024/25.
Level of Study: Masters Degree, Postgraduate
Type: Scholarship
Value: 10% reduction in the first year tuition fee
Length of Study: for 1 year
Frequency: Annual
Country of Study: Any country
Application Procedure: This award will be applied automatically to eligible University of Exeter progressing students enrolling for study in 2024/25. A separate application is not required.
Closing Date: 31 August
Additional Information: website: www.exeter.ac.uk/study/funding/award/?id=4530

For further information contact:

Stocker Rd, Exeter EX4 4PY, United Kingdom.

Tel: (44) 1392 661000

University of Geneva

University of Geneva, 24 rue du Général-Dufour, CH-1211 Genève 4, Switzerland.

Tel: (41) 022 379 71 11
Email: Excellence-Master-Sciences@unige.ch
Website: www.unige.ch/
Contact: Dean of the Faculty of Science

The University of Geneva is a public research university located in Geneva, Switzerland. It was founded in 1559 by John Calvin as a theological seminary and law school.

University of Geneva Excellence Masters Fellowships

Purpose: The Faculty of Science of the University of Geneva is an internationally recognized leading research institution.
Eligibility: Excellence Fellowship program open to outstanding and highly motivated students who wish to pursue a Master of Science degree in one of the disciplines covered by the Faculty1. Candidate selection is based on excellence.
Level of Study: Masters Degree
Type: Fellowship
Value: CHF 10,000 to CHF 15,000 per year
Application Procedure: The application is made online, from the beginning of January of each year. After registering, you will receive an e-mail containing a personal link allowing you to fill out the application form. Application: formulaire.unige.ch/outils/limesurveyfac/sciences/index.php/289872?lang=en
Closing Date: 15 March
Additional Information: website: www.unige.ch/sciences/en/enseignements/formations/masters/excellencemasterfellowships/

For further information contact:

24 rue du Général-Dufour, CH-1211 Genève 4, Switzerland.

Tel: (41) 22 379 71 11
Email: Sciences@unige.ch

University of Glasgow

Postgraduate Research Office, Research and Enterprise, University of Glasgow, Glasgow G12 8QQ, United Kingdom.

Tel: (44) 141 330 2000
Email: s.rait@enterprise.gla.ac.uk
Website: www.gla.ac.uk
Contact: Shirley Rait

The University of Glasgow is a major research led university operating in an international context, which aims to provide education through the development of learning in a research environment, to undertake fundamental, strategic and applied research and to sustain and add value to Scottish culture, to the natural environment and to the national economy.

Alexander and Dixon Scholarship (Bryce Bequest)

Purpose: The Bryce Bequest was made by the late Professor John Cameron Bryce in memory of Professor Peter Alexander, former Professor of English Literature at the University of Glasgow, and in memory of Professor W. MacNeile Dixon. The bequest supports exceptional MLitt students on any of the taught programmes in English Literature.
Eligibility: This award is only available to UK or EU applicants.
Level of Study: Masters Degree
Type: Scholarship
Value: Fee waiver (Home/EU fees) for 1 year of full time study or 2 years of part time study.
Length of Study: 3 years
Application Procedure: All applicants who wish to be considered for an Alexander and Dixon Scholarship should send a brief CV (1 page) and a statement (2 pages max) for the attention of the English Literature Convenor for Taught Postgraduate Programmes (currently Dr Matthew Sangster). The submitted documents should detail the your past record and academic achievements; discuss why you wish to pursue postgraduate studies at Glasgow; and explain how an Alexander and Dixon Scholarship would assist you in realising your ambitions. Emails should be headed 'Application: Alexander and Dixon Scholarship - [APPLICANT NAME]'. Applications should be sent to Critstudies-PGScholarships@glasgow.ac.uk.
No. of awards offered: 2
Closing Date: 21 June
Additional Information: For more information contact: Critstudies-PGScholarships@glasgow.ac.uk Website: www.gla.ac.uk/scholarships/alexanderanddixonscholarshipbrycebequest/

For further information contact:

Department Office, Department of English Literature, University of Glasgow, Glasgow G12 8QQ, United Kingdom.

Email: critstudies-pgscholarships@glasgow.ac.uk

Alexander and Margaret Johnstone Postgraduate Research Scholarships

Eligibility: Open to students intending a research degree in the faculty of arts in a department rated 5 or 5 in the research assessment exercise
Level of Study: Doctorate
Type: Research scholarship
Value: Tuition fees at the Home/European Union student rate, plus stipend of between £6,000 and £7,000
Length of Study: 3 years
Country of Study: Any country
Application Procedure: Check website for further details
Funding: Government

For further information contact:

Tel: (44) 141 330 6828
Email: e.queune@admin.gla.ac.uk

Bellahouston Bequest Fund

Eligibility: Open to postgraduate students undertaking a Masters Degree course in the faculty of arts
Level of Study: Postgraduate
Type: Scholarship
Value: £1,000
Length of Study: 1 year
Frequency: Annual
Country of Study: Any country
Application Procedure: The candidate must contact the clerk of the faculty of arts. Check website for further information
Closing Date: 17 July
Additional Information: Preference will be given to the Glaswegians www.gla.ac.uk/scholarships/alexanderanddixonscholarshipbrycebequest/

For further information contact:

Tel: (44) 141 330 2000
Email: ugs@archives.gla.ac.uk

British Federation of Women Graduates (BFWG)

Purpose: To encourage applicants to become members of the Federation to help promote better links between female graduates throughout the world
Eligibility: Open to female graduate with academic excellence. Doctoral students of all nationalities who will be studying in the United Kingdom are eligible for the scholarship
Level of Study: Postgraduate
Type: Scholarship and award
Value: £1,000–6,000
Length of Study: Four years
Frequency: Annual
Country of Study: United Kingdom
Application Procedure: Check website for further details
Closing Date: 4 March
Funding: Private
No. of awards given last year: 6
Additional Information: For further information see website Awards & Scholarships: bfwg.org.uk/bfwg2/awards-and-scholarships/ - BFWG or email awardsqueries@bfwg.org.uk website: bfwg.org.uk/bfwg2/

For further information contact:

Tel: (44) 20 7498 8037
Fax: (44) 20 7498 5213
Email: awardsqueries@bfwg.org.uk

Clark Graduate Bursary Fund for International Students at University of Glasgow

Purpose: The aim of the bursary is to support graduates of the University of Glasgow or Strathclyde studying for, or applying to study for, a subsequent degree at a university in the United Kingdom or abroad
Eligibility: Applicants can either be graduates of the University of Glasgow or Strathclyde studying for, or applying to study for, a subsequent degree at a university in the United Kingdom or abroad. Applicants must be fluent in English
Level of Study: Postdoctorate, Postgraduate, Research
Type: Postgraduate scholarships
Value: The value of the bursary normally between £500 and £1,500.
Study Establishment: Bursary is awarded in the field offered by the university
Country of Study: United Kingdom
Application Procedure: There is an annual application process. Applications can be submitted between 1st March and 1st October each year. Applications must be submitted online. Interviews of candidates selected for consideration are held in Glasgow at a Governors' meeting during November. Interviewees will usually be notified within a week of the interviews whether they will receive an award. Awards are normally paid to successful applicants before the end of the year
Closing Date: 1 May
Additional Information: For more details please visit the website scholarship-positions.com/clark-raduate-bursary-fund-international-students-university-of-glasgow-uk/2017/12/20/ www.gla.ac.uk/scholarships/clarkmileendbursaryfund/

For further information contact:

Glasgow G12 8QQ, United Kingdom.

Tel: (44) 141 330 2000
Email: clarkmileendfund@gmail.com

Glasgow Educational & Marshall Trust Award

Purpose: To offer financial support to those who have lived, or are currently living within the Glasgow Municipal Boundary
Eligibility: It is an absolute requirement that awards can only be made to persons who have lived in the city of Glasgow for a minimum of 5 years in total. Students, please note, if you came to live in Glasgow solely for the proposes of study, those years do not count. The following postcodes qualify as the city of Glasgow: G1 G2 G3, G4 G5 G11, G12 G13* G14, G15 G20 G21*, G22 G23 G31, G32* G33* G34, G40 G41 G42, G43* G44* G45, G46* G51 G52*, G53* G69*
Level of Study: Doctorate, Graduate, MBA, Postdoctorate, Postgraduate, Predoctorate, Research
Type: Studentships and bursaries
Value: Course Fees, Living Expenses, Books and Materials, Childcare Costs, Travel
Length of Study: 1 year
Study Establishment: Glasgow Educational and Marshall Trust
Country of Study: United Kingdom
Application Procedure: Check website for further details
Closing Date: 30 April
Contributor: Glasgow Educational and Marshall Trust
Additional Information: www.itpt.co.uk/glasgow-educational-marshall-trust/

For further information contact:

Tel: (44) 141 4334449
Fax: (44) 141 424 1731
Email: sloanea@hutchesons.org

U

Henry Dryerre Scholarship in Medical and Veterinary Physiology

Eligibility: Open to candidates holding a degree of a Scottish University with first class honours or, if in their final year, to be expected to achieve first class honours.
Level of Study: Postgraduate
Type: Scholarships and fellowships
Value: Varies
Frequency: Every 3 years
Country of Study: Any country
Application Procedure: The candidate must submit the application form through a member of staff on the appropriate Henry Dryerre Nomination Form.
Additional Information: website: www.postgraduatefunding.com/award-1672

For further information contact:

Tel: (44) 141 330 6828; (44) 141 330 2000
Fax: (44) 141 330 2000
Email: scholarships@glasgow.ac.uk
Website: www.gla.ac.uk/

Royal Historical Society: Postgraduate Research Support Grants

Purpose: To assist postgraduate students in the pursuit of advanced historical research
Eligibility: The candidate must be a postgraduate student registered for a research degree at United Kingdom Institute of Higher Education
Level of Study: Graduate, Research
Type: Award/Grant
Country of Study: United States of America
Application Procedure: Check website for further details
Closing Date: 12 November
Contributor: Royal Historical Society

For further information contact:

Email: m.ransom@royalhistsoc.org

Saint Andrew's Society of the State of New York Scholarship Fund

Purpose: The Saint Andrew's Society of the State of New York awards five scholarships annually, to support graduate study for one year - three scholarships for US students to study in Scotland and two scholarships for Scottish students to study in the United States.
Eligibility: See website
Level of Study: Graduate
Type: Scholarship
Value: Each scholarship is valued at US$35,000 and is granted for tuition, maintenance and travel.
Length of Study: 1 academic year
Frequency: Annual
Country of Study: United States of America
Application Procedure: Candidates apply directly to the university where they are studying in Scotland. For an application form and any further information on this scholarship opportunity, students at the University of St Andrews should email careers@st-andrews.ac.uk
No. of awards offered: 5
Closing Date: 8 February
Funding: Trusts
Contributor: Saint Andrew's Society of the State of New York
Additional Information: For further information, please visit the Society website: standrewsny.org/. Website: www.st-andrews.ac.uk/study/fees-and-funding/postgraduate/scholarships/new-york/

For further information contact:

Tel: (44) 141 330 6063
Email: careers@st-andrews.ac.uk

Stevenson Exchange Scholarships

Purpose: To promote friendly relations between the students of Scotland, Germany, France and Spain
Eligibility: Open to current or recent students of French, German or Spanish universities who intend to study at any university in Scotland
Level of Study: Postdoctorate
Type: Scholarship
Value: £250–2,000
Application Procedure: Check website for further details
Closing Date: 1 February
Additional Information: www.ed.ac.uk/student-funding/current-students/study-abroad/undergraduate/stevenson-exchange

For further information contact:

Room 1.07, Undergraduate Teaching Office, 50 George Square, Edinburgh EH8 9LD, Scotland, United Kingdom.

Tel: (44) 141 330 4241
Fax: (44) 141 330 4045
Email: delc@ed.ac.uk

Sustainability Scholarship

Purpose: The scholarship will be awarded for the fall/autumn semester of 2024 and is open to people from anywhere in the world who want to study a master's program that is helping you making the world more sustainable.
Eligibility: 1. You must have applied (or will apply) to a master's program that can help you make the world more sustainable 2. You must have applied (or will apply) for a study starting in the Fall Semester 2024 3. The degree program may not be online 4. You must meet the entry requirements for the university or graduate school, including 5. Hold a valid undergraduate degree 6. Meet language requirements for the program 7. You must hold or be eligible to apply for a relevant study visa (if applicable)
Type: Scholarship
Value: €5000
Frequency: Annual
Country of Study: Any country
No. of awards offered: 1
Closing Date: 22 September
Additional Information: www.gla.ac.uk/scholarships/sustainabilityscholarship/#

For further information contact:

Glasgow G12 8QQ, United Kingdom.

Tel: (44) 141 330 2000
Email: frederik.keller.dietz@finduddannelse.dk

The Catherine Mackichan Trust

Eligibility: Open to applications from academic centres worldwide, schools, colleges and individuals or groups
Level of Study: Research
Type: Award
Value: £500
Length of Study: 1 year
Frequency: Annual
Country of Study: Any country
Application Procedure: Check website for further details
Closing Date: 16 April
Funding: Trusts
Contributor: The Catherine Mackichan Trust
Additional Information: grants-search.turn2us.org.uk/grant/the-catherine-mackichan-trust-13908

For further information contact:

Email: peter.mcghee@vaslan.org.uk

University of Göttingen

Georg-August-University Göttingen, Wilhelmsplatz 1 (Aula), D-37073 Göttingen, Germany.

Tel: (49) 551/39 33959
Email: nina.guelcher@zvw.uni-goettingen.de
Website: www.uni-goettingen.de/
Contact: Mrs Nina Gülcher

The University of Göttingen is an internationally renowned research university with a long tradition. Founded in 1737 in the Age of Enlightenment, it feels committed to the values of social responsibility of science, democracy, tolerance and justice. In 2003, it was the first full university in Germany to be transferred to the sponsorship of a foundation under public law. With 13 faculties, it covers a diverse range of subjects in the natural sciences, humanities and social sciences as well as medicine. Around 30,000 students are spread across more than 210 courses.

Dorothea Schlozer Postdoctoral Scholarships for Female Students

Purpose: The University of Göttingen is inviting female postdocs from Germany to apply for Dorothea Schlozer Postdoctoral Scholarships. These scholarships are available to conduct a research project at the Georg-August-University
Eligibility: Female postdocs from Germany are eligible to apply. The candidate should have a very good command of English language. Therefore, the application should be written in English
Value: There will be 3 positions (TV-L 13, 100%, term of 2 years), one of which at the University Medical Center (UMG)
Length of Study: 2 years
Country of Study: Germany
Application Procedure: Applications will only be accepted through the online portal. After submitting your application you will receive an automatic confirmation of receipt via e-mail
Closing Date: 8 April
Additional Information: For more details, please visit the website www.uni-goettingen.de/de/122481.html scholarship-positions.com/dorothea-schlozer-postdoctoral-scholarships-female-students-germany/2018/02/20/

For further information contact:

Email: admin@scholarship-positions.com

U

University of Graz

Universitätsplatz 3, A-8010 Graz, Austria.

Website: www.uni-graz.at/de/
Contact: University of Graz

The University of Graz (German: Karl-Franzens-Universität Graz), located in Graz, Austria, is the largest and oldest university in Styria, as well as the second-largest and second-oldest university in Austria.

Ida Pfeiffer Scholarships

Purpose: This program is designed to give applicants the opportunity to submit an application for a waiver of tuition fees
Eligibility: 1. Regular studies at the University of Graz 2. Minimum age: 19 years 3. At the time you start mobility (not at the time of application), you have completed at least the first year of basic studies in the field of study relevant to your stay
Type: Scholarship
Length of Study: 1 year
Application Procedure: See website
Closing Date: 3 March
Additional Information: Please visit website: international.uni-graz.at/de/stud/outgoing/s-out-mprog/ida-pfeiffer-stipendium/ www.european-funding-guide.eu/other-financial-assistance/14286-ida-pfeiffer-scholarships

For further information contact:

Email: maren.leykauf@uni-graz.at

Marie Sklodowska-Curie Actions Postdoctoral Fellowships

Purpose: Fellowship is available to pursue Postdoctoral programme
Eligibility: Please visit ec.europa.eu/research/mariecurieactions/actions/postdoctoral-fellowships for eligibility criteria
Type: Fellowship
Value: Receive up to €400 for your travel costs to Austria
Country of Study: Austria
Closing Date: 1 May
Contributor: University of Graz
Additional Information: Please visit www.unica.it/unica/it/news_avvisi_s1.page?contentId=AVS93045 www.ersnet.org/professional-development/fellowships/marie-curie-post-doctoral-research-fellowships-respire

For further information contact:

Av. Sainte-Luce 4, CH-1003 Lausanne, Switzerland.

Tel: (41) 21 213 01 01

University of Guelph

University Centre, Room 437, 50 Stone Road East, Guelph, ON N1G 2W1, Canada.

Tel: (1) 519 824 4120
Email: immccorki@uoguelph.ca
Website: www.uoguelph.ca
Contact: Linda McCorkindale, Associate Registrar

The University of Guelph is renowned in Canada and around the world as a research-intensive and learner-centred institution and for its commitment to open learning, internationalism and collaboration. Their vision is to be Canada's leader in creating, transmitting and applying knowledge to improve the social, cultural and economic quality of life of people in Canada and around the world.

Arrell Scholarships

Purpose: The Institute is seeking emerging scholars who are not only academically outstanding but also passionately committed to ensuring that future generations are well fed, that diets are nutritious and equitable, and that agriculture is sustainable.
Eligibility: Students entering a graduate program in the Fall semester following the application deadline with a minimum first-class (A-) admissions average, whose research aligns with the vision of the Arrell Food Institute, and who have the support of a prospective University of Guelph faculty advisor. In cases of extenuating circumstances, students may be able to defer the start of the award, subject to approval by their graduate program and the Arrell Food Institute.
Level of Study: Doctorate, Masters Degree
Type: Scholarship
Value: Master's - US$50,000 per year; Doctoral - US$50,000 per year

Length of Study: Master's - up to 2 years; Doctoral - up to 4 years
Application Procedure: See website for details
Additional Information: Website: graduatestudies.uoguelph.ca/current/funding/scholarships/internal/arrell-scholarships

Canada-ASEAN Scholarships and Educational Exchanges for Development (SEED) – for Students

Purpose: The Government of Canada announced the Canada-ASEAN Scholarships and Educational Exchanges for Development (SEED) program to provide opportunities for students from ASEAN member states to conduct short-term study or research in Canadian post-secondary institutions in areas that contribute to the implementation of the 2030 Agenda for Sustainable Development.
Eligibility: To be eligible, you must be: 1. a citizen of an ASEAN member state A. Brunei Darussalam, Cambodia, Indonesia, Laos (Lao People's Democratic Republic (Lao PDR)), Malaysia, Myanmar, The Philippines, Singapore, Thailand, or Vietnam 2. a student enrolled full-time at a post-secondary institution in an ASEAN member state 3. paying tuition fees to that institution at the time of application and for the full duration of your exchange
Level of Study: Research
Type: Scholarship
Country of Study: Any country
Application Procedure: Canadian institutions must apply on behalf of eligible students before the deadline. See website for more Details
Closing Date: 28 March
Additional Information: Contact the scholarship administrator, the Canadian Bureau for International Education (CBIE): scholarships-bourses@cbie.ca or 613-237-4820 Website: www.educanada.ca/scholarships-bourses/can/institutions/asean-anase.aspx?lang=eng

For further information contact:

50 Stone Rd E, Guelph, ON N1G 2W1, Canada.

Tel: (1) 519 824 4120; (1) 613 237 4820
Email: scholarships-bourses@cbie.ca

Canada-CARICOM Faculty Leadership Program

Purpose: The Canada-CARICOM Faculty Leadership Program provides faculty or international liaison officers/managers from post-secondary institutions located in the CARICOM member and associate member states with short-term exchange opportunities for professional development, graduate study or research at Canadian post-secondary institutions.
Eligibility: To be eligible, you must be: 1. a citizen of one of the CARICOM member and associate member states A. Anguilla, Antigua and Barbuda, Bahamas, Barbados, Belize, Bermuda, British Virgin Islands, Cayman Islands, Dominica, Grenada, Guyana, Haiti, Jamaica, Montserrat, Saint Kitts and Nevis, Saint Lucia, Saint Vincent and the Grenadines, Suriname, Trinidad and Tobago, and Turks and Caicos 2. employed full-time as a faculty or international liaison officer/manager at a post-secondary institution in an eligible country/territory at the time of application and for the entire duration of your stay in Canada
Type: Scholarship
Country of Study: Any country
Application Procedure: Canadian institutions must apply for the scholarship on behalf of eligible candidates before the deadline. see website for more Details
Closing Date: 21 March
Additional Information: Contact the scholarship administrator, the Canadian Bureau for International Education (CBIE): scholarships-bourses@cbie.ca or 613-237-4820 website: www.educanada.ca/scholarships-bourses/can/institutions/flpp-pplpe.aspx?lang=eng

For further information contact:

50 Stone Rd E, Guelph, ON N1G 2W1, Canada.

Tel: (1) 519 824 4120; (1) 613 237 4820
Email: scholarships-bourses@cbie.ca

Emerging Leaders in the Americas Program (ELAP)

Purpose: To support the development of human capital and the next generation of leaders in the Americas while strengthening the linkages between post-secondary institutions in Canada and the Americas.
Eligibility: To be eligible, you must be: 1. a citizen of an eligible country/territory a. Caribbean: Anguilla, Antigua and Barbuda, Bahamas, Barbados, Belize, Bermuda, British Virgin Islands, Cayman Islands, Cuba, Dominica, Dominican Republic, Grenada, Guyana, Haiti, Jamaica, Montserrat, Saint Kitts and Nevis, Saint Lucia, Saint Vincent and the Grenadines, Suriname, Trinidad and Tobago, Turks and Caicos b. Central America: Costa Rica, El Salvador, Guatemala, Honduras, Nicaragua, Panama c. North America: Mexico d. South America: Argentina, Bolivia, Brazil, Chile, Colombia, Ecuador, Paraguay, Peru, Uruguay, Venezuela 2. a student enrolled full-time at post-secondary institution in an eligible country/territory 3. paying tuition fees to that

U

institution at the time of application and for the full duration of your exchange
Level of Study: Graduate, Masters Degree, Postgraduate
Type: Scholarship
Value: CA$ 8,200 for college (Master's and PhD); CA$ 11,100 (Master's and PhD)
Length of Study: six months or one year
Frequency: Annual
Country of Study: Any country
Application Procedure: Canadian institutions must apply for the scholarship on behalf of eligible students before the deadline. See website for more details
Closing Date: 21 March
Additional Information: Contact the scholarship administrator, the Canadian Bureau for International Education (CBIE): scholarships-bourses@cbie.ca or 613-237-4820. website: www.educanada.ca/scholarships-bourses/can/institutions/elap-pfla.aspx?lang=eng#tab_1528378062_3

For further information contact:

50 Stone Rd E, Guelph, ON N1G 2W1, Canada.

Tel: (1) 519 824 4120; (1) 613 237 4820
Email: scholarships-bourses@cbie.ca

Faculty Mobility for Partnership Building Program

Purpose: The Program will award short-term grants to professors to teach and/or conduct research in ELAP-eligible countries. The primary objective of the exchange should be to create new agreements with host institutions and/or to strengthen existing agreements.
Eligibility: Applicants should be full-time professors at Canadian post-secondary institutions (part-time professors and lecturers, as well as public servants (federal, provincial/territorial, municipal, or Crown corporations) are not eligible); and submit a proposal for collaboration with a post-secondary host institution in an ELAP-eligible country.
Type: Scholarship
Value: CAD 7,000.
Length of Study: eight weeks maximum
Country of Study: Any country
Closing Date: 2 December
Additional Information: www.educanada.ca/scholarships-bourses/can/institutions/elap_faculty-pfla_professeurs.aspx?lang=eng#tab_1530023127_3

For further information contact:

50 Stone Rd E, Guelph, ON N1G 2W1, Canada.

Tel: (1) 519 824 4120
Email: scholarships-bourses@cbie.ca.

Indigenous Graduate Scholarship - Fulfilling Indigenous Community Responsibilities

Purpose: The Indigenous Graduate Scholarship was established to encourage Indigenous (First Nations, Inuit, Métis) students to pursue graduate studies in any discipline.
Eligibility: Students entering graduate studies in May, September or January following the application deadline or registered in any graduate program who self-identify as First Nations, Inuit or Métis
Level of Study: Graduate, Masters Degree
Type: Scholarship
Value: up to US$5,000 year
Length of Study: one year
Application Procedure: The online Indigenous Graduate Scholarships Application is available via a Qualtrics Webform: uoguelph.eu.qualtrics.com/jfe/form/SV_1YTkRY8QWdXvQjA. Please include: 1. A statement self-identifying as Indigenous. This could be as simple as a sentence or two. 2. A 1-2 page research budget.
Closing Date: 1 February
Additional Information: Website: graduatestudies.uoguelph.ca/current/funding/scholarships/internal

For further information contact:

Website: uoguelph.eu.qualtrics.com/jfe/form/SV_1YTkRY8QWdXvQjA

Indigenous Graduate Scholarship - Leadership

Purpose: The Indigenous Graduate Scholarship was established to encourage Indigenous (First Nations, Inuit, Métis) students to pursue graduate studies in any discipline.
Eligibility: Students entering full-time graduate studies or are in semesters 1-3 of a full-time graduate application at the time of application, who self-identify as First Nations, Inuit, or Métis.
Level of Study: Doctorate, Graduate, Masters Degree
Type: Scholarship
Value: master's CA$15,000/year; doctoral CA$15,000/year
Length of Study: master's for up to 2 years; doctoral for up to 4 years
Application Procedure: 1. The online Indigenous Graduate Scholarships Application is available via a Qualtrics Webform: uoguelph.eu.qualtrics.com/jfe/form/SV_1YTkRY8QWdXvQjA. Please include: a. A statement self-identifying as Indigenous. This could be as simple as a sentence or two. b. A resume/CV c. 1-page research

proposal. 2. Two letters of support from academic and/or community-based references must also be emailed by the referees to grschol@uoguelph.ca
Closing Date: 1 February
Additional Information: Website: graduatestudies.uoguelph.ca/current/funding/scholarships/internal

For further information contact:

Email: grschol@uoguelph.ca
Website: uoguelph.eu.qualtrics.com/jfe/form/SV_1YTkRY8QWdXvQjA

Indigenous Graduate Scholarship - Merit

Purpose: The Indigenous Graduate Scholarship was established to encourage Indigenous (First Nations, Inuit, Métis) students to pursue graduate studies in any discipline.
Eligibility: Students entering full-time graduate studies or are in semesters 1-3 of a full-time graduate application at the time of application, who self-identify as First Nations, Inuit, or Métis.
Level of Study: Graduate, Masters Degree, Postgraduate
Type: Scholarship
Value: master's CA$15,000/year; doctoral CA$15,000/year
Length of Study: master's up to 2 years; doctoral up to 4 years
Application Procedure: 1. The online Indigenous Graduate Scholarships Application is available via a Qualtrics Webform: uoguelph.eu.qualtrics.com/jfe/form/SV_1YTkRY8QWdXvQjA. Please include: a. A statement self-identifying as Indigenous. This could be as simple as a sentence or two. b. A resume/CV c. 1-page research proposal. 2. Two letters of support from academic and/or community-based references must be emailed by the referees to grschol@uoguelph.ca
Closing Date: 1 February
Additional Information: Website: graduatestudies.uoguelph.ca/current/funding/scholarships/internal

Indigenous Graduate Scholarship - Top-Up

Purpose: The Indigenous Graduate Scholarship was established to encourage Indigenous (First Nations, Inuit, Métis) students to pursue graduate studies in any discipline.
Eligibility: Students holding a Tri-Agency or Ontario Graduate scholarship who are entering or already registered full-time in graduate studies in May, September or January following the application deadline, who self-identify as First Nations, Inuit or Métis
Level of Study: Doctorate, Graduate, Masters Degree
Type: Scholarship
Value: master's CA$5,000/year; doctoral CA$5,000/year
Length of Study: master's up to 2 years; and doctoral up to 4 years
Application Procedure: The online Indigenous Graduate Scholarships Application is available via a Qualtrics Webform. Please include: a. A statement self-identifying as Indigenous. This could be as simple as a sentence or two. b. A copy of your Notice of Award to the Qualtrics form for our records so we can confirm your award value/duration. If you have an OGS/QEII award, please upload a copy of your OGS offer e-mail if possible.
Closing Date: 1 February
Additional Information: Website: graduatestudies.uoguelph.ca/current/funding/scholarships/internal

International doctoral Tuition Scholarship

Eligibility: 1. International students who become permanent residents or Canadian citizens will no longer be eligible for the scholarship. 2. Incoming students who have not identified their residency status with the Office of Registrarial Services by the 14th class day are not eligible until such evidence is presented. 3. Students must maintain full-time registration and satisfactory progress in their program. 4. Not tenable with the International Graduate Tuition Scholarship, Ontario Trillium Scholarships, Brock Doctoral Scholarships, Arrell Scholarships, Vanier CGS-D, Dairy Farmers of Ontario, China Scholarship Council, CONACyT, Science without Borders or any other third party funding (e.g., workplace funding, scholarships from a home government). 5. Students who transfer from full-time to part-time status are no longer eligible to hold the award. However, should the student return to full-time status, and all other criteria are met, they will be eligible to hold the award for the remainder of the four-year period of eligibility (part-time semesters will be equated to full-time semesters on a 3:1 ratio).
Level of Study: Doctorate
Type: Scholarship
Value: CA$12,500 per year
Length of Study: up to four years
Application Procedure: No application required. Students who meet all eligibility criteria will receive the scholarship automatically.
Additional Information: Please contact the Graduate Program Assistant in the department to which you will apply (contact information available by program here: graduatestudies.uoguelph.ca/programs/list/byprogram).
Website: graduatestudies.uoguelph.ca/current/funding/scholarships/internal

Study in Canada Scholarships

Purpose: Study in Canada Scholarships aim to increase opportunities for Canadian post-secondary institutions to welcome international students from a wide range of countries and territories on short-term exchanges for study or research.
Eligibility: To be eligible, you must be: 1. a citizen of an eligible country/territory a. Asia: Bangladesh, Nepal, Taiwan b. Europe: Türkiye, Ukraine c. Middle East and North Africa: Algeria, Egypt, Jordan, Morocco, Tunisia d. Sub-Saharan Africa: Burkina Faso, Ethiopia, Ghana, Ivory Coast, Kenya, Nigeria, Rwanda, Senegal, Tanzania, Uganda 2. a student enrolled full-time at a post-secondary institution in an eligible country/territory 3. paying tuition fees to that institution at the time of application and for the full duration of your exchange
Level of Study: Graduate
Type: Scholarship
Value: CA$10,200; CA$12,700;
Length of Study: six months or one academic year.
Frequency: Annual
Country of Study: Any country
Application Procedure: Canadian institutions must apply on behalf of eligible students before the deadline. See website for more details
Closing Date: 21 March
Additional Information: Contact the scholarship administrator, the Canadian Bureau for International Education (CBIE): scholarships-bourses@cbie.ca or 613-237-4820 www.educanada.ca/scholarships-bourses/can/institutions/study-in-canada-sep-etudes-au-canada-pct.aspx?lang=eng#tab_1530023127_1

For further information contact:

50 Stone Rd E, Guelph, ON N1G 2W1, Canada.

Tel: (1) 519 824 4120; 613 237 4820
Email: scholarships-bourses@cbie.ca

The Brock Doctoral Scholarship

Purpose: To financially support Doctoral students to attain a high level of academic achievement and to make significant teaching and research contributions
Eligibility: Open to students with sustained outstanding academic performance, evidence of strong teaching and research skills, demonstrated outstanding communication skills and excellent potential for research and teaching as assessed by the College Dean.
Level of Study: Doctorate
Type: Scholarship
Value: Up to CA$120,000 (CA$10,000 per semester for up to 12 semesters)
Length of Study: 6 years
Frequency: Annual
Study Establishment: University of Guelph
Country of Study: Canada
Application Procedure: Students entering a Doctoral programme should apply to their College Dean by February 1st with a curriculum vitae, which must then be forwarded to Graduate Program Services by February 15th, with the Dean's written assessment of the candidate's research and teaching potential attached.
Closing Date: 15 February
Additional Information: website: www.postgraduatefunding.com/award-4145

For further information contact:

Email: sinclair@registrar.uoguelph.ca

University of Illinois

225 DKH, 1407 West Gregory, Urbana, IL 61801, United States of America.

Tel: (1) 217 333 8153
Website: www.uiuc.edu
Contact: Ms Diane Carson, Graduate Advising Office

Illinois students, scholars, and alumni are a community with the power to change the world. With our land-grant heritage as a foundation, we pioneer innovative research that tackles global problems and expands the human experience. Our transformative learning experiences, in and out of the classroom, are designed to produce alumni who desire to make a significant, societal impact.

Master of Business Administration Programme

Length of Study: 2 years
Application Procedure: Applicants must complete an application form supplying US$50 fee, official transcripts, TOEFL score, statement of financial support and a personal statement

For further information contact:

Tel: (1) 217 244 8019
Email: mba@uiuc.edu

University of Kent

Admissions and Partnership Services, The Registry, Canterbury, Kent CT2 7NZ, United Kingdom.

Tel: (44) 1227 764 000
Email: scholarships@kent.ac.uk
Website: www.kent.ac.uk

The University of Kent is a United Kingdom higher education institution funded by the Higher Education Funding Council for United Kingdom (HEFCE). The university provides education of excellent quality characterized by flexibility and inter disciplinarily and informed by research and scholarship, meeting the lifelong needs of diversity students.

Alumni Postgraduate Research Scholarship - Exclusively for Kent Graduates

Eligibility: 1. Hold, or be expected to hold a Bachelor's degree (1 or 2.1), or Master's degree (merit or distinction) from the University of Kent. 2. Hold an offer of a place for a full-time or part-time PhD research degree at University of Kent for the following academic year 2024/25. 3. Demonstrate that they have made a contribution to the wider University community, for example, through Students' Union activities - societies, sports, volunteering - or acting as a student representative on University committees. 4. Have excellent written and oral communication skills and be able to: a. Explain their research clearly and without jargon to non-experts. b. Convey their passion for their research to a wider audience. c. Convince the panel of their research's wider value. 5. Provide a CV. 6. Provide a supporting statement of no more than two A4 pages. Any statement exceeding this limit will not be accepted. 7. Provide an academic reference in support of the project; this will be requested if you are successful through the first round of shortlisting. 8. Act as 'ambassadors' for both the University and their subjects. 9. Be available for video interview, via Zoom, date TBC. Undergraduates applying to study at any of the University of Kent campuses (Brussels, Canterbury, Medway, Paris) are eligible to apply.
Level of Study: Postgraduate
Type: Scholarship
Value: Tuition fees at the home rate and a maintenance grant at the same rate as the UK Research Councils
Application Procedure: Eligible applicants will be able to apply through their KentVision portal in due course. All documents must be in either Microsoft Word or PDF format; documents that are not sent in this format will not be reviewed. Please do NOT send documents via Google Docs or SharePoint.
Closing Date: 9 April
Additional Information: Website: www.kent.ac.uk/scholarships/search/FNADALUMNI02

Army Medical Services

Eligibility: The Student Offer is available to candidates who have made an application for or be registered to study on one of the following programmes at the University of Kent: 1. Primary Dental Care (PDip) 2. Primary Dental Care (MSc) 3. Pharmacy (MPhil) 4. Pharmacy (PhD)
Level of Study: Masters Degree, Postdoctorate, Research
Type: Scholarship
Value: £2,500 payable upon completion of your Officer Training
Application Procedure: To take up this offer: 1. You must have made an application for or be registered to study on one of the above programmes at the University of Kent. 2. You need to join your local Army Medical Services Reserve unit and complete the first element of your soldier or officer training. For further information, contact Captain Yam Pun via email on yambahadur.pun113@mod.uk
Additional Information: Website: www.kent.ac.uk/scholarships/search/FNADARMYMS02

For further information contact:

Email: yambahadur.pun113@mod.uk

Bill Jenkins Award

Eligibility: 1. Have applied to study a Master's at the School of Social Policy, Sociology and Social Research at the University of Kent 2. Preference will be given to candidates on the MA International Social Policy 3. Study to commence in September 2024 4. Be able demonstrate financial need
Level of Study: Masters Degree
Type: Award
Value: £3,000
Application Procedure: This Scholarship is now receiving applications, which can be made via your Kent Applicant Portal following receipt of an application for admission to one of the courses detailed above. Applicants should provide a supporting statement explaining why they wish to embark upon their chosen Master's and how the Bill Jenkins Award would benefit them. The statement should not exceed 500 words.
Closing Date: 30 June

Additional Information: Website: www.kent.ac.uk/scholarships/search/FN40JENKIN01

British Federation of Women Graduates Postgraduate Awards

Eligibility: Please go to www.bfwg.org.uk and look up under 'Awards' where more information including criteria for eligibility can be found.
Level of Study: Postgraduate
Type: Award
Value: Between £1,000 and £6,000
Application Procedure: Please go to www.bfwg.org.uk and look under 'Awards & Scholarships' for details of the application process.
Closing Date: 3 March
Additional Information: Website: www.kent.ac.uk/scholarships/search/FNADFEDWOM02

Canadian Centennial Scholarship Fund

Purpose: Awards are granted to scholars from a wide range of disciplines including science, engineering, social science and humanities as well as music, creative arts and design.
Eligibility: To find out more about eligibility requirements, please see the information for students page: www.canadianscholarshipfund.co.uk/information-for-students/.
Level of Study: Postgraduate, Research
Type: Scholarship
Value: £2,000 to £5,000
Application Procedure: To find out more about the application process and required documents, please see the information for students page: www.canadianscholarshipfund.co.uk/information-for-students/.
Closing Date: 10 March
Additional Information: Website: www.kent.ac.uk/scholarships/search/FNADCANCEN02

Christine and Ian Bolt Scholarship

Purpose: Scholarships are aimed at students whose area of research has an American element and/or where the centre of expertise or an important source of research material is located in the United States of America.
Eligibility: Applicants must: 1. Hold an excellent bachelor's (1st or 2.1), or Master's degree (merit or distinction); 2. Hold an offer of a place, or be a currently registered student, for a full-time or part-time postgraduate research or taught degree at the University of Kent for the following academic year within one of the listed Academic Divisions: a. Arts and Humanities; b. Human and Social Sciences; c. Kent Business School; or d. Law, Society and Social Justice. 3. Have excellent communication skills, both written and oral, and be able to explain their project clearly and without jargon to non-experts, 4. Convey their passion for their project to a wider audience and convince the panel of the project's wider value 5. Act as 'ambassador' for both the University and their subject. For more information see website
Level of Study: Postgraduate
Type: Scholarship
Value: Up to £10,000
Application Procedure: Apply by submitting the following separate documents to scholarships@kent.ac.uk before the deadline. See website for details
Closing Date: 14 May
Additional Information: Website: www.kent.ac.uk/scholarships/search/FNADCIBOLT02

Colt Foundation Fellowships in Occupational/Environmental Health

Purpose: to enable holders to study for a PhD in occupational or environmental health at a UK university.
Eligibility: For information on criteria, please visit the website: www.coltfoundation.org.uk/phd-fellowships/
Level of Study: Postgraduate, Research
Type: Scholarship
Value: Up to £5,000 per year towards research expenses.
Frequency: Annual
Application Procedure: For information on how to apply, please visit the website: www.coltfoundation.org.uk/phd-fellowships/
Closing Date: 24 August
No. of applicants last year: Upto 4
Additional Information: Website: www.kent.ac.uk/scholarships/search/FNADCOLTFF02

Commonwealth PhD Scholarship (for High Income Countries)

Purpose: Commonwealth PhD Scholarships enable talented and motivated individuals to gain the knowledge and skills required for sustainable development, and are aimed at those who could not otherwise afford to study in the UK.
Eligibility: Please contact the CSC directly to further information: cscuk.fcdo.gov.uk/about-us/contact-us/
Level of Study: Postgraduate, Research
Type: Scholarship
Application Procedure: Please see the CSC website for further information: cscuk.fcdo.gov.uk/scholarships/high-income-commonwealth-phd-scholarships/

Contributor: The UK Department for Education (DfE)
Additional Information: Website: www.kent.ac.uk/scholarships/search/FN00COMMON01

Commonwealth Split-site Scholarship

Purpose: To widen access to UK equipment and expertise for high quality doctoral candidates from low- and middle-income Commonwealth countries, and to contribute to UK and Commonwealth higher education and research through collaboration and partnerships.
Eligibility: To apply for these Scholarships, prospective Scholars must: 1. Be a citizen of or have been granted refugee status by an eligible Commonwealth country, or be a British Protected Person 2. Be permanently resident in an eligible Commonwealth country 3. Be registered for a PhD at a university in an eligible Commonwealth country by the time your Scholarship starts (September 2024) 4. Ensure that an institutional or departmental link exists between your home university and your proposed UK university. This link must be greater than simply a collaboration between individuals – see section on 'Tenure and placement' for further details. Both supervisors must provide a supporting statement which provides further details of the link to ensure your application is eligible. 5. Be available to start your academic studies in the UK in September 2024 6. By September 2024, hold a first degree of at least upper second class (2:1) honours standard, or a lower second class degree and a relevant postgraduate qualification (usually a Master's degree) 7. Be unable to afford to study in the UK without this Scholarship
Level of Study: Postgraduate, Research
Type: Scholarship
Value: See website
Application Procedure: Applications must be made using the CSC's online application system: fs29.formsite.com/m3nCYq/rrdstgrnjg/index.html. for more information: cscuk.fcdo.gov.uk/scholarships/commonwealth-split-site-scholarships-for-low-and-middle-income-countries/
Closing Date: 2 March
Additional Information: Website: www.kent.ac.uk/scholarships/search/FNADCSCSSS01

Computing, Engineering and Mathematical Sciences Graduate Teaching Assistant PhD Studentship

Eligibility: Successful candidates will demonstrate academic excellence, outstanding research potential and ability to teach. Applicants should have, or expect to obtain, a first or upper second-class honours degree in a relevant subject, and ideally a Master's degree or equivalent. The studentships are open to Home and Overseas (including EU) students. The University of Kent requires all non-native speakers of English to hold a minimum standard of proficiency in written and spoken English before beginning a postgraduate degree.
Level of Study: Postgraduate, Research
Type: Studentship
Value: Tuition fees plus a combined maintenance grant and salary equivalent to the Research Councils UK National Minimum Doctoral Stipend
Application Procedure: When applying, students should follow the University of Kent's online application process. As part of the process, students should include the following: 1. explain reasons for study/outline research proposal 2. provide details/evidence of qualifications 3. provide details of any teaching experience 4. provide two academic references 5. provide other personal information and supporting documentation.
Closing Date: 5 March
Additional Information: Website: www.kent.ac.uk/scholarships/search/FN00CEMSGT01

Engineering and Physical Sciences Research Council EPSRC

Purpose: If you are applying as an international candidate, Kent will waive the difference between Home and International fees.
Eligibility: Successful candidates will demonstrate academic excellence and outstanding research potential. Applicants should have, or expect to obtain, a first or upper second-class honours degree in a relevant subject, and ideally a Master's degree or equivalent. The studentships are open to Home and Overseas (including EU) students. The number of international studentships awarded per cohort is capped by UKRI at 30%. To be classed as a Home student, candidates must meet the RCUK residency criteria. For details see website
Level of Study: Postgraduate
Type: Scholarship
Value: Tuition fees at the home rate and access to further research support funding
Length of Study: 3.5 years
Application Procedure: When applying, students should follow the University of Kent's online application process. As part of the process, students should include the following: 1. explain reasons for study/outline research proposal 2. provide details/evidence of qualifications 3. provide two academic references 4. provide other personal information and supporting documentation.
Closing Date: 5 March
Additional Information: Website: www.kent.ac.uk/scholarships/search/FNADEPSRCS02

EPSRC - School of Computing

Eligibility: Successful candidates will demonstrate academic excellence and outstanding research potential. Applicants should have, or expect to obtain, a first or upper second-class honours degree in a relevant subject, and ideally a Master's degree or equivalent. The studentships are open to Home and Overseas (including EU) students. The number of international studentships awarded per cohort is capped by UKRI at 30%. To be classed as a Home student, candidates must meet the RCUK residency criteria
Level of Study: Postgraduate
Type: Scholarship
Value: Tuition fees at the home rate and access to further research support funding
Length of Study: 3.5 years
Application Procedure: Please apply for a Computer Science PhD: evision.kent.ac.uk/urd/sits.urd/run/siw_ipp_lgn.login?process=siw_ipp_app&code1=RCSC000101PHFD&code2=0082 and include the following: 1. explain reasons for study/outline research proposal 2. provide details/evidence of qualifications 3. provide two academic references 4. provide other personal information and supporting documentatio
Closing Date: 5 March
Additional Information: Website: www.kent.ac.uk/scholarships/search/FN15EPSRCC01

EPSRC - School of Engineering

Purpose: The University of Kent is committed to equality, diversity, widening participation and inclusion and we endeavour to recruit students from all walks of life. We encourage enquiries and applications from all sections of the community regardless of gender, ethnicity, disability, age, sexual orientation and transgender status.
Eligibility: Successful candidates will demonstrate academic excellence and outstanding research potential. Applicants should have, or expect to obtain, a first or upper second-class honours degree in a relevant subject, and ideally a Master's degree or equivalent. The studentships are open to Home and Overseas (including EU) students. The number of international studentships awarded per cohort is capped by UKRI at 30%. For more criteria see website.
Level of Study: Postgraduate, Research
Type: Scholarship
Value: Tuition fees at the home rate and access to further research support funding.
Length of Study: 3.5 years
Application Procedure: Please apply for a PhD for one of the following programmes Electronic Engineering, Biomedical Engineering or Mechanical Engineering and include the following: 1. explain reasons for study/outline research proposal 2. provide details/evidence of qualifications 3. provide two academic references 4. provide other personal information and supporting documentation.
Closing Date: 5 March
Additional Information: Enquiries should be directed to cemsadmissions@kent.ac.uk. Website: www.kent.ac.uk/scholarships/search/FN16EPSCRE01

For further information contact:

Email: cemsadmissions@kent.ac.uk.

EPSRC - School of Mathematics, Statistics and Actuarial Science

Subjects: The University of Kent is committed to equality, diversity, widening participation and inclusion and we endeavour to recruit students from all walks of life. We encourage enquiries and applications from all sections of the community regardless of gender, ethnicity, disability, age, sexual orientation and transgender status.
Eligibility: Successful candidates will demonstrate academic excellence and outstanding research potential. Applicants should have, or expect to obtain, a first or upper second-class honours degree in a relevant subject, and ideally a Master's degree or equivalent. The studentships are open to Home and Overseas (including EU) students. The number of international studentships awarded per cohort is capped by UKRI at 30%. To be classed as a Home student, candidates must meet the RCUK residency criteria
Level of Study: Masters Degree, Postgraduate
Type: Scholarship
Value: Tuition fees at the home rate and access to further research support funding
Length of Study: 3.5 years
Application Procedure: Please apply for a PhD for one of the following programmes Actuarial Science, Mathematics or Statistics and include the following: 1. select a suitable supervisor by contacting SMSAS staff with a matching research interest, see here: www.kent.ac.uk/mathematics-statistics-actuarial-science/people 2. explain reasons for study/outline research proposal 3. provide details/evidence of qualifications 4. provide two academic references 5. provide other personal information and supporting documentation.
Closing Date: 5 March
Additional Information: Enquiries should be directed to cemsadmissions@kent.ac.uk. Website: www.kent.ac.uk/scholarships/search/FN17EPSRC001

For further information contact:

Email: cemsadmissions@kent.ac.uk

ERC-funded Studentships in Psychology: Consequences of Conspiracy Theories

Eligibility: The competition is open to applicants of all student fee paying statuses. Both of the studentships guarantee coverage of fees at the Home or International rate. Please note that current Kent PhD students are not eligible to apply.
Level of Study: Postgraduate, Research
Type: Scholarship
Value: see website
Application Procedure: Completed applications must comprise all of the following: 1. Submission of a KentVision application for a Psychology PhD place in the School of Psychology at the University of Kent including: a. A transcript of degree undergraduate and postgraduate marks to date and certificate, if available, in pdf format. b. The names and email addresses of two academic referees. References must also be received by 17.00 (UK time) on 28 February 2024. Please leave a suitable amount of time for your referees to respond to the reference request which is sent automatically upon submission of the PhD application in KentVision. c. A current CV in pdf format. 2. Submission of a 1-2 page covering letter which explains why you should be considered for one of the ERC-funded Psychology PhD studentships. This should be sent directly to hssadmissions@kent.ac.uk and should include the KentVision application ID number. If you have any specific questions about the studentships, please write to Professor Karen Douglas at k.douglas@kent.ac.uk.
Closing Date: 28 February
Additional Information: If you have any specific questions about the studentships, please write to Professor Karen Douglas at k.douglas@kent.ac.uk. Website: www.kent.ac.uk/scholarships/search/FN39PSYCON01

For further information contact:

Email: k.douglas@kent.ac.uk.

Fully Funded EPSRC Scholarships in Chemistry

Eligibility: Successful candidates will demonstrate academic excellence and outstanding research potential. Applicants should have, or expect to obtain, a first or upper second-class honours degree in a relevant subject, and ideally a Master's degree or equivalent. The studentships are open to Home and Overseas (including EU) students. The number of international studentships awarded per cohort is capped by UKRI at 30%. To be classed as a Home student, candidates must meet the RCUK residency criteria.
Level of Study: Postgraduate, Research
Type: Scholarship
Value: Tuition fees at the home rate and access to further research support funding
Length of Study: 3.5 years
Application Procedure: When applying students should follow the University of Kent's online application process: www.kent.ac.uk/courses/postgraduate/apply?utm_source=FindAPhD&utm_medium=paid_referrer&utm_content=programme-page-EPSRC&utm_campaign=PGUK2022. As part of the process, students should include the following: 1. Explain reasons for study/outline research proposal (please speak with the academic leading the project you wish to apply for) 2. Provide details/evidence of qualifications 3. Provide two academic references 4. Provide other personal information and supporting documentation.
Closing Date: 5 March
Additional Information: For further information or help with your PhD application, please contact studypgnats@kent.ac.uk Website: www.kent.ac.uk/scholarships/search/FNADFFESIC01

For further information contact:

Email: studypgnats@kent.ac.uk

Fully Funded EPSRC Scholarships in Physics

Eligibility: Successful candidates will demonstrate academic excellence and outstanding research potential. Applicants should have, or expect to obtain, a first or upper second-class honours degree in a relevant subject, and ideally a Master's degree or equivalent. The studentships are open to Home and Overseas (including EU) students. The number of international studentships awarded per cohort is capped by UKRI at 30%. To be classed as a Home student, candidates must meet the RCUK residency criteria.
Level of Study: Postgraduate, Research
Type: Scholarship
Value: Tuition fees at the home rate and access to further research support funding
Length of Study: 3.5 years
Application Procedure: When applying students should follow the University of Kent's online application process. As part of the process, students should include the following: 1. Explain reasons for study/outline research proposal (please speak with the academic leading the project you wish to apply for) 2. Provide details/evidence of qualifications 3. Provide two academic references 4. Provide other personal information and supporting documentation.
Closing Date: 5 March
Additional Information: For further information or help with your PhD application, please contact studypgnats@kent.ac.uk Website: www.kent.ac.uk/scholarships/search/FNADFFSIPH01

For further information contact:

Email: studypgnats@kent.ac.uk

Kent Lille Cotutelle: LATP Glass-ceramic Electrolytes to Advance Battery Technology for a Low Carbon Future

Eligibility: 1. Open to home and international fee paying students. Home fees only are provided, the shortfall in international fees would need to be self-funded. 2. Scholarships are available on a cotutelle (dual award) basis only. 3. Students have to spend at least 12 months at Kent and Lille.
Level of Study: Postgraduate, Research
Type: Scholarship
Value: Tuition fees and stipend at the standard Research Council rate
Application Procedure: To apply please go to www.kent.ac.uk/courses/postgraduate/4957/chemistry (PhD in Chemistry) or www.kent.ac.uk/courses/postgraduate/4958/physics (PhD in Physics). You will need to apply through the online application form on the main University website. Please note that you will be expected to provide personal details, education and employment history and supporting documentation (Curriculum Vitae, transcript of results, two academic references). Applications should state that you would like to be considered for this Kent-Lille studentship project.
Closing Date: 24 March
Additional Information: Students are welcome to make informal enquiries about the project by contacting Dr Gavin Mountjoy (g.mountjoy@kent.ac.uk) or any of the other project supervisors. website: www.kent.ac.uk/scholarships/search/FNADLATPGE01

For further information contact:

Email: g.mountjoy@kent.ac.uk

Kent Research Institute PhD Scholarships for Institute of Cyber Security for Society (iCSS)

Eligibility: Applicants to a PhD programme should normally hold a good Honours degree (First or 2:1) or a Master's Degree (at Merit or Distinction) in a relevant discipline, or the equivalent from an internationally recognised institution. In addition, programmes of study at individual schools have specific entry requirements that need to be fulfilled (for these, please check under the 'entry requirements' tab on Kent's course finder page). The University of Kent requires all non-native speakers of English to reach a minimum standard of proficiency in written and spoken English before beginning a postgraduate degree. For more information on English language requirements, please visit this page.
Level of Study: Postgraduate, Research
Type: Scholarship
Value: Annual stipend at UKRI rates, Annual tuition fees at Home rates
Application Procedure: Applicants should follow the University of Kent's online application process. As part of the process, you should include the following: 1. your reasons for study; 2. your research proposal; 3. how your research fits with iCSS's research themes and cross-cutting topics; 4. details of your qualifications (including at least all university transcripts and degree certificates); 5. two academic references; and 6. other relevant information and supporting documentation.
Closing Date: 10 April
Additional Information: Website: www.kent.ac.uk/scholarships/search/FNADICSS0001

Kent-Lille Cotutelle: Advancing Communication between Children and Paediatricians: a Cross-linguistic Contribution

Eligibility: 1. Open to home and international fee-paying students. Home fees only are provided, the shortfall in international fees would need to be self-funded. 2. Scholarships are available on a cotutelle (dual award) basis only. 3. Students have to spend at least 12 months at Kent and Lille. for more criteria see website
Level of Study: Postgraduate, Research
Type: Scholarship
Value: Tuition fees and stipend at the standard Research Council rate
Application Procedure: To apply please go to www.kent.ac.uk/courses/postgraduate/12/linguistics (PhD in Linguistics). You will need to apply through the online application form on the main University website. Please note that you will be expected to provide personal details, education and employment history and supporting documentation (Curriculum Vitae, transcript of results, two academic references). Applications should state that you would like to be considered for this Kent-Lille studentship project.
Closing Date: 24 March
Additional Information: Website: www.kent.ac.uk/scholarships/search/FNADADVCOM01

For further information contact:

Website: www.kent.ac.uk/courses/postgraduate/12/linguistics

Kent-Lille Cotutelle: Novel Neuromorphic, Radically Energy Efficient Training Algorithms for Action Recognition

Eligibility: 1. Open to home and international fee paying students. Home fees only are provided, the shortfall in international fees would need to be self-funded. 2. Scholarships are available on a cotutelle (dual award) basis only. 3. Students have to spend at least 12 months at Kent and Lille.
Level of Study: Postgraduate, Research
Type: Scholarship
Value: Tuition fees and stipend at the standard Research Council rate
Application Procedure: To apply please visit: www.kent.ac.uk/courses/postgraduate/283/computer-science (Computer Science PhD programme). You will need to apply through the online application form on the main University website. Please note that you will be expected to provide personal details, education and employment history and supporting documentation (Curriculum Vitae, transcript of results, a writing sample e.g. project report, Bachelor/Master thesis, two academic references). Applications should state that you would like to be considered for this Kent-Lille studentship project.
Closing Date: 24 March
Additional Information: For question about this project, please contact Prof. Tirilly (pierre.tirilly@univ-lille.fr) or Dominique Chu (d.f.chu@kent.ac.uk). website: www.kent.ac.uk/scholarships/search/FNADNOVELN01

For further information contact:

Email: pierre.tirilly@univ-lille.fr; d.f.chu@kent.ac.uk

Leverhulme-funded Studentship in Psychology

Eligibility: The competition is open to applicants of all student fee paying statuses; however, this studentship guarantees coverage of fees at the Home rate only. This means that EU and International students may be required to make up the difference in fees.
Level of Study: Postgraduate, Research
Type: Studentship
Value: tuition fees at the Home rate, additionally provides you with a stipend for maintenance
Length of Study: 3 Year
Application Procedure: Completed applications must comprise all of the following: 1. Submission of a KentVision application for a Psychology PhD place in the School of Psychology at the University of Kent including: a. A transcript of degree undergraduate and postgraduate marks to date and certificate, if available, in pdf format. b. The names and email addresses of two academic referees. References must also be received by 10 March 2024. Please leave a suitable amount of time for your referees to respond to the reference request which is sent automatically upon submission of the PhD application in KentVision. c. A current CV in pdf format. 2. Submission of a 1-2 page covering letter which explains why you should be considered for the Leverhulme Trust-funded Psychology PhD Studentship. In this letter, please include your research interests and how you think the data being generated by this project could be useful in pursuing them. This should be sent directly to hssadmissions@kent.ac.uk and should include the KentVision application ID number. If you have any specific questions about the scholarship, please write to Professor Heather Ferguson.
Closing Date: 10 March
Additional Information: Please direct questions about the online application process to lssjadmissions@kent.ac.uk & Questions about the studentship can be directed to lssjpgrfunding@kent.ac.uk Website: www.kent.ac.uk/scholarships/search/FN39PSYLEV01

For further information contact:

Email: lssjadmissions@kent.ac.uk; lssjpgrfunding@kent.ac.uk

Lisa Pan Marketing and Technology Scholarship

Purpose: The Lisa Pan Marketing and Technology Scholarship is an exciting new scholarship for students applying to our MSc Marketing programme and is open to all UK and International applicants.
Eligibility: To be eligible, candidates must: 1. Hold an offer to study MSc Marketing at Kent Business School for 2024 entry 2. Hold a UK first class degree (or International equivalence) ideally in a Science or Technology subject 3. Be self-funded 4. Submit a supporting statement which should discuss how the candidate could develop their interest in technology and marketing through being awarded the scholarship. These interests may include areas such as the blockchain, artificial intelligence and machine learning, social media, online gaming, cloud technologies, privacy issues, the Internet of Things, virtual reality, technology entrepreneurship, and autonomous vehicles. This list is not exhaustive but aimed as a guide. 5. Demonstrate their passion for Marketing and Technology
Level of Study: Postgraduate, Research
Type: Scholarship
Value: £11,100
Application Procedure: To apply, please use the linked application form: www.kent.ac.uk/scholarships/lisa-pan-scholarship-form.
Closing Date: 31 May
Additional Information: Website: www.kent.ac.uk/scholarships/search/FN35LSAPAN01

Martin Cook Scholarship for Humanities Students

Purpose: A generous donation has been received by the University of Kent in memory of Martin Cook. The purpose of the gift is to help support one full-time undergraduate student in the humanities.
Eligibility: 1. Open to all full-time applicants who are UK residents paying Home tuition fees. 2. Applicants must have accepted a place on a humanities undergraduate course at the University of Kent starting in September 2024 by the UCAS deadline of 30 June 2024. 3. Applicants must obtain a minimum of 136 UCAS points from A Levels or equivalent, and must fulfil the normal entry requirements for their course. 4. Applicants must demonstrate financial need and satisfy a range of socio-economic criteria 5. Applicants must be willing to act as an 'ambassador' for the University, their subject and faculty and attend University events when requested, if not in conflict with either course attendance or classes being in session. 6. Current students at the University of Kent are not eligible to apply.
Type: Scholarship
Value: £2,000
Length of Study: 3 - 4 years
Frequency: Annual
Country of Study: Any country
Application Procedure: See website
Closing Date: 30 June
Additional Information: For further information please email scholarships@kent.ac.uk. Website: www.kent.ac.uk/scholarships/search/FNADMARCOO01

For further information contact:

Giles Ln, Canterbury CT2 7NZ, United Kingdom.

Tel: (44) 1227 764000
Email: scholarships@kent.ac.uk.

Music Performance Scholarship

Eligibility: Music Scholarships/Awards are intended to recognise and encourage excellence. Applicants would usually be expected to demonstrate some or all of the following criteria when submitting their written application: 1. An advanced ABRSM grade (or equivalent, including RockSchool, Trinity or other international musical qualifications) 2. A significant musical profile whilst in school / college / university or the local community 3. Appropriate performing experience at county or national level / conservatoire, e.g. youth choir, county orchestra, wind band, jazz or big band 4. Experience in giving public performances, e.g. gigs or solo recitals, major role in musical theatre productions
Level of Study: Postgraduate, Research
Type: Scholarship
Value: The Music Performance Scholarships, worth £1,000, are awarded each year to talented instrumentalists and singers studying for any degree at the University of Kent, together with £500 worth of instrumental/singing tuition with experienced teachers.
Frequency: Annual
Application Procedure: For detailed information and application forms, please visit the Music at Kent web page: www.kent.ac.uk/music/scholarships.html
Additional Information: If you would like to discuss the Music Scholarship/Award Schemes prior to your application, contact Daniel Harding, Head of Music Performance, Tel: 01227 823625 Website: www.kent.ac.uk/scholarships/search/FNADMUSICS01

For further information contact:

Tel: (44) 1227 823625
Website: www.kent.ac.uk/music/scholarships.html

PhD in Conservation: Hunting, Consumption, and Trade of Animals in the Tropics

Purpose: This project is funded by the University of Kent. Applications are welcome from UK and International students.
Eligibility: We are looking for an enthusiastic self-motivated candidate with a strong interest in wildlife use as well as the below criteria. 1. A first degree and a Master's (at least Merit) or substantial professional experience in a relevant field is required. 2. French language skills would be beneficial. 3. Experience with field work in the tropics would be beneficial. 4. Experience analysing complex data using R would be beneficial and will be keen to develop their analytical skills.
Level of Study: Postgraduate, Research
Type: Scholarship
Value: Costs of UK home fees and stipend for three years
Length of Study: 3 years
Application Procedure: Candidates should apply using the online application form: forms.office.com/r/uDPeNeJLye, shortlisted candidates will be prompted to make a formal application via KentVision.
Closing Date: 2 January
Additional Information: For informal enquiries please contact Dr Daniel Ingram at d.j.ingram@kent.ac.uk. Website: www.kent.ac.uk/scholarships/search/FN45CONSER01

For further information contact:

Email: d.j.ingram@kent.ac.uk.

Postgrad Solutions Study Bursaries

Purpose: Kent University- Kent offers well-structured and ambitious. It provides a comprehensive package of skills development training programs, careers advice, and volunteering and paid work opportunities to enhance your career prospects in a global workplace.
Eligibility: Must have been accepted an offer of a place at your chosen institution for postgraduate study
Level of Study: Postgraduate
Type: Bursary
Value: £500
Frequency: Annual
Country of Study: Any country
Application Procedure: See full details at: www.postgrad.com/fees_and_funding/postgrad_solutions_study_bursaries/information/ See full details at: www.postgrad.com/fees_and_funding/postgrad_solutions_study_bursaries/information/
Funding: International office
Additional Information: website: www.kent.ac.uk/scholarships/search/FNADPGSOLU02

For further information contact:

The University of Kent, Canterbury, Kent CT2 7NZ, United Kingdom.

Tel: (44) 1227 764000

Resilient Reinforcement Learning for Cyber Security

Eligibility: We are looking for an enthusiastic self-motivated candidate who can demonstrate academic excellence, outstanding research potential and ability to teach. Good programming skills will be essential for this position. Applicants with a wide range of STEM expertise are encouraged to apply, e.g., computer science, engineering, applied mathematics, statistics, physics or similar. Knowledge of any of the following would be a plus: reinforcement learning, deep learning, machine learning, computational statistics, probabilistic graphical models, or artificial intelligence for cyber security applications. Applicants should have, or expect to obtain, a first or upper second-class honours degree in a relevant subject, and ideally a Master's degree or equivalent. The University of Kent requires all non-native speakers of English to hold a minimum standard of proficiency in written and spoken English before beginning a postgraduate degree. For more information on English language requirements, please visit www.kent.ac.uk/courses/postgraduate/apply/english-language-requirements.
Level of Study: Postgraduate, Research
Type: Scholarship
Value: home tuition fees plus a combined maintenance grant and salary equivalent to the Research Councils UK National Minimum Doctoral Stipend for the first three years followed by home fees and maintenance grant for a further six months.
Application Procedure: Please apply for a Computer Science PhD. As part of the process, students should include the following: 1. explain reasons for study/outline research proposal 2. provide details/evidence of qualifications 3. provide details of any teaching experience 4. provide two academic references 5. provide other personal information and supporting documentation.
Closing Date: 10 April
Additional Information: Website: www.kent.ac.uk/scholarships/search/FN15RESILI01

School of Anthropology and Conservation Research Scholarship

Purpose: The School of Anthropology and Conservation (SAC) at Kent offers a supportive, dynamic and diverse environment for creative research and learning. Our lecturers and research students are engaged in exciting projects in the UK and around the world.
Eligibility: Please see the full advert for eligibility criteria: www.kent.ac.uk/anthropology-conservation/news/8463/school-of-anthropology-and-conservation-research-scholarships-2023.
Level of Study: Postgraduate, Research
Type: Scholarship
Value: The GTAs will cover tuition fees at the UK rate plus a combined maintenance grant and salary, equivalent to the Research Councils UK National Minimum Doctoral Stipend.
Application Procedure: Please see the full advert for how to apply: www.kent.ac.uk/anthropology-conservation/news/8463/school-of-anthropology-and-conservation-research-scholarships-2023.
Closing Date: 10 March
Additional Information: Website: www.kent.ac.uk/scholarships/search/FN45SACPHD01

Signature Research Theme Scholarship: Future Human - E-scooters in the Life of the Future Human

Eligibility: We are seeking a motivated, independent, and collaborative individual, who also has the personal skills

that are conducive to working across disciplines, with the capability to translate basic research into applied practice. The successful candidate will need to recruit and work with human participants, collaborate and communicate with key stakeholders (e.g., the public, policy makers, businesses), alongside disseminating study findings to a range of audiences (e.g., academic, public, policy makers). The ability to effectively communicate in both verbal and written form is therefore a key requirement of this studentship. See Website for more details
Level of Study: Postgraduate, Research
Type: Scholarship
Value: Annual stipend at UKRI rates, Annual tuition fees at home rates
Application Procedure: Applicants should follow the University of Kent's online application process. As part of the process, you must: 1. Include details of your qualifications; 2. Include two academic references; 3. Complete an Expression of Interest form: forms.gle/LYbdQCcUN5mUTULC8.
Closing Date: 3 March
Additional Information: Website: www.kent.ac.uk/scholarships/search/FNADESCOOT01

South East ESRC DTC Funding

Purpose: To support research studies
Level of Study: Postgraduate, Research
Type: Studentship
Value: The funding will typically cover yearly maintenance (£13,863 for last year) and fees for one of the following +3 programme or 1+3
Length of Study: 3 years
Frequency: Annual
Study Establishment: The University of Kent
Country of Study: United Kingdom
Application Procedure: Applicants must complete an application form
No. of awards offered: 30–40
Closing Date: 2 February
Funding: Private
Contributor: South-East ESRC DTC
No. of awards given last year: 2
No. of applicants last year: 30–40
Additional Information: Studentships will be awarded on the basis of the academic excellence of both the candidate and the research proposal www.kent.ac.uk/scholarships/search/FNADINTAMA02

For further information contact:

Tel: (44) 1227 823085
Email: rsg@kent.ac.uk

Spatio-temporal Models for Large Citizen Science Data Sets

Eligibility: We seek a candidate with a strong quantitative background, for example an MSc in Statistics or an MSc with high statistics content, or a background in ecological modelling. Experience coding in R, or similar, is essential. An interest in conservation and ecology is advantageous. Quantitative ecologists are encouraged to apply. The University of Kent requires all non-native speakers of English to reach a minimum standard of proficiency in written and spoken English before beginning a postgraduate degree. For more information on English language requirements, please visit this page.
Level of Study: Postgraduate, Research
Type: Scholarship
Value: Annual stipend at UKRI rates, Annual tuition fees at Home rates
Application Procedure: Applicants should follow the University of Kent's online application process: evision.kent.ac.uk/urd/sits.urd/run/siw_ipp_lgn.login?process=siw_ipp_app&code1=RSTA000101PH-FD&code2=0085.
Closing Date: 17 April
Additional Information: Website: www.kent.ac.uk/scholarships/search/FN17SPATIO01

Sports Scholarships (Kent Sports Website)

Purpose: The University of Kent is committed to delivering sporting excellence and is proud to offer scholarships to students with outstanding sporting ability at both Canterbury and Medway campuses.
Eligibility: 1. Scholarships are available to elite sportsmen and women from any sport who compete (at least) at county level or equivalent. 2. Sports Scholars should be committed to representing the University of Kent in British University & College Sport (BUCS) competition and join their relevant student club. 3. Sports Scholarships are open to new undergraduate and postgraduate applicants, as well as current University of Kent students. 4. The Kent & Medway Medical School offer exclusive Sports Scholarships to their students and have a different application route on their webpage. (See note below)
Level of Study: Postgraduate, Research
Type: Scholarship
Value: £300 - £5,000
Application Procedure: Download an application form at: www.kent.ac.uk/sports/scholarships/
Closing Date: 30 April
Additional Information: Website: www.kent.ac.uk/scholarships/search/FNADSPORT001

SRT Scholarship: Future Human – Enhancing Exercise Outcomes Using Immersive Virtual Reality and Machine Learning

Purpose: The aim of this PhD programme is to optimise the use of immersive technologies (e.g., virtual reality) in supporting exercise interventions in healthy and clinical populations.
Eligibility: The call is open to candidates interested in pursuing a PhD programme at the University of Kent on a project linked to the Signature Research Theme 'Future Human'. The full title of this project is: Enhancing exercise outcomes using immersive virtual reality and machine learning interventions. It is Led by Dr Lucy Hale in the School of Sport and Exercise Sciences in collaboration with Professor Markus Bindemann in the School of Psychology and Dr Giovanni Masala & Dr Dominique Chu in the School of Computing. We particularly welcome applications from but not limited to Sport and Exercise Science (or related subjects) graduates. Knowledge or an interest in advanced data analysis, immersive technologies, and computer or data science would be advantageous.
Level of Study: Postgraduate, Research
Type: Scholarship
Value: Annual Stipend at UKRI rates, Annual tuition fees at home rates
Application Procedure: Applicants should follow the University of Kent's online application process: www.kent.ac.uk/courses/postgraduate. As part of the process, you must: 1. Include details of your qualifications; 2. Attach a separate curriculum vitae (maximum 2 pages) detailing any relevant education, training and experience to your application; 3. Include two academic references; 4. Complete an Expression of Interest form: docs.google.com/forms/d/e/1FAIpQLSfHT0fjqAsQjTVxJezWXv6y0aH4AXDYDGq2QVUtgQ2cK1ZlnQ/viewform.
Closing Date: 3 March
Additional Information: For more information about Future Human, please visit: research.kent.ac.uk/signature-research-themes/future-human/ Website: www.kent.ac.uk/scholarships/search/FNADAUGPFP01

For further information contact:

Website: www.kent.ac.uk/courses/postgraduate

The Bestway Foundation Scholarship

Purpose: This scholarship is administered and awarded exclusively by the University of Kent.
Eligibility: 1. Open to students from, and domiciled in, Pakistan 2. Applicants will be shortlisted based on their academic performance 3. Shortlisted applicants will also be considered on the basis of financial need. 4. Applicants must have received a conditional or unconditional offer for a full-time*, one year programme in one of the following disciplines by the deadline in order to be considered for the award: a. Biosciences b. Chemistry and Forensic Science c. Computing d. Mathematics, Statistics and Actuarial Science e. Physics and Astronomy 5. Candidates must be available for video interview, via Zoom, to be held on the week commencing 5th June 2024, exact date to be confirmed.
Level of Study: Postgraduate, Research
Type: Scholarship
Value: £26,000
Application Procedure: In order to apply for this scholarship you must have made an application for a programme of study at: www.kent.ac.uk/courses/postgraduate/how-to-apply/index.html.
Closing Date: 14 May
Additional Information: Please direct any queries regarding this award to scholarships@kent.ac.uk. Website: www.kent.ac.uk/scholarships/search/FNADBESTWA02

For further information contact:

Email: scholarships@kent.ac.uk
Website: www.kent.ac.uk/courses/postgraduate/how-to-apply/index.html

The Christine and Ian Bolt MA Scholarships in American Literature and Culture

Eligibility: Applicants must be resident in the UK and have been awarded an undergraduate degree in English Literature, American Studies or a related subject with a classification of 2:1 or higher by 1 September 2024. Applications will be assessed and awarded on the basis of the following: 1. Record of academic achievement 2. Motivation for study 3. Writing Sample 4. References (shortlisted candidates only) 5. Interview (shortlisted candidates only)
Level of Study: Postgraduate, Research
Type: Scholarship
Value: Tuition Fee Waiver at the UK Home rate
Application Procedure: Please submit the following separate documents to scholarships@kent.ac.uk with the subject line 'The Christine and Ian Bolt MA Scholarships in American Literature and Culture application' before the deadline: 1. Covering letter explaining why you wish to study on the MA in American Literature and Culture 2. CV 3. Transcript of academic record to date 4. Writing sample: please submit one piece of written academic work of up to 3,000 words total
Closing Date: 8 May
Additional Information: Website: www.kent.ac.uk/scholarships/search/FNADBOLTMA01

For further information contact:

Email: scholarships@kent.ac.uk

The Wellcome Trust

Purpose: The Wellcome Trust offers funding to support the brightest minds in biomedical research and the medical humanities, with the aim of improving human and animal health. We offer a wide variety of funding schemes, including Investigator Awards, fellowships and Strategic Awards, and also support several major initiatives.
Eligibility: 1. You should have a minimum of an excellent upper-second-class honours degree (or equivalent) in a relevant subject 2. Applications will not be considered from those who have already received support for their postgraduate studies from another funding body
Level of Study: Postgraduate, Research
Type: Scholarship
Value: Funding varies
Application Procedure: For enquiries about Trust grant schemes, eligibility and how to apply, closing dates, committee dates, funding policies and processes: Telephone (44) 20 7611 8888 Email: grantenquiries@wellcome.org Website: www.wellcome.ac.uk
Additional Information: Website: www.kent.ac.uk/scholarships/search/FNADWELCOM02

For further information contact:

Tel: (44) 20 7611 8888
Email: grantenquiries@wellcome.org
Website: www.wellcome.ac.uk

The Widening Participation Ambition Scholarship for University of Kent Graduates

Purpose: The University has developed a range of scholarships to support our final year undergraduate students choosing to progress to postgraduate study.
Eligibility: 1. Eligible candidates must: a. Be progressing directly from undergraduate to postgraduate study at Kent, having completed the undergraduate programme. b. Have received the Kent Financial Support Package (KFSP) during undergraduate study. c. Have received an unconditional offer for a programme by the deadline 16 July 2024. If you have not received an unconditional offer (or a conditional offer where the only outstanding condition(s) is your fee deposit and/or your final results), the application will be rejected and the next eligible candidate will be selected. 2. Postgraduate Taught programmes only. Postgraduate Research Master's students are not eligible due to its lower fee. 3. MArch students who are direct entrants from an UG degree are eligible. Postgraduate Certificate or Diploma Students are not eligible. 4. Undergraduates applying to study at any of the University of Kent campuses (Brussels, Canterbury, Medway, Paris) are eligible to apply.
Level of Study: Postgraduate, Research
Type: Scholarship
Value: £5,000 for UK students (£2,500 per year for part time students)
Application Procedure: 1. Applications for the Widening Participation Ambition Scholarship should be made via your application portal, where you will be able to view any scholarships for which you may be eligible to apply. 2. You will need to have received a formal offer for your programme in order to submit a scholarship application. 3. In order to apply for this scholarship, you will need to submit the following documents: a. CV b. x1 supporting academic or professional statement. Your programme application's First Referee will be used for this criterion. c. 200 word statement on "Why I have chosen to continue my studies at the University of Kent". d. Please upload your statement in Word or pdf format. Other formats will be rejected. e. "You will be asked to confirm by way of a check-box that we may use the demographic information you supplied to us when you started at Kent to establish your eligibility for this award.
Closing Date: 16 July
Additional Information: If you have any queries, then please contact scholarships@kent.ac.uk. Website: www.kent.ac.uk/scholarships/search/FNADWPAMBS01

For further information contact:

Email: scholarships@kent.ac.uk

University of Kent Law School Studentship

Purpose: To support research
Eligibility: Applicants should normally have obtained, or be about to obtain an undergraduate degree of at least Upper Second Class Honours level (21 or equivalent from other countries), or a postgraduate degree
Level of Study: Doctorate, Postgraduate
Type: Scholarships
Value: Maintenance grant equivalent to that offered by ESRC (£13,863 in last year) and tuition fees paid at the Home/European Union rate (£3,900 in last year)
Length of Study: Up to 3 years
Frequency: Annual
Study Establishment: University of Kent
Country of Study: United Kingdom
Application Procedure: Applications to be filled electronically at www.kent.ac.uk/law/postgraduate/research/entryreq-research.html
Closing Date: 31 January

Funding: Commercial, Government
No. of awards given last year: 8
Additional Information: See website for further details: www.kent.ac.uk/law/postgraduate/research/KLS_research_funding.html

For further information contact:

The University of Kent, Canterbury, Kent CT2 7NZ, United Kingdom.

Tel: (44) 1227 764000
Email: m.drakopoulou@kent.ac.uk

University of KwaZulu-Natal

Westville Campus, Private Bag X 54001, Durban 4000, South Africa.

Email: enquiries@ukzn.ac.za
Website: www.ukzn.ac.za/

HEARD is a leading applied research centre with a global reputation for its research, education programmes, technical services, partnerships and networks, devoted to addressing the broad health challenges of Africa. HEARD was established in 1998 and is based at the University of KwaZulu-Natal, South Africa.

Health Economics and HIV/AIDS Research Division PhD Scholarships

Purpose: Under the supervision of Professor Nana Poku and with the generous support of Sida/NORAD, HEARD is offering up to four full-time PhD Research Scholarships in any of the following key areas of strategic focus Sexual and Reproductive Health; Health Systems Strengthening and Economics of Critical Enablers in HIV Programming
Eligibility: Applicants must: 1. Hold a Master's Degree (first or upper second class pass or its equivalent). 2. Have demonstrable research experience. 3. Undertake to register for a PhD dissertation (full time) at the University of KwaZulu–Natal (UKZN). 4. Make a commitment to remain on the African continent for at least TWO years after graduation
Value: The value of each scholarship is R540,000 paid over three years
Length of Study: Scholarships will be paid in tranches over 3 years. Tranche payments will be conditional on research progress
Country of Study: South Africa
Application Procedure: Applications must be submitted to Ms Cailin Hedderwick, PhD Programme Manager (hedderwick@ukzn.ac.za). For more details, visit HEARD Website: www.opportunitiesforafricans.com/wp-content/uploads/2019/10/2020-PhD-scholarship-advert.pdf
Closing Date: 30 January
Additional Information: www.afterschoolafrica.com/43874/university-of-kwazulu-natal-health-economics-and-hiv-aids-research-division-heard-phd-scholarships-2020-for-african-students/

For further information contact:

Email: Hedderwick@ukzn.ac.za

University of Leeds

Woodhouse Lane, West Yorkshire, Leeds LS2 9JT, United Kingdom.

Tel: (44) 113 2431751
Email: security@leeds.ac.uk
Website: www.leeds.ac.uk

The University, established in 1904, is one of the largest higher education institutions in the UK. We are renowned globally for the quality of our teaching and research

Alumni Bursary

Eligibility: To be eligible you must: 1. Have previously studied at the University of Leeds at an undergraduate or postgraduate level, and this includes incoming study abroad students. See the later section further down this page to find the small number of previous courses that are not eligible for the alumni bursary. 2. Be registering for an award leading to a postgraduate qualification (with the exception of the Postgraduate Certificate in Education (PGCE)), see the full list of awards eligible for the alumni bursary. 3. Be self-financing for at least part of the cost of your tuition fees. You are deemed to be self-funding if you have support from a friend or relative, or if you are receiving a postgraduate loan from the UK government. 4. Have commenced your studies from September 2016 onwards. The bursary cannot be awarded retrospectively.
Level of Study: Graduate
Type: Bursary
Value: 10% alumni tuition fee bursary

U

Application Procedure: If you think you are eligible you need to email the relevant School or admissions contact for the course you have applied for. If you are a Masters student you can search for these in Course Search: courses.leeds.ac.uk/. For PGR applicants please contact the relevant PGR Admissions team: www.leeds.ac.uk/research-applying/doc/graduate-school-contacts.
Additional Information: Website: https://www.leeds.ac.uk/research-funding-scholarships/doc/alumni-bursary

Beit Trust Postgraduate Scholarships

Purpose: To support Postgraduate Study or research at Masters' level (MSc/MA)
Eligibility: Open to persons under 30 years of age, or 35 years for medical doctors, who are university graduates domiciled in Zambia, Zimbabwe or Malawi. Applicants must be nationals of those countries, and have an Honours degree at undergraduate level
Level of Study: Postgraduate
Type: Scholarship
Value: Academic fees, living expenses, other allowances, economy return airfares and allowance toward laptops
Length of Study: A maximum of 2 years at a South African University or 1 year at a United Kingdom University
Frequency: Annual
Study Establishment: The University of Leeds
Country of Study: United Kingdom
Application Procedure: Please see the Beit Trust website on 1 April for the new Scholarship application process. Applicants from Zimbabwe and Malawi should contact the Harare office at africa@beittrust.org.uk
No. of awards offered: 720
Closing Date: 11 February
Funding: Private
No. of awards given last year: 19
No. of applicants last year: 720
Additional Information: Zambian applicants should contact the Beit Trust United Kingdom office at: scholarships@beittrust.org.uk beittrust.org.uk/beit-trust-scholarships

For further information contact:

Tel:	(44) 1483 772575
Email:	scholarships@beittrust.org.uk

Frank Stell Scholarship

Subjects: Biology, Agricultural Science or Social and Political Science.
Purpose: To provide postgraduate scholarships for UK research students of high calibre.
Eligibility: Candidates must be commencing PhD study for the first time and hold at least a UK upper second class honours degree or equivalent. Candidates should be resident, or have parents resident within the former administrative area of the County Council of the West Riding of Yorkshire.
Level of Study: Doctorate
Type: Scholarship
Value: Fees at the UK/EU rate plus a maintenance allowance
Length of Study: Up to 3 years, subject to satisfactory progress
Frequency: Dependent on funds available
Study Establishment: University of Leeds
Country of Study: United Kingdom
Application Procedure: An application form must be completed and returned to the Postgraduate Scholarships Office by the relevant date.
Closing Date: 1 June
Funding: Trusts
Additional Information: Website: www.postgraduatefunding.com/award-1820

For further information contact:

Leeds International Piano Competition, The University of Leeds, Leeds LS2 9JT, United Kingdom.

Tel:	(44) 113 244 6586
Fax:	(44) 113 234 6106
Email:	pianocompetition@leeds.ac.uk; info@leedspiano.com
Website:	www.leeds.ac.uk/

Henry Ellison Scholarship

Purpose: The Henry Ellison Scholarship was established in 1943. The fund was bequeathed by Mr Henry Ellison of Calverley, Leeds for the promotion of research in pure and applied chemistry and physics and is intended to enable promising graduates to gain training in scientific research in the School of Chemistry or School of Physics and Astronomy
Eligibility: 1. Applicants must not have already been awarded or be currently studying for a doctoral degree 2. The awards are available for new Postgraduate Researchers undertaking full-time or part-time research study leading to the degree of PhD. PGRs who are already registered for PhD research study are excluded from applying 3. Applicants must be graduates of the University of Leeds 4. Applicants must live within a reasonable distance of the University of Leeds whilst in receipt of this Scholarship.
Level of Study: Postgraduate
Type: Scholarship
Value: A maintenance grant of £14,000 for 3 years (full-time), or £8,400 for 5 years (part-time).

Length of Study: Full-time (3 years) or part-time (5 years)
Frequency: Dependent on funds available
Study Establishment: University of Leeds
Country of Study: United Kingdom
Application Procedure: Details provided on website www.scholaships.leeds.ac.uk
Closing Date: 1 June
Funding: Trusts
Contributor: 1

For further information contact:

Woodhouse, Leeds LS2 9JT, United Kingdom.

Tel: (44) 113 243 1751
Email: maps.pgr.admissions@leeds.ac.uk or pg_scholarships@ac.uk

John Henry Garner Scholarship

Purpose: To provide postgraduate scholarships for United Kingdom and European Union research students of high calibre
Eligibility: Candidates must be from the United Kingdom or an European Union country (or eligible to pay fees at the United Kingdom rate) and be commencing PhD study for the first time. Candidates must hold at least a United Kingdom Upper Second Class Honours degree or equivalent
Level of Study: Doctorate
Type: Scholarship
Value: A maintenance grant at a rate of £14,000 for 3 years (full-time), or £8,400 for 5 years (part-time).
Length of Study: Full-time (3 years) or part-time (5 years)
Frequency: Dependent on funds available
Study Establishment: University of Leeds
Country of Study: United Kingdom
Application Procedure: Details provided on website www.scholarships.leeds.ac.uk
Closing Date: 1 June

For further information contact:

Woodhouse, Leeds LS2 9JT, United Kingdom.

Tel: (44) 113 343 34077
Email: pg_scholarships@leeds.ac.uk

Marks and Spencer - Leeds University- FCO Chevening Scholarships

Purpose: To provide postgraduate scholarships to students of high academic calibre
Eligibility: Open to candidates from Hong Kong who have obtained, or are about to obtain, a first degree of a similar standard to a United Kingdom good Upper Second Class (Honours) Degree. An adequate standard of English language is required
Level of Study: Postgraduate
Type: Scholarship
Value: Full tuition fees, maintenance allowance, books, equipment and production of dissertation
Length of Study: 1 year
Frequency: Annual
Study Establishment: The University of Leeds
Country of Study: United Kingdom
Application Procedure: By application form and acceptance onto taught course. Both application forms are available from the University and British Council (Hong Kong)
Funding: Commercial, Government
No. of awards given last year: 1
Additional Information: The address for the British Council in Hong Kong is: The Education Exchange Unit, 255 Hennessey Road, Wanchai, Hong Kong business.leeds.ac.uk/dir-record/lubs-scholarships/1355/university-of-leeds-chevening-scholarships

For further information contact:

Email: scholarships@gcu.ac.uk

Royal Academy of Engineering MSc Motorsport Scholarship Programme

Purpose: These scholarships aim to help address the under-representation of Black or mixed Black ethnic engineers and accelerate the rate of progress of change.
Eligibility: Applicants to the programme must: 1. Be from a Black or Mixed Black ethnic background. 2. Be considered as a UK student and eligible for Home fee status and have the right to live and work in the UK 3. Be applying, or have applied, to one of the eligible Master's degree courses listed below, to start in the 2024/2025 academic year. a. Aerospace Engineering MSc b. Advanced Mechanical Engineering MSc c. Automotive Engineering MSc d. Advanced Computer Science (Artifical Intelligence) MSc e. Communications and Signal Processing MSc f. Materials Science and Engineering MSc Please visit the Royal Academy of Engineering website for full eligibility criteria.
Level of Study: Masters Degree
Type: Scholarship
Value: Up to £25,000
Application Procedure: Please visit the Royal Academy of Engineering website to apply: raeng.org.uk/programmes-

U

and-prizes/programmes/uk-grants-and-prizes/support-for-education/msc-motorsport/how-to-apply.
Closing Date: 6 March
Additional Information: Website: https://eps.leeds.ac.uk/dir-record/scholarships/4554/royal-academy-of-engineering-msc-motorsport-scholarship-programme

School of Chemical and Process Engineering - International Masters Excellence Scholarship

Purpose: Our International Masters Excellence Scholarships support international students to fulfil their academic potential and contribute to the social and cultural diversity of our student community
Eligibility: To be considered for the scholarship you must: 1. be classified as an International student for tuition fee purposes 2. have applied for 2024/2025 entry for a Masters programme included in the eligible courses section 3. be a self-funding student 4. demonstrate an excellent academic track record, and be predicted to achieve or have achieved a Bachelor degree with a 2:1 (hons), based on the criteria used by the School for offer purposes, or equivalent 5. show excellent professional and personal skills evidenced through work experience and/or extracurricular activities 6. demonstrate the potential to contribute to the social and cultural diversity of our Masters programmes and student community.
Level of Study: Masters Degree
Type: Scholarship
Value: 25% tuition fee reduction
Application Procedure: Apply now by completing the online form: forms.office.com/Pages/ResponsePage.aspx?id=qO3qvR3IzkWGPlIypTW3y3HSZrCtJm5FvrG2FYO6wo1URjRZODA2VDBKWlNMMVBEVkpaOEtOWDc1OC4u. Please note that you will require your University of Leeds Application ID to proceed.
Closing Date: 12 May
No. of applicants last year: 10
Additional Information: Website: eps.leeds.ac.uk/dir-record/scholarships/4398/school-of-chemical-and-process-engineering-international-masters-excellence-scholarship

School of Chemistry – International Masters Excellence Scholarship

Purpose: Our International Masters Excellence Scholarships support international students to fulfil their academic potential and contribute to the social and cultural diversity of our student community.
Eligibility: To be considered for the scholarship you must: 1. be classified as an International student for tuition fee purposes 2. have applied for 2024/2025 entry for a Masters programme included in the eligible courses section 3. be a self-funding student 4. demonstrate an excellent academic track record, and be predicted to achieve or have achieved a Bachelor degree with a 2:1 (hons), based on the criteria used by the School for offer purposes, or equivalent 5. show excellent professional and personal skills evidenced through work experience and/or extracurricular activities 6. demonstrate the potential to contribute to the social and cultural diversity of our Masters programmes and student community.
Level of Study: Masters Degree
Type: Scholarship
Value: 10% tuition fee reduction
Application Procedure: Apply now by completing the onlinc form: forms.officc.com/Pagcs/RcsponscPage.aspx?id=qO3qvR3IzkWGPlIypTW3y3HSZrCtJm5FvrG2FYO6wo1UMlVaWTFPUE4wVDRLRk5UV1NGSFBXS0Y5Si4u. Please note that you will require your University of Leeds Application ID to proceed.
Closing Date: 12 May
Additional Information: Website: eps.leeds.ac.uk/dir/scholarships

For further information contact:

Website: forms.office.com/Pages/ResponsePage.aspx?id=qO3qvR3IzkWGPlIypTW3y3HSZrCtJm5FvrG2FYO6wo1UMlVaWTFPUE4wVDRLRk5UV1NGSFBXS0Y5Si4u

School of Civil Engineering - International Masters Excellence Scholarship

Purpose: Our Masters International Excellence Scholarships support international students to fulfil their academic potential and contribute to the social and cultural diversity of our student community.
Eligibility: To be considered for the scholarship you must: 1. be classified as an International student for tuition fee purposes 2. have applied for 2024/2025 entry for a Masters programme included in the eligible courses section 3. be a self-funding student 4. demonstrate an excellent academic track record, and be predicted to achieve or have achieved a Bachelor degree with a 2:1 (hons), based on the criteria used by the School for offer purposes, or equivalent 5. show excellent professional and personal skills evidenced through work experience and/or extracurricular activities 6. demonstrate the potential to contribute to the social and cultural diversity of our Masters programmes and student community.
Level of Study: Masters Degree
Type: Scholarship
Value: 25% tuition fee reduction

Application Procedure: Apply now by completing the online form: forms.office.com/Pages/ResponsePage.aspx?id=qO3qvR3IzkWGPlIypTW3y2RGCzpiIoJGn8byoZ0PdxZURUdHVVNDVzNCSE5WWlA2WDg4VktLUTFSOS4u. Please note that you will require your University of Leeds Application ID to proceed.
Closing Date: 12 May
No. of applicants last year: 10
Additional Information: Website: eps.leeds.ac.uk/dir/scholarships

School of Computing – International Masters Excellence Scholarship

Purpose: Our International Masters Excellence Scholarships support international students to fulfil their academic potential and contribute to the social and cultural diversity of our student community.
Eligibility: To be considered for the scholarship you must: 1. be classified as an International student for tuition fee purposes 2. have applied for 2024/2025 entry for a Masters programme included in the eligible courses section 3. be a self-funding student 4. demonstrate an excellent academic track record, and be predicted to achieve or have achieved a Bachelor degree with a First (hons), based on the criteria used by the School for offer purposes, or equivalent 5. show excellent professional and personal skills evidenced through work experience and/or extracurricular activities 6. demonstrate the potential to contribute to the social and cultural diversity of our Masters programmes and student community.
Level of Study: Masters Degree
Type: Scholarship
Value: 25% tuition fee reduction
Application Procedure: Apply now by completing the online form: forms.office.com/Pages/ResponsePage.aspx?id=qO3qvR3IzkWGPlIypTW3y2RGCzpiIoJGn8byoZ0PdxZUQzBMTEdTWlVXNkZGUldaSjJZWVA4MTZUTC4u. Please note that you will require your University of Leeds Application ID to proceed.
Closing Date: 12 May
Additional Information: Website: eps.leeds.ac.uk/dir/scholarships

School of Electronic and Electrical Engineering - International Masters Excellence Scholarship

Purpose: Our Masters International Excellence Scholarships support international students to fulfil their academic potential and contribute to the social and cultural diversity of our student community.
Eligibility: To be considered for the scholarship you must: 1. be classified as an International student for tuition fee purposes 2. have applied for 2024/2025 entry for a Masters programme included in the eligible courses section 3. be a self-funding student 4. demonstrate an excellent academic track record, and be predicted to achieve or have achieved a Bachelor degree with a First (hons), based on the criteria used by the School for offer purposes, or equivalent 5. show excellent professional and personal skills evidenced through work experience and/or extracurricular activities 6. demonstrate the potential to contribute to the social and cultural diversity of our Masters programmes and student community.
Level of Study: Masters Degree
Type: Scholarship
Value: 50% tuition fee reduction
Application Procedure: Apply now by completing the online form: forms.office.com/Pages/ResponsePage.aspx?id=qO3qvR3IzkWGPlIypTW3y3HSZrCtJm5FvrG2FYO6wo1UQk5SNzlFSERHMEQ1WUgwTkRSU1RGMTZYUy4u. Please note that you will require your University of Leeds Application ID to proceed.
Closing Date: 12 May
No. of applicants last year: 8
Additional Information: Website: eps.leeds.ac.uk/dir-record/scholarships/4523/school-of-electronic-and-electrical-engineering-international-masters-excellence-scholarship

For further information contact:

Website: forms.office.com/Pages/ResponsePage.aspx?id=qO3qvR3IzkWGPlIypTW3y3HSZrCtJm5FvrG2FYO6wo1UQk5SNzlFSERHMEQ1WUgwTkRSU1RGMTZYUy4u

School of Mathematics – International Masters Excellence Scholarship

Purpose: Our International Masters Excellence Scholarships support international students to fulfil their academic potential and contribute to the social and cultural diversity of our student community.
Eligibility: To be considered for the scholarship you must: 1. be classified as an International student for tuition fee purposes 2. have applied for 2024/2025 entry for a Masters programme included in the eligible courses section 3. be a self-funding student 4. demonstrate an excellent academic track record, and be predicted to achieve or have achieved a Bachelor degree with a First (hons), based on the criteria used by the School for offer purposes, or equivalent 5. show excellent professional and personal skills evidenced through work experience and/or extracurricular activities 6. demonstrate the potential to contribute to the social and cultural diversity of our Masters programmes and student community.
Level of Study: Masters Degree

Type: Scholarship
Value: 25% tuition fee deduction
Application Procedure: Apply now by completing the online form: forms.office.com/Pages/ResponsePage.aspx?id=qO3qvR3IzkWGPlIypTW3y2RGCzpiIoJGn8byoZ0PdxZUQk9BMEVOTTFHTzkwTEtFTFpHOUI4QUlENC4u. Please note that you will require your University of Leeds Application ID to proceed.
Closing Date: 12 May
Additional Information: Website: eps.leeds.ac.uk/dir-record/scholarships/4528/school-of-mathematics-international-masters-excellence-scholarship

School of Mechanical Engineering - International Masters Excellence Scholarship

Purpose: Our Masters International Excellence Scholarships support international students to fulfil their academic potential and contribute to the social and cultural diversity of our student community.
Eligibility: To be considered for the scholarship you must: 1. be classified as an International student for tuition fee purposes 2. have applied for 2024/2025 entry for a Masters programme included in the eligible courses section 3. be a self-funding student 4. demonstrate an excellent academic track record, and be predicted to achieve or have achieved a Bachelor degree with a 2:1 (hons), based on the criteria used by the School for offer purposes, or equivalent 5. show excellent professional and personal skills evidenced through work experience and/or extracurricular activities 6. demonstrate the potential to contribute to the social and cultural diversity of our Masters programmes and student community.
Level of Study: Masters Degree
Type: Scholarship
Value: 25% tuition fee reduction
Application Procedure: Apply now by completing the online form: forms.office.com/Pages/ResponsePage.aspx?id=qO3qvR3IzkWGPlIypTW3y3HSZrCtJm5FvrG2FYO6wo1UQ0w1OEpFNzZOQkk2SFU2U1o3MVdMQzBTQi4u. Please note that you will require your University of Leeds Application ID to proceed.
Closing Date: 12 May
Additional Information: Website: eps.leeds.ac.uk/dir-record/scholarships/4527/school-of-mechanical-engineering-international-masters-excellence-scholarship

For further information contact:

Website: forms.office.com/Pages/ResponsePage.aspx?id=qO3qvR3IzkWGPlIypTW3y3HSZrCtJm5FvrG2FYO6wo1UQ0w1OEpFNzZOQkk2SFU2U1o3MVdMQzBTQi4u

School of Physics and Astronomy - International Masters Excellence Scholarship

Purpose: Our International Masters Excellence Scholarships support international students to fulfil their academic potential and contribute to the social and cultural diversity of our student community.
Eligibility: To be considered for the scholarship you must: 1. be classified as an International student for tuition fee purposes 2. have applied for 2024/2025 entry for a Masters programme included in the eligible courses section 3. be a self-funding student 4. demonstrate an excellent academic track record, and be predicted to achieve or have achieved a Bachelor degree with a 2:1 (hons), based on the criteria used by the School for offer purposes, or equivalent 5. show excellent professional and personal skills evidenced through work experience and/or extracurricular activities 6. demonstrate the potential to contribute to the social and cultural diversity of our Masters programmes and student community.
Level of Study: Masters Degree
Type: Scholarship
Value: 10% tuition fee deduction
Application Procedure: Apply now by completing the online form: forms.office.com/Pages/ResponsePage.aspx?id=qO3qvR3IzkWGPlIypTW3y8waQspxPtVBuG5cu-qFnqFUOEtGU1pQRFU5WFdZNk9KSkQ4UkZOWEUwVy4u. Please note that you will require your University of Leeds Application ID to proceed.
Closing Date: 12 May
No. of applicants last year: 5
Additional Information: Website: eps.leeds.ac.uk/dir/scholarships

For further information contact:

Website: forms.office.com/Pages/ResponsePage.aspx?id=qO3qvR3IzkWGPlIypTW3y8waQspxPtVBuG5cu-qFnqFUOEtGU1pQRFU5WFdZNk9KSkQ4UkZOWEUwVy4u

Stanley Burton Research Scholarship

Purpose: To provide postgraduate scholarships for UK/EU research students of high calibre.
Eligibility: Candidates must be from UK or an EU country and be commencing PhD study for the first time. Candidates must hold at least a UK upper second class honours degree or equivalent.
Level of Study: Doctorate
Type: Scholarship
Value: Fees at the UK/EU rate plus a maintenance allowance
Length of Study: Up to 3 years, subject to satisfactory progress

Frequency: Dependent on funds available
Study Establishment: University of Leeds
Country of Study: United Kingdom
Application Procedure: An application form must be completed and returned to the Postgraduate Scholarships Office by the relevant date.
No. of awards offered: 1
Closing Date: 1 June
Additional Information: Website: www.postgraduatefunding.com/award-3464

For further information contact:

Woodhouse, Leeds LS2 9JT, United Kingdom.

Tel: (44) 113 244 6586
Fax: (44) 113 234 6106
Email: pg-scholarships@leeds.ac.uk; pianocompetition@leeds.ac.uk; info@leedspiano.com
Website: www.leeds.ac.uk/

The Ray and Naomi Simpson Scholarship

Eligibility: To be considered for the scholarship you must: 1. be a UK or commonwealth country student 2. demonstrate strong academic achievement, relevant experience and a clear statement of interest. 3. be a self funding or partially self funding student 4. be holding an offer for an MSc within the School of Civil Engineering for 2024/25 entry
Level of Study: Postgraduate (MSc)
Type: Scholarship
Value: £3,000 towards tuition fees, plus £1,000 towards maintenance.
Application Procedure: Apply now by completing the online form: forms.office.com/Pages/ResponsePage.aspx?id=qO3qvR3IzkWGPlIypTW3yzd24Y40KVRFgnFQx83qXC9UMDlYODMwT1oxVVE2R0VXQk9MVEs5SzZSTy4u. Please note that you will require your University of Leeds Application ID to proceed.
Closing Date: 31 July
Additional Information: Website: eps.leeds.ac.uk/dir-record/scholarships/4566/the-ray-and-naomi-simpson-scholarship

University of Leeds International Fee Bursary (Vietnam) - Information Systems/Multimedia Systems

Purpose: To provide scholarships to students of high academic calibre who wish to study in the school of computing
Eligibility: Applicants must be nationals of Vietnam and must already have obtained a good Second Class (Honours) Degree. An adequate standard of English is also required
Level of Study: Postgraduate
Type: Scholarship
Value: Academic fees
Length of Study: 1 year
Frequency: Annual
Study Establishment: The University of Leeds
Country of Study: United Kingdom
Application Procedure: Applicants must make an application in letter form to the Taught Postgraduate Secretary in the School of Computing
Closing Date: 11 June
Funding: Private
No. of awards given last year: 1

For further information contact:

International office, University of Leeds, Leeds LS2 9JT, United Kingdom.

Email: info@lubs.leeds.ac.uk

Water, Sanitation and Health Engineering MSc - International Masters Excellence Scholarship

Purpose: Our Masters International Excellence Scholarships support international students to fulfil their academic potential and contribute to the social and cultural diversity of our student community.
Eligibility: To be considered for the scholarship you must: 1. be classified as an International student for tuition fee purposes 2. have applied for 2024/2025 entry for a Masters programme included in the eligible courses section 3. be a self-funding student 4. demonstrate an excellent academic track record, and be predicted to achieve or have achieved a Bachelor degree with a 2:1 (hons), based on the criteria used by the School for offer purposes, or equivalent 5. show excellent professional and personal skills evidenced through work experience and/or extracurricular activities 6. demonstrate the potential to contribute to the social and cultural diversity of our Masters programmes and student community.
Level of Study: Masters Degree
Type: Scholarship
Value: 50% tuition fee reduction
Application Procedure: Apply now by completing the online form: forms.office.com/Pages/ResponsePage.aspx?id=qO3qvR3IzkWGPlIypTW3y2RGCzpiIoJGn8byoZ0PdxZURUdHVVNDVzNCSE5WWlA2WDg4VktLUTFSOS4u. Please note that you will require your University of Leeds Application ID to proceed.
Closing Date: 12 May

U

No. of applicants last year: 2
Additional Information: Website: eps.leeds.ac.uk/dir/scholarships

For further information contact:

Website: forms.office.com/Pages/ResponsePage.aspx?id=qO3qvR3IzkWGPlIypTW3y2RGCzpiIoJGn8byoZ0PdxZURUdHVVNDVzNCSE5WWlA2WDg4VktLUTFSOS4u

University of Leicester

University Road, Leicester LE1 7RH, United Kingdom.

Tel: (44) 162 522 522
Website: www.le.ac.uk

The University was founded as Leicester, Leicestershire and Rutland University College in 1921. The site for the University was donated by a local businessman, Thomas Fielding Johnson, in order to create a living memorial for all local people who made sacrifices during the First World War.

Alumni Discount

Eligibility: 1. taught degrees such as MA, MSc, MRes or LLM and research degrees such as PhD or MPhil 2. campus-based degrees and distance learning degrees 3. full-time courses and part-time courses
Level of Study: Masters Degree, Postgraduate
Type: Scholarship
Value: Discount of 20% of the new course fee
Application Procedure: Your scholarship will be automatically calculated when you apply for your postgraduate course. No separate application form is required.
Additional Information: Please note that this scholarship is only available for self-funding students. Website: le.ac.uk/study/postgraduates/fees-funding/scholarships-discounts/alumni

College of Science and Engineering International PGT Merit Scholarship

Purpose: University of Leicester's aim is to be a world-class research-intensive university and deliver teaching and facilitate learning of the highest quality
Eligibility: 1. Degree equivalent to a UK high upper second class degree, 2. Degree equivalent to a UK first class degree
Level of Study: Postgraduate
Type: Scholarships
Value: This merit-based scholarship, worth either £3,000 or £5,000 per year
Study Establishment: Scholarships are awarded in the field of Chemistry, Engineering, Geography, Informatics, Mathematics and Physics and Astronomy
Country of Study: United Kingdom
Application Procedure: There is no need to apply for this scholarship. Eligible students will be automatically considered. If successful, you will be notified when you submit your final results.
Closing Date: January
Additional Information: le.ac.uk/study/postgraduates/fees-funding/scholarships-discounts/cse-postgrad

For further information contact:

The University of Leicester, University Road, Leicester LE1 7RH, United Kingdom.

Email: scholarships@le.ac.uk

College of Social Sciences, Arts and Humanities Masters Excellence Scholarship

Purpose: These scholarships are intended to support applicants with excellent undergraduate records and who have the capacity to complete a Masters degree at Distinction level.
Eligibility: 1. A strong second class undergraduate degree or an equivalent overseas qualification* 2. Standard English language requirements 3. Scholarships will be awarded on the basis of the overall strength of the application - including consideration of previous academic attainment, relevant experience, references, and the personal statement 4. Available to UK applicants only 5. Available for full- or part-time campus based study (subject to availability) 6. You must be able to start in the 2024/25 academic year * or show evidence of achieving this before the start of the Masters degree
Level of Study: Masters Degree, Postgraduate
Type: Scholarship
Value: A full fee waiver and £9,000 stipend
Application Procedure: 1. Apply for a Masters course with one of the schools listed above within the University of Leicester's College of Social Sciences, Arts and Humanities and supply the relevant supporting documents for your application, including two references (including at least one academic reference), evidence of your academic qualifications, evidence that you meet our English language entry requirements (if English is not your first language), and personal

statement. 2. Complete the additional Masters Excellence Studentship application form. Your application form will be submitted to pgadmissions@leicester.ac.uk. The Masters Excellence Studentships application form will ask you to include the following: A. A brief personal statement (1,000 words maximum) that tells us why you wish to study your chosen Masters course, how your previous academic and/or professional experience has given you the skills needed for postgraduate level study and how taking this course will support your personal and/or professional development plans. B. Details of the research area and theme which you would like to pursue in a future PhD programme. 3. Applications for the scheme will be assessed by a cross-College panel using the following criteria: eligibility; academic and/or professional background in the arts and humanities; academic background; relevant professional experience (if applicable); personal statement; references.
Closing Date: 22 May
Additional Information: Informal enquiries are welcome - please contact Dr Isobel Whitelegg, email icjw1@leicester.ac.uk. Website: le.ac.uk/study/postgraduates/fees-funding/scholarships-discounts/cssah-masters-excellence

For further information contact:

Email: icjw1@leicester.ac.uk.

College of Social Sciences, Arts and Humanities Minority Ethnic Masters Scholarship

Purpose: The University of Leicester's College of Social Sciences, Arts and Humanities (CSSAH) is committed to increasing the participation of Minority Ethnic students in its postgraduate cohorts and supporting Minority Ethnic students to progress into academia as a career.
Eligibility: Candidates must: 1. hold a place on a full-time campus-based or Distance Learning Masters course at the University of Leicester beginning in September/October 2024 2. be a permanent resident* in the UK; 3. self-identify as Minority Ethnic. *People who have permanent residency in the UK are: 1. British Citizens (includes Channel Islands and Isle of Man); 2. Republic of Ireland citizens; 3. Those with Indefinite Leave to Remain (ILR); 4. EU Citizens who have been given Settled Status under the EU Settlement Scheme (same as ILR).
Level of Study: Masters Degree, Postgraduate
Type: Scholarship
Value: a full tuition fee waiver
Application Procedure: 1. Apply for a Masters course in one of the subject areas listed above within the University of Leicester's College of Social Sciences, Arts and Humanities by 3 June 2024. 2. Complete the Minority Ethnic Scholarship application form by 30 June 2024 (by 5.30 pm). The form asks you to provide a personal statement of up to 750 words which includes the following: A. why you wish to study your chosen Masters course; B. how your previous academic and/or professional experience has given you the skills needed for postgraduate level study; C. how taking this course will support your personal and/or professional development plans; D. how the course relates to your potential research project (e.g. PhD). 3. Applications will be assessed on their overall strength, taking into consideration the candidate's academic achievements to date and their personal statement.
Closing Date: 30 June
No. of applicants last year: 10
Additional Information: Informal enquiries are welcome: please contact Dr Sarah Graham, Deputy Dean of Education, CSSAH: sarah.graham@leicester.ac.uk Website: le.ac.uk/study/postgraduates/fees-funding/scholarships-discounts/cssah-minority-ethnic-masters-scholarship

For further information contact:

Tel: (44)116 252 2628
Email: sarah.graham@leicester.ac.uk

PhD Studentships in Mathematics

Eligibility: United Kingdom and European Union PhD students, who have been residents in the United Kingdom for 3 years prior to application, and fees-only funding for other European Union students
Level of Study: Doctorate, Research
Type: Studentship
Value: £14,057 in the first year, rising in successive years, and full tuition fees
Length of Study: 3.5 years
Country of Study: United Kingdom
Application Procedure: Applications can be made online and submitted to admissions office. Information on how to apply and what supporting documents needed can be found at www2.le.ac.uk/research/degrees/phd/maths/supervision

For further information contact:

Email: pgresearch@maths.ed.ac.uk

U

President's Postgraduate Scholarship Scheme

Purpose: This is a postgraduate scholarship that enables international students to get a chance to study in University of Leicester, United Kingdom
Eligibility: 1. This scholarship is for new international (non-EU) students on a full-time, taught, campus-based

Masters course starting in September 2024 or January 2025. 2. This scholarship is open to applicants who already have an offer (conditional or unconditional) to study for a Masters degree programme at the University. 3. If you receive your offer to study by 10 March 2024, please submit your scholarship application by the first deadline of 30 March 2024. If you receive your offer to study after 10 March 2024, please apply by the second deadline of 13 July 2024. 4. You cannot combine this scholarship with a full scholarship (for tuition fees and living costs) from any other source. You are able to receive only one partial scholarship from the University. If you have a partial scholarship from other sources you will still be considered for the President's Postgraduate Scholarship. 5. This scholarship is not available for distance learning courses.
Value: Value of Scholarship £3,000 in the form of reduction in tuition fees
Length of Study: 1 to 2 years
Country of Study: Any country
Application Procedure: Send your completed application by email to scholarships@le.ac.uk
No. of awards offered: 100
Closing Date: 31 July
Additional Information: le.ac.uk/study/postgraduates/fees-funding/scholarships-discounts/

For further information contact:

Tel: (44) 141 331 3000
Email: ukroenquiries@gcu.ac.uk

University of Limerick

University of Limerick, Limerick V94 T9PX, Ireland.

Tel: (353) 61 202700
Email: reception@ul.ie
Website: www.ul.ie

Kemmy Business School: PhD Scholarship

Purpose: The scholarships are based on academic merit and are a reduction in tuition fees.
Eligibility: Please note that this scholarship is only available to International students
Level of Study: Doctorate
Type: Postgraduate scholarships
Value: €1,500 per year
Frequency: Every 3 years
Country of Study: Ireland
Application Procedure: Students do not apply for the scholarship, once they apply for any of the mentioned programmes they will be automatically considered for scholarship. For further information, please contact the International Education Division: international@ul.ie
Additional Information: Website: www.ul.ie/gps/international-student/scholarships-international-students/kemmy-business-school-scholarships

For further information contact:

Email: international@ul.ie

University of Lincoln

Brayford Pool, Lincoln LN6 7TS, United Kingdom.

Tel: (44) 1522 882 000
Website: www.lincoln.ac.uk

We are placed among the top 30 universities in the UK for student satisfaction in the Guardian University Guide 2024. Employers are increasingly looking for individuals who can make a difference in today's global workplace. With our expert staff, modern facilities, close links with business, and world-leading research we aim to provide the tools you need to achieve your career aspirations.

Africa Scholarship

Purpose: The University of Lincoln's Africa Scholarship is aimed at supporting postgraduate taught students from across Africa.
Eligibility: In order to be eligible to receive the Africa Scholarship, prospective students must meet the following criteria: 1. Be a national of, or have permanent residence in, Africa. 2. Hold a Conditional or Unconditional Offer from the University of Lincoln for a full-time postgraduate taught programme commencing in September/October 2024 or January/February 2025. 3. Have been awarded, or be expected to receive, one of the following qualifications: A. A Bachelor's degree from a recognised institution with a minimum grade of 2:2 or equivalent. B. A Pre-Masters qualification from a recognised institution with a grade comparable to a 2:2. C. A Master's degree from a recognised institution with a merit grade or equivalent. Please visit your

country webpage for more detail regarding regional entry requirements that are equivalent to a 2:2.
Level of Study: Postgraduate
Type: Scholarship
Value: £4,000
Application Procedure: In addition to meeting the above criteria, prospective students must have applied to the University of Lincoln prior to the relevant deadline mentioned in website
Closing Date: 1 December
Additional Information: Further information regarding the awarding of international scholarships can be found within the University of Lincoln International Scholarships Terms and Conditions 2024-25: www.lincoln.ac.uk/media/responsive2017/international2022/University,of,Lincoln,International,Scholarships,Terms,and,Conditions,2023-24.pdf Please note that University of Lincoln International Scholarships may be subject to change. The University of Lincoln reserves the right to amend the above scholarship provision without notice. For further information, please contact the International Office: international@lincoln.ac.uk. Website: www.lincoln.ac.uk/studywithus/scholarshipsandbursaries/africascholarship/

Alumni Scholarship for Postgraduate Study

Purpose: For UK students who hold a University of Lincoln undergraduate degree or higher qualification.
Eligibility: 1. You will have previously been awarded an undergraduate degree (or equivalent qualification that leads to postgraduate study), Graduate Certificate or Graduate Diploma at the University of Lincoln. 2. You will have a student status of Home 3. You will be enrolled on the University's student management system on a University of Lincoln postgraduate taught Master's or Postgraduate research programme for the current academic year, excluding the following programmes: A. Master of Architecture Part 2 B. MSc Nursing with Registered Nurse – (Adult/Child/Mental Health) C. MSc Physiotherapy (Pre-registration) D. MSc Occupational Therapy (Pre-registration) E. MSc Social Work 4. All tuition fees and payments due to the University in relation to any previous study have been paid in full. 5. You are not already in receipt of a studentship.
Level of Study: Postgraduate, Research
Value: Upto 15% of the tuition fees
Application Procedure: No Application Required
Additional Information: Further information regarding this scholarship can be found within the Terms and Conditions for the University's Bursaries and Scholarships (PDF): www.lincoln.ac.uk/media/responsive2017/welcomeweek/BursariesAndScholarshipTermsAndConditions.pdf. Website: www.lincoln.ac.uk/studywithus/scholarshipsandbursaries/alumnischolarshipforpostgraduatestudy/

Bangladesh Scholarship

Purpose: The University of Lincoln's Bangladesh Scholarship is aimed at supporting postgraduate taught students from across Bangladesh.
Eligibility: 1. Be a national of, or have permanent residence in, Bangladesh 2. Hold a Conditional or Unconditional Offer from the University of Lincoln for a full-time postgraduate taught programme commencing in September/October 2024 or January/February 2025 3. Have been awarded, or be expected to receive, one of the following qualifications: A. A Bachelor's degree from a recognised institution with a minimum grade of 2:2 or equivalent. B. A Pre-Masters qualification from a recognised institution with a grade comparable to a 2:2. C. A Master's degree from a recognised institution with a merit grade or equivalent. Please visit your country webpage for more detail regarding regional entry requirements that are equivalent to a 2:2. In addition to meeting the above criteria, prospective students must have applied to the University of Lincoln prior to the relevant deadline outlined below.
Level of Study: Postgraduate
Type: Scholarship
Value: £4,000
Frequency: Annual
Country of Study: Any country
Application Procedure: No Application Required
Closing Date: 1 December
Additional Information: Further information regarding the awarding of international scholarships can be found within the University of Lincoln International Scholarships Terms and Conditions: www.lincoln.ac.uk/media/responsive2017/international2022/University,of,Lincoln,International,Scholarships,Terms,and,Conditions,2023-24.pdf. Website: www.lincoln.ac.uk/studywithus/scholarshipsandbursaries/bangladeshscholarship/

For further information contact:

Brayford Way, Brayford Pool, Lincoln LN6 7TS, United Kingdom.

Tel: (44) 1522 882000

Developing Futures Scholarship

Purpose: The University of Lincoln Developing Futures Scholarship is designed to help support students from the Czech Republic, Slovakia, Poland, Hungary, Romania,

U

Bulgaria, Slovenia, Croatia, Estonia, Latvia, Lithuania, Malta, and Cyprus.

Eligibility: In order to be eligible to receive the Developing Futures Scholarship, prospective students must meet the following criteria: 1. Be a national of, or have permanent residence in, one of the following countries: Czech Republic, Slovakia, Poland, Hungary, Romania, Bulgaria, Slovenia, Croatia, Estonia, Latvia, Lithuania, Malta, or Cyprus. 2. Hold a Conditional or Unconditional Offer from the University of Lincoln for a full-time undergraduate, postgraduate taught or postgraduate research programme commencing in September/October 2024 or January/February 2025. 3. Students intending to join a postgraduate taught or postgraduate research programme must have been awarded, or be expected to receive, one of the following qualifications: A. A Bachelor's degree from a recognised institution with a minimum grade of 2:2 or equivalent. B. A Pre-Masters qualification from a recognised institution with a grade comparable to a 2:2. C. A Master's degree from a recognised institution with a merit grade or equivalent. Please visit your country webpage for more detail regarding regional entry requirements that are equivalent to a 2:2. In addition to meeting the above criteria, students must have applied to the University of Lincoln prior to the relevant deadline outlined below.

Level of Study: Masters Degree, Postgraduate, Research

Type: Scholarship

Value: £5,000

Country of Study: Any country

Application Procedure: No Application Required

Closing Date: 1 December

Additional Information: Further information regarding the awarding of international scholarships can be found within the University of Lincoln International Scholarships Terms and Conditions: www.lincoln.ac.uk/media/responsive2017/international2022/University,of,Lincoln,International,Scholarships,Terms,and,Conditions,2023-24.pdf. Please note that University of Lincoln International Scholarships may be subject to change. The University of Lincoln reserves the right to amend the above scholarship provision without notice. For further information, please contact the International Office: international@lincoln.ac.uk. Website: www.lincoln.ac.uk/studywithus/scholarshipsandbursaries/developingfuturesscholarship/

For further information contact:

Brayford Way, Brayford Pool, Lincoln LN6 7TS, United Kingdom.

Tel: (44) 1522 882000
Email: international@lincoln.ac.uk

Egypt Scholarship

Purpose: The University of Lincoln's Egypt Scholarship is aimed at supporting postgraduate taught students from across Egypt.

Eligibility: In order to be eligible to receive the Egypt Scholarship, prospective students must meet the following criteria: 1. Be a national of, or have permanent residence in, Egypt. 2. Hold a Conditional or Unconditional Offer from the University of Lincoln for a full-time postgraduate taught programme commencing in September/October 2024 or January/February 2025. 3. Have been awarded, or be expected to receive, one of the following qualifications: A. A Bachelor's degree from a recognised institution with a minimum grade of 2:2 or equivalent. B. A Pre-Masters qualification from a recognised institution with a grade comparable to a 2:2. C. A Master's degree from a recognised institution with a merit grade or equivalent. Please visit your country webpage for more detail regarding regional entry requirements that are equivalent to a 2:2. In addition to meeting the above criteria, prospective students must have applied to the University of Lincoln prior to the relevant deadline outlined below.

Level of Study: Postgraduate

Type: Scholarship

Value: £5,000

Frequency: Annual

Country of Study: United Kingdom

Application Procedure: No Application Required

Closing Date: 1 December

Additional Information: Further information regarding the awarding of international scholarships can be found within the University of Lincoln International Scholarships Terms and Conditions: www.lincoln.ac.uk/media/responsive2017/international2022/University,of,Lincoln,International,Scholarships,Terms,and,Conditions,2023-24.pdf. Please note that University of Lincoln International Scholarships may be subject to change. The University of Lincoln reserves the right to amend the above scholarship provision without notice. For further information, please contact the International Office: international@lincoln.ac.uk. Website: www.lincoln.ac.uk/studywithus/scholarshipsandbursaries/egyptscholarship/

For further information contact:

Brayford Way, Brayford Pool, Lincoln LN6 7TS, United Kingdom.

Tel: (44) 1522 882000
Email: international@lincoln.ac.uk

George Major Bursaries

Purpose: George Major Bursaries aims to provide bursaries for students with disabilities.
Eligibility: The bursaries will be used to support students who have a life-long illness (see indicative list below although this is not exhaustive) where additional financial support could be used to help a student enjoy a better quality of life and have access to all aspects of their students experience. 1. Cancer 2. Heart Disease 3. Cystic fibrosis 4. HIV 5. Metabolic disorders 6. Neurodegenerative disease (i.e. multiple sclerosis) 7. Genetic conditions 8. Chronic liver disease 9. Renal disease
Level of Study: Postgraduate, Research
Type: Scholarship
Value: £1,000
Application Procedure: The bursaries will be administered by Student Services, who can be contacted by emailing studentsupport@lincoln.ac.uk.
Additional Information: Further information regarding this scholarship can be found within the Terms and Conditions for the University's Bursaries and Scholarships (PDF): www.lincoln.ac.uk/media/responsive2017/welcomeweek/BursariesAndScholarshipTermsAndConditions.pdf. Website: www.lincoln.ac.uk/studywithus/scholarshipsandbursaries/georgemajorbursaries/

For further information contact:

Email: studentsupport@lincoln.ac.uk.

Global Postgraduate Scholarship

Purpose: The Global Postgraduate Scholarship is designed to help international students to access postgraduate taught level study at the University of Lincoln.
Eligibility: To be eligible for the scholarship, students must have been awarded, or be expected to receive, one of the following qualifications: 1. A Bachelor's degree from a recognised institution with a minimum grade of 2:2 or equivalent. 2. A Pre-Masters qualification from a recognised institution with a grade comparable to a 2:2. 3. A Master's degree from a recognised institution with a merit grade or equivalent. Please visit your country webpage for more detail regarding regional entry requirements that are equivalent to a 2:2 or merit grade.
Level of Study: Postgraduate
Type: Scholarship
Value: £2,000
Frequency: Varies
Country of Study: Any country
Application Procedure: Students are not required to apply for this scholarship. You will automatically be considered for a Global Postgraduate Scholarship once you have submitted your application to study at the University of Lincoln.
Closing Date: 1 June
Funding: Trusts
Additional Information: Further information regarding the awarding of international scholarships can be found within the University of Lincoln International Scholarships Terms and Conditions: www.lincoln.ac.uk/media/responsive2017/international2022/University,of,Lincoln,International,Scholarships,Terms,and,Conditions,2023-24.pdf. Please note that University of Lincoln International Scholarships may be subject to change. The University of Lincoln reserves the right to amend the above scholarship provision without notice. For further information, please contact the International Office: international@lincoln.ac.uk. Website: www.lincoln.ac.uk/studywithus/scholarshipsandbursaries/globalpostgraduatescholarship/

For further information contact:

Brayford Way, Brayford Pool, Lincoln LN6 7TS, United Kingdom.

Tel: (44) 1522 882000
Email: international@lincoln.ac.uk

India Scholarship

Purpose: The University of Lincoln's India Scholarship is aimed at supporting postgraduate taught students from across India.
Eligibility: In order to be eligible to receive the India Scholarship, prospective students must meet the following criteria: 1. Be a national of, or have permanent residence in, India. 2. Hold a Conditional or Unconditional Offer from the University of Lincoln for a full-time postgraduate taught programme commencing in September/October 2024 or January/February 2025. 3. Have been awarded, or be expected to receive, one of the following qualifications: A. A Bachelor's degree from a recognised institution with a minimum of 2:2 or equivalent. B. A Pre-Masters qualification from a recognised institution with a grade comparable to a 2:2. C. A Master's degree from a recognised institution with a merit grade or equivalent. Please visit your country webpage for more detail regarding regional entry requirements that are equivalent to a 2:2. In addition to meeting the above criteria, prospective students must have applied to the University of Lincoln prior to the relevant deadline outlined below.

Level of Study: Postgraduate
Type: Scholarship
Value: £4,000
Length of Study: 1 year
Frequency: Varies
Country of Study: Any country
Application Procedure: No Application Required
Closing Date: 1 June
Funding: Trusts
Additional Information: Further information regarding the awarding of international scholarships can be found within the University of Lincoln International Scholarships Terms and Conditions: www.lincoln.ac.uk/media/responsive2017/international2022/University,of,Lincoln,International,Scholarships,Terms,and,Conditions,2023-24.pdf. Please note that University of Lincoln International Scholarships may be subject to change. The University of Lincoln reserves the right to amend the above scholarship provision without notice. For further information, please contact the International Office: international@lincoln.ac.uk. website: www.lincoln.ac.uk/home/studywithus/scholarshipsandbursaries/indiascholarship/

For further information contact:

Brayford Way, Brayford Pool, Lincoln LN6 7TS, United Kingdom.

Tel: (44) 1522 882000
Email: intscholarships@lincoln.ac.uk

Indonesia Scholarship

Purpose: The University of Lincoln Indonesia Scholarship is aimed at supporting high-achieving postgraduate students from across Indonesia.
Eligibility: 1. Be a national of, or have permanent residence in, Indonesia 2. Hold a Conditional or Unconditional Offer from the University of Lincoln for a full-time postgraduate taught programme 3. Have been awarded, or be expected to receive, a bachelor's degree from a recognised university with a minimum GPA score of 2.8 or equivalent 4. Meet the English language requirements of their intended programme of study
Level of Study: Postgraduate
Type: Scholarship
Value: This scholarship is valued at £5,000
Frequency: Varies
Country of Study: Any country
Closing Date: 1 June
Funding: Trusts
Additional Information: www.lincoln.ac.uk/home/studywithus/scholarshipsandbursaries/

For further information contact:

Email: intscholarships@lincoln.ac.uk

International Alumni Scholarship

Purpose: The International Alumni Scholarship is designed to support University of Lincoln graduates to pursue further studies at the University of Lincoln.
Eligibility: In order to be eligible for the International Alumni Scholarship, students must be in receipt of a Bachelor's degree from either the University of Lincoln, or an approved provider overseas, with a minimum grade of 2:2 or equivalent.
Level of Study: Postgraduate, Research
Type: Scholarship
Value: £2,000 as a tuition fee discount.
Application Procedure: You do not need to apply for this scholarship. You will automatically be considered for the International Alumni Scholarship once you have submitted your application to study at the University of Lincoln.
Additional Information: Further information regarding the awarding of international scholarships can be found within the University of Lincoln International Scholarships Terms and Conditions 2024-25: www.lincoln.ac.uk/media/responsive2017/international2022/University,of,Lincoln,International,Scholarships,Terms,and,Conditions,2023-24.pdf. Please note that University of Lincoln International Scholarships may be subject to change. The University of Lincoln reserves the right to amend the above scholarship provision without notice. For further information, please contact the International Office: international@lincoln.ac.uk. Website: www.lincoln.ac.uk/studywithus/scholarshipsandbursaries/internationalalumnischolarship/

For further information contact:

Email: international@lincoln.ac.uk

Lincoln Alumni Master of Architecture Scholarship

Purpose: The Lincoln Alumni Master of Architecture Scholarship is an award for students who have previously completed study at the University of Lincoln and are enrolling on the Master of Architecture Programme (MArch).
Eligibility: 1. You must have previously completed an undergraduate degree (or equivalent qualification that leads to postgraduate study), Graduate Certificate, or Graduate Diploma at the University of Lincoln. 2. You must have

a student status of 'Home' on the Student Information System. 3. You must be enrolled on the Student Information System, via one of the identified progression routes, on the Master of Architecture programme for the current academic year. 4. You must commence the programme in the academic year 2023/24 and be paying the full tuition fee rate of £9,250. 5. Part-time students must commence the programme in academic year 2023/24 and be paying the part-time tuition fee rate of £77 per credit point.
Level of Study: Postgraduate
Type: Scholarship
Value: £1,000 will be paid directly to the student for each year of study for each completed academic year of study, with part-time students eligible for a pro-rata payment.
Frequency: Annual
Country of Study: United Kingdom
Application Procedure: There is no need to apply, eligible students will receive this scholarship upon enrolling for the Master of Architecture programme.
Funding: Private
Additional Information: Website: https://www.lincoln.ac.uk/studywithus/scholarshipsandbursaries/lincolnalumnimasterofarchitecturescholarship/

For further information contact:

Email: intscholarships@lincoln.ac.uk

Lincoln Alumni MSc School of Health and Social Care Scholarship

Eligibility: The Lincoln Alumni MSc School of Health and Social Care Scholarship is an award for students who have previously completed study at the University of Lincoln and are enrolling one of the following programmes in 2024/25: 1. MSc Nursing with Registered Nurse (Adult) 2. MSc Nursing with Registered Nurse (Child) 3. MSc Nursing with Registered Nurse (Mental Health) 4. MSc Physiotherapy (Pre-registration) 5. MSc Occupational Therapy (Pre-registration) 6. MSc Speech and Language Therapy (Pre-registration). You will have previously completed an undergraduate degree (or equivalent qualification that leads to postgraduate study), Graduate Certificate or Graduate Diploma at the University of Lincoln, confirmed by a University of Lincoln Board of Examiners.
Level of Study: Postgraduate (MSc)
Type: Scholarship
Value: £1000 will be paid directly to the student for each year of study for each completed academic year of study, with part-time students eligible for a pro-rata payment.
Application Procedure: Please contact admissions@lincoln.ac.uk for further details.
Additional Information: Website: www.lincoln.ac.uk/studywithus/scholarshipsandbursaries/lincolnalumnihealthandsocialcarescholarship/

For further information contact:

Email: admissions@lincoln.ac.uk

Lincoln Alumni MSc Social Work Scholarship

Purpose: The Lincoln Alumni MSc Social Work Scholarship is an award for students who have previously completed study at the University of Lincoln and are enrolling on the MSc Social Work (Pre-Qualification) programme.
Eligibility: 1. You will have previously completed an undergraduate degree (or equivalent qualification that leads to postgraduate study), Graduate Certificate, or Graduate Diploma at the University of Lincoln. 2. You must commence the programme in academic year 2023/24 and be paying the full tuition fee rate of £8,100 per year if Home or £14,900 per year if International (pro-rata for part-time studies). 3. You will be enrolled on the University's Student Management System on the MSc Social Work programme 4. All tuition fees and payments due to the University in relation to any previous study have been paid in full.
Level of Study: Postgraduate
Type: Scholarship
Value: £1000 will be paid directly to the student for each year of study for each completed academic year of study, with part-time students eligible for a pro-rata payment.
Application Procedure: Please contact admissions@lincoln.ac.uk for further details.
Additional Information: Website: www.lincoln.ac.uk/studywithus/scholarshipsandbursaries/lincolnalumnimscsocialworkscholarship/

For further information contact:

Email: admissions@lincoln.ac.uk

Pakistan Scholarship

Purpose: The University of Lincoln's Pakistan Scholarship is aimed at supporting postgraduate taught students from across Pakistan.
Eligibility: In order to be eligible to receive the Pakistan Scholarship, prospective students must meet the following criteria: 1. Be a national of, or have permanent residence in, Pakistan. 2. Hold a Conditional or Unconditional Offer from the University of Lincoln for a full-time postgraduate taught programme commencing in September/October 2024 or January/February 2025. 3. Have been awarded, or be

expected to receive, one of the following qualifications: A. A Bachelor's degree from a recognised institution with a minimum grade of 2:2 or equivalent. B. A Pre-Masters qualification from a recognised institution with a grade comparable to a 2:2. C. A Master's degree from a recognised institution with a merit grade or equivalent.
Level of Study: Postgraduate
Type: Scholarship
Value: £4,000
Application Procedure: In addition to meeting the above criteria, prospective students must have applied to the University of Lincoln prior to the relevant deadline
Closing Date: 1 December
Additional Information: Website: www.lincoln.ac.uk/studywithus/scholarshipsandbursaries/pakistanscholarship/

Thailand Scholarship

Purpose: The University of Lincoln's Thailand Scholarship is aimed at supporting postgraduate taught students from across Thailand.
Eligibility: In order to be eligible to receive the Thailand Scholarship, prospective students must meet the following criteria: 1. Be a national of, or have permanent residence in, Thailand. 2. Hold a Conditional or Unconditional Offer from the University of Lincoln for a full-time postgraduate taught programme commencing in September/October 2024 or January/February 2025. 3. Have been awarded, or be expected to receive, one of the following qualifications: A. A Bachelor's degree from a recognised institution with a minimum grade of 2:2 or equivalent. B. A Pre-Masters qualification from a recognised institution with a grade comparable to a 2:2. C. A Master's degree from a recognised institution with a merit grade or equivalent. Please visit your country webpage for more detail regarding regional entry requirements that are equivalent to a 2:2. In addition to meeting the above criteria, prospective students must have applied to the University of Lincoln prior to the relevant deadline outlined below.
Level of Study: Postgraduate
Type: Scholarship
Value: £4,000
Country of Study: Any country
Application Procedure: No Application Required
Closing Date: 1 June
Additional Information: Further information regarding the awarding of international scholarships can be found within the University of Lincoln International Scholarships Terms and Conditions: www.lincoln.ac.uk/media/responsive2017/international2022/University,of,Lincoln,International,Scholarships,Terms,and,Conditions,2023-24.pdf. Please note that University of Lincoln International Scholarships may be subject to change. The University of Lincoln reserves the right to amend the above scholarship provision without notice. For further information, please contact the International Office: international@lincoln.ac.uk. Website: www.lincoln.ac.uk/studywithus/scholarshipsandbursaries/thaischolarship/

For further information contact:

Brayford Way, Brayford Pool, Lincoln LN6 7TS, United Kingdom.

Tel: (44) 1522 882000
Email: intscholarships@lincoln.ac.uk

The Lincoln 50% Global Scholarship

Purpose: The Lincoln Global Leaders Scholarship is designed to recognise the achievements and potential of international students joining the University of Lincoln in September/October 2024 or January/February 2025.
Eligibility: Students intending to join a postgraduate taught programme must be in receipt of one of the following qualifications before applying for the Lincoln Global Leaders Scholarship: 1. A Bachelor's degree from a recognised institution with a minimum grade of 2:1 or equivalent 2. A pre-Master's qualification from a recognised institution with a grade comparable to a 2:1 3. A Master's degree from a recognised institution with a merit grade or equivalent. Please visit your country webpage for more detail regarding regional entry requirements that are equivalent to a 2:1.
Level of Study: Masters Degree, Postgraduate
Type: Scholarship
Value: 50% of tuition fees
Length of Study: one year
Frequency: Varies
Country of Study: Any country
Application Procedure: In addition to meeting the above academic requirements, students must complete an International Scholarship Application Form: forms.office.com/Pages/ResponsePage.aspx?id=xEculd4FgkKDr19LRrFij8GPNxDj2cVCtsH2VGx7gjFUMFVKMFY2NkZXR0Y0TjEyQkQ0R0ExWVRXSC4u.
Funding: Trusts
Additional Information: For further information, please contact the International Office: international@lincoln.ac.uk. Website: www.lincoln.ac.uk/home/studywithus/scholarshipsandbursaries/

For further information contact:

Email: international@lincoln.ac.uk

The School of History and Heritage MA Bursary

Purpose: The School of Humanities and Heritage is pleased to be able to offer up to four bursaries, by competition, to University of Lincoln students and alumni who wish to undertake one of the MA degree programmes offered by the School (MA History, MA Medieval Studies, MA Conservation of Cultural Heritage, or MA English Literature).
Eligibility: 1. The School of Humanities and Heritage is pleased to be able to offer up to four bursaries, by competition, to University of Lincoln students and alumni who wish to undertake one of the MA degree programmes offered by the School (MA History, MA Medieval Studies, MA Conservation of Cultural Heritage, or MA English Literature). 2. Please note that the bursary is only available to current students or alumni of the University of Lincoln. 3. There is no fixed allocation per programme; bursaries will be awarded to candidates who submit the best applications.
Level of Study: Postgraduate
Type: Scholarship
Value: The School bursaries will cover fees to cover one year of full-time study
Application Procedure: Please note that the bursary is only available to current students or alumni of the University of Lincoln. Applicants are required to have applied for their MA programme of choice before submitting their application.
Closing Date: 5 May
Additional Information: For more information about this bursary, please contact our Postgraduate Team at pgenquirie s@lincoln.ac.uk or by calling (44)1522 886644. Website: https://www.lincoln.ac.uk/studywithus/scholarshipsand bursaries/theschoolofhumanitiesandheritagemabursary/

For further information contact:

Tel: (44)1522 886644
Email: pgenquiries@lincoln.ac.uk

Turkey Scholarship

Purpose: The University of Lincoln's Turkey Scholarship is aimed at supporting postgraduate taught students from across Turkey.
Eligibility: In order to be eligible to receive the Turkey Scholarship, prospective students must meet the following criteria: 1. Be a national of, or have permanent residence in, Turkey. 2. Hold a Conditional or Unconditional Offer from the University of Lincoln for a full-time postgraduate taught programme commencing in September/October 2024 or January/February 2025. 3. Have been awarded, or be expected to receive, one of the following qualifications: A. A Bachelor's degree from a recognised institution with a minimum grade of 2:2 or equivalent. B. A Pre-Masters qualification from a recognised institution with a grade comparable to a 2:2. C. A Master's degree from a recognised institution with a merit grade or equivalent. Please visit your country webpage for more detail regarding regional entry requirements that are equivalent to a 2:2.
Level of Study: Postgraduate
Type: Scholarship
Value: £4,000
Application Procedure: In addition to meeting the above criteria, prospective students must have applied to the University of Lincoln prior to the relevant deadline
Closing Date: 1 December
Additional Information: Further information regarding the awarding of international scholarships can be found within the University of Lincoln International Scholarships Terms and Conditions: www.lincoln.ac.uk/media/responsive2017/international2022/University,of,Lincoln,International,Scholarships,Terms,and,Conditions,2023-24.pdf. Please note that University of Lincoln International Scholarships may be subject to change. The University of Lincoln reserves the right to amend the above scholarship provision without notice. For further information, please contact the International Office: international@lincoln.ac.uk. Website: www.lincoln.ac.uk/studywithus/scholarshipsand bursaries/turkeyscholarship/

For further information contact:

Email: international@lincoln.ac.uk

Uruguay PhD Scholarship

Purpose: A new programme of scholarships to conduct PhD studies in Life Sciences has recently been agreed between the University of Lincoln and the Uruguay National Agency for Research and Innovation (ANII - Agencia Nacional de Investigación e Innovación).
Eligibility: A new programme of scholarships to conduct PhD studies in Life Sciences has recently been agreed between the University of Lincoln and the Uruguay National Agency for Research and Innovation (ANII - Agencia Nacional de Investigación e Innovación). 1. Must be a citizen of Uruguay Have already obtained a BSc (or equivalent) degree in an area relevant to the research fields described above. 2. A minimum of a UK equivalent to a 2:1 award is required to enter the application process
Level of Study: Postgraduate
Type: Scholarship
Value: University fees and a subsistence bursary
Length of Study: 3 Year
Country of Study: United Kingdom

Application Procedure: The applications must include a copy of the applicant's CV and a one page research statement describing research interests, ambition and briefly outline a research project. Full details are available here: www.anii.org.uy/apoyos/formacion/9/maestrias-y-doctorados-en-el-exterior-en-areas-estrategicas/.
Closing Date: 22 April
Additional Information: For additional information regarding this scholarship please contact: Email: Prof. Fernando Montealegre-Zapata: fmontealegrez@lincoln.ac.uk Website: www.lincoln.ac.uk/studywithus/scholarshipsandbursaries/uruguayphdscholarship/

For further information contact:

Tel: (44) 1522 835460
Email: fmontealegrez@lincoln.ac.uk

Vietnam Scholarship

Purpose: The University of Lincoln's Vietnam Scholarship is aimed at supporting postgraduate taught students from across Vietnam.
Eligibility: In order to be eligible to receive the Vietnam Scholarship, prospective students must meet the following criteria: 1. Be a national of, or have permanent residence in, Vietnam. 2. Hold a Conditional or Unconditional Offer from the University of Lincoln for a full-time postgraduate taught programme commencing in September/October 2024 or January/February 2025. 3. Have been awarded, or be expected to receive, one of the following qualifications: A. A Bachelor's degree from a recognised institution with a minimum grade of 2:2 or equivalent. B. A Pre-Masters qualification from a recognised institution with a grade comparable to a 2:2. C. A Master's degree from a recognised institution with a merit grade or equivalent. Please visit your country webpage for more detail regarding regional entry requirements that are equivalent to a 2:2.
Level of Study: Postgraduate
Type: Scholarship
Value: £4,000
Application Procedure: In addition to meeting the above criteria, prospective students must have applied to the University of Lincoln prior to the relevant deadline
Closing Date: 1 December
Additional Information: Further information regarding the awarding of international scholarships can be found within the University of Lincoln International Scholarships Terms and Conditions: www.lincoln.ac.uk/media/responsive2017/international2022/University,of,Lincoln,International,Scholarships,Terms,and,Conditions,2023-24.pdf. Please note that University of Lincoln International Scholarships may be subject to change. The University of Lincoln reserves the right to amend the above scholarship provision without notice. For further information, please contact the International Office: international@lincoln.ac.uk. Website: www.lincoln.ac.uk/studywithus/scholarshipsandbursaries/vietnamscholarship/

University of Liverpool

Foundation Building, Brownlow Hill,, Liverpool L69 7ZX, United Kingdom.

Tel: (44) 151 794 2000
Email: irro@liverpool.ac.uk.
Website: www.liverpool.ac.uk

For advancement of learning and ennoblement of life. This has been our mission since the University was founded in 1881. To this day, these values focus our efforts as we strive to achieve our ambitions and tackle the grand challenges of the age.

ANID CHILE

Eligibility: 1. Postgraduate taught and research students from Chile are eligible for this scholarship. 2. Residents of State of Guanajuato, Mexico, wishing to study at postgraduate taught and research levels.
Level of Study: Masters Degree, Postgraduate, Research
Type: Award
Value: 20% discount on Master's and Postgraduate Research tuition fees, excluding bench fees.
Application Procedure: See www.anid.cl/ for more information
Additional Information: Website: www.liverpool.ac.uk/study/postgraduate-taught/finance/scholarships/

Chevening Scholarships

Purpose: The University, in partnership with Chevening, is delighted to offer this generous scholarship to students who are studying a master's programme and who have future leadership potential.
Eligibility: The scholarship is open to all subjects offered as a one-year taught master's programme at the Liverpool campus.
Level of Study: Masters Degree
Type: Scholarship

Value: £18,000
Application Procedure: Applications are made via the Chevening website: www.chevening.org/apply. Apply Here: www.chevening.org/apply
Additional Information: Website: www.liverpool.ac.uk/study/postgraduate-taught/finance/scholarships/

For further information contact:

Website: www.chevening.org/apply

Commonwealth Shared Scholarship Scheme

Purpose: Commonwealth Shared Scholarships, offered in partnership with United Kingdom universities, are for developing country students who would not otherwise be able to undertake master's level study in the United Kingdom
Eligibility: The scholarship has certain eligibility criteria and other requirements, which include 1. Students who hold a first degree at either first class or upper second-class level are eligible for the award 2. The university confirms candidates are sufficiently fluent in written and oral English to pursue their proposed studies immediately 3. Scholarships are applicable to the nationals of commonwealth developing countries, who are not at present living or studying in a developed commonwealth country. 4. Students must return to their home country as soon as the award comes to an end.
Level of Study: Masters Degree
Type: Scholarship
Value: Covers tuition fees, living costs and return flights to the United Kingdom
Country of Study: United Kingdom
No. of awards offered: 5
Closing Date: 1 April
Funding: Trusts
Contributor: Department for International Development (DFID)
Additional Information: www.univariety.com/scholarship/Commonwealth-Shared-Scholarship-Scheme-University-of-Liverpool/6670280b

For further information contact:

Tel: (44) 151 794 2000

CONACYT

Purpose: The University of Liverpool has an agreement with CONACYT to support postgraduate taught and research students from Mexico.
Eligibility: You must be a Mexican national.
Level of Study: Masters Degree, Research
Type: Award
Value: 30% reduction in tuition fees
Application Procedure: Apply via: www.conacyt.mx/index.php/becas-y-posgrados
Additional Information: Website: www.liverpool.ac.uk/study/postgraduate-taught/finance/scholarships/

Dean's 20th Anniversary Scholarships

Eligibility: 1. Home (UK) and international applicants to all Management School campus-based MSc programmes, starting in autumn 2024. 2. Candidates are considered for this award based on their academic excellence, CV and personal statement. 3. Hold or be on track to obtain a First Class or equivalent in their undergraduate degree or comparable qualification, with no marks below a 2:1 (60%) or equivalent in modules relevant to their chosen postgraduate programme. 4. Work experience relevant to the programme (paid, internship, shadowing or voluntary positions) would be advantageous, as would previously studying at a highly ranked university.
Level of Study: Postgraduate (MSc)
Type: Scholarship
Value: Part fee waiver (50%)
Application Procedure: Eligible programme applicants will be considered. No separate scholarship application is necessary.
Additional Information: Website: www.liverpool.ac.uk/management/study/postgraduate-taught/scholarships/

Duncan Norman Scholarship

Purpose: The Duncan Norman Research Scholarship at the University of Liverpool was established in 2004 following the receipt of a generous donation from The Duncan Norman Charitable Trust in memory of the late Duncan Norman.
Eligibility: The Scholarship is open for application to all prospective full-time postgraduate research students irrespective of nationality, tuition fee status or subject area. It is expected that, where possible, all candidates for the Duncan Norman Research Scholarship should also have made an application to secure funding from alternate sources for a postgraduate studentship. If offered, the studentship must be accepted, and in such circumstances the Duncan Norman Research Scholarship would provide additional top up funding. The holders of the Scholarship must register for a PhD at the University of Liverpool and attend any events based in Liverpool that are organised by the Duncan Norman Charitable Trust.
Level of Study: Postgraduate, Research
Type: Scholarship
Value: 1. Competitive annual maintenance stipend of £17,000 2. Full payment of tuition fees 3. Free University

accommodation of up to £4,635 pa or an allowance of the same amount for students wishing to live off campus 4. Laptop or desktop computer of up to £1000 in value 5. Support for conference expenses of up to £500 in years 2 & 3.
Application Procedure: Download the DNRS Application Form: www.liverpool.ac.uk/media/livacuk/study/postgraduate-research/DNRS,Application,Form,2023.doc and the Duncan Norman Research Scholarship terms of award (Microsoft Award): www.liverpool.ac.uk/media/livacuk/DN,Terms,of,Award.docx.
Closing Date: 7 April
Additional Information: Website: www.liverpool.ac.uk/study/postgraduate-research/fees-and-funding/scholarships-and-awards/duncan-norman-research-schol/

FIDERH Award

Eligibility: You must be a Mexican national
Type: Award
Value: 20% reduction in tuition fees for postgraduate taught and research programmes
Country of Study: United Kingdom
Application Procedure: Please apply for funding through FIDERH: www.fiderh.org.mx/. Students who are awarded a FIDERH Graduate Loan and register at the University of Liverpool will automatically receive the award. Apply: www.fiderh.org.mx/
Additional Information: Please apply for funding through FIDERH. Students who are awarded a FIDERH Graduate Loan and register at the University of Liverpool will automatically receive the award www.liverpool.ac.uk/study/postgraduate-taught/finance/scholarships/scholarships/fiderh-award/

For further information contact:

Website: www.fiderh.org.mx/

Fulbright Scholarships

Purpose: One scholarship is available for a master's student from the US and another is available for a postgraduate research student to undertake a three to six month research stay from the US.
Eligibility: 1. US citizens 2. One scholarship is available for a master's student from the US and another is available for a postgraduate research student to undertake a three to six month research stay from the US.
Level of Study: Masters Degree
Type: Scholarship
Value: £20,000 towards tuition fees for a master's student, £2,500 monthly living stipend for a postgraduate research student.
Application Procedure: Apply via: www.fulbright.org.uk.
Additional Information: Website: www.liverpool.ac.uk/study/postgraduate-taught/finance/scholarships/

FUNED Awards

Eligibility: 1. You must be a Mexican national in receipt of a FUNED loan. 2. For Masters or Research students from Mexico in receipt of FUNED loans.
Level of Study: Masters Degree, Research
Type: Award
Value: 20% reduction in tuition fees
Application Procedure: Apply via: www.funedmx.org/.
No. of applicants last year: 10
Additional Information: Website: www.liverpool.ac.uk/study/postgraduate-taught/finance/scholarships/

Health Data Science Scholarships

Purpose: These scholarships will be awarded on a competitive basis to the strongest applicants for the MSc Health Data Science, and paid as a reduction in fees.
Eligibility: To be eligible for these scholarships, you must be awarded a place on the MSc Health Data Science programme at the University of Liverpool. You must hold, or be on track to obtain, at least a high 2:1 (65+%) in your undergraduate degree, including marks of 60+% in modules relevant to the MSc programme. Work experience relevant to Data Science (paid, internship, shadowing or voluntary positions) would be advantageous.
Level of Study: Postgraduate (MSc)
Type: Scholarship
Value: £10,850
Frequency: Annual
Country of Study: Any country
Application Procedure: Once you have secured a place on the MSc Health Data Science at the University of Liverpool, submit your CV, and a brief supporting statement (no longer than 750 words), which should outline (1) why you should receive a scholarship to study on this programme, (2) your past achievements in academic and professional activities relevant to the MSc programme, and (3) your data science experience to date and any future career plans to Prof Ruwanthi Kolamunnage-Dona (kdrr@liverpool.ac.uk).
Closing Date: 31 May
Additional Information: Website: www.liverpool.ac.uk/study/postgraduate-taught/finance/scholarships/scholarships/health-data-science-msc-scholarships/

For further information contact:

Tel: (44) 151 794 2000

Hodgson Law Scholarship

Purpose: The Trustees wish Hodgson Law Scholars to benefit from education in Liverpool with a view to encouraging the intellectual growth of promising law students and the nurturing of close links with the City of Liverpool and the Liverpool City Region.
Eligibility: 1. Academic excellence. 2. Evidence of an interest in legal and public service which may benefit the Liverpool City Region. 3. Potential and ambition for future leadership. 4. That they are not otherwise able to undertake a postgraduate degree at either institution.; Further details are available on the hodgsonlawscholarships.com/ The Scholarship is available to all prospective Overseas candidates (i.e. non UK, non EU) intending to pursue a postgraduate taught degree in law at the University of Liverpool.
Level of Study: Postgraduate
Value: £9,207
Country of Study: United Kingdom
Application Procedure: You will need to complete and submit an application form electronically to the Hodgson Selection Committee by email to hodgsonscholarship@liverpool.ac.uk.
Additional Information: Applications may also be sent by post, to the address provided on the application form. https://www.liverpool.ac.uk/postgraduate-taught/finance/scholarships/scholarships/hodgson-law-scholarship/

For further information contact:

Email: jtribe@liverpool.ac.uk

HRM Princess Sirindhorn University of Liverpool Scholarship (Thailand)

Purpose: The University is able to offer one award to a new postgraduate taught master's student from Thailand.
Eligibility: The scholarship is open to all subjects offered as a one-year taught master's programme. However, priority will be given to those students who wish to study in a subject area associated with HRH Princess Sirindhorn such as science, IT, medicine, the arts, geography, history and languages.
Level of Study: Masters Degree, Postgraduate
Type: Scholarship
Value: Full tuition fees and living stipend of £9,000
Application Procedure: Application forms will automatically be forwarded to all eligible candidates by the International Recruitment, Relations and Study Abroad Team.
Additional Information: Website: www.liverpool.ac.uk/study/postgraduate-taught/finance/scholarships/

John Lennon Memorial Scholarship

Purpose: The award is intended to support students from Merseyside who might be in financial need and enhance, among other things, awareness of global problems and environmental issues.
Eligibility: If you are a current or prospective Home postgraduate (taught and research), either born in or with very strong family connections to Merseyside and who has an academic offer from the University of Liverpool, you are eligible to apply. The award is available to all subject areas studied on the main University campus.
Type: Scholarship
Country of Study: Any country
Application Procedure: In order to apply for this award you will be required to complete an John Lennon Memorial Scholarship Form: www.liverpool.ac.uk/media/livacuk/study/postgraduate-research/JLMS,Application,Form,2023.doc. Please ensure you complete all the sections, especially the reference section. You will need to complete and submit the form by email to the Secretary to the Scholarships Sub-Committee by email to scholarships@liverpool.ac.uk. Applications may also be returned by post to the address indicated on the application form, but candidates are asked to consider the environmental impact of doing so.
Closing Date: 7 April
Additional Information: For all enquiries please contact the Secretary to the Scholarships Sub-Committee: seschol@liverpool.ac.uk. Weblink: www.liverpool.ac.uk/study/postgraduate-taught/finance/scholarships/scholarships/john-lennon-memorial-scholarship/

For further information contact:

Email: seschol@liverpool.ac.uk

JuventudEsGto

Eligibility: Residents of State of Guanajuato, Mexico, wishing to study at postgraduate taught and research levels.
Level of Study: Postgraduate, Research
Type: Award
Value: 10% discount on tuition fees, excluding bench fees
Application Procedure: See website for more details
Additional Information: Note: See www.facebook.com/JuventudEsGto/ for more information Website: www.liverpool.ac.uk/study/postgraduate-taught/finance/scholarships/

Liverpool International College (LIC) Excellence Award

Purpose: The University of Liverpool will award five University of Liverpool International College students, who achieve the highest academic excellence (minimum 75%) in their UoLIC Pre-Master's programme, the prestigious UoLIC Excellence scholarship.
Eligibility: Five students who achieve the highest academic attainment (minimum 75%) in a UoLIC Pre-Master's programme who are: progressing from UoLIC onto a University of Liverpool master's programme.
Level of Study: Masters Degree
Type: Award
Value: £5,000 tuition fee reduction
Country of Study: United Kingdom
Application Procedure: No application necessary. The award will automatically be awarded to those who meet criteria.
Additional Information: No application necessary. The award will automatically be awarded to those who meet criteria www.liverpool.ac.uk/study/postgraduate-taught/finance/scholarships/scholarships/lic-excellence-award/

For further information contact:

Email: irro@liverpool.ac.uk

Liverpool Law School Hong Kong Scholarships

Purpose: The Liverpool Law School is offering two scholarships for new international students, awarded on merit.
Eligibility: Students from Hong Kong studying a LLM programme.
Type: Scholarship
Value: £1,000 each
Application Procedure: Students do NOT need to make an extra application for the Liverpool Law School Hong Kong Bursaries. All students who have registered for either a taught or research programme will be considered automatically.
No. of applicants last year: 2
Additional Information: Website: www.liverpool.ac.uk/study/postgraduate-taught/finance/scholarships/

Liverpool Law School LLM Bursaries

Purpose: Awards will help students with their tuition fees. They are offered to encourage the best students, from the United Kingdom, Europe and internationally, to join the expanding LLM programme
Eligibility: Home, EU and international students studying a LLM programme. Liverpool Law School LLM Bursaries will be awarded on the basis of merit. Academic performance in earlier degrees they have taken, as well as any other practical or intellectual achievements, will be taken into account. Academic references will also be considered.
Type: Bursary
Value: 1. Two bursaries worth £500 each for Home students 2. Two bursaries wroth £1,000 each for international students
Application Procedure: Students do NOT need to make an extra application for the Liverpool Law School LLM Bursaries. All students who have registered for the LLM will be considered automatically. The decision of Liverpool Law School on the award of the bursaries is final.
Additional Information: Website: www.liverpool.ac.uk/study/postgraduate-taught/finance/scholarships/scholarships/liverpool-law-school-llm-bursaries/

For further information contact:

Email: irro@liverpool.ac.uk

Marshall Scholarships

Purpose: To enable intellectually distinguished young Americans, their country's future leaders, to study in the United Kingdom. 1. To help Scholars gain an understanding and appreciation of contemporary Britain
Eligibility: To qualify, candidates should 1. Be citizens of the United States of America normally resident in the United States of America. 2. Hold a doctorate in a science or engineering subject by the time they take up their Fellowship
Type: Scholarship
Value: Full tuition fee waiver for a master
Country of Study: United Kingdom
Closing Date: 30 September
Additional Information: Apply via: www.marshallscholarship.org/applications/apply www.marshallscholarship.org/apply

For further information contact:

Email: apps@marshallscholarship.org

Ministry of Education and Training Vietnam Research Awards

Purpose: 5 awards for PhD students from Vietnam will be funded by the Ministry of Education and Training (MOET), Vietnam.
Eligibility: PhD students from Vietnam
Level of Study: Postgraduate, Research
Type: Award
Value: The awards will provide a 20% reduction in fees

Application Procedure: Apply Here: en.moet.gov.vn/Pages/home.aspx For more information, visit the Ministry of Education and Training Vietnam (MOET) website: en.moet.gov.vn/.
Contributor: The Ministry of Education and Training (MOET)
No. of applicants last year: 5
Additional Information: Website: www.liverpool.ac.uk/study/postgraduate-research/fees-and-funding/scholarships-and-awards/ministry-of-education-and-training-vietnam-research-awards/

Postgraduate Opportunity Bursary

Purpose: This bursary is available to UK University of Liverpool graduates who are progressing to a standard master's course, including MRes programmes, within two years of graduation from their undergraduate degree.
Eligibility: They must be beginning a new full-time or part-time postgraduate taught master's programme (including MRes programmes) in academic year 2024/25. ii) They must be an alumnus or alumna of the University of Liverpool having completed an undergraduate degree on the Liverpool campus no earlier than session 2022/23. iii) They must have been in receipt of one of the University's Widening Access Awards during their period of undergraduate studies at the University of Liverpool.
Level of Study: Graduate, Masters Degree
Type: Award
Value: £3,000
Country of Study: Any country
Application Procedure: Applicants will be automatically selected based on their previous receipt of any of the current widening access awards at UG level within the last two academic years prior to commencement of their PGT study. No separate application is necessary.
Additional Information: For more Details see website: www.liverpool.ac.uk/study/postgraduate-taught/finance/scholarships/scholarships/postgraduate-opportunity-bursary/

For further information contact:

Tel: (44) 151 794 2000

Postgraduate Progression Award - International Students

Eligibility: The Postgraduate Progression Award is not eligible to the following groups of students: 1. Students registered with the Liverpool School of Tropical Medicine. 2. Students transferring to the University of Liverpool from partnership institutions where an alternative fee payment or scholarship arrangement has been made. For more details see website
Level of Study: Postgraduate
Type: Award
Value: £2,500 reduction in tuition fees for the first year of study
Application Procedure: You do not need to make an application to receive the Postgraduate Progression Award as it will be automatically allocated to all eligible students.
Additional Information: Website: www.liverpool.ac.uk/study/postgraduate-taught/finance/scholarships/scholarships/postgraduate-progression-award-international-students/

Postgraduate Progression Award - UK Students

Purpose: If you're a current University of Liverpool undergraduate or alumni from the UK progressing to either full or part-time new postgraduate taught programme you're eligible to receive our Postgraduate Progression Award a £1,000 reduction in tuition fees.
Eligibility: 1. Students registered with the Liverpool School of Tropical Medicine. 2. Students transferring to the University of Liverpool from partnership institutions where an alternative fee payment or scholarship arrangement has been made.
Level of Study: Graduate, Masters Degree, Postgraduate
Type: Award
Value: £1,000 reduction in tuition fees.
Frequency: Annual
Country of Study: Any country
Application Procedure: You do not need to make an application to receive the Postgraduate Progression Award as it will be automatically allocated to all eligible students.
Additional Information: Website: www.liverpool.ac.uk/study/postgraduate-taught/finance/scholarships/scholarships/postgraduate-progression-award-uk-students/

For further information contact:

Tel: (44) 151 794 2000

Sarah Barrow Bursary in Music

Purpose: The Sarah Barrow Bursary in Music is to be supportive of PG Home/UK students for whom the cost of continuing onto postgraduate study would be prohibitive.
Eligibility: 1. Applicants must be Home/UK students and able to demonstrate this. 2. Applicants are required to make a convincing case explaining why they need additional financial support. 3. Applicants are required to have applied for and successfully secured a place on the MMus performance

through the standard procedure. 4. Applicants are required to have achieved a minimum performance standard equivalent of a first class grade in their undergraduate third year final recital. University of Liverpool students who have successfully completed third year classical performance are not required to submit video performances or audition as these materials will already be on record. Candidates from outside the University will be required to submit a video of a 30 minute performance in the first instance. If appropriate they may also be invited to interview in person or online and/or required to undertake a quick study at the panel's request. For more Details see website
Level of Study: Masters Degree
Type: Bursary
Value: £6,000
Frequency: Annual
Application Procedure: Please download the Sarah Barrow Bursary for Music: www.liverpool.ac.uk/media/livacuk/schoolofthearts/documents/music/SBBMMusApplicationForm2023final.doc and return it to Ruth Minton: rkminton@liverpool.ac.uk
Closing Date: 8 July
Additional Information: For more information about the scheme or an informal discussion about the programme, please contact Ruth Minton. Details about the MMus programme can be found here: www.liverpool.ac.uk/study/postgraduate-taught/taught/music-mmus/overview/. Website: www.liverpool.ac.uk/music/study/postgraduate-taught/sarah-barrow-bursary/

For further information contact:

Email: rkminton@liverpool.ac.uk
Website: www.liverpool.ac.uk/media/livacuk/schoolofthearts/documents/music/SBBMMusApplicationForm2023final.doc

Scottish Power Scholarships

Purpose: Scottish Power is inviting future energy leaders to join their scholarship programme. The Scholarships Programme is designed to train top-calibre professionals in the energy sector, who are capable of contributing to the development of a sustainable energy model that meets the energy needs of society and promotes environmental protection.
Eligibility: Promote career opportunities available within the company Act as a STEM ambassador for the industry Introduce future scholarship applicants to the scheme Support any recruitment activities agreed on campus/virtually
Level of Study: Masters Degree, Postgraduate
Type: Scholarship
Value: £1,200 per month
Frequency: Annual
Country of Study: Any country
Application Procedure: The scholarships are for graduates and final-year students who have a permanent right to work in the UK after graduation. The following subjects are eligible: 1. Energy and Power Systems MSc (Eng) 2. Advanced Mechanical Engineering MSc 3. Environmental Assessment and Management MSc 4. Environmental and Climate Change MSc 5. Environmental Sciences MSc 6. Telecommunications and Wireless Systems MSc (Eng) 7. Big Data and High Performance Computing MSc 8. Geographic Data Science MSc 9. Sustainable Civil and Structural Engineering MSc
Additional Information: website: www.liverpool.ac.uk/study/postgraduate-taught/finance/scholarships/scholarships/scottish-power-scholarships/

For further information contact:

Tel: (44) 151 794 2000
Website: www.scottishpower.com/pages/scottishpower_foundation_scholarships.aspx

The Aziz Foundation Scholarship

Purpose: The University of Liverpool together with the Aziz Foundation are offering master's scholarships to support British Muslims who are dedicated to bringing positive change to society and have career aspirations in media and journalism, technology, sustainability and the environment, law, policy (excluding health policy) and creative content.
Eligibility: You are required to meet all of the following requirements: 1. Be eligible for Home fees status at the University 2. Be active within a Muslim community and demonstrate intimate knowledge of issues affecting British Muslim communities 3. Be able to demonstrate long-term commitment to community/societal development within Britain 4. Demonstrate that you require financial assistance in order to undertake a master's degree.
Level of Study: Masters Degree, Postgraduate
Type: Scholarship
Value: The scholarship will cover your home UK postgraduate taught programme tuition fees.
Application Procedure: Applications are submitted online, via a portal on the Aziz Foundation website: www.azizfoundation.org.uk/scholarships-application/. You will need to demonstrate active engagement in British Muslim communities, a long-term commitment to community/societal development, and a need for financial assistance in order to undertake a master's degree.
Closing Date: 30 June

Additional Information: If you have questions about the award please contact Deonne Hill, Widening Participation and Outreach Manager, via: wpscholarships@liverpool.ac.uk website: www.liverpool.ac.uk/study/postgraduate-taught/finance/scholarships/scholarships/aziz-foundation-scholarship/

For further information contact:

Email: wpscholarships@liverpool.ac.uk

The Kick It Out Scholarship

Purpose: Sky and Kick It Out have partnered with the University of Liverpool Management School to offer Scholarships to four Football Industries MBA offer holders from under-represented ethnic groups in 2024/25; as part of Sky UK's 3-year partnership with anti-racism organisation Kick it Out.
Eligibility: Please check your eligibility before making an application for this scholarship. Awards may be withdrawn if we later become aware that successful students have not met the eligibility criteria or have provided false information. Applicants must satisfy ALL of the following to be considered for this scholarship: 1. Permanently reside in the UK. 2. You must have been assessed for fee status as a 'home' student, or expect to be assessed as a 'home student'. 3. Be applying for the Football Industries MBA programme, to commence study in the 2024-25 academic year. 4. Be from an under-represented ethnic group.
Level of Study: MBA
Type: Scholarship
Value: £25,500 per year
Frequency: Annual
Country of Study: Any country
Application Procedure: Students who meet the criteria should declare their interest when applying for the Football Industries MBA Programme, as part of their personal statement. The personal statement encourages students to write between 100-200 words for each of the following sections: 1. your interest and experience in this subject area, 2. your reasons for choosing this particular programme, 3. your future aim or career plan, 4. how the programme of study enables you to achieve this, 5. why you should be considered for the Kick it Out Scholarship. Apply Here: www.liverpool.ac.uk/study/postgraduate-taught/taught/football-industries-mba/overview/
Closing Date: 30 April
No. of applicants last year: 4
Additional Information: website: www.liverpool.ac.uk/study/postgraduate-taught/finance/scholarships/scholarships/kick-it-out-scholarship/

For further information contact:

Tel: (44) 151 794 2000

The University of Liverpool and China Scholarship Council Awards

Purpose: The University of Liverpool and the China Scholarship Council are proud to be able to offer a joint scholarship programme for postgraduate research students.
Eligibility: In order to be eligible for these awards applicants must: 1. Be a Chinese national 2. Meet the requirements of the CSC – please see their website 3. Have applied for a place to study 4. Have completed bachelors or masters degree before the agreed start of PhD study.
Level of Study: Masters Degree, Postgraduate
Type: Scholarship
Value: Covers all tuition fees and research fees up to £1250 per annum
Length of Study: Up to 4 years
Application Procedure: For application process see website. CSC application form: www.liverpool.ac.uk/media/livacuk/study/CSCUniversityApplication2023.docx
Closing Date: 31 January
Contributor: The University of Liverpool & China Scholarship Council
Additional Information: For further information about applying for the scholarship, please contact scholarships@liverpool.ac.uk. Website: www.liverpool.ac.uk/study/postgraduate-research/fees-and-funding/scholarships-and-awards/the-university-of-liverpool-and-china-scholarship-council-awards/

For further information contact:

Email: scholarships@liverpool.ac.uk

Turkish Ministry of Education

Eligibility: Students from Turkey wishing to study at postgraduate taught and research levels.
Level of Study: Postgraduate, Research
Type: Award
Value: 20% discount on Master's and Postgraduate Research tuition fees, excluding bench fees.
Application Procedure: See meb.gov.tr/ for more information
Additional Information: Website: www.liverpool.ac.uk/study/postgraduate-taught/finance/scholarships/

U of L Graduate Association Hong Kong & Tung Postgraduate Scholarships

Purpose: The University is able to offer competitive scholarships for offer holders from Hong Kong, SAR and PR China for both postgraduate taught master's and research programmes.
Eligibility: 1. Students from Hong Kong or mainland China. 2. Students studying a postgraduate taught master's or research programme.
Level of Study: Masters Degree, Postgraduate, Research
Type: Scholarship
Value: Up to £5,000 or up to £10,000
Application Procedure: More about how to apply for this scholarship: www.livcrpool.ac.uk/student-administration/research-students/fees-and-funding/scholarships/tung/. Apply Here: www.liverpool.ac.uk/student-administration/research-students/fees-and-funding/scholarships/tung/
Additional Information: Website: www.liverpool.ac.uk/study/postgraduate-taught/finance/scholarships/scholarships/university-of-liverpool-hong-kong-graduate-association-scholarships/

For further information contact:

Website: www.liverpool.ac.uk/student-administration/research-students/fees-and-funding/scholarships/tung/

ULMS Attainment Award

Eligibility: Offered to Home* applicants for on-campus 2024-25 ULMS MSc programmes who have the equivalent of a First Class degree. *UK and ROI (More information: www.liverpool.ac.uk/study/undergraduate/applying/brexit/)
Level of Study: Postgraduate (MSc)
Type: Award
Value: £2,000
Application Procedure: No separate application is needed. Eligible applicants will receive the award automatically.
Additional Information: Note: This award can be combined with any ULMS or centrally-awarded funding that the applicant is eligible for, up to a maximum of a 50% fee discount. Please consult the central Scholarships and financial support pages: www.liverpool.ac.uk/study/postgraduate-taught/finance/scholarships/. Website: www.liverpool.ac.uk/management/study/postgraduate-taught/scholarships/

ULMS MBA Excellence Scholarship

Eligibility: Home*/Overseas applicants on the Liverpool MBA and the Football Industries MBA on-campus programmes. Applicants that have achieved academic and professional excellence will be considered. Candidates must hold at least a high 2:1 (65+% in their undergraduate or postgraduate degree); have four or more years of professional/managerial experience and be able to demonstrate leadership potential. For more Details: www.liverpool.ac.uk/student-administration/fees-and-finance/fee-status/definition-of-an-eu-student/
Level of Study: MBA
Type: Scholarship
Value: 50% and 30% waivers available
Application Procedure: Eligible programme applicants will be automatically considered. No separate application is necessary.
Additional Information: Website: www.liverpool.ac.uk/management/study/mba/scholarships/

ULMS MBA Latin America Excellence Scholarship

Eligibility: 1. Awarded to Latin American applicants on the Liverpool MBA programme and Football Industries MBA programme on campus programmes. 2. Eligible nationalities are: Argentina, Bolivia, Brazil, Chile, Colombia, Costa Rica, Cuba, Dominican Republic, Ecuador, El Salvador, Guatemala, Honduras, Mexico, Nicaragua, Panama, Paraguay, Peru, Puerto Rico, Uruguay, and Venezuela. 3. Applicants that have achieved academic and professional excellence will be considered. Candidates must hold at least a high 2:1 (65+% in their undergraduate or postgraduate degree); have four or more years of professional/managerial experience and be able to demonstrate leadership potential.
Level of Study: MBA
Type: Scholarship
Value: 50% fee wavier
Application Procedure: No separate application is necessary, the award is applied automatically.
Additional Information: Website: www.liverpool.ac.uk/management/study/mba/scholarships/

ULMS Progress to Postgraduate Award

Eligibility: 1. Offered to all current University of Liverpool undergraduate students (Home* and International) from any discipline, who want to progress onto one of the Management School's MSc programmes beginning in autumn 2024. 2. Full-time and part-time applicants are eligible. 3. Please visit our ULMS Progress to Postgraduate: www.liverpool.ac.uk/management/study/postgraduate-taught/progress-to-postgraduate/ information pages for more details about this award. *UK and ROI (More information: www.liverpool.ac.uk/study/undergraduate/applying/brexit/)
Level of Study: Postgraduate (MSc)

Type: Award
Value: £1,000
Application Procedure: No separate application is needed. Eligible applicants will receive the award automatically.
Additional Information: Note: This award can be combined with any ULMS or centrally-awarded funding that the applicant is eligible for, up to a maximum of a 50% fee discount, including the Postgraduate Progression Award (PPA) or Postgraduate Opportunity Bursary. Website: www.liverpool.ac.uk/management/study/postgraduate-taught/scholarships/

ULMS Southeast Asia Excellence Scholarship

Purpose: These Scholarships are allocated at the discretion of the University of Liverpool and the decision is final.
Eligibility: Candidates are considered for this award based on their academic excellence and must hold, or be on track to obtain, at least a high 21 (65+%) in their undergraduate degree, including marks of 60+% in modules relevant to their MSc programme. Work experience relevant to the programme (paid, internship, shadowing or voluntary positions) would be advantageous, as would previously studying at a highly ranked university.
Level of Study: Postgraduate
Type: Scholarship
Value: Part fee waiver (50%)
Frequency: Annual
Country of Study: Any country
Additional Information: www.liverpool.ac.uk/management/study/postgraduate-taught/scholarships/

For further information contact:

Tel: (44) 151 794 2000

ULMS West Africa Excellence Scholarship

Purpose: These Scholarships are allocated at the discretion of the University of Liverpool and the decision is final.
Eligibility: Candidates are considered for this award based on their academic excellence, CV, and personal statement.
Level of Study: Postgraduate
Type: Scholarship
Value: Part fee waiver (50%)
Frequency: Annual
Country of Study: Any country
Additional Information: www.liverpool.ac.uk/management/study/postgraduate-taught/scholarships/

For further information contact:

Tel: (44) 151 794 2000

ULMS Women in Football Scholarship

Eligibility: 1. Home*/Overseas Female applicants to the Football Industries MBA programme. 2. Applicants that have achieved academic and professional excellence will be considered. Candidates must hold at least a high 2:1 (65+% in their undergraduate or postgraduate degree); have four or more years of professional/managerial experience and be able to demonstrate leadership potential.
Level of Study: MBA
Type: Scholarship
Value: 50% Scholarships available
Application Procedure: Eligible programme applicants will be considered. No separate scholarship application is necessary.
No. of applicants last year: 2
Additional Information: Website: www.liverpool.ac.uk/management/study/mba/scholarships/

University of Liverpool Commonwealth Postgraduate Bursary

Purpose: The University of Liverpool Commonwealth Postgraduate Bursary fee reduction for students from Commonwealth countries new to studying at the University of Liverpool on master's programmes
Eligibility: Students from Commonwealth countries.
Type: Bursary
Value: £2,500 fee reduction for Commonwealth for students studying all subjects. Please note: students eligible for this scholarhsip starting in January 2024 will be entitled to the 23/24 rate of £2,000
Country of Study: Any country
Application Procedure: No application necessary, automatically awarded to those who meet criteria.
Additional Information: Website: www.liverpool.ac.uk/study/postgraduate-taught/finance/scholarships/scholarships/university-of-liverpool-commonwealth-postgraduate-bursary/

For further information contact:

Email: irro@liverpool.ac.uk

University of Liverpool International College (UoLIC) Excellence Scholarship

Purpose: The University of Liverpool will award five University of Liverpool International College students, who achieve the highest academic excellence (minimum 75%) in their UoLIC Pre-Master's programme, the prestigious UoLIC Excellence scholarship.

Eligibility: Five students who achieve the highest academic attainment (minimum 75%) in a UoLIC Pre-Master's programme who are: progressing from UoLIC onto a University of Liverpool master's programme.
Level of Study: Masters Degree
Type: Scholarship
Value: £5,000 tuition fee reduction
Application Procedure: No application necessary. The award will automatically be awarded to those who meet criteria.
Additional Information: Website: www.liverpool.ac.uk/study/postgraduate-taught/finance/scholarships/scholarships/lic-excellence-award/

University of Liverpool International College (UoLIC) Impact Progression Scholar

Purpose: In partnership with Kaplan, the University of Liverpool is offering up to 7 x £3,000 scholarships for students progressing from the University of Liverpool International College in 2024.
Eligibility: To be eligible for our Impact Progression Scholarships, students must apply for one of the Kaplan Impact Scholarships: study.kaplanpathways.com/special-scholarships/?utm_medium=email&utm_source=SFMC&utm_campaign=B2B-AG-Commercial-UKAgentDigitalDigest41 demonstrating their commitment to making an impact across issues of importance to the University and Kaplan. Themes include: 1. Sustainability 2. Women in STEM 3. Community 4. Career Focus (Employability)
Type: Scholarship
Value: £3,000 tuition fee reduction
Application Procedure: Students must apply for the Kaplan Impact Scholarships through the University of Liverpool International College: study.kaplanpathways.com/special-scholarships/?utm_medium=email&utm_source=SFMC&utm_campaign=B2B-AG-Commercial-UKAgentDigitalDigest41.
Closing Date: 15 April
Additional Information: Website: www.liverpool.ac.uk/study/postgraduate-taught/finance/scholarships/scholarships/lic-impact-progression-scholarships/#d.en.1376407

Vice-Chancellor's International Attainment Scholarship

Purpose: The Vice-Chancellor's International Attainment Scholarship (PGT) rewards high-achieving international students (including students from the EU) starting a postgraduate taught master's programme in 2024.
Eligibility: To be eligible for this award you must: 1. be liable to pay full tuition fees at the overseas/international rate 2. be starting a new postgraduate master's programme in academic year 2024 at the campus in Liverpool. 3. achieve a first class degree or equivalent qualification - as defined by the University of Liverpool and listed here: www.liv.ac.uk/study/international/first-class/. 4. The award will not be available to students who have studied at Liverpool International College, XJTLU or completed their Undergraduate degree at Liverpool, as these students have their own scholarship provision.
Level of Study: Masters Degree, Postgraduate
Type: Scholarship
Value: £2,500 tuition fee reduction
Application Procedure: You do not need to make an application to receive this scholarship. The Scholarship will be automatically allocated to all eligible students.
Additional Information: Website: www.liverpool.ac.uk/study/postgraduate-taught/finance/scholarships/scholarships/vc-international-attainment-scholarship/

Vice-Chancellor's International Attainment Scholarship for China

Purpose: This application form should only be used to apply for the above Scholarship at the University of Liverpool. Please read the following notes carefully before completing the application form.
Eligibility: Applicants must meet all the conditions as below: 1. Domiciled in PR China when applications are made 2. Have Bachelor's Degree awarded or to be awarded by a Project 211 or Project 985 university in PR China with a minimum average grade of 80% overall 3. Have accepted and paid deposit on one of the Postgraduate Taught Programmes at the University of Liverpool's campus 4. Are self-financed (which means tuition fees are to be paid by students or the parents).
Level of Study: Postgraduate
Type: Scholarship
Value: 1 (one) Full scholarship; 2 (two) £10,000 scholarships; 5 (five) £5,000 scholarships; 10 (ten) £1,000 scholarships
Frequency: Annual
Country of Study: Any country
Application Procedure: Application form: www.liverpool.ac.uk/media/livacuk/study/international/money-and-scholarships/china-vc-scholarship-application-form.pdf. Please send the completed application form in PDF file to chinarep@liv.ac.uk
No. of awards offered: 18
Additional Information: www.liverpool.ac.uk/study/postgraduate-taught/finance/scholarships/scholarships/vc-international-attainment-china/

For further information contact:

Tel: (44) 151 794 2000
Email: chinarep@liv.ac.uk

University of Manchester

Oxford Road, Manchester M13 9PL, United Kingdom.

Tel: (44) 161 306 6000
Email: hr@manchester.ac.uk
Website: www.manchester.ac.uk

A* STAR PhD Programme

Subjects: Faculty of Science and Engineering
Purpose: This programme is open to across all research areas, and will be of interest to students of the highest calibre who are keen to undertake a research project in Manchester and Singapore as part of the A*STAR Research Attachment Programme (ARAP).
Eligibility: Academic requirements: To be considered for this award you must: 1. Hold (or be about to obtain) a first class or upper second class honours degree (or international equivalent) in a related subject area. 2. Ideally hold a master's-level qualification at merit or distinction (or international equivalent), although this is not compulsory. 3. Meet academic eligibility criteria (inc. English language), if you are an international student. Nationality restrictions: 1. This funding is available to all nationalities. Other eligibility criteria: 1. To ensure the diversity of students studying at A*STAR institutions, A*STAR may apply stricter criteria to certain nationalities that may be over-represented in Singapore. As part of the offer/nomination process, The University of Manchester will select the most outstanding candidates for this programme.
Level of Study: Postgraduate, Research
Type: Scholarship
Value: 1. Tuition fees at the international rate 2. Annual maintenance stipend equivalent to UKRI minimum stipend rate 3. Airfare grants 4. Settling in allowance (Singapore) 5. Medical insurance 6. For international applicants funding will cover tuition fees and stipend only.
Length of Study: 4 years
Application Procedure: Visit our website: www.bmh.manchester.ac.uk/study/research/astar/#apply to check that you are eligbile to apply and find out more about the application process. Application form: www.bmh.manchester.ac.uk/study/research/astar/#apply
Closing Date: 24 March
Contributor: The University of Manchester Faculty of Science and Engineering
No. of applicants last year: 6
Additional Information: Contact details for enquiries: Sandra Kershaw, Recruitment and Admissions Manager, Tel: 0161 306 4826, Email: fse-pgr-admissions@manchester.ac.uk Website: www.manchester.ac.uk/study/postgraduate-research/funding/opportunities/display/?id=00000470&offset=0&sort=name&sortdir=ascending&subjectArea=&nationality=&submit=

For further information contact:

Tel: (44) 161 306 4826
Email: fse-pgr-admissions@manchester.ac.uk

Advanced Biomedical Materials CDT

Subjects: Faculty of Science and Engineering
Purpose: Our aim is to train the next generation of internationally leading postdoctoral engineers who will enable innovation between industry, clinicians and academics to address areas of national and international need
Eligibility: Academic requirements: To be considered for this award you must: 1. Hold (or be about to obtain) a UK undergraduate honours degree (or international equivalent) or a first degree with an additional master's degree (or international equivalent). 2. For international students, you must also have a minimum of 6.5 in each category with an overall average of 7.0 if you are taking the International English Language Testing System (IELTS). Nationality restrictions: This funding is available to all nationalities.
Level of Study: Postgraduate, Research
Type: Studentship
Value: 1. UKRI rate stipend and fees, international fees can be waived for successful applicants under UKRI relaxation scheme. 2. Generous travel and consumables allowance to support project of £23,000.
Length of Study: 4 years
Application Procedure: For application information please visit our Advanced Biomedical Materials CDT website: www.advanced-biomedical-materials-cdt.manchester.ac.uk/.
Closing Date: 24 February
Contributor: The Engineering and Physical Sciences Research Council (EPSRC)
No. of applicants last year: 12
Additional Information: Contact details for enquiries, Advanced Biomedical Materials CDT, Tel: (44) 161 306 5942, Email: abmcdt@manchester.ac.uk Website: www.manchester.ac.uk/study/postgraduate-research/funding/opportunities/display/?id=00000471&offset=0&sort=name&sortdir=ascending&subjectArea=&nationality=&submit=

AHRC North West Consortium Doctoral Training Partnership (NWCDTP) in the School of Arts, Languages and Cultures

Subjects: Faculty of Humanities, School of Arts, Languages and Cultures
Eligibility: 1. This award is available to existing postgraduate students. 2. This award is available to postgraduate research students in year one, applying for funding for years two and three of a PhD.
Level of Study: Postgraduate, Research
Type: Studentship
Value: covers tuition fees, maintenance stipend (the annual maintenance stipend rate for 2023-24 is £17,668) and opportunity to apply for additional funding towards fieldwork and conference costs. Additional disability allowance can be provided where appropriate. Students opting to study part-time will receive a pro rata maintenance stipend.
Length of Study: 2 - 3.5 years
Frequency: Annual
Country of Study: Any country
Application Procedure: Please refer to the application guidance on the NWCDTP website: www.nwcdtp.ac.uk/current-students/funding-prospective-students/. Application form: www.nwcdtp.ac.uk/current-students/funding-prospective-students/
Closing Date: 3 February
Contributor: AHRC North West Consortium Doctoral Training Partnership
Additional Information: Contact details for enquiries: Miss Rachel Corbishley, Postgraduate Admissions Administrator, Email: phdfunding-salc@manchester.ac.uk Website: www.manchester.ac.uk/study/postgraduate-research/funding/opportunities/display/?id=00000328&offset=0&sort=name&sortdir=ascending&subjectArea=Any&nationality=United%20Kingdom&submit=Search

For further information contact:

Postgraduate Admissions Administrator, Oxford Rd, Manchester M13 9PL, United Kingdom.

Tel: (44) 161 306 6000
Email: phdfunding-salc@manchester.ac.uk

AHRC North West Consortium Doctoral Training Partnership in the School of Environment, Education and Development

Subjects: Faculty of Humanities, School of Environment, Education and Development
Eligibility: 1. For Academic requirements Please refer to the application guidance on the SEED website. 2. This funding is available to all nationalities. 3. This award is available to existing postgraduate students. 4. This award is available to postgraduate research students in year one, applying for funding for years two and three of a PhD.
Level of Study: Postgraduate, Research
Type: Studentship
Value: The award covers tuition fees, a maintenance stipend (the annual maintenance stipend for 2023-24 is £17,668), a research training support grant and an opportunity to apply for additional funding towards overseas fieldwork, difficult language training, overseas institutional visits and internships. An additional disability allowance can be provided where appropriate. Students opting to study part-time will receive a pro-rata maintenance stipend.
Length of Study: 24-48 months.
Country of Study: Any country
Application Procedure: Please refer to the application guidance on the NWCDTP website: www.manchester.ac.uk/study/postgraduate-research/funding/opportunities/display/www.nwcdtp.ac.uk/funding-prospective-students/. Application form: www.nwcdtp.ac.uk/prospective-students/
Closing Date: 5 February
Contributor: AHRC North West Consortium Doctoral Training Partnership
Additional Information: Contact details for enquiries: Christopher Kitchen, PGR Recruitment and Admissions Officer, Email: pgr-seedfunding@manchester.ac.uk Website: www.manchester.ac.uk/study/postgraduate-research/funding/opportunities/display/?id=00000329&offset=0&sort=name&sortdir=ascending&subjectArea=Any&nationality=United%20Kingdom&submit=Search

For further information contact:

PGR Recruitment and Admissions Officer, Oxford Rd, Manchester M13 9PL, United Kingdom.

Tel: (44) (0)161 275 0807
Email: pgr-seedfunding@manchester.ac.uk

Alliance Manchester Business School PhD Studentships

Subjects: Accounting and Finance Business and Management Science, Technology and Innovation Policy
Eligibility: 1. Applicants must have obtained a First or Upper Second Class Honours degree (or equivalent) and hold or expect to obtain a Masters level qualification with Distinction. English Language requirements (where required) are IELTS 7.0, TOEFL 100 (internet based test), or Pearson Test of

English (76 or above). 2. This funding is available to all nationalities. 3. Applicants must hold an offer of study at The University of Manchester before applying for this funding.
Level of Study: Postgraduate, Research
Type: Studentship
Value: Programme tuition fees and stipend of approx. £17,668 per year
Length of Study: Up to 4 years
Frequency: Annual
Country of Study: Any country
Application Procedure: To be considered for one of these awards, candidates should submit a PhD application and indicate that they wish to be considered for this funding opportunity. Application form: www.alliancembs.manchester.ac.uk/study/phd/how-to-apply-for-a-phd/
Closing Date: 4 January
Contributor: Alliance Manchester Business School
Additional Information: Website: www.manchester.ac.uk/study/postgraduate-research/funding/opportunities/display/?id=00000346&offset=0&sort=name&sortdir=ascending&subjectArea=Any&nationality=United%20Kingdom&submit=Search

For further information contact:

Doctoral Programmes Office.

Tel:	(44) (0)161 275 1200
Email:	ambs-pgresearch@manchester.ac.uk
Website:	www.alliancembs.manchester.ac.uk/study/phd/how-to-apply-for-a-phd/

Bell Burnell Graduate Scholarship Fund

Subjects: Department of Physics & Astronomy
Purpose: The Bell Burnell Graduate Scholarship Fund is a doctoral scholarship fund provided by the Institute of Physics to encourage greater diversity in physics.
Eligibility: Academic requirements: To be nominated for this external scholarship you must: 1. Hold (or be about to obtain) a minimum of a 2i class UK Masters honours degree, or international equivalent, or a First Class Bachelor degree with an additional Masters degree, or international equivalent. 2. Applicants with a First Class Bachelor degree, or international equivalent, with proven research experience may also be considered. Nationality restrictions: This funding is available to all nationalities. Other eligibility criteria: 1. This award is available to existing postgraduate students. 2. Applicants must hold an offer of study at The University of Manchester before applying for this funding. 3. You must fall within one of the following underrepresented groups: A. Women B. Students of Black-Carribean, Black-African and other minority ethnic (BAME) heritage C. Students with disabilities, or who require additional funding to support inclusive learning D. LGBT+ students C. A student from disadvantaged background who may struggle to find the levels of funding needed to complete their studies
Level of Study: Postgraduate, Research
Type: Scholarship
Value: maximum of £36k per student; or a top-up award to support additional costs that are needed to complete a fully funded PhD. The top-up awards will have a maximum value of £10k.
Length of Study: 4 years
Application Procedure: This scholarship works on a nomination basis, the lead supervisor will consider you for nomination and will support you through the process. It is important that you have had significant contact with the supervisory team during the application process and that they are aware that you wish to be considered for funding. Your application will then be considered by a departmental funding panel. In order to be considered, you must hold an academic offer for a place on one of our PhD programmes. It is therefore essential that you apply for a place on the PhD programme of your choice as early as possible.
Contributor: Institute of Physics
No. of applicants last year: 2
Additional Information: Contact details for enquiries, Institute of Physics - Bell Burnell Fund, Tel: (44)20 7470 4800, Email: bellburnellfund@iop.org Website: www.manchester.ac.uk/study/postgraduate-research/funding/opportunities/display/?id=00000490&offset=0&sort=name&sortdir=ascending&subjectArea=&nationality=&submit=

For further information contact:

Tel:	(44)20 7470 4800
Email:	bellburnellfund@iop.org

British Council Scholarships for Women in STEM

Purpose: The University of Manchester is proud to offer five fully-funded scholarships for female students from Bangladesh, India, Nepal, Pakistan and Sri Lanka completing specific master's courses in STEM.
Eligibility: 1. be a woman, or identify as a woman; 2. be a passport holder and permanent resident of Bangladesh, India, Nepal, Pakistan or Sri Lanka; 3. be in receipt of a conditional or unconditional offer for September 2024 entry to study on an eligible postgraduate course at The University of Manchester; 4. have not previously studied at degree level or higher in the UK or lived recently in the UK; 5. have completed all components of an undergraduate degree that will enable you to gain entry on to a postgraduate

programme at a UK university, and be due to start your postgraduate programme in the UK during 2024 by the time of registration;\ 6. meet or be working towards fulfilling the English language requirement stated in your offer by the stated deadline; 7. demonstrate a case for financial support; 8. return to your country of citizenship for a minimum of two years after your scholarship award has ended; 9. demonstrate that you are active in the field of study with work experience or with a proven interest in the course area you are applying for; 10. demonstrate plans for future contribution to capacity-building and socio-economic advancement through the benefits achieved after graduating and returning to your home country; 11. demonstrate a plan and passion to engage other women and girls in STEM from your home country; 12. agree to your personal data being shared with the British Council as a condition of applying for the bursary; 13. agree to maintain contact with the British Council and act as an ambassador for the UK and engage with activities as part of a British Council Scholarships for Women in STEM alumnus during and after your study in the UK. Any involvement in these activities during your study in the UK will take up no more than five hours per term.
Level of Study: Masters Degree
Type: Scholarship
Value: see website
Application Procedure: A scholarship application form will be emailed to all relevant offer-holders by the International Office.
Closing Date: 30 April
Additional Information: Website: www.manchester.ac.uk/study/international/finance-and-scholarships/funding/women-in-stem-scholarships/

CDT in Advanced Metallic Systems

Subjects: Faculty of Science and Engineering
Purpose: Study for a PhD or EngD in Advanced Metallic Systems to explore innovative materials and manufacturing routes to increase sustainability and performance.
Eligibility: Academic requirements: To be considered for this award you must: Hold (or be about to obtain) a first class or upper second class honours honours undergraduate degree (or international equivalent) in an engineering discipline or a STEM (science, technology, engineering, maths) subject. Nationality restrictions: This funding is available to all nationalities.
Level of Study: Postgraduate, Research
Type: Studentship
Value: 1. UKRI rate stipend and fees, stipend top up of up to £5,000 per year, international fees can be waived for successful applicants under UKRI relaxation scheme. 2. Generous travel and consumables allowance to support project
Length of Study: 4 years
Application Procedure: For application information please visit the CDT in Advanced Metallic Systems website: www.sheffield.ac.uk/metallicscdt.
Closing Date: 31 July
Contributor: The Engineering and Physical Sciences Research Council (EPSRC)
No. of applicants last year: 8
Additional Information: CDT in Advanced Metallic Systems, The University of Sheffield, Tel: (44) 114 222 2000, Email: enquiries@metallicscdt.co.uk Website: www.manchester.ac.uk/study/postgraduate-research/funding/opportunities/display/?id=00000475&offset=0&sort=name&sortdir=ascending&subjectArea=&nationality=&submit=

For further information contact:

Tel: (44) 114 222 2000
Email: enquiries@metallicscdt.co.uk

CDT in Aerosol Science

Subjects: Faculty of Science and Engineering
Purpose: The CDT in Aerosol Science gives you an opportunity to undertake leading research in aerosols, and will equip you with a unique mix of skills and experiences for your future career.
Eligibility: Academic requirements: To be considered for this award you must: Depending on the subject area, hold (or be about to obtain) a first class or upper second class honours honours undergraduate degree (or international equivalent) in an area of physical science, engineering or biological science. Nationality restrictions: This funding is available to all nationalities. Application procedure: For application information please visit the CDT in Aerosol Science website: www.aerosol-cdt.ac.uk/.
Level of Study: Postgraduate, Research
Type: Studentship
Value: 1. UKRI rate stipend and fees, international fees can be waived for successful applicants under UKRI relaxation scheme. 2. Generous travel and consumables allowance to support project.
Length of Study: 4 years
Application Procedure: For application information please visit the CDT in Aerosol Science website: www.aerosol-cdt.ac.uk/.
Closing Date: 31 January
Contributor: The Engineering and Physical Sciences Research Council (EPSRC)
No. of applicants last year: 8

Additional Information: Contact details for enquiries, CDT in Aerosol Science, The University of Bristol, Tel: (44) 117 394 1649, Email: aerosol-science@bristol.ac.uk Website: www.manchester.ac.uk/study/postgraduate-research/funding/opportunities/display/?id=00000479&offset=0&sort=name&sortdir=ascending&subjectArea=&nationality=&submit=

For further information contact:

Tel: (44) 117 394 1649
Email: aerosol-science@bristol.ac.uk

CDT in Biodesign Engineering

Subjects: Faculty of Science and Engineering
Purpose: The CDT in BioDesign Engineering aims to train the next generation of leaders at the interface of biology, engineering, physical and data sciences.
Eligibility: Academic requirements: To be considered for this award you must: 1. Hold (or be about to obtain) a first class or upper second class honours honours undergraduate degree (or international equivalent). 2. Meet the English language requirements of Imperial College. Nationality restrictions: This funding is available to all nationalities.
Level of Study: Postgraduate, Research
Type: Studentship
Value: 1. UKRI rate stipend and fees, international fees can be waived for successful applicants under UKRI relaxation scheme. 2. Generous travel and consumables allowance to support project of £22,500.
Length of Study: 4 years
Application Procedure: Application procedure: For application information please visit the CDT in Biodesign Engineering website: www.imperial.ac.uk/synthetic-biology/cdt-biodesign-engineering/.
Closing Date: 31 January
Contributor: The Engineering and Physical Sciences Research Council (EPSRC)
No. of applicants last year: 10
Additional Information: Contact details for enquiries: CDT in BioDesign Engineering, Imperial College London, Tel: (44)20 7589 5111, Email: cdt-biodesign-eng@imperial.ac.uk Website: www.manchester.ac.uk/study/postgraduate-research/funding/opportunities/display/?id=00000477&offset=0&sort=name&sortdir=ascending&subjectArea=&nationality=&submit=

For further information contact:

Tel: (44)20 7589 5111
Email: cdt-biodesign-eng@imperial.ac.uk

CDT in Compound Semiconductor Manufacturing

Subjects: Faculty of Science and Engineering
Purpose: The CDT in Compound Semiconductor Manufacturing (CSM) is led by Cardiff University in partnership with the University of Manchester, University of Sheffield, and University College London.
Eligibility: Academic requirements: To be considered for this award you must: 1. Hold (or be about to obtain) a first class or upper second class honours undergraduate degree (or international equivalent) in physics, electronic or electrical engineering, or other relevant STEM subjects. 2. Have an interest in compound semiconductors and enthusiasm for the group approach. 3. Applicants with a lower second class honours undergraduate degree in physics, electronic or electrical engineering, or other relevant STEM subjects may be considered if they possess a merit or distinction at Masters-level study and/or other relevant qualifications or industry experience. Nationality restrictions: This funding is available to all nationalities.
Level of Study: Postgraduate, Research
Type: Studentship
Value: 1. UKRI rate stipend and fees, international fees can be waived for successful applicants under UKRI relaxation scheme. 2. Generous travel and consumables allowance to support project.
Length of Study: 4 years
Application Procedure: For application information please visit the CDT in Compound Semiconductor Manufacturing website: www.cdt-compound-semiconductor.org/.
Closing Date: 31 July
Contributor: The Engineering and Physical Sciences Research Council (EPSRC)
Additional Information: CDT in Compound Semiconductor Manufacturing, Cardiff University, Tel: (44) 29 2251 1593, Email: semiconductors-cdt@cardiff.ac.uk Website: www.manchester.ac.uk/study/postgraduate-research/funding/opportunities/display/?id=00000478&offset=0&sort=name&sortdir=ascending&subjectArea=&nationality=&submit=

For further information contact:

Tel: (44) 29 2251 1593
Email: semiconductors-cdt@cardiff.ac.uk

CDT in Future Innovation in NDE

Subjects: Faculty of Science and Engineering
Purpose: The FIND-CDT is a leading international centre of excellence that provides doctoral training in sensing, imaging and analysis for the vital field of Non-Destructive Evaluation (NDE).

Eligibility: Academic requirements: To be considered for this award you must: Hold (or be about to obtain) a good first class, upper second class honours honours undergraduate degree or master's (or international equivalent) in engineering or physical science. Nationality restrictions: This funding is available to all nationalities.
Level of Study: Postgraduate, Research
Type: Studentship
Value: 1. Tuition fees and stipend to cover living costs provided by EPSRC (UKRI rate stipend plus £1,500) 2. EngD students will receive a generous further top-up from their sponsor company of at least £5,000 a year.
Length of Study: 4 years
Application Procedure: For application information please visit the CDT in Future Innovation in NDE website: www.find-cdt.ac.uk/.
Contributor: The Engineering and Physical Sciences Research Council (EPSRC)
No. of applicants last year: 10
Additional Information: Contact details for enquiries, CDT in Future Innovation in NDE, The University of Bristol, Tel: (44) 117 394 1649, Email: FIND-CDT@Bristol.ac.uk Website: www.manchester.ac.uk/study/postgraduate-research/funding/opportunities/display/?id=00000480&offset=0&sort=name&sortdir=ascending&subjectArea=&nationality=&submit=

CDT in the Science and Technology of Fusion Energy

Subjects: Faculty of Science and Engineering
Purpose: The Centre for Doctoral Training in the Science and Technology of Fusion Energy is a collaboration between five of the UK's top universities (Durham University, The University of Liverpool, The University of Manchester, The University of Oxford and The University of York), working with a range of non-academic partners to train four cohorts of PhD students.
Eligibility: Academic requirements: To be considered for this award you must: Hold (or be about to obtain) a first class or upper second class honours honours undergraduate degree (or international equivalent). You do not require in-depth knowledge of fusion when you apply. Nationality restrictions: This funding is available to all nationalities.
Level of Study: Postgraduate, Research
Type: Studentship
Value: 1. UKRI rate stipend and fees, international fees can be waived for successful applicants under UKRI relaxation scheme. 2. Generous travel and consumables allowance to support project.
Length of Study: 4 years
Application Procedure: For application information please visit the CDT in Science and Technlogy of Fusion Energy website: fusion-cdt.ac.uk/.
Closing Date: 31 January
No. of applicants last year: 2
Additional Information: Contact details for enquiries: CDT in the Science and Technology of Fusion Energy, The University of York, Tel: (44)1904 324907, Email: outreach@fusion-cdt.ac.uk Website: www.manchester.ac.uk/study/postgraduate-research/funding/opportunities/display/?id=00000476&offset=0&sort=name&sortdir=ascending&subjectArea=&nationality=&submit=

China Scholarship Council - The University of Manchester Joint Scholarship for PhD Study in Alliance Manchester Business School

Subjects: Faculty of Humanities, Alliance Manchester Business School
Eligibility: Academic requirements: Candidates must meet the academic requirements for admission to the selected doctoral programme in Alliance Manchester Business School. Please see programmes website: www.alliancembs.manchester.ac.uk/study/phd/entry-requirements/ for more details. Nationality restrictions: This funding is available to students from: 1. China. Other eligibility criteria 1. Candidates will be citizens and permanent residents of the People's Republic of China at the time of application; overseas Chinese students may be eligible for application subject to CSC policy at the time; (CSC publicises the policy in October or November every year) 2. Successful candidates must return to China upon completion of their studies and/or research 3. Candidates must hold an unconditional offer from The University of Manchester. They must fulfil the relevant academic entry requirements set by their chosen School at The University of Manchester, including a high level of English language proficiency. 4. Candidates should satisfy the selection criteria set out by CSC
Level of Study: Postgraduate, Research
Type: Scholarship
Value: Tuition fees, living allowance, airfare and visa and passport application fees.
Length of Study: Three years
Application Procedure: Please submit your application via The University of Manchester online application form: www.manchester.ac.uk/study/postgraduate-research/admissions/how-to-apply/ with your supporting documents. Application form: www.alliancembs.manchester.ac.uk/study/phd/how-to-apply-for-a-phd/
Closing Date: 16 January

Additional Information: Website: www.manchester.ac.uk/study/postgraduate-research/funding/opportunities/display/?id=00000343&offset=0&sort=name&sortdir=ascending&subjectArea=&nationality=&submit=

For further information contact:

Website: www.alliancembs.manchester.ac.uk/study/phd/how-to-apply-for-a-phd/

China Scholarship Council - The University of Manchester Joint Scholarship for PhD Study in the School of Arts, Languages and Cultures

Subjects: Faculty of Humanities, School of Arts, Languages and Cultures
Eligibility: Academic requirements: Candidates must meet the academic requirements for admission to the selected doctoral programme in the School of Arts, Languages and Cultures. Please see programmes website: www.alc.manchester.ac.uk/study/postgraduate-research/programmes/ for more details. Nationality restrictions: This funding is available to students from: China. Other eligibility criteria: For full details on eligibility, please visit: www.manchester.ac.uk/study/international/country-specific-information/china-mainland/scholarships/#country-profile
Level of Study: Postgraduate, Research
Type: Scholarship
Value: Tuition fees
Length of Study: Three years
Application Procedure: You can apply online at www.manchester.ac.uk/study/postgraduate-research/admissions/how-to-apply/
Closing Date: 16 January
Additional Information: Website: www.manchester.ac.uk/study/postgraduate-research/funding/opportunities/display/?id=00000334&offset=0&sort=name&sortdir=ascending&subjectArea=&nationality=&submit=

For further information contact:

Email: phdfunding-salc@manchester.ac.uk

China Scholarship Council - The University of Manchester Joint Scholarship for PhD Study in the School of Environment, Education and Development

Subjects: Faculty of Humanities, School of Environment, Education and Development
Eligibility: 1. Academic requirements: Candidates must meet the academic requirements for admission to the selected doctoral programme in the School of Environment, Education and Development. Please see programmes website for more details. 2. Nationality restrictions: This funding is available to students from: China. 3. Other eligibility criteria: A. Candidates will be citizens and permanent residents of the People's Republic of China at the time of application; overseas Chinese students may be eligible for application subject to CSC policy at the time; (CSC publicises the policy in October or November every year) B. Successful candidates must return to China upon completion of their studies and/or research C. Candidates must hold an unconditional offer from The University of Manchester. They must fulfil the relevant academic entry requirements set by their chosen School at The University of Manchester, including a high level of English language proficiency as outlined on the University's website. D. Candidates should satisfy the selection criteria set out by CSC
Level of Study: Postgraduate, Research
Type: Scholarship
Value: Tuition fees, living allowance, airfare and visa and passport application fees
Length of Study: Three years
Application Procedure: Candidates should submit an online application: www.manchester.ac.uk/study/postgraduate-research/admissions/how-to-apply/#application for admission to The University of Manchester
Closing Date: 16 January
Contributor: The University of Manchester and China Scholarship Council
Additional Information: Contact details for enquiries: Christopher Kitchen, Postgraduate Research Recruitment and Admissions, Email: pgr-seedfunding@manchester.ac.uk Website: www.manchester.ac.uk/study/postgraduate-research/funding/opportunities/display/?id=00000335&offset=0&sort=name&sortdir=ascending&subjectArea=&nationality=&submit=

Commonwealth Scholarships and Fellowships Plan (CSFP) General Scholarship

Subjects: The University of Manchester
Eligibility: 1. Academic requirements: Upper second class honours degree or equivalent. 2. Nationality restrictions: This funding is available to students from the Commonwealth. 3. Other eligibility criteria: A. Applicants must hold an offer of study at The University of Manchester before applying for this funding. B. Open to Commonwealth citizens, refugees or British protected persons permanently resident in any Commonwealth country other then the UK. There are additional requirements for awards involving clinical training in medicine and dentistry. The Commission may require candidates to undertake the IELTS English language test as a condition of

eligibility. The Commission or host institution in the UK may require a candidate to take particular English tests and/or training in English. Some subjects and modes of study may be available/restricted depending on the award.
Level of Study: Postgraduate, Research
Type: Studentship
Value: Varies depending on type of award.
Length of Study: Varies depending on type of award.
Frequency: Annual
Application Procedure: Applicants should contact the national agency in their home country for information about how to apply: cscuk.fcdo.gov.uk/scholarships-filter-search/
Contributor: Commonwealth Scholarships and Fellowships Plan (CSFP)
No. of applicants last year: 750
Additional Information: Website: www.manchester.ac.uk/study/postgraduate-research/funding/opportunities/display/?id=00000019&offset=0&sort=name&sortdir=ascending&subjectArea=&nationality=&submit=

CONACyT Mexico Scholarships

Eligibility: Academic requirements: 1. CONACyT set the academic requirement for their scholarships. The usual promedio required by applicants is 8.5 in the Mexican system. 2. CONACyT will consider most subjects for funding, with the exception of Arts and Business. Nationality restrictions: This funding is available to students from: 1. Mexico. Other eligibility criteria: As determined by CONACyT.
Level of Study: Postgraduate, Research
Type: Studentship
Value: Varies - please see the CONACyT website for details.
Length of Study: Duration of Programme.
Application Procedure: Please see CONACyT website for details.
Contributor: CONACyT Mexico
No. of applicants last year: Variable
Additional Information: Contact details for enquiries, CONACyT, Tel: 55 5322 7708, Email: becascst@conacyt.mx Website: www.manchester.ac.uk/study/postgraduate-research/funding/opportunities/display/?id=00000244&offset=0&sort=name&sortdir=ascending&subjectArea=&nationality=&submit=

CONACyT Tuition Top-up Award

Subjects: Faculty of Science and Engineering
Eligibility: Academic requirements: To be considered for this award you must: 1. Hold (or be about to obtain) a first class honours honours undergraduate degree (or international equivalent) 2. Hold an offer letter from The University of Manchester to start a three year PhD programme (starting no later than 31 March) 3. Ideally hold a master's-level qualification at merit or distinction (or international equivalent) 4. Have some research related experience. e.g. undergraduate/master's projects, placements, internships, contributions to publications/articles, promoting research or project outcomes to a wider audience, prizes for previous work or setting up collaborations with other groups 5. Be undertaking a project which is in one the priority areas highlighted by CONACyT (please note that priority areas vary by year). Nationality restrictions: This funding is available to students from: 1. Mexico
Level of Study: Postgraduate, Research
Type: Scholarship
Value: The CONACyT Tuition Top Up Awards include tuition top ups to cover the CONACyT funding shortfall - this is calculated as: (0.7 x International fee amount) - £10.8k
Length of Study: 3 years
Application Procedure: Application procedure: Check funding page for further details
No. of applicants last year: 6
Additional Information: Contact details for enquiries: Sandra Kershaw, Recruitment and Admissions Officer, Tel: 0161 306 4826, Email: fse-pgr-admissions@manchester.ac.uk Website: www.manchester.ac.uk/study/postgraduate-research/funding/opportunities/display/?id=00000468&offset=0&sort=name&sortdir=ascending&subjectArea=&nationality=&submit=

Daiwa Scholarships in Japanese Studies

Subjects: School of Arts, Languages and Cultures
Eligibility: 1. Candidates for the Daiwa Scholarships in Japanese Studies must be British citizens who are holders of an Honours degree in Japanese Studies, defined as a programme focussing primarily on the study of Japan, and containing a substantial Japanese language component, and enrolled or enrolling in a Japanese Studies-related programme in either Japan or the UK 2. This award is available to existing postgraduate students.
Level of Study: Postgraduate, Research
Type: Scholarship
Value: The scholarship will cover tuition fees fro the programme, plus maintenance. Maintenance will be payable at a rate of £1,200 per month for periods spent in the UK, and 260,000 Yen per month for periods spent in Japan.
Length of Study: 3 Years
Country of Study: Any country
Application Procedure: Application is made directly to the Daiwa Anglo-Japanese Foundation. Application form: dajf.org.uk/scholarships/japanese-studies
No. of awards offered: 3

Closing Date: 27 January
Contributor: Daiwa Anglo-Japanese Foundation
Additional Information: Website: www.manchester.ac.uk/study/postgraduate-research/funding/opportunities/display/?id=00000453&offset=0&sort=name&sortdir=ascending&subjectArea=Any&nationality=United%20Kingdom&submit=Search

For further information contact:

Oxford Rd, Manchester M13 9PL, United Kingdom.

Tel: (44) 161 306 6000
Email: scholarships@dajf.org.uk

Dean's Doctoral Scholarship Award

Subjects: Faculty of Science and Engineering
Eligibility: 1. Academic requirements: To be considered for this award you must: A. Have submitted an application by the deadline for a PhD programme to start in September 2024. B. Hold (or expect to acheive) a first class or 2.1 UK honours undergraduate degree (or international equivalent). C. Ideally hold a master's qualification at merit or distinction (or international equivalent). D. Be able to demonstrate potential for academic research. This may include undergraduate projects, placements, internships, contributions to publications or articles, promoting research to a wider audience, prizes for previous work or stetting up collaborations with other groups. E. Be able to demonstrate involvement in broader activities, e.g. outreach, volunteering, community engagement, engagement in EDIA and other extra-curricular activities. 2. Nationality restrictions: A. This funding is available to all nationalities. 3. Other eligibility criteria: Applicants must hold an offer of study at The University of Manchester before applying for this funding. Candidates must also: A. meet English language entry requirements as specified by the Department that you are a pplying to; B. have a track record of engaging with research. This may include contributions to publications / articles, promoting your research to a wider audience, prizes for research or project work.
Level of Study: Postgraduate, Research
Type: Scholarship
Value: 1. Tuition fees at the international rate 2. Annual maintenance stipend equivalent to UKRI minimum stipend rate 3. £1000 Research Training Support Grant per year
Length of Study: 3.5 years
Application Procedure: Dean's Doctoral Scholarships work on a nomination basis, the lead supervisor will consider you for nomination and will support you through the process. It is important that you have had significant contact with the supervisory team during the application process and that they are aware that you wish to be considered for funding. In order to be considered, applicants must apply for a place on the PhD programme of your choice as early as possible before the advertised funding deadline.
Closing Date: 30 March
Contributor: The University of Manchester's Faculty of Science and Engineering
Additional Information: Website: www.manchester.ac.uk/study/postgraduate-research/funding/opportunities/display/?id=00000447&offset=0&sort=name&sortdir=ascending&subjectArea=&nationality=&submit=

Department of Mathematics Scholarship Award

Subjects: Department of Mathematics
Eligibility: 1. First class honours degree, or possibly a good upper second class honours degree in Mathematics at Masters level or an appropriate related discipline. 2. This funding is available to all nationalities. 3. This award can be held alongside other awards.
Level of Study: Postgraduate, Research
Type: Studentship
Value: Home Students Tuition Fees and Maintenance. International Students Tuition Fees Only.
Length of Study: 3.5 years
Frequency: Annual
Country of Study: Any country
Application Procedure: Applicants should highlight on their PHD application form that they wish to be considered for an EPSRC DTA Award or a Department Scholarship Award. Application form: www.manchester.ac.uk/postgraduate/howtoapply/
No. of awards offered: 6-10
Additional Information: Website: www.manchester.ac.uk/study/postgraduate-research/funding/opportunities/display/?id=00000131&offset=0&sort=name&sortdir=ascending&subjectArea=Any&nationality=United%20Kingdom&submit=Search

For further information contact:

Department of Mathematics, Oxford Rd, Manchester M13 9PL, United Kingdom.

Tel: (44) (0)161 275 5812
Email: pgr-maths@manchester.ac.uk

Department of Physics and Astronomy Diversity Enhancement Studentship

Subjects: Department of Physics & Astronomy

U

Purpose: This scholarship is open to home or EU applicants (overseas with fee waiver) from underrepresented groups, or challenging social or academic backgrounds, who are motivated to tackle, and plan to engage with, diversity enhancement in physics and astronomy.
Eligibility: 1. Academic requirements: To be considered for this studentship you must: A. Hold (or be about to obtain) a minimum of a 2i class UK Masters honours degree, or international equivalent, or a First Class Bachelor degree with an additional B. Masters degree, or international equivalent. C. Applicants with a First Class Bachelor degree, or international equivalent, with proven research experience may also be considered. 2. Nationality restrictions: This funding is available to students from the UK and EU. 3. Other eligibility criteria: Applicants must hold an offer of study at The University of Manchester before applying for this funding.
Level of Study: Postgraduate, Research
Type: Studentship
Value: 1. Tuition fees at home or international rate 2. Annual maintenance stipend equivalent to UKRI minimum stipend.
Length of Study: 3.5 years
Application Procedure: This scholarship works on a nomination basis, the lead supervisor will consider you for nomination and will support you through the process. It is important that you have had significant contact with the supervisory team during the application process and that they are aware that you wish to be considered for funding. Your application will then be considered by a departmental funding panel. In order to be considered, you must hold an academic offer for a place on one of our PhD programmes. It is therefore essential that you apply for a place on the PhD programme of your choice as early as possible.
Additional Information: Website: www.manchester.ac.uk/study/postgraduate-research/funding/opportunities/display/?id=00000489&offset=0&sort=name&sortdir=ascending&subjectArea=&nationality=&submit=

Department of Physics and Astronomy STFC Studentship

Subjects: Department of Physics & Astronomy
Purpose: This studentship is open to all nationalities and will be of interest to students who want to research physics and astronomy.
Eligibility: 1. Academic requirements: To be considered for this studentship you must: A. Hold (or be about to obtain) a minimum of a 2i class UK Masters honours degree, or international equivalent, or a First Class Bachelor degree with an additional Masters degree, or international equivalent. B. Applicants with a First Class Bachelor degree, or international equivalent, with proven research experience may also be considered. 2. Nationality restrictions: This funding is available to all nationalities.
Level of Study: Postgraduate, Research
Type: Studentship
Value: Tuition fees at home or international rate, Annual maintenance stipend equivalent to UKRI minimum stipend
Length of Study: 3.5 years
Application Procedure: Application procedure: A. Apply for a place on the PhD programme of your choice. B. Specify in your application form that you want to be considered for the 'STFC Funding' (funding section).
No. of applicants last year: Varies
Additional Information: Website: www.manchester.ac.uk/study/postgraduate-research/funding/opportunities/display/?id=00000488&offset=0&sort=name&sortdir=ascending&subjectArea=&nationality=&submit=

Dual-award between The University of Manchester and IIT Kharagpur

Subjects: Faculty of Science and Engineering
Purpose: These scholarships are open to all nationalities and across all research areas, and will be of interest to students of the highest calibre who have the commitment and desire to work on challenging research projects in a world leading research environment.
Eligibility: Academic requirements: 1. If you're an Indian national, to be considered for this award you must: A. Hold (or be about to obtain) a BTech or MSc/MTech degree from any IIT with minimum CGPA of 7.5/10. 2. If you're not an Indian national, to be considered for this award you must: A. Hold (or be about to obtain) a first class honours undergraduate degree or master's qualification (or international equivalent) in science, engineering or related field from a globally reputed university (with QS rank within 500), or minimum GPA of 3.0/4.0. Nationality restrictions: This funding is available to all nationalities. Other eligibility criteria: You must also: 1. Be able to undertake PhD studies at IIT Kharagpur from July 2024, or as soon as possible thereafter, with no requirement for a (further) visa to study in India. 2. Possess a willingness to travel to the UK to undertake two years of study based at The University of Manchester, if such travel is permitted by UK and India governments 3. Have demonstrable excellent communication skills, including in English language, a proficiency in which should be demonstrably indicated by meeting the requirements as indicated on The University of Manchester website 4. Have demonstrable suitability of academic background for the proposed project 5. Have demonstrable skills in teamworking and self-organisation 6. Have demonstrable interest and curiosity in the proposed area of research
Level of Study: Postgraduate, Research

Type: Studentship
Value: Tuition fee sponsorship and top-up awards for living costs
Length of Study: 4 years
Closing Date: 13 March
Contributor: The University of Manchester Faculty of Science and Engineering
Additional Information: Website: www.manchester.ac.uk/study/postgraduate-research/funding/opportunities/display/?id=00000482&offset=0&sort=name&sortdir=ascending&subjectArea=&nationality=&submit=

Dual-award between The University of Manchester and The University of Melbourne

Subjects: Faculty of Science and Engineering
Purpose: These scholarships are open to all nationalities and across all research areas, and will be of interest to students of the highest calibre who have the commitment and desire to work on challenging research projects in a world leading research environment.
Eligibility: 1. Academic requirements: To be considered for this award you must meet the entry requirements of both The University of Manchester and The University of Melbourne:- The University of Mancheter admissions criteria can be found under 'Available Projects: www.manchester.ac.uk/study/postgraduate-research/golden/melbourne/' and then selecting the PhD programme information for that specific project. The University of Melbourne admissions criteria can be found on their website: research.unimelb.edu.au/research-at-melbourne/melbourne-and-manchester-graduate-research-group. 2. Nationality restrictions: This funding is available to all nationalities.
Level of Study: Postgraduate, Research
Type: Studentship
Value: 1. Tuition fees, an annual stipend at the minimum Research Councils UK rate, 2. A research training grant and student travel to Melbourne.
Length of Study: 4 years
Application Procedure: Candidates looking to apply for a Manchester-based project are encouraged to contact the Manchester supervisor named under 'Availabile projects' for an initial discussion before submitting an official application form. Find out how to apply on our website: www.manchester.ac.uk/study/postgraduate-research/golden/melbourne/apply/.
Closing Date: 30 March
Contributor: The University of Manchester Faculty of Science and Engineering
Additional Information: Website: www.manchester.ac.uk/study/postgraduate-research/funding/opportunities/display/?id=00000481&offset=0&sort=name&sortdir=ascending&subjectArea=&nationality=&submit=

Engineering the Future Scholarships

Purpose: The University of Manchester's School of Engineering is proud to offer scholarship awards to academically excellent international students, commencing their postgraduate taught studies
Eligibility: 1. be a resident of a country within South Asia, South East Asia or Africa; 2. hold an offer (conditional or unconditional) for a master's level (taught) full time course – commencing in September 2024 – within The Faculty of Science and Engineering. (You will also be considered if you held an offer as part of an earlier admissions round; should you win the award, your offer will be reinstated.); 3. have completed an English Language qualification to the required standard for the course; 4. be fully registered for your chosen course by the registration deadline; 5. hold a bachelor's degree with a minimum classification of a good Upper Second class (2:1) (or international equivalent), or be on track to achieve this; 6. be self-funding (for example, not sponsored) your course and classified as an international candidate for tuition fee purposes.
Level of Study: Masters Degree
Type: Scholarship
Value: 1. One full tuition fee waiver up to £33,500. This award is for the MSc Management of Projects suite of programmes. 2. Four £10,000 partial tuition fee waivers. 3. Ten £6,000 partial tuition fee waivers.
Application Procedure: These awards require no additional application; all offer holders are considered based on academic merit. Shortlisted candidates may be contacted for further assessment in the form of a written statement.
Additional Information: If you have any questions, please get in touch: fse-scholarships@manchester.ac.uk Website: www.manchester.ac.uk/study/international/finance-and-scholarships/funding/engineering-future-scholarships/

For further information contact:

Email: fse-scholarships@manchester.ac.uk

U

EPSRC Doctoral Training Partnership (DTP)

Subjects: Faculty of Science and Engineering
Purpose: These scholarships are open to all nationalities and across all research areas. We actively encourage applicants from diverse career paths and backgrounds and from all sections of the community, regardless of age, disability, ethnicity, gender, gender expression, sexual orientation and

transgender status. In order to recruit the very best students, EPSRC allows up to 30% of DTP studentships to be allocated to International students; this is known as relaxation of residential criteria.
Eligibility: 1. Academic requirements: Please enquire with the admissions team in the department in which you intend to study as to their specific eligibility criteria. UK Research and Innovation eligibility criteria: www.ukri.org/apply-for-funding/before-you-apply/check-if-you-are-eligible-for-research-and-innovation-funding 2. Nationality restrictions: This funding is available to all nationalities.
Level of Study: Postgraduate, Research
Type: Scholarship
Value: 1. 3.5 year fully-funded studentship 2. Tuition fees at home or international rate 3. Annual maintenance stipend equivalent to UKRI minimum stipend
Length of Study: 3.5 years
Application Procedure: 1. Search our list of competition funded projects on the FindAPhD project page: www.manchester.ac.uk/study/postgraduate-research/funding/projects/ using keyword 'EPSRC DTP'. 2. Specify in the funding section of your PhD application form: www.manchester.ac.uk/study/postgraduate-research/admissions/how-to-apply/ that you wish to be considered for the EPSRC DTP. Your application will then be considered by a departmental funding panel.
Contributor: The University of Manchester Faculty of Science and Engineering
Additional Information: website: www.manchester.ac.uk/study/postgraduate-research/funding/opportunities/display/?id=00000469&offset=0&sort=name&sortdir=ascending&subjectArea=&nationality=&submit=

EPSRC Doctoral Training Partnership Studentships in Alliance Manchester Business School

Subjects: Faculty of Humanities, Alliance Manchester Business School
Eligibility: 1. Candidates must have an Upper Second class honours degree or above and a Masters degree with an overall mark of 65% or above, or an equivalent combination of qualifications and/or experience. Additionally, they are expected to meet the specific requirements of the intended PhD programme. 2. The proposed research project must be within the remit of EPSRC's research themes. Please see EPSRC website: epsrc.ukri.org/research/ourportfolio/researchareas/ for information.
Level of Study: Masters Degree, Postgraduate
Type: Studentship
Value: an annual stipend starting at approximately £15,609, and £1,000 research training support grant per year
Length of Study: 4 years
Frequency: Annual
Country of Study: Any country
Application Procedure: Application form: www.alliancembs.manchester.ac.uk/study/phd/how-to-apply-for-a-phd/
Closing Date: 21 February
Contributor: Engineering and Physical Sciences Research Council
Additional Information: Website: www.manchester.ac.uk/study/postgraduate-research/funding/opportunities/display/?id=00000341&offset=0&sort=name&sortdir=ascending&subjectArea=Any&nationality=United%20Kingdom&submit=Search

For further information contact:

Oxford Rd, Manchester M13 9PL, United Kingdom.

Tel: (44) (0)161 275 1200
Email: lynne.barlow-cheetham@manchester.ac.uk
Website: epsrc.ukri.org/research/ourportfolio/researchareas/

EPSRC Doctoral Training Partnership Studentships in the School of Arts, Languages and Cultures

Subjects: Faculty of Humanities, School of Arts, Languages and Cultures
Eligibility: 1. Candidates must have an upper second class honours degree or above and a masters degree with an overall mark of 60% or above, or an equivalent combination of qualifications and/or experience. Additionally, they are expected to meet the specific requirements of the intended PhD programme. 2. This funding is available to all nationalities. 3. The proposed research project must be within the remit of EPSRC's research themes. Candidates and supervisors should consult the EPSRC website for further details of the eligible research themes and sub-themes: epsrc.ukri.org/research/ourportfolio/researchareas/
Level of Study: Postgraduate, Research
Type: Studentship
Value: 1 studentship covering Home Tuition Fees (£4,596 in the academic year 2023-24) and an annual stipend at standard UKRI rate (£16,062 in the academic year 2023-24), plus £1000 RTSG.
Length of Study: Up to 4 years
Frequency: Annual
Country of Study: Any country
Application Procedure: Applications must be submitted to Miss Rachel Corbishley, Postgraduate Admissions Administrator. Application form: www.alc.manchester.ac.uk/study/postgraduate-research/applying/

Closing Date: 30 March
Contributor: Engineering and Physical Sciences Research Council
Additional Information: Website: www.manchester.ac.uk/study/postgraduate-research/funding/opportunities/display/?id=00000324&offset=0&sort=name&sortdir=ascending&subjectArea=Any&nationality=United%20Kingdom&submit=Search

For further information contact:

Postgraduate Admissions Administrator, Oxford Rd, Manchester M13 9PL, United Kingdom.

Tel: (44) 161 306 6000
Email: phdfunding-salc@manchester.ac.uk
Website: www.alc.manchester.ac.uk/study/postgraduate-research/applying/

EPSRC Doctoral Training Partnership Studentships in the School of Environment, Education and Development

Subjects: Faculty of Humanities, School of Environment, Education and Development
Eligibility: 1. Candidates must have an Upper Second class honours degree or above and a masters degree with an overall mark of 60% or above, or an equivalent combination of qualifications and/or experience. Additionally, they are expected to meet the specific requirements of the intended PhD programme. 2. This funding is available to all nationalities. 3. The proposed research project must be within the remit of EPSRC's research themes. Please see EPSRC website for information.
Level of Study: Postgraduate, Research
Type: Studentship
Value: Each studentship comprises tuition fees, an annual stipend starting at £16,062 for 2023/24 and £1,000 research training support grant per year for 3/3.5 years.
Length of Study: 3 years
Frequency: Annual
Country of Study: Any country
Application Procedure: 1. Submit a complete application for one of the School's PhD programmes through the University of Manchester's online application: pgapplication.manchester.ac.uk/psp/umgap/EMPLOYEE/HRMS/c/UM_GAP_MNU.UM_GAP_IDENTIFY.GBL. 2. Send an email to pgr-seedfunding@manchester.ac.uk to express interest in the scholarship and request consideration for this funding opportunity. 3. Application form: www.seed.manchester.ac.uk/study/postgraduate-research/applying/
Closing Date: 30 March
Additional Information: Website: www.manchester.ac.uk/study/postgraduate-research/funding/opportunities/display/?id=00000336&offset=0&sort=name&sortdir=ascending&subjectArea=Any&nationality=United%20Kingdom&submit=Search

For further information contact:

Christopher Kitchen, Postgraduate Research Recruitment and Admissions.

Tel: (44) (0)161 275 0807
Email: pgr-seedfunding@manchester.ac.uk
Website: pgapplication.manchester.ac.uk/psp/umgap/EMPLOYEE/HRMS/c/UM_GAP_MNU.UM_GAP_IDENTIFY.GBL

ESRC North West Social Science DTP (NWSSDTP) PhD Studentships in Alliance Manchester Business School

Subjects: Faculty of Humanities, Alliance Manchester Business School
Eligibility: 1. Please refer to the application guidance on the NWSSDTP website: nwssdtp.ac.uk/how-to-apply/ 2. This funding is available to all nationalities. 3. This award is available to existing postgraduate students. 4. This award is available to postgraduate research students in year one, applying for funding for years two and three of PhD.
Level of Study: Postgraduate, Research
Type: Studentship
Value: The award covers tuition fees, maintenance stipend (approximately £17,668 per annum)
Length of Study: 24-48 months.
Country of Study: Any country
Application Procedure: Please refer to the application guidance on the NWSSDTP website: nwssdtp.ac.uk/how-to-apply/. Application form: nwssdtp.ac.uk/how-to-apply/
Closing Date: 1 February
Additional Information: Website: www.manchester.ac.uk/study/postgraduate-research/funding/opportunities/display/?id=00000327&offset=0&sort=name&sortdir=ascending&subjectArea=Any&nationality=United%20Kingdom&submit=Search

For further information contact:

Lynne Barlow-Cheetham.

Tel: (44) (0)161 275 1200
Email: lynne.barlow-cheetham@manchester.ac.uk

ESRC North West Social Science DTP (NWSSDTP) PhD Studentships in the School of Arts, Languages and Cultures

Subjects: 1. Faculty of Humanities 2. School of Arts, Languages and Cultures
Eligibility: 1. This award is available to existing postgraduate students. 2. This award is available to postgraduate research students in year one, applying for funding for years two and three of a PhD.
Level of Study: Postgraduate, Research
Type: Studentship
Value: Subject to residential eligibility status, the award covers tuition fees, a maintenance stipend (the annual maintenance stipend for 2023-24 is £17,668)
Length of Study: 24 and 48 months
Frequency: Annual
Country of Study: Any country
Application Procedure: 1. Please refer to the application guidance here: nwssdtp.ac.uk/how-to-apply/ 2. Application form: nwssdtp.ac.uk/how-to-apply/
Closing Date: 1 February
Contributor: ESRC North West Social Sciences Doctoral Training Partnership
Additional Information: Contact details for enquiries: Miss Rachel Corbishley, Postgraduate Admissions Administrator, Email: phdfunding-salc@manchester.ac.uk Website: www.manchester.ac.uk/study/postgraduate-research/funding/opportunities/display/?id=00000160&offset=0&sort=name&sortdir=ascending&subjectArea=Any&nationality=United%20Kingdom&submit=Search

For further information contact:

Postgraduate Admissions Administrator, Oxford Rd, Manchester M13 9PL, United Kingdom.

Tel: (44) 161 306 6000
Email: phdfunding-salc@manchester.ac.uk

ESRC North West Social Science DTP (NWSSDTP) PhD Studentships in the School of Environment, Education and Development

Subjects: Faculty of Humanities, School of Environment, Education and Development
Eligibility: 1. Please refer to the application guidance on the SEED website. 2. This funding is available to all nationalities. 3. This award is available to existing postgraduate students.
Level of Study: Postgraduate, Research
Type: Studentship
Value: the award covers tuition fees, annual maintenance stipend (the annual maintenance stipend for 2023-24 is £17,668)
Length of Study: 24-48 months
Frequency: Annual
Country of Study: Any country
Application Procedure: Application form: nwssdtp.ac.uk/how-to-apply/
Closing Date: 1 February
Contributor: ESRC North West Social Sciences Doctoral Training Partnership
Additional Information: Website: www.manchester.ac.uk/study/postgraduate-research/funding/opportunities/display/?id=00000325&offset=0&sort=name&sortdir=ascending&subjectArea=Any&nationality=United%20Kingdom&submit=Search

For further information contact:

PGR Recruitment and Admissions Officer, Oxford Rd, Manchester M13 9PL, United Kingdom.

Tel: (44) (0)161 275 0807
Email: pgr-seedfunding@manchester.ac.uk

ESRC-BBSRC PhD Studentships in Biosocial Research

Subjects: School of Social Sciences
Purpose: Biosocial research is an exciting new area of study. We are seeking bright, motivated applicants to form the next cohort of students in the new Soc-B Centre for Doctoral Training (CDT) jointly funded by the Economic and Social Research Council (ESRC) and the Biotechnology and Biological Sciences Research Council (BBSRC).
Eligibility: 1. Academic requirements: A. Applicants are expected to have a First Class or Upper Second-Class Bachelor's degree and/or a Master's degree (preferably with a merit or distinction) in a social, biological, mathematical or computer science. B. See entry requirements for relevant PhD programme 2. Nationality restrictions: This funding is available to all nationalities.
Level of Study: Postgraduate, Research
Type: Studentship
Value: 1. Tuition fees for 4 years 2. Annual maintenance stipend (£17,668 for 2023/24)
Length of Study: 4 years full-time (part-time option subject to final confirmation)
Application Procedure: Application form: www.ucl.ac.uk/soc-b-biosocial-doctoral-training/how-apply-0
Closing Date: 15 January

Additional Information: Website: www.manchester.ac.uk/study/postgraduate-research/funding/opportunities/display/?id=00000354&offset=0&sort=name&sortdir=ascending&subjectArea=&nationality=&submit=

Funds for Women Graduates

Subjects: Faculty of Science and Engineering
Eligibility: 1. Academic requirements: Individual awards will have different eligibility criteria. Please check the funder's website for full details 2. Nationality restrictions: This funding is available to all nationalities. 3. Other eligibility criteria: Subject and nationality restrictions may apply for individual awards. Please see the funder's website for full details.
Level of Study: Postgraduate, Research
Type: Bursary
Value: Various grants and bursaries of differing values are available.
Length of Study: Varies from duration of the PhD to final year only.
Application Procedure: Application form: www.ffwg.org.uk/grants-bursaries-fellowships/check-eligibility-and-apply/
Additional Information: Website: https://www.ffwg.org.uk/

Future of the Academy PhD Studentship

Subjects: School of Social Sciences
Eligibility: Academic requirements: 1. Minimum Entry Requirements: A. Bachelor's (Honours) degree (or overseas equivalent) at 2:1 level or above in a cognate subject; and B. Master's degree in a cognate subject - with an overall average of 65% or above, and a minimum mark of 65% in your dissertation (or overseas equivalent) and no mark below 55% 2. Satisfying the minimum entry criteria does not automatically make applicants competitive for funding. Therefore, to be considered for internal funding, you will normally need: A. Bachelor's (Honours) degree (or overseas equivalent) at 2:1 level or above in a cognate subject (1st class highly desirable); and B. Master's degree in a cognate subject - with an overall average of 70% or above, and a minimum mark of 70% in your dissertation (or overseas equivalent). Nationality restrictions: This funding is available to all nationalities. Other eligibility criteria: Applicants must belong to one of two broad groups identified as under-represented in the Academy: 1. Black, Asian, or minority ethnic heritage (BAME), including people of a mixed race/ethnic background; 2. Low-income/lower-socio-economic background (broadly defined) or who have incurred major familial or personal financial hardship, currently or whilst growing up. This group also includes care leavers. and those who are the first generation to attend University in their family.
Level of Study: Postgraduate, Research
Type: Studentship
Value: 1. Tuition fees 2. An annual maintenance stipend
Length of Study: 3.5 years full-time or 7 years part-time
Application Procedure: Application form: documents.manchester.ac.uk/display.aspx?DocID=64320
Closing Date: 27 January
Additional Information: Website: www.manchester.ac.uk/study/postgraduate-research/funding/opportunities/display/?id=00000485&offset=0&sort=name&sortdir=ascending&subjectArea=&nationality=&submit=

Graphene NOWNANO CDT

Subjects: Faculty of Science and Engineering
Purpose: The Graphene NOWNANO Centre for Doctoral Training (CDT) was established in 2013 with UK Research Council (EPSRC) funding and is now financially supported by The University of Manchester and industry.
Eligibility: Academic requirements: To be considered for this award you must: Hold (or be about to obtain) a first class or upper second class honours honours undergraduate degree (or international equivalent) in science, engineering or biomedical disciplines. Nationality restrictions: This funding is available to all nationalities.
Level of Study: Postgraduate, Research
Type: Studentship
Value: UKRI rate stipend and fees.
Length of Study: 4 years
Application Procedure: For application information please visit our Graphene NOWNANO CDT website: www.graphene-nownano.manchester.ac.uk/.
Contributor: The University of Manchester Faculty of Science and Engineering
No. of applicants last year: 15
Additional Information: Website: www.manchester.ac.uk/study/postgraduate-research/funding/opportunities/display/?id=00000474&offset=0&sort=name&sortdir=ascending&subjectArea=&nationality=&submit=

GREAT Scholarships

Purpose: If you're considering a postgraduate degree in the UK, then a GREAT scholarship can help.
Eligibility: 1. You must be holding either a conditional or unconditional offer to study at the University to apply for The University of Manchester GREAT Scholarship. 2. Applicants should be passport holders of Bangladesh, Kenya, Mexico, Nigeria, Pakistan, Thailand or Turkey. 3. Read our full

eligibility and selection criteria: documents.manchester.ac.uk/display.aspx?DocID=64332
Level of Study: Postgraduate
Type: Scholarship
Value: Minimum of £10,000
Application Procedure: See website
Closing Date: 1 June
Additional Information: Website: www.manchester.ac.uk/study/international/finance-and-scholarships/funding/great-scholarships/

Harry Clough Bursary

Subjects: School of Arts, Languages and Cultures
Eligibility: Academic requirements: Applicants must hold or expect to achieve a Masters-level qualification, which we would expect to be at distinction level, or equivalent, and will normally have a first-class Honours degree (or non-UK equivalent). Other eligibility criteria: 1. This award can be held alongside other awards. 2. The bursary is open to new PhD students only.
Level of Study: Postgraduate, Research
Type: Bursary
Value: The award covers home tuition fees.
Length of Study: 3 year full-time programmes. Part-time is also available.
Application Procedure: Application form: documents.manchester.ac.uk/display.aspx?DocID=52015
Closing Date: 3 February
Contributor: The School of Arts, Languages and Cultures
No. of applicants last year: 1
Additional Information: Website: www.manchester.ac.uk/study/postgraduate-research/funding/opportunities/display/?id=00000347&offset=0&sort=name&sortdir=ascending&subjectArea=&nationality=&submit=

Heilbronn Doctoral Partnership (HDP) Studentship

Subjects: School of Mathematics
Purpose: These studentships are open to all nationalities and will be of interest to students who want to research pure mathematics, probability, data science, and quantum information.
Eligibility: 1. Academic requirements: To be considered for this award you must: Hold (or be about to obtain) upper second class honours undergraduate degree (or international equivalent) in pure mathematics, probability, data science, and quantum information or a related discipline. 2. Nationality restrictions: This funding is available to all nationalities. 3. Other eligibility criteria: Applicants must hold an offer of study at The University of Manchester before applying for this funding.
Level of Study: Postgraduate, Research
Type: Studentship
Value: 1. Tuition fees (for home students only) 2. Annual maintenance stipend equivalent to UKRI minimum stipend
Length of Study: 4 years
Application Procedure: Apply for a place on a relevant PhD programme of your choice prior to the advertised funding application deadline. Specify in your application form that you want to be considered for the 'Heilbronn Doctoral Partnership' (funding section).
Closing Date: 30 March
Contributor: Heilbronn Institute for Mathematical Research
No. of applicants last year: 3
Additional Information: Website: www.manchester.ac.uk/study/postgraduate-research/funding/opportunities/display/?id=00000487&offset=0&sort=name&sortdir=ascending&subjectArea=&nationality=&submit=

Indian Excellence Scholarship Award

Subjects: Faculty of Humanities, School of Arts, Languages and Cultures
Eligibility: 1. Please refer to the application guidance here: www.alc.manchester.ac.uk/study/postgraduate-research/applying/ 2. This funding is available to all nationalities. 3. This award is available to existing postgraduate students. 4. This award is available to postgraduate research students in year one, applying for funding for years two and three of a PhD.
Level of Study: Postgraduate, Research
Type: Studentship
Value: Subject to residential eligibility status, the award covers tuition fees, a maintenance stipend
Length of Study: Between 24 and 48 months
Country of Study: Any country
Application Procedure: Please refer to the application guidance here: nwssdtp.ac.uk/how-to-apply/ Application form: nwssdtp.ac.uk/how-to-apply/
Closing Date: 1 February
Additional Information: Contact details for enquiries, Miss Rachel Corbishley, Postgraduate Admissions Administrator. Website: www.eee.manchester.ac.uk/study/undergraduate/fees-and-funding/

For further information contact:

Email: phdfunding-salc@manchester.ac.uk

Integrated Catalysis (iCAT) CDT

Subjects: Faculty of Science and Engineering

Purpose: These studentships are open to all nationalities and will be of interest to students of the highest calibre who have the commitment and desire to work on challenging research projects in a world leading research environment.
Eligibility: Academic requirements: To be considered for this award you must: Hold (or be about to obtain) a first class or upper second class honours honours undergraduate degree (or international equivalent) in a relevant area of science and engineering. Nationality restrictions: This funding is available to all nationalities.
Level of Study: Postgraduate, Research
Type: Studentship
Value: 1. UKRI rate stipend and fees, regardless of nationality. 2. Generous travel and consumables allowance to support project.
Length of Study: 4 years
Application Procedure: For application information please visit our iCAT CDT website: www.icat.manchester.ac.uk/.
Contributor: The Engineering and Physical Sciences Research Council (EPSRC)
No. of applicants last year: 50
Additional Information: Website: www.manchester.ac.uk/study/postgraduate-research/funding/opportunities/display/?id=00000473&offset=0&sort=name&sortdir=ascending&subjectArea=&nationality=&submit=

James Elson Studentship

Subjects: Department of Computer Science
Purpose: This studentship is open to UK and EU nationals researching in the Department of Computer Science.
Eligibility: 1. Academic requirements: A. Candidates must at a minimum satisfy the academic requirements for entry onto PhD programmes within the Department of Computer Science. B. However, this is a highly competitive studentship and therefore both the supervisor and the final PGR interview panel will be looking for the candidate who can best demonstrate evidence of their potential to undertake their selected research project and to successfully complete the doctoral programme to the standard necessary to qualify for a PhD. 2. Nationality restrictions: This funding is available to students from the UK and EU. 3. Other eligibility criteria: Candidates should select a research project from the list of eligible projects prior to applying.
Level of Study: Postgraduate, Research
Type: Studentship
Value: 1. Tuition fees at the international rate 2. Annual maintenance stipend equivalent to UKRI minimum stipend rate
Length of Study: 3 years
Application Procedure: Candidates will be shortlisted for interview on the basis of academic quality and their preparedness for their chosen project as evidenced in their application. References and supervisor support will also be sought when shortlisting. Please contact the potential supervisor for your chosen project prior to applying. Further information can be found here: www.cs.manchester.ac.uk/study/postgraduate-research/programmes/phd/funding/james-elson/apply/.
Contributor: Department of Computer Science
No. of applicants last year: 1
Additional Information: Website: www.manchester.ac.uk/study/postgraduate-research/funding/opportunities/display/?id=00000323&offset=0&sort=name&sortdir=ascending&subjectArea=&nationality=&submit=

Joint-award between The University of Manchester and IISC Bangalore

Subjects: Faculty of Science and Engineering
Purpose: These scholarships are open to all nationalities and across all research areas, and will be of interest to students of the highest calibre who have the commitment and desire to work on challenging research projects in a world leading research environment.
Eligibility: Academic requirements: Applicants must meet entry requirements at both institutions: 1. IISc Bangalore lead projects: A. Have successfully completed the required coursework and comprehensive examination within 24 months of enrolment/joining at IISc with a minimum CGPA of 8.0/10; B. Be able to enrol in the Joint PhD Award at IISc from August 2024 or as soon as possible thereafter with no requirement for a (further) visa to study in India. 2. The University of Manchester lead projects: A. Hold (or expect to achieve) a first class or upper-second class UK honours degree (or international equivalent). B. Ideally hold a master's-level qualification at merit or distinction (or international equivalent). C. Demonstrable excellent communication skills, including in English language, a proficiency in which should be demonstrably indicated by meeting our English language requirements. Nationality restrictions: This funding is available to all nationalities. Other eligibility criteria: You must also have: 1. Willingness to travel to the partner institution to undertake 2 years of study, if such travel is permitted by UK and India governments 2. Demonstrable suitability of academic background for the proposed project 3. Demonstrable skills in teamworking and self-organisation 4. Demonstrable interest and curiosity in the proposed area of research
Level of Study: Postgraduate, Research
Type: Studentship
Value: Tuition fee sponsorship and top-up awards for living costs
Length of Study: 4 years

Closing Date: 27 April
Contributor: The University of Manchester Faculty of Science and Engineering
Additional Information: Website: www.manchester.ac.uk/study/postgraduate-research/funding/opportunities/display/?id=00000483&offset=0&sort=name&sortdir=ascending&subjectArea=&nationality=&submit=

Manchester Melbourne Dual Award

Type: Studentship
Value: Tuition fees Home/International Stipend AApprox £15,609 per year RTSG Up to £5,000 per year Travel Up to £1,250 (whole programme) Health insurance while at Melbourne
Length of Study: 3.5 years full-time or 7 years part-time
Country of Study: Any country
Closing Date: 14 March
Additional Information: Oxford Rd, Manchester M13 9PL, United Kingdom www.eee.manchester.ac.uk/study/undergraduate/fees-and-funding/

For further information contact:

Oxford Rd, Manchester M13 9PL, United Kingdom.

Tel: (44) (0) 161 275 4740
Email: daniel.davies@manchester.ac.uk

Manchester-China Scholarship Council Joint Postgraduate Scholarship Programme

Purpose: To provide scholarships to the nationals of PR China who wish to pursue their PhD at the University of Manchester
Eligibility: To be considered suitable for the joint scholarship, you must be a citizen and permanent resident of the People's Republic of China at the time of application. Overseas Chinese students may be eligible for application subject to CSC policy at the time (CSC publicises the policy in October or November every year). You must also 1. return to China upon completion of your studies and/or research; 2. hold an Upper Second class UK honours undergraduate degree (or international equivalent) from a reputable institution; 3. hold an unconditional offer letter from The University of Manchester; 4. ideally hold a master's-level qualification at merit or distinction (or international equivalent); 5. have a track record of engaging with research, which may include contributions to publications/articles, promoting your research to a wider audience, prizes for research or project work; satisfy CSC's selection criteria.
Level of Study: Doctorate, Postgraduate
Type: Scholarships
Value: Tuition fees and annual stipend of approx. £4,800
Length of Study: 3 years
Frequency: Annual
Study Establishment: University of Manchester
Country of Study: United Kingdom
Application Procedure: Applicants must complete the standard postgraduate application form and return it together with Academic transcripts, English language qualification, 2 reference letters and a research proposal
Closing Date: 15 January
Additional Information: For enquires to the China Scholarship Council, please contact Miss Zou Dongyun, Project Officer by email dyzou@csc.edu.cn

For further information contact:

Tel: (86) 10 6609 3977
Email: admissions.doctoralacademy@manchester.ac.uk

Myrtle McMyn Bursary

Subjects: School of Arts, Languages and Cultures
Eligibility: Applicants should hold an MA in a relevant subject area, with a taught course unit average of 65%, a disseration mark of 65% and no mark below 55%. They should also hold a UK BA with a 2i classification (orequivalent if studied overseas).
Level of Study: Postgraduate, Research
Type: Bursary
Value: The award covers Home tuition fees
Length of Study: 3 year
Frequency: Annual
Country of Study: Any country
Application Procedure: Application form: documents.manchester.ac.uk/display.aspx?DocID=52015
Closing Date: 3 February
No. of applicants last year: 1
Additional Information: Contact details for enquiries: Miss Rachel Corbishley, Postgraduate Admissions Administrator, Email: phdfuding-salc@manchester.ac.uk Website: www.manchester.ac.uk/study/postgraduate-research/funding/opportunities/display/?id=00000454

For further information contact:

Postgraduate Admissions Administrator, Oxford Rd, Manchester M13 9PL, United Kingdom.

Email: phdfuding-salc@manchester.ac.uk

Nuclear Energy - GREEN CDT

Subjects: Faculty of Science and Engineering
Purpose: These studentships are open to all nationalities and will be of interest to students of the highest calibre who have the commitment and desire to work on challenging research projects in a world leading research environment.
Eligibility: 1. Academic requirements: To be considered for this award you must: A. Hold (or be about to obtain) a UK undergraduate honours degree (or international equivalent) or a first degree with an additional master's degree (or international equivalent). 2. Nationality restrictions: This funding is available to all nationalities.
Level of Study: Postgraduate, Research
Type: Studentship
Value: 1. UKRI rate stipend and fees, international fees can be waived for successful applicants under UKRI relaxation scheme. 2. Generous travel and consumables allowance to support project of £22,500.
Length of Study: 4 years
Application Procedure: For application information please visit our GREEN CDT website: www.nuclear-energy-cdt.manchester.ac.uk/.
Contributor: The Engineering and Physical Sciences Research Council (EPSRC)
Additional Information: Website: www.manchester.ac.uk/study/postgraduate-research/funding/opportunities/display/?id=00000472&offset=0&sort=name&sortdir=ascending&subjectArea=&nationality=&submit=

PhD Studentships in Humanitarianism and Conflict Response

Eligibility: Applicants must hold or expect to achieve a Masters-level qualification, which we would expect to be at distinction level, or equivalent, and have a first-class Honours degree (or non-UK equivalent).
Type: Studentship
Value: Tuition fees and living allowance, the annual maintenance stipend £15,609.
Length of Study: 3 year
Country of Study: Any country
No. of awards offered: 2
Closing Date: 4 February

For further information contact:

Postgraduate Research Director: HCRI, Oxford Rd, Manchester M13 9PL, United Kingdom.

Email: nathaniel.ogrady@manchester.ac.uk, phdfuding-salc@manchester.ac.uk

Postgraduate Research Teaching Associate (PGRTA) Scholarships

Subjects: Faculty of Science and Engineering
Purpose: These hybrid scholarships are open to UK applicants across all research areas, and will be of interest to students who wish to tackle areas of key research and develop their teaching experience.
Eligibility: 1. Academic requirements A. To be considered for this award you must: Hold (or be about to obtain) upper second class honours undergraduate degree (or international equivalent). B. It would also be great if you: Held a Master's degree in a relevant field at merit or equivalent 2. Other eligibility criteria: You will also need to: A. Have applied for a PhD by the advertised funding deadline. B. Have an interest in teaching and supporting students C. Have the ability to engage and enthuse others D. Have strong team working skills E. Be able to initiative and organisational skills when working independently F. Have the capacity to work flexibly to tight deadlines G. Have strong English language proficiency. It would also be great if you: A. Had a proven track record of engaging with research B. Have relevant teaching or volunteering experience
Level of Study: Postgraduate, Research
Type: Scholarship
Value: Funding details: 1. A minimum combined teaching salary and stipend of £23,406/annum 2. All tuition fees covered 3. Transferable skills to support your career 4. Your research guided by our leading minds
Length of Study: 4-5 years
Application Procedure: PGRTA Awards work on a nomination basis, the lead supervisor will consider you for nomination and will support you through the process. For more information see website
Closing Date: 30 March
Contributor: The University of Manchester's Faculty of Science and Engineering
Additional Information: Website: www.manchester.ac.uk/study/postgraduate-research/funding/opportunities/display/?id=00000466&offset=0&sort=name&sortdir=ascending&subjectArea=&nationality=&submit=

U

President's Doctoral Scholar (PDS) Awards in the School of Arts, Languages and Cultures

Subjects: School of Arts, Languages and Cultures
Eligibility: 1. Applicants must hold or expect to achieve a Masters-level qualification, which we would expect to be at distinction level, or equivalent, and have a first-class Honours degree (or non-UK equivalent). Additional indicators of academic quality will include contributions to publications/articles, promoting your research to a wider audience, setting

up research collaborations, prizes awarded and information supplied by your referees. 2. This funding is available to all nationalities. 3. In order to apply for the PDS awards, an application for AHRC or ESRC funding must be submitted, if eligible, by the stated deadlines. Please note that current PhD students are not eligible for these awards.
Type: Studentship
Value: The award covers tuition fees and a maintenance stipend (£18,668 in 2022-23).
Length of Study: 3.5 year
Country of Study: Any country
Application Procedure: Application form: documents.manchester.ac.uk/display.aspx?DocID=52012
Closing Date: April
Additional Information: Contact details for enquiries: Miss Rachel Corbishley, Postgraduate Admissions Administrator, Email: phdfunding-salc@manchester.ac.uk Website: www.manchester.ac.uk/study/postgraduate-research/funding/opportunities/display/?id=00000331&offset=0&sort=name&sortdir=ascending&subjectArea=Any&nationality=United%20Kingdom&submit=Search

For further information contact:

Postgraduate Admissions Administrator, Oxford Rd, Manchester M13 9PL, United Kingdom.

Email: phdfunding-salc@manchester.ac.uk

President's Doctoral Scholar (PDS) Awards in the School of Environment, Education and Development

Subjects: School of Environment, Education and Development
Eligibility: 1. Applicants must hold or expect to achieve a Masters-level qualification, which we would expect to be at distinction level, or equivalent, and have a first-class Honours degree (or non-UK equivalent). Additional indicators of academic quality will include contributions to publications/articles, promoting your research to a wider audience, setting up research collaborations, prizes awarded and information supplied by your referees. 2. This funding is available to all nationalities.
Level of Study: Postgraduate, Research
Type: Studentship
Value: The award covers tuition fees and a maintenance stipend.
Length of Study: 3.5 year
Frequency: Annual
Country of Study: Any country
Application Procedure: Successful PhD and Professional Doctorate applicants are automatically considered for this funding - no further application is required.
Closing Date: 1 February
Additional Information: Contact details for enquiries: Christopher Kitchen, Recruitment and Admissions Officer, Email: PGR-SEED-Admissions@manchester.ac.uk Website: www.manchester.ac.uk/study/postgraduate-research/funding/opportunities/display/?id=00000366&offset=0&sort=name&sortdir=ascending&subjectArea=Any&nationality=United%20Kingdom&submit=Search

For further information contact:

Recruitment and Admissions Officer.

Tel: (44) 0161 275 0807
Email: PGR-SEED-Admissions@manchester.ac.uk

President's Doctoral Scholar Award

Purpose: The PDS Award will give the most outstanding students from around the world a foundation to support research training with prominent academics across a full range of subjects.
Eligibility: To be considered for this award, candidates must meet all of the following criteria: 1. hold a conditional/unconditional offer for a PhD programme to commence in September 2024; 2. hold (or are about to obtain) a first-class honours undergraduate degree (or international equivalent) from a reputable institution; 3. ideally, hold a master's-level qualification at merit or distinction (or international equivalent); 4. have a track record of engaging with research. This may include contributions to publications/articles, promoting their research to a wider audience, prizes for research or project work; 5. be interested in attending a series of exclusive events to facilitate interactions with our academic community and network with other PDS award holders.
Level of Study: Doctorate
Type: Scholarship
Value: 1. all university tuition fees at the international rate; 2. an annual stipend (at UKRI rate) plus a £1,000 stipend enhancement.
Length of Study: 3.5 years
Frequency: Annual
Country of Study: United Kingdom
Application Procedure: On your application form in the funding section, state that you intend to apply for a PDS Award. See information on potential projects and supervisors: www.bmh.manchester.ac.uk/study/research/projects/ and information on how to submit an online PhD application: www.bmh.manchester.ac.uk/study/research/apply/.

Closing Date: 28 April
Additional Information: www.bmh.manchester.ac.uk/study/research/financial-support/presidents-doctoral-scholar-awards/

For further information contact:

Oxford Rd, Manchester M13 9PL, United Kingdom.

Tel: (44) 161 306 6000
Email: EPSGradEd@manchester.ac.uk

Sasakawa Japanese Studies Postgraduate Studentship

Eligibility: 1. Please refer to the application guidance here: www.alc.manchester.ac.uk/study/postgraduate-research/applying/ 2. This funding is available to all nationalities. 3. This award is available to existing postgraduate students. 4. Current students who have already accepted an offer of a full scholarship for September 2024 entry are ineligible to apply. 5. PhD students who have already received the Sasakawa studentship may be nominated again, and receive the studentship for up to three years, through repeated awards cannot be guaranteed.
Level of Study: Postgraduate, Research
Type: Studentship
Value: studentships worth £10,000
Length of Study: 1 year
Frequency: Annual
Country of Study: Any country
Application Procedure: Interested applicants should contact Dr Peter Cave (peter.cave@manchester.ac.uk) for the application form, which should be returned to Dr Cave
No. of awards offered: 3
Closing Date: 27 February
Contributor: The School of Arts, Languages and Cultures
Additional Information: Contact details for enquiries: Dr Peter Cave, Senior Lecturer - Japanese Studies, Email: peter.cave@manchester.ac.uk Website: www.manchester.ac.uk/study/postgraduate-research/funding/opportunities/display/?id=00000348&offset=0&sort=name&sortdir=ascending&subjectArea=Any&nationality=United%20Kingdom&submit=Search

For further information contact:

Senior Lecturer - Japanese Studies, Oxford Rd, Manchester M13 9PL, United Kingdom.

Tel: (44) 161 306 6000
Email: peter.cave@manchester.ac.uk

School of Arts, Languages and Cultures PhD Studentships

Purpose: School of Arts, Languages and Cultures
Eligibility: 1. Applicants must hold or expect to achieve a Masters-level qualification, which we would expect to be at distinction level, or equivalent, and have a first-class Honours degree (or non-UK equivalent). 2. This funding is available to all nationalities. 3. MPhil students are not eligible to apply for this studentship. 4. Current PhD students are not eligible to apply for this studentship.
Level of Study: Postdoctorate
Type: Studentship
Value: The award covers tuition fees and a maintenance stipend
Length of Study: 3.5 year
Frequency: Annual
Country of Study: Any country
Application Procedure: Application form: documents.manchester.ac.uk/display.aspx?DocID=52015
Closing Date: 3 February
Contributor: The School of Arts, Languages and Cultures
Additional Information: Contact details for enquiries: Miss Rachel Corbishley, Postgraduate Admissions Administrator, Email: phdfunding-salc@manchester.ac.uk Website: www.manchester.ac.uk/study/postgraduate-research/funding/opportunities/display/?id=00000332&offset=0&sort=name&sortdir=ascending&subjectArea=Any&nationality=United%20Kingdom&submit=Search

For further information contact:

Postgraduate Admissions Administrator, Oxford Rd, Manchester M13 9PL, United Kingdom.

Tel: (44) 161 306 6000
Email: phdfunding-salc@manchester.ac.uk

School of Engineering Diversity PhD Scholarship

Subjects: School of Engineering
Purpose: This scholarship is open to students residing in the UK who are eligible for home fees and who identify as black-heritage (encompassing African, Carribean, and black-mixed heritage).
Eligibility: 1. Academic requirements: To be considered for this award you must: A. Hold (or be about to obtain) an upper second class honours undergraduate degree in one of the following disciplines (or related disciplines): Aerospace Engineering, Chemical Engineering, Civil Engineering, Computer Science, Electrical and Electronic Engineering, Engineering Project Management, Mechanical Engineering.

2. Other eligibility criteria: You must also: A. Identify as black-heritage (encompassing African, Carribean, and black-mixed heritage) B. Residing in the UK C. Be eligible for home fees
Level of Study: Postgraduate, Research
Type: Scholarship
Value: 1. 3.5 year fully-funded studentship 2. Tuition fees 3. Minimum annual stipend of £17,668 for the duration of the scholarship
Length of Study: 3.5 years
Application Procedure: Applicants for this award should apply by completing this short application: www.qualtrics.manchester.ac.uk/jfe/form/SV_9zAJSQ2q95SiSwK.
Contributor: School of Engineering
Additional Information: Website: www.manchester.ac.uk/study/postgraduate-research/funding/opportunities/display/?id=00000491&offset=0&sort=name&sortdir=ascending&subjectArea=&nationality=&submit=

School of Engineering Graduate PhD Scholarship

Subjects: School of Engineering
Purpose: This scholarship is open to current undergraduate and master's students in the Faculty of Science and Engineering, residing in the UK, who are eligible for home fees and are progressing onto postgraduate research
Eligibility: 1. Academic requirements: To be considered for this scholarship you must: A. Have, or expect to achieve, at least a 2.1 honours degree or a master's in the Faculty of Science and Engineering at The University of Manchester 2. Other eligibility criteria A. This award is available to existing postgraduate students. You must also: B. Reside in the UK C. Be eligible for home fees D. Be starting your PhD in 2024/25 in one of the following research disciplines: Aerospace Engineering, Chemical Engineering, Civil Engineering, Computer Science, Electrical and Electronic Engineering, Engineering Project Management, Mechanical Engineering
Level of Study: Postgraduate, Research
Type: Scholarship
Value: 1. 3.5 year fully-funded scholarship 2. Tuition fees at home rate 3. Minimum annual stipend of £17,668 for the duration of the scholarship
Length of Study: 3.5 years
Application Procedure: 1. Choose your research project and find your supervisor. 2. Complete your application online. 3. Specify in the funding section of your application that you wish to be considered for the School of Engineering Graduate PhD Scholarship. 4. Your application will be considered on a first-come, first-served basis. 5. Successful applicants will be invited to interview.
Contributor: School of Engineering
Additional Information: Website: www.manchester.ac.uk/study/postgraduate-research/funding/opportunities/display/?id=00000492&offset=0&sort=name&sortdir=ascending&subjectArea=&nationality=&submit=

School of Environment, Education and Development Postgraduate Research Scholarship

Eligibility: Candidates should meet the entry requirements of the School of Environment, Education and Development: 1. Bachelor degree with First Class or Upper Second Class Honours (or international equivalent) 2. Master degree with a minimum grade of 60% in the dissertation and a minimum taught average grade of 60% (or international equivalent) 3. English language proficiency if applicable - minimum of IELTS 7 overall with 7 in writing and 6 in the other subsections or TOEFL 100 overall with 25 in writing and 22 in the other subsections. Please note that existing PhD students cannot be considered for this funding. For more information see website
Level of Study: Postgraduate, Research
Type: Scholarship
Value: These awards will cover tuition fees and include annual stipends
Length of Study: 3.5 year
Frequency: Annual
Country of Study: Any country
Application Procedure: Successful PhD and Professional Doctorate applicants are automatically considered for this funding - no further application is required. Application form: www.seed.manchester.ac.uk/study/postgraduate-research/applying/
Closing Date: 1 February
Contributor: School of Environment, Education and Development
Additional Information: Website: www.manchester.ac.uk/study/postgraduate-research/funding/opportunities/display/?id=00000218&offset=0&sort=name&sortdir=ascending&subjectArea=Any&nationality=United%20Kingdom&submit=Search

For further information contact:

Postgraduate Research Recruitment and Admissions, Oxford Rd, Manchester M13 9PL, United Kingdom.

Tel: (44) 161 275 0807
Email: pgr-seedfunding@manchester.ac.uk

School of Natural Sciences Diversity PhD Scholarship

Subjects: School of Natural Sciences
Purpose: This scholarship is open to students residing in the UK who are eligible for home fees and who identify as black-heritage (encompassing African, Carribean, and black-mixed heritage).
Eligibility: 1. Academic requirements: To be considered for this award you must: A. Hold (or be about to obtain) an upper second class honours undergraduate degree in the following disciplines (or related disciplines) Chemistry, Earth and Environmental Sciences, Fashion Business Technology, Materials Science and Engineering, Mathematics or Physics and Astronomy 2. Nationality restrictions: This funding is available to students from: A. England B. Northern Ireland C. Scotland D. Wales 3. Other eligibility criteria: You must also: A. Identify as black-heritage (encompassing African, Carribean, and black-mixed heritage) B. Reside in the UK C. Be eligible for home fees
Level of Study: Postgraduate, Research
Type: Scholarship
Value: 1. 3.5 year fully-funded studentship 2. Tuition fees 3. Minimum annual stipend of £17,668 for the duration of the scholarship
Length of Study: 3.5 years
Application Procedure: Applicants for this award should apply by completing this short application: www.qualtrics.manchester.ac.uk/jfe/form/SV_9STXWcKkYL3xsiy
Closing Date: 30 March
Contributor: The University of Manchester's School of Natural Sciences
Additional Information: Website: www.manchester.ac.uk/study/postgraduate-research/funding/opportunities/display/?id=00000486&offset=1&sort=name&sortdir=ascending&subjectArea=&nationality=&submit=

School of Social Sciences - China Scholarship Council Joint Scholarship for PhD Study

Subjects: School of Social Sciences
Eligibility: 1. Academic requirements: Candidates must satisfy the entry requirements for PhD programmes in the School of Social Sciences. Further information can be obtained from the programmes website. 2. Nationality restrictions: This funding is available to students from: China 3. Other eligibility criteria. A. Applicants must hold an offer of study at The University of Manchester before applying for this funding. B. Candidates will be citizens and permanent residents of the People's Republic of China at the time of application; overseas Chinese students may be eligible for application subject to CSC policy at the time; (CSC publicises the policy in October or November every year). C. Successful candidates must return to China upon completion of their studies and/or research. D. Candidates must hold an un-conditional offer from the University of Manchester. This excludes offers conditional upon completion of a current masters degree E. Candidates should satisfy the selection criteria set out by CSC. F. PGR students who have already started a PhD are not eligible.
Level of Study: Postgraduate, Research
Type: Scholarship
Value: Tuition fees, living allowance, airfare, visa and passport application fees
Length of Study: Three years full-time
Application Procedure: Application form: www.manchester.ac.uk/study/postgraduate-research/admissions/how-to-apply/
Closing Date: 16 January
Contributor: The University of Manchester and China Scholarship Council
Additional Information: Website: www.manchester.ac.uk/study/postgraduate-research/funding/opportunities/display/?id=00000345&offset=1&sort=name&sortdir=ascending&subjectArea=&nationality=&submit=

School of Social Sciences - Economics PhD Studentships

Eligibility: 1. Please see the programme information for academic entry requirements: www.socialsciences.manchester.ac.uk/study/postgraduate-research/programmes/list/economics-phd-mres/?pg=3#course-profile. 2. This funding is available to all nationalities.
Level of Study: Postgraduate, Research
Type: Studentship
Value: Home Fees or overseas fees, £18,500 annual maintenance stipend (to be confirmed), Students can apply for certain research expenses from the Research Training Support Grant.
Length of Study: 4 or 5 years
Frequency: Annual
Country of Study: Any country
Application Procedure: Application form: www.manchester.ac.uk/postgraduate/howtoapply/
Contributor: School of Social Sciences - Economics
Additional Information: Website: www.manchester.ac.uk/study/postgraduate-research/funding/opportunities/display/?id=00000294&offset=0&sort=name&sortdir=ascending&subjectArea=Any&nationality=United%20Kingdom&submit=Search

For further information contact:

Tel: (44) 161 275 4743
Email: pgr-soss-admissions@manchester.ac.uk

School of Social Sciences - Manchester Master

Purpose: The bursaries are aimed at widening access to master's courses by removing barriers to postgraduate education for students from underrepresented groups, so applicants need to meet a number of criteria to be eligible. Last year, there were more eligible applications than places, so meeting the criteria is no guarantee of an award
Eligibility: You will need to meet all the following (plus at least one of the demographic criteria): 1. Studying for an LLM, MA, MEd, MBA, MEnt, MPH, MPhil, MRes, MSc, MSc by Research, MusM. 2. Studying a full-time one-year or part-time two-year course, for a maximum of two years. 3. Be a home student paying tuition fees and have been in the UK for at least five years prior to starting your undergraduate course. 4. Commencing your degree course in September 2024. 5. Not hold a master's qualification or higher. 6. Commenced your undergraduate course after September 2013. 7. Intercalating medical students taking a master's course are eligible to apply. Medical students should note that if they plan to intercalate and take a master's course between Years 2 and 3, they won't be eligible for undergraduate loans in Year 3. However, there will be no interruption to funding if they intercalate between Years 3 and 4, and they will be eligible for the postgraduate loan. For more information see website
Level of Study: Doctorate, Postgraduate, Postgraduate (MSc)
Type: Bursary
Value: £4,000
Length of Study: 1 year
Frequency: Annual
Country of Study: Any country
Closing Date: 31 May
Funding: International office
No. of applicants last year: 75
Additional Information: Website: www.manchester.ac.uk/study/masters/fees-and-funding/uk-student-funding/masters-bursary/

For further information contact:

School of Social Sciences, Arthur Lewis Building, The University of Manchester, Oxford Road, Manchester M13 9PL, United Kingdom.

Tel: (44) 161 306 1340
Email: myra.knutton@manchester.ac.uk

School of Social Sciences - North West Consortium Doctoral Training Partnership (AHRC NWCDTP)

Subjects: School of Social Sciences
Eligibility: See website
Level of Study: Postgraduate, Research
Type: Studentship
Value: 1. Tuition fees 2. Stipend £17,668 per annum for 2023/24
Length of Study: Upto 8 years
Application Procedure: You must also submit your programme application. This is to ensure you hold an offer of a place by the time the NWCDTP committee make their selection. Otherwise, you will not be included in the competition. Application form: www.nwcdtp.ac.uk/
Closing Date: 3 February
Contributor: AHRC North West Consortium Doctoral Training Partnership
Additional Information: Website: www.manchester.ac.uk/study/postgraduate-research/funding/opportunities/display/?id=00000316&offset=1&sort=name&sortdir=ascending&subjectArea=&nationality=&submit=

School of Social Sciences - North West Social Sciences Doctoral Training Partnership (ESRC NWSSDTP) Studentships

Subjects: School of Social Sciences
Eligibility: See Website
Level of Study: Postgraduate, Research
Type: Studentship
Value: 1. Tuition fees up to the Home rate (£4,596 for 2023/24) 2. An annual maintenance stipend (£17,668 for 2023/24) 3. Students can claim reimbursement of research expenses via the Research Training Support Grant
Length of Study: Upto 8 years
Application Procedure: Application form: nwssdtp.ac.uk/how-to-apply/
Closing Date: 1 February
Contributor: North West Social Sciences Doctoral Training Partnership
Additional Information: Website: www.manchester.ac.uk/study/postgraduate-research/funding/opportunities/display/?id=00000297&offset=1&sort=name&sortdir=ascending&subjectArea=&nationality=&submit=

School of Social Sciences - PhD Studentship with the Stuart Hall Foundation

Subjects: School of Social Sciences

Eligibility: 1. Academic requirements: Applicants are expected to have a First Class or Upper Second Class Bachelor Honours UK degree and/or a Master's degree (or overseas equivalent) minimum merit, with a minimum overall average of 65%, including 65% in dissertation and no mark below 55%) in a social science subject. For course-specific requirements please visit our website. 2. Nationality restrictions: This funding is available to all nationalities. 3. Other eligibility criteria: Applicants must hold an offer of study at The University of Manchester before applying for this funding.
Level of Study: Postgraduate, Research
Type: Studentship
Value: 1. Tuition fees for 3 years and 6 months 2. An annual maintenance stipend (£17,668 for 2022/23).
Length of Study: 3 years full-time
Application Procedure: Applicants must first submit a complete on-line PhD application: www.manchester.ac.uk/study/postgraduate-research/admissions/
Closing Date: 1 March
Contributor: School of Social Sciences
Additional Information: Website: www.manchester.ac.uk/study/postgraduate-research/funding/opportunities/display/?id=00000422&offset=1&sort=name&sortdir=ascending&subjectArea=&nationality=&submit=

School of Social Sciences - PhD Studentships

Subjects: School of Social Sciences
Eligibility: Candidates MUST normally have: 1. Bachelors (Honours) degree (or overseas equivalent) at 2:1 level or above in a cognate subject, and 2. Normally a Masters degree at 65% overall average with minimum 65% in dissertation and with no mark below 55% (or overseas equivalent) in a relevant cognate subject, preferably one with a substantial research methods component. Transcripts will be carefully scrutinised to ensure that applicants have the required background. 3. Due to the volume of applications received each year, and limited spaces, regrettably offers cannot be made to all applicants who satisfy the academic entry criteria. 4. Competition for funding is very competitive and successfully candidates normally exceed the minimum entry requirements. 5. All applicants who pass the initial assessment stage will be interviewed before any offer is confirmed. 6. This funding is available to all nationalities. 7. Funding will not be awarded to candidates who have previously received funding from any source for PhD level study at any other University.
Level of Study: Postgraduate, Research
Type: Studentship
Value: Tuition fees, An annual maintenance stipend (£17,668 per annum for 2022/23), Students can claim for certain research expenses from the Research Training Support Grant.
Length of Study: 3.5-year PhD
Frequency: Annual
Country of Study: Any country
Application Procedure: Application form: www.manchester.ac.uk/postgraduate/howtoapply/
Closing Date: April
Additional Information: Website: www.manchester.ac.uk/study/postgraduate-research/funding/opportunities/display/?id=00000293&offset=0&sort=name&sortdir=ascending&subjectArea=Any&nationality=United%20Kingdom&submit=Search

For further information contact:

Tel: (44) 161 275 4743
Email: pgr-soss-admissions@manchester.ac.uk

School of Social Sciences - President's Doctoral Scholarship (PDS)

Subjects: School of Social Sciences
Purpose: PhD programmes in the School of Social Sciences
Eligibility: 1. Academic requirements: Applicants must hold, or expect to achieve a Masters at Merit level, including 65% overall average, 65% in dissertation and no mark below 55% 2. Nationality restrictions: This funding is available to all nationalities. 3. Other eligibility criteria: Current PhD students are NOT eligible for PDS.
Level of Study: Postgraduate, Research
Type: Studentship
Value: Tuition fees and include annual stipends of approximately £16,062
Length of Study: 3.5 year full-time programmes. Part-time studentships are also available
Application Procedure: Application form: www.manchester.ac.uk/study/postgraduate-research/admissions/
Closing Date: 1 February
Contributor: School of Social Sciences
Additional Information: Website: www.manchester.ac.uk/study/postgraduate-research/funding/opportunities/display/?id=00000428&offset=1&sort=name&sortdir=ascending&subjectArea=&nationality=&submit=

U

SEED Enhancing Racial Equality Studentship

Subjects: School of Environment, Education and Development
Eligibility: Bachelor degree with First Class or Upper Second Class Honours (or international equivalent) Master degree with a minimum grade of 60% in the dissertation and a minimum taught average grade of 60% (or international equivalent). Applicants must hold an offer of study at The

University of Manchester before applying for this funding. This scholarship is open to Home (UK) applicants who identify as BAME/People of Colour.
Level of Study: Postgraduate, Research
Type: Studentship
Value: This award will cover tuition fees and include an annual stipend (£18,668 in 2022-23) for a period of three and a half years, subject to satisfactory progress.
Length of Study: 3.5 year
Country of Study: Any country
Application Procedure: Application form: www.seed.manchester.ac.uk/study/postgraduate-research/applying/
Closing Date: 1 February
Contributor: School of Environment, Education and Development
No. of applicants last year: 1
Additional Information: Website: www.manchester.ac.uk/study/postgraduate-research/funding/opportunities/display/?id=00000439&offset=0&sort=name&sortdir=ascending&subjectArea=Any&nationality=United%20Kingdom&submit=Search

For further information contact:

Postgraduate Research Recruitment and Admissions, Oxford Rd, Manchester M13 9PL, United Kingdom.

Tel: (44) 161 275 0807
Email: pgr-seedfunding@manchester.ac.uk

Talented Athlete Scholarship Scheme (TASS)

Subjects: The University of Manchester
Eligibility: 1. Academic requirements: For athletes in Higher Education they should be studying an undergraduate programme (including HND, HNC, Degree programme including Foundation Degrees) or postgraduate (Masters, Doctorate). This can be achieved by studying full time, part time or via distance learning. 2. Nationality restrictions: This funding is available to students from: A. England B. Northern Ireland C. Scotland D. Wales
Level of Study: Postgraduate, Research
Type: Scholarship
Value: £3,500
Length of Study: 1 year with an annual application
Application Procedure: Apply via website here: www.sport.manchester.ac.uk/sport-and-activity/scholarships/
Closing Date: November
Contributor: Talented Athlete Scholarship Scheme (TASS)
Additional Information: Website: www.manchester.ac.uk/study/postgraduate-research/funding/opportunities/display/?id=00000214&offset=1&sort=name&sortdir=ascending&subjectArea=&nationality=&submit=

The John Bright Fellowship

Eligibility: Applicants should hold a BA Honours degree in English literature or another relevant field with at least a 2. i classification. Applications should also hold, or be about to complete, an MA or equivalent degree in an area relevant to the proposed doctoral research.
Level of Study: Postgraduate
Type: Bursary
Value: The Award covers home tuition fees.
Length of Study: 3 year
Frequency: Annual
Country of Study: Any country
Closing Date: 4 February
Additional Information: www.manchester.ac.uk/study/postgraduate-research/funding/opportunities/display/?id=00000404&offset=0&sort=name&sortdir=ascending&subjectArea=Any&nationality=United%20Kingdom&submit=Search

For further information contact:

Postgraduate Admissions Administrator, Oxford Rd, Manchester M13 9PL, United Kingdom.

Email: phdfunding-salc@manchester.ac.uk

The Lees Scholarship

Subjects: School of Arts, Languages and Cultures
Eligibility: Applicants must meet the entry requirements for their intended programme of study. The Scholarship is awarded for PhD research in the field of Latin (including, literary, historical, philosophical and linguistic topics).
Level of Study: Postgraduate, Research
Type: Bursary
Value: The PhD bursary funds the equivalent of three years of home (full time) or 6 years of home (part time)
Length of Study: 3 years full time or 6 years part time.
Frequency: Annual
Country of Study: Any country
Application Procedure: Application form: documents.manchester.ac.uk/display.aspx?DocID=52015
No. of awards offered: 1
Closing Date: 3 February
Additional Information: Website: www.manchester.ac.uk/study/postgraduate-research/funding/opportunities/display/?id=00000353&offset=0&sort=name&sortdir=ascending&

subjectArea=Any&nationality=United%20Kingdom&submit=Search

For further information contact:

Email: phdfunding-salc@manchester.ac.uk

The University of Manchester Humanitarian Scholarships

Purpose: our Humanitarian Scholarship programme is intended to support individuals at immediate risk who have been forced to flee their homes as a direct result of armed conflict. The awards cover full tuition fees, living expenses and visas.
Eligibility: To apply for a scholarship, you must meet all of the following eligibility criteria: 1. be at serious risk as a direct result of armed conflict, and/or 2. be displaced inside your own country or have been forced to leave your home country within the last three years because of armed conflict; 3. be unable to access or complete higher education; 4. have not previously studied, at any level, in the UK or EU; 5. have received an offer of admission for entry in September 2024; 6. be able to demonstrate knowledge of, and commitment, to your chosen course; 7. have an excellent academic background. The awards are for academically outstanding students and typically this means that you are in the top 10% of your class.
Level of Study: Masters Degree
Type: Scholarship
Value: The awards cover full tuition fees, living expenses and visas
Application Procedure: For master's level courses, you can apply online: www.manchester.ac.uk/study/masters/admissions/how-to-apply/
Closing Date: 14 April
Additional Information: Website: www.manchester.ac.uk/study/international/finance-and-scholarships/funding/humanitarian-scholarship/

The University of Manchester-China Scholarship Council Joint Scholarship

Subjects: Faculty of Science and Engineering
Purpose: These scholarships are open across all research areas to those who are both Chinese citizens and permanent residents of the People's Republic of China at the time of the application.
Eligibility: Academic requirements: To be considered for this award you must: 1. Hold an upper second class UK honours undergraduate degree (or international equivalent) from a leading Chinese university 2. Hold an unconditional offer letter from The University of Manchester 3. Ideally hold a master's-level qualification at merit or distinction (or international equivalent) 4. Have a track record of engaging with research, which may include contributions to publications/articles, promoting your research to a wider audience, prizes for research or project work; Nationality restrictions: This funding is available to students from: China. Other eligibility criteria: You will also need to: 1. Be both a citizen and permanent resident of the People's Republic of China at time of application 2. Return to China upon completion of your studies and/or research 3. Satisfy CSC's selection criteria (www.csc.edu.cn/chuguo)
Level of Study: Postgraduate, Research
Type: Scholarship
Value: 1. Living allowances as prescribed by the Chinese Government, plus airfare, visa and passport fees. 2. Full tuition fees at the international rate.
Length of Study: 3.5 years
Closing Date: 13 January
Contributor: The University of Manchester Faculty of Science and Engineering
No. of applicants last year: 40
Additional Information: Website: www.manchester.ac.uk/study/postgraduate-research/funding/opportunities/display/?id=00000467&offset=1&sort=name&sortdir=ascending&subjectArea=&nationality=&submit=

University of Manchester President's Doctoral Scholar Awards (PDS Awards)

Subjects: Alliance Manchester Business School
Eligibility: 1. Applicants must have obtained a First or Upper Second Class Honours degree (or equivalent) and hold (or expect to obtain) a Masters-level qualification with Distinction. They should have a track-record of research engagement (including relevant research experience and dissemination) and/or potential for outstanding research, as demonstrated in the quality of the proposal submitted as part of the application. 2. English Language requirements (where required) are IELTS 7.0 or TOEFL 623 (100 internet based test). 3. Applicants must hold an offer of study at The University of Manchester before applying for this funding.
Level of Study: Postgraduate, Research
Type: Studentship
Value: tuition fee and stipend, £1,000 p.a.
Length of Study: 4 years
Frequency: Annual
Country of Study: Any country
Application Procedure: To be considered for one of these awards, candidates should submit a PhD application: www.alliancembs.manchester.ac.uk/study/phd/how-to-apply-for-

a-phd/ and indicate that they wish to be considered for this funding opportunity. Application form: www.alliancembs.manchester.ac.uk/study/phd/how-to-apply-for-a-phd/
No. of awards offered: 2
Closing Date: 24 February
No. of applicants last year: 2
Additional Information: Website: www.manchester.ac.uk/study/postgraduate-research/funding/opportunities/display/?id=00000285&offset=0&sort=name&sortdir=ascending&subjectArea=Any&nationality=United%20Kingdom&submit=Search

For further information contact:

Doctoral Programmes Office, Oxford Rd, Manchester M13 9PL, United Kingdom.

Tel: (44) (0)161 275 1200
Email: ambs-pgresearch@manchester.ac.uk

Usher Bursary

Subjects: School of Arts, Languages and Cultures
Eligibility: 1. Academic requirements: Please refer to the application guidance here: www.alc.manchester.ac.uk/study/postgraduate-research/applying/ 2. Nationality restrictions: This funding is available to all nationalities. 3. Other eligibility criteria: This award can be held alongside other awards.
Level of Study: Postgraduate, Research
Type: Bursary
Value: Full home tuition fees
Length of Study: 3 years
Application Procedure: Application form: documents.manchester.ac.uk/display.aspx?DocID=52015
Closing Date: 3 February
Contributor: Usher Fund in Art History
No. of applicants last year: 1
Additional Information: website: www.manchester.ac.uk/study/postgraduate-research/funding/opportunities/display/?id=00000484&offset=1&sort=name&sortdir=ascending&subjectArea=&nationality=&submit=

University of Melbourne

The University of Melbourne, Grattan Street, Parkville, VIC 3010, Australia.

Tel: (61) 3 9035 5511
Email: pg-schools@unimelb.edu.au
Website: www.unimelb.edu.au

Bryan Scholarships

Subjects: Sciences and mathematics
Purpose: This scholarship is awarded to a student who has successfully completed a Bachelor of Science at the University of Melbourne and is undertaking a Bachelor of Science (Honours) or the first year of a research training program in the Master of Science, or the Postgraduate Diploma in Science in a branch of natural science, on the basis of academic merit.
Eligibility: To be eligible for this scholarship, you must: 1. Be a University of Melbourne Bachelor of Science Graduate, 2. Be enrolled in a Bachelor of Science (Honours) or the first year of a research training program in the Master of Science, or the Postgraduate Diploma in Science in a branch of natural science. Australian / domestic student International student
Level of Study: Masters Degree, Postgraduate
Type: Scholarship
Value: up to AU$2000
Frequency: Annual
Country of Study: Any country
Application Procedure: No application is required. You will be automatically considered for this award.
No. of awards offered: 2
Additional Information: Website: scholarships.unimelb.edu.au/awards/bryan-scholarships

For further information contact:

The University of Melbourne Grattan Street, Parkville, Victoria 3010, Australia.

Tel: (61) 3 9035 5511

China Scholarship Council - University of Melbourne PhD Scholarship

Purpose: This scholarship was established by the Chinese Scholarship Council and the University of Melbourne to promote international collaboration and is awarded to citizens of the People's Republic of China wishing to undertake a Doctor of Philosophy (PhD) degree at the University of Melbourne.
Eligibility: be a citizen of the People's Republic of China have received an offer for a place in a Doctor of Philosophy (PhD) course at the University of Melbourne. This requires completion of at least a four-year undergraduate degree, with the equivalent of a minimum overall average grade of H2A (or 75%) achieved at the University of Melbourne with a significant research component. Applicants are also required to meet minimum English language requirements.

Level of Study: Doctorate
Type: Scholarship
Value: 100% fee remission and up to AU$120,000
Frequency: Annual
Country of Study: Any country
Application Procedure: There is a two-stage application process. Stage 1: Applying to the University of Melbourne for entry to the PhD. Stage 2: Applying to the CSC for the living allowance scholarship. For Detailed explanations see website
No. of awards offered: Up to 45
Closing Date: 25 February
Additional Information: Website: scholarships.unimelb.edu.au/awards/china-scholarship-council-university-of-melbourne-phd-scholarship

For further information contact:

The University of Melbourne Grattan Street, Parkville, Victoria 3010, Australia.

Tel: (61) 3 9035 5511

Coursework Access Scholarships

Purpose: A suite of coursework access scholarships is available to undergraduate and graduate students who have experienced or are experiencing compassionate or compelling circumstances.
Eligibility: 1. Be an Australian citizen or permanent resident 2. have applied for or be enrolled in an undergraduate or graduate degree by coursework at the University of Melbourne 3. have at least twelve months of full-time equivalent study remaining to complete your course 4. be experiencing compassionate or compelling circumstances (e.g. having primary care responsibilities for a dependent, medical condition, disability, or personal or financial difficulties) 5. meet the requirements for one of the following scholarships A. Hugh Kingsley Family Scholarship B. Irene and Arthur Kinsman Award for Postgraduate Studies C. Eleanor and Joseph Wertheim Scholarship
Level of Study: Graduate
Type: Scholarship
Value: AU$5,000 - AU$20,000
Frequency: Annual
Country of Study: Any country
Application Procedure: You will need to submit one application to be considered for the following scholarships: 1. Hugh Kingsley Family Scholarship 2. Irene and Arthur Kinsman Award for Postgraduate Studies 3. Eleanor and Joseph Wertheim Scholarship
No. of awards offered: 8
Closing Date: 31 January
Additional Information: Website: scholarships.unimelb.edu.au/awards/coursework-access-scholarships

For further information contact:

The University of Melbourne Grattan Street, Parkville, Victoria 3010, Australia.

Tel: (61) 3 9035 5511

Dairy Postgraduate Scholarships and Awards

Purpose: To enable students for research contributing to the technical areas relevant to dairy farming and dairy manufacturing operations
Eligibility: Open to citizens or permanent residents of Australia.
Level of Study: Postgraduate
Type: Scholarship
Value: AU$25,000 stipend plus AU$3,000 per year
Frequency: Annual
Country of Study: Australia
Application Procedure: To apply for this scholarship one must apply direct to the faculty
Closing Date: 20 October
Additional Information: Website: www.postgraduatefunding.com/award-4149

For further information contact:

Scholarships Office, Melbourne, VIC 3010, Australia.

Tel: (61) 3 8344 4000
Fax: (61) 3 8344 5104
Email: gsa@gsa.unimelb.edu.au
Website: www.unimelb.edu.au/

Diane Lemaire Scholarship

Purpose: This scholarship is made possible through a bequest from the late Diane Lemaire, who was the first woman to graduate with an engineering degree from the University of Melbourne in 1942. It's available to female PhD students in the Faculty of Engineering & IT to fund a project or proposal that will enhance the applicant's PhD and research outcomes.
Eligibility: To be eligible for this scholarship, you must: 1. identify as a female 2. be enrolled in a PhD in the Faculty of Engineering and Information Technology 3. have completed the equivalent of at least six months candidature

Level of Study: Postgraduate
Type: Scholarship
Value: AU$4,000 - AU$15,000
Frequency: Annual
Country of Study: Any country
Application Procedure: Submit an online application via the Faculty of Engineering & IT graduate research scholarships webpage.
No. of awards offered: Approximately 3
Closing Date: 30 January
Additional Information: website: scholarships.unimelb.edu.au/awards/diane-lemaire-scholarship

For further information contact:

The University of Melbourne Grattan Street, Parkville, Victoria 3010, Australia.

Tel: (61) 3 9035 5511

Dr Betty Elliott Horticulture Scholarship

Purpose: This scholarship is awarded to a student undertaking postgraduate research in the discipline of sustainability in horticulture, on the basis of demonstrated academic merit and financial need.
Eligibility: To be eligible for this scholarship, you must: 1. Be undertaking postgraduate research in the discipline of sustainability in horticulture, 2. Demonstrate financial need by filling in the application.
Level of Study: Postgraduate
Type: Scholarship
Value: Up to AU$12,000 is available to award in scholarships. This scholarship is usually awarded at around AU$3,000.
Frequency: Annual
Country of Study: Any country
Application Procedure: Apply via the link below - applications are open on a rolling basis until 30 November. Application Link: scienceunimelb.smartygrants.com.au/betty2023
No. of awards offered: 8
Closing Date: 31 March
Additional Information: Website: scholarships.unimelb.edu.au/awards/dr-betty-elliott-horticulture-scholarship

For further information contact:

The University of Melbourne Grattan Street, Parkville, Victoria 3010, Australia.

Tel: (61) 3 9035 5511

Eleanor and Joseph Wertheim Scholarship

Purpose: The Eleanor and Joseph Wertheim Scholarship was established with a bequest from Dr Eleanor Sabina Wertheim, and is offered to single, mature-aged, female undergraduate or graduate students who are experiencing disadvantaged circumstances.
Eligibility: be a single female student over 25 years of age at the time of application an Australian citizen or permanent resident have applied for or be enrolled in an undergraduate or graduate degree by coursework at the University of Melbourne have at least twelve months of full-time equivalent study remaining to complete your course be experiencing compassionate or compelling circumstances (e.g. having primary care responsibilities for a dependent, medical condition, disability, or personal or financial difficulties)
Level of Study: Graduate
Type: Scholarship
Value: Up to AU$5,000
Frequency: Annual
Country of Study: Any country
Application Procedure: You must submit a Coursework Access Scholarships application: scholarships.unimelb.edu.au/awards/coursework-access-scholarships.
No. of awards offered: 8
Closing Date: 31 January
Additional Information: Website: scholarships.unimelb.edu.au/awards/wertheim

For further information contact:

The University of Melbourne Grattan Street, Parkville, Victoria 3010, Australia.

Tel: (61) 3 9035 5511

Frank Keenan Scholarship

Purpose: This scholarship is awarded to graduate or undergraduate students studying at Burnley College, based on academic merit undertaking study relating to the advancement of services and practices of amenity and/or ornamental horticulture.
Eligibility: To be eligible for this scholarship, you must: 1. Enrolled in any undergraduate, graduate coursework, or graduate research course at the Burnley Campus. 2. Undertaking study relating to the advancement of services and practices of amenity and/or ornamental horticulture
Level of Study: Graduate
Type: Scholarship
Value: AU$1,000 - AU$3,000
Frequency: Annual
Country of Study: Any country

Application Procedure: Submit the Scholarship application: scienceunimelb.smartygrants.com.au/Keenan2023
No. of awards offered: At least 1
Closing Date: 31 March
Additional Information: Website: scholarships.unimelb.edu.au/awards/frank-keenan-scholarship

For further information contact:

The University of Melbourne Grattan Street, Parkville, Victoria 3010, Australia.

Tel: (61) 3 9035 5511

Frank Knox Memorial Fellowships

Purpose: Established in honour of the late Frank Knox to encourage scholarly exchange between the United States and the British Commonwealth, this scholarship supports graduate coursework students to undertake graduate study at Harvard University.
Eligibility: have applied directly to the relevant graduate school at Harvard University for your chosen degree program have Australian citizenship at the time of application and normally reside in Australia have graduated with a Bachelor or higher degree at an Australian university by the 2023–2024 academic year have completed the Bachelor or higher degree no earlier than 2019
Level of Study: Graduate
Type: Fellowship
Value: 100% fee remission and up to AU$60,000
Frequency: Annual
Country of Study: Any country
Application Procedure: The below documents must be submitted via the Frank Knox Memorial Fellowship application portal by 1st February: 1. Certified copies of all academic transcripts 2. Curriculum vitae 3. Personal essay (maximum 1000 words); provide an account of your academic pursuits, intellectual interests, extra-curricular activities, and the reasons for your desire to study at Harvard University; the essay should also explain your plan of study at Harvard and your future career plans. 4. Two confidential letters of recommendation
No. of awards offered: Up to 3
Closing Date: 1 February
Additional Information: website: scholarships.unimelb.edu.au/awards/frank-knox-memorial-fellowships

For further information contact:

The University of Melbourne Grattan Street, Parkville, Victoria 3010, Australia.

Tel: (61) 3 9035 5511

Friends of the Sports Association Scholarship

Purpose: Supported by the Sport Foundation Chapter, these scholarships provide cash and in-kind assistance to help aspiring High Performance student-athletes to simultaneously pursue their academic and sporting dreams.
Eligibility: To be eligible for this scholarship, you must: be a member of the relevant Melbourne University Sporting Club, represent the University in varsity competition and be competing at a junior national team level (or equivalent).
Type: Scholarship
Value: at least AU$7,000
Frequency: Annual
Country of Study: Any country
Application Procedure: Submit a completed Elite Athlete Program application form online. Further details and application form are available here: sport.unimelb.edu.au/programs/elite-athlete-program
No. of awards offered: 12
Closing Date: 13 March
Additional Information: Website: scholarships.unimelb.edu.au/awards/friends-of-the-sports-association-scholarship

For further information contact:

The University of Melbourne Grattan Street, Parkville, Victoria 3010, Australia.

Tel: (61) 3 9035 5511

Fulbright Scholarships

Subjects: All study areas
Purpose: This scholarship supports Australian students to study in the US, with varying benefits depending on your level of study.
Eligibility: 1. To be eligible for this scholarship, you must: meet the criteria listed on the Fulbright Australia website: www.fulbright.org.au/applicants/australian-applicants/ 2. Fulbright scholarships are open to Postgraduates, Postdoctoral, Professional and Senior Scholars from any field of study.
Level of Study: Postdoctorate, Postgraduate
Type: Scholarship
Value: See website
Application Procedure: Apply directly via the Fulbright Australia website: www.fulbright.org.au/applicants/.
No. of awards offered: Approximately 10
Closing Date: 1 July
Additional Information: Website: scholarships.unimelb.edu.au/awards/fulbright-scholarships#full-benefit-details

Graduate Research Scholarships

Subjects: All study areas
Purpose: Available to high-achieving students undertaking graduate research at the University of Melbourne.
Eligibility: To be eligible for this scholarship, you must: have applied for and meet the entry requirements for a graduate research degree at the University of Melbourne, or be currently enrolled in a graduate research degree at the University of Melbourne
Level of Study: Graduate
Type: Scholarship
Value: 100% fee remission and up to AU$110,000
Frequency: Annual
Country of Study: Any country
Application Procedure: No application is required. You will be automatically considered for this award. see website for details
No. of awards offered: Approximately 600
Additional Information: Website: scholarships.unimelb.edu.au/awards/graduate-research-scholarships

For further information contact:

The University of Melbourne Grattan Street, Parkville, Victoria 3010, Australia.

Tel: (61) 3 9035 5511

Graduate Women Victoria Scholarship Program

Purpose: The Graduate Women Victoria Scholarship Program is a suite of scholarships and bursaries offered to women studying at Victorian universities who have overcome or are overcoming disadvantage. The Program is offered and run by Graduate Women Victoria.
Eligibility: To be eligible for this scholarship, you must: 1. be an Australian citizen or permanent resident 2. be female 3. be enrolled in an eligible course at a Victorian university, or at the Victorian campuses of the Australian Catholic University, in the year of application 4. have overcome or are overcoming disadvantage in the pursuit of your studies.
Level of Study: Graduate
Type: Scholarship
Value: AU$3,500 - AU$9,000
Frequency: Annual
Country of Study: Any country
Application Procedure: All applicants must apply online at gwvschols.gradwomenvic.org.au/
No. of awards offered: 16
Closing Date: 31 March
Additional Information: website: scholarships.unimelb.edu.au/awards/graduate-women-victoria-scholarship-program

For further information contact:

The University of Melbourne Grattan Street, Parkville, Victoria 3010, Australia.

Tel: (61) 3 9035 5511

Hansen Scholarship

Purpose: The Hansen Scholarship is a flagship scholarship program at The University of Melbourne. From 2020, The Hansen Scholarship will be awarded to talented students whose financial circumstances present a challenge to accessing a first-class education. Recipients will be awarded accommodation, an allowance, and financial and personal support.
Eligibility: be an Australian citizen or permanent resident, and be enrolled in an Australian Year 12 or the International Baccalaureate in Australia; or have applied for or be the holder of an Australian temporary or permanent protection visa, and be enrolled in an Australian Year 12 or the International Baccalaureate in Australia; or be an Australian citizen and be enrolled in an Australian Year 12 or the International Baccalaureate outside Australia. be aged between 16 and 20 years of age in the year of application be on track to achieve a minimum Australian Tertiary Admissions Rank (ATAR) of at least 90 (or the IB equivalent) experience financial circumstances that present a challenge to attending The University of Melbourne. (e.g. you or your family receive Centrelink benefits)
Type: Scholarship
Value: Up to AU$108,000
Frequency: Annual
Country of Study: Any country
Application Procedure: See website
No. of awards offered: 20
Closing Date: 30 March
Additional Information: Website: scholarships.unimelb.edu.au/awards/hansen-scholarship

For further information contact:

The University of Melbourne Grattan Street, Parkville, Victoria 3010, Australia.

Tel: (61) 3 9035 5511

Henry and Louisa Williams Bequest

Subjects: All study areas
Purpose: The Henry and Louisa Williams Bequest was established with a gift from Alfred, Alice and Robert Williams. Scholarships provided by the fund are offered to students undertaking research in a field of study other than theology and music in the names of Henry James Williams, Frederick Charles Williams, Alice Louisa Williams, Alfred Edward Williams and Robert George Williams.
Eligibility: To be eligible for this scholarship, you must: 1. be an Australian citizen or permanent resident 2. have received an offer for a graduate research degree at the University of Melbourne and intend to undertake research in a field of study other than theology and music. 3. have not already completed a research qualification at the same or higher level as the course for which a scholarship is sought 4. not have previously received a graduate research scholarship with equivalent benefits
Level of Study: Research
Type: Scholarship
Value: AU$70,000 - AU$125,000
Frequency: Annual
Country of Study: Any country
Application Procedure: If you have applied for admission to a graduate research degree by 31 October for commencement in the following year, you will be automatically considered for this scholarships.
No. of awards offered: 10
Additional Information: website: scholarships.unimelb.edu.au/awards/henry-james-williams-scholarship

For further information contact:

The University of Melbourne Grattan Street, Parkville, Victoria 3010, Australia.

Tel: (61) 3 9035 5511

High Performance Sports Scholarship

Purpose: Supported by the Sport Foundation Chapter, these scholarships provide cash and in-kind assistance to help aspiring High Performance student-athletes to simultaneously pursue their academic and sporting dreams.
Eligibility: To be eligible for this scholarship, you must: Be a member of the relevant Melbourne University Sporting Club, represent the University in varsity competition and be competing at a senior national team level (or the equivalent).
Type: Scholarship
Value: at least AU$8,000
Frequency: Annual
Country of Study: Any country
Application Procedure: Submit a completed Elite Athlete Program application form here: sport.unimelb.edu.au/programs/elite-athlete-program.
No. of awards offered: 8
Closing Date: 13 March
Additional Information: Website: scholarships.unimelb.edu.au/awards/high-performance-sports-scholarship

For further information contact:

The University of Melbourne Grattan Street, Parkville, Victoria 3010, Australia.

Tel: (61) 3 9035 5511

Hilda Trevelyan Morrison Bequest

Purpose: This scholarship is awarded to a faculty of science student on the basis of demonstrated financial need.
Eligibility: To be eligible for this scholarship, you must: 1. Be enrolled in a Faculty of Science program, 2. Demonstrate Financial Need by completing the online Student Financial Assessment Form by no later than the 8th of March 2024
Type: Scholarship
Value: Up to AU$5,000
Frequency: Annual
Country of Study: Any country
Application Procedure: Submit a Student Financial Assessment Form: unimelb-scholarships.smartygrants.com.au/SFA
No. of awards offered: 8
Closing Date: 8 March
Additional Information: website: scholarships.unimelb.edu.au/awards/hilda-trevelyan-morrison-bequest

For further information contact:

The University of Melbourne Grattan Street, Parkville, Victoria 3010, Australia.

Tel: (61) 3 9035 5511

Indigenous Accommodation Grant

Purpose: The Indigenous Accommodation Grant is offered to Indigenous students who are residing at University Accommodation or Residential College and are ineligible for government accommodation funding or other forms of financial support.
Eligibility: To be eligible for this scholarship, you must: 1. be of Aboriginal and/or Torres Strait Islander descent, identify as Aboriginal and/or Torres Strait Islander, and be accepted as Aboriginal and/or Torres Strait Islander by the community in

which they live, or formerly lived 2. be currently enrolled in a degree at The University of Melbourne 3. be residing in one of the University of Melbourne's affiliated accommodation providers, as listed on the following webpages: Residential Colleges and other accommodation, and University Accommodation.
Type: Grant
Value: Up to AU$10,000
Frequency: Annual
Country of Study: Any country
Application Procedure: You must submit an application for the Student Grants: scholarships.unimelb.edu.au/awards/student-grants to be considered for this bursary.
No. of awards offered: 20
Closing Date: 8 March
Additional Information: Website: scholarships.unimelb.edu.au/awards/indigenous-accommodation-grant

For further information contact:

The University of Melbourne Grattan Street, Parkville, Victoria 3010, Australia.

Tel: (61) 3 9035 5511

International House Scholarship

Purpose: Live at International House residential college while studying at the University of Melbourne. This scholarship supports commencing students with a fee remission of US$7,000 at International House. It is funded by charitable giving to International House by friends and alumni.
Eligibility: International or domestic student applying to live at International House.
Type: Scholarship
Value: Up to AU$7,000
Frequency: Annual
Country of Study: Any country
No. of awards offered: 3
Closing Date: 18 January
Additional Information: https://scholarships.unimelb.edu.au/awards/international-house-scholarships

For further information contact:

The University of Melbourne Grattan Street, Parkville, Victoria 3010, Australia.

Irene and Arthur Kinsman Award for Postgraduate Studies

Purpose: The Irene and Arthur Kinsman Award for Postgraduate Studies was established with a bequest from Mavis Kinsman, and is offered to female graduates from the University of Melbourne who intend to undertake graduate study in social sciences.
Eligibility: be a female graduate of the University of Melbourne an Australian citizen or permanent resident have applied for or be enrolled in a graduate degree by coursework in Social Sciences at the University of Melbourne have at least twelve months of full-time equivalent study remaining to complete your course be experiencing compassionate or compelling circumstances (e.g. having primary care responsibilities for a dependent, medical condition, disability, or personal or financial difficulties)
Level of Study: Postgraduate
Type: Scholarship
Value: Up to AU$5,000
Frequency: Annual
Country of Study: Any country
Application Procedure: You must submit a Coursework Access Scholarships application.
No. of awards offered: Approximately 2
Closing Date: 31 January
Additional Information: Website: scholarships.unimelb.edu.au/awards/kinsman

For further information contact:

The University of Melbourne Grattan Street, Parkville, Victoria 3010, Australia.

Tel: (61) 3 9035 5511

Italian Australian Foundation Travel Scholarships

Purpose: The Italian Australian Foundation Travel Scholarship supports Faculty of Arts students of Italian descent who are planning to travel to and study in Italy.
Eligibility: To be eligible for this scholarship, you must: 1. be a student of Italian descent defined as being able to trace Italian ancestry within three generations on at least one side of the family; 2. be enrolled in a Bachelor of Arts, Diploma in Languages in Italian Studies or postgraduate course in the Faculty of Arts and wish to travel for the purpose of formal study of Italian language, culture and/or heritage; and, 3. require financial support.
Level of Study: Postgraduate
Type: Scholarship
Value: up to AU$40,000
Frequency: Annual
Country of Study: Any country
Application Procedure: Eligible applicants are required to submit the online application form including: 1. a proposal outlining the travel activities that will be undertaken; 2. a

300-500 word statement describing how you would use this scholarship, how overseas travel is relevant to your study and how it would positively impact your academic work, including how the support will assist you financially; 3. an indicative budget; 4. at least one academic reference; 5. a current statement of results; 6. proof of Italian descent (please supply a copy of your parents or grandparents' passport, birth certificate, citizenship certificate, or death certificate; the document/s does not need to be an original certified copy but the committee reserve the right to request the original at a later date if required); and, 7. any other information to support the application that may assist the committee in making its decision.
Closing Date: 10 April
Additional Information: website: scholarships.unimelb.edu.au/awards/italian-australian-foundation-travel-scholarship

For further information contact:

The University of Melbourne Grattan Street, Parkville, Victoria 3010, Australia.

Tel: (61) 3 9035 5511

Jack Keating Fund Scholarship

Purpose: This scholarship supports research students of the Melbourne Graduate School of Education who are pursuing policy research in the field of education, where the research is likely to impact on greater equality of opportunity and education outcomes and the advancement of social justice. This scholarship is awarded in the memory of Professor Jack Keating, who was a specialist in post compulsory education and training, most noted for his contribution to education policy and debates.
Eligibility: be an Australian citizen or permanent resident be a current or prospective research student (with at least a year of candidature remaining as at the closing date) of the Melbourne Graduate School of Education be pursuing policy research in the field of education where the research is likely to impact on greater equality of opportunity and education outcomes and the advancement of social justice
Level of Study: Graduate, Research
Type: Scholarship
Value: Up to AU$8,500
Frequency: Annual
Country of Study: Any country
Application Procedure: 1. Completion of application via the online application form (the application form will be available when the scholarship opens) 2. Applications are ranked by the selection committee which consists of four academics and a member of the Keating family 3. Shortlisted applicants may be invited to an interview 4. Supervisors may be contacted
No. of awards offered: 2
Closing Date: 9 February
Additional Information: Website: scholarships.unimelb.edu.au/awards/jack-keating-fund-scholarship

For further information contact:

The University of Melbourne Grattan Street, Parkville, Victoria 3010, Australia.

Tel: (61) 3 9035 5511

Jean E Laby PhD Travelling Scholarships

Purpose: This scholarship supports support PhD students in Physics for travel, preferably overseas, to enhance their research program and research experience.
Eligibility: To be eligible for this scholarship, you must: 1. Be confirmed as a PhD candidate in the School of Physics 2. Provide a short statement of endorsement from your supervisor 3. Be undertaking travel for a research related purpose. If you are requesting conference funds, you must be presenting research results.
Level of Study: Postgraduate
Type: Scholarship
Value: Up to AU$5,000
Frequency: Annual
Country of Study: Any country
Application Procedure: See website
No. of awards offered: 5
Closing Date: 31 March
Additional Information: Website: scholarships.unimelb.edu.au/awards/jean-e-laby-phd-travelling-scholarships

For further information contact:

The University of Melbourne Grattan Street, Parkville, Victoria 3010, Australia.

Tel: (61) 3 9035 5511

U

Madeleine Selwyn-Smith Memorial Scholarships

Purpose: The Madeleine Selwyn-Smith Memorial Award is open for award annually to a graduate student engaged in the conduct of research relating to arboriculture.
Eligibility: To be eligible for this scholarship, you must: Be a graduate coursework student or graduate researcher at the University of Melbourne Faculty of Science undertaking research in the discipline of arboriculture.

Level of Study: Graduate
Type: Scholarship
Value: Up to AU$3000.
Frequency: Annual
Country of Study: Any country
Application Procedure: Fill in an scholarship application form online and submit it to the Faculty of Science by the due date
No. of awards offered: 6
Closing Date: 31 March
Additional Information: Website: scholarships.unimelb.edu.au/awards/madeleine-selwyn-smith-memorial-scholarships

For further information contact:

The University of Melbourne Grattan Street, Parkville, Victoria 3010, Australia.

Tel: (61) 3 9035 5511

Melbourne Mobility Excellence Awards

Purpose: A range of awards to support students undertaking overseas study.
Eligibility: be enrolled at the University of Melbourne in either an undergraduate degree or a graduate coursework degree intend to undertake approved overseas study of 12 weeks or more (Exchange or Study Abroad) as part of your course within 12 months after the closing date have achieved a Course Weighted Average of at least 80 in your current course
Type: Award
Value: AU$2,500 - AU$4,000
Frequency: Annual
Country of Study: Any country
Application Procedure: Apply via this link: unimelb-scholarships.smartygrants.com.au/melb-mobility-excellence
No. of awards offered: 5
Closing Date: 31 May
Additional Information: website: scholarships.unimelb.edu.au/awards/melbourne-mobility-excellence-awards

For further information contact:

The University of Melbourne Grattan Street, Parkville, Victoria 3010, Australia.

Melbourne Welcome Grant

Purpose: The Melbourne Welcome Grant is aimed at assisting international students with the cost of travel and adjustment to study and life in Melbourne.
Eligibility: To be eligible for this scholarship, you must: 1. be an international student enrolled in a coursework or research course 2. have commenced your course in or before 2023 and re-enrolled for 2024. 3. have arrived in Australia between 1 December 2022 and 31 March 2024 4. not have departed Australia on or after the start of Semester 2, 2022 (26 July 2022) 5. not have previously received a Student Travel Grant or Melbourne Welcome Grant towards the cost of transitioning to study and life in Melbourne.
Level of Study: Postgraduate
Type: Grant
Value: AU$4,000.
Frequency: Annual
Country of Study: Any country
Application Procedure: You must submit an online Melbourne Welcome Grant application: unimelb-scholarships.smartygrants.com.au/melbourne-welcome-grant
No. of awards offered: over 15,000
Closing Date: 30 April
Additional Information: Website: scholarships.unimelb.edu.au/awards/melbourne-welcome-grant

For further information contact:

The University of Melbourne, Grattan Street, Parkville, Victoria 3010, Australia.

Tel: (61) 3 9035 5511

New Colombo Plan Grant

Purpose: Funded by the Department of Foreign Affairs and Trade (DFAT), the New Colombo Plan mobility program provides funding to Australian undergraduate students studying in the Indo-Pacific region.
Eligibility: To be eligible for this scholarship, you must: 1. be an Australian citizen and do not hold dual citizenship or residency rights of the host location of the mobility program 2. be enrolled in an undergraduate University of Melbourne course 3. be between 18 and 28* years of age at the commencement of the mobility program (*Aboriginal and/or Torres Strait Islander students do not need to be aged between 18 and 28.) 4. have not commenced a period of overseas study in the same host location as the mobility program 5. have not received a Melbourne Mobility Award for the same overseas program 6. have not received an Endeavour Student Exchange Grant, or the Lin Martin Scholarship 7. New Colombo Plan: A. have not received a Student Grant under more than one Semester Grant B. have not received a Student Grant under more than one Short-term Grant C. have not received a Student Grant under both a Semester Grant and a Short-term Grant for the same Mobility Project or for the

same period of travel outside of Australia. 8. be approved to participate in a University of Melbourne Overseas Program supported by New Colombo Plan funding.
Level of Study: Postgraduate
Type: Grant
Value: AU$1,000 - AU$7,000
Frequency: Annual
Country of Study: Any country
Application Procedure: 1. Short-term programs: Eligible students will apply for available NCP grants as part of their University of Melbourne application to the relevant short-term program: studyos.students.unimelb.edu.au/. 2. Semester-long exchange programs: Eligible students will apply for available NCP grants as part of their University of Melbourne application to the relevant Semester-exchange program. Only students who preference an eligible NCP host institution will submit an application.
No. of awards offered: 150
Closing Date: 1 January
Additional Information: Website: scholarships.unimelb.edu.au/awards/new-colombo-plan-grant

For further information contact:

The University of Melbourne Grattan Street, Parkville, Victoria 3010, Australia.

Tel: (61) 3 9035 5511

Rae and Edith Bennett Travelling Scholarship

Purpose: This scholarship was established with bequests from Rae and Edith Bennett, and is offered to students or graduates from the University of Melbourne who intend to undertake graduate study or research in England, Scotland Wales or Northern Ireland.
Eligibility: Open to students and graduates of the University of Melbourne who can demonstrate outstanding academic merit and promise
Level of Study: Postgraduate
Type: Scholarship
Value: Up to AU$90,000
Frequency: Annual
Country of Study: Australia
Application Procedure: Please see the website www.services.unimelb.edu.au/scholarships/research/local/available/travelling/rae
No. of awards offered: 6
Closing Date: 1 February
Funding: Private
Contributor: Rae and Edith Bennett Travelling Scholarship Fund

For further information contact:

Email: gsa@gsa.unimelb.edu.au

S.F. Pond Travelling Scholarship

Purpose: This scholarship is awarded to a postgraduate student who is undertaking research in the discipline of Forest Science.
Eligibility: Be a postgraduate student engaged in forestry research, Be undertaking a research project that requires funding for travel or fieldwork. Provide evidence of conference attendance, Provide evidence of abstract submission and acceptance, Provide a letter of invitation from your host university that confirms laboratory attendance. Outline a fieldwork expenditure budget.
Level of Study: Postgraduate
Type: Scholarship
Value: AU$2500
Frequency: Annual
Country of Study: Any country
Application Procedure: Submit scholarship application online by the due date: Submit scholarship application online by the due date
No. of awards offered: 5
Closing Date: 31 March
Additional Information: Website: scholarships.unimelb.edu.au/awards/samuel-francis-ponds-trust

For further information contact:

The University of Melbourne Grattan Street, Parkville, Victoria 3010, Australia.

Tel: (61) 3 9035 5511

Sir Arthur Sims Travelling Scholarship

Purpose: This scholarship was established in 1945 with a donation from Sir Arthur Sims, and is awarded to students who intend to pursue further study or research in subjects Ancient or Modern Languages, History, Philosophy, Physics, Chemistry, Mathematics, and Medicine in Great Britain.in.
Eligibility: To be eligible for this scholarship, you need to 1. have graduated from any Australian university or be currently enrolled at the University of Melbourne; 2. were born in any of the States or Territories of Australia or are the child of parents both of whom have been resident in Australia for a period of seven years or more such period of residence having commenced within a period of three years since the birth of the child 3. intend to undertake

a graduate degree or research in the subjects Ancient or Modern Languages, History, Philosophy, Physics, Chemistry, Mathematics, and Medicine at an educational institution in Great Britain; and 4. not have completed a course of study at the same or higher level as the proposed overseas study.
Level of Study: Graduate, Postgraduate, Research
Type: Scholarship
Value: Up to AU$48,000
Country of Study: United Kingdom
Application Procedure: See: Prestigious Travelling Scholarships: scholarships.unimelb.edu.au/awards/prestigious_travelling_scholarship
No. of awards offered: 1
Closing Date: 31 May
Funding: Private
Additional Information: Website: scholarships.unimelb.edu.au/awards/sir-arthur-sims-travelling-scholarship#:~:text=This%20scholarship%20was%20established%20in,and%20Medicine%20in%20Great%20Britain

Sir Thomas Naghten Fitzgerald Scholarship

Subjects: Medicine, dentistry, health and welfare
Purpose: For domestic medical graduates undertaking a graduate research degree in surgery through the Faculty of Medicine, Dentistry and Health Sciences. It was established with a bequest from the late Kathleen Maggie Douglas in memory of her father.
Eligibility: To be eligible for this scholarship, you must: 1. be an outstanding graduate research applicant, or enrolled graduate researcher, of the Faculty of Medicine, Dentistry and Health Sciences 2. be a medical graduate undertaking research in surgery 3. satisfy the Faculty's entry requirements for PhD
Level of Study: Graduate, Research
Type: Scholarship
Value: up to AU$7,200
Frequency: Annual
Study Establishment: University of Melbourne
Country of Study: Australia
Application Procedure: Commencing students will be automatically considered. Continuing students must complete an online application for Graduate Research Scholarships: scholarships.unimelb.edu.au/awards/graduate-research-scholarships.
No. of awards offered: 1
Funding: Government
Additional Information: Please direct your enquiries to mdhs-scholarships@unimelb.edu.au. Website: scholarships.unimelb.edu.au/awards/the-sir-thomas-naghten-fitzgerald-scholarship

For further information contact:

Email: mdhs-scholarships@unimelb.edu.au

Sport Access Scholarship

Purpose: Melbourne University Sport proudly offers students facing financial hardship with a complimentary fitness membership.
Eligibility: To be eligible for this scholarship, you must: 1. Be enrolled in a course of study with the University of Melbourne 2. Have an academic status of good standing 3. Must not be receiving subsidised Fitness Membership Access through alternative means or programs
Type: Scholarship
Value: at least AU$800
Frequency: Annual
Country of Study: Any country
Application Procedure: You must submit a complete and submit an online Sport Access Scholarship Application Form: melbourneuniversitysport.formstack.com/forms/sports_access_2023 and an online Student Financial Need Assessment: unimelb-scholarships.smartygrants.com.au/SFA by the closing date.
No. of awards offered: 150
Closing Date: 8 March
Additional Information: Website: scholarships.unimelb.edu.au/awards/sport-access-scholarship

For further information contact:

The University of Melbourne Grattan Street, Parkville, Victoria 3010, Australia.

Tel: (61) 3 9035 5511

Student Grants

Purpose: Over 150 bursaries established by various generous bequests and donations to assist students in financial need.
Eligibility: To be eligible for this scholarship, you must: 1. be enrolled at the University of Melbourne 2. provide evidence of financial need
Type: Grant
Value: AU$200 - AU$10,000
Frequency: Annual
Country of Study: Any country
Application Procedure: 1. Applications are accepted in two rounds: A. Round 1: Opens 1 January - closes 8 March B. Round 2: Opens 1 June- closes on 6 August 2. Submit an online Student Financial Assessment form: unimelb-scholarships.smartygrants.com.au/SFA in the relevant round

by the closing date. 3. The application form will only be available to access when the round is open.
No. of awards offered: 250
Closing Date: 8 March
Additional Information: Website: scholarships.unimelb.edu.au/awards/student-grants

For further information contact:

The University of Melbourne Grattan Street, Parkville, Victoria 3010, Australia.

Tel: (61) 3 9035 5511

Tertiary Access Payment

Purpose: The Tertiary Access Payment program has been developed by the Australian Government to assist undergraduate students from regional and remote areas with the costs associated with relocating and to encourage them to start tertiary study immediately after completing secondary school. The Payment is administered by Services Australia.
Eligibility: To be eligible for this scholarship, you must: 1. be an Australian citizen or permanent resident, or a New Zealand citizen 2. have completed Year 12 or equivalent 3. have applied for a University of Melbourne undergraduate course for commencement in the year following completion of Year 12 or equivalent 4. be from an inner regional, outer-regional, remote or very remote area (use the Student Regional Area Search tool to check eligibility) 5. provide evidence that your parent(s) or guardian(s) have a combined income of less than AU$250,000 or be exempt from meeting this requirement 6. be relocating to study at the University of Melbourne and your family home is at least 90 minutes by public transport from the University of Melbourne 7. be at least 16 years of age or 15 years of age if you are living independently, and no older than 22 years of age at time of starting your course
Type: Programme
Value: Up to AU$5,000
Frequency: Annual
Country of Study: Any country
Application Procedure: You must apply for the Tertiary Access Payment through Centrelink: www.servicesaustralia.gov.au/how-to-claim-tertiary-access-payment?context=53447. You can only get the payment once, and you must apply in your first year of study. Any questions about the application process should be directed to Services Australia: www.servicesaustralia.gov.au/tertiary-access-payment.
No. of awards offered: 120
Closing Date: 31 December
Additional Information: Website: scholarships.unimelb.edu.au/awards/tertiary-access-payment

For further information contact:

The University of Melbourne Grattan Street, Parkville, Victoria 3010, Australia.

Tel: (61) 3 9035 5511

The Helen Macpherson Smith Scholarships

Purpose: Established by a donation from the Helen Macpherson Smith Trust, this scholarship is available to female students undertaking research study in the two areas of Scientific and Technical disciplines. and Humanities and Social Sciences.
Eligibility: To be eligible for this scholarship, you must: 1. be an Australian citizen or permanent resident 2. have applied for and meet the entry requirements for a graduate research degree at the University of Melbourne 3. have not already completed a research qualification at the same or higher level as the course for which a scholarship is sought 4. intend to study as a full-time student unless there are compassionate or compelling circumstances that prevent full-time study 5. not have previously received a graduate research scholarship with similar benefits
Level of Study: Postgraduate
Type: Scholarship
Value: Up to AU$5,000
Frequency: Annual
Country of Study: Australia
Application Procedure: If you have applied for a Master by research or Doctorate by research degree by 31 October for commencement in the following year, you will be automatically considered for this scholarship.
No. of awards offered: 2
Funding: Trusts
Contributor: Helen Macpherson Smith Trust
Additional Information: Website: scholarships.unimelb.edu.au/awards/helen-macpherson-smith-scholarship

For further information contact:

Email: gsa@gsa.unimelb.edu.au

U

University of Melbourne Graduate Research Scholarships

Subjects: All study areas
Purpose: Available to high-achieving students undertaking graduate research at the University of Melbourne.
Eligibility: To be eligible for this scholarship, you must: have applied for and meet the entry requirements for a graduate research degree at the University of Melbourne, or be

currently enrolled in a graduate research degree at the University of Melbourne.
Level of Study: Graduate, Research
Type: Scholarships
Value: 100% fee remission and up to AU$110,000
Country of Study: Australia
Application Procedure: No application is required. You will be automatically considered for this award.
No. of awards offered: 600
Additional Information: Website: scholarships.unimelb.edu.au/awards/graduate-research-scholarships

Viola Edith Reid Bequest Scholarship

Subjects: Medicine, dentistry, health and welfare
Purpose: This scholarship, is for domestic medical graduate research students in the Faculty of Medicine, Dentistry and Health Sciences. It was established with a bequest by Viola Edith Reid.
Eligibility: To be eligible for this scholarship, you need to 1. Be an outstanding graduate research applicant, or enrolled graduate researcher, of the Melbourne Medical School within the Faculty of Medicine, Dentistry and Health Sciences 2. Be a medical graduate 3. Satisfy faculty entry requirements for PhD.
Level of Study: Postgraduate, Research
Type: Scholarship
Value: Up to AU$31,200
Frequency: Annual
Study Establishment: University of Melbourne
Country of Study: Australia
Application Procedure: No application is required. You will be automatically considered for this award.
No. of awards offered: 1
Funding: Government
Additional Information: Website: scholarships.unimelb.edu.au/awards/viola-edith-reid-bequest-scholarship

For further information contact:

Tel: (61) 8344 4019
Fax: (61) 9347 7854
Email: mdhs-scholarships@unimelb.edu.au

Wellcome Trust: Principal Research Fellowships

Purpose: The Wellcome Trust's £25.9 billion investment portfolio directly funds thousands of scientists and researchers around the world at every step from discovery to impact. The Trust's funding schemes offer grants across biomedical science, population health, medical innovation, humanities and social science, and public engagement. Principal Research Fellowships are the most prestigious of the Trust's awards and provide long-term funding for researchers of international standing
Eligibility: Have an established track record in research at the highest level. 1. Have sponsorship from an eligible host organisation in the UK or Republic of Ireland. 2. Have a research project that is within the Trust's scientific remit.
Type: Fellowship
Value: AU$725,000 - AU$1,350,000
Frequency: Annual
Country of Study: Any country
Application Procedure: Applications are online and applicants can express an interest at any time.
No. of awards offered: 10
Closing Date: 31 December
Additional Information: For enquiries, use the Trust's contact form: wellcome.ac.uk/about-us/contact-us/form-type?ref=1814 or visit The Wellcome Trust's "Principal Research Fellowships" website: wellcome.org/grant-funding/schemes/principal-research-fellowships. Website: scholarships.unimelb.edu.au/awards/wellcome-trust-principal-research-fellowships

For further information contact:

The University of Melbourne Grattan Street, Parkville, Victoria 3010, Australia.

Tel: (61) 3 9035 5511

University of Montevallo

75 College Dr, Montevallo, AL 35115, United States of America.

Tel: (1) 205 665 6000

Graduate Honors Scholarship

Subjects: English
Purpose: To award prospective English students at the University of Montevallo.
Eligibility: Note In order to be eligible for consideration, each student must have a minimum overall GPA of 3.5 on a 4.0 scale, and a minimum of 1100/old format or 302/new format on the verbal and quantitative portions of the GRE, a minimum of 407 on the MAT, or a 550 on the GMAT (for MBA students). Please note that the selection of scholarship recipients and amount of the award is made in each

department and is based upon scholarship money available to that department. A student who meets all scholarship requirements is not guaranteed an award and receiving the scholarship one semester does not guarantee an award for future semesters. Only students who have been admitted to a graduate program may be considered for the scholarship.
Type: Scholarship
Value: Varies
Frequency: Annual
Study Establishment: University of Montevallo
Country of Study: United States of America
Application Procedure: Applicants must supply a completed application; Official transcripts sent from all institutions attended; Graduate Record Examination (GRE); Miller Analogies Test (MAT), or GMAT (for MBA students) scores sent; a letter of professional intent, including a statement of career goals; three letters of recommendation covering academic ability, personal qualities, and professional qualifications
Closing Date: 1 July
Additional Information: Renewal requests are no longer required for students currently enrolled in graduate courses as completed scholarship packets are processed and sent to department chairs for review each semester. However, students who change programs or plan to apply to another program after graduation should reapply for the scholarship. www.montevallo.edu/academics/colleges/college-of-arts-sciences/department-of-english-foreign-languages/programs/english-m-a/scholarships-and-deadlines/

University of Nevada, Las Vegas (UNLV)

Graduate College, 4505 Maryland Parkway, Box 451010, Las Vegas, NV 89154-1017, United States of America.

Tel: (1) 702 895 3011
Email: gradcollege@unlv.edu
Website: www.unlv.edu
Contact: Administrative Officer

Since our first classes were held on campus in 1957, UNLV has transformed itself from a small branch college into a thriving urban research institution.

University of Nevada, Las Vegas Alumni Association Graduate Scholarships

Purpose: To reward outstanding graduate students.
Eligibility: Applicants must have completed at least 12 credits of graduate study at UNLV, have a minimum undergraduate and graduate grade point average of 3.5 and enrol for six or more graduate credits in each semester of the scholarship year.
Level of Study: Graduate, MBA
Type: Scholarship
Value: US$1,500
Length of Study: 1 year
Frequency: Annual
Study Establishment: UNLV
Country of Study: United States of America
Application Procedure: Applicants must telephone (1) 702 895 3320 or write for application forms or further information.
Closing Date: 3 March
Additional Information: Weblink: www.postgraduatefunding.com/award-3184

For further information contact:

Tel: (1) 702 895 3320
Email: gradcollege@unlv.edu
Website: www.unlv.edu/

University of Nevada, Las Vegas James F Adams/GPSA Scholarship

Purpose: To recognize the academic achievements of graduate students.
Eligibility: Applicants must have completed at least 12 credits of graduate study at UNLV, have a minimum undergraduate and graduate grade point average of 3.5 and enrol for six or more graduate credits in each semester of the scholarship year.
Level of Study: Graduate, MBA
Type: Scholarship
Value: US$1,000
Length of Study: Varies
Frequency: Annual
Study Establishment: UNLV
Application Procedure: Applicants must telephone (1) 702 895 3320, or write for application forms or further information.
Closing Date: 3 March
No. of applicants last year: 6
Additional Information: Website: www.postgraduatefunding.com/award-3185

For further information contact:

Tel: (1) 702 895 3320
Email: gradcollege@unlv.edu

University of New England (UNE)

University of New England, Elm Avenue, Armidale, NSW 2351, Australia.

Tel: (61) 2 6773 3333
Email: research@une.edu.au
Website: www.une.edu.au

UNE is internationally recognized as one of the best teaching and research universities. Yearly, the university offers students more than AU$2,500,000 in scholarships, prizes, and bursaries and more than AU$18,000,000 for staff and students involved in research. It provides distance education for the students. Its scholars and scientists have established international reputations through their contributions in areas such as rural science, agricultural economics, educational administration, linguistics and archaeology.

A S Nivison Memorial Scholarship

Eligibility: To be eligible, candidates should domestic students who are pursuing research program in one of the fields mentioned above.
Level of Study: Doctorate, Postgraduate
Type: Scholarship
Value: AU$5,000
Length of Study: 1 year
Frequency: Annual
Country of Study: Australia
Application Procedure: Check website for further details www.une.edu.au/research/research-services/hdr/hdr-scholarships/a-s-nivison-memorial-scholarship
Closing Date: 30 April
Funding: Private
Contributor: Nivison family
Additional Information: www.scholarshipdesk.com/s-nivison-memorial-scholarship-at-the-university-of-new-england-australia/

For further information contact:

Tel: (61) 2 6773 3745
Email: pgscholarships@une.edu.au

Betty J Fyffe Scholarship

Purpose: The family of Betty J Fyffe (née Cahill) were pharmacists and chemist shop owners in Tamworth and Armidale over many years. In her Will, Betty established the Elizabeth Cahill Fyffe Trust to distribute funds to support students who are training in the medical fields with the expectation that they will hopefully carry out their profession in country areas when they finish their studies.
Eligibility: 1. Australian Citizen/Permanent Resident: Applicants must be an Australian Citizen or permanent resident as defined by the Commonwealth. 2. Open to ALL new commencing and continuing students in their 1st/2nd/3rd year of the Joint Medical Program Bachelor of Medical Science / Doctor of Medicine degree. 3. Regional/Remote: You can prove that you have resided for at least 5 years consecutively or 10 years cumulatively in a rural and/or remote location (Regions defined as RA2-5), as defined by the Government Remoteness Tool 4. Degree/Discipline: The applicant is enrolling or enrolled in a Bachelor of Medical Science and Doctor of Medicine within the Joint Medical Program at the University of New England
Level of Study: Doctorate
Type: Scholarship
Value: AU$4,000
Length of Study: Maximum of three years
Frequency: Annual
Country of Study: Any country
Application Procedure: Applications for the Betty Fyffe Scholarship should be made using the UNE Scholarships Application Form: www.une.edu.au/__data/assets/pdf_file/0019/435007/UNE-SCHOLARSHIPS-APPLICATION-FORM-2023.pdf. Only complete applications will be processed, so please ensure that you have submitted all required documentation with your application. The Alumni Relations and Student Scholarships team will notify you via email when your application has been processed.
No. of awards offered: Variable
Closing Date: 6 March
Additional Information: Website: www.une.edu.au/scholarships/2023/betty-j-fyffe-scholarship

For further information contact:

Tel: (61) 2 6773 3333

Bush Children's Education Foundation Scholarship

Purpose: In 1965, the Bush Children's Education Foundation came into being, inspired by a man with true vision. His vision continues to positively change the lives of young people and their families in remote areas today.
Eligibility: 1. Australian Citizen/Permanent Resident: The applicant must be an Australian Citizen or permanent resident as defined by the Commonwealth: www.servicesaustralia.gov.au/individuals/topics/residence-descriptions/30391 2. Open to students enrolling/enrolled

in 1st year of one of the following Agriculture-related degrees at UNE: A. Bachelor of Agribusiness B. Bachelor of Agriculture/Bachelor of Business C. Bachelor of Agriculture D. Bachelor of Agricultural and Resource Economics E. Bachelor of Rural Science 3. Academic requirement: An ATAR of 70 or higher is required 4. Financial Disadvantage: Be able to demonstrate financial need 5. Regional/Remote: The applicant's residential address must be either regional or remote (RA2 – RA5) as defined by the Government Remoteness Tool
Type: Scholarship
Value: AU$5,000
Length of Study: Maximum 3 years
Frequency: Annual
Country of Study: Any country
Application Procedure: Applications for the Bush Children's Education Foundation Scholarship should be made with the UNE Scholarships Application Form: www.une.edu.au/__data/assets/pdf_file/0019/435007/UNE-SCHOLARSHIPS-APPLICATION-FORM-2023.pdf.
No. of awards offered: 1
Closing Date: 5 March
Additional Information: website: www.une.edu.au/scholarships/2023/bush-childrens-education-foundation-scholarship

For further information contact:

Tel: (61) 2 6773 3333

Cec Spence Memorial UNE Country Scholarship

Purpose: The Cec Spence Memorial UNE Country Scholarship recognises the generosity and commitment that Cec Spence demonstrated during this lifetime in supporting students attending UNE.
Eligibility: 1. Australian Citizen/Permanent Resident The applicant must be an Australian Citizen or permanent resident as defined by the Commonwealth 2. Open to applicants who are completing Year 12 and gap year/s students who are commencing university study for the first time 3. Academic requirement An ATAR of at least 86.30 is required 4. Regional/Remote The applicant's residential address must be either regional or remote as defined by the Government Remoteness Tool
Type: Scholarship
Value: AU$7,500
Length of Study: 3 Years
Frequency: Annual
Country of Study: Any country
Closing Date: 3 January
Additional Information: https://www.une.edu.au/scholarships/2023/cec-spence-memorial-une-country-scholarship

For further information contact:

Tel: (61) 2 6773 3333

Commonwealth Accommodation Scholarship

Purpose: This Scholarship is funded by the Australian Government under the Indigenous Student Success Program. The purpose of the Commonwealth Accommodation Costs Scholarships is to widen participation in on campus higher education for Aboriginal and Torres Strait Islander students. Equity programs aim to overcome educational and financial disadvantages and help everyone access their potential.
Eligibility: 1. Aboriginal and/or Torres Strait Islander: The applicant must identify as an Australian Aboriginal and/or Torres Strait Islander person and provide documentation according to the UNE Confirmation of Aboriginality and Torres Strait Islander Identity Rule 2. Open to all new and continuing students enrolled in a UNE Enabling, Undergraduate or Postgraduate (Coursework) course at the University of New England 3. Relocation to Armidale for the purpose of study: Be able to demonstrate a planned relocation for the upcoming teaching period, or a recent relocation to Armidale in the last 6 months, for the purpose of study. 4. Financial Disadvantage: Be able to demonstrate financial disadvantage. Refer to the Supporting Documentation section below for details on what qualifies.
Level of Study: Postgraduate
Type: Scholarship
Value: Up to AU$9,000
Frequency: Annual
Country of Study: Any country
Application Procedure: Apply online though the Universities Admission Centre (UAC): www26.uac.edu.au/esapply?_ga=2.160597498.656148587.1678356539-1002181168.1678356538. Only one application is required to be considered for one or more of these Commonwealth Equity Scholarships.
Closing Date: 2 February
Additional Information: Website: www.une.edu.au/scholarships/2023/commonwealth-accommodation-scholarship

For further information contact:

Tel: (61) 2 6773 3333

Commonwealth Education Costs Scholarship

Purpose: This Scholarship is funded by the Australian Government under the Indigenous Student Success Program. The purpose of the Commonwealth Education Costs Scholarships is to widen participation in higher education for Aboriginal

and Torres Strait Islander students. Equity programs aim to overcome educational and financial disadvantages and help everyone access their potential.
Eligibility: 1. Aboriginal and/or Torres Strait Islander: The applicant must identify as an Australian Aboriginal and/or Torres Strait Islander person and provide documentation according to the UNE Confirmation of Aboriginality and Torres Strait Islander Identity Rule 2. Open to all new and continuing students enrolled in a UNE Enabling, Undergraduate or Postgraduate (Coursework) course at the University of New England 3. Financial Disadvantage: Be able to demonstrate financial disadvantage. Refer to the Supporting Documentation section below for details on what qualifies.
Level of Study: Postgraduate
Type: Scholarship
Value: Up to AU$4,500
Frequency: Annual
Country of Study: Any country
Application Procedure: Apply online though the Universities Admission Centre (UAC): www26.uac.edu.au/esapply?_ga=2.201960022.656148587.1678356539-1002181168.1678356538. Only one application is required to be considered for one or more of these Commonwealth Equity Scholarships.
No. of awards offered: min 20
Closing Date: 2 February
Additional Information: Website: www.une.edu.au/scholarships/2023/commonwealth-education-costs-scholarship

For further information contact:

Tel: (61) 2 6773 3333

D.L. McMaster Fund Endowed Housing Scholarship

Purpose: This endowed scholarship is named in memory of Mr Douglas McMaster OBE, who in 1964 donated to the University of New England 2,500 acres of his property 'Inverness' for agricultural research to benefit the Warialda district and the North West Slopes.
Eligibility: Australian Citizen/Permanent Resident The applicant must be an Australian Citizen or permanent resident as defined by the Commonwealth. Open to new commencing and continuing UNE students 1. Financial Disadvantage Be able to demonstrate financial need 2. Geographic area The applicant has a permanent home address in the following state and/or geographic area/s Gwydir Shire of NSW 3. Degree/Discipline The applicant is enrolling or enrolled in one of the following degrees at the University of New England 4. Bachelor of Agriculture 5. Bachelor Rural Science 6. Bachelor of Agricultural Production and Management 7. Bachelor of Agriculture and Business 8. Bachelor of Agribusiness 10. Living in college The applicant is living or intending to live in a UNE Residential College, including St Albert's College - see Conditions section of this document for specific living requirements of this scholarship
Type: Scholarship
Value: AU$16,000 - 50% each for Residential and Tuition fees
Length of Study: 3 Years
Frequency: Annual
Country of Study: Any country
No. of awards offered: 2
Closing Date: 14 February
Additional Information: https://www.une.edu.au/scholarships/2023/d.l.-mcmaster-fund-endowed-housing-scholarship

For further information contact:

Tel: (61) 2 6773 3333

Destination Australia Program Honours Scholarship

Purpose: The University of New England has been selected by the Commonwealth Government as one of the tertiary education institutions that will award a number of Destination Australia Program (DAP) scholarships for commencement in the 2024 academic year.
Eligibility: Australian Citizen/Permanent Resident This scholarship is open to Australian citizens and permanent residents Open to students commencing Honours in Trimester 1 2024 Academic requirement An average GPA of 5.5 in their undergraduate degree is required Degree/Discipline The applicant is enrolling in a Bachelor of Science with Honours degree at the University of New England Maintain ongoing residency in the Armidale regional area as defined by the Australian Statistical Geography Standard Remoteness Structure from the Australian Bureau of Statistics for the duration of each study period.
Type: Scholarship
Value: AU$15,000
Length of Study: 1 Year
Frequency: Annual
Country of Study: Any country
No. of awards offered: 5
Closing Date: 25 February
Additional Information: www.une.edu.au/scholarships/2022/DAP-Hons-scholarship

For further information contact:

Tel: (61) 2 6773 3333

Destination Australia Program Scholarship for Masters by Coursework

Purpose: The University of New England has been selected by the Commonwealth Government as one of the tertiary education institutions that will award a number of Destination Australia Program (DAP) scholarships for commencement
Eligibility: 1. Australian Citizen / Permanent Resident / International student: This scholarship is open to Australian citizens, permanent residents and international students. 2. Open to students enrolling in a new course at UNE commencing in Trimester 1 or 2, 2024. 3. Academic requirement: An ATAR of 75 or above is required, if a school leaver OR An average GPA of 4.0 in their undergraduate degree is required, if entering postgraduate study 4. Maintain ongoing residency in the Armidale regional area as defined by the Australian Statistical Geography Standard Remoteness Structure from the Australian Bureau of Statistics for the duration of each study period. 5. Students in educationally under-represented groups (e.g. first in family, low socioeconomic status, First Nations, disability) are strongly encouraged to apply.
Level of Study: Graduate, Masters Degree
Type: Scholarship
Value: AU$15,000
Length of Study: 1, 2 & 3 year scholarships available
Frequency: Annual
Country of Study: Any country
Application Procedure: Applications for the Destination Australia Program Scholarship should be made through the Application for University of New England Scholarship/s Form: www.une.edu.au/__data/assets/pdf_file/0019/435007/UNE-SCHOLARSHIPS-APPLICATION-FORM-2023.pdf. Only complete applications will be processed, so please ensure that you have submitted all required documentation with your application. The Student Scholarships team will notify you via email when your application has been processed.
No. of awards offered: Multiple
Closing Date: 28 May
Additional Information: Website: www.une.edu.au/scholarships/2023/destination-australia-program-scholarship-2023

For further information contact:

Tel: (61) 2 6773 3333

Don and Lee Stammer Scholarship

Eligibility: 1. Australian Citizen/Permanent Resident The applicant must be an Australian Citizen or permanent resident as defined by the Commonwealth 2. The applicant is enrolled/enrolling in their 1st/2nd/3rd/4th Year 3. Academic Requirement ATAR of at least 75 (New Students) or GPA 5 (Continuing Students) 4. The scholarship is open to students who must be able to demonstrate disadvantage in one or more of the following categories Financial disadvantage Physical, Intellectual or other disability Aboriginal or Torres Strait Islander The applicant must identify as an Australian Aboriginal and/or Torres Strait Islander person and provide documentation according to the University's Confirmation of Aboriginality and Torres Strait Islander Identity Procedures The applicant can demonstrate some other hardship or life circumstance which they have overcome/are overcoming in order to pursue tertiary studies, such as being a single parent, coming from an abusive background, etc.
Type: Scholarship
Value: Minimum of AU$5,000 per annum
Frequency: Annual
Country of Study: Any country
No. of awards offered: 2
Closing Date: 3 January
Additional Information: https://www.une.edu.au/scholarships/2023/don-lee-stammer-scholarship

For further information contact:

Tel: (61) 2 6773 3333

Indigenous Master of Psychology (Clinical) Scholarship

Purpose: Financial resources are a major issue impacting tertiary study for Indigenous students. This contributes to the chronic under representation of Indigenous students in post-graduate clinical psychology programs that in turn results in Aboriginal and Torres Strait Islander psychologists making up well under 1% of the proportion of all registered psychologists.
Eligibility: visit website
Level of Study: Masters Degree
Type: Scholarship
Value: AU$15,000
Length of Study: 2 Years
Frequency: Annual
Country of Study: Any country
No. of awards offered: 2
Closing Date: 6 February
Additional Information: https://www.une.edu.au/scholarships/2023/indigenous-master-of-psychology-clinical-scholarship

For further information contact:

Tel: (61) 2 6773 3333

Max Schroder Indigenous Scholarship

Purpose: Max Schroder provided a scholarship for one Indigenous student to pursue a UNE degree. Since then, Max's ongoing support and generosity has grown the program significantly to support dozens of UNE scholars over the years.
Eligibility: 1. Australian Citizen/Permanent Resident The applicant must be an Australian Citizen or permanent resident as defined by the Commonwealth 2. Open to ALL new commencing and continuing UNE students 3. Academic requirement For continuing students an average GPA of 4.0 in their course to date is required 4. Aboriginal or Torres Strait Islander The applicant must identify as an Australian Aboriginal and/or Torres Strait Islander person and provide documentation according to the University's Confirmation of Aboriginality and Torres Strait Islander Identity Procedures 5. Financial Disadvantage Be able to demonstrate financial need 6. Regional/ Remote The applicant's residential address must be either regional or remote as defined by the Government Remoteness Tool 7. Living in college The applicant is living or intending to live in a UNE Residential College (excluding St Albert's College) - see Conditions section of this document for specific living requirements of this scholarship
Type: Scholarship
Value: AU$6,000
Frequency: Annual
Country of Study: Any country
No. of awards offered: 5
Closing Date: 13 February
Additional Information: https://www.une.edu.au/scholarships/2023/max-schroder-indigenous-scholarship

For further information contact:

Tel: (61) 2 6773 3333

Oorala Kick Start Scholarship

Purpose: This is a scholarship that is designed to help support Aboriginal and/or Torres Strait Islander students with the costs of starting their tertiary studies. The scholarship aims to promote a relationship with Oorala for school leavers who are commencing study for the first time.
Eligibility: Aboriginal or Torres Strait Islander The applicant must identify as an Australian Aboriginal and/or Torres Strait Islander person and provide documentation according to the University's Confirmation of Aboriginality and Torres Strait Islander Identity Procedures Open to applicants who are school leavers (completing Year 12 or gap year/s students in 2023) who are commencing university study for the first time. Financial Disadvantage Be able to demonstrate financial need
Type: Scholarship
Value: AU$2,000 full-time or AU$1,000 part-time
Length of Study: 1 Year
Frequency: Annual
Country of Study: Any country
No. of awards offered: 3
Closing Date: 14 February
Additional Information: https://www.une.edu.au/scholarships/2023/oorala-kick-start-scholarship

For further information contact:

Tel: (61) 2 6773 3333

Oorala Wellbeing Scholarship

Purpose: The Accessibility & Wellbeing office supports students who are living with a disability or health condition, carers of a family member, elite athletes, ADF and SES personnel, living remotely, incarcerated, or do not have access to reliable internet and online technology.
Eligibility: 1. Aboriginal or Torres Strait Islander: The applicant must identify as an Australian Aboriginal and/or Torres Strait Islander person and provide documentation according to the University's Confirmation of Aboriginality and Torres Strait Islander Identity Procedures 2. Applicant has a registered Student Access Plan with the UNE Accessibility and Wellbeing Office 3. Open to all new commencing and continuing UNE students.
Level of Study: Postgraduate
Type: Scholarship
Value: AU$500
Length of Study: One-off payment
Application Procedure: Applications for the Oorala Wellbeing Scholarship should be made through the Application for University of New England Scholarship/s Form: www.une.edu.au/__data/assets/pdf_file/0019/435007/UNE-SCHOLARSHIPS-APPLICATION-FORM-2023.pdf.
Closing Date: 4 November
Additional Information: Website: www.une.edu.au/scholarships/2023/oorala-wellbeing-scholarship2

PhD Scholarship: Weed Ecology

Purpose: To manage the species through a series of field and controlled environment experiments on emergence, growth, reproduction and spread of environment experiments on emergence, growth, reproduction and spread of fleabane species
Eligibility: Applicants must hold a Class 1 or 2A Honours (or equivalent) Degree in a suitable discipline, and be an citizen or permanent resident of Australia

Level of Study: Doctorate
Type: Scholarship
Value: AU$26,000 per year (tax free)
Length of Study: 3 years
Study Establishment: University of New England
Country of Study: Australia
Application Procedure: Applicants should send a letter outlining their suitability for the position accompanied by a brief curriculum vitae (including contact details of two referees) and a copy of their academic transcripts
Closing Date: 27 April
Funding: Government

For further information contact:

School of Rural Science and Agriculture, University of New England, Armidale, NSW 2351, Australia.

Tel: (61) 2 6773 3238
Email: bsindel@une.edu.au

Robb College Foundation Irvine Scholarship

Purpose: This scholarship recognises Dr Jim W. Irvine (the 3rd Head of College) and Mrs Sue Irvine for their outstanding contributions to the development and life of the College from 1981 to 1990.
Eligibility: 1. Open to Australian citizens, permanent residents and international students. 2. Open to continuing UNE students in their 3rd, 4th or Final year of a degree (minimum 96 completed credit points) 3. The applicant must have resided in Robb College for a minimum of two Trimesters. 4. Academic requirement: An average GPA of 4.5 or above in their course to date is required 5. The applicant is ideally an all-rounder participating in any sport and has demonstrated leadership and contributed positively to college life 6. The applicant is living in Robb College at UNE - see Conditions section of this document for specific living requirements of this scholarship
Type: Scholarship
Value: AU$6,000
Length of Study: 1 Year
Frequency: Annual
Country of Study: Any country
Application Procedure: Applications for the Robb College Foundation Irvine Scholarship should be made through the Application for University of New England Scholarship/s Form: www.une.edu.au/__data/assets/pdf_file/0019/435007/UNE-SCHOLARSHIPS-APPLICATION-FORM-2023.pdf.
No. of awards offered: 1
Closing Date: 9 January
Additional Information: Website: www.une.edu.au/scholarships/2023/robb-college-foundation-irvine-scholarship

For further information contact:

Tel: (61) 2 6773 3333

Robb College Foundation Sinclair-Wilson Scholarship

Purpose: This scholarship recognises the late Mr J D Sinclair–Wilson's leadership of the College as Head of College from 1968 to 1980 and his outstanding contributions to the cultural and academic life of the College. This Scholarship is awarded at the Academic Dinner to a College resident who has entered their second year of undergraduate studies at UNE, who has a strong academic record and can demonstrate a history of strong contribution to leadership in sporting or cultural aspects.
Eligibility: 1. Open to Australian citizens, permanent residents or international students 2. Open to students in their 2nd year of a degree (minimum 48 completed credit points) 3. The applicant must have resided in Robb College for a minimum of two Trimesters 4. Academic requirement: An average GPA of 4.5 in their course to date is required 5. The applicant has demonstrated leadership and contributed positively to college life. 6. The applicant is intending to live in Robb College at UNE - see Conditions section of this document for specific living requirements of this scholarship
Level of Study: Undergraduate
Type: Scholarship
Value: AU$4,000
Length of Study: 1 Year
Frequency: Annual
Country of Study: Any country
Application Procedure: Applications for the Robb College Foundation Sinclair-Wilson Scholarship should be made through the Application for University of New England Scholarship/s Form: www.une.edu.au/__data/assets/pdf_file/0019/435007/UNE-SCHOLARSHIPS-APPLICATION-FORM-2023.pdf.
No. of awards offered: Up to 4
Closing Date: 9 January
Additional Information: Website: www.une.edu.au/scholarships/2023/robb-college-sinclair-wilson-scholarship

For further information contact:

Tel: (61) 2 6773 3333

Robb Scholarship for Regional Planning and Development

Purpose: Robb Scholarship for Regional Planning & Development is co-funded by Octopus Investments, MAAS Group and Robb College Foundation.
Eligibility: Australian Citizen/Permanent Resident The applicant must be an Australian Citizen or permanent resident as defined by the Commonwealth. Degree/Discipline The applicant is enrolling/enrolled in one of the following courses Bachelor of Urban and Regional Planning, Diploma in Town Planning, Bachelor of Social Science, Bachelor of Sustainability, Bachelor of GeoScience, Bachelor of Rural Science, Open to New Commencing or Continuing UNE Students in their 1st/2nd/3rd/4th year of a course (including Honours) listed above, Academic requirement, New/Commencing students ATAR of 77.1, Continuing students An average GPA of 4.0 in their course to date is required.
Type: Scholarship
Value: AU$6,000 for non-Robb residents AU$9,000 if residing in Robb College for the first year AU$12,000 if residing in Robb College for returning year
Frequency: Annual
Country of Study: Any country
Closing Date: 31 January

For further information contact:

Tel: (61) 2 6773 3333

Support Fund for Students with a Disability

Purpose: The Support Fund for Students with a Disability (SFSD) (originally the Australian Foundation for Disabled Students) was established to assist undergraduate students with a disability to study at the University of New England, Armidale, NSW.
Eligibility: 1. Australian Citizen/Permanent Resident: The applicant must be an Australian Citizen or permanent resident as defined by the Commonwealth 2. Open to ALL new and continuing students in any year of an undergraduate degree (excluding Honours) 3. Academic requirement: For continuing students a minimum average GPA of 4.0 in their course to date is required 4. Financial Disadvantage: Be able to demonstrate financial need 5. Be registered with the Student Accessibility and Wellbeing Office (SAWO) at UNE
Level of Study: Undergraduate
Type: Scholarship
Value: The minimum award will be AU$1,000 and the maximum may be up to AU$8,000.
Length of Study: 1 Year
Frequency: Annual
Country of Study: Any country
Application Procedure: Applications for the Support Fund for Students with a Disability should be made through the Application for University of New England Scholarship/s Form: www.une.edu.au/__data/assets/pdf_file/0019/435007/UNE-SCHOLARSHIPS-APPLICATION-FORM-2023.pdf. Applicants must also complete and submit the Application Form for the Support Fund for Students with a Disability: www.une.edu.au/__data/assets/pdf_file/0009/398538/Support-Fund-for-Students-with-a-Disability-Form_2022_01.pdf.
No. of awards offered: Variable
Closing Date: 2 January
Additional Information: Website: www.une.edu.au/scholarships/2023/support-fund-for-students-with-a-disability

For further information contact:

Tel: (61) 2 6773 3333

Tamex Transport Scholarship

Purpose: Tamex became involved with the UNE scholarship program over 15 years ago to give the opportunity of a university education to those rural-based students who would otherwise be unable to attend university due to financial constraints.
Eligibility: 1. Australian Citizen/Permanent Resident: The applicant must be an Australian Citizen or permanent resident as defined by the Commonwealth: www.humanservices.gov.au/individuals/enablers/residence-descriptions 2. Open to applicants who are completing Year 12 and 1-year gap year students who are commencing university study for the first time 3. Financial Disadvantage: Be able to demonstrate financial need 4. Geographic area: The applicant has a permanent home address in the following state and/or geographic area/s: New England, North-West NSW or Central West NSW 5. Degree/Discipline: The applicant is enrolling in an undergraduate degree within the UNE Business School or School of Law at the University of New England 6. Living in college: The applicant is living or intending to live in a UNE Residential College, including St Albert's College - see Conditions section of this document for specific living requirements of this scholarship
Level of Study: Undergraduate
Type: Scholarship
Value: AU$6,000
Length of Study: 3 Years

Frequency: Annual
Country of Study: Any country
Application Procedure: Applications for the Tamex Transport Scholarship should be made through the Application for University of New England Scholarship/s Form: www.une.edu.au/__data/assets/pdf_file/0019/435007/UNE-SCHOLARSHIPS-APPLICATION-FORM-2023.pdf.
No. of awards offered: 1
Closing Date: 2 January
Additional Information: website: www.une.edu.au/scholarships/2023/tamex-transport-scholarship

For further information contact:

Tel: (61) 2 6773 3333

The Duncan Family Scholarship in Early Childhood Education

Purpose: Ian Duncan was fortunate to have scholarships at both Agricultural College and then at University studying Veterinary Science; he has not forgotten the generous assistance these scholarships provided.
Eligibility: 1. Australian Citizen/Permanent Resident: The applicant must be an Australian Citizen or permanent resident as defined by the Commonwealth. 2. Open to both new commencing and continuing UNE students. 3. Academic requirement: For new students, an ATAR of at least 75.00 is required. For continuing students, an average GPA of 5.0 in their course to date is required. 4. Financial Disadvantage: Be able to demonstrate financial need 5. Degree/Discipline: The applicant is enrolling or enrolled in a Bachelor of Education (Early Childhood and Primary) or Bachelor of Education (Early Childhood Teaching) degree at the University of New England.
Level of Study: Undergraduate
Type: Scholarship
Value: AU$5,000
Length of Study: 1 Year
Frequency: Annual
Country of Study: Any country
Application Procedure: Applications for the Duncan Family Scholarship in Early Childhood Scholarship should be made through the Application for University of New England Scholarship/s Form: www.une.edu.au/__data/assets/pdf_file/0019/435007/UNE-SCHOLARSHIPS-APPLICATION-FORM-2023.pdf.
No. of awards offered: 1
Closing Date: 2 January
Additional Information: website: www.une.edu.au/scholarships/2023/the-duncan-family-scholarship-in-early-childhood-education

For further information contact:

Tel: (61) 2 6773 3333

The Duncan Family Scholarship in Pharmacy

Purpose: Ian Duncan was fortunate to have scholarships at both Agricultural College and then at University studying Veterinary Science; he has not forgotten the generous assistance these scholarships provided.
Eligibility: 1. Australian Citizen/Permanent Resident: The applicant must be an Australian Citizen or permanent resident as defined by the Commonwealth 2. Open to ALL new commencing and continuing UNE students. 3. Academic requirement: For new students, an ATAR of at least 75.00 is required Or For continuing students, an average GPA of 5.0 in their course to date is required. 4. Financial Disadvantage: Be able to demonstrate financial need 5. Degree/Discipline: The applicant is enrolling or enrolled in a Bachelor of Pharmacy degree at the University of New England.
Level of Study: Undergraduate
Type: Scholarship
Value: AU$5,000
Length of Study: 1 Year
Frequency: Annual
Country of Study: Any country
Application Procedure: Applications for the Duncan Family Scholarship in Pharmacy Scholarship should be made through the Application for University of New England Scholarship/s Form: www.une.edu.au/__data/assets/pdf_file/0019/435007/UNE-SCHOLARSHIPS-APPLICATION-FORM-2023.pdf.
No. of awards offered: 1
Closing Date: 2 January
Additional Information: Website: www.une.edu.au/scholarships/2023/the-duncan-family-scholarship-in-pharmacy

For further information contact:

Tel: (61) 2 6773 3333

The William McIlrath Rural Scholarship

Purpose: The William McIlrath Rural Scholarship is established to encourage and assist rural and regional students to undertake a full-time undergraduate degree at the University of New England.
Eligibility: 1. Australian Citizen/Permanent Resident: The applicant must be an Australian Citizen or permanent resident as defined by the Commonwealth. 2. Open to applicants who are completing Year 12 and gap year/s students who are commencing university study for the first time 3. An ATAR

of at least 80 is required 4. Financial Disadvantage: Be able to demonstrate financial need 5. The applicant's permanent residential address must be either regional or remote as defined by the Government Remoteness Tool 6. The applicant is enrolling in any of the following UNE Schools: School of Science and Technology, School of Environmental and Rural Science, School of Rural Medicine, School of Health, School of Education, School of Law and UNE Business School.
Level of Study: Undergraduate
Type: Scholarship
Value: AU$10,000 in the first year, then AU$4,000 annually thereafter
Length of Study: max 5 Years
Frequency: Annual
Country of Study: Any country
Application Procedure: Applications for the William McIlrath Rural Scholarship should be made through the Application for University of New England Scholarship/s Form: www.une.edu.au/__data/assets/pdf_file/0019/435007/UNE-SCHOLARSHIPS-APPLICATION-FORM-2023.pdf.
No. of awards offered: 1
Closing Date: 29 January
Additional Information: Website: www.une.edu.au/scholarships/2023/the-william-mcilrath-rural-scholarship

For further information contact:

Tel: (61) 2 6773 3333

UNE Indigenous Medical Scholarship

Purpose: This Scholarship is a joint initiative of the Oorala Aboriginal Centre and the Faculty of Medicine and Health at UNE. The purpose of the UNE Indigenous Medical Scholarship is to attract more Indigenous students to study medicine at UNE. This scholarship will assist Indigenous students to alleviate their financial burden whilst studying Medicine at UNE.
Eligibility: 1. Aboriginal or Torres Strait Islander: The applicant must be an Australian Aboriginal and/or Torres Strait Islander student as defined by the University's Confirmation of Aboriginality and Torres Strait Islander Identity Procedures 2. Open to ALL new commencing students enrolled in the Joint Medical Program at the University of New England 3. Financial Disadvantage: Be able to demonstrate financial need
Level of Study: Undergraduate
Type: Scholarship
Value: AU$6,000
Length of Study: Duration of degree
Frequency: Annual
Country of Study: Any country
Application Procedure: Applications for the UNE Indigenous Medical Scholarship should be made through the Application for University of New England Scholarship/s Form: www.une.edu.au/__data/assets/pdf_file/0019/435007/UNE-SCHOLARSHIPS-APPLICATION-FORM-2023.pdf.
No. of awards offered: 1
Closing Date: 31 January
Additional Information: website: www.une.edu.au/scholarships/2023/une-indigenous-medical-scholarship

For further information contact:

Tel: (61) 2 6773 3333

UNE Residential Financial Assistance Scholarship

Purpose: The University of New England has established residential scholarships to encourage qualified and motivated students who may not otherwise have considered college living because of financial constraints, to reside in a UNE residential college and be involved in the college community.
Eligibility: 1. Australian Citizens and Permanent residents 2. All New Commencing students OR Continuing UNE students in any year of a degree/course who have not previously resided in a UNE college/residence. 3. Current recipients of a UNE Residential Financial Assistance scholarship seeking an extension of their scholarship. The applicant must be able to demonstrate financial need. The applicant is living or intending to live in a UNE Residential College (excludes Wright College and St Alberts College) - see Conditions section of this document for specific living requirements of this scholarship.
Level of Study: Postgraduate
Type: Scholarship
Value: 37% - 66% discount on residential fees (room only) depending on the room type and contract length. This equates to AU$3,400 for 34 weeks, up to a maximum of AU$5,000 for a 51 week contract.
Length of Study: 34-52 Weeks
Frequency: Annual
Country of Study: Any country
Application Procedure: Applications for the UNE Residential Financial Assistance Scholarship should be made online via the UNE Accommodation Portal: residences.une.edu.au/StarRezPortalX/E0D38B65/19/170/Financial_Assistance-Information_on_the_U.
No. of awards offered: maximum of 40
Closing Date: 4 January

Additional Information: Website: www.une.edu.au/scholarships/2023/residential-assistance-scholarship

For further information contact:

Tel: (61) 2 6773 3333

Wright College Scholarship

Purpose: This scholarship is to assist an undergraduate student, who is new to UNE, with their first year of accommodation costs at Wright College or Wright Village and is generously funded by the Wright College Association and the Martlet Foundation (a recognised charitable body supported by gifts and donations from the Wright College Alumni and friends).
Eligibility: 1. Australian Citizen/Permanent Resident The applicant must be an Australian Citizen or permanent resident as defined by the Commonwealth 2. Open to new commencing UNE students 3. Financial Disadvantage Be able to demonstrate financial need 4. Regional/Remote The applicant's residential address must be either regional or remote as defined by the Government Remoteness Tool 5. Living in college The applicant is living or intending to live in Wright College or Wright Village at UNE - see the Conditions section of this document for specific living requirements of this scholarship
Type: Scholarship
Value: AU$3,000
Length of Study: 1 Year
Frequency: Annual
Country of Study: Any country
No. of awards offered: 1
Closing Date: 3 January
Additional Information: https://www.une.edu.au/scholarships/2023/wright-college-scholarship

For further information contact:

Tel: (61) 2 6773 3333

Wright Honours Scholarship

Purpose: This scholarship is generously funded by the Wright College Association and the Martlet Foundation (a recognised charitable body supported by gifts and donations from the Wright College Alumni and friends).
Eligibility: 1. Australian Citizen/Permanent Resident: The applicant must be an Australian Citizen or permanent resident as defined by the Commonwealth 2. Open to ALL new commencing/continuing UNE students in their Honours year. 3. Financial Disadvantage: Be able to demonstrate financial need 4. Regional/Remote: The applicant's residential address must be either regional or remote as defined by the Government Remoteness Tool 5. Living in college: The applicant is living or intending to live in Wright College or Wright Village at UNE - see Conditions section of this document for specific living requirements of this scholarship
Type: Scholarship
Value: AU$5,000
Length of Study: 1 Year
Frequency: Annual
Country of Study: Any country
Application Procedure: Applications for the Wright Honours Scholarship should be made through the Application for University of New England Scholarship/s Form: www.une.edu.au/__data/assets/pdf_file/0019/435007/UNE-SCHOLARSHIPS-APPLICATION-FORM-2023.pdf.
No. of awards offered: 1
Closing Date: 2 January
Additional Information: Website: www.une.edu.au/scholarships/2023/wright-honours-scholarship

For further information contact:

Tel: (61) 2 6773 3333

University of New South Wales

UNSW Sydney, NSW 2052, Australia.

Tel: (61) 2 93851000
Website: www.unsw.edu.au/a

UNSW Scholarships is responsible for the administration of all undergraduate and postgraduate coursework scholarships offered at UNSW and is the point of contact for any questions relating to these scholarships. Scholarships are offered in a variety of categories and are funded by the University with the support of many generous donors and organisations. Merit Scholarships are available to recognise your academic and other achievements (such as leadership, community involvement, commitment to a program of study). Equity Scholarships provide assistance to students that may experience educational disadvantage or are from low socio-economic backgrounds, and to support access and diversity. UNSW Scholarships is home to the Elite Athlete Support Program and Sports Scholarships, including the Ben Lexcen Sports Scholarship. We also provide information on Prestigious Programs for UNSW students to undertake graduate study at overseas institutions, and manage the Australian selection process for the Robertson Scholars Leadership Program Scholarship to study at Duke University/UNC in the United States. Please search for a scholarship program that may suit you and check the eligibility, selection criteria and closing dates. Scholarships are competitive and there are less scholarships than applicants. UNSW Scholarships allows you to apply for as many scholarships as you are eligible for.

Tyree Nuclear Masters by Coursework Tuition Scholarship

Purpose: The purpose of the Scholarship is to support a diverse cohort of Tyree Scholars at Masters level that will provide a talent pipeline to an emerging nuclear industry in Australia. The scholarship will support students undertaking studies at the Masters level in the nuclear engineering program at UNSW.
Eligibility: Be an Australian Citizen, an Australian permanent resident (including Humanitarian Visa Holders) or New Zealand Citizen. Be eligible for a Commonwealth Supported Place (CSP). Must have received an offer of admission into the Master of Engineering Science (8338) in the Nuclear Engineering specialisation
Type: Scholarship
Value: AU$8,000
Frequency: Annual
Country of Study: Any country
Application Procedure: Applications are not required for this scholarship. Successful applicants will be selected based on academic merit and an offer of admission to the eligible program.
No. of awards offered: 3
Additional Information: Website: www.scholarships.unsw.edu.au/scholarships/id/1593

For further information contact:

Tel: (61) 2 9385 1000

UNSW International Scholarships

Purpose: UNSW offers a wide range of Scholarships and Awards to support International undergraduate and postgraduate coursework students commencing full-time study at UNSW
Eligibility: To be eligible, applicants must: 1. Be an International student 2. Be commencing studies in Term 3 2024 3. Must have received an offer of admission and be commencing in any UNSW undergraduate or postgraduate coursework degree program by 31 July 2024. This must include one of the following: A. Undergraduate or Postgraduate Letter of Offer (unconditional) B. Undergraduate or Postgraduate Conditional English Package Offer (UEEC) - students must be enrolled in the UNSW Institute of Languages and successfully complete the program prior to commencing studies. Additional eligibility criteria may apply. Click here to view the eligibility criteria for individual scholarships
Level of Study: Postgraduate
Type: Scholarships
Value: AU$5,000
Length of Study: 1 year
No. of awards offered: Not specified
Closing Date: 31 March
Additional Information: https://www.scholarships.unsw.edu.au/scholarships/id/1713/5886

Welcome Scholarship for Students from Refugee Backgrounds

Purpose: The Welcome Scholarship for Students from Refugee Backgrounds has been established to support talented students who are refugees on permanent visas with the opportunity to pursue tertiary education at UNSW.
Eligibility: Be commencing an eligible UNSW coursework degree program in 2024; and, Be a refugee currently holding one of the following visas Global Special Humanitarian Visa (Subclass 202) Protection Visa (Subclass 866) Refugee Visas (Subclass 200, 201, 203 and 204)
Type: Scholarship
Value: AU$10,000
Frequency: Annual
Country of Study: Any country
No. of awards offered: 1
Closing Date: 13 February
Additional Information: https://www.scholarships.unsw.edu.au/scholarships/id/1582

For further information contact:

Tel: (61) 2 9385 1000

University of New South Wales (UNSW)

UNSW Sydney, NSW 2052, Australia.

Tel: (61) 2 9385 1000
Email: scholarships@unsw.edu.au
Website: www.unsw.edu.au

University of New South Wales (UNSW) is one of Australia's leading research and teaching universities. UNSW takes great pride in the broad range and high quality of teaching programmes. UNSW's teaching gains strength, vitality and currency both from their research activities and from their international nature.

Alton & Neryda Fancourt Chapple Award

Purpose: The Alton & Neryda Fancourt Chapple Biological Science Honours Award was established to encourage students to undertake an Honours year in the School of Biological, Earth and Environmental Sciences (BEES) at UNSW.
Eligibility: To be eligible, applicants must: Be proposing to undertake a full-time Honours year in the Bachelor of Science (Advanced) or Bachelor of Science degree, majoring in any program in the School of Biological, Earth and Environmental Sciences.
Type: Award
Value: AU$2,500
Length of Study: 1 Year
Frequency: Annual
Country of Study: Any country
Application Procedure: In order to be potentially considered for this scholarship please apply via the advertisement for the School of Biological, Earth & Environmental Sciences Honours Awards (UGCA1735): www.scholarships.unsw.edu.au/scholarships/id/1279.
Additional Information: Website: www.scholarships.unsw.edu.au/scholarships/id/213

For further information contact:

Tel: (61) 2 9385 1000

Australia's Global University Award

Eligibility: To be eligible, applicants must: 1. Be an International Student; and 2. Be commencing full-time study on campus in a UNSW undergraduate or postgraduate coursework degree program (excluding UNSW Online and UNSW Canberra); and 3. Have received an offer of admission* into an eligible program for Term 2 2024. * Offers of admission must be one of the following: A. Undergraduate or postgraduate Letter of Offer (unconditional) B. Undergraduate or postgraduate Conditional English Package Offer (UEEC) - students must be enrolled in the UNSW Institute of Languages and successfully complete the program prior to commencing in Term 2 2024.
Level of Study: Postgraduate
Type: Award
Value: AU$10,000
Length of Study: one year
Application Procedure: There is no application required for this Award.
Additional Information: Website: www.scholarships.unsw.edu.au/unsw-scholarships-international-students-commencing-term-2-2023

BHP Billiton Mitsubishi Alliance (BMA) Award in Mining Engineering

Purpose: This Award aims to support a rural or remote student currently enrolled in full-time study in UNSW Bachelor of Mining Engineering.
Eligibility: To be eligible, applicants must meet all of the following criteria: 1. Be an Australian Citizen or Permanent Resident (including Humanitarian Visa Holders); and 2. Be enrolled in full-time undergraduate study (single or double degree) in Bachelor of Engineering (Honours) (Mining); and 3. Must have lived in a rural, regional or remote area within the two years prior to the start of your UNSW studies. *Check the Australian Standard Geographic Classification Remoteness Areas (ASGC-RA) system map to check your eligibility. All categories other than RA1 Major Cities of Australia are considered to be regional or remote with the exception of Hobart.
Type: Scholarship
Value: AU$6,600
Length of Study: 1 Year
Frequency: Annual
Country of Study: Any country
Application Procedure: THERE IS NO APPLICATION REQUIRED FOR THIS AWARD
No. of awards offered: 1
Additional Information: Website: www.scholarships.unsw.edu.au/scholarships/id/37

For further information contact:

Tel: (61) 2 9385 1000

Brother Vincent Cotter Endowed Honours Award

Purpose: The purpose of this application is for applicants to be potentially considered for multiple Science Faculty honours scholarships, depending on individual scholarship criteria.
Eligibility: Must be commencing full-time Honours study in Physics
Type: Award
Value: US$5,000
Length of Study: 1 Year
Frequency: Annual
Country of Study: Any country
Closing Date: 21 February
Additional Information: www.scholarships.unsw.cdu.au/scholarships/id/1579/5283

For further information contact:

Tel: (61) 2 9385 1000

CEPAR Honours Scholarship

Purpose: The ARC Centre of Excellence in Population Ageing Research (CEPAR) offers exceptional opportunities for outstanding applicants with expertise in Actuarial Studies, Demography, Economics, Epidemiology, Psychology or Sociology to join a multi-disciplinary research team committed to transforming thinking about population ageing and establishing Australia as a world leader in the field.
Eligibility: Applicants must be 1. enrolling in a 2024 4th year undergraduate Honours program with a thesis component in an Australian university and 2. undertaking research in an area directly related to the CEPAR research program under the supervision of a CEPAR Chief Investigator, Australian university based Associate Investigator or Research Fellow (for a list of Chief and Associate Investigators and Research Fellows visit www.cepar.edu.au).
Level of Study: Undergraduate
Type: Scholarship
Value: AU$5,000
Length of Study: 1 Year
Frequency: Annual
Country of Study: Any country
Application Procedure: UNSW candidates must apply online via the UNSW scholarship website (https://www.scholarships.unsw.edu.au/scholarships/id/871).
Closing Date: 20 February

For further information contact:

Tel: (61) 2 9385 1000

Craig John Hastings Smith Surveying Engineering Honours Year Award

Purpose: The purpose of the Award is to support high-achieving Honours year Surveying Engineering students at the UNSW School of Civil and Environmental Engineering.
Eligibility: To be eligible, applicants must meet all of the following criteria: 1. Be Australian Citizen, Australian Permanent Resident (including Humanitarian Visa Holders) or New Zealand Citizen 2. Be commencing full-time undergraduate study (single or double degree) in the following degree program: Surveying Engineering (Honours) 3. Be commencing Honours year
Level of Study: Undergraduate
Type: Scholarship
Value: AU$7,000
Length of Study: 1 Year
Frequency: Annual
Country of Study: Any country
Application Procedure: Applicants will be assessed on the basis of: 1. Academic Merit 2. Leadership skills (school, workplace or community) 3. Extra-curricular activities (sporting, cultural activities, volunteer/work experiences) 4. Aptitude and commitment to studies in an area of Surveying
Closing Date: 20 February
Additional Information: Website: www.scholarships.unsw.edu.au/scholarships/id/1399

For further information contact:

Tel: (61) 2 9385 1000

David Walsh Memorial Scholarship

Purpose: The David Walsh Memorial Scholarship is established for Medicine students to undertake Honours level study in developmental biology, genetics or biochemistry, and their relationship to birth defects.
Eligibility: To be eligible, applicants must: Be an undergraduate student proposing to undertake the one year Honours Program in Bachelor of Medical Science, Bachelor of Science (Advanced Science) or Science (Medicine) Honours in developmental biology, genetics or biochemistry and their relationship to developmental birth defects.
Type: Scholarship
Value: AU$5,000
Length of Study: 1 Year
Frequency: Annual
Country of Study: Any country
Closing Date: 28 February

Additional Information: Website: www.scholarships.unsw.edu.au/scholarships/id/202

For further information contact:

Tel: (61) 2 9385 1000

Easson Geha Award in Planning

Purpose: The Easson Geha Endowed Award in Planning was established to assist students undertaking their Honours year in the UNSW Arts, Architecture & Design, Bachelor of Planning program.
Eligibility: To be eligible, applicants must: Be commencing full-time Honours study in the Bachelor of Planning (Honours)(3362).
Type: Award
Value: AU$5,000
Length of Study: 1 Year
Frequency: Annual
Country of Study: Any country
Closing Date: 28 February
Additional Information: Website: www.scholarships.unsw.edu.au/scholarships/id/145#:~:text=The%20Easson%20Geha%20Endowed%20Award,Planning%20(Honours)(3362).

For further information contact:

Tel: (61) 2 9385 1000

Elias Duek-Cohen Civid Design Award

Eligibility: Must be an Australian Citizen, Permanent Resident (including Humanitarian Visa Holders) or New Zealand Citizen Be commencing full-time Honours study in the Faculty of Built Environment with a focus on making towns and cities more beautiful and workable.
Type: Award
Value: US$5,000
Length of Study: 1 Year
Frequency: Annual
Country of Study: Any country
Closing Date: 21 February
Additional Information: www.scholarships.unsw.edu.au/scholarships/id/1580/5284

For further information contact:

Tel: (61) 2 9385 1000

Emeritus Professor William Gordon Rimmer Award

Purpose: The award was established to encourage students to undertake an honours year in history.
Eligibility: Applicants must: be Australian citizens or permanent residents; be proposing to undertake an honours year in history. Selection is based on academic merit and interest in history. Preference may be given to applicants studying American or European history.
Level of Study: Undergraduate
Type: Award
Value: AU$2,500
Length of Study: 1 Year
Frequency: Annual
Country of Study: Any country
Closing Date: 28 February
Additional Information: Website: www.gooduniversitiesguide.com.au/course-provider/unsw-sydney/scholarships/emeritus-professor-william-gordon-rimmer-award

For further information contact:

Tel: (61) 2 9385 1000

Fred Katz Award

Purpose: The Fred Katz Award was established to support a recipient undertaking the Honours Year of a Bachelor of Arts (Philosophy) program.
Eligibility: To be eligible, applicants must: Be undertaking the Honours Year of a full-time Bachelor of Arts (Philosophy) program at the UNSW Faculty of Arts and Social Sciences
Type: Scholarship
Value: AU$3,000
Length of Study: 1 Year
Frequency: Annual
Country of Study: Any country
Closing Date: 7 June
Additional Information: Website: www.scholarships.unsw.edu.au/scholarships/id/181

For further information contact:

Tel: (61) 2 9385 1000

Future of Change Scholarship

Eligibility: To be eligible, applicants must: 1. Be a citizen of India, and not a permanent resident of Australia; and 2. Be residing in India prior to commencing study at UNSW for undergraduate applicants. Postgraduate applicants may have

prior residence in Australia; and 3. Have received an offer of admission* into an eligible UNSW undergraduate or postgraduate coursework degree program for Term 2 2024. * Offers of admission must be one of the following: A. Undergraduate or postgraduate Letter of Offer (unconditional); or B. Undergraduate or postgraduate Conditional English Package Offer (UEEC) - students must be enrolled in the UNSW Institute of Languages and successfully complete the program prior to commencing in Term 2 2024.
Level of Study: Postgraduate
Type: Scholarship
Value: AU$10,000 per annum
Length of Study: minimum duration of program
Application Procedure: There is no application required for this scholarship.
Additional Information: website: www.scholarships.unsw.edu.au/unsw-scholarships-international-students-commencing-term-2-2023

Future of Change Schools Excellence Bursary

Eligibility: To be eligible, applicants must: 1. Be a citizen of India, and not a permanent resident of Australia; and 2. Be residing in India prior to commencing study at UNSW for undergraduate applicants. Postgraduate applicants may have prior residence in Australia; and 3. Have received an offer of admission* into an eligible UNSW undergraduate or postgraduate coursework degree program for Term 2 2024. * Offers of admission must be one of the following: A. Undergraduate or postgraduate Letter of Offer (unconditional); or B. Undergraduate or postgraduate Conditional English Package Offer (UEEC) - students must be enrolled in the UNSW Institute of Languages and successfully complete the program prior to commencing in Term 2 2024.
Level of Study: Postgraduate
Type: Bursary
Value: AU$10,000 per annum
Length of Study: minimum duration of program
Application Procedure: There is no application required for this scholarship.
Additional Information: Website: www.scholarships.unsw.edu.au/unsw-scholarships-international-students-commencing-term-2-2023

Gail Kelly Honours Award for Business

Purpose: The purpose of the Award is to support students in their Honours year with an interest in International Business as part of the Bachelor of Economics or Commerce, and aims to decrease the amount of additional paid work a student needs while studying.
Eligibility: 1. The recipient must be commencing full-time Honours study in one of the following degrees: A. Bachelor of Commerce (Honours) B. Bachelor of Economics (Honours) 2. Be a domestic student - Australian Citizen, Permanent Resident (including Humanitarian Visa Holders) or New Zealand Citizen
Type: Scholarship
Value: AU$20,000
Length of Study: 1 Year
Frequency: Annual
Country of Study: Any country
Closing Date: 21 February
No. of applicants last year: 2
Additional Information: Website: www.scholarships.unsw.edu.au/scholarships/id/1597#:~:text=The%20purpose%20of%20the%20Award,a%20student%20needs%20while%20studying.

For further information contact:

Tel: (61) 2 9385 1000

Glencore Mining Engineering Scholarship

Purpose: The purpose of this scholarship is to scholarship is to support a current undergraduate student undertaking a Bachelor of Engineering (Honours) (Mining) degree at UNSW Sydney in their 2nd year.
Eligibility: Be an Australian Citizen, Permanent Resident (including Humanitarian Visa Holders) or New Zealand Citizen Be enrolled full-time in Bachelor of Engineering (Honours) (Mining) undergraduate degree program in the 2nd year. Enrolment in a double degree in combination with the Mining Engineering in the 2nd year is also permissible, but the tenure of the Scholarship will remain at a maximum of 4 years.
Type: Scholarship
Value: AU$10,000
Length of Study: 4 Years
Frequency: Annual
Country of Study: Any country
No. of awards offered: 1
Closing Date: 21 February
Additional Information: Website: www.scholarships.unsw.edu.au/scholarships/id/1258

For further information contact:

Tel: (61) 2 9385 1000

H.C. & M.E. Porter Memorial Endowed Award

Purpose: This scholarship is available to full-time students undertaking a degree in Chemistry, Mathematics or Physics at UNSW or at another Australian University who are proposing to transfer to complete their degree with Honours at UNSW.
Eligibility: Be proposing or currently undertaking a full-time Honours program in the Faculty of Science
Type: Award
Value: AU$8,000
Length of Study: 1 Year
Frequency: Annual
Country of Study: Any country
Additional Information: Website: www.scholarships.unsw.edu.au/scholarships/id/216

For further information contact:

Tel: (61) 2 9385 1000

Herbert Smith Freehills Law and Economics Honours Year Award

Purpose: The Herbert Smith Freehills Law and Economics Honours Year Award was established to support Honours students in Economics at the UNSW Business School.
Eligibility: Applicants must be proposing to study Honours in Economics at the UNSW Business School
Type: Award
Value: AU$5,000
Length of Study: 1 Year
Frequency: Annual
Country of Study: Any country
Closing Date: 23 February
Additional Information: Website: www.scholarships.unsw.edu.au/scholarships/id/1021

For further information contact:

Tel: (61) 2 9385 1000

Honourable Jack Beale Scholarship in Engineering

Purpose: The purpose of the Award is to support students undertaking an Honours year at the UNSW School of Civil and Environmental Engineering who demonstrate an interest in water resources and the environment.
Eligibility: To be eligible, applicants must meet all of the following criteria: 1. Be an Australian Citizen, Australian Permanent Resident (including Humanitarian Visa Holders), or a New Zealand Citizen 2. Be currently enrolled full-time undergraduate study (single or double) in one of the following degree programs: A. Civil Engineering B. Environmental Engineering 3. Be undertaking an Honours year
Type: Scholarship
Value: AU$10,000
Length of Study: 1 Year
Frequency: Annual
Country of Study: Any country
Closing Date: 20 February
Additional Information: Website: www.scholarships.unsw.edu.au/scholarships/id/49#:~:text=The%20purpose%20of%20the%20Award,water%20resources%20and%20the%20environment.

For further information contact:

Tel: (61) 2 9385 1000

Honours Award Education

Eligibility: Be commencing full-time Honours year program Education
Type: Award
Value: US$5,000
Length of Study: 1 Year
Frequency: Annual
Country of Study: Any country
Application Procedure: Sydney NSW 2052, Australia
Closing Date: 21 February
Additional Information: www.scholarships.unsw.edu.au/scholarships/id/1580/5284

For further information contact:

Tel: (61) 2 9385 1000

International Scientia Coursework Scholarship

Purpose: The scholarships and awards listed below will be automatically offered to eligible students on the basis of academic merits highlighted in the application for admission to UNSW.
Eligibility: To be eligible, applicants must: 1. Be an International Student; and 2. Be commencing full-time study on campus in a UNSW undergraduate or postgraduate coursework program (excluding UNSW Online and UNSW Canberra); and 3. Have received an offer of admission* into an eligible program for Term 2 2024 by 31 March 2024. * Offers of admission must be one of the following: A. Undergraduate or postgraduate Letter of Offer (unconditional); or B. Undergraduate or postgraduate Conditional English Package Offer (UEEC) - students must be enrolled in the UNSW Institute of Languages and

successfully complete the program prior to commencing in Term 2 2024.
Level of Study: Postgraduate
Type: Scholarship
Value: Full tuition fee scholarship paid directly towards tuition fees for the minimum duration of program. AU$20,000 per annum
Frequency: Annual
Country of Study: Any country
Application Procedure: Submit a UNSW Scholarships for International Students Commencing Term: www.scholarships.unsw.edu.au/scholarships/id/1695
Closing Date: 31 March
Additional Information: Website: www.scholarships.unsw.edu.au/unsw-scholarships international-students-commencing-term-2-2023

For further information contact:

Tel: (61) 2 9385 1000

International Student Award

Purpose: The International Student Award has been established to assist students from low income and developing countries to access education at a highly ranked Australian university.
Eligibility: To be eligible, applicants must: 1. Be an International Student; and 2. Be a citizen of an eligible country; and 3. Be commencing full-time study as a new student on campus^ in a UNSW Diploma, UNSW undergraduate or postgraduate coursework program (excluding programs offered by AGSM, UNSW Online, UNSW Canberra, UNSW Foundation Programs, Transition Program Online, any program taught in the Hexamester calendar, or Study Abroad students); and 4. Have applied and received an offer of admission* into a UNSW undergraduate or postgraduate degree program; and 5. Not be a current student of UNSW (exceptions made for those who have completed an undergraduate program at UNSW and are commencing a postgraduate program). Open to students commencing studies online in a program that is usually offered on campus. * Open to students commencing their studies at UNSW in 2024 or 2025. The Award cannot be deferred beyond 2025.
Level of Study: Postgraduate
Type: Award
Value: Provides a 15% contribution directly towards tuition fees.
Length of Study: Duration of program
Application Procedure: To apply for the UNSW International Student Award applicants must submit a personal statement of no more than 500 words outlining their reasons to study the proposed program at UNSW. New applicants can upload their personal statement through Apply Online as part of their application. Existing offer holders should upload their personal statement via Apply Online or myUNSW if you are a UNSW Foundation or UAC applicant. Apply Here: applyonline.unsw.edu.au/
Additional Information: Website: www.scholarships.unsw.edu.au/unsw-scholarships-international-students-commencing-term-2-2023

J Holden Family Foundation Honours Award in Maths and Physics

Purpose: The purpose of this application is for applicants to be potentially considered for multiple Science Faculty honours scholarships, depending on individual scholarship criteria.
Eligibility: Be proposing to undertake a full-time Honours year in the Faculty of Science, undertaking specialisation in Mathematics or Physics Be an Australian Citizen, New Zealander Citizen or Australian Permanent Resident
Type: Award
Value: AU$8,000
Length of Study: 1 Years
Frequency: Annual
Country of Study: Any country
Closing Date: 20 February
Additional Information: Website: scholarships.online.unsw.edu.au/scholarship/sc_al_search_detail.display_scholarship_details?p_scholarship_specific_id=1579

For further information contact:

Tel: (61) 2 9385 1000

John MacIntyre Honours Year Scholarship in Marine Science

Purpose: The John MacIntyre Honours Year Scholarship in Marine Science was established to encourage an undergraduate student to undertake the Bachelor of Science Honours program with a Marine Science project.
Eligibility: To be eligible, applicants must: 1. Be proposing to undertake a full-time Honours year in the Bachelor of Science program with a project specialising in Marine Science. 2. Be an Australian Citizen or Permanent Resident
Type: Award
Value: AU$5,000
Length of Study: 1 Year

Frequency: Annual
Country of Study: Any country
Additional Information: Website: www.scholarships.unsw.edu.au/scholarships/id/218

For further information contact:

Tel: (61) 2 9385 1000

Judith Robinson-Valery Honours Award in Modern Languages

Eligibility: Be commencing full-time Honours study in one of the following disciplines Asian Studies and European Studies Languages and Cultures - Chinese Studies, French Studies, German Studies, Spanish Studies, Japanese Studies, and Korean Studies Linguistics
Type: Award
Value: US$5,000
Length of Study: 1 Year
Frequency: Annual
Country of Study: Any country
Closing Date: 21 February
Additional Information: www.scholarships.unsw.edu.au/scholarships/id/1580/5284

For further information contact:

Tel: (61) 2 9385 1000

Judith Robinson-Valery Honours Award in Modern Languages

Purpose: The Judith Robinson-Valery Honours Award in Modern Languages was established to encourage students to undertake a full-time Honours language program in the school of Humanities & Language at the Faculty of Arts and Social Sciences.
Eligibility: To be eligible, applicants must: 1. Be an Australian Citizen or Permanent Resident 2. Be proposing to undertake a full-time Honours language program in the school of Humanities & Languages at the UNSW Faculty of Arts and Social Sciences.
Type: Scholarship
Value: AU$5,000
Length of Study: 1 Year
Frequency: Annual
Country of Study: Any country
Application Procedure: No application is required. This will be automatically awarded.
No. of awards offered: 1
Additional Information: Website: www.scholarships.unsw.edu.au/scholarships/id/186

For further information contact:

Tel: (61) 2 9385 1000

Late Stephen Robjohns Science Scholarship

Purpose: The purpose of the Scholarship is to support students undertaking an undergraduate program of study specialising in physics, chemistry or mathematics at UNSW Sydney.
Eligibility: To be eligible, applicants must: Be a current full-time undergraduate student in any program with a major in either Mathematics, Chemistry or Physics.
Type: Scholarship
Value: AU$12,000
Length of Study: 4 Years
Frequency: Annual
Country of Study: Any country
Closing Date: 20 February
Additional Information: Website: www.scholarships.unsw.edu.au/scholarships/id/850#:~:text=The%20purpose%20of%20the%20Scholarship,or%20mathematics%20at%20UNSW%20Sydney.&text=To%20be%20eligible%2C%20applicants%20must,either%20Mathematics%2C%20Chemistry%20or%20Physics.

For further information contact:

Tel: (61) 2 9385 1000

Malcolm Cole Indigenous Scholarship

Eligibility: Indigenous Australian (Aboriginal and Torres Strait Islander only); and Be commencing full-time undergraduate studies in the School of the Arts & Media. Enrolment in a double degree is permissible.
Type: Scholarship
Value: US$5,000
Frequency: Annual
Country of Study: Any country
Closing Date: 28 February
Additional Information: www.scholarships.unsw.edu.au/scholarships/id/1395/5455

For further information contact:

Tel: (61) 2 9385 1000

Minerals Industry Flexible First Year Scholarship (Current Students)

Purpose: The purpose of the Scholarship is to encourage the recruitment of students in the flexible first year of the Bachelor of Engineering (Honours) of high potential to transfer to the Bachelor of Engineering (Honours) in Mining Engineering.
Eligibility: Be currently enrolled as a Flexible First year student within the Faculty of Engineering, and be transferring to full-time undergraduate study (single or double) in Bachelor of Engineering (Honours) in Mining Engineering.
Type: Scholarship
Value: AU$12,000
Length of Study: Remaining minimum duration of program
Frequency: Annual
Country of Study: Any country
No. of awards offered: 1
Additional Information: website: www.unsw.edu.au/engineering/our-schools/minerals-and-energy-resources-engineering/student-life/scholarships

For further information contact:

Tel: (61) 2 9385 1000

Norman, Disney & Young Indigenous Scholarship

Eligibility: Indigenous Australian (Aboriginal and Torres Strait Islander only); and Be commencing full-time study in a Bachelor of Engineering, specialising in one of the following Mechanical and Manufacturing Engineering Mechanical Engineering Mechatronic Engineering Electrical Engineering Environmental Engineering Photovoltaics & Solar Engineering Renewable Engineering Enrolment in a double degree is permissible.
Type: Scholarship
Value: US$5,000
Length of Study: 5 Years
Frequency: Annual
Country of Study: Any country
Closing Date: 28 February
Additional Information: www.scholarships.unsw.edu.au/scholarships/id/1395/5455

For further information contact:

Tel: (61) 2 9385 1000

Oliver Correy Award

Purpose: The Oliver Correy Award was established to support a high-achieving student undertaking an Honours year in Civil Engineering.
Eligibility: To be eligible, applicants must meet all of the following criteria: 1. Australian Citizen, Australian Permanent Resident (including Humanitarian Visa Holders) or New Zealand Citizen 2. Be currently enrolled full-time undergraduate study (single or double) in the following degree program: A. Civil Engineering 3. Be enrolled in the required thesis courses over the academic year
Type: Scholarship
Value: AU$7,500
Length of Study: Duration of program (minimum)
Frequency: Annual
Country of Study: Any country
Closing Date: 20 February
Additional Information: Website: www.scholarships.unsw.edu.au/scholarships/id/1389

For further information contact:

Tel: (61) 2 9385 1000

Paradice Honours Award in Mathematics & Statistics

Purpose: The Paradice Honours Year Scholarship has been setup to encourage female students to undertake a Honours Year Program in the School of Mathematics & Statistics at UNSW.
Eligibility: To be eligible, applicants must: 1. Female 2. Undertaking an Honours Year Program in the School of Mathematics & Statistics at UNSW
Type: Award
Value: AU$5,000
Length of Study: 1 Year
Frequency: Annual
Country of Study: Any country
Application Procedure: In order to be potentially considered for this scholarship please apply via the advertisement for the Mathematics & Statistics Honours Award: www.scholarships.unsw.edu.au/scholarships/id/1276
No. of applicants last year: 1
Additional Information: website: www.scholarships.unsw.edu.au/scholarships/id/1014

For further information contact:

Tel: (61) 2 9385 1000

Peggy Bamford Award

Purpose: The purpose of the Award is to encourage UNSW students undertaking Honours or Masters by coursework in the School of Social Sciences within the Faculty or Arts, Design & Architecture to excel in their studies.

Eligibility: To be eligible, applicants must: Be commencing full-time honours year or postgraduate coursework study in the Social Sciences disciplines at the Faculty of Arts, Design & Architecture.
Type: Award
Value: AU$5,000
Length of Study: 1 Year
Frequency: Annual
Country of Study: Any country
Closing Date: 30 November
Additional Information: Website: www.scholarships.unsw.edu.au/scholarships/id/187

For further information contact:

Tel: (61) 2 9385 1000

PhD Scholarships in Environmental Microbiology

Purpose: To attract the nations strongest candidates capable of pursuing PhD studies in the genomics of environmental microorganisms.
Eligibility: This scholarship is for study in Australia for those who have achieved Honours 1 or equivalent, or Masters or equivalent. There are no restrictions on citizenship.
Level of Study: Doctorate, Postgraduate, Research
Type: Scholarship
Value: AU$35,000
Application Procedure: Check website for further details.
Closing Date: 31 March
Additional Information: Website: www.postgraduatefunding.com/award-2355

For further information contact:

Email: scholarships@unsw.edu.au
Website: www.unsw.edu.au/

Royston Honours Award in Chemical Engineering

Purpose: This Award supports Honours year students undertaking studies in the area of Chemical Engineering closely associated with Mineral Processing or Fuel Technology.
Eligibility: To be eligible, applicants must meet all of the following criteria: 1. Be an Australian Citizen, Australian Permanent Resident (including Humanitarian Visa Holders), or a New Zealand Citizen 2. Be currently enrolled full-time undergraduate study (single or double) in the following degree program: A. Bachelor of Engineering (Honours) (Chemical) 3. Be undertaking an Honours year with a research thesis in one of the following areas: Mineral Processing, Fuel Technology or similar as determined by the Head of School
Type: Scholarship
Value: AU$6,000
Length of Study: 1 Year
Country of Study: Any country
Application Procedure: Please refer to the Scholarship Application Supporting Documents for a detailed list of examples: www.scholarships.unsw.edu.au/sites/default/files/uploads/Supporting%20Documentation%20Guide%20-%20UNSW%20Scholarships.pdf.
Closing Date: 20 February
Additional Information: website: www.scholarships.unsw.edu.au/scholarships/id/170#:~:text=This%20Award%20supports%20Honours%20year,Mineral%20Processing%20or%20Fuel%20Technology.&text=Be%20currently%20enrolled%20full%2Dtime,Engineering%20(Honours)%20(Chemical)

For further information contact:

Tel: (61) 2 9385 1000

School of Mathematics and Statistics Indigenous Scholarship

Purpose: The School of Mathematics and Statistics Indigenous Scholarship aims to encourage and support Indigenous Australian students to undertake study in the School of Mathematics and Statistics at UNSW.
Eligibility: to an Australian Indigenous student who is of Aboriginal or Torres Strait Islander descent, and identifies as an Aboriginal or Torres Strait Islander, and who is: Commencing full-time study in a Bachelor of Advanced Science or Bachelor of Science (Advanced Mathematics), including dual-award degrees with a declared major in the School of Mathematics & Statistics - Bachelor of Science, Bachelor of Adv Science, Bachelor of Adv Maths, Bachelor of Data Sci and Decisions and dual degrees including one of the above.
Type: Scholarship
Value: US$5,000
Frequency: Annual
Country of Study: Any country
Application Procedure: Apply via: UNSW Scholarships online: www.scholarships.unsw.edu.au/
Additional Information: website: www.unsw.edu.au/science/our-schools/maths/student-life-resources/undergraduate/scholarships

For further information contact:

Tel: (61) 2 9385 1000

Sonja Huddle Award

Purpose: The Sonja Huddle Award was established to encourage students to undertake an Honours year in the Bachelor of Environmental Science, Bachelor of Advanced Science or Bachelor of Science program with a project specialising in earth sciences and the environment.
Eligibility: To be eligible, applicants must: 1. Be proposing to undertake a full-time Honours year in the Bachelor of Environmental Science, the Bachelor of Advanced Science or the Bachelor of Science program with a project specialising in earth science and the environment. 2. Be an Australian Citizen or Permanent Resident
Type: Award
Value: AU$5,000
Length of Study: 1 Year
Frequency: Annual
Country of Study: Any country
Application Procedure: In order to be potentially considered for this scholarship please apply via the advertisement for the School of Biological, Earth & Environmental Sciences Honours Awards (UGCA1735): www.scholarships.unsw.edu.au/scholarships/id/1279.
No. of applicants last year: 1
Additional Information: Website: www.scholarships.unsw.edu.au/scholarships/id/1035

For further information contact:

Tel: (61) 2 9385 1000

Surface Coatings Association Australia Award

Purpose: The purpose of this application is for applicants to be potentially considered for multiple Science Faculty honours scholarships, depending on individual scholarship criteria.
Eligibility: You must: 1. be enrolled in a master's by research or PhD in the School of Chemistry 2. be undertaking your research in the field of surface coatings (including pigments, polymers, corrosion, weathering, adhesion and methods of manufacture) 3. be a recipient of a primary scholarship that provides a stipend allowance.
Level of Study: Masters Degree, Postgraduate
Type: Award
Value: AU$1500
Length of Study: 1 Year
Frequency: Annual
Country of Study: Any country
Application Procedure: Apply here: sydneyuniversity.formstack.com/forms/sc0517.
Closing Date: 12 November
Additional Information: Website: www.sydney.edu.au/scholarships/d/surface-coatings-association-australia-scholarship.html

For further information contact:

Tel: (61) 2 9385 1000

The Faculty of Law Juris Doctor Scholarship for Indigenous Students

Purpose: The Juris Doctor (JD) Scholarship for Indigenous Students was established to assist high achieving Indigenous students to undertake the Juris Doctor Program at UNSW.
Eligibility: Applicants must be of Australian Aboriginal or Torres Strait Islander descent and undertaking the Juris Doctor program at UNSW.
Type: Scholarship
Value: US$10,000
Frequency: Annual
Country of Study: Any country
No. of awards offered: 2
Closing Date: 21 February
Additional Information: www.scholarships.unsw.edu.au/scholarships/id/703/5377

For further information contact:

Tel: (61) 2 9385 1000

UNSW Business School Honours Scholarship

Purpose: The UNSW Business School Honours Scholarship was established to encourage students to undertake an Honours Program offered by participating Schools in the UNSW Business School.
Eligibility: 1. Must be undertaking a relevant Honours program offered by a participating School in the UNSW Business School 2. No residency requirements 3. Please note that those who applied in 2022 are not eligible to re-apply.
Type: Scholarship
Value: AU$5,000
Length of Study: 1 Year
Frequency: Annual
Country of Study: Any country
Closing Date: 21 February

Additional Information: Website: www.scholarships.unsw.edu.au/scholarships/id/190

For further information contact:

Tel: (61) 2 9385 1000

UNSW Business School International Pathways Award

Eligibility: To be eligible, applicants must: 1. Be an International Student; and 2. Be commencing a UNSW postgraduate (Master) coursework degree program offered by UNSW Business School (excluding those offered by AGSM); and 3. Have received an offer of admission* into an eligible program for Term 2 2024 by 31 March 2024; and Have undertaken: A. A postgraduate (Master) coursework articulation pathway qualification from an approved partner institution; or B. Completed the UNSW Foundation Studies Commerce or Commerce Actuarial stream prior to commencing study at UNSW; and C. Have achieved academic excellence in the relevant program of study at the pathway partner institution or in the eligible UNSW Foundation Studies Stream;
Level of Study: Postgraduate
Type: Award
Value: AU$15,000
Length of Study: one year
Application Procedure: Submit a UNSW Scholarships for International Students Commencing Term 2: www.scholarships.unsw.edu.au/scholarships/id/1695
Closing Date: 31 March
Additional Information: Website: www.scholarships.unsw.edu.au/unsw-scholarships-international-students-commencing-term-2-2023

UNSW Law & Justice International Award

Purpose: The UNSW Law & Justice International Award has been established to encourage high quality international students to join UNSW Law & Justice programs (LLB, JD or LLM).
Eligibility: To be eligible, applicants must: 1. Be an International Student; and 2. Be commencing a UNSW Law & Justice undergraduate or postgraduate coursework degree program (LLB, JD or LLM programs); and 3. Have received an offer of admission* into an eligible program for Term 2 2024 by 31 March 2024. * Offers of admission must be one of the following: A. Undergraduate or postgraduate Letter of Offer (unconditional); or B. Undergraduate or postgraduate Conditional English Package Offer (UEEC) - students must be enrolled in the UNSW Institute of Languages and successfully complete the program prior to commencing in Term 2 2024
Level of Study: Postgraduate
Type: Award
Value: AU$10,000
Length of Study: one year
Application Procedure: Submit a UNSW Scholarships for International Students Commencing Term 2: www.scholarships.unsw.edu.au/scholarships/id/1695, 2023 (PUCA1029)
Closing Date: 31 March
Additional Information: Website: www.scholarships.unsw.edu.au/unsw-scholarships-international-students-commencing-term-2-2023

UNSW Medical Research Honours Scholarship - South Western Sydney

Purpose: The purpose of this scholarship is to encourage the highest quality candidates in undergraduate Science, Medical Science, Advanced Science and Exercise Physiology programs to consider undertaking an Honours Project in the South Western Sydney campuses of UNSW, including at the Ingham Institute for Applied Medical Research
Eligibility: Be currently enrolled in an eligible UNSW degree program Be eligible to undertake an approved Honours program offered by South Western Sydney Clinical School as part of an approved Honours program in Science, Medical Science, Advanced Science and Exercise Physiology (commencing in 2024)
Type: Scholarship
Value: AU$5,000
Length of Study: 1 Year
Frequency: Annual
Country of Study: Any country
Closing Date: 28 February
No. of applicants last year: 2
Additional Information: Website: www.scholarships.unsw.edu.au/scholarships/id/1325

For further information contact:

Tel: (61) 2 9385 1000

Viktoria Marinov Award in Art

Purpose: To financially assist female artists who are proposing to undertake the Master of Art or Master of Fine Arts course.

Eligibility: Open to female artists under the age of 35 years who are proposing to undertake the Master of Art or Master of Fine Arts course.
Level of Study: Postgraduate
Type: Award
Value: AU$7,500
Length of Study: 1 year
Frequency: Annual
Study Establishment: New South Wales, Sydney City Central and Eastern Suburbs
Country of Study: Australia
Closing Date: 30 July
Additional Information: Website: www.postgraduatefunding.com/award-2816

For further information contact:

Tel:	(61) 2 9385 0684
Email:	scholarships@unsw.edu.au
Website:	www.unsw.edu.au/

Women in Computer Science Award (WICS)

Purpose: The purpose of the Award is to support high-performing female students undertaking study in the School of Computer Science & Engineering.
Eligibility: 1. Be a Domestic student - Australian Citizen, Permanent Resident (including Humanitarian Visa Holders) or New Zealand Citizen 2. Be Female 3. The recipient must be commencing full-time undergraduate study in one of the following degree programs (single or double program): A. Bachelor of Computer Science B. Bachelor of Bioinformatics Engineering C. Bachelor of Software Engineering D. Bachelor of Computer Engineering
Type: Scholarship
Value: AU$5,000
Length of Study: 1 Year
Frequency: Annual
Country of Study: Any country
Additional Information: Website: www.scholarships.unsw.edu.au/scholarships/id/1613#:~:text=The%20purpose%20of%20the%20Award,School%20of%20Computer%20Science%20%26%20Engineering.&text=Applications%20are%20not%20required%20for%20this%20scholarship.

For further information contact:

Tel: (61) 2 9385 1000

University of Newcastle

Research Division, University of Newcastle, University Drive, Callaghan, NSW 2308, Australia.

Tel:	(61) 2 4921 5000
Email:	research@newcastle.edu.au
Website:	www.newcastle.edu.au/research/rhd/
Contact:	Office of Graduate Studies

Our research drives transformative innovation and impact.

Aboriginal and Torres Strait Islander Scholarship

Purpose: The Aboriginal and Torres Strait Islander Scholarship was established through contributions from the university, industry donors, community organisations and the annual Reconciliation Scholarship Dinner Dance.
Eligibility: To be eligible to apply for this scholarship, you will need to: 1. Be enrolled in any year of an undergraduate degree program at the University of Newcastle. 2. Be enrolled full-time. 3. Demonstrate academic progress either by the Australian Tertiary Admission Rank (ATAR) or equivalent required for entry for commencing students, or a Grade Point Average (GPA) of 4.0 for continuing students. 4. Establish your Aboriginal and/or Torres Strait Islander identity and heritage with the university as outlined here.
Level of Study: Undergraduate
Type: Scholarship
Value: AU$40,000
Frequency: Annual
Country of Study: Any country
No. of awards offered: 1
Closing Date: 15 February
No. of applicants last year: 1
Additional Information: Website: www.newcastle.edu.au/scholarships/EXT_152

For further information contact:

University Dr, Callaghan NSW 2308, Australia.

Tel: (61) 2 4921 5000

Aboriginal Housing Office Tertiary Accommodation Grants

Purpose: The NSW Government - Aboriginal Housing Office is offering Tertiary Accommodation Grants to eligible

Aboriginal and Torres Strait Islander students enrolled in full time studies with University of Newcastle.
Eligibility: To be eligible to apply for this scholarship, you will need to: 1. Establish your Aboriginal and/or Torres Strait Islander identity and heritage with the university as outlined here. 2. Be enrolled/enrolling in any year of an enabling, undergraduate, or postgraduate program on campus with University of Newcastle. Students who have accepted an offer to start study with us next year may also apply. 3. Be enrolled full-time. 4. Demonstrate that you are a social housing tenant or are experiencing housing stress and provide evidence of independent living arrangements. (housing stress is defined as an individual expending more than 40% of weekly income on housing).
Level of Study: Postgraduate
Type: Grant
Value: AU$10,000
Application Procedure: Application is via submission of this application form: www.newcastle.edu.au/__data/assets/pdf_file/0011/887393/AHOTertiaryAccomGrants_Application2023.pdf to wollotuka@newcastle.edu.au
Closing Date: 17 March
No. of applicants last year: 40
Additional Information: Website: www.newcastle.edu.au/scholarships/UNI_028

For further information contact:

Email: wollotuka@newcastle.edu.au
Website: www.newcastle.edu.au/__data/assets/pdf_file/0011/887393/AHOTertiaryAccomGrants_Application2023.pdf

Africa Excellence Scholarship

Purpose: Africa Excellence Scholarship has been established to attract high-performing international students to the University of Newcastle for study in 2023 and beyond. This is a merit-based scholarship that recognises applicants with a strong academic background and incentivises them to continue striving to be the best that they can be.
Eligibility: To be eligible to apply for this scholarship, you will need to: 1. Hold a passport from one of the 54 countries of Africa. 2. Be commencing study in an eligible undergraduate or postgraduate coursework degree program at the University (excluding ELICOS, Enabling, Non-Award, Higher Degrees by Research programs and programs delivered at offshore campuses). 3. Be an International full-fee paying student. 4. Be commencing in an eligible program at an Australian or Online campus as indicated in your Letter of Offer. 5. Not be the beneficiary of a separate University scholarship unless prior approval for special dispensation has been obtained from the university. 6. Meet all of the financial obligations of a full-fee paying international student, including the full tuition fee and other expenses for the purpose of obtaining your student visa, and in the event that eligibility for the scholarship is not maintained.
Level of Study: Postgraduate
Type: Scholarship
Value: AU$50,000
Application Procedure: No application is required for this scholarship.
No. of applicants last year: 100
Additional Information: Website: www.newcastle.edu.au/scholarships/UNI_043

Anderson-Yamanaka Scholarship

Purpose: This is a donor-funded scholarship will support a high achieving commencing student studying a Bachelor of Arts. Preference will to be given to students who are studying a language.
Eligibility: To be eligible to apply for this scholarship, you will need to: 1. Commencing study in the Bachelor of Arts (including combined degrees) with University of Newcastle. 2. Preference may be given to students planning to study Languages as part of their degree. 3. Must have completed your Year 12 Higher School Certificate OR a University of Newcastle enabling program within the two years prior to commencing your Bachelor of Arts. 4. Be enrolled full-time. 5. Have achieved a minimum ATAR (Australian Tertiary Admission Rank) or equivalent of 95 or higher, with adjustment factors NOT included. 6. Be an Australian citizen, Australian Permanent Resident (includes New Zealand Permanent Residents). 7. Not be the recipient of another University of Newcastle donor-funded or sponsored scholarship concurrently.
Level of Study: Postgraduate
Type: Scholarship
Value: AU$5,000
Application Procedure: No application is required for this scholarship.
Additional Information: Website: www.newcastle.edu.au/scholarships/EXT_286

U

Andrew Brown Sport Scholarship

Purpose: In recognition of the important role that sports and university sports clubs played in his own development and educational experience, Andrew would like to support a student to enjoy the same benefits where financial hardship may otherwise prevent them from participating in tertiary study and sports activities.

Eligibility: To be eligible to apply for this scholarship, you will need to: 1. Be enrolled in any year of an enabling program, undergraduate, or postgraduate (including Graduate Research) degree at the University of Newcastle. 2. Be a member of, and play with, a University of Newcastle sporting team. 3. Be enrolled full-time. 4. Demonstrate educational disadvantage such as carer, sole parent, financial hardship, English language difficulty, long term medical condition/disability or effects of abuse, Aboriginal and Torres Strait Islander, Out of Home Care, Refugee, or Geographic. 5. Demonstrate that the ability to study is affected, or will be affected, by financial hardship. 6. Not be the recipient of another University of Newcastle donor-funded or sponsored scholarship concurrently.
Level of Study: Postgraduate, Undergraduate
Type: Scholarship
Value: AU$4,000
Frequency: Annual
Country of Study: Any country
No. of awards offered: 1
Closing Date: 15 February
No. of applicants last year: 1
Additional Information: Website: www.newcastle.edu.au/scholarships/EXT_271

For further information contact:

University Dr, Callaghan NSW 2308, Australia.

Tel: (61) 2 4921 5000
Email: scholarships@newcastle.edu.au

ASEAN Excellence Scholarship

Purpose: The ASEAN Excellence Scholarship has been established to attract high-performing students to study at the University of Newcastle. This is a merit-based scholarship that recognises applicants with a strong academic background and incentives them to continue striving to be the best that they can be.
Eligibility: To be eligible to apply for this scholarship, you will need to: 1. Hold a passport from one of the eligible "ASEAN" countries: Brunei, Cambodia, Indonesia, Laos, Malaysia, Myanmar, Singapore, Thailand, The Philippines, Vietnam. 2. Be commencing study in an eligible undergraduate or postgraduate coursework degree program at the University (excluding ELICOS, Enabling, Non-Award, Higher Degrees by Research programs and programs delivered at offshore campuses). 3. Be an International full-fee paying student. 4. Be commencing in an eligible program at an Australian or Online campus as indicated in your Letter of Offer. 5. Not be the beneficiary of a separate University scholarship unless prior approval for special dispensation has been obtained from the university. 6. Meet all of the financial obligations of a full-fee paying international student, including the full tuition fee and other expenses for the purpose of obtaining your student visa, and in the event that eligibility for the scholarship is not maintained. 7. Not be enrolling in an excluded quota program (see selection details).
Level of Study: Postgraduate
Type: Scholarship
Value: AU$50,000
Application Procedure: No application is required for this scholarship.
Additional Information: Website: www.newcastle.edu.au/scholarships/UNI_034

Association of Consulting Surveyors Aboriginal and Torres Strait Islander Scholarship

Purpose: The Association intends for these scholarships to assist Aboriginal and Torres Strait Islander students in achieving a career in surveying and to help them maintain a connection to their communities.
Eligibility: To be eligible to apply for this scholarship, you will need to: 1. Be enrolled in any year of an undergraduate Surveying degree with the University of Newcastle. 2. Be enrolled full-time. 3. Establish your Aboriginal and/or Torres Strait Islander identity and heritage with the university as outlined here: www.newcastle.edu.au/confirmation-of-aboriginality. 4. Be a resident of NSW 5. Not be the recipient of another University of Newcastle donor-funded or sponsored scholarship concurrently.
Level of Study: Undergraduate
Type: Scholarship
Value: AU$15,000
Length of Study: Over the full 3-year tenure of the scholarship
Frequency: Annual
Country of Study: Any country
Application Procedure: No application is required for this scholarship.
No. of awards offered: 1
No. of applicants last year: 2
Additional Information: Website: www.newcastle.edu.au/scholarships/EXT_288

For further information contact:

University Dr, Callaghan NSW 2308, Australia.

Tel: (61) 2 4921 5000

Betty Josephine Fyffe Rural Allied Health, Nursing and Midwifery Scholarship

Purpose: Betty leaves this legacy as her way of trying to improve the education of doctors, nurses and allied health professionals in training with hope that some will return to the country areas to practice their profession.
Eligibility: To be eligible to apply for this scholarship, you will need to: 1. Be enrolled in any year (including honours) of a B Nursing, B Midwifery, B Physiotherapy, B Nutrition and Dietetics, B Occupational Therapy, B Medical Radiation Science, B Pharmacy degree. 2. Be enrolled full-time. 3. Demonstrate academic achievement either by an Australian Tertiary Admission Rank (ATAR) or equivalent of 90 or higher (adjustment factors included) for commencing students or a Grade Point Average (GPA) of 6.0 or higher for continuing students. 4. Have lived in a regional or remote area of Australia for at least 12 months within the two years prior to study. 5. Demonstrate activity in your local community (for example volunteering or involvement in community projects). 6. Be an Australian citizen. 7. Not be the recipient of another University of Newcastle donor-funded or sponsored scholarship concurrently.
Type: Scholarship
Value: AU$50,000
Frequency: Annual
Country of Study: Any country
No. of awards offered: 1
Closing Date: 15 February
Additional Information: Website: www.newcastle.edu.au/scholarships/EXT_256

For further information contact:

University Dr, Callaghan NSW 2308, Australia.

Tel: (61) 2 4921 5000

BMG Indigenous Music Industry Scholarship - Creative Industries

Purpose: BMG Australia is the Sydney based office of the international BMG publishing and recording business that spans Europe, the Americas and the Asia-Pacific. Their mission is to help artists and songwriters make the very most of their songs and recordings in the digital age through offering first-class creative support for their artists.
Eligibility: Be enrolled in any Bachelor program in the School of Creative Industries. Be enrolled either full-time or part-time. Establish your Aboriginal and/or Torres Strait Islander identity and heritage with the university as outlined here. Demonstrate academic progress with a Grade Point Average (GPA) of 4.0 or higher and maintain this for the duration of scholarship. Be enrolled or be willing to enroll in one of the following course codes MUSI3442 Engaging in the Music Industry, CIND3002 Project Development, CIND3003 Creative Industries Prof Project, DESN3411 Creative Studio Placement, CIND3500 Prof Project. or CMNS3450 Media Arts Project, DESN3910 Professional Creative Portfolio 20 units (Studio Z), DESN3411 Creative Studio Placement (WIL).
Level of Study: Undergraduate
Type: Scholarship
Value: AU$15,000
Frequency: Annual
Country of Study: Any country
No. of awards offered: 1
Closing Date: 22 February
No. of applicants last year: 1
Additional Information: www.newcastle.edu.au/scholarships/EXT_275

For further information contact:

University Dr, Callaghan NSW 2308, Australia.

Tel: (61) 2 4921 5000

Boeing Indigenous Engineering Scholarship

Purpose: Boeing Defence Australia is a leading Australian aerospace enterprise. With a world-class team of more than 1,800 employees at 14 locations throughout Australia and two international sites, Boeing Defence Australia supports some of the largest and most complex defence projects in Australia
Eligibility: To be eligible to apply for this scholarship, you will need to: 1. Be enrolled in 2nd, 3rd, 4th year of a Bachelor of Engineering (Software), (Computer Systems), (Electrical and Electronic), Mechatronics or (Mechanical) with the University of Newcastle. 2. Be enrolled full time (min 30 units per semester or equivalent). 3. Be studying at the Newcastle Callaghan, Newcastle City or Central Coast campus. 4. Identify as an Australian Aboriginal and/or Torres Strait Islander and be recognised as such your community. 5. Have a GPA of 4.0 or higher. 6. Be an Australian citizen; and 7. Not hold another University of Newcastle donor-funded or sponsored scholarship concurrently
Level of Study: Undergraduate
Type: Scholarship
Value: AU$6,000
Frequency: Annual
Country of Study: Any country
No. of awards offered: 1

Additional Information: Website: www.newcastle.edu.au/__data/assets/pdf_file/0009/699642/EXT_230-Boeing-Indigenous-Engineering-Scholarship.pdf

For further information contact:

University Dr, Callaghan NSW 2308, Australia.

Tel: (61) 2 4921 5000

Catherine and Peter Tay for Singapore Alumni (follow on) Scholarship

Purpose: This scholarship was established in 2018 by Catherine and Peter Tay from Singapore. It is a continuing demonstration of appreciation that 50 years earlier in 1968, Dr Peter Tay received his undergraduate education for a double degree in Industrial Engineering and Economics from the University of Newcastle through a Colombo Plan Scholarship from the Australian Government. That scholarship became a stepping stone in Peter's life-long achievements, and helped him to become what he is today.
Eligibility: To be eligible to apply for this scholarship, you will need to: 1. Be a past recipient of the Singapore Alumni Scholarship. 2. Be enrolled in any year of an undergraduate degree program at the University of Newcastle. 3. Be enrolled full-time. 4. Demonstrate educational disadvantage such as carer, sole parent, financial hardship, English language difficulty, long term medical condition/disability or effects of abuse, Aboriginal and Torres Strait Islander, Out of Home Care, Refugee, or Geographic. 5. Demonstrate academic achievement by having a Grade Point Average (GPA) of 5.0 or higher in your current program. 6. If successful, be willing to submit an essay of approximately 400 words on Singapore and one or more aspects of its people, economy, geography, history, culture, political system etc. 7. Not be the recipient of another University of Newcastle donor-funded or sponsored scholarship concurrently.
Level of Study: Undergraduate
Type: Scholarship
Value: AU$4,000
Frequency: Annual
Country of Study: Any country
Closing Date: 22 February
No. of applicants last year: 2
Additional Information: www.newcastle.edu.au/scholarships/EXT_235

For further information contact:

University Dr, Callaghan NSW 2308, Australia.

Tel: (61) 2 4921 5000

China Excellence Scholarship

Purpose: The China Excellence Scholarship has been established to attract high-performing students to study at the University of Newcastle. This is a merit-based scholarship that recognises International applicants with a strong academic background and incentives them to continue striving to be the best that they can be.
Eligibility: To be eligible to apply for this scholarship, you will need to: 1. Hold a passport from the People's Republic of China. 2. Be commencing your first program of study at the University in the current intake. 3. Be commencing study in an eligible undergraduate or postgraduate coursework degree program at the University (excluding ELICOS, Enabling, Non-Award, Higher Degrees by Research programs and programs delivered at offshore campuses). 4. Be an International full-fee paying student. 5. Be commencing in an eligible program at an Australian or Online campus as indicated in your Letter of Offer. 6. Not be the beneficiary of a separate University scholarship unless prior approval for special dispensation has been obtained from the university. 7. Meet all of the financial obligations of a full-fee paying international student, including the full tuition fee and other expenses for the purpose of obtaining your student visa, and in the event that eligibility for the scholarship is not maintained. 8. Not be enrolling in an excluded quota program (see selection details).
Level of Study: Postgraduate
Type: Scholarship
Value: AU$10,000
Length of Study: One year of study of full-time study load
Application Procedure: Scholarships are automatically applied for upon application to the University (where eligibility criteria is met). Students will receive notification of the value of their scholarship with their offer.
Additional Information: Website: www.newcastle.edu.au/scholarships/UNI_042

College of International Education International Pathways Scholarship

Purpose: This scholarship has been established as an International Pathway Scholarship for eligible students entering the University of Newcastle. It is applicable for students who have completed an applicable pathway program (Foundation Studies, Degree Transfer, Degree Transfer Extended and Pre-Master's Program) at the College of International Education and will progress to their undergraduate or postgraduate coursework degree program.
Eligibility: To be eligible to apply for this scholarship, you will need to: 1. Be an International full-fee paying student. 2. Have successfully completed a Foundation Studies, Degree Transfer, Degree Transfer Extended or Pre-Master's Program at the

University of Newcastle College of International Education as part of a packaged offer into the University. 3. Be commencing an eligible undergraduate or postgraduate coursework degree program at the University. Please note, this excludes ELICOS, Enabling, Non-Award, Higher Degrees by Research and quota-limited programs. 4. Not be the beneficiary of a separate University scholarship unless prior approval for special dispensation has been obtained from the university. 5. Meet all of the financial obligations of a full-fee paying international student, including the full tuition fee and other expenses for the purpose of obtaining your student visa, and in the event that eligibility for the scholarship is not maintained. 6. Not be enrolling in an excluded quota program (see selection details).
Level of Study: Postgraduate
Type: Scholarship
Value: 10% fee reduction for each year
Application Procedure: No application is required for this scholarship.
Additional Information: Website: www.newcastle.edu.au/scholarships/UNI_033

Crystalbrook Kingsley Environmental Scholarship

Purpose: The Crystalbrook Kingsley Environmental Scholarship will support a student with a strong passion for environmental change and practical solutions for environmental sustainability, while providing a foundation for a collaborative and long-standing relationship between Crystalbrook Collection, students and the University for the benefit of our shared sustainability goals and communities.
Eligibility: To be eligible to apply for this scholarship, you will need to: 1. Be enrolled in 3rd or 4th year of an undergraduate Honours degree focused on environmental sustainability within the School of Environmental and Life Sciences at the University of Newcastle. 2. Have an interest in practical solutions for environmental sustainability. 3. Be enrolled full-time. 4. Have a Grade Point Average (GPA) of 6.0 or higher. 5. Not be the recipient of another University of Newcastle donor-funded or sponsored scholarship concurrently.
Level of Study: Undergraduate
Type: Scholarship
Value: AU$5,000
Frequency: Annual
Country of Study: Any country
Closing Date: 15 February
No. of applicants last year: 1
Additional Information: Website: www.newcastle.edu.au/scholarships/EXT_283

For further information contact:

University Dr, Callaghan NSW 2308, Australia.

Tel: (61) 2 4921 5000

CSIRO Women in Energy Industry Placement Scholarship

Purpose: A scholarship sponsored by The Commonwealth Scientific and Industrial Research Organisation CSIRO is now available for a current first year female student studying in the Industry Placement Stream
Eligibility: To be eligible to apply for this scholarship, you will need to: 1. Be enrolled in 1st year of an eligible Engineering degree program with University of Newcastle. 2. Be enrolled full-time. 3. Demonstrate academic achievement by attaining an ATAR of 75 or higher. 4. Be female. 5. Be an Australian citizen. 6. Not be the recipient of another University of Newcastle donor-funded or sponsored scholarship concurrently.
Type: Scholarship
Value: AU$40,000
Frequency: Annual
Country of Study: Any country
No. of awards offered: 1
Closing Date: 15 February
Additional Information: Website: www.newcastle.edu.au/scholarships/ENGB_070

For further information contact:

University Dr, Callaghan NSW 2308, Australia.

Tel: (61) 2 4921 5000

Delta Electricity Scholarship

Purpose: This scholarship was established to recognise a commitment to higher education by Delta Electricity. Delta Electricity has been offering scholarships at University of Newcastle since 2007 with the intention to offer financial support to undergraduate students who study or reside in the Central Coast LGA.
Eligibility: To be eligible to apply for this scholarship, you will need to: 1. Be enrolled in an eligible program for this scholarship, being the B Enviromental Science, B Business, and Environmental, Mechanical, E&E, Chemical and Mechatronics Engineering programs. 2. Be studying at Central Coast Campus (for relevant programs) and/or be a resident of the Central Coast LGA. 3. Demonstrate academic achievement either by an Australian Tertiary Admission Rank (ATAR) or equivalent of 95 or higher for commencing students, or a Grade Point Average (GPA) of 6.0 for continuing students. 4. Be an Australian citizen, Australian Permanent Resident (includes New Zealand Permanent Residents). 5. Not be the recipient of another University of Newcastle donor-funded or sponsored scholarship concurrently.
Type: Scholarship

Value: US$5,000
Frequency: Annual
Country of Study: Any country
Closing Date: 15 February
No. of applicants last year: 1
Additional Information: Website: www.newcastle.edu.au/scholarships/EXT_001

For further information contact:

University Dr, Callaghan NSW 2308, Australia.

Tel: (61) 2 4921 5000

Dr Bill Jonas Memorial Indigenous Scholarship

Purpose: This scholarship has been established by donations made to the Dr Bill Jonas Memorial Indigenous Fund. The fund was established with donations from the Wollotuka Institute, friends, family and community members who wished to honour Dr Bill Jonas's significant contribution to Wollotuka and the University of Newcastle.
Eligibility: To be eligible to apply for this scholarship, you will need to: 1. Be enrolled in any year of any undergraduate or postgraduate degree at the University of Newcastle. 2. Be enrolled either full-time or part-time. 3. Demonstrate academic progress either by the Australian Tertiary Admission Rank (ATAR) or equivalent required for entry for commencing students, or a Grade Point Average (GPA) of 4.0 for continuing students. 4. Establish your Aboriginal and/or Torres Strait Islander identity and heritage with the university as outlined here. 5. Demonstrate educational disadvantage such as carer, sole parent, financial hardship, English language difficulty, long term medical condition/disability or effects of abuse, Aboriginal and Torres Strait Islander, Out of Home Care, Refugee, or Geographic. 6. Not be the recipient of another University of Newcastle donor-funded or sponsored scholarship concurrently.
Type: Scholarship
Value: US$5,000
Frequency: Annual
Country of Study: Any country
Closing Date: 15 February
No. of applicants last year: 1
Additional Information: Website: www.newcastle.edu.au/scholarships/EXT_261

For further information contact:

University Dr, Callaghan NSW 2308, Australia.

Tel: (61) 2 4921 5000

ELBP Start Now Scholarship

Purpose: The English Language Bridging Program (ELBP) Start Now Scholarship has been established to encourage and support international students from the regions of South East Asia, South Asia, and Africa to study ELBP plus Undergraduate or Postgraduate programs with the University of Newcastle (Australia).
Eligibility: To be eligible to apply for this scholarship, you will need to: 1. Be an international full-fee paying student from Region 2 2. Be enrolled full-time. 3. Be commencing 10 weeks ELBP plus a UON destination program. 4. Be able to meet all of the financial obligations of a full-fee paying international student, including the full tuition fee and other expenses for the purpose of obtaining a student visa for study in Australia, and in the event that continued eligibility
Level of Study: Postgraduate
Type: Scholarship
Value: AU$740
Application Procedure: No application is required for this scholarship
Additional Information: Website: www.newcastle.edu.au/scholarships/UNI_048

Friends of the University Development Studies Scholarship

Purpose: The Friends of the University were established in 1981 to foster an awareness of the university and its place in the community and to conduct activities including fundraising that promote the interests of the university. Since that time the Friends have raised over AU$1,000,000 and contributed towards scholarships, art works, music, rare books, infrastructure and more.
Eligibility: To be eligible to apply for this scholarship, you will need to: 1. Be enrolled in any year of the Bachelor of Development Studies, including Honours, with University of Newcastle. 2. Be enrolled full-time. 3. Demonstrate educational disadvantage such as carer, sole parent, financial hardship, English language difficulty, long term medical condition/disability or effects of abuse, Aboriginal and Torres Strait Islander, Out of Home Care, Refugee, or Geographic. 4. Be an Australian citizen, Australian Permanent Resident (includes New Zealand Permanent Residents). 5. Not be the recipient of another University of Newcastle donor-funded or sponsored scholarship concurrently.
Level of Study: Undergraduate
Type: Scholarship
Value: AU$4,000
Frequency: Annual
Country of Study: Any country

No. of awards offered: 1
Closing Date: 15 February
Additional Information: Website: www.newcastle.edu.au/scholarships/EXT_292

For further information contact:

University Dr, Callaghan NSW 2308, Australia.

Tel: (61) 2 4921 5000

Friends of the University Ken Gordon Memorial Honours Scholarship

Purpose: The Friends of the University were established in 1981 to foster an awareness of the university and its place in the community and to conduct activities including fundraising that promote the interests of the university. Since that time the Friends have raised over AU$1,000,000 and contributed towards scholarships, art works, music, rare books, infrastructure and more.
Eligibility: To be eligible to apply for this scholarship, you will need to: 1. Be enrolled in your 1st or 2nd year of a Business or Law program with University of Newcastle. 2. Be enrolled full-time. 3. Have an Australian Tertiary Admission Rank (ATAR) or equivalent of 75 or higher for commencing students, or a Grade Point Average (GPA) of 5.0 for continuing students. 4. Demonstrate educational disadvantage such as carer, sole parent, financial hardship, English language difficulty, long term medical condition/disability or effects of abuse, Aboriginal and Torres Strait Islander, Out of Home Care, Refugee, or Geographic. 5. Not be the recipient of another University of Newcastle donor-funded or sponsored scholarship concurrently. 6. Be an Australian citizen, Australian Permanent Resident (includes New Zealand Permanent Residents). 7. Not have previously received this scholarship.
Type: Scholarship
Value: AU$4,000
Frequency: Annual
Country of Study: Any country
Closing Date: 15 February
No. of applicants last year: 1
Additional Information: Website: www.newcastle.edu.au/scholarships/EXT_023

For further information contact:

University Dr, Callaghan NSW 2308, Australia.

Tel: (61) 2 4921 5000

Friends of the University Sport Scholarship

Purpose: To improve the quality of our sporting teams, raise the university's profile through sport, and establish a standard of excellence to complement our academic achievements
Eligibility: To be eligible to apply for this scholarship, you will need to: 1. Be enrolled in any year of an undergraduate degree or enabling program at the University of Newcastle. 2. In the scholarship award year, be a member of, and play with a University of Newcastle sporting team or represent the University in an individual or team sport. 3. Be enrolled full-time. 4. Demonstrate academic progress either by the Australian Tertiary Admission Rank (ATAR) or equivalent required for entry for commencing students, or a Grade Point Average (GPA) of 4.0 for continuing students. 5. Have attained an equivalent sporting standard in the previous 2 years of selection at district representative level in the sport for an Under 17 or older age district team as a minimum. 6. Must not be a Professional Sports Person. 7. Not have previously received this scholarship.
Level of Study: Undergraduate
Type: Scholarship
Value: AU$4,000
Frequency: Annual
Country of Study: Any country
Closing Date: 15 February
Additional Information: Website: www.newcastle.edu.au/scholarships/EXT_199

For further information contact:

University Dr, Callaghan NSW 2308, Australia.

Tel: (61) 2 4921 5000

Idemitsu Engineering Scholarship

Purpose: To support a student financially while encouraging them to pursue a career in the engineering / resources industry.
Eligibility: 1. Be enrolled in a Bachelor of Electrical or Electronic Engineering (Honours), Bachelor of Renewable Energy Engineering (Honours) or a Bachelor of Mechanical Engineering (Honours) degree. 2. Be enrolled full-time. 3. Demonstrate educational disadvantage such as carer, sole parent, financial hardship, English language difficulty, long term medical condition/disability or effects of abuse, Aboriginal and Torres Strait Islander, Out of Home Care, Refugee, or Geographic. 4. Demonstrate academic progress either by the Australian Tertiary Admission Rank (ATAR) or equivalent required for entry for commencing students, or a Grade Point Average (GPA) of 4.0 for continuing students. 5. Be an Australian citizen, Australian Permanent Resident (includes

New Zealand Permanent Residents). 6. Not have previously completed a degree. 7. Not be the recipient of another University of Newcastle donor-funded or sponsored scholarship concurrently.
Type: Scholarship
Value: AU$5,000
Frequency: Annual
Country of Study: Any country
Closing Date: 15 February
Additional Information: Website: www.newcastle.edu.au/scholarships/EXT_262

For further information contact:

University Dr, Callaghan NSW 2308, Australia.

Tel: (61) 2 4921 5000

Indigenous Education Scholarship

Purpose: These Commonwealth-funded scholarships aim to support Indigenous students with the costs of University study, particularly for those who face financial disadvantage and who are relocating from a remote or regional area.
Eligibility: To be eligible to apply for this scholarship, you will need to: 1. Be enrolled (or enrolling) in any year of an enabling, undergraduate, or postgraduate degree program at the University of Newcastle. 2. Demonstrate financial hardship by either being in receipt of a means-tested Commonwealth income support payment (such as Austudy, ABSTUDY, Youth Allowance etc), or on the basis of a comprehensive assessment. 3. Be of Australian Aboriginal and/or Torres Strait Islander descent, AND identify as an Australian Aboriginal and/or Torres Strait Islander, AND be accepted as an Aboriginal and/or Torres Strait Islander by the community in which you live or have lived. 4. Must not have previously received the full entitlement of a Commonwealth Indigenous Scholarship awarded prior to 2017 or hold this scholarship concurrently at another institution. 5. If accepting the scholarship offer, must not have received - or agrees to repay - a Student Start-up Loan, a Student Start-up Scholarship or a Relocation Scholarship or the Residential Costs option of ABSTUDY from Centrelink.
Level of Study: Postgraduate
Type: Scholarship
Value: AU$3,000
Frequency: Annual
Country of Study: Any country
No. of awards offered: 60
Closing Date: 15 February
Additional Information: Website: www.newcastle.edu.au/scholarships/GOV_EDU

For further information contact:

University Dr, Callaghan NSW 2308, Australia.

Tel: (61) 2 4921 5000

International Excellence Scholarship (Information Technology and Computer Science)

Purpose: This scholarship has been established to attract high-performing international students to the University of Newcastle for study in 2023 and beyond. This is a merit-based scholarship that recognises applicants with a strong academic background and incentivises them to continue striving to be the best that they can be.
Eligibility: To be eligible, you will need to: 1. Be commencing study in an eligible program at the University of Newcastle in 2024 and beyond at an Australian or online campus as indicated on your Letter of Offer 2. Be an International full-fee paying student. 3. Not be the beneficiary of a separate University scholarship unless prior approval for special dispensation has been obtained from the university. 4. Meet all of the financial obligations of a full-fee paying international student, including the full tuition fee and other expenses for the purpose of obtaining your student visa, and in the event that eligibility for the scholarship is not maintained.
Level of Study: Masters Degree
Type: Scholarship
Value: AU$15,000 for each year of study under full-time study load
Application Procedure: No application is required for this scholarship.
Additional Information: Website: www.newcastle.edu.au/scholarships/UNI_044

International Excellence Scholarship (Management, Accounting and Finance)

Purpose: This is a merit-based scholarship that recognises applicants with a strong academic background and incentivises them to continue striving to be the best that they can be.
Eligibility: To be eligible, you will need to: 1. Be commencing study in an eligible program at the University of Newcastle in 2024 and beyond at an Australian or online campus as indicated on your Letter of Offer 2. Be an International full-fee paying student. 3. Not be the beneficiary of a separate University scholarship unless prior approval for special dispensation has been obtained from the university. 4. Meet all of the financial obligations of a full-fee paying international student, including the full tuition fee and other expenses for

the purpose of obtaining your student visa, and in the event that eligibility for the scholarship is not maintained.
Level of Study: Postgraduate
Type: Scholarship
Value: AU$15,000 for each year of study under full-time study load
Application Procedure: No application is required for this scholarship.
Additional Information: Website: www.newcastle.edu.au/scholarships/UNI_045

Jayce and Seamus Fagan Enabling Program Scholarship

Purpose: This scholarship has been established to support a student in an enabling program with the hope that this financial support will ensure they can concentrate on their studies and achieve the results to gain entry into an undergraduate degree.
Eligibility: To be eligible to apply for this scholarship, you will need to: 1. Be enrolled in an enabling program (Open Foundation or Yapug) with the University of Newcastle. 2. Demonstrate educational disadvantage such as carer, sole parent, financial hardship, English language difficulty, long term medical condition/disability or effects of abuse, Aboriginal and Torres Strait Islander, Out of Home Care, Refugee, or Geographic.
Type: Scholarship
Value: AU$4,000
Frequency: Annual
Country of Study: Any country
Closing Date: 15 February
Additional Information: Website: www.newcastle.edu.au/scholarships/EXT_227

For further information contact:

University Dr, Callaghan NSW 2308, Australia.

Tel: (61) 2 4921 5000

Joy Ingall Scholarship for Music Studies

Eligibility: 1. Be enrolled in Bachelor of Music (including Honours) or any combined program incorporating Bachelor of Music with University of Newcastle. 2. Be enrolled full-time. 3. Demonstrate academic achievement either by an Australian Tertiary Admission Rank (ATAR) or equivalent of 75 or higher for commencing students, or a Grade Point Average (GPA) of 5.0 for continuing students. 4. Demonstrate educational disadvantage such as carer, sole parent, financial hardship, English language difficulty, long term medical condition/disability or effects of abuse, Aboriginal and Torres Strait Islander, Out of Home Care, Refugee, or Geographic. 5. Have demonstrated a high standard during performance either at entry audition or at interview for shortlisted applicants. 6. Not have previously received this scholarship. 7. Not be the recipient of another University of Newcastle donor-funded or sponsored scholarship concurrently. 8. Be an Australian Citizen or Permanent Resident.
Type: Scholarship
Value: AU$15,000
Frequency: Annual
Country of Study: Any country
Closing Date: 15 February
No. of applicants last year: 3
Additional Information: Website: www.newcastle.edu.au/scholarships/EXT_163

For further information contact:

University Dr, Callaghan NSW 2308, Australia.

Tel: (61) 2 4921 5000

Latin America ELBP Scholarship

Purpose: The Latin America ELBP Scholarship has been established to encourage and support international students from the region of Latin America to study ELBP only and ELBP plus Undergraduate or Postgraduate programs with the University of Newcastle (Australia).
Eligibility: To be eligible, you will need to: 1. Be an international full-fee paying student from Region 3. 2. Be enrolled full-time. 3. Be commencing a minimum of 10 weeks ELBP. 4. Be able to meet all of the financial obligations of a full-fee paying international student, including the full tuition fee and other expenses for the purpose of obtaining a student visa for study in Australia, and in the event that continued eligibility
Level of Study: Postgraduate
Type: Scholarship
Value: AU$1,950
Application Procedure: No application is required for this scholarship.
No. of applicants last year: 15
Additional Information: Website: www.newcastle.edu.au/scholarships/UNI_049

Onshore Excellence Scholarship

Purpose: This is a merit-based scholarship that recognises applicants with a strong academic background and

incentivises them to continue striving to be the best that they can be.
Eligibility: To be eligible, you will need to: 1. Be an Onshore student currently located in Australia. 2. Be commencing study in an eligible undergraduate or postgraduate coursework degree program at the University (excluding ELICOS, Enabling, Non-Award, Higher Degrees by Research programs and programs delivered at offshore campuses). 3. Be an International full-fee paying student. 4. Be commencing in an eligible program at an Australian or Online campus as indicated in your Letter of Offer. 5. Not be the beneficiary of a separate University scholarship unless prior approval for special dispensation has been obtained from the university. 6. Meet all of the financial obligations of a full-fee paying international student, including the full tuition fee and other expenses for the purpose of obtaining your student visa, and in the event that eligibility for the scholarship is not maintained. 7. Not be enrolling in an excluded quota program (see selection details). 8. An offshore recent graduate of the University of Newcastle who has completed all program(s) of study listed in a prior letter of offer may also meet eligibility requirements..
Level of Study: Postgraduate
Type: Scholarship
Value: AU$50,000
Application Procedure: No application is required for this scholarship.
No. of applicants last year: 100
Additional Information: Website: www.newcastle.edu.au/scholarships/UNI_035

Shaping Futures Postgraduate Scholarship

Purpose: The Shaping Futures Postgraduate Scholarship will support postgraduate coursework students, alongside our undergraduate students supported by the Shaping Futures Scholarship, to overcome adversity and educational disadvantage.
Eligibility: To be eligible, you will need to: 1. Be enrolled in any year of a postgraduate coursework degree program with the University of Newcastle where the majority of delivery is on-campus. 2. Be enrolled in a minimum of 20 units in the term of scholarship award. 3. Demonstrate educational disadvantage such as carer, sole parent, financial hardship, English language difficulty, long term medical condition/disability or effects of abuse, Aboriginal and Torres Strait Islander, Out of Home Care, Refugee, or Geographic. 4. Be residing in Australia for the duration of your degree. 5. Not be the recipient of another University of Newcastle donor-funded or sponsored scholarship concurrently.
Level of Study: Postgraduate
Type: Scholarship
Value: AU$4000
Frequency: Annual
Country of Study: Any country
Closing Date: 15 February
No. of applicants last year: 7
Additional Information: Website: Website: www.newcastle.edu.au/scholarships/EXT_272

For further information contact:

University Dr, Callaghan NSW 2308, Australia.

Tel: (61) 2 4921 5000

Shaping Futures Scholarships

Purpose: The Shaping Futures Scholarship Program was established in 2011 with the aim of helping those students who are most in need.
Eligibility: To be eligible, you will need to: 1. Be enrolled in any year of an undergraduate degree program at the University of Newcastle. 2. Be enrolled full-time. 3. Demonstrate academic progress either by the Australian Tertiary Admission Rank (ATAR) or equivalent required for entry for commencing students, or a Grade Point Average (GPA) of 4.0 for continuing students. 4. Demonstrate educational disadvantage such as carer, sole parent, financial hardship, English language difficulty, long term medical condition/disability or effects of abuse, Aboriginal and Torres Strait Islander, Out of Home Care, Refugee, or Geographic. 5. Be an Australian citizen, Australian Permanent Resident (includes New Zealand Permanent Residents). 6. Not be the recipient of another University of Newcastle donor-funded or sponsored scholarship concurrently.
Level of Study: Postgraduate
Type: Scholarship
Value: AU$4000
Frequency: Annual
Country of Study: Any country
Closing Date: 15 February
No. of applicants last year: 61
Additional Information: Website: www.newcastle.edu.au/scholarships/EXT_140

For further information contact:

University Dr, Callaghan NSW 2308, Australia.

Tel: (61) 2 4921 5000

South Asia Excellence Scholarship

Purpose: This is a merit-based scholarship that recognises applicants with a strong academic background and incentives them to continue striving to be the best that they can be.

Eligibility: To be eligible, you will need to: 1. Hold a passport from an eligble South Asia country, being Afghanistan, Bangladesh, Bhutan, India, Maldives, Nepal, Pakistan, Sri Lanka. 2. Be commencing study in an eligible undergraduate or postgraduate coursework degree program at the University (excluding ELICOS, Enabling, Non-Award, Higher Degrees by Research programs and programs delivered at offshore campuses). 3. Be an International full-fee paying student. 4. Be commencing in an eligible program at an Australian or Online campus as indicated in your Letter of Offer. 5. Not be the beneficiary of a separate University scholarship unless prior approval for special dispensation has been obtained from the university. 6. Meet all of the financial obligations of a full-fee paying international student, including the full tuition fee and other expenses for the purpose of obtaining your student visa, and in the event that eligibility for the scholarship is not maintained. 7. Not be enrolling in an excluded quota program (see selection details).
Level of Study: Postgraduate
Type: Scholarship
Value: AU$10,000 for each year of study under full-time study load, apportioned over each course taken
Application Procedure: No application is required for this scholarship.
Additional Information: Website: www.newcastle.edu.au/scholarships/UNI_036

The Margaret Senior Natural History Illustration Scholarship

Purpose: This is a donor funded scholarship established from a bequest from the late Margaret Senior to recognize excellence in an Illustration major for a University of Newcastle student.
Eligibility: To be eligible, you will need to: 1. Be completing your first year of the Visual Communication Design program with an Illustration major with University of Newcastle. 2. Be enrolled full-time. 3. Not be the recipient of another University of Newcastle donor-funded or sponsored scholarship concurrently.
Level of Study: Postgraduate
Type: Scholarship
Value: AU$5,000
Application Procedure: No application is required for this scholarship
Additional Information: Website: www.newcastle.edu.au/scholarships/EXT_099

The Parker Fellowship

Purpose: The Parker Fellowship is an annual travelling scholarship available to students studying architecture at the University of Newcastle.
Eligibility: To be eligible, you will need to: 1. Be enrolled in any year of the Bachelor of Design (Architecture) or in year 1 of the Master of Architecture with the Faculty of Engineering and Built Environment, University of Newcastle. 2. Demonstrate academic progress either by the Australian Tertiary Admission Rank (ATAR) or equivalent required for entry for commencing students, or a Grade Point Average (GPA) of 4.0 for continuing students. 3. Not have previously received this scholarship. 4. Not be the recipient of another University of Newcastle donor-funded or sponsored scholarship concurrently.
Level of Study: Masters Degree
Type: Fellowships
Value: AU$8,000
Application Procedure: Apply for this scloarship: applications.newcastle.edu.au/scholarships/
Closing Date: 15 March
No. of applicants last year: 1
Additional Information: Website: www.newcastle.edu.au/scholarships/EXT_007

University of Newcastle - Malaysian Australia Columbo Plan Commemoration (MACC) Scholarship

Purpose: The University of Newcastle, in partnership with The Malaysian Australian Alumni Council (MAAC), has established the University of Newcastle - Malaysian Australia Columbo Plan Commemoration (MACC) Scholarship to attract high-performing Malaysian students to study at the University of Newcastle.
Eligibility: To be eligible, you will need to: 1. Be a citizen of Malaysia. 2. Be commencing study in an eligible undergraduate or postgraduate coursework degree program at the University (excluding ELICOS, Enabling, Non-Award, Higher Degrees by Research programs and programs delivered at offshore campuses). 3. Not be enrolling in an excluded quota program (see selection details). 4. Be an International full-fee paying student. 5. Be commencing in an eligible program at an Australian campus as indicated in your Letter of Offer. 6. Not be the beneficiary of a separate University scholarship unless prior approval for special dispensation has been obtained from the university. 7. Meet all of the financial obligations of a full-fee paying international student, including the full tuition fee and other expenses for the purpose of obtaining your student visa, and in the event that eligibility for the scholarship is not maintained.
Level of Study: Postgraduate
Type: Scholarship
Value: AU$10,000 for each year of study under full-time study load, apportioned over each course taken
Application Procedure: No application is required for this scholarship

Additional Information: Website: www.newcastle.edu.au/scholarships/UNI_046

University of Newcastle Postgraduate Research Scholarship (UNRS Central)

Eligibility: Open to the residents of Australia and New Zealand or permanent residents who have achieved Honours 1 or equivalent and have completed at least 4 years of undergraduate study
Level of Study: Postgraduate, Research
Type: Scholarship
Value: AU$23,728 per year full-time stipend, AU$12,898 part time stipend
Length of Study: 2 years (Masters) and 3 years (PhD)
Frequency: Annual
Country of Study: Australia
Application Procedure: Check website for further details
Closing Date: 31 October
No. of applicants last year: 30
Additional Information: Website: www.postgraduatefunding.com/award-1422

For further information contact:

Research Higher Degrees, The Chancellery Eastern Wing, University Drive, 905 University Dr., State College, PA 16801, United States of America.

Tel: (61) 2 4921 6537
Fax: (61) 2 4921 6908

University of Newcastle, Australia MBA Programme

Application Procedure: Applicants must return a completed application form, with original or certified copies of official academic transcripts (not to be returned), Graduate Management Admission Test and TOEFL (if applicable) scores, the names of two referees

For further information contact:

Business Administration International Students Office University Drive, 905 University Dr., State College, PA 16801, United States of America.

Tel: (61) 4 9216 595
Fax: (61) 4 9601 766
Email: io@newcastle.edu.au

Women in Master of Business Administration (WiMBA) Scholarship

Purpose: The Newcastle Business School is proud to support aspirational and high-achieving females with the Women in MBA (WiMBA) scholarship.
Eligibility: Aspirational and high-achieving females with the Women in MBA (WiMBA)
Level of Study: MBA
Type: Scholarship
Value: AU$18,000
Application Procedure: Applications are open now on the WiMBA: www.newcastle.edu.au/about-uon/governance-and-leadership/faculties-and-schools/faculty-of-business-and-law/newcastle-business-school/study-with-us/women-in-master-of-business-administration-wimba-scholarship/page.
No. of applicants last year: 9
Additional Information: Website: www.newcastle.edu.au/scholarships/BUSLAW_021

University of Notre Dame

1124 Flanner Hall, Notre Dame, IN 46556, United States of America.

Tel: (1) 574 631 1305
Email: ndias@nd.edu
Website: www.nd.edu
Contact: Brad S Gregory, Director of the Notre Dame Institute for Advanced Study

The University of Notre Dame provides a distinctive voice in higher education that is at once rigorously intellectual, unapologetically moral in orientation, and firmly embracing of a service ethos.

Templeton Fellowships for United States of America and International Scholars at NDIAS

Purpose: With grant support from the John Templeton Foundation, the NDIAS will help chart a new course for future scholarship by offering Templeton Fellowships that encourage scholars to return to reflection on the broad questions that link multiple areas of inquiry and to do so in a manner that embraces a value-oriented interpretation of the world
Eligibility: Distinguished senior scholars with extensive records of academic accomplishment and who have had a considerable impact on their discipline are encouraged to apply. Outstanding junior scholars with academic records of

exceptional promise and whose research agendas align with the purpose and parameters of the program are also invited to apply
Type: Fellowship
Value: These distinctive fellowships offer an extraordinary measure of scholarly support, including a stipend of up to US$100,000; fully furnished faculty housing (for those who reside outside of the Michiana area); up to US$3,000 in research expenditures; a private office at the NDIAS, with a personal desktop computer and printer; etc. Check detailed information on the website
Frequency: Annual
Country of Study: United States of America
Application Procedure: Please see ndias.nd.edu/fellowships/templeton/application-instructions/
Closing Date: 15 October
Additional Information: For more information, please check at ndias.nd.edu/fellowships/templeton/

For further information contact:

Email: csherman@nd.edu

University of Nottingham

University of Nottingham, University Park, Nottingham NG7 2RD, United Kingdom.

Tel: (44) 115 951 5151
Website: www.nottingham.ac.uk
Contact: Ms Nicola Pickering, Process Manager Funding

The University of Nottingham is a community of students and staff dedicated to bringing out the best in all of its members. It aims to provide the finest possible environment for teaching, learning and research and has a world class record of success.

Developing Solutions Masters Scholarship

Purpose: The aim of the Developing Solutions Masters Scholarship is to enable and encourage academically able students from Africa, India or one of the countries of the Commonwealth
Eligibility: To apply, you must 1. be domiciled in Africa, India or one of the selected Commonwealth countries listed below 2. be classed as an overseas student for fee purposes 3. hold an offer to start a full-time masters (including MRes) in any subject area at the University of Nottingham UK in September or October 2024, within the Faculty of Engineering, Faculty of Medicine and Health Sciences, Faculty of Science or Faculty of Social Sciences
Type: Scholarship
Value: covering 50% or 100% of full-time masters tuition fees
Length of Study: 1 year
Frequency: Annual
Country of Study: United Kingdom
Application Procedure: Apply online
No. of awards offered: 105
Closing Date: 17 May
Additional Information: www.nottingham.ac.uk/pgstudy/funding/developing-solutions-masters-scholarship

For further information contact:

Tel: (44) 115 951 5151
Email: scholarship-assistant@nottingham.ac.uk

Fully-funded PhD Studentship in the School of Geography

Eligibility: Applicants must hold an offer to start a PhD research degree programme in the School of Geography between 1 October 2024 and 1 February 2025
Level of Study: Doctorate
Type: Studentship
Value: £17,668
Country of Study: United Kingdom
Application Procedure: download and complete the application form (Word): www.nottingham.ac.uk/geography/documents/geography-studentship-application.doc submit it to tara.kaur@nottingham.ac.uk
Closing Date: 14 April
Additional Information: www.nottingham.ac.uk/pgstudy/funding/fully-funded-phd-studentship-geography

For further information contact:

Email: tara.kaur@nottingham.ac.uk

Grundy Educational Trust Postgraduate Award

Eligibility: You must: 1. be intending to pursue a course leading to a career in a STEM (technologically or scientifically based) discipline in industry, commerce or the professions 2. be a citizen or resident of the United Kingdom and can show you are in need of financial assistance to fund your maintenance costs 3. hold a conditional or unconditional offer of a place to study for a postgraduate degree at the University of Nottingham.
Level of Study: Doctorate, Research
Type: Award

Value: between £1,200 and £4,800
Frequency: Annual
Country of Study: United Kingdom
Closing Date: 31 March
Additional Information: www.nottingham.ac.uk/pgstudy/funding/grundy-educational-trust-postgraduate-award

For further information contact:

Email: br-ra-dtp-funding@exmail.nottingham.ac.uk

Nottingham Developing Solutions Scholarships

Purpose: The Developing Solutions Scholarships are designed for international students who want to pursue a Master's Degree in the University of Nottingham and make a difference to the development of their home country
Eligibility: To apply, you must: 1. be domiciled in Africa, India or one of the selected Commonwealth countries 2. be classed as an overseas student for fee purposes 3. hold an offer to start a full-time masters (including MRes) at the University of Nottingham UK, studying in the Faculty of Engineering, Faculty of Medicine and Health Sciences, Faculty of Science or Faculty of Social Sciences.
Level of Study: Postdoctorate
Type: Award
Value: 50-100% of the tuition fees
Length of Study: 1 year
Frequency: Annual
Country of Study: United Kingdom
No. of awards offered: 105
Closing Date: 17 May
Funding: Foundation
Additional Information: www.nottingham.ac.uk/pgstudy/funding/developing-solutions-masters-scholarship

For further information contact:

Email: scholarship-assistant@nottingham.ac.uk

Sir Francis Hill Postgraduate Scholarship

Eligibility: Students with a conditional or an unconditional offer on a PhD research programme at the University of Nottingham, or who are currently in the first year of their PhD are eligible to apply. International students are eligible to apply but funding is only at the level of UK home fees and maintenance grant. Each school may nominate one student.
Level of Study: Doctorate, Research
Type: Scholarship
Value: £4,596 and £17,668
Length of Study: 3.5 years
Country of Study: United Kingdom
Application Procedure: Download an application form (Word document): www.nottingham.ac.uk/pgstudy/Documents/sir-francis-hill-postgraduate-award-application-form-2023.doc
Closing Date: 28 April
Additional Information: www.nottingham.ac.uk/pgstudy/funding/sir-francis-hill-postgraduate-scholarship

University of Oklahoma

College of Business Administration, Adams Hall Room 105K, Norman, OK 73019, United States of America.

Tel: (1) 405 325 4107
Email: awatkins@ou.edu
Website: www.ou.edu/
Contact: MBA Admissions Officer

Ben Barnett Scholarship

Purpose: Any full-time Art majors admitted to either the MA or MFA degree program
Eligibility: Applicant must be a full-time student in the School of Art and have a minimum 3.0 GPA and an outstanding portfolio
Level of Study: Postgraduate
Type: Scholarship
Value: Maximum of US$1,000 will be given as scholarship amount
Frequency: Annual
Country of Study: United States of America
Application Procedure: Contact Director, School of Art University of Oklahoma 520 Parrington Room 202 Normak, OK 73019 United States Phone (405) 325-2691
No. of awards offered: 16
Closing Date: 1 March
Funding: Private
Additional Information: Visit the official website for further info: www.ou.edu www.collegexpress.com/scholarships/ben-barnett-scholarship/6650/

For further information contact:

Director, School of Art University of Oklahoma, 520 Parrington, Room 202, Normak OK 73019, United States.

Email: art@ou.edu

University of Ontario

Graduate Finance and Administration, 2000 Simcoe Street, North Oshawa, Ontario L1G 0C5, Canada.

Email: pmenzies@uwo.ca
Website: ontariotechu.ca/
Contact: Office of Graduate Studies Manager.

The University of Ontario Institute of Technology is a public research university located in Oshawa, Ontario, Canada.

The Ontario Trillium Scholarships (OTS)

Purpose: To attract top international students to Ontario for PhD studies
Eligibility: An eligible applicant must have achieved a minimum of 80% in each of the last 2 most recently completed years of full-time university study, or equivalent to full-time study. Eligibility averages for competitive scholarship are rounded ONLY to the nearest decimal place
Type: Scholarship
Value: CA$40,000 annually
Length of Study: 4 years
Frequency: Annual
Country of Study: Any country
Application Procedure: Submit a complete UOIT application with supporting documentation to the Office of Graduate Studies
Closing Date: 1 April
Additional Information: Submit the PDF nomination to SGPS pmenzies@uwo.ca uwaterloo.ca/graduate-studies-postdoctoral-affairs/awards/ontario-trillium-scholarship-ots

University of Oregon

1585E, 13th Ave, Eugene, OR 97403, United States of America.

Tel: (1) 541 346 1000
Website: www.uoregon.edu

Center for AIDS Prevention Studies, Small Professional Grants for Graduate Students

Purpose: Awards will be made for the following purposes travel to conferences to present papers, travel to library, museum, and archival collections; and expenses related to book and article production and publication
Eligibility: The Center for Asian and Pacific Studies is offering awards of up to US$500 in support of the professional activities of UO graduate students studying Asia. Awards will be made for the following purposes travel to conferences to present papers, travel to library, museum, and archival collections; and expenses related to book and article production and publication
Level of Study: Postgraduate
Type: Grant
Value: Up to US$500
Frequency: Annual
Country of Study: Any country
Application Procedure: 1. To submit a proposal, please complete the online application form. 2. A brief letter of support from your advisor explaining how this activity is central to your research interests is also required. This letter can be emailed directly to Holly Lakey at lakey@uoregon.edu
Closing Date: 15 April
Funding: Private
Additional Information: caps.uoregon.edu/2010/11/03/caps-small-professional-grants-for-graduate-students/

For further information contact:

1246 University of Oregon, Eugene, OR 97403, United States of America.

Tel: (1) 541 346 5068
Email: lakey@uoregon.edu

Jeremiah Lecture Series Support

Purpose: The Center for Asian and Pacific Studies is accepting proposals from UO faculty for speakers to visit the UO and deliver a public lecture on campus
Level of Study: Postgraduate
Type: Award
Frequency: Annual
Country of Study: Any country
Application Procedure: For a hardcopy version of the application form, please contact Holly Lakey at lakey@uoregon.edu
Closing Date: 15 April
Funding: Private
Additional Information: caps.uoregon.edu/2010/10/15/proposals-for-the-jeremiah-fund-lecture-series/

For further information contact:

Email: lakey@uoregon.edu

U

University of Otago

362 Leith Street, Dunedin 9016, New Zealand.

Tel: (64) 3 479 7000
Email: university@otago.ac.nz
Website: www.otago.ac.nz

The University of Otago, founded in 1869 by an ordinance of the Otago Provincial Council, is New Zealand's oldest university. The new University was given 100,000 acres of pastoral land as an endowment and authorised to grant degrees in Arts, Medicine, Law and Music.

Alliance Group Postgraduate Scholarship

Eligibility: 1. Obtaining their first doctoral qualification 2. Domestic students 3. Undertaking research related to the improvement of livestock
Level of Study: Doctorate, Postgraduate
Type: Scholarship
Value: NZ$30,696 per annum plus domestic tuition fees waiver (excludes student services fee)
Frequency: Annual
Country of Study: New Zealand
Application Procedure: Applications for doctoral scholarships are made online through the eVision portal and can be made at any time of the year. Once you have applied for admission to your programme, you will receive an alert in your student portal inviting you to apply for a scholarship
No. of awards offered: Varies
Funding: Foundation
Additional Information: www.otago.ac.nz/study/scholarships/database/search/otago016137.html

For further information contact:

Tel: (64) 800 80 80 98
Email: scholarships@otago.ac.nz

Angus Ross Travel Scholarship in History

Purpose: Established by the family of Angus Ross in 2010, the Angus Ross Travel Scholarship in History is intended to assist PhD candidates studying history with the costs associated with off-campus field and archival research
Eligibility: Applications are open to current University of Otago PhD candidates who, as part of their PhD studies 1. are conducting historically-focused research (preference will be given to candidates primarily based in the Department of History and Art History); 2. will be conducting off-campus field or archival research in the year for which the scholarship is awarded (the year following application). Note that this scholarship is not intended to support travel to a conference. Previous recipients are not eligible to apply for the scholarship in subsequent years.
Level of Study: Postgraduate
Type: Scholarship
Value: NZ$1,000
Frequency: Annual
Country of Study: New Zealand
Application Procedure: Every applicant must submit to the Doctoral and Scholarships Office by 1 November. 1. A brief Curriculum Vitae; 2. A description of the work to be conducted with the assistance of the scholarship, and the significance this work will have for their PhD research (no more than 500 words); 3. A budget of costs associated with the work to be conducted with the assistance of the scholarship; 4. A letter of support from their PhD supervisor. The University may also access academic transcripts and evidence of PhD progress in assessing this award. In exceptional circumstances applicants may be required to attend an interview either in person or by teleconference.
Closing Date: 1 November
Funding: Foundation
Additional Information: www.otago.ac.nz/study/scholarships/database/search/otago020796.html

Brenda Shore Award for Women

Purpose: Brenda Shore was an enthusiastic, enterprising person famous for her energy and passion. Over the course of 35 years Brenda became a prominent figure in the University of Otago Botany Department, both as a researcher and teacher, until her retirement in 1983. Leading by example Brenda Shore established this fund to help support women who have that same passion and energy for the natural sciences, particularly where their research relates to the Otago, Southland or Antarctic region
Eligibility: 1. University of Otago women graduates. 2. Women graduates carrying out research related to the Otago, Southland and Antarctic area. 3. Women graduates carrying out research for a postgraduate degree at the University of Otago
Level of Study: Postgraduate
Type: Award
Value: Up to NZ$15,000 for one year (not to be used for living expenses)
Length of Study: 1 year
Frequency: Annual
Country of Study: New Zealand

No. of awards offered: Varies
Closing Date: 28 February
Funding: Foundation
Additional Information: www.otago.ac.nz/study/scholarships/database/otago014683.html

Bruggeman Postgraduate Scholarship in Classics

Eligibility: 1. Obtaining their first Master's or Doctoral qualification 2. Domestic students 3. Undertaking research in the field of Classics
Level of Study: Postgraduate
Type: Scholarship
Value: NZ$17,172 stipend per annum (Master); NZ$30,696 stipend per annum (PhD) plus domestic tuition fee waiver (excludes student services fee)
Frequency: Annual
Country of Study: New Zealand
No. of awards offered: Varies
Funding: Foundation
Additional Information: www.otago.ac.nz/study/scholarships/database/otago016143.html

For further information contact:

362 Leith Street, Dunedin North, Dunedin 9016, New Zealand.

Tel: (64) 800 80 80 98
Email: scholarships@otago.ac.nz

Diane Campbell-Hunt Memorial Award

Purpose: Diane Campbell-Hunt was a PhD candidate in the Department of Geography, funded by a Tertiary Education Commission Top Achiever Doctoral scholarship. She had completed two-thirds of her PhD programme at the time of her death. Her project looked at the long-term sustainability of fenced sanctuaries in New Zealand in a multi-disciplinary analysis ecological, economic, social, and governmental
Eligibility: 1. Be enrolled and confirmed in a PhD programme in any Department or School at the University of Otago. 2. Have had accepted a peer-reviewed academic paper (conference or journal) that contributes to New Zealand conservation (as defined above), and in which they are the lead author. 3. Not have previously been awarded the award
Level of Study: Doctorate, Postgraduate
Type: Award
Value: NZ$1,000
Frequency: Annual
Country of Study: New Zealand
Closing Date: 30 June
Funding: Foundation
Additional Information: www.otago.ac.nz/study/scholarships/database/search/otago017367.html

Douglass D Crombie Award in Physics

Purpose: Established by the University of Otago Council in memory of Mr Douglass D Crombie. This award has been made possible by a generous bequest from the late Mr Crombie for the purpose of encouraging postgraduate research in Physics. This award will be offered to an outstanding University of Otago Physics graduate intending to undertake a PhD in Physics at an overseas university
Eligibility: 1. Were born in New Zealand. 2. Graduated or will soon graduate from the University of Otago with a degree in Physics. 3. Are intending to pursue doctoral-level studies in Physics. 4. Are intending to undertake their studies at an English speaking University in an English speaking country (excluding New Zealand). 5. Have displayed outstanding academic ability
Eligible Country: New Zealand
Level of Study: Postgraduate
Type: Award
Value: NZ$7,000
Frequency: Annual
Country of Study: New Zealand
Application Procedure: 1. be born in New Zealand 2. have graduated or will soon graduate from the University of Otago with a degree in Physics 3. be intending to pursue doctoral-level studies in Physics 4. be intending to undertake their studies at an English speaking University in an English speaking country (excluding New Zealand) 5. have displayed outstanding academic ability
No. of awards offered: 1
Funding: Foundation
Additional Information: www.otago.ac.nz/study/scholarships/database/otago040266.html

For further information contact:

Scholarships Office, Graduate Research School, PO Box 56, Dunedin 9054, New Zealand.

Tel: (64) 3 479 7000
Email: scholarships@otago.ac.nz

Dr Sulaiman Daud 125th Jubilee Postgraduate Scholarship

Purpose: This scholarship was established in 1994 to mark the 125th Anniversary of the foundation of the University of

Otago, New Zealand's oldest university. The purpose of the scholarship is to assist an exceptional postgraduate research student from Malaysia to attend the University
Eligibility: 1. Unless otherwise stated in these conditions or within the schedule, doctoral and Masters' scholarships are open only to Domestic Fee Paying Students. International candidates studying for professional doctorates are eligible to apply but if awarded a scholarship the tuition fee waiver will be capped at the domestic rate. 2. In the case of applicants for a doctoral scholarship, confirmation of the scholarship is dependent on approval of their application for admission to the relevant doctoral programme and completion of the enrolment procedure. 3. In the case of applicants for a Master's scholarship, confirmation of the scholarship is dependent on approval of their application to register as a Master's candidate and completion of the enrolment procedure
Level of Study: Postgraduate
Type: Scholarship
Value: Establishment allowance of NZ$575; domestic tuition fee waiver (excludes student services fee); health insurance to the value of NZ$600; NZ$30,696 per annum stipend; educational allowance of NZ$550
Length of Study: 1 year
Frequency: Annual
Country of Study: New Zealand
No. of awards offered: 1
Funding: Foundation
Additional Information: www.otago.ac.nz/study/scholarships/database/otago020604.html

For further information contact:

P.O. Box 514070, Milwaukee, WI 53203-3470, United States of America.

Email: scholarships@otago.ac.nz

Elizabeth Jean Trotter Postgraduate Research Travelling Scholarship in Biomedical Sciences

Purpose: Established by the University of Otago Council from a generous donation in memory of Elizabeth Jean Trotter
Eligibility: Applicants must be: 1. enrolled for a PhD or in the research year of a Master's programme with primary supervision in the Otago School of Biomedical Sciences (BMS) 2. undertaking research in a Biomedical Sciences field
Level of Study: Postgraduate
Type: Fellowships
Value: Up to NZ$5,000
Length of Study: 1 year
Frequency: Annual
Country of Study: New Zealand
Application Procedure: See Website
No. of awards offered: Varies
Closing Date: 1 November
Funding: Foundation
Additional Information: Website: www.otago.ac.nz/study/scholarships/database/otago622380.html

For further information contact:

Tel: (64) 3 479 7000

Elman Poole Travelling Scholarship

Purpose: The Elman Poole Travelling Scholarship provides funds to support PhD students in their 2nd or 3rd year of study, who wish to do field work outside of New Zealand.
Eligibility: Applicants must be: 1. enrolled full-time in PhD study at the University of Otago majoring in one of the following areas: physical or biological sciences, health sciences or music 2. intending to engage in study outside of New Zealand in their second or third year of PhD study 3. New Zealand citizens or New Zealand Residence Class Visa Holders 4. under the age of 35 on 1 February in the year of application
Level of Study: Postgraduate
Type: Scholarship
Value: Maximum NZ$20,000, plus up to NZ$5,000 additional expenses
Frequency: Annual
Country of Study: New Zealand
Application Procedure: Download the Elman Poole Travelling Scholarship regulations and application information: www.otago.ac.nz/study/scholarships/otago703727.pdf
No. of awards offered: Varies
Closing Date: 1 June
Funding: Foundation
Additional Information: Website: www.otago.ac.nz/study/scholarships/database/otago014682.html

For further information contact:

St David II Building, University of Otago, PO Box 56, Dunedin 9054, New Zealand.

Freemasons Scholarships

Purpose: The Freemasons Scholarships are provided annually by Freemasons New Zealand and are administered by the Freemasons Charity
Eligibility: 1. Have a good academic report. 2. Be a New Zealand citizen or permanent resident. 3. Demonstrate

good citizenship. 4. Show leadership potential. 5. Have proven community commitment
Level of Study: Postgraduate
Type: Scholarship
Value: NZ$6,000 (University); NZ$10,000 (Postgraduate)
Frequency: Annual
Country of Study: New Zealand
No. of awards offered: 3 (University); 1 (Postgraduate)
Closing Date: 1 October
Funding: Foundation
Additional Information: https://www.otago.ac.nz/study/scholarships/database/otago020853.html

For further information contact:

Email: info@lincoln.ac.nz

Fully Funded PhD Scholarships

Purpose: Fully Funded PhD Scholarships, University of Sheffield, United Kingdom are offered to international students who attract the administration panel with their academic performance to pursue PhD programme. The candidates should have the knowledge in the English language and candidates from non-English countries should meet the abilities of the university by attaining the IELTS and other related tests. Annually the university offers five scholarships
Eligibility: 1. Eligible Countries Overseas participants are eligible. 2. Acceptable Course or Subjects The program will be awarded for the PhD degree in Quantitative Biology 3. Admissible Criteria To be eligible, the applicants must meet all the given criteria 4. Applicants must have a master's degree in a relevant area. There are three types of PhD students can apply for this grant 5. Students with a life science degree, interested in working in an experimental lab, but with a high degree of motivation to learn the fundamentals of computational biology, and to develop quantitative skills to analyze data more effectively 6. Students with a life science degree interested in working in a dry computational lab, keen to deepen their quantitative skills and broaden their horizon in terms of experimental and computational techniques 7. Students with a non-biological background (e.g. computer science, maths, physics), who are highly motivated to transition to Life Sciences
Level of Study: Masters Degree, Postgraduate
Type: Scholarship
Value: The university covers full tuition fee plus a monthly stipend to high achieving participants
Frequency: Annual
Country of Study: New Zealand
Application Procedure: Aspirants are suggested to take part in a PhD degree program at the university. And then apply for the grants through completing the online application form: career5.successfactors.eu/sfcareer/jobreqcareer?jobId=14879&company=universitdP.
No. of awards offered: 15
Closing Date: 15 October
Funding: Foundation
Additional Information: Website: scholarship-positions.com/15-fully-funded-phd-studentsnational-students-in-switzerhips-for-interland/2019/09/27/

Gilbert M Tothill Scholarship in Psychological Medicine

Purpose: Doctoral scholarships are awarded by the University Council, on the recommendation of the Senate, to candidates proceeding to a course of supervised doctoral study at this University. These scholarships are normally available only to students seeking to obtain their first doctoral qualification
Eligibility: In the case of an applicant for a doctoral scholarship who has completed a Master's degree by papers and thesis (at least 0.75 EFTS), the grades of all relevant2 advanced level papers counting towards the award of the degree and the thesis will be taken into account. An explanation of the time taken for completion of the thesis may be requested and considered by the Scholarships and Prizes Committee if the thesis has taken more than 2 EFTS (2 fulltime years) to complete
Level of Study: Postgraduate
Type: Scholarship
Value: NZ$10,000 per annum
Length of Study: 3 year
Frequency: Annual
Country of Study: New Zealand
Funding: Foundation
Additional Information: www.otago.ac.nz/study/scholarships/database/otago089208.html

For further information contact:

Email: scholarships@otago.ac.nz

Helen Rosa Thacker Scholarship in Neurological Research

Purpose: The Helen Rosa Thacker Scholarship in Neurological Research was established by Helen Rosa Thacker in 2012 to support research and teaching in the field of neurology at the University of Otago. The scholarship aims to recognise, reward and inspire a particularly good PhD student. This scholarship can be held alongside an existing scholarship. This scholarship will be awarded for one year, with a chance of extension to a second year due to outstanding progress

Eligibility: 1. a PhD in neurological research at the University of Otago 2. enrolled full-time (student) 3. a male scholar holding a New Zealand birth certificate 4. available to receive the scholarship in person and provide updates on the progress of their research
Level of Study: Postgraduate
Type: Scholarship
Value: NZ$5,000
Length of Study: 1 year
Frequency: Annual
Country of Study: New Zealand
Closing Date: 2 October
Funding: Foundation
Additional Information: Website: www.otago.ac.nz/study/scholarships/database/otago055663.html

For further information contact:

Jane Reynolds, Administrative Assistant, Brain Health Research Centre, C/- Department of Anatomy, PO Box 56, Dunedin 9054, New Zealand.

Tel: (64) 3 479 7612
Email: bhrc@otago.ac.nz

James Park Scholarship in Geology

Purpose: Masters' scholarships are awarded by the University Council, on the recommendation of the Senate, to candidates in the first year of their thesis research for a Master's degree which constitutes entry to the PhD course at this University. These scholarships are available only to students seeking to obtain their first research-based Master's qualification
Eligibility: 1. Unless otherwise stated in these conditions or within the schedule, doctoral and Masters' scholarships are open only to Domestic Fee Paying Students. International candidates studying for professional doctorates are eligible to apply but if awarded a scholarship the tuition fee waiver will be capped at the domestic rate. 2. In the case of applicants for a doctoral scholarship, confirmation of the scholarship is dependent on approval of their application for admission to the relevant doctoral programme and completion of the enrolment procedure. 3. In the case of applicants for a Master's scholarship, confirmation of the scholarship is dependent on approval of their application to register as a Master's candidate and completion of the enrolment procedure
Level of Study: Postgraduate
Type: Scholarship
Value: NZ$17,172 stipend per annum (Master); NZ$30,696 stipend per annum (PhD); domestic tuition fee waiver (excludes student services fee)
Frequency: Annual
Country of Study: New Zealand
No. of awards offered: Varies
Funding: Foundation
Additional Information: www.otago.ac.nz/study/scholarships/database/search/otago020608.html

For further information contact:

Educational Credential Evaluators, Inc., P.O. Box 514070, Milwaukee, WI 53203-3470, United States of America.

Tel: (1) 414 289 3400
Email: scholarships@otago.ac.nz

Macandrew-Stout Postgraduate Scholarship in Economics

Purpose: Established from funds made available by public subscription in memory of the late James Macandrew, member of the Council and one of the founders of the University and in 1920 by Sir Robert Stout, KCMG, Chief Justice of New Zealand
Eligibility: 1. Unless otherwise stated in these conditions or within the schedule, doctoral and Masters' scholarships are open only to Domestic Fee Paying Students. International candidates studying for professional doctorates are eligible to apply but if awarded a scholarship the tuition fee waiver will be capped at the domestic rate. 2. In the case of applicants for a doctoral scholarship, confirmation of the scholarship is dependent on approval of their application for admission to the relevant doctoral programme and completion of the enrolment procedure. 3. In the case of applicants for a Master's scholarship, confirmation of the scholarship is dependent on approval of their application to register as a Master's candidate and completion of the enrolment procedure
Level of Study: Postgraduate
Type: Scholarship
Value: NZ$17,172 stipend per annum (Master); NZ$30,696 stipend per annum (PhD); domestic student fee waiver (excludes student services fee).
Frequency: Annual
Country of Study: New Zealand
No. of awards offered: varies
Funding: Foundation
Additional Information: www.otago.ac.nz/study/scholarships/database/search/otago020612.html

For further information contact:

Educational Credential Evaluators, Inc., P.O. Box 514070, Milwaukee, WI 53203-3470, United States of America.

Tel: (1) 414 289 3400
Email: scholarships@otago.ac.nz

Noni Wright Scholarship

Purpose: Established by the University Council in association with the Guardian Trust in 2011 to provide support for Theatre Studies students to pursue postgraduate study. The scholarship was made possible by a generous endowment from the late Mrs Eleanor Wright, to honour the memory of her daughter Noni Wright, who was well known in drama circles, and had appeared on programmes for the BBC
Eligibility: Applicants must be: 1. Currently enrolled or intending to enrol for full-time study at the University of Otago in the year following the closing date 2. Intending to study for the degree of MA or MFA in Theatre Studies, or for a PhD researching a topic in Theatre Studies
Level of Study: Masters Degree, Postgraduate, Research
Type: Scholarship
Value: NZ$5,000
Length of Study: 1 year
Frequency: Annual
Country of Study: New Zealand
No. of awards offered: 1
Closing Date: 28 February
Funding: Foundation
Additional Information: Website: www.otago.ac.nz/study/scholarships/database/otago030561.html

For further information contact:

Email: scholarships@otago.ac.nz

Otago International Pathway Scholarship

Purpose: The Otago International Pathway Scholarship enables ambitious students to pursue their academic study goals, by supporting them in their preparation for further study at the University of Otago.
Eligibility: International students who are not citizens, permanent residents or resident visa holders of New Zealand or Australia*; and Have gained admission to the Foundation Studies Certificate through meeting both academic and English entry requirements, as outlined on the Otago website, and Are subject to paying international tuition fees; and Are enrolling in the Foundation Studies Certificate for the first time.
Type: Scholarship
Value: NZ$5,000 for tuition fees
Length of Study: 8 months
Frequency: Annual
Country of Study: Any country
Additional Information: https://www.otago.ac.nz/international/future-students/international-scholarships/#pathway-scholarships

For further information contact:

362 Leith Street, Dunedin North, Dunedin 9016, New Zealand.

Tel: (64) 3 479 7000

Patricia Pratt Scholarships in Musical Performance

Purpose: To assist outstanding New Zealand musical performers who have completed an honours degree in musical performance in New Zealand to continue their musical development at a renowned international music school or conservatorium. The scholarship will be awarded for classical music performance including vocal or instrumental performance or conducting
Eligibility: Applicants will be New Zealand citizens. Applicants may apply from outside New Zealand but must have resided in New Zealand for at least three of the last five years immediately preceding the year of selection. Applicants will have recently completed the requirements for an honours degree in musical performance at a New Zealand university (or an equivalent musical qualification).
Level of Study: Postgraduate
Type: Scholarship
Value: Up to NZ$45,000
Frequency: Annual
Country of Study: New Zealand
No. of awards offered: 1
Closing Date: 1 March
Funding: Foundation
Additional Information: www.otago.ac.nz/study/scholarships/database/search/otago016525.html

Postgraduate Tassell Scholarship in Cancer Research

Purpose: Doctoral scholarships are awarded by the University Council, on the recommendation of the Senate, to candidates proceeding to a course of supervised doctoral study at this University. These scholarships are normally available only to students seeking to obtain their first doctoral qualification
Eligibility: 1. Unless otherwise stated in these conditions or within the schedule, doctoral and Masters' scholarships are open only to Domestic Fee Paying Students. International candidates studying for professional doctorates are eligible to apply but if awarded a scholarship the tuition fee waiver will be capped at the domestic rate. 2. In the case of applicants for a doctoral scholarship, confirmation of the

scholarship is dependent on approval of their application for admission to the relevant doctoral programme and completion of the enrolment procedure. 3. In the case of applicants for a Master's scholarship, confirmation of the scholarship is dependent on approval of their application to register as a Master's candidate and completion of the enrolment procedure
Level of Study: Postgraduate
Type: Scholarship
Value: NZ$30,696 plus domestic tuition fee waiver
Frequency: Annual
Country of Study: New Zealand
No. of awards offered: Varies
Funding: Foundation
Additional Information: www.otago.ac.nz/study/scholarships/database/otago035878.html

For further information contact:

Email: scholarships@otago.ac.nz

Ramboll Masters Scholarship for International Students

Purpose: Ramboll Masters Scholarship for International Students provides scholarships to the students all over the world who are pursuing masters degree and diploma in engineering in all related fields of Engineering, Natural Science, Political Science, Economics or Architecture, the candidates are selected based on the academic merit considering their projects and profile, the Ramboll offers opportunities to the students by providing inspirational and longstanding solutions that strengthen the ideas of candidate and enhance the nature and future
Eligibility: To be eligible, the applicant should meet the necessary criteria such as the candidate is currently studying Engineering, Natural Science, Political Science, Economics, or Architecture subjects as one of their course studies, and is going to study abroad outside of Denmark, to be eligible to apply the applicant should be a Diploma Engineer on semester 4 – 7 or studying on a Master's level, and must be agreed to send Ramboll two travel updates during their stay abroad.
Level of Study: Masters Degree
Type: Scholarship
Value: NZ$25,000
Frequency: Annual
Country of Study: New Zealand
Closing Date: 20 April
Funding: Foundation
Additional Information: Website: scholarship-fellowship.com/ramboll-masters-scholarship-for-international-students/

Rhodes Scholarship

Eligibility: Candidates must: 1. at the closing date for applications in the year of application hold New Zealand citizenship or a New Zealand Permanent Resident Visa 2. at the closing date for applications in the year of application have spent at least five of the previous 10 years in New Zealand 3. by the time of entry to Oxford have graduated with an undergraduate degree with a GPA of 7.50/9.00.
Level of Study: Doctorate
Type: Scholarship
Value: £12,200 sterling per year personal allowance, plus fees
Length of Study: 3 years
Country of Study: United Kingdom
No. of awards offered: 3
Closing Date: 1 August
Additional Information: www.otago.ac.nz/graduate-research/scholarships/otago014758.html www.universitiesnz.ac.nz/scholarships/rhodes-scholarship-new-zealand

Senior Smeaton Scholarship in Experimental Science

Purpose: Masters' scholarships are awarded by the University Council, on the recommendation of the Senate, tocandidates in the first year of their thesis research for a Master's degree which constitutes entry to the PhD course at this University. These scholarships are available only to students seeking to obtain their first research-based Master's qualification
Eligibility: 1. Unless otherwise stated in these conditions or within the schedule, doctoral and Masters' scholarships are open only to Domestic Fee Paying Students. 3 International candidates studying for professional doctorates are eligible to apply but if awarded a scholarship the tuition fee waiver will be capped at the domestic rate. 2. In the case of applicants for a doctoral scholarship, confirmation of the scholarship is dependent on approval of their application for admission to the relevant doctoral programme and completion of the enrolment procedure. 3. In the case of applicants for a Master's scholarship, confirmation of the scholarship is dependent on approval of their application to register as a Master's candidate and completion of the enrolment procedure
Level of Study: Postgraduate
Type: Scholarship
Value: NZ$17,172 stipend per annum (Master); NZ$30,696 stipend per annum (PhD) plus domestic tuition fee waiver (excludes student services fee).
Frequency: Annual
Country of Study: New Zealand

Funding: Foundation
Additional Information: www.otago.ac.nz/study/scholarships/database/otago020614.html

For further information contact:

Educational Credential Evaluators, Inc. P.O. Box 514070, Milwaukee, WI 53203-3470, United States of America.

Tel: (1) 414 289 3400
Email: scholarships@otago.ac.nz

The Dr Stella Cullington Postgraduate Scholarship in Ophthalmology

Purpose: Established in 2014 by the Faculty of Medicine, from a generous donation from Dr Stella Cullington. Dr Cullington is a medical graduate and practised as a GP in United Kingdom and New Zealand. The Dr Stella Cullington Postgraduate Scholarship in Ophthalmology was created to support the sustainability and development of Ophthalmology Research within the academic discipline
Eligibility: 1. Be a NZ citizen or NZ permanent resident. 2. Hold a Bachelor of Medicine and Bachelor of Surgery degrees (MBChB) or an equivalent medical degree. 3. Demonstrate proof of potential academic research ability through (i) successful completion of a research Master's degree, or (ii) appropriate and equivalent prior research experience. 4. Be enrolled or intending to enrol for a MOphth or PhD at the University of Otago
Eligible Country: New Zealand
Level of Study: Postgraduate
Type: Scholarship
Value: up to NZ$5,000 per year for full-time study or NZ$2,500 per year for part-time study
Length of Study: 1 year
Frequency: Annual
Country of Study: New Zealand
No. of awards offered: 1
Funding: Foundation
Additional Information: www.otago.ac.nz/study/scholarships/database/otago597632.html

The Eamon Cleary Trust Postgraduate Study Scholarship

Purpose: Established in 2016 by the University of Otago Council from a generous donation by the Eamon Cleary Trust. The Eamon Cleary Trust Postgraduate Study Scholarship was created to support University of Otago students undertaking postgraduate research in Irish Studies. The scholarship may be used for expenses associated with postgraduate study, such as tuition fees, research expenses or travel associated with their research programme
Eligibility: 1. Be intending to enrol in a Doctoral or Research Masters programme in Irish Studies or a Coursework Masters programme in Irish Studies with a research component greater than or equal to 60 points at the University of Otago for the year of the award. 2. Have made contact to discuss satisfactory supervisory arrangements with the Eamon Cleary Professor of Irish Studies prior to submission of the application
Level of Study: Postgraduate
Type: Scholarship
Value: NZ$15,000 to NZ$27,000
Frequency: Annual
Country of Study: New Zealand
Funding: Foundation
Additional Information: www.otago.ac.nz/study/scholarships/database/otago616894.html

The Joan, Arthur & Helen Thacker Aboriginal and/or Torres Strait Islander Postgraduate Scholarship

Purpose: Established by the University of Otago Council in 2014, through the provision of funding from Helen R Thacker, this scholarship aims to support students of Aboriginal and/or Torres Strait Islander descent to undertake postgraduate studies in the field of Health Sciences at the University of Otago. The purpose of the fund is to support research and training in health sciences subjects that may have a future benefit to Aboriginal and/or Torres Strait Islander communities
Eligibility: 1. Aboriginal and/or Torres Strait Islander descent. 2. Australian citizens and residing in Australia at the time of application. 3. Planning to enrol in a postgraduate course of study in either Dental Technology, Dentistry, Oral Health, Medicine, Neuroscience, Pharmacy or Radiation Therapy at the University of Otago. 4. Planning to undertake study/research that is likely to be of future benefit to their Aboriginal and/or Torres Strait Islander community. 5. Intending to return to work in Australia after their course of study
Level of Study: Postgraduate, Research
Type: Scholarship
Value: NZ$25,000 per annum (PhD); NZ$15,000 stipend per annum (other postgraduate study); tuition fee waiver to a maximum of NZ$30,000 per annum (excludes student services fee)
Frequency: Annual
Country of Study: New Zealand
No. of awards offered: 1
Closing Date: 1 October

Funding: Foundation
Additional Information: www.otago.ac.nz/study/scholarships/database/otago106285.html

The Robinson Dorsey Postgraduate Scholarship

Purpose: The Robinson Dorsey Postgraduate Scholarship was created to support postgraduate students who are returning to university study after a break, and/or who through their personal circumstances, are not eligible for usual scholarships
Eligibility: 1. A New Zealand Citizen or New Zealand Residence Class Visa Holder 2. Enrolled or intending to enrol in a postgraduate diploma, honours degree, Master of Science or PhD degree in Physiology or Human Nutrition at the University of Otago 3. Returning to university study after a break, and/or who through their personal circumstances are not eligible for usual scholarships
Level of Study: Masters Degree, Postgraduate
Type: Scholarship
Value: NZ$25,000 full time PhD study or NZ$13,000 full time Masters', Postgraduate Diploma or Honours Study
Frequency: Annual
Country of Study: New Zealand
No. of awards offered: 1
Closing Date: 28 February
Funding: Foundation
Additional Information: www.otago.ac.nz/study/scholarships/database/otago664753.html

For further information contact:

Post to Student Administration (Scholarships), St David II Building, University of Otago, PO Box 56, Dunedin 9054, New Zealand.

Email: scholarships@otago.ac.nz

University of Helsinki Masters Scholarships

Purpose: University of Helsinki Masters Scholarships are offered to the students of international arena who are interested to pursue masters degree from the university, the scholarships offered are fully funded which includes full tuition fees, eligible candidates are selected by the committee not only based on academic criteria the committee will also consider the variety and diversity of the applicants and grant the scholarships to those coming from different backgrounds and fields of studies, the main aim hidden under the scholarship program is to create a rich and diverse learning environment at the University of Helsinki, candidates should receive an offer from the university to apply for the scholarship
Eligibility: All candidates must meet the following requirements 1. You are eligible for the Master's programme at the University of Helsinki 2. The country of your nationality is outside the EU/EEA and you meet the requirements for obtaining an entry visa and residence permit for Finland. More information at the Studyinfo. 3. You have obtained excellent results in your previous studies and can prove this in your application.
Level of Study: Postgraduate
Type: Scholarship
Value: Tuition fees range from €13,000 to €18,000.
Length of Study: 2 years
Frequency: Annual
Country of Study: Finland
Application Procedure: The scholarship application will be filled out in the same application system and simultaneously with your online application to the University of Helsinki English language Master's programmes. The possible scholarship-related documents should be delivered with the other enclosed documents of your degree application.
Closing Date: 10 January
Funding: Private
Additional Information: Tuition fee will range from €13,000 to €18,000. For further information on the scholarship, refer the below link. www.helsinki.fi/en/admissions/scholarship-programme www.afterschoolafrica.com/17865/university-helsinki-masters-scholarships/

University of Otago Academic General Practitioner Registrar PhD Scholarship

Purpose: The scholarship was created to support the sustainability and development of the Primary Health Care and General Practice academic discipline. The scholarship aims to help establish research capability among a new generation of General Practitioners by supporting the achievement of a Doctoral degree (PhD) at the University of Otago as well as vocational registration as a Fellow of the Royal New Zealand College of General Practitioners (RNZCGP)
Eligibility: 1. Be a New Zealand citizen or New Zealand Residence Class Visa Holder; 2. hold a Bachelor of Medicine and Bachelor of Surgery degrees (MBChB) or an equivalent medical degree; 3. demonstrate a formal commitment to a General Practice career by having successfully completed either (i) the General Practice Education Programme first year (GPEP1) with an above average pass in the Primary Membership Examination (PRIMEX) or (ii) a RNZCGP Fellowship; 4. have successfully completed either the 'Health Sciences Research Methods' paper (HASX417) or the

'Research Methods in General Practice' paper (GENX821), or an alternative 30 point postgraduate research methods paper with a minimum B+ grade; 5. demonstrate proof of potential academic research ability through (i) successful completion of a research Master's degree, or (ii) appropriate and equivalent prior research experience; 6. be enrolled or intending to enrol for a PhD through one of the following Departments: A. Department of Public Health & General Practice, University of Otago, Christchurch; B. Department of General Practice & Rural Health, Dunedin School of Medicine, University of Otago; C. Department of Primary Health Care & General Practice, University of Otago, Wellington.
Eligible Country: New Zealand
Level of Study: Masters Degree, Postgraduate, Research
Type: Scholarship
Value: NZ$25,000 per year for full-time study or NZ$12,500 per year for part-time study plus a tuition fee waiver for the PhD thesis paper for the period of tenure
Frequency: Annual
Country of Study: New Zealand
No. of awards offered: 1
Closing Date: 15 September
Funding: Foundation
Additional Information: Website: www.otago.ac.nz/study/scholarships/database/otago049881.html

University of Otago China Scholarship Council Doctoral Scholarship

Purpose: Masters' scholarships are awarded by the University Council, on the recommendation of the Senate, to candidates in the first year of their thesis research for a Master's degree which constitutes entry to the PhD course at this University. These scholarships are available only to students seeking to obtain their first research-based Master's qualification
Eligibility: 1. Unless otherwise stated in these conditions or within the schedule, doctoral and Masters' scholarships are open only to Domestic Fee Paying Students. International candidates studying for professional doctorates are eligible to apply but if awarded a scholarship the tuition fee waiver will be capped at the domestic rate. 2. In the case of applicants for a doctoral scholarship, confirmation of the scholarship is dependent on approval of their application for admission to the relevant doctoral programme and completion of the enrolment procedure. 3. In the case of applicants for a Master's scholarship, confirmation of the scholarship is dependent on approval of their application to register as a Master's candidate and completion of the enrolment procedure
Level of Study: Postgraduate
Type: Scholarship
Value: NZ$25,000 per year for full-time study or NZ$12,500 per year for part-time study plus a tuition fee waiver for the PhD thesis paper for the period of tenure
Frequency: Annual
Country of Study: New Zealand
No. of awards offered: Varies
Closing Date: 15 September
Funding: Foundation
Additional Information: https://www.otago.ac.nz/study/scholarships/database/otago624690.html

For further information contact:

Email: scholarships@otago.ac.nz

University of Otago City of Literature PhD Scholarship

Purpose: Masters' scholarships are awarded by the University Council, on the recommendation of the Senate, to candidates in the first year of their thesis research for a Master's degree which constitutes entry to the PhD course at this University. These scholarships are available only to students seeking to obtain their first research-based Master's qualification
Eligibility: 1. Unless otherwise stated in these conditions or within the schedule, doctoral and Masters' scholarships are open only to Domestic Fee Paying Students. 3 International candidates studying for professional doctorates are eligible to apply but if awarded a scholarship the tuition fee waiver will be capped at the domestic rate. 2. In the case of applicants for a doctoral scholarship, confirmation of the scholarship is dependent on approval of their application for admission to the relevant doctoral programme and completion of the enrolment procedure. 3. In the case of applicants for a Master's scholarship, confirmation of the scholarship is dependent on approval of their application to register as a Master's candidate and completion of the enrolment procedure
Level of Study: Postgraduate
Type: Scholarship
Value: NZ$30,696 stipend per annum (PhD) plus domestic tuition fee waiver (excludes student services fee)
Frequency: Annual
Country of Study: New Zealand
Closing Date: 30 September
Funding: Foundation
Additional Information: www.otago.ac.nz/study/scholarships/database/otago624693.html

For further information contact:

Email: scholarships@otago.ac.nz

University of Otago Doctoral Scholarships

Purpose: To fund research towards a PhD degree at the University of Otago
Eligibility: Open to applicants of any country but must be primarily resident in New Zealand during study
Level of Study: Doctorate, Research
Type: Scholarship
Value: NZ$30,696 stipend per annum stipend per annum plus a domestic tuition fees waiver for 36 months (excludes student services fee and insurance) Professional Doctorates (DClinDent, DMA, DBA, EDd) - NZ$27,000 stipend per annum plus a tuition fee waiver for up to 36 months capped at the domestic rate (excludes student services fee and insurance).
Length of Study: 3 years
Frequency: Annual
Study Establishment: The University of Otago
Country of Study: New Zealand
Application Procedure: Please visit www.otago.ac.nz/applynow
No. of awards offered: 200
No. of awards given last year: 180
Additional Information: www.otago.ac.nz/study/scholarships/database/otago014687.html

For further information contact:

Tel: (64) 800 80 80 98
Email: scholarships@otago.ac.nz

University of Otago Doctorate in Medical Education Scholarship

Purpose: Established with funding from the Otago Medical School, this scholarship is intended to provide support for clinically qualified health care professionals with an interest in medical education to undertake research at PhD level. The research must be applicable to the enhancement of the Otago MB ChB programme. The scholarship will be awarded for a three-year period; part-time PhDs will be considered. The participants will perform medical educational research in their own educational setting at University of Otago campuses in Dunedin, Christchurch or Wellington, but associated sites e.g. Invercargill, Nelson, Palmerston North, Hawkes Bay will be considered provided satisfactory supervisory arrangements can be made
Eligibility: 1. Normally be a NZ citizen or NZ permanent resident. 2. Hold a clinical health care discipline degree. Non-clinically qualified people with a strong background in Education may be considered but priority will be given to applicants from the first category. 3. Provide confirmation that this is their first doctoral qualification. 4. Be enrolled or intending to enrol for a PhD.
Level of Study: Postgraduate
Type: Scholarship
Value: NZ$25,000 stipend per annum plus a domestic tuition fees waiver
Frequency: Annual
Country of Study: New Zealand
No. of awards offered: Varies
Closing Date: 20 February
Funding: Foundation
Additional Information: www.otago.ac.nz/study/scholarships/database/otago634374.html

University of Otago International Master's Scholarship

Purpose: To assist international students in their master's thesis year of studies at the University of Otago
Eligibility: Applicants must be: 1. obtaining their first Master's qualification 2. international students 3. undertaking a thesis-based Master's
Level of Study: Masters Degree, Research
Type: Scholarship
Value: NZ$17,172 stipend per annum plus a tuition fee waiver for 1 year capped at the domestic rate for Master study (excludes student services fee and insurance)
Frequency: Annual
Country of Study: Any country
No. of awards offered: 8
Funding: Private
Additional Information: Website: www.otago.ac.nz/study/scholarships/database/search/otago014691.html

For further information contact:

Doctoral and Scholarships Office, PO Box 56, Dunedin 9054, New Zealand.

Email: university@otago.ac.uk

University of Otago Māori Doctoral Scholarship

Purpose: The University of Otago Māori Doctoral Scholarship provides funding to support Māori PhD students studying at the University of Otago.
Eligibility: Applicants must be: 1. of Māori descent 2. obtaining their first PhD qualification For more details see website
Level of Study: Doctorate, Postgraduate
Type: Scholarship

Value: NZ$30,696 stipend per annum plus a domestic tuition fees waiver for 36 months
Length of Study: For 36 months
Frequency: Annual
Country of Study: New Zealand
Application Procedure: Applications for scholarships are made online through the University's website.
No. of awards offered: Varies
Funding: Foundation
Additional Information: Website: www.otago.ac.nz/study/scholarships/database/search/otago014684.html

For further information contact:

Email: scholarships@otago.ac.nz

University of Otago Postgraduate Scholarship in Obstetrics and Gynaecology

Purpose: The Scholarship is intended to provide support for Obstetrics and Gynaecology trainees to carry out research in Obstetrics, Gynaecology and Women's Health whilst enrolled at the University of Otago for a graduate research degree, such as a Master of Medical Science (MMedSc) or Doctor of Philosophy (PhD). It is desirable, but not compulsory, that the research be carried out at the University of Otago
Eligibility: 1. Medical graduates (normally Registrars enrolled in the Royal Australian and New Zealand College of Obstetrics and Gynaecology Integrated Training Programme, or Members or Fellows of the College). 2. Enrolled in, or intending to enrol in a research Master's degree or PhD, normally towards a topic in the field of Obstetrics and Gynaecology or Women's Health
Level of Study: Postgraduate
Type: Scholarship
Value: NZ$25,000 stipend per annum, plus tuition fees (up to a maximum of NZ$9,000 per annum)
Frequency: Annual
Country of Study: New Zealand
No. of awards offered: 1
Closing Date: 28 October
Funding: Foundation
Additional Information: www.otago.ac.nz/study/scholarships/database/search/otago115047.html

University of Otago Special Health Research Scholarship

Purpose: The University of Otago Special Health Research Scholarship provides funding to support outstanding doctoral students who are contemplating a career in Health Research.
Eligibility: 1. seeking to obtain their first doctoral qualification 2. studying, or planning to study, full-time 3. undertaking health related research
Level of Study: Postgraduate
Type: Scholarship
Value: NZ$27,000 stipend per annum plus domestic tuition fees waiver (excludes student services fee and insurance)
Frequency: Annual
Country of Study: New Zealand
No. of awards offered: 1
Funding: Foundation
Additional Information: www.otago.ac.nz/study/scholarships/database/otago016136.html

For further information contact:

Tel: (64) 800 80 80 98
Email: scholarships@otago.ac.nz

Vice-Chancellor's Scholarship for International Students

Purpose: The Vice-Chancellor's Scholarships for International Students celebrate and welcome international students to the University of Otago, as valued members of our University community. This scholarship recognises the additional personal, academic and financial challenges currently faced by international students and is awarded to support students to pursue their academic goals.
Eligibility: International undergraduate students at the University of Otago, living in New Zealand, or studying online or by distance from outside of New Zealand
Type: Scholarship
Value: NZ$10,000 for tuition fees
Length of Study: 12 months – applies to the first year of study only.
Frequency: Annual
Country of Study: Any country
No. of awards offered: 1
Closing Date: 10 December
Additional Information: www.otago.ac.nz/study/scholarships/database/otago827694.html

For further information contact:

362 Leith Street, Dunedin North, Dunedin 9016, New Zealand.

Tel: (64) 3 479 7000

Waddell Smith Postgraduate Scholarship

Purpose: Masters' scholarships are awarded by the University Council, on the recommendation of the Senate, to

candidates in the first year of their thesis research for a Master's degree which constitutes entry to the PhD course at this University. These scholarships are available only to students seeking to obtain their first research-based Master's qualification
Eligibility: 1. Unless otherwise stated in these conditions or within the schedule, doctoral and Masters' scholarships are open only to Domestic Fee Paying Students. International candidates studying for professional doctorates are eligible to apply but if awarded a scholarship the tuition fee waiver will be capped at the domestic rate. 2. In the case of applicants for a doctoral scholarship, confirmation of the scholarship is dependent on approval of their application for admission to the relevant doctoral programme and completion of the enrolment procedure. 3. In the case of applicants for a Master's scholarship, confirmation of the scholarship is dependent on approval of their application to register as a Master's candidate and completion of the enrolment procedure
Level of Study: Postgraduate
Type: Scholarship
Value: NZ$2,000
Frequency: Annual
Country of Study: New Zealand
No. of awards offered: Varies
Funding: Foundation
Additional Information: www.otago.ac.nz/study/scholarships/database/otago020616.html

For further information contact:

Educational Credential Evaluators, Inc., P.O. Box 514070, Milwaukee, WI 53212, United States of America.

Email: graduate@balliol.ox.ac.uk

Williamson Medical Research PhD Scholarship

Purpose: The scholarship may be held by PhD candidates studying towards a PhD in the field of medical research. Applicants must have previously completed a medical degree and be New Zealand citizens (preference will be given to New Zealand–born applicants). The scholarship shall be awarded by the University of Council on the recommendation of the Faculty of Medicine
Eligibility: 1. Unless otherwise stated in these conditions or within the schedule, doctoral and Masters' scholarships are open only to Domestic Fee Paying Students. 3 International candidates studying for professional doctorates are eligible to apply but if awarded a scholarship the tuition fee waiver will be capped at the domestic rate. 2. In the case of applicants for a doctoral scholarship, confirmation of the scholarship is dependent on approval of their application for admission to the relevant doctoral programme and completion of the enrolment procedure. 3. In the case of applicants for a Master's scholarship, confirmation of the scholarship is dependent on approval of their application to register as a Master's candidate and completion of the enrolment procedure
Level of Study: Postgraduate
Type: Scholarship
Value: NZ$25,000
Length of Study: 3 year
Frequency: Annual
Country of Study: New Zealand
No. of awards offered: Varies
Funding: Foundation
Additional Information: www.otago.ac.nz/study/scholarships/database/otago046608.html

For further information contact:

Email: scholarships@otago.ac.nz

University of Oxford

University Offices, Wellington Square, Oxford OX1 2JD, United Kingdom.

Email: internal.communications@admin.ox.ac.uk
Website: www.ox.ac.uk/

As the oldest university in the English-speaking world, Oxford is a unique and historic institution. There is no clear date of foundation, but teaching existed at Oxford in some form in 1096 and developed rapidly from 1167, when Henry II banned English students from attending the University of Paris.

Area Studies: FirstRand Laurie Dippenaar Scholarship

Purpose: African Studies
Eligibility: Open to South African graduate applicants for the MSc African Studies
Level of Study: Postgraduate
Type: Scholarship
Value: R925,000
Length of Study: Period of fee liability
Frequency: Annual
Study Establishment: Wadham College
Country of Study: South Africa
Application Procedure: APPLY HERE: bursaries.firstrand.co.za/Bursary/FirstRandLaurieDippenaarScholarship

Closing Date: 20 February
Additional Information: Please visit the website: www.firstrand.co.za/csi/Pages/laurie-dippenaar-scholarship.aspx bursaries.firstrand.co.za/Bursary/FirstRandLaurieDippenaarScholarship?AspxAutoDetectCookieSupport=1

Atmospheric, Oceanic & Planetary Physics: STFC Studentships

Eligibility: Open to Home and European Union graduate applicants to the DPhil Atmospheric, Oceanic and Planetary Physics. To be eligible for consideration for these scholarships, applicants must be successful in being offered a place on their course after consideration of applications received by the relevant January deadline for the course
Level of Study: Doctorate
Type: Studentship
Value: Home-£8,960, Overseas-£29,700
Length of Study: 3 to 4 years
Frequency: Annual
Country of Study: Any country
No. of awards offered: 1000
Closing Date: 6 January
Additional Information: Please visit the website: www.ox.ac.uk/admissions/graduate/courses/dphil-atmospheric-oceanic-and-planetary-physics

For further information contact:

Email: F.Y.Ogrin@exeter.ac.uk

Balliol College: Balliol Economics Scholarship

Eligibility: Open to all graduate applicants to MPhil or MPhil +DPhil 2+2 in Economics. Students of any nationality applying to read for the MPhil in economics
Type: Scholarship
Value: value of the UKRI stipend for the first two years of the scholarship, third year scholarship will cover all University and College fees
Length of Study: Up to 3 years
Country of Study: United Kingdom
Application Procedure: Please see website for how to apply and more details
Closing Date: November
Additional Information: www.balliol.ox.ac.uk/media/14072/download?inline

For further information contact:

Email: graduate@balliol.ox.ac.uk

Balliol College: Brassey Italian Scholarship

Eligibility: Open to all applicants to postgraduate degrees in Modern Languages where Italian is the principal subject of study. Please see website for more details
Level of Study: Postgraduate, Research
Type: Scholarship
Value: £3,700
Length of Study: full duration of the period of fee liability for the agreed course
Country of Study: United Kingdom
Application Procedure: No separate application is required to be considered for this award.
Closing Date: November
Additional Information: www.balliol.ox.ac.uk/media/14057/download?inline

For further information contact:

Email: graduate.admissions@balliol.ox.ac.uk

Balliol College: Eddie Dinshaw Scholarship

Eligibility: Open to all graduate applicants from India for relevant areas of study
Level of Study: Postgraduate, Research
Type: Scholarship
Value: £10,000
Length of Study: Up to 3 years
Frequency: Annual
Application Procedure: Please see website for more details and how to apply
Closing Date: 23 January

For further information contact:

Email: graduate.admissions@balliol.ox.ac.uk

Balliol College: Foley-Bejar Scholarships

Eligibility: Open to all graduate applicants who a) were born in or who have one parent born in Mexico, Spain, or the Republic of Ireland, or who have a strong connection with Northern Ireland; and b) are ordinarily resident in Mexico, Spain or the Republic of Ireland. Please see website for more details
Type: Scholarship
Value: £15,500 per annum
Length of Study: 5 years
Frequency: Annual
Country of Study: United Kingdom

Application Procedure: No separate application is required to be considered for this award
Closing Date: 23 January

For further information contact:

Email: graduate@balliol.ox.ac.uk

Balliol College: McDougall Scholarship

Eligibility: Open to graduate applicants to Law
Level of Study: Graduate, Postgraduate, Research
Type: Scholarship
Value: £7,500 per annum
Length of Study: full duration of the period of fee liability
Frequency: Annual
Country of Study: United Kingdom
Application Procedure: No separate application
Additional Information: www.law.ox.ac.uk/mcdougall-scholarship

For further information contact:

Email: graduate@balliol.ox.ac.uk

Balliol College: Peter Storey Scholarship

Eligibility: Open to all applicants to Master's degrees in History. May be awarded as a fully-funded scholarship in partnership with an AHRC award or as a standalone award of £10,000 per year. Please see website for more details
Level of Study: Postgraduate, Research
Type: Scholarship
Value: £15,500 per annum
Length of Study: duration of fee liability
Country of Study: United Kingdom
Application Procedure: Please see website for more details and how to apply
Closing Date: November
Additional Information: www.balliol.ox.ac.uk/media/14066/download?inline

For further information contact:

Email: graduate@balliol.ox.ac.uk

Balliol College: Snell Scholarship

Purpose: The College seeks to elect one Scholar who has gained an offer of admission to read for a higher degree at Balliol College after completing a degree at the University of Glasgow
Eligibility: Honours graduates or in their final Honours year, applicants must have a connection with Scotland by birth (either themselves or one parent), domicile (at least three years) or education at a school in Scotland (at least three years) before admission to the University of Glasgow. Graduates of the University of Glasgow. Please see website for more details including how to apply
Type: Scholarship
Value: £15,000 per annum
Length of Study: Up to 3 years
Country of Study: United Kingdom
Closing Date: September
Additional Information: www.balliol.ox.ac.uk/sites/default/files/snell_2020.pdf

For further information contact:

Email: graduate@balliol.ox.ac.uk

Black Academic Futures Scholarship

Purpose: Academic Futures is a series of scholarship programmes that will address under-representation and help improve equality, diversity and inclusion in our graduate student body.
Eligibility: Applicants who are ordinarily resident in the United Kingdom, who are of Black or Mixed Black ethnicity and who hold an offer for either a taught or research postgraduate degree.
Type: Scholarship
Value: Each scholarship will cover your course fees in full and will provide you with a grant for living costs.
Frequency: Annual
Country of Study: United Kingdom
No. of awards offered: 30
Additional Information: www.ox.ac.uk/admissions/graduate/access/academic-futures

For further information contact:

University of Oxford, University Offices, 15 Wellington Square, Oxford OX1 2JD, United Kingdom.

Tel: (44) 1865 270000
Fax: (44) 1865 270708

Blavatnik School of Government: Africa Governance Initiative Scholarship

Eligibility: Open to all Master of Public Policy applicants who are ordinarily resident in Africa. Scholarships are

awarded on the basis of outstanding academic ability, commitment to public service, a capacity to lead, an interest in and experience of improving governance in Africa, a commitment to completing their summer project on some aspect of governance in Africa, and a commitment to return to Africa after their time at the School to continue their work on governance there
Level of Study: Postgraduate
Type: Scholarship
Value: University fee, college fee and full living expenses
Length of Study: Period of fee liability
Frequency: Annual
Country of Study: United Kingdom
Application Procedure: To apply, applicants must provide a supporting statement. Please see website for more details
Closing Date: 23 September
Additional Information: opportunitydesk.org/2019/08/01/africa-initiative-for-governance-scholarships-2020-2021/

For further information contact:

Email: inquiries@aigafrica.org

Blavatnik School of Government: African Initiative for Governance Scholarships

Purpose: Public Policy
Eligibility: Open to all Master of Public Policy applicants who are ordinarily resident in Nigeria and Ghana (and other West African nations). Scholarships are awarded on the basis of exceptional academic and leadership merit and/or potential. Applicants will usually hold an undergraduate degree from an African university. They should also intend to return to work in public service in Qualifying country for at least three years after completing their studies
Level of Study: Postgraduate
Type: Scholarship
Value: University fee, college fee and full living expenses
Length of Study: Period of fee liability
Frequency: Annual
Country of Study: Any country
Application Procedure: To apply, applicants must provide a supporting statement. Please see website for more details
Closing Date: 20 January
Additional Information: Please visit the website: www.bsg.ox.ac.uk/study/mpp/bsg-funding-options

For further information contact:

Email: enquiries@bsg.ox.ac.uk

Blavatnik School of Government: Public Service Scholarship

Purpose: Public Policy
Eligibility: Open to all Master of Public Policy applicants. Scholarships are awarded on the basis of unwavering dedication to public service, shown through an exceptional academic and professional record
Level of Study: Postgraduate
Type: Scholarship
Value: Variable, often half or full fees
Length of Study: Period of fee liability
Frequency: Annual
Country of Study: Any country
Application Procedure: To apply, applicants must provide a supporting statement. Please see website for more details
Closing Date: 10 January
Additional Information: Please visit the website: www.bsg.ox.ac.uk/study/mpp/bsg-funding-options ssc.govt.nz/assets/SSC-Site-Assets/Workforce-and-Talent-Management/Diversity-Inclusion/Blavatnik-School-of-Govt-brochure.pdf

For further information contact:

Email: enquiries@bsg.ox.ac.uk

Chevening Scholarships

Eligibility: You must 1. Be a citizen of a Chevening-eligible country or territory. 2. Return to your country of citizenship for a minimum of two years after your award has ended. 3. Have completed all components of an undergraduate degree that will enable you to gain entry onto a postgraduate programme at a UK university by the time you submit your application. This is typically equivalent to an upper second-class 21 honours degree in the UK but may be different depending on your course and university choice. 4. Have at least two years (equivalent to 2,800 hours) of work experience. 5. Apply to three different eligible UK university courses and have received an unconditional offer from one of these choices by 14 July 2024.
Level of Study: Graduate
Type: Scholarship
Value: University fee, college fee, and full living expenses
Length of Study: 1 year
Country of Study: United Kingdom
Application Procedure: Please see website for more details and how to apply
Closing Date: 1 November
Additional Information: www.ox.ac.uk/admissions/graduate/fees-and-funding/external-funding

For further information contact:

Email: international@lincoln.ac.uk

China Oxford Scholarship Fund

Purpose: The China Oxford Scholarship Fund (COSF) awards scholarships to students from the People's Republic of China, Hong Kong and Macau who have won a place for postgraduate degree studies on a full-time basis at the University of Oxford. Up to twenty scholarships are awarded annually. Preference is given to those who are studying in the United Kingdom for the first time. Successful candidates are those of the highest calibre studying in any subject. They are chosen for their academic excellence, financial need, leadership quality and their commitment to contribute to the development of China.
Eligibility: An applicant must be a national of the People's Republic of China who is ordinarily resident in China, Hong Kong or Macau. An applicant must have an official or conditional offer to pursue a postgraduate degree at Oxford University.
Level of Study: Graduate
Type: Scholarship
Value: £10,000
Frequency: Annual
Country of Study: Any country
Application Procedure: See website chinaoxford.org/?page_id=43
Closing Date: 15 April

For further information contact:

Email: application@chinaoxford.org; info@chinaoxford.org

China Scholarship Council-University of Oxford Scholarships

Subjects: All subjects
Purpose: The scholarships are supported jointly by the China Scholarship Council (on behalf of the Chinese Ministry of Education) and the University of Oxford. Another strand of this scholarship is the China Scholarship Council-PAG Oxford Scholarships. They are funded by PAG, which is one of the regions' largest Asia-focused investment managers. The scholarships enable academically excellent Chinese students to pursue doctoral studies in the Social Sciences and Mathematical, Physical and Life Sciences at the University of Oxford.
Eligibility: 1. You must be applying to start a new full-time DPhil course at Oxford. 2. You must be a national of and ordinarily resident in mainland China (not including Hong Kong or Macau). You must also be intending to return to China once your course is completed. 3. Scholarships will be awarded on the basis of academic merit, potential to become a leader in your field and potential to become a decision-maker and opinion former within China. 4. Applicants who hold deferred offers "www.ox.ac.uk/admissions/graduate/after-you-apply/your-offer-and-contract" to start in 2024–25 are not eligible to be considered for these scholarships.
Type: Scholarship
Value: The scholarship will cover 100% of course fees, a grant for living costs (at least £17,668) and one return flight from China to the UK
Length of Study: For the full duration of your fee liability for the agreed course
Frequency: Annual
Country of Study: United Kingdom
Application Procedure: See website www.ox.ac.uk/admissions/graduate/fees-and-funding/fees-funding-and-scholarship-search/china-scholarship-council-university-oxford-scholarships
No. of awards offered: Up to 20
Closing Date: January
Additional Information: Website: www.ox.ac.uk/admissions/graduate/fees-and-funding/fees-funding-and-scholarship-search/china-scholarship-council-university-oxford-scholarships

Commonwealth Shared Scholarship Scheme (CSSS)

Purpose: To support students from developing Commonwealth countries who would not otherwise be able to study in the United Kingdom
Eligibility: Applicants must: 1. be a Commonwealth citizen, refugee, or British Protected Person; 2. be permanently resident in an eligible Commonwealth country; 3. be available to start your academic studies in the UK by the start of the UK academic year in September/October 2024; 4. by September 2024, hold a first degree of either first or upper second class (2:1) classification, or lower second class (2:2) classification plus a relevant postgraduate qualification (usually a Master's degree). If you are applying for a second UK Master's degree, you will need to provide justification as to why you wish to undertake this study; 5. not have studied or worked for one (academic) year or more in a high-income country; 6. be unable to afford to study in the UK without this scholarship.
Level of Study: Postgraduate
Type: Scholarship
Value: Tuition fees, living costs, flights to UK
Length of Study: 1 year

Frequency: Annual
Country of Study: United Kingdom
Application Procedure: Candidates must apply to Oxford by completing the Graduate Application Form by Application Deadline 2. They must complete the CSSS application form and submit this to Student Funding Services by email or post by March 13th
No. of awards offered: 9
Closing Date: 13 December
Additional Information: www.ucl.ac.uk/scholarships/commonwealth-shared-scholarship-scheme

Commonwealth Shared Scholarships

Purpose: Funded by the UK Foreign, Commonwealth and Development Office (FCDO) Commonwealth Shared Scholarships enable talented and motivated individuals to gain the knowledge and skills required for sustainable development, and are aimed at those who could not otherwise afford to study in the UK.
Eligibility: You must 1. Be a citizen of or have been granted refugee status by an eligible Commonwealth country, or be a British Protected Person 2. Be permanently resident in an eligible Commonwealth country 3. Be available to start your academic studies in the UK by the start of the UK academic year in September 2024 4. By September 2024, hold a first degree of at least upper second-class (21) honours standard, or a lower second-class degree (22) and a relevant postgraduate qualification (usually a Master's degree). 5. Not have studied or worked for one (academic) year or more in a high-income country 6. Be unable to afford to study at a UK university without this scholarship 7. Have provided all supporting documentation in the required format
Type: Scholarship
Value: Stipend (living allowance) at the rate of £1,236 per month, or £1,516 per month.
Frequency: Annual
Country of Study: United Kingdom
Closing Date: March
Additional Information: cscuk.fcdo.gov.uk/scholarships/commonwealth-shared-scholarships-applications/

For further information contact:

Email: csc.safeguarding@cscuk.org.uk

Computer Science: Department Studentships

Purpose: To develop practical methods, algorithms, and tools for a use-case driven approach to system-level hardware/software formal co-verification. A key objective, and the foundation for the methodology, will be the invention of a systematic abstraction framework that closes the gap, currently unaddressed, between a system and implementation levels in co-verification
Eligibility: Open to all applicants applying for a DPhil in Computer Science
Level of Study: Doctorate
Type: Studentship
Value: Course fee, college fee and stipend
Length of Study: 3 years
Country of Study: United Kingdom
Closing Date: 10 March
Additional Information: Please visit the website: www.cs.ox.ac.uk/aboutus/vacancies/studentship.html

For further information contact:

Email: enquiries@cs.ox.ac.uk

Department of Education: Talbot Scholarship

Eligibility: Open to all applicants for DPhil in Education. Please visit website for more details
Level of Study: Doctorate
Type: Partial scholarship
Value: £15,000 per annum contribution towards fees and living expenses 35% reduction of tuition fee
Length of Study: 3 years
Frequency: Every 3 years
Country of Study: United Kingdom
Closing Date: 8 April
Additional Information: Please visit the website: www.education.ox.ac.uk/courses/d-phil/funding-opportunities/

Economic and Social Research Council: Socio-Legal Studies

Eligibility: Open to all prospective students applying for the 1 +3 MSt Socio-Legal Studies and DPhil Socio-Legal Studies, or just for the latter
Level of Study: Postgraduate
Type: Scholarship
Value: University fee, college fee, and living expenses. Fees-only award for European Union applicants
Length of Study: Period of fee liability
Frequency: Annual
Country of Study: United Kingdom
Application Procedure: Please contact the pathway representitive Professor Richard Sparks before applying r.sparks@ed.ac.uk
Closing Date: 20 January

Funding: Trusts
Additional Information: Please see website: www.law.ox.ac.uk/postgraduate/scholarships.php www.ed.ac.uk/student-funding/postgraduate/uk-eu/humanities/law/esrc-socio-legal

For further information contact:

Email: r.sparks@ed.ac.uk

Engineering and Physical Sciences Research Council (EPSRC) Doctoral Training Programme Studentships

Eligibility: Open to United Kingdom and European Union applicants for DPhil in Statistics. European Union applicants may only be eligible for a fees-only award, depending on residency requirements
Level of Study: Postgraduate
Type: Scholarship
Value: University fee, college fee and full living expenses
Length of Study: Three and a half years maximum
Frequency: Annual
Country of Study: United Kingdom
Closing Date: 20 January
Funding: Trusts
Additional Information: For more information, please visit website: www.stats.ox.ac.uk/study_here/research_degrees epsrc.ukri.org/skills/students/dta/

For further information contact:

Email: phdfunding-salc@manchester.ac.uk

English Faculty: Asian Human Rights Commission (AHRC) Doctoral Training Partnership Studentship (Master)

Eligibility: Open to all Home/European Union applicants to MSt and MPhil degrees offered by the Faculty of English. Please see website for more details
Level of Study: Postgraduate
Type: Studentship
Value: University fee, college fee, and living expenses (pro-rata for courses less than 1 year). Fees-only awards for non-United Kingdom, European Union students
Length of Study: Period of fee liability
Frequency: Annual
Country of Study: United Kingdom
Closing Date: 20 January
Funding: Trusts
Additional Information: For more information, please visit: www.humanities.ox.ac.uk/prospective_students/graduates/funding/ahrc www.humanities.ox.ac.uk/ahrc-doctoral-training-partnership#collapse395456

For further information contact:

Email: ahrcdtp@admin.ox.ac.uk

English Faculty: Cecily Clarke Studentship

Eligibility: Open to all applicants to English Medieval Studies, with preference to Middle English Philology. All students applying for English graduate courses will automatically be considered
Level of Study: Postgraduate
Type: Studentship
Value: £12,000 per year
Length of Study: Up to 2 years
Country of Study: United Kingdom
Closing Date: 24 January
Additional Information: All students applying for English graduate courses will automatically be considered. Candidates apply at the same time as they apply for admission to their postgraduate programme at the University of Oxford, using the same application form. To be considered candidates must apply by the January deadline. Please check at www.english.ox.ac.uk www.european-funding-guide.eu/scholarship/13407-cecily-clark-studentship

For further information contact:

Tel: (44) 1865 270 000

Ertegun Graduate Scholarship Programme in the Humanities

Purpose: The Humanities Division offers taught graduate and research degrees in a wide range of subjects.
Eligibility: Applications to The Mica and Ahmet Ertegun Graduate Scholarship Programme may be made by those in fields covered by the following Faculties Classics (including classical archaeology); English Language and Literature; Fine Art (DPhil in Contemporary Art History and Theory only), History (including History of Art and the History of Architecture); Linguistics, Philology and Phonetics; Medieval and Modern Languages (covering most European languages and their literature); Music; Oriental Studies (including Far Eastern and Middle Eastern Studies, and the study of a wide range of languages); Philosophy; Theology and Religion; and the interdisciplinary courses of Comparative Literature & Critical Translation, Medieval Studies, Film Aesthetics, Women's, Gender & Sexuality Studies, and Digital Scholarship
Level of Study: Doctorate, Masters Degree

Type: Scholarship
Value: £16,062
Length of Study: 1 year
Frequency: Annual
Country of Study: United Kingdom
Closing Date: 20 January
Additional Information: www.ertegun.ox.ac.uk/scholarships#tab-420046

For further information contact:

Graduate Admissions and Funding University Offices, Wellington Square, Oxford OX1 2JD, United Kingdom.

Tel: (44) 1865 270059
Fax: (44) 1865 270049
Email: graduate.admissions@admin.ox.ac.uk

Exeter College Usher-Cunningham Senior Studentship

Purpose: To support graduate study
Eligibility: 1. Be an applicant to the University of Oxford who has been offered a place for a DPhil degree in the Radcliffe Department of Medicine 2. be a graduate of an Irish University who has been normally resident in Ireland for at least three of the five years before starting at the University of Oxford 3. become a member of Exeter College and commit to remaining at Exeter College for the duration of their degree.
Level of Study: Postgraduate
Type: Studentship
Value: £14,777
Length of Study: Usually awarded for up to 3 years
Frequency: Every 3 years
Study Establishment: Exeter College, University of Oxford
Country of Study: United Kingdom
Application Procedure: Applicants must address enquiries to the Academic Administrator
Closing Date: January
Funding: Private
Contributor: An endowment
Additional Information: www.exeter.ox.ac.uk/file/2018/12/Usher-Cunningham-Medicine-2019.pdf

For further information contact:

Email: admissions@exeter.ox.ac.uk

Exeter College: Exonian Graduate Scholarship

Eligibility: 1. Be an applicant to the University of Oxford for admission to a graduate degree 2. have an offer of a place to study for a DPhil in one of the Departments in the Social 3. Sciences Division of the University 4. be awarded a UK Research Council Studentship by the University of Oxford; 5. become a member of Exeter College, and commit to remaining at Exeter College for the duration of their course.
Level of Study: Postdoctorate
Type: Fellowship
Value: Course Fees, and a grant to cover living expenses
Length of Study: Up to 3 years
Country of Study: United Kingdom
Application Procedure: Applicants must address enquiries to the Academic Administrator
Closing Date: January
Funding: Private
Additional Information: https://www.exeter.ox.ac.uk/applicants/graduates/graduate-scholarships/

For further information contact:

Exeter College, Turl St, Oxford OX1 3DP, United Kingdom.

Email: admissions@exeter.ox.ac.uk

Exeter College: Nicholas Frangiscatos Scholarship in Byzantine Studies

Eligibility: For a DPhil student in the field of Byzantine studies
Level of Study: Doctorate, Postdoctorate
Type: Fellowship
Value: £14,777
Length of Study: 1 to 3 years
Frequency: Every 3 years
Country of Study: United Kingdom
Application Procedure: Please see website for how to apply
Closing Date: 12 March
Funding: Private
Additional Information: Please check at www.exeter.ox.ac.uk/currentstudents/finance/scholarships www.exeter.ox.ac.uk/wp-content/uploads/2018/12/Nicholas-Frangiscatos-2019.pdf

For further information contact:

Email: admissions@exeter.ox.ac.uk

Felix Scholarships

Purpose: The scholarship will cover 100% of course fees, a grant for living costs (around £15,840) and one return flight from India to the UK. Awards are made for the full duration of your fee liability for the agreed course.
Eligibility: To be eligible for both the Indian and the non-Indian scholarship, you must be applying to start a new, full-time master's course or full-time DPhil course at Oxford.

U

You must not have previously studied a course at the same level as the course to which you are applying (i.e. if you already have a master's degree, you will not be considered for this scholarship if you are applying for another master's course). You must be unable to take up your place at Oxford without financial assistance.
Level of Study: Postgraduate
Type: Scholarship
Value: around £16,164
Length of Study: full duration of your fee liability for the agreed course.
Country of Study: United Kingdom
No. of awards offered: 6
Closing Date: December
Additional Information: www.ox.ac.uk/admissions/graduate/fees-and-funding/fees-funding-and-scholarship-search/felix-scholarships

For further information contact:

University of Oxford, University Offices, 15 Wellington Square, Oxford OX1 2JD, United Kingdom.

Tel: (44) 1865 270000
Fax: (44) 1865 270708

Freshfields Bruckhaus Deringer Scholarships (Law)

Purpose: To assist graduate students with fees and a living allowance
Eligibility: Varies
Level of Study: Doctorate, Postgraduate, Research
Type: Scholarships
Value: To be confirmed
Length of Study: 1 year
Country of Study: United Kingdom
Closing Date: 22 January
Additional Information: www.freshfields.com/en-gb/about-us/responsible-business/freshfields_stephen_lawrence_scholarship/

For further information contact:

Email: ContactFSLScheme@freshfields.com

Geography and the Environment: Andrew Goudie Bursary

Eligibility: Open to all applicants for MSc in Environmental Change and Management
Level of Study: Postgraduate
Type: Scholarship
Value: Up to £5,000
Length of Study: 1 year
Country of Study: United Kingdom
Closing Date: 20 January
Additional Information: www.eci.ox.ac.uk/msc/funding.html

For further information contact:

Email: support@linacre.ox.ac.uk

Geography and the Environment: Boardman Scholarship

Eligibility: Open to all applicants for MSc in Environmental Change and Management
Level of Study: Postgraduate
Type: Scholarship
Value: Up to £5,000
Length of Study: 1 year
Country of Study: United Kingdom
No. of awards offered: 1
Closing Date: 20 January
Additional Information: www.eci.ox.ac.uk/msc/funding.html

For further information contact:

Email: socialsciences@devoff.ox.ac.uk

Geography: Sir Walter Raleigh Postgraduate Scholarship

Eligibility: 1. Academic achievement and potential 2. Breadth of vision 3. Career aspirations and commitment 4. Global orientation 5. Potential as Leader/Agent/Manager of Change 6. Multi-disciplinary training in relevant fields prior to graduation (vacation jobs etc) 7. Range and depth of experience relevant to the MSc course.
Level of Study: Postgraduate
Type: Scholarship
Value: £4,000
Length of Study: 1 year
Frequency: Annual
Country of Study: United Kingdom
Application Procedure: Any person wishing to be considered for this award should follow the application procedure for admission to the degree of Master of Science in Environmental Change and Management at Oxford University, nominating Colleges of preference as detailed in the application procedure. They must, additionally, complete a separate application form which will be made available to them once

in receipt of a place on the MSc, and submit this to the College by the deadline (end of May each year).
Closing Date: May
Additional Information: www.oriel.ox.ac.uk/study-with-us/postgraduates/postgraduate-scholarships/sir-walter-raleigh-scholarship/

For further information contact:

Tel: (44) 1865 276 520
Fax: (44) 1865 286 548

Goodger and Schorstein Research Scholarships in Medical Sciences

Eligibility: Open to postdoctoral researchers from any department/institute of the Medical Sciences Division. Applicants must have completed their DPhil (at any Higher Education Institution) at the time of application and are required to work primarily in units run by the University of Oxford
Type: Scholarship
Value: up to £10,000
Country of Study: United Kingdom
Application Procedure: Please see the website for more details. Enquires may be sent by email to Aga.Bush@medsci.ox.ac.uk
Closing Date: 11 February
Additional Information: www.medsci.ox.ac.uk/research/internal-research-funding/funding-directory/goodger-and-schorstein-scholarship

For further information contact:

Email: Aga.Bush@medsci.ox.ac.uk

Green Moral Philosophy Scholarship

Subjects: Moral Philosophy
Eligibility: Open to all graduate applicants for DPhil courses in the Faculty of Philosophy. All applicants who receive a place on any graduate course automatically considered
Level of Study: Unrestricted
Type: Scholarship
Value: The value of the scholarship is to be determined by the Board of Graduate Admissions. The scholarship may not be offered on a yearly basis
Length of Study: 1 year
Country of Study: United Kingdom

For further information contact:

Email: jane.sherwood@admin.ox.ac.uk

Green Templeton College: GTC-Medical Sciences Doctoral Training Centre Scholarship

Purpose: Green Templeton College is pleased to be able to offer a top-up award for overseas students who have been awarded a Studentship for study at the Medical Sciences Doctoral Training Centre beginning in October month
Eligibility: Open to all applicants to the Medical Sciences Doctoral Training Centre with Overseas fee status
Level of Study: Doctorate
Type: Scholarship
Value: £1,000
Length of Study: Up to 4 years
Country of Study: United Kingdom
Closing Date: October
Additional Information: Please visit the website: www.gtc.ox.ac.uk/admissions/scholarships-and-awards www.gtc.ox.ac.uk/students/how-to-apply/scholarships-bursaries/

For further information contact:

Email: enquiries@msdtc.ox.ac.uk

Green Templeton College: GTC-SBS DPhil Scholarship

Purpose: In conjunction with the Saïd Business School (SBS), Green Templeton College is able to offer a scholarship for a student beginning a DPhil Management or DPhil Finance in October 2024.
Eligibility: Open to all applicants to the DPhil in Management Studies
Level of Study: Doctorate, Graduate
Type: Scholarship
Value: Full fees and annual stipend at minimum Research Council UK rate (£17,668)
Length of Study: four years
Study Establishment: Green Templeton College
Country of Study: United Kingdom
Closing Date: January
Additional Information: www.gtc.ox.ac.uk/students/how-to-apply/scholarships-bursaries/gtc-sbs-dphil-scholarships/

Hertford College: Vaughan Williams Senior Scholarship

Purpose: The Vaughan Williams Fund supports medical students with a £300 award per student towards stethoscopes and 'on the ward' textbooks

Eligibility: Open to all graduate students pursuing research in any area of study. Please see website for more details, including how to apply
Level of Study: Postgraduate
Type: Scholarship
Value: £5,000 per year with certain associated dining rights
Length of Study: Two years
Frequency: Annual
Study Establishment: Hertford
Country of Study: United Kingdom
Application Procedure: For more information, please visit www.hertford.ox.ac.uk/discover-hertford/graduates/graduate-scholarships
Closing Date: 11 March
Funding: Trusts

For further information contact:

Email: communications@hertford.ox.ac.uk

Hertford College: Worshipful Company of Scientific Instrument Makers Senior Scholarship

Eligibility: Open to DPhil applicants in all subjects. Please note applicants are expected to be involved in the design of instrumentation
Level of Study: Doctorate, Graduate
Type: Scholarship
Value: £4,000 per year with certain associated dining rights
Length of Study: 2 years
Country of Study: Any country
Application Procedure: Please see website for details of how to apply
Additional Information: Please check at www.hertford.ox.ac.uk/advertised-posts

For further information contact:

Email: college.office@hertford.ox.ac.uk

Hill Foundation Scholarships

Eligibility: Applicants who are nationals of and ordinarily resident in the Russian Federation and who are applying to any full-time master's or DPhil course at Oxford. Applicants must also have a first degree from a Russian university. Preference will be given to applicants who have not previously been enrolled in any other degree programme outside of Russia. The trustees favour candidates who demonstrate extremely high academic ability and personal and social qualities of a high order. They seek applicants who intend to develop their careers in their homeland and who wish to spend their lives in ways that are beneficial to their home society, whether in business, academic life, public service, the arts or the professions. The selection panel will use the information that applicants provide in their graduate application form to assess how they meet these criteria. Applicants who are offered this scholarship will be required to confirm that they will return to Russia for at least one year following completion of their studies in the UK. Scholarships will be awarded on the basis of academic merit.
Level of Study: Graduate, Postgraduate, Research
Type: Scholarship
Value: at least £17,668
Frequency: Annual
Country of Study: United Kingdom
No. of awards offered: 15
Closing Date: January
Additional Information: www.ox.ac.uk/admissions/graduate/fees-and-funding/fees-funding-and-scholarship-search/scholarships-a-z-listing

For further information contact:

University of Oxford, University Offices, 15 Wellington Square, Oxford OX1 2JD, United Kingdom.

Tel: (44) 1865 270000
Fax: (44) 1865 270708

Hong Kong Jockey Club Graduate Scholarships

Purpose: For students who combine outstanding academic performance with a strong commitment to serving the community
Eligibility: Open to applicants who are ordinarily resident in Hong Kong and who are applying to a full-time master's or full-time DPhil course at Oxford. Please note that DPhil courses with four years of fee liability are not eligible. Please see website for more details
Level of Study: Doctorate, Postgraduate
Type: Scholarship
Value: University fee, college fee, and full living expenses
Length of Study: 4 years
Country of Study: United Kingdom
Closing Date: January
Funding: Trusts
Additional Information: www.ox.ac.uk/admissions/graduate/fees-and-funding/fees-funding-and-scholarship-search/scholarships-a-z-listing?_ga=2.244571969.571132691.1679064314-409237753.1679064067#hkjc

For further information contact:

Email: hkjcscholarships@hkjc.org.hk

International Development: QEH Scholarship

Eligibility: Open to all graduate applicants for MPhil in Development Studies with a preference for those from Sub-Saharan Africa. Please visit departmental website for more details
Level of Study: Predoctorate
Type: Scholarship
Value: University fee, college fee, and £13,000 towards living expenses
Length of Study: 1 year
Country of Study: United Kingdom
Closing Date: 20 January
Additional Information: Please visit the website: www.qeh.ox.ac.uk/content/fees-funding

For further information contact:

Email: jane.sherwood@admin.ox.ac.uk

Ioan and Rosemary James / Mathematical Institute Scholarship

Eligibility: Open to applicants for the DPhil in Mathematics, or CDT in Mathematical Institute only
Type: Scholarship
Value: University fees (at either the Home/European Union or Overseas student rate as applicable), College fees and a maintenance stipend at the United Kingdom research council rate
Country of Study: United Kingdom
Application Procedure: Duration of full-fee liability; 3 years for DPhil and 4 years for CDT. For non-CDT students, the Mathematical Institute will provide an additional 6 months of funding from its own funds for maintenance
Closing Date: January
Additional Information: For more details, please visit website www.sjc.ox.ac.uk www.sjc.ox.ac.uk/study/undergraduate/

For further information contact:

Email: sarah.jones@sjc.ox.ac.uk

James Fairfax - Oxford-Australia Fund Scholarships

Eligibility: Applicants should normally be under 30 on January 1st in the year in which the scholarship is to be taken up, and must have a bachelor's degree with first or upper second class honours or equivalent from a recognized university
Level of Study: Graduate, Postgraduate
Type: Scholarship
Value: The scholarships provide up to £15,000 per annum
Frequency: Annual
Study Establishment: University of Oxford
Country of Study: United Kingdom
Application Procedure: Candidates for an Oxford Australia Scholarship need first to apply to Oxford University by completing the online Graduate Application form at: www.graduate.ox.ac.uk/applyonline by the relevant deadline.
Closing Date: 28 February
Funding: Individuals, Private
Contributor: Australian scholars who have studied at Oxford and, in particular, Mr James Fairfax
Additional Information: rsc.anu.edu.au/~oxford/2017%20JFOA%20Nov%2017.pdf

For further information contact:

Tel: (61) 2 6125 3578/3761
Email: jww@rsc.anu.edu.au

Jesus College: Joint Law Faculty-Jesus College BCL Scholarship

Eligibility: Open to all graduate applicants to the BCL (Bachelor of Civil Law). Please see website for further details
Level of Study: Graduate
Type: Scholarship
Value: £10,000
Length of Study: Period of fee liability
Frequency: Annual
Study Establishment: Jesus College
Country of Study: United Kingdom
No. of awards offered: 2
Closing Date: 20 January
Additional Information: Please visit the website: www.jesus.ox.ac.uk/current-students/scholarships-prizes-awards?field_subject_target_id=20&field_type_value=Graduate

For further information contact:

Email: lodge@jesus.ox.ac.uk

Joan Doll Scholarship

Subjects: MSc Environmental Change & Management only.
Purpose: This scholarship is awarded following nomination by the department. Early applications for the MSc Environmental Change & Management programme are strongly encouraged, and you are advised to make Green Templeton your preferred college on your application form, although this is not essential
Level of Study: Masters Degree

Type: Scholarship
Value: £1,500
Length of Study: one year
Frequency: Annual
Country of Study: United Kingdom
Closing Date: January
Funding: Private, University of Sheffield
Additional Information: www.gtc.ox.ac.uk/students/how-to-apply/scholarships-bursaries/joan-doll-scholarship/

Kalisher Trust-Wadham Student Scholarship

Subjects: MSc Criminology and Criminal Justice
Purpose: The scholarships are intended to encourage and assist those intending to practise at the Criminal Bar who demonstrate 'exceptional promise but modest means'
Eligibility: Applications are invited from United Kingdom residents who can demonstrate 1. Intellectual ability – demonstrated by academic performance, past work, activities and other experience. 2. Motivation to succeed at the Criminal Bar – including steps taken to acquire the personal skills required of a Barrister, and a demonstration of the will to succeed. 3. Potential as an advocate – both in oral and written skills. 4. Personal qualities – including self-reliance, independence, integrity, reliability and humanity. 5. Financial need - candidates will be asked to supply to the interview panel, in confidence, information demonstrating financial need
Level of Study: Graduate
Type: Scholarship
Value: £6,000
Frequency: Annual
Country of Study: United Kingdom
Application Procedure: In particularly to discuss their motivation to succeed at the Criminal Bar. This statement should be no more than 800 words. Application statements should be sent to tracy.kaye@crim.ox.ac.uk
Funding: Private
Additional Information: Website: www.law.ox.ac.uk/sites/files/oxlaw/kalisher_trust_scholarship.pdf

For further information contact:

The Faculty of Law, University of Oxford, St Cross Building, St Cross Road, Oxford OX1 3UL, United Kingdom.

Email: tracy.kaye@crim.ox.ac.uk

Keble College Gosden Water-Newton Scholarship

Eligibility: Open to students intending to seek ordination in a church in communion with the Church of England. Candidates must be either ordained or be able to show clear evidence of desire for ordination in the Church of England or a church in communion therewith, and be already at or intending to be registered for a postgraduate degree at Keble College, University of Oxford
Level of Study: Postgraduate
Type: Scholarship
Value: £15,000
Length of Study: Up to 3 years
Frequency: Dependent on funds available
Study Establishment: Keble College, University of Oxford
Country of Study: United Kingdom
Application Procedure: Applicants must contact the Deputy Academic Administrator at Keble College in the first instance: www.keble.ox.ac.uk/wp-content/uploads/Gwynne-Jones-App-Form-for-2023-24-entry-Gwynne.doc
No. of awards offered: 4
Closing Date: 21 January
No. of awards given last year: 2
No. of applicants last year: 4
Additional Information: www.keble.ox.ac.uk/admissions/graduates/scholarships/

For further information contact:

Keble College, Oxford OX1 3PG, United Kingdom.

Email: college.office@keble.ox.ac.uk

Keble College Gwynne-Jones Scholarship

Eligibility: This award is only for study at Keble College
Level of Study: Postgraduate
Type: Scholarship
Value: £12,500
Length of Study: Up to 3 years
Frequency: Varies
Study Establishment: Keble College, University of Oxford
Country of Study: United Kingdom
Application Procedure: Applicants must write for details: www.keble.ox.ac.uk/wp-content/uploads/Gwynne-Jones-App-Form-for-2023-24-entry-Gwynne.doc
Closing Date: 21 January
Funding: Private
Additional Information: www.keble.ox.ac.uk/admissions/graduates/scholarships/

For further information contact:

Email: college.office@keble.ox.ac.uk

Keble College Ian Palmer Graduate Scholarship in Information Technology

Eligibility: Applicants must write for details
Level of Study: Postgraduate
Type: Scholarship
Value: £3,933
Length of Study: Up to 3 years
Frequency: Dependent on funds available
Study Establishment: Keble College, University of Oxford
Country of Study: United Kingdom
Application Procedure: Applicants must write for details
Closing Date: 21 January
Funding: Private
Additional Information: www.keble.ox.ac.uk/admissions/graduates/scholarships/

For further information contact:

Email: college.office@keble.ox.ac.uk

Keble College Ian Tucker Memorial Bursary

Eligibility: Candidates must demonstrate sporting prowess principally in the field of rugby football, together with qualities that will make a contribution to both the College and University
Level of Study: Graduate
Type: Bursary
Value: £6,000
Length of Study: 1 year
Frequency: Annual
Study Establishment: Keble College, University of Oxford
Country of Study: United Kingdom
Application Procedure: Applicants must contact the Tutor for Graduates at Keble College for an application form: www.keble.ox.ac.uk/wp-content/uploads/Ian-Tucker-App-Form-for-2023-24-entry-Ian-Tucker.doc
No. of awards offered: 6
Closing Date: 21 January
No. of awards given last year: 2
No. of applicants last year: 6
Additional Information: www.keble.ox.ac.uk/admissions/graduates/scholarships/

For further information contact:

Email: college.office@keble.ox.ac.uk

Keble College Water Newton Scholarship

Eligibility: Open to students intending to seek ordination in a church in communication with the Church of United Kingdom
Level of Study: Postdoctorate, Research
Type: Scholarship
Value: £15,000
Length of Study: Up to 3 years
Frequency: Dependent on funds available
Study Establishment: Keble College, University of Oxford
Country of Study: United Kingdom
Application Procedure: Applicants must contact the Deputy Academic www.keble.ox.ac.uk/wp-content/uploads/GWN-Application-Form-for-23-24entry.doc
Closing Date: 21 January
Funding: Private
Additional Information: www.keble.ox.ac.uk/admissions/graduates/scholarships/

For further information contact:

Email: college.office@keble.ox.ac.uk

Keble College: James Martin Graduate Scholarship

Subjects: MSc in MPLS (mathematical, physical and life sciences), Medical Sciences or Environmental Science
Eligibility: Open to Home/European Union students, who can demonstrate that they are in financial need. Applicants must be intending to study for a MSc in the MPLS (Mathematical, Physical and Life Sciences) Division, Medical Sciences Division or Geography and the Environment department
Level of Study: Postgraduate
Type: Scholarship
Value: £9,000, for one year only
Length of Study: 1 year
Study Establishment: Keble College
Country of Study: Any country
Application Procedure: Please see website for further details, including how to apply
Closing Date: 21 January
Additional Information: Please visit the website: www.keble.ox.ac.uk/admissions/graduate/graduate-scholarships

For further information contact:

Email: college.office@keble.ox.ac.uk

U

Kellogg College: Bigg Scholarship in African Climate Science

Purpose: Keble seeks to award a scholarship for doctoral research into African climate science.
Level of Study: Masters Degree
Type: Scholarship

Value: £10,000
Frequency: Annual
Country of Study: Any country
Application Procedure: The scholarship can only be held at Keble College and potential applicants should apply to Keble and complete a short application form here www.keble.ox.ac.uk/admissions/graduates/scholarships/
Closing Date: 21 January

For further information contact:

Email: Richard.washington@keble.ox.ac.uk

Kellogg College: Oxford-McCall MacBain Graduate Scholarship

Purpose: The scholarship is only tenable at Kellogg College. All eligible applicants will be considered for the scholarship
Eligibility: All eligible applicants will be considered for the scholarship, regardless of which college (if any) you state as your preference on the graduate application form. However, successful applicants will be transferred to Kellogg College in order to take up the scholarship
Level of Study: Graduate
Type: Scholarship
Value: The scholarship covers course fees and provides a study support grant
Frequency: Annual
Country of Study: United Kingdom
Closing Date: 25 August
Funding: Private
Additional Information: Initially the MMF operated on a regional-based approach, with a strategy to develop and encourage best practices and policies in multiple areas related to improving the human condition scholarscareers.com/2019/02/16/oxford-mccall-macbain-graduate-scholarship/

For further information contact:

Kellogg College, 60-62 Banbury Road, Oxford OX2 6PN, United Kingdom.

Email: enquiries@kellogg.ox.ac.uk

Lady Margaret Hall: Ann Kennedy Graduate Scholarship in Law

Eligibility: Open to graduate applicants for the BCL, MJur, MSt in Legal Research or MPhil in Law at Lady Margaret Hall. The award will be made on the basis of academic excellence
Level of Study: Graduate, Postgraduate, Predoctorate
Type: Scholarship
Value: £7,000 per annum
Length of Study: 1 year
Study Establishment: Lady Margaret Hall
Country of Study: United Kingdom
Closing Date: 20 January
Additional Information: Please visit the website: www.law.ox.ac.uk/admissions/scholarships-index/college-awards-specific-law-postgraduates-index

For further information contact:

Email: enquiries@lmh.ox.ac.uk

Latin American Centre-Latin American Centre Scholarship

Eligibility: Open to all graduate applicants to the MSc in Latin American Studies from one of the CAF shareholder countries. Applicants must send an email to the Admissions Secretary requesting to be considered
Level of Study: Postgraduate
Type: Scholarship
Value: University and college fees (not living expenses)
Length of Study: 1 year (Non-renewable)
Country of Study: Any country
Application Procedure: Please visit website for more details and how to apply
Closing Date: 10 March
Additional Information: For more information, please check the websites: www.lac.ox.ac.uk/funding www.educationprogram.scholarshipcare.com/lac-caf-scholarships/

For further information contact:

Email: laclib@bodleian.ox.ac.uk

Law Faculty: David and Helen Elvin Scholarship

Eligibility: Open to all graduate applicants for the BCL and MJur. Award holders will become members of Hertford College. Please see website for more information
Level of Study: Graduate, Postgraduate
Type: Scholarship
Value: £10,000 towards course fees, college fees and living costs where appropriate

Length of Study: 1 year
Study Establishment: Hertford College
Country of Study: Any country
Closing Date: 20 January
Additional Information: Please visit the website: www.law.ox.ac.uk/postgraduate/scholarships.php

For further information contact:

Email: lawfac@law.ox.ac.uk

Law Faculty: Des Voeux Chambers

Eligibility: Open to all graduate applicants to the BCL. Preference may be shown for candidates with an interest in pursuing a career at the Hong Kong Bar. Please see website for more information
Level of Study: Postgraduate
Type: Scholarship
Value: £10,000
Length of Study: 1 year
Frequency: Annual
Country of Study: United Kingdom
Application Procedure: No separate application
Closing Date: 20 January
Funding: Trusts
Additional Information: Please check the website: www.law.ox.ac.uk/postgraduate/scholarships.php

For further information contact:

Email: pupillage@dvc.com.hk

Law Faculty: James Bullock Scholarship

Purpose: The James Bullock Scholarship was established by the Oxford Law Faculty in memory of James Bullock, partner in Pinsent Masons, who died before his time in 2015 and who did so much to support tax teaching and research in Oxford.
Eligibility: Open to all applicants for the MSc in Taxation
Level of Study: Postgraduate
Type: Scholarship
Value: £2,800 per annum
Length of Study: 2 years
Country of Study: Any country
Application Procedure: No separate application
Closing Date: 10 March
Additional Information: Please visit the website: www.law.ox.ac.uk/postgraduate/scholarships.php www.law.ox.ac.uk/content/james-bullock-scholarship

For further information contact:

Email: lawfac@law.ox.ac.uk

Law Faculty: The Peter Birks Memorial Scholarship

Purpose: To assist graduate students with fees
Eligibility: Open to all graduate applicants to BCL/MJur, MSc in Law and Finance, MSt Legal Research, MPhil Or DPhil Law. Please see website for further information
Level of Study: Graduate, Postgraduate
Type: Scholarship
Value: £5,000
Length of Study: Full fee liability period
Frequency: Annual
Country of Study: United Kingdom
Closing Date: 20 January
Additional Information: www.law.ox.ac.uk/admissions/scholarships-index/law-faculty-awards-study-any-college-index/peter-birks-memorial

For further information contact:

Email: lawfac@law.ox.ac.uk

Linacre College: Applied Materials MSc Scholarship

Purpose: To assist graduate students with fees and a living allowance
Eligibility: Open to all
Level of Study: Postgraduate
Type: Scholarship
Length of Study: 1 year

For further information contact:

School of Geography and the Environment, University of Oxford, South Parks Road, Oxford OX1 3QY, United Kingdom.

Tel: (44) 1865 285 070
Email: enquiries@ouce.ox.ac.uk

Linacre College: David Daube Scholarship

Purpose: The scholarship is available to a student reading or intending to read for a DPhil in law, and who is liable to pay fees
Eligibility: Open to all graduate applicants for the BCL and MJur
Level of Study: Postgraduate
Type: Scholarship
Value: £4,500 per year
Length of Study: Period of fee liability
Country of Study: United Kingdom
Closing Date: 12 March
Additional Information: Applicants should first secure a place on the Oxford BCL or MJur course and mark Linacre College as their chosen College. Please check at www.linacre.ox.ac.uk/Admissions/Scholarships

For further information contact:

Email: ben.nicholson@admin.ox.ac.uk

Linacre College: EPA Cephalosporin Scholarship

Subjects: Biological, medical & chemical sciences.
Purpose: To assist graduate students with fees
Eligibility: Open to all graduate students
Level of Study: Postgraduate, Research, Unrestricted
Type: Scholarship
Value: Full course fees and a stipend for living expenses
Length of Study: Period of fee liability
Country of Study: United Kingdom
Application Procedure: Eligible students are automatically considered for this award.
No. of awards offered: 2
Additional Information: www.linacre.ox.ac.uk/prospective-students/scholarships/epa-cephalosporin-scholarship

For further information contact:

Sir William Dunn School of Pathology.

Email: scholarships@linacre.ox.ac.uk

Linacre College: Hicks Scholarship

Purpose: With the initial support of several Old Members, a fund is being established to provide a College fee scholarship to a Linacre student studying for a degree in Economics
Eligibility: Open to students reading, or intending to read for a DPhil in Economics who are liable to pay fees
Level of Study: Doctorate, Postgraduate
Type: Scholarship
Value: £80,000. 1st 3 years scholarship paid out £6,486
Length of Study: Period of fee liability
Study Establishment: Linacre College
Country of Study: United Kingdom
Closing Date: 21 April
Funding: Private
Additional Information: www.linacre.ox.ac.uk/alumni-friends/current-fundgiving-projects/hicks-scholarship-fund

For further information contact:

Linacre College, St. Cross Road, Oxford OX1 3JA, United Kingdom.

Tel: (44) 1865 271 650
Email: development@linacre.ox.ac.uk

Linacre College: Hitachi Chemical Europe Scholarship

Eligibility: Preference given to applicant from China or Central/South America
Level of Study: Postgraduate
Type: Scholarship
Value: £9,000 and lasts one year
Length of Study: 1 year
Application Procedure: Eligible candidates are automatically considered for this scholarship
No. of awards offered: 1
Closing Date: 24 January
Additional Information: Please check at www.linacre.ox.ac.uk/extras/scholarships www.linacre.ox.ac.uk/prospective-students/scholarships/hitachi-chemical-environmental-scholarship

For further information contact:

Oxford University Centre for the Environment, Environmental Change Institute, South Parks Road, Oxford OX1 3QY, United Kingdom.

Email: thomas.thornton@ouce.ox.ac.uk

Linacre College: John Bamborough MSc Scholarship

Eligibility: Citizens of all nationalities are eligible to apply. In order to be eligible for these scholarships, students must be suitably qualified and be, or intending to become, a member of Linacre College.
Level of Study: Postgraduate

Type: Scholarship
Value: 100% college fees.
Length of Study: One year
Study Establishment: Linacre College
Country of Study: United Kingdom
Application Procedure: Please see website for more details, including how to apply
Closing Date: 20 April
Additional Information: Please visit the website: www.linacre.ox.ac.uk/prospective-students/scholarships scholarship-positions.com/john-bamborough-msc-scholarships-humanities-linacre-college-uk/2018/04/10/

For further information contact:

Email: scholarships@linacre.ox.ac.uk

Linacre College: Linacre Rausing Scholarship (English)

Level of Study: Research
Type: Scholarship
Value: £3,500
Length of Study: 1 to 3 years
Country of Study: United Kingdom
Application Procedure: Eligible candidates are automatically considered for this scholarship
No. of awards offered: 1
Additional Information: www.linacre.ox.ac.uk/prospective-students/scholarships/rausing-scholarship-english

For further information contact:

Email: english.office@ell.ox.ac.uk

Linacre College: Mary Blaschko Graduate Scholarship

Purpose: To enable European students to carry out research for 1 year in the department of pharmacology or the MRC anatomical neuropharmacology unit
Eligibility: Open to all graduate applicants for research degrees in the Humanities division
Level of Study: Postgraduate, Research
Type: Scholarship
Value: College fee
Length of Study: Period of fee liability
Study Establishment: Linacre College
Country of Study: United Kingdom
Application Procedure: Please see website for more details, including how to apply
No. of awards offered: 2
Additional Information: Please visit the website: www.linacre.ox.ac.uk/prospective-students/scholarships www.linacre.ox.ac.uk/prospective-students/scholarships/mary-blaschko-scholarship

For further information contact:

Email: scholarships@linacre.ox.ac.uk

Linacre College: Rausing Scholarship in Anthropology

Eligibility: Open to all graduate applicants in Anthropology
Level of Study: Research
Type: Scholarship
Value: £3,500
Length of Study: 3 years
Country of Study: United Kingdom
Application Procedure: Eligible students are automatically considered for this award.
Additional Information: Please check at www.linacre.ox.ac.uk/Admissions/Scholarships www.linacre.ox.ac.uk/prospective-students/scholarships/rausing-scholarship-anthropology

For further information contact:

Email: ben.nicholson@admin.ox.ac.uk

Linacre College: Rausing Scholarship in English

Eligibility: Open to all graduate applicants for any course in the English Faculty
Level of Study: Doctorate
Type: Scholarship
Value: £3,500
Length of Study: 1 to 3 years
Study Establishment: Linacre College
Country of Study: United Kingdom
Application Procedure: Eligible students are automatically considered for this award.
Additional Information: Please visit the website: www.linacre.ox.ac.uk/scholarships/rausing-scholarship-anthropology

For further information contact:

Email: support@linacre.ox.ac.uk

Linacre College: Raymond and Vera Asquith Scholarship

Eligibility: Open to suitably qualified students who were born in the United Kingdom, reading or intending to read for a DPhil in Humanities who are liable to pay fees and have AHRC funding
Level of Study: Doctorate, Postgraduate
Type: Scholarship
Value: £3300
Length of Study: 1 to 2 years
Country of Study: Any country
Application Procedure: Please see website for details of how to apply
Additional Information: Please check at www.linacre.ox.ac.uk/Admissions/Scholarships www.linacre.ox.ac.uk/raymond-vera-asquith

For further information contact:

Email: ben.nicholson@admin.ox.ac.uk

Linacre College: Ronald and Jane Olson Scholarship

Eligibility: Open to all graduate applicants for the MSc in Refugee and Forced Migration Studies
Level of Study: Postgraduate
Type: Scholarship
Value: The scholarship covers all fees and provides a grant for living costs of at least £17,668
Length of Study: 1 year
Study Establishment: Linacre College
Country of Study: United Kingdom
Application Procedure: Eligible students are automatically considered for this award.
No. of awards offered: 4
Closing Date: January
Additional Information: Please visit the website: www.linacre.ox.ac.uk/prospective-students/scholarships www.linacre.ox.ac.uk/prospective-students/scholarships/ronald-and-jane-olson-scholarship-refugee-studies

For further information contact:

Email: rsc-msc@qeh.ox.ac.uk

Linacre College: Women in Science Scholarship

Eligibility: Open to all graduate applicants for the DPhil in Materials who are liable to pay fees
Level of Study: Doctorate
Type: Scholarship
Value: £3,500
Length of Study: 1 year
Study Establishment: Linacre College
Country of Study: United Kingdom
No. of awards offered: 1
Closing Date: January
Additional Information: www.linacre.ox.ac.uk/scholarships/women-science-scholarship

For further information contact:

Email: support@linacre.ox.ac.uk

Lincoln College: Berrow Foundation Lord Florey Scholarships

Eligibility: Open to all graduate applicants for courses in Medical, Chemical or Biochemical Sciences of Swiss or Lichtenstein nationality who are students at, or have recently graduated from, any Swiss university, including ETHZ and EPFL, and who must not be more than five years beyond graduation from their first degree at one of these institutions (except for candidates in medicine, for whom the five years limit dates from obtaining the Federal Diploma in Medicine). Up to two awards available. Please see website for full details and application form
Level of Study: Postgraduate, Research
Type: Scholarship
Value: Course fees, college accommodation costs, and a generous living allowance.
Length of Study: Up to 3 years
Frequency: Annual
Study Establishment: Lincoln
Country of Study: United Kingdom
Application Procedure: Please see website for details of how to apply
No. of awards offered: 2
Closing Date: 30 January
Funding: Foundation
Additional Information: lincoln.ox.ac.uk/study-here/graduate-study/finance-and-funding/berrow-foundation-scholarships

For further information contact:

Email: rectors.office@lincoln.ox.ac.uk.

Lincoln College: Berrow Foundation Scholarships

Eligibility: Open to all graduate applicants of Swiss or Lichtenstein nationality who are students at, or have recently

graduated from, selected Swiss universities. Up to four awards available. Please see website for full details and application form
Level of Study: Postgraduate, Research
Type: Scholarship
Value: Course fees, college accommodation costs, and a generous living allowance.
Length of Study: Up to 3 years
Frequency: Annual
Study Establishment: Lincoln
Country of Study: United Kingdom
No. of awards offered: 5
Closing Date: 30 January
Funding: Foundation
Additional Information: lincoln.ox.ac.uk/study-here/graduate-study/finance-and-funding

For further information contact:

Email: rectors.office@lincoln.ox.ac.uk.

Lincoln College: Crewe Graduate Scholarships

Eligibility: Students, in any subject, ordinarily resident in the Dioceses of Durham and Newcastle; Northallertonshire (in North Yorkshire); Howdenshire (in Humberside); Leicestershire; Northamptonshire; and the Diocese of Oxford. Applicants must hold an offer of a place to read for a graduate degree course at an Oxford college before applying. Successful applicants holding an offer of a place at another College will be required to migrate to Lincoln College in order to take up the award.
Level of Study: Graduate, MBA, Postgraduate
Type: Scholarship
Value: £7,000
Length of Study: One year, with the possibility of renewal on applying
Frequency: Annual
Study Establishment: Lincoln College, University of Oxford
Country of Study: United Kingdom
Application Procedure: A combined application form is available www.lincoln.ox.ac.uk/uploads/files/Scholarship%20application%20form%202020.docx.
Closing Date: 1 June
Funding: Trusts
Additional Information: lincoln.ox.ac.uk/study-here/graduate-study/finance-and-funding

For further information contact:

Email: admissions@lincoln.ox.ac.uk

Lincoln College: Hartley Bursary

Eligibility: Candidates must be new or current graduate students of Lincoln College, ordinarily resident in the UK, who are studying for a degree in any humanities subject and who are in financial need.
Level of Study: Graduate
Type: Scholarship
Value: £1,200
Length of Study: 1 years
Study Establishment: Lincoln College
Country of Study: United Kingdom
Application Procedure: A combined application form is available www.lincoln.ox.ac.uk/uploads/files/Scholarship%20application%20form%202020.docx.
No. of awards offered: 1
Closing Date: 1 June
Additional Information: lincoln.ox.ac.uk/study-here/graduate-study/finance-and-funding

For further information contact:

Email: admissions@lincoln.ox.ac.uk

Lincoln College: Jermyn Brooks Graduate Award

Eligibility: 1. Candidates must be a new or current graduate student of the College in the Humanities, preferably in Modern Languages. 2. Candidates should have attained a high standard in their previous academic work.
Level of Study: Postgraduate
Type: Scholarship
Value: £2,500
Length of Study: One year
Frequency: Annual
Study Establishment: Lincoln College, University of Oxford
Country of Study: United Kingdom
Application Procedure: Application form available from Admissions Office at Lincoln College
No. of awards offered: 1
Closing Date: 1 June
Funding: Private
Additional Information: https://lincoln.ox.ac.uk/study-here/graduate-study/finance-and-funding

For further information contact:

The Admissions Office Lincoln College.

Email: info@lincoln.ox.ac.uk

Lincoln College: Lord Crewe Graduate Scholarships in the Humanities

Eligibility: Open to graduates of any United Kingdom university for all courses within the Humanities
Level of Study: Postgraduate, Research
Type: Scholarship
Value: £18,000 per year
Length of Study: Period of fee liability
Country of Study: United Kingdom
Application Procedure: Please see website for details of how to apply
Closing Date: 18 January
Additional Information: Please check at www.lincoln.ox.ac.uk/

For further information contact:

Email: info@lincoln.ox.ac.uk

Lincoln College: Lord Crewe Graduate Scholarships in the Social Sciences

Eligibility: Open to graduates of any United Kingdom university for all courses within the Social Sciences
Level of Study: Postgraduate, Research
Type: Scholarship
Value: £7,000
Length of Study: Period of fee liability
Country of Study: United Kingdom
Application Procedure: Please see website for details of how to apply
No. of awards offered: 2
Closing Date: 1 June
Additional Information: Please check at www.lincoln.ox.ac.uk/

For further information contact:

Email: info@lincoln.ox.ac.uk

Lincoln College: Overseas Graduate Entrance Scholarship

Eligibility: All non-European Union nationals
Type: Scholarship
Value: £2,300
Length of Study: 1 year
Country of Study: United Kingdom
Closing Date: 1 June
Additional Information: Successful candidates will show evidence of both academic merit and financial need. Applicants must hold a place, or an offer of a place, at Lincoln College before applying. Eligible to the nationals of Overseas testbig.com/article_items/menasseh-ben-israel-room-scholarship-israeli-students-lincoln-college-uk-2013

For further information contact:

Email: info@lincoln.ox.ac.uk

Lincoln College: Sloane Robinson Foundation Graduate Awards

Purpose: To fund those intending to pursue research programmes at Oxford
Eligibility: Any DPhil candidates in the Social Sciences
Level of Study: Graduate, MBA, Postgraduate, Research
Type: Award
Value: Fees and Stipend
Length of Study: 3 to 4 years
Frequency: Annual
Study Establishment: Lincoln College, University of Oxford
Country of Study: United Kingdom
Application Procedure: There is no separate scholarship application process or extra supporting documentation required for these awards. Based on the information supplied in your graduate application, you will be automatically considered for scholarships where you meet the eligibility criteria.
No. of awards offered: 4
Closing Date: 1 June
Funding: Foundation
Additional Information: lincoln.ox.ac.uk/study-here/graduate-study/finance-and-funding

For further information contact:

Email: info@lincoln.ox.ac.uk

Lincoln College: Supperstone Law Scholarship

Eligibility: Open to candidates reading for the BCL or the MJuris, with an emphasis or special interest in European or public law. Applicants must have an offer of a college place at Lincoln College
Level of Study: Postgraduate
Type: Scholarship
Value: £1,200
Length of Study: 1 year
Frequency: Annual
Study Establishment: Lincoln College, University of Oxford

Country of Study: United Kingdom
Application Procedure: Applicants must contact the Admissions Office at Lincoln College: lincoln.ox.ac.uk/study-here/graduate-study/finance-and-funding/application-for-graduate-awards
No. of awards offered: 1
Closing Date: 1 June
Funding: Trusts
Additional Information: lincoln.ox.ac.uk/study-here/graduate-study/finance-and-funding

Magdalen College: Perkin Research Studentship

Eligibility: For Commonwealth citizen graduates reading Chemistry.
Level of Study: Research
Type: Studentship
Value: £14,000 per annum
Length of Study: 1 years
Country of Study: United Kingdom
Application Procedure: Please see website for details of how to apply
Additional Information: Please check at www.magd.ox.ac.uk/admissions_graduate/scholarships.shtml

For further information contact:

Email: jane.sherwood@admin.ox.ac.uk

Magdalen College: Student Support Fund Graduate Grants

Eligibility: Restricted to graduate students who are already studying at Magdalen.
Level of Study: Postgraduate, Research
Type: Grant
Value: According to individual circumstances
Length of Study: 1 year, renewable after review
Country of Study: United Kingdom
Application Procedure: Application is made via an internal College application form.
Additional Information: www.magd.ox.ac.uk/considering-magdalen/graduate-study/scholarships-and-awards/#collapse10020

For further information contact:

Tel: (44) 1865 286796
Email: sean.rainey@magd.ox.ac.uk

Magdalen Hong Kong Scholarship

Eligibility: Students who are an ordinary resident of Hong Kong and are citizens of the People's Republic of China (PRC). Candidates should be intending to return to Hong Kong or the PRC on completion of their studies.
Level of Study: Postgraduate
Type: Scholarship
Value: Maximum of £40,000 per annum as a contribution towards College and University tuition fees and living expenses.
Length of Study: Up to 4 years
Country of Study: United Kingdom
Application Procedure: There is no separate application process.
Closing Date: 22 January
Additional Information: www.magd.ox.ac.uk/considering-magdalen/graduate-study/scholarships-and-awards/#collapse10040

For further information contact:

Tel: (44) 1865 276063
Email: admissions@magd.ox.ac.uk

Mansfield College: Adam von Trott Scholarship

Eligibility: Open to German nationals applying to the two year MPhil in Politics. Please see website for more details
Level of Study: Postgraduate, Research
Type: Scholarship
Value: University fee, college fee, living expenses up to €20,000 per annum
Length of Study: Duration of fee liability
Country of Study: Any country

For further information contact:

Email: avt.oxford@gmail.com

Mansfield College: Elfan Rees Scholarship

Purpose: To commencing studies towards a higher degree in the field of theology
Eligibility: Open to students on the MSt, MPhil, MLitt or DPhil in any branch of theology
Level of Study: Postdoctorate, Postgraduate, Research
Type: Scholarship
Value: Scholarship is £3,000 maintenance, paid termly in £1,000 instalments
Length of Study: Up to 2 years
Country of Study: United Kingdom

Closing Date: 1 April
Additional Information: www.mansfield.ox.ac.uk/graduate-scholarships

For further information contact:

Email: admissions@mansfield.ox.ac.uk

Medical Sciences Doctoral Training Centre: Wellcome Trust Studentship in Structural Biology

Purpose: Provides training in structural biology and related biochemical, genetic and cell biological approaches to understand molecular and cellular function
Eligibility: Open to all applicants to the DPhil in Structural Biology. All applicants are automatically considered for these awards
Level of Study: Doctorate
Type: Studentship
Value: stipend at not less than £19,919 per annum, £50,000 for research expenses, £2,500 for travel expenses
Length of Study: 4 years
Country of Study: United Kingdom
Closing Date: 1 March
Funding: Trusts
Additional Information: Please visit the website: www.medsci.ox.ac.uk/study/graduateschool/courses/dtc-structured-research-degrees/cellular-structural-biology

For further information contact:

Email: enquiries@msdtc.ox.ac.uk

Merton College Leventis Scholarship

Eligibility: Open to citizens of Greece or the Republic of Cyprus only
Level of Study: Graduate
Type: Scholarship
Value: Fees and maintenance
Length of Study: Up to 4 years depending on programme of study
Frequency: Every 2 years
Study Establishment: Merton College, University of Oxford
Country of Study: United Kingdom
Application Procedure: Further particulars and application forms are available from the Merton College website www.merton.ox.ac.uk/vacancies
No. of awards offered: 10
Closing Date: January
Funding: Private
No. of applicants last year: 10
Additional Information: Prospective applicants should refer to the college website www.merton.ox.ac.uk

For further information contact:

Merton College, Merton College, Merton Street, Oxford OX1 4JD, United Kingdom.

Email: julie.gerhardi@merton.ox.ac.uk

Merton College: Barton Scholarship

Eligibility: Open to British graduate applicants for the BCL. Awarded with the Law Faculty. No separate application required
Level of Study: Graduate, Postgraduate
Type: Scholarship
Value: £5,000 from Merton College and £5,000 from the Faculty of Law
Length of Study: 1 year
Frequency: Annual
Country of Study: United Kingdom
Application Procedure: No separate application required
Closing Date: 22 January
Additional Information: Please check at www.merton.ox.ac.uk/graduate/graduate-scholarships-2015

For further information contact:

Email: jane.sherwood@admin.ox.ac.uk

Merton College: Merton Lawyers

Eligibility: Open to graduate applicants for the BCL/MJur. No separate application required. Please see website for more details
Level of Study: Graduate, Postgraduate
Type: Scholarship
Value: £5,000 from Merton College and £5,000 from the Faculty of Law.
Length of Study: 1 year
Frequency: Annual
Study Establishment: Merton
Country of Study: United Kingdom
Closing Date: January

Additional Information: Please check the website: www.merton.ox.ac.uk/graduate/graduate-scholarships

MSc Sustainable Urban Development Programme Scholarship

Eligibility: The Scholarship will be awarded on the basis of outstanding academic and professional merit, and taking account of demonstrable commitment and ability to contribute significantly to the field of sustainable urban development. Key criteria include: (1) Academic excellence, where indicators may include: a high-level qualification in a relevant discipline (such as a first-class honours degree, US GPA of 3.7, or equivalent, distinction at Master's level, or a doctoral degree); individual marks on a student's transcript; information on a student's overall position within their cohort; and relevant published work. (2) Professional excellence: Evidence of a strong record of relevant professional achievement, and a demonstrably successful history of continuing professional development and commitment to the candidate's profession. Indicators may include the candidate's CV, personal statement, testimonials and/or professional references. (3) Motivation and potential future contribution to the field: Applications should demonstrate the potential to make an on-going professional contribution to the built environment, and to contribute significantly to sustainable urban development (either during or following completion of the MSc). Indicators may include the candidate's personal statement, interview performance and/or professional references.
Level of Study: Masters Degree, Postgraduate
Type: Scholarship
Value: The course fees for the first six terms of registration (the MSc is normally completed over two years)
Length of Study: Duration of the course
Frequency: Annual
Country of Study: United Kingdom
Application Procedure: All applicants whose completed application has been received by 20 January, 2024 and who are offered a place on the MSc will be automatically considered for the Scholarship.
No. of awards offered: 1
Closing Date: 20 January
Additional Information: For any queries about the Scholarship, please email the course team at sud@conted.ox.ac.uk. Website: www.conted.ox.ac.uk/about/msc-in-sustainable-urban-development

For further information contact:

Tel: (44) 1865 286952
Email: sud@conted.ox.ac.uk

North American Electric Reliability Corporation (NERC) Studentships in Earth Sciences

Purpose: To assist graduate students with fees and maintenance
Eligibility: Open to Home or European Union candidates usually with a 2.1 degree or higher
Level of Study: Research
Type: Studentship
Value: £5,000 per year
Length of Study: Duration of fee liability
Frequency: Annual
Country of Study: Any country
Application Procedure: 1. Upload a transcript from your current or previous study, a CV and any other documents that you feel would support your application (within 24 hours of submitting your online application you will receive a link allowing you to upload additional supporting documents). 2. Ask your referees to submit a reference for you by 29 April at the very latest. Note when you submit your application, an email will automatically be sent to your referees requesting a reference for you. This email will contain a secure link for your referee to upload a reference for you. 3. View the available projects. 4. Make an initial project enquiry by contacting supervisors directly
Closing Date: 6 January
Additional Information: The Department will have a number of NERC studentships, to be confirmed. An European Union national who has studied for an undergraduate degree at a United Kingdom university during the 3 years leading up to the application may be classed as a United Kingdom resident www.devex.com/jobs/peter-j-braam-junior-research-fellowship-in-global-wellbeing-561725

For further information contact:

Email: c.morgan@imperial.ac.uk

Nuffield College Funded Studentships

Purpose: To assist students in a postgraduate degree course
Eligibility: Open to persons with at least an Upper Second Class (Honours) Degree or equivalent
Level of Study: Postgraduate
Type: Studentship
Value: Living expenses (at £17,668 per annum)
Length of Study: up to 4 years
Frequency: Annual
Study Establishment: Nuffield College, University of Oxford
Country of Study: United Kingdom

Application Procedure: All students offered a place at Nuffield College will automatically be considered for a studentship without the need for further application, other than the University of Oxford Graduate Admissions application form
Closing Date: September
Additional Information: Requests for information should be addressed to the Academic Administrator www.nuffield.ox.ac.uk/study-here/funding-your-studies/

For further information contact:

Nuffield College, New Rd, Oxford OX1 1NF, United Kingdom.

Email: graduate.admissions@nuffield.ox.ac.uk

Nuffield College Gwilym Gibbon Research Fellowships

Purpose: To support the study of problems of government, especially by co-operation between academic and non academic persons
Eligibility: See website
Level of Study: Postdoctorate, Postgraduate, Professional development
Type: Fellowship
Value: RSIV- salary £86K to £95K per annum (including the College's academic responsibility allowance)
Frequency: Annual
Study Establishment: Nuffield College, the University of Oxford
Country of Study: United Kingdom
Application Procedure: There is no application form. In order to apply, please submit: 1. Your full contact details including email and full postal addresses, and a telephone number; 2. Your CV, including a statement of research interests, details of teaching experience, and a full list of publications (maximum 6 pages); please ensure that you draw the selection committee's attention to two article-length publications which best represent your research; 3. A covering letter or statement explaining how you meet the criteria set out above (maximum 2 pages); 4. The names and contact details (postal and e-mail addresses and telephone number) of three referees whom you have asked to submit confidential reference letters. Please ensure that your referees send their letters by the stated deadline for applications. If you would prefer a referee or referees to supply their reference only if you are being called for interview on the final short list, then you must state this in your application, alongside the details of the relevant referee. Applications and reference letters should be sent by email to academic.admin@nuffield.ox.ac.uk.
Closing Date: 9 February
No. of awards given last year: 1
Additional Information: Website: www.nuffield.ox.ac.uk/media/2407/srf_britishpolicy_fp.pdf

For further information contact:

Tel: (44) 1865 278 515
Fax: (44) 1865 278 621
Email: academic.admin@nuffield.ox.ac.uk

Nuffield Department of Clinical Medicine: LICR Studentship (Ludwig Institute for Cancer Research)

Eligibility: Minimum 21 or above, higher level English language test. Open to United Kingdom, European Union and Overseas Students
Type: Studentship
Value: All University and College fees plus stipend £16,500 per year
Length of Study: 3-4 years
Country of Study: United Kingdom
Closing Date: 26 September
Additional Information: Please check at www.ludwig.ox.ac.uk/ www.ndm.ox.ac.uk/ludwig-institute-for-cancer-research

For further information contact:

Email: webmaster@ox.ac.uk

Nuffield Department of Orthopaedics, Rheumatology and Musculoskeletal Sciences: Kennedy Trust Prize Studentships

Purpose: To provide world-class scientific training in a supportive and collaborative environment
Eligibility: Both European Union and Overseas applicants for the DPhil in Molecular and Cellular Medicine are eligible for this award. Interested applicants should have or expect to obtain a first or upper second class BSc degree or equivalent, and will also need to provide evidence of English language competence at time of application
Level of Study: Doctorate
Type: Studentship
Value: £22,000 per annum
Length of Study: 4 years
Frequency: Annual

Country of Study: Any country
Additional Information: Please visit the website: www.ndorms.ox.ac.uk/graduate-courses/kennedy-trust-prize-studentships www.ndorms.ox.ac.uk/graduate-courses/kennedy-trust-prize-studentships/how-to-apply

For further information contact:

Email: reception@kennedy.ox.ac.uk

Nuffield Department of Population Health: NDPH Scholarship

Eligibility: The department aims to provide up to two fully funded scholarships for the MSc each year. All applicants for the MSc in Global Health Science are eligible for this; the highest ranked applicants in the department are shortlisted for funding
Level of Study: Postgraduate
Type: Scholarship
Value: £18,000 per year
Length of Study: 3 years
Frequency: Annual
Country of Study: United Kingdom
Closing Date: 9 December

For further information contact:

Email: enquiries@ndph.ox.ac.uk

Nuffield Department of Primary Care Health Science: NIHR School for Primary Care Research DPhil Studentship

Purpose: The Health Sciences Research Group invites applications for NIHR School for Primary Care Research (NSPCR) PhD studentships
Eligibility: The award can only be taken up by a student enrolled on the DPhil in Primary Health Care programme in a non-clinical area
Level of Study: Doctorate
Type: Studentship
Value: An annual tax-free stipend of £16,000
Length of Study: 3 years
Frequency: Annual
Country of Study: United Kingdom
Closing Date: December
Additional Information: www.phc.ox.ac.uk/study/dphil/postgrad-study-info/spcr-funded-phd-studentships-in-primary-care-2021

For further information contact:

Radcliffe Observatory Quarter, Woodstock Road, Oxford OX2 6GG, United Kingdom.

Tel: (44) 1865 289 300

Ooni Adeyeye Enitan Ogunwusi Scholarships

Purpose: The scholarship is funded by the Imperial Majesty Oba Adéyeyè Enitan Ògúnwùsì and aims to provide funding to exceptional candidates pursuing postgraduate study of Africa
Eligibility: See website
Level of Study: Postgraduate
Type: Scholarship
Value: Course fee and a grant for living expenses of at least £ 14,777
Frequency: Annual
Country of Study: United Kingdom
Closing Date: January
Funding: Private
Additional Information: www.opportunitiesforafricans.com/ooni-adeyeye-enitan-ogunwusi-scholarships-2019/

For further information contact:

University of Oxford, University Offices, 15 Wellington Square, Oxford OX1 2JD, United Kingdom.

Tel: (44) 1865 270 000
Email: joe@advance-africa.com

Oriel College: Oriel Graduate Scholarships

Eligibility: Open to all current graduate students at the college. Please see website for more details, including how to apply
Level of Study: Postgraduate, Research
Type: Scholarship
Value: £5,000
Length of Study: Period of fee liability
Country of Study: Any country
Closing Date: 22 January
Additional Information: Scholars are entitled to dine free of charge at High Table once per week during term time. Please contact to Academic Assistant at academic.office@oriel.ox.ac.uk

For further information contact:

Email: jane.sherwood@admin.ox.ac.uk

Oriel College: Paul Ries Collin Graduate Scholarship

Eligibility: Open to current graduate students at Oriel
Level of Study: Postgraduate, Research
Type: Scholarship
Value: Annual stipend equivalent to college fee; guaranteed college room at usual charge
Length of Study: 1 year, renewable for second or third
Frequency: Annual
Country of Study: Any country
Closing Date: 27 January
Additional Information: Scholars are entitled to dine free of charge at High Table once a week during term-time mail to: academic.office@oriel.ox.ac.uk

For further information contact:

Oriel College, Oriel Square, Oxford OX1 4EW, United Kingdom.

Email: academic.office@oriel.ox.ac.uk

Oriel College: Sir Walter Raleigh Scholarship

Purpose: To assist a student studying at the Environmental Change Institute for an MSc degree in Environmental Change and Management
Eligibility: Open to all applicants to the MSc in Environmental Change and Management. Please see website for more details, including how to apply
Level of Study: Postgraduate
Type: Scholarship
Value: £4,000
Length of Study: 1 year
Frequency: Annual
Country of Study: United Kingdom
Application Procedure: Any person wishing to be considered for this award should follow the application procedure for admission to the degree of Master of Science in Environmental Change and Management at Oxford University, nominating Colleges of preference as detailed in the application procedure. They must, additionally, complete a separate application form which will be made available to them once in receipt of a place on the MSc
No. of awards offered: 1
Closing Date: May

Oriental Studies: Sasakawa Fund

Eligibility: Open to all graduate applicants in Oriental Studies, or United Kingdom applicants whose work will require some time spent in Japan
Level of Study: Postgraduate, Research
Type: Award
Value: £5,000 per year
Length of Study: Period of fee liability
Country of Study: United Kingdom
Application Procedure: An application form is available at www.orinst.ox.ac.uk/general/grants/sasakawa_fund.html
Closing Date: 18 January
Additional Information: www.nissan.ox.ac.uk/sasakawa-fund-travel-grant-at-the-faculty-of-oriental-studies

For further information contact:

Tel: (44) 1865 278 225
Fax: (44) 1865 278 190
Email: trustfunds@orinst.ox.ac.uk

Other Studentships in Earth Sciences

Eligibility: Applicants must have 2.1 degree or higher. United Kingdom students are eligible for full support, and a range of support is available for European Union and international students
Level of Study: Research
Type: Studentship
Value: University and college fees and maintenance allowance
Length of Study: Normally 3 years, which can be extended in some cases
Frequency: Dependent on funds available
Country of Study: United Kingdom
Application Procedure: Candidates are advised to apply directly to the department as advertised on the website
Closing Date: 20 January
Additional Information: The department occasionally has studentship funding associated with grants or industrial funding www.earth.ox.ac.uk/teaching/graduates/funding/

For further information contact:

Email: emmab@earth.ox.ac.uk

Oxford-Aidan Jenkins Graduate Scholarship

Eligibility: Open to applicants who are applying to any full-time course in the Faculty of English Language and Literature. Tenable at Merton College only. Please see website for more details
Type: Scholarship
Value: University fee, college fee, and full living expenses
Length of Study: Duration of fee liability
Study Establishment: Merton College
Country of Study: United Kingdom

Closing Date: 20 January
Additional Information: Please visit the website: www.ox.ac.uk/admissions/graduate/fees-and-funding/fees-funding-and-scholarship-search/scholarships-2#aidanjenkins www.european-funding-guide.eu/scholarship/13585-oxford-aidan-jenkins-graduate-scholarship

Oxford-Anderson Graduate Scholarship in History

Purpose: One full scholarship is available for applicants who are applying to any full-time graduate course in the Faculty of History within the range accepted by University College. To check whether the course you are planning to apply for is accepted by University College
Eligibility: The scholarship is only tenable at University College.
Type: Scholarship
Value: scholarship covers course fees and provides a grant for living costs
Length of Study: full duration of your fee liability for the agreed course
Frequency: Annual
Country of Study: United Kingdom
No. of awards offered: 1
Closing Date: April
Additional Information: www.ox.ac.uk/admissions/graduate/fees-and-funding/fees-funding-and-scholarship-search/scholarships-a-z-listing

For further information contact:

University of Oxford, University Offices, 15 Wellington Square, Oxford OX1 2JD, United Kingdom.

Tel: (44) 1865 270000
Fax: (44) 1865 270708

Oxford-Anderson Humanities Graduate Scholarship

Purpose: One full scholarship is available for applicants who are applying to any full-time Humanities graduate course within the range accepted by University College. To check whether the course you are planning to apply for is accepted by University College
Eligibility: The scholarship is only tenable at University College.
Type: Scholarship
Value: scholarship covers course fees and provides a grant for living costs.
Country of Study: Any country
No. of awards offered: 1
Closing Date: April
Additional Information: www.ox.ac.uk/admissions/graduate/fees-and-funding/fees-funding-and-scholarship-search/scholarships-a-z-listing

For further information contact:

University of Oxford, University Offices, 15 Wellington Square, Oxford OX1 2JD, United Kingdom.

Tel: (44) 1865 270000
Fax: (44) 1865 270708

Oxford-Angus McLeod Graduate Scholarship

Purpose: The Oxford-Angus McLeod Graduate Scholarship is available for any applicants who are applying to undertake any postgraduate Taught or Research courses offered by the Social Sciences Division for which St John's College normally accepts applications.
Eligibility: The scholarship is only tenable at St John's College
Type: Scholarship
Value: The scholarship covers course fees and a grant for living costs
Length of Study: the full duration of your fee liability for the agreed course
Frequency: Annual
Country of Study: United Kingdom
No. of awards offered: 1
Closing Date: April
Additional Information: www.sjc.ox.ac.uk/study/graduate/graduate-scholarships/

For further information contact:

University of Oxford, University Offices, 15 Wellington Square, Oxford OX1 2JD, United Kingdom.

Tel: (44) 1865 270000
Fax: (44) 1865 270708

Oxford-Ashton Graduate Scholarship in Engineering

Purpose: The scholarship is jointly funded by the University and by anonymous Old Members (alumni) of University College, in memory of Mrs J P Ashton.
Eligibility: The scholarship is only tenable at University College
Type: Scholarship

Value: scholarship covers course fees and provides a grant for living costs
Length of Study: full duration of your fee liability for the agreed course.
Frequency: Annual
Country of Study: United Kingdom
No. of awards offered: 2
Closing Date: April
Additional Information: www.ox.ac.uk/admissions/graduate/fees-and-funding/fees-funding-and-scholarship-search/scholarships-a-z-listing

For further information contact:

University of Oxford, University Offices, 15 Wellington Square, Oxford OX1 2JD, United Kingdom.

Tel: (44) 1865 270000
Fax: (44) 1865 270708

Oxford-Bellhouse Graduate Scholarship

Eligibility: Open to applicants who are ordinarily resident in the EEA or Switzerland and who are applying to the full-time DPhil in Engineering Sciences, specialising in Biomedical Engineering. The scholarship is only tenable at Magdalen College. Please see website for more details
Level of Study: Doctorate
Type: Scholarship
Value: a grant of at least £17,668 for living expenses
Length of Study: Period of fee liability
Study Establishment: Magdalen College
Country of Study: United Kingdom
Closing Date: January
Additional Information: www.magd.ox.ac.uk/considering-magdalen/graduate-study/scholarships-and-awards/#collapse10030

For further information contact:

Email: accommodation@linacre.ox.ac.uk

Oxford-Berman Graduate Scholarship

Purpose: This scholarship has been funded by a group of Old Members (alumni) in recognition of Dr Robert 'Bobby' Berman's valuable and much appreciated contribution to life at University College over more than three decades.
Eligibility: The scholarship is only tenable at University College.
Type: Scholarship
Value: The scholarship covers course fees and provides a grant for living costs.
Length of Study: full duration of your fee liability for the agreed course.
Frequency: Annual
Country of Study: United Kingdom
No. of awards offered: 1
Closing Date: April
Additional Information: www.ox.ac.uk/admissions/graduate/fees-and-funding/fees-funding-and-scholarship-search/scholarships-a-z-listing

For further information contact:

University of Oxford, University Offices, 15 Wellington Square, Oxford OX1 2JD, United Kingdom.

Tel: (44) 1865 270000
Fax: (44) 1865 270708

Oxford-Bob Thomas Graduate Scholarship in Chemistry

Purpose: Established in 2016 at University College, to assist eligible postgraduate students admitted to the Department of Chemistry, the scholarship is named in honour of Dr Robert K. Thomas and co-funded by the Department of Chemistry as well as University College Old Members. Dr Thomas was Aldrichian Praelector in Physical Chemistry and a Fellow of University College for three decades (1978-2008).
Eligibility: The scholarship is only tenable at University College.
Type: Scholarship
Value: The scholarship covers course fees and provides a grant for living costs.
Length of Study: full duration of your fee liability for the agreed course
Frequency: Annual
Country of Study: United Kingdom
No. of awards offered: 1
Closing Date: April
Additional Information: www.ox.ac.uk/admissions/graduate/fees-and-funding/fees-funding-and-scholarship-search/scholarships-a-z-listing

For further information contact:

University of Oxford, University Offices, 15 Wellington Square, Oxford OX1 2JD, United Kingdom.

Tel: (44) 1865 270000
Fax: (44) 1865 270708

Oxford-Bounden Graduate Scholarship

Purpose: The Oxford-Bounden Graduate Scholarship is available for applicants who are ordinarily resident in the United Kingdom or Republic of Ireland who are applying to any Humanities Division courses within the range accepted by Jesus College.
Eligibility: The scholarship is only tenable at Jesus College.
Type: Scholarship
Value: The scholarship covers course fees and a grant for living costs.
Frequency: Annual
Country of Study: United Kingdom
Closing Date: April
Additional Information: www.jesus.ox.ac.uk/study-here/graduate-studies/admissions/finance/oxford-bounden-graduate-scholarship/

For further information contact:

University of Oxford, University Offices, 15 Wellington Square, Oxford OX1 2JD, United Kingdom.

Tel: (44) 1865 270000
Fax: (44) 1865 270708

Oxford-Brunsfield Association of Southeast Asian Nations (ASEAN) Human Rights Graduate Scholarships

Eligibility: The Oxford-Brunsfield ASEAN Human Rights Scholarship is available for applicants who are nationals of and ordinarily resident in Brunei Darussalam, Cambodia, Indonesia, Laos, Malaysia, Myanmar (Burma), Philippines, Singapore, Thailand or Vietnam and are applying to the part-time MSt in International Human Rights Law.
Level of Study: Postgraduate
Type: Scholarship
Value: The scholarship covers course fees and a study support grant (towards your travel expenses to Oxford and other sundry expenses).
Length of Study: full duration of your fee liability for the agreed course.
Country of Study: United Kingdom
Closing Date: April
Additional Information: www.ox.ac.uk/admissions/graduate/fees-and-funding/fees-funding-and-scholarship-search/scholarships-a-z-listing?wssl=1

For further information contact:

Email: iphumrts@conted.ox.ac.uk

Oxford-C S Wu Graduate Scholarship

Purpose: The Oxford-C S Wu Graduate Scholarship is available for applicants who are applying for a full-time DPhil within Particle Physics.
Eligibility: you must be ordinarily resident in the United Kingdom or Republic of Ireland.
Type: Scholarship
Value: The scholarship covers course fees and a grant for living costs.
Country of Study: Any country
Closing Date: April
Additional Information: www.ox.ac.uk/admissions/graduate/fees-and-funding/fees-funding-and-scholarship-search/scholarships-a-z-listing

For further information contact:

University of Oxford, University Offices, 15 Wellington Square, Oxford OX1 2JD, United Kingdom.

Tel: (44) 1865 270000
Fax: (44) 1865 270708

Oxford-Calleva Scholarship

Purpose: It is intended to make available three scholarships for entry in October to applicants ordinarily resident in the European Union applying to the DPhil History (including History of Science and Medicine, and Economic and Social History), the DPhil Experimental Psychology, or the DPhil Anthropology
Eligibility: Students ordinarily resident in the EU
Level of Study: Doctorate
Type: Scholarship
Value: 100% of course fees, and a grant for living costs of at least £17,668 per annum
Frequency: Annual
Country of Study: United Kingdom
Application Procedure: The scholarship is only tenable at Linacre College. All eligible applicants will be considered for this scholarship, regardless of which college (if any) you state as your preference on the graduate application form
Closing Date: 1 January
Funding: Private
Additional Information: www.magd.ox.ac.uk/the-oxford-calleva-scholarship/

For further information contact:

Email: graduate.enquiries@magd.ox.ac.uk

U

Oxford-Carolyn and Franco Gianturco Graduate Scholarship

Purpose: The scholarship have been made possible by Carolyn Gianturco, who completed her DPhil in Musicology at the University of Oxford under the guidance of Sir Jack Westrup in 1970. Together with her husband Franco Gianturco, they have generously endowed this scholarship at Linacre College to advance research in the music field.
Eligibility: The scholarship is only tenable at Linacre College.
Level of Study: Graduate
Type: Scholarship
Value: The scholarship covers course fees and a grant for living costs.
Length of Study: 4 years
Frequency: Annual
Country of Study: United Kingdom
Closing Date: April
Additional Information: www.ox.ac.uk/admissions/graduate/fees-and-funding/fees-funding-and-scholarship-search/scholarships-a-z-listing

For further information contact:

University of Oxford, University Offices, 15 Wellington Square, Oxford OX1 2JD, United Kingdom.

Tel: (44) 1865 270000
Fax: (44) 1865 270708

Oxford-Cecil Lubbock Memorial Graduate Scholarship

Purpose: The Oxford-Cecil Lubbock Graduate Scholarship is available for applicants who are applying to the DPhil English (with preference for either Medieval or Victorian areas of research).
Eligibility: The scholarship is only tenable at Trinity College.
Level of Study: Doctorate, Postgraduate, Research
Type: Scholarship
Value: The scholarship covers course fees at the Home rate and a grant for living costs
Frequency: Annual
Country of Study: United Kingdom
No. of awards offered: 1
Closing Date: 31 August
Additional Information: www.ox.ac.uk/admissions/graduate/fees-and-funding/fees-funding-and-scholarship-search/scholarships-a-z-listing

For further information contact:

University of Oxford, University Offices, 15 Wellington Square, Oxford OX1 2JD, United Kingdom.

Tel: (44) 1865 270000
Fax: (44) 1865 270708

Oxford Centre for Islamic Studies (OCIS) Graduate Scholarships

Purpose: These scholarships have been established by the Oxford Centre for Islamic Studies to allow graduates to pursue study of benefit to the Muslim world.
Eligibility: 1. You must be applying to start a new full-time master's or DPhil course at Oxford. 2. You must be either: a.ordinarily resident in the United Kingdom and from a Muslim community (with preference given to those from a financially disadvantaged household), or b.a national of, and ordinarily resident in, Afghanistan, Albania, Algeria, Azerbaijan, Bahrain, Bangladesh, Benin, Brunei Darussalam, Burkina Faso, Cameroon, Chad, Comoros, Cote d'Ivoire, Djibouti, Egypt, Gabon, Gambia, Guinea, Guyana, India, Indonesia, Iran, Iraq, Jordan, Kazakhstan, Kuwait, Kyrgyzstan, Lebanon, Libya, Malaysia, Maldives, Mali, Mauritania, Morocco, Mozambique, Niger, Nigeria, Oman, Pakistan, Palestine, Qatar, Saudi Arabia, Senegal, Sierra Leone, Somalia, Sudan, Suriname, Syrian Arab Republic, Tajikistan, Togo, Tunisia, Turkey, Turkmenistan, Uganda, United Arab Emirates, Uzbekistan, Yemen. 3. You should be intending to return to your country of ordinary residence once your course is completed. 4. Scholarships will be awarded on the basis of academic merit. 5. You should be intending to undertake study in a field derived from or of relevance to the Islamic tradition, or which is of relevance and/or benefit to the Muslim world.
Level of Study: Doctorate, Research
Type: Scholarship
Value: 100% of course fees and a grant for living costs (at least £17,668)
Length of Study: Period of fee liability
Frequency: Annual
Country of Study: United Kingdom
Application Procedure: All
No. of awards offered: 5
Closing Date: December
Additional Information: www.ox.ac.uk/admissions/graduate/fees-and-funding/fees-funding-and-scholarship-search/oxford-centre-islamic-studies-ocis-scholarships

Oxford-Chellgren Graduate Scholarships

Purpose: The scholarship is jointly funded by the University and by Paul Chellgren, who studied at University College in 1966. Paul Chellgren is a visionary Old Member (alumnus) and an Honorary Fellow of University College.
Eligibility: The scholarship is only tenable at University College.
Type: Scholarship
Value: covers course fees and provides a grant for living costs
Length of Study: Full duration of your fee liability for the agreed course
Frequency: Annual
Country of Study: United Kingdom
No. of awards offered: 2
Closing Date: April
Additional Information: www.ox.ac.uk/admissions/graduate/fees-and-funding/fees-funding-and-scholarship-search/scholarships-a-z-listing

For further information contact:

University of Oxford, University Offices, 15 Wellington Square, Oxford OX1 2JD, United Kingdom.

Tel: (44) 1865 270000
Fax: (44) 1865 270708

Oxford-Chelly Halsey Graduate Scholarship

Purpose: The scholarship is jointly funded by the University and by generous donors to Nuffield College, who contributed funds to establish a scholarship in memory of Professor Albert Henry Halsey, best known as Chelly, an eminent sociologist and a Fellow of Nuffield College for over fifty years.
Eligibility: The scholarship is only tenable at Nuffield College.
Type: Scholarship
Value: The scholarship covers course fees and a grant for living costs.
Length of Study: full duration of your fee liability for the agreed course
Frequency: Annual
Country of Study: United Kingdom
Closing Date: May
Additional Information: www.ox.ac.uk/admissions/graduate/fees-and-funding/fees-funding-and-scholarship-search/scholarships-a-z-listing

For further information contact:

University of Oxford, University Offices, 15 Wellington Square, Oxford OX1 2JD, United Kingdom.

Tel: (44) 1865 270000
Fax: (44) 1865 270708

Oxford-Clayton Graduate Scholarship

Purpose: The scholarship is jointly funded by the University and Gerald 'David' Clayton, who came up to Merton in 1955 to read Modern History. He was a passionate musician, who was a great supporter of the Choral Foundation at Merton in his lifetime, and was a frequent visitor to College throughout his life. The Oxford-Clayton Graduate Scholarship was set up using part of a generous legacy that David left to Merton after he sadly passed away in 2014.
Eligibility: The scholarship covers course fees and a grant for living costs.
Type: Scholarship
Value: The scholarship covers course fees and a grant for living costs.
Frequency: Annual
Country of Study: Any country
Closing Date: April
Additional Information: www.ox.ac.uk/admissions/graduate/fees-and-funding/fees-funding-and-scholarship-search/scholarships-a-z-listing

For further information contact:

University of Oxford, University Offices, 15 Wellington Square, Oxford OX1 2JD, United Kingdom.

Tel: (44) 1865 270000
Fax: (44) 1865 270708

Oxford-Creat Group Graduate Scholarships

Purpose: The scholarships have been jointly funded by the University and by the Creat Group of Beijing. The Creat Group is a leading investment company with a global portfolio and partnerships with leading financial institutions in the UK and Japan. The Creat Group intends that scholars will make a considerable contribution to the development of China's economy over the course of their lifetime.

Eligibility: scholarships are available for applicants who are ordinarily resident in the People's Republic of China
Type: Scholarship
Value: The scholarship covers course fees and a grant for living costs
Length of Study: full duration of your fee liability for the agreed course
Frequency: Annual
Country of Study: United Kingdom
Closing Date: April
Additional Information: www.ox.ac.uk/admissions/graduate/fees-and-funding/fees-funding-and-scholarship-search/scholarships-a-z-listing

For further information contact:

University of Oxford, University Offices, 15 Wellington Square, Oxford OX1 2JD, United Kingdom.

Tel: (44) 1865 270000
Fax: (44) 1865 270708

Oxford-David Jones Graduate Scholarship

Purpose: The Oxford-David Jones Graduate Scholarship is available for applicants who are ordinarily resident in the United Kingdom or Republic of Ireland who are applying to undertake any postgraduate Taught or Research courses offered by the History Faculty.
Eligibility: The scholarship is only tenable at Jesus College.
Type: Scholarship
Value: The scholarship covers course fees and a grant for living costs.
Frequency: Annual
Country of Study: United Kingdom
Application Procedure: There is no separate application for this studentship; you simply need to apply for your graduate course by the relevant January deadline.
Closing Date: January
Additional Information: www.jesus.ox.ac.uk/study-here/graduate-studies/admissions/finance/oxford-david-jones-scholarship/

For further information contact:

University of Oxford, University Offices, 15 Wellington Square, Oxford OX1 2JD, United Kingdom.

Tel: (44) 1865 270000
Fax: (44) 1865 270708

Oxford-DeepMind Graduate Scholarship (Computer Science)

Purpose: The Oxford-DeepMind Graduate Scholarships (Computer Science) are available for applicants to any full-time DPhil course within, or affiliated to, the Department of Computer Science. The scholarships have been made possible through the support of DeepMind, a world leader in artificial intelligence research.
Type: Scholarship
Value: covers course fees and a grant for living costs
Length of Study: full duration of your fee liability for the agreed course
Frequency: Annual
Country of Study: United Kingdom
Closing Date: April
Additional Information: www.ox.ac.uk/admissions/graduate/fees-and-funding/fees-funding-and-scholarship-search/scholarships-a-z-listing

For further information contact:

University of Oxford, University Offices, 15 Wellington Square, Oxford OX1 2JD, United Kingdom.

Tel: (44) 1865 270000
Fax: (44) 1865 270708

Oxford-E P Abraham Research Fund Graduate Scholarships

Eligibility: applicants who are applying to the full-time DPhil in Molecular Cell Biology in Health and Disease.
Type: Scholarship
Value: covers course fees and an annual grant for living costs of at least £17,609
Length of Study: 4 years
Frequency: Annual
Country of Study: United Kingdom
No. of awards offered: 3
Closing Date: February
Additional Information: www.ox.ac.uk/admissions/graduate/fees-and-funding/fees-funding-and-scholarship-search/scholarships-a-z-listing

For further information contact:

University of Oxford, University Offices, 15 Wellington Square, Oxford OX1 2JD, United Kingdom.

Tel: (44) 1865 270000
Fax: (44) 1865 270708

Oxford-EPA Cephalosporin Graduate Scholarship

Purpose: The Oxford-EPA Cephalosporin Graduate Scholarship is available for applicants who are applying for a course within the Interdisciplinary Bioscience (BBSRC DTP). The scholarship have been funded via grants from the EPA Cephalosporin Fund and the University of Oxford.
Eligibility: The scholarship is only tenable at Linacre College.
Level of Study: Postgraduate
Type: Scholarship
Value: Full course fees and a stipend for living expenses
Length of Study: 4 years
Frequency: Annual
Country of Study: United Kingdom
Application Procedure: Eligible students are automatically considered for this award.
Closing Date: April
Additional Information: www.linacre.ox.ac.uk/scholarships/oxford-%E2%80%93-epa-cephalosporin-graduate-scholarship

For further information contact:

University of Oxford, University Offices, 15 Wellington Square, Oxford OX1 2JD, United Kingdom.

Tel: (44) 1865 270000
Fax: (44) 1865 270708

Oxford-Feltham Graduate Scholarship

Purpose: In 2016 Magdalen College launched a fundraising appeal in order to create and financially support a scholarship for students studying the Bachelor of Civil Law (BCL), a world-renowned taught graduate course in law, designed to serve outstanding law students from common law backgrounds. The scholarship is named in memory of the late John Feltham, Tutorial Fellow in Law at the College from 1965-1992. The Oxford-Feltham Graduate Scholarship was created and 2020-21 was the first year that this scholarship has been awarded.
Eligibility: The scholarship is only tenable at Magdalen College.
Type: Scholarship
Value: The scholarship covers course fees and provides a grant for living costs.
Length of Study: full duration of your fee liability for the agreed course.
Frequency: Annual
Country of Study: United Kingdom
Closing Date: April
Additional Information: www.ox.ac.uk/admissions/graduate/fees-and-funding/fees-funding-and-scholarship-search/scholarships-a-z-listing

For further information contact:

University of Oxford, University Offices, 15 Wellington Square, Oxford OX1 2JD, United Kingdom.

Tel: (44) 1865 270000
Fax: (44) 1865 270708

Oxford-Finnis Graduate Scholarship in Law

Purpose: The Oxford-Finnis Graduate Scholarship in Law was established at University College to assist eligible students admitted to the Law Faculty, in particular those working towards the Bachelor of Civil Law. This was the first law scholarship to be offered by University College, was funded by John Finnis' former pupils and Univ lawyers, and is named in honour of the 50th anniversary of his own Fellowship at the College (2016-17).
Type: Scholarship
Value: Course fees Maintenance costs
Length of Study: 1 year
Frequency: Annual
Country of Study: United Kingdom
Application Procedure: The scholarship is only tenable at University College.
Closing Date: April
Additional Information: www.ox.ac.uk/admissions/graduate/fees-and-funding/fees-funding-and-scholarship-search/scholarships-a-z-listing

For further information contact:

University of Oxford, University Offices, 15 Wellington Square, Oxford OX1 2JD, United Kingdom.

Tel: (44) 1865 270000
Fax: (44) 1865 270708

Oxford-Hackney BCL Graduate Scholarship

Purpose: The Oxford-Hackney BCL Graduate Scholarship is available for applicants to the full-time Bachelor of Civil Law (BCL). The scholarships have been funded by the University and by a collection of Wadham College alumni, in honour of Jeffrey Hackney, the College's Fellow in Law from 1976-2008 and an extremely prominent and much-loved tutor.
Eligibility: The scholarship is only tenable at Wadham College.

Type: Scholarship
Value: covers course fees and a grant for living costs
Length of Study: full duration of your fee liability for the agreed course
Frequency: Annual
Country of Study: United Kingdom
Closing Date: June
Additional Information: www.ox.ac.uk/admissions/graduate/fees-and-funding/fees-funding-and-scholarship-search/scholarships-a-z-listing

For further information contact:

University of Oxford, University Offices, 15 Wellington Square, Oxford OX1 2JD, United Kingdom.

Tel: (44) 1865 270000
Fax: (44) 1865 270708

Oxford-Hoffmann Graduate Scholarships

Purpose: Fondation Hoffmann is a Swiss-based grant making institution supporting the emergence and expansion of concrete projects which address global problems in today's societies
Eligibility: Open to applicants who are applying to any full or part-time course within the Medical Science Division. Tenable at Jesus College only
Level of Study: Graduate
Type: Scholarship
Value: covers course fees and a grant for living costs
Length of Study: full duration of your fee liability for the agreed course
Frequency: Annual
Study Establishment: Jesus College
Country of Study: United Kingdom
Closing Date: April
Additional Information: www.ox.ac.uk/admissions/graduate/fees-and-funding/fees-funding-and-scholarship-search/scholarships-a-z-listing?wssl=1

Oxford-Hoffmann Graduate Scholarships in Medical Sciences

Purpose: The Oxford-Hoffmann Graduate Scholarships in Medical Sciences are available for any applicants who are applying to study within the Medical Sciences Division. The scholarships have been made possible through the support of André Hoffmann, who is an entrepreneur, investor and philanthropist. Mr Hoffmann studied economics at St Gallen University and holds an MBA from INSEAD.
Eligibility: The scholarship is only tenable at Jesus College.
Type: Scholarship
Value: covers course fees and a grant for living costs
Length of Study: full duration of your fee liability for the agreed course
Frequency: Annual
Country of Study: Any country
Closing Date: April
Additional Information: www.ox.ac.uk/admissions/graduate/fees-and-funding/fees-funding-and-scholarship-search/scholarships-a-z-listing

For further information contact:

University of Oxford, University Offices, 15 Wellington Square, Oxford OX1 2JD, United Kingdom.

Tel: (44) 1865 270000
Fax: (44) 1865 270708

Oxford-ID Travel Group Foundation Bonham-Carter Graduate Scholarship

Purpose: The scholarship is available to applicants who are applying to a full-time or part-time graduate master's. Preference should be given to courses in the Social Sciences Division (except the Saïd Business School), within the range accepted by Christ Church.
Eligibility: The scholarship is only tenable at Christ Church. All eligible applicants will be considered for this scholarship, regardless of which college (if any) you state as your preference on the graduate application form. However, successful applicants will be transferred to Christ Church in order to take up the scholarship.
Type: Scholarship
Value: The scholarship covers course fees and a grant for living costs £14,777
Frequency: Annual
Country of Study: United Kingdom
Application Procedure: There is no separate application process for this scholarship: to be considered, submit your application for graduate study by the relevant January deadline for your course
Closing Date: January
Additional Information: idtravelfoundation.org/oxford-scholarship

For further information contact:

University of Oxford, University Offices, 15 Wellington Square, Oxford OX1 2JD, United Kingdom.

Tel: (44) 1865 270000
Fax: (44) 1865 270708

Oxford-Indira Gandhi Graduate Scholarships

Purpose: Three full scholarships are available for applicants who are ordinarily resident in India. You must be applying for one of the eligible full-time or part-time master's courses listed below or for a DPhil course with proposed research in the eligible areas of study.
Eligibility: The scholarship is only tenable at Somerville College.
Type: Scholarship
Value: course fees and a grant for living costs
Length of Study: full duration of your fee liability for the agreed course
Frequency: Annual
Country of Study: United Kingdom
No. of awards offered: 2
Closing Date: May
Additional Information: www.ox.ac.uk/admissions/graduate/fees-and-funding/fees-funding-and-scholarship-search/scholarships-a-z-listing

For further information contact:

University of Oxford, University Offices, 15 Wellington Square, Oxford OX1 2JD, United Kingdom.

Tel: (44) 1865 270000
Fax: (44) 1865 270708

Oxford-Intesa Sanpaolo Graduate Scholarship

Purpose: Intesa Sanpaolo is one of Italy's leading banks, with a proud record of corporate philanthropy across a range of global priorities, including educational programmes aimed at driving social change.
Eligibility: 1. Female candidates. 2. Tenable at Green Templeton College only. All eligible applicants will be considered for the scholarship, regardless of which college (if any) you state on your offer acceptance form. However, successful applicants will be transferred to Green Templeton College to take up the scholarship.
Type: Scholarship
Value: £17,668
Length of Study: 5 Years
Frequency: Annual
Country of Study: United Kingdom
Application Procedure: No additional application is needed. We will use the details you supply in your MBA application form. A complete MBA application must be submitted by the deadline.
No. of awards offered: 7
Closing Date: 4 January
Additional Information: www.sbs.ox.ac.uk/oxford-experience/scholarships-and-funding/oxford-intesa-sanpaolo-mba-graduate-scholarship

For further information contact:

University of Oxford, University Offices, 15 Wellington Square, Oxford OX1 2JD, United Kingdom.

Tel: (44) 1865 270000
Fax: (44) 1865 270708

Oxford – Intesa Sanpaolo MBA Graduate Scholarships

Purpose: This scholarship is funded by Intesa Sanpaolo in partnership with Oxford University and Green Templeton College. The award is only tenable at Green Templeton College. There is no additional application process for this scholarship; we will use the details provided in your MBA application form to determine eligibility.
Eligibility: 1. Open to female candidates. 2. Tenable at Green Templeton College only. All eligible applicants will be considered for the scholarship, regardless of which college (if any) you state on your offer acceptance form. Selection is carried out by Green Templeton College, in collaboration with Saïd Business School.
Type: Scholarship
Value: £17,668.
Length of Study: 5 years
Country of Study: United Kingdom
Application Procedure: No additional application is needed. We will use the details you supply in your MBA application form. A complete MBA application must be submitted by the deadline.
No. of awards offered: 7
Closing Date: 4 January
Additional Information: www.sbs.ox.ac.uk/oxford-experience/scholarships-and-funding/oxford-intesa-sanpaolo-mba-graduate-scholarship

Oxford-Jeffrey Cheah Graduate Scholarship

Purpose: The scholarship is jointly funded by the University and Tan Sri Dato' Seri Dr Jeffrey Cheah. Tan Sri Jeffrey is the founder and chairman of the Sunway Group, founding trustee of the Jeffrey Cheah Foundation, and is an Honorary Fellow of Brasenose College.
Eligibility: The scholarship is only tenable at Brasenose College.

U

Type: Scholarship
Value: The scholarship covers course fees and provides a grant for living costs.
Frequency: Annual
Country of Study: Any country
No. of awards offered: 1
Closing Date: April
Additional Information: www.ox.ac.uk/admissions/graduate/fees-and-funding/fees-funding-and-scholarship-search/scholarships-a-z-listing

For further information contact:

University of Oxford, University Offices, 15 Wellington Square, Oxford OX1 2JD, United Kingdom.

Tel: (44) 1865 270000
Fax: (44) 1865 270708

Oxford-Kaifeng Graduate Scholarship

Purpose: The Oxford-Kaifeng Graduate scholarships are available for applicants who are ordinarily resident and nationals of the People's Republic of China (excluding Hong Kong and Macau SAR). Preference will be given to those applying to courses in the order listed History of Art; other Humanities Division courses; Social Science Division courses. Candidates must also demonstrate potential leadership qualities.
Eligibility: Applicants who are ordinarily resident and nationals of the People's Republic of China (excluding Hong Kong and Macau SAR).
Type: Scholarship
Value: The scholarship covers course fees and a grant for living costs.
Length of Study: ull duration of your fee liability for the agreed course.
Country of Study: United Kingdom
Closing Date: April
Additional Information: www.ox.ac.uk/admissions/graduate/fees-and-funding/fees-funding-and-scholarship-search/scholarships-a-z-listing

For further information contact:

University of Oxford, University Offices, 15 Wellington Square, Oxford OX1 2JD, United Kingdom.

Tel: (44) 1865 270000
Fax: (44) 1865 270708

Oxford-Ko Cheuk Hung Graduate Scholarship

Purpose: The Oxford-Ko Cheuk Hung Graduate Scholarship is available for applicants who are ordinarily resident in UK and who are applying to the MSt Traditional China.
Eligibility: The scholarship is only tenable at St Cross College. All eligible applicants will be considered for this scholarship, regardless of which college (if any) you state as your preference on the graduate application form. However, successful applicants will be transferred to St Cross College in order to take up the scholarship.
Type: Scholarship
Value: covers course fee and a grant for living costs
Length of Study: full duration of your fee liability for the agreed course
Country of Study: United Kingdom
Closing Date: March
Additional Information: www.ox.ac.uk/admissions/graduate/fees-and-funding/fees-funding-and-scholarship-search/scholarships-a-z-listing

For further information contact:

University of Oxford, University Offices, 15 Wellington Square, Oxford OX1 2JD, United Kingdom.

Tel: (44) 1865 270000
Fax: (44) 1865 270708

Oxford-Leon E and Iris L Beghian Graduate Scholarships

Purpose: The scholarship is jointly funded by the University and by a donation from the estate of Leon and Iris Beghian. Leon Beghian came to Magdalen College in 1938 to study Physics. After scientific research during the war, he graduated with a first-class degree in 1947, and then undertook a DPhil at Oxford before progressing to a distinguished career in Physics in the USA.
Eligibility: The scholarship is only tenable at Magdalen College. You must have been ordinarily resident in the UK for at least five years prior to the start of your course.
Type: Scholarship
Value: covers course fees and provides a grant for living costs
Length of Study: full duration of your fee liability for the agreed course
Frequency: Annual
Country of Study: United Kingdom
No. of awards offered: 2
Closing Date: April

Additional Information: www.ox.ac.uk/admissions/graduate/fees-and-funding/fees-funding-and-scholarship-search/scholarships-a-z-listing

For further information contact:

University of Oxford, University Offices, 15 Wellington Square, Oxford OX1 2JD, United Kingdom.

Tel: (44) 1865 270000
Fax: (44) 1865 270708

Oxford-Louis Curran Graduate Scholarship

Purpose: The Oxford-Louis Curran Graduate Scholarship is available for applicants who are applying for a course within the Faculty of Music (with a preference for the DPhil in Music). The scholarship was established in memory of the late Professor Louis Curran, who read Musicology at Linacre College and left a generous bequest to Linacre College to support the study of music.
Eligibility: The scholarship is only tenable at Linacre College.
Type: Scholarship
Value: The scholarship covers course fees and a grant for living costs.
Country of Study: Any country
Closing Date: April
Additional Information: www.ox.ac.uk/admissions/graduate/fees-and-funding/fees-funding-and-scholarship-search/scholarships-a-z-listing

For further information contact:

University of Oxford, University Offices, 15 Wellington Square, Oxford OX1 2JD, United Kingdom.

Tel: (44) 1865 270000
Fax: (44) 1865 270708

Oxford-Mary Jane Grefenstette Graduate Scholarship

Eligibility: Open to all applicants applying for a DPhil in Computer Science or Philosophy, specialising in the cross-over between the subjects. Tenable at Hertford College only. Please see website for more details
Level of Study: Postgraduate
Type: Scholarship
Value: £14,057
Length of Study: Period of fee liability
Frequency: Annual
Study Establishment: Hertford
Country of Study: United Kingdom
Application Procedure: For more information, please check the website www.ox.ac.uk/admissions/graduate/fees-and-funding/fees-funding-and-scholarship-search/scholarships-3#grefenstette
Closing Date: 22 January
Funding: Trusts

For further information contact:

Email: enquiries@cs.ox.ac.uk

Oxford-Murray Graduate Scholarship

Purpose: One full scholarship is available for applicants who are applying to one of the following full-time courses MSt in Greek and/or Latin Languages and Literature, MPhil in Greek and/or Latin Languages and Literature, MSt in Greek and/or Roman History, MPhil in Greek and/or Roman History.
Eligibility: The scholarship is only tenable at Wadham College.
Type: Scholarship
Value: costs of the course fees for the normal period of fee liability of the award-holder's programme
Frequency: Annual
Country of Study: United Kingdom
No. of awards offered: 1
Closing Date: 1 May
Additional Information: www.ox.ac.uk/admissions/graduate/fees-and-funding/fees-funding-and-scholarship-search/scholarships-a-z-listing

For further information contact:

University of Oxford, University Offices, 15 Wellington Square, Oxford OX1 2JD, United Kingdom.

Tel: (44) 1865 270000
Fax: (44) 1865 270708

Oxford-Nicholas Bratt Graduate Scholarship

Purpose: The Oxford-Nicholas Bratt Graduate Scholarship is available for any applicants who are applying to undertake any postgraduate Taught or Research courses offered by the Mathematical, Physical and Life Sciences (MPLS) Division (except for those offered by the Mathematical Institute), in which St John's College accepts applications.
Eligibility: Unless otherwise stated, you will be considered automatically for these scholarships if: 1. You are applying to start a new graduate course; 2. You submit your course

application by the relevant January admissions deadline; 3. You are subsequently offered a place after consideration of applications received by the deadline; 4. Your application is not placed on a waiting list or held back after the January admissions deadline to be re-evaluated against applications received by the March admissions deadline; and 5. You meet the eligibility criteria.
Type: Scholarship
Value: The scholarship covers course fees and a grant for living costs.
Frequency: Annual
Country of Study: United Kingdom
Closing Date: 8 January
Additional Information: www.ox.ac.uk/admissions/graduate/fees-and-funding/fees-funding-and-scholarship-search/scholarships-a-z-listing

For further information contact:

University of Oxford, University Offices, 15 Wellington Square, Oxford OX1 2JD, United Kingdom.

Tel: (44) 1865 270000
Fax: (44) 1865 270708

Oxford-Nizami Ganjavi Graduate Scholarships

Purpose: The University of Oxford is home to a dedicated centre for the study of Azerbaijan, the Caucasus and Central Asia, thanks to generous philanthropic support from the British Foundation for the Study of Azerbaijan and the Caucasus (BFSAC)
Eligibility: Open to applicants applying for any full or part-time DPhil or Master's course offered by the Humanities or Social Sciences Division where the course content relates to the study of the history, languages and cultures of Azerbaijan, the Caucasus and Central Asia. Please see the website for further details, including how to apply
Level of Study: Graduate
Type: Scholarship
Frequency: Annual
Study Establishment: covers course fees and a grant for living costs
Country of Study: United Kingdom
Closing Date: April
Funding: Private
Contributor: full duration of your fee liability for the agreed course
Additional Information: www.scholarshipdesk.com/oxford-mitsui-co-europe-plc-full-graduate-scholarships-uk/

For further information contact:

Tel: (44) 1865 270 000
Fax: (44) 1865 270 708

Oxford-Oak Foundation Clinical Medicine

Eligibility: 1. The candidates applying for Oxford-Oak Foundation Clinical Medicine, should be residents of Nepal, Zimbabwe, Kenya or Vietnam. 2. The scholarship is jointly funded by the University f Oxford and the Oak Foundation to make an impact on infectious disease research around the world. 3. Open to residents of Nepal, Zimbabwe, Kenya or Vietnam.
Level of Study: Doctorate
Type: Scholarship
Value: £14,553 towards college fees, course fees, and living costs
Country of Study: United Kingdom
Closing Date: 1 May
Additional Information: www.country.scholarshipcare.com/oxford-oak-foundation-clinical-medicine/

Oxford-Oxford Thai Foundation Graduate Scholarship

Purpose: The scholarship is jointly funded by the University and The Oxford Thai Foundation. The Oxford Thai Foundation is a scholarship programme to help promising young professionals from Thailand in the broader field of public policy to pursue advanced degrees at the University of Oxford. The programme wishes to create a strong network of future thinkers and leaders, built on mutual respect and trust developed during their time at Oxford, as well as through activities organised by the Foundation upon their return to Thailand. The goal is a more cohesive and equitable society, built on an inclusive public policy development platform.
Eligibility: Scholarship is available for applicants who are ordinarily resident in Thailand and intending to return there after graduation.
Type: Scholarship
Value: covers course fee and a grant for living costs.
Length of Study: full duration of your fee liability for the agreed course
Frequency: Annual
Country of Study: United Kingdom
Closing Date: May
Additional Information: www.ox.ac.uk/admissions/graduate/fees-and-funding/fees-funding-and-scholarship-search/scholarships-a-z-listing

For further information contact:

University of Oxford, University Offices, 15 Wellington Square, Oxford OX1 2JD, United Kingdom.

Tel: (44) 1865 270000
Fax: (44) 1865 270708

Oxford-Particle Physics Graduate Scholarship

Purpose: The scholarship has been made possible through the support of an anonymous donor, with the aim of supporting an outstanding thinker of tomorrow undertaking research in the field of experimental particle physics.
Eligibility: Open to applicants who are applying to the full-time DPhil Particle Physics course
Level of Study: Doctorate
Type: Scholarship
Value: University fee, college fee, and full living expenses
Length of Study: Duration of fee liability
Country of Study: United Kingdom
Closing Date: 1 March
Additional Information: Please visit the website: www.ox.ac.uk/admissions/graduate/fees-and-funding/fees-funding-and-scholarship-search/scholarships-3#particlephysics www.ox.ac.uk/admissions/graduate/courses/dphil-particle-physics?wssl=1

For further information contact:

Email: contact@physics.ox.ac.uk

Oxford-Patrick Duncan Graduate Scholarships

Purpose: The scholarship is jointly funded by the University, St Antony's College and the family of Patrick Duncan (1918-67), who was a South African political activist with a particular interest in sustainable development.
Eligibility: You will be considered automatically for these scholarships if: 1. You are applying to start a new graduate course; 2. You submit your course application by the relevant January admissions deadline; 3. You are subsequently offered a place after consideration of applications received by the deadline; 4. Your application is not placed on a waiting list or held back after the January admissions deadline to be re-evaluated against applications received by the March admissions deadline.
Level of Study: Graduate
Type: Scholarship
Value: The scholarship covers course fees and a grant for living costs.
Length of Study: Full duration of your fee liability for the agreed course.
Frequency: Annual
Country of Study: United Kingdom
No. of awards offered: 1
Closing Date: January
Additional Information: www.ox.ac.uk/admissions/graduate/fees-and-funding/fees-funding-and-scholarship-search/scholarships-a-z-listing

For further information contact:

University of Oxford, University Offices, 15 Wellington Square, Oxford OX1 2JD, United Kingdom.

Tel: (44) 1865 270000
Fax: (44) 1865 270708

Oxford-Percival Stanion Graduate Scholarship in Biochemistry

Eligibility: Open to applicants who are applying to the DPhil Biochemistry or MSc by Research Biochemistry. Tenable at Pembroke College only. Please see the website for more details
Level of Study: Doctorate, Postgraduate
Type: Scholarship
Value: University fee, college fee, and a grant for living costs
Length of Study: Period of fee liability
Study Establishment: Pembroke College
Country of Study: United Kingdom
Closing Date: 6 January
Additional Information: Please visit the website: www.ox.ac.uk/admissions/graduate/fees-and-funding/fees-funding-and-scholarship-search/scholarships-3#percivalstanion www.pmb.ox.ac.uk/oxford-percival-stanion-graduate-stories

For further information contact:

St Aldate's, Oxford OX1 1DW, United Kingdom.

Tel: (44) 1865 276444
Fax: (44) 1865 276418
Email: ioannis.vakonakis@bioch.ox.ac.uk

U

Oxford-Pershing Square Graduate Scholarships

Purpose: Established in 2014, the Pershing Square Scholarships provide up to six full awards covering both the Master's and the MBA degrees. Scholars can pursue any of the partnering Master's degrees and combine it with our MBA.

Eligibility: You will be considered in order of priority for the scholarship: 1. New applicants to the Oxford 1+1 MBA programme 2. You must be admitted to a 1+1 MBA partnering programme and to the MBA prior to the selection process (waitlisted or re-evaluated applicants will not be considered) 3. If you apply to any full-time one-year Master's course that is not currently part of the official list of 1+1 MBA partnering programmes, and to the MBA (as a separate application)
Level of Study: Masters Degree
Type: Scholarship
Value: £17,668 per year
Length of Study: 2 years
Country of Study: United Kingdom
No. of awards offered: 6
Closing Date: 4 January
Additional Information: www.sbs.ox.ac.uk/oxford-experience/scholarships-and-funding/oxford-pershing-square-graduate-scholarships

For further information contact:

University of Oxford, University Offices, 15 Wellington Square, Oxford OX1 2JD, United Kingdom.

Tel: (44) 1865 270000
Fax: (44) 1865 270708

Oxford-Qatar-Thatcher Graduate Scholarships

Purpose: The scholarship is jointly funded by the University and the Thatcher Development Programme at Somerville College. The late Lady Thatcher studied Chemistry at Somerville College Oxford from 1943 to 1946 and received bursary and scholarship support from the College.
Eligibility: The scholarship is only tenable at Somerville College. Countries Algeria, Bahrain, Egypt, Iraq, Jordan, Kuwait, Lebanon, Libya, Morocco, Oman, Palestine, Qatar, Saudi Arabia, Sudan, Syria, Tunisia, United Arab Emirates, Yemen.
Type: Scholarship
Value: course fees and a grant for living costs
Length of Study: full duration of your fee liability for the agreed course
Frequency: Annual
Country of Study: United Kingdom
Closing Date: April
Additional Information: www.ox.ac.uk/admissions/graduate/fees-and-funding/fees-funding-and-scholarship-search/scholarships-a-z-listing, https://www.some.ox.ac.uk/funding-and-opportunities/graduate-scholarships/the-oxford-qatar-thatcher-graduate-scholarships/

For further information contact:

University of Oxford, University Offices, 15 Wellington Square, Oxford OX1 2JD, United Kingdom.

Tel: (44) 1865 270000
Fax: (44) 1865 270708

Oxford-Radcliffe Graduate Scholarships

Purpose: The scholarships are unique to University College, supported by an historic £10m gift from a group of the College's Old Members, the largest single gift received by the college in modern times.
Type: Scholarship
Value: Covers course fees and provides a grant for living costs
Length of Study: Full duration of your fee liability for the agreed course.
Frequency: Annual
Country of Study: United Kingdom
No. of awards offered: 13
Closing Date: April
Additional Information: www.ox.ac.uk/admissions/graduate/fees-and-funding/fees-funding-and-scholarship-search/scholarships-a-z-listing

For further information contact:

University of Oxford, University Offices, 15 Wellington Square, Oxford OX1 2JD, United Kingdom.

Tel: (44) 1865 270000
Fax: (44) 1865 270708

Oxford Refugee Scholarship

Purpose: The Oxford Refugee Scholarship is available for applicants applying to any one year full-time master's course, or two-year part-time master's course, at Oxford.
Eligibility: Hold an offer to commence a master's degree at the University of Oxford in 2024/25 for a one-year full-time course or two-year part-time course. Have been displaced within, or beyond, their home country due to conflict or violation of human rights, such as persecution. Further details will be published at the start of the application process for this scholarship. Face barriers to progressing their education and have limitations on the financial support for their university studies. Have not previously completed a degree at the same level (master's) for which they are making an application.
Type: Scholarship

Value: covers course fees up to a total of £40,000 and provides a grant for living costs
Length of Study: 1 to 2 years
Frequency: Annual
Country of Study: United Kingdom
Closing Date: 14 May
Additional Information: www.ox.ac.uk/admissions/graduate/fees-and-funding/fees-funding-and-scholarship-search/scholarships-a-z-listing

For further information contact:

University of Oxford, University Offices, 15 Wellington Square, Oxford OX1 2JD, United Kingdom.

Oxford-Richards Graduate Scholarships

Purpose: The scholarships have been made possible through the support of the University and David Richards' generous bequest. David Richards (1939–2015) studied at Wadham College from 1961 and was a distinguished alumnus and Foundation Fellow of the College.
Eligibility: The scholarship is only tenable at Wadham College.
Type: Scholarship
Value: The scholarship covers course fees and a grant for living costs.
Length of Study: full duration of your fee liability for the agreed course
Frequency: Annual
Country of Study: United Kingdom
No. of awards offered: 3
Closing Date: June
Additional Information: www.ox.ac.uk/admissions/graduate/fees-and-funding/fees-funding-and-scholarship-search/scholarships-a-z-listing

For further information contact:

University of Oxford, University Offices, 15 Wellington Square, Oxford OX1 2JD, United Kingdom.

Tel: (44) 1865 270000
Fax: (44) 1865 270708

Oxford-Robert and Soulla Kyprianou Graduate Scholarship

Purpose: The University of Oxford is currently accepting applications for the Oxford-Robert and Soulla Kyprianou Program. This fully-funded scholarship is exclusively open to students from Republic of Cyprus
Eligibility: Open to applicants ordinarily resident in the Republic of Cyprus, applying for any full- or part-time master's or DPhil course offered by Brasenose College. This scholarship is open to applicants who are ordinarily resident in the Republic of Cyprus and who are applying for a full- or part-time master's or DPhil course, within the range accepted by Brasenose College
Level of Study: Doctorate, Postgraduate
Type: Scholarship
Value: covers course fees and provides a grant for living costs
Length of Study: Period of fee liability
Study Establishment: Brasenose College
Country of Study: United Kingdom
Closing Date: April
Additional Information: www.ox.ac.uk/admissions/graduate/fees-and-funding/fees-funding-and-scholarship-search/scholarships-a-z-listing#urquhart

For further information contact:

Email: contact@scholarshipdesk.com

Oxford-Rothermere American Institute Graduate Scholarship

Eligibility: Open to applicants who are ordinarily resident in the EEA and who are applying to a full- or part-time DPhil in History, specialising in American History. The scholarship is ordinarily tenable at University College. Please see website for more details
Level of Study: Doctorate
Type: Scholarship
Value: covers course fees and a grant for living costs
Length of Study: Period of fee liability
Study Establishment: University College
Country of Study: United Kingdom
Closing Date: April
Additional Information: www.ox.ac.uk/admissions/graduate/fees-and-funding/fees-funding-and-scholarship-search/scholarships-a-z-listing#urquhart

For further information contact:

Email: enquiries@rai.ox.ac.uk

Oxford-Ryniker Lloyd Graduate Scholarship

Purpose: The scholarship has been made possible through the support of the University and a generous legacy donation from Robert Lloyd. He cared deeply about supporting postgraduate students and scientific research, in commemoration

of Eleanor Ruth Ryniker and Somerville alumna Elizabeth Lloyd.
Eligibility: The scholarship is only tenable at Somerville College.
Type: Scholarship
Value: covers course fees and a grant for living costs
Length of Study: full duration of your fee liability for the agreed course
Frequency: Annual
Country of Study: United Kingdom
Closing Date: April
Additional Information: www.ox.ac.uk/admissions/graduate/fees-and-funding/fees-funding-and-scholarship-search/scholarships-a-z-listing

For further information contact:

University of Oxford, University Offices, 15 Wellington Square, Oxford OX1 2JD, United Kingdom.

Tel: (44) 1865 270000
Fax: (44) 1865 270708

Oxford-Sheikh Mohammed bin Rashid Al Maktoum Graduate Scholarship

Purpose: The scholarships are available to applicants who are applying to any full-time Master's and DPhil courses, except the Master of Business Administration (MBA). You should be intending to return to one of the eligible countries on completion of your studies.
Eligibility: The Oxford-Sheikh Mohammed bin Rashid Al Maktoum Graduate Scholarships are available for applicants who are nationals of and ordinarily resident in one of the following countries Algeria, Bahrain, Comoros, Djibouti, Egypt, Iraq, Jordan, Kuwait, Lebanon, Libya, Mauritania, Morocco, Oman, Palestine, Qatar, Saudi Arabia, Somalia, Sudan, Syria, Tunisia, United Arab Emirates, and Yemen.
Type: Residency
Value: Covers course fees and a grant for living costs
Length of Study: Full duration of your fee liability for the agreed course
Frequency: Annual
Country of Study: United Kingdom
Closing Date: June
Additional Information: www.ox.ac.uk/admissions/graduate/fees-and-funding/fees-funding-and-scholarship-search/scholarships-a-z-listing

For further information contact:

University of Oxford, University Offices, 15 Wellington Square, Oxford OX1 2JD, United Kingdom.

Tel: (44) 1865 270000
Fax: (44) 1865 270708

Oxford-Sir Anwar Pervez Graduate Scholarships

Purpose: The scholarship is funded by the Imperial Majesty Oba Adéyeyè Enitan Ògúnwùsì and aims to provide funding to exceptional candidates pursuing postgraduate study of Africa
Eligibility: 1. Open to applicants ordinarily resident in Pakistan, who have not previously studied for an HE qualification outside of Pakistan. 2. Candidates can be applying for any graduate course. Scholars to be selected on the basis of academic merit and financial need. Please see the website for further details
Level of Study: Postgraduate
Type: Scholarship
Value: Covers course fees and provides a grant for living costs
Length of Study: Full duration of your fee liability for the agreed course
Frequency: Annual
Country of Study: United Kingdom
Application Procedure: For more information, please check the website www.ox.ac.uk/admissions/graduate/fees-and-funding/fees-funding-and-scholarship-search/scholarships-3#pervez
Closing Date: April
Funding: Trusts
Additional Information: www.ox.ac.uk/admissions/graduate/fees-and-funding/fees-funding-and-scholarship-search/scholarships-a-z-listing?wssl=1

For further information contact:

Tel: (44) 1865 611 530
Email: enquiries@devoff.ox.ac.uk

Oxford-Swire Graduate Scholarship

Purpose: The scholarship is jointly funded by the University and by Sir John Swire, who is a distinguished Old Member (alumnus) and Honorary Fellow of University College.
Eligibility: Open to all applicants for any full- or part-time master's and DPhil courses in the Faculty of History, within the range accepted by University College
Level of Study: Doctorate, Postgraduate
Type: Scholarship
Value: Covers course fees and provides a grant for living costs

Length of Study: full duration of your fee liability for the agreed course
Country of Study: United Kingdom
Closing Date: April
Additional Information: www.ox.ac.uk/admissions/graduate/fees-and-funding/fees-funding-and-scholarship-search/scholarships-a-z-listing#urquhart

For further information contact:

Email: swirescholarships@jsshk.com

Oxford-Thatcher Graduate Scholarships

Purpose: The scholarship is jointly funded by the University and the Thatcher Development Programme at Somerville College. The late Lady Thatcher, studied Chemistry at Somerville College Oxford from 1943 to 1946 and received bursary and scholarship support from the College.
Eligibility: The scholarship is only tenable at Somerville College.
Type: Scholarship
Value: The scholarship covers course fees and a grant for living costs and a travel allowance.
Length of Study: Duration of fee liability for the course
Frequency: Annual
Country of Study: United Kingdom
No. of awards offered: 3
Closing Date: April
Additional Information: www.some.ox.ac.uk/funding-and-opportunities/graduate-scholarships/the-oxford-thatcher-graduate-scholarships/

For further information contact:

University of Oxford, University Offices, 15 Wellington Square, Oxford OX1 2JD, United Kingdom.

Tel: (44) 1865 270000
Fax: (44) 1865 270708
Email: scholarships.funding.officer@some.ox.ac.uk

Oxford-TrygFonden Graduate Scholarship

Purpose: Up to three full scholarships are available for applicants who are ordinarily resident in Denmark and who are applying for one of the following courses (preference will be given to courses in the order listed) MSc Evidence-Based Social Intervention and Policy Evaluation; MSc Education, with a speciality in Research Training
Eligibility: Open to applicants ordinarily resident in Denmark who are applying to various master's courses. One full scholarship is available for applicants who are ordinarily resident in Denmark and who are applying for one of the following courses (preference will be given to courses in the order listed) MSc Evidence-Based Social Intervention and Policy Evaluation; MSc Education, with a speciality in Research Training
Level of Study: Postgraduate
Type: Scholarship
Value: It covers the expenditure of about £14,777 (students on part-time courses will receive a study support grant instead)
Length of Study: Period of fee liability
Frequency: Annual
Country of Study: Any country
Application Procedure: 1. The eligibility criteria will be applied automatically, using the details you provide in the relevant sections of the graduate application form (for example, your country of ordinary residence and your previous education institutions), to determine whether you are eligible. 2. Selection is based on academic merit, unless specified otherwise. Some of the scholarships are only tenable at specific colleges. Unless specified otherwise, you do not need to select that college as your preference on the graduate application form. All eligible applicants will be considered, regardless of which college (if any) you state as your preference. However, successful applicants will be transferred to the relevant college in order to take up the scholarship
Closing Date: April
Funding: Private
Additional Information: Please check the website: www.ox.ac.uk/admissions/graduate/fees-and-funding/fees-funding-and-scholarship-search/scholarships-3#trygfonden

For further information contact:

Tel: (44) 1865 270 000
Fax: (44) 1865 270 708

Oxford-University College-Burma Graduate Scholarship

Purpose: The scholarship is jointly funded by the University and a syndicate of generous donors to University College.
Eligibility: The scholarship is only tenable at University College.
Type: Scholarship
Value: The scholarship covers course fees provides and a grant for living costs.
Frequency: Annual
Country of Study: Any country
Closing Date: April

Additional Information: www.ox.ac.uk/admissions/graduate/fees-and-funding/fees-funding-and-scholarship-search/scholarships-a-z-listing

For further information contact:

University of Oxford, University Offices, 15 Wellington Square, Oxford OX1 2JD, United Kingdom.

Tel: (44) 1865 270000
Fax: (44) 1865 270708

Oxford-Wadham Graduate Scholarships for Disabled Students

Purpose: Scholarships are awarded to applicants who have demonstrated excellent academic ability, who will contribute to the University's ground-breaking research, and who will go on to contribute to the world as leaders in their field, pushing the frontiers of knowledge
Eligibility: Open to all applicants applying to any full- and part-time master's courses offered by Wadham College, who have a disability as defined by the Equality Act and determined by the University's Disability Advisory Service
Level of Study: Postgraduate
Type: Scholarship
Value: Full Tuition + Stipend
Frequency: Annual
Study Establishment: Wadham College
Country of Study: Any country
Closing Date: 15 January
Funding: Trusts

For further information contact:

Email: graduate.admissions@wadham.ox.ac.uk

Oxford-Weidenfeld and Hoffmann Scholarships and Leadership Programme

Purpose: The Oxford-Weidenfeld and Hoffman Scholarship and Leadership Programme supports outstanding students from transition and emerging economies throughout Africa
Eligibility: Open to applicants from selected countries to selected courses. Please see website for more details and how to apply, including closing dates
Level of Study: Postgraduate
Type: Scholarship
Value: £17,668
Frequency: Annual
Country of Study: United Kingdom
Closing Date: May
Funding: Trusts
Additional Information: For more information, please check the website: www.graduate.ox.ac.uk/weidenfeld-oxford www.ox.ac.uk/admissions/graduate/fees-and-funding/fees-funding-and-scholarship-search/weidenfeld-hoffmann-scholarships-and-leadership-programme

For further information contact:

Weidenfeld-Hoffmann Trust, Saïd Business School, Park End Street, Oxford OX1 1HP, United Kingdom.

Email: info@whtrust.org

Oxford-Wolfson-Ancient History Graduate Scholarship

Eligibility: Open to applicants ordinarily resident in the EEA or Switzerland, applying for any graduate course in Ancient History, preferably with a focus on economics and banking. Tenable at Wolfson College only. Please see website for more details
Level of Study: Postgraduate
Type: Scholarship
Value: University fee, college fee, and full living expenses
Length of Study: Period of fee liability
Frequency: Annual
Study Establishment: Wolfson
Country of Study: United Kingdom
Application Procedure: For more information, please check the website www.ox.ac.uk/admissions/graduate/fees-and-funding/fees-funding-and-scholarship-search/scholarships-3#wolfsonancienthistory
Closing Date: 22 January
Funding: Trusts

For further information contact:

Wolfson College, Linton Road, Oxford OX2 6UD, United Kingdom.

Oxford-Wolfson-Marriott Graduate Scholarships

Purpose: The scholarships have been made possible through the support of the late Dr Frances Marriott (a University lecturer in biomathematics and taught statistics and a Fellow of Wolfson College) and by departments and faculties.
Eligibility: The scholarship is only tenable at Wolfson College.
Type: Scholarship
Value: The scholarship covers course fees and a grant for living costs.

Frequency: Annual
Country of Study: Any country
Additional Information: www.ox.ac.uk/admissions/graduate/fees-and-funding/fees-funding-and-scholarship-search/scholarships-a-z-listing

For further information contact:

University of Oxford, University Offices, 15 Wellington Square, Oxford OX1 2JD, United Kingdom.

Tel: (44) 1865 270000
Fax: (44) 1865 270708

Pembroke College Jose Gregorio Hernandez Award of the Venezuelan National Academy of Medicine

Eligibility: Open to nationals of Venezuela. Students must be nominated by the Venezuelan National Academy of Medicine and then accepted by the General Medical Council
Level of Study: Postgraduate
Type: Stipendiary
Value: Full fees and maintenance
Length of Study: 1 year, renewable for a further year
Frequency: Dependent on funds available
Study Establishment: Pembroke College, University of Oxford
Country of Study: United Kingdom
Application Procedure: Applicants must write or email the Admissions Secretary for details
Funding: Private

For further information contact:

Pembroke College, Cambridge CB2 1RF, United Kingdom.

Email: admissions@pmb.ox.ac.uk

Pembroke College: Gordon Aldrick Scholarship

Purpose: To assist scholars in Chinese cultural studies
Eligibility: Open to candidates beginning a two or three-year research degree at Oxford
Level of Study: Research
Type: Scholarship
Value: £5,000 per year towards college fee and contribution towards living expenses
Length of Study: Tenable for up to three years whilst the recipient is liable to pay University and College fees. Automatically renewed each year if satisfactory academic progress is made
Frequency: Annual
Country of Study: Any country
Application Procedure: Intending candidates should apply in Section L of the Oxford University graduate application form or notify the Admissions & Access Officer at Pembroke
Closing Date: 3 May

For further information contact:

Email: jane.sherwood@admin.ox.ac.uk

Pembroke College: Tokyo Electric Power Company (TEPCO) Scholarship

Eligibility: Open to all graduate applicants specialising in studies of Japanese literature, art or history. Please see website for details of how to apply.
Level of Study: Research
Value: £5,000 per year towards college fee and contribution towards living expenses
Length of Study: Period of fee liability
Country of Study: United Kingdom
Closing Date: 3 May

For further information contact:

Email: ben.nicholson@admin.ox.ac.uk

Philosophy Faculty-Wolfson College Joint Scholarship

Eligibility: Open to Home/European Union graduate applicants to DPhil courses in the Faculty of Philosophy. Eligible applicants for these courses are automatically considered. Please see website for more information
Level of Study: Postgraduate
Type: Scholarship
Value: £5,000
Frequency: Annual
Study Establishment: Wolfson
Country of Study: United Kingdom
Application Procedure: Applications for Wolfson Bursaries and Scholarships should be submitted on the form that will become available after mid-December here www.wolfson.cam.ac.uk/postgraduate-study/fees-funding/postgraduate-studentship-application
No. of awards offered: 1
Closing Date: 1 May
Funding: Trusts

For further information contact:

Email: graduatestudies@mml.cam.ac.uk

Pirie-Reid Scholarships

Purpose: Pirie-Reid is a small trust fund which is used for scholarships benefiting Scottish students coming to Oxford. The Pirie-Reid trust fund is managed by Wells Fargo in San Francisco.
Eligibility: 1. Candidates should be applying to start a new graduate course at Oxford. 2. This scholarship is open to candidates studying for degree-bearing courses, with the exception of Postgraduate Certificate and Postgraduate Diploma courses. 3. Please ensure you meet the requirements for entry to your course, including English language requirements. 4. Students must have been or must currently be domiciled or educated in Scotland. 5. Preference is given to students who have not studied at Oxford before.
Level of Study: Graduate, Postgraduate
Type: Scholarship
Value: University and college fees normally at the home rate plus maintenance grant, subject to assessment of income from other sources
Length of Study: Renewable from year to year, subject to satisfactory progress and continuance of approved full-time study
Frequency: Annual
Study Establishment: University of Oxford
Country of Study: United Kingdom
Application Procedure: Electronically
Closing Date: 20 January
Funding: Private
Additional Information: Website: scholarship-positions.com/2012-pirie-reid-scholarship-for-graduate-studies-at-oxford-university-uk/2011/10/03/, https://www.ox.ac.uk/admissions/graduate/fees-and-funding/fees-funding-and-scholarship-search/scholarships-a-z-listing#trygfonden

For further information contact:

Email: student.funding@admin.ox.ac.uk

Radcliffe Department of Medicine: RDM Scholars Programme

Eligibility: Open to basic science applicants of any nationality applying for projects based within the Radcliffe Department of Medicine. Please see additional information on personal statement on the RDM webpage
Level of Study: Doctorate
Type: Scholarship
Value: £18,000 per annum
Length of Study: 4 years
Frequency: Annual
Country of Study: Any country
Closing Date: 10 January
Additional Information: For more details, please visit www.rdm.ox.ac.uk/rdm-scholars-programme www.european-funding-guide.eu/other-financial-assistance/13805-rdm%C2%A0scholars-programme

For further information contact:

Email: graduate.enquiries@rdm.ox.ac.uk

Radiation Oncology & Biology: Departmental Studentships

Purpose: To provide comprehensive preparation for a career in research or industry, whether in radiobiology, protection or the advancement of cancer treatments
Eligibility: Open to home/European Union and overseas students
Level of Study: Postgraduate, Research
Type: Studentship
Value: University and college fees at the home/European Union rate, stipend, research expenses and support with travel to conferences
Length of Study: Up to 4 years
Frequency: Annual
Country of Study: Any country
Closing Date: 10 January
Contributor: Cancer Research United Kingdom (United Kingdom) or Medical Research Council (MRC)
Additional Information: The Medical Research Council (MRC) awards have residency requirements www.ox.ac.uk/admissions/graduate/courses/msc-radiation-biology?wssl=1

For further information contact:

Tel: (44) 1865 617410
Email: graduate.studies@oncology.ox.ac.uk

Roche-Law Faculty Scholarship

Eligibility: Open to all graduate applicants to BCL/MJur, MSc in Law and Finance, MSt Legal Research, MPhil or DPhil Law. Award holders will become members of New College. Please see website for more information
Level of Study: Doctorate, Graduate, Postgraduate, Research
Type: Scholarship
Value: £10,000 pa
Length of Study: Full fee liability period
Study Establishment: New College

Country of Study: Any country
Application Procedure: No separate application
Closing Date: January
Additional Information: Please visit the website: www.law.ox.ac.uk/admissions/graduate-scholarships/new-college-roche-scholarship

For further information contact:

Email: student.finance@new.ox.ac.uk

Sasakawa Fund Scholarships

Purpose: The scholarships will be awarded to applicants who are Japanese nationals currently on a course or starting a course at Oxford University, or alternatively to students from the UK or other countries currently on a course or starting a course at Oxford University which requires some period of study in Japan.
Level of Study: Doctorate, Graduate, Postgraduate
Type: Scholarship
Value: £10,000
Length of Study: 1 to 3 years
Frequency: Annual
Study Establishment: University of Oxford
Country of Study: United Kingdom
Application Procedure: Please complete the Scholarship Application Form, along with 1. one reference (to be sent by the referee directly) 2. a Curriculum Vitae 3. a statement of research interests (of no more than six pages) including an outline and research proposal (for research degree applicants only) OR 4. a personal statement (of no more than six pages - for taught degree applicants only).
Closing Date: 31 March
Contributor: Japan Shipbuilding Industry Foundation
Additional Information: www.nissan.ox.ac.uk/the-sasakawa-fund-scholarships-faculty-of-oriental-studies

For further information contact:

Email: trustfunds@orinst.ox.ac.uk

Sasakawa Postgraduate Studentship in Japanese Studies

Purpose: As part of the five-year programme designed to support the study of Japan in the UK at postgraduate level, which the Nippon Foundation and the Great Britain Sasakawa Foundation re-launched in 2018, East Asian Studies at the University of Leeds invites applications from suitably qualified candidates who wish to pursue a taught MA programme in Film Studies with a focus on Japanese cinema, a MA by research (MAR) in Japanese Studies or a PhD in Japanese Studies starting October 2024.
Eligibility: These scholarships are available for students studying either MA Film Studies with a focus on Japanese cinema, MA by Research in Japanese Studies or a PhD in Japanese studies. The Sasakawa Postgraduate studentships are open to both UK and international students. In general, non-UK nationals intending to do a MA or a MAR are eligible only if they are settled in the UK or have been ordinarily resident for at least three years immediately preceding the start of their MA or MAR course. This does not apply to PhD studentship candidates.
Level of Study: Masters Degree, Postgraduate
Type: Studentship
Value: £10,000
Country of Study: Any country
Application Procedure: Please see website for more details, including how to apply
Closing Date: 3 March
Additional Information: Website: ahc.leeds.ac.uk/dir-record/scholarships/1480/sasakawa-postgraduate-studentships-in-japanese-studies

For further information contact:

Tel: (44) 20 7074 5094/5091
Email: scholarships@soas.ac.uk

Saven European Scholarships

Purpose: The Saven European Scholarships have been created by a generous gift from Mr Bjorn Saven to support graduate students who are applying to Oxford to undertake a full-time Masters or DPhil course from the following countries: Austria, Belgium, Bulgaria, Estonia, Finland, France, Germany, Greece, Luxembourg, Poland, Portugal or Sweden.
Eligibility: Graduate students who are applying to Oxford to undertake a full-time Masters or DPhil course from the following countries: Austria, Belgium, Bulgaria, Estonia, Finland, France, Germany, Greece, Luxembourg, Poland, Portugal or Sweden. Only ordinary residents and nationals of the country, who have also completed their undergraduate degree in that country, are eligible.
Level of Study: Masters Degree
Type: Scholarship
Value: The value of the award will be £25,000 for a one-year Master course or £30,000 in total for a multiple year course.
Frequency: Annual
Country of Study: Any country
Additional Information: Website: www.ox.ac.uk/admissions/graduate/fees-and-funding/fees-funding-and-scholarship-search/scholarships-a-z-listing

For further information contact:

University of Oxford, University Offices, 15 Wellington Square, Oxford OX1 2JD, United Kingdom.

Tel: (44) 1865 270000
Fax: (44) 1865 270708

Saïd Foundation Oxford Scholarships

Purpose: The scholarship will cover course fees, a grant for living costs (of at least £15,609) and flights to and from the UK at the start and end of your course. Awards are made for the full duration of your fee liability for the agreed course.
Eligibility: You must be applying to start a new full-time master's courses at Oxford, and be of Jordanian, Lebanese, Palestinian or Syrian nationality and ordinarily resident in Jordan, Lebanon, Syria, Palestine or Israel. You should be intending to return to one of these countries on completion of your course to apply your new skills and knowledge.
Level of Study: Masters Degree
Type: Scholarship
Value: Course fees, a grant for living costs and flights to and from the UK at the start and end of your course
Length of Study: Full duration of your fee liability for the agreed course
Country of Study: Any country
Application Procedure: In order to be considered for this scholarship, you must: (1) Apply to the Saïd Foundation by 28 October 2024. (2) Submit your application for graduate study to the University of Oxford by the relevant December or January deadline for your course. See the relevant course page for the deadline applicable to your course.
Closing Date: 28 October
Additional Information: Website: www.ox.ac.uk/admissions/graduate/fees-and-funding/fees-funding-and-scholarship-search/scholarships-a-z-listing

For further information contact:

University of Oxford, University Offices, 15 Wellington Square, Oxford OX1 2JD, United Kingdom.

Tel: (44) 1865 270000

School of Anthropology and Museum Ethnography: Peter Lienhardt/Philip Bagby Travel Awards

Eligibility: Open to new and current Anthropology students who are hoping to fund research/travel. Please see website for more details, including closing dates and how to apply
Level of Study: Postgraduate
Type: Scholarship
Value: Up to £1,000 for travel/small research projects only
Length of Study: Ad hoc
Frequency: Annual
Country of Study: United Kingdom
Application Procedure: For more information, please check the website www.anthro.ox.ac.uk/prospective-students/funding/travel-grants/
Closing Date: 22 January
Funding: Trusts

For further information contact:

Email: information@anthro.ox.ac.uk

Sir William Dunn School of Pathology: Departmental PhD Prize Studentships

Value: £17,285 per annum
Length of Study: 4 years
Frequency: Annual
Country of Study: Any country
Closing Date: 3 December

For further information contact:

Tel: (44) 1865 275 500
Email: finance@path.ox.ac.uk

Social Policy and Intervention: Barnett House-Nuffield Joint Scholarship

Eligibility: Open to all applicants applying for the DPhil Social Policy at the Department of Social Policy and Intervention and Nuffield College
Value: Course fee, college fee, maintenance
Length of Study: 3 years
Country of Study: Any country
Closing Date: October
Additional Information: For more details, please visit www.spi.ox.ac.uk/study-with-us/funding.html www.spi.ox.ac.uk/departmental-scholarships#collapse401546

For further information contact:

Tel: (44) 1865 280734
Email: admissions@spi.ox.ac.uk

Social Policy and Intervention: Barnett Scholarship

Purpose: To assist graduate students with fees.

Eligibility: Open to all applicants for the DPhils in Social Policy and Social Intervention.
Level of Study: Research
Type: Scholarship
Value: £20,000 per year
Length of Study: 3 years
Country of Study: Any country
Application Procedure: Applications can be made by post or e-mail on the appropriate application form together with an up to date CV and a piece of recent written work (e.g. course essay, draft chapter, paper, journal article). Please visit website for more details and how to apply.
Additional Information: Website: www.postgraduatefunding.com/award-2530

For further information contact:

Tel: (44) 18 6527 0000
Fax: (44) 18 6527 0708
Email: admissions@oriel.ox.ac.uk

Somerville College Janet Watson Bursary

Eligibility: Open to graduates from the United States of America who are in need of financial assistance
Level of Study: Postgraduate
Type: Bursary
Value: £2,000, £3,500 p.a
Length of Study: 1 year, with possibility of renewal for second year
Study Establishment: Somerville College, the University of Oxford
Country of Study: United Kingdom
Application Procedure: Applicants must contact the Assistant College Secretary
No. of awards offered: 1
Funding: Private

For further information contact:

Email: sara.kalim@some.ox.ac.uk

St Antony's College Ali Pachachi Scholarship

Purpose: To assist candidates pursue doctoral study in any discipline in the humanities or social sciences with a primary focus on the social and political issues confronting the modern Middle East
Eligibility: St Antony's doctoral students
Level of Study: Doctorate, Research
Value: £7,500 towards fees and maintenance
Length of Study: One year
Country of Study: Any country
Application Procedure: Please check the website for further details
Additional Information: scholarshipandinternship.blogspot.com/2011/10/st-antonys-college-scholarships.html

For further information contact:

The Director, Middle East Centre, St Antony's College, 62 Woodstock Rd, Oxford OX2 6JF, United Kingdom.

Email: mec@sant.ox.ac.uk

St Antony's College - Swire Scholarship

Purpose: The Swire Scholarships at St Antony's are generously funded by the Swire Charitable Trust, founded by John Swire &; Sons. These scholarships are available to graduate students demonstrating exceptional academic merit
Eligibility: The scholarships are open to applicants who are permanent residents of Japan, China or Hong Kong and have completed the majority of their formal education in their country of permanent residency. The Scholarships will be awarded primarily on academic merit, although financial need may be taken into account. Applicants must apply for admission to a full-time graduate course of study that is offered by St Antony's College to start in current and upcoming year
Level of Study: Graduate
Type: Scholarship
Value: 100% of the course fees, a grant for living costs of £17,442 per year.
Frequency: Annual
Country of Study: Japan
Closing Date: 1 March
Funding: Private
Additional Information: https://www.sant.ox.ac.uk/prospective-students/fees-and-funding/scholarships-new-students/swire

For further information contact:

Email: funding@sant.ox.ac.uk

U

St Antony's College Wai Seng Senior Research Scholarship

Purpose: The Scholarship is tenable at St Antony's College for two years and is open to all matriculated students of the University of Oxford working for a Doctor of Philosophy degree in fields such as modern history, social sciences
Level of Study: Doctorate

Type: Scholarship
Value: An annual maintenance grant of £9,000. approved University and College fees up to the value of £15,000
Length of Study: 2 years
Frequency: Every 2 years
Study Establishment: St Antony's College, University of Oxford
Country of Study: United Kingdom
Application Procedure: See www.sant.ox.ac.uk
Closing Date: 3 March
Funding: Individuals
Additional Information: www.sant.ox.ac.uk/research-centres/asian-studies-centre/scholarships/wai-seng-senior-research-scholarship

For further information contact:

Email: asian@sant.ox.ac.uk

St Catherine's College: Poole Scholarship

Purpose: To assist students who are or will be reading for an Oxford University DPhil, MLitt or MSc by research degree
Eligibility: British nationals of good character studying for a DPhil. Limited SCR dining rights and guaranteed 2 years' single accommodation at current room rate
Level of Study: Graduate, Research
Type: Scholarship
Value: £2,500 per annum
Length of Study: Up to 3 years while student is liable for fees
Frequency: Dependent on funds available
Study Establishment: St Catherine's College, University of Oxford
Country of Study: United Kingdom
Application Procedure: See www.stcatz.ox.ac.uk

For further information contact:

Fax: (44) 1865 271 768
Email: academic.registrar@stcat2.ox.ac.uk

St Catherine's College Glaxo Scholarship

Eligibility: Open to graduates who have a confirmed place in the Oxford University 2nd BM or the accelerated graduate entry medicine course
Level of Study: Graduate
Type: Scholarship
Value: £3,300 per year
Length of Study: Up to 2 years
Frequency: Annual
Study Establishment: St Catherine's College, University of Oxford
Country of Study: United Kingdom
Application Procedure: Please see www.stcatz.ox.ac.uk/prospective-students/postgraduate-admissions/student-finance-and-scholarships/ for full details including how to apply
Closing Date: 24 February
Additional Information: www.stcatz.ox.ac.uk/prospective-students/postgraduate-admissions/student-finance-and-scholarships/

For further information contact:

St Catherine's College, Manor Rd, Oxford OX1 3UJ United Kingdom.

Email: college.office@stcatz.ox.ac.uk

St Catherine's College: College Scholarship (Arts)

Eligibility: Open to DPhil, MLitt, and MSc by Research applicants and students in the Humanities and Social Sciences Divisions
Level of Study: Doctorate, Postgraduate, Research
Type: Scholarship
Value: £3,300 per annum
Length of Study: up to 3 years
Frequency: Annual
Study Establishment: St Catherine's College, University of Oxford
Country of Study: United Kingdom
Application Procedure: Please see www.stcatz.ox.ac.uk/prospective-students/postgraduate-admissions/student-finance-and-scholarships/ for full details including how to apply
Closing Date: 24 February
Funding: Private
Additional Information: Please see www.stcatz.ox.ac.uk/prospective-students/postgraduate-admissions/student-finance-and-scholarships/

For further information contact:

Fax: (44) 1865 271 700
Email: college.office@stcatz.ox.ac.uk

St Catherine's College: College Scholarship (Sciences)

Eligibility: Open to DPhil and MSc by research applicants and students in the Mathematical, Physical and Life Sciences Division and Medical Sciences Division
Level of Study: Doctorate, Postgraduate, Research
Type: Scholarship

Value: £3,300 per annum
Length of Study: up to 3 years
Frequency: Annual
Study Establishment: St Catherine's College, University of Oxford
Country of Study: United Kingdom
Application Procedure: Please see www.stcatz.ox.ac.uk/prospective-students/postgraduate-admissions/student-finance-and-scholarships/ for full details including how to apply
Closing Date: 24 February
Funding: Private
Additional Information: Please see www.stcatz.ox.ac.uk/prospective-students/postgraduate-admissions/student-finance-and-scholarships/

For further information contact:

Email: college.office@stcatz.ox.ac.uk

St Catherine's College: Ghosh Graduate Scholarship

Eligibility: Open to BPhil, MFA, MSt, MSc by Coursework or MPhil in the Humanities Division.
Level of Study: Postgraduate, Predoctorate
Type: Scholarship
Value: £5,000 per annum
Length of Study: one or two years
Study Establishment: St Catherine's College, University of Oxford
Country of Study: United Kingdom
Application Procedure: Please see www.stcatz.ox.ac.uk/prospective-students/postgraduate-admissions/student-finance-and-scholarships/ for full details including how to apply
Closing Date: 24 February
Funding: Private
Additional Information: Please see www.stcatz.ox.ac.uk/prospective-students/postgraduate-admissions/student-finance-and-scholarships/

For further information contact:

Email: college.office@stcatz.ox.ac.uk

St Catherine's College: Leathersellers' Company Scholarship

Eligibility: Open to DPhil and MSc by Research applicants and students in the MPLS Division and Department of Biochemistry who have studied at a European (including United Kingdom) university
Level of Study: Doctorate, Postgraduate, Research
Type: Scholarship
Value: £3,500 per annum
Length of Study: Up to 3 years
Frequency: Annual
Study Establishment: St Catherine's College, University of Oxford
Country of Study: United Kingdom
Application Procedure: Please see www.stcatz.ox.ac.uk/prospective-students/postgraduate-admissions/student-finance-and-scholarships/ for full details including how to apply
Closing Date: 24 February
Funding: Private
Additional Information: Please see www.stcatz.ox.ac.uk/prospective-students/postgraduate-admissions/student-finance-and-scholarships/

For further information contact:

Email: college.office@stcatz.ox.ac.uk

St Catherine's College: Overseas Scholarship

Eligibility: Open to Overseas fee status DPhil, MLitt and MSc by research applicants and students
Level of Study: Doctorate, Postgraduate, Research
Type: Scholarship
Value: £3,300 per annum
Length of Study: Up to 3 years
Frequency: Annual
Study Establishment: St Catherine's College, University of Oxford
Country of Study: United Kingdom
Application Procedure: Please see www.stcatz.ox.ac.uk/prospective-students/postgraduate-admissions/student-finance-and-scholarships/ for full details including how to apply
Closing Date: 24 February
Funding: Private
Additional Information: Please see www.stcatz.ox.ac.uk/prospective-students/postgraduate-admissions/student-finance-and-scholarships/

For further information contact:

Email: college.office@stcatz.ox.ac.uk

St Cross College: E.P. Abraham Scholarships

Purpose: St Cross College is a graduate college of the University of Oxford. It offers an outstanding academic

environment dedicated to the pursuit of excellence within the Collegiate University
Eligibility: Open to all graduate applicants for research degrees in the chemical, biological/life and medical sciences. Please visit website for more details, including how to apply
Level of Study: Postgraduate
Type: Scholarship
Value: £5,000 per year towards college fee, and the remainder towards living expenses
Length of Study: Up to three years
Frequency: Annual
Study Establishment: St Cross College
Country of Study: United Kingdom
Application Procedure: For more information, please check the website www.stx.ox.ac.uk/prospective-students/funding-support/ep-abraham-scholarships-chemical-biologicallife-and-medical
Closing Date: 24 May
Funding: Trusts

For further information contact:

Email: master.pa@stx.ox.ac.uk

St Cross College: Graduate Scholarship in Environmental Research

Purpose: St Cross College, jointly with the Oxford NERC Doctoral Training Program in Environmental Research, offers the following scholarship for students in this Doctoral Training Programme (DTP) at the University of Oxford - the DTP recruits to three subject streams The Physical Climate; Biodiversity, Ecology & Evolutionary Processes and the Dynamic Earth - Surface Processes and Natural Hazards.
Eligibility: The Scholarship is open to all candidates and covers the cost of the course fee at the Home/Republic of Ireland level for the duration.
Eligible Country: Any Country
Level of Study: Doctorate, Research
Type: Scholarship
Value: Covers the cost of the course fee at the Home/Republic of Ireland level for the duration. Overseas students with UKRI funding may be eligible for Home fee status.
Length of Study: Up to 3 years
Country of Study: United Kingdom
Application Procedure: No separate application is required and all eligible offer-holders will be considered for this award.
Closing Date: January
Additional Information: For more details, please visit website www.stx.ox.ac.uk/graduate-scholarship-in-environmental-research

For further information contact:

61 St Giles, Oxford OX1 3LZ, United Kingdom.

Email: bursar@stx.ox.ac.uk

St Cross College: HAPP MPhil Scholarship in the History of Science

Subjects: DPhil in the History of Physics in the Faculty of History or a DPhil in the Philosophy of Physics in the Faculty of Philosophy
Purpose: The successful Scholar will be expected to engage with the termly activities of the St Cross Centre for the History and Philosophy of Physics (HAPP).
Value: £10,000 per annum
Length of Study: three years
Country of Study: Any country
Application Procedure: No separate application is required and all eligible offer-holders will be considered automatically
Closing Date: October

For further information contact:

Email: admissions-academic@stx.ox.ac.uk

St Cross College: MPhil Scholarships in the Humanities and Social Sciences

Purpose: St Cross College offers two MPhil Scholarships for students studying at the University of Oxford for an MPhil degree in any of the humanities and social science disciplines or for the BPhil degree in Philosophy.
Eligibility: Open to all applicants for MPhil degrees in the Humanities and the Social Sciences or for the BPhil degree in Philosophy. The scholarships are tenable at St Cross College only
Level of Study: Predoctorate
Type: Scholarship
Value: £5,000 per annum
Length of Study: 2 years
Study Establishment: St Cross College
Country of Study: United Kingdom
Application Procedure: No separate application is required and all eligible offer-holders will be considered for these awards.
Closing Date: January
Additional Information: www.stx.ox.ac.uk/mphil-scholarships-in-the-humanities-and-social-sciences

For further information contact:

St Cross College, St Giles, Oxford OX1 3LZ, United Kingdom.

Tel: (44) 1865 278 458
Fax: (44) 1865 278 484
Email: admissions-academic@stx.ox.ac.uk

St Cross College: Oxford-Ko Cheuk Hung Graduate Scholarship

Eligibility: Open to applicants who are ordinarily resident in the EEA or Switzerland and who are applying for the full-time MSt Chinese Studies
Level of Study: Postgraduate
Type: Residency
Value: Tuition fees, college fees and a grant towards living expenses
Length of Study: Period of fee liability
Frequency: Annual
Study Establishment: St Cross
Country of Study: United Kingdom
Application Procedure: For more information, please check the website www.ox.ac.uk/admissions/graduate/fees-and-funding/fees-funding-and-scholarship-search/scholarships-3#kocheukhung
Closing Date: March
Funding: Trusts
Additional Information: www.ox.ac.uk/admissions/graduate/fees-and-funding/fees-funding-and-scholarship-search/scholarships-a-z-listing?wssl=1

For further information contact:

Tel: (44) 1865 278 490
Email: master@stx.ox.ac.uk

St Cross College: The Harun Ur Rashid Memorial Scholarship

Eligibility: Open to applicants (who are normally resident in Bangladesh) for MPhil degrees in the Humanities and the Social Sciences or for the BPhil degree in Philosophy. Please visit website for more details including how to apply. The candidates applying for the Harun Ur Rashid Memorial Scholarship, should have an outstanding academic ability. The applicants should apply for a two-year Master's (MPhil) course to the University of Oxford. The candidates who have already been accepted by another Oxford college are not eligible.
Value: £6,000 per annum
Length of Study: 2 years
Country of Study: Any country
Application Procedure: www.stx.ox.ac.uk/prospective-students/funding-support/harun-ur-rashid-memorial-scholarship
Closing Date: 23 March
Additional Information: For more details, visit website www.stx.ox.ac.uk/prospective-students/funding-support/harun-ur-rashid-memorial-scholarship www.scholarshipcare.com/scholarship/the-harun-ur-rashid-memorial-scholarship/

For further information contact:

Email: master@stx.ox.ac.uk

St Cross College: The Robin & Nadine Wells Scholarship

Purpose: To provide financial assistance to an academically meritorious graduate student who has been accepted into both an accredited one year's Masters programme at the University of Oxford and St Cross College and are unable to secure funding elsewhere
Eligibility: Open to all applicants for one-year Master's courses who are unable to secure funding from elsewhere
Level of Study: Postgraduate
Type: Scholarship
Value: £5,000 for one year
Length of Study: 1 year
Frequency: Annual
Study Establishment: St Cross College
Country of Study: United Kingdom
Application Procedure: Please visit website for more details, including how to apply
Closing Date: 21 June

St Edmund Hall: Peel Award

Eligibility: Open to all students applying for Master of Fine Art at the Ruskin School
Level of Study: Postgraduate
Type: Scholarship
Value: £1,000
Length of Study: 1 year
Frequency: Annual
Study Establishment: St Edmund Hall
Country of Study: Any country
Additional Information: www.seh.ox.ac.uk/study/undergraduate/fees-and-funding/scholarships-and-prizes-undergraduates

For further information contact:

Email: lawfac@law.ox.ac.uk

St Edmund Hall: William Asbrey BCL Studentship

Purpose: The William Asbrey scholarship is worth £10,000, is jointly funded by St Edmund Hall and the Law Faculty, and is available to all BCL applicants. There is no separate application procedure.
Eligibility: Open to all graduate applicants to the BCL
Value: £10,000
Length of Study: 1 year
Country of Study: United Kingdom
Additional Information: www.seh.ox.ac.uk/study/postgraduate/postgraduate-scholarships

For further information contact:

Queen's Lane, Oxford OX1 4AR, United Kingdom.

Tel: (44) 1865 279000
Email: lodge@seh.ox.ac.uk

St Edmund Hall: William R. Miller Postgraduate Award

Purpose: To assist graduate students with fees and accommodation
Eligibility: A rent-free college room for one academic year offered to a student entering the first or second year of a research degree (DPhil or MRes)
Level of Study: Postgraduate, Research
Type: Award
Value: £6,000 pa
Length of Study: 1 year
Frequency: Annual
Country of Study: Any country
Application Procedure: Please see website for more details, including how to apply
Closing Date: 20 January
Additional Information: www.seh.ox.ac.uk/study/postgraduate/postgraduate-scholarships

For further information contact:

Queen's Lane, Oxford OX1 4AR, United Kingdom.

Tel: (44) 1865 279000
Email: jane.sherwood@admin.ox.ac.uk

Standard Bank Africa Chairman's Scholarships

Purpose: The scholarships have been funded through the support of the Standard Bank of South Africa. Standard Bank is committed to enable and empower scholars to become effective leaders in Africa.
Eligibility: Residents of Angola, Botswana, Cote d'Ivoire, Democratic Republic of the Congo, Ethiopia, Ghana, Kenya, Lesotho, Malawi, Mauritius, Mozambique, Namibia, Nigeria, South Africa, South Sudan, Swaziland, Tanzania, Uganda, Zambia or Zimbabwe. The scholarship is only tenable at Wadham College.
Type: Scholarship
Value: The scholarship covers course fees and a grant for living costs.
Country of Study: Any country
Closing Date: July
Additional Information: www.ox.ac.uk/admissions/graduate/fees-and-funding/fees-funding-and-scholarship-search/scholarships-a-z-listing

For further information contact:

University of Oxford, University Offices, 15 Wellington Square, Oxford OX1 2JD, United Kingdom.

Tel: (44) 1865 270000
Fax: (44) 1865 270708

Standard Bank Derek Cooper Africa Scholarship

Eligibility: Open to applicants who are ordinarily resident in one of the following countries Angola, Botswana, Cote d'Ivoire, Democratic Republic of the Congo, Ghana, Kenya, Lesotho, Malawi, Mauritius, Mozambique, Namibia, Nigeria, South Africa, South Sudan, Swaziland, Tanzania, Uganda, Zambia or Zimbabwe. Preference will be given to nationals of Angola, Ghana, Kenya, Mozambique, Nigeria, South Africa and South Sudan. You must also be applying to start any full-time, 1 year taught master's course within the Mathematical, Physical and Life Sciences, Social Sciences, or Humanities Divisions
Level of Study: Postgraduate
Type: Scholarship
Value: £21,000 pa
Length of Study: Period of fee liability
Frequency: Annual
Country of Study: United Kingdom
Closing Date: 27 April
Funding: Trusts

For further information contact:

Tel: (44) 20 7405 7686
Email: graduates@standardbank.co.za

Statistical Science (EPSRC and MRC Centre for Doctoral Training) Studentships

Eligibility: Open to United Kingdom and European Union applicants for Statistical Science (EPSRC and MRC CDT)
Level of Study: Doctorate, Research
Type: Studentship
Value: £22,356
Length of Study: 4 years
Frequency: Annual
Country of Study: Any country
Closing Date: 20 January
Funding: Trusts
Additional Information: For more information, please check the website: www.stats.ox.ac.uk/study_here/research_degrees

For further information contact:

Email: ri@fgv.br

Synthetic Biology Doctorate Training Centre EPSRC/ BBSRC Studentships

Eligibility: Open to United Kingdom applicants for all MPLS subjects. Other European Union nationals are eligible for a fees-only award. It is recommended that students submit a CV directly to us prior to making a full application. Please visit website for more information
Level of Study: Postgraduate
Type: Scholarship
Value: £21,703
Length of Study: Four years
Frequency: Annual
Country of Study: United Kingdom
Application Procedure: For more information, please check the website www.dtc.ox.ac.uk/
Funding: Trusts

For further information contact:

Email: dtcenquiries@dtc.ox.ac.uk

Templeton College MBA Scholarship

Level of Study: MBA
Type: Scholarship
Value: £17,668
Length of Study: 1 year
Frequency: Annual
Study Establishment: Templeton College, the University of Oxford
Country of Study: United Kingdom
Application Procedure: Applicants must contact the Academic Administrator
Closing Date: January
Additional Information: www.gtc.ox.ac.uk/students/how-to-apply/scholarships-bursaries/oxford-intesa-sanpaolo-mba-graduate-scholarships/

For further information contact:

Email: admissions@templeton.ox.ac.uk

The Christopher Welch Scholarship in Biological Sciences

Eligibility: Open to all DPhil applicants applying for a project falling within the broad topic of Biological Sciences in Departments in the Medical Science, the Department of Plant Sciences and the Department of Zoology. Enquires may be sent by email to ga.Bush@medsci.ox.ac.uk.
Level of Study: Graduate
Value: 1. Payment of fees 2. a maintenance grant (currently min £20,000 pa in years 1 to 4) 3. Research Support Grant of £5,000 per annum in years 1, 2 and 3
Length of Study: 3 years
Country of Study: Any country
Closing Date: 8 January
Additional Information: www.medsci.ox.ac.uk/study/graduateschool/application-process/funding/the-christopher-welch-scholarship-in-biological-sciences

For further information contact:

Email: aga.bush@medsci.ox.ac.uk

U

The John Brookman Scholarship

Purpose: The aim of the scholarship is to encourage the study of Music.
Eligibility: 1. Eligible Countries: Students from the UK are eligible to apply for this scholarship. 2. Entrance Requirements: The Scholarship is open to those reading for and those who have applied to read for, a graduate degree at the University of Oxford in any subject, and who as John Brookman Scholar will participate in the musical life of the College.

3. English Language Requirements: Applicants must have sufficient knowledge of the language of instruction of the host university.
Level of Study: Graduate
Type: Scholarship
Value: The Scholarship will be offered at a value of the college fee (£3,112 for 2018/19) per annum.
Frequency: Annual
Country of Study: Any country
Application Procedure: Please email the Graduate Administrator a full CV detailing: academic and musical qualifications and experience; the graduate course that you are following or to which you have applied; and the names of two referees.
Closing Date: 23 March
Funding: Private
Additional Information: Website: scholarship-positions.com/john-brookman-graduate-scholarship-university-oxford-uk/2018/01/31/

The Khazanah Asia Scholarship in Collaboration with Ancora Foundation

Purpose: Initiated through a generous benefaction from Mr. Gita Irawan Wirjawan, this scholarship provides one year's tuition, fees, and expenses
Eligibility: Applicants should have; (a) a confirmed acceptance at the Environmental Change Institute, Oxford University; (b) an excellent academic record with a first degree equivalent to a good Second Class (Upper) Honors or a GPA of at least 3.5; (c) a very good command of the English language; (d) a commercial or industrial background and a deep interest in the environment; (e) assessed to have outstanding potential for leadership in government, business, or civil society after graduation
Level of Study: Graduate
Type: Scholarship
Value: Up to £28,500
Frequency: Varies
Country of Study: Any country
Application Procedure: Each fellowship is tenable for one-year only for full-time students on the Master of Science in Environmental Change and Management program. The successful candidate is expected to complete his/her studies within the tenable period. Each scholarship will cover the following Tuition and other compulsory fees (as specified by Oxford University); Monthly stipend; and Return air-ticket (economy class)
Closing Date: 6 December
Funding: Private
Additional Information: www.heysuccess.com/opportunity/Khazanah-Asia-Scholarship-Programme-21462

For further information contact:

Equity Tower, 41st Floor Sudirman Central Business District (SCBD), Jl. Jend. Sudirman Kav. 52-53, Lot 9, Jakarta 12190 Indonesia.

Email: inquiry@ancorafoundation.com

Theology and Religion: AHRC Doctoral Training Partnership Studentships

Level of Study: Graduate
Value: University fee, college fee and full living expenses. Fees-only awards for non-United Kingdom, European Union students
Length of Study: Period of fee liability
Country of Study: Any country
Application Procedure: Open to all graduate applicants for the DPhil degree offered by the Faculty of Theology and Religion. Please see website for more details
Closing Date: 20 January
Additional Information: For more details, please visit www.humanities.ox.ac.uk/prospective_students/graduates/funding/ahrc www.humanities.ox.ac.uk/ahrc-doctoral-training-partnership#collapse395446

For further information contact:

Email: theo.pgresearchadmissions@durham.ac.uk

Trinity College Birkett Scholarship in Environmental Studies

Eligibility: Open to any graduate accepted for the MSc
Level of Study: Postgraduate, Research
Type: Scholarship
Value: £7,000
Length of Study: 1 year
Frequency: Annual
Study Establishment: Trinity College, University of Oxford
Country of Study: United Kingdom
Application Procedure: Applicants must contact the Academic Administrator for details
No. of awards offered: 2
Closing Date: 31 August

For further information contact:

Trinity College, Broad St, Oxford OX1 3BH, United Kingdom.

Email: jane.sherwood@admin.ox.ac.uk

Trinity College Junior Research Fellowship

Purpose: To promote and encourage research among those at the start of an academic career
Eligibility: Open to suitably qualified candidates having some research experience (e.g. a completed doctoral thesis)
Level of Study: Doctorate, Postdoctorate
Value: £34,304 p.a, an allowance of up to £1520 p.a
Length of Study: 3 years, non renewable
Frequency: Annual
Study Establishment: Trinity College, University of Oxford
Country of Study: United Kingdom
Application Procedure: Please see application form on Trinity College website www.trinity.ox.ac.uk
Closing Date: 28 January
Additional Information: www.trin.cam.ac.uk/vacancies/junior-research-fellowships/

For further information contact:

Email: academic.administrator@trinity.ox.ac.uk

Trinity College: Michael and Judith Beloff Scholarship

Purpose: To assist graduate students with fees
Eligibility: Open to all graduate applicants for the BC-L. Preference given those intending to practise at the Bar of United Kingdom and Wales
Level of Study: Postgraduate
Type: Scholarship
Value: £10,000 p.a.
Length of Study: 1 year
Frequency: Annual
Country of Study: United Kingdom
Application Procedure: Please note interest on application form. Please see website for details of how to apply
Closing Date: October
Additional Information: Please check at www.trinity.ox.ac.uk/pages/admissions/loans-grants-and-bursaries.php www.trinity.ox.ac.uk/postgraduate-study/postgraduate-application/postgraduate-scholarships/

For further information contact:

Email: Student.Funding@law.ox.ac.uk

University College: Chellgren

Purpose: Applicants must have a place on a postgraduate programme at University College, Oxford. Scholarships can be awarded to students embarking on any postgraduate programme. However, prospective economics students are given preference
Eligibility: Open to all graduate applicants in Economics. Applicants must have a place on a postgraduate programme at University College, Oxford
Level of Study: Postgraduate
Type: Scholarship
Value: £4,000 per year
Length of Study: Up to 3 years
Frequency: Annual
Study Establishment: University
Country of Study: United Kingdom
Application Procedure: Please see website for more details, including how to apply
Closing Date: January
Funding: Trusts
Additional Information: For more information, please check the website: www.univ.ox.ac.uk/postgraduate/financial_1/scholarships_and_studentships/

University College: Loughman

Purpose: To assist graduate students with fees.
Eligibility: Open to all graduate applicants that can demonstrate potential to make significant contributions to College life through extra-academic pursuits (arts, sports, community service, etc.).
Level of Study: Postgraduate, Research
Type: Scholarship
Value: £4,000 per year
Length of Study: Period of fee liability
Frequency: Annual
Study Establishment: University
Country of Study: United Kingdom
Application Procedure: Please see website for details of how to apply.
Funding: Trusts
Additional Information: For more information, please check the website: www.univ.ox.ac.uk/postgraduate/financial_1/scholarships_and_studentships/

For further information contact:

Email: john.loughman@ucd.ie

University Hardship Fund

Purpose: The University Hardship Fund aims to assist students who experience unexpected financial difficulties due to

circumstances which could not have been predicted at the start of their course
Eligibility: Students can apply to the University Hardship Fund (UHF) if they are experiencing unexpected and unforeseeable financial difficulties
Level of Study: Graduate
Type: Funding support
Value: £8,000
Frequency: Annual
Country of Study: Any country
Application Procedure: Students should contact their college hardship officer to request an application form and discuss their application. The hardship officer varies across colleges but could be your Senior Tutor, Bursar or Academic Administrator. Complete application forms should be submitted by the student or their college to Student Fees and Funding as soon as possible and by the appropriate deadline listed below. The form includes sections for the student, tutor or supervisor and college hardship officer to complete, and applications will only be considered when all sections and evidence have been received
Closing Date: 28 April
Funding: Trusts
Additional Information: www.ox.ac.uk/students/fees-funding/assistance/hardship/uhf?wssl=1

For further information contact:

Email: graduatefunding@admin.cam.ac.uk

Vicky Noon Educational Foundation Oxford Scholarships

Purpose: This scholarship is not open to candidates applying for postgraduate certificate or postgraduate diploma courses, or non-matriculated courses.
Eligibility: You should be intending to return to Pakistan once your course is completed. If you have previously studied outside Pakistan you will not normally be considered unless there are exceptional circumstances which explain why you have studied abroad.
Type: Scholarship
Value: The size and duration of awards vary according to each scholar circumstances.
Frequency: Annual
Country of Study: United Kingdom
No. of awards offered: 2
Closing Date: January
Additional Information: www.ox.ac.uk/admissions/graduate/fees-and-funding/fees-funding-and-scholarship-search/scholarships-a-z-listing

For further information contact:

University of Oxford, University Offices, 15 Wellington Square, Oxford OX1 2JD, United Kingdom.

Tel: (44) 1865 270000
Fax: (44) 1865 270708

Wadham College: Beit Scholarship

Level of Study: Postgraduate
Type: Scholarship
Value: University fee, college fee, and full living expenses plus a stipend in line with that offered by the equivalent UK research council.
Length of Study: 1 year
Country of Study: United Kingdom
Application Procedure: Open to graduate applicants for 1-year Masters courses who are ordinarily resident in Malawi, Zambia or Zimbabwe. Please see website for further details, including how to apply
No. of awards offered: 1
Closing Date: January
Additional Information: For more details, please visit website https://www.wadham.ox.ac.uk/finance/graduate-scholarships

For further information contact:

Email: graduate.admissions@wadham.ox.ac.uk

Wadham College: Donner Canadian Foundation Law Scholarship

Purpose: The Donner Canadian Scholarship is awarded to Canadian graduates intending to undertake the BCL or MJur at the University of Oxford as a member of Wadham College. This prize is available on an annual basis and is awarded on the basis of academic excellence and aptitude
Eligibility: Any applicant to the BCL or MJur who is ordinarily resident in Canada.
Type: Scholarship
Value: £22,000 towards fees or living expenses
Length of Study: One year
Frequency: Annual
Country of Study: Any country
Funding: Trusts
Additional Information: Please note that the scholarship will not cover the full cost for the BCL or MJur, and the selected candidate, like all other applicants offered places in the College, will be required to demonstrate to the College that they have sufficient funds to cover the additional costs.

Website: www.wadham.ox.ac.uk/finance/graduate-scholarships

For further information contact:

Tutor for Graduates, Wadham College, Parks Road, Oxford OX1 3PN, United Kingdom.

Email: senior.tutor@wadh.ox.ac.uk

Wadham College: John Brookman Scholarship

Purpose: To assist an organisation scholar who has been given admission to read for a higher degree in the university
Eligibility: The Scholarship is open to those reading for and those who have applied to read for, a graduate degree at the University of Oxford in any subject, and who as John Brookman Scholar will participate in the musical life of the College.
Level of Study: Postgraduate, Research
Type: Scholarship
Value: Equivalent to college fee (£3,112 for 2022)
Length of Study: Duration of fee liability
Frequency: Annual
Study Establishment: Wadham College, University of Oxford
Country of Study: United Kingdom
Application Procedure: Applicants should send a full curriculum vitae detailing their academic and musical qualifications and experience; the graduate course that they are following, or to which they have applied; and the names of two referees, either by post to the Tutor for Graduates. Applicants should also request referees to submit their references (using the same contact details as listed above) by the same date. A successful candidate will take up his/her scholarship from October 1st
Closing Date: 23 March
Funding: Trusts
Contributor: Endowed by late E.W.M. Brookman, an old member of the college, in memory of his son, John M. Brookman (1926–1980)

For further information contact:

Email: admissions@wadh.ox.ac.uk

Wadham College: Peter Carter Taught Graduate Scholarship in Law

Purpose: The Taught Graduate Scholarship in Law is available to graduate students of exceptional academic merit embarking on the BCL or MJur at Wadham College and is available to law graduates of any university
Eligibility: Open to all graduate applicants for the BCL or MJur. Please see website for details
Level of Study: Graduate, Postgraduate
Type: Scholarship
Value: £12,500
Length of Study: 1 year
Study Establishment: Wadham College
Country of Study: Any country
Application Procedure: Please visit the website www.wadham.ox.ac.uk/students/graduate-students/graduate-finance/graduate-scholarships
Closing Date: January
Additional Information: Please visit the website: https://www.wadham.ox.ac.uk/finance/graduate-scholarships for more information. The scholarship can be used to defray in part University fees, College fees and/or maintenance of the Scholar during their period of study. It does not cover all fees so you will have to demonstrate sufficient funds for additional costs llm-guide.com/scholarships/peter-carter-taught-graduate-scholarship-in-law-201

For further information contact:

Email: admissions@wadh.ox.ac.uk

Weatherall Institute of Molecular Medicine: WIMM Prize Studentship

Level of Study: Graduate
Value: All fees and living expenses of £18,000 per annum
Length of Study: 4 years
Country of Study: United Kingdom
Application Procedure: Open to applicants of any nationality applying for projects advertised on the WIMM website. Applicants must quote scholarship reference code H816027
Closing Date: 1 June
Additional Information: For more details, visit website www.imm.ox.ac.uk/wimm-prize-studentship-2017 www.rdm.ox.ac.uk/study-with-us/funding-options/wimm-prize-studentships

For further information contact:

University of Oxford, Level 6, West Wing John Radcliffe Hospital, Headington, Oxford OX3 9DU, United Kingdom.

Email: graduate.enquiries@rdm.ox.ac.uk

Weidenfeld-Hoffmann Scholarships and Leadership Programme

Purpose: The Weidenfeld-Hoffmann Scholarships and Leadership Programme cultivates the leaders of tomorrow by

providing outstanding university graduates and professionals from developing and emerging economies with the opportunity to pursue fully-funded graduate studies at the University of Oxford, combined with a comprehensive programme of leadership development, long-term mentoring and networking.
Eligibility: You must be applying to start a new graduate course at Oxford. Please visit the website to see the complete list of eligible courses and country of residence
Level of Study: Postgraduate
Type: Scholarship
Value: £17,668
Length of Study: Period of fee liability
Frequency: Annual
Country of Study: United Kingdom
Application Procedure: Please see website for more details, including how to apply
Closing Date: April
Funding: Trusts
Additional Information: For more information, please check the website: www.graduate.ox.ac.uk/weidenfeld-hoffmann

For further information contact:

Email: info@whtrust.org

Weidenfeld-Hoffmann Scholarships and Leadership Programme

Purpose: The Weidenfeld-Hoffmann Scholarships and Leadership Programme cultivates the leaders of tomorrow by providing outstanding university graduates and professionals from developing and emerging economies with the opportunity to pursue fully-funded graduate studies at the University of Oxford, combined with a comprehensive programme of leadership development, long-term mentoring and networking
Eligibility: visit website
Type: Scholarship
Value: £17,668
Country of Study: Any country
Closing Date: April
Additional Information: www.ox.ac.uk/admissions/graduate/fees-and-funding/fees-funding-and-scholarship-search/weidenfeld-hoffmann-scholarships-and-leadership-programme

For further information contact:

University of Oxford, University Offices, 15 Wellington Square, Oxford OX1 2JD, United Kingdom.

Tel: (44) 1865 270000
Fax: (44) 1865 270708

Wolfson Postgraduate Scholarships in the Humanities

Purpose: The Wolfson Postgraduate Scholarships in the Humanities are available for applicants who are applying to a full or part-time DPhil course in history, languages or literature.
Eligibility: To be considered for this scholarship, you must be ordinarily resident in the United Kingdom or Republic of Ireland.
Type: Scholarship
Value: The scholarship covers course fees at the Home rate only.
Frequency: Annual
Country of Study: Any country
Closing Date: April
Additional Information: www.ox.ac.uk/admissions/graduate/fees-and-funding/fees-funding-and-scholarship-search/scholarships-a-z-listing

For further information contact:

University of Oxford, University Offices, 15 Wellington Square, Oxford OX1 2JD, United Kingdom.

Tel: (44) 1865 270000
Fax: (44) 1865 270708

Worcester College: C. Douglas Dillon Scholarship

Eligibility: Open to graduate applicants for 1 year or 2-year courses in the fields of Politics, Diplomacy, Governance and International Relations. Please see website for more details, including eligible courses and how to apply
Level of Study: Graduate
Value: £10,000
Length of Study: 1 or 2 years
Country of Study: Any country
Closing Date: 3 March
Additional Information: For more details, visit website www.worc.ox.ac.uk/applying/graduates/graduate-scholarships www.worc.ox.ac.uk/sites/default/files/ad_c_douglas_dillon_scholarship_2020-21.pdf

For further information contact:

Tel: (44) 1865 278300
Email: graduate.enquiries@worc.ox.ac.uk

Worcester College: Drue Heinz Scholarship

Level of Study: Graduate

Value: £10,000
Length of Study: 1 year
Country of Study: Any country
Application Procedure: Open to graduate applicants in the Humanities. Preference given to international applicants. Please see website for more details, including how to apply
Closing Date: 5 March
Contributor: Worcester

For further information contact:

Email: graduate.enquiries@worc.ox.ac.uk

Worcester College: Ogilvie Thompson Scholarships

Purpose: To assist graduate students with fees
Eligibility: Open to incoming graduates who have been undergraduates at Worcester within the last two years and have not undertaken any graduate work at Oxford or elsewhere
Type: Scholarships
Value: £10,000 towards the full cost of fees and maintenance
Length of Study: 1 year
Country of Study: United Kingdom
Closing Date: 5 March

For further information contact:

Tel: (44) 1865 278300
Email: graduate.enquiries@worc.ox.ac.uk

University of Paris-Saclay

3 rue Joliot Curie, Building Breguet, (F-) 91190 Gif-sur-Yvette, France.

Website: www.universite-paris-saclay.fr/

Born of the combined will of universities, grandes écoles and research organizations, Université Paris-Saclay is one of the major European and world universities, covering the sectors of Science and Engineering, Life Sciences and Health, and Humanities and Social Sciences. Its scientific policy closely associates research and innovation, and is expressed in both basic and applied sciences to respond to major societal challenges.

Université Paris-Saclay International Master's Scholarships

Purpose: Université Paris-Saclay aims to promote access for international students to its Master's programmes, provided by its faculties, component-institutions and associated universities, and to make it easier for highly-qualified international students to join the University, especially for those wishing to develop an academic project through research up to the doctoral level.
Eligibility: 1. Students admitted to a Paris-Saclay University Master's programme delivered by one of the following institutions: AgroParisTech, CentraleSupelec, ENS Paris-Saclay, INSTN-CEA, IOGS, UEVE, UPSaclay, UVSQ. Among these students, only those who answer one of the following criteria are eligible to apply: 2. Newly arrived international students, aged 30 and less during the course of the selection year. 3. Students of foreign nationality living on the French soil for less than a year, previously or currently enrolled in a training course or internship that does not lead to certification. 4. Students of foreign nationality living on the French soil for less than a year, taking language classes (type FFL). 5. Students who have lived in France in the past, within the framework of a mobility programme during their studies (e.g. Erasmus Mundus Joint Master's Degrees, exchange programme...) that did not lead to certification.
Level of Study: Masters Degree
Type: Scholarship
Value: The scholarship will be suspended if internship wages exceed €700/month
Length of Study: 1 or 2 years
Frequency: Annual
Study Establishment: Université Paris-Saclay, France
Country of Study: France
Application Procedure: 1) Selected students will automatically be sent a link by email to an online application form. Upon reception of this email, students wishing to apply will need to complete the online application form and provide (mandatory) the names and contact details of two referees who would be willing to submit a reference for the candidate (director of studies, professor, internship coordinator...). 2) Each of the two referees named by the candidate will be sent a link by email to an online recommendation form. They will be asked to complete and submit the form prior to the closing day of the scholarship call. The candidate will automatically be informed when each referee has submitted the form. 3) The application file for a scholarship will be considered complete when both recommendation forms have been submitted by the referees. Please note: the candidate will not receive a message confirming that the application is complete. It is up to the candidate to ensure both referees

complete and submit the form by the deadline given in the invitation email.
Closing Date: 12 May
Funding: Government
Additional Information: Website: www.universite-paris-saclay.fr/en/admission/bourses-et-aides-financieres/international-masters-scholarships-program-idex

For further information contact:

Email: international-master-scholarship.idex@universite-paris-saclay.fr

University of Pretoria

Private Bag X20, Hatfield 0028, South Africa.

Tel: (27) 12 420 3111
Email: ssc@up.ac.za
Website: www.up.ac.za/

The University of Pretoria (UP) was established in 1908 with just four professors and 32 students, in a little house called Kya Rosa. Today, it is one of the largest research universities in South Africa. UP has transformed into a dynamic university community of staff and students who come from a range of diverse backgrounds and cultures showcasing South African and global societies. The University was born from a vision to create a space for quality education and for new ideas to flourish. Over the course of its existence, and through different phases of political power and social change, UP has been resilient in its commitment to academic quality.

Africa Cosmos Education Trust Bursary Application

Eligibility: See website For Details: www.up.ac.za/funding/attachment/3129924/africa-cosmos-education-trust-bursary-agreement-2023 & www.up.ac.za/funding/attachment/3129929/africa-cosmos-education-trust-bursarypolicy-2023
Level of Study: Postgraduate
Type: Bursary
Application Procedure: Application: www.up.ac.za/funding/attachment/3129914/africa-cosmos-education-trust-bursary-application-2023
Closing Date: 17 March
Additional Information: Website: www.up.ac.za/funding/3129890/africa-cosmos-education-trust-bursary-application-2023

For further information contact:

Email: miffy.moodley@lsacademies.co.za; jessie.radebe@lsacademies.co.za

Commonwealth PhD Scholarships

Purpose: Commonwealth PhD Scholarships are for candidates from low and middle income Commonwealth countries, for full-time doctoral study at a United Kingdom university. Commonwealth PhD Scholarships are for candidates from low and middle income Commonwealth countries, for full-time doctoral study at a United Kingdom university
Eligibility: 1. Applicants should be citizens of Commonwealth countries (excluding South African students). 2. Applicants must conduct their studies at the University of Pretoria. 3. They must have completed the degree that will give them admission to a doctoral programme a maximum of 3 years prior to their application for the University of Pretoria Commonwealth Doctoral Scholarship. 4. They must not be older than 35 years of age at the time of application. Masters students currently registered at the University of Pretoria are not eligible for the Doctoral Scholarship
Level of Study: Doctorate
Type: Scholarship
Value: The value of the Doctoral Scholarships will be R120,000. This amount must be used to cover accommodation and living cost, medical aid and books/stationery. For detailed information, please visit website
Country of Study: South Africa
Application Procedure: The mode of applying is electronically or by post
Closing Date: 28 August
Contributor: University of Pretoria
Additional Information: Website: www.up.ac.za/funding/3085161/2023-up-phd-commonwealth-scholarship

For further information contact:

Email: eas@cscuk.org.uk

Ek Brown Of Monaltrie Animal Sanctuary Trust Bursary

Eligibility: 1. Degree programme in Veterinary Science (BVSc) (2nd year +++) 2. Students must have completed the first year of study successfully. 3. Students who are SA Citizens, from KwaZulu Natal may apply for the bursary. 4. Previous EK Brown bursary holders may apply again. 5. Preference will be given to applicants who demonstrate interest in Equine Studies and who intend to practice in KZN.
Level of Study: Postgraduate

Type: Bursary
Value: R30 000
Application Procedure: 1. Application for UP financial aid – submitted & verified as complete 2. Curriculum Vitae 3. Full academic record 4. Motivational letter – indicate why you should be considered for this award. 5. Declaration of other funding that applicant is receiving for the financial year and/or applications for funding in process. Submit your documents via e-mail to jeanne.goosen@up.ac.za.
Closing Date: 15 March
Contributor: UP Internal Bursary
Additional Information: Website: www.up.ac.za/funding/3128700/ek-brown-of-monaltrie-animal-sanctuary-trust-bursary-2023

For further information contact:

Email: jeanne.goosen@up.ac.za

Fulbright Foreign Student Funding

Purpose: Scholarships to work towards your Master's or PhD studies in the United States
Eligibility: 1. Be a South African citizen or a permanent resident (minimum 5 years). 2. For Non-Degree (Visiting Student Researcher) studies: Must be registered for a PhD with a South African university. 3. Have a four-year Bachelor's degree, BTech degree or a three-year Bachelor's degree plus honors year when applying for Master's. 4. Have a Master's degree when applying for a Doctoral degree.
Level of Study: Postgraduate
Type: Scholarship
Application Procedure: For more details & application: za.usembassy.gov/fulbright-foreign-student-program/
Closing Date: 1 May
Additional Information: Website:https: www.up.ac.za/funding/3131281/2024-to-2025-fulbright-foreign-student-funding

Scholarship for Sustainable Energy Development

Eligibility: 1. Full-time master's students 2. From a developing country 3. Pursuing studies in any field related to sustainable energy development (renewable energy, advanced electricity technologies, public policy...)
Level of Study: Masters Degree
Type: Scholarship
Value: R10,000 /year
Length of Study: for at most 2 years
Application Procedure: Information and application: globalelectricity.org/scholarship
Closing Date: 7 April
Additional Information: Website: www.up.ac.za/funding/3123748/scholarship-for-sustainable-energy-development

Western Australian Premiers Scholarship

Purpose: The Program will focus on attracting new students from priority target markets, studying in a range of fields that are linked to priority sectors and industries for Western Australia.
Eligibility: To be eligible, applicants must: 1. Have received a letter of offer for a new enrolment as an onshore international student, undertaking full-time studies in a postgraduate program (minimum two years) at one of Western Australia's five Universities, commencing in Semester 2 2024, or a start date after 30 June 2024 applicable to the student's course of study (for PhD students). 2. Have not commenced nor completed previous studies in Western Australia in 2023 or Semester 1, 2024. 3. Have met the criteria to obtain an international student visa for study in Australia, arriving in the State of Western Australia (the State) and commencing studies onshore in Semester 2 2024. 4. Be commencing studies directly in a postgraduate program and not via a packaged, foundation or English language pathway. 5. Be prepared to decline any other scholarships they may have been previously granted by the University, State or Commonwealth if successful in being awarded a WA Premier's University Scholarship. 6. Be applying to the University as an international fee-paying student. 7. Be a citizen of one of the following countries: A. Brazil B. ColombiaC. Hong Kong D. Japan E. Kenya F. India G. Indonesia H. Republic of Korea (South Korea) I. Singapore J. South Africa K. The Philippines L. Vietnam M. Zimbabwe
Level of Study: Postgraduate
Type: Scholarship
Value: R50,000 each
Frequency: Annual
Application Procedure: The application and decision process for the WA Premier's University Scholarship will be administered by each participating Western Australian University. Applicants will apply directly to the University in which they plan to enrol. Each University will determine the documentation required to be provided from applicants in order to assess and evaluate applications. This will be a competitive process. The specific Scholarship application information for each of the universities will be provided prior to applications being opened, and will be accessible on wa.gov.au
Closing Date: 31 May

Additional Information: Website: www.up.ac.za/funding/3133158/western-australian-premiers-scholarship-2023

University of Pune

Institute of Bioinformatics & Biotechnology (IBB), Ganeshkhind, Pune, Maharashtra 411007, India.

Tel: (91) 20 2569 2039
Email: director@bioinfo.ernet.in
Website: www.unipune.ernet.in
Contact: Director

The University stands for humanism and tolerance, for reason for adventure of ideas and for the search of truth. It stands for the forward march of the human race towards even higher objectives. If the universities discharge their duties adequately then it is well with the nation and the people–Jawaharlal Nehru.

Department of Biotechnology (DBT) Junior Research Fellowship

Subjects: Biotechnology and Applied Biology
Purpose: To support candidates pursuing research in areas of biotechnology and applied biology
Eligibility: 1. Candidates should appear for BET examination and only for three attempts during their career within the prescribed age limit. 2. Candidates who have completed eligibility qualification in a year will be eligible to appear for BET examination in that year and two subsequent years. Students who have passed after 01st Jan 2015 or will appear for the final exam of qualifying degree for this year is eligible. 3. Students with M.Sc/M.Tech/M.V.Sc degree with Biotechnology as the main subject e.g. Biotechnology, specialization such as Agricultural, Animal/Veterinary, Medical, Marine, Industrial, Environmental, Pharmaceutical, Food, Bio-resources Biotechnology, Biochemical Engineering, Bio-sciences and Biotechnology, Bioinformatics and M.Sc Molecular & Human Genetics and M.Sc Neuroscience as well as B.Tech / B.E in Biotechnology (4-year course after 10+2) recognized by UGC/AICTE are eligible for this exam. 4. Candidates with minimum 60% for general and OBC category and SC/ST/PH candidates with 55% of the total marks (equivalent grade) are only eligible 5. Age Limit: The applicants should be below the age of 28 years for open category as on 28th February. Age relaxation of 5 years (up to 33 years) for SC/ST/PH and women candidates and 3 years (31st years) for OBC candidates will be given.
Level of Study: Research
Type: Fellowship
Value: Stipend of Rs 25,000/- or Rs 28,000/- per month plus HRA as per DST guidelines and research contingency of Rs.30,000/- per year.
Length of Study: For 3 years and extended to 2 more years based on performance
Frequency: Annual
Study Establishment: University of Pune
Country of Study: India
Application Procedure: Candidates should register and apply online in the prescribed application form available at the institute website www.bcil.nic.in. The details about the application process, filling the online application form, payment of application fees and uploading of required documents/certificates and the examination are available on the website. General/OBC candidates have to pay an application fee of Rs.1000/- and SC/ST/PH categories are exempted from payment of application fees. The application fees is payable either online or offline according to the details given in the web site for completion of application process.
Contributor: Biotech Consortium India Limited.
Additional Information: career.webindia123.com/career/scholarships/scholarships_india/dbt-junior-research-fellowship/index.htm

For further information contact:

Department of Biotechnology, University of Pune, Pune, Maharashtra 411007, India.

Tel: (91) 20 2569 4952, 2569 2248
Email: jkpal@unipune.ernet.in

University of Queensland

Research and Postgraduate Studies, Cumbrae-Stewart Building, Brisbane, St Lucia, QLD 4072, Australia.

Tel: (61) 7 3365 1111
Email: scholarships@research.uq.edu.au
Website: www.uq.edu.au

The University of Queensland maintains a world-class, comprehensive programme of research and research training, underpinned by state-of-the-art infrastructure and a commitment to rewarding excellence. As one of Australia's premier universities, UQ attracts researchers and students of outstanding calibre.

Dr Rosamond Siemon Postgraduate Renal Research Scholarship

Purpose: To support a research higher degree candidate to undertake multidisciplinary, collaborative research into renal disease, repair and regeneration
Eligibility: Open to candidates who are enroled or intend to enrol in a research higher degree at the University of Queensland and who demonstrate a high level of academic achievement and ability
Level of Study: Postgraduate
Type: Scholarship
Value: AU$30,000 per year (a stipend of AU$25,000 and a direct research cost allowance of AU$5,000)
Length of Study: 3 years and 6 months
Frequency: Annual
Country of Study: Australia
Application Procedure: Applicants must send a proposed research project description, certified copies of academic transcripts, academic curriculum vitae, including publications and 3 letters of recommendation
Closing Date: 31 August
Funding: Individuals
Contributor: Dr Rosamond Siemon
Additional Information: Research Scholarships Referee Report Form can be used. This can be accessed from www.uq.edu.au/grad-school/scholarship-forms

For further information contact:

Research Scholarships, Office of Research and Postgraduate Studies, The University of Queensland, St Lucia, QLD 4072, Australia.

Email: postgrad-office@imb.uq.edu.au

Herdsman Fellowship in Medical Science

Purpose: The fellowship is open to graduates in medicine or related health sciences enrolled full-time for a PhD on a topic related to the medical problems of the aged.
Eligibility: Applicants must be graduates in medicine or related health sciences, enrol full-time for a PhD, and be undertaking a research topic related to the medical problems of the aged.
Level of Study: Postgraduate
Type: Fellowship
Value: AU$22,860 per year
Length of Study: Fellowship shall initially be for 1 year but may be extended by the commitee for further terms of 1 year up to a total of 3 years
Country of Study: Australia
Application Procedure: Applications must consist of: covering letter addressing the Herdsman Fellowship Rules, in particular point 2, academic Curriculum vitae, 2 referee reports. No strict format is required; however the Research Scholarships generic Referee Report may be used.
No. of awards offered: 1
Closing Date: 31 August
Contributor: Maintained by the income from a bequest of AU$2,60,000 from Mrs Rose Herdsman
No. of awards given last year: 1
No. of applicants last year: 1
Additional Information: website: www.postgraduatefunding.com/award-655

For further information contact:

Faculty of Health Sciences, University of Queensland, St Lucia, QLD 4072, Australia.

Email: scholarships@research.uq.edu.au
Website: www.uq.edu.au/

PhD Scholarship in Immunology and Immunogenetics

Purpose: To provide the foundations for the development of treatments based on the genetic findings.
Eligibility: Open to a dynamic, intelligent and diligent PhD candidate (Australian or international) with either a clinical or a relevant basic science background to take forward the project.
Level of Study: Doctorate
Type: Scholarship
Value: AU$25,000 per year
Length of Study: 3 years
Frequency: Annual
Study Establishment: The University of Queensland
Country of Study: Australia
Application Procedure: Candidates must contact Prof. Brown for more information
Closing Date: 3 September
No. of applicants last year: 1
Additional Information: website: www.postgraduatefunding.com/award-2337

For further information contact:

Tel: (61) 7 3240 2870
Email: scholarships@research.uq.edu.au

The Constantine Aspromourgos Memorial Scholarship for Greek Studies

Subjects: Arts, humanities and social sciences
Purpose: To assist a research higher degree student studying at least 1 area of Greek studies
Eligibility: You're eligible if you 1. have a bachelor's or a master's degree.; And you're either 2. undertaking a UQ postgraduate program involving studies that relate to at least one area of Greek studies (ancient, Byzantine or modern) in 1. language 2. culture 3. literature 4. history 5. archaeology 6. society 7. religion 8. economics 9. politics 10 geography (a Greek studies program) 3. a UQ graduate undertaking a Greek studies program at another university.
Level of Study: Postgraduate
Type: Scholarship
Value: Approx. AU$5,000
Length of Study: 1 year
Frequency: Annual
Country of Study: Australia
Application Procedure: Apply using the online application form
No. of awards offered: 1
Closing Date: October
Funding: Individuals
Additional Information: The Scholarship is also open to candidates who are undertaking the programme as a student of another university acceptable to the committee, or this university, provided that some part of the programme involves studies at another university scholarships.uq.edu.au/scholarship/constantine-aspromourgos-memorial-scholarship-greek-studies#qt-scholarship_tabs-foundation-tabs-1

For further information contact:

Faculty of Arts, Forgan Smith Building, The University of Queensland, St Lucia, QLD 4072, Australia.

Tel: (61) 7 3365 1333
Email: scholarships@hass.uq.edu.au

University of Queensland PhD Scholarships for International Students

Purpose: Students must have achieved an entry level OP minimum of 11 or the equivalent if originating from another Australian state or territory or for continuing students has a GPA of at least 4.0.
Eligibility: 1. Eligible Countries: Australian and Permanent Residents or NZ citizens and International students are eligible to apply. 2. Eligible Course or Subjects: The scholarship will be awarded in the Agribusiness, agriculture, environment and science, Engineering, architecture and planning, and information technology, Health, Humanities, education, psychology, music, business, and social sciences.
Level of Study: Postgraduate
Type: Scholarship
Value: Available amount for UQ PhD scholarships is AU$27,596 per annum (2019 rate), indexed annually, tuition fees, Overseas Student Health Cover (OSHC).
Study Establishment: View projects by area Agribusiness, Agriculture, Environment, and Science Engineering, Architecture and Planning, and Information Technology Health Humanities, Education, Psychology, and Music Business, economics, and law (coming soon)
Country of Study: Australia
Application Procedure: See the website.
Closing Date: 31 December
Additional Information: For more details please visit the website scholarship-positions.com/uq-phd-scholarships-international-students-australia/2018/03/06/

For further information contact:

Email: graduateschool@uq.edu.au

Walter and Eliza Hall Scholarship Trust Opportunity Scholarship for Nursing

Purpose: This scholarship supports financially disadvantaged students who are studying nursing.
Eligibility: 1. Domestic undergraduate nursing student 2. Financially disadvantaged background
Level of Study: Undergraduate
Type: Scholarship
Value: AU$10,000
Length of Study: 3 yearS
Frequency: Annual
Country of Study: Any country
Application Procedure: Apply here: sydneyuniversity.formstack.com/forms/walter_eliza_hall_trust.
No. of awards offered: 2
Closing Date: 31 October
Funding: Private
Additional Information: website: www.sydney.edu.au/scholarships/c/walter-eliza-hall-trust-opportunity-scholarship-nursing.html

For further information contact:

Brisbane, St Lucia, QLD 4072, Australia.

Email: nmsw.scholarship@uq.edu.au

University of Reading

Whiteknights, PO Box 217, Reading RG6 6AH, United Kingdom.

Tel: (44) 1189 875 123
Email: student.recruitment@reading.ac.uk
Website: www.rdg.ac.uk
Contact: Student Financial Support Office

The University of Reading offers postgraduate taught and research degree courses in all the traditional subject areas except medical sciences. Vocational courses are also offered. Research work in many areas is of international renown.

AHRC South, West and Wales Doctoral Training Partnerships

Purpose: The AHRC SWW2 DTP funding allows for innovative doctoral support, including the development of broader skills such as partnership working and language skills, and experience in working outside academia through industry and international placements.
Eligibility: Applications are open to UK and international applicants. AHRC funding covers tuition fees at the UK/Republic of Ireland rate; for international candidates offered a AHRC award, the difference between UK/Republic of Ireland and international fees will be covered by the University of Reading. Students who have already commenced doctoral study may apply for funding for the remainder of their study, providing that, at the start of the AHRC award, they will have at least 50% of their period of study remaining (excluding the fourth "writing up" year (or part time equivalent).
Level of Study: Doctorate
Value: Covering fees at the UK/Republic of Ireland rate and provide a maintenance grant (stipend), the current (2023/24) level of which is £17,668 for full-time study.
Application Procedure: See website
Closing Date: 16 January
Additional Information: For further information and advice about these studentships, please contact the Graduate School by emailing doctoralstudentshipsofficer@reading.ac.uk. Website: www.reading.ac.uk/graduate-school/funding/phd-studentships/sww-dtp

Alumni Discounts

Eligibility: View full details of the eligibility criteria and terms and conditions: www.reading.ac.uk/alumni/-/media/alumni/files/pdfs/alumni_discount_tc_and_cs_-_jun_2020.pdf
Level of Study: Masters Degree
Value: discount is worth £1,500 and is applied to the first year of tuition fees in the case of full-time students or split over two years (£750 per year) for part-time studies.
Application Procedure: There is no need to apply for the discount - it is applied automatically for eligible students.
Additional Information: Website: www.reading.ac.uk/graduate-school/funding/phd-studentships

For further information contact:

Email: pgadmissions@reading.ac.uk

China Scholarship Council Studentships

Eligibility: Specific eligibility criteria can be found on the CSC website: www.csc.edu.cn/ and include the following. 1. Candidates must be citizens and permanent residents of the People's Republic of China at the time of application. 2. Candidates must not be working abroad at the time of application. 3. Successful candidates must return to China upon completion of their studies and/or research. 4. Candidates must hold an academic offer from the University to commence study in the relevant academic year. They must, therefore, fulfil the relevant academic entry requirements set by the University of Reading, including a high level of English language proficiency. 5. Candidates must be intending to pursue study/research in one of the priority academic areas identified by the University of Reading and CSC. 6. Candidates must satisfy the selection criteria set out by CSC and complete the documentation required by the CSC.
Level of Study: Postgraduate
Type: Studentship
Value: The tuition fee and a £1,000 per year training and development allowance, while CSC funding provides an annual living allowance that includes overseas student health cover and visa application fees.
Application Procedure: To be considered for these awards, you must apply online for admission to the University of Reading by Friday 6th January 2024, stating in the application that you are applying for a University of Reading/China Scholarship Council joint scholarship. Indicate on your admissions application (when prompted for details of the funding you are applying for) that you wish to be considered for the China Scholarship Council studentships. Please spell out in full, as there are other organisations that use the abbreviation CSC.
Closing Date: 6 January

Additional Information: Website: www.reading.ac.uk/graduate-school/funding/phd-studentships/china-scholarship-council

Earth System Prediction Doctoral Training Programme

Purpose: AFESP is establishing a long-term Doctoral Training Programme to develop skills in the fundamental new research across the physical, mathematical and computational sciences that will be required to address next-generation challenges in Earth system prediction and operational weather and climate forecasting. PhD students will be trained and embedded within the overall AFESP programme.
Eligibility: See website
Level of Study: Postgraduate
Type: Programme
Value: Cover tuition fees, research-training costs and a stipend for up to three-and-a-half years for living costs
Length of Study: The maximum duration of funding is four years
Application Procedure: Please apply using the AFESP application form: www.reading.ac.uk/graduate-school/-/media/project/uor-main/schools-departments/graduate-school/documents/phd-application-form_earth-system-prediction_20122022.docx?la=en&hash=17D28CCAA8BFCAB864062F26F8AD9D30. Applications should be submitted to AFESP-DTP@reading.ac.uk
Closing Date: 31 January
Additional Information: Website: www.reading.ac.uk/graduate-school/funding/phd-studentships/earth-system-prediction-doctoral-training-programme

For further information contact:

Email: AFESP-DTP@reading.ac.uk

ESRC SeNSS Doctoral Training Partnerships Studentships

Purpose: The University of Reading is part of the South East Network for Social Sciences (SeNSS), a prestigious doctoral training partnership funded by the Economic and Social Research Council (ESRC).
Eligibility: In order to receive ESRC studentship funding you must meet the eligibility criteria set out by the ESRC; see SeNSS eligibility criteria (senss-dtp.ac.uk/application-faqs) for further information. Individual departments can advise about the English language requirements for your chosen PhD programme at Reading. Applications are open to UK and international applicants. ESRC and University of Reading funding covers tuition fees at the UK/Republic of Ireland rate; for international candidates offered a SeNSS award, the difference between UK/Republic of Ireland and international fees will be covered by the University of Reading. The studentships do not fund professional doctorates (e.g. DBA, EdD) or PhD by distance.
Level of Study: Postgraduate
Type: Studentship
Value: UKRI stipend / living allowance (currently £17668 for 2022/3), tuition fees at the UK/Republic of Ireland rate and provide innovative and challenging doctoral training in an interdisciplinary research environment.
Length of Study: three- (PhD) or four-year awards (master's and PhD) and on a full- or part-time basis.
Application Procedure: See website
Additional Information: Website: www.reading.ac.uk/graduate-school/funding/phd-studentships/esrc-senss-dtp

Felix Scholarships

Purpose: The Felix Scholarship scheme is available to high achieving students from India and other developing countries pursuing postgraduate studies at the University of Reading.
Eligibility: To be eligible for all the Felix Scholarships offered, you must be applying to start a full-time postgraduate degree at the University of Reading. You must be able to demonstrate academic excellence and financial need and are expected by the Trust to return to work in your home country after completing your studies. For the scholarship for Indian citizens, the following eligibility criteria apply: 1. You must be an Indian national and not currently be living or studying outside of India. 2. You must have not previously studied for one year or more outside India. 3. You must have at least a first-class bachelor's degree from an Indian university or comparable institution. Those with an upper second-class degree at a bachelor's level may be considered if they hold a first-class degree at master's level. 4. You must not hold a degree from a university outside of India. 5. This scholarship is available to students pursuing either a PhD or master's. For the scholarship for students from developing countries, the following eligibility criteria apply: 1. You must have at least a first-class bachelor's degree from a university or comparable institution. Those with an upper second-class degree at a bachelor's level may be considered if they hold a first-class degree at master's level. 2. You must not hold a degree from a university outside of your home country. 3. Please note that this scholarship is for master's level only.
Level of Study: Masters Degree, Postgraduate
Type: Scholarship

Value: Cover tuition fees at the international rate and provide a stipend (maintenance grant) to cover living expenses (around £15,038)
Length of Study: Up to three years
Application Procedure: Only those candidates who have been accepted for admission will be considered for short listing. You can apply online for a master's or PhD on our website: www.risisweb.reading.ac.uk/si/sits.urd/run/siw_ipp_lgn.login?process=siw_ipp_app&code1=P_ADM&code2=0001.
Closing Date: 30 January
Additional Information: Please note, candidates who already hold a master's degree cannot apply for a master's degree scholarship.

International PhD Studentships

Purpose: The University is pleased to announce a range of international PhD studentships available for October 2024 start. These are available for highly qualified applicants for research within the science, life sciences, social sciences and arts and humanities areas.
Eligibility: Funding is only open to international candidates. Candidates will be required to meet the language requirements specified by their School/Department upon entry. Due to the nature of the studentships where training and support will be directly available via the university, we only invite applications for students wishing to study at one of the University of Reading campuses. Unfortunately, we cannot support other modes of study, such as by distance.
Level of Study: Postgraduate
Type: Studentship
Value: A subsistence grant (stipend) broadly in line with the UKRI minimum stipend. The 2022/23 stipend rate is £17,668. tuition fees at the international rate a £1,000 per annum training and development allowance.
Length of Study: three years
Frequency: Annual
Country of Study: Any country
Application Procedure: See website www.reading.ac.uk/graduate-school/funding/phd-studentships/international-phd-studentships
Closing Date: 9 January
Additional Information: Weblink: www.reading.ac.uk/graduate-school/funding/phd-studentships/international-phd-studentships

For further information contact:

Doctoral Studentships Officer.

Email: doctoralstudentshipsofficer@reading.ac.uk

Regional PhD Bursaries

Purpose: The University of Reading is delighted to offer a number of PhD bursaries to support residents of Reading and the surrounding area to achieve their highest academic potential, enhance their professional prospects and pursue research in an area they are passionate about.
Eligibility: These bursaries are available for either part-time or full-time PhD research in a broad range of subject areas. Applicants must permanently reside in Reading or within 25 miles of the University and demonstrate a connection to the region. Candidates must satisfy the normal entry requirements for PhD study at Reading (normally an upper second class undergraduate degree or a master's degree, depending on the subject area). This scheme is not open to students who have already started a PhD at the University of Reading.
Level of Study: Postgraduate
Type: Bursary
Value: Up to five years for part-time study or up to three years full-time study.
Length of Study: cover the full cost of tuition fees at the UK/Republic of Ireland rate. This is not provided as a cash bursary.
Application Procedure: See Website
Closing Date: 2 May
Additional Information: Website: www.reading.ac.uk/graduate-school/funding/phd-studentships/regional-bursaries

For further information contact:

Email: doctoralstudentshipsofficer@reading.ac.uk

Self-funded PhD Scholarships

Purpose: The Department of Meteorology is pleased to announce the introduction of PhD scholarships for self-funding applicants who meet the eligibility criteria outlined on this page, and who are starting their PhD
Eligibility: Applicants will need to meet all of the following requirements: 1. be self-funding or have a studentship/scholarship that does not provide sufficient funding for the student's entire tuition fee and their reasonable living costs 2. be in possession of a formal PhD offer of admission from the University of Reading, including meeting the language requirements specified by the School upon entry.
Level of Study: Postgraduate
Type: Scholarship
Value: £1,000 per year for UK (home) students, £3,000 per year for international students, to be awarded as a bursary directly allocated to the PhD student.
Length of Study: up to three years for full-time students and up to four years for part-time students.

Application Procedure: 1. Before applying, please read our guidance on how to apply and entry requirements. 2. Submit an application for admission to our PhD in Atmosphere, Oceans and Climate or PhD in Space Weather and Solar-Terrestrial Physics, via our online admissions portal. 3. In the 'Scholarships applied for' box that appears within the Funding Section of your online application, please quote "Reading Department of Meteorology PhD Scholarships" in order for your application to be considered.
Additional Information: Website: www.reading.ac.uk/graduate-school/funding/phd-studentships

University International Research Studentships

Subjects: All subject areas are eligible
Eligibility: Open to nationals of countries outside of the UK
Level of Study: PhD
Type: Studentship
Value: All tuition fees and a grant for living costs
Length of Study: Up to 3 years
Frequency: Annual
Study Establishment: University of Reading
Country of Study: United Kingdom
Application Procedure: Contact Jonathan Lloyd at the University Graduate School
No. of awards offered: Varies
Closing Date: 1 January
Contributor: University of Reading

For further information contact:

Tel: (44) 118 378 6839
Email: j.d.lloyd@reading.ac.uk

University of Reading Dorothy Hodgkin Postgraduate Award

Eligibility: Open to nationals of either India, Mainland China, Hong Kong, Russia or a country in the developing world only
Level of Study: Postgraduate
Type: Scholarship
Value: All tuition fees and a grant for living costs
Length of Study: 1 year; 3 years
Frequency: Annual
Study Establishment: University of Reading
Country of Study: United Kingdom
Application Procedure: Contact the Jonathan Lloyd at the faculties of science and life science
Closing Date: 6 May
Additional Information: www.european-funding-guide.eu/awardprize/11552-dorothy-hodgkin-postgraduate-awards-dhpa

For further information contact:

Tel: (44) 1183 788 341
Email: j.d.lloyd@reading.ac.uk

University of Reading MSc Intelligent Buildings Scholarship

Purpose: In order to be considered for this Scholarship you must hold the offer of a place on the MSc Intellegent Buildings course.
Eligibility: In order to be considered for this Scholarship you must hold the offer of a place on the MSc Intelligent Buildings course
Level of Study: Postgraduate
Type: Scholarship
Value: £3,000
Length of Study: 1 year
Frequency: Annual
Study Establishment: University of Reading
Country of Study: United Kingdom
Application Procedure: Contact Gulay Ozkan, Programme Coordinator at the School of Construction Management and Engineering.
No. of awards offered: 1
Closing Date: 30 August
Contributor: The Happold Trust
No. of awards given last year: 1
No. of applicants last year: 1
Additional Information: Website: www.postgraduatefunding.com/award-2608

For further information contact:

Tel: (44) 11 8987 5123
Fax: (44) 11 8931 4404
Email: student.recruitment@reading.ac.uk

Wilkie Calvert Co-supported PhD Studentships

Purpose: This scheme is aimed at supporting professionals to undertake PhD research, on a part-time basis, which will both support their own career development and be of strategic importance to their employer.
Eligibility: Candidates: 1. will normally be expected to hold an undergraduate degree (at the 2:1 level or equivalent) and a master's degree. This requirement may be waived where candidates have a body of relevant professional experience 2. will normally be UK or Republic of Ireland nationals.

Those who are not eligible for UK/Republic of Ireland fee status may apply, but they would be liable to provide the additional funding required to cover the international fee rate. They would also be required to meet the standard English Language requirements.

Level of Study: Postgraduate

Type: Studentship

Value: finding the funding to cover the cost of their fees gaining support from their employers, particularly in terms of time for study and for attending supervision meetings or training sessions.

Application Procedure: In order to apply for an award, candidates should: 1. Seek the support of their employer and consult with them about their specific research proposal; gain a letter of support from their employer. 2. Contact the relevant University of Reading School/Department to ensure that they would be prepared to support an application in the proposed area; candidates are encouraged to consult their prospective supervisor about the research proposal prior to submitting an application if possible 3. Apply online for a place of admission (and have a PhD place confirmed) at the University by the deadlines given above. 4. Complete a Wilkie Calvert Studentships application form (Word document, 0.4 MB): www.reading.ac.uk/graduate-school/-/media/project/uor-main/schools-departments/graduate-school/documents/wilkie_calvert_phd_applicationform_2021.docx?la=en&hash=05FAA75777DC6F212AB07C13A660C5A3.

Closing Date: 2 May

Additional Information: Website: www.reading.ac.uk/graduate-school/funding/phd-studentships/wilkie-calvert

University of Regina

University of Regina, 3737 Wascana Parkway, Regina, SK S4S 0A2, Canada.

Email: ask.us@uregina.ca
Website: www.uregina.ca/

The U of R is here for you through every step of your educational journey: 1. Excellent mental, academic, and physical wellness support systems. 2. An active commitment to working with Indigenous partners to reconcile our past. 3. Valuable hands-on work placements for real-world experience.

Master of Indigenous Education

Purpose: The Master of Indigenous Education degree aims to 1. Prepare students as leaders in pedagogical practice in Indigenous Education. 2. Provide students with the required skills, knowledge, and competencies needed to become effective Indigenous educators. 3. Prepare students to conduct research with Indigenous peoples 4. Provide students with opportunities to learn, to understand, and to experience different forms and systems of Indigenous knowledge; and 5. Equip students with the competencies and abilities to integrate Indigenous knowledge into school curricula.

Eligibility: See website

Level of Study: Postgraduate

Type: Funding support

Frequency: Annual

Country of Study: Any country

Closing Date: 15 October

Funding: Private

Additional Information: www.uregina.ca/education/Programs1/Graduate-Degree-Programs/Masters_Degree/mied.html

For further information contact:

Tel: (44) 3065 854 502
Email: Grad.Studies@uregina.ca

University of Sheffield

The University of Sheffield, Western Bank, Sheffield S10 2TN, United Kingdom.

Tel: (44) 114 222 2000
Website: www.shef.ac.uk
Contact: Graduate Office

The University of Sheffield is a research led university offering research supervision, taught courses and professional training in engineering and physical sciences, biologies, environmental sciences, humanities, social sciences, medical and health sciences. Many departments have funding council accreditation and scholarships and bursaries may be available.

Economic and Social Research Council (ESRC) White Rose Doctoral Training Partnership (DTP) and Faculty Scholarships

Purpose: The University is part of the ESRC White Rose Doctoral Training Partnership - a collaboration between the Universities of Leeds, Sheffield, York, Sheffield Hallam, Hull, Bradford and Manchester Metropolitan University and offers a range of ESRC Postgraduate Scholarships

U

Eligibility: See Website
Level of Study: Graduate, Postgraduate
Type: Scholarship
Value: Tuition Fees, an annual stipend and research training support grant
Frequency: Annual
Study Establishment: University of Sheffield
Country of Study: Any country
No. of awards offered: 3
Closing Date: 14 May
Funding: Private
Additional Information: www.sheffield.ac.uk/postgraduate/phd/scholarships/esrc

For further information contact:

Email: internationalscholarships@sheffield.ac.uk

Gaza-Palestine Postgraduate Taught Scholarship

Purpose: We're pleased to offer one scholarship for a taught postgraduate student from Gaza.
Eligibility: To apply and be considered for the scholarship you must: 1. be a citizen of Gaza 2. be self-funding and classified as overseas for tuition fee purposes 3. hold a conditional or unconditional offer from the University of Sheffield before the application deadline to study a full-time postgraduate taught Master's course starting in September 2024.
Level of Study: Postgraduate
Type: Scholarship
Value: The scholarship covers the cost of tuition, accommodation in a single occupant en-suite room in University halls of residence and a maintenance award of £4,000.
Application Procedure: Apply for a Gaza-Palestine Postgraduate Taught Scholarship: finance.ssid.shef.ac.uk/apply/2023-gaza-palestine-postgraduate-taught-scholarship-application-form
Closing Date: 31 May
Additional Information: Website: www.sheffield.ac.uk/international/fees-and-funding/scholarships/postgraduate/gaza

Hossein Farmy Scholarship

Purpose: The Hossein Farmy Scholarship was founded by the late Hossein Farmy, a graduate of the University's former Department of Mining. It is available for students pursuing research related to mining. This includes the geological, engineering, scientific and technological aspects of mining, and the archaeological, economic, historical, legal and social aspects of mining and the mining industry.
Eligibility: 1. You should be intending to pursue a course of research related to mining. 2. You should have, or expect to achieve, a first or upper second class UK honours degree or equivalent qualifications gained outside the UK in an appropriate area of study. 3. You should be registering on your first year of doctoral study with the University
Level of Study: Graduate
Type: Scholarship
Value: tuition fees and provides an annual, tax-free maintenance stipend at the standard UK Research Council rate (currently £17,668 for 22/23).
Country of Study: United Kingdom
Closing Date: 30 April
Additional Information: If you have any questions about scholarships please see our FAQs or email pgr-scholarships@sheffield.ac.uk. Website: www.sheffield.ac.uk/postgraduate/phd/scholarships/hossein-farmy

For further information contact:

Email: pgr-scholarships@sheffield.ac.uk

Intake Education Taiwan Scholarship

Purpose: The University of Sheffield and Intake Education Taiwan are delighted to offer a joint scholarship exclusively for students from Taiwan.
Eligibility: The following eligibility criteria apply: 1. You must have applied to the University of Sheffield through Intake Education Taiwan 2. You must have an offer of a place to study on a one year taught Masters degree programme at the University of Sheffield, starting in September 2024 3. You must be a Taiwanese national or permanently domiciled in Taiwan 4. You must be classified as overseas for fee purposes
Level of Study: Masters Degree
Type: Scholarship
Value: £2,000 towards the cost of tuition fees
Length of Study: for one year of study
Application Procedure: Apply Here: intake.education/tw/scholarship/university-sheffield
Closing Date: 31 May
Contributor: Intake Education Taiwan
Additional Information: Website: www.sheffield.ac.uk/international/fees-and-funding/scholarships/postgraduate/intake

International Merit Postgraduate Scholarship

Purpose: Each scholarship is a competitive award worth 25% of the original tuition fee for a postgraduate taught programme starting in September 2024. The scholarships are available to all new international (non-EU) students who meet the eligibility criteria

Eligibility: Your programme must commence at the University of Sheffield in autumn 2024. 1. Distance learning courses are ineligible for a merit scholarship. 2. You must receive an offer for a course studied in full at the University of Sheffield. Masters programmes split between the University of Sheffield and a partner institution are not eligible to apply for a scholarship. 3. All Crossways courses and Erasmus Mundus courses are ineligible for a merit scholarship. 4. For tuition fee purposes you must be self-funded and required to pay the overseas tuition fee. 5. You must not be a sponsored student. 6. For scholarship purposes all MArch programmes are considered as postgraduate taught programmes and are not eligible for undergraduate scholarships. 7. Anyone studying a Masters/integrated PhD programme is eligible for a merit scholarship in the Masters element of the programme only. 8. These scholarships are not applicable to any postgraduate courses where the higher clinical fee is applicable. This includes, but is not exclusive to, the following courses: A. DClinDent Orthodontics B. MClinDent in Orthodontics C. DClinDent Endodontics D. MClinDent in Paediatric Dentistry E. DClinDent Periodontics F. MMedSci in Diagnostic Oral Pathology G. DClinDent Prosthodontics 9. The University of Sheffield reserves the right to review and change scholarship provision.

Level of Study: Postgraduate

Value: 25% of the original tuition fee for a postgraduate taught programme

Country of Study: Any country

Application Procedure: See website

Closing Date: 15 May

Additional Information: Website: www.sheffield.ac.uk/international/fees-and-funding/scholarships/postgraduate/international-merit-postgraduate-scholarship

For further information contact:

Email: l.a.tarrant@sheffield.ac.uk

NCUK Postgraduate Taught Scholarships

Purpose: We are pleased to offer the NCUK Postgraduate Taught Scholarship 2024 to new international students joining the University of Sheffield for a taught masters in September 2024 from an NCUK Study Centre.

Eligibility: 1. You must hold an offer to study a full-time or part-time postgraduate taught course before 16:00 (UK time) on 16 June 2024. 2. You must accept an offer to study a full-time or part-time postgraduate taught programme at the University of Sheffield before 16:00 (UK time) on 16 June 2024. 3. Your programme must commence at the University of Sheffield in September 2024. 4. Distance learning courses are ineligible for a merit scholarship. 5. Postgraduate Diploma (PGDip) and Postgraduate Certificate (PGCert) courses are ineligible for this scholarship. 6. You must receive an offer for a course studied in full at the University of Sheffield. Masters programmes split between the University of Sheffield and a partner institution are not eligible to apply for a scholarship. 7. All Crossways courses and Erasmus Mundus courses are ineligible for this scholarship. 8. For tuition fee purposes you must be self-funded and required to pay the overseas tuition fee rate. You must not be a sponsored student. 9. For scholarship purposes all MArch programmes are considered as postgraduate taught programmes and are not eligible for undergraduate scholarships. 10. Anyone studying a Masters/integrated PhD programme is eligible for a merit scholarship in the Masters element of the programme only. 11. You must be studying a pre-masters qualification at an NCUK Centre, in any country. 12. These scholarships are not applicable to any postgraduate courses where the higher clinical fee is applicable, this includes, but is not exclusive to the following courses: A. DClinDent Orthodontics B. MClinDent in Orthodontics C. DClinDent Endodontics D. MClinDent in Paediatric Dentistry E. DClinDent Periodontics F. MMedSci in Diagnostic Oral Pathology G. DClinDent Prosthodontics 13. The University of Sheffield reserves the right to review and change scholarship provision.

Level of Study: Postgraduate

Type: Scholarship

Value: Upto £2,500

Application Procedure: No additional scholarship application is required, if you meet the eligibility and award criteria below the scholarship will be applied as a tuition fee discount.

Closing Date: 16 June

Additional Information: Website: www.sheffield.ac.uk/international/fees-and-funding/scholarships/postgraduate/ncuk-postgraduate-taught-scholarships

Postgraduate Taught Sheffield Scholarship

Purpose: To offer the Postgraduate Taught Sheffield Scholarship to international students starting a taught masters programme in September

Eligibility: See website

Type: Scholarship

Value: The scholarship is worth £2,000 for courses in the Faculty of Arts and Humanities and Faculty of Social Sciences and £2,500 for courses in the Faculty of Engineering, Faculty of Medicine, Dentistry and Health, and Faculty of Science.

Country of Study: United Kingdom

Application Procedure: No additional scholarship application is required, if you meet the eligibility and award criteria below the scholarship will be applied as a tuition fee discount.
No. of awards offered: 100
Closing Date: 18 June
Additional Information: Website: www.sheffield.ac.uk/international/fees-and-funding/scholarships/postgraduate/international-postgraduate-taught-scholarship

For further information contact:

Email: eurec@sheffield.ac.uk

Sanctuary Scholarships

Purpose: The University of Sheffield offers Sanctuary Scholarships for those who have sought refuge in the UK - for example, students who have been displaced or affected by the Russian invasion of Ukraine, a conflict in their home country or have another reason for their forced migration to the UK.
Eligibility: 1. Have been granted humanitarian protection or limited leave to remain in the UK, be a dependant or partner of someone with humanitarian protection or limited leave to remain, or you or your parent/guardian or partner are an asylum seeker and have submitted a claim within the UK for refugee status and have not yet received a decision from the Home Office on that application. 2. Have applied for asylum on arrival in the UK, and before you have applied for a place at university. 3. Currently attend a school, college or community/voluntary group that will provide a reference in support of your application. 4. Hold an offer from the University of Sheffield to study an undergraduate or postgraduate taught course starting in September 2024.** 5. Be studying at degree level in the UK for the first time (applicable to undergraduate students only)*. *Please contact the Student Fees and Funding Team if you have withdrawn from a previous course. ** Students who require a foundation or conversion course as part of their offer to study at the University should contact us to discuss their eligibility.
Level of Study: Postgraduate
Type: Scholarship
Value: Cover the cost of tuition and provide a £9,840 award to support living costs for each year of study.
Application Procedure: Apply for a Sanctuary Scholarship: finance.ssid.shef.ac.uk/apply/2023-sanctuary-scholarships-application-form
Closing Date: 3 July
No. of applicants last year: 5
Additional Information: Website: www.sheffield.ac.uk/funding/sanctuary-scholarships

Sheffield Postgraduate Scholarships

Purpose: The scholarships are for students who meet at least one of our widening participation criteria and/or students who achieve a first in their undergraduate degree. If your application is successful you can use the scholarship towards fees or living expenses, the choice is yours
Eligibility: You can apply for a scholarship if you meet all of the following four criteria 1. You'll be studying a taught postgraduate course full-time or part-time for a maximum of four years. 2. You're paying the 'home' rate of fees. 3. You're not already qualified at masters level or higher. 4. You're self funded. Courses funded by the NHS or the Initial Teacher Training bursary, or courses that are eligible for undergraduate funding such as integrated masters are not eligible.; And one or both of the following: 1. You're from a group that is evidentially under-represented among the institution's taught masters population - see the widening participation criteria below. 2. You've already achieved or currently predicted a first class undergraduate degree - see the academic merit criteria below.
Level of Study: Postgraduate
Type: Scholarship
Value: £10,000 each
Country of Study: United Kingdom
Application Procedure: Apply for a Sheffield Postgraduate Scholarship: finance.ssid.shef.ac.uk/apply/2023-sheffield-postgraduate-scholarship-application-form
Closing Date: 9 May
No. of applicants last year: 100
Additional Information: Website: www.sheffield.ac.uk/postgraduate/taught/funding/scholarships

For further information contact:

Tel: (44) 1142221319
Email: funding@sheffield.ac.uk

Sir Sze-yuen Chung Postgraduate Merit Scholarship

Purpose: We are delighted to offer 1 Sir Sze-yuen Chung Scholarship to a student that is a national of or permanently domiciled in Hong Kong SAR.
Eligibility: 1. You must hold an offer to study a full-time or part-time postgraduate taught course at the University of Sheffield. 2. Your programme must commence at the University of Sheffield in September 2024. 3. You must be a national of or permanently domiciled in Hong Kong SAR. 4. Distance learning courses are ineligible for a merit scholarship. 5. You must receive an offer for a course studied in full at the University of Sheffield. Masters programmes split between

the University of Sheffield and a partner institution are not eligible to apply for a scholarship. 6. All Crossways courses and Erasmus Mundus courses are ineligible for a merit scholarship. 7. For tuition fee purposes you must be self-funded and required to pay the overseas tuition fee. You must not be a sponsored student. 8. For scholarship purposes all MArch programmes are considered as postgraduate taught programmes and are not eligible for undergraduate scholarships. 9. Anyone studying a Masters/integrated PhD programme is eligible for a merit scholarship in the Masters element of the programme only. 10. These scholarships are not applicable to any postgraduate courses where the higher clinical fee is applicable, this includes, but is not exclusive to the following courses: A. DClinDent Orthodontics B. MClinDent in Orthodontics C. DClinDent Endodontics D. MClinDent in Paediatric Dentistry E. DClinDent Periodontics F. MMedSci in Diagnostic Oral Pathology G. DClinDent Prosthodontics 11. The University of Sheffield reserves the right to review and change scholarship provision.
Level of Study: Masters Degree, Postgraduate
Type: Scholarship
Value: worth 25% of the original tuition fee
Application Procedure: You can apply for this scholarship through an online application form and is accessed via MUSE (our online portal for applicants). If you are eligible, you'll receive an email inviting you to apply after you have been offered a place on a course at The University of Sheffield. You will also be considered for a range of other scholarships by applying through the same form.
Closing Date: 15 May
Additional Information: Website: www.sheffield.ac.uk/international/fees-and-funding/scholarships/postgraduate/sir-sze-yuen-chung-postgraduate-merit-scholarship

The Sheffield MBA Scholarship Scheme

Purpose: Sheffield University Management School is looking for talented and ambitious professionals who will contribute to the continuous success of our Sheffield MBA.
Eligibility: As part of the application process, the admissions team will assess the application, including the personal statement. Candidates will be also assessed by their performance at their interview with the MBA admissions team. 1. Applicants to the scholarship are required to hold any offer to study the Sheffield MBA, conditional or unconditional. 2. Applicants who have been offered a place through the exceptions process cannot be considered for a scholarship.
Level of Study: MBA
Type: Scholarship
Value: £10,000
Application Procedure: You do not need to complete a separate application for the scholarship. All candidates who are offered a place on the full-time MBA will automatically be considered for our MBA scholarship. Please read our guidance before you submit your MBA application. MBA application guidance: www.sheffield.ac.uk/management/sheffield-mba/how-apply
No. of applicants last year: 2
Additional Information: Website: www.sheffield.ac.uk/management/sheffield-mba/scholarship-scheme

The University of Sheffield Africa Scholarship

Purpose: In partnership with the University of Sheffield Africa Scholarship Trust, the Department of Geography is pleased to offer one scholarship for a postgraduate taught student from Africa.
Eligibility: 1. You must have an offer to study on one of the following courses starting in September 2024 at the University of Sheffield A. MA International Development B. MSc Environmental Change and International Development C. MPH International Development 2. You must be classified as overseas for tuition fee purposes. 3. You must be self-funded to receive this award, i.e. not funded by a research council, government, private enterprise, charity or any similar organisation. 4. You must not already hold a qualification equal to or higher than a Masters. 5. You must not have already studied outside of your home country. 6. This scholarship cannot be awarded in conjunction with any other funding awards, either from the University of Sheffield or external sources. 7. Your mode of attendance must be full time. 8. Receipt of the scholarship is subject to successfully meeting any condition(s) attached to your offer before the deadline provided by the Admissions Service. 9. Receipt of the scholarship is subject to successfully receiving a visa to study at the University in September 2024. 10. You must be a national of or permanently domiciled in an African country.
Level of Study: Masters Degree, Postgraduate
Type: Scholarship
Value: 1. A full tuition 2. fee waiver Maintenance stipend
Application Procedure: See website
Closing Date: 24 May
Additional Information: Website: www.sheffield.ac.uk/international/fees-and-funding/scholarships/postgraduate/usas

White Rose Studentships

Purpose: The WRDTP provides access to a range of training and development opportunities across the partner institutions, as well as the opportunity to be part of an interdisciplinary social sciences network incorporating academic and non-academic partners.

Eligibility: 1. These studentships are only available to applicants to Sheffield Institute of Education (SIoE) and the Centre for Regional Economic and Social Research (CRESR). 2. For 1+3 and +3 awards, applicants must hold at least a UK upper second class honours degree or equivalent. 3. Applicants applying for a +3 award must demonstrate that they have already completed the full social sciences research methods training requirements at masters level. See the WRDTP website for more information. 4. UKRI have confirmed that international students will be eligible for all UKRI-funded postgraduate studentships from the start of the 2022/23 academic year. Further information can be found through the WRDTP website. 5. Where English is not your first language, you must show evidence of English language ability to the following minimum level of proficiency: an overall IELTS score of 7.0 or above, with at least 7.0 in each component or an accepted equivalent. Please note that your test score must be current, i.e. within the last two years. 6. Please note that students must be resident close to the University at which they are registered and we would expect there to be direct contact between the student and supervisor. This applies to full-time and part-time students.
Level of Study: Postgraduate, Research
Type: Studentship
Value: 1. Tuition fees 2. A PhD stipend at the standard Sheffield Hallam PhD stipend rate (this is aligned with the net Real Living Wage and the current rate for academic year 2022/23 is £18,178 per annum) 3. A research training support grant where eligible
Length of Study: 3.5 years of full-time study (6 years part-time).
Frequency: Annual
Study Establishment: One of the three White Rose Universities
Application Procedure: Candidates can check the website for further details
Closing Date: 25 January
Additional Information: Website: www.shu.ac.uk/research/degrees/phd-scholarships/white-rose-dtp-scholarships

For further information contact:

Email: fdsresearch@shu.ac.uk

University of South Australia

GPO Box 2471, Adelaide, SA 5001, Australia.

Tel: (61) 8 8302 6611/3615
Email: research.international@unisa.edu.au
Website: www.unisa.edu.au

The University of South Australia is an innovative and successful institution with a distinctive profile. It is committed to educating professionals, creating and applying knowledge and serving the community.

Ability Grants for Research Degree Students

Purpose: The Ability Grant recognises that research degree students with a disability may face additional research-related costs, such as the need for specialised equipment, transport costs or other support to enable them to complete their research project. They may also have limited ability to earn additional income whilst studying.
Eligibility: 1. Ability Grants are open to enrolled UniSA research degree students who have had their research proposal approved and are in the research phase of their degree. Students may be enrolled either part or full-time. 2. Applicants must have an Access Plan with UniSA arranged through a Disability Adviser 3. A supporting statement will be required from the student's Principal Supervisor. On receipt of the application, Graduate Research will contact the Supervisor to comment on: A. how the applicant would benefit from the grant B. the likelihood of the applicant completing the research project.
Level of Study: Research
Type: Scholarship
Value: Grants of up to AU$3,000 are available to help fund mobility, special equipment at home or other types of assistance specific to your disability during the conduct of the research.
Application Procedure: Application form: www.unisa.edu.au/siteassets/research/forms/abilitygrantappform.pdf
Additional Information: Enquiries: Graduate Research Candidature Team: research.students@unisa.edu.au Website: www.unisa.edu.au/research/degrees/scholarships/for-current-research-degree-students/ability-grants/

Aboriginal Enterprise Research Scholarship

Purpose: The University of South Australia offers the scholarship with stipends to domestic applicants.
Eligibility: Australian Aboriginal and/or Torres Strait Islander applicants
Level of Study: Research
Type: Scholarship
Value: Maximum RTP rate of AU$46,653 per annum (2023 rate)
Application Procedure: Scholarship benefits and conditions (www.unisa.edu.au/siteassets/episerver-6-files/global/research/scholarships/scholarship-benefits-and-conditions-

2022.pdf). Please contact us for more information: www.unisa.edu.au/research/degrees/#contact.
Additional Information: Website: www.unisa.edu.au/research/degrees/scholarships/domestic-student-scholarships/

Completion Scholarships

Purpose: Completion scholarships provide funding of up to six months living allowance. They are directed primarily towards research degree students who are enrolled part-time.
Eligibility: Research degree students must: 1. currently be enrolled at UniSA in either a doctoral degree by research or a masters by research 2. have completed their data collection or equivalent 3. be in the writing-up stage 4. be within their candidature time AND 1. if part-time, or working, provide evidence that time release is available to work on the writing-up on a full-time basis 2. not hold a living allowance scholarship 3. not be a continuing UniSA academic staff member.
Level of Study: Research
Type: Scholarship
Value: Funding of up to six months living allowance
Length of Study: Up to a maximum of six months
Application Procedure: First, check that you are eligible. Completion Scholarship Application Form: www.unisa.edu.au/siteassets/research/forms/application-for-completion-scholarship.pdf 1. Your application should be no more than two pages, plus a proposed work plan. In the work plan, address how your thesis will be completed within no more than six months of commencement of the scholarship. 2. You must obtain the support of your Principal Supervisor (or Associate Supervisor) for the application. 3. The Supervisor will forward your application to the Dean: Research for a decision. 4. The Dean: Research will forward your application to SAS to confirm eligibility. A panel assists with the selection of successful candidates.
Closing Date: 1 August
Additional Information: Website: www.unisa.edu.au/research/degrees/scholarships/for-current-research-degree-students/completion-scholarships/

Enterprise Research Scholarship

Purpose: The University of South Australia offers the scholarship with stipends to domestic applicants.
Eligibility: You must read the Scholarship Benefits and Conditions (www.unisa.edu.au/siteassets/episerver-6-files/global/research/scholarships/scholarship-benefits-and-conditions-2022.pdf) before accepting an offer from us. These conditions apply to all domestic students who accept an offer from us. You can also view our Research Degrees and Research Training Program (RTP) Scholarships policy: i.unisa.edu.au/policies-and-procedures/university-policies/academic/ab-59/.
Level of Study: Masters Degree, Postgraduate, Research
Type: Scholarship
Value: The total stipend is at least AU$28,854 per annum
Length of Study: over 3 years for PhD students and over 2 years for masters by research students
Application Procedure: Applications are made online via a project that has an assigned scholarship. View our step by step guide on how to apply: www.unisa.edu.au/research/degrees/how-to-apply/.
Additional Information: Your question might be answered on the RTP FAQs website: www.dese.gov.au/research-training-program-frequently-asked-questions-students. If not, please contact us: www.unisa.edu.au/research/degrees/#contact. Website: www.unisa.edu.au/research/degrees/scholarships/university-wide-scholarships-for-australian-research-degree-applicants/

Fee-relief Scholarships

Purpose: Fee-relief scholarships are available to candidates who have exceeded the funding period for their candidature.
Eligibility: To apply for a fee-relief scholarship, you must: 1. currently be enrolled at UniSA in either a doctoral degree by research or a masters by research 2. have completed your data collection or equivalent 3. be enrolled as a domestic student. International students are not eligible for this scholarship 4. be in the writing-up stage 5. not be a continuing UniSA academic staff member. 6. not be in Bad Financial Standing from a previous Research Period
Level of Study: Doctorate, Masters Degree, Research
Type: Scholarship
Value: 1. Doctoral students are exempt from tuition fees for up to the equivalent of 4 years full-time. 2. Masters by research students are exempt from tuition fees for up to the equivalent of 2 years full-time.
Application Procedure: Complete and submit the application form. You will need to provide a detailed work plan of activities, including tasks and dates, to complete the thesis within the period of the fee-relief scholarship. Application to go overtime/Fee Relief scholarship- Online form: bpi.unisa.edu.au/suite/sites/application-to-go-overtime-fee
Additional Information: Website: www.unisa.edu.au/research/degrees/scholarships/for-current-research-degree-students/

Ferry Scholarship

Purpose: To promote study and research into the scientific fields of physics and chemistry.

Eligibility: Open only to the citizens of Australia below the age of 25 who have achieved Honours 1 or equivalent.
Level of Study: Postgraduate
Type: Scholarship
Value: AU$7,500 per year
Length of Study: 1 year
Frequency: Annual
Application Procedure: Applicants must apply directly to the university. Check the website for further details.
Closing Date: 31 March
Contributor: Late Cedric Arnold Seth Ferry
Additional Information: Website: www.postgraduatefunding.com/award-4060

For further information contact:

Tel: (61) 8302 3967
Email: jenni.critcher@unisa.edu.au

International Research Tuition Scholarship (IRTS)

Purpose: International Research Tuition Scholarships (IRTS) are awarded to international students on the basis of academic merit and demonstrated research capability, and who will be supported during their degree by a full living stipend supported by external funding, e.g a recognised sponsor or external scholarship awarding body.
Eligibility: In addition to meeting UniSA's eligibility criteria, applicants must be: 1. Commencing international research degree students 2. High quality with demonstrated research capability, as assessed by UniSA 3. Be supported by a strong supervisory panel(with end-user adviser on the supervisory panel, where appropriate), and be enrolled in a research-rich environment 4. In receipt of (or been awarded) a fully externally funded stipend scholarship, or in receipt of a living stipend supported by external funding*. *Note: the living stipend needs to be in the form of an externally funded scholarship administered through the University or in agreement with an industry partner, sponsorship body or organisation.
Level of Study: Research
Type: Scholarship
Value: total fee-waiver
Length of Study: maximum of 4 years
Application Procedure: International students with an external sponsorship or scholarship can apply for any listed projects. Some applicants may have additional conditions stipulated by their sponsorship or scholarship provider, and may need to develop their own project with a UniSA supervisor. You can find more information about this here: www.unisa.edu.au/research/degrees/how-to-apply/create-a-research-project/.
Additional Information: Website: www.unisa.edu.au/research/degrees/scholarships/university-wide-scholarships-for-international-applicants/

International Travel Grants

Purpose: The purpose of the grant is to provide the opportunity for research degree students to gain an international perspective that enhances their research experience and improves their thesis by undertaking research or work with world class institutional or industry partners in overseas locations.
Eligibility: 1. Must be currently enrolled at the University of South Australia for a Doctoral degree and be in their second or early third year of candidacy (or an equivalent period part-time) 2. should have had their research proposal accepted and have the appropriate ethics and/or safety clearances 3. must have a supervisory panel that meets university requirements: i.unisa.edu.au/SysSiteAssets/policies-and-procedures/docs/research/procedure-ab-58-p2-_2021_clean.pdf 4. must be making satisfactory progress and is likely to complete their degree within the required timeframe 5. is to provide evidence of the way the research and thesis will be enhanced by the visit overseas 6. must have gained unqualified support from the supervisor for the proposed overseas visit 7. is to provide confirmation from the overseas institution that arrangements have been finalised or are in the process of being finalised 8. must indicate how contact will be maintained with the supervisor and the University whilst overseas. 9. travel must be undertaken in the year of the travel grant being awarded
Level of Study: Research
Type: Grant
Value: up to AU$3000.00 towards travel and living expenses and any additional expenses will need to be negotiated and supported by the Supervisory panel
Application Procedure: Application www.unisa.edu.au/siteassets/research/forms/travelgrant-application_2023.docx Please note: sections to be completed by the student, principal supervisor and Dean of Research (or delegate). Fully signed and supported applications must be sent to research.students@unisa.edu.au
Closing Date: 24 March
No. of applicants last year: approximately 3
Additional Information: Website: www.unisa.edu.au/research/degrees/scholarships/for-current-research-degree-

students/research-degree-international-travel-grants–student-mobility/#value

Research Training Program domestic (RTPd) Scholarship

Purpose: The University of South Australia offers the scholarships with stipends to domestic applicants.
Eligibility: You must read the Scholarship Benefits and Conditions (www.unisa.edu.au/siteassets/episerver-6-files/global/research/scholarships/scholarship-benefits-and-conditions-2022.pdf) before accepting an offer from us. These conditions apply to all domestic students who accept an offer from us. You can also view our Research Degrees and Research Training Program (RTP) Scholarships policy: i.unisa.edu.au/policies-and-procedures/university-policies/academic/ab-59/.
Level of Study: Masters Degree, Postgraduate, Research
Type: Scholarship
Value: The total stipend is at least AU$28,854 per annum
Length of Study: over 3 years for PhD students and over 2 years for masters by research students
Application Procedure: Applications are made online via a project that has an assigned scholarship. View our step by step guide on how to apply: www.unisa.edu.au/research/degrees/how-to-apply/.
Additional Information: Enquiries: Your question might be answered on the RTP FAQs website: www.dese.gov.au/research-training-program-frequently-asked-questions-students. If not, please contact us: www.unisa.edu.au/research/degrees/#contact. Website: www.unisa.edu.au/research/degrees/scholarships/university-wide-scholarships-for-australian-research-degree-applicants/

Research Training Program International Scholarships in Australia (RTPI)

Purpose: Research Training Program international (RTPi) Scholarships are funded by the Australian Government and awarded to international students on the basis of academic merit and research potential. These scholarships include a stipend (living allowance) and a fee offset for a limited time.
Eligibility: To international students see website for more details
Level of Study: Research
Type: Scholarship
Value: The total stipend is at least AU$28,854 per annum
Length of Study: Upto 3 years
Country of Study: Any country
Application Procedure: Applications are made online via a project that has an assigned scholarship. View our step by step guide on how to apply.: www.unisa.edu.au/research/degrees/how-to-apply/
Closing Date: 31 August
Funding: Government
Additional Information: Your question might be answered on the RTP FAQs website: www.dese.gov.au/research-training-program-frequently-asked-questions-students. If not, please contact us: www.unisa.edu.au/research/degrees/#contact. Website: www.unisa.edu.au/research/degrees/scholarships/university-wide-scholarships-for-international-applicants/

For further information contact:

Tel: (61) 8 8302 5880 or (61) 8 8302 0828
Email: research.degrees@unisa.edu.au

University of South Wales

Pontypridd Wales NP18 3YG, United Kingdom.

Tel: (44) 8455 767 778
Email: enquiries@southwales.ac.uk
Website: www.southwales.ac.uk

The University of Wales, Newport, has been involved in higher education for more than 80 years, and its roots go back even further to the first Mechanics Institute in the town, which opened in 1841.

USW Postgraduate Alumni Discount

Eligibility: The discount will be automatically applied to your tuition fee account if you meet all of the following requirements: 1. Be considered by the University to be a Home student. 2. Hold an Honours Degree ** from the University of South Wales* 3. Enrol and be studying an eligible full or part time taught/online *** MA, MSc, LLM MBA, DBA programme, at a University of South Wales campus (Treforest, Glyntaff, Cardiff, Newport) during the 2024/25 academic year. *This includes graduates from the University of South Wales, University of Glamorgan, University of Wales Newport, the Polytechnic of Wales, Royal Welsh College of Music and Drama. **If you graduated with an integrated Masters for your undergraduate degree e.g. MComp,

U

MChiro, MEng, with the University of South Wales you would be eligible for the discount if you are undertaking an eligible postgraduate course.
Level of Study: Postgraduate
Value: 20% reduction in tuition fees
Application Procedure: For further information or advice on the Alumni Discount, please contact either the Revenue Team Revenue@southwales.ac.uk or Student Money Advice Team scholarships@southwales.ac.uk
Additional Information: Website: www.southwales.ac.uk/study/fees-and-funding/postgraduate-fees-and-funding/#scholarships

USW Postgraduate Ethnicity Equality Bursary

Purpose: The University of South Wales is offering 10 bursaries to postgraduate students commencing their studies in the academic year and have self-identified as one of the following ethnic groups under the following headings as per the UK government published list: Black, African, Caribbean, or Black British, Mixed or Multiple Ethnic Groups, Asian or Asian British, Other Ethnic Group.
Eligibility: To be eligible, you will need to meet all of the criteria below: 1. Self-identify as one of the ethnic groups under the following headings on this published UK Government list: 2. Mixed or Multiple Ethnic Groups 3. Asian or Asian British 4. Black, African, Caribbean, or Black British 5. Other Ethnic Group* 6. Have applied for entry to a full-time USW postgraduate course lasting 1 or more academic years starting in the 2024-25 academic year. 7. Applied for a course studying on a University of South Wales campus (Treforest, Glyntaff, Cardiff or Newport) 8. Be a UK home student liable for the UK home rate of tuition fees and eligible for Student Finance from the UK government (SFE/SFW/SFNI/SAAS). 9. Be enrolled full-time on a taught postgraduate course at time of payment in November 2024
Level of Study: Postgraduate
Type: Bursary
Value: £1,000
Length of Study: First year of study
Application Procedure: To apply for the bursary, please click here: forms.office.com/Pages/ResponsePage.aspx?id=fP6q5RuXt0qwORQa02rOwI3TarcUytdNtMseK-U9yTRUOTRLUE42REU4N1A5SldPMEg1VU1FUjdHSS4u Please ensure that you have applied for a course before applying for the bursary.
Closing Date: 7 July
No. of applicants last year: 10
Additional Information: Website: www.southwales.ac.uk/study/fees-and-funding/postgraduate-fees-and-funding/#scholarships

USW Postgraduate Sanctuary Scholarship

Purpose: The Sanctuary Scholarship will support two successful postgraduate applicants with tuition fees waived for the duration of their postgraduate studies and a scholarship to assist with course related costs.
Eligibility: To be eligible you must be assessed by USW as having one of the following immigration status's: 1. Be a Person Seeking Asylum 2. Limited Leave to Remain (as a result of an Asylum application) 3. Be the partner/dependent included on the application of a person of any of the above groups* * Spouses/civil partners must have been the spouse/civil partner on the date on which the asylum application was made. Children/step-children must have been aged under 18 on the date on which the asylum application was made. For more information see website
Level of Study: Postgraduate
Type: Scholarship
Value: Full tuition fees costs of an eligible full time taught on campus postgraduate degree
Length of Study: Duration of your original programme or until such a point that you become eligible to apply for UK government student financial support, at which point scholarship recipients must apply for this support.
Application Procedure: Once you have received and accepted a conditional or unconditional offer on to a full-time taught on campus postgraduate degree, you will be sent an email containing a link to apply for the USW Postgraduate Sanctuary Scholarship. The email will be sent to the email address listed on your course application to the University.
Closing Date: 7 July
No. of applicants last year: 2
Additional Information: Website: www.southwales.ac.uk/study/fees-and-funding/postgraduate-fees-and-funding/#scholarships

USW Refugee Sanctuary Scheme

Purpose: The USW Postgraduate Refugee Sanctuary Scheme provides support to a limited number of eligible refugees via free English language tuition prior to starting a postgraduate course at the University.
Eligibility: See Website to check eligibility
Level of Study: Postgraduate
Value: Cover the full tuition fee costs for the Pre-sessional English Language Programme
Length of Study: 15 weeks or less duration
Application Procedure: You will be sent an email containing a link to an online application form once you have been offered a place on a course. The email will be sent to the email address listed on your course application to the University.

Additional Information: Website: www.southwales.ac.uk/study/fees-and-funding/postgraduate-fees-and-funding/#scholarships

University of Southampton

University of Southampton, University Road, Southampton SO17 1BJ, United Kingdom.

Tel: (44) 238 059 5000
Email: admissns@soton.ac.uk
Website: www.soton.ac.uk
Contact: Student Marketing Office

Join our community of staff, students and researchers at the University of Southampton. As a global top 100 university, our expert academics and wide range of study options will help you achieve your goals.

Chevening Scholarships

Purpose: Funded by the UK Foreign and Commonwealth Office and partner organisations, Chevening provides fully-funded scholarships, leaving you free to focus on achieving your academic goals and enjoying the experience of a lifetime.
Eligibility: Postgraduate students from more than 160 countries can apply for this scholarship (excluding USA). Use the following link to find the awards available in your country/territory.
Level of Study: Postgraduate
Type: Scholarship
Application Procedure: Find out more and apply using the Chevening website: www.chevening.org/.
Additional Information: Website: www.southampton.ac.uk/courses/funding/scholarships-awards.page

China Scholarship Council Scholarships

Purpose: Each year the China Scholarship Council (CSC) offers scholarships to Chinese students who wish to study a degree programme outside China. The University of Southampton is recognised by the China Scholarship Council as a partner institute.
Eligibility: To apply for this scholarship you must: 1. be a Chinese national 2. be younger than 35 when you apply 3. meet one of the following academic criteria: A. be studying a Bachelor or Masters at a top Chinese university (for example, 211 Group, 985 Group or highly ranked by subject area B. or be studying a Masters, having obtained a Master's degree in an overseas (non-Chinese) University within a year by the time of the application (not including those who have already returned to China), or first year of a PhD in an overseas University. For the latter, CSC funding starts from the second year of study C. or have already obtained a bachelor degree and be currently working in China D. candidates can not be those who have already obtained a PhD degree 4. usually have an academic achievement of 80-85% or above in your current studies 5. have received an offer of a PhD place from the University of Southampton 6. have met the University's English language requirements at the time of application
Level of Study: Postgraduate
Type: Scholarship
Value: full tuition fees subject to successful application for a CSC award for living costs.
Frequency: Annual
Application Procedure: 1. Identify a research area: www.southampton.ac.uk/courses/research-postgraduate.page or academic supervisor for your research topic 2. Contact the Faculty Postgraduate Research Admissions team: www.southampton.ac.uk/studentadmin/admissions/contact-us.page or your proposed supervisor to find out about CSC scholarship opportunities. 3. Apply for a PhD programme: www.southampton.ac.uk/study/postgraduate-research/apply. Please state in your application that you wish to apply for China Scholarship Council funding. We recommend that you submit your application by 31 December.
Closing Date: 31 December
Additional Information: Website: www.southampton.ac.uk/courses/funding/scholarships-awards.page

Fulbright Awards

Purpose: Fulbright Awards are scholarships for American students wanting to study abroad. Each year we offer one of these awards to a student wanting to study a master's degree at the University of Southampton.
Eligibility: To apply for this scholarship you must meet the Fulbright eligibility requirements: us.fulbrightonline.org/about/eligibility
Level of Study: Masters Degree, Postgraduate
Type: Scholarship
Value: full tuition fees and a monthly stipend
Application Procedure: 1. Choose your master's degree programme: www.southampton.ac.uk/courses/taught-postgraduate.page at Southampton. 2. Apply using our online postgraduate application form: www.southampton.ac.uk/courses/how-to-apply/postgraduate-applications.page.
3. Apply to Fulbright: www.fulbright.org.uk/fulbright-awards/exchanges-to-the-uk/postgraduates/university-of-southampton.

Additional Information: You can find more information about the application process and timelines on the US Fulbright website: us.fulbrightonline.org/.

GREAT Scholarship

Purpose: The GREAT Scholarships 2024 programme, launched by the British Council together with 49 UK universities, supports postgraduate students from Bangladesh, China, Egypt, Ghana, Kenya, India, Indonesia, Malaysia, Mexico, Nigeria, Pakistan, Thailand, Turkey and Vietnam to access world-class UK higher education opportunities.
Eligibility: To apply for this scholarship, you must have an admissions offer letter for a postgraduate taught master's programme from one of the programmes listed above and hold a Nigerian passport.
Level of Study: Masters Degree, Postgraduate, Postgraduate (MSc)
Type: Scholarship
Value: £10,000 issued as a tuition fee reduction
Application Procedure: 1. Apply to an eligible masters level programme at the University of Southampton using the online form. In order to avoid disappointment you are advised to complete and submit your programme application as soon as possible in order for you to be able to receive the required admissions offer letter for you to then submit an expression of interest form for the scholarship by the deadline. 2. Complete the scholarship expression of interest form, which can be accessed here: app.geckoform.com/public/?_gl=1*1ktamr4*_ga*MTAxMTczMjA3LjE2Nzg3ODYzNzQ.*_ga_51YK64STMR*MTY3ODc4NjM3NC4xLjEuMTY3ODc4ODI4Ni41Ny4wLjA.*_ga_BGQ2PL3BJ8*MTY3ODc4NjM3NC4xLjEuMTY3ODc4ODI5Ny4wLjAuMA..#/modern/21FO00fmriwtlf00dausl6lx3y.
Closing Date: 31 May
Additional Information: Website: www.southampton.ac.uk/courses/funding/scholarships-awards/great-scholarship-nigeria.page

Honor Frost Foundation Masters and/or Doctoral Awards in Maritime Archaeology

Purpose: The Foundation's mission is to promote the advancement and research, including publication, of maritime archaeology with particular focus on the eastern Mediterranean
Eligibility: 1. The successful candidate must demonstrate a genuine interest in maritime archaeology and would be expected to develop the subject in their home country upon their return. 2. The successful candidate will also be required to submit annual reports on their progress to the Honor Frost Foundation and contribute towards the Foundation's activities during the duration of their studies, including supporting the annual lecture. 3. The MA Scholarship requires a good 21 honours degree (or equivalent) in either archaeology or a related discipline. You must be a citizen of Cyprus, Lebanon, Egypt or Syria
Level of Study: Postgraduate
Type: Award
Value: an annual stipend of £15,000 with an additional travel fund of £1,000
Frequency: Annual
Country of Study: Any country
Application Procedure: The MA Scholarship requires a good 21 honours degree (or equivalent) in either archaeology or a related discipline. You must be a citizen of Cyprus, Lebanon, Egypt or Syria. The MA scholarship is tenable for one year, commencing September, at an annual stipend of £15,000 with an additional travel fund of £1,000, which can be drawn as required during your study. Tuition fees will also be paid directly to the University at the appropriate fee rate. There may also be the opportunity to continue to PhD, fully funded, for a further 3 years on completion of the MA/MSc. Application for this studentship is by CV; a sample of written work (4,000 words, max); and a personal statement of up to 800 words explaining why you feel you are suitable for the MA or PhD scholarship. Please also arrange for two academic references to be sent independently by the deadline
Closing Date: 15 May
Funding: Private
Additional Information: educaloxy.com/honor-frost-foundation-masters-andor-doctoral-awards-in-maritime-archaeology,i6125.html

For further information contact:

Email: lkb@soton.ac.uk

Marshall Scholarship

Purpose: Marshall Scholarships are for American students of high ability who want to study in the UK. Marshall Scholars are identified as future leaders and ambassadors who will strengthen the relationship between the UK and the US.
Eligibility: To apply for this scholarship you must meet the Marshall eligibility requirements: www.marshallscholarship.org/applications/eligible.
Level of Study: Doctorate, Masters Degree, Postgraduate
Type: Scholarship
Value: 1. your tuition fees 2. your cost of living expenses 3. an annual book grant 4. a thesis grant 5. research and daily travel grants 6. travel to and from the United States 7. a payment to support a dependent spouse, if applicable
Length of Study: up to 2 years
Application Procedure: 1. Choose a suitable master's: www.southampton.ac.uk/courses/taught-postgraduate.page or

doctoral degree: www.southampton.ac.uk/courses/research-postgraduate.page programme at Southampton. 2. Apply using our online postgraduate application form: www.southampton.ac.uk/courses/how-to-apply/postgraduate-applications.page. 3. Apply to the Marshall Commission: www.marshallscholarship.org/applications/apply
Additional Information: You can find more information about this scholarship on the Marshall Scholarship website: www.marshallscholarship.org/. Website: www.southampton.ac.uk/courses/funding/scholarships-awards.page

Merit Scholarships for International Postgraduates

Eligibility: Available to international postgraduate students on eligible courses.
Level of Study: Postgraduate
Type: Scholarship
Value: Ranging from £1,000 to £8,000
Application Procedure: They are awarded automatically to students who meet the eligibility criteria. For full details, see the relevant scholarship page: www.southampton.ac.uk/study/fees-funding/scholarships/merit-postgraduate.
Additional Information: www.southampton.ac.uk/courses/funding/scholarships-awards.page

Wellcome Master's Programme Awards in Humanities and Social Science

Purpose: The Wellcome Master's Programme Awards in Humanities and Social Science scholarship scheme aims to train humanities and social science researchers from low and middle-income countries in Global Health.
Eligibility: Applicants must have evidence of excellent academic achievement, with the minimum of a BSc/BA grade equivalent to a UK 2i or first. In addition, applicants must: 1. Be a UK national or national of a low, lower-middle or upper-middle income country as defined by the World Bank for the 2024 fiscal year. 2. Have some research experience or have clear plans for a career in research 3. Have received an unconditional offer for the MSc in Global Health commencing in September 2024 4. Have obtained the relevant English Language qualifications if necessary
Level of Study: Postgraduate (MSc), Research
Type: Programme
Value: Full tuition fees and a stipend of £16,000
Length of Study: One year
Application Procedure: 1. Apply to the MSc in Global Health(www.southampton.ac.uk/courses/global-health-masters-msc): When applying please ensure you choose the MSc Global Health programme in the Faculty of Social Sciences NOT the MSc Public Health (Global Health Pathway) as this programme is not eligible for the scholarship award. 2. After you have received an unconditional offer, complete the scholarship application form available here: app.geckoform.com/public/?_gl=1*1h1ddpn*_ga*MTAxMTczMjA3LjE2Nzg3ODYzNzQ.*_ga_51YK64STMR*MTY3ODc4NjM3NC4xLjEuMTY3ODc4ODkzMC41Mi4wLjA.*_ga_BGQ2PL3BJ8*MTY3ODc4NjM3NC4xLjEuMTY3ODc4ODk1OC4wLjAuMA..#/modern/21FO00fmrlwc4e00iwfezmeb97.
Closing Date: 17 May
Additional Information: Website: www.southampton.ac.uk/courses/funding/scholarships-awards/wellcome-scholarship.page

Xiamen University PhD Scholarships

Purpose: The University of Southampton has a partnership with Xiamen University. Each year we offer several fully-funded PhD scholarships to students from the university.
Eligibility: To apply, you must: 1. currently be completing your bachelor's studies at Xiamen University 2. successfully apply for a scholarship for living costs from the Chinese Scholarship Council: www.csc.edu.cn/chuguo or another source
Level of Study: Postgraduate
Type: Scholarship
Value: Covers full tuition fee costs for each year of your PhD programme
Application Procedure: 1. Identify a suitable PhD programme 2. Contact the Faculty PhD Admissions team to discuss a suitable project and/or potential supervisor for the research topic, and any deadline for applications 3. Make a PhD application to the University of Southampton using the online postgraduate application form, including appropriate documents and a research proposal if required 4. Allow sufficient time for the Admissions team to process the application and make a decision. 5. To be nominated, candidates must either have received an offer of a PhD place or have firm confirmation of support from a potential supervisor and made an application 6. Apply to the Talent Service Office at Xiamen University. Only applicants who are selected and nominated by the Talent Office will be eligible
Closing Date: December
Additional Information: You can find more information about this scholarship on the Chinese Scholarship Council's website: www.csc.edu.cn/chuguo. You can also read the Xiamen Scholarships Applicant Guidance (PDF): www.southampton.ac.uk/~assets/doc/Courses/%E9%99%84%E4%BB%B67%20Xiamen%20UoS%20PhD%20scholarships%202023%20-%20Applicant%20guidance.pdf. Website: www.southampton.ac.uk/courses/funding/scholarships-awards.page

University of Stirling

University of Stirling, Stirling FK9 4LA, United Kingdom.

Tel: (44) 1786 473171
Email: international@stir.ac.uk
Website: www.stir.ac.uk

Since our founding in 1967, the University of Stirling has always been driven by transformative thinking and a spirit of innovation. Our mission is to do everything we can to give our students the knowledge and expertise to make their impact in the world.

Commonwealth Scholarships and Fellowships Programme

Purpose: If you are from one of the Commonwealth countries you may be eligible for an award for our postgraduate taught and research courses.
Eligibility: If you are from one of the Commonwealth countries (not the Commonwealth of Independent States) you may be eligible for this scheme.
Level of Study: Postgraduate, Research
Type: Scholarship
Value: covers tuition fees, travel and living expenses
Length of Study: up to three years
Application Procedure: For application enquiries, contact the The British Council: www.britishcouncil.org/ in your country, or contact their information Centre.
Additional Information: Website: www.stir.ac.uk/scholarships/?page=1&nationality=&subject=!padrenullquery&level=Postgraduate%20Research&feestatus=

Institute for Advanced Studies Studentships

Eligibility: We welcome expressions of interest from all candidates who meet the University's entry criteria for Postgraduate Research degrees. We especially welcome expressions of interest from people from groups that have been under-represented in the UK Post Graduate Research community in the past, including people from ethnic minorities, women, disabled people, and people from care-experienced or socio-economically disadvantaged backgrounds. Recommendations for the offer of a studentship will be made by a panel of senior members of the University that will consider all applications from qualified candidates, supported by an adviser on equality, diversity and inclusion. The panel will consider a range of criteria, focusing on candidates' academic excellence, evidence of advanced methodological skills and capacity to undertake a major piece of independent research at doctoral level.
Level of Study: Postgraduate, Research
Type: Studentship
Value: 1. A number of 3-year full-time equivalent PhD studentships on a fully-funded basis (fees and stipend at the UKRI rate) 2. Fee waivers 3. Cash bursaries for students who already hold funding awards for fees
Application Procedure: Read more on our Institute for Advanced Studies Studentships homepage: www.stir.ac.uk/research/research-degrees/institute-for-advanced-studies-studentships/. For full details of how to submit an expression of interest and project proposal, read our Institute for Advanced Studies Studentships guide for applicants: www.stir.ac.uk/research/research-degrees/institute-for-advanced-studies-studentships/guide-for-applicants/.
Closing Date: 14 April
Additional Information: Website: www.stir.ac.uk/scholarships/general/institute-for-advanced-studies-studentships/

The Anne Wingate Paterson Scholarship

Purpose: Awards will be made to individuals with a place on a postgraduate programme for the study and prevention of child abuse and neglect.
Eligibility: Awards will be made to individuals with a place on a postgraduate programme at a UK higher education institution
Level of Study: Postgraduate, Research
Type: Scholarship
Value: £5,000
Application Procedure: Full details and application form are available on the Association of Child Protection Professionals website: www.childprotectionprofessionals.org.uk/anne-paterson-scholarship.
Additional Information: Website: www.stir.ac.uk/scholarships/social-sciences/anne-wingate-paterson-scholarship/

University of Strathclyde

McCance Building, 16 Richmond Street, Glasgow G1 1XQ, United Kingdom.

Tel: (44) 141 552 4400
Email: r.livingston@mis.strath.ac.uk
Website: www.strath.ac.uk

Asylum Seeker Scholarship

Purpose: The scholarship is open to prospective undergraduate and taught postgraduate students of the University of Strathclyde. The scholarship meets the cost of your tuition fees and includes an allowance for essential study-related expenditure.
Eligibility: 1. Applications will be considered from potential students who: A. hold a conditional or unconditional offer to study at the University of Strathclyde for 2024-2025 (September start courses); and B. have submitted, or are the dependant of someone who has submitted, an application to the Home Office for recognition as a Refugee under the 1951 UN Convention on the Status of Refugees (hereafter "The Convention") and not yet received a final decision from the Home Office on that application; or C. have been offered leave to remain in the UK on the grounds of Article 8 of the European Convention on Human Rights provided that the student has not become eligible for Student Support from the relevant student funding body in Scotland, England, Wales or Northern Ireland. 2. Applicants must live within the Glasgow area at the point of application as housing costs are not covered by the scholarship. Applications will only be accepted from prospective students outwith the Glasgow area if they submit written evidence of appropriate accommodation arrangements at the point of application. 3. Applications will also be considered from students who have already started their course of study but have subsequently applied for asylum and can no longer access their original funding. In these cases it will be necessary to establish that the original funding for study is no longer available and applicants will be required to provide supporting evidence.
Level of Study: Postgraduate
Type: Scholarship
Value: Cost of tuition fees and essential study costs
Length of Study: Length of course, or until eligible for state funding
Application Procedure: Asylum Seeker Scholarship application criteria: www.strath.ac.uk/media/ps/sees/studentfinance/Asylum_Seeker_Scholarship_-_application_criteria.pdf Please read the above application criteria before submitting an application form. Asylum Seeker Scholarship application form: www.strath.ac.uk/media/ps/sees/studentfinance/Asylum_Seeker_Scholarship_application_form.docx Completed forms should be returned by email to: asylum-scholarship@strath.ac.uk
Closing Date: 28 May
No. of applicants last year: Variable
Additional Information: Website: www.strath.ac.uk/studywithus/scholarships/asylumseekerscholarship/

For further information contact:

Email: asylum-scholarship@strath.ac.uk

British Council Scholarships for Women in STEM

Purpose: The British Council is the UK's international organisation for cultural relations and educational opportunities. They build connections, understanding and trust between people in the UK and other countries through arts and culture, education and the English language
Eligibility: see website
Level of Study: Postgraduate (MSc)
Type: Scholarship
Value: Full costs of study - tuition fees, monthly stipend etc
Length of Study: The scholarship will last for the duration of the one year MSc
Application Procedure: 1. Applications should be made to the Faculty of Engineering at the University of Strathclyde. A. Application form: forms.office.com/e/j4UwKDSghM 2. You must demonstrate in your application that: A. You are active in your desired field of study with work experience or with a proven interest in the programme area you are applying for B. You are willing to demonstrate future contribution to capacity-building and socio-economic advancement through the benefits achieved after graduating from UK higher education and returning your home country C. You can demonstrate a plan and passion to engage other women and girls in STEM from your home country D. If you are awarded a scholarship, you agree to maintain contact with the British Council and act as an ambassador for the UK and engage with activities as part of a British Council Scholarships for Women in STEM alumnus during and after your study in the UK. Any involvement in these activities during your study in the UK will take up no more than five hours per term. 3. You agree that your personal data being shared with the British Council as a condition of applying for the bursary.
Closing Date: 31 March
No. of applicants last year: 5
Additional Information: Website: www.strath.ac.uk/studywithus/scholarships/britishcouncilwomeninstem/

Childcare Funding

Purpose: Full-time eligible students attending University will be able to apply for help with registered childcare costs from the Childcare Fund. Children must be under 15, or under 17 if they have special educational needs. Childcare fund awards are in the form of a grant and are in addition to any other funding a student receives.
Eligibility: See website
Level of Study: Postgraduate
Type: Funding support
Value: Various
Application Procedure: 1. Students have to apply to the childcare fund each semester. The current application is to

cover semester 1 childcare. Students who apply for support with semester 1 childcare will be contacted when applications open for semester 2. 2. You complete the application form and your childcare provider(s) complete Annex A detailing what childcare they have been asked to provide and the cost. Application and Annex A for semester 1 childcare: Online Application: studentsupport.strath.ac.uk/finsup/

Closing Date: 31 May

Additional Information: Website: www.strath.ac.uk/studywithus/scholarships/childcarefund/

Dean's Global Research Award

Purpose: The Faculty of Humanities & Social Sciences is pleased to invite applications from excellent international students with original research proposals for the Dean's Global Research Award for commencing study in October 2024.

Eligibility: You should have, or be expected to obtain, a first-class honours degree and/or a master's degree with distinction. IELTS Academic (minimum overall band score of 6.5 or higher for Education, gained within 2 years prior to commencing PhD study) or equivalent.

Level of Study: Postgraduate, Research

Type: Award

Value: International fee

Length of Study: 3 years

Application Procedure: Step 1: identify a supervisor Step 2: application further Details see website

Closing Date: 31 March

Additional Information: Website: www.strath.ac.uk/studywithus/scholarships/deansglobalresearchaward202324-internationalcandidatesonlydgra/

Discretionary Fund

Purpose: Are you struggling to cover your essential living costs? The Discretionary Fund awards are non - repayable top ups to your standard student support such as student loan. If you are a home student or from the rest of UK you might be eligible for support from the fund.

Eligibility: 1. A registered full or part time Undergraduate or Postgraduate student at the University of Strathclyde 2. Studying a course with a normal credit load of 30 credits or more 3. Applied for and had their application assessed for all statutory funding, including maintenance loans, to which they are entitled (typically SAAS support, the equivalent support from other funding bodies in the rest of the UK. 4. Is UK domiciled and meets residency criteria set out in the Education (Access Funds) (Scotland) Determination 2013, or is eligible to receive maintenance support under legislation applicable in other parts of the UK 5. The fund cannot make awards to assist students with travel costs related to periods of exchange or study abroad 6. The fund cannot make awards to assist with tuition fees *Full eligibility can be found in the University of Strathclyde Discretionary Fund Assessment Guidance.

Level of Study: Postgraduate, Research

Type: Funding support

Value: Various

Length of Study: One off award

Application Procedure: Complete the Application for Financial Support form if you wish to apply for financial support. You only need to submit one application (and one set of supporting documents) and our assessing team will assess your circumstances and eligibility across all of the funds we administer (Housing Support Fund, Mature Students Hardship Fund, The Lady Eileen McDonald EU & International Student Fund and Discretionary Fund). Please complete the application, ensure you include all income and expenditure. We cannot assess an incomplete application. You must provide all the documents needed or your application will be delayed. Please provide photocopies, originals will not be returned. Application for Financial Support: studentsupport.strath.ac.uk/finsup University of Strathclyde Discretionary Fund Assessment Guidance: www.strath.ac.uk/media/ps/sees/studentfinance/University_of_Strathclyde_Discretionary_Fund_Assessment_Guidance_V.1.2.pdf

Closing Date: 7 July

Additional Information: Funding and Financial Support Team: financial-support@strath.ac.uk (44) 141 548 2753 Website: www.strath.ac.uk/studywithus/scholarships/discretionaryfund/

Emergency Aid Fund

Purpose: The Funding and Financial Support Team administer a short-term, interest-free emergency loan facility to assist in cases of serious and immediate financial hardship.

Eligibility: A loan from the fund is at the discretion of the adviser after assessing the student's situation against the following criteria: 1. Applicants must be a registered students on a graduating course with the University of Strathclyde 2. The loan must be to meet essential expenditures that cannot be deferred until receipt of other income (such as student loan, stipend, wages). The student may be asked to supply supporting evidence showing the need for the loan. 3. Emergency loans will not be issued to fund tuition fees/tuition fee arrears, library fines, or any other money owed to another area of the University. The student should be advised to discuss a payment plan with the relevant area. 4. The student must demonstrate a means of repaying the loan such as wages, student loan, stipend, parental contributions, discretionary

fund installment, or discretionary fund award if in the adviser's view the application will result in an award. The student must be able to supply supporting evidence showing their ability to repay from disposable income. 5. A realistic time scale for repaying the loan must be agreed upon, this is usually within 90 days. 6. If you are in the final year of your course you are not eligible to apply for an emergency loan after the course end date regardless of your graduation date. It is important that loans are repaid by the agreed date so that we can continue to assist other students in financial difficulty. You will not be permitted to graduate if you have any outstanding debts to the University. You may be refused a loan if you have no source of income.
Level of Study: Postgraduate, Research
Type: Funding support
Value: Varies
Application Procedure: You can apply for an emergency loan through the financial support portal by following this link: studentsupport.strath.ac.uk/finsup/.
Closing Date: 1 January
Additional Information: Website: www.strath.ac.uk/studywithus/scholarships/emergencyaidfund/

EU Engagement Scholarships Postgraduate Taught Courses

Purpose: We are delighted to announce our EU Engagement Scholarships to support full-time students commencing postgraduate taught courses in 2024. The scholarships will be available to those EU applicants who would have previously been eligible for Home (Scottish/EU) fee status but, because of Brexit, will now be classified as being eligible for International fee status
Eligibility: 1. The scholarships will be available to those EU applicants who would have previously been eligible for Home (Scottish/EU) fee status but, because of Brexit, will now be classified as being eligible for International fee status. 2. Your application for study will be checked for eligibility when you apply, therefore you do not need to make a separate application for this scholarship. 3. The scholarships will be automatically applied to: 4. EU nationals and their dependant family members who are self-funding and: A. are resident in the European Economic Area, Switzerland or the UK at the time of application; and B. are classed as international for tuition fee purposes; and C. are entering a full time degree undergraduate or postgraduate taught Masters programmes in 2024 5. This scholarship does not apply to students classified as Home or RUK for tuition fee purposes.
Level of Study: Postgraduate, Research
Type: Scholarship
Value: up to £10,000
Application Procedure: Your application for study will be checked for eligibility when you apply, therefore you do not need to make a separate application for this scholarship.
Closing Date: 30 September
Additional Information: Website: www.strath.ac.uk/studywithus/scholarships/euengagementscholarshipspostgraduatetaughtcourses/

Faculty of Engineering International Scholarships Postgraduate

Purpose: We offer a number of scholarships for our Faculty of Engineering applicants joining postgraduate taught and postgraduate research courses in academic year 2024/25.
Eligibility: See website
Level of Study: Postgraduate
Type: Scholarship
Value: Typically £3,670
Length of Study: Varies
Application Procedure: CLICK HERE TO APPLY FOR THE SCHOLARSHIPS USING OUR ONLINE APPLICATION FORM: news.strath.ac.uk/p/2AB5-6DY/faculty-of-engineering-international-scholarships-2023-24 You should write no more than 500 words on why you should receive a Faculty of Engineering International Scholarship. The application process Step 1 - Apply for the engineering course of your choice Step 2 - Receive an offer letter for your degree course Step 3 – Submit the scholarship application form Step 4 - If you're successful, you'll receive your scholarship offer letter via email.
Closing Date: 18 August
Additional Information: Website: www.strath.ac.uk/studywithus/scholarships/engineeringinternationalscholarships-pg202324/

Faculty of Humanities & Social Sciences: International Scholarships Postgraduate Taught

Purpose: We offer several scholarships for our Faculty of Humanities & Social applicants joining postgraduate taught programmes in academic year 2024/25.
Eligibility: See website
Level of Study: Postgraduate
Type: Scholarship
Value: £2,500 - £5,000
Length of Study: One year
Closing Date: 31 July
Additional Information: For further information contact: E: hass-pg-selection@strath.ac.uk Website: www.strath.ac.uk/studywithus/scholarships/humanitiessocialsciencesinternationalscholarship202324postgraduate/

For further information contact:

Email: hass-pg-selection@strath.ac.uk

Faculty of Science Health & Care Futures MSc and PhD Scholarships for NHS Employees

Purpose: A number of 25% tuition fee scholarships are available to new MSc and PhD students who are currently employed by one of our NHS partners, through the University's Health & Care Futures: www.strath.ac.uk/workwithus/healthcarefutures/ initiative.
Eligibility: Check website
Level of Study: Postgraduate (MSc), Research
Type: Scholarship
Value: 25% tuition fee scholarships are available
Application Procedure: Candidates who meet the eligibility criteria should contact science-scholarships@strath.ac.uk for application details.
Additional Information: Website: www.strath.ac.uk/studywithus/scholarships/facultyofsciencehealthcarefuturesmscandphdscholarshipsfornhsemployees/

Faculty of Science Masters Scholarship for International Students

Purpose: Scholarships will be awarded on a competitive basis to candidates who demonstrate excellent academic performance (current and/ or previously gained) and any relevant extra-curricular or professional experience.
Eligibility: In order to be considered for a Faculty of Science International Masters Scholarship, candidates must: 1. Be a new, international fee-paying student holding an offer of admission for a full-time, taught masters degree in the Faculty of Science for the 2024/2025 academic year. 2. Be self-funded. Students who receive full scholarships, for example from a government office or embassy, will not be eligible.
Level of Study: Masters Degree, Postgraduate
Type: Scholarship
Value: £4,000- £6,000
Length of Study: 1 Year
Application Procedure: A link to the scholarship application form will be included in an applicant's offer of admission.
Closing Date: 3 July
No. of applicants last year: Up to 150
Additional Information: Website: www.strath.ac.uk/studywithus/scholarships/facultyofsciencemastersscholarshipsforinternationalstudents202324/

Faculty of Science Masters Scholarship for UK Students

Purpose: Scholarships will be awarded on a competitive basis to candidates who complete a scholarship application form and can demonstrate excellent academic performance (current and/ or previously gained) and any relevant extra-curricular or professional experience.
Eligibility: In order to be considered for a Faculty of Science Masters Scholarship for UK Students, candidates must: 1. Be a new student holding an offer of admission for a taught masters degree in the Faculty of Science for the 2024/2025 academic year. 2. Be eligible for tuition fees at the Home or RUK fee rate.
Level of Study: Postgraduate
Type: Scholarship
Value: £1,250
Length of Study: 1 Year
Application Procedure: A link to the scholarship application form will be included in an applicant's offer of admission.
Closing Date: 3 July
No. of applicants last year: Up to 60
Additional Information: For more information email: science-scholarships@strath.ac.uk Website: www.strath.ac.uk/studywithus/scholarships/facultyofsciencemastersscholarshipsforukandroistudents202324/

For further information contact:

Email: science-scholarships@strath.ac.uk

Faculty of Science Scholarship for Online Masters Students

Purpose: Scholarships will be awarded on a competitive basis to candidates who demonstrate excellent academic performance (current and/ or previously gained) and any relevant extra-curricular or professional experience.
Eligibility: In order to be considered for a Faculty of Science Online Masters Scholarship, candidates must: 1. be a new student holding an offer of admission for an online MSc in the Department of Mathematics and Statistics for the 2024/2025 academic year. 2. be self-funded. Students who receive full scholarships, for example from a government office or embassy, will not be eligible.
Level of Study: Postgraduate
Type: Scholarship
Value: £1,500
Length of Study: 3 years
Application Procedure: A link to the scholarship application form will be included in an applicant's offer of admission
Closing Date: 3 September

Additional Information: For more information email: science-scholarships@strath.ac.uk Website: www.strath.ac.uk/studywithus/scholarships/facultyofsciencescholarshipsforonlinemastersstudents202324/

For further information contact:

Email: science-scholarships@strath.ac.uk

Faculty of Science Scholarship for the PgCert in Fundamentals in Forensic Science

Purpose: Scholarships will be awarded on a competitive basis to candidates who demonstrate excellent academic performance (current and/ or previously gained) and any relevant extra-curricular or professional experience.
Eligibility: In order to be considered for a Faculty of Science Scholarship for the PgCert Fundamentals in Forensic Science, candidates must: 1. be a new student holding an offer of admission for the PgCert Fundamentals in Forensic Science in the Faculty of Science for the 2024/2025 academic year. 2. be self-funded. Students who receive full scholarships, for example from a government office or embassy, will not be eligible.
Level of Study: Postgraduate
Type: Scholarship
Value: £500
Length of Study: 1 year
Application Procedure: A link to the scholarship application form will be included in an applicant's offer of admission.
Closing Date: 3 September
Additional Information: For more information about the course, take a look at MSc Fundamentals in Forensic Science: www.strath.ac.uk/courses/postgraduatetaught/fundamentalsinforensicscience/. For more information email: science-scholarships@strath.ac.uk

For further information contact:

Email: science-scholarships@strath.ac.uk

FIDERH

Purpose: FIDERH is a federal loan administered by the Bank of Mexico to support Mexican students in funding their postgraduate studies.
Eligibility: The fee discount will be applied to those who have successfully been awarded the FIDERH loan for graduate studies at Strathclyde.
Level of Study: Postgraduate, Research
Type: Funding support
Value: 15% tuition fee discount
Application Procedure: Application for the FIDERH loan can be made through FIDERH: www.fiderh.org.mx/.
Additional Information: Contact us: Melissa McGrady, Senior International Recruitment Officer: melissa.mcgrady@strath.ac.uk Website: www.strath.ac.uk/studywithus/scholarships/fiderh/

Finn Randall Travel Award

Purpose: In memory of Finn Randall – an alumnus of Strathclyde University and an intrepid traveller – this award was established to assist one registered undergraduate or postgraduate student of the University with the cost of a particular scheme of travel which is considered to be the most enterprising and the most relevant to their course of study.
Eligibility: 1. The Finn Randall Travel Award is granted to one Strathclyde student to assist them with a planned non-compulsory travel, undertaken to enrich the applicant's interests and skills within their field of study. 2. The purpose, region, and duration of the travel are entirely up to the applicant. 3. The Award is open to all current registered Undergraduates and Postgraduates of the University of Strathclyde. 4. Applicants must be a registered student at the University at the time of the proposed travel. 5. The award is not for travel to the University, conference travel, research, fieldwork or any travel directly associated with, or part of, a course/programme/PhD. 6. Applications for travel that has already taken place, or incomplete applications, will not be considered. 7. The proposed travel should commence sometime after the deadline for applications has passed. 8. If you are uncertain whether your planned travel would be eligible for the Award, please see the "Further Information" tab for examples of previous winners, or email us at rkes-pgrfunding@strath.ac.uk with your query.
Level of Study: Postgraduate, Research
Type: Award
Value: £300
Application Procedure: 1. A completed Finn Randall Travel Award Application Form (www.strath.ac.uk/media/students/postgraduate/pgro/Finn_Randall_Travel_Award_2023_Application_Form.docx) 2. A CV to include your school and university records, academic or other distinctions gained and interests and extra-curricular activities. 3. A brief statement from an appropriate member of academic staff who is able to comment on the significance of your travel plans in relation to your course of study – this could be the Head of Department, course tutor, or supervisor (as appropriate). This can be provided on Section 4 of the application form, or as a separate document.
Closing Date: 31 March
Additional Information: If you have any queries regarding the Finn Randall Travel Award please contact the PGR

U

Funding Team by email at rkes-pgrfunding@strath.ac.uk Website: www.strath.ac.uk/studywithus/scholarships/finnrandalltravelaward/

For further information contact:

Email: rkes-pgrfunding@strath.ac.uk

Fraser of Allander Institute Scholarships for MSc Applied Economics

Purpose: Scholarships are available to join the MSc Applied Economics programme
Eligibility: 1. The closing date is 3rd August 2024 and applications to be considered for these scholarships should be submitted by then. Successful candidates will be notified shortly thereafter. 2. Candidates must be self-funded (ie. not in receipt of any funding from any other scholarships, employer sponsorship, etc) and already hold an offer of a place on the Full Time Msc Applied Economics programme for entry September 2024. 3. Candidates interested in applying should provide a maximum 1000 word statement demonstrating, through their ideas, experience and future career plans (including their reasoning for joining the MSc Applied Economics) why they should be awarded this scholarship. Candidates will also be considered on the overall quality of their application and financial need. *These Scholarships are only available to students who are classified Home fee status - ie: Scotland, Rest of the UK or EU with Settled Status*
Level of Study: Postgraduate (MSc)
Type: Scholarship
Value: £6,000
Country of Study: United Kingdom
Application Procedure: Candidates interested in applying should provide a maximum 1,000 word statement demonstrating, through their ideas, experience and future career plans (including their reasoning for joining the MSc Applied Economics) why they should be awarded this scholarship. Candidates will also be considered on the overall quality of their application and financial need. The mode of applying is online. Please visit website www.sbs.strath.ac.uk/apps/scholarships/economics/applied-economics.asp
No. of awards offered: 6
Closing Date: 3 August
Additional Information: For more information about the programme, please visit Applied Economics (MSc). Website: www.strath.ac.uk/studywithus/scholarships/fraserofallanderinstitutefaihomeeuscholarshipsformscappliedeconomics/

For further information contact:

Email: sbs.admissions@strath.ac.uk

Global Research Scholarship Programme (Faculty of Humanities & Social Sciences)

Purpose: As part of its longstanding commitment to growing its population of excellent postgraduate researchers, the University is offering a number of Global Research Scholarships.
Eligibility: 1. Candidates must demonstrate an excellent academic record. For Doctoral study, this should comprise a First-Class undergraduate degree (or equivalent); and/or a relevant Master's degree with Merit/Distinction, and/or evidence of equivalent achievement. (Students with an Upper Second Class degree (or equivalent) and a Masters, with an outstanding proposal, may also apply) 2. MPhil and MRes applicants are only required to have an undergraduate degree at First or Upper Second Class 3. candidates must demonstrate strong research potential (evidenced by the research proposal and academic references) and a clear fit between their research interests and the research strengths of one of the Schools and/or subject areas in the Faculty of Humanities and Social Sciences
Level of Study: Postgraduate, Research
Type: Scholarship
Value: Full tuition fees
Length of Study: 1. PhD/EdD: 3 years full-time 2. DEdPsy: 2 years full-time only 3. MPhil/MRes: 1 year full-time
Application Procedure: You must have a conditional offer of study before the closing date to be considered for this award. Step 1: identify a supervisor To begin this process you should identify a potential supervisor for your project from the staff listed on the 'supervisor' tab on the website of your chosen subject area - listed under "Eligible programmes" above. You may contact potential supervisors by email to ask if they would be able to supervise your proposed project. Step 2: application Prospective students who receive and accept an offer of admission will be eligible to apply for a Global Research Scholarship. Prospective students can apply for this award if they are self-funded. These scholarships cannot be combined with any other Strathclyde University award.
Closing Date: 31 March
Additional Information: Website: www.strath.ac.uk/studywithus/scholarships/globalresearchscholarshipprogramme/

Global Research Scholarship Programme – Faculty of Science

Purpose: As part of its longstanding commitment to growing its population of excellent postgraduate researchers, the University of Strathclyde is offering up to 15 full tuition fee scholarships for outstanding PhD students commencing their studies in the Faculty of Science in October 2024.

Eligibility: In order to be considered for a Global Research Scholarship, candidates must: 1. be a new, international fee-paying student holding an offer of admission for a full-time PhD in the Faculty of Science for the 2024/2025 academic year. 2. have achieved excellent grades in their academic studies to date. 3. be committed to their field of study. 4. be able to start their PhD studies in October 2024.
Level of Study: Postgraduate, Research
Type: Scholarship
Value: Full tuition fees
Length of Study: 3 years
Application Procedure: Step 1: identify a supervisor and submit an application for PGR study if you have not already done so Please refer to the website in your chosen subject area for potential supervisors and email them to discuss your research interests. Step 2: submit an application for a Global Research Scholarship award. Once you have an offer of admission, please complete the GRS application jointly with your chosen supervisor. for further information see website
Closing Date: 31 March
No. of applicants last year: up to 15
Additional Information: Website: www.strath.ac.uk/studywithus/scholarships/globalresearchscholarshipprogramme202324-facultyofscience/

Housing Support Fund

Purpose: The Housing Support Fund is provided by the University to address urgent student housing needs.
Eligibility: Registered students of the University shall be eligible to apply to the Fund if they meet the following criteria: 1. A payment from the fund would make a significant contribution to your ability to continue your studies successfully; and 2. You have an urgent housing need that can be addressed through an award by the fund; and 3. You are unable to meet the immediate costs of your housing needs through your existing funding.
Level of Study: Postgraduate, Research
Type: Funding support
Value: Varies
Length of Study: One off award
Application Procedure: 1. Complete the Application for Financial Support form if you wish to apply for financial support. You only need to submit one application (and one set of supporting documents) and our assessing team will assess your circumstances and eligibility across all of the funds we administer (Housing Support Fund, Mature Students Hardship Fund, University of Strathclyde Covid-19 Hardship Fund, The Lady Eileen McDonald EU & International Student Fund and Discretionary Fund). 2. Please complete the application, ensure you include all income and expenditure. We cannot assess an incomplete application. You must provide all the documents needed or your application will be delayed. Please provide photocopies, originals will not be returned. Application for Financial Support: studentsupport.strath.ac.uk/finsup University of Strathclyde Discretionary Fund Assessment Guidance: www.strath.ac.uk/media/ps/sees/studentfinance/University_of_Strathclyde_Discretionary_Fund_Assessment_Guidance_V.1.2.pdf
Closing Date: 1 January
No. of applicants last year: Varies
Additional Information: Funding and Financial Support Team: financial-support@strath.ac.uk (for enquiries only) Website: www.strath.ac.uk/studywithus/scholarships/housingsupportfund/

Humanities & Social Sciences: Student Excellence Awards

Purpose: The Faculty of Humanities & Social Sciences is pleased to invite applications from excellent students with original research proposals for the University of Strathclyde Student Excellence Awards for commencing study on 1 October 2024.
Eligibility: You must have, or be expected to obtain, a first-class honours degree and a master's degree with distinction/merit. Candidates from outside the UK will be considered but will be required to pay the difference between the Home and EU/International fee.
Level of Study: Postgraduate, Research
Type: Award
Value: Home fee & stipend
Length of Study: 3 years full-time (home & international) or 6 years part-time (home only)
Application Procedure: You must have a conditional offer of study before the closing date to be considered for this award. Step 1: identify a supervisor Step 2: application See website for further details
Closing Date: 31 March
No. of applicants last year: 7
Additional Information: Website: www.strath.ac.uk/studywithus/scholarships/humanitiessocialsciencesstudentexcellenceawards2324/

Humanities and Social Sciences Home Postgraduate Taught Performance Sport Scholarship

Purpose: The HaSS Home Taught Postgraduate Performance Sport Scholarship aims to enable talented student-athletes who are regularly competing at International level to follow a dual career. Consequently, the programme provides academic flexibility (where feasible), World-Class sports science

and medical support, and financial assistance towards training and competition costs.
Eligibility: All applicants must be competing in a Sportscotland-recognised sport, and priority will be given to students competing in a BUCS-sport who can demonstrate the potential to contribute toward the University's objective of being ranked in the top 20 in the UK. In addition, all applicants should be competing at least at Junior, if not senior, International level. Furthermore, we actively encourage students competing at an elite level within disability sport and our new £31m Sports Facility is fully-accessible.
Level of Study: Postgraduate
Type: Scholarship
Value: £1,000 (+ up to £3,750* in-kind support)
Application Procedure: Please apply through the online form: strath.eu.qualtrics.com/jfe/form/SV_bIW66SQoeF9kyWO.
Closing Date: 3 April
No. of applicants last year: 4
Additional Information: If you require any further information / guidance, please contact: Dave Sykes, Performance Sport Manager via email (dave.sykes@strath.ac.uk). Website: www.strath.ac.uk/studywithus/scholarships/hasshomepostgraduatetaughtperformancesportscholarship/

Humanities and Social Sciences International Postgraduate Taught Performance Sport Scholarship

Purpose: The HaSS International Taught Postgraduate Performance Sport Scholarship aims to enable talented student-athletes who are regularly competing at International level to follow a dual career. Consequently, the programme provides academic flexibility (where feasible), World-Class sports science and medical support, and financial assistance towards training and competition costs.
Eligibility: All applicants must be competing in a Sport Scotland-recognised sport, and priority will be given to students competing in a BUCS-sport who can demonstrate the potential to contribute toward the University's objective of being ranked in the top 20 in the UK. In addition, all applicants should be competing at least at Junior, if not senior, International level. Furthermore, we actively encourage students competing at an elite level within disability sport and our new £31m Sports Facility is fully-accessible.
Level of Study: Postgraduate
Type: Scholarship
Value: £3,000 (+ up to £3,750* in-kind support)
Application Procedure: Please apply through the online form: strath.eu.qualtrics.com/jfe/form/SV_bIW66SQoeF9kyWO. Scholarships bursaries privacy notice: www.strath.ac.uk/strathclydesport/scholarshipsbursariesprivacynotice/ Please note, that once started, you will not be able to pause and revisit your application. Therefore, prior to starting your application, it is advisable to watch the following short five-minute application help video: strath-my.sharepoint.com/:v:/g/personal/dave_sykes_strath_ac_uk/EY053CxLOtZEjmSPSgWonxMBvsjlReD3azPa8DfOWMt1WA?e=eHkGe3attached, which walks you through all the questions you will be required to answer. Please then use this guide to have all details to hand, prior to commencing your application.
Closing Date: 3 April
Additional Information: If you require any further information / guidance, please contact: Dave Sykes, Performance Sport Manager via email (dave.sykes@strath.ac.uk). Website: www.strath.ac.uk/studywithus/scholarships/hassinternationalpostgraduatetaughtperformancesportscholarship/

Humanities and Social Sciences RUK Postgraduate Taught Performance Sport Scholarship

Purpose: The HaSS RUK Postgraduate Taught Performance Sport Scholarship aims to enable talented student-athletes who are regularly competing at International level to follow a dual career. Consequently, the programme provides academic flexibility (where feasible), World-Class sports science and medical support, and financial assistance towards training and competition costs.
Eligibility: All applicants must be competing in a Sport Scotland-recognised sport, and priority will be given to students competing in a BUCS-sport who can demonstrate the potential to contribute toward the University's objective of being ranked in the top 20 in the UK. In addition, all applicants should be competing at least at Junior, if not senior, International level. Furthermore, we actively encourage students competing at an elite level within disability sport and our new £31m Sports Facility is fully-accessible.
Level of Study: Postgraduate
Type: Scholarship
Value: £1,000 (+ up to £4,750* in-kind support)
Application Procedure: Please apply through the online form: strath.eu.qualtrics.com/jfe/form/SV_bIW66SQoeF9kyWO. Scholarships bursaries privacy notice: www.strath.ac.uk/strathclydesport/scholarshipsbursariesprivacynotice/ Please note, that once started, you will not be able to pause and revisit your application. Therefore, prior to starting your application, it is advisable to watch the following short five-minute application help video: strath-my.sharepoint.com/:v:/g/personal/dave_sykes_strath_ac_uk/EY053CxLOtZEjmSPSgWonxMBvsjlReD3azPa8DfOWMt1WA?e=eHkGe3attached, which walks you through all the questions you will be required to answer. Please then use this guide to have all details to hand, prior to commencing your application.
Closing Date: 3 April

Additional Information: If you require any further information / guidance, please contact: Dave Sykes, Performance Sport Manager via email (dave.sykes@strath.ac.uk). Website: www.strath.ac.uk/studywithus/scholarships/hassruk postgraduatetaughtperformancesportscholarship/

International Strathclyde Prestige Award for Excellence in Business Translation and Interpreting in United Kingdom

Purpose: Applications are open for Strathclyde Prestige Award for Excellence in Business Translation & Interpreting. The scholarship is available to the international student to pursue a master degree program.
Eligibility: Eligible Course or Subjects: The scholarship will be awarded in the field of Business Translation & Interpreting Eligibility Criteria: To be eligible, the applicants must meet all the following criteria: 1. To apply for this scholarship, the applicants must be available to commence their academic studies in the UK by the start of the academic year in September 2. The candidates must hold a first degree at first class or upper second class honors, or equivalent and an academic offer to study MSc Business Translation & Interpreting. For more information see website
Level of Study: Masters Degree, Postgraduate
Type: Award
Value: £5000
Frequency: Annual
Country of Study: United Kingdom
Application Procedure: To apply, the applicants must submit an online application through the link: r1.dotmailer-surveys.com/432p4736-ae3nzoab.
Closing Date: 31 May
Funding: Private
Additional Information: website: o3schools.com/international-strathclyde-prestige-award-for-excellence-in-business-translation-interpreting-in-uk/

For further information contact:

Email: hass-pg-enquiries@strath.ac.uk

Law Postgraduate Community Bursary

Purpose: The Faculty of Humanities & Social Sciences is offering a £700 fee reduction for applicants to the LLM Criminal Justice & Penal Change, LLM Human Rights Law and LLM Mediation and Conflict Resolution degree programmes who are working at any third sector/NGO organisation in the field of criminal justice and penal change, human rights or conflict resolution.
Eligibility: To be eligible for this award applicants must: 1. Be working in a paid or voluntary role at any third sector/NGO organisation in the field of criminal justice and penal change, human rights or conflict resolution at the time of their application. 2. Be available to commence their academic studies in the UK by the start of the academic year in September 2024. 3. Hold an unconditional academic offer to the LLM Criminal Justice & Penal Change, LLM Human Rights Law or LLM Mediation and Conflict Resolution.
Level of Study: Postgraduate
Type: Bursary
Value: £700
Length of Study: 1 year
Application Procedure: To apply for this award, please contact stewart.coubrough@strath.ac.uk. Please be able to provide a reference from a colleague in the the third sector/NGO organisation as part of your application. This will usually take the form of an email from the organisation confirming that you work with them (in a paid or voluntary capacity).
Closing Date: 31 August
No. of applicants last year: Unlimited
Additional Information: Contact us: Email: stewart.coubrough@strath.ac.uk Website: www.strath.ac.uk/studywithus/scholarships/lawpostgraduatecommunitybursary/

Mac Robertson Travelling Scholarship

Purpose: The aim of the funding is to enrich and further the award-holder's academic experience and research achievements.
Eligibility: 1. The Mac Robertson Travel Scholarship is open to all current registered postgraduate research students (PhD, MRes, MPhil, MSc by Research or similar) at the University of Strathclyde and the University of Glasgow. 2. The Scholarship is open to students from all academic disciplines. 3. Travel will not be funded within 6 months of starting or within 6 months prior to the applicant's expected thesis submission date, with the exception of students completing a 1 year Masters degree. 4. Students who have already submitted or will have submitted before or during the planned travel are ineligible to apply. 5. Minimum length of trip is 2 months, with a maximum stay of 12 months. 6. Applicants to the Mac Robertson Travel Scholarship should show how their research is relevant to both the University of Glasgow and Strathclyde University and how it may contribute to further collaborative research between these two universities. It should be made clear in your application how the intended trip will be additional to and not essential to the completion of the applicant's research degree. 7. Applicants must meet all of the relevant conditions outlined above.

U

Level of Study: Postgraduate, Research
Type: Scholarship
Value: Up to £4,000
Length of Study: 2-12 months
Frequency: Annual
Study Establishment: University of Strathclyde
Country of Study: United Kingdom
No. of awards offered: 3
Closing Date: 29 April
Funding: Individuals
Contributor: Mac Robertson
Additional Information: All queries about the Mac Robertson Travel Scholarship should be directed to the University of Glasgow's PGR Service - pgr@glasgow.ac.uk.

For further information contact:

Email: pgr@glasgow.ac.uk.

Mature Students Hardship Fund

Eligibility: Registered students of the University shall be eligible to apply to the Fund if they meet the following criteria: 1. are aged 21 or over at the start of their current course of study. 2. started their course with an appropriate funding arrangement in place but have fallen into hardship 3. if eligible, have applied to the Discretionary Fund for support 4. If eligible, have applied for all statutory funding (Student loan, bursary, cost of living grant) 5. or they have been recommended for support from the Fund by the Student Support Team on the basis of urgent or exceptional circumstances 6. a payment from the fund will make a significant contribution to the student's ability to continue their studies successfully.
Level of Study: Postgraduate, Research
Type: Funding support
Value: Varies, £500-£1000
Length of Study: One off award
Application Procedure: 1. Complete the Application for Financial Support form if you wish to apply for financial support. You only need to submit one application (and one set of supporting documents) and our assessing team will assess your circumstances and eligibility across all of the funds we administer (Housing Support Fund, Mature Students Hardship Fund, University of Strathclyde Covid-19 Hardship Fund, The Lady Eileen McDonald EU & International Student Fund and Discretionary Fund). 2. Please complete the application, ensure you include all income and expenditure. We cannot assess an incomplete application. You must provide all the documents needed or your application will be delayed. Please provide photocopies, originals will not be returned. Application for Financial Support: studentsupport.strath.ac.uk/finsup. University of Strathclyde Discretionary Fund Assessment Guidance: www.strath.ac.uk/media/ps/sees/studentfinance/University_of_Strathclyde_Discretionary_Fund_Assessment_Guidance_V.1.2.pdf
Closing Date: 1 January
No. of applicants last year: Varies
Additional Information: Website: www.strath.ac.uk/studywithus/scholarships/maturestudentshardshipfund/

Postgraduate Research Travel Award

Purpose: The Postgraduate Research (PGR) Travel Award can be requested by current, registered doctoral students for travel to conferences where the student will either present papers or speak to a poster exhibit. Only one award can be granted per student for the duration of their PhD.
Eligibility: To be eligible for the PGR Travel Award, applicants must be a full-time or part-time registered doctoral student at the University of Strathclyde at the time of their intended travel. In order for the purpose of the intended travel to be eligible, applicants must have been accepted to present their own research undertaken at the University of Strathclyde at a conference in the form of a paper or a poster.
Level of Study: Postgraduate, Research
Type: Scholarship
Value: Dependant on destination
Application Procedure: Please complete the PGR Travel Award application form: strath.sharepoint.com/sites/rkes/SitePages/Postgraduate-Research-(PGR)-Travel-Award.aspx (available on RKES Portal) and return a signed version as a PDF file to rkes-pgrfunding@strath.ac.uk Applications must be submitted prior to the start of the intended travel. Retrospective applications will not be considered.
No. of applicants last year: ~70
Additional Information: For further information concerning the PGR Travel Award, please contact rkes-pgrfunding@strath.ac.uk

For further information contact:

Email: rkes-pgrfunding@strath.ac.uk

ScottishPower International Master's Scholarship Programme

Purpose: This programme, which is aimed at graduates and final-year students, aims to promote excellence in the training of new generations and foster the employability of young people in sectors of the future.
Eligibility: Through its International Master's Scholarship Programme ScottishPower are looking to develop a new

generation of people with enthusiasm for learning, desire to innovate, and aspiration to transform the energy industry. 1. Applicants must be in possession of, or expect to receive, a Bachelor with Honours at a minimum 2:1 (or equivalent) or Master's degree from a recognised university on submission of the application. If the applicant is still in the final year of the academic course 2023-2024, the grant will be contingent upon the applicant securing the university degree at the determined level at the end of the academic cycle in June/July 2024. 2. Applicants must follow the usual application procedure for the UK University they wish to attend. Applications submitted by students who have not submitted an application will be rejected during the selection process. 3. Applicants may not receive any remuneration, wages or be in receipt of any scholarship, financial aid or other award of a similar nature from institutions and public or private foundations during the period that the scholarship is awarded for. 4. Candidates who have previously been awarded a scholarship by ScottishPower, the ScottishPower Foundation or any of the other companies within the Iberdrola group are not eligible to apply.
Level of Study: Masters Degree, Postgraduate
Type: Scholarship
Value: Full tuition fees and a monthly payment of £1,200
Length of Study: 1 year
Application Procedure: Applications can be made online via the ScottishPower website: www.scottishpower.com/pages/scottishpower_masters_scholarships.aspx.
Closing Date: 31 March
No. of applicants last year: 14 throughout the UK
Additional Information: Contact us: ScottishPower International Master's Scholarship Programme Website: www.strath.ac.uk/studywithus/scholarships/scottishpowermasters scholarships/

Strathclyde Alumni Scholarship: Postgraduate Taught

Purpose: We are delighted to offer our Strathclyde graduates a 15% tuition fee discount on postgraduate taught courses running in September and January. All alumni will be eligible for the discount, including those who have studied at Strathclyde on an exchange or study abroad programme.
Eligibility: We are delighted to offer our Strathclyde graduates a 15% tuition fee discount on postgraduate taught courses running in September and January. All alumni will be eligible for the discount, including those who have studied at Strathclyde on an exchange or study abroad programme. Please visit the 'how to apply' tab for details. Please note: this discount cannot be used in conjunction with any other scholarship offer.
Level of Study: Postgraduate
Type: Scholarship
Value: 15% tuition fee discount
Application Procedure: To apply please contact the relevant faculty stating the programme you have applied for along with your applicant number: 1. Engineering: eng-admissions@strath.ac.uk 2. Humanities and Social Sciences: hass-pg-enquiries@strath.ac.uk 3. Science: science-scholarships@strath.ac.uk 4. Strathclyde Business School: sbs.admissions@strath.ac.uk
Additional Information: Website: www.strath.ac.uk/studywithus/scholarships/strathclydealumnischolarshipmasters/

Strathclyde Business School Full Time MBA Deans Excellence Awards

Purpose: The Deans Excellence Awards will be awarded to candidates who demonstrate in their Scholarship application, MBA programme application and interview; exceptional professional/managerial/leadership experience and career development, excellent academic performance and who will significantly contribute to the overall academic, cultural and experiential profile of the programme cohort.
Eligibility: Applicants must hold an offer of a place on the Full-time MBA September 2024 programme in order to be considered. Awards will only be made to candidates who have undergone a successful interview. MBA Scholarship applications are invited from exceptional candidates who are prepared to act as ambassadors for the Strathclyde FT MBA. Who can demonstrate through their ideas outlined in their scholarship and programme application aswell as their interview how they would contribute to bring the class together through teamwork to create community, from the outset, in order to achieve the ultimate learning (and social) experience for the group as a whole. Leadership/management skills or potential, overall quality of the programme application and financial need will also be considered
Level of Study: Postgraduate
Type: Award
Value: 50% of Full Time MBA tuition fee
Application Procedure: *You must have an offer to study our MBA in Glasgow with Strathclyde Business School before applying for a scholarship. Any incorrect or false application numbers entered will render the application ineligible for consideration* **Duplicate applications will not be considered. Any standard or clearly template-based SOP/Personal Statement/Duplicate Programme essay answers uploaded will be disregarded and the application not considered for a Scholarship** Due to volume of applications, only successful applicants will be notified but all applications received will remain under consideration until the closing date. Please complete this MBA Scholarship

application form: www.sbs.strath.ac.uk/apps/scholarships/mba/september-2023/ and submit your supporting statement.
Closing Date: 31 July
Additional Information: Please contact sbs.admissions@strath.ac.uk with any queries. Website: www.strath.ac.uk/studywithus/scholarships/strathclydebusinessschoolmbadeansexcellenceawards/

Strathclyde Business School Full Time MBA Scholarships

Eligibility: MBA Scholarship and progamme applications are invited from exceptional candidates who are prepared to act as ambassadors for the Strathclyde FT MBA. Who can demonstrate through their ideas outlined in their application and interview how they would contribute to bring the class together through teamwork to create community, from the outset, in order to achieve the ultimate learning (and social) experience for the group as a whole. Leadership/management skills or potential, overall quality of the application and financial need will also be considered.
Level of Study: MBA, Postgraduate
Type: Scholarship
Value: Between £7,000 and £15,000 dependent on experience.
Application Procedure: *You must have an offer to study an MBA in Glasgow with Strathclyde Business School before applying for a scholarship. Any incorrect or false application numbers entered will render the application ineligible for consideration* **Duplicate applications will not be considered. Any standard or clearly template-based SOP/Personal Statement/Duplicate Programme essay answers uploaded will be disregarded and the application not considered for a Scholarship** Due to volume of applications, only successful applicants will be notified but all applications received will remain under consideration until the closing date. Please complete this MBA Scholarship application form and submit your supporting statement.
Closing Date: 31 July
No. of applicants last year: Up to 20
Additional Information: Website: www.strath.ac.uk/studywithus/scholarships/sbsfulltimembascholarshipsseptember2023/

Strathclyde Business School Home Postgraduate Taught Performance Sport Scholarship

Purpose: The SBS Home Taught Postgraduate Performance Sport Scholarship aims to enable talented student-athletes who are regularly competing at International level to follow a dual career. Consequently, the programme provides academic flexibility (where feasible), World-Class sports science and medical support, and financial assistance towards training and competition costs.
Eligibility: All applicants must be competing in a Sport Scotland-recognised sport, and priority will be given to students competing in a BUCS-sport who can demonstrate the potential to contribute toward the University's objective of being ranked in the top 20 in the UK. In addition, all applicants should be competing at least at Junior, if not senior, International level. Furthermore, we actively encourage students competing at an elite level within disability sport and our new £31m Sports Facility is fully-accessible.
Level of Study: Postgraduate
Type: Scholarship
Value: £1,750-£2,000 (+ up to £3,750* in-kind support)
Application Procedure: Please apply through the online form: strath.eu.qualtrics.com/jfe/form/SV_bIW66SQoeF9kyWO. Scholarships bursaries privacy notice: www.strath.ac.uk/strathclydesport/scholarshipsbursariesprivacynotice/ Please note, that once started, you will not be able to pause and revisit your application. Therefore, prior to starting your application, it is advisable to watch the following short five-minute application help video: strath-my.sharepoint.com/:v:/g/personal/dave_sykes_strath_ac_uk/EY053CxLOtZEjmSPSgWonxMBvsjlReD3azPa8DfOWMt1WA?e=eHkGe3attached, which walks you through all the questions you will be required to answer. Please then use this guide to have all details to hand, prior to commencing your application.
Closing Date: 3 April
Additional Information: If you require any further information / guidance, please contact: Dave Sykes, Performance Sport Manager via email (dave.sykes@strath.ac.uk). Website: www.strath.ac.uk/studywithus/scholarships/sbshomepostgraduatetaughtperformancesportscholarship/

Strathclyde Business School International Postgraduate Taught Performance Sport Scholarship

Purpose: The SBS International Taught Postgraduate Performance Sport Scholarship aims to enable talented student-athletes who are regularly competing at International level to follow a dual career. Consequently, the programme provides academic flexibility (where feasible), World-Class sports science and medical support, and financial assistance towards training and competition costs.
Eligibility: All applicants must be competing in a Sport Scotland-recognised sport, and priority will be given to students competing in a BUCS-sport who can demonstrate the potential to contribute toward the University's objective of being ranked in the top 20 in the UK. In addition, all

applicants should be competing at least at Junior, if not senior, International level. Furthermore, we actively encourage students competing at an elite level within disability sport and our new £31m Sports Facility is fully-accessible.
Level of Study: Postgraduate
Type: Scholarship
Value: £2,500-£3,250 (+ up to £3,750* in-kind support)
Application Procedure: Please apply through the online form: strath.eu.qualtrics.com/jfe/form/SV_bIW66SQoeF9kyWO. Scholarships bursaries privacy notice: www.strath.ac.uk/strathclydesport/scholarshipsbursariesprivacynotice/ Please note, that once started, you will not be able to pause and revisit your application. Therefore, prior to starting your application, it is advisable to watch the following short five-minute application help video: strath-my.sharepoint.com/:v:/g/personal/dave_sykes_strath_ac_uk/EY053CxLOtZEjmSPSgWonxMBvsjlReD3azPa8DfOWMt1WA?e=eHkGe3attached, which walks you through all the questions you will be required to answer. Please then use this guide to have all details to hand, prior to commencing your application.
Closing Date: 3 April
No. of applicants last year: up to four
Additional Information: If you require any further information / guidance, please contact: Dave Sykes, Performance Sport Manager via email (dave.sykes@strath.ac.uk). Website: www.strath.ac.uk/studywithus/scholarships/sbsinternationalpostgraduatetaughtperformancesportscholarship/

Strathclyde Business School Masters Scholarships for International Students

Purpose: Strathclyde Business School is delighted to be able to offer a number of Masters Scholarships
Eligibility: Candidates must be self-funded (ie. not in receipt of any funding from any other scholarships, employer sponsorship, etc) and already hold an offer of a place on one of our Full Time Msc programmes for entry September 2024: www.strath.ac.uk/business/postgraduate/ and also be deemed International with regards to Fee Status. See website for more details
Level of Study: Masters Degree, Postgraduate
Type: Scholarship
Value: Varies by course fee - Between £9,000 and £10,000
Application Procedure: *You must have an offer to study a Full Time Postgraduate course with Strathclyde Business School before applying for a scholarship. Any incorrect or false application numbers entered will render the application ineligible for consideration* **Duplicate applications will not be considered. Any standard or clearly template-based SOP/Personal Statement/Duplicate Programme essay answers uploaded will be disregarded and the application not considered for a Scholarship** Due to volume of applications, only successful applicants will be notified but all applications received will remain under consideration until the closing date. Please complete this Scholarship application form: www.sbs.strath.ac.uk/apps/scholarships/masters/september-2023/ and submit your supporting statement.
Closing Date: 31 July
No. of applicants last year: Up to a maximum of 35
Additional Information: Please contact sbs.admissions@strath.ac.uk with any queries. Website: www.strath.ac.uk/studywithus/scholarships/strathclydebusinessschoolmastersforinternationalstudents/

Strathclyde Business School Masters Scholarships for Scottish/UK Students

Purpose: Strathclyde Business School is delighted to be able to offer a number of Masters Scholarships
Eligibility: Candidates must be self-funded (ie. not in receipt of any funding from any other scholarships, employer sponsorship, etc) and already hold an offer of a place on one of our MSc September 2024 full-time programmes: www.strath.ac.uk/business/postgraduate/ and also be deemed Scotland/UK (Home) with regards to Course Fee Status. For more information see website
Level of Study: Masters Degree, Postgraduate
Type: Scholarship
Value: Varies by Course fee - Between £4000 and £5000
Application Procedure: All candidates holding an offer of a place one of our FT MSc programmes: www.strath.ac.uk/business/postgraduate/ will automatically be considered, therefore no separate scholarship application is required.
Closing Date: 31 August
No. of applicants last year: Multiple
Additional Information: Please contact sbs.admissions@strath.ac.uk with any queries. Website: www.strath.ac.uk/studywithus/scholarships/strathclydebusinessschoolmastersforscottishukstudents/

Strathclyde Business School RUK Postgraduate Taught Performance Sport Scholarship

Purpose: The SBS RUK Taught Postgraduate Performance Sport Scholarship aims to enable talented student-athletes who are regularly competing at International level to follow a dual career. Consequently, the programme provides academic flexibility (where feasible), World-Class sports science and medical support, and financial assistance towards training and competition costs.
Eligibility: All applicants must be competing in a Sport Scotland-recognised sport, and priority will be given to

students competing in a BUCS-sport who can demonstrate the potential to contribute toward the University's objective of being ranked in the top 20 in the UK. In addition, all applicants should be competing at least at Junior, if not senior, International level. Furthermore, we actively encourage students competing at an elite level within disability sport and our new £31m Sports Facility is fully-accessible.
Level of Study: Postgraduate
Type: Scholarship
Value: £1,500-£2,000 (+ up to £4,750* in-kind support)
Application Procedure: Please apply through the online form: strath.eu.qualtrics.com/jfe/form/SV_bIW66SQoeF9kyWO. Scholarships bursaries privacy notice: www.strath.ac.uk/strathclydesport/scholarshipsbursariesprivacynotice/ Please note, that once started, you will not be able to pause and revisit your application. Therefore, prior to starting your application, it is advisable to watch the following short five-minute application help video: strath-my.sharepoint.com/:v:/g/personal/dave_sykes_strath_ac_uk/EY053CxLOtZEjmSPSgWonxMBvsjlReD3azPa8DfOWMt1WA?e=eHkGe3attached, which walks you through all the questions you will be required to answer. Please then use this guide to have all details to hand, prior to commencing your application.
Closing Date: 3 April
No. of applicants last year: up to four
Additional Information: If you require any further information / guidance, please contact: Dave Sykes, Performance Sport Manager via email (dave.sykes@strath.ac.uk). Website: www.strath.ac.uk/studywithus/scholarships/sbsrukpostgraduatetaughtperformancesportscholarship/

Strathclyde Business School – Global Research Scholarships

Purpose: Strathclyde Business School are offering ten full fee scholarships for outstanding students seeking to join our PhD programme
Eligibility: 1. evidence of ability to self-fund living costs for duration of studies (as this is a fee-only scholarship) 2. a first-class or upper second-class UK Honours degree, or overseas equivalent, in a relevant discipline from a recognised academic institution. 3. if English isn't your first language, you'll need an IELTS score of 6.5 or equivalent. 4. not be in receipt of any other Scholarship
Level of Study: Postgraduate
Type: Scholarship
Value: Fee Waiver for Home/International students
Application Procedure: During the application you'll be asked for the following: 1. your full contact details 2. transcripts and certificates of all degrees 3. proof of English language proficiency if English isn't your first language 4. two references, one of which must be academic 5. research proposal of up to 1,500 words in length, demonstrating potential contribution both in theory and practice; please use our Postgraduate Research Proposal Outline and attach this with your application
Closing Date: 31 May
Additional Information: Interested candidates should contact the SBS PGR office at sbs-pgradmissions@strath.ac.uk Website: www.strath.ac.uk/studywithus/scholarships/globalresearchscholarships/

Strathclyde Research Studentship Scheme (SRSS)

Purpose: Strathclyde Research Studentship Scheme (SRSS) doctoral studentships are available annually for excellent students and excellent research projects. There are two main sources of funding: Central University funding, and the Engineering and Physical Sciences Research Council - Doctoral Training Partnership (EPSRC - DTP) funding.
Eligibility: Funding is provided for students with a good honours degree at a first- or upper second-class level, awarded within a relevant cognate discipline. Faculties may stipulate a first class honours degree
Level of Study: Postgraduate, Research
Type: Studentship
Value: Home fees and stipend at UKRI rate
Length of Study: Between 3 and 3.5 years
Application Procedure: Applications are made by academic supervisors and, in the first instance, interested candidates should contact the department/supervisor they are interested in working with.
No. of applicants last year: 100
Additional Information: Website: www.strath.ac.uk/studywithus/scholarships/strathclyderesearchstudentshipschemesrss/

The Lady Eileen McDonald EU & International Student Fund

Purpose: The fund is to assist EU and International Students who have fallen into financial hardship after starting their course. If you started your course with suitable funding in place and now find yourself in financial hardship you could be eligible to apply.
Eligibility: Registered students of the University shall be eligible to apply to the Fund if they meet the following criteria: 1. You have fallen into financial hardship after starting your course of study with an appropriate funding arrangement in place 2. You are not eligible to apply to the

University Discretionary Fund by virtue of your residence status 3. A payment from the fund would make a significant contribution to your ability to continue your studies successfully; and 4. You are unable to meet your immediate living costs through your existing funding. The level of award will be judged on a case to case basis. Awards are around £300-£500 and are intended to meet immediate short term living costs. Because of this the fund cannot be used to replace a regular income. Awards will normally be made in the form of a grant.
Level of Study: Postgraduate, Research
Type: Funding support
Value: £300-£500
Length of Study: One off award
Application Procedure: 1. Complete the Application for Financial Support form if you wish to apply for financial support. You only need to submit one application (and one set of supporting documents) and our assessing team will assess your circumstances and eligibility across all of the funds we administer (Housing Support Fund, Mature Students Hardship Fund, University of Strathclyde Covid-19 Hardship Fund, The Lady Eileen McDonald EU & International Student Fund and Discretionary Fund). 2. Please complete the application, ensure you include all income and expenditure. We cannot assess an incomplete application. You must provide all the documents needed or your application will be delayed. Application for Financial Support: studentsupport.strath.ac.uk/finsup. University of Strathclyde Discretionary Fund Assessment Guidance: www.strath.ac.uk/media/ps/sees/studentfinance/University_of_Strathclyde_Discretionary_Fund_Assessment_Guidance_V.1.2.pdf
Closing Date: 1 January
No. of applicants last year: Varies
Additional Information: Funding and Financial Support Team: financial-support@strath.ac.uk (for enquiries only) Website: www.strath.ac.uk/studywithus/scholarships/theladyeileenmcdonaldeuinternationalstudentfund/

University of Strathclyde - British Council GREAT Scholarships (Environmental Science and Climate Change)

Purpose: In partnership with the British Council and the GREAT Britain Campaign, The University of Strathclyde, Faculty of Engineering is offering 3 scholarships to students in India, Malaysia and Thailand applying for postgraduate courses in the areas of environmental sciences and climate change.
Eligibility: There are 3 scholarships available - one for India, one for Malaysia and one for Thailand. Please note students should be passport holders of these countries. For more information see website.
Level of Study: Postgraduate
Type: Scholarship
Value: £10,000
Length of Study: One year MSc study
Application Procedure: Click here to apply using the online application form: news.strath.ac.uk/p/2AB5-5YE/great-scholarship-engineering-2023.
Closing Date: 1 June
No. of applicants last year: 3
Additional Information: For more information email eng-scholarships@strath.ac.uk. Website: www.strath.ac.uk/studywithus/scholarships/greatscholarships-engineering/

University of Strathclyde - British Council GREAT Scholarships 2024 for Justice and Law - China, Ghana, Malaysia, Pakistan

Purpose: In partnership with the British Council and the GREAT Britain campaign, the University of Strathclyde, Faculty of Humanities and Social Sciences is offering four GREAT Scholarships for Justice and Law.
Eligibility: In order to be deemed eligible for the GREAT Scholarship for justice and law, candidates must: 1. Be available to commence academic studies in the UK by the start of the academic year in September 2024. 2. Have paid their tuition fee deposit before 28 June 2024. 3. Register as an international, fee-paying student and should be passport holders of China, Ghana, Malaysia, Pakistan. 4. Have an offer of study for a full-time, postgraduate law programme at the University of Strathclyde. This scholarship is only available on the following programmes: LLM Law, LLM/MSc Criminal Justice and Penal Change; LLM/MSc Mediation and Conflict Resolution; LLM Global Environmental Law and Governance; LLM Human Rights Law; LLM International Commercial Law; LLM Construction Law.
Level of Study: Postgraduate
Type: Scholarship
Value: £10,000
Length of Study: 1 year
Application Procedure: To apply for this scholarship, please complete the following application form: Scholarship application form > >r1.dotdigital-pages.com/p/2P47-EF1/great-scholarships-law-2023
Closing Date: 1 June
No. of applicants last year: 4
Additional Information: For further information contact: E: studywithus-hass@strath.ac.uk. Website: www.strath.ac.uk/studywithus/scholarships/greatscholarshipsforjusticeandlaw/

University of Strathclyde Performance Sport Scholarship

Purpose: The University of Strathclyde Performance Sport Scholarship Programme aims to enable talented student-athletes who are regularly competing at International level to follow a dual career. Consequently, the programme provides academic flexibility (where feasible), World-Class sports science and medical support, and financial assistance towards training and competition costs.
Eligibility: All applicants must be competing in a Sport Scotland-recognised sport, and priority will be given to students competing in a BUCS-sport who can demonstrate the potential to contribute toward the University's objective of being ranked in the top 20 in the UK. In addition, all applicants should be competing at least at Junior, if not senior, International level.
Level of Study: Postgraduate, Research
Type: Scholarship
Value: up to £1,000 (+ up to £3,750* in-kind support)
Application Procedure: Please apply through the online form: strath.eu.qualtrics.com/jfe/form/SV_bIW66SQoeF9kyWO. Scholarships bursaries privacy notice: www.strath.ac.uk/strathclydesport/scholarshipsbursariesprivacynotice/ Please note, that once started, you will not be able to pause and revisit your application. Therefore, prior to starting your application, it is advisable to watch the following short five-minute application help video: strath-my.sharepoint.com/:v:/g/personal/dave_sykes_strath_ac_uk/EY053CxLOtZEjmSPSgWonxMBvsjlReD3azPa8DfOWMt1WA?e=eHkGe3attached, which walks you through all the questions you will be required to answer. Please then use this guide to have all details to hand, prior to commencing your application.
Closing Date: 3 April
No. of applicants last year: Varies (circa 65)
Additional Information: We offer 3-tiers of Scholarship awards (GOLD, SILVER and BRONZE). See further information on the packages: www.strath.ac.uk/strathclydesport/performancesport/sportsscholarships/performancesportsscholarshipprogramme/. Website: www.strath.ac.uk/studywithus/scholarships/performancesportscholarship/

Wellcome Trust Master's Programme Award for the MSc Health History

Purpose: The Centre for Social History of Health & Healthcare Glasgow invites applications for studentships funded by the Wellcome Trust.
Eligibility: To be eligible for this award applicants must: 1. Have a live application for the full-time MSc Health History at the University of Strathclyde, to begin study in September 2024 2. Be strongly committed to building a research career in the Medical Humanities. The Centre for the Social History of Health and Healthcare Glasgow is committed to building a diverse and inclusive research environment, so welcomes applications from all sections of the community, in the UK, the EU, and around the world.
Level of Study: Postgraduate
Type: Award
Value: Fees, stipend and research travel budget/fees and a research travel budget
Length of Study: 1 year
Application Procedure: To apply please provide the following: 1. A brief CV of no more than one side of A4 that outlines information and achievements relevant to this opportunity. If the outcome of your first degree is yet to be decided please include a transcript of your Honours level marks to date and the title of your dissertation project. If your first degree has been awarded please include the transcript of marks and the title of your dissertation project. 2. A clear proposal of no more than 300 words for a Master's-level research project which is likely to form the foundation for doctoral study. State the central research question and the reasons why the project is likely to provide highly original outcomes in the field. 3. The name and address of two academic referees. These should be willing to provide a statement of support for your application if contacted. All completed applications should be sent to Caroline Marley (caroline.marley@strath.ac.uk). A selection committee will meet to consider applications later that month.
Closing Date: 17 April
Additional Information: Website: www.strath.ac.uk/studywithus/scholarships/cshhhglasgowwellcometrustmastersprogrammeawardmschealthhistory/

University of Surrey

University of Surrey, Guildford GU2 7XH, United Kingdom.

Tel: (44) 1483 689498
Email: centreforwellbeing@surrey.ac.uk
Website: www.surrey.ac.uk/

The University of Surrey is a global community of ideas and people, dedicated to life-changing education and research. With a beautiful and vibrant campus, we provide exceptional teaching and practical learning to inspire and empower our students for personal and professional success.

Biodiverse Nature Prescriptions and Mental Health

Purpose: The aim of this PhD study is to understand the mental health benefits of contact with biodiversity in order to create a 'biodiverse nature prescription'.
Eligibility: Applicants are expected to hold a minimum of an upper second-class honour's degree (65 per cent or above) in psychology (or a related discipline) and a master's degree in a relevant subject with a pass of 65 per cent or above.
Level of Study: Masters Degree, Postgraduate
Type: Studentship
Value: 1. Full tuition fee cover 2. Stipend of c £17,000 p.a. 3. £3,000 Research Training Support Grant
Length of Study: 3.5 years
Application Procedure: Applications should be submitted via the Psychology PhD programme page on the "Apply" tab. Please clearly state the studentship title and supervisor on your application. In place of a research proposal you should upload a document stating the title of the project that you wish to apply for, the name of the relevant supervisor and a personal statement. The statement should explain how your previous experience has prepared you for doctoral research and this project in particular. Explain how this PhD will support your career aspirations (maximum 500 words). Apply Here: www.surrey.ac.uk/postgraduate/psychology-phd
Closing Date: 31 March
Additional Information: Website: www.surrey.ac.uk/fees-and-funding/studentships/biodiverse-nature-prescriptions-and-mental-health

Brunei GREAT Scholarship

Eligibility: In order to be eligible, applicants must: 1. Be a citizen of the GREAT target country (i.e. Brunei) 2. Have an undergraduate degree that will enable you to gain entry onto a postgraduate programme at a UK university 3. Be motivated and academically able to follow and benefit from a UK postgraduate taught course 4. Be active in the field with work experience or with a proven interest in the proposed subject area 5. Meet the English language requirement of the UK HEI 6. Be willing to embody the UK Higher Education experience, by attending lectures and tutorials and engaging with extra-curricular activities, and act as an ambassador for UK Higher Education, by promoting the value of studying at a UK HEI 7. Be willing to establish an engagement with the UK as a scholar, through personal and academic fulfilment 8. Represent the high standards of the GREAT brand by becoming an advocate for scholarships 9. Be willing to attend a networking event of all UK-based GREAT scholars, to discuss experiences and capture perceptions of studying in the UK 10. Be willing to demonstrate future contribution to capacity-building and socio-economic advancement through the benefits achieved after graduating from UK higher education 11. Be willing to maintain contact with the British Council and act as an ambassador for the GREAT scholarships, by sharing experiences of studying in the UK with future GREAT scholars 12. As an alumnus of the GREAT scholarship, willing occasionally to speak to potential candidates about his or her own experience of studying in the UK.
Level of Study: Postgraduate
Type: Scholarship
Value: £10,000
Application Procedure: Applicants must complete the scholarship application form: forms.office.com/pages/responsepage.aspx?id=kyaQa3QQqkCeldiURqLrtRY446xu34NLq8sGrttPqJdURE1FN1dITjExUlIyR1JaOUU0R1VFS0xDRy4u&web=1&wdLOR=cC19B88AE-2CC8-418F-A2FC-88D69B237483.
Closing Date: 1 April
Additional Information: For all enquiries regarding this scholarship, please contact Annie Kennington - international@surrey.ac.uk. Website: www.surrey.ac.uk/fees-and-funding/scholarships-and-bursaries/brunei-great-scholarship-2023

Development of Next-generation Microfluidic Technology Device for Detection of Circulating Cancer Cells

Purpose: An exploration into new microfluidic technologies for cancer diagnosis.
Eligibility: Due to the interdisciplinary nature of the work, we are happy to consider graduates with degrees in engineering, physics, chemistry or life sciences. You will need to meet the minimum entry requirements for our PhD programme: www.surrey.ac.uk/postgraduate/biomedical-engineering-phd#entry. This studentship is for UK students only.
Level of Study: Graduate
Type: Studentship
Value: 1. UKRI standard stipend (£16,062 for 2022-23) 2. UK fees.
Length of Study: 3.5 years
Application Procedure: Applications should be submitted via the Biomedical Engineering PhD programme page: www.surrey.ac.uk/postgraduate/biomedical-engineering-phd. In place of a research proposal you should upload a document stating the title of the project that you wish to apply for and the name of the relevant supervisor.
Closing Date: 1 August
Contributor: The University of Surrey and ANGLE PLC

Additional Information: Website: www.surrey.ac.uk/fees-and-funding/studentships/development-next-generation-microfluidic-technology-device-detection-circulating-cancer-cells

Discounts for Surrey Graduates

Eligibility: Students graduating in the summer of 2024 may be eligible, as well as alumni from previous years, on receipt of evidence of the award from Surrey and where we can identify that you actually studied in Guildford. Students from SII DUFE are eligible for this scheme. Associated Institution students are not eligible. This scheme is not available to modular self-pacing students.
Level of Study: Graduate
Value: 20 per cent discount
Application Procedure: The University will identify eligible students, so there is no application form for this scheme. For more information see website
Closing Date: 1 March
Additional Information: If you have any enquiries regarding this matter, please contact the Fees and Funding team: feesandfunding@surrey.ac.uk. Website: www.surrey.ac.uk/fees-and-funding/scholarships-and-bursaries/discounts-surrey-graduates-2023

International Excellence Award (Postgraduate)

Purpose: This prestigious award recognises academic excellence and is awarded to selected students starting a masters degree at the University of Surrey
Eligibility: In order to be eligible applicants must: 1. Be an overseas fee-paying student 2. Hold an offer to study a full-time masters programme (excluding MBA) 3. Be self-funded (you must be paying for your studies independently rather than being sponsored or in receipt of another scholarship) 4. This Scholarship is not open to students from Surrey International Study Centre (SISC) 5. Applicants in receipt of the International Excellence Award will not be eligible for the alumni discount as the value of this award is higher.
Level of Study: Postgraduate
Type: Award
Value: £5,000 fee waiver
Application Procedure: You must have an offer from the University to complete the Scholarship application form. Applications without a valid student ID and offer will not be assessed. Please email international@surrey.ac.uk if you have any queries about this scholarship. Apply Here: forms.office.com/r/pSAvwkhgn0
Closing Date: 31 May
Additional Information: Website: www.surrey.ac.uk/fees-and-funding/scholarships-and-bursaries/international-excellence-award-postgraduate-2023

Smart Flooring Solutions for Fall Protection

Purpose: This studentship will investigate how novel flooring materials address the challenges of balance and gait in an older population.
Eligibility: A 2.1 degree or above in a relevant subject at undergraduate or taught postgraduate level. This project is funded for UK-based students. In exceptional circumstances, applications may be considered from high-calibre overseas students. However, current funding is only guaranteed for those students who are UK-based. International applicants will need to demonstrate their high-calibre in addition to meeting all entry requirements: www.surrey.ac.uk/postgraduate/engineering-materials-phd#entry.
Level of Study: Postgraduate
Type: Studentship
Value: University fees and a stipend (£15,400) for 3 years in addition to £1,000 per annum to be spent on research and training for the student.
Length of Study: 3 Years
Application Procedure: 1. Formal applications can be made through our Biomedical Engineering PhD programme: www.surrey.ac.uk/postgraduate/biomedical-engineering-phd page. In your application you must mention this studentship in order to be considered. 2. Informal applicant enquiries are recommended prior to submission and can be directly made to Dr Iman Mohagheghian: www.surrey.ac.uk/people/iman-mohagheghian. 3. Applications should be made through the University's website. Applications made by email cannot be considered. 4. All applications must include a current CV, transcripts for most relevant undergraduate and, where applicable, postgraduate qualifications, two references or contact details for two referees.
Closing Date: 24 July
Additional Information: Website: www.surrey.ac.uk/fees-and-funding/studentships/smart-flooring-solutions-fall-protection

Studentship in Physical Sciences

Purpose: The aim of this project is to determine the microscopic length scales that control the macroscopic rheology using novel magnetic resonance imaging and optical light scattering techniques in combination with conventional tools
Eligibility: You are required to have a First, 21 or merit in a masters degree in a physical sciences subject. If English is not your first language you are required to have an IELTS of 6.5 or above. United Kingdom and European Union

candidates are eligible to apply. Activities at the Cambridge centre focus on the development of new science and technology for well construction, with an emphasis on drilling and automation

Level of Study: Graduate

Type: Studentship

Frequency: Annual

Country of Study: Any country

Application Procedure: In order to apply for this studentship, kindly contact Noelle Hartley, Centre Manager for the EPSRC CDT in MiNMaT Greater understanding of the hierarchy of relevant structural lengths from the nanoscale to the macroscale will enable the design of improved complex fluid formulations with predictable rheological properties. N.Hartley@surrey.ac.uk

Closing Date: 30 April

Funding: Private

For further information contact:

Tel: (44) 1483 683467
Email: N.Hartley@surrey.ac.uk

Surrey MBA Scholarship Competition

Eligibility: The competition is open to anyone who meets the entry requirements to the Executive MBA: www.surrey.ac.uk/postgraduate/master-business-administration-mba#entry.

Level of Study: MBA

Type: Competition

Value: value up to and including 100% of the programme fees, and two runner-up prizes of 75%

Application Procedure: Entrants should follow the standard application process and to be considered for the scholarship competition are required to also submit a 1,000 word discussion essay on one of the following subjects to mba@surrey.ac.uk: 1. Glass ceilings in the workplace – gender and representation challenges for 21st century business. 2. Growth that doesn't cost the Earth – should companies support national or global sustainability initiatives, even if there are no direct benefits to the business (and why)?

Closing Date: 8 May

Additional Information: For information about the Scholarship Competition email mba@surrey.ac.uk. Website: www.surrey.ac.uk/fees-and-funding/scholarships-and-bursaries/surrey-mba-scholarship-competition-2023

Ted Adams Trust Nursing Scholarship

Purpose: Supporting mature students (25 years and over) living in Guildford and surrounding areas who want to study adult, mental health, children's nursing or midwifery at the University of Surrey.

Eligibility: To be considered for the Ted Adams Trust Scholarship for Student Nurses applicants must meet the following criteria: 1. Be a mature student (25 years old or over) 2. Applying to study one of the following courses at the University of Surrey: A. Nursing Studies (Registered Nurse Mental Health Nursing) BSc (Hons) B. Nursing Studies (Registered Nurse Adult Nursing) BSc (Hons) C. Nursing Studies (Registered Nurse Children and Young People Nursing) BSc (Hons) D. Midwifery (Registered Midwife) BSc (Hons) E. Nursing Studies (Registered Nurse - Adult Nursing) PGDip F. Nursing Studies (Registered Nurse - Mental Health) PGDip 3. Have been living in Guildford or the surrounding area for at least three years 4. Require financial assistance to be able to pursue a career in nursing.

Level of Study: Postgraduate

Type: Scholarship

Value: £3,000 each year of study up to a total of £9,000.

Length of Study: maximum of three years

Application Procedure: To apply for the Ted Adams Trust Scholarship please download an application form: www.surrey.ac.uk/sites/default/files/2023-02/application-form-ted-adams2023.docx. Complete the form and then email it to the Bursaries and Scholarships Team: bursariesandscholarships@surrey.ac.uk.

Closing Date: 31 March

Additional Information: For further information please visit the Ted Adams Trust website: www.tedadamstrust.org.uk/scholarships.htm or contact Bursaries and Scholarships team: bursariesandscholarships@surrey.ac.uk. Website: www.surrey.ac.uk/fees-and-funding/scholarships-and-bursaries/ted-adams-trust-nursing-scholarship-2023

For further information contact:

Email: bursariesandscholarships@surrey.ac.uk

Women in Leadership Scholarship: Surrey MBA

Purpose: Our Women in Leadership scholarship is open to female candidates who can demonstrate their contribution to business and a drive to support other female candidates in the future

Eligibility: In order to be eligible: 1. You must hold a lower second-class degree or equivalent, alternatives may be considered, see entry criteria for more information. 2. You must be a UK, EU or Internationanl student 3. You must be self-funded, or receiving a partial sponsorship or loan 4. You must be studying full or part time 5. You must be studying Full Time MBA or Executive MBA 6. EU and overseas' students must comply with the English language requirements (IELTS Academic: 6.5 overall grade with 6.0 in each element or equivalent).

U

Level of Study: MBA
Type: Scholarship
Value: covers 10 – 50% of the tuition fee
Application Procedure: In order to apply for the Women in Leadership Scholarship all applicants need to complete a programme application for one of our MBA programmes: www.surrey.ac.uk/postgraduate/master-business-administration-mba and under go an informal interview.
Closing Date: 1 November
Additional Information: For application enquiries, please contact MBA@surrey.ac.uk. Website: www.surrey.ac.uk/fees-and-funding/scholarships-and-bursaries/women-leadership-scholarship-surrey-mba-2023

University of Sussex

University of Sussex, Sussex House, Falmer, Brighton BN1 9RH, United Kingdom.

Tel: (44) 1273 606 755
Email: information@sussex.ac.uk
Website: www.sussex.ac.uk
Contact: Mr Terry O'Donnell

For over 60 years the aim of our courses, research, culture and campus has been to stimulate, excite and challenge. So from scientific discovery to global policy, from student welfare to career development, Sussex innovates and takes a lead. And today, in every part of society and across the world, you will find someone from Sussex making an original and valuable contribution.

be.AI Leverhulme Doctoral Scholarships (Leverhulme Trust)

Eligibility: You must be a PhD applicant, who is applying for a place with one of the participating schools (Life Sciences, Informatics, Psychology, Media Arts and Humanities).
Level of Study: Postgraduate
Type: Scholarship
Value: As a be.AI student, you will have your PhD tuition fees and living allowance covered for 3.5 years. You will also have access to further funds for research expenses.
Length of Study: 3.5 years
Application Procedure: To apply for one of the advertised projects, or to propose your own, you should apply for a PhD place at Sussex: www.sussex.ac.uk/study/phd/apply using the online PhD application system www.sussex.ac.uk/study/phd/apply/log-into-account.
Additional Information: Website: www.sussex.ac.uk/study/phd/doctoral/funding-support/leverhulme-doctoral-scholarships

Chancellor's Masters Scholarship

Purpose: Chancellor's Masters Scholarships are available for First Class graduates from the UK or Ireland.
Eligibility: To be eligible for this scholarship, you must: 1. have studied a Bachelors (Hons) at a UK or Irish university and hold, or expect to achieve, a First 2. have accepted an offer of a place on an eligible full time or part time Masters course to start in September 2024
Level of Study: Masters Degree
Type: Scholarship
Value: £3,000 for UK students or £5,000 for international students
Application Procedure: To be considered for the Chancellors Masters Scholarship, you need to have received and accepted an offer of a place on an eligible Masters at Sussex and hold, or expect to achieve, a First Class UK or Irish Bachelors degree. To apply for the scholarship, you are required to provide a statement of academic interests. You should include information about: 1. your previous academic achievement and excellence 2. your academic and career aspirations after you have completed your Masters 3. any work or extra-curricular activity you have undertaken that relates to your Masters. APPLY ONLINE: www.sussex.ac.uk/study/fees-funding/masters-scholarships/apply-for-the-chancellors-masters-scholarship
Closing Date: 1 August
No. of applicants last year: 100
Additional Information: Contact us: scholarships@sussex.ac.uk Website: www.sussex.ac.uk/study/fees-funding/masters-scholarships/view/1463-Chancellor-s-Masters-Scholarship

Chancellor's International Scholarship

Purpose: Applications are invited for University of Sussex to international postgraduate students who can demonstrate academic excellence
Eligibility: To be eligible for this scholarship you must: 1. be classified as overseas for fee purposes. 2. have accepted a place on a full time eligible Masters, commencing at the University of Sussex in September 2020. 3. have excellent grades (UK first class or equivalent) 4. have clear and specific goals with defined links to your course. As there are limited scholarships available, this scholarship is extremely competitive.
Level of Study: Masters Degree, Postgraduate

Type: Scholarship
Value: 50% tuition fee reduction
Country of Study: Any country
Application Procedure: 1. To be considered for the Chancellors International Scholarship, you need to have received and accepted an offer of a place on an eligible Masters at Sussex. There is guidance about how to apply for a Masters on our website. 2. To apply for the scholarship, you are required to provide a statement of academic interests. You should include information about: A. your drive and ambitions B. your potential for positive impact when you return to your home country C. any relevant work experience, skills or extra-curricular activity that relate to your ambitions and/or chosen course 3. To be considered, you will need to demonstrate excellent grades in your most recent qualification (i.e. a first class degree if you are studying in the UK). You do not need to have completed your qualification, however, as we can make conditional scholarship offers. 4. Please complete the application form online: Apply for the Chancellor's International Scholarship(archive.sussex.ac.uk/study/fees-funding/masters-scholarships/apply-for-the-chancellors-international)
Closing Date: 1 May
Contributor: University of Sussex
No. of applicants last year: 25
Additional Information: Contact us: scholarships@sussex.ac.uk Website: www.sussex.ac.uk/study/fees-funding/masters-scholarships/view/1005-Chancellor%E2%80%99s-International-Scholarship

Consortium for the Humanities and the Arts (CHASE)

Purpose: We co-ordinate the Consortium for the Humanities and the Arts (South-East England) – a Doctoral Training Partnership which funds PhD scholarships and PhD training events and programmes. If you are an arts and humanities student, and you are successful with your CHASE scholarship application, you'll receive support with fees and access to further funds for research expenses.
Eligibility: If you are an arts and humanities student, and you are successful with your CHASE scholarship application, you'll receive support with fees and access to further funds for research expenses.
Level of Study: Postgraduate
Type: Scholarship
Value: This includes support for: 1. travel to national and international conferences 2. placements, and collaborations with partners 3. specific training/professional development activities (e.g. language support) 4. monitoring public engagement with your research 5. fieldwork 6. publishing your research and commercialisation.
Application Procedure: 1. Choose your PhD degree. You must apply for a PhD in the Arts and Humanities to be eligible for the scholarship. See our PhD degrees. 2. Make contact with your potential supervisor to discuss your research area. See our guide on finding a supervisor. 3. Apply to Sussex using our online application system (applications must be submitted by the deadline on our scholarships advertisement). Find out how to apply to Sussex. 4. Indicate on your academic application form that you intend to apply for a CHASE scholarship. 5. If your application to study at Sussex is approved, we will send you a link to an online application form for the CHASE scholarship. 6. The application must be submitted in full, including your research proposal, supervisor statement and two references (incomplete applications will not be accepted). The deadline for CHASE applications is on our scholarships advertisement.
Additional Information: Website: www.sussex.ac.uk/study/phd/doctoral/funding-support/chase

Engineering and Physical Sciences Research Council (EPSRC) Doctoral Training Partnership

Purpose: You may be eligible to apply for projects funded by the Sussex EPSRC Doctoral Training Partnership if you are conducting research in a number of subject areas (listed below). You receive support with fees, living costs and have access to further funds for research expenses.
Eligibility: EPSRC scholarships are open to you if you are conducting research in one of the following Departments: 1. Science and Technology Policy Research Unit 2. Engineering 3. Informatics 4. Chemistry 5. Mathematics 6. Quantum Physics.
Level of Study: Research
Type: Scholarship
Value: Fees, living costs and have access to further funds for research expenses.
Application Procedure: 1. Projects supported by EPSRC funding at Sussex are advertised on this page, and throughout the year on our scholarships database. You apply for one of these scholarships using our online application system. Find out how to apply to Sussex. 2. You must indicate on your academic application form that you intend to apply for a EPSRC scholarship, giving the title of the project. You may be invited to an interview as part of your application for an EPSRC scholarship.
Additional Information: Find out more about EPSRC: www.epsrc.ac.uk/ Website: www.sussex.ac.uk/study/phd/doctoral/funding-support/epsrc

PhD Studentships in Mathematics

Eligibility: 1. Applicants must hold, or expect to hold, at least a UK upper second class degree (or non-UK equivalent qualification) in Mathematics, or a closely-related area, or else a lower second class degree followed by a relevant Master's degree. 2. This award is open to UK students only.
Level of Study: Doctorate, Postgraduate, Research
Type: Studentship
Value: 1. Fully-paid tuition fees for three and a half years at the home fee status. 2. A tax-free bursary for living costs for three and a half years (£17,668 per annum in 2022/23). 3. Additional financial support is provided to cover short-term and long-term travel. 4. If you are not a UK national, nor an EU national with UK settled/pre-settled status, you will need to apply for a student study visa before admission.
Length of Study: 3.5 years
Country of Study: United Kingdom
Application Procedure: Apply through the University of Sussex on-line system. www.sussex.ac.uk/study/phd/apply/log-into-account. We advise early application as the position will be filled as soon as a suitable applicant can be found. Due to the high volume of applications received, you may only hear from us if your application is successful.
Closing Date: 14 March
Contributor: University of Sussex, United Kingdom
Additional Information: If you have practical questions about the progress of your on-line application or your eligibility, contact Cara Gathern at mps-pgrsupport@sussex.ac.uk Website: archive.sussex.ac.uk/study/scholarships/1582-PhD-Studentship-in-Mathematics-Numerical-methods-in-dynamical-systems

For further information contact:

Email: pgresearch@maths.ed.ac.uk

SoCoBio Doctoral Training Partnership (Biotechnology and Biological Sciences Research Council)

Purpose: The University of Sussex is a member of the SoCoBio Doctoral Training Partnership, funded by the Biotechnology and Biosciences Research Council (BBSRC).
Eligibility: Check Website
Level of Study: Doctorate, Research
Type: Scholarship
Value: PhD tuition fees and living allowance
Length of Study: 4 Years
Application Procedure: 1. You must apply to the SoCoBio programme rather than directly for a specific project as the final choice of PhD project and of PhD supervisor is made during year one. Details of potential PhD projects and of how to apply are the SoCoBio system are on the SoCoBio website and are listed on the scholarships database: www.sussex.ac.uk/study/fees-funding/phd-funding. 2. In tandem you can also apply for a PhD place at Sussex using our online application system: www.sussex.ac.uk/study/apply/logintoaccount. 3. Find out how to apply to Sussex: www.sussex.ac.uk/study/phd/apply 4. You must indicate on your application form that you intend to apply for a SoCoBio scholarship, giving the title of the project. 5. You will be invited to an interview as part of your application for a SoCoBio scholarship.
Additional Information: Website: www.sussex.ac.uk/study/phd/doctoral/funding-support/socobio-doctoral-training-partnership

Sussex Graduate Scholarship

Eligibility: To be eligible for this scholarship, you must: 1. Be graduating from Sussex in 2024 with a First Class or Upper Second Class Bachelors degree 2. Have accepted an offer of a place on an eligible Masters, either part time or full time, to start in September 2024
Level of Study: Masters Degree
Type: Scholarship
Value: £3,000
Application Procedure: This scholarship is not automatic. Eligible applicants need to register interest in this scholarship through the postgraduate application system when you accept an offer of a place to study. No confirmation will be sent, as the scholarship is awarded automatically to all eligible applicants that register for the scholarship on time. More information see website
Closing Date: 30 September
Additional Information: Contact us: scholarships@sussex.ac.uk Website: www.sussex.ac.uk/study/fees-funding/masters-scholarships/view/1507-Sussex-Graduate-Scholarship

Sussex Malaysia Scholarship

Purpose: The aim of the Sussex Master Scholarship is to enable and encourage academically able students from Malaysia
Eligibility: To be eligible for this scholarship, you must: 1. be a Malaysian national 2. be classified as overseas for fee purposes 3. be self-financing 4. have accepted an offer to study an eligible Masters course at Sussex
Level of Study: Masters Degree, Postgraduate
Type: Scholarships
Value: £3,000 tuition fee reduction.

Length of Study: 2 years
Country of Study: United Kingdom
Application Procedure: Register your interest in the scholarship through the postgraduate application system when you accept our offer of a place on an eligible Masters course. If you applied through one of our overseas representatives, you will need to ask them to do this for you. You will only be able to accept one University of Sussex scholarship. more details see website
No. of awards offered: Unlimited
Closing Date: 31 January
Contributor: University of Sussex
Additional Information: Contact us: scholarships@sussex.ac.uk Website: archive.sussex.ac.uk/study/scholarships/1167-Sussex-Malaysia-Scholarship

For further information contact:

Email: scholarships@sussex.ac.uk

University of Sussex Chancellor's International Scholarships

Purpose: A limited number of scholarships are available to international applicants. These are highly competitive and only applicants with excellent academic achievement and potential will be considered. If you have excellent grades to date, you can apply for a scholarship after you have received an offer to study an eligible Bachelors or Masters at the University of Sussex in 2024.
Eligibility: To be eligible for this scholarship, you must: 1. Be classified as 'overseas' for fee purposes 2. Be taking up a place on a full time Masters degree, starting September 2024 3. Be self-financing 4. Have excellent academic grades
Level of Study: Masters Degree
Type: Scholarships
Value: £5,000
Country of Study: United Kingdom
Application Procedure: The scholarship application will ask you for- 1. Personal details- such as applicant number, name, email address. 2. Education details- if you are currently studying or have finished studying, your predicted or final grade. 3. A 500 word (maximum) supporting statement to answer the following – "Describe your academic achievements to date and your ambitions for the future. Why should you receive this scholarship and what impact will receiving the scholarship have on your time at Sussex and when you return home?" For more information see website
No. of awards offered: 60
Closing Date: 26 April
Additional Information: Website: www.sussex.ac.uk/study/fees-funding/masters-scholarships/view/1475-Chancellor-s-International-Scholarships

For further information contact:

Email: study@sussex.ac.uk

University of Sydney

Scholarships and Financial Support Service, Jane Foss Russell Building, G02, Sydney, NSW 2006, Australia.

Tel: (61) 2 8627 1444
Email: scholarships.officer@sydney.edu.au
Website: www.sydney.edu.au
Contact: Manager

Education for all, leadership for good. Progressive thinking, breaking with convention, challenging the status quo and improving the world around us are in our DNA.

Aboriginal and Torres Strait Islander Pharmacy Scholarship Scheme

Purpose: The aim of this scholarship scheme is to encourage Aboriginal and Torres Strait Islander students to undertake undergraduate or graduate entry studies in pharmacy at an Australian university.
Eligibility: To be eligible to apply for the Aboriginal and Torres Strait Islander Pharmacy Scholarship Scheme, students must be: 1. An Australian citizen or permanent resident 2. Of Aboriginal and/or Torres Strait Islander descent 3. Enrolled (or accepted for enrolment) as a full-time student at an Australian university in an undergraduate or graduate degree that leads to a registrable qualification as a Pharmacist 4. A member of their university's student Rural Health Club or the university's affiliated Rural Health Club 5. Not currently in receipt of a scholarship under the Rural Pharmacy Scholarship Scheme.
Level of Study: Graduate
Type: Scholarship
Value: maximum of AU$60,000
Length of Study: 4 Years
Additional Information: Website: www.ppaonline.com.au/programs/aboriginal-and-torres-strait-islander/aboriginal-and-torres-strait-islander-pharmacy-scholarship-scheme

AE and FAQ Stephens Scholarship

Purpose: Supporting research work in any faculty or discipline
Eligibility: 1. Be an Australian citizen, Australian permanent resident or New Zealand citizen and eligible to be considered for RTP Stipend Scholarships 2. be undertaking full-time Masters by Research or PhD studies
Level of Study: Research
Type: Scholarship
Value: RTP Stipend Rate
Frequency: Annual
Application Procedure: No separate application required. Highly ranked eligible applicants for the RTP/UPA will be automatically considered.
Additional Information: Website: www.sydney.edu.au/scholarships/e/ae-faq-stephens-scholarship.html

AHURI Postgraduate Scholarship Top-up

Purpose: This scholarship aims to attract new postgraduate students to AHURI National Housing Research Program (NHRP).
Eligibility: You must: 1. be a domestic or international student 2. hold an RTP or University of Sydney primary stipend scholarship 3. All other criteria are outlined in the Guidelines.
Level of Study: Postgraduate
Type: Scholarship
Value: AU$7000 p.a.
Length of Study: Upto 3 years
Application Procedure: 1. Download and complete the application form (www.sydney.edu.au/content/dam/corporate/documents/scholarships/2023-nhrp-scholarship-top-up-application-form.docx.docx). 2. Completed applications are to be emailed to Dr Laruence Troy, Director USyd AHURI Research Centre laurence.troy@sydney.edu.au. 3. Please refer to the 2024 application guidelines (www.sydney.edu.au/content/dam/corporate/documents/scholarships/2023-nhrp-scholarship-top-up-guidelines.pdf.pdf) for more information.
Closing Date: 10 March
Additional Information: Website: www.sydney.edu.au/scholarships/e/ahuri-postgraduate-scholarship-top-up.html

Alexander Hugh Thurland Scholarship

Eligibility: Open to the graduates from other universities with relevant degree.
Level of Study: Doctorate, Postgraduate, Research
Type: Scholarship
Value: AU$24,653 per year
Length of Study: 2 years for Masters by research candidates and 3 years with a possible 6-month extension for research doctoral candidates
Frequency: Dependent on funds available
Study Establishment: The University of Sydney
Country of Study: Australia
Application Procedure: Check website www.sydney.edu.au/agriculture for further details.
Funding: Trusts
Additional Information: Website: www.postgraduatefunding.com/award-1575

For further information contact:

Tel: (61) 2 8627 1002
Fax: (61) 2 8627 1099
Email: pg@agric.usyd.edu.au

Australian Government RTP Scholarship (Domestic)

Purpose: The Australian Government Research Training Program (RTP) scholarships provide financial assistance to domestic students enrolled in or commencing a postgraduate research degree.
Eligibility: You must: 1. be an Australian citizen, Australian permanent resident or New Zealand citizen 2. have an outstanding record of academic achievement and research potential 3. have an unconditional offer of admission or be currently enrolled in a Masters by Research or PhD at the University of Sydney. Note: Applicants who are undertaking their first PhD degree will be the first priority to be considered for Research Training Program Scholarships.
Level of Study: Research
Type: Scholarship
Value: AU$37,207 pa
Application Procedure: Apply per key deadlines. RTP stipend scholarships are awarded in November, February and June. Therefore, you must submit all required documentations for your admission application, and Research Experience evidence (if applicable) to be considered in the relevant award timeline. Please note that you may be notified of your RTP scholarship outcome at a different time to receiving your offer of study. Further Details see website
Additional Information: Website: www.sydney.edu.au/scholarships/e/australian-government-rtp-scholarship-domestic.html

Australian Government RTP Scholarship (International)

Purpose: Postgraduate research scholarships
Eligibility: You must: 1. be a commencing or enrolled international postgraduate research student 2. have an outstanding record of academic achievement and research potential 3. have an unconditional offer of admission or be currently enrolled in a master's by research or PhD at the University of Sydney.
Level of Study: Postgraduate
Type: Scholarship
Value: AU$37,207 p.a.
Application Procedure: Refer to the application and award timeline: www.sydney.edu.au/scholarships/e/australian-government-rtp-scholarship-international.html#timeline table below for details.
Contributor: Australian government
Additional Information: Website: www.sydney.edu.au/scholarships/e/australian-government-rtp-scholarship-international.html#timeline

Australian Rotary Health Indigenous Health Scholarship

Purpose: This scholarship supports Aboriginal and/or Torres Strait Islander students undertaking an undergraduate or postgraduate coursework degree at the Faculty of Medicine and Health.
Eligibility: You must: 1. identify as an Aboriginal and/or Torres Strait Islander person as defined in the University of Sydney's Confirmation of Aboriginal and Torres Strait Islander Identity Policy 2015 2. be an Australian citizen 3. be enrolled, or have an unconditional offer of admission into an undergraduate or postgraduate coursework degree within the Faculty of Medicine and Health 4. have completed at least one year of tertiary study at an Australian University 5. be in a proposed course of study that contributes significant benefit to the needs of the Aboriginal community.
Level of Study: Postgraduate
Type: Scholarships
Value: AU$5000 p.a.
Application Procedure: Apply here: australianrotaryhealth.org.au/programs/program-applications/.
Closing Date: 17 February
Additional Information: Weblink: www.sydney.edu.au/scholarships/c/australian-rotary-health-indigenous-health-scholarship.html

China Scholarship Council Postgraduate Research Scholarship

Purpose: This scholarship supports international students with an unconditional offer to study a PhD at the University of Sydney.
Eligibility: You must: 1. be willing to apply for admission, have applied for admission, have an conditional or unconditional offer of admission, or be currently enrolled in a PhD but yet to commence at the University of Sydney 2. be a citizen of the People's Republic of China 3. at the time of application, not be: A. working or studying in Australia B. aged over 35 years 4. satisfy any additional selection criteria set out by the China Scholarship Council.
Level of Study: Postgraduate, Research
Type: Scholarship
Value: Tuition fees, livng allowance, airfares, visa application costs and OSHC
Application Procedure: Apply here: sydneyuniversity.formstack.com/forms/csc.
Closing Date: 31 January
Additional Information: Website: www.sydney.edu.au/scholarships/e/china-scholarship-council-research-programs-scholarship.html

China Scholarship Council Postgraduate Research Visiting Scholarship

Purpose: This scholarship supports postgraduate students in China to undertake research at the University of Sydney.
Eligibility: You must: 1. be a citizen of the People's Republic of China 2. not working or studying in Australia at the time of application 3. be under 35 years of age 4. be currently enrolled in a postgraduate degree in China and remain enrolled for the duration of your intended research period at the University of Sydney 5. meet the University of Sydney's English language proficiency requirements for admission, as demonstrated by an IELTS test completed no more than two years prior to the course start date 6. satisfy the Australian Government Department of Immigration and Border Protection requirements for the issue of a student visa for postgraduate research 7. complete a formal application for admission to a Visiting Researcher Program (VRP) course at the University of Sydney and receive an Unconditional Offer of Admission 8. satisfy any additional selection criteria set out by the China Scholarship Council.
Level of Study: Postgraduate

Type: Scholarship
Value: Various
Application Procedure: Apply here: sydneyuniversity.formstack.com/forms/csc.
Closing Date: 31 January
Additional Information: Website: www.sydney.edu.au/scholarships/e/china-scholarship-council-research-programs-visiting-scholarship.html

China Scholarship Council Research Programs Visiting Scholars

Purpose: This fellowship supports early career research scholars from leading Chinese research universities to conduct research at the University of Sydney.
Eligibility: You must: 1. be a citizen of the People's Republic of China 2. not be working or studying in Australia at the time of application 3. hold a Doctorate degree 4. satisfy the University of Sydney English-language proficiency requirements.
Level of Study: Doctorate
Type: Fellowship
Value: Various
Application Procedure: See Website
Additional Information: Website: www.sydney.edu.au/scholarships/e/china-scholarship-council-research-programs-visiting-scholars-scholarship.html

Cicada Innovations Postgraduate Research Placement Scholarship

Purpose: This scholarship financially supports PhD students accepted into the Cicada Innovations Placement.
Eligibility: 1. be enrolled in a PhD at the University of Sydney 2. have successfully completed at least one year's equivalent of full-time study in your PhD 3. have been selected to undertake a six-month placement with the Cicada Innovations Company through the University of Sydney in research periods 3 and 4, 2019.
Level of Study: Postgraduate
Type: Scholarship
Value: AU$16,666
Length of Study: for five months
Application Procedure: Apply here: sydneyuniversity.formstack.com/forms/cicada.
Additional Information: Website: www.sydney.edu.au/scholarships/e/cicada-innovations-postgraduate-research-placement-scholarship.html

Commencing Scholarship in Art Curating or Museum and Heritage Studies

Purpose: A postgraduate scholarship
Eligibility: You must: 1. be a domestic student 2. identify as an Aboriginal and/or Torres Strait Islander person as defined in the University of Sydney's Confirmation of Aboriginal and Torres Strait Islander Identity Policy 2015. 3. have an unconditional offer of admission or having commenced in the current year in one of the following degrees within the Faculty of Arts and Social Sciences at the University of Sydney on a full-time or part-time basis: A. Graduate Certificate in Art Curating B. Graduate Diploma in Art Curating C. Master of Art Curating D. Graduate Certificate in Museum and Heritage Studies E. Graduate Diploma in Museum and Heritage Studies or F. Master of Museum and Heritage Studies.
Level of Study: Postgraduate
Type: Scholarship
Value: Upto AU$10,000 per annum
Length of Study: up to one year
Application Procedure: Apply here: sydneyuniversity.formstack.com/forms/sc4205.
Closing Date: 14 April
Additional Information: Website: www.sydney.edu.au/scholarships/b/commencing-scholarship-in-art-curating-or-museum-and-heritage-st.html

Data61 PhD Scholarships

Purpose: At CSIRO's Data61, we aim to develop top-quality doctoral students who will prosper in careers in Australia's data-skilled workforce. Our PhD scholarship program provides opportunities for outstanding postgraduate students with demonstrated academic and research excellence to further their careers at one of Australia's most trusted organisations.
Eligibility: Applications are open to: 1. domestic and international students who current live in Australia 2. international students overseas at the time of application, who hold a visa to study in Australia. In addition to the above criteria, you must: 1. hold a first-class honours (H1) Bachelor's degree or equivalent in the relevant research area (completed or near completion) 2. have applied for admission to a PhD program at an Australian university or have completed less than 12 months study in a PhD program at an Australian university at the start of the scholarship's commencement period 3. have a university supervisor who confirms they are willing and able to supervise you listed in your application, as Data61 does not organise your academic supervisor 4. not already

hold a PhD degree 5. be ready to commence within the specific time and period noted in the advertisement.
Level of Study: Postgraduate
Type: Scholarship
Value: A full scholarship includes a base stipend at the Australian Government Research Training (RTP) Program base rate supplemented with a top-up scholarship of AU$10,000 per annum.
Application Procedure: Opportunities are advertised twice each year, usually April-June and September-October. Bookmark the CSIRO Studentships and Scholarships: jobs.csiro.au/go/Students/990500/ website to find out when applications open and create a personal profile to apply.
Additional Information: Website: www.csiro.au/en/careers/Scholarships-student-opportunities/Postgraduate-programs-and-Scholarships/Data61-scholarships

Dean's International Postgraduate Research Scholarships

Purpose: Scholarships are available to undertake a research doctorate degree (PhD) programme
Eligibility: To be eligible, the applicants must meet all the given criteria 1. have an offer of admission for full-time studies in a master's by research or doctor of philosophy (PhD) 2. be currently enrolled either a. the final year of at least a four-year bachelor's degree in science or relevant discipline area, b. an equivalent degree at a non-Australian university, with at least 25% of the final year of the degree being a research component 3. have achieved a minimum weighted average mark (WAM) equivalent to a grade of 85 not be an Australian citizen or permanent resident, or a New Zealand citizen 4. apply for a Research Training Program (RTP) Fee Offset and Stipend scholarship
Level of Study: Postgraduate
Value: The scholarship consists of the full cost of academic tuition fees plus a stipend equivalent to an Australian Postgraduate Award indexed annually
Length of Study: 3 years
Study Establishment: Faculty of Science
Country of Study: Australia
Application Procedure: International students (except Australia or New Zealand) can apply for these postgraduate research scholarships. An annual stipend allowance equivalent to the Research Training Program (RTP) stipend rate indexed annually
Closing Date: 30 April
Additional Information: For more details, visit website scholarship-positions.com/deans-international-postgraduate-research-scholarships-in-australia-2015-2016/2015/03/03/scholarship-positions.com/deans-international-postgraduate-research-scholarship-at-the-university-of-sydney-australia/2019/02/01/

Dr Abdul Kalam International Postgraduate Scholarships

Purpose: Celebrating Dr Abdul Kalam's commitment to education, and his endeavours to support outstanding students to develop as future leaders.
Eligibility: 1. Applicants must be an international student and have an unconditional offer of admission for a masters by coursework program in the Faculty of Engineering and Information Technologies. 2. Applicants must have achieved a minimum distinction average (equivalent to 75 at the University of Sydney) in their undergraduate studies. 3. Students who have already commenced their postgraduate studies in the Faculty, or students transferring from another postgraduate program are not eligible.
Level of Study: Masters Degree, Postgraduate
Type: Scholarship
Value: 50% off tuition fees
Length of Study: 1 year
Frequency: Annual
Country of Study: United States of America
Application Procedure: Application link: sydney.edu.au/scholarships/postgraduate/faculty/engineering-it.shtml#KALPG
Additional Information: Website: postgradaustralia.com.au/institutions/university-of-sydney-usyd/scholarships/dr-abdul-kalam-international-postgraduate-scholarship

For further information contact:

Tel: (61) 2 8627 1444
Fax: (61) 2 9351 7082
Email: engineering.scholarships@sydney.edu.au

Graduate Certificate in Human and Community Services Tuition Scholarship

Purpose: This scholarship supports Aboriginal and/or Torres Strait Islander students studying a Graduate Certificate in Human and Community Services (Interpersonal Trauma).
Eligibility: You must: 1. identify as an Aboriginal or Torres Strait Island person as defined in the University of Sydney's Confirmation of Aboriginal and Torres Strait Islander Identity Policy 2015: sydney.edu.au/policies/showdoc.aspx?recnum=PDOC2014/364&RendNum=0 2. have an

unconditional offer of admission to study in the Graduate Certificate in Human and Community Services (Interpersonal Trauma) within the Sydney School of Education and Social Work at the University of Sydney 3. be a non-ECAV pathway student.
Level of Study: Graduate, Postgraduate
Type: Scholarship
Value: Tuition fees for 2 semesters
Application Procedure: Apply here: sydneyuniversity.formstack.com/forms/gcihacs_it_tuition_fee_scholarship.
Closing Date: 17 February
Additional Information: Website: www.sydney.edu.au/scholarships/b/graduate-certificate-in-human-and-community-services-scholarship.html

Grants-in-aid (GIA)

Purpose: Supporting international field work for student researchers. Grants-in-aid are available to provide students with travel grants to support short-term research trips overseas.
Eligibility: You must be: 1. an Australian citizen or permanent resident 2. enrolled full-time in a higher degree by research at the University of Sydney.
Level of Study: Research
Type: Grant
Value: Value determined by selection committee
Application Procedure: Apply here: sydneyuniversity.formstack.com/forms/gia_application_form.
Closing Date: 23 March
Additional Information: Website: www.sydney.edu.au/scholarships/e/grants-in-aid.html

Greta Davis Equity Scholarship for Musically Talented Students

Purpose: A scholarship for students studying performance
Eligibility: 1. have an unconditional offer of admission or being currently enrolled full time in a coursework or research degree at the University of Sydney Conservatorium of Music, 2. be studying performance, 3. be able to demonstrate that you meet at least one of the below criteria: A. hold asylum seeker or refugee status, B. identify as Aboriginal and/or Torres Strait Islander person as defined in the University of Sydney's Confirmation of Aboriginal and Torres Strait Islander Identity Policy, and/or C. financial hardship.
Level of Study: Research
Type: Scholarship
Value: AU$10,000 per annum
Length of Study: 4 Year
Application Procedure: To apply for a Sydney Conservatorium of Music Equity Scholarship please complete the online application form here: sydneyuniversity.formstack.com/forms/music_equity when applications open.
Closing Date: 31 March
Additional Information: Website: www.sydney.edu.au/scholarships/a/greta-davis-equity-scholarship-for-musically-talented-students.html

Indigenous Health Promotion – Social and Emotional Wellbeing Scholarship

Purpose: A postgraduate scholarship
Eligibility: You must: 1. be commencing in the Graduate Diploma in Indigenous Health Promotion (Social and Emotional Wellbeing) at the University of Sydney 2. be enrolled in a Commonwealth supported place, and 3. not have previously recieved this scholarship.
Level of Study: Postgraduate
Type: Scholarship
Value: AU$12,500
Application Procedure: No application required. Eligible applicants are automatically considered.
Additional Information: Website: www.sydney.edu.au/scholarships/c/indigenous-health-promotion-social-and-emotional-wellbeing.html

International Postgraduate Research Scholarships (IPRS) Australian Postgraduate Awards (APA)

Purpose: To support candidates with exceptional research potential
Eligibility: Open to suitably qualified graduates eligible to commence a higher degree by research. Australia and New Zealand citizens and Australian permanent residents are not eligible to apply
Level of Study: Doctorate, Postgraduate, Research
Type: Scholarship
Value: Tuition fees for IPRS, and an Australian Postgraduate Award for AU$24,653 per year
Length of Study: 2 years for the Master's by research candidates, and 3 years with a possible 6-month extension for PhD candidates
Frequency: Annual
Study Establishment: The University of Sydney
Country of Study: Australia
Application Procedure: Applicants must complete an application form for admission available from the International Office
Closing Date: 15 December
Funding: Government
Contributor: Australian Government and University of Sydney
No. of awards given last year: 34

Additional Information: Website: www.postgraduate funding.com/award-1500

For further information contact:

Tel: (61) 2 8627 8358
Fax: (61) 2 8627 8387
Email: research.training@sydney.edu.au

Leslie Rich Scholarship

Purpose: This Scholarship is to provide financial assistance to a Higher Degree Research student who is undertaking research in Alzheimer's Disease.
Eligibility: You must: 1. domestic or international student 2. have an unconditional offer of admission or being currently enrolled to study in a Master's by Research or PhD at the University of Sydney. 3. hold a First-class Honours degree or Equivalent Degree or a Master's degree. 4. a recipient of a primary scholarship from the University of Sydney that provides a stipend allowance. 5. provide a research proposal related to Alzheimer's Disease.
Level of Study: Research
Type: Scholarship
Value: AU$7,500p.a.
Length of Study: duration of degree
Application Procedure: Apply here: sydneyuniversity. formstack.com/forms/leslie_rich.
Closing Date: 9 January
Additional Information: Website: www.sydney.edu.au/ scholarships/e/leslie-rich-scholarship.html

Master of Business Administration Programme

Length of Study: 1 year
Application Procedure: Applicants must complete an application form supplying official transcripts and a Graduate Management Admission Test score
Closing Date: 31 October

For further information contact:

Tel: (61) 2 9351 0038
Fax: (61) 2 9351 0099
Email: gsbinfo@gsb.usyd.edu

Postgraduate Research Scholarship in Better Outcomes for Inflammatory Arthritis

Purpose: This scholarship supports students undertaking research in Inflammatory Arthritis.
Eligibility: You must: 1. an Australia Citizen, New Zealand Citizen, or an Australian Permanent Resident. 2. an unconditional offer of admission to undertake PhD on a full-time basis at the Faculty of Medicine and Health. 3. hold an Honours degree (First Class) or a First Class Honours Equivalent Degree or a Master's degree with a substantial research component. 4. be willing toundertake research into improving inflammatory arthritis outcomes under the supervision of Professor Lyn March.
Level of Study: Postgraduate
Type: Scholarship
Value: AU$35,950 p.a.
Length of Study: 3.5 years
Application Procedure: Apply here: sydneyuniversity. formstack.com/forms/sc4322.
Closing Date: 31 March
Additional Information: Website: www.sydney.edu.au/ scholarships/c/postgraduate-research-scholarship-in-better-outcomes-for-inflamm.html

Postgraduate Research Scholarship in Health Literacy and Optimising the Assessment of Written Health Information

Purpose: This scholarship is to support an outstanding PhD scholar to undertake research to optimise the assessment of written health information and to investigate the impact of grade reading level on consumer outcomes, under the supervision of Professor Kirsten McCaffery, Dr Danielle Muscat and Dr Julie Ayre.
Eligibility: You must: 1. domestic student. 2. have an unconditional offer of admission or being currently enrolled to undertake PhD on a full-time basis at the School of Public Health within the Faculty of Medicine and Health at the University of Sydney. 3. hold an Honours degree (First Class) or a First Class Honours Equivalent Degree or a Master's degree with substantial research experience in social science and/or public health. 4. willing to conduct research into the use of CACS for the primary prevention of cardiovascular disease, as part of a broader program of work on improved detection and treatment of people at high risk of cardiovascular disease (CVD) under the supervision of Associate Professor Katy Bell and Dr Carissa Bonner.
Level of Study: Postgraduate
Type: Scholarship
Value: AU$35, 950 p.a.
Length of Study: up to 3.5 years
Application Procedure: Apply here: sydneyuniversity. formstack.com/forms/sc4050.
Closing Date: 10 March
Additional Information: Website: www.sydney.edu.au/ scholarships/e/postgraduate-research-scholarship-in-health-

literacy-and-optimising-the-assessment-of-written-health-information.html

Sydney International Student Award (Africa)

Purpose: This award recognises the academic achievements of applicants from eligible countries in Africa.
Eligibility: To be eligible for this award, you must: 1. be an international student 2. be a citizen from the eligible countries in Africa (dual Australian and New Zealand citizens are not eligible) 3. receive admission into a full-time undergraduate coursework, postgraduate coursework, or postgraduate research degree, commencing in 2024.* 4. not be an Australian or New Zealand citizen, or a permanent resident of Australia 5. not have already started a degree at the University of Sydney at the time that you apply for the award. However, you are eligible if you are completing a degree here and are applying for the award with a second degree.
Level of Study: Postgraduate
Type: Award
Value: 20% contribution to tuition fees
Application Procedure: 1. Apply for your chosen degree 2. Submit a personal statement Further details see website
Additional Information: Website: www.sydney.edu.au/scholarships/e/sydney-international-student-award-africa.html

Sydney International Student Award (Bangladesh)

Purpose: This award recognises the academic achievements of applicants from Bangladesh.
Eligibility: To be eligible for this award, you must: 1. be an international student 2. be a Bangladesh citizen (dual Australian and New Zealand citizens are not eligible) receive admission into a full-time undergraduate coursework, postgraduate coursework, or postgraduate research degree, commencing in 2024.* 3. not be an Australian or New Zealand citizen, or a permanent resident of Australia 4. not have already started a degree at the University of Sydney at the time that you apply for the award. However, you are eligible if you are completing a degree 5. here and are applying for the award with a second degree. *This award is not available for the Master of Business Administration (MBA), Executive MBA (EMBA), study abroad, executive education programs, or courses offered in distance mode or to students participating in a Law Dual Degree pathway program.
Level of Study: Postgraduate
Type: Award
Value: 20% contribution to tuition fees
Application Procedure: 1. Apply for your chosen degree: As part of the application process, you will be asked to select your nationality. If you are a citizen of an eligible country, you will be prompted to upload a personal statement. 2. Submit a personal statement: As part of the application process for your chosen degree, you will be asked to submit a personal statement using the template to apply for the Award. Further details see website
Additional Information: Website: www.sydney.edu.au/scholarships/e/sydney-international-student-award-bangladesh.html

Sydney International Student Award (Central Asia)

Purpose: This award recognises the academic achievements of applicants from eligible countries in Central Asia.
Eligibility: To be eligible for this award, you must: 1. be an international student 2. be a citizen from eligible countries in Central Asia (dual Australian and New Zealand citizens are not eligible) 3. receive admission into a full-time undergraduate coursework, postgraduate coursework, postgraduate research degree, commencing in 2024.* 4. not be an Australian or New Zealand citizen, or a permanent resident of Australia 5. not have already started a degree at the University of Sydney at the time that you apply for the award. However, you are eligible if you are completing a degree here and are applying for the award with a second degree. *This award is not available for the Master of Business Administration (MBA), Executive MBA (EMBA), study abroad, executive education programs, or courses offered in distance mode or to students participating in a Law Dual Degree pathway program.
Level of Study: Postgraduate
Type: Award
Value: 20% contribution to tuition fees
Application Procedure: How to apply: 1. Apply for your chosen degree: As part of the application process, you will be asked to select your nationality. If you are a citizen of an eligible country, you will be prompted to upload a personal statement. 2. Submit a personal statement: As part of the application process for your chosen degree, you will be asked to submit a personal statement using this template to apply for the Award. In this personal statement, you will be asked to: A. Tell us about yourself (maximum 200 words) B. Tell us what has inspired you to apply to the University (maximum 200 words) C. Tell us what you want to achieve with your studies at the University or how it will help you to achieve your goals (maximum 200 words).
Additional Information: Website: www.sydney.edu.au/scholarships/e/sydney-international-student-award-central-asia.html

Sydney International Student Award (India)

Purpose: This award recognises the academic achievements of applicants from India.
Eligibility: To be eligible for this award, you must: 1. be an international student 2. be an Indian citizen (dual Australian and New Zealand citizens are not eligible) 3. receive admission into a full-time undergraduate coursework, postgraduate coursework, or postgraduate research degree, commencing in 2024.* 4. not be an Australian or New Zealand citizen, or a permanent resident of Australia 5. not have already started a degree at the University of Sydney at the time that you apply for the award. However, you are eligible if you are completing a degree here and are applying for the award with a second degree. *This award is not available for the Master of Business Administration (MBA), Executive MBA (EMBA), study abroad, executive education programs, or courses offered in distance mode or to students participating in a Law Dual Degree pathway program.
Level of Study: Postgraduate
Type: Award
Value: 20% contribution to tuition fees
Application Procedure: 1. Apply for your chosen degree: As part of the application process, you will be asked to select your nationality. If you are a citizen of an eligible country, you will be prompted to upload a personal statement. 2. Submit a personal statement: As part of the application process for your chosen degree, you will be asked to submit a personal statement using this template to apply for the Award. In this personal statement, you will be asked to: A. Tell us about yourself (maximum 200 words) B. Tell us what has inspired you to apply to the University (maximum 200 words) C. Tell us what you want to achieve with your studies at the University or how it will help you to achieve your goals (maximum 200 words).
Additional Information: Website: www.sydney.edu.au/scholarships/e/sydney-international-student-award-india.html

Sydney International Student Award (Indonesia)

Purpose: This award recognises the academic achievements of applicants from Indonesia.
Eligibility: To be eligible for this award, you must: 1. be an international student 2. be an Indonesian citizen (dual Australian and New Zealand citizens are not eligible) 3. receive admission into a full-time undergraduate coursework, postgraduate coursework, or postgraduate research degree, commencing in 2024.* 4. not be an Australian or New Zealand citizen, or a permanent resident of Australia 5. not have already started a degree at the University of Sydney at the time that you apply for the award. However, you are eligible if you are completing a degree here and are applying for the award with a second degree. *This award is not available for the Master of Business Administration (MBA), Executive MBA (EMBA), study abroad, executive education programs, or courses offered in distance mode or to students participating in a Law Dual Degree pathway program.
Level of Study: Postgraduate
Type: Award
Value: 20% contribution to tuition fees
Application Procedure: 1. Apply for your chosen degree: As part of the application process, you will be asked to select your nationality. If you are a citizen of an eligible country, you will be prompted to upload a personal statement. 2. Submit a personal statement: As part of the application process for your chosen degree, you will be asked to submit a personal statement using this template to apply for the Award. In this personal statement, you will be asked to: A. Tell us about yourself (maximum 200 words) B. Tell us what has inspired you to apply to the University (maximum 200 words) C. Tell us what you want to achieve with your studies at the University or how it will help you to achieve your goals (maximum 200 words).
Additional Information: Website: www.sydney.edu.au/scholarships/e/sydney-international-student-award-indonesia.html

Sydney International Student Award (Malaysia)

Purpose: This award recognises the academic achievements of applicants from Malaysia.
Eligibility: To be eligible for this award, you must: 1. be an international student 2. be a Malaysian citizen (dual Australian and New Zealand citizens are not eligible) 3. receive admission into a full-time undergraduate coursework, postgraduate coursework, postgraduate research degree, commencing in 2024.* 4. not be an Australian or New Zealand citizen, or a permanent resident of Australia 5. not have already started a degree at the University of Sydney at the time that you apply for the award. However, you are eligible if you are completing a degree here and are applying for the award with a second degree. *This award is not available for the Master of Business Administration (MBA), Executive MBA (EMBA), study abroad, executive education programs, or courses offered in distance mode or to students participating in a Law Dual Degree pathway program.
Level of Study: Postgraduate
Type: Award
Value: 20% contribution to tuition fees
Application Procedure: 1. Apply for your chosen degree: As part of the application process, you will be asked to select

your nationality. If you are a citizen of an eligible country, you will be prompted to upload a personal statement. 2. Submit a personal statement: As part of the application process for your chosen degree, you will be asked to submit a personal statement using this template to apply for the Award. In this personal statement, you will be asked to: A. Tell us about yourself (maximum 200 words) B. Tell us what has inspired you to apply to the University (maximum 200 words) C. Tell us what you want to achieve with your studies at the University or how it will help you to achieve your goals (maximum 200 words).
Additional Information: Website: www.sydney.edu.au/scholarships/e/sydney-international-student-award-malaysia.html

Sydney International Student Award (South and Central America)

Purpose: This award recognises the academic achievements of applicants from eligible countries in South and Central America (including Mexico and the Caribbean).
Eligibility: To be eligible for this award, you must: 1. be an international student 2. be a citizen from eligible countries in South and Central America (dual Australian and New Zealand citizens are not eligible) 3. receive admission into a full-time undergraduate coursework, postgraduate coursework, or postgraduate research degree, commencing in 2024.* 4. not be an Australian or New Zealand citizen, or a permanent resident of Australia 5. not have already started a degree at the University of Sydney at the time that you apply for the award. However, you are eligible if you are completing a degree here and are applying for the award with a second degree. *This award is not available for the Master of Business Administration (MBA), Executive MBA (EMBA), study abroad, executive education programs, or courses offered in distance mode or to students participating in a Law Dual Degree pathway program.
Level of Study: Postgraduate
Type: Award
Value: 20% contribution to tuition fees
Application Procedure: 1. Apply for your chosen degree: As part of the application process, you will be asked to select your nationality. If you are a citizen of an eligible country, you will be prompted to upload a personal statement. 2. Submit a personal statement: As part of the application process for your chosen degree, you will be asked to submit a personal statement using this template to apply for the Award. In this personal statement, you will be asked to: A. Tell us about yourself (maximum 200 words) B. Tell us what has inspired you to apply to the University (maximum 200 words) C. Tell us what you want to achieve with your studies at the University or how it will help you to achieve your goals (maximum 200 words).
Additional Information: Website: www.sydney.edu.au/scholarships/e/sydney-international-student-award-central-south-and-central-america.html

Sydney International Student Award (South Korea)

Purpose: This award recognises the academic achievements of applicants from South Korea.
Eligibility: To be eligible for this award, you must: 1. be an international student 2. be a South Korean citizen (dual Australian and New Zealand citizens are not eligible 3. receive admission into a full-time undergraduate coursework, postgraduate coursework, or postgraduate research degree, commencing in 2024.* 4. not be an Australian or New Zealand citizen, or a permanent resident of Australia 5. not have already started a degree at the University of Sydney at the time that you apply for the award. However, you are eligible if you are completing a degree here and are applying for the award with a second degree. *This award is not available for the Master of Business Administration (MBA), Executive MBA (EMBA), study abroad, executive education programs, or courses offered in distance mode or to students participating in a Law Dual Degree pathway program.
Level of Study: Postgraduate
Type: Award
Value: 20% contribution to tuition fees
Application Procedure: 1. Apply for your chosen degree: As part of the application process, you will be asked to select your nationality. If you are a citizen of an eligible country, you will be prompted to upload a personal statement. 2. Submit a personal statement: As part of the application process for your chosen degree, you will be asked to submit a personal statement using this template to apply for the Award. In this personal statement, you will be asked to: A. Tell us about yourself (maximum 200 words) B. Tell us what has inspired you to apply to the University (maximum 200 words) C. Tell us what you want to achieve with your studies at the University or how it will help you to achieve your goals (maximum 200 words).
Additional Information: Website: www.sydney.edu.au/scholarships/e/sydney-international-student-award-south-korea.html

Sydney International Student Award (Sri Lanka)

Purpose: This award recognises the academic achievements of applicants from Sri Lanka.

Eligibility: To be eligible for this award, you must: 1. be an international student 2. be a Sri Lankan citizen (dual Australian and New Zealand citizens are not eligible) 3. receive admission into a full-time undergraduate coursework, postgraduate coursework, or postgraduate research degree, commencing in 2024.* 4. not be an Australian or New Zealand citizen, or a permanent resident of Australia 5. not have already started a degree at the University of Sydney at the time that you apply for the award. However, you are eligible if you are completing a degree here and are applying for the award with a second degree. *This award is not available for the Master of Business Administration (MBA), Executive MBA (EMBA), study abroad, executive education programs, or courses offered in distance mode or to students participating in a Law Dual Degree pathway program.
Level of Study: Postgraduate
Type: Award
Value: 20% contribution to tuition fees
Application Procedure: 1. Apply for your chosen degree: As part of the application process, you will be asked to select your nationality. If you are a citizen of an eligible country, you will be prompted to upload a personal statement. 2. Submit a personal statement: As part of the application process for your chosen degree, you will be asked to submit a personal statement using this template to apply for the Award. In this personal statement, you will be asked to: A. Tell us about yourself (maximum 200 words) B. Tell us what has inspired you to apply to the University (maximum 200 words) C. Tell us what you want to achieve with your studies at the University or how it will help you to achieve your goals (maximum 200 words).
Additional Information: Website: www.sydney.edu.au/scholarships/e/sydney-international-student-award-sri-lanka.html

Sydney International Student Award (Vietnam)

Purpose: This award recognises the academic achievements of applicants from Vietnam.
Eligibility: To be eligible for this award, you must: 1. be an international student 2. be a Vietnamese citizen (dual Australian and New Zealand citizens are not eligible) 3. receive admission into a full-time undergraduate coursework, postgraduate coursework, or postgraduate research degree, commencing in 2024.* 4. not be an Australian or New Zealand citizen, or a permanent resident of Australia 5. not have already started a degree at the University of Sydney at the time that you apply for the award. However, you are eligible if you are completing a degree here and are applying for the award with a second degree. *This award is not available for the Master of Business Administration (MBA), Executive MBA (EMBA), study abroad, executive education programs, or courses offered in distance mode or to students participating in a Law Dual Degree pathway program.
Level of Study: Postgraduate
Type: Award
Value: 20% contribution to tuition fees
Application Procedure: 1. Apply for your chosen degree: As part of the application process, you will be asked to select your nationality. If you are a citizen of an eligible country, you will be prompted to upload a personal statement. 2. Submit a personal statement: As part of the application process for your chosen degree, you will be asked to submit a personal statement using this template to apply for the Award. In this personal statement, you will be asked to: A. Tell us about yourself (maximum 200 words) B. Tell us what has inspired you to apply to the University (maximum 200 words) C. Tell us what you want to achieve with your studies at the University or how it will help you to achieve your goals (maximum 200 words).
Additional Information: Website: www.sydney.edu.au/scholarships/e/sydney-international-student-award-vietnam.html

Sydney Scholars India Equity Scholarship

Purpose: A scholarship for postgraduate students
Eligibility: You must: 1. be an Indian citizen and current residents of slum communities in Delhi, India where ASHA Society works, 2. be an international student, 3. have applied for a postgraduate coursework degree, 4. be a new student. Note: You will also need to meet the requirements set by ASHA.
Level of Study: Postgraduate
Type: Scholarship
Value: Up to AU$60,000
Application Procedure: No application required. Nominations will be made by the Asha Community Health and Development Society (ASHA).
Additional Information: Website: www.sydney.edu.au/scholarships/e/sydney-scholars-india-equity-scholarship0.html

The Gregg Indigenous Scholarship

Purpose: A scholarship for Aboriginal and Torres Strait Islander students
Eligibility: You must: 1. identify as an Aboriginal and/or Torres Strait Islander person as defined in the University of Sydney's Confirmation of Aboriginal and Torres Strait Islander Identity Policy 2015. 2. be enrolled or have applied to study a coursework degree in the Sydney Conservatorium of Music, at the time of scholarship application submission.

Note: Confirmation of Aboriginal or Torres Strait Islander identity will be part of the application process. Preference will be given to applicants who can demonstrate financial need.
Type: Scholarship
Value: AU$20,000
Application Procedure: Apply here: sydneyuniversity.formstack.com/forms/gregg_in_music.
Closing Date: 20 March
Additional Information: Website: www.sydney.edu.au/scholarships/d/gregg-indigenous-scholarship.html

The Paulette Isabel Jones PhD Completion Scholarship

Purpose: A postgraduate research scholarship
Eligibility: You must: 1. be a currently enrolled HDR student 2. have completed at least 6 research periods of candidature if you are MPhil student and 12 research periods of candidature if you are a Phd student, at the time of application 3. have a reasonable expectation of submitting your thesis within 6 months from commencement of the award, i.e. 31st August 2024 4. have obtained a satisfactory rating for your most recent Annual Progress Evaluation. * Applicants who submit their thesis on or before 23 March 2024, are not eligible for the scholarship.
Level of Study: Postgraduate, Research
Type: Scholarship
Value: AU$7,000
Length of Study: For 3 months
Application Procedure: Apply here: sydneyuniversity.formstack.com/forms/sc3979_sc3999.
Closing Date: 23 March
Additional Information: Website: www.sydney.edu.au/scholarships/e/the-paulette-isabel-jones-phd-completion-scholarship.html

The Steglick Indigenous Women's Scholarship

Purpose: An undergraduate or postgraduate scholarship
Eligibility: You must: 1. be a female student 2. identify as an Aboriginal and/or Torres Strait Islander person as defined in the University of Sydney's Confirmation of Aboriginal and Torres Strait Islander Identity Policy 2015 3. be enrolled in, or have applied for admission to a full-time undergraduate or postgraduate degree in the fields of teaching, education or health. Note: Preference will be given to applicants who are from rural, remote or regional areas in Australia and/or can demonstrate financial disadvantage.
Level of Study: Postgraduate
Type: Scholarship
Value: AU$6000
Application Procedure: Apply here: sydneyuniversity.formstack.com/forms/steglick.
Closing Date: 21 March
Additional Information: Website: www.sydney.edu.au/scholarships/c/steglick-indigenous-womens-scholarship.html

University of Sydney International Scholarship

Purpose: A postgraduate research scholarship
Eligibility: You must: 1. be a commencing or enrolled international student 2. have an outstanding record of academic achievement and research potential 3. have an unconditional offer of admission or be currently enrolled in a master's by research or PhD at the University of Sydney.
Level of Study: Postgraduate, Research
Type: Scholarship
Value: AU$37,207 p.a.
Application Procedure: Current students can apply here: sydneyuniversity.formstack.com/forms/rtp_current_students, applications are open all year round, however, deadlines mentioned here: www.sydney.edu.au/scholarships/domestic/postgraduate-research/australian-government-research-training-program.html apply.
Additional Information: Website: www.sydney.edu.au/scholarships/e/university-sydney-international-scholarship.html

Vice-Chancellor's International Scholarships Scheme

Purpose: A scholarship for exceptional international students
Eligibility: You must: 1. be an international student 2. have applied for but not yet commenced a bachelor's degree or a coursework master's degree that is a CRICOS registered award program usually delivered onshore at the University of Sydney 3. receive an unconditional offer of admission by the relevant close date.
Level of Study: Masters Degree
Type: Scholarship
Value: Up to US$40,000
Application Procedure: No application is required, as all eligible students who have secured an unconditional offer of admission, will be automatically considered
Closing Date: 19 June
Additional Information: Website: www.sydney.edu.au/scholarships/e/vice-chancellor-international-scholarships-scheme.html

University of Tasmania

Private Bag 45, Hobart, TAS 7001, Australia.

Tel: (61) 3 6226 2999
Email: scholarships@research.utas.edu.au
Website: www.utas.edu.au
Contact: Graduate Research Unit

The University of Tasmania was officially founded on January 1st 1890, by an Act of the Colony's Parliament and was only the fourth university to be established in 19th century Australia. The university represents areas of significant research strengths and substantial teaching endeavours.

Cancer Council Tasmania Honours Scholarship

Purpose: These scholarships are generously provided by Cancer Council Tasmania in recognition of SeaRoad, the family of Pat Campbell and the Mazengarb family to support a student to undertake an Honours research project in any area of cancer.
Eligibility: Available to a full-time student undertaking a Honours research project in Semester 1, 2024 in any area that focuses on cancer, this may include behavioural, prevention, detection and supportive care.
Level of Study: Research
Type: Scholarship
Value: AU$10,000
Length of Study: 1 year
Frequency: Annual
Country of Study: Any country
Application Procedure: Check website for further details
Closing Date: 31 January
Additional Information: www.cancerwa.asn.au/cancer-research/i-am-a-cancer-researcher/funding/honours-masters-scholarships/

For further information contact:

Tel: (61) 3 6226 4832
Email: g.m.woods@utas.edu.au

Centre of Excellence in Ore Deposits PhD Scholarships

Purpose: For students to study within one of the five major programs of the centre location, formation, discovery, recovery or technology
Eligibility: Open to students undertaking PhD research in the specified fields. Applicants require either an MSc in geology/geophysics or a first or upper second–class honours degree. Some experience in the minerals industry is preferred but not essential
Level of Study: Postgraduate
Value: AU$20,000 - AU$30,000 depending on qualifications and experience
Length of Study: 3 and a half years
Additional Information: www.utas.edu.au/codes/available-rhd-projects

For further information contact:

Tel: (61) 3 6226 2892
Email: j.mcphie@utas.edu.au

Master of Business Administration Programme

Length of Study: Varies
Application Procedure: Applicants must contact The University of Tasmania Graduate School of Management for an application form

For further information contact:

Tel: (61) 2 2078 37
Fax: (61) 2 2078 62
Email: International.Office@admin.utas.edu.au

North Hobart Football Club Peter Wells Scholarships

Purpose: To support North Hobart players while at UTAS
Eligibility: One scholarship available to a north-western/northern student and one to a southern student with good academic records and who are available to play for the NHFC while studying at UTAS
Type: Scholarship
Value: AU$3,000
Length of Study: 1 year
Frequency: Annual
Country of Study: Any country
Closing Date: 31 October
Contributor: The late Peter Wells

For further information contact:

Email: International.Scholarships@utas.edu.au

Tasmania Honours Scholarships

Purpose: These honours scholarships are provided by the University of Tasmania to encourage excellent students to continue their study at honours level.
Eligibility: Available to students who are commencing an Honours course in any discipline in Semester 1, 2024. Selection will be based on academic merit.
Type: Scholarship
Value: Up to AU$10,000
Length of Study: 1 year (full-time study)
Frequency: Annual
Country of Study: Any country
Application Procedure: Applicants should apply online. All potential honours students should make contact with the Honours Coordinator in their discipline to discuss interests and options.
Closing Date: 31 January
Additional Information: Website: info.scholarships.utas.edu.au/AwardDetails.aspx?AwardId=41

For further information contact:

Email: Scholarships.Referee@utas.edu.au

Tasmania University Cricket Club Scholarship

Purpose: This scholarship is made available through the generosity of past members and supporters of the Tasmanian University Cricket Club (TUCC). It will support a student with good academic achievements who can also demonstrate a talent and commitment to cricket as demonstrated by performance in school, club and representative competitions. The selected student must be prepared to play for the TUCC in the coming season.
Eligibility: Available to a commencing or current student who can demonstrate a talent and commitment to cricket. Selection will based on the following five criteria 1. Cricket skill ie representative levels and success at those levels; 2. Academic achievement and potential to succeed at university; 3. Leadership skills and experiences; 4. Cricket involvement eg coaching; 5. Community involvement. The selected student must be playing for, or be able to play for, the TUCC in the coming season. Potential applicants may also wish to visit the Cricket website (www.tucc.org.au/) to gain a better understanding about the club and its goals.
Type: Scholarship
Value: AU$3,000
Length of Study: 1 year
Frequency: Annual
Country of Study: Any country
Application Procedure: Apply online prior to closing date. Applications cannot be submitted after closing date. As applicants will be assessed on the quality of application, all questions should be answered in full. Please ensure care is taken with spelling and grammar.
Closing Date: 6 March
Contributor: Supporters and past players of the Tasmania University Cricket Club
Additional Information: info.scholarships.utas.edu.au/AwardDetails.aspx?AwardId=281

For further information contact:

Email: chas.rose@gmail.com

Tasmanian Government Mining Honours Scholarships

Purpose: To encourage geological research at CODES on topics that are relevant to the Tasmanian minerals industry
Eligibility: Open to students undertaking research in the field of geology, with relevance to the Tasmanian minerals industry. Specialization in one or more of ore deposit geology, igneous petrology, volcanology, structure, sedimentology, geochemistry or geophysics. Applicants require at least a credit average in geology units at the second or third year levels
Level of Study: Research
Type: Scholarship
Value: AU$5,000; AU$8,000 depending on qualifications and experience
Length of Study: 1 year
Frequency: Annual
Application Procedure: Applicants can apply through the Tasmania Honours Scholarship application form downloaded from the website
Closing Date: 31 October
Contributor: Mineral Resources Tasmania

For further information contact:

Tel: (61) 3 6226 2815
Email: garry.davidson@utas.edu.au

Tasmanian Government Mining PhD Scholarship

Purpose: To encourage geological research undertaken at the ARC Centre of Excellence in Ore Deposits (CODES) on topics relevant to the Tasmanian minerals industry
Eligibility: The following eligibility criteria apply to this scholarship 1. The scholarship is open to domestic (Australian and New Zealand) and international candidates.

2. The Research Higher Degree must be undertaken on a full-time basis. 3. Applicants must already have been awarded a First Class Honours degree or hold equivalent qualifications or relevant and substantial research experience in an appropriate sector. 4. Applicants must be able to demonstrate strong research and analytical skills
Level of Study: Doctorate, Research
Type: Scholarship
Value: AU$18,000–25,000 depending on qualifications and experience
Length of Study: 3 and a half years
Frequency: Annual
Country of Study: Any country
Contributor: Mineral Resources Tasmania

For further information contact:

Tel: (61) 3 6226 2819
Email: anita.parbhakar@utas.edu.au

University of Technology Sydney (UTS)

PO Box 123, Broadway, Ultimo, NSW 2007, Australia.

Tel: (61) 2 9514 1659
Email: clg.postgraduate@uts.edu.au
Website: www.uts.edu.au/
Contact: UTS Institute for Public Policy and Governance

The University of Technology Sydney (UTS) is a thriving university located in the centre of Sydney, one of the world's most desirable and multicultural cities.

UTS Institute for Public Policy and Governance Postgraduate Scholarship

Purpose: To support commencing University of Technology Sydney (UTS) Master of Local Government students by assisting them financially.
Eligibility: To be eligible for the Scholarship, an applicant must meet all of the following criteria: 1. Australian or New Zealand citizen, or the holder of an Australian permanent resident visa or permanent humanitarian visa; and 2. Must have submitted an application and met the entry requirements for admission to the UTS Institute for Public Policy and Governance Master of Local Government degree by coursework degree; and 3. Must be commencing the UTS Institute for Public Policy and Governance Master of Local Government program; and 4. Must not have completed any study under any other postgraduate courses within the UTS Institute for Public Policy and Governance; and 5. Intend to enrol into a minimum of 12 credit points/session in the session immediately following the Scholarship selection; and 6. All candidates must apply using the online UTS online Scholarship Application form to be eligible (see below).
Eligible Country: Australia, New Zealand
Level of Study: Postgraduate
Type: Scholarship
Value: The maximum value of this scholarship is AU$5,000 for each recipient
Length of Study: 1 year
Frequency: Annual
Country of Study: Australia
Application Procedure: Please note that Scholarship applicants must first submit an application for the UTS Master of Local Government to be considered for the Scholarship. To apply for the Master course, please request an application form from the Institute at postgraduate-at-uts.edu.au or on (61) 2 9514 1659.
No. of awards offered: 2
Closing Date: 6 March
Funding: Government
Additional Information: The UTS Institute for Public Policy and Governance (UTS:IPPG) Postgraduate Scholarship was designed to support local government professionals seeking to broaden their knowledge and skills through postgraduate study and to recognize the diverse pathways to a local government career armacad.info/university-of-technology-sydney-institute-for-public-policy-and-governance-postgraduate-scholarship-2017-australia

For further information contact:

Email: Alan.Morris@uts.edu.au

University of Texas

School of Public Health Health, Science Center, PO Box 20186, Houston, TX 77225, United States of America.

Contact: Mr Robert E Roberts

Harry Ransom Center: Research Fellowships

Purpose: The fellowships are awarded for projects that require substantial on-site use of its collections
Eligibility: All applicants, with the exception of dissertation fellowship applicants, must have a PhD or be an independent

U

scholar with a substantial record of achievement; if the PhD is in-progress, the proposal and letters of recommendation must clearly indicate a June 1st, completion in order to be eligible for fellowships. Dissertation fellowship applicants must be doctoral candidates engaged in dissertation research by the time of application. United States of America citizens and foreign nationals are eligible to apply. Previous recipients of Ransom Center fellowships are eligible to reapply after two full academic years have passed. All things being equal, however, preference is given to applicants who have not previously held a Ransom Center fellowship
Type: Research fellowship
Value: stipends of US$3,500 per month
Frequency: Annual
Country of Study: United States of America
Application Procedure: Fellowships must be submitted electronically through an online fellowship account on the Ransom Center's website
Closing Date: 31 March

For further information contact:

Email: ransomfellowships@utexas.edu

Mobility Scooters Direct Scholarship Program

Purpose: Mobility Scooters Direct provides a US$1,500 scholarship each year to selected students who apply to the program
Eligibility: 1. Must be enrolled in a minimum of 6 hours undergraduate or 3 hours graduate at an accredited University or College. 2. Must have taken at least 40 undergraduate credit hours or 10 graduate credit hours. 3. Must have proof of a declared major. 4. Must demonstrate involvement on campus or in the community of attended University or College. 5. Must attach one letter of recommendation on official letterhead. 6. You must be at least 18 years of age to apply. 7. You must be currently enrolled at your college or university during the time of submission. 8. You must have a 3.0 GPA or higher
Level of Study: Graduate
Type: Programme grant
Value: US$1,500
Frequency: Annual
Country of Study: Any country
Application Procedure: The below details have to be included in the application. 1. Your first & last name, ph. number & email address(s). 2. Statement or transcript of your Grade Point Average (GPA). Letter of recommendation should have the below entities. 1. All applicants must meet certain criteria outlined below and submit an application via email or United States mail. 2. Applicants are also required to provide a letter of recommendation from a teacher, professor or counselor from the school being attended by the applicant
Funding: Private

For further information contact:

4135 Dr. M.L. King Jr Blvd. Store D21, Ft. Myers, FL 33916, United States of America.

Email: help@mobilityscootersdirect.com

University of Tokyo

9-7-3, Akasaka TK 107-0052, Japan.

Tel: (81) 3 6271 4368
Website: www.u-tokyo.ac.jp/en/
Contact: Fujixerox Co., Ltd., Kobayashi Fund, c/o Fuji Xerox

The University of Tokyo aims to be a world-class platform for research and education, contributing to human knowledge in partnership with other leading global universities. The University of Tokyo aims to nurture global leaders with a strong sense of public responsibility and a pioneering spirit, possessing both deep specialism and broad knowledge.

Kobayashi Research Grants

Purpose: Grants are available to pursue research programme
Eligibility: International students from Asia, Oceania countries/regions. 1. Note the Asia-Pacific countries and regions as referred to here, it shows the following countries and regions
Type: Grant
Value: Maximum of ¥1,200,000 /person
Country of Study: Japan
Application Procedure: Please download the application documents and instructions for sending at the following link www.fujixerox.com/eng/company/social/pdf/1.pdf
Closing Date: 28 February
No. of awards given last year: 39
Additional Information: research.nd.edu/our-services/funding-opportunities/faculty/internal-grants-programs/kobayashi-travel-fund/

For further information contact:

International Liaison Office Room 120, Environmental Studies Building 5-1-5 Kashiwanoha, Kashiwa, Chiba 277-8563, Japan.

University of Twente

Universiteit Twente, Drienerlolaan 5, NL-7522 Enschede, Netherlands.

Tel: (31) 53 489 9111
Email: info@utwente.nl
Website: www.utwente.nl/en

ASML Henk Bodt Scholarship

Purpose: The ASML Henk Bodt Scholarship supports a talented technical student who has completed (or is about to complete) the Bachelor of Science programme, and who is further motivated to pursue a 2 years full-time Master of Science degree in technical and scientific disciplines at the University of Twente
Eligibility: To qualify for a ASML Henk Bodt Scholarship, candidates must at least fulfill the following basic requirements Bachelor of Science diploma, academic transcripts of each academic year from the BSc programme, cumulative Grade Point Average of at least 80% of the scale maximum of all courses of the BSc program, MSc programme admission letter from the University of Twente, up-to-date curriculum vitae
Type: Scholarship
Value: The scholarship will provide financial support for the entire duration of the Master's degree (2-year period) which covers the full tuition fee and living expenses, approx. €22,000 per year
Length of Study: 2 years
Frequency: Annual
Country of Study: Any country
Closing Date: 1 March
Additional Information: Check details at www.utwente.nl/internationalstudents/scholarshipsandgrants/all/asml_henk_bodt_scholarship/ www.utwente.nl/en/news/2015/4/41467/asml-technology-scholarships

For further information contact:

Tel: (81) 40 268 6572
Email: scholarships@asml.com

Holland Scholarship

Purpose: The Holland Scholarship is a scholarship for excellent students from non-European Union/EEA countries, applying for a Bachelor or Masters programme at the University of Twente
Eligibility: Open to non-European Union/EEA countries. In order to be eligible for a Holland Scholarship, you should meet all the requirements as follows your programme starts in the current academic year; you have not studied in the Netherlands before for a full degree (e.g. a Bachelor's or Master's degree); you are from a non-European Union/EEA country; you are an excellent student (i.e. CGPA of 7.5 (out of 10)); etc. Please check complete eligibility criteria at
Type: Scholarship
Value: € 5,000
Length of Study: 1 year
Country of Study: Any country
Application Procedure: In order to apply for this scholarship, you already need to be (provisionally) admitted to one of the qualifying Bachelor or Master programmes
Closing Date: 1 May
Additional Information: www.utwente.nl/en/education/scholarship-finder/holland-scholarship-university-of-twente/#applicationrequirements

For further information contact:

Email: study@utwente.nl

Kipaji Scholarship

Purpose: University Twente Scholarships (UTS) are scholarships for excellent students from both EU/EEA and non-EU/EEA countries, applying for a graduate programme (MSc) at the University of Twente.
Eligibility: In order to be eligible for a the University of Twente Scholarship, you should meet all the requirements below Application for an UT scholarship is a procedure separate from the application for course entry at the University of Twente. Regardless of funding, you will need to gain an admission letter first. You have been (provisionally) admitted to one of the qualifying UT Master programmes starting in the academic year 2024/2025 (September). Please note After completion of your application, it may take up to 8 weeks before you receive the results. You must have a studentnumber. You have not graduated from a UT (under) graduate programme; You comply with the conditions for obtaining an entry visa in the Netherlands (if applicable); You comply with the general English language test requirement Academic IELTS 6.5 (or TOEFL iBT of 90) and an additional 6.0 (TOEFL iBT 20) on the subscore of speaking skills You are not eligible for a Dutch study loan; The University Twente Scholarship is a scholarship for excellent students. Typically this means that you belong to the best 5 to 10 % of your class
Level of Study: Masters Degree
Type: Scholarships

Value: € 12,000
Length of Study: 2 year
Frequency: Annual
Country of Study: Netherlands
Application Procedure: You have to apply for a Master's programme first. Once you applied for a Master's programme and received a (conditional) admission letter, you can apply for the scholarship with your student number. UTS is not available for Dutch and/or current UT students. This programme is also not available for Master's programmes at the Faculty of Geo-Information Science and Earth Observation (ITC).
No. of awards offered: Approximately 50
Closing Date: 1 May
Additional Information: www.utwente.nl/en/education/scholarship-finder/kipaji-scholarship/#application requirements

Orange Tulip Scholarship (OTS) China

Purpose: The Orange Tulip Scholarship (OTS) offers talented students from China the opportunity to obtain a Masters degree at the University of Twente. The scholarship programme is highly selective, offering two scholarships for the current academic year
Eligibility: 1. You have the Chinese nationality and you live in China 2. You have a degree from a non-Dutch university 3. You have not previously studied or worked in the Netherlands 4. You have been admitted to a Master's programme at the School of Business and Economics or the Faculty of Law
Level of Study: Graduate
Type: Scholarship
Value: €24,000. The scholarship consists of a reduction of the institutional tuition fee for non-EEA students (to €2,083)
Country of Study: Any country
Application Procedure: Applications should be submitted to the Netherlands Education Support Office (NESO) China. Visit their website for more information about the requirements for the Orange Tulip Scholarship (OTS), or send an email to ots@nesochina.org
Closing Date: 1 April
Additional Information: www.ru.nl/currentstudents/during-your-studies/@924838/orange-tulip-scholarship-china/ www.utwente.nl/en/education/scholarship-finder/university-of-twente-scholarship/#application-deadlines-details

Orange Tulip Scholarship (OTS) Indonesia

Purpose: The Orange Tulip Scholarship (OTS) offers talented students from Indonesia the opportunity to obtain a Master degree at the University of Twente
Level of Study: Graduate
Type: Scholarship
Value: € 22,000
Length of Study: 2 year
Country of Study: Any country
Application Procedure: Apply online osiris.utwente.nl/inkomend/WelkomPagina.do?proces=%20OTS-SCHOLAR-1
No. of awards offered: 5
Closing Date: 1 May
Additional Information: Please visit www.utwente.nl/en/education/scholarship-finder/orange-tulip-scholarship-indonesia/

For further information contact:

Email: study@utwente.nl

Professor de Winter Scholarship

Purpose: Professor de Winter and Mrs. de Winter were highly involved in UT programmes and with 'their' students. Their heirs continue to be involved in their honour by awarding a scholarship of €7,500 to an excellent female student. The Professor de Winter Scholarship is provided by the inheritors of Professor de Winter and his wife. Professor de Winter was one of the founders of the research and education department of the 'Technische Hogeschool Twente' - which later became the University of Twente.
Eligibility: The student must have obtained an average grade of 7 (out of 10) at the end of the third quartile of the first year of the programme; The student must have obtained at least 50% of European Credits at the end of the third quartile of the first year programme; The student must have obtained 90% of European Credits before start of the second year programme.
Level of Study: Masters Degree
Type: Scholarships
Value: €7,500 per year for the full duration of your Master's programme.
Length of Study: 2 year
Country of Study: Netherlands
Application Procedure: You cannot apply for a Professor de Winter scholarship yourself. You need to be nominated by your faculty, after you have applied for the University of Twente Scholarship (UTS)
Closing Date: 1 May
Additional Information: www.utwente.nl/en/education/scholarship-finder/professor-de-winter-scholarship/#eligible-programmes-and-countries

For further information contact:

Email: study@utwente.nl

University of Verona

Via S. Francesco, 22, I-37129 Verona, Italy.

Tel: (39) 45 802 8588
Contact: University of Verona

The University of Verona is a university located in Verona, Italy. It was founded in 1982 and is organized in 12 Departments.

Invite Doctoral Programme

Subjects: Life and Health Sciences
Purpose: The INVITE doctoral programme aims to encourage each student's intellectual curiosity and support the acquisition of critical thinking skills by training them in the use of innovative theoretical tools and practical methods
Value: Living allowance €2,000/month for 36 months, mobility allowance €600/month for 36 months, family allowance €150/month for 36 months
Country of Study: Italy
Closing Date: 16 April
Additional Information: www.timeshighereducation.com/unijobs/minisites/university-of-verona/the-invite-doctoral-programme/

For further information contact:

Email: invite@ateneo.univr.it

University of Waikato

Private Bag 3105, Hamilton, New Zealand.

Tel: (64) 7 856 2889 ext. 6723
Email: scholarships@waikato.ac.nz
Website: www.waikato.ac.nz/asd/groups/scholarships.shtml
Contact: Ms Maureen Phillips, Assistant Manager, Scholarships

The Mission of the University of Waikato is to be the New Zealand leader in the business of knowledge. The business of knowledge includes the development of new knowledge, the transmission and dissemination of knowledge, and the assembling and structuring of knowledge.

Acorn Foundation Eva Trowbridge Scholarship

Subjects: Any
Purpose: To support the people of Tauranga and the Western Bay of Plenty community
Eligibility: For students who are 25 years or older who reside in the areas administered by Tauranga City Council or Western Bay of Plenty District Council, and in 2024 will be studying at the University of Waikato Tauranga Campus.
Type: Scholarship
Value: NZ$3,000 per year
Length of Study: 1 year
Frequency: Annual
Country of Study: New Zealand
Closing Date: 31 August
Contributor: Acorn Foundation
Additional Information: Contact the School of Graduate Research: www.waikato.ac.nz/scholarships/contact

For further information contact:

Te Mata Kairangi School of Graduate Research, The University of Waikatom Private Bag 3105, Hamilton, 3240, New Zealand.

Tel: (64) 7 858 5096
Email: scholarships@waikato.ac.nz

Evelyn Stokes Memorial Doctoral Scholarship

Subjects: Arts & Social Sciences
Eligibility: To be eligible, applicants must: 1. be currently enrolled in a Doctor of Philosophy (PhD) in the Geography or Environmental Planning programmes, in the School of Social Sciences at the University of Waikato. 2. have a minimum grade point average of A- in the most recent year of full-time study. 3. be seeking to obtain their first doctoral qualification. 4. Submit a complete application. 5. Applicants employed on a permanent or full-time basis with the University of Waikato are not eligible to apply unless the position is as a sessional assistant, or similar.
Level of Study: Doctorate
Type: Scholarship
Value: NZ$10,000 per year
Length of Study: 3 years
Frequency: Annual
Study Establishment: University of Waikato
Country of Study: New Zealand
Application Procedure: Check website for further details
Closing Date: 1 February
Funding: Private
Additional Information: The Scholarship will end on the completion of doctoral study, or after 3 years, whichever is the

earlier date, provided that the candidate is enroled during this time in an appropriate programme of studies. Completion takes place when the postgraduate studies committee has accepted the report of the examiners and recommends the awarding of the degree www.waikato.ac.nz/scholarships/s/evelyn-stokes-memorial-doctoral-scholarship

For further information contact:

Te Mata Kairangi School of Graduate Research, The University of Waikato, Private Bag 3105, Hamilton, 3240, New Zealand.

Tel: (64) 7 858 5096
Email: scholarships@waikato.ac.nz

Lee Foundation Grants

Eligibility: 1. Applicable to students who are pursuing a full-time undergraduate degree programme at the Institute. 2. Singapore Citizens or Permanent Residents. 3. Preference will be given to applicants who are hindered by financial difficulties where a lack of financial assistance will result in a discontinuation of their studies
Type: Grant
Value: NZ$500
Application Procedure: Application dates & submission instructions can be found www.singaporetech.edu.sg/fees/bursaries-study-grants
Additional Information: Grants are awarded on the basis of above average academic performance www.singaporetech.edu.sg/lee-foundation-study-grant

For further information contact:

10 Dover Drive, 138683, Singapore.

Tel: (65) 6592 1189
Fax: (65) 6592 1190

Tauranga Campus Research Masters Scholarship

Purpose: At this university, candidates can study a broad range of subjects to shape a qualification that matches to their strengths and career interests. It helps the candidate with career planning, developing a CV and cover letters, interview skills, enhancing their employability skills.
Eligibility: To be eligible for consideration applicants must: 1. have applied to enrol, or be planning to enrol, full-time1 in a thesis of 90-points or more as part of their first master's degree at the University of Waikato and based in Tauranga; 2. A minimum Grade Point Average (GPA) of A- is expected. Normally, GPA calculations will be based on the equivalent of the applicant's last two years of full-time study. 3. Applicants must have made contact with a potential University of Waikato master's thesis supervisor; and 4. be a New Zealand citizen, permanent resident or an international student. 4a. International students must have completed at least 120-points of study at a New Zealand university in order to be eligible for this Scholarship.
Level of Study: Postgraduate
Type: Scholarship
Value: Up to NZ$23,000
Frequency: Annual
Country of Study: New Zealand
Closing Date: 30 April
Funding: International office
Additional Information: www.waikato.ac.nz/scholarships/s/tauranga-campus-research-masters-scholarship

For further information contact:

Te Mata Kairangi School of Graduate Research, The University of Waikato, Private Bag 3105, Hamilton 3240, New Zealand.

Tel: (64) 7 858 5096

University of Waikato Masters Research Scholarships

Subjects: Any
Purpose: To encourage research at the University, principally by assisting with course-related costs
Eligibility: To be eligible, applicants must: 1. be enrolled in, or intending to enrol full-time in their first master's degree including a 593 (90-point thesis) or 594 (120-point thesis)1; 2. have had contact with a potential University of Waikato master's thesis supervisor (the potential supervisor may be asked to confirm their involvement with the applicant's research); and 3. have not applied for this Scholarship before, i.e., applicants may only apply once. 4. The Scholarship is open to NZ Citizens, NZ Permanent residents, NZ Resident Class Visa holders or Australian Citizens/Permanent Residents domiciled in NZ, and international students. International students must have completed at least 120-points of study at a New Zealand university (by the closing date of the round in which they are applying).
Level of Study: Postgraduate
Type: Research grant
Value: NZ$12,000 to NZ$15,000

Length of Study: 1 year
Frequency: Annual
Country of Study: New Zealand
Closing Date: 30 April
Additional Information: Should a student also hold another fees scholarship, the University of Waikato Masters Research Scholarship will pay the balance of any fees (up to NZ$3,500) www.waikato.ac.nz/scholarships/s/university-of-waikato-research-masters-scholarship

For further information contact:

Te Mata Kairangi School of Graduate Research, The University of Waikato, Private Bag 3105, Hamilton 3240, New Zealand.

Tel: (64) 7 858 5096
Email: scholarships@waikato.ac.nz

University of Wales, Bangor (UWB)

Bangor North Wales, Bangor, Wales, Gwynedd LL57 2DG, United Kingdom.

Tel: (44) 12 4838 2025/18
Email: admissions@bangor.ac.uk
Website: www.bangor.ac.uk
Contact: The Student Recruitment Unit

The University of Wales, Bangor (UWB) is the principal seat of learning, scholarship and research in North Wales. It was established in 1884 and is a constituent institution of the Federal University of Wales. The University attaches considerable importance to research training in all disciplines and offers research studentships of a value similar to those of other United Kingdom public funding bodies.

Gold and Silver Scholarships

Purpose: To provide financial support to full-time students on all MSc, MBA and MA programmes
Eligibility: Open to applicants who wish to apply for a postgraduate MBA or MA degree programme included in the scholarship scheme
Level of Study: MBA, Postgraduate
Type: Scholarship
Value: Gold Scholarship £5,000 per year. Silver Scholarship £2,000 per year
Length of Study: 1 year
Frequency: Annual
Study Establishment: Bangor University
Country of Study: United Kingdom
Application Procedure: There is no application form for scholarships. Candidates who wish to be considered for the awards should include a letter listing their main academic and personal achievements together with a short essay on why they have chosen to study at Bangor and a curriculum vitae. For further information contact at law.pg@bangor.ac.uk
Closing Date: 1 July
Funding: Government
Additional Information: PLEASE NOTE: your application form will NOT be accepted without a CV www.bangor.ac.uk/business/study-with-us/postgraduate-funding/en

For further information contact:

Tel: (44) 1248 382 644
Fax: (44) 1248 383 228
Email: b.hamilton@bangor.ac.uk

MSc Bursaries

Eligibility: Open to applicants with good second class honours degree in sports science or health and to students with a 22 degree or a degree from a different academic area will also be considered
Level of Study: Postgraduate
Type: Bursary
Value: £2,500 (United Kingdom/European Union students); £3,500 (non-European Union international students)
Length of Study: 1 year (full-time); 2 years (part-time); 30 weeks full-time (diploma)
Frequency: Dependent on funds available
Study Establishment: Bangor University
Country of Study: United Kingdom
Application Procedure: Complete a Postgraduate Application Form with a four page (maximum) curriculum vitae or resumé. Refer to the website for further details or mail to postgraduate@bangor.ac.uk
Closing Date: 30 June
Contributor: Bangor University
Additional Information: £1,000 internal bursaries to former SHES (or related disciplines) students (who have 1st class undergraduate degree). £1,000 internal assistantships in addition to the other bursaries aimed at the very best students www.bangor.ac.uk/business/study-with-us/postgraduate-funding/en

For further information contact:

Tel: (44) 1248 383 493
Email: mscsport@bangor.ac.uk

Santander Taught Postgraduate Scholarships

Purpose: The Santander Group awards a number of 1 year undergraduate and taught postgraduate scholarships to current Bangor University students
Eligibility: The scholarship fund aims to reward the most academically gifted students from countries that are supported by the Santander Universidades scheme. The award will be given to students from the following 11 countries Argentina, Brazil, Chile, Colombia, Mexico, Portugal, Puerto Rico, Spain, Uruguay and Venezuela. To be eligible for the postgraduate scholarship you will have to have studied within a University which is part of the Santander Universidades Scheme
Type: Scholarship
Value: £3,000 to £4,166
Length of Study: 1 year
Application Procedure: Application forms and guidance notes for the Santander Scholarship Scheme are available on the University website www.bangor.ac.uk/scholarships/santander.php.en
Closing Date: 10 December

For further information contact:

University of St Andrews, St Katharine's West, The Scores, St Andrews KY16 9AX, United Kingdom.

Tel: (44) 1334 46 2254
Fax: (44) 1334 46 2254
Email: admissions@st-andrews.ac.uk

University of Warwick

Tel: (44) 2476 523 523
Website: www.warwick.ac.uk
Contact: Project Officer, Postgraduate Scholarships

The University of Warwick offers an exciting range of doctoral, research-based and taught Master's programmes in the humanities, sciences, social sciences and medicine. In the 2001 Research Assessment Exercise, Warwick was ranked 5th in the United Kingdom for research quality. Postgraduate students make up around 35% of Warwick's 18,000 students. The University is located in the heart of United Kingdom, adjacent to the city of Coventry and on the border with Warwickshire.

Sociology Departmental MA Scholarship

Purpose: 10 awards of £5,000 are available for students commencing MA study in the Sociology department in Autumn. The award will automatically be deducted from the winners' tuition fees.
Eligibility: 1. Open to applicants on all Sociology taught Masters programmes. 2. You must submit your application to the MA programme before submitting your scholarship application. 3. Successful candidates must obtain an offer from the university before taking up the award. 4. Candidates may apply concurrently to other funding sources; however, successful candidates who receive major tuition funding elsewhere will be disqualified.
Level of Study: Postgraduate
Type: Scholarship
Value: £5000
Length of Study: 2 year
Frequency: Annual
Country of Study: United Kingdom
Closing Date: 30 June
Funding: Foundation
Additional Information: https://warwick.ac.uk/fac/soc/sociology/prospectivestudents/postgraduate/taughtcourses/funding/mascholarship/

For further information contact:

Social Sciences Building, The University of Warwick, Coventry CV4 7AL, United Kingdom.

Email: socpgt@warwick.ac.uk

University of Waterloo

200 University Avenue West, Waterloo, ON N2L 3G1, Canada.

Email: rchild@uwaterloo.ca
Website: uwaterloo.ca/

Mitacs Accelerate Fellowship

Purpose: The Mitacs Accelerate Fellowship provides a long-term funding and internship option for undergraduates, master's and PhD students. Recipients can also access professional development training that helps them ensure project success and gain in-demand career skills.
Level of Study: Masters Degree, Postgraduate
Type: Fellowship
Value: Upto CA$106,666

Length of Study: Upto 48 months (4 years)
Frequency: Annual
Country of Study: Any country
Application Procedure: New proposals submitted to Mitacs will be reviewed and approvals will be determined per our standard course of business, with funding start dates expected beginning from April 1, 2024. All award approvals are subject to funding availability.
Funding: Private
Additional Information: Mitacs Program contact: Amanda Green at agreen@mitacs.ca Website: uwaterloo.ca/research/mitacs-accelerate-fellowship

For further information contact:

Tel: (1) 519 888 4567
Email: accelerate@mitacs.ca

University of West London

Website: www.uwl.ac.uk

International Ambassador Scholarships

Purpose: The International Ambassador Scholarship recognises and provides financial support for outstanding students who wish to act as ambassadors for the University of West London
Eligibility: Applicants must be 1. An offer holder for an undergraduate or postgraduate course at UWL, to commence study in September 2024. This means that you must have already applied for a course of study at this university and you must have already received an official offer from one of our admissions officers. 2. A self-funded overseas full fee-paying paying student (please note EU applicants are not eligible). The International Ambassador Scholarship will be awarded on a competitive basis to candidates who demonstrate enthusiasm and the ability to be an excellent international student ambassador.
Level of Study: Graduate
Type: Scholarship
Value: £2,000 to £5,000
Length of Study: 1 year
Frequency: Annual
Country of Study: United Kingdom
Application Procedure: To be considered for the scholarship, you must have been offered a place to study on a full-time undergraduate or postgraduate course at the University of West London
Closing Date: 11 July
Funding: Private
Contributor: University of West London
Additional Information: Official Scholarship Website: www.uwl.ac.uk/courses/undergraduate-study/fees-and-funding/bursaries-and-scholarships www.scholars4dev.com/8119/international-ambassador-scholarships-university-west-london/

For further information contact:

Tel: (44) 20 8231 2914
Email: int.app@uwl.ac.uk

University of Western Australia

35 Stirling Highway, Crawley, WA 6009, Australia.

Tel: (61) 8 9380 2490, 8 6488 6000
Email: general.enquiries@uwa.edu.au
Website: www.uwa.edu.au

Since its establishment in 1911, the University of Western Australia has helped to shape the careers of more than 75,000 graduates. Their success reflects the UWA's balanced coverage of disciplines in the arts, sciences and professions.

Master of Business Administration Programme

For further information contact:

Tel: (61) 9 3803 939
Fax: (61) 9 3824 071
Email: icweb@acs.edu.au

U

University of Western Sydney

Office of Research Services, Hawkesbury Campus, Building H3, Locked Bag 1797, Penrith South DC, NSW 1797, Australia.

Tel: (61) 2 4570 1463
Email: t.mills@uws.edu.au
Website: www.uws.edu.au
Contact: Ms Tracey Mills, Research Scholarships Development Officer

Master of Business Administration Programme

Length of Study: 1–5 years
Application Procedure: Applicants must complete an application form supplying a TOEFL score
Closing Date: January
Additional Information: www.uwa.edu.au/study/courses/master-of-business-administration-intensive

For further information contact:

Tel: (61) 2 9685 9297
Fax: (61) 2 9685 9298
Email: international@uws.edu.au

University of Westminster

309 Regent Street, London W1B 2HW, United Kingdom.

Tel: (44) 20 7911 5000 Exts 66257, 66258, 66259
Email: scholarships@westminster.ac.uk
Website: www.westminster.ac.uk

The University of Westminster is proud of its generous scholarship programme, which benefits both United Kingdom and international students. Full details are available on our website www.westminster.ac.uk/scholarships

Brian Large Bursary Fund

Purpose: To provide financial support to United Kingdom students that are studying full time on the Transport and Planning MSc
Eligibility: Applicants must have been accepted for a full time Masters course in transport for 2020/21. While no minimum level of first degree is required, the Trustees expect young graduates to have at least a 2.2, preferably a 2.1. However, they are willing to relax that requirement for outstanding mature students.
Type: Funding support
Value: £8,000
Country of Study: United Kingdom
Application Procedure: If you are interested in applying for one of these bursaries please contact Dr. Enrica Papa, the Course Leader of MSc Transport Planning at papa@westminster.ac.uk
Closing Date: 12 July
Additional Information: For more information, visit the: www.blbf.co.uk/services environment.leeds.ac.uk/dir-record/scholarships/665/the-brian-large-bursary-fund

Fully Funded Master Scholarship

Purpose: To study a full-time master degree in a subject within the School of Media, Arts and Design at the university
Type: Scholarship
Value: € 10 000
Country of Study: Any country
Application Procedure: For application, please visit website www.westminster.ac.uk/about-us/faculties/westminster-school-of-media-arts-and-design/departments
Closing Date: 31 October
Additional Information: www.afterschoolafrica.com/624/university-of-westminster-international/

For further information contact:

Email: graduate.admissions@cs.ox.ac.uk

Higher Education Scholarship Palestine (HESPAL) Scholarships

Purpose: The University of Westminster is working in partnership with the British Council to provide a Higher Education Scholarship for a Palestinian (HESPAL); that is, to support a junior academic at a Palestinian University wishing to study a one-year masters programme or a three-year PhD research programme in the United Kingdom
Eligibility: To be eligible for this scholarship, you must 1. be a resident citizen of Palestinian Territories 2. be currently employed by a Palestinian university and nominated by this university 3. have a Bachelor's degree from a Palestinian University with a minimum grade of very good (and equivalent to at least a 2.1 Bachelor's degree from the UK) 4. sign a written undertaking to return to Palestine and work in your university on completion of your degree
Level of Study: Masters Degree
Type: Scholarship
Value: Full tuition fee award, pre-departure briefing from the British Council, arrival allowances, thesis allowances and a monthly allowance to cover living expenses
Frequency: Annual
Country of Study: Any country
Application Procedure: Applications are made through the British Council in the Palestinian Territories. Find out more on the British Council website
No. of awards offered: 2
Closing Date: January

Additional Information: www.britishcouncil.ps/en/study-uk/scholarships/hespal

For further information contact:

Email: tom.sperlinger@bristol.ac.uk

Rees Jeffrey Road Fund

Purpose: To support financially for education, research and physical road transport-related projects in accordance with the founding Trust Deed
Level of Study: Masters Degree
Type: Bursary
Value: £10,000
Frequency: Annual
Study Establishment: Universities Birmingham, Cardiff, Hertfordshire, Imperial College, Leeds, Newcastle, Nottingham, Salford, Southampton, University College London (UCL), University of the West of England (UWE), Westminster
Country of Study: United Kingdom
Application Procedure: Applications are made on behalf of students by Universities listed, where departents are providing Transport Masters courses. Students are not able to apply directly for funding themselves.
Closing Date: July
Additional Information: For more information visit the Rees Jeffreys website www.reesjeffreys.co.uk/bursaries/

For further information contact:

Email: Secretary@reesjeffreys.org

University of Westminster GREAT Scholarships

Eligibility: To be eligible, applicants must meet all of the following conditions: 1. Be an Overseas student for fee purposes from (and residing in) Egypt, Ghana or Vietnam and have an offer for a place on a full-time postgraduate course at the University of Westminster starting in September 2024 2. Have a minimum UK equivalent 2:1 Honours Degree.
Type: Scholarship
Value: £10,000
Length of Study: 1 year
Country of Study: United Kingdom
Application Procedure: Please return your completed application form including any required supporting evidence as pdf attachments to: m.davies1@westminster.ac.uk (Egyptian students), m.parzych01@westminster.ac.uk (Ghanaian students), b.kelhar@westminster.ac.uk (Vietnamese students). www.westminster.ac.uk/sites/default/public-files/general-documents/GREAT%20Scholarships%20Application%20Form%202023%20%283%29.docx
No. of awards offered: 3
Closing Date: 19 June
Additional Information: www.westminster.ac.uk/study/fees-and-funding/scholarships/university-of-westminster-great-scholarships

Westminster Full-Fee Masters Scholarships for International Students

Purpose: The Westminster University offers full tuition fee scholarships to prospective postgraduate applicants from any country
Eligibility: You must hold an offer for a full-time Masters Program at the University of Westminster. The main scholarship criteria are: Equivalent to a UK First Class Honours degree and financial need.
Level of Study: Doctorate, Postgraduate
Type: Scholarship
Value: Full tuition fee award only
Country of Study: United Kingdom
Application Procedure: You should only apply for a scholarship once you have applied for admission and successfully been offered a place (either conditional or unconditional) on the course you wish to study. To apply for a scholarship, you will need to download and complete the relevant scholarship application form and submit it together with supporting documents by post
Closing Date: 12 October
Additional Information: For more details visit official scholarship Website: www.westminster.ac.uk/study/prospective-students/fees-and-funding/scholarships/international-postgraduate-scholarships/westminster-full-fee-scholarship Weblink: www.scholars4dev.com/8785/full-tuition-fee-waivers-international-students-westminster-university/

For further information contact:

Email: course-enquiries@westminster.ac.uk

U

Westminster Vice-Chancellor's Scholarships

Purpose: The Westminster Vice-Chancellor's Scholarships, the university's most prestigious award, is aimed at fully funding a student from a developing country to study a full-time masters degree at the University
Eligibility: You must be an international student from a developing country and hold an offer for a full-time Undergraduate degree at University of Westminster. The main

criteria are United Kingdom First Class Honours degree, financial need and development potential
Level of Study: Postgraduate
Type: Scholarship
Value: Full tuition fee waivers, accommodation, living expenses and flights to and from London
Frequency: Annual
Study Establishment: University of Westminster
Country of Study: United Kingdom
Application Procedure: It is important to visit the official website to access the application form and for detailed information on how to apply for this scholarship
Closing Date: 31 May
Additional Information: For more details, please visit official scholarship website: www.westminster.ac.uk/study/prospective-students/fees-and-funding/scholarships/international-postgraduate-scholarships/vice-chancellor-scholarship www.scholarshiproar.com/westminster-vice-chancellors-scholarships/

University of Winnipeg

515 Portage Avenue, Winnipeg, R3B 2E9, Canada.

Website: www.uwinnipeg.ca

The University of Winnipeg Manitoba Graduate Scholarships (MGS)

Purpose: Applications are open for the University of Winnipeg Manitoba Graduate Scholarships (MGS) organized by the University of Winnipeg. These scholarships are open to the students who are enrolled or plan to enroll as a full-time student in a master's program at the University of Winnipeg
Eligibility: 1. Have achieved a minimum GPA of 3.75 in the last 60 credits hours of study. 2. Be in a pre-master's program and/or entering the first or second year of an eligible master's program as of May or September of the current year or January of the upcoming year. 3. Be enrolled in or plan to enroll in as a full-time student in a master's program.
Level of Study: Postdoctorate, Postgraduate
Type: Scholarship
Value: CA$15,000
Length of Study: 1 year
Frequency: Annual
Country of Study: Any country
Application Procedure: Apply online www.uwinnipeg.ca/graduate-studies/docs/uwmgs-application+checklist-revisedjan2019-2.pdf
Closing Date: 1 March
Funding: Foundation
Additional Information: If you have any questions, or require additional information, please contact the Graduate Studies Office via email; gradstudies@uwinnipeg.ca Website: www.uwinnipeg.ca/graduate-studies/docs/uwmgs-regulations-and-instructions-guide-jan2019.pdf

For further information contact:

Email: gradstudies@uwinnipeg.ca

Weweni Future Scholars Award

Eligibility: You are eligible to apply for this award if you meet the following criteria: 1. You are accepted to begin your first year of a PhD program 2. You are a University of Winnipeg alumnus/alumna 3. You have Indigenous ancestry.
Type: Award
Value: CA$12,750
Length of Study: 2 years
Country of Study: Canada
Closing Date: 15 September
Additional Information: www.uwinnipeg.ca/graduate-studies/funding/weweni-future-scholars-award.html

For further information contact:

Email: c.garland@uwinnipeg.ca

University of Wollongong (UOW)

Northfields Ave, Wollongong, NSW 2522, Australia.

Tel: (61) 2 4221 3555
Email: scholarships@uow.edu.au
Website: www.uow.edu.au

The University of Wollongong (UOW) is a university of international standing with an enviable record of achievement in teaching and research. It enjoys a significant international research profile, attracting more Australian Research Council funding per student that any other Australian university. Over 850 postgraduate students are enrolled of which 30% are overseas students.

University of Wollongong Sydney Business School Bursary Scheme

Purpose: The University of Wollongong (UOW) is offering Sydney Business School Bursary Scheme for students commencing master's courses. The bursaries offer a 15% reduction of the tuition fee per trimester of the study of applied

Eligibility: The bursary will apply to the following citizenships only India, Nepal, Vietnam, Pakistan, Indonesia, Sri Lanka, Bangladesh, Thailand, Iran, Kenya, Mongolia, Nigeria, Cambodia, Zimbabwe, Myanmar and Ghana

Value: The bursaries offer a 15% reduction of the tuition fee per trimester of the study of applied

Study Establishment: Bursaries are awarded to study the subjects offered by the university

Country of Study: Australia

Application Procedure: You do not have to make a separate application for a bursary, as it will be awarded automatically when you receive an offer for an eligible course and meet scholarship requirements. Applicants will receive a bursary notification and Terms and Conditions of their bursary at the same time as their offer of admission into their course

Additional Information: For more details please visit the website sydneybusinessschool.edu.au/content/groups/public/@web/@gsb/documents/doc/uow247217.pdf scholarship-positions.com/uow-sydney-business-school-bursary-scheme-australia/2017/07/27/

For further information contact:

Email: business-enquiries@uow.edu.au

University of Wollongong in Dubai (UOWD)

Blocks 5 & 15, Knowledge Village, PO Box 20183, Dubai, United Arab Emirates.

Tel: (971) 4 367 2400
Email: info@uowduabi.ac.ae

The UOWD in Dubai, established in 1993, is one UAE's oldest and most prestigious universities. The university strives to provide a fertile environment for bright young minds to flourish, and maintains a long and proud tradition of excellence in education.

University of Wollongong in Dubai Postgraduate Scholarships

Purpose: To reward the academically outstanding postgraduates

Eligibility: 1. Applications are open to students of any citizenship. 2. Applications are open to new (entry level) students only who will be undertaking full time study. 3. Applicants must have achieved the minimum grades as listed in the Curriculum table below. 4. Applicants must meet all of the academic and admission criteria to be admitted to the University and be intending to enrol in the relevant session for which they have applied.

Level of Study: Postgraduate

Type: Scholarship

Value: 15% to 25% of tuition fees each semester

Frequency: Annual

Study Establishment: University of Wollongong in Dubai

Country of Study: United Kingdom

Application Procedure: Contact the University

No. of awards offered: 2

Closing Date: 5 January

No. of awards given last year: 1

Additional Information: For further information regarding UOWD Scholarships you can contact Student Recruitment on +9714 278 1800 or info@uowdubai.ac.ae www.uowdubai.ac.ae/postgraduate-programs/scholarships-new-students

For further information contact:

Tel: (971) 4 278 1800
Email: info@uowdubai.ac.ae

University of York

Graduate Schools Office, Heslington, York Y010 5DD, United Kingdom.

Tel: (44) 1904 320 000
Email: graduate@york.ac.uk
Website: www.york.ac.uk
Contact: Mr Philip Simison

The University of York offers postgraduate degree courses in archaeology, art history, biology, biochemistry, chemistry, communication studies, computer science, economics, educational studies, electronics, English, environment, health sciences, history, language and linguistics, management, mathematics, medieval studies, music, philosophy, physics, politics, psychology, social policy, social work, sociology and women's studies.

China Scholarships Council Joint Research Scholarships

Purpose: The scholarships are open to Chinese nationals intending to begin a PhD in the current and upcoming

academic year. They will be awarded on the basis of academic merit and CSC priorities
Eligibility: 1. You must be a citizen and permanent resident of the People's Republic of China at the time of application. 2. You must hold an unconditional offer* for a full-time PhD degree programme at the University of York, commencing in Autumn 2024. 3. You are eligible to apply if you have an outstanding ATAS certificate as your only offer condition. 4. You must fulfil any English language requirements of your offer by 7 February 2024. 5. You must satisfy the eligibility and selection criteria set out by the CSC (csc.edu.cn). *If you are currently studying the final year of a bachelor or Masters degree, you are eligible to apply for the scholarship if you hold a conditional offer, where the only condition is the successful completion of your degree or the receipt of your ATAS certificate. If your offer is still conditional on fulfilling English language requirements, you cannot apply.
Level of Study: Postgraduate, Research
Type: Scholarship
Value: 100% of tuition fees for the full duration of the CSC funding period, a grant and uk visa fees
Length of Study: 3 years
Frequency: Annual
Country of Study: United Kingdom
Application Procedure: Check the details online. www.york.ac.uk/study/postgraduate-research/funding/china-scholarships/
No. of awards offered: 10
Closing Date: 6 February
Funding: Private
Additional Information: www.york.ac.uk/study/postgraduate-research/funding/china-scholarships/

For further information contact:

Tel: (44) 1904 323534
Email: international@york.ac.uk

Overseas Research Scholarship (ORS)

Purpose: For applicants commencing PhD study at the University of York. Applicants must be liable to pay the overseas rate of tuition fee
Eligibility: Students must be outstanding academically and have the support of their chosen department at York. You must hold an offer for PhD study to be eligible to apply
Level of Study: Doctorate
Type: Scholarship
Value: The scholarship will pay the full overseas tuition fee and a stipend of £5,000 per year for each year of successful study
Country of Study: United Kingdom
Application Procedure: Please visit external link: www.york.ac.uk/study/international/fees-funding/scholarships/ to apply.
Closing Date: 30 April
Additional Information: Please email: international@york.ac.uk Website: www.postgraduatefunding.com/award-1518

For further information contact:

Sally Baldwin Buildings, Block B, Heslington, York YO10 5DD, United Kingdom.

Tel: (44) 1904 324043
Fax: (44) 1904 324142
Email: student-financial-support@york.ac.uk
Website: www.york.ac.uk/study/international/fees-funding/scholarships/

Scholarship for Overseas Students

Subjects: All subjects except MBBS (Medicine), GEMMA, CASPPER and Mundus MAPP.
Purpose: For applicants commencing study of any taught subject (excluding students applying to the Hull York Medical School) at any level as a full-time student at the University of York. Applicants must be liable to pay the overseas rate of tuition fee.
Eligibility: This is a competitive scholarship based on academic merit and financial need. You must hold an offer for academic study to be eligible to apply.
Level of Study: Postgraduate
Type: Scholarship
Value: The scholarship is worth one-quarter (25%) of the overseas tuition fee for each year of successful study
Frequency: Annual
Country of Study: United Kingdom
Application Procedure: Please visit www.york.ac.uk/study/international/fees-funding/academic-excellence-scholarships/
Closing Date: 30 April
Additional Information: Please email for further information. international@york.ac.uk

For further information contact:

Email: international@york.ac.uk

White Rose University Consortium Studentships

Purpose: Each year York collaborates with the Universities of Leeds and Sheffield to be able to offer a number of studentships in each of the three universities

Eligibility: In order to be eligible you must have applied for a place on a full time PhD programme in the relevant Department. Have or expect to obtain a first or upper second class honours degree or equivalent prior to commencing the PhD degree
Level of Study: Doctorate
Type: Studentship
Value: A full Research Council equivalent stipend £14,057. Rates for current year were not set at time of publication. A fee waiver at the Home/European Union rate (Overseas candidates are welcome to apply but would need to fund the difference between Home/European Union fee rate and international fee rate.). A Research Support Grant £900
Frequency: Annual
Country of Study: United Kingdom
Application Procedure: Please visit www.york.ac.uk/study/postgraduate/fees-funding/research/white-rose-studentships/
Closing Date: 24 January
Additional Information: Contact research-student-admin@york.ac.uk

For further information contact:

Email: s.wilson@york.ac.uk

Wolfson Foundation Scholarships

Purpose: The University is delighted to be offering Wolfson Scholarships in the Humanities for the second year as part of a national Arts funding scheme
Eligibility: The Wolfson Postgraduate Scholarships in the humanities will be awarded to outstanding students who demonstrate the potential to make an impact on their chosen field. Wolfson Scholarships will be awarded solely on academic merit. In order to be eligible you must have applied for and be in receipt of an offer of a place on a full time PhD programme in the relevant department (some departments may be able to accept applications on the basis of a programme application without an offer, please speak to your prospective department to confirm). Expect to begin your PhD studies in October. Have or expect to obtain a first or upper second class honours degree or equivalent prior to commencing the PhD Have completed a masters level qualification before commencing the PhD.
Level of Study: Doctorate, Postgraduate, Research
Type: Scholarship
Value: Covers tuition fees, £30,000
Length of Study: 3 years
Frequency: Annual
Country of Study: United Kingdom
Application Procedure: Please visit www.york.ac.uk/study/postgraduate/fees-funding/postgraduate/wolfson/
No. of awards offered: 3
Closing Date: 27 January
Additional Information: www.st-andrews.ac.uk/study/fees-and-funding/postgraduate/scholarships/wolfson-postgraduate/

For further information contact:

Tel: (44) 1904 325962
Email: lola.boorman@york.ac.uk

US Department of Energy

Email: The.Secretary@hq.doe.gov
Website: www.energy.gov/

Department of Energy Computational Science Graduate Fellowship Krell Institute

Subjects: Engineering and the physical, computer, mathematical or life sciences
Purpose: To help ensure a supply of scientists and engineers trained to meet workforce needs; to make Department of Energy laboratories available to fellows for work experiences; to strengthen ties between the national academic community and Department of Energy laboratories; and to make computational science careers more visible.
Eligibility: 1. Undergraduate seniors 2. Applicants with no more than B.S. or B.A. degrees who are not enrolled in graduate school 3. First-year graduate students (M.S. degree or Ph.D. students without an M.S. degree) 4. Enrolled M.S. degree students beyond their first year provided that they plan full-time, uninterrupted study toward a Ph.D. at: 1) a different academic institution, OR 2) in a different academic department 5. Applicants with no more than M.S. degrees who are not currently enrolled AND who will not have been enrolled in graduate school for two years prior to resuming graduate studies 6. First-year Ph.D. students with an M.S. degree provided that they 1) completed the M.S. degree within two years at a different academic institution, 2) completed the M.S. degree within two years in a different academic department, OR 3) prior to current enrollment, they had not been enrolled in graduate school for at least two years
Level of Study: Graduate, Masters Degree, Postgraduate
Type: Fellowship
Value: 1. A yearly stipend of US$45,000 2. Payment of full tuition and required fees during the appointment period (at any accredited U.S. university) 3. An annual US$1,000 professional development allowance 4. Up to four years of

U

total support, depending on renewal 5. A twelve-week practicum experience at one of 21 DOE national laboratories or sites, including access to DOE supercomputers 6. A rigorous program of study that ensures fellows have solid backgrounds in a scientific or engineering discipline plus computer science and applied mathematics 7. An annual program review for fellows, alumni, university and DOE laboratory staff, held each summer in the Washington, D.C. area
Frequency: Annual
Country of Study: United States of America
Application Procedure: Eligible candidates have the option to apply: www.krellinst.org/csgf/how-apply/apply-now for either the DOE CSGF Science & Engineering Track or the DOE CSGF Math/CS Track. Access the Online Application: www.krellinst.org/csgf/how-apply/apply-now
Closing Date: 18 January
Additional Information: www.krellinst.org/csgf/

The Energy Efficiency and Renewable Energy (EERE) Science and Technology Policy (STP) Fellowships

Subjects: Engineering; Physical Sciences
Purpose: The Energy Efficiency and Renewable Energy (EERE) Science and Technology Policy (STP) Fellowships serve as a next step in the educational and professional development of scientists and engineers by providing opportunities to participate in policy-related projects at DOE's Office of Energy Efficiency and Renewable Energy in Washington, D.C. Participants will become part of a group of highly-trained scientists and engineers with the education, background, and experience to be part of the workforce that supports the DOE's mission in the future.
Eligibility: Advanced degree in engineering or physical sciences; Knowledge of energy efficiency concepts, technologies and RD&D programs, specifically those related to HVAC, refrigeration, refrigerants, and/or building energy efficiency
Type: Fellowship
Value: Selected candidates will receive a stipend as support for their living and other expenses during this appointment. Stipend rates are determined by EERE officials and are based on the candidate's academic and professional background. Relocation expenses, not to exceed US$5,000, incurred in relocating from the participant
Length of Study: Varies
Study Establishment: Office of Energy Efficiency and Renewable Energy (EERE) Building Technologies Office (BTO)
Country of Study: United States of America
Application Procedure: Via website at www.zintellect.com/Account/ApplicantRegister/4347; A complete application consists of An application Transcript(s) - For this opportunity, an unofficial transcript or copy of the student academic records printed by the applicant or by academic advisors from internal institution systems may be submitted. Selected candidate may be required to provide proof of completion of the degree before the appointment can start. A current resume/curriculum vitae (CV) The resume/CV must include the following Basic applicant Information Name, address, phone, email, and other contact information. Work & Research Experience List all work and research experiences beginning with current or most recent. Include the name of the employer, location, position held, and time period involved. Leadership Experience List experiences (e.g., work, civic, volunteer, research) that demonstrate your leadership skills. Detail your role, type of experience, organization, location, and duration. Educational History List all institutions from which you received or expect to receive a degree, beginning with current or most recent institution. Include the name of the academic institution, degree awarded or expected, date of awarded or expected degree, and academic discipline. Honors & Awards List in chronological order (most recent first) any awards or public recognitions. Include the name of awarding institution, title of the award or honor, and date of award or honor. All documents must be in English or include an official English translation.
Additional Information: Quote reference code in all correspondence: DOE-EERE-STP-BTO-2018-1202 www.zintellect.com/Opportunity/Details/DOE-EERE-STP-BTO-2018-1202

For further information contact:

Email: DOE-RPP@orau.org

Utrecht University

Heidelberglaan 8, NL-3584 CS Utrecht, Netherlands.

Tel: (31) 30 253 35 50
Email: studievoorlichting@uu.nl
Website: www.uu.nl

Utrecht University stands for broad and interdisciplinary education. Students at Utrecht University learn to look beyond the boundaries of their fields of study and work together in interdisciplinary projects. The education programmes are modern and innovative. Students and high-ranking scientists work together on a better future.

Utrecht Excellence Scholarships for International Students

Purpose: The Utrecht Excellence Scholarship (UES) is a highly selective programme for talented international students from outside the European Economic Area (EEA = the EU countries, Iceland, Liechtenstein and Norway) who wish to study for a master's degree at Utrecht University.
Eligibility: To be eligible for a Utrecht Excellence Scholarship, you must meet the following criteria: 1. You must belong to the top 10% of your graduating class. 2. You must not hold an EU/EEA passport and not be eligible for support under the Dutch study grant and loan system. 3. You must have completed your secondary school and/or bachelor's degree outside the Netherlands. 4. You must have applied for an international master's programme with a start date of 1 September 2024. Not all programmes participate. Please check Master's programme > Tuition fees and financial support to see if the Utrecht Excellence Scholarship is mentioned as a scholarship opportunity.
Level of Study: Graduate, Postgraduate
Type: Scholarship
Value: 1. the tuition fee, or 2. the tuition fee plus the income required for a period of one year linked to a residence permit for study as determined by the IND (Immigration and Naturalisation Service).
Frequency: Annual
Country of Study: The Netherlands
Application Procedure: After submitting an application (or applications) for a UES eligible master's programme before the stated deadline, non-EU/EEA students will have the opportunity to submit an application for one Utrecht Excellence Scholarship from 1 November 2023. You will see the UES application(s) in your OSIRIS Online Application account dashboard. Click view/edit for the UES linked (related process) to the programme you wish to apply for, upload the requested proof of belonging to the top 10% of your class, answer the questions and submit the application.
No. of awards offered: 25
Closing Date: 31 January
Funding: Private
Additional Information: Official Scholarship Website: www.uu.nl/masters/en/general-information/international-students/financial-matters/grants-and-scholarships/utrecht-excellence-scholarships

For further information contact:

Email: study@uu.nl

U

V

Vascular Cures

274 Redwood Shores Parkway, #717, Redwood City, CA 94065, United States of America.

Tel: (1) 650 368 6022
Email: info@vascularcures.org
Website: vascularcures.org/

Vascular Cures is the only US national non-profit representing millions of patients with vascular disease. For more than 30 years, it has transformed patient lives through support of innovative research and programs that advance patient-centered healthcare.

Wylie Scholar Program

Subjects: Vascular health
Purpose: Vascular Cures' Wylie Scholar Program is building a pipeline of innovators in vascular health. We provide 3-year career development grants to outstanding young vascular surgeon-scientists who combine active patient care with academic research. The award supports crucial research that enables them to compete for future research funding.
Eligibility: Candidates must hold a full-time faculty appointment as a vascular surgeon with active privileges at a medical school accredited by the Liaison Committee on Medical Education in the United States or the Committee for the Accreditation of Canadian Medical Schools in Canada.
Level of Study: Research
Type: Grant
Value: US$50,000
Length of Study: 3 years
Frequency: Annual
Country of Study: United States of America or Canada
Application Procedure: Scholarship website: static1.squarespace.com/static/633ba514bb0a7342b4a41bc8/t/63aa175798941c251e97ecaa/1672091479974/Wylie+Scholar+Application+2023.pdf
Closing Date: 1 March
No. of awards given last year: 1
Additional Information: www.vascularcures.org/2023-wylie-scholar-application

For further information contact:

Email: grants@vascularcures.org

Victoria University

PO Box 14428, Melbourne, VIC 8001, Australia.

Tel: (61) 3 9919 4000
Website: www.vu.edu.au/

We are one of Australia's few dual-sector universities. Today, we have over 40,000 enrolled higher education, and vocational education and training students studying on our campuses. Being a dual-sector university means that our students can easily pathway from vocational education to higher education - such as from a certificate or diploma course through to an undergraduate degree or even a postgraduate qualification by coursework or research.

Victoria University Research Scholarships

Purpose: To support students undertaking Master's research and research Doctorates
Eligibility: Open to citizens or permanent residents of Australia who have achieved Honours 1 or equivalent having

Palgrave Macmillan (ed.), *The Grants Register 2024*,
https://doi.org/10.1057/978-1-349-96073-6

studied at or currently studying at Victoria University of Technology
Level of Study: Postgraduate
Type: Scholarship
Value: Tuition fees and a living allowance (stipend) to assist graduate research students with the costs of their study.
Length of Study: 1 year
Frequency: Annual
Study Establishment: Victoria University
Country of Study: Australia
Closing Date: 31 October
Additional Information: www.vu.edu.au/study-at-vu/fees-scholarships/scholarships/graduate-research-scholarships

For further information contact:

Tel: (61) 3 9688 4659
Fax: (61) 3 9688 4559
Email: Lesley.Birch@vu.edu.au

Women in Sport Scholarships

Purpose: This scholarship is a legacy of the fundraising assistance Dr Susan Alberti AC provides to the Victoria University Women in Sport centre. Her contributions help us to strengthen sport career pathways for women, and advance workforce development through education.
Eligibility: To be eligible, you must meet these criteria: 1. be an Australian citizen or permanent resident. 2. be enrolled at VU in an undergraduate or postgraduate study in sport. 3. reside in Australia. 4. have experienced barriers and challenges in your academic and personal life that have prevented you from accessing/completing tertiary study. 5. be able to clearly articulate your career aspirations in sport.
Level of Study: Postgraduate
Type: Scholarship
Value: US$2000 per annum
Length of Study: 2 years
Country of Study: Any country
Application Procedure: 1. Documentation supporting your application must include: a. CV (maximum 2 pages). b. contact details of a referee to support the application. c. personal statement (500 words). 2. The personal statement must: a. demonstrate how this scholarship may help you overcome a barrier to access study. b. articulate the reason (s) for selecting your chosen undergraduate or postgraduate course in sport. c. clearly explain how being a recipient of a VU Women in Sport scholarship will assist you to achieve your career aspirations and development.
Additional Information: www.vu.edu.au/study-at-vu/fees-scholarships/scholarships/women-in-sport-scholarship

Victoria University of Wellington

PO Box 600, Wellington 6140, New Zealand.

Tel: (64) 4 472 1000
Email: info@vuw.ac.nz
Website: www.wgtn.ac.nz/

Te Herenga Waka—Victoria University of Wellington was founded in 1897. A civic university is one that values close involvement with the social, cultural, and economic life of its city and region.

Therle Drake Postgraduate Scholarship

Subjects: Music
Purpose: The scholarship is for postgraduate classical performance overseas study and application should be made in the year for which the project is planned. While the terms of the bequest are that preference be given to a piano student, other applicants will be considered.
Eligibility: 1. Applicants must be enrolling or have enrolled for postgraduate study at Te Kōkī New Zealand School of Music at Te Herenga Waka - Victoria University of Wellington. 2. The scholarship can involve the student attending a short course; or attending and/or participating in a concert and/or masterclass in Europe, North America or Australia. 3. The scholarship is open to New Zealand citizens, permanent residents and international students.
Level of Study: Postgraduate
Type: Scholarship
Value: NZ$15,000
Length of Study: 1 year
Frequency: Annual
Country of Study: New Zealand
Application Procedure: A completed online application must be submitted by 4.30 pm on the closing date. Late or incomplete applications will not be accepted. Any required supporting documentation (including references) must also be received by 4.30 pm on the closing date in order for the application to be considered. Applications will normally open one month prior to the closing date.
No. of awards offered: 1
Closing Date: 15 March
Funding: Private
Additional Information: www.wgtn.ac.nz/scholarships/current/therle-drake-postgraduate-scholarship#:~:text=The%20Therle%20Drake%20Postgraduate%20Scholarship,given%20to%20a%20piano%20student.

For further information contact:

Tel: (64) 800 04 04 04
Email: scholarships-office@vuw.ac.nz; pg-research@vuw.ac.nz; summer-research@vuw.ac.nz

Vice-Chancellor's Strategic Doctoral Research Scholarships

Purpose: To encourage and support doctoral study (PhD) at Victoria University of Wellington. Victoria University of Wellington offers scholarships to those about to begin their doctoral studies. These scholarships are awarded on academic merit are open to New Zealand and international students in any discipline.
Eligibility: These scholarships are open to graduates of any university within or outside of New Zealand who intend to enrol full time for a Doctorate (PhD) or who have commenced their doctoral study at Victoria University of Wellington. Please note: It is very important to refer to the website for regulations and further process requirements regarding an application for this scholarship.
Level of Study: Doctorate
Type: Scholarship
Value: NZ$29,500 stipend annually plus tuition fees.
Length of Study: 3 Years
Frequency: Annual
Study Establishment: Victoria University
Country of Study: New Zealand
Application Procedure: Information on applying to do a Doctorate at Victoria University of Wellington and apply for funding to do so is also available from the Wellington Faculty of Graduate Research website. General information about doctoral study is also available from this website.
No. of awards offered: 110
Closing Date: 1 November
Contributor: Victoria University
Additional Information: Closing Date(s): Three rounds each year closing 1 March, 1 July and 1 November. For more information www.wgtn.ac.nz/scholarships/current/wellington-doctoral-scholarships

For further information contact:

Tel: (64) 800 04 04 04
Email: scholarships-office@vuw.ac.nz; pg-research@vuw.ac.nz; summer-research@vuw.ac.nz

Victoria Hardship Fund Equity Grants for International Students in New Zealand

Purpose: These grants are to encourage students who are facing financial hardship to continue in their studies at Te Herenga Waka—Victoria University of Wellington. The grants will be awarded on the basis of financial need and satisfactory academic commitment and progress. The Grants are intended to assist with ongoing costs related to study.
Eligibility: Applications are open to all students who are currently studying at Te Herenga Waka—Victoria University of Wellington, including domestic, international, undergraduate, postgraduate, part-time, and full-time students. Applicants must be enrolled in the trimester they are applying for, e.g., students who apply for round 1 must be enrolled in trimester 1 of the same year.
Level of Study: Doctorate, Graduate, Masters Degree, Postgraduate
Type: Grant
Value: Up to NZ$2,000 for one or two trimesters
Frequency: Annual
Study Establishment: Victoria University of Wellington
Country of Study: New Zealand
Application Procedure: Apply online. Required supporting documentation 1. A personal statement (max 500 words) outlining your financial difficulties and your personal circumstances and study goals. 2. Proof of your income (details of specific documents required are on online application).
Closing Date: 18 October
Additional Information: Closing Date(s): 1 February, 8 June and 18 October. They are not intended for tuition fees. The award may be paid in instalments. For more information www.wgtn.ac.nz/scholarships/current/hardship-fund-equity-grants.

For further information contact:

Tel: (64) 800 04 04 04
Email: scholarships-office@vuw.ac.nz; pg-research@vuw.ac.nz; summer-research@vuw.ac.nz

Victoria Tongarewa Scholarship

Purpose: The Tongarewa Scholarship ("the Scholarship") celebrates the University's commitment to our international student community. This is a partial fee-based scholarship that will be put towards your tuition fees for one year of study.
Eligibility: Applicants must be 1. International students who are paying full international fees. 2. Entering their first year of an undergraduate degree or entering a postgraduate degree.

Applicants can be entering a postgraduate degree programme at Victoria University of Wellington.
Level of Study: Masters Degree, Postgraduate, Research
Type: Scholarship
Value: NZ$5,000 or NZ$10,000
Frequency: Annual
Country of Study: New Zealand
Application Procedure: Apply online.
No. of awards offered: 19
Closing Date: 30 November
Additional Information: Closing Date(s): 1 June (For Trimester 2), 30 November (For Trimester 1), 1 September (For Trimester 3). For more details www.wgtn.ac.nz/scholarships/current/tongarewa-scholarship

For further information contact:

Tel: (64) 800 04 04 04
Email: scholarships-office@vuw.ac.nz; pg-research@vuw.ac.nz; summer-research@vuw.ac.nz

Wellington Graduate Award

Purpose: The Wellington Graduate Award encourages undergraduate students to proceed to graduate study and to research degrees
Eligibility: 1. Applications are sought from those who are eligible at the time of application, or who will have become eligible by the start of Trimester 2 the following year, to enrol for a Master's degree by thesis worth 90 points or more. This will be either a one-year Master's programme in which the student will undertake a thesis worth 90 points or more, or Part 2 Master's degree in which the student will take a thesis course worth 90 points or more. The Master's thesis will usually have the course code 591 or 592. 2. For avoidance of doubt, eligibility includes students who are taking a portfolio course that is worth 90 points or more, and is administered under the University's Master's by Thesis regulations (see section 6 of those regulations). 3. Students who are taking a 60 points dissertation course are not eligible. 4. Students would normally be expected to have completed a Bachelor's degree or Master's degree Part 1 demonstrating academic achievement equivalent to a GPA of at least 7.0 from a New Zealand university. Applicants must be aware that a GPA of 7.0 is a minimum requirement and that the University Research Scholarships Committee has discretion to use a higher bar if there are more applications than funding available. 5. Scholarships will be awarded solely on the basis of academic merit by the University Research Scholarships Committee, a sub-committee of the University Research Committee.
Level of Study: Masters Degree, Postgraduate
Type: Scholarship
Value: The scholarship comprises a NZ$15,000 tax free stipend for one year plus tuition fees
Length of Study: One year
Frequency: Annual
Study Establishment: Victoria University of Wellington
Country of Study: New Zealand
Application Procedure: A completed online application must be submitted by 4.30 pm on the closing date. Late or incomplete applications will not be accepted. Any required supporting documentation (including references) must also be received by 4.30 pm on the closing date in order for the application to be considered. Applications will normally open one month prior to the closing date. If no application link is provided below, check back again closer to the closing date. Contact us www.wgtn.ac.nz/scholarships/scholarships-office if you have any queries.
Closing Date: 1 November
Additional Information: www.wgtn.ac.nz/scholarships/current/wellington-graduate-award

For further information contact:

Tel: (64) 800 04 04 04
Email: scholarships-office@vuw.ac.nz; pg-research@vuw.ac.nz; summer-research@vuw.ac.nz

Wellington Master's by Thesis Scholarship

Purpose: To encourage postgraduate research at Te Herenga Waka—Victoria University of Wellington, the University offers scholarships to students about to begin a full-time, research-focussed Master's degree.
Eligibility: 1. Applications are sought from those who are eligible at the time of application, or who will have become eligible by the start of Trimester 2 the following year, to enrol for a Master's degree by thesis worth 90 points or more. This will be either a one-year Master's programme in which the student will undertake a thesis worth 90 points or more, or Part 2 Master's degree in which the student will take a thesis course worth 90 points or more. The Master's thesis will usually have the course code 591 or 592. 2. For avoidance of doubt, eligibility includes students who are taking a portfolio course that is worth 90 points or more, and is administered under the University's Master's by Thesis regulations (see section 6 of those regulations). 3. Students who are taking a 60 points dissertation course are not eligible.

4. Students would normally be expected to have completed a Bachelor's degree or Master's degree Part 1 demonstrating academic achievement equivalent to a GPA of at least 7.0 from a New Zealand university. Applicants must be aware that a GPA of 7.0 is a minimum requirement and that the University Research Scholarships Committee has discretion to use a higher bar if there are more applications than funding available. 5. Scholarships will be awarded solely on the basis of academic merit by the University Research Scholarships Committee, a sub-committee of the University Research Committee.
Level of Study: Masters Degree, Postgraduate
Type: Scholarship
Value: The scholarship comprises a NZ$15,000 tax free stipend, plus tuition fees for one year
Length of Study: One year
Frequency: Annual
Study Establishment: Victoria University of Wellington
Country of Study: New Zealand
Application Procedure: A completed online application must be submitted by 4.30 pm on the closing date. Late or incomplete applications will not be accepted. Any required supporting documentation (including references) must also be received by 4.30 pm on the closing date in order for the application to be considered. Applications will normally open one month prior to the closing date. If no application link is provided below, check back again closer to the closing date. Contact us www.wgtn.ac.nz/scholarships/scholarships-office if you have any queries.
No. of awards offered: Varies
Closing Date: 1 November
Additional Information: www.wgtn.ac.nz/scholarships/current/wellington-masters-by-thesis-scholarship

For further information contact:

Tel: (64) 800 04 04 04
Email: scholarships-office@vuw.ac.nz; pg-research@vuw.ac.nz; summer-research@vuw.ac.nz

Villa I Tatti and the Museo Nacional del Prado

Via di Vincigliata 26, I-50135 Florence, Italy.

Tel: (39) 55 603 251
Email: info@itatti.harvard.edu
Website: itatti.harvard.edu/
Contact: Villa I Tatti

Villa I Tatti, The Harvard University Center for Italian Renaissance Studies is a center for advanced research in the humanities located in Florence, Italy, and belongs to Harvard University. It also houses a library and an art collection, and it is the site of Italian and English gardens.

I Tatti/Museo Nacional del Prado Joint Fellowship

Purpose: A fellowship designed to support early and mid-career scholars in the field of art history, with preference given to advanced research projects that address the relationship between Spain and Italy (including transnational connections and dialogues with Latin America) during the Renaissance, broadly understood historically to include the period from the 14th to the 17th century.
Eligibility: At the time of application, scholars must have a PhD in hand and will be asked to upload a scan of the certificate. Applicants must be conversant in English and Spanish and have at least a reading knowledge of Italian, with a solid background in Italian and/or Spanish and Latin American studies. Each successful candidate must be approved by both the Museo Nacional del Prado and Villa I Tatti and will spend the fall term (mid-September – mid-December) at the Museo del Prado in Madrid supported by Centro de Estudios Europa Hispánica and the spring term (January-June) at Villa I Tatti in Florence. During both terms, it must be possible for Fellows to carry out most of their research with the resources available in the city where they are resident. Priority will be given to applicants with no previous association with either I Tatti or the Museo del Prado. Renewals, repeats, or deferments of this Fellowship are not granted. The Fellow will be expected to carry out original research on the topic for which they have been awarded their Fellowship.
Level of Study: Postdoctorate
Type: Fellowship
Value: For Spring term, the stipend is US$4,000 per month, plus a one-time supplement (maximum US$1,500) towards relocation expenses supported by Villa I Tatti. For Fall term, the stipend is €3000 per month, supported by the Centro de Estudios Europa Hispánica.
Length of Study: One academic year
Frequency: Annual
Country of Study: Any country
Application Procedure: Applications must be written in English and must be submitted electronically. Please visit website.
Closing Date: 15 November
Additional Information: itatti.harvard.edu/i-tattimuseo-nacional-del-prado-joint-fellowship

Villa I Tatti and the Warburg Institute School of Advanced Study

Via di Vincigliata 26, I-50135 Florence, Italy.

Tel: (39) 55 603 251
Email: info@itatti.harvard.edu
Website: itatti.harvard.edu/
Contact: Villa I Tatti

Villa I Tatti - The Harvard University Center for Italian Renaissance Studies (Florence, Italy) and the Warburg Institute School of Advanced Study at the University of London, England.

Warburg - I Tatti Joint Fellowship

Purpose: Villa I Tatti - The Harvard University Center for Italian Renaissance Studies in Florence, Italy, and the Warburg Institute School of Advanced Study at the University of London offer a joint, residential fellowship for early and mid-career scholars in the field of history, with preference given to advanced research projects that address the history of science and knowledge related to early modern Italy, including transnational connections between Italy and other cultures. Scholars can also apply to work on the transmission and circulation of ideas, objects, and people during the Renaissance, into and beyond the Italian peninsula, or on the historiography of the Italian Renaissance, including the rebirth of interest in the Renaissance in later periods.
Eligibility: At the time of application, scholars must have a PhD in hand and will be asked to upload a scan of the certificate. They may not be working on a second PhD at the time of application. Applicants must be conversant in English and have at least a reading knowledge of Italian, with a solid background in Italian Renaissance Studies. Each successful candidate must be approved by both the Warburg Institute and Villa I Tatti and will spend the fall term (September – December) at the Warburg Institute in London and the spring term (January-June) at Villa I Tatti in Florence. During both terms, it must be possible for Fellows to carry out most of their research with the resources available in the city where they are resident. Priority will be given to applicants with no previous association with either I Tatti or the Warburg Institute. Renewals, repeats, or deferments of this Fellowship are not granted. The fellow will be expected to carry out original research on the topic for which they have been awarded their fellowship. Applications will not be accepted from candidates proposing to revise their doctoral dissertation for publication.
Level of Study: Postdoctorate
Value: For Spring Term The stipend is US$4,000 per month, plus a one-time supplement (maximum US$1,500) towards relocation expenses. For Autumn Term The stipend is £1,500 per month.
Frequency: Annual
Country of Study: Any country
Application Procedure: Applications must be written in English and must be submitted electronically. Please visit website.
Closing Date: 15 November
Additional Information: itatti.harvard.edu/warburgi-tatti-joint-fellowship

Villa I Tatti: The Harvard University Center for Italian Renaissance Studies

Via di Vincigliata 26, I-50135 Florence, Italy.

Tel: (39) 55 603 251
Email: info@itatti.harvard.edu
Website: itatti.harvard.edu/

Villa I Tatti, The Harvard University Center for Italian Renaissance Studies is a center for advanced research in the humanities located in Florence, Italy, and belongs to Harvard University. It also houses a library and an art collection, and it is the site of Italian and English gardens.

Berenson Fellowship

Subjects: Post-doctoral reasearch on "Italy in the World." Projects should address the transnational dialogues between Italy and other cultures (e.g. Latin American, Mediterranean, African, Asian etc.) during the Renaissance, broadly understood historically to include the period from the 14th to the 17th century.
Purpose: This Fellowship, made possible by The Lila Wallace – Reader's Digest Fund, is designed for scholars who explore "Italy in the World." I Tatti offers Fellows the precious time they need to pursue their studies with a minimum of obligations and interruptions together with a maximum of scholarly resources–a combination that distinguishes the Harvard Center from similar institutions.
Eligibility: At the time of application, scholars must have a PhD in hand and will be asked to upload a scan of the certificate. They may not be working on a second PhD at the time of application. Applicants must be conversant in English and have familiarity with Italian. Priority will be given to early and mid-career scholars. I Tatti welcomes applications

from scholars from all nations and gives special consideration to candidates without regular access to research materials and facilities in Italy
Level of Study: Postdoctorate
Value: The stipend is NZ$4,200 per month, plus a one-time supplement (maximum NZ$1,500) towards relocation expenses
Length of Study: 4-6 months
Frequency: Annual
Country of Study: Italy
Application Procedure: Applications can be written in English or Italian and must be submitted electronically.
No. of awards offered: 4
Closing Date: 20 November
Funding: Private
Contributor: The Lila Wallace - Reader's Digest Fund
Additional Information: For more information itatti.harvard.edu/berenson-fellowship

Craig Hugh Smyth Fellowship

Purpose: The Craig Hugh Smyth Fellowship is designed for curators and conservators pursuing advanced research in any aspect of the Italian Renaissance.
Eligibility: Applicants should be scholars who work for an educational or cultural institution as a curator or conservator. They may apply to carry out research on behalf of their home institution or propose projects relating to their personal research interests. Applicants must be conversant in English and have familiarity with Italian. Priority will be given to early and mid-career scholars. It must be possible for applicants to carry out most of their research in Florence. I Tatti welcomes applications from scholars from all nations and gives special consideration to candidates without regular access to research materials and facilities in Italy.
Level of Study: Research
Value: The stipend is US$4,200 per month, plus a one-time supplement (maximum US$1,500) towards relocation expenses
Length of Study: 4–6 months
Frequency: Annual
Country of Study: Italy
Application Procedure: Applicants should indicate their preference between fall (September through December) and winter-spring (January through June). Applications can be written in English or Italian and must be submitted electronically. Please refer website.
No. of awards offered: 2
Closing Date: 20 November
Additional Information: itatti.harvard.edu/craig-hugh-smyth-fellowship

David and Julie Tobey Fellowship

Subjects: This fellowship supports research on drawings, prints, and illustrated manuscripts from the Italian Renaissance, and especially the role that these works played in the creative process, the history of taste and collecting, and questions of connoisseurship. Proposals on a variety of subjects with a substantive component of research on drawings, prints, and illustrated manuscripts done on paper or parchment types are welcome.
Purpose: The Fellowship supports research on drawings, prints, and illustrated manuscripts from the Italian Renaissance, and especially the role that these works played in the creative process, the history of taste and collecting, and questions of connoisseurship.
Eligibility: At the time of application, scholars must have a PhD in hand and will be asked to upload a scan of the certificate. They may not be working on a second PhD at the time of application. Applicants must be conversant in English and have familiarity with Italian. Priority will be given to early and mid-career scholars. It must be possible for applicants to carry out most of their research in Florence. I Tatti welcomes applications from scholars from all nations and gives special consideration to candidates without regular access to research materials and facilities in Italy.
Level of Study: Postdoctorate
Value: The stipend is US$4,200 per month, plus a one-time supplement (maximum US$1,500) towards relocation expenses
Length of Study: 4–6 months
Frequency: Annual
Country of Study: Italy
Application Procedure: Applications can be written in English or Italian and must be submitted electronically.
No. of awards offered: 1
Closing Date: 20 November
Additional Information: itatti.harvard.edu/david-and-julie-tobey-fellowship

Fellowship in the Digital Humanities

Subjects: Projects can address any aspect of the Italian Renaissance, broadly understood historically to include the period from the 14th to the 17th century, and geographically to include transnational dialogues between Italy and other cultures (e.g. Latin American, Mediterranean, African, Asian, etc.). Projects should apply digital technologies such as mapping, textual analysis, visualization, or the semantic web to topics in fields such as art and architecture, history, literature, material culture, music, philosophy, religion, and the history of science.

Purpose: A fellowship to support research of scholars in the humanities or social sciences, librarians, archivists, and data science professionals whose research interests or practice cut across traditional disciplinary boundaries and actively employ technology in their work.
Eligibility: Applicants must be conversant in English and have familiarity with Italian. At the time of application, a PhD is required for scholars in the humanities and social sciences. A Master's degree is required for librarians, archivists, and data science professionals. A background in programming, library sciences, computer graphics, computational linguistics, or other fields relevant to digital humanities research is highly desirable. Candidates should possess the technical skills to carry out their project at the time of application, and it must be possible for applicants to carry out most of their research in Florence. Priority will be given to early and mid-career scholars. I Tatti welcomes applications from scholars from all nations and gives special consideration to candidates without regular access to research materials and facilities in Italy.
Level of Study: Doctorate, Masters Degree
Value: The stipend is US$4,200 per month, plus a one-time supplement (maximum US$1,500) towards relocation expenses.
Length of Study: 4–6 months
Frequency: Annual
Country of Study: Italy
Application Procedure: Applicants should indicate their preference between fall (September through December) and winter-spring (January through June). Applications must be written in English and must be submitted electronically.
No. of awards offered: 2
Closing Date: 15 November
Contributor: The Fellowship in the Digital Humanities is generously supported in part by the Samuel H. Kress Foundation.
Additional Information: itatti.harvard.edu/fellowship-digital-humanities

I Tatti Fellowship

Subjects: Post-doctoral research in any aspect of the Italian Renaissance, broadly understood historically to include the period from the 14th to the 17th century and geographically to include transnational dialogues between Italy and other cultures (e.g. Latin American, Mediterranean, African, Asian etc.).
Purpose: A Fellowship to support post-doctoral research in any aspect of the Italian Renaissance.
Eligibility: Scholars must hold a PhD, dottorato di ricerca, or an equivalent degree. They must be conversant in either English or Italian and able to understand both languages. They should be in the early stages of their career, having received a PhD between 2012–2022 and have a solid background in Italian Renaissance studies. Candidates may not be working on a second PhD at the time of application. In the event that a candidate holds two doctoral degrees, the eligibility dates (PhD certificate dated between January 1, 2012 and December 31, 2022, inclusive) apply to the more recent degree.
Level of Study: Postdoctorate
Value: US$60,000, plus relocation supplement and housing or housing supplement
Length of Study: 1 year
Frequency: Annual
Country of Study: Italy
No. of awards offered: 15
Closing Date: 22 October
Additional Information: itatti.harvard.edu/i-tatti-fellowship

Mellon Fellowship in Digital Humanities

Eligibility: A PhD is required for scholars in the humanities and social sciences; in exceptional cases, applications from advanced PhD (ABD) students will be considered. A Master's degree is required for librarians, archivists, and data science professionals. A background in programming, library sciences, computer graphics, computational linguistics, or other fields relevant to digital humanities research is highly desirable. Candidates should possess the technical skills to carry out their project at the time of application
Type: Residential fellowships
Value: Up to US$4,000 per month plus a one-time supplement (Max US$1,500)
Length of Study: 4–6 months
Frequency: Annual
Country of Study: Italy
Application Procedure: Please check at itatti.harvard.edu/mellon-fellowship-digital-humanities
Closing Date: 14 December
Contributor: Andrew W. Mellon Foundation

Villa I Tatti - Bogaziçi University Joint Fellowship

Subjects: This fellowship focusses on the interaction between Italy and the Byzantine Empire (ca. 1300 to ca. 1700) and aims to foster the development of research on Late Byzantine-Italian relations by supporting early-career scholars whose work explores Byzantium's cross-cultural contacts in the late medieval and early modern Mediterranean world through the study of art, architecture, archaeology, history, literature, material culture, music, philosophy, religion, or science.

Purpose: Villa I Tatti - The Harvard University Center for Italian Renaissance Studies (VIT, Florence) and the Byzantine Studies Research Center of Bogaziçi University (BSRC, Istanbul) offer a joint, residential fellowship to support research on the interaction between Italy and the Byzantine Empire (ca. 1300 to ca. 1700). This collaboration aims to foster the development of research on Late Byzantine-Italian relations by supporting early-career scholars whose work explores Byzantium's cross-cultural contacts in the late medieval and early modern Mediterranean world through the study of art, architecture, archaeology, history, literature, material culture, music, philosophy, religion, or science.
Eligibility: The VIT-BSRC Joint Fellowship is offered for candidates who have received a PhD in or after 2012. Candidates must be conversant in English and have at least a reading knowledge of Italian. They must have a solid background in Italian Renaissance and/or Byzantine Studies. Each successful candidate must be approved by both the BSRC and VIT and will spend the fall term (September - December) at Bogaziçi University in Istanbul and the spring term (January-June) at Villa I Tatti in Florence. During both terms, it must be possible for Fellows to carry out most of their research with the resources available in the city where they are resident. Priority will be given to applicants with no previous association with VIT or BSRC.
Level of Study: The VIT-BSRC Joint Fellowship is offered for candidates who have received a PhD in or after 2012.
Type: Residential Fellowship
Value: The stipend for the autumn semester in Istanbul is US$1,800 per month, plus a one-time supplement (maximum US$1,500) towards airfare to/from Istanbul. The stipend for the spring semester in Italy is US$4,200 per month plus a one-time supplement (maximum US$1,500) towards relocation expenses. An additional US$1,000 per month will be offered to offset rental costs, if applicable.
Length of Study: One academic year.
Frequency: Annual
Country of Study: Fellows will spend the fall term (September - December) in Istanbul and the spring term (January - June) in Florence.
No. of awards offered: 1
Closing Date: 15 November
Additional Information: itatti.harvard.edu/fellowships

Wallace Fellowship

Subjects: Post-doctoral research on historiography and impact of the Italian Renaissance in the Modern Era (19th-21st centuries). Projects can address the historiography or impact of the Renaissance on any field, including art and architecture, landscape architecture, history, literature, material culture, music, philosophy, religion, and science.
Purpose: A Fellowship to support post-doctoral research on the historiography and impact of the Italian Renaissance in the Modern Era (19th–21st centuries).
Eligibility: At the time of application, scholars must have a PhD in hand and will be asked to upload a scan of the certificate. They may not be working on a second PhD at the time of application. Applicants must be conversant in English and have familiarity with Italian. Priority will be given to early and mid-career scholars. Projects can address the historiography or impact of the Renaissance on any field, including art and architecture, landscape architecture, history, literature, material culture, music, philosophy, religion, and science. It must be possible for applicants to carry out most of their research in Florence. I Tatti welcomes applications from scholars from all nations and gives special consideration to candidates without regular access to research materials and facilities in Italy.
Level of Study: Postdoctorate
Value: The stipend is US$4,200 per month, plus a one-time supplement (maximum US$1,500) towards relocation expenses.
Length of Study: 4–6 months
Frequency: Annual
Country of Study: Italy
Application Procedure: Applicants should indicate their preference between fall (September through December) and winter-spring (January through June). Applications can be written in English or Italian and must be submitted electronically.
No. of awards offered: 4
Closing Date: 20 November
Funding: Private
Contributor: The Lila Wallace - Reader's Digest Fund.
Additional Information: itatti.harvard.edu/wallace-fellowship

Vinaver Trust

Email: bonnie.millar@nottingham.ac.uk
Website: www.internationalarthuriansociety.com/
Contact: Bonnie Millar, Website Editor

The Vinaver Trust was established in 1981, when the British Branch of the International Arthurian Society, at the urging of Eugène Vinaver, formerly professor of medieval French at Manchester University, and Cedric Pickford, professor of Medieval French at the University of Hull, found the British Branch had earned an astonishingly large sum in royalties from endorsing Arthurian plates for a Swiss ceramics firm, Atelier Arts.

Barron Bequest

Subjects: Any field of Arthurian studies
Purpose: To support postgraduate research in Arthurian studies
Eligibility: Open to graduates of any university in the British Isles, including those of the Republic of Ireland.
Level of Study: Postgraduate
Type: Grant
Value: £1,250 as a contribution to postgraduate fees
Frequency: Annual
Country of Study: United Kingdom, Republic of Ireland
Application Procedure: There is no standard application form. Instead, a leaflet is available giving details of information to be supplied by applicants in typed or word-processed form. The leaflet is available in electronic form and available via the website. Alternatively copies of the leaflet can be obtained from Professor Jane Taylor.
Closing Date: 30 April
Funding: Trusts
Contributor: The Eugène Vinaver Memorial Trust
Additional Information: For more information www.internationalarthuriansociety.com/british-branch/view/awards

For further information contact:

Professor Jane Taylor, Garth Head, Penruddock, Penrith, Cumbria CA11 0QU, United Kingdom.

Email: jane.taylor@durham.ac.uk

Volkswagen Foundation

Kastanienallee 35, D-30519 Hannover, Germany.

Tel: (49) 511 8381 0
Email: info@volkswagenstiftung.de
Website: www.volkswagenstiftung.de/en
Contact: VolkswagenStiftung

The Volkswagen Foundation is a non-profitmaking foundation established under private law in 1961. The Foundation owes its existence to a treaty between the Government of the Federal Republic of Germany and the State of Lower Saxony. The Volkswagen Foundation (VolkswagenStiftung) is the largest private research funder and one of the major foundations in Germany. Since 1962 the Foundation has granted more than 5.3 billion euros of funding for over 33,000 projects. Foundation capital amounts to 3.5 billion euros. The Volkswagen Foundation (VolkswagenStiftung) is dedicated to the support of the humanities and social sciences as well as science and technology in higher education and research.

Volkswagen Foundation Freigeist Fellowships

Purpose: The Freigeist funding initiative provides an opportunity for outstandingly qualified, creative and independent early career researchers to conduct their own research. It aims to encourage exceptional research personalities to embark on visionary, risk-taking research projects at the intersections between established fields of research.
Eligibility: Anyone can apply who identifies with the goals of a 'Freigeist' Fellowship and whose proposed research project fits in with the aims pursued by the Freigeist initiative. Candidates must, however, conform to the following conditions 1. Their doctorate must have been obtained no longer than four years ago but at least one year previously (with regard to the date of the defense relative to the deadline of the initiative). 2. The Fellowship must be integrated within a university or an extra-mural research institution in Germany. 3. Candidates must already have changed their academic environment and moved to a new location – at the latest when starting the Fellowship. A return to the working context of the doctorate will only be accepted under exceptional circumstances. 4. A previously completed research sojourn abroad, at the latest integrated in the proposed research project.
Level of Study: Doctorate, Postdoctorate
Type: Fellowship
Value: The scope of funding foresees a funding period of up to eight years in two funding phases (5 + 3 years or 6 + 2 years) with total funding of up to €2.2 million
Length of Study: 8 years
Frequency: Annual
Country of Study: Germany
Application Procedure: Applications can be submitted online via the Electronic Application System of the Volkswagen Foundation. Please refer website.
No. of awards offered: 10 to 15
Closing Date: 1 April
Additional Information: Persons who obtained their doctorate (date of defense) less than one year ago as of April 1st are not eligible to apply. For more information www.volkswagenstiftung.de/en/funding/our-funding-portfolio-at-a-glance/freigeist-fellowships

W

W.F. Albright Institute of Archaeological Research

26 Salah ed-Din Street, P.O. Box 19096, Jerusalem 9711049, Israel.

Tel: (972) 2 628 8956
Email: albrightinstitute@aiar.org
Website: www.aiar.org/

The W.F. Albright Institute of Archaeological Research is a non-profit organization formed to engage in and facilitate research on the history and cultures of the Near East, to document and preserve evidence from the ancient world as a cultural resource, and to educate the public about the history and cultures of the region.

Sean W. Dever Memorial Prize

Purpose: The W.F. Albright Institute of Archaeological Research in Jerusalem announces the Sean W. Dever Memorial Prize call for papers.
Eligibility: Authors must be Ph.D. candidates in the semester in which the winner is announced (Spring).
Level of Study: Doctorate, Postdoctorate
Type: Prize
Value: US$750
Frequency: Annual
Country of Study: Israel
Application Procedure: Scholarship website: https://aiar.org/available-fellowships
Closing Date: 1 February
Funding: Private

Wageningen University

P.O. Box 9101, NL-6700 HB Wageningen, Netherlands.

Tel: (31) 317 480 100
Website: www.wur.nl/en/wageningen-university.htm
Contact: Wageningen University and Research

Wageningen University & Research is a collaboration between Wageningen University and the Wageningen Research foundation. 'To explore the potential of nature to improve the quality of life' - that is the mission of Wageningen University & Research.

Africa Scholarship Programme

Purpose: The Africa Scholarship Program (ASP) has been initiated by Wageningen University and Research to give talented and motivated students from Africa the opportunity to study at the university in Wageningen.
Eligibility: 1. You are a citizen of an African country. 2. You are an excellent student with a First class honours degree or a GPA of 80% or higher in a Bachelor degree. 3. You have applied for one the master's programmes of Wageningen University and Research.
Level of Study: MBA, Masters Degree, Postgraduate, Postgraduate (MSc)
Type: Scholarship
Length of Study: 2 years
Frequency: Annual
Country of Study: Any country
No. of awards offered: 10
Closing Date: 15 January

Palgrave Macmillan (ed.), *The Grants Register 2024*,
https://doi.org/10.1057/978-1-349-96073-6

Funding: Foundation
Additional Information: Only candidates who have been invited for the ASP selection have received an e-mail. If you have not received an invitation to apply for this scholarship, you have not been selected to participate. www.wur.nl/en/education-programmes/master/practical-information-masters/scholarships-for-international-masters-students/africa-scholarship-programme.htm

For further information contact:

Tel: (1) 800 311 6823
Email: walmartdependent@applyISTS.com

Anne van den Ban Fund

Purpose: The Anne van den Ban Fund allows promising students from developing countries to follow a MSc education at Wageningen University.
Eligibility: International students from developing countries starting an MSc programme in September 2024
Level of Study: Postgraduate (MSc)
Type: Funding support
Value: Full and partial scholarships.
Application Procedure: This scholarship is based on invitation.
Closing Date: 15 May
Additional Information: For more information see website: https://www.wur.nl/en/benefactors/more-information-1/information-for-applicants/anne-van-den-ban-fund.htm

DUO - Study Grant (only for EU-students)

Eligibility: Students under 30 who have the Dutch nationality or a residence permit type II, III, IV of V.
Level of Study: Postgraduate (MSc)
Type: Scholarship
Value: Partial scholarship or loan.
Application Procedure: see website: duo.nl/particulier/international-student/
Additional Information: Website: www.wur.nl/en/education-programmes/master/practical-information-masters/scholarships-for-international-masters-students.htm

Excellence Programme (MSc/Non-EEA)

Purpose: The Excellence Programme is initiated by Wageningen University & Research to attract excellent students for a Master's programme, and who might have the potential to do a PhD after their MSc graduation. In Wageningen or elsewhere.
Eligibility: 1. You come from a country outside the European Economic Area (and Switzerland) 2. You have applied for one of the MSc programmes at Wageningen University & Research before 1 February 2023. Please see: How can I apply for the master's programme? 3. You have a high GPA of 80% or higher. A First Class honours BSc graduation or equivalent is required 4. One or two letter(s) of recommendation uploaded during your MSc application; written by a dean, teacher or academic supervisor that demonstrates your affinity and talent for academic research
Level of Study: Masters Degree, Postgraduate (MSc)
Type: Scholarship
Value: 1. A tuition fee waiver for the duration of the programme (24 months) 2. A budget for one seminar in Europe (travel, stay, registration fee) 3. A budget for participation in the 'Future Potential programme'
Length of Study: 24 months
Application Procedure: 1. If you feel that that the requirements above apply to you, you can apply for an MSc programme and, after being unconditionally admitted, we might invite you to participate in the Excellence Programme selection procedure. 2. For the MSc application please see: How can I apply for the master's programme? (Non EU/EFTA): www.wur.nl/en/Education-Programmes/master/Apply-for-a-Master-programme/Apply-for-a-Master-programme-non-EUEFTA.htm 3. A list of Wageningen University MSc programmes can be found here: www.wur.nl/en/Education-Programmes/master.htm
Closing Date: 1 February
No. of applicants last year: 10
Additional Information: For more information see website: www.wur.nl/en/education-programmes/master/practical-information-masters/scholarships-for-international-masters-students/excellence-programme.htm

Holland Scholarship for international Master Students

Purpose: The scholarship is meant for international students from one of the selected countries outside the European Economic Areas (EEA) who wish to pursue a bachelor's or master's degree in Holland.
Eligibility: 1. You are an excellent applicant from Australia, Brazil, Canada, Chile, Colombia, Costa Rica, Ecuador, Guatemala, Honduras, India, Indonesia, Japan, Mexico, New Zealand, Peru, South Africa, South Korea, Taiwan, Thailand, Turkey, United Kingdom, United States or Vietnam. 2. You have (un-)conditional admission to one of our on campus MSc programmes. 3. You did not participate in a degree programme in the Netherlands before. * Students

with a double nationality (EU and Non-EEA nationality) must contact the Student Service Centre to check whether they are eligible for a scholarship.
Level of Study: Masters Degree, Postgraduate (MSc)
Type: Scholarship
Value: Upto €15.000
Application Procedure: The form will be available to invited students only. Eligible students will receive an e-mail about the application process. You could be eligible for this scholarship if you meet the criteria mentioned above.
Closing Date: 1 May
Contributor: The Ministry of Education, Culture and Science
Additional Information: For more information see website: www.wur.nl/en/education-programmes/master/practical-information-masters/scholarships-for-international-masters-students/holland-scholarship-programme.htm

Orange Tulip Scholarship

Purpose: The Orange Tulip Scholarship Programme is organised by Nuffic Neso and gives talented students, both bachelor's as master's students, the opportunity to study at Wageningen University & Research.
Eligibility: 1. You are admitted to a master's programme at Wageningen University & Research 2. Meet the English language proficiency requirement: www.wur.nl/en/education-programmes/master/practical-information-masters/apply-for-a-master-programme.htm for your master's programme 3. You are a citizen of one the mentioned Neso countries and currently not studying or working already in the Netherlands 4. You have a nationality as a result of which you are not eligible for the lower European tuition fees 5. You will start next year with a master's programme at Wageningen University & Research
Level of Study: Masters Degree
Type: Scholarship
Value: Reduction of 25% on the regular tuition fee for non-EU/EFTA students.
Length of Study: For two study years
Application Procedure: The procedure and application link: 1. Nuffic Neso India: www.studyinholland.nl/finances/orange-tulip-scholarship-programme/ots-india/apply-for-ots-india 2. Nuffic Neso Indonesia: www.studyinholland.nl/finances/orange-tulip-scholarship-programme/ots-indonesia/apply-for-ots-indonesia
Closing Date: 1 May
Additional Information: Note: The Orange Tulip Scholarship is not a full scholarship. So, be aware that it does not include living costs. Website: www.wur.nl/en/education-programmes/master/practical-information-masters/scholarships-for-international-masters-students/orange-tulip-scholarship.htm

Wageningen University Fellowship Programme

Purpose: With the WU Fellowship Programme, Wageningen University & Research aims to attract talented students with a non-EEA nationality by offering them financial support by means of waiving some or all of the tuition fees.
Eligibility: International MSc students from outside the European Economic Area (including Switzerland) starting an MSc programme in September 2024
Level of Study: Postgraduate (MSc)
Type: Fellowship
Value: Full or partial tuition fee support.
Application Procedure: This scholarship is based on co-financing with funds and organisations.
Closing Date: 1 February
Additional Information: For more Details: www.wur.nl/en/education-programmes/master/practical-information-masters/scholarships-for-international-masters-students.htm

Warsaw Agricultural University The International Institute of Management and Marketing in Agri-Business (IZMA)

Nowoursynowska 166, PL-02 787 Warsaw, Poland.

Tel: (48) 22 59 31 000
Email: izma@sggw.waw.pl
Website: www.sggw.pl/en/
Contact: MBA Admissions Officer

The Warsaw University of Life Sciences is the largest agricultural university in Poland, established in 1816 in Warsaw. The University is since 2005 a member of the Euroleague for Life Sciences which was established in 2001.

Warsaw Agricultural University MBA in Agribusiness Management

Length of Study: 2–5 years
Application Procedure: Applicants must supply an application form together with the following transcripts from previous institutions, a leaving school certificate, three passport photos, a certificate of physical fitness, relevant identification documents. All documents must be translated into Polish by an official translator.

For further information contact:

Tel: (48) 22 843 9751
Fax: (48) 22 843 1877
Email: majewski@alpha.sggw.waw.pl

Washington University

Graduate School of Arts and Sciences, Box 1186, 1 Brookings Drive, St. Louis, MO 63130-4899, United States of America.

Tel: (1) 314 935 5000
Email: graduateartsci@wustl.edu
Website: www.wustl.edu/
Contact: Dr Nancy P. Pope, Associate Dean

Washington University has grown to be a world-class research university with our roots firmly in St. Louis. We have come together throughout our mutual history, creating benefits and opportunities for everyone in the community.

Olin School of Business Washington University MBA Programme

Purpose: Our Program Focuses on Practicing and Mastering Management Concepts.
Eligibility: 1. Admission to the Olin MBA Program is competitive. 2. Each applicant is carefully considered by the Olin Admissions Committee-using both objective and subjective criteria-and there is no formula used to arrive at a decision. 3. Rather, the Admissions Committee takes a holistic approach to candidate evaluation with specific interest in your academic ability, professional potential, leadership qualities, communication and interpersonal skills, demonstrated achievements, motivation, and diversity.
Level of Study: MBA, Masters Degree
Type: Programme
Length of Study: 2 years
Frequency: Annual
Country of Study: Any country
Application Procedure: 1. Resume. 2. Three required essays. 3. Standardized test scores. 4. Academic transcripts and One professional recommendation.
Closing Date: 24 March
Additional Information: There is no application fee for the Full-time MBA Program. olin.wustl.edu/EN-US/academic-programs/professional-mba/admissions/tuition-and-financial-aid/Pages/default.aspx

Washington American Indian Endowed Scholarship

Purpose: The American Indian Endowed Scholarship (AIES) helps financially needy students with close social and cultural ties to an American Indian community in the state of Washington. Students can use the scholarships at public colleges and many independent colleges in Washington. The program prioritizes upper-division and graduate-level students, but all applicants are considered.
Eligibility: Applicants must meet the following criteria 1. Demonstrate financial need based on a completed FAFSA (Free Application for Federal Student Aid). 2. Meet Washington State residency requirements for financial aid. 3. Intend to enroll full-time as an undergraduate or graduate student at a participating public or private college or university in Washington State fall term of the application year. 4. Intend to use their education to benefit the American Indian community in Washington State. 5. Not pursue a degree in theology. 6. Have not yet received a total of five years of this scholarship
Level of Study: Graduate
Type: Scholarship
Value: US$500 to US$2,000
Length of Study: Up to 5 years
Frequency: Annual
Country of Study: United States of America
Application Procedure: 1. Read the application and instruction sheet. 2. Compile and complete the required attachments. 3. Complete and sign the AIES application form. 4. Print and mail the application and required attachments to the WSAC address printed on the application form, postmarked by March 1, 2024.
No. of awards offered: Varies
Closing Date: 1 March
Funding: Private
Additional Information: Website: wsac.wa.gov/american-indian-endowed-scholarship#eligibility-requirements

Wellcome Trust

Gibbs Building, 215 Euston Road, London NW1 2BE, United Kingdom.

Tel: (44) 20 7611 8888
Email: grantenquiries@wellcome.ac.uk
Website: www.wellcome.ac.uk

The Wellcome Trust's mission is to foster and promote research with the aim of improving human and animal health.

The Trust funds most areas of biomedical research and funds research in the history of medicine, biomedical ethics, public engagement of science.

Four-year PhD Studentship Programmes

Purpose: This scheme offers graduates outstanding training in scientific research.
Eligibility: You can apply for a studentship on one of Wellcome's four-year programmes if you're a graduate or student who has, or expects to obtain, a degree (or equivalent for EU and overseas candidates) in a relevant subject. Candidates with other relevant qualifications or research experience may also be eligible. For more information about eligibility, contact the individual programmes listed in the 'How to apply' section on this page.
Level of Study: Postgraduate, Research
Type: Studentship
Value: Studentship stipend, fees and other costs
Length of Study: 4 years
Country of Study: Any country
Application Procedure: To apply for a Four-year PhD Studentship in Science, contact one of the programmes mentioned in webpage. Please don't apply to Wellcome.
Funding: Trusts
Additional Information: For more informations: wellcome.org/grant-funding/schemes/four-year-phd-programmes-studentships-basic-scientists

For further information contact:

Email: 4yrphd@wellcome.ac.uk

International Training Fellowships

Purpose: This scheme offers nationals of low- and middle-income countries the opportunity to receive training at postgraduate or postdoctoral level.
Eligibility: 1. You're a national of a low- or middle-income country 2. Your proposed research focuses on a health priority in a low- or middle-income country 3. You have sponsorship from an eligible host organisation in a low- or middle-income country apart from mainland China. 4. You must want to undertake a guided period of research so that you can consolidate your existing experience and explore new areas of research. 5. You must have a PhD and be an early-career researcher or have a degree in a relevant subject and some initial research experience or be a clinically qualified doctor (and be qualified to enter higher specialist training), vet, dentist or clinical psychologist, and have some initial research experience.
Level of Study: Postgraduate
Type: Fellowship
Value: Usually £15,000 to £300,000 for salary, fees and research expenses.
Length of Study: 3 year
Frequency: Annual
Application Procedure: You must submit your application through the Wellcome Trust Grant Tracker (WTGT).
Closing Date: 9 July
Funding: Trusts

For further information contact:

Gibbs Building, 215 Euston Road, London NW1 2BE, United Kingdom.

Tel: (44) 20 7611 5757

Learned Society Curation Awards

Purpose: These awards support learned society publishers who want to explore new ways of signalling the significance of published research outputs in an open and transparent manner.
Level of Study: Research
Type: Award
Value: Up to £200,000
Length of Study: 3 year
Frequency: Annual
Application Procedure: You must submit your application through the Wellcome Trust Grant Tracker (WTGT).
Closing Date: 20 April
Funding: Trusts
Additional Information: Website: wellcome.org/grant-funding/schemes/learned-society-curation-awards-closed

For further information contact:

Gibbs Building, 215 Euston Road, London NW1 2BE, United Kingdom.

Tel: (44) 20 7611 5757
Email: openresearch@wellcome.ac.uk

Master's Awards

Purpose: This scheme enables scholars to undertake basic training in research and methods through a 1-year Master's course in medical history and humanities.
Eligibility: You should have a minimum of an excellent upper-second-class honours degree (or equivalent) in a relevant subject. Applications will not be considered from

those who have already received support for their postgraduate studies from another funding body.
Level of Study: Postgraduate, Research
Type: Award
Value: The award is for 1 year. It includes the student's stipend and all compulsory university and college fees at the United Kingdom home postgraduate student level. Fees at the overseas rate will not be provided.
Frequency: Annual
Application Procedure: All enquiries about Master's Awards should be made directly to the relevant institution.
Closing Date: 1 May
Funding: Trusts

For further information contact:

Tel: (44) 20 7611 5757
Email: MHgrants@wellcome.ac.uk

Master's Studentships in Humanities and Social Science

Purpose: This scheme enables researchers to undertake humanities or social science Master's courses in any area of health.
Eligibility: You can apply to one of the Master's programmes that we fund if you want to develop humanities or social science research skills and train in an area of health. You can apply before you graduate, but you must have obtained your degree (or equivalent) before taking up the award. Find out more about eligibility by going to the websites of the programmes
Level of Study: Masters Degree, Postgraduate
Type: Studentship
Value: Studentship stipend and fees covered
Length of Study: 1 year
Application Procedure: Please don't apply to Wellcome. Instead, you should apply directly to one of the programmes below that mentioned in webpage
Additional Information: Website: wellcome.org/grant-funding/schemes/masters-studentships-humanities-and-social-science

Research Fellowships

Purpose: Due to the multidisciplinary nature of research on the social and ethical aspects of biomedicine and healthcare, Research Fellowships may provide postdoctoral researchers with support to enable them to obtain research training, either in a new discipline or in a new aspect of their own field, e.g. a humanities scholar who wishes to be trained in social science. In such cases, the requested training must form a substantial component of the proposed research and should not normally be available via the standard funding routes, e.g. by learning new skills as a postdoctoral researcher on a project grant. The requested training should also include methodologies and skills that are new to the applicant. Research training provision can include participation in taught courses, and periods spent in other research groups gaining practical, technical or other skills for introduction to the sponsor's or individual's own group.
Eligibility: You are eligible to apply if you are a postdoctoral scholar who is not in a tenured or otherwise long-term established post. Fellowships must be held at a United Kingdom, Irish or low- or middle-income country institution. You will also be expected to have been awarded your PhD before you are eligible to apply. Applications from candidates who are still awaiting their viva by the time of the full application will not normally be accepted.
Level of Study: Research
Type: Fellowship
Value: An award will not normally exceed £250,000, exclusive of any standard Wellcome Trust allowances. Fellowships provide a salary, plus appropriate employer's contributions. Essential research expenses, including travel and fieldwork, are available, as is a set amount for travel to conferences, seminars and other meetings of a scholarly nature.
Length of Study: 3 years
Application Procedure: Preliminary applications should be made in writing, and include a brief curriculum vitae and full publication list; details of research proposed (maximum of 1 page); a letter of support from the head of department in which you will be working; the approximate cost of the proposal, broken down into equipment and project running expenses.
Funding: Trusts

For further information contact:

Tel: (44) 20 7611 5757
Email: MHgrants@wellcome.ac.uk

Research Fellowships in Humanities and Social Science

Purpose: This scheme supports postdoctoral researchers in health-related humanities and social sciences who do not hold established academic posts.
Level of Study: Postdoctoral

Type: Fellowship
Value: Salary and research expenses covered.
Length of Study: 3 year
Frequency: Annual
Application Procedure: You must submit your application through the Wellcome Trust Grant Tracker (WTGT).
Closing Date: 10 September

For further information contact:

Gibbs Building, 215 Euston Road, London NW1 2BE, United Kingdom.

Tel: (44) 20 7611 5757
Email: hss@wellcome.ac.uk.

Senior and Intermediate Research Fellowship for International Students

Purpose: The aim of the fellowship is to support outstanding researchers of any nationality, either medically qualified or science graduates, who wish to pursue a research career in an academic institution in India.
Eligibility: 1. This competition is open for basic science/veterinary researchers with 4–15 years of post-PhD research experience; applicant can have a PhD in any discipline of science. 2. Applicants are advised to choose the most appropriate scheme based on their qualification, research experience, track record, and aspirations. They may refer to the guidance notes, provisions, and mandates of the schemes. The Office reserves the right to advise on the suitability of the scheme. 3. There are no age or nationality restrictions. The applicant need not be resident in India while applying but should be willing to relocate to and work in India. 4. A salaried position or commitment towards a salaried position at the Host Institution is not required.
Type: Research
Value: The 5-year Fellowship provides: 1. Competitive personal salary support 2. Generous and flexible funds for research 3. Funds to develop international collaborations
Study Establishment: Fellowship is awarded to support biomedical research that is relevant to human and animal welfare.
Country of Study: India
Application Procedure: Preliminary Application forms shall be launched at the India Alliance online application System (IASys): grants.indiaalliance.org/Login/. We will assess your eligibility and competitiveness; if suitable, we will invite you to submit a full application for the subsequent steps of review and interview.
Closing Date: 1 March
Additional Information: For further information on these Fellowships, please click here. Queries may be addressed to info@indiaalliance.org website www.indiaalliance.org/news/sif-call-for-applications

For further information contact:

Email: info@wellcomedbt.org

Senior Fellowships in Public Health and Tropical Medicine

Purpose: Senior Fellowships in Public Health and Tropical Medicine: The scheme supports outstanding researchers from developing countries to establish themselves as leading investigators at an academic institution in a developing country location.
Eligibility: You must be a national or legal resident of a developing country, and be either a: 1. Graduate in a subject relevant to public health or tropical medicine (for example; biomedical or social science, veterinary medicine, physics, chemistry or mathematics) with a PhD and at least five years' postdoctoral experience, or 2. Medical graduate with a higher qualification equivalent to membership of the UK Royal College of Physicians, or be recognised as a specialist within a relevant research area, and have at least five years' research experience. Applicants who do not have a PhD but who are educated to first degree or Master's level and have substantial research experience, as evidenced by their publication record, may be considered.
Level of Study: Postgraduate, Research
Type: Fellowship
Value: A basic salary; research expenses (e.g. consumables, equipment, collaborative travel, research assistance, technical support), training costs where appropriate and justified; an inflation/flexible funding allowance and support to attend scientific meetings; and contributions to costs of the project that are directly incurred by the overseas institution may also be provided.
Length of Study: Up to 5 years
Application Procedure: Applications are considered three times a year. For further information on application process, see: Senior Fellowships in Public Health and Tropical Medicine Website: www.wellcome.ac.uk/News/2011/index.htm
Funding: Trusts
Additional Information: website: www.advance-africa.com/Fellowships-in-Public-Health-and-Tropical-Medicine.html

For further information contact:

Tel: (44) 20 7611 5757
Email: sciencegrants@wellcome.ac.uk

The Hub Award

Purpose: The Hub Award brings researchers and creative professionals together at Wellcome Collection to work as a collaborative residency.
Type: Award
Value: Flexible funding, up to £1 million
Length of Study: 1 to 2 year
Frequency: Annual
Application Procedure: You must submit your application through the Wellcome Trust Grant Tracker (WTGT).
Closing Date: 20 February
Additional Information: Website: wellcome.org/grant-funding/schemes/hub-award

For further information contact:

Gibbs Building, 215 Euston Road, London NW1 2BE, United Kingdom.

Tel: (44) 20 7611 5757

Training Fellowships in Public Health and Tropical Medicine

Purpose: This scheme provides researchers from low- and middle-income countries - who are at an early stage in the establishment of their research careers - with opportunities for research experience and high-quality research training in public health and tropical medicine. Research projects should be aimed at understanding and controlling diseases (either human or animal) of relevance to local, national or global health. This can include laboratory-based molecular analysis of field or clinical samples, but projects focused solely on studies in vitro or using animal models will not normally be considered under this scheme.
Eligibility: Applications are only accepted in the Public Health and Tropical Medicine Interview Committee remit. This covers research on infectious and non-communicable diseases within the fields of public health and tropical medicine that is aimed at understanding and controlling diseases (either human or animal) of relevance to local, national or global health. You must be a national or legal resident of a low- and middle-income country and should be either: 1. A graduate in a subject relevant to public health or tropical medicine (e.g. biomedical or social science, veterinary medicine, physics, chemistry or mathematics) with a PhD and no more than three years' postdoctoral experience, or 2. A medical graduate with a higher qualification equivalent to membership of the UK Royal Colleges of Physicians (i.e. qualified to enter higher specialist training) and some initial research experience. Applicants may also apply if they do not have a PhD, but have a clinical, basic or Master's degree and some initial research experience, with the expectation that they will register for a PhD.
Level of Study: Postgraduate, Research
Type: Fellowship
Value: see website
Length of Study: 3 years
Application Procedure: You are required to complete and submit a preliminary application form (Word 236kB) by the published deadline. The form should be emailed to e-mail: phatic@wellcome.ac.uk. Completed forms will normally be assessed within one month of the preliminary deadline. If the preliminary application meets the scheme's requirements, you will be invited to submit a full application.
Closing Date: 27 November
Funding: Trusts
Additional Information: website: www.postgraduatefunding.com/award-781

For further information contact:

Tel: (44) 20 7611 8888
Email: contact@wellcome.ac.uk; phatic@wellcome.ac.uk

Translation Fund

Purpose: Translation Awards are response-mode funding designed to bridge the funding gap in the commercialisation of new technologies in the biomedical area.
Eligibility: Projects must address an unmet need in healthcare or in applied medical research, offer a potential new solution, and have a realistic expectation that the innovation will be developed further by the market. Institutions Eligible institutions are not-for-profit research institutions, including those funded by the Medical Research Council, Cancer Research United Kingdom, and Biotechnology and Biological Sciences Research Council, in the United Kingdom. Institutions are normally required to sign up to a short funding agreement and the Grant Conditions. Companies We are able to use our charitable monies to fund commercial companies to meet our charitable objectives through programme-related investment (PRI). For further details please refer to our policy on PRI. Companies will normally be expected to sign up to specific terms relating to the scheme. Overseas organizations United Kingdom organizations may contract or collaborate with overseas organizations. Although overseas organizations are not eligible for Translation Awards, some proposals may be invited for consideration as a Strategic Translation Award (including Seeding Drug Discovery). Overseas organizations should contact Technology Transfer staff about their proposed project in the first instance. Principal applicants and coapplicants applicants should normally hold a position of

responsibility within the eligible organization and be able to sign up to or comply with the conditions or terms of an award. In addition, postdoctoral research assistants–whether seeking their own salary as part of the grant proposal, funded by the Wellcome Trust on another grant, or funded by another agency–are eligible for coapplicant status if they make a significant contribution to a research proposal and have agreement from their funding agency. Other eligibility information Disciplines outside biomedicine – researchers from disciplines outside biomedicine can apply providing the application of research is designed to facilitate or meet a need in healthcare. For example, the application of physics, chemistry, computing, engineering and materials science to the development of medical products is entirely appropriate. Healthcare need in an area that is not commercially attractive. We are committed to the translation of research into practical healthcare benefits across the full spectrum of disease. Disease areas neglected by industry because of the lack of a return on investment pose a particular problem, but imaginative ways forward can sometimes be developed (e.g. public-private partnerships such as the Medicines for Malaria Venture). Intellectual property rights (IPR)/publications – if there are any restrictions on IPR or publications arising from your research, you must provide a written statement that details them. Restrictions on intellectual property may affect your eligibility to apply to the Trust. Please refer to our Grant Conditions.
Level of Study: Research
Type: Award
Value: The important criterion is to develop the innovation to the point at which it can be adopted by another party. Providing it is adequately justified, modest equipment purchase and maintenance costs may be included in a Translation Award application. Building or refurbishment expenditure will not normally be considered. Applications may not include requests for academic institutional overheads. If you hold a tenured university post, you may not re-charge your salary (in full or part) to a Translation Award.
Application Procedure: A preliminary application form must be completed and sent to Technology Transfer by the published deadline. Preliminary applications are subject to a triage for shortlisting for the full application stage. Applications will be considered by the Technology Transfer Challenge Committee (TTCC), which meets twice a year. Full applications will be invited following the triage meeting. Shortlisted applicants will be invited to submit a full application and will be subject to international peer review and due diligence. Applicants will be expected to make a presentation on their proposal to the TTCC. Unless otherwise advised, this will be at the next scheduled meeting of the TTCC.
Funding: Trusts
Additional Information: www.erc-online.eu/financial-support/translation-fund/

For further information contact:

Tel: (44) 20 7611 5757
Fax: (44) 20 7611 8857
Email: innovations@wellcome.ac.uk

University Awards

Purpose: This scheme allows universities to attract outstanding research staff by providing support for up to 5 years, after which time the award holder takes up a guaranteed permanent post in the university. A monograph and other substantial publications are expected to result from an award, so teaching and other non-research commitments are expected to be minimal during the period of full Wellcome Trust support.
Eligibility: You must be nominated by your prospective head of department and have an undertaking from the head of the institution, vice-chancellor, principal or dean that your personal support will be taken over by the institution at the end of the award. Support is normally available only at lecturer level, although in exceptional cases awards to senior-lecturer level may be possible.
Level of Study: Research
Type: Award
Value: Up to 5 years' support is available, providing your full salary for 3 years, 50% in the fourth year and 25% in the fifth year. Travel expenses to attend meetings are provided for 5 years, but research expenses are provided for the first 3 years of the award only.
Application Procedure: Initial enquiries about the scheme may be made by you (the potential candidate) or a department in an institution. These enquiries should be followed by a preliminary application from you by email or post including an explicit statement from the head of the institution, vice-chancellor or dean demonstrating the institution's commitment to the history of medicine field, and a statement confirming that the institution will provide 50% salary costs in year four, 75% in year 5 and full salary thereafter; curriculum vitae and full publication list; an outline of no more than two pages of the proposed project; a letter of support from the head of department, including a statement on your expected teaching/administrative load for the 5-year period (this can be sent by separate cover); the approximate cost of the proposal, broken down into your salary, equipment and project running costs.
Funding: Trusts
Additional Information: www.studentaffairs.ku.edu/university-awards

For further information contact:

Tel: (44) 20 7611 5757
Email: MHgrants@wellcome.ac.uk

Wellcome Discovery Awards

Purpose: This scheme provides funding for established researchers and teams from any discipline who want to pursue bold and creative research ideas to deliver significant shifts in understanding that could improve human life, health and wellbeing.
Eligibility: You can apply for a Wellcome Discovery Award if you are a researcher who wants to pursue bold and creative research ideas. You must aim to make a major contribution to your research field by: 1. generating significant shifts in understanding and/or 2. developing methodologies, conceptual frameworks, tools or techniques that could benefit health-related research.
Level of Study: Research
Type: Award
Length of Study: Maximum 8 years
Country of Study: Any country
Application Procedure: See website for application process & application link: wtgrants.wellcome.org/Login.aspx?ReturnUrl=/
Closing Date: 11 April
Additional Information: website: wellcome.org/grant-funding/schemes/discovery-awards

For further information contact:

Tel: (44) 20 7611 5757

Wellcome Early-Career Awards

Purpose: This scheme provides funding for early-career researchers from any discipline who are ready to develop their research identity. Through innovative projects, they will deliver shifts in understanding that could improve human life, health and wellbeing. By the end of the award, they will be ready to lead their own independent research programme.
Eligibility: You can apply to this scheme if you are an early-career researcher and you are ready to design, plan and deliver your own innovative research project that aims to: 1. advance understanding in your field and/or 2. develop methodologies, conceptual frameworks, tools or techniques that could benefit health-related research.
Level of Study: Postgraduate
Type: Award
Value: Up to £400,000
Length of Study: 5 years
Frequency: Annual
Country of Study: Any country
Application Procedure: see website for application procedure. Appication form: wtgrants.wellcome.org/Login.aspx?ReturnUrl=/
Closing Date: 18 May
Additional Information: Website: https://wellcome.org/grant-funding/schemes/early-career-awards

For further information contact:

Tel: (44) 20 7611 5757

Wellcome Trust and NIH Four-Year PhD Studentships

Purpose: This scheme provides opportunities for the most promising postgraduate students to undertake international, collaborative four-year PhD training based in both a United Kingdom/Republic of Ireland (RoI) academic institution and the intramural campus of the National Institutes of Health at Bethesda (Maryland, United States of America).
Eligibility: You should be a United Kingdom/European Economic Area (EEA) national with (or be in your final year and expected to obtain) a first- or upper-second-class honours degree or an equivalent EEA graduate qualification. You must have 1. A suitable doctoral supervisor at an eligible academic host institution in the United Kingdom or Republic of Ireland. The host institution must be able to confer doctoral degrees; 2. A suitable supervisor at a NIH institute. The NIH supervisor should hold a tenured or tenured-track position for the proposed period of the award and should be willing to provide funding for the student whilst at the NIH.
Level of Study: Doctorate, Research
Type: Studentship
Value: The studentship is awarded for 4 years with support provided by the Wellcome Trust (in the United Kingdom/Republic of Ireland) and the NIH (in the United States of America). Our funding will provide support for the student's stipend, PhD fees, college fees (if required) and a contribution towards research costs.
Length of Study: 4 year
Frequency: Annual
Application Procedure: The application form should be completed and submitted by the closing date. An electronic copy (as a Word document) should be emailed to wtnih@wellcome.ac.uk
Funding: Trusts

For further information contact:

Wellcome Trust-NIH PhD Studentships, Wellcome Trust, Gibbs Building, 215 Euston Road, Bloomsbury, London NW1 2BE, United Kingdom.

Email: wtnih@wellcome.ac.uk

Wellcome Trust-POST Fellowships in Medical History and Humanities

Purpose: This scheme enables a PhD student or junior fellow funded through the Wellcome Trust Medical History and Humanities (MHH) programme to undertake a 3-month fellowship at the Parliamentary Office of Science and Technology (POST).
Eligibility: Applicants should be in the second or third year of their PhD or in the first year of a fellowship funded by the MHH Programme. POST is a strictly non-partisan organization. Wellcome Trust-POST Fellows will be required to abstain from any lobbying or party political activity, and generally uphold the principles of parliamentary service, including a commitment to confidentiality, during their time with the Office. All provisionally selected candidates must sign a declaration to this effect. They must also receive security clearance from the parliamentary security authorities as a condition of finally taking up the fellowship.
Level of Study: Postdoctorate, Research
Type: Fellowship
Value: The successful applicant will receive a fully funded 3-month extension to their PhD or fellowship award. While placements typically last 3-months, they may be extended under exceptional circumstances. If the successful applicant is not within reasonable daily travelling distance to POST in London, the Wellcome Trust will consider paying travel and accommodation costs up to a maximum of £2,000.
Frequency: Annual
Application Procedure: An application should include the application form, your curriculum vitae, a letter of support from your sponsor/supervisor and a summary of a proposed topic for a POST publication. The summary should be no longer than 1,000 words and should demonstrate why you think this subject would be of particular parliamentary interest; how the training you have received and your research to date will enable you to carry out this work; your ability to write in a style suitable for a parliamentary (rather than an academic) audience.
Closing Date: 23 November
Funding: Trusts
Additional Information: Check website for more details www.studentaffairs.ku.edu/university-awards

For further information contact:

Tel: (44) 20 7611 5757
Email: MHgrants@wellcome.ac.uk

Wells Mountain Foundation

25 Main Street, Bristol, VT 05443, United States of America.

Tel: (1) 877 318 6116
Website: www.wellsmountaininitiative.org/

WMF is a non-profit, tax-exempt charity qualified of the US Internal Revenue Code. Wells Mountain Foundation has as its focus education, which they believe is the key building block to success in all other endeavors, literacy, the essential tie to the knowledge contained in the written word, and community, the core entity, just beyond the family, critical to building a compassionate and effective society.

Woodcock-Munoz Foundation Empowerment Through Education Scholarships

Purpose: The Foundation believes in the power and importance of community service; therefore, all scholarship participants are required to volunteer for a minimum of 100 hours a year.
Eligibility: WMF's ideal candidate is a student, male or female, from a country in the developing world, who: 1. Successfully completed a secondary education, with good to excellent grades 2. Is 35 or under on 1 March 2024 3. Will be studying in his or her country or another country in the developing world* 4. Is pursuing his or her first bachelor's degree or diploma 5. Will be enrolled in a program of study that will benefit the community and/or contribute to the continued growth and advancement of his or her home country 6. Plans to live and work in his or her own country after graduation 7. Has demonstrated his or her commitment to giving back and has volunteered prior to applying 8. May have some other funds available for his or her education, but will not be able to go to pursue his or her tertiary degree without financial assistance
Level of Study: Graduate
Type: Scholarship
Value: Average of US$1,500 for tuition and fee, books and materials.
Frequency: Annual
Country of Study: United States of America
Application Procedure: To apply for the Empowerment Through Education (ETE) program, you must submit a complete application via the online scholarship application

portal (preferred method) or via postal mail to the Foundation's office. The Empowerment Through Education online application will be available from 1 December 2023 to 1 March 2024. It is important to visit the official website (link found below) to access the application form and for detailed information on how to apply for this scholarship.
Closing Date: 1 March
Funding: Private
Additional Information: Official Scholarship Website: www.wellsmountainfoundation.org/our-programs/scholarships/ website: www.scholars4dev.com/5802/wmf-scholarships-for-developing-country-students/

Wenner-Gren Foundation for Anthropological Research

655 Third Avenue, 23rd Floor, New York, NY 10017, United States of America.

Tel: (1) 212 683 5000
Email: inquiries@wennergren.org
Website: www.wennergren.org

The Wenner-Gren Foundation is a private operating foundation dedicated to providing leadership in support of anthropology and anthropologists worldwide.

Conference and Workshop Grant

Purpose: This grant program supports meetings and events that promote the development of inclusive communities of anthropologists and advance significant and innovative research.
Eligibility: Doctorates in Anthropology, Doctorates in Related Fields, Independent Scholars. For more information see website
Level of Study: Doctorate
Type: Grant
Value: The maximum Conference and Workshop Grant is US$20,000
Application Procedure: To present your conference or workshop in the best possible light, please follow all instructions for completing your application. Use all the available space to describe your event. If you have questions, contact us at applications@wennergren.org or (1) 212 683 5000. You may access the application portal for conferences here: www.tfaforms.com/4970704. The application portal for workshops is here: www.tfaforms.com/4971305.
Closing Date: 1 December
Additional Information: Website: wennergren.org/program/conference-and-workshop-grant/

For further information contact:

Tel: (1) 212 683 5000
Email: applications@wennergren.org

Dissertation Fieldwork Grant

Purpose: Our goal is to support vibrant and significant work that furthers our understanding of what it means to be human. There is no preference for any methodology, research location, topic, or subfield.
Eligibility: Applicants must be enrolled in a doctoral program (or equivalent, if outside the U.S.). Qualified students of any nationality or institutional affiliation may apply. Applicants must designate a dissertation advisor or other scholar from the same institution who will take responsibility for supervising the project. To receive an award, applicants must fulfill all of their program's doctoral degree requirements, other than the dissertation/thesis, before the start date listed on their application form. Successful applicants must provide proof from their department that they have completed all the necessary coursework and exams. Unsuccessful applicants are welcome to reapply. But as part of their resubmission, they must explain how they have addressed the reviewers' concerns, along with any changes to their plans.
Level of Study: Doctorate, Research
Type: Grant
Value: The maximum Dissertation Fieldwork Grant is US$25,000
Length of Study: No limit to the duration
Application Procedure: To present your project in the best possible light, please follow all instructions for completing your application. Use all the available space to describe your project. If you have questions, contact us at applications@wennergren.org or (1) 212 683 5000. See website for more information. You may access the application portal here: www.tfaforms.com/4978023.
Closing Date: 1 May
Additional Information: Website: wennergren.org/program/dissertation-fieldwork-grant/

For further information contact:

Tel: (1) 212 683 5000
Email: applications@wennergren.org

Engaged Research Grant

Purpose: This program supports research partnerships that empower those who have historically been the subjects of anthropological research, rather than researchers themselves. Designed in alliance with individuals who have borne the impact of marginalization, these partnerships bring together scholars and their interlocutors in an effort to expand anthropological knowledge, combat inequality, and help communities flourish. The program supports projects that will make a significant contribution to anthropological conversations through collaboration and engagement.
Eligibility: Doctoral Students, Doctorates in Anthropology, Doctorates in Related Fields, Independent Scholars. for more information see website
Level of Study: Doctorate, Research
Type: Research grant
Value: The maximum Engaged Research Grant is US$25,000
Length of Study: There is no limit to the duration of the grant
Application Procedure: To present your project in the best possible light, please follow all instructions for completing your application. If you have questions, contact us at applications@wennergren.org or (1) 212 683 5000.
Closing Date: 1 August
Additional Information: Website: wennergren.org/program/engaged-research-grant/

For further information contact:

Tel: (1) 212 683 5000
Email: applications@wennergren.org

Global Initiatives Grant

Purpose: Global Initiatives Grants help support innovative projects that benefit the discipline as a whole by creating the conditions for anthropologists to do better work. We look for initiatives in which a small amount of money can have a wide and lasting impact, building capacity for the discipline to thrive.
Eligibility: Applicants of any nationality or country of residence may apply. Applicants must have a PhD in anthropology at the time of application and be affiliated with a school or organization that can carry forward the lessons learned through the project. We are eager to receive applications from individuals based in countries, regions, and communities where anthropology is disadvantaged or under threat. Although we welcome applications from teams of scholars, the primary organizer must hold a doctorate in anthropology or a related field. Graduate students are welcome to act as co applicants, but they must be listed as such for the purpose of the grant. Applicants from all nationalities and institutional locations are welcome to apply.
Level of Study: Doctorate, Postgraduate
Type: Grant
Value: Between US$5,000 to US$20,000
Application Procedure: To present your project in the best possible light, please follow all instructions for completing your application. Use all the available space to describe your project. If you have questions, contact Judy Kreid at internationalprograms@wennergren.org or (1) 212 683 5000. You may access the application portal here: www.tfaforms.com/4966592.
Closing Date: 15 May
Additional Information: Website: wennergren.org/program/global-initiatives-grant/

Hunt Postdoctoral Fellowships

Purpose: To support the writing-up of already completed research.
Eligibility: 1. Applicants must have a Ph.D. or equivalent at the time of application. 2. Applicants should be no more than ten years beyond their PhD, with allowances made for periods of caregiving, and have a doctorate in anthropology or an equivalent field. 3. Qualified scholars are eligible without regard to nationality, institutional, or departmental affiliation although preference is given to applicants who are untenured or do not yet have a permanent academic position. 4. The Hunt Postdoctoral Fellowship is to support a continuous period of full-time academic writing. The research that forms the basis of the writing project is expected to be completed at the time of application. In special circumstances and with prior approval of the Foundation, recipients may use part of their stipend for a minor research component if necessary to complete their proposed publication/s. No research funds in addition to the basic stipend are available as part of the Hunt Postdoctoral Fellowship. 5. The fellowship may be used to support the preparation of a book or monograph manuscript, journal articles, book chapters, or a combination of these forms of publication. 6. The Foundation cannot accept an application from a prior grantee unless all requirements of a previous grant have been completed. Please contact the Foundation for more information if this situation applies. 7. Prior recipients of Hunt Postdoctoral Fellowships are not eligible to apply for a second fellowship for a different writing project. 8. Hunt Postdoctoral Fellowship applications that were unsuccessful in a prior funding cycle may be resubmitted only twice. A resubmission statement explaining how the application is different from the prior application and how the referees' comments have been addressed must accompany resubmitted applications. 9. If a fellowship is awarded, the applicant must agree to comply with the

Requirements and Conditions of the Hunt Postdoctoral Fellowship.
Level of Study: Postdoctorate
Type: Fellowship
Value: Up to US$40,000
Length of Study: Nine-month
Frequency: Annual
Country of Study: Any country
Application Procedure: Applications can be downloaded from the website and must be submitted online. See website www.wennergren.org/programs/hunt-postdoctoral-fellowships/application-procedures
No. of awards offered: 89
Closing Date: 1 May
No. of awards given last year: 9
No. of applicants last year: 89

For further information contact:

Email: applications@wennergren.org

Post-PhD Research Grant

Purpose: Our goal is to support vibrant and significant work that furthers our understanding of what it means to be human.
Eligibility: Doctorates in Anthropology, Doctorates in Related Fields, Independent Scholars
Level of Study: Postdoctorate, Research
Type: Research grant
Value: The maximum Post-PhD Research Grant is US$25,000
Application Procedure: To present your project in the best possible light, please follow all instructions for completing your application. Use all the available space to describe your project. If you have questions, contact us at applications@wennergren.org or (1) 212 683 5000.
Closing Date: 1 November
Additional Information: website: wennergren.org/program/post-phd-research-grant/

For further information contact:

Tel: (1) 212 683 5000
Email: applications@wennergren.org

SAPIENS Public Scholars Training Fellowship

Eligibility: Doctoral Students, Doctorates in Anthropology, Independent Scholars. Applicants must be pursuing a research area that coincides with that year's theme. Applicants must be ABD Ph.D. students who have completed dissertation research and are currently enrolled in an anthropology degree program, have a Ph.D. in anthropology, and/or have an appointment in an anthropology department. Preference will be given to early career scholars. Qualified applicants of any nationality or institutional affiliation may apply. We also welcome applicants who hold or in the process of applying for Wenner-Gren Foundation grants.
Level of Study: Doctorate, Postgraduate
Type: Fellowship
Value: US$2,500 award upon completion of the fellowship
Application Procedure: To present yourself in the best possible light, please follow all instructions for completing the application, which must be in English. If you have questions, contact us at editor sapiens.org.
Closing Date: 15 July
Additional Information: For more information see website: wennergren.org/program/sapiens-public-scholars-training-fellowship/

Wadsworth African Fellowship

Purpose: Wadsworth African Fellowships provide funding for African students pursuing a PhD or equivalent doctoral degree at South African universities where they can receive international-level training in anthropology, including archaeology and biological anthropology.
Eligibility: This program is intended for African scholars who may not otherwise be able to pursue a doctoral degree in anthropology. They must be citizens and residents of an African country at the time of application. They must also be members of an underrepresented group in academic anthropology and archaeology. see website for more information
Level of Study: Doctorate, Postgraduate
Type: Fellowship
Value: The US$20,000 annual fellowship can be used toward travel, living expenses, tuition, income taxes, student fees, insurance, books, research costs, and any other relevant expenditures
Frequency: Annual
Application Procedure: The Foundation awards one Wadsworth African Fellowship annually. To present yourself in the best possible light, please follow all instructions for completing your application. Use all the available space to make your case. If you have questions, contact us at applications@wennergren.org or (1) 212 683 5000. You may access the application portal here: www.tfaforms.com/4938400.
Closing Date: 15 December
No. of applicants last year: 1

Additional Information: Website: wennergren.org/program/wadsworth-african-fellowship/

For further information contact:

Tel: (1) 212 683 5000
Email: applications@wennergren.org

Wadsworth International Fellowship

Purpose: The program's goal is to extend and strengthen international ties and deepen anthropological expertise globally.
Eligibility: Applicants must be from countries with limited opportunities for advanced training in anthropology. Candidates must have an application for doctoral admission pending at their chosen host institution at the time they apply for this award. The host institution must provide high-quality training in anthropology and have a strong international reputation. It may be located anywhere in the world. Successful applicants will be in residence at the host institution during the study and training component of their fellowship. For more information see website.
Level of Study: Doctorate, Postgraduate
Type: Fellowship
Value: The US$20,000 annual fellowship can be used toward travel, living expenses, tuition, income taxes, student fees, insurance, books, research costs, and any other relevant expenditures
Frequency: Annual
Application Procedure: The Foundation awards about five Wadsworth International Fellowships annually. To present yourself in the best possible light, please follow all instructions for completing your application. Use all the available space to make your case. If you have questions, contact us at applications@wennergren.org or (1) 212 683 5000. You may access the application portal here: wennergren.org/program/wadsworth-international-fellowships/.
Closing Date: 1 March
No. of applicants last year: 5
Additional Information: Website: wennergren.org/program/wadsworth-international-fellowships/

For further information contact:

Tel: (1) 212 683 5000
Email: applications@wennergren.org

Wenner-Gren Fellowship in Anthropology and Black Experiences

Purpose: The purpose of this fellowship is to expand the anthropological conversation and build capacity in anthropology as a career and field of study, amplifying perspectives previously underrepresented in the discipline.
Eligibility: This opportunity is open to anthropology PhDs of all ranks. Qualified scholars with U.S. citizenship or residency are welcome to apply.
Level of Study: Doctorate, Postgraduate
Type: Fellowship
Value: Stipend of US$50,000
Length of Study: 9 months
Application Procedure: Doctorates in Anthropology, Doctorates in Related Fields, Independent Scholars. The application process is administered by SAR. All application materials must be submitted through the SAR online application system. Emailed, mailed, or faxed application materials, including letters of recommendation, will not be accepted. Supplementary materials will not be considered. In fairness to all applicants, we do not grant on- or off-campus interviews. If you have questions, contact Wenner-Gren at inquiries@wennergren.org or (1) 212 683 5000, or SAR at scholar@sarsf.org or (1) 505 954 7201.
Closing Date: November
Additional Information: Website: wennergren.org/program/wenner-gren-fellowship-in-the-anthropology-of-black-experiences/

For further information contact:

Tel: (1) 212 683 5000; (1) 505 954 7201
Email: inquiries@wennergren.org; scholar@sarsf.org

Wharton School

Vance Hall, Suite 111, 3733 Spruce Street, Philadelphia, PA 19104-6340, United States of America.

Tel: (1) 215 898 6183
Email: mba.admissions@wharton.upenn.edu
Website: www.wharton.upenn.edu/mba/catalog

The Wharton School of the University of Pennsylvania was a remarkable innovation when Joseph Wharton, a self-educated 19th-century industrialist, first proposed its establishment more than 135 years ago. Wharton School has continued innovating to meet mounting global demand for new ideas, deeper insights, and transformative leadership.

Wharton Executive MBA Programme

Length of Study: 2 years
Country of Study: Any country
Application Procedure: Applicants may apply online or contact Wharton for information.

For further information contact:

The Wharton School Executive MBA Programme, University of PA, 224 Steinberg Conference Centre, 255 South 38th Street, Philadelphia, PA 19104-6359, United States of America.

Tel: (1) 215 898 5887
Fax: (1) 215 898 2598
Email: wemba-admissions@wharton.upenn.edu

Whitehall Foundation, Inc.

PO Box 3423, Palm Beach, FL 33480, United States of America.

Tel: (1) 561 655 4474
Email: email@whitehall.org
Website: www.whitehall.org
Contact: Ms Catherine Thomas, Corporate Secretary

The Whitehall Foundation, Inc. through its programme of grants and grants-in-aid, assists scholarly research in the life sciences. It is the Foundation's policy to assist those dynamic areas of basic biological research that are not heavily supported by federal agencies or other foundations with specialized missions.

Whitehall Foundation Grants-in-Aid

Purpose: To better understand behavioural output or brain mechanisms of behaviour.
Eligibility: Open to researchers at the assistant professor level who have experienced difficulty in competing for research funds as they have not yet become firmly established. Senior scientists may also apply.
Level of Study: Research
Type: Research grant one year
Value: Up to US$30,000
Length of Study: 1 year
Frequency: Annual
Country of Study: United States of America
Application Procedure: Applicants must contact the Foundation.
Funding: Private
Additional Information: For up to date policy, application information and important calendar deadlines please refer to the website www.whitehall.org/applying/

For further information contact:

Email: email@whitehall.org

Whitehall Foundation Research Grants

Purpose: To better understand behavioural output or brain mechanisms of behaviour.
Eligibility: Open to established scientists of all ages working at accredited institutions in the United States of America. The principal investigator must hold no less than the position of assistant professor, or the equivalent, in order to make an application. The Foundation does not award funds to investigators who have substantial existing or potential support.
Level of Study: Research
Type: Research grant one year
Value: US$30,000–US$75,000 per year.
Length of Study: Up to 3 years
Frequency: Annual
Country of Study: Any country
Application Procedure: Please visit web-site @ www.whitehall.org
Funding: Private
Additional Information: For up to date policy, application information and important calendar deadlines, please refer to the website www.whitehall.org/grants/

For further information contact:

Email: email@whitehall.org

Wilfrid Laurier University

75 University Avenue West, Waterloo, ON N2L 3C5, Canada.

Tel: (1) 519 884 1970
Email: webservices@wlu.ca.
Website: www.wlu.ca
Contact: Mr Al Hecht, International Relations

Laurier traces its roots to the opening of the Evangelical Lutheran Seminary in Waterloo more than 100 years ago in 1911. We have gone through several changes since then, and in 1973 our name changed from Waterloo Lutheran University to Wilfrid Laurier University. A Laurier education is about building the whole person: mind, body and spirit. We believe that your university career must lead to more than just a job to be considered a success; Laurier creates engaged and aware citizens in a culture that inspires lives of leadership and purpose.

Viessmann/Marburg Travel Scholarship

Purpose: To assist students wanting to study in Germany.
Level of Study: Postgraduate
Type: Scholarship
Value: €767
Length of Study: 1 year
Frequency: Annual
Study Establishment: An approved place of study in Marburg.
Country of Study: Germany
Application Procedure: Contact University
Closing Date: 2 July
Additional Information: Website: www.postgraduatefunding.com/award-1567

For further information contact:

Tel: (1) 519 884 1970
Fax: (1) 519 886 9351
Email: webmaster@wlu.ca

Wilfrid Laurier University President

Purpose: To reward significant contribution to the community as a volunteer or to the discipline as a scholar.
Eligibility: Full-time undergraduate students entering year 1. Minimum overall average of 95% in best six Grade 12 U and/or Grade 12 M courses or Ontario Academic Credits (OACs) (or equivalent).
Level of Study: Postgraduate
Type: Scholarship
Value: CA$23,000 (CA$3,000 1st year; renewable based on academic performance for up to 4 years at CA$5,000 per year) 4th year of renewal eligibility for approved 5-year undergraduate programs only.
Length of Study: 1 year
Frequency: Annual
Study Establishment: Laurier University
Country of Study: Canada
Application Procedure: Apply online.
Funding: Trusts
Contributor: Dr Neale H. Taylor

For further information contact:

Email: fgps@wlu.ca

Wingate Scholarships

2nd Floor, 20-22 Stukeley Street, London WC2B 5LR, United Kingdom.

Tel: (1) 800 755 5550
Email: enquiries@wingate.org.uk
Website: www.wingatescholarships.org.uk
Contact: Ms Sarah Mitchell, Administrator

Wingate Scholarships have been offered by the Foundation since 1988. The first significant donation by the Foundation was in the late 1970s and was to the Royal London Hospital. It also funds an annual Book Prize in association with the Jewish Quarterly. There are currently six trustees, four from the family, who meet quarterly to decide on which organisations or projects, which have applied for grants, should receive them.

Wingate Scholarships

Purpose: To fund creative or original work of intellectual, scientific, artistic, social or environmental value and advanced music study.
Eligibility: Open to United Kingdom, Commonwealth, former Commonwealth, Israeli. Also open to European Union and Council of Europe country citizens provided that they are and have been resident in the United Kingdom for at least 3 years at start of award. Applicants must be over 24 years of age. No upper age limit is prescribed. No academic qualifications are necessary. Applications must be made in United Kingdom from a valid United Kingdom address.
Level of Study: Doctorate, Postdoctorate, Postgraduate, Research
Type: Scholarship
Value: Costs of a project, which may last for up to 3 years, to a maximum of United Kingdom £10,000 in any 1 year.
Length of Study: 1–3 years
Frequency: Annual
Study Establishment: Any approved institute or independent research

Country of Study: Any country
Application Procedure: Applicants must be living in United Kingdom during the period of application. Applications from a valid United Kingdom address only are acceptable. Applicants must complete online application form from the website. Applicants must be able to satisfy the Scholarship Committee that they need financial support to undertake the work projected, and show why the proposed work (if it takes the form of academic research) is unlikely to attract Research Council, British Academy or any other major agency funding if they are United Kingdom applicants. All applications require two references to be submitted independently. Guidance is available on the website.
No. of awards offered: 228
Closing Date: 1 February
Funding: Foundation
Contributor: HHW Foundation
No. of awards given last year: 39
No. of applicants last year: 228
Additional Information: The scholarships are not awarded for professional qualifications, taught courses or electives, or in the following subject areas: performing arts, fine art, business studies. Practising musicians (not composers) are eligible for advanced training, but apart from that, all applicants must have projects that are personal to them and involve either creative or original work. Only postgraduate students in their final two years can apply for scholarships to enable them to undertake field work, or in exceptional circumstances where an award has been withdrawn or closed, to complete a PhD. Applications for studies or projects undertaken post doctorally are eligible, but not postdoctoral fellowship posts per se. Applicant must be based in United Kingdom when applying www.tau.ac.il/acad-sec/grantsite/abroad/britania%20wingate.htm

For further information contact:

Email: emma@shrimsley.com

Winston Churchill Foundation of the United States of America

600 Madison Avenue, Suite 1601, New York, NY 10022-1737, United States of America.

Tel: (1) 212 752 3200
Email: info@churchillscholarship.org
Website: www.churchillscholarship.org
Contact: Mr Michael Morse, Executive Director

Carl Gilbert, chairman of the Gillette Company, became the first Chairman of the Winston Churchill Foundation of the United States, which was established as a 501 (c) (3) US charity in 1959. In its early years, the Foundation made small travel grants to Churchill Overseas Fellows, distinguished senior faculty who would spend one year at the College. In the 1980s, funding was raised during gala dinners at which the Foundation granted the Churchill Award to an individual who has made outstanding contributions exemplifying Churchill's attributes and ideals. Today, the Scholarship is supported through a combination of the Foundation's investment reserves and through individual donations.

Churchill Scholarship

Purpose: The Churchill Scholarship provides funding to American students for a year of Master's study at the University of Cambridge, based at Churchill College. The program was set up at the request of Sir Winston Churchill in order to fulfill his vision of United States–United Kingdom scientific exchange with the goal of advancing science and technology on both sides of the Atlantic, helping to ensure our future prosperity and security.
Eligibility: Please check eligibility before you apply https://www.churchillscholarship.org/the-scholarship#About-The-Scholarship
Type: Fellowship/Scholarship
Value: US$65,000
Length of Study: 1 year
Frequency: Annual
Country of Study: United Kingdom
Application Procedure: Must be nominated by undergraduate institution.
No. of awards offered: 18
Closing Date: 1 November
No. of awards given last year: 15
No. of applicants last year: 105
Additional Information: https://www.churchillscholarship.org/the-scholarship#About-The-Scholarship

For further information contact:

600 Madison Avenue, Suite 1601, New York, NY 10022, United States of America.

Tel: (1) 212 752 3200
Email: info@churchillscholarship.org

Winterthur

Winterthur Museum, Garden and Library, 5105 Kennett Pike, Winterthur, DE 19735, United States of America.

Tel: (1) 800 448 3883
Email: tourinfo@winterthur.org
Website: www.winterthur.org
Contact: Thomas A. Guiler, Manager and Instructor, Academic Programmes

Winterthur is set amidst a 1,000-acre preserve of rolling meadows and woodlands. Designed by du Pont, its 60-acre naturalistic garden is among America's best, with magnificent specimen plantings and massed displays of color. Graduate programs and a preeminent research library make Winterthur an important center for the study of American art and culture.

Winterthur Dissertation Research Fellowships

Purpose: To encourage the use of Winterthur's collections for critical inquiry that will further the understanding of American history and visual and material culture.
Level of Study: Research
Type: Fellowship
Value: US$7,000 per semesters
Length of Study: 1–2 semesters
Frequency: Annual
Country of Study: United States of America
Application Procedure: Applicants can download application form from the website.
Closing Date: 15 January
Funding: Foundation
Contributor: Winterthur
No. of awards given last year: 4
Additional Information: www.winterthur.org/education/academic-programs/research-fellowships/fellowships-available/

For further information contact:

Winterthur Museum Garden & Library, 5105 Kennett Pike, Winterthur, DE 19735, United States of America.

Email: academicprograms@winterthur.org

Winterthur Postdoctoral Fellowships

Purpose: To encourage the use of Winterthur's collections for critical inquiry that will further the understanding of American history and visual and material culture.
Eligibility: Open to scholars who hold the PhD degree, pursuing advanced research.
Level of Study: Postdoctorate, Research
Type: Fellowships
Value: Up to US$4,500 per month.
Length of Study: 4 months
Frequency: Annual
Country of Study: United States of America
Application Procedure: Applicants can download the application form from the website.
Closing Date: 15 January
Funding: Foundation
Contributor: Winterthur
No. of awards given last year: 2
Additional Information: www.winterthur.org/education/academic-programs/research-fellowships/fellowships-available/

For further information contact:

Winterthur Museum Garden & Library, 5105 Kennett Pike, Winterthur, DE 19735, United States of America.

Tel: (1) 800 448 3883
Email: tguiler@winterthur.org.

Winterthur Research Fellowships

Purpose: To encourage the use of Winterthur's collections for critical inquiry that will further the understanding of American history and visual and material culture.
Eligibility: Open to scholars pursuing advanced research.
Level of Study: Research
Type: Fellowship
Value: US$1,750 per month
Length of Study: 1–3 months
Frequency: Annual
Country of Study: United States of America
Application Procedure: Applicants can download the application form from the website.
Closing Date: 15 January
Funding: Foundation
Contributor: Winterthur
No. of awards given last year: 21

For further information contact:

Email: researchapplication@winterthur.org

Wolf Blass Wines International

97 Sturt Highway, Nuriootpa, SA 5355, Australia.

Tel: (61) 8 8568 7311
Email: visitorcentre@wolfblass.com.au
Website: www.wolfblass.com.au/brands/wolfblass/index.asp

Wolf Blass Wines International is a public listed company and one of the Australia's top sellers of red and white wine.

Wolf Blass Australian Winemaking Independent Study Scholarship

Purpose: To support independent study related to winemaking in Australia.
Eligibility: Open to culinary professional to conduct research and writing related to Australian winemaking and culinary traditions.
Type: Scholarship
Value: AU$5,000
Country of Study: Australia
Application Procedure: All applicants are required to include a project proposal, an itemized budget detailing the use of this award and a tentative travel schedule with dates and locations. Check website for further details.
Additional Information: Applicant is additionally required to provide a current resume to qualify for this scholarship https://www.unisa.edu.au/research/degrees/Scholarships/Wolf-Blass-Scholarship/

Wolfsonian-Florida International University

1001 Washington Avenue, Miami Beach, FL 33139, United States of America.

Tel: (1) 305 531 1001
Email: info@thewolf.fiu.edu
Website: www.wolfsonian.org
Contact: Mr Jonathan Mogul, Fellowship Co-ordinator

The Wolfsonian-Florida International University or The Wolfsonian-FIU, located in the heart of the Art Deco District of Miami Beach, Florida, is a museum, library and research center that uses its collection to illustrate the persuasive power of art and design. For fifteen years, The Wolfsonian has been a division within Florida International University.

Research Fellowships

Purpose: Each fellow broadens public access to Wolfsonian collection items and enriches our collective knowledge about its artifacts by sharing takeaways and discoveries in new projects.
Eligibility: U.S. and international
Level of Study: Doctorate, Masters Degree
Type: Fellowship
Value: A stipend, Round-trip travel, Accommodations (if non-local), Access to the collection and collections staff.
Length of Study: 3 to 4 weeks
Country of Study: United States of America
Application Procedure: Scholarship website: webforms.fiu.edu/view.php?id=748326
Closing Date: 31 December
Additional Information: wolfsonian.org/research/fellowships/

For further information contact:

Email: research@thewolf.fiu.edu

Wolfsonian-FIU Fellowship

Purpose: To conduct research on the Wolfsonian's collection of objects and library materials from the period 1885 to 1945, including decorative arts, works on paper, books and ephemera.
Eligibility: The programme is open to holders of Master's or doctoral degrees, PhD candidates, and to others who have a record of significant professional achievement in relevant fields.
Level of Study: Doctorate, Postdoctorate, Professional development
Type: Fellowship
Value: A stipend, accommodations, round-trip travel
Length of Study: 3–4 weeks
Frequency: Annual
Study Establishment: The Wolfsonian-Florida International University.
Country of Study: United States of America
Application Procedure: Applicants must complete an application form and submit this with three letters of recommendation. Contact the Fellowship Co-ordinator for details and application materials. Applicants may also download programme information and an application form from the website www.wolfsonian.fiu.edu/education/research

No. of awards offered: 26
Closing Date: 31 December
No. of awards given last year: 5
No. of applicants last year: 26
Additional Information: https://wolfsonian.org/research/fellowships/

For further information contact:

Tel: (1) 305 535 2613
Email: research@thewolf.fiu.edu

Women's Studio Workshop (WSW)

722 Binnewater Lane, PO Box 489, Rosendale, NY 12472, United States of America.

Tel: (1) 845 658 9133
Email: info@wsworkshop.org
Website: www.wsworkshop.org
Contact: Ms Ann Kalmbach, Executive Director

WSW is an artist-run workshop with facilities for printmaking, papermaking, photography, book arts and ceramics. WSW supports the creation of new work through studio residency and annual book arts grant programmes and an ongoing subsidized fellowship programme.

Artists Fellowships at WSW

Purpose: To provide a time for artists to explore new ideas in a dynamic and co-operative community of women artists in a rural environment.
Eligibility: Open to women artists only.
Level of Study: Unrestricted
Type: Fellowship
Value: The award includes on-site housing and unlimited access to the studios. Cost to artists will be US$200 per week, plus their own material.
Length of Study: Each fellowship is 3–6 weeks long. Fellowship opportunities are from September to June.
Frequency: Annual
Study Establishment: WSW
Country of Study: United States of America
Application Procedure: Applicants must complete an application form, available on request or online at the website. One-sentence summary plus half-page description of proposed project, resume, 10 slides plus slide script, self addressed stampe envelope for return of materials.
No. of awards offered: 100
Closing Date: 15 October
Funding: Government, Private
Contributor: Private foundations
No. of awards given last year: 25
No. of applicants last year: 100

Women's Studio Workshop Internships

Purpose: To provide opportunities for young artists to continue development of their work in a supportive environment, while learning studio skills and responsibilities.
Eligibility: 1. Experience in at least two of the following areas: silkscreen, letterpress, printmaking, papermaking, book arts, or graphic design 2. Ability to prioritize tasks and work independently as well as collaboratively 3. Excellent communication skills 4. Enthusiasm for working with many different people in a studio environment
Level of Study: Unrestricted
Type: Internship
Value: All internships include a private room in WSW's on-campus Anne Atwood House and a stipend of US$600/month.
Frequency: Annual
Study Establishment: WSW
Country of Study: United States of America
Application Procedure: Application must include: 1. Cover letter 2. Resume 3. Name and contact information for 3 references 4. Up to ten images of recent work (digital specifications here) 5. An image script, which should include the title, medium, dimension, and date of each image
No. of awards offered: 150
Closing Date: 1 April
Funding: Government, Private
Contributor: Private foundations
No. of awards given last year: 6
No. of applicants last year: 150
Additional Information: www.wsworkshop.org/residencies/studio-internship/

Woodrow Wilson National Fellowship Foundation

104 Carnegie Center, Suite 301, Princeton, NJ 08540, United States of America.

Tel: (1) 609 452 7007
Website: www.woodrow.org/about/fellows/

The Woodrow Wilson National Fellowship Foundation identifies and develops the best minds for the nation's most important challenges. The fellowships are awarded to enrich human resources, work to improve public policy, and assist organizations and institutions in enhancing practice in the United States and abroad.

The Millicent C. McIntosh Fellowship

Purpose: These fellowships are specifically intended for recently tenured faculty who would benefit from additional time and resources.
Level of Study: Postgraduate
Type: Fellowship
Value: A US$15,000 stipend
Length of Study: 1 year
Frequency: Annual
Application Procedure: Contact the Foundation.
Closing Date: 31 March
Funding: Private
Contributor: Gladys Krieble Delmas Foundation.

For further information contact:

Tel: (1) 609 452 7007 ext. 301
Email: mcintoshfellowship@woodrow.org

Woodrow Wilson MBA Fellowship in Education Leadership

Purpose: To address the United States' twin educational achievement gaps–the one between the nation's lowest performing and its best schools, as well as the one between the nation's best schools and their top international competitors. The Fellowship seeks both to prepare leaders who can bring all American schools up to world-class levels of performance and to develop a new gold standard for preparing education leaders.
Eligibility: Fellows commit to serve for 3 years in approved school or district leadership positions within their states.
Level of Study: Postgraduate
Type: Fellowship
Value: Fellows will receive a stipend to cover tuition for the MBA program and other expenses.
Length of Study: 13 to 15 months of full-time study
Frequency: Annual
Country of Study: Any country
Application Procedure: Fellows must be nominated by a local education leader/colleague before they are eligible to apply. Contact information buntrock@woodrow.org
Closing Date: December
Additional Information: If you have already been nominated, see the respective pages for the WW MBA Fellowship at MSOE www.msoe.edu/community/academics/business/page/2311/mba-in-education-leadership-overview, www.woodrow.org/mobile/fships/ww-ed-mba/

For further information contact:

Email: buntrock@woodrow.org

Woodrow Wilson Teaching Fellowship

Eligibility: The Woodrow Wilson Teaching Fellowship seeks to attract talented, committed individuals with science, technology, engineering, and mathematics (STEM) backgrounds – including current undergraduates, recent college graduates, midcareer professionals, and retirees – into teaching in high-need secondary schools. A qualified applicant should demonstrate a commitment to the program and its goals; have United States citizenship or permanent residency; have attained, or expect to attain by 30 June, a bachelor's degree from an accredited United States college or university; have majored in and/or have a strong professional background in an STEM field; have achieved a cumulative undergraduate grade point average (GPA) of 3.0 or better on a 4.0 scale (negotiable for applicants from institutions that do not employ a 4.0 GPA scale). Note Prior teaching experience does not exclude a candidate from eligibility. All applications are considered in their entirety and selection is based on merit.
Level of Study: Graduate
Type: Fellowship
Value: US$30,000-US$32,000 stipend, with tuition arrangements varying by campus in Georgia, Indiana, and New Jersey. (Once Fellows are certified teachers at the end of the first year, they obtain salaried employment in high-need schools.)
Length of Study: 12–18 months plus 3-year teaching commitment
Frequency: Annual
Study Establishment: Fellowship is only available for use at specific schools in Indiana (Ball State University, Indiana University-Purdue University Indianapolis, Purdue University, and the University of Indianapolis); Michigan (Eastern Michigan University, Grand Valley State University, Michigan State University, University of Michigan, Wayne State University, Western Michigan University); and Ohio (John Carroll University, Ohio State University, University of Akron, and University of Cincinnati).
Country of Study: Any country
Application Procedure: Online application procedure and supporting documents. See www.wwteachingfellowship.org
No. of awards offered: 1690

Funding: Foundation, Government, Private
Contributor: Ohio STEM, Lilly Endowment Inc., W K Kellogg Foundation, Choose Ohio First.
Additional Information: University of Dayton and University of Toledo are also included in study establishment www.woodrow.org/fellowships/ww-teaching-fellowships/

For further information contact:

Email: wwteachingfellowship@woodrow.org

Woods Hole Oceanographic Institution (WHOI)

266 Woods Hole Road, Woods Hole, MA 02543-1050, United States of America.

Tel: (1) 508 289 2252
Email: information@whoi.edu
Website: www.whoi.edu/education
Contact: Janet Fields, Coordinator

The Woods Hole Oceanographic Institution is dedicated to advancing knowledge of the ocean and its connection with the Earth system through a sustained commitment to excellence in science, engineering, and education, and to the application of this knowledge to problems facing society. This is essential not only to advance knowledge about our planet, but also to ensure society's long-term welfare and to help guide human stewardship of the environment. WHOI researchers are also dedicated to training future generations of ocean science leaders, to providing unbiased information that informs public policy and decision-making.

Postdoctoral Scholar Program

Purpose: Eighteen-month Postdoctoral Scholar awards are offered to recipients of new or recent doctorates in the fields of chemistry, engineering, geology, geophysics, mathematics, meteorology, physics, and biology as well as oceanography. The awards are designed to further the education and training of the applicant with primary emphasis placed on the individual's research promise.
Eligibility: In order to be eligible for one of these awards, applicants must have received their doctoral degree no more than 3 years before their start date. A doctoral degree is required at the time of appointment, but not at the time of application. It is also expected that candidates will have a command of the English language. The following groups are not eligible for the Scholar competition: MIT-WHOI Joint Program Students; those holding any type of WHOI appointment at the post-doctorate level during the 12 months prior to December 31st of the Scholar application year; and those with more than 12 total months as a WHOI guest student, or who have a formal doctoral (co)advisor who is a WHOI employee.
Level of Study: Postdoctoral
Type: Fellowship
Value: US$61,200 per year
Length of Study: 18 months
Frequency: Annual
Study Establishment: Woods Hole Oceanographic Institution
Country of Study: United States of America
Closing Date: 15 October
Additional Information: Website: www.whoi.edu/what-we-do/educate/postdoctoral/postdocs-scholar-fellowship-appointments/apo-postdoctoral-scholar/

Worcester College

Walton Street, Oxford OX1 2HB, United Kingdom.

Tel: (44) 1865 278300
Email: lodge@worc.ox.ac.uk
Website: www.worc.ox.ac.uk/

We are situated in the heart of Oxford, with its many attractions and amenities, yet behind the College walls lie 26 acres of beautiful, tranquil gardens, and we are fortunate to be the only College with an on-site sports field.

C Douglas Dillon Graduate Scholarship

Subjects: MPhil Politics (Comparative Government), MPhil Politics (European Politics and Society), MPhil Politics (Political Theory), MSc Politics Research, MSc Political Theory Research, MPhil International Relations, MSc Global Governance and Diplomacy
Eligibility: Open to all graduate applicants
Level of Study: Graduate
Type: Scholarship
Value: £10,000 per annum
Length of Study: two years
Frequency: Annual
Country of Study: Any country
Application Procedure: Application process: www.worc.ox.ac.uk/sites/default/files/files/page/ad_c_douglas_dillon_scholarship_2023-24.pdf

Closing Date: 4 March
Additional Information: website: www.worc.ox.ac.uk/applying/graduates/graduate-scholarships

For further information contact:

Email: graduate.enquiries@worc.ox.ac.uk

Drue Heinz Scholarship

Eligibility: Open to all graduate applicants for courses in the Humanities in which Worcester College admits students and who specify Worcester College as their first choice College.
Level of Study: Graduate
Type: Award
Value: Up to a maximum of £10,000 per annum
Length of Study: One year
Frequency: Annual
Country of Study: Any country
Application Procedure: for application process: www.worc.ox.ac.uk/sites/default/files/files/page/ad_drue_heinz_scholarship_2023-24.pdf
Closing Date: 3 March
Additional Information: website: www.worc.ox.ac.uk/applying/graduates/graduate-scholarships

For further information contact:

Email: graduate.enquiries@worc.ox.ac.uk

Ogilvie Thompson Scholarship

Subjects: All subjects
Purpose: The purpose of the Ogilvie Thompson Scholarship is to enable people to apply for graduate study knowing that if they are not successful in securing funding from elsewhere they will be provided with some financial assistance.
Eligibility: Students who are already members of Worcester College and currently in their final year of undergraduate study or who have taken finals within the last two years but have not undertaken any graduate study since (either at Oxford or at another university). Open to all subjects. Please see the further details about this scholarship in the link on the right.
Level of Study: Graduate
Type: Award
Value: Up to a maximum of £10,000
Length of Study: One year
Frequency: Annual
Country of Study: Any country
Application Procedure: For application process: www.worc.ox.ac.uk/sites/default/files/files/page/ad_ogilvie_thompson_scholarship_2023-24.pdf
No. of awards offered: 1
Closing Date: 3 March
Additional Information: website: www.worc.ox.ac.uk/applying/graduates/graduate-scholarships

For further information contact:

Email: graduate.enquiries@worc.ox.ac.uk

World Bank Institute

1818 H Street, NW, Washington, DC 20433, United States of America.

Tel: (1) 202 473 1000
Email: pic@worldbank.org
Website: www.worldbank.org
Contact: Communications Officer

One of the largest sources of funding and knowledge for transition and development councils; The World Bank uses its financial resources, staff and extensive experience to help developing countries reduce poverty, increase economic growth and improve their quality of life.

World Bank Grants Facility for Indigenous Peoples

Purpose: To support sustainable and culturally appropriate development projector planed and implemented by and for Indigenous People.
Eligibility: Applicant must be an Indigenous People's community or not-for-profit/non-governmental Indigenous People's organization, must be legally registered in the country of grant implementation, the country must be eligible to borrow from the World Bank (IBRD and/or IDA). Applicant should have an established bank account in the name of the applicant organization and should demonstrate internal controls to govern the use of funds. Applicant should not have received a grant from the Grants Facility for Indigenous Peoples in the previous 2 years.
Level of Study: Professional development, Research
Type: Grant

Value: Proposed project budget requests should range between US$10,000 and US$30,000 and include a minimum contribution of 20% of the total project cost.
Frequency: Annual
Application Procedure: A complete application, not more than 10 pages, should be submitted.
Closing Date: 15 November
Contributor: The World Bank
Additional Information: www.siteresources.worldbank.org/INTINDPEOPLE/948158-1113428433802/20662536/englishcall.pdf

For further information contact:

Fax: (1) 202 522 1669
Email: indigenouspeoples@worldbank.org

World Bank Scholarships Program

Purpose: The World Bank Scholarships Program contributes to the World Bank Group's mission of forging new dynamic approaches to capacity development and knowledge sharing in the developing world.
Eligibility: Eligibility criteria details for each call are provided in the respective call for application guidelines. Please note that the eligibility criteria is strictly adhered to and there are no exceptions.
Level of Study: Masters Degree, Postgraduate
Type: Scholarship
Frequency: Annual
Country of Study: Any country
Closing Date: 31 January
Funding: Private

World Federation of International Music Competitions

104, rue de Carouge, CH-1205 Genéve, Switzerland.

Tel: (41) 22 321 36 20
Email: fmcim@fmcim.org
Website: www.wfimc.org/

The World Federation of International Music Competitions contributes to the vibrancy of the music world by representing leading international music competitions and supporting them with valuable services and guidelines.

International Beethoven Piano Competition, Vienna

Purpose: To encourage the artistic development of young pianists.
Level of Study: Unrestricted
Type: Competition
Value: €50,000
Frequency: Annual
Country of Study: Any country
Application Procedure: Apply online through the website www.beethoven-comp.at
Closing Date: 28 April
Funding: Private

World Learning

1015 15th Street, NW 7th Floor, Washington, DC 20005, United States of America.

Tel: (1) 202 408 5420
Email: info@worldlearning.org
Website: www.worldlearning.org

World Learning is a 501(c)(3) international nonprofit organization that focuses on international development, education, and exchange programs. The School for International Training (SIT) was established in 1964. SIT filled a need of returned Peace Corps volunteers by offering a graduate degree in International Development. The Vermont campus originally consisted of a small collection of dorms around a Carriage House on a scenic farm on the north end of Brattleboro. These early Peace Corps volunteers took lessons in foreign languages with materials and teachers from the language training from their service, and The School for International Training began to expand its offerings.

School for International Training (SIT) Master of Arts in Teaching Program

Purpose: To prepare language teachers committed to professional development and service in their field.
Eligibility: Open to persons of any nationality who are preparing for a language teaching career. Awards are available only to students studying at the School for International Training.
Level of Study: Graduate
Type: Scholarship
Value: Varies

Length of Study: A period that includes a time of student teaching and homestay. The programme is offered in a 1 year or 2 Summer format designed for working professionals.
Frequency: Annual
Study Establishment: SIT
Country of Study: Any country
Application Procedure: Applicants must complete an institutional financial aid application and should contact the Financial Aid Office for further details, by email at finaid@sit.edu
Additional Information: Students master technical teaching methodologies through language classroom practice, on campus coursework and a supervised teaching internship. Further information is available on the website www.sit.edu/mat

For further information contact:

Email: tesol@rennert.com

Worshipful Company of Musicians

1 Speed Highwalk, Barbican, London EC2Y 8DX, United Kingdom.

Tel: (44) 20 7496 8980
Email: clerk@wcom.org.uk.
Website: www.wcom.org.uk

The Worshipful Company of Musicians is one of the Livery Companies of the City of London. Its history dates back to at least 1350. We are also known as The Worshipful Company of Musicians.

Carnwath Scholarship

Purpose: To support young pianists.
Eligibility: Open to any person permanently resident in the United Kingdom and 21–25 years of age. The scholarship is intended only for the advanced student who has successfully completed a solo performance course at a college of music.
Level of Study: Postgraduate
Type: Scholarship
Value: £4,150 per year
Length of Study: Up to 2 years
Frequency: Every 2 years
Country of Study: United Kingdom
Application Procedure: Applicants must be nominated by principals of the Royal Academy of Music, the Guildhall School of Music, the Royal Northern College of Music, the Royal Scottish Academy of Music, Trinity College of Music, London College of Music, the Welsh College of Music, the Birmingham School of Music or the Royal College of Music. No application should be made directly to the Worshipful Company of Musicians.
Closing Date: 30 April
Funding: Private
Additional Information: website: www.postgraduatefunding.com/award-418

For further information contact:

Email: clerk@wcom.org.uk

Writtle University College

Lordship Road, Writtle, Chelmsford CM1 3RR, United Kingdom.

Tel: (44) 1245 424 200
Email: info@writtle.ac.uk
Website: writtle.ac.uk/

Writtle University College is one of the largest land-based university colleges in the United Kingdom; it is also one of the oldest. Set in the Essex countryside on a 220 hectare estate, Writtle, previously known as Writtle College, provides FE and HE programmes.

Elinor Roper Scholarship

Purpose: The Elinor Roper Scholarship offers five £1,000 scholarship awarded for Taught Master's programme in Crop Production or Post Harvest Technology.
Eligibility: To be considered for a Writtle University College Elinor Roper Scholarship award, students must be Home students and must apply by completing the ERS application form. This application must include a written statement of between 500 – 800 words detailing the value the applicant expects to gain from study on the Master's programme and the way in which they anticipate using the experience after graduation to further their chosen career. If you have a "conditional offer" the scholarship will only be awarded if the conditions are met. Any applicant who defers entry will have to submit a new application for the academic year their studies will commence. Current Writtle University College Postgraduate students are not eligible to apply. The value of the scholarship will be deducted from the tuition fee invoice. It will be a condition of the scholarship that the successful

applicant agrees to provide a student profile detailing their experience on the programme to be used in publications for the purpose of marketing Writtle University College and/or inclusion in the "University College Alumni Association" publication.
Level of Study: Masters Degree
Type: Scholarship
Value: £1,000
Frequency: Annual
Country of Study: Any country
Application Procedure: All applicants must be new Writtle University College home students and will need to apply by completing the relevant application form. Download an application 1. This application must include a written statement of between 500 – 800 words detailing the value the applicant expects to gain from study on the Master's programme and the way in which they anticipate using the experience after graduation to further their career. 2. A "conditional offer" the scholarship will only be awarded if the conditions are met. 3. Any applicant who defers entry will have to submit a new application for the academic year their studies will commence. 4. Current Writtle University College Postgraduate students are not eligible to apply. 5. The value of the scholarship will be deducted from the tuition fee invoice. 6. It will be a condition of the scholarship that the successful applicant agrees to provide a student profile detailing their experience on the programme to be used in publications for the purpose of marketing Writtle University College and/or inclusion in the "University College Alumni Association" publication. 7. This can either be on a full-time or part-time basis.
Funding: Private
No. of awards given last year: 31 August

For further information contact:

Student Finance, Writtle University College, Writtle, Chelmsford, Essex CM1 3RR, United Kingdom.

Tel: (44) 1245 424200
Email: student.finance@writtle.ac.uk

Elinor Roper Scholarship 2024

Purpose: The Elinor Roper Scholarship is awarded for Taught Master's programme in Crop Production or Post Harvest Technology. The Writtle University College provides students with the options of being able to study certain courses on a part-time basis.
Eligibility: To be considered for a Writtle University College Elinor Roper Scholarship award, students must be Home students and must apply by completing the ERS application form. This application must include a written statement of between 500 - 800 words detailing the value the applicant expects to gain from study on the Master's programme and the way in which they anticipate using the experience after graduation to further their chosen career. If you have a "conditional offer", the scholarship will only be awarded if the conditions are met. Any applicant who defers entry will have to submit a new application for the academic year their studies will commence. Current Writtle University College students are not eligible to apply. The value of the scholarship will be deducted from the tuition fee invoice. It will be a condition of the scholarship that the successful applicant agrees to provide a student profile detailing their experience on the programme to be used in publications for the purpose of marketing Writtle University College and/or inclusion in the "University College Alumni Association" publication.
Level of Study: Masters Degree, Postgraduate, Postgraduate (MSc)
Type: Scholarship
Value: £1,000
Frequency: Annual
Country of Study: United Kingdom
Application Procedure: All applicants must be new Writtle University College Home students and will need to apply by completing the relevant application form. Download an application (ERS2024).
No. of awards offered: Limited
Closing Date: 31 August
Contributor: Writtle University
Additional Information: Website: writtle.ac.uk/scholarships.cfm?Scholarship=147&nohead=1&nofooter=1

For further information contact:

Email: student.finance@writtle.ac.uk

Postgraduate International Scholarships

Purpose: Scholarships are available for pursuing postgraduate programme.
Eligibility: Students who meet the entry requirements, and who are accepted on a taught postgraduate course at Writtle University College, are eligible to apply for this award. Students must complete the application form to be considered for the award.
Type: Scholarship
Value: For taught MA/MSc courses, the award will be worth £1,000; for MA conversion students the award will be delivered within the conversion year ONLY, as per the terms and conditions set out below.
Length of Study: 2 years
Frequency: Annual
Country of Study: Any country

W

Application Procedure: Visit website. Applications to be sent to: admissions@writtle.ac.uk
Closing Date: 31 July
Contributor: Writtle University
Additional Information: https://writtle.ac.uk/International-Fees

For further information contact:

Email: admissions@writtle.ac.uk

Postgraduate Progression Award

Purpose: This Scholarship is available to ALL new Postgraduate students, commencing their studies
Eligibility: These scholarships are only available to Writtle University College undergraduate students who meet all of the following criteria 1. A Writtle University College undergraduate student completing your course in 2022/23 or 2023/24 academic years. 2. Meet the entry requirements of the full-time or part time postgraduate course. 3. Begin a Writtle University College postgraduate programme in autumn 2024. 4. The closing date for applications is 31st August 2024.
Level of Study: Postgraduate
Type: Award
Value: £1,000 cash award for Home students or £1900 for International and EU students
Length of Study: one academic year
Frequency: Annual
Country of Study: European Union
Application Procedure: Applications to be sent to student.finance@writtle.ac.uk
Closing Date: 31 August
Funding: Private
Additional Information: Website: writtle.ac.uk/scholarships.cfm?Scholarship=175&nohead=1&nofooter=1

For further information contact:

Email: student.finance@writtle.ac.uk

The Colegrave Seabrook Foundation

Eligibility: There are no specific criteria for application, though most students will be enrolled or about to be enrolled on a full-time horticultural course at a horticultural college or university. Preference will, however, be given to candidates who meet the following criteria: 1. Focus of studies on ornamental commercial horticulture, especially with an emphasis on the bedding, container, pot plant and cut flower sectors. 2. Are seeking to make careers in the field of commercial ornamental horticulture. 3. Show demonstrable talent, as evidenced by grades achieved and by tutors' assessments.
Type: Scholarship
Value: up to £1,000
Application Procedure: Applications to be sent to: info@colegraveseabrookfoundation.org.uk
Closing Date: 31 January
No. of applicants last year: 5
Additional Information: website: writtle.ac.uk/scholarships.cfm?Scholarship=170&nohead=1&nofooter=1

Vice-Chancellor International Postgraduate Scholarship

Eligibility: 1. Have a received a conditional/unconditional offer to study on a FULL-TIME programme at the University College by 1st July 2024. 2. Be self-funding and must be confirmed as an overseas student for fee paying purposes. 3. Only one scholarship award can be made per student and the award cannot normally be held in conjunction with other awards. 4. Have met / or be progressing well to meet the necessary Student Visa requirements in accordance with UKVI. 5. Not be in receipt of funding discounts for fees from external bodies such as local Government, charities or private organisations. 6. Complete the online 'VC Scholarship application form' as soon as possible after their application and no later than 1st July 2024. All information, which will be used for consideration, must be presented on the application form. 7. Successful recipients of the Vice-Chancellor's Scholarship will be required to act as an ambassador for the University for the duration of your studies, which may involve but is not limited to the following: representing WUC at open events, contributing to marketing and promotional materials, participating in international student events, acting as a mentor to fellow students and contributing to/creating a blog to report on your experience at WUC.
Level of Study: Postgraduate
Type: Scholarship
Value: £3000 per annum
Application Procedure: A step-by-step guide to applying: 1. Make your application to Writtle University College following guidance, application form: forms.office.com/r/JTBLkJNH49. 2. Once you have received an offer to study with us you should check the eligibility criteria to ensure you are eligible to apply for the Vice-Chancellor's Scholarship. 3. When you are in receipt of an offer for an eligible undergraduate or postgraduate course, you will be able to apply for the Vice-Chancellor's Scholarship. We will email you with an invitation to our online form to apply for the scholarship. 4. Submit your application for the Vice-Chancellor's scholarship by providing confirmation of your qualifications as well

as your personal statement demonstrating your outstanding attributes, both personal and academic, how you have demonstrated commitment to your chosen industry and subject specialism and how you will use your Writtle University College degree to achieve your future ambitions. You will also need to commit to act as an ambassador to Writtle University College to help drive increased student recruitment and support for other international students.

Closing Date: 1 July
Additional Information: Please note that any agents fees will be calculated on the discounted fee invoice (% commission will be based on the fee invoice after deducting award). Tuition fee discount will be deducted from the final tuition fee instalment invoice which is payable in December. Website: writtle.ac.uk/Scholarships-&-Bursaries-23-24

X

Xavier Labor Relations Institute -Xavier School of Management

C. H. Area (East), Jamshedpur, Jharkhand 831001, India.

Tel: (91) 657 398 3329, 3330
Email: admis@xlri.ac.in
Website: www.xlri.ac.in

XLRI - Xavier School of Management is a management school founded in 1949 by the Society of Jesus and based in Jamshedpur, Jharkhand, India.

Fellow Programme in Management (FPM) at Xavier Labor Relations Institute

Purpose: The programme aims to train prospective scholars to become highly skilled and innovative researchers and teachers in various aspects of management. It primarily aims at preparing students for careers as faculty members at premier academic institutions and for positions outside academia requiring advanced research and analytical capabilities
Eligibility: The basic eligibility to apply for admission to the FPM is either 1. a BE / B. Tech. degree or its equivalent with at least 60% marks (50% for SC/ST candidates) obtained after after completing higher secondary education (10+2) or equivalent, and followed by at least 2 years of relevant work experience, OR 2. a bachelor's degree / equivalent of minimum three years duration with at least 60% marks (50% for SC/ST candidates) after completing higher secondary education (10+2) or equivalent, and followed by post-graduation (MBA/Master's degree in any discipline) from a university or a centre of higher learning in India / abroad with at least 55% marks (50% for SC/ST candidates), OR 3. an integrated master's degree of four / five years in any discipline, with at least 55% marks (50% for SC/ST candidates), obtained after completing higher secondary education (10+2) or equivalent, OR 4. a professional qualification like CA, ICWA or CS with at least 55% marks (50% for SC/ST candidates)
Study Establishment: Fellowship is available for pursuing full-time, residential doctoral programme
Country of Study: India
Application Procedure: See the website
Closing Date: 15 January

Xerox Foundation

6th Floor/PO Box 4505, 45 Glover Avenue, Norwalk, CT 06856-4505, United States of America.

Tel: (1) 800 275 9376
Email: D.Garvin.Byrd@xerox.com
Website: www.xerox.com
Contact: Dr Joseph M. Cahalan

Xerox Foundation is a US$15.7 billion technology and services enterprise that helps businesses deploy Smarter Document Management strategies and find better ways to work. Its intent is to constantly lead with innovative technologies, products and services that customers can depend upon to improve business results.

Xerox Technical Minority Scholarship

Purpose: To provide funding to minority students enroled in one of the technical sciences or engineering disciplines
Eligibility: Open to citizens of the United States or visa-holding permanent residents of African American, Asian, Pacific Island,

Palgrave Macmillan (ed.), *The Grants Register 2024*,
https://doi.org/10.1057/978-1-349-96073-6

Native American, Native Alaskan or Hispanic descent. Applicants must have grade point average of 3.0 or better
Level of Study: Postgraduate
Type: Scholarship
Value: Scholarships amount vary from US$1,000–US$10,000
Frequency: Annual
Country of Study: United States of America
Application Procedure: Applicants must submit the completed application form along with a curriculum vitae
Closing Date: 30 September
Additional Information: worldscholarshipforum.com/xerox-technical-minority-scholarship/

For further information contact:

Xerox Technical Minority Scholarship Programme office.

Email: xtmsp@rballiance.com

Y

Yale Center for British Art

1080 Chapel Street, New Haven, CT 06510-2302, United States of America.

Tel: (1) 203 432 2800
Email: ycba.info@yale.edu
Website: britishart.yale.edu/

Founded by Paul Mellon (Yale College, Class of 1929), the Yale Center for British Art is the largest museum outside of the United Kingdom devoted to British art. Located in the final building designed by Louis I. Kahn, the YCBA is a focal point for modernist architecture. It is free and open to all.

Andrew W Mellon Fellowship

Purpose: To promote the study of British art
Eligibility: Open to foreign students enrolled for a higher degree at a British or other non-American university
Level of Study: Postgraduate
Type: Fellowship
Value: US$15,000 plus return airfare from London, health benefits and travel expenses up to US$1,000
Length of Study: 1 year
Frequency: Annual
Study Establishment: The Yale Center for British Art
Country of Study: United States of America
Application Procedure: There is no application form. Please submit name, address, telephone number, CV listing professional experience, education and publications, three page outline of research proposal, and two confidential letters of recommendation.
No. of awards offered: 2
Closing Date: 15 January
Funding: Private

For further information contact:

Email: bacinfo@minerva.cis.yale.edu

Yale School of Management (SOM)

Edward P. Evans Hall, 165 Whitney Avenue, New Haven, CT 06511-3729, United States of America.

Tel: (1) 203 432 9637
Email: jonathan.weisberg@yale.edu
Website: som.yale.edu/
Contact: Jonathan Weisberg, Managing Director of Communications

Yale Corporation approved the creation of a School of Organization and Management founded in 1976. The school changed its name to the Yale School of Management in 1994. The mission of the Yale School of Management is educating leaders for business and society. Across its portfolio of degree programs, Yale SOM educates purposeful leaders who pursue their work with integrity; who are equipped to contribute to all sectors of society–public, private, nonprofit, and entrepreneurial; and who understand complexity within and among societies in an increasingly global world.

Arthur Liman Public Interest Law Fellowship

Purpose: Through the work of faculty, students, and Fellows, the Liman Center aims to improve the ability of individuals and groups to obtain fair treatment under the law. Since 1997, the Center has launched hundreds of public sector legal careers, undertaken innovative research to generate

Palgrave Macmillan (ed.), *The Grants Register 2024*,
https://doi.org/10.1057/978-1-349-96073-6

meaningful change, and supported communities, in the hopes of contributing to a more just legal system.
Eligibility: Graduates of law schools who have done work thereafter are eligible to apply. Individuals who have held other fellowships, including those sponsored by the Liman Center, are eligible.
Level of Study: Graduate
Type: Fellowship
Frequency: Annual
Country of Study: United States of America
Application Procedure: Applications for 2024–2025 Liman Law Fellowships will be accepted online via the YLS Public Interest Fellowship Common Application: https://law.yale.edu/centers-workshops/arthur-liman-center-public-interest-law/yale-law-school-fellowship/apply
Closing Date: 3 February
No. of awards given last year: 10
Additional Information: website: law.yale.edu/centers-workshops/arthur-liman-center-public-interest-law/fellowships/liman-law-fellowships

For further information contact:

Anna Van Cleave, Liman Center Director.

Tel: (1) 203 436 3520
Email: anna.vancleave@yale.edu

Yanshan University

No. 438 West Hebei Avenue, Hebei 066004, Qinhuangdao, China.

Tel: (86) 335 8057070
Email: international@ysu.edu.cn
Website: english.ysu.edu.cn/

Yanshan University (YSU) is a member of the Cooperation Consortium of Beijing High Technology Universities. The mission of YSU is to aim at achieving and maintaining excellence in its teaching and research.

China Scholarship Council Scholarships

Purpose: China Scholarship Council (CSC), entrusted by the Ministry of Education of the People's Republic of China (MOE), is responsible for the enrollment and the administration of Chinese Government Scholarship programs. CSC offer a wide variety of academic programs in science, engineering, agriculture, medicine, economics, legal studies, management, education, history, literature, philosophy, and fine arts for scholarship recipients at all levels.
Eligibility: 1. Applicants must be non-Chinese citizens and be in good health. 2. Education background and age limit: A. Applicants for undergraduate program must have senior high school diploma with good academic performance and be under the age of 25. B. Applicants for master's degree program must have bachelor's degree and be under the age of 35. C. Applicants for doctoral degree program must have master's degree and be under the age of 40. D. Applicants for Chinese language training program must have senior high school diploma and be under the age of 35. Chinese language is the only subject available. E. Applicants for general scholar program must have completed at least two years of undergraduate study and be under the age of 45. All subjects including Chinese language are available. F. Applicants for senior scholar program must have master's degree or above, or hold academic titles of associate professor or above, and be under the age of 50.
Type: Scholarship
Frequency: Annual
Country of Study: China
Application Procedure: Applicants shall apply to Chinese diplomatic missions or dispatching authorities between January and April every year.
Closing Date: April
Additional Information: For more details: english.ysu.edu.cn/info/1160/2158.htm

For further information contact:

HE Ling, JI Hongyue.

Tel: (86) 335 8047570
Email: study@ysu.edu.cn

Chinese Government Scholarship Program

Purpose: Chinese Government Scholarship Program is established by the Ministry of Education of P.R. China (MOE) in accordance with educational exchange agreements or understandings reached between the Chinese government and the governments of other countries, organizations, education institutions and relevant international organizations to provide both full scholarships and partial scholarships to international students and scholars.
Eligibility: 1. Applicants must be non-Chinese citizens and be in good health. 2. Education background and age limit: a. Applicants for undergraduate program must have senior high school diploma with good academic performance and be under the age of 25. b. Applicants for master's degree program must have bachelor's degree and be under the age of 35. c. Applicants for doctoral degree program must have master's degree and be under the age of 40. d. Applicants for Chinese

language training program must have senior high school diploma and be under the age of 35. Chinese language is the only subject available. e. Applicants for general scholar program must have completed at least two years of undergraduate study and be under the age of 45. All subjects including Chinese language are available. f. Applicants for senior scholar program must have master's degree or above, or hold academic titles of associate professor or above, and be under the age of 50.

Level of Study: Doctorate, Masters Degree, Postgraduate
Type: Scholarship
Value: See website
Length of Study: Upto Year
Frequency: Annual
Country of Study: China
Application Procedure: See website
Funding: Government
Additional Information: Website: english.ysu.edu.cn/info/1160/2158.htm

For further information contact:

HE Ling, JI Hongyue.

Tel: (86) 335 8047570
Email: study@ysu.edu.cn

Confucius Institute Scholarship

Purpose: This scholarship is offered to study Chinese language and culture in more than 150 Chinese Universities. CIS scholarship includes tuition and lodging fees, medical insurance and a monthly allowance for personal expenses.
Eligibility: Confucius Institute Scholarships are offered for specific doctoral studies, research stays, participation in international conferences, Chinese language and culture courses. If you are interested in scholarships offered for postgraduates and researchers you can take a look here: ccsp.chinese.cn/.
Level of Study: Doctorate, Research
Type: Scholarship
Value: Upto ¥3,000 per month
Country of Study: Any country
Application Procedure: See Website
Closing Date: May
Additional Information: Website: scholarshiproar.com/confucius-institute-scholarship/

For further information contact:

Tel: (86) 335 8095518, (86) 335 8096708
Email: study@ysu.edu.cn

Hebei Provincial Government Scholarship

Purpose: The Hebei Provincial Government awards scholarships to international students studying degree programs in Colleges and Universities located in Hebei Province. Application is open to undergraduate, master's and doctoral level students of all fields of study.
Eligibility: For master students: 1. Bachelor degree or its equivalent 2. HSK Level 5 with a minimum score of 180. For Doctoral Students: 1. Master's degree 2. HSK Level 5 with a minimum score of 180 Or IELTS with a minimum score of 6.0
Level of Study: Doctorate, Masters Degree
Type: Scholarship
Value: Master's Students ¥15,000/year; Doctoral Students: ¥20,000/year
Length of Study: Period of Academic Study
Frequency: Annual
Country of Study: Any country
Application Procedure: The documents provided by the applicants are required to be true, correct and complete. They include 1. Apvip 2. Scanned copy of passport data page 3. Scanned copies of valid HSK score report or IELTS score report 4. Notarized photocopy of highest diploma certificate and academic transcripts. Current students must also provide proof of expected graduation issued by the university. 5. Study or research plan. Master's or doctoral applicants are required to submit study or research plansin Chinese or English. 6. Recommendation letters. Master's and Doctoral applicants are required to provide two (2) reference letters from professors or associate professors. 7. Applicants for music studies are requested to submit a CD of theirown work, while applicants for fine arts must submit a DVD of their own work(two sketches, two color paintings and two other works). 8. Applicants under the age of 18 shall provide guarantee letters signed by their entrusted legal guardians in China. 9. Applicants shall also provide any additional documents required by the university.; Documents in languages other than Chinese or English must be attached with notarized Chinese or English translations.
Additional Information: website: cice.hebtu.edu.cn/a/en/SPrograms/HBGScholarship/

For further information contact:

International Students Admissions Office, 20 E. South 2nd Ring Road, Yuhua District, Shijiazhuang City, Hebei Province, China.

Tel: (86) 311 80789542
Email: scholarship@mail.hebtu.edu.cn; studyinhnu@mail.hebtu.edu.cn

Yanshan University Doctoral Scholarships

Purpose: The aim of the scholarships is to provide financial help to the students who are coming to study doctoral programs in China.
Eligibility: 1. Applicants must be non-Chinese citizens with a foreign passport and be in good health. 2. Applicants for doctoral degree programmust have a diploma of master's degree and be under the age of 40.
Level of Study: Doctorate
Type: Scholarship
Value: The scholarship covers 1. Registration fee, tuition fee, and accommodation fee for dormitory on campus. 2. Monthly allowance ¥ 1,400 for 12 months/year. 3. One–off settlement subsidy ¥ 2,000
Length of Study: 3 to 4 years
Frequency: Annual
Country of Study: China
Application Procedure: 1. Application Form for YSU Scholarship; 2. Copy of passport (the photo page); 3. YSU admission application form international students (with a photograph of the applicant); 4. Certified educational records, degree certificates or diplomas, and academic transcripts (photocopy); 5. Curriculum vitae or resume; 6. Physical examination form for foreigners; 7. Copy of HSK-5 certificate; 8. Personal statement; 9. Two letters of recommendation from professors or associated professors. Please send completed application to mailing address.
Closing Date: 20 May
Additional Information: Please visit website for more information: english.ysu.edu.cn/info/1160/2161.htm

For further information contact:

He Ling, College of International Exchange, Yanshan University, 438 Hebei Street, Hebei Province 066004, Qinhuangdao, China.

Tel: (86) 335 8047570, (86) 335 8053537
Email: study@ysu.edu.cn

Yanshan University Scholarship Program for International Students

Purpose: Scholarships are available for pursuing Master Degree programs.
Eligibility: 1. Applicants must benon-Chinese citizens with a foreign passport and be in good health; 2. Applicants for doctoral degree programmust have a diploma of master's degree and be under the age of 40. 3. Awardees ofChinese Government Scholarship, Confucius Institute Scholarship and otherscholarships will be not accepted for this Scholarship program.
Level of Study: Doctorate, Postgraduate
Type: Scholarship
Value: The scholarship covers 1. registration fee,tuition fee, and accommodation fee for dormitory on campus. 2. Monthly allowance ¥ 1,400 for 12 months/year. 3. One–off settlement subsidy ¥ 2,000.
Length of Study: 3 to 4 years
Frequency: Annual
Country of Study: China
Application Procedure: See website
Closing Date: 20 May
Funding: Government
Additional Information: For more information: english.ysu.edu.cn/info/1160/2161.htm, www.campuschina.org/content/details3_121468.html

For further information contact:

He Ling, Ji Hongyue, College of International Exchange, Yanshan University, 438 Hebei Street, Hebei Province 066004, Qinhuangdao, China.

Tel: (86) 335 8047570, (86) 335 8053537
Fax: (86) 335 8583078
Email: study@ysu.edu.cn

Yidisher Visnshaftlekher Institut Institute for Jewish Research

15 West 16th Street, New York, NY 10011-6301, United States of America.

Tel: (1) 212 246 6080
Email: info@yivo.org
Website: www.yivo.org/

YIVO is all these things: a research institute, an institution of higher learning, an adult education organization, a cultural organization, and a world-renowned library and archive. Mission: To preserve, study, share, and perpetuate knowledge of the history and culture of East European Jewry worldwide.

Abraham and Rachela Melezin Fellowship

Purpose: To support doctoral and postdoctoral research on Jewish educational networks in Lithuania, with emphasis on pre-war Vilna and the Vilna region
Eligibility: The Abraham and Rachela Melezin Fellowship supports doctoral or post-doctoral research in the field of Lithuanian Jewish history

Level of Study: Doctorate, Postdoctorate
Type: Fellowship
Value: US$1,500
Length of Study: 1–3 months
Frequency: Annual
Study Establishment: YIVO Library and Archives
Country of Study: United States of America
Application Procedure: For most up-to-date information see this page www.petersons.com/scholarship/abraham-and-rachela-melezin-fellowship-111_153684.aspx
Closing Date: 31 December
Additional Information: Website: gradfund.rutgers.edu/awards/abraham-rachela-melezin-fellowship/

Abram and Fannie Gottlieb Immerman and Abraham Nathan and Bertha Daskal Weinstein Memorial Fellowship

Purpose: The Abram and Fannie Gottlieb Immerman and Abraham Nathan and Bertha Daskal Weinstein Memorial Fellowship in Eastern European Jewish Studies, the Abraham and Rachela Melezin Memorial Fellowship and the Maria Salit-Gitelson Tell Memorial Fellowship support original doctoral or post-doctoral research in the field of Lithuanian Jewish history for a period of two to three months of research at the YIVO Library and Archives.
Eligibility: For those engaged in PhD dissertation research in archives and libraries of the Baltic states with preference given to research on the Jews of Courland and Latvia
Level of Study: Doctorate, Research
Type: Fellowship
Value: US$4,000
Length of Study: Period of two to three months of research
Frequency: Every 2 years
Application Procedure: Applicants must send a cover letter, curriculum vitae, research proposal and 2 letters of support through regular mail, fax or email. A written summary of one's research is required
Closing Date: 31 December
Funding: Private
Additional Information: www.yivo.org/List-of-Fellowships

For further information contact:

YIVO Institute for Jewish Research, 15 West 16 Street, New York, NY 10011, United States of America.

Aleksander and Alicja Hertz Memorial Fellowship

Purpose: The Aleksander and Alicja Hertz Memorial Fellowship and the Samuel and Flora Weiss Research Fellowship and the Maria Salit-Gitelson Tell Memorial Fellowship support doctoral or post-doctoral research on Polish-Jewish history in the modern period, particularly Jewish-Polish relations, including the Holocaust period, and Jewish contributions to Polish literature and culture.
Level of Study: Doctorate, Postdoctorate
Type: Fellowship
Value: US$4,000
Length of Study: 1–3 months
Frequency: Annual
Country of Study: United States of America
Application Procedure: Applicants must send their curriculum vitae, research proposal and 2 letters of support through regular mail, fax or email. A written summary of one's research is required
Closing Date: 1 February
Additional Information: www.yivo.org/List-of-Fellowships

Dina Abramowicz Emerging Scholar Fellowship

Purpose: To support a significant scholarly publication that may encompass the revision of a doctoral dissertation
Eligibility: The Dina Abramowicz Emerging Scholar Fellowship is intended for post-doctoral research on a topic in Eastern European Jewish Studies.
Level of Study: Postdoctorate
Type: Fellowship
Value: US$3,000
Length of Study: Period of two to three months
Frequency: Annual
Country of Study: Any country
Application Procedure: Applicants must send their curriculum vitae, a research proposal and 2 letters of support through regular mail, fax or email
Closing Date: 1 February
Additional Information: www.yivo.org/List-of-Fellowships

Dora and Mayer Tendler Fellowship

Purpose: Dedicated to doctoral or post-doctoral research in American Jewish history, with special consideration given to scholars working on some aspect of the Jewish labor movement.
Eligibility: Graduate applicants must carry out original research in the field of Jewish studies and give a written summary of the research carried out
Level of Study: Doctorate, Postdoctorate
Type: Fellowship
Value: US$5,000
Length of Study: 3 months

Frequency: Annual
Study Establishment: YIVO collections
Country of Study: United States of America
Application Procedure: For most up-to-date information see this page www.yivo.org/list-of-fellowships#~text=The%20Rose%20and%20Isidore%20Drench,of%20the%20Jewish%20labor%20movement
Closing Date: 31 December
Additional Information: A public lecture at the end of the tenure of the Fellowship is optional www.yivo.org/List-of-Fellowships

For further information contact:

Email: eportnoy@yivo.cjh.org

Joseph Kremen Memorial Fellowship

Purpose: Dedicated to assist an undergraduate, graduate or post-graduate researcher in the fields of Eastern European Jewish arts, music and theater.
Eligibility: A written summary of one's research is required
Level of Study: Postgraduate, Research
Type: Fellowship
Value: US$5,000
Length of Study: Two to Three months
Frequency: Annual
Country of Study: Any country
Application Procedure: Applicants must send their curriculum vitae, research proposal and 2 letters of support by regular mail, fax or email
Closing Date: 1 February
Additional Information: www.yivo.org/List-of-Fellowships

Maria Salit-Gitelson Tell Memorial Fellowship

Purpose: To support original doctoral or postdoctoral research in the field of Lithuanian Jewish history, the city of Vilnus in particular, at the YIVO Library and Archives
Eligibility: Applicants must carry out original doctoral or postdoctoral research in the field of Lithuanian Jewish history and give a public lecture at the end of the tenure of the Fellowship
Level of Study: Doctorate, Postdoctorate
Type: Fellowship
Value: US$7,000
Length of Study: 1–3 months
Frequency: Annual
Study Establishment: YIVO Library and Archives
Country of Study: United States of America
Application Procedure: Applicants must send a cover letter, curriculum vitae, research proposal and 2 letters of support through regular mail, fax or email
Closing Date: 1 February
Additional Information: www.yivo.org/List-of-Fellowships

Natalie and Mendel Racolin Memorial Fellowship

Purpose: To support original doctoral or post-doctoral research in the field of East European Jewish studies.
Eligibility: Applicants must carry out original doctoral or postdoctoral research in the field of East European Jewish history and give a public lecture at the end of the tenure of the Fellowship
Level of Study: Doctorate, Postdoctorate
Type: Fellowship
Value: US$20,000
Length of Study: 3 months
Frequency: Annual
Study Establishment: YIVO Library and Archives
Country of Study: United States of America
Application Procedure: Applicants must send a cover letter, curriculum vitae, research proposal and 2 letters of support through regular mail, fax or email
Closing Date: 1 February
Additional Information: www.yivo.org/List-of-Fellowships

Professor Bernard Choseed Memorial Fellowship

Purpose: To financially support original doctoral or post-doctoral research in the field of East European Jewish studies.
Eligibility: Applicants are required to give a public lecture
Level of Study: Doctorate, Postdoctorate
Type: Fellowship
Value: US$20,000
Length of Study: 3 months
Frequency: Annual
Country of Study: United States of America
Application Procedure: Applicants must submit a curriculum vitae, a research proposal and 2 letters of support through regular mail, fax or email
Closing Date: 1 February
Additional Information: www.yivo.org/List-of-Fellowships

Rose and Isidore Drench Memorial Fellowship

Purpose: Dedicated to doctoral or post-doctoral research in American Jewish history, with special consideration given to scholars working on some aspect of the Jewish labor movement.

Eligibility: Applicants are required to give a public lecture
Level of Study: Doctorate, Postdoctorate
Type: Fellowship
Value: US$5,000
Length of Study: 3 months
Frequency: Annual
Country of Study: Any country
Application Procedure: Applicants must submit their curriculum vitae, a research proposal and 2 letters of support through regular mail, fax or email
Closing Date: 1 February
Additional Information: www.yivo.org/List-of-Fellowships

Samuel and Flora Weiss Research Fellowship

Purpose: To support doctoral or post-doctoral research on Polish-Jewish history in the modern period, particularly Jewish-Polish relations, including the Holocaust period, and Jewish contributions to Polish literature and culture.
Eligibility: Applicants must carry out original research on the destruction of Polish Jewry or on Polish-Jewish relations during the Holocaust period and give a written summary of the research carried out. The research should result in a scholarly publication
Level of Study: Doctorate, Postdoctorate
Type: Fellowship
Value: US$4,000
Length of Study: Three months
Frequency: Annual
Country of Study: Any country
Application Procedure: Applicants must send a cover letter, curriculum vitae, research proposal and 2 letters of support through regular mail, fax or email
Closing Date: 1 February
Additional Information: www.yivo.org/List-of-Fellowships

For further information contact:

Tel: (1) 212 294 613
Email: pglasse@yivo.cjh.org

Vivian Lefsky Hort Memorial Fellowship

Purpose: To assist an undergraduate, graduate or postgraduate researcher in Eastern European Jewish literature.
Eligibility: Applicants must carry out original doctoral or postdoctoral research in Yiddish literature and give a public lecture at the end of the tenure of the Fellowship
Level of Study: Doctorate, Postdoctorate
Type: Fellowship
Value: US$4,000
Length of Study: 2 to 3 months
Frequency: Annual
Study Establishment: YIVO Library and Archives
Country of Study: United States of America
Application Procedure: Applicants must send a cover letter, curriculum vitae, research proposal and 2 letters of support through regular mail, fax or email
Closing Date: 1 February
Additional Information: www.yivo.org/List-of-Fellowships

Vladimir and Pearl Heifetz Memorial Fellowship in Eastern European Jewish Music

Purpose: To assist undergraduate, graduate and postgraduate researchers defray expenses connected with research in YIVO's music collection at the YIVO Archives and Library
Eligibility: Undergraduate, graduate and postgraduate researchers who will carry on research in YIVO's music collection at the YIVO Archives and Library
Level of Study: Graduate, Postgraduate
Type: Fellowship
Value: US$1,500
Frequency: Annual
Study Establishment: YIVO's music collection
Country of Study: United States of America
Application Procedure: Applicants must send a cover letter, curriculum vitae, research proposal and 2 letters of support through regular mail, fax or email
Closing Date: 31 December
Funding: Foundation
Additional Information: www.yivo.org/List-of-Fellowships

Workmen's Circle/Dr Emanuel Patt Visiting Professorship

Purpose: To support three months of post-doctoral research at the YIVO Library and Archives and a public lecture by the visiting faculty member.
Level of Study: Postdoctorate
Type: Professorship
Value: US$5,000
Length of Study: 3 months
Frequency: Annual
Country of Study: United States of America
Application Procedure: Applicants must send a covering letter, curriculum vitae, research proposal and 2 letters of support through regular mail, fax or email
Closing Date: 31 December
Additional Information: The visiting faculty member should give a public lecture at the end of the award's tenure www.yivo.org/list-of-fellowships

Subject and Eligibility Guide to Awards

AGRICULTURE, FORESTRY AND FISHERY

General
Agricultural business
Agricultural economics
Agriculture and farm management
Agronomy
Animal husbandry
 Sericulture
Crop production
Fishery
 Aquaculture
Food science
 Brewing
 Dairy
 Fish
 Harvest technology
 Meat and poultry
 Oenology
Forestry
 Forest biology
 Forest economics
 Forest management
 Forest pathology
 Forest products
 Forest soils
Horticulture and viticulture
Soil and water science
 Irrigation
 Soil conservation
 Water management
Tropical agriculture
Veterinary science

ARCHITECTURE AND TOWN PLANNING

General
Architectural and environmental design
Architectural restoration
Landscape architecture
Regional planning
Rural planning
Structural architecture
Town planning

ARTS AND HUMANITIES

General
Archaeology
Classical languages and literatures
 Classical Greek
 Latin
 Sanskrit
Comparative literature
History
 Ancient civilisations
 Contemporary history
 Medieval studies
 Modern history
 Prehistory
Linguistics
 Applied linguistics
 Grammar
 Logopedics
 Phonetics
 Psycholinguistics
 Semantics and terminology
 Speech studies
Modern languages
 African Languages
 Afrikaans
 Altaic languages
 Amerindian languages
 Arabic
 Austronesian and oceanic languages
 Baltic languages
 Celtic languages
 Chinese
 Danish
 Dutch

Palgrave Macmillan (ed.), *The Grants Register 2024*,
https://doi.org/10.1057/978-1-349-96073-6

English
Eurasian and North Asian languages
European languages (others)
Finnish
Fino Ugrian languages
French
German
Germanic languages
Hebrew
Hungarian
Indian languages
Indic languages
Iranic languages
Italian
Japanese
Korean
Modern Greek
Norwegian
Portuguese
Romance languages
Russian
Scandinavian languages
Slavic languages (others)
Spanish
Swedish
Native language and literature
Philosophy
Ethics
Logic
Metaphysics
Philosophical schools
Translation and interpretation
Writing (authorship)

BUSINESS ADMINISTRATION AND MANAGEMENT

General
Accountancy
Business and commerce
Business computing
Business machine operation
Finance, banking and investment
Human resources
Institutional administration
Insurance
International business
Labour/industrial relations
Management systems
Marketing
Public relations
MBA
Personnel management
Private administration
Public administration
Real estate
Secretarial studies

EDUCATION AND TEACHER TRAINING

General
Adult education
Continuing education
Educational science
Curriculum
Distance education
Educational administration
Educational and student counselling
Educational research
Educational technology
Educational testing and evaluation
International and comparative education
Philosophy of education
Teaching and learning
Higher education teacher training
Nonvocational subjects education
Education in native language
Foreign languages education
Humanities and social science education
Literacy education
Mathematics education
Physical education
Science education
Pre-school education
Primary education
Secondary education
Special education
Bilingual/bicultural education
Education of foreigners
Education of natives
Education of specific learning disabilities
Education of the gifted
Education of the handicapped
Education of the socially disadvantaged
Staff development
Teacher trainers education
Vocational subjects education
Agricultural education
Art education
Commerce/business education
Computer education
Health education
Home economics education
Industrial arts education
Music education
Technology education

ENGINEERING

General
Aeronautical and aerospace engineering
Agricultural engineering
Automotive engineering
Bioengineering and biomedical engineering
Chemical engineering
Civil engineering
Computer engineering
Control engineering (robotics)
Electrical and electronic engineering
Energy engineering
Engineering drawing/design
Environmental and sanitary engineering
Forestry engineering
Hydraulic engineering
Industrial engineering
Marine engineering and naval architecture
Materials engineering
Measurement/precision engineering
Mechanical engineering
Metallurgical engineering
Mining engineering
Nanotechnology
Nuclear engineering
Petroleum and gas engineering
Physical engineering
Production engineering
Safety engineering
Sound engineering
Surveying and mapping science

FINE AND APPLIED ARTS

General
Art criticism
Art history
  Aesthetics
Art management
Cinema and television
Dance
Design
  Display and stage design
  Fashion design
  Furniture design
  Graphic design
  Industrial design
  Interior design
  Textile design
Drawing and painting
Handicrafts
Music
  Conducting
  Jazz and popular music
  Music theory and composition
  Musical instruments
  Musicology
  Opera
  Religious music
  Singing
Photography
Religious art
Sculpture
Theatre

HOME ECONOMICS

General
Child care/child development
Clothing and sewing
Consumer studies
House arts and environment
Household management
Nutrition

LAW

General
Air and space law
Canon law
Civil law
Commercial law
Comparative law
Criminal law
European community law
History of law
Human rights
International law
Islamic law
Justice administration
Labour law
Maritime law
Notary studies
Private law
Public law
  Administrative law
  Constitutional law
  Fiscal law

MASS COMMUNICATION AND INFORMATION SCIENCE

General
Communication arts
Documentation techniques and archiving
Journalism
Library science
Mass communication
Media studies
Museum management
Museum studies
Public relations and publicity
Radio/television broadcasting
Restoration of works of art

MATHEMATICS AND COMPUTER SCIENCE

General
Actuarial science
Applied mathematics
Artificial intelligence
Computer science
Statistics
Systems analysis

MEDICAL SCIENCES

- General
- Acupuncture
- Biomedicine
- Chiropractic
- Dental technology
  - Prosthetic dentistry
- Dentistry and stomatology
  - Community dentistry
  - Oral pathology
  - Orthodontics
  - Periodontics
- Forensic medicine and dentistry
- Health administration
- Homeopathy
- Medical auxiliaries
- Medical technology
- Medicine
  - Anaesthesiology
  - Cardiology
  - Dermatology
  - Endocrinology
  - Epidemiology
  - Gastroenterology
  - Geriatrics
  - Gynaecology and obstetrics
  - Haematology
  - Hepathology
  - Nephrology
  - Neurology
  - Oncology
  - Ophthalmology
  - Otorhinolaryngology
  - Paediatrics
  - Parasitology
  - Pathology
  - Plastic surgery
  - Pneumology
  - Psychiatry and mental health
  - Rheumatology
  - Tropical medicine
  - Urology
  - Venereology
  - Virology
- Midwifery
- Nursing
- Optometry
- Osteopathy
- Pharmacy
- Podiatry
- Public health and hygiene
  - Dietetics
  - Social/preventive medicine
  - Sports medicine
- Radiology
- Rehabilitation and therapy
- Traditional eastern medicine
- Treatment techniques

NATURAL SCIENCES

- General
- Astronomy and astrophysics
- Biological and life sciences
  - Anatomy
  - Biochemistry
  - Biology
  - Biophysics and molecular biology
  - Biotechnology
  - Botany
  - Embryology and reproduction biology
  - Genetics
  - Histology
  - Immunology

Limnology
Marine biology
Microbiology
Neurosciences
Parasitology
Pharmacology
Physiology
Plant pathology
Toxicology
Zoology
Chemistry
Analytical chemistry
Inorganic chemistry
Organic chemistry
Physical chemistry
Earth sciences
Geochemistry
Geography (scientific)
Geology
Geophysics and seismology
Mineralogy and crystallography
Palaeontology
Petrology
Marine science and oceanography
Meteorology
Arctic studies
Arid land studies
Physics
Atomic and molecular physics
Nuclear physics
Optics
Solid state physics
Thermal physics

RECREATION, WELFARE, PROTECTIVE SERVICES

General
Civil security
Criminology
Environmental studies
Ecology
Environmental management
Natural resources
Waste management
Wildlife and pest management
Fire protection science
Leisure studies
Military science
Parks and recreation
Peace and disarmament
Police studies
Social welfare and social work
Social and community services
Sports
Sociology of sports
Sports management
Vocational counselling

RELIGION AND THEOLOGY

General
Church administration (pastoral work)
Comparative religion
Esoteric practices
History of religion
Holy writings
Religious education
Religious practice
Religious studies
Agnosticism and atheism
Ancient religions
Asian religious studies
Christian religious studies
Islam
Judaic religious studies
Sociology of religion
Theology

SERVICE TRADES

General
Cooking and catering
Cosmetology
Hotel and restaurant
Hotel management
Retailing and wholesaling
Tourism

SOCIAL AND BEHAVIOURAL SCIENCES

General
Econometrics
Economic and finance policy
Economic history
Economics
Industrial and production economics
International economics
Taxation
Ancient civilisations (egyptology, assyriology)
Anthropology

Ethnology
Folklore
Cognitive sciences
Cultural studies
African American
African studies
American
Asian
Canadian
Caribbean
East Asian
Eastern European
European
Hispanic American
Indigenous studies
Islamic
Jewish
Latin American
Middle Eastern
Native American
Nordic
North African
Pacific area
South Asian
Southeast Asian
Subsahara African
Western European
Demography and population
Development studies
Geography
Heritage preservation
International relations
Political science and government
Comparative politics
Psychology
Clinical psychology
Development psychology
Educational psychology
Experimental psychology
Industrial and organisational psychology
Personality psychology
Psychometrics
Social psychology
Rural studies
Sociology
Comparative sociology
Futurology
History of societies
Social institutions
Social policy
Social problems
Urban studies
Women's studies

TRADE, CRAFT AND INDUSTRIAL TECHNIQUES

General
Building technologies
Electrical and electronic equipment and maintenance
Food technology
Graphic arts
Printing and printmaking
Publishing and book trade
Heating, and refrigeration
Laboratory techniques
Leather techniques
Mechanical equipment and maintenance
Metal techniques
Optical technology
Paper and packaging technology
Textile technology
Wood technology

TRANSPORT AND COMMUNICATIONS

General
Air transport
Marine transport and nautical science
Postal services
Railway transport
Road transport
Telecommunications services
Transport economics
Transport management

ANY SUBJECT

Any Country

AAA Northeast Scholarship, 1003
Aarhus University Scholarships, 6
The Abdullah Al-Mubarak Al-Sabah Foundation BRISMES Scholarships, 263
Aberdeen International Masters Scholarship, 1214
Aboriginal and Torres Strait Islander Pharmacy Scholarship Scheme, 1561
Academic Excellence Award: Postgraduate, 830
Academic Excellence International Masters Scholarship, 1304
Acadia Graduate Scholarship/Acadia Graduate Teaching Assistantships, 14
Acorn Foundation Eva Trowbridge Scholarship, 1579
Adelle and Erwin Tomash Fellowship in the History of Information Processing, 347
Adelphi University Full-Time Transfer Merit Award, 16

Adolf Fassbender Travel Fellowship Award, 337
Advanced Clinician Scientist Fellowship, 311
Africa Postgraduate Regional Scholarship, 1305
Ahmanson Veterans Scholarship, 210
AHO Tertiary Accommodation Grants, 349
AHRC South, West and Wales Doctoral Training Partnerships, 1521
AHURI Postgraduate Scholarship Top-up, 1562
AIMS@JCU Scholarship, 673
The Alan Howard Scholarship, 616
Alexander Hugh Thurland Scholarship, 1562
Alex C P Chu Trade for Training Scholarship, 788
Allianz Care Scholarship, 164
Alumni Bursary, 1335
The Alumni Bursary, 812
Alumni Discounts, 1342, 1521
Alumni Discount Scheme, 943
Alumni 10% Fee Tuition Discount, 830
Alumni 25% Fee Tuition Discount, 831
Alumni Heritage Graduate Scholarship (AHGS), 1220
Alumni Loyalty Scholarship, 555
Alumni Postgraduate Research Scholarship-Exclusively for Kent Graduates, 1323
Alumni Scholarship, 1284
Ambassadors Fund for Cultural Preservation Small Grants Competition, 483
The Amelia and John Kentfield PhD Scholarships, 616
American Association of University Women International Fellowships, 51
American Institute of Certified Public Accountants/Robert Half Student Scholarship Award, 670
American Library Association John Phillip Immroth Memorial Award, 82
Ampère Excellence Scholarships for International Students, 456
Amsterdam Excellence Scholarships (AES), 1223
Amsterdam Science Talent Scholarship (ASTS), 1223
ANID (Becas Chile), 966
Anna Schiller Scholarship, 988
The Anne Seagrim Accommodation Scholarships, 616
Anne van den Ban Fund, 1604
Annual Hazards and Disasters Student Paper Competition, 879
Annual Meetings Travel and Hotel Subsidies, 458
The Applications of Nanotechnology in Prevention of Chemotherapy-induced Hearing Impairment, 408
Arturo Falaschi Postdoctoral Fellowships 2023, 652
Arturo Falaschi Short-term PhD Fellowships–March 2023, 652
Arturo Falaschi Short-term Postdoctoral Fellowships, 652
Asian Development Bank Japan Scholarship, 1226
Asian Development Bank-Japan Scholarship Program, 875
The ASID Educational Foundation/Irene Winifred Eno Grant, 118
Associated Colleges of the Midwest/the Great Lakes Colleges Association Faculty Fellowships, 892
Association of Commonwealth Universities Titular Fellowships, 376
Association of Firearm and Tool Mark Examiners Scholarship, 400
A*Star Graduate Scholarship, 20
Aston Dean, 149
Asylum Seeker Scholarship, 1539
Athens State University Phi Theta Kappa Transfer Scholarship, 152
Auckland University of Technology Vice Chancellor Doctoral Scholarship, 154
Australia Awards, 1266
Australian Eye and Ear Health Survey, 766
Australian Federation of University Women-Western Australian-Foundation Bursary, 167
Australian Government Research Training Program (AGRTP) Stipend Scholarship, 1266
Australian Government RTP Scholarship (International), 1563
Australian National University Doctoral Fellowships, 172
Australian National University Excellence Scholarship Program, 173
Australian Postgraduate Award, 509
Australia's Global University Award, 1415
Austria: Erasmus+ Master in Research and Innovation in Higher Education (MARIHE) Programme, 593
AUT Doctoral Scholarships, 154
Awards for Current Students-The Bath Spa University International Travel Fund, 181
Awards for Current Students-The Extra-curricular Activity Fund, 182
Awards for Current Students-The Harbutt Fund, 182
Awards for Current Students-The Porthleven Prize, 182
Awards for Current Students-The Wilfred Southall Sustainability Awards, 183
Awarua Trust Scholarship, 154
Azerbaijan: Non-Aligned Movement (NAM) Scholarship, 594
Bailey Bequest Bursary, 639, 789
Banting Postdoctoral Fellowships, 289
Barron Prize, 240
BASF (Ludwigshafen/Germany), 967
Basil O'Connor Starter Scholar Research Award, 784
Bass Connections–Collaborative Project Expeditions, 441
Baxter International Foundation Grants, 16
Bayreuth International Graduate School of African Studies Sandwich Scholarship Programme, 187
Beit Trust Grants, 191
Belgian Technical Cooperation Scholarships, 194

Ben Barnett Scholarship, 1440
The Bestway Foundation Scholarship, 1333
BFWG Academic Awards, 247
Bibliographical Society of America-Harry Ransom Center Pforzheimer Fellowship in Bibliography, 203
Bielefeld Science Award, 208
Bilkent Industrial Engineering Fellowship, 208
Bilkent MIAPP Fellowship, 209
Bilkent Turkish Literature Fellowship, 209
BIPOC Postgraduate Essay Award, 236
2023-24 Bloomsbury Colleges PhD Studentship-Project 2, 744
BOF postdoctoral fellowships, 569
Bonnart Trust Master's Studentships, 221
Boulton Fellowship, 799
Bournemouth University Dean, 227
Bournemouth University Dean's Scholarship–The Media School, 227
Bowler Ravensdown Scholarship in Soil Science, 639
Brenda Shore Award for Women, 1442
Bridge to Independence Award Program, 1113
BRISMES Early Career Development Prize, 262
British-American Chamber of Commerce Awards, 551
British Association for Japanese Studies Postgraduate Studentships, 238
British Federation of Women Graduates (BFWG), 1315
British Federation of Women Graduates Postgraduate Awards, 1324
British Federation of Women Graduates Scholarships, 247
British Institute at Ankara Research Scholarship, 254
British Society for Antimicrobial Chemotherapy Overseas Scholarship, 262
The Brock Doctoral Scholarship, 1322
Bruggeman Postgraduate Scholarship in Classics, 1019
Brunei Darussalam: Government of Brunei Darussalam Scholarship, 594
Brunel Family Discount Terms and Conditions, 266
Brunel Santander International Scholarship, 266
The Business School Dean's Scholarship, 229
Cameron Beyer Scholarship, 509
Canada-CARICOM Faculty Leadership Program, 1319
Canada Graduate Scholarships–Michael Smith Foreign Study Supplements Program, 880
Canadian Embassy Faculty Enrichment Program, 285
Canadian Federation of University Women/A. Vibert Douglas Fellowship, 658
Canadian Institutes of Health Research Gold Leaf Prizes, 289
Canadian Tobacco Control Research Initiative Planning Grants, 1127
Cardiff Business School-ESRC Wales DTP Fully Funded General Studentships (Economics), 323
Cardiff Business School Scholarships in Business and Management and Economics, 324
Cardiff India scholarships, 324
Cardiff School of Mathematics–PhD Studentships, 325
Cardiff School of Music–PhD Studentships, 326
Cardiff University PhD Studentship in European Studies, 328
Career Development Award, 659
Career Development Fellowship, 312
Career Establishment Award, 312
Career Transition Fellowships, 864
Carnegie PhD Scholarships, 1295
Cartmel College Postgraduate Studentship, 556, 705
Cartmel College Scholarships, 706
Casinomucho Research Scholarship (CSR), 334
Catalyst Award, 364
Catherine and Peter Tay for Singapore Alumni (follow on) Scholarship, 1430
Catherine Baxter Dairy Scholarship, 640
The Catherine Mackichan Trust, 1317
CBC Literary Prizes, 270
CDU Vice-Chancellor's International High Achievers Scholarships, 348
Center for AIDS Prevention Studies, Small Professional Grants for Graduate Students, 1441
Centre de Sciences Humaines Post-Doctoral Fellowship, 344
CEPAR Honours Scholarship, 1416
Chancellor, 651
Chancellor's International Scholarship, 1558
Chancellor's Research Scholarship, 1163
Charles Sturt University Postgraduate Research Studentships (CSUPRS), 351
Chemistry Department Scholarship for students of Black heritage, 609
Chevening Scholarships, 1535
Chevening Scholarship scheme (External Scholarship), 228
Chiang Ching Kuo Foundation Doctoral Fellowships, 357
Childcare Funding, 1539
Children of Alumni Award, 968
China Scholarship Council Cambridge Scholarships, 1262
China Scholarship Council-Massey University PhD Scholars Programme, 790
China Scholarship Council Scholarships, 1636
Chinese Government Scholarship Program, 1636
Chris and Gina Grubb Ornithology Scholarship, 351
Chulalongkorn University (Thailand) LAW Scholarships, 1291
Church Matching Scholarship, 210
Cicada Innovations Postgraduate Research Placement Scholarship, 1564
Civil and Structural Engineering PhD Scholarship, 402
Civil Engineering Dixon Scholarship, 609
Civil Engineering Skempton Scholarship, 609
Clara Collet Departmental Scholarships, 1202
Clare Hall Research Fellowships in the Arts and Social Sciences, 365

Clarendon Scholarship, 1139
Claude Leon Foundation Postdoctoral Fellowship, 366
Clem Hill Memorial Scholarship, 640
Clinical Management of Pain Scholarship, 1296
Clinical & Public Health Research Fellowships-Early Career Fellowship, 617
Clinical & Public Health Research Fellowships-Intermediate Fellowship, 618
Clinical & Public Health Research Fellowships-Senior Fellowship, 618
Co-funded Monash Graduate Scholarship (CF-MGS), 821
Coimbra Group Scholarship Programme for Young Researchers from the European Neighbourhood, 367
Collaborative Offline & Online Platform for Research EuroTechPostdoc Fellowships for International Students at European Universities, 504
College of International Education International Pathways Scholarship, 1430
College of Science and Engineering International PGT Merit Scholarship, 1342
Commonwealth Distance Learning Scholarships, 1296
Commonwealth Masters Scholarships, 446
Commonwealth PhD Scholarship (for High Income Countries), 1324
Commonwealth PhD Scholarships, 1516
Commonwealth Scholarships, 242, 1226
Commonwealth Scholarships and Fellowships Plan (CSFP) General Scholarship, 1369
Commonwealth Scholarships and Fellowships Programme, 1538
Commonwealth Scholarships for Developing Countries, 446
Commonwealth Shared Scholarship Scheme (CSSS), 1202, 1353, 1458, 1459
Commonwealth Shared Scholarships-PGT, 446
Commonwealth Split-Site Doctoral Scholarships, 447
Commonwealth Split-site Scholarship, 1325
Community Bridging Services (CBS) Inc Scholarship, 522
Community Support Grants, 390
Completion Scholarships, 1531
Computing, Engineering and Mathematical Sciences Graduate Teaching Assistant PhD Studentship, 1325
CONACyT Mexico Scholarships, 1370
Conference Attendance Support for Postgraduate Students, 238
Conference/Seminar/Workshop Grants, 358
Conference Travel Grants, 1240
Conseil Européen Pour la Recherche Nucléaire Summer Student Programme, 380
Conservation Guest Scholars, 567
Consortium for Advanced Research Training in Africa PhD Fellowships, 382
Consortium for Applied Research on International Migration Postdoctoral Talent Fellowship, 382
Cook School of Intercultural Studies Graduate Grant, 211
Cooperative Research Center for Water Quality and Treatment Young Water Scientist of the Year Scholarship, 383
Council Scholarship, 510
County College Travel Award, 556
CQUniCares Emergency Grant, 339
CQUniversity/Industry Collaborative Grants Scheme, 340
Cranfield Global Manufacturing Leadership Masters Scholarship, 394
Cranfield Sub-Saharan Africa Merit Scholarship, 394
C. Ravi Ravindran Outstanding Doctoral Thesis Award, 1075
Crohn's & Coltis Foundation Research Fellowship Awards, 396
Crohn's & Coltis Foundation Senior Research Award, 396
Croucher Innovation Awards, 398
Croucher Science Communication Studentships, 398
Croucher Senior Research Fellowships, 399
CSU Foundation Persistence Scholarship, 352
CSU give-Research Scholarship, 352
Cultural Learnings: Strengthening Aboriginal children's wellbeing, 403
Curtin Business School Doctoral Scholarship, 403
Daad-Master Studies, 436
The Dalai Lama Trust Scholarship, 413
Daphne Jackson Fellowships, 485
Data61 PhD Scholarships, 1564
David Phillips Fellowships, 216
Davis Scholarship, 846
Deakin Alumni Discount, 420
Deakin International Scholarship, 421
Deakin University Postgraduate Research Scholarship (DUPR), 422
Deakin University Postgraduate Research Scholarships (DUPRS), 422
Deakin Vice-Chancellor's International Scholarship, 423
Dean's 20th Anniversary Scholarships, 1353
DeepMind PhD Scholarships, 1296
DeepMind Scholarship-Department of Computing, 609
Defence Research and Development Canada Postgraduate Scholarship Supplements, 881
De Montfort University Awards to Women for Final Year Doctoral Research, 414
The Dennis Mock Student Leadership Award, 1079
Dennis William Moore Scholarship, 1268
Departmental Scholarships-Chemical Engineering, 610
Department of Bioengineering Scholarship (MRes), 610
Department of Bioengineering Scholarship (MSc), 610
Design School Scholarships, 753
Destination Australia, 511
Destination Australia Scholarships-International Students, 699
Deutsche Forschungsgemeinschaft Mercator Programme, 432

Deutsche Forschungsgemeinschaft Research Training Groups, 433
Deutscher Akademischer Austauschdienst (German Academic Exchange Service) Scholarships, 1272
Developing Solutions Masters Scholarship, 1439
Diane Campbell-Hunt Memorial Award, 1443
Dilmah Tea International Study Award, 791
Discounts for Surrey Graduates, 1556
Dissertation Planning Grants, 78
Dissertation Research Scholarship, 565
Diversity Scholarship, 742
Doctoral Completion Award, 1076
Doctoral Scholarships, 201, 1227
Dorothy Hodgkin Postgraduate Award, 1242
Doshisha University Graduate School Reduced Tuition Special Scholarships for Self-Funded International Students, 439
Doshisha University Graduate School Scholarship, 439
Doshisha University Merit Scholarships for Self-Funded International Students, 440
Doshisha University Reduced Tuition Scholarships for Self-Funded International Students, 440
Dr Andres Petrasovits Fellowship in Cardiovascular Health Policy Research, 585
Drever Trust MSc Scholarships, 1297
Dr Lloyd John Ogilvie Scholarships, 1296
Dr Sulaiman Daud 125th Jubilee Postgraduate Scholarship, 1443
Dr Theo George Wilson Scholarship, 611
Dual Credit Scholarship, 721
Dulcie Bowman Memorial Scholarship, 1227
Duncan Norman Scholarship, 1353
Dunkeld Refugee and Asylum Seeker, 511
Early Career Fellowships, 725
Earthwatch Field Research Grants, 455
ECCO-AOCC Visiting Travel Grant, 498
ECCO Global Grant-New, 497
ECCO Grant, 497
ECCO Pioneer Award, 498
École Normale Supérieure International Selection Scholarships, 455
Economic and Social Research Council (ESRC) White Rose Doctoral Training Partnership (DTP) and Faculty Scholarships, 1525
Economics: MSc Applied Training Scholarships (International), 1292
Economics 50% Scholarships: Thammasat University (Thailand), 1291
ECU-DBCA Kings Park Science Industry PhD Scholarship, 470
E4D Continuing Education Scholarship, 479
Edinburgh Business School PhD Management Scholarship, 592
Edinburgh Dental Institute MSc Scholarship, 1297
Edinburgh Doctoral College Scholarships, 1297
Edinburgh Global Online Distance Learning Masters Scholarship, 1297
Edinburgh Global Online Distance Learning Scholarships, 1298
Edinburgh Global Online Learning Masters Scholarships, 1298
Edinburgh Global Research Scholarship, 1298
Edouard Morot-Sir Fellowship in French Studies, 628
Educational Testing Service Summer Internships in Programme Direction, 477
EDUFI Fellowship, 519
Edward E. Hildebrand Research Fellowship, 196
Eiffel Scholarships in France for International Students, 548
Elphinstone PhD Scholarships, 1216
Elspeth D. Rostow Memorial Graduate Fellowship, 1169
Emergency Aid Fund, 1540
Emergency Grants for United Kingdom and International Women Graduates, 554
Emergency Medicine Foundation Grants, 552
Emerging Leaders Awards, 848
Emeritus Fellowships, 725
Emile Boutmy Scholarships, 1106
Emmy Noether Programme, 433
Employment-Based Postgraduate Programme, 670
Endeavour Postgraduate Leadership Award, 436
Energy Futures Lab Widening Participation Scholarship, 611
Engerman-Goldin Prize, 459
Engineering and Physical Sciences Research Council (EPSRC), 612, 1325
Enterprise Partnership Scheme, 671
The Enterprise Showcase Fund, 185
EPA-IRC Government of Ireland Postgraduate Scholarship Programme, 491
EPFL PhD Excellence Program, 457
EPSRC Centres for Doctoral Training, 217
EPSRC-School of Computing, 1326
EPSRC-School of Engineering, 1326
EPSRC-School of Mathematics, Statistics and Actuarial Science, 1326
Erasmus University Holland Scholarship, 1013
ERC-funded Studentships in Psychology: Consequences of Conspiracy Theories, 1327
Ernest Rutherford Fellowship, 1101
Ernst Mach Grant for Young Researchers, 535
ESRC SeNSS Doctoral Training Partnerships Studentships, 1522
Essex Global Partner Scholarship, 1306
Eta Sigma Phi Summer Scholarships, 492
ETH4D Doctoral Mentorship Programme, 479
ETH4D Research Challenges, 480
ETH4D Seed Grants, 480

European Committee for Treatment and Research in Multiple Sclerosis-MAGNIMS Fellowship in Magnetic Resonance Imaging in MS, 496
European Travelling Scholarships, 240
EuroTechPostdoc, 504
Evans Fund, 1242
Evonik Stiftung Scholarships, 505
Excellence in Education Scholarship, 1292
Excellence Scholarships for Postgraduate Study, 1234
The Exeter MBA Better World Scholarship, 1311
External Sources of Funding, 707
The Eynesbury College High Achiever Progression Scholarship, 1218
The Eynesbury College International Scholarship, 1219
Faculty Mobility for Partnership Building Program, 1320
Faculty of Science Masters Scholarship for International Students, 1155
Fee-relief Scholarships, 1531
Felix Scholarships, 1461
Fellow Programme in Management (FPM) at Xavier Labor Relations Institute, 1633
Ferrari Innovation Team Project Scholarship, 518
FfWG Foundation Grants, 554
FfWG-Foundation Grants for Women Graduates, 556, 707
Fieldwork Bursary, 256
Finn Randall Travel Award, 1543
Fitzwilliam College Charlton Studentships, 1243
Fitzwilliam College: Cleaver-Wang Studentship, 1244
Fitzwilliam College: E D Davies Scholarship, 1244
Fitzwilliam College Graduate Scholarship, 1243
Fitzwilliam College: Lee Kuan Yew PhD Studentships, 1245
Fitzwilliam College Research Fellowship, 1243
Fitzwilliam College: The Hong Leong–Lee Kuan Yew Masters Scholarship, 1246
Fitzwilliam Masters Studentship, 1246
Flinders University Research Scholarships (FURS), 554
Foundation Commencing Scholarships, 512
Foundation Continuing Scholarships, 513
Foundation Grants, 554
Foundation HDR Scholarships, 513
Four-year PhD Studentship Programmes, 1607
Free University of Berlin and Peking University Joint Postdoctoral Fellowship, 548
French Association of University Women (AFFDU) Grants, 248
Fulbright Postdoctoral Scholarship in All Disciplines, 551
Fulbright Scholarship, 1227
Full Tuition International Relations Scholarships, 174
Fully Funded EPSRC Scholarships in Chemistry, 1327
Fully Funded EPSRC Scholarships in Physics, 1327
Fully Funded PhD Scholarships, 1445
Furness Studentship, 708
Future Finance (Private Student Loans), 708
Fylde College-Travel Award, 556
Gallman-Parker Prize, 460
Gates Cambridge Scholarship, 561
General Research Grants: Scholarships, 1172
George Major Bursaries, 1347
The George Melhuish Postgraduate Scholarship, 1211
George Pepler International Award, 1073
German Academic Scholarship Foundation, 189
Getty Scholar Grants, 568
Gilbert Chinard Fellowships, 628
Gilchrist Fieldwork Award, 569
Girton College: Doris Woodall Studentship, 1247
Girton College Graduate Research Scholarship, 1246
Girton College: Ida and Isidore Cohen Research Scholarship, 1247
Girton College: Irene Hallinan Scholarship, 1247
Girton College Overseas Bursaries, 1247
Girton College: Ruth Whaley Scholarship, 1248
Girton College: Sidney and Marguerite Cody Studentship, 1248
Girton College: Stribling Award, 1249
Girton College: The Diane Worzala Memorial Fund, 1249
Girton College: The Dinah James Scholarship, 1249
Girton College: The Joyce Biddle Scholarship, 1250
Girton College: The Postgraduate Research Scholarship, 1250
Girton College: Travel Grant, 1251
Global Ambassador Scholarship Programme (GASPR), 766
Global Challenges Research Fund Networking Grants, 12
Global Citizenship Scholarship, 1284
Global Excellence Scholarship, 150, 1285
Global Excellence Scholarships-Postgraduate Taught (Masters), 1311
Global Opportunity Fellowship (GO: AFRICA), 581
Global Partnership Network Masters Scholarships, 1007
Global Postgraduate Scholarship, 1347
Global Talent Fellowships, 1292
Godfrey Tyler Scholarship in Economics, 1139
Gold and Silver Scholarships, 1581
Gonville and Caius College Gonville Bursary, 1251
Gonville and Caius College Michael Miliffe Scholarship, 1251
Goodrich Scholarship Program, 847
Gordon David Family Scholarship, 464
Gottfried Wilhelm Leibniz Prize, 434
Governor General Gold Medal, 1077
Graduate Council Fellowships, 1220
Graduate Division Caregiver Grant, 197
Graduate Research Scholarships, 1203, 1394
Graduate Research Scholarships for Cross-disciplinary Training (One-Year), 1203
Graduate Student Stipend, 1077
'Green Futures' Postgraduate Taught Scholarships, 1311

Greta Davis Equity Scholarship for Musically Talented Students, 1566
Greyfriars Postgraduate Scholarship, 985
Hardiman PhD Scholarships, 872
Hardship Support Fund, 754
Harmon Chadbourn Rorison Fellowship, 628
Harry Crossley Master, 1153
Harry Ransom Center: Research Fellowships, 1575
Harry S. Truman Book Award, 580
Harry S Truman Library Institute Research Grant, 580
Harry S Truman Library Institute Scholar's Award, 580
Hatfield Lioness Scholarship, 448
Health Research Council (HRC) Summer Studentships (Ethics), 641
Heart and Stroke Foundation of Canada Research Fellowships, 586
Hebei Provincial Government Scholarship, 1637
The Hector and Elizabeth Catling Doctoral Award, 258
Heilongjiang Provincial Government Scholarships, 682
Heinrich Boll Scholarships in Germany for International Students, 588
Helen E. Akers Postgraduate Scholarship, 641
Hélène La Rue Scholarship in Music, 1139
Hellman Fellows Fund, 1239
Henry Rudolf Meisels Bursary Awards, 713
Heriot-Watt Expo Award, 592
Heritage Scholarship, 722
Hertford College: Worshipful Company of Scientific Instrument Makers Senior Scholarship, 1464
Heseltine Ecology Bursary, 641
High-End Instrumentation (HEI) Grant Program, 859
Higher Education Scholarships (International), 1217
Holland Government Scholarship/Upcoming Year for School of Management, 1014
Holland Scholarship, 577
Hong Kong and Shanghai Banking Corporation School of Oriental and African Studies Scholarships, 1094
The Horowitz Foundation for Social Policy, 603
Housing Support Fund, 1545
The Hub Award, 1610
Hudson and McGowan Scholarship, 642
Hugh Last Fund and General Fund, 1130
The Hugh Martin Weir Prize, 1219
The Humane Research Trust Grant, 605
Humanitarian Scholarship–The University of Dundee, 1289
Humboldt Talent Travel Awards, 606
Hunt Postdoctoral Fellowships, 1615
ICGEB Short-Term PhD Fellowships, 653
ICGEB Short-Term Postdoctoral Fellowships, 654
ICGEB Smart Fellowships, 654
ICTS Post Doctoral Program, 655
Ida Smedley MacLean Fellowship, 658
IDeA Networks of Biomedical Research Excellence (INBRE) (P20 Clinical Trial Optional), 859
Indian Arts Partner Scholarship, 771
Indian Council of Medical Research Centenary-Postdoctoral Fellowship, 620
Indigenous Graduate Scholarship-Fulfilling Indigenous Community Responsibilities, 1320
Indigenous Graduate Scholarship-Leadership, 1320
Indigenous Graduate Scholarship-Merit, 1321
Indigenous Graduate Scholarship-Top-Up, 1321
Indonesia: Kemitraan Negara Berkembang (Developing Countries Partnership) Scholarship, 597
IndusInd Foundation Scholarship for Postgraduate Students, 625
Industry Fellowships, 1051
Informatics Global PhD Scholarships, 1299
Institute Career Path Fellowships, 218
Institute for Advanced Studies on Science, Technology and Society Fellowship Programme, 629
Institute for Advanced Studies Studentships, 1538
Institute for Supply Management Professional Research Development Grant, 634
Institute of Education, University of London Centenary Masters Scholarships, 1204
Institut Européen d'Administration des Affaires MBA Programme, 627
Institution of Engineering and Technology Travel Awards, 647
International Alumni Scholarship, 1348
International Ambassador Scholarships, 1583
International Business Machines Herman Goldstine Postdoctoral Fellowship, 650
International Business Machines PhD Fellowship Program, 650
International College Dundee Progressing with Excellence Scholarship (Taught Postgraduate), 1289
International Development*: Full Fees Scholarship, 1292
International Development*: Scholarships for Students from Bangladesh, 1293
International Development*: Scholarships for Students from Colombia, 1293
International Development*: Scholarships for Students from India, 1293
International Development*: Scholarships for Students from Japan, 1293
International Development*: Scholarships for Students from South Korea, 1294
International Development*: Scholarships for Students from Sub Saharan Africa, 1294
International Excellence Scholarships, 267, 675, 1158
International Exchanges, 1051
International Fellowships, 555, 725

International Institute for Management Development MBA Merit Scholarships, 661
International Merit Award, 811
International Merit Postgraduate Scholarship, 1527
International Merit Scholarships, 748
International Office Postgraduate Scholarship, 971
International Partner Scholarship, 183
International PhD Student Positions in Mathematics, Sweden, 902
International Postgraduate Research Scholarship at Queensland University of Technology, 974
International Postgraduate Research Scholarships (IPRS), 166
International Postgraduate Research Studentship (IPRS) at Murdoch University in Australia, 831
International Postgraduate Scholarships–Taught Master's Programmes, 1236
International Postgraduate Taught Merit Scholarship, 416
International Recruitment Office Scholarship, 183
International Research Training Program Scholarship (IRTPS), 676
International Research Tuition Scholarship (IRTS), 1532
International Road to Research Scholarship-Session 2 2023, 772
International Scholarship Award Program, 417
International Scholarships at University of Derby, 1283
International School of Crystallography Grants, 663
International Scientia Coursework Scholarship, 1419
International Student Aid Grant, 211
International Student Award, 1420
International Student Grant, 918
International Student PGT Scholarship, 959
International Training Fellowships, 1607
International Travel Grants, 1532
International Welcome Scholarships (IWS), 832
IOE Centenary Doctoral Scholarships, 1204
Islamic Cooperation Organization International Internship Program, 671
The ISST Scholarship, 616
IT Support Fund, 556
IT University of Copenhagen State Scholarships, 672
Ivan Morris Memorial Prize, 239
Izaak Walton Killam Memorial Scholarship, 1222
Izaak Walton Killam Predoctoral Fellowships, 1238
The James Callaghan Scholarships, 1160
James Cook University Postgraduate Research Scholarship, 676
Jane's Travel and Research Grant Prizes and Awards, 230
Janet Watson Scholarship, 613
Jan-Georg Deutsch Scholarship in African Studies, 1140
Japanese Studies Event Top-Up Funding, 239
Japan: MEXT Scholarships, 597
Japan Society for the Promotion of Science (JSPS) Fellowship, 1121
Jayce and Seamus Fagan Enabling Program Scholarship, 1435
Jean Kennoway Howells Scholarship, 466
JEP MSc Progression Scholarship, 1289
Jeremiah Lecture Series Support, 1441
Joan Dingley Memorial Scholarship in Mycology, 642
John and Pat Hume Doctoral Scholarships, 874
The John Bright Fellowship, 1388
John Crump Studentship, 239
John Grey Hall of Residence Scholarship, 677
John Hodgson Pastoral Science Scholarship, 642
John L Paterson Postgraduate Design Scholarship, 1299
The John Morrison Memorial Fund for Hellenic Maritime Studies, 258
Joint Japan World Bank Graduate Scholarship Program, 693
Julie Alley Bursary, 642
Justin G. Schiller Prize, 204
Kate Edger Educational Charitable Trust-Expenses/Class Materials Awards, 156
Keble College Gwynne-Jones Scholarship, 1466
Keeling Scholarship, 1205
Kellogg College: Oxford-McCall MacBain Graduate Scholarship, 1468
Kemmy Business School: PhD Scholarship, 1344
Kent-Lille Cotutelle: Advancing Communication between Children and Paediatricians: a Cross-linguistic Contribution, 1328
Kent Lille Cotutelle: LATP Glass-ceramic Electrolytes to Advance Battery Technology for a Low Carbon Future, 1328
Kent-Lille Cotutelle: Novel Neuromorphic, Radically Energy Efficient Training Algorithms for Action Recognition, 1329
Kent Research Institute PhD Scholarships for Institute of Cyber Security for Society (iCSS), 1328
The Khazanah Asia Scholarship in Collaboration with Ancora Foundation, 1510
Killam Doctoral Scholarships, 1238
Kings College: Stipendiary Junior Research Fellowships, 1252
Kipaji Scholarship, 1577
The Kirby Laing International Scholarships, 1303
The Knossos Research Fund, 258
The Lady Eileen McDonald EU & International Student Fund, 1552
Lancaster Enabling Access Fund, 557, 709
Lancaster Opportunity and Access Fund (LOAF) (for UK, EU & International), 710
La Trobe Greater China Scholarship, 700
La Trobe Jordan Scholarship, 701

La Trobe Latin America Scholarship, 701
La Trobe South Asia Scholarship, 702
La Trobe South East Asia Scholarship, 702
La Trobe Turkey Scholarship, 702
L B Wood Travelling Scholarship, 1277
Learned Society Curation Awards, 1607
Lee Kuan Yew School of Public Policy Graduate Scholarships (LKYSPPS), 876
Lesbian, Gay, Bisexual and Transgender+Allies Scholarship, 418
Leslie Rich Scholarship, 1567
Leverhulme Doctoral Scholarships, 725
Leverhulme-funded Studentship in Psychology, 1329
Leverhulme International Professorships, 726
Leverhulme Trade Charities Trust, 557
Liaoning Medical University Postdoctoral Fellowship for International Students at MCMP, 758
Linacre College: Applied Materials MSc Scholarship, 1469
Linacre College: John Bamborough MSc Scholarship, 1470
Lincoln College: Overseas Graduate Entrance Scholarship, 1474
The Lincoln 50% Global Scholarship, 1350
Lindemann Trust Fellowship, 487
Liverpool International College (LIC) Excellence Award, 1356
Liverpool Law School LLM Bursaries, 1356
LLM: E-Fellows Scholarship Programme, 1294
Lockheed Martin Corporation Scholarship for Freshmen, 739
London Metropolitan University Refugee Scholarship, 741
Lone Parents Child Care Grant, 710
Long-Term Fellowship, 499
Lonsdale College Travel Grant, 710
Loyola Marymount University MBA Programme, 758
2023-24 LSHTM Next Generation Scholars, 746
The Lt. Col Jack Wishart Scholarship, 1303
Lucy Cavendish College: Enterprise Studentship, 1252
Lucy Cavendish College: Lord Frederick Cavendish Studentship, 1253
Lucy Cavendish College: Research Fellowships, 1253
Maastricht University Holland Euregion Refugee Scholarship, 764
Maastricht University Holland-High Potential scholarship, 764
The Macmillan-Rodewald Studentship, 258
Macquarie University Alumni Scholarship, 773
Macquarie Vice-Chancellor's International Scholarships, 776
Mac Robertson Travelling Scholarship, 1547
Magdalen College: Student Support Fund Graduate Grants, 1475
Magnusson Awards, 571
Main Fund-International Projects, 232
Major Jeremiah P. Murphy Scholarship, 1004
Manchester Melbourne Dual Award, 1380
Marian Madison Gypsy Lore Society Young Scholar's Prize, 575
Marie Sklodowska-Curie Actions Postdoctoral Fellowships, 1318
The Mary Isabel Sibley Fellowship, 955
Massey University Doctoral Scholarship, 643, 793
Master Excellence Fellowships, 457
Master Mind Scholarships, 569, 1189, 1224
Master of Business Administration Business Excellence Scholarships, 896
Master of Business Administration Global Ambassador Scholarship, 150
Master of Business Administration Programme, 603, 635, 876, 1322
Master of Public Health Scholarship, 571
A Master of Science Degree Scholarship, 1186
Masters Achievement Scholarships, 449
Master Scholarships for International Students, 815
Masters (PGT) EU Scholarship, 1307
Masters Excellence Scholarship, 1308
Masters International Scholarships, 449
Mature Students Hardship Fund, 1155, 1548
Max-Planck-Society Research Scholarships, 798
Maxwell King PhD Scholarship, 824
Maynooth University Teaching Studentships, 875
Maypole Fund Grants for Women, 16
MBPhD Studentships, 252
Melbourne Mobility Excellence Awards, 1398
Melbourne Welcome Grant, 1398
Mellon Mays Predoctoral Research Grants, 1122
Merit International Postgraduate Scholarship, 471
Merit Scholarships for International Postgraduates, 1537
MFL Scholarship applications, 243
Michael and Alice Kuhn Summer Fellowships, 1170
The Millicent C. McIntosh Fellowship, 1624
Minerva Scholarship Fund, 718
Ministry of Foreign Affairs and International Cooperation Scholarships for Foreign and Italian Students, 816
Mitacs Accelerate Fellowship, 1582
Mobility Scooters Direct Scholarship Program, 1576
MRes Scholarships, 1158
MSc Fellowships and PhD Fellowships, 582
Murray and Terry Scholarship, 644
Music Performance Scholarship, 1330
Music Scholarships-Organ Scholarship, 602
National Fellowship and Scholarship for Higher Education of ST Students, 914
National Institute of General Medical Sciences Research Project Grants (R01), 860
National Library of Medicine Investigator Initiated Project Grant, 862
National Research Foundation Visiting Fellowships, 866

National Sun Yat-sen University International Fellowship, 870
NATS Artist Awards, 849
NCUK Postgraduate Taught Scholarships, 1527
Nederlandse Taalunie Scholarship, 1207
Netherlands Organization for International Cooperation in Higher Education-Natural Family Planning Fellowships for PhD Studies, 915
Newcastle University-English Language Excellence Scholarships (Business School Masters), 896
Newcastle University International Postgraduate Scholarship (NUIPS), 898
Newcastle University Overseas Research Scholarship (NUORS), 898
Newcastle University-Vice-Chancellor's Excellence Scholarships-Postgraduate, 897
Newcastle Vice-Chancellor's Global Scholarships-Postgraduate, 899
Newton Advanced Fellowships, 13
Newton International Fellowships, 13, 1051
Newton Mobility Grants, 235
New York State Council on the Arts/New York Foundation for the Arts Artist Fellowship, 888
New Zealand Agency for International Development Scholarship (NZDS)–Open Category, 1229
New Zealand International Doctoral Research (NZIDRS) Scholarship, 1230
NFR FRN Grants for Scientific Equipment, 1162
NFR Travel Grants, 1162
Ngarimu VC and 28th (Māori) Battalion Memorial Scholarships, 474
The Nita Curtis Scholarship, 509
NKA Ellen Gleditsch Scholarship, 249
Norman Fiering Fund, 683
Nottingham Developing Solutions Scholarships, 1440
Nuffield College Funded Studentships, 1477
NUS Research Scholarship, 877
Ogilvie Thompson Scholarship, 1626
Onshore Excellence Scholarship, 1435
Ontario Graduate Scholarship (OGS), 922
Ontario Graduate Scholarship (OGS) Program, 923
Ontario Ministry of Education and Training Graduate Scholarship Programme, 925
The Ontario Trillium Scholarships (OTS), 1441
The Optical Society, Amplify Scholarship, 841
Oriel and Institute for New Economic Thinking (INET) Graduate Scholarship, 939
Oriel College: Oriel Graduate Scholarships, 1479
Oriel College: Paul Ries Collin Graduate Scholarship, 1480
Oriel Graduate Student Scholarships for Academic Merit, 940
Osborn Research Studentship, 1254
Otago International Pathway Scholarship, 1447
Overseas Research Scholarship (ORS), 1588
Overseas Scholarship, 1147
Oxford-Berman Graduate Scholarship, 1482
Oxford-Chellgren Graduate Scholarships, 1485
Oxford-Chelly Halsey Graduate Scholarship, 1485
Oxford-Clayton Graduate Scholarship, 1485
Oxford-Intesa Sanpaolo Graduate Scholarship, 1489
Oxford-Jeffrey Cheah Graduate Scholarship, 1489
Oxford-Patrick Duncan Graduate Scholarships, 1493
Oxford-Pershing Square Graduate Scholarships, 1493
Oxford Refugee Scholarship, 1494
Oxford-Ryniker Lloyd Graduate Scholarship, 1495
Oxford-University College-Burma Graduate Scholarship, 1497
Oxford-Wadham Graduate Scholarships for Disabled Students, 1498
Oxford-Weidenfeld and Hoffmann Scholarships and Leadership Programme, 1498
Paton Masser Memorial Fund, 241
The Paulette Isabel Jones PhD Completion Scholarship, 1572
The Peel Trust Studentship, 558, 712
Pembroke College: College Research Studentships, 1254
Pembroke College: MPhil Studentship for Applicants from the Least Developed Countries, 1254
Peninsula College of Medicine and Dentistry PhD Studentships, 950
The PEN Translation Fund Grants, 959
Perfect Storms: Leverhulme Doctoral Scholarships, 1300
Peterhouse: Research Studentships, 1257
PGR Hardship Fund (for UK, EU & International), 711
Phase II Scholarships, 202
Phase I scholarships, 202
PhD Excellence Scholarships for International Students at Walailak University, Thailand, 902
PhD Fellowship, 540
PhD in Conservation: Hunting, Consumption, and Trade of Animals in the Tropics, 1330
13 PhD International Studentships at Northumbria University in UK, 901
PhD International Studentships in Physical Layer Algorithm Design in 6G Non-Terrestrial Communications, UK, 903
PhD Scholarship Programs, 176
PhD Scholarships, 1173
PhD Scholarship-Transitioning to Caring Economies Through Transformative Community Investment, 644
PhD Studentship in Predicting Higher-Order Biomarker Interactions Using Machine Learning, 1300
PhD Studentship in the Field of Machine Learning in Medical Imaging, 613
PhD Studentship Opportunities in Environment and Health, 614
PhD Studentships in Humanitarianism and Conflict Response, 1381

Phi Beta Kappa Graduate Fellowships for Academic Distinction, 199
Philip Leverhulme Prizes, 726
Postdoc Fellowship for Research Abroad-Bioscience and Basic Biomedicine, 914
Postdoctoral Earth and Planetary Sciences Fellowship, 845
Postdoctoral Fellowship in Health Outcomes Research, 956
Postdoctoral Fellowship Program, 478
Postgrad Solutions Study Bursaries, 1331
Postgraduate Access Awards (United Kingdom-Fee Only), 711
Postgraduate Care Leaver Bursary Terms and Conditions, 267
Postgraduate International Scholarships, 1629
Postgraduate Masters Scholarships in the School of Geography, Politics and Sociology, 899
Postgraduate Progression Award, 1630
Postgraduate Progression Award-International Students, 1357
Postgraduate Research EU Scholarship, 1308
Postgraduate Research Travel Award, 1548
Postgraduate Scholarship for Bath Spa University Alumni, 184
Postgraduate Scholarships (ABS), 150
Postgraduate Taught Sheffield Scholarship, 1527
Predoc Scholarships, 201
Predoctoral Fellowships, 1116
President, 651
President of Ireland Young Research Award (PIYRA), 1104
President's Doctoral Scholar Award, 1382
President's Fund, Edinburgh Association of University Women, 1301
President's Graduate Fellowship, 877
President's PhD Scholarships, 614
President's Postgraduate Scholarship Scheme, 1343
Principal Career Development PhD Scholarship, 1301
Principal's Studentship, 1257
Priority Programme Awards, 1157
Professor de Winter Scholarship, 1578
Provost's Postdoctoral Fellowship Program, 890
Public Scholars, 856
Queen's Loyalty Scholarship, 973
Queen's Transfer Fund, 450
Radboud Encouragement Scholarship, 975
Radboud Scholarship Programme, 976
Radboud Scholarship Programme for International Students, 976
Radboud Scholarships Programme for Masters Students, 977
Radcliffe Department of Medicine: RDM Scholars Programme, 1500
Rae and Edith Bennett Travelling Scholarship, 1399
Regents' Junior Faculty Fellowships, 638
Regional Impact Scholarship (MBA), 900
Regional PhD Bursaries, 1523
Reliance Foundation Global Internship, 633
Research Council of Norway Senior Scientist Visiting Fellowship, 991
Research Fellowships, 1622
Research Grants on Education: Small, 1138
Research Leadership Awards, 726
Research@Pickett Community Outreach and Engagement Voucher Program, 444
Research Student Conference Travel Grants semester 2, 2024, 532
Research Training Fellowships for Nurses and Allied Health Professionals, 253
Research Training Program International Scholarships in Australia (RTPI), 1533
Resilient Reinforcement Learning for Cyber Security, 1331
Rhodes Scholarship, 1006, 1448
The Rhona Beare Award, 1259
The Richard Bradford McConnell Fund for Landscape Studies, 258
RMIT-CSIRO PhD International Scholarship in Mineral Resources and Environmental Science, Australia, 906
The Robin & Nadine Wells Scholarship, 1141
Roche-Law Faculty Scholarship, 1500
Romania: Romanian State Scholarships, 598
Rosemead School of Psychology Graduate Grant, 212
Royal Holloway Principal's Masters Scholarship, 1042
Royal Irish Academy Senior Visiting Fellowships, 1045
Royal Society of Edinburgh Personal Research Fellowships, 1054
RSE Research Network Grants, 1055
RSE Research Workshop Grants, 1055
RSE Small Research Grants, 1056
RSL Queensland Scholarships, 678
RSM non-EEA Scholarship of Excellence (MSc), 1013
Rubicon Programme, 883
Rudolf Diesel Industry Fellowship, 630
Ruth First Scholarship, 450
Saint Louis University International MBA Programme, 1084
Sallie Mae Student Loans, 711
Sam and Nina Narodowski PhD International Scholarships in Australia, 904
Sanctuary Scholarships, 1528
Sandbox Student Grant Program, 1078
Santander Scholarships, 451
Santander Work Based Learning Scholarship, 812
Sasakawa Japanese Studies Postgraduate Studentship, 1383
Scalable Parallelism in the Extreme (SPX), 869
Scholar-in-Residence Program, 436
Scholarly Editions and Scholarly Translations, 856
Scholarship for Overseas Students, 1588
Scholarships for Masters (ICP Connect), 192
School of Arts Master's Bursaries and Studentships, 222

School of Chemical and Process Engineering-International Masters Excellence Scholarship, 1338
School of Chemistry–International Masters Excellence Scholarship, 1338
School of Civil Engineering-International Masters Excellence Scholarship, 1338
School of Computing–International Masters Excellence Scholarship, 1339
School of Divinity Postgraduate Masters Scholarships, 1302
School of Electronic and Electrical Engineering-International Masters Excellence Scholarship, 1339
School of Environment, Education and Development Postgraduate Research Scholarship, 1384
School of Languages & Social Studies PhD, 150
School of Mathematics–International Masters Excellence Scholarship, 1339
School of Mechanical Engineering-International Masters Excellence Scholarship, 1340
School of Physics and Astronomy-International Masters Excellence Scholarship, 1340
School of Social Sciences-Economics PhD Studentships, 1385
School of Social Sciences-Manchester Master, 1386
Science and Technology Facilities Council (STFC), 615
Science Foundation Ireland Career Development Award (CDA), 1104
Science Foundation Ireland Investigator Programme, 1105
Scotland's Saltire Scholarships, 572
ScottishPower International Master's Scholarship Programme, 1548
Sean W. Dever Memorial Prize, 1603
Self-funded PhD Scholarships, 1523
Senior Smeaton Scholarship in Experimental Science, 1448
SG and JG Scholarship (MIT Melbourne), 515
SG and JG Scholarship (MIT Sydney), 515
SG and JG Scholarships (Mt Helen), 516
Shaping Futures Postgraduate Scholarship, 1436
Shapoorji Pallonji Scholarships, 1095
Sheffield Postgraduate Scholarships, 1528
The Shell Centenary Scholarship Fund, Netherlands, 1168
Shell Centenary Scholarships and Shell Centenary Chevening Scholarships at Edinburgh, 1302
Signature Research Theme Scholarship: Future Human-E-scooters in the Life of the Future Human, 1331
Singapore International Graduate Award (SINGA), 20
Sir Francis Hill Postgraduate Scholarship, 1440
Sir George Jessel Studentship in Mathematics, 1209
Sir Paul Callaghan Doctoral Scholarship in Chemistry and Physics, 645
Sir Richard Stapley Educational Trust Grants, 1114
Sir William Dunn School of Pathology: Departmental PhD Prize Studentships, 1502
Snowdon Masters Scholarships, 557, 970
SOAS Sanctuary Scholarship, 1096
Social Work Bursary, 711
Society for the Scientific Study of Sexuality Student Research Grants, 1132
SoCoBio Doctoral Training Partnership (Biotechnology and Biological Sciences Research Council), 1560
Solidarity Grants, 499
South Asia Program Junior Fellowship, 634
South East ESRC DTC Funding, 1332
Special Project Grants, 253
Special Research Fund-Doctoral Scholarship, 569
Sponsored Student Grant, 780
Sport Leadership Grants for Women Program, 177
Square Mile International Scholarship, 418
SRT Scholarship: Future Human–Enhancing Exercise Outcomes Using Immersive Virtual Reality and Machine Learning, 1333
Staff Scholarship-Continuing, 516
Staff Scholarship-International, 516
Starting Investigator Research Grant (SIRG), 1105
St Catherine's College: College Scholarship (Sciences), 1504
St Catherine's College: Ghosh Graduate Scholarship, 1505
St Catherine's College: Leathersellers' Company Scholarship, 1505
St Catherine's College: Overseas Scholarship, 1505
St Catherine's College: Poole Scholarship, 1504
St Cross College: The Harun Ur Rashid Memorial Scholarship, 1507
St Cross College: The Robin & Nadine Wells Scholarship, 1507
St Edmund Hall: William Asbrey BCL Studentship, 1508
St Edmund Hall: William R. Miller Postgraduate Award, 1508
Stellenbosch Merit Bursary Award, 1153
Stellenbosch Rector's Grants for Successing Against the Odds, 1154
St John's College Benefactors' Scholarships for Research, 1258
Strathclyde Alumni Scholarship: Postgraduate Taught, 1549
Strathclyde Business School–Global Research Scholarships, 1552
Strathclyde Business School Home Postgraduate Taught Performance Sport Scholarship, 1550
Strathclyde Business School International Postgraduate Taught Performance Sport Scholarship, 1550
Strathclyde Business School Masters Scholarships for International Students, 1551
Strathclyde Business School RUK Postgraduate Taught Performance Sport Scholarship, 1551
Strathclyde Research Studentship Scheme (SRSS), 1156, 1552
Student Employability Fund, 451
Student Grants, 1400

Study in Australia-Northern Territory Scholarships, 168
Sully Scholarship, 1210
Summer Research Fellowship, 445
Summer Stipends, 856
Susana Menendez Bright Future Scholarship, 577
Sussex Graduate Scholarship, 1560
Sustainability Scholarship, 1317
Sustainable Tourism CRC–Climate Change PhD Scholarship, 678
The Swedish Institute Study Scholarships (SISS), 1161
Swinburne University Postgraduate Research Award (SUPRA), 1163
Sydney Campbell Undergraduate Scholarship, 794
Talbot School of Theology Graduate Grant, 213
Tasmania Honours Scholarships, 1574
Tasmania University Cricket Club Scholarship, 1574
Taught Postgraduate Scholarships, 873
Tel Aviv University Scholarships, 1169
Templeton College MBA Scholarship, 1509
Templeton Fellowships for United States of America and International Scholars at NDIAS, 1438
Test Scholarships for International Students at Free University of Berlin, Germany, 905
Thames and Hudson Scholarship, 1211
Think Big Postgraduate Scholarships, 1237
Transformer Scholarship, 225
Translational Awards, 253
Transmission Fund, 590
Travel Awards for National Travel, 648
Travel Grants, 192
Travelling Bursaries for Presentation at Overseas Meetings, 242
Trinity College Birkett Scholarship in Environmental Studies, 1510
Trinity College Junior Research Fellowship, 1511
Trobe Excellence Scholarships, 700
TUM Global Visiting Professor Program, 630
Turkey Government Scholarships, 1188
Turkey: Türkiye Scholarships, 600
UC International Alumni Scholarship, 1267
UC International Course Merit Scholarship, 1267
UC International High Achiever Scholarship, 1267
UC International Merit Scholarship, 1267
UKRI Centres for Doctoral Training in Artificial Intelligence, 220
UKRI Policy Fellowships 2024, 879
ULMS Attainment Award, 1360
ULMS Progress to Postgraduate Award, 1360
ULMS Southeast Asia Excellence Scholarship, 1361
ULMS West Africa Excellence Scholarship, 1361
ULMS Women in Football Scholarship, 1361
Ulysses, 671
UM Academic Achievement Scholarship, 765
UM Brightlands Talent Scholarship, 766
UniBE International, 1234
Union College Board of Trustees Scholarship, 1190
United States: Fulbright Foreign Student Program, 601
Université Paris-Saclay International Master's Scholarships, 1515
University Awards, 1611
University College London Department Awards for Graduate Students, 1212
University College: Loughman, 1511
University Hall Eurest Overseas Study Scholarship, 534
University Hardship Fund, 1511
The University of Adelaide Global Citizens Scholarship, 1219
University of Alberta Graduate Entrance Scholarship, 1222
University of Alberta Graduate Recruitment Scholarship, 1223
The University of Auckland International Doctoral Fees Bursary, 1232
University of Auckland International Doctoral Scholarship, 1232
University of Auckland International Student Excellence Scholarship, 1232
University of Auckland Research Masters Scholarships, 1233
University of Bologna Study Grants for International Students, 1235
University of British Columbia Graduate Fellowship (UGF), 1238
University of Canterbury Doctoral Scholarship, 1280
University of East Anglia International Development Scholarships, 1294
University of Edinburgh-KU Leuven PhD Studentship, 1303
University of Exeter Alumni Scholarship, 1312
University of Exeter Class of 2024 Progression Scholarship, 1313
University of Helsinki Masters Scholarships, 1450
University of Kent Law School Studentship, 1334
University of Liverpool Commonwealth Postgraduate Bursary, 1361
University of Liverpool International College (UoLIC) Excellence Scholarship, 1361
University of Liverpool International College (UoLIC) Impact Progression Scholar, 1362
The University of Manchester Humanitarian Scholarships, 1389
University of Manchester President's Doctoral Scholar Awards (PDS Awards), 1389
University of Melbourne Graduate Research Scholarships, 1401
University of Nevada, Las Vegas Alumni Association Graduate Scholarships, 1403
University of Nevada, Las Vegas James F Adams/GPSA Scholarship, 1403

University of Otago China Scholarship Council Doctoral Scholarship, 1451
University of Otago City of Literature PhD Scholarship, 1451
University of Otago Doctoral Scholarships, 1452
University of Otago International Master's Scholarship, 1452
University of Strathclyde Performance Sport Scholarship, 1554
University of Sussex Chancellor's International Scholarships, 1561
University of Sydney International Scholarship, 1572
The University of Winnipeg Manitoba Graduate Scholarships (MGS), 1586
University of Wollongong in Dubai Postgraduate Scholarships, 1587
UNSW International Scholarships, 1414
USW Postgraduate Alumni Discount, 1533
USW Postgraduate Sanctuary Scholarship, 1534
USW Refugee Sanctuary Scheme, 1534
Vanne Trompf Scholarship, 517
Vercille Voss Scholarship, 658
Vice-Chancellor International Postgraduate Scholarship, 1630
Vice Chancellor's Centenary Research Scholarship (VCRS), 1163
Vice-Chancellor's International Attainment Scholarship, 973, 1362
Vice-Chancellor's International Scholarship, 151, 186
Vice-Chancellors International Scholarship (VCIS)-Korea University, 780
Vice-Chancellors International Scholarship (VCIS)-Pontificia Universidad Javeriana, 781
Vice-Chancellor's International Scholarships Scheme, 1572
Vice-Chancellor's Scholarship for International Students, 1453
Vice-Chancellor's Strategic Doctoral Research Scholarships, 1595
Victorian International Research Scholarships, 166
Victoria Tongarewa Scholarship, 1595
Viessmann/Marburg Travel Scholarship, 1619
Vietnam Scholarships–Ho Chi Minh City University and National Economics University, Hanoi, 1295
Visby Programme Scholarships, 1162
Voice Pedagogy Award, 849
The Vronwy Hankey Memorial Fund for Aegean Studies, 259
Vronwy Hankey Memorial Travel Award for Pre-Doctoral Students, 260
Waddell Smith Postgraduate Scholarship, 1453
Wadham College: Beit Scholarships, 1512
Wadham College: John Brookman Scholarship, 1513
Wai-man Woo Scholarship, 517
Walter and Eliza Hall Scholarship Trust Opportunity Scholarship for Nursing, 1520
Warsaw Agricultural University MBA in Agribusiness Management, 1605
Washington American Indian Endowed Scholarship, 1606
Water, Sanitation and Health Engineering MSc-International Masters Excellence Scholarship, 1341
Watson Fellowship, 1006
Weatherall Institute of Molecular Medicine: WIMM Prize Studentship, 1513
Weidenfeld-Hoffmann Scholarships and Leadership Programme, 1513, 1514
Welcome Scholarship for Students from Refugee Backgrounds, 1414
Wellcome Trust-POST Fellowships in Medical History and Humanities, 1613
Wellcome Trust 4-Year PhD Programme Studentships, 1304
Wellington Graduate Award, 1596
Wellington Master's by Thesis Scholarship, 1596
Weweni Future Scholars Award, 1586
Wharton Executive MBA Programme, 1618
White Rose University Consortium Studentships, 1588
The Widening Participation Ambition Scholarship for University of Kent Graduates, 1334
Wilfrid Laurier University President, 1619
Wilkie Calvert Co-supported PhD Studentships, 1524
William Blake Trust Bursary, 1212
The William P. Van Wagenen Fellowship, 885
William Ross Murray Scholarship, 1097
Winter Pilot Award, 1113
Witherby Publishing Scholarship, 470
Wolfsonian-FIU Fellowship, 1622
Woodcock-Munoz Foundation Empowerment Through Education Scholarships, 1613
Wood Whistler Prize and Medal, 1260
Worcester College: Drue Heinz Scholarship, 1514
Worcester College: Ogilvie Thompson Scholarships, 1515
World Bank Scholarships Program, 1627
World Citizen Talent Scholarship for International Students, 577
WOTRO DC Fellowships, 883
Xiamen University PhD Scholarships, 1537
Yanshan University Doctoral Scholarships, 1638
Yanshan University Scholarship Program for International Students, 1638
4-Year Studentship, 317
Zhengzhou University President Scholarships, 19

African Nations

Academy of Research and Higher Education Scholarships, 1213
AfOx-Linacre Humanities Scholarship, 731
AfOx-Linacre Norman and Ivy Lloyd Scholarship, 731
AfOx-Linacre Trapnell Scholarship, 731

Africa Excellence Scholarship, 1427
Africa: Mwalimu Julius Nyerere African Union Scholarship, 593
Africa: Next Einstein Forum (NEF) Fellows Programme, 593
African Graduate Fellowships, 120
African Peacebuilding Network Fellowships, 1121
African Peacebuilding Network (APN) Residential Postdoctoral Fellowship Program, 1120
African Scholarships, 461
Africa Scholarship, 1344
Africa Scholarship Programme, 1603
Allan and Nesta Ferguson Scholarships, 1092
Alumni Loyalty Scholarship, 704
Arthington-Davy Grants for Tongan Students for Postgraduate Study, 1242
Ashinaga Scholarships, 142
Australia Awards Scholarships, 430
Beit Trust Postgraduate Scholarships, 191, 1336
British Institute in Eastern Africa Minor Grants, 255
British Petroleum Research Bursaries for PhD Study, 1261
British Petroleum Research Bursaries for Postgraduate Study, 1262
Chevening Scholarships, 1457
Chile: Nelson Mandela Scholarships, 361
Citadel Capital Scholarship, 965
Coimbra Group Short Stay Scholarship Programme for Young Researchers, 367
Cranfield Merit Scholarship in Leadership and Management, 394
Creating Better Futures Masters Scholarship for African Students, 751
The Cultural Diaspora, 269
Curtin International Scholarships-Alumni and Family Scholarship, 403
Curtin International Scholarships–Merit Scholarship, 403
Cusanuswerk–Organization of the German Bishops' Conference Promoting Gifted Catholic Students, 187
Dean's International Postgraduate Research Scholarships, 1565
Developing World Education Fund Scholarships for PhD Study, 1263
Development Trust Africa Scholarships, 753
Diversity100 PhD Studentships, 222
Early Bird Acceptance Grant-International Students, 700
Eastern and Southern Africa Scholarship, 462
Egypt Scholarship, 1346
ELBP Start Now Scholarship, 1432
Eldred Scholarship, 733
Engineering the Future Scholarships, 1373
Ferguson Scholarships, 149
Fulbright Scholarship Program for Nigerians, 551
40 Fully-Funded Postgraduate Scholarships at Newcastle University in the United Kingdom, 901
Glenmore Medical Postgraduate Scholarship, 1298
GREAT Egypt Scholarship, 464
GREAT Kenya Scholarship, 464
GREAT Scholarships, 571, 1203, 1282, 1306, 1377, 1536
Griffith Remarkable Scholarship, 574
H3Africa Global Health Bioinformatics Research Training Program, 536
Holland Scholarship, 1577
Holland Scholarship for international Master Students, 1604
Institut Européen d'Administration des Affaires Nelson Mandela Endowment Scholarships, 627
International Institute of Tropical Agriculture Research Fellowships, 662
International Merit Stipend, 676
International Student Academic Excellence Scholarship, 574
International Student Academic Merit Scholarship, 575
KSP Fund for Innovative Projects, 1107
La Trobe International Scholarship, 701
La Trobe University Offshore Online Bursary, 703
La Trobe University OSHC Grant, 703
Leicester Castle Business School Full Postgraduate Scholarship, 417
Leiden University Fund-Lutfia Rabbani Scholarship Fund, 715
Lund University Global Scholarship, 760
Macquarie University AU$5,000 Regional Scholarship, 773
Mauritius: Mauritius-Africa Scholarship Scheme, 598
Middle East and North Africa Scholarship, 467
Netherlands Fellowship Programmes, 452
New Zealand: Scholarships for International Tertiary Students and Commonwealth Scholarship, 598
Next Gen Fellowship Program for Sub-Saharan African Countries, 333
The Oriel Graduate Scholarship for Sub-Saharan African Scholars, 940
Oxford–Linacre African Scholarship, 735
Oxford-Oak Foundation Clinical Medicine, 1492
Oxford-Qatar-Thatcher Graduate Scholarships, 1494
Pathway to Victoria Scholarship, 703
Regional Scholarship-International Students, 704
Regional Victoria Experience Bursary, 704
Santander Formula Scholarship, 811
Santander Mobility Scholarship, 811
Santander Taught Postgraduate Scholarships, 1582
SOAS Research Scholarship, 1096
Standard Bank Africa Chairman's Scholarships, 1508
Standard Bank Derek Cooper Africa Scholarship, 1508
Study in Canada Scholarships, 1322
Sydney International Student Award (Africa), 1568

University College London-AET Undergraduate International Outreach Bursaries, 1212
University International Research Studentships, 1524
The University of Sheffield Africa Scholarship, 1529
University of Westminster GREAT Scholarships, 1585
USW Postgraduate Ethnicity Equality Bursary, 1534
Vice Chancellor's Africa Scholarship, 1290
Vice-Chancellors International Scholarship, 332
VLIR-UOS Training and Masters Scholarships, 193
West Africa Scholarship, 470
WE-STAR Fellowships, 655

Asian Countries

Academy of Research and Higher Education Scholarships, 1213
AIBS Bangladeshi Graduate Student Fellowship, 79
AIBS Professional Development Fellowships for Bangladeshi Scholars, 79
Alumni Loyalty Scholarship, 704
Anning Morgan Bursary, 1310
Armenian International Women, 133
ArtsLink Independent Projects, 335
ArtsLink Projects, 336
ArtsLink Residencies, 336
The Arturo Falaschi ICGEB Predoctoral Fellowships ICGEB Trieste International PhD Programme, 655
Arturo Falaschi PhD Fellowships, 652
ASEAN AU$10,000 Early Acceptance Scholarship, 766
ASEAN Excellence Scholarship, 1428
Association of Management Development Institutions in South Asia Doctoral Fellowships, 147
Association of Management Development Institutions in South Asia Postdoctoral Fellowship, 148
Australia Awards Scholarships, 430
Australian National University-Study Canberra India Scholarship for Postgraduate and Undergraduates in Australia, 173
Balliol College: Eddie Dinshaw Scholarship, 1455
Bangladesh Ministry of Public Affairs (MoPA), 767
Bangladesh Scholarship, 1345
Birkbeck International Merit Scholarships, 221
British Chevening Cambridge Scholarships for Postgraduate Study (Indonesia), 1261
British Chevening Malaysia Cambridge Scholarship for PhD Study, 1261
British Petroleum Research Bursaries for PhD Study, 1261
British Petroleum Research Bursaries for Postgraduate Study, 1262
Brunei GREAT Scholarship, 1555
Bupa Foundation Annual Specialist Grant, 268
Cambridge Trust Scholarships, 411
Canada-ASEAN Scholarships and Educational Exchanges for Development (SEED)–for Students, 1319
Canadian Prime Minister's Awards for Publishing (CPMA), 282
Charles Wallace India Trust, 1262
Chevening Scholarships, 1457
Chiang Ching Kuo Foundation for International Scholarly Exchange Publication Subsidies, 358
China Elite Scholarship, 767
China Excellence Scholarship, 1430
China Key Partnership Cotutelle Stipend Scheme, 768
China Oxford Scholarship Fund, 1458
China Scholarship Council, 751
China Scholarship Council (CSC)-Deakin University Joint Funding Program, 419
China Scholarship Council, PhD Studentship, 591
China Scholarship Council Postgraduate Research Scholarship, 1563
China Scholarship Council Postgraduate Research Visiting Scholarship, 1563
China Scholarship Council Research Programs Visiting Scholars, 1564
China Scholarship Council (CSC) Scholarship, 1215
China Scholarship Council Scholarships, 1535
China Scholarship Council Studentships, 1521
China Scholarship Council-University of Melbourne PhD Scholarship, 1390
China Scholarships Council Joint Research Scholarships, 1587
Corpus Christi Research Scholarship, 1262
Curtin International Scholarships-Alumni and Family Scholarship, 403
Curtin International Scholarships–Merit Scholarship, 403
Cusanuswerk–Organization of the German Bishops' Conference Promoting Gifted Catholic Students, 187
Daiwa Foundation Small Grants, 411
The Dalai Lama Foundation Graduate Scholarship Program, 413
Deakin India 20% Postgraduate Bursary, 420
Dean's International Postgraduate Research Scholarships, 1565
Developing World Education Fund Scholarships for PhD Study, 1263
Diversity100 PhD Studentships, 222
Dr. Suguru Furuichi Memorial Scholarship General Information, 917
Early Bird Acceptance Grant-International Students, 700
ELBP Start Now Scholarship, 1432
Engineering the Future Scholarships, 1373
Erasmus Mundus Scholarship Programme, 621
Felix Scholarships, 1094, 1522
Ferguson Scholarships, 149

Fitzwilliam College: Quantedge–Lee Kuan Yew Masters Scholarship, 1245
Foundation for Liberal and Management Education University Scholars Program, 545
Fulbright Distinguished Awards in Teaching Program for International Teachers, 1192
Fulbright-Nehru Academic and Professional Excellence Fellowships, 1194
Full-Tuition Fees Waiver for MPhil/PhD Students, 345
40 Fully-Funded Postgraduate Scholarships at Newcastle University in the United Kingdom, 901
Future of Change Scholarship, 1417
Future of Change Schools Excellence Bursary, 1418
Girton College: The Chan and Mok Graduate Scholarship, 1249
Girton College: The Girton Hong Kong Founder's Scholarship, 1250
The Girton Singapore Scholarship, 1259
Global Wales Postgraduate Scholarship, 329
The Goa Education Trust (GET) Scholarships, 243
Great Eastern Scholarship (All Subjects), 1147
GREAT India Scholarship, 464
GREAT Pakistan Scholarship, 464
GREAT Scholarship-Bangladesh, 1285
GREAT Scholarships, 571, 1203, 1282, 1306, 1377, 1536
GREAT Scholarship–Sri Lanka, 1285
Griffith Remarkable Scholarship, 574
Higher Education Commission Pakistan Scholarship, 754
Higher Education Scholarship Palestine (HESPAL) Scholarships, 1584
Holland Scholarship, 1577
Holland Scholarship for international Master Students, 1604
Hong Kong Jockey Club Graduate Scholarships, 1464
HRM Princess Sirindhorn University of Liverpool Scholarship (Thailand), 1355
Ian Kay Scholarships, 465
ICGEB PhD and POSTDOC Fellowships, South Africa, 653
ICGEB PhD Fellowships, 653
India GREAT Scholarship, 416
Indian Institute of Science Bangalore Kishore Vaigyanik Protsahan Yojana Fellowships, 623
Indian Institute of Technology Ropar Institute Postdoctoral Fellowship, 623
India Scholarship, 1347
Indonesia Endowment Fund for Education (LPDP), 895
Indonesia Scholarship, 1348
Intake Education Taiwan Scholarship, 1526
International Merit Stipend, 676
International Postgraduate Scholarships, 1095
International Student Academic Excellence Scholarship, 574
International Student Academic Merit Scholarship, 575
Jawaharlal Nehru Memorial Trust Commonwealth Shared Scholarships, 1263
Joint Postgraduate Scholarship Program, 1218
KC Wong Postdoctoral Fellowships, 361
K C Wong Postgraduate Scholarship Programme, 361
Khazanah–INCEIF Scholarship, 651
Kiran Mazumdar-Shaw Scholarship, 514
Kobayashi Research Grants, 1576
Korea Foundation Fellowship, 1107
Korea-Japan Cultural Association Scholarship, 1108
KSP Fund for Innovative Projects, 1107
Lady Meherbai D. TATA Education Trust, 1167
La Trobe Greater China Scholarship, 700
La Trobe International Scholarship, 701
La Trobe South Asia Scholarship, 702
La Trobe South East Asia Scholarship, 702
La Trobe University Offshore Online Bursary, 703
La Trobe University OSHC Grant, 703
Lawrence Ho Scholarship, 466
The Lee Family Scholarships, 617
Lee Foundation Grants, 1580
Leicester Castle Business School Full Postgraduate Scholarship, 417
Liverpool Law School Hong Kong Scholarships, 1356
Lund University Global Scholarship, 760
Macquarie University AU$5,000 Regional Scholarship, 773
Magdalen Hong Kong Scholarship, 1475
Manchester-China Scholarship Council Joint Postgraduate Scholarship Programme, 1380
Marks and Spencer-Leeds University-FCO Chevening Scholarships, 1337
Ministry of Education and Science of the Republic of Lithuania Scholarships for Studies and Research Work, 814
Ministry of Education and Training Vietnam Research Awards, 1356
Ministry of Education (Malaysia) Scholarships for Postgraduate Study, 1264
Ministry of Science, Technology and the Environment Scholarships for Postgraduate Study (Malaysia), 1264
Mongolia AU$10,000 Early Acceptance Scholarship, 776
Nanyang Technological University HASS International PhD Scholarship (HIPS) for Singaporean Students, 835
Narotam Sekhsaria Postgraduate Scholarship, 837
National Centre for Promotion of Employment for Disabled People (NCPEDP) Rajiv Gandhi Postgraduate Scholarship Scheme, 621
Nehru Trust for the Indian Collections V&A Cambridge DFID Scholarship, 1265
Netherlands Fellowship Programmes, 452
Newcastle University Scholarship–Thailand-GREAT, 898
Orange Tulip Scholarship, 765, 975, 1605
Orange Tulip Scholarship (OTS) Indonesia, 1578
Overseas Koreans Scholarship, 1108
Oxford and Cambridge Society of Bombay Cambridge DFID Scholarship, 1265

Oxford-Creat Group Graduate Scholarships, 1485
Oxford-Indira Gandhi Graduate Scholarships, 1489
Oxford-Oak Foundation Clinical Medicine, 1492
Oxford-Oxford Thai Foundation Graduate Scholarship, 1492
Oxford-Sir Anwar Pervez Graduate Scholarships, 1496
Pakistan Scholarship, 468, 1349
Pathway to Victoria Scholarship, 703
Philip Chui East Asia Scholarship, 515
Pok Rafeah Cambridge Scholarship, 1265
Post-doctoral Fellows and Visiting Scholars, 425
Postgraduate Research Funding-China, 873
Prime Minister's Fellowship Scheme for Doctoral Research, 1099
Prime Minister's Research Fellowship Scheme, 963
Regional Office Scholarship-India, 185
Regional Office Scholarships-China, 185
Regional Scholarship-International Students, 704
Regional Victoria Experience Bursary, 704
The Royal Bank of Scotland International Scholarship, 742
Santander Formula Scholarship, 811
Santander Mobility Scholarship, 811
Sasakawa Fund Scholarships, 1501
Scotland's Saltire Scholarship, 468
The Sievert Larsson Scholarship, 1110
Sir Sze-yuen Chung Postgraduate Merit Scholarship, 1528
South Asia AU$10,000 Early Acceptance Scholarship, 779
South Asia Excellence Scholarship, 1436
South Asian Scholarships at Edinburgh Napier University, 468
South East Asia Scholarship, 469
South Korea A$10,000 Early Acceptance Scholarship, 779
St Antony's College-Swire Scholarship, 1503
Stephen and Anna Hui Fellowship, 615
Study in Canada Scholarships, 1322
StuNed Scholarship, 719
Sussex Malaysia Scholarship, 1560
Sydney International Student Award (Bangladesh), 1568
Sydney International Student Award (Central Asia), 1568
Sydney International Student Award (India), 1569
Sydney International Student Award (Indonesia), 1569
Sydney International Student Award (Malaysia), 1569
Sydney International Student Award (South Korea), 1570
Sydney International Student Award (Sri Lanka), 1570
Sydney International Student Award (Vietnam), 1571
Sydney Scholars India Equity Scholarship, 1571
Tauranga Campus Research Masters Scholarship, 1580
Thailand Scholarship, 1350
Tibawi Trust Awards, 1097
Turkish Ministry of Education, 1359
United Kingdom-India Year of Culture Great Postgraduate Scholarships, 1234
University International Research Studentships, 1524
University of Leeds International Fee Bursary (Vietnam)-Information Systems/Multimedia Systems, 1341
The University of Liverpool and China Scholarship Council Awards, 1359
The University of Manchester-China Scholarship Council joint scholarship, 318
University of Newcastle-Malaysian Australia Columbo Plan Commemoration (MACC) Scholarship, 1437
University of Reading Dorothy Hodgkin Postgraduate Award, 1524
University of Strathclyde-British Council GREAT Scholarships (Environmental Science and Climate Change), 1553
University of Waikato Masters Research Scholarships, 1580
University of Westminster GREAT Scholarships, 1585
University of Wollongong Sydney Business School Bursary Scheme, 1586
U of L Graduate Association Hong Kong & Tung Postgraduate Scholarships, 1360
USW Postgraduate Ethnicity Equality Bursary, 1534
Vice-Chancellors China Scholarship Scheme, 332
Vice Chancellor's Indonesia Scholarship, 1290
Vice-Chancellor's International Attainment Scholarship for China, 1362
Vice-Chancellors International Scholarship, 332
Vice Chancellor's Mainland China Scholarship, 1290
Vice Chancellor's Scholarship, 592
Vice Chancellor's South Asia Scholarship, 1291
Vicky Noon Educational Foundation Oxford Scholarships, 1512
Vietnam Scholarship, 426, 470, 1352
Visiting Scholars Funding Schemes, 333
VLIR-UOS Training and Masters Scholarships, 193
Water MSc Scholarship for Students from Malawi and Vietnam, 395
Westminster Full-Fee Masters Scholarships for International Students, 1585
Westminster Vice-Chancellor's Scholarships, 1585
Yalda Hakim Graduate Scholarship for Female Afghan Scholars, 940

Asia-Pacific Countries

Australia Awards Scholarships, 430
Banting Postdoctoral Fellowships, 280
Curtin International Scholarships-Alumni and Family Scholarship, 403
Curtin International Scholarships–Merit Scholarship, 403
Early Bird Acceptance Grant-International Students, 700
Griffith Remarkable Scholarship, 574
Holland Scholarship, 1577
International Institute for Population Sciences Diploma in Population Studies, 662
International Student Academic Excellence Scholarship, 574

International Student Academic Merit Scholarship, 575
Kobayashi Research Grants, 1576
La Trobe International Scholarship, 701
La Trobe University Offshore Online Bursary, 703
La Trobe University OSHC Grant, 703
Lund University Global Scholarship, 760
Massey University Pacific Success Scholarship for Doctoral Students, 644
Pathway to Victoria Scholarship, 703
Regional Scholarship-International Students, 704
Regional Victoria Experience Bursary, 704
University International Research Studentships, 1524
Utrecht Excellence Scholarships for International Students, 1591

Australia

AAA Graduate Education Scholarships, 52
Aboriginal and Torres Strait Islander Scholarship, 1426
Aboriginal and Torres Strait Islander Staff Scholarship, 508
Aboriginal Enterprise Research Scholarship, 1530
Aboriginal Housing Office Tertiary Accommodation Grants, 1426
Aboriginal social and emotional wellbeing Scholarship, 418
Adelaide Postgraduate Coursework Scholarships, 1216
AE and FAQ Stephens Scholarship, 1562
Alex Raydon Scholarship for Refugee or Migrant Students, 821
The Applications of Drugs in Enhancing Scaffold-associated Healing in the Middle Ear, 407
Arrow Energy-JCU Go Further Indigenous Tertiary Scholarships, 674
Australia-India Strategic Research Fund (AISRF), 175
Australian Biological Resources Study Postgraduate Scholarship, 402
Australian Federation of University Women SA Inc. (AFUW-SA) Diamond Jubilee Scholarship, 1217
Australian Government RTP Scholarship (Domestic), 1562
Australian Health Inequities Program Research Scholarship, 520
Australian Health Inequities Program University Research Scholarship, 521
Australian Postgraduate Awards, 349
Australian Security Intelligence Organisation Scheme, 169
Bupa Foundation Annual Specialist Grant, 268
Burralga Yumba Bursary, 674
Bush Children's Education Foundation Scholarship, 1404
The Capstone Editing Conference Travel Grant for Postgraduate Research Students, 158
The Capstone Editing Early Career Academic Research Grant for Women, 158
Care-leavers Scholarship (Continuing), 510
Care-leavers Scholarships (Commencing), 510
Carol Lynette Grant (Prowse) Scholarship, 510
Cec Spence Memorial UNE Country Scholarship, 1405
Central West Medical Association Medical Student Scholarship, 350
Charles Sturt Accommodation Equity Scholarship, 351
Chinese Government Scholarship Water and Environmental Research Scholarships, 346
Chris and Gina Grubb Ornithology Scholarship, 351
Colin and Eleanor Bourke Indigenous Postgraduate Scholarship, 822
Commonwealth Accommodation Scholarship, 1405
Commonwealth Education Costs Scholarship, 1405
Commonwealth Indigenous Support Scholarship, 822
Coursework Access Scholarships, 1391
CQUniversity Indigenous Australian Postgraduate Research Award, 339
CQUniversity Womens Equal Opportunity Research Award, 340
Curtin University Postgraduate Scholarship (CUPS), 404
David M. Livingstone (Australia) Scholarship, 1263
Deadly Education Scholarships-Aboriginal and Torres Strait Islanders, 511
Deakin Funded Scholarship Program, 420
Destination Australia Program Honours Scholarship, 1406
Destination Australia Program Scholarship for Masters by Coursework, 1407
Diamond Jubilee Bursary, 522
Disability, Mental Health and Carers: National Disability Conference Initiative, 167
Don and Lee Stammer Scholarship, 1407
Dr Bill Jonas Memorial Indigenous Scholarship, 1432
Eleanor and Joseph Wertheim Scholarship, 1392
Emergency Equity Grant, 353
Enterprise Research Scholarship, 1531
Evidence-Based Approach to Improve Insulin Sensitivity in Horses, Using Dietary Ingredients, 353
Expensive Commonwealth Criminal Cases Fund (ECCCF), 169
First Nations Accommodation and Relocation Scholarship, 353
First Nations Education Costs Scholarship, 353
Frank Knox Memorial Fellowships, 1393
Friends of the University Development Studies Scholarship, 1432
Friends of the University Ken Gordon Memorial Honours Scholarship, 1433
Fulbright Scholarships, 1393
Full-time Scholarship (Australian Government's Research Training Program), 354
The General Sir John Monash Awards, 408
Graduate Women Victoria Scholarship Program, 1394
Grants-in-aid (GIA), 1566
The Gregg Indigenous Scholarship, 1571

Hansen Scholarship, 1394
Henry and Louisa Williams Bequest, 1395
Holland Scholarship, 1577
Holland Scholarship for international Master Students, 1604
Honours Scholarship HECS Exempt Award, 354
Hume Multiversity Scholarship, 423
Ian Alexander Gordon Scholarship, 513
Indigenous Accommodation Grant, 1395
Indigenous Commonwealth Accommodation Scholarship, 525
Indigenous Commonwealth Accomodation Top-up Scholarship, 526
Indigenous Commonwealth Education Costs Scholarship, 526
Indigenous Education Costs Scholarship, 675
Indigenous Education Scholarship, 1434
Indigenous Macquarie University Research Excellence Scholarship, 771
Indigenous Research Training Program Scholarship (RTPSI), 675
Indigenous Student On-Campus Accommodation Scholarship, 675
Institute of Health and Biomedical Innovation Awards, 974
International House Scholarship, 1396
International Leadership Scholarship, 224
International Postgraduate Research Scholarships (IPRS) Australian Postgraduate Awards (APA), 1566
International Stand Out Scholarship, 224
International student support scholarship, 355
Isobella Foundation Scholarship, 513
James Fairfax-Oxford-Australia Fund Scholarships, 1465
John Cassim Scholarship, 355
John Eales Rugby Excellence Scholarship, 225
Lund University Global Scholarship, 760
Macquarie University Higher Study Scholarship-Full time rate, 774
Macquarie University Higher Study Scholarship-Part time rate, 775
Macquarie University Postgraduate Loyalty Scheme 10% Sponsorship, 775
Mary MacKillop Today First Nations Tertiary Scholarship, 424
Max Schroder Indigenous Scholarship, 1408
May Mills Scholarship for Women, 527
MPhil Scholarship–Reconnecting to Rivers: Urban Water & Water Sensitive Urban Design, 406
Nan Tien Institute Postgraduate Scholarship, 834
Narre Warren South Bendigo Bank Scholarship, 514
National Disability Insurance Scheme Jobs and Market Fund Round 1, 169
New Colombo Plan Grant, 1398
North Hobart Football Club Peter Wells Scholarships, 1573
Novel Concept Awards, 850
Online Student Representative Committee Post-Graduate Scholarship, 355
Oorala Kick Start Scholarship, 1408
Oorala Wellbeing Scholarship, 1408
Pembroke College: The Pembroke Australian Scholarship, 1256
PhD Elevate Scholarship-CQUniversity and Surf Lifesaving Queensland, 342
Postgraduate Equity Scholarship, 355
Pratt Foundation Bursary (IES), 166
Professor Lowitja O'Donoghue Indigenous Student Postgraduate Research Scholarship, 530
Reconciliation SA Aboriginal Education Leaders Fund Postgraduate Research Scholars, 531
Research Administration Assistants Postdoctoral Award, 343
Research Training Program domestic (RTPd) Scholarship, 1533
Residential School Equity Grant, 356
RMIT-CSIRO PhD International Scholarship in Mineral Resources and Environmental Science, Australia, 906
Robb College Foundation Irvine Scholarship, 1409
Robb College Foundation Sinclair-Wilson Scholarship, 1409
Roberta Sykes Bursary, 1011
Roberta Sykes Scholarship, 1012
Rural and Regional Enterprise Scholarships (RRES), 515
Santa Singh and Balwant Kaur Scholarship, 825
Scots Australian Council Scholarships, 406
Shaping Futures Scholarships, 1436
Staff Scholarship-Domestic, 516
Starter Support Scholarship, 407
The Steglick Indigenous Women's Scholarship, 1572
Support Fund for Students with a Disability, 1410
Technology Equity Grant, 356
Tertiary Access Payment, 1401
UNE Residential Financial Assistance Scholarship, 1412
University Hall Dean's Scholarship, 534
University International Research Studentships, 1524
University of Newcastle Postgraduate Research Scholarship (UNRS Central), 1438
University of Queensland PhD Scholarships for International Students, 1520
Utrecht Excellence Scholarships for International Students, 1591
UTS Institute for Public Policy and Governance Postgraduate Scholarship, 1575
Victoria University Research Scholarships, 1593
Western Australian Premiers Scholarship, 1517
The William McIlrath Rural Scholarship, 1411
Women's Leadership and Development Program (WLDP)-Women's Economic Security Grant Guidelines, 168
Wright College Scholarship, 1413
Wright Honours Scholarship, 1413

Canada

Banting Postdoctoral Fellowships, 280, 289
Canada-Brazil Awards-Joint Research Projects, 280
Canada-China Scholars, 282
Canada Council for the Arts Molson Prizes, 275
Canada Graduate Scholarships–Doctoral Program, 1126
Canada Graduate Scholarships–Master's Program, 1126
Canada Graduate Scholarships-Master's (CGS M) Program, 881
Canada-Japan Literary Awards, 270
Canada Postgraduate Scholarships (PGS), 881
Canadian Alumni Scholarship, 732
Canadian Federation of University Women Bourse Georgette Lemoyne, 279
Canadian Initiatives For Nordic Studies (CINS) Graduate Scholarship, 1221
Canadian Institutes of Health Research Gold Leaf Prizes, 289
Chiang Ching Kuo Foundation for International Scholarly Exchange Eminent Scholar Lectureship, 357
Clarendon Canadian National Scholarship, 733
Collaborative Research, 625
ConocoPhillips Canada Centennial Scholarship Program, 1196
Curtin International Scholarships-Alumni and Family Scholarship, 403
Curtin International Scholarships–Merit Scholarship, 403
The Davies Charitable Foundation Fellowship, 414
Dean's International Postgraduate Research Scholarships, 1565
The Dennis Mock Graduate Scholarship, 1079
Early Bird Acceptance Grant-International Students, 700
Emerging Leaders in the Americas Program (ELAP), 283
ESC Ed Becker Conference Travel Awards, 489
Fessenden-Trott Scholarship, 1197
Foundation Grant Program, 289
Fulbright Canada Scholarship, 1076
40 Fully-Funded Postgraduate Scholarships at Newcastle University in the United Kingdom, 901
Governor General's Literary Awards, 271
Griffith Remarkable Scholarship, 574
Holland Scholarship, 1577
Holland Scholarship for international Master Students, 1604
Horatio Alger Association Canadian Scholarships, 275
International doctoral Tuition Scholarship, 1321
International Student Academic Excellence Scholarship, 574
International Student Academic Merit Scholarship, 575
Japan Society for the Promotion of Science Postdoctoral Fellowships, 882
Japan Society for the Promotion of Science Postdoctoral Fellowships for North American and European Researchers (Short-term), 680
John Hirsch Prizes, 272
John Hobday Awards in Arts Management, 273
Killam Research Fellowships, 273
La Trobe International Scholarship, 701
La Trobe University Offshore Online Bursary, 703
La Trobe University OSHC Grant, 703
Lund University Global Scholarship, 760
Multiple Sclerosis Society of Canada Scholarship Programs: John Helou Scholarship, 1197
Naim Mehlab Student Travel Award, 377
Natural Sciences and Engineering Research Council of Canada-Postdoctoral Fellowship Program, 1112
North American Postgraduate Scholarship, 467
NSERC Indigenous Student Ambassadors, 882
Ontario Graduate Scholarship Program, 925
Organization of American States (OAS) Fellowships Programs, 283
Pathway to Victoria Scholarship, 703
Pierre Elliott Trudeau Foundation Doctoral Scholarships, 957
The Pierre Elliott Trudeau Foundation Scholarship, 1081
Regional Scholarship-International Students, 704
Regional Victoria Experience Bursary, 704
Research Grants & Fellowships, 946
Ruth Watson Henderson Choral Composition Competition, 363
School of Graduate Studies F. A. Aldrich Award, 809
Scotland's Saltire Scholarship, 468
Senior Women Academic Administrators of Canada Awards, 1078
SSHRC Doctoral Fellowships, 1127
University International Research Studentships, 1524
Utrecht Excellence Scholarships for International Students, 1591
Vanier Canada Graduate Scholarships, 290
Vice-Chancellors International Scholarship, 332
Wadham College: Donner Canadian Foundation Law Scholarship, 1512

Caribbean Countries

Academy of Research and Higher Education Scholarships, 1213
Canada-CARICOM Faculty Leadership Program, 281
The Cultural Diaspora, 269
Curtin International Scholarships-Alumni and Family Scholarship, 403
Curtin International Scholarships–Merit Scholarship, 403
Diversity100 PhD Studentships, 222
Early Bird Acceptance Grant-International Students, 700
Emerging Leaders in the Americas Program (ELAP), 1319
Griffith Remarkable Scholarship, 574
International Student Academic Excellence Scholarship, 574
International Student Academic Merit Scholarship, 575
La Trobe International Scholarship, 701

La Trobe University Offshore Online Bursary, 703
La Trobe University OSHC Grant, 703
Lund University Global Scholarship, 760
Netherlands Fellowship Programmes, 452
Pathway to Victoria Scholarship, 703
Regional Scholarship-International Students, 704
Regional Victoria Experience Bursary, 704
Santander Formula Scholarship, 811
Santander Mobility Scholarship, 811
University International Research Studentships, 1524
USW Postgraduate Ethnicity Equality Bursary, 1534
Vice-Chancellors International Scholarship, 332

Central American Countries

Canada-CARICOM Faculty Leadership Program, 281
Chiang Ching Kuo Foundation for International Scholarly Exchange Eminent Scholar Lectureship, 357
Netherlands Fellowship Programmes, 452
Sydney International Student Award (South and Central America), 1570
Utrecht Excellence Scholarships for International Students, 1591

Central European Countries

Alumni Loyalty Scholarship, 704
ArtsLink Independent Projects, 335
ArtsLink Projects, 33
CGES Research and Travel Award, 230
Curtin International Scholarships-Alumni and Family Scholarship, 403
Curtin International Scholarships–Merit Scholarship, 403
Deutsche Forschungsgemeinschaft Collaborative Research Centres, 432
Early Bird Acceptance Grant-International Students, 700
Excellence Initiative, 434
German Historical Institute Collaborative Research Program for Postdoctoral Scholars, 566
Griffith Remarkable Scholarship, 574
Humboldt Postdoc Scholarships, 605
Ida Pfeiffer Scholarships, 1318
International Student Academic Excellence Scholarship, 574
International Student Academic Merit Scholarship, 575
Japan Society for the Promotion of Science Postdoctoral Fellowships for North American and European Researchers (Short-term), 680
John G. Diefenbaker Award, 272
Jozef Tischner Fellowships, 697
La Trobe International Scholarship, 701
La Trobe University Offshore Online Bursary, 703
La Trobe University OSHC Grant, 703
Lincoln College: Berrow Foundation Scholarships, 1472
Lund University Global Scholarship, 760
Oxford Colleges Hospitality Scheme for East European Scholars, 926
Pathway to Victoria Scholarship, 703
Regional Scholarship-International Students, 704
Regional Victoria Experience Bursary, 704
Transatlantic Doctoral Seminar in German History, 567
UCLouvain-CSC PhD Co-funding Fellowship Competition 2023, 335
University International Research Studentships, 1524
Volkswagen Foundation Freigeist Fellowships, 1602

East European Countries

Andrew W Mellon Foundation Fellowships, 108
ArtsLink Independent Projects, 335
ArtsLink Projects, 336
Curtin International Scholarships-Alumni and Family Scholarship, 403
Curtin International Scholarships–Merit Scholarship, 403
Cusanuswerk–Organization of the German Bishops' Conference Promoting Gifted Catholic Students, 187
Early Bird Acceptance Grant-International Students, 700
Griffith Remarkable Scholarship, 574
International Student Academic Excellence Scholarship, 574
International Student Academic Merit Scholarship, 575
La Trobe International Scholarship, 701
La Trobe University Offshore Online Bursary, 703
La Trobe University OSHC Grant, 703
Lund University Global Scholarship, 760
Oxford Colleges Hospitality Scheme for East European Scholars, 926
Pathway to Victoria Scholarship, 703
Regional Scholarship-International Students, 704
Regional Victoria Experience Bursary, 704
Ukrainian students Scholarships, 757
Union for International Cancer Control American Cancer Society International Fellowships for Beginning Investigators (ACSBI), 284
University International Research Studentships, 1524
Vice-Chancellors International Scholarship, 332

European Countries

Aboriginal and Torres Strait Islander Scholarship Program, 401
Africa Cosmos Education Trust Bursary Application, 1516
Al Fog Bergljot Kolflats Stipendfond, 910
Alice Brown PhD Scholarships, 1295
ArtsLink Independent Projects, 335
ArtsLink Projects, 336
ArtsLink Residencies, 336
Avicenna-Studienwerk, 187
Balliol College: Foley-Bejar Scholarships, 1455
Barron Bequest, 494

Berkeley-Hasselt Research Fellowship, 194
Birkbeck International Merit Scholarships, 221
Bourses Scholarships, 488
British Petroleum Research Bursaries for PhD Study, 1261
British Petroleum Research Bursaries for Postgraduate Study, 1262
Bupa Foundation Annual Specialist Grant, 268
Canada-CARICOM Faculty Leadership Program, 281
CGES Research and Travel Award, 230
Chevening Scholarships, 1352
Clark Graduate Bursary Fund for International Students at University of Glasgow, 1315
The Cultural Diaspora, 269
Curtin International Scholarships-Alumni and Family Scholarship, 403
Curtin International Scholarships–Merit Scholarship, 403
Dean's International Postgraduate Research Scholarships, 1565
Developing Futures Scholarship, 1345
Doctoral and Postdoctoral Research Fellowships, 566
Dorothea Schlozer Postdoctoral Scholarships for Female Students, 1317
DUO-Study Grant (only for EU-students), 1604
Early Bird Acceptance Grant-International Students, 700
Early Career Fellowship, 256
Erasmus Trustfonds Scholarship, 1013
Ernst Ludwig Ehrlich Studienwerk, 188
ETH4D Research to Action Grants, 480
EU Engagement Scholarships Postgraduate Taught Courses, 1541
Europe AU$10,000 Early Acceptance Scholarship, 770
Evangelisches Studienwerk Villigst, 188
Excellence Programme (MSc/Non-EEA), 1604
Glasgow Educational & Marshall Trust Award, 1315
Glasgow School for Business and Society Scholarship, 570
Griffith Remarkable Scholarship, 574
Henry Dryerre Scholarship in Medical and Veterinary Physiology, 1316
Holland Scholarship, 1187
Holland Scholarship for international Master Students, 1604
International Family Discounts (IFD), 895
International Student Academic Excellence Scholarship, 574
International Student Academic Merit Scholarship, 575
John Lennon Memorial Scholarship, 1355
Justus & Louise van Effen Excellence Scholarships, 1187
La Trobe International Scholarship, 701
La Trobe University Offshore Online Bursary, 703
La Trobe University OSHC Grant, 703
Lund University Global Scholarship, 760
LUSTRA+ Scholarship, 718
Macquarie University AU$5,000 Regional Scholarship, 773
Manfred Wörner Fellowship, 907
Merton College Leventis Scholarship, 1476
Ministry of Education and Science of the Republic of Lithuania Scholarships for Studies and Research Work, 814
Netherlands Fellowship Programmes, 452
NFR Travel Grants, 1162
The Norway-America Association Awards, 913
The Norway-America Association Graduate & Research Stipend, 913
Oxford-David Jones Graduate Scholarship, 1486
Oxford-Richards Graduate Scholarships, 1495
Oxford-Sheikh Mohammed bin Rashid Al Maktoum Graduate Scholarship, 1496
Oxford-Thatcher Graduate Scholarships, 1497
Oxford-Wolfson-Marriott Graduate Scholarships, 1498
Pathway to Victoria Scholarship, 703
Pembroke College: The Monica Partridge Studentship, 1256
Pirie-Reid Scholarships, 1500
Postgraduate Master's Loan Scheme (Students from United Kingdom and non-United Kingdom European Union Countries), 899
Regional Scholarship-International Students, 704
Regional Victoria Experience Bursary, 704
R.J. Hunter Research Bursary Scheme, 1044
Romanian State Scholarships, 599
Saint Andrew's Society of the State of New York Scholarship Fund, 1316
Santander Formula Scholarship, 811
Santander Masters Scholarship, 1309
Santander Taught Postgraduate Scholarships, 1582
Saven European Scholarships, 1502
Södertörn University Tuition Fee Waive, 1134
St Andrews Society of New York Scholarships, 334
St Cross College: Oxford-Ko Cheuk Hung Graduate Scholarship, 1507
Stevenson Exchange Scholarships, 1316
Study in Canada Scholarships, 1322
Swedish Institute Scholarships for Global Professionals (SISGP), 1160
Swiss Government Excellence Scholarships for Foreign Scholars and Artists, 1152
Talented Athlete Scholarship Scheme (TASS), 1388
Taught Master's Scholarships, 875
Three-year Researcher Project with International Mobility, 992
The Torskeklubben Stipend, 913
Trustee Funds (Curatorenfondsen), 719
UCL Masters Bursary, 1212
UFL Jan de Limpens Scholarship, 765
ULMS MBA Excellence Scholarship, 1360
Union for International Cancer Control American Cancer Society International Fellowships for Beginning Investigators (ACSBI), 284

United Nations Educational, Scientific and Cultural Organization-ROSTE Long-term Postgraduate Training Course, 14
University International Research Studentships, 1524
University of Reading Dorothy Hodgkin Postgraduate Award, 1524
Utrecht Excellence Scholarships for International Students, 1591
Wageningen University Fellowship Programme, 1605
Wellcome Trust and NIH Four-Year PhD Studentships, 1612
Wingate Scholarships, 1619

European Union

Academy of Korean Studies Postgraduate Bursaries, 1092
Annual Fund Postgraduate Scholarships, 695
Arts Humanities Research Council Collaborative Doctoral Partnership PhD Studentship, 1215
Bournemouth University Vice-Chancellor's Scholarship–Most Promising Postgraduate Applicant, 227
Cardiff Business School-ESRC Wales DTP Fully Funded General Studentships (Economics), 323
Cardiff School of Medicine–PhD Studentships, 326
Cardiff School of Medicine–PhD Studentships (Department of Surgery), 326
Churches Together in Britain and Ireland, 556
Curtin International Scholarships-Alumni and Family Scholarship, 403
Curtin International Scholarships–Merit Scholarship, 403
Data Visualisation Design, Ambiguity & Decision Making in Megaprojects: EPSRC Studentship, 462
De Montfort University PhD Scholarships, 414
Early Bird Acceptance Grant-International Students, 700
Engineering and Physical Sciences Research Council Standard Research Studentships, 485
Ernst Ludwig Ehrlich Studienwerk, 188
European Union Postgraduate Scholarship, 463
European Union Visiting Students Scholarship, 463
EU Transition Scholarships, 741
Excellence Programme (MSc/Non-EEA), 1604
Glasgow School for Business and Society Scholarship, 570
Global Wales Postgraduate Scholarship, 329
Griffith Remarkable Scholarship, 574
Holland Scholarship, 1187
Holland Scholarship for international Master Students, 1604
Improving Project Delivery: ESRC Studentship, 465
International Student Academic Excellence Scholarship, 574
International Student Academic Merit Scholarship, 575
Japan Society for the Promotion of Science Postdoctoral Fellowships for North American and European Researchers (Short-term), 680
John Henry Garner Scholarship, 1337
Justus & Louise van Effen Excellence Scholarships, 1187
La Trobe International Scholarship, 701
La Trobe University Offshore Online Bursary, 703
La Trobe University OSHC Grant, 703
Liver Group PhD Studentship, 1205
Liverpool Law School LLM Bursaries, 1356
Masters (PGT) EU Scholarship, 1307
Master's Scholarship, 263
National Health Service Bursaries, 1207
Pathway to Victoria Scholarship, 703
Perren Studentship, 1207
PhD Fees-only Bursaries, 1159
13 PhD International Studentships at Northumbria University in UK, 901
PhD Studentship in Organisms and Environment at Cardiff University, 330
PhD Studentships in Mathematics, 1343
Postgraduate Masters Scholarships in the School of Geography, Politics and Sociology, 899
Regional Scholarship-International Students, 704
Regional Victoria Experience Bursary, 704
Södertörn University Tuition Fee Waive, 1134
Stanley Burton Research Scholarship, 1340
Statistical Science (EPSRC and MRC Centre for Doctoral Training) Studentships, 1509
Swansea University Masters Scholarships, 1159
Swansea University PhD Scholarships, 1159
Synthetic Biology Doctorate Training Centre EPSRC/BBSRC Studentships, 1509
Theology and Religion: AHRC Doctoral Training Partnership Studentships, 1510
University International Research Studentships, 1524
University of Edinburgh-KU Leuven PhD Studentship, 1303
Vice Chancellor's EU Scholarship, 1290
Wageningen University Fellowship Programme, 1605
Wellcome Trust and NIH Four-Year PhD Studentships, 1612
Wingate Scholarships, 1619

Latin America

Birkbeck International Merit Scholarships, 221
Coimbra Group Scholarship Programme for Young Professors and Researchers from Latin American Universities, 366
Curtin International Scholarships-Alumni and Family Scholarship, 403
Curtin International Scholarships–Merit Scholarship, 403
Cusanuswerk–Organization of the German Bishops' Conference Promoting Gifted Catholic Students, 187
Deakin Latin America Scholarship, 421
Early Bird Acceptance Grant-International Students, 700
Latin America–Creative and Culture Scholarships, 184
Latin America ELBP Scholarship, 1435
La Trobe International Scholarship, 701

La Trobe Latin America Scholarship, 701
La Trobe University Offshore Online Bursary, 703
La Trobe University OSHC Grant, 703
Lund University Global Scholarship, 760
Macquarie University AU$5,000 Regional Scholarship, 773
Pathway to Victoria Scholarship, 703
Regional Scholarship-International Students, 704
Regional Victoria Experience Bursary, 704
ULMS MBA Latin America Excellence Scholarship, 1360
University International Research Studentships, 1524
VLIR-UOS Training and Masters Scholarships, 193

Middle East

The Abdul Aziz Al Ghurair Refugee Education Fund, 7
The Alan Howard Scholarship, 616
Australia Awards Scholarships, 430
Birkbeck International Merit Scholarships, 221
British Petroleum Research Bursaries for PhD Study, 1261
British Petroleum Research Bursaries for Postgraduate Study, 1262
Bupa Foundation Annual Specialist Grant, 268
Curtin International Scholarships-Alumni and Family Scholarship, 403
Curtin International Scholarships–Merit Scholarship, 403
Cusanuswerk–Organization of the German Bishops' Conference Promoting Gifted Catholic Students, 187
David Gritz Scholarship, 1106
Developing Futures Scholarship, 1345
Diversity100 PhD Studentships, 222
Durham Palestine Educational Trust, 447
Early Bird Acceptance Grant-International Students, 700
40 Fully-Funded Postgraduate Scholarships at Newcastle University in the United Kingdom, 901
Gaza-Palestine Postgraduate Taught Scholarship, 1526
GREAT Scholarships, 1377
GREAT Turkey Scholarship, 465
Griffith Remarkable Scholarship, 574
International Merit Stipend, 676
International Postgraduate Gaza Scholarships, 958
International Student Academic Excellence Scholarship, 574
International Student Academic Merit Scholarship, 575
La Trobe International Scholarship, 701
La Trobe Jordan Scholarship, 701
La Trobe Turkey Scholarship, 702
La Trobe University Offshore Online Bursary, 703
La Trobe University OSHC Grant, 703
Leiden University Fund-Lutfia Rabbani Scholarship Fund, 715
Lund University Global Scholarship, 760
Macquarie University AU$5,000 Regional Scholarship, 773
Merton College Leventis Scholarship, 1476
Middle East and North Africa Scholarship, 467
Minerva Fellowship, 813
Minerva Short-Term Research Grants, 814
Netherlands Fellowship Programmes, 452
Oxford-Qatar-Thatcher Graduate Scholarships, 1494
Oxford-Robert and Soulla Kyprianou Graduate Scholarship, 1495
Oxford-Sheikh Mohammed bin Rashid Al Maktoum Graduate Scholarship, 1496
Pathway to Victoria Scholarship, 703
The Prof. Rahamimoff Travel Grants for Young Scientists, 445
Regional Scholarship-International Students, 704
Regional Victoria Experience Bursary, 704
Saïd Foundation Oxford Scholarships, 1502
Said Scholarship, 450
Santander Formula Scholarship, 811
Santander Mobility Scholarship, 811
Study in Canada Scholarships, 1322
Turkey Scholarship, 469, 1351
University International Research Studentships, 1524
Vice-Chancellors International Scholarship, 332

New Zealand

Aboriginal Enterprise Research Scholarship, 1530
Access & Rural Women New Zealand Scholarship, 153
AE and FAQ Stephens Scholarship, 1562
Allan Kay Undergraduate Memorial Scholarship, 789
Auckland University of Technology and Cyclone Computers Laptop and Tablet Scholarship, 153
Auckland University of Technology Post Graduate Scholarships, 153
Australian Biological Resources Study Postgraduate Scholarship, 402
Australian Government RTP Scholarship (Domestic), 1562
Australian Health Inequities Program Research Scholarship, 520
Australian Health Inequities Program University Research Scholarship, 521
Australian Postgraduate Awards, 349
Bamforth Postgraduate Scholarship, 942
BayTrust Bruce Cronin Scholarship, 321, 789, 1199, 1272
Betty Loughhead Soroptimist Scholarship Trust, 155
Bing, 789
Brian Aspin Memorial Scholarship, 639, 790
Bupa Foundation Annual Specialist Grant, 268
C. Alma Baker Postgraduate Scholarship, 790
The Capstone Editing Conference Travel Grant for Postgraduate Research Students, 158
The Capstone Editing Early Career Academic Research Grant for Women, 158
Care-leavers Scholarship (Continuing), 510
Care-leavers Scholarships (Commencing), 510

Carol Lynette Grant (Prowse) Scholarship, 510
Central West Medical Association Medical Student Scholarship, 350
Charles Fleming Senior Scientist Award, 1050
Charles Sturt Accommodation Equity Scholarship, 351
Chris and Gina Grubb Ornithology Scholarship, 351
The Claude McCarthy Fellowships, 1279
Clifford Wallace Collins Memorial Trust Scholarship, 321
Collin Post Memorial Scholarship in Sculpture, 640
CQUniversity Womens Equal Opportunity Research Award, 340
Curtin International Scholarships-Alumni and Family Scholarship, 403
Curtin International Scholarships–Merit Scholarship, 403
Curtin University Postgraduate Scholarship (CUPS), 404
C V Fife Memorial Scholarship, 639
Cypress-Fairbanks Independent School District/CIHR Doctoral and Postdoctoral Research Awards, 287
Damon Runyon Clinical Investigator Award, 308
Deakin Funded Scholarship Program, 420
Destination Australia Scholarship (Master of Research), 340
Destination Australia Scholarship-International Students, 401, 404
Destination Australia Scholarships, 348
The Diamond Education Grant, 394
Discrete Cosine Transform Māori and Pacific Mature Student Doctoral Scholarship, 155
Doctoral Fellowships, 358
Dr. A. Vibert Douglas Fellowship, 287
Economic & Social Research Council (1+3) Sociology Studentship, 329
Emergency Equity Grant, 353
Energy Education Trust of New Zealand Masterate Scholarship, 640, 791
Enterprise Research Scholarship, 1531
Ernest William File Scholarship, 1273
FAR Postgraduate Scholarship, 640, 791
Fibrosis in IBD Research Initiative, 397
Foundation Grant Program, 289
Frank Knox Memorial Fellowships at Harvard University, 1273
Freemasons Scholarships, 1444
French-Australian Cotutelle, 404
Fulbright New Zealand General Graduate Awards, 156
Full-Time MBA at Copenhagen Business School, 383
Future Conservationist Awards, 381
Garrick Latch Postgraduate Travel Grants, 641
Gary Metz Research Fellowship, 337
Governor General's Performing Arts Awards, 271
Graduate School of Arts and Sciences International Travel Fellowships, 369
Graduate Women Canterbury (Inc.) Trust Board Scholarship, 1275
Graduate Women Manawatu Postgraduate Scholarship, 792
Graduate Women North Shore Branch Scholarship, 792
GREAT Scholarships, 329
Gulbali Institute PhD Scholarships, 354
Harold Jones and Frances Murray Research Fellowship, 337
Henry Kelsey Scholarship, 1199
Holland Scholarship, 1577
Holland Scholarship for international Master Students, 1604
Honours Scholarship HECS Exempt Award, 354
HOPE Foundation Scholarship for Research on Ageing, 641
Hume Multiversity Scholarship, 423
Hunter Postgraduate Scholarship, 405
Ian Alexander Gordon Scholarship, 513
International Onshore Postgraduate Support Scholarship, 406
International Postgraduate Research Scholarships (IPRS) Australian Postgraduate Awards (APA), 1566
International Student Scholarship, 341
International Student Scholarship–Regional, 341
Isobella Foundation Scholarship, 513
Joan Yvonne Lowndes Award, 272
Josef Breitenbach Research Fellowship, 338
Joseph S. Stauffer Prizes, 276
The Julia Child Endowment Fund Scholarship, 400
Junior Scholar Grants, 359
The Kate Edger Educational Charitable Trust Masters Degree Award, 1232
Kenneth J. Botto Research Fellowship, 338
Kupe Leadership Scholarships, 1233
Lawson Robinson Hawke's Bay A&P Scholarship, 319
L.B. Wood Travelling Scholarship, 319
Lecture Series Grants, 359
Leonard Condell Farming PhD Scholarship, 643
Leonard Condell Farming Postgraduate Scholarship, 643
Lighthouse Vision Trust Scholarship, 1269
Lloyd J. Old STAR Program, 310
Lois Turnbull Postgraduate Scholarship, 643
Lovell and Berys Clark Scholarships, 643
Lund University Global Scholarship, 760
Macquarie University Higher Study Scholarship-Full time rate, 774
Macquarie University Higher Study Scholarship-Part time rate, 775
Māori and Pacific Graduate Scholarships (Masters/Honours/PGDIP), 1228
Marie Curie Fellowships for Early Stage Training at CERN, 380
Master of Research Elevate Scholarship-CQUniversity and Surf Lifesaving Queensland, 341
Menzies Global Leader Scholarship, 348
Merit Grants Scheme, 342
Naim Mehlab Student Travel Award, 377
Nanyang Technological University MBA Programme, 348
Narre Warren South Bendigo Bank Scholarship, 514

Nelson Algren Awards, 360
New Zealand Pacific Scholarships, 891
Online Student Representative Committee Post-Graduate Scholarship, 355
Outreach Grant, 286
Peter Densem Postgraduate Scholarship, 644
PhD Elevate Scholarship-CQUniversity and Surf Lifesaving Queensland, 342
PhD Research Scholarships, 330
PhD Scholarship as part of an International ARC-Discovery Research Project, 343
PhD scholarships in Economics, 384
Photographic Arts Council-Los Angeles (PAC-LA) Research Fellowship, 338
Postgraduate Equity Scholarship, 355
Postgraduate Merit Scholarship, 406
Pre Admissions Scholarships, 346
President, 317
Prince of Wales' Cambridge International Scholarship, 1277
Publication Subsidies, 359
Pukehou Poutu Scholarship, 1278
Rare Epilepsy Partnership Award, 364
Refugee Study Awards, 603
Research Grants, 360
Research Training Program domestic (RTPd) Scholarship, 1533
Research Training Program (RTP) Stipend Scholarship, 343
Residential School Equity Grant, 356
Robin Rousseau Memorial Mountain Achievement Scholarship, 363
The Robinson Dorsey Postgraduate Scholarship, 1450
Rural and Regional Enterprise Scholarships (RRES), 515
Scholar Grants, 360
Scots Australian Council Scholarships, 406
Seed Grants Scheme, 344
Shirtcliffe Fellowship, 474, 1200
Sir Alan Stewart Postgraduate Scholarships, 793
Sir Douglas Myers Scholarship, 1278
Staff Scholarship-Domestic, 516
Sustainable Transitions Team Research Initiative 2024, 378
Technology Equity Grant, 356
Tertiary Access Payment, 1401
Todd Walker Research Fellowship, 338
University Hall Dean's Scholarship, 534
University International Research Studentships, 1524
University of Newcastle Postgraduate Research Scholarship (UNRS Central), 1438
University of Otago Māori Doctoral Scholarship, 1452
University of Queensland PhD Scholarships for International Students, 1520
Ursula Henriques Scholarships, 332
Utrecht Excellence Scholarships for International Students, 1591
UTS Institute for Public Policy and Governance Postgraduate Scholarship, 1575
Vice-Chancellors EU Scholarship, 332
Victoria Hardship Fund Equity Grants for International Students in New Zealand, 1595
Vocational Education and Training (VET) Distinction Scholarship, 349
W.D. Farr Endowment Fund Grants, 377
William Georgetti Scholarships, 1167, 1200
Woodrow Wilson Visiting Fellows, 387
Woolf Fischer Scholarship, 1281
Zonta Club of South Auckland Area Study Award, 159
Zonta International Canterbury Tertiary Education Scholarship, 737

North American Countries

ANID CHILE, 1352
Balliol College: Foley-Bejar Scholarships, 1455
Banco de Mexico FIDERH Scholarship, 266
Bishop Thomas Hoyt Jr Fellowship, 368
Chevening Scholarships, 1457
Chiang Ching Kuo Foundation for International Scholarly Exchange Eminent Scholar Lectureship, 357
CONACYT, 1353
CONACYT Scholarship, 769
The Cultural Diaspora, 269
Curtin International Scholarships-Alumni and Family Scholarship, 403
Curtin International Scholarships–Merit Scholarship, 403
Dean's International Postgraduate Research Scholarships, 1565
Doctoral and Postdoctoral Research Fellowships, 566
Early Bird Acceptance Grant-International Students, 700
FIDERH, 1543
FIDERH Award, 1354
FIDERH Scholarship, 770
FUNED Awards, 1354
FUNED Scholarship, 770
GREAT Scholarships, 1203, 1377, 1536
Griffith Remarkable Scholarship, 574
Holland Scholarship, 1577
International Student Academic Excellence Scholarship, 574
International Student Academic Merit Scholarship, 575
JuventudEsGto, 1355
La Trobe International Scholarship, 701
La Trobe University Offshore Online Bursary, 703
La Trobe University OSHC Grant, 703
Lund University Global Scholarship, 760
Mexican CONACYT-Macquarie University Postgraduate Research Scholarships, 776
Mexico Scholarship, 467
Pathway to Victoria Scholarship, 703

Regional Scholarship-International Students, 704
Regional Victoria Experience Bursary, 704
Samuel H Kress Joint Athens-Jerusalem Fellowship, 109
Santander Formula Scholarship, 811
Santander Masters Scholarship, 1309
Santander Mobility Scholarship, 811
SEP Scholarship, 779
University International Research Studentships, 1524
Utrecht Excellence Scholarships for International Students, 1591

North European Countries

Denmark-America Foundation Grants, 427
Japan Society for the Promotion of Science Postdoctoral Fellowships for North American and European Researchers (Short-term), 680
William Charnley Anglo-Danish Scholarship, 125

Oceania

The AUT Queen Elizabeth II Diamond Jubilee Doctoral Scholarship, 1231
Dean's International Postgraduate Research Scholarships, 1565
Holland Scholarship, 1577
International Merit Stipend, 676
The Jackson Family Foundation Scholarship, 1231
Kobayashi Research Grants, 1576
Utrecht Excellence Scholarships for International Students, 1591

Russia

British Petroleum Research Bursaries for PhD Study, 1261
British Petroleum Research Bursaries for Postgraduate Study, 1262
Chevening Scholarships, 1457
Hill Foundation Scholarships, 1464
Japan Society for the Promotion of Science Postdoctoral Fellowships for North American and European Researchers (Short-Term), 680
Leicester Castle Business School Full Postgraduate Scholarship, 417
Macquarie University AU$5,000 Regional Scholarship, 773
Orange Tulip Scholarship, 765, 1605

South Africa

The Arturo Falaschi ICGEB Predoctoral Fellowships ICGEB Trieste International PhD Programme, 655
Arturo Falaschi PhD Fellowships, 652
Azerbaijan: Azerbaijan Diplomatic Academy University Scholarship, 989
Botswana Insurance Holdings Limited Trust Thomas Tlou Scholarship for Master Programme, 226
Brunei Darussalam: Government of Brunei Darussalam Scholarship, 594
Chile: Nelson Mandela Scholarships, 361
Claude Leon Foundation Postdoctoral Fellowship, 366
Curtin International Scholarships-Alumni and Family Scholarship, 403
Early Bird Acceptance Grant-International Students, 700
Eastern and Southern Africa Scholarship, 462
Ek Brown Of Monaltrie Animal Sanctuary Trust Bursary, 1516
Embassy of France in South Africa Master Scholarship Programme, 595
France: French Embassy and Saint-Gobain Master Scholarship, 596
Fulbright Foreign Student Funding, 1517
Griffith Remarkable Scholarship, 574
Hansi Pollak Scholarship, 1136
Hungary: Stipendium Hungaricum for South Africa, 596
ICGEB PhD and POSTDOC Fellowships, South Africa, 653
ICGEB PhD Fellowships, 653
Innovation Masters and Doctoral Scholarships, 865
International Student Academic Excellence Scholarship, 574
International Student Academic Merit Scholarship, 575
Ireland: Kader Asmal Fellowship Programme, 597
Isie Smuts Research Award, 1136
La Trobe International Scholarship, 701
La Trobe University Offshore Online Bursary, 703
La Trobe University OSHC Grant, 703
Lund University Global Scholarship, 760
National Research Foundation Free-standing Masters and Doctoral Scholarships, 866
National Research Foundation Targeted Research Awards Competitive Industry Programme, 866
Next Gen Fellowship Program for Sub-Saharan African Countries, 333
Orange Tulip Scholarship, 765, 1605
Pathway to Victoria Scholarship, 703
Regional Scholarship-International Students, 704
Regional Victoria Experience Bursary, 704
Russia: Scholarships for South Africans, 599
Spain: Student and Staff Exchange between South Africa and Spain, 599
Standard Bank Africa Chairman's Scholarships, 1508
Standard Bank Derek Cooper Africa Scholarship, 1508
Sweden: Swedish Institute Scholarships for South Africa (SISSA), 600
University International Research Studentships, 1524
Vice-Chancellors International Scholarship, 332
Vrije University Amsterdam-NRF Desmond Tutu Doctoral Scholarships, 867

South American Countries

Academy of Research and Higher Education Scholarships, 1213
ANII Becas, 966
Brazil Scholarship, 462
Canada-Brazil Awards-Joint Research Projects, 280
Canada-CARICOM Faculty Leadership Program, 281
Canada-Chile Leadership Exchange Scholarship, 282
Chevening Scholarships, 1457
Chiang Ching Kuo Foundation for International Scholarly Exchange Eminent Scholar Lectureship, 357
COLFUTURO Scholarships, 768, 968
Colombia Scholarship, 462
The Cultural Diaspora, 269
Curtin International Scholarships-Alumni and Family Scholarship, 403
Curtin International Scholarships–Merit Scholarship, 403
Deakin International COLFUTURO Bursary, 421
Early Bird Acceptance Grant-International Students, 700
Girton College: Maria Luisa de Sanchez Scholarship, 1248
Griffith Remarkable Scholarship, 574
Holland Scholarship, 1577
Holland Scholarship for international Master Students, 1604
International Club of Boston College Cambridge Scholarship, 1263
International Student Academic Excellence Scholarship, 574
International Student Academic Merit Scholarship, 575
Latin America Scholarship, 466
La Trobe International Scholarship, 701
La Trobe University Offshore Online Bursary, 703
La Trobe University OSHC Grant, 703
Lund University Global Scholarship, 760
Netherlands Fellowship Programmes, 452
Pathway to Victoria Scholarship, 703
Regional Scholarship-International Students, 704
Regional Victoria Experience Bursary, 704
Santander Formula Scholarship, 811
Santander Masters Scholarship, 1309
Santander Mobility Scholarship, 811
Santander Taught Postgraduate Scholarships, 1582
Sydney International Student Award (South and Central America), 1570
University International Research Studentships, 1524
Utrecht Excellence Scholarships for International Students, 1591
Vice-Chancellors International Scholarship, 332

South European Countries

John R. Mott Scholarship, 686

United Kingdom

Academy of Korean Studies Postgraduate Bursaries, 1092
The ACE Foundation Scholarship, 125
Ageing Research Development Awards, 215
AHRC South, West and Wales Doctoral Training Partnerships, 1521
Alice Brown PhD Scholarships, 1295
Alumni Loyalty Scholarship, 704
Alumni Postgraduate Scholarships, 705
Alumni Scholarship for Postgraduate Study, 1345
Annual Fund Postgraduate Scholarships, 695
Artificial Intelligence Innovation to Accelerate Health Research, 215
Artificial Intelligence Research to Enable UK's Net Zero Target, 215
Arts Humanities Research Council Collaborative Doctoral Partnership PhD Studentship, 1215
Awards for Current Students-The Taunton Maids Bursary, 182
BA/Leverhulme Small Research Grants, 233
Balliol College: Snell Scholarship, 1456
BAPRAS Pump Priming Fund for Clinical Trials, 240
The Bartlett Promise PhD Scholarship, 1211
BBSRC Brazil Pump-Priming Award, 215
BBSRC International Travel Award Scheme, 215
BBSRC Standard Research Grant, 216
Black Academic Futures Scholarship, 1456
Bond University United Kingdom Excellence Scholarship in Australia, 223
Bournemouth University Vice-Chancellor's Scholarship–Most Promising Postgraduate Applicant, 227
Bowland College–Willcock Scholarships, 705
British Academy/Cara/Leverhulme Researchers at Risk Research Support Grants, 233
British Academy Conferences, 233
British Association for American Studies Postgraduate and Early Career Short-Term Travel Awards, 236
British Institute in Eastern Africa Minor Grants, 255
Bupa Foundation Annual Specialist Grant, 268
Cancer Research United Kingdom LRI Graduate Studentships, 312
Cardiff School of Medicine–PhD Studentships, 326
Cardiff School of Medicine–PhD Studentships (Department of Surgery), 326
Carnegie Trust: St Andrew's Society Scholarships, 1155
Chancellor's Masters Scholarship, 1558
The Christine and Ian Bolt MA Scholarships in American Literature and Culture, 1333
Churches Together in Britain and Ireland, 556, 706
Churchill Fellowship, 1171
Collaborate with Researchers in Luxembourg, 216
College of Social Sciences, Arts and Humanities Masters Excellence Scholarship, 1342
College of Social Sciences, Arts and Humanities Minority Ethnic Masters Scholarship, 1343
Commonwealth Shared Scholarship Scheme at United Kingdom Universities, 375

Cornwall Heritage Trust Scholarship, 1311
County College Scholarships, 706
County College Studentship, 706
Curtin International Scholarships-Alumni and Family Scholarship, 403
Curtin International Scholarships–Merit Scholarship, 403
Daiwa Foundation Small Grants, 411
Daphne Jackson Fellowship, 216
Data Visualisation Design, Ambiguity & Decision Making in Megaprojects: EPSRC Studentship, 462
DeepMind Scholarships-Department of Life Sciences, 610
De Montfort University PhD Scholarships, 414
Denmark Liberation Scholarships, 125
Design Engineering PhD Scholarships (DEPS), 611
Develop a UK Digital Twinning Research Community with a NetworkPlus, 217
Develop Basic Technologies in Sensing and Imaging, 802
Diagnostics and Surveillance of Antimicrobial resistance (JPIAMR), 217
Discovery Programme Foundation Awards, 314
Discretionary Fund, 1540
Dowden Scholarship, 1305
Early Bird Acceptance Grant-International Students, 700
Economic and Social Research Council Studentships, 753
Edinburgh Dental Institute MSc Scholarship, 1297
Edinburgh Doctoral College Scholarships, 1297
Emergency Grants, 554
Engineering and Physical Sciences Research Council Standard Research Studentships, 485
Explore the Requirements of Exascale Software for UK Science, 217
Forensic Science for the Justice System Sandpit, 218
Friends of Israel Educational Foundation Academic Study Bursary, 549
Geoffrey Leech Departmental MA scholarship, 708
Global Challenges Research Fund Challenge-led Grants (GCRF), 1051
Global Professorships, 231
Griffith Remarkable Scholarship, 574
Grizedale College Awards Fund, 708
GROW Your Future Careers Bursary, 709
Grundy Educational Trust Postgraduate Award, 1439
Historic Royal Palaces Heritage Scholarships, 970
Holland Scholarship, 1577
Holland Scholarship for international Master Students, 1604
Impact Focussed Supergen Hubs in Bioenergy, Networks and ORE, 218
Improving Project Delivery: ESRC Studentship, 465
Inspiring Success Scholarship, 754
International Student Academic Excellence Scholarship, 574
International Student Academic Merit Scholarship, 575
Irish Research Council Scholarships-Ulysses, 872
John Henry Garner Scholarship, 1337
John L Paterson Postgraduate Design Scholarship, 1299
John Speak Trust Scholarships, 229
Keble College Gosden Water-Newton Scholarship, 1466
Keble College Water Newton Scholarship, 1467
Kennedy Scholarships, 694
Knowledge Asset Grant Fund: Expand 2023, 878
Knowledge Transfer Partnership, 218
La Trobe International Scholarship, 701
La Trobe University Offshore Online Bursary, 703
La Trobe University OSHC Grant, 703
Leverhulme Trade Charities Trust, 710
Leverhulme Trade Charities Trust Postgraduate Bursaries, 755
Lincoln College: Crewe Graduate Scholarships, 1473
Liver Group PhD Studentship, 1205
London Goodenough Association of Canada Scholarship Program, 739
London Scholarships, 755
The Lorch Foundation MSc Student Bursary, 395
Lund University Global Scholarship, 760
Martin Cook Scholarship for Humanities Students, 1330
Master's Compare Postgraduate Scholarship, 184
National Health Service Bursaries, 1207
Natural Environment Research Council Research Grants, 878
Novel, Low-emission Food Production Systems: Feasibility Studies, 218
Novel, Low-emission Food Production Systems: Industrial Research, 218
Ove Arup Foundation Award, 125
Oxford-David Jones Graduate Scholarship, 1486
Oxford-Leon E and Iris L Beghian Graduate Scholarships, 1490
Pandemic Preparedness: Lessons to Learn from COVID-19 across the G7, 235
Pathway to Victoria Scholarship, 703
Perren Studentship, 1207
PhD Fees-only Bursaries, 1159
PhD Studentship in Organisms and Environment at Cardiff University, 330
PhD Studentships in Mathematics, 1343
Population Health Improvement Network of Clusters, 219
Postgraduate Masters Scholarships in the School of Geography, Politics and Sociology, 899
Postgraduate Opportunity Bursary, 1357
Postgraduate Opportunity Scholarships, 900
Postgraduate Progression Award-UK Students, 1357
Postgraduate Research EU Scholarship, 1308
Professor Sir Malcolm Grant Postgraduate Scholarship, 1207
Protected and Controlled Environment (PACE) Horticulture, 219
The Ray and Naomi Simpson Scholarship, 1341
Regional Scholarship-International Students, 704
Regional Victoria Experience Bursary, 704
Research Assistance Awards, 237
Research Development Fellowships, 219

Research Fellowships, 726
Research for a Plastics Circular Economy: Full Proposal Stage, 219
R.J. Hunter Research Bursary Scheme, 1044
RSE Fulbright Scholar Award, 1055
Sanctuary Scholarship, 1309
Sandpit: Novel Computing for UK Defence and Security, 220
Santander Masters Scholarship, 1309
SOAS Master's Scholarship, 1095
SOAS Research Scholarship, 1096
Stanley Burton Research Scholarship, 1340
Statistical Science (EPSRC and MRC Centre for Doctoral Training) Studentships, 1509
Strathclyde Business School Masters Scholarships for Scottish/UK Students, 1551
Students Awards Agency for Scotland Postgraduate Students' Allowances Scheme (PSAS), 966
Study Abroad Studentship, 727
Sustainable Bio-based Materials and Manufacture: Feasibility Study, 220
Swansea University Masters Scholarships, 1159
Swansea University PhD Scholarships, 1159
Synthetic Biology Doctorate Training Centre EPSRC/BBSRC Studentships, 1509
Thomas Witherden Batt Scholarship, 1211
Travel Fellowships, 253
Trinity College: Michael and Judith Beloff Scholarship, 1511
UCL Masters Bursary, 1212
UKRI Policy Fellowships 2023, 220
UKRI Policy Fellowships 2024, 879
UKRI-SBE Lead Agency Opportunity, 220
University College: Chellgren, 1511
University of Edinburgh-KU Leuven PhD Studentship, 1303
University of Exeter Chapel Choir Choral and Organ Scholarship, 1312
USW Postgraduate Ethnicity Equality Bursary, 1534
Utrecht Excellence Scholarships for International Students, 1591
Visiting Professorships, 727
Wellcome Trust and NIH Four-Year PhD Studentships, 1612
William Charnley Anglo-Danish Scholarship, 125
Wingate Scholarships, 1619

United States of America

Abell Foundation-For Small Grant Requests, 9
Abell Foundation-Grant Requests Greater than US$10,000, 9
Abilene Christian University National Merit Finalist or Semifinalist Scholarship, 9
Abilene Christian University Valedictorian/Salutatorian Scholarship, 10
Academia Resource Management Postgraduate Fellowship, 11
Access Missouri Financial Assistance Program, 818
American Association of University Women Career Development Grants, 50
American Association of University Women Case Support Travel Grants, 50
American Association of University Women Community Action Grants, 50
American Association of University Women Selected Professions Fellowships, 52
American Foundation of RHBNC International Excellence Scholarship, 1039
American Institute of Certified Public Accountants Fellowship for Minority Doctoral Students, 696
American-Scandinavian Foundation Scholarships (ASF), 910
Arthur L. Norberg Travel Fund, 347
Associated Women for Pepperdine (AWP) Scholarship, 988
Association of Flight Attendants Annual Scholarship, 147
Belgian American Educational Foundation (B.A.E.F.), 191
Benjamin A. Gilman International Scholarship Program, 372
Berkeley-Hasselt Research Fellowship, 194
Berreman-Yamanaka Award for Himalayan Studies, 631
Bhattacharya Graduate Fellowship, 632
The Bibliographical Society of America-American Society for Eighteenth-Century Studies Fellowship for Bibliographical Studies in the Eighteenth Century, 205
The Bibliographical Society of America-Pine Tree Foundation Fellowship in Hispanic Bibliography, 206
The Bibliographical Society of America-Rare Book School Fellowship, 206
The Bibliographical Society of America Short-term Fellowships, 206
Bodha Pravaham Fellowship, 632
Boren Fellowships, 225
Boren Scholarship, 226
British Marshall Scholarships, 893
Canadian Embassy Graduate Student Fellowship Program, 286
Canadian Embassy (United States of America) Research Grant Program, 285
Canadian Women Artists' Award, 888
Cardiff University Marshall Scholarship, 327
Carter Roger Williams Scholarship, 1004
Cataract Fire Company #2 Scholarship, 1004
CBCF Congressional Summer Internship Program, 378
CBCF NREI Historically Black Colleges and Universities (HBCU) Scholarship, 379
CBC Spouses Education Scholarship, 378
Center for British Studies Grants, 195
Charlie Trotter's Culinary Education Foundation Culinary Study Scholarship, 356
Chiang Ching Kuo Foundation for International Scholarly Exchange Eminent Scholar Lectureship, 357
CIEE-Gilman Go Global Grant, 230

Columbia College of Missouri Boone County Endowed Award, 368
Council of American Overseas Research Centers Multi-Country Research Fellowship Program for Advanced Multi-Country Research, 386
Council on Foreign Relations International Affairs Fellowship in Japan, 389
Culture of Health Prize, 1010
Curtin International Scholarships-Alumni and Family Scholarship, 403
Curtin International Scholarships–Merit Scholarship, 403
CVS Health Pharmacy Scholarship, 1183
The Daniel Gerber Sr, Medallion Scholarship, 565
Dean's International Postgraduate Research Scholarships, 1565
Denmark-America Foundation Grants, 427
Dissertation Fellowship in Hazards, Risks, and Disaster, 879
DOE Office of Science Graduate Student Research (SCGSR) program, 195
Dolores Zohrab Liebmann, 196
Early Bird Acceptance Grant-International Students, 700
Everett And Florence Drumright Scholarship, 917
Fellowship Program, 78
Fellowships for Study of Research in Belgium, 192
Fibrosis in IBD Research Initiative, 397
FLAS Fellowship (Academic Year), 368
Ford Foundation Dissertation Fellowship, 539
Ford Foundation Predoctoral Fellowships for Research-Based PhD or ScD Programs in United States of America, 538
Ford Foundation Senior Fellowship, 838
Foreign Language and Area Studies Fellowship, 369
The Fredson Bowers Award, 207
Fulbright Awards, 1535
Fulbright Commission (Argentina) Awards for United States Lecturers and Researchers, 550
Fulbright-Durham University Award, 448
The Fulbright-Edinburgh University Award, 1196
Fulbright/Maastricht University Award, 763
Fulbright New Zealand General Graduate Awards, 156
Fulbright Scholar-in-Residence, 550
Fulbright Scholarships, 1354
40 Fully-Funded Postgraduate Scholarships at Newcastle University in the United Kingdom, 901
Garden Club of America Summer Scholarship in Field Botany, 559
George A. and Eliza Gardner Howard Foundation, 563
George F. Wellik Scholarship, 132
Georges Lurcy Fellowship for Study in France, 197
The Gerber Foundation Merit Scholarship, 565
German Historical Institute Collaborative Research Program for Postdoctoral Scholars, 566
Global International and Area Studies Grants, 197
Global Wales Postgraduate Scholarship, 329
Griffith Remarkable Scholarship, 574
Hart Fellowship, 632
Hitchings-Elion Postdoctoral Fellowships for United States Scientist, 861
Holland Scholarship, 1577
Holland Scholarship for international Master Students, 1604
HSF Scholarship, 1177
Institute of International Studies (IIS) Dissertation Fellowships, 198
International Need-Based Tuition Awards and Graduate Student Family Grants, 198
International Student Academic Excellence Scholarship, 574
International Student Academic Merit Scholarship, 575
Japan Society for the Promotion of Science Postdoctoral Fellowships for North American and European Researchers (Short-term), 680
Jefferson Science Fellowship, 839
Jozef Tischner Fellowships, 697
La Trobe International Scholarship, 701
La Trobe University Offshore Online Bursary, 703
La Trobe University OSHC Grant, 703
League of United Latin American Citizens National Educational Service Centers National Scholarship Fund, 761
Leicester Castle Business School Full Postgraduate Scholarship, 417
Long-Term Fellowships, 892
Luce Scholarship, 199
Lund University Global Scholarship, 760
Maharaj Kaul Memorial Trust, 633
The Marine Corps Scholarship, 785
Marshall Scholarships, 243, 448, 787, 970, 1356, 1536
McNair Graduate Fellowships, 1220
Michael P. Metcalf Memorial Fund and Christine T. Grinavic Adventurer, 1004
Mike M. Masaoka Congressional Fellowship, 681
MS Clinical Mentorship for Medical Students, 864
Multi-Country Research Fellowship, 387
Naval Sea Systems Command (NAVSEA) and Strategic Systems Programs Scholarship, 76
New Work Projects Grants, 579
The Next Generation: Leadership in Asian Affairs Fellowship, 851
North American Postgraduate Scholarship, 467
Norwegian Emigration Fund, 912
Norwegian Marshall Fund, 912
Norwegian Thanksgiving Fund Scholarship, 912
Outstanding Paper Prize, 633
Pathway to Victoria Scholarship, 703
The Paul & Daisy Soros Fellowship for New Americans, 949
Pembroke College Jose Gregorio Hernandez Award of the Venezuelan National Academy of Medicine, 1499
Pfizer Scholars Grants in Clinical Epidemiology, 954

Pfizer Scholars Grants in Clinical Psychiatry, 954
Pfizer Scholars Grants in Clinical Rheumatology, 954
Pfizer Scholars Grants in Pain Medicine, 954
Polish National Alliance of Brooklyn, United States of America, Inc. Scholarship, 697
Postdoctoral Fellowship in Health Outcomes Research, 956
The Prof. Rahamimoff Travel Grants for Young Scientists, 445
Rangel Graduate Fellowship Program, 891
Rauschenberg Emergency Grants, 889
Regional Scholarship-International Students, 704
Regional Victoria Experience Bursary, 704
Research Fellowships, 1622
Research Grants & Fellowships, 946
Saint Andrew's Society of the State of New York Scholarship Fund, 1316
School of Education Graduate Grant, 212
Scotland's Saltire Scholarship, 468
Sea Grant/NOAA Fisheries Graduate Fellowship, 870
Social Science Research Council Eurasia Program Postdoctoral Fellowships, 1123
Social Science Research Council Eurasia Program Teaching Fellowships, 1124
Somerville College Janet Watson Bursary, 1503
Soroptimist International Founder Region Women's Fellowships, 200
Stephen Feinberg Scholars Scholarship Program, 380
Thurgood Marshall College Fund Scholarships, 1183
TMCF All Around Scholarship, 1182
Tortuga Study Abroad Scholarship, 231
Transatlantic Doctoral Seminar in German History, 567
TREC: Institutional Postdoctoral Training Award, 307
TREC: Pilot Study Award, 307
UC President's Pre-Professoriate Fellowship, 200
University International Research Studentships, 1524
USA Transfer Scholarship, 185
Utrecht Excellence Scholarships for International Students, 1591
Vice-Chancellors International Scholarship, 332
The Wendell Alton Moats and Virginia Evelyn Moats Scholarship for Business, 213
The White House Fellowship, 1178
White House Fellowships, 962

West European Countries

Curtin International Scholarships-Alumni and Family Scholarship, 403
Curtin International Scholarships–Merit Scholarship, 403
Early Bird Acceptance Grant-International Students, 700
Griffith Remarkable Scholarship, 574
International Student Academic Excellence Scholarship, 574
International Student Academic Merit Scholarship, 575
La Trobe International Scholarship, 701
La Trobe University Offshore Online Bursary, 703
La Trobe University OSHC Grant, 703
Lund University Global Scholarship, 760
Minerva Fellowship, 813
Minerva Short-Term Research Grants, 814
Pathway to Victoria Scholarship, 703
Regional Scholarship-International Students, 704
Regional Victoria Experience Bursary, 704
University International Research Studentships, 1524

AGRICULTURE, FORESTRY AND FISHERY

GENERAL

Any Country

Arrell Scholarships, 1318
AsureQuality Seed Technology Scholarship, 638
The Council of Scientific and Industrial Research/TWAS Fellowship for Postdoctoral Research, 1180
Dreamfields Farm Agricultural Scholarship, 791
Fulbright Distinguished Chair in Science, Technology, and Innovation (CSIRO), 551
Hurley Fraser Postgraduate Scholarship, 792
Kress Conservation Fellowships, 1085
Marshal Papworth Scholarships in Agriculture for Developing Countries, 786
PhD Elevate Scholarship-CQUniversity and CRC for Developing Northern Australia Partnership-Climate Change (External), 342
Robert E. Thunen Memorial Scholarships, 200
Sir John Logan Campbell Agricultural Scholarship, 793
TWAS-COMSTECH Science in Exile PhD Fellowship Programme for Displaced and Refugee Scientists, 1180

African Nations

Africa Land and Food Masters Fellowship, 1016
Austrian Academy of Sciences, 4-months Trimester at Egerton University, Kenya, 178
The Beacon Scholarship, 331
Seed Grant for New African Principal Investigators (SG-NAPI), 1179

Asian Countries

Fulbright-Nehru Doctoral Research Fellowships, 1195
Fulbright-Nehru Postdoctoral Research Fellowships, 1195
Korea New Zealand Agricultural Cooperation Scholarships (KNZACS), 473
National Bioscience Awards for Career Development (NBACD), 428
S. Ramachandran-National Bioscience Award for Career Development, 428
Tata Innovation Fellowship, 429

Australia
Buninyong Community Bank Scholarship, 509
HeART of the Basin Scholarship, 340
Playford Trust: Playford Trust: PhD Scholarships, 530
Water Corporation Scholarship in Biosolids Research, 408
Canada
Dr Lloyd M. Dosdall Memorial Scholarship, 489
European Countries
Bayer Foundation Scholarships, 186
New Zealand
Buninyong Community Bank Scholarship, 509
Kitchener Memorial Scholarship, 1269
Leonard Condell Farming Postgraduate Scholarship, 793
United Kingdom
Frank Stell Scholarship, 1336
United States of America
Rudolf Steiner Foundation Seed Fund, 17
Western Center for Agricultural Health and Safety, 1240

AGRICULTURAL BUSINESS

Any Country
Alistair Betts Scholarship, 638, 788
Australia
Australian Banana Growers' Council Mort Johnston Scholarship, 674
D.L. McMaster Fund Endowed Housing Scholarship, 1406

AGRICULTURAL ECONOMICS

Any Country
A S Nivison Memorial Scholarship, 1404

AGRICULTURE AND FARM MANAGEMENT

Australia
Australian Banana Growers' Council Mort Johnston Scholarship, 674
AGRONOMY
Asian Countries
China Scholarships, 620

ANIMAL HUSBANDRY

Any Country
Bell-Booth Dairy Research Scholarship, 789
Australia
Samuel & Eileen Gluyas Fellowship, 678
Australia
Alliance Group Postgraduate Scholarship, 1442
New Zealand
Samuel & Eileen Gluyas Fellowship, 678
New Zealand
Alliance Group Postgraduate Scholarship, 1442
SERICULTURE
Asian Countries
China Scholarships, 620

CROP PRODUCTION

Any Country
Elinor Roper Scholarship, 1628
Elinor Roper Scholarship 2024, 1629
Australia
Australian Banana Growers' Council Mort Johnston Scholarship, 674
Biology of Annual Ryegrass Scholarship, 350

FISHERY

Any Country
Ministry of Fisheries PG Scholarships in Quantitative Fisheries Science, 815
OFAH/Fleming College Fish & Wildlife Scholarship, 924
Ontario Federation of Anglers & Hunters/Oakville and District Rod & Gun Club Conservation Research Grant, 924
RFRC Graduate Student Fellowship Awards, 1221

FOOD SCIENCE

Any Country
Continuing Medical Education Beef Industry Scholarship, 851
University of Copenhagen International PhD Fellowships in Food Biotechnology, Denmark, 905
European Countries
Collaborative Project to Meet Societal and Industry-related Challenges, 990
United States of America
Cabot Scholarships, 886

DAIRY

Any Country
Catherine Baxter Dairy Scholarship, 790
Australia
Dairy Postgraduate Scholarships and Awards, 1391

HARVEST TECHNOLOGY

Any Country
Elinor Roper Scholarship, 1628
Elinor Roper Scholarship 2024, 1629

OENOLOGY

Any Country
Wolf Blass Australian Winemaking Independent Study Scholarship, 1622
New Zealand
Bragato Research Fellowship, 790

FORESTRY

Any Country
Canadian Forest Service Graduate Supplements, 1126
McKelvey Award, 1270
S.F. Pond Travelling Scholarship, 1399

FOREST PRODUCTS

Any Country
Wood Technology Research Centre–Postgraduate Scholarships, 1271

HORTICULTURE AND VITICULTURE

Any Country
The Colegrave Seabrook Foundation, 1630
Dr Betty Elliott Horticulture Scholarship, 1392
Frank Keenan Scholarship, 1392
Grants for Orchid Research, 91
Herb Society of America Research Grant, 591
Horticulture NZ Undergraduate Scholarships, 792
Madeleine Selwyn-Smith Memorial Scholarships, 1397
Royal Horticultural Society Financial Awards, 1043
Stanley Smith (UK) Horticultural Trust Awards, 1151
Turners and Growers Undergraduate Scholarships, 794
Zespri Innovation Scholarships, 737
Australia
Casella Family Brands PhD Scholarship, 350
New Zealand
Casella Family Brands PhD Scholarship, 350
Farmers Union Scholarship, 640
Zespri Innovation Scholarships, 737
United Kingdom
Blaxall Valentine Bursary Fund, 1043
Royal Horticulture Society Bursary Scheme, 1044
United States of America
The Garden Club of America Hope Goddard Iselin Fellowship in Public Horticulture, 560

SOIL AND WATER SCIENCE

Any Country
Bowler Ravensdown Scholarship in Soil Science, 789
The Kenneth E. Grant Scholarship, 1135
STRI Postdoctoral Research in Hydrology, 1120
North American Countries
American Water Works Association Abel Wolman Fellowship, 121
WATER MANAGEMENT
Australia
2024 Great Artesian Basin Lynn Brake Scholarship, 520
TROPICAL AGRICULTURE
Caribbean Countries
Scholarship Opportunities Linked to CATIE, 1186
Central American Countries
Scholarship Opportunities Linked to CATIE, 1186
North American Countries
Scholarship Opportunities Linked to CATIE, 1186
South American Countries
Scholarship Opportunities Linked to CATIE, 1186
United States of America
RaMP-UP-Research and Mentoring Program–Understanding and Preserving Tropical BioDiversity Fellowship, 1120

VETERINARY SCIENCE

Any Country
2023-24 Bloomsbury Colleges PhD Studentship-Project 2, 744
Collaborative Project relating to Antimicrobial Resistance from a One Health Perspective, 990
Intermediate Fellowship, 619
Joan Berry Fellowships in Veterinary Science-Postgraduate, 642
Medical Research Council Clinical Research Training Fellowships, 803
Medical Research Council Clinician Scientist Fellowship, 804
Medical Research Council Senior Clinical Fellowship, 804
Senior and Intermediate Research Fellowship for International Students, 1609
Senior Fellowship, 619
Universities Federation for Animal Welfare Student Scholarships, 1198
Asian Countries
Early Career Fellowship, 618
Australia
Samuel & Eileen Gluyas Fellowship, 678
European Countries
Harry Steele-Bodger Memorial Travelling Scholarship, 263
European Union
Cardiff Institute of Tissue Engineering and Repair (CITER)–EPSRC Studentship, 324
New Zealand
Samuel & Eileen Gluyas Fellowship, 678
United Kingdom
Cardiff Institute of Tissue Engineering and Repair (CITER)–EPSRC Studentship, 324
Harry Steele-Bodger Memorial Travelling Scholarship, 263
Medical Research Council/RCOG Clinical Research Training Fellowship, 805

ARCHITECTURE AND TOWN PLANNING

GENERAL

Any Country
A-AA Austrian Studies Scholarship Award, 180

Architecture, Building and Civil Engineering Scholarships, 750
Byera Hadley Travelling Scholarships, 887
Easson Geha Award in Planning, 1417
Edilia and Francois-Auguste de Montequin Fellowship in Auguste de Montequin Fellowship Architecture, 1133
Graduate Scholarship, 144
Lincoln Alumni Master of Architecture Scholarship, 1348
Madbury Road Design Success Award Scholarship, 132
Max Brauer Award, 25
The Parker Fellowship, 1437
Rae and George Hammer Memorial Visiting Research Fellowship, 1218
Ramboll Masters Scholarship for International Students, 1448
Resource Management Law Association of New Zealand Masters Scholarship, 157
Robert E. Thunen Memorial Scholarships, 200
The Royal Scottish Academy John Kinross Scholarships to Florence, 1049
University of Reading MSc Intelligent Buildings Scholarship, 1524
Villa I Tatti-Bogaziçi University Joint Fellowship, 1600
Wallace Fellowship, 1601
African Nations
The Beacon Scholarship, 331
GREAT Scholarships-Egypt, 1286
GREAT Scholarships-Ghana, 1286
GREAT Scholarships-Kenya, 1287
Asian Countries
Fulbright-Nehru Doctoral Research Fellowships, 1195
Fulbright-Nehru Master's Fellowships, 1195
Fulbright-Nehru Postdoctoral Research Fellowships, 1195
Geddes Scholarship, 1087
GREAT Scholarships-China, 1286
GREAT Scholarships-India, 1287
GREAT Scholarships–Indonesia, 1287
GREAT Scholarships–Malaysia, 1288
GREAT Scholarships–Pakistan, 1288
GREAT Scholarships–Thailand, 1288
Australia
Arcadia Landscape Architecture Scholarship in Landscape Architecture Design, 1046
Australian Building Codes Board Research Scholarship, 1216
Client Service Excellence Award, 887
Elias Duek-Cohen Civid Design Award, 1417
HeART of the Basin Scholarship, 340
Robb Scholarship for Regional Planning and Development, 1410
Canada
J.B.C. Watkins Award: Architecture, 271
Prix de Rome in Architecture-Emerging Practitioners, 274
Prix de Rome in Architecture-Professional, 276
United Kingdom
Bartlett School of Planning Centenary Scholarship, 1201
Cardiff University MSc/Diploma in Housing Studentship, 327
Department of Communities and Local Government (formally Office of the Deputy Prime Minister), 1202
Giles Worsley Travel Fellowship, 260
Rome Scholarship in Architecture, 261
United States of America
Congressional Black Caucus Foundation Spouses Visual Arts Scholarship, 379

ARCHITECTURAL AND ENVIRONMENTAL DESIGN

European Countries
Design Alumni Bursary, 752

LANDSCAPE ARCHITECTURE

Any Country
Wallace Fellowship, 1601
Canada
Ronald J. Thom Award for Early Design Achievement, 276

ARTS AND HUMANITIES

GENERAL

Any Country
A-AA Austrian Studies Scholarship Award, 180
ACLS Emerging Voices Fellowships, 62
AHRC: Chase Doctoral Training Partnership, 221
AHRC North West Consortium Doctoral Training Partnership in the School of Environment, Education and Development, 1364
Alexander and Margaret Johnstone Postgraduate Research Scholarships, 1314
Ampère & MILYON Excellence Scholarships for International Students, 456
Ana Hatherly Graduate Student Research Grant, 638
Anderson-Yamanaka Scholarship, 1427
Andrew W Mellon Fellowship, 1635
Andrew W. Mellon Foundation/ACLS Early Career Fellowships Program Dissertation Completion Fellowships, 63
Asian Cultural Council Humanities Fellowship Program, 144
Associate Alumni Bursary, 967
Australian Academy of the Humanities Visiting Scholar Programmes, 163
Awards for Faculty at Hispanic-Serving Institutions, 853
be.AI Leverhulme Doctoral Scholarships (Leverhulme Trust), 1558
Beinecke Scholarship, 190
Bellahouston Bequest Fund, 1314

Berlinski-Jacobson Graduate Scholarship (Humanities & Social Sciences), 1146
The Camargo Core Program, 269
Canadian Centennial Scholarship Fund, 1324
China Scholarship Council Scholarships, 968
China Scholarship Council-The University of Manchester Joint Scholarship for PhD Study in the School of Arts, Languages and Cultures, 1369
Christine and Ian Bolt Scholarship, 1324
College Scholarship (Arts), 1146
Commencing Scholarship in Art Curating or Museum and Heritage Studies, 1564
Consortium for the Humanities and the Arts (CHASE), 1559
The Constantine Aspromourgos Memorial Scholarship for Greek Studies, 1520
The Dean of Humanities, Arts & Social Sciences Excellence Scholarship, 986
Dean's Global Research Award, 1540
Digital Humanities Advancement Grants, 645
Drake Lewis Graduate Scholarship for Art History, 1306
Drue Heinz Scholarship, 1626
EPSRC Doctoral Training Partnership Studentships in Alliance Manchester Business School, 1374
EPSRC Doctoral Training Partnership Studentships in the School of Arts, Languages and Cultures, 1374
EPSRC Doctoral Training Partnership Studentships in the School of Environment, Education and Development, 1375
Ertegun Graduate Scholarship Programme in the Humanities, 1460
ESRC North West Social Science DTP (NWSSDTP) PhD Studentships in Alliance Manchester Business School, 1375
ESRC North West Social Science DTP (NWSSDTP) PhD Studentships in the School of Arts, Languages and Cultures, 1376
ESRC North West Social Science DTP (NWSSDTP) PhD Studentships in the School of Environment, Education and Development, 1376
Exeter College: Nicholas Frangiscatos Scholarship in Byzantine Studies, 1461
Faculty of Humanities & Social Sciences: International Scholarships Postgraduate Taught, 1541
Fully Funded Master Scholarship, 1584
Ghosh Graduate Scholarship (Humanities), 1147
Global Research Scholarship Programme (Faculty of Humanities & Social Sciences), 1544
Grants for ANS Summer Seminar in Numismatics, 91
GSAS Summer Language Fellowships for International Students, 370
Gulf Research Program Science Policy Fellowships, 1175
Harvard Travellers Club Permanent Fund, 581
Humanities and Social Sciences Home Postgraduate Taught Performance Sport Scholarship, 1546
Humanities and Social Sciences Postgraduate Scholarships, 894
Humanities and Social Sciences RUK Postgraduate Taught Performance Sport Scholarship, 1546
Humanities St Cross College UK BAME PGT Studentship, 1140
Indian Excellence Scholarship Award, 1378
Institute for Advanced Studies in the Humanities Postdoctoral Fellowships, 1299
International PhD Awards, 971
Lancaster Master's Scholarship, 709
Leigh Douglas Memorial Prize, 262
Lincoln College: Jermyn Brooks Graduate Award, 1473
Lincoln College: Lord Crewe Graduate Scholarships in the Humanities, 1474
Lindt Dissertation Fellowship, 370
MPhil Scholarships in the Humanities and Social Sciences, 1140
National Endowment for the Humanities Post-Doctoral Fellowships, 729
National Research Foundation Fellowships for Postdoctoral Research, 865
Newton International Fellowships, 234
Oxford-Anderson Humanities Graduate Scholarship, 1481
Paul Mellon Centre Rome Fellowship, 261
Program in African American History (PAAH) Mellon Postdoctoral Fellowships, 729
Radcliffe Institute Fellowship, 977
Research Fellowships in Humanities and Social Science, 1608
Robinson College: Lewis Graduate Scholarship, 1258
School of Social Sciences and Humanities International PhD Studentships in UK, 905
Short-Term EFEO Postdoctoral Contracts, 537
Skinner Fund, 1053
Social Science Research Council International Dissertation Research Fellowship, 1124
St Antony's College Ali Pachachi Scholarship, 1503
St Catherine's College: College Scholarship (Arts), 1504
St Cross College: MPhil Scholarships in the Humanities and Social Sciences, 1506
University of California, Los Angeles (UCLA) Sardar Patel Award, 1239
University of Leicester Future 50 PhD Scholarship: "Latinx in the UK: Identity, Visibility and British Latinx Studies," 237
Villa I Tatti-Bogaziçi University Joint Fellowship, 1600
Visiting Fellowships, 259
Wallace Fellowship, 1601
Wellcome Master's Programme Awards in Humanities and Social Science, 1537
Wilfrid Knapp Scholarship (Arts), 1148
The William Sanders Scarborough Fellowships, 106
Wolfson Foundation Scholarships, 1589

African Nations
The Beacon Scholarship, 331
Humanities & Social Sciences: Student Excellence Awards, 1545
Indonesian Arts and Culture Scholarship, 816
Respective Government Fellowships, 986
Zentrum Moderner Orient and Berlin Graduate School of Muslim Cultures and Societies Visiting Research Fellowship, 201
Asian Countries
China Scholarship Council-The University of Manchester Joint Scholarship for PhD Study in Alliance Manchester Business School, 1368
China Scholarship Council-The University of Manchester Joint Scholarship for PhD Study in the School of Environment, Education and Development, 1369
Dissertation Fellowships for ROC Students Abroad, 358
Fulbright-Nehru Master's Fellowships, 1195
GREAT Scholarships India, 243
Indonesian Arts and Culture Scholarship, 816
Oxford-Kaifeng Graduate Scholarship, 1490
Research Fellowships for Young Researchers, 680
Serendib Community Cultural Association Sri Lanka Bursary, 425
Zentrum Moderner Orient and Berlin Graduate School of Muslim Cultures and Societies Visiting Research Fellowship, 201
Asia-Pacific Countries
Indonesian Arts and Culture Scholarship, 816
Australia
Council of Catholic School Parents (NSW) Indigenous Postgraduate Scholarship (IES), 165
The Helen Macpherson Smith Scholarships, 1401
Humanities & Social Sciences: Student Excellence Awards, 1545
Indigenous Pathways Advance Queensland VET Scholarship, 341
The John Mulvaney Fellowship, 163
Malcolm Cole Indigenous Scholarship, 1421
Canada
The Coburn Award, 274
Humanities & Social Sciences: Student Excellence Awards, 1545
International Council for Canadian Studies Graduate Student Scholarships, 283
Social Sciences and Humanities Research Council Impact Awards, 1078
SSHRC Impact Awards, 1127
SSHRC Postdoctoral Fellowships, 1128
The Winter 2022 Gift Competition, 414
East European Countries
Humanities & Social Sciences: Student Excellence Awards, 1545
European Countries
Alfred Toepfer Natural Heritage Scholarships, 25
Arts and Humanities Research Council Studentships, 1093
Barron Bequest, 1602
Berkeley-Austria Research Fellowship, 194
Council of American Overseas Research Centers Andrew W. Mellon East-Central European Research Fellows, 386
John and Pat Hume Research Scholarships, 874
Open Society Institute's Global Supplementary Grant Program (Grant SGP), 926
Oxford-Bounden Graduate Scholarship, 1483
Swiss National Science Foundation Fellowships for Prospective Researchers, 1164
W.D.E. Coulson & Toni M. Cross Aegean Exchange Program, 106
European Union
Arts and Humanities Research Council Studentships, 1093
English Faculty: Asian Human Rights Commission (AHRC) Doctoral Training Partnership Studentship (Master), 1460
Indonesian Arts and Culture Scholarship, 816
John and Pat Hume Research Scholarships, 874
Oxford-Calleva Scholarship, 1483
Middle East
Humanities & Social Sciences: Student Excellence Awards, 1545
Zentrum Moderner Orient and Berlin Graduate School of Muslim Cultures and Societies Visiting Research Fellowship, 201
New Zealand
Humanities & Social Sciences: Student Excellence Awards, 1545
Masters/Honours/PGDIP Scholarships, 1229
Sasakawa Young Leaders Fellowship Fund Research Scholarship-Masters and PhD, 736
North American Countries
American School of Classical Studies at Athens Fellowships, 98
Humanities & Social Sciences: Student Excellence Awards, 1545
North European Countries
Humanities & Social Sciences: Student Excellence Awards, 1545
Oceania
Humanities & Social Sciences: Student Excellence Awards, 1545
Indonesian Arts and Culture Scholarship, 816
South American Countries
Sasakawa Young Leader Fellowship (SYLFF) Program, 1090
United Kingdom
The Anglo-Norse Dame Gillian Brown Postgraduate Scholarship, 126
Daphne Jackson Fellowships, 1101

English Faculty: Asian Human Rights Commission (AHRC) Doctoral Training Partnership Studentship (Master), 1460
Greyfriars Postgraduate Scholarship, 984
Linacre College: Raymond and Vera Asquith Scholarship, 1472
Lincoln College: Hartley Bursary, 1473
Net Zero Policy Programme, 234
Oxford-Bounden Graduate Scholarship, 1483
Policy Insight Case Studies, 235
United States of America
American Council of Learned Societies Digital Extension Grants, 1133
American Council of Learned Societies/New York Public Library (NYPL) Fellowships, 63
American Schools of Oriental Research W.F. Albright Institute of Archaeological Research/National Endowment of the Humanities Fellowships, 108
CAORC-NEH Senior Research Fellowship, 385
Council of American Overseas Research Centers (CAORC) Fellowships for Advanced Multi-Country Research, 109
Council of American Overseas Research Centers Neh Research Fellowships, 386
Foreign Language and Area Studies Awards, 196
Humanities & Social Sciences: Student Excellence Awards, 1545
Rudolf Steiner Foundation Seed Fund, 17
Social Science Research Council Eurasia Program Predissertation Training Fellowships, 1123
Title VIII-Supported Summer Research Grant, 694
West European Countries
Foundation Praemium Erasmianum Study Prize, 548

ARCHAEOLOGY

Any Country
Albright Institute of Archaeological Research (AIAR) Annual Professorship, 107
American School of Classical Studies at Athens Advanced Fellowships, 98
American School of Classical Studies at Athens Research Fellowship in Environmental Studies, 99
American School of Classical Studies at Athens Research Fellowship in Faunal Studies, 99
American School of Classical Studies at Athens Research Fellowship in Geoarchaeology, 99
American School of Classical Studies at Athens Summer Sessions, 99
Awards for Faculty at Historically Black Colleges and Universities, 854
Awards for Faculty at Tribal Colleges and Universities, 854
C. Brian Rose AIA/DAI Exchange Fellowships, 128
Cotsen Traveling Fellowship for Research in Greece, 100
The Elizabeth Catling Memorial Fund for Archaeological Draughtsmanship, 257
Fowler-Merle Smith Summer Scholarship for Teachers, 101
Graduate Scholarship, 144
Honor Frost Foundation Grants, 234
The John and Bryony Coles Bursary (Student Travel Award), 962
John R. Coleman Traveling Fellowship, 129
Kress Publications Fellowships, 102
Malcolm H. Wiener Laboratory for Archaeological Science Senior Fellowship, 102
Malcolm H. Wiener Laboratory Postdoctoral Fellowship, 103
Malcom H. Wiener Laboratory for Archaeological, 103
Master's Degree Awards in Archaeology, 1206
National Endowment for the Humanities (NEH) Fellowships, 104
Open Scholarship for Summer Sessions, 104
Open Scholarship for the Summer Session and Summer Seminars, 104
Postgraduate Research Award (PGRA), 171
Richard Brookdale Scholarship, 677
Simon Keay Award in Mediterranean Archaeology, 261
A S Nivison Memorial Scholarship, 1404
The Tim Collins Scholarship for the Study of Love in Religion, 984
Villa I Tatti-Bogaziçi University Joint Fellowship, 1600
Wiener Laboratory Predoctoral Fellowship, 106
Wiener Laboratory Research Associate Appointment, 107
Asian Countries
CSC-Leiden University Scholarship, 714
Australia
Jacqui Thorburn and Family Bursary for Indigenous Archaeology and Cultural Heritage Management, 527
Canada
Anna C. & Oliver C. Colburn Fellowships, 127
Archaeological Institute of America (AIA) Anna C. and Oliver C. Colburn Fellowships, 100
Harriet and Leon Pomerance Fellowship, 128
Regular Member Fellowships, 105
European Countries
Archaeology of Portugal Fellowship, 127
The Archaeology Of Portugal Fellowship, 129
Harry Bikakis Fellowship, 101
Hector and Elizabeth Catling Bursary, 256
Middle East
Honor Frost Foundation Masters and/or Doctoral Awards in Maritime Archaeology, 1536
Jacob Hirsch Fellowship, 102
Martin Harrison Memorial Fellowship, 254
North American Countries
Harry Bikakis Fellowship, 101

South Africa
Leiden University South Africa Scholarship-University of Cape Town, 716
Leiden University South Africa Scholarship-University of Pretoria, 716
Leiden University South Africa Scholarship-University of the Western Cape, 717
LUF International Study Fund (LISF), 717
Mandela Scholarship Fund, 718
United Kingdom
Postgraduate History and Archaeology Studentship, 331
United States of America
Anna C. & Oliver C. Colburn Fellowships, 127
Archaeological Institute of America (AIA) Anna C. and Oliver C. Colburn Fellowships, 100
Council of American Overseas Research Centers Multi Country Research Fellowships, 101
Harriet and Leon Pomerance Fellowship, 128
Jacob Hirsch Fellowship, 102
Olivia James Traveling Fellowship, 129
Regular Member Fellowships, 105

CLASSICAL LANGUAGES AND LITERATURES

Any Country
AHRC North West Consortium Doctoral Training Partnership (NWCDTP) in the School of Arts, Languages and Cultures, 1364
American School of Classical Studies at Athens Advanced Fellowships, 98
American School of Classical Studies at Athens Summer Sessions, 99
Andrew W. Mellon Foundation Masters & Doctoral Scholarships, 1007
Bedford Society Scholarship, 1040
Chinese-English Translation Scholarships, 1305
Cotsen Traveling Fellowship for Research in Greece, 100
The Dr Ethel M. Janes Memorial Scholarship in Education, 809
Ernest Hemingway Research Grants, 685
FfWG-Theodora Bosanquet Bursary for Women Graduates, 707
Guy Butler Research Award, 1008
Harry Clough Bursary, 1378
The Lees Scholarship, 1388
Master of Arts Scholarship in Applied Language Studies or Professional Language Studies, 156
Myrtle McMyn Bursary, 1380
Oxford-Nizami Ganjavi Graduate Scholarships, 1492
Pembroke College: Tokyo Electric Power Company (TEPCO) Scholarship, 1499
President's Doctoral Scholar (PDS) Awards in the School of Arts, Languages and Culture, 1381
Rae and George Hammer Memorial Visiting Research Fellowship, 1218
Samuel H Kress Joint Athens-Jerusalem Fellowship, 105
School of Arts, Languages and Cultures PhD Studentships, 1383
The School of History and Heritage MA Bursary, 1351
St. Louis Mercantile Library Prize, 204
The Tim Collins Scholarship for the Study of Love in Religion, 984
Usher Bursary, 1390
Asian Countries
China Scholarships, 620
Fulbright-Nehru Doctoral Research Fellowships, 1195
Fulbright-Nehru Postdoctoral Research Fellowships, 1195
Australia
Sir Arthur Sims Travelling Scholarship, 1399
Canada
John Charles Polanyi Prizes, 1077
Regular Member Fellowships, 105
European Countries
Wolfson Postgraduate Scholarships in the Humanities, 1514
United Kingdom
Daiwa Scholarships in Japanese Studies, 1370
Theodora Bosanquet Bursary, 249
Wolfson Postgraduate Scholarships in the Humanities, 1514
United States of America
Lilly Fellows Program in the Humanities and the Arts, 1006
Regular Member Fellowships, 105
Weiss/Brown Publication Subvention Award, 892
CLASSICAL GREEK
African Nations
Scholarships for a Summer Seminar in Greek Language and Culture, 574
Asian Countries
Scholarships for a Summer Seminar in Greek Language and Culture, 574
East European Countries
Scholarships for a Summer Seminar in Greek Language and Culture, 574
European Countries
Oxford-Murray Graduate Scholarship, 1491
Scholarships for a Summer Seminar in Greek Language and Culture, 574
Middle East
Scholarships for a Summer Seminar in Greek Language and Culture, 574
United States of America
Scholarships for a Summer Seminar in Greek Language and Culture, 574

SANSKRIT

Any Country
Brough Sanskrit Awards, 1093

COMPARATIVE LITERATURE

Any Country
Andrew W. Mellon Foundation Masters & Doctoral Scholarships, 1007
Bedford Society Scholarship, 1040
FfWG-Theodora Bosanquet Bursary for Women Graduates, 707
Graduate Scholarship, 144
Guy Butler Research Award, 1008
The Louis Cha Scholarship, 1141
Pembroke College: Tokyo Electric Power Company (TEPCO) Scholarship, 1499
Rae and George Hammer Memorial Visiting Research Fellowship, 1218
The School of History and Heritage MA Bursary, 1351
St. Louis Mercantile Library Prize, 204
Villa I Tatti-Bogaziçi University Joint Fellowship, 1600
Vivian Lefsky Hort Memorial Fellowship, 1641
Wallace Fellowship, 1601
Asian Countries
China Scholarships, 620
Fulbright-Nehru Doctoral Research Fellowships, 1195
Fulbright-Nehru Postdoctoral Research Fellowships, 1195
Canada
John Charles Polanyi Prizes, 1077
European Countries
Oxford-Murray Graduate Scholarship, 1491
European Union
Alexander and Dixon Scholarship (Bryce Bequest), 1314
United Kingdom
Alexander and Dixon Scholarship (Bryce Bequest), 1314
Theodora Bosanquet Bursary, 249
United States of America
Lilly Fellows Program in the Humanities and the Arts, 1006
Weiss/Brown Publication Subvention Award, 892

HISTORY

Any Country
AHRC Chase PhD Studentship Narratives of Fall: The Archive and Art Collection of the Nineteenth Century Foundling Hospitale, 221
ALA Library History Round Table Davis Article Award, 928
Albright Institute of Archaeological Research (AIAR) Annual Professorship, 107
American School of Classical Studies at Athens Advanced Fellowships, 98
American School of Classical Studies at Athens Summer Sessions, 99
Angus Ross Travel Scholarship in History, 1442
Balliol College: Peter Storey Scholarship, 1456
Bedford Society Scholarship, 1040
Berenson Fellowship, 1598
Bielefeld Graduate School in History and Sociology Start-up Doctoral Scholarships, 208
Boughton PhD Scholarship, 222
China Residency Program, 928
Cotsen Traveling Fellowship, 100
Cotsen Traveling Fellowship for Research in Greece, 100
Craig Hugh Smyth Fellowship, 1599
David and Julie Tobey Fellowship, 1599
Donald & Margot Watt Bursary Fund (FASS Only), 706
The Eleonore Koch Fund, 1309
FfWG-Theodora Bosanquet Bursary for Women Graduates, 707
Fowler-Merle Smith Summer Scholarship for Teachers, 101
150 Fully Funded PhD Degree Scholarships for International Students, 503
Germany Residency Program, 930
Getty Pre-and Postdoctoral Fellowships and GRI-NEH Postdoctoral Fellowships, 568
Goethe-Institut Postdoctoral Fellowship for International Students, 572
Harry S Truman Library Institute Dissertation Year Fellowships, 579
I Tatti Fellowship, 1600
I Tatti/Museo Nacional del Prado Joint Fellowship, 1597
James H. Billington Fellowship, 694
The Japan Residencies Program, 937
Joan Burns Memorial Scholarship in History, 1276
John A. S. Grenville PhD Studentship in Modern Jewish History and Culture, 720
John Higham Research Fellowship, 932
Keith Hawkins Graduate Research Scholarship in English or American Legal History, 939
Kress Publications Fellowships, 102
Lerner-Scott Prize, 933
Library Associates Fellowship, 683
Library Company of Philadelphia Dissertation Fellowships, 728
The Louis Cha Scholarship, 1141
Louis Pelzer Memorial Award, 933
Master of Arts in Art Museum and Gallery Studies Scholarship, 895
Max Planck Institute for the History of Science Postdoctoral Fellowship in Germany, 796
Media@McGill Postdoctoral Fellowship, 800
Mellon Fellowship in Digital Humanities, 1600
National Endowment for the Humanities (NEH) Fellowships, 104

New South Wales Indigenous History Fellowship, 141
Ontario Bicentennial Award, 238
Open Scholarship for Summer Sessions, 104
Open Scholarship for the Summer Session and Summer Seminars, 104
Oxford-Anderson Graduate Scholarship in History, 1481
Oxford-Radcliffe Graduate Scholarships, 1494
Oxford-Rothermere American Institute Graduate Scholarship, 1495
Oxford-Swire Graduate Scholarship, 1496
Pembroke College: The Thornton Graduate Studentship in History, 1256
Pembroke College: Tokyo Electric Power Company (TEPCO) Scholarship, 1499
Phillips Fund for Native American Research, 94
Presidents' Travel Fund, 935
Ray Allen Billington Prize, 935
The Reese Fellowship for American Bibliography and the History of the Book in the Americas, 207
Richard Chattaway Scholarship, 1208
Ruth and Lincoln Ekstrom Fellowship, 683
Samuel H Kress Joint Athens-Jerusalem Fellowship, 105
Stanton-Horton Award for Excellence in National Park Service History, 936, 938
St. Louis Mercantile Library Prize, 204
Tachau Teacher of the Year Award, 936
Theodora Bosanquet Bursary, 555
The Tim Collins Scholarship for the Study of Love in Religion, 984
Villa I Tatti-Bogaziçi University Joint Fellowship, 1600
Wallace Fellowship, 1601
Warburg-I Tatti Joint Fellowship, 1598
Winterthur Dissertation Research Fellowships, 1621
Winterthur Postdoctoral Fellowships, 1621
Winterthur Research Fellowships, 1621
Zuckerman Dissertation Fellowship, 371

African Nations

GREAT Scholarships-Egypt, 1286
GREAT Scholarships-Ghana, 1286
GREAT Scholarships-Kenya, 1287
Haywood Doctoral Scholarship, 1299

Asian Countries

Fulbright-Nehru Doctoral Research Fellowships, 1195
Fulbright-Nehru Postdoctoral Research Fellowships, 1195
GREAT Scholarships-China, 1286
GREAT Scholarships-India, 1287
GREAT Scholarships–Indonesia, 1287
GREAT Scholarships–Malaysia, 1288
GREAT Scholarships–Pakistan, 1288
GREAT Scholarships–Thailand, 1288

Australia

Bruggeman Postgraduate Scholarship in Classics, 1443
Emeritus Professor William Gordon Rimmer Award, 1417
New South Wales Premier's History Awards, 141
Sir Arthur Sims Travelling Scholarship, 1399

Canada

Mary McNeill Scholarship in Irish Studies, 972
Regular Member Fellowships, 105

European Countries

Barron Bequest, 1602
Harry Bikakis Fellowship, 101
Oxford-Wolfson-Ancient History Graduate Scholarship, 1498
Royal Historical Society: Postgraduate Research Support Grants, 1316
Wolfson Postgraduate Scholarships in the Humanities, 1514

European Union

Master of Arts in Art Museum and Gallery Studies Scholarship, 895

New Zealand

Bruggeman Postgraduate Scholarship in Classics, 1443

North American Countries

Harry Bikakis Fellowship, 101

United Kingdom

Black Academic Futures DPhil Scholarship in History, 938
Brian Harris Scholarship, 1040
Master of Arts in Art Museum and Gallery Studies Scholarship, 895
Postgraduate History and Archaeology Studentship, 331
Theodora Bosanquet Bursary, 249
Wolfson Postgraduate Scholarships in the Humanities, 1514

United States of America

The Charles J. Tanenbaum Fellowship in Cartographical Bibliography, 207
Council of American Overseas Research Centers Multi Country Research Fellowships, 101
David N. Keightley Fellowship, 195
Gerald D. and Norma Feldman Graduate Student Dissertation Fellowship, 197
Helmut Kohl Award in German and European Studies, 198
History of Art Institutional Fellowships, 1084
Huggins-Quarles Award, 930
The James Madison Memorial Fellowship, 782
Japanese Residencies for United States of America Historians, 931
John D'Emilio LGBTQ History Dissertation Award, 932
Lilly Fellows Program in the Humanities and the Arts, 1006
Mary McNeill Scholarship in Irish Studies, 972
National Endowment for the Humanities American Research Institute in Turkey-National Endowment for the Humanities Fellowships for Research in Turkey, 97
Paul J. Alexander Memorial Fellowship, 199
Regular Member Fellowships, 105
Richard W. Leopold Prize, 935
Summer Seminar in Germany, 567

ANCIENT CIVILISATIONS

Any Country

American Schools of Oriental Research Mesopotamian Fellowship, 108

MEDIEVAL STUDIES

Any Country

Dr Pirkko Koppinen Scholarship, 1041
English Faculty: Cecily Clarke Studentship, 1460
The School of History and Heritage MA Bursary, 1351

MODERN HISTORY

Any Country

Aleksander and Alicja Hertz Memorial Fellowship, 1639
Hodson Trust-John Carter Brown Library Fellowship, 682
Samuel and Flora Weiss Research Fellowship, 1641
St Antony's College Wai Seng Senior Research Scholarship, 1503

United Kingdom

Browning Fund Grants, 234

PREHISTORY

Any Country

JCB J. M. Stuart Brown Graduate Fellowship, 682
The John and Bryony Coles Bursary (Student Travel Award), 962
Prehistoric Society Conference Fund, 961
Research Fund, 961
To Support Research in the Prehistory of the Aegean and Its Connections with the East Mediterranean, 259

LINGUISTICS

Any Country

Beyond Segments: Towards a Lexical Model for Tonal Bilinguals, 767
Chinese-English Translation Scholarships, 1305
Fitzwilliam College: Robert Lethbridge Scholarship in Modern Languages, 1246
Lucy Cavendish College: Mastermann-Braithwaite Studentship, 1253
McGill University PhD Studentships in Neurolinguistics, 800
Phillips Fund for Native American Research, 94
A S Nivison Memorial Scholarship, 1404
The Tim Collins Scholarship for the Study of Love in Religion, 984

Asian Countries

Fulbright-Nehru Doctoral Research Fellowships, 1195
Fulbright-Nehru Postdoctoral Research Fellowships, 1195

United States of America

Boren Fellowships for Graduate Students, 230

MODERN LANGUAGES

Any Country

AHRC North West Consortium Doctoral Training Partnership (NWCDTP) in the School of Arts, Languages and Cultures, 1364
Chinese-English Translation Scholarships, 1305
The Dr Ethel M. Janes Memorial Scholarship in Education, 809
Fitzwilliam College: Robert Lethbridge Scholarship in Modern Languages, 1246
Harry Clough Bursary, 1378
The Lees Scholarship, 1388
Master of Arts Scholarship in Applied Language Studies or Professional Language Studies, 156
Master of Arts (Taught Masters) Scholarships in the School of Modern Languages, 895
Myrtle McMyn Bursary, 1380
Oxford-Nizami Ganjavi Graduate Scholarships, 1492
President's Doctoral Scholar (PDS) Awards in the School of Arts, Languages and Culture, 1381
School of Arts, Languages and Cultures PhD Studentships, 1383
The Tim Collins Scholarship for the Study of Love in Religion, 984
Usher Bursary, 1390

Asian Countries

Fulbright-Nehru Doctoral Research Fellowships, 1195
Fulbright-Nehru Postdoctoral Research Fellowships, 1195

Australia

Judith Robinson-Valery Honours Award in Modern Languages, 1421
Sir Arthur Sims Travelling Scholarship, 1399

European Countries

Wolfson Postgraduate Scholarships in the Humanities, 1514

United Kingdom

Daiwa Scholarships in Japanese Studies, 1370
Wolfson Postgraduate Scholarships in the Humanities, 1514

United States of America

Blakemore Freeman Fellowships for Advanced Asian Language Study, 223
Critical Language Scholarship Program, 1177
Lilly Fellows Program in the Humanities and the Arts, 1006

AFRICAN LANGUAGES

Any Country

Rhodes University African Studies Centre (RASC), 1009

ARABIC

Any Country

Pembroke College: Graduate Studentships in Arabic and Islamic Studies (including Persian), 1254

CHINESE

Any Country
Bernard Buckman Scholarship, 1093
Confucius Institute Scholarship, 1637
Judith Robinson-Valery Honours Award in Modern Languages, 1421
Asian Countries
China Scholarships, 620
United States of America
Blakemore Freeman Fellowships for Advanced Asian Language Study, 223
Chinese Language Fellowship Program, 851

ENGLISH

Any Country
Bedford Society Scholarship, 1040
English Faculty: Cecily Clarke Studentship, 1460
English Scholarships, 753
Graduate Honors Scholarship, 1402
Guy Butler Research Award, 1008
Linacre College: Linacre Rausing Scholarship (English), 1471
Linacre College: Rausing Scholarship in English, 1471
Oxford-Aidan Jenkins Graduate Scholarship, 1480
Oxford-Cecil Lubbock Memorial Graduate Scholarship, 1484
African Nations
ELICOS Scholarship, 700
GREAT Scholarships-Egypt, 1286
GREAT Scholarships-Ghana, 1286
GREAT Scholarships-Kenya, 1287
Asian Countries
ELICOS Scholarship, 700
GREAT Scholarships-China, 1286
GREAT Scholarships-India, 1287
GREAT Scholarships–Indonesia, 1287
GREAT Scholarships–Malaysia, 1288
GREAT Scholarships–Pakistan, 1288
GREAT Scholarships–Thailand, 1288
Asia-Pacific Countries
ELICOS Scholarship, 700
Canada
ELICOS Scholarship, 700
Caribbean Countries
ELICOS Scholarship, 700
Central European Countries
ELICOS Scholarship, 700
East European Countries
ELICOS Scholarship, 700
European Countries
ELICOS Scholarship, 700
Rausing Scholarship in English, 735
European Union
ELICOS Scholarship, 700
Latin America
ELICOS Scholarship, 700
Middle East
ELICOS Scholarship, 700
North American Countries
ELICOS Scholarship, 700
South Africa
ELICOS Scholarship, 700
South American Countries
ELICOS Scholarship, 700
United Kingdom
ELICOS Scholarship, 700
United States of America
ELICOS Scholarship, 700
West European Countries
ELICOS Scholarship, 700

EUROPEAN LANGUAGES (OTHERS)

United States of America
Fellowships for Intensive Advanced Turkish Language Study in Istanbul, Turkey, 97

FRENCH

Any Country
Judith Robinson-Valery Honours Award in Modern Languages, 1421
Australia
Language Assistantships in France and New Caledonia, 481
West European Countries
Lucy Cavendish College: Evelyn Povey Studentship, 1252

GERMAN

Any Country
Judith Robinson-Valery Honours Award in Modern Languages, 1421

ITALIAN

Any Country
Balliol College: Brassey Italian Scholarship, 1455
South European Countries
Italian Australian Foundation Travel Scholarships, 1396

JAPANESE

Any Country
Judith Robinson-Valery Honours Award in Modern Languages, 1421
New Zealand
Barbara Mito Reed Award, 1272

United Kingdom
Daiwa Scholarships, 412
United States of America
Blakemore Freeman Fellowships for Advanced Asian Language Study, 223

KOREAN

Any Country
Judith Robinson-Valery Honours Award in Modern Languages, 1421
Sochon Foundation Scholarship, 1096
United States of America
Blakemore Freeman Fellowships for Advanced Asian Language Study, 223

MODERN GREEK

Any Country
American School of Classical Studies at Athens Advanced Fellowships, 98
Summer Intensive Course in modern Greek Language Scholarship, 132
United States of America
Council of American Overseas Research Centers Multi Country Research Fellowships, 101

SPANISH

Any Country
Judith Robinson-Valery Honours Award in Modern Languages, 1421

NATIVE LANGUAGE AND LITERATURE

Any Country
AHRC North West Consortium Doctoral Training Partnership (NWCDTP) in the School of Arts, Languages and Cultures, 1364
Bedford Society Scholarship, 1040
Chinese-English Translation Scholarships, 1305
FfWG-Theodora Bosanquet Bursary for Women Graduates, 707
Harry Clough Bursary, 1378
The Lees Scholarship, 1388
Library Associates Fellowship, 683
Myrtle McMyn Bursary, 1380
Oxford-Nizami Ganjavi Graduate Scholarships, 1492
Pembroke College: Tokyo Electric Power Company (TEPCO) Scholarship, 1499
President's Doctoral Scholar (PDS) Awards in the School of Arts, Languages and Culture, 1381
School of Arts, Languages and Cultures PhD Studentships, 1383
The School of History and Heritage MA Bursary, 1351
St. Louis Mercantile Library Prize, 204
Theodora Bosanquet Bursary, 555
Usher Bursary, 1390
Asian Countries
China Scholarships, 620
European Countries
Oxford-Murray Graduate Scholarship, 1491
Wolfson Postgraduate Scholarships in the Humanities, 1514
European Union
Alexander and Dixon Scholarship (Bryce Bequest), 1314
United Kingdom
Alexander and Dixon Scholarship (Bryce Bequest), 1314
Daiwa Scholarships in Japanese Studies, 1370
Theodora Bosanquet Bursary, 249
Wolfson Postgraduate Scholarships in the Humanities, 1514
United States of America
Weiss/Brown Publication Subvention Award, 892

PHILOSOPHY

Any Country
Bedford Society Scholarship, 1040
Boughton PhD Scholarship, 222
Donald & Margot Watt Bursary Fund (FASS Only), 706
The Eleonore Koch Fund, 1309
Frank Chapman Sharp Memorial Prize, 93
Fred Katz Award, 1417
Green Moral Philosophy Scholarship, 1463
HAPP Scholarship in the History & Philosophy of Physics, 1140
The Pamela Sue Anderson Studentship for the Encouragement of the Place of Women in Philosophy, 984
Ruth First Scholarship, 1010
The Tim Collins Scholarship for the Study of Love in Religion, 984
Villa I Tatti-Bogaziçi University Joint Fellowship, 1600
Wallace Fellowship, 1601
Zuckerman Dissertation Fellowship, 371
African Nations
GREAT Scholarships-Egypt, 1286
GREAT Scholarships-Ghana, 1286
GREAT Scholarships-Kenya, 1287
Asian Countries
GREAT Scholarships-China, 1286
GREAT Scholarships-India, 1287
GREAT Scholarships–Indonesia, 1287
GREAT Scholarships–Malaysia, 1288
GREAT Scholarships–Pakistan, 1288
GREAT Scholarships–Thailand, 1288
Australia
Co-op Bookshop Scholarship, 165
Sir Arthur Sims Travelling Scholarship, 1399
European Countries
American Council of Learned Societies Humanities Program in Belarus, Russia and Ukraine, 62

Oxford-Mary Jane Grefenstette Graduate Scholarship, 1491
European Union
Philosophy Faculty-Wolfson College Joint Scholarship, 1499
New Zealand
Canterbury Scholarship, 321
Russia
American Council of Learned Societies Humanities Program in Belarus, Russia and Ukraine, 62
United States of America
Lilly Fellows Program in the Humanities and the Arts, 1006

ETHICS

Any Country
Centre for Bioethics and Emerging Technologies PhD Funding, 1148
Greenwall Fellowship Program, 687
Hoover Fellowships for International Scholars, 335

TRANSLATION AND INTERPRETATION

Any Country
Chin Communications Master of Interpreting and Translation Studies Scholarship, 821
HLC MA in Chinese-English Translating and Interpreting Scholarships, 1282
Translation Competition, 123
Latin America
Latin America Scholarship, 1307

WRITING (AUTHORSHIP)

Any Country
Avery O. Craven Award, 928
Charles Fleming Publishing Award, 1050
Civil War and Reconstruction Book Award, 928
Darlene Clark Hine Award, 929
David Montgomery Award, 929
Donald & Margot Watt Bursary Fund (FASS Only), 706
Ellis W. Hawley Prize, 929
Frank Chapman Sharp Memorial Prize, 93
Frederick Jackson Turner Award, 930
James A. Rawley Prize, 931
James Russell Lowell Prize, 819
Katherine Singer Kovacs Prize, 819
Lawrence W. Levine Award, 932
Liberty Legacy Foundation Award, 933
Mark Mills Award, 89
Merle Curti Award in American Intellectual History, 934
Merle Curti Intellectual History Award, 934
Merle Curti Social History Award, 934
Miles Franklin Literary Award, 1186
Minnesota Historical Society Research Grant, 817
Modern Language Association Prize for a First Book, 820
Modern Language Association Prize for Independent Scholars, 820
Social Science Research Council Summer Institute on International Migration, 1124
Spencer Foundation Dissertation Fellowship Program, 1138
Willi Paul Adams Award, 937
African Nations
Miles Morland Foundation Writing Scholarship, 813
Canada
Aid to Scholarly Journals, 1125
Berlin Program Fellowship, 1121
Central European Countries
Berlin Program Fellowship, 1121
United Kingdom
Royal Literary Fund Grant, 1045
United States of America
Berlin Program Fellowship, 1121
Mary Nickliss Prize in United States Women's and/or Gender History, 934
SSRC/ACLS Eastern European Program Dissertation Fellowships, 1125

BUSINESS ADMINISTRATION AND MANAGEMENT

GENERAL

Any Country
Advancing Women in Leadership Scholarship (MBA), 893
Alliance Manchester Business School PhD Studentships, 1364
American Association of University Women (AAUW) International Fellowships, 49
Blockchain in Business and Society Scholarships, 968
Business and Management Postgraduate Scholarships, 968
Business, Economics & Law Postgraduate Academic Excellence Scholarship, 155
Christine and Ian Bolt Scholarship, 1324
College of Business Government and Law PhD Top-up, 522
Discover Business at Dundee, 1284
The Durham University Business School's Dean's Scholarship, 452
Edward & Susan Wilson Graduate Scholarship in Business, 1115
Faculty PhD Scholarships, 319
Francis Regan Student Scholarship, 525
Future Leaders Postgraduate Scholarship, 1235
Global Excellence Scholarships, 165
Grants, 1173
Green Templeton College: GTC-SBS DPhil Scholarship, 1463
Harvard/Newcomen Postdoctoral Award, 906
International Excellence Scholarship (Management, Accounting and Finance), 1434

International Strathclyde Prestige Award for Excellence in Business Translation and Interpreting in United Kingdom, 1547
LLM in International Trade Law–Contracts and Dispute Resolution–Scholarships, 1213
Massey Business School-PhD Scholarships, 643
Master in Business Analytics Scholarships, 449
The Material Handling Education Foundation, 794
MSc Psychology with a Specialisation in Business Scholarship, 1156
National Assessment of Educational Progress (NAEP) Internships, 478
Peter E. Liberti and Judy D. Olian Scholarship, 1116
Presidential Scholarships for Students of Black Heritage, 615
RHBNC Trust Scholarship, 1042
Robinson Scholarship, 557
School of Business and Economics Scholarships, 756
Stewart Hamilton Scholarship, 661
Think Big About Innovation Scholarships, 1237
UNSW Business School International Pathways Award, 1425

African Nations

The Beacon Scholarship, 331
GREAT-Imperial College London Scholarship, 613
GREAT Scholarships-Egypt, 1286
GREAT Scholarships-Ghana, 1286
GREAT Scholarships-Kenya, 1287

Asian Countries

Chandigarh University Scholarships in India, 346
China Scholarship Council-The University of Manchester Joint Scholarship for PhD Study in Alliance Manchester Business School, 1368
GREAT-Imperial College London Scholarship, 613
GREAT Scholarships-China, 1286
GREAT Scholarships-India, 1287
GREAT Scholarships–Indonesia, 1287
GREAT Scholarships–Malaysia, 1288
GREAT Scholarships–Pakistan, 1288
GREAT Scholarships–Thailand, 1288

Australia

Anthony Costa Foundation Arts Management Scholarship, 419
Co-op Bookshop Scholarship, 165
Delta Electricity Scholarship, 1431
George Fairfax Arts Management Scholarship in Association with the Sue Nattrass Arts Management Fund, 423
Postgraduate Petroleum Engineering Scholarship, 472
Tamex Transport Scholarship, 1410
UNSW Business School Honours Scholarship, 1424

Canada

Bank of Montréal Pauline Varnier Fellowship, 377

European Countries

Dean's Award for Enterprise, 752
Dean's Award for Enterprise Scholarship, 758
Noord-Limburg Region Scholarship-FHML and SBE, 764

New Zealand

Anthony Costa Foundation Arts Management Scholarship, 419
George Fairfax Arts Management Scholarship in Association with the Sue Nattrass Arts Management Fund, 423

United States of America

American Association of University Women (AAUW) American Fellowships, 48
American Association of University Women (AAUW) Career Development Grants, 49
Center for Advancing Opportunity Doctorial Fellowship, 1182
SEED Awards, 306

ACCOUNTANCY

Any Country

Doctoral Fellowship Program, 427
Global Accounting and Finance Scholarship, 1236
HKBU Fully Funded International Postgraduate Scholarship, 19
Reserve Bank of New Zealand Scholarships, 992
The Robert W. and Charlotte Bitter Graduate Scholarship Endowment, 819
The Roger Perry Memorial Scholarship, 993
Women in Central Banking Scholarship, 993

Asian Countries

Research School of Accounting India Merit Scholarships, 174

New Zealand

Māori and Pacific Islands Scholarship, 992
Reserve Bank of New Zealand Scholarships for International Students, 993

South Africa

Nicholas Iain Paumgarten Scholarship for Postgraduate Studies in Accounting, 1009

United States of America

American Institute of Certified Public Accountants Fellowship for Minority Doctoral students, 81
Maryland Association of Certified Public Accountants Scholarship, 787

BUSINESS AND COMMERCE

Any Country

Doshisha University Doctoral-Program Young Researcher Scholarship, 439
Robinson Scholarship, 711

Australia

Gail Kelly Honours Award for Business, 1418

New Zealand

Gail Kelly Honours Award for Business, 1418

FINANCE, BANKING AND INVESTMENT

Any Country
Al-Maktoum College Hamdan Bin Rashid Award, 1283
Al-Maktoum College Living Support Bursary, 1283
Global Accounting and Finance Scholarship, 1236
Library Company of Philadelphia Postdoctoral Research Fellowship, 729
PhD scholarships in Finance, 384
Reserve Bank of New Zealand Scholarships, 992
The Roger Perry Memorial Scholarship, 993
Steve Weston and Trust Scholarships, 1289
Tax Institute of America Doctoral Dissertations in Government and Taxation, 871
Women in Central Banking Scholarship, 993
Asian Countries
W L 'Bill' Byrnes Global Scholarship, 617
Australia
Women in Finance and Economics Scholarship, 426
European Countries
Candriam Scholarship, 763
New Zealand
Māori and Pacific Islands Scholarship, 992
Reserve Bank of New Zealand Scholarships for International Students, 993

INTERNATIONAL BUSINESS

Any Country
Al-Maktoum College Hamdan Bin Rashid Award, 1283
Al-Maktoum College Living Support Bursary, 1283
European Countries
Candriam Scholarship, 763
United States of America
The Thomas R. Pickering Foreign Affairs Fellowship, 1177

LABOUR/INDUSTRIAL RELATIONS

Any Country
Institute for Labour Market Policy Evaluation Post Doctoral Scholarship, 631

MANAGEMENT SYSTEMS

Any Country
Council of Supply Chain Management Professionals Distinguished Service Award, 388
Council of Supply Chain Management Professionals Doctoral Dissertation Award, 388
Doshisha University Doctoral-Program Young Researcher Scholarship, 439
George A. Gecowets Graduate Scholarship Program, 387
HKBU Fully Funded International Postgraduate Scholarship, 19
Post-Doctoral Fellowship, 622
Supply Chain Innovation Award, 388
Asian Countries
Manju Mehrotra Scholarship, 1041
Postdoctoral Research Fellowship (PDRF), 622
United States of America
R. Gene Richter Scholarship Program, 635

MARKETING

Any Country
Doctoral Dissertation Proposal Competition, 785
Lisa Pan Marketing and Technology Scholarship, 1329
Mary Kay Doctoral Dissertation Award, 11
MSc International Fashion Marketing Scholarship, 571
African Nations
Chevening Partner Scholarship scheme, 228
Asian Countries
Chevening Partner Scholarship scheme, 228
European Union
Glasgow School for Business and Society Postgraduate EU scholarships for MSc International Fashion Marketing, 570

MBA

Any Country
Akhtarali H. Tobaccowala Fellowship, 517
Alumni Scholarship for the Master of Business Administration (MBA), 699
China: One Belt One Road Scholarship, 595
Dominican College of San Rafael MBA in Strategic Leadership, 437
The Durham MBA (Full-time) Scholarships, 451
The Durham MBA (Online) Scholarships, 451
Escola Superior d'Administració i Direcció d'Empreses (ESADE) MBA Scholarships, 492
The Essex MBA Early Bird Discount, 1310
European Excellence Scholarship (MBA), 894
Executive MBA Programme, 1281
Executive MBA Scholarship, 415
The Exeter MBA SDG Scholarships, 1312
Global MBA Alumni Scholarship, 771
Global MBA International Scholarship Fund, 416
Harold Taber MBA Scholarship, 211
Institut Européen d'Administration des Affaires Jewish Scholarship, 627
Jeanne and Charles Rider Graduate Fellowship, 1115
Leicester Castle Business School MBA Scholarship, 418
Master of Business Administration Global Leaders Scholarship, 424
Master of Business Administration Programme, 677, 1137, 1277, 1289, 1573, 1584
Monash Mt Eliza Business School Executive MBA Programme, 821

Nabil Boustany Scholarships, 1253
Olin School of Business Washington University MBA Programme, 1606
Ossian R. MacKenzie Teaching Award, 1115
Oxford Brookes University MBA Programme, 943
Oxford–Intesa Sanpaolo MBA Graduate Scholarships, 1489
Oxford-Pershing Square Graduate Scholarships, 1493
Petra Och Kail Erik Hedborgs Stiftelse Scholarship, 1154
The Robert W. and Charlotte Bitter Graduate Scholarship Endowment, 819
Royal Holloway, University of London MBA Programme, 1043
The Sheffield MBA Scholarship Scheme, 1529
Strathclyde Business School Full Time MBA Deans Excellence Awards, 1549
Strathclyde Business School Full Time MBA Scholarships, 1550
Surrey MBA Scholarship Competition, 1557
Syracuse University Executive MBA Programme, 1165
Syracuse University MBA, 1165
University of Alberta MBA Programme, 1223
University of Auckland Executive MBA Programme, 1233
University of Newcastle, Australia MBA Programme, 1438
Women in Leadership Scholarship: Surrey MBA, 1557
Women in Master of Business Administration (WiMBA) Scholarship, 1438
African Nations
Dapo Olagunju Scholarship, 733
Institut Européen d'Administration des Affaires Goldman Sachs Scholarship for African Nationals, 627
Asian Countries
China Scholarships, 620
Orange Tulip Scholarship (OTS) China, 1578
Rotterdam School of Management Master of Business Administration Asia & Australia Regional Scholarship, 1013
Singapore Education–Sampoerna Foundation MBA in Singapore, 836
Spring Management Development Scholarship (MDS), 836
Australia
Rotterdam School of Management Master of Business Administration Asia & Australia Regional Scholarship, 1013
Trimester 2-Rob Riley MBA Memorial Scholarship, 408
European Countries
Sainsbury Management Fellowships, 1016
European Union
Sainsbury Management Fellowships, 1016
Middle East
Rotterdam School of Management Master of Business Administration Asia & Australia Regional Scholarship, 1013
New Zealand
Rotterdam School of Management Master of Business Administration Asia & Australia Regional Scholarship, 1013
North American Countries
Consejo Nacional de Ciencia y Tecnologia (CONACYT) Scholarships, 1154
Oceania
Rotterdam School of Management Master of Business Administration Asia & Australia Regional Scholarship, 1013
South American Countries
The Swedish Foundation for International Cooperation in Research and Higher Education (STINT) Scholarship, 1154
United Kingdom
Browns Restaurant Scholarships, 1266
Sainsbury Management Fellowships, 1016
United States of America
The Thomas R. Pickering Foreign Affairs Fellowship, 1177

PUBLIC ADMINISTRATION

Any Country
Christine Mirzayan Science & Technology Policy Graduate Fellowship Program, 864
United States of America
WGRG Foundation Terri Grier Memorial Scholarship, 1183

REAL ESTATE

Any Country
Appraisal Institute Education Trust Minorities and Women Education Scholarship, 126
Property Institute of New Zealand Postgraduate Scholarship, 1230

EDUCATION AND TEACHER TRAINING

GENERAL

Any Country
AHRC North West Consortium Doctoral Training Partnership in the School of Environment, Education and Development, 1364
Department of Education: Talbot Scholarship, 1459
Faculty Early Career Development Program (CAREER), 868
Faculty PhD Scholarships, 319
Guy Butler Research Award, 1008
Honours Award Education, 1419
Marian D'Eve Memorial Scholarship, 322
Marie Clay Literacy Trust Literacy Learning Research Award, 1229

Mary Jane Oestmann Professional Women, 89
Oxford-TrygFonden Graduate Scholarship, 1497
Postdoctoral Scholar Program, 1625
President's Doctoral Scholar (PDS) Awards in the School of Environment, Education and Development, 1382
School for International Training (SIT) Master of Arts in Teaching Program, 1627
The Tim Collins Scholarship for the Study of Love in Religion, 984
University Distinguished Teaching Awards, 890
Woodrow Wilson MBA Fellowship in Education Leadership, 1624
African Nations
The Beacon Scholarship, 331
GREAT Scholarships-Egypt, 1286
GREAT Scholarships-Ghana, 1286
GREAT Scholarships-Kenya, 1287
Asian Countries
Chandigarh University Scholarships in India, 346
Daiwa Foundation Awards, 411
Fulbright-Nehru Doctoral Research Fellowships, 1195
Fulbright-Nehru Master's Fellowships, 1195
Fulbright-Nehru Postdoctoral Research Fellowships, 1195
GREAT Scholarships-China, 1286
GREAT Scholarships-India, 1287
GREAT Scholarships–Indonesia, 1287
GREAT Scholarships–Malaysia, 1288
GREAT Scholarships–Pakistan, 1288
GREAT Scholarships–Thailand, 1288
Asia-Pacific Countries
Fujitsu Scholarship Program for Asia-Pacific Region, 549
Australia
Council of Catholic School Parents (NSW) Indigenous Postgraduate Scholarship (IES), 165
The Duncan Family Scholarship in Early Childhood Education, 1411
Jack Keating Fund Scholarship, 1397
Canada
Jim Bourque Scholarship, 130
The Winter 2022 Gift Competition, 414
European Countries
Collaborative Project to Meet Societal and Industry-related Challenges, 990
Researcher Project for Scientific Renewal, 991
United Kingdom
Daiwa Foundation Awards, 411
SEED Enhancing Racial Equality Studentship, 1387
United States of America
American Studies (Lecturing Award), 550
Center for Advancing Opportunity Doctorial Fellowship, 1182
Fujitsu Scholarship Program for Asia-Pacific Region, 549
John Dana Archbold Fellowship Program, 911
Rudolf Steiner Foundation Seed Fund, 17

ADULT EDUCATION

Any Country
Albert and Alexis Dennis Donation, 788

CONTINUING EDUCATION

Any Country
Abraham Lincoln High School Alumni Association, 10
Azure Dillon 4-H Memorial Scholarship, 958
Carnegie PhD Scholarships, 333
David Baumgardt Memorial Fellowship, 720
Fritz Halbers Fellowship, 720
Research Project Grants, 727
European Countries
The Professional Development Award, 913
United Kingdom
Ray Y. Gildea Jr Award, 1038
United States of America
Ray Y. Gildea Jr Award, 1038

EDUCATIONAL SCIENCE

Any Country
Bossing-Edwards Research Scholarship Award, 846
The British & Foreign School Society, 232
CFUW 100th Anniversary Legacy Fellowship funded by the Charitable Trust, 287
Clifton Ware Group-Voice Pedagogy Award, 847
Distinguished Scholarship, 846
Educational Testing Service Postdoctoral Fellowships, 476
Educational Testing Service Summer Internship Program in Research for Graduate Students, 476
Educational Testing Service Sylvia Taylor Johnson Minority Fellowship in Educational Measurement, 477
Endeavour Research Fellowship for International Applicants, 483
Engineering for Development (E4D) Doctoral Scholarship Programme, 479
The Engineering for Development (E4D) Doctoral Scholarship Programme, 481
Envision Equity Grants, 852
Ethnic Minority Foundation Grants, 493
German Business Foundation, 189
Harvard Travellers Club Permanent Fund, 581
Institute for Student Achievement Summer Internship in Program Monitoring & Evaluation, 478
Institute of Education Postgraduate Pathway Scholarship, 642
Javits-Frasier Scholars Program, 847
Joan Frey Boytim Awards for Independent Teachers, 848
Konrad-Adenauer-Stiftung, 190
Learning & Leadership Grants, 852
The Lien Foundation Scholarship for Social Service Leaders, 837
Los Alamos Graduate Research Assistant Program, 749

Master of Indigenous Education, 1525
National Union of Teachers Page Scholarship, 853
North Central Association for Counselor Education and Supervision Research Grant Awards, 907
Student Achievement Grants, 852
2023 Summer Research and Measurement Sciences (RMS) Internship program, 475
University of Newcastle International PhD Scholarships in Geomicrobial Biosensors, Australia, 905
Wallace Scholarships for Tertiary Student Research, 481
Australia
Ministry of Foreign Affairs (France) International Teaching Fellowships, 482
Ministry of Foreign Affairs (France) Stage de la Réunion (One Month Scholarships), 482
Prince Charles Hospital Foundation's PhD Scholarship, 963
European Union
FINS Student Loans, 707
United Kingdom
FfWG Grants-Emergency Grant, 247
FfWG Grants-Foundation Grant, 248
Main Fund-UK Projects, 232
United States of America
AICPA Legacy Scholarships, 210
Ford Foundation Fellowship Programs, 838
Ford Foundation Predoctoral Diversity Fellowships, 196
Fulbright Awards, 570
James W. Tyra Memorial Scholarship, 908
John Dana Archbold Fellowship, 834

EDUCATIONAL TECHNOLOGY

Any Country
Council on Library and Information Resources Postdoctoral Fellowship, 390

INTERNATIONAL AND COMPARATIVE EDUCATION

United Kingdom
Nicholas Hans Comparative Education Scholarship, 636

TEACHING AND LEARNING

United Kingdom
The Birts Scholarship, 825
United States of America
Alliance for Clinical Research Excellence and Safety Teacher Scholarship Award, 64

NONVOCATIONAL SUBJECTS EDUCATION

HUMANITIES AND SOCIAL SCIENCE EDUCATION

Any Country
Fowler-Merle Smith Summer Scholarship for Teachers, 101
Tachau Teacher of the Year Award, 936

PHYSICAL EDUCATION

Any Country
College Scholarship (Sciences), 1146
Performance Analysis Scholarship, 176
Wilfrid Knapp Scholarship (Sciences), 1148

SCIENCE EDUCATION

United States of America
James Bryant Conant Award in High School Chemistry Teaching, 61
PRE-SCHOOL EDUCATION
Australia
Early Childhood Scholarships, 511
New Zealand
Early Childhood Scholarships, 511
SECONDARY EDUCATION
United Kingdom
Ray Y. Gildea Jr Award, 1038
United States of America
Ray Y. Gildea Jr Award, 1038

SPECIAL EDUCATION

Any Country
James Samuel Gutshall Scholarship (Viola Vestal Coulter Foundation), 212
Marian D Eve Memorial Scholarship, 1270

TEACHER TRAINERS EDUCATION

Any Country
Arabic Language Teacher Training scholarships programme, 242
School Teacher Fellowship, 257

VOCATIONAL SUBJECTS EDUCATION

Any Country
Tohmae Pa Scholarships, 516

ENGINEERING

GENERAL

Any Country
Acute Generalized Exanthematous Pustulosis Fellowship, 670
AfterCollege STEM Inclusion Scholarship, 18
AMS-AAAS Mass Media Fellowship, 85
Bert Enserink Scholarship EPA, 1187
BHW Women in STEM Scholarship, 1177
British Council Scholarships for Women in STEM, 1539

Canadian Centennial Scholarship Fund, 1324
CDT in Advanced Metallic Systems, 1366
CDT in Aerosol Science, 1366
CDT in Biodesign Engineering, 1367
CDT in Compound Semiconductor Manufacturing, 1367
CDT in Future Innovation in NDE, 1367
CDT in the Science and Technology of Fusion Energy, 1368
China Scholarship Council Scholarships, 968
Christine Mirzayan Science & Technology Policy Graduate Fellowship Program, 864
Churchill Scholarship, 1620
College of Engineering and Computer Science: College Postgraduate International Award, 173
College of Engineering and Computer Science: College Postgraduate International Honours Award, 173
CONACyT Tuition Top-up Award, 1370
The Council of Scientific and Industrial Research/TWAS Fellowship for Postdoctoral Research, 1180
Council of Scientific and Industrial Research/TWAS Fellowship for Postgraduate Research, 1178
Cross-Disciplinary Fellowships, 659
Dean's Doctoral Scholarship Award, 1371
Department of Energy Computational Science Graduate Fellowship Krell Institute, 1589
Development of Next-generation Microfluidic Technology Device for Detection of Circulating Cancer Cells, 1555
Dhaka PhD Scholarships, 969
Diane Lemaire Scholarship, 1391
Directorate for Education and Human Resources Core Research, 867
Doshisha University Doctoral-Program Young Researcher Scholarship, 439
Dr Abdul Kalam International Postgraduate Scholarships, 1565
Dual-award between The University of Manchester and IIT Kharagpur, 1372
Dual-award between The University of Manchester and The University of Melbourne, 1373
Duke/NCCU Collaborative Translational Research Awards, 442
East Gippsland Water Scholarship, 512
The Energy Efficiency and Renewable Energy (EERE) Science and Technology Policy (STP) Fellowships, 1590
Engineering and Physical Sciences Research Council (EPSRC) Doctoral Training Partnership, 1559
EPSRC Doctoral Training Partnership (DTP), 1373
Expanding Capacity in Quantum Information Science and Engineering (ExpandQISE), 909
Faculty of Engineering International Scholarships Postgraduate, 1541
Fitzwilliam College Leathersellers, 1243
Fulbright Distinguished Chair in Science, Technology, and Innovation (CSIRO), 551
Funds for Women Graduates, 1377
GeneTex Scholarship Program, 562
Government of Ireland Postgraduate Scholarship Programme, 671
Graphene NOWNANO CDT, 1377
The Gulf Research Program's Early-Career Research Fellowship, 1175
HAPP MSc Scholarship in the History of Science, 1139
Industrial CASE Studentships, 1101
Institution of Engineering and Technology Postgraduate Scholarship for an Outstanding Researcher, 647
Integrated Catalysis (iCAT) CDT, 1378
International Centre for Theoretical Sciences S. N. Bhatt Memorial Excellence Research Fellowship, 656
International Engineering MSc Studentship, 330
International Master of Engineering (Professional) Scholarship, 676
Joint-award between The University of Manchester and IISC Bangalore, 1379
Landis Young Member Engineering Achievement, 89
Mary Jane Oestmann Professional Women, 89
Master of Professional Engineering International Scholarship, 824
Mott MacDonald Charitable Trust Scholarships, 828
MS Engineering and Science Fellowship Program, 1176
National Research Foundation Fellowships for Postdoctoral Research, 865
National Science Foundation Research Traineeship (NRT) Program, 869
National University of Singapore Design Technology Institute Scholarship, 876
Natural Sciences and Engineering Research Council of Canada Industrial Post-Graduate Scholarships (IPS), 1112
Nuclear Energy-GREEN CDT, 1381
Operations and Power Division Scholarship Award, 89
The Optical Society, Chang Pivoting Fellowship, 841
Oxford-Ashton Graduate Scholarship in Engineering, 1481
Packard Fellowships for Science and Engineering, 413
Performance Analysis Scholarship, 176
PhD Engineering and Science Fellowship, 1176
PhD Opportunity-Engineering, 644
PhD Scholarship: Digital Modelling of Apple for Quality Prediction, 645
PhD Science Fellowship, 1176
Postdoctoral Scholar Program, 1625
Postgraduate Research Award (PGRA), 171
Postgraduate Research Teaching Associate (PGRTA) Scholarships, 1381
PPARC Standard Research Studentship, 1103
Presidential Scholarships for Students of Black Heritage, 615
Program Grants, 660
Ramboll Masters Scholarship for International Students, 1448

Research Internships in Science and Engineering (RISE), 436
Resource Management Law Association of New Zealand Masters Scholarship, 157
RHT Bates Postgraduate Scholarship, 1052
Robert Noyce Teacher Scholarship Program, 869
Royal Academy Engineering Professional Development, 1015
Royal Academy Sir Henry Royce Bursary, 1016
Ruth L. Kirschstein National Research Service Award (NRSA) Individual Postdoctoral Fellowship, 861
Science and Engineering Research Board Distinguished Fellowship, 1100
S.N Bose Scholar Program, 1099
Society of Women Engineers Past Presidents Scholarships, 1134
TWAS-COMSTECH Science in Exile PhD Fellowship Programme for Displaced and Refugee Scientists, 1180
United Arab Emirates: Khalifa University Postgraduate Scholarships, 600
University of Sydney: Data Science Scholarships, 124
Western Digital Scholarship Program, 1112
Woodrow Wilson Teaching Fellowship, 1624
Young Investigator Grant, 660

African Nations

Austrian Academy of Sciences, 4-months Trimester at Egerton University, Kenya, 178
The Beacon Scholarship, 331
Brewer Street Scholarship, 732
Deakin STEM Scholarship, 422
GREAT-Imperial College London Scholarship, 613
OWSD PhD Fellowships for Women Scientists, 1179
Seed Grant for New African Principal Investigators (SG-NAPI), 1179
Xerox Technical Minority Scholarship, 1633

Asian Countries

British Council Scholarship for Women in STEM Terms and Conditions, 266
British Council Scholarships for Women in STEM, 446, 1365
Chandigarh University Scholarships in India, 346
Daiwa Foundation Awards, 411
Deakin STEM Scholarship, 422
GREAT-Imperial College London Scholarship, 613
Manju Mehrotra Scholarship, 1041
National Post Doctoral Fellowship (N-PDF), 1098
OWSD PhD Fellowships for Women Scientists, 1179
Ramanujan Fellowship, 1099
Science and Engineering Research Board Overseas Postdoctoral Fellowship (OPDF), 1100
Science and Engineering Research Board Women Excellence Award, 1100
The University of Manchester-China Scholarship Council Joint Scholarship, 1389
Xerox Technical Minority Scholarship, 1633

Asia-Pacific Countries

OWSD PhD Fellowships for Women Scientists, 1179
Xerox Technical Minority Scholarship, 1633

Australia

AGL Jungurra Wunnik Scholarship, 508
Engineering (Honours) Masters Accelerated Pathway, 823
Faculty of Science and Engineering Research Awards (FSERA), 523
Flinders University and Defence Science: Defence Science Partnership Grant, 524
HeART of the Basin Scholarship, 340
Indigenous Pathways Advance Queensland VET Scholarship, 341
Meredith Doig Scholarship, 514
Victoria Fellowships, 430

Canada

American Society for Photogrammetry and Remote Sensing Robert N. Colwell Memorial Fellowship, 113
Canada's Distinguished Dissertation Awards, 1075
Engineers Canada-Manulife Scholarship, 486
Engineers Canada's National Scholarship Program, 486
Engineers Canada-TD Insurance Meloche Monnex, 487
NSERC Postgraduate Scholarships-Doctoral Program, 882

Caribbean Countries

OWSD PhD Fellowships for Women Scientists, 1179

European Countries

John and Pat Hume Research Scholarships, 874
Leathersellers' Company Scholarship (Sciences), 1147

European Union

John and Pat Hume Research Scholarships, 874

Latin America

OWSD PhD Fellowships for Women Scientists, 1179

New Zealand

AGL Jungurra Wunnik Scholarship, 508
The Dick and Mary Earle Scholarship in Technology, 1279
Engineering (Honours) Masters Accelerated Pathway, 823
Faculty of Science and Engineering Research Awards (FSERA), 523
Flinders University and Defence Science: Defence Science Partnership Grant, 524
Meredith Doig Scholarship, 514

North American Countries

British Council Scholarships for Women in STEM, 608

Oceania

Toloa Scholarships for Pacific STEM Scholars, 158

Pacific Islands

University of Canterbury Pasifika Doctoral Scholarship, 1103

South American Countries

British Council Scholarships for Women in STEM, 608

United Kingdom

Daiwa Foundation Awards, 411
Daphne Jackson Fellowships, 1101
Leathersellers' Company Scholarship (Sciences), 1147

Multidisciplinary Project Award, 315
Oriel DPhil Scholarship in Engineering Science, 939
Postgraduate Masters Scholarships, 649
Royal Academy of Engineering MSc Motorsport Scholarship Programme, 1337
School of Engineering Diversity PhD Scholarship, 1383
School of Engineering Graduate PhD Scholarship, 1384
Spencer Wilks Postgraduate Masters Scholarships, 649
United States of America
American Society for Engineering Education Helen T Carr Fellowship Program, 110
American Society for Photogrammetry and Remote Sensing Robert N. Colwell Memorial Fellowship, 113
Department of Defense-National Defense and Science Engineering Fellowships, 195
Foundation for Science and Disability Student Grant Fund, 546
Graduate Student Grant, 546
Marshall Sherfield Fellowships, 787
MEDxColloquia, 443
MEDx Engineering, Environment, and Health 2022 Request for Proposals, 443
National Defense Science and Engineering Graduate Fellowship Program, 111
National Institute of Justice's Graduate Research Fellowship Program, 199
Office of Naval Research Summer Faculty Research Program, 112
Xerox Technical Minority Scholarship, 1633

AERONAUTICAL AND AEROSPACE ENGINEERING

Any Country
Aeronautical and Automotive Engineering Scholarships, 749
Astridge Postgraduate Research Scholarship, 648
A. Verville Fellowship, 1118
The Aviation Space Writers Foundation Award, 1117
Charles A Lindbergh Chair in Aerospace History, 844, 1117
Charles A. Lindbergh Chair in Aerospace History, 1118
France: ISAE-SUPAERO Scholarship Programmes, 596
Guggenheim Fellowship, 844
Mercer Memorial Scholarship in Aeronautics, 1229
National Air and Space Museum, 1119
National Air and Space Museum Aviation/Space Writers Award, 845
Asian Countries
Space Environment Research Centre Scholarships, 1137
Australia
Destination Australia Scholarship, 1046
Space Environment Research Centre Scholarships, 1137
United States of America
American Society for Engineering Education Air Force Summer Faculty Fellowship Program, 110
Space Environment Research Centre Scholarships, 1137
United States Air Force Academy/National Research Council Summer Faculty Research Program (SFFP), 21

AUTOMOTIVE ENGINEERING

Any Country
Spencer Wilks Scholarship/Fellowship, 649

BIOENGINEERING AND BIOMEDICAL ENGINEERING

Any Country
Career Development Awards, 213
Diversity Lecture Award, 214
Lab on Bag: Bioengineering a Device for Blood Diagnostics, 772
Multi Scale Biomechanical Investigations of the Intervertebral Disc, 528
Robert A. Pritzker Distinguished Lecture Award, 214
Shu Chien Achievement Award, 214
African Nations
GREAT Scholarships-Egypt, 1286
GREAT Scholarships-Ghana, 1286
GREAT Scholarships-Kenya, 1287
Asian Countries
Fulbright-Nehru Doctoral Research Fellowships, 1195
Fulbright-Nehru Postdoctoral Research Fellowships, 1195
GREAT Scholarships-China, 1286
GREAT Scholarships-India, 1287
GREAT Scholarships–Indonesia, 1287
GREAT Scholarships–Malaysia, 1288
GREAT Scholarships–Pakistan, 1288
GREAT Scholarships–Thailand, 1288
European Countries
Oxford-Bellhouse Graduate Scholarship, 1482
European Union
Cardiff Institute of Tissue Engineering and Repair (CITER)–EPSRC Studentship, 324
United Kingdom
Cardiff Institute of Tissue Engineering and Repair (CITER)–EPSRC Studentship, 324
United States of America
Postdoctoral Research Fellowship, 588

CHEMICAL ENGINEERING

Any Country
American Chemical Society Award for Encouraging Disadvantaged Students into Careers in the Chemical Sciences, 55
American Chemical Society Award for Encouraging Women into Careers in the Chemical Sciences, 55
Chemical Engineering Scholarships, 750
Doctoral New Investigator (DNI) Grants, 437

Dow Agrosciences Bursary in Chemical Engineering, 1268
Master's Degree Awards in Biochemical Engineering, 1206
Research Degree Scholarship in Chemical Engineering, 1208
Australia
Corrosion Research Postgraduate Scholarships, 822
Delta Electricity Scholarship, 1431
Doctor of Philosophy Scholarship-Corrosion in Alumina Processing, 823
Royston Honours Award in Chemical Engineering, 1423
New Zealand
Corrosion Research Postgraduate Scholarships, 822
Doctor of Philosophy Scholarship-Corrosion in Alumina Processing, 823
Royston Honours Award in Chemical Engineering, 1423
United Kingdom
ExxonMobil Excellence in Teaching Awards, 1015
United States of America
Graduate Fellowships for Science, Technology, Engineering, and Mathematics Diversity, 573

CIVIL ENGINEERING

Any Country
Architecture, Building and Civil Engineering Scholarships, 750
Associated General Contractors of America The Saul Horowitz, Jr. Memorial Graduate Award, 144
Building Research Association of New Zealand (BRANZ) Scholarship, 639
HDR Scholarship-Geotechnical Engineering PhD Scholarship, 405
HDR Scholarship in Structural Vibration Control, 405
Park and Paulay Scholarship, 1270
Scottish Power Masters Scholarships, 572
African Nations
GREAT Scholarships-Egypt, 1286
GREAT Scholarships-Ghana, 1286
GREAT Scholarships-Kenya, 1287
Asian Countries
GREAT Scholarships-China, 1286
GREAT Scholarships-India, 1287
GREAT Scholarships–Indonesia, 1287
GREAT Scholarships–Malaysia, 1288
GREAT Scholarships–Pakistan, 1288
GREAT Scholarships–Thailand, 1288
Australia
Australian Building Codes Board Research Scholarship, 1216
Craig John Hastings Smith Surveying Engineering Honours Year Award, 1416
Oliver Correy Award, 1422
PhD Scholarship in Material Science and/or Civil Engineering, 530
Wellington Shire Council Scholarship, 517
New Zealand
Craig John Hastings Smith Surveying Engineering Honours Year Award, 1416
Oliver Correy Award, 1422
PhD Scholarship in Material Science and/or Civil Engineering, 530
Wellington Shire Council Scholarship, 517

COMPUTER ENGINEERING

Any Country
Royal Melbourne Institute of Technology PhD Scholarship in the School of Electrical and Computer Engineering, 1047
Australia
Boeing Indigenous Engineering Scholarship, 1429
Women in Computer Science Award (WICS), 1426
New Zealand
Women in Computer Science Award (WICS), 1426
United States of America
Graduate Fellowships for Science, Technology, Engineering, and Mathematics Diversity, 573
CONTROL ENGINEERING (ROBOTICS)
Australia
Honours/Masters Scholarship for AI, User Interface or Robotics, 525
United States of America
National Robotics Initiative 2.0: Ubiquitous Collaborative Robots (NRI-2.0), 910

ELECTRICAL AND ELECTRONIC ENGINEERING

Any Country
Hudswell International Research Scholarship, 646
Institute of Electrical and Electronics Engineers Fellowship in the History of Electrical and Computing Technology, 637
Leslie H. Paddle Scholarship, 648
Leverhulme (LINCS) PhD Scholarship, 972
Mechanical, Electrical and Manufacturing Engineering Scholarships, 756
PhD in Mechatronics, 1163
RHBNC Trust Scholarship, 1042
Royal Melbourne Institute of Technology PhD Scholarship in the School of Electrical and Computer Engineering, 1047
Scottish Power Masters Scholarships, 572
African Nations
GREAT Scholarships-Egypt, 1286
GREAT Scholarships-Ghana, 1286
GREAT Scholarships-Kenya, 1287
Asian Countries
GREAT Scholarships-China, 1286
GREAT Scholarships-India, 1287

GREAT Scholarships–Indonesia, 1287
GREAT Scholarships–Malaysia, 1288
GREAT Scholarships–Pakistan, 1288
GREAT Scholarships–Thailand, 1288
Australia
Boeing Indigenous Engineering Scholarship, 1429
Delta Electricity Scholarship, 1431
Idemitsu Engineering Scholarship, 1433
Norman, Disney & Young Indigenous Scholarship, 1422
United States of America
Charles LeGeyt Fortescue Fellowship, 637
Graduate Fellowships for Science, Technology, Engineering, and Mathematics Diversity, 573

ENERGY ENGINEERING

Any Country
Demonstration of Energy & Efficiency Developments (DEED)-Technical Design Project, 96
Energy Futures Lab Overseas Scholarship for Development, 611
Master of Energy Systems Management (MESM) Scholarships, 449
Project Specific-Energy and Natural Resources Innovation and Technology Research Initiative (International), 777
Scholarship for Sustainable Energy Development, 1517
ScottishPower Masters Scholarships, 572
Scottish Power Scholarships, 1358
Asian Countries
Fulbright-Nehru Doctoral Research Fellowships, 1195
Fulbright-Nehru Postdoctoral Research Fellowships, 1195
Australia
Idemitsu Engineering Scholarship, 1433
Norman, Disney & Young Indigenous Scholarship, 1422
European Countries
Collaborative Project to Meet Societal and Industry-related Challenges, 990
Knowledge-building Project for Industry, 990
North European Countries
Postdoctoral Scholarship in Solar Fuels at KTH, 698
South Africa
Air-Conditioning, Heating, and Refrigeration Institute MSc Scholarship, 22
United Kingdom
Aziz Foundation/Imperial College Sustainable Energy Futures Scholarship, 607
Brown Family Bursary, 1201
United States of America
Art Rosenfeld Award for Energy Efficiency, 194
ENGINEERING DRAWING/DESIGN
European Countries
Design Alumni Bursary, 752

ENVIRONMENTAL AND SANITARY ENGINEERING

Any Country
Royal Academy Sir Angus Paton Bursary, 1015
Stellenbosch Fellowship in Polymer Science, 1153
Australia
Delta Electricity Scholarship, 1431
Honourable Jack Beale Scholarship in Engineering, 1419
Norman, Disney & Young Indigenous Scholarship, 1422
New Zealand
Honourable Jack Beale Scholarship in Engineering, 1419
United Kingdom
Brown Family Bursary, 1201
United States of America
Graduate Fellowships for Science, Technology, Engineering, and Mathematics Diversity, 573

INDUSTRIAL ENGINEERING

Any Country
Industrial CASE-Plus Studentship, 1102
The Material Handling Education Foundation, 794
African Nations
GREAT Scholarships-Egypt, 1286
GREAT Scholarships-Ghana, 1286
GREAT Scholarships-Kenya, 1287
Asian Countries
GREAT Scholarships-China, 1286
GREAT Scholarships-India, 1287
GREAT Scholarships–Indonesia, 1287
GREAT Scholarships–Malaysia, 1288
GREAT Scholarships–Pakistan, 1288
GREAT Scholarships–Thailand, 1288
Australia
CSIRO Women in Energy Industry Placement Scholarship, 1431
Sugar Industry Postgraduate Research Scholarships (SPRS), 1157
United Kingdom
PPARC Communications/Media Programme, 1102
MARINE ENGINEERING AND NAVAL ARCHITECTURE
Canada
John W. Davies Scholarship, 1133
United States of America
American Society of Naval Engineers (ASNE) Scholarship, 1091
John W. Davies Scholarship, 1133

MATERIALS ENGINEERING

Any Country
American Nuclear Society Mishima Award, 87
American Nuclear Society Utility Achievement Award, 87

Engen Conservation, 1118
Henry DeWolf Smyth Nuclear Statesman Award, 88
Materials Scholarships, 755
Perovskite and Quantum Dot Opto-electronic Devices, 777
Asian Countries
Fulbright-Nehru Doctoral Research Fellowships, 1195
Fulbright-Nehru Postdoctoral Research Fellowships, 1195
Australia
Corrosion Research Postgraduate Scholarships, 822
Doctor of Philosophy Scholarship-Corrosion in Alumina Processing, 823
PhD Scholarship in Material Science and/or Civil Engineering, 530
European Countries
Leathersellers' Company Scholarship (Sciences), 1147
New Zealand
Corrosion Research Postgraduate Scholarships, 822
Doctor of Philosophy Scholarship-Corrosion in Alumina Processing, 823
PhD Scholarship in Material Science and/or Civil Engineering, 530
United Kingdom
Brown Family Bursary, 1201
Leathersellers' Company Scholarship (Sciences), 1147
Smart Flooring Solutions for Fall Protection, 1556
United States of America
Graduate Fellowships for Science, Technology, Engineering, and Mathematics Diversity, 573

MECHANICAL ENGINEERING

Any Country
Mechanical, Electrical and Manufacturing Engineering Scholarships, 756
PhD in Mechatronics, 1163
Scottish Power Masters Scholarships, 572
African Nations
GREAT Scholarships-Egypt, 1286
GREAT Scholarships-Ghana, 1286
GREAT Scholarships-Kenya, 1287
Asian Countries
GREAT Scholarships-China, 1286
GREAT Scholarships-India, 1287
GREAT Scholarships–Indonesia, 1287
GREAT Scholarships–Malaysia, 1288
GREAT Scholarships–Pakistan, 1288
GREAT Scholarships–Thailand, 1288
Australia
Australian Research Council Australian Postgraduate Award Industry–Alternative Engine Technologies, 974
Boeing Indigenous Engineering Scholarship, 1429
Corrosion Research Postgraduate Scholarships, 822
Doctor of Philosophy Scholarship-Corrosion in Alumina Processing, 823
Idemitsu Engineering Scholarship, 1433
Norman, Disney & Young Indigenous Scholarship, 1422
New Zealand
Australian Research Council Australian Postgraduate Award Industry–Alternative Engine Technologies, 974
Corrosion Research Postgraduate Scholarships, 822
Doctor of Philosophy Scholarship-Corrosion in Alumina Processing, 823
United Kingdom
ExxonMobil Excellence in Teaching Awards, 1015
James Clayton Lectures, 648
United States of America
Elisabeth M and Winchell M Parsons Scholarship, 119
Graduate Fellowships for Science, Technology, Engineering, and Mathematics Diversity, 573
Marjorie Roy Rothermel Scholarship, 119

MINING ENGINEERING

Any Country
Hossein Farmy Scholarship, 1526
Minerals Industry Flexible First Year Scholarship (Current Students), 1422
Steve Weston and Trust Scholarships, 1289
Australia
BHP Billiton Mitsubishi Alliance (BMA) Award in Mining Engineering, 1415
Glencore Mining Engineering Scholarship, 1418
New Zealand
Glencore Mining Engineering Scholarship, 1418

NUCLEAR ENGINEERING

Any Country
American Nuclear Society Mishima Award, 87
American Nuclear Society Utility Achievement Award, 87
Australian Institute of Nuclear Science and Engineering Awards, 170
Early Career Researcher Grant (ECRG), 171
Henry DeWolf Smyth Nuclear Statesman Award, 88
Honours Scholarship, 171
John R. Lamarsh Scholarship, 88
Landis Public Communication and Education Award, 88
Residential Student Scholarship (RSS), 172
SAAFE Program, 482
Samuel Glasstone Award, 90
Australia
Tyree Nuclear Masters by Coursework Tuition Scholarship, 1414
New Zealand
Tyree Nuclear Masters by Coursework Tuition Scholarship, 1414
United States of America
Verne R Dapp Memorial Scholarship, 90

PETROLEUM AND GAS ENGINEERING

Any Country
Establishing the Source of Gas in Australia's Offshore Petroleum Basins Scholarship, 404
Postgraduate Petroleum Engineering Scholarship, 472
Steve Weston and Trust Scholarships, 1289
African Nations
GREAT Scholarships-Egypt, 1286
GREAT Scholarships-Ghana, 1286
GREAT Scholarships-Kenya, 1287
Shell Petroleum Development Company Niger Delta Postgraduate Scholarship, 1209
Asian Countries
GREAT Scholarships-China, 1286
GREAT Scholarships-India, 1287
GREAT Scholarships–Indonesia, 1287
GREAT Scholarships–Malaysia, 1288
GREAT Scholarships–Pakistan, 1288
GREAT Scholarships–Thailand, 1288
Australia
Common Data Access MSc Petroleum Data Management Scholarships, 1216
European Countries
Collaborative Project to Meet Societal and Industry-related Challenges, 990
Knowledge-building Project for Industry, 990
Researcher Project for Scientific Renewal, 991
United Kingdom
ExxonMobil Excellence in Teaching Awards, 1015

PRODUCTION ENGINEERING

Australia
Norman, Disney & Young Indigenous Scholarship, 1422

SURVEYING AND MAPPING SCIENCE

Australia
Association of Consulting Surveyors Aboriginal and Torres Strait Islander Scholarship, 1428
Craig John Hastings Smith Surveying Engineering Honours Year Award, 1416
New Zealand
Craig John Hastings Smith Surveying Engineering Honours Year Award, 1416

FINE AND APPLIED ARTS

GENERAL

Any Country
A-AA Austrian Studies Scholarship Award, 180
Artists Fellowships at WSW, 1623
The Aviation Space Writers Foundation Award, 1117
Aziz Foundation Masters Scholarships, 1310
Bickerton-Widdowson Trust Memorial Scholarship, 1267
Canadian Centennial Scholarship Fund, 1324
The Dean of Humanities, Arts & Social Sciences Excellence Scholarship, 986
Durham University Arts Management Group, 447
Ethel Rose Overton Scholarship, 1268
Faculty PhD Scholarships, 319
Good Ideas-Artist Led Projects, 139
Guy Butler Research Award, 1008
International Opportunities Funding, 139
International PhD Awards, 971
Lancaster Master's Scholarship, 709
Lindt Dissertation Fellowship, 370
Master of Arts in Art Museum and Gallery Studies Scholarship, 895
Master of Cultural & Creative Practice Scholarships (Art & Design), 157
Radcliffe Institute Fellowship, 977
Royal Over-Seas League Travel Scholarship, 1048
The Royal Scottish Academy John Kinross Scholarships to Florence, 1049
St Edmund Hall: Peel Award, 1507
The Tim Collins Scholarship for the Study of Love in Religion, 984
Viktoria Marinov Award in Art, 1425
Visiting Fellowships, 259
Vital Knowledge-Artists' Mentoring Scheme, 139
Women's Studio Workshop Internships, 1623
African Nations
The Beacon Scholarship, 331
Indonesian Arts and Culture Scholarship, 816
Asian Countries
Daiwa Foundation Awards, 411
Indonesian Arts and Culture Scholarship, 816
Kalakriti Fellowship in Indian Classical Dance, 1087
Serendib Community Cultural Association Sri Lanka Bursary, 425
Sher-Gil Sundaram Arts Foundation: Installation Art Grant, 1108
Asia-Pacific Countries
Indonesian Arts and Culture Scholarship, 816
Australia
Aboriginal and Torres Strait Islander Arts Fellowship, 159
Aboriginal and Torres Strait Islander Arts Skills and Arts Development, 159
Aboriginal and Torres Strait Islander New Work Grant, 159
AGL Jungurra Wunnik Scholarship, 508
Asialink Residency Program, 140
Indigenous Pathways Advance Queensland VET Scholarship, 341
The Red Ochre Award, 161
Visions of Australia: Regional Exhibition Touring Fund, 161
Western Sydney Artists Fellowship, 887

William Thomas Williams Postgraduate Scholarship, 679
Canada
The Coburn Award, 274
Jean A. Chalmers Fund for the Crafts, 272
Peter Dwyer Scholarships, 274
Saidye Bronfman Award, 284
European Countries
Arts Council of Ireland Artist-in-the-Community Scheme, 136
Creative Arts Alumni Bursary, 752
Croatian Arts and Cultural Exchange Croatia, 140
European Union
Indonesian Arts and Culture Scholarship, 816
Master of Arts in Art Museum and Gallery Studies Scholarship, 895
Middle East
AICF Sharett Scholarship Program, 33
New Zealand
AGL Jungurra Wunnik Scholarship, 508
Grant Lingard Scholarship, 1275
Masters/Honours/PGDIP Scholarships, 1229
Oceania
Indonesian Arts and Culture Scholarship, 816
United Kingdom
Artists at Work, 136
Arts Council of Wales Artform Development Scheme, 136
Arts Council of Wales Pilot Training Grants Scheme, 138
Awards for Current Students-The Betty and Peter McLean Prize, 181
Cultural Enterprise Service Grant, 139
Daiwa Foundation Awards, 411
The Gane Trust Travel Award, 185
Master of Arts in Art Museum and Gallery Studies Scholarship, 895
United States of America
Arts Innovator Award, 134
Congressional Black Caucus Foundation Spouses Visual Arts Scholarship, 379
Fellowship Awards, 134
Grants for Artist Projects (GAP), 134
Harpo Foundation Grants for Visual Artists, 579
Ohio Arts Council Individual Excellence Awards, 919
Rudolf Steiner Foundation Seed Fund, 17

ART CRITICISM

Any Country
Graduate Scholarship, 144
Kurt Weill Prize, 698

ART HISTORY

Any Country
A&A Masters Higher Degree Research Award, 172
Forum Transregional Studies Postdoctoral Fellowships for International Students, 540
Graduate Scholarship, 144
Interpretive Fellowships at Art Museums, 1085
Joseph Kremen Memorial Fellowship, 1640
Kurt Weill Prize, 698
Pembroke College: The Lander Studentship in the History of Art, 1256
United States of America
Lilly Fellows Program in the Humanities and the Arts, 1006

AESTHETICS

Any Country
Ertegun Graduate Scholarship Programme in the Humanities, 1460

ART MANAGEMENT

Any Country
Graduate Scholarship, 144
Australia
Anthony Costa Foundation Arts Management Scholarship, 419
George Fairfax Arts Management Scholarship in Association with the Sue Nattrass Arts Management Fund, 423
New Zealand
Anthony Costa Foundation Arts Management Scholarship, 419
George Fairfax Arts Management Scholarship in Association with the Sue Nattrass Arts Management Fund, 423

CINEMA AND TELEVISION

Any Country
A&A Masters Higher Degree Research Award, 172
Erik Barnouw Award, 929
Ertegun Graduate Scholarship Programme in the Humanities, 1460
Garrick Scholarship, 463
Graduate Scholarship, 144
"Made in NY" Women's Film, TV and Theatre Fund, 888
OZCO Visual Arts Fellowship, 160
Robert E. Thunen Memorial Scholarships, 200
Robert McKee International Screenwriting Scholarships, 985
Sasakawa Postgraduate Studentship in Japanese Studies, 1501
Visual Arts New Work, 161
Visual Arts Skills and Arts Development, 162
Asian Countries
Fulbright-Nehru Doctoral Research Fellowships, 1195
Fulbright-Nehru Postdoctoral Research Fellowships, 1195
Australia
The Dreaming Award, 160

South American Countries
Invertimos en el Talento de los Colombianos (ICETEX) Artistas Jovenes Scholarships, 183
United Kingdom
Arts Council of Wales Awards for Career Development of Individual Visual Artists and Craftspeople, 137
Arts Council of Wales Awards for Individual Visual Artists and Craftspeople, 137
Sasakawa Postgraduate Studentship in Japanese Studies, 1501
Wales One World Film Festival Grant, 139
United States of America
Commissioning Music/United States of America, 807
Harriet Hale Woolley Scholarship, 536
Irving and Yvonne Twining Humber Award for Lifetime Artistic Achievement, 135
SOLA Awards, 135
Twining Humber Award, 135

DANCE

Any Country
Graduate Scholarship, 144
Kurt Weill Prize, 698
The Rebecca Skelton Scholarship, 983
RHBNC Trust Scholarship, 1042
Sybil Shearer Fellowship: Dancemakers, 983
Asian Countries
Fulbright-Nehru Doctoral Research Fellowships, 1195
Fulbright-Nehru Postdoctoral Research Fellowships, 1195
Madhobi Chatterji Memorial Fellowship, 1088
Australia
The Dreaming Award, 160
Playing Australia: Regional Performing Arts Touring Fund, 160
Canada
Jacqueline Lemieux Prize, 271
European Countries
American Council of Learned Societies Humanities Program in Belarus, Russia and Ukraine, 62
Russia
American Council of Learned Societies Humanities Program in Belarus, Russia and Ukraine, 62
United Kingdom
Arts Council of Wales Awards for Career Development of Individual Visual Artists and Craftspeople, 137
Arts Council of Wales Awards for Individual Visual Artists and Craftspeople, 137
Arts Council of Wales Community Touring Night Out, 137
Arts Council of Wales Performing Arts Projects, 138
Community Dance Wales Grants, 138
Welsh Independent Dance Grant, 139
United States of America
Commissioning Music/United States of America, 807
Irving and Yvonne Twining Humber Award for Lifetime Artistic Achievement, 135
SOLA Awards, 135
Twining Humber Award, 135

DESIGN

Any Country
A&A Masters Higher Degree Research Award, 172
Donald & Margot Watt Bursary Fund (FASS Only), 706
OZCO Visual Arts Fellowship, 160
Visual Arts New Work, 161
Visual Arts Skills and Arts Development, 162
African Nations
GREAT Scholarships-Egypt, 1286
GREAT Scholarships-Ghana, 1286
GREAT Scholarships-Kenya, 1287
Asian Countries
Fulbright-Nehru Doctoral Research Fellowships, 1195
Fulbright-Nehru Postdoctoral Research Fellowships, 1195
GREAT Scholarships-China, 1286
GREAT Scholarships-India, 1287
GREAT Scholarships–Indonesia, 1287
GREAT Scholarships–Malaysia, 1288
GREAT Scholarships–Pakistan, 1288
GREAT Scholarships–Thailand, 1288
Australia
The Dreaming Award, 160
European Countries
Design Alumni Bursary, 752
South American Countries
Invertimos en el Talento de los Colombianos (ICETEX) Artistas Jovenes Scholarships, 183
United States of America
Harriet Hale Woolley Scholarship, 536

FASHION DESIGN

Any Country
Hessnatur Foundation Scholarship, 492
Asian Countries
GREAT Scholarships India, 243
United Kingdom
Awards for Current Students-The Doris Southcott Bursary, 181
GRAPHIC DESIGN
European Countries
Arts Council of Ireland Frameworks Animation Scheme, 136

INTERIOR DESIGN

Any Country
Interior Design-Masters of Arts by Research, 1047

TEXTILE DESIGN

United Kingdom
Awards for Current Students-The Doris Southcott Bursary, 181

DRAWING AND PAINTING

Any Country
A&A Masters Higher Degree Research Award, 172
Abbey Scholarship in Painting, 260
The Barns-Graham Travel Award, 1048
David and Julie Tobey Fellowship, 1599
Graduate Scholarship, 144
The Margaret Senior Natural History Illustration Scholarship, 1437
OZCO Visual Arts Fellowship, 160
The RSA David Michie Travel Award, 1049
Visual Arts New Work, 161
Visual Arts Skills and Arts Development, 162
Asian Countries
China Scholarships, 620
Fulbright-Nehru Doctoral Research Fellowships, 1195
Fulbright-Nehru Postdoctoral Research Fellowships, 1195
Australia
The Dreaming Award, 160
European Countries
American Council of Learned Societies Humanities Program in Belarus, Russia and Ukraine, 62
Russia
American Council of Learned Societies Humanities Program in Belarus, Russia and Ukraine, 62
United Kingdom
Abbey Harris Mural Fund, 7
Arts Council of Wales Awards for Career Development of Individual Visual Artists and Craftspeople, 137
Arts Council of Wales Awards for Individual Visual Artists and Craftspeople, 137
The Royal Scottish Academy William Littlejohn Award for Excellence and Innovation in Water-Based Media, 1049
United States of America
Harriet Hale Woolley Scholarship, 536
Irving and Yvonne Twining Humber Award for Lifetime Artistic Achievement, 135
Recharge Foundation Fellowship for New Surrealist Art, 889
SOLA Awards, 135
Twining Humber Award, 135

HANDICRAFTS

Any Country
A&A Masters Higher Degree Research Award, 172
Graduate Scholarship, 144
OZCO Visual Arts Fellowship, 160
Visual Arts New Work, 161
Visual Arts Skills and Arts Development, 162
Asian Countries
Fulbright-Nehru Doctoral Research Fellowships, 1195
Fulbright-Nehru Postdoctoral Research Fellowships, 1195
Australia
The Dreaming Award, 160
United Kingdom
Arts Council of Wales Awards for Career Development of Individual Visual Artists and Craftspeople, 137
Arts Council of Wales Awards for Individual Visual Artists and Craftspeople, 137
United States of America
Harriet Hale Woolley Scholarship, 536
Irving and Yvonne Twining Humber Award for Lifetime Artistic Achievement, 135
SOLA Awards, 135
Twining Humber Award, 135

MUSIC

Any Country
Allen Senior Scholarship (Music), 1146
Arts Council of Wales Music Projects Grants, 138
Beatrice Ratcliffe Postgraduate Scholarship in Music, 1226
Bournemouth University Music Scholarships, 227
Carolyn and Franco Gianturco Scholarship in Music, 732
Eckhardt-Gramatté National Music Competition, 271
Farina Thompson Charitable Trust Music Scholarship, 1269
Joseph Kremen Memorial Fellowship, 1640
Kurt Weill Prize, 698
Music Scholarships, 592
POP Awards, 590
Postgraduate Awards, 590
Rae and George Hammer Memorial Visiting Research Fellowship, 1218
Reardon Postgraduate Scholarship in Music, 1230
RHBNC Trust Scholarship, 1042
Royal College of Organists Various Open Awards, 1030
Royal Over-Seas League Annual Music Competition, 1047
Rudolph Ganz Fellowship, 892
Sybil Tutton Awards, 590
Therla Drake Postgraduate Scholarships, 517
Van L. Lawrence Fellowship, 849
Villa I Tatti-Bogaziçi University Joint Fellowship, 1600
Vladimir and Pearl Heifetz Memorial Fellowship in Eastern European Jewish Music, 1641
Wallace Fellowship, 1601
Asian Countries
Fulbright-Nehru Doctoral Research Fellowships, 1195
Fulbright-Nehru Postdoctoral Research Fellowships, 1195
Madhobi Chatterji Memorial Fellowship, 1088
Mani Mann Fellowship, 1088

Pt. Vasant Thakar Memorial Fellowship, 1089
Australia
BMG Indigenous Music Industry Scholarship-Creative Industries, 1429
The Dreaming Award, 160
Elizabeth Pearse Music Scholarship, 674
Joy Ingall Scholarship for Music Studies, 1435
Paul Lowin Prizes-Song Cycle Prize, 949
Playing Australia: Regional Performing Arts Touring Fund, 160
University of Adelaide Research Scholarship-The Elder Conservatorium of Music, 1220
Western Sydney Artists, 142
Canada
Musical Instrument Bank, 273
European Countries
American Council of Learned Societies Humanities Program in Belarus, Russia and Ukraine, 62
Oxford-Louis Curran Graduate Scholarship, 1491
Wingate Scholarships, 1619
European Union
Cardiff University PhD Music Studentship, 327
Wingate Scholarships, 1619
New Zealand
Anne Bellam Scholarship, 1225
Elman Poole Travelling Scholarship, 1444
The Judith Clark Memorial Fellowships, 1280
The Kate Edger Educational Charitable Trust Vinka Marinovich Award in Music, 1232
The Kia Ora Foundation Patricia Pratt Music Scholarship, 1280
Kia Ora Foundation Patricia Pratt Scholarship, 1199, 1276
Kiwi Music Scholarship, 1200, 1276
Patricia Pratt Scholarships in Musical Performance, 1447
Therle Drake Postgraduate Scholarship, 1594
University of Adelaide Research Scholarship-The Elder Conservatorium of Music, 1220
Russia
American Council of Learned Societies Humanities Program in Belarus, Russia and Ukraine, 62
South American Countries
Invertimos en el Talento de los Colombianos (ICETEX) Artistas Jovenes Scholarships, 183
United Kingdom
Arts Council of Wales Community Touring Night Out, 137
Arts Council of Wales Performing Arts Projects, 138
Cardiff University PhD Music Studentship, 327
Headley Trust Scholarship, 1041
The John Brookman Scholarship, 1509
Sarah Barrow Bursary in Music, 1357
Wingate Scholarships, 1619
United States of America
Harriet Hale Woolley Scholarship, 536
Lilly Fellows Program in the Humanities and the Arts, 1006
Weiss/Brown Publication Subvention Award, 892

CONDUCTING

Any Country
The Leonard Freestone Scholarship, 1031
The Peter Wiles Scholarship, 1031
Royal College of Organists Various Open Award Bequests, 1030
United States of America
Commissioning Music/United States of America, 807

MUSICAL INSTRUMENTS

Any Country
Carnwath Scholarship, 1628
Clara Haskil International Piano Competition, 365
Gold, Silver and Bronze Medals, 945
The Harry Moreton Memorial Scholarship, 1031
International Beethoven Piano Competition, Vienna, 1627
International Carl Flesch Violin Competition, 268
The Leonard Freestone Scholarship, 1031
Music Scholarships-Choral Scholarship, 601
Music Scholarships-Orchestral Scholarships, 602
National Association of Teachers of Singing Art Song Competition Award, 848
The Peter Wiles Scholarship, 1031
Queen Elisabeth International Music Competition of Belgium, 965
Royal College of Organists Scholarships and Awards, 1030
Royal College of Organists Various Open Award Bequests, 1030
Australia
David Paul Landa Memorial Scholarships for Pianists, 141
Canada
Virginia Parker Prize, 277
New Zealand
Alex Lindsay awards, 788

MUSICOLOGY

Any Country
Graduate Scholarship, 144
Oxford-Carolyn and Franco Gianturco Graduate Scholarship, 1484

MUSIC THEORY AND COMPOSITION

Any Country
Jules Leéger Prize for New Chamber Music, 276
Robert Fleming Prize, 274
United States of America
American Society of Composers, Authors and Publishers Foundation Morton Gould Young Composer Awards, 117

Commissioning Music/United States of America, 807
JP Morgan Chase Regrant Program for Small Ensembles, 808

OPERA

Any Country
Wigmore Hall/Independent Opera International Song Competition, 124
United States of America
Commissioning Music/United States of America, 807

SINGING

Any Country
Loren L Zachary National Vocal Competition for Young Opera Singers, 748
Music Scholarships-Choral Scholarship, 1042
Queen Elisabeth International Music Competition of Belgium, 965
Wigmore Hall/Independent Opera International Song Competition, 124
United States of America
JP Morgan Chase Regrant Program for Small Ensembles, 808

PHOTOGRAPHY

Any Country
A&A Masters Higher Degree Research Award, 172
Aaron Siskind Foundation-Individual Photographer's Fellowship, 142
Center for Creative Photography Ansel Adams Research Fellowship, 337
Graduate Scholarship, 144
Hearst Fellowships, 585
Individual Photographer, 7
OZCO Visual Arts Fellowship, 160
Visual Arts New Work, 161
Visual Arts Skills and Arts Development, 162
Asian Countries
Fulbright-Nehru Doctoral Research Fellowships, 1195
Fulbright-Nehru Postdoctoral Research Fellowships, 1195
India Habitat Centre Fellowship for Photography, 620
Australia
The Dreaming Award, 160
Canada
Duke and Duchess of York Prize in Photography, 271
United Kingdom
Arts Council of Wales Awards for Career Development of Individual Visual Artists and Craftspeople, 137
Arts Council of Wales Awards for Individual Visual Artists and Craftspeople, 137
Ashley Family Foundation MA Photography Scholarship, 143
United States of America
Harriet Hale Woolley Scholarship, 536
Irving and Yvonne Twining Humber Award for Lifetime Artistic Achievement, 135
SOLA Awards, 135
Twining Humber Award, 135

SCULPTURE

Any Country
A&A Masters Higher Degree Research Award, 172
The Barns-Graham Travel Award, 1048
OZCO Visual Arts Fellowship, 160
Visual Arts New Work, 161
Visual Arts Skills and Arts Development, 162
Asian Countries
China Scholarships, 620
Fulbright-Nehru Doctoral Research Fellowships, 1195
Fulbright-Nehru Postdoctoral Research Fellowships, 1195
Australia
The Dreaming Award, 160
United Kingdom
Arts Council of Wales Awards for Career Development of Individual Visual Artists and Craftspeople, 137
Arts Council of Wales Awards for Individual Visual Artists and Craftspeople, 137
United States of America
Harriet Hale Woolley Scholarship, 536
Irving and Yvonne Twining Humber Award for Lifetime Artistic Achievement, 135
SOLA Awards, 135
Twining Humber Award, 135

THEATRE

Any Country
Donald & Margot Watt Bursary Fund (FASS Only), 706
Graduate Scholarship, 144
Joseph Kremen Memorial Fellowship, 1640
Kurt Weill Prize, 698
"Made in NY" Women's Film, TV and Theatre Fund, 888
Noni Wright Scholarship, 1447
Philip Parsons Young Playwright's Award, 142
Rae and George Hammer Memorial Visiting Research Fellowship, 1218
RHBNC Trust Scholarship, 1042
Asian Countries
Fulbright-Nehru Doctoral Research Fellowships, 1195
Fulbright-Nehru Postdoctoral Research Fellowships, 1195
Australia
The Dreaming Award, 160
Playing Australia: Regional Performing Arts Touring Fund, 160

Canada
Walter Carsen Prize for Excellence in the Performing Arts, 277
European Countries
American Council of Learned Societies Humanities Program in Belarus, Russia and Ukraine, 62
Russia
American Council of Learned Societies Humanities Program in Belarus, Russia and Ukraine, 62
United Kingdom
Arts Council of Wales Barclays Stage Partners, 137
Arts Council of Wales Community Touring Night Out, 137
Arts Council of Wales Performing Arts Projects, 138
United States of America
Commissioning Music/United States of America, 807
Lilly Fellows Program in the Humanities and the Arts, 1006
Weiss/Brown Publication Subvention Award, 892

HOME ECONOMICS

GENERAL

Any Country
American Association of Family and Consumer Sciences National Fellowships in Family and Consumer Sciences, 44
American Association of Family and Consumer Sciences New Achievers Award, 45
MSc Scholarship for Women, 613
Ruth O Brian Project Grant, 45
African Nations
The Beacon Scholarship, 331
Australia
Doctoral Research on Family Relationships, 511
United States of America
Jewell L. Taylor National Graduate Fellowship, 45
Margaret E. Terrell National Graduate Fellowship, 45

CHILD CARE/CHILD DEVELOPMENT

Any Country
The Anne Wingate Paterson Scholarship, 1538

NUTRITION

Any Country
AFZ Giles Scholarship, 1214
Arnold Klopper Scholarship, 1215
Arrell Scholarships, 1318
School for Policy Studies International Postgraduate Scholarships, 1237
United Kingdom
Pace Award, 244
United States of America
Healthy Eating Research, 1011

LAW

GENERAL

Any Country
AALL Research Fund: An Endowment Established by Lexisnexis, 46
Academic Excellence Scholarship (International), 227
Academic Excellence Senior Status Law Scholarship, 1304
AIPLEF Sidney B. Williams Scholarship, 1172
American Association of Law Libraries LexisNexis/John R Johnson Memorial Scholarship Endowment, 46
American Association of Law Libraries Scholarship (Type II), 47
Arthur Liman Public Interest Law Fellowship, 1635
Aziz Foundation Masters Scholarships, 1310
Balliol College: McDougall Scholarship, 1456
Bedford Society Scholarship, 1040
Business, Economics & Law Postgraduate Academic Excellence Scholarship, 155
California Senate Fellows, 1083
Cardiff University School of Law and Politics-ESRC Wales DTP General Studentships-Empirical Studies in Law, 328
Children's Rights Scholarship, 713
Children's Rights Scholarship 2, 714
Christine and Ian Bolt Scholarship, 1324
Christine Mirzayan Science & Technology Policy Graduate Fellowship Program, 864
College of Business Government and Law PhD Top-up, 522
Doshisha University Doctoral-Program Young Researcher Scholarship, 439
Economic and Social Research Council: Socio-Legal Studies, 1459
Evan Lewis-Thomas Law Studentships, 1109
Faculty of Law Masters International Scholarship, 823, 824
Fitzwilliam College: Fitzwilliam Society JRW Alexander Law Book Grants, 1244
Francis Regan Student Scholarship, 525
Freshfields Bruckhaus Deringer Scholarships (Law), 1462
Friedrich-Naumann-Stiftung, 188
150 Fully Funded PhD Degree Scholarships for International Students, 503
Gonville and Caius College W M Tapp Studentship in Law, 1251
GREAT Scholarship for Justice and Law, 1307
Herchel Smith Scholarship in Intellectual Property, 969
Hodgson Law Scholarship, 1355
Jesse M. Unruh Assembly Fellowship Program, 1083
Joseph Hume Scholarship, 1205

Lady Margaret Hall: Ann Kennedy Graduate Scholarship in Law, 1468
Law Faculty: David and Helen Elvin Scholarship, 1468
Law/Faculty Graduate Scholarship (FGS), 876
Law Faculty Scholarships, 1140
Law Faculty: The Peter Birks Memorial Scholarship, 1469
Linacre College: David Daube Scholarship, 1470
Lionel Murphy Endowment Postgraduate Scholarship, 737
LLM in European Law Scholarship, 1300
LLM in International Trade Law–Contracts and Dispute Resolution–Scholarships, 1213
Lucy Cavendish College: Becker Law Scholarships, 1252
Master of the Rolls Scholarship for Commonwealth Students, 1205
Merton College: Merton Lawyers, 1476
Michael Wong Pakshong Bursary, 1237
Mr and Mrs Kenny Lam's Graduate Scholarship (Law), 1147
Oxford-Finnis Graduate Scholarship in Law, 1487
Pembroke College: The Ziegler Graduate Studentship in Law, 1257
Reserve Bank of New Zealand Scholarships, 992
Resource Management Law Association of New Zealand Masters Scholarship, 157
The Roger Perry Memorial Scholarship, 993
Steve Weston and Trust Scholarships, 1289
The Tim Collins Scholarship for the Study of Love in Religion, 984
UC Te Kaupeka Ture Faculty of Law PhD Fees Scholarship, 1271
UK, CI and ROI Student Scholarships-Academic Achievement Scholarship, 229
UNSW Law & Justice International Award, 1425
Wadham College: Peter Carter Taught Graduate Scholarship in Law, 1513
Women in Central Banking Scholarship, 993
Yuill Scholarship, 175
African Nations
The Beacon Scholarship, 331
Bournemouth University–GREAT Scholarships 2023, 227
Canon Collins Scholarship for Distance Learning Master of Laws (LLM), 318
Children's Rights Scholarship 3, 714
GREAT Scholarships-Egypt, 1286
GREAT Scholarships-Ghana, 1286
GREAT Scholarships-Kenya, 1287
University of Strathclyde-British Council GREAT Scholarships 2024 for Justice and Law-China, Ghana, Malaysia, Pakistan, 1553
Asian Countries
CSC-Leiden University Scholarship, 714
GREAT Scholarship for Justice and Law, 1204, 1307
GREAT Scholarship for Justice & Law-Thailand, 1285
GREAT Scholarships-China, 1286
GREAT Scholarships-India, 1287
GREAT Scholarships–Indonesia, 1287
GREAT Scholarships–Malaysia, 1288
GREAT Scholarships–Pakistan, 1288
GREAT Scholarships–Thailand, 1288
Orange Tulip Scholarship (OTS) China, 1578
Swaantje Mondt Fund Law and Society Scholarship, 719
Tinson Fund Scholarship for Law, 1310
University of Strathclyde-British Council GREAT Scholarships 2024 for Justice and Law-China, Ghana, Malaysia, Pakistan, 1553
Australia
Co-op Bookshop Scholarship, 165
Dodson Indigenous Juris Doctor Scholarship, 823
The Faculty of Law Juris Doctor Scholarship for Indigenous Students, 1424
Lionel Murphy Endowment Postgraduate Scholarship, 737
Sir John Salmond Scholarship for Students from Australia and New Zealand, 1210
Tamex Transport Scholarship, 1410
Canada
French Language Scholarship, 288
The Right Honorable Paul Martin Sr. Scholarship, 288
European Countries
Tinson Fund Scholarship for Law, 1310
European Union
Kyle Scholarship, 971
Middle East
Bournemouth University–GREAT Scholarships 2023, 227
New Zealand
Francis Martin Baillie Reynolds Scholarship in Law to Oxford, 1273
Māori and Pacific Islands Scholarship, 992
New Zealand Law Foundation Ethel Benjamin Scholarship (For Women), 1200, 1277
Reserve Bank of New Zealand Scholarships for International Students, 993
Sir John Salmond Scholarship for Students from Australia and New Zealand, 1210
South Africa
Canon Collins Scholarship for Distance Learning Master of Laws (LLM), 318
Graça Machel scholarship, 715
Kuiper-Overpelt Study Fund, 715
Leiden University South Africa Scholarship-University of Cape Town, 716
Leiden University South Africa Scholarship-University of Pretoria, 716
Leiden University South Africa Scholarship-University of the Western Cape, 717
LUF International Study Fund (LISF), 717
Mandela Scholarship Fund, 718

United Kingdom
Kyle Scholarship, 971
Postgraduate Essay Award, 237
United States of America
Sir Frederick Pollock Scholarship for Students from North America, 1209

CIVIL LAW

Any Country
Grants, 1173
Jesus College: Joint Law Faculty-Jesus College BCL Scholarship, 1465
Law Faculty: Des Voeux Chambers, 1469
Merton College: Barton Scholarship, 1476
Oxford-Feltham Graduate Scholarship, 1487
Oxford-Hackney BCL Graduate Scholarship, 1487

CRIMINAL LAW

Any Country
Criminology Scholarships for Foreign Researchers in Germany, 795
Soros Justice Fellowships, 927
United States of America
Center for Advancing Opportunity Doctorial Fellowship, 1182

HISTORY OF LAW

Any Country
Keith Hawkins Graduate Research Scholarship in English or American Legal History, 939
Postdoctoral and Research Scholarships at MPIeR in Germany, 797
European Countries
Harry Bikakis Fellowship, 101
North American Countries
Harry Bikakis Fellowship, 101

HUMAN RIGHTS

Any Country
Abba P. Schwartz Research Fellowship, 684
Asian Countries
Oxford-Brunsfield Association of Southeast Asian Nations (ASEAN) Human Rights Graduate Scholarships, 1483

INTERNATIONAL LAW

Any Country
Abba P. Schwartz Research Fellowship, 684
Asian Countries
Fulbright-Nehru Master's Fellowships, 1195
Oxford-Brunsfield Association of Southeast Asian Nations (ASEAN) Human Rights Graduate Scholarships, 1483

JUSTICE ADMINISTRATION

Any Country
Soros Justice Fellowships, 927

LABOUR LAW

Any Country
Law Postgraduate Community Bursary, 1547

PUBLIC LAW

Any Country
Lincoln College: Supperstone Law Scholarship, 1474

FISCAL LAW

Any Country
Law Faculty: James Bullock Scholarship, 1469

MASS COMMUNICATION AND INFORMATION SCIENCE

GENERAL

Any Country
The Council of Scientific and Industrial Research/TWAS Fellowship for Postdoctoral Research, 1180
Eugene Garfield Doctoral Dissertation Fellowship, 203
Fellowship in the Digital Humanities, 1599
Fulbright Distinguished Chair in Science, Technology, and Innovation (CSIRO), 551
Keble College Ian Palmer Graduate Scholarship in Information Technology, 1467
PPARC Communications/Media Programme, 1102
RHBNC Trust Scholarship, 1042
RHT Bates Postgraduate Scholarship, 1052
University of Sydney: Data Science Scholarships, 124
African Nations
The Beacon Scholarship, 331
OWSD PhD Fellowships for Women Scientists, 1179
Asian Countries
Fulbright-Nehru Master's Fellowships, 1195
OWSD PhD Fellowships for Women Scientists, 1179
Serendib Community Cultural Association Sri Lanka Bursary, 425
Asia-Pacific Countries
OWSD PhD Fellowships for Women Scientists, 1179
Australia
Information Technology Postgraduate Scholarship, 824
Canada
Edward S. Rogers Sr. Graduate Student Fellowships, 1076
Caribbean Countries
OWSD PhD Fellowships for Women Scientists, 1179

Latin America
OWSD PhD Fellowships for Women Scientists, 1179
New Zealand
Information Technology Postgraduate Scholarship, 824

DOCUMENTATION TECHNIQUES AND ARCHIVING

Any Country
Mellon Fellowship in Digital Humanities, 1600
Workmen's Circle/Dr Emanuel Patt Visiting Professorship, 1641
Canada
Society of American Archivists' Mosaic Scholarship Opportunity, 936
European Countries
W.D.E. Coulson & Toni M. Cross Aegean Exchange Program, 589
United States of America
Society of American Archivists' Mosaic Scholarship Opportunity, 936

JOURNALISM

Any Country
Asia Journalism Fellowship, 835
Aziz Foundation Masters Scholarships, 1310
The Aziz Foundation Scholarship, 1358
Barbara Jordan Baines Report Fellowship Fund, 1169
Engen Conservation, 844
Fully Funded Master Scholarship at Hong Kong Baptist University, 602
Guy Butler Research Award, 1008
Hearst Fellowships, 585
Knight-Bagehot Fellowships in Economics and Business Journalism at Columbia University, 372
Reham al-Farra International Scholarship in Journalism, 228
Thomson Foundation Scholarship, 1181
Asian Countries
Prabha Dutt Fellowship, 1089
United States of America
Carlos M. Castaeda Journalism Scholarship, 553

LIBRARY SCIENCE

Any Country
Accelerating Promising Practices for Small Libraries, 645
American Association of Law Libraries James F Connolly LexisNexis Academic and Library Solutions Scholarship, 46
American Association of Law Libraries LexisNexis/John R Johnson Memorial Scholarship Endowment, 46
American Association of Law Libraries Scholarship (Type II), 47
American Library Association Beta Phi Mu Award, 202
American Library Association Carroll Preston Baber Research Grant, 81
American Library Association Loleta D. Fyan Grant, 82
American Library Association Shirley Olofson Memorial Awards, 83
American Library Association W. David Rozkuszka Scholarship, 83
American Library Association YALSA/Baker and Taylor Conference Grant, 83
Center for Creative Photography Ansel Adams Research Fellowship, 337
Chartered Institute of Library and Information Professionals International Library and Information Group Alan Hopkinson Award, 657
Clark-Huntington Joint Bibliographical Fellowship, 1241
Council on Library and Information Resources Postdoctoral Fellowship, 390
Dixie Electric Membership Corporation New Leaders Travel Grant, 83
Frank B. Sessa Scholarships for Continuing Professional Education of Beta Phi Mu Members, 203
International Federation of Library Associations and Institutions Green Library Award, 657
International Studies Research Lab, 632
Mellon Fellowship in Digital Humanities, 1600
Native American Library Services: Enhancement Grants, 646
Workmen's Circle/Dr Emanuel Patt Visiting Professorship, 1641
Asia-Pacific Countries
Native Hawaiian Library Services, 646
Canada
American Library Association Miriam L Hornback Scholarship, 83
Canadian Library Association Library Research and Development Grants, 290
MLA Doctoral Fellowship, 801
Spectrum Initiative Scholarship Program, 84
European Countries
W.D.E. Coulson & Toni M. Cross Aegean Exchange Program, 589
Middle East
Dr. Shawky Salem Conference Grant, 657
United States of America
American Library Association Miriam L Hornback Scholarship, 83
Bancroft Library Study Awards, 194
MLA Doctoral Fellowship, 801
Spectrum Initiative Scholarship Program, 84

MASS COMMUNICATION

Any Country
Asian Communication Resource Centre (ACRC) Fellowship Award, 835

BEA Research Grant, 264
Communication and Media Scholarships, 751

MEDIA STUDIES

Any Country
AMS-AAAS Mass Media Fellowship, 85
Aziz Foundation Masters Scholarships, 1310
The Aziz Foundation Scholarship, 1358
Communication and Media Scholarships, 751
Ruth First Scholarship, 1010
Australia
Malcolm Cole Indigenous Scholarship, 1421
University of Adelaide Research Scholarship-The Elder Conservatorium of Music, 1220
New Zealand
University of Adelaide Research Scholarship-The Elder Conservatorium of Music, 1220
United Kingdom
Digital Media Programme Bursary, 1203

MUSEUM STUDIES

Any Country
BIAA-ANAMED Joint Fellowship in Heritage Studies, 97
Collections Study Award, 961
Graduate Scholarship, 144
Inspire! Grants for Small Museums, 646
Interpretive Fellowships at Art Museums, 1085
Kress Conservation Fellowships, 1085
European Countries
W.D.E. Coulson & Toni M. Cross Aegean Exchange Program, 589

RADIO/TELEVISION BROADCASTING

Any Country
Abe Voron Award, 264
BEA Research Grant, 264
John Bayliss Award, 265
Kenneth Harwood Outstanding Dissertation Award, 265
Library of American Broadcasting Foundation Award, 265
Thomson Foundation Scholarship, 1181
Vincent T. Wasilewski Award, 265

MATHEMATICS AND COMPUTER SCIENCE

GENERAL

Any Country
Abdus Salam ICTP Fellowships, 8
Acute Generalized Exanthematous Pustulosis Fellowship, 670
AfterCollege STEM Inclusion Scholarship, 18
AHA Postdoctoral Fellowship, 76
Alan Tayler Scholarship (Mathematics), 1146
Ampère & MILYON Excellence Scholarships for International Students, 456
BHW Women in STEM Scholarship, 1177
Bilkent Mathematics Fellowship, 209
Biomechanics Postgraduate Scholarship (General Sports), 176
British Council Scholarships for Women in STEM, 1539
Bryan Scholarships, 1390
Canadian Centennial Scholarship Fund, 1324
CDT in Advanced Metallic Systems, 1366
CDT in Aerosol Science, 1366
CDT in Biodesign Engineering, 1367
CDT in Compound Semiconductor Manufacturing, 1367
CDT in Future Innovation in NDE, 1367
CDT in the Science and Technology of Fusion Energy, 1368
China Scholarship Council Scholarships, 968
Christine Mirzayan Science & Technology Policy Graduate Fellowship Program, 838
College Scholarship (Sciences), 1146
Computational and Methodological Breakthroughs in High Dimensional Statistical Modelling for Complex Data, 768
Computer Science Scholarships, 1041
CONACyT Tuition Top-up Award, 1370
Cross-Disciplinary Fellowships, 659
Croucher Foundation PhD Scholarships and Postdoctoral Fellowships, 398
The David Caminer Postgraduate Scholarship in Business Computing, 812
Dean's Doctoral Scholarship Award, 1371
Department of Energy Computational Science Graduate Fellowship Krell Institute, 1589
Department of Mathematics Scholarship Award, 1371
Dhaka PhD Scholarships, 969
Directorate for Education and Human Resources Core Research, 867
Dirichlet International Postdoctoral Fellowship at Berlin Mathematical School in Germany, 202
Dual-award between The University of Manchester and IIT Kharagpur, 1372
Dual-award between The University of Manchester and The University of Melbourne, 1373
Earth System Prediction Doctoral Training Programme, 1522
The Edward & Isabel Kidson Scholarship, 1279
Ely M. Gelbard Graduate Scholarship, 88
Engineering and Physical Sciences Research Council (EPSRC) Doctoral Training Partnership, 1559
EPSRC Doctoral Training Partnership (DTP), 1373
Faculty of Science Scholarship for Online Masters Students, 1542
Faculty PhD Scholarships, 319
Fitzwilliam College Leathersellers, 1243
Fulbright Distinguished Chair in Science, Technology, and Innovation (CSIRO), 551

Funds for Women Graduates, 1377
GeneTex Scholarship Program, 562
Government of Ireland Postgraduate Scholarship Programme, 671
Graphene NOWNANO CDT, 1377
H.C. & M.E. Porter Memorial Endowed Award, 1419
Heilbronn Doctoral Partnership (HDP) Studentship, 1378
Ilona Takacs Scholarship, 513
Institution of Engineering and Technology Postgraduate Scholarship for an Outstanding Researcher, 647
Integrated Catalysis (iCAT) CDT, 1378
International Centre for Theoretical Sciences S. N. Bhatt Memorial Excellence Research Fellowship, 656
International Mathematical Union Visiting Mathematician Programme, 663
Internships and Industry Fund for Computer Science, 448
Ioan and Rosemary James/Mathematical Institute Scholarship, 1465
IT Kharagpur Post Doctoral Fellowship, 623
Joint-award between The University of Manchester and IISC Bangalore, 1379
Lancaster Master's Scholarship, 709
Late Stephen Robjohns Science Scholarship, 1421
LMS Early Career Fellowships 2021-22 with support from the Heilbronn Institute for Mathematical Research (HIMR) and UKRI, 740
MacGillavry Fellowships, 1224
Mathematical Sciences Scholarship, 756
Monica Hulse Scholarship, 1206
MS Catalyzing Advocacy in Science and Engineering (CASE) Workshop, 86
National University of Singapore Design Technology Institute Scholarship, 876
Nuclear Energy-GREEN CDT, 1381
NZ-GRADS New Zealand Global Research Alliance Doctoral Scholarship, 473
The Optical Society, Deutsch Fellowship, 842
Oxford-Nicholas Bratt Graduate Scholarship, 1491
Packard Fellowships for Science and Engineering, 413
Paradice Honours Award in Mathematics & Statistics, 1422
PhD Scholarship: Digital Modelling of Apple for Quality Prediction, 645
Postdoctoral Fellowships in Mathematics at Harish-Chandra Research Institute, 578
Postdoctoral Scholar Program, 1625
Postgraduate Research Teaching Associate (PGRTA) Scholarships, 1381
Research/Visiting Scientist Fellowships, 18
Reserve Bank of New Zealand Scholarships, 992
RHBNC Trust Scholarship, 1042
RHT Bates Postgraduate Scholarship, 1052
Robert Noyce Teacher Scholarship Program, 869
Roger Helm Scholarship in Pure Mathematics, 322
The Roger Perry Memorial Scholarship, 993
Royal Society EPSRC BBSRC and Rolls Royce PLC Industry Fellowships, 485
RuralKids GPS–Delivering Equitable Care to Children in Rural NSW, 778
Schrödinger Scholarship Scheme, 615
Singapore International Graduate Award, 836
Singapore-MIT Alliance Graduate Fellowship, 877
Sir James Lighthill Scholarship, 1210
Society for Immunotherapy of Cancer Scholarship, 10
Tim and Margaret Bourke PhD Scholarships, 174
Trinity College: Studentships in Mathematics, 1259
TWAS-COMSTECH Science in Exile PhD Fellowship Programme for Displaced and Refugee Scientists, 1180
TWAS-SN Bose Postgraduate Fellowship Programme, 1181
University of Canterbury Mathematics and Statistics Scholarship, 323
University of Geneva Excellence Masters Fellowships, 1313
University of Sydney: Data Science Scholarships, 124
Western Digital Scholarship Program, 1112
Wilfrid Knapp Scholarship (Sciences), 1148
Women in Central Banking Scholarship, 993
Women in Science Scholarship, 736
Woodrow Wilson Teaching Fellowship, 1624

African Nations

The Beacon Scholarship, 331
Deakin STEM Scholarship, 422
GREAT-Imperial College London Scholarship, 613
GREAT Scholarships-Egypt, 1286
GREAT Scholarships-Ghana, 1286
GREAT Scholarships-Kenya, 1287
Microsoft Research European PhD Scholarship Programme, 810

Asian Countries

Advanced Biomedical Materials CDT, 1363
A* STAR PhD Programme, 1363
British Council Scholarship for Women in STEM Terms and Conditions, 266
British Council Scholarships for Women in STEM, 446, 1365
China Scholarship Council-University of Oxford Scholarships, 1458
Daiwa Foundation Awards, 411
Deakin STEM Scholarship, 422
Fulbright-Nehru Doctoral Research Fellowships, 1195
Fulbright-Nehru Postdoctoral Research Fellowships, 1195
GREAT-Imperial College London Scholarship, 613
GREAT Scholarships-China, 1286
GREAT Scholarships-India, 1287
GREAT Scholarships–Indonesia, 1287
GREAT Scholarships–Malaysia, 1288
GREAT Scholarships–Pakistan, 1288
GREAT Scholarships–Thailand, 1288

Ramanujan Research Studentship in Mathematics, 1257
Ramanujan Research Studentship in Mathematics at Trinity College, Cambridge, 1258
The University of Manchester-China Scholarship Council Joint Scholarship, 1389
Australia
AGL Jungurra Wunnik Scholarship, 508
Asia Pacific Institute of Information Technology_IT PhDs in Grid Computing, 1216
HeART of the Basin Scholarship, 340
Indigenous Pathways Advance Queensland VET Scholarship, 341
J Holden Family Foundation Honours Award in Maths and Physics, 1420
Masters Scholarship in Scotland, 406
Meredith Doig Scholarship, 514
School of Mathematics and Statistics Indigenous Scholarship, 1423
Sir Arthur Sims Travelling Scholarship, 1399
Victoria Fellowships, 430
European Countries
Cecil King Travel Scholarship, 740
John and Pat Hume Research Scholarships, 874
Microsoft Research European PhD Scholarship Programme, 810
European Union
John and Pat Hume Research Scholarships, 874
Keble College: James Martin Graduate Scholarship, 1467
The Von Kaven Awards, 435
Middle East
Kuwait Program at Sciences Po Excellence Scholarship for Arab Students and Kuwait Nationals, 947
Microsoft Research European PhD Scholarship Programme, 810
New Zealand
AGL Jungurra Wunnik Scholarship, 508
Asia Pacific Institute of Information Technology_IT PhDs in Grid Computing, 1216
Māori and Pacific Islands Scholarship, 992
Meredith Doig Scholarship, 514
Reserve Bank of New Zealand Scholarships for International Students, 993
North American Countries
American Meteorological Society Centennial Fellowships in Mathematics, 85
British Council Scholarships for Women in STEM, 608
Oceania
Toloa Scholarships for Pacific STEM Scholars, 158
South Africa
Leiden University South Africa Scholarship-University of Cape Town, 716
Leiden University South Africa Scholarship-University of Pretoria, 716
Leiden University South Africa Scholarship-University of the Western Cape, 717
LUF International Study Fund (LISF), 717
Mandela Scholarship Fund, 718
South American Countries
British Council Scholarships for Women in STEM, 608
United Kingdom
Cecil King Travel Scholarship, 740
Daiwa Foundation Awards, 411
Keble College: James Martin Graduate Scholarship, 1467
PhD Studentships in Mathematics, 1560
United States of America
AMS Congressional Fellowship, 85
Department of Defense-National Defense and Science Engineering Fellowships, 195
Foundation for Science and Disability Student Grant Fund, 546
Graduate Fellowships for Science, Technology, Engineering, and Mathematics Diversity, 573
Graduate Student Grant, 546
Howard Hughes Medical Institute Gilliam Fellowships for Advanced Study, 604
National Energy Technology Laboratory Methane Hydrates Fellowship Program (MHFP), 840
National Institute of Justice's Graduate Research Fellowship Program, 199
NRC Research Associate Programs (RAP), 840
NRC Research Associateship Programs (RAP), 840
United States Air Force Academy/National Research Council Summer Faculty Research Program (SFFP), 21
Winston Churchill Foundation Scholarships, 200

ARTIFICIAL INTELLIGENCE

Any Country
DeepMind Scholarship, 969
Doctor of Philosophy Scholarship-Artificial Intelligence in Medicine and Healthcare, 769
Postgraduate Conversion Courses in AI and Data Science Scholarships, 1308
Asian Countries
Manju Mehrotra Scholarship, 1041
Australia
Honours/Masters Scholarship for AI, User Interface or Robotics, 525

COMPUTER SCIENCE

Any Country
College of Engineering and Computer Science: College Postgraduate International Award, 173
College of Engineering and Computer Science: College Postgraduate International Honours Award, 173
Computer Science: Department Studentships, 1459

Computer Science Scholarships, 751
Cross-Disciplinary Fellowships, 659
DeepMind Scholarship, 969
G B Battersby-Trimble Scholarship in Computer Science, 1274
International Excellence Scholarship (Information Technology and Computer Science), 1434
Leverhulme (LINCS) PhD Scholarship, 972
Mellon Fellowship in Digital Humanities, 1600
Oxford-DeepMind Graduate Scholarship (Computer Science), 1486
Performance Analysis Scholarship, 176
PhD (via MPhil) International Studentships in Cyber Security in UK, 902
PhD Science Fellowship, 1176
Postgraduate Conversion Courses in AI and Data Science Scholarships, 1308
Program Grants, 660
S.N Bose Scholar Program, 1099
Young Investigator Grant, 660

African Nations

Chevening Partner Scholarship scheme, 228
Seed Grant for New African Principal Investigators (SG-NAPI), 1179

Asian Countries

Chevening Partner Scholarship scheme, 228

Asia-Pacific Countries

Microsoft Fellowship, 810

European Countries

Oxford-Mary Jane Grefenstette Graduate Scholarship, 1491

European Union

Computer Science Scholarship, 149
James Elson Studentship, 1379

United Kingdom

Computer Science Scholarship, 149
Daphne Jackson Fellowships, 1101
James Elson Studentship, 1379
Women in Computing Master's Scholarship, 617

United States of America

Graduate Fellowships for Science, Technology, Engineering, and Mathematics Diversity, 573

STATISTICS

Any Country

Ellis R. Ott Scholarship for Applied Statistics and Quality Management, 113
Member Scholarship in Statistics, 1206
Pierre Robillard Award, 1152
Spatio-temporal Models for Large Citizen Science Data Sets, 1332

European Countries

Leathersellers' Company Scholarship (Sciences), 1147

European Union

Engineering and Physical Sciences Research Council (EPSRC) Doctoral Training Programme Studentships, 1460

United Kingdom

Engineering and Physical Sciences Research Council (EPSRC) Doctoral Training Programme Studentships, 1460
Leathersellers' Company Scholarship (Sciences), 1147

MEDICAL SCIENCES

GENERAL

Any Country

AACR Clinical Oncology Research (CORE) Training Fellowships, 2
Acromegaly/Growth Hormone Excess Research, 951
Acute Generalized Exanthematous Pustulosis Fellowship, 670
AFZ Giles Scholarship, 1214
AHA Postdoctoral Fellowship, 76
Alberta Heritage Foundation for Medical Research Part-Time Studentship, 22
Alberta Innovates-Health Solutions Postgraduate Fellowships, 22
Alzheimer's Association Research Fellowship (AARF), 27
Alzheimers Drug Discovery Foundation Grants Program, 32
American Cancer Society International Fellowships for Beginning Investigators, 53
Arnold Klopper Scholarship, 1215
Australian-American Health Policy Fellowship, 374
Beyond Segments: Towards a Lexical Model for Tonal Bilinguals, 767
2023–24 Bloomsbury Colleges PhD Studentship-Project 2, 744
Breast Cancer Competitive Research Grant Program, 952
CAMS Summer Research Fellowship Scholarship, 362
Canadian Centennial Scholarship Fund, 1324
Cancer Research Fund of the Damon Runyon-Walter Winchell Foundation Research Fellowships for Physician Scientists, 308
Carson Northern Territory Medical Program Scholarship, 521
CDT in Advanced Metallic Systems, 1366
CDT in Aerosol Science, 1366
CDT in Compound Semiconductor Manufacturing, 1367
CDT in Future Innovation in NDE, 1367
CDT in the Science and Technology of Fusion Energy, 1368
Cell and Oligonucleotide Therapy Fellowship with AstraZeneca, 802
China Scholarship Council Scholarships, 968

Chinese American Medical Society Scholarship Program, 362
Christine Mirzayan Science & Technology Policy Graduate Fellowship Program, 838, 864
The Christopher Welch Scholarship in Biological Sciences, 1509
Clinical Assistant Professorships, 397
Clinical Research Training Fellowship, 484
Clinician Scientist Fellowship, 313, 947
Collaborative Project relating to Antimicrobial Resistance from a One Health Perspective, 990
Commonwealth Infection Prevention and Control Scholarship, 1284
CONACyT Tuition Top-up Award, 1370
The Council of Scientific and Industrial Research/TWAS Fellowship for Postdoctoral Research, 1180
Croucher Foundation PhD Scholarships and Postdoctoral Fellowships, 398
Dean's Doctoral Scholarship Award, 1371
Developing Novel Genetic Disease Models for Dementia-International, 769
Dhaka PhD Scholarships, 969
Directorate for Education and Human Resources Core Research, 867
Discovery Programme Awards, 313
Doctor of Philosophy Scholarship-Artificial Intelligence in Medicine and Healthcare, 769
Doshisha University Doctoral-Program Young Researcher Scholarship, 439
Dual-award between The University of Manchester and IIT Kharagpur, 1372
Ellison-Cliffe Travelling Fellowship, 1060
Emergency Medicine Section: Innovation in ED Education for Students, 1060
Emergency Medicine section: Innovation in ED Education for Trainers, 1060
Emergency Medicine Section: Innovation in ED Education Prize, 1060
Emergency Medicine Section: Students' Prize for Students, 1060
Emergency Medicine Section: Students' Prize for Trainers, 1061
Environmental Sustainability in Life Sciences and Medical Practice, 802
EPSRC Doctoral Training Partnership (DTP), 1373
Eugene Garfield Research Fellowship, 800
Executive Dean's Postgraduate Scholarship, 512
Exeter College Usher-Cunningham Senior Studentship, 1461
Experimental Medicine, 803
Faculty Grant Program, 1174
Faculty of Medicine Master, 612
Faculty of Science Health & Care Futures MSc and PhD Scholarships for NHS Employees, 1542
Fulbright Distinguished Chair in Science, Technology, and Innovation (CSIRO), 551
Funds for Women Graduates, 1377
GeneTex Scholarship Program, 562
Gertrude Ardagh Holmes Bursary Fund, 1275
Gina M. Finzi Memorial Student Summer Fellowship Program, 760
Global Health Research Initiative Program for New Foreign Investigators (GRIP), 683
Goodger and Schorstein Research Scholarships in Medical Sciences, 1463
Government of Ireland Postgraduate Scholarship Programme, 671
Graduate Studentships, 23
Graphene NOWNANO CDT, 1377
Green Templeton College: GTC-Medical Sciences Doctoral Training Centre Scholarship, 1463
Greenwall Fellowship Program, 687
Gulf Research Program Science Policy Fellowships, 1175
Harkness Fellowships in Healthcare Policy and Practice, 374
Health Economics and HIV/AIDS Research Division PhD Scholarships, 1335
Heart and Stroke Foundation of Canada New Investigator Research Scholarships, 585
History of Medicine Society: Norah Schuster Essay Prize, 1062
Indian Health Service Health Professions Scholarship Program, 624
Innovative Grants, 689
Institution of Engineering and Technology Postgraduate Scholarship for an Outstanding Researcher, 647
Integrated Catalysis (iCAT) CDT, 1378
Intermediate Clinical Research Fellowships, 251
International Centre for Theoretical Sciences S. N. Bhatt Memorial Excellence Research Fellowship, 656
James H. Graham Award of Merit, 1033
J C Bose National Fellowship, 1098
Josiah Charles Trent Memorial Foundation Endowment Fund, 443
Lancaster Master's Scholarship, 709
Life Sciences Research Foundation Postdoctoral Fellowships, 730
Linacre College: EPA Cephalosporin Scholarship, 1470
Lindt Dissertation Fellowship, 370
Macquarie University Centre for the Health Economy (MUCHE) Industry Funded Higher Degree Research (HDR) Scholarships, 773
Master's Awards, 1607
Medical Research Council Clinical Research Training Fellowships, 803
Medical Research Council Clinician Scientist Fellowship, 804

Medical Research Council Industrial CASE Studentships, 804
Medical Research Council Senior Clinical Fellowship, 804
Medical Research Council Senior Non-Clinical Fellowship, 805
Medical Research Council Special Training Fellowships in Health Services and Health of the Public Research, 805
Military Medicine Colt Foundation Research Prize, 1064
National Library of Medicine Publication Grant Program, 862
National Science Foundation Research Traineeship (NRT) Program, 869
National University of Singapore Design Technology Institute Scholarship, 876
Newton International Fellowships, 234
Nuclear Energy-GREEN CDT, 1381
Nuffield Department of Primary Care Health Science: NIHR School for Primary Care Research DPhil Studentship, 1479
NZ-GRADS New Zealand Global Research Alliance Doctoral Scholarship, 473
Occupational Medicine Section Malcolm Harrington Prize, 1065
Ontario Women's Health Scholars Award, 923
The Optical Society, Deutsch Fellowship, 842
Oxford-EPA Cephalosporin Graduate Scholarship, 1487
Oxford-Hoffmann Graduate Scholarships, 1488
Oxford-Hoffmann Graduate Scholarships in Medical Sciences, 1488
Packard Fellowships for Science and Engineering, 413
Part the Cloud Translational (PTC) Research for Alzheimer's Disease Program, 30
Patient Safety Section: Student and Trainees' Prize, 1069
Pfizer Visiting Professorships Program, 955
PhD International Studentships in Control of Mitosis in Calcium in Mammalian Cells, UK, 903
Postdoctoral Fellowship in Translational Medicine, 956
Postdoctoral Fellowships, 689
Postdoctoral Research Fellowships for Physicians, 604
Postgraduate Research Scholarship in Health Literacy and Optimising the Assessment of Written Health Information, 1567
Postgraduate Research Teaching Associate (PGRTA) Scholarships, 1381
Presidential Scholarships for Students of Black Heritage, 615
Primary Care Training and Enhancement-Physician Assistant Program, 584
Project Grant Program, 289
Research Grants, 1142
Robert Noyce Teacher Scholarship Program, 869
Royal College AMS Donald Richards Wilson Award for CanMEDS Integration, 1033
Royal College Award for Early-Career Leadership, 1034
Royal Society EPSRC BBSRC and Rolls Royce PLC Industry Fellowships, 485
Ruth L. Kirschstein National Research Service Award (NRSA) Individual Postdoctoral Fellowship, 861
Savoy Foundation International Grant, 1090
Savoy Foundation Postdoctoral and Clinical Research Fellowships, 1091
Senior and Intermediate Research Fellowship for International Students, 1609
The Sergievsky Award For Epilepsy Health Equity And Diversity, 553
Sexuality & Sexual Health Section: Medical Student Essay Prize, 1070
Sexuality & Sexual Health Section: Trainee Essay Prize, 1070
Singapore International Graduate Award, 836
Singapore-MIT Alliance Graduate Fellowship, 877
Sleep Medicine Section: Student Essay Prize, 1071
Society of Nuclear Medicine Pilot Research Grants in Nuclear Medicine/Molecular Imaging, 473
St. Baldrick's International Scholars, 1143
St. Baldrick's Scholars, 1144
St Catherine's College Glaxo Scholarship, 1504
St Cross College: E.P. Abraham Scholarships, 1505
Trainees' Committee John Glyn Trainees' Prize, 1071
University of Geneva Excellence Masters Fellowships, 1313
University of Otago Special Health Research Scholarship, 1453
UNSW Medical Research Honours Scholarship-South Western Sydney, 1425
Viola Edith Reid Bequest Scholarship, 1402
Wellcome Trust: Principal Research Fellowships, 1402
Wilfrid Knapp Scholarship (Sciences), 1148
Women in Science Scholarship, 736
African Nations
Deakin STEM Scholarship, 422
GREAT-Imperial College London Scholarship, 613
Score Africa/Allan & Nesta Ferguson Charitable Trust Scholarship, 1209
Seed Grant for New African Principal Investigators (SG-NAPI), 1179
Asian Countries
Advanced Biomedical Materials CDT, 1363
A* STAR PhD Programme, 1363
British Council Scholarship for Women in STEM Terms and Conditions, 266
British Council Scholarships for Women in STEM, 446, 1365
CSC-Leiden University Scholarship, 714
Daiwa Foundation Awards, 411
Deakin STEM Scholarship, 422
GREAT-Imperial College London Scholarship, 613
GREAT Scholarships India, 243

National Bioscience Awards for Career Development (NBACD), 428
National Post Doctoral Fellowship (N-PDF), 1098
Ramanujan Fellowship, 1099
S. Ramachandran-National Bioscience Award for Career Development, 428
Tata Innovation Fellowship, 429
The University of Manchester-China Scholarship Council Joint Scholarship, 1389
Australia
Advanced Community Care Scholarship, 520
Austin Taylor Indigenous NT Medical Program Scholarship, 520
Betty J Fyffe Scholarship, 1404
Choosing the Way Forward: Addressing the Post-Parental Housing Transition Needs with Intellectual Disability and Their Older Family Carers, 521
Co-designing Culturally Relevant End of Life Care in Cancer, 768
Developing Novel Genetic Disease Models for Dementia-Domestic, 769
FMC Foundation Research Scholarship, 525
Harkness Fellowships in Health Care Policy, 374
HeART of the Basin Scholarship, 340
Indigenous Pathways Advance Queensland VET Scholarship, 341
The Joan, Arthur & Helen Thacker Aboriginal and/or Torres Strait Islander Postgraduate Scholarship, 1449
Macquarie University Centre for the Health Economy (MUCHE) Industry Funded Higher Degree Research (HDR) Scholarships-Domestic, 774
Masters Scholarship in Scotland, 406
National Health and Medical Research Council: Primary Health Care Postgraduate Research Scholarships, 529
Northern Territory Territory Medical Program Aboriginal and Torres Strait Islander Bursary, 529
PhD Scholarship-NHMRC People Support Grants-Postgraduate Scholarships, 424
Playford Trust: Playford Trust: PhD Scholarships, 530
Postgraduate Research Scholarship in Better Outcomes for Inflammatory Arthritis, 1567
Postgraduate Scholarships for Interdisciplinary Bioethics Research, 345
Professor Michael Kidd AM Scholarship, 531
Repatriation General Hospital Department of Rehabilitation and Aged Care: Medical Research Scholarship, 532
Sir Thomas Naghten Fitzgerald Scholarship, 1400
South Australian Department of Health Research Award, 533
Victoria Fellowships, 430
Canada
Canada's Distinguished Dissertation Awards, 1075
John Charles Polanyi Prizes, 1077
MLA Doctoral Fellowship, 801
Paralyzed Veterans of America Fellowships in Spinal Cord Injury Research, 945
Savoy Foundation Studentships, 1091
The Winter 2022 Gift Competition, 414
Central European Countries
Lincoln College: Berrow Foundation Lord Florey Scholarships, 1472
European Countries
Bayer Foundation Scholarships, 186
Collaborative Project to Meet Societal and Industry-related Challenges, 990
EPA Cephalosporin Scholarship, 733
Health Data Science Scholarships, 1354
John and Pat Hume Research Scholarships, 874
Oxford–EPA Cephalosporin Graduate Scholarship, 735
Partner with researchers in Switzerland, 806
Polish School of Medicine Memorial Fund Scholarships, 1301
Researcher Project for Scientific Renewal, 991
European Union
Child Health Research Appeal Trust Studentship, 1201
John and Pat Hume Research Scholarships, 874
Keble College: James Martin Graduate Scholarship, 1467
Middle East
Kuwait Program at Sciences Po Excellence Scholarship for Arab Students and Kuwait Nationals, 947
New Zealand
The Auckland Medical Aid Trust Scholarship, 322
BCEF Future Regional Doctors Scholarship, 350
Choosing the Way Forward: Addressing the Post-Parental Housing Transition Needs with Intellectual Disability and Their Older Family Carers, 521
Elman Poole Travelling Scholarship, 1444
Harkness Fellowships in Health Care Policy, 374
Postgraduate Research Scholarship in Better Outcomes for Inflammatory Arthritis, 1567
Repatriation General Hospital Department of Rehabilitation and Aged Care: Medical Research Scholarship, 532
Senior Health Research Scholarships, 1230
University of Otago Doctorate in Medical Education Scholarship, 1452
Williamson Medical Research PhD Scholarship, 1454
North American Countries
British Council Scholarships for Women in STEM, 608
Medical Student Research Grant, 979
South Africa
Leiden University South Africa Scholarship-University of Cape Town, 716
Leiden University South Africa Scholarship-University of Pretoria, 716

Leiden University South Africa Scholarship-University of the Western Cape, 717
LUF International Study Fund (LISF), 717
Mandela Scholarship Fund, 718
South American Countries
British Council Scholarships for Women in STEM, 608
United Kingdom
Australian-American Health Policy Fellowship, 374
Biomarker Project Awards, 311
Child Health Research Appeal Trust Studentship, 1201
Daiwa Foundation Awards, 411
Doctor of Philosophy Studentship, 806
Early Detection and Diagnosis Primer Award, 314
Experimental Medicine Award, 314
Keble College: James Martin Graduate Scholarship, 1467
Medical Elective Funding and Annual Essay Competition, 721
Medical Research Council/RCOG Clinical Research Training Fellowship, 805
Medical Research Scotland Sponsored Daphne Jackson Trust Fellowships, 807
Pre-doctoral Research Bursary, 315
Resuscitation Council (United Kingdom) Research & Development Grant, 994
Vera Down Research Grant, 256
United States of America
American Board of Emergency Medicine Fellowship, 837
The Commonwealth Fund Mongan Fellowship in Minority Health Policy, 375
Department of Defense-National Defense and Science Engineering Fellowships, 195
Harold Amos Medical Faculty Development Program, 1010
Howard Hughes Medical Institute Gilliam Fellowships for Advanced Study, 604
John E Fogarty Foreign Funded Fellowship Programs, 684
Life Sciences Research Foundation, 730
MLA Doctoral Fellowship, 801
National Energy Technology Laboratory Methane Hydrates Fellowship Program (MHFP), 840
National Foundation for Infectious Diseases Postdoctoral Fellowship in Nosocomial Infection Research and Training, 856
National Institute of Justice's Graduate Research Fellowship Program, 199
National Library of Medicine Fellowship in Applied Informatics, 861
NRC Research Associate Programs (RAP), 840
NRC Research Associateship Programs (RAP), 840
Paralyzed Veterans of America Fellowships in Spinal Cord Injury Research, 945
Postdoctoral Fellowship in Translational Medicine, 956
Research Fellowship, 589
Winston Churchill Foundation Scholarships, 200

BIOMEDICINE

Any Country
Awards Supported by the San Antonio Nathan Shock Center, 1085
Basil Reeve DPhil Scholarship in Physical or Biomedical Sciences, 938
Biostatistics/Informatics Junior Faculty Award, 863
Diana Jacobs Kalman/AFAR Scholarships for Research in the Biology of Aging, 65
Elizabeth Jean Trotter Postgraduate Research Travelling Scholarship in Biomedical Sciences, 1444
Greenwall Fellowship in Bioethics, 839
Morgan E. Williams MRes Scholarship in Helminthology, 330
National Health and Medical Research Council Equipment Grants, 857
National Library of Medicine Postdoctoral Informatics Research Fellowships, 862
National Road Safety Authority Individual Postdoctoral Fellowships (F32), 860
NLM Research Grants in Biomedical Informatics and Data Science, 863
Pembroke College: The Bristol-Myers Squibb Graduate Studentship in the Biomedical Sciences, 1255
Research Fellowships, 1608
Translation Fund, 1610
The Wellcome Trust, 1334
African Nations
GREAT Scholarships-Egypt, 1286
GREAT Scholarships-Ghana, 1286
GREAT Scholarships-Kenya, 1287
Asian Countries
GREAT Scholarships-China, 1286
GREAT Scholarships-India, 1287
GREAT Scholarships–Indonesia, 1287
GREAT Scholarships–Malaysia, 1288
GREAT Scholarships–Pakistan, 1288
GREAT Scholarships–Thailand, 1288
Australia
Flinders and Nourish Ingredients Industry PhD Scholarship: Medical Biotechnology, Microbial Bioprocessing, 523
Middle East
Daniel Turnberg Travel Fellowships, 12
New Zealand
Flinders and Nourish Ingredients Industry PhD Scholarship: Medical Biotechnology, Microbial Bioprocessing, 523
United Kingdom
Daniel Turnberg Travel Fellowships, 12
Sir Henry Dale Fellowships, 1053
United States of America
Gilbert S. Omenn Fellowship, 839

DENTAL TECHNOLOGY

Australia
Winifred E. Preedy Postgraduate Bursary, 534

DENTISTRY AND STOMATOLOGY

Any Country
Army Medical Services, 1323
British Dental Association/Dentsply Student Support Fund, 244
Doctor TMA Pai PhD Scholarships for International Students at Manipal University, 783
Oral & Maxillofacial Surgery Section: UMAX Poster Prize for students, 1066
Oral & Maxillofacial Surgery Section: UMAX Poster Prize for trainers, 1066
Australia
National Health and Medical Research Council Medical and Dental Postgraduate Research Scholarships, 528
Winifred E. Preedy Postgraduate Bursary, 534
European Union
BMDST-RSM Student Elective Awards, 1057
Cardiff Institute of Tissue Engineering and Repair (CITER)–EPSRC Studentship, 324
Oceania
John and Janice King Bursary, 676
United Kingdom
BMDST-RSM Student Elective Awards, 1057
Cardiff Institute of Tissue Engineering and Repair (CITER)–EPSRC Studentship, 324
Oral & Maxillofacial Surgery Section: Short Paper Prize, 1065

FORENSIC MEDICINE AND DENTISTRY

Any Country
Clinical Forensic and Legal Medicine Section Poster Competition, 1058
Clinical Forensics and Legal Medicine: Postgraduate Poster Prize, 1058
Faculty of Science Scholarship for the PgCert in Fundamentals in Forensic Science, 1543
African Nations
GREAT Scholarships-Egypt, 1286
GREAT Scholarships-Ghana, 1286
GREAT Scholarships-Kenya, 1287
Asian Countries
GREAT Scholarships-China, 1286
GREAT Scholarships-India, 1287
GREAT Scholarships–Indonesia, 1287
GREAT Scholarships–Malaysia, 1288
GREAT Scholarships–Pakistan, 1288
GREAT Scholarships–Thailand, 1288

HEALTH ADMINISTRATION

Any Country
Albert W Dent Graduate Student Scholarship, 547
The Council of Scientific and Industrial Research/TWAS Fellowship for Postdoctoral Research, 1180
Foster G McGaw Graduate Student Scholarship, 547
The Gulf Research Program's Early-Career Research Fellowship, 1175
Master's Studentships in Humanities and Social Science, 1608
Program Administrator Award for Excellence, 1033
Research Fellowships, 1608
Research Fellowships in Humanities and Social Science, 1608
TWAS-COMSTECH Science in Exile PhD Fellowship Programme for Displaced and Refugee Scientists, 1180
Wellcome Discovery Awards, 1612
Wellcome Early-Career Awards, 1612
Wellcome Trust Master's Programme Award for the MSc Health History, 1554
Australia
Australian Rotary Health Indigenous Health Scholarship, 1563
Canada
Savoy Foundation Studentships, 1091

MEDICINE

Any Country
Adrian Tanner Prize, 1056
Advanced Postdoctoral Fellowships, 688
The Anne Rowling Clinic Regenerative Neurology Scholarships, 1302
Canadian Research Awards for Specialty Residents (Medicine, Surgery), 1032
Career Development Awards, 688
Career Development Bridge Funding Program, 441
Carl W Gottschalk Research Scholar Grant, 119
Chronic, Noncommunicable Diseases and Disorders Research Training (NCD-Lifespan), 535
Clinical Immunology & Allergy President's Prize, 1058
Cutlers' Surgical Prize, 1036
David Walsh Memorial Scholarship, 1416
Doctor TMA Pai PhD Scholarships for International Students at Manipal University, 783
Duke Cancer Institute/Duke Microbiome Center Joint Partnership Pilot Award, 442
Duke/NCCU Collaborative Translational Research Awards, 442
Education Research Grant, 1128
Ethicon Foundation Fund, 1036
Ethicon Foundation Fund Travelling Fellowship, 1021
Ethicon Travel Award, 1035

European Calcified Tissue Society/Servier Fellowship, 495
The Gulf Research Program's Early-Career Research Fellowship, 1175
HAPP MSc Scholarship in the History of Science, 1139
The Helena Anna Henzl-Gabor Young Women in Science Fund for Postdoctoral Scholars Travel Grant, 1149
Herdsman Fellowship in Medical Science, 1519
Hertford College: Vaughan Williams Senior Scholarship, 1463
Internal Studentships Past and Current Year, 799
International Medical Educator of the Year Award, 1032
International Resident Leadership Award, 1032
The Katharine McCormick Advanced Postdoctoral Scholar Fellowship to Support Women in Academic Medicine, 1150
Kristin Sivertz Resident Leadership Award, 1033
Lesley Shorne Memorial Scholarship, 527
Master's Awards, 1607
Medical and Graduate Student Preceptonship, 1000
Medical Research Council Career Development Award, 803
National Institute for Health and Care Excellence Scholarships, 858
Pain Medicine Section: Andrew Lawson Prize, 1068
Pain Medicine Section: Andrew Lawson Prize for Trainers, 1068
Palliative Care Section MSc/MA Research Prize, 1068
Physician Scientist Fellowship, 438
Radiology SA Scholarship, 531
Rebecca Davies Clinician Researcher Fellowship, 691
Research Training Grant, 1129
School of Medicine (SoM) Bridge Funding Program, 444
School of Medicine Dean's Postdoctoral Fellowship, 1149
Sir Ratanji Dalal Research Scholarship, 1035
Solomon Awards, 1138
The Stroke Association Research Project Grants, 1157
Surgery Section Norman Tanner Prize and Glaxo Travelling Fellowship, 1071
Venous Forum: Annual Meeting Prize, 1072
The Walter V. and Idun Berry Postdoctoral Fellowship Program, 1150

African Nations

African Association for Health Professions Education and Research, 535

Australia

AMA Queensland Foundation Medical Scholarships, 673
Australian Orthopaedic Association Joint University Scholarship, 674
National Health and Medical Research Council Medical and Dental Postgraduate Research Scholarships, 528
Neville and Di Bertalli Bush Placement Scholarship, 424
PhD Scholarship for Vascular and Metabolic Research, 529
Sir Arthur Sims Travelling Scholarship, 1399
UNE Indigenous Medical Scholarship, 1412

Canada

Duncan Graham Award for Outstanding Contribution to Medical Education, 1032
Royal College Dr. Thomas Dignan Indigenous Health Award, 1034
Stanford Postdoctoral Recruitment Initiative in Sciences and Medicine (PRISM), 1149
Wylie Scholar Program, 1593

European Countries

Critical Care Medicine Section: Audit and Quality Improvement Project Prize, 1059
Moynihan Travelling Fellowship, 148

European Union

BMDST-RSM Student Elective Awards, 1057

Middle East

Daniel Turnberg Travel Fellowships, 12

New Zealand

AMA Queensland Foundation Medical Scholarships, 673
Australian Orthopaedic Association Joint University Scholarship, 674
Neville and Di Bertalli Bush Placement Scholarship, 424
University of Otago Academic General Practitioner Registrar PhD Scholarship, 1450

North American Countries

Stanford Postdoctoral Recruitment Initiative in Sciences and Medicine (PRISM), 1149

Oceania

John and Janice King Bursary, 676

United Kingdom

BMDST-RSM Student Elective Awards, 1057
Catastrophes & Conflict Forum Medical Student Essay Prize, 1057
Critical Care Medicine Section: Audit and Quality Improvement Project Prize, 1059
Cutlers' Surgical Fellowship, 1036
Daniel Turnberg Travel Fellowships, 12
Moynihan Travelling Fellowship, 148
Ronald Raven Barbers, 1037

United States of America

American Head and Neck Society-American Cyronics Society Career Development Award, 74
Career Development Bridge Funding Award: K Bridge, 996
Career Development Bridge Funding Award: K Supplement, 996
Career Development Bridge Funding Award: R Bridge, 997
Career Development in Geriatric Medicine Award, 997
CBCF Louis Stokes Health Scholars Program, sponsored by United Health Foundation, 379
Dr. Marie E. Zakrzewski Medical Scholarship, 697
Foundation for Science and Disability Student Grant Fund, 546
Graduate Student Grant, 546
Lawren H. Daltroy Health Professional Preceptorship, 1000

MEDxColloquia, 443
MEDx Engineering, Environment, and Health 2022 Request for Proposals, 443
Post-Doctoral Training in Genomic Medicine Research, 444
Stanford Postdoctoral Recruitment Initiative in Sciences and Medicine (PRISM), 1149

CARDIOLOGY

Any Country
British Heart Foundation-Daphne Jackson Fellowships, 249
Career Re-entry Research Fellowships, 250
Clinical Research Leave Fellowships, 250
Clinical Study Grants, 250
Firkin PhD Scholarship, 167
Grants-in-Aid of Research and Development, 585
Heart Research United Kingdom Translational Research Project Grants, 586
Immediate Postdoctoral Basic Science Research Fellowships, 251
New Horizon Grants, 252
Non-Clinical PhD Studentships, 252
Novel and Emerging Technologies (NET) Grants, 587
PhD Studentship, 587
Scotland Grant, 587
Transthyretin Amyloidosis (ATTR) Competitive Grant Program/ASPIRE, 955
United Kingdom
Cardiology Section Presidents Prize, 1057
Josephine Lansdell Research Grant, 255

DERMATOLOGY

Any Country
Centre de Recherches et d'Investigations Epidermiques et Sensorielles Research Award, 344
Dermatology Clinicopathological Meetings, 1059
Dermatology Section: Hugh Wallace Essay Prize, 1059
Canada
Gary S. Gilkeson Career Development Award, 759
European Countries
Dermatology Section: Trainee Research Prize, 1059
United Kingdom
Dermatology Section: Trainee Research Prize, 1059
United States of America
Gary S. Gilkeson Career Development Award, 759

ENDOCRINOLOGY

Any Country
Career Support and Travel Grants, 690
Conference Grants, 688, 690
Early-Career Patient-Oriented Diabetes Research Awards, 689
EFSD/Lilly Young Investigator Research Award Programme, 494
European Association for the Study of Diabetes-ADA Transatlantic Fellowships, 494
Industry Discovery & Development Partnerships, 689
Pathway to Stop Diabetes Diabetes Initiator Award, 64
Strategic Research Agreement, 690
Australia
Connellan Airways Trust Diabetes Management and Education Scholarship, 522
JDRF PhD Top-up Scholarships 2024, 690
Mediserve Northern Territory Diabetes Management and Education Scholarship, 528
Canada
AHNS Endocrine Surgery Section Eisai Research Grant Policies, 71
AHNS Endocrine Surgery Section Stryker Research Grant Policies, 72
United States of America
AHNS Endocrine Surgery Section Eisai Research Grant Policies, 71
AHNS Endocrine Surgery Section Stryker Research Grant Policies, 72

EPIDEMIOLOGY

Any Country
Ecology and Evolution of Infectious Diseases Initiative (EEID), 539
Epidemiology & Public Health Young Epidemiologists Prize, 1061
Pfizer Scholar, 953
St Cross MSc Scholarship in Global Health Science and Epidemiology, 1141
United Kingdom
Reducing Global Health Non-communicable Disease Risk for Young People, 806

GASTROENTEROLOGY

Any Country
AACR-Debbie's Dream Foundation Career Development Award for Gastric Cancer Research, 3
AGA-Moti L. & Kamla Rustgi International Travel Awards, 543
American Gastroenterological Association-Elsevier Pilot Research Award, 543
American Gastroenterological Association Fellowship to Faculty Transition Awards, 543
American Gastroenterological Association Research Scholar Awards, 544
Anastomotic Leak Grant, Special Limited Project Grant, 114
Coloproctology John of Arderne Medal, 1059

Crohn's & Coltis Foundation Career Development Award, 396
European Crohn's and Colitis Organisation Fellowship, 498
Gastroenterology & Hepatology Section: Gut Club Prize, 1061
General Surgery Resident Research Initiation Grant, 115
International Spinal Research Trust, 1138
Limited Project Grant (LPG), 6
Lustgarten Foundation-AACR Career Development Award for Pancreatic Cancer Research, in Honor of John Robert Lewis, 5
Lustgarten Foundation-AACR Career Development Award for Pancreatic Cancer Research, in honor of Ruth Bader Ginsburg, 6
Medical Student Research Initiation Grant, 116
Research in Robotic Surgical Technology Grant, 116
Training in Research Methodology Grant, 116
Australia
Investigation of the Human Intestinal Nervous System, 526
Canada
Career Development Award, 114
International Fellowship Grant, 115
North American Countries
AGA Abstract Award for Health Disparities Research, 541
AGA-APFED Abstract Award in Eosinophilic GI Diseases, 542
AGA Fellow Abstract Award, 541
AGA Student Abstract Award, 542
American Gastroenterological Association/American Gastroenterological Association-Eli & Edythe Broad Student Research Fellowship(s), 545
American Gastroenterological Association R Robert and Sally D Funderburg Research Scholar Award in Gastric Cancer, 544
United States of America
Career Development Award, 114
Core Fellowships and Grants, 385
International Fellowship Grant, 115

GERIATRICS

Any Country
Alzheimer's Association Clinician Scientist Fellowship (AACSF) Program, 25
Alzheimer's Association Clinician Scientist Fellowship to Promote Diversity (AACSF-D), 26
Alzheimer's Association Leveraging Model & Data Resources to Advance Alzheimer's and Dementia Discovery Program (ALZ Discovery Grant Program), 26
Alzheimer's Association Research Fellowship to Promote Diversity (AARF-D), 27
Alzheimer's Association Research Grant (AARG), 27
Alzheimer's Association Research Grant-New to the Field (AARG-NTF), 28
Alzheimer's Association Research Grant to Promote Diversity (AARG-D), 28
Alzheimer's Association Research Grant to Promote Diversity-New to the Field (AARG-D-NTF), 29
American Federation for Aging Research/Pfizer Research Grants in Metabolic Control and Late Life Diseases, 65
American Federation for Aging Research Research Grants for Junior Faculty, 65
Diana Jacobs Kalman/AFAR Scholarships for Research in the Biology of Aging, 65
Duke Aging Center–Busse Research Awards, 442
Geriatrics & Gerontology Section: Clinical Audit and Governance Prize, 1062
Geriatrics & Gerontology Section: President's Essay Prize for Students, 1062
Geriatrics & Gerontology Section: President's Essay Prize for Trainers, 1062
Geriatrics & Gerontology Section: Trainees' Prize, Clinical Presentations, 1062
Geriatrics & Gerontology Section: Trainees' Prize, Clinical Presentations for Trainers, 1062
Glenn Foundation for Medical Research Postdoctoral Fellowships in Aging Research, 66
New Connections: Increasing Diversity, 29
The Paul Beeson Career Development Awards in Aging Research for the Island of Ireland, 66
Pilot Grants, 393
The Sagol Network GerOmic Award for Junior Faculty Eligibility Criteria, 66
Sex and Gender in Alzheimer's (SAGA 23) Award Program, 30
The Zenith Fellows Award Program (Zenith), 31
Australia
Association of American Railroads Janssen Cilag Dementia Research Grant, 31
Association of American Railroads Rosemary Foundation Travel Project Grant-Dementia Research, 32
Cheryl Ann Keatley Scholarship, 521
Rosemary Foundation Travel Grant, 32
New Zealand
Hope Selwyn Foundation Scholarship, 1228
Rosemary Foundation Travel Grant, 32
United Kingdom
James Mellon DPhil Scholarship in Longevity Research, 939

GYNAECOLOGY AND OBSTETRICS

Any Country
Bernhard Baron Travelling Fellowship, 1019
Biomedical Catalyst: Developmental Pathway Funding Scheme (DPFS), 801

Eden Travelling Fellowship in Obstetrics and Gynaecology, 1019
Edgar Gentilli Prize, 1019
Ethicon Student Elective Award, 1021
Florence and William Blair Bell Research Fellowship, 1021
Green-Armytage and Spackman Travelling Scholarship, 1022
Health and Population Innovation Fellowship Program, 960
John Lawson Prize, 1022
Malcolm Black Travel Fellowship, 1023
Obstetrics & Gynaecology Section: Dame Josephine Barnes Award, 1064
Obstetrics & Gynaecology Section: Herbert Reiss Trainees' Prize, 1064
Overseas Fund, 1023
Professor Geoffrey Chamberlain Award, 1024
Royal College of Obstetricians and Gynaecologists Edgar Research Fellowship, 1024
Royal College of Obstetricians and Gynaecologists Research Training Fellowships, 1025
Royal College of Obstetricians and Gynaecologists WellBeing Grants, 1025
Sims Black Travelling Proffesorship, 1025
University of Otago Postgraduate Scholarship in Obstetrics and Gynaecology, 1453
William Blair Bell Memorial Lecture, 1026
Canada
Rural Maternity Care Doctoral Student Fellowship, 1074
European Countries
American Gynecological Club/Gynaecological Visiting Society Fellowship, 71
Endometriosis Millenium Fund, 1020
Herbert Erik Reiss Memorial Case History Prize, 1022
Kolkata Eden Hospital Annual Prize, 1023
Peter Huntingford Memorial Prize, 1024
Tim Chard Case History Prize, 1026
Women's Visiting Gynaecological Club Prize, 1027
United Kingdom
Action Medical Research Project Grants, 15
Action Medical Research Training Fellowship, 15
American Gynecological Club/Gynaecological Visiting Society Fellowship, 71
Annual Academic Award, 1018
Elizabeth Garrett Anderson Hospital Charity Travelling Fellowship in Memory of Anne Boutwood, 1020
Endometriosis Millenium Fund, 1020
Herbert Erik Reiss Memorial Case History Prize, 1022
Kolkata Eden Hospital Annual Prize, 1023
Maternity & the Newborn Forum: Basil Lee Bursary for Innovation in Communication, 1063
Maternity & the Newborn Forum: Wendy Savage Bursary, 1064
Peter Huntingford Memorial Prize, 1024
Target Ovarian Cancer Essay Prize, 1025
Women's Visiting Gynaecological Club Prize, 1027
United States of America
American Gynecological Club/Gynaecological Visiting Society Fellowship, 71
National Early Detection of Ovarian Cancer Research Awards 2020, 817

HAEMATOLOGY

Any Country
Canadian Blood Services Graduate Fellowship Program, 278
Fanconi Anemia Research Fund Award, 508
RUNX1 Early Career Investigator Grants, 24
Canada
ASH Scholar Award, 117
BloodTechNet Award Program, 277
Canadian Blood Services Graduate Fellowship Program, 278
Elianna Saidenberg Transfusion Medicine Traineeship Award, 278
Postdoctoral Fellowship Program, 279
United States of America
ASH Scholar Award, 117

HEPATHOLOGY

Any Country
American Gastroenterological Association Research Scholar Awards, 544
Gastroenterology & Hepatology Section: Gut Club Prize, 1061

NEPHROLOGY

Any Country
Allied Health Professional Fellowship (Clinical), 695
International Society of Nephrology Fellowship Awards, 664
International Society of Nephrology Travel Grants, 664
International Society of Nephrology Visiting Scholars Program, 665
Nephrology Section Rosemarie Baillod Clinical Award, 1064
Canada
Gary S. Gilkeson Career Development Award, 759
United States of America
Gary S. Gilkeson Career Development Award, 759

NEUROLOGY

Any Country
AACR-Sontag Foundation Brain Cancer Research Fellowship, 5
AANS International Visiting Surgeon Fellowship, 47
A. B. Baker Award for Lifetime Achievement in Neurologic Education, 36

Alzheimer's Association Clinician Scientist Fellowship (AACSF) Program, 25
Alzheimer's Association Clinician Scientist Fellowship to Promote Diversity (AACSF-D), 26
Alzheimer's Association Leveraging Model & Data Resources to Advance Alzheimer's and Dementia Discovery Program (ALZ Discovery Grant Program), 26
Alzheimer's Association Research Fellowship to Promote Diversity (AARF-D), 27
Alzheimer's Association Research Grant (AARG), 27
Alzheimer's Association Research Grant-New to the Field (AARG-NTF), 28
Alzheimer's Association Research Grant to Promote Diversity (AARG-D), 28
Alzheimer's Association Research Grant to Promote Diversity-New to the Field (AARG-D-NTF), 29
Ataxia United Kingdom PhD Studentship, 152
Ataxia United Kingdom Research Grant, 152
Cerebrovascular Traveling Fellowship, 883
Clinical Neurosciences Gordon Holmes Prize, 1058
Clinical Neurosciences President's Prize, 1058
The CURE Epilepsy Award, 364
CV Section/CNS Foundation Young Investigator Research Grant, 884
Directed Residency Scholarships, 884
Dr. George C. Cotzias Memorial Fellowship, 92
Graduate School of Brain Science Special Scholarship, 440
Morton Cure Paralysis Fund Research Grant, 826
Motor Neurone Disease Association Non-Clinical Fellowship Awards, 826
Motor Neurone Disease Association Research Project Grants, 827
Multiple Sclerosis Society of Canada Donald Paty Career Development Award, 829
Multiple Sclerosis Society of Canada Postdoctoral Fellowship Award, 829
Neilsen SCIRTS Postdoctoral Fellowship Grants, 391
New Connections: Increasing Diversity, 29
NREF Clinical Fellowship Grant, 884
NREF Research Fellowship Grant, 885
NREF Young Clinician Investigator Award, 885
Postdoctoral Fellowship Awards, 679
Postdoctoral Fellowships, 393
Research Grants, 93
Ruth K. Broad Biomedical Research Foundation-Ellen Luken Student Awards, 444
Sex and Gender in Alzheimer's (SAGA 23) Award Program, 30
Studies and Demonstration Projects, 393
Studying Post-translational Protein Modifications in Brain Function and Disease-International, 780
Transthyretin Amyloidosis (ATTR) Competitive Grant Program/ASPIRE, 955
The Zenith Fellows Award Program (Zenith), 31

Australia

Association of American Railroads Janssen Cilag Dementia Research Grant, 31
Association of American Railroads Rosemary Foundation Travel Project Grant-Dementia Research, 32
Investigation of the Human Intestinal Nervous System, 526
The Jack Loader Top-Up Scholarship, 533
Project Specific Scholarship-Investigating Neuron-glia Interactions in MND/ALS, 778
Rosemary Foundation Travel Grant, 32
Studying Post-translational Protein Modifications in Brain Function and Disease-Domestic, 780

Canada

SCIRTS Pilot Research Grants, 392

European Countries

Motor Neurone Disease Association PhD Studentship Award, 827

New Zealand

Helen Rosa Thacker Scholarship in Neurological Research, 1445
Rosemary Foundation Travel Grant, 32

North American Countries

Neurosurgery Research and Education Foundation Research Fellowship, 47
William P Van Wagenen Fellowship, 48

United Kingdom

MND Pre-Fellowship Scheme, 826
Motor Neurone Disease Association PhD Studentship Award, 827
Parkinson's UK drug accelerator grant, 948
Parkinson's UK non-drug approaches grant, 948
Parkinson's UK project grant, 948

United States of America

SCIRTS Pilot Research Grants, 392
Taking Flight Award, 364

ONCOLOGY

Any Country

AACR-Bayer Stimulating Therapeutic Advances through Research Training (START) Grants, 2
AACR Cancer Disparities Research Fellowships, 1
AACR-Debbie's Dream Foundation Career Development Award for Gastric Cancer Research, 3
AACR NextGen Grants for Transformative Cancer Research, 2
AACR-Novocure Career Development Awards for Tumor Treating Fields Research, 3
AACR-Novocure Tumor Treating Fields Research Grants, 4
AACR-Sontag Foundation Brain Cancer Research Fellowship, 5
Alice Ettinger Distinguished Achievement Award, 43

American Association for Cancer Research Anna D. Barker Basic Cancer Research Fellowship, 38
American Association for Cancer Research-AstraZeneca Stimulating Therapeutic Advancements through Research Training (START) Grants, 40
American Association for Cancer Research Career Development Awards, 39
American Association for Cancer Research Gertrude B. Elion Cancer Research Award, 39
American Association for Cancer Research NextGen Grants for Transformative Cancer Research, 40
Ann and Sol Schreiber Mentored Investigator Award, 942
The Bosarge Family Foundation-Waun Ki Hong Scholar Award for Regenerative Cancer Medicine, 6
Breast Cancer Research Foundation-AACR Career Development Awards to Promote Diversity and Inclusion, 5
The Cancer Council NSW Research Project Grants, 296
Cancer Council Tasmania Honours Scholarship, 1573
Cancer Research Institute Irvington Postdoctoral Fellowship Program, 308
Career Development Program-Fellow, 723
Career Development Program-Special Fellow, 723
Clinical and Laboratory Integration Program, 309
Clinical Innovator, 309
Clinical Trial Award, 313
Doctoral Scholarships, 920
Edgar Gentilli Prize, 1019
European Society of Surgical Oncology Training Fellowships, 500
Immuno-Informatics Postdoctoral Fellowship, 309
Individual Investigator Research Awards (IIRA), 301
Individual Investigator Research Awards for Cancer in Children and Adolescents (IIRACCA), 301
Individual Investigator Research Awards for Clinical Translation (IIRACT), 302
Individual Investigator Research Awards for Computational Systems Biology of Cancer (IIRACSBC), 303
LCRF Research Grant on Disparities in Lung Cancer, 759
Leukaemia Foundation PhD Scholarships, 722
Leukaemia Foundation Postdoctoral Fellowship, 722
Leukemia Research Foundation New Investigator Research Grant, 724
Lustgarten Foundation-AACR Career Development Award for Pancreatic Cancer Research, in Honor of John Robert Lewis, 5
Lustgarten Foundation-AACR Career Development Award for Pancreatic Cancer Research, in honor of Ruth Bader Ginsburg, 6
Master's Scholarships, 920
Melville Trust for Care and Cure of Cancer Research Fellowships, 808
Melville Trust for Care and Cure of Cancer Research Grants, 808
National Cancer Institute Immunotherapy Fellowship, 298
North West Cancer Research Fund Research Project Grants, 908
Nuffield Department of Clinical Medicine: LICR Studentship (Ludwig Institute for Cancer Research), 1478
NWCR & Tenovus PhD Studentship Award, 909
Oncology Doctoral Scholarships, 920
Oncology Nursing Society Breast Cancer Research Grant, 921
Oncology Nursing Society Foundation Research Grant Awards, 921
Oncology Research Grant, 921
Oncology Section Sylvia Lawler Prize, 1065
Pfizer Scholar, 953
Postdoctoral Fellowships for Training in Cancer Research, 650
Postgraduate Tassell Scholarship in Cancer Research, 1447
POST Program Grants, 23
Prostate Cancer Research Centre-NSW, 163
QuadW Foundation-AACR Fellowship for Clinical/Translational Sarcoma Research, 41
Rex Elliot Wegener Memorial Fund for Mesothelioma Research, 533
RUNX1 Early Career Investigator Grants, 24
Sally Crossing AM Award, 296
Sandy Purl Mentorship Scholarship, 922
Senior Cancer Research Fellowship, 316
SITC-Bristol Myers Squibb Postdoctoral Cancer Immunotherapy Translational Fellowship, 298
SITC-Merck Cancer Immunotherapy Clinical Fellowship, 298
SITC-Nektar Therapeutics Equity and Inclusion in Cancer Immunotherapy Fellowship, 299
Society for Immunotherapy of Cancer-Amgen Cancer Immunotherapy in Hematologic Malignancies Fellowship Award, 299
Strong Arm of Georgia Scholarship, 723
Technology Impact Award, 310
Therapeutic Catalyst, 316
Australia
Cancer Council's Beat Cancer Project, 297
FMC Foundation Pink Ribbon Ball Committee Breast Cancer Research Scholarship, 524
Margaret Fay Fuller Scholarship: Margaret Fay Fuller PhD top up Scholarship, 527
National Breast Cancer Foundation Doctoral Scholarship, 850
PhD Scholarships, 297
Pilot Study Grants, 850
East European Countries
Union for International Cancer Control International Oncology Nursing Fellowships (IDNF), 284

European Countries
European Society of Surgical Oncology Training Fellowships, 500
Union for International Cancer Control International Oncology Nursing Fellowships (IDNF), 284
European Union
Radiation Oncology & Biology: Departmental Studentships, 1500
North American Countries
American Gastroenterological Association R Robert and Sally D Funderburg Research Scholar Award in Gastric Cancer, 544
United Kingdom
Action Cancer Project Grant, 15
Biology to Prevention Award, 311
Cancer Immunology Project Awards, 312
Multidisciplinary Project Award, 315
Target Ovarian Cancer Essay Prize, 1025
Tim Chard Case History Prize, 1026
United States of America
Cancer Screening and Early Detection, 300
Clinical and Laboratory Integration Program, 309
Colorectal Cancer Screening Coordinating Center, 300
Dissemination of CPRIT-Funded Cancer Control Interventions, 300
Immuno-Informatics Postdoctoral Fellowship, 309
Individual Investigator Research Awards for Prevention and Early Detection (IIRAP), 303
LCRF Research Grant on Disparities in Lung Cancer, 759
The Mesothelioma Cancer Alliance Scholarship, 723
National Cancer Institute Immunotherapy Fellowship, 298
National Early Detection of Ovarian Cancer Research Awards 2020, 817
Recruitment of Established Investigators, 303
Recruitment of First-Time, Tenure-Track Faculty Members, 304
Research Training Awards (RTA), 304
SITC-Genentech Women in Cancer Immunotherapy Fellowship, 298
Texas Regional Excellence in Cancer Award, 306
TREC: Major Instrumentation Award, 307

OPHTHALMOLOGY

Any Country
Canadian National Institute for the Blind Winston Gordon Award, 292
Cardiff School of Optometry and Vision Sciences–PhD Studentship, 326
CEHC Masters Scholarships in Public Health for Eye Care, 373
Chanchlani Global Vision Research Award, 292
The E. (Ben) & Mary Hochhausen Access Technology Research Award, 293
Fight for Sight, 518
2023–24 Lieutenant Colonel Henry Kirkpatrick Scholarship, 745
Ophthalmology Section Travelling Fellowships, 1065
PhD Studentships, 519
Royal College of Ophthalmologists-Bayer Research Award, 1029
Australia
National Health and Medical Research Council Centre of Clinical Eye Research: PhD Scholarships, 528
Canada
Canadian National Institute for the Blind Baker Applied Research Fund, 291
Canadian National Institute for the Blind Baker Fellowship Fund, 291
Canadian National Institute for the Blind Baker New Researcher Fund, 291
CNIB Barbara Tuck MacPhee Award, 292
Gretzky Scholarship Foundation for the Blind Youth of Canada, 293
Ross Purse Doctoral Fellowship, 293
European Countries
Glaucoma UK and The Royal College of Ophthalmologists Research Award, 1028
Patrick Trevor-Roper Undergraduate Award, 1029
New Zealand
The Dr Stella Cullington Postgraduate Scholarship in Ophthalmology, 1449
Susan Barnes Memorial Scholarship, 322
United Kingdom
Bayer Educational Grant Awards, 1027
Essay Prize for Foundation Doctors, 1027
Glaucoma UK and The Royal College of Ophthalmologists Research Award, 1028
Keeler Scholarship, 1028
National Health Service Education for Scotland Primary Care Ophthalmology Scholarship, 1300
Nettleship Medal, 1028
Patrick Trevor-Roper Undergraduate Award, 1029
Sir William Lister/Dorey Bequest, 1114
The Ulverscroft David Owen Award, 1029

OTORHINOLARYNGOLOGY

Any Country
AHRF Discovery Grants, 74
American Academy of Otolaryngology-Head and Neck Surgery Translational Innovator Award, 72
American Head and Neck Society Endocrine Research Grant, 73

American Head and Neck Society Pilot Research Grant, 73
American Head and Neck Society Surgeon Scientist Career Development Award (with AAOHNS), 73
Laryngology & Rhinology Travel and Equipment Grants, 1063
Otology Section: Matthew Yung Short Paper and Poster Prize, 1067
Otology Section: Training Scholarships, 1067
Australia
Ember Venning Postgraduate Research Scholarship in Speech Pathology and Audiology, 523
Canada
American Otological Society Research Training Fellowships, 92
European Countries
Laryngology & Rhinology Section: Rhinology Essay Prize, 1063
Laryngology & Rhinology Section: Short Paper and Poster Prize, 1063
United Kingdom
Laryngology & Rhinology Section: Rhinology Essay Prize, 1063
Laryngology & Rhinology Section: Short Paper and Poster Prize, 1063
Otology Section Norman Gamble Grant, 1067
United States of America
American Head and Neck Society Young Investigator Award (with AAOHNS), 73
American Otological Society Research Training Fellowships, 92
Bernard & Lottie Drazin Memorial Grants, 75
Meniere's Disease Grant, 75

PAEDIATRICS

Any Country
AACAP Pilot Research Award for Attention Disorders, 33
AACAP Pilot Research Award for Early Career Faculty and Child and Adolescent Psychiatry Fellows, 34
AACAP Pilot Research Award for Learning Disabilities, 34
Advocacy Training Grants, 36
European Young Investigator Award, 433
Paediatrics & Child Health Section: Overseas Bursary, 1067
Paediatrics & Child Health Section: President's Prize for Students, 1068
Paediatrics & Child Health Section: President's Prize for Trainers, 1068
Paediatrics & Child Health Section Trainees Tim David Prize, 1067
Pilot Research Award for General Psychiatry Residents, 35
POST Program Grants, 23
Canada
American Academy of Pediatrics Resident Research Grants, 37
United Kingdom
Action Medical Research Project Grants, 15
Action Medical Research Training Fellowship, 15
United States of America
American Academy of Pediatrics Resident Research Grants, 37
Novice Research Awards, 564

PATHOLOGY

Any Country
Awards Supported by the San Antonio Nathan Shock Center, 1085
Gillson Scholarship in Pathology, 1132
Polycystic Kidney Disease Foundation Grant-In-Aid, 960
Student Research Fund, 146
Australia
Dr Rosamond Siemon Postgraduate Renal Research Scholarship, 1519

PLASTIC SURGERY

Any Country
Fellowship Travelling Bursary, 241
Student Bursaries, 241
United Kingdom
British Association of Plastic Reconstructive and Aesthetic Surgeons European Travelling Scholarships, 240

PNEUMOLOGY

Any Country
CHEST Foundation Grants, 62
Respiratory Medicine Section: Foundation Year and Internal Medicine Trainee Award, 1069
Respiratory Medicine Section: Respiratory Specialist Registrar Award, 1070
Rex Elliot Wegener Memorial Fund for Mesothelioma Research, 533
United Kingdom
Respiratory Medicine Section: Student Award, 1070
United States of America
Lung Health (LH) Research Dissertation Grants, 84

PSYCHIATRY AND MENTAL HEALTH

Any Country
AACAP Pilot Research Award for Attention Disorders, 33
AACAP Pilot Research Award for Early Career Faculty and Child and Adolescent Psychiatry Fellows, 34
AACAP Pilot Research Award for Learning Disabilities, 34

The AACAP Rieger Psychodynamic Psychotherapy Award, 36
Alzheimer's Association Clinician Scientist Fellowship (AACSF) Program, 25
Alzheimer's Association Clinician Scientist Fellowship to Promote Diversity (AACSF-D), 26
Alzheimer's Association Leveraging Model & Data Resources to Advance Alzheimer's and Dementia Discovery Program (ALZ Discovery Grant Program), 26
Alzheimer's Association Research Fellowship to Promote Diversity (AARF-D), 27
Alzheimer's Association Research Grant (AARG), 27
Alzheimer's Association Research Grant-New to the Field (AARG-NTF), 28
Alzheimer's Association Research Grant to Promote Diversity (AARG-D), 28
Alzheimer's Association Research Grant to Promote Diversity-New to the Field (AARG-D-NTF), 29
American Foundation for Suicide Prevention Distinguished Investigator Awards, 67
Applied Research Competition, 927
Blue Sky Focus Grant, 67
Distinguished Investigator Grant, 68
Linked Standard Research Grant, 68
MQ Fellows Awards 2023, 828
New Connections: Increasing Diversity, 29
Pilot Innovation Grants, 68
Pilot Research Award for General Psychiatry Residents, 35
Postdoctoral Fellowship, 69, 180
Psychiatry Section Mental Health Foundation Research Prize, 1069
Sex and Gender in Alzheimer's (SAGA 23) Award Program, 30
Short-Term Risk Focus Grant, 69
Standard Research Grant, 69
The Zenith Fellows Award Program (Zenith), 31

Australia

Aboriginal Social and Emotional Wellbeing Scholarship, 1046
Association of American Railroads Janssen Cilag Dementia Research Grant, 31
Association of American Railroads Rosemary Foundation Travel Project Grant-Dementia Research, 32
Australian Rotary Health PhD Scholarships–Post Traumatic Stress Disorder (PTSD), 1217
The Jack Loader Top-Up Scholarship, 533
Professor Ross Kalucy Indigenous Well-Being Scholarship, 531
Rosemary Foundation Travel Grant, 32

Canada

Autism Scholars Award, 1074

New Zealand

Rosemary Foundation Travel Grant, 32

United States of America

Arc of the United States Research Grant, 127
Harriet Hale Woolley Scholarship, 536
National Board for Certified Counselors Minority Fellowship Program for Mental Health Counselors, 1073

RHEUMATOLOGY

Any Country

American College of Rheumatology/REF Arthritis Investigator Award, 995
American College of Rheumatology REF Rheumatology Scientist Development Award, 995
Amgen Fellowship Training Award, 995
Clinical Research Fellowships, 133
Fellowship Training Award for Workforce Expansion, 998
Innovative Research Award, 999
Innovative Research Award for Community Practitioners, 999
Mentored Nurse Practitioner/Physician Assistant Award for Workforce Expansion, 1001
Nuffield Department of Orthopaedics, Rheumatology and Musculoskeletal Sciences: Kennedy Trust Prize Studentships, 1478
Orthopaedics Section FOSC (Future Orthopaedic Surgeons Conference) Prize for Research for Students, 1066
Orthopaedics Section FOSC (Future Orthopaedic Surgeons Conference) Prize for Research for Trainers, 1066
Orthopaedics Section: President's Prize, 1067
Orthopaedics Section President's Prize Papers, 1066
Paula de Merieux Fellowship Training Award, 1001
Rheumatology & Rehabilitation Section: Barbara Ansell Prize, 1070
Rheumatology & Rehabilitation Section: Eric Bywaters Prize, 1070
Royal National Orthopaedic Hospital Special Trustees Research Training Scholarship, 1208
Training Graduate PhD Salary Award (TGP), 810

Canada

Gary S. Gilkeson Career Development Award, 759

New Zealand

Henry Kelsey Scholarship, 1275

United States of America

American College of Rheumatology/REF Arthritis Investigator Award, 998
Friedenberg Mentored Clinician Scientist Grant, 941
Gary S. Gilkeson Career Development Award, 759
Grants Programs, 941
Health Professional Online Education Grant, 999
Rheumatology Future Physician Scientist Award, 1002
Scientist Development Award, 1002

TROPICAL MEDICINE

Any Country

Senior Fellowships in Public Health and Tropical Medicine, 1609

Training Fellowships in Public Health and Tropical Medicine, 1610

African Nations

American University of Beirut Mediterranean Scholarships, 120

Asian Countries

American University of Beirut Mediterranean Scholarships, 120

UROLOGY

Any Country

National Institute of Diabetes and Digestive and Kidney Diseases (NIDDK)/AFUD Intramural Urology Research Training Program, 70

Prostate Cancer Research Centre-NSW, 163

Research Scholar Awards, 121

Urology, 1071

Urology Professor Geoffrey D Chisholm CBE Communication Prize, 1071

Urology Section Professor John Blandy Essay Prize for Medical Students, 1072

Urology Section: Secretary's Prize, 1072

United Kingdom

Urology Section: Malcolm Coptcoat Spring Short Papers Prize, 1072

Urology Section Winter Short Papers Prize (Clinical Uro-Radiological Meeting), 1072

MIDWIFERY

Any Country

Royal College of Midwives Annual Midwifery Awards, 1017

Ruth Davies Research Bursary, 1017

Australia

Betty Josephine Fyffe Rural Allied Health, Nursing and Midwifery Scholarship, 1429

NURSING

Any Country

AACN Impact Research Grant, 43

AACN-Sigma Theta Tau Critical Care Grant, 44

Agilent Technologies-AACN Critical-Care Nursing Research Grant, 44

Agilent Technology Critical Care Nursing Research Grant, 21

Association of Perioperative Registered Nurses Scholarship Program, 148

Doctoral Scholarships, 920

Education Grants, 1018

The Fulbright-Edinburgh Napier University Scholar Award, 469

Heart and Stroke Foundation of Canada New Investigator Research Scholarships, 586

H 15 GRANT: Early Career Research Grant, 42

H-21 Grant: Established Scholar Research Grant, 42

H 31 Grant: Pre-Doctoral Research Grant, 42

Master's Scholarships, 920

National Institute for Health and Care Excellence Scholarships, 858

Oncology Doctoral Scholarships, 920

Oncology Nursing Society Breast Cancer Research Grant, 921

Oncology Nursing Society Foundation Research Grant Awards, 921

Oncology Research Grant, 921

Sandy Purl Mentorship Scholarship, 922

Sigma Theta Tau International/Association of Operating Room Nurses Foundation Grant, 1110

Sigma Theta Tau International/Association of Perioperative Registered Nurses Foundation Grant, 1111

Sigma Theta Tau International/Rehabilitation Nursing Foundation Grant, 1111

Ted Adams Trust Nursing Scholarship, 1557

African Nations

African Association for Health Professions Education and Research, 535

GREAT Scholarships-Egypt, 1286

GREAT Scholarships-Ghana, 1286

GREAT Scholarships-Kenya, 1287

Asian Countries

Chevening Partner Scholarship scheme, 228

GREAT Scholarships-China, 1286

GREAT Scholarships-India, 1287

GREAT Scholarships–Indonesia, 1287

GREAT Scholarships–Malaysia, 1288

GREAT Scholarships–Pakistan, 1288

GREAT Scholarships–Thailand, 1288

Australia

Aboriginal Social and Emotional Wellbeing Scholarship, 1046

Anthea Jane Wilson Scholarship, 419

Betty Josephine Fyffe Rural Allied Health, Nursing and Midwifery Scholarship, 1429

Cheryl Ann Keatley Scholarship, 521

Repatriation General Hospital Department of Rehabilitation and Aged Care: Nursing Research Scholarship, 532

Middle East

Chevening Partner Scholarship scheme, 228

New Zealand

Anthea Jane Wilson Scholarship, 419

Repatriation General Hospital Department of Rehabilitation and Aged Care: Nursing Research Scholarship, 532
United Kingdom
Lincoln Alumni MSc School of Health and Social Care Scholarship, 1349
Mary Seacole Leadership and Development Awards, 1018
Queen's Nursing Institute Fund for Innovation and Leadership, 970
United States of America
Harry & Lula McCarn Nurses Scholarship, 1171
Nursing Scholarships, 1005

OPTOMETRY

New Zealand
HC Russell Memorial Postgraduate Scholarship, 1227

PHARMACY

Any Country
Army Medical Services, 1323
Call for Nominations for Urdang Medal and Kremers Award, 122
Doctor TMA Pai PhD Scholarships for International Students at Manipal University, 783
National Institute for Health and Care Excellence Scholarships, 858
Australia
Betty Josephine Fyffe Rural Allied Health, Nursing and Midwifery Scholarship, 1429
The Duncan Family Scholarship in Pharmacy, 1411
European Countries
Linacre College: Mary Blaschko Graduate Scholarship, 1471
United Kingdom
Develop New Approaches to Small Molecule Medicine, 802

PUBLIC HEALTH AND HYGIENE

Any Country
Applied Programme Grants (APRO) 2023, 582
Bupa Foundation Medical Research Grant for Health at Work, 268
Bupa Foundation Medical Research Grant for Information and Communication, 268
Colt Foundation Fellowships in Occupational/Environmental Health, 1324
Drake Lewis Graduate Scholarship for Health and Human Sciences, 1306
Epidemiology & Public Health Young Epidemiologists Prize, 1061
Ethnic Minority Foundation Grants, 493
Faculty PhD Scholarships, 319
General Practice with Primary Healthcare John Fry Prize, 1061
Growth Hormone Research, 953
Harvard Travellers Club Permanent Fund, 581
HRB Postdoctoral Fellowships-Applying Research into Policy and Practice (ARPP) 2023, 583
HRB Postdoctoral Fellowships-Clinician Scientist Fellowships (CSF) 2023, 583
2023-24 LSHTM Fund Scholarship, 746
National Health and Medical Research Council Public Health Travelling Fellowships, 857
National Institute for Health and Care Excellence Scholarships, 858
Nuffield Department of Population Health: NDPH Scholarship, 1479
Patient-Centered Outcomes Challenge Award, 956
Research Leaders Awards, 584
SAAFE Program, 482
Senior Fellowships in Public Health and Tropical Medicine, 1609
Student Research Scholarship in Occupational Hygiene, 873
Three-year Fully Funded PhD Scholarship in Public Health, 401
Training Fellowships in Public Health and Tropical Medicine, 1610
African Nations
Chevening Partner Scholarship scheme, 228
2023–24 GSK Scholarships for Future Health Leaders, 745
Jeroen Ensink Memorial Fund Scholarship, 747
University of Cape Town Masters Scholarships in Public Health, 1281
Asian Countries
Chevening Partner Scholarship scheme, 228
Fulbright-Nehru Doctoral Research Fellowships, 1195
Fulbright-Nehru Master's Fellowships, 1195
Fulbright-Nehru Postdoctoral Research Fellowships, 1195
Jeroen Ensink Memorial Fund Scholarship, 747
2023–24 Kuberbhai Shivabhai Desai Trust Scholarship, 745
Australia
National Health and Medical Research Council Public Health Postgraduate Scholarships, 529
Professor Ross Kalucy Indigenous Well-Being Scholarship, 531
R Douglas Wright Awards, 857
Tom and Dorothy Cook Scholarships in Public Health and Tropical Medicine, 678
Canada
Competitive Research, 626
Institut de Recherche Robert-Sauvéen Santéet en Sécurité du Travail Graduate Studies Scholarship and Postdoctoral Fellowship Program, 626
United Kingdom
Excellence in Diversity PhD Scholarships, 317
Helen H Lawson Research Grant, 255

DIETETICS

Australia

Betty Josephine Fyffe Rural Allied Health, Nursing and Midwifery Scholarship, 1429

SPORTS MEDICINE

Any Country

Sports Physiology Postgraduate Scholarship-Fatigue and Recovery, 178

Australia

Adolescent Health and Performance Scholarship, 164

Sports Medicine Fellowship Program, 178

United Kingdom

Sport, Exercise and Health Sciences Alumni Bursary, 757

RADIOLOGY

Any Country

Alice Ettinger Distinguished Achievement Award, 43

Derek Harwood-Nash International Education Scholar Grant, 978

Education Project Award, 978

Lucy Frank Squire Distinguished Resident Award in Diagnostic Radiology, 43

Radiological Society of North America Education Seed Grant, 979

Radiological Society of North America Research Resident/Fellow Program, 981

Radiology: BSHNI Annual Oral Presentation, 1069

Research Seed Grant, 982

African Nations

GREAT Scholarships-Egypt, 1286

GREAT Scholarships-Ghana, 1286

GREAT Scholarships-Kenya, 1287

Asian Countries

GREAT Scholarships-China, 1286

GREAT Scholarships-India, 1287

GREAT Scholarships–Indonesia, 1287

GREAT Scholarships–Malaysia, 1288

GREAT Scholarships–Pakistan, 1288

GREAT Scholarships–Thailand, 1288

European Countries

Radiology Section: Finzi Prize, 1069

North American Countries

Radiological Society of North America Institutional Clinical Fellowship in Cardiovascular Imaging, 980

Radiological Society of North America Medical Student Grant Program, 980

Radiological Society of North America Research Resident Program, 980

Radiological Society of North America Research Scholar Grant Program, 981

Research Scholar Grant, 982

United Kingdom

Radiology Section: Finzi Prize, 1069

REHABILITATION AND THERAPY

Australia

Betty Josephine Fyffe Rural Allied Health, Nursing and Midwifery Scholarship, 1429

Repatriation General Hospital Department of Rehabilitation and Aged Care: Health Professionals Research Scholarship, 531

New Zealand

Repatriation General Hospital Department of Rehabilitation and Aged Care: Health Professionals Research Scholarship, 531

United Kingdom

Lincoln Alumni MSc School of Health and Social Care Scholarship, 1349

NATURAL SCIENCES

GENERAL

Any Country

Acute Generalized Exanthematous Pustulosis Fellowship, 670

AfterCollege STEM Inclusion Scholarship, 18

AHA Postdoctoral Fellowship, 76

ASML Henk Bodt Scholarship, 1577

Beyond Segments: Towards a Lexical Model for Tonal Bilinguals, 767

BHW Women in STEM Scholarship, 1177

Biomechanics Postgraduate Scholarship (General Sports), 176

British Council Scholarships for Women in STEM, 1539

Brother Vincent Cotter Endowed Honours Award, 1416

Bryan Scholarships, 1390

Canadian Centennial Scholarship Fund, 1324

CDT in Advanced Metallic Systems, 1366

CDT in Aerosol Science, 1366

CDT in Biodesign Engineering, 1367

CDT in Compound Semiconductor Manufacturing, 1367

CDT in Future Innovation in NDE, 1367

CDT in the Science and Technology of Fusion Energy, 1368

China Scholarship Council Scholarships, 968

Christine Mirzayan Science & Technology Policy Graduate Fellowship Program, 838

Churchill Scholarship, 1620

Communicator Award, 432

CONACyT Tuition Top-up Award, 1370

Council of Scientific and Industrial Research/TWAS Fellowship for Postgraduate Research, 1178

Croucher Foundation PhD Scholarships and Postdoctoral Fellowships, 398
Dean's Doctoral Scholarship Award, 1371
Dhaka PhD Scholarships, 969
Directorate for Education and Human Resources Core Research, 867
Doshisha University Doctoral-Program Young Researcher Scholarship, 439
Dual-award between The University of Manchester and IIT Kharagpur, 1372
Dual-award between The University of Manchester and The University of Melbourne, 1373
Duke/NCCU Collaborative Translational Research Awards, 442
EPSRC Doctoral Training Partnership (DTP), 1373
Faculty of Science Masters Scholarship for International Students, 1542
Faculty PhD Scholarships, 319
Funds for Women Graduates, 1377
GeneTex Scholarship Program, 562
Global Research Scholarship Programme–Faculty of Science, 1544
Government of Ireland Postgraduate Scholarship Programme, 671
Graphene NOWNANO CDT, 1377
Heinz Maier–Leibnitz Prize, 434
Hilda Trevelyan Morrison Bequest, 1395
Ilona Takacs Scholarship, 513
Industrial Transformation Training Centre in Facilitated Advancement of Australia's Bioactive-International, 771
Institution of Engineering and Technology Postgraduate Scholarship for an Outstanding Researcher, 647
Integrated Catalysis (iCAT) CDT, 1378
International Centre for Theoretical Sciences S. N. Bhatt Memorial Excellence Research Fellowship, 656
IT Kharagpur Post Doctoral Fellowship, 623
J C Bose National Fellowship, 1098
Joint-award between The University of Manchester and IISC Bangalore, 1379
Lancaster Master's Scholarship, 709
Lindt Dissertation Fellowship, 370
The Lorraine Allison Memorial Scholarship, 131
Lucy Cavendish College: Dorothy and Joseph Needham Studentship, 1252
Max Planck Institute for the History of Science Postdoctoral Fellowship in Germany, 796
National Research Foundation Fellowships for Postdoctoral Research, 865
National Science Foundation Research Traineeship (NRT) Program, 869
National University of Singapore Design Technology Institute Scholarship, 876
Natural Sciences and Engineering Research Council of Canada Industrial Post-Graduate Scholarships (IPS), 1112
Newton International Fellowships, 234
Nuclear Energy-GREEN CDT, 1381
NZ-GRADS New Zealand Global Research Alliance Doctoral Scholarship, 473
The Optical Society, Deutsch Fellowship, 842
Packard Fellowships for Science and Engineering, 413
Postdoctoral Fellowships, 1116
Postgraduate Research Teaching Associate (PGRTA) Scholarships, 1381
PPARC Standard Research Studentship, 1103
Presidential Scholarships for Students of Black Heritage, 615
Ramboll Masters Scholarship for International Students, 1448
Research Internships in Science and Engineering (RISE), 436
Resource Management Law Association of New Zealand Masters Scholarship, 157
Robert Noyce Teacher Scholarship Program, 869
Royal Society EPSRC BBSRC and Rolls Royce PLC Industry Fellowships, 485
Science and Engineering Research Board Distinguished Fellowship, 1100
Singapore International Graduate Award, 836
Singapore-MIT Alliance Graduate Fellowship, 877
University of Geneva Excellence Masters Fellowships, 1313
Ursula M. Händel Animal Welfare Prize, 435
Villa I Tatti-Bogaziçi University Joint Fellowship, 1600
Wallace Fellowship, 1601
Western Digital Scholarship Program, 1112
Women in Science Scholarship, 736
Woodrow Wilson Teaching Fellowship, 1624
World Citizen Talent Scholarship, 656
African Nations
Austrian Academy of Sciences, 4-months Trimester at Egerton University, Kenya, 178
The Beacon Scholarship, 331
Deakin STEM Scholarship, 422
GREAT-Imperial College London Scholarship, 613
KSP Joint Research Projects, 1107
Kuwait Excellence Scholarship for Arab Students and Kuwait Nationals, 1107
OWSD PhD Fellowships for Women Scientists, 1179
Asian Countries
Advanced Biomedical Materials CDT, 1363
A* STAR PhD Programme, 1363
British Council Scholarship for Women in STEM Terms and Conditions, 266
British Council Scholarships for Women in STEM, 446, 1365
Daiwa Foundation Awards, 411
Deakin STEM Scholarship, 422
GREAT-Imperial College London Scholarship, 613

KSP Joint Research Projects, 1107
Kuwait Excellence Scholarship for Arab Students and Kuwait Nationals, 1107
OWSD PhD Fellowships for Women Scientists, 1179
Research Fellowships for Young Researchers, 680
Science and Engineering Research Board Overseas Postdoctoral Fellowship (OPDF), 1100
Science and Engineering Research Board Women Excellence Award, 1100
The University of Manchester-China Scholarship Council Joint Scholarship, 1389
Asia-Pacific Countries
OWSD PhD Fellowships for Women Scientists, 1179
Australia
AGL Jungurra Wunnik Scholarship, 508
Alex Gusbeth Scholarship, 509
Faculty of Science and Engineering Research Awards (FSERA), 523
HeART of the Basin Scholarship, 340
Indigenous Pathways Advance Queensland VET Scholarship, 341
Industrial Transformation Training Centre in Facilitated Advancement of Australia's Bioactive-Domestic, 771
Masters Scholarship in Scotland, 406
Meredith Doig Scholarship, 514
Sediment and Asphaltite Transport by Canyon Upwelling-Top Up Scholarship, 407
Victoria Fellowships, 430
Canada
Canada's Distinguished Dissertation Awards, 1075
L'Oréal Canada For Women in Science Research Excellence Fellowships, 1197
NSERC Postgraduate Scholarships-Doctoral Program, 882
Caribbean Countries
OWSD PhD Fellowships for Women Scientists, 1179
Central European Countries
Copernicus Award, 432
Heisenberg Programme, 435
European Countries
John and Pat Hume Research Scholarships, 874
School of Natural Sciences Diversity PhD Scholarship, 1385
Studentship in Physical Sciences, 1556
European Union
John and Pat Hume Research Scholarships, 874
Latin America
OWSD PhD Fellowships for Women Scientists, 1179
Middle East
Kuwait Program at Sciences Po Excellence Scholarship for Arab Students and Kuwait Nationals, 947
New Zealand
AGL Jungurra Wunnik Scholarship, 508
Alex Gusbeth Scholarship, 509
Faculty of Science and Engineering Research Awards (FSERA), 523
Meredith Doig Scholarship, 514
Sediment and Asphaltite Transport by Canyon Upwelling-Top Up Scholarship, 407
The Sir Hugh Kawharu Masters Scholarship for Innovation in Science, 1053
North American Countries
British Council Scholarships for Women in STEM, 608
Oceania
Toloa Scholarships for Pacific STEM Scholars, 158
South Africa
Leiden University South Africa Scholarship-University of Cape Town, 716
Leiden University South Africa Scholarship-University of Pretoria, 716
Leiden University South Africa Scholarship-University of the Western Cape, 717
LUF International Study Fund (LISF), 717
Mandela Scholarship Fund, 718
South American Countries
British Council Scholarships for Women in STEM, 608
United Kingdom
Daiwa Foundation Awards, 411
Faculty of Science Masters Scholarship for UK Students, 1542
School of Natural Sciences Diversity PhD Scholarship, 1385
Studentship in Physical Sciences, 1556
United States of America
Council of American Overseas Research Centers (CAORC) Fellowships for Advanced Multi-Country Research, 109
Department of Defense-National Defense and Science Engineering Fellowships, 195
Foundation for Science and Disability Student Grant Fund, 546
Graduate Student Grant, 546
Howard Hughes Medical Institute Gilliam Fellowships for Advanced Study, 604
Marshall Sherfield Fellowships, 787
National Defense Science and Engineering Graduate Fellowship Program, 111
National Energy Technology Laboratory Methane Hydrates Fellowship Program (MHFP), 840
National Institute of Justice's Graduate Research Fellowship Program, 199
NRC Research Associate Programs (RAP), 840
NRC Research Associateship Programs (RAP), 840
Office of Naval Research Summer Faculty Research Program, 112
United States Air Force Academy/National Research Council Summer Faculty Research Program (SFFP), 21
Winston Churchill Foundation Scholarships, 200

ASTRONOMY AND ASTROPHYSICS

Any Country

Basil Reeve DPhil Scholarship in Physical or Biomedical Sciences, 938
Bell Burnell Graduate Scholarship Fund, 1365
The Council of Scientific and Industrial Research/TWAS Fellowship for Postdoctoral Research, 1180
Department of Physics and Astronomy STFC Studentship, 1372
Frank and Doris Bateson Memorial Graduate Scholarship, 1269
Fred. L. Scarf Award, 70
Fulbright Distinguished Chair in Science, Technology, and Innovation (CSIRO), 551
Hubble Fellowships for Postdoctoral Scientists, 843
Joint Institute for Laboratory Astrophysics Postdoctoral Research Associateship and Visiting Fellowships, 687
MacGillavry Fellowships, 1224
PhD Studentships in Astrophysics Research Centre, 972
Research Corporation (United States of America) Research Innovation Awards, 989
TWAS-COMSTECH Science in Exile PhD Fellowship Programme for Displaced and Refugee Scientists, 1180

Canada

European Space Agency's Postdoctoral Internal Research Fellowship Programme, 501

European Countries

European Space Agency's Postdoctoral Internal Research Fellowship Programme, 501

European Union

Atmospheric, Oceanic & Planetary Physics: STFC Studentships, 1455
Department of Physics and Astronomy Diversity Enhancement Studentship, 1371

United Kingdom

Atmospheric, Oceanic & Planetary Physics: STFC Studentships, 1455
Department of Physics and Astronomy Diversity Enhancement Studentship, 1371

United States of America

Graduate Fellowships for Science, Technology, Engineering, and Mathematics Diversity, 573
Hubble Fellowships for Postdoctoral Scientists, 843

BIOLOGICAL AND LIFE SCIENCES

Any Country

Alton & Neryda Fancourt Chapple Award, 1415
American Chemical Society Ahmed Zewail Award in Ultrafast Science and Technology, 54
be.AI Leverhulme Doctoral Scholarships (Leverhulme Trust), 1558
Bedford Society Scholarship, 1040
Bell Burnell Graduate Scholarship Fund, 1365
Biostatistics/Informatics Junior Faculty Award, 863
Charles Parsons Energy Research Award, 872
Christine Mirzayan Science & Technology Policy Graduate Fellowship Program, 864
Collaborative Project relating to Antimicrobial Resistance from a One Health Perspective, 990
College Scholarship (Sciences), 1146
Department of Energy Computational Science Graduate Fellowship Krell Institute, 1589
Developing Novel Genetic Disease Models for Dementia-International, 769
Development of Next-generation Microfluidic Technology Device for Detection of Circulating Cancer Cells, 1555
Duke Cancer Institute/Duke Microbiome Center Joint Partnership Pilot Award, 442
Enabling Discovery through GEnomic Tools (EDGE), 868
The Energy Efficiency and Renewable Energy (EERE) Science and Technology Policy (STP) Fellowships, 1590
Engineering and Physical Sciences Research Council (EPSRC) Doctoral Training Partnership, 1559
Environmental Sustainability in Life Sciences and Medical Practice, 802
Fitzwilliam College Leathersellers, 1243
ICGEB-Elettra Sincrotrone Trieste International Fellowship Programme, 654
Invite Doctoral Programme, 1579
Linacre College: EPA Cephalosporin Scholarship, 1470
Long-Term Fellowships, 659
MacGillavry Fellowships, 1224
Macrosystems Biology and NEON-Enabled Science (MSB-NES), 868
Oxford-EPA Cephalosporin Graduate Scholarship, 1487
Oxford-Nicholas Bratt Graduate Scholarship, 1491
PhD International Studentships in Control of Mitosis in Calcium in Mammalian Cells, UK, 903
PhD Science Fellowship, 1176
Ruth L. Kirschstein National Research Service Award (NRSA) Individual Postdoctoral Fellowship, 861
Schrödinger Scholarship Scheme, 615
St Cross College: E.P. Abraham Scholarships, 1505
Wilfrid Knapp Scholarship (Sciences), 1148

Asian Countries

China Scholarship Council-University of Oxford Scholarships, 1458
ICGEB Postdoctoral Fellowships, 653
International PhD Studentships, 1522
S. Ramachandran-National Bioscience Award for Career Development, 428

Australia

Australian Biological Resources Study (ABRS) National Taxonomy Research Grant Program, 168
Calver Family Scholarship, 831

Developing Novel Genetic Disease Models for Dementia-Domestic, 769
The Joyce W. Vickery Research Fund, 738
European Countries
EPA Cephalosporin Scholarship, 733
European Molecular Biology Organisation Award for Communication in the Life Sciences, 499
Oxford–EPA Cephalosporin Graduate Scholarship, 734
European Union
Engineering and Physical Sciences Research Council Studentships for Biophotonics, 329
Keble College: James Martin Graduate Scholarship, 1467
Swansea University Research Excellence Scholarship, 1159
Middle East
European Molecular Biology Organisation Award for Communication in the Life Sciences, 499
New Zealand
Elman Poole Travelling Scholarship, 1444
South American Countries
Uruguay PhD Scholarship, 1351
United Kingdom
Engineering and Physical Sciences Research Council Studentships for Biophotonics, 329
Excellence in Diversity PhD Scholarships, 317
Frank Stell Scholarship, 1336
Keble College: James Martin Graduate Scholarship, 1467
Swansea University Research Excellence Scholarship, 1159
United States of America
Research Fellowship, 589
ANATOMY
African Nations
GREAT Scholarships-Egypt, 1286
GREAT Scholarships-Ghana, 1286
GREAT Scholarships-Kenya, 1287
Asian Countries
GREAT Scholarships-China, 1286
GREAT Scholarships-India, 1287
GREAT Scholarships–Indonesia, 1287
GREAT Scholarships–Malaysia, 1288
GREAT Scholarships–Pakistan, 1288
GREAT Scholarships–Thailand, 1288

BIOCHEMISTRY

Any Country
Agnes Fay Morgan Research Award, 668
Gladys Anderson Emerson Scholarship, 668
IUBMB Mid-Career Research Fellowships, 666
IUBMB Tang Education Fellowships, 666
IUBMB Travel Fellowships, 667
Oxford-Percival Stanion Graduate Scholarship in Biochemistry, 1493
PROLAB Fellowships, 667
Robert Logan Memorial Bursary, 677
Wood-Whelan Research Fellowships, 667
Central European Countries
Lincoln College: Berrow Foundation Lord Florey Scholarships, 1472
European Countries
Leathersellers' Company Scholarship (Sciences), 1147
United Kingdom
Leathersellers' Company Scholarship (Sciences), 1147
United States of America
Herman Frasch Foundation Grant, 60

BIOLOGY

Any Country
Awards Supported by the San Antonio Nathan Shock Center, 1085
Centre for Bioethics and Emerging Technologies PhD Funding, 1148
The Council of Scientific and Industrial Research/TWAS Fellowship for Postdoctoral Research, 1180
Fulbright Distinguished Chair in Science, Technology, and Innovation (CSIRO), 551
Lorna Casselton Memorial Scholarships in Plant Sciences, 1140
Medical Sciences Doctoral Training Centre: Wellcome Trust Studentship in Structural Biology, 1476
Postdoctoral Scholar Program, 1625
Roland Stead Postgraduate Scholarship in Biology, 1278
Stanley Smith (UK) Horticultural Trust Awards, 1151
TWAS-COMSTECH Science in Exile PhD Fellowship Programme for Displaced and Refugee Scientists, 1180
African Nations
Seed Grant for New African Principal Investigators (SG-NAPI), 1179
Asian Countries
Janaki Ammal-National Women Bioscientist Award, 428
Australia
Australian Postgraduate Award Industry Scholarships within Integrative Biology, 973
European Countries
Bayer Foundation Scholarships, 186
United Kingdom
Dax Copp Travelling Fellowship, 636
Early-stage Frontier Bioscience Research, 217
United States of America
RaMP-UP-Research and Mentoring Program–Understanding and Preserving Tropical BioDiversity Fellowship, 1120

BIOPHYSICS AND MOLECULAR BIOLOGY

Any Country
Cardiff School of Chemistry–Master's Bursaries, 325

The Council of Scientific and Industrial Research/TWAS Fellowship for Postdoctoral Research, 1180
IUBMB Mid-Career Research Fellowships, 666
IUBMB Tang Education Fellowships, 666
IUBMB Travel Fellowships, 667
Morgan E. Williams MRes Scholarship in Helminthology, 330
Oxford-E P Abraham Research Fund Graduate Scholarships, 1486
PROLAB Fellowships, 667
Wood-Whelan Research Fellowships, 667
United States of America
Immersive Training in the Glycosciences-Fellowship, 858

BIOTECHNOLOGY

Any Country
Department of Biotechnology (DBT) Junior Research Fellowship, 1518
Postgraduate Research Award (PGRA), 171
Translation Fund, 1610
Asian Countries
Janaki Ammal-National Women Bioscientist Award, 428
National Bioscience Awards for Career Development (NBACD), 428
Australia
Flinders and Nourish Ingredients Industry PhD Scholarship: Medical Biotechnology, Microbial Bioprocessing, 523
Rowe Scientific Foundation Scholarship, 425
New Zealand
Flinders and Nourish Ingredients Industry PhD Scholarship: Medical Biotechnology, Microbial Bioprocessing, 523

BOTANY

Any Country
American Museum of Natural History Collection Study Grants, 87
The Anne S. Chatham Fellowship, 559
B.A. Krukoff Fellowship in Systematics, 967
The Christopher Welch Scholarship in Biological Sciences, 1509
ECU-DBCA Kings Park Science Industry PhD Scholarship, 471
Grants for Orchid Research, 91
International PhD Fellowships in Environmental Chemistry, Denmark, 901
PhD Scholarship: Digital Modelling of Apple for Quality Prediction, 645
Asian Countries
China Scholarships, 620
International College of Auckland PhD Scholarship in Plant Sciences, 1228
European Countries
Giacomo Vaciago Scholarship, 734
International PhD Fellowships in Environmental Chemistry, Denmark, 901
New Zealand
Hutton Fund, 1051
United States of America
The Garden Club of America Fellowship in Tropical Botany, 560
The Zeller Summer Scholarship in Medicinal Botany, 560

GENETICS

Any Country
Global Hemophilia ASPIRE, 953
PhD International Scholarships in Quantitative Genetics of Senescence in Seychelles Warblers, Netherlands, 903
PhD Scholarship in Immunology and Immunogenetics, 1519
Polycystic Kidney Disease Foundation Grant-In-Aid, 960
Postdoctoral Research Fellowships, 409
Research Proposals, 409
The Walter V. and Idun Berry Postdoctoral Fellowship Program, 1150
Asian Countries
China Scholarships, 620
United Kingdom
Alan Emery Prize, 1057
United States of America
Texas CONNECT for Cancer Prevention Study Awards, 306

IMMUNOLOGY

Any Country
Cancer Research Institute Irvington Postdoctoral Fellowship Program, 308
Center for Alternatives to Animal Testing Grants Programme, 687
Clinical Immunology & Allergy President's Prize, 1058
United States of America
Cancer Research Institute Irvington Postdoctoral Fellowship Program, 308

LIMNOLOGY

Any Country
Austrian Academy of Sciences, MSc Course in Limnology and Wetland Ecosystems, 179
African Nations
Austrian Academy of Sciences, Short Course-Tropical Limnology, 179

MARINE BIOLOGY

Any Country
ER Walker Bequest Bursary, 675

Peter Baker Fellowship, 784
PhD Elevate Scholarship–CQUniversity and FutureFeed Pty Ltd Partnership (External), 342
Australia
Joyce and George Vaughan Bequest Scholarship, 677
New Zealand
Joyce and George Vaughan Bequest Scholarship, 677

MICROBIOLOGY

Any Country
Graduate School of Brain Science Special Scholarship, 442
International Collaboration to Address Antimicrobial Resistance, 803
PhD Scholarships in Environmental Microbiology, 1423
Australia
Flinders and Nourish Ingredients Industry PhD Scholarship: Medical Biotechnology, Microbial Bioprocessing, 523
William Macleay Microbiology Research Fund, 738
New Zealand
Flinders and Nourish Ingredients Industry PhD Scholarship: Medical Biotechnology, Microbial Bioprocessing, 523
North American Countries
American Society for Microbiology Microbe Minority Travel Awards, 112

NEUROSCIENCES

Any Country
Clinical Neurosciences Gordon Holmes Prize, 1058
Clinical Neurosciences President's Prize, 1058
The Council of Scientific and Industrial Research/TWAS Fellowship for Postdoctoral Research, 1180
Graduate School of Brain Science Special Scholarship, 440
Max Planck Institute-CBS Postdoctoral Position in Neuroscience of Pain Perception in Germany, 797
McGill University PhD Studentships in Neurolinguistics, 800
Postdoctoral Fellowship Awards, 679
Postdoctoral Research Training, 496
Ruth K. Broad Biomedical Research Foundation–Ellen Luken Student Awards, 444
TWAS-COMSTECH Science in Exile PhD Fellowship Programme for Displaced and Refugee Scientists, 1180
Asian Countries
Fulbright-Nehru Doctoral Research Fellowships, 1195
Fulbright-Nehru Postdoctoral Research Fellowships, 1195

PHARMACOLOGY

Any Country
Awards Supported by the San Antonio Nathan Shock Center, 1085
Postdoctoral Research Bursary for Clinical Trainees, 315
United Kingdom
Develop New Approaches to Small Molecule Medicine, 802

PHYSIOLOGY

Any Country
American Physiological Society Minority Travel Fellowship Awards, 94
Awards Supported by the San Antonio Nathan Shock Center, 1085
Postgraduate Scholarship-Physiology (Biochemistry/Haematology), 177
Postgraduate Scholarship Program-Physiology (Quality Control), 177
Sports Physiology Postgraduate Scholarship-Fatigue and Recovery, 178
Canada
John Charles Polanyi Prizes, 1077
PLANT PATHOLOGY
European Countries
Leathersellers' Company Scholarship (Sciences), 1147
United Kingdom
Leathersellers' Company Scholarship (Sciences), 1147

TOXICOLOGY

Any Country
Alan and Helene Goldberg In Vitro Toxicology Grants, 686
Alleghery-ENCRC Student Research Award, 1184
Center for Alternatives to Animal Testing Grants Programme, 687
Colgate-Palmolive Grants for Alternative Research, 1184
Food Safety SS Burdock Group Travel Award, 1185
Regulation and Safety SS Travel Award, 1185
Robert L. Dixon International Travel Award, 1185
School of Life and Health Sciences Postgraduate Masters Scholarships-Commonwealth Shared Scholarship Scheme, 151

ZOOLOGY

Any Country
American Museum of Natural History Collection Study Grants, 87
The Christopher Welch Scholarship in Biological Sciences, 1509
ER Walker Bequest Bursary, 675
Marcia Brady Tucker Travel Award, 92
Canada
Biological Survey of Canada Scholarship, 488
Danks Scholarship, 489
Dr Lloyd M. Dosdall Memorial Scholarship, 489
Graduate Research Travel Scholarships, 489
John H. Borden Scholarship, 490

Keith Kevan Scholarship, 490
Postgraduate Scholarships, 490
European Countries
Leathersellers' Company Scholarship (Sciences), 1147
New Zealand
Hutton Fund, 1051
United Kingdom
Leathersellers' Company Scholarship (Sciences), 1147

CHEMISTRY

Any Country
Agnes Fay Morgan Research Award, 668
Alfred Burger Award in Medicinal Chemistry, 53
American Chemical Society Ahmed Zewail Award in Ultrafast Science and Technology, 54
American Chemical Society Award for Creative Research and Applications of Iodine Chemistry, 54
American Chemical Society Award for Encouraging Disadvantaged Students into Careers in the Chemical Sciences, 55
American Chemical Society Award for Encouraging Women into Careers in the Chemical Sciences, 55
American Chemical Society Award in Colloid Chemistry, 56
American Chemical Society National Awards, 56
American Chemical Society Priestley Medal, 57
American Chemical Society Stanley C. Israel Regional Award for Advancing Diversity in the Chemical Sciences, 57
American Museum of Natural History Collection Study Grants, 87
Anna Louise Hoffman Award for Outstanding Achievement in Graduate Research, 668
Basil Reeve DPhil Scholarship in Physical or Biomedical Sciences, 938
Betty Wignall Scholarship in Chemistry, 1268
Carolyn and Franco Gianturco Scholarship in Theoretical Chemistry, 732
Chemistry Scholarships, 750
The Council of Scientific and Industrial Research/TWAS Fellowship for Postdoctoral Research, 1180
Cross-Disciplinary Fellowships, 659
Development of Next-generation Microfluidic Technology Device for Detection of Circulating Cancer Cells, 1555
Doctoral New Investigator (DNI) Grants, 437
Engineering and Physical Sciences Research Council (EPSRC) Doctoral Training Partnership, 1559
Ernest Guenther Award in the Chemistry of Natural Products, 59
Fitzwilliam College Leathersellers, 1243
Frederic Stanley Kipping Award in Silicon Chemistry, 59
Fulbright Distinguished Chair in Science, Technology, and Innovation (CSIRO), 551
Gladys Anderson Emerson Scholarship, 668
Glenn T. Seaborg Award for Nuclear Chemistry, 60
H.C. & M.E. Porter Memorial Endowed Award, 1419
Henry Ellison Scholarship, 1336
Iota Sigma Pi National Honorary Member Award, 669
Ipatieff Prize, 60
Irving Langmuir Award in Chemical Physics, 60
Late Stephen Robjohns Science Scholarship, 1421
Linacre College: EPA Cephalosporin Scholarship, 1470
MacGillavry Fellowships, 1224
Magdalen College: Perkin Research Studentship, 1475
National Honorary Member, 669
Oxford-Bob Thomas Graduate Scholarship in Chemistry, 1482
Oxford-EPA Cephalosporin Graduate Scholarship, 1487
PhD Science Fellowship, 1176
PhD Studentship in Liquid Metal Catalysts for Green Fuels, Australia, 904
Postdoctoral Fellowships in Conservation Science, 568
Postdoctoral Scholar Program, 1625
Program Grants, 660
Research Corporation (United States of America) Research Innovation Awards, 989
RHT Bates Postgraduate Scholarship, 1052
Royal Society of Chemistry Journals Grants for International Authors, 1054
Schrödinger Scholarship Scheme, 615
S.N Bose Scholar Program, 1099
St Cross College: E.P. Abraham Scholarships, 1505
Surface Coatings Association Australia Award, 1424
TWAS-COMSTECH Science in Exile PhD Fellowship Programme for Displaced and Refugee Scientists, 1180
TWAS-SN Bose Postgraduate Fellowship Programme, 1181
Violet Diller Professional Excellence Award, 669
Young Investigator Grant, 660
African Nations
Seed Grant for New African Principal Investigators (SG-NAPI), 1179
Asian Countries
China Scholarship Council-University of Oxford Scholarships, 1458
Fulbright-Nehru Doctoral Research Fellowships, 1195
Fulbright-Nehru Postdoctoral Research Fellowships, 1195
GREAT Scholarships India, 243
Linacre College: Hitachi Chemical Europe Scholarship, 1470
Australia
Corrosion Research Postgraduate Scholarships, 822
Doctor of Philosophy Scholarship-Corrosion in Alumina Processing, 823
Ferry Scholarship, 1531
Ferry Scholarship–UniSA, 1217
PhD Studentship in Liquid Metal Catalysts for Green Fuels, Australia, 904

Rowe Scientific Foundation Scholarship, 425
Sir Arthur Sims Travelling Scholarship, 1399
Canada
Award for Research Excellence in Materials Chemistry, 296
Canadian National Committee/IUPAC Travel Awards, 295
John Charles Polanyi Prizes, 1077
Central American Countries
Linacre College: Hitachi Chemical Europe Scholarship, 1470
Central European Countries
Lincoln College: Berrow Foundation Lord Florey Scholarships, 1472
European Countries
Bayer Foundation Scholarships, 186
EPA Cephalosporin Scholarship, 733
Leathersellers' Company Scholarship (Sciences), 1147
Oxford–EPA Cephalosporin Graduate Scholarship, 734
European Union
Keble College: James Martin Graduate Scholarship, 1467
New Zealand
Corrosion Research Postgraduate Scholarships, 822
Doctor of Philosophy Scholarship-Corrosion in Alumina Processing, 823
South American Countries
Linacre College: Hitachi Chemical Europe Scholarship, 1470
United Kingdom
Keble College: James Martin Graduate Scholarship, 1467
Leathersellers' Company Scholarship (Sciences), 1147
United States of America
Graduate Fellowships for Science, Technology, Engineering, and Mathematics Diversity, 573
Herman Frasch Foundation Grant, 60
James Bryant Conant Award in High School Chemistry Teaching, 61

ANALYTICAL CHEMISTRY

Any Country
American Chemical Society Award in Chromatography, 56
Award in Chemical Instrumentation, 58
Award in Spectrochemical Analysis, 58
United States of America
Pfizer Graduate Travel Awards in Analytical Chemistry, 61

INORGANIC CHEMISTRY

Any Country
F. Albert Cotton Award in Synthetic Inorganic Chemistry, 59

ORGANIC CHEMISTRY

Any Country
American Chemical Society Award for Creative Work in Synthetic Organic Chemistry, 55
American Chemical Society Roger Adams Award in Organic Chemistry, 57
Arthur C. Cope Scholar Awards, 57

PHYSICAL CHEMISTRY

Any Country
Peter Debye Award in Physical Chemistry, 61

EARTH SCIENCES

Any Country
Albert Maucher Prize in Geoscience, 431
Alton & Neryda Fancourt Chapple Award, 1415
Basil Reeve DPhil Scholarship in Physical or Biomedical Sciences, 938
Bedford Society Scholarship, 1040
Bernd Rendel Prize in Geoscience, 431
The Council of Scientific and Industrial Research/TWAS Fellowship for Postdoctoral Research, 1180
GHI Fellowships at the Horner Library, 566
MacGillavry Fellowships, 1224
Marie Tharp Visiting Fellowships, 372
National Geographic Conservation Trust Grant, 381
Other Studentships in Earth Sciences, 1480
PhD Science Fellowship, 1176
Postgraduate Research Award (PGRA), 171
S.N Bose Scholar Program, 1099
TWAS-COMSTECH Science in Exile PhD Fellowship Programme for Displaced and Refugee Scientists, 1180
Walter Heywood Bryan Scholarship for International Students in Australia, 781
African Nations
Seed Grant for New African Principal Investigators (SG-NAPI), 1179
Asian Countries
Fulbright-Nehru Doctoral Research Fellowships, 1195
Fulbright-Nehru Postdoctoral Research Fellowships, 1195
Australia
Robb Scholarship for Regional Planning and Development, 1410
Sonja Huddle Award, 1424
European Countries
European Science Foundation Response of the Earth System to Impact Processes (IMPACT) Mobility Grants, 500
European Union
Atmospheric, Oceanic & Planetary Physics: STFC Studentships, 1455
North American Electric Reliability Corporation (NERC) Studentships in Earth Sciences, 1477
United Kingdom
Atmospheric, Oceanic & Planetary Physics: STFC Studentships, 1455

Enabling Fund for Non-Fieldwork Expenses, 222
ExxonMobil Excellence in Teaching Awards, 1015
Leathersellers' Company Scholarship (Sciences), 1147
North American Electric Reliability Corporation (NERC) Studentships in Earth Sciences, 1477
United States of America
American Meteorological Society Graduate Fellowships, 86
Frontier Research in Earth Sciences (FRES), 442

GEOCHEMISTRY

Any Country
Tasmanian Government Mining Honours Scholarships, 1574
GEOGRAPHY (SCIENTIFIC)
Any Country
Fulbright Distinguished Chair in Science, Technology, and Innovation (CSIRO), 551
Phyllis Mary Morris Bursaries, 1237
Visiting Geographical Scientist Program, 146
Walters Kundert Fellowship, 1039
United States of America
Association of American Geographers NSF International Geographical Union Conference Travel Grants, 146

GEOLOGY

Any Country
The Betty Mayne Scientific Research Fund for Earth Sciences, 738
Centre of Excellence in Ore Deposits PhD Scholarships, 1573
Fulbright Distinguished Chair in Science, Technology, and Innovation (CSIRO), 551
James Park Scholarship in Geology, 1446
Marie Morisawa Award, 563
Postdoctoral Scholar Program, 1625
Steve Weston and Trust Scholarships, 1289
Tasmanian Government Mining Honours Scholarships, 1574
Tasmanian Government Mining PhD Scholarship, 1574
Australia
James Stewart Bequest (Geology), 514
Central American Countries
Graduate Student Research Grants, 562
J. Hoover Mackin Award, 563
New Zealand
Hutton Fund, 1051
James Stewart Bequest (Geology), 514
North American Countries
Graduate Student Research Grants, 562
J. Hoover Mackin Award, 563
United States of America
Graduate Fellowships for Science, Technology, Engineering, and Mathematics Diversity, 573

GEOPHYSICS AND SEISMOLOGY

Any Country
Postdoctoral Scholar Program, 1625
Tasmanian Government Mining Honours Scholarships, 1574

MINERALOGY AND CRYSTALLOGRAPHY

Any Country
Mineral and Rock Physics Graduate Research Award, 71
European Countries
Olga Kennard Research Fellowship Scheme, 1052
European Union
Olga Kennard Research Fellowship Scheme, 1052
Middle East
Olga Kennard Research Fellowship Scheme, 1052

PALAEONTOLOGY

Any Country
American Museum of Natural History Collection Study Grants, 87

PETROLOGY

Any Country
Mineral and Rock Physics Graduate Research Award, 71
Tasmanian Government Mining Honours Scholarships, 1574

MARINE SCIENCE AND OCEANOGRAPHY

Any Country
Christchurch City Council Antarctic Scholarship, 1272
Fulbright Distinguished Chair in Science, Technology, and Innovation (CSIRO), 551
Gateway Antarctica's Ministry of Foreign Affairs and Trade Scholarship in Antarctic and Southern Ocean Studies, 1274
Heather Leaity Memorial Award, 1227
Peter Baker Fellowship, 784
Postdoctoral Scholar Program, 1625
Asian Countries
MarTERA Call, 784
Australia
Calver Family Scholarship, 831
John MacIntyre Honours Year Scholarship in Marine Science, 1420
European Countries
Collaborative Project to Meet Societal and Industry-related Challenges, 990
MarTERA Call, 784
Researcher Project for Scientific Renewal, 991
Researcher Project for Young Talents, 991

European Union
Atmospheric, Oceanic & Planetary Physics: STFC Studentships, 1455
South Africa
MarTERA Call, 784
United Kingdom
Atmospheric, Oceanic & Planetary Physics: STFC Studentships, 1455

METEOROLOGY

Any Country
The Edward & Isabel Kidson Scholarship, 1279
Kellogg College: Bigg Scholarship in African Climate Science, 1467
PhD Student Scholarship in Atmospheric Science, 873
Postdoctoral Scholar Program, 1625
Researcher Project for Young Talents, 991
Asian Countries
Fulbright-Kalam Climate Fellowships for Doctoral Research, 1193
Fulbright-Kalam Climate Fellowships for Postdoctoral Research, 1194
United States of America
American Meteorological Society Graduate Fellowships, 86
Fulbright-Kalam Climate Fellowships for Doctoral Research, 1193

ARCTIC STUDIES

Any Country
The H.M. Ali Family Educational Award, 131
The Jennifer Robinson Memorial Scholarship, 131
Researcher Project for Scientific Renewal, 991
Canada
Arctic Institute of North America Grants-in-Aid, 130
United States of America
Arctic Institute of North America Grants-in-Aid, 130

ARID LAND STUDIES

Any Country
George Mason Sustainable Land Use Scholarship, 641

PHYSICS

Any Country
Abdus Salam ICTP Fellowships, 8
American Chemical Society Ahmed Zewail Award in Ultrafast Science and Technology, 54
American Museum of Natural History Collection Study Grants, 87
Basil Reeve DPhil Scholarship in Physical or Biomedical Sciences, 938
Christine Mirzayan Science & Technology Policy Graduate Fellowship Program, 864
The Council of Scientific and Industrial Research/TWAS Fellowship for Postdoctoral Research, 1180
Cross-Disciplinary Fellowships, 659
Department of Physics and Astronomy STFC Studentship, 1372
Development of Next-generation Microfluidic Technology Device for Detection of Circulating Cancer Cells, 1555
The Edward & Isabel Kidson Scholarship, 1279
Engineering and Physical Sciences Research Council (EPSRC) Doctoral Training Partnership, 1559
European Synchrotron Radiation Facility Postdoctoral Fellowships, 502
European Synchrotron Radiation Facility Thesis Studentships, 502
Fitzwilliam College Leathersellers, 1243
Fulbright Distinguished Chair in Science, Technology, and Innovation (CSIRO), 551
HAPP Scholarship in the History & Philosophy of Physics, 1140
H.C. & M.E. Porter Memorial Endowed Award, 1419
Henry Ellison Scholarship, 1336
Institute for Particle and Nuclear Physics MSc Prize Scholarships, 465
Irving Langmuir Award in Chemical Physics, 60
Jean E Laby PhD Travelling Scholarships, 1397
Late Stephen Robjohns Science Scholarship, 1421
Linacre College: Women in Science Scholarship, 1472
MacGillavry Fellowships, 1224
Max Planck Institute-DS Gauss Postdoctoral Fellowships for International Students, 796
Oxford-Nicholas Bratt Graduate Scholarship, 1491
Oxford-Particle Physics Graduate Scholarship, 1493
PhD Scholarship: Digital Modelling of Apple for Quality Prediction, 645
PhD Science Fellowship, 1176
Physics Scholarships, 756
Postdoctoral Fellowships in Conservation Science, 568
Postdoctoral Scholar Program, 1625
Program Grants, 660
Research Corporation (United States of America) Research Innovation Awards, 989
RHBNC Trust Scholarship, 1042
RHT Bates Postgraduate Scholarship, 1052
Ruth L. Kirschstein National Research Service Award (NRSA) Individual Postdoctoral Fellowship, 861
Schrödinger Scholarship Scheme, 615
St Cross College: HAPP MPhil Scholarship in the History of Science, 1506
TWAS-COMSTECH Science in Exile PhD Fellowship Programme for Displaced and Refugee Scientists, 1180
TWAS-SN Bose Postgraduate Fellowship Programme, 1181

University of Sydney: Data Science Scholarships, 124
Welch Scholarship, 665
Young Investigator Grant, 660
African Nations
Seed Grant for New African Principal Investigators (SG-NAPI), 1179
Asian Countries
China Scholarship Council-University of Oxford Scholarships, 1458
Conseil Européen Pour la Recherche Nucléaire-Japan Fellowship Programme, 380
Earth System Prediction Doctoral Training Programme, 1522
Fulbright-Nehru Doctoral Research Fellowships, 1195
Fulbright-Nehru Postdoctoral Research Fellowships, 1195
Postdoctoral Fellowships in Physics at Harish-Chandra Research Institute, 578
Australia
Corrosion Research Postgraduate Scholarships, 822
Ferry Scholarship, 1531
Ferry Scholarship–UniSA, 1217
J Holden Family Foundation Honours Award in Maths and Physics, 1420
Raman LiDAR Spectroscopy Techniques for Remote Sensing of Subsurface Water Properties, 778
Sir Arthur Sims Travelling Scholarship, 1399
Canada
John Charles Polanyi Prizes, 1077
European Countries
Oxford-C S Wu Graduate Scholarship, 1483
European Union
Cardiff School of Chemistry–MSc Studentships in Computing in the Physical Sciences, 325
Department of Physics and Astronomy Diversity Enhancement Studentship, 1371
Engineering and Physical Sciences Research Council Studentships for Biophotonics, 329
Keble College: James Martin Graduate Scholarship, 1467
New Zealand
Corrosion Research Postgraduate Scholarships, 822
Douglass D Crombie Award in Physics, 1443
Elman Poole Travelling Scholarship, 1444
United Kingdom
Alvin Li-Shen Chua Memorial Scholarship, 607
Department of Physics and Astronomy Diversity Enhancement Studentship, 1371
Engineering and Physical Sciences Research Council Studentships for Biophotonics, 329
Keble College: James Martin Graduate Scholarship, 1467
Leathersellers' Company Scholarship (Sciences), 1147
Multidisciplinary Project Award, 315
Oxford-C S Wu Graduate Scholarship, 1483
United States of America
Graduate Fellowships for Science, Technology, Engineering, and Mathematics Diversity, 573

NUCLEAR PHYSICS

Any Country
American Nuclear Society Mishima Award, 87
American Nuclear Society Utility Achievement Award, 87
Australian Institute of Nuclear Science and Engineering Awards, 170
Early Career Researcher Grant (ECRG), 171
Henry DeWolf Smyth Nuclear Statesman Award, 88
Honours Scholarship, 171
John R. Lamarsh Scholarship, 88
Landis Public Communication and Education Award, 88
Mary Jane Oestmann Professional Women, 89
Operations and Power Division Scholarship Award, 89
Residential Student Scholarship (RSS), 172
Samuel Glasstone Award, 90
United States of America
Verne R Dapp Memorial Scholarship, 90
OPTICS
Any Country
The Optical Society, Optica Women Scholars, 842
Australia
Centre for Lasers and Applications Scholarships, 767

RECREATION, WELFARE, PROTECTIVE SERVICES

GENERAL

African Nations
The Beacon Scholarship, 331
Asian Countries
Women as Cyber Leaders Scholarship, 395

CIVIL SECURITY

Any Country
Mershon Center Graduate Student Grants, 918
Thesis, Dissertation and Institutional Research Awards, 426
Asia-Pacific Countries
Freyberg Scholarship, 1199
Australia
National Security College Entry Scholarship for Aboriginal and Torres Strait Islander Students, 174
Canada
Freyberg Scholarship, 1199
New Zealand
Freyberg Scholarship, 1199
United States of America
Center for Defense Information Internship, 338

Freyberg Scholarship, 1199
Rocky Talkie Search and Rescue Award, 38

CRIMINOLOGY

Any Country
Bedford Society Scholarship, 1040
College of Business Government and Law PhD Top-up, 522
Criminology Scholarships for Foreign Researchers in Germany, 795
Francis Regan Student Scholarship, 525
Thesis, Dissertation and Institutional Research Awards, 426
United Kingdom
Kalisher Trust-Wadham Student Scholarship, 1466

ENVIRONMENTAL STUDIES

Any Country
African Forest Forum (AFF) Research Fellowships, 17
AHRC North West Consortium Doctoral Training Partnership in the School of Environment, Education and Development, 1364
Alton & Neryda Fancourt Chapple Award, 1415
American Alpine Club Research Grants, 37
American Chemical Society Award for Creative Advances in Environmental Science and Technology, 54
Aziz Foundation Masters Scholarships, 1310
Climate Data Expeditions: Climate + Health–Request for Proposals, 441
Crystalbrook Kingsley Environmental Scholarship, 1431
Duke Cancer Institute/Duke Microbiome Center Joint Partnership Pilot Award, 442
Duke/NCCU Collaborative Translational Research Awards, 442
Ecology and Evolution of Infectious Diseases Initiative (EEID), 539
Environment and Sustainability Research Grants, 1037
Evelyn Stokes Memorial Doctoral Scholarship, 1579
Fitzwilliam College: Peter Wilson Estates Gazette Studentships, 1245
Fulbright Distinguished Chair in Science, Technology, and Innovation (CSIRO), 551
Geography and Environment Scholarships, 754
Geography and the Environment: Andrew Goudie Bursary, 1462
Geography and the Environment: Boardman Scholarship, 1462
George Mason Sustainable Land Use Scholarship, 791
Heinrich-Böll-Stiftung, 189
Horizons Regional Council Sustainable Land Use Scholarships-Year 1 & Year 2 Students, 792
International PhD Fellowships in Environmental Chemistry, Denmark, 901
Joan Doll Scholarship, 1465
LUF-SVM Fund, 717
MSc Scholarships in Sustainability, Enterprise and the Environment, 1141
Natural Environment Research Council Independent Research Fellowships (IRF), 878
PhD in Sustainability Science, 1191
President's Doctoral Scholar (PDS) Awards in the School of Environment, Education and Development, 1382
Research Grants, 37
Royal Academy Sir Angus Paton Bursary, 1015
Ruth L. Kirschstein National Research Service Award (NRSA) Individual Postdoctoral Fellowship, 861
School of Geography and the Environment Commonwealth Shared Scholarship, 735
ScottishPower Masters Scholarships, 572
Stanley Smith (UK) Horticultural Trust Awards, 1151
The Tim Collins Scholarship for the Study of Love in Religion, 984
United Nations Educational, Scientific and Cultural Organization(UNESCO)/International Sustainable Energy DeISEDC Co-Sponsored Fellowships Programme, 1190
Walters Kundert Fellowship, 1039
African Nations
Austrian Academy of Sciences, 4-months Trimester at Egerton University, Kenya, 178
GREAT Scholarships-Egypt, 1286
GREAT Scholarships-Ghana, 1286
GREAT Scholarships-Kenya, 1287
Norman & Ivy Lloyd Scholarship/Commonwealth Shared Scholarship, 734
Oxford Commonwealth Trapnell Scholarship, 734
Showa Denko Environmental Scholarship, 736
Asian Countries
China Scholarships, 620
Fulbright Indo-American Environmental Leadership Program, 1193
Fulbright-Kalam Climate Fellowships for Doctoral Research, 1193
Fulbright-Kalam Climate Fellowships for Postdoctoral Research, 1194
Fulbright-Nehru Master's Fellowships, 1195
GREAT Scholarships-China, 1286
GREAT Scholarships-India, 1287
GREAT Scholarships–Indonesia, 1287
GREAT Scholarships–Malaysia, 1288
GREAT Scholarships–Pakistan, 1288
GREAT Scholarships–Thailand, 1288
National Bioscience Awards for Career Development (NBACD), 428
Royal Society South East Asia Rainforest Research Project-Travel Grants, 1053
S. Ramachandran-National Bioscience Award for Career Development, 428

Tata Innovation Fellowship, 429
Australia
Buninyong Community Bank Scholarship, 509
Calver Family Scholarship, 831
Delta Electricity Scholarship, 1431
HeART of the Basin Scholarship, 340
Max Day Environmental Science Fellowship Award, 162
Playford Trust: Playford Trust: PhD Scholarships, 530
Sonja Huddle Award, 1424
Canada
Danks Scholarship, 489
Jim Bourque Scholarship, 130
European Countries
Candriam Scholarship, 763
Collaborative Project to Meet Societal and Industry-related Challenges, 990
Giacomo Vaciago Scholarship, 734
International PhD Fellowships in Environmental Chemistry, Denmark, 901
Researcher Project for Scientific Renewal, 991
St Cross College: Graduate Scholarship in Environmental Research, 1506
European Union
Fully-Funded PhD Studentship in Sustainable Place-Making, 329
Keble College: James Martin Graduate Scholarship, 1467
Royal Society South East Asia Rainforest Research Project-Travel Grants, 1053
New Zealand
Anne Reid Memorial Trust Scholarship, 320
Buninyong Community Bank Scholarship, 509
North European Countries
Awards for American Universities and Colleges to host Norwegian lecturers, 122
South American Countries
Showa Denko Environmental Scholarship, 736
United Kingdom
Brown Family Bursary, 1201
Fully-Funded PhD Studentship in Sustainable Place-Making, 329
Keble College: James Martin Graduate Scholarship, 1467
SEED Enhancing Racial Equality Studentship, 1387
United States of America
Environmental Leadership Fellowships, 491
Fulbright-Kalam Climate Fellowships for Doctoral Research, 1193

ECOLOGY

Any Country
Austrian Academy of Sciences, MSc Course in Limnology and Wetland Ecosystems, 179
Heatherlea Bursary, 709
Outreach Grant, 245
Research Grants, 245
Smithsonian Environmental Research Center Graduate Student Fellowship, 1117
Training & Travel Grants, 246
Asian Countries
Indira Gandhi Institute of Development Research-International Development Research Centre Scholarships and Fellowships for Asian Countries Students, 624
European Union
Swansea University Research Excellence Scholarship, 1159
United Kingdom
Swansea University Research Excellence Scholarship, 1159

ENVIRONMENTAL MANAGEMENT

Any Country
Oriel College: Sir Walter Raleigh Scholarship, 1480
Sir Walter Raleigh MSc Scholarship in Environmental Change and Management, 940
St Cross MSc Scholarship in Biodiversity, Conservation and Management, 1141

NATURAL RESOURCES

Any Country
The Geoffrey F. Bruce Fellowship in Canadian Freshwater Policy, 1080
The Kenneth E. Grant Scholarship, 1135
Luke Pen Fund-Honours Scholarships, 471
Melville H. Cohee Student Leader Conservation Scholarship, 1135
Project Specific-Energy and Natural Resources Innovation and Technology Research Initiative (International), 777
Smithsonian Environmental Research Center Graduate Student Fellowship, 1117
Australia
Common Data Access MSc Petroleum Data Management Scholarships, 1216
2024 Great Artesian Basin Lynn Brake Scholarship, 520
Caribbean Countries
Scholarship Opportunities Linked to CATIE, 1186
Central American Countries
Scholarship Opportunities Linked to CATIE, 1186
North American Countries
Scholarship Opportunities Linked to CATIE, 1186
South American Countries
Scholarship Opportunities Linked to CATIE, 1186

WASTE MANAGEMENT

Any Country
Smithsonian Environmental Research Center Graduate Student Fellowship, 1117

WILDLIFE AND PEST MANAGEMENT

Any Country
OFAH/Fleming College Fish & Wildlife Scholarship, 924
Ontario Federation of Anglers & Hunters/Oakville and District Rod & Gun Club Conservation Research Grant, 924
Project Specific Scholarship-Improving Integrated Pest Management with Genome Editing, 777
Smithsonian Environmental Research Center Graduate Student Fellowship, 1117
Australia
PhD Scholarship: Weed Ecology, 1408

MILITARY SCIENCE

Asia-Pacific Countries
Freyberg Scholarship, 1199
Australia
National Security College Entry Scholarship for Aboriginal and Torres Strait Islander Students, 174
Canada
Freyberg Scholarship, 1199
New Zealand
Freyberg Scholarship, 1199
United States of America
American Society for Engineering Education Air Force Summer Faculty Fellowship Program, 110
Freyberg Scholarship, 1199
Naval Research Laboratory Post Doctoral Fellowship Program, 111
United States Air Force Academy/National Research Council Summer Faculty Research Program (SFFP), 21

PEACE AND DISARMAMENT

Any Country
Jennings Randolph Program for International Peace Dissertation Fellowship, 1191
Jennings Randolph Program for International Peace Senior Fellowships, 1192
Matsumae International Foundation Research Fellowship Program, 795
Peace and Disarmament Education Trust (PADET), 157
Canada
Graduate Research Awards for Disarmament, Arms Control and Non-Proliferation, 539

POLICE STUDIES

Australia
National Security College Entry Scholarship for Aboriginal and Torres Strait Islander Students, 174

SOCIAL WELFARE AND SOCIAL WORK

Any Country
Bedford Society Scholarship, 1040
Indigenous Health Promotion–Social and Emotional Wellbeing Scholarship, 1566
Marie Clay Literacy Trust Literacy Learning Research Award, 1229
PhD Social Work Scholarship at University of Edinburgh in United Kingdom, 1300
School for Policy Studies International Postgraduate Scholarships, 1237
African Nations
GREAT Scholarships-Egypt, 1286
GREAT Scholarships-Ghana, 1286
GREAT Scholarships-Kenya, 1287
Asian Countries
GREAT Scholarships-China, 1286
GREAT Scholarships-India, 1287
GREAT Scholarships–Indonesia, 1287
GREAT Scholarships–Malaysia, 1288
GREAT Scholarships–Pakistan, 1288
GREAT Scholarships–Thailand, 1288
Australia
Aboriginal Social and Emotional Wellbeing Scholarship, 1046
Volunteer Grants, 169
New Zealand
Shirley Gilliver Memorial Fund Grant, 678
United Kingdom
Lincoln Alumni MSc Social Work Scholarship, 1349
Social Work Bursary, 561
United States of America
Emerson National Hunger Fellows Program, 1005

SOCIAL AND COMMUNITY SERVICES

Any Country
Koshland Young Leader Awards, 1086
Robert Westwood Scholarship, 1087

SPORTS

Any Country, 812
Andrew Brown Sport Scholarship, 1427
Biomechanics Postgraduate Scholarship (General Sports), 176
BU Sport Scholarship, 228
Daryl Jelinek Sporting Scholarship, 752
DMU Sport Scholarship, 415
Doshisha University Doctoral-Program Young Researcher Scholarship, 439
Friends of the Sports Association Scholarship, 1393
Friends of the University Sport Scholarship, 1433

High Performance Sports Scholarship, 1395
Keble College Ian Tucker Memorial Bursary, 1467
Loughborough Sports Scholarships, 755
MSc Bursaries, 1581
Performance Analysis Scholarship, 176
Postgraduate Scholarship-Biomechanics (Swimming), 177
Sport Access Scholarship, 1400
Sports Scholarships, 1043
Sports Scholarships (Kent Sports Website), 1332
University of Strathclyde Performance Sport Scholarship, 1156

Australia

Elite Athlete Scholarship, 352, 512
Hancock Prospecting Swimming Excellence Scholarship, 224
Indigenous Sporting Excellence Scholarships, 176
Women in Sport Scholarships, 1594

Canada

Newcastle University-United States of America Athlete Scholarship, 897
The Winter 2022 Gift Competition, 414

New Zealand

Elite Athlete Scholarship, 352, 512

United Kingdom

The Kick It Out Scholarship, 1359

United States of America

Newcastle University-United States of America Athlete Scholarship, 897

RELIGION AND THEOLOGY

GENERAL

Any Country

American Atheists Chinn Scholarships, 987
American Atheists O'Hair Award, 987
Aziz Foundation Scholarships, 750
CSJR Postgraduate Student Bursary, 1094
Donald & Margot Watt Bursary Fund (FASS Only), 706
Ertegun Graduate Scholarship Programme in the Humanities, 1460
Harry Crossley Doctoral Fellowship, 1152
Hsing Yun Education Foundation (HYEF) Scholarship for International Students, 833
International Prize, 537
Religion, Spirituality, and Democratic Renewal Fellowship, 1122
The Rev Dr Norma P Robertson Scholarship, 1303
Sidney Topol Fellowship in Nonviolence Practice, 231
The Tim Collins Scholarship for the Study of Love in Religion, 984
Villa I Tatti-Bogaziçi University Joint Fellowship, 1600
VP Kanitkar Memorial Scholarship, 1097
Wallace Fellowship, 1601

African Nations

The Beacon Scholarship, 331

Australia

Co-op Bookshop Scholarship, 165
Hsing Yun Education Foundation (HYEF) Scholarship for Domestic Students, 833

New Zealand

Hsing Yun Education Foundation (HYEF) Scholarship for Domestic Students, 833

United States of America

Lilly Fellows Program in the Humanities and the Arts, 1006

CHURCH ADMINISTRATION (PASTORAL WORK)

Any Country

Fitzwilliam College: Hirst-Player Scholarship, 1245

HOLY WRITINGS

Any Country

Albright Institute of Archaeological Research (AIAR) Annual Professorship, 107
Fitzwilliam College: Gibson Scholarship, 1244

RELIGIOUS STUDIES

CHRISTIAN RELIGIOUS STUDIES

Any Country

Acts 17 Scholarship, 210
Federal TEACH Grant, 211
Oriel Graduate Scholarship in Science and Religion, 939

ISLAM

Any Country

Pembroke College: Graduate Studentships in Arabic and Islamic Studies (including Persian), 1254

African Nations

Oxford Centre for Islamic Studies (OCIS) Graduate Scholarships, 1484

Asian Countries

Oxford Centre for Islamic Studies (OCIS) Graduate Scholarships, 1484

European Countries

Oxford Centre for Islamic Studies (OCIS) Graduate Scholarships, 1484

Middle East

Oxford Centre for Islamic Studies (OCIS) Graduate Scholarships, 1484

United Kingdom
Oxford Centre for Islamic Studies (OCIS) Graduate Scholarships, 1484

JUDAIC RELIGIOUS STUDIES

Any Country
Ephraim Urbach Post Doctoral Fellowship, 809

THEOLOGY

Any Country
Diaconia Graduate Fellowships, 950
Doshisha University Doctoral-Program Young Researcher Scholarship, 439
Evangelical Lutheran Church in America Educational Grant Program, 505
Fitzwilliam College: Hirst-Player Scholarship, 1245
Fitzwilliam College: Shipley Studentship, 1246
Luce Fellowships, 1130
Mansfield College: Elfan Rees Scholarship, 1475
Pembroke College: The Bethune-Baker Graduate Studentship in Theology, 1255
United Kingdom
Westminster College Lewis and Gibson Scholarship, 1259

SERVICE TRADES

GENERAL

Any Country
The Culinary Trust Scholarship, 712
Toyota Earth Day Scholarship Program, 363
African Nations
The Beacon Scholarship, 331

COOKING AND CATERING

Any Country
Hospitality Maine Scholarships, 604
L' Academie de Cuisine Culinary Arts Scholarship, 399
Zwilling, J.A. Henckels Culinary Arts Scholarship, 400
United States of America
The Bibliographical Society of America-Pine Tree Foundation Fellowship in Culinary Bibliography, 205
Russ Casey Scholarship, 782

HOTEL AND RESTAURANT

United States of America
Cabot Scholarships, 886

TOURISM

Any Country
National Tour Association (NTA) Luray Caverns Graduate Research Scholarship, 871
Savoy Educational Trust Scholarships, 742
Australia
Visions of Australia: Regional Exhibition Touring Fund, 161

SOCIAL AND BEHAVIOURAL SCIENCES

GENERAL

Any Country
ACLS Emerging Voices Fellowships, 64
ALA Library History Round Table Davis Article Award, 928
Ampère & MILYON Excellence Scholarships for International Students, 456
Andrew W. Mellon Foundation/ACLS Early Career Fellowships Program Dissertation Completion Fellowships, 63
Associate Alumni Bursary, 967
Beinecke Scholarship, 190
Berlinski-Jacobson Graduate Scholarship (Humanities & Social Sciences), 1146
Boughton PhD Scholarship, 222
Call for Proposals: Narratives in Public Communications, 950
Canadian Centennial Scholarship Fund, 1324
China Scholarship Council Scholarships, 968
Christine and Ian Bolt Scholarship, 1324
Christine Mirzayan Science & Technology Policy Graduate Fellowship Program, 864
College Scholarship (Arts), 1146
Commencing Scholarship in Art Curating or Museum and Heritage Studies, 1564
The Constantine Aspromourgos Memorial Scholarship for Greek Studies, 1520
Copenhagen Business School PhD Scholarship on IT Management, 383
The Dean of Humanities, Arts & Social Sciences Excellence Scholarship, 986
Dean's Global Research Award, 1540
Doshisha University Doctoral-Program Young Researcher Scholarship, 439
Duke/NCCU Collaborative Translational Research Awards, 442
Economic and Social Research Council: Socio-Legal Studies, 1459
ESRC-BBSRC PhD Studentships in Biosocial Research, 1376
Evelyn Stokes Memorial Doctoral Scholarship, 1579
Exeter College: Exonian Graduate Scholarship, 1461
Fletcher Graduate Scholarship (International Development & Social Enterprise), 1146

Future of the Academy PhD Studentship, 1377
The Geoffrey F. Bruce Fellowship in Canadian Freshwater Policy, 1080
Global Research Scholarship Programme (Faculty of Humanities & Social Sciences), 1544
GSAS Summer Language Fellowships for International Students, 370
The Gulf Research Program's Early-Career Research Fellowship, 1175
HAPP MSc Scholarship in the History of Science, 1139
Humanities and Social Sciences Home Postgraduate Taught Performance Sport Scholarship, 1546
Humanities and Social Sciences Postgraduate Scholarships, 894
Institute for Advanced Studies in the Humanities Postdoctoral Fellowships, 1299
International PhD Awards, 971
J C Bose National Fellowship, 1098
Lancaster Master's Scholarship, 709
Leigh Douglas Memorial Prize, 262
Leverhulme (LINCS) PhD Scholarship, 972
Lincoln College: Lord Crewe Graduate Scholarships in the Social Sciences, 1474
Lincoln College: Sloane Robinson Foundation Graduate Awards, 1474
The Lorraine Allison Memorial Scholarship, 131
Michael Wong Pakshong Bursary, 1237
MPhil Scholarships in the Humanities and Social Sciences, 1140
National Research Foundation Fellowships for Postdoctoral Research, 865
Newton International Fellowships, 234
Northeast Florida Phi Beta Kappa Alumni Association Scholarship, 909
Nosce Scholarship, 734
Oxford-Angus McLeod Graduate Scholarship, 1481
Oxford-ID Travel Group Foundation Bonham-Carter Graduate Scholarship, 1488
Oxford-TrygFonden Graduate Scholarship, 1497
Postgraduate Ambassador Studentship, 572
PPARC Communications/Media Programme, 1102
Radcliffe Institute Fellowship, 977
Religion, Spirituality, and Democratic Renewal Fellowship, 1122
School of Social Sciences and Humanities International PhD Studentships in UK, 905
School of Social Sciences-North West Consortium Doctoral Training Partnership (AHRC NWCDTP), 1386
School of Social Sciences-North West Social Sciences Doctoral Training Partnership (ESRC NWSSDTP) Studentships, 1386
School of Social Sciences-PhD Studentships, 1387
School of Social Sciences-PhD Studentship with the Stuart Hall Foundation, 1386
School of Social Sciences-President's Doctoral Scholarship (PDS), 1387
Short-Term EFEO Postdoctoral Contracts, 537
Social and Policy Studies Scholarships, 757
Social Science Research Council International Dissertation Research Fellowship, 1124
Society for the Psychological Study of Social Issues Grants-in-Aid Program, 1131
St Catherine's College: College Scholarship (Arts), 1504
St Cross College: MPhil Scholarships in the Humanities and Social Sciences, 1506
University of California, Los Angeles (UCLA) Sardar Patel Award, 1239
Visiting Fellowships, 259
Wellcome Master's Programme Awards in Humanities and Social Science, 1537
Whitehall Foundation Grants-in-Aid, 1618
White Rose Studentships, 1529

African Nations

The Beacon Scholarship, 331
Zentrum Moderner Orient and Berlin Graduate School of Muslim Cultures and Societies Visiting Research Fellowship, 201

Asian Countries

China Scholarship Council-University of Oxford Scholarships, 1458
CR Parekh Fellowship, 743
CSC-Leiden University Scholarship, 714
Dissertation Fellowships for ROC Students Abroad, 358
International PhD Studentships, 1523
Oxford-Kaifeng Graduate Scholarship, 1490
Research Fellowships for Young Researchers, 680
School of Social Sciences-China Scholarship Council Joint Scholarship for PhD Study, 1385
Sir Ratan Tata Postdoctoral Fellowship, 743
Social Science Research Council Abe Fellowship Program, 1122
Zentrum Moderner Orient and Berlin Graduate School of Muslim Cultures and Societies Visiting Research Fellowship, 201

Australia

Graduate Certificate in Human and Community Services Tuition Scholarship, 1565
The Helen Macpherson Smith Scholarships, 1401
Irene and Arthur Kinsman Award for Postgraduate Studies, 1396
Peggy Bamford Award, 1422
Robb Scholarship for Regional Planning and Development, 1410

Canada

Aid to Scholarly Journals, 1125
International Council for Canadian Studies Graduate Student Scholarships, 283

Savoy Foundation Studentships, 1091
Social Sciences and Humanities Research Council Impact Awards, 1078
SSHRC Impact Awards, 1127
SSHRC Postdoctoral Fellowships, 1128
European Countries
Alfred Toepfer Natural Heritage Scholarships, 25
Berkeley-Austria Research Fellowship, 194
Council of American Overseas Research Centers Andrew W. Mellon East-Central European Research Fellows, 386
John and Pat Hume Research Scholarships, 874
Open Society Institute's Global Supplementary Grant Program (Grant SGP), 926
Swedish Institute Scholarships for the Western Balkans Programme, 1160
W.D.E. Coulson & Toni M. Cross Aegean Exchange Program, 106
European Union
Cardiff University PhD Social Sciences Studentship, 328
John and Pat Hume Research Scholarships, 874
Middle East
Swedish-Turkish Scholarship Programme for PhD Studies and Postdoctoral Research, 1161
Zentrum Moderner Orient and Berlin Graduate School of Muslim Cultures and Societies Visiting Research Fellowship, 201
New Zealand
Sasakawa Young Leaders Fellowship Fund Research Scholarship-Masters and PhD, 736
Oceania
Raewyn Good Study Award for Māori and Pasifika Social Science Research, 1052
South Africa
Leiden University South Africa Scholarship-University of Cape Town, 716
Leiden University South Africa Scholarship-University of Pretoria, 716
Leiden University South Africa Scholarship-University of the Western Cape, 717
LUF International Study Fund (LISF), 717
Mandela Scholarship Fund, 718
The Swedish Institute Study Scholarships for South Africa, 1161
South American Countries
Sasakawa Young Leader Fellowship (SYLFF) Program, 1090
United Kingdom
The Anglo-Norse Dame Gillian Brown Postgraduate Scholarship, 126
Cardiff University PhD Social Sciences Studentship, 328
Daphne Jackson Fellowships, 1101
ESRC/SSRC Collaborative Visiting Fellowships, 1121
Net Zero Policy Programme, 234
Policy Insight Case Studies, 235
United States of America
American Council of Learned Societies Digital Extension Grants, 1133
American Council of Learned Societies/New York Public Library (NYPL) Fellowships, 63
Council of American Overseas Research Centers (CAORC) Fellowships for Advanced Multi-Country Research, 109
ESRC/SSRC Collaborative Visiting Fellowships, 1121
Fellowships for Advanced Social Science Research on Japan, 855
Fellowships Open Book Program, 855
Gerald D. and Norma Feldman Graduate Student Dissertation Fellowship, 197
Helmut Kohl Award in German and European Studies, 198
National Endowment for the Humanities Fellowships, 855
NEH-Mellon Fellowships for Digital Publication, 855
Social Science Research Council Abe Fellowship Program, 1122
Social Science Research Council Eurasia Program Predissertation Training Fellowships, 1123
Title VIII-Supported Summer Research Grant, 694
Whitehall Foundation Research Grants, 1618
West European Countries
Foundation Praemium Erasmianum Study Prize, 548

ECONOMIC HISTORY

Any Country
Alexander Gerschenkron Prize, 458
Alice Hanson Jones Biennial Prize, 458
The Allan Nevins Prize in American Economic History, 460
Arthur H Cole Grants-in-Aid, 459
Early Stage Dissertation Grants, 459
Gyorgy Ranki Biennial Prize, 460
Harvard/Newcomen Postdoctoral Award, 906
Jonathan Hughes Prize, 460
The Lindert-Williamson Biennial Prize, 461

ECONOMICS

Any Country
American Institute for Economic Research Summer Fellowship, 77
Balliol College: Balliol Economics Scholarship, 1455
Bedford Society Scholarship, 1040
Business, Economics & Law Postgraduate Academic Excellence Scholarship, 155
Doctor of Philosophy Scholarship in Globalisation and International Economics, 1214
Economics: MSc Academic and Professional Scholarships (International), 1292
Faculty PhD Scholarships, 319
Fitzwilliam College: Peter Wilson Estates Gazette Studentships, 1245

150 Fully Funded PhD Degree Scholarships for International Students, 503
Global Economics Postgraduate Scholarship, 1236
Grants, 1173
GUS LIPSCHITZ BURSARY, 1008
Herbert Smith Freehills Law and Economics Honours Year Award, 1419
HKBU Fully Funded International Postgraduate Scholarship, 19
Hobart Houghton Research Fellowship, 1008
Hoover Fellowships for International Scholars, 335
India: Export-Import Bank of India BRICS Economic Research Award, 596
Knight-Bagehot Fellowships in Economics and Business Journalism at Columbia University, 372
Linacre College: Hicks Scholarship, 1470
Lindt Dissertation Fellowship, 370
LLM in International Trade Law–Contracts and Dispute Resolution–Scholarships, 1213
Macandrew-Stout Postgraduate Scholarship in Economics, 1445
Makabongwe Ndzwayiba Bursary, 1009
Program in Early American Economy and Society (PEAES) Post-Doctoral Fellowships, 729
Reserve Bank of New Zealand Scholarships, 992
The Roger Perry Memorial Scholarship, 993
Ruth First Scholarship, 1010
Shorenstein Fellowships in Contemporary Asia, 1109
A S Nivison Memorial Scholarship, 1404
Steve Weston and Trust Scholarships, 1289
Teaching Assistantships (Economics), 1210
The Tim Collins Scholarship for the Study of Love in Religion, 984
William Moore Gorman Graduate Research Scholarship, 1212
Women in Central Banking Scholarship, 993

African Nations

Canon Collins Trust Scholarships, 741

Asian Countries

Fulbright-Nehru Doctoral Research Fellowships, 1195
Fulbright-Nehru Master's Fellowships, 1195
Fulbright-Nehru Postdoctoral Research Fellowships, 1195
Indira Gandhi Institute of Development Research-International Development Research Centre Scholarships and Fellowships for Asian Countries Students, 624

Australia

American Planning Association(I)-Innovation, Competition and Economic Performance, 402
Gail Kelly Honours Award for Business, 1418
HeART of the Basin Scholarship, 340
Pembroke College: The Grosvenor-Shilling Bursary in Land Economy, 1255
Women in Finance and Economics Scholarship, 426

Canada

John Charles Polanyi Prizes, 1077

European Countries

Candriam Scholarship, 763

New Zealand

American Planning Association(I)-Innovation, Competition and Economic Performance, 402
Auckland Council Chief Economist's Research Scholarship in Economics, 1271
Auckland Council Research Scholarship in Urban Economics, 1198
Fulbright-Platinum Triangle Scholarship in Entrepreneurship, 736
Gail Kelly Honours Award for Business, 1418
Gordon Watson Scholarship, 1199
Māori and Pacific Islands Scholarship, 992
Reserve Bank of New Zealand Scholarships for International Students, 993

South Africa

Canon Collins Trust Scholarships, 741

United Kingdom

Fraser of Allander Institute Scholarships for MSc Applied Economics, 1544

United States of America

Gerald D. and Norma Feldman Graduate Student Dissertation Fellowship, 197
Helmut Kohl Award in German and European Studies, 198
The Thomas R. Pickering Foreign Affairs Fellowship, 1177

ANCIENT CIVILISATIONS (EGYPTOLOGY, ASSYRIOLOGY)

Any Country

American Schools of Oriental Research Mesopotamian Fellowship, 108

ANTHROPOLOGY

Any Country

American Museum of Natural History Collection Study Grants, 87
Conference and Workshop Grant, 1614
Cultural Anthropology Program Senior Research Awards, 867
Dissertation Fieldwork Grant, 1614
Engaged Research Grant, 1615
Global Initiatives Grant, 1615
Harvard Travellers Club Permanent Fund, 581
Linacre College: Rausing Scholarship in Anthropology, 1471
Lindt Dissertation Fellowship, 370
Post-PhD Research Grant, 1616
Rausing Scholarship in Anthropology, 735
Ruth First Scholarship, 1010

SAPIENS Public Scholars Training Fellowship, 1616
School of Anthropology and Conservation Research Scholarship, 1331
Skinner Fund, 1053
The Tim Collins Scholarship for the Study of Love in Religion, 984
VP Kanitkar Memorial Scholarship, 1097
Wadsworth International Fellowship, 1617
William Wyse Studentship in Social Anthropology, 1260
African Nations
GREAT Scholarships-Egypt, 1286
GREAT Scholarships-Ghana, 1286
GREAT Scholarships-Kenya, 1287
Wadsworth African Fellowship, 1616
Asian Countries
Fulbright-Nehru Doctoral Research Fellowships, 1195
Fulbright-Nehru Postdoctoral Research Fellowships, 1195
GREAT Scholarships-China, 1286
GREAT Scholarships-India, 1287
GREAT Scholarships–Indonesia, 1287
GREAT Scholarships–Malaysia, 1288
GREAT Scholarships–Pakistan, 1288
GREAT Scholarships–Thailand, 1288
Australia
Three Nations Conference Award, 323
European Countries
Linacre Anthropology Scholarship, 734
European Union
Oxford-Calleva Scholarship, 1483
Research Degree Scholarships in Anthropology, 1208
Middle East
School of Anthropology and Museum Ethnography: Peter Lienhardt/Philip Bagby Travel Awards, 1502
United Kingdom
Research Degree Scholarships in Anthropology, 1208
United States of America
Council of American Overseas Research Centers Multi Country Research Fellowships, 101
Wenner-Gren Fellowship in Anthropology and Black Experiences, 1617

ETHNOLOGY

Any Country
Phillips Fund for Native American Research, 94
European Countries
American Council of Learned Societies Humanities Program in Belarus, Russia and Ukraine, 62
Russia
American Council of Learned Societies Humanities Program in Belarus, Russia and Ukraine, 62

COGNITIVE SCIENCES

Any Country
International Prize, 537
JSMF Opportunity Awards, 679
Max Planck Institute-CBS Postdoctoral Position in Neuroscience of Pain Perception in Germany, 797
West European Countries
Doctor of Philosophy and Postdoctoral Positions-Investigating Sensory Aspects of Human Communication, 798

CULTURAL STUDIES

Any Country
A-AA Austrian Studies Scholarship Award, 180
AHRC North West Consortium Doctoral Training Partnership (NWCDTP) in the School of Arts, Languages and Cultures, 1364
Confucius Institute Scholarship, 1637
Grants for Public Projects, 123
Guy Butler Research Award, 1008
Harry Clough Bursary, 1378
Harvard Travellers Club Permanent Fund, 581
James H. Billington Fellowship, 694
The Lees Scholarship, 1388
Library Associates Fellowship, 683
Lingenfelter Doctoral Fellowship, 212
Memorial Fund of 8 May, 911
Myrtle McMyn Bursary, 1380
Oriental Studies: Sasakawa Fund, 1480
Oxford-Nizami Ganjavi Graduate Scholarships, 1492
Paul Mellon Centre Rome Fellowship, 261
Petro Jacyk Program, 951
President's Doctoral Scholar (PDS) Awards in the School of Arts, Languages and Culture, 1381
School of Arts, Languages and Cultures PhD Studentships, 1383
The School of History and Heritage MA Bursary, 1351
Sidney Topol Fellowship in Nonviolence Practice, 231
The Tim Collins Scholarship for the Study of Love in Religion, 984
University of Leicester Future 50 PhD Scholarship: "Latinx in the UK: Identity, Visibility and British Latinx Studies," 237
Usher Bursary, 1390
African Nations
Canon Collins Trust Scholarships, 741
Asian Countries
Daiwa Foundation Awards, 411
Asia-Pacific Countries
Fujitsu Scholarship Program for Asia-Pacific Region, 549

Australia
Jacqui Thorburn and Family Bursary for Indigenous Archaeology and Cultural Heritage Management, 527
Canada
Edward S. Rogers Sr. Graduate Student Fellowships, 1076
European Countries
American Council of Learned Societies Humanities Program in Belarus, Russia and Ukraine, 62
Collaborative Project to Meet Societal and Industry-related Challenges, 984
Researcher Project for Scientific Renewal, 991
North European Countries
Awards for American Universities and Colleges to host Norwegian lecturers, 122
Russia
American Council of Learned Societies Humanities Program in Belarus, Russia and Ukraine, 62
South Africa
Canon Collins Trust Scholarships, 741
United Kingdom
Daiwa Foundation Awards, 411
Daiwa Scholarships in Japanese Studies, 1370
United States of America
Boren Fellowships for Graduate Students, 230
Fujitsu Scholarship Program for Asia-Pacific Region, 549
Gerald D. and Norma Feldman Graduate Student Dissertation Fellowship, 197
Summer Seminar in Germany, 567
University of California at Los Angeles Institute of American Culture (IAC) Postdoctoral/Visiting Scholar Fellowships, 1241
Weiss/Brown Publication Subvention Award, 892

AFRICAN STUDIES

Any Country
Area Studies: FirstRand Laurie Dippenaar Scholarship, 1454
Rhodes University African Studies Centre (RASC), 1009
African Nations
Ooni Adeyeye Enitan Ogunwusi Scholarships, 1479

AMERICAN

Any Country
China Residency Program, 928
Dora and Mayer Tendler Fellowship, 1639
JCB J. M. Stuart Brown Graduate Fellowship, 682
Omohundro Institute-NEH Postdoctoral Fellowship, 919
Rose and Isidore Drench Memorial Fellowship, 1640
Winterthur Dissertation Research Fellowships, 1621
Winterthur Postdoctoral Fellowships, 1621
Winterthur Research Fellowships, 1621

CANADIAN

Any Country
Distinguished Dissertation Award, 145
Donner Medal in Canadian Studies, 145

EAST ASIAN

Asian Countries
Daiwa Scholarships in Japanese Studies, 412
Australia
Western Australian Government Japanese Studies Scholarships, 429
New Zealand
Barbara Mito Reed Award, 1272
United Kingdom
Oxford-Ko Cheuk Hung Graduate Scholarship, 1490

EASTERN EUROPEAN

Any Country
Dina Abramowicz Emerging Scholar Fellowship, 1639
Joseph Kremen Memorial Fellowship, 1640
Natalie and Mendel Racolin Memorial Fellowship, 1640
Professor Bernard Choseed Memorial Fellowship, 1640
Vivian Lefsky Hort Memorial Fellowship, 1641

EUROPEAN

Any Country
American School of Classical Studies at Athens Summer Sessions, 99
The Eamon Cleary Trust Postgraduate Study Scholarship, 1449
Samuel H Kress Joint Athens-Jerusalem Fellowship, 105
Canada
Mary McNeill Scholarship in Irish Studies, 972
South European Countries
Italian Australian Foundation Travel Scholarships, 1396
United States of America
Helmut Kohl Award in German and European Studies, 198
Mary McNeill Scholarship in Irish Studies, 972

HISPANIC AMERICAN

Caribbean Countries
Latin American Centre-Latin American Centre Scholarship, 1468
European Countries
Latin American Centre-Latin American Centre Scholarship, 1468
Latin America
Latin American Centre-Latin American Centre Scholarship, 1468

INDIGENOUS STUDIES

Any Country
Australian Institute of Aboriginal and Torres Strait Islander Studies Conference Call for papers, 170
New South Wales Indigenous History Fellowship, 141
Phillips Fund for Native American Research, 94
Rae and George Hammer Memorial Visiting Research Fellowship, 1218
World Bank Grants Facility for Indigenous Peoples, 1626

ISLAMIC

Any Country
Pembroke College: Graduate Studentships in Arabic and Islamic Studies (including Persian), 1254

JEWISH

Any Country
Abraham and Rachela Melezin Fellowship, 1638
Aleksander and Alicja Hertz Memorial Fellowship, 1639
Dina Abramowicz Emerging Scholar Fellowship, 1639
Dora and Mayer Tendler Fellowship, 1639
Joseph Kremen Memorial Fellowship, 1640
Maria Salit-Gitelson Tell Memorial Fellowship, 1640
Natalie and Mendel Racolin Memorial Fellowship, 1640
Professor Bernard Choseed Memorial Fellowship, 1640
Rose and Isidore Drench Memorial Fellowship, 1640
Samuel and Flora Weiss Research Fellowship, 1641
Vivian Lefsky Hort Memorial Fellowship, 1641
European Countries
Abram and Fannie Gottlieb Immerman and Abraham Nathan and Bertha Daskal Weinstein Memorial Fellowship, 1639

MIDDLE EASTERN

Any Country
Samuel H Kress Joint Athens-Jerusalem Fellowship, 105
United States of America
W. F. Albright Institute of Archaeological Research/National Endowment for the Humanities Fellowship, 110

SOUTH ASIAN

United States of America
American Institute of Bangladesh Studies Junior Fellowship, 79
American Institute of Bangladesh Studies Pre-Dissertation Fellowships, 80
American Institute of Bangladesh Studies Senior Fellowship, 80
American Institute of Bangladesh Studies Travel Grants, 80

SOUTHEAST ASIAN

African Nations
Indonesian Arts and Culture Scholarship, 816
Asian Countries
Indonesian Arts and Culture Scholarship, 816
Asia-Pacific Countries
Indonesian Arts and Culture Scholarship, 816
European Union
Indonesian Arts and Culture Scholarship, 816
Oceania
Indonesian Arts and Culture Scholarship, 816

WESTERN EUROPEAN

West European Countries
Lucy Cavendish College: Evelyn Povey Studentship, 1252

DEMOGRAPHY AND POPULATION

Any Country
2023-24 Basia Zaba Memorial Scholarship, 744
United Kingdom
Prevention and Population Research Programme Award, 315

DEVELOPMENT STUDIES

Any Country
African Forest Forum (AFF) Research Fellowships, 17
International Development: QEH Scholarship, 1465
MSc Sustainable Urban Development Programme Scholarship, 1477
Ruth First Scholarship, 1010
The Tim Collins Scholarship for the Study of Love in Religion, 984
African Nations
Arthington Davy Scholarship, 1225
European Countries
Collaborative Project in Global Health, 990
Researcher Project for Scientific Renewal, 991

GEOGRAPHY

Any Country
Albright Institute of Archaeological Research (AIAR) Annual Professorship, 107
Bedford Society Scholarship, 1040
Evelyn Stokes Memorial Doctoral Scholarship, 1579
Fulbright Distinguished Chair in Science, Technology, and Innovation (CSIRO), 551
Fully-funded PhD Studentship in the School of Geography, 1439
Geography and Environment Scholarships, 754
Geography: Sir Walter Raleigh Postgraduate Scholarship, 1462

Geography Students Conference Fund, 1274
Harvard Travellers Club Permanent Fund, 581
Phyllis Mary Morris Bursaries, 1237
Resource Management Law Association of New Zealand Masters Scholarship, 157
School of Geography and the Environment Commonwealth Shared Scholarship, 735
The Tim Collins Scholarship for the Study of Love in Religion, 984
Visiting Geographical Scientist Program, 146
African Nations
GREAT Scholarships-Egypt, 1286
GREAT Scholarships-Ghana, 1286
GREAT Scholarships-Kenya, 1287
Asian Countries
GREAT Scholarships-China, 1286
GREAT Scholarships-India, 1287
GREAT Scholarships–Indonesia, 1287
GREAT Scholarships–Malaysia, 1288
GREAT Scholarships–Pakistan, 1288
GREAT Scholarships–Thailand, 1288
European Union
Fully-Funded PhD Studentship in Sustainable Place-Making, 329
30th International Geographical Congress Award, 1037
United Kingdom
Fully-Funded PhD Studentship in Sustainable Place-Making, 329
Geographical Club Award, 1038
Innovative Geography Teaching Grants, 1038
30th International Geographical Congress Award, 1037
United States of America
Association of American Geographers NSF International Geographical Union Conference Travel Grants, 146

HERITAGE PRESERVATION

Any Country
BIAA-ANAMED Joint Fellowship in Heritage Studies, 97
Honor Frost Foundation Grants, 234
PhD scholarship in Craft, Technology and Entrepreneurship, 383
School of Anthropology and Conservation Research Scholarship, 1331
Asian Countries
Fulbright-Nehru Doctoral Research Fellowships, 1195
Fulbright-Nehru Postdoctoral Research Fellowships, 1195
Australia
Jacqui Thorburn and Family Bursary for Indigenous Archaeology and Cultural Heritage Management, 527
South European Countries
Italian Australian Foundation Travel Scholarships, 1396

INTERNATIONAL RELATIONS

Any Country
Abba P. Schwartz Research Fellowship, 684
Bedford Society Scholarship, 1040
Cardiff University School of Law and Politics-ESRC-funded PhD Studentship in Politics and International Relations, 328
Carnegie Endowment Junior Fellows Program, 1005
Doctor of Philosophy Scholarships in the Social Sciences, 503
Jennings Randolph Program for International Peace Dissertation Fellowship, 1191
Jennings Randolph Program for International Peace Senior Fellowships, 1192
Josiah Charles Trent Memorial Foundation Endowment Fund, 443
Linacre College: Ronald and Jane Olson Scholarship, 1472
Marjorie Kovler Research Fellowship, 685
Worcester College: C. Douglas Dillon Scholarship, 1514
African Nations
GREAT Scholarships-Egypt, 1286
GREAT Scholarships-Ghana, 1286
GREAT Scholarships-Kenya, 1287
Asian Countries
China Scholarships, 620
Fulbright-Nehru Master's Fellowships, 1195
GREAT Scholarships-China, 1286
GREAT Scholarships-India, 1287
GREAT Scholarships–Indonesia, 1287
GREAT Scholarships–Malaysia, 1288
GREAT Scholarships–Pakistan, 1288
GREAT Scholarships–Thailand, 1288
Shorenstein Fellowships in Contemporary Asia, 1109
Canada
The W. L. Mackenzie King Scholarships, 1081
European Countries
Collaborative Project in Global Health, 990
Researcher Project for Scientific Renewal, 991
New Zealand
Gordon Watson Scholarship, 1199
North European Countries
Awards for American Universities and Colleges to host Norwegian lecturers, 122
United States of America
Arthur M. Schlesinger, Jr. Fellowship, 685
International Affairs Fellowship for Tenured International Relations Scholars, 389

POLITICAL SCIENCE AND GOVERNMENT

Any Country
Abba P. Schwartz Research Fellowship, 684
Bedford Society Scholarship, 1040

Bilkent International Relations Fellowship, 209
Bilkent Political Science Fellowship, 209
Blavatnik School of Government: Public Service Scholarship, 1457
Canadian Parliamentary Internship Programme, 294
Cardiff University School of Law and Politics-ESRC-funded PhD Studentship in Politics and International Relations, 328
C Douglas Dillon Graduate Scholarship, 1625
College of Business Government and Law PhD Top-up, 522
David N. Lyon Scholarship in Politics–The Politics of Sex and Gender Equality in Diverse Societies, 938
Francis Regan Student Scholarship, 525
French Association of University Women (AFFDU) Monique Fouet Grant, 248
Friedrich-Ebert-Stiftung, 188
150 Fully Funded PhD Degree Scholarships for International Students, 503
Harry Crossley Doctoral Fellowship, 1152
Heinrich-Böll-Stiftung, 189
Institute for Advanced Studies in the Humanities (The Institute for Advanced Studies in the Humanities)-SSPS (School of Social and Political Science) Research Fellowships, 629
Jesse M. Unruh Assembly Fellowship Program, 1083
Konrad-Adenauer-Stiftung, 190
Linacre College: Ronald and Jane Olson Scholarship, 1472
Lindt Dissertation Fellowship, 370
LLM in International Trade Law–Contracts and Dispute Resolution–Scholarships, 1213
Marjorie Kovler Research Fellowship, 685
Nuffield College Gwilym Gibbon Research Fellowships, 1478
Ontario Bicentennial Award, 238
Petro Jacyk Program, 951
Politics and International Studies Scholarships, 756
Ramboll Masters Scholarship for International Students, 1448
Ruth First Scholarship, 1010
School for Policy Studies International Postgraduate Scholarships, 1237
St Antony's College Ali Pachachi Scholarship, 1503
Theodore C. Sorensen Research Fellowship, 685
The Tim Collins Scholarship for the Study of Love in Religion, 984
Vincent Lemieux Prize, 295
Worcester College: C. Douglas Dillon Scholarship, 1514
African Nations
Blavatnik School of Government: Africa Governance Initiative Scholarship, 1456
Blavatnik School of Government: African Initiative for Governance Scholarships, 1457
GREAT Scholarships-Egypt, 1286
GREAT Scholarships-Ghana, 1286
GREAT Scholarships-Kenya, 1287
Asian Countries
China Scholarships, 620
Fulbright-Nehru Doctoral Research Fellowships, 1195
Fulbright-Nehru Master's Fellowships, 1195
Fulbright-Nehru Postdoctoral Research Fellowships, 1195
GREAT Scholarships-China, 1286
GREAT Scholarships-India, 1287
GREAT Scholarships–Indonesia, 1287
GREAT Scholarships–Malaysia, 1288
GREAT Scholarships–Pakistan, 1288
GREAT Scholarships–Thailand, 1288
Indira Gandhi Institute of Development Research-International Development Research Centre Scholarships and Fellowships for Asian Countries Students, 624
Shorenstein Fellowships in Contemporary Asia, 1109
Canada
The Hydro One Aboriginal Award for Graduate Studies in Public Policy and Administration, 1080
Ontario Legislature Internship Programme, 294
European Countries
Collaborative Project to Meet Societal and Industry-related Challenges, 990
Rosa-Luxemburg-Stiftung, 190
United Kingdom
Frank Stell Scholarship, 1336
United States of America
Gerald D. and Norma Feldman Graduate Student Dissertation Fellowship, 197
Helmut Kohl Award in German and European Studies, 198
The James Madison Memorial Fellowship, 782
Norman Y. Mineta Fellowship, 681
The Thomas R. Pickering Foreign Affairs Fellowship, 1177
WGRG Foundation Terri Grier Memorial Scholarship, 1183
West European Countries
Mansfield College: Adam von Trott Scholarship, 1475

COMPARATIVE POLITICS

Any Country
Doctor of Philosophy Scholarships in the Social Sciences, 503

PSYCHOLOGY

Any Country
Alzheimer's Association Clinician Scientist Fellowship (AACSF) Program, 25
Alzheimer's Association Clinician Scientist Fellowship to Promote Diversity (AACSF-D), 26
Alzheimer's Association Leveraging Model & Data Resources to Advance Alzheimer's and Dementia Discovery Program (ALZ Discovery Grant Program), 26

Alzheimer's Association Research Fellowship (AARF), 27
Alzheimer's Association Research Fellowship to Promote Diversity (AARF-D), 27
Alzheimer's Association Research Grant (AARG), 27
Alzheimer's Association Research Grant-New to the Field (AARG-NTF), 28
Alzheimer's Association Research Grant to Promote Diversity (AARG-D), 28
Alzheimer's Association Research Grant to Promote Diversity-New to the Field (AARG-D-NTF), 29
American Foundation for Suicide Prevention Distinguished Investigator Awards, 67
be.AI Leverhulme Doctoral Scholarships (Leverhulme Trust), 1558
Bedford Society Scholarship, 1040
Beyond Segments: Towards a Lexical Model for Tonal Bilinguals, 767
Biodiverse Nature Prescriptions and Mental Health, 1554
Blue Sky Focus Grant, 67
The Clara Mayo Grants, 1131
Dissertation Research Grants, 95
Distinguished Investigator Grant, 68
ECTRIMS Allied Health Professional Fellowship, 495
F.J. McGuigan Early Career Investigator Research Grant on Understanding the Human Mind, 95
Gilbert M Tothill Scholarship in Psychological Medicine, 1445
Javits-Frasier Scholars Program, 847
Linked Standard Research Grant, 68
Macquarie University PhD Scholarship in Knowledge Acquisition and Cognitive Modelling, 775
Max Planck Institute-CBS Postdoctoral Position in Neuroscience of Pain Perception in Germany, 797
McGill University PhD Studentships in Neurolinguistics, 800
MSc Psychology with a Specialisation in Business Scholarship, 1156
New Connections: Increasing Diversity, 29
PhD (via MPhil) International Studentships in Cyber Security in UK, 902
Pilot Innovation Grants, 68
Postdoctoral Fellowship, 69, 180
School of Life and Health Sciences Postgraduate Masters Scholarships-Commonwealth Shared Scholarship Scheme, 151
The Sergievsky Award For Epilepsy Health Equity And Diversity, 552
Sex and Gender in Alzheimer's (SAGA 23) Award Program, 30
Short-Term Risk Focus Grant, 69
Standard Research Grant, 69
The Zenith Fellows Award Program (Zenith), 31
African Nations
GREAT Scholarships-Egypt, 1286
GREAT Scholarships-Ghana, 1286
GREAT Scholarships-Kenya, 1287
Asian Countries
Fulbright-Nehru Doctoral Research Fellowships, 1195
Fulbright-Nehru Postdoctoral Research Fellowships, 1195
GREAT Scholarships-China, 1286
GREAT Scholarships-India, 1287
GREAT Scholarships–Indonesia, 1287
GREAT Scholarships–Malaysia, 1288
GREAT Scholarships–Pakistan, 1288
GREAT Scholarships–Thailand, 1288
Australia
Aboriginal Social and Emotional Wellbeing Scholarship, 1046
Association of American Railroads Janssen Cilag Dementia Research Grant, 31
Association of American Railroads Rosemary Foundation Travel Project Grant-Dementia Research, 32
Doctor of Philosophy APA(I) Police-Mental Health Scholarship, 822
Professor Ross Kalucy Indigenous Well-Being Scholarship, 531
Rosemary Foundation Travel Grant, 32
Canada
Doctoral Dissertation Grant Program (Fahs-Beck Scholars), 507
Faculty/Post-Doctoral Grant Program (Fahs-Beck Fellows), 507
European Union
Fully-Funded PhD Studentship in Sustainable Place-Making, 329
New Zealand
Doctor of Philosophy APA(I) Police-Mental Health Scholarship, 822
Rosemary Foundation Travel Grant, 32
United Kingdom
Fully-Funded PhD Studentship in Sustainable Place-Making, 329
International Student Merit Scholarship, 958
United States of America
Arc of the United States Research Grant, 127
Doctoral Dissertation Grant Program (Fahs-Beck Scholars), 507
Eileen J Garrett Scholarship, 946
Faculty/Post-Doctoral Grant Program (Fahs-Beck Fellows), 507
Fulbright-Freud Visiting Lecturer of Psychoanalysis, 552
West European Countries
Doctor of Philosophy and Postdoctoral Positions-Investigating Sensory Aspects of Human Communication, 798

CLINICAL PSYCHOLOGY

Australia
Indigenous Master of Psychology (Clinical) Scholarship, 1407

DEVELOPMENT PSYCHOLOGY

Any Country
Esther Katz Rosen Fund Grants, 95
John and Polly Sparks Early Career Grant for Psychologists Investigating Serious Emotional Disturbance (SED), 96

EXPERIMENTAL PSYCHOLOGY

European Union
Oxford-Calleva Scholarship, 1483

PSYCHOMETRICS

Any Country
Educational Testing Service Harold Gulliksen Psychometric Fellowship Program, 475
Harold Gulliksen Psychometric Research Fellowship, 477

SOCIAL PSYCHOLOGY

United States of America
Greater Good Science Center Graduate Fellowships, 198

RURAL STUDIES

Any Country
A S Nivison Memorial Scholarship, 1404
Australia
D.L. McMaster Fund Endowed Housing Scholarship, 1406

SOCIOLOGY

Any Country
Bielefeld Graduate School in History and Sociology Start-up Doctoral Scholarships, 208
Bill Jenkins Award, 1323
Doctor of Philosophy Scholarships in the Social Sciences, 503
Lindt Dissertation Fellowship, 370
Ruth First Scholarship, 1010
Saving Lives: Mapping the Influence of Indigenous LGBTIQ + Creative Artists-International, 779
Sociology Departmental MA Scholarship, 1582
Soros Equality Fellowship, 926
The Tim Collins Scholarship for the Study of Love in Religion, 984
Zuckerman Dissertation Fellowship, 371
Asian Countries
Fulbright-Nehru Doctoral Research Fellowships, 1195
Fulbright-Nehru Postdoctoral Research Fellowships, 1195
Australia
Saving Lives: Mapping the Influence of Indigenous LGBTIQ + Creative Artists-Domestic, 778
Three Nations Conference Award, 323
European Countries
American Council of Learned Societies Humanities Program in Belarus, Russia and Ukraine, 62
Rosa-Luxemburg-Stiftung, 190
European Union
Fully-Funded PhD Studentship in Sustainable Place-Making, 329
Russia
American Council of Learned Societies Humanities Program in Belarus, Russia and Ukraine, 62
United Kingdom
Fully-Funded PhD Studentship in Sustainable Place-Making, 329
SOCIAL POLICY
Any Country
Social Policy and Intervention: Barnett House-Nuffield Joint Scholarship, 1502
Social Policy and Intervention: Barnett Scholarship, 1502

URBAN STUDIES

Any Country
Lost Cities Funding Programme, 1172
MSc Sustainable Urban Development Programme Scholarship, 1477
Terrell Blodgett Fellowship for Government Services in Urban Management and Finance, 1170
The Tim Collins Scholarship for the Study of Love in Religion, 984
Asian Countries
Fulbright-Nehru Doctoral Research Fellowships, 1195
Fulbright-Nehru Postdoctoral Research Fellowships, 1195

WOMEN'S STUDIES

Any Country
American Association of University Women/International Federation of University Women International Fellowships, 246
Azure Dillon 4-H Memorial Scholarship, 958
Ertegun Graduate Scholarship Programme in the Humanities, 1460
Ethnic Minority Foundation Grants, 493
Asian Countries
Fulbright-Nehru Doctoral Research Fellowships, 1195
Fulbright-Nehru Master's Fellowships, 1195
Fulbright-Nehru Postdoctoral Research Fellowships, 1195
United Kingdom
Hilda Martindale Trust Awards, 601

United States of America
American Association of University Women Eleanor Roosevelt Fund Award, 51

TRADE, CRAFT AND INDUSTRIAL TECHNIQUES

GENERAL

African Nations
The Beacon Scholarship, 331
Xerox Technical Minority Scholarship, 1633
Asian Countries
Xerox Technical Minority Scholarship, 1633
Asia-Pacific Countries
Xerox Technical Minority Scholarship, 1633
United States of America
Xerox Technical Minority Scholarship, 1633

FOOD TECHNOLOGY

Any Country
Interdisciplinary Doctoral Studentships in Food Systems: UKFS-CDT, 267
International Dairy-Deli-Bakery Association Graduate Scholarships, 656
United Kingdom
Interdisciplinary Doctoral Studentships in Food Systems: UKFS-CDT, 267

GRAPHIC ARTS

PRINTING AND PRINTMAKING

Any Country
The Barns-Graham Travel Award, 1048

PUBLISHING AND BOOK TRADE

Any Country
Charles Fleming Publishing Award, 1050
Guggenheim Fellowships, 1119
South Africa
South African Council for English Education's EX-PCE Bursary, 1136

OPTICAL TECHNOLOGY

Any Country
The Optical Society, Chang Pivoting Fellowship, 841
The Optical Society, Corning Women in Optical Communications Scholarship, 841
The Optical Society, Foundation Fellowships, 842

WOOD TECHNOLOGY

Any Country
Wood Technology Research Centre–Postgraduate Scholarships, 1271

TRANSPORT AND COMMUNICATIONS

GENERAL

Any Country
Ability Grants for Research Degree Students, 1530
Brian Large Bursary Fund, 1584
Rees Jeffrey Road Fund, 1585
The Ship Smart Annual Scholarship, 133
African Nations
The Beacon Scholarship, 331
European Countries
Collaborative Project to Meet Societal and Industry-related Challenges, 990
Knowledge-building Project for Industry, 990
European Union
Cardiff School of City and Regional Planning–Master's Bursaries, 325
United Kingdom
Cardiff School of City and Regional Planning–Master's Bursaries, 325

AIR TRANSPORT

Any Country
Wolf Aviation Fund Grants Program, 24
Australia
Destination Australia Scholarship, 1046

TELECOMMUNICATIONS SERVICES

Canada
Jim Bourque Scholarship, 130

Index of Awards

A
A. B. Baker Award for Lifetime Achievement in Neurologic Education, 36
A. Verville Fellowship, 1118
A-AA Austrian Studies Scholarship Award, 180
AAA Graduate Education Scholarships, 52
AAA Northeast Scholarship, 1003
AACAP Pilot Research Award for Attention Disorders, 33
AACAP Pilot Research Award for Early Career Faculty and Child and Adolescent Psychiatry Fellows, 34
AACAP Pilot Research Award for Learning Disabilities, 34
The AACAP Rieger Psychodynamic Psychotherapy Award, 36
AACN Impact Research Grant, 43
AACN-Sigma Theta Tau Critical Care Grant, 44
AACR-Bayer Stimulating Therapeutic Advances through Research Training (START) Grants, 2
AACR Cancer Disparities Research Fellowships, 1
AACR Clinical Oncology Research (CORE) Training Fellowships, 2
AACR-Debbie's Dream Foundation Career Development Award for Gastric Cancer Research, 3
AACR NextGen Grants for Transformative Cancer Research, 2
AACR-Novocure Career Development Awards for Tumor Treating Fields Research, 3
AACR-Novocure Tumor Treating Fields Research Grants, 4
AACR-Sontag Foundation Brain Cancer Research Fellowship, 5
AALL Research Fund: An Endowment Established by LexisNexis, 46
A&A Masters Higher Degree Research Award, 172
AANS International Visiting Surgeon Fellowship, 47
Aarhus University Scholarships, 6
Aaron Siskind Foundation-Individual Photographer's Fellowship, 142
Abba P. Schwartz Research Fellowship, 684
Abbey Harris Mural Fund, 7
Abbey Scholarship in Painting, 260
The Abdul Aziz Al Ghurair Refugee Education Fund, 7
The Abdullah Al-Mubarak Al-Sabah Foundation BRISMES Scholarships, 263
Abdus Salam ICTP Fellowships, 8
Abell Foundation-For Small Grant Requests, 9
Abell Foundation-Grant Requests Greater than US$10,000, 9
Aberdeen International Masters Scholarship, 1214
Abe Voron Award, 264
Abilene Christian University National Merit Finalist or Semifinalist Scholarship, 9
Abilene Christian University Valedictorian/Salutatorian Scholarship, 10
Aboriginal and Torres Strait Islander Arts Fellowship, 159
Aboriginal and Torres Strait Islander Arts Skills and Arts Development, 159
Aboriginal and Torres Strait Islander New Work Grant, 159
Aboriginal and Torres Strait Islander Scholarship, 1426
Aboriginal and Torres Strait Islander Scholarship Program, 401
Aboriginal and Torres Strait Islander Staff Scholarship, 508
Aboriginal Housing Office Tertiary Accommodation Grants, 1426
Aboriginal Social and Emotional Wellbeing Scholarship, 1046
Aboriginal social and emotional wellbeing Scholarship, 418
Abraham and Rachela Melezin Fellowship, 1638
Abraham Lincoln High School Alumni Association, 10
Abram and Fannie Gottlieb Immerman and Abraham Nathan and Bertha Daskal Weinstein Memorial Fellowship, 1639
Academia Resource Management Postgraduate Fellowship, 11
Academic Excellence Award: Postgraduate, 830
Academic Excellence International Masters Scholarship, 1304
Academic Excellence Scholarship (International), 227
Academic Excellence Senior Status Law Scholarship, 1304
Academy of Korean Studies Postgraduate Bursaries, 1092
Academy of Research and Higher Education Scholarships, 1213
Acadia Graduate Scholarship/Acadia Graduate Teaching Assistantships, 14
Accelerating Promising Practices for Small Libraries, 645
Access Missouri Financial Assistance Program, 818
Access & Rural Women New Zealand Scholarship, 153
The ACE Foundation Scholarship, 125
ACLS Emerging Voices Fellowships, 62
Acromegaly/Growth Hormone Excess Research, 951
Action Cancer Project Grant, 15
Action Medical Research Project Grants, 15
Action Medical Research Training Fellowship, 15
Acts 17 Scholarship, 210
Acute Generalized Exanthematous Pustulosis Fellowship, 670
Adelaide Postgraduate Coursework Scholarships, 1216
Adelle and Erwin Tomash Fellowship in the History of Information Processing, 347
Adelphi University Full-Time Transfer Merit Award, 16
Adolescent Health and Performance Scholarship, 164
Adolf Fassbender Travel Fellowship Award, 337
Adrian Tanner Prize, 1056
Advanced Biomedical Materials CDT, 1363
Advanced Clinician Scientist Fellowship, 311
Advanced Community Care Scholarship, 520
Advanced Postdoctoral Fellowships, 688
Advancing Women in Leadership Scholarship (MBA), 893
Advocacy Training Grants, 36
Aeronautical and Automotive Engineering Scholarships, 749
AfOx-Linacre Humanities Scholarship, 731
AfOx-Linacre Norman and Ivy Lloyd Scholarship, 731
AfOx-Linacre Trapnell Scholarship, 731
Africa: Mwalimu Julius Nyerere African Union Scholarship, 593
Africa: Next Einstein Forum (NEF) Fellows Programme, 593
Africa Excellence Scholarship, 1427
Africa Land and Food Masters Fellowship, 1016
African Association for Health Professions Education and Research, 535
African Forest Forum (AFF) Research Fellowships, 17
African Graduate Fellowships, 120

Palgrave Macmillan (ed.), *The Grants Register 2024*,
https://doi.org/10.1057/978-1-349-96073-6

African Peacebuilding Network Fellowships, 1121
African Peacebuilding Network (APN) Residential Postdoctoral Fellowship Program, 1120
African Scholarships, 461
Africa Postgraduate Regional Scholarship, 1305
Africa Scholarship, 1344
Africa Scholarship Programme, 1603
AfterCollege STEM Inclusion Scholarship, 18
AFZ Giles Scholarship, 1214
AGA Abstract Award for Health Disparities Research, 541
AGA-APFED Abstract Award in Eosinophilic GI Diseases, 542
AGA Fellow Abstract Award, 541
AGA-Moti L. & Kamla Rustgi International Travel Awards, 543
AGA Student Abstract Award, 542
Ageing Research Development Awards, 215
Agilent Technologies-AACN Critical-Care Nursing Research Grant, 44
Agilent Technology Critical Care Nursing Research Grant, 21
AGL Jungurra Wunnik Scholarship, 508
Agnes Fay Morgan Research Award, 668
AHA Postdoctoral Fellowship, 76
Ahmanson Veterans Scholarship, 210
AHNS Endocrine Surgery Section Eisai Research Grant Policies, 71
AHNS Endocrine Surgery Section Stryker Research Grant Policies, 72
AHO Tertiary Accommodation Grants, 349
AHRC: Chase Doctoral Training Partnership, 221
AHRC Chase PhD Studentship Narratives of Fall: The Archive and Art Collection of the Nineteenth Century Foundling Hospitale, 221
AHRC North West Consortium Doctoral Training Partnership (NWCDTP) in the School of Arts, Languages and Cultures, 1364
AHRC North West Consortium Doctoral Training Partnership in the School of Environment, Education and Development, 1364
AHRF Discovery Grants, 74
AIBS Bangladeshi Graduate Student Fellowship, 79
AIBS Professional Development Fellowships for Bangladeshi Scholars, 79
AICF Sharett Scholarship Program, 33
AICPA Legacy Scholarships, 210
Aid to Scholarly Journals, 1125
AIMS@JCU Scholarship, 673
AIPLEF Sidney B. Williams Scholarship, 1172
Air-Conditioning, Heating, and Refrigeration Institute MSc Scholarship, 22
Akhtarali H. Tobaccowala Fellowship, 517
ALA Library History Round Table Davis Article Award, 928
Alan and Helene Goldberg In Vitro Toxicology Grants, 686
Alan Emery Prize, 1057
The Alan Howard Scholarship, 616
Alan Tayler Scholarship (Mathematics), 1145
Alberta Heritage Foundation for Medical Research Part-Time Studentship, 22
Alberta Innovates-Health Solutions Postgraduate Fellowships, 22
Albert and Alexis Dennis Donation, 788
Albert Maucher Prize in Geoscience, 431
Albert W Dent Graduate Student Scholarship, 547
Albright Institute of Archaeological Research (AIAR) Annual Professorship, 107
Aleksander and Alicja Hertz Memorial Fellowship, 1639
Alexander and Dixon Scholarship (Bryce Bequest), 1314
Alexander and Margaret Johnstone Postgraduate Research Scholarships, 1314
Alexander Gerschenkron Prize, 458
Alex C P Chu Trade for Training Scholarship, 788
Alex Gusbeth Scholarship, 509
Alex Lindsay awards, 788
Alex Raydon Scholarship for Refugee or Migrant Students, 821
Al Fog Bergljot Kolflats Stipendfond, 910
Alfred Burger Award in Medicinal Chemistry, 53
Alfred Toepfer Natural Heritage Scholarships, 25
Alice Brown PhD Scholarships, 1295
Alice Ettinger Distinguished Achievement Award, 43
Alice Hanson Jones Biennial Prize, 458
Alistair Betts Scholarship, 638, 788
Allan and Nesta Ferguson Scholarships, 1092
Allan Kay Undergraduate Memorial Scholarship, 789
The Allan Nevins Prize in American Economic History, 460
Alleghery-ENCRC Student Research Award, 1184
Allen Senior Scholarship (Music), 1146
Alliance for Clinical Research Excellence and Safety Teacher Scholarship Award, 64
Alliance Group Postgraduate Scholarship, 1442
Alliance Manchester Business School PhD Studentships, 1364
Allianz Care Scholarship, 164
Allied Health Professional Fellowship (Clinical), 695
Al-Maktoum College Hamdan Bin Rashid Award, 1283
Al-Maktoum College Living Support Bursary, 1283
Alton & Neryda Fancourt Chapple Award, 1415
Alumni 10% Fee Tuition Discount, 830
Alumni 25% Fee Tuition Discount, 831
Alumni Bursary, 749, 1335
The Alumni Bursary, 812
Alumni Discounts, 1342, 1521
Alumni Discount Scheme, 943
Alumni Heritage Graduate Scholarship (AHGS), 1220
Alumni Loyalty Scholarship, 555, 704
Alumni Postgraduate Research Scholarship-Exclusively for Kent Graduates, 1323
Alumni Postgraduate Scholarships, 705
Alumni Scholarship, 1284
Alumni Scholarship for Postgraduate Study, 1345
Alumni Scholarship for the Master of Business Administration (MBA), 699
Alvin Li-Shen Chua Memorial Scholarship, 607
Alzheimer's Association Clinician Scientist Fellowship (AACSF) Program, 25
Alzheimer's Association Clinician Scientist Fellowship to Promote Diversity (AACSF-D), 26
Alzheimer's Association Leveraging Model & Data Resources to Advance Alzheimer's and Dementia Discovery Program (ALZ Discovery Grant Program), 26
Alzheimer's Association Research Fellowship (AARF), 27
Alzheimer's Association Research Fellowship to Promote Diversity (AARF-D), 27
Alzheimer's Association Research Grant (AARG), 27
Alzheimer's Association Research Grant-New to the Field (AARG-NTF), 28
Alzheimer's Association Research Grant to Promote Diversity (AARG-D), 28
Alzheimer's Association Research Grant to Promote Diversity-New to the Field (AARG-D-NTF), 29
Alzheimers Drug Discovery Foundation Grants Program, 32
AMA Queensland Foundation Medical Scholarships, 673
A Master of Science Degree Scholarship, 1186
Ambassadors Fund for Cultural Preservation Small Grants Competition, 483
The Amelia and John Kentfield PhD Scholarships, 616
American Academy of Otolaryngology-Head and Neck Surgery Translational Innovator Award, 72
American Academy of Pediatrics Resident Research Grants, 37
American Alpine Club Research Grants, 37
American Association for Cancer Research Anna D. Barker Basic Cancer Research Fellowship, 38

American Association for Cancer Research-AstraZeneca Stimulating Therapeutic Advancements through Research Training (START) Grants, 40
American Association for Cancer Research Career Development Awards, 39
American Association for Cancer Research Gertrude B. Elion Cancer Research Award, 39
American Association for Cancer Research NextGen Grants for Transformative Cancer Research, 40
American Association of Family and Consumer Sciences National Fellowships in Family and Consumer Sciences, 44
American Association of Family and Consumer Sciences New Achievers Award, 45
American Association of Law Libraries James F Connolly LexisNexis Academic and Library Solutions Scholarship, 46
American Association of Law Libraries LexisNexis/John R Johnson Memorial Scholarship Endowment, 46
American Association of Law Libraries Scholarship (Type II), 47
American Association of University Women (AAUW) American Fellowships, 48
American Association of University Women Career Development Grants, 50
American Association of University Women (AAUW) Career Development Grants, 49
American Association of University Women Case Support Travel Grants, 50
American Association of University Women Community Action Grants, 50
American Association of University Women Eleanor Roosevelt Fund Award, 51
American Association of University Women/International Federation of University Women International Fellowships, 246
American Association of University Women International Fellowships, 51
American Association of University Women (AAUW) International Fellowships, 49
American Association of University Women Selected Professions Fellowships, 52
American Atheists Chinn Scholarships, 987
American Atheists O'Hair Award, 987
American Board of Emergency Medicine Fellowship, 837
American Cancer Society International Fellowships for Beginning Investigators, 53
American Chemical Society Ahmed Zewail Award in Ultrafast Science and Technology, 54
American Chemical Society Award for Creative Advances in Environmental Science and Technology, 54
American Chemical Society Award for Creative Research and Applications of Iodine Chemistry, 54
American Chemical Society Award for Creative Work in Synthetic Organic Chemistry, 55
American Chemical Society Award for Encouraging Disadvantaged Students into Careers in the Chemical Sciences, 55
American Chemical Society Award for Encouraging Women into Careers in the Chemical Sciences, 55
American Chemical Society Award in Chromatography, 56
American Chemical Society Award in Colloid Chemistry, 56
American Chemical Society National Awards, 56
American Chemical Society Priestley Medal, 57
American Chemical Society Roger Adams Award in Organic Chemistry, 57
American Chemical Society Stanley C. Israel Regional Award for Advancing Diversity in the Chemical Sciences, 57
American College of Rheumatology/REF Arthritis Investigator Award, 995
American College of Rheumatology REF Rheumatology Scientist Development Award, 995
American Council of Learned Societies Digital Extension Grants, 1133
American Council of Learned Societies Humanities Program in Belarus, Russia and Ukraine, 62
American Council of Learned Societies/New York Public Library (NYPL) Fellowships, 63
American Federation for Aging Research/Pfizer Research Grants in Metabolic Control and Late Life Diseases, 65
American Federation for Aging Research Research Grants for Junior Faculty, 65
American Foundation for Suicide Prevention Distinguished Investigator Awards, 67
American Foundation of RHBNC International Excellence Scholarship, 1039
American Gastroenterological Association/American Gastroenterological Association-Eli & Edythe Broad Student Research Fellowship(s), 545
American Gastroenterological Association-Elsevier Pilot Research Award, 543
American Gastroenterological Association Fellowship to Faculty Transition Awards, 543
American Gastroenterological Association Research Scholar Awards, 544
American Gastroenterological Association R Robert and Sally D Funderburg Research Scholar Award in Gastric Cancer, 544
American Gynecological Club/Gynaecological Visiting Society Fellowship, 71
American Head and Neck Society-American Cyronics Society Career Development Award, 74
American Head and Neck Society Endocrine Research Grant, 73
American Head and Neck Society Pilot Research Grant, 73
American Head and Neck Society Surgeon Scientist Career Development Award (with AAOHNS), 73
American Head and Neck Society Young Investigator Award (with AAOHNS), 73
American Institute for Economic Research Summer Fellowship, 77
American Institute of Bangladesh Studies Junior Fellowship, 79
American Institute of Bangladesh Studies Pre-Dissertation Fellowships, 80
American Institute of Bangladesh Studies Senior Fellowship, 80
American Institute of Bangladesh Studies Travel Grants, 80
American Institute of Certified Public Accountants Fellowship for Minority Doctoral Students, 81, 696
American Institute of Certified Public Accountants/Robert Half Student Scholarship Award, 670
American Library Association Beta Phi Mu Award, 202
American Library Association Carroll Preston Baber Research Grant, 81
American Library Association John Phillip Immroth Memorial Award, 82
American Library Association Loleta D. Fyan Grant, 82
American Library Association Miriam L Hornback Scholarship, 83
American Library Association Shirley Olofson Memorial Awards, 83
American Library Association W. David Rozkuszka Scholarship, 83
American Library Association YALSA/Baker and Taylor Conference Grant, 83
American Meteorological Society Centennial Fellowships in Mathematics, 85
American Meteorological Society Graduate Fellowships, 86
American Museum of Natural History Collection Study Grants, 87
American Nuclear Society Mishima Award, 87
American Nuclear Society Utility Achievement Award, 87
American Otological Society Research Training Fellowships, 92
American Physiological Society Minority Travel Fellowship Awards, 94
American Planning Association(I)-Innovation, Competition and Economic Performance, 402

American-Scandinavian Foundation Scholarships (ASF), 910
American School of Classical Studies at Athens Advanced Fellowships, 98
American School of Classical Studies at Athens Fellowships, 98
American School of Classical Studies at Athens Research Fellowship in Environmental Studies, 99
American School of Classical Studies at Athens Research Fellowship in Faunal Studies, 99
American School of Classical Studies at Athens Research Fellowship in Geoarchaeology, 99
American School of Classical Studies at Athens Summer Sessions, 99
American Schools of Oriental Research Mesopotamian Fellowship, 108
American Schools of Oriental Research W.F. Albright Institute of Archaeological Research/National Endowment of the Humanities Fellowships, 108
American Society for Engineering Education Air Force Summer Faculty Fellowship Program, 110
American Society for Engineering Education Helen T Carr Fellowship Program, 110
American Society for Microbiology Microbe Minority Travel Awards, 112
American Society for Photogrammetry and Remote Sensing Robert N. Colwell Memorial Fellowship, 113
American Society of Composers, Authors and Publishers Foundation Morton Gould Young Composer Awards, 117
American Society of Naval Engineers (ASNE) Scholarship, 1091
American Studies (Lecturing Award), 550
American University of Beirut Mediterranean Scholarships, 120
American Water Works Association Abel Wolman Fellowship, 121
Amgen Fellowship Training Award, 995
Ampère Excellence Scholarships for International Students, 456
Ampère & MILYON Excellence Scholarships for International Students, 456
AMS-AAAS Mass Media Fellowship, 85
AMS Congressional Fellowship, 85
Amsterdam Excellence Scholarships (AES), 1223
Amsterdam Science Talent Scholarship (ASTS), 1223
Ana Hatherly Graduate Student Research Grant, 638
Anastomotic Leak Grant, Special Limited Project Grant, 114
Anderson-Yamanaka Scholarship, 1427
Andrew Brown Sport Scholarship, 1427
Andrew W. Mellon Foundation/ACLS Early Career Fellowships Program Dissertation Completion Fellowships, 63
Andrew W. Mellon Foundation Masters & Doctoral Scholarships, 1007
Andrew W Mellon Fellowship, 1635
Andrew W Mellon Foundation Fellowships, 108
The Anglo-Norse Dame Gillian Brown Postgraduate Scholarship, 126
Angus Ross Travel Scholarship in History, 1442
ANID (Becas Chile), 966
ANID CHILE, 1352
ANII Becas, 966
Anna C. & Oliver C. Colburn Fellowships, 127
Anna Louise Hoffman Award for Outstanding Achievement in Graduate Research, 668
Ann and Sol Schreiber Mentored Investigator Award, 942
Anna Schiller Scholarship, 988
Anne Bellam Scholarship, 1225
Anne Reid Memorial Trust Scholarship, 320
The Anne Rowling Clinic Regenerative Neurology Scholarships, 1302
The Anne S. Chatham Fellowship, 559
The Anne Seagrim Accommodation Scholarships, 616
Anne van den Ban Fund, 1604
Anning Morgan Bursary, 1310
Annual Academic Award, 1018
Annual Fund Postgraduate Scholarships, 695
Annual Hazards and Disasters Student Paper Competition, 879
Annual Meetings Travel and Hotel Subsidies, 458
Anthea Jane Wilson Scholarship, 419
Anthony Costa Foundation Arts Management Scholarship, 419
The Applications of Drugs in Enhancing Scaffold-associated Healing in the Middle Ear, 407
The Applications of Nanotechnology in Prevention of Chemotherapy-induced Hearing Impairment, 408
Applied Programme Grants (APRO) 2023, 582
Applied Research Competition, 927
Appraisal Institute Education Trust Minorities and Women Education Scholarship, 126
Arabic Language Teacher Training scholarships programme, 242
Arcadia Landscape Architecture Scholarship in Landscape Architecture Design, 1046
Archaeological Institute of America (AIA) Anna C. and Oliver C. Colburn Fellowships, 100
Archaeology of Portugal Fellowship, 127
The Archaeology Of Portugal Fellowship, 129
Architecture, Building and Civil Engineering Scholarships, 750
Arc of the United States Research Grant, 127
Arctic Institute of North America Grants-in-Aid, 130
Area Studies: FirstRand Laurie Dippenaar Scholarship, 1454
Armenian International Women, 133
Army Medical Services, 1323
Arnold Klopper Scholarship, 1215
Arrell Scholarships, 1318
Arrow Energy-JCU Go Further Indigenous Tertiary Scholarships, 674
Arthington-Davy Grants for Tongan Students for Postgraduate Study, 1242
Arthington Davy Scholarship, 1225
Arthur C. Cope Scholar Awards, 57
Arthur H Cole Grants-in-Aid, 459
Arthur L. Norberg Travel Fund, 347
Arthur Liman Public Interest Law Fellowship, 1635
Arthur M. Schlesinger, Jr. Fellowship, 685
Artificial Intelligence Innovation to Accelerate Health Research, 215
Artificial Intelligence Research to Enable UK's Net Zero Target, 215
Artists at Work, 136
Artists Fellowships at WSW, 1623
Art Rosenfeld Award for Energy Efficiency, 194
Arts and Humanities Research Council Studentships, 1093
Arts Council of Ireland Artist-in-the-Community Scheme, 136
Arts Council of Ireland Frameworks Animation Scheme, 136
Arts Council of Wales Artform Development Scheme, 137
Arts Council of Wales Awards for Career Development of Individual Visual Artists and Craftspeople, 137
Arts Council of Wales Awards for Individual Visual Artists and Craftspeople, 137
Arts Council of Wales Barclays Stage Partners, 137
Arts Council of Wales Community Touring Night Out, 137
Arts Council of Wales Music Projects Grants, 138
Arts Council of Wales Performing Arts Projects, 138
Arts Council of Wales Pilot Training Grants Scheme, 138
Arts Humanities Research Council Collaborative Doctoral Partnership PhD Studentship, 1215
Arts Innovator Award, 134
ArtsLink Independent Projects, 335
ArtsLink Projects, 336
ArtsLink Residencies, 336
The Arturo Falaschi ICGEB Predoctoral Fellowships ICGEB Trieste International PhD Programme, 655
Arturo Falaschi PhD Fellowships, 652
Arturo Falaschi Postdoctoral Fellowships 2023, 652
Arturo Falaschi Short-term PhD Fellowships–March 2023, 652
Arturo Falaschi Short-term Postdoctoral Fellowships, 652
ASEAN AU$10,000 Early Acceptance Scholarship, 766

ASEAN Excellence Scholarship, 1428
Ashinaga Scholarships, 142
Ashley Family Foundation MA Photography Scholarship, 143
ASH Scholar Award, 117
Asia Journalism Fellowship, 835
Asialink Residency Program, 140
Asian Communication Resource Centre (ACRC) Fellowship Award, 835
Asian Cultural Council Humanities Fellowship Program, 144
Asian Development Bank Japan Scholarship, 1226
Asian Development Bank-Japan Scholarship Program, 875
Asia Pacific Institute of Information Technology_IT PhDs in Grid Computing, 1216
The ASID Educational Foundation/Irene Winifred Eno Grant, 118
A S Nivison Memorial Scholarship, 1404
Associate Alumni Bursary, 967
Associated Colleges of the Midwest/the Great Lakes Colleges Association Faculty Fellowships, 892
Associated General Contractors of America The Saul Horowitz, Jr. Memorial Graduate Award, 144
Associated Women for Pepperdine (AWP) Scholarship, 988
Association of American Geographers NSF International Geographical Union Conference Travel Grants, 146
Association of American Railroads Janssen Cilag Dementia Research Grant, 31
Association of American Railroads Rosemary Foundation Travel Project Grant-Dementia Research, 32
Association of Commonwealth Universities Titular Fellowships, 376
Association of Consulting Surveyors Aboriginal and Torres Strait Islander Scholarship, 1428
Association of Firearm and Tool Mark Examiners Scholarship, 400
Association of Flight Attendants Annual Scholarship, 147
Association of Management Development Institutions in South Asia Doctoral Fellowships, 147
Association of Management Development Institutions in South Asia Postdoctoral Fellowship, 148
Association of Perioperative Registered Nurses Scholarship Program, 148
A*Star Graduate Scholarship, 20
A* STAR PhD Programme, 1363
Aston Dean, 149
Astridge Postgraduate Research Scholarship, 648
AsureQuality Seed Technology Scholarship, 638
Ataxia United Kingdom PhD Studentship, 152
Ataxia United Kingdom Research Grant, 152
Athens State University Phi Theta Kappa Transfer Scholarship, 152
Atmospheric, Oceanic & Planetary Physics: STFC Studentships, 1455
Auckland Council Chief Economist's Research Scholarship in Economics, 1271
Auckland Council Research Scholarship in Urban Economics, 1198
The Auckland Medical Aid Trust Scholarship, 322
Auckland University of Technology and Cyclone Computers Laptop and Tablet Scholarship, 153
Auckland University of Technology Post Graduate Scholarships, 153
Auckland University of Technology Vice Chancellor Doctoral Scholarship, 154
Austin Taylor Indigenous NT Medical Program Scholarship, 520
Australia Awards, 1266
Australia Awards Scholarships, 430
Australia-India Strategic Research Fund (AISRF), 175
Australian Academy of the Humanities Visiting Scholar Programmes, 163
Australian-American Health Policy Fellowship, 374
Australian Banana Growers' Council Mort Johnston Scholarship, 674
Australian Biological Resources Study (ABRS) National Taxonomy Research Grant Program, 168
Australian Biological Resources Study Postgraduate Scholarship, 402
Australian Building Codes Board Research Scholarship, 1216
Australian Eye and Ear Health Survey, 766
Australian Federation of University Women SA Inc. (AFUW-SA) Diamond Jubilee Scholarship, 1217
Australian Federation of University Women-Western Australian-Foundation Bursary, 167
Australian Government Research Training Program (AGRTP) Stipend Scholarship, 1266
Australian Health Inequities Program Research Scholarship, 520
Australian Health Inequities Program University Research Scholarship, 521
Australian Institute of Aboriginal and Torres Strait Islander Studies Conference Call for papers, 170
Australian Institute of Nuclear Science and Engineering Awards, 170
Australian National University Doctoral Fellowships, 172
Australian National University Excellence Scholarship Program, 173
Australian National University-Study Canberra India Scholarship for Postgraduate and Undergraduates in Australia, 173
Australian Orthopaedic Association Joint University Scholarship, 674
Australian Postgraduate Award Industry Scholarships within Integrative Biology, 973
Australian Postgraduate Awards, 349, 509
Australian Research Council Australian Postgraduate Award Industry–Alternative Engine Technologies, 974
Australian Rotary Health PhD Scholarships–Post Traumatic Stress Disorder (PTSD), 1217
Australian Security Intelligence Organisation Scheme, 169
Australia's Global University Award, 1415
Austria: Erasmus+ Master in Research and Innovation in Higher Education (MARIHE) Programme, 593
Austrian Academy of Sciences, MSc Course in Limnology and Wetland Ecosystems, 179
Austrian Academy of Sciences, Short Course—Tropical Limnology, 179
Austrian Academy of Sciences 4-months Trimester at Egerton University, Kenya, 178
AUT Doctoral Scholarships, 154
Autism Scholars Award, 1074
The AUT Queen Elizabeth II Diamond Jubilee Doctoral Scholarship, 1231
Avery O. Craven Award, 928
The Aviation Space Writers Foundation Award, 1117
Avicenna-Studienwerk, 187
Award for Research Excellence in Materials Chemistry, 296
Award in Chemical Instrumentation, 58
Award in Spectrochemical Analysis, 58
Awards for American Universities and Colleges to host Norwegian lecturers, 122
Awards for Current Students-The Bath Spa University International Travel Fund, 181
Awards for Current Students-The Betty and Peter McLean Prize, 181
Awards for Current Students-The Doris Southcott Bursary, 181
Awards for Current Students-The Extra-curricular Activity Fund, 182
Awards for Current Students-The Harbutt Fund, 182
Awards for Current Students-The Porthleven Prize, 182
Awards for Current Students-The Taunton Maids Bursary, 182
Awards for Current Students-The Wilfred Southall Sustainability Awards, 183
Awards for Faculty at Hispanic-Serving Institutions, 853
Awards for Faculty at Historically Black Colleges and Universities, 854
Awards for Faculty at Tribal Colleges and Universities, 854
Awards for United States Lecturers and Researchers Fulbright Commission (Argentina), 550
Awards Supported by the San Antonio Nathan Shock Center, 1085
Awarua Trust Scholarship, 154

Azerbaijan: Azerbaijan Diplomatic Academy University Scholarship, 989
Azerbaijan: Non-Aligned Movement (NAM) Scholarship, 594
Aziz Foundation/Imperial College Sustainable Energy Futures Scholarship, 607
Aziz Foundation Masters Scholarships, 1310
The Aziz Foundation Scholarship, 1358
Aziz Foundation Scholarships, 750
Azure Dillon 4-H Memorial Scholarship, 958

B

B.A. Krukoff Fellowship in Systematics, 967
Bailey Bequest Bursary, 639, 789
BA/Leverhulme Small Research Grants, 233
Balliol College: Balliol Economics Scholarship, 1455
Balliol College: Brassey Italian Scholarship, 1455
Balliol College: Eddie Dinshaw Scholarship, 1455
Balliol College: Foley-Bejar Scholarships, 1455
Balliol College: McDougall Scholarship, 1456
Balliol College: Peter Storey Scholarship, 1456
Balliol College: Snell Scholarship, 1456
Bamforth Postgraduate Scholarship, 942
Banco de Mexico FIDERH Scholarship, 266
Bancroft Library Study Awards, 194
Bangladesh Ministry of Public Affairs (MoPA), 767
Bangladesh Scholarship, 1345
Bank of Montréal Pauline Varnier Fellowship, 377
Banting Postdoctoral Fellowships, 280, 289
BAPRAS Pump Priming Fund for Clinical Trials, 240
Barbara Jordan Baines Report Fellowship Fund, 1169
Barbara Mito Reed Award, 1272
The Barns-Graham Travel Award, 1048
Barron Bequest, 494, 1602
Barron Prize, 240
The Bartlett Promise PhD Scholarship, 1211
Bartlett School of Planning Centenary Scholarship, 1201
BASF (Ludwigshafen/Germany), 967
2023-24 Basia Zaba Memorial Scholarship, 744
Basil O'Connor Starter Scholar Research Award, 784
Basil Reeve DPhil Scholarship in Physical or Biomedical Sciences, 938
Bass Connections–Collaborative Project Expeditions, 441
Baxter International Foundation Grants, 16
Bayer Educational Grant Awards, 1027
Bayer Foundation Scholarships, 186
Bayreuth International Graduate School of African Studies Sandwich Scholarship Programme, 187
BayTrust Bruce Cronin Scholarship, 321, 789, 1199, 1272
BBSRC Brazil Pump-Priming Award, 215
BBSRC International Travel Award Scheme, 215
BBSRC Standard Research Grant, 216
BCEF Future Regional Doctors Scholarship, 350
The Beacon Scholarship, 331
BEA Research Grant, 264
Beatrice Ratcliffe Postgraduate Scholarship in Music, 1226
Bedford Society Scholarship, 1040
Beinecke Scholarship, 190
Beit Trust Grants, 191
Beit Trust Postgraduate Scholarships, 191, 1336
Belgian American Educational Foundation (B.A.E.F.), 191
Belgian Technical Cooperation Scholarships, 194
Bellahouston Bequest Fund, 1314
Bell-Booth Dairy Research Scholarship, 789
Bell Burnell Graduate Scholarship Fund, 1365
Ben Barnett Scholarship, 1440
Benjamin A. Gilman International Scholarship Program, 372
Berenson Fellowship, 1598
Berkeley-Austria Research Fellowship, 194
Berkeley-Hasselt Research Fellowship, 194
Berlin Program Fellowship, 1121
Berlinski-Jacobson Graduate Scholarship (Humanities & Social Sciences), 1146
Bernard Buckman Scholarship, 1093
Bernard & Lottie Drazin Memorial Grants, 75
Bernd Rendel Prize in Geoscience, 431
Bernhard Baron Travelling Fellowship, 1019
Berreman-Yamanaka Award for Himalayan Studies, 631
Bert Enserink Scholarship EPA, 1187
The Bestway Foundation Scholarship, 1333
Betty J Fyffe Scholarship, 1404
Betty Josephine Fyffe Rural Allied Health, Nursing and Midwifery Scholarship, 1429
Betty Loughhead Soroptimist Scholarship Trust, 155
The Betty Mayne Scientific Research Fund for Earth Sciences, 738
Betty Wignall Scholarship in Chemistry, 1268
Beyond Segments: Towards a Lexical Model for Tonal Bilinguals, 767
BFWG Academic Awards, 247
Bhattacharya Graduate Fellowship, 632
BHP Billiton Mitsubishi Alliance (BMA) Award in Mining Engineering, 1415
BHW Women in STEM Scholarship, 1177
BIAA–ANAMED Joint Fellowship in Heritage Studies, 97
The Bibliographical Society of America-American Society for Eighteenth-Century Studies Fellowship for Bibliographical Studies in the Eighteenth Century, 205
Bibliographical Society of America-Harry Ransom Center Pforzheimer Fellowship in Bibliography, 203
The Bibliographical Society of America-Pine Tree Foundation Fellowship in Culinary Bibliography, 205
The Bibliographical Society of America-Pine Tree Foundation Fellowship in Hispanic Bibliography, 206
The Bibliographical Society of America-Rare Book School Fellowship, 206
The Bibliographical Society of America Short-term Fellowships, 206
Bickerton-Widdowson Trust Memorial Scholarship, 1267
Bielefeld Graduate School in History and Sociology Start-up Doctoral Scholarships, 208
Bielefeld Science Award, 208
Bilkent Industrial Engineering Fellowship, 208
Bilkent International Relations Fellowship, 209
Bilkent Mathematics Fellowship, 209
Bilkent MIAPP Fellowship, 209
Bilkent Political Science Fellowship, 209
Bilkent Turkish Literature Fellowship, 209
Bill Jenkins Award, 1323
Bing, 789
Biological Survey of Canada Scholarship, 488
Biology of Annual Ryegrass Scholarship, 350
Biology to Prevention Award, 311
Biomarker Project Awards, 311
Biomechanics Postgraduate Scholarship (General Sports), 176
Biomedical Catalyst: Developmental Pathway Funding Scheme (DPFS), 801
Biostatistics/Informatics Junior Faculty Award, 863
BIPOC Postgraduate Essay Award, 236
Birkbeck International Merit Scholarships, 221
The Birts Scholarship, 825
Bishop Thomas Hoyt Jr Fellowship, 368
Black Academic Futures DPhil Scholarship in History, 938
Black Academic Futures Scholarship, 1456
Blakemore Freeman Fellowships for Advanced Asian Language Study, 223

Blavatnik School of Government: Africa Governance Initiative Scholarship, 1456
Blavatnik School of Government: African Initiative for Governance Scholarships, 1457
Blavatnik School of Government: Public Service Scholarship, 1457
Blaxall Valentine Bursary Fund, 1043
Blockchain in Business and Society Scholarships, 968
BloodTechNet Award Program, 277
2023-24 Bloomsbury Colleges PhD Studentship-Project 2, 744
Blue Sky Focus Grant, 67
BMDST-RSM Student Elective Awards, 1057
BMG Indigenous Music Industry Scholarship-Creative Industries, 1429
Bodha Pravaham Fellowship, 632
Boeing Indigenous Engineering Scholarship, 1429
BOF postdoctoral fellowships, 569
Bond University United Kingdom Excellence Scholarship in Australia, 223
Bonnart Trust Master's Studentships, 221
Boren Fellowships, 225
Boren Fellowships for Graduate Students, 230
Boren Scholarship, 226
The Bosarge Family Foundation-Waun Ki Hong Scholar Award for Regenerative Cancer Medicine, 6
Bossing-Edwards Research Scholarship Award, 846
Botswana Insurance Holdings Limited Trust Thomas Tlou Scholarship for Master Programme, 226
Boughton PhD Scholarship, 222
Boulton Fellowship, 799
Bournemouth University Dean, 227
Bournemouth University Dean's Scholarship–The Media School, 227
Bournemouth University–GREAT Scholarships 2023, 227
Bournemouth University Music Scholarships, 227
Bournemouth University Vice-Chancellor's Scholarship–Most Promising Postgraduate Applicant, 227
Bourses Scholarships, 488
Bowland College–Willcock Scholarships, 705
Bowler Ravensdown Scholarship in Soil Science, 639, 789
Bragato Research Fellowship, 790
Brazil Scholarship, 462
Breast Cancer Competitive Research Grant Program, 952
Breast Cancer Research Foundation-AACR Career Development Awards to Promote Diversity and Inclusion, 5
Brenda Shore Award for Women, 1442
Brewer Street Scholarship, 732
Brian Aspin Memorial Scholarship, 639, 790
Brian Harris Scholarship, 1040
Bridge to Independence Award Program, 1113
BRISMES Early Career Development Prize, 262
British Academy/ Cara/ Leverhulme Researchers at Risk Research Support Grants, 233
British Academy Conferences, 233
British-American Chamber of Commerce Awards, 551
British Association for American Studies Postgraduate and Early Career Short-Term Travel Awards, 236
British Association for Japanese Studies Postgraduate Studentships, 238
British Association of Plastic Reconstructive and Aesthetic Surgeons European Travelling Scholarships, 240
British Chevening Cambridge Scholarships for Postgraduate Study (Indonesia), 1261
British Chevening Malaysia Cambridge Scholarship for PhD Study, 1261
British Council Scholarship for Women in STEM Terms and Conditions, 266
British Council Scholarships for Women in STEM, 446, 608, 1365
British Dental Association/Dentsply Student Support Fund, 244
British Federation of Women Graduates (BFWG), 1315
British Federation of Women Graduates Postgraduate Awards, 1324
British Federation of Women Graduates Scholarships, 247
The British & Foreign School Society, 232
British Heart Foundation-Daphne Jackson Fellowships, 249
British Institute at Ankara Research Scholarship, 254
British Institute in Eastern Africa Minor Grants, 255
British Marshall Scholarships, 893
British Petroleum Research Bursaries for PhD Study, 1261
British Petroleum Research Bursaries for Postgraduate Study, 1262
British Society for Antimicrobial Chemotherapy Overseas Scholarship, 262
The Brock Doctoral Scholarship, 1322
Brother Vincent Cotter Endowed Honours Award, 1416
Brough Sanskrit Awards, 1093
Brown Family Bursary, 1201
Browning Fund Grants, 234
Browns Restaurant Scholarships, 1266
Bruggeman Postgraduate Scholarship in Classics, 1019, 1443
Brunei Darussalam: Government of Brunei Darussalam Scholarship, 594
Brunel Family Discount Terms and Conditions, 266
Brunel Santander International Scholarship, 266
Bryan Scholarships, 1390
Bseisu-Imperial College London Scholarships/Chevening-Bseisu Scholarship, 608
Building Research Association of New Zealand (BRANZ) Scholarship, 639
Buninyong Community Bank Scholarship, 509
Bupa Foundation Annual Specialist Grant, 268
Bupa Foundation Medical Research Grant for Health at Work, 268
Bupa Foundation Medical Research Grant for Information and Communication, 268
Burralga Yumba Bursary, 674
Bush Children's Education Foundation Scholarship, 1404
Business, Economics & Law Postgraduate Academic Excellence Scholarship, 155
Business and Management Postgraduate Scholarships, 968
The Business School Dean's Scholarship, 229
BU Sport Scholarship, 228
Byera Hadley Travelling Scholarships, 887

C

Cabot Scholarships, 886
California Senate Fellows, 1083
Call for Proposals: Narratives in Public Communications, 950
C. Alma Baker Postgraduate Scholarship, 790
Calver Family Scholarship, 831
The Camargo Core Program, 269
Cambridge Trust Scholarships, 411
Cameron Beyer Scholarship, 509
CAMS Summer Research Fellowship Scholarship, 362
Canada-ASEAN Scholarships and Educational Exchanges for Development (SEED)–for Students, 1319
Canada-Asia-Pacific Awards, 280
Canada-Brazil Awards-Joint Research Projects, 280
Canada-CARICOM Faculty Leadership Program, 281, 1319
Canada-CARICOM Leadership Scholarships Program, 281
Canada-Chile Leadership Exchange Scholarship, 282
Canada-China Scholars, 282
Canada Council for the Arts Molson Prizes, 275
Canada Graduate Scholarships–Doctoral Program, 1126
Canada Graduate Scholarships–Master's Program, 1126
Canada Graduate Scholarships-Master's (CGS M) Program, 881
Canada Graduate Scholarships–Michael Smith Foreign Study Supplements Program, 880

Canada-Japan Literary Awards, 270
Canada Postgraduate Scholarships (PGS), 881
Canada's Distinguished Dissertation Awards, 1075
Canadian Alumni Scholarship, 732
Canadian Blood Services Graduate Fellowship Program, 278
Canadian Centennial Scholarship Fund, 1324
Canadian Embassy Faculty Enrichment Program, 285
Canadian Embassy Graduate Student Fellowship Program, 286
Canadian Embassy (United States of America) Research Grant Program, 285
Canadian Federation of University Women/A. Vibert Douglas Fellowship, 658
Canadian Federation of University Women Bourse Georgette Lemoyne, 279
Canadian Forest Service Graduate Supplements, 1126
Canadian Initiatives For Nordic Studies (CINS) Graduate Scholarship, 1221
Canadian Institutes of Health Research Gold Leaf Prizes, 289
Canadian Library Association Library Research and Development Grants, 290
Canadian National Committee/IUPAC Travel Awards, 295
Canadian National Institute for the Blind Baker Applied Research Fund, 291
Canadian National Institute for the Blind Baker Fellowship Fund, 291
Canadian National Institute for the Blind Baker New Researcher Fund, 291
Canadian National Institute for the Blind Winston Gordon Award, 292
Canadian Parliamentary Internship Programme, 294
Canadian Prime Minister's Awards for Publishing (CPMA), 282
Canadian Research Awards for Specialty Residents (Medicine, Surgery), 1032
Canadian Tobacco Control Research Initiative Planning Grants, 1127
Canadian Women Artists' Award, 888
The Cancer Council NSW Research Project Grants, 296
Cancer Council's Beat Cancer Project, 297
Cancer Immunology Project Awards, 312
Cancer Research Fund of the Damon Runyon-Walter Winchell Foundation Research Fellowships for Physician Scientists, 308
Cancer Research Institute Irvington Postdoctoral Fellowship Program, 308
Cancer Research United Kingdom LRI Graduate Studentships, 312
Cancer Screening and Early Detection, 300
Candriam Scholarship, 763
Canon Collins Scholarship for Distance Learning Master of Laws (LLM), 318
Canon Collins Trust Scholarships, 741
Canterbury Scholarship, 321
CAORC-NEH Senior Research Fellowship, 385
The Capstone Editing Conference Travel Grant for Postgraduate Research Students, 158
The Capstone Editing Early Career Academic Research Grant for Women, 158
Cardiff Business School-ESRC Wales DTP Fully Funded General Studentships (Economics), 323
Cardiff Business School Scholarships in Business and Management and Economics, 324
Cardiff India scholarships, 324
Cardiff Institute of Tissue Engineering and Repair (CITER)–EPSRC Studentship, 324
Cardiff School of Chemistry–Master's Bursaries, 325
Cardiff School of Chemistry–MSc Studentships in Computing in the Physical Sciences, 325
Cardiff School of City and Regional Planning–Master's Bursaries, 325
Cardiff School of Mathematics–PhD Studentships, 325
Cardiff School of Medicine–PhD Studentships, 326
Cardiff School of Medicine–PhD Studentships (Department of Surgery), 326
Cardiff School of Music–PhD Studentships, 326
Cardiff School of Optometry and Vision Sciences–PhD Studentship, 326
Cardiff University Marshall Scholarship, 327
Cardiff University MSc/Diploma in Housing Studentship, 327
Cardiff University PhD Music Studentship, 327
Cardiff University PhD Social Sciences Studentship, 328
Cardiff University PhD Studentship in European Studies, 328
Cardiff University School of Law and Politics-ESRC-funded PhD Studentship in Politics and International Relations, 328
Cardiff University School of Law and Politics-ESRC Wales DTP General Studentships-Empirical Studies in Law, 328
Cardiology Section Presidents Prize, 1057
Career Development Awards, 114, 213, 659, 688
Career Development Bridge Funding Award: K Bridge, 996
Career Development Bridge Funding Award: K Supplement, 996
Career Development Bridge Funding Award: R Bridge, 997
Career Development Bridge Funding Program, 441
Career Development Fellowship, 312
Career Development in Geriatric Medicine Award, 997
Career Development Program-Fellow, 723
Career Development Program-Special Fellow, 723
Career Establishment Award, 312
Career Re-entry Research Fellowships, 250
Career Support and Travel Grants, 690
Career Transition Fellowships, 864
Care-leavers Scholarship (Continuing), 510
Care-leavers Scholarships (Commencing), 510
Carlos M. Castaeda Journalism Scholarship, 553
Carl W Gottschalk Research Scholar Grant, 119
Carnegie Endowment Junior Fellows Program, 1005
Carnegie PhD Scholarships, 333, 1295
Carnegie Trust: St Andrew's Society Scholarships, 1155
Carnwath Scholarship, 1628
Carol Lynette Grant (Prowse) Scholarship, 510
Carolyn and Franco Gianturco Scholarship in Music, 732
Carolyn and Franco Gianturco Scholarship in Theoretical Chemistry, 732
Carson Northern Territory Medical Program Scholarship, 521
Carter Roger Williams Scholarship, 1004
Cartmel College Postgraduate Studentship, 556, 705
Cartmel College Scholarships, 706
Casella Family Brands PhD Scholarship, 350
Casinomucho Research Scholarship (CSR), 334
Catalyst Award, 364
Cataract Fire Company #2 Scholarship, 1004
Catastrophes & Confiict Forum Medical Student Essay Prize, 1057
Catherine and Peter Tay for Singapore Alumni (follow on) Scholarship, 1430
Catherine Baxter Dairy Scholarship, 640, 790
The Catherine Mackichan Trust, 1317
CBCF Congressional Summer Internship Program, 378
CBCF Louis Stokes Health Scholars Program, sponsored by United Health Foundation, 379
CBCF NREI Historically Black Colleges and Universities (HBCU) Scholarship, 379
CBC Literary Prizes, 270
CBC Spouses Education Scholarship, 378
C. Brian Rose AIA/DAI Exchange Fellowships, 128
C Douglas Dillon Graduate Scholarship, 1625
CDT in Advanced Metallic Systems, 1366
CDT in Aerosol Science, 1366
CDT in Biodesign Engineering, 1367
CDT in Compound Semiconductor Manufacturing, 1367
CDT in Future Innovation in NDE, 1367

CDT in the Science and Technology of Fusion Energy, 1368
CDU Vice-Chancellor's International High Achievers Scholarships, 348
Cecil King Travel Scholarship, 740
Cec Spence Memorial UNE Country Scholarship, 1405
CEHC Masters Scholarships in Public Health for Eye Care, 373
Cell and Oligonucleotide Therapy Fellowship with AstraZeneca, 802
Center for Advancing Opportunity Doctorial Fellowship, 1182
Center for AIDS Prevention Studies, Small Professional Grants for Graduate Students, 1441
Center for Alternatives to Animal Testing Grants Programme, 687
Center for British Studies Grants, 195
Center for Creative Photography Ansel Adams Research Fellowship, 337
Center for Defense Information Internship, 338
Central West Medical Association Medical Student Scholarship, 350
Centre de Recherches et d'Investigations Epidermiques et Sensorielles Research Award, 344
Centre de Sciences Humaines Post-Doctoral Fellowship, 344
Centre for Bioethics and Emerging Technologies PhD Funding, 1148
Centre for Lasers and Applications Scholarships, 767
CEPAR Honours Scholarship, 1416
Cerebrovascular Traveling Fellowship, 883
CFUW 100th Anniversary Legacy Fellowship funded by the Charitable Trust, 287
CGES Research and Travel Award, 230
Chancellor, 651
Chancellor's Research Scholarship, 1163
Chanchlani Global Vision Research Award, 292
Chandigarh University Scholarships in India, 346
Charles A Lindbergh Chair in Aerospace History, 844, 1117, 1118
Charles Fleming Publishing Award, 1050
Charles Fleming Senior Scientist Award, 1050
The Charles J. Tanenbaum Fellowship in Cartographical Bibliography, 207
Charles LeGeyt Fortescue Fellowship, 637
Charles Parsons Energy Research Award, 872
Charles Sturt Accommodation Equity Scholarship, 351
Charles Sturt University Postgraduate Research Studentships (CSUPRS), 351
Charles Wallace India Trust, 1262
Charlie Trotter's Culinary Education Foundation Culinary Study Scholarship, 356
Chartered Institute of Library and Information Professionals International Library and Information Group Alan Hopkinson Award, 657
Chemical Engineering Scholarships, 750
Chemistry Department Scholarship for students of Black heritage, 609
Chemistry Scholarships, 750
Cheryl Ann Keatley Scholarship, 521
CHEST Foundation Grants, 62
Chevening Partner Scholarship scheme, 228
Chevening Scholarships, 1352, 1457
Chevening Scholarship scheme (External Scholarship), 228
Chiang Ching Kuo Foundation Doctoral Fellowships, 357
Chiang Ching Kuo Foundation for International Scholarly Exchange Eminent Scholar Lectureship, 357
Chiang Ching Kuo Foundation for International Scholarly Exchange Publication Subsidies, 358
Child Health Research Appeal Trust Studentship, 1201
Children of Alumni Award, 968
Children's Rights Scholarship, 713
Children's Rights Scholarship 2, 714
Children's Rights Scholarship 3, 714
Chile: Nelson Mandela Scholarships, 361
China: Chinese Government Scholarship, 594
China: One Belt One Road Scholarship, 595
China Elite Scholarship, 767
China Excellence Scholarship, 1430
China Key Partnership Cotutelle Stipend Scheme, 768
China Oxford Scholarship Fund, 1458
China Residency Program, 928
China Scholarship Council, 751
China Scholarship Council, PhD Studentship, 591
China Scholarship Council Cambridge Scholarships, 1262
China Scholarship Council (CSC)-Deakin University Joint Funding Program, 419
China Scholarship Council-Massey University PhD Scholars Programme, 790
China Scholarship Council (CSC) Scholarship, 1215
China Scholarship Council Scholarships, 968, 1636
China Scholarship Council-The University of Manchester Joint Scholarship for PhD Study in Alliance Manchester Business School, 1368
China Scholarship Council-The University of Manchester Joint Scholarship for PhD Study in the School of Arts, Languages and Cultures, 1369
China Scholarship Council-The University of Manchester Joint Scholarship for PhD Study in the School of Environment, Education and Development, 1369
China Scholarship Council-University of Melbourne PhD Scholarship, 1390
China Scholarship Council-University of Oxford Scholarships, 1458
China Scholarships, 620
Chin Communications Master of Interpreting and Translation Studies Scholarship, 821
Chinese American Medical Society Scholarship Program, 362
Chinese-English Translation Scholarships, 1305
Chinese Government Scholarship Program, 1636
Chinese Government Scholarship Water and Environmental Research Scholarships, 346
Chinese Language Fellowship Program, 851
Choosing the Way Forward: Addressing the Post-Parental Housing Transition Needs with Intellectual Disability and Their Older Family Carers, 521
Chris and Gina Grubb Ornithology Scholarship, 351
Christchurch City Council Antarctic Scholarship, 1272
The Christine and Ian Bolt MA Scholarships in American Literature and Culture, 1333
Christine and Ian Bolt Scholarship, 1324
Christine Mirzayan Science & Technology Policy Graduate Fellowship Program, 838, 864
Chronic, Noncommunicable Diseases and Disorders Research Training (NCD-Lifespan), 535
Chulalongkorn University (Thailand) LAW Scholarships, 1291
Churches Together in Britain and Ireland, 556, 706
Churchill Fellowship, 1171
Churchill Scholarship, 1620
Church Matching Scholarship, 210
CIEE-Gilman Go Global Grant, 230
Citadel Capital Scholarship, 965
Civil and Structural Engineering PhD Scholarship, 402
Civil Engineering Dixon Scholarship, 609
Civil Engineering Skempton Scholarship, 609
Civil War and Reconstruction Book Award, 928
Clara Collet Departmental Scholarships, 1202
Clara Haskil International Piano Competition, 365
The Clara Mayo Grants, 1131
Clare Hall Research Fellowships in the Arts and Social Sciences, 365
Clarendon Canadian National Scholarship, 733
Clarendon Scholarship, 1139
Clark Graduate Bursary Fund for International Students at University of Glasgow, 1315

Clark-Huntington Joint Bibliographical Fellowship, 1241
Claude Leon Foundation Postdoctoral Fellowship, 366
The Claude McCarthy Fellowships, 1279
Clem Hill Memorial Scholarship, 640
Client Service Excellence Award, 887
Clifford Wallace Collins Memorial Trust Scholarship, 321
Clifton Ware Group-Voice Pedagogy Award, 847
Climate Data Expeditions: Climate + Health–Request for Proposals, 441
Clinical and Laboratory Integration Program, 309
Clinical Assistant Professorships, 397
Clinical Forensic and Legal Medicine Section Poster Competition, 1058
Clinical Forensics and Legal Medicine: Postgraduate Poster Prize, 1058
Clinical Immunology & Allergy President's Prize, 1058
Clinical Innovator, 309
Clinical Management of Pain Scholarship, 1296
Clinical Neurosciences Gordon Holmes Prize, 1058
Clinical Neurosciences President's Prize, 1058
Clinical & Public Health Research Fellowships-Early Career Fellowship, 617
Clinical & Public Health Research Fellowships-Intermediate Fellowship, 618
Clinical & Public Health Research Fellowships-Senior Fellowship, 618
Clinical Research Fellowships, 133
Clinical Research Leave Fellowships, 250
Clinical Research Training Fellowship, 484
Clinical Study Grants, 250
Clinical Trial Award, 313
Clinician Scholar Educator Award, 998
Clinician Scientist Fellowship, 313, 947
CNIB Barbara Tuck MacPhee Award, 292
The Coburn Award, 274
Co-designing Culturally Relevant End of Life Care in Cancer, 768
Co-funded Monash Graduate Scholarship (CF-MGS), 821
Coimbra Group Scholarship Programme for Young Professors and Researchers from Latin American Universities, 366
Coimbra Group Scholarship Programme for Young Researchers from the European Neighbourhood, 367
Coimbra Group Short Stay Scholarship Programme for Young Researchers, 367
The Colegrave Seabrook Foundation, 1630
COLFUTURO Scholarship, 768
Colfuturo Scholarships, 968
Colgate-Palmolive Grants for Alternative Research, 1184
Colin and Eleanor Bourke Indigenous Postgraduate Scholarship, 822
Collaborate with Researchers in Luxembourg, 216
Collaborative Offline & Online Platform for Research EuroTechPostdoc Fellowships for International Students at European Universities, 504
Collaborative Project in Global Health, 990
Collaborative Project relating to Antimicrobial Resistance from a One Health Perspective, 990
Collaborative Project to Meet Societal and Industry-related Challenges, 990
Collaborative Research, 625
Collections Study Award, 961
College of Business Government and Law PhD Top-up, 522
College of Engineering and Computer Science: College Postgraduate International Award, 173
College of Engineering and Computer Science: College Postgraduate International Honours Award, 173
College of International Education International Pathways Scholarship, 1430
College of Science and Engineering International PGT Merit Scholarship, 1342
College of Social Sciences, Arts and Humanities Masters Excellence Scholarship, 1342
College of Social Sciences, Arts and Humanities Minority Ethnic Masters Scholarship, 1343
College Scholarship (Arts), 1146
College Scholarship (Sciences), 1146
Collin Post Memorial Scholarship in Sculpture, 640
Colombia Scholarship, 462
Coloproctology John of Arderne Medal, 1059
Colorectal Cancer Screening Coordinating Center, 300
Colt Foundation Fellowships in Occupational/Environmental Health, 1324
Columbia College of Missouri Boone County Endowed Award, 368
Commissioning Music/United States of America, 807
Common Data Access MSc Petroleum Data Management Scholarships, 1216
Commonwealth Accommodation Scholarship, 1405
Commonwealth Distance Learning Scholarships, 1296
Commonwealth Education Costs Scholarship, 1405
The Commonwealth Fund Mongan Fellowship in Minority Health Policy, 375
Commonwealth Indigenous Support Scholarship, 822
Commonwealth Infection Prevention and Control Scholarship, 1284
Commonwealth Masters Scholarships, 446
Commonwealth PhD Scholarship (for High Income Countries), 1324
Commonwealth Scholarship, 242, 1226
Commonwealth Scholarships and Fellowships Plan (CSFP) General Scholarship, 1369
Commonwealth Scholarships for Developing Countries, 446
Commonwealth Shared Scholarships, 1459
Commonwealth Shared Scholarship Scheme (CSSS), 1202, 1353, 1458
Commonwealth Shared Scholarship Scheme at United Kingdom Universities, 375
Commonwealth Shared Scholarships-PGT, 446
Commonwealth Split-Site Doctoral Scholarships, 447
Commonwealth Split-site Scholarship, 1325
Communication and Media Scholarships, 751
Communicator Award, 432
Community Bridging Services (CBS) Inc Scholarship, 522
Community Dance Wales Grants, 138
Community Support Grants, 390
Competitive Research, 626
Computational and Methodological Breakthroughs in High Dimensional Statistical Modelling for Complex Data, 768
Computer Science: Department Studentships, 1459
Computer Science Scholarships, 149, 751, 1041
Computing, Engineering and Mathematical Sciences Graduate Teaching Assistant PhD Studentship, 1325
CONACYT, 1353
CONACyT Mexico Scholarships, 1370
CONACYT Scholarship, 769
CONACyT Tuition Top-up Award, 1370
Conference and Workshop Grant, 1614
Conference Attendance Support for Postgraduate Students, 238
Conference Grants, 688, 690
Conference/Seminar/Workshop Grants, 358
Conference Travel Grants, 1240
Confucius Institute Scholarship, 1637
Congressional Black Caucus Foundation Spouses Visual Arts Scholarship, 379
Connellan Airways Trust Diabetes Management and Education Scholarship, 522
ConocoPhillips Canada Centennial Scholarship Program, 1196
Conseil Européen Pour la Recherche Nucléaire-Japan Fellowship Programme, 380
Conseil Européen Pour la Recherche Nucléaire Summer Student Programme, 380

Consejo Nacional de Ciencia y Tecnologia (CONACYT) Scholarships, 1154
Conservation Guest Scholars, 567
Consortium for Advanced Research Training in Africa PhD Fellowships, 382
Consortium for Applied Research on International Migration Postdoctoral Talent Fellowship, 382
Continuing Medical Education Beef Industry Scholarship, 851
Cook School of Intercultural Studies Graduate Grant, 211
Co-op Bookshop Scholarship, 165
Cooperative Research Center for Water Quality and Treatment Young Water Scientist of the Year Scholarship, 383
Copenhagen Business School PhD Scholarship on IT Management, 383
Copernicus Award, 432
Core Fellowships and Grants, 385
Cornwall Heritage Trust Scholarship, 1311
Corpus Christi Research Scholarship, 1262
Corrosion Research Postgraduate Scholarships, 822
Cotsen Traveling Fellowship, 100
Cotsen Traveling Fellowship for Research in Greece, 100
Council of American Overseas Research Centers Andrew W. Mellon East-Central European Research Fellows, 386
Council of American Overseas Research Centers (CAORC) Fellowships for Advanced Multi-Country Research, 109
Council of American Overseas Research Centers Multi-Country Research Fellowship Program for Advanced Multi-Country Research, 386
Council of American Overseas Research Centers Multi Country Research Fellowships, 101
Council of American Overseas Research Centers Neh Research Fellowships, 386
Council of Catholic School Parents (NSW) Indigenous Postgraduate Scholarship (IES), 165
The Council of Scientific and Industrial Research/TWAS Fellowship for Postdoctoral Research, 1180
Council of Scientific and Industrial Research/TWAS Fellowship for Postgraduate Research, 1178
Council of Supply Chain Management Professionals Distinguished Service Award, 388
Council of Supply Chain Management Professionals Doctoral Dissertation Award, 388
Council on Foreign Relations International Affairs Fellowship in Japan, 389
Council on Library and Information Resources Postdoctoral Fellowship, 390
Council Scholarship, 510
County College Scholarships, 706
County College Studentship, 706
County College Travel Award, 556
Coursework Access Scholarships, 1391
CQUniCares Emergency Grant, 339
CQUniversity Indigenous Australian Postgraduate Research Award, 339
CQUniversity/Industry Collaborative Grants Scheme, 340
CQUniversity Womens Equal Opportunity Research Award, 340
Craig Hugh Smyth Fellowship, 1599
Craig John Hastings Smith Surveying Engineering Honours Year Award, 1416
Cranfield Global Manufacturing Leadership Masters Scholarship, 394
Cranfield Merit Scholarship in Leadership and Management, 394
Cranfield Sub-Saharan Africa Merit Scholarship, 394
C. Ravi Ravindran Outstanding Doctoral Thesis Award, 1075
Creating Better Futures Masters Scholarship for African Students, 751
Creative Arts Alumni Bursary, 752
Criminology Scholarships for Foreign Researchers in Germany, 795
Critical Care Medicine Section: Audit and Quality Improvement Project Prize, 1059
Critical Language Scholarship Program, 1177
Croatian Arts and Cultural Exchange Croatia, 140
Crohn's & Coltis Foundation Career Development Award, 396
Crohn's & Coltis Foundation Research Fellowship Awards, 396
Crohn's & Coltis Foundation Senior Research Award, 396
Cross-Disciplinary Fellowships, 659
Croucher Foundation PhD Scholarships and Postdoctoral Fellowships, 398
Croucher Innovation Awards, 398
Croucher Science Communication Studentships, 398
Croucher Senior Research Fellowships, 399
CR Parekh Fellowship, 743
Crystalbrook Kingsley Environmental Scholarship, 1431
CSC-Leiden University Scholarship, 714
CSIRO Women in Energy Industry Placement Scholarship, 1431
CSJR Postgraduate Student Bursary, 1094
CSU Foundation Persistence Scholarship, 352
CSU give-Research Scholarship, 352
The Culinary Trust Scholarship, 712
Cultural Anthropology Program Senior Research Awards, 867
The Cultural Diaspora, 269
Cultural Enterprise Service Grant, 139
Cultural Learnings: Strengthening Aboriginal children's wellbeing, 403
Culture of Health Prize, 1010
The CURE Epilepsy Award, 364
Curtin Business School Doctoral Scholarship, 403
Curtin International Scholarships-Alumni and Family Scholarship, 403
Curtin International Scholarships–Merit Scholarship, 403
Curtin University Postgraduate Scholarship (CUPS), 404
Cusanuswerk–Organization of the German Bishops' Conference Promoting Gifted Catholic Students, 187
Cutlers' Surgical Fellowship, 1036
Cutlers' Surgical Prize, 1036
C V Fife Memorial Scholarship, 639
CV Section/CNS Foundation Young Investigator Research Grant, 884
CVS Health Pharmacy Scholarship, 1183
Cypress-Fairbanks Independent School District/CIHR Doctoral and Postdoctoral Research Awards, 287

D

Daad-Master Studies, 436
Dairy Postgraduate Scholarships and Awards, 1391
Daiwa Foundation Awards, 411
Daiwa Foundation Small Grants, 411
Daiwa Scholarships, 412
Daiwa Scholarships in Japanese Studies, 412, 1370
The Dalai Lama Foundation Graduate Scholarship Program, 413
The Dalai Lama Trust Scholarship, 413
Damon Runyon Clinical Investigator Award, 308
The Daniel Gerber Sr, Medallion Scholarship, 565
Daniel Turnberg Travel Fellowships, 12
Danks Scholarship, 489
Daphne Jackson Fellowships, 216, 485, 1101
Dapo Olagunju Scholarship, 733
Darlene Clark Hine Award, 929
Daryl Jelinek Sporting Scholarship, 752
Data Visualisation Design, Ambiguity & Decision Making in Megaprojects: EPSRC Studentship, 462
David and Julie Tobey Fellowship, 1599
David Baumgardt Memorial Fellowship, 720
The David Caminer Postgraduate Scholarship in Business Computing, 812
David Gritz Scholarship, 1106
David M. Livingstone (Australia) Scholarship, 1263
David Montgomery Award, 929

David N. Keightley Fellowship, 195
David N. Lyon Scholarship in Politics–The Politics of Sex and Gender Equality in Diverse Societies, 938
David Paul Landa Memorial Scholarships for Pianists, 141
David Phillips Fellowships, 216
David Walsh Memorial Scholarship, 1416
The Davies Charitable Foundation Fellowship, 414
Davis Scholarship, 846
Dax Copp Travelling Fellowship, 636
Deadly Education Scholarships-Aboriginal and Torres Strait Islanders, 511
Deakin Alumni Discount, 420
Deakin Funded Scholarship Program, 420
Deakin India 20% Postgraduate Bursary, 420
Deakin International COLFUTURO Bursary, 421
Deakin International Scholarship, 421
Deakin Latin America Scholarship, 421
Deakin STEM Scholarship, 422
Deakin University Postgraduate Research Scholarship (DUPR), 422
Deakin University Postgraduate Research Scholarships (DUPRS), 422
Deakin Vice-Chancellor's International Scholarship, 423
The Dean of Humanities, Arts & Social Sciences Excellence Scholarship, 986
Dean's 20th Anniversary Scholarships, 1353
Dean's Award for Enterprise, 752
Dean's Award for Enterprise Scholarship, 758
Dean's Doctoral Scholarship Award, 1371
DeepMind PhD Scholarships, 1296
DeepMind Scholarship, 969
DeepMind Scholarship-Department of Computing, 609
DeepMind Scholarships-Department of Life Sciences, 610
Defence Research and Development Canada Postgraduate Scholarship Supplements, 881
Delta Electricity Scholarship, 1431
Demonstration of Energy & Efficiency Developments (DEED)-Technical Design Project, 96
De Montfort University Awards to Women for Final Year Doctoral Research, 414
De Montfort University PhD Scholarships, 414
Denmark-America Foundation Grants, 427
Denmark Liberation Scholarships, 125
The Dennis Mock Graduate Scholarship, 1079
The Dennis Mock Student Leadership Award, 1079
Dennis William Moore Scholarship, 1268
Departmental Scholarships-Chemical Engineering, 610
Department of Bioengineering Scholarship (MRes), 610
Department of Bioengineering Scholarship (MSc), 610
Department of Communities and Local Government (formally Office of the Deputy Prime Minister), 1202
Department of Defense-National Defense and Science Engineering Fellowships, 195
Department of Education: Talbot Scholarship, 1459
Department of Mathematics Scholarship Award, 1371
Department of Physics and Astronomy Diversity Enhancement Studentship, 1371
Department of Physics and Astronomy STFC Studentship, 1372
Derek Harwood-Nash International Education Scholar Grant, 978
Dermatology Clinicopathological Meetings, 1059
Dermatology Section: Hugh Wallace Essay Prize, 1059
Dermatology Section: Trainee Research Prize, 1059
Design Alumni Bursary, 752
Design Engineering PhD Scholarships (DEPS), 611
Design School Scholarships, 753
Destination Australia, 511
Destination Australia Program Honours Scholarship, 1406
Destination Australia Program Scholarship for Masters by Coursework, 1407
Destination Australia Scholarship (Master of Research), 340
Destination Australia Scholarship-International Students, 401, 404
Destination Australia Scholarships, 348, 1046
Destination Australia Scholarships-International Students, 699
Deutsche Forschungsgemeinschaft Collaborative Research Centres, 432
Deutsche Forschungsgemeinschaft Mercator Programme, 432
Deutsche Forschungsgemeinschaft Research Training Groups, 433
Deutscher Akademischer Austauschdienst (German Academic Exchange Service) Scholarships, 1272
Develop a UK Digital Twinning Research Community with a NetworkPlus, 217
Develop Basic Technologies in Sensing and Imaging, 802
Developing Futures Scholarship, 1345
Developing Novel Genetic Disease Models for Dementia-Domestic, 769
Developing Novel Genetic Disease Models for Dementia-International, 769
Developing Solutions Masters Scholarship, 1439
Developing World Education Fund Scholarships for PhD Study, 1263
Development Trust Africa Scholarships, 753
Develop New Approaches to Small Molecule Medicine, 802
Dhaka PhD Scholarships, 969
Diaconia Graduate Fellowships, 950
Diagnostics and Surveillance of Antimicrobial resistance (JPIAMR), 217
The Diamond Education Grant, 394
Diamond Jubilee Bursary, 522
Diana Jacobs Kalman/AFAR Scholarships for Research in the Biology of Aging, 65
Diane Campbell-Hunt Memorial Award, 1443
Diane Lemaire Scholarship, 1391
The Dick and Mary Earle Scholarship in Technology, 1279
Digital Humanities Advancement Grants, 645
Digital Media Programme Bursary, 1203
Dilmah Tea International Study Award, 791
Dina Abramowicz Emerging Scholar Fellowship, 1639
Directed Residency Scholarships, 884
Directorate for Education and Human Resources Core Research, 867
Dirichlet International Postdoctoral Fellowship at Berlin Mathematical School in Germany, 202
Disability, Mental Health and Carers: National Disability Conference Initiative, 167
Discover Business at Dundee, 1284
Discovery Programme Awards, 313
Discovery Programme Foundation Awards, 314
Discrete Cosine Transform Mâori and Pacific Mature Student Doctoral Scholarship, 155
Dissemination of CPRIT-Funded Cancer Control Interventions, 300
Dissertation Fellowship in Hazards, Risks, and Disaster, 879
Dissertation Fellowships for ROC Students Abroad, 358
Dissertation Fieldwork Grant, 1614
Dissertation Planning Grants, 78
Dissertation Research Grants, 95
Dissertation Research Scholarship, 565
Distinguished Dissertation Award, 145
Distinguished Investigator Grant, 68
Distinguished Scholarship, 846
Diversity100 PhD Studentships, 222
Diversity Lecture Award, 214
Diversity Scholarship, 742
Dixie Electric Membership Corporation New Leaders Travel Grant, 83
D.L. McMaster Fund Endowed Housing Scholarship, 1406
DMU Sport Scholarship, 415
Doctoral and Postdoctoral Research Fellowships, 566
Doctoral Completion Award, 1076

Doctoral Dissertation Grant Program (Fahs-Beck Scholars), 507
Doctoral Dissertation Proposal Competition, 785
Doctoral Fellowship Program, 427
Doctoral Fellowships, 358
Doctoral New Investigator (DNI) Grants, 437
Doctoral Research on Family Relationships, 511
Doctoral Scholarships, 201, 920, 1227
Doctor of Philosophy and Postdoctoral Positions-Investigating Sensory Aspects of Human Communication, 798
Doctor of Philosophy APA(I) Police-Mental Health Scholarship, 822
Doctor of Philosophy Scholarship-Artificial Intelligence in Medicine and Healthcare, 769
Doctor of Philosophy Scholarship-Corrosion in Alumina Processing, 823
Doctor of Philosophy Scholarship in Globalisation and International Economics, 1214
Doctor of Philosophy Scholarships in the Social Sciences, 503
Doctor of Philosophy Studentship, 806
Doctor TMA Pai PhD Scholarships for International Students at Manipal University, 783
Dodson Indigenous Juris Doctor Scholarship, 823
DOE Office of Science Graduate Student Research (SCGSR) program, 195
Dolores Zohrab Liebmann, 196
Dominican College of San Rafael MBA in Strategic Leadership, 437
Donald & Margot Watt Bursary Fund (FASS Only), 706
Don and Lee Stammer Scholarship, 1407
Donner Medal in Canadian Studies, 145
Dora and Mayer Tendler Fellowship, 1639
Dorothea Schlozer Postdoctoral Scholarships for Female Students, 1317
Dorothy Hodgkin Postgraduate Award, 1242
Doshisha University Doctoral-Program Young Researcher Scholarship, 439
Doshisha University Graduate School Reduced Tuition Special Scholarships for Self-Funded International Students, 439
Doshisha University Graduate School Scholarship, 439
Doshisha University Merit Scholarships for Self-Funded International Students, 440
Doshisha University Reduced Tuition Scholarships for Self-Funded International Students, 440
Douglass D Crombie Award in Physics, 1443
Dow Agrosciences Bursary in Chemical Engineering, 1268
Dowden Scholarship, 1305
Dr. A. Vibert Douglas Fellowship, 287
Dr. George C. Cotzias Memorial Fellowship, 92
Dr. Marie E. Zakrzewski Medical Scholarship, 697
Dr. Shawky Salem Conference Grant, 657
Dr. Suguru Furuichi Memorial Scholarship General Information, 917
Drake Lewis Graduate Scholarship for Art History, 1306
Drake Lewis Graduate Scholarship for Health and Human Sciences, 1306
Dr Andres Petrasovits Fellowship in Cardiovascular Health Policy Research, 585
Dr Betty Elliott Horticulture Scholarship, 1392
Dr Bill Jonas Memorial Indigenous Scholarship, 1432
Dreamfields Farm Agricultural Scholarship, 791
The Dreaming Award, 160
The Dr Ethel M. Janes Memorial Scholarship in Education, 809
Drever Trust MSc Scholarships, 1297
Dr Lloyd John Ogilvie Scholarships, 1296
Dr Lloyd M. Dosdall Memorial Scholarship, 489
Dr Pirkko Koppinen Scholarship, 1041
The Dr Stella Cullington Postgraduate Scholarship in Ophthalmology, 1449
Dr Sulaiman Daud 125th Jubilee Postgraduate Scholarship, 1443
Dr Theo George Wilson Scholarship, 611
Drue Heinz Scholarship, 1626
Dual-award between The University of Manchester and IIT Kharagpur, 1372
Dual-award between The University of Manchester and The University of Melbourne, 1373
Dual Credit Scholarship, 721
Duke Aging Center–Busse Research Awards, 442
Duke and Duchess of York Prize in Photography, 271
Duke Cancer Institute / Duke Microbiome Center Joint Partnership Pilot Award, 442
Duke Microbiome Center Development Grants, 442
Duke/NCCU Collaborative Translational Research Awards, 442
Dulcie Bowman Memorial Scholarship, 1227
The Duncan Family Scholarship in Early Childhood Education, 1411
The Duncan Family Scholarship in Pharmacy, 1411
Duncan Graham Award for Outstanding Contribution to Medical Education, 1032
Duncan Norman Scholarship, 1353
Dunkeld Refugee and Asylum Seeker, 511
DUO-Study Grant (only for EU-students), 1604
The Durham MBA (Full-time) Scholarships, 451
The Durham MBA (Online) Scholarships, 451
Durham Palestine Educational Trust, 447
Durham University Arts Management Group, 447
The Durham University Business School's Dean's Scholarship, 452

E

The E. (Ben) & Mary Hochhausen Access Technology Research Award, 293
E4D Continuing Education Scholarship, 479
The Eamon Cleary Trust Postgraduate Study Scholarship, 1449
Early Bird Acceptance Grant-International Students, 700
Early Career Fellowship, 256, 618
Early Career Fellowships, 725
Early-Career Patient-Oriented Diabetes Research Awards, 689
Early Career Researcher Grant (ECRG), 171
Early Childhood Scholarships, 511
Early Detection and Diagnosis Primer Award, 314
Early Detection and Diagnosis Programme Award, 314
Early Stage Dissertation Grants, 459
Early-stage Frontier Bioscience Research, 217
Earthwatch Field Research Grants, 455
Easson Geha Award in Planning, 1417
Eastern and Southern Africa Scholarship, 462
East Gippsland Water Scholarship, 512
ECCO-AOCC Visiting Travel Grant, 498
ECCO Global Grant-New, 497
ECCO Grant, 497
ECCO Pioneer Award, 498
Eckhardt-Gramatté National Music Competition, 271
Ècole Normale Supérieure International Selection Scholarships, 455
Ecology and Evolution of Infectious Diseases Initiative (EEID), 539
Economic and Social Research Council: Socio-Legal Studies, 1459
Economic and Social Research Council Studentships, 753
Economics: MSc Academic and Professional Scholarships (International), 1292
Economics: MSc Applied Training Scholarships (International), 1292
Economics 50% Scholarships: Thammasat University (Thailand), 1291
Economic & Social Research Council (1+3) Sociology Studentship, 329
ECTRIMS Allied Health Professional Fellowship, 495
ECU-DBCA Kings Park Science Industry PhD Scholarship, 470, 471
Eden Travelling Fellowship in Obstetrics and Gynaecology, 1019
Edgar Gentilli Prize, 1019
Edilia and François-Auguste de Montequin Fellowship in Iberian and Latin American Architecture, 1133

Edinburgh Business School PhD Management Scholarship, 592
Edinburgh Dental Institute MSc Scholarship, 1297
Edinburgh Doctoral College Scholarships, 1297
Edinburgh Global Online Distance Learning Masters Scholarship, 1297
Edinburgh Global Online Distance Learning Scholarships, 1298
Edinburgh Global Online Learning Masters Scholarships, 1298
Edinburgh Global Research Scholarship, 1298
Edouard Morot-Sir Fellowship in French Studies, 628
Educational Testing Service Harold Gulliksen Psychometric Fellowship Program, 475
Educational Testing Service Postdoctoral Fellowships, 476
Educational Testing Service Summer Internship Program in Research for Graduate Students, 476
Educational Testing Service Summer Internships in Programme Direction, 477
Educational Testing Service Sylvia Taylor Johnson Minority Fellowship in Educational Measurement, 477
Education Grants, 1018
Education Project Award, 978
Education Research Grant, 1128
EDUFI Fellowship, 519
Edward E. Hildebrand Research Fellowship, 196
The Edward & Isabel Kidson Scholarship, 1279
Edward S. Rogers Sr. Graduate Student Fellowships, 1076
Edward & Susan Wilson Graduate Scholarship in Business, 1115
EFSD/Lilly Young Investigator Research Award Programme, 494
Egypt Scholarship, 1346
Eiffel Scholarships in France for International Students, 548
Eileen J Garrett Scholarship, 946
ELBP Start Now Scholarship, 1432
Eldred Scholarship, 733
Eleanor and Joseph Wertheim Scholarship, 1392
The Eleonore Koch Fund, 1309
Elianna Saidenberg Transfusion Medicine Traineeship Award, 278
Elias Duek-Cohen Civid Design Award, 1417
ELICOS Scholarship, 700
Elinor Roper Scholarship, 1628
Elinor Roper Scholarship 2024, 1629
Elisabeth M and Winchell M Parsons Scholarship, 119
Elite Athlete Scholarship, 352, 512
The Elizabeth Catling Memorial Fund for Archaeological Draughtsmanship, 257
Elizabeth Garrett Anderson Hospital Charity Travelling Fellowship in Memory of Anne Boutwood, 1020
Elizabeth Jean Trotter Postgraduate Research Travelling Scholarship in Biomedical Sciences, 1444
Elizabeth Pearse Music Scholarship, 674
Ellison-Cliffe Travelling Fellowship, 1060
Ellis R. Ott Scholarship for Applied Statistics and Quality Management, 113
Ellis W. Hawley Prize, 929
Elman Poole Travelling Scholarship, 1444
Elphinstone PhD Scholarships, 1216
Elspeth D. Rostow Memorial Graduate Fellowship, 1169
Ely M. Gelbard Graduate Scholarship, 88
Embassy of France in South Africa Master Scholarship Programme, 595
Ember Venning Postgraduate Research Scholarship in Speech Pathology and Audiology, 523
Emergency Equity Grant, 353
Emergency Grants, 554
Emergency Grants for United Kingdom and International Women Graduates, 554
Emergency Medicine Foundation Grants, 552
Emergency Medicine Section: Innovation in ED Education for Students, 1060
Emergency Medicine section: Innovation in ED Education for Trainers, 1060
Emergency Medicine Section: Innovation in ED Education Prize, 1060
Emergency Medicine Section: Students' Prize for Students, 1060
Emergency Medicine Section: Students' Prize for Trainers, 1061
Emerging Leaders Awards, 848
Emerging Leaders in the Americas Program (ELAP), 283, 1319
Emeritus Fellowships, 725
Emeritus Professor William Gordon Rimmer Award, 1417
Emerson National Hunger Fellows Program, 1005
Emile Boutmy Scholarships, 1106
Emmy Noether Programme, 433
Employment-Based Postgraduate Programme, 670
Enabling Discovery through GEnomic Tools (EDGE), 868
Enabling Fund for Non-Fieldwork Expenses, 222
Endeavour Postgraduate Leadership Award, 436
Endeavour Research Fellowship for International Applicants, 483
Endometriosis Millenium Fund, 1020
Energy Education Trust of New Zealand Masterate Scholarship, 640, 791
Energy Futures Lab Overseas Scholarship for Development, 611
Energy Futures Lab Widening Participation Scholarship, 611
Engaged Research Grant, 1615
Engen Conservation, 844, 1118
Engerman-Goldin Prize, 459
Engineering and Physical Sciences Research Council (EPSRC), 612, 1325
Engineering and Physical Sciences Research Council (EPSRC) Doctoral Training Programme Studentships, 1460
Engineering and Physical Sciences Research Council Standard Research Studentships, 485
Engineering and Physical Sciences Research Council Studentships for Biophotonics, 329
The Engineering for Development (E4D) Doctoral Scholarship Programme, 479, 481
Engineering (Honours) Masters Accelerated Pathway, 823
Engineering the Future Scholarships, 1373
Engineers Canada-Manulife Scholarship, 486
Engineers Canada's National Scholarship Program, 486
Engineers Canada-TD Insurance Meloche Monnex, 487
English Faculty: Asian Human Rights Commission (AHRC) Doctoral Training Partnership Studentship (Master), 1460
English Faculty: Cecily Clarke Studentship, 1460
English Scholarships, 753
Enterprise Partnership Scheme, 671
The Enterprise Showcase Fund, 185
Environmental Leadership Fellowships, 491
Environmental Sustainability in Life Sciences and Medical Practice, 802
Environment and Sustainability Research Grants, 1037
Envision Equity Grants, 852
EPA Cephalosporin Scholarship, 733
EPA-IRC Government of Ireland Postgraduate Scholarship Programme, 491
EPFL PhD Excellence Program, 457
Ephraim Urbach Post Doctoral Fellowship, 809
Epidemiology & Public Health Young Epidemiologists Prize, 1061
EPSRC Centres for Doctoral Training, 217
EPSRC Doctoral Training Partnership (DTP), 1373
EPSRC Doctoral Training Partnership Studentships in Alliance Manchester Business School, 1374
EPSRC Doctoral Training Partnership Studentships in the School of Arts, Languages and Cultures, 1374
EPSRC Doctoral Training Partnership Studentships in the School of Environment, Education and Development, 1375
EPSRC-School of Computing, 1326
EPSRC-School of Engineering, 1326

EPSRC-School of Mathematics, Statistics and Actuarial Science, 1326
Erasmus Mundus Scholarship Programme, 621
Erasmus Trustfonds Scholarship, 1013
Erasmus University Holland Scholarship, 1013
ERC-funded Studentships in Psychology: Consequences of Conspiracy Theories, 1327
Erik Barnouw Award, 929
Ernest Guenther Award in the Chemistry of Natural Products, 59
Ernest Hemingway Research Grants, 685
Ernest Rutherford Fellowship, 1101
Ernest William File Scholarship, 1273
Ernst Ludwig Ehrlich Studienwerk, 188
Ernst Mach Grant for Young Researchers, 535
Ertegun Graduate Scholarship Programme in the Humanities, 1460
ER Walker Bequest Bursary, 675
ESC Ed Becker Conference Travel Awards, 489
Escola Superior d'Administració i Direcció d'Empreses (ESADE) MBA Scholarships, 492
ESRC-BBSRC PhD Studentships in Biosocial Research, 1376
ESRC North West Social Science DTP (NWSSDTP) PhD Studentships in Alliance Manchester Business School, 1375
ESRC North West Social Science DTP (NWSSDTP) PhD Studentships in the School of Arts, Languages and Cultures, 1376
ESRC North West Social Science DTP (NWSSDTP) PhD Studentships in the School of Environment, Education and Development, 1376
ESRC/SSRC Collaborative Visiting Fellowships, 1121
Essay Prize for Foundation Doctors, 1027
Essex Global Partner Scholarship, 1306
The Essex MBA Early Bird Discount, 1310
Establishing the Source of Gas in Australia's Offshore Petroleum Basins Scholarship, 404
Esther Katz Rosen Fund Grants, 95
Eta Sigma Phi Summer Scholarships, 492
ETH4D Doctoral Mentorship Programme, 479
ETH4D Research Challenges, 480
ETH4D Research to Action Grants, 480
ETH4D Seed Grants, 480
Ethel Rose Overton Scholarship, 1268
Ethicon Foundation Fund, 1036
Ethicon Foundation Fund Travelling Fellowship, 1021
Ethicon Student Elective Award, 1021
Ethicon Travel Award, 1035
Ethnic Minority Foundation Grants, 493
Eugene Garfield Doctoral Dissertation Fellowship, 203
Eugene Garfield Research Fellowship, 800
European Association for the Study of Diabetes-ADA Transatlantic Fellowships, 494
European Calcified Tissue Society/Servier Fellowship, 495
European Committee for Treatment and Research in Multiple Sclerosis-MAGNIMS Fellowship in Magnetic Resonance Imaging in MS, 496
European Crohn's and Colitis Organisation Fellowship, 498
European Excellence Scholarship (MBA), 894
European Molecular Biology Organisation Award for Communication in the Life
Sciences, 499
European Molecular Biology Organisation Award for Communication in the Life Sciences, 499
European Science Foundation Response of the Earth System to Impact Processes (IMPACT) Mobility Grants, 500
European Society of Surgical Oncology Training Fellowships, 500
European Space Agency's Postdoctoral Internal Research Fellowship Programme, 501
European Synchrotron Radiation Facility Postdoctoral Fellowships, 502
European Synchrotron Radiation Facility Thesis Studentships, 502
European Travelling Scholarships, 240
European Union Postgraduate Scholarship, 463
European Union Visiting Students Scholarship, 463
European Young Investigator Award, 433
Europe AU$10,000 Early Acceptance Scholarship, 770
EuroTechPostdoc, 504
EU Transition Scholarships, 741
Evangelical Lutheran Church in America Educational Grant Program, 505
Evangelisches Studienwerk Villigst, 188
Evan Lewis-Thomas Law Studentships, 1109
Evans Fund, 1242
Everett And Florence Drumright Scholarship, 917
Evidence-Based Approach to Improve Insulin Sensitivity in Horses, Using Dietary Ingredients, 353
Evonik Stiftung Scholarships, 505
Excellence in Diversity PhD Scholarships, 317
Excellence in Education Scholarship, 1292
Excellence Initiative, 434
Excellence Programme (MSc/Non-EEA), 1604
Excellence Scholarships for Postgraduate Study, 1234
Executive Dean's Postgraduate Scholarship, 512
Executive MBA Programme, 1281
Executive MBA Scholarship, 415
Exeter College: Exonian Graduate Scholarship, 1461
Exeter College: Nicholas Frangiscatos Scholarship in Byzantine Studies, 1461
Exeter College Usher-Cunningham Senior Studentship, 1461
The Exeter MBA Better World Scholarship, 1311
The Exeter MBA SDG Scholarships, 1312
Expanding Capacity in Quantum Information Science and Engineering (ExpandQISE), 909
Expensive Commonwealth Criminal Cases Fund (ECCCF), 169
Experimental Medicine, 803
Experimental Medicine Award, 314
Explore the Requirements of Exascale Software for UK Science, 217
External Sources of Funding, 707
ExxonMobil Excellence in Teaching Awards, 1015
The Eynesbury College High Achiever Progression Scholarship, 1218
The Eynesbury College International Scholarship, 1219

F

F. Albert Cotton Award in Synthetic Inorganic Chemistry, 59
Faculty Early Career Development Program (CAREER), 868
Faculty Grant Program, 1174
Faculty Mobility for Partnership Building Program, 1320
The Faculty of Law Juris Doctor Scholarship for Indigenous Students, 1424
Faculty of Law Masters International Scholarship, 823, 824
Faculty of Medicine Master, 612
Faculty of Science and Engineering Research Awards (FSERA), 523
Faculty of Science Masters Scholarship for International Students, 1155
Faculty PhD Scholarships, 319
Faculty/Post-Doctoral Grant Program (Fahs-Beck Fellows), 507
Fanconi Anemia Research Fund Award, 508
Farina Thompson Charitable Trust Music Scholarship, 1269
Farmers Union Scholarship, 640
FAR Postgraduate Scholarship, 640, 791
Federal TEACH Grant, 211
Felix Scholarships, 1094, 1461
Fellow Programme in Management (FPM) at Xavier Labor Relations Institute, 1633
Fellowship Awards, 134
Fellowship in the Digital Humanities, 1599
Fellowship Program, 78
Fellowships for Advanced Social Science Research on Japan, 855

Fellowships for Intensive Advanced Turkish Language Study in Istanbul, Turkey, 97
Fellowships for Study of Research in Belgium, 192
Fellowships Open Book Program, 855
Fellowship Training Award for Workforce Expansion, 998
Fellowship Travelling Bursary, 241
Ferguson Scholarships, 149
Ferrari Innovation Team Project Scholarship, 518
Ferry Scholarship–UniSA, 1217
Fessenden-Trott Scholarship, 1197
FfWG Foundation Grants, 554
FfWG-Foundation Grants for Women Graduates, 556, 707
FfWG Grants-Emergency Grant, 247
FfWG Grants-Foundation Grant, 248
FfWG-Theodora Bosanquet Bursary for Women Graduates, 707
Fibrosis in IBD Research Initiative, 397
FIDERH Award, 1354
FIDERH Scholarship, 770
Fieldwork Bursary, 256
Fight for Sight, 518
FINS Student Loans, 707
Firkin PhD Scholarship, 167
First Nations Accommodation and Relocation Scholarship, 353
First Nations Education Costs Scholarship, 353
Fitzwilliam College: Cleaver-Wang Studentship, 1244
Fitzwilliam College: E D Davies Scholarship, 1244
Fitzwilliam College: Fitzwilliam Society JRW Alexander Law Book Grants, 1244
Fitzwilliam College: Gibson Scholarship, 1244
Fitzwilliam College: Hirst-Player Scholarship, 1245
Fitzwilliam College: Lee Kuan Yew PhD Studentships, 1245
Fitzwilliam College: Peter Wilson Estates Gazette Studentships, 1245
Fitzwilliam College: Quantedge–Lee Kuan Yew Masters Scholarship, 1245
Fitzwilliam College: Robert Lethbridge Scholarship in Modern Languages, 1246
Fitzwilliam College: Shipley Studentship, 1246
Fitzwilliam College: The Hong Leong–Lee Kuan Yew Masters Scholarship, 1246
Fitzwilliam College Charlton Studentships, 1243
Fitzwilliam College Graduate Scholarship, 1243
Fitzwilliam College Leathersellers, 1243
Fitzwilliam College Research Fellowship, 1243
Fitzwilliam Masters Studentship, 1246
F.J. McGuigan Early Career Investigator Research Grant on Understanding the Human Mind, 95
FLAS Fellowship (Academic Year), 368
Fletcher Graduate Scholarship (International Development & Social Enterprise), 1146
Flinders and Nourish Ingredients Industry PhD Scholarship: Medical Biotechnology, Microbial Bioprocessing, 523
Flinders University and Defence Science: Defence Science Partnership Grant, 524
Flinders University Research Scholarships (FURS), 524
Florence and William Blair Bell Research Fellowship, 1021
FMC Foundation Pink Ribbon Ball Committee Breast Cancer Research Scholarship, 524
FMC Foundation Research Scholarship, 525
Food Safety SS Burdock Group Travel Award, 1185
Ford Foundation Dissertation Fellowship, 539
Ford Foundation Fellowship Programs, 838
Ford Foundation Predoctoral Diversity Fellowships, 196
Ford Foundation Predoctoral Fellowships for Research-Based PhD or ScD Programs in United States of America, 538
Ford Foundation Senior Fellowship, 838
Foreign Language and Area Studies Awards, 196
Foreign Language and Area Studies Fellowship, 369
Forensic Science for the Justice System Sandpit, 218
Forum Transregional Studies Postdoctoral Fellowships for International Students, 540
Foster G McGaw Graduate Student Scholarship, 547
Foundation Commencing Scholarships, 512
Foundation Continuing Scholarships, 513
Foundation for Liberal and Management Education University Scholars Program, 545
Foundation for Science and Disability Student Grant Fund, 546
Foundation Grant Program, 289
Foundation Grants, 554
Foundation HDR Scholarships, 513
Foundation Praemium Erasmianum Study Prize, 548
Four-year PhD Studentship Programmes, 1607
Fowler-Merle Smith Summer Scholarship for Teachers, 101
France: French Embassy and Saint-Gobain Master Scholarship, 596
France: ISAE-SUPAERO Scholarship Programmes, 596
Francis Martin Baillie Reynolds Scholarship in Law to Oxford, 1273
Francis Regan Student Scholarship, 525
Frank and Doris Bateson Memorial Graduate Scholarship, 1269
Frank B. Sessa Scholarships for Continuing Professional Education of Beta Phi Mu Members, 203
Frank Chapman Sharp Memorial Prize, 93
Frank Keenan Scholarship, 1392
Frank Knox Memorial Fellowships, 1393
Frank Knox Memorial Fellowships at Harvard University, 1273
Frank Stell Scholarship, 1336
Fred. L. Scarf Award, 70
Frederick Jackson Turner Award, 930
Frederic Stanley Kipping Award in Silicon Chemistry, 59
Fred Katz Award, 1417
The Fredson Bowers Award, 207
Freemasons Scholarships, 1444
Free University of Berlin and Peking University Joint Postdoctoral Fellowship, 548
French Association of University Women (AFFDU) Grants, 248
French Association of University Women (AFFDU) Monique Fouet Grant, 248
French-Australian Cotutelle, 404
French Language Scholarship, 288
Freshfields Bruckhaus Deringer Scholarships (Law), 1462
Freyberg Scholarship, 1199
Friedenberg Mentored Clinician Scientist Grant, 941
Friedrich-Ebert-Stiftung, 188
Friedrich-Naumann-Stiftung, 188
Friends of Israel Educational Foundation Academic Study Bursary, 549
Friends of the Sports Association Scholarship, 1393
Friends of the University Development Studies Scholarship, 1432
Friends of the University Ken Gordon Memorial Honours Scholarship, 1433
Friends of the University Sport Scholarship, 1433
Fritz Halbers Fellowship, 720
Frontier Research in Earth Sciences (FRES), 442
Fujitsu Scholarship Program for Asia-Pacific Region, 549
Fulbright Awards, 570
Fulbright Canada Scholarship, 1076
Fulbright Distinguished Awards in Teaching Program for International Teachers, 1192
Fulbright Distinguished Chair in Science, Technology, and Innovation (CSIRO), 551
Fulbright-Durham University Award, 448
The Fulbright-Edinburgh Napier University Scholar Award, 469
The Fulbright-Edinburgh University Award, 1196
Fulbright-Freud Visiting Lecturer of Psychoanalysis, 552
Fulbright Indo-American Environmental Leadership Program, 1193

Fulbright-Kalam Climate Fellowships for Doctoral Research, 1193
Fulbright-Kalam Climate Fellowships for Postdoctoral Research, 1194
Fulbright/Maastricht University Award, 763
Fulbright-Nehru Academic and Professional Excellence Fellowships, 1194
Fulbright-Nehru Doctoral Research Fellowships, 1195
Fulbright-Nehru Master's Fellowships, 1195
Fulbright-Nehru Postdoctoral Research Fellowships, 1195
Fulbright New Zealand General Graduate Awards, 156
Fulbright-Platinum Triangle Scholarship in Entrepreneurship, 736
Fulbright Postdoctoral Scholarship in All Disciplines, 551
Fulbright Scholar-in-Residence, 550
Fulbright Scholarship, 1227
Fulbright Scholarship Program for Nigerians, 551
Fulbright Scholarships, 1354, 1393
Full-Time MBA at Copenhagen Business School, 383
Full-time Scholarship (Australian Government's Research Training Program), 354
Full-Tuition Fees Waiver for MPhil/PhD Students, 345
Full Tuition International Relations Scholarships, 174
Fully Funded EPSRC Scholarships in Chemistry, 1327
Fully Funded EPSRC Scholarships in Physics, 1327
Fully Funded Master Scholarship at Hong Kong Baptist University, 602
150 Fully Funded PhD Degree Scholarships for International Students, 503
Fully-Funded PhD Studentship in Sustainable Place-Making, 329
Fully-funded PhD Studentship in the School of Geography, 1439
Fully Funded PhD Scholarships, 1445
40 Fully-Funded Postgraduate Scholarships at Newcastle University in the United Kingdom, 901
Funds for Women Graduates, 1377
FUNED Awards, 1354
FUNED Scholarship, 770
Furness Studentship, 708
Future Conservationist Awards, 381
Future Finance (Private Student Loans), 708
Future Leaders Postgraduate Scholarship, 1235
Future of Change Scholarship, 1417
Future of Change Schools Excellence Bursary, 1418
Future of the Academy PhD Studentship, 1377
Fylde College-Travel Award, 556

G

Gail Kelly Honours Award for Business, 1418
Gallman-Parker Prize, 460
The Gane Trust Travel Award, 185
The Garden Club of America Fellowship in Tropical Botany, 560
The Garden Club of America Hope Goddard Iselin Fellowship in Public Horticulture, 560
Garden Club of America Summer Scholarship in Field Botany, 559
Garrick Latch Postgraduate Travel Grants, 641
Garrick Scholarship, 463
Gary Metz Research Fellowship, 337
Gary S. Gilkeson Career Development Award, 759
Gastroenterology & Hepatology Section: Gut Club Prize, 1061
Gates Cambridge Scholarship, 561
Gateway Antarctica's Ministry of Foreign Affairs and Trade Scholarship in Antarctic and Southern Ocean Studies, 1274
G B Battersby-Trimble Scholarship in Computer Science, 1274
Geddes Scholarship, 1087
General Practice with Primary Healthcare John Fry Prize, 1061
General Research Grants: Scholarships, 1172
The General Sir John Monash Awards, 408
General Surgery Resident Research Initiation Grant, 115
GeneTex Scholarship Program, 562
The Geoffrey F. Bruce Fellowship in Canadian Freshwater Policy, 1080
Geoffrey Leech Departmental MA scholarship, 708
Geographical Club Award, 1038
Geography: Sir Walter Raleigh Postgraduate Scholarship, 1462
Geography and Environment Scholarships, 754
Geography and the Environment: Andrew Goudie Bursary, 1462
Geography and the Environment: Boardman Scholarship, 1462
Geography Students Conference Fund, 1274
George A. and Eliza Gardner Howard Foundation, 563
George A. Gecowets Graduate Scholarship Program, 387
George F. Wellik Scholarship, 132
George Fairfax Arts Management Scholarship in Association with the Sue Nattrass Arts Management Fund, 423
George Major Bursaries, 1347
George Mason Sustainable Land Use Scholarship, 641, 791
The George Melhuish Postgraduate Scholarship, 1211
George Pepler International Award, 1073
Georges Lurcy Fellowship for Study in France, 197
Gerald D. and Norma Feldman Graduate Student Dissertation Fellowship, 197
The Gerber Foundation Merit Scholarship, 565
Geriatrics & Gerontology Section: Clinical Audit and Governance Prize, 1062
Geriatrics & Gerontology Section: President's Essay Prize for Students, 1062
Geriatrics & Gerontology Section: President's Essay Prize for Trainers, 1062
Geriatrics & Gerontology Section: Trainees' Prize, Clinical Presentations, 1062
Geriatrics & Gerontology Section: Trainees' Prize, Clinical Presentations for Trainers, 1062
German Academic Scholarship Foundation, 189
German Business Foundation, 189
German Historical Institute Collaborative Research Program for Postdoctoral Scholars, 566
Germany Residency Program, 930
Gertrude Ardagh Holmes Bursary Fund, 1275
Getty Pre-and Postdoctoral Fellowships and GRI-NEH Postdoctoral Fellowships, 568
Getty Scholar Grants, 568
GHI Fellowships at the Horner Library, 566
Ghosh Graduate Scholarship (Humanities), 1147
Giacomo Vaciago Scholarship, 734
Gilbert Chinard Fellowships, 628
Gilbert M Tothill Scholarship in Psychological Medicine, 1445
Gilbert S. Omenn Fellowship, 839
Gilchrist Fieldwork Award, 569
Giles Worsley Travel Fellowship, 260
Gillson Scholarship in Pathology, 1132
Gina M. Finzi Memorial Student Summer Fellowship Program, 760
Girton College: Doris Woodall Studentship, 1247
Girton College: Ida and Isidore Cohen Research Scholarship, 1247
Girton College: Irene Hallinan Scholarship, 1247
Girton College: Maria Luisa de Sanchez Scholarship, 1248
Girton College: Ruth Whaley Scholarship, 1248
Girton College: Sidney and Marguerite Cody Studentship, 1248
Girton College: Stribling Award, 1249
Girton College: The Chan and Mok Graduate Scholarship, 1249
Girton College: The Diane Worzala Memorial Fund, 1249
Girton College: The Dinah James Scholarship, 1249
Girton College: The Girton Hong Kong Founder's Scholarship, 1250
Girton College: The Joyce Biddle Scholarship, 1250
Girton College: The Postgraduate Research Scholarship, 1250
Girton College: Travel Grant, 1251
Girton College Graduate Research Scholarship, 1246
Girton College Overseas Bursaries, 1247

The Girton Singapore Scholarship, 1259
Gladys Anderson Emerson Scholarship, 668
Glasgow Educational & Marshall Trust Award, 1315
Glasgow School for Business and Society Postgraduate EU scholarships for MSc International Fashion Marketing, 570
Glasgow School for Business and Society Scholarship, 570
Glaucoma UK and The Royal College of Ophthalmologists Research Award, 1028
Glencore Mining Engineering Scholarship, 1418
Glenmore Medical Postgraduate Scholarship, 1298
Glenn Foundation for Medical Research Postdoctoral Fellowships in Aging Research, 66
Glenn T. Seaborg Award for Nuclear Chemistry, 60
Global Accounting and Finance Scholarship, 1236
Global Ambassador Scholarship Programme (GASPR), 781
Global Challenges Research Fund Challenge-led Grants (GCRF), 1051
Global Challenges Research Fund Networking Grants, 12
Global Citizenship Scholarship, 1284
Global Economics Postgraduate Scholarship, 1236
Global Excellence Scholarship, 150, 1285
Global Excellence Scholarships, 165
Global Excellence Scholarships-Postgraduate Taught (Masters), 1311
Global Health Research Initiative Program for New Foreign Investigators (GRIP), 683
Global Hemophilia ASPIRE, 953
Global Initiatives Grant, 1615
Global International and Area Studies Grants, 197
Global MBA Alumni Scholarship, 771
Global MBA International Scholarship Fund, 416
Global Opportunity Fellowship (GO: AFRICA), 581
Global Partnership Network Masters Scholarships, 1007
Global Postgraduate Scholarship, 1347
Global Professorships, 231
Global Talent Fellowships, 1292
Global Wales Postgraduate Scholarship, 329
The Goa Education Trust (GET) Scholarships, 243
Godfrey Tyler Scholarship in Economics, 1139
Goethe-Institut Postdoctoral Fellowship for International Students, 572
Gold, Silver and Bronze Medals, 945
Gonville and Caius College Gonville Bursary, 1251
Gonville and Caius College Michael Miliffe Scholarship, 1251
Gonville and Caius College W M Tapp Studentship in Law, 1251
Goodger and Schorstein Research Scholarships in Medical Sciences, 1463
Good Ideas-Artist Led Projects, 139
Goodrich Scholarship Program, 847
Gordon David Family Scholarship, 464
Gordon Watson Scholarship, 1199
Gottfried Wilhelm Leibniz Prize, 434
Government of Ireland Postgraduate Scholarship Programme, 671
Governor General Gold Medal, 1077
Governor General's Literary Awards, 271
Governor General's Performing Arts Awards, 271
Graça Machel scholarship, 715
Graduate Council Fellowships, 1220
Graduate Division Caregiver Grant, 197
Graduate Fellowships for Science, Technology, Engineering, and Mathematics Diversity, 573
Graduate Honors Scholarship, 1402
Graduate Research Awards for Disarmament, Arms Control and Non-Proliferation, 539
Graduate Research Scholarships, 1203, 1394
Graduate Research Scholarships for Cross-disciplinary Training (One-Year), 1203
Graduate Research Travel Scholarships, 489
Graduate Scholarship, 144
Graduate School of Arts and Sciences International Travel Fellowships, 369
Graduate School of Brain Science Special Scholarship, 440
Graduate Student Grant, 546
Graduate Student Research Grants, 562
Graduate Studentships, 23
Graduate Student Stipend, 1077
Graduate Women Canterbury (Inc.) Trust Board Scholarship, 1275
Graduate Women Manawatu Postgraduate Scholarship, 792
Graduate Women North Shore Branch Scholarship, 792
Graduate Women Victoria Scholarship Program, 1394
Grant Lingard Scholarship, 1275
Grants, 1173
Grants for ANS Summer Seminar in Numismatics, 91
Grants for Artist Projects (GAP), 134
Grants for Orchid Research, 91
Grants for Public Projects, 123
Grants-in-Aid of Research and Development, 585
Grants Programs, 941
Graphene NOWNANO CDT, 1377
2024 Great Artesian Basin Lynn Brake Scholarship, 520
Great Eastern Scholarship (All Subjects), 1147
GREAT Egypt Scholarship, 464
Greater Good Science Center Graduate Fellowships, 198
GREAT-Imperial College London Scholarship, 613
GREAT India Scholarship, 464
GREAT Kenya Scholarship, 464
GREAT Pakistan Scholarship, 464
GREAT Scholarship-Bangladesh, 1285
GREAT Scholarship for Justice and Law, 1204, 1307
GREAT Scholarship for Justice & Law-Thailand, 1285
GREAT Scholarships, 329, 571, 1203, 1282, 1306, 1377
GREAT Scholarships-China, 1286
GREAT Scholarships-Egypt, 1286
GREAT Scholarships-Ghana, 1286
GREAT Scholarships India, 243
GREAT Scholarships-India, 1287
GREAT Scholarships–Indonesia, 1287
GREAT Scholarships-Kenya, 1287
GREAT Scholarships–Malaysia, 1288
GREAT Scholarships–Pakistan, 1288
GREAT Scholarship–Sri Lanka, 1285
GREAT Scholarships–Thailand, 1288
GREAT Turkey Scholarship, 465
Green-Armytage and Spackman Travelling Scholarship, 1022
'Green Futures' Postgraduate Taught Scholarships, 1311
Green Moral Philosophy Scholarship, 1463
Green Templeton College: GTC-Medical Sciences Doctoral Training Centre Scholarship, 1463
Green Templeton College: GTC-SBS DPhil Scholarship, 1463
Greenwall Fellowship in Bioethics, 839
Greenwall Fellowship Program, 687
Gretzky Scholarship Foundation for the Blind Youth of Canada, 293
Greyfriars Postgraduate Scholarship, 984, 985
Griffith Remarkable Scholarship, 574
Grizedale College Awards Fund, 708
Growth Hormone Research, 953
GROW Your Future Careers Bursary, 709
Grundy Educational Trust Postgraduate Award, 1439
GSAS Summer Language Fellowships for International Students, 370
2023-24 GSK Scholarships for Future Health Leaders, 745
Guggenheim Fellowships, 844, 1119
Gulbali Institute PhD Scholarships, 354
Gulf Research Program Science Policy Fellowships, 1175
The Gulf Research Program's Early-Career Research Fellowship, 1175
GUS LIPSCHITZ BURSARY, 1008

Guy Butler Research Award, 1008
Gyorgy Ranki Biennial Prize, 460

H

H3Africa Global Health Bioinformatics Research Training Program, 536
H 15 GRANT: Early Career Research Grant, 42
H-21 Grant: Established Scholar Research Grant, 42
H 31 Grant: Pre-Doctoral Research Grant, 42
Hancock Prospecting Swimming Excellence Scholarship, 224
Hansen Scholarship, 1394
Hansi Pollak Scholarship, 1136
HAPP MSc Scholarship in the History of Science, 1139
HAPP Scholarship in the History & Philosophy of Physics, 1140
Hardiman PhD Scholarships, 872
Hardship Support Fund, 754
Harkness Fellowships in Health Care Policy, 374
Harkness Fellowships in Healthcare Policy and Practice, 374
Harmon Chadbourn Rorison Fellowship, 628
Harold Amos Medical Faculty Development Program, 1010
Harold Gulliksen Psychometric Research Fellowship, 477
Harold Jones and Frances Murray Research Fellowship, 337
Harold Taber MBA Scholarship, 211
Harpo Foundation Grants for Visual Artists, 579
Harriet and Leon Pomerance Fellowship, 128
Harriet Hale Woolley Scholarship, 536
Harry Bikakis Fellowship, 101
Harry Clough Bursary, 1378
Harry Crossley Doctoral Fellowship, 1152
Harry Crossley Master, 1153
Harry & Lula McCarn Nurses Scholarship, 1171
The Harry Moreton Memorial Scholarship, 1031
Harry Steele-Bodger Memorial Travelling Scholarship, 263
Harry S Truman Library Institute Dissertation Year Fellowships, 579
Harry S Truman Library Institute Research Grant, 580
Harry S Truman Library Institute Scholar's Award, 580
Hart Fellowship, 632
Harvard/Newcomen Postdoctoral Award, 906
Harvard Travellers Club Permanent Fund, 581
Hatfield Lioness Scholarship, 448
Haywood Doctoral Scholarship, 1299
H.C. & M.E. Porter Memorial Endowed Award, 1419
HC Russell Memorial Postgraduate Scholarship, 1227
HDR Scholarship-Geotechnical Engineering PhD Scholarship, 405
HDR Scholarship in Structural Vibration Control, 405
Headley Trust Scholarship, 1041
Health and Population Innovation Fellowship Program, 960
Health Data Science Scholarships, 1354
Health Economics and HIV/AIDS Research Division PhD Scholarships, 1335
Health Professional Online Education Grant, 999
Health Research Council (HRC) Summer Studentships (Ethics), 641
Healthy Eating Research, 1011
Hearst Fellowships, 585
Heart and Stroke Foundation of Canada New Investigator Research Scholarships, 585
Heart and Stroke Foundation of Canada Nursing Research Fellowships, 586
Heart and Stroke Foundation of Canada Research Fellowships, 586
HeART of the Basin Scholarship, 340
Heart Research United Kingdom Translational Research Project Grants, 586
Heatherlea Bursary, 709
Heather Leaity Memorial Award, 1227
Hebei Provincial Government Scholarship, 1637
Hector and Elizabeth Catling Bursary, 256
The Hector and Elizabeth Catling Doctoral Award, 258
Heilbronn Doctoral Partnership (HDP) Studentship, 1378
Heilongjiang Provincial Government Scholarships, 682
Heinrich Boll Scholarships in Germany for International Students, 588
Heinrich-Böll-Stiftung, 189
Heinz Maier–Leibnitz Prize, 434
Heisenberg Programme, 435
The Helena Anna Henzl-Gabor Young Women in Science Fund for Postdoctoral Scholars Travel Grant, 1149
Helen E. Akers Postgraduate Scholarship, 641
Helen H Lawson Research Grant, 255
The Helen Macpherson Smith Scholarships, 1401
Helen Rosa Thacker Scholarship in Neurological Research, 1445
Hellman Fellows Fund, 1239
Helmut Kohl Award in German and European Studies, 198
Henry and Louisa Williams Bequest, 1395
Henry DeWolf Smyth Nuclear Statesman Award, 88
Henry Dryerre Scholarship in Medical and Veterinary Physiology, 1316
Henry Ellison Scholarship, 1336
Henry Kelsey Scholarship, 1199, 1275
Henry Rudolf Meisels Bursary Awards, 713
Herbert Erik Reiss Memorial Case History Prize, 1022
Herbert Smith Freehills Law and Economics Honours Year Award, 1419
Herb Society of America Research Grant, 591
Herchel Smith Scholarship in Intellectual Property, 969
Heriot-Watt Expo Award, 592
Heritage Scholarship, 722
Herman Frasch Foundation Grant, 60
Hertford College: Vaughan Williams Senior Scholarship, 1463
Hertford College: Worshipful Company of Scientific Instrument Makers Senior Scholarship, 1464
Heseltine Ecology Bursary, 641
Hessnatur Foundation Scholarship, 492
High-End Instrumentation (HEI) Grant Program, 859
Higher Education Commission Pakistan Scholarship, 754
Higher Education Scholarships (International), 1217
High Performance Sports Scholarship, 1395
Hilda Martindale Trust Awards, 601
Hilda Trevelyan Morrison Bequest, 1395
Hill Foundation Scholarships, 1464
Historic Royal Palaces Heritage Scholarships, 970
History of Art Institutional Fellowships, 1084
History of Medicine Society: Norah Schuster Essay Prize, 1062
Hitchings-Elion Postdoctoral Fellowships for United States Scientist, 861
HKBU Fully Funded International Postgraduate Scholarship, 19
HLC MA in Chinese-English Translating and Interpreting Scholarships, 1282
The H.M. Ali Family Educational Award, 131
Hobart Houghton Research Fellowship, 1008
Hodgson Law Scholarship, 1355
Hodson Trust-John Carter Brown Library Fellowship, 682
Hélène La Rue Scholarship in Music, 1139
Holland Government Scholarship/Upcoming Year for School of Management, 1014
Holland Scholarship, 577, 1187
Holland Scholarship for international Master Students, 1604
Hong Kong and Shanghai Banking Corporation School of Oriental and African Studies Scholarships, 1094
Hong Kong Jockey Club Graduate Scholarships, 1464
Honor Frost Foundation Grants, 234
Honourable Jack Beale Scholarship in Engineering, 1419
Honours Award Education, 1419
Honours/Masters Scholarship for AI, User Interface or Robotics, 525
Honours Scholarship, 171
Honours Scholarship HECS Exempt Award, 354

Hoover Fellowships for International Scholars, 335
HOPE Foundation Scholarship for Research on Ageing, 641
Hope Selwyn Foundation Scholarship, 1228
Horatio Alger Association Canadian Scholarships, 275
Horizons Regional Council Sustainable Land Use Scholarships-Year 1 & Year 2 Students, 792
The Horowitz Foundation for Social Policy, 603
Horticulture NZ Undergraduate Scholarships, 792
Hospitality Maine Scholarships, 604
Howard Hughes Medical Institute Gilliam Fellowships for Advanced Study, 604
HRB Postdoctoral Fellowships-Applying Research into Policy and Practice (ARPP) 2023, 583
HRB Postdoctoral Fellowships-Clinician Scientist Fellowships (CSF) 2023, 583
HRM Princess Sirindhorn University of Liverpool Scholarship (Thailand), 1355
HSF Scholarship, 1177
Hsing Yun Education Foundation (HYEF) Scholarship for Domestic Students, 833
Hsing Yun Education Foundation (HYEF) Scholarship for International Students, 833
The Hub Award, 1610
Hubble Fellowships for Postdoctoral Scientists, 843
Hudson and McGowan Scholarship, 642
Hudswell International Research Scholarship, 646
Huggins-Quarles Award, 930
Hugh Last Fund and General Fund, 1130
The Hugh Martin Weir Prize, 1219
The Humane Research Trust Grant, 605
Humanitarian Scholarship–The University of Dundee, 1289
Humanities and Social Sciences Postgraduate Scholarships, 894
Humanities St Cross College UK BAME PGT Studentship, 1140
Humboldt Postdoc Scholarships, 605
Humboldt Talent Travel Awards, 606
Hume Multiversity Scholarship, 423
Hungary: Stipendium Hungaricum for South Africa, 596
Hunter Postgraduate Scholarship, 405
Hunt Postdoctoral Fellowships, 1615
Hurley Fraser Postgraduate Scholarship, 792
Hutton Fund, 1051
The Hydro One Aboriginal Award for Graduate Studies in Public Policy and Administration, 1080

I

Ian Alexander Gordon Scholarship, 513
Ian Kay Scholarships, 465
ICGEB-Elettra Sincrotrone Trieste International Fellowship Programme, 654
ICGEB PhD and POSTDOC Fellowships, South Africa, 653
ICGEB PhD Fellowships, 653
ICGEB Postdoctoral Fellowships, 653
ICGEB Short-Term PhD Fellowships, 653
ICGEB Short-Term Postdoctoral Fellowships, 654
ICGEB Smart Fellowships, 654
ICTS Post Doctoral Program, 655
Ida Pfeiffer Scholarships, 1318
Ida Smedley MacLean Fellowship, 658
IDeA Networks of Biomedical Research Excellence (INBRE) (P20 Clinical Trial Optional), 859
Idemitsu Engineering Scholarship, 1433
Ilona Takacs Scholarship, 513
Immediate Postdoctoral Basic Science Research Fellowships, 251
Immersive Training in the Glycosciences-Fellowship, 858
Immuno-Informatics Postdoctoral Fellowship, 309
Impact Focussed Supergen Hubs in Bioenergy, Networks and ORE, 218
Improving Project Delivery: ESRC Studentship, 465
India: Export-Import Bank of India BRICS Economic Research Award, 596
India GREAT Scholarship, 416
India Habitat Centre Fellowship for Photography, 620
Indian Arts Partner Scholarship, 771
Indian Council of Medical Research Centenary-Postdoctoral Fellowship, 620
Indian Excellence Scholarship Award, 1378
Indian Health Service Health Professions Scholarship Program, 624
Indian Institute of Science Bangalore Kishore Vaigyanik Protsahan Yojana Fellowships, 623
Indian Institute of Technology Ropar Institute Postdoctoral Fellowship, 623
India Scholarship, 1347
Indigenous Accommodation Grant, 1395
Indigenous Commonwealth Accommodation Scholarship, 525
Indigenous Commonwealth Accomodation Top-up Scholarship, 526
Indigenous Commonwealth Education Costs Scholarship, 526
Indigenous Education Costs Scholarship, 675
Indigenous Education Scholarship, 1434
Indigenous Graduate Scholarship-Fulfilling Indigenous Community Responsibilities, 1320
Indigenous Graduate Scholarship-Leadership, 1320
Indigenous Graduate Scholarship-Merit, 1321
Indigenous Graduate Scholarship-Top-Up, 1321
Indigenous Macquarie University Research Excellence Scholarship, 771
Indigenous Master of Psychology (Clinical) Scholarship, 1407
Indigenous Pathways Advance Queensland VET Scholarship, 341
Indigenous Research Training Program Scholarship (RTPSI), 675
Indigenous Sporting Excellence Scholarships, 176
Indigenous Student On-Campus Accommodation Scholarship, 675
Indira Gandhi Institute of Development Research-International Development Research Centre Scholarships and Fellowships for Asian Countries Students, 624
Individual Investigator Research Awards (IIRA), 301
Individual Investigator Research Awards for Cancer in Children and Adolescents (IIRACCA), 301
Individual Investigator Research Awards for Clinical Translation (IIRACT), 302
Individual Investigator Research Awards for Computational Systems Biology of Cancer (IIRACSBC), 303
Individual Investigator Research Awards for Prevention and Early Detection (IIRAP), 303
Individual Photographer, 7
Indonesia: Kemitraan Negara Berkembang (Developing Countries Partnership) Scholarship, 597
Indonesia Endowment Fund for Education (LPDP), 895
Indonesian Arts and Culture Scholarship, 816
Indonesia Scholarship, 1348
IndusInd Foundation Scholarship for Postgraduate Students, 625
Industrial CASE-Plus Studentship, 1102
Industrial CASE Studentships, 1101
Industrial Transformation Training Centre in Facilitated Advancement of Australia's Bioactive-Domestic, 771
Industrial Transformation Training Centre in Facilitated Advancement of Australia's Bioactive-International, 772
Industry Discovery & Development Partnerships, 689
Industry Fellowships, 1051
Informatics Global PhD Scholarships, 1299
Information Technology Postgraduate Scholarship, 824
Innovation Masters and Doctoral Scholarships, 865
Innovative Geography Teaching Grants, 1038
Innovative Grants, 689
Innovative Research Award, 999

Innovative Research Award for Community Practitioners, 999
Inspire! Grants for Small Museums, 646
Inspiring Success Scholarship, 754
Institut de Recherche Robert-Sauvé en Santé et en Sécurité du Travail Graduate Studies Scholarship and Postdoctoral Fellowship Program, 626
Institute Career Path Fellowships, 218
Institute for Advanced Studies in the Humanities Postdoctoral Fellowships, 1299
Institute for Advanced Studies in the Humanities (The Institute for Advanced Studies in the Humanities)-SSPS (School of Social and Political Science) Research Fellowships, 629
Institute for Advanced Studies on Science, Technology and Society Fellowship Programme, 629
Institute for Labour Market Policy Evaluation Post Doctoral Scholarship, 631
Institute for Particle and Nuclear Physics MSc Prize Scholarships, 465
Institute for Student Achievement Summer Internship in Program Monitoring & Evaluation, 478
Institute for Supply Management Professional Research Development Grant, 634
Institute of Education, University of London Centenary Masters Scholarships, 1204
Institute of Education Postgraduate Pathway Scholarship, 642
Institute of Electrical and Electronics Engineers Fellowship in the History of Electrical and Computing Technology, 637
Institute of Health and Biomedical Innovation Awards, 974
Institute of International Studies (IIS) Dissertation Fellowships, 198
Institut Européen d'Administration des Affaires Goldman Sachs Scholarship for African Nationals, 627
Institut Européen d'Administration des Affaires Jewish Scholarship, 627
Institut Européen d'Administration des Affaires MBA Programme, 627
Institut Européen d'Administration des Affaires Nelson Mandela Endowment Scholarships, 627
Institution of Engineering and Technology Postgraduate Scholarship for an Outstanding Researcher, 647
Institution of Engineering and Technology Travel Awards, 647
Integrated Catalysis (iCAT) CDT, 1378
Interdisciplinary Doctoral Studentships in Food Systems: UKFS-CDT, 267
Interior Design-Masters of Arts by Research, 1047
Intermediate Clinical Research Fellowships, 251
Intermediate Fellowship, 619
Internal Studentships Past and Current Year, 799
International Affairs Fellowship for Tenured International Relations Scholars, 389
International Alumni Scholarship, 1348
International Beethoven Piano Competition, Vienna, 1627
International Business Machines Herman Goldstine Postdoctoral Fellowship, 650
International Business Machines PhD Fellowship Program, 650
International Carl Flesch Violin Competition, 268
International Centre for Theoretical Sciences S. N. Bhatt Memorial Excellence Research Fellowship, 656
International Club of Boston College Cambridge Scholarship, 1263
International Collaboration to Address Antimicrobial Resistance, 803
International College Dundee Progressing with Excellence Scholarship (Taught Postgraduate), 1289
International College of Auckland PhD Scholarship in Plant Sciences, 1228
International Council for Canadian Studies Graduate Student Scholarships, 283
International Dairy-Deli-Bakery Association Graduate Scholarships, 656
International Development*: Full Fees Scholarship, 1292
International Development: QEH Scholarship, 1465
International Development*: Scholarships for Students from Bangladesh, 1293
International Development*: Scholarships for Students from Colombia, 1293
International Development*: Scholarships for Students from India, 1293
International Development*: Scholarships for Students from Japan, 1293
International Development*: Scholarships for Students from South Korea, 1294
International Development*: Scholarships for Students from Sub Saharan Africa, 1294
International doctoral Tuition Scholarship, 1321
International Engineering MSc Studentship, 330
International Excellence Scholarship (Information Technology and Computer Science), 1434
International Excellence Scholarship (Management, Accounting and Finance), 1434
International Excellence Scholarships, 267, 675, 1158
International Exchanges, 1051
International Family Discounts (IFD), 895
International Federation of Library Associations and Institutions Green Library Award, 657
International Fellowship Grant, 115
International Fellowships, 525, 725
30th International Geographical Congress Award, 1037
International House Scholarship, 1396
International Institute for Management Development MBA Merit Scholarships, 661
International Institute for Population Sciences Diploma in Population Studies, 662
International Institute of Tropical Agriculture Research Fellowships, 662
International Leadership Scholarship, 224
International Master of Engineering (Professional) Scholarship, 676
International Mathematical Union Visiting Mathematician Programme, 663
International Medical Educator of the Year Award, 1032
International Merit Award, 811
International Merit Scholarships, 748
International Merit Stipend, 676
International Need-Based Tuition Awards and Graduate Student Family Grants, 198
International Office Postgraduate Scholarship, 971
International Onshore Postgraduate Support Scholarship, 406
International Opportunities Funding, 139
International Partner Scholarship, 183
International PhD Awards, 971
International PhD Fellowships in Environmental Chemistry, Denmark, 901
International PhD Student Positions in Mathematics, Sweden, 902
International Postgraduate Gaza Scholarships, 958
International Postgraduate Research Scholarship at Queensland University of Technology, 974
International Postgraduate Research Scholarships (IPRS), 166
International Postgraduate Research Studentship (IPRS) at Murdoch University in Australia, 831
International Postgraduate Scholarships, 1095
International Postgraduate Scholarships–Taught Master's Programmes, 1236
International Postgraduate Taught Merit Scholarship, 416
International Prize, 537
International Recruitment Office Scholarship, 183
International Research Training Program Scholarship (IRTPS), 676
International Resident Leadership Award, 1032
International Road to Research Scholarship-Session 2 2023, 772
International Scholarship Award Program, 417

International Scholarships at University of Derby, 1283
International School of Crystallography Grants, 663
International Scientia Coursework Scholarship, 1419
International Society of Nephrology Fellowship Awards, 664
International Society of Nephrology Travel Grants, 664
International Society of Nephrology Visiting Scholars Program, 665
International Spinal Research Trust, 1138
International Stand Out Scholarship, 224
International Student Academic Excellence Scholarship, 574
International Student Academic Merit Scholarship, 575
International Student Aid Grant, 211
International Student Award, 1420
International Student Grant, 918
International Student Merit Scholarship, 958
International Student PGT Scholarship, 959
International Student Scholarship, 341
International Student Scholarship–Regional, 341
International student support scholarship, 355
International Studies Research Lab, 632
International Training Fellowships, 1607
International Welcome Scholarships (IWS), 832
Internships and Industry Fund for Computer Science, 448
Interpretive Fellowships at Art Museums, 1085
Invertimos en el Talento de los Colombianos (ICETEX) Artistas Jovenes Scholarships, 183
Investigation of the Human Intestinal Nervous System, 526
Ioan and Rosemary James / Mathematical Institute Scholarship, 1465
IOE Centenary Doctoral Scholarships, 1204
Iota Sigma Pi National Honorary Member Award, 669
Ipatieff Prize, 60
Ireland: Kader Asmal Fellowship Programme, 597
Irene and Arthur Kinsman Award for Postgraduate Studies, 1396
Irish Research Council Scholarships-Ulysses, 872
Irving and Yvonne Twining Humber Award for Lifetime Artistic Achievement, 135
Irving Langmuir Award in Chemical Physics, 60
Isie Smuts Research Award, 1136
Islamic Cooperation Organization International Internship Program, 671
Isobella Foundation Scholarship, 513
The ISST Scholarship, 616
Italian Australian Foundation Travel Scholarships, 1396
I Tatti Fellowship, 1600
I Tatti/Museo Nacional del Prado Joint Fellowship, 1597
IT Kharagpur Post Doctoral Fellowship, 623
IT Support Fund, 557
IT University of Copenhagen State Scholarships, 672
IUBMB Mid-Career Research Fellowships, 666
IUBMB Tang Education Fellowships, 666
IUBMB Travel Fellowships, 667
Ivan Morris Memorial Prize, 239
Izaak Walton Killam Memorial Scholarship, 1222
Izaak Walton Killam Predoctoral Fellowships, 1238

J

J. Hoover Mackin Award, 563
Jack Keating Fund Scholarship, 1397
The Jack Loader Top-Up Scholarship, 533
The Jackson Family Foundation Scholarship, 1231
Jacob Hirsch Fellowship, 102
Jacqueline Lemieux Prize, 271
Jacqui Thorburn and Family Bursary for Indigenous Archaeology and Cultural Heritage Management, 527
James A. Rawley Prize, 931
James Bryant Conant Award in High School Chemistry Teaching, 61
The James Callaghan Scholarships, 1160
James Clayton Lectures, 648
James Cook University Postgraduate Research Scholarship, 676
James Elson Studentship, 1379
James Fairfax-Oxford-Australia Fund Scholarships, 1465
James H. Billington Fellowship, 694
James H. Graham Award of Merit, 1033
James Kreppner Award, 278
The James Madison Memorial Fellowship, 782
James Mellon DPhil Scholarship in Longevity Research, 939
James Park Scholarship in Geology, 1446
James Russell Lowell Prize, 819
James Samuel Gutshall Scholarship (Viola Vestal Coulter Foundation), 212
James Stewart Bequest (Geology), 514
James W. Tyra Memorial Scholarship, 908
Janaki Ammal-National Women Bioscientist Award, 428
Jane's Travel and Research Grant Prizes and Awards, 230
Janet Watson Scholarship, 613
Jan-Georg Deutsch Scholarship in African Studies, 1140
Japan: MEXT Scholarships, 597
Japanese Residencies for United States of America Historians, 931
Japanese Studies Event Top-Up Funding, 239
The Japan Residencies Program, 937
Japan Society for the Promotion of Science (JSPS) Fellowship, 1121
Japan Society for the Promotion of Science Postdoctoral Fellowships, 882
Japan Society for the Promotion of Science Postdoctoral Fellowships for North American and European Researchers (Short-term), 680
Javits-Frasier Scholars Program, 847
Jawaharlal Nehru Memorial Trust Commonwealth Shared Scholarships, 1263
Jayce and Seamus Fagan Enabling Program Scholarship, 1435
J.B.C. Watkins Award: Architecture, 271
JCB J. M. Stuart Brown Graduate Fellowship, 682
J C Bose National Fellowship, 1098
JDRF PhD Top-up Scholarships 2024, 690
Jean A. Chalmers Fund for the Crafts, 272
Jean E Laby PhD Travelling Scholarships, 1397
Jean Kennoway Howells Scholarship, 466
Jeanne and Charles Rider Graduate Fellowship, 1115
Jefferson Science Fellowship, 839
The Jennifer Robinson Memorial Scholarship, 131
Jennings Randolph Program for International Peace Dissertation Fellowship, 1191
Jennings Randolph Program for International Peace Senior Fellowships, 1192
JEP MSc Progression Scholarship, 1289
Jeremiah Lecture Series Support, 1441
Jeroen Ensink Memorial Fund Scholarship, 747
Jesse M. Unruh Assembly Fellowship Program, 1083
Jesus College: Joint Law Faculty-Jesus College BCL Scholarship, 1465
Jewell L. Taylor National Graduate Fellowship, 45
J Holden Family Foundation Honours Award in Maths and Physics, 1420
Jim Bourque Scholarship, 130
The Joan, Arthur & Helen Thacker Aboriginal and/or Torres Strait Islander Postgraduate Scholarship, 1449
Joan Berry Fellowships in Veterinary Science-Postgraduate, 642
Joan Burns Memorial Scholarship in History, 1276
Joan Dingley Memorial Scholarship in Mycology, 642
Joan Doll Scholarship, 1465
Joan Frey Boytim Awards for Independent Teachers, 848
Joan Yvonne Lowndes Award, 272
John A. S. Grenville PhD Studentship in Modern Jewish History and Culture, 720
The John and Bryony Coles Bursary (Student Travel Award), 962
John and Janice King Bursary, 676
John and Pat Hume Doctoral Scholarships, 874

John and Pat Hume Research Scholarships, 874
John and Polly Sparks Early Career Grant for Psychologists Investigating Serious Emotional Disturbance (SED), 96
John Bayliss Award, 265
The John Bright Fellowship, 1388
John Cassim Scholarship, 355
John Charles Polanyi Prizes, 1077
John Crump Studentship, 239
John Dana Archbold Fellowship, 834
John Dana Archbold Fellowship Program, 911
John D'Emilio LGBTQ History Dissertation Award, 932
John Eales Rugby Excellence Scholarship, 225
John E Fogarty Foreign Funded Fellowship Programs, 684
John G. Diefenbaker Award, 272
John Grey Hall of Residence Scholarship, 677
John H. Borden Scholarship, 490
John Henry Garner Scholarship, 1337
John Higham Research Fellowship, 932
John Hirsch Prizes, 272
John Hobday Awards in Arts Management, 273
John Hodgson Pastoral Science Scholarship, 642
John Lawson Prize, 1022
John Lennon Memorial Scholarship, 1355
John L Paterson Postgraduate Design Scholarship, 1299
John MacIntyre Honours Year Scholarship in Marine Science, 1420
The John Morrison Memorial Fund for Hellenic Maritime Studies, 258
The John Mulvaney Fellowship, 163
John R. Coleman Traveling Fellowship, 129
John R. Lamarsh Scholarship, 88
John R. Mott Scholarship, 686
John Speak Trust Scholarships, 229
John W. Davies Scholarship, 1133
Joint-award between The University of Manchester and IISC Bangalore, 1379
Joint Institute for Laboratory Astrophysics Postdoctoral Research Associateship and Visiting Fellowships, 687
Joint Japan World Bank Graduate Scholarship Program, 693
Joint Postgraduate Scholarship Program, 1218
Jonathan Hughes Prize, 460
Josef Breitenbach Research Fellowship, 338
Joseph Hume Scholarship, 1205
Josephine Lansdell Research Grant, 255
Joseph Kremen Memorial Fellowship, 1640
Joseph S. Stauffer Prizes, 276
Josiah Charles Trent Memorial Foundation Endowment Fund, 443
Joyce and George Vaughan Bequest Scholarship, 677
The Joyce W. Vickery Research Fund, 738
Joy Ingall Scholarship for Music Studies, 1435
Jozef Tischner Fellowships, 697
JP Morgan Chase Regrant Program for Small Ensembles, 808
JSMF Opportunity Awards, 679
The Judith Clark Memorial Fellowships, 1280
Judith Robinson-Valery Honours Award in Modern Languages, 1421
Jules Léger Prize for New Chamber Music, 276
The Julia Child Endowment Fund Scholarship, 400
Julie Alley Bursary, 642
Junior Scholar Grants, 359
Justin G. Schiller Prize, 204
Justus & Louise van Effen Excellence Scholarships, 1187
JuventudEsGto, 1355

K

Kalakriti Fellowship in Indian Classical Dance, 1087
Kalisher Trust-Wadham Student Scholarship, 1466
Kate Edger Educational Charitable Trust-Expenses / Class Materials Awards, 156
The Kate Edger Educational Charitable Trust Masters Degree Award, 1232
The Kate Edger Educational Charitable Trust Vinka Marinovich Award in Music, 1232
The Katharine McCormick Advanced Postdoctoral Scholar Fellowship to Support Women in Academic Medicine, 1150
Katherine Singer Kovacs Prize, 819
KC Wong Postdoctoral Fellowships, 361
K C Wong Postgraduate Scholarship Programme, 361
Keble College: James Martin Graduate Scholarship, 1467
Keble College Gosden Water-Newton Scholarship, 1466
Keble College Gwynne-Jones Scholarship, 1466
Keble College Ian Palmer Graduate Scholarship in Information Technology, 1467
Keble College Ian Tucker Memorial Bursary, 1467
Keble College Water Newton Scholarship, 1467
Keeler Scholarship, 1028
Keeling Scholarship, 1205
Keith Hawkins Graduate Research Scholarship in English or American Legal History, 939
Keith Kevan Scholarship, 490
Kellogg College: Bigg Scholarship in African Climate Science, 1467
Kellogg College: Oxford-McCall MacBain Graduate Scholarship, 1468
Kemmy Business School: PhD Scholarship, 1344
Kennedy Scholarships, 694
The Kenneth E. Grant Scholarship, 1135
Kenneth Harwood Outstanding Dissertation Award, 265
Kenneth J. Botto Research Fellowship, 338
Kent-Lille Cotutelle: Advancing Communication between Children and Paediatricians: a Cross-linguistic Contribution, 1328
Kent Lille Cotutelle: LATP Glass-ceramic Electrolytes to Advance Battery Technology for a Low Carbon Future, 1328
Kent-Lille Cotutelle: Novel Neuromorphic, Radically Energy Efficient Training Algorithms for Action Recognition, 1329
Kent Research Institute PhD Scholarships for Institute of Cyber Security for Society (iCSS), 1328
Khazanah–INCEIF Scholarship, 651
The Kia Ora Foundation Patricia Pratt Music Scholarship, 1280
Kia Ora Foundation Patricia Pratt Scholarship, 1199, 1276
The Kick It Out Scholarship, 1359
Killam Doctoral Scholarships, 1238
Killam Research Fellowships, 273
Kings College: Stipendiary Junior Research Fellowships, 1252
Kiran Mazumdar-Shaw Scholarship, 514
The Kirby Laing International Scholarships, 1303
Kitchener Memorial Scholarship, 1269
Kiwi Music Scholarship, 1200, 1276
Knight-Bagehot Fellowships in Economics and Business Journalism at Columbia University, 372
The Knossos Research Fund, 258
Knowledge Asset Grant Fund: Expand 2023, 878
Knowledge-building Project for Industry, 990
Knowledge Transfer Partnership, 218
Kolkata Eden Hospital Annual Prize, 1023
Konrad-Adenauer-Stiftung, 190
Korea Foundation Fellowship, 1107
Korea-Japan Cultural Association Scholarship, 1108
Korea New Zealand Agricultural Cooperation Scholarships (KNZACS), 473
Koshland Young Leader Awards, 1086
Kress Conservation Fellowships, 1085
Kress Publications Fellowships, 102
Kristin Sivertz Resident Leadership Award, 1033
KSP Fund for Innovative Projects, 1107

KSP Joint Research Projects, 1107
2023-24 Kuberbhai Shivabhai Desai Trust Scholarship, 745
Kuiper-Overpelt Study Fund, 715
Kupe Leadership Scholarships, 1233
Kurt Weill Prize, 698
Kuwait Excellence Scholarship for Arab Students and Kuwait Nationals, 1107
Kuwait Program at Sciences Po Excellence Scholarship for Arab Students and Kuwait Nationals, 947
Kyle Scholarship, 971

L
Lab on Bag: Bioengineering a Device for Blood Diagnostics, 772
L' Academie de Cuisine Culinary Arts Scholarship, 399
Lady Margaret Hall: Ann Kennedy Graduate Scholarship in Law, 1468
Lady Meherbai D. TATA Education Trust, 1167
Lancaster Enabling Access Fund, 557, 709
Lancaster Master's Scholarship, 709
Lancaster Opportunity and Access Fund (LOAF) (for UK, EU & International), 710
Landis Public Communication and Education Award, 88
Landis Young Member Engineering Achievement Award, 89
Language Assistantships in France and New Caledonia, 481
Languages, 1246
Laryngology & Rhinology Section: Rhinology Essay Prize, 1063
Laryngology & Rhinology Section: Short Paper and Poster Prize, 1063
Laryngology & Rhinology Travel and Equipment Grants, 1063
Late Stephen Robjohns Science Scholarship, 1421
Latin America–Creative and Culture Scholarships, 184
Latin America ELBP Scholarship, 1435
Latin American Centre-Latin American Centre Scholarship, 1468
Latin America Scholarship, 466, 1307
La Trobe Excellence Scholarships, 700
La Trobe Greater China Scholarship, 700
La Trobe International Scholarship, 701
La Trobe Jordan Scholarship, 701
La Trobe Latin America Scholarship, 701
La Trobe South Asia Scholarship, 702
La Trobe South East Asia Scholarship, 702
La Trobe Turkey Scholarship, 702
La Trobe University Offshore Online Bursary, 703
La Trobe University OSHC Grant, 703
Law Faculty: David and Helen Elvin Scholarship, 1468
Law Faculty: Des Voeux Chambers, 1469
Law Faculty: James Bullock Scholarship, 1469
Law Faculty: The Peter Birks Memorial Scholarship, 1469
Law/Faculty Graduate Scholarship (FGS), 876
Law Faculty Scholarships, 1140
Lawrence Ho Scholarship, 466
Lawrence W. Levine Award, 932
Lawren H. Daltroy Health Professional Preceptorship, 1000
Lawson Robinson Hawke's Bay A&P Scholarship, 319
L B Wood Travelling Scholarship, 319, 1277
LCRF Research Grant on Disparities in Lung Cancer, 759
League of United Latin American Citizens National Educational Service Centers National Scholarship Fund, 761
Learned Society Curation Awards, 1607
Learning & Leadership Grants, 852
Leathersellers' Company Scholarship (Sciences), 1147
Lecture Series Grants, 359
The Lee Family Scholarships, 617
Lee Kuan Yew School of Public Policy Graduate Scholarships (LKYSPPS), 876
The Lees Scholarship, 1388
Leicester Castle Business School Full Postgraduate Scholarship, 417
Leicester Castle Business School MBA Scholarship, 418
Leiden University Fund-Lutfia Rabbani Scholarship Fund, 715
Leiden University South Africa Scholarship-University of Cape Town, 716
Leiden University South Africa Scholarship-University of Pretoria, 716
Leiden University South Africa Scholarship-University of the Western Cape, 717
Leigh Douglas Memorial Prize, 262
Leonard Condell Farming PhD Scholarship, 643
Leonard Condell Farming Postgraduate Scholarship, 643, 793
The Leonard Freestone Scholarship, 1031
Lerner-Scott Prize, 933
Lesbian, Gay, Bisexual and Transgender+Allies Scholarship, 418
Lesley Shorne Memorial Scholarship, 527
Leslie H. Paddle Scholarship, 648
Leukaemia Foundation PhD Scholarships, 722
Leukaemia Foundation Postdoctoral Fellowship, 722
Leukemia Research Foundation New Investigator Research Grant, 724
Leverhulme Doctoral Scholarships, 725
Leverhulme-funded Studentship in Psychology, 1329
Leverhulme International Professorships, 726
Leverhulme (LINCS) PhD Scholarship, 972
Leverhulme Trade Charities Trust, 557, 710
Leverhulme Trade Charities Trust Postgraduate Bursaries, 755
Liaoning Medical University Postdoctoral Fellowship for International Students at MCMP, 758
Liberty Legacy Foundation Award, 933
Library Associates Fellowship, 683
Library Company of Philadelphia Dissertation Fellowships, 728
Library Company of Philadelphia Postdoctoral Research Fellowship, 729
Library of American Broadcasting Foundation Award, 265
The Lien Foundation Scholarship for Social Service Leaders, 837
2023-24 Lieutenant Colonel Henry Kirkpatrick Scholarship, 745
Life Sciences Research Foundation, 730
Life Sciences Research Foundation Postdoctoral Fellowships, 730
Lighthouse Vision Trust Scholarship, 1269
Lilly Fellows Program in the Humanities and the Arts, 1006
Limited Project Grant (LPG), 115
Linacre Anthropology Scholarship, 734
Linacre College: Applied Materials MSc Scholarship, 1469
Linacre College: David Daube Scholarship, 1470
Linacre College: EPA Cephalosporin Scholarship, 1470
Linacre College: Hicks Scholarship, 1470
Linacre College: Hitachi Chemical Europe Scholarship, 1470
Linacre College: John Bamborough MSc Scholarship, 1470
Linacre College: Linacre Rausing Scholarship (English), 1471
Linacre College: Mary Blaschko Graduate Scholarship, 1471
Linacre College: Rausing Scholarship in Anthropology, 1471
Linacre College: Rausing Scholarship in English, 1471
Linacre College: Raymond and Vera Asquith Scholarship, 1472
Linacre College: Ronald and Jane Olson Scholarship, 1472
Linacre College: Women in Science Scholarship, 1472
The Lincoln 50% Global Scholarship, 1350
Lincoln Alumni Master of Architecture Scholarship, 1348
Lincoln Alumni MSc School of Health and Social Care Scholarship, 1349
Lincoln Alumni MSc Social Work Scholarship, 1349
Lincoln College: Berrow Foundation Lord Florey Scholarships, 1472
Lincoln College: Berrow Foundation Scholarships, 1472
Lincoln College: Crewe Graduate Scholarships, 1473
Lincoln College: Hartley Bursary, 1473
Lincoln College: Jermyn Brooks Graduate Award, 1473
Lincoln College: Lord Crewe Graduate Scholarships in the Humanities, 1474

Lincoln College: Lord Crewe Graduate Scholarships in the Social Sciences, 1474
Lincoln College: Overseas Graduate Entrance Scholarship, 1474
Lincoln College: Sloane Robinson Foundation Graduate Awards, 1474
Lincoln College: Supperstone Law Scholarship, 1474
Lindemann Trust Fellowship, 487
The Lindert-Williamson Biennial Prize, 461
Lindt Dissertation Fellowship, 370
Lingenfelter Doctoral Fellowship, 212
Linked Standard Research Grant, 68
Lionel Murphy Endowment Postgraduate Scholarship, 737
Lisa Pan Marketing and Technology Scholarship, 1329
Liver Group PhD Studentship, 1205
Liverpool International College (LIC) Excellence Award, 1356
Liverpool Law School Hong Kong Scholarships, 1356
Liverpool Law School LLM Bursaries, 1356
LLM: E-Fellows Scholarship Programme, 1294
LLM in European Law Scholarship, 1300
LLM in International Trade Law–Contracts and Dispute Resolution–Scholarships, 1213
Lloyd J. Old STAR Program, 310
LMS Early Career Fellowships 2021-22 with support from the Heilbronn Institute for Mathematical Research (HIMR) and UKRI, 740
Lockheed Martin Corporation Scholarship for Freshmen, 739
Lois Turnbull Postgraduate Scholarship, 643
London Goodenough Association of Canada Scholarship Program, 739
London Metropolitan University Refugee Scholarship, 741
London Scholarships, 755
Lone Parents Child Care Grant, 710
Long-Term Fellowship, 499
Long-Term Fellowships, 659, 892
Lonsdale College Travel Grant, 710
The Lorch Foundation MSc Student Bursary, 395
L'Oréal Canada For Women in Science Research Excellence Fellowships, 1197
Loren L Zachary National Vocal Competition for Young Opera Singers, 748
Lorna Casselton Memorial Scholarships in Plant Sciences, 1140
The Lorraine Allison Memorial Scholarship, 131
Los Alamos Graduate Research Assistant Program, 749
Lost Cities Funding Programme, 1172
Loughborough Sports Scholarships, 755
The Louis Cha Scholarship, 1141
Louis Pelzer Memorial Award, 933
Lovell and Berys Clark Scholarships, 643
Loyola Marymount University MBA Programme, 758
2023-24 LSHTM Fund Scholarship, 746
2023-24 LSHTM Next Generation Scholars, 746
The Lt. Col Jack Wishart Scholarship, 1303
Luce Fellowships, 199, 1130
Lucy Cavendish College: Becker Law Scholarships, 1252
Lucy Cavendish College: Dorothy and Joseph Needham Studentship, 1252
Lucy Cavendish College: Enterprise Studentship, 1252
Lucy Cavendish College: Evelyn Povey Studentship, 1252
Lucy Cavendish College: Lord Frederick Cavendish Studentship, 1253
Lucy Cavendish College: Mastermann-Braithwaite Studentship, 1253
Lucy Cavendish College: Research Fellowships, 1253
Lucy Frank Squire Distinguished Resident Award in Diagnostic Radiology, 43
LUF International Study Fund (LISF), 717
LUF-SVM Fund, 717
Luke Pen Fund-Honours Scholarships, 471
Lund University Global Scholarship, 760
Lung Health (LH) Research Dissertation Grants, 84
Lustgarten Foundation-AACR Career Development Award for Pancreatic Cancer Research, in Honor of John Robert Lewis, 5
Lustgarten Foundation-AACR Career Development Award for Pancreatic Cancer Research, in honor of Ruth Bader Ginsburg, 6
LUSTRA+ Scholarship, 718

M

Maastricht University Holland Euregion Refugee Scholarship, 764
Maastricht University Holland-High Potential scholarship, 764
Macandrew-Stout Postgraduate Scholarship in Economics, 1446
MacGillavry Fellowships, 1224
The Macmillan-Rodewald Studentship, 258
Macquarie University Alumni Scholarship, 773
Macquarie University AU$5,000 Regional Scholarship, 773
Macquarie University Centre for the Health Economy (MUCHE) Industry Funded Higher Degree Research (HDR) Scholarships, 773
Macquarie University Centre for the Health Economy (MUCHE) Industry Funded Higher Degree Research (HDR) Scholarships-Domestic, 774
Macquarie University Higher Study Scholarship-Full Time Rate, 774
Macquarie University Higher Study Scholarship-Part Time Rate, 775
Macquarie University PhD Scholarship in Knowledge Acquisition and Cognitive Modelling, 775
Macquarie University Postgraduate Loyalty Scheme 10% Sponsorship, 775
Macquarie Vice-Chancellor's International Scholarships, 776
Macrosystems Biology and NEON-Enabled Science (MSB-NES), 868
Madbury Road Design Success Award Scholarship, 132
"Made in NY" Women's Film, TV and Theatre Fund, 888
Madeleine Selwyn-Smith Memorial Scholarships, 1397
Madhobi Chatterji Memorial Fellowship, 1088
Magdalen College: Perkin Research Studentship, 1475
Magdalen College: Student Support Fund Graduate Grants, 1475
Magdalen Hong Kong Scholarship, 1475
Magnusson Awards, 571
Maharaj Kaul Memorial Trust, 633
Main Fund-International Projects, 232
Main Fund-UK Projects, 232
Major Jeremiah P. Murphy Scholarship, 1004
Makabongwe Ndzwayiba Bursary, 1009
Malcolm Black Travel Fellowship, 1023
Malcolm Cole Indigenous Scholarship, 1421
Malcolm H. Wiener Laboratory for Archaeological Science Senior Fellowship, 102
Malcolm H. Wiener Laboratory Postdoctoral Fellowship, 103
Malcom H. Wiener Laboratory for Archaeological Science Research Associate Appointments, 103
Manchester-China Scholarship Council Joint Postgraduate Scholarship Programme, 1380
Manchester Melbourne Dual Award, 1380
Mandela Scholarship Fund, 718
Manfred Wörner Fellowship, 907
Mani Mann Fellowship, 1088
Manju Mehrotra Scholarship, 1041
Mansfield College: Adam von Trott Scholarship, 1475
Mansfield College: Elfan Rees Scholarship, 1475
Marcia Brady Tucker Travel Award, 92
Margaret E. Terrell National Graduate Fellowship, 45
Margaret Fay Fuller Scholarship: Margaret Fay Fuller PhD top up Scholarship, 527
The Margaret Senior Natural History Illustration Scholarship, 1437
Marian D Eve Memorial Scholarship, 1270
Marian D'Eve Memorial Scholarship, 322
Marian Madison Gypsy Lore Society Young Scholar's Prize, 575

Maria Salit-Gitelson Tell Memorial Fellowship, 1640
Marie Clay Literacy Trust Literacy Learning Research Award, 1229
Marie Curie Fellowships for Early Stage Training at CERN, 380
Marie Morisawa Award, 563
Marie Sklodowska-Curie Actions Postdoctoral Fellowships, 1318
Marie Tharp Visiting Fellowships, 372
The Marine Corps Scholarship, 785
Marjorie Kovler Research Fellowship, 685
Marjorie Roy Rothermel Scholarship, 119
Mark Mills Award, 89
Marks and Spencer-Leeds University-FCO Chevening Scholarships, 1337
Marshall Scholarships, 243, 448, 787, 970, 1356
Marshall Sherfield Fellowships, 787
Marshal Papworth Scholarships in Agriculture for Developing Countries, 786
MarTERA Call, 784
Martin Cook Scholarship for Humanities Students, 1330
Martin Harrison Memorial Fellowship, 254
The Mary Isabel Sibley Fellowship, 955
Mary Jane Oestmann Professional Women, 89
Mary Kay Doctoral Dissertation Award, 11
Maryland Association of Certified Public Accountants Scholarship, 787
Mary MacKillop Today First Nations Tertiary Scholarship, 424
Mary McNeill Scholarship in Irish Studies, 972
Mary Nickliss Prize in United States Women's and/or Gender History, 934
Mary Seacole Leadership and Development Awards, 1018
Massey Business School-PhD Scholarships, 643
Massey University Doctoral Scholarship, 643, 793
Massey University Pacific Success Scholarship for Doctoral Students, 644
Master Excellence Fellowships, 457
Master in Business Analytics Scholarships, 449
Master Mind Scholarships, 569, 1189, 1224
Master of Arts in Art Museum and Gallery Studies Scholarship, 895
Master of Arts Scholarship in Applied Language Studies or Professional Language Studies, 156
Master of Arts (Taught Masters) Scholarships in the School of Modern Languages, 895
Master of Business Administration Business Excellence Scholarships, 896
Master of Business Administration Global Ambassador Scholarship, 150
Master of Business Administration Global Leaders Scholarship, 424
Master of Business Administration Programme, 603, 635, 677, 876, 1137, 1277, 1289, 1322
Master of Cultural & Creative Practice Scholarships (Art & Design), 157
Master of Energy Systems Management (MESM) Scholarships, 449
Master of Professional Engineering International Scholarship, 824
Master of Public Health Scholarship, 571
Master of Research Elevate Scholarship-CQUniversity and Surf Lifesaving Queensland, 341
Master of the Rolls Scholarship for Commonwealth Students, 1205
Masters Achievement Scholarships, 449
Master's Awards, 1607
Master Scholarships for International Students, 815
Master's Compare Postgraduate Scholarship, 184
Master's Degree Awards in Archaeology, 1206
Master's Degree Awards in Biochemical Engineering, 1206
Masters (PGT) EU Scholarship, 1307
Masters Excellence Scholarship, 1308
Masters/Honours/PGDIP Scholarships, 1229
Masters International Scholarships, 449
Master's Scholarship, 263
Masters Scholarship in Scotland, 406
Master's Scholarships, 920
Master's Studentships in Humanities and Social Science, 1608
The Material Handling Education Foundation, 794
Materials Scholarships, 755
Maternity & the Newborn Forum: Basil Lee Bursary for Innovation in Communication, 1063
Maternity & the Newborn Forum: Wendy Savage Bursary, 1064
Mathematical Sciences Scholarship, 756
Matsumae International Foundation Research Fellowship Program, 795
Mature Students Hardship Fund, 1155
Mauritius: Mauritius-Africa Scholarship Scheme, 598
Max Brauer Award, 25
Max Day Environmental Science Fellowship Award, 162
Max Planck Institute-CBS Postdoctoral Position in Neuroscience of Pain Perception in Germany, 797
Max Planck Institute-DS Gauss Postdoctoral Fellowships for International Students, 796
Max Planck Institute for the History of Science Postdoctoral Fellowship in Germany, 796
Max-Planck-Society Research Scholarships, 798
Max Schroder Indigenous Scholarship, 1408
Maxwell King PhD Scholarship, 824
May Mills Scholarship for Women, 527
Maynooth University Teaching Studentships, 875
Maypole Fund Grants for Women, 16
MBPhD Studentships, 252
McGill University PhD Studentships in Neurolinguistics, 800
McKelvey Award, 1270
McNair Graduate Fellowships, 1220
Mechanical, Electrical and Manufacturing Engineering Scholarships, 756
Media@McGill Postdoctoral Fellowship, 800
Medical and Graduate Student Preceptonship, 1000
Medical Elective Funding and Annual Essay Competition, 721
Medical Research Council Career Development Award, 803
Medical Research Council Clinical Research Training Fellowships, 803
Medical Research Council Clinician Scientist Fellowship, 804
Medical Research Council Industrial CASE Studentships, 804
Medical Research Council/RCOG Clinical Research Training Fellowship, 805
Medical Research Council Senior Clinical Fellowship, 804
Medical Research Council Senior Non-Clinical Fellowship, 805
Medical Research Council Special Training Fellowships in Health Services and Health of the Public Research, 805
Medical Research Scotland Sponsored Daphne Jackson Trust Fellowships, 807
Medical Sciences Doctoral Training Centre: Wellcome Trust Studentship in Structural Biology, 1476
Medical Student Research Grant, 979
Medical Student Research Initiation Grant, 116
Mediserve Northern Territory Diabetes Management and Education Scholarship, 528
MEDx Colloquia, 443
MEDx Engineering, Environment, and Health 2022 Request for Proposals, 443
Melbourne Mobility Excellence Awards, 1398
Melbourne Welcome Grant, 1398
Mellon Fellowship in Digital Humanities, 1600
Mellon Mays Predoctoral Research Grants, 1122
Melville H. Cohee Student Leader Conservation Scholarship, 1135
Melville Trust for Care and Cure of Cancer Research Fellowships, 808
Melville Trust for Care and Cure of Cancer Research Grants, 808
Member Scholarship in Statistics, 1206
Memorial Fund of 8 May, 911
Meniere's Disease Grant, 75

Mentored Nurse Practitioner/Physician Assistant Award for Workforce Expansion, 1001
Menzies Global Leader Scholarship, 348
Mercer Memorial Scholarship in Aeronautics, 1229
Meredith Doig Scholarship, 514
Merit Grants Scheme, 342
Merit International Postgraduate Scholarship, 471
Merle Curti Award in American Intellectual History, 934
Merle Curti Intellectual History Award, 934
Merle Curti Social History Award, 934
Mershon Center Graduate Student Grants, 918
Merton College: Barton Scholarship, 1476
Merton College: Merton Lawyers, 1476
Merton College Leventis Scholarship, 1476
The Mesothelioma Cancer Alliance Scholarship, 723
Mexican CONACYT-Macquarie University Postgraduate Research Scholarships, 776
Mexico Scholarship, 467
MFL Scholarship applications, 243
Michael and Alice Kuhn Summer Fellowships, 1170
Michael P. Metcalf Memorial Fund and Christine T. Grinavic Adventurer, 1004
Michael Wong Pakshong Bursary, 1237
Microsoft Fellowship, 810
Microsoft Research European PhD Scholarship Programme, 810
Middle East and North Africa Scholarship, 467
Mike M. Masaoka Congressional Fellowship, 681
Miles Franklin Literary Award, 1186
Miles Morland Foundation Writing Scholarship, 813
Military Medicine Colt Foundation Research Prize, 1064
The Millicent C. Mclntosh Fellowship, 1624
Mineral and Rock Physics Graduate Research Award, 71
Minerals Industry Flexible First Year Scholarship (Current Students), 1422
Minerva Fellowship, 813
Minerva Scholarship Fund, 718
Minerva Short-Term Research Grants, 814
Ministry of Education and Science of the Republic of Lithuania Scholarships for Studies and Research Work, 814
Ministry of Education and Training Vietnam Research Awards, 1356
Ministry of Education (Malaysia) Scholarships for Postgraduate Study, 1264
Ministry of Fisheries PG Scholarships in Quantitative Fisheries Science, 815
Ministry of Foreign Affairs and International Cooperation Scholarships for Foreign and Italian Students, 816
Ministry of Foreign Affairs (France) International Teaching Fellowships, 482
Ministry of Foreign Affairs (France) Stage de la Réunion (One Month Scholarships), 482
Ministry of Science, Technology and the Environment Scholarships for Postgraduate Study (Malaysia), 1264
Minnesota Historical Society Research Grant, 817
MLA Doctoral Fellowship, 801
Mlori and Pacific Graduate Scholarships (Masters/Honours/PGDIP), 1228
Mlori and Pacific Islands Scholarship, 992
MND Pre-Fellowship Scheme, 826
Modern Language Association Prize for a First Book, 820
Modern Language Association Prize for Independent Scholars, 820
Monash Mt Eliza Business School Executive MBA Programme, 821
Mongolia AU$10,000 Early Acceptance Scholarship, 776
Monica Hulse Scholarship, 1206
Morgan E. Williams MRes Scholarship in Helminthology, 330
Morton Cure Paralysis Fund Research Grant, 826
Motor Neurone Disease Association Non-Clinical Fellowship Awards, 826
Motor Neurone Disease Association PhD Studentship Award, 827
Motor Neurone Disease Association Research Project Grants, 827
Mott MacDonald Charitable Trust Scholarships, 828
Moynihan Travelling Fellowship, 148
MPhil Scholarship–Reconnecting to Rivers: Urban Water & Water Sensitive Urban Design, 406
MPhil Scholarships in the Humanities and Social Sciences, 1140
MQ Fellows Awards 2023, 828
Mr and Mrs Kenny Lam's Graduate Scholarship (Law), 1147
MRes Scholarships, 1158
MS Catalyzing Advocacy in Science and Engineering (CASE) Workshop, 86
MSc Fellowships and PhD Fellowships, 582
MSc International Fashion Marketing Scholarship, 571
MS Clinical Mentorship for Medical Students, 864
MSc Psychology with a Specialisation in Business Scholarship, 1156
MSc Scholarship for Women, 613
MSc Scholarships in Sustainability, Enterprise and the Environment, 1141
MSc Sustainable Urban Development Programme Scholarship, 1477
MS Engineering and Science Fellowship Program, 1176
Multi-Country Research Fellowship, 387
Multidisciplinary Project Award, 315
Multiple Sclerosis Society of Canada Donald Paty Career Development Award, 829
Multiple Sclerosis Society of Canada Postdoctoral Fellowship Award, 829
Multiple Sclerosis Society of Canada Scholarship Programs: John Helou Scholarship, 1197
Multi Scale Biomechanical Investigations of the Intervertebral Disc, 528
Murray and Terry Scholarship, 644
Musical Instrument Bank, 273
Music Performance Scholarship, 1330
Music Scholarships, 592
Music Scholarships-Choral Scholarship, 601, 1042
Music Scholarships-Orchestral Scholarships, 602
Music Scholarships-Organ Scholarship, 602
Myrtle McMyn Bursary, 1380

N

Nabil Boustany Scholarships, 1253
Naim Mehlab Student Travel Award, 377
Nan Tien Institute Postgraduate Scholarship, 834
Nanyang Technological University HASS International PhD Scholarship (HIPS) for Singaporean Students, 835
Nanyang Technological University MBA Programme, 348
Narotam Sekhsaria Postgraduate Scholarship, 837
Narre Warren South Bendigo Bank Scholarship, 514
Natalie and Mendel Racolin Memorial Fellowship, 1640
National Air and Space Museum, 1119
National Air and Space Museum Aviation/Space Writers Award, 845
National Assessment of Educational Progress (NAEP) Internships, 478
National Association of Teachers of Singing Art Song Competition Award, 848
National Bioscience Awards for Career Development (NBACD), 428
National Board for Certified Counselors Minority Fellowship Program for Mental Health Counselors, 1073
National Breast Cancer Foundation Doctoral Scholarship, 850
National Cancer Institute Immunotherapy Fellowship, 298
National Centre for Promotion of Employment for Disabled People (NCPEDP) Rajiv Gandhi Postgraduate Scholarship Scheme, 621
National Defense Science and Engineering Graduate Fellowship Program, 111

National Disability Insurance Scheme Jobs and Market Fund Round 1, 169
National Early Detection of Ovarian Cancer Research Awards 2020, 817
National Endowment for the Humanities American Research Institute in Turkey-National Endowment for the Humanities Fellowships for Research in Turkey, 97
National Endowment for the Humanities Fellowships, 855
National Endowment for the Humanities (NEH) Fellowships, 104
National Endowment for the Humanities Post-Doctoral Fellowships, 729
National Energy Technology Laboratory Methane Hydrates Fellowship Program (MHFP), 840
National Fellowship and Scholarship for Higher Education of ST Students, 914
National Foundation for Infectious Diseases Postdoctoral Fellowship in Nosocomial Infection Research and Training, 856
National Geographic Conservation Trust Grant, 381
National Health and Medical Research Council: Primary Health Care Postgraduate Research Scholarships, 529
National Health and Medical Research Council Centre of Clinical Eye Research: PhD Scholarships, 528
National Health and Medical Research Council Equipment Grants, 857
National Health and Medical Research Council Medical and Dental Postgraduate Research Scholarships, 528
National Health and Medical Research Council Public Health Postgraduate Scholarships, 529
National Health and Medical Research Council Public Health Travelling Fellowships, 857
National Health Service Bursaries, 1207
National Health Service Education for Scotland Primary Care Ophthalmology Scholarship, 1300
National Honorary Member, 669
National Institute for Health and Care Excellence Scholarships, 858
National Institute of Diabetes and Digestive and Kidney Diseases (NIDDK)/AFUD Intramural Urology Research Training Program, 70
National Institute of General Medical Sciences Research Project Grants (R01), 860
National Institute of Justice's Graduate Research Fellowship Program, 199
National Library of Medicine Fellowship in Applied Informatics, 861
National Library of Medicine Investigator Initiated Project Grant, 862
National Library of Medicine Postdoctoral Informatics Research Fellowships, 862
National Library of Medicine Publication Grant Program, 862
National Post Doctoral Fellowship (N-PDF), 1098
National Research Foundation Fellowships for Postdoctoral Research, 865
National Research Foundation Free-standing Masters and Doctoral Scholarships, 866
National Research Foundation Targeted Research Awards Competitive Industry Programme, 866
National Research Foundation Visiting Fellowships, 866
National Road Safety Authority Individual Postdoctoral Fellowships (F32), 860
National Robotics Initiative 2.0: Ubiquitous Collaborative Robots (NRI-2.0), 910
National Science Foundation Research Traineeship (NRT) Program, 869
National Security College Entry Scholarship for Aboriginal and Torres Strait Islander Students, 174
National Sun Yat-sen University International Fellowship, 870
National Tour Association (NTA) Luray Caverns Graduate Research Scholarship, 871
National Union of Teachers Page Scholarship, 853
National University of Singapore Design Technology Institute Scholarship, 876
Native American Library Services: Enhancement Grants, 646
Native Hawaiian Library Services, 646
NATS Artist Awards, 849
Natural Environment Research Council Independent Research Fellowships (IRF), 878
Natural Environment Research Council Research Grants, 878
Natural Sciences and Engineering Research Council of Canada Industrial Post-Graduate Scholarships (IPS), 1112
Natural Sciences and Engineering Research Council of Canada-Postdoctoral Fellowship Program, 1112
Naval Research Laboratory Post Doctoral Fellowship Program, 111
Naval Sea Systems Command (NAVSEA) and Strategic Systems Programs Scholarship, 76
Nederlandse Taalunie Scholarship, 1207
NEH-Mellon Fellowships for Digital Publication, 855
Nehru Trust for the Indian Collections V&A Cambridge DFID Scholarship, 1265
Neilsen SCIRTS Postdoctoral Fellowship Grants, 391
Nelson Algren Awards, 360
Nephrology Section Rosemarie Baillod Clinical Award, 1064
Netherlands Fellowship Programmes, 452
Netherlands Organization for International Cooperation in Higher Education-Natural Family Planning Fellowships for PhD Studies, 915
Nettleship Medal, 1028
Net Zero Policy Programme, 234
Neurosurgery Research and Education Foundation Research Fellowship, 47
Neville and Di Bertalli Bush Placement Scholarship, 424
Newcastle University-English Language Excellence Scholarships (Business School Masters), 896
Newcastle University International Postgraduate Scholarship (NUIPS), 898
Newcastle University Overseas Research Scholarship (NUORS), 898
Newcastle University Scholarship–Thailand-GREAT, 898
Newcastle University-United States of America Athlete Scholarship, 897
Newcastle University-Vice-Chancellor's Excellence Scholarships-Postgraduate, 897
Newcastle Vice-Chancellor's Global Scholarships-Postgraduate, 899
New Colombo Plan Grant, 1398
New Connections: Increasing Diversity, 29
New Horizon Grants, 252
New South Wales Indigenous History Fellowship, 141
New South Wales Premier's History Awards, 141
Newton Advanced Fellowships, 13
Newton International Fellowships, 13, 234, 1051
Newton Mobility Grants, 235
New Work Projects Grants, 579
New York State Council on the Arts/New York Foundation for the Arts Artist Fellowship, 888
New Zealand: Scholarships for International Tertiary Students and Commonwealth Scholarship, 598
New Zealand Agency for International Development Scholarship (NZDS)–Open Category, 1229
New Zealand International Doctoral Research (NZIDRS) Scholarship, 1230
New Zealand Law Foundation Ethel Benjamin Scholarship (For Women), 1200
New Zealand Law Foundation Ethel Benjamin Scholarship (for Women), 1277
New Zealand Pacific Scholarships, 891
The Next Generation: Leadership in Asian Affairs Fellowship, 851
Next Gen Fellowship Program for Sub-Saharan African Countries, 333
NFR FRN Grants for Scientific Equipment, 1162
NFR Travel Grants, 1162
Ngarimu VC and 28th (Mlori) Battalion Memorial Scholarships, 474
Nicholas Hans Comparative Education Scholarship, 636

Nicholas Iain Paumgarten Scholarship for Postgraduate Studies in Accounting, 1009
The Nita Curtis Scholarship, 533
NKA Ellen Gleditsch Scholarship, 249
NLM Research Grants in Biomedical Informatics and Data Science, 863
Non-Clinical PhD Studentships, 252
Noni Wright Scholarship, 1447
Noord-Limburg Region Scholarship-FHML and SBE, 764
Norman, Disney & Young Indigenous Scholarship, 1422
Norman Fiering Fund, 683
Norman & Ivy Lloyd Scholarship/Commonwealth Shared Scholarship, 734
Norman Y. Mineta Fellowship, 681
North American Electric Reliability Corporation (NERC) Studentships in Earth Sciences, 1477
North American Postgraduate Scholarship, 467
North Central Association for Counselor Education and Supervision Research Grant Awards, 907
Northeast Florida Phi Beta Kappa Alumni Association Scholarship, 909
Northern Territory Territory Medical Program Aboriginal and Torres Strait Islander Bursary, 529
North West Cancer Research Fund Research Project Grants, 908
The Norway-America Association Awards, 913
The Norway-America Association Graduate & Research Stipend, 913
Norwegian Emigration Fund, 912
Norwegian Marshall Fund, 912
Norwegian Thanksgiving Fund Scholarship, 912
Nosce Scholarship, 734
Nottingham Developing Solutions Scholarships, 1440
Novel, Low-emission Food Production Systems: Feasibility Studies, 218
Novel, Low-emission Food Production Systems: Industrial Research, 218
Novel and Emerging Technologies (NET) Grants, 587
Novel Concept Awards, 850
Novice Research Awards, 564
NRC Research Associate Programs (RAP), 840
NRC Research Associateship Programs (RAP), 840
NREF Clinical Fellowship Grant, 884
NREF Research Fellowship Grant, 885
NREF Young Clinician Investigator Award, 885
NSERC Indigenous Student Ambassadors, 882
NSERC Postgraduate Scholarships-Doctoral Program, 882
Nuclear Energy-GREEN CDT, 1381
Nuffield College Funded Studentships, 1477
Nuffield College Gwilym Gibbon Research Fellowships, 1478
Nuffield Department of Clinical Medicine: LICR Studentship (Ludwig Institute for Cancer Research), 1478
Nuffield Department of Orthopaedics, Rheumatology and Musculoskeletal Sciences: Kennedy Trust Prize Studentships, 1478
Nuffield Department of Population Health: NDPH Scholarship, 1479
Nuffield Department of Primary Care Health Science: NIHR School for Primary Care Research DPhil Studentship, 1479
Nursing Scholarships, 1005
NUS Research Scholarship, 877
NWCR & Tenovus PhD Studentship Award, 909
NZ-GRADS New Zealand Global Research Alliance Doctoral Scholarship, 473

O

Obstetrics & Gynaecology Section: Dame Josephine Barnes Award, 1064
Obstetrics & Gynaecology Section: Herbert Reiss Trainees' Prize, 1064
Occupational Medicine Section Malcolm Harrington Prize, 1065
Ocean Studies, 1274
OFAH/Fleming College Fish & Wildlife Scholarship, 924
Office of Naval Research Summer Faculty Research Program, 112
Ogilvie Thompson Scholarship, 1626
Ohio Arts Council Individual Excellence Awards, 918
Olga Kennard Research Fellowship Scheme, 1052
Olin School of Business Washington University MBA Programme, 1606
Oliver Correy Award, 1422
Olivia James Traveling Fellowship, 129
Omohundro Institute-NEH Postdoctoral Fellowship, 919
Oncology Doctoral Scholarships, 920
Oncology Nursing Society Breast Cancer Research Grant, 921
Oncology Nursing Society Foundation Research Grant Awards, 921
Oncology Research Grant, 921
Oncology Section Sylvia Lawler Prize, 1065
Online Student Representative Committee Post-Graduate Scholarship, 355
Onshore Excellence Scholarship, 1435
Ontario Bicentennial Award, 238
Ontario Federation of Anglers & Hunters/Oakville and District Rod & Gun Club Conservation Research Grant, 924
Ontario Graduate Scholarship (OGS) Program, 922, 923, 925
Ontario Legislature Internship Programme, 294
Ontario Ministry of Education and Training Graduate Scholarship Programme, 925
The Ontario Trillium Scholarships (OTS), 1441
Ontario Women's Health Scholars Award, 923
Ooni Adeyeye Enitan Ogunwusi Scholarships, 1479
Oorala Kick Start Scholarship, 1408
Oorala Wellbeing Scholarship, 1408
Open Scholarship for Summer Sessions, 104
Open Scholarship for the Summer Session and Summer Seminars, 104
Open Society Institute's Global Supplementary Grant Program (Grant SGP), 926
Operations and Power Division Scholarship Award, 89
Ophthalmology Section Travelling Fellowships, 1065
The Optical Society, Amplify Scholarship, 841
The Optical Society, Chang Pivoting Fellowship, 841
The Optical Society, Corning Women in Optical Communications Scholarship, 841
The Optical Society, Deutsch Fellowship, 842
The Optical Society, Foundation Fellowships, 842
The Optical Society, Optica Women Scholars, 842
Oral & Maxillofacial Surgery Section: Short Paper Prize, 1065
Oral & Maxillofacial Surgery Section: UMAX Poster Prize for students, 1066
Oral & Maxillofacial Surgery Section: UMAX Poster Prize for trainers, 1066
Orange Tulip Scholarship, 765, 975, 1605
Organization of American States (OAS) Fellowships Programs, 283
Oriel and Institute for New Economic Thinking (INET) Graduate Scholarship, 939
Oriel College: Oriel Graduate Scholarships, 1479
Oriel College: Paul Ries Collin Graduate Scholarship, 1480
Oriel College: Sir Walter Raleigh Scholarship, 1480
Oriel DPhil Scholarship in Engineering Science, 939
The Oriel Graduate Scholarship for Sub-Saharan African Scholars, 940
Oriel Graduate Scholarship in Science and Religion, 939
Oriel Graduate Student Scholarships for Academic Merit, 940
Oriental Studies: Sasakawa Fund, 1480
Orthopaedics Section: President's Prize, 1067
Orthopaedics Section FOSC (Future Orthopaedic Surgeons Conference) Prize for Research for Students, 1066
Orthopaedics Section FOSC (Future Orthopaedic Surgeons Conference) Prize for Research for Trainers, 1066
Orthopaedics Section President's Prize Papers, 1066

Osborn Research Studentship, 1254
Ossian R. MacKenzie Teaching Award, 1115
Otago International Pathway Scholarship, 1447
Other Studentships in Earth Sciences, 1480
Otology Section: Matthew Yung Short Paper and Poster Prize, 1067
Otology Section: Training Scholarships, 1067
Otology Section Norman Gamble Grant, 1067
Outreach Grant, 245, 286
Outstanding Paper Prize, 633
Ove Arup Foundation Award, 125
Overseas Fund, 1023
Overseas Koreans Scholarship, 1108
Overseas Scholarship, 1147
OWSD PhD Fellowships for Women Scientists, 1179
Oxford-Aidan Jenkins Graduate Scholarship, 1480
Oxford and Cambridge Society of Bombay Cambridge DFID Scholarship, 1265
Oxford-Anderson Graduate Scholarship in History, 1481
Oxford-Anderson Humanities Graduate Scholarship, 1481
Oxford-Angus McLeod Graduate Scholarship, 1481
Oxford-Ashton Graduate Scholarship in Engineering, 1481
Oxford-Bellhouse Graduate Scholarship, 1482
Oxford-Berman Graduate Scholarship, 1482
Oxford-Bob Thomas Graduate Scholarship in Chemistry, 1482
Oxford-Bounden Graduate Scholarship, 1483
Oxford Brookes University MBA Programme, 943
Oxford-Brunsfield Association of Southeast Asian Nations (ASEAN) Human Rights Graduate Scholarships, 1483
Oxford-Calleva Scholarship, 1483
Oxford-Carolyn and Franco Gianturco Graduate Scholarship, 1484
Oxford-Cecil Lubbock Memorial Graduate Scholarship, 1484
Oxford Centre for Islamic Studies (OCIS) Graduate Scholarships, 1484
Oxford-Chellgren Graduate Scholarships, 1485
Oxford-Chelly Halsey Graduate Scholarship, 1485
Oxford-Clayton Graduate Scholarship, 1485
Oxford Colleges Hospitality Scheme for East European Scholars, 926
Oxford Commonwealth Trapnell Scholarship, 734
Oxford-Creat Group Graduate Scholarships, 1485
Oxford-C S Wu Graduate Scholarship, 1483
Oxford-David Jones Graduate Scholarship, 1486
Oxford-DeepMind Graduate Scholarship (Computer Science), 1486
Oxford-E P Abraham Research Fund Graduate Scholarships, 1486
Oxford-EPA Cephalosporin Graduate Scholarship, 735, 1487
Oxford-Feltham Graduate Scholarship, 1487
Oxford-Finnis Graduate Scholarship in Law, 1487
Oxford-Hackney BCL Graduate Scholarship, 1487
Oxford-Hoffmann Graduate Scholarships, 1488
Oxford-Hoffmann Graduate Scholarships in Medical Sciences, 1488
Oxford-ID Travel Group Foundation Bonham-Carter Graduate Scholarship, 1488
Oxford-Indira Gandhi Graduate Scholarships, 1489
Oxford-Intesa Sanpaolo Graduate Scholarship, 1489
Oxford–Intesa Sanpaolo MBA Graduate Scholarships, 1489
Oxford-Jeffrey Cheah Graduate Scholarship, 1489
Oxford-Kaifeng Graduate Scholarship, 1490
Oxford-Ko Cheuk Hung Graduate Scholarship, 1490
Oxford-Leon E and Iris L Beghian Graduate Scholarships, 1490
Oxford–Linacre African Scholarship, 735
Oxford-Louis Curran Graduate Scholarship, 1491
Oxford-Mary Jane Grefenstette Graduate Scholarship, 1491
OZCO Visual Arts Fellowship, 160

P

Pace Award, 244
Packard Fellowships for Science and Engineering, 413
Paediatrics & Child Health Section: Overseas Bursary, 1067
Paediatrics & Child Health Section: President's Prize for Students, 1068
Paediatrics & Child Health Section: President's Prize for Trainers, 1068
Paediatrics & Child Health Section Trainees Tim David Prize, 1067
Pain Medicine Section: Andrew Lawson Prize, 1068
Pain Medicine Section: Andrew Lawson Prize for Trainers, 1068
Pakistan Scholarship, 468, 1349
Palliative Care Section MSc/MA Research Prize, 1068
The Pamela Sue Anderson Studentship for the Encouragement of the Place of Women in Philosophy, 984
Pandemic Preparedness: Lessons to Learn from COVID-19 across the G7, 235
Paradice Honours Award in Mathematics & Statistics, 1422
Paralyzed Veterans of America Fellowships in Spinal Cord Injury Research, 945
Park and Paulay Scholarship, 1270
The Parker Fellowship, 1437
Parkinson's UK drug accelerator grant, 948
Parkinson's UK non-drug approaches grant, 948
Parkinson's UK project grant, 948
Partner with researchers in Switzerland, 806
Part the Cloud Translational (PTC) Research for Alzheimer's Disease Program, 30
Pathway to Stop Diabetes Diabetes Initiator Award, 64
Pathway to Victoria Scholarship, 703
Patient-Centered Outcomes Challenge Award, 956
Patient Safety Section: Student and Trainees' Prize, 1069
Paton Masser Memorial Fund, 241
Patricia Pratt Scholarships in Musical Performance, 1447
Patrick Trevor-Roper Undergraduate Award, 1029
Paula de Merieux Fellowship Training Award, 1001
The Paul Beeson Career Development Awards in Aging Research for the Island of Ireland, 66
The Paul & Daisy Soros Fellowship for New Americans, 949
Paul J. Alexander Memorial Fellowship, 199
Paul Lowin Prizes-Song Cycle Prize, 949
Paul Mellon Centre Rome Fellowship, 261
Peace and Disarmament Education Trust (PADET), 157
The Peel Trust Studentship, 558, 712
Peggy Bamford Award, 1422
Pembroke College: College Research Studentships, 1254
Pembroke College: Graduate Studentships in Arabic and Islamic Studies (including Persian), 1254
Pembroke College: MPhil Studentship for Applicants from the Least Developed Countries, 1254
Pembroke College: The Bethune-Baker Graduate Studentship in Theology, 1255
Pembroke College: The Bristol-Myers Squibb Graduate Studentship in the Biomedical Sciences, 1255
Pembroke College: The Grosvenor-Shilling Bursary in Land Economy, 1255
Pembroke College: The Lander Studentship in the History of Art, 1256
Pembroke College: The Monica Partridge Studentship, 1256
Pembroke College: The Pembroke Australian Scholarship, 1256
Pembroke College: The Thornton Graduate Studentship in History, 1256
Pembroke College: The Ziegler Graduate Studentship in Law, 1257
Peninsula College of Medicine and Dentistry PhD Studentships, 950
The PEN Translation Fund Grants, 959
Perfect Storms: Leverhulme Doctoral Scholarships, 1300
Performance Analysis Scholarship, 176
Perovskite and Quantum Dot Opto-electronic Devices, 777
Perren Studentship, 1207
Peter Baker Fellowship, 784
Peter Debye Award in Physical Chemistry, 61
Peter Densem Postgraduate Scholarship, 644
Peter Dwyer Scholarships, 274

Peter E. Liberti and Judy D. Olian Scholarship, 1116
Peterhouse: Research Studentships, 1257
Peter Huntingford Memorial Prize, 1024
The Peter Wiles Scholarship, 1031
Petra Och Kail Erik Hedborgs Stiftelse Scholarship, 1154
Petro Jacyk Program, 951
PGR Hardship Fund (for UK, EU & International), 711
Phase II Scholarships, 202
Phase I scholarships, 202
PhD Elevate Scholarship-CQUniversity and CRC for Developing Northern Australia Partnership-Climate Change (External), 342
PhD Elevate Scholarship–CQUniversity and FutureFeed Pty Ltd Partnership (External), 342
PhD Elevate Scholarship-CQUniversity and Surf Lifesaving Queensland, 342
PhD Engineering and Science Fellowship, 1176
PhD Excellence Scholarships for International Students at Walailak University, Thailand, 902
PhD Fees-only Bursaries, 1159
PhD Fellowship, 540
PhD in Conservation: Hunting, Consumption, and Trade of Animals in the Tropics, 1330
PhD in Mechatronics, 1163
PhD in Sustainability Science, 1191
PhD International Scholarships in Quantitative Genetics of Senescence in Seychelles Warblers, Netherlands, 903
13 PhD International Studentships at Northumbria University in UK, 901
PhD International Studentships in Control of Mitosis in Calcium in Mammalian Cells, UK, 903
PhD (via MPhil) International Studentships in Cyber Security in UK, 902
PhD International Studentships in Physical Layer Algorithm Design in 6G Non-Terrestrial Communications, UK, 903
PhD Opportunity-Engineering, 644
PhD Research Scholarships, 330
PhD Scholarship: Digital Modelling of Apple for Quality Prediction, 645
PhD Scholarship: Weed Ecology, 1408
PhD Scholarship as part of an International ARC-Discovery Research Project, 343
PhD Scholarship for Vascular and Metabolic Research, 529
PhD scholarship in Craft, Technology and Entrepreneurship, 383
PhD Scholarship in Material Science and/or Civil Engineering, 530
PhD Scholarship-NHMRC People Support Grants-Postgraduate Scholarships, 424
PhD Scholarship Programs, 176
PhD Scholarships, 297, 1173
PhD scholarships in Economics, 384
PhD Scholarships in Environmental Microbiology, 1423
PhD scholarships in Finance, 384
PhD Scholarship-Transitioning to Caring Economies Through Transformative Community Investment, 644
PhD Science Fellowship, 1176
PhD Social Work Scholarship at University of Edinburgh in United Kingdom, 1300
PhD Student Scholarship in Atmospheric Science, 873
PhD Studentship in Liquid Metal Catalysts for Green Fuels, Australia, 904
PhD Studentship in Organisms and Environment at Cardiff University, 330
PhD Studentship in Predicting Higher-Order Biomarker Interactions Using Machine Learning, 1300
PhD Studentship in the Field of Machine Learning in Medical Imaging, 613
PhD Studentship Opportunities in Environment and Health, 614
PhD Studentships, 519, 587
PhD Studentships in Astrophysics Research Centre, 972
PhD Studentships in Humanitarianism and Conflict Response, 1381
PhD Studentships in Mathematics, 1343
Phi Beta Kappa Graduate Fellowships for Academic Distinction, 199
Philip Chui East Asia Scholarship, 515
Philip Leverhulme Prizes, 726
Philip Parsons Young Playwright's Award, 142
Phillips Fund for Native American Research, 94
Photographic Arts Council-Los Angeles (PAC-LA) Research Fellowship, 338
Phyllis Mary Morris Bursaries, 1237
Physician Scientist Fellowship, 438
Physics Scholarships, 756
Pierre Elliott Trudeau Foundation Doctoral Scholarships, 957
The Pierre Elliott Trudeau Foundation Scholarship, 1081
Pierre Robillard Award, 1152
Pilot Grants, 393
Pilot Innovation Grants, 68
Pilot Research Award for General Psychiatry Residents, 35
Pilot Study Grants, 850
Playford Trust: Playford Trust: PhD Scholarships, 530
Playing Australia: Regional Performing Arts Touring Fund, 160
Pok Rafeah Cambridge Scholarship, 1265
Policy Insight Case Studies, 235
Polish National Alliance of Brooklyn, United States of America, Inc. Scholarship, 697
Polish School of Medicine Memorial Fund Scholarships, 1301
Politics and International Studies Scholarships, 756
Polycystic Kidney Disease Foundation Grant-In-Aid, 960
POP Awards, 590
Population Health Improvement Network of Clusters, 219
Postdoc Fellowship for Research Abroad-Bioscience and Basic Biomedicine, 914
Postdoctoral and Research Scholarships at MPIeR in Germany, 797
Postdoctoral Earth and Planetary Sciences Fellowship, 845
Post-doctoral Fellows and Visiting Scholars, 425
Post-Doctoral Fellowship, 622
Postdoctoral Fellowship Awards, 679
Postdoctoral Fellowship in Health Outcomes Research, 956
Postdoctoral Fellowship in Translational Medicine, 956
Postdoctoral Fellowship Program, 279, 478
Postdoctoral Fellowships, 69, 180, 393, 689, 1116
Postdoctoral Fellowships for Training in Cancer Research, 650
Postdoctoral Fellowships in Conservation Science, 568
Postdoctoral Fellowships in Mathematics at Harish-Chandra Research Institute, 578
Postdoctoral Fellowships in Physics at Harish-Chandra Research Institute, 578
Postdoctoral Research Bursary for Clinical Trainees, 315
Postdoctoral Research Fellowship (PDRF), 622
Postdoctoral Research Fellowships, 409, 588
Postdoctoral Research Fellowships for Physicians, 604
Postdoctoral Research Training, 496
Postdoctoral Scholar Program, 1625
Postdoctoral Scholarship in Solar Fuels at KTH, 698
Post-doctoral Study Grants, 537
Post-Doctoral Training in Genomic Medicine Research, 444
Postgrad Solutions Study Bursaries, 1331
Postgraduate Access Awards (United Kingdom-Fee Only), 711
Postgraduate Ambassador Studentship, 572
Postgraduate Awards, 590
Postgraduate Care Leaver Bursary Terms and Conditions, 267
Postgraduate Conversion Courses in AI and Data Science Scholarships, 1308
Postgraduate Equity Scholarship, 355
Postgraduate Essay Award, 237

Postgraduate History and Archaeology Studentship, 331
Postgraduate International Scholarships, 1629
Postgraduate Master's Loan Scheme (Students from United Kingdom and non-United Kingdom European Union Countries), 899
Postgraduate Masters Scholarships, 649
Postgraduate Masters Scholarships in the School of Geography, Politics and Sociology, 899
Postgraduate Merit Scholarship, 406
Postgraduate Opportunity Bursary, 1357
Postgraduate Opportunity Scholarships, 900
Postgraduate Petroleum Engineering Scholarship, 472
Postgraduate Progression Award, 1630
Postgraduate Progression Award-International Students, 1357
Postgraduate Progression Award-UK Students, 1357
Postgraduate Research Award (PGRA), 171
Postgraduate Research EU Scholarship, 1308
Postgraduate Research Funding-China, 873
Postgraduate Research Teaching Associate (PGRTA) Scholarships, 1381
Postgraduate Scholarship–Biomechanics (Swimming), 177
Postgraduate Scholarship for Bath Spa University Alumni, 184
Postgraduate Scholarship–Physiology (Biochemistry/Haematology), 177
Postgraduate Scholarship Program–Physiology (Quality Control), 177
Postgraduate Scholarships, 490
Postgraduate Scholarships (ABS), 150
Postgraduate Scholarships for Interdisciplinary Bioethics Research, 345
Postgraduate Tassell Scholarship in Cancer Research, 1447
Post-PhD Research Grant, 1616
POST Program Grants, 23
PPARC Communications/Media Programme, 1102
PPARC Royal Society Industry Fellowships, 1102
PPARC Standard Research Studentship, 1103
Prabha Dutt Fellowship, 1089
Pratt Foundation Bursary (IES), 166
Pre Admissions Scholarships, 346
Predoc Scholarships, 201
Predoctoral Fellowships, 1116
Pre-doctoral Research Bursary, 315
Prehistoric Society Conference Fund, 961
President, 317, 651
Presidential Scholarships for Students of Black Heritage, 615
President of Ireland Young Research Award (PIYRA), 1104
President's Doctoral Scholar Award, 1382
President's Doctoral Scholar (PDS) Awards in the School of Arts, Languages and Cultures, 1381
President's Doctoral Scholar (PDS) Awards in the School of Environment, Education and Development, 1382
President's Fund, Edinburgh Association of University Women, 1301
President's Graduate Fellowship, 877
President's PhD Scholarships, 614
President's Postgraduate Scholarship Scheme, 1343
Presidents' Travel Fund, 935
Prevention and Population Research Programme Award, 315
Prevention and Population Research Project Award, 316
Primary Care Training and Enhancement-Physician Assistant Program, 584
Prime Minister's Fellowship Scheme for Doctoral Research, 1099
Prime Minister's Research Fellowship Scheme, 963
Prince Charles Hospital Foundation's PhD Scholarship, 963
Prince of Wales' Cambridge International Scholarship, 1277
Principal Career Development PhD Scholarship, 1301
Principal's Studentship, 1257
Priority Programme Awards, 1157
Prix de Rome in Architecture-Emerging Practitioners, 274
Prix de Rome in Architecture-Professional, 276
The Prof. Rahamimoff Travel Grants for Young Scientists, 445
The Professional Development Award, 913
Professor Bernard Choseed Memorial Fellowship, 1640
Professor Geoffrey Chamberlain Award, 1024
Professor Lowitja O'Donoghue Indigenous Student Postgraduate Research Scholarship, 530
Professor Michael Kidd AM Scholarship, 531
Professor Ross Kalucy Indigenous Well-Being Scholarship, 531
Professor Sir Malcolm Grant Postgraduate Scholarship, 1207
Program Administrator Award for Excellence, 1033
Program Grants, 660
Program in African American History (PAAH) Mellon Postdoctoral Fellowships, 729
Program in Early American Economy and Society (PEAES) Post-Doctoral Fellowships, 729
Project Grant Program, 289
Project Specific-Energy and Natural Resources Innovation and Technology Research Initiative (International), 777
Project Specific Scholarship-Improving Integrated Pest Management with Genome Editing, 777
Project Specific Scholarship-Investigating Neuron-glia Interactions in MND/ALS, 778
PROLAB Fellowships, 667
Property Institute of New Zealand Postgraduate Scholarship, 1230
Prostate Cancer Research Centre-NSW, 163
Protected and Controlled Environment (PACE) Horticulture, 219
Provost's Postdoctoral Fellowship Program, 890
Psychiatry Section Mental Health Foundation Research Prize, 1069
Pt. Vasant Thakar Memorial Fellowship, 1089
Publication Subsidies, 359
Public Scholars, 856
Pukehou Poutu Scholarship, 1278
Pfizer Graduate Travel Awards in Analytical Chemistry, 61
Pfizer Scholar, 953
Pfizer Scholars Grants in Clinical Epidemiology, 954
Pfizer Scholars Grants in Clinical Psychiatry, 954
Pfizer Scholars Grants in Clinical Rheumatology, 954
Pfizer Scholars Grants in Pain Medicine, 954
Pfizer Visiting Professorships Program, 955

Q

QuadW Foundation-AACR Fellowship for Clinical/Translational Sarcoma Research, 41
Queen Elisabeth International Music Competition of Belgium, 965
Queen's Loyalty Scholarship, 973
Queen's Nursing Institute Fund for Innovation and Leadership, 970
Queen's Transfer Fund, 450

R

R. Gene Richter Scholarship Program, 635
Radboud Encouragement Scholarship, 975
Radboud Scholarship Programme, 976
Radboud Scholarship Programme for International Students, 976
Radboud Scholarships Programme for Masters Students, 977
Radcliffe Institute Fellowship, 977
Radiological Society of North America Education Seed Grant, 979
Radiological Society of North America Institutional Clinical Fellowship in Cardiovascular Imaging, 980
Radiological Society of North America Medical Student Grant Program, 980
Radiological Society of North America Research Resident/Fellow Program, 981
Radiological Society of North America Research Resident Program, 980
Radiological Society of North America Research Scholar Grant Program, 981

Radiology: BSHNI Annual Oral Presentation, 1069
Radiology SA Scholarship, 531
Radiology Section: Finzi Prize, 1069
Rae and Edith Bennett Travelling Scholarship, 1399
Rae and George Hammer Memorial Visiting Research Fellowship, 1218
Raewyn Good Study Award for Mlori and Pasifika Social Science Research, 1052
Raman LiDAR Spectroscopy Techniques for Remote Sensing of Subsurface Water Properties, 778
Ramanujan Fellowship, 1099
Ramanujan Research Studentship in Mathematics, 1257
Ramanujan Research Studentship in Mathematics at Trinity College, Cambridge, 1258
Ramboll Masters Scholarship for International Students, 1448
RaMP-UP-Research and Mentoring Program–Understanding and Preserving Tropical BioDiversity Fellowship, 1120
Rangel Graduate Fellowship Program, 891
Rare Epilepsy Partnership Award, 364
Rauschenberg Emergency Grants, 889
Rausing Scholarship in Anthropology, 735
Rausing Scholarship in English, 735
Ray Allen Billington Prize, 935
The Ray and Naomi Simpson Scholarship, 1341
Ray Y. Gildea Jr Award, 1038
R Douglas Wright Awards, 857
Reardon Postgraduate Scholarship in Music, 1230
Rebecca Davies Clinician Researcher Fellowship, 691
The Rebecca Skelton Scholarship, 983
Recharge Foundation Fellowship for New Surrealist Art, 889
Reconciliation SA Aboriginal Education Leaders Fund Postgraduate Research Scholarship, 531
Recruitment of Established Investigators, 303
Recruitment of First-Time, Tenure-Track Faculty Members, 304
The Red Ochre Award, 161
Reducing Global Health Non-communicable Disease Risk for Young People, 806
The Reese Fellowship for American Bibliography and the History of the Book in the Americas, 207
Refugee Bursary, 1308
Refugee Study Awards, 603
Regents' Junior Faculty Fellowships, 638
Regional Impact Scholarship (MBA), 900
Regional Office Scholarship-India, 185
Regional Office Scholarships-China, 185
Regional Scholarship-International Students, 704
Regional Victoria Experience Bursary, 704
Regular Member Fellowships, 105
Regulation and Safety SS Travel Award, 1185
Reham al-Farra International Scholarship in Journalism, 228
Reliance Foundation Global Internship, 633
Religion, Spirituality, and Democratic Renewal Fellowship, 1122
Repatriation General Hospital Department of Rehabilitation and Aged Care: Health Professionals Research Scholarship, 531
Repatriation General Hospital Department of Rehabilitation and Aged Care: Medical Research Scholarship, 532
Repatriation General Hospital Department of Rehabilitation and Aged Care: Nursing Research Scholarship, 532
Research Administration Assistants Postdoctoral Award, 343
Research Assistance Awards, 237
Research Corporation (United States of America) Research Innovation Awards, 989
Research Council of Norway Senior Scientist Visiting Fellowship, 991
Research Degree Scholarship in Chemical Engineering, 1208
Research Degree Scholarships in Anthropology, 1208
Research Development Fellowships, 219
Researcher Project for Scientific Renewal, 991
Researcher Project for Young Talents, 991
Research Fellowship, 589, 1622
Research Fellowships, 726, 1608
Research Fellowships for Young Researchers, 680
Research Fellowships in Humanities and Social Science, 1608
Research for a Plastics Circular Economy: Full Proposal Stage, 219
Research Fund, 961
Research Grants, 37, 93, 245, 360, 1142
Research Grants & Fellowships, 946
Research Grants on Education: Small, 1138
Research in Robotic Surgical Technology Grant, 116
Research Internships in Science and Engineering (RISE), 436
Research Leaders Awards, 584
Research Leadership Awards, 726
Research@Pickett Community Outreach and Engagement Voucher Program, 444
Research Project Grants, 727
Research Proposals, 409
Research Scholar Awards, 121
Research Scholar Grant, 982
Research School of Accounting India Merit Scholarships, 174
Research Seed Grant, 982
Research Student Conference Travel Grants semester 2, 2024, 532
Research Training Awards (RTA), 304
Research Training Fellowships for Nurses and Allied Health Professionals, 253
Research Training Grant, 1129
Research Training Program (RTP) Stipend Scholarship, 343
Research/Visiting Scientist Fellowships, 18
Reserve Bank of New Zealand Scholarships, 992
Reserve Bank of New Zealand Scholarships for International Students, 993
Residential School Equity Grant, 356
Residential Student Scholarship (RSS), 172
Resilient Reinforcement Learning for Cyber Security, 1331
Resource Management Law Association of New Zealand Masters Scholarship, 157
Respective Government Fellowships, 986
Respiratory Medicine Section: Foundation Year and Internal Medicine Trainee Award, 1069
Respiratory Medicine Section: Respiratory Specialist Registrar Award, 1070
Respiratory Medicine Section: Student Award, 1070
Resuscitation Council (United Kingdom) Research & Development Grant, 994
The Rev Dr Norma P Robertson Scholarship, 1303
Rex Elliot Wegener Memorial Fund for Mesothelioma Research, 533
RFRC Graduate Student Fellowship Awards, 1221
RHBNC Trust Scholarship, 1042
Rheumatology Future Physician Scientist Award, 1002
Rheumatology & Rehabilitation Section: Barbara Ansell Prize, 1070
Rheumatology & Rehabilitation Section: Eric Bywaters Prize, 1070
Rhodes Scholarship, 1006, 1448
Rhodes University African Studies Centre (RASC), 1009
The Rhona Beare Award, 1259
RHT Bates Postgraduate Scholarship, 1052
The Richard Bradford McConnell Fund for Landscape Studies, 258
Richard Brookdale Scholarship, 677
Richard Chattaway Scholarship, 1208
Richard W. Leopold Prize, 935
The Right Honorable Paul Martin Sr. Scholarship, 288
R.J. Hunter Research Bursary Scheme, 1044
RMIT-CSIRO PhD International Scholarship in Mineral Resources and Environmental Science, Australia, 906
Robb College Foundation Irvine Scholarship, 1409
Robb College Foundation Sinclair-Wilson Scholarship, 1409

Robb Scholarship for Regional Planning and Development, 1410
Robert A. Pritzker Distinguished Lecture Award, 214
Roberta Sykes Bursary, 1011
Roberta Sykes Scholarship, 1012
Robert E. Thunen Memorial Scholarships, 200
Robert Fleming Prize, 274
Robert L. Dixon International Travel Award, 1185
Robert Logan Memorial Bursary, 677
Robert McKee International Screenwriting Scholarships, 985
Robert Noyce Teacher Scholarship Program, 869
The Robert W. and Charlotte Bitter Graduate Scholarship Endowment, 819
Robert Westwood Scholarship, 1087
The Robin & Nadine Wells Scholarship, 1141
Robin Rousseau Memorial Mountain Achievement Scholarship, 363
Robinson College: Lewis Graduate Scholarship, 1258
The Robinson Dorsey Postgraduate Scholarship, 1450
Robinson Scholarship, 557, 711
Rocky Talkie Search and Rescue Award, 38
Roger Helm Scholarship in Pure Mathematics, 322
The Roger Perry Memorial Scholarship, 993
Roland Stead Postgraduate Scholarship in Biology, 1278
Romania: Romanian State Scholarships, 598
Romanian State Scholarships, 599
Rome Scholarship in Architecture, 261
Ronald J. Thom Award for Early Design Achievement, 276
Ronald Raven Barbers, 1037
Rosa-Luxemburg-Stiftung, 190
Rose and Isidore Drench Memorial Fellowship, 1640
Rosemary Foundation Travel Grant, 32
Rosemead School of Psychology Graduate Grant, 212
Ross Purse Doctoral Fellowship, 293
Rotterdam School of Management Master of Business Administration Asia & Australia Regional Scholarship, 1013
Rowe Scientific Foundation Scholarship, 425
Royal Academy Engineering Professional Development, 1015
Royal Academy of Engineering MSc Motorsport Scholarship Programme, 1337
Royal Academy Sir Angus Paton Bursary, 1015
Royal Academy Sir Henry Royce Bursary, 1016
The Royal Bank of Scotland International Scholarship, 742
Royal College AMS Donald Richards Wilson Award for CanMEDS Integration, 1033
Royal College Award for Early-Career Leadership, 1034
Royal College Dr. Thomas Dignan Indigenous Health Award, 1034
Royal College of Midwives Annual Midwifery Awards, 1017
Royal College of Obstetricians and Gynaecologists Edgar Research Fellowship, 1024
Royal College of Obstetricians and Gynaecologists Research Training Fellowships, 1025
Royal College of Obstetricians and Gynaecologists WellBeing Grants, 1025
Royal College of Ophthalmologists-Bayer Research Award, 1029
Royal College of Organists Scholarships and Awards, 1030
Royal College of Organists Various Open Award Bequests, 1030
Royal College of Organists Various Open Awards, 1030
Royal Historical Society: Postgraduate Research Support Grants, 1316
Royal Holloway, University of London MBA Programme, 1043
Royal Holloway Principal's Masters Scholarship, 1042
Royal Horticultural Society Financial Awards, 1043
Royal Horticulture Society Bursary Scheme, 1044
Royal Irish Academy Senior Visiting Fellowships, 1045
Royal Literary Fund Grant, 1045
Royal Melbourne Institute of Technology PhD Scholarship in the School of Electrical and Computer Engineering, 1047
Royal National Orthopaedic Hospital Special Trustees Research Training Scholarship, 1208
Royal Over-Seas League Annual Music Competition, 1047
Royal Over-Seas League Travel Scholarship, 1048
The Royal Scottish Academy John Kinross Scholarships to Florence, 1049
The Royal Scottish Academy William Littlejohn Award for Excellence and Innovation in Water-Based Media, 1049
Royal Society EPSRC BBSRC and Rolls Royce PLC Industry Fellowships, 485
Royal Society of Chemistry Journals Grants for International Authors, 1054
Royal Society of Edinburgh Personal Research Fellowships, 1054
Royal Society South East Asia Rainforest Research Project-Travel Grants, 1053
Royston Honours Award in Chemical Engineering, 1423
The RSA David Michie Travel Award, 1049
RSE Fulbright Scholar Award, 1055
RSE Research Network Grants, 1055
RSE Research Workshop Grants, 1055
RSE Small Research Grants, 1056
RSL Queensland Scholarships, 678
RSM non-EEA Scholarship of Excellence (MSc), 1013
Rubicon Programme, 883
Rudolf Diesel Industry Fellowship, 630
Rudolf Steiner Foundation Seed Fund, 17
Rudolph Ganz Fellowship, 892
RUNX1 Early Career Investigator Grants, 24
Rural and Regional Enterprise Scholarships (RRES), 515
RuralKids GPS–Delivering Equitable Care to Children in Rural NSW, 778
Rural Maternity Care Doctoral Student Fellowship, 1074
Russ Casey Scholarship, 782
Russia: Scholarships for South Africans, 599
Ruth and Lincoln Ekstrom Fellowship, 683
Ruth Davies Research Bursary, 1017
Ruth First Scholarship, 450, 1010
Ruth K. Broad Biomedical Research Foundation–Ellen Luken Student Awards, 444
Ruth L. Kirschstein National Research Service Award (NRSA) Individual Postdoctoral Fellowship, 861
Ruth O Brian Project Grant, 45
Ruth Watson Henderson Choral Composition Competition, 363

S

S. Ramachandran-National Bioscience Award for Career Development, 428
SAAFE Program, 482
The Sagol Network GerOmic Award for Junior Faculty Eligibility Criteria, 66
Said Scholarship, 450
Saidye Bronfman Award, 284
Sainsbury Management Fellowships, 1016
Saint Andrew's Society of the State of New York Scholarship Fund, 1316
Saint Louis University International MBA Programme, 1084
Sallie Mae Student Loans, 711
Sally Crossing AM Award, 296
Sam and Nina Narodowski PhD International Scholarships in Australia, 904
Samuel and Flora Weiss Research Fellowship, 1641
Samuel & Eileen Gluyas Fellowship, 678
Samuel Glasstone Award, 90
Samuel H Kress Joint Athens-Jerusalem Fellowship, 105, 109
Sanctuary Scholarship, 1309

Sandbox Student Grant Program, 1078
Sandpit: Novel Computing for UK Defence and Security, 220
Sandy Purl Mentorship Scholarship, 922
Santander Formula Scholarship, 811
Santander Masters Scholarship, 1309
Santander Mobility Scholarship, 811
Santander Scholarships, 451
Santander Work Based Learning Scholarship, 812
Santa Singh and Balwant Kaur Scholarship, 825
SAPIENS Public Scholars Training Fellowship, 1616
Sarah Barrow Bursary in Music, 1357
Sasakawa Japanese Studies Postgraduate Studentship, 1383
Sasakawa Young Leader Fellowship (SYLFF) Program, 1090
Sasakawa Young Leaders Fellowship Fund Research Scholarship-Masters and PhD, 736
Saving Lives: Mapping the Influence of Indigenous LGBTIQ+ Creative Artists-Domestic, 778
Saving Lives: Mapping the Influence of Indigenous LGBTIQ+ Creative Artists-International, 779
Savoy Educational Trust Scholarships, 742
Savoy Foundation International Grant, 1090
Savoy Foundation Postdoctoral and Clinical Research Fellowships, 1091
Savoy Foundation Research Grants, 1091
Savoy Foundation Studentships, 1091
Scalable Parallelism in the Extreme (SPX), 869
Scholar Grants, 360
Scholar-in-Residence Program, 436
Scholarly Editions and Scholarly Translations, 856
Scholarship, 510, 597, 1211, 1217, 1219, 1267, 1280, 1405, 1428, 1432, 1455
Scholarship Opportunities Linked to CATIE, 1186
Scholarships for Americans to Study in Norway, 913
Scholarships for a Summer Seminar in Greek Language and Culture, 574
Scholarships for Masters (ICP Connect), 192
School for International Training (SIT) Master of Arts in Teaching Program, 1627
School for Policy Studies International Postgraduate Scholarships, 1237
School of Anthropology and Conservation Research Scholarship, 1331
School of Arts, Languages and Cultures PhD Studentships, 1383
School of Arts Master's Bursaries and Studentships, 222
School of Business and Economics Scholarships, 756
School of Chemical and Process Engineering-International Masters Excellence Scholarship, 1338
School of Chemistry–International Masters Excellence Scholarship, 1338
School of Civil Engineering-International Masters Excellence Scholarship, 1338
School of Computing–International Masters Excellence Scholarship, 1339
School of Divinity Postgraduate Masters Scholarships, 1302
School of Education Graduate Grant, 212
School of Electronic and Electrical Engineering-International Masters Excellence Scholarship, 1339
School of Engineering Diversity PhD Scholarship, 1383
School of Engineering Graduate PhD Scholarship, 1384
School of Environment, Education and Development Postgraduate Research Scholarship, 1384
School of Geography and the Environment Commonwealth Shared Scholarship, 735
School of Graduate Studies F. A. Aldrich Award, 809
The School of History and Heritage MA Bursary, 1351
School of Languages & Social Studies PhD Bursaries, 150
School of Life and Health Sciences Postgraduate Masters Scholarships–Commonwealth Shared Scholarship Scheme, 151
School of Mathematics and Statistics Indigenous Scholarship, 1423
School of Mathematics–International Masters Excellence Scholarship, 1339
School of Mechanical Engineering-International Masters Excellence Scholarship, 1340
School of Medicine (SoM) Bridge Funding Program, 444
School of Medicine Dean's Postdoctoral Fellowship, 1149
School of Natural Sciences Diversity PhD Scholarship, 1385
School of Physics and Astronomy-International Masters Excellence Scholarship, 1340
School of Social Sciences and Humanities International PhD Studentships in UK, 905
School of Social Sciences-China Scholarship Council Joint Scholarship for PhD Study, 1385
School of Social Sciences-Economics PhD Studentships, 1385
School of Social Sciences-Manchester Master, 1386
School of Social Sciences-North West Consortium Doctoral Training Partnership (AHRC NWCDTP), 1386
School of Social Sciences-North West Social Sciences Doctoral Training Partnership (ESRC NWSSDTP) Studentships, 1386
School of Social Sciences-PhD Studentships, 1387
School of Social Sciences-PhD Studentship with the Stuart Hall Foundation, 1386
School of Social Sciences-President's Doctoral Scholarship (PDS), 1387
School Teacher Fellowship, 257
Schrödinger Scholarship Scheme, 615
Science and Engineering Research Board Distinguished Fellowship, 1100
Science and Engineering Research Board Overseas Postdoctoral Fellowship (OPDF), 1100
Science and Engineering Research Board Women Excellence Award, 1100
Science and Technology Facilities Council (STFC), 615
Science and Technology Facilities Council Postgraduate Studentships, 1103
Science Foundation Ireland Career Development Award (CDA), 1104
Science Foundation Ireland Investigator Programme, 1105
Scientist Development Award, 1002
SCIRTS Pilot Research Grants, 391
SCIRTS Senior Research Grants, 392
Score Africa/Allan & Nesta Ferguson Charitable Trust Scholarship, 1209
Scotland Grant, 587
Scotland's Saltire Scholarships, 468, 572
Scots Australian Council Scholarships, 406
ScottishPower Masters Scholarships, 572
Scottish Power Scholarships, 1358
Sea Grant/NOAA Fisheries Graduate Fellowship, 870
Sean W. Dever Memorial Prize, 1603
Sediment and Asphaltite Transport by Canyon Upwelling-Top Up Scholarship, 407
SEED Awards, 306
SEED Enhancing Racial Equality Studentship, 1387
Seed Grant for New African Principal Investigators (SG-NAPI), 1179
Seed Grants Scheme, 344
Senior and Intermediate Research Fellowship for International Students, 1609
Senior Cancer Research Fellowship, 316
Senior Fellowship, 619
Senior Fellowships in Public Health and Tropical Medicine, 1609
Senior Health Research Scholarships, 1230
Senior Smeaton Scholarship in Experimental Science, 1448
Senior Women Academic Administrators of Canada Awards, 1078
SEP Scholarship, 779
Serendib Community Cultural Association Sri Lanka Bursary, 425
The Sergievsky Award For Epilepsy Health Equity And Diversity, 552
Sex and Gender in Alzheimer's (SAGA 23) Award Program, 30

Sexuality & Sexual Health Section: Medical Student Essay Prize, 1070
Sexuality & Sexual Health Section: Trainee Essay Prize, 1070
S.F. Pond Travelling Scholarship, 1399
SG and JG Scholarship (MIT Melbourne), 515
SG and JG Scholarship (MIT Sydney), 515
SG and JG Scholarships (Mt Helen), 516
Shaping Futures Postgraduate Scholarship, 1436
Shaping Futures Scholarships, 1436
Shapoorji Pallonji Scholarships, 1095
The Shell Centenary Scholarship Fund, Netherlands, 1168
Shell Centenary Scholarships and Shell Centenary Chevening Scholarships at Edinburgh, 1302
Shell Petroleum Development Company Niger Delta Postgraduate Scholarship, 1209
Sher-Gil Sundaram Arts Foundation: Installation Art Grant, 1108
The Ship Smart Annual Scholarship, 133
Shirley Gilliver Memorial Fund Grant, 678
Shirtcliffe Fellowship, 474, 1200
Shorenstein Fellowships in Contemporary Asia, 1109
Short-Term EFEO Postdoctoral Contracts, 537
Short-Term Risk Focus Grant, 69
Showa Denko Environmental Scholarship, 736
Shu Chien Achievement Award, 214
Sidney Topol Fellowship in Nonviolence Practice, 231
The Sievert Larsson Scholarship, 1110
Sigma Theta Tau International/Association of Operating Room Nurses Foundation Grant, 1110
Sigma Theta Tau International/Association of Perioperative Registered Nurses Foundation Grant, 1111
Sigma Theta Tau International/Rehabilitation Nursing Foundation Grant, 1111
Signature Research Theme Scholarship: Future Human-E-scooters in the Life of the Future Human, 1331
Significant Achievement in Sport, 812
Simon Keay Award in Mediterranean Archaeology, 261
Sims Black Travelling Proffesorship, 1025
Singapore Education–Sampoerna Foundation MBA in Singapore, 836
Singapore International Graduate Award (SINGA), 20, 836
Singapore-MIT Alliance Graduate Fellowship, 877
Sir Alan Stewart Postgraduate Scholarships, 793
Sir Arthur Sims Travelling Scholarship, 1399
Sir Douglas Myers Scholarship, 1278
Sir Francis Hill Postgraduate Scholarship, 1440
Sir Frederick Pollock Scholarship for Students from North America, 1209
Sir George Jessel Studentship in Mathematics, 1209
Sir Henry Dale Fellowships, 1053
The Sir Hugh Kawharu Masters Scholarship for Innovation in Science, 1053
Sir James Lighthill Scholarship, 1210
Sir John Logan Campbell Agricultural Scholarship, 793
Sir John Salmond Scholarship for Students from Australia and New Zealand, 1210
Sir Paul Callaghan Doctoral Scholarship in Chemistry and Physics, 645
Sir Ratanji Dalal Research Scholarship, 1035
Sir Ratan Tata Postdoctoral Fellowship, 743
Sir Richard Stapley Educational Trust Grants, 1114
Sir Thomas Naghten Fitzgerald Scholarship, 1400
Sir Walter Raleigh MSc Scholarship in Environmental Change and Management, 940
Sir William Lister/Dorey Bequest, 1114
SITC-Bristol Myers Squibb Postdoctoral Cancer Immunotherapy Translational Fellowship, 298
SITC-Genentech Women in Cancer Immunotherapy Fellowship, 298
SITC-Merck Cancer Immunotherapy Clinical Fellowship, 298
SITC-Nektar Therapeutics Equity and Inclusion in Cancer Immunotherapy Fellowship, 299
Skinner Fund, 1053
Sleep Medicine Section: Student Essay Prize, 1071
Smithsonian Environmental Research Center Graduate Student Fellowship, 1117
S.N Bose Scholar Program, 1099
Snowdon Masters Scholarships, 557, 970
SOAS Master's Scholarship, 1095
SOAS Research Scholarship, 1096
SOAS Sanctuary Scholarship, 1096
Sochon Foundation Scholarship, 1096
Social and Policy Studies Scholarships, 757
Social Science Research Council Abe Fellowship Program, 1122
Social Science Research Council Eurasia Program Postdoctoral Fellowships, 1123
Social Science Research Council Eurasia Program Predissertation Training Fellowships, 1123
Social Science Research Council Eurasia Program Teaching Fellowships, 1124
Social Science Research Council International Dissertation Research Fellowship, 1124
Social Science Research Council Summer Institute on International Migration, 1124
Social Sciences and Humanities Research Council Impact Awards, 1078
Social Work Bursary, 561, 711
Society for Immunotherapy of Cancer-Amgen Cancer Immunotherapy in Hematologic Malignancies Fellowship Award, 299
Society for Immunotherapy of Cancer Scholarship, 10
Society for the Psychological Study of Social Issues Grants-in-Aid Program, 1131
Society for the Scientific Study of Sexuality Student Research Grants, 1132
Society of American Archivists' Mosaic Scholarship Opportunity, 936
Society of Nuclear Medicine Pilot Research Grants in Nuclear Medicine/Molecular Imaging, 473
Society of Women Engineers Past Presidents Scholarships, 1134
Södertörn University Tuition Fee Waive, 1134
SOLA Awards, 135
Solidarity Grants, 499
Solomon Awards, 1138
Sonja Huddle Award, 1424
Soroptimist International Founder Region Women's Fellowships, 200
Soros Equality Fellowship, 926
Soros Justice Fellowships, 927
South African Council for English Education's EX-PCE Bursary, 1136
South Asia AU$10,000 Early Acceptance Scholarship, 779
South Asia Excellence Scholarship, 1436
South Asian Scholarships at Edinburgh Napier University, 468
South Asia Program Junior Fellowship, 634
South Australian Department of Health Research Award, 533
South East Asia Scholarship, 469
South East ESRC DTC Funding, 1332
South Korea A$10,000 Early Acceptance Scholarship, 779
Space Environment Research Centre Scholarships, 1137
Spain: Student and Staff Exchange between South Africa and Spain, 599
Spatio-temporal Models for Large Citizen Science Data Sets, 1332
Special Project Grants, 253
Special Research Fund-Doctoral Scholarship, 569
Spectrum Initiative Scholarship Program, 84
Spencer Foundation Dissertation Fellowship Program, 1138
Spencer Wilks Postgraduate Masters Scholarships, 649
Spencer Wilks Scholarship/Fellowship, 649
Sponsored Student Grant, 780
Sport, Exercise and Health Sciences Alumni Bursary, 757
Sport Access Scholarship, 1400

Sport Leadership Grants for Women Program, 177
Sports Medicine Fellowship Program, 178
Sports Physiology Postgraduate Scholarship–Fatigue and Recovery, 178
Sports Scholarships, 1043
Sports Scholarships (Kent Sports Website), 1332
Spring Management Development Scholarship (MDS), 836
Square Mile International Scholarship, 418
SRT Scholarship: Future Human–Enhancing Exercise Outcomes Using Immersive Virtual Reality and Machine Learning, 1333
SSHRC Doctoral Fellowships, 1127
SSHRC Impact Awards, 1127
SSHRC Postdoctoral Fellowships, 1128
SSRC/ACLS Eastern European Program Dissertation Fellowships, 1125
St. Baldrick's International Scholars, 1143
St. Baldrick's Scholars, 1144
St. Louis Mercantile Library Prize, 204
Staff Scholarship-Continuing, 516
Staff Scholarship-Domestic, 516
Staff Scholarship-International, 516
Standard Research Grant, 69
St Andrews Society of New York Scholarships, 334
Stanford Postdoctoral Recruitment Initiative in Sciences and Medicine (PRISM), 1149
Stanley Burton Research Scholarship, 1340
Stanley Smith (UK) Horticultural Trust Awards, 1151
Stanton-Horton Award for Excellence in National Park Service History, 936, 938
Starter Support Scholarship, 407
Starting Investigator Research Grant (SIRG), 1105
St Cross MSc Scholarship in Biodiversity, Conservation and Management, 1141
St Cross MSc Scholarship in Global Health Science and Epidemiology, 1141
Stellenbosch Fellowship in Polymer Science, 1153
Stellenbosch Merit Bursary Award, 1153
Stellenbosch Rector's Grants for Successing Against the Odds, 1154
Stephen and Anna Hui Fellowship, 615
Stephen Feinberg Scholars Scholarship Program, 380
Stevenson Exchange Scholarships, 1316
Steve Weston and Trust Scholarships, 1289
Stewart Hamilton Scholarship, 661
St John's College Benefactors' Scholarships for Research, 1258
Strategic Research Agreement, 690
Strathclyde Research Studentship Scheme (SRSS), 1156
STRI Postdoctoral Research in Hydrology, 1120
The Stroke Association Research Project Grants, 1157
Strong Arm of Georgia Scholarship, 723
Student Achievement Grants, 852
Student Bursaries, 241
Student Employability Fund, 451
Student Grants, 1400
Student Research Fund, 146
Student Research Scholarship in Occupational Hygiene, 873
Students Awards Agency for Scotland Postgraduate Students' Allowances Scheme (PSAS), 966
Studies and Demonstration Projects, 393
Study Abroad Studentship, 727
Study in Australia-Northern Territory Scholarships, 168
Study in Canada Scholarships, 1322
Studying Post-translational Protein Modifications in Brain Function and Disease-Domestic, 780
Studying Post-translational Protein Modifications in Brain Function and Disease-International, 780
StuNed Scholarship, 719
Sugar Industry Postgraduate Research Scholarships (SPRS), 1157
Sully Scholarship, 1210
Summer Intensive Course in modern Greek Language Scholarship, 132
2023 Summer Research and Measurement Sciences (RMS) Internship program, 475
Summer Research Fellowship, 445
Summer Seminar in Germany, 567
Summer Stipends, 856
Supply Chain Innovation Award, 388
Support Fund for Students with a Disability, 1410
Surface Coatings Association Australia Award, 1424
Surgery Section Norman Tanner Prize and Glaxo Travelling Fellowship, 1071
Susana Menendez Bright Future Scholarship, 577
Susan Barnes Memorial Scholarship, 322
Sustainability Scholarship, 1317
Sustainable Bio-based Materials and Manufacture: Feasibility Study, 220
Sustainable Tourism CRC–Climate Change PhD Scholarship, 678
Sustainable Transitions Team Research Initiative 2024, 378
Swaantje Mondt Fund Law and Society Scholarship, 719
Swansea University Masters Scholarships, 1159
Swansea University PhD Scholarships, 1159
Swansea University Research Excellence Scholarship, 1159
Sweden: Swedish Institute Scholarships for South Africa (SISSA), 600
The Swedish Foundation for International Cooperation in Research and Higher Education (STINT) Scholarship, 1154
Swedish Institute Scholarships for Global Professionals (SISGP), 1160
Swedish Institute Scholarships for the Western Balkans Programme, 1160
The Swedish Institute Study Scholarships (SISS), 1161
The Swedish Institute Study Scholarships for South Africa, 1161
Swedish-Turkish Scholarship Programme for PhD Studies and Postdoctoral Research, 1161
Swinburne University Postgraduate Research Award (SUPRA), 1163
Swiss Government Excellence Scholarships for Foreign Scholars and Artists, 1152
Swiss National Science Foundation Fellowships for Prospective Researchers, 1164
Sybil Shearer Fellowship: Dancemakers, 983
Sybil Tutton Awards, 590
Sydney Campbell Undergraduate Scholarship, 794
Syracuse University Executive MBA Programme, 1165
Syracuse University MBA, 1165

T

Tachau Teacher of the Year Award, 936
Taking Flight Award, 364
Talbot School of Theology Graduate Grant, 213
Talented Athlete Scholarship Scheme (TASS), 1388
Tamex Transport Scholarship, 1410
Target Ovarian Cancer Essay Prize, 1025
Tata Innovation Fellowship, 429
Taught Master's Scholarships, 875
Taught Postgraduate Scholarships, 873
Tax Institute of America Doctoral Dissertations in Government and Taxation, 871
Teaching Assistantships (Economics), 1210
Technology Equity Grant, 356
Technology Impact Award, 310
Tel Aviv University Scholarships, 1169
Templeton Fellowships for United States of America and International Scholars at NDIAS, 1438
Terrell Blodgett Fellowship for Government Services in Urban Management and Finance, 1170
Tertiary Access Payment, 1401

Test Scholarships for International Students at Free University of Berlin, Germany, 905
Texas CONNECT for Cancer Prevention Study Awards, 306
Texas Regional Excellence in Cancer Award, 306
Thailand Scholarship, 1350
Thames and Hudson Scholarship, 1211
Theodora Bosanquet Bursary, 249, 555
Theodore C. Sorensen Research Fellowship, 685
Therapeutic Catalyst, 316
Therla Drake Postgraduate Scholarships, 517, 1594
Thesis, Dissertation and Institutional Research Awards, 426
Think Big About Innovation Scholarships, 1237
Think Big Postgraduate Scholarships, 1237
The Thomas R. Pickering Foreign Affairs Fellowship, 1177
Thomas Witherden Batt Scholarship, 1211
Thomson Foundation Scholarship, 1181
Three Nations Conference Award, 323
Three-year Fully Funded PhD Scholarship in Public Health, 401
Three-year Researcher Project with International Mobility, 992
Thurgood Marshall College Fund Scholarships, 1183
Tibawi Trust Awards, 1097
Tim and Margaret Bourke PhD Scholarships, 174
Tim Chard Case History Prize, 1026
The Tim Collins Scholarship for the Study of Love in Religion, 984
Tinson Fund Scholarship for Law, 1310
Title VIII-Supported Summer Research Grant, 694
TMCF All Around Scholarship, 1182
Todd Walker Research Fellowship, 338
Tohmae Pa Scholarships, 516
Toloa Scholarships for Pacific STEM Scholars, 158
Tom and Dorothy Cook Scholarships in Public Health and Tropical Medicine, 678
The Torskeklubben Stipend, 913
Tortuga Study Abroad Scholarship, 231
To Support Research in the Prehistory of the Aegean and Its Connections with the East Mediterranean, 259
Toyota Earth Day Scholarship Program, 363
Trainees' Committee John Glyn Trainees' Prize, 1071
Training Fellowships in Public Health and Tropical Medicine, 1610
Training Graduate PhD Salary Award (TGP), 810
Training in Research Methodology Grant, 116
Training & Travel Grants, 246
Transatlantic Doctoral Seminar in German History, 567
Transformer Scholarship, 225
Translational Awards, 253
Translation Competition, 123
Translation Fund, 1610
Transmission Fund, 590
Transmission of Immunodeficiency Viruses: Postdoctoral Research Position, 961
Transthyretin Amyloidosis (ATTR) Competitive Grant Program/ ASPIRE, 955
Travel Awards for National Travel, 648
Travel Fellowships, 253
Travel Grants, 192
Travelling Bursaries for Presentation at Overseas Meetings, 242
TREC: Institutional Postdoctoral Training Award, 307
TREC: Major Instrumentation Award, 307
TREC: Pilot Study Award, 307
Trimester 2-Rob Riley MBA Memorial Scholarship, 408
Trinity College: Studentships in Mathematics, 1259
Trustee Funds (Curatorenfondsen), 719
TUM Global Visiting Professor Program, 630
Turkey: Türkiye Scholarships, 600
Turkey Government Scholarships, 1188
Turkey Scholarship, 469, 1351
Turkish Ministry of Education, 1359
Turners and Growers Undergraduate Scholarships, 794
TWAS-COMSTECH Science in Exile PhD Fellowship Programme for Displaced and Refugee Scientists, 1180
TWAS-SN Bose Postgraduate Fellowship Programme, 1181
Twining Humber Award, 135
Tyree Nuclear Masters by Coursework Tuition Scholarship, 1414

U

UC International Alumni Scholarship, 1267
UC International Course Merit Scholarship, 1267
UC International High Achiever Scholarship, 1267
UC International Merit Scholarship, 1267
UCL Masters Bursary, 1212
UCLouvain-CSC PhD Co-funding Fellowship Competition 2023, 335
UC President's Pre-Professoriate Fellowship, 200
UC Te Kaupeka Ture Faculty of Law PhD Fees Scholarship, 1271
UFL Jan de Limpens Scholarship, 765
UK, CI and ROI Student Scholarships-Academic Achievement Scholarship, 229
Ukrainian students Scholarships, 757
UKRI Centres for Doctoral Training in Artificial Intelligence, 220
UKRI Policy Fellowships 2023, 220
UKRI Policy Fellowships 2024, 879
UKRI-SBE Lead Agency Opportunity, 220
ULMS Attainment Award, 1360
ULMS MBA Excellence Scholarship, 1360
ULMS MBA Latin America Excellence Scholarship, 1360
ULMS Progress to Postgraduate Award, 1360
ULMS Southeast Asia Excellence Scholarship, 1361
ULMS West Africa Excellence Scholarship, 1361
ULMS Women in Football Scholarship, 1361
The Ulverscroft David Owen Award, 1029
Ulysses, 671
UM Academic Achievement Scholarship, 765
UM Brightlands Talent Scholarship, 766
UNE Indigenous Medical Scholarship, 1412
UNE Residential Financial Assistance Scholarship, 1412
UniBE International, 1234
Union College Board of Trustees Scholarship, 1190
Union for International Cancer Control American Cancer Society International Fellowships for Beginning Investigators (ACSBI), 284
Union for International Cancer Control International Oncology Nursing Fellowships (IDNF), 284
United Arab Emirates: Khalifa University Postgraduate Scholarships, 600
United Kingdom-India Year of Culture Great Postgraduate Scholarships, 1234
United Nations Educational, Scientific and Cultural Organization-ROSTE Long-term Postgraduate Training Course, 14
United Nations Educational, Scientific and Cultural Organization (UNESCO)/International Sustainable Energy DeISEDC Co-Sponsored Fellowships Programme, 1190
United States: Fulbright Foreign Student Program, 601
United States Air Force Academy/National Research Council Summer Faculty Research Program (SFFP), 21
Universities Federation for Animal Welfare Student Scholarships, 1198
University Awards, 1611
University College London-AET Undergraduate International Outreach Bursaries, 1212
University College London Department Awards for Graduate Students, 1212
University Distinguished Teaching Awards, 890
University Hall Dean's Scholarship, 534

University Hall Eurest Overseas Study Scholarship, 534
The University of Adelaide Global Citizens Scholarship, 1219
University of Adelaide Research Scholarship-The Elder Conservatorium of Music, 1220
University of Alberta Graduate Entrance Scholarship, 1222
University of Alberta Graduate Recruitment Scholarship, 1223
University of Alberta MBA Programme, 1223
University of Auckland Executive MBA Programme, 1233
The University of Auckland International Doctoral Fees Bursary, 1232
University of Auckland International Doctoral Scholarship, 1232
University of Auckland International Student Excellence Scholarship, 1232
University of Auckland Research Masters Scholarships, 1233
University of Bologna Study Grants for International Students, 1235
University of British Columbia Graduate Fellowship (UGF), 1238
University of California, Los Angeles (UCLA) Sardar Patel Award, 1239
University of California at Los Angeles Institute of American Culture (IAC) Postdoctoral/Visiting Scholar Fellowships, 1241
University of Canterbury Doctoral Scholarship, 1280
University of Canterbury Mathematics and Statistics Scholarship, 323
University of Canterbury Pasifika Doctoral Scholarship, 1103
University of Cape Town Masters Scholarships in Public Health, 1281
University of Copenhagen International PhD Fellowships in Food Biotechnology, Denmark, 905
University of East Anglia International Development Scholarships, 1294
University of Edinburgh-KU Leuven PhD Studentship, 1303
University of Exeter Alumni Scholarship, 1312
University of Exeter Chapel Choir Choral and Organ Scholarship, 1312
University of Exeter Class of 2024 Progression Scholarship, 1313
University of Geneva Excellence Masters Fellowships, 1313
University of Helsinki Masters Scholarships, 1450
University of Kent Law School Studentship, 1334
University of Leeds International Fee Bursary (Vietnam)-Information Systems/Multimedia Systems, 1341
University of Leicester Future 50 PhD Scholarship: "Latinx in the UK: Identity, Visibility and British Latinx Studies," 237
The University of Liverpool and China Scholarship Council Awards, 1359
University of Liverpool Commonwealth Postgraduate Bursary, 1361
University of Liverpool International College (UoLIC) Excellence Scholarship, 1361
University of Liverpool International College (UoLIC) Impact Progression Scholar, 1362
The University of Manchester-China Scholarship Council Joint Scholarship, 1389
The University of Manchester-China Scholarship Council joint scholarship, 318
The University of Manchester Humanitarian Scholarships, 1389
University of Manchester President's Doctoral Scholar Awards (PDS Awards), 1389
University of Melbourne Graduate Research Scholarships, 1401
University of Nevada, Las Vegas Alumni Association Graduate Scholarships, 1403
University of Nevada, Las Vegas James F Adams/GPSA Scholarship, 1403
University of Newcastle, Australia MBA Programme, 1438
University of Newcastle International PhD Scholarships in Geomicrobial Biosensors, Australia, 905
University of Newcastle-Malaysian Australia Columbo Plan Commemoration (MACC) Scholarship, 1437
University of Newcastle Postgraduate Research Scholarship (UNRS Central), 1438
University of Otago Academic General Practitioner Registrar PhD Scholarship, 1450
University of Otago China Scholarship Council Doctoral Scholarship, 1451
University of Otago City of Literature PhD Scholarship, 1451
University of Otago Doctoral Scholarships, 1452
University of Otago Doctorate in Medical Education Scholarship, 1452
University of Otago International Master's Scholarship, 1452
University of Otago Mlori Doctoral Scholarship, 1452
University of Otago Postgraduate Scholarship in Obstetrics and Gynaecology, 1453
University of Otago Special Health Research Scholarship, 1453
University of Strathclyde Performance Sport Scholarship, 1156
University of Sydney: Data Science Scholarships, 124
UNSW Business School Honours Scholarship, 1424
UNSW Business School International Pathways Award, 1425
UNSW International Scholarships, 1414
UNSW Law & Justice International Award, 1425
UNSW Medical Research Honours Scholarship-South Western Sydney, 1425
U of L Graduate Association Hong Kong & Tung Postgraduate Scholarships, 1360
Urdang Medal and Kremers Award, 122
Urology, 1071
Urology Professor Geoffrey D Chisholm CBE Communication Prize, 1071
Urology Section: Malcolm Coptcoat Spring Short Papers Prize, 1072
Urology Section: Secretary's Prize, 1072
Urology Section Professor John Blandy Essay Prize for Medical Students, 1072
Urology Section Winter Short Papers Prize (Clinical Uro-Radiological Meeting), 1072
Ursula Henriques Scholarships, 332
Ursula M. Händel Animal Welfare Prize, 435
Uruguay PhD Scholarship, 1351
USA Transfer Scholarship, 185
Usher Bursary, 1390

V

Vanier Canada Graduate Scholarships, 290
Van L. Lawrence Fellowship, 849
Vanne Trompf Scholarship, 517
Venous Forum: Annual Meeting Prize, 1072
Vera Down Research Grant, 256
Vercille Voss Scholarship, 658
Verne R Dapp Memorial Scholarship, 90
Vice-Chancellor International Postgraduate Scholarship, 1630
Vice Chancellor's Africa Scholarship, 1290
Vice Chancellor's Centenary Research Scholarship (VCRS), 1163
Vice-Chancellors China Scholarship Scheme, 332
Vice-Chancellors EU Scholarship, 332
Vice Chancellor's EU Scholarship, 1290
Vice Chancellor's Indonesia Scholarship, 1290
Vice-Chancellor's International Attainment Scholarship, 973, 1362
Vice-Chancellor's International Attainment Scholarship for China, 1362
Vice-Chancellor's International Scholarship, 151, 186, 332
Vice-Chancellors International Scholarship (VCIS)-Korea University, 780
Vice-Chancellors International Scholarship (VCIS)-Pontificia Universidad Javeriana, 781
Vice Chancellor's Mainland China Scholarship, 1290
Vice Chancellor's Scholarship, 592
Vice-Chancellor's Scholarship for International Students, 1453
Vice Chancellor's South Asia Scholarship, 1291
Vice-Chancellor's Strategic Doctoral Research Scholarships, 1595
Victoria Fellowships, 430
Victoria Hardship Fund Equity Grants for International Students in New Zealand, 1595
Victorian International Research Scholarships, 166

Victoria Tongarewa Scholarship, 1595
Victoria University Research Scholarships, 1593
Viessmann/Marburg Travel Scholarship, 1619
Vietnam Scholarship, 426, 470, 1352
Vietnam Scholarships–Ho Chi Minh City University and National Economics University, Hanoi, 1295
Viktoria Marinov Award in Art, 1425
Villa I Tatti-Boğaziçi University Joint Fellowship, 1600
Vincent Lemieux Prize, 295
Vincent T. Wasilewski Award, 265
Viola Edith Reid Bequest Scholarship, 1402
Violet Diller Professional Excellence Award, 669
Virginia Parker Prize, 277
Visby Programme Scholarships, 1162
Visions of Australia: Regional Exhibition Touring Fund, 161
Visiting Fellowships, 259
Visiting Geographical Scientist Program, 146
Visiting Professorships, 727
Visiting Scholars Funding Schemes, 333
Visual Arts New Work, 161
Visual Arts Skills and Arts Development, 162
Vital Knowledge-Artists' Mentoring Scheme, 139
Vivian Lefsky Hort Memorial Fellowship, 1641
Vladimir and Pearl Heifetz Memorial Fellowship in Eastern European Jewish Music, 1641
VLIR-UOS Training and Masters Scholarships, 193
Vocational Education and Training (VET) Distinction Scholarship, 349
Voice Pedagogy Award, 849
Volkswagen Foundation Freigeist Fellowships, 1602
Volunteer Grants, 169
The Von Kaven Awards, 435
VP Kanitkar Memorial Scholarship, 1097
Vrije University Amsterdam-NRF Desmond Tutu Doctoral Scholarships, 867
The Vronwy Hankey Memorial Fund for Aegean Studies, 259
Vronwy Hankey Memorial Travel Award for Pre-Doctoral Students, 260

W

W. F. Albright Institute of Archaeological Research/National Endowment for the Humanities Fellowship, 110
The W. L. Mackenzie King Scholarships, 1081
Waddell Smith Postgraduate Scholarship, 1453
Wadsworth African Fellowship, 1616
Wadsworth International Fellowship, 1617
Wageningen University Fellowship Programme, 1605
Wai-man Woo Scholarship, 517
Wales One World Film Festival Grant, 139
Wallace Fellowship, 1601
Wallace Scholarships for Tertiary Student Research, 481
Walter Carsen Prize for Excellence in the Performing Arts, 277
Walter Heywood Bryan Scholarship for International Students in Australia, 781
Walters Kundert Fellowship, 1039
The Walter V. and Idun Berry Postdoctoral Fellowship Program, 1150
Warburg-I Tatti Joint Fellowship, 1598
Warsaw Agricultural University MBA in Agribusiness Management, 1605
Washington American Indian Endowed Scholarship, 1606
Water, Sanitation and Health Engineering MSc-International Masters Excellence Scholarship, 1341
Water Corporation Scholarship in Biosolids Research, 408
Water MSc Scholarship for Students from Malawi and Vietnam, 395
Watson Fellowship, 1006
W.D. Farr Endowment Fund Grants, 377
W.D.E. Coulson & Toni M. Cross Aegean Exchange Program, 106, 589
Weiss/Brown Publication Subvention Award, 892
Welch Scholarship, 665
Welcome Scholarship for Students from Refugee Backgrounds, 1414
Wellcome Discovery Awards, 1612
Wellcome Early-Career Awards, 1612
The Wellcome Trust, 1334
Wellcome Trust: Principal Research Fellowships, 1402
Wellcome Trust 4-Year PhD Programme Studentships, 1304
Wellcome Trust and NIH Four-Year PhD Studentships, 1612
Wellcome Trust-POST Fellowships in Medical History and Humanities, 1613
Wellington Graduate Award, 1596
Wellington Master's by Thesis Scholarship, 1596
Wellington Shire Council Scholarship, 517
Welsh Independent Dance Grant, 139
The Wendell Alton Moats and Virginia Evelyn Moats Scholarship for Business, 213
Wenner-Gren Fellowship in Anthropology and Black Experiences, 1617
West Africa Scholarship, 470
WE-STAR Fellowships, 655
Western Australian Government Japanese Studies Scholarships, 429
Western Center for Agricultural Health and Safety, 1240
Western Digital Scholarship Program, 1112
Western Sydney Artists, 142
Western Sydney Artists Fellowship, 887
Westminster College Lewis and Gibson Scholarship, 1259
WGRG Foundation Terri Grier Memorial Scholarship, 1183
Wharton Executive MBA Programme, 1618
Whitehall Foundation Grants-in-Aid, 1618
Whitehall Foundation Research Grants, 1618
The White House Fellowship, 1178
White House Fellowships, 962
The Widening Participation Ambition Scholarship for University of Kent Graduates, 1334
Wiener Laboratory Predoctoral Fellowship, 106
Wiener Laboratory Research Associate Appointment, 107
Wigmore Hall/Independent Opera International Song Competition, 124
Wilfrid Knapp Scholarship (Arts), 1148
Wilfrid Knapp Scholarship (Sciences), 1148
Wilfrid Laurier University President, 1619
William Blair Bell Memorial Lecture, 1026
William Blake Trust Bursary, 1212
William Charnley Anglo-Danish Scholarship, 125
William Georgetti Scholarships, 1167, 1200
William Macleay Microbiology Research Fund, 738
The William McIlrath Rural Scholarship, 1411
William Moore Gorman Graduate Research Scholarship, 1212
The William P. Van Wagenen Fellowship, 886
William P Van Wagenen Fellowship, 48
William Ross Murray Scholarship, 1097
The William Sanders Scarborough Fellowships, 106
Williamson Medical Research PhD Scholarship, 1454
William Thomas Williams Postgraduate Scholarship, 679
William Wyse Studentship in Social Anthropology, 1260
Willi Paul Adams Award, 937
Wingate Scholarships, 1619
Winifred E. Preedy Postgraduate Bursary, 534
Winston Churchill Foundation Scholarships, 200
The Winter 2022 Gift Competition, 414
Winter Pilot Award, 1113
Winterthur Dissertation Research Fellowships, 1621
Winterthur Postdoctoral Fellowships, 1621
Winterthur Research Fellowships, 1621
Witherby Publishing Scholarship, 470
W L 'Bill' Byrnes Global Scholarship, 617
Wolf Aviation Fund Grants Program, 24

Wolf Blass Australian Winemaking Independent Study Scholarship, 1622
Wolfsonian-FIU Fellowship, 1622
Women as Cyber Leaders Scholarship, 395
Women in Central Banking Scholarship, 993
Women in Computer Science Award (WICS), 1426
Women in Computing Master's Scholarship, 617
Women in Finance and Economics Scholarship, 426
Women in Finance and Economics Scholarship Program, 472
Women in Master of Business Administration (WiMBA) Scholarship, 1438
Women in Science Scholarship, 736
Women in Sport Scholarships, 1594
Women's Leadership and Development Program (WLDP)-Women's Economic Security Grant Guidelines, 168
Women's Studio Workshop Internships, 1623
Women's Visiting Gynaecological Club Prize, 1027
Woodcock-Munoz Foundation Empowerment Through Education Scholarships, 1613
Woodrow Wilson MBA Fellowship in Education Leadership, 1624
Woodrow Wilson Teaching Fellowship, 1624
Woodrow Wilson Visiting Fellows, 387
Wood Technology Research Centre–Postgraduate Scholarships, 1271
Wood-Whelan Research Fellowships, 667
Wood Whistler Prize and Medal, 1260
Woolf Fischer Scholarship, 1281
Workmen's Circle/Dr Emanuel Patt Visiting Professorship, 1641
World Bank Grants Facility for Indigenous Peoples, 1626
World Bank Scholarships Program, 1627
World Citizen Talent Scholarship, 656
World Citizen Talent Scholarship for International Students, 577
WOTRO DC Fellowships, 883
Wright College Scholarship, 1413
Wright Honours Scholarship, 1413
Wylie Scholar Program, 1593

X

Xerox Technical Minority Scholarship, 1633

Y

Yalda Hakim Graduate Scholarship for Female Afghan Scholars, 940
Yanshan University Doctoral Scholarships, 1638
Yanshan University Scholarship Program for International Students, 1638
4-Year Studentship, 317
Young Investigator Grant, 660
Yuill Scholarship, 175

Z

The Zeller Summer Scholarship in Medicinal Botany, 560
The Zenith Fellows Award Program (Zenith), 31
Zentrum Moderner Orient and Berlin Graduate School of Muslim Cultures and Societies Visiting Research Fellowship, 201
Zespri Innovation Scholarships, 737
Zhengzhou University President Scholarships, 19
Zonta Club of South Auckland Area Study Award, 159
Zonta International Canterbury Tertiary Education Scholarship, 737
Zuckerman Dissertation Fellowship, 371
Zwilling, J.A. Henckels Culinary Arts Scholarship, 400

Index of Awarding Organisations

A

AACR-American Association for Cancer Research, 1
Aarhus University, 6
Aaron Siskind Foundation, 7
Abbey Harris Mural Fund, 7
Abdul Aziz Al Ghurair Foundation for Education, 7
Abdus Salam International Centre for Theoretical Physics (ICTP), 8
Abell Foundation, 8
Abilene Christian University, 9
Abraham Lincoln High School, 10
Academia Resource Management (ARM), 11
Academy of Marketing Science Foundation, 11
Academy of Medical Sciences, 12
Academy of Sciences of the Czech Republic, 13
Acadia University, 14
Action Cancer, 14
Action Medical Research, 15
Adelphi University, 16
Advance Africa, 16
African Forest Forum (AFF), 17
African Mathematics Millennium Scientific Initiative, 17
After School Africa, 18
Agency for Science, Technology and Research (A*STAR), 20
Agilent Technology and American Association of Critical Care Nurses, 21
Air-Conditioning, Heating, and Refrigeration Institute, 22
Air Force Office of Scientific Research (AFOSR), 21
Alberta Innovates Health Solutions, 22
Alex's Lemonade Stand Foundation, 23
Alfred L and Constance C Wolf Aviation Fund, 24
Alfred Toepfer Foundation, 25
Alzheimer's Association, 25
Alzheimer's Australia, 31
Alzheimer's Drug Discovery Foundation (ADDF), 32
America–Israel Cultural Foundation (AICF), 33
American Academy of Child and Adolescent Psychiatry, 33
American Academy of Neurology (AAN), 36
American Academy of Pediatrics (AAP), 36
American Alpine Club (AAC), 37
American Association for Cancer Research (AACR), 38
American Association for the History of Nursing (AAHN), 41
American Association for Women Radiologists (AAWR), 42
American Association of Critical-Care Nurses (AACN), 43
American Association of Family and Consumer Sciences (AAFCS), 44
American Association of Law Libraries (AALL), 45
American Association of Neurological Surgeons (AANS), 47
American Association of University Women (AAUW), 48
American Association of University Women Educational Foundation, 50
American Australian Association (AAA), 52
American Cancer Society (ACS), 53
American Chemical Society (ACS), 53
American College of Chest Physicians, 62
American Council of Learned Societies (ACLS), 62
American Council on Rural Special Education (ACRES), 63
American Diabetes Association (ADA), 64
American Federation for Aging Research (AFAR), 64
American Foundation for Suicide Prevention (AFSP), 67
American Foundation for Urologic Disease, Inc. (AFUD), 70
American Geophysical Union (AGU), 70
American Gynecological Club, 71
American Head and Neck Society (AHNS), 71
American Hearing Research Foundation-AHRF, 74
American Heart Association (AHA), 76
American Indian Science and Engineering Society, 76
American Institute for Economic Research (AIER), 77
American Institute for Sri Lankan Studies (AISLS), 77
American Institute of Bangladesh Studies (AIBS), 79
American Institute of Certified Public Accountants (AICPA), 81
American Library Association (ALA), 81
American Lung Association, 84
American Mathematical Society, 85
American Meteorological Society (AMS), 86
American Museum of Natural History (AMNH), 86
American Nuclear Society (ANS), 87
American Numismatic Society (ANS), 90
American Orchid Society, 91
American Ornithologists' Union (AOU), 91
American Otological Society (AOS), 92
American Parkinson Disease Association, 92
American Philosophical Association (APA), 93
American Philosophical Society, 94
American Physiological Society (APS), 94
American Psychological Association Minority Fellowship Program (APA/MFP), 95
American Psychological Foundation (APF), 95
American Public Power Association (APPA), 96
American Research Institute in Turkey (ARIT), 96
American-Scandinavian Foundation (ASF), 122
American School of Classical Studies at Athens (ASCSA), 98
American Schools of Oriental Research (ASOR), 107
American Society for Engineering Education (ASEE), 110
American Society for Microbiology (ASM), 112
American Society for Photogrammetry & Remote Sensing (ASPRS), 113
American Society for Quality (ASQ), 113
American Society of Colon and Rectal Surgeons, 114
American Society of Composers, Authors and Publishers Foundation, 117
American Society of Hematology, 117
American Society of Interior Designers (ASID) Educational Foundation, Inc., 118

Palgrave Macmillan (ed.), *The Grants Register 2024*,
https://doi.org/10.1057/978-1-349-96073-6

American Society of Mechanical Engineers (ASME International), 118
American Society of Nephrology (ASN), 119
American University in Cairo (AUC), 120
American University of Beirut, 120
American Urological Association, 121
American Water Works Association (AWWA), 121
American Woman's Society of Certified Public Accountants, 122
Analytics India, 124
Anglo-Austrian Music Society, 124
Anglo-Danish Society, 124
Anglo-Norse Society, 125
Appraisal Institute Education Trust, 126
Archaeological Institute of America, 127
Arc of the United States, 126
Arctic Institute of North America (AINA), 130
Aristotle University of Thessaloniki, 132
Arizona Community Foundation, 132
Arizona State University College of Business, 132
Armenian International Women's Association, 133
Arthritis Research United Kingdom, 133
Artist Trust, 134
Arts Council of Ireland, 136
Arts Council of Wales, 136
Arts International, 140
Arts NSW, 140
Artwork Archive, 142
Ashinaga, 142
Ashley Family Foundation, 143
Asian Cultural Council (ACC), 143
Associated General Contractors of America (AGC), 144
Association for Canadian Studies in the United States, 145
Association of American Geographers (AAG), 145
Association of Clinical Pathologists, 146
Association of Flight Attendants, 147
Association of Management Development Institutions in South Asia (AMDISA), 147
Association of Perioperative Registered Nurses Foundation, 148
Association of Surgeons of Great Britain and Ireland, 148
Aston University, 149
Ataxia United Kingdom, 152
Athens State University, 152
Auckland University of Technology University of Technology, 153
Australia Council for the Arts, 159
Australian Academy of Science, 162
Australian Academy of the Humanities (AAH), 163
Australian Bio Security-CRC (AB-CRC), 163
Australian Catholic University (ACU), 164
Australian Centre for Blood Diseases (ACBD), 166
Australian Department of Science, 167
Australian Federation of University Women (AFUW), 167
Australian Government Research Training Scholarships, 168
Australian Institute of Aboriginal and Torres Strait Islander Studies (AIATSIS), 170
Australian Institute of Nuclear Science and Engineering (AINSE), 170
Australian National University (ANU), 172
Australian Research Council (ARC), 175
Australian Sports Commission (ASC), 175
Austrian Academy of Sciences, 178
Austro-American Association of Boston, 180
Autism Speaks, 180

B

Bath Spa University, 181
Bayer AG, 186
Bayreuth International Graduate School of African Studies (BIGSAS), 186
Beinecke Scholarship Program, 190
Beit Trust (Zimbabwe, Zambia and Malawi), 191
Belgian American Educational Foundation (B.A.E.F.), 191
Belgian Flemish University, VLIR-UOS, 192
Belgian Technical Cooperation agency (BTC), Ghent University, 193
Berkeley Graduate Division, 194
Berlin Graduate School Muslim Cultures and Societies, 201
Berlin Mathematical School, 201
Beta Phi Mu Headquarters, 202
Bibliographical Society of America (BSA), 203
Bielefeld University, 208
Bilkent University, 208
Biola University, 210
Biomedical Engineering Society (BMES), 213
Biotechnology and Biological Sciences Research Council (BBSRC), 214
Birkbeck, University of London, 221
Blakemore Foundation, 223
Bond University, 223
Boren Awards, 225
Botswana Insurance Holdings Limited Trust, 226
Bournemouth University, 226
Bradford Chamber of Commerce and Industry, 229
Brandeis University, 230
British Academy, 233
British Association for American Studies (BAAS), 236
British Association for Canadian Studies (BACS), 237
British Association for Japanese Studies, 238
British Association of Plastic Reconstructive and Aesthetic Surgeons (BAPRAS), 239
British Council, 242
British Dental Association, 244
British Dietetic Association, 244
British Ecological Society (BES), 245
British Federation of Women Graduates (BFWG), 246
British & Foreign School Society, 231
British Heart Foundation (BHF), 249
British Institute at Ankara (BIAA), 254
British Institute in Eastern Africa, 254
British Medical Association (BMA), 255
British School at Athens, 256
British School at Rome (BSR), 260
British Society for Antimicrobial Chemotherapy, 261
British Society for Middle Eastern Studies, 262
British Veterinary Association, 263
Broadcast Education Association, 264
Brunel University London, 266
Budapest International Music Competition, 267
Bupa Foundation, 268

C

Camargo Foundation, 269
Canada Council for the Arts, 270
Canadian Association of Broadcasters (CAB), 275
Canadian Blood Services (CBS), 277
Canadian Breast Cancer Research Alliance (CBCRA), 279
Canadian Bureau for International Education (CBIE), 280
Canadian Cancer Society Research Institute (CCSRI), 284
Canadian Crafts Council, 284
Canadian Embassy (United States of America), 285
Canadian Federation of University Women (CFUW), 286
Canadian Foundation for the Study of Infant Deaths, 287
Canadian Institute for Advanced Legal Studies, 287
Canadian Institutes of Health Research, 289
Canadian Library Association (CLA), 290

Canadian National Institute for the Blind (CNIB), 291
Canadian Political Science Association, 294
Canadian Society for Chemical Technology, 295
Canadian Society for Chemistry (CSC), 296
Cancer Council N.S.W, 296
Cancer Council South Australia, 297
Cancer Immunotherapy, 298
Cancer Prevention and Research Institute of Texas-CPRIT, 299
Cancer Research Fund of the Damon Runyon-Walter Winchell Foundation, 307
Cancer Research Institute, 308
Cancer Research United Kingdom, 311
Cancer Research United Kingdom Manchester Institute, 317
Canon Collins Trust, 318
Canterbury Christ Church, University College, Graduate School, 319
Canterbury Historical Association, 319
Cardiff University, 323
Carnegie Corporation of New York, 333
Carnegie Trust, 333
Casino Mucho, 334
Catholic University of Louvain, 335
CEC Artslink, 335
Center for Creative Photography (CCP), 337
Center for Defense Information (CDI), 338
Central Queensland University, 339
Centre de Recherches et d'Investigations Epidermiques et Sensorielles, 344
Centre De Science Humaines (CSH), 344
Centre for Clinical Research Excellence, 345
Centre for Environment Planning and Technology University, 345
Centre for Groundwater Studies (CGS), 346
Chandigarh University, 346
Charles Babbage Institute (CBI), 347
Charles Darwin University, 347
Charles Darwin University (CDU), 348
Charles Sturt University (CSU), 349
Charlie Trotter Culinary Education Foundation, 356
Chiang Ching Kuo Foundation for International Scholarly Exchange, 357
Chicago Tribune, 360
Chilean International Cooperation Agency, 361
China Scholarship Council, 361
Chinese American Medical Society (CAMS), 362
Chinook Regional Career Transitions for Youth, 363
Choirs Ontario, 363
Citizens United in Research for Epilepsy (CURE), 364
Clara Haskil Competition, 365
Clare Hall Cambridge, 365
Claude Leon Foundation, 366
Coimbra Group, 366
Collegeville Institute for Ecumenical and Cultural Research, 367
Columbia College of Missouri, 368
Columbia GSAS, 368
Columbia University, 371
Commonwealth Eye Health Consortium, 373
Commonwealth Fund, 373
Commonwealth Scholarship and Fellowship Plan, 375
Commonwealth Scholarship Commission in the United Kingdom, 376
Community Foundation for Calderdale, 376
Concordia University, 377
Congressional Black Caucas Foundation, 378
Conseil Européen Pour la Recherche Nucléaire European Organization for Nuclear Research, 380
Conservation Leadership Programme, 381
Conservation Trust, 381
Consortium for Advanced Research Training in Africa (CARTA), 382
Consortium for Applied Research on International Migration, 382
Cooperative Research Centre for Water Quality and Treatment (CRCWQT), 382
Copenhagen Business School, 383
Core, 385
Council of American Overseas Research Centers (CAORC), 385
Council of Independent Colleges, 387
Council of Logistics Management, 387
Council of Supply Chain Management Professionals (CSCMP), 388
Council on Foreign Relations (CFR), 389
Council on Library and Information Resources (CLIR), 390
Craig H. Neilsen Foundation, 390, 393
Cranfield University, 394
Crohn's and Colitis Foundation of America, 396
Croucher Foundation, 397
Culinary Trust, 399
Curtin University, 400
Curtin University of Technology, 401
Cystinosis Research Foundation, 409

D

Daiwa Anglo-Japanese Foundation, 411
Dalai Lama Foundation, 412
David & Lucile Packard Foundation, 413
Davies Charitable Foundation, 413
Deakin University, 418
Defense Personnel Security Research Center, 426
Deloitte Foundation, 427
De Montfort University, 414
Denmark-America Foundation, 427
Department of Biotechnology, 428
Department of Education Services, 429
Department of Foreign Affairs and Trade, 430
Department of Innovation, Industry and Regional Development, 430
Deutsche Forschungsgemeinschaft (DFG), 431
Deutscher Akademischer Austauschdienst, 435
Deutsches Museum, 436
Diabetes United Kingdom, 436
Doctoral New Investigator (DNI) Grants, 437
Dominican College of San Rafael, 437
Doris Duke Charitable Foundation (DDCF), 438
Doshisha University, 439
Duke University, 441
Durham University, 446
Dutch Ministry of Foreign Affairs, 452

E

Earthwatch Institute, 455
École Normale Supérieure (ENS), 455
École Normale Supérieure de Lyon, 456
Ecole Polytechnique Federale de Lausanne, 457
Economic History Association (EHA), 458
Edinburgh Napier University, 461
Edith Cowan University, 470
Educational Testing Service (ETS), 475
Education and Research Foundation for the Society of Nuclear Medicine (SNM), 472
Education.govt.nz, 474
Education New Zealand (ENZ), 473
Eidgenössische Technische Hochschule Zurich, 479
Electoral Commission New Zealand, 481
Embassy of France in Australia, 481
Embassy of the United States in Kabul, 483
Endeavour Research Fellowship, 483

Engineering and Physical Sciences Research Council (EPSRC), 484
Engineers Canada, 486
English-Speaking Union (ESU), 487
Entente Cordiale Scholarships, 488
Entomological Society of Canada (ESC), 488
Environmental Leadership Program, 491
Environmental Protection Agency, 491
Escola Superior d'Administració i Direcció d'Empreses (ESADE), 492
ESMOD Berlin, 492
Eta Sigma Phi, 492
Ethnic Minority Foundation, 493
Eugène Vinaver Memorial Trust, 493
European Association for the Study of Diabetes, 494
European Calcified Tissue Society, 495
European Committee for Treatment and Research in Multiple Sclerosis (ECTRIMS), 495
European Crohn's and Colitis Organisation, 497
European Molecular Biology Organization (EMBO), 499
European Science Foundation (ESF), 500
European Society of Surgical Oncology (ESSO), 500
European Space Agency, 501
European Synchrotron Radiation Facility (ESRF), 501
European University Institute (EUI), 503
EuroTech Universities Alliance, 503
Evangelical Lutheran Church in America (ELCA), 505
Evonik Foundation, 505

F
Fahs-Beck Fund for Research and Experimentation, 507
Fanconi Anemia Research Fund, Inc., 507
Federation University Australia, 508
Fellowship Program in Academic Medicine, 517
Ferrari, 518
Fight for Sight, 518
Finnish National Agency for Education-EDUFI, 519
Flinders University, 519
Fogarty International Center, 535
Fondation des Etats-Unis, 536
Fondation Fyssen, 537
Fondation Jeunesse Internationale, Ecole Franchaise d'Extreme-Orient, 537
Ford Foundation, 538
Foreign Affairs and International Trade Canada, 538
Forgarty International Center, 539
Forum Transregional Studies, 540
Foundation for Digestive Health and Nutrition, 540
Foundation for Liberal and Management Education University, 545
Foundation for Science and Disability, Inc., 546
Foundation of the American College of Healthcare Executives, 546
Foundation Praemium Erasmianum, 547
Freie Universitat Berlin and Peking University, 548
French Ministry of Foreign Affairs, 548
Friends of Israel Educational Foundation, 549
Fujitsu, 549
Fulbright Commission (Argentina), 550
Fulbright Foundation (United Kingdom), 550
Fundacion Educativa Carlos M. Castaneda, 553
Fund for Epilepsy, 552
Funds for Women Graduates, 553
Fylde College, 555

G
Garden Club of America, 559
Gates Cambridge Trust, 560
General Social Care Council, 561
GeneTex, 562
Geological Society of America (GSA), 562
George A and Eliza Gardner Howard Foundation, 563
Gerber Foundation, 564
German Academic Exchange Service (DAAD), 565
German Historical Institute, 566
Getty Foundation, 567
Ghent University, 568
Gilchrist Educational Trust (GET), 569
Glasgow Caledonian University, 570
Goethe-Institut, 572
Graduate Fellowships for Science, Technology, Engineering, and Mathematics Diversity, 573
Greek Ministry of National Education and Religious Affairs, 573
Griffith University, 574
Gypsy Lore Society, 575

H
Hague University of Applied Sciences, 577
Harish-Chandra Research Institute, 578
Harpo Foundation, 578
Harry S Truman Library Institute, 579
Harvard Business School, 581
Harvard Travellers Club, 581
Health Canada, 582
Health Research Board (HRB), 582
Hearst Corporation, 585
Heart and Stroke Foundation, 585
Heart Research United Kingdom, 586
Heinrich Boll Foundation, 587
Helen Hay Whitney Foundation, 588
Hellenic Pasteur Institute, 589
Help Musicians United Kingdom, 590
Herb Society of America, Inc., 591
Heriot-Watt University, 591
Higher & Education South Africa, 593
Hilda Martindale Educational Trust, 601
Hong Kong Baptist University, 602
Horowitz Foundation for Social Policy, 603
Hosei University, 603
Hospitality Maine, 604
Howard Hughes Medical Institute (HHMI), 604
Humane Research Trust, 605
Humboldt University of Berlin, 605

I
Imperial College of Science, Technology and Medicine, 607
India Alliance, 617
India Habitat Centre, 619
Indian Council of Medical Research, 620
Indian Education Department, 620
Indian Institute of Management, Calcutta, 622
Indian Institute of Management Ranchi, 622
Indian Institute of Science Bangalore (IISc), 622
Indian Institute of Technology Kharagpur, 623
Indian Institute of Technology Ropar, 623
Indian School of Business, 624
Indira Gandhi Institute of Development Research, 624
IndusInd Foundation, 625
Institut de Recherche Robert-Sauvé en Santé et en Sécurité du Travail (IRSST), 625
Institute for Advanced Studies in the Humanities, 629

Institute for Advanced Studies on Science, Technology and Society (IAS-STS), 629
Institute for Advanced Study (IAS) Technical University of Munich, 630
Institute for Labour Market Policy Evaluation (IFAU), 631
Institute for South ASIA Studies UC Berkeley, 631
Institute for Supply Management (ISM), 634
Institute of Behavioural Science (IBS), University of Colorado at Boulder, 635
Institute of Biology, 636
Institute of Education, 636
Institute of Electrical and Electronics Engineers History Center, 637
Institute of European Studies, 637
Institute of Fundamental Sciences, Massey University, 638
Institute of Museum and Library Services, 645
Institut Européen d'Administration des Affaires, 627
Institut Français d'Amérique, 628
Institution of Engineering and Technology (IET), 646
Institution of Mechanical Engineers (IMechE), 648
International Arctic Research Center Fellowships for Cancer Research, 649
International Business Machines Corporation, 650
International Centre for Education in Islamic Finance (INCEIF), 651
International Centre for Genetic Engineering and Biotechnology (ICGEB), 651
International Centre for Theoretical Sciences, 655
International Dairy-Deli-Bakery Association, 656
International Education Specialist, 656
International Federation of Library Associations and Institutions WLIC, 657
International Federation of University Women (IFUW), 658
International Furnishings and Design Association Education Foundation, 658
International Human Frontier Science Program Organization (HFSP), 659
International Institute for Management Development (IMD), 661
International Institute for Population Sciences (IIPS), 661
International Institute of Tropical Agriculture (IITA), 662
International Mathematical Union (IMU), 663
International School of Crystallography, E Majorana Centre, 663
International Society of Nephrology (ISN), 664
International Union for Vacuum Science and Technology (IUVSTA), 665
International Union of Biochemistry and Molecular Biology (IUBMB), 666
Iota Sigma Pi, 667
Iowa State University, 669
Iowa State University of Science and Technology, 670
Irish Research Council, 670
Islamic Cooperation Organization (OIC), 671
IT University of Copenhagen, 672

J
James Cook University, 673
James S. McDonnell Foundation, 679
Japanese American Citizens League (JACL), 681
Japan Society for the Promotion of Science (JSPS), 680
Jiamusi University, 681
John Carter Brown Library at Brown University, 682
John E Fogarty International Center (FIC) for Advanced Study in the Health Sciences, 683
John F. Kennedy Library Foundation, 684
John R. Mott Scholarship Foundation, 686
Johns Hopkins University, 686
Joint Institute for Laboratory Astrophysics (formerly Joint Institute for Laboratory Astrophysics), 687
Juvenile Diabetes Foundation International/The Diabetes Research Foundation, 688
Juvenile Diabetes Research Foundation-JDRF, 690

K
Keio University, 693
Kennan Institute, 694
Kennedy Memorial Trust, 694
Kidney Research United Kingdom, 695
Kingston University, 695
Klynveld Peat Marwick Goerdeler Foundation, 696
Kosciuszko Foundation, 696
Kungliga Tekniska Högskolan Royal Institute of Technology, 697
Kurt Weill Foundation for Music, 698

L
Lancaster University, 704
La Trobe University, 699
Le Cordon Bleu Australia, 712
Leeds International Pianoforte Competition, 713
Leiden University, 713
Leo Baeck Institute (LBI), 720
Lepra Health in Action, 721
LeTourneau University, 721
Leukaemia Foundation, 722
Leukemia & Lymphoma Society, 723
Leukemia Research Foundation (LRF), 724
Leverhulme Trust, 724
Library Company of Philadelphia, 728
Life Sciences Research Foundation (LSRF), 730
Linacre College, 731
Lincoln Memorial University, 736
Linnean Society of New South Wales, 737
Lock Heed Martin, 739
London Goodenough Association of Canada, 739
London Mathematical Society, 740
London Metropolitan University, 741
London School of Business & Finance, 742
London School of Economics and Political Science (LSE), 743
London School of Hygiene & Tropical Medicine-LSHTM, 744
London South Bank University, 748
Loren L Zachary Society for the Performing Arts, 748
Los Alamos National Laboratory (LANL), 749
Loughborough University, 749
Loughborough University Business School, 758
Loyola Marymount University, 758
Ludwig-Maximilian University, 758
Lung Cancer Research Foundation, 759
Lupus Foundation of America, 759
Luton Business School, University of Luton, 760

M
Maastricht University, 763
Macquarie University, 766
Magna Carta College, 781
Maine Restaurant Association, 782
Managed Care Organization, 782
Manipal University in India, 783
March of Dimes, 784
Marine Biological Association, 784
Marines' Memorial Association, 785
Marketing Science Institute (MSI), 785
Marshall Aid Commemoration Commission, 787

Marshal Papworth, 786
Maryland Association of Certified Public Accountants, 787
Massey University, 788
Materials Research Society, 794
Matsumae International Foundation (MIF), 795
Max Planck Institute, 795
Max Planck Institute for Dynamics and Self-Organization, 796
Max Planck Institute for European Legal History, 797
Max Planck Institute for Human Cognitive and Brain Sciences, 797
Max Planck Research Group Neural Mechanisms of Human Communication, 798
Max Planck Society, 798
McGill University, 799
Media@McGill, 800
Medical Library Association (MLA), 800
Medical Research Council (MRC), 801
Medical Research Scotland, 806
Meet The Composer, Inc., 807
Melville Trust for Care and Cure of Cancer, 808
Memorial Foundation for Jewish Culture, 809
Memorial University of Newfoundland (MUN), 809
Microsoft Research, 810
Middlesex University London, 811
Miles Morland Foundation, 813
Minerva Stiftung, 813
Ministry of Education and Science Republic of Latvia (MESRL), 814
Ministry of Fisheries, 814
Ministry of Foreign Affairs, 815
Ministry of Foreign Affairs and International Cooperation, 815
Ministry of Foreign Affairs of the Republic of Indonesia, 816
Minnesota Historical Society (MHS), 817
Minnesota Ovarian Cancer Alliance (MOCA), 817
Missouri Department of Higher Education, 818
Missouri State University, 818
Modern Language Association of America (MLA), 819
Monash Mount Eliza Business School, 821
Monash University, 821
Montessori St Nicholas Centre, 825
Morton Cure Paralysis Fund, 825
Motor Neurone Disease Association, 826
Mott MacDonald Charitable Trust, 827
MQ Mental Health, 828
Multiple Sclerosis Society of Canada (MSSC), 829
Murdoch University, 830

N

Nansen Fund, 834
Nan Tien Institute, 833
Nanyang Technological University (NTU), 834
Narotam Sekhsaria Foundation, 837
National Academies, 837
National Aeronautics and Space Administration (NASA), 843
National Air and Space Museum (NASM), Smithsonian Institution, 843
National Association for Core Curriculum, Inc., 845
National Association for Gifed Children, 846
National Association of Teachers of Singing (NATS), 847
National Breast Cancer Foundation (NBCF), 850
National Bureau of Asian Research (NBR), 851
National Cattleman Foundation, 851
National Education Association (NEA) Foundation, 852
National Education Union (NEU), 853
National Endowment for the Humanities (NEH), 853
National Foundation for Infectious Diseases (NFID), 856
National Health and Medical Research Council (NHMRC), 857
National Heart, Lung, and Blood Institute, 858
National Institute for Health and Care Excellence (NICE), 858
National Institute of General Medical Sciences (NIGMS), 859
National Institutes of Health, 860
National Library of Medicine (NLM), 861
National Multiple Sclerosis Society (MS), 863
National Research Council (NRC), 864
National Research Foundation (NRF), 865
National Science Foundation (NSF), 867
National Sea Grant College, 870
National Sun Yat-Sen University (NSYSU), 870
National Tax Association, 871
National Tour Association, 871
National University of Ireland, Maynooth, 874
National University of Ireland Galway, 871
National University of Singapore (NUS), 875
Natural Environment Research Council (NERC), 878
Natural Hazards Center-University of Colorado, 879
Natural Sciences and Engineering Research Council of Canada (NSERC), 880
Netherlands Organization for Scientific Research (NWO), 883
Neurosurgery Research & Education Foundation (NREF), 883
Newberry Library, 891
Newcastle University, 893
Newcastle University in the United Kingdom, 901
Newcomen Society of the United States, 906
New England Culninary Institute (NECI), 886
New South Wales Architects Registration Board, 886
New South Wales Ministry of the Arts, 887
New York Foundation for the Arts (NYFA), 887
New York University, 889
New York University Academic and Science, 890
New Zealand Aid Programme, 891
North Atlantic Treaty Organization (NATO), 907
North Central College, 907
North Dallas Bank & Trust Company, 908
Northeastern University, 909
Northeast Florida Phi Beta Kappa Alumni Association, 909
North West Cancer Research Fund, 908
Norway–the Official Site in the United States, 910
Novo Nordisk A/S, 914
Novo Nordisk Foundation, 914
Nuffic, 915

O

Office of International Affairs at Ohio State University (OIA), 917
Ohio Arts Council, 918
Omohundro Institute of Early American History and Culture, 919
Oncology Nursing Society Foundation (ONS), 920
Ontario Council on Graduate Studies (OCGS), 922
Ontario Federation of Anglers & Hunters (OFAH), 924
Ontario Ministry of Education and Training, 924
Ontario Student Assistance Program (OSAP), 925
Open Society Foundation-Sofia, 925
Organization for Autism Research (OAR), 927
Organization of American Historians (OAH), 927
Organization of American States (OAS), 937
Oriel College, 938
Orthopaedic Research and Education Foundation (OREF), 941
Otaru University of Commerce, 941
Ovarian Cancer Research Fund, 942
Oxford Brookes University, School of Business, 942

P

Paloma O Shea Santander International Piano Competition, 945
Paralyzed Veterans of America (PVA), 945
Parapsychology Foundation, Inc., 946

Paris School of International Affairs (PSIA), 947
Parkinson's United Kingdom, 947
Paul & Daisy Soros Fellowships for New Americans, 948
Paul Lowin Prizes, 949
Peninsula School of Medicine and Dentistry, 949
Penn State, College of Communications, 950
Perkins School of Theology, 950
Petro Jacyk Central & East European Resource Centre (PJRC), 951
Pfizer, 951
Phi Beta Kappa Society, 955
PhRMA Foundation, 956
Pierre Elliott Trudeau Foundation, 957
Pine Tree State 4-H Foundation, 957
Plymouth University, 958
Poets Essayists Novelists American Center, 959
Polycystic Kidney Disease Foundation, 960
Population Council, 960
Prehistoric Society, 961
President's Commission on White House Fellowships, 962
Prime Minister's Research Fellowship, 963
Prince Charles Hospital Foundation's, 963

Q
Qalaa Holdings Scholarship Foundation (QHSF), 965
Queen Elisabeth International Music Competition of Belgium, 965
Queen Margaret University, 966
Queen Mary, University of London, 966
Queensland University of Technology (QUT), 973
Queen's Nursing Institute, 970
Queen's University of Belfast, 971

R
Radboud University Nijmegen, 975
Radcliffe Institute for Advanced Study, 977
Radiological Society of North America, Inc. (RSNA), 978
Ragdale, 982
Rebecca Skelton Fund, 983
Regent's Park College, 984
Regent's University London, 985
Regional Institute for Population Studies, 986
Religious Scholarships, 987
Republic of South Africa, 988
Research Corporation for Science Advancement, 989
Research Council of Norway, 989
Reserve Bank of New Zealand, 992
Resuscitation Council (United Kingdom), 994
Rheumatology Research Foundation, 994
Rhode Island Foundation, 1003
Rhodes College, 1005
Rhodes Trust, 1006
Rhodes University, 1007
Roberta Sykes Indigenous Education Foundation, 1011
Robert Wood Johnson Foundation, 1010
Rotterdam School of Management, Erasmus Graduate School of Business, 1014
Rotterdam School of Management Erasmus University, 1012
Royal Academy of Engineering, 1015
Royal Agricultural University, 1016
Royal College of Midwives, 1017
Royal College of Nursing Foundation, 1017
Royal College of Obstetricians and Gynaecologists (RCOG), 1018
Royal College of Ophthalmologists, 1027
Royal College of Ophthalmologists-Bayer Research, 1029
Royal College of Organists (RCO), 1030
Royal College of Physicians and Surgeons of Canada (RCPSC), 1032
Royal College of Surgeons, 1034
Royal College of Surgeons of United Kingdom, 1035
Royal Geographical Society (with the Institute of British Geographers), 1037
Royal Holloway, University of London, 1039
Royal Horticultural Society (RHS), 1043
Royal Irish Academy, 1044
Royal Literary Fund RLF, 1045
Royal Melbourne Institute of Technology University, 1045
Royal Over-Seas League ARTS, 1047
Royal Scottish Academy (RSA), 1048
Royal Society, 1050
Royal Society of Chemistry, 1054
Royal Society of Edinburgh, 1054
Royal Society of Medicine (RSM), 1056
Royal Town Planning Institute (RTPI), 1073
Rural Health Information Hub, 1073
Rural Maternity Care Research, 1074
Ryerson University, 1074

S
Sacramento State, 1083
Saint Louis University, 1084
Samuel H. Kress Foundation, 1084
San Antonio Nathan Shock Center, 1085
San Francisco Foundation (SFF), 1086
San Francisco State University (SFSU), 1086
Sanskriti Pratishthan, 1087
Sasakawa Fund, 1090
Savoy Foundation, 1090
Scholarship Foundation of the League of Finnish-American Societies, 1091
School of Oriental and African Studies (SOAS), 1092
Science and Engineering Research Board, 1098
Science and Technology Facilities Council (STFC), 1100
Science Foundation Ireland, 1104
Sciences Po, 1106
Seoul National University, 1107
Sher-Gil-Sundaram Arts Foundation, 1108
Shorenstein Asia-Pacific Research Center (APARC), 1109
Sidney Sussex College, 1109
Sievert Larsson Foundation, 1110
Sigma Theta Tau International, 1110
Silicon Valley Community Foundation, 1111
Simon Fraser University, 1112
Simons Foundation, 1113
Sir Richard Stapley Educational Trust, 1114
Sir William Lister/Dorey Bequest, 1114
Smeal College of Business, 1115
Smithsonian Environmental Research Center (SERC), 1116
Smithsonian Institution-National Air and Space Museum, 1117
Smithsonian National Air and Space Museum, 1118
Smithsonian Tropical Research Institution (STRI), 1119
Social Science Research Council (SSRC), 1120
Social Sciences and Humanities Research Council of Canada (SSHRC), 1125
Society for Academic Emergency Medicine Foundation, 1128
Society for Promotion of Roman Studies, 1129
Society for the Arts in Religious and Theological Studies (SARTS), 1130
Society for the Psychological Study of Social Issues (SPSSI), 1130
Society for the Scientific Study of Sexuality (SSSS), 1131
Society of Apothecaries of London, 1132
Society of Architectural Historians (SAH), 1132
Society of Naval Architects and Marine Engineers, 1133
Society of Women Engineers (SWE), 1134
Södertörn University, 1134

Soil and Water Conservation Society (SWCS), 1135
South African Association of Women Graduates (SAAWG), 1135
South African Council for English Education (SACEE), 1136
Southern Cross University, 1137
Space Environment Research Centre (SERC), 1137
Spencer Foundation, 1137
Spinal Research, 1138
Stanford University, 1148
Stanley Smith (United Kingdom) Horticultural Trust, 1151
State Secretariat for Education, Research and Innovation SERI, 1151
Statistical Society of Canada, 1152
St. Baldricks Foundations, 1142
St. Catherine's College-University of Oxford, 1145
St Cross College, 1139
Stellenbosch University, 1152
St John's College, 1141
St. Mary's University, 1148
Stockholm School of Economics, 1154
Strathclyde University, 1155
Stroke Association, 1156
Sugar Research Australia-SRA, 1157
Swansea University, 1158
Swedish Institute, 1160
Swedish Natural Science Research Council (NFR), 1162
Swinburne University of Technology, 1162
Swiss National Science Foundation (SNSF), 1164
Syracuse University, 1164

T

Tata Trusts, 1167
Technische Universiteit Delft (TUD), 1168
Tel Aviv University (TAU), 1168
Te Pôkai Tara Universities New Zealand, 1167
Texas LBJ School, 1169
The Churchill Fellowship, 1170
The Community Foundation of South Alabama, 1171
The Foundation for Advancement of Diversity in IP Law, 1171
The Gerda Henkel Foundation, 1172
The Lynde and Harry Bradley Foundation, 1173
The Marfan Foundation, 1174
The National Academies of Sciences, Engineering and Medicine, 1175
The National GEM Consortium, 1176
The National Hispanic Scholarship Fund, 1177
The Thomas R. Pickering Foreign Affairs Fellowship Program, 1177
The White House, 1178
Third World Academy of Sciences (TWAS), 1178
Thomson Foundation, 1181
Thurgood Marshall College Fund (TMCF), 1182
Toxicology Education Foundation (TEF), 1184
Transport Research Laboratory, 1185
Tropical Agricultural Research and Higher Education Center (CATIE), 1186
Trust Company, 1186
TU Delft, 1187
Turkiye Scholarships Burslari, 1188

U

UHasselt University, 1189
Union College, 1190
United Nations Educational, Scientific and Cultural Organization (UNESCO), 1190
United Nations University-Institute for the Advanced Study of Sustainability (UNU-IAS), 1191
United States-India Educational Foundation (USIEF), 1192
United States Institute of Peace (USIP), 1191
United States-United Kingdom Fulbright Commission, 1196
Universities Canada, 1196
Universities Federation for Animal Welfare (UFAW), 1198
Universities New Zealand, 1198
University College London, 1201
University Commission for Development Academy of Research and Higher Education Scholarships, 1213
University Institute of European Studies, 1213
University of Aarhus, 1213
University of Aberdeen, 1214
University of Adelaide, 1216
University of Alabama, 1220
University of Alaska Fairbanks (UAF), 1221
University of Alberta, 1221
University of Amsterdam, 1223
University of Antwerp, 1224
University of Auckland, 1225
University of Auckland Business School, 1233
University of Bath, 1234
University of Bern, 1234
University of Bologna, 1235
University of Bristol, 1235
University of British Columbia (UBC), 1238
University of California, Berkeley, 1240
University of California, Los Angeles(UCLA) Center for 17th and 18th Century Studies and the William Andrews Clark Memorial Library, 1240
University of California, Los Angeles(UCLA) Institute of American Cultures (IAC), 1241
University of California at Los Angeles (UCLA) Center for India and South Asia, 1239
University of California Berkeley-Haas School, 1239
University of Cambridge, 1241
University of Cambridge (Cambridge Commonwealth Trust, Cambridge Overseas Trust, Gates Cambridge Trust, Cambridge European Trust and Associated Trusts), 1261
University of Cambridge, Judge Business School, 1266
University of Canberra, 1266
University of Canterbury, 1268
University of Canterbury, Department of Management, 1271
University of Cape Town, 1281
University of Delaware, 1281
University of Derby, 1282
University of Dundee, 1283
University of East Anglia (UEA), 1291
University of Edinburgh, 1295
University of Essex, 1304
University of Exeter, 1310
University of Geneva, 1313
University of Glasgow, 1314
University of Göttingen, 1317
University of Graz, 1318
University of Guelph, 1318
University of Illinois, 1322
University of Kent, 1323
University of KwaZulu-Natal, 1335
University of Leeds, 1335
University of Leicester, 1342
University of Limerick, 1344
University of Lincoln, 1344
University of Liverpool, 1352
University of Manchester, 1363
University of Melbourne, 1390
University of Montevallo, 1402
University of Nevada, Las Vegas (UNLV), 1403
University of Newcastle, 1426
University of New England (UNE), 1404

University of New South Wales (UNSW), 1413, 1415
University of Notre Dame, 1438
University of Nottingham, 1439
University of Oklahoma, 1440
University of Ontario, 1441
University of Oregon, 1441
University of Otago, 1442
University of Oxford, 1454
University of Paris-Saclay, 1515
University of Pretoria, 1516
University of Pune, 1518
University of Queensland, 1518
University of Reading, 1521
University of Regina, 1525
University of Sheffield, 1525
University of Southampton, 1535
University of South Australia, 1530
University of South Wales, 1533
University of Stirling, 1538
University of Strathclyde, 1538
University of Surrey, 1554
University of Sussex, 1558
University of Sydney, 1561
University of Tasmania, 1573
University of Technology Sydney (UTS), 1575
University of Texas, 1575
University of Tokyo, 1576
University of Twente, 1577
University of Verona, 1579
University of Waikato, 1579
University of Wales, Bangor (UWB), 1581
University of Warwick, 1582
University of Waterloo, 1582
University of Western Australia, 1583
University of Western Sydney, 1583
University of West London, 1583
University of Westminster, 1584
University of Winnipeg, 1586
University of Wollongong (UOW), 1586
University of Wollongong in Dubai (UOWD), 1587
University of York, 1587
US Department of Energy, 1589
Utrecht University, 1590

V

Vascular Cures, 1593
Victoria University, 1593
Victoria University of Wellington, 1594
Villa I Tatti and the Museo Nacional del Prado, 1597
Villa I Tatti and the Warburg Institute School of Advanced Study, 1598
Villa I Tatti: The Harvard University Center for Italian Renaissance Studies, 1598
Vinaver Trust, 1601
Volkswagen Foundation, 1602

W

Wageningen University, 1603
Warsaw Agricultural University The International Institute of Management and Marketing in Agri-Business (IZMA), 1605
Washington University, 1606
Wellcome Trust, 1606
Wells Mountain Foundation, 1613
Wenner-Gren Foundation for Anthropological Research, 1614
W.F. Albright Institute of Archaeological Research, 1603
Wharton School, 1617
Whitehall Foundation, Inc., 1618
Wilfrid Laurier University, 1618
Wingate Scholarships, 1619
Winston Churchill Foundation of the United States of America, 1620
Winterthur, 1621
Wolf Blass Wines International, 1622
Wolfsonian-Florida International University, 1622
Women's Studio Workshop (WSW), 1623
Woodrow Wilson National Fellowship Foundation, 1623
Woods Hole Oceanographic Institution (WHOI), 1625
Worcester College, 1625
World Bank Institute, 1626
World Federation of International Music Competitions, 1627
World Learning, 1627
Worshipful Company of Musicians, 1628
Writtle University College, 1628

X

Xavier Labor Relations Institute-Xavier School of Management, 1633
Xerox Foundation, 1633

Y

Yale Center for British Art, 1635
Yale School of Management (SOM), 1635
Yanshan University, 1636
Yidisher Visnshaftlekher Institut Institute for Jewish Research, 1638